TURNER PUBLISHING COMPANY
Paducah, Kentucky

TURNER PUBLISHING COMPANY
The Front Line of Military History Books
412 Broadway, P.O. Box 3101
Paducah, Kentucky 42002-3101
(502) 443-0121

Library of Congress Catalog
Card No.: 94-060421
ISBN:1-56311-142-X

Printed in the United States of America
Limited Edition

*Photo, title page: Consolidated B-24J "Liberator." Three
aircraft over England during World War II (NASM Photo).
John Fry Productions. (Courtesy of John F. Curcio)*
Photo, this page: Courtesy of James Kotupish

TABLE OF CONTENTS

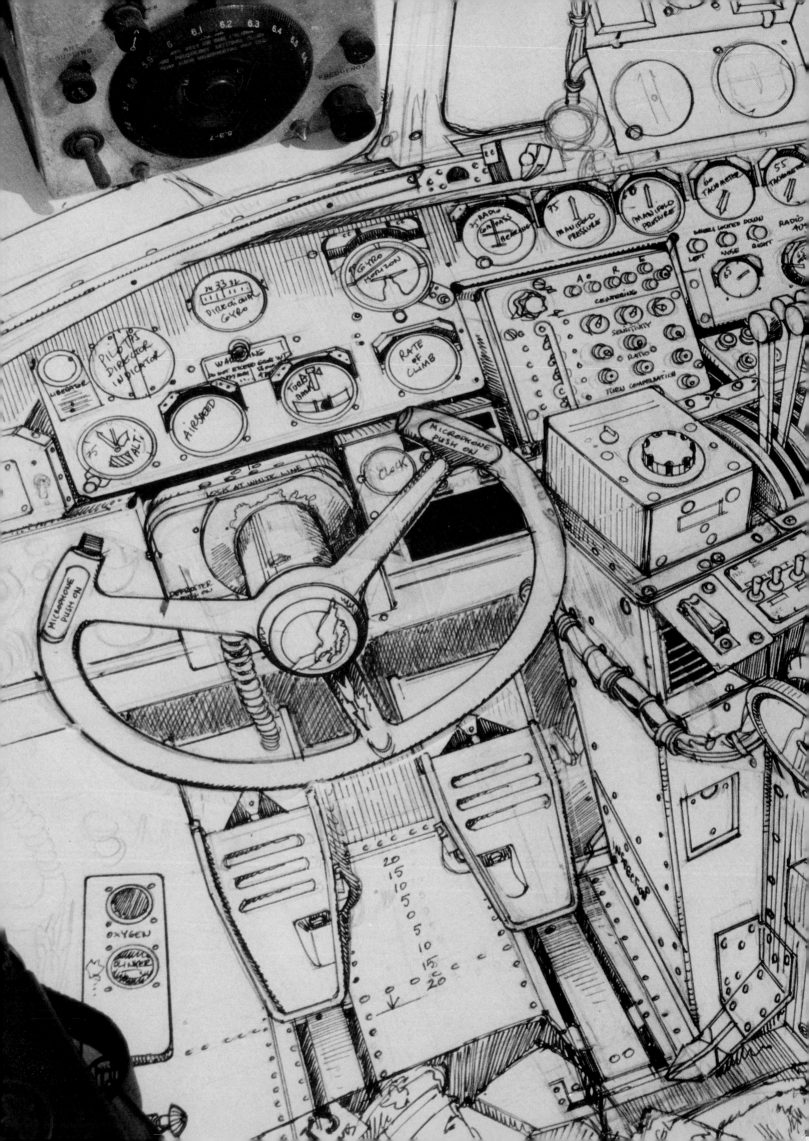

FRENCH
PHRASE BOOK
SEPTEMBER 28, 1943

The B-24 "Liberator" cockpit rendition in the making on Jean-Luc Beghin's drawing board.

John B. Conrad, President
Second Air Division Association

It is difficult for me to express my feelings of honor and pride in serving such an outstanding group as your president. I am proud to have been associated with and a part of you for 50 years. It was 50 years ago, in early 1944, that I was transferred into the 2nd Bomb Division from the 8th Air Force Pathfinders, the 482nd Bomb Group (PFF) at Alconbury.

When we try to look back 50 years it is hard to remember so many details of the operation. This might be a good thing because there are some memories that are not so pleasant to remember. In looking at the personal log that I kept at that time, when many of our targets were aircraft plants and ball bearing factories, I found that I sometimes referred to our combat missions as "raids" and that I recorded the number of the B-24 flown each mission as "Ship No." Differences in terminology since then may exist, but between then and now there are no incongruities in our comradeship and concern for each other.

We were tied together by an organizational chart depicting the 2nd Air Division's combat wings, fighter and bomber groups and squadrons. A stronger tie, whether we were on flying status or ground duty, was the B-24 Liberator, which served so many so well. Another less tangible but continuing tie is our mutual love and respect for the English people among whom our air bases were located in Norfolk.

The comradeship of those days will never be forgotten, nor will the pride that we shared in helping to bring the war to a successful conclusion. It is our continuing concern for each other that built this Association into what it is today—a vehicle that arranges for communication between comrades and places and times for fellowship at our annual conventions and regional reunions.

Another continuing tie is the 2nd Air Division's Memorial Room in Norwich Central Library. The concept and initial contributions to the Memorial were provided by personnel still on active duty in England at the end of the war. The Memorial was dedicated and began serving the public in 1963.

Thereafter, contributions by members of this Association added substantially to the funds of the Trust supporting it. More recently the American Librarian Fund was inaugurated to provide for an American librarian at the memorial.

Additionally, we are prepared to support and participate in the development of memorial centers in this country including the 8th Air Force Heritage Center now under way near Savannah, GA. This facility will include a depository for our memorabilia and historical records for use by future generations.

Finally, we have a continuing and ongoing tie among us, the veterans, and the Heritage League memberships now consisting of our spouses, children, grandchildren and other family members. This organization has the potential to perpetuate the memory of our comrades killed in action and the part the rest of us filled in bringing World War II to a successful conclusion.

Perhaps this book, principally composed of biographical sketches of our members and detailed histories of the units in which we served, will be another reminder of our comradeship and concern one for the other.

John B. Conrad

John B. Conrad
President

Brigadier General Milton W. Arnold, U.S.A.F. Retired

The surviving members of the 2nd Air Division, who probably number 25,000 today, are carrying with them the satisfaction and the pride that they were a major part of the greatest air force of all times. The 2nd Air Division, at its peak strength, totaled over 44,000 people. During the period 1942 through 1945, more than 60,000 served. In 1944, when there was a shortage of manpower in the ground forces after the invasion in Europe, the 2nd Air Division furnished over 8,000 troops to the ground forces. In spite of this reduction of one third of the 2nd Air Division troops to the ground forces, the demand was for a greater number of daily bomber and fighter sorties, which demand was efficiently accomplished. In late 1944 and 1945, bombing was the most accurate and our fighters took control of the air over western Europe.

There were scores of heroes almost daily. The aerial gunners, who flew missions in 1943 without adequate protection, were exposed to temperatures as low as minus 60 degrees Fahrenheit. For several months the Division suffered greater losses from frostbite than from enemy action. At the same time, the unsung heroes were the ground crews who performed repair and routine maintenance in a superior manner, most of which was accomplished on uncovered and unheated hardstands with little sleep and practically no rest. Over 6,600 from all walks of life gave their lives as members of the division, that the rest of us Americans and hopefully the world would live in peace. It was a great experience and it is a privilege to have served with you, young Americans, who grew up as mature men and women while members of the 2nd Air Division, 8th Air Force USAAF, and my thoughts salute you for your unselfish service to our country.

"Delectable Doris" and crew make final preparations.

Dave Turner, President - Turner Publishing Company

It is a great honor for me, as an Air Force veteran and publisher, to have been a part of preserving the history of the 8th Air Force and specifically the 2nd Air Division, USAAF, 1942-1945. It was in Savannah, Georgia at the 50th Anniversary of the 8th Air Force that I had the privilege of being introduced to Mr. Richard M. Kennedy, Past President of the Second Air Division Association. As a result of that encounter, this book commemorating and preserving the history of the 2nd Air Division, is now a reality.

The 2nd Air Division history covers the era of World War II which was crucial to the freedom that was imminently threatened by Nazi Germany. The striking photographs help document that history. Most of them were supplied by 2nd Air Division veterans. Likewise, recorded in these pages are the "Special Stories." These are first hand accounts written by the veterans who were there, telling in their own words their description of the fears, tears, and triumphs of the battle of the skies in Europe and Africa. Also enclosed is the Roll of Honor which lists the fallen comrades of the 2nd Air Division. This book is a memorial to those who gave the ultimate sacrifice in the cause of freedom. Finally, between the covers of this volume are nearly 1,900 personal biographies and photographs of 2nd Air Division veterans. Indeed, their legacy is given in these pages to be remembered as those who have fought so gallantly and survived.

My personal thanks is extended to Mr. John B. Conrad, President of the Second Air Division Association, and to the editorial review board of Mr. C. N. "Bud" Chamberlain, Chairman; Mr. Charles Freudenthal; Mr. Gene Hartley; and Mr. Jordan Uttal. It has been a distinction to work together with these gentlemen. I want to thank every Association member who chose to contribute to the history in this book. I also wish to commend Mr. Robert J. Martin, Chief Editor at Turner Publishing Company, for an excellent job in coordinating such a large project as this book turned out to be. To all the veterans of the 2nd Air Division and to their families, I give my sincerest gratitude for your service to keep America strong and free. God bless you.

In kind regards,

Dave Turner
President

"Little Friends" pilots discuss route and strategy.

13

Witchcraft dropping 1000 pound bombs on Berlin mission.
(Courtesy of Vince Re)

General History

The 2nd Air Division, USAAF, 1942-1945

by Raymond E. Strong and Jordan R. Uttal

The 2nd Air Division was activated at Detrick Field, Maryland, as the 2nd Bombardment Wing on June 7, 1942, under the command of Brig. Gen. James P. Hodges. It was redesignated as the 2nd Bombardment Division on September 13, 1943, and further redesignated as the 2nd Air Division on January 1, 1945.

After a short period of training at Detrick Field, a cadre of the Headquarters and Headquarters Squadron of the 2nd Bombardment Wing (2BW) moved to Fort Dix, New Jersey, and then to the Port of Embarkation for transport on the *Queen Elizabeth* to England.

Their first station as of September 7, 1942, was at Old Catton, near Norwich, Norfolk, the major city of East Anglia. Very soon thereafter, headquarters moved to Horsham St. Faith, a permanent Royal Air Force Base with very desirable operating and living quarters. More than a year later, in December 1943, Headquarters moved again to Ketteringham Hall, a private estate six miles south of Norwich. It became the scene of the division's greatest growth and success.

Indeed, from a few small acorns grew a mighty oak! In September 1942 the 2nd Bomb Wing had assigned to it the newly arrived 44th Bomb Group, and three months later the 93rd Bomb Group. The latter also had arrived in September, was originally assigned to the 1st Bomb Wing, but reassigned to the 2nd Bomb Wing in December.

The Second Bomb Wing combat operations commenced with the first mission flown by the 44th on November 7, 1942, followed by 35 more missions up to June 1943. The 93rd, on the other hand, flew its first mission on October 9, 1942 (1st Bomb Wing). This was the first mission flown by USAAF Liberators from an English base, and indeed the first mission on which 100 American heavy bombers took part.

Following a series of attacks on submarine pens along the French coast, and anti-submarine patrols over the Bay of Biscay, came the reassignment of the 93rd to the 2nd Bomb Wing. However, only one squadron stayed in England while the other three were loaned to the 9th Air Force in North Africa. They returned to the 2nd Bomb Wing in February 1943.

From this small start, the 2nd Air Division developed into an extremely powerful strike force, dropping bombs on enemy installations in all parts of Europe, from Norway in the north to the shores of the Mediterranean in the south, and from Poland and Rumania in the east to the shores of the Atlantic in the west.

The third B-24 Group, the 389th, came into the 2nd Bomb Wing in late June 1943. The fourth, the 392nd, arrived in August. From November 1943 through April 1944, 10 more bomb groups were added, raising the total to 14. They were the 445th, 446th, 448th, 453rd, 458th, 466th, 467th, 489th, 491st and

Taxiing around perimeter to runway to take off for a mission at Shipham. These are the first planes to be used by the 44th BG at Shipdham. (Courtesy of Howard Landers)

August 1, 1943, low level raid on the Ploesti (Rumania) oil fields. (Courtesy of Joseph Taddonio, Jr., 93rd)

492nd. Further, as of September 15, 1944, five fighter groups from the 8th Fighter Command were also assigned to the division for operational control.

At the time of its total growth, the maximum total strength of the 2nd Air Division was close to 9,000 officers and 45,000 enlisted personnel. However, due to rotation of crews and replacement of casualties, the total number of military personnel of all categories passing through the division is estimated as close to 150,000 during its history in World War II.

No sooner had the 389th arrived, late in June 1943, than it, and the two veteran 2nd Bomb Wing groups, the 44th and 93rd, went off to North Africa to join with two other B-24 groups, the 98th and 378th of the 9th Air Force, to prepare for and execute the August 1, 1943, low level raid on the Ploesti (Rumania) oil fields. As has been stated many times in World War II histories, that mission stands out as a unique example of heroism and sacrifice on the part of all participants. Indeed, five Medals of Honor were awarded for this mission, four of them were to 2nd Bomb Wing personnel, Col. Leon W. Johnson, 44th; Lt. Col. Addison E. Baker and Maj. John L. Jerstad, 93rd; and 2nd Lt. Lloyd H. Hughes, 389th. The awards to Baker, Jerstad and Hughes were posthumous.

Eighth Air Force plans for the growth of all three of its divisions were proceeding at a rapid pace. To prepare for the arrival, housing, administration, training, and operational control of the 11 more bomb groups, the personnel of 2nd Bomb Wing Headquarters were augmented by the arrival of 14th Bomb Wing Headquarters from the United States in early June. Each section of headquarters welcomed the arrival of the badly needed newcomers.

In late June a contingent of approximately 60 WACs arrived. These young ladies were all volunteers, eager to make their contribution. Indeed they did, serving throughout the headquarters with distinction. Their numbers were increased within a year to 150.

These additions, and subsequent 1944 and 1945 arrivals, raised the headquarters strength to nearly 250 officers and 900 enlisted personnel.

After the three groups of the 2nd Bomb Wing returned from North Africa, where they had participated in many more attacks against the enemy, they were joined by the 392nd Bomb Group which flew its first mission on September 9, 1943. Three November arrivals, the 445th, 446th, and 448th flew their first missions on December 13, 16, and 22 respectively. To conclude 1943, in late December, along came the 453rd (first mission February 5, 1944). The air over East Anglia grew thicker with the sight and sounds of the redoubtable Liberators.

January 1944 saw the arrival of the 458th (first mission February 24) which was followed by two groups in March, the 466th and 467th (first missions, March 22 and April 10). The 492nd Bomb Group arrived in April (first mission May 11), and the final two arrived in May, the 489th and 491st (first missions May 30 and June 2 respectively).

As noted above the 2nd Bomb Wing was redesignated as the 2nd Bombardment Division (2BD) in September 1943. Air operations continued against the enemy all through the period of massive growth in strength and destructive power. Indeed, the division was a major contributor to the overall strategic bombing campaigns established by Allied Command against transportation networks, weapon component manufacturing centers, oil supply lines, airfields and other types of targets.

Each group, in addition to its four bomb squadrons, had its own Headquarters Squadron and all the necessary support units, i.e. service groups, sub-depot groups, station complement squadrons, quartermaster companies, military police companies, engineer fire fighter platoons, finance, chemical, and ordnance companies, medical dispensaries and so on. All personnel at each station, air crew and ground support personnel, bomb squadron or attached service section took pride in their identification with their respective bomb groups. And so they should have!

As the 2nd Bombardment Division grew, a restructuring into combat bomb wings (CBWs) took place from September 1943 through January 1944 as follows:

2nd Combat Bomb Wing was comprised of the 389th, 445th, and 453rd Bomb Groups with Headquarters at Hethel under the command of Brig. Gen. Milton W. Arnold.

14th Combat Bomb Wing was comprised of the 44th, 392nd, and 492nd Bomb Groups with Headquarters at Shipdham under the command of Brig. Gen. Leon W. Johnson.

20th Combat Bomb Wing was comprised of the 93rd, 446th, and 448th Bomb Groups, with Headquarters under the command of Brig. Gen. Jack Wood, succeeded by Brig. Gen. Ted Timberlake.

96th Combat Bomb Wing was comprised of the 458th, 466th, and 467th Bomb Groups with Headquarters at Horsham St. Faith, under the command of Brig. Gen. Walter R. Peck.

95th Combat Bomb Wing was comprised of the 489th and 491st Bomb Groups with Headquarters at Halesworth and was under the command of Brig. Gen. Frederick R. Dent Jr., succeeded by Col. Irvine A. Rendle. However, this combat bomb wing was deactivated in August 1944 with the 489th reassigned to the 20th Combat Bomb Wing, and the 491st to the 14th Combat Bomb Wing, from which the 492nd was withdrawn.

The 2nd Bombardment Wing and 2nd Bombardment Division were continuously under the command of Brig. Gen. (later Maj. Gen.) James P. Hodges from its activation in 1942 until August 1944 when command was assumed by Maj. Gen. William E. Kepner.

On September 15, 1944, the 65th Fighter Wing which was comprised of the 4th, 56th, 355th, 361st, and 479th Fighter Groups, all formerly under the direction of 8th Fighter Command, was transferred to the operational control of the 2nd Bombardment Division. The fighter groups, since their arrivals in the theater over the period from October 1942 through May 1944, had been serving with valor, distinction and sacrifice as support for the heavy bomb groups of all three divisions. The term "little friends" does not do justice to the role they played in protecting, to the best of their ability, the crews of the bomber groups for whom they were always a welcome sight. In fact, in addition to those vital duties, they caused considerable havoc with raids on airfields and other tactical targets.

And so grew the 2nd Air Division, from two groups in December 1942 to three as of June 1943, to eight as of December 1943, and to 14 as of June 1944. In the last half of 1944 the number of bomb groups was reduced to 12 due to the redeployment back home of the 489th for B-29 training, and the deactivation of the 492nd due to probably the heaviest losses in a three month period that any group in the theater sustained. However, in that same time frame, the 65th Fighter Wing was added; and with that composition, 12 bomb groups and five fighter groups, the 2nd Air Division carried on its responsibilities with distinction through the end of hostilities in the ETO.

It is a matter of great pride to the personnel of the 2nd Air Division that in spite of the far greater attention and publicity given to its companions in arms of the 1st and 3rd Divisions (B-17 Fortresses), the B-24 Liberator Groups of the 8th Air Force, on their almost 95,000 sorties flown, represented a force of almost 1,000,000 men (10 men per sortie) striking at the enemy. The almost 200,000 tons of bombs dropped on enemy targets by 2nd Air Division groups wrought intense misery on the enemy.

Most important, relative to the most significant operational measurement factor, bombing accuracy, after leading the 1st and 3rd Divisions in the last quarter of 1943 and trailing them during all of 1944, the 2nd Air Division led the 8th Air Force in three of the last four months of operations. Actually, in the last month, April 1944, the 2nd Air Division's bombing accuracy reached its all time high with 58% of its bombs striking within 1,000 feet and 79% within 2,000 feet of the aim point.

This was a tribute to the incessant efforts of Generals, Hodges and Kepner, the combat wing commanders, the group commanders, and of course, the air crews, to concentrate on bombing accuracy. Their efforts were successful because of the teamwork of all concerned with operations. They, in turn were backed up by tens of thousands of ground support personnel. This is described in the 2nd Air Division Statistical Summary of Operations, passed on by Gen. Kepner to 8th Air Force Headquarters in May 1945 as follows:

"It is obvious that the ground crews worked valiantly to service the 94,441 sorties. The low mechanical and equipment noneffective rate is testimony to the quality of that service. The ordnance, chemical and armament crews who loaded more than 200,000 tons of bombs, the intelligence briefing and interrogations of more than 400 missions, the communications personnel, the clerks, the cooks, the drivers, the quartermaster activities, weather, and medical service, all merged into a team that made the 2nd Air Division one of the most potent and effective fighting forces in the world. But, the striking power of this force rests primarily with the combat crews whose deeds of heroism, devotion to duty and skilled airmanship were legion. To the officers and men of the combat crews who flew the Liberators, Mustangs and Thunderbolts we dedicate this 'story in figures' to their achievements."

The division attacked 1,049 separate targets, 605 by more than one squadron and 444 by one squadron or less. There were two targets in France that were attacked 28 times, and six in Germany that were attacked 63 times. The pride of accomplishment and achievement grew stronger with each passing month in all the men and women of the division.

However, there was an ever present realiza-

Louis Morris, Howard Landers and Ralph Stine preparing to supply bombs for a mission of the 44th Bomb group. This was a bomb storage area at Shipdham. (Courtesy of Howard D. Landers)

Second Bombardment Division Commanders. **Seated, L to R:** *B/Gen. Jack W. Wood, 20th CBW; B/Gen. Leon W. Johnson, 14th CBW; B/Gen. Walter R. Peck 96th CBW; M/Gen. William E. Kepner, 2nd BD; B/Gen. E.J. Timberlake, 20th CBW; B/Gen. Jesse Auton, 65th FW; B/Gen. Milton W. Arnold, 2nd CBW.* **First row, standing:** *Col. Lorin L. Johnson, 392nd; Col. Eugene H. Snavely, 44th BG; Col. E.W. Napier, 489th BG, Col. Fred H. Miller, 491st BG; Col. Leland G. Fiegel, 93rd BG; Col. Gerry Mason, 448th BG; L/C Roy B. Caviness, 361st FG; L/C Everett W. Stewart, 355th FG; L/C C.H. Kinnard, 4th FG.* **Back row:** *Col. James H. Isbell, 458th BG; Col. Albert G. Shower, 467th BG; Col. Luther J. Fairbanks, 466th BG; Col. Laurence M. Thomas, 453rd BG; Col. Ramsay D. Potts, 389th BG; Col. W.W. Jones, 445th BG; missing from picture, 56th FB, 446th BG.*

tion of the horrendous cost in human life that accompanied the taste of victory. Each dangerous take off from the bases in England, through the problems of bad weather and crowded air space, the strong enemy flak and fighter attacks, the ever present danger of mid-air collision, and the sometimes unsuccessful efforts to return to bases in damaged aircraft, resulted in the deaths of almost 6,700 brave young men of the bombardment and fighter groups of the 2nd Air Division. Each of them was mourned from 1942 through 1945, and they are remembered to this day in 1994, and will be for all time.

The story of the 2nd Air Division would not be complete without mentioning its Memorial, unique in U.S. military history. Its story is told elsewhere, but it should be known that in the 2nd Air Division Memorial Room, located in the Norwich Central Library there exists a 2nd Air Division Roll of Honor, beautifully inscribed by talented calligraphers, in which the names of the 6,674 are recorded with respect and affection. They represent a major foundation of the history of the 2nd Air Division USAAF.

The division headquarters evolved, from its activation as a small group of officers and enlisted personnel (most only recently having come into the Army, and only a very few with any prior service) into a large, complex, but highly professional team working to assist the combat bomb wings, groups, and squadrons prepare the combat crews for their very dangerous missions. Many of those who were a part of this team have commented in recent years on the caliber, the dedication and the determination of their colleagues. They treasure the fact that they have remained lifetime friends.

The addition of casuals, from time to time, and particularly the addition to headquarters' staff of some of the best and most talented individuals from the groups who had completed their combat missions, and had a very special understanding of the problems of the combat crews, all contributed significantly to the high quality of this team. Many division headquarters' personnel believe that the experience they gained from working within this great organization was of enormous value to them as they returned to civilian careers or if they remained in the military.

The story of the 2nd Air Division USAAF (World War II) has not and will not be forgotten. For the veterans there will always be the feeling of pride in having served their country well in a just cause. They, and the fallen comrades, will be remembered through the 2nd Air Division Memorial Room, the Memorial Trust of the 2nd Air Division USAAF, and the ongoing efforts of the 2nd Air Division Association and its Heritage League Auxiliary here, and the "Friends of the 2nd Air Division Memorial" in East Anglia.

Editorial Note: *Messrs. Strong and Uttal served at division headquarters, 32 months and 27 months respectively. Ray Strong was assistant adjutant general, and Jordan Uttal was division photo officer and statistical control officer. Both served two terms as president of the 2nd Air Division Association of which they and several others were co-founders.*

THE SECOND AIR DIVISION ASSOCIATION

Born 1948...Still Thriving 1994

Jordan R. Uttal

When the thousands of 2nd Air Division personnel returned to the United States in 1945 from their World War II service in England, it is highly

The bombed out skeletons of Hamburg, Germany. Note church by lake, untouched, in the center of devastation. Photo taken by Lt. Roger Hicks in June 1945. (Courtesy of Roger Hicks)

2ADA Officers, Executive Committee, Group Vice Presidents and Committee Chairmen. Hilton Head, November 1993. Bottom row, L to R: Bill Nothstein (Treasurer 466th); Bill Beasley (V.P. 492nd); Rick Rokicki (V.P. 458th); Marvin Speidel (V.P. 446th); Dave Patterson (Secretary 445th); Hap Chandler (V.P. 491st); Bud Chamberlain (489th Chmn. Oversight Comm.). Seated: Fred Thomas (392nd Chmn. Nominating); Bill Robertie (44th Editor Journal); Ralph Elliot (V.P. 467th); Oak Mackey (V.P. 392nd); John Conrad (President 392nd); Evelyn Cohen (Hqs. V.P. Membership); Norma Beasley (Asst. to Editor 44th); Hazel Robertie, Ray Pytel (V.P. 445th). 3rd row: Cater Lee (V.P. 448th); Dick Kennedy (448th Liason 8th Heritage Ctr.); Floyd Mabee (93rd Outgoing Exec. V.P.); Ray Strong (Hqs. V.P.); Neal Sorensen (V.P. 489th); Wib Clingan (V.P. 453rd); Bud Koorndyk (2AD Rep. to Governors); Jordan Uttal (Honorary President). Back row: Geoff Gregory (467th Chmn. Awards); Paul Steichen (V.P. 93rd); Jim Reeves (Hqs. Chmn. Planning); Gene Hartley (V.P. 389th); Chuck Walker (445th Exec. V.P.); Earl Wassom (V.P. 466th). Note: Ten of the above, Rokicki, Patterson, Chamberlain, Thomas, Robertie, Kennedy, Strong, Koorndyk, Uttal and Reeves are Past Presidents.

doubtful that there was much, if any, thought given to anything but getting on with their lives. At the same time, there is no doubt that many felt that, sooner or later, they would establish contact with their crew mates and other close friends made during service days. But a spark was lit in 1946 and the fire caught. It burned slowly at first, but as this is being written in late 1993, it is still growing.

As it happened in August 1946, seven 2nd Air Division Headquarters veterans (some of them with prior group experience) came together for a party in Chicago. They had such a good time that they

decided to try to reach as many more as they could for a 2nd Air Division convention/reunion. All they had to work with was a Division Headquarters officer roster, and from that alone, the first convention was held, in Chicago, on the weekend of Oct. 1, 1948.

Former 2nd Air Division colleagues came from coast to coast and border to border. This convinced the group that they were on the right track and a second attempt was made in 1949, again in Chicago. It was a happy accident that while the troops were gathering it was learned that the WAC contingent was also meeting. They were asked to join, and it is widely acknowledged that the 2nd Air Division Association has benefitted greatly from the continuing participation of these ladies who became loyal members and tireless workers. Indeed, for decades, Evelyn Cohen has served as membership vice president and convention chair. Several others have served as association pilot officers and committee personnel. The attendees at the 1989 convention will long remember the beautiful quilt, hand made, and raffled off by the WAC ladies for the benefit of the American Librarian Fund.

At the 1948 convention it was decided to create bylaws establishing the 2nd Air Division Association as a non-profit veterans organization chartered in Illinois. The original objectives were to perpetuate the friendships made during 2nd Air Division service in the ETO in World War II and to advocate an effective military establishment. It was the feeling, originally, that the memorial to which we had subscribed was in competent hands. And so it was, and always has been. It wasn't until 1952 that it was learned that our help was needed. From that time on the most important objective became supporting, in every way possible, the dedicated and devoted efforts of the Board of Governors of the Memorial Trust of the 2nd Air Division USAAF in Norwich.

To each of the British friends in England who have served on the board and to everyone at the library who has maintained the Memorial Room, unending gratitude is owed. Those 2nd Air Division Association members who have visited the Memorial know what a splendid achievement it represents.

In June 1963, the association convention was held in Norwich for the dedication of the memorial. What a memorable ceremony it was! Those who were fortunate enough to attend it, and any of the subsequent Norwich conventions in 1972, 1975, 1979, 1983, 1987, and 1990 have become even more convinced of the importance of the association's primary mission, the support of this memorial to the 6,674 division personnel who gave their lives, and indeed to all who served.

Over the years, and particularly since the early 1970s, donations from 2nd Air Division Association members of money and books and permanent endowments have enabled the Board of Governors to expand the use and purpose of the memorial to the point where it truly is a "living memorial," such as no other sponsored by any American military unit. It is a "window on America" as it was originally intended to be, a memorial originally funded by 2nd Air Division personnel, supported almost exclusively by former 2nd Air Division personnel and administered by friends who have served as governors, the Norwich Central Library staff, and the Norfolk County Council.

Going back to the beginning, the 2nd Air Division Association charter made eligible for membership anyone who served with 2nd Air Division Headquarters and with any of the units of the 2nd Air Division in England in World War II. This included the 14 bomber groups and the five fighter groups, all assigned and attached support units, enlisted and officer personnel and the Red Cross. From the very beginning, continuing efforts were made to reach personnel from all the units.

It is a matter of pride that the membership has grown from about 100 in 1948 to our present 8,000 (1993). Further, twice a month, the membership vice president submits a "new member" report. The September 1993 report shows the addition of 37 new members against the regrettable loss of 10 old comrades. The group vice presidents have played a prominent role over the years in achieving this remarkable growth in membership.

So the start in Chicago in 1948, with a nucleus of headquarters personnel, has expanded to all units of the division. Indeed the success of the 2nd Air Division Association has served as an example to and a stimulus for many other Air Force veterans organizations.

The association has had 46 conventions throughout the United States and England. Ten of them were held in Chicago; seven in Norwich; five in Washington, D.C.; four in Pennsylvania; three in Ohio; two each in New York City, California, Colorado and South Carolina; and one each in Massachusetts, Michigan, New Jersey, Nevada, North Carolina, Tennessee, Texas, Virginia and Wisconsin. Missouri is scheduled for 1994.

All seven of the conventions in Norwich have been heart warming demonstrations of the wonderful friendship that has endured between the people of East Anglia and those who served there and who were privileged to partake of the hospitality and affection extended so sincerely.

Every successful organization in any field requires competent and dedicated leadership. The 2nd Air Division Association has had 37 individuals who have served as president these past 46 years. It is sad indeed that eight of them have passed away. Those who knew them (Bill Brooks, Dick Clough, John Cunningham, Ken Darney, John Karoly, Howard Moore, Chappie Seward and Percy Young) remember them fondly.

These leaders have represented many different job assignments during service in England. Twelve of them were pilots, five of them radio operator/gunner/engineers, a division bombardier, group bombardier, two group navigators, division chaplain, and various ground assignments. They

492nd BG Crew: Top photo - Standing, L to R: Murrell E. Hollopeter, Bombardier; Oliver W. Chapman, Navigator; Donald L. Taylor, Pilot; Wallace R. Hunt, Copilot. Kneeling, L to R: Wayne M. Fisher, Ball Turret; James P. McCrory, Radio; Sygmunt B. Jarosz, Engineer; Jake P. Suddath, Tail Gunner; John A. Evans, Waist Gunner; Edward Samuel, Top Turret. Photo taken in 1944. Bottom photo - Men in same position as above photo, taken in 1983. (Courtesy of James P. McCrory)

have ranged in rank from corporal to major general, and served with 12 of our bomb groups and headquarters.

Always backing them up, there have been association officers, group vice presidents, and an ever changing executive committee. Also, since 1972, the association has been represented on the Board of Governors of the Memorial Trust. Regardless of what these leaders did during the war, or what their military rank may have been, each of them has served all of the 2nd Air Division Association members, keeping the association zeroed in on its objectives, keeping the flame burning, keeping the memories alive and remembering the fallen.

Most recently the association leadership has exerted strong efforts and accomplished the "last mission," to further perpetuate the objectives by raising funds to provide an American librarian to serve the 2nd Air Division Memorial under the direction of the Board of Governors. In addition, the 2nd Air Division Association encourages assistance to the Memorial Trust by the Heritage League, on this side, and the Friends of the 2nd Air Division Memorial, in East Anglia.

The growth and the achievements of the 2nd Air Division Association represent an enduring expression of respect, friendship and affection for each other, and particularly for the almost 6,700 brave young men who did not return to their loved ones.

THE UNIQUE 2ND AIR DIVISION MEMORIAL

by Jordan R. Uttal, Division Headquarters

Scattered throughout England there are memorials of various kinds at 61 of the 122 base areas used during World War II by the 8th Air Force. They consist of memorial plaques made of stone, brick, metal and concrete. There are obelisks, benches, village signs, church signs, church windows and statues. All are appropriately, solemnly and justifiably dedicated to the men of a particular group who gave their lives during the war.

Indeed, there are others on the continent, in different theaters and here in the United States, similarly raised in testimony to the service and sacrifices of Americans in all branches of the service.

Unique among them all is the living memorial, the 2nd Air Division Memorial Room located in Norwich, in the Norwich Central Library.

A splendid description of this achievement was given in 1988 by the Cultural Attache at the American Embassy in London. Dr. Ronald Clifton, a career diplomat, was, from 1987 to 1991, a member of the Board of Governors of the Memorial Trust of the 2nd Air Division USAAF. Writing of his prior foreign service, he stated that he had visited many other American memorials abroad which did not offer the tangible dimension, the real touch or the reminder that the books and displays of the 2nd Air Division Memorial do. He concluded, "For 20 years now I have worked abroad with American libraries as part of our public diplomacy. None have served the United States better than the 2nd Air Division Memorial in Norwich."

How did all this come about? The idea for the creation of a memorial to the over 6,600 men of the 2nd Air Division killed in combat related duty was conceived by three senior officers of the division, Col. Fred Bryan (Headquarters 2nd Air Division), Brig. Gen. Milton W. Arnold (C.G. 2nd Combat Bomb Wing) and Lt. Col. Ion Walker (467th Bomb Group). The concept was heartily endorsed by the Division Commanding General, Maj. Gen. William E. Kepner. An appeal for funds to all division personnel just after V-E day raised the amazing sum of 20,916 pounds sterling within three weeks.

In June 1945, the Memorial Trust of the 2nd Air Division USAAF was created under British law, to be supervised for all time, by the British Charity Commission. The monies were handed over to this trust with the assurance that the Charity Commission would see to it that as long as there was income, there would be materials purchased for the memorial. Eighteen years later, the Norwich Central Library was finally completed, and the 2nd Air Division Memorial Room was opened and dedicated on June 13, 1963.

It contained the Roll of Honor and a collection of books covering every facet of American life. Outside the Memorial Room, a Memorial Fountain was built, containing the 8th Air Force insignia, and stones from each of the 50 States. At the outset, no plans were made for the future funding of the Memorial Capital Trust Fund, the income from which was to provide for the desired perpetuity of this tribute to the service and sacrifices of 2nd Air Division personnel. However in 1948, the 2nd Air Division Association was formed, and since the early 1970s its members have contributed generously.

The Board of Governors is comprised of 13 members, two of whom, according to the 1945 Declaration of Trust, are to be appointees of the Ameri-

Memorial Room. (Courtesy of Jordan R. Uttal)

2nd Air Division Memorial Room located in Norwich, England.(Courtesy of Jordan R. Uttal)

Memorial Fountain outside the Memorial Room. (Courtesy of Jordan R. Uttal)

FOUNDING MEMBERS OF
2ND AIR DIVISION ASSOCIATION 1946/48

Henry Brandt	93rd/Headquarters
Henry X. Dietch	Headquarters
Clem Kowalczyk	446th/Headquarters
Jim LaPonsie	Headquarters
Howard Moore	Headquarters
Raymond Strong	Headquarters
Jordan R. Uttal	Headquarters
Percy C. Young	Headquarters

PRESIDENTS OF 2ND AIR DIVISION ASSOCIATION

Year	Name	2nd Air Division Unit
1948	Howard W. Moore	Headquarters
1949	Father Edward Seward	Headquarters
1950	John Cunningham	Headquarters
1951	Raymond E. Strong	Headquarters
1952	Raymond E. Strong	Headquarters
1953	Jordan R. Uttal	Headquarters
1954	Percy C. Young	Headquarters
1955	Fen Marsh	Headquarters
1956	Stephen Posner	445th
1957	Richard Clough	389th
1958	Stephen Posner	445th
1959	Percy C. Young	Headquarters
1960	Dean Moyer	Headquarters
1961	John Karoly	Headquarters
1962	Charles Stine	445th
1963	Jordan R. Uttal	Headquarters
1964/65	Warren Alberts	Headquarters/93rd
1965/66	Warren Alberts	Headquarters/93rd
1966/67	Charles Merrill	93rd
1967/68	John Jacobowitz	466th
1968/69	John Jacobowitz	466th
1969/70	Paul Trissel	389th
1970/71	Ken Darney	467th
1971/72	Joseph Whittaker	Headquarters/392nd
1972/73	William Robertie	44th
1973/74	William Robertie	44th
1974/75	William Brooks	466th
1975/76	Goodman Griffin	44th
1976/77	Earl Zimmerman	389th
1977/78	J.T. Long	392nd
1978/79	E.A. Rokicki	458th
1979/80	H.C. Henry	44th
1980/81	David G. Patterson	445th
1981/82	Vincent La Russa	467th
1982/83	Andrew Low	453rd
1983/84	Charles Freudenthal	489th
1984/85	J. Fred Thomas	392nd
1985/86	E. Bud Koorndyk	389th
1986/87	James H. Reeves	Headquarters
1987/88	Carl Alexanderson	491st
1988/89	C.N. Chamberlain	489th
1989/90	Francis Di Mola	445th
1990/91	Richard M. Kennedy	448th
1991/92	Richard M. Kennedy	448th
1992/93	John B. Conrad	392nd
1993/94	John B. Conrad	392nd
1994/95	Charles L. Walker	445th

can Ambassador. In addition, since 1972 the 2nd Air Division Association has had a representative serving on the board. The governors, in close cooperation with the Norfolk County Council continue to administer the memorial. Day to day work has been provided by the Central Library staff, and since 1985, by a temporary American librarian (1985), a Fulbright scholar librarian (1986-1988); a library aide, Tony North (1986-1991); an American archivist, Dr. Martin Levitt, PhD. (1991-1992) and by the current trust American librarian, Phyllis Dubois, along with two part-time American aides.

Through the years, since the opening in 1963, the memorial has benefitted greatly from the devoted efforts of British librarians Philip Hepworth, Joan Benns Smith, Colin Sleath and their county librarian colleagues. Currently, Hilary Hammond, director of arts and libraries for Norfolk County, is proving of tremendous assistance to the efforts of the governors and the trust librarian.

In the years since 1963, the objectives of the memorial have broadened to take account of newer library practices, i.e., the provision of audio and video cassettes and other materials in current use. Also it has developed that the 2nd Air Division Memorial has become the repository of group archives and written memorabilia.

Through the generosity of the 2nd Air Division Association members, and particularly the astute and proficient management of funds by the Board of Governors, the trust capital asset market value, as of April 1993 amounted to close to 400,000 pounds! The trust capital fund is designed to generate income to pay for new books, periodicals, cassettes and other expenses.

Second Air Division Association members have further demonstrated their generosity and dedication to the memory of the 2nd Air Division and all its personnel by helping to raise a sum of $550,000.00 which, in accordance with the 2nd Air Division Association/Fulbright Memorial Library Award Agreement, is invested in the United States. The income from this American Librarian Fund is designed to provide a permanent American presence in the memorial. At present, it is accumulating interest against the day when the Board of Governors and Fulbright agree to start the program for which the fund was created.

Quoting again from Dr. Clifton, he said in 1991 when he left his post in London, "Once again, the veterans of the 2nd Air Division have scored a point, and placed a marker in history. The decision to establish an endowment fund for the Memorial Librarian Award is as far sighted as the creation of the 2nd Air Division Memorial Trust at the end of World War II."

Special recognition must be given to the dedicated service of all of our British friends who have served on the Board of Governors of the trust. Among them in 1993 is one of the original 1945 governors, Mrs. Michael (Anne) Barne, and the present chairman (on the board since 1957 and chairman since 1975) Mr. T.C. Eaton.

Quoting from another source, this time the Norwich *Eastern Evening News* of Monday, June 28, 1993, the 2nd Air Division Memorial is described as "the biggest American Library in Britain. There are others in universities, but we are unique, a point of reference for people all over the country."

To the best of our knowledge there is no other similar living memorial of any unit of U.S. Armed Forces. The 2nd Air Division memorial is truly unique and 2nd Air Division Association members may justifiably be proud of this permanent reminder of the division's existence, its achievements, and the sacrifice of so many wonderful young men.

Unfortunately, the unique 2nd Air Division Memorial and Central Library in which it was housed were essentially destroyed by a tragic fire on August 1, 1994.

THE LIBERATOR
ORIGINS AND EVOLUTION

by Philip A. St. John, PhD

In the beginning of 1939 Gen. Henry Harley "Hap" Arnold, chief of the Army Air Corps, invited the Consolidated Aircraft Company of San Diego, CA (now Convair Division of General Dynamics) to submit a design for a heavy bomber. It was to be superior in carrying capacity and range to the Boeing B-17 which was then the mainstay of the Air Corps' heavy bombers, and had been flying since 1935. Consolidated's chief designer, Isaac M. "Mac" Laddon, and his design team began immediately to lay out the design for a four-engined aircraft (Consolidated's Model 32 - they had already begun to look at this project months before the Air Corps' request) that would have a maximum speed of 300 miles per hour, and cruise at a speed near 280 miles per hour. It was to carry a bomb load (apparently unspecified) over a normal operating range of 3,000 miles at an altitude of 35,000 feet.

The Air Corps' review of Laddon's design and performance data resulted in a contract for a prototype to be built and test flown as soon as possible. The design incorporated several unusual features. The wing was designed by David R. Davis (the now famous "Davis Wing") for its high efficiency. It was longer than the B-17s wing (110 feet versus 103.8 feet), very narrow at its root (14 feet), and with a thick cross-section or camber. This high aspect ratio shape proved to have a very favorable lift to drag ratio. It was relatively flexible compared to the broad root and more rigid wing of the B-17. It was to be mounted in the "shoulder" position, would have Fowler flaps, recesses for the retractable main wheels, and 2400 gallon capacity fuel tanks. The wing area was 1048 square feet, almost 400 square feet less than that of the B-17.

The fuselage of the original design was 63 feet long and was lumbering and boxy in appearance compared to the sleek shape of the B-17. In later models of the B-24 series (G, H, and J) the fuselage would be 7'5" wide at the wing root and 10'5" deep at the bomb bays. Bomb bay doors were unique in that they were of a roller design (not unlike the old roll top desk) which opened and closed by sliding along vertical tracks. Two bomb bays were provided by the design.

The landing gear was of the tricycle type (a first in heavy bombers) with two wing-mounted main wheels and a single nose wheel beneath the cockpit, all retractable. The tail surfaces were designed in a twin fin configuration supported by a horizontal tail surface 26 feet long and 9 feet wide (in later models). On the ground, the twin fins towered to 17'11." Most of these dimensions were somewhat smaller in the prototype B-24; the wing and tail were actually "borrowed" from Consolidated's Model 31 flying boat then under construction. The Model 32 allowed a few hand aimed .30 caliber machine guns for defense.

The prototype airplane, Air Corps type B-24, thundered down the runway on its first 17 minute flight on Dec. 29, 1939. The Air Corps had already placed an order for seven YB-24s for evaluation, and ordered another 38 B-24As. The prototype loaded weight would be up to 47,000 pounds but later models in the long series were to be considerably heavier - 65,000 pounds in the J model - as various types of equipment, dictated by combat demands, were added.

The engines chosen for this airplane, early dubbed the Liberator, were the 14 cylinder, double bank Pratt & Whitney Twin Wasp model R-1830-33 with a peak output of 1200 horsepower at takeoff. They would soon be equipped with an exhaust-driven turbo super-charger of General Electric design to compress the thin air at high altitudes into oxygen starved engines. Several other more advanced models of the R-1830 were to be used in later B-24 models. Buick built many of the engines used in the H and J models. These power plants were tough, reliable, and were easily maintained by experienced ground crews. Many of these engines are still flying today.

France, already falling to the German onslaught, placed the first order for production B-24s in early June, 1940, totaling 120 units, and the British followed with an order of 164. These export aircraft were designated the LB-30. Britain took over this order when all French resistance failed. They were to be delivered during 1941. The first six (designated LB-30A) were actually the Air Corps' YB-24, given up to the British, and were used as transports to bring Canadian and British ferry crews back to Canada. The next 20 aircraft (LB-30Bs) built at San Diego were the first to see combat. Called the Liberator I, they were fitted with four 20 millimeter cannons and quickly proved their worth in Britain's desperate struggle to survive the German submarine menace. (The name "Liberator" seems to have been chosen in a company name contest, but others say it was a British idea.)

The next 139 export models of the LB-30 (the Liberator II) were to go to the Royal Air Force. The Liberator II was an elongated version of the B-24 (the nose was extended three feet). It had a four-gun top turret over the aft bomb bay, a two-gun tail turret, and twin guns at each waist position. All guns were the light .303 caliber weapon. Most of these IIs were assigned to the 120 Squadron of the RAF Coastal Command. The 139 unit order was completed at the end of December, 1941. Some had their armament removed and flew with the Return Ferry Service, British Overseas Airways Corporation, Qantas, and other airlines. Winston Churchill's personal transport, the "Commando," was the second Liberator II manufactured. Four LB-30s were sent to Africa (of 16 scheduled) and saw action against Rommel's tank forces beginning in January 1942. The USAF stopped export of the remaining 12 following entry of the United States into the war.

One YB-24 and eight B-24As were built (of the 38 ordered) and the USAAF took delivery of these through June of 1941. Most of these aircraft were assigned to Ferry Command, forerunner of the Air Transport Command, flying between Canada and the British Isles. One of these pioneered the South Atlantic route to Africa (later to be an essential link between the United States and the Mediterranean Theater of Operations). Two were assigned to reconnaissance of Japanese-held bases in the South Pacific; one arrived at Hickam Field, Honolulu on December 5th and was destroyed on the ground by the Japanese carrier-based attack on Pearl Harbor two days later. Because of its long range, one was chosen to fly the Harriman mission to Moscow in September, 1941.

Following the entry of the United States into World War II, the Army Air Force commandeered 74 undelivered Liberator IIs and assigned them to various bases (Alaska, Hawaii, Panama). Three of

Just one of many 44th Bomb Group B-24s and her crew — "The Lemon Drop" with Sgts. Huff, Ingram, Banta, Hayes and Gavin in the back and 2nd Lt. Haworth, Capt. Phillips, 2nd Lt. Scarlett and lst Lt. LaFleur in front. (Photo courtesy of R.H. Phillips)

B-24 in flight photographed from above. (Photo courtesy of Ray L. Summa)

23

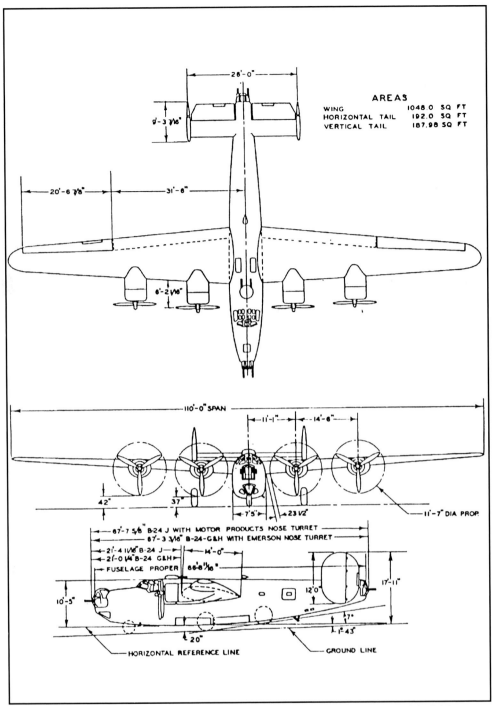

AREAS

WING	1048.0 SQ FT
HORIZONTAL TAIL	192.0 SQ FT
VERTICAL TAIL	187.98 SQ FT

The diagrams and cutaways (above and below) illustrate the specs and arrangement of the B-24.

the Liberator IIs sent to the Far East attacked a Japanese base on Celebes (Kendari, on the southeast coast) on January 17, 1942. This bombing attack - 41 days after the Pearl Harbor massacre - is the first documented attack of Liberators manned by American crews. Japanese fighters damaged two of these, forcing one to ditch and the other to crash land short of its base. The next model in the Liberator series was the XB-24B which had self-sealing fuel tanks, added armor, and - most important - turbo superchargers for the Pratt & Whitneys. This model introduced the oval cowling with its two side oil cooler ducts. Apparently only one experimental model was built. This was followed by the B-24C which was fitted with a Martin top turret mounted just behind the cockpit, a Consolidated-designed tail turret, and a Bendix bottom turret (later discontinued). All turrets mounted twin .50 caliber M-2 machine guns. Only nine of the C models were built, eight being delivered by the end of December 1941.

The C model was followed by the B-24D and with this model, mass production began at Consolidated's San Diego and Fort Worth, Texas, plants. 2,415 Ds were built at San Diego, and 303 at Fort Worth. Douglas Aircraft, a subcontractor, built 10Ds at its Tulsa, Oklahoma plant. These D models underwent various armament modifications, much of it in the field. The first production run had a single hand aimed gun in the nose and single gun firing downward through camera hatch just aft of the bomb bays. Later model Ds added two more nose guns, two waist guns, and eventually a Sperry ball turret replaced the camera hatch gun. All of these were .50 caliber weapons, 10 in all on most B-24Ds. The gross weight at take-off was now over 60,000 pounds.

The first D models to see combat were a flight of 12 Liberators, the so-called HALPRO Force, that bombed the Ploesti, Romania, oil refinery complex on June 12, 1942. This high altitude mission preceded by more than a year the much publicized (and costly) low level attack on Ploesti on August 1, 1943. (More of the HALPRO strike later).

The British took delivery of some D models also, calling them Liberator IIIs or IIIAs depending on the type of equipment. Almost all went to the Coastal Command. The U.S. Navy's B-24Ds were redesignated PB4Y-1s and production models of this aircraft were fitted with the distinctive ball-shaped Erco turret in the nose. In all, 1,450 PB4Y-1s were delivered to the Navy, corresponding to B-24 models D, J, and M.

By this time the 90th "Jolly Roger" Bomb

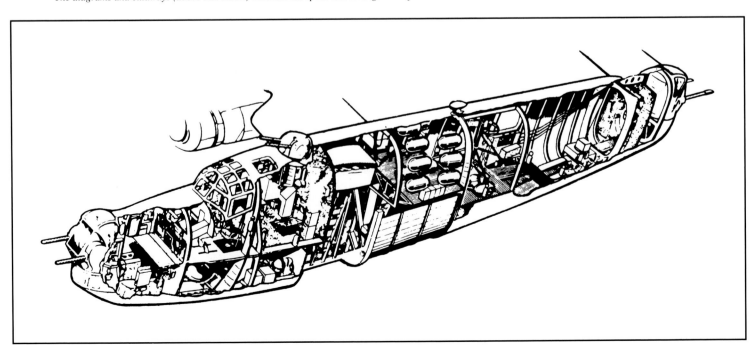

Group of the 5th Air Force in the Southwest Pacific had already experimented with installing a Consolidated tail turret in the nose of its B-24Ds. In later G models and those following, nose turrets would be installed during assembly. Next in the series was the B-24E which had only minor modifications from the D model. At this time only Consolidated and Douglas were fabricating the B-24 series, but with the E model, the Ford Motor Company was licensed as a third manufacturer. Ford, at its gigantic Willow Run plant in Ypsilanti, MI, starting in September of 1942, built 490Es; Consolidated and Douglas built a combined total of 311 more at the Fort Worth and Tulsa plants. One XB-24F was built, a D model, testing new deicing equipment.

A fourth manufacturer now entered into B-24 production: North American Aviation with its plant in Dallas, Texas. Beginning in March, 1943, North American built all 430B-24Gs, the next in the series. The first 25 of these models were slightly modified Es but, beginning in November 1943, the remaining 405 were equipped with the electrically powered Emerson nose turret. These 405 were equivalent to the next model in the series, the Hs, but North American's aircraft were not redesignated.

The B-24H models, of which 738 were built by Consolidated at Fort Worth, were identical to the later G models with the Emerson turret. Ford built 1,780Hs at Willow Run and Douglas built another 582 at its Tulsa facilities.

The next model in the series, the J (there was no "I" model) was built in greater numbers than any other model of B-24s. Almost identical to the H, some J models went to the Navy still designated as the PB4Y-1 some (about 200) to the RAF, and still others were refitted for reconnaissance. The J was the first model to do away with the camouflage paint that characterized all previous production aircraft. The J model alone constituted more than one-third of all the B-24 type airplanes built between 1940 and 1945. Ford built 1,587 Js at Willow Run, Consolidated built 2,792 at San Diego and 1,558 at Fort Worth, North American built 536 at Dallas, and Douglas, 205 at Tulsa. In all, 6,678 B-24Js went into service.

The B-24L was fitted with a lighter more easily operated tail turret but otherwise was nearly identical to the J models. The new turret was some 200 pounds lighter in weight and its arc of fire was increased. 1,250 L models were built by Ford and another 417 turned out by Consolidated's San Diego plant.

Next in the series was the B-24M, nearly identical to the L model with the new tail turret, but with an improved aileron control 'boost' feature which significantly eased the handling of the big Lib in high altitude formation flying, particularly above 20,000 feet. The M models also had designed into its control system a 'formation stick' device that was interfaced with the C-1 autopilot. Although this feature was much more sensitive than the control column, few pilots felt confident enough in it to use it consistently in formation flying. Notwithstanding, pilots who flew the M model report that it was much smoother to handle than any of the previous models. Ford and Consolidated (San Diego) built 2,593 Ms and this was the final mass production run of the long B-24 series.

A single XB-24K was built in 1943. It was a D model whose twin tail was replaced by a single, centered, very tall (26 feet 9 inches) fin and rudder. This modification proved to add stability and inflight control compared to the twin fin configuration, and it was decided to discontinue manufacture of the classic twin fin models in April of 1944. Designated as the B-24N by the Air Force, only eight of these were built when Liberator production ceased in May of 1945. However, the Navy had placed an order for 1,370 single tailed Libera-

Fort Worth Assembly line: San Diego, B-24D-95-CO aircraft on a modification line before the Ft. Worth plant started production. (Photo by Robert Blair, courtesy A.I. Hall)

tors, which it named the Privateer with the designation PB4Y-2. Of these, 736 were delivered by the end of hostilities in August 1945. These aircraft were so markedly different from the classic B-24 design however, the two probably should not be mentioned in the same breath.

To this point we have been following the evolution of the B-24 primarily as a machine designed for combat. But the design was a versatile one and the airplane was to be used and flown in many different configuration to perform a variety of functions.

The C-87 was the Air Force designation for the transport version of the B-24. Known as the Liberator Express, the first C-87s were modified D models and in all, 286 C-87s came off Consolidated's Fort Worth assembly lines. In various configurations, the C-87, with a row of seven low-placed windows on each side of the fuselage and a large cargo door on the left side, was usually flown by a crew of four or five. It could carry up to 20 passengers or be reconfigured with 10 sleeper berths or, as purely a cargo ship, could lift 12,000 pounds of anything that could be fitted through the doors. It was usually flown with no heavy armament and without bomb bay equipment or bomb bay doors. C-87s saw duty in all theaters of war including flying the "Hump" in the China-Burma-India (CBI) Theater of Operations. The Navy's cargo version was the single-tailed Privateer, designated the RY-3.

The C-109 was a bomber-modified tanker with fuselage fuel tanks in the bomb bays. Some 109s saw service in the CBI Theater flying gasoline to supply B-29s based at Chengtu, China. It was not an overly successful operation. Two hundred B-24s were converted to the tanker configuration. One B-24D was modified to carry 14 machine guns and 11,000 rounds of ammunition (normal armament was 10 machine guns and 5,000 rounds in most models). It was designated the XB-41 by the Air Force and was to be flown as a bomber escort. With the arrival of long-range fighter escorts (the P-38, P-47, and P-51) the XB-41 never went into operation.

Another modification of the B-24 allowed its function as a long range reconnaissance plane. These bore the designation F-7 and could be configured with up to 20 cameras. Some of these were modi-

fied J models; 213 F-7 types were made. The AT-22 was a D model modified as a training aircraft for flight engineers, and then as the TB-24 when remodified as a gunnery trainer. Five AT-22s were built. Two additional models in the long B-24 series were built, both as experimental modifications. The XB-24P (there was no "O" model in the series) was modified from a D model to research methods of fire control, and the XB-24Q was a modified L model to research the use of a radar-controlled tail turret. One of each was built.

It is difficult to arrive at a totally accurate figure for the final number of B-24 type aircraft built before and during World War II. There were so many modifications of existing aircraft one can easily be trapped into counting one airplane twice (or more times). If we can add up all the B-24 type aircraft built of all models, A through M and including the Liberators I, II, and III, the C-87s and the Navy's PB4Y-1 (but not the single-tailed Privateer, or the C-109s that were converted Ds and Es), we arrive at a number quite close to 18,500. No other four-engined aircraft built during this period approached this production figure (fewer than 13,000 B-17s were built). In fact, no other American airplane ever built, before, during, or since World War II, military or civilian, of any number of engines, approaches the number of B-24s that went into service. Peak inventories of the Armed Forces' B-24s that could be put up at any one time occurred in the Fall of 1944 when perhaps 7,000 were on hardstands and ready to fly. Almost 1,000 of these were in the Pacific area.

A B-24D ready for combat had a 1942 price tag of $304,391. By 1944, mass production methods (Ford rolled out a B-24E every 55 minutes) had reduced the price to $215,516. If we are allowed to use some intermediate price tag - say, $250,000 each over the five years of production - and use a conservative number of 18,000 manufactured, we come up with a total cost for these B-24s of $4.5 billion. The B-29s that finally finished off Japan's war effort cost $639,000 each, nearly three times the last models built of the B-24. The eight-jet B-52 "Stratofortress" cost $7 million each. That's 32 of the final B-24 models. Whatever accounting gymnastics one chooses to use, the B-24 was worth every penny.

2ᴰ BOMB DIVISION
IDENTIFICATION MARKINGS
C.W.'S   G R O U P S

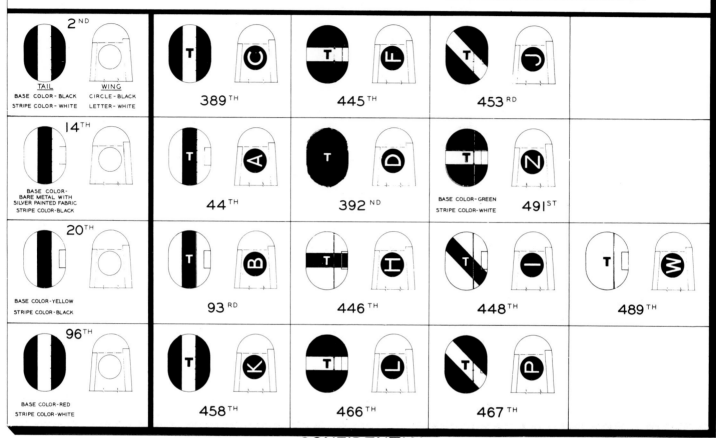

2ND TAIL / WING — BASE COLOR - BLACK, STRIPE COLOR - WHITE, CIRCLE - BLACK, LETTER - WHITE	389ᵀᴴ (T / C)	445ᵀᴴ (T / F)	453ᴿᴰ (T / J)
14ᵀᴴ BASE COLOR - BARE METAL WITH SILVER PAINTED FABRIC, STRIPE COLOR - BLACK	44ᵀᴴ (T / A)	392ᴺᴰ (T / D)	491ˢᵀ BASE COLOR - GREEN, STRIPE COLOR - WHITE (T / N)
20ᵀᴴ BASE COLOR - YELLOW, STRIPE COLOR - BLACK	93ᴿᴰ (T / B)	446ᵀᴴ (T / H)	448ᵀᴴ (T / I) / 489ᵀᴴ (T / W)
96ᵀᴴ BASE COLOR - RED, STRIPE COLOR - WHITE	458ᵀᴴ (T / K)	466ᵀᴴ (T / L)	467ᵀᴴ (T / P)

REPRODUCED BY 942ND ENGR AVN TOPO BN
325TH PWR   US AR

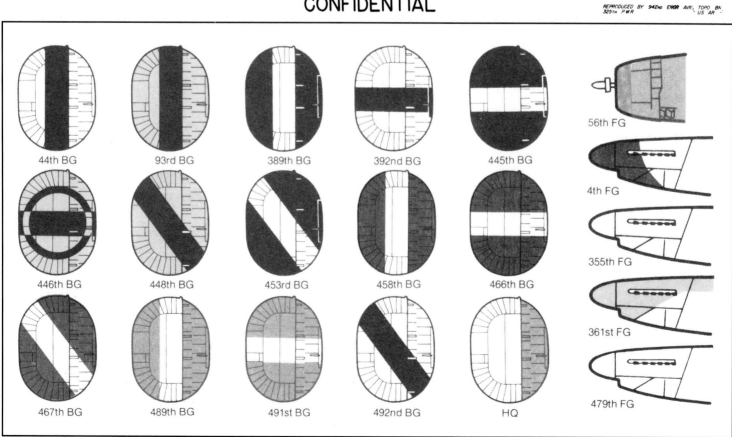

44th BG   93rd BG   389th BG   392nd BG   445th BG   56th FG

446th BG   448th BG   453rd BG   458th BG   466th BG   4th FG

355th FG

361st FG

467th BG   489th BG   491st BG   492nd BG   HQ

479th FG

Prior to August 15, 1944 wing compositions were as follows: **2nd Wing** — 389th BG, 445th BG, 453rd BG; **14th Wing** — 44th BG, 392nd BG, 492nd BG; **20th Wing** — 93rd BG, 446th BG, 448th BG; **95th Wing** — 489th BG, 491st BG; **96th Wing** — 458th BG, 466th Bg, 467th BG.

44TH BOMB GROUP (H)
The Flying Eightballs
by Will Lundy

The 44th Bombardment Group (H) was among the first of what might be termed the "expansion" groups. The 29th Bomb Group from which the 44th was activated was the very first of the new groups activated at Langley Field, Virginia. The 29th came to MacDill Field as soon as it was activated. The 44th Bomb Group is proud of its record as being the oldest of the new groups.

The 44th was organized under S.O. #11 dated January 13, 1941, under paragraph 14 and 15 Tampa, Florida, and was activated on January 15, 1941. Lt. Col. Melvin B. Asp assumed command of this group which included Headquarters and Headquarters Squadron, 66th, 67th, and 68th Squadrons. Original squadron commanding officers were: Maj. Olds, Headquarters and Headquarters Squadron; Capt. Edward J. Timberlake, 66th Bomb Squadron; Maj. George R. Acheson, 67th Bomb Squadron; and Capt. Samford, 68th Bomb Squadron.

On February 10, 1942, the group arrived at Barksdale Field, Louisiana to become an Operational Training Unit. Later in that same month the 44th was split, helping to form the newly activated 98th Bomb Group, and in March sent many more men to that same group. They also helped form the 92nd Bomb Group, and on March 26 helped form the 93rd Bomb Group with 587 personnel.

Popular Lt. Col. Frank H. Robinson assumed command of the 44th Bomb Group, soon to lead us into mortal combat. Further transfers of personnel occurred on May 27 when 656 men helped form the new 90th Bomb Group.

On June 20, 10 organizations were attached to the 44th. They were: Finance Detachment AG 2, 34th Signal Platoon, 755th Quartermaster (Trk-colored), 164th Quartermaster Platoon SC AVN, 722nd Ordnance Co. AVN AB, 447th Ordnance Co. AVN (B), 537th Chemical Platoon AFSC, 874th Chemical Platoon (AB), 134th Chemical Platoon (Airdrome-Colored) and the 708th Chemical Platoon AFSB, totaling about 2,400 enlisted personnel to process. It is believed most, if not all, remained at Barksdale Field.

Transfer to Will Roger's Field, Oklahoma, was begun on June 20, 1942, where the group began training in earnest for overseas combat duty. On July 1, the Headquarters and Headquarters Squadron, with some personnel forming the 404th Bomb Squadron, joined with 20 flying officers who were assigned for administration, plus the 14th Reconnaissance Squadron. The 404th was sent on Detached Service (DS) to Alaska in early August, never to return to group.

About August 28 the ground echelon departed Will Rogers to Fort Dix, New Jersey, for overseas duty, and on the 29th, the air echelon went to Grenier Field, New Hampshire, composed of about 120 officers and 148 enlisted men. Both echelons joined again on October 10, 1942, at Shipdham Airfield after the ground echelon spent one month at Cheddington waiting. Twenty-seven new B-24D aircraft were readied for combat at Station 115, Shipdham.

The 44th Bomb Group, 8th Air Force, began combat operations on November 7 only a short time after the 93rd Bomb Group flew its first combat mission in the B-24 Liberator. Three hundred and forty four operational missions were flown between then and April 25, 1945. During that period of 30 months more than 18,000 tons of high explosives and incendiaries were dropped on targets in 11 separate countries with two detached service periods flying out of North Africa. Group gunners shot down 357 enemy aircraft, with a loss of 153 Liberators,

plus 75 others crashing or being salvaged. Seventy-two planes returned to the Zone of the Interior (ZOI) at the completion of the war in Europe. Several Liberators completed over 100 missions, with three completing over 120, and one, *Iron Corset*, completing 129. Group combat men who paid the supreme price, numbered 858 killed in action and still missing in action.

This group won two Distinguished Unit Citations, one for its part in the great air battle of Kiel, May 14, 1943; with a second such honor for the famous low-level Liberator attack on the Ploesti oil fields in Romania on August 1, 1943.

Two officers flying with the group were awarded the Medal of Honor, Brig. Gen. (then Colonel) Leon W. Johnson, of Moline, Kansas, for leading the group into Ploesti; and the late Lt. Col. Leon Vance (489th), for heroism displayed while flying with our group's plane and crew on June 5, 1944.

The 506th Bomb Squadron arrived during late February and early March 1943 to become our permanent fourth squadron. Its first mission was flown on March 22 with the loss of one plane.

The group, along with the 93rd Bomb Group, were pioneers in the air war over Europe. The winter of 1942-43 was most difficult due to the need to improve conditions, develop and make modifications to the B-24, and work "on the line" under blackout conditions with no heat, or shelter. Combat men suffered the bitter cold of winter at high altitude with inadequate flying suits and very poor oxygen equipment, machine guns which froze up due to congealing oil, and superchargers which failed due to mechanical regulators. Group planes, along with a few from the 93rd Bomb Group, mostly provided tail cover for the small formations of B-17s. Except for the arrival of the nine 506th Squadron planes and crews, no replacements for our losses were received until late April 1943. Many ground crew personnel volunteered and became replacement combat crew men. It was late September 1943 before sufficient numbers of replacement planes and combat crews arrived to bring the group to full complement.

In early June the group was taken off operations to prepare for the low-level attack on Ploesti, leaving on detached service for North Africa on June 26, 1943. Fifteen missions were flown from Benina Main, Libya, with 338 sorties, 871 tons of bombs dropped, and 108 enemy aircraft destroyed. Included in these totals were 36 planes attacking Ploesti oil fields in Romania, with the loss of 11 aircraft, two of which were interned in Turkey.

A second Detached Service to Africa was made in mid-September to Ounda No. 1, near Tunis. Four missions were flown against the Axis, with the last one dated October 1, 1943, against Weiner-Neustadt in Austria. Like Ploesti, this one proved most difficult, losing seven aircraft to enemy action.

44th Bomb Group (H) Commanding Officers:

Lt. Col. Melvin B. Asp	January 15, 1941- May 8, 1941
Maj. Hugh P. Rush	May 8, 1941- March 27, 1942
Lt. Col. Frank H. Robinson	March 27, 1942- January 4, 1943
Col. Leon W. Johnson	January 4, 1943- September 3, 1943
Lt. Col. James T. Posey	September 3, 1943- December 3, 1943
Col. Frederick R. Dent	December 4, 1943- March 29, 1944
Col. John H. Gibson	March 29, 1944- August 15, 1944
Col. Eugene H. Snavely	August 15, 1944- April 13, 1945
Col. Vernon C. Smith	August 13, 1945- August, 1945

Attachments:

14th Combat Bomb Wing
18th Weather Station
50th Station Complement
208th Finance
464th Sub-Depot Class 1
806th Chemical
1132nd Quartermaster Co. Serv. Group
1287th Military Police Co. AVN
1646th Ordnance Co.Maintenance and Supply
2033rd Engineer Co.Fire Fighting Plt.
RAF Detachment-Liaison

The 44th's last mission was flown to Hallein, Austria, on April 25, 1945, with a formation of 30 aircraft. Excellent bombing results were achieved with no losses and very little damage to our aircraft.

Combat crews began returning to the States on May 25 via the northern route under Air Trans-

68th Squadron Ordnance, 44th Bomb Group. Alfred Adkins, Michael Bolza, Robert A. Coffman, Albert J. Diana, Chester A. Dunbar, Clifford A. David, Clarence A. Glowski, Harvey E Hoffman, George A. Kilford, Howard D. Landers, Louis W. Morris, James S. Musser, Frederick Quisenberry, George A. Rose, Arthur F. Rooks, Phillip E. Scott, Albert N. Sinkus, Joseph R. Siska, Michael A. Straccioni, Ralph J. Stine, Casemer Uzarowski, Jr., Herbert W. Waltz, Walter El Winiarski, Walter J. Synoweic. (Courtesy of Howard Landers)

port Command supervision. One aircraft with 16 men onboard crashed in northwestern Scotland, killing 10 crew members and six non-44th combat passengers. Our ground echelon boarded the *Queen Mary* (the same ship that brought them in 1942) June 15, 1945.

Unlike most returning 2nd Air Division groups, the 44th remained active, became a bomb wing, and currently is active as a missile wing in South Dakota. However, it is slated for deactivation in early 1994.

FIRSTS: First USAAF group to be equipped with B-24 Liberators; first Liberator group to attack the enemy-in U.S. waters; first group in 8th Air Force to be awarded a DUC (for May 14, 1943); sustained highest missing in action loss of 8th Air Force B-24 groups; claimed more enemy fighters than any other 8th Air Force B-24 group.

STATIONS: Cheddington-September 11, 1942 to October 9, 1942 (66BS Air Ech. on October 10, 1942). Shipdham-October 10, 1942 to June 15, 1945 (temporary stations in North Africa; Benina Main, Libya; June 28, 1943 to August 25, 1943 and Ounda No. 1, Tunis; September 19, 1943 to October 4, 1943).

FIRST MISSION: November 7, 1942
LAST MISSION: April 25, 1945
TOTAL MISSIONS: 343 (18 from NA)
TOTAL CREDIT SORTIES: 8,009
TOTAL BOMB TONNAGE: 18,980 tons
A/C MIA: 153
OTHER OP. LOSSES: 39
E/A CLAIMS: 330-74-69

MAJOR AWARDS: Two Distinguished Unit Citations: May 14, 1943; Kiel (66, 67 and 506BS) August 1, 1943; Ploesti. Medal of Honor: Col. Leon W. Johnson, August 1, 1943.

CLAIMS TO FAME: First USAAF group to be equipped with B-24 Liberators. Operated from England for longer period than any other B-24 group. Sustained highest MIA loss of 8AF B-24 groups. First group in 8AF to be awarded a DUC (for May 14, 1943).

THE "CIRCUS" AND THE "EIGHTBALLS"

submitted by Will Lundy

In the 8th Air Force's early combat history, Liberators were in a minority whose exploits were frequently over-shadowed by those of the more numerous Fortresses. Even in later months when numbers equalized, the Liberator never quite achieved the same prominence as its team-mate. The Fortress was bestowed with a certain romanticism due to the very nature of its development as the prime weapon of Air Corps pre-war bombardment plans: the Liberator had no such background; neither could it compete visually with the gracious curvey lines of the refined Boeing. Characterized by two large vertical stabilizers and a deep slab-sided fuselage, it brought forth such derogatory sobriquets as "Pregnant Cow" or Banana Boat" from the Fortress men. Liberator men retorted with "Glamour Girl and "Medium Bomber" for the B-17; they did not themselves find their charges lacking in aesthetic qualities and were quick to point out the advantages of being able to fly fast, further, and with a much heavier bomb load than the vaunted Fortress; facts that made the B-24 the most sought after aircraft in the American inventory by late 1942.

The first true Liberator group was the 44th which, having mastered the new bomber, was given the task of forming and training other groups. Its first offspring went to the Middle East, the second eventually found its way to the United Kingdom, and the third was dispatched to the Pacific. Thereafter the 44th was relieved of training duties and sent to England where its protege, the 93rd, The Traveling Circus, had already entered combat. Not until September 1943 were more Liberator bomber groups to join the 44th and 93rd in operations from the United Kingdom for others, originally scheduled to arrive earlier, were diverted to the Pacific fronts and a good proportion of new aircraft were diverted to an anti-submarine role.

In the early days, the two United Kingdom based groups were as distant in their careers as in their fortunes. The 44th followed the Fortresses over Northern Europe and suffered severely, so that even the B-17 men referred to them as "the jinx B-24 outfit." Conversely, the 93rd had the lowest operational loss rate of all six groups in 8th Bomber Command. This group took its turn across the channel, hunted U-boats in the Bay of Biscay, experimented with "blind bombing" techniques, and also "wintered" in Africa. Diverse activities and locations earned the group the title "Ted's Travelling Circus".

Crew of the Princess Charlotte, 66th Squadron, 44th Bomb Group. Front row, L to R: Richard J. Comey, Pilot; Thomas Drysdale, Copilot; John J. Harmonowski, Bombardier; Louis Trouve, Navigator. Back row, L to R: Richard H. Walker, Tail Gunner; Quentin Hall, Art. Radio Operator and Waist Gunner; Albert Greenberg, Radio Operator; Adelbert D. Franklin, Flight Engineer and Top Turret Operator; Stanley Rosinski, Waist Gunner; Dale Neitzel, Ball Turret Operator. (Courtesy of Richard J. Comey)

A formation of the 44th Bomb Group over England. (Courtesy of Howard Landers)

The 44th dubbed itself "The Flying Eightballs" and was unique in the 8th Air Force for a group design painted on the noses of its aircraft.

After an initial baptism of fire and loss over Lille on October 9, 1942, the 93rd fared comparatively well. Sent out on eight further occasions up to December, no B-24s were lost by enemy action although some of these missions were not without incident. Only small forces were dispatched, for on November 25 the group's 330th Bomb Squadron was ordered to Holmsley South, Hampshire, for anti-submarine patrols under the direction of RAF Coastal Command. The 409th Bomb Squadron was similarly detached, but after aiding in the fruitless search for a 97th Group Fort that had disappeared while carrying Brig. Gen. Asa Duncan (the 8th's first commander) to Africa, it was withdrawn from Holmsley South after a brief stay and returned to Alconbury. The 330th's task during the crucial stages of the North African landings was to assist in convoy protection and for a month their aircraft scanned the Bay of Biscay, in flights of up to 12 hours endurance. Although opportunities to attack enemy shipping did not arise, sighting reports were sent in on a U-boat and five enemy surface vessels. Skirmishes with hostile aircraft occurred twice during November, the most spectacular on the 21st when a B-24, piloted by squadron commander Maj. Ramsey Potts, was confronted with five JU-88s. It did not prove the easy kill the enemy apparently anticipated, for their somewhat clumsy approach resulted in two being shot down and a third damaged before the Liberator escaped. While no loss was sustained through enemy action on patrol work, one B-24 on a routine flight crashed at Porlock Bay, Somerset on October 30, killing the crew.

Although currently committed to training the air units for North Africa, the 8th's 2nd Bomb Wing,

44th Bomb Group/66th Squadron. George Insley's crew - standing, L to R: Rudy Jandreau, Thomas Edmonds, Paul Kettle, John Young, Allen Deutsch, George Federlin. Kneeling: unidentified, Capt. George Insley, Lt. Milton Finestrin, Lt. Leonard Dwelle. (Courtesy of George Insley)

located in Norfolk, was selected to control all Liberator groups, and early in November it was announced that the 93rd would soon transfer to this organization. While still at Alconbury on November 13, King George VI paid the first of his many visits in 8th Air Force stations, and Col. Timberlake showed His Majesty around *Teggie Ann*, then regarded as the group's "lead ship."

This is one of the original planes of the 44th Bomb Group which was named Lemon Drop. It came through the Ploesti Raid and several other raids. Later Lemon Drop was retired and stripped up to be used as a lead ship for formation. (Courtesy of Howard D. Landers)

93RD BOMB GROUP (H)
The Traveling Circus
courtesy of Charles J. Weiss

This mini-history cannot do justice to the great part the 93rd Group played in making the world a better place in which to live.

The War in Europe was already in "full swing." On December 7, 1941, "A day that will live in infamy," the USA entered the conflict. On March 1, 1942, the 93rd Bomb Group was activated.

Barksdale Army Air Base, Louisiana, was the site where it all began. Four squadrons, the 328th, 329th, 330th and 19th Recon Squadron (subsequently to become the 409th) were formed. The cadre of the 93rd was made up mainly of personnel reassigned from the 98th Bomb Group and the 44th Bomb Group.

In May 1942 the 93rd was assigned to Fort Myers Air Field, Florida, mostly sand and tents with a few temporary "shacks" thrown in for good measure. It was here that training began in earnest to make it combat ready. Its aircraft—the consolidated B-24. Training by all personnel in their respective jobs was only to last about three months. Bombing, navigation, armament, communications, intelligence and every operation necessary to prepare for combat was practiced. Interesting to note that Hitler's U-boats "Wolf Pack" were sinking U.S. and Allied ships just off our shores—only a few miles from our training area. On one of the long-range navigational training missions a B-24 loaded a few depth charges in the bomb bay, and by fortuitous "luck" on the over-the-water leg of the mission, sighted and destroyed one of Hitler's "Best."

In August 1942 the 93rd had completed training and moved to Alconbury RAF Airfield, Cambridgeshire, England. Training continued for air and ground crews, in new B-24 aircraft. Familiarization with RAF procedures, close formation flying, communications procedures, armament methods, intelligence, maintenance, and new support facilities were the orders of the day. In other words everyone was very busy in order to be ready for combat operations.

On October 9, 1942, the 93rd flew its first combat mission. This was the first time that B-24 aircraft had participated in the European Theater of Operations. It flew six missions to U-boat pens in France in the effort to neutralize the U-boat threat in the North Atlantic which was causing heavy losses to Allied war-support shipping.

' In early December 1942, the 328th, 330th and 409th squadrons were temporarily assigned to the 12th Air Force with station at Tafaroui, Algeria, to assist in stemming the threat for the planned takeover of North Africa by Field Marshal Rommel's forces. Most of the missions were hampered by heavy rains and logistic support problems. The three squadrons were then temporarily transferred to the 9th Air Force and stationed at Gambut, Libya, to assist in the bombing of targets in Italy, Sicily and Tunisia.

Meanwhile, back in England, the 329th Squadron moved to Hardwick Airdrome #104 which was to become the permanent home of the 93rd. There was no doubt, because of the its operational flexibility, that it would become known as "Ted's Traveling Circus." (Ted from its commander, Edward Timberlake Jr.)

In February 1943, the three squadrons returned to Hardwick. In June 1943, the 329th Squadron, which also had been temporarily moved to Flixton Air Field, Bungay, Suffolk, also returned to Hardwick.

The 93rd had been training for low-level bombing, and on June 25, 1943, it once again departed for Bengazi, Libya, North Africa. After 17 missions to targets in Sicily and Italy, they participated in the August 1, 1943, low-level raid on the Ploesti Oil Refineries in Romania. The 93rd suffered heavy losses (of the 37 B-24s which took off, 32 reached the target area, one was shot down short of the target, 11 were lost over the target, two aborted on take-off and two collided in a cloud bank and crashed). An estimated 42% of the refining capacity was destroyed. After several more strikes on enemy airdromes and marshalling yards in Germany and Italy, they returned on August 24, 1943, to England.

After only two missions from England the 93rd once again was ordered back to Tunis, North Africa. Again against targets in southern Germany and Italy.

On October 2, 1943, they returned to Hardwick and flew missions to Norway, Poland, Germany and France before the year came to an end.

In May 1944, in a prelude to the invasion of the continent, they began bombing tactical targets. Activity was stepped up with the 93rd flying 27 missions in June (the 329th Squadron made eight additional strikes). Many of the missions were directed against gun positions. On June 6 (D-day) the targets were bridges, choke-points, enemy airdromes and rocket installations along the coast of France.

In July 1944 the 93rd resumed its bombing of strategic targets in Germany and France. On July 13, 1944 the 93rd completed its 200th mission, the first heavy bombardment group to have completed 200 missions. On November 25, 1944, they then again established another record, the first heavy bomb group to complete 300 missions.

Between August 29 and September 10, 1944, the group flew many mercy and support missions, carrying food and freight to the people of France and to allied armies.

During Christmas time, the group assisted the invasion forces by bombing railheads, choke points, and marshalling yards. It was at this time our army ground troops were surrounded by German tanks and infantry (The Battle of the Bulge).

During the first few months of 1945 the 93rd continued bombing both strategic and tactical targets. Its experience with low-level flying held it in good stead when it provided low-level drops in support of the Rhine River crossings. Until the end of the war, it concentrated on bombing enemy airfields. The last mission flown by the 93rd was on April 25, 1945. This was the 391st mission.

By June 15, 1945, all elements of the 93rd Bomb Group had departed for the USA.

As a matter of interest, the 93rd Bomb Group continued in existence. In July 1945, at Pratt AAF, KS, it was refitted with B-29 aircraft, and planned for subsequent redeployment to the Pacific Theater of Operations.

By December 1945, war in the Pacific had already ended, and the 93rd was assigned to Clovis AA Field, where it continued its training. By May 1946 the group had only 10 personnel assigned, and by October it was reduced to two individuals.

In May 1947, the 93rd had been transferred to Castle AAB, California, where it began to receive new life.

During 1948 the 93rd was fully manned and into advanced phases of operational training. (It had lost the 409th Squadron to the 44th Bomb Group.) Between May and August they were assigned to Kadena Air Base, Okinawa for training.

In June 1949 the group began receiving B-50 aircraft and by January 1950 it had its full complement of aircraft.

Between July 1950 and January 1951, the group was temporarily assigned training missions while stationed at Mildenhall AFB, England.

On February 10, 1951, back at Castle AFB, California, the group was reduced to a "Records Unit," one officer and one airman (for historical purposes).

The group's tactical squadrons were assigned to the 93rd Bombardment Wing for operations, and, on June 16, 1952, at Castle AFB, California, the 93rd Bombardment Group was inactivated.

(Most of the information above has been extracted from reports prepared by the USAF Historical Division of the Research Studies Institute, Maxwell AFB, Alabama.)

93RD BOMB GROUP (H)
2nd Air Division, 8th USAF Memorial Dedication at Hardwick Aerodrome 104
courtesy of Charles J. Weiss

The following inscriptions are those which appear on the memorial stone:

93rd Bombardment Group (Heavy)
328th, 329th, 330th, and 409th Squadrons
  and attached units

20th Combat Wing-2nd Air Division
8th United States Army Air Force
From this Airfield and others in England
And North Africa,
The 93rd Group flew a total of 391 combat
    missions
In support of the Allied
War Effort during World War II
These missions were flown from
9 October 1942 until 25 April 1945

This monument is dedicated to the memory
Of those lost in the war
And to the survivors who helped
achieve ultimate peace and victory

Two Medals of Honor
Two Presidential Unit Citations:
For North Africa and Ploesti

Battles and Campaigns
American Theater - Antisubmarine, ATO -
Air Combat - EAME Theater - Air Offensive,
Europe - Antisubmarine, ETO - Egypt-Libya -
Ploesti - Tunisia - Naples Foggia - Sicily -
Normandy - Northern France - Rhineland -
Ardennes-Alsace - Central Europe

Dedicated 25th of May 1987

(The 8th Air Force, 93rd Bomb Group and
Squadron. Insignias as well as two 2B-24 aircraft
are engraved on the stone.)

Africa - 1943, 93rd Bomb Group. (Courtesy of H.W. Feichter)

389TH BOMB GROUP (H)
The Flying Scorpions
by H.H. 'Chris' Christensen

Constituted as the 389th Bombardment Group
(H) on December 19, 1942, the group was assigned
to the 8th Air Force on June 11, 1943, the third group
assigned to the 2nd Bomb Wing (later 2nd Air Division) in England. It was based at Army Air Force
Station 114, Hethel, Norfolk, England. The group
was deployed temporarily to Berka Four (Benghazi
No. 10), Libya, Africa, from July 3 to August 25,
1943, and to Massicault, Tunisia, Africa, from September 19 to October 3, 1943. Operations resumed
from England in October 1943 until April 1945,
concentrated primarily on strategic objectives in
France, the low countries and Germany.

93rd Bomb Group, B-24s on a mission. (Courtesy of H.W. Feichter)

The group participated in the intensive air campaign against the German aircraft industry during
Big Week, February 20-25, 1944. Support and
interdictory missions were flown, bombing gun batteries and airfields, during the Normandy invasion,
June 1944. Enemy positions were hit to aid the
breakthrough at St. Lo, July 1944. Storage depots
and communication centers were among the targets
during the Battle of the Bulge, December 1944. Following the last combat mission, relief missions dropping food, medicine and supplies over Holland were
flown April-May, 1945.

Combat missions flown were 321, totalling
7,579 sorties and 17,548 tons of bombs dropped.
Enemy aircraft claimed destroyed were 209 with
an additional 31 probable and 45 damaged. The
group had 116 aircraft missing in action and experienced 37 other operational losses for a total of 153
airplanes. Planes damaged by enemy action which
crashed or ditched into the water or crashed in England were listed as "accidents" and counted as operational losses.

Many of the airplanes which returned to base
with combat damage were repaired and flew additional missions. Many individual aircraft received
combat damage on each of several missions. On

93rd Bomb Group in the desert of Africa. (Courtesy of H.W. Feichter)

Early "D" Model, 1943 B-24 with no ball turret or nose turret. 389th Bomb Group. (Courtesy of Russell Leslie)

Col. Burton (top left) and some of the ground crew of the 565th Squadron of the 389th Bomb Group. (Courtesy of Russell Leslie)

389th Bomb Group crew photo, 565th Squadron. (Courtesy of Russell Leslie)

some missions a majority of airplanes received combat damage. Some damaged airplanes which returned to base were declared uneconomical to repair and were salvaged for parts.

Most airplanes missing in action had 10-man crews which became Prisoners of War (POW), Killed in Action (KIA) or remained Missing in Action (MIA) depending on the circumstances. Some crew members were rescued or escaped from operational loss airplanes, but many were killed or became MIA. Some of the damaged aircraft returned to base with wounded or dead crew members aboard.

Air crew members received hundreds of decorations including Air Medals, Distinguished Flying Crosses, Silver Stars, Purple Hearts, and one Medal of Honor. The Medal of Honor was awarded posthumously to Lt. Lloyd H. Hughes for his participation in the Ploesti mission.

The 389th participated in many of the combat actions of World War II including the following campaigns:

Sicilian Campaign
July 9, 1943-August 17, 1943

Air Combat Ploesti-Romania
August 1, 1943

Naples-Foggia Campaign
August 18, 1943-September 9, 1943

Air Offensive Europe
July 1, 1943-June 5, 1944

Normandy Campaign
June 6, 1944-July 24, 1944

Northern France Campaign
July 25, 1944-September 14, 1944

Rhineland Campaign
September 15, 1944-March 21, 1945

Ardennes Campaign
December 16, 1944-Jananuary 25, 1945

Central Europe Campaign
March 22, 1945-April 25, 1945

The group was formed at Davis-Monthan Field, Tucson, Arizona. It trained at Biggs Field, El Paso, Texas, and Lowry Field, Denver, Colorado. The air echelon received its new airplanes and then departed Lowry Field for England beginning June 13, 1943. Most of the planes, crews and passengers had arrived at Hethel, England, by June 25, 1943. The passengers included key squadron and group personnel. The air echelon travelled by way of Lincoln, Nebraska, where airplane modifications were performed. They then flew to Great Britain via the North Atlantic route departing the United States from either Presque Isle or Bangor, Maine. Most crews stopped at either Gander, Newfoundland, or Goose Bay, Labrador, both being in Canada. At least one crew flew from Maine to Ireland, non-stop. The North Atlantic route allowed for emergency or weather delay landings in Greenland, Iceland, and/ or Ireland. Most of the 389th airplanes stopped at one or more of these locations.

The ground echelon departed from Denver, Colorado, by train on June 5, 1943, and traveled to Camp Kilmer, New Jersey. They boarded the *Queen Elizabeth* on June 30, sailed on July 1, and arrived in Scotland July 6, 1943. The people in the ground echelon were surprised to learn that the air echelon had been deployed to Africa while they were on the *Queen Elizabeth*.

Most of the maintenance personnel used during the first African deployment were loaned from either the 44th Bombardment Group (H) or the 93rd Bombardment Group (H). The men temporarily assigned included a crew chief and a mechanic for each airplane, a group engineering officer, squadron engineering officers, and a small number of other personnel. The 389th had excellent maintenance in Africa using these people. They rejoined their original groups on return from Africa, with the exception of Thomas W. Landrum who was permanently assigned as group engineering officer.

During the first African deployment, the group flew its seventh mission as part of the low level attack on the Steaua Romania refinery at Campina, Romania, a part of the Ploesti raid of August 1, 1943. The 389th participation is best summarized from the official AAFRH-3 report which stated in part, "Colonel Wood's force, much the least experienced of the five participating groups, succeeded in reaching the target area with all aircraft that had been dispatched. Of the four groups which actually attacked selected targets, its losses were lightest, and it completely destroyed its target." Four crews were lost and two others were interned in Turkey.

Probably the most familiar 389th airplane was the *Green Dragon*. This airplane with its broad diagonal green and yellow stripes on the fuselage, wing and tail, and with many green lights, was used to help assemble the group formation in the early dawn and above the clouds. The airplane was modified from an early model B-24 with narrow blade propellers. It flew four missions with the 93rd before being judged unsuitable for combat, and transferred to the 389th.

The 389th was assigned the responsibility of providing radar bombing "pathfinder" crews and aircraft for the 2nd Bomb (later Air) Division. These crews and airplanes led all 2nd Division radar bombing operations for several months beginning in early 1944. The "handmade" equipment was in short supply and difficult to maintain.

On April 22, 1944, about 20 enemy aircraft flew into England with the 2nd Bomb Division force returning from a mission to Hamm, Germany. During the action which followed, one of the group airplanes went off the runway and after narrowly missing the control tower, went through the nearby radar maintenance building and burst into flames. Many scarce radar spare parts and vital test equipment were destroyed. However, group personnel managed to keep providing pathfinder aircraft to the combat wings of the 2nd Bomb Division.

The 389th leadership was of the highest calibre. Commanding officers of the group included:

Maj. David B. Lancaster, Jr.	November 30, 1942-May 4, 1943
Col. Jack W. Wood	May 16, 1943-December 29, 1943
Col. Milton W. Arnold	December 30, 1943-March 28, 1944
Col. Robert B. Miller	March 29, 1944-August 16, 1944
Col. Ramsey D. Potts	August 17, 1944-December 3, 1944
Col. John B. Herboth Jr. (MIA)	December 4, 1944-April 7, 1945
Lt. Col. Chester Morneau	April 9, 1945-April 13, 1945
Lt. Col. Jack Merrell	April 14, 1945-June 1945

The group was cited many times for having the best maintenance in the division. One squadron in the group was named best squadron in the division. The group was awarded a Presidential Unit Citation for participation in the 1943 Ploesti mission. Ground personnel of the 389th, including the several units attached to the group, received many awards for meritorious service including at least one Legion of Merit.

Successful 389th operation required the dedication, skills and hard work of many people in addition to the crews who flew the airplanes on their missions. Each individual was necessary and important, and singly and collectively earned shares of the credit for the successful bombing operations conducted by the group: Official records contain many references to the contributions of assigned individuals.

Here listed are the Hethel organizational elements, including those units attached to the 389th:

Headquarters 389th Bombardment Group (H)
564th Bombardment Squadron
565th Bombardment Squadron
566th Bombardment Squadron
567th Bombardment Squadron
327th Service Group, Detachment A (attached)
79th Service Group (attached)
463rd Sub-Depot (attached)
48th Station Complement (attached)
1215th Quartermaster Company (attached)
1200th Military Police Company (attached)
2032nd Engineer Aviation Firefighter Platoon (attached)
209th Finance Company (attached)
1750th Ordnance Company (attached)
255th Medical Dispensary (attached)

The group received its orders to return to the United States soon after the last combat mission. In addition to all the activities to close down the base, it was necessary to modify the airplanes to get them in shape for the flight back across the Atlantic. This effort was completed and airplanes started to leave Hethel on May 19, 1945. The ground echelon left Bristol on May 30, 1945, on the USS *Cristobal*, arriving in New York City June 8, 1945. Most personnel were given leave and the group was reestablished at Charleston Army Air Field, South Carolina, June 12, 1945. The group was never again fully manned. It was inactivated on September 13, 1945, after the war had been concluded.

The 389th Bombardment Group (H) existed for less than 1,000 days.

392ND BOMB GROUP (H)
The Crusaders
by Delmar C. Johnson

The 392nd Bombardment Group (H) was assigned to the USAAF's 8th Air Force (The Mighty Eighth) in England during July 1943. The 8th was the USAAF's heavy bombardment arm operating in Northern and Central Europe. The group was comprised of the 576th, 577th, 578th and 579th Bombardment Squadrons and was equipped with B-24 aircraft. Its early history began with activation at Davis-Monthan Army Air Field, Tucson, Arizona, on January 26, 1943. The cadre moved to Biggs Field, El Paso, Texas, in March, where the buildup to operational strength began. In early April the group moved to Alamogordo AAF, New Mexico, where training and strength buildup continued until July 1943.

On July 18, 1943, the ground echelon departed for overseas by train and ship, arriving in England July 30, 1943. The air echelon, with 36 aircrews (nine per squadron), moved to Topeka AAF, Kansas, July 10, 1943. This was just after having been equipped with new B-24Es at Alamogordo. Departure from Topeka for a combat theater was delayed while the group was reequipped with a new model,

A plane would be loaded with 40 of these 300 lb. demolition bombs. (Courtesy of Howard D. Landers)

The 392nd Bomb Group carried 52 of these 100 lb. bombs per plane. (Courtesy of Howard D. Landers)

the B-24H. Thus, the 392nd had the distinction of being the first USAAF group to be equipped with B-24s having "factory production" nose turrets. After one crew was lost in a training accident at Topeka, the remaining 35 air crews started flying to England about mid-August via the North Atlantic route. All crews arrived safely by August 21, 1943. The 392nd Bomb Group was the fourth of 19 B-24 bombardment groups to be assigned to the 8th Air Force. Fourteen of those were in what became the 2nd Air Division.

In England, the 392nd was assigned briefly to the 202nd Combat Bombardment Wing, then permanently to the 14th Combat Bomb Wing. Both were in the 2nd Bomb Division, subsequently designated as the 2nd Air Division, and consisting entirely of B-24 groups. The group named "The Crusaders," was based at 8th Air Force Station 118 about 20 miles west of Norwich in Norfolk, East Anglia. The airfield was named Wendling, after the parish in which the runways and taxiways were located. Living and administrative quarters were mostly located in adjoining Beeston.

Following are some significant facts of the 392nd's combat history. The group flew a total of 285 combat missions over North and Central Europe. The first on September 9, 1943, to a Luftwaffe Air Base at Abbeville, France, and the last one, April 25, 1945, to a marshalling yard at Hallien, Austria. It flew 7,060 aircraft sorties (one plane flying one combat mission) and delivered a total of 17,452 tons of bombs. Among its notable achievements were an award of the Distinguished Unit Citation and, despite heavy losses, a bombing accuracy better than the 2nd Air Division average during its first nine months of operation. Claims for destroyed enemy aircraft totalled 238; 144 confirmed, 45 probable and 49 unconfirmed. Total B-24 aircraft lost were 184, of which 127 were missing in action and 57 to other combat related causes. Only one other 8th Air Force B-24 group lost more aircraft/crews. Commanding officers of the 392nd Bomb Group during its World War II service were (in order): Col. Irvine A. Rendle, Col. Lorin L. Johnson and Lt. Col. Lawrence G. Gilbert.

The group's Distinguished Unit Citation was awarded for its February 24, 1944, attack on an aircraft factory at Gotha, Germany. When the 2nd Bomb Division's lead group made an erroneous turn,

the 392nd continued on the correct heading becoming the de facto leader of most of the 2nd Bomb Division groups. Despite sustained heavy Luftwaffe attacks for two and one-half hours into and from the target, bombing accuracy was outstanding-97 percent of their bombs impacted within 2,000 feet of the aiming point. The factory, contributing nearly one third of German's twin engine fighter production, was severely damaged and never did fully recover. The group lost seven planes on this mission, plus two airmen killed and one wounded in the planes that did return.

The 392nd's heaviest loss of the war was to come three weeks later on March 18, 1944. This was a return trip to aircraft factories at

Friedrichshafen, Germany, two days after an unsuccessful, uneventful trip. Cloud cover had prevented dropping any bombs. This second trip was to be far different. Initially, two planes were lost in a collision over France going in, then it was uneventful until the target area. With the 44th Bomb Group leading, the 14th Combat Bomb Wing was about 30 minutes late at the target and missed its fighter escort rendezvous. Since this target was at extreme fighter range, the escort hadn't been able to wait around for its late arrival. German ground defenses and Luftwaffe fighters had been alerted by the various other groups arriving on schedule and well ahead of this wing.

The 392nd went through heavy flak on the

392nd Bomb Group, Crew 4570. First row, L to R: S/Sgt. Leo J. Purcell, Waist Gunner; T/Sgt. Gerald Rubin, Radio Op./Spare Gunner; T/Sgt. Michael J. Roberts, Flt. Eng./Top Turret Gunner; S/Sgt. Talbert Dunn, Tail Gunner; S/Sgt. John T. Johnson, Jr., Waist Gunner; S/Sgt. John Kirol, Ball Turret Gunner. Second row, L to R: 1st Lt. Vernon H. Stillwagon, Navigator; 1st Lt. Frank Koza, Pilot; 1st Lt. Rollin Wilcoxson, Copilot; 1st Lt. Arthur A. Solomon, Bombardier. (Courtesy of Frank Koza)

392nd Bomb Group 579th Squadron with the B-24, Rose of Juarez.. (Courtesy of William C Jensen)

Bombs Away! 392nd Bomb Group, 578th Squadron. (Courtesy of Milton Planche)

June 1943, a B-24 of the 392nd Bomb Group flying formation wingship. (Courtesy of Milton M. Planche)

L to R: Guy Spinelli and Kenneth O'Boyle of the 578th Armament Section 392nd Bomb Group loading fragmentation bombs. 100th mission, D-Day Invasion of France. (Courtesy of Gaetao Spinelli)

bomb run, with a number of its planes coming off the target crippled. Shortly thereafter, a swarm of FW-190s and ME-109s attacked. By the time 8th Air Force P-38s could respond to calls for help, at least three attacks had been pressed home, with gaggles of five or six Luftwaffe fighters flying line-abreast through the formation. When the P-38s arrived, they found the formation decimated. With the enemy fighters driven off, only seven planes, all badly damaged, were left to struggle back to England. A total of 14 planes were lost to fighters, flak and collision. Apparently three damaged planes

did manage to make their way to Switzerland. The last surviving plane landed at 1645, thus ending the 392nd's most tragic mission by far.

The group's last mission on April 25, 1945, was an attack on railroad marshalling yards at Hellein, Austria, near Salzburg, with no losses. With the war in Europe over, group personnel were redeployed to the U.S. by sea and air during June 1945. The group was subsequently inactivated September 13, 1945, at Charleston, South Carolina, where it was retraining in B-29s for deployment to the Pacific and action against Japan. During the 1950s, squadrons of the 392nd were reactivated as missile training units of the Strategic Air Command.

Shortly after World War II ended, a memorial monument, with commemorative plaques, was erected in tribute to the 1,553 casualties suffered by the group, including 764 killed in action. The idea for such a memorial was conceived and implemented by Joseph Bush, 392nd executive officer, with the help of other 392nd members. For many years it was the only such memorial in England commemorating a B-24 group. It stands on the Beeston Road at the site of what was then the main gate, near the west end of the east-west runway. After being refurbished it was rededicated in the Fall of 1989, with many 392nd veterans, their families, English people and dignitaries attending the moving ceremonies.

The 392nd Bomb Group Memorial Association, and English friends of the group, accomplished the excellent refurbishing with help from many others. The first officers of the association included: Lawrence G. Gilbert, president; William H. Richards, vice-president, Newsletter; Carrol W. Cheek, vice-president, Memorial; and Gilbert R. Bambauer, secretary-treasurer. A fund has been established to provide perpetual care for this memorial.

The staff of the 392nd Bomb Group (H) during the service in the 8th Air Force included:

HEADQUARTERS 392ND BOMB GROUP (H)

Commanding Officers: Irvine A. Rendle, Lorin L. Johnson, Lawrence G. Gilbert

Deputy Commanding Officers: Lorin L. Johnson;, Lawrence G. Gilbert

Operations Officers: Lawrence G. Gilbert, Malcom K. Martin

Executive Officer: Joseph Bush

Group Adjutant: John Fritsche

Group Navigator: Kenneth Q. Paddock

Group Bombardiers: Joseph B. Whittaker, Harold F. Weiland

Group Flight Surgeon: Robert M. Holland

Group Chaplain: Donald B. Clark

Sub-Depot Officer: James W. Wall

576th Bomb Squadron (H)

Commanding Officers: Clyde T. Gray, Charles L. Lowell, Leonard B. Barnes, Olen F. Levell Jr.

Operations Officers: Joseph Gurney, Henry W. Miller

Executive Officer: Edmund R. Dilworth

577th Bomb Squadron (H)

Commanding Officers: William V. Taylor, Clinton F. Schoolmaster, Jacque L. Francine, Harley Sather, James N. McFadden

Operations Officers: Thomas R. Donaldson, Leonard B. Barnes, Melvin H. Graper, Samuel C. Smith

Executive Officer: Willard T. Pennington

These 40 lb. fragmentation bombs were loaded 40 to a plane. 392nd Group Ordnance and Armament Bomb Display. (Courtesy of Howard D. Landers)

An incendiary cluster bomb of the 392nd Group Ordnance and Armament Bomb Display. (Courtesy of Howard D. Landers)

578th Bomb Squadron (H)

Commanding Officers: Warren E. Polking, George C. Player Jr.

Operations Officers: Clinton F. Schoolmaster, Gordon MacLean, Clifford E. Edwards, George H. Taylor, Claude Allen, J.D. Long, Allen Duff

Executive Officers: Daniel P. Lieblich, Robert E. Lane

579th Bomb Squadron (H)

Commanding Officers: Donald Appert, Myron H. Keilman

Operations Officers: Myron H. Keilman, Charles C. Holloman, Harrison Cassell, Harold Dawson

Executive Officers: Albert B. Huber, Peter A. Zahm

Support Echelons Assigned/Attached to the 392nd Bomb Group (H)

465th Sub-Depot (Class I)
10th Station Complement Squadron
1217th Quartermaster Service Group (RS)
1825th Ordnance S & M Company (Avn.)
1287th Military Police, Detachment "A"
806th Chemical Company (AO), Detachment "A"
586th Army Postal Unit
208th Finance Detachment
2101st Engineer Fire-Fighting Platoon

Author's Note: There may be some omissions/errors in the listing of 392nd staff members. It was compiled largely from memories of various 392nd members, including my own, and a few records.

As a navigator, my 392nd career began when my first crew, Thomas R. McKee, pilot, was assigned to the 578th Squadron April 3, 1943, at Biggs Field, Texas. With my second crew, Rex L. Johnson, pilot, it was ended abruptly by a FW-190 on the March 18, 1944 Friedrichshafen mission. Liberation from POW status was achieved April 29, 1945 at Moosburg, Germany.

Crew of Rowe D. Bowen, 445th Bomb Group, 701st Bomb Squadron. (Courtesy of Lowell D. Harris)

445th Bomb Group B-24s dropping bombs on German target. (Courtesy of John O. Goffe)

445TH BOMB GROUP (H)

by Chuck Walker

The 445th Bomb Group was activated per War Department letter AG 302.2 dated March 20, 1943. The group prepared for combat with B-24 Liberators under the guidance of Commanding Officer Lt. Col. Robert H. Terrill. The group began forming at Boise, Idaho. Training continued at Wendover, Utah, and Sioux City, Iowa. The most publicized personnel assignment was that of Capt. Jimmy Stewart as commanding officer of the 703rd Squadron. Maj. Stewart was transferred to another group in March 1944, and in May 1945, Col. Stewart became commanding officer of the 2nd Combat Bombardment Wing. (Stewart always a strong supporter of the Air Force, remained active in the Air Force Reserves after the war and ultimately retired as a brigadier general).

The ground echelon sailed from New York aboard the *Queen Mary* on October 27, 1943, arriving in Scotland November 2. Meanwhile the air echelon of 62 combat crews accompanied by 248 other aircraft maintenance and flying personnel proceeded by air via the southern route to England for service with the 8th Air Force. The group moved into a former RAF base at Tibenham, Norfolk County, where the newly attached 462nd Sub-Depot personnel assisted the maintenance crews in preparing the aircraft for combat.

On December 13, 1943, the 445th Bomb Group flew its first combat mission: 15 aircraft were dispatched of which 12 bombed U-boat installations at Kiel, Germany, with excellent results. No losses were sustained.

The group participated in the Allied campaign against the German aircraft industry during Big Week, February 20-25, 1944, and was awarded the Presidential Unit Citation for outstanding performance of duty during their February 24, 1944, attack on the ME-110 assembly and component plant at Gotha, Germany. The group lost 13 of the 25 aircraft that attacked the target. Gunners of the 445th were officially credited with 21 enemy aircraft destroyed, two aircraft probably destroyed and seven damaged.

Quoting from the Presidential Unit Citation: "On February 24, 1944, this group (445th) participated...in an attack on the Gothaer Waggonfabric, A.G. located at Gotha, Germany...attacking bombers met and overcame the fiercest and most determined resistance the enemy was able to muster in defense of this target, so vital to his ability to wage war. Unprotected by friendly fighter cover, the 445th Bomb Group (H) was under almost continuous attack from enemy aircraft for a period of two hours and 20 minutes...anti-aircraft fire was hurled at the formation along the route to and from the target...For one hour and 20 minutes before "bombs away" savage attacks were made by single and twin-engined enemy fighters in a vain attempt to keep the bombers from reaching their target. On the actual bomb run, fierce and relentless attacks were unable to keep the bombers from accomplishing their task. For another hour after bombing, the group continued to be the object of ferocious fighter attacks. The target was located and bombed with extreme accuracy and devastating results. This enemy air force suffered a most telling blow. The courage, zeal and perseverance shown by the crew members of the 445th...on this occasion were in accordance with the highest traditions of the military service of the United States and reflect great credit on themselves and the group, and the Army Air Forces."

The group operated primarily as a strategic bombardment organization striking such targets as industries in Osnabruck, synthetic oil refineries in Lutzkendor, chemical works in Ludwigshafen, marshalling yards at Hamm, airfields at Munich, an ammunition plant at Duneberg, underground oil storage facilities at Ehmen, and factories at Munster. The group occasionally flew interdictory and support missions.

Flying the "Ramblin Wreck," Samuel F. Miller's crew, 700th Squadron, became the first 445th crew to complete their tour of combat duty.

445TH FOR THE RECORD

Missions flown	280
Sorties flown	6,323
Airmen killed in action	576
Aircraft lost	138
Enemy aircraft destroyed	80
Enemy aircraft probably destroyed	35
Enemy aircraft damaged	31
Tons of bombs dropped	16,262

MOST HEAVILY BOMBED TARGETS

Target	No. Missions
Brunswick, Germany	10
Siracourt, France	9
Magdenburg, Germany	7
Koblenz, Germany	6
Saarbrucken, Germany	5
Bonnieres, France	6
Munster, Germany	5
Hamburg, Germany	3
Hamm, Germany	5
Berlin, Germany	5
Bremen, Germany	3
Kassel, Germany	3
Kiel, Germany	4
Gotha, Germany	3

BATTLE HONORS

The following are the campaigns for which the 445th Bomb Group was given official battle participation credit: Air Offensive Europe; Normandy; Northern France; Rhineland; Ardennes; Central Europe.

MEDALS AWARDED TO MEMBERS OF THE GROUP

Distinguished Service Cross	1
Legion of Merit	1
Silver Star	13
Bronze Star	60
Distinguished Flying Cross	1,041
Oak Leaf Cluster to DFC	51
Soldier's Medal	6
Air Medal	12,938
Oak Leaf Cluster to Air Medal	6,409
Purple Heart	114*
Oak Leaf Cluster to Purple Heart	3
Croix de Guerre (French)	5
Croix de Guerre (French) to the Group	1

*This does not include medals presented to next of kin of members who were killed in action.

Lest their supreme sacrifice be forgotten, surviving 445th Bomb Group members have, in the years since World War II, perpetuated the memory of their lost comrades by their participation in the best of all memorials, the 2nd Air Division Memorial Room in the Central Library, Norwich, England.

The 445th celebrated the completion of its 100th mission on the sixth-month anniversary of its first mission, December 13, 1943. By D-day, 57 of the original 62 aircraft with which the 445th had begun combat operations had been lost.

The 445th helped prepare for the invasion at Normandy by bombing airfields, V-1 (Buzz Bomb) sites and other crucial targets. The group's 89th, 90th, 91st and 92nd missions were flown on D-day, June 6, 1944, against shore installations and supported ground forces at St. Lo by striking enemy defenses in July 1944, and flew plane loads of gasoline to a French airfield near the front on September 17, 1944, in support of Patton's forces which had outdistanced its supplies.

On July 24, 1944, Col. Terrill was transferred to 2nd Bomb Division A-3. Col. William W. Jones became the 445th commanding officer. The 445th regretted losing Col. Terrill, but were proud of his promotion. Col. Jones was well known as he had been with the group from its inception, first as group operations officer and then as deputy commanding officer.

September 27, 1944, began much like many other days in England that year: rain and low ceilings. The group's 169th mission was routinely launched but in a few hours it was learned that this was not just another raid into Germany. It was the most tragic day in the history of the 445th, and was the most disastrous raid for a single group in 8th Air Force history. The assigned target was Kassel, Germany. Thirty ships set out for the target. The route was 8/10 - 10/10 undercast. After reaching the I.P. the group made a target identification error and mistakenly headed for Gottingen, Germany, which was approximately 30 degrees to the north of course and bombed Gottingen which is approximately 25 miles northeast of Kassel. Bombs landed just short of Gottingen. The group not fully realizing they were off course, proceeded to turn off the target per mission plan which placed them, unescorted, 8-10 miles east of the intended route, thus separating them from the bomber stream and friendly fighter cover. In less than five minutes, 25 bombers were shot down by waves of an estimated 100 plus FW-190s and ME-109s. Twenty five of our aircraft were shot down during the brief attack, two bellied in at airfields in France, one crash landed in Belgium, two crash landed at Manston, England, and one crashed near Tibenham while attempting to land. Only four returned to Tibenham.

In the words of Paul Dickerson, the left waist gunner on Cecil Isom's crew, (703rd Squadron); "In waves of 10 and 15, FW-190s poured in on us. Machine guns were firing...everywhere B-24s, ME-109s and FW-190s were falling. Some were blazing, some were smoking and some were blown to bits. The air was full of parachutes, Pandemonium reigned! A German with a black parachute drifted by our right waist window. Bill Wagner took a bead on him, then looked at me. I said, 'no,' and Wagner let him drift by. An ME-109 drifted up on our left wing. I could see the pilot plainly. He was so close. One burst and I had him...Then all was quiet. We waited for the kill. We knew that we could last no longer. We were dead men and we knew it. By then there remained only about seven of the original formation. Three were too crippled to fight back. We were helpless and hopeless. But the Germans didn't come back. There wasn't much left of them either. Then we saw a most beautiful sight and we knew then why the Germans did not come back. The sight of our fighters was unmistakable. Of course there wasn't much to rescue. At 1000 hours we were a squadron of 10. At 1006 we were a squadron of two. This trauma, this lifetime, this eternity lasted only five minutes. When we returned to our base we found the plane in front of us firing red flares for an emergency landing, there were injured

Back row, L to R: Floyd Crago, Copilot; William M. Hill, Pilot; B. Sugarman, Navigator; Robert Crossland, Radio Operator; Robert Evans, Nose Gunner. Front row, L to R: Paul S. Hahn, Gunner; Sam Boyko, Engineer; James Shows, Tail Gunner; J. Stockdale, Gunner. Taken at the 445th Base. (Courtesy of William M. Hill)

445th Bomb Group, 702nd Bomb Squadron. Standing, L to R: Bill Sorgel, Copilot; Max Taylor, Pilot; "Jeep" Warren; Mack Shumate, Navigator. Kneeling, L to R: Don Anderson, Flight Engineer; Bill Zoller, Tail Gunner; Bud Williams, Radio; John Knizeski, Waist; Al Stuart, Nose; Bob Libby, Waist. (Courtesy of John M. Knizeski, Jr.)

onboard. The tower wanted to know where the rest of the group was ... we told them that we were the group."

The 445th could muster only 10 combat serviceable aircraft the next day (September 28). Undaunted, they returned to Kassel.

The 445th flew its last mission of World War II, number 280, on April 25, 1945: 19 aircraft took off, 19 aircraft bombed the target and 19 aircraft returned safely to Tibenham. The target was Salzburg, Austria.

The 445th established an enviable record as one of the very best bombardment groups in the 8th Air Force, demonstrated by its bombing accuracy, the

long hours of labor under very adverse weather conditions, its ground crews dedicated to their task of keeping the aircraft combat ready and the bravery and skill of the air crews which never turned back no matter how devastating the enemy attack. The administrative sections kept the base glued together and morale high. Everyone bitched about the weather, food in the mess hall, rationing of items at the PX, the lack of hot water in the latrines, and too few passes; but isn't that what all good GIs are supposed to do?

The 445th Bomb Group (H) returned to the United States during May-June 1945 and was inactivated on September 12, 1945.

446TH BOMB GROUP (H)
Bungay Buckeroos

by Marvin H. Speidel

The 446th Bomb Group (H), destined to become "The Bungay Buckaroos" and "The D-day Leaders," was activated at Davis-Monthan Field, Tucson, Arizona, on April 1, 1943, under the command of Lt. Col. Arthur Y. Snell. The personnel assigned to the group in its initial stages were drawn largely from the 39th Bomb Group (H) at Davis-Monthan with additional personnel from the Clovis, AAF, New Mexico, and from other 2nd Air Force stations. On April 20, 1943, equipment was shipped to the group at Alamogordo, New Mexico, which was expected to be its permanent station. Key personnel and four complete model crews were ordered to AAFSAT at Orlando, Florida for specialized training before conducting the group's regular phase training. The group cadre was then moved to Montbrook Field, Florida, where they completed five successful missions under actual field conditions. On May 26, 1943, the group received orders to move to Lowry Field, Denver, Colorado. There it completed its phase training under less than satisfactory conditions, suffering the loss of three crews in air accidents and two aerial gunners on the ground, one to a blood infection and one to a propeller accident.

On September 27, 1943, Col. Jacob J. Brogger assumed command of the 446th when Col. Snell was relieved on orders from Headquarters 16th Bombardment Operational Training Wing, Tucson, Arizona. Col. Brogger took the group overseas with the following group and squadron leaders: Lt. Col. Frederick J. Knorre, deputy group commander; Maj. Karl B. Greenlee, executive officer; Capt. Cooper F. Hawthorne, 704th Squadron Commander; 1st Lt. William A. Schmidt, 704th Squadron Operations; Capt. Solomon Cutcher, 705th Squadron Commander; 1st Lt. Arthur H. Aull, 706th Squadron Operations; Capt. Hugh C. Arnold, 707th Squadron

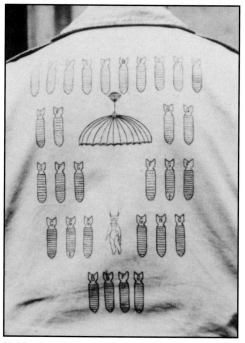

Field Jacket of Ernest D. Little, 446th Bomb Group, 705th Bomb Squad. The "†" on the bottom of the 19th bomb is for Lt. Homer S. Gentry, KIA on 4-11-44, Bernberg, Germany. The "E" on the bottom of the bottom of the 22nd bomb is for when the Germans followed us home from Hamm, Germany and shot down a number of our planes in the dark. The parachute is for bailout in Africa, July 7th, 1943. (Courtesy of Ernest D. Little)

Commander; 1st Lt. Oscar F. Fowler, 707th Squadron Operations. Over the time of the 446th Bomb Group's combat service in Europe, the following men were promoted and served in one or more of the above leadership positions as attrition brought about changes due to wounds, becoming prisoners of war, completion of combat tours, and movement to other assignments: Floyd B. Mitchell, Myers B. Cather, Edward L. Sheeley, Arthur C. Quattlebaum, William D. Kyle, Frank Yochem, Thomas W. Spurgin, William B. Cozard and Vincent J. Loyeto.

On October 24, 1943, an advance party was flown to England by the Air Transport Command where it visited other bases and surveyed the new station in preparation for the arrival of the entire group. Those in the party were followed in short order by the ground echelon on the *Queen Mary* and the air echelon via the southern route from Lincoln, Nebraska, to Borinquen Field, Puerto Rico; Waller Field, Trinidad; Belem, Brazil; Natal, Brazil; Dakar, French West Africa and Marrakech, Morocco. On the last leg to Station 125, Flixton near Bungay, Suffolk, England, one plane was shot down by FW-190s and JU-88s and one was lost to flak when it strayed off course and flew over the Brest Peninsula thereby receiving an early introduction to enemy action.

The group's first mission was to Bremen on December 16, 1943, and was followed by missions to such targets as: the U-boat installations at Kiel, the port at Bremen, a chemical plant at Ludwigshafen, a ball-bearing factory at Berlin, an aero-engine plant at Rostock, an aircraft factory at Munich, the marshalling yards at Coblenz, an oil refinery at Hamburg, and a synthetic oil plant at Politz among its total of 273 missions including its last one to Salzburg on April 25, 1945. Its most famous mission occurred on D-day, June 6, 1944, when, in company with a 389th H2X aircraft, it was chosen to lead the 8th Air Force for the early morning coastal bombings that preceded the invasion landings. In addition, the group flew in support of ground troops at both Caen and St. Lo; carried flour and medical supplies to the French civilians at Orleans, France; made a supply drop near Nijmegen, Holland; bombed bridges, marshalling yards, and road junctions during the Battle of the Bulge; and made supply drops to airborne and ground troops during the Allied assault at the crossing of the Rhine. All told the groups campaigns included: the Air Offensive over Europe, Normandy, Northern France, the Rhineland, Ardennes-Alsace and Central Europe.

Col. Brogger was wounded by ground fire on September 18, 1944, during the low level supply drop to 1st Army paratroopers near Nijmegen, Holland. He was hospitalized, relieved of command and returned to the States. Col. Troy W. Crawford became group CO and was later shot down by gunners from his own 446th Bomb Group. While flying in a Mosquito on the April 4, 1945, mission to Wesendorf Airfield near Berlin to monitor the formation, he attempted to enter the formation for protection from attacking FW-190s and 15 ME-262s. The Mosquito was mistaken for one of the jets in as much as it was on what seemed to be a regular pursuit curve between two ME-262s and was hit by 446th gunners. This forced Col. Crawford and his pilot to bail out. He was rescued from a German interrogation center and returned to the States as a former POW. He was replaced by Col. William A. Schmidt who had been part of the original cadre of the group and who then served as 446th Bomb Group C.O. until the time of its deactivation at Sioux Falls, South Dakota, on August 28, 1945.

The group lost a total of 65 planes with 447 of its men killed in action while dropping 16,818.95 tons of bombs on its 273 missions during which its gunners destroyed 37 enemy aircraft.

The group was redesignated the 446th Bomb Group (VH) and allotted to the Reserve. It was re-

activated on March 26, 1948, ordered to active duty May 1, 1951, and assigned to the Strategic Air Command. It was deactivated June 25, 1951 and redesignated as the 446th Troop Carrier Group (Medium), allotted to the Reserve, and activated on May 25, 1955. It continues to serve in this capacity at McCord AFB, Spokane, Washington.

The 446th Bomb Group Association, Inc. has been formed to perpetuate its history, to hold reunions, to provide comradeship and to foster the esprit de corps of the 446th. It also maintains and supports its memorial at the USAF Museum, Dayton, Ohio; the memorial gates and benches at St. Marys Church, Flixton, England, where its Roll of Honor is installed; a second Roll of Honor in the 2nd Air Division Memorial Room at the Norwich Central Library, Norwich, England, and the restored B-24J in the 446th Bomb Group's yellow and black tail colors, at the Pima Air Museum in Tucson, Arizona. The association also publishes a quarterly newsletter, *The Beachbell Echo* and holds an annual reunion in addition to joining in the annual 2nd Air Division convention.

The 446th Bomb Group (H) was composed of the 704th, 705th, 706th and 707th Bomb Squadrons during Worl War II and included the following service units:

Detachment 'A' 1248th MP Co. (Avn.)
460th Sub-Depot Class I
558th Army Postal Unit
559th Army Postal Unit
2967th Finance Department
212th Finance Section
2035th Engineer Aviation Fire Fighting Plt.
1214th QM Co. Service Group Avn. (RS)
Detachment 'A' 885th Chemical Co.
1821st Ordnance Supply and Maintenance Co. (Avn.)
25th Station Complement Sqdn. (SP)
260th Medical Dispensary Avn. (RS)
378th Air Service Group
Group HQ and HQ Sqdn.
815th Air Engineering Sqdn.
639th Materiel Sqdn.

The story of a B-24 in the 704th Bomb Squadron, 446th Bomb Group, which was destined to become one of the most famous Liberators of the 8th Air Force began in Denver, Colorado, like the group did. S/Sgt. Ronald Gannon of Zanesville, Ohio, was a waist gunner on Lt. Casteel's model crew. He was tall, good looking and a crack shot, but before the group went overseas something happened to Ronnie. His coordination seemed to leave him and on the skeet range he began missing targets that were once easy for him. Finally, he went to the base hospital at Lowry field where he died of the same slow paralyzing disease which caused the death of baseball great, Lou Gehrig. His pilot and crew named their aircraft *Ronnie* and flew it across the Atlantic as part of the original group. Ironically, the plane at first seemed to follow the tragic pattern of its namesake. Four times *Ronnie* took off and, due to engine trouble, returned without completing a mission. Beginning to have a reputation as a lemon, the plane was turned over to Crew Chief Mike Zyne who worked long hours and got the bugs out. *Ronnie* went on to fly well over 100 missions including 79 consecutively without an abort. This was the heavy bomber record at that time. This special B-24 was returned to the States after the end of hostilities as one of the few aircraft of the original group to survive the war.

Another unusual B-24 in the 446th Bomb Group was *Werewolf/Princess O'Rourke*. The crew of Lt. Wylie had named their Liberator *Werewolf* while in training at Lowry Field. They were approached by a Hollywood publicity team to use the name *Princess O'Rourke* as a temporary name in order to publicize the 1943 movie *Princess O'Rourke* starring Jane Wyman. The story was about a Scottish Terrier named *Princess O'Rourke*, so the name went on along with a painting of a black Scottish Terrier. The aircraft went overseas keeping both names, one on each side of the fuselage making it what may well have been the only plane to fly combat with two names. It was lost on the April 11, 1944 mission to Bernberg, Germany.

Medals Presented To Group Members

One Distinguished Service Cross, one Legion of Merit, 13 Silver Stars, 60 Bronze Stars, 1,041 Distinguished Flying Crosses, 51 Oak Leaf Clusters to Distinguished Flying Crosses, six Soldier's Medals, 2,938 Air Medals, 6,409 Oak Leaf Clusters to Air Medals, 114* Purple Hearts, three Oak Leaf Clusters to Purple Hearts, five Croix de Guerres (French).

*This does not include medals presented to next of kin of group personnel who were killed in action.

Battle Honors

The following are the battles and campaigns for which the 446th Bomb Group was given official battle participation credit as outlined in War Department General Orders:

Air Offensive, Europe, Combat zone, European Theater of Operations exclusive of the land areas of the United Kingdom and Iceland. Time limitation, July 4, 1942 to June 5, 1944.

Normandy, Time limitation, June 6, 1944 to July 24, 1944.

Northern France, European Theater of Operations exclusive of land areas of the United Kingdom and Iceland. Time limitation, July 25, 1944 to September 14, 1944.

Rhineland, Combat zone. Those portions of France, Belgium, Holland, Luxembourg, and Germany east of the line: Franco-Belgian frontier to four degrees east longitude, thence south along that meridian to 47 degrees latitude, thence east along that parallel to five degrees east longitude, thence south along that meridian to the Mediterranean Coast. Time limitation, September 15, 1944 to March 21, 1945.

Ardennes, Combat zone. The area forward of the line: Euskirchen-Eupen (inclusive), Liege (exclusive), east bank of Meuse River to its intersection with the Franco-Belgian Border, thence south and east along this border and the southern border of Luxembourg. Time limitation, September 15, 1944 to March 21, 1945.

Central Europe, Combat zone. The areas occupied by troops assigned to the European Theater of Operations, United States Army, which lie beyond a line 10 miles west of the Rhine River between Switzerland and the Waal River until March 28, 1945 (inclusive), and thereafter beyond the east bank of the Rhine. Time limitation, March 22, 1945 to May 11, 1945.

448TH BOMB GROUP (H)

by Leroy Engdahl

The beginning of the 448th Bomb Group was at Gowen Field, Boise, Idaho in May 1943. After a short period at the Orlando School, the group began operations at Wendover, Utah where personnel were assigned to expand the group.

The advance phases of training took place at Sioux City, Iowa. This was during the months of September, October and part of November 1943.

It wasn't until just prior to final staging at Herington, Kansas, where aircraft were assigned, that ground crews, establishment staff and combat crews were completed. The training was hurried and incomplete, but the big push was on to start the serious bombardment of Germany and occupied Europe.

The group commander was Col. James McK Thompson, 37 years of age, a regular Army officer. His background, like many others, was primarily in twin engine aircraft.

The operations officer was Capt. Ronald Kramer from Denver, Colorado, 23 years of age and a pre-war private pilot. He had been a B-17 instructor pilot.

The assistant operations officer was 1st Lt. John Grunow. Grunow was a 1942 graduate of Columbia University and an experienced four engine pilot on B-24s. Both Kramer and Grunow had previously served as test pilots.

The intelligence officer was Capt. Seul Arnold, 46 years old and a World War I retread who served in France in 1918. He was a lawyer in civilian life.

The unit's deputy commander was Maj. Hubert Stonewall Judy Jr., a graduate of the University of Oklahoma, who was called to active duty from the Officers Reserve Corps in the wake of Pearl Harbor. He was a very experienced B-24 pilot and an engineer.

The ground executive officer was Lt. Col. Carl Elver and the base adjutant was Capt. Ken Parkinson.

Each of the four squadrons of the 448th (712th, 713th, 714th, 715th) had a full complement of officers and enlisted men. The group staff was also complete.

In late November records were checked, wills and allotments were made out to dependents, and final medical checks were completed. The air echelon departed in 64 planes from Morrison Field in South Florida with 14 men in each plane.

For the over ocean-flight, group commander, Col. J. McK Thompson was assigned to Lts. Graham Guyton and Tom Allen's plane along with engineering officer, Capt. John Laws, together with assistant executive officer, Maj. Patterson, and Lt. Minor Morgan.

Their destination was Puerto Rico. After two hours in the air each pilot was to open his sealed orders to find out his final destination and route. The southern route was designated as it was late November and the weather wasn't very friendly.

The route took them from Puerto Rico to Trinidad or Georgetown, to Belem, Brazil and to Natal, Brazil. One pilot had his left arm severed at Georgetown in a landing accident. His was the first of four planes to be lost en route to England.

From Natal they flew to Dakar, West Africa over 1,200 miles across the Atlantic with all the other planes arriving okay. At Dakar the pilots landed for their first time on steel mats.

After a flight to Marrakech, Morroco, the crews were given a much needed rest before their final briefing for their long flight to England.

At Marrakech the 448th lost two planes and all 14 aboard each. One plane heavily laden with fuel stalled on take off. This was 2nd Lt. John P. Rhodes in *Fink Jink*.

The second mishap occurred to 2nd Lt. Joseph W. Shank who lost an engine about 75 miles out. It being a night take off, they missed the field at Marrakech in an attempted return and flew into the Atlas Mountains.

The weather had been pretty bad for the previous five days and all planes that landed in England at St. Mawgan Airfield had been grounded.

All the planes that left Marrakech had been accounted for except that of 2nd Lt. Robert C. Ayrest.

Later, after several planes had reached their final destination at Seething about 11 miles southeast of Norwich, it was learned that Lt. Ayrest's plane had a forced landing in Wales and the aircraft was completely wrecked and burned, with all crewman safe. Fate was not to be nice to Lt. Ayrest as he was later killed in an attempt to avoid a collision in the air near the base along with several others. The stress on the plane, in avoiding the collision, broke it into two pieces at the rear of the bomb bay.

It was soon determined that more training was necessary before sending this group into combat against the Germans. Formation flying had to be especially addressed, procedures in a combat zone were a must to become familiar with and an intense brushing up was undertaken.

Violations of some procedures could draw friendly fire from nervous British ground gunners as the Germans had several downed American planes in flying order and occasionally used them to penetrate British air space.

Procedures also had to be learned by the ground echelon which had arrived via the *Queen Elizabeth* out of New York and which landed at the Firth of Clyde near Glasgow, Scotland.

The ground echelon consisted of the 862nd Chemical Company Air Operations; 123rd Quarter Master Company; 58th Station Complement Squadron which handled the control tower; 262nd Medical Dispensary (aviation); 459th Sub Depot; 2102nd Engineer Aviation Fire Fighting Platoon; 1193rd Military Police Company and the 1596th Ordnance Supply and Maintenance Company. In all, there were around 3,000 men.

The 448th's first combat mission was flown on December 22, 1943, to Osnaburck, Germany. This was the same day that the last of the group's B-24s finally arrived from the States.

Twenty six aircraft took off, but due to bad weather and inexperienced pilots 13 returned early without having made the formation.

The weather was so bad that the entire 20th Combat Wing, made up of the 448th, the 446th at Bungay and the 93rd at Hardwick, was very confused. However, they finally made wing formation by the time they reached the Dutch coast.

The 448th suffered its first combat losses there. Second Lieutenant David E. Manning was shot down and all the crew was killed. First Lieutenant Ed Hughey Jr. fell out of formation and was hit immediately. All were killed except the assistant engineer and top turret gunner. Lieutenant Joe Smith's plane was bombed by one of our own during the turmoil over the target. No parachutes were seen as the plane plummeted to earth. In addition, five other 448th planes were severely damaged. To make things even worse, when the target was photographed two days later it showed no damage to the target. It was a bitter start for the 448th.

Losses continued between 10 and 12 percent for the 2nd Bomb Division and the 448th until late April 1944 when the 8th Air Force began to control the sky.

Until the end of the war in Europe the 448th did not suffer more than two losses per mission, with the exceptions of the Wesel raid on March 24, 1945, when three planes were lost; the Buchen raid on March 25, 1945, when the group suffered four losses; and the Berlin raid of April 19, 1944, on which the 448th suffered six planes lost.

The first airman of the original 448th combat crews to complete his tour was 1st Lt. Leroy Engdahl, then of Brady, Texas. He finished his 30th mission on May 11, 1944, on a mission to Mulhouse, France. The 448th had lost 75 bombers to combat and accidents prior to this, so it was a real morale boost for the group to finally get an airman through his tour.

In all, during the 448th time in the ETO, the

Crew B-16, March Field 1944. Carl Wysochanski AEG, Charles Yoho ROG, William Watling AG, Rheo Swiggum AG, Joseph Autobee AAG, Edaward Malkowski AG,Harold Gully P, John Reynolds CP, Francis Walsh B, Elton Shull N, assigned to this crew before going to ETO, 713 Sqdn. 448th Bomb AAF 146, Seething, England. (Courtesy of Elton M. Shull)

group flew 262 missions, lost 146 planes, and had 462 of its men killed.

One of the 448th officers, Lt. Joe McConnell, who served as a navigator in early 1945, returned to the States, became a pilot and was the leading jet ace in the Korean conflict with 16 kills. He lost his life while serving as a test pilot at Edwards AFB.

The 448th had four commanders during its period of operation in the ETO: Col. James McK Thompson from May 1943 to April 1944; Col. Gerry Mason from April 1944 to November 1944; Col. Charles B. Westover from November 1944 to May 1945 and; Lt. Col. Lester F. Miller from May 1945 until the return to the States.

The 448th had six of its officers go on to become general officers. In no particular order: Brig. Gen. Hubert S. Judy, Maj. Gen. Lester F. Miller (living), Lt. Gen. William W. Snavely (living), Gen. Charles B. Westover, Maj. Gen. James Jones (living) and Maj. Gen. William Hayes.

The 448th Bomb Group Association has held group reunions since 1985, and returned to England in 1984, 1987, and 1992. Granite memorials have been established at the old air base, the village of Seething churchyard, and at Wright Patterson AFB. Their World War II Control Tower which serves as a popular museum has been restored. The base is owned and operated by the Waveney Flying Group at old station No. 146. Members have established wonderful friendships with many of the British in Seething and Norwich.

Past officers of the 448th Bomb Group Association are: Kenneth Englebrecht (living), Joseph Michalczyk (deceased), Leroy Engdahl (living), Gail Irish (deceased), Cater Lee (living).

We are proud to have been a part of the 8th Air Force and to have contributed to the defeat of the German War Machine.

453RD BOMB (H) GROUP

courtesy of Don Olds

The 453rd Bombardment Group (H) was organized by the 2nd Bomber Command, pursuant to the order of the 2nd Air Force, Colorado Springs, Colorado, dated June 22, 1943. Special orders, dated June 22, 1943, released Col. Joseph A. Miller, 0-18211, from assignment and designated him as the commanding officer of the 453rd Bomb Group (H), Gowen Field, Boise, Idaho. On June 29, 1943, Col. Miller assumed command of said group at Gowen Field.

Four B-24s were assigned, one for each squadron, and on July 21, the entire cadre moved to Pinecastle AAF, located directly south of Orlando, Florida. On July 23 they flew their first simulated attack on some docks and a warehouse area at Wilmington. The 453rd dispatched five B-24s (one on loan). Two returned to base from a point about 60 miles west of Charleston because of bad weather, but the other three reached their target. On July 30, the group flew its seventh and final practice mission in Florida. Four planes took off and all attacked the primary target. This final mission was planned and briefed by the staff of the 735th Bomb Squadron, commanded by Maj. Robert Harris.

By this time it had been definitely determined that the group would be stationed, at least temporarily, at Pocatello, Idaho. Travel began on Saturday, July 31. No unusual occurrence accompanied the prescribed TPA travel, or the travel by military airplane, with the possible exceptions that the automobiles were strained to make Pocatello by the following Friday. However, travel by troop train was made more interesting by the fact that Capt. John C. McFadden, in command, missed the train twice; first at Denver, and next at Cheyenne. However, he managed to make Pocatello with his troops. Someone suggested that he caught his train in one instance by going to the highway and thumbing a ride on a truck.

Meanwhile, the group cadre at Gowen field, performed the usual garrison duties from the time the group was organized, until orders to move. During the waiting period, rumors prevailed as to the future home of the group. Wendover, Utah; Bruning and Lincoln, Nebraska; and Salt Lake City were among the places wagered on by many. Finally, the orders came directing movement by troop train to Pocatello. Wives drove automobiles because TPA was not authorized. Maj. Hayden Trigg of the 732nd was train commander.

The base at Pocatello was not prepared to take care of an additional heavy bombardment group, but everything possible was done to assign comfortable living quarters and working facilities. Flying missions were run in every squadron and training for future tasks was the constant call and endeavor. Several flights were made by group and squadron officers to Wendover, Utah, to visit OTU groups, then in second and third phase training in order to get ideas as to the best methods. Programs for crew and maintenance training, including ground school, were planned and prepared.

It was assumed and assured that the group would not remain at Pocatello for second and third phase training, and there was much speculation as to where the organization might be sent. Finally, March AA Field, Riverside, California, was appointed the new home of the 453rd Bomb Group. Col. Miller, accompanied by other staff members, visited March AA Field and gave to the group a picture of what might be expected at its new home. The advance party left by troop train on September 22 and proceeded to make the arrangements that could be made for the arrival of the crews, planes and main train movements.

Many new crews were assigned to the group during the last days at Pocatello and the remainder arrived shortly after headquarters was established at March AAF. These crews were not evenly trained. some had very little training in the planes and this added to the task of creating a trained group. The tactical training was planned and handled in the squadron throughout the first and second phases.

The group POM inspection was held on November 13 and 15, and on November 16 it was announced at group staff meeting that it had been successfully passed. It was understood that the rigid training would continue and the regular third-phase plans carried out during the remainder of the time at March AAF.

The 453rd Bomb Group left March by rail on December 2, 1943 and arrived at Camp Kilmer, New Jersey POE on December 7, 1943. They were quickly put through the final processing and boarded their ship, the mighty *Queen Elizabeth*, on December 13 bound for England. The remainder of the trip was made by train and the first section arrived at Station No. 144, Old Buckenham on the morning of December 23. The second section arrived the next day. After a day or so of getting settled, the 453rd was beginning to set up its new home for operations against the Axis.

While the ground echelon was moving overseas by boat, the air echelon traveled to Hamilton Field, California. They were processed there and received their new airplanes. From Hamilton Field the air echelon moved brokenly across the southern sector of the United States and flew to their new station by the southern route. Terrible weather conditions caused some delay at different points along the route, but the first contingent arrived at Station 144 soon after the first of the year.

The arriving men of the 453rd Bomb Group found their new home near Old Buckenham, Norfolk, England, in a turmoil. The prevailing weather conditions of rain, snow and cold wind made the base a quagmire. Minor cases of colds and flu took a big toll and men were issued overshoes to counteract the mud.

As each squadron came in, it set up its own operational offices on the line. Each department had its own separate installations, except intelligence and communications which were consolidated at group headquarters. The group began operations February 5, 1944, with its first mission being the airfield at Tours, France. Lt. Voskian crashed on take off claiming the lives of eight crew members. The rest of the mission was successful and all of its planes returned safely.

On February 20, 24 planes took off on their seventh mission to bomb Brunswick, Germany. All planes returned safely, save one. Lt. Albert Lane's crew was shot down, becoming the first crew to be lost to enemy fire.

On February 22, the group performed its ninth mission with 28 planes. The target was an aircraft assembly plant at Gotha, Germany. Lt. Ingram and his entire crew, flying 42-64138, were lost on this mission. This was only the group's second loss, but there were many more to follow.

March 6, 1944, was a historic day. Berlin felt the sting of the first daylight attack. Four of the planes sent out by the 453rd failed to return. Lt. Cripe and his crew of the 734th Squadron, along with the Lt. Tobin of the 733rd went down over enemy territory. Lts. Crockett of the 733rd and Meek of the 735th ditched their planes in the channel. Lt. Joseph Cyr was the lone survivor of Lt. Meek's crew and Lts. George Nacos and Orvis Martin, and S/Sgts. William Talbot and Max Martin were picked up with Lt. Crockett.

On April 8, the group suffered its heaviest loss in a single raid to date. Of 32 dispatched, seven failed to return. Heavy flak and severe enemy fighter attacks took a heavy toll, but the bombing results were excellent. The target for that day was Brunswick. Lts. Joe DeJarnette and James Bingaman of the 732nd, Lts. August Bergman and Fred Brady of the 733rd, Lt. Robert Swigert of the 734th and Lts. Jack Dixon and Jay Wells of the 735th were lost with their crews.

April 22 saw 26 planes depart for the marshalling yards at Hamm, Germany. Due to a late take off, landings were made in total darkness and many aircraft had encounters with intruders. Lt. James Munsey's ship was hit by a JU-88 off the English coast and crashed in flames just after making landfall at Southwold. The bodies of Lt. Munsey and Lt. Robert Crall, the co-pilot, were found dead. T/Sgt. Grover Conway was last seen dropping into the water about 50 feet offshore. Lts. Leon Helfand and Arthur Orlowski, S/Sgts. Ralph McClure and Kenneth Laux and Sgt. Norman Brown escaped with burns and other injuries. In July of 1944, Lt. Munsey received the Distinguished Flying Cross posthumously for his selfless devotion to his comrades.

On May 8, one month to the day since the 453rd had attacked Brunswick with such great loss, the episode was repeated with still greater loss. Capt. Low, commanding officer of the 735th Squadron, led the group which in turn led the 2nd Air Division and the entire 8th Air Force. Of a total of 27 planes dispatched, only 17 returned safely to home base. Lt. Jones and Lt. Asbury crash landed at Watton after ordering the rest of the crew to bail out. Lt. Catlin experienced a similar landing at Hardwick, injuring S/Sgt. Bates, the ball turret gunner. Those lost with their own crews were, Lts. Richard Witton and Ray Keith of the 732nd; Lt. Fred Parker of the 733rd, Lts. Dean Hart, John Banks and Thomas Stilbert of the 734th; and Lts. John McKay and Endicott Lovell of the 735th Squadron.

Zero-hour, 0628, June 6, 1944; code word, Mairsey-Doats; target, complete destruction of the enemy forces' installations on the shore line between LeHavre and Cherbourg and as far inland as the city of Caen. Secondary targets: any railroad, enemy troop concentration or road junction further inland. Precise timing was of the utmost importance. The invasion of Europe was on. Throughout the whole day of June 6, despite the worsening weather, planes took off and landed, helping to make this the greatest day in the history not only of the group, but of the entire 8th Air Force as well. In all, four complete missions were flown by the group. A total of 70 planes were dispatched against the targets of St. Laurent, St. Lo, Caen and Coutances. They continued to pound France in June.

One of the 453rd's replacement B-24s. They were natural metal finish (NMF). This one displays the new tail markings. Black fin with black diagonal stripe. (Courtesy of Donald J. Olds)

Of 33 missions credited to the group in June, only five were done somewhere other than France. During the month, four aircraft were lost, Capt. George Baatz, Lt. Williams, Lt. Raiser, and Lt. Kolb, who was forced down in Sweden.

July 5, 1944, the 100th mission was flown exactly five months after commencing operations. The 100th mission was celebrated by a dance at the Aero Club that night. During the month, most bombing was routine and results varied. Bad weather often necessitated the use of PFF equipment. Losses were significant. in this one month, three command pilots were lost; Capt. Beckett, Capt. Boreske, and Maj. Low on the 31st. Other planes suffered battle damage and were forced to make emergency landings on the continent and at various airfields around England.

Twenty-four targets were attacked in August, again mostly in France. Losses were down, however. On the 11th, Lt. Freed was forced to ditch his plane on his way home, and Lt. Stanchfield was also lost to heavy flak on the 16th.

Lt. Dean Mills' crew was the only loss during the month of September. On September 18, 19 and 20, the 453rd went into the hauling and/or trucking business. The group dispatched 52 planes carrying supplies, landing at Clastres, France. On the 18th, they sent planes full of five gallon cans of gasoline, blankets on the 19th, and flour and other rations on the 20th.

In approximately eight months of operations, the group had lost 40 crews over Germany. Forty men were interned in Sweden and 13 in Switzerland, seven had escaped and returned to the home base. Of the crews that had crash landed or ditched, 42 had survived, some had been grounded, others had gone on flying. Seventeen men had evaded the Germans after bailing out over enemy territory. Thirty five had been reported killed in action, 136 prisoners of war and 266 missing in action. This is the unfortunate price of war.

October saw two crews lost. Lt. James Emerson's plane was bombed by the group above him and exploded. Only one of the crew members survived. Lt. Lloyd Carter was lost to flak on the 19th. Several ground crew chiefs were awarded medals in October for meritorious achievement. They had sent out several Libs day after day without an abort. Also, Maj. Robert D. Coggeshall was awarded the Distinguished Flying Cross in recognition of the 733rd Squadron going 82 consecutive missions without a loss. Maj. Coggeshall was Squadron Commanding Officer of the 733rd and had been with the group from its beginning.

Weather had begun to take control of flying in November. Only 14 missions were flown by the group during the month. El Flako, had never aborted in 77 missions and always returned its crew safely. But on her 78th, she took a direct flak hit, broke in half and went down. The entire crew, flying their first mission, was lost, victims of a cruel trick of fate.

December saw the group fly its fewest missions since February, an even dozen. Hitler could thank the ETO weather for that. Nevertheless, the group did establish a 2nd Division record by putting 62 Liberators over the target on Christmas Eve. December showed no operational losses to the enemy, but Lt. Brown's crash on take off on the 27th, left only three survivors.

The group put on a huge Christmas party for 1,250 British children from surrounding villages. They were served ice cream and cake and were entertained with some animated cartoons. Everyone had a good time.

Mission No. 197, the first of the new year, had a tragic beginning. Lt. Judd of the 735th Squadron, leading the group, crashed while attempting to take off. The plane slipped off the runway, slithered across the frozen field unable to rise or stop and crashed into two parked planes. The planes sustained only minor damage, but nine of the 11 man crew lost their lives. Undaunted by the tragedy, the planes continued to take off from the treacherous runway. Six aircraft succeeded in taking to the air but the eighth, piloted by Lt. V. E. Smith of the 733rd Squadron, while trying to test the runway slid off bringing his plane to a stop on the rough frozen field. Watching from the control tower, Col. Thomas, group commander, prevented further loss of lives and equipment by ordering a halt to the proceedings.

January 5, 1945, the group established a record of which it could be rightly proud. On that day, the group accomplished its 200th mission, exactly 11 months from the date it had performed its first mission. The group managed only 13 missions during the month. They were grounded by inclement weather and at one stretch, flew only one mission in 13 days. No aircraft were lost to hostile fire during the month.

453rd Bomb Group, Golden Gaboon ... Showing the letter J in the circle. The original group marking. It crashed on the Old Buckenham runway after the mission of May 30, 1944 and was consumed by fire. (Courtesy of Donald J. Olds)

Crew of Diana-Mite, 734th Bomb Squadron, 453rd Bomb Group, "Old Buckenham." Front, L to R: Richard Sutton, Copilot; Salvadore A. Moriello, Pilot; Charles Brannigan, Navigator; Richard Webb, Bombardier. Rear, L to R: Daniel Hoien, Left Waist; Ross Walters, Engineer; George Ion, Nose Gunner; Robert Viets, Tail Gunner; Joseph Hancock, Radio Operator; Roger R. Hann, Right Waist Gunner. (Courtesy of Roger Hahn)

Crew of the 733rd Squadron from October 1944 through May 1945. The top photo was taken January 1, 1945 and the bottom photo was taken June 1990. Pictured are: Carl Lessing, Pilot; Bill Hailey, Copilot; Verl Anderson, Bombardier; Jim Wilcox, Navigator; George Giovannani, Engineer; Fred Talley, Radio Operator; Carloton Mann, Gunner; Donald Nell, Gunner; Ed Winick, Gunner; Jack Harris, Gunner. They flew 25 missions with the 453rd Bomb Group. (Courtesy of Jack Harris)

February of 1945 came in very quietly. The year's shortest month observed 16 missions, 12 recorded in the last 15 days. February 5 marked one year of operations completed against the enemy. To celebrate, a ground party was held at the Aero Club. The club was packed for an evening of dancing and merriment for the GI's and their dates. Also, in February, an entire crew was lost during an assembly crash. Two B-24s ditched in the North Sea, returning from their missions, losing a total of 10 men. On the ninth, Lt. Glass and Lt. Rollins were involved in a landing pattern collision which resulted in the death of Lt. Rollins and his entire 11 man crew.

For its contribution to the successful conclusion of the war, the 453rd flew 25 missions in March, the greatest total since that memorable June in 1944. Carrying the string of missions which began on February 21 well into March, the group performed five missions in the first five days of the month to establish the enviable record of 14 missions on 14 consecutive days. Considerably better than half of the months missions resulted in visual bombing with

excellent results. None of our planes were lost until the 31st, and again it was the nemesis Brunswick. Lt. Richard Bussell was hit by jet aircraft and had two engines knocked out. He trailed the formation and finally dropped out and made a crash landing, killing two on board. Lt. Bussell was the first crew lost to enemy aircraft in 10 months. Lt. Owens Hopper was seen going down at the Dutch Coast on the way to the target. Eleven chutes were counted indicating all on board had escaped.

April ushered in more gloomy days. The weather kept the group grounded for the first three days. On April 4, the target was an airfield at Wessendorf. German fighters made an appearance but concentrated their attack on other groups. The 453rd escaped with but a few holes in their planes. April 10 saw the seventh mission performed in seven days, to the Luftwaffe's experimental base at Rechlin. About 10 miles from Hittenberge, the group ran into intense flak and Lt. William Powell's Lib received a direct hit and went down in flames. It was to be the last 453rd plane lost to the enemy

and it carried eight of the 11 man crew to their deaths.

On April 11, the 453rd Bomb Group wrote finis to its operation in the ETO. It flew its 259th and final mission against a rail junction at Amberg. After the mission, the group was stood down permanently and verbal orders to prepare to move were received on the 12th. With the cessation of operations on April 13, 1945, the group was afforded a unique opportunity to catch up on maintenance and repair work. This period of non-activity lasted almost a week. On April 19 orders came through from Headquarters, ETO, alerting the organization for departure from the theater. We were to be one of the "redeployed units" destined for duty in the Pacific Theater, after all personnel had been given thirty days R&R leaves and furloughs in the USA.

By May 5, all of the group aircraft had been accepted by technical inspectors of the groups which were to receive them, and all organizational property was packed and crated, ready for shipment.

V-E day arrived on May 8, as well as our movement orders. Victory in Europe was really good news for us, as it meant that we saw the successful conclusion of the job we had directed our efforts to for the past two years. Also, we could now be departing the European Theater with no regrets about leaving in the middle of a fight. We took our last look at Old Buckenham at about 1000 hours and boarded the troop train which was to take us to the POE at Southampton, England.

The 453rd Bomb Group, along with the other organizations, embarked on the Naval Transport, USS *Hermitage*, on May 9, 1945. We got under-

453rd Bomb Group, 735th Bomb Squadron. Standing L to R: Long, Fresberg, Hegwood, Thurman, Moffsinger, Ruble. Kneeling L to R: Green, Parcells, Plasmati, Brady, Turner. (Courtesy of Orvile K. Long)

way on our journey back to the USA on May 13. After an uneventful crossing, we docked at Boston Harbor at about 1400 hours on May 23. By 2000 hours, we had disembarked and were speeding on yet another troop train, toward Camp Myles Standish. Onboard we were served doughnuts and fresh milk by the American Red Cross. For many, this was the first fresh milk in over 18 months. Everyone agreed that the United States was a fine place to be.

The next day the whole organization had been segregated by reception station groups, and were entertained to their new stations where they were to receive their 30 days R&R leaves. They were to rejoin the group at the Army Air Field at Fort Dix, New Jersey, some 30 days in the future.

Upon reporting back to the air base, it was learned that our organization was to be disbanded and all personnel were to be placed in the Air Transport Command. Personnel were shipped out each day to stations all over the United States: Dallas, St. Joseph, Reno, Long Beach, Palm Springs, Great Falls, etc.," the best damn outfit in the Army Air Force splitting up."

The 453rd Bomb Group activated June 29, 1943, completed its assigned mission and was officially deactivated September 15, 1945. Another organization, another chapter, in the annuals of the United States at war.

458TH BOMB GROUP (H)

by George A. Reynolds

The creation of a new, heavy bombardment group composed of four existing bombardment squadrons, the 752nd, 753rd, 754th and 755th, began in March 1943. The number 458 was specified on or about April 24, and this unit was activated July 1, 1943, at Wendover, Utah. Personnel and hardware assembly started at Gowen Field, Boise, Idaho, July 28. Training was accomplished at airfields in Boise, Orlando and Pinecastle, Florida, Kearns, Salt Lake City and Wendover, Utah and Tonopah, Nevada.

Project 92336 reassigned the 458th to the European Theater of Operations (ETO). Its ground echelon left Tonopah by rail January 1, 1944 en route to New York's Port of Embarkation and the USS *Florence Nightingale* for their overseas journey. They arrived at Greenock, Scotland, January 31 and

their base, Army Air Forces Station 123, Horsham St. Faith, Norfolk County, England, February 1. This airdrome had been a permanent Royal Air Force facility and soon the new arrivals were attracting envy from some of their peers stationed in lesser quality quarters throughout East Anglia.

Aircrews departed Tonopah for Hamilton Field, California to pick up new and additional B-24s. They flew their "Liberators" to England via Brazil and West Africa, joining the support elements on the home base February 18. Additional personnel training and aircraft modifications began immediately as this fledgling group prepared for its coming aerial battles.

The 458th's first combat assignment came February 24 in flying a diversionary mission along the Dutch coast to draw enemy fighters away from Germany while experienced units struck deep into the enemy's homeland. A similar mission was flown the next day along the French coast. Initial bombing sorties began March 2 with a strike on Frankfurt, Germany. All ships returned to base. Then on March 6 the 458th flew in the first mission the 8th Air Force completed on Berlin. Five crews did not return from this one—the highest loss total of any mission for the remainder of its combat tour.

On June 6, D-day was a hectic one for the group in flying three missions with 59 aircraft being dispatched. As weather conditions improved during summer, operations increased and the 458th completed 100 missions before June expired.

During the month of May a cadre of personnel brought a specialized and highly classified project to Horsham to test a new, revolutionary weapon for the 8th Air Force. Ten crews, initially, were to deliver a cargo of "controllable" bombs on bridges and other selected targets in preparations for the D-day invasion of fortress Europe. Those bombs were named AZ (imuth) ON (ly) and amounted to a projectile whose course could be altered after it was released from the aircraft.

The Azon Bomb consisted of a unit with a radio receiver bolted to a standard 1,000-pound bomb which replaced ordinary fins. After release from the bomb bay, bombardiers used a transmitter in the aircraft to correct azimuth errors while the projectile fell by activating moveable fins on the control unit. Range errors could not be changed, however. This weapon also employed a flare of different colors, and the controller had to observe the bomb's flight path down to the objective. Weather conditions over the continent were not at all favorable

for this type activity during its test period. But one practice run and 13 actual Azon missions were made before the project was discontinued in September. Under ideal conditions, Azon Bombs proved to be a very effective weapon for use in pinpoint bombing requirements more than saturation-type bombing. But more importantly, the testing pointed the way for use in other "smart" bomb projects in future years.

When September arrived, Allied ground forces were making rapid advances across Europe as they pushed the enemy back toward his homeland. Progress was so good, in fact, America's 3rd Army was outrunning its own supply sources, and gasoline for its armored vehicles became in critically short supply. All of the 2nd Air Division heavy bomber groups, including the 458th, suspended bombing operations, stripped their aircraft down to bare essentials and began hauling fighter auxiliary tanks filled with gasoline instead of bombs.

The 458th flew 13 of those "truckin" missions to Lille, Clastres and St. Dizier, France, in delivering 727,160 gallons of fuel to the doughboys. Aircraft were manned with skeleton crews, and they flew at minimum altitudes to avoid detection by enemy radar. The airmen received no mission credit for these flights, and all expressed more apprehension over carrying the volatile gasoline than a full load of bombs. A total of 494 aircraft were dispatched for "truckin" operations, of which six were lost in accidents. Four others were damaged and had to be salvaged.

On April 15, 1945, the 458th participated in an unusual sortie to Royan, France. More than 120,000 enemy troops were still occupying an area along the Gironde Estuary that French forces had been unable to clear out. Further ground action appeared to be very costly and lengthy. Aircrews loaded containers of "jellied gasoline" into their bomb bays and flew the mission. This was the first use of napalm in the ETO, and it was successful. The group's last mission occurred on April 25 with a strike on a railroad target at Bad Reichenhall, Germany, and it proved to be one of the few "milk runs" this Group had.

The mellow rumble of Liberator radial engines was very prominent over the East Anglia countryside on June 14 as aircrews began taking off for the USA and possibly Pacific war zones. Air traffic controllers in the Horsham control tower would no longer respond to radio calls for "Hulking." Once again, the ground echelon went by sea for their return voyage home when they boarded the *Queen Mary* on July 6 for New York. Following R&R leave, the unit reported to Walker Field, Kansas, then to March Field, California for B-29 transition. But Japan surrendered before advance training could begin and the group was officially deactivated October 17, 1945.

The 458th tally sheet, for its 14-month overseas tour, includes 230 combat, 14 Azon bomb, 13 truckin and two diversionary missions. It delivered 13,168 tons of bombs and recorded 28 enemy fighter "kills" plus several more probables. Just prior to D-day, the group led the entire 2nd Bomb Division in bombing accuracy.

The 458th won no awards from the Army Air Forces nor the 8th Air Force although it had a prominent role in every major air campaign in the ETO after arriving for duty. It was cited four times by the 2nd Air Division for outstanding accomplishments. First for completing 100 missions by June 1944. Secondly for destroying a bridge at Blois St. Dennis, France on June 11 that was vital to the enemy. Thirdly for completing 200 missions by March 1945, and fourthly, in the period of September 1944-February 1945, for "a very low level of venereal diseases—lower than other stations and the 8th Air Force as a whole."

In September 1944 General Order 3982 awarded the 458th a Distinguished Unit Citation. However, on November 9, 1944, the Group was dispatched to Metz, France, on a mission in atmospheric conditions whereby any conceivable aerial mishap might occur. One did! Some bombs from 458th aircraft landed on American forces engaged in ground fighting and prestigious powers demanded retribution. It came swiftly, in December, by a revocation of the Distinguished Unit Citation Order, but it remained for almost a sadistic length of time and manner. There is no evidence of the order nor its revocation in official group records now. But there are entries on individual's WD AGO Form 100 (Honorable Discharge) to verify the award.

The 96th Combat Bombardment Wing was composed of the 458th, 466th and 467th Groups, and their aircraft markings were: fire engine-red ovals with a white stripe bearing a red, squadron radio call letter. The 458th had a vertical stripe, the 466th horizontal and the 467th diagonal from front to back. A figure/letter grouping just aft of the waist window designated individual squadrons. The 458th Squadrons were: 752nd - 7V, 753rd - J4, 754th - Z5, and 755th - J3.

Initial markings for all 2nd Air Division aircraft were similar, but featured a large group letter in black on a white disc applied to the ovals. A change in markings occurred after the olive drab paint scheme on aircraft gave way to the natural metal finish in about April 1944. The 458th's letter

was K, and it also appeared on the upper surface of the right wing.

Major campaigns the 458th participated in were: Air Offensive, Europe, March 2-June 5, 1944; Normandy, June 6-July 24, 1944; Northern France, July 25-September 14, 1944; Rhineland, September 16, 1944-March 21, 1945; Ardennes, December 16, 1944-January 25, 1945; Central Europe, March 22-April 25, 1945.

Support units attached to the 458th were: 60th Station Complement Sq., 469th Sub Depot, 1105th Quartermaster Company, 258th Medical Dispensary, 211th Finance Section, 2016th Aviation Fire Fighter Platoon, 1119th Military Police Company, 130th Army Postal Unit, 858th Chemical Company, 1686th Ordnance Supply and Material Company, and 18th Weather Sq. Late in the tour several of these units were combined into the 377th HQ and Base Service Sq.

Commanding officers of the 458th and their tenure were: Lt. Col. Robert F. Hardy of Flint, Michigan, July 28-December 16, 1943; Col. James H. Isbell of Union City, Tennessee, December 16, 1943-March 10, 1945 (Col. Isbell was the first officer in the 8th Air Force to command a single unit through 200 missions). Col. Allen F. Herzberg of Houston, TX, March 10-August 13, 1945; Capt. Patrick Hayes (?)-August 13...

Commanding officers of the squadrons were: 752nd-Maj. John J. LaRoche, Maj. Walter H. Williamson and Maj. John A. Hensler; 753rd-Capt.

Elman J. Beth, Maj. Frederick M. O'Neill, Maj. John A. Hensler and Maj. Charles N. Breeding; 754th-Capt. Estle P. Henson, Maj. Theodore J. Bravakis and Maj. Daniel H. Phillips; 755th-Lt. Col. Donald C. Jamison and Maj. Valin R. Woodward.

Operations officers were: Maj. Bruno W. Feiling and Lt. Col. Walter H. Williamson (incomplete). Medical officers were: William M. Routon, MD; Nathaniel T. Ballou, MD; and Seymour I. Shapiro, MD (incomplete). Dental officers: Porter R. Danford, DDS (incomplete).

Staff Sgt. Wells N. Gardner was a 46-year old gunner assigned to the 458th and completed more than 25 missions. He was also a World War I veteran and glider pilot. Sgt. DeSales Glover was also a gunner in the group. He completed six combat missions, including the March 6, 1944 strike on Berlin. Then he was found to be only 16-years old after enlisting in the AAF at 14. He was returned to the U.S. and discharged (honorable). Thus the 458th has a rightful claim on having perhaps the youngest and oldest warriors of the air war in its ranks.

Twin brothers serving in the armed forces in World War II was not unusual. However, when they both were assigned to the same organization, especially as crew members on the same aircraft, it was very unusual. Don and John Echols flew a number of missions together, but Don picked up a flak wound and their togetherness ended. Both left the military on a happy note.

One of the most renowned B-24 Liberators in

458th Bomb Group, 2nd Air Div., 8th USAF. Gabriels crew taken in front of "Gashouse Mouse," July 1944. Standing L to R: Fountaine Beale, Right Waist Gunner; Mel Johnston, Left Waist Gunner; William Sweigel, Radio Operator; Wayne Walker, Flight Engineer; John Curcio, Tail Turret Gunner; John Barbour, Ball Turret Gunner. Kneeling: Anthony Gianforti, Copilot; Gene Gabriel, Pilot; John Stem, Bombardier; Robert Gordon, Navigator.

458th Bomb Group, 754th Bomb Squadron returning from a mission. Notice the coast in the background. (Courtesy of Ernest Kelly)

Pilot Royce Glenn and crew #71 of the 458th Bomb Group on their return from bombing mission to Germany. (Courtesy of Royce B. Glenn)

the ETO flew with the 458th. *Final Approach,* serial 42-52457 was an H model in the 752nd Squadron. It was built by Ford at Willow Run, Michigan and modified at the Bechtel-McCone-Parsons Center in Birmingham, Alabama. Its original crew gave it this nickname reminiscent of a landing back in the U.S. after the war was won. The ship flew 113 missions before turning back from battle on an abort. She was lost on her 123rd mission April 9, 1945, at Lechfeld, Germany. One crewman was killed on this flight, and became the only known casualty among airmen flying the bomber. Master Sgt. H.R. Hill and his assistant, Sgt. E.H. Klase, had maintained *Final Approach* to perfection under the most harrowing weather and operational conditions imaginable. Their work was the epitome of the 458th personnel's attitude in general toward winning the war. This group's airmen never turned back from battle because of enemy action.

Target disparity for the 458th missions were (targets of opportunity have been omitted and numbers are approximate): airfields, 39; aircraft plants, 15; marshaling yards, 52; miscellaneous (factories, bridges, etc.), 54; no ball (V-1 rocket sites), 11; oil facilities, 19; troops/gun emplacements, 8; waterways, 3.

This narrative is dedicated to those 275 members of the 458th Bombardment Group who paid the ultimate price in service to our country.

466TH BOMB
GROUP (H)
The Flying Deck

by Barkey Hovesepian, edited by Mac Meconis

Fifty years ago, the 466th Bomb Group was activated at Alamogordo, New Mexico, and became part of the 96th Combat Wing of the 2nd Air Division of the 8th Air Force in the U.S. Army. Many of the crews were formed at Clovis, New Mexico, after completing flight training at bases throughout the U.S. Initial combat training as a group began at what is now the Salt Lake City Municipal Airport in Utah. Final training and complete group formation flights were completed at the Alamogordo base.

After being rated as combat ready, 62 Liberator B-24 aircraft and crews left the United States for England by way of the southern route, from West Palm Beach, Florida, to Belem, Brazil, to Dakar, Senegal, and to Marrakech, Morocco. Another over-

night skirting around Spain and west of France brought the 466th Cadre to various fields in England, from which they were escorted to their Attlebridge Station 120 base a few miles northwest of the East Anglia town of Norwich.

Major Beverly Steadman, commander of the advance units, had gone ahead to welcome the early B-24 arrivals, first of which was John Woolnough's crew 715 to officially activate the 466th. Colonel Arthur J. Pierce arrived soon afterwards with the Sharrett crew which flew the southern route. One crew was lost in the South Atlantic crossing.

The 466th Bomb Group flew its first combat mission on March 22, 1944, to Berlin, the longest initial assault ever flown by any unit in the history of the European Theater and one of the heaviest daylight bombardments on record of the German capital. General James H. Doolittle gave them an official commendation for that achievement. Two aircraft of the 786th Squadron were lost over Berlin and 13 crew survivors became POWs for the remainder of the war.

By the time the 466th had flown its 10th mission on April 13, losses were 18 aircraft and their crews. A total of 107 crewmen were killed, 63 were POWs and 10 were interned in Switzerland. On April 8, during a mission to Brunswick in Germany, six B-24s were lost to ME-109 German fighter attacks and anti-aircraft flak.

On July 25, 1944, the 466th Bomb Group led the entire 8th Air Force to bomb German fortifications around the city of St. Lo in France from which the U.S. Army achieved a breakthrough afterwards. The saturation bombing of the target earned the lead pilot, navigator and bombardier the French Croix de Guerre for their flying skills.

In August 1944, the 2nd Air Division Headquarters cited the 466th Bomb Group for distinguished and outstanding performance of duty from March 22 through August 9, during which time the group attacked 41 targets in Germany and 59 in occupied Continental Europe. 466th Bomb Group gunners were credited with destroying more than 25 enemy aircraft during that period.

According to eminent 8th Air Force historian Roger Freeman, the 785th Squadron of the 466th Bomb Group flew consecutive missions from March 24 through July 24 without incurring the loss of any of its aircraft. This was a record achievement in the entire 8th Air Force.

The identifying mark on the 466th Bomb Group's aircraft was originally a large letter "L" on the rudders, upper right wing and lower left wing surfaces. A color scheme was later adopted for all 2nd Air Division aircraft, with the 466th sporting red tails with a horizontal white stripe. The "L" was retained on the wings. Squadron markings on the fuselage were: T9 (784th), 2U (785th), U8 (786th), and 6L (787th). Cowling colors were: 784-red, 785-blue, 786-yellow and 787-white.

The 466th Bomb Group flew a total of 231 combat missions with 5,693 sorties during its 8th Air Force service in Europe during 1944 and 1945. (A sortie is one aircraft on one mission.) They dropped nearly 13,000 tons of bombs for an average of two tons per sorties. The 466th was one of the three groups in the 96th Combat Wing which were taken off operations from September 12 through September 30, 1944 to haul low octane gasoline to Clastres, Lille and St. Dizier in France.

The 96th Combat Wing completed 320 sorties during the gasoline flights, with the loss of 30 men killed, 17 in practice missions, 12 in gas missions and one ground man. Total losses for the 466th Bomb Group from March 22, 1944 to April 25, 1945 were 333 KIA, 171 POWs, eight evaded capture and 27 were interned. There were 233 aircraft assigned to the group at one time or another: 98 B-24s, two P-47s and one P-38. Seventy-two were lost in combat or from other operational causes, 83 aircraft were written off as war-weary and unrepairable, and 72 were returned to the Continental U.S. in "Operation Home Run." A B-24 known as *Black Cat* was the last aircraft lost in combat on April 21, 1945.

The gas haul missions found 466th Bomb Group morale rather low, as the combat crews felt they were being wasted, since only a skeleton crew of five was used, with the bombardier and four gunners left at home. The active crews received no recognition, but were able to brag about how much their ships could haul to help the war effort. Major John Jacobowitz was in charge of 14 ships from the 466th and 12 from the 458th Bomb Group. He was one of the first to fly his plane with 218 GI cans to Clastres for the 1st Army tanks. Later, the war-weary rejects were fitted with fabricated tanks to fit the large bomb bays in order to carry more gas.

The 466th Bomb Group celebrated the first anniversary of the group from August 22, 1943, simultaneously with its 100th mission party. The officers of the 466th obtained 150 forty-gallon barrels of English beer as a present to the group's enlisted men and an estimated 1,000 British women and girls were invited to the 100th mission party held on August 18, 1944.

On the same day, the newly built chapel was dedicated by the group, and Col. Joseph West spoke to the attendees. An All-Girl Swing Session was held in the North Hangar and later Glenn Miller's orchestra arrived to play for the party. The "Flying Deck" Glee Club also made its first appearance at the event, led by M/Sgt. Henry Bamman.

When the 466th reached its 200th mission anniversary, a party also was held with the cooperation of Red Cross women and girls who came out for a two-day celebration. During the party, a turnabout called for the enlisted men to be off duty and the officers to do all the detailed work such as cooking and washing dishes like GIs on KP duty. Both noon and evening meals were served by officers who also acted as bartenders in the evening. There was an air circus, a dance, floor show and movie. Another band concert was held the second day, another floor show and a dance that evening. It was a celebration to unwind all the tension of the previous months of tense combat times.

There were 3,000 men on the 466th Bomb Group base at one time or another during its operations. Approximately one half returned to the U.S. by air, 20 in each of 78 aircraft involved in the movement. In the 784th Squadron there were 18 aircraft, with only 15 men to each. The planes were modified with wooden platforms in the bomb bays and with the ball turrets removed. As added insurance, the crew chiefs rode in their own aircraft. Before departure, there were ditching drills for everyone, as well as briefing for pilots and navigators. Lieutenant Colonel Jennison of Group Operations flew out in the last plane to leave the 466th base on June 10, 1945. A writer for *Yank Magazine* rode with Capt. Stu Peace and wrote an article which appeared in the 1945 issue of *Liberty* magazine. The flight took the group from Attlebridge to Valley, Wales, to Meeks Field in Iceland and then to Goose Bay, Labrador, and finally to Bradley Field in Connecticut. The war had then ended and the 466th Bomb Group was officially inactivated on October 17, 1945.

After the war, in May 1945, Maj. Gen. William E. Kepner who commanded the 2nd Air Division, presented the City of Norwich a trust fund of 20,000 pounds sterling from his division's members for the construction and maintenance of a Memorial Room in the city's proposed Central Library Building. The library was dedicated on June 13, 1963, and became the flame that founded and nourished the 2nd Air Division Association, which by 1967 had 46 members from the 466th Bomb Group.

In June of 1971, Lt. Col. John H. Woolnough visited the old 466th base at Attlebridge to find that the field had become the largest turkey farm in the world, "Bernard Matthews, Ltd." and that the control tower, in excellent condition, was its corporate office.

A few years later in Florida, 100 former 466th Bomb Group members formed the group's association with John Woolnough as president. Articles of Incorporation were filed on January 5, 1987, as a non-profit veterans organization, with all former group members automatically part of the association. To date, over 1,300 former 466thers have been found and listed in the group's roster. Several memorials also have been erected by the group in England and in the U.S.

467TH BOMB GROUP (H)
The Rackheath Aggies

The 467th BG (H), with its four squadrons, the 788th, 789th, 790th and 791st Bomb Squadrons (H), was constituted on May 29, 1943, by War Department Secret Instructions and assigned to the 2nd Air Force for training. The group and squadrons were activated August 1, 1943, at Wendover Army Air Field, Utah, to train in consolidated B-24 Liberator heavy bombers.

The cadre of 35 officers and 155 enlisted men from the 470th Bomb Group (H) at Mountain Home, Idaho AAF, assembled on orders of September 9, 1943. On September 12, 1943, the air echelon of group and squadron flying officers and key operational and intelligence personnel proceeded to the Army Air Force School of Applied Tactics in Orlando, Florida, under command of Capt. Garnet B. Palmer, group operations officer. The ground echelon remained at Mountain Home AAF with the command of group and squadrons by 1st Lt. James A. Seccaffico. This command was not relinquished until October 17, 1944.

The air echelon was joined at Orlando, by Group Commander Col. Frederic E. Glantzberg and Deputy Group Commander Lt. Col. Albert J. Shower.

In October, the air echelon returned to Salt Lake City AAF, Utah, while the ground echelon arrived at Camp Kearns, Utah. Col. Glantzberg assumed command of the 467th on October 17, 1943, but stayed as commander only until October 24, 1943, when he was relieved and assigned as group commander of the 461st Bomb Group (H). Lt. Col. Shower became group commander, and he was the last commander of the group. Lt. Col. Allen F. Herzberg joined the group in October as deputy commander. On the last day of October the group was ordered to Wendover AAF, Utah, for phase training.

It took troop trains to transport the group from Camp Kearns to Wendover AAF. Wendover was on the Utah-Nevada border and was deficient in most

466th Bomb Group, 784th Squadron. Fall of 1944, Attlebridge mission to Karlsruche, Germany. (Courtesy of Frank Mathews)

466th Bomb Group, 785th Squadron. (Courtesy of Pate Given, Jr.)

467th Bomb Group (H)
Station 145, Rackheath,
Norfolk, England
March 11, 1944-July 6, 1945

Col. Albert J. Shower, USAAF, Commanding

Constituted	May 29, 1943
Activated	August 1, 1943
Pre-operational Training	Sept. 9, 1943-January 20, 1944
Departure Overseas Began	February 12, 1944
Assigned to 2nd Air (Bomb) Wing	March 11, 1944
Arrival Station 145 Rackheath	March 11, 1944
First Combat Mission	April 10, 1944
100th Combat Mission	August 18, 1944
Transporting Supplies/Gasoline	Sept. 11, 1944-October 2, 1944
200th Combat Mission	March 22, 1945
212th Last Combat Mission	April 25, 1945
The War Ends in Europe—VE Day	May 8, 1945
Depart Station 145 for U.S.	June 12, 1945-July 6, 1945
Redesignated Very Heavy	September 10, 1945

Battle Participation Credits:

American Theater	December 7, 1941-March 1946
Air Offensive Europe	July 4, 1942-June 5, 1944
Normandy	June 7, 1944-July 25, 1944
Northern France	July 25, 1944-September 14, 1944
Rhineland	September 15, 1944-March 21, 1945
Ardennes—Alsace	December 16, 1944-January 25, 1945
Central Europe	March 22, 1945-May 11, 1945

Assigned or attached to the group were the following squadrons and ancillary units:

788th Bomb Sqdn. (H) 1st Organization	August 1, 1943-May 10, 1944
788th Bomb Sqdn. (H) 2nd Organization	August 12, 1944-September 10, 1945
789th Bomb Sqdn. (H)	August 1, 1943-September 10, 1945
790th Bomb Sqdn. (H)	August 1, 1943-September 10, 1945
791st Bomb Sqdn. (H)	August 1, 1943-September 10, 1945
1229th QM Co. Service Group (AVN)	September 10, 1943
862nd Chemical Co. (AO), Detachment "A"	November 11, 1943
74th Station Complement Sqdn., Aviation (RS)	November 12, 1943
1451st Ordnance Supply Maint. Co. (AVN)	November 15, 1943
2105th Engineer (AVN) Fire Fighting Plt.	December 8, 1943
470th Sub-Depot	January 7, 1944
207th Finance Section	January 18, 1944
1286th Military Police Co. (AVN)	February 3, 1944
259th Medical Dispensary Aviation (RS)	September 22, 1944
*375th Air Service Group, HQ	April 15, 1945
*375th Base Service Sqdn.	April 15, 1945
*812th Air Engineering Sqdn.	April 15, 1945
*636th Air Material Sqdn.	April 15, 1945

*All ancillary units except 862nd Chemical Company formed into these four units and remained assigned until redesignation.

---

expected amenities since construction of it was not completed. The training aircraft available were old, "war wearies," and maintenance was made extra difficult due to the weather conditions. The group set to work, however, with dispatch and single purposefulness toward going overseas. Personnel continued to arrive and the rosters were constantly changing. From the top down, the right man was being sought for every job. Transferred to the group on November 3 were twenty-three crews, consisting of pilot, copilot, navigator, engineer, radio operator and one career gunner, from the 18th Replacement Wing. On November 6 twenty, ten men crews arrived from the 470th Bomb Group (H) with three aircraft. The remainder of November was concerned with the continuing organization of the group and squadrons and completion of the first phase of training wherein pilots/copilots were certified, crew orientation and training progressed, and four squadrons flew 262 sorties and 900-plus hours. At the month's end there were 390 officers, 1,660 enlisted men and seventeen aircraft, B-24D's, in the group.

In December the second phase of training was completed for the bombardiers. The squadrons flew 652 sorties (fourteen additional aircraft, B-24s, were received in the first week of December), dropped 1,621 practice bombs and made 177 camera attacks. Two aircraft and twenty-five crewmen were lost in a mid-air collision on Christmas Eve day.

The third and last phase of training was completed for the navigators by January 20, 1944, with 396 sorties flown; 1,125 bombs dropped and 250,000 rounds of ammunition fired. In this phase, three crews and aircraft were lost in crashes.

The inspection team to qualify the group for overseas service arrived January 17, and the group flew its Preparation For Overseas Movement Mission (POM) on January 18, which was unacceptable to the inspectors. Additional training was accomplished in the remainder of January and February toward a second POM inspection.

This inspection, though not entirely satisfactory, nevertheless did not stop the ground echelon and 108 aircrew personnel from departing on February 12, 1944, to the port of embarkation at Camp Shanks, New Jersey, while the air echelon flew to Herington AAF, Kansas, for further practice missions and a final POM inspection. With one major glitch, the POM inspector's aircraft aborted the mission, the group passed, and on February 26 and 27 the air echelon was en route to Morrison AAF, Florida, to begin its overseas flights. On arrival at Morrison, they came under command of the Air Transport Command for direction to their overseas destination via the southern ferry route: Waller Field, Trinidad; Belem, Brazil; Fortaleza and Natal, Brazil; Dakar; Marrakech, Morocco; Prestwick, Scotland; Valley and Mangan, Wales; then to Rackheath. One crew ferrying an Air Transport Command B-24 was lost in a take off accident at Agadir, Morocco, and a crew and group aircraft were lost in a crash in the Atlas Mountains of North Africa.

Fifty-eight group aircraft and crews arrived at Rackheath from March 8, 1944, through March 26, 1944. One aircraft was rendered unfit for further flight after landing downwind on Rackheath on March 20.

The ground movement, in the meantime, boarded the SS Frederick Lykes, a C-3 freighter converted to troop transport, at New York on February 28, 1944, and sailed the following day in convoy. The Lykes arrived in Glasgow, Scotland, on March 10. The echelon boarded trains for the overnight trip to Rackheath, where they arrived on March 11.

Rackheath, Station 145, was constructed on the estate of Sir Edward Stracy, Bart. Construction was accomplished by John Laing and Son, Ltd. at a cost of approximately one million pounds (four million plus dollars). Accommodations for 500 officers and 2,400 enlisted men were provided in 10 living sites. The living standards were not up to those that had been experienced on domestic bases. There was no sewerage system, for instance. Ablution buildings in the living areas had running water but "honeypot" toilets. Bathing was available only in the communal area, generally some distance from the living area.

Sleeping quarters were Nissen Huts, half-barrel corrugated steel shells over concrete floors with wooden ends and two windows and a door on each end. The principal entrance had a light screen, box-like affair attached. These held 12 to 16 in very crowded conditions. Other housing were prefabricated concrete structures (Seco huts), generally quarters for the more permanent personnel. The other buildings of the base were also of the Nissen or Seco type, large Nissens for the mess halls, large Secos for briefing and headquarters type functions.

The living and operational sites were scattered to the west of the airfield and were sited to take advantage of the terrain and growth thereon for camouflage purposes. Blast (bomb) shelters, open to top, brick-lined, in earth mound, were scattered randomly throughout the living and working areas. A communal site, somewhat centrally located, had officers and flight EM messes and bath buildings. Close by was the Red Cross area, PX, gymnasium and station theater.

The airfield proper was a class A-type (Air Ministry Directorate-General of Works), standard for heavy bomber requirements. The main runway, N-S (actually 030 degrees and 210 degrees) was 6,000 feet in length, the intersecting runways, NE-SW (100 degrees and 280 degrees) and SE-NW (140 degrees and 320 degrees) were 4,800 feet long. All runways were 150 feet wide. The taxiway (perimeter track) was 2.7 miles long and 50 feet wide. Runways and perimeter track were of screeded concrete construction (it was rumored that London rubble was incorporated into the concrete). Fifty loop (spectacle) hard standings were constructed around the perimeter track, some held more than one plane (concrete also in most cases).

The field had Mark II type lighting with runway lights, not taxiways however. Pole mounted lights, a sufficient distance away from the field to provide a proper landing circuit, circled the field with other pole mounted lights leading into the runways for either right or left hand landing patterns. An instrument landing system localizer was later installed south of the north landing runway.

Major structures on the field were the two T-2 hangars, 120' wide by 240' long by 39' high, sufficiently wide for the 110' wing spread of the B-24. One was at the technical site, the other on the east of the field. Aviation gasoline was provided from two 100,000 gallon storage facilities, one on the southwest of the field, the other on the east near Salhouse Station.

The group that went overseas was not self-sufficient in itself but required the services of the several ancillary organizations already assigned to the base. These were:

The 1229th Quartermaster Company Service Group (AVN) was first on the base on September 10, 1943. Its duties included all quartermaster clothing and equipment for all enlisted men on the base, all expendable items (stationery, office supplies), all subsistence, all solid fuels, ground petroleum products, laundry and dry cleaning, local purchases, rail movement of personnel and quartermaster salvage operations.

Detachment A 862nd Chemical Company (AO) arrived on November 11, 1943. They maintained 23,000 square feet of chemical bomb storage for incendiary bombs, colored grenades (pyrotechnics) and sky markers. Half of the detachment worked with the squadron ordnance sections in loading conventional ordnance. Over 1,570 tons of incendiaries were dropped by the group from the 630 ton stock maintained. It was also responsible for gas attack training and chemical gas use.

The 74th Station Complement Squadron AVN (RS) arrived next, on November 12, 1943. It operated the base, the telephone exchange, fire department, post office, electrical installations and other utilities, utilizing the other ancillary organizations and 467th Bomb Group personnel.

Assigned on November 15, 1943, was the 1451st Ordnance Supply and Maintenance Company (AVN). This company maintained over 300 vehicles from jeeps to 4,000 gallon fuel trailers, including the 2,600-ton bomb dump with bombs for various purposes weighing from 100 pounds to 2,000 pounds. It stored and dispensed all ammunition and maintained all aircraft guns, over 650 .5 caliber machine guns, and all ground ordnance. For vehicle maintenance they built their own 35 feet wide by 96 feet long Bentley building with nearly 3,500 square feet of work area under the roof.

The beginning of the 2105th Engineer (AVN) Fire Fighting Platoon was five enlisted men from the 74th Station Complement Squadron and four RAF personnel on December 8, 1943. Ten enlisted men arrived from the 2031st E.(A) FFP in February 1944 and the 2105th was activated on April 10, 1944, with one officer, 16 assigned EM and six on special duty from the 74th SCS. Its duties varied from alert and rescue operations during flying periods, to maintenance of fire extinguishers, to extinguishing over 64 on-base fires, to training ground personnel in basic fire fighting, to practicing in dry runs all manner of fire fighting techniques.

The 470th Sub-Depot was activated on January 7, 1944. Five officers and 87 enlisted men, machinists, mechanics, instrument technicians, clerks, etc. were assigned. The sub-depot built, repaired, and supplied the needed parts and equipment necessary to keep the bombers and the men who flew in them in the air. Their machine shop, welding shop, paint shop, instrument shop, propeller shop, supply sections, etc. were the best in the division.

The 270th Finance Section was activated on January 18, 1944. They handled all assigned personnel payroll including all base pay information, deductions, allotments, etc.

Finally, the 1286th Military Police Company

(AVN) was assigned on February 3, 1944. Their responsibility was all base security.

The 259th Medical Dispensary Aviation (RS), had Station Sick Quarters ready on December 25, 1943, for use by the Medical Section. With the arrival of the group in March 1944, the medical section was reorganized along the lines of a Station Hospital, incorporating the squadron medical personnel into the total medical facility. The 259th eventually had a surgeon, four medical officers, one dental officer, technicians for pharmacy, laboratory, x-ray, medical and dental, two ambulance drivers and several clerks (no nurses ever assigned).

All of the above auxiliary units on the field were inactivated (except Detachment A, 862nd Chemical Company (AO) on April 15, 1945, and reorganized and activated into the 375th Air Service Group, composed of a Headquarters and Base Service Squadron, the 812th Air Engineering Squadron, and the 636th Air Material Squadron.

Mess facilities were manned by personnel from the squadrons on arrival of the group. These persons were assigned permanently to the facilities and provided four meals: breakfast, dinner, supper and a late meal for everyone on the base.

Upon assignment to the 2nd Bombardment, later 2nd Air Division on March 11, 1944, Lt. Col. Shower was named station commanding officer, Lt. Col. Herzberg became air executive officer with responsibility of operations and intelligence, and Lt. Col. Ion S. Walker became ground executive officer with responsibility of base maintenance, personnel and supply.

The first mission of the group was April 10 against an aircraft assembly plant at an airfield at Bourges, France. Thirty aircraft were dispatched, carrying six 1,000-pound SAP (Semi-Armour Piercing) bombs each. All reached the target, but four failed to drop their bombs due to mechanical problems. Lt. Col. Shower led the two-squadron group effort, and Maj. Walter R. Smith, group operations officer led the second squadron. The group returned and flew over the base in perfect formation; 30 dispatched, 30 returned, a feeling of joy, pride and relief for those who stayed behind. Neither flak nor fighters had been encountered, so the crews on the first mission had had a "milk run." The bombing results were judged very good, with only one aircraft's six bombs falling outside the target area.

Fifteen missions were flown in April, one more was recalled. Mission two, on April 11, was the group's first attack into Germany, with 36 aircraft in three squadrons dispatched and effective. Results

Brindisi, Italy — 1945. 467th Bomb Group, the original 788th Bomb Squadron, now the 801st plus additional men. (Courtesy of Curtice Fry)

were good, moderate flak encountered, enemy fighter seen but did not attack, but one crew was lost in a crash landing in England, resulting in the first seven of the group killed in action.

A late afternoon take off on April 22 of 28 aircraft to a marshalling (rail) yard at Hamm, Germany, resulted in very good results by the Shower led group. However, the return to England was after dark, and German aircraft followed the bombers back to England, shooting down two of the group's aircraft with deaths of 15 crewmen. A bomb, dropped by the intruders on a hardstand near the south end of the field, resulted in one ground airman killed in action and one wounded in action.

Mission 16, the group's first to Berlin, on April 29, had a long-lasting effect on the group. Twenty-eight aircraft were dispatched and 26 attacked the general target area. Three aircraft were lost with 31 airmen, 13 killed in action, 17 prisoners of war, and one evadee. Among the prisoners of war was Maj. Robert L. Salzarulo, commanding officer of the 788th Bomb Squadron.

Replacements began arriving in April. The first replacement to gain mission credit is first noted as aircraft commander on April 29, 1944. Fifteen replacement crews flew their first missions in May, 17 in June and 21 in July. By the end of July, the group had flown 86 missions and original nonlead crews were finishing their tours of 30 missions. Eleven crews had been lost due to combat operations.

In August, the group flew 20 missions. Six missions were flown in September, five effective, prior to the group being "stood down" to ferry supplies, principally gasoline, to France.

Upon resuming combat missions on October 3, 1944, the group flew six missions.

On October 13, 1944, a change in squadron responsibilities occurred. Prior to that date, each squadron trained and provided its own lead crews. From that date forward, group lead crew responsibility was placed with 791st Bomb Squadron (H). Many crew assignments changed at this time as squadron lead crews were transferred to the 791st and wing crews of the 791st were transferred to the other three squadrons. In the remainder of October there were eight missions flown.

There were 12 missions, all effective, flown in November.

In December, 15 effective missions were flown. On December 11 the group dispatched 47 aircraft with 46 effective. On December 24, 1944, the group dispatched 63 aircraft, including *Pete The POM Inspector II* assembly ship. One aircraft returned early. Of the 62 aircraft attacking the targets (Duan, Gerolstein and Ober), each flew an average of 6.15 hours and consumed an average of 1,790 gallons of aircraft gasoline each, a total of 111,000 gallons for the mission. On December 29, mission 151 was launched in very adverse weather conditions, zero ceiling-zero visibility. Eight aircraft took off and completed the mission, two crashed on take off with the loss of 15 killed in action and four seriously wounded. Two others were severely damaged on take off. One had to be abandoned in flight while the other crashed on landing at another airfield.

In January 1945, 12 missions were launched, all effective. There were 17 missions in February. The second greatest number of missions, 24 all effective, and the largest number of aircraft dispatched, 709, occurred in March. In the 25 days of combat operations in April, 15 missions were launched. In total, the group launched 221 missions sorties and is credited with 212 missions. (The group is credited with 212 missions; the difference in numbers occurred when mission recalls without penetrating enemy territory were counted in the group but not in the Wing). This number took only 357 days of combat.

The earlier assigned crews sometimes flew three, four and five missions in a row. Later it was the normal practice in the 467th for a crew to fly two combat missions and one practice mission in a four-day time span. The fourth day was, except for Sunday, for ground schools, for pilots link trainers, celestial navigation trainers with the navigator, for gunners, skeet and/or other gunnery trainers. Some administrative flights were scheduled on the non-combat flight days, slow time of aircraft engines, pick up of replacement aircraft, etc. Typically, the initial crews assigned to the group flew 30 missions, later this was increased to 35 missions. In fact, there was no maximum number of missions required to be flown, all air crews technically were relieved due to combat fatigue and not number of missions. It was the practice to relieve pilots, copilots, navigators, bombardiers, radio operators and aerial engineers after the number of missions above. Ball, nose, tail and waist gunners were generally relieved when their crew pilot finished his missions, even though they may not have had the number of missions noted above.

The total number of ground personnel assigned to the group has not been found. Estimated from available records, primarily in orders returning the group to the Zone of the Interior in June 1945 are the following:

Group Headquarters	115
375th Air Service Group	227
636th Air Material Squadron	130
788th Bomb Squadron (H)	305
789th Bomb Squadron (H)	309
790th Bomb Squadron (H)	306
791st Bomb Squadron (H)	295
812th Air Engineers	238
862nd Chemical Company	67
Total	1,992

Transfers in and out of the group are known to have occurred but such orders have not been available. A major transfer, probably not replaced, were 126 ground echelon transferred in January/February 1945 to infantry training to replace ground force losses in the Battle of Ardennes-Alsace of December 1944 and January 1945. Enlisted personnel quarters would be another indicator. The maximum number reported as quartered was 2,464. Air echelon enlisted would have been maximum approximately 560 for 94 aircrews, leaving 1,900 in enlisted ground echelon. Ground echelon units officers numbered 106 in June 1945.

There has been made a compilation of the names of all who were assigned or attached to the 467th from overseas movement to return to the United States, in number nearly 5,200. It is believed this listing is possibly 200 to 300 short of completion and probably will never be complete.

The last Table of Organization Roster of officer personnel for group headquarters detachment and the four bombardment squadrons shows as follows:

	Authorized	Actual	Rated*
Headquarters	32	43	9
788th	107	118	104
789th	114	111	98
790th	113	119	105
791st	113	114	102
Total	481	487	399

*Rated-pilot, navigator or bombardier

This table of organization was prior to the reorganization of squadrons on or about May 17, 1945 in preparation for return to the Zone of the Interior and is probably typical for the months October 1944 through April 1945.

In the 15 months the group was at Rackheath, principal personnel assignments had very little change. Key positions and assigned officers were:

Group Commander, Col. Albert J. Shower
August 1943-August 1945

Air Executive Officer, Lt. Col. Allen F. Herzberg
October 1943-October 1944*

Air Executive Officer, Lt. Col. James J. Mahoney
October 11, 1944-August 1945

Operations Officer, Lt. Col. Walter R. Smith Jr.

Ground Executive, Lt. Col. Ion S. Walker
September 22, 1944-August 1945

Group Bombardier, 1st Lt. John L. Low Jr.

Group Bombardier, 1st Lt. Robert E. Dolan

Group Bombardier, Capt. William C. Evans

Group Navigator, Maj. Capers A. Holmes Jr.

Intelligence, Maj. Edward M. Ogden

Adjutant, Maj. George W. Darnell

Engineering, Maj. Walter R. Giesecke

470th Sub-Depot, Lt. Col. Frank F. Creager

Other group headquarters table of organization officers were aerial gunnery, aerial photo, air inspector, air sea rescue, chaplain, communications, dental, enlisted mess, legal, ordnance, personal equipment, officers mess, photo, public relations, radar, special services, statistical, supply, surgeon, transportation and weather.

Lt. Col. Herzberg was transferred to the 96th Combat Wing as operations officer. On March 10, 1945 he became commanding officer of the 458th Bomb Group (H).

The squadron table of organizations mirrored that of the group to an extent but where the group had 30 table of organization positions, the squadrons had only 13. The squadrons, like the group, had little change in key personnel in the preparation for and the oversea period. Key squadron personnel were:

788th (First Organization)

Maj. Robert L. Salzarulo	April 29, 1944
Maj. Leonard M. McManus	May 10, 1944

788th (Second Organization):

Lt. Col. James J. Mahoney	August 12, 1944-October 11, 1944
Maj. John J. Taylor	October 11, 1944-August 1945

789th

Maj. Garnet B. Palmer	March 1945
Maj. Robert S. Sieler	March 1945-August 1945

790th

Maj. Fred E. Holdrege	February 27, 1945
Maj. Eugene W. Veverka	February 27, 1945-August 1945

Lt. Col. Albert L. Wallace Jr. August 1945

Aircraft assigned to the group, not including those temporarily transferred in for the September 1944 gasoline trucking operation, are estimated as high as 194.

New aircraft began being assigned to the group soon after its arrival at Station 145 from depots where modifications to ETO standards had been performed.

One of the first aircraft acquired was a "war-weary" B-24D from the 44th Bomb Group (H) to be used as an "assemble on" ship for combat and practice missions. Painted distinctively with large yellow circles surrounded by red borders, the tail white with a large, black, block letter group identifier P on it and with a large illuminated P on each side of the fuselage. This ship was usually first off on missions to fly to the assembly point and there to fly the race track assembly pattern while the group assembled on it. It also fired pyrotechnic flares in the group identification colors while in its role. With the group assembled the ship would return to base, except in one instance. On December 24, 1944, when the group mounted a maximum effort of 62 aircraft (all that were flyable at that time), *Pete the POM Inspector*, the name given the aircraft, with a skeleton crew, armed only with 30 caliber carbines, went with the group to the target.

It was probably the intention that each heavy bombardment squadron would have 16 aircraft as the table of organization provided for 16 crew chiefs. The squadrons of the 467th were each similar in aircraft line maintenance personnel. There was a group engineering officer over the whole aircraft maintenance operation working through engineering officers in each squadron. Each squadron, in turn, had a line chief who had under him three flight chiefs. There were 16 crew chiefs with three or four aircraft and engine mechanics assigned to him, one an assistant crew chief. Specialists in armament, inspection, instruments, propellers and sheet metal, generally two of each and a welder worked at the direction of the line chief with the aircraft ground crews as needed. The Squadron Tech Center provided support for auto pilot, bomb sight and radio problems. Routinely each aircraft received a preflight and daily inspection by the crew who also performed the 25, 50 and 100 hour inspections. Engine changes at 250 to 300 hours were performed on the hardstand and repairs, except major structural damage which was done at the Sub-Depot, were also done on the line. Engine changes and repairs required were done by the crews with help of the specialists as required without regard to hour or hours required, the aircraft were brought back to flying condition a soon as possible in all cases. Because the squadrons had generally more than 16 aircraft, several crews in each squadron had two aircraft to maintain. The work was hard, the hours long. Only through the dedication of these maintenance crews was the group able to consistently have the best maintenance record in the 2nd Air Division and for several periods the best in the whole 8th Air Force.

After the initial aircraft, all H models, the group began receiving J models which required the maintenance crews to learn of them and their variations from the H models on the line. Later L and M models were received and following hostilities many aircraft were assigned to the group, some new, some castoffs from other groups and each had to be prepared for the flight back to the United States. The aircraft maintenance crews received a deserved honor in that the majority of the passengers on these flights were from their ranks.

The 467th had no one hero but did have a "hero" aircraft and crew that maintained it. *Witchcraft,* a B-24H, Serial number 42-52534 of all the 790th Bomb Squadron (H) flew on the first group mission and on the next to last, a total of 130 missions without once failing to reach its assigned target, the record for 8th Air Force Liberators. Her ground crew consisted of Crew Chief Joe Rameriz, Assistant George Dong, Mechanics Ray Betcher, Walt Elliott and Joe Vetter, a real "league of nations" representation. Much credit has to be given to the crews who flew *Witchcraft* to the record, they never turned back before reaching the target for mechanical or personnel reasons, *Witchcraft* received over 300 flak holes, had 13 engine changes, had to go to the Sub-Depot twice for repairs; but in her remarkable career, not a man was injured or killed in her. *Witchcraft* returned to the United States in June 1945, one of five original group aircraft that did so. Following the war, example Allied aircraft were displayed in Paris at the base of the Eiffel Tower. Representing the B-24 was one painted in the 467th and 790th colors carrying on its nose the *Witchcraft* caricature and named *Witchcraft II.*

The 467th was destined to become a B-24 Liberator Heavy Bombardment Group slated for operations in the European or Mediterranean Theater of Operations. The cadre training was oriented toward missions in either of these theaters. Phase training was toward high altitude, massed formation missions. In January 1944, when Lt. Col. Herzberg was sent with advance party to Station 145 Rackheath, England, at least a select few group and squadron command staff would have been told of the group's ultimate destination. The ground echelon sailing from New York could have been going to either theater. The air echelon flying from Florida did not know their destination until one hour into the first leg of their flight, to Waller Field, Trinidad.

On arrival at station 145 Rackheath, the group became the third group of the 96th Combat Wing, 2nd Bomb Division (later Air Division, January 1, 1945), 8th Air Force of the United States Strategic Air Forces in Europe (USSTAF). Commanding the 8th at that time and to the end of hostilities in Europe was Lt. James H. Doolittle, commanding USSTAF was Lt. Gen. Carl Spaatz.

The missions of the 8th as the 467th began its combat tour were in compliance with the pointblank directive of June 10, 1943, directing the then 8th Bomber Command to destroy the German aviation industry and secure air superiority over the continent. Beginning with Blitz Week, July 20, 1943, German aircraft industries, assembly plants, ball bearing works and GAF airfields had been attacked repeatedly, in some missions with very high losses to the 8th. These pointblank missions resulted in little loss of German aircraft production but GAF reaction to these raids confronting increased Allied escort fighters caused severe losses to the GAF in manpower. In the first four months of 1944 nearly 1,700 GAF pilots were lost in combat, losses the GAF were never able to replace. Fighter range to escort the bombers were Spitfires-100 mile radius, P-47 Thunderbolts-250 to 300 miles, P-38 Lightnings, to be phased out to P-51s 350 to 400 miles and the P-51 Mustang to 600 miles, the escorts could go anywhere the bombers went. The 467th was seldom attacked by GAF fighters due to the excellent formation integrity insisted upon by group and squadron commanders, and rehearsed in practice missions that were briefed and flown, observed and critiqued just as the combat missions. German antiaircraft artillery (AAA) became an increasing menace as the Germans withdrew from occupied areas to their own country, they brought their "flak" (AAA) with them in retreat and the concentrations of guns at various targets were sometimes in the hundreds. Missions against chemical plants did reduce the ammunition available to these guns in the latter days and they became somewhat less of the menace than they had been when the group began its missions. Radar countermeasures, including fixed and variable frequency pulse generators to counter the GAF gun laying radar and aluminum foil chaff also reduced the "flak" effectiveness, especially when missions were flown over undercast conditions.

So the group in April participated in the "winding down" of Operation Pointblank and the beginning of Crossbow, the code name for the effort to eliminate German vengeance weapon (V-1s) sites in France and the Low Countries.

The invasion of France had been postponed from May to June 1944 to allow the isolation of the coming invasion sites from rail and road traffic by interdiction (tactical) missions against these transportation targets and against airfields within range of the GAF fighters and bombers of the invasion sites. This effort was at the direction of Supreme Headquarters, Allied Expeditionary Forces (SHAEF) and included 101 rail centers in Northern France and the Low Countries to be hit with 41,000 tons of bombs by the Eighth and RAF. Prior to D-day, June 6, 1944, these rail centers had been subject to 71,000 tons of bombs and not one GAF airfield was operable in Normandy. Twenty-two bridges across the lower Seine River were also priority targets. When weather conditions prevented operations toward the above objectives, the Eighth was released to strategic bombing of industrial targets, oil industries, aircraft and air depot targets in Germany. June's missions were mostly tactical with only six strategic missions in the 29 missions flown by the group in the month. Only 19 missions were flown in July, of which 11 were strategic types. Of the 20 missions of August, nine were strategic and the major number of those against oil or air related targets. Crossbow missions ended for the Eighth on August 31, the group had flown only seven of this type mission to that date.

On August 18, the group flew its 100th mission, in just 140 days, a 2nd Bomb (Air) Division record. Sorties flown numbered 2,375 bombs delivered, 5,500 tons. Aircraft losses totaled only 27, the lowest rate of loss in the 8th Air Force, with 46 men killed in action, 45 wounded in action and 182 missing in action.

In September there were only five combat missions, all strategic, into Germany, against transportation and oil industry targets. On September 11, the group and 96th Combat Wing, went off operations to begin ferrying food and medical supplies to Orleans-Bracy Airfield in France, later to Clastres Airfield in France. From September 20 to October 2 the B-24s were equipped to haul 80 octane gasoline to the rapidly advancing Allied armies in France. In the period the 96th delivered 2.12 million gallons, the 467th 664,000 gallons of that.

Back to combat missions on October 3, the 14 missions of October, 12 of November and the first seven of December were each strategic, each into Germany with 21 against transportation, four against airfields, six against the oil industry, one area bombing at Cologne and one mission credit toward Koblenz in which no bombs were dropped.

Tactical, interdiction missions, against transportation centers and airfields, in support of Allied ground forces in the Battle of Ardennes-Alsace (Battle of the Bulge) began December 24 with 8th Air Force mission 760, the largest air strike of the war. There were 2,034 heavy bombers launched, 1,874 effective along with 768 P-51s and 50 P-47s for escort, 780 effective. The 467th launched 63 aircraft, 62 effective except one of those was the group assembly ship which carried no bombs. The group's targets were three rail junction. An additional six tactical missions were flown in December and the first seven of January 1945 were also tactical.

From January 14, through the last mission of the group and the 8th Air Force on April 25, 1945, there were 60 missions launched, 58 effective, all but four were strategic. Operation Clarion, a major assault on German canal, rail and road communications began on February 22, 1945. The group after January 14, 1945 flew 26 attacks on marshaling (rail) yards and four on highway bridges, canals and viaducts. Other missions were to 10 oil targets, two U-Boat building yards, two armor building facilities including one at Berlin, eight airfields or air depots including four oriented toward jet fighters/interceptors, two industrial targets, a mission to Brunswick that was recalled as the group approached Dummer Lake, Germany, and one against the German Army Headquarters at Zossen, Germany. Of the four tactical missions, two were in support of Varsity, the Allied assault across the Rhine River and were

467th Bomb Group Executive officers, E.T.O. 1944. Rackheath Airbase, England. (Courtesy of Phil Day and Al Welters)

against GAF airfield in Western Germany. The other two were against German pockets of resistance in the Pointe de Grave/Royan, France, area that denied the Allies the use of the port facilities at Bordeaux. On April 15, the group launched 29 aircraft including four lead ships in a three squadron effort. Effective were 26 aircraft dropping 4 x 2,000 pounds bombs each, all of which landed within 1,000 feet of the MP (main point of impact), 55 percent within 500 feet. This proved to be the best bomb record by any 8th Air Force group on any mission of the war.

The following day 25 aircraft undertook the longest mission of the group, an average 9:05 hours per aircraft, to carry napalm (jellied gasoline) bombs to the same area. Of unknown capacity, these cardboard cylinders had very poor ballistics and the bombing effort, rated fair, was the only use of napalm by 8th Air Force bombers.

The group mission 200 came on March 22, 1945 and was celebrated with a large "stand-down"

party. The day after the 200th mission party, the group was still celebrating with a big "beer bust" and watching P-47 and P-51 exhibition teams in an air show of stunt flying. A less experienced pilot in a P-51 wandered by and attempted a slow roll at 100 feet, lost control and crashed in the Red Cross gym area. The party was soon over, no one felt like celebrating further.

What did the group accomplish in its 13 months of combat? It flew 212 combat missions in 357 combat days, 5,538 combat sorties, an average of 26 aircraft effective per mission and dropped 13,353 tons of bombs, 2.4 tons per aircraft sortie. Aircraft lost in action numbered only 29, the lowest loss rate of any group of the Eighth but we suffered 242 killed in action or killed in the line of duty. Aircraft losses in accidents numbered 20. Enemy aircraft claims were six destroyed, five probably destroyed, two damaged. The group set the unsurpassed record for bombing accuracy and had the

best overall standing for bombing accuracy in the Eighth. The group had the highest overall aircraft availability record in the 2nd Air Division, was always high in effective aircraft launched, and had low mechanical failures and/or aborted missions. The motor pool had an extremely low accident rate, the photo section received citations for photos secured, the best kept airplane in the division was from the 467th, the 789th Bomb Squadron (H) had a record 45 missions, 371 sorties without loss of aircraft or crewmen in the period April 21 to June 20, 1944. Decorations and promotions, the group received its share of the former, probably not enough of the latter.

In summary, as our combat history drew to a close, the commanding general of the 96th Combat Wing wrote to Col. Shower: "The records clearly indicate the continuous outstanding performance of the 467th group in all phases of operation. Most commendable is the absence of any slumps in your

467th BG Crew, front row, L to R: T/Sgt. Lory Tognarini, Radio Operator; S/Sgt. Warren O'Neal, Waist Gunner;S/Sgt. Edmond Laczynski, Ball Turret Gunner/Waist; S/Sgt. Allan L. Francis, Tail Turret Gunner; S/Sgt. James H. Eberline, Nose Turret Gunner. Second row, L to R: T/Sgt. Stephen H. Arnold, Engineer/Top Turret Gunner; Lt. James G. Buck, Navigator; Lt. Henry E. Meyer, Copilot; Lt. S.T. Gray, Jr., Pilot/AC Commander. (Courtesy of S.T. Gray, 467th)

bombing records. You have been at or near the top throughout. It is proof of the initiative, tenacity of purpose and drive exercised by you and your command."

The mission of the 467th was to put bombs on targets. This was done consistently, with exceptional precision. We are very proud of what we did. Many who were with us did not survive. We shall never forget them. And toward this end we have the 467th Bombardment Group (H) Association, Limited, which presently has nearly 1,300 veterans of the group as members. Our efforts in memorials to the group and to its casualties are in San Diego, at the Air Force Academy, at the Air Force Museum, at the 8th Air Force Museum, in the 2nd Air Division Memorial Room in Norwich, England, and at the former site of station 145, Rackheath. We will continue to honor our group and our casualties in similar efforts to the last man.

489TH BOMB GROUP (H)

courtesy of Neal E. Sorensen

489th Bomb Group Commanders

Col. Ezekiel W. Napier	October 20, 1943-February 4, 1945
Lt. Col. Robert E. Kolliner	February 5, 1945-April 10, 1945
Col. Paul C. Ashworth	April 11, 1945-October 17, 1945

844th Squadron Commanders

Capt. Harold D. Feil	October 12, 1943-December 31, 1943

Capt. Paul B. Woodward	January 1, 1944-October 17, 1945

(promoted to major August 1, 1944)

845th Squadron Commanders

Capt. Willis B. Sawyer	October 12, 1943-October 27, 1943
Capt. Maurice L. Minette	October 28, 1943-December 14, 1943
Maj. Byron B. Webb	December 15, 1943-July 25, 1944

(promoted to lieutenant colonel, March 1, 1944)

Capt. Lewis W. Tanner	July 26, 1944-October 17, 1945

(promoted to major, July 18, 1944)

846th Squadron Commanders

Capt. Thayer C. Harper	October 12, 1943-November 10, 1944

(promoted to major, February 2, 1944)

Maj. Ralph B. Conner	November 11, 1944-June 30, 1945
Maj. Thayer C. Harper	July 1, 1945-October 17, 1945

847th Squadron Commander

Capt. Arvo E. Lohela	October 12, 1943-March 1, 1945

(promoted to major, March 6, 1944)

(Squadron inactivated "within 15 days before March 17, 1945," exact date unknown)

489TH BOMB GROUP (H)

Charles H. Freudenthal

Constituted as 489th Bombardment Group (H) on September 14, 1943, it was activated on October 1, 1943. It trained with B-24s at Wendover, Utah, moved to England during April-May 1944, and was assigned to the 2nd Bomb Division. The group entered combat on May 30, 1944, and during the next few days concentrated on targets in France in preparation for the Normandy invasion.

In an attack against coastal defenses near Wimereaux on June 5, 1944, the group's lead plane was seriously crippled by enemy fire, its pilot was killed and the deputy group commander, Lt. Col. Leon R. Vance Jr., who was commanding the formation, was severely wounded. Although his right foot was practically severed, Vance took control of the plane, led the group to a successful bombing of the target and managed to fly the damaged aircraft to the coast of England, where he ordered the crew to bail out. Believing a wounded man had been unable to jump, he ditched the plane in the channel and was rescued. For his action during this mission, Vance was awarded the Medal of Honor.

The group supported the landings in Normandy on June 6, 1944, and afterward bombed coastal defenses, airfields, bridges, railroads and V-weapon sites in the campaign for France. It began flying missions into Germany in July, and engaged primarily in bombing strategic targets such as factories, oil refineries and storage plants, marshalling yards and airfields in Ludwigshafen, Magdeburg,

Brunswick, Saarbrücken and other cities until November 1944. Other operations included participation in the saturation bombing of German lines just before the breakthrough at St. Lo in July, carrying food to the liberated French and to Allied forces in France during August and September and dropping food and ammunition to U.S. Forces in Holland in support of Operation Market Garden later in September.

The 489th returned to the U.S. in December 1944 to prepare for redeployment to the Pacific Theater, and in March 1945 was redesignated 489th Bombardment Group (Very Heavy), equipped with B-29s. The group was alerted for movement overseas in the summer of 1945, but the war with Japan ended before the group left the U.S. and it was inactivated on October 17, 1945.

Stations: Wendover Field, Utah, October 1, 1943-April 3, 1944; Halesworth, England, c. May 1-November 1944; Lincoln AAFld, Nebraska, c. December 17, 1944; Great Bend AAFld, Kansas, c. February 28, 1945; Davis-Monthan Field, Arizona, April 3, 1945; Fairmont AAFld, Nebraska, c. July 13, 1945; Ft. Lawton, Washington, August 23, 1945; March Field, California, September 2,-October 17, 1945

Campaigns: American Theater, Air Offensive Europe, Normandy, Northern France, Rhineland

Motto: "Ex Tenebris Lux Veritatis" translates to "Out of darkness the light of truth."

From the Diary of Lt. Frank W. Skrzynski, April 1944

"One hour from Morrison Field, it is now the 24th. We open the secret orders and our final destination is Prestwick, Scotland, to join the 8th Air Force. This is OK with us as we're not very crazy about the tropics. Most of the trip to Trinidad is in pitch blackness, so we couldn't enjoy the beauty of the Caribbean much. Most of our flying is at 9,000 to 11,000 feet, and it's mighty cool up here. When we land, the heat is terrific. After travelling 1,700 miles in about nine hours and 45 minutes we landed at Waller Field. This is the first foreign country I've been to besides Canada and Mexico. The town of Port of Spain is 28 miles away, but being transient personnel we are restricted to the base. The Officers Club is the first club we've been to where we can buy mixed drinks without supplying our own liquor. They had some very good scotch on sale for $5.50 a bottle. I couldn't afford that, but I did buy a bottle of Seagram's VO for $2.50 a fifth. The fellows really got feeling good, including myself, and it's lucky we bombardiers don't do a thing on this trip. That night we were briefed for the trip to Val de Caex Field, near Belem, Brazil, a distance of about 1,000 miles.

We were awakened at 0200, and at 0400 we were off on another jaunt. The days are very hot and you have to watch out for malaria and sleep under netting, as there are various pests to look out for. Just as we were getting into the plane I was bitten by a snake when I picked up a bag of mine. It was dark of course, and I couldn't see it, but the two fang marks are in my middle right hand finger. It couldn't have been poisonous, because nothing has happened yet.

April 1944-The day is the 29th, the time 0715, and we have just left Eknes Field at Dakar, Africa. We took off from Fortaleza at 2050 on the eve of the 27th and flew over the Atlantic in a little over 11 hours. We were warned about there being enemy subs on our route but we never saw any. We landed at Dakar about 1110 their time, and this was about the worst field we'd hit. In fact it is the worst. The runways are steel mats and there is a red dust blowing all the time. The field is right near the ocean so it is

very cool here. Malaria is quite high, so extreme precautions have to be taken. The mess and lodgings are free, and are terrible. Everything is rationed at the PX and all business is done with the French African 'Franc.' Everyone was glad to leave the place. We are now on our way to Casablanca. This and the hop to Scotland will be our last major hops. The trip is over miserable country and we can thank our lucky stars we weren't forced down. We reached Marrakech, French Morocco, about 1430. Did I say Dakar was lousy? Well, this place runs a close second, if not first.

On Sunday the 30th, we were allowed to go into town for five hours. All the stores were closed, and if they had been open you couldn't do much as the goods for sale were worthless, with absurd prices. At night we loaded more ammunition on the ship as the trip to England is quite dangerous. Now we have 100 rounds per gun. We left at 2330 and headed for merry old England."

From the Diary of Copilot Richard Stenger 847th Squadron

July 7, 1944-Early morning take off (our 20th mission) for a JU-88 fuselage factory at Aschersleben, Germany. The 1st and 3rd Divisions also went to targets in the same 50 mile area, so with all the bombers, plus our fighter escort, it looked like a Mummer's parade. The flak was no bother at all until we got to the target. Then...

From some distance away, I could see the dark clouds of black smoke coming up at the squadrons ahead of us. Then I started seeing white flashes and rather large orange-red bursts of fire with black smoke and balls of fire and smoke dropping downward. Also little black specks buzzing all through and around the advance formations.

In about three minutes we were right on the edge of it. A huge ball of German fighters (I say ball because they weren't in formation, but about two hundred just flying along together) had taken a pass at a B-24 squadron, and for 12 bombers lost, they shot down two fighters. Our P-51s had seen them though, and were on their tails just as they went through the formation, and then started the greatest melee and fastest action and mess that I ever imagined possible.

P-51s were chasing Me-109s all over the place. We were right close then, on our bombing run, and

a lot of the 109s came at our formation and through it trying to shake the Mustangs off, but they followed them right through.

I saw an Me-109 go across our bow with a P-51 right behind him. The 109 did a chandelle to the right, and just at the top of it the 51 got him. There was a burst of flame and black smoke and the Me-109 stopped in mid-air and dropped like a stone. Then a bunch of six or eight fighters (mixed) came in about 0130 level. And I mean they were fast. I saw them about 1,500 yards out, and before I could blink my eyes an Me-109 went under our right wing, with a P-51 about 20 yards behind him followed by a couple of 109s and 51s. The Me-109 blew up right behind us and we believe Shafer got him. I also saw a P-51 being chased by four Me-109s. The Mustang ran away from them and 15 P-38s came over about 3,000 feet above the Me's and peeled off on them - zip, zip, zip, zip - the Jerries never even saw them. About the same time, some P-47s joined the fracas.

All this that I saw took place in the seven or eight minutes we were in the area, and bombers and fighters were dropping like flies in a flit-sprayed room. I'll wait until I see the newspapers before I guess how many went down.

I would draw this conclusion. The first squadron that the GAF jumps can be written off; then it's even for a couple of minutes, and then our fighters erase or chase them off. The whole operation lasting from five to 10 minutes.

Just one bomber in our group got it; Kimbrough. Eight chutes were seen to open, and none of the Jerries had time to follow them even if they had wanted to. Another ship was hit by a 20mm shell, and they came back with the dome of the top turret and the gunner's head missing.

We have tomorrow off, so I guess I'll sleep late.

From the Diary of Tail Gunner Bill Campbell, 846th Squadron, Tail Gunner
Ludwigshaven, July 31, 1944

Well, today was the day. If I live to be 1,000 years old I'll never forget it. I still can't see how we got back. The infantry must have it rough, but I can see the air forces have their troubles too. I never knew I could make myself so small. I'd tuck my legs up under me and pull my flak helmet down to

489th Bomb Group, 844th Squadron, Crew #6. (Courtesy of James Fetterly)

my shoulders. We came in over Antwerp and picked up some medium flak there, but they weren't sighted in on us, but the trail flight got the hell knocked out of it. After we passed through, it was clear for a while, then when we hit the bomb run we caught hell for half an hour. The first ship to go down was in the high element to our right. One crew had 31 missions, and I saw it get a direct hit between number three and four engines. The wing fell off and it went into a flat spin; then the tail broke off and it disappeared in the clouds. No one got out.

The PFF lead ship had a smoke bomb on fire in the bomb bay, and one man bailed out; his chute caught onto the ship, he broke loose and fell 22,000 feet. What a drop! He wasn't 50 feet from our right wing, and I could see it just like a picture show. The thing happened so fast a man just can't imagine how tragic it is. Three ships went down and some are still missing.

I can't understand how I can possibly make 35 missions without going nuts, even if I don't go down. The sky was black as far as the eye could see; little black puffs that look harmless as hell but creep up as silent as the wind. It appears as if you can reach out and touch each puff. But when you can hear it, is when it's really bad. The whole ship shakes and rocks like it has hit a pocket. We picked up a few holes, and I can't for the life of me understand why it didn't look like a sieve. This mission today was the toughest they've had for a long time, and it had

to be our first. But it sure as hell won't be our last, as we are alerted tonight again. Today we went to Ludwigshaven, and if that's the target for tomorrow I'll stay home. I'm so tired I can hardly move. I sat in the tail without moving for seven hours and 30 minutes, six hours on oxygen.

Four hours till it's time to get up again.

From the Diary of Staff Sgt. Arthur G. Cressler
Shot down Aug. 6, 1944

August 6, 1944—Awakened at 0315. Just Mac and I because we were to fly *Cookie*, our forming ship. Got to briefing room and we were listed in the formation, so we were off to Hamburg. Our target was oil installations and storage tanks west of the city. An "88" went through #2 engine and exploded just as it broke through the top of the nacelle. A miracle saved Mac because the burst that started the fire in #2 also wrecked the turret controls and made a mess out of his flak helmet, plus cutting his oxygen line. Bailed out about 12:10 p.m. I landed in a small wheat field close by the town of Stade, and was picked up by farmers after I took about 10 steps toward nearby woods. Later picked up Mac, Jack and Fred, then marched to nearby 'love camp' and then to a Luft base at Stade. We were interrogated, searched and placed in solitary confinement. After about two hours, I was called out and Mac and I helped Nick into my cell. He had two bad legs as a result of his jump. We got straw mattresses and spent the night in a large room with 30 to 35 men, where we found Hank and Mark. The next morning we were served cold coffee and it tasted terrible. At noon we got soup which contained potatoes, cabbage and turnips. For supper we got a millet soup, similar to cream of wheat but not as tasty. The morning of the eighth we were awakened to be moved. We got into a bus and met Buck and Ty. Went to Hamburg, where we were put on a train; passed through Hanover and Frankfurt, and all places were practically level. Arrived at a Dulag Luft station at Oberursel, which is appropriately called the Flea Center.

Mac, Mark and I carried Nick practically all the way from the train station, a distance of about three miles. We were put in a small cell, 10 to 11 men, and given two slices of bread. Next morning we got two more slices of bread. Had some horrible soup for dinner, but I forced mine down. That night we got two slices of bread and some sickly tea. Shipped out next morning on two more slices bread and coffee. Left at 0630, arriving at Wetzlar at 1400. Here we received Red Cross capture parcels containing pajamas, long underwear, three pair socks, four handkerchiefs, sweater, shirt, razor and blades, soap, toothbrush, vitamin pills, toilet tissue, etc.

August 20, 1944-Went to church this morning. Wasn't much of a service but it helped us a lot as our hearts were all in it. Very thankful Jerry didn't take my prayer book, as it is sure comforting and strengthening to read prayers from it each night and to read the Mass on Sundays. Lots of the fellows are wounded and burnt. Sure wish we knew if Willie is alright. We know he got out of the ship, but don't know about after that. Got 110 loaves of bread yesterday, to last 293 men for 12 meals. Some diet!

September 1, 1944-Hope Uncle Joe is on German soil like he said. He is reported in three or four different places. All day the Jerries have been running around in dress uniforms. Heard a lot of artillery fire during the early evening and all night. Spent practically all day inside due to air alerts, seven or eight. Jerries dug foxholes all around our fence. Two platoons moved into valley south of camp. Trucks, tanks, guns, etc., moving south on road east of camp and continued all night. Firing let up about daybreak. Rumor, equipment from Belgium to France?

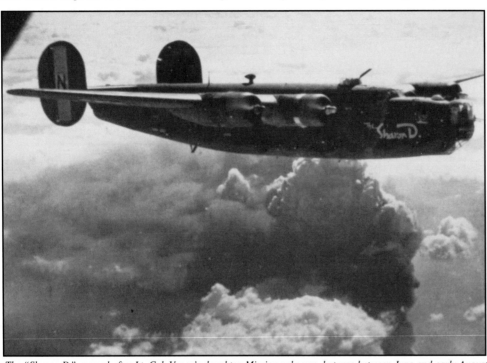

The "Sharon D.", named after Lt. Col. Vance's daughter. Mission unknown, but was between June and early August 1944, since plane has green and white tail colors of the 95th Wing. (Courtesy of C.H. Freudenthal, 489th)

Air Crew #4356. Taken June 16, 1944 just before take-off to Lincoln, Nebraska from Gowen Field, Boise, Idaho. En route to combat duty in European Theaters of Operations in England via Bangor, Maine, Goose Bay, Labrador, Reykjavik, Iceland and Shannon, Ireland. Bottom row, L to R: Sgt. Carl Olander, R. Waist Gunner; Sgt. "Monk" Wendell, Armorer/ Upper Turret Gunner; T/Sgt. Mike Koczan, Engineer/Left Waist Gunner; S/Sgt. Hugh McMonagle, Radio Operator; Sgt. Ed Blosel, Assistant Eng./Nose Gunner; Sgt. Sammy Stralo, Tail Gunner. Top row L to R: 2nd Lt. Jack Brainard, Copilot; 2nd Lt. Arnie Klopp, Bombardier; 2nd Lt. Dewey Edwards, Navigator; 2nd Lt. Mike Brienza, Pilot. First overseas assignment; advanced gunnery school, Greencastle, Ireland, then to 855th Bomb Sqdn., 491st Bomb Group, 2nd Air Div., 8th Air Force, Metfield, England.

B-24 "Pappy's Persauders" #44-40144. B-24J Convair Vultee out of San Diego, CA. The original crew of this aircraft, piloted by 1st Lt. Dwight L. Turner, Sr., flew 31 combat missions from June 2, 1944 to August 27 1944. The next crew to fly this aircraft, then commanded by Lt. Eckard, were shot down by flak over Misburg, Germany on September 12, 1944. (Courtesy of Mark M. Turner and Norman J. Canfield, 491st)

December 25, 1944-Christmas Day! Yesterday and today we were on parole. Lockup wasn't until one o'clock the 24th and midnight tonight. Each man got a #2 Christmas parcel, which was very nice. Marty gave Man a can of jam and me a can of cheese. We gave him some dates I fixed up with nuts and rolled in sugar. I made some dressing-bread, pate, onions, salt and turkey, which tasted pretty good. Sang carols at midnight on the 24th. Willie gave Man and me one and a half box of crackers each.

From the Diary of Steve Havanec

Flight Engineer, 845TH Squadron

October 7, 1944-Got up at 0330, ate and briefed at 0430. Went to communion after briefing. I do every time we're going on a raid. We took off at 0805. We were supposed to bomb an oil refinery at Magdeburg, but they had a smoke screen over the town, and the flak was very, very heavy, so the Command Pilot "Iron Balls" took us over the secondary target, a chemical explosive plant at Clausthal-Zellerfeld, 25 miles from Magdeburg. It was the first time it was ever hit, as it was only discovered by photo recon planes yesterday. We carried six 1,000 pound demolition bombs. What a beautiful sight it was. The whole town was up in flames when the chemicals started to pop. The plant is probably leveled now, 'cause everybody hit it. We were 25,500 feet above the target. When bombs away was yelled it was 35 below zero. On one of the bombs I wrote "To Adolf with love and kisses, Helen Larkin," and on another I wrote, "To Schicklegruber Happy Landings, Ann Palck." There were more than 2,000 planes on this raid. They all didn't hit the same target though. I'm very tired, so I'll hit the sack. We're up again for tomorrow.

Crew of B-24 "Pappy's Persuaders." Back row L to R: R. Fogliani, Waist Gunner; U.H. Anderson, Bombardier; T.R. Allen, Navigator; Robert Fogarty, Copilot; Dwight L. Turner, Pilot; P. Gafford, Waist Gunner. Front row, L to R: R.S. Kimberly, Radio Operator; W.T. Kay, Top Turret Gunner; B. Zatkovic, Tail Gunner; N.J. Canfield, Ball Turret Gunner. (Courtesy of Norman J. Canfield, 491st)

491ST BOMB GROUP (H)
Foreword

The outstanding success of the 491st Bomb Group (H) is due in large part to the inspired leadership of Col. (Maj. Gen.) Frederic H. Miller Jr. who assumed command in June 1944 and was transferred to Headquarters, USSTAF in December 1944. Gen. Miller provided the management expertise and leadership required to run a "green" untried group into an outstanding battle hardened force.

No story of the 491st is complete without a tribute to the continuity of leadership provided by Lt. Col. (Gen.) Jack G. Merrell, one of the first officers assigned to the group and deputy commander from October 1943 until March 1945 when he left to take command of the 389th Group. Jack Merrell was one of the young, inspired officers whose rise to the top of the post-war Air Force was forecast by his outstanding combat and leadership record.

The squadron commanders, Ken Strauss (852nd), Harry Stepheg (853rd), Col. Parmelee (854th) and Escor Watts (855th) came from anti-submarine duty to squadron command in Pueblo. They held these commands, serving with distinction, through training and combat. Their efforts played a large part in the group's record.

491ST BOMB GROUP (H)
The Ringmasters

"No other group was ever committed to action so fast and flew so many missions in so short a time, achieving such fine results." (Quote is from the 14th Combat Wing, 8th Air Force, final report, June 1945).

The last heavy bomber group to be assigned to the 2nd Bomb Division, 8th Air Force, the 491st made an indelible mark in the air in Europe. The 491st is proud to be known as : "The Last And The Best."

Our commanding officer as we trained in Pueblo and went overseas was Lt. Col. Carl T. Goldenberg, a great commanding officer who really got a 'promotion' when he was replaced and sent to a fighter squadron. His replacement, Col. Frederic H. Miller, was just what the 491st needed and his guidance from June to October 1944 made us an outstanding outfit. Our deputy commanding officer, Lt. Col. Jack G. Merrell, from fall of 1943 until April 1945, was the group's backbone and a good part of the glue that held us together during trying times. Jack moved on to become commanding officer of the 389th Bomb Group.

The 491st Bomb Group (H) was 'born' in September 1943 at Tucson, Arizona, and with the addition of a squadron from Alamagordo, New Mexico, became a four squadron group. After a lot of movement to various bases, the group moved to Pueblo, Colorado, and with its full complement of crews we started operating as a group. Many of our crews had already trained for up to three months as crews. Now at Pueblo, our air crews along with the support people trained for almost four months. With the prior experience, our air crews became very efficient at formation flying plus the bombardier, navigator, engineers, radio operators and gunners honed their skills. Some crews had over six months of training behind them.

The ground support echelons left for England April 1 and the flight crews started leaving on April 25, flying the southern route from Florida to Trinidad, Belem, Fortalaza, Dakar, Marrakech, and then on to England and our new base at Metfield in East Anglia. Our first aircraft arrived on May 9 and the balance of the 72 aircraft came in the following three weeks with only a few mechanical problems en route. Our navigators enjoyed going for "real" with their celestial navigation of three long, overwater flights.

The 491st was assigned to the 95th Combat Wing of the 2nd Air Division, 8th Air Force. In May we trained for combat flying in Europe, a new ball game for the air crews and the ground support personnel. The 491st was scheduled to go operational on June 10, 1944, but on June 2, 1944, we were alerted and flew our first combat mission to bomb an airfield at Bretigney, France. We sent 26 B-24s, lost our first crew in combat, and had our first taste of war. Returning to Metfield at night was not a great experience for 35 aircraft, many with their first battle damage. The Bill Evans crew, our first combat loss bailed out in the target area. Four crew members became prisoners of war, four were picked up by the French Underground and were later returned to England. The navigator, Malcolm Blue, and the ball turret gunner, George Lemay, were killed in their chutes by gunfire from the airfield.

During the month of June 1944, we flew 29 missions in 29 days with 749 sorties — more than any other B-24 group in the 8th Air Force. During

Standing, L to R: 2nd Lt. Grove, 1st Lt. Figal, Capt. Dougan, Lt. Col. Goldenberg, Capt. Joe Moffitt, Capt. Hayduk. Kneeling, L to R: M/Sgt. Freeman, M/Sgt. Redfern, T/Sgt. Lauritzen, T/Sgt. Judson. (Courtesy of Alfred Hayduk, 491st)

the last two weeks of June, the 491st led the 2nd Air Division in tonnage of bombs dropped, hours of combat flown, number of sorties per assigned crews, number of sorties per assigned aircraft, lowest loss of aircraft and lowest loss of personnel. We set these records in spite of being a new group, last to receive mission information, and all bomb loading accomplished without electric bomb hoists.

In the summer of 1944, the 491st adopted the name and patch "The Ringmasters." We are still today, "The Ringmasters."

July 1944: The 491st flew 15 missions, 474 sorties, six aircraft lost on missions plus 24 aircraft lost in a bomb dump explosion.

July 15, 1955, was a memorable day for the 491st in Metfield. Our bomb dump blew up. Five trucks delivering bombs to the dump had very impatient drivers. According to a sixth driver who was not involved, they decided to unload their trucks by backing fast and then braking, allowing the bombs to drop off the truck. Mistake, the bombs were RDX, 500 pounds with the power of 750 pounds and very unstable if bumped or dropped. The crater was 25 feet deep by 75 feet in diameter plus over 700 tons of bombs were destroyed or made unusable for operations. Five drivers and their trucks were blown up and their parts scattered in the debris. At the Air Force Museum in Dayton, Ohio, there is a display of a bomb casing wrapped around a shoe. No doubt the shoe belonged to one of the unfortunate men who 'kicked' the bombs off the tailgate that day.

It took three days to create a new bomb dump and repair the worse damage. The group lost 24 B-24s and most of the pressure sensitive instruments on the remaining aircraft. There was a lot of building damage on the base plus some windows broken in the villages.

On July 24, 1944, the 491st had two missions to bomb in front of the ground troops from medium altitude of 15,000 feet. It was not a fun trip with heavy flak until the bombs hit. We had no losses and after the bombing our ground troops were able to 'break out' from St. Lo, France.

August 1944: Nineteen missions with 545 sorties and the loss of four B-24s in combat. The big change was on August 15 and 16 when we moved to our new base at North Pickenham and left the 95th Combat Wing to become part of the 14th Combat Wing headed by Gen. Leon Johnson. We were a fortunate group. We did worry about losing our "lucky tails." The green and white tail fins that we all thought had brought us good luck. Fortunately we

were able to keep them until January 1945 when we changed to the silver and black tails.

On August 24, 1944 in a mission to Hanover, Germany, the Norman J. Rogers crew bailed out. The nine man crew were all captured with Nose Gunner William Adams wounded in the arm, Engineer Forrest Brinistool wounded in the abdomen and William A. Dumont with a broken ankle. The Germans walked the eight survivors (Brinistool was hospitalized) through Russelsheim, Germany, where the citizens urged on by two women and the local Nazis stoned and beat them. When no life signs were evident, the Germans loaded them on a cart and took them to the town cemetery. They then proceeded to 'finish off' the crew when they were interrupted by an air raid siren. They left and two survivors, Sidney E. Brown and William M. Adams got out of the cart and hid. They then proceeded west until captured again four days later. Brown, Adams and Brinistool survived.

The murders first became known in March 1945 when the 3rd Army took the town. French and Polish slave laborers told the authorities. In June 1945 the Army War Crimes branch investigated the incident and with the help of the mayor and other citizens of Russelsheim got the full story and proceeded to prosecute the guilty. On July 25, 1945 the trial was held and nine men and women were pronounced guilty. Six were hanged and the others sentenced to 15 years at hard labor.

The 491st lost several men when we thought they had gotten out of their crippled aircraft yet were never found.

On August 27, 1944, the Yurcina crew became our first crew to complete their missions.

September 1944: 14 missions and 380 sorties with combat losses of nine B-24s. Official records show a loss of nine aircraft for the month but don't show our many losses over friendly territory. We lost many aircraft and men from battle damage where the plane crashed in friendly territory. Also, some take offs, landings and weather related accidents add to our losses.

German flak has become increasingly heavier and more accurate as our ground troops advance.

On September 18, 1944, we sent 41 aircraft to Eindhoven, Holland, to support our ground troops in the Market Garden offensive. We dropped supplies at low level with disastrous results. The German troops threw everything at us including small arms fire. All our crews were thrilled at the reception by the Dutch people who were out in the streets obviously cheering. We lost two aircraft in the drop area and four aircraft in friendly territory, plus every B-24 had battle damage, plus many wounded. Many planes came back with leaves, branches, etc. stuck in the fuselage. One B-24 came back with a fence post stuck in the fuselage and trailing some barbed wire. The lower you flew, the safer it was.

October 1944: We flew 15 missions and 434 sorties with one combat loss from flak. At Hamm, Germany, on October 2, 1944, the Means crew had just two survivors who became prisoners of war.

On October 14, 1944, we had a V-1 (buzz bomb) alert and one traveled over the base at about 200 feet. When it cleared the base and danger was past, Gale Johnson (duty flight control officer) announced the all clear. The V-1 hit a few miles from our base shortly after the all clear and our commanding officer came out of his shelter just as it went off. He dove back into the wet bunker on his stomach. Ugh! He gave Gale a great 'chewing out' but this was a very funny situation to all who remember.

November 1944: 14 missions, 282 sorties and a loss of 16 B-24s at Misburg, Germany, on November 26, 1944. The 491st had three squadrons, 28 aircraft and after uncovering at the IP, approximately 100 FW-190s attacked, first the 853rd Bomb Squadron downing the entire squadron of nine aircraft, then they went after the 854th Bomb Squadron and shot down six aircraft plus a seventh that crashed later near Brussels. The battle went on for over 20 minutes until we received help from our fighter support. The 491st was given confirmed credit for seven enemy aircraft destroyed, 11 damaged, and three probables. This does not include the 16 aircraft that failed to return.

Interestingly, three 'Ringmasters' bailed out on November 26, 1944, for the third time. Dale Allan and Charles Miller became prisoners of war and Robert Brennen was killed in action.

There were no dry eyes in North Pickenham that afternoon when we finally realized what had happened. Sixteen aircraft, 16 crews, 160 friends were all gone. Vince Cahill remembers that the chapel was very crowded that night. (It was a Sunday.)

December 1944: 13 missions, 305 sorties with two losses. Weather, our greatest enemy, became an even more serious foe in December with the Battle of the Bulge. The weather prevented us from hitting the German targets just when the ground forces urgently needed our support. From December 13 to 23, 1944, we were briefed almost every day and aircraft loaded, and then we sat in the planes until the mission was scrubbed because of weather. A few times we were able to get off the ground but then called back because of weather on the continent. On December 23, 1944, we sent 17 aircraft to bomb the rail junction at Ahrweiler, Germany, by H2X.

On December 24, 1944, the weather cleared enough to get off the ground and we went for a maximum effort with 50 B-24s for our target at Wittlich, Germany.

On December 31, 1944, we completed our last mission of 1944 with 26 aircraft to Neuweld, Germany, a bridge. With seven months of combat, we had flown 121 missions; 2,403 sorties; 32,328 personnel sorties; dropped 8,722 tons of bombs; delivered supplies to the ground troops; 461 men completed their tours and returned stateside, with a loss of 42 aircraft (combat). Our bombing record had been second to none and our losses were low to compare favorably with all other groups in the 8th Air Force.

The 491st Bomb Group (H) completed its 100th mission on November 9, 1944, and had a celebration on December 1, 1944, with a three day stand down. The party was outstanding.

January 1945: 13 missions, 252 sorties and one loss. An original crew, Dean Strain leading the 14th Combat Wing, was shot down by flak over Hamburg, Germany, with 12 men, no survivors.

On January 5, 1945, the 491st was scheduled for a mission to Munster, Germany. The weather was even worse than normal with heavy snow and icing conditions. An over-eager commanding officer, not accepting the senior flight control officer's recommendations, ordered take off. The first B-24 off crashed near Swaffham with no survivors; the second B-24, Wright, barely got off; the Sweet crew started but could only get 50 feet off the ground. They crashed into some fir trees about one-half mile off the runway and the crew although badly bruised with some broken bones did survive. Next, McKenzie took off and made it. Finally, common sense prevailed and the mission was scrubbed.

February 1945: 14 missions, 373 sorties and one loss. In addition, we lost one B-24 on a ferry trip. The Goeking crew hit a mountain and eight were killed with two survivors.

Our missions were becoming longer as our ground troops fought their way into Germany. We were flying over eight hours per mission now.

During January and February, the 491st was called upon to supply 177 men to go through a fast course to become infantry men. The losses at Battle of the Bulge caused a shortage. In addition, there was a shortage of blankets and every bed was checked and all excess shipped to our ground troops. It was a very cold winter.

March 1945: 26 missions, 581 sorties and four combat losses.

The German Luftwaffe was still active and on March 4 and 5, 1945, they bombed and strafed our base with no damage to us.

On March 24, 1945, we again flew a low level supply mission to Wesel, Germany, to supply British troops. We lost three B-24s plus five B-24s landed at other bases with battle damage and wounded on board.

On missions of March 30, 1945, the Siek crew had to ditch in the North Sea and only two crewmen survived even though a PBY followed them down and landed next to the B-24 at once. This is

Front row, L to R: Eugene Porter, Waist Gunner; William P. Mitchell, Waist Gunner; Ed Hohman, Radio Operator; Byron R. Jones, Engineer; Hilton P. Ritch, Tail Gunner. Back row: Lt. Fleming, Pilot; Lt. Pitts, Copilot; Lt. Cal. Shahbaz, Bombardier/Navigator; Bill Hickey, Nose Gunner. (Courtesy of Edward J. Hohman, 491st)

Crew 3-0-114, 852nd Squadron, 491st Group. Standing L to R: Dudley Friday, P; Roy Gabrielson, CP; Edward Wood, N; Daniel Hurley, B; Charles Bates, G; John Shay, G. Front row, L to R: Arthur Degennaro, E.G.; Francis Rondinone, G; Name unknown, C.D.; Donald Birnbaumer, G; David Allen, R.O. (Courtesy of Dudley Friday, 491st)

only one of several we lost in ditching, but this incident ended up being our last operational loss.

April 1945: 13 missions, 293 sorties and no operational loss.

April 25, 1945, we flew our last mission to Bad Reichenhall, Germany, hitting the railroad facilities with 28 B-24s. The war was over.

With the war over, we flew "trolley missions" at low altitude over areas in Europe that we had bombed to give our ground support men a chance to see what their work had enabled the flying crews to do. The bombing results were awesome from low altitude.

May 1945: The 491st air crews plus 10 to 12 passengers per plane were flying home. The staff and operations personnel boarded the *Queen Mary* and arrived home the first week of July.

June 1, 1945, the 491st was alerted for deployment to the Pacific. Everyone was given 30-day leave and then would reassemble at McCord AAF for transition into B-29s or B-32s and join the war in the Pacific. Fortunately, the war with Japan ended in August and in September the 491st became a part of history.

Reunions: Many "Ringmasters" had been taking part in 2nd Air Division reunions for many years. On November 1, 1989, the group met in Savannah, Georgia, to incorporate and become an organization-The 491st Bomb Group (H) Association, Inc. (It was only through the efforts of "Hap' Chandler that this happened.)

As a group many have attended several reunions in England. We have dedicated group memorials at Metfield, North Pickenham and at the Air Force Museum in Dayton. In September 1993 we dedicated a memorial at the Air Force Academy in Colorado Springs.

The 491st flew 187 missions plus many transport missions ferrying supplies to the ground troops.

Lest we forget...there was a cost. The 491st Bomb Group lost almost 700 men killed in action, and an unknown number who were injured and/or ended up as prisoners of war.

492ND BOMB GROUP (H)
The Happy Warriors
Station 143 - North
Pickenham, England
by Henry Gendreizig

In 1920 the Flying Club of Baltimore was organized for reserve officers of that city. The club became part of the Maryland National Guard as the 104th Observation Squadron. At the beginning of World War II, the 104th became part of the antisubmarine patrol used along the east coast. In early 1942, the 104th operated out of the Atlantic City Municipal Airport. On October 17, 1942, the unit was designated the 517th Bombardment Squadron and on November 29, 1942, became the 12th Antisubmarine Squadron and Maj. Joshua Rowe became the commanding officer. He was one of the original Baltimoreans. A month later, it started operations from Langley Field and stayed there until September 19, 1943. Before leaving Langley, a new commanding officer, Lt. Col. Sheffeld, was assigned.

On September 19, 1943, the 12th Anti-submarine Squadron was transferred to Blythe, California. Upon arriving at Blythe, a new commanding officer, Lt. Col. Carl Goldenburg, was assigned. On October 1, 1943, it was designated the 859th Bombardment Squadron (H), and also designated as the cadre source for the new heavy 492nd Bomb Group, activated on the same date at Clovis Army Air Field, New Mexico. The crews that came from Langley (as cadre for the 492nd) did not go to Clovis. They stayed at Blythe until departing for AAFSAT (AAF

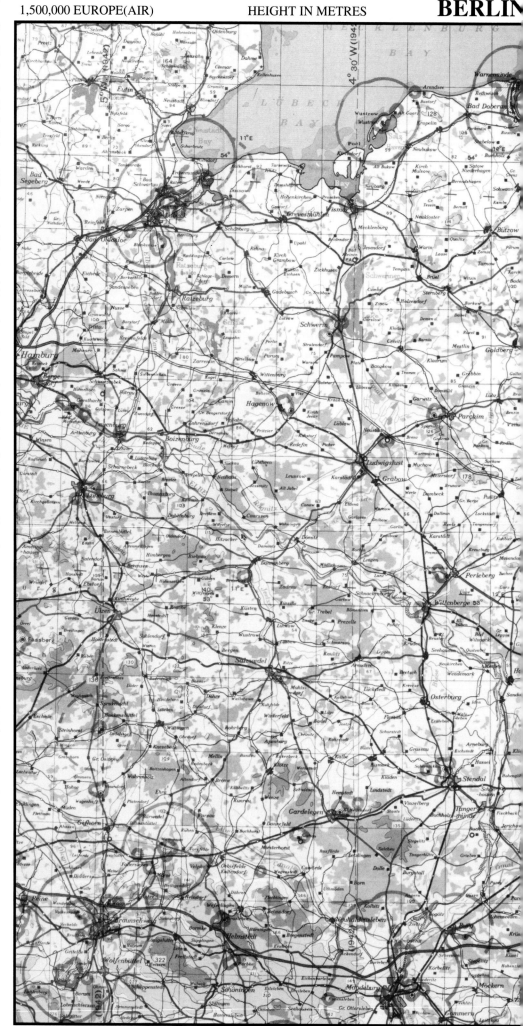

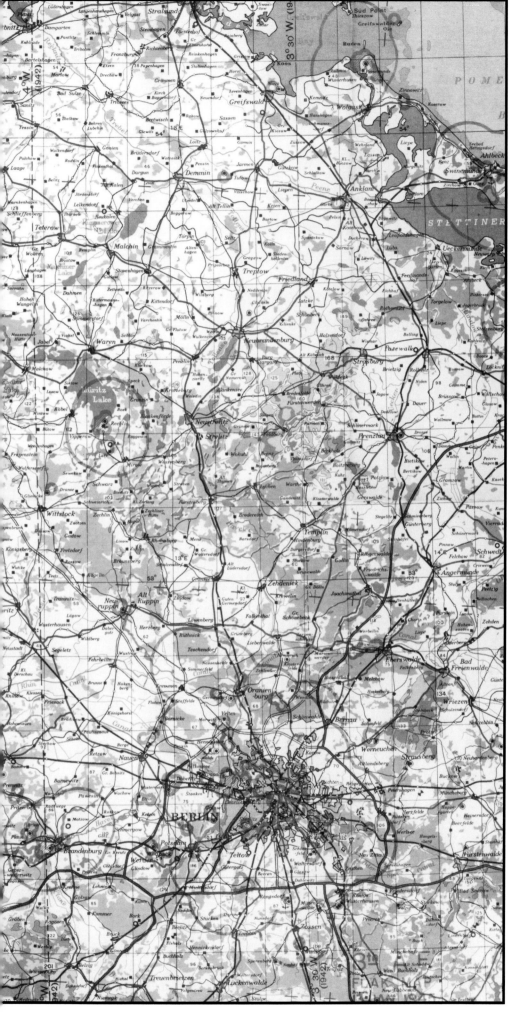

8th Air Force Flak Map, 13 Jan. 1945. (Courtesy of Dick Martin)

School of Applied Tactics) at Orlando, Florida, on November 3, 1943. At this point, another commanding officer, Col. Arthur Pierce, was assigned to the unit. He went through AAFSAT with the crews and went with the crews from Orlando to Alamogordo Army Air Field, New Mexico. Squadron ground personnel moved to Clovis and on October 27, 1943, the 856th, 857th and 858th Squadrons were activated with personnel from the 25th Anti-submarine Squadron stationed at Jacksonville, Florida.

On December 31, 1943, the temporary commander of the 492nd was Maj. Louis C. Adams. The original group commander, Col. Arthur J. Pierce, departed to assume command of the 466th Bomb Group (B-24) on December 17, 1943. The permanent commander, Lt. Col. Eugene H. Snavely, was appointed January 1944. The commander of the 856th Bomb Squadron (H) was Maj. John F. Losee, the commander of the 857th Bomb Squadron (H) was Maj. Donald H. Heaton, the commander of the 858th Bomb Squadron (H) was Maj. Robert Hambaugh and the commander of the 859th Bomb Squadron (H) was Maj. James J. Mahoney.

In early January 1944, 20 crews were assigned to the 492nd from the 39th Combat Crew Training School at Davis-Monthan. On January 27, 1944, 16 more crews arrived from the 331st CCTS at Casper, Wyoming. These were supplemented on January 26, 1944, by 24 more crews from Casper and four from the 29th CCTS at Boise, Idaho, bringing the group up to full strength. Of the entire group, 32 crews failed the ORI (Operation Readiness Inspection) and were declared "not sufficiently advanced to fit in with the rest of the group." In early March 1944 they were exchanged for a like number of crews from the 330th CCTS at Biggs Field, Texas. The replacement crews had pilots who had many hundreds of hours flying B-24s. With this high level of pilot experience, the 492nd was able to: (1) complete their training ahead of schedule, and (2) move from Alamogordo to North Pickenham without loss or mishap.

Flyaway B-24s departed for Herington, Kansas, April 1-4, 1944. After several days at Herington spent modifying and preparing the planes for combat, they departed for Morrison Field, West Palm Beach, Florida. From there to Waller Field, Trinidad, then on to Wales and finally on April 18, 1944, home field at North Pickenham, England.

Practice missions were conducted May 4, 7, and 8, 1944, and a full dress rehearsal on May 10, 1944, assembling 40 aircraft with the 2nd Air Division. The first mission was flown May 11, 1944, against the marshalling yards at Mulhouse, France. The 492nd finished the month of June as a three squadron group, for on June 19 the 858th was ordered to the 8th Air Force Composite Command.

Maj. Robert Hambaugh, the 858th commander, accompanied the men to their new station at Harrington. The 492nd flew its last daylight combat mission (89 days from start to finish) number 66 against Ostend, Belgium on August 7, 1944, and then were deactivated. The original 492nd was broken up and its personnel assigned to a variety of units in the 8th Air Force. With a few exceptions, all crews with less than 15 missions were assigned to the 859th Squadron, Lt. Col. Mahoney went with them. Twenty-nine crews in all went to Rackheath where they became the 788th Bomb Squadron, 467th Bomb Group.

An official quote regarding the 492nd, "No other bombardment group in U.S. history every lost as many aircraft in combat in so short a time." Not counting losses to accidents or crash landings, the 492nd lost 52 aircraft in almost exactly three months of combat operations. Killed in action (KIA) were 530 personnel and missing in action (MIA) 58 personnel. A total of 3,643 tons of bombs were dropped during the 66 missions.

BIG FRIEND - LITTLE FRIENDS

To doubt that a special relationship existed between bomber crews and fighter pilots is to be misinformed, indeed. On the other hand, giving it meaningful expression is at least challenging. However, a letter from a 445th Bomb Group pilot to a 361st Fighter Group "Little Friend" sums it up eloquently.

July 19, 1944

Dear Capt. Cole:

Frankly I am not too good at writing letters of gratitude—in fact a letter of gratitude would never adequately cover the feeling I and my crew have for you and your wingman. This is just a brief note from one pilot to another pilot both fighting a war under fairly comparative circumstances.

My crew are full of praise for me and what I did to get them home. But I am passing the buck to you in this case because if it hadn't been for your calm, cool assistance and encouragement I simply couldn't have brought that ship home. We had a tough time on that ship, what with two engines out, fire and panic amongst my new crew—and I had some snap decisions to make which, thanks to you, were correct. It is not the easiest thing in the world to decide to nurse a crippled ship directly over the Calais flak belt at 10,000 feet. But I knew you two lads were out there pulling for us—and you would be a witness to our fate, ditching or otherwise, if they did manage to knock us down.

Captain, there are no atheists on my crew and believe me The Lord and I had a little chat over there in the target area. You were an answer to a prayer, and just what I needed to put my guts at ease and give me the encouragement to take the fighting chance. I have known since my first mission that those "little friends" we see over Europe are our guardian angels but never had I realized just how big a job you chaps really do—"over and beyond the line of duty" I think the Army puts it. I can never thank you enough and I don't possibly see how I can return the favor. All of the praise that was heaped on me by the commanding officers here I am passing on to you triple-fold.

On behalf of my crew I want to wish you the best of luck and God speed during the balance of your tour. The drinks are on me any time you want to drop in here for a visit."

1/Lt. William C. Riemer
445th Bombardment Group
Pilot of a B-24 Liberator named *TAHELENBAK*.

THE LITTLE FRIENDS
65th Fighter Wing
by George M. Epperson, Lt. Colonel, USAF, Retired

Commanding Officer, Brig. Gen. Jesse Auton. Based at Saffron Walden.

The fighter history of the 2nd Bomb Division/Air Division actually starts with the assignment of the 65th Fighter Wing specifically to the 2nd Bomb Division on September 15, 1944.

Prior to September 15, 1944, Eighth Air Force fighter groups were under the operational control of VIII Fighter Command through three fighter wings, the 65th, 66th, and 67th. On that date, the fighter wings were transferred to bomb divisions. The 67th Fighter Wing was assigned to the First Bomb Division; the 65th Fighter Wing went to the Second Bomb Division, and the 66th Fighter Wing to the Third Bomb Division. The bomb divisions, with both bombardment and fighter groups, were organized on the concept that, as integrated fight-

ing units, with sub-depots and strategic air depots, they could be moved individually to the Far East to pursue the war against Japan. However, this never became necessary.

Each fighter wing was comprised of five fighter groups together with administrative and operational headquarters. Operationally, the fighter wings remained on a level with the combat bomb wings already operating under the bomb divisions. Administratively the fighter wing paralleled the bombardment group since the combat bomb wings had no administrative function.

The 65th Fighter Wing of the Second Bomb and Air Division was located at Saffron Walden, Essex in an old grammar school built in 1881 and requisitioned by the Royal Air Force at the outbreak of World War II; it has since reverted to its original mission. Through its collocated 52nd Fighter Control Squadron, ALL Eighth Air Force fighters on operational missions were controlled by the 65th Fighter Wing. A control room converted from a gymnasium was used for this purpose. It also remains and is used as originally intended.

Additionally, the 65th Fighter Wing, in close coordination with the Royal Air Force, controlled ALL air-sea rescue operations for the Eighth Air Force, both, bombers and fighters. This operation was also carried out in the Saffron Walden control room; the operational unit was the 5th Emergency Rescue Squadron, initially at Boxted, near Colchester, and later at Halesworth. It was equipped with B-17s and P-47s modified to drop life rafts or dinghies and with 0A-10s that could land on water.

Although there were interim changes, the five fighter groups ultimately assigned to and under the operational control of the 65th Fighter Wing were the 4th Fighter Group at Debden, a few miles south of Saffron Walden, formerly the Eagle Squadron of the Royal Air Force, initially equipped with Spitfires, then as the 4th Group with P-47s and finally with P-51s; the 56th Fighter Group at Boxted, with P-47s, the only Eighth Air Force fighter group to retain the P-47; the 355th Fighter Group at Steeple Morden, west of Royston, with P-51s; the 361st Fighter Group at Little Walden, a few miles north of Saffron Walden, with P-51s; and the 479th Fighter Group at Wattisham, northwest of Ipswich, initially with P-38s and then converted to P-51s.

In combat with the German Luftwaffe, total claims of the five fighter groups of the 65th Fighter

Wing were 1,959 1/2 aircraft destroyed in the air and 1,666 1/2 destroyed on the ground. The 65th Fighter Wing was surely the most important fighter wing in the Eighth Air Force from the standpoint of operational responsibilities. Were its fighters, along with those of the other two fighter wings, merely used for bomber support, "Big Friends" and "Little Friends?" Not at all! A very large number of locomotives and rolling stock, marshalling yards, bridges, viaducts, Rhine River barges, convoys, and airfields felt the sting of fighter-dropped bombs of .50 caliber and 20 millimeter ammunition. The number of German aircraft destroyed on the ground attests to the fact that the fighters were not always at high altitude on bomber escort.

In his magnificent book, "The Mighty Eighth," Roger Freeman summed it all up. "Probably the greatest single contribution of the Eighth Air Force to victory in Europe was the star part its fighters played in attaining combat superiority in continental air space."

Maj. John Trevor Godfrey, of Woonsocket, RI, 336th Squadron was acclaimed to have the sharpest eyes in the group with 18 enemy aircraft shot down in the air and 12.60 destroyed on the ground. (Courtesy of Dick Martin)

Ralph Kidd Hofer, "Kidd," Salem, Missouri, 334th Squadron, July 2, 1944. (Courtesy of Dick Martin)

Lt. Paul H. Skogstad, 335th Fighter Squadron, 4th Fighter Group, at Debden, England in 1945. (Courtesy of Dick Martin)

4TH FIGHTER GROUP
The Eagles
submitted by Ray L. Shewfelt

Commanding Officers: Col. Edward W. Anderson, Col. Donald J.M. Blakeslee, Lt. Col. Harry J. Dayhuff, Col. Chesley C. Peterson, Lt. Col. Claiborne H. Kinnard Jr. and Col. Everett W. Stewart. Based at Debden.

In September 1942, the 4th Fighter Group came into being with the integration of the three Eagle Squadrons (RAF) into the USAAF. No. 71 Eagle Squadron (ES) became the 334th Fighter Squadron; No. 121 ES became the 335th Fighter Squadron; and No. 133 ES became the 336th Fighter Squadron.

They continued to fly Spitfires for several months until they converted to P-47s to become the first 8th Air Force Fighter Group to fly the Thunderbolt. On July 28, 1943, the group was carrying external 200 gallon tanks. Although they were not pressurized and would not feed at high altitude, it enabled them to penetrate into German airspace and catch the Luftwaffe by surprise. They attacked 45-plus enemy aircraft and accounted for three ME-109s and six FW-190s.

On October 23, 1943, Group CO, Lt. Col. Chesley Peterson (ex RAF), was promoted to colonel at the age of 23. What a responsibility! This was a man who was washed out of USAAC flying training for lack of flying aptitude. Until the end of the year, replacement pilots were Americans from other RAF units integrated into the USAAF. Starting in January 1944, American-trained replacements started to arrive. On February 28, 1944 the 4th Fighter Group flew its first mission in P-51s to become the first of 14 8th Air Force groups to be equipped with the Mustang. Its teething troubles proved to be very aggravating but the P-51 would be the turning point in the air war over Europe. When it was provided with two 108 gallon wing tanks, the Mustang had the range to go anywhere in Europe with the bombers. It was also an excellent fighting machine.

The 4th Fighter Group received the Distinguished Unit Citation for destroying 323 enemy aircraft in the 50 day period March 5 to April 24, 1944. On June 21, 1944, the group flew escort for three combat wings of B-17s, the first shuttle mission to Russia. Five pilots were lost on the mission.

Major Pierce McKennon, CO of 335th Fighter Squadron, was shot down on March 18, 1945, while strafing Neubrandenburg A/D. Lt. George Green landed, picked him up, and successfully brought him back to Debden. Technically McKennon is listed as lost and evaded.

The 4th Fighter Group was in a long time rivalry with the 56th Fighter Group for the greatest number of victories and the first to reach the 1,000 mark to include both air and ground. As of the end of hostilities, the 4th did in fact top this mark, but to achieve this, 241 pilots are listed as missing in action.

56TH FIGHTER GROUP
from Air Force Combat Units of World War II

Constituted as 56th Pursuit Group (Interceptor) on November 20, 1940. Activated on January 15, 1941. Equipped with P-39s and P-40s. Trained, participated in maneuvers, served as an air defense organization, and functioned as an operational training unit. Redesignated 56th Fighter Group in May 1942. Received P-47s in June and began training for combat. Moved to England, December 1942-January 1943. Assigned to 8th Air Force. Continued training for several weeks. Entered combat with a fighter sweep in the area of St. Omer on April 13, 1943, and during the next two years destroyed more enemy aircraft in aerial combat than any other fighter group of 8th Air Force. Flew numerous missions over France, the Low Countries, and Germany to escort bombers that attacked industrial establishments, V-weapons sites, submarine pens, and other targets on the continent. Also strafed and dive-bombed airfields, troops, and supply points; attacked the enemy's communications; and flew counter-air patrols. Engaged in counter-air and interdictory missions during the invasion of Normandy in June 1944. Supported Allied forces for the break through at St. Lo in July. Participated in the Battle of the Bulge, December 1944-January 1945. Helped to defend the Remagen bridge-head against air attacks in March 1945. Received a Distinguished Unit Citation for aggressiveness in seeking out and destroying enemy aircraft and for attacking enemy air bases, February 20-March 9, 1944. Received another Distinguished Unit Citation for strikes against anti-aircraft positions while supporting the airborne attack on Holland in September 1944. Flew last combat mission on April 21, 1945. Returned to the U.S. in October. Inactivated on October 18, 1945. Activated on May 1, 1946. Equipped with P-47 and P-51 aircraft; converted to F-80s in 1947. Redesignated 56th Fighter Interceptor Group in January 1950. Converted to F-86 aircraft. Inactivated on February 6, 1952.

Redesignated 56th Fighter Group (Air Defense). Activated on August 18, 1955. Assigned to Air Defense Command and equipped with F-86s.

Squadrons. 61st: 1941-1945; 1946-1952. 62nd: 1941-1945; 1946-1952; 1955-. 63rd: 1941-1945; 1946-1952; 1955-.

Stations: Savannah, GA, January 15, 1941; Charlotte, NC, May 1941; Charleston, SC, December 1941; Bendix, NJ, January 1942; Bridgeport, CT, c. July 7-December 1942; Kings Cliffe, England, January 1943; Horsham St Faith, England, c. April 6, 1943; Halesworth, England, c. July 9, 1943; Boxted, England, c. April 19, 1944-October 1945; Camp Kilmer, NJ, c. October 16-18, 1945. Selfridge Field, MI, May 1, 1946-February 6, 1952. O'Hare International Airport, IL, August 18, 1955.

Commanders. Unknown, January-June 1941; Lt. Col. Davis D. Graves, June 1941; Col. John C. Crosthwaite, c. July 1, 1942; Col. Hubert A. Zemke, September 1942; Col. Robert B. Landry, October 30, 1943; Col. Hubert A. Zemke, January 19, 1944; Col. David C. Schilling, August 12, 1944; Lt. Col.

Lucian A. Dade Jr., January 27, 1945; Lt.Col. Donald D. Renwick, August 1945-unknown. Col David C. Schilling, May 1946; Lt. Col. Thomas D. DeJarnette, August 1948; Lt. Col. Irwin H. Dregne, 1949; Lt. Col. Francis S. Gabreski, 1950; Col. Earnest J. White Jr., 1951-unknown. Unknown, 1955-.

Campaigns. American Theater; Air Offensive, Europe; Normandy; Northern France; Rhineland; Ardennes-Alsace; Central Europe.

Decorations. Distinguished Unit Citation: ETO, February 20-March 9, 1944; Holland, September 18, 1944.

Insigne. Shield: Tenne on a chevron azure fimbriated or two lightning flashes chevronwise of the last. Motto: Cave Tonitrum-Beware of the Thunderbolt. (Approved April 4, 1942).

355TH FIGHTER GROUP
submitted by Ray Shewfelt

Commanding officers: Col. William J. Cummings Jr., Lt. Col. Everett W. Stewart, Lt. Col. Claiborne H. Kinnard Jr. Based at Steeple Morden.

The 355th Fighter Group flew its first operational mission on September 14, 1943 under the guidance of Maj. Phillip Tukey of the 56th Fighter Group. For the first six months, the group was equipped with P-47s and became quite proficient at bomber escort duties. They also flew some dive bombing missions but with no great success. In March 1944, the 355th converted to P-51s and acquired the range to penetrate deeper into Germany where they were able to reach choice strafing targets.

On April 5, 1944, led by Col. "Wild Bill" Cummings, the 355th made strafing attacks against Oberpfaffenhofen A/D, Landsburg A/D and four other airdromes in the area SW of Munich. The attack was made through a swirling snowstorm and heavy flak. The results were 51 enemy aircraft destroyed and 81 damaged. Three pilots were lost. This mission resulted in the award of the Distinguished Unit Citation. On August 18, Captain Bert Marshall, while leading the 354th Squadron was hit by flak and forced to crash land. His element leader, Lt. Royce Preist, landed in an adjacent field, threw out his parachute and had Marshall climb in. With Marshall sitting on his lap, he brought the plane back to Steeple Morden. This was the first of two known successful rescues.

On September 17, 1944, the 355th Fighter Group with a four squadron strength, 64 aircraft, flew escort for the 3rd Bomb Division's B-17s on Operation Frantic VII. This was the last of four shuttle missions the 8th Air Force flew to Russia, Italy and return. Two pilots, including Lt. Roberts Peters, were lost in combat over Poland.

Upon return, the four squadron leaders were awarded the Polish Cross of Valor by the Polish government in exile in England. Subsequently, all pilots received the award. In 19 months of combat, 175 planes and pilots were missing in action. Of this, 90 pilots were killed in action, the majority in strafing operations.

361ST FIGHTER GROUP
YELLOW JACKETS
8TH AIR FORCE
World War II
Historical Summary
from a history by Steve Gotts, kindness of Arthur F. Trilli

The 361st Fighter Group was activated on Feb. 10, 1943, at Richmond Army Air Field in Virginia. It was comprised of personnel from the 327th Fighter Group and commanded by Maj. Thomas

Jonathan Jackson Christian Jr. By this time Maj. Christian, great-grandson of Gen. "Stonewall" Jackson, was already an experienced combat veteran from action against the Japanese in the Philippines and the Solomon Islands. Three months later the group moved to Langley Field, Virginia, and began training in Republic P-47 Thunderbolts.

In July 1943, the group moved to Camp Springs Army Air Field, Maryland, where most of its flying training and ground school was completed. Later, the group's three fighter squadrons, the 374th, 375th and 376th were detached to Milville Army Air Field, New Jersey, for gunnery training.

On September 28, 1943, 36 P-47s led by Lt. Col. Christian left Camp Springs on a cross-country training flight to Harding Field, Baton Rouge, Louisiana. They stopped at Charlotte, North Carolina; Atlanta, Georgia; and Meridian, Mississippi. Meanwhile, the group's ground echelon started moving men and equipment back to Richmond Army Air Field to begin final preparations for overseas movement. The flight returned from Baton Rouge on Oct. 6, 1943. By the end of that month, the P-47s were transferred back to the 327th Fighter Group as overseas preparations continued.

On November 10, 1943, an advanced echelon comprising Maj. Joseph J. Kruzel, Capt. Wallace E. Hopkins and Lt. J.L. Griffith flew to England to prepare for the group's move to the European Theater of Operations (ETO). All other personnel departed on the following day for the Camp Shanks, New York staging area. Twelve days later, they, too, headed for England aboard the liner *Queen Elizabeth*. After arriving in the Clyde early on November 29th, an overnight train journey brought the group to RAF Bottisham, six miles east of the famous university town of Cambridge. The base was in the process of being enlarged so enlisted personnel were dispersed in Bottisham village and the officer's quarters were established at Bottisham Hall, the Jenyns family home.

During December, supplies and new P-47s arrived almost daily and operational readiness assumed the highest priority. On January 3, 1944, RAF Bottisham was handed over officially to the group and redesignated Army Air Force Station F-374. This took place in a formal ceremony in which Lt. Col. Christian received the station from Wing Commander J.R.T. Bradford, OBE, Officer Commanding RAF Snailwell.

After a number of practice missions and with a total of 57 Thunderbolts on hand, the 361st was declared operational on January 15, 1944. The first mission was flown on January 21 with 52 aircraft (eight suffered mechanical problems) to an assigned patrol west of St. Omer in France. All returned safely.

Following the January 21st mission, 440 more were flown through April 20, 1945, including 80 with the 2nd Bombardment Division (later 2nd Air Division). The group was assigned to the 2nd Bomb Division from September 15, 1944, through the war's end with the air echelon assigned briefly to the 9th Air Force from December 24, 1944, through January, 1945, and, again, to the 8th Fighter Command from February 1 through April 9, 1945. The group also was transferred to Little Walden on September 26, 1944, and returned there on April 10 after more than three months on the continent.

Some Highlights From The Yellow Jacket History

PERFORMANCE: During the group's 441 missions, 15,209 sorties were flown for an average of 34.5 aircraft per mission. Pilot losses were 63 with 117 aircraft losses. Against this, there were 208.5 air victories, 11 probables and 62.5 damaged. On the ground, 111.9 enemy aircraft were destroyed,

one probable and 68.5 damaged. Decorations awarded were 1,623 including three Distinguished Service Crosses, one Air Force Cross, seven Silver Stars and 201 Distinguished Flying Crosses.

LOSSES: Heaviest one-day losses occurred on June 19, 1944 due to bad weather. Six P-51s went down costing the lives of five pilots. Slated for a bomber escort mission over France, the group found itself near Vire at 22,000 feet contending with a thick shifting overcast covering the entire area. In his efforts to climb over it, Group Leader Lt. Col. Joseph K. Kruzel nearly collided with a B-17. Realizing operating conditions were impossible, Kruzel ordered an immediate recall, but amid the confusion the losses were suffered, likely due to midair collisions.

GROUND CREWS: An important secret to the success of any flying unit is the skill of the ground crews which work long and hard to keep them flying. This was especially true during the group conversion from P-47s to P-51s in May 1944. Ground crews wasted no time becoming accustomed to the new aircraft and its Rolls-Royce Packard Merlin power plant. The relative ease of this conversion was enhanced by men like S/Sgt. Arthur F. Trilli who was awarded the Bronze Star for his performance. A portion of his citation reads as follows:

"...for exceptionally meritorious conduct in the performance of outstanding service during the period January 21 to May 1, 1944. S/Sgt. Trilli has zealously pursued his duties as airplane crew chief in such a manner as to keep his airplane operational for 81 continuous missions and for a total of 188 hours of operational flying. During this period, S/Sgt. Trilli;'s airplane has not returned early for either mechanical or other reasons."

It is interesting to note that during the two weeks prior to complete conversion to P-51s, the group flew 546 sorties for a 42 per-day average with only one loss. This speaks well for both ground and air crews.

LEADERSHIP: Success of any military organization is critically dependent upon quality leadership. The 361st was no different. Group Commanding Officer Col. Thomas J.J. Christian Jr. led his unit on dive bombing and strafing missions against rail transportation targets in France on August 12, 1944. He was seen to score hits on marshalling yards at Arras, but thereafter contact was lost. German records disclose that he died from injuries the day following his crash, but his final resting place remains a mystery. This was a severe blow

to the men of the 361st as reported by Group Historical Officer, Capt. O'Mara: "Words are but silent testimony to the efficiency and admirable qualities of leadership displayed by this officer. His loss is noted in reverent tribute by all who had the pleasure to know, or serve under him."

GOOD NEWS/BAD NEWS: September 27, 1944, was a bittersweet day. Bitter for the 445th bombers and sweet for the 361st fighters. Led by the 445th Bomb Group, 315 2nd Bomb Division B-24s gathered for an attack on the Henschel engine and vehicle assembly plants at Kassel in central Germany. The 65th Fighter Wing provided 218 fighter escorts including 45 P-51s of the 361st. A navigational error at the initial point and again at the target, isolated the 445th from the main force and subjected it to fierce Luftwaffe attacks from the infamous Sturmgruppen. As the Germans broke through the bomber formation, the 376th Squadron spotted them and intervened. By the time it was over, 25 to 37 445th aircraft had been shot down and five more had crash landed. But, thanks to the 361st, this Luftwaffe victory came at the cost of 18 of their aircraft destroyed and seven damaged. This 361st performance was exceeded only by its November 26, 1944, victory of 23 kills, two probables and nine damaged with one loss.

There are other fitting highlights one might quote in tribute to the "Yellow Jackets," but space limitations must prevail. Suffice it to say that the group returned to the U.S. on November 9, 1945,

Gen. Dwight D. Eisenhower awarding DSCs to Col. Donald J. M. Blakeslee and Maj. Donald Gentile, 4th FG, 1944. (Courtesy of Dick Martin)

Courtesy of Dick Martin.

Я американец

"**Ya Amerikánets**" (*Pronounced as spelt*)

Пожалуйста сообщите сведения обо мне в Американскую Военную Миссию в Москве

Please communicate my particulars to American Military Mission Moscow

via the *Queen Mary* and was deactivated at Camp Kilmer, New Jersey, the next day.

PERSONNEL: Succeeding Col. Christian as group commanding officer were the following: Col. Ronald F. Fallows, Lt. Col. Roy B. Caviness, Lt. Col. Joseph J. Kruzel, Col. Junius W. Dennison Jr., Col. John D. Landers.

Support units on the base and their commanders were as follows:

468th Service Sqdn.
    Lt. Matthew W. Marvin
2118th Fire Fighting Platton
    Lt. Charles Gerstein
66th Station Complement Squadron
    Lt. Robert C. Tyler
1598th Ordnance Company
    Lt. James C. Beal
1184th Military Police Company
    Lt. Lawrence M. Ferguson
1073rd Quartermaster Company
    Lt. Edville G. Lemoine

1097th Signal Co.
    Capt. Richard W. Steinnmetz
Det. "A" HQ 50th Service Group
    Capt. Enos C. Throop

479TH FIGHTER GROUP
Riddle's Raiders

submitted by Ray Shewfelt

Commanding Officers: 1/Col Kyle L. Riddle and Col. Hubert A. Zemke.

The 479th moved into its base at Wattisham near Ipswich on May 15, 1944. This was an old prewar permanent RAF facility with brick buildings and a good 4800 foot concrete main runway. The group was operational in just 11 days and flew its first mission with 34 P-38s on a sweep over Holland and Belgium. By D-day, they were doing normal escort, dive bombing and strafing operations. On July 29, 1944, Capt. Arthur Jeffrey encountered and possibly shot down the first Me-163 rocket fighter. While strafing NE of Paris on August 10, the group CO, Lt. Col. Riddle was hit and crash-landed. Two days later, Col. Hubert Zemke, CO of the 56th Fighter Group, assumed command of the 479th Group. On August 18, Col. Zemke led the 434th and 435th Squadrons on a strafing attack on Nancy/Essey A/D resulting in 43 enemy aircraft destroyed and 25 damaged. The group converted to P-51 "Spamcans" and the 435th Squadron flew its first mission on September 13. On September 26 with Col. Zemke leading a mixed P-38 and P-51 formation on an MEW controlled sweep, the 479th engaged in what was possibly the greatest aerial battle to date and claimed 29 enemy aircraft destroyed and eight damaged.

On what was to be his last mission before being grounded and assuming a desk job at 65th Wing Headquarters, Col. Zemke was lost when he went into a spin in turbulent weather. A wing came off the plane and he baled out. The 8th Air Force's greatest air tactician became a Prisoner of War. In the last two weeks of operations of the war, the 479th Group destroyed over 150 German aircraft on strafing operations.

On April 25, 1945, Lt. Hilton O. Thompson shot down an AR-234 to score the last victory of the war.

2ND SCOUTING FORCE

submitted by Ray L. Shewfelt

Commanding officers: Lt. Col. John A. Brooks III and Lt. Col. Frank B. Elliott. Based at Steeple Morden.

The 2nd Scouting Force was a Provisional Squadron assigned to the 355th Fighter Squadron for logistical and maintenance support but under direct operational control of the 2nd Bomb Division/Air Division.

It was a unique P-51 fighter equipped squadron, commanded by a B-24 bomber pilot. The air executive officer was also a B-24 pilot staff officer and there were eight additional B-24 lead crew pilots who had completed their operational tour. The balance of the flying personnel consisted of 12 fighter pilots drawn from all five groups of the 65th Fighter Wing. An Intelligence officer and two experienced bomber navigators completed the squadron.

The primary mission was penetration, target and withdrawal weather reporting approximately 30 minutes preceding the bomber force in direct communication with the bomber commander. An additional task was free-lance escort of stragglers. The Scouting Force flew 136 missions. Two pilots were missing in action.

The Scouts flew in weather that kept fighter forces on the ground. Its success in bad weather is due to the instrument flying ability of the bomber pilots and the ability of the fighter pilots to fly tight formation. On November 26, 1944, a formation of four led by Capt. Robert V. Whitlow, 458th Bomb Group with 1st Lt. William Whalen and 1st Lt. George Ceglarski of the 4th Fighter Group intercepted an attacking flight of FW-190s and accounted for five victories. The pilots were awarded the Silver Star. On February 9, 1945, the CO, Lt. Col. John A. Brooks III, and his wingman, Lt. Whalen, in a two-man action, attacked 60 enemy aircraft, accounted for two victories each and broke up the entire German formation. Col. Brooks' strategy was to go through the entire formation and get the leader first. For this action, he was awarded the Distinguished Service Cross. The Scouting Force had a total of 14 victories, but they were cited most for their invaluable weather reporting which enabled the bomber forces to maneuver well in advance of the weather and to know in advance if the targets were covered or clear.

5TH EMERGENCY RESCUE SQUADRON

submitted by Ray L. Shewfelt

The 5th ERS was originally based with the 56th Fighter Group at Boxted. It was a provisional squadron manned by support personnel and pilots on detached service from 16 different VIII Fighter Command stations. The unit was equipped with 25 war weary P-47s carrying a dinghy pack under each wing and smoke marker. It was armed with only four of the normal eight .50 machine guns. The squadron colors were red, white and blue bands painted around the cowling and the squadron identifier letters on the side of the fuselage were 5F. When 8th Air Force missions were airborne, these planes patrolled the North Sea to act as spotters for any aircraft that were unable to reach England and forced to ditch. They worked in conjunction with RAF rescue facilities.

In January 1945, the 5th ERS moved to Halesworth where they received six OA-10 Catalinas. They then had the capability of making actual rescue pickups at sea. In March, several B-17s carrying lifeboats were assigned.

"Candy is always handy ..."

SPECIAL STORIES

North American P-51D "Mustang" by Jean-Luc Beghin.

44TH BOMB GROUP
First Combat Mission
by George R. Insley

It was mid-August 1943 when we first arrived at the 44th Bomb Group in Shipdham, England. We were sent to combat training for a couple of weeks and when we returned we found most of the group had gone to the African area to do some missions with the 9th Air Force. It was during their absence that we were sent on our first mission. Six new crews joined forces with another group for our "baptism of fire." The target in Poland was a German battleship or its supply link. My position was low left and last in "Purple Heart Corner." It was a long mission. I recorded 9:50 hours of flight time.

The course took us over the North Sea, crossing Denmark, and flying over the sea to Poland. In Denmark the anti-aircraft gunners were waiting for us. They were putting up a wall for us to fly through. Everything was new to us, the unknown and scary. As soon as I saw the flak, my feet were dancing on the rudder pedals and I was all over the sky (who me scared?) and yet trying to stay in formation. The way I was flying the fighters couldn't have hit me if they tried to, and they were going to try. Well, we flew through those black clouds and on to Poland. We climbed up to our assigned altitude and began our bomb run. The flak was larger caliber, bigger explosions, blacker smoke. It was right at our altitude. They were putting it right in front of me. The shell exploded and we instantly hit the smoke and what a noise the explosions made. It was many missions after this one before I heard flak again, though we had it on every mission. Those gunners on the battleship were really top notch.

We experienced our first flak, and first sound of flak explosions. Our first attack was a running battle with twin engine fighters which zeroed in on our element. The fighters that came up were black, so we presumed that they were night fighters. Fortunately, they were not overly aggressive. Here we were two groups, one B-17 and one B-24, flying parallel. When the fighters showed up, the B-24 leader slid our formation in under the B-17s for more protection, as well as more defense against the fighters. Where did they attack? You guessed it, in my corner, low left and last. So you can see why they called it Purple Heart Corner. My tail gunner, George Federlin, shot up all of his ammo and the waist gunner took more ammo to him. The fighters shot up all of their ammo, landed, refueled, reloaded and came up again to have another go at us. I didn't see any fighters go down, nor did we lose any, though I saw one engine with a little smoke from something damaged.

About 50 miles west of Denmark, the fighters broke off attacking, going back to their base. Suddenly I felt the ship yaw, and I saw the fuel pressure of #4 drop to zero, so I feathered #4 and called over the intercom about the engine emergency. Just then #3 pressure dropped and I feathered that one, then #1&2 dropped off—sure was quiet, but everyone was too busy scrambling as I rang the emergency bell in preparation for ditching the plane in the North Sea. The engineer dropped out of the top turret and into the bomb bay to find the radio operator there pointing at the fuel shut off valves. The engineer turned the valves on and we had power again. We were going down at 2,000' a minute and it looked like it was going to be a cold swim. What happened? The engineer had been transferring fuel when the fighters attacked. After they left us, the engineer asked the radio operator to shut off the transfer pumps, which were behind the bomb bay, instead he mistakenly closed the fuel shut off valves, which were in the front of the bomb bay. Thankfully we didn't have to try our life rafts. We had lost several

thousand feet of altitude as well as distance so we never did catch up with the formation before it got back to England. That was the first mission of the 48 that we flew in the 20 months we were in England. Glad that they weren't all like this first one.

Combat Mission #25 November 10, 1944
courtesy of E. Jay Spencer

The target was in Hanau, Germany, near Frankfurt, probably an industrial plant. Lt. Spencer flew in the #4 position (the center of the formation and logical aiming point for enemy ack-ack gunners). The flak was intense and accurate that day, resulting in 20 holes in the plane (N-bar). During the bombing run, Lt. Spencer's waist gunner, George Schofield, was hit in the lower jaw and began bleeding profusely. It was the nose turret gunner, Tom Stewart, who went from the front of the plane, all the way to the back to administer first aid to Schofield. Lt. Spencer received permission to leave the squadron and got fighter escort on the way back to England. By flying in a gradual descent, he was able to increase his speed enough to keep up with the fighters and return to base approximately one hour ahead of his squadron. Yellow flares were fired in the landing pattern, to signal injured aboard. Ambulances and medical personnel met the plane at the hard stand. The entire crew visited Schofield in the hospital the next day. (Lt. Spencer later learned that Schofield required multiple operations over the next several years to reconstruct his face.) The crew was given the next 10 days off before the next combat mission, as was the custom when a crew member was badly injured. Schofield was replaced on the crew by Abercrombie, an armament gunner.

To Feather Or Not To Feather
by James L. Whittle Jr. (44th)

I was the co-pilot of a crew that was assigned to the 506th Bomb Squadron in early November 1944. About halfway through our tour I was checked out as an aircraft commander (1st pilot) and flew the remaining missions with either my own crew or my original crew. We flew either 25 or 28 missions (depending on which crew we were talking about) with that squadron through the end of the war in Europe. After our last combat mission and before the 44th returned to the U.S., we were required to make several training flights to fulfill the ATC requirements for an over water flight.

On one such flight, on which I went along as the copilot with my original crew, we spent four or five hours accomplishing some of those requirements, and were returning to Shipdham from a flight to south England when it was decided that practicing some emergency procedures would fulfill part of those requirements. One of the drills was to practice feathering procedure to test the pilot's reaction to engine failure and the subsequent change in flying characteristics, etc. We were probably at 4,000 or 5,000 feet, with lots of airspeed since we were descending to our base at Shipdham, so that the loss of one engine would create no danger at all. One outboard engine was feathered with nothing more than a slight drop in airspeed. As soon as that simulated emergency was under control, the opposite outboard engine was feathered.

That simulated emergency too was handled with no difficulty because of the experience of the pilot and the higher than normal airspeed due to our descent. From that point on, things get a little vague, but I believe that a pretense was made of feathering one of the two remaining engines and in fact, I think that the feathering button was momentarily de-

pressed but without any intent of actually feathering it.

Everything happened very quickly and unexpectedly. When the feathering button was pulled out, it should have either stopped the feathering and returned it to normal, or if it had actually feathered, it should have immediately unfeathered. Neither of those things happened, which caused us to reach for an outboard button to unfeather them. Neither of those worked either (Murphy's Law). After a few futile attempts to unfeather them, our attention turned to finding the nearest airfield.

From the co-pilot's seat, I remembered seeing an airfield off our right wing. I took over the controls since I was in the best position to see the field. We were rapidly losing both airspeed and altitude, and in a matter of minutes we would be on the ground—airfield or not. The events happened so fast that there was no time to alert the three airmen in the rear of the aircraft, nor did we even have time to broadcast a "MAYDAY."

Fortunately our flight engineer, radio operator and one gunner who were in the back, realized there was an emergency when they saw the feathered props and took up the appropriate positions for a crash landing. We now had emergency military power on the one remaining engine (#3), and though I'm certain we exceeded the max boost limit, it was a constant fight to keep from stalling.

I had managed to get lined up with the runway, and since the field had been off the right wing, it meant making two turns into the one good engine. Although we were lined up with the runway, it was a question whether we would make it before our altitude and airspeed ran out.

One of the last things I remember was wondering whether we would be able to top the big trees which loomed before us and the overrun. The airspeed was just slightly above stalling speed and my last thought was that if I hauled back on the yoke at the very last moment in hopes of zooming over the tree tops, would I be able to get the nose back down quickly enough to keep from stalling. None of us remembered what happened in those last few moments, but we obviously had not gotten over the trees because my very next recollection was that we were on the ground.

Through a haze I can remember seeing our navigator walking (or trying to walk) and complaining about his back. He had been standing between the pilot's seats and things happened so fast that he was still in that position when we impacted and was propelled through the bullet proof glass that surrounded the cockpit.

My next hazy recollection was opening my eyes in a hospital bed and feeling as though every bone in my body was broken. Fortunately the only broken things were a rib and a tooth. With considerable effort, I turned my head enough to see that the patient next to me was our navigator, who had broken his back and was encased in plaster of paris from his neck to his hips, and would remain in that cast through his ocean voyage back to the States. The first pilot sustained the most severe injuries, which included the shattering of most of the bones in his face, and head injuries which were life threatening at that time. Injuries to the three airmen in the rear of the plane were limited to cuts and bruises and did not require hospitalization.

It seems hardly possible that any of us survived, especially since the trees had sheered off our outer wings between #1 and #2 engines on the one side and between #3 and #4 on the other. This "short wing" modification has a tendency to be very unstable. Since the B-24 had a "wet wing," the ruptured fuel cells allowed 115/145 fuel to drop precariously onto the whitehot #3 supercharger impellor from the moment of impact with the trees until the arrival of the crash crew, which had no warning of our impending crash. To further complicate matters, the crashed cockpit delayed the extrication of the first pilot and myself from the aircraft.

To this day, no one has been able to explain why none of the props would unfeather, although probably somewhere there is an accident report on file which makes an attempt at it. More important, though, at this time, is that none of us has ever been able to determine just which field we crashed on. All we know is that it was near, but not at Shipdham. Neither our medical records, nor the official Air Force photos of the crash, gives any clue to the name of that field. The accident occurred on the afternoon of May 11, 1945, and the plane was a new "M" model which we had been scheduled to return to the States. The tail marking was C and the aircraft number was 450698 with the letters "GJ" on the side of the fuselage. *(Shortly after the story was published in the 2nd Air Division Journal, I received*

two letters from England from two different people who presented documents to prove that the location of the crash site was Watton Air Base, just a few miles south of our home base at Shipdham.)

Although Don Edkins (1st pilot), Ed Smith (navigator) and I, all recovered from our injuries to the extent that we were able to carry on normal lives, we all suffered various degrees of physical incapacity.

93RD BOMB GROUP
Sixteen And Counting
by James (Jim) Rutherford, L/Col. USAF, RET

The first 15 missions aboard the B-24 "U.S. Express" were rather routine. We had accumulated about 261 flak fragment holes in the aircraft, had no fighter activity, and had lost only seven of our planes. This is not to be construed that we weren't

scared to death on a few occasions, but like most other crew members, we hid our fears as best as we could.

Number 16 was to be different. I was to fly my first mission as a lead pilot, in a different airplane and with new faces in all aircraft positions. The night before the mission was a cold, dreary one, with rain pouring down, a hint of winter exerting itself with patches of fog and human breath hanging in the air for prolonged periods. Sleep did not come easy. In fact, when the CQ made his entrance into our Nissen hut, the majority of us were still turning in the hammock shaped cots. "Is it 3:30 already?" I asked. "Yes sir. Time to rise and shine, if you will pardon the expression," he answered.

The usual ritual followed. Put on a robe, grab the toilet kit, put on some boots, a trench coat and trudge through the wetness 100 yards to the latrine for a quick shave, shower and tooth massage. I noted as I pulled the comb through my hair that globs of hair remained in the comb. Oh, Gad! Losing my hair already.

Back to the hut, dress and over to the mess hall for some delicious dehydrated (powdered) eggs, almost cooked bacon and burned toast. This morning there were no complaints. We ate quietly, and quickly. Later, I couldn't remember if I had eaten or not.

The taxi trucks were waiting outside and we clambered aboard. We yawned in silence as each truck meandered its way from the Upper WAF's site to the briefing area. The rain still came down, occasionally in torrents.

At our lockers we began adding clothing, gear and Mae Wests. Had we all lost our voices? Not so. Once inside the smoke-filled briefing room, noting our mission slot depicted on the aluminum airplanes on the wall, we found our seats and a low rumble of voices began to mesh into a crescendo of unintelligible sounds until "Attention" was called. Once again it was church quiet.

B-24D, 23819 "Rugged Buggy" flown by Jim O'Brien, 44th Bomb Group, after 21 missions. shot down May 14, 1943 over Kiel, Germany. (Courtesy of James O'Brien)

B-24H, 2nd Bomb Division, 14th Combat Wing, 44th Bomb Group, 67th Squadron, AAF Station 115, Shipdham, England. Crewman servicing plane unknown. Front row, L to R: Intelligence Officer (Interrogating) unknown; Robert P. Knowles, Pilot; John E. Butler, Navigator; Francis T. Ryan, Engineer; Michael A. Powers, Radio Operator; Henry E. Lavallee, Armorer, Gunner; John A. Fenn, Bombardier; Howard H. Robb, Copilot. Back row: William S. Guess, Tail Gunner; Russell B. Lindsey, Nose Gunner. Picture taken after returning from D-Day bombing mission, June 6, 1944. (Courtesy of Howard H. Robb)

93rd Bomb Group crewman gets a haircut in Africa. (Courtesy of H.W. Feichter)

44th Bomb Group control tower, Shipdham, England, 1944. (Courtesy of Albert (Ed) Jones)

Anticipation and anxiety began to rise as the colonel and his staff walked down the aisles, heels hitting hard into the floor as they came. As his left foot hit the briefing stage, the colonel voiced, "At ease." We sat and waited.

After a few words of praise and other baloney, the main speaker, our operations officer, walked over to the map, neatly covered as usual with a pull-down roll of window shade. He raised the shade and the murmur once again brought the room out of the doldrums. There were more red areas on that map than on the inside of a Texas watermelon.

Osnabruck

We had heard of it before, although I had never been there. Wasn't that supposed to be a nice ski area, or a quiet hideaway to spend the winter weekend? Maybe so, but not today.

We could expect fighter activity from the coastline to the I.P., after the target and back to the coastline. Flak was "programmed" to be heavy to intense with both barrage and tracking a strong possibility. Weather would clear before the I.P., altitude to be 23,500 for the lead squadron and fighter escort to be P-51s and P-47s from the coast to the target. None upon withdrawal, as they would be downstairs on the lookout for their old friends—Jerry.

Off we headed to the locker room again to pick up the most important pieces of equipment—the flak jackets and hard helmets. They weighed a ton until the flak began popping, and then they were hardly noticeable and almost felt inadequate.

Our bombardier today, Capt. Briggs, was an old hat at war, having completed 28 missions to date. He only spread the flak jacket (and one extra one) on the floor beneath him. He held the one part of the apron over his "treasure chest" as he termed it, just for precautions.

Captain Mathison, Lt. Whitman and their command pilot reminded the others that "when the flak starts, just remember that they are shooting at us." "Yeah," someone said. "But, they are hitting us."

Into the jeeps and convoyed to the proper plane at the dispersal areas. The crew chief and his men were always cheerful and helpful. We generally provided them with our left over K rations or candy bars on our return and they always looked forward to the treat.

Today, we visually checked the plane over as if it were a new and strange craft to us. I believe that I looked at every rivet and flange twice. We boarded, checked all equipment and sat, waiting for the minute hand to reach 0610 hours. On cue we started our engines. Each one caught timely and sounded superb.

Then, the long, slow taxi gauntlet began. We were second today, as deputy lead of the group. I had never been this close to the #1 ship before. It was a strange, awe-inspiring feeling. Past the Control Tower, where the commander and his staff, plus a few uninvited guests stood, to the north end of runway 18/36. No one off the edge of the taxiway so far.

Engines began to hum as we checked magnetos, power, instruments, radio equipment and uttered another prayer.

The *Ball O'Fire*, a stripped down B-24 with huge orange strips painted vertically around the fuselage, had taken off an hour earlier, and while making the usual elliptical pattern at altitude, reported cloud base at 200 feet with tops at 20,000 feet. Excellent for forming, I thought.

It's another thrill in the Davis wing plane to get to the first 1,000 feet. I had seen several B-24s settle back to the ground after takeoff, into a ball of fire. The artificial horizon, with its slow erection system, was the culprit, they said. Thank God, I had had a number one instrument instructor back at Liberal, Kansas, who taught (brain-washed) us to use the artificial horizon only as a cross check and to rely on more than any one instrument. Many lives were saved following those simple words of wisdom.

Captain Mathison, on cue of a green flare shot from the tower, applied power and began his roll. We quickly filled his vacant spot at the extreme end of the runway, to wait for our turn. I could see the flames from under as he turned the supercharger on about halfway down the runway. He was airborne none too soon, it seemed. We were heavy today. Rain fell by the buckets full. Visibility was good and we could see about a half mile.

Green flare and we rolled. Full power, everything O.K., speed picked up, #8 position on the supercharger and we were moving like a freight train going downhill. Airborne and no tree limbs in the landing gear as we crossed the boundary of the airfield. Gear came up quickly (if it ever did that), flaps up and into the soup. Straight ahead for one minute, left turn to 045 degrees and on the way to Buncher Eight, near the coast. Out over the North Seas, heading 090 degrees to 15,000 feet, turn left to 270 degrees and continue climbing to 22,000 feet. As we broke through the last layer of clouds, we could see the *Ball O'Fire* dead ahead in his pattern, firing an occasional yellow-yellow flare, used today for identification.

We cut off his turn and joined on the right wing seconds after the lead ship arrived. *Ball O'Fire* dropped back, continued the pattern and firing flares until the first squadron was formed—loosely. Each turn found us flying through our own contrails, so we inched up another 500 feet. At last came the time to depart and we headed out over the North Sea.

Hundreds of other B-24s were still forming into squadrons and into groups, all over England. It may not be a good mission for us, but it certainly was not a good day for Germany, with all those planes in the skies.

We meshed into the stream of bombers, closed up our formations and off we sailed, the low elements barely above the snow white clouds. We were the fifth group in the stream, and I could see the others, ahead, barging on in what appeared to be tight formations.

Out over the water now, the order came by "waggle of wings" to loosen up the formation and to test the airborne weapons. A verbal warning to all gunners to insure that no weapon was to be pointed in the direction of any aircraft, and to commence testing.

The airplane shuddered from the recoil of the 50 calibers, as each gunner aimed purposely into space. Smoke and the smell of gun powder filled the airplane interior. It is an odor that one will never forget, much like remembering the odor of spilled hydraulic fluid, only better on one's nerves.

Close in the formation, we were nearing the enemy coast. A gunner on another flight on another day chanced to remark, "If that guy's wing was any closer to me, I could change that little red light in the wing tip." Tight formations were mandatory to provide more concentrated fire power against enemy fighters. It also gave you the false impression of being "next to your mother's protective bosom"—and thus much safer.

"This is Big Bear Leader. Watch for bandits and maintain radio silence for now. Over and Out." Although there had been a minimum of radio transmissions, it seemed deathly quiet for the next few minutes. Were the F-90s, ME-210s, etc. coming up to meet us? All eyes scanned the horizon, back and forth, up and down. Nothing. Maybe we would be lucky today. Only Little Friends—everywhere. Lovely.

Suddenly, in the far distance at 12 o'clock, we saw the first bursts of flak. As more bursts showed up, it appeared to be tracking the first group, but much lower. I guessed that the idle gunners were no longer idle, but were dispensing chaff by the ton. We bored on as time seemed to stand still. The navigator reported that we were on course, on time, and would be coming up for a turn to the initial point (IP) soon. Still, no fighters. "Relax," I told myself. "It's no different from some of the other times."

Group after group turned toward the I.P. and now we were turning. Fly close, relax, and pray (not necessarily in that order). The AFCE was blinking and ready to be engaged, if necessary. All engines running smoothly, oil pressure, oxygen, everything fine.

"Over initial point and bombardier working." The navigator had given way to allow the bombardier more working room and to take control, if need be.

The flak was heavier now and black clouds were forming up ahead. Then, a red ball of fire and two planes were heading down in flames. We hoped that chutes would begin opening soon. I knew that about 60 miles farther we would be over the target area and in the midst of the flak concentration. Enemy fighters should not appear now.

WHAM! Black smoke appeared from nowhere. Bursts of AA shells exploded dead ahead. Looked like a polka dot of black and white. Barrage firing. A wall nearly 500 feet across and 1,000 feet vertical. Now it was getting solid. The next second it was red, red fire intermixed in the black. That meant close. The fuselage was peppered. The wings were taking hits. I hung in close to the lead plane, trying to keep my eyes in one direction only.

The next second, a shell exploded in the #3 engine of the lead plane, my left window crashed, and I felt a blow in the center of my chest just below the collar bone line. That #3 engine appeared to have been sliced off with a huge knife. It fell below the plane, waiting for someone to hit it. The lead was in a sudden 45 degree bank toward us. I yanked the control column back as I applied more power and the co-pilot increased mixture and RPM. We were at the edge of the stalling point. I relaxed the yoke and dropped the left wing slightly. I called the tail gunner. "Are we clear of all planes yet?" "Yes sir, Skipper. We're clear." I leveled out and asked him, "Where are the other planes?" "All over the sky," he said.

AFCE turned on, I called "This is Big Bear Deputy. We've started a left 360 degree turn. Get back in as fast as you can." I continued the slow turn and the Germans probably couldn't figure out what we were doing. Bursts were all over the sky and fortunately hitting where we had been.

After the full 360, all planes were tucked in. We fell behind the group which had been in back of us and bombardier called "Center the PDI."

The run was short, but long enough to be buffeted, and hit many times by the Ack Ack. My left arm was now deadened. I didn't feel any pain, but wondered if I had been hit. I took off my right glove, put my hand under my flight suit and felt around. No warm blood. I pulled my hand out. No blood. Then I realized that I had been flying so long that my left arm was simply asleep. What a relief. Now, get those bombs on target, put up with the winds rushing in the window and get back home.

Two chutes were spotted below us. Another and then another. White chutes, black flak, red hot centers. Fuselage taking a beating. Sounded like metal chairs being thrown against a tin wall.

"Bombs away." What music. I turned left, dropped the nose and as we swung around, I got a glimpse of the formations yet to come. Those Krauts will run out of ammo today, I thought. There must be over 2,000 airplanes behind us.

Back out over the water, oxygen masks unhitched, cigarettes lighted, we all began to feel more at ease and out came some K rations. I wasn't hungry, just thirsty and thankful.

Over the English coast we were able to skim in under the clouds at 3,000 feet. Past the Buncher and straight to Hardwick.

The "Old Man" wanted a tight formation when we came home, so we really tightened it up. We dropped to 1,000 feet, passed over the field and broke into squadrons for landing.

Taxiing around perimeter to runway to take off for a mission at Shipdham. These are the first planes to be used by the 44th Bomb Group at Shipdham. (Courtesy of Howard D. Landers and C.W. Lundy)

Screech. That B-24 was the easiest plane to land I had flown to date. We cleared the runway and while taxiing in, took a look at the others in the pattern. Red-red flares were popping everywhere, three B-24s on three engines each. Ambulances and fire trucks raced into position. The final airplane landed. We had lost a total of three planes and 30 good men!

The crew chief smiled his usual smile. He counted some of the holes in the plane and said, "I'll have those holes and that window replaced and ready to go for tomorrow's mission."

"Tomorrow," I said. Yes, I guess there will be a tomorrow. And hopefully, many more after that.

Captain Mathison's crew and the other two crews all landed in a safe combat zone, were treated and came back to Hardwick safely, I am told. They got back after I had left, I suppose.

The crew members began a search for the piece of shrapnel that had come through my window and hit my chest protector 1/2 inch below the top of it. The crew chief found the piece of metal on the floor in back of the co-pilot's seat. It was 1 1/2 inches long, 1/4 inch wide and lightly curved. Inside, where the thread marks are, were three initials—USA.

I'm so grateful they didn't read JER.

Osnabruck

by Glenn A. Tessmer (93rd)

I flew the B-24 as first pilot and as co-pilot. In this mission to Osnabruck, I was slated to be lead copilot with 1st Lt. Whitman in command. About 8-10 hours before T.O., Capt. Mathison advised me he would take my place. This was just fine with me as I was not very happy in the lead position or, in fact, in the B-24. The crew disposition then resolved to Lt. Whitman, left seat and Capt. Mathison as command pilot, right seat. As Lt. Col. Rutherford's story unfolds (he was flying deputy lead position) the lead aircraft (Whitman) sustained a direct hit on #3 engine, detaching it completely from the aircraft. This was in the vicinity of the I.P. Lt. Rutherford (at that time) narrowly averted a midair collision with the disabled aircraft. He then skillfully took over the lead position, got the group back together and bombed the target successfully.

I'm sorry to report that all of Whitman's crew, with the exception of the R.O. and a waist gunner, went down and were KIA in the resulting crash. I was able, many years ago, to get the German and USAF MACR (which was on file in Suitland, Maryland DCA area at the time) to verify this.

After this rather close encounter, and after a three day pass, I continued on as copilot with Lt. Rosacher and his crew. This got me out of the lead position and seemed a little safer (was there such a thing?). Anyway, P-51s were in the offing, and that after finishing a bomber tour, sounded just great. Alas, it was not to be. Mission 24 came to a climactic affair. Just inside the I.P. (target Dortmund) an engine prop went to full flat pitch (ran away) and would not feather. We dropped the bombs roughly in the target area and then started a long trek out of Germany alone, all the while slowly losing altitude and trying to avoid known flack areas. Along the way, #2 engine followed the same pattern as #1! The situation now rapidly deteriorated. Engines #1 and #2 assumed full flat pitch, wouldn't feather and were putting a tremendous drag and yaw on the aircraft. Engines #1 and #2 were critical engines and failure of these two necessitated both feet on the right rudder, plus rudder trim, and lots of push! (Never could understand why the aircraft did not incorporate a mechanical servo rudder trim boost tab.) We followed the coast line southwestward, staying perhaps five miles outside the shore line, not daring a channel crossing now, and even thinking we might get out of the occupied area before we were too low to bail out. I alerted the crew to this possibility, telling

them to make sure their parachutes were on and secure. Then, just to keep things interesting, #1 engine caught fire and a few minutes later #4 followed the pattern of #1 and #2. We now concluded we were having a bad day. Schowen Island and 2,000 feet came about the same time no choice but to bail out over the island. To my surprise, the island was still held by the Germans. No doubt about this as we were shot at all the way down in the parachutes. And I thought I was going to enjoy this parachute jump!

More surprises followed. The abandoned aircraft, with no one now holding the rudders, continued a diving left turn, picked up speed and started to climb right back at me. That's quite a sight. All four propellers churning the air and looking you right in the face. I just hoped it would descend faster than me. Perhaps a thousand feet separated us when it stalled out, dove below me and crashed, bursting into flames. My first thought, my hat is in there.

We were quickly surrounded by German soldiers (this area was part of the North Sea defense wall), who informed me the Canadians were less than five miles away (on the mainland), "The Fortunes of War."

After the war, I found that this run away propeller problem was not an uncommon one. Experienced crews seemed to get into this configuration by not having to juggle the throttles as much to stay in formation and therefore the oil in the prop domes did not circulate through the oil system and that in turn allowed the oil to congeal (in the domes) and therefore no prop. control.

A hair raising high speed boat run at night, all blacked out, was the start of a long journey by train and butane powered trucks into the depths of the Third Reich, eventually ending at Stalag XIII at Nurnburg. En route, a very well dressed civilian asked me, in perfect English, after he checked with a guard (I speak a little German, so I knew what was coming) one question, "Was I a Christian?" I have occasionally pondered that one over the years and hope he has too.

The other memorable quote was from the aircraft crew chief just before we boarded on this last mission, "I wish this airplane was in hell and I had a receipt for it."

All crew members survived this ordeal.

The Dilemma Of The Trailing Wire Antenna

by Michael J. Donahue (93rd)

The trailing wire antenna was one type of radio antenna found on a B-24 Liberator bomber. It

was used for long range radio transmission on medium or low frequencies. It was 150 feet of fine flexible copper wire wound around a spool type reel and weighted at the trailing end by a 10 pound lead weight. When not in use the weighted end fit flush against the fuselage on the undercarriage of the bomber. When long range transmission was necessary, the reel type mechanism, located in the radio compartment, was cranked out so that the weighted wire trailed below and behind the plane. In the training manual it reads, "Know your length of the antenna with which you are operating. Full transmission may save the life of your crew."

Now let me take you back in time to where this story begins. It's Sept. 30, 1944. The war in Europe is going well against the Nazis. On this day our plane, a B-24 heavy bomber called, *Ma's Worry,* will lead the 2nd Air Division of the 8th Air Force to a target in Hamm, Germany.

Major Brown and Capt. Spencer of the 409th Squadron, 93rd Bomb Group will be the lead pilots. This bombing mission will be our 17th.

My duties as a radio-operator gunner during this eight hour mission were to send and receive coded messages to division headquarters in England. Take off and assembly from our base at Hardwick went well. With the group together, we crossed the English Channel at 0800 hours. Flying over enemy territory at 25,000 feet we picked up heavy flak on the bomb run and over the target. After the bombs were dropped on the target, it was time for me to send a strike report back to our base in England. For this long range transmission, I cranked out the trailing wire antenna to its full length. With the bombs gone and the plane much lighter, our air speed must have increased. The training manual warned us not to reel out the antenna if the air speed exceeds 240 mph. This could have been the cause of the problem that now plagued me.

With the transmission completed I proceeded to reel the wire into my radio compartment. About one quarter of the way in, the wire became a tangled, twisted mess on the spool of the reel. There was no way I could reel the wire in any further. Over 100 feet of twisted line trailed helplessly behind the bomber. I tried feverishly to untangle the twisted mess. Working with heavy gloves on made it very difficult. I wouldn't dare remove them because of the sub-zero cold my fingers would stick fast to the metal wire.

Over the loud noise of the plane's engines, I could hear the bursts of flak and the thump of the 50 caliber machine guns fired by our gunners as the German fighter planes flew through our formation. World War II was going on around me as I worked to free this bloody wire. I imagined I could see the

Dec. 24, 1944, en route to I.P. Ahrweiler, Germany. Note radar dome on lead aircraft. (Courtesy of Glenn Tessmer)

damn weighted wire swinging and swaying below our bomber and finally crashing into the flight deck of the plane below us. That could really hurt somebody and needless to say it would cause great concern to the pilot and crew of the other bomber.

I could also visualize the wire getting caught and winding around the turning props of the bomber below us, thus causing the right side of our plane's fuselage to be ripped apart. This could result in the loss of our plane as well as the whole crew. If the crew ever found this out they would kill me.

The radio operator's manual states, "WARNING: The trailing wire antenna must be reeled in before landing." If we land with that turkey trailing behind us, there's a good possibility that it might bounce off of the runway and come crashing through the waist window inflicting serious injuries upon our tail gunner. Walter Borland would never forgive me if I let a thing like that happen.

I reached a decision. I must cut the wire and released the antenna from the plane. Consider first what might happen when you drop that heavy weight on the innocent people below. Don't be an idiot; for God's sake, you're worried about dropping a 10 lb. weight when your bomber just released three tons of bombs. Besides this is war, that's not cream puffs they're shooting at you. What about the bomber flying on your wing, taking a direct hit and going down in flames? Don't forget about your last pass in London. Remember how those buzz bombs and V-2s kept you awake all night. Cut the damm thing and get back to your duties.

The pilot called me on the intercom. In a loud voice he says, "What the hell are you doing, have you sent in that strike report?" Now I am really nervous, hope he doesn't find out what's going on. He has enough trouble trying to feather a prop of a dead, shot-up engine.

My God, that burst of flak was close. I have got to take this flak suit off. It's 60° below zero, but I am sweating like a bull. It's a good thing I am on oxygen, my breathing is rapid. Better turn up the valve a little.

Wham! Flak hits the dome of the top turret gun, Plexiglass comes falling down around me. I look up into the turret where "Neadue,"the engineer is sitting. I fear the worst, but he is OK. The shrapnel passed through the dome and hit Ned in the flak helmet.

Once again I looked at the tangled mess of wire and realized the situation had not got any better. Kelly the navigator called me on the intercom and wanted a position report. Now I have got to cut the wire and switch to the fixed wire antenna. With a firm grasp

on the wire with the pliers I applied the right amount of pressure and cut the wire. In a flash the end of the wire disappeared and, along with the heavy weight, fell to earth.

Again my imagination began to run away with me. I visualized the weight crashing throught a huge round stained glass window in an ancient old cathedral somewhere in Germany. In a few seconds I would have destroyed a work of art that had endured for centuries. Then again, it might have dropped on an oil refinery, blown up a munition dump, or discouraged and interrupted a German field marshall in his endeavors to seduce a beautiful young maiden.

Anyway its gone and good riddance. It will be a cold day in hell before I use that damn antenna again!

All in all it was a successful mission. We destroyed the target and the group returned with minimum casualties.

Although there is no evidence in the files or the record books of the 8th Air Force, that any of these events or happenings ever took place, I believe that after I released that trailing wire antenna I should have received some credit for saving our plane from destruction and possibly the lives of our crew. Destroying the oil refinery and blowing up a munitions dump is doubtful and would be difficult to prove. I would like to take credit for putting that oversexed German Field Marshall out of his misery. About the stained glass window, well it was probably broken anyway.

After all these years, I wonder what ever happened to that leaded weight and where it finally ended up. I am not really sure, and I would not swear to it, but when I watched President Reagan and the German Chancellor walk through the SS Military Cemetery in Bitburg, Germany, for a second I thought I saw hanging in the background a rusted old trailing wire antenna weight with a twisted length of tarnished copper wire hanging peacefully from a huge tree limb in the cemetery.

389TH BOMB GROUP IN NORTH AFRICA

by Gene Hartley

For this story, I solicited memories from men who were with the 389th Bomb Group during assignment to North Africa while preparing for the Ploesti raids.

An interesting quote, "The planners for Tidal Wave must have needed more bombers in a hurry,

so they sent bombers and air crews overseas without the maintenance personnel following on the *Queen Mary*." This quote must refer to the first 389th B24s arriving in England (probably from Lowry). The Group barely touched down in England, being immediately deployed to North Africa. Due to the shortage of man power, two maintenance men for each plane were detached from the 44th Bomb Group and "temporarily" assigned to the 389th. These men remained with the group from departing Hethel until the Group returned from the desert.

The 389th flew from Hethel to Portreath, near Land's End, England on July 1, 1943. In addition to the 10 man crews, each plane carried maintenance people and their tools and equipment. On July 2, they were some 10 hours in the air as they flew to Oran, Algeria. The route carried them out to longitude 10° west, then southward to Portugal, and from there eastward through the Strait of Gibralter to Oran. Many of the crews reported their first look at flak as they made their way through the Strait. July 3, another nine hour flight to Benghazi, searching from the air for a place to land. They located a couple of graders smoothing off a strip in the desert, and came on in.

The base consisted of one runway cut out of the Libyan desert. Outside of a mess tent, there was nothing there. Choking heat, high temperatures, heavy dust, a great place to go camping.

Upon arriving you were issued a canvas folding cot, two GI blankets, a mattress cover (no mattress), and a mosquito netting. You teamed up with three other guys to put up a four man tent and move in. For some, the first few nights were spent in the open on the desert. There were not enough tents available.

Slit trenches were dug around all tents. They were necessary to jump into in case of a raid. Many fell into them at night, as the nights in Africa were like, DARK.

One gunner, an adventurous soul, somehow came up with a bicycle which he rode each evening to the shower. He once ventured to Benghazi. Coming back late at night, he could not find his tent. He yelled for a tentmate, and 20 responded. He visited half the tents in the area before he found home.

The mess was in one huge tent, catering to all ranks. You were served in your mess kit. Some of the delicacies included powdered eggs, Spam, dehydrated potatoes, mutton, canned veggies, canned fruit cocktail. One could wash it down with warm powdered lemonade. The bread was a favorite food as the cooks had tables around the outside of the tent with plenty of jam and peanut butter. All food was served with a little sand.

Everyone washed his own utensils in three barrels of water outside the eating area. The first barrel was soapy and the other two were for rinsing. After a few washings, all three barrels looked the same. The last guys to eat might better let their gear go unwashed.

A favorite past-time after the evening meal was to fashion some kind of paddle, and get into the contest of swatting locusts. They flew around the mess tent in hordes at sunset. You could hear the SPLATS of the locusts hitting the paddles all over the place, and the heavy swingers counting, 101, 102, etc., etc. It is doubtful that anyone knows who might have held the record.

To make things more exciting for the diners, some GI, as he was leaving the mess tent, would kick a tent stake, which resulted in hundreds of locusts, clinging to the underside of the tent, becoming dislodged and falling into mess kits.

An old story. You can tell a rookie from an old timer by the way he acts when confronted with locusts in the mess kit. The rookie will stop eating, get up, and leave the mess tent. An old timer will remove the locusts and continue eating. The old

B-24 landing on desert, 389th Bomb Group. (Photo by Earl Zimmerman)

Men cleaning utensils after their meal, 389th Bomb Group, North Africa. (Photo by Earl Zimmerman)

Theatre and briefing, 389th Bomb Group. (Photo by Earl Zimmerman)

timer cannot eat until he has a few in his mess kit, and will on occasion throw a few in his food so he feels at home.

The latrines were made from 55 gallon drums cut in half, and provided with a wooden seat and hinged cover made from crate lumber. To clean them, seats and covers were removed. Oil was added and ignited. When the fire burned out and there was time to cool, the seats and cover were added, and all was ready for the next day's use. Not uncommon to look out over the desert from your tent and see many men, all ranks, contemplating their future from the top of a 50 gallon can.

The latrines, regardless of their design, were essential. So many came down with some form of dysentery. The medics provided us with "lister bags" for safe drinking water. A "lister bag" was made of rubberized fabric to contain treated water. It was suspended from a tripod in the middle of the tent and had several push button taps around the base of the bag. Much chlorine was added to the water. It tasted awful. After the sun came up, it was hot enough to shave.

The only way one could get cold water or ice was to fill empty metal ammo boxes with water, load them in bomb bays, and go for a "training flight" over 20,000 feet with bomb bay doors cracked open. After an hour or so, we would have our ice. On occasion, the cook would load up a B-24 with cases of fruit juice to take aloft for ice cold drinks.

The call goes out, heading for the beach, all bathers get with the program. You ride a few miles to the beach, have a few hours splashing around, and return to the base to line up for chow and more locust bashing. That night, you can't sleep, the salt tightens up your skin, you itch and wonder from where all the fleas have come. The next day, another call for the beach, but only one guy goes.

Take a shower? Sure! Walk about two miles each way and by the time you get back, you're dirty. Scorpions were a constant hazard. As long as you checked your shoes before putting them on in the morning, you'd be all right. Many are of the opinion that the name, 389th Sky (or Flying) Scorpions, resulted from the battles the guys had with the things. It is probably quite true.

Paul Burton, Bud Doyle, Felix Dunagan, Cal Fager, Ray Nathe, Andy Opsata, Ben Walsh, and Earl Zimmerman, men who were there, contributed to this story.

From England To Africa

by Peter J. Rice, radioman, 389th BG, 567th BS

Our group, the 389th, left Hethel, England, for our assignment in Africa. After a fuel stop at French Morocco, we lumbered into our desert base at Bengazi, which was then called Italian Libra. My recollection of this area was of just a surrounding desert.

Our home barracks were tents that had to have good anchorage, because the night winds were very strong crossing that area. What I remembered most in this desolate desert is fighting the war of insects. The flies actually shared our mess kit meals with us. It was a constant brushing them away to get a mouthful of food. However, I shall never forget the Arabs who awaited our leftover food. It seems that they were immune to the flies on their face and body.

Water was very scarce and had to be trucked to our desert home. Dysentery was very common and our GI 55-gallon drum toilets were in constant use.

We did have one outlet in this desolate desert and that was the Mediterranean Sea, which was an approximately six or seven mile trip. What a refreshing and cleansing feeling to swim in this beautiful blue sea. But this feeling was lost when we had to return to our constant sand dust base.

Any special rations we received (candy, cookies or any foods) we learned in a hurry not to hide or conserve. The policy had become to eat the goodies right away. Because, no matter how they were boxed or wrapped, it was impossible to save for the next day; the mass of ants would take over like the blight. We had another cute animal that lived with us and that was the kangaroo rat. We would only see them in the black of night. However, they would freeze and play dead when we focused our flashlights on them, very much like our possum's. They stood four to seven inches in height and they were a perfect miniature of the Australian kangaroo.

All the above happened a week or 10 days before July 9, 1943. That date I do recall because it was the first mission assigned to our 389th Bomb Group.

As a group of fresh Yanks just arriving overseas, we wondered where the enemy was and were anxious to get this war over with.

I shall never forget that first mission. The target: the airdrome on the isle of Crete; this was near Greece. The Germans were still in control of this area and we were anxious to come into battle with them.

We took off from our Bengazi base. It was a beautiful formation; here we were at 25,000 feet overlooking the blue Mediterranean and the boot of Italy. What a sight!

With no sign of the enemy, we sighted our target and dispensed our bombs. All of a sudden, as we turned for our base, a flock of ME-109s were all over our group. This is when we knew that we were in war. Both planes on either side of us went down aflame towards the sea. I did not see any of the crew get out of the plane on our right wing; the plane on our left wing was tilted on its wing. I can remember seeing four chutes opening, one of which I thought was the radio man's (He did not have his straps buckled properly). I can still see him clutching at the air. I do not recall how many planes were lost that day, but I do know we paid the price and knew we were in a serious war and a killing one.

We remained at this base for seven more missions, the seventh mission was the low level attack Aug. 1, 1943 on Ploesti oil fields in Romania. That mission I shall never forget, because it was one of the toughest missions of the war. Another reason I shall never forget is because it was on my 28th birthday. I believe we lost 77 aircraft on this flight and it was one of the biggest losses during the war.

Our eighth mission from this area was on Aug. 13, 1943, and the target was the Messerschmitt fighter plant at Wiener Neustadt in Austria.

Returning to our home base at Hethel, England was like a trip to paradise to us. Although we had a lot of tough missions ahead of us, we were glad to be home, and our favorite expression was "Bengazi was a good place to be from."

The Dukes

by Mr. and Mrs. Reuben D. Duke

The twins, Lt. Allenby K. Duke (A.K.) and Lt. Reuben D. Duke (R.D.), served together in the Army Air Force from enlistment in the Reserves on May 22, 1942 in San Antonio, TX to active duty November 26, 1942, until A.K. was killed in action on August 8, 1944. This includes Aerial Gunnery School; Preflight Ground School in Houston, TX; Bombardier School in Big Spring, TX, where they graduated in Class 43-17 as second lieutenants on Dec. 3, 1943.

In January 1944 they were sent to March Field, CA, a B-24 Liberator Bomber Transition School. A.K. was assigned to Lt. Clarence Craft's crew as bombardier and R.D. was assigned to Lt. Loyd Berger's crew as bombardier. They completed Transition School and were sent to Hamilton Field, San Francisco, then to Camp Kilmer, NJ.

On May 2, 1944 they boarded a troop ship and joined the largest convoy of ships to cross the Atlantic. They landed in Scotland on May 14, 1944 and entrained to England, along with their crews. They were assigned to the 389th Bomb Group, located on Hethel Air Field near Norwich, England. A.K. and R.D. ended up in different squadrons, but they were together in the 389th Bomb Group until the death of A.K. on August 8, 1944. A.K. was on his 17th mission and in the wing lead plane synchronizing on a tactical support target in France when he was killed by anti-aircraft fire. Seven of his missions were as lead bombardier. He was buried in the U.S. Cemetery in Cambridge, England. His body was returned to San Antonio, Texas, Mission Burial Park, after the war ended.

R.D. completed 30 combat missions, 13 missions were as the lead bombardier on lead Pathfinder missions.

Twenty Minutes Over Germany

Ken "Deacon" Jones (389th)

At a 389th Bomb Group reunion in June, 1993, a famous flyer and piano player from the 389th "O" Club, Bob Meuse, told a banquet story. It was an emotional experience to hear Bob tell the story, from the viewpoint of a witness, of losing the Jones crew over Karlsruhe, Germany on Dec. 11, 1944.

With the help of war time notes and the clarity of vague memory, historic details of this event are recalled with some consistency of truth.

The mission got off to a bad start that winter day. Take-off was delayed 20 minutes. The bad omens were frost on the wings and heavy ground fog. The heavily laden bomber was reluctant to leave the ground and used up nearly all of the main runway. Homing on Buncher 6, we climbed slowly up over 10,000 feet through dense clouds to get on top of the thick overcast.

The 8th Air Force was putting up a maximum effort, with nearly 1,600 bombers and more than 800 fighters. The Jones crew was flying mission #2 on the right wing of Don Armstrong and Bob Meuse in the high right element of the high right squadron.

At the briefing, S-2 said we would run into some black clouds over the target. At 1220 hours, on the bomb run to Maxilliansau RR Bridge, four flak bursts exploded under our left wing knocking out both engines on that side. I screamed, "salvo, salvo!" into the mike.

The concussion of the 88s going off and the 2,000 pound bombs going out threw us up and to the right. The left wing went up, then down, as we skidded and yawed back to the left. I slammed bottom rudder and aileron to avoid a mid-air collision with other ships in the squadron.

According to witnesses, Bob Meuse and other Armstrong crew members, "The B-24 rolled over on its back and sort of split-s'ed out of formation. Then it went into a steep, vertical spin. The B-24 disappeared, spinning out of control, into the under-cast at 15,000 feet...There were no parachutes..." The BBC might report, "One of our aircraft is missing."

(Excerpts from Consolidated Aircraft Manual: *Maneuvers Prohibited.* Spins - The airplane was not designed for...a spin condition, and structural failure could result from spins. Dive - Air loads build up rapidly on any large airplane...the inertia of a heavy body in motion resists efforts to change the direction of that motion...it takes some time and considerable force to flare out of this rate of descent...")

Maintaining group integrity was important. However, there wasn't time to request permission from Bourbon Leader to leave the formation. The throttles were pulled back as we entered the spin. In a desperate struggle with heavy controls, we lost over 8,000 feet from bombing altitude. The airplane did not respond. It took the combined strength of both pilots, with both feet on the right rudder to stop the spin.

Centrifugal force pinned each crewman at his position with a dreadful fear of dying helpless. The spin recovery was the standard 1-2-3, in a time ma-

chine, with agonizingly slow results. 1. Pop the wheel forward to break the stall. 2. Apply full opposite rudder to stop the rotation. 3. After the airplane stops spinning, back pressure on the wheel to pull out of the dive.

We were in the soup on primary flight instruments. It was a link trainer nightmare. The gyros had tumbled on the artificial horizon and directional compass.

The airspeed showed an indicated 375 mph in the dive and this B-24 was red-lined at 275 mph max. Using superhuman strength, we nearly blacked out from G-forces on pulling out of the dive. An iron grip on the control wheel crushed my class ring. We could hear rivets popping in the wings and thought the wings would come together over our heads. "Things are tough all over boys - then it's going to get worse."

The vacuum control for the instrument group was switched from #2 engine to #1. The #2 engine was dead - windmilling and could not be feathered. #1 had the turbo controls shot off and the engine was running away, out of control, on RPM over 3,000. Shrapnel punched a number of small holes and one large hole in the left main gas tank. There was considerable leakage and siphoning of fuel. Severe vibrations from windmilling #2 prop threatened to tear #2 engine from the engine mounts or throw detached prop blades through the cockpit.

In one split second, the efficient Nazis had modified our European tour bus with 200 or so odd sized fresh air vents.

In December, 1944, the European winter was the most appalling weather in 50 years. The entire continent was socked-in with dense clouds, and there was no possibility of a normal or forced landing anywhere on the continent. You keep flying or bail out. The homeward journey was made in blind flight. We said a lot of prayers and made some promises to the Lord.

Thankfully, there were no wounded. Navigator Pat (Wiley) Patterson had his throat mike shaved from his neck by a piece of flak.

I read a piece on bravery concerning the fact that it was a shame the beautiful girls could not see how brave the boys were in the frozen skies over Germany. In our case the truth was that if the damaged #1 engine stopped running, we would lose vacuum to our flight instruments. We would then auger in and never get to see any girls, beautiful or not. We were apprehensive rather than brave in combat. Bravery was learning to eat the food in the messhall or taking a cold shower outside in the winter time.

For a while, we continued to slowly lose another 9,000 feet of altitude because of extreme drag from the windmilling prop. There was little hope of sitting down to a candle-lit supper of stringy Argentina mutton at Hethel Army Air Base that night. The gunners had been evacuated from turrets and they clipped on their chutes. The gas fumes were very strong.

Eventually, lack of engine oil and friction caused #2 engine to seize and freeze in a stopped position. Not feathered, the props still caused lots of drag but we could now maintain altitude. The radio operator called "Darky" on the CW radio for a QDM heading to confirm our homeward course. This pleased some crew members as this was another step of insurance to lower that risk of not having to miss four o'clock tea.

A miracle then occurred, where for one brief moment we could bring the runaway RPM on #1 engine back with the toggle switch, once to 2100 and then couldn't regulate it again because of damage. The RPM was back within tolerance and the high cylinder head temperature started back to normal.

Above all else, our chances of growing one day

Lt. A.K. Duke (left) and Lt. R.D. Duke in Norwich, England. (Courtesy of Reuben D. Duke)

older depended upon a questionable #1 engine and flight instruments to carry on. There was no horizon for visual reference. The value of USAAF instrument flight training was that we were depriving the Germans of 10 Yanks as uninvited guests of the 3rd Reich.

The airplane flew catty-wumpus, with the left wing held high and strong right rudder to counteract the hard push of two good engines on the right side. Our legs shook and ached with fatigue from holding hard rudder pressure.

Survival prospects began to look better. "Backward, oh backward, move time in your flight. Make me a boy again just for tonight." One relaxed crew member suggested a RON (Remain Over Night) at Gay Paree to see the French Can Can Girls. This fantasy received 10 affirmative votes. The weather cancelled the vote, as a landing in France was out of the question.

We tried for home base on the remaining fuel. Unseen by friend or foe, a solitary bird of war left Germany, crossed into France and flew onward, across the English Channel from Calais to Dover, following the ancient path of the Normans to Ye Olde England. Outside of a two-second glimpse of Calais before clouds rolled in again, there was no sight of land and only occasional breaks in thick clouds over an empty sea. Ditching prospects were grim to speculate about with a 10-minute life expectancy in icy waters.

"They say there's a 24 leaving Calais,
Bound for old limey shore.
Its laden with petrified men,
Laying prone and so scared on the floor."

Old Q- of the 567th Bomb Squadron brought us all the way home, through 10/10s clouds and five snow and ice storms on two and a half engines with punctured de-icer boots. Over France, propellers slinging ice pellets played a tattoo on the side of the fuselage and that added to our anxiety. (One B-24 expert said the Davis wing wouldn't hold enough ice to chill your drink. He was wrong.)

"With six QDMs and some bloody luck,
We made the limey shore.
The cloud was eleven-tenths,
Right on the deck,
And tried bloody hard to be more.
They dug up a windmill and six thatch roof shacks,
When they traced us back to landfall.
Now, there'll be no promotion,
This side of the ocean,
So cheer up my lads, Bless them all."

A radio transmission was made about 25 miles out. Pussface Tower, named after Stan Greer's cat at Hethel Army Air Base, was notified about a straight-in approach. Flying through scud clouds at 500 feet, the gear was lowered early to check for possible damage. There was no latch indication that the right main gear was locked down. We couldn't tell if the tires were inflated.

The radio compass was on zero. Red flares were fired when we had the runway in sight. Other mission aircraft were in the traffic pattern from a squadron peel off. Home never looked so good.

As we started the let-down on final approach, we got cut off by a hot pilot wearing a white silk scarf. Score one more disappointment for the 11th of December. "Cheer up my lads, Bless 'em all!"

The wounded Baker Two Four/Queenie Bar was only one minute to touchdown. It just wasn't cricket to cut us off and out of our one opportunity to land in one piece. There was this mental image of a disabled B-24H ploughing through a hedgerow and scaring the hell out of some farmer's chickens. I said a four letter "S" word that doesn't rhyme with "Oh mercy." Struggling for a little altitude, our ship buzzed the aircraft landing beneath us and the main runway. "Pussface...Crewhand Queenie...going around." (We hope!)

Some unkind words were said about the other pilot's ancestry and his mother's pedigree. The throttles were rammed to the gate on emergency military power. Suspended by a thin thread of prayer, Q- made a low continuous circle to the right, away from the weak side, to a safe landing at 1515 hours. The right gear did not collapse.

We killed #3 engine and taxied in to the hard stand. The ship was spun around to face the perimeter strip and we shut down the power on those wonderful Pratt and Whitney engines.

Hours of suspense ended with a warm kiss on the cold fuselage of a Queen. Relief was like compressed air escaping from an over-inflated tire. This is the kind of excitement that brings out the crowds. A few dedicated members of our fan club gathered at the hard stand to count flak holes. Some technical words were spoken to a concerned crew chief. Then the air crew of Q- hastily departed for debriefing and several glasses of adult beverage to smooth out the bumps.

Later that evening, a uniformed messenger from the 567th Squadron popped into the Nissen Hut. The operations officer, Capt. Fred Mauch, informed us we were alerted for tomorrow's mission. We turned kind of green around the gills. None of us rejoiced in that announcement. After a long moment, I said we were scared sick but we would go. It was said like we had a choice. There were some things you just had to do.

All of this soldiering in the U.S. Army Air Force was for the gal back home, for mom and apple pie and to stop a madman named Hitler.

The personal war diary of the late Bill Dunne of the Armstrong crew, dated December 11, 1944 - Mission 12B reads in part: "Lost ship flying our right wing..." Lost is defined as; losing interest in glory at the height of the frolic. Apathy is measured by the metallic content of man made clouds over the target. Explosive creations by the flak gunner's society sometimes results in sudden departure from a tight formation.

Words to a song had new meaning now. "I wanted wings until I got the gosh-darned things, Now I don't want them anymore."

We all had a few sleepless hours, until 0300 hours, to muster the courage to go out again. Those who didn't know how to pray had a lot of time to practice. If we had not gone the next day, we would never fly again.

The invincibility of youth was shattered by the sound and the fury of war. There was a new awareness and sensitivity about life. No one talked about that because you might come unraveled by talking about it. The unwritten code, like the West Point motto, was duty, honor and country. There was no other alternative except to be a willing participant and to do your utmost to end the war.

There is a heartfelt expression of eternal gratitude to the Man upstairs for a miracle and our survival. We are grateful for memories of the fighting green dragons and those magical ground support folks of the 389th Bomb Group. Special thanks to Bob Meuse and the producers of the greatest airplane ever built, the B-24 Liberator.

Buy War Bonds and Keep Em Flying Yank.

392ND BOMB GROUP I Remember: The Big Week

by Col. Myron H. Keilman

I remember the Big Week and the day the 392nd earned the Distinguished Unit Citation.

General Jimmy Doolittle took command of the 8th Air Force on January 1, 1944. At group and squadron level we were quite impressed. We all felt we knew the famous aviator; if not from his airplane racing days, from his leading the famous Tokyo bombing raid. We didn't realize that at that moment his orders were "Win the air war and isolate the battlefield." In other words - destroy the Luftwaffe and cut off the beaches of Normandy for the invasion.

By February 20 our group had been alerted, briefed, and taxied for take-off nearly every morning since Gen. Doolittle took command. There we waited for hours in the dense fog before the red flare signal of "Mission Cancelled" was fired from the control tower.

Then back to the airplane's dispersal pad; back to the dank Nissen huts; back to the damp, ice-cold cots for needed sleep and tomorrow's alert. "Damn the foggy weather, damn the war, and damn Gen. Doolittle, too." After those early hour breakfasts, the mess sergeant had to pick up the general's portrait from a face-down position in the middle of the floor and rehang it in its respected place. Disrespect? Yes, but who wants to be rousted out at 0300 hours, day in and day out, just to sit in the fog? We couldn't win the war doing this, and you didn't have to be a general to see that the weather was unfit to fly a bombing mission - were our glum thoughts.

The weather had been so adverse during January and to February 20, our group had flown only 16 missions; most of them were no-ball strikes against buzz-bomb (V-1 missiles) launching sites. Then came a streak of decent weather and an all out air offensive against the German Luftwaffe factories. Five great air battles were fought over Germany on February 20, 21, 22, 24 and 25, 1944. They have gone down in 8th Air Force annuals as the "Big Week."

Maximum efforts by 8th Air Force's 1,000 bombers (B-17s and B-24s) and fighters were made during those five days against airplane manufacturing and component plants at Tutow, Rostock, and Straslund on the Baltic Sea coast; Magdeburg, Augsburg, Bernberg, Oschersleben, Leipzig, Brunswick, Gotha, Furth, Halberstaddt, Schweinfurt, Regensburg, and Stuttgart in central and eastern Germany. Five hundred and fifty German fighters were declared shot down, 170 B-17s and B-24s, and 33 friendly fighters were lost.

The Royal Air Force (RAF) Halifax and Lancaster bombers got in their "licks", too. At night, they dropped block-busters and fire bombs on the cities of Leipzig, Schweinfurt and Augsburg, causing great fire storms and devastation.

On the first day, Sunday, February 20, the 2nd Air Division's B-24s struck at Brunswick and Magdeburg. Cloud cover was a big problem. The 392nd had to bomb Helmstedt as a target of opportunity. The results were rated as fair and we lost one airplane. The B-17s managed to get in destructive strikes on airplane plants at Leipzig, Bernberg, and Oschersleben. Twenty-five bombers and four fighters were lost; 153 Germans shot down.

On the 21st, clouds covered the big targets; so the main scheduled targets were airfields. My group bombed the fighter base at Verden, Holland, northeast of Arnhem. The bombing results were good, but we lost another airplane and crew. Nineteen bombers and five fighters went down with 60 Germans.

The 22nd, our target was Gotha, but the mission was recalled because of weather conditions, and no bombs were dropped. Some B-24 groups did strike targets of opportunity in Holland and West Germany. The B-17s did the same. Fifteenth Air Force in Italy struck the Regensburg plants.

Weather in England on the 23rd caused a standdown for all of 8th Air Force; however, the 15th Air Force struck Weiner Neustadt factories.

On the fifth day, Thursday, February 24, most

of Germany was clear of clouds, and formations of 860 B-17s and B-24s struck deep. Nearly 800 P-47s, P-38s, and P-51s provided protective fighter cover for the bombers. The 2nd Bomb Division target was the big Messerschmitt airplane plant at Gotha, 420 miles due east of the White Cliffs of Dover.

Our briefing for the attack on Gotha was at 0630 hours. It was our group's 40th mission; so we took it all in stride. To most of us it meant another mission to be accomplished against a total of 25, then back home to the safety of the ZI (Zone of Interior). Remember? The intelligence officer briefed on the importance of the big plant to German's ability to carry on the air war; on the fact that it was heavily defended by big 88 and 110 millimeter anti-aircraft artillery like we faced over Bremen, Kiel, and Wilhelmshaven, and we were certain to encounter heavy fighter attacks all across enemy territory. Four hundred miles in and 400 miles out.

After drawing our escape and evasion kits, donning our heated flying suits, gathering up our oxygen masks, flak helmets, Mae Wests, and parachutes we climbed aboard two and one-half ton trucks for a cold ride to our airplane's dispersal pad. It was still very dark as we made our airplane inspection, checking all the engine cowling for loose Dzus fasteners; the turbines of the superchargers; the propeller blades pushing them through to release any piston hydraulic lock; the fuel cells for being "topped-off" and their caps for security; the guns and turrets; ammunition quantity of 500 rounds for each of the ten, 50 caliber machine guns; the Sperry bombsight; the twelve, 500-pound bombs, their shackles, fuses and safety wires; the oxygen supply and regulators; signal flares; camera and many other things. Remember?

At 0810 hours we started engines. At 0815 the lead ship taxied to take-off position. At 0830 the green flare from the control tower signaled "take-off!" It was breaking dawn.

Lead crew Pilot Jim McGregor "revved-up" his engines, checked the instruments, released the brakes and rolled. Thirty-one B-24H's followed at 30 second intervals.

In the clear at 12,000 feet, the lead ship fired red-yellow identification flares. Flying deputy lead, I pulled into position on his right wing, and the group formed over radio beacon "21" into three squadrons. Then it flew the wing triangular assembly pattern to Kings Lynn.

Leading the 14th Combat Wing, we fell into number two position of the 2nd Bomb Division's bomber stream over Great Yarmouth. Heading east over the channel and climbing to 18,000 feet, our gunners test fired their guns. We penetrated enemy territory just north of Amsterdam. At 235 miles an hour true air speed over the Zuider Zee, our streaming vapor trails signaled our presence and our intent. It was a thrilling moment. Onward over Dummer Lake, past our future Osnabruck target, southeast past Hanover's bombed-out airfields our big formations hurried.

Paralleling our course to the right were the B-17 formations of the 1st Bomb Division heading for their tough old ball-bearing works at Schweinfurt. Over the North Sea, the 3rd Bomb Division "forts" were en route to their Baltic coast targets. P-47 fighters covered us to the vicinity of Hanover, then P-38s and P-51s orbited over us to Gotha. Luftwaffe fighters made attempts to penetrate our formations but "our little friends" kept them at a distance and when opportunity prevailed, dove in for a "kill." Using our thick vapor trails as a screen, the Germans often struck from below and from behind to shoot up any lagging bomber.

Bending southeastward toward Gotha, the white snowy earth looked cold and lifeless; only the large communities, rail lines, and an autobahn

stood out in relief. Fighter attacks became more persistent. By the time we reached our initial point (IP) to start our bomb run, the sky about our three squadrons was full of busy P-38s and P-51s, fending off the Germans. I remember how they dove past the lead ship in pursuit of Messerschmitts and Focke-Wulf's making head on attacks. Our gunners got in a lot of shooting, too. The staccato of the turrets' twin 50s vibrated throughout the airplane. It was real scary.

The weather was clear as a bell as we turned to the target. Red flares from the lead ship signaled bomb bay doors were open. The bombardier removed the heated cover blanket from the bombsight. (Bombsights had heated blankets before people did. Remember?) He checked his gyroscope's stabilization, and all bombing switches on. Our high and low squadrons fell intrail and all seemed great. Then Pilotage Navigator Kennedy, in the nose turret, observed the lead wing formations veering from the target heading. A fast and anxious cross-check with Lead Crew Navigator Swangren and with a recheck of compass heading and reference points, they assured Command Pilot Lorin Johnson that the target was dead ahead. Thirty years later, I don't know where the 2nd Bomb Division leader wound up, and I've forgotten which group and wing it was, but at that moment the 392nd leading the 14th Combat Wing was "on course, on target." Within minutes Lead Bombardier Good called over the interphone, "I've got the target!" Lead Pilot McGregor checked his flight instruments for precise 18,000 feet altitude and 160 miles per hour indicated air speed, and carefully levelled the airplane on auto-pilot. Then he called back, "On airspeed, on altitude. You've got the airplane." Making a final level of his bombsight, Good took over control of steering the airplane with the bombsight.

The lead bombardier's target folder didn't contain a snowy, winter view of the Messerschmitt aircraft works. He had to use his keen judgement and trained skills in discerning the briefed aiming point. Only his one eye peering through the bombsight optics could determine where to place the crosshairs. He could and did give a commentary to the command pilot and crew of what he saw and what he was doing in steering the lead airplane and formation of bombers to the bomb release point, but only he knew for sure what was viewed through that bombsight.

At 18,000 feet it was 40 degrees below zero, but the bombardier never felt the cold as his fingers delicately operated the azimuth and range controls. He cross-checked all the bomb and camera switches to the on position, especially the radio bomb release (RBR) signal switch that would release all the bombs of the other airplanes in the formation simultaneously. There wasn't a cloud in the sky.

When the flak started bursting near the formation, Lt. Good had already attained a synchronized bombing run with the wind drift "killed" and the cross-hair holding steady on the aiming point of the great manufacturing complex. The bombsight indicies crossed and "Bombs away!" Beautiful!

While the camera was recording the impact of the bombs, Lt. McGregor took over and swung the formation to the outbound heading and the rally point.

In spite of the new accurate flak from the 88 and 110 millimeter anti-aircraft artillery, the 2nd and 3rd squadron bombardiers, Lt. Ziccarrelli and Lt. Jackson, steered their squadrons to the precise bomb delivery points, too. Of 32 B-24s that took off that morning, 29 delivered 348, 500-pound bombs, precisely on the Gotha factory as briefed. Outstanding!

The bombs were smack on target, but the battle wasn't over. No sooner had the wing left the target's flak than we were accosted by German fighters

again. Strung out in trail and with some planes slowed down from flak damage, our three squadrons became vulnerable to vicious attacks. For the next hour and more, Messerschmitt, Folke Wulf and Junker fighters worked us over until our fighters could fend them off.

As deputy command pilot, I frequently changed off flying formation with the airplane commander to keep occupied and not have to watch the Jerries press their blazing gun attacks. The interphone was alive with excited calls of enemy action; head on passes and tail attacks; in singles and in "gaggles;" rockets, 20mm cannon, and even some cables were thrown at us. Seven of our B-24s were shot down. Many of us were shot up, but it was not all one-sided. The gunners of the 22 airplanes that returned accounted for 16 German fighters.

At 1530, seven hours after take-off, the battle weary group landed back at Wendling; 8th Air Force lost 50 bombers and 10 fighters; 155 German fighters were shot down.

The very next day, Friday, February 25, the target areas were again clear, and the 2nd Bomb Division struck the aircraft plant at Furth, near Nuernberg. The 14th Wing with the 392nd's two squadrons of 22 B-24s bombed it with excellent results. In spite of the nine hour long deep penetrations, our group did not suffer a loss. The "Forts" successfully struck aircraft plants at Regensburg, Augsburg and Stuttgart. The 8th lost 33 bombers and three fighters; the Germans lost 70.

This ended the famous "Big Week," Gen. Doolittle had struck the Luftwaffe a devastating blow and all but won the air war. Within a couple more months, through persistent bombing of air fields and railroad marshalling yards, shooting the German fighters in the air and on the ground in France, Belgium and Western Germany, the battlefield of Normandy was isolated. The stage was set for the great invasion of the continent on D-day, June 6, 1944. Remember?

On April 20, 1945, our group adjutant, Major "Jack" Fritsche, sent the following notice to all units of our group:

"The 392nd Bombardment Group has been awarded the Distinguished Unit Citation for outstanding performance of duty in armed conflict with the enemy on February 24, 1944, when the group virtually destroyed their assigned target at Gotha, Germany."

War Department General Order #37, 1945, that awarded the Distinguished Unit Badge to all individuals who were assigned to the 392nd reads in part "The destruction of this high priority target (Gotha) was a serious blow to the German air force and was a contributing factor to its impotency during the invasion of Continental Europe."

A Day To Remember
by Jim Maris (392nd)

August 3 was briefed as a "No Ball" mission that we expected to be a milk run. We were assigned an alternate airplane called *Fords Folly*, and departed Wendling at 4:00 p.m. We penetrated the coast at 23,000 feet, and the lead bombardier missed the target. Since we had no flak or fighters, he elected to take the group around for another run on the V-1 launch site that was our target.

This allowed the enemy to activate several batteries of mobile anti-aircraft guns, and as we passed over the I.P. (initial point), they started firing on the 392nd. Our wing men later told us that the first burst of four exploded 300 feet low and behind us. The next burst of four took us out of the lead of the lower element. They said our B-24 disappeared in a cloud of smoke and they could see it being blown up and over on its back above the formation. I had set up the Minneapolis Honeywell electric auto pilot on standby earlier in the mission, and with the aircraft inverted and badly damaged, I activated the auto pilot, which righted the B-24 and gave us a chance to assess the damage. One engine was gone, another was running away with the controls severed, and the third was sitting out there stripped of its cowling, supercharger blown away, but still running. A heavy odor of aviation fuel permeated the cockpit, and all electrical systems were deactivated.

The recovery was accomplished at 18,000 feet on a westerly heading, approaching the coast. Since we had been hit along the coast where the swimmers cross the channel at its narrowest point, the cockpit crew elected to attempt to get back to England, rather than bail out over France. The flight engineer was told to go to the various stations and tell them to prepare for the crossing by throwing out everything that we could toss. They were to then rig parachutes at the waist windows to use for air brakes upon landing, if we could make it back to a field in England.

As we became stable, I finally managed to feather the runaway engine. Later we found the only control out to the runaway engine that wasn't severed was the circuit to the feathering pump. We calculated that with the rate of descent we had established, we should come over the English coast with about 2,000 feet of altitude remaining. We then approached the Continental Coast; more flak hit our limping B-24 which sustained more damage. The waist gunner came forward to tell us that the right wing had a hole big enough to drop a man through, and the fuel cells in that area were ruptured and dumping fuel. This allowed fuel to follow the spars into the fuselage and was the reason we were experiencing the fuel in the cockpit area.

Two Spitfires came into formation with us, signaling that we should follow them. We gave them a thumbs up, and continued throwing everything loose out of the airplane. Some of our wing men had punched the emergency channel when they saw us recover and head for England. They had requested help for us, so that German fighters couldn't pick us off on our way back.

We were at 1800 feet as the Spits led us over the coast of England, near the mouth of the Thames River. We could see a dark black column of smoke ahead, and we assumed the British had lit a tire fire, which they sometimes did to mark a field to help to burn off fog. The smoke was rising from Manston, the crash recovery base near the British coast. The Spits peeled off with a waggle of their wings, and we started to prepare for landing. The flight engineer and the crew in the nose released the lock and kicked out the nose gear. They then went back to the bomb bay to crank down the mains. They rigged a safety device out of parachute harness, and one at a time, they'd go out in the bomb bay and crank until they would nearly pass out from the raw fuel and fumes. The cranker would be pulled back in and another crew member would go out into the bomb bay and crank. On downwind we were down to about 900 feet and the gear was not clear down. One of the crew was at the rear of the cockpit keeping me informed of the progress.

The crew in the rear portion of the aircraft had rigged the parachutes in the waist windows and had sat down with their backs against the crash belt. Turning on base, I glanced out of the left side window and was alarmed to see that the column of black smoke was from a B-24 that had crashed about halfway down the recovery runway. In the cockpit the bombardier, navigator, top turret gunner and flight engineer had assumed their crash positions, immediately behind the pilots' seats. Turning on final approach, I had to allow for no flaps, damaged wing surface, no hydraulics, and a cockpit full of gas fumes. The B-24 had been at altitude for several hours and the outer surfaces were deeply chilled.

When the B-24 passed through 400 feet, the windows clouded up with condensed moisture and immediately froze in a thin covering of ice. Forward visibility was immediately cut off, and I immediately threw open the small weather window on the left and reached out, getting one good scrape across the corner of the windshield. I didn't recall this action, but Herb, the navigator, described the instant response later as the crew was debriefed.

Peeking through the iced windshield and judging height with glances out the side, I brought the B-24 in on the crash recovery runway. There were no brakes and the tires were losing air, but the B-24 tracked straight and rolled to a stop just a few feet short of the burning B-24. The crew had been well drilled on evacuation, and as the pilots shut everything down they went out through the bomb bay. As I ducked down out of the bomb bay, I ran into the crew waiting to see if everyone was getting out. I yelled, "Run before it blows!" and they took off like they were shot.

About 200 feet down the runway, we stopped and turned to look at the dying B-24 that had so valiantly brought us home. Fuel was dripping from the wings and the fuselage and the tires were now flat. The wing had a hole through it big enough to drop a man through and later we counted 85 holes from nose to tail. Our guardian angel must have been riding with us, since not a crew member had been hit. We did have several suffering from gas fume inhalation, extreme soreness from extensive cranking on the main gear, and I was in a state of nervous stress from the pressure of the last couple of hours. Captain English, the officer in charge of the crash crew, debriefed the crew and complimented them

WACs christening "G.I. Jane," February, 1944, Wendling, England. (Courtesy of John Rickey)

392nd Bomb Group, 576th Squadron. (Courtesy of Virgil H. Popson)

on a job well done. The medical staff asked everyone to go to the infirmary for checkups and a night of rest.

In the dressing room, where the crew was removing its flying clothes, flak vests, etc., the doctor stopped me and asked to check my badly bruised left side. I had repeatedly been checking my left side for signs of blood on the flight over the channel, because I felt like I'd been hit by something. The flak vest was checked; one of the steel squares near the bruised area was badly bent and in the cloth near the bent piece of metal was a small piece of flak shrapnel. When checking the B-24 the next day, a hole in the left side of the cockpit was identified as where the shrapnel had penetrated the aircraft and hit me in the side. Fortunately the flak vest had stopped its travel, because the doctor said it would have gone on to my heart if it had not been stopped by the small square of steel. I kept the small piece of the flak vest and the shrapnel, and they're a part of my collection of memories from my B-24 days.

The crew was worried about Blondie, and I called the 392nd asking them to feed our mascot and to please not strip our Quonset, for we were in fact okay and would be back to base in a day or so, as soon as they would release us. There was a B-24 there that had been repaired and needed to be taken back to Norwich, and I had said our crew would take it back.

We settled down in the infirmary to try to sleep, and soon the nurse came in and asked us all to put on our robes and follow her out into a revetment at the building's rear. She explained that the Germans sent their V-1 planes over every night at the same time, and they'd be over the coast at 2330 hours. Sure enough, the sky lit up at 2330 hours and to the west we could see the searchlights lighting up the V-1 as it crossed the coast. Antiaircraft fire was tracking the V-1 as it approached the airfield. About this time, a battery of four antiaircraft guns in the revetment next to the one we were in started firing and frightened us all more than the day's mission had. Suddenly a green flare was fired, guns ceased firing, and an unfamiliar whine filled the air.

Flashing into the cone of light was a twin tailed airplane like one we had never seen. It appeared to have no propellers, and the strange high-pitched whine continued. The sleek twin-tailed fighter moved into close formation with the V-1, and when properly positioned, the pilot raised his wing up under the wing of the V-1, upsetting the gyros of the V-1 auto pilot, and it immediately went into a spiral, crashing out on the airfield with a roar that

sent us all down to the dirt behind the revetment wall. Enough was enough; we all retreated to the infirmary and were given something to help us sleep. The 3rd was certainly a day we'd all remember.

One Of Ten

by S.J. Maloukis Jr. (392nd)

We made numerous bombing missions into Germany, but my most memorable was my 22nd and last mission. This mission would go down in our group's history as one of the 10 roughest ever flown in terms of aircraft lost (6) and air crew casualties (60). We were flying in formation to our target when we flew through some clouds. Anyone who knows about formation flying knows how dangerous that is. It took only about 20 seconds but it seemed like 20 minutes. The formation came out of the clouds in pretty good shape, proceeded on to its target, dropped its bombs and had headed home when it flew through the same clouds again. Well, as soon as we hit the clouds the formation spread out all over the sky. When we came out, they were waiting for us. Our tail gunner called out "FWs at 5 and 7 high and 5 and 7 low" and he started firing. I was sitting down tossing out chaff. I jumped up and looked out the window and there was an ME-109 flying along side of us, I grabbed my machine gun and fired a burst and the next thing I knew I was on my back on the floor. I jumped up and grabbed my gun again but the fighter was gone. The fighter escort took care of the rest of the enemy.

Our pilot put the plane in a steep dive and we thought we were going down, so I grabbed my chute, snapped it on and headed for the escape hatch, which was a mass of twisted metal from the shells hitting it. I struggled with it for what seemed like an eternity and finally got it opened. I looked back at Tom, the other gunner, who in his haste had picked up his chute by the rip cord, and had it all gathered up in his arms. I knew he couldn't bail out like that, so I crawled to the rear of the ship and got the spare chute and gave it to him. I looked out the escape hatch and thought, "it's a long way down."

By this time the plane had leveled off and was flying on even keel so we thought we had better stick around for awhile. My right foot was starting to hurt, so I looked down and there was a hole the size of a quarter in my sheep skin flying boot. I pulled off my boot, two pair of wool socks, my electrically heated boot and a pair of cotton socks. There

was a hole where the joint of my little toe was supposed to be. About then our flight engineer came back to see what had happened to us, since our intercom was shot out, along with several control cables, most of our oxygen was gone, one engine was gone and the other on the right wing was sputtering. He put sulfa powder on my foot and gave me a shot of morphine, which helped. Our badly damaged B-24 limped back to England, barely making the coast. We lost most of the hydraulic fluid and they had to hand pump the flaps and landing gear down. I found out later that the copilot was flying the plane and he put it down with one of the smoothest landings we had ever felt. We didn't have any brakes so we had to let the plane coast to a stop.

They put me in the hospital and were getting ready to operate on my foot when I looked over at the X-rays they had taken and noticed the slug. I asked the Doc if those were my X-rays and he said yes, so I asked him to save me that slug, which he did. It turned out to be the bottom part of a 20mm cannon shell from one of those FWs. I still carry it today, my memento of the war.

B-24 Starduster

by Willis L. Miller (392nd)

I would like to relate some of the experiences of the B-24 "Starduster" crew which flew with the 392nd Bomb Group, 577th and 579th Squadrons, Wendling, England. The crew was composed of Willis Miller, Jim Cassity, Jack Crane, Joe Mohr, Frank Prach, Hal Hagopian, Les Walters, Bill Moles and Alan Pace. Frank Gillett, Rudy Boettcher, and Red Sprowls joined us when we became a radar or "mickey" crew. Our crew chief was Earl French (Frenchy) who worked tirelessly to keep us in the air. All of our missions were memorable, but some more than others.

Our first mission was quite an introduction to combat flying. We had just arrived at the 392nd and had been told that we would not fly for about two weeks. However, on July 6, 1944 we were awakened and told to come to briefing. Our mission that day was Kiel, Germany, and we were assigned to an old junker called *Trips Daily*. We had difficulty climbing to the altitude designated and were told to look for the group shooting yellow flares. It appeared everyone had yellow flares that day. We eventually found our group about the time we left the English coast line and immediately dropped into the "tail end Charley" slot that had been assigned to us. We were not able to keep up with the group, so we dropped our bombs some time after the rest of the group. It was apparent that if we kept using the fuel we were consuming in trying to keep up with the group, we would not have enough to return to our base. With our right stabilizer gone and one engine inoperative, our only choice was to get into the clouds to keep the German naval gunners from shooting us down and the German fighters trying to finish us off. Our navigator had no idea where we were, so we decided to try time and distance and just prayed we would break out over friendly territory. We were fortunate, and found ourselves over Scotland, losing altitude, low on fuel, and hoping we could make our base. We were able to make our base but found that all of our clothes and personal belongings had been taken. The rest of our group had run into enemy fighters and flak and a large number of our group did not return. This was quite an initiation into combat!

As the lead for the group on July 19, 1944 we headed to the rail yards at Kassel, Germany, which turned out to be a mission that was quite a lot out of the ordinary. We were on the bomb run and seconds from bombs away when Jack Crane, our bombardier, noticed that the 578th Squadron was directly below us and out of position. He asked what he should do and we decided to hold the bombs and not jeopardize any crews below us. It was expedient that we remain in the flow with the rest of the planes and so deviated slightly, with the group following us, and dropped the bombs on what appeared to be a sugar beet factory south of Germunden and along the railroad. When the bombs hit, the whole sky seemed alive with flying debris and we wondered what the innocent sugar beet factory really was. On our return both Lorin Johnson and Leon Johnson were very upset that we were the only group that did not drop on the primary target. Later the strike photos and intelligence revealed it was one of the main ammunition storage dumps.

The 577th Squadron was called in to do a low level supply mission on September 18, 1944 to the 82nd Airborne Division that had been dropped in the early morning at Best, Holland, and were in trouble. We had not trained for the low level mission and so were surprised that we were going. I had just returned to the base from leave, and as I came to the gate was told to get in the jeep and that I was flying a mission that day. I was stripped of my clothes, put on my flying suit, and climbed into the plane without benefit of a briefing. Since my copilot had not returned from leave, Benny Hunsacker flew as my copilot, reading me the necessary information regarding the mission as we took off. As we approached the mainland we could see that the German army had broken the dikes, had moved barges on the Wilhelmina Canal equipped with guns and had armed soldiers in the windmills who were putting a lot of shells into our plane. At that point we dropped below the top of the windmills and had to go up and over the power lines. Rudy Boettcher was in the nose and was absolutely sure we were going to hit the lines. He threw his papers up in the air and was prepared for the worst. The gunners were ordered to shoot at every windmill as we approached, and we watched the German soldiers jumping out of them for a 15 foot fall to the ground. The farmers were driving their wagons loaded with hay, and most of them had lost control of their horses which were scared to death, although the farmers were waving. The school children, on their way home from school, were waving orange handkerchiefs/bandanas which was refreshing to see. However, we were there for more serious business. As we approached the drop area, the squadron in front of us had two planes go down; the lead and deputy lead, and about that time a P-47 fighter pointed his nose at us. We gave the order to the gunners to shoot. When we got back to our base, my crew informed me that there was someone wanting to see me. I had been making out a Form One report for Frenchy in regards to some damage to our plane. When I came out, this person who was still in his flight suit without any identification, was obviously very upset and was "chewing" us out. Later, in debriefing, the same individual was with our commanding officer and he introduced himself. It was Gen. Kepner, and he was standing in front of a directive that he had signed which instructed us to shoot at any plane that came and turned its nose into our plane - which he acknowledged. He explained that the lead plane's pilot was a friend of his, and he was trying to determine what had happened to him. He apologized to us and was a friend of our crew from then on.

October 12, 1944, our 15th mission took us to Osnabruck. We were approaching the target and our bombardier, Jack Crane, had just pushed his protective goggles up so that he could get a closer look at the bomb sight when we took a direct hit which blew the glass out of the nose and flak went into Jack's eyes. Our nose navigator, Rudy Boettcher, was sitting out in the front with no protection, Jack was badly hurt, Jim Cassity, copilot, and I were knocked out. We came to with Benny Hunsacker,

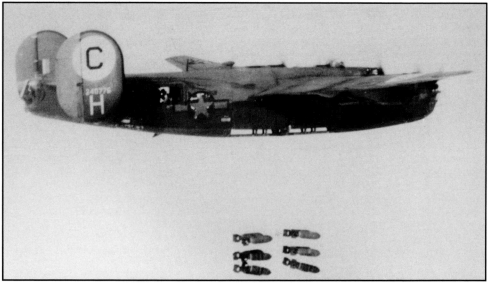

"Old Blister Butt," B-24-D. (Courtesy of Andrew Opsata)

who was along for the ride that day, hitting us on the back of the head to get us to regain consciousness from the concussion of the hit. We had lost two engines, one was out of control and the other one was still operating. When I regained consciousness, we were in a spin and Jim and I had to use every bit of strength that we had to get the ship under control. Fortunately for us, we were in the clouds and were able to avoid any action from the fighters and did make it back to the base. However, we were not sure that we could make it back, so the order was given for the enlisted men to bail out. We never knew until about 30 years later why the order was ignored. A visit from Bill Moles told Jack and me that some of the crew had forgotten their parachutes that day so the decision was to stay with the plane. Flying without a parachute is not supposed to happen at any time. Jack had several operations on his eyes and today with corrective lenses has good eyesight.

On the return from one of our missions in the summer of 1944, we put down our landing gear and upon landing discovered that we had a flat tire. This caused our plane to veer off the side of the runway, and rather than using the brakes and possibly wiping out our plane, we destroyed all of the new landing lights that had just been installed at some expense. We did not know that the inspector general was in the tower when we did this. He came up to us in debriefing and congratulated us for protecting and preserving the flyability of the plane.

Many more stories can be told but there will be others with experiences that should be included for posterity to read. I find it an opportunity to thank all of the members of my crew for their concerted effort to help in doing our job well, answering the dictates of our government to serve in the Army Air Force, and to return to our homes and families and enjoy the rest of our lives in the greatest country in the world, the United States of America.

I Remember 689

by Myron H. Keilman (392nd BG)

B-24D, #123689, was assigned to the 392nd Bombardment Group in August 1943. It had been classified "war weary" as later model airplanes became available, and it was no longer suitable for combat operations. With its distinguished markings its new mission was to lead the group in assembling the large 18 airplane formations on combat missions. While firing the designated colored flares, it orbited the radio beacon at the assigned assembly altitude until all airplanes were assembled in their assigned positions and it was time for the group to depart for the wing rendezvous.

No doubt the distinguished paint job was an experiment by some "always thinking" person— the idea being that the three silhouettes would make the real airplane difficult to discern and cause confusion to German fighter pilots as they dove their Messerschmitts and Focke-Wulfs at our bombing formations. To say the least, the idea never caught on—689 was one of a kind.

It was a 1941 vintage B-24D—the same model I piloted in 1942 on ocean patrol missions from Ecuador to the Galapagos Islands in defense of the Panama Canal. Perhaps it was one of the original 44th Bomb Group airplanes that came to England in October 1942. Perhaps 689 flew on the first bombing mission to Germany (Emden) January 23, 1943 when a FW-190 collided with the deputy lead airplane and it, with my brother, Bombardier Paul Keilman, crashed into the North Sea from 20,000 feet.

As a squadron operations officer and then a squadron commander, I don't remember that it actually served to lead the group in its assembly. That was the job of the lead crew with its command pilot.

As in the case of all old airplanes, upon the departure of the 392nd from England in June 1945, 689 was flown to Burtonwood for reclamation (scrap). It is entirely possible that the aluminum alloy of its wings, struts, wheels, skin, ribs, and empennage are still being utilized to this day in British homes, restaurants and sculleries.

Addendum: The scheme to return Army Air Force personnel to the United States on combat airplanes was never employed. I don't know how all 8th Air Force ground echelon people (they were called troops) came home, but the officers and airmen (they were called soldiers) of the 392nd, with those of other groups of the 2nd Air Division, boarded the *Queen Mary* on June 15, 1945. In five days 14,526 servicemen arrived in New York for a heroes' welcome. I was proud to be the 392nd Troop Commander.

I remember: The *Queen* never had to zig-zag in defense against Nazi submarines, and it was a very smooth voyage. We had life-boat drill once a day. We were fed two meals a day. We gambled money away in never ending games of Red Dog. Remember?

445TH BOMB GROUP
September 27, 1944
by Jack M. Erickson

September 27, 1944 began like most other days at the air base at Tibenham. It showed signs of rain as I plodded through the mud from the mess hall to the briefing room. Once everyone had arrived and were seated, the briefing got under way. The curtain was drawn back to expose the map revealing our target for today. Colored strings attached to the map indicated the routes we were to fly both to and from the target. The 445th was to mount a maximum effort mission, which would be 37 Liberators loaded with 1,000 pound general purpose (GP) bombs. Our target was the Henschel Aircraft Plant at Kassel, Germany.

When the briefing ended, I attended the radio operators briefing to receive the assigned codes of the day, as well as the operating frequencies schedule and the special instructions of the day.

Afterwards, I picked up my flight gear, parachute, Mae West, and donned my heated flying suit. I climbed aboard a 6x6 and was delivered to hard stand #40 where our assigned aircraft was parked. The plane was a B-24H still in olive drab paint. The name on the nose was *Ole Baldy*. I believe it was probably one of the oldest Liberators still operational in our group. The bulk of the planes were newer J models and were in the natural shining aluminum finish.

At the hard stand I joined the rest of the crew, which included Lt. Bill Golden, pilot; Lt. Bob Christie, copilot; Lt. Ed Boomhower, navigator; Lt. Ted Boecher, bombardier; T/Sgt. Earl Romine, engineer; Sgt. Bob Bagley, armor/gunner; Sgt. Ed Feltus, gunner; and Sgt. Norman Stewart, tail gunner.

Lt. Golden told the crew that the 445th would be leading the 2nd Combat Wing until we turned at the IP for the target.

Our crew had been reduced from 10 men to nine inasmuch as the Sperry ball turrets had been removed to reduce weight, and allow the aircraft to fly at a higher ceiling. We had been assured that the Luftwaffe was kaput, therefore the belly turret was not needed. How wrong that decision turned out to be.

Once at the aircraft, each crewman began the pre-flight inspection of those items falling into his area of responsibility. I pre-flighted all of the radio gear and pre-tuned the SCR-287 transmitter to the assigned frequency. I made sure that a flak suit and a flak helmet had been delivered to my station. I then tested my oxygen mask and plugged my electrical heated flying suit in to make sure it heated properly. It gets mighty cold at 23,000 feet. Next I checked out my Mae West to be sure it contained live CO2 cartridges. Once I was satisfied that it was in good working order, I put it on. Next I strapped

on my parachute harness and sat down at my radio position all set for another mission.

The crew chief had completed the pull through of the engines and Lt. Golden now started the #3, then the rest of the engines in proper sequence. They coughed and sputtered and emitted lots of smoke, but those big Pratt and Whitneys soon roared to life. The engines were warmed up running at 1,000 RPMs until the oil temperature reached 40 to 60 degrees centigrade.

The wheel chocks were pulled by the ground crew and we taxied away from the hard stand and got in line for take-off. Finally, we reached the end of the runway and Lt. Golden gave the engines their final run-up. The magnetos were checked, the flaps extended and the cowl flaps closed. All hatches and the bomb bay doors were secured. The brakes were released and the throttles pushed wide open and our big bird plodded down the runway to reach the 130 mph take-off speed. Soon we were leaving the ground and were airborne. The landing gear was retracted-up and locked.

Once airborne, I entered the take off time on my radio log. I then zero-beat the SCR 287 transmitter to the assigned frequency and loaded the fixed antenna. I tested the intercom system by calling each position individually and then the all station call. Everything tested okay.

For the next hour or so we continued our climb to the assembly area and once above the overcast we spotted our buncher ship and soon joined the formation for our flight to Germany.

The mission was now pretty much routine, as we had gone through this many times before, and I expected this to be a pretty normal mission with some heavy flak in the target area. A few hours later I was to find out that this was not just another mission. As it turned out, this was to be the most tragic mission in the 445th's history and probably the most disastrous raid for any single group in the AAF's history.

The weather over Germany was 10/10ths overcast and the lead navigator had to rely on navigational aids to locate the target. Upon reaching what was thought to be the initial point (IP) of the bombing run, the group turned and headed for the target. Later I was to learn that the group had missed the IP and was headed for Gottingen which was approximately 30 miles northeast of Kassel. Bomb bay doors were opened and on the signal from the lead bombardier the bombs were dropped, falling about a half mile short of Gottingen. Bomb strike observations could not be made due to the dense cloud

cover. The group now turned and circled, setting a course that would join up with the main stream of the 2nd Combat Wing for our return flight. Due to the navigational error on the IP, the group was well out of the main bomber stream, and we were on our own without fighter escort. After about 10 minutes of routine flying, we were suddenly attacked by Focke Wulf 190 fighters of the Luftwaffe's Gruppe II of Jagdeschwader 4, one of Germany's elite fighter groups. More than 100 FW190s attacked the group from below, making a head on assault in waves 10 planes wide. They had come up from beneath our formation without being observed and made their frontal attack on our vulnerable under belly.

I first saw the FW190s from the window at my radio position. They flashed by from front to rear so fast I could hardly identify them. Everywhere I looked I saw the Swatiska marked aircraft. The sky seemed to be full of them. In horror I saw our right wingman's Liberator take many hits. Debris was showering from the B-24. As it started to peel off, it suddenly broke in two just aft of the wing, and the two pieces plummeted toward the earth some 20,000 feet below. I did not see any parachutes emerge from the flaming pieces, and I assume all aboard went to their deaths.

Pivoting my stool around, I looked out through the windshield between Lt. Golden and Lt. Christie just as the lead ship of our element disintegrated. Debris from the stricken bomber was streaming back straight toward our aircraft. Instinctively I put my arms up to shield my face. I don't believe that any of the debris hit our ship as the slip stream apparently carried it above us.

The voices of our gunners were screaming fighter locations over the intercom, "Bandit at three o'clock low, enemy fighter at ten o'clock high, etc." All eight 50 caliber machine guns on our plane were firing bursts of API ammunition in an attempt to stave off the enemy fighters. Our Liberator began to shake and vibrate from the recoil of the machine gun fire.

From what I learned later, the group's gunners did a great job, and inflicted heavy losses on the Luftwaffe attackers. The 445th gunners were officially credited with the destruction of 23 FW-190s and an additional five probables. These kills, however, only represented the toll credited to the returning and surviving crews. It was known for certain that other losses were inflicted by the crews that did not make it back to base to report their hits.

Suddenly our plane shuddered as it took hits in the #3 engine. From my vantage point directly below the engine, I saw a cloud of black smoke pour out into the slip stream and metal parts flying through the air as the engine came to a stop. Lt. Golden immediately feathered the prop. A few seconds later the plane shook again as the tail turret took a direct hit by a 20mm cannon shell. Sgt. Norman Stewart, the tail gunner, was gravely wounded and removed from the shattered turret by Sgts. Bagley and Feltus.

As I looked out through my window, I saw many B-24s falling in flames. I saw several parachutes blossom out, but not nearly enough for the number of crewmen who had manned the planes going down.

In a subsequent attack, our right wing was hit in the flap area by cannon shells and a large hole was opened up near the trailing edge of the wing. I could see wires and hoses dangling into the slipstream. Lts. Golden and Christie fought the controls to keep our aircraft from going out of control.

I turned on the Liaison transmitter and quickly keyed an SOS to our home base relaying the destruction of the 445th from the Luftwaffe's onslaught.

As the intercom system was knocked out, I arose from my stool and stood next to Lt. Golden. He told me tell the crew to bail out. I nodded to him

Crew of "Miss Judy." (Courtesy of Lester E. Hix, 467th)

and turned to where Sgt. Romine was operating the Martin upper turret, located directly above my radio position. I grabbed him by the leg and gave it a quick tug. When he looked down at me, I motioned for him to jump. I then opened the door on the flight deck that led to the bomb bay and saw Bagley and Feltus looking toward me from the waist position. I signaled to them to abandon the aircraft. They quickly hooked Stewart's parachute rip cord to a static line and dropped him out through the camera hatch. They both immediately followed him out.

Lowering myself to the catwalk below the flight deck, I grabbed the bomb bay opener handle and tried to open the doors. Apparently the hydraulic system had been knocked out, for the doors didn't budge. I remembered that in case of a hydraulic failure, there was a hand crank located on the cat walk at the center of the bomb bay. I edged my way to the emergency crank and began to turn it. The doors started up but soon I couldn't move them any more. As I recall, the opening on each side of the bomb bay was only about two feet wide. No sooner had I opened the doors when Sgt. Romine dove through the opening. He was followed a few seconds later by Lt. Christie.

I then crawled along the cat walk to the nose of the plane. I opened the doors to the nose turret and helped Lt. Boecher climb out. I told both him and Lt. Boomhower to bail out through the nose wheel hatch, then quickly crawled back to the flight deck and observed Lt. Golden still at the controls. I climbed up beside him and told him that everyone else had jumped. He told me to go and I gave him a salute and turned toward the half opened bomb bay. That was the last time I ever saw him.

In the brief seconds it took me to reach the open bomb bay, the fact that I had not had my parachute inspected or repacked since my first mission flashed through my mind. Would it open and function properly? All bomber crewmen were issued detachable chest type chutes with the exception of the pilot and co-pilot who used back packs. Since my first mission to Strasbourg, when I was nearly knocked out of the open bomb bay by a piece of flak while releasing a hung up bomb with my chest chute lying on the flight deck, I had worn a seat type chute that I had scrounged and had kept in my locker. Luckily I had been wearing my flak vest and was not injured by the spent flak, although it knocked the wind out of me. I had not turned in my chute for repacking for fear of losing it. As I prepared to jump, I said a little prayer that the chute would function properly. I then dove through the opening head first. As soon as I hit the slip stream, my helmet and oxygen mask were ripped from my head. I had neglected to buckle the chin strap.

I resisted the urge to pull the ripcord at this altitude without a portable oxygen mask and bail out bottle, and took a free fall which seemed like an eternity to me. As I fell, I saw a chute far below me. I was rapidly catching up to it. The ground now seemed to rush up and I could distinguish farm houses, fields and trees below. At approximately 2,000 feet I pulled the rip cord. About two seconds later I felt a sharp, strong jolt as the canopy blossomed and bit the air. It was very reassuring to look up and see the large white expanse above me. The sudden deceleration caused my right flying boot to keep on going and I ended up with only the heated boot liner on my right foot.

I had often heard that parachutists never remember what they do with the ripcord after the chute opens. Mine was still in my hand and by God, I was going to remember what I did with mine. I stuffed it into the rear pocket of my flight suit.

As I drifted earthward, I watched the chute below me descend and land in an open area between two wooded areas. Approaching the ground, my chute drifted me right over the heads of a group of farm workers. I was barely 100 feet above them, but not one of them looked up or saw me. My chute carried me over a clump of woods where I descended into the trees where my chute snagged on the top of a pine tree and the canopy collapsed. I was left dangling about 20 feet above the ground. Grabbing the shroud lines with my right hand, I tried to lift my weight off my harness so that I could unsnap the leg harness straps with my left hand. Without warning, the limb that had snagged the chute suddenly let go and I fell to the ground, chute and all. I landed so heavily on my feet that my knees were jammed up under my chin. I apparently passed out for a few moments and when I came to I had a terrific pain in my lower back. When I stood up the pain was more acute and it was difficult to walk. I got down on my hands and knees, gathered up my chute, and buried it beneath the pine needles and leaves that I gathered from around me. I then crawled to the edge of the woods where I could see the clearing and saw the other chutist walking across the field. I picked up a dead tree limb that was laying on the ground and using it as a crutch I stood up and yelled at him. I hobbled out of the woods toward him, and it was not until I had exposed my position, that I saw a uniformed man holding a shotgun some yards behind the other airman. It was too late for me to change direction as the armed man had seen me. He waved his arm motioning me to continue over to his location. As I approached, I was very surprised to see that the other chutist was Lt. Bob Christie, our copilot.

I now took a closer look at our captor. He was wearing a funny shaped hat that was curved to fit the rear of his head like a skull cap and it had a circular crown in the front. The front of the hat was embellished with a large silver like sunburst badge. He wore a greenish gray military like tunic over riding breeches and polished knee high boots. He was an elderly man, probably in his 60s. He appeared to be very nervous and his shotgun shook as he covered Christie and me. With one hand he gave us a pat search but could find no weapons. Air crewmen in the 8th Air Force did not carry side arms at this stage of the war. We had all turned in our Colt 45 Automatics in early August this year. He did pull the rip cord from my pocket and by the expression on his face I could tell he was puzzled as to what it

was. Perhaps he thought it was some kind of a secret weapon. In a somewhat shaken voice he said to us, "For you der var is uber."

As it turned out, he was the local policeman, in fact, he was the only one in the area. He motioned to me to put down the limb I had been using for a crutch and for me to sit down on the ground. He then took Lt. Christie into the woods where I had landed to retrieve my parachute. They shortly returned with it. Apparently, I had not hidden it as well as I thought I had. He motioned for Christie to carry me piggy back, while he gathered up both chutes that he half carried and half dragged, and we started off for the local village about a quarter of a mile away.

Upon arrival in the tiny village, we were taken directly to the local jail which consisted of one small cell with a barred door and window. The cell contained two straw ticks on wooden frames. The jailer was a jovial, robust woman about 40 years old. She and the policeman quickly searched us and confiscated all of our belongings. In my case it included my GI issued wrist watch, a pack of Camel cigarettes and my cigarette lighter. The jailer was quite friendly and after the policeman departed, I coaxed her into giving me back two of my Camels that they had confiscated. I learned that the Germans called them Zigerettens. Christie and I sat down for a much needed smoke, the first since before take-off that morning. As the longest day in my life came to a close and darkness settled in, the jailer brought us each a bowl of very thin barley soup. After this, we settled down on the straw ticks to try to get some sleep, wondering what tomorrow would bring.

The entire air battle that day had lasted less than five minutes. Twenty five of the 445th 37 Liberators had been shot down at the scene of the attack. In addition, two B-24s had crashed in France, two more at Manston in England and a fifth had crashed in the vicinity of our home base at Tibenham. Only seven of the 37 Libs that bombed the target were able to make it home.

The original group casualty list showed one killed, 13 wounded and 236 crewman missing in action (MIA). By the time the war was over and the 445th was departing England, the status of the 236 MIAs indicated only 15 officers and 63 NCOs were prisoners of war (POWs). Only 13 were officially

"J" of the 489th B.G., 845th Squadron over Schulau oil refineries (Hamburg), Aug. 6, 1944. (Courtesy of C.H. Freudenthal)

G.M. Collar, POW photo taken at Stalag Luft I, Oct. 1944. Barth, Pommern, on the Baltic Sea. (Courtesy of G.M. Collar)

listed as killed in action (KIA). The group never learned the fate of the remaining 145 MIAs, and it must now be presumed that most of them had also been killed in action and their bodies never recovered or identified.

American P-51 fighters responding to the SOS finally appeared on the scene, too late to provide protection or cover for the 445th, although they did manage to destroy a number of the Luftwaffe fighter planes.

According to news reports, American P-51 fighters of the 376th Fighter Squadron, 361st Fighter Group responded to my SOS, too late to protect the bulk of the 445th Libs. The P-51s led by 1st Lt. Victor Bocquin were able to intercept several of the heavily armed FW-190s of Stormgruppe 11 JG4 and its ME-109 escorts. In an air battle that was fought between 24,000 feet and the deck, the 376th pilots in their yellow nosed P-51s shot down 18 of the enemy aircraft and probably prevented the complete annihilation of the 445th forces. One pilot, 1st Lt. William Beyer, shot down five FW-190s and Lt. Boquin destroyed three. The total of 18 credited victories by the 361st Group set a record for the total number of victories by a single group on a single day's operation.

Kassel Report
submitted by 2nd Lt. Eric W. Smith Jr.

I was with the 445th Bomb Group, 702nd Squadron, bombardier navigator and assigned to Lt. Myron Donald's crew.

The following is a description of my participation in the Kassel raid. It draws on my poorly recorded notes written shortly after the war and my very hazy memory after 48 years. I wish that I had responded to the request for data that later became the Kassel Mission Report. And I really wish that I had attended the Kassel Mission Memorial service. But I didn't, and I apologize.

The battle actually started several days before September 27, 1944, when two German jets whizzed through our formation, verifying the fact that our ball turrets had been removed. I had never seen a jet before. They didn't fire on us, just observed.

The Kassel mission started in the usual fashion. Although I was always apprehensive during missions, I had no premonition of the disaster to come. We followed our lead, dropped our bombs, and (I thought) were rallying to head home. I have no conception of the passage of time during the battle. German fighters (probably ME 109s) were making a frontal attack from about 11:00 o'clock slightly low. Then there was another pass. We were hit badly, our intercom was out, no verbal instructions, so I left my station to see what damage we had sustained. The plane was out-of-control in a spiraling glide. The tunnel was the biggest blow torch I'd ever seen. I was certain the plane would blow momentarily. I helped our bombardier, Lt. Ira Weinstein, out of the nose turret and out of the nose wheel hatch. I then grabbed my chest-chute and took the plunge.

The sky was full of crippled bombers, fighters, and parachutes. I decided to free fall out of this mess and set about doing what I should have done before leaving the plane. I buckled my chute on, but could not get my harness buckled in front. I was falling face down and my eyes were tearing from the slip-stream. By spreading my arms I was able to flip over on my back. The "crowd" was thinning out somewhat, but I decided to fall through the cloud cover before popping my chute. The clouds extended from approximately 5,000 to 6,000 feet. A fighter whizzed by and I started tumbling in the slip-stream. Extending my arms again and twisting returned me to the face-up position where I could look up and down, surveying the situation.

When I emerged from the clouds, I could see wooded areas, fields, and even people looking up. I almost waited too long. I popped at approximately 1,000 feet, closed rapidly on Mother Earth, took one wide swing and hit the ground. People were advancing. I unbuckled my chute and retreated to the woods nearby, jogged down a slight slope and took cover in a thicket to assess the situation. The Germans did not follow, probably thinking I was armed, which I wasn't. My escape kit had a map and several compasses, so I selected a heading to Denmark. The Thuringer Forest was remarkably clear of underbrush. I started jogging and soon came upon two Polish DPs cutting down a tree. We tried to communicate, but my escape kit didn't include Polish. I continued on my own and eventually tired. I took some pep pills (Benzadrine, I think) and continued on toward Denmark. At dark I stumbled on a fallen tree, crawled to the end and burrowed into the roots for concealment, planning to awake at dawn to continue my escape.

This wasn't to be. When the Benzadrine wore off, I slept like a log. I awoke about noon to the sound of a barking dog and the laughter of Volkspolice. I was captured. These were good guys, very ancient. Armed with very long and equally ancient guns similar to those used by our mountaineers of old. They marched me down the mountain to a collection station and protected me from the understandably irate citizens clustered around.

I am hazy on how I got to Dulag Luft, or even where it is located. We walked partway. By now there were maybe 20 or 30 captured airmen, including many wounded. (I was slightly wounded, but didn't know it.) Somewhere along this trek we walked through a village. In the middle of the town square was a statue of Johann Wolfgang Goethe. This might have been Erfurt, not too far from where I believe we were shot down.

We arrived at Dulag Luft after dark, in the rain, and were assembled in formation in a courtyard without protection from the rain. For reasons completely unknown to me, I was appointed squad leader, taken inside and interrogated. I was told that "my men" would be brought in out of the rain as soon as I revealed my unit number and location. However, I stuck strictly to "name, rank, and serial number" and eventually wore that guy out. I never learned what happened to "my men." The rest of the interrogation consisted of a chat and cigarette with the "nice" guy, threats from the "bullies," and Nazi zealots displaying swastikas. I was amused because this entire charade was identical to that portrayed in a training film we viewed in England.

I was put in solitary confinement for several days, then transferred to Stalag Luft 1 (on the beautiful North Sea) near Barth. That trip was memorable because our buddies in England bombed the rail yard in Frankfurt am Main while we were in it. They were so accurate, the Germans detached us from the engine, ran for cover, and left us to hope we wouldn't get hit. We weren't, but our car would bounce up and then down as a shock wave travelled down the tracks.

The rest is history. I cherish the experience, but do not want to ever repeat it. My kriege days are over.

William L. Vance Jr.
by Judy Vance Garren

Following is a story of my search for the missing link of my father's life, his time spent in service during the war, and for someone who might have known him.

I was 18 months old when my father was killed. He was home when I was born and received a short three day furlough in August 1944, just before going overseas. I have tried so hard to remember him... I have a vague picture in my distant memory of sitting in a chair in my Grandmother's living room, being held by a man in uniform, and getting ice cream on his uniform. Although I had two uncles who were also in the service at that time, I hold on to the belief that this was my father, William L. Vance Jr. (Chub). His last request to his mother was that she care for my mother and me until he returned. I lived with my grandmother until I was 16 years old. I used to ask her about my father, but it would make her cry, so I finally stopped asking. She told me she had some things in her cedar chest belonging to my father that she wanted me to have after her death.

When I lost my dear Grandmother in 1984, only then was I able to have the mementos she had saved for me: his high school annual, a boxing trophy, photographs, his medals, report cards from grade school and the folded flag that was on his casket at funeral services long after the war. Also included was a typed sheet listing nine men, the crew of my father's plane: 1st Lt. John D. Barringer Jr., 2nd Lt. Robert D. Levy, Flight Officer Paul J. Juliano, 2nd Lt. Norman F. Brunswig, S/Sgt. Joseph F. Black, S/Sgt. Eugene J. Sullivan, Sgt. Roland C. Lyons Jr., Sgt. Eldon R. Personette, and Sgt. William L. Vance Jr. Among these items also were letters from the War Department, giving me enough information to begin my search for anything I could find about my father, but more importantly, anyone who knew him during the war.

I wrote to the National Personnel Records Center in St. Louis, only to learn that my father's military records had been destroyed in a fire in 1973. I was able to obtain recently declassified microfilm from Maxwell AFB, which confirmed that my father and the entire crew, had in fact, gone down with the plane, and all but two, my father and one other, were interred in a mass grave.

In February 1984 a co-worker, who was a WWII veteran, supplied me with a roster from the 2nd Air Division Association, and I wrote a letter to approximately 150 members of the 445th Bombardment Group, picked at random. Unfortunately, none of the people I contacted had known my father, but the wonderful, warm letters I received in response became as treasured to me as if they had been my father's best friend.

One of those letters went to Buddy Cross in Amarillo, Texas. He hadn't known my father, but he offered to request my letter be included in the next 2nd Air Division Association quarterly newsletter. Still no luck. In September Buddy wrote that he would be attending the 2nd Air Division Association reunion in Palm Springs in October and would continue to search for someone who knew my father.

On October 24, 1984, I received a letter from Ford P. Tracey, Saratoga, California. He was the original pilot and flew the first eight combat missions with my father's crew. The crew was then transferred to Lt. Barringer to become a lead crew. Mr. Tracey sent me some photographs of the crew, which to my astonishment, matched the photographs from my grandmother's cedar chest. We corresponded back and forth, and in March of 1988, my husband and I flew to California to meet Ford and his wife personally. When he opened the door, I immediately felt that I was with "family," and as we embraced, I knew I had found someone very special. Ford Tracey gave me something not another human on earth could give me, a piece of my father's life. He visited with my husband and me in Tennessee in October of 1989, and I was so terribly saddened by his death in 1991. There is no way I could ever describe what our friendship meant to me.

One member of the crew, Sgt. Herman F. Zimmer, the ball turret gunner, was not listed with those that were killed. According to Ford Tracey, Zimmer was ill and did not go on the November 26 mission. He was later assigned as gunnery training NCO in the 445th. My search continues for Herman F. Zimmer.

446TH BOMB GROUP
A Day To Remember! D-Day

by Robert A. Jacobs

The Tannoy sounded at 0230 hours on June 5, 1944, as the crew of the *Liberty Run* was awakened to fly its 24th mission. Originally from the 93rd Bomb Group, Lt. Litwiller's crew has been selected for PFF (pathfinder) training with the 564th Bomb Squadron of the 389th Bomb Group, Hethel in April 1944. I was the DR navigator. Our remaining missions were flown out of Hethel as a PFF crew flying lead or deputy lead for other groups, but most often with the 93rd. This mission was to the Pas de Calais area, a most welcome short haul with no fighters and little flak observed.

We returned to Hethel just after noon and learned that hot water was available in the "ablutions." This was an infrequent occurrence, and most of us made a beeline for the showers. While bathing, our crew was paged on the Tannoy, told to report to the briefing room immediately, ready to fly (which we did) to Flixton, home of the 446th Bomb Group. There we were met by armed MPs and taken to a secured building. Upon entry we were informed that tomorrow, June 6, 1944, was "D" day. To say that we were excited would be a gross understatement. This was what we had been waiting for and the adrenalin was flowing. Our mission was to lead the 446th Bomb Group to bomb the invasion beaches of Normandy, immediately prior to the ground assault. During the briefing we learned that the 446th was to lead the 8th Air Force on the first "D" day strike.

We took off at 0220, climbed to 10,000 feet, and circled in our prescribed forming area while our engineer fired the specific colored signal flares as the 446th aircraft assembled in formation behind us. The mission went precisely as planned with the briefed undercast necessitating bombing by H2X radar. As we approached the French coast, the radar navigator called me over to look at his PPI scope. It

showed clearly the vast armada of the invasion fleet standing just off the coast of Normandy, a thrilling sight even on radar. As we crossed the coast, the airborne commander, Col. J.J. Brogger, was flying off our wing. Bombs were away at 0600! We led our formation back to Bungay via Portland Bill and returned to Hethel.

As we started to undress for a well-deserved rest, we were again paged and subsequently told to get over to Bungay for another mission. We had been up for some 36 hours and we were running on reserve energy. During the briefing, the flight surgeon gave each of us a pill with the instruction to take it only. "...when you feel you can no longer keep awake..."

Shortly after take-off my eyelids began to get very heavy. Since we were again leading aircraft of the 446th Bomb Group, I needed to have all faculties clear so I took my pill. Shortly thereafter, all signs of weariness disappeared and I was again able to perform my navigation tasks. We flew to Coutances, dropped our bombs and returned to the English coast without incident, above a solid undercast. At landfall, I gave the pilot a heading for Bungay and relaxed.

The next thing that I recall was being shaken rather violently by my engineer. He finally managed to convey that the pilot was calling me over the intercom. The pill had worn off and I had fallen sound asleep. My pilot informed me that he had been directed by the British Ground Controllers to circle and let down below the clouds so that our formation could be identified visually. There was fear of German intruder aircraft. The formation was now at 1,000 feet and the pilot wanted a new heading for Bungay. There I was, the lead navigator, feeling half drugged, without the foggiest notion of our position. What to do? I told him to contact the deputy lead and obtain a heading from his navigator while I attempted to sort out where we were. We were apparently too low to receive GEE because I could not pick up any station clearly. By this time it was dark so the pilotage navigator in the nose turret could not help.

The heading obtained from the deputy lead put us on a track due east. My first action was to find out exactly when the formation let-down started; thus, I was able to compute a very rough DR position. Around this point I drew a circle whose radius was the maximum distance we could have travelled from the let-down area. We were somewhere in the circle, about 50 to 80 miles due west of London and heading straight for Piccadilly according to my best estimate. I called the pilot and told him to monitor frequency 6440 for balloon barrage squeakers.

In the meantime I continued to work with the GEE set and was finally able to pick up one station. Just about then the pilot called on the intercom to tell me he had picked up the squeaker transmissions. I immediately gave him a new heading for Bungay. Then for the first and only time during my combat tour, I used the single station homing procedure that we had been taught at Cheddington when our crew first arrived in the U.K. It worked beautifully, and we came across the blue perimeter lights of Flixton just as the second blip aligned with the first. The second station had come in about 10 minutes out of Bungay. A quick peel-off and we were back on the ground at Hethel, time 2345. It had been a very long day!

"Banger" Crew
#302-7-65

by Irving Day (446th)

Banger was a faithful old friend named after his pilot and his bombardier, who brought their brides to Lowry Field following their marriages during pre-embarkation leave (presumably because

bombs go "Bang!" when deployed). On April 11, 1944, *Banger* was recovering from battle damage, so this crew was assigned to B-24H 42-7572 *"Werewolf/Princess O'Rourke."* *Werewolf* was so named by his regular crew of Capt. James M. Wylie and the right side nose art depicted a ferocious black wolf. While still training in Denver, a publicity crew for Jane Wyman's movie *Princess O'Rourke* came to Lowry seeking a typical patriotic backdrop to lure the patrons of 1943. With proper permission, they painted the second name on the left side nose together with a picture of a cute black Scotty puppy named Princess O'Rourke. They took their pictures with a pup obtained from a Denver pet store, presented the dog to the crew, and departed. Soon, plane, crew and "Princess" were en route to England.

So on that fateful April 11, what was probably the only B-24 Liberator with two names and nose arts, was destroyed by enemy anti-aircraft fire near Dummer Lake, Germany. Lt. Tuck's crew bailed out and were quickly rounded up. A second 446th aircraft, *Brown Noser*, piloted by 1st Lt. Kermit A. Fuchs was lost at that same location, but only the bombardier, 2nd Lt. Philip R. Wescott got out.

Shortly after capture, these crewmen were taken to the sites of three crashed bombers and were required to remove the remains of the crews killed in the action. It is believed that Lt. Wescott participated in recovering bodies of his fellow crewmen; an experience which haunted him for the short remainder of his life.

These five officers sweated out the 13 months of hostilities in North Compound I of Stalag Luft I, Barth, Pomerania, Germany. The NCOs were held in other camps and endured many hardships before final repatriation.

Banger and *Werewolf* are both listed in the Honor Crew section of the Collings Foundation's B-24J "All American" which many have seen during its tours of the U.S. Irving Day is listed as lead crew bombardier and Marin Stoddard Day (Irv's bride) is honored in the Distinguished Flying Command section as representative of the many ladies on the home front who waited and worried while their menfolk were facing the perils of war. Irv's principal souvenirs of World War II are his parachute rip cord handle and his Caterpillar Club pin.

For You The War
Is Over

by E. Sherman (446th)

It was July 20, 1944, the place was Flixton Estate, home of the 446th Bomb Group, a couple of miles south of Bungay in East Anglia, England. The mission for the next day was rocket launching sites in the Pas de Calais region of France. These missions were known as "milk runs" because of their short duration and the bomb release point being out over the English Channel. Glen, Nelson and I had attended a special briefing in the evening, as we were to lead the 446th Bomb Group.

When we walked into the briefing room early on the morning of the 21st (my 25th birthday), the long red tape on the briefing map really set us back. It extended deep into southern Germany. The target was Munich, not the rocket launch sites. This was a nasty twist. We could be late for my party at the club that night (little did we know then that we would miss all the fun). This was to be Glen's last mission, #30. Lead crew personnel were required to fly five fewer missions because we only flew when we led our squadron and/or the group. This put us way behind regular crews in missions flown over a given length of time. We still acquired ample flying time, being scheduled to fly the weather plane, group forming plane and pre-flighting our plane the day before we were scheduled to lead. The rest of the crew had 27 missions. This was our 28th mission

(Courtesy of Russell R. Leslie, 389th)

together. We felt good about each other. I considered Nelson Segraves to be the equal of any bombardier I had known. Glen Hoffman was an excellent navigator. The enlisted men were tops. There were T/Sgt. Lutes, flight engineer; T/Sgt. Kopcynski, radio operator; and gunners: S/Sgts. Jackson, Olson, McDonald and Clay. And on this mission the copilot was Lt. Hand and our group navigator, Capt. C. Ballard was in the nose turret to do dead reckoning navigation.

So off we go on a scheduled 10 hour mission instead of the four and a half hour "milk run" we had hoped for. Our planned altitude was 21,000 feet, but as we crossed into Germany, we encountered a high weather front. Visibility dropped fast and the other groups faded out of sight. We tried to climb over the weather, but the plane topped out at 25,500 feet and responded to the controls like a drunk whale, while the clouds persisted. I decided to turn back and find a "target of opportunity." Occasionally we saw puffs of flak in the clouds, but never quite close enough to hear the bursts. It was an eerie situation. As we completed our 180° turn and let down, we broke into the clear at 20,000 feet. I looked around to see how many planes were still with us. It appeared that our squadron was alone, and, according to the waist gunners, we had picked up a few planes from other groups.

Glen checked the map and then exclaimed that immediately ahead of us was a bridge crossing an unknown river. This was to be our "target of opportunity." The bomb bay doors were opened and we made a straight run on the bridge. Our bombs were on target, according to those who could see the results.

Now let's get home. We were the first planes to be returning "thru the pass" (over Ostend) on this day. The first bursts occurred just as we started our let down toward the channel. It put an oil leak in #1 engine and Glen said he had been hit in the back by a fragment. I immediately started a slow turn to the left (you can't forget your formation) and feathered the damaged engine. Two more shells exploded under the plane, probably killing those below the flight deck level and setting fire to the plane. The copilot got out of his seat and disappeared into the smokey radio compartment. The intercom was dead and the

flying controls nonexistent. I got out of my seat, but had forgotten to remove my oxygen mask and was jerked back. After I released myself, I turned into the radio compartment full of flame which again drove me back to my seat. After a short interval, I looked again and the compartment was clear. I got up, took two steps, when I remembered that we were close to the channel. Again I returned to my seat, this time to get my "Mae West" life jacket from behind the seat and realized I still had my flak vest on. I removed the flak vest, donned the "Mae West" and returned to an empty radio compartment. The bomb bay was closed but the top hatch was open. I put my upper body out the hatch and my parachute hung up. (I had the only seat pack left in our group). I experienced no sensation of air passing by and somehow I was finally free falling. (I had always felt that the plane turned over, but subsequent information that it blew up convinced me that that was what set me free of the plane.) I counted to six and pulled the rip cord. It opened at what I guessed to be about 12,000 feet over the Scheldt Estuary. I guided my parachute by tentatively pulling on the shroud lines. This skill paid off, and I guided my chute right over a chimney. Fortunately the houses on the isle of Tholen were built close to the ground, and I managed to kick away from the chimney. I landed alongside the house with my toes just barely touching the ground. Friendly people rushed up to assist me in getting out of the chute harness. They brought a chair and a glass of water. (What a relief to escape the chute leg straps. The descent had taken what seemed like forever.) Then as if by signal, everyone disappeared and moments later German soldiers came running from both ends of the narrow lane. They were reasonably friendly and put me in a 1939 Ford converted to a charcoal burning engine. We visited several locations where parts of the plane had hit. (Shortly after I opened my parachute, a part of the plane I took to be an aileron fluttered down on fire and descending faster then my chute, another near miss as it was less than 25 feet away.) They then took me to a "dugout" where Sgt. Lutes was also brought. We were told that Lt. Hand was dead. Sgt. Lutes told me that the bomb bay was on fire so he opened the top hatch when Lt. Hand appeared. He started out the top hatch and collapsed, so Sgt. Lutes

pushed him out and followed him. Sgt. Kopcynski was still looking for his chest pack parachute when Lutes jumped. (Subsequent info from Sgt. Kopcynski after the war was that he also went out the top hatch and hit one of the rudders. He spent the remainder of the war in a German hospital and was permanently crippled. This explains why the radio deck was vacant when he made his escape.) Lutes noticed that my flight jacket right sleeve was covered with blood. It wasn't mine so it must have been Lt. Hand's. He must have suffered a bad wound. The rest of the crew never got out. Why not? Maybe killed or severely wounded by the flak bursts. Sgt. Lutes was untouched. I just suffered second degree burns on my face and hair. Sgt. Kopcynski would also have been okay if he hadn't hit the tail on leaving the plane. What's called the flight deck was the place to be to survive, but not for Lt. Hand. Who decided who is to live or die? Is it fate, chance or God's hand?

While waiting for their orders, one of the soldiers (who turned out to be conscripted Austrians) gave me a sort of yellowish colored coarse bar to eat. It tasted awful and after one bite I hid the rest. He also returned my cigarettes and lighter. Shortly after, a Nazi officer appeared and started berating the soldiers. Though I didn't understand German, much was obvious by his tone of voice. However, I did manage to understand "Yankee schweinhundt" as he slapped a cigarette out of my mouth and confiscated the package and Zippo lighter laying close by. He then laid considerable verbal abuse on me, but my ignorance of the language was my protection.

They put Sgt. Lutes and me in the local jail for the night. The next day we were driven to a prison in Arnhem, Holland. After five days of solitary, we and several other POWs were placed on a train for our journey along the beautiful Rhine River to "Dulag Luft" at Frankfurt am Main, Germany. It was a clearing house for all POWs. Five days in solitary in a very compact cell (5X9) was followed by interrogation by a gregarious German who had my complete military history at his fingertips.

The following day, I was transferred to an open compound and saw Sgt. Lutes for the last time. The next morning we were shipped out to our final home for the duration. My destination was Barth, Germany, about 90 miles north of Berlin. The new home was called Stalag Luft I. Several members of my group were permanent POWs. My face had healed, the weather was fine, and my friends needed a short-stop for their fast pitch softball team (equipment furnished by the YMCA), and the Red Cross food parcels provided an adequate, if not exciting diet. We even played a tough game of two hand touch football that the Germans finally stopped because of broken or bent limbs.

Along about November the "Country Club" atmosphere ended. The war was going badly for the Germans (our secret radio and internal communications system kept us abreast). The Allied air strikes were bringing German trains to a standstill, and, with that, no Red Cross food parcels or packages from home. Now our daily sustenance was a slab of very coarse brown bread (about one inch thick) and a handful of dehydrated vegetables with an occasional bowl of wormy barley and ersatz coffee.

When the Russians overran the Barth area, they tore down our fences and gave us meat (horse or cow, no one cared) and released a cache of Red Cross food parcels found at the camp headquarters. We finally ate well again. But the devious politics of the Communists started their "Cold War" tactics and for three weeks they would not permit our Air Force to fly in planes to evacuate us. Finally it happened. Those beautiful B-17s (even to a B-24 pilot) landed at a nearby airfield and we marched over to board them and fly to Camp Lucky Strike in France. "Home Alive in '45."

448TH BOMB GROUP
Flying Back On A Time Capsule

by Ben S. Daniel (448th)

After 45 years (1945-1990), I have made the "command decision" to blow the whistle for a referee time-out, to reflect, to collect my thoughts and share some memories of my World War II Army Air Corps flying crew, as a tribute to them, especially to my pilot Forrest F. Anderson, also a member of the 2nd Air Division Association, 448th Bombardment Group.

Our air crew, of which names follow, met one another for the first time in August 1944 in Omaha, Nebraska: Forrest F. Anderson, pilot, Gallantin, Tennessee; Arthur R. Seat Jr., copilot, Virgiline, Virginia; Frank W. Leonard, navigator, Meridan, Idaho; Jerome Brown, bombardier, Chicago, Illinois; Harry Hutchinson, engineer, Dayton, Ohio; Ben S. Daniel, radio gunner, Chicago, Illinois; Charles E. Schmucker, aerial gunner, Denver, Colorado; John W. Wideman, aerial gunner, Woodstock, Illinois; Elberon G. Andrews, aerial gunner, Cortland, Ohio; Douglas J. Fowler, aerial gunner, Atlanta, Georgia.

Like any military formation, our crew was made up of persons from all walks of life. We learned very quickly that the main purpose, the objective and bottom line, was that the group conduct itself in a team effort by executing its duties and responsibilities in a cohesive military manner. We were assigned to three months of intensive combat air crew training exercises at Casper, Wyoming. These consisted of continued ground school training in respective responsibilities for related emergency procedures, of flying at different periods within the day, of formation flying, as well as bombing and aerial gunnery exercises. This was the crucial time period to determine if our combat alertness and our ability to act and react under all possible combat situations met the requirements. We got to know one another, officers and enlisted men, during this intense period, as to our personalities, strengths and weaknesses. As I recall we were a group of happy "characters," enjoying our camaraderie. (I sincerely hope my group will have the opportunity to read this article. As of this date they are not all members of the 2nd Air Division Association.) Our pilot, 2nd Lt. Forrest F. Anderson, was our leader and we respected him highly as an individual, an officer and an expert flyer. In flying the great B-24, he had a perfect record of making each landing on the first attempt. We graduated from combat air crew training at Casper, Wyoming in the fall of 1944, and were immediately ordered to Topeka, Kansas to pick up our B-24M Liberator Bomber.

It was a strange feeling when we arrived at Topeka, Kansas to see the beautiful new B-24s lined up, wondering which would be assigned to us. In due time we were assigned to bomber serial #44-50718. I often wonder where it is today? During this time the song, *Rum 'n Coke*, made famous by the Andrews Sisters was very popular and without hesitation we named our new B-24 after the song. We had our crew photograph taken with the inscription, "Rum 'n Coke" on both sides of the aircraft, and mailed it to the Andrews Sisters for their autograph. Either we had the wrong address or our photograph got lost in the shuffle or... who knows why; we did not get it back. After a week of flying the *Rum 'n Coke* to become familiar with this aircraft, we were ordered to Grenier Field, New Hampshire for an overseas assignment. I remember the comfortable and confident feeling each time I heard the four Pratt & Whitney engines start, taxi and take off in the "Wild Blue Yonder." During the morning we took off for Grenier Field. Before takeoff, we borrowed a jeep to carry a load on the plane, consisting of enough barrack mattresses for the crew to rest for the eventual long journey to the 8th Air Force in England. As the radio operator, I purposely selected special radio programs with the popular music of the time so the crew could listen and relax on the flight between Topeka, Kansas and Grenier Field, New Hampshire, which took about three hours. They appreciated the selections.

As we flew from Kansas to New Hampshire, crossing part of this great country of ours, we enjoyed the scenery and commented on its majestic beauty. Landing at Grenier Field was a thrill and a first for most of us. It was a short lay-over, for the following morning we were briefed for our flight to Goose Bay, Labrador. Whoever heard of Goose Bay, Labrador?

As we lined up for take-off that morning, our pilot, Lt. Anderson, reminded us we were leaving the United States. I don't recall what prevailed—excitement, thrill and/or fright? That afternoon we landed at Goose Bay, Labrador, after flying over parts of beautiful Canada. At Goose Bay we were briefed, shown a film on what we would expect to see on approaching our next stop at Bluie West #1, Greenland. The various fjords were pointed out as checkpoints, on our approaching to the landing field. We stayed at Bluie West #1 for several days because of bad weather conditions and prepared for our next flight to Reykjavik, capital of Iceland. (Who would guess in future years it would be the meeting place for President Reagan and Mr. Gorbachev.) During our stay at Bluie West #1, we were captivated by the beautiful Northern Lights in the evening. What a beautiful and unforgettable sight, and to think the other half of the earth was in full daylight. After our short stay at Bluie West #1, we took off for Reykjavik, Iceland, crossing the cold North Atlantic Ocean, and landed at Reykjavik within a few hours. We were restricted to the air base, since we were subject to an immediate call. After a day, we were briefed for our final destination—Valley, Wales.

Between Iceland and Valley, Wales, we realized that we were finally in a combat zone. We arrived at Valley and were very disappointed when we had to give up the *Rum 'n Coke* for a plane modified for combat missions. Our crew immediately took a train to Blackpool for an assignment to a bomb group. Regretfully, here we had to bid farewell to F/O Jerome Brown, our bombardier, who was reassigned to another group, since the 8th Air Force was converting navigators to "togglers" (bomb load was released by a navigator after observing the lead bombardier trigger the action.) So our navigator, Lt. Frank Leonard, had a dual role on our missions, primarily a navigator and a "toggler" during the bomb run over the target.

At Blackpool we were assigned to the 20th Combat Wing, 448th Bombardment Group (Heavy), 713th Bombardment Squadron (Heavy), which was located at Seething Airfield near Norwich (northeast part of England). Two crews of enlisted men occupied each small barrack. Our crew replaced a bomber crew which had been shot down over Magdeburg, Germany. It was a strange feeling, walking into the barracks as a replacement crew to meet the crew whose friends had been shot down. We got to know each other and became close friends over a period of time. During this period we flew on practice missions over the English countryside and as weather observers over the North Sea.

Our first bombing mission was to be over Brunswick, Germany. The frightening thrill was checking our 50 caliber machine guns the night before the mission, arising early the following morning, having breakfast, listening intently to our briefing, attending our respective religious services, picking up our flight gear, getting in a truck and riding out to our assigned B-24J. No enemy over the target that day, but a lot of flak from below. We had made our first run!

Our second bombing mission ended in a comedy of errors. The assigned target was an ordnance depot in Bayreuth, Germany. Because of adverse weather conditions over England, each plane took off and flew independently south of England, passing over the White Cliffs of Dover. At this point, I realized that my radio transmitter and receiver were not operating effectively. At the same time, our navigator, Lt. Leonard, indicated his radar equipment was inoperative. But we continued on with a left turn to form with our squadron, group and combat wing over France. Above France, after getting into an attack formation, we turned north toward Germany. However, the bad weather over England had entered the air space over continental Europe, forcing our bombing units to disperse and abort the mission. On our way back to England, without our radio and radar equipment operating effectively, we decided to land at the 361st P-51 Fighter Group in Mons, Belgium, near the French border. We were served lunch, while our radio and radar equipment were repaired by the ground crew specialists. We extended our thanks for the hospitality shown by the fighter group personnel and took off for our home base in England. I identified our aircraft over the English Channel with the Main Control Radio Contact of the 8th Air Force, and received permission to continue to our base at Seething Airfield. We dropped our bomb load over the English Channel to avoid any possible explosion on landing. After landing, we were directed to taxi to a stall (parking space) about a half a mile from the control tower. At the same time, other planes from our group were returning from a similar fate. We waited for over an hour for a truck to pick us and our flying gear up. This is when the day's comedy of errors almost ended in a tragedy. We were all frustrated for lack of attention from the control tower to send someone to get us back to the debriefing room. For some unknown reason, I returned to our plane, got the Very (flare) pistol, and shot it in the air to get the tower's attention. As the colored flare descended, it began drifting in the direction of the gasoline trucks that were refueling our parked planes. I quickly blew the whistle, which all combat flying crews wear on the collar of their flight jackets to keep the crew together in the event of a bail-out over a body of water. The high pitch alerted the crew and it was every man for himself, fleeing in every direction, including the refueling crew. I froze unable to move while I watched this pending explosion, but "thank God" the descending flare overshot the refueling truck and three planes in their respective stalls by 20 yards. For me, it was a long ride back to our debriefing room.

Later, Lt. Anderson calmly read off the "riot act" to our navigator and myself for the day's events. (We should have checked our radio and radar equipment before take-off that morning.) It was only our second combat mission attempt but we matured in a hurry.

Our remaining missions involved much flak and several encounters with ME-109s (propeller driven) and ME-262s (jet propulsion driven). At times during slack periods, just for laughs, we recalled our second mission and how we almost caused a disaster. We flew our group's final combat mission on April 25, 1945, attacking the marshaling yards in Salzburg, Austria. That mission was over eight hours, including five hours of oxygen usage. It was a successful one.

The war ended in Europe within two weeks of our final combat mission. Thereafter it was a countdown of when we would return home, despite rumors that we would be flying directly to the conflict in the Pacific Theater. It did not happen. During the next few months, the planes were serviced

L to R: Dale Downs, Don Webster, Chas. Healy, Dick Beaulieu, Sonny Howard, Gabe Signorelli, Harold Smith, Al Jenkins, Bill Ruth, Len Armstrong. Horsham St. Faith, Norwich, England, Sept. 26, 1944. (Courtesy of Charles F. Healy)

to return home. In the meantime, we flew ground personnel at low level over continental Europe to observe the devastation that took place over the years. A frightening sight for all of us.

Finally, the day arrived for us to return home. Our first stop was the Azores in mid-Atlantic Ocean, and then on to Bangor, Maine. An additional 10 ground personnel returned with each air crew. It was a new experience for all of us. We landed on United States soil in June 1945 and were given 30 day furloughs. We regrouped in Sioux Falls, South Dakota, where I first attended radio school. While here, in August 1945, the war with Japan ended. We were then reassigned to different air bases before being discharged.

In closing, I want to thank my pilot, Forrest F. Anderson for his leadership and flying ability, and my air crew for being an important part of a major step towards patriotism and team effort, which I consider strengthened my values and continued to work for me in my lifetime. Also a heartfelt thanks to the charter members and officers of the 2nd Air Division Association for having the foresight and vision to create this opportunity to have our moments of reflection and keep our story alive.

God bless us, everyone.

Account Of Crew 64, 715th Sqdn., 448th BG

by Douglas Skaggs

This is an account of several events during World War II which shaped the lives of 10 young men from various parts of the country and ranging in age from 18 to 25 years. Just 14 months of our lives together forged a strong bond which has blossomed over the years. Some of our experiences will be familiar to many other crews while some may be rather uncommon. We survived two crash landings, once when the plane ran out of fuel and the other when the plane was shot up and on fire. During our 30 combat missions, one member was killed by flak, one was shot through the leg by an ME-109 .30 calibre slug, a flak burst showered splinters into the face of another member, two others suffered frost bite, while another escaped with only minor burns, but painful bruises from one of the crash landings.

Most of our crew members were instructors in their specialties and were experienced in the B-17 before being assigned to the crew. Flight Engineer George Glevanik, for example, was an instructor in aircraft mechanics, hydraulics and emergency equipment as well as a B-17 flight engineer instructor. He had also survived a crash when the pilot of his B-17 lost control on landing, bounced off the runway into a parked B-17 and crashed head-on into the paint shop. Both the plane and shop caught on fire and there were several casualties, but he was unharmed.

Our crew may have been the only 2nd AD "original," "Model," "Lead" crew to stay intact throughout a combat tour.

The 448th Group was formed May 25, 1943 at Gowen Field in Boise, Idaho with Col. James M. Thompson as the commander. The nucleus of a Model crew was selected for each of the four squadrons; Crew #1 for the 712th and our Crew #4 (later #64) for the 715th.

From Boise we went to Orlando to attend the School of Applied Tactics; to Wendover Field, Utah for further training and to round out our crew members; thence to Sioux City, Iowa for final training before going overseas.

While at Sioux City, Engineer George Glevanik went with another crew to Kansas to pick up a new plane, with less than eight hours flying time, which was to be our (Crew 64) combat plane to take overseas. Upon his return early the next morning, he turned over the manuals etc. to Operations and went to the barracks for some sleep. However, he was awakened a short time later with instructions to join his crew now at the flight line for a training flight. Upon his arrival, the other members had completed their pre-flights, started the engines, and were ready for the mission. Ground personnel assured Glevanik that the plane had been re-serviced, re-fueled, and was ready to go. This training mission was to be rather extensive; including cross-country navigation, practice bomb runs, and low-level air-to-ground gunnery. Therefore, he made a quick engine check, boarded the plane and double checked the fuel gages before the flight.

As we were completing the last phase of the mission, low-level gunnery, Glevanik and Navigator Don Todt made another check of fuel consumption. The sight gages showed normal consumption with some 1600 gallons remaining in the tanks, enough for several hours of flying. However, as we started a power climb towards cruising altitude, the engines began to sputter. We leveled off while Glevanik rechecked the engine instruments, fuel level, etc., which all looked just fine. But again as we started to climb, the engines began to miss; whereupon Glevanik reported "fuel problems" and "head for the nearest field."

Todt usually spotted emergency fields on his charts and quickly gave a heading to the only nearby airfield. This was a small field near Vermillion, South Dakota, some 30 miles northwest of Sioux City. We soon lost two engines and Glevanik tried feeding all tanks into the remaining two engines. Todt sighted the airfield just as the last two engines were sputtering to a stop. This "emergency air field" turned out to be a flat alfalfa field with no prepared landing strip. We managed to head into it upwind for a dead-stick landing but we soon ran out of airfield. The adjoining field was a similar flat hay field which appeared to be separated only by a wire fence, but as we rapidly approached we could see that it was several inches higher and there was a drainage ditch along the far side of the fence.

Copilot Ben Baer had locked the brakes but the green alfalfa provided little traction. Glevanik called to release the brakes and kill the master switch but as we hit the fence and ditch, both the left gear and nose wheel collapsed. We managed to steer the fuselage between two haystacks almost straight ahead where the right wing hit close to the top of one haystack and bounced over it while the left wing and #1 engine hit the other, smaller, haystack and went through it.

Moments later, as we came to a stop just beyond the haystacks, nine young men covered with hay and dust scrambled from the plane (Tail Gunner Bill Jackson was on furlough at this time). We were a bit shaken up but no one needed medical treatment.

In a few minutes some local ranchers and their wives began to arrive with first aid equipment, sandwiches, and drinks. They were very hospitable and helped us call the base. Base personnel, including the base engineering officer, began to arrive some time later. Glevanik made it a point to show the fuel gages to the engineering officer and it was later determined that they gave faulty readings due to an air lock. This plane had to be salvaged but we learned to always, and personally, check the fuel tanks and top them off if they were not completely filled.

This crash landing occurred about midafternoon on October 4, 1943. Possibly the Board of Inquiry thought we had done a fairly good job as three weeks later Pilot Skaggs was promoted to first lieutenant and Engineer Glevanik was promoted to master sergeant.

The Missing Of The Ludendorff Bridge

by Thomas L. McQuoid (448th)

On the last day of 1944, the 448th Bomb Group (H), 715th Bomb Squadron, was assigned the task of destroying the Ludendorff Bridge at Remagen, Germany. Fifty-six B-17, Flying Fortresses had missed it the day before. The destruction of the bridge was considered to be very important to stalling the advance of the German ground forces. The Ludendorff Bridge was one of the few major bridges still intact across the Rhine River. It was a principal supply and reinforcement route for the Wehrmacht offensive through the Ardennes in their effort to split the Allied forces; therefore, it was very important to block that route. Starting on December 28 the bridge was a target for both B-17s and B-24s for six consecutive days. The English weather had moderated somewhat allowing the bombers to take off, but bombing conditions in Germany were poor. The Remagen Bridge from an altitude of about twenty thousand feet presented a very small target even for visual bombing, much less on Gee-H radar. Those conditions undoubtedly accounted for the unsuccessful strikes from the Fortresses and Liberators.

General Patton's tanks had made a break through in the German lines to the west of Bastogne. General Bradley's forces were pressing the Germans from the south, west and north while Field Marshal Montgomery's 30 Corps was squeezing from the north in what became known as the "Battle of the Bulge." If the Germans were stalled and contained, the Allied Forces could close the pincers and pummel them at will. They would have no alternative but to surrender which, of course, "would end the war much sooner and save countless Allied troops." **NOTE:** (A favorite bombing mission motivation.)

We were a relatively small flight of aircraft dispatched to knock out that particular bridge. Other B-24 bomb groups were on their way to hit bridges at Koblenz/Gus, Euskirchen, Irlich and Engers with eventual success. It was unusual for a squadron to be on its own in the heart of the Rhine River Valley. That was where the 88mm and 105mm anti-aircraft batteries were as thick as mushrooms on a new golf course. The pilots of the ME-109s and FW-190s were continually showing their dislike for intruders into this industrial area. If they were up in force, a lonesome squadron would be dessert for the taking. Its funny how thoughts like that run through your mind when you are placed in a dangerous situation.

Well, we tried hard. As copilot, I had a good view of the target area through the broken clouds below. Flak was moderate - no Luftwaffe. Why? My idea was that they thought we were decoys and did not want to activate a trap. They were most likely too busy harassing the "Bomb Line." We were flying right wing off the lead aircraft. 1st Lt. Richard "Dick" Neurer, bombardier/navigator, (Cumberland, Wisconsin) of 1st Lt. Daniel "Dan" Durbin's (Louisville, Kentucky) crew was tracking the target along with the leader. Dick was to drop when the lead aircraft released its bombs along with the white flare signal. Things were looking pretty good. Steady - coming up on the target - watch for the flare - got it - Drop! Drop! Bombs Away! Trouble was a cloud obscured the bridge seconds before the drop. Result - explosions on both sides of the bridge, but none on it. We missed the damn bridge! Dick was even more upset because he had the bridge dead on the cross hairs before he had to yield to the lead bombardier. Nothing left to do but make it back to the base at Seething.

The interesting point of this story is that just a little more than two months later (March 7) the general staff of the Allied Forces was expounding on the speedy and brilliant tactical maneuvering which created great confusion among the German troops, resulting in saving the Ludendorff Bridge. It was the only bridge left standing over the Rhine River in that most strategic area. The Germans had retreated to the east side and had the bridge mined for destruction when the "Yanks" arrived. The detachment responsible for the detonation of the charges under the bridge had failed to do so. The bridge was quickly taken at a great cost in combat losses.

To "end the war much sooner and save countless Allied troops" by destroying the bridge, according to the 448th Bomb Group briefing was, in time, replaced by the General Staff with the account of the speedy tactical maneuvers weighed against the stated "remote possibility" of finding any bridge intact. The Ludendorff Bridge had withstood a terrible bombardment by both the "Yanks" and the Germans within the span of a few weeks. It became the lonely bridge that spanned the Rhine River; "the traditional defensive barrier to the heart of Germany." Our troops attacked the Germans head on, withstood their counter attacks, and pushed them farther and farther east into Germany. Within a mat-

ter of a few months, the Allied Forces had secured the "Festung Europa" victory. The "Missing of the Ludendorff Bridge" (not its destruction) contributed considerably to the success of the Allied war effort and saved the lives of countless Allied troops.

P.S.: The Ludendorff Bridge had been shelled and bombed by the retreating Germans, which weakened it considerably. "On March 17, 1945, the center span (the one which had been damaged by the unsuccessful attempt to blow the bridge on March 7) fell into the river. It carried with it a number of our fine engineers, some of whom we were unable to rescue from the icy waters of the river." By that time, the engineers had built, and the troops were using treadway bridges to cross the river.

Saved By The Seat Of My Pants - April 21, 1944
by Art Steele (448th)

The Mission Attempt when Lt. S.D. Ausfresser (Ausie) was lost at sea.

This day the cloud cover was thousands of feet thick in the formation assembly area over East Anglia. The B-24s would reach the area by following a race-track course into and out of a buncher radio beacon (#24 Hemsby). The track our group was assigned to extended out over the North Sea. After single take-offs from Seething, the B-24s, in trail and on instruments, started to climb to cloud free altitude. I (the bombardier) and navigator "Ausie" went to our stations in the forward compartment. I would don my flak vest and flak helmet, lift myself into the Emerson nose turret, and plug into the intercom, oxygen system, and the electric heated suit outlet. Ausie would close the door to the turret.

In theory, you could release the door from inside the turret, but with all the extra equipment on it would take some doing. After a lot of scratching and orientation to my surroundings, the aircraft was still in a climb mode, on instruments, in the soup, and I was praying for a break-out into the clear. After grinding away for some minutes at maximum power settings and around the 12,000 foot level the noise level of the slipstream increased, and the warning bell (one ring) sounded.

I started unplugging things and I felt the door give way. Ausie had released the turret door. By the time I had popped the release on my flak vest and lifted myself out of the turret, I could see Ausie exiting through the nose wheel well.

I did not hear the second bell ring for bail out, in fact it was not given. I buckled on my chest pack parachute and had my feet pressuring at the slipstream ready for push-off into space. I had my escape kit in my left rear pants pocket. It caught on a canvas tie down post. The canvas wall which separated the nose wheel well from the rest of the forward compartment was removed for combat missions.

I was getting set for another try and I saw the bomb load being salvoed, so I knew I was not alone in the aircraft. I pulled myself away from the bailout position and crawled through the tunnel to the flight deck where things were very tense, but no one other than Ausie had left the ship. About the same time I got to the flight deck, we broke into the clear over the North Sea. We had lost power on the climb and had fallen off into tight spiral.

I don't recall the altitude at which we broke out, but I think it was below 2,000 feet. Jack W. O'Brien, the pilot, called the Air Sea Rescue and started a search pattern coordinated with an Air-Sea Rescue plane with which we also established visual contact. We searched for several hours with some other B-24s which were available as our original mission had been recalled. We found no trace of Ausie.

When we returned to the Quonset hut, there on Ausie's inspection ready cot was an unopened letter from his bride of six months.

448TH BOMB GROUP
Tid Bits
by Cater Lee

No organization consisting of around three thousand men and women, especially in wartime, can exist without humor, sadness, heroism, exceptional skill, and just plain good luck.

The 448th was no exception. Here are some known examples.

Charles Cupp's plane was shot completely into two separate pieces. The tail section was going one way and the front of the plane was in a powerful dive heading violently toward the earth.

Staff Sergeant Charles Cupp was in the front of the plane. By some stroke of luck, the plane somehow turned upside down and with the bombbay doors being open, he managed to get out and was the only one of the crew to survive.

At the time he was flying, all combat crewmen carried 45 caliber pistols. Luckily, Charles had not put a clip in his pistol that day. When he landed, he was mobbed by a large gathering of German civilians who had him down, stomping and hitting him with their fists or anything they could muster. One German youth, about 16 or so, got Charles' pistol, held it to Charles' head and tried to fire it. Luck was with Charles as the pistol was not loaded.

Again, after Charles had given up against such odds, he played dead. Two German soldiers soon appeared, dispersing the crowd and saving his life.

The other good fortune was that one of the planes in the formation had a camera and caught the picture of the plane as it separated and was heading downward. This was one of the most outstanding pictures of the air war in Europe; this picture, along with a nice lengthy write up, is on display at the Air Force Museum at Wright/Patterson AFB at Dayton, Ohio.

Charles, his wife, and two daughters, have gone back to a reunion at the base in Seething where Charles showed them around what was his home until he became a POW. Charles and his family have attended several other reunions.

Another of our enlisted men, who just recently passed away in early 1994, was Master Sergeant Williard L. Cobb who was a tail gunner on Lieutenant John McCune's (now lieutenant colonel retired) crew who flew the *Maid of Orleans* in Squadron #715, Crew #63. On a mission over Germany, their plane was attacked, not by one, but by four Focke-Wulf 190s in separate passes; Sergeant Cobb was severely wounded three times by shrapnel from 20mm cannon shells. He managed a makeshift bandage and stayed at his station, shooting down each of the four FW 190s on separate passes.

His extreme skill was witnessed below by French citizens, who sent a report through their underground, noting the date, time and serial number of the plane; this was later traced back to the plane of Lieutenant McCune and Sergeant Cobb.

On a previous mission Master Sergeant Cobb got another German fighter making five in all.

Later, after recovery at his English base, two French soldiers representing Charles de Gaulle came to the base; and with permission from the base commander, took him to London where he was personally honored by General Charles de Gaulle with the Croix de Guerre, Avec Etoile de Bronze. He was recommended for the Silver Star by his pilot, Lieutenant McCune, but was awarded the Distinguished Flying Cross. Later on, Master Sergeant Cobb was named the outstanding enlisted man of the 448th Bomb Group. What a guy! We will sure miss him; it's too bad we didn't all get to meet him and give our personal thanks and gratitude for his heroism and devotion to duty.

Now for a humorous story that wasn't humorous at the time.

Pilot "Commanche" Wahnee, full blooded Commanche Indian from Oklahoma and a graduate of Oklahoma State University, and copilot Stu Barr and their crew were forced to bail out over France. Stu Barr and Elliott of Pasadena, Texas, escaped capture and were helped by the French Underground.

They made their initial escape from the pursuing Germans by running into a heavily wooded forest. Here they spent several days with numerous other evaders who were fed by the Underground until they could be taken care of individually.

Captain (RET) Stu Barr adds humor in telling of this episode. He says he had the advantage over his German pursuers as he had dry ground to run on. We all know what he meant. Stu is retired and living in Ocala, Florida.

Another interesting story about one of our 448th veterans is Robert Brokstein who lives in Ohio.

Bob is now 85 years old, and since he was an enlisted man, his story is worth telling. When the war started, Bob was a graduate lawyer and should have been taken into the JAG, but somehow Uncle Sam didn't make him that offer. Being in his mid-30s, he didn't even have to go in the service; but he wanted to be near the action, and arrived by boat in December 1944 in England during the Battle of the Bulge. He served in the map section helping to lay out the bomb routes.

Bob is now 85 and has several health problems and, like many of us, watches the TV programs showing WWII activities. Hopefully, he will be able to attend the 448th Group's 11th consecutive annual association reunion in Boston, September 1 through 5, 1994, where he will be recognized as being the oldest enlisted survivor in our group.

453RD BOMB GROUP
Bail Out!
by Wilbur Stites (453rd)

What was it like to get shot down and have to bail out, is a question I'm sometimes asked. "Well, it was exciting," I sometimes reply.

Facetious? Flippant? I don't mean it that way. But how can I describe the thoughts and emotions that flood the mind and senses in a situation like that? If you've ever had the experience, you know what it's like. If not, you'll probably never understand, no matter how hard I try to explain. But if you're interested, I'll give it a try.

For me it happened on October 17, 1944. We were on our 23rd bombing mission. Target: the railroad marshalling yards at Cologne, Germany. We were flying "Lucky Penny II," a gleaming silvery B-24 that had been assigned to us after her first crew completed their tour of missions. The first "Lucky Penny" had been shot down with a crew other than the one to which she had been assigned.

Classified as a "Heavy" bomber in World War II, the B-24 with its thin, narrow wing mounted high

(Courtesy of Russell R. Leslie, 389th)

on the full-bodied fuselage and its twin vertical stabilizers (rudders) was one of the most distinctive planes in the sky. The four supercharged 1,200 horsepower engines powered the 56,000 pound combat loaded plane, including its 10-man crew, to altitudes up to 30,000 feet. Cruising at 165 miles an hour, the plane could deliver 6,000 pounds of bombs on round trip missions to targets more than a thousand miles away. Nose, top, and tail turrets, each with twin .50 caliber machine guns plus single .50 caliber guns swivel-mounted on each side, gave the plane a total defensive fire power of some 6,000 rounds a minute.

The B-24 was a tough, airplane, capable of dealing out and absorbing an astonishing amount of punishment. But it was not invulnerable. The heavy barrages of anti-aircraft fire and determined mass attacks by enemy fighters took a heavy toll of Liberators and crews during the war in the skies over Europe.

"We" were "Lofton's crew" of the 453rd Bomb Group, based at Old Buckenham near Norwich in East Anglia. Ours was one of 14 groups of B-24s assigned to the 2nd Bomb Division. Our crew members were William Lofton, pilot; Bruce (Joe) Florea, copilot; Leonard Lonigan, navigator; Thomas Welch, bombardier; Hilliard (Eddie) Edwards, engineer; Johnnie Miller, radio operator; Edward Paulsen, nose gunner; Winford Pace, right waist gunner; Elden Gould, tail gunner; and Wilbur Stites, left waist gunner. We had an additional crew member on this mission, Edward Rosenberg, assigned to monitor the German radio frequencies as an intelligence gathering tactic. Gould was flying with us as replacement for our regular tail gunner, Robert Hon, who was temporarily grounded with a touch of the flu.

Our take-off from the base was uneventful and we rendezvoused with the 30 or so other planes from the 453rd Group and took up our customary position in the "slot," the rear-most plane in one of the four plane diamond-shaped elements. The elements formed the group, flying together in close formation in order to achieve a tight bomb pattern on the target and to provide concentrated fire power from our guns against enemy fighter attacks.

We approached the target at the usual 20,000 foot altitude, flying over a solid cloud undercast about 5,000 feet below our formation. We reached the IP (initial point) and made the prescribed 45 degree left turn to begin the 12-minute bomb run to the target.

As we made our turn, I looked ahead through my Plexiglass window and saw a thick cloud of black smoke from anti-aircraft shells bursting over the target. The black cloud was measled with red-orange flashes from new-bursting shells. Hitler's antiaircraft gunners were sending up a reception for us we weren't going to like.

I heard the bomb bay doors rumble open. From here on we were committed. Fly straight and level. No evasive maneuvers that would throw the bombs off target.

I thought of other missions we had flown. Ludwigshaven, Hamburg, Hannover, Kassel, Dessau, and the others, 22 of them so far. A total of 35 needed to complete our tour. How many more times could we do this and get through it? Would we make it this time? Would I make it this time?

Now we are into it. Flak is all around us. I watch the bright flashing fire of breaking shells. I hear the c-r-r-ump-whump of the close explosions and feel the big plane tremble and shudder from the shock waves. I hear the ping and spang of flak fragments whanging into and through the fuselage like gravel hitting a tin roof.

I feel the familiar sweat of fear begin to trickle down my face and back. Fear? You bet! I doubt that any man can honestly disclaim fear when faced with this kind of mortal danger. But you control the fear. To lose control is to panic and panic is the prelude to disaster.

I glance down at Win Pace crouched on the floor of the fuselage busily stuffing fist-sized bundles of "chaff" into the small porthole in the side of the plane. The thin strips of metal foil, looking like Christmas tinsel, scatter in the slipstream and drift down through the thin air. This stuff is supposed to cloud the Germans' radar screens and interfere with their flak accuracy. I always wondered why we bothered, since it never seemed to do any good. But it was required on bomb runs, so we did it.

Win returns my look. His eyes above the oxygen mask are bright with question and concern. He can't see the flak breaking outside from his position so he gives me our prearranged signal by rapidly

idly opening and closing the fingers on his free hand. "How bad is the flak?" he wants to know. I signal back by nodding my head and rapidly opening and closing my fingers several times. "Yes, Win, there's a lot of flak," is my signal. Win keeps shoving chaff out the porthole, faster now. I can't help grinning behind my own mask. The chaff is supposed to be thrown at a measured pace, but when Win gets the signal from me that there's a lot of flak he always throws it faster, as if this might make it do more good. Of course, it doesn't.

Nobody says anything on the interphone. One of the disciplines of our crew is to maintain interphone silence on the bomb run. It's important not to clutter the interphone with extraneous conversation that might interfere with emergency communications.

We're about half way through the bomb run now. Suddenly, there is a tremendous sound of rending, tearing metal. The plane lurches violently, peels over on its left wing and heads down toward the clouds below. The big plane is mortally stricken. A cannon shell whistles up through the bomb bay, bursts through the fuselage and explodes above, sending a hail of jagged metal fragments into the body, wings, and engines. Edwards, in his top turret reported later that he saw the fuselage open up in front of his eyes like rolling back the top of a sardine can.

At that point, a lot of things happened at once.

The interphone crackled to life. "Bombs away, Tom!" It was Lofton signaling Welch to drop the bombs. Tom flipped the emergency toggle switch and bombs, thankfully all 12 of them, released from their shackles and fell away from the plane. The last thing we wanted right then was a 500-pound bomb hung up in our bomb bay.

The plane continued its downward slant toward the clouds with a vapor trail of gasoline spewing out behind. Some of the gas lines had been ruptured by flak fragments and gas was leaking out of the breaks and streaming out behind. Crews in other planes in the formation who saw us disappear into the clouds thought the gas vapor trail was smoke. They assumed we were on fire with no chance to survive.

Lofton and Florea fought with the controls and managed to pull the plane out of its dive into level flight again. But all four engines were running rough and we continued to lose altitude. Lofton asked for Lonigan to give him a heading for Belgium, with the hope that we could set down on an airfield in American occupied territory. He then called for an interphone crew check. One by one they reported in and, miraculously, no one was hurt.

By now Edwards had scrambled out of his top turret and began trying to stop gas from leaking from the ruptured lines snaking along the bulkhead walls inside the bomb bay. Using pieces of cloth handed to him from the flight deck by Johnnie Miller, he did what he could to stop the leaks, but it wasn't enough. Eddie had to balance precariously on the narrow catwalk of the open bomb bay, working with one hand while clinging to the bomb racks with the other. No parachute. There was no room to wear it in the close confines of the bomb bay. We didn't feel that we dared to close the bomb bay doors for fear that doing so might cause a spark that would ignite the gas fumes and blow us out of the sky. Edwards was awarded the Distinguished Flying Cross for his heroic actions performed in the face of deadly peril.

While this was happening, the rest of us were busy jettisoning whatever heavy items we could sacrifice in an effort to lighten the load to help keep the plane in the air. We opened emergency hatches to be prepared for bail-out and to ventilate the plane as much as possible. We disconnected electrically heated flying suits, most of the interphone connec-

tions, and whatever other non-essential electrical equipment we could. Again, we were trying to minimize the possibility of an electric spark that would surely set the gas vapors aflame.

We had been losing altitude steadily and suddenly broke out of the clouds at an altitude of about 1,000 feet. I looked out of my left waist window at the ground so close below and saw several heavy vehicles, tanks and armored trucks, parked in a wooded area and covered with camouflage netting.

Just then, four bursts of flak exploded directly in front of me at a distance of about a hundred yards. Whoever was down there with those vehicles was shooting at us. I punched my interphone button (mine was the one we kept operative in the waist compartment of the plane). "Waist to pilot," I said. "Flak at nine o'clock level."

"Roger," Lofton acknowledged and hauled back on the control column. He managed to coax the struggling ship back into the clouds and out of sight of the gunners below.

But there was more to come. A few minutes later we again settled out of the clouds and immediately I saw a string of fiery tracer shells zip under the left wing and the two engines on that side. "Waist to pilot, tracers flying under #1 and 2 engines."

"Roger, waist," said Bill again and again he managed to pull the plane back into the cloud cover.

Once again we broke below the clouds at an altitude of only about 900 feet. The plane was lumbering, engines were faltering, cutting in and out intermittently. Gallant *Lucky Penny II* had come to the end of her career.

My earphones crackled, "Pilot to crew - bail out! bail out! bail out!"

I whirled from my place at the window and shouted to the others in my compartment. "Bail out! Lofton says bail out!" We already had our parachutes snapped in place on the chest clamps of our harnesses ready to go, and out we went.

When my turn came, I crouched at the edge of the two-foot square escape hatch in the floor of the compartment. I saw a man go past the hatch opening, arms and legs pumping as if swimming in the air. Someone from one of the forward sections of the plane, I couldn't tell who. He disappeared from view to the rear of the plane.

I somersaulted out the escape hatch like roll-

Low altitude practice, Prior to supply drop at Nijmegen, Holland. (Courtesy of Carroll A. Berner, 93rd)

"Jamaica" crashed in France nine days after D-Day, 1944. (Courtesy of Clyde M. Fauley, 466th)

Col. James Stewart interrogates the crew of the 453rd Bomb Group after returning from a mission. (Photo courtesy of Kenneth Englebrecht)

ing into the water from the edge of a swimming pool. The windstream caught me and turned me over and around so that I was lying stretched out on my back as if lying in bed. I watched *Lucky Penny II* fly away from me, rear her nose in the air, then flip to her left and dive to the ground. She disappeared behind a high wooded hill with a thunderous crash and explosion. A black column of smoke boiled up from the spot where she hit.

I saw no parachutes come out. Who got out and who didn't?

I grabbed the metal ring of my parachute, gave it a yank, and threw it from me in the same motion. I watched it spiral away and thought, "Darn, I should have hung onto that for a souvenir."

My chute popped open with a sound like bursting a paper bag blown full of air. It stopped me with a jolt that racked my whole body. "Pulled too quick," I thought, "Should have waited until I slowed." My body was still traveling at the same speed as the plane, about 165 miles an hour. The human body will slow to about 125 mph, then continue to fall at about that rate of speed. But at the same instant I knew I had done the right thing. At only 900 feet there's very little time to delay opening your chute or you'll hit the ground before it can open.

The chute blossomed above me (a beautiful sight at that moment), turned me around and started pulling me forward and down toward the ground. Below and ahead I saw a man dangling from an open chute. I could recognize the tall, slim figure of Rosenberg, our German radio monitor. He was waving his arms frantically and yelling, "Help! Help!" at the top of his voice. I thought, "Shut up, you dummy, you'll have every German in the country coming in on us." He drifted on, disappearing behind some trees, and I never saw him again, although I later learned that he had landed safely.

Now the ground was coming up fast. An open meadow on a sloping hillside. No trees to slam into or hang up in. In an instant, I hit. Hard. I pitched forward and rolled over and over I don't know how many times. I came to rest flat on my back just like I'd been when I pulled the rip cord to open the chute.

I got my breath back, sat up and took stock. Everything seemed to be OK, except for a pretty severe pain in my neck. Later x-rays showed no broken bones; it was just a bad sprain that left me with a sore neck for a few days.

All at once, I realized I was surrounded by a dozen people in civilian clothes. Who were they and how did they get here so fast? They were jabbering at me in a language I didn't understand. But then I recognized some words, "Boche? American?" as they pointed at me. And, "Belgique, Belgique," as they pointed at themselves.

I tapped my chest. "American," I said.

"Oh, American, American, bon, American." they echoed, a mixture of relief and gladness in their voices.

With that, those fine folks began checking me for injuries, helped me to my feet, got me untangled from the parachute shroud lines and proffered cigarettes.

At that point, two American sergeants in a jeep came rolling onto the scene. Where did they come from and how did they get here so fast?

It turned out we had come down near the little town of Malmedy in Belgium. This was shortly before the Battle of the Bulge was due to break out and we had made it into Allied occupied territory by a distance of about a mile.

The American sergeants, from an ordnance company camp nearby, took me to their camp and into their care. I was delighted to find they also had picked up Johnnie Miller and Len Lonigan. But no one had information about any other members of our crew and we were deeply concerned about and worried about them.

A couple days later, the American soldiers drove us in an open-top "scout car" to Brussels from where a C47 troop plane flew us back to our base at Old Buckenham.

Three days after we had gone down, we walked into our hut at our air base, to the surprise and delight of the other crew with whom we shared the hut. We found them busily packing our personal belongings to send home. They had seen us go down into the clouds and thought we were lost. Some 10 missions later, that crew went down with no survivors. We had the sad duty of sending their personal belongings home.

Remarkably, all 11 members of our crew of that fateful mission to Cologne survived with no major injuries. Just a few scrapes, bruises and sprains. We were given seven days rest leave to get ourselves back together, then back to flying again. I completed my full tour of 35 missions, as did most of the other members of our crew.

Sadly, we lost our pilot, Bill Lofton. He suf-

fered an unfortunate accident on our air base when he fell and fractured both forearms. Of course, he was unable to fly for several weeks and during that time we finished our missions with other pilots. Later, Lofton was killed when his plane crashed during a training flight at the airbase.

So, what was it like to get shot down and have to bail out?

Well, it was exciting.

Mission With A Surprise Ending

by Bob Lambert (453rd)

How many of you from the 453rd remember a B-24 plane named the *Lonesome Polecat*? As a replacement crew we inherited this wonderful plane in May 1944. After many successful missions, with a number of close calls, we flew its last mission with Jimmy Woolley as our pilot and me as the radio man. Our crew picture with this plane and some formation missions are in the book *In Search Of Peace.*

I am not sure but I believe this mission was over Hamburg, Germany; if not, it was another large city where the sky was black with flak. During our bombing run we were hit several times and lost an engine. As we pulled away from the formation, a second engine on the opposite wing began to cough and act up. A short time later we lost the second engine and gradually began to lose altitude, but since we were over enemy territory, our pilot felt it was best to see how far we could go.

After what seemed like an eternity, we finally could see the English Channel. I was told to send an SOS, as we probably could not make it across the channel. I pressed so hard on the key (thinking the signal would go farther) that it broke off and I had to quickly jury-rig an alternative and kept on sending SOSs until I received a response. Then I continued a signal so they could obtain a fix on our location.

While doing this, the crew was ordered to throw everything out of the plane that was not fastened down. Out went the guns, ammunition, equipment, etc. In the excitement even a gunner's parachute was tossed out (what a shock!). Plans were quickly made that if we were to jump, Barney Feeney (a waist gunner) would take Jack Day with him and the two would go down together on one chute.

Even with the loss of weight, we were still losing altitude and getting closer to the water. Jump or ditch? As we got even closer to the water we prepared to ditch. We then saw the coast of England in the distance and counted our blessings. Maybe we could reach shore and land somewhere on the beach area. However it was felt it would be safer to ditch and then swim ashore.

As we were thinking ditch, our pilot saw a patch of grass he thought we could make and headed for that. We barely cleared the surrounding trees and our pilot was able to land our shot-up B-24 on the grassy area. We all climbed out and kissed the ground. When we looked up we found we were surrounded by British Troops with Tommy-guns and rifles pointed right at us. They stated in English and in German that we were under arrest. Naturally we were surprised and spoke to them in English. They paid no attention and ordered us to put our hands behind our heads and marched us to a hidden building. As we did we saw many strange planes strategically placed under an umbrella of trees with camouflage netting over some of them. We were ushered into a room and they asked for the commander of our aircraft. They took our pilot away while we were still being guarded by British Troops.

After what seemed like hours, our pilot came in saying that we had landed on a very secret British Royal Air Force experimental aircraft base. They thought we were German spies flying in on a captured American plane. Our 2nd Bomb Division Headquarters cleared us as Americans returning from a mission.

The British then became friendly and furnished us with tea and crumpets. Later we were led to a waiting bus that returned us to our base at Old Buckenham for debriefing, food and bed. We all counted our Blessings being very thankful we were alive and "Home." We then finished our tour of missions in a plane called *Dolly* or *Dolly's Sister*.

James Stewart And He Went To War All The Way

Briefing, Winter 1974

If they gave Academy Awards for superior performance in a B-24, Jimmy Stewart would have won one of these too!

While actor Stewart was said to typify the thousands the entertainment industry sent into uniform during World War II, there were but a rare few whose performances came anywhere near his. He was singled our for special mention because he was among the first to go but has never received the publicity deserved for being the best of those that went!

It seems appropriate for *Briefing* to mention that Jimmy Stewart was expertly wrestling with the controls of a B-24 in leading his bomb group over heavily-defended targets in Europe long before Billie Joe Hawkins of TV ever got his first case.

Universally favorable reaction to the actor in uniform and his contributions to the war effort as a squadron commander and group operations officer in the 8th Air Force was his only reward for a job well done.

James Maitland Stewart, in February 1941, ambled into a Los Angeles recruiting station and applied for the Army Air Corps. He owned his own plane; had logged 400 hours in the air.

In any case, the Army turned him down. He weighed only 147 pounds—10 pounds too light for his gangling six feet four.

Stewart embarked on a diet of candy, beer and bananas. In one uncomfortable month he brought his displacement up to standard. Before he could enlist, however, his draft number came up. "First lottery I ever won," he drawled, and boarded a streetcar to the induction center on March 22, 1941.

(Courtesy of William Greer, 389th)

He was a typical raw recruit. Fast dressing, after an early rising, was difficult for "a morning piddler by nature and long habit." Dress was fraught with menace for legs the length of his.

Like other soldiers, too, he did his share of griping. But he learned to like the Army, and he plugged hard at his job.

In due time he mastered the ground routine, was transferred to pilot training and, nine months after induction, won his wings and a commission as a second lieutenant.

Following further training, Stewart served as a flying instructor in AT-9s and B-17s at fields in California, New Mexico and Idaho. Then, in August 1943, he joined the 445th B-24 group at Sioux City, Iowa as squadron commander of the 703rd Bomb Squadron. Four months later the group, assigned to the 8th Army Air Force, flew the Atlantic to Tibenham, East Anglia, England. Stewart now held the rank of captain.

Second motion picture star to be sent to the European Theater (after Clark Gable), he was the first to do active combat flying there.

As squadron commander, he piloted his bomber (which was later named *Nine Yanks and a Jerk* on its first raid. Target: Bremen.

Stewart soon proved himself a capable flying officer, unruffled, and determined under fire. In January 1944 he was made a major—a rank he had previously refused to accept until, as he said, "my junior officers get promoted from lieutenants."

When the 453rd Liberator group, one of the 445th's two sisters, wanted the best "ops" officer they could find, Maj. Stewart was chosen.

In two months the group led its division in bombing efficiency. That helped win Stewart an appointment as combat wing chief of staff to Brig. Gen. Edward Timberlake; by then (July 1944), he had led his outfit on 14 missions over enemy territory in Europe.

He led the 2nd Combat Wing (389th, 445th and 453rd groups) to Berlin on March 22, 1944.

His men shared his pride when he won the Air Medal with Oak Leaf Cluster and, later, the Distinguished Flying Cross. They approved when he was made a lieutenant colonel.

In May 1945 they heard even better news: Jim Stewart was now a colonel and was commander of the 2nd Combat Bomb Wing.

In all, Col. Stewart was credited with 20 combat missions, all as command pilot. He returned to the States as a full colonel in 1945. In the intervening years, he was promoted to brigadier general in the USAF Reserve—the rank he held upon retirement.

General Stewart says of the B-24, "I remember the B-24 very well and, although it came out of the war with a rather questionable reputation for some reason, I think most of those who flew the airplane have a very soft spot in their hearts for the machine.

"I learned four engine operation in the B-17, but while I was instructing in that airplane, the change was suddenly made to the B-24. The transition didn't seem at all difficult, which speaks well for the bird.

"In combat, the airplane was no match for the B-17 as a formation bomber above 25,000 feet; but, from 12,000 to 18,000 feet the airplane did a fine job."

Forget The Enemy - Beware Of The "Friendlies"

by Dwight Bishop (453rd)

It was early in my tour that I learned there was much more danger 'out there' than enemy flak or fighters. Flak I saw plenty of, but fighters, none! It was on my fourth mission, July 7, 1944, mission nearly over, coming off the 'enemy' coast when it happened. Everything was going well, and I wanted to see the scenery below, so copilot Walter Mahanay was driving. We were #3 in the lead squadron, so I was standing by on fighter channel. I felt the airplane take a sudden lurch upwards, and thinking of the high right element above, pushed forward on the wheel as I turned to look at Mahanay and switched to intercom.

All I heard was unintelligible yelling, especially from the nose gunner, John Portoghese. I soon learned that our group had met another group at the same altitude on a reciprocal heading. Both lead planes started down to evade, so Mahanay, bless his soul, went up. The two lead planes collided and were the only ones lost—that was enough.

On Mission #16, August 26, 1944, I was flying group deputy lead, and after 'bombs away,' lost #3 engine. With the briefing admonitions about ditching in the North Sea in mind, I would play it safe. Held about 9,000' altitude and headed for the narrowest part of the channel. The lovely coast of England was well in sight, when a line of flak appeared across my course. I made a correction to starboard and told engineer John Fiel to fire a flare of the 'colors of the day.' The line of flak appeared again, a little closer. It had to come from British batteries, but why? I turned further to starboard, and now Navigator Max Marcus told me we were too close to the Thames Estuary, which was "never, never land" forbidden to all aircraft.

On either a practice mission or aircraft check flight, can't remember which, the landing was memorable! I was in the landing pattern at Old Buc, gear and some flaps down, when I saw a gaggle of B-17s at our altitude and coming straight at us. The designers of the B-24 did not plan the maneuver I made, nor did they engineer the 'Lib' to be able to do it. Throttles full forward (and then some) and haul back on the wheel. I remember seeing the 'rate of climb' indicator momentarily reading 1,000'/ minute, as we 'leap-frogged' above the 17s. But normally, the B-17s were on our side.

On Mission #18, October 17, 1944, my first PFF lead, the target was marshalling yards. After the group strung out in squadrons in trail, Bob Dault, radar operator, said he had the target on the scope. Seconds later, the bomber stream began to angle off to the left. Now what? Do I follow the stream and shake Bob's confidence, or do I trust him and his training? I decided to go with Bob's call, and kept an eye on the rest of the group. We were still on the bomb run when the rest of the group made a right turn and would fly over us. Now the big question was, 'Have they dropped?' Relief that day was spelled "Bomb Bays Closed."

The most hair-raising experience with 'friendlies' came when I aborted a mission and was trying to land at Old Buc in bad visibility. If I was close enough to the field to see the runway flares, I could not make the turn to final approach. If I was out far enough to make the turn, I could not see the flares. Then came to mind something taught in the States, the Procedure Turn. You fly over the field on the reverse of the landing heading, make a timed dog-leg at 45 degrees from your heading, then a timed turn to the opposite side to come back to your landing heading, in line with the runway. While doing this, the bombardier, Ed Dekker, told me he looked up at trees. Then I saw IT! A B-24 passing from right to left in front of us, in a slight climb. I could not go down, or up or turn. I knew I would hit it right behind the wing, no way out.

The next thing I remember, it was gone and we were still flying. Dekker leaned over my shoulder and said "Dewey, let's get out of here." I agreed.

I got some altitude where I could see, and was directed to a base in western England. Now comes the strange part. On the landing approach, the boys in the back room (waist) were making book on how many times and how high the 'shook-up' skipper would bounce on this landing. During the discussions, Portoghese looked out the window, then said, "Forget it guys; we're on the ground." I never did make a smoother landing. I met Marcus at the So. California dinner, March 1991, and he told me we suffered a bent radio antenna from this escapade.

I believed back then, and I believe now, that during these events, neither I nor Mahanay was in control of the plane. Some Supreme Being, Force, Power, Spirit - call it what you will - was taking care of us. For a long time, I wondered why I had been protected. A few years ago, I realized that maybe another crew member was being protected, and I was just lucky enough to "go along for the ride." The crew members not previously mentioned were: tail turret, John Baillie; pilotage navigator, Clyde Colvin; top turret, Joe Ferrara; radio, Ray Rogala; ball turret (and Chief Chaff Chucker), George (Ed) Yarbrough.

458TH BOMB GROUP
The Mission I Missed
by Milt Jay

When I returned to our quarters the night of March 17, 1945, everyone was asleep, expecting the wake up jeep to stop by in a few hours, so I quietly turned in, but not before eating two hot tamales from our home-stocked larder. I awakened later and stumbled through the back door, violently vomiting. God, I was sick! Claude McConnell, our engineer, woke up and shooed me over to the infirmary. The Flight Surgeon, muttering about food poisoning, grounded me for a day.

"Rise and shine, guys. 3700 gallons topped and four 2000 pounders." The jeep took off and my buddies grumbled into their clothes, ate a mission breakfast, ambled over to briefing, donned their flight gear and flew off to Berlin. Feeling much better by 3 p.m., I made my way over to the tower building to watch the mission return. I stood next to the man with a check-off list and, when the roar of the engines faded and he turned to leave, I asked if Mitchell (pilot) came in. He looked at his list and replied, "Nope, I don't have him here. Go down to Squadron Operations, kid, they probably know where he is.

They didn't! They told me my crew had been hit and dropped out of formation, and hadn't been heard from since. I plopped into an ancient easy chair and began to silently cry. The sensation of guilt was a choking lump in my throat. I had let down my crew. I should have been with them, no matter what.

For the next four hours, I sat there numb. Everything was hushed, with the phone occasionally ringing and being quietly answered, until that one wonderful call, "Hey, Milt, your crew crash-landed at Brussels and everybody is OK." A cheer resounded. I got up and almost fell over, I had hardly moved all that time. To say I was ecstatic would be an understatement. Four days later they flew in. We were so happy to see each other we never got into the details of the mission which, as strange as it may seem, I learned of only a few years ago. In 1985, I wrote to Ray Peters (copilot) and Claude, asking some question about the mission. For the first time, I revealed to Ray what I had experienced when they didn't return. The following is what he wrote to me:

"Milt, I've written as much as I recall of our March 18, 1945 mission over Berlin. I've sent it to "Mac" in the hope that he can fill in parts that are lost to me. There are three things that stand out:

1. Over the target there was a formation high above us crossing to the left. There were several parachutes. I was so concerned one chap was going to get caught by our 3 and 4 props. Another parachute was dead ahead, but he must have cleared under us. I'll never forget the fleeting glimpse of the man's legs and body rippling by just above the right wing. Some time during that frightening moment, we felt a thud and slight lift; that must have been it.

2. After the loss of oil in #3 and the electric lines had been cut, we couldn't feather the prop so it windmilled off track, eating its way into the cowling. It was oscillating badly; the yellow tips just outside my window were snarling like a mad dog.

3. The prop finally came off, coming directly towards the cockpit, but the armor plating deflected it downward. The spinning motion sawed a 3 1/2' x 11' slash through the nose, cut the hydraulics and electric lines and started a fire, which Claude extinguished.

Allen (navigator) told me that he and Weiler (bombardier) were on their knees looking through the plastic, doing a bit of navigation, when the prop passed just inches from their feet. One end struck the rudder pedal slides an awful blow. My feet and legs went numb and the small of my back hurt terribly. There was no blood and I could sort of lift my knees, so I was sure I was OK.

Milt, I never gave it a thought as to how you must have felt when we didn't come back. Man, that must have been a terrible empty lost feeling. All of us wished you could have been along for the experience since no one was hurt. It was really a superb chance to see how everyone pulled together. It would have made you feel good. You deserved to be there, really wish you had been along.

There just wasn't any reason for you to be on a guilt trip. If you had known we were going to have a rough mission, you would have gone on the

B-24J, 855th Bomb Sqdr., 1945. (Courtesy of J.A. Homsher)

(Courtesy of W. Cranson, 392nd)

mission, nothing would have stopped you. This I'm positive of and I'd bet my last dollar on it."

A few years ago, Claude and his wife, Mary Jane, visited us and he revealed a few more details. Before the prop came off, the vibration was so bad, Mitchell told Claude to ready the crew to bail out at the sound of the bell. Claude told Mitch, "I can't bail out." "Why?" "Because my chute is soaked with hydraulic fluid from the battle damage." Claude then told me, "Mitch looked straight at me and said, "OK, Claude, you and I will take her down." Then the prop came off, the vibration stopped and three engines kept going. Number two started to lose power and finally quit and the ship continued to lose altitude. The navigation charts had blown out the gash, but the navigator was able to give a heading towards the front lines. Then they picked up a railroad going their way. Suddenly, the sky was filled with flak. Racing beneath them was a train with a flat car carrying an .88 which was popping away at them. They veered off and finally made Brussels, which we had captured a few weeks before. With the hydraulics out, they cranked down the wheels but had no flaps or brakes when they went in. Everyone ran to the tail in order to drag down the tail skid as a brake. They ran out of runway and plowed into the mud, which finally stopped them. They all sat there for a moment, breathing a sigh of relief, with 25 gallons of fuel left in the tank. And so ended the mission I missed.

The Death Of A Lady

by Herman A. Peacher (458th)

This is the account of *Flak Magnet's* last mission and what happened to her crew. This frightening experience is narrated by Herman Peacher (tail turret) with the input of the rest of the crew.

We were Crew #33, members of the original 458th Bomb Group, 753rd Bomb Squadron. The crew consisted of: 1st Lt. George N. Spaven, pilot; 2nd Lt. Robert Zedeker, co-pilot; 2nd Lt. Peter Kowal, navigator; 2nd Lt. James F. Martinson, Bombardier; T/Sgt. James H. Wedding, Engineer/top turret; S/Sgt. Cedric C. Cole, radio operator; S/Sgt. James L. Fittinger, nose turret; S/Sgt. Lawrence J. Scheiding, ball turret; Sgt. Robert L. Allen, waist gunner; S/Sgt. Herman A. Peacher, tail turret.

It was Saturday, April 22, 1944. We were called out twice but the missions were aborted. The third time, later in the day, we got the green light. Our primary target was Hamm, Germany, a huge marshaling yard. Takeoff was without incident. At approximately 1936 hours at 20,500 feet we started the bomb run to the target. Less than two minutes later, before release of the bombs, Crew #33 were to wish their ship bore a name other than *Flak Magnet*.

According to Wedding (engineer): "I observed a crippled B-17 off our starboard wing being escorted by a P-47 and heading back towards England. This sighting gave me a certain sense of security. If we should get hit, that fighter escort would be available. However, shortly after this sighting, along with other crew members I noticed the flak barrage boxing us in. The first box was low, but dead ahead. The second was high, but still dead ahead. The third boxed the aircraft at 8 o'clock, 11 o'clock, 2 o'clock, and 4 o'clock. The fifth projectile penetrated the fuselage in the front bomb bay area and into the center wing section, penetrating the three main fuel cells feeding #2 engine. The 88 mm projectile ex-

ited just aft of the life raft hatch slightly on the starboard top of the fuselage. A huge hole opened up with part of the fuselage skin flapping like a half opened tin can."

There was a torrential downpour of gasoline in the bomb bay. Without hesitation, Wedding jumped from the top turret to the flight deck and into the bomb bay entrance. He immediately opened the bomb bay doors to dispense with the gasoline in hopes that it would clear out the fumes and eliminate the chance of fire. At this instant we were a flying bomb. Wedding had checked the fuel gauge and confirmed that the three fuel tanks that were hit were empty. He put #2 engine on crossfeed. He estimated we lost 550 gallons of gasoline but there appeared to be enough fuel to get back to England. Cole, the radio operator, tried to call in fighter cover but to no avail.

In the meantime the intercom from the waist cackled; "We are soaked and waist deep in gas! Let's get the hell out of here!" Allen (waist gunner), Scheiding (ball turret) and Martinson (bombardier) bailed out of the waist windows. As for me (Peacher, tail turret), nothing came over the intercom to alert me. I was watching fuel streaming off the right hand stabilizer and getting more uneasy by the minute. I glanced around and saw a pair feet disappear out of the waist window. I immediately doubled up in a ball and rolled backwards out of the turret. We were carrying a big electric camera in the entrance hatch. That was where I elected to go out. All the corrugations in the floor and every depression was full of gasoline. It was also running out the camera hatch. When I exited the hatch, the door caught me around the knees. I hung head down for an instant until I kicked loose. According to Armstrong, engineer on

Dreamboat, our wing man, it looked like I was holding on with my hands and was afraid to let go.

Fittinger (nose turret) was called back to the bomb bay to see if he could release the bombs. The only way they could be released was with a screw driver. He managed to get rid of three or four bombs. He was working with a walk-around oxygen bottle which lasts about three minutes. This bottle ran out and another was given to him by Cole and Wedding who were in the bomb bay with him.

A FW-190 made a firing pass from about 5 o'clock and above. Bullets riddled the tail section and glanced off the remaining bombs. The #2 engine was also set on fire. Fittinger was getting groggy again so Wedding and Cole got his chute, snapped it to his harness and pushed him off the catwalk. Cale and Wedding bailed out the bomb bay opening.

Zedeker (copilot) recalls: "I thought we had been hit by more flak because of stuff flying around the cockpit. Then I saw the FW-190 peeling off to the right of us. He circled around and ahead of us and lined up about 10 or 11 o'clock for a frontal attack. I got up and said to George Spaven (pilot). "Let's get out of here." I looked back but he had not moved. I slapped him on the shoulder and said, "Come on." He nodded and then all hell broke loose. There were tracers and pieces of aircraft flying everywhere. George was hit numerous times because the instrument panel had disintegrated. If it had not been for the armor plate on the pilot and copilot seats, I would not have made it either. George slumped over the controls. I jumped down on the catwalk and bailed out."

Kowal, the navigator, had opened the nose wheel doors. This was his escape hatch. As he started through the opening the green earth below turned red from tracers. After this stopped he bailed out. As he and Zedeker, hanging in their chutes, glanced back at the crippled Flak Magnet, there was a big flash and explosion. Both wings blew off and disintegrated. The fuselage lowered her nose and slipped down to earth, shielding George Spaven who made the supreme sacrifice.

In 1946 Spaven's mother received this word from Washington taken from captured German records: "1st Lt. George Napier Spaven Jr. was shot down by enemy flak April 22, 1944, a short distance from Hoetmar, District of Waredorf, Prussia. He was interred April 23, 1944 at 10:00 a.m. at the communal cemetery, Hoetmar, Grave #2.

The rest of the crew, after interrogation and several instances of beatings and mistreatment, were sent to different POW camps. There were numerous injuries to the crew. Some were sent to Luft 3 and others to Stalag Luft 17B. I (Peacher) was sent to Obermassfeld where my badly broken ankle was put in a cast after a period of 20 days. Later I was sent to Luft IV, then to Luft I POW camp. Starvation was the worst part of our internment.

All crew members are still surviving today, despite various health conditions, with the exception of Robert Allen, who passed away approximately three years ago. Ours was an ordinary crew, but to me, very special and the best. We have a bond stronger than blood relations.

A 2nd Air Division Navigator's Memories

by R.E. Bateman (458th)

It always started out about 3 a.m. it seemed; an operations enlisted man opening the door to our room (pilots and the navigator of a crew usually bunked three to a room) and saying "Lt. Wilburn? Your crew is on the mission today. Briefing at 0430." Tex Wilburn or Bob Henn would ask, "How many gallons?" and the reply, "2700" was followed by three groans, as 2700 meant a long, long day ahead,

a deep penetration mission to a distant German target.

We immediately rose and washed up, with the thought "Is this going to be the last day of my life?" But spirits rose with some breakfast, usually powdered eggs, bread and jam, a spot of meat, coffee or powdered milk. Then to general briefing, where the days target and routes in and out were displayed on a wall-sized map of northwestern Europe, marked with colored ribbon.

Briefing officers then described the target and the bomb run approach, potential German fighter aircraft reaction, heaviness of flak to expect, meteorological situation at several altitudes, and weather front locations, and motions during the eight to eight and a half hours we would be in the air, and the latest positions of the German front lines on the ground. Briefing concluded with a short prayer by the chaplain. Then followed special briefings for the pilots and for the navigators.

In the navigators' briefing, routes were plotted on Mercator charts or Lambert conformal charts, or on special maps, drawn and printed from aerial photographs, and which showed every detail of terrain, woods, railroads, cities, highways, rivers, etc. These maps were for use during those rare periods when the ground was visible from 23000 feet, the operational mission altitude at which we usually flew.

Planned timings at turning points, Initial Point (IP) at the beginning of the short bomb run up to the target, planned time of "Bombs Away," all these times were added to the charts and the navigator's log books. The latest intelligence on new German flak concentrations and fighter plane strength were given. When complete mission data had been recorded and briefing ended, we went off to supply to draw flying equipment.

Proper dressing for a mission was a matter of some importance. A missed detail could mean the difference between serious, incapacitating injury due to cold and frostbite, and if shot down, to treatment as a POW, or to execution as an Allied underground agent. For the latter reason, we always wore full uniform between our long johns and our outer flying clothes.

Outer flying clothes consisted of a full-length, heated, thin suit, complete with silk gloves, which worked like a heated blanket. These gloves were

worn so that if we had to remove our outer gauntlet, like gloves to clear a jammed gun, pry loose a bomb hung up on a shackle, or otherwise touch any metal, our hands and fingers would not instantly freeze tightly to the bitterly cold metal. On top of the thin heated suit, we wore thick, cloth, padded pants and jacket, thick, leather sheepskin lined flying boots and a thin leather helmet sometimes with large goggles. We always wore a greenish-rubber oxygen mask, and an Army steel helmet.

A lot of the time, I'm afraid, we didn't smell too good. Our inner flying clothes became sweat-soaked; our outer-heavy clothes oil stained, and there was no such thing as a cleaner's establishment, due to the wartime shortage of cleaning solvents and soap. Sometimes kind English ladies could be persuaded by our aromatic condition, and a well-earned fee, to do a washing and spot cleaning for us, to our heartfelt thanks.

Lastly, at supply we were each issued a parachute and an "escape kit." These escape kits were composed of a thin plastic box about six inches by eight inches by one inch thick. They were waterproof and of a size that fitted exactly into a special pocket of our thick outer flying trousers, in the shin area. The boxes were curved so as to conform to the rounded contour of the lower leg. Each box contained, as I remember, a tiny compass (no more than one-fourth inch in diameter) and a map of northwestern Europe, printed on both sides of an approximately 12-inch by 12-inch thin silk cloth, showing every known German POW camp, all the major cities, etc. This thin silk map could be folded and compressed to an unbelievably small volume.

The escape kit also contained two or three small gold coins, a morphine syrette for pain, no-doz tablets, aspirin, and atabrine tablets for purifying water and a couple of hard candies. There was also a tiny printed paper with foreign languages phrases on it. I remember the Russian phrase, "Ya Amarikanyets," I am an American. There may have been other things in the escape kits, I may have forgotten after 48 years.

Having dressed, we headed for trucks to take us out to the hard stands on the field where our planes were parked. They were already gassed up, full of bombs and ammunition, with full supplies of oxygen. Included were the "walk-around" bottles, which

John O. Bennett crew, Topeka, KS, March 1944. Top, L to R: Rodney Erxleben, Co-Pilot; Richard Dixon, Bombardier; John Bennett, Pilot; Frank Frederill, Navigator. Bottom: Lee Garson, Tailgunner; Amador Espinosa, Waist Gunner; Richard Hoyt, Radio Operator; Charles Turner, Engineer; Coleman Pinkerton, Belly Gunner. (Courtesy of Lee Garson, 445th)

were not glass bottles but metal canisters with rounded hemispherical ends. These could be plugged in to an airman's own mask, if he had to unplug from the planes oxygen system and move away from his position to render first aid, etc. The aircraft's system had all been checked out by that plane's ground crew, including the electrical system on which everything depended.

We all carried our parachutes in one hand, except the two pilots who wore theirs as backpacks. The navigators also carried their briefcases, which contained their charts and maps, books, rulers, dividers, and our indispensable E-6B "computer," which was a hand-held slide rule-type, analog device on which a navigator could very quickly solve a wind triangle without resort to plane trigonometrical formulas and a lot of arithmetic.

Having arrived at the plane, we stowed equipment aboard, checked guns and gun belts, checked bomb fuses, oxygen and other systems, then waited for time to "start engines." A few moments of last minute conversation, a final cigarette and urination, some nervous jokes, then aboard for engines start, taxi out into line, and, on the green light from the tower, take-off.

Assembly of the group's aircraft and the mission's bomber stream now took place; proceeding out over the English coast and over the freezing water of the North Sea, we flew in a large, spiralling, climbing flight until all the group's aircraft could "tack on" to the formation behind the lead aircraft. We were already visible on German radar. Then, each group in turn joined the bomber stream, and we departed the English coast for Nazi Germany.

At the height of its power, the U.S. 8th Air Force bomber stream of up to 1400 heavy bombers was 300 miles long and took two hours to pass a point on the ground.

On take-off, the navigator sat in a space on the flight deck, near the flight engineer and the radioman, and behind the two pilots. After we were well airborne, he stepped down through a hole in the flight deck, just in front of the bomb bay, into a 12-15 foot plywood enclosed passage. This passage led past the nose wheel and forward into the navigator's compartment and to the nose turret. The compartment was just ahead and below the pilots in their seats on the flight deck and was fitted on each side with a large metal box holding the belts of machine gun ammunition for the nose turret. Above each of these two boxes was a Plexiglass bubble window, just large enough to stick one's steel helmet into if one wanted to look outside directly below the plane. Also in the compartment, underneath the nose turret, were clear, flat, Plexiglass windows offering a view below, ahead, and to the sides.

A small fold down plywood board about chest high and about 18 inches by 15 inches in size was the navigator's work place. The navigator spent almost the entire mission standing up, facing backward to the direction of flight, working on this tiny table.

On entering the compartment, the navigator first hooked up his intercom wires so he could communicate with the rest of the crew. He stowed his parachute on top of one of the metal ammunition boxes within easy reach. He attached his oxygen mask to his helmet, where it hung away from his face until he clipped it to the other side of his helmet. At 10,000 to 12,000 feet all crew members went on oxygen for the next six hours or so. He also plugged in the wires for his heated suit for later use. During the mission his parachute stayed on the top of the ammunition container, and he hoped that if he needed to clip it on to the parachute harness he wore, that there would be time to do so. If, due to battle damage, the plane went out of control and into a violent spin with its centrifugal force and he could not reach his parachute to get out, too bad!

In addition to everything else, he wore an inflatable "Mae West" to keep him afloat if the crew had to ditch in the North Sea or the English Channel.

Lastly, he had available a flak suit, which was a kind of serape which he could drape over himself hanging down front and back. It was made of rough canvas into which dozens of small pockets had been sewn, each containing a small plate of hardened steel, thus giving some degree of protection from the many red hot, jagged fragments of flak shells from the very effective German 88 millimeter antiaircraft gun. In actuality, wearing a flak suit was impractical due to the intercom wires, oxygen tube, Mae West, and parachute harness over the bulky outer-clothing, so the flak suit was usually placed on the floor or elsewhere to prevent flak fragments from entering the compartment.

As we departed the English coast, we began climbing on course, gaining a thousand feet of altitude every few minutes.

One of the navigator's most useful instruments over England and the channel was the "Gee Box." This was a Loran-type electronic set, only of much shorter range. It measured the tiny differences in time of reception of radio signals from a pair of stations on the ground, the loads of a constant difference being a hyperbolic curve across the map of the English countryside and channel. By also tuning in another pair of Gee stations, a second hyperbolic curve was obtained where the two hyperbolics crossed was the position of the plane (to simplify slightly).

Unfortunately, as was discovered on the first mission, after a few minutes of climbing on course toward Germany, over all of Germany and much of France, Belgium and the Netherlands, the Germans had electronically "jammed" the Gee signal frequencies, and this device for position finding became useless for the rest of the mission.

Because of this, a navigator was extremely busy while Gee was still working, deriving the wind direction and velocity every 2,000 feet of altitudes or so. It was surprising how well this technique worked. As we ascended, the wind and our drift angle grew greater, and racked around several degrees in direction. By the time the mission altitude of 23,000 feet was reached, a surprisingly good determination of the winds at altitude could be made. Forecast winds, given at briefing, were seldom accurate enough to be of any use.

The reason this technique was so very important was that, with the exception of the lead plane and deputy lead plane, which had radar equipment not available to the other navigators for the rest of the mission beyond Gee, frequently six hours or more, we were usually entirely dependent on dead reckoning.

There were a few days, when for short periods of time, the ground was visible and we could get our position by identifying features of the terrain below, cities, rivers, auto-bahns, etc. But there were many days when the cloud coverage below was total and 10-10th coverage above, too. At such times, an accurate knowledge of the wind speed and direction was critical, in case we had to come back to England alone.

But when the weather situation over Germany was troubled, with complex interplay of fronts, it was very tricky indeed to maintain even an approximately accurate knowledge of position.

A complicating factor in the dead reckoning was the fact that, for all except the lead plane, there was no such thing as "the heading" or "the airspeed." The reason for this was that, as the pilots attempted to fly a close formation, they were continually kicking rudder and advancing or retarding the throttles. The result was that the navigator's air speed meter and compass, instead of remaining at fixed values,

in fact varied continually by several degrees and by several knots of airspeed. The navigator was thus forced to watch airspeed and compass continually, taking quick, five-minute averages of both airspeed and compass reading. These averages were usually pretty good, but over several hours, errors did build up in the dead reckoning, errors only occasionally corrected by identification of some kind of land mark on the ground.

And so we proceeded into Germany. The mission course consisted of perhaps a dozen dog legs of varying lengths. There were a couple of reasons for this: (1) We could conceal until the last possible minute the identity of the target. This concealment affected the German fighter plane controllers' deployment and timing of their fighter groups and (2) by fragment changes of course we could avoid, as much as possible, flying over heavily defended flak areas. Avoidance was never completely possible; targets were always surrounded by many, sometimes hundreds or even thousands of the big 88 millimeter flak guns, aided by their radars. At Berlin, for example, the flak defended area was 40 miles wide and 60 miles long; we were briefed that there were at least 5,000 of the 88s known from aerial photos to be taken.

Further errors were introduced when we had to change course to a new dog leg. The planes on the outer part of the turn had to fly the turn in a large curve, of radius several miles. During such a turn, the navigator could only guess at the radius and his position at the completion of the turn, since in those days there was no known way of navigating while flying a curved path over the ground.

Of course, celestial navigation was not possible since we were flying in the daytime, and even then sometimes had total cloud coverage above us as well as below us. This happened on a mission to Nuremberg. Almost always, if the sun was visible, no other celestial body was also to be seen, so no celestial position fix was possible. Also the course dog legs were short enough that to "shoot" a celestial fix, to compute it out, and to plot it, was impractical.

Always there was the terrible cold. Our planes weren't heated, and the temperature inside was the same as it was outside, and when the bomb bays were open, it was plenty breezy, too.

That winter of 1944-1945 was, it was said later, the coldest winter northwestern Europe had experienced in 20 years. Temperatures at our altitude were commonly around 40°-50° below zero, centigrade; on one mission I remember seeing the air temperature thermometer at the bottom of its graduated range of 60° below, centigrade. This works out to 76° below zero Fahrenheit. I don't know how much colder than that it got that day.

There tended to be two main trends in the mission courses used by the 8th Air Force, and the 2nd Air Division, on daylight missions, easterly, and trending southeasterly in late 1944 and 1945.

The easterly route, sometimes termed the 8th Air Force Highway, proceeded through a gap in the flak defenses near Alkmaar, the Netherlands, on the Dutch coast, and easterly past Amsterdam, Fwolle, Osnabruck, Minden, Hannover, Braunschweig, Magdeburg, and on to Berlin; or turning north to Emden, Wilhelmshaven or Hamburg; or turning south to Merseburg and Leipzig.

The southeasterly routes took the bomber stream to Cologne, Frankfurt, Nuremburg, Ingolstedt, Augsburg and Munich.

At times the flak was sporadic; at other times the flak gunners would throw up great walls of flak ahead and on each side of the bomber stream. We would no sooner fly through one wall than another would appear ahead. This went on until we eventually flew out of range of those particular batteries.

Our group attacked the oil refineries at

Magdeburg, on the Elbe River, twice, on missions several weeks apart. After our first encounter with the flak guns at Magdeburg, we were naively sure that that was where the flak gunner's schools were located, and that the guns on the ground were all manned by instructor gunners, because the flak was so accurate there. We half-seriously believed that they could not only pick which group of B-24s they wanted to hit, but a particular engine on a particular plane. It was spooky to our young minds.

On a mission to Berlin, to the Borsig Tank Works in the western part of the city, when our group arrived on the bomb run, the clouds below had largely broken up, it was about 8/10ths clear, and as we approached the city, thousands of flashes of light appeared on the ground, like sunlight glinting off water. It was eerie, until after a second or two, we realized that those were the muzzle flashes of the flak guns defending the city. They could see us equally clearly, and for a while it was a tense time flying through those huge artillery barrages. Inevitably, we had losses of aircraft and crews.

At Hallendorf, south of Braunschweig, we attacked the Hermann Goering Steel Works, a particularly satisfying target for us, since Goering was head of the German Air Force, the Luftwaffe.

Like the flak, German fighter attacks on our formations could be sporadic. At times we never saw a German fighter plane, but from radio reports up ahead in the bomber stream we could hear that those groups were getting hit hard. It was a great lottery as to which groups in the long bomber stream were attacked by the fighters. The concentrated firepower of our formations was crucial to our survival; if a bomber took battle damage and lost one or more engines and couldn't keep up, and had to cut corners at turns or leave the formation entirely, that crew was in deep trouble and often times doomed.

German fighter tactics varied widely. Sometimes they would attack on a broad front from directly ahead. At other times single fighters would slant in from the side in curving attacks on a plane, then break off the attack and roll out and down through the formation.

One day I heard our own guns going, and looked out to the right, and was surprised to see a ME-109 flying parallel to our plane no more than 50 yards away and firing at a B-24 up ahead. Our gunners got him, but the bomber went down.

Later in the war, a favored German fighter tactic was to mount several large rockets under each wing of their 109s or Focke-Wulf 190s, then to approach a bomber formation and while still outside the range of the bombers' guns, launch these rockets into the formations with a large salvo. The effect on the bombers was like flying through a great artillery barrage.

On a few occasions, RAF radio monitors reported overhearing the German fighter controllers ordering their fighters to ram the bombers.

We saw the first jet fighters (ME-262) and the first rocket-powered fighter (ME-163), but they did not appear in great enough numbers to be effective. Their performance was awesome for the time-750 miles an hour versus 155 for the bombers and 450 for the Allied fighter planes.

Despite the intensity of German fighters and flak resistance, no bomber stream was ever turned back from its targets. Once launched, the bomber stream was relentless.

On a mission to Nuremberg, deep in southern Germany, one of the terrible sights in the history of war developed. Nurenberg was the city that hosted the great Nazi party rallies in the huge amphitheater designed by Speer. It was the shrine of Naziism, famous throughout Germany, attended by hundreds of thousands of fanatical Nazi party members. The mission was a big one, probably close to the maximum of 1400 heavy bombers, and a thou-

The 68th Squadron preparing bombs for loading. (Courtesy of Howard D. Landers, 44th)

sand fighters as escort. The weather was 10/10ths over the city; it could not be seen.

The timings of arrivals were a little off; so many planes arrived to bomb through the clouds below that many groups had to leave the bomber stream and circle for half an hour, just waiting their turn to bomb! German resistance was ineffective. The knowledge of what those tens of thousands of bombs must be doing to that city below gave one the feeling of witnessing one of the great tragedies of the history of warfare. The Germans had indeed achieved Gotterdamerung, the twilight of their Gods, at Nuremberg that day.

Accidents were common, a bomb hung up in the bomb bay after the other bombs had gone down. It had to be pried loose by a crew man, usually the radioman, standing out in the windy open bomb bay, clutching whatever he could to keep himself from falling out of the plane.

Most of the planes in the formations had no bombardiers; the whole group depended on the bombardiers in the lead and deputy lead planes. On the bomb run, the other navigators set up the intervalometers which released the bombs in the proper sequence. Each navigator then watched the lead plane; when he saw its bombs start falling from its bomb bay, he flipped a switch on his own bomb panel. This started his own plane's sequential release of its bomb load. The navigator watched the indicator lights on his electrical panel; if the lights did not flicker out in sequence, the navigator then released the entire bomb load at the same time with a six foot long steel salvo handle attached to the bomb panel.

On one mission we were only 30 seconds or so away from bomb release, when to my horror, I saw another bomber group directly below us, slowly sliding across our flight path under our bombs. I called the pilot, whose radio could reach the lead plane, which in turn contracted the group below us. When they looked directly upward into our yawning bomb bays only three or four hundred yards above them—consternation. You wouldn't believe fully laden bombers could maneuver like that. An impending disaster in the skies, fortunately averted at literally the last second.

Three times we had to come home alone. Once on the climb on course our plane fell out of the sky, fully loaded with gas and bombs, over the English Channel. Our pilots fought desperately to regain control, and eventually did so, a few thousand feet short of the water. To this day no one knows what happened.

I gave the pilot a heading to a small airfield called Bradwell Bay, where, I learned later, RAF

Mosquito Intruder aircraft were based. We landed safely even though their runways were short. After an afternoon of beer in the local pub, thanking our lucky stars, we discovered the place had filled up with attractive young English women, in the uniform of the ATS, Auxiliary Territorial Service, We were amazed to learn they they "manned" many of the anti-aircraft guns batteries protecting London from the Germans V-2 "buzz bombs." Some of these girl gun crews had excellent records of V-1s shot down.

A second time we came home alone was the day the weather was so atrocious over England that there was no hope of assembling the mission. Some genius then decided we should assemble over eastern France where the weather was supposedly clear at 20,000 feet. So we climbed out on course in total fog until we reached the "splasher" (radio beacon) in eastern France. but was it clear at altitude as predicted? Still total, thick fog right up to the windows—nothing could be seen. After circling, looking for the other thousand planes, which we could hear all around us, we saw nothing. After half an hour of this Russian roulette in the sky, we got out of there, found a small fighter field in France and landed, later returning to England that day. That day's mission never did get assembled, but there were mid-air collisions between bombers.

The third time we came home alone, we were on a mission in north Germany, lost an engine to flak or malfunction, I forget which, and had to leave the formation. We flew northward across the German north coast and out over the North Sea, past the island of Helgoland. Sixty to eighty miles offshore we turned west; I got some accurate fixes from bearings taken on the clouds over the Frisian Islands, the islands themselves being obscured from view, and so safely home to Norwich, England. We were very lucky not to have attracted the attention of German fighter planes.

We flew three missions to the Ardennes during the Battle of the Bulge. Entire bomb groups were assigned to destroy intersections of roads running through the forested mountain valleys of eastern Belgium, Luxembourg and the Eifel section of Germany. The object was to destroy the road net behind the German lines in the Ardennes, so as to obstruct the movement of the German panzer columns and their supply columns. These missions were flown at low altitude and planes were lost to German ground fire. I saw a B-24 bomber close to us on the left take a hit from an 88 gun, just behind the bomb bay. The 88 shell broke the plane in two and both pieces went end over end and into the ground a few seconds later. The fuel tanks and bomb load went up in a huge explosion and fire. The whole thing happened in just a few seconds.

On the usual high-altitude mission, after leaving German airspace, we began to let down on course back to Norfolk County. Gradually, the deadly cold abated, leaving a large ball of ice frozen to the lower part of the oxygen mask where my breath had frozen with oxygen tube and intercom wires embedded in the ice.

But we did not relax our guard, German intruder aircraft had a nasty habit of attacking unwary planes returning to base, even while they were in the landing pattern. Any plane of any type, even Allied planes which approached us were tracked alertly by our guns.

On landing and taxiing back to our hard stand parking areas, we were met by trucks and carried back to the debriefing rooms. While waiting for our turn to report results of the mission, planes seen going down, chutes counted and their locations, enemy activity on the ground, fighter aircraft and flak encountered and any other pertinent intelligence, we usually had a shot of whiskey served by one or two real American Red Cross girls.

After debriefing, we turned in equipment and went to our rooms to clean up, put on Class A uniform, and go to supper, which was much like breakfast, only plus brussel sprouts.

After supper it was a couple of beers in the club plus, later, maybe some sausage and rye bread snacks, and a movie.

Occasionally, I would go into Norwich, then a city of about 130,000. There were dance halls there where one could get a drink, meet an English girl and enjoy a few dances together. I met some fine young English women at one particular dance hall, called the Samson and Hercules Club after statues of these historical figures, which served as columns holding up the roof of the entrance to the club. We called it, after those columns, the Muscle Club.

I was impressed by these young English women. They were well-behaved, sensible, reserved yet friendly, doing their best under the heavy restrictions of wartime rationing. Many of them served in the British forces and had fine records as service women. All in all, they were admirable girls. We were so young, barely out of our teens, and living day after day in a situation where one never knew if the next few hours would be one's last. It made all the normal life forces burn uncommonly brightly. One result was the number of good marriages, many of which endure to this day.

After a few hours of dancing and perhaps some hot fish and chips on the cold walk home, we arrived at her door. Then maybe a good night kiss, her wishes for good luck on the next day's mission and the walk back to the base, for a few short hours of sleep before that middle of the night knock on the door.

466TH BOMB GROUP
A Salute To My Flight Engineer

by J.W. Tikey (466th)

Tech. Sgt. Ivan S. Roberts was my flight engineer on B-24 *Slick Chick*, and later in 1944 on our various Pathfinder craft. My crew (those who still correspond) lost track of Ivan after we returned to the States, so we don't know if he's still living. But I remember him well because we owe our lives to this laid back, extremely loyal, Ozark-talking fellow crewman - even before we flew one combat mission out of England.

In early February 1944, after phase training in Casper, Wyoming and Alamogordo, New Mexico, we embarked for our combat base in Attlebridge, England, via the southern route (Herington, Kansas; West Palm Beach, Florida; Trinidad; Belem, Brazil; Fortaleza, Brazil; Dakar, Senegal; Marrakech, Morocco; and Prestwick, Scotland). This narrative essentially covers our leg from Fortaleza, some 2,200 plus miles over the South Atlantic, to Dakar. Aboard that evening were: J.W. Tikey, pilot; Richard Smith, co-pilot; Henry Tevelin, navigator; Francis Spigelmire, bombardier; Ivan Roberts, flight engineer; Frank Simek, radio operator; Marlow Jovaag, waist gunner; Boyd Condon, ball turret; Bernard Massing, tail gunner; and Frank Bois, waist gunner.

We spent two days in Fortaleza and were confined to the base awaiting better weather conditions. We finally were told to take off around 10 p.m. one evening in early February, with the warning that we would hit one of those numerous, huge South Atlantic storms and that the best penetration would be at 9,000 to 11,000 feet. Not to worry, they said!

About midnight we hit it, and it was a vicious one, tossing us around like a feather! We had to go straight through because we didn't have radar then and couldn't skirt around it.

My airplane had a Sperry A-5 auto-pilot aboard, but since the altitude control was "wired" off for technical reasons, I chose not to engage it and flew manually. (Probably a mistake because automatic rudder and aileron control would have helped. I later spent 36 years working for Sperry.)

Thunder! Lightning! Tremendous wind gusts! Up and down! Spigelmire, my bombardier, was praying like crazy. Weren't we all! This huge storm lasted two to three hours. But here's the scary part. After about an hour of this buffeting, I noticed the #3 engine manifold pressure slowly, slowly dropping from 30 inches. Here's where Roberts came into the picture, and he started frantically to try to resolve the reason for this ever so slow drop. We could never have made it to Dakar from our position on three engines. We would have run out of gas.

The #3 manifold pressure was down to 12 inches and I was thinking of feathering, when Roberts, thank God and praise the Lord, found the trouble. He removed the #3 oil dilution fuse and the pressure started a slow rise up to normal. The shaking and super G's on the plane caused a short in the system. With the benefit of hindsight, the malfunction probably occurred in the #3 oil dilution switch in the cockpit. It was "off" but "shorted" to "on" because of the storm.

There was no reason for Ivan to suspect this trouble, and why he pulled that fuse, God only knows. This was truly a miracle!

Gas was steadily pouring into the #3 engine oil manifold and would have caused an engine failure and/or a fire. The tremendous rains must have helped to curtail a fire.

Specifically, on the B-24, some gas was normally poured into the oil system in small amounts for cold weather starting. Overdilution causes sludge and carbon to be loosened in the engine, causing oil lines to clog and oil screens to collapse. A very dangerous condition.

Lt. Pastovich's plane, another in the 466th Group on this Dakar leg, lost one engine, then two, and never made it. Immediately upon landing and refueling, we helped search for this plane and absolutely no trace of it was found.

So, Tech. Sgt. Ivan S. Roberts, wherever you are, many, many thanks for what you accomplished on that dastardly night. You saved our crew—pure and simple.

Truthfully, I can say that this midnight to 3 a.m. episode in early February 1944 was my most frightening World War II experience. No combat mission compared to it.

The Bet At Barth

by Earl Wassom (466th)

In peacetime, it was not, at its best, a resort area by any stretch of the imagination. In war, it was hell. The place was called Barth, a prisoner of war camp located only a few miles south of the Baltic Sea in Northern Germany. It was the place where downed aircrews were interned, after having been captured by the enemy. This experience was one which was dreaded by anyone who flew combat.

Barth had 10,000 airmen interned there, divided into four administrative compounds of 2,500 each. These were elite and quality men, leaders and brave American youths. The German authorities took pride in the fact that they held captive three outstanding American fighter pilot aces with a com-

Lt. Gen. James Doolittle, CG, 8th Air Force awards decoration to Maj. Gen. William E. Kepner CG, 2nd Air Division at Ketteringham Hall. January 1945. (Courtesy of Jordan Uttal)

Cockpit of B-24, crew and bomb group unknown. (Courtesy of James G. Kotapish, 453rd)

bined total of 63 3/4 enemy aircraft destroyed ("kills") by these three men alone, and a bomber pilot who had received the highest military award his country could confer, the Medal of Honor. There were thousands of other internees who were equally brave and effective in their adversarial role in the war. Each was held in high honor and regard by his country. One of these "guests of the Germans" at Barth was Kenneth Powell of Nashville, Tennessee. More about Kenneth later.

Internment brought suffering beyond belief; the unending frigid weather, the unpredictable behavior of the guards, inadequate food, lice, sickness, boredom, death by starvation or by exposure. Yet there were times when the spirits of the prisoners of war were lifted. It was always through their own methods of creativity and ingenuity that this happened.

One ongoing "high" was when each new contingent of "guests" arrived in the camp. Up-to-date information became immediately available. It was true that the illegal radio, smuggled into the camp piece-by-piece, was a source of information from the BBC (British Broadcasting Company). But, the reports brought in by these new prisoners of war gave fresh, unbiased running accounts of how the war was progressing on both the Eastern Front with the Russians and the Western Front. Reports from eye witnesses of D-day, the Normandy landings, the liberation of Paris, the deliverance of the Lowlands, Patton's rapid dash across Europe towards the Rhine River, the increasing numbers of new bombers and fighters appearing on the British bases and in the air overhead brought silent but exuberant joy and hope to Barth's imprisoned guests.

As optimism flourished, small group conversation centered on the war's end and their freedom. Liberation was on everyone's lips. The war was indeed winding down! Talk of being home for Christmas became a utopian dream. Although all embraced the dream, not all were optimistic. This difference in opinion brought about the "bet at Barth." A wager was on. New life came to the camp. But what was there to wager? There was no money, no freedom or three day passes to London, no material possessions for the loser to forfeit, no points or promotions to be gained or lost.

Kenneth Powell, now living in Nashville, Tennessee, was shot down on his third mission. After a brush with death, a series of internments in differ-

ent prisoner of war camps, interrogations and threats by his captors, he eventually ended up in Barth. He was one among many who were always speculating on how long the war would last. He tells the following story with relish because he was an eyewitness to the whole event!

In a heated conversation, two men got carried away in their claims. An optimistic airman bet a pessimistic one on the following terms, "If we aren't home by Christmas, I will kiss your ass (not the mule kind) before the whole group formation right after head-count on Christmas morning." They shook hands, the bet was on! Well, the optimist hadn't counted on the Battle of the Bulge in early December. Consequently the war was prolonged and they were still in Barth on Christmas Day, 1944.

Christmas morning was cold, there was snow on the ground and frigid air was blowing in off the Baltic Sea. The body count for the compound began, each man was counted off, ein, zwei, drei, vier, funf, sechs, sieben, acht. Under ordinary circumstances, when the counting is completed and the German guards are satisfied that everyone is accounted for, the group splits up and everyone goes to their barracks. But this time, everybody stayed in formation. The two betting "Kriegies" walked out of the formation and went into the barracks. No one else moved! The guards were puzzled. They didn't know what was going on. Soon, the two men came out of the barracks. One was carrying a bucket of water with a towel over the other arm. The second one marched to the front of the formation, turned his back toward the assembled troops and guards, pulled down his pants and stooped over. The other took the towel, dipped it in the soapy water and washed his posterior. The whole formation was standing there looking and laughing. The German guards and dignitaries of Barth stood gazing in amazement, they didn't know what was going on! Then the optimist bent over and kissed his opponent on the rear! A mighty cheer went up from over 2,000 men. Then the puzzled guards joined in on the fun.

Nothing changed on Christmas Day, the same black bread and thin soup, sparse as it was. Yet it was a good day. As evening fell, the weather worsened, the barracks were cold, the last of the daily allotted coal briquettes were reduced to nothing but ash. Boredom was settling in for another long miserable night. Suddenly, the door opened, and a voice

shouted, "The curfew has been lifted for tonight! We're going to have a Christmas service over in the next compound." The weather was bitterly cold, the new fallen snow crunched under the feet of the men as they quickly shuffled towards their congregating comrades in the distance.

The nightly curfew always kept the men inside; this Christmas night's reprieve allowed them to be outside after dark for the first time. Above, the stars were shining brightly and high in the northern skies the dim flickering of Aurora Borealis added a magical touch as the troops assembled. Gratitude was felt in their hearts, a lone singer led out with one of the world's most loved and known carols. Others joined in and soon there was joyful worship ringing throughout the camp.

Silent night! Holy night!
All is calm, all is bright...

The German guards marching their assigned beats stopped in their tracks, they turned their heads toward the music. The words were unfamiliar but they recognized the tune, after all, *Stille Nacht, Heilige Nacht* was composed by a German. They loosened up, smiled, and joined in the celebration, the praise became bilingual.

Round yon virgin mother and Child
Cinsam wacht nurdas traute hoch heilige Paar
Holy Infant, so tender and mild
Holder Knabe im lockigen Hoiar,
Sleep in heavenly peace, sleep in heavenly peace.
Schlaf in himmlischer ruh', Schlaf in himmlischer ruh'.

The bet at Barth had paid off. Everyone had won! As the words of the carol rang in their hearts, there was literal fulfillment. Tonight they would sleep in peace. War and internment did not have the power to destroy the meaning and beauty of this special day.

It was Christmas. They were not at home. But they declared, "Next year we will be! All of us!" And they were!

Notes From The Log Of J.O. Auman (466th)

The 10-man B-24 combat crew put together at Casper, Wyoming, in September of 1943, with Lt. Robert H. Taylor, pilot, was a mischievous, untested, but dedicated bunch of typical young Americans. We were from all over the United States: New York, Texas, Oklahoma, West Virginia, Pennsylvania, Illinois, etc. We all had completed our flying training, engineering, radio navigation, and armorer schooling weeks before and were now ready (they told us) for our overseas three-phase training.

For the next three grueling months, our crew flew almost daily on missions that sometimes lasted up to 11 hours over the coldest states of the union at the wettest and windiest time of the year.

At that time, servicemen were rather new to the Casper area and were made very welcome by local society. It did not take our crew long to establish a home-away-from-home in a honky tonk establishment called "The Crystal Bar," where we found plenty of excitement playing cards, shooting dice, and drinking cheap booze.

Although Taylor was anything but our father or commander, he could fly a B-24 Liberator better than anyone on the field. His positive attitude about life and perfect control on take offs, landings, down drafts, or whatever gave the crew plenty of reasons to want to be with our pilot.

Our copilot, George R. Snowdon, was a well-educated engineer who kept close tabs on Taylor.

Together they kept the boxcar within its limits and balanced at all times.

John Lindenmeyer, our navigator, was replaced by Sol Rosenbaum, when we left Wyoming for Alamogordo, New Mexico. We were then joined by the newly activated 466th Bomb Group in late November, the same week Col. Arthur J. Pierce took command.

It was Capt. Ralph S. Bryant, a graduate of the Virginia Military Institute (a strict disciplinarian), who directed our final high altitude close formation flying those last weeks at Alamogordo.

Crew #607 (as we were now designated) took delivery of our Ford-built boxcar in mid-February of 1944 with sealed orders to transport ourselves to the European Theater of Operations via South America and Africa.

On our way to West Palm Beach, Florida, from Herington, Kansas, we made a pass over Birmingham, Alabama, the hometown of our waist gunner, Charles Culverhouse.

The following day we flew south to Waller Field in Trinidad. The next two airfields were newly built strips on the east coast in the jungles of South America. We flew to Dakar under darkness and cooler air, landing at dawn on a field south of the city.

Marrakech was our last staging before England. We spent two weeks waiting for the weather to clear in the north. This time off in the sun gave all the bomber crews time to paint nose art and names on their aircraft. Crew #607 decided on the name *Queen of Hearts* which was in keeping with the group's theme "The Flying Deck."

We touched down at Valley, Wales, on a rainy afternoon early in March. The next day we flew into Station #120 near Attlebridge, and became part of the 2nd Bomb Division and the 8th Air Force.

The group lost two aircraft at the very start of its first mission when they collided in the fog near our airfield.

We flew deputy lead to a German airfield near Biarritz, France, and made a perfect run west to east over the target, but nobody dropped any bombs. The command pilot on this mission was Maj. Asastacio; and, at this point he directed the flight to come around again to drop its bombs. We did, with fair results, and with antiaircraft bursts exploding at our exact altitude.

Al Rapuano was the outstanding crew member on our second mission when he claimed some good solid hits on a Luftwaffe FW-190 coming at us on a pursuit curve. He sobered up a bit when we landed, and he found his parachute on the hard stand where he left it that morning.

The most excitement on our third mission was a hit we took on the tail turret and rudder assembly by a fighter's phosphorous cannon burst that burned holes clean through everything it splattered.

Some of our missions started as early as 0230 hours, when we were awakened by a loud NCO truck driver. On two of our missions to South Germany, we saw the Alps and on one occasion we almost went to Switzerland with mechanical trouble.

Returning home after dark on our eighth mission, the English shore batteries opened up on our tail-end flight. It was our radio operator, William E. Ward, who, at our pilot's instructions, quickly made contact with someone and stopped the would-be disaster.

On our 10th mission, we were chased into the Liepzig area by fighters until we reached the city limits. Then the antiaircraft gunners shot us up until we came out the other side where the Luftwaffe came after us again.

On our way out, our tail gunner, Harm J. Krull, ran out of luck when he was hit with a large piece of shrapnel that lodged in his groin. We landed with two engines that day.

We flew our D-day mission late in the morning at about 15,000 feet. The clouds were scattered and visibility was good. Our group flew over the entire Normandy landing area, and we had a good pattern on the target.

The target on our 17th mission was an aircraft assembly plant at Eisenach, Germany. Again, we made a bulls-eye on the target, but it was in the wrong town. Russell F. Taylor (top turret) claimed later that we hit a large bread factory.

Rapuano and I volunteered to fly with another crew that was short three men on August 9. The pilot was Lt. Godbout, an excellent officer and a good PFF lead pilot. Our prime target that day was near Stuttgart, where we experienced an intense antiaircraft barrage. Later, on our way out, just south of Cologne, four sharp bursts that exploded below and behind us took both our wing men down. The Liberator on our left was Lt. Keyes, who called Godbout and told him that they were leaving the formation with major damage and wounded aboard. They crash landed in Holland about 45 minutes later, killing several of their crew.

The deputy lead on our right was Capt. Harry B. McGregor, one of the group's most admired flyers. His airplane fell off with a wing broken off, and his ship burst into flames immediately. We saw no one get out.

Our tail gunner, Edward Lukanic, also a volunteer on that day's mission, and I both had our legs shattered from the same burst that took the others down. We landed safely and were taken to the 65th General Hospital. Ed and I would have stuck around for more of the action, but it wasn't in the cards.

467TH BOMB GROUP
The Battles of Splasher 5
April 1944 - August 1944
by 1st Lt. Howard W. Johnson, 790th Sqdn.,
467th BG, 2nd AD, 8th AF (later Col. USAFR, RET)

World War II pilots who flew "the Hump" have emphasized the hazards of flying between India and China where the clouds have "rocks" in them. The 467th Bomb Group, and all 8th Air Force pilots flying combat missions from England in 1944 could emphasize similar weather hazards. The clouds over England did not have rocks in them. They had airplanes, lots of airplanes; under, in, and over the clouds. I submit that English weather and air traffic were greater hazards than the flak and the occasional German fighters that we encountered.

Adding to the constant hazard of collisions was the fact that we usually used only one major electronic "lighthouse," Splasher 5, located several miles north of Rackheath on the North Sea coast, towards which or away from which all of our pilots flew ADF courses to reach assembly altitudes or to let down after missions.

Formation assembly procedures, if possible, were to form at an assigned altitude over Splasher 5. If there were clouds at this altitude, we formed at whatever altitude necessary to get above the clouds. There were almost always clouds. During my entire tour at Rackheath, I rarely glimpsed the sun from the ground.

When assembly of the group aircraft had to be effected above the clouds (most of the time) our planes took off at 30-second intervals. When gear and flaps were up and a rate of climb of 300 feet per minute (FPM) at 155 miles per hour was established, we made a single needle width turn, if necessary, to 33 degrees magnetic heading (this was the actual heading of Runway 3), continuing to maintain the rate of climb and airspeed. At 5,000 feet, we made a single needle width turn to the left, still climbing and rolled out on a heading of 210 degrees magnetic. Climbing upwards, at 7,000 feet a turn to 30

degrees magnetic; at 9,000 feet a turn back to 210 degrees; 11,000 feet a turn; 13,000 feet, turn, and so on until we reached the top of the overcast. We then continued climbing to assembly altitude in a like manner and finally homed in on Splasher 5 while looking for the group formation assembly ship, *Pete, the POM Inspector*, which displayed the group assembly colors and flew a racetrack course over the beacon.

The return to base almost always involved Splasher 5. After leaving enemy-held territory, the group would "home" in on the splasher, letting down to 500 feet above the cloud tops. We returned to the racetrack around it again and the ships in order, first up, first down, leave the formation, at one minute intervals, home to the Splasher, then out to sea on a 53 degrees magnetic heading, letting down at 500 FPM at 160 miles per hour. At 5,000 feet we turned left and flew toward the splasher on an ADF (Aural Direction Finder Radio Aid) heading, still at 500 FPM and 160 miles per hour, to break out under the clouds (hopefully) before reaching the coast line. Then inland to pick up the Cromer-North Walsham-Worstead-Wroxham railroad line that would lead us to the base perimeter lighting and around the circuit to the left to the active landing runway.

Our crew, in addition to myself as pilot, included Bob Moulton as copilot, Don Kaynor as navigator (transferred early to a lead crew), Jack Merritt as bombardier-navigator (Don Kaynor was replaced by additional training for Jack plus a G box), Dave Baumhover as flight engineer, Roger Rafford as radio operator, Glenn Permann originally as ball turret gunner later waist gunner, Guenter Staedicke and Harold Peek as waist gunners and Woodrow Spacek as tail gunner.

Our plane, acquired at Wendover, Utah flown to England via South America and Africa, brought us home safely from 13 combat missions with me as airplane commander. We named the plane *Ruth Marie* for my wife, who shared the problems and the challenges of our lives at Mountain Home, Wendover, and Herington, Kansas.

On D-day our crew fought the Battle of Splasher 5 and Buncher 15 twice (the group flew three missions). When a pre midnight briefing was scheduled on June 5 (D-day evening), we knew something was up, not only because of the timing of the briefing, but because when we entered the briefing room we noticed the presence of a one-star general, Gen. Peck.

We rarely had a general in attendance at a 467th Bomb Group briefing, I am sure that this was one mission all of us wanted to fly, to be part of history on the long-awaited D-day. Plans were to have some 1,000 airplanes in the skies over England and France prior to and during the Normandy landings.

I recall we had one-way traffic on D-day eve and D-day. Our planes took off and formed up over Splasher 5. We then headed north to Scotland, then turned south on course to Normandy, then west past the Jersey Isles and then north, back to England. This was the special airways traffic control procedure set up for the D-day missions.

On D-day morning we took off long before dawn and made our race track pattern to Splasher 5. To find our place in the formation we had to recognize flashlight signals from the tail of the aircraft on which we were to fly formation. Somehow we did and we were over the beaches at the time of the landings.

I will always remember that on the way back, our radio operator, Roger Rafford, handed me earphones to listen to Gen. Dwight Eisenhower announcing the Normandy landings to an excited world. But our day was not over. On return and some rest, we took off for a second mission, the group's third of the day. Our return again involved a one-way traffic pattern as we had for the earlier mission. We let down to stay beneath a lowering ceiling and on arrival over England flew through the traffic patterns of many bases south of Rackheath on the aircraft carrier that was the island England.

The final challenge for this day came on arrival near Rackheath when the usually silent radio announced "bandits in the area." This meant that all lights on aircraft and on the ground were extinguished. Once more I headed for Splasher 5 and then out over the North Sea for a while. Returning to Splasher 5 and thence toward Rackheath, I was delighted to see perimeter lights for the various airfields again visible. Bob Moulton, always reliable, announced that he thought he saw the perimeter lights of Rackheath. He was right, and we landed about 24 hours after Gen. Peck's original briefing.

Flak Meeting Frags = Can Opener

by Arthur L. Prichard (467th)

About 3:30 a.m. on June 12, 1944, our crew, which was a lead crew of the 791st Squadron of the 467th Bomb Group, was awakened and told to attend a 0500 hours briefing for a mission to be flown that day. We were not supposed to fly, but the lead crew that was to fly was "stood down" because the pilot was indisposed after a poker game that had lasted long into the night.

After getting into the lucky clothes that most crew members saved for missions, we went to the mess hall for a sumptuous meal of Farmers Glory and dried milk—remember that stuff? It came in a bag like dog food. The first man at the table got the powder and the rest got diluted water.

Back to the Nissen huts, where we ate half of a candy bar. We always saved the other half because we knew we had to make it back to eat it.

The "field order," was in, the string had been strung on the mission board, etc., and as we sat down on the benches for briefing, everything was ready. As the curtain was pulled back, we saw that the string was not a long one and sighed with relief. This was six days after D-day and they had us flying missions that would help protect the beachheads and ships offshore. Today it was to Evreux, France to destroy the airfield so German fighters could not use it as a base to harass our invasion troops.

After the briefing, weather, flak maps, etc., I picked up the escape kits and joined the others in putting on flight gear. We were transported to the hardstand of #237, a new B-24H that had been delivered a few days before. Our original plane, *Gerocko*, was getting patched up, so it would stay on the ground today.

We pulled the props through, loaded up, started them up and awaited taxi instructions. When the call came, we taxied out second in line as we were deputy lead. After the customary wait, take-off time arrived, number one started rolling and we all took off in that long line and climbed out over Splasher 5. *Pete the POM Inspector*, the 467th group assembly ship, was circling and we formed on it, taking up our assigned position in the formation which slid into the slot of the groups heading out.

It was a partly cloudy day and as we passed over the French coast we could see the ships offshore and the Higgins boats shuttling from them to the shore.

On this mission, our planes were loaded, some with high explosives, some with incendiary, some with delayed action and some with fragmentation bombs. We were carrying frags. We encountered no opposition on the way in, but as we turned at the IP and started making our run we discovered that the airfield was defended by one battery of four anti-aircraft guns. They fired the familiar pattern of four bursts with little effectiveness as far as we were concerned at the time. As we opened the bomb bay doors and dropped our load, we saw the first of the black bursts of another salvo, a little ahead and high on the left. I had a feeling then that something was about to happen. The fourth burst hit our bombs, which exploded. I had been looking out at the wing before the blast, and had just glanced at the instrument panel as they blew and when I looked out again it looked like someone had been working up and down the wing with a can opener.

All positions checked in and no one had been hit, so we were feeling pretty lucky. We had the doors closed and were heading back. Lt. Charles Grace, the pilot had it all re-trimmed and all was going well, I thought, until I checked the gauges. We were losing oil pressure on #4 engine. Chuck gave me the signal to feather the prop, so I raised the guard and hit the feathering button, pulled off the power, etc., and shut it down. We had just gotten it trimmed again when I noticed the oil pressure was falling fast on #3. We conferred for a few seconds and Chuck said feather it, so I shut it down. A B-24 is not noted for flying very well on two engines, especially when they are on the same side. We had all the trim cranked in and were both standing on the left rudder to stay on course. I dropped about 10 degrees of flaps to help keep us afloat and Chuck had advanced power on the two remaining engines when I saw that #2 was running hot and the oil pressure was fluctuating. No way were we about to feather another prop, so Chuck opened the cowl flaps and we kept plugging along.

We were dropping down and falling behind the formation and feeling just a little lonesome back there. I was monitoring the command channel on the radio and being a confirmed coward at heart, I pushed the button and said "Lincoln Green leader (our code word for the day), this is Lincoln Green deputy." After awhile he said, "Lincoln Green deputy, what is your position?" I told him we were about 5,000 feet below and six or seven miles back. No answer at that time was just like goodbye. So after a while I said, "How about some fighter support." Still no answer, but about five or six minutes later the right waist gunner reported bogies at three o'clock. All positions were alerted, but they turned out to be four P-51 Mustangs and a beautiful sight they were. They stayed out of range for a couple of minutes, then slipped in closer and took up their positions—two on each side of us. We were escorted by them for the next 100 or so miles until we neared the coast, then they waggled their wings, waved and flew off for more exciting duties.

On the way in over the coast, we had seen a partially built airstrip near the beach, so we decided to look for it because we knew we could never make it back to England. Near Caen, we were subjected to fire from the ground and we turned northeast, then swung left to the coast. When we spotted the strip, I instructed the crew members to prepare to bail out, which was not new to them as they had done it once before. Flying parallel to the beach, everyone except Lt. Grace, Sgt. Bernard Solinsky, the engineer and I, jumped. Solinsky then went to the waist position where he waited till the gear was lowered. He announced that they were down and locked and he too jumped.

As we approached the strip that was being built by the Royal Engineers, they started putting up a barrage balloon which forced us to make an abrupt right turn into two dead engines, then a sweeping turn to the left to come in on the opposite end of the strip. On our short final approach, I tried to put down more flaps with the wobble pump as I found that the hydraulic system was inoperative, but I didn't have any luck. Looking ahead, we saw that there were 40 or 50 men working on the strip who were apparently unaware of our approach. Finally a soldier with a "Bren" gun fired it in the air and these men scrambled to get out of the way. One guy climbed off a bulldozer and ran, leaving it on the strip. As we touched down on the sandy surface at about 100 mph, things went fine for about 200 feet, then it started to veer to the right. When it had about reached the point where we were going to lose it, the only remaining good engine hit the dozer, tearing the engine loose but it straightened us out. We applied the brakes (having only one push left) and slowed it down somewhat, until we hit a bump of about two feet at the end of the worked on area. This jumped us up a little and we went through a hedgerow into the next field full of cows. We stopped just short of these animals and as that B-24 stopped, I popped my safety belt, got out of the chute harness, opened the top hatch,

Back row, L to R: Hal D. Farmer, B; Thomas F. Ryan, N; William G. Ritter, CP; Robert C. Knablein, P. Front row, L to R: Norman P. Bergh, E; Nicola C. Rutigliano, W; Nicholas Rizak, W; Harold A. Barnes, TG; Murry Kramer, R; Glenn L. Barr, BT. Topeka, KS, April 1944. (Courtesy of Robert Knablein, 44th)

"Sack-Time Sally," 565th Sqdn., 389th Bomb Group. (Courtesy of Russell R. Leslie, 389th)

climbed out, ran down the left wing and jumped to the ground. I heard the patter of feet and looked up in time to see Lt. Grace jump off and land beside me.

What do you say at a time like this? I said to Chuck, "That was a hell of a wild ride," and he just nodded his head in agreement.

While we were standing there, there was a shrill whistling and swishing sound followed by an explosion. Chuck said "What the hell is that?" We found out immediately, it was artillery fire.

The Germans had been unable to get planes up as spotters and probably knew a strip was being prepared, so they zeroed in on us on the way up. Luckily we had come in hot and had ended up a considerable distance off the end of the strip, so the shells fell on the strip and not on us. We had taken refuge behind a stump and when the barrage stopped, we stood up and saw several men running toward us, followed by a jeep. In that jeep was the maddest man I saw all the time I was in the ETO. He was Wing Commander Brown of the Royal Canadian Air Force who was to bring his planes in the next day. While yelling about his strip being blown up, he got to the point of being nearly distasteful.

About that time, Chuck and I felt that we were responsible only to God and Col. Albert Showers, in that order. So we told the wing commander that all we really wanted at the time was to get back to Rackheath, so he drove off in a huff. The 467th Bomb Group had the distinction of having the first four engined aircraft to land on freed French soil.

Memories Of The 8th Air Force "Surprise" Attack on Hamm, Germany
April 22, 1944
by Maj. Kenneth L. Driscoll, USAF (Ret.) (467th)

Why am I writing this article 48 years after the events happened? Here is why:

A couple of years ago I heard about the 467th and 801st/492nd Bomb Group Associations. During 1944 I had flown five daylight B-24 bombing missions with the 467th Bomb Group and 30 secret night missions with the 801st/492nd Bomb Group dropping spies and supplies to support the French underground forces.

I joined both associations, have gone to their reunions, have received their quarterly newsletters,

and bought and read the two books written that best describe the history of both groups: *The 467th Bombardment Group, September 1943-June 1945* and *The Carpetbaggers, America's Secret War in Europe* by Ben Parnell, which describes the secret night missions of the 801st/492nd Group.

Because of my renewed interest in both groups, I have recently been reminiscing about the various missions that I flew from April through August 1944.

One mission in particular stands out above the other 34, the 467th Bomb Group mission to Hamm, Germany on April 22, 1944. That was my crews third combat mission.

Headquarters, 8th Air Force, decided to pull a "surprise" attack on Germany. Our target was the railroad marshalling yards at Hamm, Germany.

The "surprise" was that the 8th Air Force was to hit the target about an hour before dark and catch the Germans unprepared to retaliate with anti-aircraft guns (flak) and fighters.

After bombing the target, we were to fly in formation back to the coastline. Upon reaching the North Sea coastline, darkness would be setting in.

At our afternoon briefing, our instructions were that when it got dark, we were to break formation, turn on our running lights and each crew was on its own to return to base.

The group aircraft took off as scheduled late in the afternoon/early evening. My squadron, the 788th, was not leading the group. My crew was flying number two position (deputy lead) in the squadron formation. I do not recall who our squadron lead pilot was.

The group got into formation at about 24,000 feet at the assigned radio beacon north of our base, Rackheath. At the designated time, the group turned east and joined other groups flying in formation at the division assembly line. When we crossed the North Sea, our altitude was approximately 27,000 feet.

After landfall, we saw some flak bursts in the distance but no enemy fighters. About 10 minutes prior to reaching the IP (a point above the ground from which a straight bomb run was made to the target) our plane got hit by flak which disabled the #2 engine. I dropped back out of formation, lost some air speed but was able to hold altitude. We dropped back about 200 yards from the formation before we had #2 prop feathered (the front edge of the propeller blades pointed forward to reduce drag), mixture controls full rich, propellers in maximum

RPM and the throttles full forward. We were too far over enemy territory to turn back. A single B-24, with one engine out, flying alone, would be an inviting and easy target for enemy fighter aircraft.

Luckily, I had been able to maintain altitude. With full power on the three good engines, I was able to catch up to and rejoin the formation. Another aircraft had pulled into my vacated position and I pulled into the open spot at the back of the 788th formation. With the extra power on the three engines, I did not have any trouble staying in formation.

Within a couple of minutes, we got to the IP and the various flights got in trail position for the bomb run.

After dropping the bombs, the flights turned right off the target and reformed into the normal group formation configuration for the return flight.

The flight to the coast was routine with the exception of having to keep extra power on the three good engines to enable us to keep in formation.

Just prior to reaching the coast in semi-darkness, enemy anti-aircraft guns shot up some tracer shells at us. They resembled the bright white Roman candles used at Fourth of July celebrations. There were 10 or 15 of them. I saw them passing nearby to the right of us. They were going straight up. Because my field of vision was cut-off at the top of the copilots window, I could not follow them up. I had never seen anything like that before.

Shortly thereafter, we crossed the coastline and headed back across the North Sea. When we were out over the water about 15 miles, darkness was becoming a reality.

I decided to break out of the formation a little early due to the fact that I had been pulling excessive power on the three good engines while in formation, and did not want to risk losing another one at night over the North Sea. I wasn't sure how far a B-24 would fly on two engines and I did not want to find out.

Shortly after dropping back out of formation, we turned on our running lights and started a very slow descent. This allowed me to reduce the power and take the strain off the three good engines.

When full darkness came, I started to fly by instruments, which was normal procedure on night flights over water. The navigator, Lt. Harold Pantis, kept getting electronic fixes. He kept us all informed, over the intercom, as to when we would make landfall near Great Yarmouth, and the estimated time of arrival (ETA) over our base at Rackheath. We did not see the lights of other aircraft. The formation had pulled ahead and dispersed in front of us. They were flying faster than we were.

Lt. Pantis who was superior at his work, gave me a few small corrections as we kept our slow letdown to the English coast.

There was radio silence.

Just about when our ETA over the coast was up, the navigator called and said we were then crossing the coastline. The night was very dark and there was a 100 percent blackout on the ground. We could not see the coastline or anything on land. He gave me the heading to the base and an ETA which was only minutes away. I told the crew to get into their normal positions for landing (ball turret up, tail gunner out, waist guns secured, etc). The navigator was to stay in place in the front of the aircraft until the base was in sight.

When the ETA at the base was up, the navigator called over the intercom and said that the base was directly below us. I banked the aircraft to the left and looked down. I could see absolutely no base lights or runway lights—everything was blacked out.

The city of Norwich was located about eight miles southwest of the air base. At Norwich, barrage balloons were up to protect the city from low flying German bombers. We had to avoid flying over the blacked out city or risk being off course and having a cable from a balloon knock us down, or being fired upon by the anti-aircraft guns protecting the city.

While circling around near the base, some other aircraft were also flying around with running lights on. No aircraft had an assigned altitude. We were on our own.

Horsham St. Faith, another B-24 base in our wing and division, was located about eight miles to the west of our base. We could not see any lights at that base either.

We did not have an alternate airport assigned during the briefing.

There was still radio silence. The control tower did not send out any instructions. I do not remember if I, or any other pilots flying around, broke radio silence. If one of us did, the tower did not respond.

With headings supplied by the navigator, I made about six passes across the blacked out base. The entire countryside was very dark with no lights or landmarks visible.

I then told the navigator that we would fly northeast for five minutes and then make a 180 degree turn and head back to the base. I thought that by flying straight and level for that period of time, the navigator would be able to better reconfirm our exact position in relation to the base.

After making the 180 degree turn, he gave me the heading and ETA back to Rackheath. When the ETA was up, he again stated that the base was below us. I then began to circle to the left again but the base was still not in sight.

By this time, I was getting quite concerned. We had been flying for about three hours with an engine out; Norwich, with its barrage balloons and anti-aircraft guns was close by; other aircraft were milling around in the darkness; no alternate airport to go to; no radio contact with the tower and no lights on the ground to indicate our base and runway. The whole countryside was still blacked out.

Luckily, fuel was not yet a problem. We had taken off with a full load of gas and the flight to Hamm was not a long one.

After circling about three more times, all of a sudden the runway lights were turned on. I immediately entered a normal traffic pattern. As usual, landing lights were turned on during the final approach. The tower still maintained radio silence.

We landed and rolled to near the end of the runway, turned right on to a taxiway, turned off our landing lights and started to taxi back to our parking area. Periodically, the landing lights were turned on for a very short time to assist me in taxiing the aircraft in. These lights were not designed for full time ground operation and would burn out quickly with prolonged use.

When we got about halfway down to our parking area, military personnel in a jeep flagged us down and I stopped the aircraft. We were then informed that German fighters and fighter bombers were in the area and had hit the base. The German planes had intermingled in the darkness with the 8th Air Force planes coming back across the North Sea and were not detected when crossing the English coast.

We shut off all lights and, due to the extreme darkness, proceeded slowly to our parking area. Needless to say, after shutting down the three engines, we evacuated the plane in a hurry.

We were told later at the debriefing that German aircraft had come across the base, strafed it, and dropped two bombs. One enlisted man, who had been visiting friends at the base, was killed, and five aircraft had not yet returned. It was not known at that time if they had been shot down by the intruding German aircraft or had landed at some other

8th Air Force base in East Anglia. Each aircraft had a 10 man crew.

Early the next morning, I went down to the squadron operations building to get clued in as to what had happened the night before and to find out the status of the five missing planes. I was told that three had landed safely at other bases and two were shot down close by with no survivors. One was shot down northwest of the base by a German fighter and the other shot down by anti-aircraft fire near the base.

Just by chance, both first pilots on each of the downed aircraft (Lts. Jack Skinner and James Roden) had been close friends of mine from our early days of training at Wendover, UT. In my opinion, Lt. Roden was the best formation flying pilot that I had ever known. I felt a great personal loss upon hearing of both their deaths.

I never learned why the tower did not break radio silence and instruct us to turn off our lights, scatter in a northerly direction and return in a half hour or so. It is possible that the first few returning aircraft were advised of the situation. At that time, I estimated that we were about eight to 10 minutes away and 20 to 25 miles out from the base. With VHF radios, we should have been able to pick-up tower transmissions at that distance.

The German fighters probably did not try to shoot down any of our aircraft while intermingled with us coming in over the North Sea. That action would have been detected and their surprise attack ruined. Our incoming aircraft would have been alerted and appropriate dispersal information given to us. The ground bases and antiaircraft gun sites would also have been alerted earlier.

We had no fighter protection while flying over the North Sea. Our normal excellent fighter escort was provided by P-38, P-47 and P-51 day fighter type aircraft while flying over the continent. We did not have any night fighters since the 8th Air Force had always flown during the daytime and there was no apparent requirement for them.

There were about 1,000 B-17s and B-24s crossing the coastline en route to about 30 to 35 8th Air Force bases in East Anglia.

If the German fighter type aircraft had enough fuel and ammunition, all their pilots could have returned to Germany as aces or double aces. This was a fighter pilots dream—to be undetected among

hundreds of enemy bombers flying at night with their running lights on and their guns secured (unmanned for landing).

I do not know how many bombers the 8th Air Force lost that night. I do know that our group lost two and there were probably about 30 to 35 groups flying.

To the best of my knowledge, the 8th Air Force never made any more of these "surprise" early evening missions over the continent.

PATHFINDER OPERATIONS

by Arnold J. Dovey and John B. Conrad (392nd)

Early radar navigation-blind bombing systems, known as H2S and OBOE were succeeded in 1943 by an improved version, AN/APS-15, code named "H2X" or "Mickey," developed at the Massachusetts Institute of Technology. The first plane modified to be equipped with H2X, a B-17, arrived at the 482nd Bomb Group (PFF), Station 102, Alconbury, England in September 1943. But the number needed for operational use and training did not arrive until early 1944, when 26 equipped B-17Gs and 14 equipped B-24Hs were received.

The 482nd Bomb Group (PFF) was composed of three squadrons rather than the four usually assigned to bomb groups. Each squadron trained navigators for the bomb (later air) division to which it was assigned. The 814th Bomb Squadron trained B-24 Pathfinder navigators for the 2nd Bomb Division.

The SOP for H2S and OBOE led missions extended to early H2X led missions with the PFF bomber proceeding from Alconbury to the host group scheduled to lead the division or wing. Its crew participated in the host group briefing, taking the wing commander and lead navigator aboard the PFF bomber. A DR navigator furnished by the host group flew in the deputy PFF aircraft if one was assigned. All other personnel on the PFF bombers were furnished by the PFF squadron involved. On the bomb run, Aldis lamp signals and smoke flares informed the formation if it was to be a visual or blind bomb drop and when to salvo bombs. Succeeding groups bombed on smoke trails left by the groups ahead. In order to achieve a more accurate

Harry Carls' crew. Front, L to R: Robert McCoy (G), LaVerne Graf (CP), David O'Connor (B), Harry Carls (P), Robert Lawser (G). Back: Frank McKever (E), Robert Knight (G), Leo Scheeler (RO), Tom Bouley (N), Vince Muti (G). (Courtesy of Charles Freudenthal, 489th)

concentration of bombs it was obvious that a PFF lead was needed for each group.

In January 1944, the first contingent of navigator trainees arrived at Alconbury, some with preliminary radar navigation training received at the 1st Sea Search Attack Group at Langley Field, Virginia. The plan was to initially form a PFF squadron in each division with the 564th Bomb Squadron of the 389th Bomb Group at Hethel chosen for this honor in the 2nd Bomb Division. In February, each group in each division sent two crews to Alconbury for training, and upon completion in mid-March crews from 2nd Bomb Division groups and 12 new H2X equipped B-24s were transferred to the 564th Bomb Squadron. Whenever possible, the crews selected to lead specific groups were those who were on detachment to the 564th Bomb Squadron from that group.

In addition to the known value in finding check points and correcting navigation errors over clouds on the way to the target, it was found the H2X navigator could pinpoint with some accuracy industrial targets situated beside cities or shore lines. Direction, drift, distance to the target and sighting angles could be provided to the bombardier for synchronization of the bombsight. The bombs would be released automatically as if it was a visual drop. This coordinated method was soon shown to improve visual bombing. In cloud breaks, the bombardier could take over visually with only minor corrections.

In early May 1944, a second PFF squadron was established in each division with the 66th Bomb Squadron in the 44th Bomb Group at Shipdham serving as such in the 2nd Bomb Division. By August there were PFF squadrons in each combat wing and by December all groups had their own PFF aircraft.

Graduates of Army Air Forces Advanced Navigation Schools received the MOS and rating of "1034-Navigator." This MOS rating was retained by those who later received radar navigation training at the 1st Sea Search Attack Group at Langley Field, Virginia. However, upon completion of the 482nd Bomb Group Pathfinder School, the MOS and rating were amended to read "1038-Radar Navigator."

An early policy in developing lead crews required each bomber squadron to name and maintain four of its most experienced crews as crews eligible to lead missions. The key figures in a lead crew were the pilot, navigator and bombardier and the command pilot (sometimes occupying the co-pilot's seat) serving as task force commander on any particular mission. The introduction of H2X brought about changes in the composition of lead crews.

Lead crews now carried three navigators; the crew's regular navigator as DR navigator, the radar (PFF) navigator and the pilotage navigator. In H2X equipped B-24s, the DR navigator was stationed on the flight deck immediately behind the pilot and the radar navigator was also on the flight deck immediately behind the co-pilot. The command pilot occupied a jump seat between the two pilots and two navigators. The pilotage navigator flew with a map in the nose turret. The radio operator position and equipment were relocated over the bomb bay, accessible from the waist of the aircraft.

By late summer, 1944, mostly bombardiers, MOS and rating "1035-Bombardier," were being recruited to fill the increasing demands for H2X trainees. At the end of the European war, the MOS and rating had been amended to "0142 Radar Observer, Bombardment H2X." Those who also received training in the spring of 1945 in EAGLE, an improved and enhanced system, acquired an MOS of "0142-EAGLE."

The landmark success of the blind H2X bombing of Bremen on July 29, 1944 by 1,200 bombers led by a PFF ship was immediately commended tele- graphically by General Hodges, the division commander. It was followed by extensive coverage in the then-classified publication, *Target Victory.*

489TH BOMB GROUP
Bomb Baby Couldn't Swim
by Morgan G. Higham

0330
Aug. 5, 1944
Halesworth, England

Charge of quarters came into the Nissen hut, shook my shoulder and said, "Lieutenant, your crew is flying today."

I got out of bed, woke up my copilot, navigator, and bombardier, and we dressed as quietly as possible because the other crew in the hut was not scheduled to fly. We walked over to the mess hall and saw the usual breakfast of green powdered eggs, powdered milk, burnt toast and marmalade. A truck took us over to the locker and briefing room, where we dressed in our flying clothes, got together as a crew, and went into the briefing room.

As usual the map on the wall was covered so we could not see the target, the routes to be flown, the formation position we were to fly, or any of the other information we would need to know. We sat there guessing what the target might be and what the flak would be like and if it might be, one of the targets we had been to in the last few days.

This was to be the fifth day in a row we were scheduled to fly and we were a little leery of returning to any of the same areas. On the first day we bombed Rouen, France. The second and third days sent us to Avesnes Chaussey, France and on the fourth day we went to Wismar, Germany. When the colonel and the briefing officers came in and we all settled down, the map was uncovered and we saw the target was Brunswick, Germany.

Then 2nd Lt. Robert E. Vickers and his crew in mid 1944 (later assigned to 392nd Bomb Groups, 2A Div., 14 CBW, 8th Air Force, England. Rear: Vickers, D.E. Schwarzer, K.E. Roberts, R.E. Shaner. Front: E.S. Markham, R.S. Moore, W.R. Nock, J.A. Carter, R.S. Leinweber and W.A. Henthorn. (Photo courtesy of R.E. Vickers)

"Rugged But Right" (Courtesy of M.O. Holmen, 448th)

"Angel Eyes" (Courtesy of Ernest Kelly, 458th)

After the briefing we picked up our chutes and were trucked out to our assigned plane. The ground crew was working on the plane and had been all night, trying to repair the damage from the day before. When the time came to start the engines, we were still not in the plane and the engineering officer came along and told us we would not be able to fly the plane as repairs could not be made in time. I asked him to notify the motor pool to send a truck to the hard stand, and we began to load our equipment in it.

A captain was in the front of the truck and he informed me that there was a plane over in the 846th Squadron that was ready to fly with all bombs loaded but no crew assigned. We were to take that plane and join the formation in our originally assigned position. We drove over to the assigned hard stand and began our preflight checkout in a hurry as most of the planes in the group were already airborne.

The plane we were to fly was named *Bomb Baby* and had been worked on for engine problems. Number two engine had been giving them trouble on previous missions, but it had been test flown and declared ready to go. We finished the check list, started the engines, and taxied out for take off. We were the only plane left so were given the green light and had a rolling start down the runway.

We were quickly airborne and climbing without any problems. As soon as I had given the crew the order to put on their masks, #2 engine started losing power. By increasing power on the other engines, we were able to catch up with the formation and got into our assigned position. The group was flying near the end of the division formation and there were a lot of contrails and bumpy air pockets to fly through, which made it difficult to stay in formation with one underpowered engine.

The flight across Germany was uneventful and we reached the IP north of Brunswick without flak or fighter opposition. As the group turned south and could see the target area, we could see a solid cone of black antiaircraft fire over the city of Brunswick with the bombers ahead of us flying into the cone. There were enemy fighters attacking the bombers (most of them with our own fighter protection chasing them) and some planes were going down. At least one plane was on fire. The sight of parachutes opening below us was enough to make most of us shrink into our little metal seats hoping we would not be the next ones to be hit.

As we neared the target we noticed the smoke coming up from the ground was varied colors, red, green, orange, and blue. We later learned that a chemical factory had been hit.

The formation was tightened up and bomb bay doors opened, which in the rough air made close formation flying a real problem. The smoke bomb fell from the lead ship and our bombardier shouted "bombs away!" At that moment we were hit by flak and the plane dropped out of formation and out of my control. After falling a few thousand feet we were able to get control of the plane.

After heading west, I called for a crew check. None of the crew had been hit, but the plane itself had many holes in it. We had been hit by two shells, one near the right side of the bomb bay and the other in the center of the right wing. The report from the tail section was that the right side of the bomb bay was riddled and there were many holes in the rest of the back end. The engineer reported from his top turret that there was a large hole between #3 and #4 engines. He reported that we had lost some of our fuel and we needed to conserve as much as possible.

The rest of the planes in the formation had disappeared to the west high above us. We were alone over the middle of Germany—a lonely feeling, indeed. I switched the radio to "C" channel and as soon as I could get a break in the chatter, called for help from any "little friend" in the area. I gave our position and within a few minutes two P-47s appeared on my wings and said they would stay with us as long as they could.

The engineer once again warned me we were low on fuel, and I made the decision to dump all excess baggage. I throttled back as far as possible and the men in the tail section reported they had dumped their guns, ammunition, and anything else they didn't need. While all this was going on, we hadn't paid too much attention to our heading until suddenly four bursts of flak appeared a few hundred yards in front of the plane. I made a sharp turn to the right. The left waist gunner reported four more bursts on our original heading, but that was all we saw. Later we found out that we were approaching the front lines and it was probably German army troops shooting at us.

We turned west again and the navigator gave us a heading for the base. As we approached the Zuider Zee in Holland our fighter escorts told me that they would have to leave us as they were also low on gas and would have just enough to get back to their base. I thanked them and told them we thought we would be all right as we could see the white cliffs of Dover to the south.

I throttled back some more and started a slow descent to an altitude where we could take off our oxygen masks. I called Air-Sea Rescue and told them our position and our problem. They said they had our position and would keep in touch. Again the engineer said we were low on fuel and in a few minutes added, "Sir, I think we are out of gas."

He was right, and the four engines stopped one right after the other. I pushed the alarm button and told the crew to bail out. I called "May Day" to Air-Sea Rescue and they told me to stand by. I just couldn't do that.

I put the plane in a bank to the right so we might be closer together in the water and had just unhooked my seat belt when my copilot, Eddie Gruber, came rushing back and asked if I needed help to get out. I told him to go ahead, I would be right behind him. As we reached the bomb bay, he stopped and we found our radio operator sitting in the bomb bay holding on to one of the girders. He was not going to jump. Eddie grabbed his leg and I stamped on his hands and we threw him out of the plane.

Then Eddie jumped. It appeared we were so low that none of us would be able to make it. I pulled the "D" ring on my parachute just as I jumped. I felt the chute pop open and then I hit the water. As I came up to the surface of the water, the plane crashed just a few hundred yards away. It seemed to explode as it hit. I got out of my parachute and inflated my Mae West and then started to look for help. None of my crew was in sight.

At this point I had to make a big decision. It was getting late in the afternoon and the fog was rolling in from the north. One of the first things we were taught to do was get rid of our boots and shoes. I wore a size 13 shoe and for over three years had been having trouble getting shoes in my size, so I decided to keep my shoes on. I figured that if I was rescued, I wouldn't be able to get another pair of shoes to fit, and if I wasn't, it wouldn't matter anyway.

The swells in the water were four to six feet high and one moment I would be down between the two walls of water and the next moment I'd be on top with visibility for miles to the south. The fog was getting closer on the north. There were many boats I could see in the distance and each time I was on top of a swell, I would holler and wave my arms, but it didn't appear that anyone could see me. A British Air-Sea Rescue plane buzzed me and dropped a green dye marker near me so I knew that someone had seen me. I was about in the middle of the water between Holland and England and I knew I couldn't swim that far. I was worried about all the men I had ordered to jump.

After I had been in the water for what seemed to be hours, but was probably two at the most, I nearly gave up hope. All the boats seemed to be so far away and none headed in my direction. I was still hollering and waving when I heard someone else holler. I looked back and saw a boat coming up in back of me. It was a British motor torpedo boat that had been on its way to Holland to attack a Germany convoy that was sneaking up the coast line. As they approached the Dutch coast, they lost an engine and the squadron commander gave orders to go back to base. At the same time, my men had started jumping right over the boat.

Four of my men were already in the boat and when the officer found out I was the pilot, he asked me how many men had jumped. I told him 10. He got on his radio and could account for nine of the men. He asked me what I wanted to do. As the plane wreckage was so close, we decided to go over there to see if by chance the 10th man had not made it out of the plane.

As we neared the wreckage we could see all of the small walk-around oxygen bottles from the plane floating in the wreckage. The bottles were about the size of a man's head and we checked each one, hoping it was only a bottle. About this time the fog rolled over us and we couldn't see five feet away from the boat. I told the officer we might as well go in to his base as we wouldn't be able to see anything until morning anyway. He headed for his base and as we got close to the shore, the fog lifted and we could see without any problem. As we pulled in to the dock at Yarmouth Naval Base, there was a man standing at the end who started running up as we started to get out of the boat.

It was our missing 10th man, the bombardier, Lt. Davis. He had been picked up by a small fishing boat that didn't have a radio and as soon as he was rescued, the captain had headed for the base and dropped him off. He had quite a story to tell. When he jumped from the plane he was swinging in his chute and hit the water on a down swing and wrenched his back. He was all tangled up in his parachute shroud lines and had to take out his knife and cut himself free. When he finally was free, he inflated his Mae West, which promptly deflated as he had cut it while cutting his shroud lines. He said that between his hurt back and the cold water he was near the end of his endurance when the fishing boat picked him up.

We were given a meal and put to bed in a large dormitory where we were the only occupants. A couple of hours later our squadron commander, Maj. Paul Woodward, and two more of the squadron staff came in to the dormitory to visit us and see if we were all right. They had heard that I had ditched the plane and were all excited until they found out I had not ditched and had bailed out all of the crew. They said they were glad we were all OK and that we would be brought back to the base in the morning. I could tell they were disappointed that I had not had a successful ditching, but I was one happy person because all of my crew were safe.

In the morning there was a knock on the dormitory door and three women of the Royal navy came into the room bringing us tea before we got out of bed. I was informed that the admiral desired the crew to come and have breakfast with him and his staff. The ten of us, dirty, unshaven and with clothes still damp from the day before, went into the admiral's dining room where he and his staff, all dressed in their clean, bright navy uniforms, sat at every other chair around the table. I sat at the admiral's right side, and my copilot sat on his left, with the rest of the crew between the staff around the table. They served us a breakfast that was delicious and included fresh eggs, which most of us had not seen since arriving in England.

After breakfast the admiral asked me to come into his office. He showed me a large map that covered one wall of the office. He explained that it was a large scale map of his area of responsibility in the North Sea and that we had bailed out in his area. There were hundreds of pins in the map and he told me that each one indicated where they had rescued plane crew members or sank an enemy ship or depth charged an enemy submarine. Each color pin had a special meaning for him and he could tell stories about many of them.

He had asked me to his office to find out if we had seen a B-17 in trouble in our flight across the water. I told him that we had seen one flying a mile or so to the north of us, but it didn't seem to be in any particular trouble outside of having one engine feathered. Because we had been busy with our own problems we hadn't paid that much attention to it. He said that it was probably the one that had called in a May Day, and they had not been able to find anything but a big oil slick on the heading on which they had reported to be flying. The admiral was a real gentleman, and we certainly appreciated the way we were treated.

About 10 o'clock in the morning of August 6, a truck arrived and took us back to Halesworth. As we arrived they took us right to the main hangar and we were told we could watch the USO entertainment before reporting for interrogation. The entertainment was Glen Miller and his orchestra, which we enjoyed for nearly two hours.

Before being assigned to me, most of my crew (six of them) had been members of a crew that had been hit on a mission June 22 over France. Before reaching England the plane crashed in the sea south of London. The pilot, navigator, and one of the gunners didn't jump and were killed in the crash. The others were picked up by the RAF Air-Sea Rescue launches. Our reluctant radio operator was one of these men. He couldn't swim and the thoughts of going into the water again made him freeze in the bomb bay. Eddie Gruber and I decided to ignore the problem we had had with the unwilling crewman, and neither of us mentioned it at the interrogation.

Ten of us came back very happy, but one didn't make it, because *Bomb Baby* couldn't swim.

The crew members who had jumped in the water for the second time were sent home. I was given a quart of whiskey and a three-day pass. I visited my old glider unit which was stationed in Scotland and when I returned I was placed with another crew, and Eddie Gruber became a first pilot.

Where Did Everybody Go?

by Theodore Maruschak (489th)

We were going to haul 2,000-pound "blockbusters" that day. It was the first time I had seen one, and it was monstrous in comparison to the 100-pound and 500-pound bombs we had previously been carrying.

It was business as usual. After briefing, we drew our electrically-heated suits, parachutes and guns. The top turret was my position. For those unfamiliar with the preparation for installing guns in the turrets, a word of explanation:

The caliber 50 guns are air cooled. The perforated cooling jackets covering the gun barrels are mounted on the gun-operating frame and remain on the turret. The standard operating procedure after each mission was to remove the barrel and bolt assembly from the turret, clean and oil it, and store it on a rack in the armament shack. On the next mission the guns, already oiled, were taken from the rack and installed inside the cooling jackets on the turret. In order to install the guns, it was necessary first to unlatch the turret seat, which was hinged in the back, allowing the front of the seat to drop down for access to the turret. Then the cooling jackets were elevated about 45 degrees. With the bolt stud in position, the barrel and bolt assembly were inserted into the jacket and rammed into place. If the barrel and bolt assembly were correctly aligned, a spring snapped into place, holding the assembly locked in position; if not, the whole assembly fell back out.

Because the bolt assembly was very slippery from light oil, and located at the opposite end of the barrel, it was difficult to ram it into the cooling jacket. If the assembly did not latch, it was necessary to lower it, re-align, and try again. We used paper towels to set the oily mechanism down on the flight deck if necessary. I was always reluctant to set them down because the oily bolt assembly could pick up dirt which could jam the gun. I had devised a way to install both guns at the same time to avoid setting them down. Sometimes it worked; sometimes it didn't. The method was to cradle both gun assemblies across the forearms, parallel to, and spaced the same distance apart, as the elevated cooling jackets. Then, carefully, I would insert both barrels simultaneously into the cooling jackets far enough to stay momentarily while I grasped the end of the bolt of one gun and rammed it in. With one gun in place, it was easy to install the other one, using both hands.

I had persuaded Charley Herrick, our left waist gunner, to help me if I failed to insert the guns on the first try. Since the single waist gun was easily installed, he usually had time to help.

Coffee break on the line at Halesworth, Summer 1944. (Courtsy of C.H. Freudenthal, 489th)

565th Squadron, 389th Bomb Group. (Courtsy of Russell R. Leslie, 389th)

This was not to be one of my better efforts at installing the guns. At the first try, the left gun failed to latch, and continued to do so after several tries. In order to avoid removing the guns and placing them on the flight deck, I was still holding the guns half way into the cooling jackets when I called, "Hey, Charley, I need a hand." No answer. By that time, many of the planes were beginning to warm up, and although ours was not yet started, I knew that I could hardly expect Charley to hear me above all the din. While I was waiting, the pilot and co-pilot went out the bomb bay door, saying something to me as they went by. I couldn't hear what they said, and assumed they were leaving for a quick cigarette before starting engines.

Finally, reluctantly, I pulled the guns out, laid them on the flight deck, and went to look for Charley. By the time I got out of the bomb bay, there was an eerie silence.

All the planes had quit warming up, and there was not a body in sight. There were no planes in the air, either. I had a strange feeling that I shouldn't be hanging around here. But where to go? There were not much in the way of shelter nearby. Finally, I spotted a small tree about 30 yards away, so I sprinted towards it. It was grossly inadequate, as I saw even before I got there. It had no leaves, even though it was about eight to 10 feet tall, and very thin, about six to eight inches in diameter. But it was the only cover available, so I took it. Once behind the little tree, I began to look around. The armament shack was about 50 yards away, and for a moment, I considered making a dash for it; but reconsidered when it occurred to me that any building would attract a bombing or strafing attack like a magnet attracts iron. So I stayed put, poorly concealed by the tree, peering out once in a while trying to find out what was going on. Still no planes, no people, no gunfire, only silence.

After some time had elapsed, I noticed several dark-green clad bodies walking towards their assigned planes. Among them was my pilot, who asked, "Didn't you hear me say 'let's get out of here?'" I told him I hadn't heard him above the noise, and assumed he was going out for a quick smoke before starting engines. He told me that Col. Webb said he had set a new world record for the 100-yard dash.

Then followed the explanation: In order to minimize the chances of the enemy obtaining information on the super-secret Norden bomb sight, the plane carrying the bomb sight carried bombs fitted with white phosphorus canisters, which left a very visible white plume when the bombs were released. I had seen it many times. The following bombers released their loads upon reaching the marker plumes. Panic began when someone saw a large cloud of red smoke billowing from the bomb bays of one of the planes. One of the bombs had either fallen from the rack, or been dropped in the process of loading, setting off the red phosphorus marker. It was near enough for the crew to see, and no one was interested enough to investigate the source. I could not see it because there is no window on the left side of the B-24, behind the pilot.

The canister was eventually removed, and normal operations were resumed.

Shot Down Over France

by Stan Biskup (489th)

(Lt. Biskup was the navigator on 42-94864, flying the slot position in the lead element of the lead squadron on June 2, 1944.)

As we were approaching the secondary target, there was very heavy flak and the plane was really bouncing around. I was crouched by the bomb bay doors with my hand on the salvo release lever. When I heard Dean Davidson's "bombs away," I pushed the lever down.

Our #3 engine was sputtering, which I didn't like, but I went back to navigating, noting in the log the areas where the flak was heaviest. Jim Bebout feathered #3, and we kept dropping farther and farther behind the formation and losing altitude. We got down to 17,000 feet and I could see the French coast ahead. I made an entry: "2,200-13 minutes to English coast." Then the coastal flak opened up and we took a direct hit in the bomb bay area. Through my oxygen mask I could smell gasoline, and I heard Dean on the intercom hollering for someone to open the nose turret door for him. Sometimes it stuck and couldn't be opened from the inside.

I opened the door and when I turned around, there were flames coming in from the hatchway that led to the flight deck. I immediately unclamped the two parachutes from the left side, handed one to Dean, sat down in front of the escape hatch, put my chute on the floor, and pulled the red emergency handle to open the door. As fast as I could, I took off my flak helmet, oxygen mask, flak jacket and throat mike, unplugged the heated suit cord, grabbed the chute, and snapped the right ring to the body harness.

I don't remember jumping, but I sensed the plane passing over me. I was holding on to the chute and tumbling through the air. When I stopped tumbling I snapped the left chute ring to the harness, checking both sides to be sure it was fastened securely. I was falling on my back, feet up, spiralling counterclockwise. I hadn't opened the chute yet, waiting to get closer to the ground. When I wanted to see how high I was I would put out my left hand, slow down the rotation, look over my right shoulder, and tell myself "still plenty high."

Before long I saw in sharp detail a horse-drawn wagon on an asphalt road and a bunch of trees off to the side. I figured I was close enough to the ground then, so I pulled the rip cord. The chute opened up beautifully, with only a slight jerk; I was amazed at the silence. I tugged on the shroud lines to help control my direction, and the last 100 feet or so came up fast.

I landed in a clearing, about 150 yards from the trees, quickly gathered up the chute, unhooked it, and threw it into some low bushes along with my Mae West and boots. Crouching down in the tall grass I began to move toward the trees when I saw a German soldier coming from that direction, shouting something that sounded like "Comrade." I crouched lower, and started to move again when I heard another voice shouting something I couldn't understand. I looked up and saw four German soldiers about 20 yards away, carrying burp guns, and running toward me. One was yelling and waving a potato-masher type of hand grenade. I stood up and waited.

They closed in and one began searching me, asking about a pistol. I brushed his hands away, saying "No pistol." They motioned for me to follow them, and we soon came to a small town, where I was led into a large home and down some stairs to a lower level. One of my captors turned the crank on a telephone and shouted a stream of words into the mouthpiece. I figured he was talking to his headquarters, but it struck me funny that they shouted so much. When he finished talking, I was taken to a front room which had a table and a few chairs...I asked them what the name of the town was, and somehow I got them to understand. One of them brought out a road map and pointed to Ancourt. I still had my escape kit with me, and figured this information would be important if I could escape somehow. They asked my name and rank, which I told them. One brought a cup of milk and drank some (I guess to show me it wasn't poisoned) and offered it to me. I drank it.

Before long an automobile arrived. It had four doors and no top, and we rode in it along a narrow winding road for abut 12 miles, to some sort of building. It was dark by this time, and I was led up a flight of stairs into a long narrow room where there were two German officers and several enlisted men. One of the officers asked my name, rank, and serial number, which I gave. Then he asked me where I was from. I told him Chicago, but that wasn't what he wanted to know. He said, "Hell, you couldn't have flown from Chicago!"

"Oh yes," I said, "We fly here every day, take pictures, and then return to Chicago." He knew I was joking, of course. In German then, he told a soldier to search me. I cooperated by emptying everything from my pockets on to the table, but earlier I had put my escape kit in my woolen olive-drab scarf, and I held this in my hand while being searched, and later laid it on the table. They didn't find the kit, but got real interested in a religious packet from my girlfriend. There were some religious medallions in it, and a note from my aunt written in Polish. One of them translated it into German for the others, then asked me if I could speak Polish. I told him I could, and he said I must have a very nice aunt.

About this time, a soldier opened a door at the end of the room and in walked George Murphy and

First row, L to R: Sgt. W.A. Carpenter, Gunner; S/Sgt. W.C. Colvin, Ball Gunner; Sgt. J.I. Lowe, Gunner; S/Sgt. J.C. Mitchell, Ass't Eng. & Gunner. Second row, L to R: T/Sgt. J.A. Kozlowitz, Engineer; 2nd Lt. H.W. Wedaa, Bombardier; 2nd Lt. L.R. Maddock, Navigator; 2nd Lt. W.R. Graf, Pilot; unidentified; S/Sgt. W.E. Stevenson, Radio Op. (Courtesy of Floyd J. Pugh, 467th)

Dave Gullett. They were as amazed as I was. After a few more questions the interrogation ended and we were taken to an underground concrete bunker, into a large room that had three straw mattresses on the floor. Two soldiers were left to guard us and an electric light bulb was left on all night. Murphy and Gullett said they could hardly believe their eyes when they saw me, because they thought I had been trapped in the nose section. I hadn't seen Dean (Davidson), but thought he got out right after me. In fact, he was in such a hurry that he probably kicked me out. None of us knew anything about the rest of the crew, except that Murphy had heard Jim Bebout give the order to prepare to ditch.

There was an air raid that night and heavy bombing shook the ground and scared the hell out of our guards and us. The next morning, June 3, we got up, washed our faces at the sink in the corner, and were given some dark bread for breakfast. About 1100 hours an officer told us we were to go with him, and we were put in an old Army truck along with three guards and taken on a short ride into the countryside. We stopped on the highway in an area of open fields, and as I looked out I was amazed to see the tail section of our plane in the distance, along with engines and part of a wing.

The officer went to examine the wreckage, which appeared to be about 300 yards out. The next thing I knew, one of the guards was motioning us to step off the highway and through the bushes. "My God," I thought, "are they going to shoot us here?" As I stepped off the road, however, I looked down and saw two bodies in a shallow pit. I turned away, almost sickened by the sight of two of our crew mates. The Germans wanted us to load the bodies on the truck, but we couldn't do it. We asked for the officer and there was some conversation among them, then two of the guards went through the bushes and returned carrying one body wrapped in a parachute. Gritting our teeth and with tears in our eyes, we helped to load both bodies on the truck. It was only a short drive to a small cemetery, near either Ancourt or Envermeu, I'm not sure. The Germans carried the bodies into a small brick building and the officer motioned us to come inside. As we reached the doorway, we could see four corpses on the concrete floor. On each of their chests were civilian photos from the escape kits and their identification tags. We identified them as Don Meehan and Don Harris, gunners; Robert Smith, radio operator; and Don Bruening, copilot.

Before we left, an old Frenchman came to us, and with tears in his eyes, tried to tell us something in French. We couldn't understand him, so he lit a match, showed two fingers, and said "Comrade." We took it to mean that two of our crew must have crashed with the plane and their bodies burned. It must have been Bebout and Trewartha, we were sure, and this left only Dean Davidson, the bombardier, unaccounted for.

In mid-April of 1945, after a three-week march across country from a prisoner of war camp at Numberg to another one at Moosburg, north of Munich, I finally ran into Dean. He told me that when he saw me pick up my chute and snap on the right side, he just couldn't wait any longer, so he put his foot to my back and shoved me out. He slid out right behind me, landed safely, and wasn't captured. Some French people found him the next day and took him to a safe hiding place, later turning him over to the underground. The day after that, however, he had an attack of appendicitis, and since there was nothing the French could do for him, they arranged for him to be captured. The Germans rushed him to a hospital and removed his appendix. They actually saved his life.

491ST BOMB GROUP
Ghosts Of The Past
North Pickenham, England
September 21, 1984
by Arnold Schonberg

Standing on the crumbling overgrown runway, a drizzle falling from an overcast sky, the western horizon brightened a bit by the setting sun, one's meditation is jolted by the sharp report of a "start engines flare." The crawling line of 34 ton "Liberators" pregnant with tons of high explosive move toward the downwind end of the active runway, four engines in a muffled roar. The whirling propellers blowing the heavy dew in vortices, persistent beads of moisture clinging to windshield, as they await take off.

A green flare, and the ground seems to tremble as the first "Liberator" rumbles down the runway, barely outlined in the dim grey morning light. Its engines reach a crescendo as it thunders off the end of the 6,000 foot runway followed at 30 second intervals by another and another until the entire 36 aircraft, the normal operating strength of the 8th Air Force's 491st Bomb Group is airborne.

In the silent sky over this now tranquil British landscape, one could "see" the old "war horses" climbing into the past to do battle.

This peaceful airfield, disturbed only by the wail of the wind, was once a battle front; the men and machinery suffering the attrition of air combat as they inflicted the same on "The Third Reich."

The machines and buildings are pretty much all gone. The men of the combat crews are not, many rest in peace at Cambridge and elsewhere in Europe; their valiant effort remembered today.

Last Operational Loss
submitted by Joe K. Fortney

The week leading up to March 30, 1945, the missions were all scrubbed because of the weather. We have spent most of the time listening to the radio news. Targets are harder to come by now, they have to be visual, because we don't know just where our ground forces are. Field Marshal Montgomery is driving ahead against bitter resistance north of the Ruhr. The biggest of all the gains are by Gen. Patton's 3rd Army. He left Frankfurt and is now 60 miles beyond the Rhine and driving toward Schweinfurt.

Finally, on March 30, the weather cleared well enough so that 21 B-24s of the 491st Bomb Group were dispatched to Wilhelmshaven to attack the submarine pens. We know that none of the Allied Troops have gone this far. The 853rd Squadron is leading the group in. The Ray Trapp crew, is flying as deputy group lead. They climb to 23,000 feet to start the bomb run. It is 43 degrees below zero, the coldest weather since back in February. There is a five tenths cloud cover in the target area so they make a PFF (radar) bomb run plus using a visual assist. The group put 64 tons of high explosive bombs on the submarine pens with good results. There was moderate but accurate flak all down the bomb run. Most of the group's aircraft received some flak damage. None of the enemy fighters were reported in our area.

Lt. Robert H. Siek, of the 855th Bomb Squadron was flying *Heavenly Body* (42-110155). This aircraft was one of the original planes of the 852nd Bomb Squadron. They must have taken some serious hits from the flak because they were observed leaving the formation with one engine out. Other problems apparently were present because the B-24 should have been able to maintain altitude and stay with the formation, especially after releasing its bomb load. Losing altitude constantly, it soon became clear that they could not make it back to England. Ditching became inevitable, so the radio operator sent out the word. An Air-Sea Rescue unit was alerted and a PBY (Catalina) was on the scene right away. In fact, the PBY followed *Heavenly Body* down as she hit the icy cold waters of the North Sea.

EDITORS NOTE: The above portion is taken pretty much word for word from the Frank Lewis diary. From here on, the information was gained from letters and accounts by Ed Lorengi, a previous member of their crew, by Sgt. Brigham and by the mother of Lt. Robert Siek.

It was later learned that *Heavenly Body* had lost two engines on one side which made it extremely difficult to control. Adding to the problem, the sea was very rough this day. As the old B-24 neared the water to touch down, a huge wave caught one of the wing tips and caused it to cartwheel and break apart. B-24s did not ditch very well. The thing that made them such good bombers and payload carriers, made them also vulnerable to ditching at sea.

The rescue team of the PBY tried desperately to save the ditched crew. There again, the rough sea made it terribly difficult to locate and retrieve survivors. Miraculously, two of the crew were saved, S/Sgt. William P. Brigham and T/Sgt. Shepard L. Miller. The rescue team searched diligently, trying to find more survivors, but the rough seas made the job all but impossible.

Those who were lost included Pilot 2nd Lt. Robert H. Siek, Co-pilot 2nd Lt. William M. LaCaillade, Bombardier 2nd Lt. Harold E. Nelson, Engineer S/Sgt. Darrence R. Siebert, Radio Operator S/Sgt. Oliver J. Bowen, Tail Gunner S/Sgt. Ray F. Fortney and Gunner Sgt. John E. Wargo.

It was later learned that the "Mae Wests" were faulty. Some partially worked, some didn't work at all.

While Sgt. Brigham was still in the water, he saw Sgt. Siebert swimming near a piece of wing which was still floating. He watched the wing and Siebert disappear under the water. He then found the pilot, Lt. Siek, floating face down. He turned him over only to discover that he was dead.

By now, Sgt. Brigham himself was almost overcome by the cold water and near passing out when a pole appeared over him from the PBY. He reached up and grabbed it. It took three men to pull him out of the water because of the weight of his heavy, wet flying suit. Sgt. Miller must have been hauled aboard the PBY earlier.

Now, another problem faced them. They were 20 miles from the Danish coast, which was occupied by the Germans, and the sea was too rough for take-off in the PBY. Another message was sent out for help. A British ship received the SOS and four and one-half hours later arrived for their rescue.

The men of the PBY and the two B-24 survivors were transferred to the ship by attaching a line between the two craft. They then towed a dingy back and forth, bringing the men to the ship. Once everyone was on board, the PBY was shelled until it sank. From there, the survivors were taken to a British hospital.

This was the last operational loss for the 491st. Less than a month later hostilities ceased.

Mission #7 — Schwabisch Hall
Sept. 13, 1944
submitted by Robert Ostrander

Briefing at 0400 hours and we were aroused at 0300. Our target was a jet-propelled airport for ME-262s. We were carrying 12 x 500 GPs and the limit of gas. It was going to be a long haul and I hated that kind of mission. We took off at dawn and flew #7 that day. Assembly was at 7,000 feet and we took off on course.

We were over Allied occupied territory for a long time. We ran into some weather and I was all set to go up to 26,000 feet. Some of the group got lost and could not find us, some aborted, and the rest of us journeyed on. We encountered some flak over the Rhine and I didn't like it. It was too accurate. I noticed the engines were acting up and that gave me cause for concern.

As we penetrated deeper into Germany, things started getting more tense. I flew the bomb run and it was a long one. I thought they would never drop them, but they finally went out and I thought that was all. We found out that we had to circle the target and make another run because one of the groups hadn't dropped its bombs, and that really teed us all off. Fortunately, nothing eventful happened.

As we left the target, our "little friends" were all around us and they sure looked good. We passed over Luxembourg, which was supposed to be Allied territory, and then all hell broke loose. They had us down to a "gnats eyelash" no matter what kind of evasive action we took.

I saw two planes collide and split right in two.

I saw a waist gunner at his station but there was no tail assembly. I thought we were goners for sure. They hit #2 and I hit the feathering button—what a sickening feeling. We dropped out of formation and everything looked pretty good for the moment. Our engineer transferred the fuel and then found out we didn't have any hydraulic systems.

We got out over the channel and everything seemed to go haywire. The props on #1, 3 and 4 were all running away and I kept hitting them simultaneously. We got over England and found that all important 10,000 foot runway at Woodbridge. Butler started circling into the bad engine and that really got to me. We were letting down at 2,500 feet per minute and then everything seemed to stop—"no nothing." I knew we couldn't get into Woodbridge so I showed him another field which we could make. Our power being completely gone, we had to make a dead stick landing.

We had to lose 3,000 feet and Butler couldn't control it alone, so I jumped on the controls (what there were) with him and pumped down the flaps at the same time.

As we were making our final approach, it looked as though arrows were pointing down the runway. We were fogging up badly and didn't notice that the "arrows" were concrete obstructions, half a wheel with a spoke down the middle. With no power I thought we were goners. It was all Butler and I could do to try and raise the plane off the runway. Our left landing gear clipped the obstruction and we hit the ground at about a 30 degree angle. We slid along in a circular direction and finally came to a stop 180 degrees from our original heading. We piled out of the plane as fast as we could from all different openings and cleared the wreck as fast as possible. Everybody got out in pretty good shape with only minor bumps and scratches. I hurt my back in the crash and Ed Kamarainen (radio operator) was limping on a twisted ankle. Bob Trombley (tail gunner) bumped his head somewhere along the line as a little red welt was blossoming on his cranium. In the excitement, I forgot to turn off the switches, but I took care of this problem after I discarded my flying gear. Rosie (waist gunner) was cut up again—poor kid.

We went over to headquarters and called the base to advise them of our "horrendous landing."

Butler stayed with the British and the rest of us returned to the wreck to pick up our gear. We didn't realize how lucky we were until we inspected the wreck. The #1 engine prop was laying about 45 feet out in front of the plane and the bomb bay was crumpled like an accordion. We had been hit very hard by flak; holes penetrating the ship everywhere, it looked like a sieve. We all picked up a souvenir of some sort.

The British treated us like kings again. The doc checked us all out for whatever we complained about and then we chowed down for a well-deserved meal. We sacked out in the clinic and they had me under a heat lamp until they came down to pick us up.

Upon return to the base everybody was overjoyed to see us, thinking that we had been shot down. It felt good to be back at the ranch. We got the flak shack out of the ordeal and I thought it would do everybody good.

I think our 10th man is God. What's next?

A Christmas To Remember
by C.W. (Bill) Getz

Not all was grim and grey in England during World War II. There were moments of relaxation, moments of fun. These were important moments to escape the high-pulse-rate activities of combat. Most leaves were spent in London, that exciting center of England with its many lures of shops, shows and shenanigans.

It was during one of those forays (to attend church and visit museums, of course, mother) that I was presented with a truly rare opportunity. It was Dec. 5, 1944 and I was in London for a two-day leave from my air base located at Steeple Morden, a small village a few miles south of Cambridge, and home to the 355th Fighter Group and the 2nd Bomb Division Scouting Force. Although I was still assigned to the 491st Bomb Group with 31 missions behind me, I had been able to finagle my way into the P-51 equipped Scouting Force. The scouts were former lead-crew bomber pilots who had completed their bomber missions and now were the combat eyes of the 2nd Bomb Division mission commander. Fighter pilots from various 8th Air Force units (God bless 'em) were assigned to the Scout-

Donald Rhinehart, Pilot; unidentified, Bombardier; Hugh E. Evans, Navigator; George L. Hugo, Copilot; John S. Carroll, Nose Gunner; Max Burger, Tail Gunner; Wilbur Mansell, Engineer; Bob Brune, Waist Gunner; Marian (Sandy) Craig, Waist Gunner; Robert L. Anderson, Radio Operator. (Courtesy of John S. Carroll, 445th)

ing Force to protect the bomber pilots. We were all on detached service from our bomb groups. That is another story reported elsewhere in this book.

On this fateful day, I was in the Red Cross Officers Club in London. By chance I talked to an "elderly" lady volunteer (she was probably forty-ish, but then I was only 20!). I don't remember the lady's name, and she was indeed, a "Lady," spelled with a capital "L," as in a title. She was an American by birth and had married an English peer. Her war effort was to serve in the Red Cross.

During our interesting conversation, she asked if I knew of any American officers who might be free for Christmas. She said that a friend of hers, Lord Derwent, a non-flying RAF officer, wished to invite several American officers to spend Christmas with him at his estate near Scarborough, north of the Wash. It sounded exciting and different. She went on to say that Lord Derwent was a widower of 45, whose wife had been the daughter of Romania's army chief of staff, Gene. D. Iliesco. No children from the marriage. Lord Derwent's wife had died in 1941. I told the lady I could be available. She gave me instructions and later I was able to obtain a few days leave.

On December 23, I took a train to Scarborough as directed. At the station I hired a cab to take me to Hackness Hall. It was several miles out of town. As we drove up the tree-lined driveway, the manor house came into view. It was large by any standard, but the initial impression was not of great size since a good part of it was hidden by trees. The walls were covered with vines, minus their summertime foliage, looking much like the veins on some giant prehistoric creature. Terrible thought.

As we drove to the entrance, the front door opened as if on signal, and two men came out, both dressed casually, but one with more elegance than the other. The elegant one opened the cab door and said, "Welcome to Hackness Hall. I'm Baron Derwent," and his hand was proffered to shake. I introduced myself as I shook his hand. In a casual manner, he introduced the other man, who it turned out was butler, custodian, general handyman, and together with his wife, who was the cook and maid, were the only permanent occupants of this 100-room mansion. I was also surprised to learn that I was the only American officer that would be present for the holiday. There was another guest, but that comes later.

The butler, who I shall call Edward, took my bag and disappeared before I even noticed my bag was gone. After a few pleasantries were exchanged, we walked into the manor doorway through an arched, grey stone passage leading to a huge, two-story entrance hall. On the opposite side, a massive stairway rose to the second level balcony that wrapped three sides of the hall. Again, stone was the dominant material, and a massive chandelier hung in the center. There were several doors opening off the entrance hall, and I could see several more off the wrap-around balcony. This place was straight out of a movie set.

We were greeted inside by two ladies, one with a small "l," and the other with a capital "L." The small "l" being the custodian's wife and the other, a woman introduced as Lady George Cholmondeley, pronounced "Chumley," an old friend of the family's. The name Cholmondeley is very famous in England by virtue of the family of the Marquess of Cholmondeley. Lady Cholmondeley was a divorcee, and it was never clear to me whether she had been married to the Marquess or his son George (dad was also a George). I am reasonably certain it was the son. Lady Cholmondeley's son had been a military aide to the Duke of Kent, brother of the king. Her son died with the Duke aboard a military plane that crashed in Scotland in December of 1942. She had to be in her mid-40s, closer to 50 I would guess,

since I later learned that when she was a little girl, she had sat on the lap of Queen Victoria who died in 1901. I also learned that Lady Cholmondeley knew Winston Churchill.

We talked for a few moments, and Lord Derwent then suggested that I might like to freshen up and change from my uniform into something more comfortable. Edward led me up the stairs to my bedroom, and what a room it was: an unlit fireplace, large, solid oak bed and furniture, all period antiques, of course. They became antiques by growing old with the manor. What first impressed me was the fact that my change of clothes were already laid out on the bed, and all of my clothes had been unpacked and put away before I got to the room. I had not noticed that Edward had left us downstairs to accomplish this task. There was a bathroom off the bedroom, a surprise in such an ancient house, but an update done in the 1920s, I was informed by Edward. The fixtures were of that era.

After bathing and dressing, I went downstairs and Lord Derwent and Lady Cholmondeley took me on a short tour of the house. Oh yes, Lady Cholmondeley called Lord Derwent, "George," a familiarity he never invited with me, nor did I volunteer. His actual name was George Harcourt Vanden-Bempde-Johnstone, the Baron Derwent. I say "short tour" because most of the manor had been closed after half had been occupied by a British army communications school. Upstairs, near my bedroom, there were several stairs leading to a half level. On that level, and in keeping with my first impression of the manor, was a movie set bedroom which Lord Derwent called "the queen's bedroom" because Queen Mary had once slept there. The canopied bed was on a raised dias, and it was quite an elegant room. There were other bedrooms, but I am not sure of the number.

Downstairs in the entrance hall, Lord Derwent approached a doorway directly across from the entrance way. The room we entered, like all rooms so far, was huge and stretched for at least 40 feet. It had high ceilings, and three sides were panelled. Down the center was a table that could seat 20 to 30 people. The wall opposite the entrance was ceiling to floor windows looking out upon an expanse of snow-covered lawn, sloping down towards a small lake where I could see two swans gliding on the water, even on this cold December day. There was a massive stone fireplace to our left, opposite the wall with the windows. At the far end, to our left, there was a door leading to other parts of the manor that I never got to see. Lord Derwent explained that this room at one time was the manor's "great hall" and now served as the dining room.

Lord Derwent led us to the right towards a panelled wall, reached out and touched something, and a hidden door opened and we stepped into a vaulted ceiling room that was obviously the library. It too had a high window looking out upon the sloping lawn. When the door was closed, it was hidden by bookshelves. Later, Lord Derwent said that he really never knew why his ancestors made the entrance and exit from the room a secret. He suspected that it was either aesthetics, or, in the days of horses and carriages, visitors would come for days because of the great distances, and the lord of the manor may have wished to have a secret escape to be by himself. Whatever the truth, it was an impressive room and where we spent the bulk of our time. On the far wall to the right of the entrance, was another mammoth stone fireplace, the walk-in variety, and a wonderful warm fire was burning. Up until that time, every room was quite cold, and we wore sweaters or jackets. Of course there was no central heating, and the principal reason we stayed most of the time in the library was because it was the only room kept heated. There were electrical heaters in the bedrooms and bath, but the fireplaces

were not used. Fuel of any kind was very limited and rationed.

On Christmas day, we were sitting in the library with a warm, cozy fire, enjoying fine conversation, when it became time for me to go with several villagers on a hunt. I was loaned a pair of superb English hunting boots my size, that I had selected from a large collection of boots, and a truly outstanding English shotgun from Lord Derwent's impressive gun collection.

We left the library through the secret door, heading to the door that led into the entrance hall. To the left of this doorway was a beautifully carved, antique sideboard, above which was a large tapestry of one of Lord Derwent's ancestors. As Lord Derwent passed this piece of furniture, he picked up an object and handed it to me with the salutation, Merry Christmas.

The object was an 18th century, tortoise shell and sterling reading glass. You can imagine my pleasant surprise, but also my embarrassment because I had not thought to bring presents. That reading glass is one of my prized possessions.

After a glorious three days, it was time to return to the real world. Lord Derwent and Lady Cholmondeley would be going to London on the same train with me. It was necessary to change trains, and I believe it was at the city of Leeds, but not certain. Anyway, the station had a hotel above it, and since we had a two-hour layover, Lord Derwent wished to check his bags with the hotel until we were ready to go. I remember we had to climb a long, very wide marble stairway from the rail station into the hotel lobby. Lord Derwent approached the clerk at the desk and asked if he could check our bags for a short time. The clerk, not too politely, replied in his best indifferent manner that it was against the policy of the hotel to store transient luggage.

At this point, the five foot 10 inch Lord Derwent grew about six inches, looked down upon the clerk, and in his best cultured, aristocratic, quiet but commanding voice said, my dear sir, I am Lord Derwent, and my family have been staying at this hotel for 200 years. I don't think it is asking too much to accommodate such a small request, or should I be speaking to your superior? Or at least words to that effect. And what an effect! As Lord Derwent grew six inches, the clerk shrunk by an equal amount. You could really see the class distinction emerge. Needless to say, the luggage was stored until departure time for our train to London.

I never saw Lord Derwent again after leaving him in London. He died in 1949 from causes I do not know. A sad and lonesome life in his later years. He never fully recovered from the loss of his wife. His younger brother, by one year, inherited the title, and it has since gone to his son. I continued a yearly Christmas letter exchange with Lady Cholmondeley. In 1963 she visited us at our home in Los Altos Hills, California, and died not too many years afterwards, but that is another and very interesting story.

Yes, it was a Christmas to remember. Time out from the war, and an experience that I will never forget. As they say, war is hell, but the friendships one makes during such difficult times are the gifts of angels.

492ND BOMB GROUP In Das Hornissen Nest

by Elvern Seitzinger

On June 20, 1944, we were awakened and told that we were going on a mission. I do not recall the exact hour that we were called, but I do remember that take-off was 0430 hours. So it must have been around 0300 hours. We gathered our gear, went to breakfast and then to briefing where we learned that

"The Duchess" and pilot Maj. William O'Donnell. (Courtesy of Mike Martin)

our target was to be the synthetic oil refinery at Politz, Germany. This was to be a maximum effort mission. Many of us had been to this target on May 29 and knew that it could be a tough mission. On the May 29 mission many aircraft were forced to ditch in the North Sea and there were many casualties. We were therefore told at briefing that if we ran into any trouble and if it was questionable that we could make it back to England, we were to try and get into Sweden. This is really all I remember about the briefing that was out of the ordinary.

We took off at about 0430 hours, formed the formation and left the coast of England at about 0615 hours, flying at an altitude of 7,500 feet. We continued at this altitude about half way across the North Sea and then started to climb. We crossed the enemy coast just south of the Danish-German border at an altitude of 21,000 feet. At this time we saw a few friendly fighters. We also saw a lot of flak over Helgoland. Shortly after we crossed the mainland and were out over the Baltic Sea one of our aircraft, piloted by Lt. Velarde, was forced to abort. He would be the only aircraft of the 856th Squadron of the 492nd Bomb Group to return to England that day.

As we continued on, flying over the Baltic Sea, our squadron, flying in the low left position, drifted to the left in a right-hand turn. As I recall, we were some 10 minutes from the IP when we made the turn. Because we were out of position and did not have the firepower of the rest of the group, the German fighters chose to attack. Reports that I have since read indicate that our fighter protection was some two minutes late in arriving on the scene. The fighters came in from the rear, probably about the eight o'clock position, made a 360 degree turn and came in for a second pass and left. Reports that I have more recently read indicate that the German fighters left when our fighters appeared on the scene. I believe that after the first pass, our Squadron Leader Nick Kehoe and our plane were the only two aircraft in our squadron still flying.

We were flying in #4 position. Both of our wing-men went down on fire. I saw the #3 man in the low left element get hit and the end of the wing from the outboard engine out was shot off. He flipped over upside down, in perfect position in the formation, and went down. This is also about the last that I saw of our squadron leader. There was a lot of smoke coming out of his aircraft and he went down. I remember calling the tail gunner, John Simpson, and asking him if the balance of the for-

mation was formed on us. He informed me that we were all alone. The rest of the squadron was gone. We had lost #4 engine so we feathered the prop. Our #3 engine was running but was not responding to the controls the way that it should. I believe that it had gone to the automatic three-quarter power setting. We had a bad gas leak in the left wing and our hydraulic tank had been hit. There was a lot of gasoline and oil getting into the bomb bay and the rear of the aircraft. At this point the copilot, Kent Dickson, and I, do not recall events the same way. As I recall, the bomb bay doors were opened and the bombs were dropped from the pilot's pedestal. The bombs went away OK but we could not get the bomb bay doors closed again. As Kent recalls the situation, the bombs did not go away and he went into the bomb bay and manually released each bomb. He also reports that we must have been hit after the bomb bay doors were open because there was a bullet hole through the open door and the side of the fuselage. There was no exit hole to show that the bullet had gone out.

During the attack, I saw ME-210s and ME-410 German fighters. It was also reported that there were ME-109 fighters present. In a recent letter that I have read it was reported that ME-262s, twin jet fighters, fired rocket missiles into the squadron. Kent Dickson noted that rockets were being fired into the squadron during the attack.

In the time that was spent dropping bombs and feathering an engine and taking stock of our damage, we lost some 5,000 feet of altitude. We found that by using high-power settings and flying at about 140 mph we could maintain altitude. We could also see very heavy flak over the target area so we elected to turn inside the group and hope to get back with our group when they left the coast and came back out over the Baltic Sea. Because we had lost altitude and were flying at a slower speed, we never did find our group or any other group that we could join for the return flight. As we approached Denmark on the return flight, we filled the sight gauges and found that we had 300 gallons of gasoline in the tanks. It was also determined at this time that we had a gas leak near #3 engine. So we decided our best chance was to head north to Sweden. Andy Gall, navigator, gave me a heading and we headed for Sweden.

We crossed the Swedish coast near Ystano at about 15,000 feet and headed toward Malmo, Sweden. The airfield we were looking for was a large grass field and we were not able to immediately locate it. About that time three Swedish fighters came up and escorted us to the field. They signaled for us to land. We tried to lower our landing gear but found that the main gear would not lock in place and the nose wheel had to be lowered manually. The engineer, John Kristynik, with the help of the radio operator, Clyde Dorsey, and others, tried in vain to get the main gear to lock in place using the hand crank. I tried to rock the wings to get the gear to lock in place but the Swedish fighters were so close I could not rock the aircraft enough to do any good. All this time they were signaling us to land. I kept nodding my head indicating that we were going to land.

About this time I decided that if we were going to get out of this alive our best bet was to bail out. If we tried to land and the gear folded up our chances of survival were next to none. So I gave the signal to stand by to bail out. The waist gunner, Arthur Suter, called on the intercom and said that his parachute was soaked with gasoline and oil and that he did not trust it to bail out. The ball turret gunner, Don Wehaber, said that his chute was in the same condition. So I decided that anyone who wanted to bail out could go ahead and that we would try to land the airplane. No one bailed out and all took crash positions. By this time the nose gunner, Tom Kelly, was out of his turret which had been hit causing him trouble trying to get out.

All the time this was going on, the Swedish fighter pilots were motioning to us to land, and according to Andy Gall they were not smiling anymore.

After the decision was made to land, we had to make a couple of more decisions. The airfield, as I have said, was a large grass field, no runways, and was built up on two sides and had parked aircraft and hangars on the third side. We did not know if we had any brakes. One accumulator showed pressure and one did not. If we landed into the wind and had no brakes, we were going to run into something, so I elected to land down-wind and roll out into a field if the brakes failed. This was, of course, assuming that the gear would hold up. If it folded, it would not make much difference. My hope was that if the main gear folded, the nose wheel would hold up until we lost speed and then we would ground loop.

The second decision we made was to land dead stick. With #4 feathered and #3 not responding to the controls, we had wound a lot of trim in to keep the aircraft flying straight and level. If we were to make a normal landing, by killing the power after we had broken our glide, there was the possibility of losing control momentarily and dropping a wing. If it hit the ground we were in big trouble.

So we got our altitude down to about 5,000 feet and I told Kent to kill the power. We trimmed the aircraft to fly straight and level and made a large turn losing altitude and got in position to make a 90 degree approach. Kent started pumping down flaps with the hand pump and we did get something over 20 degrees of flap. We made our approach at about 130 mph and touched down well within the boundary of the field. As soon as the main gear touched down I hit the brakes and held them. The brakes did hold. There was enough pressure for one application. The main gear did not collapse and we slid the wheel an estimated 3,000 feet before coming to a stop. We did not see them from the air but we had landed in a direction that was headed for a pile of stacked oil drums. However, we stopped some 50 yards short of them.

I looked out of the window and saw a pick-up truck loaded with people coming toward us. I called the crew on the intercom and told them that I would get out first. I got out of my seat, down onto the catwalk and ducked out of the bomb bay. As I ducked out the bomb bay I saw someone enter the bomb bay from the opposite side. I also saw that the aircraft was surrounded by armed guards. My first thought was, we have come to the wrong place. At that moment, someone asked "Who is the captain of the aircraft?" I ducked back inside and answered that I was. He stuck out his hand and said "Welcome to Sweden, do not destroy the aircraft." He had barely said these words when Kent hit the button to blow up the IFF. The Swedish officer said "There goes the radio." We did not blow up the IFF in the air because of the oil and gasoline in that area.

I indicated that I was the first to get out of the aircraft once we had landed. John Kristynik tells me that this is not true. He got out before I did but when he saw those guns pointed at him he scrambled back into the aircraft.

We were loaded into the truck and taken to the headquarters building where we were locked in a large conference-type room. While we were in this room we were joined by Nick Kehoe and John Losee. Nick was flying squadron lead for the 856th Squadron, and John Losee was flying 492nd Group lead with Joe Harris. Due to some mix-up or faulty bomb sight John Losee and Joe Harris wound up leading the 2nd Bomb Division that day. There had been a fire in Nick Kehoe's plane and his crew had bailed out over the Baltic Sea. He had flown to Sweden, turned the plane around, headed it out to sea and bailed out. The plane did crash in Sweden with no one aboard. John Losee and Joe Harris had lead the formation over the target through heavy flak. Their plane was badly damaged by flak and since there was no chance of getting back to England they chose to land at Malmo.

On this same day some 10 or 12 other crews who had problems also chose to land in Sweden.

Late in the day of June 20 we were taken from the conference room, fed and marched to the city jail. We spent one night in the city jail and the next day were moved by train to a barbed wire enclosed stockade near Falun, Sweden. As I recall, we spent some two or three nights in this facility. While we were there we were each interviewed by a representative from the American Embassy. I believe that this was to establish our identity. We were then moved by bus to Ratvik, Sweden, where I was to spend the next four months at Pensionnat Ledalshoiden. On the night of November 7, I was flown from the Stockholm Airport to Scotland and from there to England and back to New York City on December 3, 1944. Some of the crew members came back at the same time I did, but some who were working at the embassy or reprocessing airplanes remained there until the following year.

Crew of Sknappy: Pilot Elvern Seitzinger; Co-pilot Willis Kent Dickson; Navigator Andy Gall; Engineer Gunner John Kristynik; Nose Turret Marion T. Kelly (Tom); and Squadron Commander John Losee.

North Sea Bailout
May 29, 1944
Lt. W. Prewitt's Combat
Crew #1644 - B-24

submitted by Charles M. Trout

We were doing fine until we ran into flak over the target. We were hit pretty bad. The copilot was hit but his flak suit prevented injury.

The #4 engine started throwing oil at about two gallons per minute. The engine was still putting out power until the oil pressure reached 20 PSI and then it was feathered by the copilot. I checked the gasoline and it was very low. I transferred the remaining fuel from #4 tank and we were still low on fuel. We thought we could make it to the English coast, weren't sure.

The radio operator started to send SOS signals as we knew we were low on fuel and couldn't make it; so we started throwing out everything that was loose or that could be taken loose. While we were doing that, two of the planes from our squadron stayed with us, but we were flying too slow for them to stay behind so they left. The radio operator was still sending SOS signals but couldn't tell if he was being heard, for his receiver was shot out, also the trailing wire antenna was knocked off by flak. Then, two P-38s started circling us and stayed with us till they saw there was no hope for us and left.

We knew we would have to ditch or bail out, for our fuel was awful low (about three minutes). The crew decided to bail instead of crash. Water was rough with big breakers. Then the pilot heard "boat in area" when he called "Mayday, Mayday." The rescue boat was below us. We all said a prayer and I was first to jump. I tried two ways to jump, but neither was satisfactory so I stood up and dove out like diving into water.

When the propellor and slip stream hit me it took my breath and threw me around roughly. When I was down low enough for clearance and everything got quiet, I pulled the rip cord but nothing happened. The chute didn't open. I reached in and pulled the pilot chute out. Everything came out of the pack and I stopped with a sudden jerk, looked up and was very pleased to see that nice white parachute above me. I looked around and saw more chutes but didn't count them.

Then I saw the plane circle which gave me a funny feeling, for I thought it was going to spin down among us. But the pilot was just getting closer to the rescue boat before leaving the planes and he was the last man out. The plane started to descend slowly on a straight course and #2 went out when the pilot left.

I looked down and seemed to be 100 feet above water but hit very quickly, a second or two. Don't know how far I went under but came up immediately. When the cold water got through my clothes it took my breath. I struggled for about 10 minutes before I finally got enough breath, but breathing was

Maj. George Carpenter, 335th Commanding Officer (Courtesy of Dick Martin)

John Sipek posing on Gabby Gabreski's airplane at Halesworth. (Courtesy of John J. Sipek)

almost impossible due to breaking waves right on top of me. I unbuckled my chute harness and thought I was rid of it until it started pulling me under. I said another prayer and something made me think of a knife I had in my pocket. I cut everything I could to get free but could not get down far enough to cut it off my feet as my strength was gone. I gave up hope when I couldn't see the rescue boat, but the it came to me in about 35 or more minutes. Boy was I glad to see the boat! They threw me a rope and I hung on and was pulled to a rope ladder. Three Air-Sea Rescue men tried to pull me up but couldn't, and had to use a hoist. The rescue team told me to save my strength as I didn't have much left. They put me on deck and told me to go below. I had to crawl, so they carried me, cut my clothes off, gave me dry ones, then had to dress me. I couldn't help myself at all, shaking like a leaf in a a hail storm. I was given a hearty welcome by the survivors already picked up. One handed me a cigarette which took the salt water taste out of my mouth. When everybody who could be found, was picked up they gave us hot tea and brandy to drink so we would get warmed up, and later hot soup and bread and butter. It sure tasted good. We hadn't eaten for a long time. The boat headed for shore and when we got there, we were led in prayer for the missing crewman by the chaplain. We felt bad about losing him for he was a great guy.

We stayed there a few days and were treated like kings. When we finally got back to our home base most of our clothes were gone, divided out but we got them all back. The best news was we all would get a week's rest at a Red Cross sponsored rehab center.

I thank God I am alive today.

Fighter Sweep To Beauvais, France
August 18, 1944
submitted by Dick Martin (Maj. John Trevor Godfrey, 336th Sqdn. gave this report)

Our flight was shooting up trucks. I guess the Germans were tired of us shooting up their equipment because they put up everything they had. I was trying to shoot down the ME-109 ahead of me when his buddy got me from behind. It took a matter of seconds. My wings were riddled and the left wing guns' fairing door was gone. Blood had splattered on the canopy. The instrument panel was plastered, with only the compass operating properly. I headed north towards Debden, wide open while hugging the fields and trees.

The ME-109 followed me for about three minutes, firing all the while. When you have to fly dangerously low, you can do it if you have to. I assume the German pilots had been briefed for them not to stray from their group; we had a lot of P-51s in the area. I was on the trees when my engine quit. I had plenty of speed as I pulled up to bail out. As I leveled off, I realized I was too low to bail out. All I saw below me were trees until I noticed a small field 45 degrees off to my left. I had no decision to make. I had to land in that field. I let down in a very heavy glide. I could tell that I had to stretch it to make the field.

My right turn into the field brought shuddering to my plane, which indicated that my air speed was too low and I was stalling out. I'm sure my plane scraped the top of that last tree. With wheels up, I crashed landed. What a sudden stop! I hopped out of the cockpit and started running into the woods. About a mile away I met this lady who led me to a farm house. I stayed with the family about 24 days. They had little to eat but they shared the food with me.

The Canadian 1st Army came through the area.

I returned to London for physicals and debriefing. Doctors removed two pieces of shrapnel from my right arm but left the third one in. I don't remember why, since I still have it. The armor plate behind me spared my life. After three days we were allowed to tour London but were told not to leave the city. Later I caught the train and returned to Debden. what a wing-ding we had that night! Freddy Glover was now the 336th Squadron Commanding Officer and promoted to major.

Debden had been an RAF field with permanent buildings and three huge hangars. The three ready huts were quickly installed metal buildings. The large brick building contained sleeping rooms, a bar, dining room, lounge. This was home. There were two floors. The bed rooms were small with two twin beds. My room was on the first floor. The food was great. Real eggs for breakfast. Elderly Englishmen, called "bat-men" kept our rooms in good shape and woke us on the mornings we had a mission. Softball was played on the parade grounds in front of the main building. Small British trucks took us to our ready rooms. A nice way to fight a war.

The Debden control tower was called Dicton. My plane radio designation was Becky 45. My ground crew was great; the crew chief was Sgt. Oscar Garrison from Elizabethton, Tennessee. The plane was designated VF-G. The group leader was called "Horseback." Being a newly arrived pilot, I normally flew wing. Normally, climbing up or letting down through dense clouds, vertigo developed. A terrible feeling. You had to fly in close to your lead plane or you would lose sight of it. When vertigo developed, you felt your plane was in a steep turn and I found I would hold a slight right rudder condition. Flying on instruments was not too bad, but overlapping your leader's wing tip so as to keep him in sight is a little too much.

On almost every mission you would have to climb in thick clouds, let down in clouds, or both. I recall on one mission, we were returning to base and "Horseback" radioed that we would let down. After we broke out from the low hanging clouds, someone yelled "balloons!" We had let down into the middle of the balloons surrounding London. Planes flew off in every direction. Today, it is funny; but then not so funny. Steel cables held each balloon, that was the problem. I don't recall that we lost any planes but it is a wonder we didn't.

I returned to France in 1987 and saw the farm family again. The two girls, Simone and Denise, were there as well as Robert who is my age. These three were at the farm in 1944. The old man and woman had died. Twenty-two persons met me when I drove up in the rental car. They had an interpreter who sat by me in the kitchen. It's a good thing because I could not communicate with them otherwise. We ate and drank wine and cider and kissed on both cheeks until the wee hours. I stayed with them for two days. It was a joyous occasion for me. I left and toured the entire invasion coast and yes, I went back to see Mont St. Michel. I walked up the steep cobblestone road; quite a sight. I took rolls of film with me on the trip.

4TH FIGHTER GROUP
335th Squadron
submitted by Dick Martin

On April 13, 1944, the 4th Fighter Group was up again and headed toward Schweinfurt on a bomber support mission. As they arrived in the Limburg area they heard the bombers reporting a very heavy attack from enemy fighters, and hurried to help out the bombers. Within a few moments they encountered 20-25 enemy fighters and engaged them at 24,000 feet. The pilots of all three squadrons did battle and sent five enemy fighters crashing to the earth at a cost of two of their own. The FW-190 that Maj. George Carpenter, 335th Squadron Commanding Officer, encountered, was flown by a wily veteran of the Luftwaffe who tried a number of maneuvers. First the German tried diving away into the cloud cover to get away, but Carpenter orbited a few moments and then saw the Focke-Wulf off to his left. Almost immediately they turned toward each other for a head-on attack. Maj. Carpenter's encounter report stated, "I got my burst in first apparently and hit him in his engine and right wing. I broke then to avoid his fire and when I saw him again he was smoking considerably. Later he stopped smoking though. I went after him again and we got in a tight circle for a few minutes. The E/A could not turn with me without losing altitude though, and eventually I got him." One more well placed burst sent the 190 down to a fiery crash.

With four victories in the last five days, Carpenter had raised his total to 12 and was clearly establishing himself as one of the 4th's most talented pilots, and a candidate for top scoring honors.

The mission of April 18 was a ramrod to Berlin, a very heavily defended area, which would more than likely offer Maj. Carpenter the opportunity to add to his score. The narrative for this mission is based on his recollection and entries made in his log book by Capt. Julius Toy, the squadron S-3 officer. "I was leading the 335th on a bomber escort to the Berlin area. In the vicinity of Rathenow I bounced a squadron of BF-109s and was flabbergasted when the plane I was firing at did not go down. I stupidly flew past him with my mouth wide open, I presume, and he swung up over my tail and let me have it. I took violent evasive action then, but I had already been hit (apparently one of the 109s he had attacked did go down, because Lt. Hunt confirmed a kill and another 109 damaged for him—logbook entry). I deliberately spun down to a low level, smoking badly but with no body wounds fortunately. There I found myself in a head-on battle with an FW-190. He didn't hurt me and at the time I didn't think I'd hurt him, but Lt. Goodwyn confirmed the kill for me. However, by now my engine temperature was up on the red and I was leaving a thick trail of smoke so I bailed out rather than taking a chance of catching fire. I might have tried to make it home, if it hadn't been so far, but I was only about 60 miles west of Berlin.

"I was picked up a few minutes after landing and wound up two or three weeks later in Stalag Luft 3 at Sagen. This is the same camp as the movie *Stalag 17* was about. My arrival at Stalag 3 was just a few weeks after the "great escape" and I guess the executions tempered any ideas of escape we may have had. I remained here until December 1944 and then we were moved south as the Russians approached. We were finally liberated from a camp near Munich during the last days of the war."

After being liberated, Maj. Carpenter returned briefly to Debden and had a reunion with the few of his friends that still were there. By this time most of his pilot friends had either gone down or rotated, but he was able to see his crew chief, S/Sgt. Walter Behm. They remained close friends and continued to visit each other after the war. Before he left to come home, Carpenter was able to pick up his gun-camera films and learn that he had ranked seventh within the group in aerial victories.

Unlike many of his fellow pilots from the 4th, George Carpenter did not elect to remain in the post-war Air Force, but instead decided to get married and resume his college career. In 1946 he returned to England to marry his girl, and then brought her back to the United States. In 1956 he graduated from the Kirksville College of Osteopathic Medicine. He has practiced medicine in Tennessee since then.

LIBERATORS AND FLYING FORTRESSES

by Jean-Luc R. Beghin

(Editor's Note: Mr. Beghin's illustrations appear on pages 4-5 and 68-69. For information on attaining his lithographs write Jean-Luc Beghin, 6420 West 80th PL., Los Angeles, CA 90045)

The streetcar stopped in the middle of the country, between Brussels and Waterloo (Belgium). My grandmother took my hand and we ran through an open field. It was a beautiful sunny day in 1944. I was five years old. I remember being flat on my back and looking straight up at many, many silvery little "fishes" high in the dark blue sky. My grandmother was seated in the grass next to me.

"Regarde les Forteresses Volantes, elles vont bombarder les boches! lls ont ce ce qu'ils meritent!" Look at the Flying Fortresses, they are on their way to bomb the boches! They are getting what they deserve!"

I couldn't really see what those "Forteresses Volantes" looked like. I was imagining real castles with soldiers manning the parapets. I wondered how such a big thing could stay in the sky and concluded that my grandmother was right: "Les Americains sont fantastiques!" "The Americans are fantastic!"

Over the years I have often wondered how good she was in aircraft recognition. She would look at the formations and say: "Des Liberators!" or "Des Forteresses Volantes!" I suspect that she like to pronounce the word "Liberator" a lot, a very encouraging name indeed. Alas for our "Little Friends," when it came to Allied fighters, they were all "Spitfires" to her! The Merlin might have been the culprit!

It has been 50 years now but the sound, the vibration, the excitement caused by an American bomber formation is forever engraved in my memory. When the barracks occupied by the Germans in Brussels were bombed by the 8th Air Force, I remember being in the basement of my mother's house with a lot of women praying. I put an aluminum pan on my head and watched little pieces of cement and plaster falling from the ceiling. Lots of windows were blown off but no bombs fell outside of the barracks perimeter.

That certainly was high altitude precision bombing. When the siren would sound the "All clear," I would run to the street, like all the other boys from the neighborhood, and pick up a maximum of shrapnel. The best place to find those was in the rain gutters of the houses. I would also pick up strange aluminum ribbons (windows/chaff) scattered all over the place. One day, my grandfather showed me a little magazine dropped by "les Americains" over Brussels. I don't remember the content but I will always remember the cover photograph: a burning B-24 with its right wing breaking off.

Being a five year old in Brussels in 1944 was an experience rich in sensations. When

Jean-Luc Beghin saluting, in the arms of Sgt. Louis Silver (British Army). His grandmother is next to him, Brussels 1944. (Courtesy of Jean-Luc Beghin)

Belgium was liberated by the American, British and Canadian armies, my world was suddenly filled with colorful Allied flags, white stars, new words, and the unique smell of Lucky Strikes and Camels. My home was alive with a constant flow of GIs and Tommies and at the piano, my mother played boogie woogie and swing tunes.

I swallowed my first piece of chewing gum during this time and discovered the pleasures of Hershey and Milky Way bars. For months I was taken to school in a jeep or sometimes even in a Bren carrier. In 1945 I saw my first movie: *Pinocchio* (Disney's very best). I was finally able to touch a "Forteresse Volante" and a "Mustang" when they were put on public display in Brussels. This was like a trip to Disneyland before such a place ever existed.

When people would ask me what I wanted to be when I grow up I would invariably answer "an American!" This childhood dream of becoming a U.S. citizen was proudly realized in 1987.

It is no wonder that my love for aviation and the U.S. Army Air Force found its source in all the fascinating flying machines crisscrossing the skies of Belgium during WWII. I had already started drawing airplanes in kindergarten and continued throughout my school years. At 10 I went to my first air show near Brussels. Armed with my Agfa camera, I took my very first pictures of airplanes (the USAF Skyblazers F-80s).

Drafted in 1960, I served for one year as an illustrator for the Belgian equivalent of *Yank Magazine*. My greatest pleasure was to draw and to drive an army jeep. In 1969 I was put in charge of the aviation section of *Spirou Magazine*, a weekly published in Belgium, France, Switzerland and Canada. I also became the official "GAF View-Master" aerial photographer in Europe.

In 1970, I signed a contract with the Belgian Air Force and started working for the BAF flight safety magazine. This gave me the opportunity to fly as a passenger-photographer in a variety of aircraft: TF-104 "Starfighter," "T-Bird," and "Fouga Magister" to name a few. My other childhood dream came true when my friend Pierre Dague (an Air France 747 pilot) gave me an unforgettable 20 minutes of combat maneuvers in a P-51D "Mustang" (1992).

My first visit to the United States took place in 1972 when I went to Cape Kennedy to see the Apollo 16 lift off. Back in Belgium I started specializing in cockpit renditions and developed my "You are in the cockpit" perspective.

In 1976 we, my wife Rita-Marie and our three children, Nathalie, Caroline and Jean-Francois, moved to California. Since then my main ambition has been to illustrate the history of the U.S. Army Air Force mostly by way of cockpit view perspectives.

When we arrived in California in 1976, I was hoping to be allowed to join the National Guard and have the privilege of wearing the uniform of the U.S. Armed Forces. It didn't happen. I was 37, two years over the limit.

If I wasn't able, in 1945 to ask all sorts of questions of my heroes, I have since met many of them. We visited with General Doolittle in Carmel, with Tony LeVier (P-38 Demonstration pilot) in Burbank, with Edgar Schmued (designer of the P-51) in Palos Verdes, with Kelly Johnson (designer of the P-38, F-80, F-104 etc.) in Los Angeles... I always find it fascinating to meet, 50 years later, the GIs and the Air Force people who played such an important role in my life. Their story is unique. They are the American Spirit at its best. I am grateful for this opportunity to thank them all.

"A" (or "B") Wing - System used by the 20th Wing, after the 489th joined, of dividing the four groups into two manageable wings of two groups each.

A5 - Automatic pilot system manufactured by the Sperry Co.

AA - Anti-aircraft.

AAFSAT - Army Air Force School of Applied Tacticts, Orlando, Florida.

Ack-Ack - British term for anti-aircraft fire; derived from the sound of the firing.

ADF - Automatic direction finder.

APU - Auxiliary power unit. A generator to provide power to start engines, or to be used in case of main generator failure in flight.

Bandit - Enemy fighter aircraft.

Blue Bomb - A 100 lb. practice bomb, filled with sand. So called because of its color.

Bogey - or Bogie - Unidentified aircraft.

Boundary for Gross Errors - A line around a target at a given distance from the center of the target, beyond which any bombing errors are considered gross errors.

Buncher - A surface-based low power radio beacon used for positioning a number of aircraft over a given point. Used mainly in assembling formations.

C1 - Automatic pilot system manufactured by Minneapolis-Honeywell.

CBW - Combat Bomb Wing.

Chaff - Narrow metallic strips which, dropped from aircraft, created false signals on ground radar scopes.

Cluster - A collection of small bombs held together by an adapter. When used in the sense of an award, as "oak leaf cluster," it signifies another award of that particular medal.

Command pilot - As used in this book, a pilot, usually senior in grade, assigned to fly with the lead crew as mission commander.

DAL - Division assembly line.

Darky - A network of low-powered radio stations to advise pilots of their approximate location.

DP - Displaced person.

DUC - Distinguished Unit Citation.

E/A - Enemy aircraft.

Element - In the 8th Air Force, three planes in formation.

ETA - Estimated time of arrival.

ETO - European Theater of Operations.

ETR - Estimated Time of Return.

Field Order - An operation order.

Flak - German anti-aircraft fire. Derived from German title "Flieger Abwehr Kanone."

Flak Vest (Also flak suit or jacket) - A jacket or vest of heavy fabric containing metal plates, for protection against flak. Could be one or wo parts, depending on needs of the person wearing it.

FO - Field Order.

FPM - Feet Per Minute (ascent or descent).

Frag Order - From "Fragmentary operation order." A section of an operation order.

FW-190 - German single engine fighter built by Focke-Wulf.

GCA - Ground Controlled Approach - a precision instrument landing system.

GEE (or GH) - A medium distance radio navigation system or aid. Aircraft position is determined by measuring the difference in the time of arrival of synchronized pulses broadcast by a master and two slave stations. Developed by the British before WWII.

GP - General Purpose. Generally used for "general purpose bomb."

Gross Error - A bombing error beyond an arbitrarily determined distance from the desired point of impact.

H2S - RAF 10 cm. frequency airborne terrain scanning radar used initially by 8th AF Pathfinder crews. Nicknamed "Stinky."

H2X - Airborne radar blind bombing and navigational system. In a B-24 it was installed in the well formerly occupied by the ball turret.

IFF - Identification Friend or Foe (A coded beacon carried by all allied aircraft).

IP - Initial Point. The point at which the bomb run started.

Jamming - The use of electronic transmissions to disrupt radio or radar transmissions.

JU88 - A twin-engined German aircraft used both as a dive bomber and a level bomber.

Lager - German word, meaning "storehouse."

Mae West - Popular name for inflatable life vest.

Maypole - Code word for aircraft which went to target area in advance of the formation and sent back weather information.

ME109 - German single-engine fighter aircraft built by Messerschmitt.

ME410 - German twin-engined ground support or light bomber aircraft.

Mickey - Short for Mickey Mouse. Slang term for various airborne radar sets. Mickey Man - the operator, radar navigator.

MOS - Military Occupational Speciality.

MP - Military Police or Manifold Pressure.

MPI - Mean Point of Impact. The mean, or geometrical center of the bombing pattern, excluding gross errors.

NCO - Noncommissioned officer.

Nickel Bombs - Propaganda leaflets.

NOBALL, or No-Ball - Term for pilotless bomb (V1 and V2) launching site targets.

OBOE - First "blind bombing" radar adopted by the 8th AF from the RAF and later abandoned. It was extremely accurate within 250 miles. Depended on two ground stations.

PFF - Pathfinder Force.

POM - Preparation for overseas movement. Final readiness inspection.

POW - Prisoner of War.

PPI - Plan position indicator (radar screen).

PSI - Pounds per square inch (such as manifold pressure).

Purple Heart Corner - Position for the last plane in a formation; generally the outside plane in the last element of the high squadron. So called because of its vulnerability to enemy attack.

Put-Put - Slang term for the Auxiliary Power Unit.

R&R - Rest and recreation.

RDX - Cyclonite - a white crystalline explosive having high sensitivity and explosive power.

RON - Remain overnight.

RPM - Revolutions per minute.

S-ing (Essing) - To make a track in the air resembling the letter S; a maneuver used to increase distance from formation ahead.

Salvo - Simultaneous release of all bombs.

Scrub - Cancel.

Sortie - One mission by one aircraft.

Splasher - A non-directional homing beacon which broadcast simultaneously on three frequencies, each with its own identifying code. Useful only over England.

Stand Down (Stood Down) - Off operational status.

T/O - Table of organization. The list of personnel and equipment authorized for a unit. (T/O & E).

Tail-end Charlie - The last element of a formation. See Purple Heart Corner. Also a term for the tail gunner.

TDY - Temporary duty.

Time Hack - Synchronization of watches by a person counting off seconds to a specified hour or minute. Also called "time tick."

TPA - Travel by private auto authorized.

V-1 - Abbreviation for "Vergeltungswaffe Uns," generally called "buzz bomb." A robot bomb with wings, horizontal and vertical stabilizers, rudder and elevators. Powered by a pulse jet engine. Had auto pilot, speed of 360 mph, range 150 miles and flew at 2-3000 feet altitude.

V-2 - A liquid fueled, rocket 46 feet long. Developed 60,000 lbs. thrust and speed of 3600 mph. Fuel supply exhausted in 60 sec. Reached 60 miles in altitude and came down at 1500 mph.

VHF - Very high frequency.

Window - See Chaff. Orgin of word apparently a matter of code.

Second Air Division Roll of Honor

As of June 1993

2nd Air Division Memorial Room ... Norwich Central Library, Norwich, England

The names recorded include personnel of the 14 Bombardment Groups and five Fighter Groups of the 2nd Air Division who were killed in action or in line of combat related duty, preparing for, during, or immediately after combat operations against the enemy during the dates of Group Assignment to the 2nd Air Division (2nd Bomb Wing or 2nd Bomb Division) through and including the date of the last mission, 27 April 1945.

44th Bomb Group

Acheson, Leonard E.	11029463	T/Sgt
Allen, George P.	11021584	S/Sgt
Anderson, James	12029395	T/Sgt
Andes, Ivan A.	14092185	Cpl
Andrino, Robert L.	0.818803	2/Lt
Armstrong, Reed	39827450	T/Sgt
Arnold, Lowell L.	35488682	T/Sgt
Austin, William E.	39019202	Sgt
Avendano, Joseph Jr.	0.724581	Capt
Bailey, Silas	13117076	S/Sgt
Baker, Addison E.	0.280827	Lt.Col
Baker, John G.	39337528	Sgt
Barnes, James L.	12030272	T/Sgt
Bartlett, Richard E.	19056154	S/Sgt
Batson, Arthur	14041220	M/Sgt
Baughman, Kenneth D.	0790930	1/Lt
Baumann, Leo F.	0824076	1/Lt
Bedwell, Philip G.	15101741	S/Sgt
Bell, Virgil R.	T.190735	F/O
Bennett, Charles E.	17037959	T/Sgt
Berger, Robert W.	15140423	S/Sgt
Biggers, Charles E.	0431240	Maj
Bins, Robert F.	0683895	1/Lt
Blais, Clifford A.	31179330	S/Sgt
Blakenship, George	0.696197	1/Lt
Bloom, William R.	19146431	Sgt
Boaze, Clyde K.	13032141	S/Sgt
Bolle, Raymond E.	14066349	S/Sgt
Bonnom, Donald E.	35170034	Sgt
Boone, Ruel K.	6923409	S/Sgt
Boswell, Joe E.	T.000153	F/O
Bournazos, Gregory	0.736752	2/Lt
Bowman, John P.	0.428650	Capt
Boyd, Robert H.	32607560	S/Sgt
Boyle, John J.	0669969	1/Lt
Bradford, William H.	0822628	2/Lt
Brannon, Ted	0660324	1/Lt
Bray, Vernon C.	13032844	S/Sgt
Brown, Jerold W.	15085748	T/Sgt
Brown, Robert L.	0.724587	1/Lt
Brown, Vern C.	0761868	2/Lt
Brunisholz, Jacob A.	32237551	S/Sgt
Bundy, James F.	39548880	S/Sgt
Byerman, Harry E.	35506495	S/Sgt
Byers, Benjamin O.	T190737	F/O
Byrd, Thomas O.	35367815	S/Sgt
Caldwell, Franklin B.	0.685437	2/Lt
Cambria, Salvatore M.	12204418	S/Sgt
Caplan, Benjamin	10600460	Sgt
Carrier, Robert E.	17154598	S/Sgt
Carriker, Raymond R.	38318506	T/Sgt
Carter, Cornelius J.	37581160	S/Sgt
Cassell, Harry Jr.	0756835	2/Lt
Cates, Charles L.	0670501	2/Lt
Cathcart, Raymond P.	15083861	T/Sgt
Chamberlain, Alfred	0736473	1/Lt
Christiansen, H.L.	6665827	T/Sgt
Chrysler, Franklin L.	32545310	Sgt
Ciccarelli, George T.	12045259	Sgt
Clifford, Wilbert L.	19060150	S/Sgt
Coats, Wesley P.	16115540	Sgt
Cochran, Glenn R.	0736840	2/Lt
Coffelt, James R.	34189424	S/Sgt
Colby, Paul E.	16079881	T/Sgt
Coleman, Idus F.	34243641	T/Sgt
Collins, John E.	34083034	S/Sgt
Collins, Nelson R.	T190646	F/O
Conoway, Merrill J.	3298111	S/Sgt
Cott, James E.	0789244	Capt
Cottingham, Harry	39169796	S/Sgt
Coury, Charles J.	36566693	S/Sgt
Cowden, John H.	18071001	S/Sgt
Cozzone, Joseph J.	33325578	S/Sgt

Cramer, Stephen H.	0717391	2/Lt
Crawford, Kenneth E.	0749426	2/Lt
Creadon, George R.	35276843	S/Sgt
Creasey, Glenn A.	35656392	Sgt
Crimmins, John D.	34167965	T/Sgt
Crisp, John B.	0789235	1/Lt
Crouthamel, Edgar S.	0749544	2/Lt
Crumley, Jim M.	14040230	Sgt
Cummings, Ralph W.	0733155	1/Lt
Daly, Herbert B.	13030084	T/Sgt
Daugherty, Paul P.	18120876	Sgt
Davis, Frank F.	0681027	2/Lt
Davis, Parkman W.	0660334	1/Lt
Davis, Robert W.	35037523	Cpl
Davison, Cornelius J.	12221225	S/Sgt
Dee, John T.	13037150	Sgt
Defreese, William A.	34261039	S/Sgt
Dekeyser, Harold J.	0734318	2/Lt
Demaroney, Stephen	12039355	S/Sgt
Dennis, Clifton E. Jr.	15071253	S/Sgt
Derx, William L.	0724393	1/Lt
Deshazo, Albert P.J.	34708766	Sgt
Deshotel, James A.	14063277	Pvt
Detoris, James	32174174	Sgt
Dick, Edward H.	13021873	Sgt
Dickson, Howard L.	0344438	1/Lt
Dimuzio, James	13039158	S/Sgt
Dinkins, Frank O.	37074959	T/Sgt
Domke, Carl A.	16046275	T/Sgt
Donze, Leo A.	0453327	1/Lt
Doyal, Faine M.	0798988	2/Lt
Doyle, Joseph R.	13039348	S/Sgt
Duer, Richard W.	13042736	S/Sgt
Dunne, Edward T.	0822147	2/Lt
Durbin, John L.	34473300	S/Sgt
Eby, Lester J.	39531654	S/Sgt
Echols, Quilla J.	14142340	S/Sgt
Ehrhart, Kenneth V.	6553476	T/Sgt
Elder, Henry M.	35038972	S/Sgt
Elliott, Wilber H.	35259633	S/Sgt
Erness, Walter R.	0415977	2/Lt
Ervin, William C.	34036553	T/Sgt
Essell, James A.	02072669	2/Lt
Faith, Edgar C.	18070690	S/Sgt
Farwell, Donald C.	0706828	1/Lt
Ferrell, Leon E.	38542833	Sgt
Fish, Sanford W.	0806422	2/Lt
Fisher, Robert H. Jr.	12141953	S/Sgt
Fortin, Charles A.	31152090	T/Sgt
Franke, William J.	32781973	Sgt
Franks, Jesse D.	0734444	1/Lt
Frey, John L.	35739127	T/Sgt
Friedlander, Emanuel	0669397	2/Lt
Frobish, Eldon C.	0706050	1/Lt
Frost, Earl L.	32144678	S/Sgt
Fuller, Harold L.	32494328	Sgt
Fulmer, Henry D. Jr.	0691639	1/Lt
Galbraith, Robert L.	17182000	S/Sgt
Gallaway, Leonard N.	37296350	S/Sgt
Gareau, Reuben L.	6798108	S/Sgt
Garrott, Carl N.	0789241	2/Lt
Garrow, Herbert J.	32551821	S/Sgt
Geer, John H.	0690206	Capt
Geiss, Robert E.	0676463	2/Lt
Gewehr, Ralph P.	0416295	Capt
Gibson, James W.	38569609	Sgt
Gifford, Ralph E.	36424034	S/Sgt
Gilbert, Howard R.	0660343	2/Lt
Gill, James L.	0660344	1/Lt
Giusti, Mario R.	0717646	2/Lt
Glass, Ira A.	35807205	S/Sgt
Glickman, Harold	19160384	S/Sgt

Glover, Farlan D.	34103972	M/Sgt
Glut, Frank C.	0766870	1/Lt
Goodman, Edwin J.	32279309	Sgt
Gordoni, Charles K.	13124793	S/Sgt
Grafe, Lee J.	39298675	S/Sgt
Graff, Robert J.	12075899	S/Sgt
Grant, Robert D.	0660347	1/Lt
Gray, Leon L.	13172229	Cpl
Greenfeld, Herman	12203930	S/Sgt
Grenwis, F.A. Jr.	0734896	2/Lt
Grinde, John H.	36241507	T/Sgt
Guess, Richard L.	13024823	S/Sgt
Gutman, Hirschel L.	0743238	1/Lt
Hagey, Robert E.	15103517	S/Sgt
Hagler, Henry A.	34765572	S/Sgt
Haller, Edward J.	39090167	T/Sgt
Handelman, Jacob W.	32568167	Sgt
Hanna, Harold J.	36021887	M/Sgt
Hanson, Ralph L.	0728862	2/Lt
Hanson, William F.	11096127	S/Sgt
Hardin, James R.	0790954	1/Lt
Harrington, John F.	0822432	1/Lt
Harris, Jack D.	0532892	1/Lt
Harrison, James M.	01541695	2/Lt
Hawkins, Thaddeus I. Jr.	0789772	1/Lt
Hayden, John H.	0311882	Col
Hayes, Roger W.	0737946	2/Lt
Henry, Leo L.	36693813	S/Sgt
Heskamp, Carl G.	0700929	2/Lt
Hickey, James R.	12177551	S/Sgt
Hickman, Cleveland D.	0727870	Capt
Hoderlein, Loren J.	35669691	T/Sgt
Hodgeman, John J.	38444079	S/Sgt
Hoffman, John R.	0808545	2/Lt
Holsomback, James E.	14079358	S/Sgt
Homnick, Frederick H.	13025960	T/Sgt
Horasanian, Haig	02074432	2/Lt
Horwitz, Roy	36734374	T/Sgt
Houseman, Murray F.	0929406	2/Lt
Howard, Henry H. Jr.	39019629	T/Sgt
Hughes, John R.	32468888	S/Sgt
Hughes, Robert A.	14095137	S/Sgt
Humphreys, Arthur S.	32475422	S/Sgt
Hurlburt, Richard C.	32245254	S/Sgt
Husten, James S.	0728790	1/Lt
Hutchens, Charles R.	0735381	1/Lt
Hutchinson, Amos M.	0436139	1/Lt
Ipher, Claude H.	0736224	1/Lt
Jacobson, Stanley	0686433	2/Lt
Jerstad, John L.		Maj
Johns, Claude L.	34803367	Sgt
Johnson, Edward F.	33226027	Cpl
Johnson, Robert A.	0724624	1/Lt
Johnson, Thaddeus C. Jr.	0750390	2/Lt
Jones, Jack S.	0435687	Capt
Jones, Oliver C. Jr.	13075961	Cpl
Juraschek, Theodore	T61913	F/O
Kaluzsa, Robert E.	0660366	1/Lt
Kammerer, Clayton C.	35125371	S/Sgt
Kasparian, Jack W.	19099178	T/Sgt
Keller, Edward L.	14063239	T/Sgt
Kennedy, Michael G.	0664319	1/Lt
Kennon, Munford	13023145	T/Sgt
Key, James R. Jr.	37041316	S/Sgt
Kibler, Alvin M.	0712410	2/Lt
Kilmer, T.J.	18085232	S/Sgt
King, Willis D.	14005640	S/Sgt
Kirken, Paul	13040527	S/Sgt
Kirkpatrick, Louis B.	14057097	T/Sgt
Kirlin, William H. Jr.	13099531	T/Sgt
Kish, Ernest J.	13038776	Sgt
Kleinsteuber, H.E.	0724438	1/Lt

Kleyman, Paul W.	35222504	Sgt
Klovis, Steve T.	35335109	Sgt
Koehn, Wilfred J.	0795263	1/Lt
Koon, Loren J.	02044710	2/Lt
Kraft, William C.	33409323	S/Sgt
Krall, Edward J.	0712598	1/Lt
Krugel, Stanley S.	20142120	T/Sgt
Krummert, Elmer C.	33693808	S/Sgt
Kudej, Elmer	35316181	S/Sgt
Kunin, Irving E.	0885946	2/Lt
Kunze, Owen L.	0435803	Capt
LaField, Jack R.	0670138	2/Lt
Lambert, Albert R.	34118415	T/Sgt
Lane, Harold M.	19077898	S/Sgt
Lang, Jack E.	17031466	T/Sgt
Lange, Erhardt C.	36281846	S/Sgt
Lara, Lupe H.	19176766	T/Sgt
Larsen, Jack J.	16077477	Sgt
Larsen, John M.	19179996	Sgt
Larson, George W.	0733666	1/Lt
Larson, Herman B.	37307236	S/Sgt
LaVearne, Morris	14027065	T/Sgt
Lawruszko, Joseph G.	31338770	Sgt
Lee, Robert E.	16060729	T/Sgt
Lemoine, Earl P.	34232459	S/Sgt
Leskis, Adam G.	36305804	Sgt
Lewis, Carl W.	35276798	Sgt
Lewis, Frank T. Jr.	0724629	2/Lt
Lewis, Thomas W.	0727892	2/Lt
Lill, Gordon T.	14035471	M/Sgt
Liller, Charles E.	33384212	S/Sgt
Linman, William A.	0683190	Capt
Locker, R.K.	0813135	2/Lt
Lofgren, Maurice A.	0727895	Capt
Logan, Paul F.	19059721	S/Sgt
Lotito, John Jr.	6995530	M/Sgt
Lovasik, Leo E.	33278427	T/Sgt
Lowery, William H.	0797340	2/Lt
Loyd, Henry C. Jr.	16041529	T/Sgt
Lozowski, William	0704843	1/Lt
Lucas, Bernard R.	17054970	T/Sgt
Luglio, Benjamin J.	12012650	S/Sgt
Lynch, Robert L.	0727896	2/Lt
Lynvill, Harry J.	0801138	2/Lt
Maciejczak, Richard	36809248	S/Sgt
Mahoney, David J. Jr.	0698895	2/Lt
Major, William H.	15104438	Sgt
Makin, Charles W. Jr.	0798147	2/Lt
Makinster, Chester D.	0680468	1/Lt
Makley, Donald D.	0718008	2/Lt
Malloy, Edwin J.	32237395	S/Sgt
Marriott, Cleland G.	0724633	2/Lt
Marsh, William A.	0660382	2/Lt
Marshel, James H. Jr.	0702469	1/Lt
Martin, Estell Q.	0660383	2/Lt
Martin, Jay W.	37632502	Cpl
Marulli, Anthony G.	0709418	1/Lt
Maruna, John J.	12145589	S/Sgt
Marx, Robert W.	0817244	1/Lt
Massart, Armand R.	33278362	T/Sgt
Mathison, Paul L.	0421779	Capt
Mayers, Irving	16036197	S/Sgt
McArthur, Donald A.	19103418	S/Sgt
McBride, Ralph J. Jr.	0435962	1/Lt
McCallen, Jack R.	33292995	T/Sgt
McCartie, Walter W.	0742182	1/Lt
McCauley, Joseph J. Jr.	0678377	1/Lt
McCorkle, T.V.	0735148	2/Lt
McCray, George H.	0681550	2/Lt
McDermott, Thomas F.	31057180	T/Sgt
McDonald, John H. Jr.	11139062	S/Sgt
McDonough, John M.	0735328	2/Lt
McFetrich, Robert L.	0744154	2/Lt
McGibony, John L.	14120341	Sgt

McGlashan, William	0807920	2/Lt
McGowan, Frank B.	0768823	2/Lt
McKanna, Frederick E. Jr.	0719115	2/Lt
McKelvey, William W.	T190580	F/O
McKethen, Beuford A.	0749177	2/Lt
McMahon, Vincent O.	11044159	S/Sgt
McManus, Thomas M.	15084943	Sgt
McNeeley, Samuel E.	15069860	T/Sgt
McNew, Harold L.	35580866	S/Sgt
McPeters, Foster C.	0734124	1/Lt
McQueen, Paul H.	13055768	S/Sgt
Mead, Carl J.	35406158	S/Sgt
Mecartea, Rexford W.	0760811	1/Lt
Medling, Stephen V. Jr.	17031048	T/Sgt
Meline, Robert C.	37437555	S/Sgt
Merlino, John J.	39037732	T/Sgt
Miller, David C.	13023198	T/Sgt
Miller, Leroy L.	13034155	Sgt
Mlot, Eugene J.	16060659	S/Sgt
Moore, Charles T.	0435976	Capt
Moya, Jose E.	0412949	1/Lt
Mullin, Clair F.	0699707	2/Lt
Murphy, Woodrow B.	39020765	S/Sgt
Musco, Gelrose	11043853	S/Sgt
Myers, Billie B.	18166363	S/Sgt
Nagle, William J.	12049897	S/Sgt
Nalett, Walter E.	16150102	S/Sgt
Nelson, Ronald L.	12036525	S/Sgt
Newell, Robert A.	T.128882	F/O
Nicholson, Louis M.	0.32649	2/Lt
Norris, Earl Jr.	0698756	2/Lt
Novick, Edwin S.	12177972	S/Sgt
O'Brien, Charles M.	12167930	S/Sgt
O'Brien, John F.	0753021	2/Lt
Odell, John J. Jr.	14092229	Pfc
Oliffe, Victor E.	0731644	1/Lt
Olsen, Oscar I.	16001771	M/Sgt
Olson, Theodore H.	0669387	1/Lt
Orwig, Paul E.	13172142	S/Sgt
Oser, Albert H.	11045730	S/Sgt
Papp, Joseph V.	01030281	2/Lt
Parker, Thomas H.	0738018	1/Lt
Parks, Bethel	6669185	S/Sgt
Parsonage, Franklin C.	0801031	2/Lt
Parsons, George L.	11045036	S/Sgt
Pas, Cornelius	13089615	Sgt
Paschal, John F. Jr.	0660391	1/Lt
Pastroff, Kenneth R.	12051123	Sgt
Patullo, Carmine C.	12132268	T/Sgt
Pearson, Edgar J.	32356111	S/Sgt
Peltier, William L.	11043876	Sgt
Perkins, Frank E. Jr.	14185528	Sgt
Petersen, Donald E.	0714829	2/Lt
Pettigrew, Fred D.	18215700	S/Sgt
Pezzella, Alfred W.	0659584	1/Lt
Phelps, Gene R.	36183733	S/Sgt
Piazza, Joseph P.	19090232	Sgt
Picard, James R.	33670945	S/Sgt
Pickett, Eldon B.	18046539	Sgt
Pietruccioli, Michael A.	0684192	2/Lt

Pinion, Jack E.	34044974	S/Sgt
Pinner, George A.	0660393	1/Lt
Piotrowski, Raymond H.	0683205	2/Lt
Pitt, Wade L.	02062285	2/Lt
Poe, Robert J.	0678452	2/Lt
Pollick, Robert	31168016	S/Sgt
Porter, Clarence R.	0412876	Lt/Col
Porter, Enoch M. Jr.	0734132	1/Lt
Porterfield, Charles L.	0736344	2/Lt
Powell, James M.	0817267	1/Lt
Powell, Mitchell W.	38181478	T/Sgt
Prather, William H.	T190608	F/O
Prekel, Stephen C.	13025825	Pvt
Presson, Charles L.	0797603	2/Lt
Price, Willard H.	35140685	S/Sgt
Pryor, John W.	0730600	1/Lt
Purdy, Earl R.	39826840	S/Sgt
Purdy, Harry M.	0702334	2/Lt
Rabinovitz, Allan F.	0685721	2/Lt
Race, Walter C.	39234251	S/Sgt
Rambo, Lester C.	16023523	Sgt
Reagan, George A.	39249488	S/Sgt
Redmond, William J.	32465910	S/Sgt
Reed, Heil R.	15324246	T/Sgt
Reid, Elgin J.	14124751	S/Sgt
Reiquam, Harvey M.	17113941	S/Sgt
Remias, Stephen	12137453	Sgt
Renk, Stanley E.	02071696	2/Lt
Reuter, George J.	0659913	1/Lt
Riddle, Alpheus H.	15115573	S/Sgt
Reiss, Lynn C. Jr.	0437652	1/Lt
Riggs, Benjamin F.	0737661	Capt
Riley, John C.	0519127	2/Lt
Rinne, Kenneth L.	17038531	T/Sgt
Robbins, Edward L.	0677572	1/Lt
Roberts, Hubert W.	0681478	2/Lt
Roberts, James V.	37191032	S/Sgt
Rodriguez, Lawrence D.	39542809	S/Sgt
Roggenkamp, Norman A.	0799463	Capt
Roop, Thomas C.	38192091	Sgt
Roper, Hugh R.	0432129	Capt
Rose, John S.	14161717	S/Sgt
Rose, Virgil Jr.	02044655	2/Lt
Roznos, Joseph M.	0743100	1/Lt
Rubin, Edward J.	16047688	S/Sgt
Rudisill, John C.	12165742	S/Sgt
Rueckert, William G.	0420521	1/Lt
Rule, Junior J.	0740281	2/Lt
Sabin, Paul	0.685027	2/Lt
Sager, Robert W.	0716897	2/Lt
Salva, Henry R.	0708104	1/Lt
Sanders, Walter W.	0700550	2/Lt
Savage, Harry R.	0667434	1/Lt
Schluter, George R.	0821422	Capt
Schmoller, William	0711807	1/Lt
Schoenberger, Richard H.	0789817	1/Lt
Schreiner, Albert A.	0805532	2/Lt
Schroeder, Robert F.	0735117	2/Lt
Schulties, Elton J.	36212498	Cpl
Schwartz, Morton H.	T190571	F/O
Scott, Peter	0772526	2/Lt
Scott, Richard S.	0902398	Capt

Segars, Henry K. Jr.	0352171	Maj
Seger, James L.	38440425	T/Sgt
Seibel, Julius R.	0735933	2/Lt
Self, Billy H.	18084642	Sgt
Sena, Harold M.	11045631	S/Sgt
Serum, Phillip T. Jr.	34231686	S/Sgt
Seson, Loren F.	0683872	2/Lt
Shannon, Robert H.	0437644	Capt
Shaw, Elwyn H.	0693705	1/Lt
Sheinfine, Sheldon	12191016	S/Sgt
Shively, Harley C.	0667442	2/Lt
Simpson, Joseph G.	0659920	1/Lt
Sipe, Clinton P.	0.661037	1/Lt
Skall, John D.	16038668	Sgt
Skinner, Clifton A.	33352664	Sgt
Slate, Irven G.	6984772	T/Sgt
Sliwa, Edwin J.	36034853	S/Sgt
Sloan, George E.	37343040	Sgt
Smith, Adrian H.	32454962	S/Sgt
Smith, Byron W.	37144913	Sgt
Smith, Walter D.	38009131	T/Sgt
Snyder, Waldon L. Jr.	0795658	2/Lt
Sorrell, Charles G.	0660412	2/Lt
Spedding, Edward W.	0767677	2/Lt
Speier, Charles B.	17154551	S/Sgt
Springer, Walter Jr.	32367016	S/Sgt
Staats, William A. Jr.	12057225	T/Sgt
Stafford, Clifford A.	37211296	T/Sgt
Stafford, Morton O. Jr.	13029264	S/Sgt
Stainker, John J.	13125583	S/Sgt
Staller, Manon E.	13027598	T/Sgt
Stamper, David L.	0798077	2/Lt
Stamper, Teddy	35448195	S/Sgt
Stearns, Jay W.	35515624	Sgt
Stefano, Victor N.	33296451	T/Sgt
Stehnach, Harry R.	13023095	S/Sgt
Stellhorn, Edwin S.	0716988	S/Lt
Stercher, Charles O.	15070128	S/Sgt
Stevens, Neil	0661042	1/Lt
Stevenson, Joe A.	32478604	S/Sgt
Stone, Ray H. Jr.	35222366	Cpl
Strait, Delmont W.	33397482	Sgt
Strickland, Carl F.	34162882	Sgt
Sullivan, Gerard E.	20119380	S/Sgt
Sullivan, Paul C.	11098543	Pfc
Sutton, George M. Jr.	0423859	2/Lt
Sweet, Vincent S.	32255510	S/Sgt
Sykes, John F.	0427969	1/Lt
Talley, Eugene Z.	0678495	2/Lt
Tardif, Hubert R.	0731694	1/Lt
Thomas, James N.	34179394	S/Sgt
Thompson, Augustus B.	38044692	T/Sgt
Thornton, Eddie R.	34261388	S/Sgt
Threadgill, Dave T.	38432542	T/Sgt
Timmer, Robert	0.2044427	2/Lt
Todd, Floyd E.	37016458	Sgt
Tompkins, Merl F.	0740044	2/Lt
Tompkins, Raymond M.	32383208	Sgt
Torrey, Arthur M.	33111291	S/Sgt
Trainor, Peter F. Jr.	11048793	S/Sgt
Trask, Robert M.	0.806012	2/Lt

Traut, Robert L. Jr.	0708157	2/Lt
Tucker, Marvin L.	02057461	2/Lt
Tucker, Trenton T.	19170139	S/Sgt
Turner, Carlus	0604211	1/Lt
Turner, Omar A.	0669815	Capt
Tushla, Harold R.	0660935	1/Lt
Uffleman, Walter D.	13022801	T/Sgt
Underdahl, Milton H.	17079431	S/Sgt
Van Cleef, Arthur A.	32385827	Sgt
Van Dervort, John C.	13013578	T/Sgt
Van Winkle, Warren O.	0.805710	1/Lt
Vogelstein, Henry	12186135	S/Sgt
Wagner, James L.	0748852	1/Lt
Wahrheit, William D.	32504330	S/Sgt
Waldmann, C.H. Jr.	38161435	S/Sgt
Walker, Rex S.	0.679412	2/Lt
Wallace, Dana K.	0886647	1/Lt
Walzel, Leland H.	0739638	2/Lt
Ward, Robert B.	0885296	1/Lt
Ward, Thurban L.	0734855	2/Lt
Wardell, Jack F.	0733116	2/Lt
Watson, Orland J.	18065065	Sgt
Watters, William R.	0560451	1/Lt
Waxler, Hyman	31140364	S/Sgt
Weander, Robert A.	37661457	T/Sgt
Weinberg, Gerald	32323397	T/Sgt
Weir, Lloyd C.	37069387	M/Sgt
Wenrick, Vaun D.	35255135	T/Sgt
White, Bob M.	0523103	2/Lt
White, Clifford E.	18050232	S/Sgt
White, John B. Jr.	0660949	1/Lt
White, Kenneth J.	0734857	1/Lt
White, L.H.	36171704	T/Sgt
Whitefield, Edwin L.	07977431	1/Lt
Whitman, Nathaniel	0455162	1/Lt
Whitten, Frank H.	34801322	S/Sgt
Wiegand, Benjamin C.	15195393	T/Sgt
Wiesler, Warren S.	0769237	2/Lt
Wile, Ralph W.	15011113	T/Sgt
Wilkinson, George B.	0.2044441	2/Lt
Williams, Farris E.	38697702	Cpl
Williams, W.J. 2nd	0.023443	Capt
Windle, Alfred I.	17030885	T/Sgt
Wojciechowski, S.A.	35303040	S/Sgt
Wolfe, Merle F.	16034774	T/Sgt
Wolfe, Vail S.	15333057	S/Sgt
Wood, William O.	14061912	S/Sgt
Woodward, Edward J.	0691554	2/Lt
Wright, Ivan M.	36371317	T/Sgt
Wurzer, Joseph M.	0.561173	1/Lt
Yaus, David	0679440	1/Lt
Young, Frank	18068258	S/Sgt
Young, Robert C.	0.820873	1/Lt
Zablocki, Walter A.	36048468	T/Sgt
Zaion, Carl E.	36616099	S/Sgt
Zielaskowski, A.M.	39303459	T/Sgt

93rd Bomb Group

Ackerman, Edward	0.798720	2/Lt
Adams, Carl E.	34735355	S/Sgt
Adams, Howard F.	0.023946	Capt
Adams, Richard W.	14120178	S/Sgt
Adams, Victor J.	32323620	S/Sgt
Aguirre, Adolph P.	39251163	Sgt
Aho, Augustus	31121510	Sgt
Airoldi, John A.	0.759546	2/Lt
Albert, Frank L.	0.800804	1/Lt
Albine, Robert L.	13087450	S/Sgt
Alford, Iceal W.	0.790924	2/Lt
Allen, Norbert G.	37480256	S/Sgt
Almlie, Harlan C.	0.676714	1/Lt
Altemus, William B.	0.2045026	2/Lt
Andello, David F.	15016119	S/Sgt
Anderhalt, Virgil J.	13060226	S/Sgt
Anderson, Everett P.	0.885575	1/Lt
Anderson, William N.	0.411678	Maj
Andris, Eugene E.	16028769	S/Sgt
Appledorn, Thomas J.	15087738	S/Sgt

Arcamone, Frank	32540668	S/Sgt
Archambault, W.S.	0738953	2/Lt
Arnold, Ernest F.	17035780	Sgt
Artym, Frank Jr.	16171652	S/Sgt
Ashwell, Harold L.	14042027	T/Sgt
Augenstene, J.A. Jr.	0.789432	1/Lt
Ayers, John T.	0.734779	2/Lt
Bair, Kenneth O.	35566053	Sgt
Bakalo, Michael	0.699752	1/Lt
Baker, Wallace P.	0.734296	2/Lt
Balca, Michael J	15070162	S/Sgt
Bales, James H.	34283420	T/Sgt
Ballangrud, Norris S.	0681300	1/Lt
Balsley, Lucius M.	39175097	S/Sgt
Banning, Charles E.	12012298	S/Sgt
Barber, Thomas G. Jr.	34163105	S/Sgt
Barefoot, Charles L.	0.1995911	1/Lt
Barnett, Edward	0.730337	2/Lt
Baron, Ernest F.	39832837	T/Sgt
Barth, David	42069644	Sgt

Bartmess, Thomas E.	0726980	1/Lt
Bartol, Stockton R.	0.680595	1/Lt
Bateman, Walter R.	0.796281	1/Lt
Battenberg, Walter R.	36832427	S/Sgt
Baum, Paul F.	0685420	2/Lt
Bauman, Francis A.	39020115	T/Sgt
Baxter, Orus Jr.	18193549	T/Sgt
Bayless, Herbert L.	0.768414	1/Lt
Bean, Loran M. Jr.	0756831	2/Lt
Beggs, William A.	38345296	S/Sgt
Behnke, George C.	32736648	Sgt
Beirne, Milton R.	0699505	2/Lt
Bell, Robert J.	11106940	Sgt
Bellard, Harold W.	0.675984	1/Lt
Belsky, George	33300775	S/Sgt
Bennett, James W.	0.7009747	2/Lt
Bentcliff, Clifford J.	0815806	1/Lt
Berg, Albert H.	19074273	Cpl
Berkstresser, G.B.	18104589	T/Sgt
Bernstein, David G.	39234569	S/Sgt
Besse, Wilson P.	38194491	S/Sgt

Bessen, Theodore		S/Sgt
Bethke, Elmer J.	16077154	S/Sgt
Bettley, Conrad R. Jr.	11113894	S/Sgt
Beverly, Paul E.	18045226	S/Sgt
Billings, Fred M. Jr.	0.411918	1/Lt
Billings, James R.	0.676728	1/Lt
Binienda, Walter	11032802	Cpl
Birge, Edward E.	14080954	T/Sgt
Bittner, Harry H.	16063878	Sgt
Blackley, William W.J.	0.680842	2/Lt
Blaine, Robert W.	0423910	1/Lt
Blake, Foster A.	11055810	S/Sgt
Blanchard, Theodore A.	11038400	S/Sgt
Bledsoe, Jesse W.	0718848	2/Lt
Blitz, Aulis L.	33204357	S/Sgt
Bloomfield, Philip J.	12067159	S/Sgt
Boersma, John A.	6770674	Cpl
Bogan, Robert D.	37264830	S/Sgt
Boggess, Boyd Jr.	33213653	S/Sgt
Bohnisch, Carl A.	08067891	1/Lt
Bolin, James O.	0424895	1/Lt

Bolster, Harry T.	35397686	S/Sgt
Bonham, Robert W.	15125248	S/Sgt
Borgstrom, Rolon D.	39917713	Sgt
Boutin, Albert L. Jr.	13551111	Sgt
Bowie, Donald	11013585	S/Sgt
Bradshaw, Eugene T.	0.717169	1/Lt
Brady, Lloyd J.	37232782	S/Sgt
Braswell, Homer H.	14105559	S/Sgt
Breakey, Karl D.	33408973	S/Sgt
Breniser, Norman A.	39092835	S/Sgt
Brenner, Joseph L.	0.727081	S/Lt
Brewer, Frederick K.	32448986	T/Sgt
Brewer, Scott E.	39826187	S/Sgt
Brisson, Willard C.	34857923	Cpl
Bronstein, George	0.523516	2/Lt
Brooks, Robert L.	15099670	S/Sgt
Broome, Garland R.	34623016	Sgt
Brown, George F. Jr.	0831104	2/Lt
Brown, Harry H. Jr.	15327559	S/Sgt
Brown, James M. Jr.	34316177	S/Sgt
Brown, John C.	0727307	2/Lt
Brown, Richard C.	0.727161	2/Lt
Brown, Walter L.	18063845	S/Sgt
Bruce, James C. Jr.	0547126	1/Lt
Bruce, W.B.	14159347	S/Sgt
Bryant, Charles W.	0727309	2/Lt
Bryl, Edward B.	10601101	S/Sgt
Buckley, Francis X.	13124177	Sgt
Buechsenstein, John L.	0739538	2/Lt
Buhl, Vernon	39621427	Sgt
Bukholts, John J.	0.669980	1/Lt
Burge, Harold L.	0697098	1/Lt
Burk, William J.	14091412	Sgt
Burns, Harry B.	13044534	T/Sgt
Burroughs, Sydney M.	0661588	2/Lt
Burton, Gerald C.	14092298	S/Sgt
Butler, Richard J.	13044499	S/Sgt
Byers, Clifford L.	37704580	Sgt
Caldwell, Paul D.	0727313	2/Lt
Callahan, Cornelius	32316551	T/Sgt
Calvin, William A.	7010352	S/Sgt
Camp, John D.	0.717380	1/Lt
Canfield, Dale K.	0.727170	2/Lt
Canfield, Ivan	0.670498	2/Lt
Cantrell, Eugene H.	0.678158	2/Lt
Capizzi, Thomas F.	32533914	T/Sgt
Cargile, Nolan B.	0427211	1/Lt
Cargill, Lawrence E.	37464353	T/Sgt
Carlton, Clyde W.	14037452	S/Sgt
Carroll, John M.	11019924	T/Sgt
Castellotti, Paul E.	0671279	1/Lt
Cate, Richard E.	20366318	Sgt
Celentano, Louis S.	0703026	1/Lt
Chalan, Andy	13145502	S/Sgt
Chandler, Max E.	0.2059456	2/Lt
Chapman, Robert D.	32142986	T/Sgt
Charleson, Norman	0740744	1/Lt
Charletta, Henry	6890102	M/Sgt
Chase, Dudley S.	01051904	1/Lt
Childers, James C.	19087800	T/Sgt
Chorzelski, Michel	T.190738	F/O
Christenson, George E.	37281658	S/Sgt
Christenson, Neil W.	17037502	T/Sgt
Christian, Charles M.	14094288	S/Sgt
Christian, James W.	14266875	T/Sgt
Churchill, Douglas E.	16108271	S/Sgt
Cianciolo, Michael A.	34288192	S/Sgt
Cieply, Eugene B. Jr.	32491716	Sgt
Clarey, Howard A. Jr.	0676748	1/Lt
Clark, Fredrick W.	11033143	S/Sgt
Clark, Raymond C.	0748571	2/Lt
Clark, Thomas W.	12100209	Sgt
Clark, William N. Jr.	35229520	S/Sgt
Clemons, Archie D.	15013217	T/Sgt
Click, George	15115001	S/Sgt
Clossen, William E.	31088145	Pvt
Cobane, William E.	0735857	1/Lt
Coe, George C.	37020898	S/Sgt
Cole, Edward A.	0691634	2/Lt
Cole, Woodrow W.	0.741099	1/Lt
Coll, William F.	13051982	T/Sgt
Collins, Richard K.	0393514	1/Lt
Confer, Charlie H.	35371803	S/Sgt
Congelli, Joseph P.	0.748579	2/Lt
Cook, Floyd R.	0.747217	1/Lt
Cook, Harold C.	0.662333	2/Lt
Cook, Roy	15337089	S/Sgt
Cool, Albert B.	0.808958	1/Lt

Cooney, Woodrow J.	35307188	T/Sgt
Cooper, Harold E.	38149230	T/Sgt
Cooper, Warren H.	0829129	2/Lt
Cordes, Thomas H.	12100258	Sgt
Corsilli, Gene	32466233	Sgt
Cottington, Orna E.	20649538	T/Sgt
Couvillion, Wilbert	38494335	Sgt
Cowan, Henry Jr.	31240322	Sgt
Cox, Sargent S.	0.734314	1/Lt
Craig, James W.	13004719	S/Sgt
Cramer, Thomas R.	0.23925	Maj
Crandell, Leonard J.	0720197	1/Lt
Crane, Paul M.	13046804	S/Sgt
Crane, Walter W.	0785168	1/Lt
Crawford, George A.	0.727320	2/Lt
Crawford, Michael C.	34267452	S/Sgt
Crigger, William C.	16041926	S/Sgt
Crocker, John L. Jr.	34430758	S/Sgt
Croll, William B.	02058627	2/Lt
Crook, Thomas W. Jr.	13040353	Sgt
Crowl, Wayne D.	0741141	1/Lt
Crump, Arch M.	34133119	T/Sgt
Crump, John W.	36318179	T/Sgt
Cunningham, Jonathan M.	0.789237	1/Lt
Currelli, Rocco A.	0.670981	2/Lt
Curry, Francis X.	33361905	T/Sgt
Curry, Thomas R.	0.682150	2/Lt
Curtis, Herman M.	0.748585	1/Lt
Dailey, Max E.	0795211	2/Lt
Dalto, John	32707708	Sgt
D'Amico, Anthony	38197204	S/Sgt
Daniels, Carl E.	32669213	Sgt
Dantzler, Robert T.	0207265	2/Lt
D'Armour, John P.	36146758	S/Sgt
Darnoll, Raymond L.	36066774	S/Sgt
Davidowitz, Edward	T.122578	F/O
Davis, Bryan C.	34248744	Sgt
Davis, Donald A.	36343869	T/Sgt
Davis, James E.	34146466	T/Sgt
Davis, Milton H.	0691878	2/Lt
Davis, Richard H.	0723022	2/Lt
Dayball, Julian H.	0701907	1/Lt
Daywalt, Harry A. Jr.	0.796325	1/Lt
Deal, Manford S.	36175723	S/Sgt
Deavenport, Thomas G.	0.443161	2/Lt
Decker, Donald R.	02044424	2/Lt
Dewald, George M.	13124616	S/Sgt
Diaz, Aribal C.	34530358	Sgt
Dick, Charles S.	31033519	Sgt
Dickinson, John L.	32453614	T/Sgt
Dillahunty, Jack C.	18160347	T/Sgt
Dittmer, Arthur H.	0818843	2/Lt
Dobbins, Maurice H.	16055011	S/Sgt
Dobson, Edward M.	0668216	1/Lt
Doherty, Robert L.	13039292	S/Sgt
Doka, Michael	36148552	S/Sgt
Dolan, Charles Jr.	08258084	2/Lt
Doria, Frank N.	12039389	S/Sgt
Douthit, William E.	34261978	S/Sgt
Downey, John J. III	12193464	S/Sgt
Dubard, James D. Jr.	0410225	1/Lt
Ducki, Stanley H.		S/Sgt
Dudrich, John	0684699	2/Lt
Duke, Benjamin F.	6376260	M/Sgt
Dunajecz, Hugo Jr.	32313726	S/Sgt
Duncan, Joseph B.	33281841	S/Sgt
Dunn, Edward K.	12126659	S/Sgt
Dunn, Robert F.	0670043	2/Lt
Durand, Frederick W.	16021949	S/Sgt
Eberhardt, B.J. Jr.	0681359	2/Lt
Eckert, Otto	36337535	S/Sgt
Ede, Hubert J.	0729151	1/Lt
Edgerton, Eugene C.	31281654	S/Sgt
Edmonds, David	0734660	2/Lt
Edmonson, Roger W.	18218286	S/Sgt
Egle, Ralph W.	0739926	2/Lt
Ela, Deforest L.	31157299	S/Sgt
Elkin, Alton M.	38132105	T/Sgt
Elliott, Eugene L.	3137886	Sgt
Ellis, John T.	0.676452	2/Lt
Ellison, Coy B.	0789240	1/Lt
Emery, Albert W.	6245362	T/Sgt
Erickson, Charles R.	0742572	2/Lt
Erwin, Roy B. Jr.	0.437436	1/Lt
Fagan, Frederick E. Jr.	33235530	T/Sgt
Falls, Charles E.	14055946	S/Sgt

Fann, Irwin	0798775	2/Lt
Farrell, John A.	0755660	1/Lt
Fassl, Richard	0.741498	2/Lt
Faulkner, James L.	34927059	Sgt
Faust, David F.	32297428	Sgt
Feeney, Larry L.	39466210	T/Sgt
Feichter, Herschel H.	35162685	Sgt
Ferguson, Earl F.	0740093	2/Lt
Ferrel, Frank C.	18075492	T/Sgt
Fidares, Nicholas J.	42068546	Sgt
Fields, Edwin D.	33522224	T/Sgt
Finder, Sheldon	0.733298	2/Lt
Fink, Ivan W.	33574486	S/Sgt
Fish, George E.	0803799	2/Lt
Fiskum, Lowell A.	0713157	1/Lt
Flaugh, Harold E.	0681534	2/Lt
Fleenor, Beattie	0.430993	Capt
Flynn, Robert K.	0727327	1/Lt
Fleshman, Lewis J.	12035273	S/Sgt
Folsom, Glenn E.		1/Lt
Ford, Herrell E.	0.665672	Capt
Forest, George W.	0695641	2/Lt
Forrest, Richard P.	0676584	2/Lt
Forrest, Robert E.	0727979	2/Lt
Fouts, Virgil R.	0437434	1/Lt
Fowls, Ralph A.	0717050	1/Lt
Fox, Frederick W.	67076003	T/Sgt
Frangos, Theodore W.	12036607	S/Sgt
Franklin, Charles B.	0789463	1/Lt
Franson, Quinten A.	0707579	2/Lt
Frazee, Winthrop T.	0727328	2/Lt
Fredericks, Adrian E.	0734663	2/Lt
Frye, Richard E.	39092033	S/Sgt
Funkhouse, Eugene H.	35495933	S/Sgt
Fuxa, Ernest C.	18194853	S/Sgt
Gaffney, William J.	12143699	S/Sgt
Galasso, Anthony L.	33288265	T/Sgt
Galindo, Ruben R.	39252107	T/Sgt
Gallagher, Joseph W.	31071580	Sgt
Gandy, Guy E.	18085234	T/Sgt
Garrard, James M.	14070592	S/Sgt
Garrett, James J.	31388309	Sgt
Garrett, Kenneth O.	35431908	S/Sgt
Garrett, Wayne D.	39294443	Sgt
Garza, Raul	38541707	Sgt
Gasperetti, Raymond	39043892	Sgt
Gatens, Frederick B.	0672946	2/Lt
Gates, Jack A.	0663253	2/Lt
Gaziukevicz, Albert	11054081	Sgt
Gempel, Charles L.	0704835	1/Lt
Gentry, Rowland M.	0727983	Capt
Gentry, William H.	39389081	T/Sgt
Gerick, Michael	33038923	S/Sgt
Germolus, Irvin E.	39047565	S/Sgt
Gibby, Cola G.	19055445	S/Sgt
Giffin, John S.	0805903	1/Lt
Gilbert, Joseph D.	34339959	S/Sgt
Gilbert, Robert N.	15102189	S/Sgt
Gilligan, Eugene G.	18110321	S/Sgt
Girard, Louis V.	0885282	1/Lt
Glasscock, Kenneth J.	37197914	S/Sgt
Gleason, Robert J.	13049367	Sgt
Gleichenhaus, Seymour	0.702411	2/Lt
Glemboski, Stanley	36196901	S/Sgt
Goddard, Cecil D.	34265714	S/Sgt
Goldman, Arthur	0671345	1/Lt
Goldman, Carl S.	14046874	S/Sgt
Gomez, John P.	12144218	S/Sgt
Goo, William L.Y.	0711390	1/Lt
Goode, Armel M.	38235476	S/Sgt
Gooden, Ray C.	33442228	S/Sgt
Goodfellow, George E.	11042195	T/Sgt
Goodman, Earl E.	11011586	T/Sgt
Goodnow, Edward W.	0.794123	1/Lt
Goodwin, Henry G. Jr.	0675337	2/Lt
Goolsby, Ray K.	13066720	S/Sgt
Gordon, Rhodes C.		S/Sgt
Gosline, Roy E.	14069419	S/Sgt
Gotts, Howard F.	12055796	Sgt
Grabowski, Barney J.	20641515	S/Sgt
Gradwohl, Jacob	19005806	Sgt
Graff, Andrew C.	37428100	T/Sgt
Graham, Sidney W.	39381894	T/Sgt
Grant, Reginald D.	0.727334	2/Lt
Greathouse, Vincent L.	37181135	T/Sgt
Greattinger, Gordon	16048131	S/Sgt
Green, Donald	35462147	S/Sgt
Green, William F.	0700447	2/Lt

Greno, Paul J.	0817662	1/Lt
Grett, Gerald L.	37120507	S/Sgt
Griffin, Curtis S.	0727211	Capt
Griffith, Warren W.	0828160	2/Lt
Grimes, George G.	0885961	1/Lt
Gritsonis, Nicholas	16034619	S/Sgt
Grogg, Emil L.	33566080	S/Sgt
Gross, Gole H.	39167088	S/Sgt
Gross, Morton P.	0727336	2/Lt
Grushkevich, Aron	32501788	Sgt
Gunter, Noah	14195404	Sgt
Haaf, Howard S.	18081540	Sgt
Hacker, William E.	0531342	2/Lt
Haggerty, James J.	13011885	S/Sgt
Hagmann, Paul A.	39393257	Sgt
Hall, Clifton C.	18157469	S/Sgt
Hall, Franklin P.	14044753	S/Sgt
Hall, Kenneth E.	11114148	S/Sgt
Hall, Kenneth H.	35323302	T/Sgt
Hambright, Archibald	0.795241	2/Lt
Hammond, Charles P.		Sgt
Hammontree, James A.	14161472	Sgt
Hannan, William J.	0727337	2/Lt
Hansen, James E.	0671429	2/Lt
Hantober, Manuel		S/Sgt
Hardwick, Robert E.	0.746482	2/Lt
Harleman, Richard E.	0799767	1/Lt
Harmon, Howard K.	0556125	2/Lt
Harms, Roy C.	0.384490	1/Lt
Harper, James A.	0681402	2/Lt
Harth, William H. Jr.	0731509	2/Lt
Havens, Leycester D.	38202168	S/Sgt
Hawkes, Hazen E.		Sgt
Hayman, Richard D.	35610332	S/Sgt
Haynes, Wiley W. Jr.	34572318	Sgt
Hegedus, Stephen L.	36233606	S/Sgt
Heim, Harry J.	17031110	T/Sgt
Heisserer, Arthur J.	15320098	S/Sgt
Heller, Clayton E.	17058569	S/Sgt
Helphrey, Aaron L.	39013517	Sgt
Henderson, C.P. Jr.	0665686	Capt
Henderson, Gordon W.	0817211	2/Lt
Henson, Forrest O.	0.736858	1/Lt
Herman, Bernard L.	0817213	2/Lt
Hersh, George P.	0.670542	2/Lt
Hess, William H.	15095142	T/Sgt
Hester, Milton Jr.	18076405	S/Sgt
Hibbs, Leo R.	35809558	Sgt
Higgins, Bernard A.	19080947	T/Sgt
Higgins, Hartwell Jr.	14094125	Sgt
Hill, Herbert S. Jr.	11088586	S/Sgt
Hilley, James A.	34117856	Sgt
Hinds, Donald A.	16054355	S/Sgt
Hine, Thomas L.	0692312	1/Lt
Hinkle, Glenn E.	0752855	2/Lt
Hinshaw, Frank T.	0.430978	Capt
Hites, Harold B.	17129255	T/Sgt
Hobbs, Herbert J. Jr.	34117537	S/Sgt
Hobbs, John C.	0828430	2/Lt
Hoffman, Leo J. Jr.	13173425	S/Sgt
Hoffman, Walter G.T.	19176656	S/Sgt
Hogan, Harry C.	37009698	T/Sgt
Holabaugh, John W.	1311012	T/Sgt
Holland, Earl M.	37299913	T/Sgt
Hook, Robert D.	0789472	1/Lt
Hoover, James K.	0.20444432	2/Lt
Houchens, George B. Jr.	15339517	S/Sgt
Houle, Joseph L.	0526201	1/Lt
Houston, Rowland B.	0727991	Capt
Hovey, Glenn C.	0676805	2/Lt
Howell, Malcolm C.	0727992	1/Lt
Howington, Hartwell	0800356	1/Lt
Howley, Robert M.	19144166	S/Sgt
Howser, Earl P.	0864127	1/Lt
Hubbard, Gaylord F.	37120505	Sgt
Hummer, William M.	0783265	2/Lt
Hurst, Clifford C. Jr.		S/Sgt
Hybarger, Tom P.	0666673	1/Lt
Idlet, Philip D.	17015167	Sgt
Iorgov, George W.	18025712	S/Sgt
Israel, Carl T.	0735871	2/Lt
Irwin, John F.	37071188	S/Sgt
Jacobs, Myron G.	0700615	2/Lt
Janiszewski, Ervin R.	16092729	S/Sgt
Jarrett, Daniel D.	0.6833457	2/Lt
Jarvis, Harry L. Jr.	0.024050	Capt

Jeffrey, George L.	15071093	S/Sgt
Jeffs, Robert H.	0.681994	2/Lt
Jefson, Harold E.	3810413	Sgt
Jesson, Max M.	38267506	S/Sgt
Jester, Donald E.	17023590	T/Sgt
John, Glenn G.	39236097	S/Sgt
Johnson, Earl T.	0799569	1/Lt
Johnson, Farmer A. Jr.	T.01010	F/O
Johnson, Guy W.	0681431	1/Lt
Johnson, Melvin J.	0749695	1/Lt
Johnson, Vernie F.	39021986	S/Sgt
Johnston, David W. Jr.	18021146	S/Sgt
Johnston, Frederick V.	0675349	2/Lt
Johnston, William P.	0738559	2/Lt
Jones, Linwood F.	34258309	S/Sgt
Jones, Norman H.	37049716	T/Sgt
Jones, Parke H. Jr.	0674587	1/Lt
Jones, Philip G.	36726983	S/Sgt
Jones, Shirley A.	39680958	Sgt
Jorgensen, Roy G.	0679073	2/Lt
Kaitala, Henry B.	0727999	2/Lt
Kallal, Lawrence B.	16051552	S/Sgt
Kasten, Richard J.	0683831	1/Lt
Katz, Ervin	16144626	S/Sgt
Keilman, Paul H.	0727349	1/Lt
Kempowicz, John J. Jr.	13004024	S/Sgt
Kenner, James D. Jr.	0766282	2/Lt
Kennon, Dan	38102848	T/Sgt
Kennon, Wyatt S.	0661626	1/Lt
Kent, Earl C.	0.442942	1/Lt
King, James L.	0681117	2/Lt
Kirkey, Vernon O.	31166867	S/Sgt
Kiser, Willard	32836806	Sgt
Klingle, Roy L.	39303276	S/Sgt
Klose, Kenneth A.	37276328	S/Sgt
Kobler, James K.	36322554	T/Sgt
Koehler, Harold F.	15019186	S/Sgt
Konstand, Gus	0794428	Capt
Kosch, Emil M.	7024614	S/Sgt
Kramp, Leonard J.	12052800	S/Sgt
Krauss, Charles E.	33338303	T/Sgt
Kraynik, Daniel J.	32934067	Sgt
Kreissig, Oscar	11010544	T/Sgt
Kretzer, Harold	37116421	T/Sgt
Krutsch, Henry	16067220	Sgt
Kushinski, Edward W.	16004932	T/Sgt
Lafleur, Robert A.	0727351	Capt
Lambert, Leonard F. Jr.	18202589	Sgt
Landahl, Howard K.	0677785	1/Lt
Landreth, Calvin F.	15104217	S/Sgt
Landry, Henry C.	31143933	Sgt
Larsen, George N.	0744855	2/Lt
Larson, John H.	19108009	S/Sgt
Latimer, Byron H.	0.674210	2/Lt
Laucamp, Robert L.	17071305	S/Sgt
Laurence, Ralph C.	36124604	S/Sgt
Lawley, Woodrow	34198246	Sgt
Lawyer, Donald A.	33244873	S/Sgt
Leary, James J.	0.724442	1/Lt
Lehnhausen, Edward C.	0764355	1/Lt
Leisinger, W.L. Jr.	37068883	Sgt
Lentz, Herbert B.	0709412	2/Lt
Lester, Julian V.	17047877	Sgt
Levake, John W.	19186283	S/Sgt
Leverich, William F.	37224192	T/Sgt
Lewis, Carl R.	33185548	S/Sgt
Lewis, James E. Jr.	33577302	S/Sgt
Liddell, James M.	0807917	2/Lt
Light, Edwin C.	38047888	T/Sgt
Lilley, Robert F.	17035867	Sgt
Lindau, Edward W.	36012770	S/Sgt
Linvill, Harry J.	0.801138	2/Lt
Lippert, Rexford W.	0662346	1/Lt
Lipten, David	0670144	2/Lt
Littell, Clyde	16041884	T/Sgt
Little, William K.	0.728290	1/Lt
Loflin, William E.	0.1996114	2/Lt
Logan, Donald J.	35564011	Sgt
Long, J.B.	0438007	1/Lt
Long, Winfield V.	34113530	S/Sgt
Lopez, Charles R.	37722472	S/Sgt
Lopez, Victor A.	18135755	T/Sgt
Lough, Robert L.	T.126827	F/O
Loveday, William	0.796406	2/Lt
Lund, Hilmer C.	37138610	S/Sgt
Lundstrom, John V.	35372611	S/Sgt
Lunenfeld, Raymond C.	0789480	1/Lt

Lytle, Leslie L.	39328109	Sgt
MacDonald, Donald W.	022367	Maj
Mace, Glenn E. Jr.	17151925	S/Sgt
Mackey, John L.	0662351	1/Lt
Maiko, Andrew	11041425	Sgt
Malone, Hugh J.	15062923	S/Sgt
Maloy, Aubrey J.	34335159	S/Sgt
Maneval, Weldon H.	0750204	2/Lt
Mann, Dale B.	33237141	T/Sgt
Mansfield, Joe	18000247	S/Sgt
Marcouiller, Gordon L.	0749680	2/Lt
Markus, Edward R.	32536008	S/Sgt
Marquez, Gabriel A.	18029077	S/Sgt
Maruszewski, Frank A.	13038809	S/Sgt
Maschmeyer, Gene E.	38511707	S/Sgt
Masci, Peter J. Jr.	32635601	S/Sgt
Mathisen, Gary M.	0735418	1/Lt
Matthews, Leslie C.	0.676589	2/Lt
Mattis, Daniel A.	32453451	T/Sgt
Mauk, Charles N.	0685346	2/Lt
Mauldin, Charles W.	14107505	T/Sgt
May, Gordon L.	15102491	S/Sgt
Mayen, Thomas C.	0.726923	2/Lt
Mayes, Robert H.	0742181	2/Lt
Maynard, Donald W.	11104466	Cpl
Maynard, George H.	0800011	1/Lt
Mays, Richard B.	0.727901	Capt
Mazure, Louis A.	0442977	Capt
McArthur, Earl R.	11017929	Sgt
McArtor, John L.	13023200	S/Sgt
McBryde, William H.	34665208	S/Sgt
McCabe, Ernest G.	36303257	S/Sgt
McCandless, Donald G.	13038391	S/Sgt
McCarty, Glenn D.	37203889	Sgt
McCloud, Merwin K.	0728009	2/Lt
McCord, Gerald D.	39084175	S/Sgt
McCormick, John F.	0728010	2/Lt
McCoy, Bill	0418136	Capt
McCoy, Richard J.	12165291	S/Sgt
McCracken, John Jr.	01102377	1/Lt
McCrady, Leo V. Jr.	17056134	S/Sgt
McDaris, Frederick F.	0719113	2/Lt
McFaddin, Robert E.	0.801029	2/Lt
McGeary, Meredyth F.	0748729	1/Lt
McGinnis, Donald C.	16039337	S/Sgt
McGuire, Thomas J.	0817721	2/Lt
McKenna, James P.	0693866	1/Lt
McKenna, Raymond H.	31155162	S/Sgt
McKinsey, Thomas E.	18061219	S/Sgt
McLeod, Stanley M.	0728012	2/Lt
McMackin, Charles G.	11046450	S/Sgt
McWhorter, Lamer	34442753	S/Sgt
Mears, William G.	3102079	Sgt
Mears, William J.	37282895	T/Sgt
Meehan, William E. Jr.	0793810	1/Lt
Mercer, George W.	16070123	S/Sgt
Merrigan, John	10601009	S/Sgt
Meskinis, Joseph M.	33355549	S/Sgt
Meyers, Walter A.	37373208	T/Sgt
Michener, Byron R.	0.734812	2/Lt
Mickey, James D.	35305177	S/Sgt
Mickey, Marvin R.	18037185	Sgt
Milhousen, George R.	37133211	S/Sgt
Milillo, Antonio	31158071	S/Sgt
Miller, Arthur L.	0818724	2/Lt
Miller, Kent F.	T.60679	F/O
Milligan, Wallace D.	14128805	T/Sgt
Mills, John D.		2/Lt
Millward, Warren F.	13092560	S/Sgt
Mindelsohn, Joseph	17037191	T/Sgt
Minogue, John F.	0734111	2/Lt
Mitchell, Edward R.	0728013	Capt
Monahan, Eugene	0734485	2/Lt
Monteleone, Edward G.	39841223	S/Sgt
Moore, Kenneth H.	0727249	1/Lt
Moore, Robert L.	34407173	T/Sgt
Morgan, Elmer R.	0.715788	2/Lt
Moriarty, Clifford F.	0679201	1/Lt
Morin, Joseph E.	20108491	S/Sgt
Morris, Harold L.	12157658	S/Sgt
Mortenson, Douglas W.	0.768169	1/Lt
Moss, Benjamin M.	0.793744	1/Lt
Muirhead, Edger P.	18188771	S/Sgt
Murach, Stanley Jr.	31104988	Sgt
Murphy, William T.	0801142	2/Lt
Murray, Richard R.	14064053	S/Sgt
Murry, George B.	18162590	T/Sgt
Musgrave, Forest M.	0677847	1/Lt

Must, John A.	0801384	2/Lt
Myers, Billie B.	18166363	S/Sgt
Myers, Rudy S. Jr.	18170066	S/Sgt
Myres, Max M.	0.2044895	2/Lt
Naber, Julius V.	37263649	S/Sgt
Nalipa, Stanley G.	15324363	Sgt
Nappier, Vernon D.	37438712	S/Sgt
Nash, Travis E.	36851997	S/Sgt
Navas, Frank	0730577	2/Lt
Navish, Kenneth C.	35052331	S/Sgt
Nedde, Sarkice T.	31360823	Sgt
Nelson, Arthur L.	36378877	S/Sgt
Nelson, Duane E.	0728017	2/Lt
Nelson, Milo G.	37286816	S/Sgt
Nesbit, Alden C.	0678381	2/Lt
Neutze, Robert E. Jr.	0755738	2/Lt
Newport, Walter N.	36199864	S/Sgt
Newton, Roger J.	31254221	Sgt
Nielson, Thomas W.	0676493	1/Lt
Nigro, Joe	15090564	S/Sgt
Nix, Robert A.	16067324	Pfc
Niznok, Steve	35307431	S/Sgt
Nome, Albert A.	35544549	Sgt
Nordquist, Richard K.	16020714	T/Sgt
Nored, George L.	14060975	T/Sgt
Norman, Lawrence C.	0.733087	Capt
Norquist, John E.	0747876	1/Lt
Novelli, Joseph R.	16068174	S/Sgt
Nowak, Andrew B.	35326545	T/Sgt
Oakley, Warren W.	0740893	1/Lt
O'Donnell, Hugh	T.65165	F/O
O'Donnell, Louis	12158116	S/Sgt
Ogilvie, Robert B. Jr.	32736724	T/Sgt
O'Hara, Henry H.	32436174	S/Sgt
Ohler, Bernard A.	13135813	T/Sgt
Oliphant, Rufus A. Jr.	0397270	1/Lt
Oliver, George H. Jr.	0819153	1/Lt
Olsen, George E.	32561391	Sgt
Olson, Stanley F.	0730588	1/Lt
O'Neal, Charles E.	13104794	S/Sgt
O'Neill, Ricard F.	0798225	1/Lt
Orbach, Norris F.	0698138	2/Lt
Osburn, Richard R.	0678132	2/Lt
Ostenson, Jack N.	6569189	S/Sgt
Ottman, Harry L.	36236878	S/Sgt
Palmer, Frederick H.	0730291	1/Lt
Palys, Joseph E.	31129150	T/Sgt
Papadopulos, John G.	0.743260	2/Lt
Parker, George H.	34265961	T/Sgt
Parker, George J.	0699237	1/Lt
Parker, Stephen E. Jr.	11045788	S/Sgt
Parker, Victor	33586476	Sgt
Parrott, Darrell	35576329	S/Sgt
Passantino, Thomas J. Jr.	39537767	S/Sgt
Passavant, Frank A.	0678758	2/Lt
Patterson, Russell W.	13151627	T/Sgt
Paxton, William A. Jr.	12155754	S/Sgt
Pedersen, Nels W.	0689636	1/Lt
Pelczar, Matthew R.	36725277	S/Sgt
Penisten, John H.	0.732866	2/Lt
Perko, Everett J.	0.744085	2/Lt
Permar, Everett E.	35497759	T/Sgt
Pest, David	14130256	Sgt
Peterson, Clifford C.	0806899	2/Lt
Peterson, Maurice J.	19079103	T/Sgt
Peterson, Ray O.	36609092	S/Sgt
Peterson, Robert E.	0421662	1/Lt
Pharis, Charles W.	34268115	T/Sgt
Phelps, John E.	0747138	2/Lt
Phillips, Allen W.	32612831	S/Sgt
Phillips, Chester L.	0421129	Capt
Phillips, Edward W.	18063461	S/Sgt
Phillips, Elvin L.	19011888	Sgt
Phillips, Philip P.	0662366	1/Lt
Phillips, Robert L.	T.125025	F/O
Pierson, Glen C.	39175146	Sgt
Pilch, Stanley Jr.	35316138	S/Sgt
Pimentel, Robert E.	0.735107	2/Lt
Plaszczykowski, Edward M.	0688396	2/Lt
Playford, Joseph E.	11052136	S/Sgt
Podojil, Robert J.	0720346	1/Lt
Pohlmeyer, Robert L.	15097510	Sgt
Pollmann, Edward C.	35672481	Sgt
Poole, Elmer H.	3266534	S/Sgt
Poole, William A.	0789500	1/Lt
Porter, Donald C.	11042360	T/Sgt

Porter, James M.	37212167	S/Sgt
Post, Herbert F.	16109394	T/Sgt
Potter, Joseph H. Jr.	0736345	2/Lt
Povich, George	33675477	S/Sgt
Powell, Samuel F.	39826734	S/Sgt
Pownall, Otis H.	20733281	Sgt
Prekopie, Michael L.	33289063	S/Sgt
Price, Clyde E.	0398584	Capt
Price, George B.	12034269	T/Sgt
Prince, Bertis R.	0700389	2/Lt
Propst, Halbert W.	0793166	1/Lt
Purdue, Paul F.	0686492	2/Lt
Rabb, Harold M.	18218358	S/Sgt
Radu, Charles	35317454	S/Sgt
Railing, Alton S.	35338599	S/Sgt
Ramsey, Floyd F.	0.742896	1/Lt
Ramsey, Ivan W.	35255507	S/Sgt
Randles, Ward M.	39092316	T/Sgt
Raniello, John V.	31269979	S/Sgt
Raspotnik, Leonard L.	17042564	T/Sgt
Rawls, Malcolm	0661659	2/Lt
Ray, Thomas C.	34280331	S/Sgt
Reasons, John W.	34194483	S/Sgt
Reback, Sanford A.	0.796598	2/Lt
Reed, Ralph E.	0.832006	2/Lt
Reedy, Wilbur R.	17033225	S/Sgt
Reeves, Clarence D.	13046428	S/Sgt
Reeves, Robert H.	0755597	1/Lt
Reichenbach, Theodore H.	6860263	T/Sgt
Reid, James W.	0.796599	1/Lt
Reilly, Michael J.	12051207	S/Sgt
Rhodes, Carl E.	0747318	2/Lt
Rhodes, Lewis W.	0807052	2/Lt
Rich, Fred A.	39276079	T/Sgt
Richardson, Paul	0752904	1/Lt
Richardson, William M.	0687496	2/Lt
Riche, Wilson A.	32143092	T/Sgt
Rieger, Martin A.	32414057	S/Sgt
Ries, Robert P.	35669582	S/Sgt
Ritter, Frederick M. Jr.	0719431	1/Lt
Rizzo, Anthony F.	35292580	Sgt
Roach, Jack H.	0.733357	1/Lt
Roach, James E.	17147154	S/Sgt
Roach, William A. Jr.	0.791505	1/Lt
Robbins, Robert E.	35369184	Sgt
Roberts, Gilman N.	0686402	2/Lt
Robinson, Adelbert M.	35166552	T/Sgt
Robinson, Edwin T.	38013153	S/Sgt
Robinson, Frederick A.	12171724	S/Sgt
Robinson, Harry R.	13053844	S/Sgt
Robison, Jack C.	15330702	S/Sgt
Rodgers, Harold R.	0684197	2/Lt
Roetto, Lawrence J.	0727264	2/Lt
Rogers, Fred B.	37235533	Sgt
Rogers, Raymond R.	35451439	Sgt
Romeo, Santo	14023217	T/Sgt
Roop, Eugene W.N.	14158075	S/Sgt
Rosenstein, Jacob	31145138	S/Sgt
Rossi, Walter Jr.	0.797402	2/Lt
Russell, Eldo A.	18070094	T/Sgt
Russell, James F.	0.812315	2/Lt
Russell, Lloyd E.	37224426	S/Sgt
Russell, Robert P.	0797076	2/Lt
Saenger, Lester E.	0734982	2/Lt
Salvo, Alberto	11045878	Sgt
Sanders, James E.	0700988	2/Lt
Satterfield, Channing N.	20631208	S/Sgt
Scarborough, John I.	0730624	2/Lt
Schappert, Thomas F.	20317133	Sgt
Schettler, William J.	39092894	T/Sgt
Schexnayder, Joseph L.	0.684807	2/Lt
Schiess, Charles F.	32529351	S/Sgt
Schmitz, Norbert J.	35224546	S/Sgt
Schoer, Walter B.	39826757	S/Sgt
Schuyler, Robert E.	0682125	2/Lt
Schwab, Harold	0.733360	1/Lt
Scott, Layton W.	3946884	Sgt
Scott, Wayne S.	0206605	2/Lt
Scott, William	0.796608	2/Lt
Scriven, Dale R.	0733106	2/Lt
Scrivner, Thomas E.	0728030	1/Lt
Scudday, Bernie L.	0682906	1/Lt
Seaman, Robert H.	0.663420	2/Lt
Seiler, Walter J.	0678476	2/Lt
Semons, Earl N.	35420784	S/Sgt
Serum, Philip T. Jr.	34231666	S/Sgt
Sevick, Stephen F.	12044639	T/Sgt

Shaeffer, Clair P.	33187932	T/Sgt
Shafer, Farren F.	0.796611	2/Lt
Shafer, Raymond C.	35354093	S/Sgt
Shaffer, Donald E.	0678477	2/Lt
Shambarger, Walter B.	0700998	1/Lt
Shaw, Charles M.	0.661667	Capt
Shaw, John W.	17155882	S/Sgt
Shea, John J.	37046013	Sgt
Sheehan, William J.	12124435	S/Sgt
Sheldon, Stanley W.	11116435	T/Sgt
Sheridan, Charles M.	0401892	2/Lt
Sherwoo, Lawrence J.	39261528	S/Sgt
Short, Emerson D.	35339045	Sgt
Shufritz, John	35333691	T/Sgt
Schultz, Robert E.	33442877	Sgt
Sicard, Edward P.	31284222	Sgt
Siecke, Eldon D.	17165143	Sgt
Siegel, Louis	0678397	2/Lt
Siegert, Paul C.	17175511	S/Sgt
Silversten, Kenneth C.	37109907	Sgt
Singer, Paul S.	0736038	2/Lt
Smilnyek, Andrew J.	13085488	S/Sgt
Smith, Allen D.	13038405	M/Sgt
Smith, Charles A.	14165246	S/Sgt
Smith, Donald M.	39094553	Sgt
Smith, Harry G.	35370944	S/Sgt
Smith, Joseph R. Jr.	0813456	2/Lt
Smith, Louis F.	31311918	S/Sgt
Smith, Malcolm R.	33452262	Sgt
Smith, Nick B.	35456291	S/Sgt
Smith, Robert F.	1702692	S/Sgt
Smith, Robert M.	13027651	M/Sgt
Smith, Thomas P.	T.126546	F/O
Smith, William L.	0805997	2/Lt
Snell, Dalton R.	17032555	T/Sgt
Snider, Edwon R.	34435403	S/Sgt
Snow, Clarence W.	37219104	Sgt
Sobotka, Frank W. Jr.	0799486	1/Lt
Sofferman, Abe	32436994	T/Sgt
Somerville, Richard V.	0727054	2/Lt
Sondag, Willis	17068404	S/Sgt
Southern, William A.	0886976	2/Lt
Sowers, Richard J.	679676	2/Lt
Sparks, John T.	0661040	2/Lt
Spears, Milford L.	37136575	S/Sgt
Spier, Robert J.	16063102	Sgt
Spelts, Martin E.	0680326	2/Lt
Spink, Harold W.	0678399	2/Lt

Spivey, Joseph B. Jr.	34303915	T/Sgt
Springs, Charles E.	34598241	Sgt
Srowbek, Pravdomil	35324375	S/Sgt
Staib, Henry T.	0808172	2/Lt
Stamos, Robert G.	0.730646	1/Lt
Staples, Robert L.	39453890	T/Sgt
Starr, Charles L.	T.190606	F/O
Starr, Henry P.	13031489	S/Sgt
Starring, Alfred A.	0732121	1/Lt
Steadhan, Roy J.	0668816	1/Lt
Steele, Arthur M.	19170304	Sgt
Stein, William F.	0.792650	1/Lt
Steinke, Arthur A.	39204852	S/Sgt
Steinke, Donald H.	0807537	1/Lt
Steinmiller, Wilbert R.	12239759	S/Sgt
Stell, Charles E.	18187261	Sgt
Stenborn, Harry W.	0667449	2/Lt
Stephanovic, Ruben J.	13169810	S/Sgt
Stephens, Raymond C.	18074552	T/Sgt
Stephenson, Theodore	38120882	T/Sgt
Steptoe, Thomas F. Jr.	33133951	T/Sgt
Stern, Jerome J.	16105797	T/Sgt
Stewart, Edwin M.	39090749	S/Sgt
Stewart, Verne C.	38148621	S/Sgt
Stickel, Robert J.	16097147	Sgt
Stigora, Joseph H.	0734393	2/Lt
Stoffel, Glenn C.	17108124	S/Sgt
Strait, Ralph E.	13074162	S/Sgt
Strally, Samuel R.	32734072	S/Sgt
Stubbs, Alvan E.	0679687	2/Lt
Sufka, Edward	37161475	S/Sgt
Sullivan, Francis A.	11037492	T/Sgt
Sullivan, Kenneth E.	35562810	S/Sgt
Sullivan, Maxwell W. Jr.	0.24058	1/Lt
Sullivan, Wilfred C.	35457629	T/Sgt
Suskind, Saul	6979809	T/Sgt
Swanson, Clark E.	0728034	2/Lt
Swensson, Berthel	0733133	1/Lt
Swetlik, William M.	16133615	S/Sgt
Szabo, Paul A. Jr.	36113560	S/Sgt
Szaras, Marion J.	32475471	S/Sgt
Tabor, James A.	0.736908	2/Lt
Tate, Joseph S. Jr.	0.024034	Lt/Col
Taylor, Oran J.	18062096	T/Sgt
Taylor, Russell C.	39196030	Sgt
Tenney, Ross A.	0728767	1/Lt
Tenosky, Andy J.	16072477	S/Sgt

Terwey, Alphonse J.	37281321	S/Sgt
Testa, Arthur F.	35520803	Sgt
Thielen, Charles M.	0.701346	2/Lt
Thompson, Edward J.	16038586	S/Sgt
Thurman, Homer A.	37211941	Sgt
Tiller, Homer M.	38101171	Sgt
Timme, Arthur C.	12092338	Sgt
Titus, Dudley G.	0556131	2/Lt
Tkachuk, John	35312760	T/Sgt
Toepel, Arthur C.	0752794	1/Lt
Tomer, Frank J.	0693433	2/Lt
Torrou, Victor T.	0.738921	2/Lt
Towning, John L.	39542241	S/Sgt
Townsend, Raymond H. Jr.	0670670	1/Lt
Travis, William C.	0.736049	2/Lt
Trolese, Alexander	0743297	2/Lt
Turnbull, John I.	0399733	Lt/Col
Tyler, Leo M.	17155940	S/Sgt
Van Cleef, Arthur A.	21285817	S/Sgt
Van Oyen, Harold D.	37144043	S/Sgt
Ventura, Anthony J.	32551956	T/Sgt
Vogt, Robert K.	13030085	T/Sgt
Voorhies, Henry H.	38263445	Sgt
Walker, Joseph H.	14135751	T/Sgt
Wapensky, Russell A.	13056108	Sgt
Ward, Edwin M. Jr.	0204503	2/Lt
Ward, Joe F.	34107345	T/Sgt
Ward, Kenneth P.	0716788	2/Lt
Warne, Gideon W.	0.404099	Capt
Warren, Lester D.	13078765	S/Sgt
Warwick, Isley B.	37290897	S/Sgt
Weaver, Lewis R.	35401274	S/Sgt
Weekley, Pharis E.	0.673652	2/Lt
Weems, Manuel H.	18053822	Sgt
Weiner, Stanley C.	0.674819	2/Lt
Weinman, Edward I.	32828525	S/Sgt
Weiser, Samuel S.	12033349	T/Sgt
Wellman, Harrison W. IV	02065203	2/Lt
Welsh, William F.	11015413	Sgt
Wenke, Raymond G.	16150461	S/Sgt
Wernicki, Edward A.	32765359	T/Sgt
Wessman, Helge E.	32432466	S/Sgt
West, John W.	35917694	S/Sgt
Westcott, Gerald S.	0.808918	1/Lt
Whalen, Jack V.	16162293	S/Sgt
Wheatly, Harold J.	0675979	1/Lt

Whitaker, Coleman S.	0.885920	1/Lt
White, Benjamin F. Jr.	11027878	Sgt
White, Gene W.	16018747	Sgt
Wieser, Jerry H.	39247916	S/Sgt
Wilborn, Everette W. Jr.	0.729393	1/Lt
Wilkes, Charles E.	0728042	2/Lt
Wilkinson, Oscar H.	0426964	Capt
Williams, Bill F.	0.435716	1/Lt
Williams, Charles E.	36451793	S/Sgt
Williams, Don J.	18037070	S/Sgt
Williams, Richard H.	12031124	T/Sgt
Williams, Fruitt H.	18037355	S/Sgt
Wilson, Dale P.	18019784	S/Sgt
Wilson, Edward R.	T.74	F/O
Wilson, James L.	14124998	S/Sgt
Wilson, Stanley	12060904	T/Sgt
Winfree, Julian E. Jr.	34431710	Sgt
Winger, George W.	0602848	2/Lt
Wise, Solomon I.	37135114	S/Sgt
Witkin, Leonard	0.701359	2/Lt
Wolf, Frederick T.	36233230	T/Sgt
Wood, Fred D. Jr.	13119193	S/Sgt
Wood, Hal N.	18113166	Sgt
Wood, Thomas M.	18015826	Sgt
Woods, Howard C.	37374038	T/Sgt
Woody, Robert E.	34010090	T/Sgt
Woolfe, Chester R.	35036742	Sgt
Worth, Woodrow N.	0683521	1/Lt
Wright, Raymond E.	35474099	S/Sgt
Wulff, Orville L.	0.675462	1/Lt
Wycheck, Joseph E.	13116002	T/Sgt
Yeatts, Roy J.	20364881	T/Sgt
Yoakum, Arthur M.	36068208	S/Sgt
Yocco, Dominic P.	12024064	T/Sgt
Young, Robert E.	0734863	2/Lt
Young, William C.	36743059	Sgt
Young, William H.	0.717013	1/Lt
Youse, Charles M.	33498702	Sgt
Yurick, Chester W.	31140518	T/Sgt
Zajicek, James L.	0698812	2/Lt
Zdonick, Michael P.	31169351	S/Sgt
Ziegler, Norbert J.	17129592	S/Sgt
Zimmer, Floyd H.	17029368	S/Sgt
Zoller, Harper F. Jr.	36529756	S/Sgt
Zwicker, Henry R.	0728529	1/Lt

389th Bomb Group

Aaronian, Tzolac A.	31365447	S/Sgt
Acevedo, Arthur	0.743156	1/Lt
Ackerson, Joseph R.	32910805	S/Sgt
Adovasio, James A.	35382569	S/Sgt
Aguayo, George	19039660	T/Sgt
Akin, John H.	38394444	S/Sgt
Alexander, Harry N.	0767721	1/Lt
Alsop, Wilber R. Jr.	0.708356	2/Lt
Amador, Louis L.	39115008	S/Sgt
Anchondo, Rudolph O.	19067148	T/Sgt
Andersen, Anders K.	0.856406	1/Lt
Anderson, William M.	17154409	S/Sgt
Angert, Richard K.	02074562	2/Lt
Ansel, William N.	0829388AC	2/Lt
Apel, Billy G.	17034892	T/Sgt
Aplington, William L.	36765437	T/Sgt
Arrington, John R. Jr.	0819382	1/Lt
Asher, Richard E.	0678137	2/Lt
Atkins, Cornelius J.	T.131118	F/O
Autry, John C.	34314701	S/Sgt
Baas, William L.	35453716	T/Sgt
Baker, Brenton W.	33205519	T/Sgt
Baker, Lester G. Jr.	0723929	2/Lt
Balin, Edward L.	31277594	S/Sgt
Balsam, Irving J.	12183535	S/Sgt
Bamford, George H.	0764175	1/Lt
Barry, Edward A.	0671214	2/Lt
Bartle, Theodore F.	02005728	2/Lt
Barton, Robert C.	0.760959	2/Lt
Bates, William P.	0735507	Capt
Beck, Orville E.	16095812	T/Sgt
Becker, Abe A.	35309153	Sgt
Becker, Otto W.	0.688163	1/Lt
Belanger, Alton C.	0735024	1/Lt
Bell, Robert K.	15331795	S/Sgt
Bengford, Norbert B.	37677323	S/Sgt
Benko, George E.	0714616	1/Lt

Berg, Walter W.	15098043	T/Sgt
Bilowich, William	13132271	S/Sgt
Bird, Robert R.	0675026	2/Lt
Blakeman, Warren R.	0.675161	2/Lt
Blanton, William E.	35210470	T/Sgt
Blazis, Arthur J.	0.722265	2/Lt
Blooke, Robert B.	0.709758	1/Lt
Bloznelis, John D.	0735163	2/Lt
Bockelman, Arthur C.	35453357	S/Sgt
Bonnar, Robert W.	0.711119	1/Lt
Boone, William E.	0.556607	Capt
Booth, Thomas C.	39828475	S/Sgt
Borgens, Harold E.	37035483	S/Sgt
Borgfeld, H.O.	01825472	2/Lt
Bossetti, Leroy R.	0671863	1/Lt
Bowman, Philip A.	18108660	S/Sgt
Boynton, Hugh	31239474	S/Sgt
Bremer, Donald R.	0710437	2/Lt
Brewer, Carl E.	17169052	S/Sgt
Brewer, Walter D.	34872455	S/Sgt
Brown, John E.	31257981	S/Sgt
Brown, Kenneth E.	0703936	2/Lt
Brown, Lester L.	0711334	2/Lt
Brown, Paul R.	0822632	2/Lt
Brown, Robert G.	17113824	T/Sgt
Brown, Virgil F.	37224234	S/Sgt
Brozek, Joseph J.	11107169	S/Sgt
Brumbaugh, L.W.	17089566	S/Sgt
Brumley, Lowell R.	0.748344	1/Lt
Brun, Edward B.	32871347	S/Sgt
Bryson, William M.	17155781	Sgt
Bsharah, Fred	02065328	2/Lt
Bucher, William M.	36814876	T/Sgt
Buchholtz, Kenneth J.	16021705	S/Sgt
Budai, William J.	35337676	S/Sgt
Bush, Edward W.	0674928	2/Lt
Butler, Arthor E. Jr.	18194717	T/Sgt
Byram, Lon J.	0734307	1/Lt

Caldwell, Kenneth M.	01699045	Maj
Calloway, Robert M.J.	35706087	T/Sgt
Campbell, P.W. Jr.	0.747977	1/Lt
Cannon, Robert J.	16085631	S/Sgt
Caplinger, George R.	15318621	S/Sgt
Carlson, Robert G.	0785568	2/Lt
Carmichael, Orville T.	39092359	Sgt
Carraro, William J. Jr.	0.678680	2/Lt
Casey, Harry W.	0735171	1/Lt
Champion, Robert E.	15323898	S/Sgt
Chappell, Herschell R. Jr.	0.815075	1/Lt
Chelini, Enrico J.	0674468	2/Lt
Chmiel, Benny M.	33920867	S/Sgt
Chouinard, Merton L.	0716355	2/Lt
Christiansen, John C.	0.752916	1/Lt
Clark, Clyde R.	17000468	S/Sgt
Coats, Donald E.	36742208	S/Sgt
Cobb, Jay W.	18231704	T/Sgt
Colford, Whitson P.	33190973	T/Sgt
Collins, Donald P.	0676356	2/Lt
Collins, Floyd S.	6575333	T/Sgt
Comerchero, Henry	32712711	S/Sgt
Connors, Jack M.	0.728833	1/Lt
Contra, Albert J.	02063160	1/Lt
Cooper, Earl T.	0667950	1/Lt
Coots, Jimmie K.	0687995	2/Lt
Copodonna, Joseph S.	0817632	2/Lt
Core, Willis B.	0693354	1/Lt
Cornell, Gene F.	33512324	S/Sgt
Coumatos, James M.	12085799	T/Sgt
Courtney, Marcus V.	0796782	1/Lt
Cowan, Thomas	T135873	F/O
Cowan, Thomas J.	6877750	S/Sgt
Cressman, William	42131258	S/Sgt
Criss, Albert H.	0764247	1/Lt
Crock, George S.	02063571	2/Lt
Crotty, Gerald E.	19181308	S/Sgt
Crouse, Carl E.	0692377	1/Lt

Culig, Walter F.	13156088	S/Sgt
Cuozzo, Robert P.	31306249	S/Sgt
Curtis, Stephen B.	02073073	2/Lt
Dailey, Wendell L.	0740760	1/Lt
Dallas, Bob C.	0.721653	1/Lt
Dalton, Dean H.	0.424924	Capt
Danis, Joseph Jr.	13132354	T/Sgt
Danneker, John H.	33508557	S/Sgt
Dare, Daniel R.	36859625	S/Sgt
Davis, Charles W.	0716715	1/Lt
Day, Glendon L.	11104055	Sgt
De Buona, B.J.	12185546	S/Sgt
Declisur, Arthur C.	0688513	1/Lt
Delariviere, Guy G.	32610489	S/Sgt
Denton, Harord V.	33541272	T/Sgt
Dewitt, Charles A.	32465122	S/Sgt
Dicks, Rosslyn E.	15081589	T/Sgt
Dicosol, Don N.	0733540	1/Lt
Dierks, Fred W.	18167797	T/Sgt
Dillon, James Jr.	35637059	S/Sgt
Dively, Morgan L.	33249217	S/Sgt
Dobson, John J.	0702023	2/Lt
Dodd, Harrison J. Jr.	12203113	T/Sgt
Dorofachuk, John	32454483	T/Sgt
Dorsett, Adelbert E.	0689520	1/Lt
Dotter, Robert L.	13895266	S/Sgt
Dout, Boyd L.	0670984	1/Lt
Dowdy, John C.	33066623	T/Sgt
Driver, Robert R.	18009315	S/Sgt
Duke, Allenby K.	0699062	1/Lt
Dunoon, James P.J.	0673509	2/Lt
Dunnings, John H.	32808739	S/Sgt
Early, Paul D.	33433893	S/Sgt
Early, Stanton A.	34268846	T/Sgt
Eberly, Walter E.	33240653	T/Sgt
Eckelbecker, George W.	36978544	S/Sgt

Edgar, George M.	16003372	T/Sgt
Eline, Sidney W.	0804311	1/Lt
Elliott, Earle D.	14126404	S/Sgt
Ellwart, Richard J.	36633443	T/Sgt
Elwood, Lewis N.	35613569	S/Sgt
Emery, William K.	39095551	Cpl
Empie, Elmer W.	02074682	2/Lt
Englehardt, Jack B.	0798772	2/Lt
Espinoza, Benjamin F.	38165504	T/Sgt
Evans, Glenn W.	0678627	2/Lt
Evans, Thomas B. Jr.	34845769	Sgt
Faircloth, William T.	0769110	1/Lt
Falco, Pasquale	0729253	2/Lt
Fawcett, Frank E.	0.2061914	2/Lt
Felbinger, Andrew E. Jr.	0700721	2/Lt
Feliz, Ralph P.	39118959	S/Sgt
Ferryman, Lee D.	0809941	2/Lt
Field, Philip C.	T.65963	F/O
Finnie, James M.	37303177	T/Sgt
Fiorentino, Joseph T.	13153046	S/Sgt
Fite, Francis H.	34723486	S/Sgt
Flannery, Robert M.	33626105	T/Sgt
Flatter, Samuel W.	35406134	T/Sgt
Fletcher, Alvin E.	0699518	2/Lt
Fletcher, Marion E.	0735070	1/Lt
Floyd, Werner H. Jr.	0703004	2/Lt
Forster, Elden G.	37519303	T/Sgt
Foshey, Richard H.	31068914	S/Sgt
Fox, Owen U.	33689392	S/Sgt
Fraveca, Thomas P.	0735072	1/Lt
Freedman, Arnold E.	0663250	1/Lt
Freeman, Harold F.	37135298	T/Sgt
French, George D.	0678525	1/Lt
Fritz, Lucius H.	0677705	2/Lt
Frogge, Lester C.	15393927	S/Sgt
Frye, Benjamin A. Jr.	14190259	S/Sgt
Fuerst, Michael J.	0735073	2/Lt
Fuller, Donald M.	0817656	2/Lt
Galley, Clifford R.	0804643	2/Lt
Gallop, Abraham A.	12090467	T/Sgt
Galloway, John W.	0685581	1/Lt
Gantus, John M.	19080438	M/Sgt
Garabedian, James V.	36554974	S/Sgt
Garda, Trenton E.	0.2000262	1/Lt
Garrett, Paull	0388758	Maj
Gayden, Quitman M. Jr.	0886805	1/Lt
Gerome, Quindo L.	33343947	T/Sgt
Giarrantano, John J.	0671340	1/Lt
Ginn, Bayard V.	0719919	2/Lt
Glenn, Jack H.	0711388	2/Lt
Glidewell, Paul C.	34603439	S/Sgt
Gluck, Leo E.	31124447	T/Sgt
Gold, John E.	0685249	1/Lt
Goodall, Edward M.	39188102	S/Sgt
Goodman, Sidney H.	0754836	2/Lt
Gordon, Richard P.	15109231	S/Sgt
Graalum, Milton L.	17025635	S/Sgt
Graham, Harvey G.	31427549	S/Sgt
Gramling, C.J. Jr.	0741165	2/Lt
Granados, Jack C.	39288223	S/Sgt
Gray, George C.	14165972	T/Sgt
Green, Berryman Jr.	33533373	S/Sgt
Greenspan, Herman	0780257	2/Lt
Grolic, William I.	02069006	2/Lt
Guillory, Francis	18170893	T/Sgt
Guimond, Everal A.	0671427	Capt
Gustafson, Richard P.	0814493	2/Lt
Haaf, Howard S.	18081540	S/Sgt
Haase, William M.	35548986	S/Sgt
Hambel, Lawrence A.	35424780	T/Sgt
Hansen, Orville A.	37580184	Sgt
Harger, Jack	38209229	S/Sgt
Harman, Hayes Jr.	0741516	2/Lt
Harris, William C.	14178207	T/Sgt
Hartley, Joseph Jr.	33790487	S/Sgt
Harvey, John B.	0682116	2/Lt
Hatton, Lloyd A.	0682031	2/Lt
Haydock, Robert L.	36257880	S/Sgt
Hebert, Kenneth C.	18149871	S/Sgt
Heitler, Julius	42041178	S/Sgt
Helms, James L.	14153911	T/Sgt
Henderson, Clarence W.	33326052	S/Sgt
Henke, Charles J.	0700729	2/Lt
Herboth, John B. Jr.	0.021198	Col
Herfel, Arthur C.	36832925	S/Sgt
Hess, Robert M.	13079306	T/Sgt
Hickerson, Fain L.	39916877	S/Sgt
Hicks, Robert W.	35726538	S/Sgt
Hill, James V. Jr.	18226786	S/Sgt
Hodges, Curtis E.	37623179	S/Sgt
Hoffman, Virgil L.	14081963	T/Sgt
Hollis, Terrell L.	0718184	2/Lt
Hollowell, Robert M.	38121247	S/Sgt
Holly, Robert W.	35568251	S/Sgt
Holroyd, George K.	16053349	T/Sgt
Hoover, Paul N.	39128872	T/Sgt
Hopkins, Robert H.M.	11099029	S/Sgt
Horecny, Joseph G.	0741344	1/Lt
Housley, Earl S.	38603232	S/Sgt
Howard, Charles H.	0675069	2/Lt
Howard, Oren J.	15382336	T/Sgt
Howell, Bethel B.	35496352	Sgt
Huebner, Dwayne H.	37661087	Sgt
Hughes, Carl V.	34021953	S/Sgt
Hughes, Lloyd H.	0666292	2/Lt
Hughes, Richard E.	39184971	T/Sgt
Hunnefeld, Edwin D.	15338788	S/Sgt
Hunter, William F.	0792598	1/Lt
Hurst, Herbery W.	35493173	S/Sgt
Hutchens, Marion A.	0563375	2/Lt
Hymes, Milton L. Jr.	0703098	2/Lt
Irving, John W.	0717216	1/Lt
Jackson, Leon J.	14125720	Sgt
Jackson, Theodore M.	16111393	S/Sgt
Janis, Arthur M.	0.826181	2/Lt
Jeremias, Albert M.	0.698888	2/Lt
Johnson, Donald G.	17143786	S/Sgt
Johnson, Raymond E.	0711213	2/Lt
Jollimore, John C.	3650983	T/Sgt
Jones, Cecil	18118845	S/Sgt
Josewski, Harold G.	37320893	S/Sgt
Judd, Stephen P.	0683019	2/Lt
Kaczmarek, Marion J.	36863620	T/Sgt
Kaems, Robert H.	36455734	S/Sgt
Kaems, Robert H.	0711416	1/Lt
Kagan, Myron H.	0823612	1/Lt
Kalinowsky, Eugene	11105754	S/Sgt
Kalligeros, Val J.	0811398	2/Lt
Kantlehner, William A.	35686142	S/Sgt
Karnes, Cecil W.	39240092	S/Sgt
Karpinko, Paul W.	0818285	2/Lt
Kase, Louis N.	3059883	T/Sgt
Kaufman, Robert P.	33250955	S/Sgt
Kaufmann, Martin J.	42091683	S/Sgt
Keener, Howard D.	13090679	S/Sgt
Kercher, Maurice J.	0735395	1/Lt
Kilcannon, Patric D.	0743031	2/Lt
Kinard, Henry G.	38383499	S/Sgt
King, Robert W.	0653962	Sgt
Kley, Ralph L.	0822467	1/Lt
Koch, Louis F.	13113265	T/Sgt
Krouskup, Roger W.	19092680	S/Sgt
Krueger, Francis L.	18074093	T/Sgt
Kuehle, Richard G.	37261327	S/Sgt
Kunkel, John A.	13029003	T/Sgt
Kurtz, John H.	0804688	2/Lt
Labaff, Albert F. Jr.	6153313	Sgt
Lacourse, Victor	36586506	S/Sgt
Lalanze, Eugene A.	33684980	T/Sgt
Lambert, Clifton F.	0824144	1/Lt
Lambert, James V.	32398109	S/Sgt
Landrum, Fred L.	34871843	S/Sgt
Lastrapes, Robert	15072927	T/Sgt
Latten, Maynard A.	6917758	T/Sgt
Leahey, Robert H.	0808090	2/LT
Leatherwood, William E.	14133777	S/Sgt
Leggett, Edgar A.	0698736	1/Lt
Leggett, Harold F.	11116727	S/Sgt
Lehmann, Alfred A.	36741460	T/Sgt
Lejeune, Edward G.	34235964	T/Sgt
Leneghan, Robert W.	35528813	S/Sgt
Lenti, Neal M.	0673594	2/Lt
Lesnak, Edward	13012429	M/Sgt
Lewis, Lonnie	34420141	S/Sgt
Lewman, George L.	6575877	S/Sgt
Liscomb, Leon S.	32940809	S/Sgt
Litman, Emanuel A.	12155557	S/Sgt
Little, Thomas C.	6382133	T/Sgt
Litz, Paul	33773452	S/Sgt
Lloyd, Myron C.	0671379	1/Lt
Loebs, Herbert H.	0742347	1/Lt
Longdo, Joseph H.	12157777	S/Sgt
Looy, Harry W.	32083731	S/Sgt
Lovelady, Milbern F.	38209916	S/Sgt
Lucas, Jimmie D.	34670472	S/Sgt
Luther, John A.	33887792	S/Sgt
Machia, Allen M.	6121916	S/Sgt
Mackey, Walter A.	0734805	1/Lt
Magellan, Arthur M.	39719226	S/Sgt
Maloney, John P.	32397916	T/Sgt
Maricic, Joseph A.	39240092	S/Sgt
Marine, Gerald R.	35632851	S/Sgt
Martin, Edward J.	19188449	Cpl
Martin, Leslie W.	33360580	T/Sgt
Martin, Stanley E.	31403710	S/Sgt
Martinez, Arthur S.	39854394	Sgt
Maruca, Jerry L.	33305573	S/Sgt
Marzolf, Martin E.	19062460	S/Sgt
Mathisen, Ralph J.	39699654	T/Sgt
Matthews, Essman G.	13079143	T/Sgt
Mattson, Carl A.	0797156	1/Lt
Maxham, Henry G.	6130880	S/Sgt
McAuliffe, Robert J.	0693693	1/Lt
McClanahan, Francis C.	39826965	T/Sgt
McCollum, Robert T.	0695508	2/Lt
McConnell, James J.	0734945	1/Lt
McCord, Willard W.	T.3078	F/O
McCormack, Henry M. Jr.	18232463	S/Sgt
McCormick, John B.	0.661952	Capt
McCoy, James T.	32329956	S/Sgt
McGhiey, Daniel J.	36446322	T/Sgt
McGraw, John J.	0666317	1/Lt
McKeon, Eugene F.	0678732	2/Lt
McLellan, Beverly W.	34168141	T/Sgt
McLoughlin, A. John	0734948	2/Lt
McMullin, James O. Jr.	0675099	1/Lt
McNair, Robert W.	12075494	T/Sgt
McWhirter, Oscar F.	14121417	T/Sgt
Mendelsohn, Marvin R.	0796566	1/Lt
Merkle, Christian W. Jr.	32012959	S/Sgt
Metcalf, Clarence J.	35064889	S/Sgt
Michalk, Paul L.	0709950	1/Lt
Miller, Kenneth J.	37160335	S/Sgt
Miller, Robert T.	33662483	Sgt
Mirando, Pasquale P.	32515508	Sgt
Mitchell, Claude H. Jr.	18036992	S/Sgt
Mitten, William L.	0744736	2/Lt
Mix, Joseph E.	39083291	T/Sgt
Moniak, Edward C.	36316858	S/Sgt
Monzingo, Jake S.	18209608	T/Sgt
Moore, Arlon D.	6295620	S/Sgt
Moore, Leroy H.	38506216	S/Sgt
Moore, Russell I.	0701628	2/Lt
Mosco, Marvin	0734818	1/Lt
Mosher, Harvey R.	0777766	1/Lt
Moyers, Samuel W.	33655977	S/Sgt
Mueller, Robert J. Jr.	37608089	S/Sgt
Mulcahy, John J.	T.123056	F/O
Mullins, Richard M.	0698592	2/Lt
Munroe, Stewart W. Jr.	0734964	2/Lt
Murphy, Gerald E.	35166638	S/Sgt
Murray, James R.	32560877	S/Sgt
Muskrat, Harvey R.	0466591	1/Lt
Nadler, Frank E.	0679642	1/Lt
Neal, Stuart L.	0806499	2/Lt
Neilson, David H.	36005588	T/Sgt
Neithercutt, Homer G.	38231010	Cpl
Nichols, Joy W.	17045673	S/Sgt
Nitsch, Cletus T.	33180313	S/Sgt
Nolan, James F.	0796583	1/Lt
Oberst, Herman J.	17132396	T/Sgt
O'Brien, Donald F.	0783083	1/Lt
Odegard, Alfred W.	19072135	Pfc
Odorisio, Raffelea C.	6998051	S/Sgt
Olson, Elmer R.	33581286	T/Sgt
Olson, Silas E.	35455073	S/Sgt
O'Neil, Charles O. Jr.	02065901	2/Lt
Oppenlander, Charles F.	33312357	S/Sgt
O'Rourke, Edward J.	0826273	1/Lt
Osborne, Charles E.	36479859	S/Sgt
Osteen, Albert P.	0693697	2/Lt
Owens, Richard V.	38399220	T/Sgt
Owings, William V.	34509001	T/Sgt
Pacetti, Herbert J.	38248500	Pvt
Parmley, Marion C.	37536572	S/Sgt
Parramore, George F.I	33221489	S/Sgt
Paskowsky, Nicholas	35912017	Sgt
Patterson, Charles F.	0742772	2/Lt
Peabody, Robert A.	02070454	2/Lt
Peale, Randolph M.	0693311	2/Lt
Pellegrino, Mario	12025811	S/Sgt
Penfield, Howard R.	37413509	S/Sgt
Peters, Clyde J.	0680373	2/Lt
Peterson, Ralph L.	37206029	S/Sgt
Peterson, Roger E.	0707106	2/Lt
Pfarr, Albert W. Jr.	33731869	S/Sgt
Pfeiffer, Hubert D.	36693836	T/Sgt
Pharo, Vaughn O.	20652820	S/Sgt
Phifer, Forest H.	0734829	1/Lt
Pierson, Kenneth B.	15330781	S/Sgt
Pitak, Bronislaus C.	32394265	S/Sgt
Pohl, Gilbert J.	0796433	1/Lt
Polevka, Walter P.	35057495	S/Sgt
Poma, John F.	0805977	2/Lt
Pounds, Willie G.	34815202	S/Sgt
Powell, William R.	37228394	S/Sgt
Powers, Bernard M.	35368344	S/Sgt
Preis, Charles M.	0701642	2/Lt
Price, Raymond E.	0820820	1/Lt
Pucko, Martin J. Jr.	0799250	2/Lt
Pupacko, Alexander	0706967	2/Lt
Quantrell, Charles B.	0797389	2/Lt
Rachel, Theodore E.	0717110	2/Lt
Raines, Lewis H.	14022765	S/Sgt
Ratchford, Robert H.	14180663	T/Sgt
Ray, John H. Jr.	34274593	S/Sgt
Raynie, Harold T.	0679654	2/Lt
Reece, Claude N.	0801147	1/Lt
Reed, Alton	34709451	S/Sgt
Reed, Jack O.	38166972	S/Sgt
Reed, Kenneth O.	0416197	1/Lt
Reed, Norman S.	13025701	S/Sgt
Reese, Glen W.	0742899	1/Lt
Reid, Wallace L.	34333383	S/Sgt
Reynolds, Jack T.	36444088	S/Sgt
Rhine, James E.	0.820824	1/Lt
Ricci, Arthur J.	31311683	T/Sgt
Rich, Edgar A.	17080324	S/Sgt
Rickner, Roy R.	0666080	1/Lt
Rightmire, Elmer G.	0678459	2/Lt
Riser, William C.	34847945	Sgt
Roach, Walter W.	34659179	S/Sgt
Robinson, L.E. Jr.	02008941	2/Lt
Rodek, Alex M.	T.125225	F/O
Rodenberg, Elmer E.	0661966	1/Lt
Rogers, Julian J.	35695706	S/Sgt
Rolly, George P.	0.426922	1/Lt
Ronn, Ernest J.	19100622	S/Sgt
Roodman, Harold	0796603	1/Lt
Rosas, Milton L.	0811249	2/Lt
Rosengren, Edward C.	36586590	T/Sgt
Ross, Richard R.	0.687074	2/Lt
Rossi, Alfred P. Jr.	33322203	Sgt
Rossignol, Fred W.	36516657	S/Sgt
Rowland, James R.	34456773	S/Sgt
Runchey, Charles F. Jr.	16010815	T/Sgt
Rutledge, George W.	0805682	2/Lt
Ryan, Francis X.	31360326	S/Sgt
Ryles, Jack E.	0823697	2/Lt
Sachs, Johnny W.	37450975	S/Sgt
Safier, Joseph M.	0692342	1/Lt
Sager, Richard M.	39318635	T/Sgt
Santomiery, Anthony	820070	2/Lt
Sarber, Robert W.	13109000	S/Sgt
Saunders, Harold L.	34350273	T/Sgt
Saunderson, George M.	0780732	2/Lt
Savage, Robert S.	32471120	S/Sgt
Sawyer, William C.	33541196	S/Sgt
Schermerhorn, William H.	12095865	S/Sgt
Schiavone, Joseph T.	33670634	T/Sgt
Schultz, Lars F.	0.735932	2/Lt
Schumacher, Robert J.	36268696	S/Sgt
Scott, Everett G.	16006298	S/Sgt
Scott, George W.	16018506	S/Sgt
Scott, Kenneth R.	12201443	S/Sgt
Selser, Joseph K.	33623178	S/Sgt
Senff, Robert J.	0797410	2/Lt
Sequin, John L.	18218040	T/Sgt
Sewell, Clyde S. Jr.	0749333	1/Lt
Sharp, Howard E.	6552835	S/Sgt
Shaver, Thomas L.	4120849	T/Sgt
Shelton, Marvin W. Jr.	38505228	S/Sgt

Shepherd, John C.	0747341	1/Lt
Sheraski, Richard	36840153	S/Sgt
Sherman, Donald F.	39168442	T/Sgt
Sherman, Oral T.	15084316	S/Sgt
Sherry, George R.	0.684201	2/Lt
Shinglar, John P.	31167929	S/Sgt
Skinner, Marvin W.	19147119	S/Sgt
Slape, Howard P.	38237253	S/Sgt
Slaughter, Jack E.	0678482	1/Lt
Sloan, Robert F.	12038467	T/Sgt
Smith, Francis H.	35566285	S/Sgt
Smith, George E.	0716978	1/Lt
Smith, Jack E.	18081681	T/Sgt
Smith, Mack H.	34450737	S/Sgt
Smith, Stanley H.	11082353	T/Sgt
Smith, Vernon E. Jr.	19160620	T/Sgt
Snider, Jack O.	33566191	Pvt
Snodgrass, Niel R.	0768849	2/Lt
Snyder, Max J.	39243194	S/Sgt
Solberg, John F.	17079300	S/Sgt
Solomon, Herbert	0796614	1/Lt
Sosa, Robert S.	0.751851	1/Lt
Sosnecke, Stephen R.	32716378	S/Sgt
Spadafora, Onofrio F.	12129244	T/Sgt
Spivey, Charles H.	38172933	T/Sgt
Springer, John H.	17152029	S/Sgt
Stachow, Benny S.	36506252	S/Sgt
Stachowiak, John A.	37295907	T/Sgt
Stanton, John F.	31306570	S/Sgt
Statton, Louis T.	0720597	2/Lt
Stearns, Ernest C.	35211879	S/Sgt
Sternstein, Ira J.	T.134524	F/O
Stewar, Forre T.W.	0927699	2/Lt
Stewart, James T.	14137499	S/Sgt
Stine, Adolphus D.	34770491	S/Sgt
Storrick, Roy L.	0715057	2/Lt
Stout, John E.	35493173	S/Sgt
Straesemeier, William R.	15103012	S/Sgt
Strange, William H.	33503587	T/Sgt
Strayhan, Stephen T.	34155276	T/Sgt
Suelflow, Frank F. Jr.	16116239	S/Sgt
Sullivan, Edward	39683668	S/Sgt
Surico, Victor P.	0928832	2/Lt
Sutter, Andrew J.	16056573	S/Sgt
Sweeney, Philip J.	0734706	2/Lt
Sylvester, William E.	12203136	T/Sgt
Tackett, Robert W.	39540641	S/Sgt
Taylor, Robert M. Jr.	33429006	Sgt
Taylor, Roger L.	0531331	1/Lt
Taylor, Walter E.	38203684	T/Sgt
Tennant, Robert T.	0744873	2/Lt
Terlesky, Frank	33289712	T/Sgt
Thackray, Francis J.	0799270	2/Lt
Tharpe, Marshall A.	18134525	S/Sgt
Thillman, Howard F.	0738945	2/Lt
Thom, Wilfred J.	0755158	1/Lt
Thomas, Abraham B.	32464078	S/Sgt
Thomas, Gordon H.	35532630	S/Sgt
Thomas, Joseph F.	0692094	2/Lt
Thompson, Ansley E.	34200583	S/Sgt
Thompson, Harold M.	39092072	T/Sgt
Thompson, Seth A.	0673645	2/Lt
Thornton, Stanley B.	34477212	T/Sgt
Tiedemann, John R.	01166634	1/Lt
Tingle, Charles T.	34087137	S/Sgt
Titus, Fern M.	0431068	Capt
Toles, William	0736046	1/Lt
Tomlinson, Robert W.	0721256	2/Lt
Tourison, Charles W.	0676827	2/Lt
Treat, Matthew F.	12144019	S/Sgt
Tucker, Walter L.	0.821380	2/Lt
Turnipseed, Donald E.	35368158	T/Sgt
Tuxbury, Fred S.	16043699	S/Sgt
Valentine, Harold H.	16031475	T/Sgt
Van De Voorde, Rene G.	0722901	1/Lt
Van Heest, Howard E.	12077713	S/Sgt
Van Weald, Eric B.J.	39380462	S/Sgt
Vancil, Jessie C.	36579752	S/Sgt
Vitale, Felice J.	12143705	S/Sgt
Vollbrecht, Eric W.	36817435	T/Sgt
Vunak, George J.	33714524	S/Sgt
Wagner, Jack E.	33506689	S/Sgt
Waldrop, Howard J.	34814519	S/Sgt
Walker, Bernard	12159500	S/Sgt
Walsh, John R.	0718037	1/Lt
Ward, Harry D.	0708972	2/Lt
Ward, John E.	38439328	S/Sgt
Ward, John J.	13146654	S/Sgt
Webb, Willis L.	0680779	S/Lt
Weems, Manuel H.	18053822	Sgt
Wells, George W. Jr.	18115929	T/Sgt
Werner, Conrad	T.126548	F/O
West, William W.	0.749372	2/Lt
Wetherby, Clyde B.	31340851	T/Sgt
Wheatley, Dwight C.	11084846	T/Sgt
Whitaker, Glenn M.	37619020	S/Sgt
Whitehurst, Alan E.	33641916	S/Sgt
Wilder, Henry C.	35432378	T/Sgt
Wilhite, David L.	0.405475	Capt
Williams, Dale E.	0.677381	1/Lt
Williams, Ralph P.	37728008	S/Sgt
Williams, Taffy J.	34771167	T/Sgt
Wilson, Avis	13035110	S/Sgt
Wince, Walter E.	13032848	S/Sgt
Wood, Joseph W.	31219716	T/Sgt
Wright, Haskell W.	38107451	T/Sgt
Wyatt, Jack L.	0.684100	1/Lt
Wylie, Kenneth C.	31261735	S/Sgt
Wyman, Elroy F.	0735946	2/Lt
Wyrwas, Leonard E.	33252656	S/Sgt
Yacona, Frank	36670995	S/Sgt
Yarbrough, James R.	34333129	S/Sgt
Yelvington, Thomas M.	6254835	S/Sgt
Yoders, Roland E.	0812721	1/Lt
Young, Howard E. Jr.	0.832311	2/Lt
Zagula, Julian M.	0707575	2/Lt
Zavorski, Joseph A. Jr.	0688771	1/Lt

392nd Bomb Group

Abshier, Arthur L.	17121589	S/Sgt
Adago, Dominick R.	12126336	S/Sgt
Adam, Billy	37433788	S/Sgt
Allen, Phillip	36343835	T/Sgt
Ammon, Robert H.	13096618	S/Sgt
Amodeo, Frank A.	32199278	Pfc
Amoss, Ralph T.	0.727885	Capt
Anderson, Charles R.	0.702880	2/Lt
Anderson, John B.	0691210	2/Lt
Anderson, Thomas L.	0.747165	2/Lt
Appert, Donald A.	0424875	Maj
Apple, Odis L. Jr.	18184135	S/Sgt
Archambeau, Alfred P.	20101348	Sgt
Arnold, Leroy D.	17034183	S/Sgt
Astleford, Charles E.	02058389	2/Lt
Auchinbaugh, C.L.	35567868	S/Sgt
Babb, Lonnie L. Jr.	0696192	2/Lt
Backus, Donald G.	13114075	T/Sgt
Baetz, Robert E.	0828902	2/Lt
Baker, Morton	32701560	T/Sgt
Baldwin, William L.J.	0718989	2/Lt
Bandura, Norbert A.	0690033	2/Lt
Barber, Kenneth A.	0.697524	2/Lt
Barker, Glynn E.	18184197	Cpl
Barnes, Leonard J.	0737932	Maj
Barnett, Joseph V.	0.672297	2/Lt
Bartholomew, Daniel	1313945	S/Sgt
Bartnowski, Matthew A.	32462661	S/Sgt
Barton, Harold T.	17070107	Sgt
Barton, Paul F.	0761796	2/Lt
Bass, Louis F.	0807662	2/Lt
Bass, Ralph T. Jr.	14158107	S/Sgt
Bauer, Herbert P.	33187531	T/Sgt
Baum, William J.	15337665	Sgt
Becker, John L.	0.805240	2/Lt
Bedore, Cletus P.	0.722982	2/Lt
Belden, Don C.	37240498	S/Sgt
Benson, Robert J.	0767976	2/Lt
Benz, Robert F.	0767467	2/Lt
Berezovsky, Alex	32115943	T/Sgt
Berglund, Bernard J.	16168255	Sgt
Berlin, William	0735160	2/Lt
Bernard, Leo E.	11052803	S/Sgt
Berquist, Earl J.	36584370	Sgt
Bertsch, Paul J.	35402908	S/Sgt
Bettis, Roy W.	37484761	Sgt
Beutler, Kenneth L.	35608098	Sgt
Biakis, Michael J.	02062964	2/Lt
Billingsley, Glenn R.	0807666	2/Lt
Bingham, Milford O.	0551348	2/Lt
Birnbaum, Stanford I.	0702364	2/Lt
Bishop, Robert R.	0.682775	2/Lt
Bixby, Gerald C.	12214457	Sgt
Blaida, John M.	16176158	S/Sgt
Blakeley, Willis G.	0721022	2/Lt
Bleickhardt, Frank C.	31253257	S/Sgt
Blekkenk, John H. Jr.	32675803	S/Sgt
Blong, James T.	36296588	Sgt
Board, Harold J.	36698943	Cpt
Bogardus, Levan I.	19088347	Sgt
Bolick, Henry P. Jr.	0.735739	1/Lt
Bond, James W.	0712369	2/Lt
Bondar, Nicholas D.	0742408	2/Lt
Bonnassiolle, John P.	19140409	Sgt
Books, Dallas O.	0416988	1/Lt
Boord, Wayne M.	15377335	S/Sgt
Bowman, Frederic N.	36455556	S/Sgt
Bowyer, Dewey O. Jr.	36884697	Sgt
Boyce, Elzie L.	38435071	S/Sgt
Boyd, Robert E.	17029961	T/Sgt
Bradford, Thomas M.	34650587	S/Sgt
Brandes, Arony H.	0.684938	2/Lt
Bratcher, Carey E.	0678673	2/Lt
Breithaupt, H.A. Jr.	16148145	S/Sgt
Brown, Gilbert R.	14054449	S/Sgt
Brown, James S.	11034006	T/Sgt
Brown, John T.	34337613	Sgt
Brown, Kenneth O.	36253519	T/Sgt
Brown, Robert T.	18124325	S/Sgt
Brown, Warren L.	32372078	Cpl
Bryan, Walter F.	31169197	S/Sgt
Buchert, William L.	15394146	S/Sgt
Buchheit, Edward L.	39315106	S/Sgt
Burke, James E.	6957060	T/Sgt
Burnett, Warren H.	12066823	S/Sgt
Butzmann, Ralph O.E.	16049684	T/Sgt
Buzzi, Harold G.	0682061	2/Lt
Byars, Allen C.	35610529	Sgt
Byler, Harvey J.	35514174	T/Sgt
Byrd, Jimmie C.	18090074	S/Sgt
Cade, George W. Jr.	39549070	T/Sgt
Cagle, William C.	14166143	S/Sgt
Callaghan, George P.	0744684	2/Lt
Callejas, Francisco	38495747	S/Sgt
Campbell, Donald G.	0734422	2/Lt
Campbell, George L. Jr	32424712	T/Sgt
Cannon, Leslie F.	35223322	S/Sgt
Carrington, William	34782864	Sgt
Carroll, Joyce B.	37083040	S/Sgt
Carter, Henry C.	38328720	S/Sgt
Cashen, Edward J.	0692369	2/Lt
Cashman, Clair A.	33252194	S/Sgt
Castaneda, Jose A.	38440725	S/Sgt
Castiglione, Joseph	32477917	S/Sgt
Castor, James R.	19179967	Sgt
Cattano, Joseph V.	0678408	2/Lt
Caufield, John J.	0757769	2/Lt
Causey, Warren W.	35726907	S/Sgt
Cavell, Dominick F.	32433382	S/Sgt
Chatterton, Gale A.	37576019	S/Sgt
Chapman, Lorn E.	15330287	T/Sgt
Chinchilla, Francis P.	0695802	1/Lt
Chiodo, Michael A.	35530766	Sgt
Chojecki, John M.	36355990	T/Sgt
Christian, Norman R.	0.696208	2/Lt
Cicora, Anthony F.	0445910	2/Lt
Cieply, Edward J.	0.705321	2/Lt
Cinquina, Enrico A.	42068209	S/Sgt
Clapper, Elwin E.	0812829	2/Lt
Clark, Frank C.	36517558	T/Sgt
Clark, James V. Jr.	17064404	Sgt
Clifford, William W.	0678174	1/Lt
Cobb, Calvin J. Jr.	14107831	S/Sgt
Coble, A.D.		S/Sgt
Coday, Donald S.	19092547	S/Sgt
Coe, John D.	0703945	2/Lt
Cohen, Jack M.	0687812	2/Lt
Cole, Monell A.	34606042	S/Sgt
Coleman, Alvin D. Jr.	02072649	2/Lt
Coleman, Vincent S.	0672939	2/Lt
Comeau, Eugene L. Jr.	0818833	1/Lt
Connolly, Martin T.	32499804	T/Sgt
Connor, Daniel Jr.	13097803	T/Sgt
Cook, Bill J.	T.122209	F/O
Coolidge, Donald B.	12201815	T/Sgt
Cooper, Joe P.	38185839	T/Sgt
Cooper, Samuel L. Jr.	38043205	S/Sgt
Coplin, Guy R.	35647687	S/Sgt
Cothran, James W.	34652746	Sgt
Coudriet, Frederick	33289787	S/Sgt
Cowely, John C.	34588794	T/Sgt
Cox, Robert B.	0.688931	2/Lt
Crabbe, Charles W.	12129506	T/Sgt
Craig, James D.	35418557	S/Sgt
Cristofaro, Gus J.	13046539	S/Sgt
Cullins, Thomas F.	31315355	S/Sgt
Cumming, Robert B.	38429250	Sgt
Cummings, Francis J.	0673057	2/Lt
Cunningham, William	36350809	S/Sgt
Dalton, Gerald M.	0675562	2/Lt
Daoust, Wallace W.	0797484	1/Lt
Darling, Lockwood	11066024	T/Sgt
Davenport, Bobby J.	38513012	Sgt
Davis, Roy W.	14158397	S/Sgt
Davis, William R.	0822649	2/Lt
Dawson, Jennings B.	0716379	2/Lt
Day, Walter N.	32447507	S/Sgt
Deal, Fred F. Jr.	34035675	S/Sgt
Deaton, James A.	36824423	Cpt
Deck, Glenn A.	37704513	Sgt
Decker, Jack C.	0721658	2/Lt
Delaney, Paul E.	11102474	S/Sgt
Della, Betta P.J.	37416250	S/Sgt
Dellitt, John J.	0676442	2/Lt
Demery, Robert F.	37666738	S/Sgt
Demontier, Herbert O.	0738626	2/Lt
Derrick, Pete E.	20828430	S/Sgt
Desimone, Peter P.	31084545	S/Sgt
Dickison, William G.	12030573	Sgt
Dickson, James W.	0677680	1/Lt
Digman, Thomas Jr.	0690553	2/Lt
Dinda, Bernard F.	35310893	S/Sgt
Dinsmore, Robert S.	0798073	2/Lt
Dinsmore, Walter F.	33252527	S/Sgt
Dmoch, Thaddeus, S.	12201499	T/Sgt
Dodd, James R.	0720219	2/Lt
Donaldson, Claude D.	0791573	1/Lt
Doolittle, David R.	31329911	T/Sgt
Doty, Amos E.	34506780	S/Sgt
Doub, Harry G. Jr.	33204984	S/Sgt
Doyle, Charles C. Jr.	0677031	2/Lt
Draper, James W.	18165905	S/Sgt
Dreher, John F.	35339934	S/Sgt
Dudley, William R.	35360460	S/Sgt
Dudziak, Teddy	0793067	2/Lt
Dufour, Joseph L.	14036724	Pvt
Dunlap, Virgil N.	17128694	S/Sgt
Durrance, Edward E.	0478603	2/Lt
Edward, Demur S.	39528562	S/Sgt
Egler, Martin G.	35057102	S/Sgt
Ellinger, C.F.		2/Lt
Elliott, Malcolm L.	34364077	T/Sgt
Ellis, John D.	0742144	2/Lt
Emerson, Herbert B. Jr.	11086911	S/Sgt
Englebrecht, Louis C.	33378957	Sgt
Epstein, Morris	32981974	Sgt
Erickson, Clifford W.	37322109	S/Sgt
Etheridge, Mart T.	0676236	2/Lt
Euwer, Charles T. Jr.	0711367	2/Lt
Faas, John E.	0693655	2/Lt
Farlow, Lynn B.	14171008	S/Sgt
Farnwalt, Walter H.	35666075	S/Sgt
Farrar, Robert E.	12169916	S/Sgt
Feldman, Alfred	02043724	1/Lt
Felsenthal, Charles L.	0691489	2/Lt
Feran, John E.	0742146	1/Lt
Ferrell, Edward D.	35598911	Cpl

126

Reed, John W. 4th	0691542	2/Lt
Reese, Robert L.	0.807513	1/Lt
Reese, William J.	14059987	T/Sgt
Reeves, Walter E.	14079106	Sgt
Reilly, Bernard A.	13029378	S/Sgt
Reilly, Christopher	32350670	S/Sgt
Reindehl, Wilbur T.	0684988	2/Lt
Reljac, Joseph G.	33037480	S/Sgt
Replogle, Wendell G.	0752697	2/Lt
Reynolds, Hugh D.	17021496	S/Sgt
Ricci, Joseph A.	0692821	2/Lt
Rice, Thomas L.	14185624	S/Sgt
Rich, Nicholas P.	39275931	Sgt
Richards, Earl B. Jr.	33548157	Sgt
Richards, William J.	0713225	2/Lt
Richardson, Frank E.	0679225	2/Lt
Richer, Ernest R.	18129940	S/Sgt
Richmond, Thomas C. Jr.	36894889	S/Sgt
Rigby, Clyde W.	0743208	2/Lt
Roberts, Truman F.	38451074	S/Sgt
Robinson, James W.	33158520	S/Sgt
Robinson, William F.	34686356	T/Sgt
Roetzel, Peter B.	0819175	1/Lt
Rogers, Charles J. Jr.	18170152	S/Sgt
Rogers, Gerald E.	0806152	2/Lt
Rooney, George W.	32425139	T/Sgt
Roper, Donald W.	15382509	S/Sgt
Rorer, Frank H.	33248466	T/Sgt
Rosenfeld, Carl B.	12146184	T/Sgt
Ross, Herbert J.	35444733	S/Sgt
Ross, John A.	0690826	2/Lt
Rowe, George F.	0751678	2/Lt
Rowlett, Robert W.	37388907	Sgt
Rudd, Charles R.	0696395	1/Lt
Rudnitsky, Bud E.	12139763	S/Sgt
Rueffer, Arthur P.	0.805680	2/Lt
Ryan, James L. Jr.	0801091	2/Lt
Sabaca, Joseph J.	39124395	Sgt
Sablitz, Paul	31453650	Sgt
Sabolish, George	33672718	S/Sgt
Sackal, Ward M.	11041277	T/Sgt
Sackeli, Angelo	12029836	T/Sgt
Saltzman, Robert L.	36870105	S/Sgt
Sambanis, George	31181659	Sgt
Sander, Lewis L. Jr.	02069216	2/Lt
Sands, Ralph D.	17123357	S/Sgt
Scalet, Joseph	18019953	T/Sgt
Schaefer, Creighton E.	6297493	S/Sgt
Schaefer, Lee A.	35670281	Sgt
Schaumberg, Gunther	32982665	S/Sgt
Schenkenberger, Jacob	35607640	S/Sgt
Schilling, John E.	0444761	2/Lt
Schilter, Norman J.	36257684	S/Sgt
Schmelzle, Oliver G. Jr.	33357306	Sgt
Schmid, Frank F.	36042420	S/Sgt
Schmidt, Arthur N.	32611279	Sgt
Schmidt, Elmer A.	37264511	S/Sgt
Schoelerman, Harold A.	0832251	2/Lt
Schoolmaster, Clinton F.	0435705	Maj
Schroeder, Harold R.	0677891	2/Lt
Schuster, William H.	0.829570	2/Lt
Scudder, Monroe A.	32889943	Sgt
Sederquist, Donald L.	0.677897	2/Lt
Seifert, Robert B.	13125074	S/Sgt
Selden, Frederick	36347326	Sgt
Senk, John J.	32460576	S/Sgt
Serrette, Robert L.	39462064	S/Sgt
Sekavec, Roy G.	32297993	T/Sgt
Shaefer, Jack O.	33668985	S/Sgt
Sharpe, William G.	0742613	1/Lt
Shea, Paul F.	0797618	1/Lt
Shearer, Martin G.	0801094	2/Lt
Shelley, Joe H.	0691299	1/Lt
Shelton, Orville W. Jr.	0814422	1/Lt
Shelton, William L.	0742532	1/Lt
Sheppard, William B.	13036735	S/Sgt
Shere, Fred C. Jr.	0745956	2/Lt
Sheridan, James J.	0755239	2/Lt
Sherman, Phillip	0688114	2/Lt
Sherwood, Walter B.	0670634	1/Lt
Shiffer, James L.	33355074	S/Sgt
Sholander, Carl T.	0778976	2/Lt
Siggs, Peter S.	0673633	2/Lt
Simila, Wilho	36554540	S/Sgt
Simons, Lee	0734752	2/Lt
Simpson, James F.	38237805	S/Sgt
Simpson, Vernon H.	17032158	S/Sgt
Skaggs, Robert L.	0692833	2/Lt
Slack, George E.	11089594	T/Sgt
Slama, Alex R.	19066725	T/Sgt
Slowik, John E.	0434025	Capt
Smith, Brian T.	0672467	1/Lt
Smith, Clifford E.	T.2533	F/O
Smith, Heber J.	0677910	2/Lt
Smith, Orville L.	38047861	T/Sgt
Smith, Ralph C.	18084615	T/Sgt
Smith, Richard E.	0743210	1/Lt
Smith, Willis H.	39326004	Sgt
Smittle, Floyd D.	0736733	2/Lt
Snyder, Robert O.	0682375	1/Lt
Soda, Michael J.	36639021	T/Sgt
Sokol, Alexander R.	12182357	S/Sgt
Somerhalder, Walter	T.6919	F/O
Sopchak, John	12169305	S/Sgt
Sorrells, John F.	14170070	Sgt
Spalding, Robert E.	13128569	S/Sgt
Spencer, William A.	0762960	2/Lt
Sporrey, Richard F.	0742622	2/Lt
Stalsby, Samuel C.	T.2041	F/O
Stancik, Martin	39240262	T/Sgt
Stankan, Paul C.	0678653	2/Lt
Stauder, James B.	0350317	Capt
Steele, Wayne M.	0692348	2/Lt
Steinmetz, Douglas R.	0797630	1/Lt
Stella, George F. Jr.	32587425	Sgt
Stevens, Hirschall M.	35423747	S/Sgt
Stewart, James M.	0738046	2/Lt
Stoltz, Clarence W.	0689397	2/Lt
Storey, Harold D.	0806006	2/Lt
Stover, Arthur R. Jr.	0755124	2/Lt
Stratton, Charles R. Jr.	0759735	2/Lt
Stricker, Donald H.	20722380	S/Sgt
Strother, Charles E.	14091858	Sgt
Sullivan, Edward Jr.	11116306	Sgt
Surls, David L.	36335093	S/Sgt
Swangren, Roy	0676167	Capt
Swanson, Arthur W.	32566314	Sgt
Talley, Edgar R.	34817268	S/Sgt
Tantum, William R.	32077912	S/Sgt
Taylor, Adraine L.	14141134	Sgt
Taylor, Ralph E. Jr.	02044872	1/Lt
Telken, Henry F.	0820855	2/Lt
Thom, Fred S.	6547418	T/Sgt
Thomas, James W.	18136291	T/Sgt
Thompson, Robert E.	17070811	Sgt
Thomson, Virgil E.	0679391	T/Sgt
Thornton, Marion Jr.	34720103	T/Sgt
Thrall, Leo C.	37254188	T/Sgt
Timm, Henry R.	36592289	Sgt
Tollok, Robert C.	33799148	Cpl
Tomak, James E.	16086428	S/Sgt
Torres, Edward J.	36459522	S/Sgt
Townsend, Edward S.	13158260	Sgt
Trappe, William H.A.	33552475	Sgt
Tremlett, Robert S.	32659672	S/Sgt
Trivison, Joseph R.	15354276	S/Sgt
Troutman, Edward A.	35352584	S/Sgt
Troxel, Davis G. Jr.	13125653	S/Sgt
Trumpy, Egidus	34125913	T/Sgt
Tschudy, Evan E.	0735002	1/Lt
Tubbs, Herbert L.	12215173	S/Sgt
Tucker, Herbert L.	32428508	S/Sgt
Tufts, Aubert M.	0755611	2/Lt
Turner, Dwight L.	0748500	2/Lt
Tweten, Ernest A.	37301968	S/Sgt
Tyler, Ace W.	0685176	1/Lt
Tynes, David D. Jr.	15086916	T/Sgt
Usry, William F. Jr.	0799104	1/Lt
Valley, Wilbur L.	0699277	2/Lt
Van Alstine, Nathan J.	17096735	S/Sgt
Vandervort, Robert M.	35579237	Sgt
Vasquez, Paul	39545676	S/Sgt
Vavra, Charles E.	37675010	S/Sgt
Verzyl, Rayford R.	12129678	S/Sgt
Victor, Albert I.	0689414	2/Lt
Viosca, Randall C.	18150956	S/Sgt
Vowels, Leroy J.	17069768	S/Sgt
Wade, Burton L.	0709867	2/Lt
Wagner, Frederick J.	32516123	S/Sgt
Wagonseller, Robert V.	33366140	T/Sgt
Walker, Charles S.	02065200	2/Lt
Walker, Thomas G.	0797649	2/Lt
Wall, John J.	0684087	2/Lt
Walla, Mitchell A.	32317543	S/Sgt
Wallace, Frank C.	39458008	T/Sgt
Walley, Henry P.	0.805712	2/Lt
Ward, Milton E.	0733004	1/Lt
Wargo, Michael A.	0736738	1/Lt
Warner, Charles W.	0.721268	2/Lt
Wasserstein, Hyman	0676186	2/Lt
Watkins, Howard D. Jr.	0433617	Capt
Watson, Harry Q.	15329848	T/Sgt
Weeks, Harvey H. Jr.	15071843	Sgt
Wehunt, John W.	34572821	Sgt
Weiner, Harry D.	32078947	S/Sgt
Weise, Everett H.	0818254	2/Lt
Weiss, Daniel B.	0.806021	2/Lt
Weiss, Jonas E.	T.2540	F/O
Welch, Roy E.	33089729	S/Sgt
Weller, Christian S.	38254660	S/Sgt
Wells, Virgil W.	35473605	S/Sgt
Wendorf, Jack A.	0744114	2/Lt
Wheeler, Bernard J.	0.682383	2/Lt
Wheeler, Merwin	39261144	Sgt
White, Edward I.	0736812	1/Lt
Whitnah, Joseph C.	0.735004	2/Lt
Whitt, Clyde G.	34604263	S/Sgt
Wieland, J.L.		2/Lt
Wilcox, Delmar R.	0.679426	2/Lt
Wilde, Allison H.	0.669823	2/Lt
Wilkinson, Harold C.	15324832	T/Sgt
Willhite, Max R.	37214580	T/Sgt
Williams, James L. Jr.	34802898	S/Sgt
Williamson, C.R. Jr.	0.689585	2/Lt
Willig, Norman K.	19169393	S/Sgt
Wilson, Fonzy M. Jr.	39690607	S/Sgt
Wilson, James C.	34307348	S/Sgt
Wilson, William E.	0689430	2/Lt
Wimer, French P.	0708602	2/Lt
Winkler, Robert D.	0.748870	2/Lt
Winzenburg, George T.	0.801048	2/Lt
Wishbow, Gabriel E.	0688770	2/Lt
Wisley, Robert L.	15331683	S/Sgt
Wohlstrom, T.C. Jr.	31143711	T/Sgt
Wolfer, Anthony J.	32360421	S/Sgt
Womer, Wiliam S.	15074670	S/Sgt
Woods, Don P.	0705873	2/Lt
Wooton, Warren J.	32362084	T/Sgt
Worcester, Charles E.	16080760	T/Sgt
Wunderlin, Carl F.	0.819445	2/Lt
Wyatt, Bert W.	0526045	2/Lt
Wyatt, Raymond I.	0674259	2/Lt
Yarbrough, W.L. Jr.	0.2043712	2/Lt
Yarbrough, William L.	14137621	S/Sgt
York, Roy M.	18120451	T/Sgt
Yorra, Marshall S.	32445483	S/Sgt
Young, Robert L. Jr.	0.699299	2/Lt
Zeigler, Richard H.	0779280	2/Lt
Zeman, Milan R.	T.61361	F/O
Zerangue, Felix A.	18151481	S/Sgt
Zimmermann, Seymour	11115346	S/Sgt
Zimpelman, John G.	35316999	T/Sgt
Zinini, Olympio C.	0759786	2/Lt
Zschiesche, Charles	38134584	T/Sgt
Zubay, Steve M.	33284889	S/Sgt

445TH BOMB GROUP

Aaron, William	11072501	S/Sgt
Abraham, Daniel A.	0717365	2/Lt
Abrams, Marvin A.	16133614	T/Sgt
Ahlin, Henry T.	37566950	S/Sgt
Ajello, Louis P.	0722971	2/Lt
Aldrich, Frederick N.	11010715	S/Sgt
Allen, Harold P.	0.772248	2/Lt
Alvarez, Edward	T.131775	F/O
Anderson, John B.	0747189	1/Lt
Andrews, Sherman J.	0712473	2/Lt
Angelo, Julius T.	31341437	S/Sgt
Appleton, Daniel H.	0681770	2/Lt
Archer, Lewis M.	39697413	T/Sgt
Armstrong, Truman Jr.	0773278	2/Lt
Aronov, Jerome L.	0726972	1/Lt
Arricotti, Joseph L.	13104959	Sgt
Attison, Cecil L.	14182361	T/Sgt
Austin, George R.	0716698	2/Lt
Bailey, Herbert E.	0.712477	2/Lt
Bald, Edward W.	36483972	T/Sgt
Banta, Donald V.	39543116	T/Sgt
Barben, Laurence G.	0771270	2/Lt
Barker, John W.	0416977	Capt
Barker, Phillip N.	20748601	S/Sgt
Barks, Arthur E.	0.687923	2/Lt
Barnes, Clarence A.	6246832	T/Sgt
Barnes, Herman R.	33896770	S/Sgt
Barnum, William	0.808499	2/Lt
Barringer, John D. Jr.	0763904	1/Lt
Barrios, Wade J.	18170716	S/Sgt
Bateman, Henry F.	34921690	Sgt
Bateman, Herbert M.	0716591	2/Lt
Bates, Lyman M. Jr.	02015334	2/Lt
Bates, Robert C.	32732366	S/Sgt
Bean, Herbert	19059131	Sgt
Beasley, Jack P.	13075881	S/Sgt
Becker, John J.	0768984	2/Lt
Becker, Sidney	0741226	2/Lt
Beggs, William L.	12169851	Sgt
Belouski, Roy A.	36440654	T/Sgt
Bergquist, Glenn R.A.	18120232	T/Sgt
Bidney, Joseph R.	32582773	S/Sgt
Billings, Elton J.	36420856	T/Sgt
Black, Joseph F.	39414426	S/Sgt
Blake, Richard M.	0.828371	2/Lt
Blanchard, Stewart E.	0434070	Capt
Block, Ernest	37583567	Sgt
Blomberg, Robert A.	0681317	2/Lt
Blumencranz, Harold J.	0795188	1/Lt
Bode, Ralph H.	16117549	S/Sgt
Boleski, Donald J.	33516148	T/Sgt
Bolin, Roy E.	0705107	2/Lt
Boone, Howard D.	12072650	T/Sgt
Boyd, Robert E.	17029961	T/Sgt
Boykin, William L. Jr.	0772784	2/Lt
Bozich, Michael	33291350	Sgt
Brainard, Newell W.	081929	2/Lt
Brandt, Charles K.	32790542	S/Sgt
Breecher, Donald W.	0713104	2/Lt
Brent, Donald E.	0747730	1/Lt
Bridgeo, James L.	31370167	S/Sgt
Brimley, Vincent	35564238	T/Sgt
Brindley, Kenyon	0685071	2/Lt
Briskin, Solon R.	02009001	2/Lt
Broadway, Henry Jr.	38420812	Sgt
Brodeur, Raymond A.	02056852	2/Lt
Bronstein, Phillip	13152993	T/Sgt
Brotherton, Robert C.	17155157	S/Sgt
Brower, Ross B.	0.717330	2/Lt
Brunswig, Norman F.	0722691	2/Lt
Bulger, Martin P. Jr.	0744971	2/Lt
Burdette, Arthur E.	34444828	S/Sgt
Bush, Lloyd W.	38300826	S/Sgt
Byars, James R.	34606613	T/Sgt
Byrd, Olen C.	381185808	S/Sgt
Callahan, John H.	38176324	S/Sgt
Calzonetti, Peter J.	32078302	Sgt
Campbell, Thomas J.	0801975	2/Lt
Cantor, Milton	12192833	Sgt
Caplane, Christ E. Jr.	12192668	S/Sgt
Carey, Leo A.	0542523	2/Lt
Carlisle, Thurston C.	0400669	Capt
Carlson, Robert F.	0801358	2/Lt
Carrillo, Edward	39280371	Sgt
Carroll, William T.J.	18242379	Sgt
Carver, John J.	0785164	2/Lt
Casser, Bryard J.	02072690	2/Lt
Cassero,Frank M.	32677375	S/Sgt
Castillo, Roland F.	14136043	Sgt
Cathey, Lewis T.	38274441	S/Sgt
Celani, Silvio E.	33898207	Sgt
Chilton, John H.	0811015	2/Lt
Christensen, Thomas	02043754	1/Lt
Churchill, Lyle L.	32675603	T/Sgt
Cicchetti, John F.	31343559	T/Sgt
Clabaugh, Martin E.	15329328	S/Sgt
Clapps, Ralph T.	0.806965	2/Lt
Clark, Albert J.	33733116	S/Sgt

Clark, Russell E.	35366464	T/Sgt
Clarkson, Billie T.	14161016	T/Sgt
Cleary, Thomas H. Jr.	42010197	S/Sgt
Clemmens, Charles H.	0744688	2/Lt
Cohea, Monroe C.	6258030	S/Sgt
Cohen, Howard	32887236	Sgt
Cohen, Seymour B.	T.129118	F/O
Colacino, Philip J.	32574551	T/Sgt
Collison, Gerald D.	0681872	2/Lt
Conner, Thomas B. Jr.	0803564	1/Lt
Constable, John S.	0.803566	1/Lt
Constantinos, N.A.	0813332	2/Lt
Cooper, Edward T.	35563465	S/Sgt
Corbin, Edward B.	0680411	2/Lt
Cornell, John R.	12189324	S/Sgt
Cornwall, Charles E.	32609009	S/Sgt
Cornwell, Gilber B.	39121492	S/Sgt
Contron, Frederick J.	11101278	T/Sgt
Costain, Phillip M.	024887	Capt
Costley, Francis W.	0713001	2/Lt
Cottrell, Glynn O.	36567820	Pfc
Cowell, Earl F.	37407603	S/Sgt
Cowgill, John W.	0703710	2/Lt
Coy, Jack W.	15120028	S/Sgt
Crabtree, Kelly	34451524	Sgt
Craig, Otis D.	32956491	S/Sgt
Crespolini, Americo	33609563	S/Sgt
Crowley, James J.	31241510	Sgt
Cyrek, Adam J.	0734315	1/Lt
Dahlstrom Joseph E.	13039511	T/Sgt
Dale, Daniel J.	T125565	F/O
Daly, William F.	12182320	S/Sgt
Dana, Phil C.	0687556	1/Lt
Dargan, Virgil V.	32912948	T/Sgt
Davis, Frank C. Jr.	0687931	2/Lt
Dekalb, Lyle R.	0886414	2/Lt
Del Pero, Otto D.	19149684	S/Sgt
Denny, Hugh S.	14196476	S/Sgt
Dent, John D.	0769013	2/Lt
Derdzenki, Walter	12200169	S/Sgt
Desmond, William J.	0803163	1/Lt
Destro, Anthoy L.	0732613	2/Lt
Dewey, Donald C.	37442329	S/Sgt
Dickey, Robert M.	15132373	T/Sgt
Dickman, Donald E.	15374061	T/Sgt
Diercks, William J.	12076970	S/Sgt
Dittmar, Robert A.	12194287	S/Sgt
Doggett, Earl T.	34496322	S/Sgt
Donahue, John J.	33524628	T/Sgt
Donald, Myron H.	0696339	1/Lt
Doriot, Jack Z. Jr.	16065022	T/Sgt
Douglas, James M.	32887504	Sgt
Driscoll, William	0800852	Capt
Dunmire, James O.	0684450	2/Lt
Dusting, Raymond J.	12131164	S/Sgt
Eberhardt, Edward Jr.	0806822	2/Lt
Eckard, Robert A.	0691969	2/Lt
Edward, R.L.	38505945	T/Sgt
Edwards, Charles D.	12180032	S/Sgt
Edwards, J.S. Jr.	14103615	Sgt
Elder, John R.	38188018	T/Sgt
Elder, Oliver B.	0817826	1/Lt
Elliott, Glenn O.	33873474	S/Sgt
Elliott, William L.	14176674	T/Sgt
Ellis, John R.	32931619	Sgt
Emens, Theodore N.	0706717	2/Lt
Engebretson, Phillip W.	02057268	1/Lt
Entzminger, George H.	37233780	T/Sgt
Erickson, Leonard E.	16076605	S/Sgt
Farina, Joe	39292548	S/Sgt
Fermyn, Charles J.	17127514	T/Sgt
Ferrini, Ferdinand B.	0691882	2/Lt
Ferrizzi, Samuel A.	13126284	S/Sgt
Fertig, Richard W.	12184649	S/Sgt
Fields, James T.	19186421	T/Sgt
Fischer, Paul G.W.	0687936	2/Lt
Flach, Ferdinand E.	37540396	Sgt
Flanagan, John	33705549	Sgt
Flanzer, Charles P.	0886643	2/Lt
Fleming, Carl Jr.	0420584	Lt/Col
Fleming, William J.	37527992	S/Sgt
Fletcher, Ernest R.	33718905	T/Sgt
Flickner, William E.	0768856	2/Lt
Folkner, Francis H.	33361283	S/Sgt
Forster, Carl W.	33832889	S/Sgt
Forsythe, Robert E.	16128311	Sgt
Francisco, Antonio Jr.	32361445	S/Sgt
Frasch, John E.	0735559	1/Lt
Fratta, Andrew	12121322	T/Sgt
Frederiksen, Tage R.	32858310	Sgt
Freybler, James R.	0716855	2/Lt
Fry, Phillip A.	0742416	1/Lt
Fussa, Michael J.	12182555	T/Sgt
Gall, Richard F.	0712794	2/Lt
Garnett, Nelson J.	31166748	T/Sgt
Gayford, Gerald B.	32580330	S/Sgt
Geiszler, Martin Jr.	0768064	2/Lt
George, Raymond J.	32738606	S/Sgt
Gfelner, Joseph F.	0745076	1/Lt
Gifford, Robert O.	0808033	2/Lt
Gilbert, F.H. Jr.	12220123	Sgt
Gilfoil, Joseph H.	31270331	S/Sgt
Gillette, Henry A.	0829458	2/Lt
Gingrich, Albert H.	35552990	S/Sgt
Globis, Edward H.	0826923	2/Lt
Goemaat, Johannes	42182830	S/Sgt
Gohl, Rudolph W.	19146550	S/Sgt
Golden, William F.	0807838	2/Lt
Golub, Eugene E.	02065979	2/Lt
Gordon, Henry J. Jr.	31307157	S/Sgt
Gordon, James B.	0685932	1/Lt
Gore, Marion E.	0806978	2/Lt
Graper, Orland R.	17181742	Sgt
Gray, Thomas	0742578	2/Lt
Greenwell, Joseph C.	0389470	Capt
Groves, Earl B.	32581359	T/Sgt
Gurstella, Joe	0818860	2/Lt
Gunning, John	6243398	M/Sgt
Gutowsky, Joe A.	36262079	S/Sgt
Hamilton, Vincent P.	0712560	1/Lt
Hankin, Morris	0687943	2/Lt
Hansen, Donald	0806440	2/Lt
Hansen, Francis E.	37450637	S/Sgt
Hansen, Robert N.	0700609	2/Lt
Hanson, Gordon E.	01703112	2/Lt
Hardy, James T.	0806441	2/Lt
Harrell, Ralph W.	34408527	S/Sgt
Harris, Norman A.	0713176	2/Lt
Harris, Richard L.	36695963	Sgt
Hautman, Edward F.	0697358	1/Lt
Hawkins, Lyle M.	36258456	T/Sgt
Hayes, Herbert L.	35138433	Sgt
Hein, Donald L.	33563157	T/Sgt
Helms, Russell S.	38290554	T/Sgt
Helpes, Robert R.	39567121	S/Sgt
Hengesbach, F.E. 3rd	0722488	2/Lt
Hennessy, John P.	0700151	1/Lt
Henrikson, Henry J.	T.124757	F/O
Henry, Alfred W.	02065119	2/Lt
Henry, Harold G.	37184118	T/Sgt
Hert, Carl J.	0887066	1/Lt
Hess, Calvin F.	35057106	T/Sgt
Hewitt, Richard W.	01824315	2/Lt
Hickey, Raymond J.	31231588	T/Sgt
Hines, Howard E.	0705235	1/Lt
Hoffman, Ferdinand	0709378	2/Lt
Hogan, Hugh F.	02060290	2/Lt
Hogan, Paul X.	31368856	Sgt
Holland, Keil G.	0723976	2/Lt
Hollis, Norman A.	39562159	S/Sgt
Holloway, Henry	36482069	T/Sgt
Hosmer, Richard H.	0808061	2/Lt
Houston, Francis 3rd	13200504	Sgt
Howard, Clifton H.	01998582	1/Lt
Howell, S.E. Jr.	38487753	S/Sgt
Howell, William L.	0761102	2/Lt
Huffman, Lee R.J.	34203002	Sgt
Hurt, Brian J.	14052620	S/Sgt
Hutton, Ernest H.	0749847	2/Lt
Hynes, Edwin J.	11115893	Sgt
Imhoff, Robert C.	19199767	S/Sgt
Ische, Raymond E.	0700886	1/Lt
Johns, De Vere J.	0693501	2/Lt
Johnson, Edward J.	32874288	S/Sgt
Johnson, Gordon W.	0800893	2/Lt
Johnson, Olin D.	37682457	Sgt
Johnson, Robert D.	37472160	T/Sgt
Johnson, William H.J.	0671366	1/Lt
Johnston, Robert C.	0826183	2/Lt
Jones, Edison E.	18171634	S/Sgt
Jones, John E.	0826992	2/Lt
Jones, Owen G.	33211631	S/Sgt
Jordan, John W. Jr.	0578111	2/Lt
Juliano, Paul J.	T126230	F/O
Kanyak, John	13060299	Sgt
Kaster, Robert G.	37334260	T/Sgt
Kielar, Anthony	12096135	T/Sgt
Kilborn, Bruce O.	0665046	1/Lt
Kilmen, Walter	11033000	Sgt
Kimmey, Robert M.	16169817	T/Sgt
King, James V.	33552460	S/Sgt
King, Wesley C.	6978159	T/Sgt
Kiser, Robert Q.	0679077	2/Lt
Klepzig, Robert B.	12130326	T/Sgt
Klingler, George P.J.	02043727	1/Lt
Klopfenstein, Richard P.	0721119	1/Lt
Knapp, Wendell R.	12030094	S/Sgt
Koenig, William H.	0823880	2/Lt
Kogan, Aaron	0723103	2/Lt
Kolasinski, Felix W.	35331002	Sgt
Koppitz, John R.	33401873	T/Sgt
Koupal, Lambert E.	02072788	2/Lt
Kovanes, Alvern G.	15374913	S/Sgt
Kritz, Frederick H.	32579664	S/Sgt
Kulp, Merlin F.	0687949	2/Lt
Kusterko, Walter W.	0828715	2/Lt
Lacronda, Anthony J.	33139787	Pvt
Lamar, John A.	0744282	2/Lt
Lanier, Sidney T.	18024236	S/Sgt
Lapolla,Anthony J. Jr.	0801136	1/Lt
Larsen, Donald W.	39571317	S/Sgt
Larsen, Garth B.	0806467	2/Lt
Larsen, Lars E.	32778375	Sgt
Last, Orville F.	36254829	T/Sgt
Lavelle, Francis J.	12080864	T/Sgt
Leahy, John H.	36372162	T/Sgt
Leary, George J.	01170052	1/Lt
Lecari, John E.	0752005	2/Lt
Lello, Sylvester V.	31145800	S/Sgt
Leyy, Robert D.	0825915	2/Lt
Lewis, Henry C. Jr.	0407017	1/Lt
Limes, Edward W.	35669600	S/Sgt
Linder, Hal F.	0823646	2/Lt
Linkletter, George B.	33539866	S/Sgt
Lloyd, Gilbert D.	34430946	Sgt
Locilenti, Vincent	0687952	2/Lt
Long, Robert M.	33515646	Sgt
Looney, Alfred J.	0803235	1/Lt
Lotoszinski, Henry W.	0684532	2/Lt
Love, Benjamin L.	0683558	2/Lt
Love, Jack B.	18122516	S/Sgt
Luce, Wallace C.	35528409	S/Sgt
Luhmann, Alfred H.	32466039	S/Sgt
Luongo, Michael J.	0711225	2/Lt
Lupher, Harry M. Jr.	02005737	2/Lt
Lyons, Roland C. Jr.	33543987	Sgt
Macdonald, Donald K.	0827020	1/Lt
Mackin, Joseph R.	32607581	S/Sgt
Mahoney, John F.	31312836	S/Sgt
Mallery, James M.	0722338	1/Lt
Maluda, James	31128500	Sgt
Manley, Roland J.	33188117	Sgt
Mann, Milo R.	36591267	S/Sgt
Marshall, Robert L.	13111851	T/Sgt
Martens, Arthur H.	16119040	S/Sgt
Martin, Andrew J.	31173238	T/Sgt
Martin, Dwight L.	36867143	Sgt
Martin, Edward R.	35589596	Pfc
Mascolo, Camillo E.	0433967	2/Lt
Mathews, Clyde F.	36775334	Sgt
Matthews, Gilbert E.	13108281	Sgt
McAfee, Harold G.	0745817	2/Lt
McAnally, Elworth B.	38136014	T/Sgt
McCargar, Elwyn R.	12169319	S/Sgt
McCollum, Francis A.	33794888	S/Sgt
McCormick, Richard E.	34118802	T/Sgt
McCoy, Daniel F.	0744987	2/Lt
McCoy, Dan W.	0740232	Maj
McDonnell, Joseph E.	6950489	T/Sgt
McDonough, Alfred G. Jr.	0695478	2/Lt
McDonough, Denis B.	39270852	S/Sgt
McEntee, James L.	35056796	S/Sgt
McGuinness, George V.	32705194	Sgt
McGuire, John J.	32810991	Sgt
McLain, Richard N.	33808283	S/Sgt
McMahon, John M.	02056433	2/Lt
McManamon, Joseph G.	33349168	T/Sgt
McMasters, Robert E.	0749484	2/Lt
McMeekin, Robert W.	0745154	2/Lt
McNeill, Harold G.	0773188	2/Lt
McPartland, Lee E.	0823508	2/Lt
Meeks, Kenneth L.	0706890	2/Lt
Mercier, Harold M.	0699562	2/Lt
Metcalf, Earle G.	0800383	1/Lt
Miller, Robert O.	0806880	1/Lt
Milliken, Leighton E.	31101464	S/Sgt
Minor, Howard K.	36761097	Sgt
Mischel, Sigmund	19162503	Sgt
Modlin, Lawrence A.	37536367	S/Sgt
Moeller, Frank J.	12087399	S/Sgt
Monnett, James R.	35373326	S/Sgt
Montgomery, Shelley D.	6281320	S/Sgt
Mootz, Frederick L.	32912698	Sgt
Moran, William H. Jr.	0550458	1/Lt
Morris, Richard P.	0695761	2/Lt
Morris, Wiliam A.	38564249	S/Sgt
Morse, Stanley H.	32672315	S/Sgt
Mosher, Roland F.	0836627	2/Lt
Moss, George S.	33719171	Sgt
Motts, Ross E.	35634126	S/Sgt
Moynihan, Robert C.	0749730	2/Lt
Mulligan, William J.	17013623	T/Sgt
Murphy, Vance H.	06299220	2/Lt
Musbach, Harold W.	37237715	S/Sgt
Neal, Stanley R.	0675864	1/Lt
Neher, John B. Jr.	37722061	S/Sgt
Nelson, Norman M.	0679101	1/Lt
Newell, Loren C.	12137525	T/Sgt
Newsome, Luther J.	14137323	S/Sgt
Newton, Eugene L.	36441261	S/Sgt
Noble, William P. Jr.	0817729	2/Lt
Nolan, William H.	32442513	Sgt
Oaks, William	39227106	S/Sgt
Ochevsky, Louis	39280567	S/Sgt
Odom, Everett M.	14165120	S/Sgt
Oleson, Robert W.	39618538	Sgt
Olson, Harold W.	0705779	2/Lt
Oswald, Robert B.	0673929	2/Lt
Owens, James C.	34351234	T/Sgt
Pakestein, Charles G.	42000885	S/Sgt
Palmer, Charles C. Jr.	19083921	T/Sgt
Panconi, Victor J.	39099421	S/Sgt
Parker, Gordon B.	0677555	2/Lt
Parsons, Richard L.	32286303	S/Sgt
Patterson, James E.	17157473	T/Sgt
Patterson, Milton A.	0740902	2/Lt
Paulus, Fred A.	35758806	S/Sgt
Paulus, Raymond J.	37573772	S/Sgt
Pavelko, Joseph J.	13125175	S/Sgt
Pear, Richard J.	0805972	2/Lt
Perry, Thomas B.	0694894	2/Lt
Personette, Eldon R.	37568985	Sgt
Peters, William H.	0683630	2/Lt
Peterson, Darling L.	02064310	1/Lt
Phillips, Robert G.	0718743	2/Lt
Picarelli, Francis D.	42090135	Sgt
Pietz, Milton F.	17071942	S/Sgt
Pile, Porter M.	0709140	2/Lt
Pohl, Irving C.	11101970	S/Sgt
Porter, Robert L.E.	0688779	2/Lt
Potts, Herbert	0702333	2/Lt
Price, William F.	0687960	1/Lt
Priebe, Walter	35534289	Sgt
Prisinzano, Emilio T.	32553927	T/Sgt
Radatta, James J.	33180860	S/Sgt
Radtke, Earl P.	35550065	S/Sgt
Raroha, Richard A.	0675288	1/Lt
Reaves, Dudley W.	16169115	S/Sgt
Reeder, Donald E.	33729001	Sgt
Reeves, Lonnie E.	14142588	S/Sgt
Reid, James W.	11027448	S/Sgt
Relyea, Floyd K.	32662360	T/Sgt
Reno, Arlec T.	0692340	1/Lt
Rice, Donald F.	T.7068	F/O
Rice, George M.	34589407	S/Sgt
Richardson, Sydney B.	0806908	2/Lt
Riedel, Arno C.	35900510	Sgt
Rispoli, Vincent J.	42058472	Sgt
Ritz, James A.	12003690	S/Sgt
Robbins, Oscar Jr.	35371021	T/Sgt
Rogalski, Francis J.	32392353	Sgt
Rogers, Layne Jr.	0449098	1/Lt
Rosati, Joseph A.	121312895	T/Sgt
Rose, Robert A.	0752940	2/Lt
Rosenthal, Harry	12157354	S/Sgt
Ross, James D.	15046678	T/Sgt

Rouse, Robert K.	0711482	1/Lt
Rundell, Robert M.	0686694	2/Lt
Ruppert, John C.	10601043	S/Sgt
Salmon, Bonifacio P.	19179289	S/Sgt
Samuels, Samuel	0682868	2/Lt
Santerian, Edward	33786092	S/Sgt
Saunders, John C.	0798588	1/Lt
Scala, Hector V.	0552862	2/Lt
Schaen, James W.	0554062	1/Lt
Schaich, Wilfred J.	35579267	S/Sgt
Schellhas, William L.	0699572	2/Lt
Schultz, Edwin W. Jr.	18219851	S/Sgt
Schultz, Raymond P.	0824921	1/Lt
Schum, Walter B.	33569394	S/Sgt
Schuyler, Keneth O.	16155718	S/Sgt
Sears, Thomas H.	0824923	1/Lt
Sechler, Roy W.	T62887	F/O
Sedlak, Edward J.	6660953	S/Sgt
Seeds, Andrew G.	0700553	2/Lt
Selin, Robert L.	T129303	F/O
Serpico, Frank R.	0.801152	2/Lt
Shaffer, Glenn H.	33764321	S/Sgt
Shay, Robert E.	37467644	S/Sgt
Shell, Fred L.	0800951	1/Lt
Shelley, Parks R. Jr.	39325367	Sgt
Sheppard, John J.	12155930	S/Sgt
Short, Ronald R.	13084225	S/Sgt
Shrum, Melvin R.	33415392	S/Sgt
Shurtz, William E.	0742790	1/Lt
Silverman, Conrad	0685748	2/Lt
Silverman, Irving	122021197	T/Sgt
Sirl, Joseph F.	0773006	2/Lt
Skalski, Chester F.	32460986	Cpl
Skeats, Kenneth J.	12120200	T/Sgt
Skjeie, David P.	0743114	1/Lt

Sloan, Ralph D.	T.122201	F/O
Small, Asha P.	33382794	S/Sgt
Smeltzer, Eldon L.	0678484	2/Lt
Smets, Orvile P.	0713603	2/Lt
Smisek, Milton C.	17037617	S/Sgt
Smith, Charles E.	16076352	T/Sgt
Smith, Douglas P.	39559850	S/Sgt
Smith, Herbert A.	13033024	T/Sgt
Smith, Jasper T.	38037255	T/Sgt
Snyder, James O.	15099660	Sgt
Snyder, Lafayette G.	0670276	2/Lt
Somers, Raymond H.	0.723833	1/Lt
Soule, James B.	16106982	S/Sgt
Speers, Edward J.	0819198	1/Lt
Spingler, John L.	T.125579	F/O
Stacey, Kenneth L.	15329773	T/Sgt
Stanfield, S.D. Jr.	14192749	Sgt
Stearns, Arthur E.	0711502	2/Lt
Steen, Robert W.	0805357	2/Lt
Steinmann, Bill H.	12083516	S/Sgt
Steinseifer, Ernest E.	19169595	T/Sgt
Stephens, William C.	16084038	T/Sgt
Stephenson, Gordon O.	32439032	T/Sgt
Stewart, Norman J.	16189151	Sgt
Stochl, William B.	0742031	2/Lt
Stonestreet, Charles G.	14074400	T/Sgt
Strickland, Jennis M.	0797634	1/Lt
Strychasz, Walter A.	0753167	2/Lt
Suitch, John J.	0.661151	1/Lt
Sullivan, Eugene J.	11069588	S/Sgt
Sutherland, Harold E.	0817862	1/Lt
Swanson, Girard H.	0682737	2/Lt
Swanson, Sidney D.	0737493	1/Lt
Szeles, Edward A.	12218466	Sgt
Tansey, Raymond E.	32453046	S/Sgt

Tarant, George	35095994	S/Sgt
Tarbert, John A.	6947526	S/Sgt
Tatum, Frank W.	33533442	S/Sgt
Taylor, Raymond H.	19069643	T/Sgt
Taylor, Truman L.	32845445	Sgt
Teasdale, Clark A.	0804535	2/Lt
Tenney, Clesen H. Jr.	0827078	2/Lt
Thompson, George E.N.	33710797	Sgt
Thompson, William A.	0827839	2/Lt
Timmons, William K.	37230256	S/Sgt
Tinklepaugh, Arthur J.	06995382	2/Lt
Tocket, Louis T.	35216173	T/Sgt
Triolo, Peter C.	32568587	T/Sgt
Triplett, James M.	39202130	T/Sgt
Truax, Don W.	0679257	2/Lt
Tubergen, Gray V. Jr.	0821812	2/Lt
Tucker, Dacus T. Sr.	34648550	S/Sgt
Tucker Leslie J.	36696770	Sgt
Tunstall, Ensign M. Jr.	33422272	S/Sgt
Ulmer, Frank H.	15338510	Sgt
Umdleby, Loran A.	0769082	2/Lt
Vance, William L. Jr.	34778642	Sgt
Varty, Robert M.	39264256	S/Sgt
Vergos, Charles	01996085	2/Lt
Vernor, Richard W.	36479868	T/Sgt
Vetri, Angelo C.	33551980	S/Sgt
Vickers, Frank S.	11128297	S/Sgt
Wages, Earl R.	34848594	S/Sgt
Waldron, Gordon F.	36459147	S/Sgt
Walston, Walter J.	18218241	S/Sgt
Walters, Lloyd T.	36829966	Sgt
Walton, Leigh A.	31169485	T/Sgt
Wampler, Roy M.	13122404	S/Sgt

Warman, Leslie E.	0817797	2/Lt
Waterfield, Lewis	02008902	2/Lt
Watt, Hugh D.	16149860	S/Sgt
Watts, Woodard C.	34366107	S/Sgt
Weatherly, Charles E.	38436326	Sgt
Weaver, Robert H.	0687097	2/Lt
Wegiel, Walter F.	02057781	2/Lt
Weingaertner, R.F.	02005791	2/Lt
West, W.D. Jr.	18171808	S/Sgt
Wheeler, Clare L.	36816304	Sgt
Wigley, Eugene C.	38369073	S/Sgt
Wilcox, Harman C.	35570357	T/Sgt
Wilkins, Joseph A.	16134684	T/Sgt
Wilkins, Robert R.	0690022	2/Lt
Willett, John P. Jr.	0432218	1/Lt
Williams, James J.	0673846	2/Lt
Williams, Everette J.	14164570	S/Sgt
Williams, James A.	0421854	1/Lt
Williams, William H.	T.131513	F/O
Wills, Ralph G.	08271111	2/Lt
Wilson, Calvin H.	11116628	S/Sgt
Winters, Richard A.	0555703	1/Lt
Wise, John F.	39465098	S/Sgt
Wolfe, Perry W.	0558011	2/Lt
Woodbury, Howard V.	37019026	Sgt
Yates, William G.	0825056	2/Lt
Yerkes, Walter L. Jr.	0679442	2/Lt
Yurkowsky, Michael	0673850	2/Lt
Zenner, Harold P.	0815044	1/Lt
Zielinski, Donald F.	0674741	2/Lt
Zornow, Dale F.	0722412	2/Lt
Zudeck, Alfred	0712446	2/Lt

446TH BOMB GROUP

Adams, Joseph B.	0731007	1/Lt
Adams, Stephen E.	13142937	S/Sgt
Aitken, Dean G.	36480191	S/Sgt
Algee, Robert D.	34635602	Sgt
Allaman, Walter R. Jr.	0697975	2/Lt
Allen, L.V.	0684216	1/Lt
Allen, Robert W.	0.831628	2/Lt
Anderson, Carl R.	31406435	Sgt
Anderson, James H.	T.134528	F/O
Andrews, Jerome C.	0.826062	2/Lt
Arata, Joseph A.	36870870	Sgt
Ashwurth, Edwin R.	12191094	Sgt
Ayd, Charles J.	13141112	Cpl
Backlund, Carl G.	37562624	Sgt
Baczek, Rudolph F.	31384867	S/Sgt
Bagwell, Emmett D.	34476923	T/Sgt
Ballard, Calvin T.	0434031	Capt
Bane, William A.	0763900	1/Lt
Baringer, Ralph E.	37549093	Cpl
Barkell, Colin F.	0708388	2/Lt
Barksdale, John M.	0821932	2/Lt
Barley, George K.	33762577	T/Sgt
Barnycastle, L.C.	0685258	1/Lt
Baron, Walter S.	31133831	S/Sgt
Barron, John R.	0.825542	1/Lt
Bart, Louis	12190218	S/Sgt
Baucom, Hoover C.	34772366	T/Sgt
Baxa, Leonard J.	0.752474	2/Lt
Beasley, Dale D.	02059149	2/Lt
Bedford, Howard E.	T.125801	F/O
Belk, Woodrow W.	34606942	S/Sgt
Bensuk, John A.	0682688	2/Lt
Berry, Emil Jr.	0662430	1/Lt
Bettner, John A.	02065494	2/Lt
Bialecki, Adolph C.	31159853	Sgt
Bickel, Myron B.	15128159	Sgt
Biddinger, Harold F.	42033851	S/Sgt
Binder, Clyde L.	33321486	S/Sgt
Birkbeck, Anthony S.	12076263	T/Sgt
Blackwood, James C.	0.747194	1/Lt
Blair, Michael P.	35724206	Sgt
Bloyd, William L.	18193941	S/Sgt
Blumberg, Harold G.	0720144	2/Lt
Bohen, Roy N.	19139011	S/Sgt
Bonaiuto, Anthony P.	0.2061334	2/Lt
Boulds, Joseph S.	0728164	1/Lt
Bourque, John J. Jr.	0819951	2/Lt
Boyles, Charles D.	34637444	Cpl
Bridges, Floyd L.	0703436	2/Lt

Brisbois, Maynard O.	13136520	S/Sgt
Brockman, Wilson M.	34648666	S/Sgt.
Brooks, Robert F.	0717741	2/Lt
Brossett, A.C.	38519103	S/Sgt
Brown, Royal F.	13180809	Pfc
Buckingham, Charles F.	0684681	2/Lt
Buncy, Floyd A.	12169883	Cpl
Burch, Charles O.	34351659	Sgt
Burdette, Arthur E.	34444828	S/Sgt
Burns, Thomas A.	0708789	2/Lt
Burt, Donald A.	11085378	Sgt
Cahill, John W.	19163408	T/Sgt
Calhoun, Jimmy L.	34395707	S/Sgt
Callahan, John H.	38176324	S/Sgt
Callahan, Patrick T.	39619200	Cpl
Campbell, Thomas E.J.	0834576	2/Lt
Canant, Amuel B.	0.747575	1/Lt
Capps, Milton L.	14053223	S/Sgt
Card, Orville F.	0768439	2/Lt
Carlsom, Elmer F.	36721086	S/Sgt
Carlson, William C.	02074333	2/Lt
Carmody, John T.	0752481	2/Lt
Carnahan, Raymond G.	33695297	S/Sgt
Carr, Jay G.	0685294	1/Lt
Case, Wayne I.	0684274	1/Lt
Casey, James E.	0676547	2/Lt
Cegelka, Chester E.	31324609	S/Sgt
Champlain, James T.	0706808	2/Lt
Cheek, Earle C.	0692295	1/Lt
Cheffer, Donald J.	0559068	1/Lt
Chism, Christopher M.	33327770	T/Sgt
Christensen, K.C.	0720437	2/Lt
Christman, John R.	35166341	Sgt
Civitarese, William	31230294	S/Sgt
Clay, John T.	34185329	S/Sgt
Clifton, William J.	16171859	T/Sgt
Cline, Peter R.	0677664	2/Lt
Cole, James L.	0699650	2/Lt
Cole, James W.	0831923	2/Lt
Collings, Robert R.	37232003	S/Sgt
Collins, Jimmie D. 3rd	0819966	2/Lt
Concannon, George E.	0701569	2/Lt
Coyle, Edward F. Jr.	31120863	S/Sgt
Coyle, Leo R. Jr.	31321370	S/Sgt
Crandall, Allan E.	15332370	Sgt
Culbertson, Harry E.	0811175	2/Lt
Culliton, Kieran P.	11121972	T/Sgt
Culp, Herbert C.	0697106	2/Lt
Cushing, John L.	0712516	2/Lt

Dale, James E.	0692767	1/Lt
Dargaczewski, Edwin J.	37482009	Sgt
Davies, James B.	07070424	2/Lt
Davis, John Y.	T.134650	F/O
Dawson, Richard W.	11131588	S/Sgt
De Rosa, Anthony R.	32997569	S/Sgt
De Rosa, John A.	39207368	Sgt
Decker, Bill L.	39918350	Cpl
Del Mastro, Jack T.	12185724	S/Sgt
Dellose, Carl J.	32488682	Sgt
Dellow, Kenneth H.	0819974	1/Lt
Denning, Clifford L.	0751592	1/Lt
Dezeeuw, John A.	16109449	Sgt
Diaz, Felix	37677247	S/Sgt
Dickson, John B.	0828391	2/Lt
Diercouff, Jean M.	0699991	1/Lt
Douglass, Charles N.	18052441	S/Sgt
Dzanaj, John B.	0817642	2/Lt
Edgar, Rogers M.	42000121	S/Sgt
Eibel, Albert R.	35599245	Sgt
Ege, Ray B.	39397829	T/Sgt
Epstein, Morris	0685299	2/LT
Fashbaugh, Keith R.	36165020	Sgt
Faulk, Alfred W.	34917619	Cpl
Fenster, Herbert	14109156	T/Sgt
Fetterhoff, Willard	36595057	Sgt
Fisher,Raymond L.	0708361	2/Lt
Flaherty, Patrick J.	12090834	T/Sgt
Fleischer, Frank E.	32579651	Sgt
Flynn, James T.	32573852	Sgt
Freda, Anthony R.	0708435	1/Lt
Free, Robert J.	0820987	1/Lt
Fuchs, Kermit A.	0806252	1/Lt
Fuller, Wendell E.	33539943	S/Sgt
Fuller, William E.	12131504	S/Sgt
Fulmer, Henry D. Jr.	0691639	1/Lt
Gallagher, Edward J.	32875666	T/Sgt
Garber, Marvin W.	0678230	1/Lt
Gauder, Merlin P.	02059148	2/Lt
Gegelka, Chester E.	31324609	S/Sgt
Gentry, Homer S. Jr.	0733456	1/Lt
Getman, William D.	0820995	2/Lt
Gilbreath, Robert E.	0685002	2/Lt
Gill, Thomas H.	0665001	2/Lt
Gilleland, Jack L.	0706732	2/Lt
Gladstein, Harold	0826921	2/Lt
Glanzrock, Murray G.	14083453	S/Sgt

Glass, Waldo W.	12098859	T/Sgt
Gochnauer, Carl P.	13102042	T/Sgt
Goletz, Robert E.	0823355	2/Lt
Good, John B.	0695053	2/Lt
Gore, John B.	35141246	Sgt
Graf, Earl A.	42027033	Sgt
Grant, Glenn O.	34357797	T/Sgt
Greenfield, George	02070016	2/Lt
Griffeth, Elwood L.	20146788	T/Sgt
Griffith, George E.D.	39410722	S/Sgt
Grigsby, Cecil K.	15334533	S/Sgt
Grisco, Henry M.	33465251	T/Sgt
Haak, August C.	16175492	Sgt
Hackworth, Harold G.	35793446	Sgt
Hafner, George M.	0752488	1/Lt
Hagesteary, Arthur W.	02005882	2/Lt
Hahnert, Calvin G.	35341785	S/Sgt
Hall, John N.	39064481	T/Sgt
Hand, John E. Jr.	0817328	1/Lt
Haran, James P. Jr.	0704196	1/Lt
Harbin, Foster P.	0674760	2/Lt
Harkins, John L.	15323515	T/Sgt
Harris, Donald E.	16075876	T/Sgt
Hart, Raymond L.	38564324	Cpl
Hasson, Solomon R.	32423449	Cpl
Hathaway, Robert	33668234	S/Sgt
Haught, Thomas M.	0714068	2/Lt
Haydel, Earl J.	38497056	Cpl
Helfer, Clifton C.	0743014	1/Lt
Hensley, David S.	18232782	Sgt
Hess, Charles J.	32626095	S/Sgt
Hilderbrand, Robert R.	33834349	Sgt
Hill, Charles E.	14163634	S/Sgt
Hill, Willard A. Jr.	0808995	1/Lt
Hirsch, Howard S.	02008855	2/Lt
Hoffman, Glenn W.	0741175	1/Lt
Hohenstein, Werner E.	37097337	Sgt
Holderman, Earl T.	T.132938	F/O
Holly, Earl B.	38342888	S/Sgt
Holt, Wilburn L.	38333212	S/Sgt
Hood, Alva W.	39682113	T/Sgt
Horn, Robert	13189410	Sgt
Howington, Luchous L.	38387966	S/Sgt
Hoyal, Lewis R.	38461510	S/Sgt
Hunter, Hugh R.	0801472	1/Lt
Husted, William F.	20226647	Sgt
Illik, Adam F.	36260667	S/Sgt
Ilstad, John E.	0826396	2/Lt

Ingraham, Robert F.	32676533	Sgt
Inlow, Burdett S.	0826456	Capt
Jackson, Euylse E.	14161707	S/Sgt
Jacobs, Frederick W.	14202685	S/Sgt
Jacobson, Syndey C.	0742719	2/Lt
Jakubiec, Frank A.	36866938	T/Sgt
Janik, Frank J.	36597649	T/Sgt
Jennings, Charles E.	15104665	Sgt
Jensen, Clark H.	01011266	1/Lt
Joachim, Harris W.	0752206	2/Lt
Jolley, Lowell T.	36602742	T/Sgt
Jones, Raymond	35390310	S/Sgt
Kant, Charles W.	0687856	2/Lt
Keefe, Thomas C.	20123765	S/Sgt
Kellogg, Randford W.	0831720	1/Lt
Kelly, Thomas R.	12203532	S/Sgt
Kendall, August R.	39118289	S/Sgt
Kerns, Harold C.	0.682699	2/Lt
Kidwel, Robert P.	0683835	2/Lt
Kiefer, Howard W.	0707935	1/Lt
Kieley, Adrian W.	32228136	S/Sgt
King, Melvin G.	15134627	S/Sgt
Kjelgren, Orley E.	37304698	S/Sgt
Koenig, Roland P.	36228535	S/Sgt
Kostrey, George H.	0713790	2/Lt
Kozielski, Ignatius M.	0752868	1/Lt
Kramer, Francis A.	17160399	S/Sgt
Krauss, Wade H.	0673201	2/Lt
Krolikowski, Henry L.	16077421	S/Sgt
Labonte, Raymond A.	31281440	S/Sgt
Lajoie, Robert W.	0830622	2/Lt
Lanier, Ernest B.	34762732	S/Sgt
Lanphere, Claude C.	0751363	1/Lt
Larson, Harold J.	0804689	1/Lt
Lee, Earl W.	11091482	T/Sgt
Leedy, Lewis B. Jr.	13002013	T/Sgt
Letterman, John M. Jr.	38185636	S/Sgt
Levine, Ernest	T129423	F/O
Lloyd, Clarence B. Jr.	0817709	2/Lt
Lofgren, Laurence R.	0720290	1/Lt
Long, Thomas B.	0742739	2/Lt
Looney, Joe C.	34732554	S/Sgt
Lovig, Ejner P.	31333242	S/Sgt
Lubomski, Joseph F.	13168192	Sgt
Luchinskas, Charles	33345067	T/Sgt
Luchko, Andrew L.	32949009	Cpl
Ludwick, Julian F.	19078541	S/Sgt
Lutz, Francis E. Jr.	0385299	1/Lt
Mack, Huler	02057345	1/Lt
Makosky, Thomas	33610533	S/Sgt
Mangiaracina, P.J.	0701941	1/Lt
Markus, Joseph R.	36636142	Sgt
Mars, Antigon O.	0808096	1/Lt
Martin, Allan R.	13111504	T/Sgt
Martinec, Robert J.	36678809	S/Sgt
Masters, William E.	34714083	S/Sgt
Maxwell, Jack A.	14056809	Pvt
May, Kenneth R.	15338702	S/Sgt
Mayer, Roswell S.	T121928	F/O
McAdam, Francis J.	32489273	S/Sgt
McCarthy, James F.	31384192	Sgt
McCreary, Raymond E.	0712634	2/Lt
McCutchen, Jay D.	0679636	1/Lt
McDonald, William A.	11117390	S/Sgt
McGlogan, Francis J.	0716917	2/Lt
McGowan, Gale B.	0764405	1/Lt
McHugh, Edward M.	32772200	S/Sgt
McKay, William A.	T063996	F/O
McKinley, Robert A. Jr.	35578530	S/Sgt
McMillen, Raymond E.	11141085	Cpl
McNeil, James P.	37480668	Sgt
McNutt, Maurice H.	33670928	T/Sgt
Meisle, Charles R.	13077714	S/Sgt
Mellgren, Roderick	42030300	S/Sgt
Mellott, George R.	33733002	S/Sgt
Merriman, James A.	0740246	1/Lt
Micken, Robert B.	13067988	S/Sgt
Mikolajewski, Alvin	0835043	2/Lt
Mikus, Chester	0688084	2/Lt
Miller, Cecil F.	0742193	2/Lt
Miller, Joseph M.	0766330	1/Lt
Miller, Robert E.	15344589	Sgt
Mincks, Fred E. Jr.	0706068	2/Lt
Mitchell, Norwood	37394688	S/Sgt
Morrissey, Pearce J.	31110865	T/Sgt
Mosckou, Chris Jr.	35370783	S/Sgt
Moseman, Herman R.	34268784	T/Sgt
Mullane, Martin J.	0760654	1/Lt
Murphy, George J. Jr.	0768173	2/Lt
Murray, Marshall J.	37394557	S/Sgt
Muse, Rex W.	0813044	2/Lt
Myers, Robert L.	33354202	S/Sgt
Nace, William R.	15333820	S/Sgt
Nappi, Ralph P.	32430048	Pfc
Narducci, Albert	33829674	S/Sgt
Neamon, Leon	0684119	1/Lt
Neumer, Robert A.	0707969	2/Lt
Nicholson, John D.	0696953	2/Lt
Nitterour, Harry L.	13098821	S/Sgt
Norton, William D.	34449229	S/Sgt
Novak, Sylvester M.	33795725	Sgt
Nunn, William	0761176	2/Lt
Nye, Leon C.	32995232	S/Sgt
Nytzak, William	32278507	Sgt
O'Bryan, John W. Jr.	0761999	2/Lt
O'Connor, William T. 2nd	0833198	2/Lt
O'Dell, Frederick J.	15300850	Sgt
Odom, Melville W.	14137267	S/Sgt
Olson, Leiding C.	39540933	S/Sgt
Osborne, Stephen W.	18121413	Sgt
O'Shields, Theodore B.	14029280	T/Sgt
Ostrander, Lawson K.	16153770	Sgt
Ousley, Joe B.	18076448	S/Sgt
Owens, Harold	38274476	Sgt
Pankowski, Karl J.	35064905	S/Sgt
Paragone, Christopher J.	31368874	Sgt
Parlowe, Louis S.	0739112	2/Lt
Peck, Charles A.	39414451	Sgt
Peck, George E.	31332334	Sgt
Pellicci, Pasquale M.	02069889	2/Lt
Penfield, John W.	02064308	1/Lt
Perry, James M.	15330497	Sgt
Perry, Richard R.	31369924	Cpl
Perry, Willard F.	36591162	T/Sgt
Peterla, William	0.2061204	2/Lt
Petrus, Richard M.	17148812	Sgt
Phillips, Joe W.	0721198	2/Lt
Phillips, Lewis W.	33234767	T/Sgt
Pietzsch, Frank H. Jr.	38456350	S/Sgt
Popilek, Henry A.	32361311	S/Sgt
Potis, Wilfred D.	01300378	1/Lt
Prendergast, Edward F.	31367024	S/Sgt
Profe, Siegfried C.	12153910	S/Sgt
Pulsipher, Lewis E.	16119118	Sgt
Quigley, Richard J.	32078529	Sgt
Rachal, James L.	38385559	S/Sgt
Radle, George E.	39011819	S/Sgt
Randall, Arthur G.	12029909	Pvt
Rathbun, Raymond W.	16144727	S/Sgt
Ray, William H.	0472987	1/Lt
Rayner, William G.	01289804	1/Lt
Redzek, Joseph T.	33673320	Cpl
Reignier, Paul A.	31406363	S/Sgt
Renner, Jack	37352735	S/Sgt
Rigg, Kenneth R.	12086297	Sgt
Ringer, Howard G.	13169444	T/Sgt
Ridley, Albert G.	0736891	1/Lt
Robbins, Charles A.	35662548	S/Sgt
Robblee, Loring J.	31202044	S/Sgt
Robinson, Wesley 3rd	0747959	2/Lt
Roeder, Irvin C.	15382181	S/Sgt
Rowe, Glen E.	0.699774	1/Lt
Rubin, Herbert	0699503	2/Lt
Rubin, Martin	T133004	F/O
Russell, Joseph W. Jr.	11070383	T/Sgt
Sabarich, Joseph J.	13022777	T/Sgt
Saint, Garnett E. Jr.	38453184	S/Sgt
Salat, Samuel	32179083	Sgt
Samuel, Frank S.	39195013	T/Sgt
Sauran, John D.	32139936	Sgt
Sawyer, William A.	18163248	S/Sgt
Schilling, Gunter W.	32856310	T/Sgt
Schneider, Marvin D.	02058269	2/Lt
Schoonmaker, Seymour C.	32502701	Sgt
Schopfer, Percy H.	0742785	1/Lt
Scott, Orval B.	16147911	S/Sgt
Scurlock, Walter B.	37395772	Sgt
Seagraves, Nelson T.	0666088	1/Lt
Selleg, Harold B.	36680738	S/Sgt
Sexton, Harvey L.	0785430	2/Lt
Shafer, Herbert E.	35451359	T/Sgt
Shaffer, Ralph V.	0706001	1/Lt
Sharp, Perry R.	0717113	2/Lt
Sheets, James E.	T.129990	F/O
Shelton, Mark D.	15112817	Sgt
Siegle, Ralph L.	38564166	Cpl
Silbo, Lee A.	0.860576	Capt
Simon, John W.	0805995	1/Lt
Simonian, Peter E.	02065920	2/Lt
Skinner, Robert S.	0778979	2/Lt
Smith, Harold A. Jr.	0780748	2/Lt
Smith, Jack D.	39343758	Sgt
Smith, Joe M.	T.001024	F/O
Smith, John G.	17096517	Sgt
Smith, Warren E.	36734147	Sgt
Smith, Welborn H.	14141453	S/Sgt
Solomon, Melvin S.	38540343	T/Sgt
Springstead, Earl R.	37353631	S/Sgt
Stalder, Kenneth J.	15335659	S/Sgt
Staton, Jack W.	35654944	Sgt
Steele, Desmond E.	0705834	2/Lt
Steeves, Robert L.	31426496	Sgt
Steinmetz, Harry H.	19073739	T/Sgt
Steldt, Robert C.	0698612	2/Lt
Stevens, Lyle	0701013	2/Lt
Stewart, Richard E.	38367894	T/Sgt
Strain, Samuel G.	17160787	Sgt
Strathern, Bernard R.	0706555	2/Lt
Stricklan, Harry F.	34730790	S/Sgt
Sweigart, Jacob C.	13091805	Sgt
Tabak, John	32058748	S/Sgt
Teetsel, Jerry E.	6671731	S/Sgt
Terenzio, Alphonse J.	33804804	S/Sgt
Terhaar, Jay A.	16148196	Sgt
Theisen, Raymond G.	37357305	Sgt
Tillman, Harvey K. Jr.	14046468	Sgt
Tillotson, Bennie F.	17065729	S/Sgt
Todd, John S.	35090214	S/Sgt
Tompkins, Alva J.	0823738	1/Lt
Tungeitt, Charles W.	35697455	Sgt
Turner, Harold W.	0674019	1/Lt
Turner, James R.	18194571	Sgt
Van Patten, Gail R.	17161004	T/Sgt
Vaughan, Clifford H.	0824013	2/Lt
Virden, Alfred H.	17114316	S/Sgt
Voellinger, Fred B. Jr.	33352355	S/Sgt
Vossler, John J.	38540632	T/Sgt
Wagner, Clyde E. Jr.	13067304	T/Sgt
Walder, Paul R.	36841007	Sgt
Wall, Walter E.	31410514	Sgt
Warren, Melvin E.	38213631	S/Sgt
Wass, Darrell A.	39862730	S/Sgt
Watkins, William J.	34349037	T/Sgt
Watson, Lawrence W.	36485720	S/Sgt
Wayne, James H.	36058502	S/Sgt
Whitaker, Lawrence A.	0831304	2/Lt
Whitton, Morgan H.	11035660	S/Sgt
Wigfield, Harold O.	13145997	S/Sgt
Wilkins, Glen O.	19180218	T/Sgt
Williams, Bobby J.	0752541	2/Lt
Winkelman, Paul	32708219	Sgt
Worsham, Edgar A. Jr.	0799702	2/Lt
Wrzesinski, Henry T.	36689702	S/Sgt
Wyatt, Charles E. Jr.	38399233	T/Sgt
Yorio, William R.	32890001	Cpl
Youngman, Allen R.	0.2068065	2/Lt
Yurka, Edward R.	37034682	Sgt
Zeller, Robert L.	0691341	1/Lt
Zemonek, Ted	35767441	Sgt
Zimmer, Charles F.	0.672264	2/Lt
Zweier, George J.	32893572	Sgt

448th Bomb Group

Acido, Norman F.	19174760	S/Sgt
Adams, Ara J.	0.2000376	1/Lt
Adelizzi, Angelo A.	16036369	S/Sgt
Alexander, George S.	0.869037	2/Lt
Allen, George L.	34580133	S/Sgt
Allen, Geroe C.	0684457	2/Lt
Allen, Harry J.	39621301	S/Sgt
Allen, Henry W.	14187838	S/Sgt
Allen, Luther E. Jr.	0805711	2/Lt
Alvis, Russell B.	13094122	Sgt
Ambrosini, Harry J.	19003327	T/Sgt
Anderson, Bernard W.	16069755	S/Sgt
Anderson, Carl	19185853	S/Sgt
Anderson, Truman K.	18167649	T/Sgt
Angelo, Arthur	11100398	T/Sgt
Anthony, Alden P.	0808492	2/Lt
Arluck, Jack	33426161	Sgt
Armstrong, Bernard F.	0745028	2/Lt
Askew, Josh K.	34503344	Sgt
Aucker, Harold L.	37115617	Sgt
Ausfresser, Seymour	0.669946	1/Lt
Ayrest, Robert C.	0.680984	2/Lt
Babini, Louis D.	31420626	Cpl
Backhaus, Albert H.	38273742	S/Sgt
Bair, Parke J.	13095286	Sgt
Ball, Roy E.	35595557	S/Sgt
Banas, Bernard J.	T.65103	F/O
Barber, Roy D.	14040228	T/Sgt
Barney, Hulick H.	39857402	S/Sgt
Barneycastle, L.C.	0685258	1/Lt
Bass, Robert V.	0688162	2/Lt
Beanland, Harold H.	02063146	2/Lt
Bell, James T.	0769089	2/Lt
Benoit, Adley V.	38486715	Sgt
Bergum, Arne O.	0747568	2/Lt
Beverlin, Dellas D.	36707999	Sgt
Bienapfl, John A.	0744233	2/Lt
Biggerstaff, Jim	0676535	2/Lt
Bilyk, John	0873020	2/Lt
Binkley, Raymond T.	0706675	1/Lt
Blanton, Charlie L.	39394021	S/Sgt
Blashe, Oryn M.	36841206	Sgt
Bookamer, Walter D.	13109114	S/Sgt
Boss, Edward F.	33227643	Sgt
Boula, Frank E.	36619461	S/Sgt
Bowers, Joe P.	0711120	2/Lt
Bradley, Ulmer E. Jr.	34333520	S/Sgt
Bramhall, Aaron R.	0.683897	2/Lt
Brenner, Fred	0687928	2/LT
Brewer, Gilman P. Jr.	20102011	S/Sgt
Briquelet, Gordon F.	36826978	S/Sgt
Brittingham, Donald	13141526	S/Sgt
Brown, Charles E.	16076433	Sgt
Brown, Millard L.	15171462	S/Sgt
Brown, Paul E.	33380722	S/Sgt
Bullard, Sam	0692604	2/Lt
Bunday, Raymond E.	0721341	2/Lt
Burke, Raymond G.	36730017	Sgt
Butler, Robert D.	0772937	2/Lt
Buxton, John M.	0705311	2/Lt
Callahan, Woodrow	6964020	T/Sgt
Campbell, Rawland	19169499	S/Sgt
Campbell, Robert L.J.	0406707	Maj
Canning, Leroy J.	13151539	S/Sgt
Carcelli, William	0692476	2/Lt
Carlson, Carl M.	T.1686	F/O
Carr, Floyd D.	34132932	S/Sgt
Cashin, Robert J.	37553432	T/Sgt
Casto, Olvie O. Jr.	0722944	2/Lt
Chaffin, Joseph C.	0797265	1/Lt
Charette, Albee G.	0687515	2/Lt
Chormley, Jack A.	32626123	T/Sgt
Ciolek, Kenneth	36180354	Sgt
Clark, Charles V.	35233954	Sgt
Clark, James G.	0796780	1/Lt
Cole, Albert P.	12228133	S/Sgt
Concepcion, Ernesto	32886753	Sgt
Conway, Theodore J.J.	0703454	2/Lt
Coolman, Dean E.	16159504	Sgt
Corziatti, Joe K.	18194485	T/Sgt
Crow, Malcolm W.	38446782	S/Sgt
Crumbley, Calvin C.	34686327	T/Sgt

Curio, Louis W.	12120417	S/Sgt
Cuthbert, William B.	0687930	2/Lt
Daley, John N.	0.801257	2/Lt
Dailey, James W. Jr.	38236448	T/Sgt
Daman, Charles H.	39463945	Sgt
Dansereau, Armand J.	31439980	Sgt
Davidson, Lester E.	0739076	1/Lt
Davis, Roy W.	0681347	2/Lt
Davis, William S.	14135368	Sgt
Deal, Philip A.	61915668	Cpl
Dean, William C. Jr.	39555534	S/Sgt
Deffner, Joseph B.	32675587	S/Sgt
Delay, Harold L.	19188393	S/Sgt
Denning, David H.	34870892	Sgt
Desoto, Kenneth H.	19186251	Sgt
Dickey, Harvey L. Jr.	18226840	Sgt
Dolecek, Victor D.	0697998	2/Lt
Dougherty, Daniel B.	12164002	Sgt
Drone, Richard E.	0717044	2/Lt
Dunham, William D.	34303305	S/Sgt
Durant, A.M. Jr.	0834771	2/Lt
Durant, William H.	35623918	Sgt
Duval, Albert F.	0716390	2/Lt
Easterling, Ernest R.	14130012	S/Sgt
Eckrosh, Floyd D.	17097350	S/Sgt
Edgerton, Henry Y. Jr.	02061656	2/Lt
Edman, Lawrence M.	0740775	1/Lt
Edson, Harlan R.	02065971	2/Lt
Edwards, Jacob E.	18000037	T/Sgt
Edwards, Samuel	32738235	Pfc
Ellis, Calvin J. Jr.	0689455	1/Lt
Fager, Peter J.	39617321	S/Sgt
Fahr, George S.	0697831	2/Lt
Falconi, Allessandro L.	31231533	S/Sgt
Fallert, Emmett E.	16144615	Sgt
Faris, Eber D.O.	0751289	2/Lt
Feingold, Leonard H.	0688744	2/Lt
Fena, William G.	0679487	2/Lt
Ferguson, William F.	0681366	2/Lt
Ferrari, Bernard X.	0717048	2/Lt
Feyti, John J.	20248174	S/Sgt
Fiego, Nicholas A.	33084134	S/Sgt
Fields, James E.	0769111	1/Lt
Finberg, Maurice M.	37573487	Sgt
Fitch, William D. Jr.	0717419	2/Lt
Ford, Walter H.	0717420	2/Lt
Foss, John R.	34707354	Sgt
Foster, Thomas A.E.	0741894	2/Lt
Foster, Thomas K.	0744267	2/Lt
Fourneyron, Matthew F. Jr.	12162824	S/Sgt
Fowler, Harold E.	34677771	Sgt
Fox, Edward A.	0808980	2/Lt
Francis, Francis E.	37236298	S/Sgt
Freeman, Francis E.	37236298	S/Sgt
French, Frank L.	0689147	2/Lt
Friedman, Stanley	0688184	2/Lt
Gartman, Woodrow W.	14040410	S/Sgt
Gauthier, Henry I.	31147965	S/Sgt
Genarlsky, Frank R.	0886510	1/Lt
George, Patrick H.	19022087	T/Sgt
Gerber, John R.	35225207	Sgt
Getz, Richard	12034631	T/Sgt
Ghormley, Jack A.	32626123	T/Sgt
Gikas, Miltiades C.	31258989	S/Sgt
Gilmore, James H. Jr.	14185681	Sgt
Ginevan, Donald G.	0817832	2/Lt
Gleason, James E. Jr.	31302882	Sgt
Goodpasture, Morgan	T.61188	F/O
Greene, George C.	31333352	Sgt
Greenwade, Billy R.	0820260	2/Lt
Grogan, Frank E. Jr.	14124065	T/Sgt
Grossman, Edward J.	32931086	Sgt
Grubbs, Roland L.	37488400	Sgt
Grubisa, George J.	32916135	Sgt
Guynes, James W. Jr.	0831159	2/Lt
Guyton, Graham G.	0390541	1/Lt
Hamblin, Herschel O.	13062783	S/Sgt
Hammond, James M. Jr.	34816783	Sgt
Handzlik, Edwin F.	36585389	Sgt
Hanson, Edward E.	0820006	1/Lt
Hardin, James R.	17077107	S/Sgt
Harwood, Thomas H.	34374445	S/Sgt
Hasiak, Henry S.	0702043	2/Lt
Hauver, Roland T.	02008958	2/Lt
Haynes, Harold C.	39712761	Sgt
Heard, John M.	02069015	1/Lt
Helm, George H.	0674042	2/Lt
Helvey, Wesley V.	0805916	2/Lt
Hershiser, Alden J.	0768545	1/Lt
Higgins, Eugene E.	36273563	Sgt
Hill, Charles D.	0379552	1/Lt
Hill,Glenn D.	17147109	Sgt
Hill, John A.	36576975	Sgt
Hinckley, Howard D.	0771716	2/Lt
Hines, Thomas H.	33560393	Sgt
Hipps, Charles F.	3325398	S/Sgt
Hogan, Thomas R.	13116127	Sgt
Holesa, John J.	15072502	T/Sgt
Holland, Robert F.	12171282	Sgt
Hudson, Robert P. Jr.	32176645	T/Sgt
Hughey, Edward D. Jr.	0677748	2/Lt
Hurton, Paul J.	31427378	Sgt
Indorf, Archie B.	35595495	S/Sgt
Jackson, William E.J.	15102452	S/Sgt
Jackson, Zachariah F.	0681101	2/Lt
Jacobsen, Edwin S.	0684114	2/Lt
Johnson, Bertil S.	35099877	S/Sgt
Johnson, Kenneth D.	36696966	Sgt
Johnson, Mabron P.	18007370	T/Sgt
Johnson, Norman H.	36740128	S/Sgt
Jones, Robert J.	12093034	Sgt
Jordan, Max R.	0725740	1/Lt
Juliano, Saverio J.	T134418	F/O
Kadehjian, Aram G.	T132946	F/O
Kaplan, Selwyn	12088705	T/Sgt
Kardys, Bronislaw J.	31252333	Sgt
Kary, John V.	19071394	S/Sgt
Kasbarian, Harry	0688359	2/Lt
Kasprzak, Joseph F.	13155970	S/Sgt
Keegstra, Donald	0679887	2/Lt
Kelley, Francis J. Jr.	11103783	S/Sgt
Kelly, John J.	32782047	S/Sgt
Kelly, Leon E.	34671680	S/Sgt
Kelly, Walter T.	14040497	T/Sgt
Kiehn, Donald R.	35898639	Sgt
Kindt, Harold L.	13094588	S/Sgt
Kittredge, Abraham J.	0745907	2/Lt
Klum, Philip H.	12186879	S/Sgt
Knight, Raymond F.	0744532	2/Lt
Kocheran, Alex	33414605	Cpl
Kolokow, Irving	12189812	Sgt
Koon, Curtis L.	33252697	T/Sgt
Korte, Jerome A.	36477450	Sgt
Kracyla, Henry J.	32488180	Sgt
Kraft, Alton L.	0702055	1/Lt
Krammer, Danile J.	13028896	T/Sgt
Kropp, John M.	36819181	Sgt
Krueger, Ardell F.	36292349	S/Sgt
Kubinski, Henry	36555495	S/Sgt
Kuzminski, Anthony J.	11101473	S/Sgt
Lackey, David E.	15082537	S/Sgt
Laing, Richard B.	19164878	Sgt
Lake, Allan L.	02060318	1/Lt
Lane, Harold J.	15383034	Sgt
Lane, Horace B.	0771451	2/Lt
Lang, Harold L.	39704462	Sgt
Lariviere, John E.	0886809	1/Lt
Larson, James M.	02061983	2/Lt
Lepley, Howard P.	13137364	T/Sgt
Lerner, Herbert M.	0771943	2/Lt
Levey, Paul D.	36654552	Sgt
Long, Andrew P.	32186301	S/Sgt
Loprete, William A.	0807004	1/Lt
Loughlin, Thomas A.J.	36851964	Sgt
Loyd, Ira H.	36431449	S/Sgt
Lunt, James C.	19064266	T/Sgt
Lyon, Edgar E.	16033854	S/Sgt
Mains, Robert L.	0680467	1/Lt
Majestic, Arthur B.	0701940	2/Lt
Major, Harold Jr.	02067316	2/Lt
Malwitz, Willard R.	19175397	S/Sgt
Manning, David E.	0745722	2/Lt
Markiewicz, Edward A.	0677543	2/Lt
Marsh, David T.	33300005	S/Sgt
Marshall, Clarence R.	33231924	S/Sgt
Martin, Leon H.	02074515	2/Lt
Mathews, James P. Jr.	34829996	Sgt
Matula, Frank J.	12100312	Sgt
Maxton, Marion C.	37205700	S/Sgt
Mazur, Irving	12036294	S/Sgt
Mazzagatti, Philip	38420922	T/Sgt
McCleary, Donald C.	01314163	2/LT
McClellan, Wendell R.	38285507	S/Sgt
McCoy, Donald M.	35763351	Cpl
McCoy, John C.	02057337	2/Lt
McFarland, Hugh Jr.	02059558	2/Lt
McGinnis, Edward E.	39208597	Sgt
McGlone, John E.	32202248	S/Sgt
McKinley, Frederick T.	02074504	2/Lt
McLaughlin, James W.	32440514	T/Sgt
McMahan, Lewis A.	18182755	S/Sgt
McNarmara, Thomas M.	16088447	S/Sgt
Meents, Edward P. Jr.	0750812	2/Lt
Meier, Elmer P.	0815366	2/Lt
Merkling, John L.	0683045	2/Lt
Merkovich, Frank S.	3684180	Sgt
Merrill, Horman M.	23498186	Sgt
Mezzetti, Peter A.	12034349	Sgt
Michels, Carroll A.	01844474	1/Lt
Mied, Arthur F.	16000220	T/Sgt
Mielke, Henry E.	07754750	2/Lt
Miltner, Robert F.	30927755	S/Sgt
Mitchell, John H.	32910987	Sgt
Mize, Thomas N.	0773427	2/Lt
Monefeldt, Leonard H.	0681460	Capt
Moran, Joseph E.	15337063	Sgt
Mroczek, Elmer J.	35065303	Sgt
Mufson, Philip	0684181	2/Lt
Mull, Joseph H. Jr.	14174063	Pvt
Murphy, Ebonezer J.	0772446	2/Lt
Murphy, Edward C. Jr.	35370754	S/Sgt
Murphy, Kenneth J.	0687958	2/Lt
Neidig, Harold S.	0684182	2/Lt
Nelson, John B.	39275415	S/Sgt
Newton, Lloyd E.	18110354	S/Sgt
Nichols, Elton L.	38518612	Sgt
Nickerosn, Joseph F.	35572323	Sgt
Nissen, Charles C.	32589610	T/Sgt
Novichenk, Paul	15323363	T/Sgt
Nystrom, Robert J.	0715412	2/Lt
O'Brien, John R.	12187452	S/Sgt
Oden, Howard M.	0735439	2/LT
Odiorne, Edward A.	35582659	S/Sgt
O'Neil, Paul G.	0771113	2/Lt
O'Neil, Ralph F.	0886634	2/Lt
Oppelt, Harry J.	0.801356	1/Lt
Opper, Henry J.	12125979	S/Sgt
Ostarello, Umberto F.	36604398	S/Sgt
Overy, Dale W.	35296070	Sgt
Packer, Cyrus	18130544	S/Sgt
Palicki, Robert F.	0808887	2/Lt
Parks, James W.	18217836	Cpl
Parks, Joseph F.	38579450	Sgt
Parsons, Jerry M.	16035535	T/Sgt
Payne, Charles C.	34737456	Sgt
Payne, Donald A.	13178062	S/Sgt
Pempek, Albert A.	0699905	2/Lt
Perkowski, Michael	32826132	S/Sgt
Peterson, Irria J.	38174375	Sgt
Peterson, Warren N. Jr.	0928144	1/Lt
Petula, George	12183208	S/Sgt
Phillips, Frank S.	02043738	Capt
Phillips, John S.	17057058	Sgt
Pickering, Everett R.	02067346	2/Lt
Pinkus, Robert F.	0661557	1/Lt
Pitts, Cherry C.	0679115	1/Lt
Pogge, Georg H.	0718794	2/Lt
Pollard, Billie C.	38425993	S/Sgt
Pomfret, Joseph	0810214	2/Lt
Ponge, William F.	0807869	2/Lt
Postemsky, Edmond G.	0821075	2/Lt
Prabucku, Bernard D.	32731039	S/Sgt
Prieb, Kenneth W.	17131824	S/Sgt
Prior, Virgle V.	37653038	S/Sgt
Pulcipher, Eugene V.	0750685	2/Lt
Quinlan, Denis C.	32456595	S/Sgt
Resnikoff, Harold	18231595	S/Sgt
Rigg, Robert W.	39549975	S/Sgt
Rikard, Robert F.	0706903	2/Lt
Risner, Homer C.	38333496	Sgt
Robinson, Ernest W. Jr.	14055978	T/Sgt
Robinson, James R.	35756585	Cpl
Rogers, Francis G.	0687768	2/Lt
Rogers, William W.	02007843	2/Lt
Romanosky, Chester J.	13056696	S/Sgt
Roorda, Delwin D.	0.2062050	2/Lt
Rosenthal, Myron	36869665	Sgt
Savo, Enrico	32805787	Sgt
Scanlon, Edgar C. Jr.	0701312	2/Lt
Schierbrock, James J.	0699776	2/Lt
Schierenbeck, Edmund A.	37547985	Pvt
Schilling, John E.	36841583	Sgt
Schlorman, Louis J.	35622664	Sgt
Schmidt, Charles R.	0750861	2/Lt
Schoonmaker, Frederick A.	32734039	S/Sgt
Schroeder, Harlyn H.	0826014	1Lt
Schroeder, Russell F.	0704067	2/Lt
Schrom, Clifford R.	0679664	2/Lt
Scott, Thomas V.	0785138	2/Lt
Seiders, Pinkney W.	0751847	2/Lt
Shank, Joseph W. Jr.	0743108	2/Lt
Shipp, Charles A.	18025053	T/Sgt
Skiedar, Joseph Jr.	33431803	Sgt
Slack, Robert W.	39912946	Sgt
Slepin, Jerome	0689676	2/Lt
Sloan, Charles E.	0689766	2/Lt
Smarinsky, Irving	0710613	1/Lt
Smidy, James S.	33667892	Sgt
Smith, Castleton D.	0750225	1/Lt
Smith, Harvey E.	34516429	S/Sgt
Smith, Howard M.	17038532	S/Sgt
Smith, Salem A. Jr.	0688978	2/Lt
Souyers, Kenneth D.	0406033	Maj
Spadafore, Albert N.	11090413	S/Sgt
Spell, Ira L.	14188306	Sgt
Spellman, Carl E.	37368208	Sgt
Sprueill, Robert B.	14080837	Sgt
Stalland, Knute P.	07218575	1/Lt
Steffan, Joseph F.	0719786	2/Lt
Stennes, John J.	0694456	2/Lt
Stevens, Sumner W.	0670285	2/Lt
Stine, Everett F.	0689683	2/Lt
Stone, Robert B.	0689684	2/Lt
Strawn, Harold E.	13029830	Sgt
Sullivan, John J.	0696718	2/Lt
Swanson, Charles P.	0717118	2/Lt
Szudarek, Severyn G.	01998528	2/Lt
Tarkington, Taylor L.	18177172	Sgt
Taylor, Carl C.	39835597	S/Sgt
Taylor, Ear. L.	37498287	S/Sgt
Tennant, Marion A.	35382677	S/Sgt
Thompson, James McKay	0.017992	Col
Thompson, Robert W.	17066011	S/Sgt
Thurber, Raymond L.	0689693	2/Lt
Tod, Frederick W.	0776133	1/Lt
Togman, Edward F.	35596301	S/Sgt
Towles, Raymond S.	0.2045237	1/Lt
Turner, Arlin W.	18140043	S/Sgt
Turner, Robert Jr.	38519135	Sgt
Turpin, Harold C.	0.807541	1/Lt
Urban, James E.	35527301	Sgt
Vajgyl, James L.	35527301	Sgt
Van Deventer, Stuart D.	38588932	Sgt
Vetter, Harry F.	16088083	S/Sgt
Villare, Anthony C.	35969619	Sgt
Vinson, Sammie D.	14177911	Sgt
Wais, Dan A.	356788495	Sgt
Walasik, Anthony	33034529	S/Sgt
Wallenda, John Jr.	35514944	S/Sgt
Wann, Keith D.	39117819	S/Sgt
Ward, Leon A. Jr.	19203253	S/Sgt
Warke, William A.	0.693082	1/Lt
Warnock, Roland D.	0731707	2/Lt
Warren, William A.	18028026	T/Sgt
Wasara, Tolvo A.	15133297	Sgt
Waters, Herman L.	34587603	Sgt
Weisenburgh, C.P.	0689706	2/Lt
Weishaar, Eugene C.	36704194	S/Sgt
Werner, Samuel	12156211	T/Sgt
Westrick, Paul E.	02062099	1/Lt
White, Harold E.	0747535	2/Lt
Wilder, Charles W. Jr.	0.683886	2/Lt
Wilhelm, Lawrence M.	37604384	Sgt
Wilkins, Robert J.	0.2066088	2/Lt
Wilson, Charles W.	0704863	2/Lt
Wilson, Howard L.	33215816	S/Sgt
Wilson, Jap R. Jr.	18076005	S/Sgt

Wilson, Stanley L.	39550446	S/Sgt
Wittenberg, Herman	13124383	Sgt
Wright, Anderson C.	33836022	S/Sgt
Wright, Gordon W.	12072510	S/Sgt
Wright, William A. Jr.	32848722	Sgt
Yarnell, Robert H.	35668792	S/Sgt
Yates, Joseph A. Jr.	13184568	S/Sgt
Yiengert, Walter A.	0742103	2/Lt
Young, John B.	T134801	F/O
Young, Maynard H.	31152846	Sgt
Zemba, Joseph M.	33427181	Sgt
Zierdt, Kenneth A.	17064455	Sgt
Zimmerman, Theodore R.	0.2058344	2/Lt

453rd Bomb Group

Acton, William J.	19106292	Sgt
Adkins, Robert W.	38469484	S/Sgt
Allen, Henry H. Jr.	14120001	Sgt
Amburn, E.W. Jr.	34037562	S/Sgt
Amtzis, Melvin	12124267	Sgt
Anderson, Richard C.	35599969	S/Sgt
Anderson, Russell C.	0.818800	2/Lt
Andrew, Ralph W.	0.785364	2/Lt
Archibald, C.E. Jr.	02061325	2/Lt
Baatz, George L.	0.742108	Capt
Baker, Barrett L.	0687664	2/Lt
Ball, Henery E.	31417304	Sgt
Barnhill, Elmo V.	37625383	Sgt
Bartholemew, Harry H.	0751795	1/Lt
Basick, Bill B.	0712752	1/Lt
Batchelder, Rodger F.	31366007	S/Sgt
Bedard, Velmore V.	19094404	S/Sgt
Bell, Henry F.	31417304	Sgt
Beltz, Robert A.	16115157	S/Sgt
Bentley, Lloyd E.	12044972	S/Sgt
Bergman, August V.	0.681312	1/Lt
Bey, Melbourne F.	3303649	T/Sgt
Bingaman, James K.	07335513	1/Lt
Blackwell, Kenneth J.	32181241	S/Sgt
Boehm, Michael A.	0688576	2/Lt
Bolger, Stephen J.	33596911	T/Sgt
Bolsover, William E.	0811319	2/Lt
Bonner, Joe B.	16120375	T/Sgt
Borden, Allen D.	11089501	T/Sgt
Borenstein, Samuel D.	0.797253	1/Lt
Bouldin, John F. Jr.	38437601	S/Sgt
Boxman, Howard F.	15334542	S/Sgt
Brady, Fred G. Jr.	0745598	1/Lt
Bready, Frank B. 3rd	33551743	S/Sgt
Bringardner, E.W. Jr.	35627175	Sgt
Brown, Roscoe C.	0705307	1/Lt
Bryan, Clifford J.	34766271	T/Sgt
Burgess, Robert E.	0752603'	2/Lt
Bull, Edmund P.	12220410	Sgt
Burns, Loris E.	36200825	Sgt
Burns, Robert L.	19175110	S/Sgt
Burns, Thomas E.	34314384	S/Sgt
Byers, Paul R.	15121806	Sgt
Caldwell, C.W. Jr.	34601630	S/Sgt
Callahan, Francis E.	0690365	2/Lt
Carman, William R.	36475684	S/Sgt
Carmack, Walter R.	16149074	S/Sgt
Carney, Charles J.	0700699	2/Lt
Castle, William J. Jr.	19161850	S/Sgt
Cay, Raymond L. Jr.	14083082	S/Sgt
Cetwinski, Myron P.	16145712	S/Sgt
Chapman, Maurice E.	36406966	S/Sgt
Chappell, William S. Jr.	18090460	
Check, Earl E.	02005832	2/Lt
Cheek, William C.	13117162	Sgt
Chiancone, Jim V.	15340373	T/Sgt
Chilcoat, James M.	0688917	2/Lt
Chovancak, Edward V.	0.688918	2/Lt
Clements, Claude M.	20367977	Sgt
Coburn, Olaf A. Jr.	31012958	T/Sgt
Coffenberry, B.R. Jr.	0692372	1/Lt
Coffin, Bruce P.	31289065	T/Sgt
Cofield, Curtis H.	0383708	Maj
Cole, Willis W.	39407665	S/Sgt
Conard, Ray H.	0429609	Capt
Connor, Edgar J.	12206364	Sgt
Conway, Grover G.	15016537	T/Sgt
Corban, James J.	33072963	S/Sgt
Corwin, James A.	12186545	T/Sgt
Cozza, Salvatore E.	31299728	S/Sgt
Crall, Robert O.	0687469	2/Lt
Crown, Richard L.	0695631	2/Lt
Crumpler, Thomas P.	33528007	S/Sgt
Crupi, Vincent N.	0688510	2/Lt
Cullinan, Paul W.	32549566	S/Sgt
Cummings, Vernon F.	36280103	T/Sgt
Cunniff, Peter M.	11117354	T/Sgt
Czeslawski, Raymond C.	16003633	T/Sgt
Daniel, Henry B. Jr.	02069661	2/LT

Dash, Leonard C.	13170728	T/Sgt
Davis, J.B.	18098761	T/Sgt
Decusati, Joseph	11103083	Sgt
Dejarnette, Joe A.	0742139	1/Lt
Deleon, Manuel C.	18060438	Sgt
Deleon, Vernon C.	39044447	S/Sgt
Dempsey, Earl W.	33627823	Sgt
Dieckhoff, Fred H.	17072410	Sgt
Diederich, Raymond J.	36408229	S/Sgt
Dierdorf, Oren W.	35560884	S/Sgt
Dietrich, James A.	33708562	Sgt
Dick, James B. Jr.	19181027	T/Sgt
Dineen, Maurice A.	0688935	2/Lt
Dock, Marvin L.	0738828	2/Lt
Dolin, Irving	0688178	2/Lt
Donaway, Morton F.	T.63389	F/O
Doninger, Fred A.	15113233	T/Sgt
Duncan, Lawrence M.	0828981	1/Lt
Durborow, John B.	0811037	2/Lt
Easterling, William T.	0805792	2/Lt
Edgett, Albert H.	37228561	S/Sgt
Ege, Arthur E.	16003433	S/Sgt
Eicher, Lawrence L.	37536932	S/Sgt
Eisenbach, Robert W.	0760269	2/Lt
Ellingson, Joelbert W.	0826898	2/Lt
Ellis, Lewis C. Jr.	0687472	S/Lt
Emerson, James F.	0886039	1/Lt
Emmons, Rufus	20452188	S/Sgt
England, Walter R.	34776142	Sgt
Entrikin, George S.	16054012	S/Sgt
Erker, Edward C.	11081850	S/Sgt
Eubank, John P. Jr.	33599361	T/Sgt
Fallacaro, Dominic	0688518	2/Lt
Farmer, Charles R.	32580459	T/Sgt
Farrell, Edward J.	0690642	2/Lt
Felbarth, Peter	16112428	Sgt
Filipiak, Edmund C.	0717022	2/Lt
Finkle, Melvin	9688693	2/Lt
Fisher, Fred L. Jr.	35527280	Sgt
Flatt, Roy F.	0756210	2/Lt
Foster, James B. Jr.	18029956	Sgt
Franke, Carl F.	0688695	2/Lt
Freed, Warren D.	0701062	2/Lt
Friedhaber, John H.	0826907	2/Lt
Fuller, Harrel W.	18183278	T/Sgt
Gallagher, Joseph F.	13029717	S/Sgt
Garrett, Mack O.	38244011	T/Sgt
Gengler, Frank T.	0693033	1/Lt
Gilbert, James G. Jr.	0833518	2/Lt
Gilbreath, Ray	0743441	2/Lt
Gill, Hiram A.	34531052	Sgt
Gilles, Glenn E.	17029033	S/Sgt
Gilligan, John E.	0772164	2/Lt
Ginstrom, Arthur W.	31385451	S/Sgt
Goff, Kyle R.	0688696	2/Lt
Golbski, James	17068513	S/Sgt
Gordon, Fred	0809351	2/Lt
Grady, William C.	17068065	T/Sgt
Granko, George R.	13128056	T/Sgt
Gray, George A.	17155974	S/Sgt
Green, James N.	16061207	S/Sgt
Gricas, William J.	33037722	S/Sgt
Gustafson, Swan E.	0761080	2/Lt
Hall, Robert Jr.	0814300	2/Lt
Halliburton, J.G. 3rd	0690648	2/Lt
Hamilton, James W.W.	0681398	1/Lt
Hankins, William E.	14181812	T/Sgt
Hannon, Joseph P.	0707444	2/Lt
Harbin, Frederick E. Jr.	35583089	S/Sgt
Harris, John H.	0688974	2/Lt
Hathorne, Clyde	34279645	T/Sgt
Hauser, William A.	37217578	S/Sgt
Hebert, Alvin L.	18150304	S/Sgt
Heike, Martin C.	36622254	T/Sgt
Hendricks, John C.	36581016	Sgt
Hendrix, Clarence L. Jr.	38405695	Sgt
Hensley, Edward J.	14168640	S/Sgt
Hensley, Edwin J.	14168683	S/Sgt

Hills, Kenyon G.	11102662	S/Sgt
Hitzfield, Charles W.	0714702	2/Lt
Hokanson, David O.	0801467	2/Lt
Holbert, Rowland F.J.	0433047	1/Lt
Holden, Robert W.	11110883	T/Sgt
Hooper, Allison L.	33609561	S/Sgt
Horgan, Daniel A.	0814320	2/Lt
Horn, Abraham I.	12164163	T/Sgt
House, Matthew J.K.	0701603	2/Lt
Hovenesian, John E.	31390259	S/Sgt
Hurley, Charles M.	34678984	S/Sgt
Hynes, John J.	6979723	T/Sgt
Indovina, Louis P.	12208096	S/Sgt
Ingram, Richard N.	0745569	2/Lt
Isakson, Carl	0715224	2/Lt
Ives, Rodney B.	0683826	1/Lt
Jacobs, David M.	T62924	F/O
Johnson, Earl L.	0713962	2/Lt
Johnson, Sidney A.	39098477	S/Sgt
Jones, James R.	0811091	2/Lt
Jones, Willard P.	34355548	S/Sgt
Judd, Alan C.	0.821032	1/Lt
Jurka, John	36626906	Cpl
Kaplan, Arthur	32612462	T/Sgt
Kasitz, Kenneth K.	37480958	S/Sgt
Katz, Saul	38387437	S/Sgt
Keathley, Thomas H.	17159588	T/Sgt
Keefe, Thomas W.	31248226	S/Sgt
Keefer, Edwin T.	T135765	F/O
Kemp, Edward K.	0329382	Maj
Kiner, Martin L.	33243195	T/Sgt
Kloeppel, Paul E.	0745698	1/Lt
Klyap, Harry J.	0769141	2/Lt
Koch, William A.	36622412	S/Sgt
Kulesza, Casimir W.	33599888	S/Sgt
Kuzelka, George F. Jr.	0812612	1/Lt
Labin, James L. Jr.	35867431	Sgt
Lampassi, Adamo G.J.	11130840	Sgt
Lamy, Arthur F.	0694385	1/Lt
Larriverre, Clyde R.	19182542	Sgt
Larson, Alfred W.	33598302	S/Sgt
Larson, Willard R.	0685251	2/Lt
Laughlin, John W. Jr.	0688367	2/Lt
Lawry, Donald C.	0690455	2/Lt
Layman, George S.	38404158	S/Sgt
Layser, Lester W.	13144771	S/Sgt
Leach, Harold W. Jr.	11035891	S/Sgt
League, William A.	0811098	2/Lt
Lefever, Frank W.	39264617	S/Sgt
Lehman, Josiah E.	34263814	S/Sgt
Leighton, Harold A.J.	32833504	Sgt
Lien, Alivin	0661507	Capt
Lillibridge, Wayne T.	35420842	S/Sgt
Litton, Frank J.	17089345	Sgt
Lofton, William E.	0699686	1/Lt
Logan, Boyd W.	18192910	Sgt
Logerfo, Peter S.	32824706	S/Sgt
Lovell, Endicott R.J.	0663531	1/Lt
Luciano, Salvatore A.	11130075	S/Sgt
Lueke, Francis C.	37628745	S/Sgt
Mackenzie, John D.	39687667	S/Sgt
Mackey, Maurice P.	18183067	S/Sgt
Martin, William C.	35563471	T/Sgt
Mayer, Frank A.	13027837	S/Sgt
McCook, Robert S.	0811417	2/Lt
McCormick, Arthur Jr.	0689479	2/Lt
McCormick, Robert W.	0834847	2/Lt
McGue, Jason H.	18084195	S/Sgt
McKee D. Robert	0.808872	2/Lt
McKee, James F.	34645430	T/Sgt
McKenzie, John E.	0701259	2/Lt
McKinney, John F.	18118550	T/Sgt
McNally, Stephen G.	0755032	2/Lt
Meek, Herman J.	0745140	2/Lt
Mercurio, Robert T.	12226249	S/Sgt
Meyers, James J.	6909552	S/Sgt
Milano, Joe	39193565	S/Sgt

Miller, David H.	0.743626	2/Lt
Mills, Dean M.	0813552	1/Lt
Mishaga, Frank	T123187	F/O
Mitchell, Elmer R. Jr.	0827906	2/Lt
Mitchell, John T.	13119139	S/Sgt
Moore, James E.	0755732	2/Lt
Morgan, Thomas H. Jr.	34504322	S/Sgt
Morris, Lonnie O.	18154535	T/Sgt
Morrow, Cletus E.	0755231	1/Lt
Mourer, Ralph L.	37341296	S/Sgt
Munsey, James S.	0686583	1/Lt
Murray, Thomas F. 3rd	33668217	S/Sgt
Myers, Jack T.	13134490	S/Sgt
Naumoff, Walter	6877612	S/Sgt
Neily, Robert W.	39277430	Sgt
Neumunz, Alfred R.	0723658	2/Lt
Nichols, Don E.	37412148	S/Sgt
Nichols, Donald G.	32731104	Sgt
Nichel, Hans	02065815	2/Lt
Nolan, Thomas E.	19175010	Sgt
Norton, Elwin S. Jr.	0719135	2/Lt
Nosal, Thomas E.	31313046	S/Sgt
Nurczyk, Raymond M.	02069096	2/Lt
Oakes, Harold G.	11015918	S/Sgt
Okane, Thomas J. Jr.	12086771	Sgt
Olsen, Kenneth U.	13200766	S/Sgt
Parker, Fred V.	0735812	2/Lt
Parker, John C.	16195394	Sgt
Patsey, Thomas L.	33614546	S/Sgt
Perrin, Robert L. Jr.	13172108	Sgt
Pessica, Charles J.	17067397	S/Sgt
Peters, Milford F.	37651155	Sgt
Peterson, George B.	17155279	Sgt
Peterson, Paul W. Jr.	02064314	2/Lt
Pfeifer, Ellis T.	13107274	S/Sgt
Phillips, James E.	34645238	S/Sgt
Pierce, Don B.	0755195	2/Lt
Pilcher, James E.	14025137	T/Sgt
Pittman, James J.	34701152	S/Sgt
Plyler, Freeman W.	14196484	S/Sgt
Poladian, Leo J.	0735920	2/Lt
Polokoff, Harold R.	02073211	2/Lt
Portella, Antonio R.	39858829	Sgt
Powell, William H. Jr.	0830916	2/Lt
Prazenica, Joseph F.	33300142	S/Sgt
Prudhon, Robert J.	0711472	2/Lt
Pryor, Roy L.	19176551	T/Sgt
Quigley, Howard M.	17061010	S/Sgt
Rakouska, Robert L.	36659512	Sgt
Ramirez, Manuel A.	19109222	S/Sgt
Reed, Wallace A.	37498459	S/Sgt
Redman, James N.	39701651	S/Sgt
Reintgen, Edward L.	13086963	Sgt
Richards, Gwillam	33873189	T/Sgt
Richardson, John N.J.	33634715	Sgt
Rilett, Joseph K.	36452147	Sgt
Robertson, Donald E.	37381791	S/Sgt
Robinson, McCalvin Jr.	14105531	S/Sgt
Robinson, Murray D.	02063476	2/Lt
Rogers, Chancy A.	36809373	S/Sgt
Rogers, Floyd R.	14124788	S/Sgt
Rollins, Robert G.	0556606	1/Lt
Rosamond, David R.	20272638	Sgt
Ross, Charles F.	18171319	S/Sgt
Ross, Jack	0.809730	2/Lt
Rottle, George H.	39183947	S/Sgt
Roy, Sandford G.	14134581	T/Sgt
Rubin, Malcolm H.	0780364	2/Lt
Rudloff, Charles M.	0811250	2/Lt
Salihar, Robert F.	36352822	T/Sgt
Sallee, Frank E.	0769182	1/Lt
Sanford, Frederick K.	0692079	2/Lt
Sang, Donald W.	32767945	Sgt
Santora, Peter	12180353	S/Sgt
Schmidt, Robert L.	0716965	2/Lt
Schulz, Herbert R.	36806809	S/Sgt

Seed, Walton T.	39191421	S/Sgt
Sharp, James E.	32589454	S/Sgt
Sherer, John G.	0679668	1/Lt
Sills, Joseph F.	33568877	T/Sgt
Skidgell, John W.	0663672	1/Lt
Sliff, Donald R.	6555937	S/Sgt
Smith, Dean R.	18148306	S/Sgt
Soine, Elmer T.	35635050	S/Sgt
Spies, John A.	16051635	S/Sgt
Stanchfield, Milton A.	0810965	2/Lt
Starbuck, Willie L.	17073731	S/Sgt
Stathes, Ernest G.	0712356	2/Lt
Steele, Dewey D.	42023252	Sgt
Stern, Martin	0743530	2/Lt
Stevenson, Robert L.	0713901	2/Lt
Streeter, Lee H.	0691068	2/Lt
Stump, Max E.	0718979	1/Lt
Surowiec, Henry	32888680	T/Sgt
Suter, Godfrey B.	13093849	S/Sgt
Swan, Maurice L.	37654230	S/Sgt
Swigert, Robert R.	0792174	1/Lt
Thomas, Walter J.	19011555	S/Sgt
Tobin, Patrick D. Jr.	0746483	1/Lt
Todd, Charles D.	0716996	2/Lt
Toll, Carl W.	16134597	Sgt
Townsend, Barney L.	0.687784	2/Lt
Trapani, Eugene	39556171	S/Sgt
Truax, Reginald H.	34788082	Sgt
Tye, Francis R.	0737902	2/Lt
Tyree, James E.	33648634	Sgt
Urschalitz, Norbert A.	0686514	2/Lt
Vartanian, Vanig	02064687	2/Lt
Villalobos, Jose M.	39566022	S/Sgt
Vincze, Frank J.	6941171	Sgt
Vittori, Quinto B.	36559483	S/Sgt
Volkman, Thomas F.	0707453	2/Lt
Walker, James B.	18127901	S/Sgt
Wallace, David D.	0811267	2/Lt
Ward, Russell A.	0748047	1/Lt
Warnke, Harold H.	0927676	2/Lt
Watson, John A.	16151240	S/Sgt
Watson, Walter F.	0.687725	2/Lt
Watts, Lawrence E.	19176176	S/Sgt
Webber, Elton Q.	12302297	M/Sgt
Weidlich, Roy H.	12049894	S/Sgt
Wells, Jay	0666388	1/Lt
Wertz, Trall W.	13089659	T/Sgt
Wheeler, James W.	0717002	2/Lt
White, Arthur E.	0811480	2/Lt
Whitehurst, C.S. Jr.	13119908	S/Sgt
Whitus, Albert J.	36586907	S/Sgt
Williams, Hubert W.	18098608	Sgt
Williams, Robert B.	11008440	T/Sgt
Williamson, Billy L.	38395737	S/Sgt
Wright, Donald E.	31257480	S/Sgt
Yeary, Hubert	33521159	S/Sgt
Yoder, Gerald B.	37440169	S/Sgt

458th Bomb Group

Abshire, Wilbert	18171009	S/Sgt
Adams, Dewey R. Jr.	35682763	Sgt
Adamson, John D.	0.739644	2/Lt
Adkins, Jimmie K.	37505143	S/Sgt
Akin, Arthur C. Jr.	0.710395	2/Lt
Amlung, Robert F.	T.137262	F/O
Amon, Harold E.	0698859	2/Lt
Anderson, Lewis L.	0.2072401	2/Lt
Arnold, Richard E.	15116810	S/Sgt
Ash, Merlin T.	39278839	T/Sgt
Ausman, Homer F.	T.061267	F/O
Bail, Alex C.	33671177	S/Sgt
Bair, Eugene A.	33498514	S/Sgt
Bambick, Lewis T.	0717317	2/Lt
Barnicle, Francis A. Jr.	31304867	S/Sgt
Barton, Kenneth C.	0663831	1/Lt
Bechtel, Russell J.	0704452	1/Lt
Bengry, Harry S. Jr.	0.811316	2/Lt
Bingaman, Robert C.	13092759	S/Sgt
Blednick, Leonard W.	01011890	1/Lt
Bloomberg, Paul	0717031	2/Lt
Bockelman, Edward H.	36659687	Sgt
Bogusch, Jack L.	0.24747	Capt
Boorse, Allen Jr.	T062414	F/O
Bourquin, Hubert D.	35471974	Sgt
Bowman, Wesley C.	34678095	Sgt
Brewer, Homer C.	15065248	S/Sgt
Bryant, Joseph C.	0771659	1/Lt
Butler, James C.	34664373	S/Sgt
Burke, James H.	13035338	S/Sgt
Butsch, James A.	17079921	Sgt
Byrnes, Martin J.	12186397	S/Sgt
Caffey, Jerome T.	34612556	Sgt
Callahan, Charles W.	T.122775	F/O
Campbell, George L. Jr.	32424712	T/Sgt
Carlstrum, Chester R.	19186336	S/Sgt
Carriero, Leonard J.	32810749	Sgt
Carter, Charlie W.	14167672	S/Sgt
Casey, William F.	33632023	Sgt
Caudell, Frederick M.	34674937	Sgt
Centola, Edward O.	0706697	1/Lt
Chapman, Rollin E.	35224326	Sgt
Charles, Lorinzo D.	37494596	S/Sgt
Ciotti, Enrico R.	33787934	S/Sgt
Cisek, Edward W.	11115616	Sgt
Cleary, John J.	19086604	Sgt
Clark, Richard B.	19019740	S/Sgt
Clark, Robert V.	18109267	Sgt
Clayborn, John A.	0.2065134	2/Lt
Coburn, Harold	0.2056553	2/Lt
Corlito, Anthony J.	31203718	T/Sgt
Couch, Robert G. Jr.	0672335	2/Lt
Craddock, Harold C.	15338346	S/Sgt
Craig, Robert A.	0697769	1/Lt
Curland, William H.	0.760589	2/Lt
Czernecki, Edvard V.	16118978	Sgt
Danielson, Wayne B.	15333425	S/Sgt
Darden, Wesley R. Jr.	34708338	Sgt
Daskam, Charles S.	T.122613	F/O
Davis, Charles E.	0.712775	2/Lt
Davis, Donald E.	16075299	S/Sgt
Daw, Clarence C.	14163539	S/Sgt
Dempsey, Gordon A.	12136682	Sgt
Denton, Walter R.	39320527	T/Sgt
Depuy, William C.	32382904	T/Sgt
Detty, Max L.	35215912	Sgt
Diehl, Stanley E.	0718579	2/Lt
Dodgen, Robert M.	34573258	Sgt
Doelling, Lawrence L.	0.768482	2/Lt
Dolce, Louis R.	32929744	S/Sgt
Donahue, Jack F.	37499710	Sgt
Dooley, Ralph J.	0821971	2/Lt
Douroumes, George J.	37681450	S/Sgt
Downer, Roy H.	18098007	Sgt
Drahos, Victor C.	35913669	Sgt
Duffy, James J.	35683062	S/Sgt
Duke, William A.	0.825602	2/Lt
Dulmage, Paul L.	12080395	S/Sgt
Dunaway, Earl C.	18191706	Sgt
Egan, John P.	0694863	2/Lt
Felthouse, Frank G.	19110388	Sgt
Fiebiger, Raymond C.	19087765	S/Sgt
Finn, Robert T.	12121403	Sgt
Fitzgerald, William	0698879	2/Lt
Flaugher, Harold J.	35791387	S/Sgt
Found, Howard E.	37493308	S/Sgt
Frazer, Charles Jr.	18232071	Sgt
Frederick, William R.	0705924	2/Lt
Freeman, Billy L.	38269438	Sgt
Funderburk, Marion E.	34649689	T/Sgt
Fuqua, William J.R.	0817192	2/Lt
Gabay, Eugene T.	32825102	Sgt
Garcia, Baldamore	39289589	Sgt
Garner, James D.	02056374	2/Lt
Gast, John A.	36448807	S/Sgt
Gebhart, George F.	13096043	Sgt
Gibson, Rex M.	02061679	2/Lt
Gibson, Samuel T.	0795456	1/Lt
Giesen, Charles A.	0764647	1/Lt
Gilbert, Cecil A.	18123941	S/Sgt
Gittelman, Bernard F.	13078789	Sgt
Glass, Tommy	38202709	T/Sgt
Goldstein, Harry	12038179	Sgt
Gorman, Paul E.	0723515	2/Lt
Gozora, Rudolph G.	42010515	Sgt
Griffith, Leland G.	0743236	Capt
Gruner, Leslie J.	T131834	F/O
Halsted, Maynard T.	17155618	S/Sgt
Hammel, Gerard B.	12121125	Sgt
Hammer, Raymond C.	16065811	S/Sgt
Hammersmith, Otto B. Jr.	0688669	2/Lt
Hardeman, Glen O.	39197606	T/Sgt
Hart, Addison E.	12082020	T/Sgt
Hartle, Deral D.	37405503	S/Sgt
Hecht, Leo W. Jr.	0832140	2/Lt
Herman, Fred B.	T.002118	F/O
Hendon, Edward C.	34681404	S/Sgt
Herzik, Frank W.	0663519	1/Lt
Hetzler, Harold W.	T.185414	F/O
Hiebert, John E.	39265138	Sgt
Hier, Henry C.	0698012	2/Lt
Hightower, John S.	0811665	2/Lt
Hoffstot, Harvey L.	33420062	S/Sgt
Hoskins, Charles P.	31296463	Sgt
Howell, Harold H.	0747418	2/Lt
Hulse, John N.	0752859	2/Lt
Humke, Herbert H.	0822170	2/Lt
Hunt, Daniel F. Jr.	0823592	2/Lt
Hunter, Raymond L.	15043105	T/Sgt
Hyland, Vincent P.	32261418	Sgt
Imundo, Rocco L.	32337250	Sgt
Jewett, Allen K.	0928696	2/Lt
Jones, Harold N.	38435950	S/Sgt
Jones, Johnie J.	38106801	S/Sgt
Jones, Russell B.	17156534	S/Sgt
Kamenski, Mitchell A.	32484628	Sgt
Kendall, William M.	0695597	2/Lt
Kesselheim, Howard	32881226	Pfc
Key, Howell D.	38213692	Cpl
Kilikowski, George T.	36719296	S/Sgt
Kingsley, Paul E.	02045233	2/Lt
Kirby, John W.	34543643	S/Sgt
Kirby, Robert H.	33723443	Sgt
Kluck, Allen R.	17078898	S/Sgt
Koehn, George J.	0699679	2/Lt
Konarski, Anthony L.	32012519	Sgt
Labbee, Carroll J.	31325501	S/Sgt
Lack, Jesse H.	0694883	2/Lt
Lacock, Russell J.	18031748	Sgt
Lademan, Marvin J.	16160272	Sgt
Lambert, Robert S.	T.1535	F/O
Larsen, Lincoln A.	0805847	1/Lt
Leake, Robert L.	33733468	Sgt
Lee, Carl P.	14123992	T/Sgt
Lenart, Casimer P.	0828009	2/Lt
Lent, Leon B. Jr.	0819834	2/Lt
Levine, Robert L.	0717085	2/Lt
Levron, Emile J.	38382568	Pfc
Lobo, Howard J.	0815179	2/Lt
Long, Grover M.	T.2599	F/O
Lorusso, Albert J.	0716487	2/Lt
Lowman, Willard L.	14092318	Sgt
Lowry, Richard G.	35599337	Sgt
Luna, Jose J.	38583501	Sgt
Lund, Wallace D.	37678657	Sgt
Lunsford, Lewis W.	35797784	Sgt
Lynde, Howard W.	17024585	S/Sgt
Macy, Paul L.	35902661	Sgt
Maki Tono, J.	0711451	2/Lt
Marburger, Joseph O.	0707955	1/Lt
Marino, Michael F.	34503062	Sgt
Marr, Glen W. Jr.	0827872	2/Lt
Marr, Westford E.	11042316	Sgt
Marshall, Melvin C.	0752764	2/Lt
Marty, George B.	39118992	T/Sgt
May, Charles E. III	12226449	Sgt
McCarthy, Richard O.	32745523	S/Sgt
McCrary, Delbert E.	0699434	2/Lt
McGlynn, Harold R.	15076042	S/Sgt
McHargue, Magnus V.	34354603	T/Sgt
McKenna, Francis X.	13153383	T/Sgt
McLaughlin, Norman	33595732	Sgt
McMains, Jesse L.	0683737	2/Lt
McNeely, Donald J.	0712868	1/Lt
McNeely, John D.	38511715	Sgt
McSwain, Rufus G.	0836898	2/Lt
Miller, Clayton L.	37314739	S/Sgt
Mire, Edward J. Jr.	38495346	Sgt
Moleck, Stephen T.	13172193	S/Sgt
Monroe, Archibald B. Jr.	0.834852	2/Lt
Moodie, David W.	13082005	Sgt
Moore, Henry S. Jr.	34288034	Sgt
Morrone, Peter F.	31324040	Sgt
Morrow, Virgil O.	37231073	Sgt
Moses, Richard L.	0810111	2/Lt
Mott, Robert D.	38412820	S/Sgt
Murray, James R.	35274255	Sgt
Musa, James H.	12199353	T/Sgt
Nabe, Edgar C.	38400028	Sgt
Nelson, Harold A.	39693919	T/Sgt
Nelson, Oscar B.	19030249	S/Sgt
Nemeth, James	32450063	S/Sgt
Newcomb, Glen E.	17110595	T/Sgt
Newell, Harold L.	12171334	S/Sgt
Nicolai, Louis	0749733	2/Lt
Nietzel, William E.	12143376	Pfc
Noblitt, Charles G.	0811874	1/Lt
Oder, Clifford L.	34407107	Sgt
O'Hara, John B.	0699322	2/Lt
Palmer, Robert A.	37572343	Sgt
Paolella, Michael A.	35926411	Sgt
Pappas, Mike R.	39694042	S/Sgt
Parkinson, Sterlin W.	14056683	S/Sgt
Pearce, William R.	12158599	T/Sgt
Peckham, Charles H. Jr.	0834870	2/Lt
Peters, Neil A.J.	0747178	2/Lt
Phillips, John A.	32494276	S/Sgt
Piasecki, Henry J.	0751840	2/Lt
Picard, Norman J.	31286410	Sgt
Prentice, Clarence M.	38022058	Sgt
Quirk, Don P.	35169768	S/Sgt
Rasmussen, Stanley G.	36193532	S/Sgt
Raughley, Harry S.	32751782	S/Sgt
Reeves, Ellis E.	14142633	T/Sgt
Reiley, Glen V.	13048158	S/Sgt
Richey, Earl S.	39125139	T/Sgt
Rickert, William F.	37659663	S/Sgt
Root, Joseph S. Jr.	T.001545	F/O
Rosenthal, Sidney	0688403	2/Lt
Rupp, Allan C.	33935486	Sgt
Russell, Everett E.	36612622	S/Sgt
Sasserson, Stanley G.	0.820071	2/Lt
Schlipf, Vincent P.	02063481	2/Lt
Schmidt, Frederick	36739281	Sgt
Schramm, John H.	31254148	Sgt
Schuman, George W.	0743952	1/Lt
Seale, Thomas F.	34810167	Sgt
Seaman, Paul K.	0904197	2/Lt
Seymour, Ulysses G.	3214373	S/Sgt
Sheren, Sidney	32818617	S/Sgt
Silverman, Arthur	11113807	S/Sgt
Smith, Leroy	32391649	S/Sgt
Smith, Richard B.	34582950	S/Sgt
Soesbe, James P.	0716983	2/Lt
Sonnefeld, Louis J.	T.001745	F/O
Sowles, Edwin E.	37443523	S/Sgt
Spaven, George N. Jr.	0.531628	1/Lt
Staub, Fred L.	0690870	2/Lt
Stawiarski, Harry	0694899	2/Lt
Steele, James	37523322	S/Sgt
Steanrd, Charles E.J.	11071476	Sgt
Stiles, Fred E.	15334471	Sgt
Stodden, Richard B.	0812327	S/Lt
Stroup, Joseph M.	0745849	1/Lt

Szarko, Joseph E.	0816001	2/Lt
Szoke, Joseph J.	01049366	1/Lt
Tamboer, Harry L.	32557920	S/Sgt
Thorpe, William L.	0812008	2/Lt
Tomlinson, Raymond F.	39126276	Sgt
Torkelson, Roy A.	19070665	S/Sgt
Torres, William E.	0716780	1/Lt
Totten, David R.	0.2059134	2/Lt
Tripp, Max S.	39911035	Sgt
Tucker, John R.	0767914	2/Lt
Vacha, Joseph J.	0716998	2/Lt
Vlahos, Charles	32630849	S/Sgt
Von Bergen, Ralph W.	37341753	S/Sgt
Wadsworth, Paul A.	38345079	S/Sgt
Wagner, Theodore F.	0811473	2/Lt
Waldrep, Preston M.J.	14072172	S/Sgt
Wall, Charles D.	0713030	2/Lt
Ward, Robert L.	34776546	Sgt
Webster, William A.	0699283	2/Lt
Wiehage, Frederick G.	37619122	Sgt
Wilson, Marvin T.	14098082	S/Sgt
Wishinski, Ben	33486153	S/Sgt
Wood, Leonard E.	15313758	Sgt
Zlotorzynski, Raymond J.	36896451	Sgt
Zonker, Jack B.	36455971	S/Sgt

466th Bomb Group

Abbott, Robert R.	35553545	S/Sgt
Adams, Warren B.	37380320	S/Sgt
Adler, Sheldon L.	0820188	2/Lt
Akens, Ernest L.	38451507	S/Sgt
Allender, Warren M.	0747186	1/Lt
Aloisi, Alfred	36035236	Sgt
Amich, Aleck A.	36267435	S/Sgt
Archer, John S. Jr.	0809346	1/Lt
Bailey, Carl E.	0691860	2/Lt
Bailey, Quinton E.	0705285	2/Lt
Barrett, Jerome	12157563	T/Sgt
Barrett, Lewis L.	37499930	S/Sgt
Bass, James T.	14020893	T/Sgt
Baus, Paul Jr.	0773284	2/Lt
Bedford, Howard E.	T.125801	F/O
Bednarski, John	37175101	S/Sgt
Bell, Thomas L.	0817617	1/Lt
Belleville, Earl W.	16115324	S/Sgt
Benagh, William S.	14161884	T/Sgt
Bender, Fred G.	15014464	Sgt
Boles, Gerald D.	39275720	S/Sgt
Bosserman, Walter D.	13048202	S/Sgt
Boulter, Roland C.	0.698649	2/Lt
Bowen, Walter M.	0710552	2/Lt
Brand, Gilley T.	0742671	2/Lt
Brennan, John C.	12206828	S/Sgt
Brennan, Robert H.	0927713	2/Lt
Brill, Paul	0692285	2/Lt
Brookshier, Kenneth G.	38395408	T/Sgt
Brown, Robert E.	0691714	2/Lt
Brosey, Paul W.	13095343	T/Sgt
Brunner, Joseph J.	0682287	2/Lt
Bryant, Ralph S.	0437192	Capt
Burke, Joseph R.	36398227	S/Sgt
Burleson, Clarence A. Jr.	18109940	S/Sgt
Byers, Clay	0673769	1/Lt
Call, Donald	35537880	T/Sgt
Callahan, John E.	36857228	Sgt
Carney,Hall G.	T.121945	F/O
Caskey, Loran D.	12168685	Sgt
Cassada, Kenneth	14161673	Sgt
Cave, Elmore Jr.	0820717	2/Lt
Cavern, Clinton H.	0686987	2/Lt
Charbonneau, Paul E.	37546605	T/Sgt
Chavis, Thomas P.	0722414	2/Lt
Childress, John M.	14012009	Pvt
Church, Frank C.	37503992	S/Sgt
Ciaramitaro, Frank	36577178	S/Sgt
Clark, Richard H.	0700860	1/Lt
Cockey, John O. Jr.	0433478	Maj
Cockrill, Elijah L.J.	0699140	2/Lt
Connors, Leonard T.	31248530	T/Sgt
Conway, John F. Jr.	02077206	2/Lt
Copley, Burnis	15170553	S/Sgt
Coultry, Douglas F.	39571478	S/Sgt
Council, Robert H.	0768008	2/Lt
Cowan, Glenn R.	35366956	Sgt
Crawford, James F.	14074517	Sgt
Crowley, Terence H.	0716371	2/Lt
Cunningham, Richard H.	31355789	Sgt
Cushenberry, Ivan L.	37239598	T/Sgt
Davis, James L.	34118321	S/Sgt
Damiani, Joseph F.E.	0.817635	2/Lt
Deck, Frederick J. Jr.	0823816	2/Lt
Delhagen, Frederick E.	32571240	Sgt
Diamond, Louis A.	01297007	2/Lt
Dickerman, Paul	0822395	2/Lt
Didomenico, John R.	0542110	2/Lt
Dillard, Patrick H.	18242486	Sgt
Dobkin, Milton M.	0716383	2/Lt
Douglas, Seaton T.	T.125539	F/O
Dragoon, Samuel	12041050	T/Sgt
Dunham, Marcus V.	0702392	2/Lt
Dwyer, William R.	0678523	1/Lt
Eaton, James R.	14147637	Sgt
Eclov, Claire W.	17113343	S/Sgt
Elliott, Charles R.	18040993	Sgt
English, Albert W.	16122131	Sgt
English, Ross K.	13134647	T/Sgt
Erdman, Roland H.	37652358	Sgt
Estes, Samuel E.	38563944	S/Sgt
Estle, Dale R.	37652527	S/Sgt
Evanoff, Earl A.	15354078	S/Sgt
Faires, Wallace	18106250	S/Sgt
Falk, Robert I.	32677413	Sgt
Farrington, Richard J.	0713376	1/Lt
Feeley, Augustus R.	0716396	2/Lt
Fein, Howard	0685822	2/Lt
Feltz, Ernest F.	35552186	Sgt
Fike, David S.	0746069	2/Lt
Fleming, Ralph W.	33633153	Sgt
Flower, Owen C.	39256481	Sgt
Foley, Thomas J.	0829614	2/Lt
Fortin, Joseph C.	31288971	T/Sgt
Forton, Stephen W. Jr.	16064435	S/Sgt
Fountain, Robert H.	35579199	S/Sgt
Foushee, William C.	0687576	1/Lt
Fowler, William E.	37558091	T/Sgt
French, John J.	0686143	1/Lt
Gardner, Gene	39910035	S/Sgt
Garner, Noble F.	18046832	T/Sgt
Garret, Robert L.	0.803596	2/Lt
Gates, John L.	35761330	S/Sgt
Gautreau, Robert D.	11114896	S/Sgt
Gilbert, Floyd A.	35467761	T/Sgt
Giorchino, Edward B.	02044436	Capt
Good, Orville S.	14182501	Sgt
Goodhand, George M.	12225449	S/Sgt
Goodner, Howard G.	34726638	T/Sgt
Goodwin, William M.J.	0703237	2/Lt
Gordon, John F.	35508372	S/Sgt
Gordon, Robert G.	0776283	2/Lt
Gorky, Herman	31281616	S/Sgt
Gossling, Walter B. Jr.	13199972	Sgt
Gottschalk, Verner A.	18198159	S/Sgt
Graboski, George F.	12090093	Sgt
Gregory, Robert W.	13093280	Sgt
Griffin, Donal C.	0437329	1/Lt
Grover, George F.	16066436	S/Sgt
Gum, Robert A.	0808989	2/Lt
Hain, Wilbur R.	33187738	Sgt
Haire, Jack C.	39905122	S/Sgt
Hammond, Phillip R.	0699611	2/Lt
Handy, Grover L.	13103779	Sgt
Hanlon, Fearon J.	20753112	Sgt
Harris, Homer Y.	0801596	1/Lt
Harris, Leon F.	02062661	2/Lt
Hartley, Joseph Jr.	0811377	1/Lt
Haseman, Harry E.	0820758	2/Lt
Hatfield, Orlie A. Jr.	0682117	2/Lt
Hawkins, Arnold F.	17129099	Sgt
Hazen, Fred P.	0.692001	2/Lt
Hendrickson, Harrold H.	16130535	Sgt
Hennig, Raymond M.	18217568	T/Sgt
Hergenhan, William N.	39690153	S/Sgt
Hittner, Stanley T.	16153472	T/Sgt
Hochheiser, Bernard	32014067	S/Sgt
Horton, Gerrard	18176834	Sgt
Hudson, Phillip	32187019	T/Sgt
Hughes, Thomas F. Jr.	32473824	S/Sgt
Hurst, Leroy F.	0769129	2/Lt
Igoe, Peter P.	0712143	2/Lt
Ivey, Teddy F.	0759811	2/Lt
Jackson, William L.	33240758	S/Sgt
Jaeger, William C.	12120058	T/Sgt
Jaffee, John J.	15374197	Sgt
Johnson James H.	0750996	2/Lt
Jones, Tice L.	18194593	S/Sgt
Jordan, Sandlin J. Jr.	38340583	Sgt
Joubert, Clifford L. Jr.	19139967	Sgt
Julian, William M. Jr.	14160074	S/Sgt
Jungers, Eugene D.	37656676	Sgt
Kack, Melvin J.	39272358	T/Sgt
Karatkiewicz, John L.	33346452	T/Sgt
Kaspshak, Edward F.	0811824	2/Lt
Kaushep, Otto M.	33567642	T/Sgt
Kayden, Frank	13084055	T/Sgt
Kayser, Forest E.	35644785	Sgt
Kempner, Leo	32609270	S/Sgt
Kent, William R.	12175811	T/Sgt
Kern, Edward D.	12209752	T/Sgt
Kerrigan, George F.	36647340	S/Sgt
Kessenger, Kenneth R.	0664404	2/Lt
Keyes, Ernest A.	0818882	2/Lt
Kirkelie, Robert F.	39569512	Sgt
Kjar, Ferdinand M.	02072356	2/Lt
Klotz, Marion F.	34535508	T/Sgt
Knoll, Edmund B.	T.131306	F/O
Kolaya, Theodore V.	0777709	2/Lt
Korba, John	T.066007	F/O
Kraft, Clinton W.	15016413	S/Sgt
Lange, William	0755705	1/Lt
Langenmayr, Kenneth W.	0815934	2/Lt
Langer, Laurence J.	0674685	1/Lt
Lankford, Earl K.	34369622	S/Sgt
Laurich, John J.	39549631	S/Sgt
Lawrence, Carrol H.	39461143	S/Sgt
Lehman, Robert J.	38395312	S/Sgt
Lewis, Marshall E. Jr.	0701934	1/Lt
Lindemuth, Robert F.	0431696	1/Lt
Lindhe, William C.	0673394	1/Lt
Lipnicki, Theodore B.	32766074	Sgt
Littleton, Freddie H.	0742297	2/Lt
Lombardo, Leonard J.	18186538	Sgt
Long, Eugene A.	36647620	Sgt
Lovell, Lewis G.	35653311	Sgt
Lund, Rolfe D.	39560152	S/Sgt
Lundquist, Robert M.	0766305	2/Lt
Lundquist, Steve S.	36643016	S/Sgt
Lunsford, William E.	34262692	S/Sgt
Mabee, Theodore W.	36692659	S/Sgt
Macdonald, John C.	0526631	1/Lt
Mackinnon, Donald W.	11114041	S/Sgt
Madara, James E.	0735889	1/Lt
Mallory, William	15078777	Sgt
Martinson, Robert G.	19055675	S/Sgt
Mason, Marney T. Jr.	0663450	2/Lt
Mazur, Joseph Z.	12174007	T/Sgt
McCarville, Louis J.	3680501	T/Sgt
McCord, George M.	37651218	Sgt
McCoy, Dennis J.	13092006	Sgt
McElhinney, Horace A.	0812843	2/Lt
McGaughy, Bruce B.	16081156	S/Sgt
McGinnis, Joseph R.	37521982	Sgt
McGrady, John F.	02068427	2/Lt
McGregor, Harry B.	0664417	Capt
Miller, Paul E.	16056129	T/Sgt
Minard, Herbert F.	0716929	2/Lt
Mintz, Irvin D.	11050850	S/Sgt
Mogford, Robert J.	0664034	1/Lt
Molengraft, Joseph H.	01574488	2/Lt
Monroe, Richard C. Jr.	0694495	2/Lt
Morgan, Henry R.	1608890	S/Sgt
Mulkern, John P.	0693525	2/Lt
Morris, Glen W. Jr.	0.749729	2/Lt
Mullins, James D.	0698323	2/Lt
Morrow, Tom J.	33290445	Sgt
Mulone, Anthony V.	13040923	S/Sgt
Munstermann, Raymond C.	37164070	S/Sgt
Murphy, John C.	0768886	1/Lt
Murray, Raleigh P.	16016615	S/Sgt
Myers, William C.	33733666	Sgt
Nemecek, William J.	0.817506	2/Lt
Newell, Max A.	0685347	1/Lt
Noe, George E.	0739110	2/Lt
O'Brien, John G. Jr.	0698757	2/Lt
Olson, Russell L.	0763320	2/Lt
Orlando, Alfred F.	32326982	S/Sgt
Ott, Robert A.	17055601	S/Sgt
Owens, Maurus C.	0706793	1/Lt
Palmer, Leonard C.	0707100	2/Lt
Patterson, Archie W.	33831218	Sgt
Paulos, James A.	19069617	Cpl
Peck, Norman	0703301	1/Lt
Perella, John Jr.	02064309	2/Lt
Peterson, Leon A.	39393714	T/Sgt
Peterson, Robert E.	16054935	S/Sgt
Pfeifer, Frank D.	13127433	Sgt
Phillips, Worthington W.	07510311	2/Lt
Philo, Edward B.	36450215	S/Sgt
Pieper, William A.	12206973	Sgt
Piergies, Edward E.	0707181	2/Lt
Pinto, Prosper F.	0750837	2/Lt
Pohle, Armand W.	0860321	2/Lt
Pung, Theodore G.	20647748	S/Sgt
Radich, Bogan	17051503	S/Sgt
Ratliff, Ernest H.	34792971	Sgt
Reed, David K.	0713025	2/Lt
Regan, John A.	0828526	1/Lt
Rodriguez, Herminian Jr.	13130693	Sgt
Rohne, Harry R.	37605202	Sgt
Rose, Philip M.	0689170	2/Lt
Ross, Philip	0833591	2/Lt
Russell, Frank R.	0699569	2/Lt
Russell, Gordon R. Jr.	0693531	2/Lt
Russo, Joseph	32465821	S/Sgt
Ruzicka, James J.	0705810	2/Lt
Sambol, Zvonlimir P.	36735304	Sgt
Samburg, Jerome R.	33558860	S/Sgt
Saunders, William H.	0685394	1/Lt
Shaddy, Robert E.	37483851	Sgt
Shinder, Raymond F.	0694807	1/Lt
Short, Robert C.	36687933	Sgt
Siegel, Herman	T.1929	F/O
Sinclair, Gordon H.	0752085	2/Lt
Skaggs, B.B.	0.025526	Capt
Slager, Eldon A.	39270687	S/Sgt
Sloberne, Tony J.	35417201	Cpl
Smith, J.W. Jr.	38397871	T/Sgt
Smith, Burton J.	0691823	1/Lt
Smith, James B.	0.701007	1/Lt
Snyder, Perry J.	32668405	S/Sgt
Smith, Ormond B.	0.817793	2/Lt
Somerville, David G.	16151554	T/Sgt
Sokalski, Alfred D.	32738895	Pfc
Spitz, Jack G.	14085504	S/Sgt
Stack, John F.	32893684	Sgt
Stevens, Edward E.	34615033	Sgt
Stewart, Edwin A.	39907345	Sgt
Stiles, Lowell D.	33560157	S/Sgt
Strickler, Paul J.	13157252	S/Sgt
Sturdevant, Harry E. Jr.	0751049	2/Lt
Stutzman, Edward L.	0712694	2/Lt
Suchiu, John	0425057	1/Lt
Sullivan, Monte V.	0679689	2/Lt
Sundquist, Gordon O.	16169905	Sgt
Swartz, Andrew L.	33843958	Sgt
Terry, William J.	0.532947	2/Lt
Thomas, Harry R.	33592743	Sgt
Thompson, Charles E.	36195604	S/Sgt

Thompson, Milton E.	34724732	Sgt
Trescott, Kenneth C.	19045786	Sgt
Van Munster, Richard C.	0715874	2/Lt
Verges, Maurice T. Jr.	18138306	S/Sgt
Vickers, Ernest H. Jr.	0500223	2/Lt
Vogel, Robert R.	0684814	1/Lt
Weeklund, Oscar A.	0690016	1/Lt
Welch, Robert E.	32928551	S/Sgt
Welde, Charles D.	0717121	2/Lt
Walker, George H.	15069416	T/Sgt
Wells, Earl A.	34059454	S/Sgt
Wentz, William F.	17069660	T/Sgt
White, John L.	39137594	Sgt
Whited, Burl E.	15200812	S/Sgt
Whitt, John N.	0765864	2/Lt
Wiard, John de Forest	0447910	2/Lt
Williams, Archibald, L. Jr.	0813627	1/Lt
Williams, Olen G.	38214822	S/Sgt
Wilson, Ralph H.	17124441	Sgt
Winn, Jake G.	34793188	Sgt
Wlaters, Jack P.	T.3146	F/O
Wollstein, R.S. Jr.	0692597	1/Lt
Wunder, John H.	0693444	2/Lt
Wunderlich, Adam E.	0817869	2/Lt
Yarbrough, George M. Jr.	14122726	Sgt
Young, Clay L. Jr.	34465056	T/Sgt
Zielinski, Raymond	0698508	2/Lt
Zierk, Wayne H.	39410875	S/Sgt
Zoff, Vernon L.	17079363	Sgt
Zyb, Chester A.	36649609	Sgt

467th Bomb Group

Abell, James W. Jr.	0707758	2/Lt
Alier, Louis A.	0668694	2/Lt
Allen, Raymond	32854699	T/Sgt
Appel, Carl S. Jr.	20346713	S/Sgt
Atley, Duane E.	0541847	2/Lt
Ayers, Frank E.	36874787	Sgt
Benner, Richard E.	33620398	T/Sgt
Bertsch, David E.	37550502	Sgt
Beseny, John M.	12152256	S/Sgt
Biggs, John H.	18183567	S/Sgt
Bishop, Carl S.	17096995	S/Sgt
Borchick, Frank	13171042	T/Sgt
Boucher, James R.	35544768	S/Sgt
Boyer, Thomas A.	33506619	S/Sgt
Brannan, George H.	14142695	S/Sgt
Brzezowski, Stanley E.	32862091	S/Sgt
Burns, Rufus R.	0697986	2/Lt
Byers, Lewis E.	37730501	Sgt
Caluori, Ernest	0668552	1/Lt
Carchietta, John A.	12155216	S/Sgt
Cardin, Fleurian P.	20122634	Sgt
Carter, George E.	16079462	S/Sgt
Cassels, Hugh R.	14188966	S/Sgt
Chilver, Harold R.	0735049	1/Lt
Christian, Lewis C.	02062455	2/Lt
Close, Duane E.	16137453	Sgt
Collins, Richard J.	0717387	2/Lt
Coltey, Edward Z.	0817390	2/Lt
Condon, Edward H.	0668899	2/Lt
Corbin, Samuel R.	35000370	S/Sgt
Countey, David J.	T.127423	F/O
Coven, Albert B.	32236493	S/Sgt
Creighton, Richard C.	39277316	S/Sgt
Dadig, Albert S. Jr.	33687001	Sgt
Davis, Harris P.	34802136	S/Sgt
Dahlin, Alex R.	0.687997	2/Lt
Deavis, Robert H.	0685779	2/Lt
Delavan, Robert E.	0703961	2/Lt
Dellarocca, Don	32718821	T/Sgt
Dery, Sylvio L.	11018088	T/Sgt
Detwiler, John K.	17056460	Sgt
Dick, James A.	12134759	T/Sgt
Doole, Roy J.	0697014	2/Lt
Dore, Joseph A.	32902673	Sgt
Dreksler, Edward J.	16118911	S/Sgt
Eaton, Raymond J.	14182367	T/Sgt
Ellefson, John N.	16082474	S/Sgt
Erickson, Floyd W.	37586060	Sgt
Evancich, Frank G.	17090272	Sgt
Ferguson, James G.	0685571	2/Lt
Fiedler, Charles A.	01059447	2/Lt
Finger, Samuel	12121751	S/Sgt
Fisher, Robert C.	32489271	S/Sgt
Fitzjarrell, Edmond M.	6829037	T/Sgt
Ford, Thomas M. Jr.	0688775	2/Lt
Foster, David W.	0673349	1/Lt
Frearon, Joseph F.	31308952	Sgt
Fuller, George E.	34782039	T/Sgt
Gage, Dan R.	33702555	S/Sgt
Gallagher, Joseph M.	T.063297	F/O
Geddes, Duncan A.	31373892	Sgt
Gensert, Thomas A.	35766187	S/Sgt
Geschel, Walter K.	T.125292	F/O
Gillett, Thornton R.	0819513	2/Lt
Gitlitz, Seymour M.	0716648	2/Lt
Godshalk, Goerge R. Jr.	0691891	1/Lt
Gorczewski, Anthony J.	13128132	Sgt
Greble, William E.	0817426	2/Lt
Green, Gene S.	15899864	Cpl
Grinkiavicus, M.	6146241	T/Sgt
Grooms, Edward C.	0703244	1/Lt
Guzik, Chester M.	36757416	Sgt
Hagist, Richard S.	T.129815	F/O
Haines, Luke M.	38239988	S/Sgt
Hall, William H.	0761083	2/Lt
Hamilton, George S.	36733219	S/Sgt
Hanks, Weldon M.	0825849	2/Lt
Hardick, Peter Jr.	13098304	S/Sgt
Harrison, Charles D.	0795738	2/Lt
Harshbarger, K.N. Jr.	14119246	S/Sgt
Hatkoff, Nathan M.	0823853	2/Lt
Heffner, Stephen A.	36593076	S/Sgt
Helton, Edwin W.	0687592	1/Lt
Herring, Algy L.	18041706	S/Sgt
Hill, Leroy M.	18168713	S/Sgt
Hinkebein, Glen L.	17038895	S/Sgt
Hird, Robert A.	42012613	S/Sgt
Hope, Edward W.	16013749	Sgt
Horak, Richard E.	37551321	S/Sgt
Houston, Earl L.	0809002	2/Lt
Howe, James R.	36810652	S/Sgt
Hudson, Donald H.	0703999	2/Lt
Hudson, Dennis J.	0820750	1/Lt
Janss, Alfred H.	T131842	F/O
Kalienko, Stanley J.	36638265	S/Sgt
Kay, Glenn C.	0717070	2/Lt
Kells, Sherwood L.	32740090	S/Sgt
Kelly, Howard J.	6871367	Pvt
Kennedy, Joseph J.	32791462	S/Sgt
Ketchel, Dale K.	17100468	T/Sgt
Kirby, Joseph W. Jr.	T.125615	F/O
Klemas, Joseph J.	32865318	S/Sgt
Knowles, Charles L. Jr.	18189980	S/Sgt
Koller, Karl J.	16107813	Sgt
Koley, Stanley P.	35230981	Sgt
Kotraba, George J.	0817698	2/Lt
Kovalenko, Walter W.	6949073	T/Sgt
Kowalski, Robert F.	36643616	S/Sgt
Kramer, William R.	0673200	2/Lt
Landis, Wellington E.	0811674	2/Lt
Lifschitz, George	12043462	T/Sgt
Lloyd, Howard A.	13153786	Sgt
Loberg, Denver C.	37632701	Sgt
Ludka, Richard J. Jr.	0694919	2/Lt
Luna, Paul D.	17164726	S/Sgt
Lund, Joseph R.	36640174	S/Sgt
Macdonald, James G.	0813538	2/Lt
Manley, Leo J.	32934716	Sgt
Margiosso, Carmine	12037871	S/Sgt
Marshall, James M.	20329202	S/Sgt
Martin, Gordon R.	37586765	Sgt
Masiak, Robert J.	16024163	S/Sgt
Mason, Warren W.	0813543	2/Lt
Massey, Luther E.	37236779	S/Sgt
Materewicz, Edward R.	13189418	Sgt
Maxey, J.H.	0699694	2/Lt
McArthur, John T. Jr.	T.125913	F/O
McCamish, Benjamin F. Jr.	33522081	S/Sgt
McCartney, Sumner A.	0711732	2/Lt
McGlynn, Bernard A.	32938814	Sgt
McGonigle, Charles D.	31299531	S/Sgt
McGrath, Vincent J. Jr.	12176066	Sgt
McVicar, Donald T.	15118711	S/Sgt
Meredith, Oliver E. Jr.	33553487	Sgt
Michalak, Eugene	36636021	Cpl
Mikulin, John	35050245	S/Sgt
Milliron, George W.	0698135	2/Lt
Mills, George W.	0821329	1/Lt
Miney, Daniel E.	32691808	Pvt
Missiras, Theologos	T.125528	F/O
Montgomery, Robert E. Jr.	39278490	Sgt
Montick, Albert	32597713	Sgt
Moore, Bill F.	0794442	1/Lt
Morehouse, Roland	36460730	Sgt
Mosser, Edward J.	0799919	1/Lt
Murphy, John J.	31060787	S/Sgt
Nelson, Maurice E.	0699712	2/Lt
O'Hara, John H.	39114719	S/Sgt
O'Malley, John F. Jr.	35354136	Sgt
Onischuk, Alek	31409559	Sgt
Orr, Riley E.	17033340	S/Sgt
Ostander, Lyle M.	36125105	T/Sgt
Pattengall, Malcom N. Jr.	0709962	2/Lt
Peacock, Charles L.	14066493	T/Sgt
Perreault, Joseph V.	11051138	T/Sgt
Peters, Richard C.	36578724	S/Sgt
Pheneger, Clifford A.	T.125782	F/O
Pontius, Darlton W.	17099290	T/Sgt
Porter, Leon F.	0829294	1/Lt
Prendergast, James R.	T128582	F/O
Prewitte, William V.	0795075	1/Lt
Price, Arthur D.	37504269	S/Sgt
Quigley, James	37558348	Sgt
Rachford, Clarence J.	35418713	S/Sgt
Rainault, Roger B.	0716532	2/Lt
Rankin, Warren C.	35575827	T/Sgt
Reed, Russell E.	33490867	S/Sgt
Reeves, Clarence F.	34440004	Sgt
Reid, Alvah D.	01014777	2/Lt
Reid, Stalie C. Jr.	0796884	1/Lt
Rinesmith, John W.	35635053	S/Sgt
Ritchey, Ernest M.	39184843	Sgt
Robinson, James E.	0754771	2/Lt
Roden, James A.	0686277	2/Lt
Rostkowski, Leonard	36872957	Sgt
Russell, Raymond T.	18063422	S/Sgt
Sager, Leonard G.	32225485	S/Sgt
Sanderford, Dan M.	0716962	2/Lt
Schellhas, Kurt F.	0713676	2/Lt
Schlomowitz, Sol	0817280	2/Lt
Schneider, Norman E.	36745005	S/Sgt
Sefca, Martin Jr.	0807790	1/Lt
Shepherd, Russell E.	35140511	S/Sgt
Sherrill, William M.	0717274	2/Lt
Shurtz, Guy F.	T.130602	F/O
Sies, Walter M.	36457521	Sgt
Skinner, Jack M.	0745205	2/Lt
Smith, John	0716775	2/Lt
Smith, John W.	0789824	Capt.
Snook, Oliver W.	0755774	2/Lt
Snyder, Philip A.	33353620	S/Sgt
Spangler, Richard B.	39565202	S/Sgt
Steinbrenner, Millard C.	33604292	S/Sgt
Stephens, Rufus B.	0795501	1/Lt
Stewart, Jehu F.	0821185	2/Lt
Stokes, Otto W.	T.129466	F/O
Story, James W.	38411714	S/Sgt
Stuckman, Charles L.	0809063	2/Lt
Swanberg, Amos M.	36775112	Sgt
Teague, Eugene J.	0750886	2/Lt
Ulerick, James E.	35147691	S/Sgt
Underwood, James F.	0813090	1/Lt
Ungerer, Maynard M. Jr.	0827088	1/Lt
Van Tress, H.P. Jr.	0722400	1/Lt
Van Veen, Francis P.	32487830	S/Sgt
Vaught, Bertie M. Jr.	38533632	Sgt
Violette, Louis J.	31064175	S/Sgt
Walinski, Walter	32939214	Sgt
Walker, William E.	38540845	Sgt
Walther, George H.	15103216	S/Sgt
Wassow, Frank C.	6862503	Sgt
Waterman, Robert P.	17165557	S/Sgt
Watson, John T.	31309579	Sgt
Weindel, Arthur L.	31148036	Sgt
Weinrich, Arnold A.	T064932	F/O
Wells, Robert A.	01826181	2/Lt
Wickerham, George B.	0716797	2/Lt
Wilder, Emmett L.	0743802	2/Lt
Wilkins, William F.	35547107	S/Sgt
Williams, Abel J.	39456073	S/Sgt
Williams, Floyd D.	18042480	S/Sgt
Williams, Robert L.	39292848	Sgt
Williams, Robert L.	15313806	Sgt
Wilson, Robert E.	0694991	2/Lt
Wilson, William B.	15171152	2/Lt
Wilt, Joseph T.	35045793	S/Sgt
Winebrenner, Paul J.	02056764	2/Lt
Woods, Willard T. Jr.	35876150	S/Sgt
Worby, Henry J.	36726002	T/Sgt
Young, Lloyd C.	35338878	S/Sgt
Younkin, Louis E.	0716804	2/Lt
Zielinski, Edward S.	36736239	S/Sgt

489th Bomb Group

Abelson, Sidney	20349443	T/Sgt
Adams, Robert E.	33746691	Sgt
Aiken, John M. Jr.	0710865	2/Lt
Allan, Evan E.	0764162	2/Lt
Anderson, Bruce D.	37706629	Sgt
Anderson, Robert H.	37652943	Sgt
Andrews, Frank	11128115	Sgt
Baker, Montee R.	0666119	1/Lt
Barbone, Patrick J.	32458130	Sgt
Bartlett, Frank W. Jr.	T061902	F/O
Baumgarten, Clarence G.	13044104	S/Sgt
Bebout, James H.	0693835	2/Lt
Bekowies, Alfred	16039355	S/Sgt
Bender, Frank	36041774	Sgt
Benedict, McCrea	0748054	2/Lt
Bigham, Karl R.	39410188	Sgt
Bishop, Wallace J.	0816216	2/Lt
Blackburn, James W.	0692851	2/Lt
Blake, William M. Jr.	0820943	2/Lt
Blanton, Jack P.	0731444	1/Lt
Bonitz, Nicholas J.	33150771	S/Sgt
Brian, Donald C.	34711245	T/Sgt
Briseno, Rosalio Jr.	37471255	Sgt
Brooks, Elvin V.	T.61720	F/O
Bruening, Donald H.	0818269	2/Lt
Brustein, Irving	32204889	Pvt
Burke, John R.	0818101	2/Lt
Butler, Robert R. Jr.	33638093	S/Sgt
Carew, Colin A.P.	11116858	S/Sgt
Cheyne, Roland M.	36400291	2/Sgt
Clendenning, Robert Jr.	0700797	1/Lt
Coward, Kenneth W.	35681168	Sgt
Coxen, Vernon R.	33622495	S/Sgt
Crompton, John H.	36656922	Sgt

Crowther, John J.	T.061828	F/O
Culkin, Lawrence P.	0667491	1/Lt
Dalton, William A. Jr.	0716376	2/Lt
Deats, Raymond C.	0699399	2/Lt
Debes, Jerry C.	0751893	2/Lt
Dede, Robert R.	12127074	Sgt
Deyo, Virgil E.	32850955	S/Sgt
Deyoung, Elmer	0698531	2/Lt
Dixon, Robert E.	33419829	Sgt
Dodds, Thomas N.	37497927	Sgt
Doherty, Loyola F.	0723316	2/Lt
Earnhardt, Fred G.	34598162	Sgt
Eastburn, Linford W.	32952613	Sgt
Etheridge, James C.	T.062260	F/O
Everhart, Virgil	15097676	S/Sgt
Fabiani, Albert J.	12153894	Sgt
Fallet, Thomas M.	0706826	2/Lt
Fierro, Peter M.	0802734	2/Lt
Florcyk, Edwin A.	0790501	1/Lt
Forslin, Henery E.	37560065	Sgt
Fox, William K.	39911207	S/Sgt
Francis, Lewis C.	T.185022	F/O
Frank, Jack S.	0713161	2/Lt
Friedenthal, Isidore L.	0695418	2/Lt
Fulks, Frank W.	0697627	1/Lt
Furden, Harry L.	39294386	Sgt
Garber, Joseph	0703978	2/Lt
Giuliani, Augustine L.	T.062040	F/O
Gommels, Glenn E.	37677284	Sgt
Goshtoian, Andrew	01995850	1/Lt
Greenberg, Stanley	0696362	1/Lt
Grime, James F.	11071378	Pvt
Gunderson, Jerome A. Jr.	37660284	S/Sgt
Gunn, Michael K.	17133630	Pfc
Hamilton, Edward L.	0693557	2/Lt
Hall, John C. Jr.	0446807	2/Lt
Hammett, George L.	34656412	Sgt
Hahn, Burton F.	0686150	2/Lt

Hanson, Stanley C.	0706094	2/Lt
Harris, Donald C.	35049809	S/Sgt
Harvey, Loy M.	34263034	S/Sgt
Hatton, Charles R.	34688934	T/Sgt
Helitzke, Joseph L.	18118688	S/Sgt
Henning, Frederick B.	42015496	Sgt
Hensley, Everett E.	15067242	Sgt
Herndon, Roy E.	17122516	T/Sgt
Hibbard, Milton	0693042	2/Lt
Holbert, Donald V.	32690632	S/Sgt
Holitzke, Joseph L.	18118688	S/Sgt
Holoka, John Jr.	7020757	T/Sgt
Hoover, Ralph E.	0716732	2/Lt
Houtchens, James W.	0706178	2/Lt
Hughes, John P.	12190234	S/Sgt
Hurley, Robert J.	0704342	2/Lt
Isles, Peter J.	13108325	S/Sgt
Jacobs, Maurice	0739100	2/Lt
Jansen, Leonard R.	31292338	Sgt
Jones, Thomas E.	0693787	2/Lt
Kader, Eugene I.	36559970	S/Sgt
Kantner, Edward R.	20322365	Sgt
Kapnick, Albert W.	6948978	T/Sgt
Keene, Theodore C.	17019800	S/Sgt
Keene, Theodore C.	17019800	S/Sgt
Kirbelis, Adolph	13041835	S/Sgt
Klecker, Robert H.	0709924	2/Lt
Klein, John N.	0700020	2/Lt
Lane, Alfred G.	38038471	Sgt
Lerner, Charles	0819124	2/Lt
Lithander, Lee B.	0705724	2/Lt
Lovelace, Claude T.	0806474	1/Lt
Lovely, Bob M.	38366300	S/Sgt
Lowther, William E.	34164188	S/Sgt
Madson, Leroy G.	0429966	Capt
McClain, Robert C.	33670501	Sgt
McCracken, Robert A.	01288263	1/Lt
McCullough, Neal D.	18155838	Sgt

McGeachie, John	32730811	S/Sgt
McIntosh, Lige	35451161	T/Sgt
Meehan, Ronald E.	11071531	S/Sgt
Miller, Samuel H. Jr.	31204873	Sgt
Montgomery, William B.	0693305	1/Lt
Morse, Richard W.	32674279	S/Sgt
Moss, Eugene E.	01287387	1/Lt
Moyer, Ernest R.	35223040	Sgt
Navarro, Antonio	39689581	S/Sgt
Neuling, Owen J.	15081714	T/Sgt
Panciera, Louis Jr.	31071457	S/Sgt
Pellini, Aldo L.	39204986	S/Sgt
Peterson, Eugene M.	37546676	S/Sgt
Phifer, Marion Jr.	0717267	2/Lt
Pickett, Paul J.	0694940	2/Lt
Please, Thomas M.	0807044	Capt
Pomles, Harry	0801391	1/Lt
Poole, Chester C.	0717953	2/Lt
Rath, Charles A.	0771529	2/Lt
Redden, Paul W.	19171031	Sgt
Risovich, Joseph	0754852	1/Lt
Roberts, Gilbert R.	0698347	2/Lt
Rogers, Doyle H.	37498799	S/Sgt
Roy, William R.	12002651	S/Sgt
Ruffini, Francis D.	12053044	S/Sgt
Ruiz, Frank S. Jr.	39418509	Sgt
Rutner, Francis W.	0668784	2/Lt
Sackett, Floyd L.	19151125	Cpl
Safy, Joseph	0752506	1/Lt
Salyer, Elbert H.	39298041	Sgt
Savage, Robert D.	0705997	1/Lt
Scofield, George A.	39566372	Pvt
Shaffer, Chester D.	33505591	S/Sgt
Sherwood, Philip B.	0794704	1/Lt
Slattery, Patrick J.	36809675	Sgt
Slein, John J.	0811254	1/Lt
Smith, Glen L.	36466092	S/Sgt
Smith, Robert C.	20637944	S/Sgt

Snead, Jack T.	15047723	S/Sgt
Sokoloski, Raymond P.	T.124017	F/O
Sombke, Howard O.	1698930	2/Lt
Springer, Walter S.	0821373	2/Lt
Steffan, Heinz G.	13090574	S/Sgt
Stensrud, Dale B.	17155439	S/Sgt
Stephens, William E.	0697715	2/Lt
Sterbenz, Frank T.	0698934	2/Lt
Stock, Henry L.	38460975	Sgt
Stodtmeister, Fred H.	39834869	S/Sgt
Stoughton, Harry A. Jr.	35626124	S/Sgt
Sund, Gilman L.	0759829	1/Lt
Suskey, Edward N.	33471004	S/Sgt
Taber, Elwyn L. Jr.	0659411	Capt
Tankersley, John F.	0811261	1/Lt
Torok, Geza	33688154	Sgt
Thornburg, Raymond C.	34594995	S/Sgt
Trewartha, James N.	16156658	T/Sgt
Udzick, Joseph W.	17146129	Sgt
Vance, Leon R. Jr.	0022050	Lt/Col
Van Winkle, John D.	0801159	1/Lt
Walker, Gerald R.	35370875	Sgt
Waldie, Doanld A.	0824016	2/Lt
Walsh, Kevin	32879830	S/Sgt
Watson, Julian A.	16176405	Sgt
Wawrzyninkowski, R.H.	36815048	Sgt
Weidemann, John B.	0717328	2/Lt
Weinstein, Charles	32993724	Sgt
Wendte, Elmer O.	39165888	T/Sgt
White, Robert J.	0428889	Capt
Whitty, Gerlad R.	0823751	2/Lt
Winter, Ralph L.	17070398	Sgt
Wisinski, Anthony J.	6949122	S/Sgt
Woolen, Bryan W. Jr.	0818316	2/Lt
Zaprola, George E.	13126746	Sgt
Zaragoza, Peter	12128453	S/Sgt
Zetteck, Richard R.	36654623	S/Sgt

491ST BOMB GROUP

Adkins, Chester	0.925956	2/Lt
Allen, David C.	38281424	T/Sgt
Allen, Edward R.	02062417	2/Lt
Anderson, Laverne G.	17154654	T/Sgt
Austin, Elmore L.	31340848	Sgt
Bailey, Arthur F.	0.694302	1/Lt
Baker, Robert S.	0.820880	1/Lt
Barnes, Fletcher	0.819726	2/Lt
Bauer, Herman C.	0.718214	1/Lt
Bemis, Elmer H.	31261913	T/Sgt
Bennett, David N. Jr.	0.686214	1/Lt
Bennett, Irwin	12191577	Sgt
Binetti, Ceasar R.	32277804	T/Sgt
Blair, Joseph F.	0.806391	1/Lt
Blount, Jesse F.	0.710548	2/Lt
Blue, Malcolm L.	0.702888	2/Lt
Bock, Frank E.	0.706678	2/Lt
Boling, William R.	34766825	S/Sgt
Borger, Frederick F. Jr.	33623530	S/Sgt
Bovey, Bruce D.	T.128551	F/O
Bowen, Oliver J.	34916524	S/Sgt
Boyer, Joseph L.	37261239	T/Sgt
Brater, Elmer R.	02070242	2/Lt
Brennan, Robert J.	0.716708	2/Lt
Brown, James W.	0.719549	1/Lt
Buchanan, Grover L.	18169943	S/Sgt
Buchholz, Raymond F.	36297048	S/Sgt
Burke, Donald T.	02061423	2/Lt
Burnett, Robert J.	15313690	S/Sgt
Butler, Marvin W.	0.742060	1/Lt
Byrnes, Hartwell P.	34872984	S/Sgt
Byrne, William H.	0.814244	1/Lt
Callahan, Frank Jr.	11016788	T/Sgt
Carlisle, William L.	17115091	T/Sgt
Carmichael, L.H.	35898770	Sgt
Carr, Delbert B.	19182823	S/Sgt
Carr, Mason C.	14184562	T/Sgt
Carson, Harold N.	16067208	T/Sgt
Caruso, John F.	36876521	S/Sgt
Clark, John L.	0.818605	2/Lt

Cole, Jesse W.	34854210	S/Sgt
Corona, George H.	39122650	S/Sgt
Costello, Frank R.	35928074	S/Sgt
Craig, Ronald M.	37731515	S/Sgt
Crane, Thomas R.	32757283	S/Sgt
Cuff, Martin J.	20724554	T/Sgt
Dance, James W. Jr.	33226840	S/Sgt
Datthyn, Lester J.	32675105	Sgt
Davies, Joseph L.	0552857	2/Lt
Delaney, Michael J.	0809331	1/Lt
Denham, Howard E.	34767797	Sgt
Derence, Leonard A.	33697311	S/Sgt
Deweber, Dewey H.	38436457	T/Sgt
Dextraze, Roland U.	0.698674	1/Lt
Difilippo, Joseph	32952888	T/Sgt
Duerr, George M.	32710949	S/Sgt
Dumont, William A.	31267637	Sgt
Eldridge, John W.	32935514	T/Sgt
Elliott, Solon W. Jr.	34052697	S/Sgt
Engel, George H.	0.723332	S/Sgt
Eshleman, Edgar R. Jr.	2065140	2/Lt
Evans, Wayne Jr.	0.666018	2/Lt
Evers, James L.	34588582	S/Sgt
Feinberg, Robert	0.2009166	2/Lt
Finnegan, Maurice R.	31298846	S/Sgt
Flick, Earl F.	33497736	S/Sgt
Fenner, Donald W.	36688616	S/Sgt
Fortney, Roy F.	35813911	S/Sgt
Foster, Edwin W.	0.696225	2/Lt
Fox, Paul	0.794389	1/Lt
Frack, Carl W.	33621138	Sgt
Fuhr, Francis E.	0.695737	1/Lt
Fulbright, Thomas R.	38416536	S/Sgt
Fulkerson, William H.	17045556	S/Sgt
Fuller, Gordon B.	39131096	S/Sgt
Funk, Richard W.	0699663	2/Lt
Gallant, Thomas E.	21049329	Sgt
Gardner, Harold G.	39552662	S/Sgt
Geppert, Carl L.	0.2058157	2/Lt

Goodacre, Charles F.	02063237	S/Lt
Grange, Lloyd V.	0707426	2/Lt
Granat, John R.	0754955	1/Lt
Greenberg, Albert A.	32608219	T/Sgt
Hadraski, Eugene W.	0827498	2/Lt
Harris, Paul I.	37469457	S/Sgt
Hasselbrinck, Glen C.	35709449	S/Sgt
Hawkins, Francis S.	12122898	T/Sgt
Haynes, James L.	7003484	T/Sgt
Hecht, Lee H.	17175438	S/Sgt
Heib, John N.	39203497	T/Sgt
Hess, Robert W.	12099180	Sgt
Higley, Lester R.	32729766	S/Sgt
Hirsch, Norman F.	0.709375	1/Lt
Hite, John P.	0448833	2/Lt
Hixson, Charles E.	34505462	S/Sgt
Hoffman, Adrian W.	34508821	S/Sgt
Holler, David R.	16044779	S/Sgt
Holzapfel, Charles E.	33423282	S/Sgt
Hoos, Henry A.	32668197	T/Sgt
Huber, Robert L.	0.704205	2/Lt
Hudson, John A.	39300660	S/Sgt
Hunter, David L.	34636844	Sgt
Hunter, James K.	0799024	Capt
Hutson, Cecil E.	18127645	T/Sgt
Jackson, Arnold S.	36376240	S/Sgt
Jamison, William J.		S/Sgt
Jarrett, Robert N.	15065925	Sgt
Johnson, Guy S.	0717659	2/Lt
Johnson, Woodrow G.	0702443	1/Lt
Jones, Clyde V.	33552445	Sgt
Kantzler, Conrad L.	0805163	1/Lt
Kelley, Joseph L.	37654681	Sgt
Kingsbury, Daniel O.	11084041	S/Sgt
Kingsland, Kenneth S.	31379109	Sgt
Krivonak, Michael	0.702867	2/Lt
Kunkel, William D.	38528720	Sgt
Lacaillade, William M.	0833137	2/Lt

Laenau, Herbert H.	39707962	Sgt
Lahaye, Edward J.	T.122552	F/O
Lane, George W.	0687484	2/Lt
Lefurjah, Keith E.	0713020	1/Lt
Lehr, Leo R.	11034382	S/Sgt
Lehtonen, Unto J.	02068422	2/Lt
Leibenhaut, Martin	12032965	S/Sgt
Lemay, Raymond G.	11057587	Sgt
Lepitre, David A.	02065082	2/Lt
Levack, Edward A.	02065164	2/Lt
Lewis, Percival M. 3rd	32949579	Sgt
Liebfeld, Sig	0745916	1/Lt
Lindhout, Richard H.	0682435	1/Lt
Lord, Gordon L.	39460796	S/Sgt
Lowman, Vern J.	17070851	Sgt
Luisi, Vito	11011113	Sgt
MacCallum, David E.	31370018	Sgt
Mahoney, Bernard F.	0739149	2/Lt
Mann, Kenneth M.	39342592	S/Sgt
Manter, Paul W.	31321694	T/Sgt
Markham, Sheldon P.	33710884	Sgt
Marko, Andrew	31409763	Sgt
Martillotta, Joseph P.	0-1996083	1/Lt
Martin, Johnnie H. Jr.	18201716	T/Sgt
Maxwell, Britt D. Jr.	34678301	S/Sgt
McCarrick, Chester E.	13088430	S/Sgt
McCloud, Cecil L.	14159474	T/Sgt
McClung, Evan L.	0694012	2/Lt
McDaniel, Melvin L.	35806187	Sgt
McKee, Raymond O.	38309651	S/Sgt
McKinney, Charles O.	14105221	S/Sgt
McKinstry, Vernon L. Jr.	0463894	1/Lt
Meadows, Charles A.	0.822766	2/Lt
Means, Daniel W.	0705750	2/Lt
Meerdo, William P.	36889459	Sgt
Melnikoff, Nicholas A.	0706300	2/Lt
Meng, Harold R.	0702472	2/Lt
Mewbourne, James F.	14170963	Sgt
Miller, Jerry R.	0768164	2/Lt
Miller, John R.	16168605	S/Sgt
Miller, Lester	T.1678	F/O

Milligan, Woodrow W.	34502412	Sgt
Minard, Oliver W.	T123017	F/O
Mitchell, Anthony B.	0659391	Capt
Mohundro, James H.	T.062957	F/O
Montalbano, Barto J.	32692213	T/Sgt
Moore, Bueron H.	35722709	S/Sgt
Moore, Mitchell H.	14137474	S/Sgt
Moussette, Alfred D.	0526032	1/Lt
Muhlhenrich, Randolph H.		Sgt
Murray, John P.	121935506	S/Sgt
Myers, George C.	0829279	2/Lt
Nagel, Robert E.	0827034	2/Lt
Negrin, Carl	32823090	Sgt
Neigh, William E.	12050436	T/Sgt
Nelson, Harold E.	01825246	2/Lt
Nietzke, Kenneth R.	36818829	Sgt
Nimmer, George J.	33797269	S/Sgt
Noon, Lendeth P.	32801820	T/Sgt
Norman, James B.	14141309	Sgt
O'Brien, Thomas R.	02062692	2/Lt
O'Connor, Raymond J.	39379326	T/Sgt
Odell, Paul C.	0772993	2/Lt
Oury, Neol A.	0199832	2/Lt
Page, Lloyd G.	14028376	S/Sgt
Parker, Harry B.	0694701	1/Lt
Patrick, Pete Jr.	33741746	T/Sgt
Patten, George K.	0754761	1/Lt
Patterson, Edward L.	T4454	F/O
Peak, Bernard E.	36556265	S/Sgt
Peterson, Walter B.	11998168	T/Sgt

Phelps, William F.	0706899	1/Lt
Philips, Donald E.	38104457	Sgt
Piatt, James B.	17169561	S/Sgt
Poulsen, Anker F.	0830695	2/Lt
Procita, Gerald	T.131754	F/O
Rachler, Paul R. Jr.	12156937	S/Sgt
Raybould, Theodore	35876057	S/Sgt
Rea, Tony L.	38579892	Sgt
Reese, William L.	0703016	1/Lt
Reffner, Francis M.	327535928	Sgt
Reutener, William E.	15140449	S/Sgt
Rhodes, Raymond R.	18166759	T/Sgt
Richards, Robert	6564934	S/Sgt
Ricker, Lincoln S.	32013166	S/Sgt
Rivera, Frank B.	11110234	Sgt
Roberts, Franklin R.	0696517	1/Lt
Robert, Herman, E. Jr.	02058550	2/Lt
Robinson, David A. Jr.	T.64139	F/O
Roe, Frank C.	T129192	F/O
Rogers, Norman J. Jr.	0820907	2/Lt
Romberger, Donald U.	33187130	S/Sgt
Rowan, Sammy T.	0814978	2/Lt
Rudolph, Warren H.	37551416	Sgt
Ruppel, Arthur J.	13075832	T/Sgt
Ryan, Troy L.	34622806	S/Sgt
Saborido, Donald	12225927	Sgt
Schatzel, Walter O.	42091484	Sgt
Schmill, Bill H.	17055962	Sgt
Schopa, Rudolph C.	36440623	S/Sgt
Schulz, Fred J.	32523617	S/Sgt
Schweitzer, Albert W.	36760668	Sgt

Schwensen, Justus Jr.	0685283	Capt
Seibert, Dorrence R.	33507511	S/Sgt
Sekul, John N.	0824262	2/Lt
Sharp, Fletcher E.	0811149	1/Lt
Shea, Max R.	0818542	2/Lt
Shepherd, Elmore W.	32755264	S/Sgt
Siek, Robert H.	0.827744	2/Lt
Simmons, Warren L.	02063526	2/Lt
Simon, Arthur D.	19147969	S/Sgt
Singley, John H.	0707445	2/Lt
Slade, David H.	15047177	S/Sgt
Sloane, Edward F.	32786393	Sgt
Smith, George H. Jr.	0714209	2/Lt
Sparrow, Robert W.	0.697508	1/Lt
Starr, Irving B.	32995257	S/Sgt
Staymates, Arden E.	13090142	Sgt
Steinman, Elmer	32775794	S/Sgt
Steward, Russell C.	35892782	S/Sgt
Stewart, Wayne E.	0.811152	Capt
Stovall, Henry P.	35869219	S/Sgt
Strain, Dean B.	0806007	Capt
Sutcliffe, Charles B.	13098893	T/Sgt
Sutton, Bill H. Jr.	0780446	2/Lt
Swanby, Glenn T.	39276091	S/Sgt
Swanson, Earl A.	16078837	Sgt
Taibl, Howard A.	12063192	T/Sgt
Taylor, Lee A.	35772070	S/Sgt
Toelle, Herman	36758126	Sgt
Tolin, Thomas S.	0570547	2/Lt
Tomkins, Raymond L.	38563633	Sgt
Triplett, Philip J.	33645162	Sgt
Tufenkjian, Haigus	T125660	F/O

Turner, John E.	32502645	T/Sgt
Tybarsky, Edward B.	13108280	Sgt
Volden, Morris J.	0689416	2/Lt
Vukovich, Matthew Jr.	0714786	2/Lt
Wagers, Harold R.	35872381	Sgt
Wais, William R.	0771846	2/Lt
Wakeman, Fred M.	19188580	S/Sgt
Walker, Floyd A. Jr.	02058592	2/Lt
Walker, Joseph B. III	0713810	2/Lt
Warczak, John S. Jr.	0696926	1/Lt
Warford, Norman G.	35703424	T/Sgt
Wargo, John E.	33693424	Sgt
Watkins, Robert L.	15097758	S/Sgt
Watters, Sidney A. Jr.	38405759	Sgt
Waxman, Benjamin	13200781	Sgt
Weck, William F.	0694824	2/Lt
Weible, Kenneth F.	37356037	Sgt
Weiss, Alvin S.	0.1549865	2/Lt
Williams, Marshall E.	18219340	S/Sgt
Williams, Thomas D.J.	13100227	Sgt
Willoughby, Joseph E.	0761485	1/Lt
Wilson, Andy T.	0.662013	1/Lt
Wimett, Theron S.	11038448	2/Sgt
Wynn, James J.	0771205	1/Lt
Yergey, Richard F.	33831532	Sgt
Yergey, Stanley A.	0717010	1/Lt
Yuzwa, Samuel	6716563	S/Sgt
Zadoorian, Harry	36145716	T/Sgt

492nd Bomb Group

Abbott, Franklin D.J.	663450	1/Lt
Allen, Charles W.	39555395	T/Sgt
Allessio, Charles J.	02072605	2/Lt
Allison, Robert C.	33080694	S/Sgt
Alm, William K.	33588138	S/Sgt
Alseth, George M. Jr.	0.930046	2/Lt
Ambrose, George		1/Lt
Anderson, Jean R.	0834342	2/Lt
Anderson, Kermit W.	0692846	2/Lt
Anderson, Lloyd L.	0.716315	2/Lt
Anderson, Richard B.	12017424	T/Sgt
Andrew, Darrell B.	39276787	T/Sgt
Augustine, Lynn P.	33425807	S/Sgt
Bachman, Harold M.	0.699111	2/Lt
Baker, Charles S.	35848400	Sgt
Barber, Bradford F.	14107943	S/Sgt
Barbkecht, Arthur H.	T.131397	F/O
Barnett, Harry	32874175	Sgt
Bashor, Wilford D.	39276440	S/Sgt
Bassing, Charles H.	0759163	2/Lt
Beasley, Herman E.	14151017	S/Sgt
Becker, George G.	12190316	T/Sgt
Bellamy, Roy E.	0.702220	2/Lt
Berkoff, Lawrence	0823270	2/Lt
Biggins, John A.	35168253	Sgt
Black, Charles H.	35797246	Sgt
Bliss, Jack M.	T.125474	F/O
Bocksberger, Alfred C.	0696318	2/Lt
Boeschenstein, A.C.	16086523	S/Sgt
Boling, Charles R.	18034362	S/Sgt
Bolte, Evert C.	37237094	S/Sgt
Booth, Ernest E.	34235335	S/Sgt
Boren, Mose C. Jr.	19106534	Sgt
Bosch, Richard A.	0783238	2/Lt
Bowen, Leslie E.	33702585	Sgt
Brackins, Donald L.	34706951	S/Sgt
Bradbury, George F.	0.699118	1/Lt
Brague, Roger J.	0807813	2/Lt
Brantley, Haywood E.	0808358	2/Lt
Bratz, Dale N.	36074107	S/Sgt
Brdecka, Vince J.	18186703	S/Sgt
Bronson, John E.	0-760438	2/Lt
Brown, Donald W.	39278285	S/Sgt
Brown, Jack R.	14054449	T/Sgt
Brown, Milton E.	08125402	2/Lt
Brown, Oliver W.	13100808	S/Sgt
Bruton, Earl J.	0702228	2/Lt
Brzozowski, John S.	32789437	S/Sgt
Bullinger, Albert O.	20723918	S/Sgt
Burns, Loren R.	36595146	Sgt
Byers, Leon A.	18242246	S/Sgt

Byrne, Austin P.	025011	Capt
Calicchio, Frank A.	31294399	T/Sgt
Campion, Fabian M.	37547174	T/Sgt
Cantor, Samuel M.	0676350	2/Lt
Carroll, James P.	0.804367	1/Lt
Cary, John L.	0697099	2/Lt
Cavanaugh, G.S. Jr.	15394280	S/Sgt
Cazzell, Leslie C.	38380728	Sgt
Cervantes, Francis I.	0703606	2/Lt
Chartier, Maurice C.	11044366	S/Sgt
Chressanthis, James	32941976	Sgt
Clark, Robert H.	0779789	2/Lt
Coates, James O.	34381779	T/Sgt
Conner, Fairce	351228260	S/Sgt
Contioso, Alfred A.	39038529	S/Sgt
Cotey, Robert L.	17121422	S/Sgt
Cotton, Joseph	0814402	2/Lt
Couch, Donald F.	42121538	Sgt
Covington, William L.	0816245	2/Lt
Cox, William E.	0.819970	1/Lt
Curtis, John R.	0-789884	1/Lt
Dauman, Alfred H.	0715729	1/Lt
Davis, Earl A.	0813477	2/Lt
Debowski, Joseph M.	13057528	S/Sgt
Debrular, Edward P.	35547122	S/Sgt
Delprete, Ralph F.	33609861	Sgt
Devine, George H. Jr.	32752185	S/Sgt
Devisser, Henry O.	1709027	S/Sgt
Devries, Alfons A.	36420245	T/Sgt
Dibble, Leon G. Jr.	0467431	1/Lt
Dichter, Lester	0699145	2/Lt
Dooling, William B.J.	11112104	Sgt
Dublisky, Martin	T.006954	F/O
Dukes, Julian E.	14140516	T/Sgt
Dydio, John J.	T.132890	F/O
Eagan, Robert A.	38497416	Sgt
Eason, William W.	34767010	Sgt
Eatherton, G.L. Jr.	37401269	S/Sgt
Edwards, Charles H.	0719592	2/Lt
Edwards, Fred W.	0724298	Capt
Edwards, John A.	39927521	Sgt
Edwards, Richard E.	T.132896	F/O
Ehrnman, Bowen T. Jr.	0699364	2/Lt
Eickhoff, Arthur G.	37721506	Sgt
Elliot, William W.	33686693	Pvt
Elmore, Gordon W.	16113201	T/Sgt
Ester, Elbert E.	39553701	S/Sgt
Estrach, Calman T.	0828127	2/Lt
Fabisiak, Theodore F.	32586872	S/Sgt

Farris, Presley E.	35128655	T/Sgt
Fleming, Richard W.	0819782	2/Lt
Flood, Robert J.	33567786	S/Sgt
Ford, Russell J.	33262604	Sgt
Foster, John F.	20756379	Sgt
Furniss, Riley J.	14134425	S/Sgt
Gaul, Clyde E.	15130667	S/Sgt
Gaulke, Frederick D.	0811064	1/Lt
Gault, John T.	33684921	S/Sgt
Gerlott, John C.	33610203	Sgt
Gillet, Jack S.	39272172	Sgt
Gleason, Irving C.	0.702265	2/Lt
Gouge, Robert R.	02068089	2/Lt
Graf, Eugene J. Jr.	33750770	Sgt
Green, Richard L.	T.132922	F/O
Grill, Mark R.	0708877	2/Lt
Grimm, Clarence W. Jr.	36802488	T/Sgt
Guy, George F. Jr.	14180873	Sgt
Hadden, Eugene H.	0808538	1/Lt
Hale, Chalmer M.	35262594	Sgt
Hamrick, James H.	35768846	Sgt
Hankin, Armond L.	0695814	2/Lt
Harmon, Raymond C.	16111441	Sgt
Harris, Roscoe E. Jr.	0747262	1/Lt
Hart, John C. Jr.	0698011	2/Lt
Hedges, Robert E.	0685606	2/Lt
Henry, William E.	17087062	Sgt
Herbert, Lloyd H.	0811381	2/Lt
Hernandez, Elias M.	38428503	S/Sgt
Higgins, John M.	T.061853	F/O
Hirschman, Gerald E.	0699931	2/Lt
Hollub, Eugene J.	38462432	Sgt
Holmes, Albert W.	0717139	2/Lt
Houser, Willie G.	38040770	Sgt
Hudiberg, Dale B.	39133839	Sgt
Hudson, William H.	0829029	1/Lt
Husbands, James H.	34649137	S/Sgt
Imparato, Joseph A.	0833120	2/Lt
Ippolito, Charles J.	12190364	T/Sgt
Jackson, Robert C.	0718102	2/Lt
Jacobs, Bernard P.	0718323	2/Lt
Jezior, Julius	35046846	S/Sgt
Johnson, Marshal W.	16080176	Sgt
Jones, Kyle B.	34728758	S/Sgt
Kalata, Vincent J.	16145063	Sgt
Kaspar, Arnold R.	0760327	2/Lt
Kaufman, Richard C.	0-693788	2/Lt

Kavanaugh, William P.	31420148	S/Sgt
Keedwell, Roger C.	0762574	2/Lt
Keller, Stanley J.	0704006	2/Lt
Kent, Dennis C. Jr.	18167684	S/Sgt
Kern, Morton J.	0550453	2/Lt
Kerr, Richard L.	35685305	S/Sgt
Kilpatrick, D.M. Jr.	0449356	1/Lt
Klasztorwski, A.B.	36501096	Sgt
Kline, Vincent M.	17087187	Sgt
Knight, Lester W.	0711424	2/Lt
Knowles, Richard A.	36860188	Sgt
Kofink, Frederick C.	0822921	1/Lt
Kossey, Theodore G.	32142243	T/Sgt
Krear, Richard S.	0709928	2/Lt
Krueger, Wallace	T.123129	F/O
Kuhlmeier, Theodore F.	37678262	Sgt
Kuhn, Howard C.	39412101	T/Sgt
Kussman, Edward W.	37261765	Sgt
Lague, Gerard A.	11111884	S/Sgt
Larivee, Francis E.	11038832	S/Sgt
Laslo, William E.	35600810	T/Sgt
Lee, Carl E. Jr.	0758500	1/Lt
Lemke, Frederick	0696381	1/Lt
Lewis, James L.	01699505	Capt
Lewis, William E. Jr.	39120406	S/Sgt
London, Edwin	T.128655	F/O
Lowblad, Charles T.	39329860	Cpl
Lupton, Charles R. Jr.	34674793	Sgt
Lutonsky, Luke F.	0659951	1/Lt
Magee, Thomas J. Jr.	0699349	2/Lt
Majchrzak, Clarence A.	32732947	T/Sgt
Majors, Merrill E. Jr.	T.003896	F/O
Manello, James M.	33495365	S/Sgt
Manfredi, Joseph A.	17070859	S/Sgt
Marangas, Stephen J.	0773413	1/Lt
Marcus, Frank E. Jr.	0823411	2/Lt
Marino, Mario A.	0783156	1/Lt
Martino, John A.	15017680	S/Sgt
Masano, Paul	38588615	Sgt
Matalamki, Wiljo J.	37543694	T/Sgt
Materna, Andrew	36634999	T/Sgt
Mathers, Creagh B. Jr.	14182562	Sgt
Matthews, James D.	38506486	Sgt
Matzen, Clifford W.	19024665	S/Sgt
Maxwell, Robert W.	0823426	1/Lt
Mazur, Victor H.	32670642	S/Sgt
McElyea, Robert H.	33479192	T/Sgt
McKee, Philip	36647268	Sgt
McKeen, Wilbur L.	0704570	2/Lt
McKoy, George C.	0689318	2/Lt

Name	Serial	Rank
McLaughlin, W.F.	12186503	T/Sgt
McMullen, Wesley F.	31196750	S/Sgt
McMurray, David P.	0796852	1/Lt
McPhillips, Herbert J.	31262090	Sgt
Melotte, James O.	14136533	Sgt
Mendenhall, William C.	35625420	Sgt
Metzger, George D.	0703285	2/Lt
Meyer, Henry H.	0702311	2/Lt
Meyer, Leonard H.H.	0702313	2/Lt
Mihocik, Milan J.	T.002701	F/O
Miller, Doyle C.	36302423	Sgt
Minihan, Thomas J.	20301527	S/Sgt
Miskevics, Charles J.	0704037	2/Lt
Mitchell, Joe D.	37651857	S/Sgt
Monahan, William J.	0833178	1/Lt
Moncy, William H.	18191727	S/Sgt
Monroe, John D.	0796426	1/Lt
Moore, Charles P.	0.694471	1/Lt
Moore, William A.	16116739	Sgt
Morrow, James G.	34703623	Sgt
Mueller, Vernon D.	0814947	2/Lt
Muller, Henry G.	0694930	2/Lt
Murray, Alvin M.	0809026	2/Lt
Nelson, Joe D.	0764926	1/Lt
Newman, Clayton J.	0.807773	1/Lt
Norton, Richard R. Jr.	0696869	2/Lt
Novotny, Herbert M.	36584465	S/Sgt
Nursall, Laurene H.	39549573	S/Sgt
Ochs, Leroy L.	0702323	2/Lt
Oliver, Henry F.	38692469	Sgt
Page, John J.	0707799	2/Lt
Parnell, Garrett C.J.	38341096	S/Sgt
Pascaul, Raymond	0668755	1/Lt
Patrinos, Frederick	36838989	Sgt
Patterson, Roy E. Jr.	38369850	Sgt
Paulsen, Richard M.	36455782	S/Sgt
Pearce, Iren R.	34474369	S/Sgt
Pelkey, Ernest E.	0341359	Capt
Pellegerini, Anthony	02068457	2/Lt
Peltz, Vincent	37471329	S/Sgt
Phinney, Judson E. Jr.	0831267	2/Lt
Pierce, Douglas E.	14098584	S/Sgt
Pirtle, James G.	39328818	S/Sgt
Pleasant, Douglas N.	17072038	S/Sgt
Polansky, Henry L.	0721858	2/Lt
Pope, Arthur		2/Lt
Powell, Joe C. Jr.	18198212	S/Sgt
Pratt, Charles C.	0687761	2/Lt
Proaps, John C.	19089738	S/Sgt
Ray, Leonard J.	20349559	T/Sgt
Ray, Reuben W.	18165452	Sgt
Raymond, Peter B.	32349111	Sgt
Redhair, Robert		2/Lt
Redinger, Ruben	36455599	Sgt
Reed, Jack S.	38449949	S/Sgt
Reeves, Eugene	18200715	S/Sgt
Reidell, George L.	32545918	Sgt
Reilly, Edward F. Jr.	0675290	1/Lt
Reyes, Miguel A.	39857267	Sgt
Richardson, Earl M.	0676494	1/Lt
Roads, Carl B. Jr.	0675120	1/Lt
Robertson, Uriel	34598778	Sgt
Rocha, Peter		2/Lt
Roe, Hiram A.	0683539	2/Lt
Rogers, James P.	0429700	1/Lt
Rogers, Edwin F.	16074978	S/Sgt
Rogers, James P.	0-492700	1/Lt
Rogers, John A.	T.135809	F/O
Rosen, Benjamin	0762947	2/Lt
Rosey, Jack	0697761	2/Lt
Royal, Lee	38365574	Sgt
Rutrick, David	32655396	Sgt
Rybarczyk, Luke S.	0668786	2/Lt
Sachtleben, Raymond	0811444	1/Lt
Salmons, Henery E.	0717148	1/Lt
Santini, Angelo	42003573	Sgt
Schaffert, Harry M.	0854918	1/Lt
Schlosser, Walter O.	16083944	S/Sgt
Schmaltz, Daniel W.	16080530	S/Sgt
Schmelyun, Calvin W.	33553905	S/Sgt
Schonfeld, Abraham	0810512	2/Lt
Schultz, William W.	0695542	2/Lt
Schwegel, Howard J.	35120394	S/Sgt
Seufert, William J.	35789596	T/Sgt
Shaw, William R.	0830988	1/Lt
Sheafer, Val D. Jr.	0718030	2/Lt
Sheely, William F.	14084971	S/Sgt
Shelledy, Fayette	39144844	Sgt
Shepherd, Richard P.	0823720	2/Lt
Simmonds, Albert F.	32937987	Sgt
Skadden, Wayman B.	39408365	S/Sgt
Skwara, Ernest C.	0746915	2/Lt
Smickle, F.W. Jr.	0785613	2/Lt
Smiley, Elmer J.	0808600	1/Lt
Smith, Graham T. Jr.	14174661	Sgt
Snyder, Franklin W.	15126090	S/Sgt
Sonner, Warren R.	0815005	2/Lt
Spyker, Jack H.	36453523	Sgt
Stallings, George D.	0706907	2/Lt
Stamerra, Salvatore E.	33422124	S/Sgt
Stein, Lester	0547173	2/Lt
Stevens, Fred J.	14176419	S/Sgt
Stevens, William K.	31268922	Sgt
Stiglitz, Hyman L.	11045879	T/Sgt
Stillfrew, Lowell S.	16076369	S/Sgt
Stolberg, John M.	0723733	2/Lt
Stone, Alton R.	02070174	2/Lt
Stpierre, Arthur M.	11038830	S/Sgt
Strauss, Murray D.	12180273	S/Sgt
Stuckey, James W.	12167320	S/Sgt
Stuckey, John	38389577	Sgt
Sumowski, Henry J.	31276731	Sgt
Swan, Jack J.	36454360	Sgt
Swisher, Chester M.	0857221	2/Lt
Tarpey, Timothy N.	0696273	2/Lt
Taylor, Colin V.	0701504	2/Lt
Taylor, Robert E.	0696528	2/Lt
Telfer, Leonard F.	0810071	2/Lt
Tetzloff, Lionel A.	17109621	S/Sgt
Thivener, Chester L.	35647426	S/Sgt
Tilton, Charles A.	32619543	T/Sgt
Toepper, Miles L	36655469	S/Sgt
Tomlinson, Douglas J.	0703343	2/Lt
Tosi, Julian	39414390	Sgt
Touron, Prosper J.	39043904	S/Sgt
Tracey, Patrick A.	32316370	S/Sgt
Tresemer, Edward C.	0434010	Maj
Trotta, Michael J.	12158002	Sgt
Turner, Leslie L.	31318529	T/Sgt
Vilelli, Frank A.	37563633	S/Sgt
Vincent, Arthur F.	0.550854	2/Lt
Walker, Connie O. Jr.	0821120	2/Lt
Watson, Ernest L.	0817307	2/Lt
Wells, Grant L.	39832925	S/Sgt
Wells, Millard C. Jr.	0808625	2/Lt
Wensel, Harry L.	12031247	S/Sgt
Wilkie, William M.	12174218	S/Sgt
Willard, Eugene F.	19193373	S/Sgt
Williams, Ralph S.	34382012	S/Sgt
Wilson, Charles		S/Sgt
Wing, John G.	35325157	T/Sgt
Wolfersberger, R.G.J.	36466780	Sgt
Wrobel, Glen R.	0702090	2/Lt
Yandoh, Thomas E.	0550440	2/Lt
Yankovich, John J.	0691849	2/Lt
Zahn, John H. Jr.	0703866	2/Lt
Zeigler, Paul L.	13031389	T/Sgt
Zinkand, Thomas	0832313	1/Lt
Zipfel, Robert N.	0702999	2/Lt
Zwinge, Joseph W. Jr.	39412668	T/Sgt

4TH FIGHTER GROUP

Name	Serial	Rank
Alfred, Carl R.	0661172	Capt
Anderson, Stanley M.	0885096	Capt
Arnold, Harvie J.	0706332	2/Lt
Barnes, George W.	02044944	1/Lt
Bates, William D.	T.126017	F/O
Boock, Robert A.	0885186	1/Lt
Boren, Stephen R.	0706574	2/Lt
Boyce, Ralph G.	0758928	2/Lt
Boyles, Frank R.	0885130	Capt
Brandenburg, James H.	02044945	1/Lt
Buchholz, Robert C.	0720770	1/Lt
Byrd, James T. Jr.	0705539	2/Lt
Carpenter, Leroy A.J.	0423822	Capt
Cole, Leon J. Jr.	0705493	2/Lt
Conley, John T.	0705549	2/Lt
Cooper, Robert J.	0707664	2/Lt
Cox, William A.	T.122255	F/O
Dahlen, Kermit O.	0695158	2/Lt
Dailey, Leo	0701075	2/Lt
Davis, Albert J.	0701076	Capt
Davis, Harry L.	0830418	2/Lt
Davis, Robert O.	0802261	1/Lt
Delnero, Carmeno J.	0767148	2/Lt
Emerson, Donald R.	0813134	Capt
Fiedler, Clemens A.	02044917	1/Lt
Fischer, Robert G.	0705570	2/Lt
Fraser, Robert B.	0885408	1/Lt
Frederick, Harold H.	0812408	1/Lt
Freeburger, Edward P.		1/Lt
Gallion, Frank D.	T.190742	F/O
Garbey, Cecil E.	0758793	2/Lt
Goetz, Joseph	T.122269	F/O
Grimm, Cheater P.	0885280	2/Lt
Hall, Frederick D.	0825433	2/Lt
Herter, Glenn A.	02044891	1/Lt
Hewes, Charles D.	0727460	Capt
Hill, Dean J.	0756576	1/Lt
Hobert, Robert D.	0885236	Capt
Hofer, Ralph K.	02045177	1/Lt
Homuth, Robert H.	0756584	1/Lt
Howard, C.G.	0706400	2/Lt
Hunt, William W.	0756593	1/Lt
Hustwit, Earl F.	0705503	
Iden, Paul S.	0817033	2/Lt
Jones, Frank C. Jr.	0659133	Capt
Kakerbeck, Robert L.	0816875	2/Lt
Kaminski, Rudolph B.	0813173	1/Lt
Kaul, Henry A.	0825449	1/Lt
Kelly, William P.	0885198	Capt
King, Gerrett C.	0885481	1/Lt
Kingham, Lloyd G.	0886110	1/Lt
Kolter, Mark H.	0501413	2/Lt
Lang, Joseph L.	0686643	Capt
Leaf, Dale B.	0885233	1/Lt
Lehman, Peter G.	02044893	1/Lt
Lewis, Ralph E.	0826699	2/Lt
Logan, George H. Jr.	0694168	1/Lt
Lutz, John F.	0885136	1/Lt
McGrattan, Bernard	02044954	Capt
McMinn, Richard D.	0885135	Capt
Mead, Charles Y.	0826476	2/Lt
Merritt, Frederick D.	0885493	1/Lt
Mitchellweis, John J.	0885217	2/Lt
Netting, Conrad J.	0694174	2/Lt
Noon, Harry B.	0699021	2/Lt
Patterson, Rufus L.	0815755	2/Lt
Pierce, Leonard R.	0813221	1/Lt
Powell, Jap A.	0885396	2/Lt
Rasmussen, Herman S.	0762408	2/Lt
Richards, Robert H.	02044979	2/Lt
Rosenson, Bernard J.	0661804	1/Lt
Ross, Harold L. Jr.	0694264	1/Lt
Ryerson, Leonard T.	0885137	2/Lt
Santos, Paul G.	0887825	1/Lt
Saunders, Ralph W.	0812491	2/Lt
Savage, Morton R.		1/Lt
Schlegel, Albert L.	02044921	Capt
Scott, James F.	0694188	1/Lt
Seifert, Robert H.	0694189	2/Lt
Senecal, Arthur J.	0887832	1/Lt
Sharp, Thomas S.	0759091	1/Lt
Sibbert, Frank T.	0759095	1/Lt
Skilton, Ernest R.	0810584	1/Lt
Smith, Donald E.	0817116	2/Lt
Smith, Homer C.	0834315	2/Lt
Smith, Kenneth B.	0694193	2/Lt
Smith, Walter Jr.	T.190716	F/O
Smith, William B.	02044874	Capt
Smolinsky, Frank J.	0885174	2/Lt
Sobanski, Winslow M.	0885191	Maj
Stallings, Robert L.	0433048	1/Lt
Stepp, Malta L. Jr.	0885155	Capt
Steppe, Edward J.	0697594	2/Lt
Tussey, Robert S.	0693176	1/Lt
Vandervate, H. Jr.	0792182	1/Lt
Villinger, George K.	02044899	1/Lt
Vozzy, Nicholas W.	0707754	2/Lt
Wallace, Alvin O.		1/Lt
Werner, Leonard,R.	0796249	1/Lt
Whalen, Edmund D.	0886143	1/Lt
White, Robert W.	0887026	2/Lt
Wyman, Burt C.	02044430	1/Lt

56TH FIGHTER GROUP

Name	Serial	Rank
Aheron, Frank R.	0829607	2/Lt
Albright, Edward M. Jr.	0-790606	1/Lt
Allayaud, Donald	0829608	2/Lt
Allen, John R.	0711896	2/Lt
Allison, Richard H.	0659214	1/Lt
Baker, Wyman A.	0821833	2/Lt
Barnum, Eugene E. Jr.	0659222	Capt
Barron, Louis T.	0661178	2/Lt
Batson, Samuel K.	0714845	2/Lt
Bokina, Carl J.	0806789	1/Lt
Bradford, Robert J.	0432047	Capt
Buchmiller, Lowell C.	0774008	2/Lt
Cagle, Oscar L. Jr.	0-824410	2/Lt
Calmes, Alben G.	T.003423	F/O
Carlson, Charles E.	0706483	2/Lt
Choate, George R. Jr.	0-552299	2/Lt
Dahl, Max H.	0832354	2/Lt
Del Corso, Joseph A.	T.063224	F/O
DeMars, Jack D.	0714894	2/Lt
DeMayo, Julius	0-770200	2/Lt
Dimmick, Allen E.	0422899	1/Lt
Dyar, Roger B.	0430926	Capt
Eby, Merle C.	0429058	Capt
Egan, Joseph L. Jr.	0790815	Capt
Evans, Alfred D. Jr.	0816081	2/Lt
Fisher, Byron J.	0-716087	2/Lt
Frazier, John F.	0710086	1/Lt
Hall, Robert S.	0830455	2/Lt
Healy, Robert F.	0-714914	2nd Lt
Hedke, Jack D.	0716126	2/Lt
Henry, Albert L.	0-715537	2nd Lt

Name	Serial	Rank	Name	Serial	Rank	Name	Serial	Rank	Name	Serial	Rank
Hines, Luther P. Jr.	0716135	1/Lt	Lightfoot, Edward B.	0708191	1/Lt	Raymond, Elwood D.	0-814757	2nd Lt	Tettemer, Don	0793592	2/Lt
Hoffman, William R.	0715544	1/Lt							Townsend, Earl L.	0826568	2/Lt
			Magel, David M.	0763676	1/Lt	Scherz, Willard C.	0767398	1/Lt	Tuttle, Richard B.	0830584	2/Lt
Kruer, Edward J.	0793635	2/Lt	McMinn, Evan D.	0886834	1/Lt	Smith, Kenneth L.	0446936	1/Lt			
						Spicer, Harold E.	0-708344	2/Lt	Wetherbee, Robert H.	0429198	Capt
Lambert, James H. Jr.	15063471	Sgt	Osborne, William J.	0712026	2/Lt	Stevens, Gordon S.	0792651	Capt	Windmayer, F.C.	0736446	2/Lt
Langdon, Lloyd M.	0686860	2/Lt				Stitt, Paul W.	0830115	2/Lt	Wither, James S.	0802093	2/Lt
Lewis, John E.	T.192076	F/O	Pitts, Walter H.	0-770393	2/Lt	Stovall, William H. Jr.	0716271	1/Lt			
Lewis, Kenneth K.	0688273	2/Lt	Pruden, Harry M. Jr.	0736351	2/Lt				Zychowski, Albin P.	0704806	2/Lt

355TH FIGHTER GROUP

Name	Serial	Rank	Name	Serial	Rank	Name	Serial	Rank	Name	Serial	Rank
Barab, Bernard R. Jr.	0796643	1/Lt	Folcer, John M.	0758787	1/Lt	Lanphier, John	0672633	2/Lt	Pipher, Frank L. Jr.	0799632	2/Lt
Barger, Clarence R.	02045165	1/Lt	Foster, Thomas J.	0758789	1/Lt	Lee, Charles M.	08102448	1/Lt	Plowman, Gilbert M.	0820657	2/Lt
Beaty, Wendell W.	0664498	Capt	Fritts, Herbert E.	01634776	2/Lt	Lowder, James P. Jr.	0812740	1/Lt			
Beckman, Jack M.	02045225	Capt	Fuller, Leonard B.	0694235	1/Lt				Rafferty, Kevin G.	0424727	Capt
Bookout, Elbert B.	3823918	Sgt				Maben, Eugene W. Jr.	0672641	2/Lt	Rankin, Chauncey H.	0671764	1/Lt
			Goth, Robert A.	0719305	1/Lt	Martyn, Donald M.	0687387	1/Lt	Reeves, Willis W. Jr.	0821781	2/Lt
Carlson, Edwin O.	0671499	1/Lt	Gowing, Franklin R.	0695315	2/Lt	McCraw, Lawrence E.	0796001	1/Lt	Riggs, John D. Jr.	0706445	1/Lt
Christensen, W.M. Jr.	0758944	2/Lt	Graczyk, Michael E.	0821694	1/Lt	McCurry, Charles R.	0821520	2/Lt	Rothenberg, Daniel S.	0687399	2/Lt
Coleman, Ralph L.	0694221	1/Lt	Guerrant, John Jr.	0695056	2/Lt	McDonald, Norman E.	0432082	Capt			
Collins, Clark	0671504	1/Lt				McNally, Donald B.	0672639	1/Lt	Sawchuk, Peter M.	0801341	2/Lt
Cooper, Randolph W.	02057566	1/Lt	Haraburda, Edward F.	0767212	1/Lt	Michela, Frank	0821608	2/Lt	Stalcup, Oran H.	0766749	1/Lt
Costigan, James J.	01030137	1/Lt	Hardee, Sellers S.	05242410	1/Lt	Mills, Newell F. Jr.	0827247	1/Lt	Sweat, Charles H.	0796222	1/Lt
Crabb, Robert L.	0710450	1/Lt	Harvey, Everett P.	18078158	Cpl	Momberger, William H.	0525127	1/Lt			
Culp, Harold F.	0673323	1/Lt	Hill, Byron L.	0671539	1/Lt	Monahan, Harold L.	0821531	1/Lt	Taylor, Thomas J.	0823174	1/Lt
			Hillman, Howard K.	0693135	1/Lt				Truel, Thomas F. Jr.	0819218	1/Lt
Daves, Richard C.	0708666	2/Lt	Hollman, Nils E. Jr.	0693209	2/Lt	Neal, Thomas F. Jr.	0672658	Capt			
Davis, Henry W.	T.123235	F/O	Hornickel, William E.	0707695	1/Lt	Norman, Robert L.	0797697	1/Lt	Vigna, Joseph J.	0697072	1/Lt
Dean, Ralph L.	0796666	1/Lt	Huish, Heber M.	0816820	2/Lt				Vincent, Roland L.	0796240	1/Lt
Delnegro, Alfred J.	0673328	1/Lt	Hull, James C.	0795961	1/Lt	Olson, Norman E.	0660186	Capt			
Dentu, Victor E.	0758778	2/Lt				Onoris, Edward	0799623	1/Lt	Wambier, Charles A.	T.000996	F/O
Dickson, James B.	0795918	Capt	Jacobson, Donald J.	0812432	1/Lt	Orr, Benjamin F. Jr.	0759066	1/Lt	Watson, Chester W.	T.000998	F/O
Donovan, James J.	0799956	2/Lt							Weber, Wilson B.	0665474	2/Lt
Demers, Raymond F.	0671516	1/Lt	Kelley, Charles W.	0826462	2/Lt	Packard, Hudson F.	0813212	1/Lt	White, Bob G.	0725235	1/Lt
			Ksanznak, Thomas A.	0697039	1/Lt	Patterson, Gilbert L.	0813217	2/Lt	Williams, Edward R.	T.061692	F/O
Easterly, William S.	0795921	Capt				Peters, Robert O.	0442108	1/Lt	Woertz, Jack J.	0796053	1/Lt
Ekstrom, Carl F.	0660122	Capt	Lake, Joseph E.	0793000	Capt	Phillips, George W.	0796024	1/Lt	Woolard, Marion L.	0886802	1/Lt
Ellison, John C.	0705563	1/Lt	Lambert, Howard L. Jr.	0025631	Capt	Pilmore, John J. Jr.	0693203	1/Lt			

361ST FIGHTER GROUP

Name	Serial	Rank	Name	Serial	Rank	Name	Serial	Rank	Name	Serial	Rank
Adams, Robert G.	0820187	1/Lt	Durbin, Richard M.	0416226	Capt	Kinnaird, Eubene W.	0673385	1/Lt	Rogers, James A.	0814041	2/Lt
Amason, Ethelbert F.	0676715	1/Lt				Knupp, Daniel F.	0824654	2/Lt			
Armsby, Sherman	0814628	1/Lt	Eason, James A.	0705561	1/Lt				Sadinski, John J.	0733994	1/Lt
Arrants, Clyde A.	0763456	2/Lt	Elliott, Miles E.	0758783	2/Lt	Lamb, Leo H.	0824657	2/Lt	Sargent, Walter H.	0806766	2/Lt
						Latimer, Joe L.	0520631	Capt	Staples, William V.	0821799	2/Lt
Berge, Glennt	0673303	1/Lt	Feller, Charles H.	0441802	Capt	Layton, Calab J.	0798660	1/Lt	Stolzy, Robert J.	0678970	1/Lt
Bosyk, Harry G.	0821447	2/Lt	Ford, Delmar R.	0720829	1/Lt						
						McKivett, Charles C.	0768186	2/Lt	Todd, Collier W. Jr.	0814788	2/Lt
Callaway, David L.	0674033	1/Lt	Geck, Robert E.	0710093	2/Lt	Merritt, George L. Jr.	0335212	Maj			
Christiansen, Francis	0726331	1/Lt	Glover, Woodrow W.	0568313	1/Lt	Moore, Charles E.	0686762	2/Lt	Wade, Russell D.	0674349	Capt
Clement, Robert C.	0820461	2/Lt	Guckeyson, John W.	0024959	Capt				Weaver, Dennis B.	0680973	2/Lt
Conroy, John J.	11100588	Sgt				Narvis, Charles W.	0698999	1/Lt	Wherry, Warren D.	0814808	2/Lt
Cook, Alfred B. Jr.	0763502	2/Lt	Hogelin, Cornelius G.	T.061492	F/O	Nazzarett, Daniel B.	0803434	2/Lt	Wilson, John R. Jr.	02059387	2/Lt
Crandell, Jack S.	0814656	2/Lt				Norman, James M. Jr.	0803437	1/Lt	Wolfe, Joseph B.	0704794	1/Lt
			Jackson, Deane E.	T.063456	F/O						
Dahl, Milton A.	0710053	2/Lt	Johnson, Denzil R.	18162817	Cpl	Perry, Lawrence B.	0803447	1/Lt	Zelinsky, Robert M.	0832540	2/Lt
Dellinger, Donald D.	0820239	2/Lt							Zieske, Clarence E.	0482345	1/Lt
Downey, Lawrence E.	0677997	1/Lt	Kapr, Joseph V.	0700275	2/Lt	Rautenbush, William	0803453	1/Lt			
Duncan, Albert C.	0678845	1/Lt	Kenoyer, Russell E.	0721424	2/Lt						

479TH FIGHTER GROUP

Name	Serial	Rank	Name	Serial	Rank	Name	Serial	Rank	Name	Serial	Rank
Clarke, William D.	0661192	1/Lt	Hymans, Robert B.	0719350	2/Lt	Neumann, Walter A.	0763313	1/Lt	Schoen, Charles F. Jr.	0825774	2/Lt
									Scordino, Anthony J.	0832823	1/Lt
Daniels, James K.	34058754	S/Sgt	King, Raymond E.	T.62723	F/O	Ontko, Andrew R.	6645381	M/Sgt	Stott, Donald H.	0856208	1/Lt
Donnell, John C. Jr.	0767155	1/Lt	Krauss, Harold F. Jr.	0057642	2/Lt				Sullivan, John A.	0423966	Maj
						Pigg, Robert N.	0758054	1/Lt			
Granville, Chester W.	0760289	1/Lt	Malone, Jay C.	0767304	Capt	Red, Douglas L.	0822265	1/Lt	Trabucco, Thomas F.	0406062	Maj
			Marlowe, Wendell H.	0824530	1/Lt	Remling, Milton L.	0660520	1/Lt			
Hurtig, Edward L.	0824493	1/Lt	McGahan, Chester	0789485	1/Lt	Sands, Thurman E.	0832497	2/Lt	Vassuer, Peter C.	0763422	1/Lt

HARRY C AARON, 489TH
FRANK W AARONSON, 445TH
JOHN G ABAJIAN, 93RD
LTC LELAND ABBEY RET, 492ND, 467TH
LTC BERNARD ABEL RET, 93RD
PETER T ABELL, 445TH
TOD ABELMAN, 491ST, AM
JOE L ABERNATHY, 467TH
LTC LEN ABRAMOWITZ RET, 458TH, 489TH
BERNARD ABRAMS, 44TH
MANNY ABRAMS, 392ND
PAUL ABRAMS, HDQ, AM
HERBERT ACHTERBERG, 466TH
ILA ACHTERBERG, SM
JAMES M ACKERMAN, 392ND
JOSEPH V ACTON, 389TH
ABNER L ADAMS, 446TH
BRUCE L ADAMS, 389TH
DAVID A ADAMS, 93RD
FRANK J ADAMS JR, 44TH
GEORGE W ADAMS, 491ST
JACK W ADAMS, 491ST
JAMES A ADAMS JR, 389TH, AM
LTC JAMES L ADAMS RET, 93RD
JOHN H ADAMS, 392ND
ORA R ADAMS, 453RD
STEPHEN P ADAMS, SM
W DEAN ADAMS, 466TH
WILLIAM B ADAMS, 453RD
MILTON ADAMSKY, 389TH
DR JACK C ADAMSON, 392ND
ERNEST J ADCOCK, 445TH
LUCIUS R ADES, 389TH
HARRY M ADIE, 93RD
AMOS B ADKINS, 453RD
GEORGE F ADKINS, 458TH
RICHARD E ADKINS, 93RD
NORWOOD ADLER, 448TH
WILLARD E ADLER, 453RD
DR JAMES M ADOVASIO, 389TH, AM
LENA ADOVASIO, 389TH, AM
BOYD D ADSIT, 392ND
LOUIS J AFFINITO, 392ND
ROBERT J AFTON SR, 489TH
CHESLEY B AGEE, 93RD
SAM AGIN, 446TH
MICHAEL P AGRESTA, 458TH
JOSEPH L AGRIESTI, 489TH
MIKE AGUIRRE, 453RD
HARRY L AHLBORN, 93RD
EINAR AHLMAN, 93RD
GEORGE W AHLSEN, 458TH
CARL W AHRENDT, 448TH
EUGENE A AICHROTH, 467TH
CHARLES E AILLET, 458TH
EDWARD M AINSWORTH, 491ST
DELMAR E AKERLEY, 448TH
W A AKINS, 93RD
BRIAN ALBERGHINI, 445TH, AM
MARK W ALBERGHINI, 445TH, AM
PAUL M ALBERGHINI, 445TH, AM
ROY E ALBERGHINI, 445TH
THERESA ALBERGHINI, 445TH, AM
TOD ALBERGHINI, 445TH, AM
ARTHUR A ALBERT, 458TH
BRUCE W ALBERT, 453RD
JOAN R ALBERT, 458TH, AM
LUCIEN ALBERT, 458T
WARREN E ALBERTS, HDQ, 93RD
HAROLD ALBERTSON, 467TH
ANTHONY ALBINO, 392ND
DONALD L ALBION, 453RD
A RICHARD ALBRECHT, 448TH
LTC CARL H ALBRIGHT RET, 446TH
HARRY J ALBRIGHT, 93RD
JACK D ALBRIGHT, 489TH, 389TH
PETE ALDEN, SM

RICHARD ALDRICH, 453RD
LTC WILLIAM S ALDRIDGE RET, 44TH
MAX K ALDWORTH, 448TH
ALLEN B ALEXANDER, 392ND
MAJ BERT F ALEXANDER RET, 93RD
LTC CYRUS J ALEXANDER RET, 448TH
EDWIN J ALEXANDER JR, 492ND, 467TH
GEORGE N ALEXANDER, 93RD
LOREN R ALEXANDER, 448TH
PHILIP A ALEXANDER, 489TH
ROBERT S ALEXANDER, 446TH
THOMAS J ALEXANDER, 392ND
CARL I ALEXANDERSON, 491ST
BERNARD A ALFRED, 453RD
JOHN E ALFRIEND, 93RD
JOSEPH D ALIFFI, 453RD
DALE E ALLAN, 491ST
MAJ PETER J D ALLATT RET, 93RD
EARL H ALLEBACH, 491ST
CHARLES R ALLEN, 453RD
DONALD C ALLEN, 458TH
EDGAR J ALLEN, 93RD
EVERETT S ALLEN, 458TH
GERALD O ALLEN, 458TH
HENRY W ALLEN, 392ND
JANET ALLEN, SM
DR LYNN D ALLEN, 467TH
PAUL S ALLEN, 93RD
ROBERT M ALLEN, 453RD
SIDNEY B ALLEN JR, 448TH
THOMAS R ALLEN, 491ST
WAYNE B ALLEN, 445TH
JOHN D ALLENBAUGH, 466TH
DONALD H ALLES, 445TH
FLOYD C ALLEY, HDQ
JACK R ALLEY, 453RD
DONALD A ALLISON, 445TH
SM/SGT OLLIN F ALLISON RET, 491ST
RAYMOND ALNOR, 489TH
JOHN F ALONSO, 445TH
JULIO ALONSO, 453RD
WILLIAM ALPERN, 467TH
GERALD ALPORT, 466TH
JAMES C ALTHOFF, SM
JOHN T ALTMAN, 44TH
DAVE ALTSHULER, 389TH
EINO ALVE, 453RD
LYLE G ALVERSON, 453RD
ALBERT A ALVES, 93RD
RICHARD O ALVESTAD, 458TH
LTC GENE P ALVORD RET, 93RD
FRANK AMADOR, 389TH, AM
HENRY R AMAR, 453RD
HAROLD A AMES, 389TH
ERNEST E AMMONS, 491ST
L C AMMONS, SM
JOSEPH E AMREIN, 446TH
RICHARD H AMSTUTZ, 93RD
ANGIE ANAPOL, 65FW
PAUL C ANDERSEN, 389TH
ANER R ANDERSON, 392ND
ARTHUR G ANDERSON, 467TH
BERNARD I ANDERSON, 445TH
BRUCE J ANDERSON, 448TH
BURKE I ANDERSON, 489TH
CLARENCE A ANDERSON, 491ST
EDWARD J ANDERSON, 453RD
EDWARD L ANDERSON, 93RD
EDWARD V ANDERSON, 448TH
FORREST F ANDERSON, 448TH
GEORGE C ANDERSON JR, 445TH
GERALD ANDERSON, 446TH
HAROLD E ANDERSON, 466TH
HENRY A ANDERSON, 448TH
HERMAN J ANDERSON, 458TH
HUGH V ANDERSON, 389TH

JAMES J ANDERSON, 453RD
LAWRENCE E ANDERSON, 448TH
LLOYD E ANDERSON, 93RD
COL MARVIN J ANDERSON RET, 446TH
PAUL I ANDERSON, 389TH
LTC RALPH N ANDERSON RET, 467TH
ROBERT L ANDERSON, 453RD
UNO H ANDERSON, 491ST
VERL D ANDERSON, 453RD, 466TH
W G ANDERSON, 93RD
WILLIAM D ANDERSON, 446TH
ROBERT J ANDRES, 44TH
ANDREW J ANDRESEN, 448TH
EINAR A ANDRESEN, 389TH
LLOYD B ANDREW, 458TH
MARVIN E ANDREWS, 492ND
VINCENT C ANGELORO, 489TH
ROBERT ANGLE, 448TH
LTC SAMUEL T ANGUISH RET, 448TH
BILLIE ASH ANKENY, HDQ
JAMES R ANSLOW, 467TH
WILLIAM ANSON, 489TH
MILTON P ANSTEY, 392ND
ROBERT I ANTHONY, 44TH
ADRIAN ANTONELLE, 389TH
ARTHUR S ANTONIEWICZ, 491ST
FRANK ANTONUCCI, 93RD, 491ST
MURRAY R APFELBAUM, 448TH
GEORGE M APGAR JR, 44TH
EDWARD W APPEL, 445TH, 93RD, 389TH, 56FG
IRVING H APPEL, 453RD
LEON APPEL, 466TH
CARL W APPELIN, 44TH
MAJ LEONARD APTER RET, 453RD
JOE L ARAIZA, 446TH
JOE ARCANGELI, 44TH
ROBERT M ARCHAMBAULT, 489TH, 445TH
JOHN W ARCHER, HM
BRUNO A ARCUDI, 453RD
PHILIP P ARDERY, 389TH
KENNETH L ARDREY, 44TH
HENRY ARIAS SR, 458TH
ROBERT E ARMBRUSTER, 458TH
LTC PAUL E ARMENTROUT RET, 446TH
ROY D ARMENTROUT, 489TH
PRESTON L ARMOND, 93RD
LESTER A ARMS, 492ND, 44TH
LTC CHARLES L ARMSTRONG RET, 44TH, 389TH
HAROLD G ARMSTRONG, 458TH
HENRY ARNAUD, 445TH
LESLIE P ARNBERGER, 458TH
CALVIN D ARNETT, 466TH
JOHN W ARNOLD, 392ND
B/GEN MILTON W ARNOLD RET, 389TH, HDQ
LTC R F ARNOLD RET, 44TH
WILLIAM D ARNOLD, 448TH
WILLIAM ARONOFF, 466TH
COL ALFRED ASCH RET, 93RD
GEORGE J ASCHINGER, 491ST
RAYMOND S ASH, 458TH
ROBERT I ASH, 458TH
ROBERT T ASH, 448TH
WILLIAM T ASH, 65FW
GEORGE T ASHEN, 392ND
HARRY J ASTLEY, 446TH
HENRY V ATHERTON, 448TH
CHARLES N ATKINS, 44TH
LTC E RICHARD ATKINS RET, SM
FRANCIS R ATKINS, 458TH
ROBERT F ATKINS, 453RD
DONALD G ATKINSON, 458TH
JAMES C ATKISON OD, 93RD

CHARLES E ATON, 93RD
JAMES O ATTAWAY SR, 448TH
ROBERT W ATTENBOROUGH, 458TH
LTC LYNN E ATWOOD RET, 491ST
RUPERT J A AUBREY-COUND, SM
VICTOR E AUCHARD, 445TH
GEORGE A AUDETTE, 467TH
LTC LEONARD S AUGER RET, 389TH
JUNIOR L AUGHENBAUGH, 445TH
MERLYN AUGSBERGER, 467TH
CHARLES A AULGUR, 389TH
JAMES O AUMAN, 466TH
JUNIOR AUSTIN, 453RD
LAURIN D AUSTIN, 392ND
WAYNE L AUSTIN, 458TH
WILLIAM D AUSTIN, 492ND
JOSEPH M AUTOBEE, 448TH
EDWARD AVENA, 446TH
BALDWIN C AVERY, 445TH, 389TH
LEONARD AVONA, 93RD
ROBERT S AYERS, HDQ
ROBERT H AYRES, 389TH
JOE BAADSGAARD, 458TH
MICHAEL R BAAS, 389TH, AM
KEITH L BABCOCK, 446TH
WILLARD E BABCOCK, 93RD
ROBERT C BACHER, 491ST
FRANKLYN BACHMAN, 491ST
LAWRENCE W BACHMAN, 392ND
HENRY J BACKOWSKI, 445TH, 492ND
T/SGT LEONARD W BACLE, SM
GEORGE W BACON, 392ND
WARREN T BACZIK, 466TH
CHARLES H BADER, 392ND
HOMER H BADGETT, 389TH, 453RD
REINHARDT BAEHR, 93RD
LTC LESTER J BAER RET, 453RD
RICHARD E BAGG, SM
W HOWARD BAGGETT, 446TH
WALTER G BAGLEY, 458TH
JEROME E BAIER, 453RD, 467TH
BERNARD W BAIL MD, 44TH
DONALD C BAILEY, 392ND
GEORGE W BAILEY, 93RD
LLOYD E BAILEY, 458TH
MIKE BAILEY, HM
RICHARD F BAILEY, 453RD
WAYNE D BAILEY, 492ND
JOHN H BAILLIE, 453RD
SAM BAIN, 93RD
ROBERT H BAIRD, 445TH
LOUIS W BAJGIER, 44TH
ALLEN J BAKER, 44TH
BURTON C BAKER, 453RD
CHARLES T BAKER, 489TH
CLARENCE E BAKER, 44TH
EDWIN C BAKER, 93RD
FRANK D BAKER, 466TH, AM
GEORGE D BAKER, 93RD
GORDON M BAKER, 389TH
JAMES R BAKER, 44TH
LAWRENCE J BAKER, 466TH
LEE M BAKER, 489TH
MAJ LOVELL E BAKER JR RET, 466TH
ORVILLE C BAKER, 445TH
RAYMOND H BAKER, 44TH
ROBERT E BAKER, 467TH
SHELDON BAKER, 453RD
WILLIE T BAKER, 458TH
WALTER S BALA, 453RD
PHILIP E BALCOMB, 446TH
MELVIN W BALDUS, 453RD
ARCHIE W BALDWIN, 466TH
CARL D BALDWIN, 448TH
LTC DONALD C BALDWIN RET, 453RD
KENNETH BALDWIN, 445TH

MILES S BALDWIN, 448TH
WILLIAM C BALDWIN, 466TH
JOHN F BALES JR, 492ND, 467TH
EDWARD A BALGA SR, 93RD
JOHN R BALL, 389TH
ORVILLE P BALL, 445TH
OWEN K BALL, 453RD, 492ND, 467TH
WALLACE J BALLA, 44TH, 14CW
PAUL BALLAM-DAVIES, SM
B E BALLARD JR, 458TH
JAMES E BALLARD, 445TH
JAMES F BALLARD JR, 467TH
COL WILBUR A BALLENTINE RET, 489TH
CARL E BALLY, 445TH
GILBERT R BAMBAUER, 392ND
THOMAS K BAMFORD, 93RD
HENRY A BAMMAN, 93RD
NORBERT J BANASZAK, 392ND
RHODA U BANDLER, HDQ, AM
WALTER E BANDLOW, 467TH
BILLY BANDY, 93RD, AM
RALPH BANEY, 389TH
COL BILL B BANIAS RET, 453RD
ANDREW BANKO, 466TH
JACK L BARAK, 448TH
CLEON M BARBER, 392ND
EDWARD R BARBER, 445TH
ERNEST H BARBER, 392ND
JAMES B BARBER, 44TH
JAMES R BARBER, 446TH
BRUNO L BARBI, 446TH
BRUNO L BARBI, 446TH
S/SGT HAROLD J BARDELL RET, 458TH
REV NORMAN BARDSLEY, SM
EVERETT G BAREFOOT, 445TH
SAM BARGAMIAN, 93RD
DR GEORGE W BARGER, 392ND
LEO G BARGER, 491ST
LOUIS G BARGOUT, 93RD
LAWRENCE W BARHAM, 448TH
STEVE F BARILICH, 467TH
JOHN R BARILLARO, 458TH
HUGH M BARINEAU, 458TH
HENRY M BARKER, 453RD
SUSIE BARKER, SM
LEWIS E BARLEY, 453RD
ARCHIE R BARLOW JR, 44TH
COL HARVEY P BARNARD JR RET, 93RD
SHERIDAN & MARY BARNARD, 445TH, AM
MRS ANNE BARNE, BG
ALBERT J BARNEBEE, 448TH, 491ST, 492ND
ALBERT R BARNES, 458TH
T/SGT ED BARNES, 445TH
HAROLD A BARNES, 44TH
RAYMOND W BARNES, 445TH
ROBERT C BARNES, 445TH
WADE D BARNES, 467TH
WILBUR E BARNES, 453RD
WILLIAM T BARNES JR, 467TH
K W BARNET, 448TH
DAVID BARON, 466TH
RAYMOND A BARR, 466TH
CLARENCE J BARRAS, 489TH
JOSEPH A BARRELLA, 446TH, 491ST
JAMES E BARRETT, 389TH
RALPH BARRETT, 44TH
STEVE BARRETT, SM
WILLIAM R BARRETT, 392ND
JOHN A BARRON, 445TH
DONALD P BARRY, 93RD
JOHN E BARRY, 446TH
COL LEARNED W BARRY RET, 467TH
WILLIAM T BARRY JR, 392ND
FORREST E BARTAY, 44TH

MAURICE A BARTELL, 389TH, 458TH
WESLEY J BARTELT, 453RD
COL CARL C BARTHEL RET, 93RD, HDQ
FLOYD R BARTHEL, 467TH
MERLE S BARTHMAN, 458TH
ARVIN J BARTLETT, 467TH
CLARENCE W BARTON, 93RD
EDWARD J BARTON, 44TH
LESTER BARTON, 453RD
TROY A BARTON, 389TH
JOHN R BASCH, 489TH
HORACE BASKIN, 489TH
PHILIP BASKIN, 448TH
SUSAN BASOM, 392ND AM
MAURICE K BASON, 445TH
LTC EARL F BASSETT RET, 392ND
CHARLES R BASTIEN, 448TH, 492ND
FRANK B BATA, 44TH
RICHARD E BATEMAN, 458TH
EDWARD M BATES, 93RD
JANICE BATES, 467TH, AM
MARK A BATTLES, 489TH
CLIFFORD H BAUER, 44TH
MARY E BAUGHMAN, 93RD, AM
HOWARD H BAUM, HDQ
J LANTZ BAUM, 446TH
GORDON H BAUMANN, 389TH
LOUIS R BAUMANN, 389TH
COL ROBERT P BAUMANN JR RET, 466TH
COL HAYNES M BAUMGARDNER RET, 491ST
LTC VERNON A BAUMGART RET, 392ND
DONALD F BAUMLER, 445TH
ROY N BAXTER, 389TH
NIGEL BAYNE, SM
COL RICHARD C BAYNES RET, 466TH
JAMES C BAYNHAM, 445TH
JACK E BAZER, 93RD
M/SGT JOSEPH T BEACH RET, 93RD
CLIFFORD L BEAL, 453RD, 392ND
GEORGE V BEAMAN, 448TH
RALPH P BEAMAN, 492ND
CORMAN H BEAN, 445TH
ELROY W BEANEY, 467TH
ARTHUR BEAR JR, 93RD
ROBERT W BEAR, 458TH
CHARLES W BEARD, 492ND
JESSE T BEARD, 458TH
CRAIG A BEASLEY, 492ND, AM
FRANCIS A BEASLEY, 492ND
W H & NORMA BEASLEY, 492ND
WILLIS H BEASLEY III, 492ND, AM
ROBERT J BEATSON, 392ND
FRANK G BEATTY, 467TH, 492ND, 479TH
EMIL G BEAUDRY, 467TH, 448TH
JEAN A BEAULIEU, 448TH
RAYMOND D BEAULIEU, 467TH
RICHARD P BEAULIEU, 458TH
DENNIS L BEAVERS, 466TH
JOHN R BEAVERS, 44TH
EDWARD BEBENROTH, 453RD
FRED BECCHETTI, 445TH
RAYMOND J BECHTOLD, 467TH
CHARLES H BECK, 445TH
DONALD F BECK, 448TH, 489TH
FRANK W BECK, 458TH
ALLEN BECKER, 466TH
EDWIN D BECKER, 453RD
JOHN R BECKER, 392ND
LESTER W BECKER, 389TH
LOREN W BECKER, 445TH
PETER S BECKER, 453RD
RALPH S BECKER, 44TH
ROBERT L BECKER, 467TH
SAM BECKER, 446TH
WILLIAM R BECKER, 466TH
GEORGE E BECKERMAN MD, 44TH
WILLIAM R BECKLEY, 458TH
EDGAR H BECKMAN, 453RD
RONALD S BECKSTROM, 458TH

LUTHER L BEDDINGFIELD, 392ND
CHARLES P BEDNARIK, 467TH
CAPT WILLIAM R BEE RET, 44TH
DR FLOYD E BEEL, 389TH
LAWRENCE J BEELER, 453RD
RALPH BEGGS, 466TH
PAUL BEGSTROM, 389TH, AM
CLIFFORD H BEHEE, 389TH
LTC JOHN M BEHRMANN RET, 93RD
HARRY J BEIERSCHMITT, 489TH
DANIEL BEIGHTOL, 93RD
RAYMOND S BEIGHTS MD, 489TH
EARL H BEITLER, 466TH
JOHN R BEITLING, 389TH
STANLEY T BEKERITIS, 467TH
LAWRENCE BELANGER, 467TH
JAMES E BELCHER, 492ND, 466TH
EARL D BELISLE, 467TH
PETER S BELITSOS, 445TH
ANTHONY V BELL, 467TH
JAMES D BELL, 448TH
DR JAMES J BELL, 448TH
JOHN W BELL, 392ND
WALTER M BELL JR, 392ND
WILBUR E BELL, SM
WESLEY BELLESON, 458TH
R E BELLGARDT, 492ND
DAVID R BELLIS, 491ST
THOMAS S BELOVICH, 446TH
IRVING BELSKY, 389TH
MELVIN BELSON, 389TH
RICHARD H BELTER, 93RD
RALPH & VIRGINIA BELWARD RET, 489TH
JAMES F BELWOOD, 93RD
RAYMOND E BENCE, 445TH
ROBERT L BENEDICT, 44TH
DALE E BENESH, 453RD
JAMES E BENHAM, 467TH
FRANK BENJAMIN, 448TH
JOSEPH A BENJAMIN, 448TH
HUGH M BENNETT, 491ST
JAMES E BENNETT JR, 392ND
JOHN E BENNETT, 491ST
MILTON W BENNETT, 458TH
RAY J BENNETT, 489TH
SIDNEY E BENNETT SR, 389TH
THOMAS E BENT, 453RD
LTC WILLIAM L BENTO RET, 466TH
WILLIAM D BENTON, 389TH, AM
LEONARD S BENTSON, 389TH
HAROLD E BENVENUTI, 448TH
BLASE J BENZIGER, 448TH
ROY BEQUETTE, 446TH
CLAYTON L BERDAN, 458TH
ARTHUR J BERG, 392ND
CLAYTON J BERG, 448TH
DONALD E BERG, 453RD
LEROY C & GLORIA BERG, 453RD
VICTOR E BERG, 491ST
LAWRENCE BERGAMIN, 389TH
ANDREW H BERGER, 448TH, 389TH, 93RD, 489TH
ARTHUR J BERGER, 453RD
LAWRENCE BERGER JR, 448TH
RICHARD G BERGER, 453RD
LTC LOYD BERGER RET, 389TH
COL ROBERT M BERGER RET, 392ND
WILLIAM C BERGER, 44TH
JOSEPH O BERGERON, 93RD
PAUL O BERGMAN, 93RD
SYLVESTER BERGMAN, 389TH
OTEY R BERKELEY, 489TH
HAROLD BERMAN, 466TH
EARL W BERNARD, 448TH
CARROLL A BERNER, 93RD
JACK E BERNER SR, 467TH
ARTHUR BERNSTEIN, HDQ
STANLEY J BERRIMAN, 93RD
FREDERICK J BERRY, 491ST
LTC JACK E BERRY RET, 446TH
LTC JAMES E BERRY RET, 448TH
JAMES W BERRY, 489TH
WILLIAM A BERRY, 93RD, 389TH
RONALD W BERRYHILL, 448TH
BENJAMIN J BERTALOT, 467TH

ARTHUR P BERTANZETTI, 489TH
ANTONIO E BERTAPELLE, 445TH
COL A L BERTHELSON RET, 389TH
HAZEL L BERTHIAUME, 392ND, AM
EDWARD L BERTHOLD, 445TH
MERRILL G BERTHRONG, 44TH
PETER G BERTHRONG, 44TH, AM
FRANK J BERTRAM, 445TH
WILLIAM B BERTRAND, 453RD
JOHN J BERZAI, 453RD
JOHN F BEST, 453RD
RICHARD H BEST, 448TH
EMIL B BESTEN, 458TH
RAYMOND A BETCHER, 467TH
RAYMOND W BETHEL MD, 44TH
E DALE BETHELL, 389TH
HENRY G BETHKE, 489TH
G W BETTES, 448TH
BERT A BETTS, 458TH
FREMONT A BETTS, 489TH
HARRY E BETTS, 448TH
HENRY C BETZ, 93RD, 44TH
ROBERT E BETZ, 458TH
DR JACK T BEVERLY, 467TH
CHARLES L BEVINS, 458TH
ROBERT BEVIS DMD, 453RD
PAUL N BEYERL, 448TH
MARTIN F BEZON, 467TH
CARL T BIANCO, 453RD
RAYMOND R BIANUCCI, 392ND
LTC J RAY BICKEL RET, 467TH
J M BICKLEY, 93RD
ROBERT J BICKNELL, 491ST
LTC ROBERT W BIEBER RET, 93RD
ROBERT B BIECK, 453RD
ALBERT H BIEL, 453RD
WALTER BIELANSKI, 389TH
FLOYD M BIENIEK, 446TH
PAUL L BIGANDT, 453RD, 466TH
JOHN A BIGNOLI, 489TH, 445TH
BRUNO BIGOLIN, 93RD
LTC FRANCIS E BIGOS RET, 446TH
EDWARD P BIICHLE, 93RD
LTC BEDFORD B BILBY RET, 389TH
WILLIAM R BILES, 392ND
COL FRANK E BILLETER SR RET, 389TH
WILLIAM R BILLING, 492ND
CHARLES W BILLINGS, 448TH
ROBERT L BILLINGS, 389TH
LTC HAL E BILYEU RET, 93RD, HDQ
GLENN W BINDER, 389TH
DONALD E BING, 389TH
WARREN T BIRCKHEAD, 389TH
DR LUTHER S BIRD, 93RD
DONALD V BIRDSALL, 448TH
JACK A BIRKLAND, 448TH
FRANCIS P BIRMINGHAM, 458TH
ROBERT C BIRMINGHAM, 458TH
ALEXANDER F BIRNIE, SM
HELEN BISBING, 467TH, AM
RICHARD O BISCHOFF DDS, 458TH
LESTER BISE, 448TH, 491ST
ALBERT J BISHOP, 448TH
C ROGER BISHOP, 93RD
CECIL J BISHOP, 446TH
DEAN K BISHOP, 389TH
DONALD M BISHOP, 453RD
DWIGHT W BISHOP, 453RD
G W BISHOP, 491ST
GORDON D BISHOP, 446TH
HAROLD E BISHOP, 448TH
MELVIN L BISHOP, 453RD
ROSALIND BISKIND, 93RD, ARC
STANLEY J BISKUP, 489TH
JOSEPH F BISSON, 93RD
MAURICE H BITTLER, 458TH
NELSON W BIVENS, 93RD
HOWARD E BJORK, 392ND
EDWARD BLACK, 445TH
GEORGE G BLACK JR, 93RD, AM
RICHARD E BLACK SR, 491ST

JOHN T BLACKIS, 389TH, 93RD
FRANK W BLACKMON, 489TH
EMIL D BLACKORBY, 491ST
BURTON N BLACKWELL, 491ST
F M BLACKWELL, 467TH
G RILE BLACKWOOD, HDQ
PETE BLAIR, 448TH
LEWIS D BLAIS, 453RD
JULIAN W BLAKE, 448TH, 389TH
SIDNEY H BLAKE, 453RD
RICHARD G BLAKELOCK, 93RD
RAYWOOD H BLANCHARD, 489TH
PATRICK F BLANCO SR, 492ND
MELVIN L BLAND, 467TH
LEWIS D BLANICH, 467TH
WILLIAM M BLANTON, HDQ
CHARLES BLATCHLEY, 44TH
PAUL S BLATERIC, 93RD
LTC JAMES L BLILIE RET, 389TH
THOMAS C J BLISARD, 458TH
HAZEL I BLISS, HDQ
VINCENT H BLISS, 389TH
LEONARD H BLOCK, 389TH
HOWARD F BLOHM, 389TH
EDWARD J BLOOM, 389TH
JOHN BLOOM, 445TH
JAMES A BLOOMER, 389TH
JOHN D BLOOMER, SM
EDWARD W BLOSEL, 491ST
MALVIN N BLOTCHER, 446TH, 44TH
RALPH W BLOWER, 492ND
WARREN A BLOWER SR, 446TH
ALLAN G BLUE, 492ND, AM
ALLEN L BLUM, 458TH
ROBERT BLUMENFELD, 466TH
LTC JOHN H BLUMENSTOCK RET, 466TH
ROBERT F BOBERG, 389TH
ROBERT O BOCHEK, 93RD
DONALD E BODIKER, 448TH
FRANCIS S BODINE, 489TH
BEN BODZIAK, 445TH
ROBERT L BOEBEL, 466TH
HAROLD F BOEHM, 489TH
WARREN K BOERNER, 93RD, 389TH
MAJ FRANKLIN BOESCH RET, 446TH
PHILIP BOGATER, 392ND, AM
NEAL L BOGGS, 491ST
ROY M BOGGS, 44TH
WALTER P BOGUSZ, 467TH
EDWIN P BOGUTSKI, 446TH
DOROTHY M BOISCLAIR, 389TH, AM
ARCADE J BOISSELLE, 467TH, 492ND
HOWARD L BOLDT, 445TH
ERNEST J BOLDUC, 453RD
OLIVER J BOLDUC, 389TH
JOSEPH L BOLGER, 453RD
VERNAL L BOLINE, 389TH
LTC RAY M BOLL RET, 448TH
GLENN L BOLLING, 448TH
MARJORIE BOLLSCHWEILER, 448TH, AM
ALBERT BONACCI, 448TH
JOSEPH C BONANNO, 392ND
ROLAND F BONEWITZ, 491ST
ROBERT E BONEY, 392ND
HARRY K BONFIELD, 448TH
PAUL E BONNELL, 389TH
CHARLES W BONNER, 448TH
GEORGE H BONNER, 448TH
EDWIN L BOOK, 446TH
CLAY U BOOKER, 93RD
JAMES F BOOKER, 453RD
GEORGE N BOOKWALTER, 489TH
CLOYED BOOMERSHINE, 466TH
EDMUND F BOOMHOWER, 44TH
DANIEL BOONE, 453RD
PAUL V BOOS, 492ND
DAYTON A BOOSTROM, 446TH
CHARLES H BOOTH JR, 458TH
LTC CLARENCE F BOOTH RET, 489TH
ROBERT O BOOTH, 389TH
WILLIAM P BOOTH, 446TH

JOHN J BORAH, 44TH
D H BORCHERDING, 93RD
GERALD H BORDEN DDS, 446TH
PAUL J BORDEWICH, 389TH, 445TH
NICHOLAS BORDNICK, 453RD
JOHN H BOREN, 491ST
HERBERT C BORGMANN, 93RD
DAVID D BORLAND, 389TH
HERBERT BORNSTEIN, 93RD
SIGMUND BOROWICZ, 448TH
M/SGT PETER J BORRACCINI RET, 392ND
MARTIN J BORROK, 389TH
VIRGINIA BORSHOFF, 93RD, AM
ROBERT G BORST, 466TH
EDWARD C BORTMESS, 446TH
RICHARD BORTON, 467TH
CHESTER A BOSHINSKI, 446TH
JOHN P BOSKO, 467TH
CHARLES J BOSSHARDT, 458TH
VINCENT L BOSSLEY, 466TH
HAROLD F BOSTIC, 389TH
FRANK T BOSTWICK, 466TH
ROBERT D BOSWORTH, 448TH
LTC HAROLD BOTH JR RET, 492ND
OWEN N BOTTOMLEY, 489TH
RICHARD E BOTTOMLEY, 44TH, 392ND, 14CW
B DALE BOTTOMS, 448TH
ANDREW R BOUCHARD, 491ST
GERARD J BOUCHER, 458TH
RICHARD C BOUCHER, 445TH
OSCAR J BOUDREAUX, 389TH
THOMAS O BOULEY, 489TH
W B BOURLAND JR, 93RD
JAMES S BOURNE, 448TH
COLBY J BOUSFIELD, 489TH
FRANCIS L BOUSQUET, 93RD
LIONEL O BOUSQUET, 489TH
M/SGT ROBERT BOUTAIN RET, 93RD
ROY J BOUTTE, SM
PETER R BOVE, 491ST
GEORGE BOVIE, 445TH
REX L BOWEN, 445TH
ROWE D BOWEN JR, 445TH
WILLIAM H BOWEN, 392ND
L S BOWERS, 445TH
HOBERT G BOWLBY, 445TH
LTC THEODORE E BOWLES RET, 93RD
JAMES L BOWMAN, 492ND, 467TH
AARON BOXER, 491ST
WILLIAM C BOYANOWSKI, 445TH
HENRY L BOYD, 458TH
KENNETH A BOYD, 491ST
ROBERT B BOYD, 466TH
CHARLES N BOYER, 93RD
PAUL B BOYER, 446TH
JAMES F BOYLAN JR, 466TH
DANIEL J BOYLE, 389TH
JAMES J BOYLE III, 489TH
ROBERT N BOYLE, 489TH
LARENCE R BOZEMAN, 445TH
CHARLES J BOZIC, 446TH
BILL J BRACKSIECK, 458TH
MERRILL G BRADLEE, 466TH
FLOYD H BRADLEY JR, 445TH
HENRY J BRADLEY, 489TH
HERBERT A BRADLEY, 453RD
JOSEPH F BRADLEY, 93RD
RICHARD H BRADLEY, 466TH
E CHRIS BRAEUNIG, 446TH
STEWART BRAGDON, 453RD
WILLIAM R BRAGG, 467TH
JOHN S BRAINARD, 491ST
JAMES L BRAMAN, 392ND
CLARENCE BRAML, 453RD
PRESTON BRANCH, 458TH
GLENN J BRANDENBURG, 93RD
LLOYD H BRANDENBURG JR, 492ND
MAURICE L BRANDENBURGER, 445TH
FINIS L BRANDON, 491ST
HENRY B BRANDT, 448TH
HENRY W BRANDT, 93RD, HDQ

ROBERT M BRANDT, 448TH, AM
WAYNE BRANSCOME, 467TH
JAMES E BRANSON, 44TH
RICHARD S BRANTLEY, 93RD
JAMES E BRANTON, 467TH
ROBERT B BRATZEL SR, 44TH
ALFRED C BRAUER, 458TH
GEORGE BRAUER, 392ND
JULIAN L BRAUN, 492ND
FRED S BRAUSE JR, 446TH
REX A BRAWLEY, 467TH
MARTIN BREDVIK, 466TH
CHARLES N BREEDING, 453RD, 458TH
ROBERT H BREITENFELD, HDQ
FRANCIS W BRENNAN, 44TH
ROBERT W BRENNAN, 392ND
WILLIAM T BRENNER, 466TH
JOHN A BRESNAHAN, 93RD
JEAN F BRESSLER, 44TH, 14CW
CAPT JEFFREY E BRETT, 448TH, AM
FRED R BREUNINGER, 446TH
COL DONALD W BREWER RET, 458TH
HAROLD E BREWER, 446TH
HUGHES H BREWER, 389TH
EDWARD M BREWSTER, 453RD, 392ND, 389TH
GAINES BREWSTER, 489TH
JAMES P BREWTON, 389TH, 453RD, 467TH
DOUGLAS D BRICE, 44TH
HAROLD E BRICE, 458TH
GEORGE A BRIDGEMAN, 93RD
DAVID I BRIDGERS, 466TH
H C BRIDGES JR, 445TH
LTC LESTER BRIDGES RET, 491ST
COL ROBERT D BRIENT RET, 389TH
MICHAEL A BRIENZA, 491ST
JESSE B BRIGGS, 492ND
JEROME BRILL, 458TH
STANLEY BRILL, 446TH
ERNEST W BRINDLE JR, 491ST
JOHN B BRINSON JR MD, 467TH
GEORGE K BRITE, 489TH
TOM BRITTAN, SM
CHARLES L BRITTON, 389TH
CHARLES BROAD, 389TH
CHARLES E BROADWATER, 453RD
JAMES F BROCK, 467TH
MARION BROCKETT, 467TH, AM
ROBERT O BROCKMAN, 448TH
MATTHEW L BROCKMEYER, 445TH
REUBEN BROCKWAY, 453RD
JOHN J BRODY, 489TH
COL S DAN BRODY RET, 453RD
ROBERT B BROKSTEIN, 448TH
FREDERICK H BROMM, 445TH
H J BRONAUGH, 489TH
LTC HERBERT B BRONNER RET, 491ST
J EUGENE BROOKS, 467TH
B/GEN JOHN A BROOKS III RET, 20TH, HDQ, 93RD, 389TH
THOMAS A BROOKS, 466TH
FRED M BROSHACK SR, 458TH
NELSON E BROTT, 44TH
CORTLAND L BROVITZ, 466TH
WILBUR C BROWER, 491ST
ADAM BROWN, 392ND
COL ALBERT J BROWN RET, 445TH
ANDREW V BROWN, 453RD
BEN A BROWN, 466TH
CARL L BROWN, 492ND
CLEMENT W BROWN, 467TH
CURTIS H BROWN, 445TH
DAVID G BROWN, 44TH
COL DELLAS A BROWN RET, 44TH
M/SGT EARL D BROWN RET, HDQ
LTC EDWIN C BROWN JR RET, 491ST
ERNEST D BROWN, 44TH
FORREST D BROWN, 467TH
GEORGE C BROWN, 93RD

GEORGE L BROWN, 466TH
MRS GILL BROWN BR LIBRARIAN, SM
LTC GLENN O BROWN RET, 448TH
HAROLD R BROWN, 389TH
HARRY R BROWN, 44TH
IVAN D BROWN, 489TH
JAMES S BROWN, 492ND
JOHN R BROWN, 93RD, 44TH
JOSEPH R BROWN, 458TH
KENNETH P BROWN, 492ND
L L BROWN JR, 93RD
LEO BROWN, 389TH
PATRICK L BROWN JR, 466TH, AM
RICHARD E BROWN, 453RD
RUAL B BROWN JR, 467TH
COL THERMAN D BROWN RET, 93RD
THOMAS B BROWN, 458TH
THOMAS F BROWN, 446TH
W H & ESTELLE BROWN, 453RD
WILFORD BROWN, 389TH
WILLIAM C BROWN, 448TH
WILLIAM M BROWN, 93RD
WILLIAM P BROWN, 448TH
WILLIAM R BROWN, 446TH
CLIFTON BROWNE, 389TH
ALBERT E BROWNING, 44TH
FREDERICK P BROWNING, 44TH
JAMIE E BROWNING, 446TH
ORVILLE T BROWNING, 389TH
SAMUEL E BRUBAKER, 448TH
VIRGINIA STOKES BRUBAKER, 453RD, AM
REX L BRUDOS, 458TH
RALPH F BRUEGGEMANN, 467TH
FELIX B BRUGNONI, 93RD
MYRTLE BRULAND, 445TH, AM
BIRTO R BRUMBY, 458TH
CHARLES H BRUMETT, 93RD
DANIEL L BRUNDAGE, 453RD
ELLIOT B BRUNER, 458TH
JAMES L BRUNER, 466TH
SAVERIO BRUNI, 445TH
LOUIS L BRUNNEMER, 491ST
ALFRED F BRUNNER, 489TH
HOWARD E BRUNNER, 44TH
JOSEPH BRUNNER JR, 389TH
JOHN C BRUNO, 448TH
ROBERT J BRUNST, 445TH
ANNE DALEY BRUSSELMANS, SM
CHESTER BRUZINSKI, 93RD
DENISE BRYAN, HDQ, AM
LOREN D BRYAN, 489TH
DOUGLAS J BRYANT, 3SAD
HARRY M BRYANT SR, 448TH
JACK BRYANT, 445TH, 93RD
M E BRYANT, 389TH
STANTON H BRYDEN, 448TH
MAJ EDDIE BRYSON RET, 467TH
WILBUR C BRYSON, 448TH
EDWARD E BUBB, 458TH
WALTER T BUBB, 467TH
WILLIAM A BUCHECKER, 467TH
KENNETH L BUCHNER, 44TH
ROBERT D BUCK, 491ST
ROBERT H BUCK, 489TH
FRANK L BUCKHOLDER, 93RD
PETER BUCKINGHAM, SM
PAUL E BUCKLES, 392ND
ALYN D BUCKLEY, 453RD
CHARLES A BUCKLEY, 392ND
WILLIAM BUCKLEY, 491ST
COL WILLIAM S BUCKMASTER RET, 489TH
JOHN E BUECHELER, 392ND
PHILIP G BUFFINTON, 93RD
LTC T W BUHLER RET, 44TH
WAYNE BUHRMANN, 389TH
HAROLD W BUKER JR, 489TH
ARTHUR P BUKOVEN, 93RD
FLOYD L BULL, 392ND
WILLIAM L BULLARD, 448TH
JIM BULLOCK, 93RD, AM
DONALD F BULS, 491ST
RICHARD H BUNCH JR, 489TH
BRADFORD BUR, 491ST, AM
LOUIS J BUR, 491ST
MILTON F BURCHETT, 448TH

DARRELL BURCHFIELD, 491ST
HAROLD W BURDEKIN, 491ST
RICHARD M BURGART, 491ST
JACK W BURGE, 446TH
COL CARL E BURGET RET, 466TH
WALTER M BURKARD, 93RD
JOHN T BURKE, 445TH, 389TH, 453RD
JOHN BURKHARDT, 453RD
HOWARD M BURKHART, 44TH
JOHN & LOIS BURKHOLDER, 453RD
HAROLD A BURKS, 93RD
NORMA F BURMAN, HDQ, 458TH AM
ROBERT F BURNES, 453RD, 467TH
KENNETH K BURNETT, 489TH
LTC EDWARD L BURNETTA RET, 448TH
EMMETT J BURNS JR, 44TH
JOHN P BURNS, 489TH
S/SGT JOHN T BURNS RET, 448TH
NORMAN E BURNS, 389TH, 492ND, 44TH
ROBERT N BURNS, 392ND
W J BURRESS, 44TH
ALVIN M BURRIS, 93RD
JAMES A BURRIS, 93RD
AUSTIN J BURROWS, 453RD
EUGENE K BURSON, 93RD
HARRIS M BURSTYN, 467TH
WILLARD S BURT, 458TH
LEWIS P BURTIS, 458TH
JESSE M BURTON, 44TH
COL PAUL T BURTON RET, 389TH
ROBERT B BURTON, 93RD, AM
EDWARD M BURTSAVAGE, 44TH
WILLIAM T BURTT, 445TH
ALBERT A BURY, 392ND, 44TH
STEPHEN H BURZENSKI, 448TH
ROBERT E BUSBEY, 453RD
MAJ JAMES N BUSBY RET, 458TH
JOHN G BUSCHMAN, 392ND
CLYDE H BUSH, 448TH
HARRY F BUSH, 93RD
COL JOSEPH BUSH RET, 392ND
HOWARD C BUSSE, 93RD
MARIE F BUSSING, 445TH, AM
EUGENE BUSZTA, 445TH
EDWARD A BUTLER, 448TH
J RICHARD BUTLER, 458TH
JAMES B BUTLER, 389TH
JOHN E BUTLER, 44TH
JOHN W BUTLER, 93RD
NEVILLE BUTLER, SM
COL RICHARD D BUTLER RET, 44TH
DONALD L BUTTERFIELD, 93RD
GENE W BUTTS, 392ND
JAMES M BUZICK, 392ND
HOYT C BYARS, 389TH
JOHN J BYCZKOWSKI, 93RD
PAMELA NELSON BYERS, 491ST, 389TH AM
DANIEL R BYNUM, 389TH
ROBERT L BYNUM, 445TH
ARTHUR W CABLE, 93RD
ALFRED W CACCESE, 453RD
JOHN V CADDEN, 445TH
LTC JOHN R CADLE JR RET, 93RD
WILLIAM M CAGNEY, 446TH
JOHN H CAHILL, 389TH
COL VINCENT S CAHILL JR RET, 491ST
S G CAIN, 446TH
EDWARD A CAIRNS, 446TH
THOMAS J CALDEN, 491ST, 44TH
MARGARET CALDERALO, 466TH, AM
CHARLES H CALDWELL, 467TH
ELLIS J CALFEE, 93RD
BETTY SHEARER CALHOUN, HDQ
ELLIOTT W CALISCH, 466TH
ROBERT S CALKINS, 93RD, 448TH
ORLAND CALL, 389TH
ARCHIE P CALLAHAN, 489TH
CURTIS W CALLAHAN, 389TH
ELEANOR M CALLIHAN, HDQ
JACK R CALLISON, 448TH

BYRON B CALOMIRIS, 491ST
GEORGE E CALTRIDER JR, 392ND
OLINDO CALVANO, 445TH
JUDGE DONALD CAMBELL, SM
MICHAEL J CAMBON, 466TH
LTC RALPH J CAMBURN RET, 448TH
COL WILLIAM R CAMERON RET, 44TH
THOMAS J CAMPANA SR, 445TH
CHARLES R CAMPBELL, 389TH
GERALD M CAMPBELL, 492ND, 44TH
H ALBERT CAMPBELL JR, 389TH, 453RD
JAMES F CAMPBELL, 491ST
JAMES W CAMPBELL, 446TH
JOSEPH N CAMPBELL, 466TH
LEROY CAMPBELL, 389TH
ROBERT W CAMPBELL, 491ST, 93RD
THOMAS W CAMPBELL, 445TH
WILLIAM M CANADAY, 446TH
COL T H CANADY JR, 458TH
HERMAN S CANFIELD, 392ND
NORMAN J CANFIELD, 491ST
DOMENICK CANNETTI, 44TH
CHARLES F CANNON, 466TH
LAWRENCE CANTWELL, 44TH
SAM CAPITANO JR, 3SAD
SEBASTIAN A CAPOBIANCO, 93RD
EUGENE S CAPODAGLI, 445TH
EMANUEL CAPPELLO, 392ND
ROLAND R CAPPIELLO, 466TH
JOSEPH CAPOSSELA, 492ND, 467TH
JOHN M CAPPS, 466TH
ANTHONY P CAPUTO, 491ST
MICHAEL CAPUTO, 467TH
LYLE E CARBAUGH, HDQ
JOSEPH L CARBONE, 93RD
WARREN G CARDEN, 489TH
ALEJANDRO CARDENAS, 458TH
JOHN S CARDOZA JR, 453RD
LTC THOMAS J M CARDWELL RET, 44TH
ALLAN J CAREY JR, 448TH
CHARLES M CAREY, 446TH
LTC THEODORE R CAREY RET, 453RD
BERTIL CARLBERG, 44TH
DR RICHARD CARLISLE, 445TH, AM
LUETTA G CARLS, 489TH, AM
CHARLES E CARLSON, SM
DONALD A CARLSON, 466TH
GLENN D CARLSON, 458TH
JAMES R CARLSON, 392ND
K WILLIAM CARLSON, 389TH
RAYMOND L CARLSON, 466TH
ROBERT CARLSON, 466TH
ROY W CARLSON, 453RD
WILLIAM A CARLSON, 448TH
ODIS F CARMICHAEL, 44TH
CHARLES H CARN, 448TH
FRANK D CARNEY, 389TH
MALCOLM S CARNEY III, 446TH
GUY D CARNINE, 392ND
PAUL J CARON, 389TH
LTC ARTHUR W CARPENTER RET, 93RD
RICHARD B CARPENTER DDS, 44TH
RICHARD H CARPENTER, SM
FREDERICK W CARR, 489TH
MAJ NEIL K CARR RET, 453RD
ANTHONY J CARRA, 466TH
LESTER J CARRICK, 44TH
LUCY CARRIGAN, 458TH, AM
HEATH H CARRIKER, 466TH
CHARLES J CARROLL, 93RD
HUGH B CARROLL, 489TH
JOHN F CARROLL, 453RD
JOHN S CARROLL, 445TH
JOHN T CARROLL, 392ND
RALPH L CARROLL, 93RD
RICHARD S CARROLL, 453RD, 466TH

RAPHAEL E CARROW, 445TH
HERBERT D CARSON JR, 44TH
JOHN H CARSTENS, 44TH
CALVIN J CARTER, 392ND
CHARLES R CARTER, 458TH
CLARENCE E CARTER, 458TH
DAN J CARTER, 489TH
JAMES A CARTER, 492ND
JOHN F CARTER JR, 458TH
LLOYD C CARTER, 453RD
ROBERT N CARTER, 492ND
WALLACE A CARTER, 448TH
WARNER B CARTER, 44TH
NICHOLAS CARUSO, 93RD
NICHOLAS A CARUSO, 93RD
ERWIN L CARVIN, 466TH
CHARLES E CARY, 44TH
JOHN F CASCIO, 448TH
E HENRY CASE, 448TH
WILLIAM D CASE, 392ND
WILLIAM L CASE, 458TH
GEORGE S CASEY, 467TH
NORMAN CASEY, 389TH
ROBERT J CASEY, 491ST
ROBERT L CASH, 492ND
HARRY D CASKEY, 93RD
LTC EDGAR P CASON RET, 467TH
DOROTHY CASSADY, 448TH, AM
ANTHONY J CASSINO, 453RD
JAMES CASSITY, 392ND
FRANK CASTELLI, 44TH
RICHARD CASTERLINE, 448TH
LTC DONALD O CASTLE RET, 445TH
MARTIN B CASTLE, 389TH
OLIN D CASTLE, 392ND
DONALD E CASTOE, 466TH
CARMINE J CASUCCI, 446TH
ALFRED W CATALDO, 44TH
AUBREY P CATES, 448TH
WILLIS O CATHCART JR, 445TH
COL MYERS B CATHER RET, 446TH
LTC JOHN W CATHEY RET, 448TH
JAMES W CATON DO, 446TH
CHESTER CATULLI, 392ND
JAMES B CAULFIELD, 44TH, 492ND
VINCENT CAUTERO, 448TH
BILL L CAUTHON, 445TH
GORDON R CAVE, 489TH
CHARLES R CAVENY, 466TH
MAJ DENNIS D CAVIT, 389TH, AM
J J CECIL DVM, 466TH
LOUIS CEPELAK, 448TH
WILLIAM F CETIN, 392ND
DANIEL I CHADBOURNE, 466TH
STEPHEN J CHADNOCK, 489TH
JOE E CHADWICK, 93RD
THOMAS L CHAFFEE, 492ND, 44TH
C N & ANN CHAMBERLAIN, 489TH
C N CHAMBERLAIN III, 489TH, AM
JENNIFER M CHAMBERLAIN, 489TH, AM
DR JOHN E CHAMBERLAIN, 458TH
MERVIN A CHAMBERLAIN, 453RD
RICHARD J CHAMBERLAIN, 389TH
JACK G CHAMBERS, 445TH
VELERIA L CHAMBERS, 93RD, AM
JEAN M CHAMBLIN, 392ND
DONALD L CHAMPAGNE, 489TH
DONALD P CHAMPLAIN, 446TH, AM
BERTHA CHANDLER, HM
F C CHANDLER JR, 491ST, 489TH
FLORENCE CHANDLER, HDQ
LAWRENCE R CHANDLER, 448TH
O C CHANDLER, 389TH
GEORGE D CHANT, 389TH
C J CHANY, 446TH
GLEN R CHAPEL, 489TH
ROBERT F CHAPIN, 389TH
BARBARA J CHAPMAN, 458TH, AM
BYRON D CHAPMAN, 458TH
LTC EDMAN L CHAPMAN RET, 448TH
HOWARD M CHAPMAN, 3SAD
JACK W CHAPMAN, 491ST

JAMES W CHAPMAN, 446TH
JOHN J CHAPMAN III, SM
SM/SGT KEITH W CHAPMAN RET, 392ND
OLIVER W CHAPMAN, 492ND
WILLIAM R CHAPMAN, 467TH
WALTER J CHAPPAS, 467TH
DARWIN T CHARLES, 458TH
JAMES M CHARLTON, 458TH
DONALD V CHASE, 44TH
GEORGE T CHASE, 93RD
FAY CHAUVIN, 44TH
CARROLL W CHEEK, 392ND
N R CHEEK, 44TH
GEORGE D CHENAIL, 392ND
JAMES M CHENAULT, 489TH
GUY P CHENEY, 93RD
HERBERT CHESKIN, 466TH
GEORGE J CHIAPPETTA, SM
WILLIAM E CHILDERS, 453RD
HOYTT CHILDRESS, 466TH
GEORGE CHIMPLES, 458TH
CARL D W CHINBERG, 93RD
GEORGE K CHIPMAN, 453RD
EDDIE JOE CHOATE, 445TH
FRANK J CHOWANSKI, 44TH
GREGORY L CHRIST, 491ST
DUANE G CHRISTENSEN, 448TH
H H CHRISTENSEN, 389TH
M C CHRISTENSEN, 467TH
SEYMOUR K CHRISTENSEN, 491ST
WARREN CHRISTENSEN, 93RD
CLYDE CHRISTIAN, 389TH
DAVID E CHRISTIAN, 44TH
HAROLD E CHRISTMAN, 392ND
EDWARD J CHU, 448TH
GEORGE E CHURCH, 467TH
HUBERT M CHURCH, 458TH
FRANK L CHURNSIDE, 489TH
FRANK CHYBOWSKI, 389TH
PAUL CIACCIO, 445TH
ROSE M CIANCITTO, 467TH, AM
MICHAEL R CIANO, 445TH
ALFRED L CIESLIGA, 445TH
ALFRED R CIMEI, 445TH, 458TH
EDWIN R CISINSKI, 44TH
CARL CITRON, 466TH
CARL W CLADER JR, 489TH
LEIGH A CLAFLIN, 93RD
COL CHARLES E CLAGUE JR RET, 93RD
CLIMPSON B CLAPP, 93RD
E W CLAREY, 492ND, 467TH
MAXINE CLAREY, 492ND, 467TH AM
ALFORD G CLARK, 93RD
CHARLES S CLARK, 446TH
EDGAR D CLARK, 389TH, 445TH, 453RD, 44TH
FARRIS L CLARK, 489TH
FORREST S CLARK, 44TH
GAYNELL CLARK, 389TH, AM
GENE S CLARK, 93RD, AM
GEORGE F CLARK JR, 389TH, AM
GEORGE H CLARK, 458TH
HAROLD L CLARK, 445TH
LTC JOHN N CLARK RET, 44TH
KENNETH F CLARK, 491ST
LUTHER E CLARK, 453RD
PAUL J CLARK, 44TH
RINGERT CLARK, 448TH, AM
ROBERT A CLARK, 491ST
ROBERT C CLARK, 445TH
ROBERT E CLARK, 458TH
THAINE A CLARK, 448TH
WILLIAM K CLARK, 458TH
WILLIAM W CLARK, 458TH
ALAN B CLARKE, 392ND
EDDIE D CLARKE, SM
JACK C CLARKE, 392ND
LEONARD O CLARKE, 93RD
L H CLAUSEN, 44TH
T/SGT CHARLES H CLAWSON RET, 467TH
RALPH O CLAYPOOLE JR, 458TH
HENRY C CLAYTON, 445TH
GEORGE M CLEARY, 389TH

CHARLES T CLEATON, 93RD
FRANK O CLEMENS, 389TH
CARROLL H CLEMENT, 389TH
EUGENE H CLEMENT, 93RD
LTC HARRY W CLEMENT RET, 446TH
J FRANK CLEMENTS, 458TH
JAMES H CLEMENTS, 44TH
L RUSSELL CLEMENTS, 466TH
COIT J CLEMMER, 392ND
YALE L CLEMMO, 93RD
JOHN W CLERKIN, 466TH
LTC HOWARD R CLEVELAND RET, 93RD
ALBERT E CLIMER, 445TH
GERALD G CLINCH, 492ND, 44TH, 93RD
ROBERT M CLINE, 489TH
WALTER M CLINE, 458TH
WILBUR L CLINGAN, 453RD
RALPH B CLIZER, 458TH
JOHN T CLOGHESSY JR, 466TH
JOHN A CLONINGER, 93RD
H K CLOSE, 467TH
HAROLD F CLOSZ JR, 448TH
PHILIP B CLOUD, 458TH
ROBERT S CLOUD, 466TH
DONALD K CLOVER, 392ND
COL JOHN P CLOWRY RET, 446TH
RICHARD K CLUPHF, 453RD
LTC ROBERT E CLYBURN RET, HDQ
DOROTHY M CMAYLO, 489TH, AM
PAUL J COAPMAN, 491ST
M/SGT CLIFTON D COATNEY RET, 458TH
WILLIS E COBB JR, 467TH
ROBERT S COBURN, 489TH
MICHAEL A COCCHIOLA, 448TH
WESLEY COCHELL, 389TH
VICTOR COCHRAN, 489TH, AM
J MARION COCHRANE, 489TH
R L COCKRELL, 448TH
JAMES W CODDINGTON, 44TH
JAMES G COFFEY, 467TH
JOHN R COFFEY, 389TH
J D COFFMAN, 489TH
RAYMOND L COHEE, 448TH
BENJAMIN COHEN, 492ND
EVELYN & LILLIAN COHEN, HDQ
IRWIN B COHEN, 93RD, 389TH, 445TH
LOUIS COHEN, 445TH
SAMUEL COHEN, 93RD
SEYMOUR COHEN, 453RD
ROBERT R COINTEPOIX, 466TH
ROBERT N COKER, 491ST
S/SGT ALLEN COLBAUGH RET, 466TH
ROYCE V COLBY, 491ST
OWEN J COLDIRON, 389TH
CEDRIC C COLE, 458TH
LTC HOWARD W COLE RET, 453RD
CMSGT LEONARD T COLE RET, 453RD
TAYLOR W COLE, 56FG
FRANCIS T COLEMAN, 458TH
HARRY J COLEMAN, 491ST
PRESCOTT W COLEMAN, 445TH
WILLIAM C COLEMAN, 458TH
WILLIAM E COLEMAN, 445TH
CARL F COLERICK, 491ST
CARROLL COLEY, 458TH
HOMER L COLEY, 458TH
RICHARD O COLEY, 445TH
MICHAEL A COLICIGNO, 466TH
GEORGE M COLLAR, 445TH
RALPH T COLLIANDER, 453RD
FRANCIS L COLLIER, 445TH
BILLY C COLLINS, 389TH
EDGAR S COLLINS, 467TH
LTC FRED A COLLINS RET, 93RD
MAJ JAMES M COLLINS RET, 389TH, 93RD, 2CW, 20CW
JOHN D COLLINS, 467TH
PATRICK L COLUCCI, 44TH
WILLIAM R COLVARD, 458TH
BARRY T COLVIN, HDQ

CLYDE C COLVIN, 453RD
JOHN A COLVIN, 392ND
RALPH L COLVIN, 453RD
WALTER C COLVIN, 467TH
LESTER D COMER, 389TH
PHILIP E COMERFORD, 489TH
RICHARD J COMEY, 44TH
DAN COMINGORE, 93RD
DUANE COMPORT, 467TH
A LEON COMPTON, 458TH
CLYDE COMPTON, 93RD
BOYD A CONDON, 466TH
JACK CONDON, 445TH
GEORGE W CONDRY, 467TH
SANFORD A CONE, 458TH
GORDON H CONGDON MD, 446TH
WILLIS G CONKLE, 448TH
CHARLES P CONLEY, 93RD
F W CONLEY, 445TH
JAMES M CONLEY, 392ND
MAJ JOHN V CONLON RET, 93RD
WALTER CONNEELY, 453RD
LEE R CONNER, 448TH
LEO M CONNER, 448TH
MRS PAT CONNICK, HDQ, AM
GARTH D CONNOLE, 448TH
G PETER CONNOLLY III, 446TH
ROBERT C CONNOLLY, 445TH
JOHN B CONRAD, 392ND, 44TH
ROBERT E CONRAD JR, 445TH
WARREN P CONRAD, 489TH
ED CONROY, 466TH
VALERIA BRINEGAR CONROY, HDQ
GEORGE A CONSTABLE, 448TH
HARRY S CONSTABLE, 448TH
CLAYTON W CONTE, 445TH
DONALD R CONWAY, 458TH
ALFRED P COOK, 446TH
CALVIN B COOK, 446TH
LTC CARL L COOK JR RET, 445TH
FRANK J COOK, 466TH
JAMES R COOK, 448TH
MARION E COOK, 93RD
NORMAN C COOK, 445TH, 492ND
ROBERT J COOK SR, 489TH
WALTER W COOK, 453RD
LTC WARREN G COOK RET, 458TH
WENDELL L COOK, 458TH
GEORGE D COOKSEY JR, 448TH
PAUL R COOL, 445TH
CM/SGT VERNON V COOL RET, 389TH
JAMES G COOLEY, 93RD
MYLES E COOLIDGE, 467TH
ARTHUR I COOPER, 389TH
CHARLES L COOPER, 445TH
LTC FLOYD C COOPER JR RET, 466TH
JACK L COOPER, 448TH
JAMES D COOPER, 3SAD
JAMES R COOPER, 448TH
MORRIS M COOPER, 448TH
DAVID P COPE, 389TH
ROBERT D COPP, 392ND
ARCHIE J CORAN, 453RD
HELEN DIALPHONSO CORBETT, HDQ
ARTHUR J CORBIN, 93RD
PAUL CORBISIERO, 453RD
ANTHONY C CORBO, 453RD
COL MICHAEL CORCORAN JR RET, 93RD, 389TH
CM/SGT HURSHELL E CORDELL RET, 446TH
DALE T CORDER, 448TH
WILLIAM W CORDRAY, 448TH
MAX CORENMAN, 448TH
CLARK L COREY, 489TH
RUTH CORKERN, 389TH, AM
H LAWSON CORLEY, 446TH
JOHN M CORLISS, 446TH
CLARENCE I CORNELIUS, 446TH
CHARLES S CORNELL, 93RD
FOREST CORNETT, 389TH
D HULON CORNETTE, 458TH
JOSEPH CORO, 44TH
ANTHONY CORRADETTI, 467TH

GEORGE W CORRAR, 466TH
ROBERT A CORRELL, 389TH
STANLEY CORRINGTON, 389TH
CARMELO COSENTINO, 392ND
JOHN H COSGRIFF, 467TH
JOHN J COSTA, 491ST
JOSEPH A COSTA, 392ND
GEORGE COSTAGE, 458TH
LTC BASIL COSTAS RET, 453RD
COL BENNY L COSTELLO RET, 458TH
CHARLES COTEL, 491ST
FRANK COTNER, 466TH
LTC GEORGE P COTNOIR RET, 491ST
RALPH A COTTON, 489TH
FRANCIS L COUNE, 44TH
HENRY W COUNTS, HDQ
MORRIS R COUNTS, 491ST
ROY F COUNTS, 491ST
WILLIAM H COUNTS, 467TH
DOYLE COURINGTON, 467TH, 492ND
LTC HOWARD A COURTNEY RET, 448TH
PAUL E COVENEY, 448TH
BARBARA J COVERDALE, HDQ, AM
RAYMOND D COVERT, 491ST
GERALD L COVEY, 458TH
JOSEPH T COVONE, 93RD
ROBERT J COWAN, SM
W A COWAN, 453RD
LTC DAVID W COWEN RET, 453RD
JOHN P COWGER, 453RD
CHARLES W COX, 467TH
ERNEST J COX, 389TH
HERBERT S COX, 466TH
JAMES W COX, 489TH, AM
COL LUTHER C COX RET, 93RD
MARVIN V COX, 458TH
MICHAEL COX, SM
MORGAN K COX, 466TH
PATRICK R COX, SM
WILLIAM L COX, 445TH
ROY P COXWELL, 491ST
HENRY J COYLE JR, 458TH
S M COZART, 389TH
JAMES F CRADDOCK, 44TH
C H CRAFT, 389TH
LTC HARRY N CRAFT RET, 458TH
JOE D CRAFT, 453RD
ARTHUR CRAFTON JR, 392ND
CHARLES O CRAIG, 445TH
WILLIAM C CRAIG, 491ST
R ROBERT CRAMER, HDQ
C LEE CRANDELL, 467TH
RALPH B CRANDELL, 445TH
GEORGE E CRANE, 448TH
GEORGE S CRANE, 446TH
HARRY F CRANE, 445TH
JACKSON B CRANE, 392ND
WALTER N CRANSON, 392ND
ARTHUR B CRAWFORD, 489TH
WILLIAM J CRAWFORD, 389TH
DALE CRAY, 446TH
EDWARD J CREEDEN, 4FG, 56FG
WILLIAM D CREEDMORE, 93RD
WILLIAM J CREEGGAN, 466TH
WILLIAM M CREEL, 445TH
WINIFRED CRESSLER, 489TH, AM
MILDRED L CREWS, 492ND, AM
QUINNIE Q CREWS, 44TH
VANCE E CRIDLING DO, 467TH
HUBERT R CRIPE, 453RD
LTC ROY D CRIST RET, 96CW, HDQ
CALVIN D CRISWELL, 458TH
JOSEPH J CROCHER, 389TH
D C CROCKETT, 448TH
DONALD L CROFT, 445TH
ARTHUR M CROMARTY, 453RD
PAUL J CROMER, 389TH
ERNIE CROMIE, SM
MARY CRONBERGER, 466TH, AM
LTC FRANK D CROOK RET, 446TH
ROBERT E CROSBY, 458TH
HARRY G CROSLAND, 446TH
E O CROSS, 445TH

FRANK K CROSS, 389TH
JOHN CROSS, 467TH
KENNETH C CROSS, 446TH
LUTHER B CROSS, 453RD
WAYNE O CROSSAN, 467TH
ROBERT CROSSLAND, 445TH
H CURT CROUCH, 445TH
ALEX J CROW, 453RD
JOHN W CROWE, 491ST
RICHARD A CROWELL, 389TH
RICHARD K CROWELL, 392ND
ROBERT K CROWELL, 392ND
J NEIL CROWLEY, 453RD
WALLACE D CROXFORD, 453RD
W L CRUM, 389TH
WILLIAM H CRUM, 453RD
LYMAN CRUMRIN, 389TH, 453RD
OSCAR S CRUTCHFIELD, 448TH
WILLIAM CSAKAI, 466TH
CHARLES B CUDD JR, 44TH
ROGER E CUDDEBACK, 44TH, 448TH
M/SGT WILLIAM M CULIN RET, 93RD
LTC ARTHUR V CULLEN RET, 44TH
SIDNEY A CULLINGTON, SM
THOMAS R CULPEPPER, 448TH
MELVIN CULROSS, 467TH, 492ND
COL W TEMPLE CUMISKEY RET, 389TH
FRANK L CUMMINGS, 392ND
JAMES F CUMMINGS JR, 448TH
LLOYD R CUMMINGS, 389TH
CARMAN CUNNINGHAM, 389TH
FRANCIS A CUNNINGHAM, 466TH
JOHN F CUNNINGHAM, 489TH
WILLIAM P CUNNINGHAM, 458TH
CHARLES E CUPP JR, 448TH
JOHN F CURCIO, 458TH
JOSEPH D CURCIO, 389TH
DEREK CURRALL, 446TH
JOHN E CURRAN, 389TH
THOMAS CURRIE JR, 44TH
COL DEANE G CURRY RET, 446TH
FOREST L CURRY, 389TH
GENE M CURRY, 389TH
EDWARD J CURTIN, 492ND
LOUIS T CURTIS JR, 467TH
ORVILLE D CURTIS, 489TH, 44TH
WILBUR C CUSHING, 93RD
JOHN F CUSHMAN, 448TH
HAROLD CUTLER, 489TH
DONALD W CUTTER, 389TH
ALBERT R CWIKLINSKI, 445TH
VICTOR CZARNECKI, 44TH
FRANCIS P CZELUSNIAK, 448TH
EMILIO D'ABRAMO, 458TH
DOMENICK D'ADAMO JR, 389TH
PRIMO D'ALESSANDRO, 392ND
JOHN F D'AMELIO, 392ND
DAVID D D'AMICO, 44TH
ALFONSO M D'APUZZO, 93RD
CHARLES E D'ARCY, 389TH
DONALD A D'LUGOS, 466TH
JOHN G DAHLEM, 446TH
DEAN W DAHLKE, 389TH
MAJ LES DAHN RET, 489TH
SIDNEY H DAILEY, 446TH
FRED A DALE, 445TH
JOHN K DALGLEISH, 489TH
HOMER DALLACQUA, 453RD
ALOYSIUS DALLMEYER, 453RD
MAJ EDGAR A DALTON RET, 445TH, 389TH
ROBERT J DALTON, 44TH
JOE C DAMIANO, 445TH
THORNTON H DAMON, 448TH
BURTON D DANE, 448TH
CHARLES E DANFORD 111, 389TH
DEBORAH DANFORD, 458TH, AM
PORTER R DANFORD DDS, 458TH
BENJAMIN S DANIEL, 448TH
BENJAMIN W DANKOSKY, 458TH
JOHN DANKS, 389TH
BILL M DANLEY, 389TH
EDWARD K DANTLER, 458TH
JOSEPH J DAPOLITO, 492ND
ROY E DARBY, 491ST

ALFRED R DARBYSHIRE, 492ND
COL ROD G DARELIUS RET, 466TH
VICTOR DARILEK, 389TH
LEWIS R DARLIN, 466TH
JOSEPH F DARNELL JR, 392ND
DOROTHY N DARNEY, 467TH, AM
CAPT KENNETH A DARNEY JR, 467TH, AM
EUGENE B DARR, 446TH
HARRY H DARRAH, 389TH, HDQ
HARRY N DARTZ, 446TH
EVAN L DASTRUP, 467TH
STANLEY DASZCZYSAK, HDQ
VIVIAN J DAUDEL, 445TH, AM
JOSEPH F DAUENHAUER, 466TH
JAMES W DAUGHERTY, 93RD
NED A DAUGHERTY, 445TH
EDWARD DAVAJIAN, 389TH, 491ST
MATTHEW J DAVAN SR, 458TH
WILLIAM F DAVENPORT, 446TH
HAROLD L DAVEY, 392ND
JAMES F DAVEY, 392ND
CALVIN DAVIDSON, 93RD
FRANK DAVIDSON, 453RD
KEITH R DAVIDSON, 93RD, AM
LLOYD S DAVIDSON, 445TH
WILLIAM I DAVIDSON, 448TH
MRS FRANCES DAVIES, BG
LLOYD A DAVIES DDS, 467TH
CHARLES J DAVILLA, 389TH
ADDISON C DAVIS, 44TH, 492ND
ERNEST T DAVIS, 489TH
FAY L DAVIS, 467TH
FLOYD R DAVIS, 491ST
FRED E DAVIS, 466TH
GAYLORD W DAVIS, 93RD
GLENN DAVIS, 392ND
HAROLD A DAVIS, 445TH
HOWARD L DAVIS, 445TH
JAMES M DAVIS, 489TH
JOHN S DAVIS, 448TH, 389TH, 489TH
LLOYD G DAVIS, 446TH
LYNN M DAVIS, 489TH, AM
MARTIN B DAVIS, 491ST
MARVIN R DAVIS, 467TH
MARVIN R DAVIS, 448TH
ROBERT D DAVIS, 392ND
ROBERT T DAVIS, 448TH
LTC ROBERT W DAVIS SR RET, 458TH
VIRGINIA TOMLIN DAVIS, HDQ
WALTER S DAVIS, 489TH
MAJ WILLARD M DAVIS RET, 389TH
ERLING DAWES, 445TH
THOMAS R DAWES, 458TH
CM/SGT E W DAWLEY RET, 93RD
ROBERT L DAWSON, 389TH
DONALD B DAY, 491ST
FRANK S DAY, 15AF, SM
IRVING & MARIN DAY, 446TH
IRVING & MARIN DAY, 446TH
PHILLIP G DAY, 467TH, 492ND
WILLIAM L DAY, 491ST
KENNETH DEAGMAN, 467TH
WILLIAM J DEAL, 466TH
HARRY R DEAN, 491ST
JACK DEAN, 453RD
JOSEPH H DEAN JR, 489TH
LAWRENCE E DEAN, 458TH
RICHARD M DEAN, 453RD
ROBERT L DEAN, 44TH
BERNARD V DEANY, 491ST
LTC CHARLES E DEARING RET, 389TH
ROBERT A DEASY, 489TH
ANTHONY DEBENEDICTUS, 389TH
ANTHONY DEBIASSE JR, 467TH
LOUIS J DEBLASIO, 44TH
MICHAEL J DEBRINO SR, 93RD
JOHN S DECANI, 489TH
ARTHUR F DECKER, 448TH
SYLVIA G DECKTOR, 448TH, AM
FRANK DECOLA, 448TH
ARTHUR J DECOSTER, 93RD

ANDREW J DECUSATI, 453RD, AM
CHARLES C DEDECKER, 458TH
ALBERT J DEDENBACH, 445TH
WARREN L DEDRICKSON, 466TH
CHARLES R DEEGAN, 458TH
ROSTEN R DEFRATES, 392ND
ANTHONY DEGENNARO, 458TH
MERIEL KOORNDYK DEGRAAF, 389TH, AM
LTC GEORGE J DEGRAFF RET, 389TH
GEORGE DEGROOT, 448TH
ALAN DEHAVEN, 453RD
M/SGT LEE ROY V DEHOFF RET, 392ND
FRED H DEIBER, 467TH
JOSEPH D DEIGERT, 389TH
COL ARIE P DEJONG RNLAF, SM
IVO M DEJONG, SM
LTC DARIO A DEJULIO RET, 458TH
ROBERT DEKERF, 467TH
HENRY A DEKEYSER, 392ND
EDWARD N DEKKER JR, 453RD
JOHN J DELACH, 392ND
GEORGE W DELACY, 44TH
SAMUEL J DELCAMBRE, 93RD
ERNEST J DELIA, 448TH
ALFRED DELLA ROCCO, 389TH
HENRY DELLANO, 489TH
MARC DELLEFEMINE, 466TH
DOMINIC J DELPERUTO, 44TH
JOHN W DELURY, 453RD
RUSSELL C DEMARY, 453RD
PAT DEMAS, 446TH
JOHN R DEMBECKI, 458TH
WILLIAM J DEMETROPOULOS, 448TH
MEL W DEMMIN, 466TH
COL RUSSELL D DEMONT RET, 93RD
JOHN DEMSHOCK, 445TH
ROBERT DENEAL, 453RD
FREDERICK M DENEFFE JR, 458TH
HERMIONE BEABER DENKER, HDQ
ROBERT E DENNEY, 492ND
WILLIAM E DENT JR, 389TH
RICHARD L DENTON, 446TH
WILLIAM J DENTON JR, 389TH
FREDERICK DEPALMA, 392ND
CHARLES A DEPPERSCHMIDT, 446TH
LTC PAUL W DEPPERT RET, 389TH
JOHN P DEREN, 448TH
CHARLES F DERR, 445TH
GLORIA M DERR, 467TH, AM
LTC MERRITT E DERR RET, 44TH
JULES DESCAMPS SR, 44TH
DR DANIEL J DESJARDIN, 458TH
ROLAND A DESJARDINS, 445TH
GEORGE DESMARAIS, 453RD
A T DESMEDT, 448TH
PAUL J DESMOND, 458TH
MAX DESONNE, 392ND
ROBERT E DETAR, 489TH
ROY M DETTINGER, 467TH
LOUIS E DEUTSCH JR, 446TH
FRANK J DEVER JR, 466TH
ROBERT P DEVER, 453RD, 467TH
LTC HAROLD O DEVERICK RET, 446TH
ARTHUR T DEVINCENZI, 489TH
HENRY DEVINE, 448TH
MELVIN H DEVISH, 491ST
HENRY M DEVITO, 93RD
ROY M DEVLIN, HDQ
DAVID F DEVOL, 93RD
MAJ EDWARD B DEVON RET, 93RD
ERNEST G DEVRIES, 458TH
COL HARTLEY C DEWEY RET, 446TH
WILLIAM R DEWEY, 445TH
AL DEXTER, 389TH
LOUIS DEZARLO, 492ND
ARTHUR DICEY JR, 389TH
ROBERT L DICKEN SR, 491ST

REV PAUL M DICKERSON, 445TH
HAZEL L DICKINSON, 448TH, AM
COL GEORGE W DICKS RET, 458TH
TOMMIE F DICKSON, 453RD
HARRY DICUS, 489TH
GERARD R DIEFFENBACH, 466TH
HAROLD E DIEGEL, 458TH
EARL E DIEHL, 458TH
GLENN A DIEL, 389TH
JUDGE HENRY X DIETCH, HDQ, 491ST
G O DIETRICH, 466TH
RICHARD L DIETRICK, 489TH
HAROLD L DIETZ, 466TH
WALTER C DIETZGEN, 458TH
MALCOLM O DIKE, 466TH
RUSSELL C DILL, 389TH
CLYDE J DILLON, 389TH
T/SGT PAUL R DILLON RET, 93RD
ROBERT L DILLON, 93RD
VERNICE DILLON, 467TH, 492NDAM
WILLIAM DILLON, 467TH, 492ND
ALBERT DILORENZO, 448TH
WILLIAM K DIMARZO, SM
CARL M DIMEDIO, 453RD
NELSON L DIMICK, 445TH
RALPH C DIMICK, 448TH
JOSEPH L DIMINO, 389TH
FRANCIS & ELIZABETH DIMOLA, 445TH
LESLIE H DINING, 467TH
MAJ ALBERT D DIPAOLA RET, 479FG
ROBERT L DIRCKS, 491ST
PAUL F DIRKER, 458TH
LTC DONALD W DISBROW RET, 448TH
JAMES P DISHAROON JR, 491ST
NORMAN DISNEY, 491ST
BERNARD L DISPENZA, 389TH
V HOWARD DITCH, 446TH
EDWARD J DITTLINGER, 445TH
OCLE D DIVELBISS, 489TH
CHARLES C DIXON, 448TH
JOHN M DIXON, 448TH
RICHARD V DIXON, 445TH
PAUL A DLUGOSCH, 389TH
T W DOBBS, 446TH
HENRY W DOBEK, 445TH
JAMES DOBRAVEC, 445TH
EDWARD M DOBSON, 44TH, AM
ODELL F DOBSON, 392ND
J C COLTER DODMAN, 389TH
WILLIAM F DOERNER, 93RD
WILLIAM J DOHONEY, 491ST
AMOS B DOLLIVER, 93RD
HARRY DOMBALAGIAN, 467TH, 489TH
STANLEY DOMBKOWSKI, 446TH, 491ST
CHARLES G DOMEK, 458TH
MICHAEL J DONAHUE DDS, 93RD
WILLIAM H DONALDSON, 446TH
JAMES V DONATELLO, 453RD
HELENE L DONDERO, 458TH, AM
RICHARD B DONDES, 466TH, AM
GEORGE DONG, 467TH
JAMES & MARGARET DONLEY, 448TH
HUGH J DONLON, 467TH
JOHN M DONNELLY, 392ND
JAMES R DONOVAN, 458TH
JOSEPH J DONOVAN, 453RD
DR R T DONOVAN DC, 389TH
ROBERT K DOOLING, 93RD, 492ND
LEE A DOOLITTLE, 44TH, 392ND, 453RD
VIRGIL DOPSON, 392ND
WARREN E DOREMUS, 491ST
LTC HAROLD H DORFMAN RET, 448TH
ROBERT M DORRIETY, 489TH
A B DORSMAN JR, 446TH
NEVILLE B DORTCH, 489TH
JOHN J DOSKOCZ, 466TH
LEE DOTSON, 445TH

A F DOUGAN MD, 491ST
DAVID J DOUGHERTY, 491ST
RALPH E DOUGHERTY, 446TH
FRANK DOUGLAS, 446TH
LIVINGSTON C DOUGLAS, 491ST
W GORDON DOUGLAS, 14CW
LTC GERALD E DOUGLASS RET, 392ND
ARNOLD J DOVEY, 392ND
ANTHONY P DOVIDIO, 453RD
WARREN E DOW, 466TH
WILLIAM H DOWDEN JR, 389TH
WILLIAM C DOWDY, 389TH, AM
ROBERT M DOWELL, 448TH
JAMES E DOWLING, 445TH
LTC SAMUEL F DOWLING RET, 445TH
WILLIAM G DOWLING, HDQ
THOMAS F DOWNEY, 458TH
WILLIAM M DOWNEY, 389TH
BERNARD J DOYLE, 458TH
CHARLES W DOYLE, 389TH
FRANCIS P DOYLE, 389TH
JAMES DOYLE, SM
THOMAS J DOYLE, 492ND
VAIDEN U DOZIER, 448TH
CHRIS C DRACOPOULOS, 492ND, 491ST
ALDRICH A DRAHOS, 448TH
WALTER M DRAKE, 479FG
MAJ MILES B DRAWHORN RET, 448TH
BEN E DRENTH, 458TH
LLOYD DREXLER, 491ST
JOSEPH A DRIGGS, 458TH
ERROLL DRINKWATER, 389TH
BERNARD F DRISCOLL, 389TH
KENNETH L DRISCOLL, 467TH
ROLAND B DRISCOLL, 389TH
EDWARD A DROUIN, 448TH
JOSEPH DRUCKER, 446TH
WILLIAM E DRUMEL, 44TH
ROBERT J DRUMMOND, 445TH
LLOYD A DRURY, 448TH
LEON B DUBIN, 445TH
GEORGE DUBINA, 389TH
LEONARD DUBINSKI, 445TH
PHYLLIS M DUBOIS, SM
LTC RET ROBERT & IRMA DUBOWSKY, 44TH
WILLIAM J DUCEY, 491ST
MILTON DUCHARME, 389TH
ROBERT G DUCHARME, 445TH
FRANK O DUDLEY, 467TH
KENNETH DUFAULT, 466TH
ALLEN L DUFF, 392ND
DENNIS DUFFIELD, SM
EDWARD C DUFFY JR, 491ST
WILLIAM DUFFY, 44TH
WILLIAM C DUFFY, 445TH
RAYMOND H DUFLON, 389TH
WILFRED P DUFOUR, 93RD
DONALD H DUGMORE, 458TH
CHARLIE DUGOSH, 448TH, 389TH
GUS A DUHON, 458TH
CLIFFORD C DUKE, 466TH
LOUIS A DUKE, 489TH
REUBEN D DUKE, 389TH
DONALD W DUKEMAN, 93RD
LTC GEORGE E DUKES RET, 492ND, HDQ
GLASCO E DUKES, 446TH
TROY K DUMAS, 448TH
LUCILLE DUMITRAS, 491ST, AM
DONALD D DUMOULIN, 453RD
FELIX DUNAGAN, 44TH, 389TH
BYRON E DUNBAR, 491ST, 492ND
JOHN L DUNBAR, 446TH
WALTER W DUNBAR, 44TH
JAMES J DUNCAN, 491ST
JULIAN A DUNCAN, 448TH
WARREN W DUNCAN, 448TH
CHARLES T DUNGAR, SM
GORDON N DUNHAM, 489TH
HAROLD D DUNHAM, 392ND
JAMES J DUNLAY, 93RD
JAMES H DUNN, 93RD
MAURICE B DUNN, 467TH
SAMUEL C DUNN, 93RD

B C DUNNAM, 467TH, 492ND
NORMAN R DUNPHE, 448TH
RAY J DUNPHY, 392ND
GEORGE P DUPONT, 448TH
WILLIAM E DUPREE, 448TH
JAMES F DUPREY JR, 93RD
ALFRED C DUPUIS, 448TH
IRVING C DUPUIS, 392ND
FRANK V DURANTE, 93RD
LTC DANIEL R DURBIN RET, 448TH
EARLE P DURLEY JR, 448TH, 491ST
E NORMAN DURRELL, 389TH
HOWARD C DURYEA, 446TH
EDMUND DUTKEVITCH, 491ST
DON A DUVALL, 453RD
BLAINE DUXBURY, 44TH
EUGENE J DWORACZYK, 448TH
PAUL F DWYER, 448TH
COL GEORGE T DWYRE RET, 458TH
CHARLES E DYE, 392ND
HOWARD W DYE JR, 467TH
DALE H DYER, 458TH
LTC MAURICE L DYER RET, 44TH
RAYMOND L DYER, 446TH
LTC JAMES P DYKE RET, 453RD
ROBERT W DYMACEK, 389TH
CHARLES H DYOTT, 458TH
ARTHUR J DYSON, 466TH
JOSEPH G DZENOWAGIS, 467TH
BRUNO DZIOBAK, 445TH
WILLIAM A EAGLESON JR, 453RD
THOMAS G EAKES, 448TH
JAMES O EALY, 453RD
PHILIP R EARL, 392ND
WALTER M EASDON, 453RD
JERRY R EASON, 389TH, AM
WALTER GLEN EASON, 389TH
WILLIAM F EASTLAND, 492ND, 467TH
CLYDE B EATON JR, 392ND
R BARTLETT EATON JR, 467TH
T C EATON, BG
HENRY W EBELING, 448TH
HOWARD R EBERSOLE, 392ND
W A EBERSVILLER, 93RD
BERNARD ECHT, 44TH
LTC RAYMOND O ECK RET, 93RD
HAROLD C ECKELBERRY, 445TH
RICHARD H ECKMAN, 445TH
GEORGE C ECONOMAKI, 44TH
ROBERT H EDDINGS, 44TH, 389TH
FREDERICK E EDELL, 389TH
WALTER A EDGEWORTH, 453RD
THOMAS J EDGINGTON, 392ND
W DON EDKINS, 44TH
WILLIAM J EDKINS, 458TH
GROVER A EDMISTON, 389TH
F A EDMONDSON, 489TH
HOWARD W EDMUNDS, 446TH
ROY H EDMUNDSON, 392ND
GERALD D EDWARDS, 492ND
JACK P EDWARDS, 448TH
COL JOHN S EDWARDS RET, 445TH
JOSEPH EDWARDS, 453RD
JOSEPH W EDWARDS SR, 466TH
NORMAN M EDWARDS, 491ST
PAUL H EDWARDS, 492ND
RAY N EDWARDS JR, 466TH
ROBERT LEE EDWARDS, 467TH
TOM N EDWARDS, 491ST
WINNIFRED B EDWARDS, 446TH, AM
CARLOS A EFFERSON, 458TH, ARC
ARTHUR J EGAN, 392ND
JAMES A EGAN, 453RD, AM
ROBERT L EGAN, 392ND, 93RD, 389TH
MAJ HOWARD O EGGE RET, 489TH
PAUL S EGGLESTON JR, 448TH
VICTOR EHLERT, 446TH
CLEM C EHMET, 466TH
ROBERT EHRENSPERGER, 491ST

JUNE R EHRLICH, 467TH, 492ND AM
FRANK J EIBEN, 93RD
WALTER H EICHENSEHR, 44TH
ROBERT E EIDELSBERG, 458TH
GEORGE L EIFEL JR, 458TH
ISRAEL EIFERMAN, 492ND
L ROBERT EINHEUSER, 448TH
HENRY EIRICH, 445TH
COL E F W EISEMANN RET, 446TH
SEYMOUR F EISENBERG, 445TH
ROBERT P EISENHAURE, 466TH
SEYMOUR EISENSTAT, 491ST
GILBERT O EISERMANN, 392ND
LTC FRED J EISERT RET, 458TH
ARTHUR EISNER, 492ND
ALLEN EK, 453RD
FRANK E EKAS, 453RD
JOSEPH EKASALA, 448TH
CHARLES B ELBERT, 389TH
JUDGE S J ELDEN, 392ND
MARY F WILLIAMS ELDER, HDQ
LEROY ELFSTROM, 445TH
DONALD R ELGAS, HDQ, 93RD
MORRIS ELISCO, 453RD
GEORGE W ELKINS, 448TH
JAMES T ELKINS, 453RD
KLEMMET P ELLEFSON, 466TH
ROY ELLENDER, 445TH
MELVIN ELLER, 392ND
LAWRENCE M ELLINGSEN, 44TH
EDWARD J ELLIOTT, 453RD
B/GEN FRANK B ELLIOTT RET, 466TH, 355FG, 4FG
MAJ RALPH H ELLIOTT RET, 467TH
RICHARD H ELLIOTT, 448TH
THOMAS C ELLIOTT, 445TH
LEONARD ELLIS, 44TH
LEWIS N ELLIS, 389TH
BURRELL M ELLISON JR, 392ND
HENRY W ELLISON, 467TH
ROBERT L ELLISON, 44TH, 491ST
EDMONDE J ELLWART, 491ST
ALBERT G ELLWEIN, 445TH
THOMAS H ELMORE, 44TH
JAMES ELOFF, 458TH
LTC THOMAS F ELSEN RET, 467TH
FRANK J ELSTON, 489TH
ROBERT C ELSTON, 392ND
JOSEPH J ELWOOD, 448TH
JOHN O EMBICH, 491ST
RONALD P EMBICK, 446TH
EARLINE EMBREY, HDQ
DONALD R EMMEL, 491ST
MICHAEL R EMRICH, 446TH
FRED J ENCK, 467TH
THOMAS A ENDECOTT, 491ST
HAROLD E ENGBERG, 466TH
LTC LEROY ENGDAHL RET, 448TH
HERMAN ENGEL, 448TH
KENNETH W ENGELBRECHT, 448TH
EMIL A ENGELMAN, 489TH
JAMES T ENGLEMAN, 445TH
DONALD R ENGLER, 489TH
VICTOR E ENGLERT, 389TH
ALEX ENGLESE, 458TH
BERT A ENGSTROM, 446TH
JAMES A ENNIS, 448TH, 93RD
LLOYD L ENNIS, 466TH
DONALD F EPHLIN, 458TH
CARL E EPTING JR, 467TH
LTC FRANK J ERBACHER RET, 448TH
HAROLD G ERBE, 489TH
CHARLES J ERCEGOVAC, 467TH
RAOUL C ERDMAN, 448TH
FREDERICK H ERDMANN, 458TH
EDMUND M ERICKSON, 492ND
HARVEY G ERICKSON, 467TH
JACK M ERICKSON, 445TH
ROBERT M ERICKSON, 446TH
1ST LT ERIC E ERICSON RET, 93RD
GERTRUDE PREGIZER ERIKSEN, HDQ
EDGAR R ERIKSON, 467TH

WILLIAM L ERKERT JR, 458TH
LEON ERNSTER, SM
ALBERT ERRAMOUSPE, 491ST
JULIAN S ERTZ, 44TH
JAMES W ERWIN, 453RD
E RICHARD ESENWEIN JR, 392ND
CLYDE C ESKRIDGE JR, 389TH
BILLY J ESPICH, 448TH
AMADOR B ESPINOSA, 445TH
EDWIN L ESSEX, 389TH
WEEMS E ESTELLE, 392ND, 492ND
CHARLES L ESTES, 389TH
LOUISE ETHERIDGE, 389TH, AM
LEWIS L EUBANKS, 389TH
CHARLES & CAREY EVANS, 458TH
FRANKLIN B EVANS, 445TH
HARL B EVANS, 93RD
COL JAMES C EVANS RET, 445TH
LTC JAMES W EVANS RET, 458TH
ROBERT E EVANS, 458TH
BENJAMIN L EVERETT, 448TH
LAWRENCE W EVERETT, 458TH
WILLIAM E EVERETT, 458TH
GEORGE G EVERHART, 93RD
PATRICIA J EVERSON, SM
ANDREW EWANUS, 389TH
HUGH EWING JR, 448TH
ROBERT P EWING, 448TH
TRUMAN D EWING, 93RD
ROBERT FACTOR, 453RD
HENRY FAGAN, 467TH, 389TH
MICHAEL A FAGEN, 491ST
LTC C E FAGER RET, 389TH
THOMAS A FAHEY, 453RD
LIONEL FAHRER, 389TH
LTC DUANE G FAIR RET, 458TH
LTC PHILIP M FAIRCHILD RET, 93RD, 44TH
CREED R FAIRFIELD, 458TH
EDWARD L FALADA, 392ND
HAROLD M FALIK, 466TH
ALBERT J FALKE, 389TH
HENRY D FALLER, 44TH
HUGH D FALLON, 448TH
A J FALSONE, 389TH
JOHN V FANELLI, 389TH
W R FANNING, 489TH
JAMES J FARLEY, 458TH
WALTER FARMER, 448TH
FRANCIS FARNELLO, 448TH
ROY J FARNSWORTH, 445TH
HERBERT E FARRELL, 93RD
JAMES F FARRELL, 467TH
FRANCIS A FARRIS, 44TH
JAMES R FARRIS, 453RD
PAT FARRIS, 448TH
LTC GEORGE E FARSCHMAN RET, 448TH
KARL E FASICK, 492ND
W C FASON, 446TH
HARRIET S FAU, HDQ
ROBERT B FAUGHT, 446TH
JOHN H FAULDS, 446TH
CLYDE M FAULEY, 466TH
IRVING R FAULKNER, 392ND
W D FAULKNER, 453RD
HAROLD G FAUST JR, 44TH
LOWELL E FAUST, 392ND
JOHN F FAY, 466TH
RAYMOND C FAY, 44TH
STEPHEN FECHO, 466TH
FRANK W FEDERICI, 445TH
FRANCIS P FEENEY, 453RD
LEO F FEENEY, 467TH
LTC THOMAS J FEENEY RET, 44TH
COL HAROLD W FEICHTER RET, 93RD
GEORGE D FEIL, 467TH
JACK FEINGOLD, 93RD
ROBERT S FEIST, 458TH
NORMAN W FELBINGER, 467TH
A J FELDMAN, 389TH
ROBERT J FELONEY, 389TH
JOSEPH R FELTON, 453RD
MAJ RAY H FENDER RET, 389TH, 445TH

FRED FENNEWALD, 448TH
PAUL J FENOGLIO, 453RD
FRED C FENSKE, 445TH
PETER F FERDINAND, 389TH
FRANK FERENC, 392ND
ANDREW FERGUSON, SM
KENNETH J FERLAND, 453RD
NICHOLAS A FERRANT JR, 389TH
COL VICTOR J FERRARI RET, 392ND
WILLIAM B FERRARO, 93RD
ROBERT A FERRATO, 453RD
HOBART G FERREE, 467TH
DANIEL B FERREIRA, 44TH
CHARLES R FERRELL, 458TH
GEORGE A FERRELL JR, 458TH
COL ROBERT L FERRELL RET, 458TH
LOUIE M FERRERO, 448TH
PARMELY T FERRIE, 448TH
JOSEPH J FERRIS, 445TH
C ARTHUR FERWERDA, 93RD
ROBERT H FESMIRE DDS, 492ND
SMS ARTHUR FETSKOS RET, 445TH
JAMES J FETTERLY, 489TH
CHARLES E FETTERMAN, 466TH
WALTER FIALKEWICZ, 392ND
LAWRENCE R FICK, 458TH
BENJAMIN P FIELDS, 93RD
BOBBY FIELDS, SM
DON C FIELDS MD, 467TH
WILLIAM G FIELDS JR, 445TH
V W FILLBACH, 44TH
GEORGE H FINCH, 448TH
WALTER E FINDLEY, 489TH
HYMAN FINE, 491ST
LTC PAUL B FINE RET, 489TH, 491ST
MARVIN A FINGER JR, 446TH
JOHN H FINITZER, 93RD
LTC C W FINK RET, 453RD
ROBERT L FINKLE, 491ST
DERMOT G FINLAY, 93RD
BEN W FINLEY, 445TH
CHARLES D FINN, 467TH
EUGENE J FINN, 453RD
THEODORE L FINNARN, 93RD, AM
WILLIAM H FINNEGAN, 446TH
JOHN V FINNERAN, 492ND, 467TH
RALPH FINNICUM, 93RD
JOHN A FINO, 389TH
ELMER M FISCHER, 445TH
MAJ LEROY J FISCHER RET, 458TH
MONTFORD R FISCHER, 453RD
ARTHUR L FISH, 458TH
ARTHUR H FISHER, 467TH
BERNARD V FISHER, 446TH, 389TH
DANIEL FISHER, 466TH
GILBERT W FISHER, 445TH
JOSEPH J FISHER, 458TH
LTC ROBERT L FISHER RET, 44TH, HDQ, 492ND
VIRGIL L FISHER, 458TH
WAYNE FISHER, 492ND
BERNARD FISHMAN, 445TH
ROBERT B FISK, 44TH
RALPH J FISKOW, 466TH
JAMES E FITZGERALD, 389TH
JOHN H FITZGERALD, 491ST
WILLIAM J FITZGERALD, 389TH
WALTER J FITZMAURICE, 44TH
JOHN W FITZSIMMONS, 492ND
JOSEPH H FLAGLER JR, 491ST
LEWIS C FLAGSTAD, 445TH
JOSEPH E FLAHERTY, 44TH, HDQ
THOMAS A FLAHERTY, 44TH
GLORIA A FLAMMANG, 491ST, AM
VIOLES L FLANARY, 93RD
DONALD V FLANDERS, 448TH
THOMAS J FLANNERY, 448TH
VICTOR B FLATT, 453RD, AM
ERNEST R FLECK, 392ND
JAMES M FLEEHR, 389TH
FREDERICK D FLEMING, 458TH
JACK E FLEMING, 445TH
JOHN L FLEMING, SM

JOSEPH S FLEMING, 446TH
ROBERT G FLETCHER, 458TH
W B FLETCHER JR, 93RD
CARROLL F FLEWELLING, 392ND
ROBERT F FLIGG, 467TH, AM
KAY FLINDERS, 448TH, AM
MAJ EUGENE A FLINT RET, 93RD
CATHY FLOOD, 458TH, AM
THOMAS FLORIO, 445TH
THOMAS W FLOYD, 492ND, 467TH
FRANCIS L FLUHARTY, 453RD
JAMES R FLYNN, 445TH
THOMAS F FOGARTY, 466TH
SCOTT FOGG, 458TH
CARSIE E FOLEY, 458TH
GEORGE W FOLLAND, 44TH
GLENN R FOLLWEILER, 93RD
ALEC FONTANA, 389TH
ROBERT M FOOSE, SM
LTC BEN F FOOTE RET, 392ND
HENRY J FORBES, 458TH
CHARLES C FORCE, 389TH
DONALD E FORD, 389TH
DONALD M FORD, 448TH
KENNETH G FORD, 467TH
MORGAN L FORD, 466TH
RALPH E FORD, 453RD
DAVID W FORESMAN, 93RD
JOHN D FORGET, 448TH
JOHN S FORMON, 491ST, AM
JAMES G FORREST, 446TH
JAMES W FORREST, 44TH
LARRY P FORREST, 458TH
PETER S FORREST, 466TH
CHARLES FORST, 491ST
DONALD O FORSYTH, 446TH
JOHN C FORSYTH, 389TH
JOSEPH J FORTI, 93RD
LEO J FORTIN, 448TH
JOE K FORTNEY, 491ST, AM
CLARENCE FOSDICK, 448TH
C EUGENE FOSMARK, 448TH
EDGAR J FOSS, 492ND
HOMER L FOSTER, 458TH
JOHN D FOSTER, 489TH, 93RD
JOHN P FOSTER, 389TH
KENNETH L FOSTER, 446TH
MELVIN F FOSTER, 453RD
LTC RICHARD O FOSTER RET, 466TH
WILLIAM R FOSTER, 445TH
WILLIS A FOSTER, 458TH
LOUIS A FOURNIER, 453RD
ROBERT M FOUST, 44TH
FRANKLIN A FOUTCH, 458TH
C RICHARD FOUTCHE, 448TH
VAN W FOWERS, 448TH
CARMEN J FOX, 93RD
GEORGE FOX JR, 93RD
JAMES B FOX, 453RD
JOHN R FOX, 389TH
KENNETH J FOX, SM
LEONARD C FOX, 467TH
ROBERT E FOX, 448TH
ROGER A FOX, 467TH
WAYNE O FOX, 446TH
WILLIAM H FOX, 492ND
FRANK A FRAGNITO, 93RD
LEO FRANCESCONI, 93RD
JACK C FRANCIS, 389TH
JACK T FRANCIS, 44TH
JAMES L FRANCIS DDS, 445TH
LESLIE R FRANCIS, 492ND
WILLIAM FRANCIS, 93RD
EDWIN W FRANK JR, 453RD
HALBERT FRANK, 491ST
LTC RICHARD H FRANK RET, 445TH
ROBERT H FRANKE, 392ND, AM
WARREN D FRANKIAN, 446TH
EMMA LOU FRANKLIN, 44TH, AM
DONALD A FRASER, 458TH
LTC DONALD W FRASER RET, 467TH, 492ND
G W FRASER, 93RD
BURT FRAUMAN, 458TH
Z W FRAUSTO, 453RD
EDWARD E FRAZIER, 467TH
LESTER J FRAZIER, 392ND

ROBERT C FRAZIER, 458TH
JOHN R FREANEY, 448TH
LAWRENCE N FREAS, 389TH
PAUL FREDRITZ, HDQ
WILLIAM A FREEBOROUGH, 44TH
EUGENE FREED, 446TH
FRED M FREEMAN JR, 446TH
GEORGE H FREEMAN, 491ST
GEORGE N FREEMAN, 445TH
COL GILBERT R FREEMAN RET, 93RD
CMS J B FREEMAN RET, 392ND
ROGER A FREEMAN, BG
TANNER H FREEMAN JR, 491ST
VERLON W FREEMAN, 458TH
WALTER H FREEMAN, 458TH
WESLEY B FREEMAN, 44TH
PAUL M FREEZE, 448TH
LOUIS FREIBERG, 458TH
HARRY D FREIVOGEL, 448TH
LLOYD G FRETWELL, 44TH
PHILLIP A FRETZ, 44TH
LTC RET CHARLES & H FREUDENTHAL, 489TH
DONALD C FREUDENTHAL, 489TH, 44TH
JOHN J FREY, 392ND
THORPE L FRIAR, 448TH, 489TH
LTC DUDLEY E FRIDAY RET, 491ST
J L FRIDELL, 93RD
LOUIS FRIEDMAN, 453RD
MATTHEW E FRIEDMAN, 466TH
MURRAY D FRIEDMAN, 93RD
ROBERT L FRIEDMAN, 389TH
DR S TOM FRIEDMAN, 389TH
ROBERT E FRIEND, 491ST
DONALD L FRIESEN, 458TH
WILFRED J FRIGGE, 446TH, 491ST
LESTER FRISBIE, 453RD
BARNEY E FRISCH, 446TH
DALE L FRITSCH, 492ND
JOHN FRITSCHE, 392ND
HAROLD W FRITZLER, 491ST
PETER A FRIZZELL, SM
VICTOR H FROBERG, 389TH
RAYMOND H FRONES, 458TH
H A FROST, 458TH, AM
ROBERT J FROST, 458TH
CURTICE B FRY, 467TH
COL REX D FRYER RET, HDQ, 446TH
HARRISON L FUGATE, 445TH, 492ND
HAYDEN W FULLBRIGHT, 491ST
MICHAEL J FULLER, 448TH
OWEN D FULLER, 445TH
MAJ ELLIS I FULLWILER RET, 93RD
JOHN FULMER, 491ST
SPENCER M FULP, 44TH
ROBERT W FUNK, 448TH
VINCENT L FURE, 93RD
SHERMAN F FUREY JR, 448TH
ROBERT G FURGESON, 446TH
HAROLD J FURLONG, 93RD
W B FURMAN JR, 445TH
EARL FURNACE, 448TH
REX L FURNESS, 448TH
FRANK FURRELLE, 458TH
ROBERT U FURRY, 448TH
MARTIN D FURST, 93RD
LLOYD G FURTHMYER, 446TH
MIKE FUSANO, 44TH, 14CW
BERNARD T FUSCO, 448TH
HARRY S FUTOR, HDQ
CHARLES S GABRUS, 489TH
FRANK W GADBOIS, BG
THEODORE W GADBOIS, 389TH
GIGLIO GADO, 93RD
LLOYD J GAEL, 389TH
JOSEPH L GAFFEY, 44TH, 392ND
ERICH A GAGEL, 458TH
FRANK T GAINES, 489TH
ROSS W GAINEY, 458TH
JACOB E GAIR, 467TH
RAYMOND GAJEWSKI, 392ND
LTC ELIAS J GALAINI JR RET, 446TH

ANTHONY T GALGANO, 389TH
EDWARD F GALIOTO, 93RD
CHARLES C GALLAGHER JR,
445TH
J WALTER GALLAGHER JR, 445TH
JAMES M GALLAGHER, 389TH
JOHN R GALLAGHER, 392ND
WARREN W GALLAGHER, 392ND
DONALD L GALLANT, 445TH
ELBERT H GALLATIN, 44TH
RUEZ R GALLERANI, 466TH
THOMAS A GALLIGHER, 491ST
JOHN GALLO, 448TH
LOUIS J GALLO, 491ST
ROBERT A GALLUP, 445TH
CARLO GALVAGNO, 466TH
RICHARD R GALVIN, 93RD
WILLIAM R GAMBLE, 448TH
HENRY L GANCARZ, 446TH
DONALD M GANNETT, 467TH
SMGT GENE GANNON RET, 448TH
JOHN E GANNON, 446TH
LTC GERALD GANAPOLE RET,
446TH
DELBERT R GARDNER, 467TH
HORACE J GARDNER, 448TH
JESSE GARDNER, 448TH
ROBERT S GARDNER, 392ND
ROY T GARDNER, 445TH
WALTER H GARDNER, 489TH
DOUGLAS C GARNER, 93RD
EUGENE R GARNER, 93RD, 389TH
HERMAN S GARNER, 392ND
JUDY VANCE GARREN, 445TH, AM
EARL V GARRETT, 489TH
EUGENE A GARRETT, 467TH
HOWARD L GARRETT, 392ND
WILLIAM L GARRETT, 453RD
ALEX S GARRISON, 446TH
ROGER L GARRISON, 466TH
BEN C GARSIDE, 389TH
LEE GARSON, 445TH
LTC HOWARD W GARVIN RET,
446TH
AUGUST J GARY, 489TH
NICK E GARZA, 44TH
O H GASAWAY JR, 453RD
DAVID C GASKIN, 445TH
EUGENE GASKINS, 448TH
RAYMOND J GASPERI, 491ST
MATTHEW J GASPERICH, 489TH
MARVIN GASSTER MD, 445TH
ROBERT H GAST, 489TH
DONALD R GASTON, 93RD
JOHN GATELY, 44TH
HAROLD GATES, 392ND
ROBERT L GATES, HDQ
CHARLES A GAUDET, 93RD
JACK GAUNTZ, 491ST
GEORGE O GAUTHIER, 491ST
CMS WILLIAM A GAUTNEY RET,
448TH
ERNEST M GAVITT, 492ND
BRUCE D GAW, 445TH
RAYMOND GAWRONSKI, 445TH
SANFORD F GAYLORD MD, 489TH
TOM G GEANNAKAKES, 389TH
DONALD G GEARY, 446TH
GERTRUDE GEBAROFF,
458TH, AM
GERALD J GEBAUER, 467TH
NORBERT N GEBHARD, 389TH
DONALD M GEDATUS, 491ST
JOHN GEDZ, 448TH
MARLIN O GEHRKE, 489TH
ROBERT F GEIGER, 458TH
RICHARD F GELVIN, 445TH
LTC HENRY G GENDREIZIG RET,
492ND
MILTON GENES, 389TH
DOUG GENGE, SM
CLARENCE R GENTLE, 466TH
ARTHUR N GENTRY, 467TH
ANDREW GEORGE, 44TH, AM
ERNEST A GEORGE, 389TH
FRANK H GEORGE, 93RD
REX H GEORGE, 448TH
ROBERT R GEORGE, 458TH
WILLIAM D GEORGE, 448TH

DONALD C GEPHARD, 392ND
ELMO W GEPPELT, 458TH
CAROL J GERARD, 93RD, AM
EARL GERARD, 467TH
CLARENCE E GERBER, 44TH
GEORGE D GERBER, 467TH
THE REV A RAYMOND GERE III,
44TH, AM
HARRIS G GERHARD JR, 446TH
ROBERT C GERLACH DC, 467TH
JOSEPH G GERMAN, 448TH
NOBLE GERMANY, 448TH
ALVA J GERON, 93RD
JACK C GERRARD, 466TH
JOHN W GERRITY, 466TH
JULIUS I GERSON, 446TH
GERALD GERSTEN, 392ND
OSCAR A GERSTUNG, 491ST
LAWRENCE C GESCHKE, HDQ
SHIRLEE PASKOFF GETLIN, HDQ
BOARDMAN G GETSINGER JR,
448TH
CHARLES R GETTY, 389TH
DR CHARLES W GETZ, 491ST
RICHARD G GHASTER, 453RD
RICHARD J GHERE, 446TH
PASCAL J GIALLELLA, 448TH
FRANCIS A GIANOLI, 453RD,
446TH
ALBERT GIARDINA, 389TH
NANCY GIBBONS, 453RD, AM
HENRY E GIBBS SR, 491ST
T C GIBBS, 93RD
W L GIBBS, 448TH
ROGER C GIBLIN, 467TH
DOROTHY P GIBSON, 389TH, AM
FRANK H GIBSON, 446TH
FRANK R GIBSON, 448TH
HENRY B GIBSON, 445TH
HENRY W GIBSON MD, 446TH
LTC JACK A GIBSON RET, 453RD
B/GEN JACK H GIBSON RET,
44TH, HDQ
MAJ NEVIN H GIBSON RET, 93RD,
491ST, 492ND
C/MSGT NEWELL R GIBSON RET,
458TH
STEPHEN E GIBSON, 93RD, AM
RALPH L GIDDISH, 44TH
PAUL M GIDEL, 492ND
RALPH GIESECKE, 467TH
REV HAROLD R GIETZ, 492ND,
HDQ, 93RD
GEORGE O GIGSTAD, 446TH
PATRICIA L GIGSTAD, 446TH, AM
ELMAR W GIGSTEAD, 446TH
FREDERICK A GILBERT, 93RD
LAWRENCE G GILBERT, 392ND
THOMAS D GILBERT, 93RD
LTC WILLIAM W GILBERT RET,
448TH
LLOYD W GILES, 491ST
ROBERT L GILES, 458TH
LTC JAMES V GILILLAND RET,
489TH
HAROLD J GILL, HDQ
JOSEPH F GILL, 445TH
MATHIAS A GILLES, 389TH
EDMON E GILLESPIE, 93RD
S HAZARD GILLESPIE, HDQ
DONALD A GILLIES, 453RD
JOHN GILLOTTE, 389TH
JOHN E GILMORE, 93RD
STEPHEN GILMORE, 492ND,
445TH
LTC VERNON L GILMORE RET,
448TH
AMISA M GILPATRICK, 458TH
JAMES R GINN, 458TH
SALVATORE GIOMBARRESE,
453RD
DOMINIC GIORDANO, 458TH
JOSEPH G GIORDANO, 93RD
FRANK GIOSTA, 467TH
JOSEPH F GIOVANINI, 448TH
GEORGE V GIOVANNONI SR,
453RD
HOWARD W GIPE, 448TH
PATE E GIVEN, 466TH

ARTHUR M GIVENS, 44TH
LTC CARL J GJELHAUG RET,
446TH
WILLIAM E GLABAU, 491ST
GENE B GLADWELL, 93RD
JOHN GLAGOLA JR, 458TH
ROBERT G GLASS, 389TH
FRANCIS E GLASSER, SM
MARVIN L GLASSMAN, 489TH,
93RD
AARON H GLATT, 458TH
RICHARD J GLAUNER, 93RD
WILLIAM GLAZER, 44TH
RALPH J GLENN JR, 93RD, 446TH
ROYCE B GLENN, 458TH
S PARKS GLENN, 466TH
COL BERNARD U GLETTLER RET,
44TH, 392ND, HDQ
GEORGE GLEVANIK, 448TH
DAVID P GLICK, 489TH
HERBERT W GLICK, 93RD
LEON R GLICK, 93RD
LEWIS L GLICK, 453RD
NATHANIEL GLICKMAN, 44TH,
93RD
JACK GLICKSMAN, 448TH
BENJAMIN J GLIDDEN JR, 491ST
H EVERETT GLIDDEN, 44TH
CARL GLOSKEY, 467TH
HARRY M GLOSS JR, 93RD
LTC C HOWARD GLOVER JR RET,
448TH
CARL B GLOVER, 392ND
JULIA B GLUT, 93RD, AM
JACK G GNEITING, 453RD, 466TH
WILMER E GOAD, 448TH
LTC JOHN F GOAN RET, 445TH
JAMES V GOAR, 392ND
LTC NEIL M GOBRECHT RET,
466TH
DAVID H GODAIR, 489TH
HENRY J GODEK, 389TH
LAVAR GODFREY, 44TH
HARRY F GODGES, 453RD
LUTHER E GODWIN, 389TH
SAMUEL F GODWIN, 466TH
GEORGE GOEHRING, 389TH
PAUL E GOEKEN, 448TH
CARL GOELTENBODT, 489TH
KARL G GOFF, 445TH
COL LYMAN H GOFF JR RET,
491ST
DR MARVIN T GOFF, 448TH
JOHN O GOFFE, 445TH
MELVIN A GOLDBERG, 489TH
NATHAN K GOLDBERG, 446TH
FRANK J GOLDCAMP, 492ND,
389TH
BILLY W GOLDEN, 453RD
JOHN W GOLDEN JR, 491ST
PHIL GOLDEN, 93RD
W H GOLDEN, 453RD
THEODORE GOLDFARB, SM
GEORGE G GOLDMAN, 93RD
JOHN D GOLDSBERRY, 389TH
EDWARD GOLDSMITH, 467TH,
445TH, 492ND
STUART GOLDSMITH, 458TH
JACK GOLDSTEIN, 44TH
MEL GOLDSTEIN, 458TH, AM
STANLEY P GOLDSTEIN, 466TH
EDWARD G GOLDSTONE, 44TH
ROBERT L GOLEN, 453RD
RAUL C GOLTARA, 466TH
RALPH GOLUBOCK, 44TH
LTC VINCENT GONZALEZ RET,
389TH
DONALD F GOOD, 467TH
LLOYD A GOODALE, 466TH
ERNEST W GOODE, 389TH
KENNETH E GOODING, 448TH
EDWARD J GOODMAN, 448TH
GEORGE A GOODMAN, 489TH
DWAYNE E GOODWIN, 445TH
JOHN J GOODWIN, 392ND
BRUNO GORA, 445TH
BURTON GORBACK, 392ND
HERBERT GORDON, 446TH
ROBERT E GORDON, 466TH

ROBERT J GORDON, 489TH, 93RD
ROBERT W GORDON, 458TH
ROBERT A GORE, 446TH
EUGENE J GORMAN, 392ND
KENNETH M GORRELL, 458TH
GEORGE B GOSNEY, 491ST
COL ERNEST E GOSSETT RET,
492ND, 44TH
CHARLES T GOTHAM, 491ST
ARNOLD GOTTLIEB, 458TH
FRANK T GOTTMAN, 453RD
CHRIS GOTTS, SM
G LIONEL GOUDREAULT, 458TH
WALLACE L GOULET, 446TH
THEODORE O GOULSON, 458TH
LTC PAUL E GOURD RET, 467TH,
492ND
LTC TED GOURLEY SR RET, 93RD
DONALD A GOWANS, 491ST
MARIE D GOWER, 392ND, AM
MOSES J GOZONSKY, 93RD
LEONARD E GRAB, 492ND, 445TH
R A GRABOWSKI, 448TH
LTC CHARLES W GRACE RET,
467TH
HENRY T GRADY JR, 466TH
JACK GRADY, 44TH
MICHAEL G GRADY, 458TH
WILLIAM H GRADY, 491ST
DALE W GRAEF, 44TH
GAYLORD W GRAF, 448TH
LAVERNE S GRAF, 489TH
WILLIAM C GRAFF, 389TH
EVERETT GRAHAM, 466TH
JAMES H GRAHAM, 458TH
LEWIS R GRAHAM, 44TH
JANE GRAHLMANN, 458TH, AM
MAJ LOUIS F GRAMANDO RET,
489TH
JOSEPH P GRANGER, 466TH,
93RD, 44TH
JACKSON W GRANHOLM, 458TH
JAMES R GRANT, 453RD
RICHARD A GRANT, 458TH
THOMAS P GRANT JR, 446TH
PAUL A GRANTHAM, 389TH
PAUL C GRASSEY, 446TH
IRVIN GRATCH, 466TH
JAMES V GRATTA, 44TH
LAWRENCE E GRAUPNER, 445TH
CHARLES I GRAVES, 93RD
DAVID G GRAY, 93RD, AM
ELDON E GRAY, 445TH
S T GRAY JR, 467TH
VAN L GRAY, 93RD
LORELLA GREASER, 491ST, AM
STEVE B GRECO, 458TH
ALAN L GREEN, 389TH
DOMINICK J GREEN, 389TH
FRANCIS W GREEN, 389TH
COL FRANK R GREEN RET,
492ND, 44TH
GILBERT F GREEN, 492ND
LTC JAMES A GREEN RET, 392ND
PATRICK GREEN, 453RD, AM
THOMAS E GREEN, 489TH
LIONEL GREENBERG, 448TH
SOL GREENBERG, 389TH
LTC DAVID A GREENE RET, 392ND
JOHN C GREENE, 446TH
LTC KERMIT Q GREENE RET,
458TH
MILTON GREENFIELD, 448TH
CARL R GREENSTEIN, 93RD
DONALD GREER, 446TH
STANLEY C GREER, 389TH
WILLIAM GREER, 389TH
PAUL R GREGG, 44TH
BILLY GREGORY, 448TH
GEOFFREY G & TERRY
GREGORY, 467TH
KENNETH GREGORY, 467TH, AM
WALTER GREGORZAK, 489TH
GEORGE R GREIFF, 492ND
MURRAY GREIFF, 93RD
WILFRID E GRENIER, 389TH
LEO F GRETHEN, 44TH
FRANK J GREW, 448TH
ANTHONY GREY, 93RD

THEODORE K GREY, 44TH
JAMES A GRIBBLE, 466TH
CHARLES L GRIBI, 458TH
FRED V GRIEP, 467TH
ROBERT F GRIES, 392ND
LTC CHARLES G GRIFFIN RET,
491ST
GEORGE A GRIFFIN, 458TH
COL GOODMAN G GRIFFIN RET,
44TH
IVY B GRIFFIN, 458TH
MYRON S GRIFFIN, 93RD
COL RICHARD E GRIFFIN RET,
392ND
DONALD GRIFFITH, 445TH
ROCKFORD C GRIFFITH, 44TH
A GEORGE GRIFFITHS, 446TH
HAROLD GRIFFITHS, 392ND
JAMES GRIFFITHS, 466TH
WILLIAM J GRIFFITHS, 458TH
CARL S GRIGG, 93RD
THOMAS J GRIMA, 389TH
ARTHUR V GRIMES, 44TH
FRANK B GRIMES, 466TH
BEN E GRIMM, 445TH
RICHARD J GRIMM, 44TH
ROY H GRIMM, 392ND
RASCOE S GRISHAM, 93RD
LORENZO GRISWOLD, 445TH
TRUMAN L GRISWOLD, 445TH
WILLIAM N GROESBECK, 466TH
GENE R GROLL, 458TH
WILLIAM L GROS, 93RD
CARL W GROSHELL, 491ST
EARL B GROSS, 392ND
GEORGE A GROSS, 93RD
SEYMOUR GROSSMAN, 445TH
JOSEPH I GROSSO, 389TH
GLENN A GROTE, 389TH
WILBERT L GROTE, 458TH
WALTER O GROTZ, 445TH
STEWART H GROVE, 44TH
M/SGT HAYWOOD B GROVES
RET, 466TH
KARL G GRUBE, 44TH
CLINTON A GRUBER, 93RD
HARRY H GRUENER, 93RD
LTC ROYAL D GRUMBACH RET,
448TH
JOHN E D GRUNOW, 448TH
MICHAEL P GUERRETTE,
458TH, AM
COL ALFRED J GUETLING RET,
453RD
WILLIAM GUEVARA, 448TH
FREDINAND J GUIDA, 458TH
GEORGE V GUILFORD, 44TH
JOHN A GUION, 491ST
HERMAN GULBRANSON JR,
446TH
KENNETH L GULLEKSON, 489TH
DAVID H GULLETT, 93RD
WILLIAM A GULLEY, 489TH
JOHN S GUMZ, 389TH
ROBERT H GUNDERSON, 458TH
PETER M GUNNAR, 453RD
JAMES T GUNNELL, 453RD
JOHN C GUNNING, 491ST
ROBERT J GUNTON, 467TH
CHARLES GUPTON, 467TH
STANLEY M GURNEY, 93RD, AM
ALBIN A GUSCIORA, 392ND
CARL GUSTAFSON, 93RD, 453RD
DAVID A GUSTAFSON, 448TH
DEAN L GUSTAVSON, 491ST
LTC STANLEY GUTERMAN RET,
458TH
JOSEPH M GUTHRIE, 448TH
JAMES P GUTTILLA, 467TH
EARL J GUY, 44TH
COL ROY E GUY RET, 466TH
IRENE T GUZIK, 44TH, AM
MAJ THEODORE GUZIK RET,
93RD
JAMES T GWALTNEY, 448TH
CECIL C GWENNAP, 448TH
FRANK GYIDIK, 56FG
FRED J HAAF JR, 458TH
ERNEST J HAAR, 467TH, 492ND

LLOYD S HABECK, 458TH
RICHARD H HABEDANK, 44TH
ROBERT F HACKER, 491ST, 492ND
RICHARD H HACKETT, 93RD
GEORGE W HACKLING, 389TH
THOMAS S HACKMAN, 458TH
DANIEL HACKU, 458TH
V LLOYD HADLEY, 466TH
JOSEPH W HAENN, 467TH
RICHARD A HAFT, 44TH
DUGALD J HAGADONE, 458TH
LOUIS F HAGAN, 93RD
WILLIAM H HAGAN, 491ST
RICHARD M HAGER, 44TH, 448TH
H A HAGOPIAN, 392ND
VIRGINIA HAGOPIAN, 93RD, AM
ALAN HAGUE, SM
ROGER R HAHN, 453RD
FREDERICK J HAHNER, 448TH
HOMER L HAILE, 489TH
SAM HAILEY, 448TH
WILLIAM E HAILEY, 453RD
JOHN A HAINES, 458TH
JAMES H HAIR, 392ND
OTIS F HAIR, 93RD
CARLTON L HAKANSON, 458TH, 93RD, 466TH
GEORGE V HALAPY, 93RD
CHARLES J HALBERT, 44TH, 93RD, 392ND, 491ST
STEPHEN J HALCISAK, 389TH
CHARLES N HALDER JR, 389TH
GEORGE H HALE, 446TH
ROBERT H HALE, 448TH
PAUL HALECKI, 446TH
ANDREW E HALEY, 445TH
LOUIS A HALEY, 458TH
WILLIAM HALFHILL, 448TH
BENJAMIN P HALL, 93RD
BRONNIE F HALL, 93RD, AM
DUDLEY T HALL, 448TH
EARL A HALL, 392ND
GEORGE E HALL, 392ND
HAROLD B HALL, 458TH
HARRY D HALL, 392ND
LEE HALL, 93RD
MAURICE G HALL, 44TH
MILTON A HALL, 489TH
ROBERT J HALL, 489TH
WILLIAM B HALL, 446TH
ABRAHAM S HALLER, 389TH
ALLAN P HALLETT, 389TH
HOWARD G HALLGARTH, 93RD
JAMES HALLIGAN, 453RD
JAMES J HALLIGAN, 453RD
L JACK HALLMAN, 467TH
ROBERT P HALLORAN, 467TH
GEORGE B HALLOWELL JR, 467TH
HORACE E HALPIN, 467TH
MILTON O HALSNE, 392ND
JOAN HALVORSON, 453RD, AM
CHARLES R HAM, 445TH
EDGAR O HAMEL, 44TH
DALE E HAMILTON, 467TH
EDWARD C HAMILTON, HDQ
HOWARD HAMILTON, 491ST
WILLIAM I HAMILTON, 491ST
WORTH O HAMILTON, 448TH
DAVID L HAMLIN, 453RD
HARTIS P HAMLIN, 93RD
NORMAN E HAMLIN, 467TH
STANLEY E HAMMELL, 458TH
LTC JOHN D HAMMER RET, 44TH
WILLIAM A HAMMES, 448TH
STEPHEN T HAMMOCK, 445TH
GEORGE E HAMMOND, 389TH
HILARY HAMMOND, SM
CHARLES W HAMPP, 467TH
THERON D HAMPTON, 489TH
J R HANAHAN, 93RD
JOHN HANCHAR, 446TH
MAJ ROBERT W HANCOCK RET, 446TH
ARTHUR A HAND, 44TH
COL CLARENCE B HAND RET, SM
MARY CATHERINE HANDLY, 445TH, AM

EDWARD A HANDY, 466TH
MARION K HANEY, 44TH
ALLAN S HANKS, 491ST
THOMAS E HANLEY, 458TH
EDWARD F HANLON, 489TH
EDWARD T HANNA, 446TH
LTC LOWELL J HANNA RET, 467TH
PAUL & FRANCES HANNAFEY, 467TH
M MIKE HANNAN, 489TH
MICK HANOU, SM
BLAINE H HANSELL, 489TH
EDWIN L HANSELMAN, 489TH
LTC BERNARD HANSEN RET, 448TH
COL HAROLD E HANSEN RET, 93RD
HELMER L HANSEN, 467TH
LAWRENCE A HANSEN, 491ST
LTC ROBERT W HANSEN RET, 458TH
RUSSELL J HANSEN, 491ST
ALBERT L HANSON, 458TH, 466TH, 467TH, 96CW
RICHARD F HANSON, 445TH
ROBERT L HANSON, 466TH
ROBERT O HANSON, 453RD
WINFIELD F HANSSEN, 389TH
FRANK HANZALIK, 453RD
HERBERT M HAPE, 93RD
ARLAND HARBERT, 445TH
JAMES G HARBILAS, 389TH
GEORGE W HARDEN, 466TH
LTC HAROLD C HARDESTY RET, 448TH
WALTER D HARDIEK, 389TH
WALTON HARDIN, 489TH
BERNERD N HARDING, 492ND
FRANKLIN HARDT, 489TH
LESTER C HARDWICK, 453RD
HAROLD HARDY, 466TH
RICHARD W HARDY, 392ND
ROBERT E HARE, 446TH
FRANK F HARHAY, 491ST
CHARLES L HARKINS, 489TH
THOMAS H HARKNESS, 489TH
R D HARLAND, 458TH
GEORGE L HARLOW, 445TH
JOHN J HARMONOWSKI, 44TH, 467TH, 95TH
ROBERT G HARNED, 392ND
HERMAN I HARNEY, 458TH
JOHN P HARNEY, 466TH
JAMES A HARPER, 392ND
JAMES A HARPER, 458TH
JOHN P HARPER, 492ND
ROBERT L HARPER, 448TH, 453RD
WESLEY E HARPER, 458TH
LTC HUGH J HARRIES RET, 448TH
C HERBERT HARRIGAN, 448TH
RUSSELL I HARRIMAN, 453RD
RUSSELL J HARRIMAN, 453RD
VERNON J HARRIMAN, 93RD
BONNIE HATTEN & JACK HARRINGTON, 467TH, AM
CRAIG W HARRINGTON, 467TH
R W HARRINGTON, 466TH
RICHARD J HARRINGTON, 448TH
ARTHUR HARRIS, 389TH
CLIFFORD HARRIS, 448TH
EVAN HARRIS, SM
JACK HARRIS, 453RD
JOE L HARRIS, 492ND
KURT HARRIS, 93RD
LTC LOWELL D HARRIS RET, 445TH
MARC E HARRIS, 44TH, AM
MORGAN K HARRIS, 93RD
NORMAN HARRIS, 389TH
LTC RICHARD D HARRIS RET, 458TH
ROBERT B HARRIS, 389TH
SAM HARRIS, 93RD
THEODORE J HARRIS, 489TH
ALFRED B HARRISON JR, 446TH
DOROTHY MCD HARRISON, 93RD, ARC
PAUL P HARRISON, 448TH

EDWIN I HARSHBARGER, 448TH
DEAN H HART, 453RD
FRANK J HART, 44TH
TOM P HART, 445TH
WILDRICK HART, 392ND
WINFRED H HART JR, 466TH
CHARLES W HARTER, 467TH
DALE V HARTGERINK, 44TH
CHESTER W HARTLEY, 448TH
DONALD C HARTLEY, 489TH
GENE G HARTLEY, 389TH
HOWARD J HARTLEY, 466TH
ROBERT L HARTLIEB, 93RD
ROBERT L HARTLIEB, 93RD
GLEN P HARTMAN, 93RD
MORGAN E HARTMAN, 453RD
HAROLD F HARTNER, 445TH
M/SGT CHARLES W HARTNEY RET, 467TH
CONRAD HARTSCH, 389TH
RICHARD W HARTSWICK, 458TH
DEWITT T HARTWELL SR, 389TH
EDWIN J HARTWICK, 392ND
BROWNIE G HARVATH, 458TH
ARTHUR J HARVEY JR, SM
ARTHUR R HARVEY, 492ND
JOHN HARVEY, SM
MACK H HARVEY, 467TH
ROBERT D HARVEY, 44TH
ROBERT R HARVEY, 491ST
WAYNE I HARVEY, 44TH
LLOYD M HARWOOD, 466TH
PAUL HARWOOD, 93RD
STEPHANIE HASSELBACK, HDQ
LAWRENCE L HASSELL, 491ST
LTC JAMIEL HASSEN RET, 467TH
ADAM J HASTAK, 93RD
DAVID J HASTINGS, BG
HERBERT A HASTINGS, 44TH
HERBERT L HASTINGS, 453RD
THOMAS F HASTINGS, 467TH
ROBERT L HATFIELD, 389TH
DR SCOTT HATHORN JR, 458TH
CHERYL W HATLEY, 448TH, AM
CLYDE S HATLEY, 492ND
CLYDE W HATLEY SR, 448TH
CLYDE W HATLEY JR, 448TH, AM
NICK HATTEL, 389TH
PAUL V HATTEN, 467TH
BOYD L HATZELL, 448TH
ANDREW J HAU, 448TH
LLOYD A & CARMEN HAUG, 467TH
GLENN HAUGHN, 489TH
M E HAUSE, 44TH
WILLIS J HAUSE, 446TH
GEORGE HAUSLAIB, 448TH, 489TH
HERSHEL J HAUSMAN, 448TH
STEPHEN HAVANEC, 489TH
HENRY HAVRE, 389TH
CHESTER T HAVRICK, 466TH
GEOFFREY HAWKER, SM
LTC HORACE P HAWKES RET, 445TH
E MUNROE HAWKINS, 466TH
LTC EARLE V HAWKINS RET, 44TH
WILLIAM F HAWKINS, 44TH
CARL O HAWORTH, 44TH
FRANCIS E HAWTHORNE, 389TH
KIRKWOOD S HAWTHORNE, 389TH, AM
CHARLES A HAY, 446TH
JACK W HAYDEN, 389TH
THEODORE E HAYDON, 458TH
ALFRED G HAYDUK, 491ST
EVERETT G HAYES, 446TH
HENRY R HAYES, 93RD
JUNE HAYES, 389TH, AM
M/GEN WILLIAM R HAYES RET, 448TH
CHARLES W HAYES-HALLIDAY, SM
CLAIRE B HAYNIE, 389TH
HAROLD E HAYS, 453RD
JOE HAYS, 446TH
KIRBY HAYWARD, 458TH
HOWARD F HAYWOOD, 392ND
LTC ROBERT R HAYZLETT RET, 458TH

M/SGT WALTER L HAZELTON RET, 44TH
BERNARD E HEAD JR, 491ST
COL CHARLES W HEAD JR RET, 445TH
NEAL L HEAD, 389TH
GERALD A HEADE, 93RD
KENNETH A HEALING, 392ND
ANN HEALY, 467TH, AM
CHARLES F HEALY, 458TH
HENRY M HEARN, 392ND
DONALD M HEATH, 453RD
WILLIAM L HEATH, 389TH
CALVIN L HEBENSTREIT, 458TH
B P HEBERT, 458TH
LEO E HEBERT JR, 93RD
MAURICE G HEBERT, 389TH, 491ST
WALTER T HEBRON, 392ND
ROBERT HEDGELON, 44TH
PAUL H HEDGES, 389TH
CHARLES L HEDRICK, 389TH, 453RD, 489TH
FRANCIS E HEFFNER, 93RD
RON HEFFNER, 389TH, AM
JAMES O HEFLEY, 491ST
OSWALD A HEID, 389TH
WILLIAM B HEIERMAN, 445TH
LARRY HEIMBINDER, 446TH
MAJ CARL R HEIN RET, 458TH
EMIL M HEIN, 467TH
FRANK J HEINECKE, 458TH
JOSEPH C HEINEMANN, 446TH
MAJ SAMUEL N HEINFLING RET, 491ST
ROSCOE HEINS DDS, 458TH
WILLIAM G HELBLING, 389TH
OTTO J HELDOBLER, 489TH
LEON HELFAND, 453RD
C JACK HELFRECHT, 458TH
LOWDON HELLER, 467TH
PEDER HELLER, 389TH
WILLIAM D HELLER, 392ND
RUSSELL F HELLWIG, 491ST
BRUCE G HELMER, 389TH, 445TH
PHILIP J HELMSTADT, 446TH
THEODORE W HELWEG, 93RD
LAWRENCE HEMMEL, 93RD
RAY F HEMRICH, 458TH, 96CW, HDQ
PHIL HEMSTED JR, 446TH
FRANK HENDERSHOT, 453RD
AUBREY D HENDERSON, 392ND
CHRISTINE COLLINS HENDERSON, HDQ
E H & HELEN HENDERSON, 389TH
MAJ MILTON A HENDERSON RET, 392ND
RICHARD L HENDERSON, 448TH
MARVIN E HENDRICKSON, 466TH
PERRY M HENEGAR, 458TH
ALBERT HENKE, 467TH
LESTER HENKE, 93RD, AM
DONALD HENLEY JR, 56FG
THOMAS H HENLEY MD, 445TH
PRESTON G HENMAN, 446TH
ROBERT A HENN, 458TH
JOHN J HENNESSEY, 491ST
JOHN E HENNESSY, 448TH
JOHN C HENNING, 392ND
LTC GEORGE R HENRIET RET, 44TH
H C & MARY HENRY, 44TH
WILLIAM HENSEN, 467TH
WILLIAM T HENSEY JR, 448TH
LTC BAXTER W HENSLEY RET, 467TH
HOWELL W HENSON, 445TH
WILMER K HENSON, 453RD
ROBERT H HEPLER, 489TH
GUNTHER C HEPPRICH, 458TH
MARION E HERBST, 389TH, 466THAM
RICHARD L HERMAN, 446TH, AM
SIDNEY HERMAN, 489TH
LEASK HERMANN, 93RD
ROBERT E HERMANN, 458TH
WALTER S HERN JR, 446TH
T P HERNANDEZ, 448TH

TOMMY HERNANDEZ SR, 93RD
GEORGE A HEROPOULOS, 448TH
CINDY HERRMAN, 453RD, AM
JOSEPH F HERRMAN, 44TH
NORMAN HERSCHBEIN, 93RD
ALFRED HERSH, 392ND
MAJ ROBERT J HERTELL RET, 448TH
COL ALLEN F HERZBERG RET, 467TH, 458TH, 96CW
FRED M HESS, 453RD
JOSEPH HESS, 489TH
MERLE L HESS, 467TH
RAYMOND A HESS, HDQ
RAYMOND A HESS, HDQ
JOHN E HESSERT, 445TH
NORRIS B HESTER, 445TH
LTC DELBERT R HETRICK RET, 446TH
HERMAN H HETZEL, 458TH
H E HETZLER, 389TH
RICHARD W HEVENER JR, 446TH
JACK HEVERLY, 389TH
LARRY M HEWIN, 93RD
JOHN C HEWITT, 93RD
JAMES O HEY, 446TH
WILLIAM HEYBURN II, 44TH
SETH HEYWOOD, 453RD
AL K HIBBERT, 93RD
DONALD T HICKEY, 389TH
JAMES R HICKEY, HDQ
WILLIAM J HICKEY, 491ST
RICHARD HICKMAN, 93RD
BILLIE C HICKS, 491ST, AM
CLYDE F HICKS, 389TH
DONALD E HICKS, HDQ, 5ERS
MARVIN W HICKS, 448TH
ROGER F HICKS, 458TH
WILLIAM F HICKS, 453RD, 458TH
ROBERT E HIEMSTRA, 458TH
WILLARD W HIGDON, 458TH
GEORGE L HIGGINS JR, 458TH
LOUIS B HIGGINS, 491ST
MORGAN G HIGHAM, 489TH
WILLIAM H HIGHTOWER, 392ND
WALTER F HILBERG, HDQ
DALE D HILBERT, 491ST
ALLEN C HILBORN, 458TH
JOHN R HILDEBRAN, 453RD
JOHN J HILDEBRAND, 448TH
LAWRENCE C HILDEBRAND, 392ND
ARTHUR G HILL, 446TH
GEORGE R HILL, 44TH
GLENN U HILL, 466TH
HOWARD R HILL, 458TH
LOUIS C HILL, 361ST
MICHAEL J HILL, 448TH
O K HILL, 44TH
PATRICIA T HILL, 93RD, AM
RICHARD G HILL, 44TH
T WALLACE HILL, 44TH
WILLIAM M HILL, 44TH
LEONARD R HILLEBRAND 93RD
ROBERT D HILLER, 448TH
SCOTT HILLIARD, 446TH
HUGH Q HILLICK, 466TH
CHARLES C HILLIS, 458TH
JAMES A HILLIS, 489TH
THEODORE G HILLS, 489TH
LTC DAVID M HILLSTROM RET, 489TH, AM
JOHN N HILTON, 467TH
CARL E HIMES, 448TH
ROBERT L HIMES, 466TH
HOWARD R HINCHMAN, 93RD, 389TH
REV CHRISTOPHER J HINCKLEY, 489TH
ROBERT H HINCKLEY JR, 458TH
LTC AURELIUS S HINDS II RET, 448TH
WALTER R HINDS, 491ST
ROBERT P HINE, 467TH
DR JAMES S HINER, 458TH
CLARENCE W HINES, 44TH
CHARLES J HINNEN, 466TH
WILLIAM O HINRICH, 93RD
HOWARD C HINRICHS, 445TH

BERNARD J HINZ, 458TH
BEN J HITE, 445TH
LESTER E HIX, 467TH
ANTHONY P HMURA, 445TH
ROBERT I HOAR, 453RD
GEORGE D HOBKIRK, 467TH
COL THOMAS B HOBSON JR RET, 44TH
HENRY HOCKER, 489TH
DEXTER L HODGE, 44TH
JOSEPH A HODGE, 467TH
COL H WAYNE HODGES RET, 489TH
JAMES P HODGES III, HDQ, AM
LLOYD N HODGES, 445TH
ROY F HODGES, 389TH
HENRY F HOECKEL JR, 489TH
RALPH F HOEHN, 491ST
ROY HOELKE, 389TH
HAL & VIRGINIA HOERNER, HDQ
RALPH E HOERR, 489TH
ROBERT H HOESSLER JR, 389TH
HOWARD F HOESTEREY, 389TH
RICHARD T HOEY, 458TH
LTC CHARLES A HOFFMAN RET, 93RD
EUGENE A HOFFMAN, 93RD
LTC FRANCIS J HOFFMAN RET, 489TH
GEORGE A HOFFMAN, 392ND
COL GEORGE D HOFFMAN RET, 491ST
R C HOFFMAN, 458TH
RICHARD H HOFFMAN, 392ND
THOMAS J HOFFMAN, 466TH, AM
FRANK O HOFMEISTER, 445TH
EDWARD J HOGAN, 446TH
JAMES T HOGARTH, 467TH
MARVIN L HOGE, 458TH
CARL A HOGEL, 445TH
MARVIS HOGEN, 453RD
HARLEY L HOGSTROM, 491ST
DAVID W HOGUE, 453RD
DWIGHT N HOHL, 445TH
EDWARD J HOHMAN, 491ST
JACK HOINE, 458TH
JAMES H HOLBEN, 458TH
KENNETH C HOLCOMB, 458TH
STANLEY HOLCOMB, 446TH
J MALCOLM HOLCOMBE, 389TH
GLENN W HOLDER, 93RD
FRED E HOLDREGE, 467TH
STRICKLAND J HOLETON, 389TH
JOHN J HOLJENCIN, 93RD
JENNIFER HOLLAND GRP LIBRARIAN, SM
WILLIAM H HOLLAND, 389TH
ELMER J HOLLIBAUGH, 389TH
FREDERICK J HOLLIEN JR, 392ND
JOSEPH F HOLLYWOOD JR, 448TH
WILLIAM J HOLM, 491ST
JAMES R HOLMAN, 458TH
LESTER HOLMAN, 389TH
HARRY G HOLMBERG, 448TH
MAURICE O HOLMEN, 448TH
DR ERNEST C HOLMER, 44TH
COL BILLIE J HOLMES RET, 93RD
COL CAPERS A HOLMES RET, 467TH
EDWARD T HOLMES, 392ND
H W HOLMES, SM
JOSEPH E HOLMES, 448TH, 389TH, 489TH
MARVIN D HOLMES, 466TH
THOMAS G HOLMES, 392ND
W TOM HOLMES JR, 44TH
EDWARD L HOLMGREN, 458TH
JOHN S HOLODAK, 458TH
DEWEY A HOLST, 448TH
COL CARL H HOLT RET, 448TH
FRANK W HOLT, 453RD
KENNETH HOLT, 93RD
SUE HOLT GRP LIBRARIAN, SM
DONALD L HOLTER, 448TH
ROBERT J HOLTMEIER, 467TH
CHARLTON H HOLTZ, 44TH
JOSEPH W HOLUB, 389TH
JOHN J HOLZINGER, 392ND

JOHN F & IRENE HOMAN, 489TH
PAUL E HOMAN, 448TH
ELMER M HOMELVIG, 448TH
JOSEPH A HOMSHER, 491ST
WELLONS B HOMUTH, 446TH
PETER HOMYOCK, 491ST
WILLIAM HONECKER, 458TH
WILLIAM C HONECKER, 458TH
ROBBIE B HONEYCUTT JR, 458TH
ROBERT J HONEYCUTT, 445TH
DALE W HONIG, 467TH
FREDERICK J HONOLD, 458TH
MAJ MARK R HONTZ RET, 93RD
JOSEPH F HOOD, 458TH
PAUL E HOOD, 93RD
BENJAMIN R HOOKER JR, 458TH
CLARENCE H HOOKS, 446TH
MAURICE L HOOKS, 448TH
IRA A HOOPER, 489TH
ODELL HOOPER, 453RD
EDWARD HOOTON JR, 467TH
EDWIN R HOOVER, 448TH
JAMES A HOOVER, 392ND
MICHAEL C HOOVER, 466TH
MORRIS L HOOVER, 93RD
RICHARD C HOOVER, 392ND
RICHARD R HOPKINS, 458TH
THAYER HOPKINS, 458TH
JOHN J HORAN, 466TH
ARNOLD L HORELICK, 491ST
CREIGHTON L HORN, 489TH
THOMAS J HORN, 392ND
PETER G HORNER, SM
WILLIAM G HORNEY JR, 466TH
EARL W HORNTVEDT, 448TH
CHARLES C HORTON, 492ND
DEWEY A HORTON, 453RD
HOWARD F HORTON, 446TH
PAUL E HORVATH, 467TH, AM
ROBERT B HOSMER, 466TH
WILLIAM H HOSPER, 446TH
FRANK E HOSTETTER, 392ND
JOHN W HOTTINGER, 448TH
JAMES L HOUGH, 44TH
ALAN N HOUGHTON, 448TH
GLENN HOUGHTON, 446TH
HAROLD HOULIHAN, 453RD
EUGENE R HOUSEMAN, 445TH
EUGENE HOUSER, 489TH
ROSS S HOUSTON, 491ST
SYD HOVDE, 466TH
BARKEV A HOVSEPIAN, 466TH
CECIL R HOWARD, 491ST
DAL HOWARD, 389TH
LTC RET ELDRIDGE D HOWARD, 446TH
GEORGE E HOWARD, 448TH
GEORGE T HOWARD JR, 458TH
JOHN D HOWARD, 466TH
JOHN N HOWARD, 458TH
KELLY E HOWARD, 458TH
LEWIS B HOWARD, HDQ
DR ROBERT M HOWARD, 466TH
ROY A HOWARD JR, 44TH
SAMUEL K HOWARD, 44TH
ARTHUR W HOWE, HDQ
LAVERNE R HOWE, 453RD
DOUGLAS D HOWELD, SM
ALONZO E HOWELL JR, 466TH
ARTHUR K HOWELL, 448TH
C J HOWELL, 448TH
DURWARD R HOWELL, 491ST
LEONARD R HOWELL JR, 389TH
RICHARD H HOWELL MD, 445TH
JOHN B HOWENSTEIN, 392ND
HARRY J HOWES, 361FG
ALSTON H HOWRY, 492ND
VINCENT E HOYER, 448TH
JOHN H HOYLE, 467TH
HUGH H HOYT, 453RD, 93RD
RALPH L HOYT JR, 458TH
JOSEPH A HRUBY, HDQ
RICHARD J HRUBY, 44TH
DELPH HRUSKA, 389TH
JOSEPH W HUBEN, 467TH
DAVID E HUBLER, 56FG
VIRGIL R HUDDLESTON, 446TH
CHARLES A HUDDLESTUN, 445TH
ROBERT D HUDNALL, 458TH

COL J DENNIS HUDSON RET, 492ND, 467TH
JAMES C HUDSON, 491ST
DONALD B HUDSPETH, 389TH
ANTHONY W & FRANCES HUDZIK, 489TH
GILMORE E HUEBNER, 453RD
DONALD HUEMOELLER, 93RD
MAX L HUFFMAN, 93RD
GALE P HUFFORD, 93RD
LEON C HUGGARD, 458TH
GEORGE K HUGHEL, 93RD, HDQ, 14CW
COLS CHAS & MARILYNN HUGHES RET, 44TH, HDQ
LLOYD W HUGHES, 453RD
ROBERT M HUGHES, 453RD
ROBERT W HUGHES, 467TH
VIRGIL HUGHES, 458TH
WALTER F HUGHES DVM, 93RD
WILLIAM D HUGHES, 389TH
COL WILLIAM E HUGHES RET, 466TH
LEWIS A HUISMAN, 453RD, 389TH
MAJ DANIEL L HULBURD RET, 491ST
ROBERT F HULL, 491ST
STEPHEN S HULL, 445TH, 93RD, 389TH
RUSSELL L HULSEY, 93RD
RICHARD P HUMPHREY JR, 389TH
ROBERT D HUMPHREY, 93RD
ELMER G HUMPHREYS, 458TH
WILLIAM W HUMPHRIES, HDQ
WAYNE F HUNER, 389TH
COL BEN W HUNSACKER RET, 392ND
LTC ARTHUR S HUNT RET, 448TH
HUBERT A HUNT, 448TH
ROBERT H HUNT, 389TH
LTC ROBERT A HUNTER RET, 458TH
WENDELL M HUNTER, 446TH
EDWARD M HUNTON, HDQ
CHARLES H HUNTOON, 453RD
WESTON D HUNTRESS, 458TH
JOHN B HURD, 93RD
Q C HURDLE, 491ST
IRENE HURNER, 453RD, AM
O FRANK HURST, 44TH
ROBERT G HURST, 448TH
CLIFTON V HURT, 93RD
LEW S HURTIG, 458TH
HARRY E HUSTER, 448TH
CHARLES E HUSTON, 467TH
BERNARD L HUTAIN, 446TH
HAROLD W HUTCHCROFT, 392ND
ERNEST J HUTCHINS, 458TH
JOHN A HUTCHINS, 458TH
JACK E HUTCHINSON, 389TH
RUPERT I HUTCHINSON, 491ST
WILLIAM C HUTCHISON, 466TH
DANIEL C HUTTO, 446TH
JOSEPH L HUTTON, 491ST
PAUL J HUTZ, 392ND
MERLE H HUYCKE, 489TH
CARL HVAMBSAL, 44TH
CHARLES T HVASS, 389TH
LEWIS R HYDE, 448TH
DR G RICHARD HYRE, 392ND
JERRY J IANNUCCI, 446TH
VETO A IAVECCHIA, 389TH
CHARLES E ILES, 453RD
JACK M ILFREY, SM
LTC FRANK E INDORF JR RET, 44TH
GARY A INDRE, 446TH, AM
HAROLD INGEBRIGTSEN, 448TH
JOHN J INGRAM JR, 458TH
EDWARD INMAN, BG
GEORGE R INSLEY, 44TH
JOSEPH A INTERMOR, 453RD
ARTHUR K IRELAND, 467TH
ALANSON L IRISH, 491ST
ARVIN L IRISH, 44TH
SHIRLEY W IRWIN, 445TH
WILLIAM R ISAACS, 389TH

COL H HARDING ISAACSON, 467TH, 492ND
WESLEY ISAACSON, 448TH
B/GEN JAMES H ISBELL RET, 458TH
EMERSON Y ISHMAEL, 458TH
WILLIAM F B ISINGER, 458TH
MORTON U ISRAEL, 446TH
A B IVERSON, 392ND
RICHARD D IVES, 489TH
RUSSELL IVES, SM
JEROME D IVICE, 491ST
DAVID IVINS BR LIBRARIAN, SM
COL NICHOLAS JABBOUR RET, 491ST
STANLEY F JACEWICZ, 93RD
CHARLES E JACKSON, 467TH
CHARLES W JACKSON, 445TH
LTC EDGAR JACKSON RET, 453RD
FOREST O JACKSON, 466TH
HARVEY JACKSON, 93RD, 392ND
JAMES H JACKSON, 453RD
JOSEPH M JACKSON, 44TH
RALPH B JACKSON, 453RD
REX J JACKSON, 389TH
RODNEY E JACKSON, 446TH
THOMAS H JACKSON JR, 93RD
WILLIAM E JACKSON, 458TH
JOHN M JACOBOWITZ MD, 466TH
DAVID L G JACOBS, 44TH
FRANK C JACOBS, 389TH
JOHN C JACOBS, 448TH
JOHN JACOBS JR, 44TH
COL JOHN W JACOBS RET, 489TH
COL ROBERT A JACOBS RET, 93RD
ROBERT C JACOBS, 453RD
ROBERT H JACOBS, 445TH
ROY D JACOBS, 448TH
ROY L JACOBS, 446TH
RALPH T JACOBSEN, 389TH
ARTHUR S JACOBSON, 467TH
CHARLES H JACOBSON, 392ND
ERLAND J JACOBSON, 44TH
LAWRENCE D JACOBSON, 392ND
NATHAN M JACOBSON, 446TH
LEWIS R JACOBUS, 458TH
CAPT EDOUARD J JACQUES RET, 458TH
ALEX E C JAHNKE, 453RD
WALTER G JAMBECK, 389TH
DANIEL L JAMES, 4FG
COL HAROLD L JAMES RET, 389TH
THOMAS K JAMES, 93RD
WILLIAM S JAMESON, 458TH
WILLIAM K JANN, 448TH
MAJ STANLEY A JANNERS RET, 389TH
HAROLD E JANSEN, SM
JOHN R JANSEN, 489TH, 467TH
DON E JANSS, 93RD
RICHARD J JANSSEN, 489TH
LESLIE C JANTZ, 389TH
FRANK C JANUSZ, 446TH
LOUIS JAQUES JR, 492ND
KENT JAQUITH, 93RD, AM
HARRY D JARRETT, 446TH
HENRY G JASKULSKI, 466TH
BERNARD J JAWORSKI SR, 448TH
DANIEL R JEDRZEJEWSKI, 448TH
THOMAS F JEFFERS, 458TH
HAROLD L JEFFERSON, 389TH
HAROLD L JEFFERSON, 389TH
MAJ DONALD N JEFFERY RET, 489TH
JAY H JEFFRIES JR, 453RD
OREN L JEFFRIES JR, 93RD
VERNON E JEFFRIES, 458TH
WAYNE JEGLUM, 489TH
DONALD R JENKINS, 44TH
HARRY W JENKINS, 44TH
WILLIAM S JENKINS, HDQ
ALFRED A JENNER, BG
THELO M JENNY, 44TH
ALDON H JENSEN, 392ND
ARTHUR H JENSEN, 392ND
NORMAN W JENSEN, 445TH

R S JENSEN, 445TH
ROBERT E JENSEN, SM
WILLIAM C JENSEN, 392ND
GEORGE H JEPSON, 448TH
RALPH M JEROME, 467TH
ROY T JEROME, 458TH
WENDELL L JESKE, 453RD
NATHANIEL H JETER, 44TH
CLAYTON M JEWETT, 467TH
JOHN JIRCITANO, 458TH, 389TH
CHARLES R JOECKEL, 492ND
EMMANUEL J JOGLUS, 491ST
JOHN E JOHANNESSEN, SM
GUS JOHANSEN, 491ST
ANTHONY J JOHN, 389TH
ALFRED E JOHNS, 453RD
NORMAN P JOHNS, 491ST
A DONALD JOHNSON, 448TH, 93RD
ALBERT C JOHNSON JR, 448TH
ALLAN M JOHNSON, 448TH
ARCHIE L JOHNSON, HDQ
ARTHUR JOHNSON, 93RD
BEN W JOHNSON JR, 448TH
BILLY SHEELY JOHNSON, 492ND, AM
CARL W JOHNSON, 492ND, 467TH
CECIL D JOHNSON, 93RD
CECIL G JOHNSON, 458TH
CLINT JOHNSON JR, 453RD, 492ND, 467TH
DALE L JOHNSON, 93RD
DEAN H JOHNSON MD, 467TH
DELMAR C JOHNSON, 392ND
DONALD JOHNSON, 44TH
EDWARD C JOHNSON, 489TH
EINO E JOHNSON, 491ST
ELIZABETH JOHNSON, 93RD, AM
FLOYD L JOHNSON, 446TH
LTC FON E JOHNSON RET, 445TH
FRANK H JOHNSON, 467TH
FRANKLIN L JOHNSON, 491ST
FREDERICK M JOHNSON, 93RD
GALE M JOHNSON, 491ST
GEORGE A JOHNSON, 389TH
GEORGE F JOHNSON, 445TH
COL GEORGE H JOHNSON RET, 93RD
GLORIA JOHNSON, 453RD, AM
GLYN JOHNSON, 489TH
HENRY K JOHNSON, 392ND
COL HOWARD W JOHNSON RET, 467TH
JEFF J JOHNSON, 458TH
LTC JOSEPH S JOHNSON RET, 389TH
KENNETH C JOHNSON, 448TH
KENNETH W JOHNSON, 389TH
LEM JOHNSON, 453RD
LEROY J JOHNSON, 489TH
LESLIE E JOHNSON, 491ST
LTC ODELL H JOHNSON RET, 453RD
OLIVE DIFFENDERFFER JOHNSON, HDQ
OLIVER D JOHNSON, 458TH
OTHO S JOHNSON JR, 445TH
RAYMOND D JOHNSON, 392ND
RICHARD M JOHNSON, 445TH
ROBERT A JOHNSON, 453RD
ROBERT W JOHNSON, 44TH
ROLAND W JOHNSON, 458TH
ROY W JOHNSON, 44TH
ROYNA R JOHNSON, 458TH, AM
STANLEY H JOHNSON, 448TH
STANLEY J JOHNSON, 389TH
THOMAS D JOHNSON, 448TH
THURSTON E JOHNSON, 448TH
WALTER J JOHNSON, 445TH
WALTER J JOHNSON, 448TH
WALTER L JOHNSON, 466TH
MAJ WARREN A JOHNSON RET, 4FG
WILLIAM F JOHNSON, 466TH
B L JOHNSTON, 467TH
DOYLE C JOHNSTON, 458TH
FLOYD JOHNSTON, 448TH
G B JOHNSTON JR, 467TH
JAMES & AUDREY JOHNSTON, 467TH

JOSEPH E JOHNSTON, 44TH, 491ST

WARREN D JOHNSTON, 458TH

MARVIN A JONAS, 93RD

ROBERT F JONAS, 466TH

MILDRED JONASSON, 389TH, AM

ALBERT E JONES, 44TH

ALBERT V JONES, 445TH

LTC ARTHUR H JONES RET, 446TH

BRECK M JONES, 458TH

T/SGT CHRISTOPHER JONES, 445TH, AM

COLIN N JONES, 93RD

DEWITT C JONES III, 453RD

DONALD K JONES, 93RD

EDWARD H JONES, 466TH

ELWOOD M JONES JR, 491ST

EVAN JONES, 492ND, 93RD

EVERETT R JONES JR, 466TH, 458TH

FAUNTLEY M JONES, 445TH

FRANCIS G JONES, 446TH

FRED JONES, 392ND

GREGG R JONES, 93RD, AM

HARLEY M JONES, 445TH

HENRY O JONES, 445TH

HOWARD P JONES JR, 93RD

J LIVINGSTON & TINA JONES, HDQ

JACK R JONES, 453RD

M/GEN JAMES H JONES RET, 448TH, 491ST

JEROME K JONES, 392ND

JESSE T JONES, 466TH

JOHN H JONES, 392ND

JOHN J JONES, 458TH

KEITH H JONES, 445TH

KENNETH D JONES, 389TH

LTC LEO L JONES RET, 467TH

LEON A JONES, 392ND

MARY M JONES, 44TH, AM

RAYMOND C JONES, 453RD

RICHARD W JONES, 446TH

ROBERT JONES, 458TH

ROBERT E JONES, 458TH, 389TH, 453RD

ROBERT T JONES, 389TH

SAMUEL W JONES, 466TH

THOMAS F JONES, 458TH

WELDON A JONES, 489TH

WILLIAM R JONES JR, 448TH

WILLIAM W JONES, 445TH

PATRICIA A S JONSON, 448TH, AM

JEROME N JOONDEPH, 446TH

DAVID S JORDAN, 458TH

ELMER A JORDAN, 466TH

JOHN A JORDAN, 448TH

ROBERT W JORDAN, 453RD

MAJ ARTHUR W JORGENSEN RET, 44TH

RALPH C JORGENSEN, 44TH

LAWRENCE JOSEPH, 453RD

MARVIN JOSEPH, 448TH

PAUL S JOSEPH, 93RD

SAUL M JOSEPH, 93RD, 491ST

FRANK A JOSEPHSON, 458TH

GEORGE E JOSTEN, 65FW

RUSS JOURNIGAN, 491ST

MARLOW A JOVAAG, 466TH

WILLIAM C JOY, 453RD

JAMES L JOYCE, 491ST

WILLIAM C JOYCE JR, 453RD

GEORGE G JUDD, 392ND

DAVID T JUDY, 93RD

GEORGE L JUDY, 491ST

MAE S JUDY, 448TH, AM

JOHN & GLORIA JULIAN, 93RD

COL CLARENCE A JUNGMAN RET, 489TH

COL BILL J JURCZYN RET, 392ND

HENRY F JURGENS, 392ND

ROBERT H JURGENS, 489TH

STANLEY S KADIN, 489TH

JOHN G KAFALAS, 458TH

FRED KAGAN, 93RD

CHARLES E KAGY, 467TH

WILLIAM J KAHLE, 446TH, 389TH

GEORGE E KALB, 491ST

HARRY KALIONZES DDS, 392ND

OLIVER O KALKE, 44TH

JOHN J KALLAS, 392ND

ARTHUR G KALTENBACH, 458TH

JOHN A KAMACHO, 392ND

EDWIN E KAMARAINEN, 491ST

ROY E KAMPFE, 392ND

JOHN J KANE, 389TH

WILLIAM P KANE, 445TH

LOREN F KANNENBERG, 44TH, 467TH

NORMAN W KANWISHER, 489TH, 448TH

STEVEN KANY, 491ST

JOHN KANYUCK, 389TH

ANDREW KAPI JR, 467TH

MORRIS KAPLAN, 93RD

ARNOLD KAPNICK, 448TH

RUSSELL J KAPP, 93RD

MICHAEL KARAS, 392ND

GEORGE KARDOS, 389TH, 453RD

ALBERT H KARELS, 93RD

GEORGE G KARIAN, 93RD

GEORGE KARNAHAN, 93RD

CHRIS KARRAS, 491ST

JOSEPH S KASACJAK, 448TH

ROBERT E KASEMAN, 492ND, 467TH

LTC JOHN KASSAB RET, 453RD

GERALD J KATHOL, 445TH

SIDNEY KATZ, 467TH

COL THEODORE KATZ RET, 389TH

RALPH E KAUFFMAN, 93RD

CHARLES F KAUFMANN, 445TH

ROBERT PAUL KAY, 44TH

THOMAS C KAY, 44TH

THEODORE S KAYAS, 491ST

THEODORE J KAYE, 445TH

DONALD D KAYNOR, 467TH

JOHN KAZANJIAN, 489TH

EDMOND KAZMIRZAK, 44TH

WILLIAM D KEAN, 489TH

JOHN J KEANE, 453RD

GEORGE O KEARNEY, 453RD

DALE E KEARNS, 389TH

LOUIS L KEARNS, 392ND

LTGEN JAMES M KECK RET, 458TH, 491ST

JOHN H KEDENBURG, 392ND

LTC JAMES H KEEFFE JR RET, 389TH

JAMES P KEEL, 458TH

GEORGE P KEENAN, 453RD

B/GEN KENNETH E KEENE RET, 93RD, 466TH

THOMAS J KEENE, 448TH

WILLIAM B KEENE, 389TH

RALPH H KEENEY, 491ST

THOMAS E KEENEY, 392ND

LAWRENCE E KEERAN, 448TH

JOHN L KEEVER, 93RD

COL MYRON H KEILMAN RET, 392ND

JOHN F KEILT, 93RD

MELVIN K KEIM, 458TH

MORRIS J KEITH, 392ND

RAY K KEITH, 453RD

HARRY A KELLEHER, 93RD

DONALD W KELLER, 453RD

JOHN H KELLER JR, 446TH

LTC JOHN W KELLER RET, 448TH

LUCIEN D KELLER, 392ND

STANLEY C KELLER, 93RD

STANLEY KELLETT, 479TH

COL CHARLES A KELLEY RET, 446TH

ERNEST J KELLEY, 448TH

GEORGE R KELLEY, 389TH

HOWARD D KELLEY, 445TH

IRA C KELLEY, 491ST

MARION T KELLEY, 492ND

ABSOLAM H KELLY, 44TH

ERNEST L KELLY, 458TH

JAMES W KELLY, 448TH

JOSEPH E KELLY, 93RD

PAUL L KELLY, 446TH

RAYMOND F KELLY, 489TH, 389TH

ROBERT J KELLY, 489TH, 445TH

WILLIAM D KELLY, 458TH

IRVING N KELSEY, 466TH

RICHARD G KELSO, 445TH

ALBERT R KEMP, 458TH

JOHN F KENDIG, 389TH

EARL R KENNEDY, 448TH

EDWARD J KENNEDY, 458TH

JACK K KENNEDY, 458TH

JAMES F KENNEDY, 467TH

JOHN R KENNEDY, 489TH

JOSEPH T KENNEDY, 458TH

RAY C KENNEDY, 448TH, AM

RICHARD L KENNEDY, 448TH, AM

RICHARD M KENNEDY, 448TH

ROLLA M KENNEDY, 445TH

CHARLES B KENNING, 445TH

JAMES C KENNON, 93RD

RAY KENTRA, SM

MELVIN L KENYON, 458TH

JOHN L KEPPEL, 491ST

JOHN G KERASOTES, 448TH

JOHN T KERLER, 93RD

BENTLEY KERN, 389TH

FRED KERNISS, 448TH

JOHN D KERNODLE, 489TH

PERRY KERR, 466TH

TONY KERRISON, SM

KURT G KERSTEN, 446TH

COL DONALD L KESSLER RET, 467TH

JOSEPH A KESSLER, 489TH

ROBERT F KESSLER, 448TH

WALTER W KETRON, 389TH

VERNON E KEY, 492ND

TOM KEYAHIAN, 491ST

ROBERT J KEYES, 44TH

ARTHUR KIDD, 458TH

CHESTER W KIDD JR, 489TH

FREDERICK KIDD, 93RD

ALAN K KIDDER, 491ST

JAMES N KIDDER, 445TH

NORMAN C KIEFER, 44TH

EARL E KIEFFER, 467TH

RALPH W KIEFFER, 392ND

JAMES & RICKY KIERNAN, HDQ

SHARON D KIERNAN, 489TH, AM

LLOYD W KILMER, 389TH

RICHARD B KIMBALL SR, 448TH

ROBERT E KIMBALL, 445TH, 492ND

JESSIE B KIMBERLY, 491ST, AM

LAURENCE B KIMBROUGH, 489TH

EDWIN N KIMMEL, 466TH

JOSEPH V KIMMEY, 389TH

DONALD R KINARD, 389TH

EARL E KINDER, 445TH

CARL KINDSFATER, 448TH, 491ST

DON L KING, 389TH

DONOVAN F KING, 93RD, 448TH

EDWARD W KING, 467TH

EUGENE L KING, 446TH

F L KING, 458TH

JAMES B KING, 489TH

LTC JOSEPH C KING RET, 446TH

LEONARD J KING, 453RD, 467TH

PAUL R KING, BG

RUFUS K KING, 93RD

HENRY W KINGSBERY, 446TH

JACK KINGSBERY, 458TH

M/SGT RET FLOYD KINGSLEY, 467TH, 492ND

ALAN W KINGSTON, 453RD

DALE F KINKEL, 458TH

FRANK T KINKER JR, 458TH

TIM W KINNALLY, 458TH

JOHN C KINNARD SR, 389TH

JOHN E KINNEY, 446TH

M DWAYNE KINSELL, 389TH

ED KIPPERS, SM

HARLICE E KIRBY, 448TH

JOHN E KIRBY, 44TH

ROBERT W KIRBY, 489TH

ROBERT W KIRBY JR, 389TH

WILLIAM C KIRK III, 491ST

JAMES S KIRKLAND, 467TH

WILLIS H KIRKTON, 467TH

THOMAS G KIRKWOOD JR, 392ND

WILLIAM F KIRNER, 448TH

ROBERT J KIRSCHLING, 44TH

PHYLLIS KIRSCHNER, 467TH, AM

WALLACE E KIRSCHNER, 44TH

MARSHALL L KISCH, 448TH

SILAS H KISER, 389TH

BERNARD F KISSELL, 458TH

JAMES L KISSLING, 389TH

ALVIS O KITCHENS, 445TH

MARVIN S KITE, 44TH

JOHN & RITA KIVLEHAN, 446TH

CHARLES L KLAUMAN, 389TH

DAVID H KLAUS, SM

CARLTON R KLEEMAN, 445TH

ARTHUR C KLEIDERER, 44TH

EDWARD E KLEIN, 458TH

EUGENE KLEIN, 453RD

JACOB KLEIN, 445TH

WARREN J KLEIN, 453RD

HOWARD H KLEINER, 93RD

KENNETH R KLEINSHROT, 389TH, 453RD, 467TH

JOHN J KLEMP, 389TH

ROBERT E KLINDT, 389TH

JACK A KLINEDINST, 453RD

WALTON H KLING, 389TH

HOWARD KLINGBEIL, 491ST

JULIUS M KLINKBELL, 466TH, 389TH

ALBERT C KLIPPERT JR, 389TH

ORVILLE H KLITZKE, 445TH

WILLARD E KLOCKOW MD, 453RD

SARA JANE KLOPFER, 389TH, AM

WALTER G KLOSE, 389TH

ROBERT C KNABLEIN, 44TH

JOHN R KNAPEK, 389TH

MARK I KNAPP, 445TH

ROBERT L KNAPP SR, 466TH

LEE F KNEPP, 492ND

LORIN G KNIERIEMEN, 467TH

MARVIN E KNIESE, 389TH

ROBERT L KNIGHT, 489TH

HOMER C KNISLEY, 458TH

JOHN M KNIZESKI JR, 445TH

CHARLES M KNOEDLER, 93RD

COL FREDERICK J KNORRE JR RET, 446TH

GEORGE W KNOTT, 492ND

HAROLD M KNOX, 458TH

JOHN J KNOX, 445TH

JOHN W KNOX, 445TH

RALPH B KNOX, 44TH

COL BRUCE B KNUTSON RET, 446TH

RICHARD A KOCH MD, 458TH

WILLIAM K KOCH, 489TH, 445TH

DANIEL J KOCIS SR, 491ST

MICHAEL M KOCZAN, 491ST

DOROTHY KOENIG, 458TH, AM

ROMAN R KOENIG, 389TH

JOHN G KOEPPER, 389TH

GEORGE P KOERNER, 458TH

HARRY E KOESTER, 44TH

GORDON H KOHLER, 448TH

JOSEPH F KOHLER, 446TH

OLAF E KOLARI, 389TH

REV DONALD F KOLB, 453RD

CASIMIR J KOLEZYNSKI, 458TH

EDWARD S KOLODZIEJ, 453RD

IRVING E KOLTUN, 492ND, 445TH

WILLIAM J KOMAREK, 93RD

ADOLPH KOMER, 466TH

WARREN KOOKEN, 44TH

DONLEY R KOON, 458TH

SM/SGT WILLIAM C KOON RET, 491ST

CHARLES M KOONTZ, 448TH

E BUD KOORNDYK, 389TH, 93RD

ROBERT A KOORNDYK, 389TH, AM

THOMAS D KOORNDYK, 389TH, AM

JULIUS KOPEC, 448TH

CYRIL C KOPECKY, 446TH

RAYMOND H KOPECKY, 392ND

CHARLES KOPPERNOLLE, 466TH

COL ROBERT J KORDA RET, 44TH

GEORGE KOSIER, 458TH

NORBERT KOSIN, 466TH

MICHAEL L KOSTAN, 453RD

JAMES G KOTAPISH SR, 453RD

ARTHUR KOTH, 448TH

LLOYD F KOTH, 467TH

CHARLES KOTIS, 467TH

JOHN KOVACIC, 389TH

PETER KOWAL, 389TH

STANLEY KOWAL, 458TH

JOHN KOWALCZUK JR, 458TH

EDWARD KOWALSKI, 445TH

LTC FRANK KOZA RET, 392ND

LEONARD R KOZAREK, 93RD

JOHN F KRAEGER, 466TH

JULIUS E KRAEMER, 491ST

ROBERT KRAFT, 492ND, 467TH

WILLILAM R KRAHAM, 445TH

DAVID KRAKOW, 458TH, AM

STEVE KRALJ, 446TH

ROBERT H KRALL, 453RD

RONALD KRAMER, 448TH, AM

WILLIAM D KRAMER, 458TH

FRANK KRANTZ, 389TH

ANTON C KRASOVEC, 491ST

JOSEPH A KRATOCHVIL, 446TH

JAMES J KRATOSKA, 389TH

LOUIS C KRAUS, 389TH

EARL F KRAUSE, 389TH

JOHN D KRAUSE, 458TH

JOHN D KRAUSE II, 458TH, AM

MERLE N KRAUSS, 491ST

OSCAR R KREBS, 93RD

WILLIAM K KREBS, 448TH

M/GEN HOWARD E KREIDLER RET, 445TH, 2CW

IRVING KREISMAN, 392ND

RUDOLPH KREMER, 453RD

DANIEL P KREMP, 93RD

HAROLD E KREN, 466TH

ROBERT L KRENTLER, 453RD

FRED KREPSER, 448TH

ALLEN R KRETSCHMAR, 458TH

ADOLPH R KRIEGER, 491ST

JASON W KRITIKOS, 448TH, AM

FRANK A KROB, 453RD

JOSEPH C KROBOTH, 389TH

GORDON M KROEBAR, 491ST

ARTHUR KROECKER JR, 389TH

DOROTHY REIM KROGMANN, HDQ

GERTRUDE KROHN, 44TH, AM

ROBERT W KROLL, 445TH

EDWARD E KROMER, 93RD, 466TH

CLARENCE W KRONBETTER, 448TH

JOHN KRPAN, 458TH

ROBERT O KRUEGER, 44TH

VICTOR W KRUEGER, 458TH

HARRY C KRUSE, 392ND

VITOLD P KRUSHES, 392ND

LEON S KRUSZEWSKI, 491ST

EUGENE V KRUTY, 392ND

JOHN KRYMSKI, SM

HENRY W KUBACEK, 467TH

GEORGE A KUBES, 44TH

VARA CHRISTIAN KUBLY, HDQ

PAUL J KUCHINSKI SR, 467TH

MAJ CHARLES J KUEHL RET, 491ST

GERALD KUHLMANN, 389TH

LTC DONALD K KUHN RET, 445TH

MARION A KUJAWSKI, 491ST

JOSEPH A KUKLEWICZ, 44TH

NICK KUKLISH, 466TH

DAVID L KUKLOK, 44TH

LAURITZ S KULSTAD, 446TH

DONALD E KUNKLE, 389TH

ANDREW K KUNSTLER, 392ND

HENRY KUNSTLER, 448TH

HAROLD L KUNZE, 446TH

GINO KUNZLE, SM

STANLEY J KUPECKI, 389TH

WALTER K KURK, 448TH

GUS C KURKOMELIS, 392ND

CLARENCE P KURTZ, 467TH

WAYNE M KURTZ, 448TH

CARL F KUSBIT, 491ST

DAVID E KUSCHNER, 3SAD

JAKE D KVETON JR, 389TH

GERALD K KVISTBERG MD, 392ND

FRANCIS X KYLE, 453RD
JOHN A KYLE, SM
COL WILLIAM D KYLE JR RET, 446TH
NORMAN LABARBERA, 491ST
DONALD E LACHANCE, 392ND
ROBERT D LACKAMP, 458TH
COL EDWIN B LACKENS RET, 467TH
EDWIN C LACKER, 466TH
EDWARD V LADAS DMD, 448TH
LTC LOUIS J LADAS RET, 448TH
LAVERAN A LADOUCEUR, 389TH
PAUL LAFAY, 389TH
HENRY A LAFORET, 445TH
DONALD S LAHER JR, 389TH
LEE T LAIN JR, 448TH
NELSON R LAKE, 453RD
NORMAN L LAKEY, 458TH
FRED LAKNER, 93RD
FORREST H LAM, 93RD
J ROBERT LAMADE, 445TH
BERNARD J LAMANTIA, 453RD
JOHN P LAMAR, 489TH
CHARLES F LAMARCA, 446TH
DONALD R LAMB, 93RD
ROBERT E LAMB, 458TH, 389TH
HERBERT G LAMBERT, 453RD, HDQ
ROBERT W LAMBERT, 453RD
ROBERT T LAMBERTSON, 448TH
HAROLD P LAMBOUSY, 458TH
GORDON W LAMERS, 458TH
ARTHUR J LAMONTAGNE, 93RD
LTC ROBERT D LAMY RET, 466TH
DONALD LANCE, 93RD
GLENDON LANDER, 489TH
HOWARD D LANDERS, 44TH, 492ND, 392ND
JOSEPH L LANDERS, 458TH, 392ND
WALTER F LANDERS JR, 458TH
LLOYD LANDIS, 489TH
WILMER D LANDON, 93RD
CHARLES A LANDRUM, 389TH
THOMAS W LANDRUM, 44TH
FORREST E LANE, 446TH, 458TH
GRACE E LANE, 453RD, AM
HAROLD H LANE, 389TH
IRWIN LANE, 448TH
JACK H LANE, 491ST
ROBERT E & MARILYN LANE, 392ND
ROBERT M LANE, 448TH, AM
WILLIAM C LANE, 458TH
CRYSTAL LANG, 448TH
HENRY A LANGBAUER, 389TH
STANLEY LANGCASKEY, 44TH
LTC ROBERT E LANGENFELD RET, 453RD
ARTHUR J LANGSDORF JR, 489TH
REV CHARLES W LANHAM, 466TH
EDWARD R LANHAM, 56FG
ROGER L LANIER, 93RD
ELMER L LANINI, 458TH
ALFRED S LANKUS, 458TH
HAROLD E LANNING, 491ST
PAUL E LANNING, 389TH
HUBERT J LANSLEY, 458TH
WILLIAM F LANTZ, 448TH
JOSEPH L LAPIERRE, 489TH
BERT J LAPOINT 111, 448TH
GEORGE A LAPRATH, 389TH
JOHN E LARGEN, 392ND
PHILIP D LARIVIERE, 448TH
JOHN E LARKIN, 389TH
LTC JOSEPH W LARKIN RET, 446TH
OLIVER S LAROUCHE, 93RD
BIRDIE SCHMIDT LARRICK, 392ND, ARC
EDWARD W LARSEN, 458TH
LTC EDWIN C LARSON RET, 489TH
HAROLD R LARSON, 445TH
M D LARSON, 93RD, HDQ
ORVILLE R LARSON, 491ST
RAYMOND O LARSON, 446TH

RICHARD A LARSON, 44TH
ROBERT S LARSON, 446TH
EMILIAN LARUE, 392ND
VINCENT D LARUSSA, 467TH
HENRY A LASCO, 44TH
WILLIAM F LASETER, 489TH
ELWOOD I LASH, 389TH
THOMAS A LASKOWSKI, 44TH
ELDRED G LASSINS, 392ND
ALAN T LAST, SM
JACK LASWELL, 445TH
G G LASZLO, 467TH
DARRELL W LATCH, 458TH
PAUL W LATENSER, 93RD, 389TH, 445TH
LYLE B LATIMER, 44TH
COL HENRY J LATIMORE JR RET, 491ST
WILLIAM LAUER, HDQ
GREGORY L LAUGHLIN, 445TH
WALTER J LAUGHLIN, 467TH
WALTER J LAUT, 489TH
COL HARRIS Y LAUTERBACH RET, 458TH
MICHAEL A LAVERE, 458TH
FRANCIS M LAVERY, 467TH
GORDON F LAW, 467TH, 389TH
STEPHEN V LAWNICKI, 448TH
WALTER V LAWRENCE, 44TH
WILLIAM C LAWRENCE, 458TH
ORAL LAWS, 389TH
ROBERT S LAWSON, 44TH
SEIBERT E LAY, 489TH
GEORGE W LAYRITZ, 445TH
SAMUEL H LAYTON, 392ND
BERNARD J LAZENSKY, 491ST
CHARLES E LEACH, 389TH
COL MILES R LEAGUE RET, 93RD
ARTHUR H LEARY JR, 491ST
WILMER H LEAS, 492ND
BRUCE C LEATHERY, 389TH
C DOUGLAS LEAVENWORTH, 453RD
LTC ROY D LEAVITT RET, 445TH
ELLIS C LEBO, 44TH
JOSEPH H LEBOEUF, 453RD
ARTHUR E LEBOVITZ, 448TH
JACOB LEBOVITZ, 448TH
JOHN P LECHMAN, 389TH
VINCENT J LECHMAN, 389TH, AM
ARTHUR S LEDFORD, 44TH
CATER LEE, 448TH
DEREK LEE, SM
FRANK W LEE, 491ST
HARRY M LEE, 453RD
COL JOHN L LEE JR RET, 93RD
W WARREN LEE, 93RD
WILLIAM K LEE, 466TH
DONALD W LEEDY, 44TH
COL WILLIAM LEESBURG RET, 389TH
FELIX LEETON, 389TH
HERMAN LEFCO, 453RD
LANI LEFCORT, 389TH, AM
JOHN LEFEVER, 491ST
ROBERT C LEFEVER, 466TH
SIMON LEGGETT, SM
THOMAS A LEGGETT, 492ND
COL L NELSON LEGGETTE RET, 491ST
CARLETON C LEGREID, 93RD
GEORGE J LEHMAN, 491ST
ROBERT J LEHNHAUSEN, 44TH
GEORGE D LEHOUX, 389TH, 491ST
WILLIAM P LEIBENSPERGER, 448TH
GEORGE B LEIGHNINGER, 445TH
ALBERT H LEIGHTON, 389TH
GEORGE LEININGER, 445TH
ROGER L LEISTER, 467TH, 492ND
GEORGE W LEITCH, 466TH
LESTER S LEITERMAN, 466TH
WILLIAM L LEITZEL, 44TH
C J LELEUX, 448TH, 491ST
WILLIAM D LEMKOWITZ, 446TH
LTC HENRY P LEMMEN RET, 467TH
WADE LEMMONS, HDQ

WALLACE LEMMONS, 389TH
F H LEMONDS JR, 389TH
J R LEMONS JR, 445TH
BERNARD T LENAHAN, 489TH
BURTON H LENHART, 93RD
JAMES T LENNON, 389TH
JAMES A LENOIR, 491ST
ROBERT L LENT, 93RD
STANLEY J LENTOWICZ, 458TH
JOSEPH E LENTZ JR, 44TH
STERLING LENTZ, 445TH
JOHN C LEO, 489TH
DEAN A LEONARD, 489TH
LEROY R LEONARD, 445TH
DR PAUL T LEONARD, 448TH
T/SGT RICHARD B LEONARD RET, 453RD
CLEMENT F LEONE, 445TH
LOUIS J LEONE, 466TH
HERBERT S LEOPOLD DDS, 466TH
SALVATORE S LEOTTA, 491ST
BERNARD A LEPOER JR, 467TH
CARL J LEPON, 491ST
ALEX J LEPORE, 93RD
JOHN D LEPPERT JR, 491ST
COL RALPH I LESLIE RET, 389TH
RUSSELL R LESLIE, 389TH
CARL J LESSING, 453RD, 466TH
ALBERT LESTER, 392ND
LEO D LESTER, 56FG
GEORGE E LETLOW, 448TH
COL HERBERT T LEVACK RET, 446TH
OLEN F LEVELL JR, 392ND
DANIEL C LEVERNIER, 93RD
WILLARD LEVIN, 392ND
DON D LEVINE, 453RD
HOWARD LEVINE, SM
ISRAEL LEVINE, 389TH
NORMAN LEVINE, 489TH
SHERMAN LEVITT, 491ST
PAUL S LEVY, 392ND
STANLEY M LEVY, 489TH
BEN F LEWALLEN JR, 453RD
T R LEWANDOWSKI, 446TH
JOSEPH S LEWIN, 392ND
CHARLES A LEWIS, 458TH
FRANK H LEWIS, 491ST
HARRY L LEWIS JR, 466TH
JAMES L LEWIS, 389TH
PAUL C LEWIS, 389TH
R V LEWIS JR, 491ST
VERNON LEWIS, 446TH
HAROLD H LIBBY, 445TH
NEVILLE D LIBBY, 93RD
ROBERT M LIBBY, 445TH
SI LIBERMAN, 466TH
LEO LIEBER, 458TH
RICHARD J LIEDAHL, 448TH
HOWARD L LIENEMANN, 448TH
WALTER C LIENEMANN, 392ND
COL HERBERT M LIGHT JR RET, 44TH
HAROLD E LIGHTCAP, 44TH
ROSEMARY BIEL LIGHTY, 453RD, AM
WILLIAM S LILES, 93RD
HENRY W LILJEDAHL, 491ST
FRANK P LIMBERT, 458TH
EDWIN G LIMSTRONG, 453RD
ELMER LINCOLN, 453RD
RICHARD G LIND, 458TH
VERNON A LINDBERG, 392ND
HAROLD R LINDEMULDER, 446TH
LEE M LINDERMUTH, 467TH
MORTEN G LINDGREN JR, 44TH
HOWARD S LINDHART, 466TH
FRANCIS L LINDQUIST, 93RD
CALVIN T LINDSAY, 389TH
ARTHUR C LINDSEY, 466TH
ADAIR T LINDSTROM, 453RD
JOHN A LINFORD, 445TH
RICHARD G LINGENBERG, 489TH
GEORGE P LINGS, 453RD
TIM M LINIHAN, 389TH
RICHARD T LINN, 489TH
JOSEPH LINSK, 458TH
THOMAS S LINTON, 491ST

KENNETH W LINTZ, 392ND
NORMAN LINVILLE, 44TH
JOSEPH A LIPOSKY, 93RD
MORRIS J LIPP, 467TH
MARY FRANCES LIPPER, 44TH, AM
MARSHALL LISIESKY, 389TH
FRANK LITCH, 389TH
JAMES A LITCHFIELD, 466TH
ERNEST D LITTLE, 446TH
FRANKLIN D LITTLE, 389TH
KYLE D LITTLE, 93RD
ROBERT E LITTLE, 389TH, 491ST
RICHARD E LITTLEFIELD, 445TH, 389TH
JAMES W LITTLEFORD, 467TH
ROY K LITTLEJOHN, 448TH
LESTER J LITWILLER, 93RD
HENRY M LIVELY, 445TH
ARTHUR V LIVINGSTON JR, 446TH
WILLIAM J LIZUT, 458TH
ROBERT LLOYD, 448TH
VERNON H LLOYD, 389TH
WILLIAM J LOADHOLTES, 489TH
WILLIAM H LOBB, 446TH
SETH L LOBDELL, 489TH
MAJ RICHARD D LODGE RET, 467TH
REV ALFRED M LOEHR, 458TH
LOUIS LOEVSKY, 466TH
WALTER L LOFGREN, 446TH, AM
JAMES H LOFTIS, 44TH
THOMAS B LOFTUS, 491ST
ED T LOGAN, 93RD
COL GRAHAM A LOGAN JR RET, 453RD
JOHN J LOGAN, 467TH
FRANCIS H LOGSDON, 44TH
ALPHONSE J LOGUIDICE, 445TH
ARVO E LOHELA, 489TH
WILLIAM R LOHNES, 489TH
JACK E LOMAN, 44TH
ROBERT LOMAX, SM
PAUL C LONDON, 93RD
DEREK K LONG, 448TH, AM
EARL C LONG, 93RD
ELDON LONG, 445TH
EUGENE H LONG, 467TH
J D & EMILY LONG, 392ND
JAMES J LONG, 453RD, 466TH
JOSEPH H LONG, 467TH
O K LONG, 453RD
ROBERT C LONG, 448TH
ROBERT R LONG, 489TH
ROBERT W LONG, 458TH
THOMAS R LONG, 467TH
VERNON R LONG, 489TH
WARREN H LONG, 93RD
WILLIAM M LONG, 491ST
WILLIAM S LONG, 392ND
JOSEPH LONGO, 448TH
JAMES E LONGSTRETH, 446TH
HORACE M LOO, 489TH
ANTON J LOOMAN, 467TH
LTC RICHARD T LOOMS RET, 448TH
ROBERT M LOONEY, 389TH
AL LOPEZ, 93RD
EDWIN L LORD, 445TH
JOHN B LORD, 44TH
LINDA G LORD, 458TH, AM
JAMES J LORENZ, 466TH
LINDA LORING, 93RD, ARC
ROBERT L LORING, 93RD
LTC ROBERT C LORY RET, 392ND
JOHN F LOSEE, 492ND
RAYMOND C LOSEY, 44TH
RAYMOND E LOTKO, 467TH
CHARLES F LOTSCH, 93RD
ROY H LOTTERHOS, 392ND
LOU'S DONUT SHOP, SM
RICHARD L LOUGEE, 458TH
ROBERT J LOUGHRAN, 489TH
GEORGE W LOUTSCH, 93RD
CLARENCE E LOVE, 467TH
THOMAS S LOVE JR, HDQ
LTC LEO L LOVEL RET, 448TH
ELLIOTT H LOVELACE, 453RD

EDWARD B LOVELL, 491ST
HELEN LOVELL, 44TH, AM
HAROLD A LOVGREN, 44TH
M/GEN ANDREW S LOW RET, 453RD
KEITH M LOWDER, 93RD
MARY M LOWE, 445TH, AM
THOMAS C LOWE, 445TH, AM
WILLIAM C LOWE, 458TH, AM
GERALD LOWENTHAL, 44TH
LEON A LOWENTHAL, 44TH
COL FRANKLIN D LOWN JR RET, 93RD
DONALD C LOWRY, 491ST
ROBERT B LOWRY, 458TH
ELBERT F LOZES, 448TH
VINCENT J LOZOWICKI, 389TH
ANDREW LUBNICK, 458TH
HARRY T LUCAS JR, 458TH
JOHN S LUCAS, 93RD
DOUGLAS T LUCE SR, 492ND
ROBERT L LUCHTMAN, 453RD
GUENTHER E LUCKENBACH, 445TH
JOHN L LUDDEN, 448TH
CHARLES L LUDOLFF, 453RD
ARTHUR H LUDWIG, 446TH
GLADYS LUDWIG, HDQ, AM
JOHN L LUFT, 458TH
CLARENCE A LUHMANN, 445TH
M/GEN ROBERT P LUKEMAN RET, 467TH
ROBERT J LUMPKIN, 453RD
COL HAROLD G LUND RET, HDQ
RICHARD S LUNDBERG, 466TH
ARTHUR E LUNDBURG, 445TH
HARRY C LUNDEEN, 491ST
ROY J LUNDQUIST, 389TH
C WILL LUNDY, 44TH
DAVID E LUNDY, 93RD, 446TH
MARVIN C LUNSFORD, HDQ
JOHN R LUPO, 489TH
ALVIN M LUSK, 448TH
EDWARD T LUSZCZ, 448TH
BERTRAND E LUTZ, 448TH
CARL D LUTZ, 445TH, 453RD
ROY W LYBROOK DVM, 489TH
JOHN E LYDAY MD, 445TH
FRANCIS J LYDEN, 448TH
M/GEN L E LYLE RET, SM
JOHN M LYMAN, 467TH
GEORGE H LYMBURN, 445TH
RAYMOND J LYNCH, 453RD
ROBERT J LYNCH, 466TH
THOMAS B LYNCH, 389TH
WAYNE LYND, 489TH
MARGUERITE LYNES, 445TH, AM
MATHEW H LYNN, 44TH
RALPH LYNN JR, 466TH
GEORGE T LYONS, 445TH
HOWARD A LYONS, 389TH
JOHN LYONS, 492ND, 44TH
RAY LYTLE, 458TH
WOOLSEY LYTTLE, 93RD
FLOYD & DOROTHY MABEE, 93RD
HAROLD F MABEE, 93RD, 44TH
EDWIN A MACASLAN, 446TH
RALPH L MACCARONE, 467TH
HARRY E MACDERMAID, 453RD
GORDON W MACDONALD, 491ST
HOWARD J MACDONALD, 489TH
JAMES E MACDONALD, 446TH
JOHN A MACDONALD, 491ST
JOHN M MACDONALD, 448TH
CLIFFORD M MACDOUGALL, 44TH
MALCOLM J MACGREGOR, 445TH
MALCOLM B MACINTIRE, 467TH
ARCHIE A MACINTYRE, 492ND
FABIAN S MACK, 445TH
OAK MACKEY, 93RD
RANDALL R MACKEY, 392ND, AM
MORTON MACKS, 93RD, 2CW
CHRISTOPHER MACMICHAEL, 489TH
JAMES MACNEW, 453RD
HOWARD S MACREADING, 93RD
LTC LEROY C MACTAVISH RET, 392ND
ROBERT C MACY, 446TH

JOSEPH M MADDEN, 448TH
BURTON D MADISON, 453RD
GILBERT MAGAZINER, 44TH
WALLACE MAGAZINER, 453RD, 389TH
JOHN M MAGEE, SM
ROBERT L MAGER, 389TH
HENRY M MAGGENTI, 448TH
DANIEL MAGID, 453RD
ARTHUR C MAGILL, 93RD
RICHARD L MAGNUSON, 467TH
WILLIAM J MAGUIRE JR, 389TH
HAROLD E MAHAFFEY, 93RD
FRANCIS X MAHANEY, 44TH
CLEM L MAHER, 448TH
LTC WILLIAM P MAHER RET, 445TH
FRED MAHNKEN, 446TH
EDWARD F MAHONEY, 467TH
JAMES J MAHONEY, 492ND, 467TH
JOHN E MAHONEY, 467TH
LTC ELMO E MAIDEN RET, 466TH
KARL I MAIJALA, 466TH
CLAUDE L MAINE, 467TH
JOHN MAINHOOD, 445TH
WILLIAM D MAISENHELDER, 446TH
EDWARD C MAJEWSKI, 448TH
GEORGE J MAKIN JR, 389TH
WALTER A MAKOWSKI, 446TH
BERNARD C MALEWISKI, 448TH
ROBERT W MALLETT, 446TH
ROBERT S MALLICK JR, 453RD, 467TH
JOHN F MALLOY, 392ND
CLIFFORD R MALMSTROM, 489TH, 389TH
GEORGE H MALO, 466TH
EARL L MALONE MD, 491ST
GIRD M MALONE, 448TH
JOHNIE R MALONE, 467TH
MAURICE L MALONE, 467TH
O M MALONE, 93RD
LTC WALLACE R MALONE RET, 446TH
S J MALOUKIS JR, 392ND
ANTHONY J MAMMOLITE, 389TH
PHILIP MANCOFF, 44TH
MICHAEL A MANCUSO, 392ND
CHARLES S MANERI, 491ST
JULES R MANGANO, 93RD
WILLIAM MANGLER, 489TH
IRVING B MANIN, 448TH
GEORGE MANLEY, 93RD
CARLTON E MANN, 453RD
DELBERT MANN, 467TH, 491ST
HAROLD J MANN MD, 93RD
JOHN L MANN, 445TH
ADDISON B MANNING, 467TH
CHARLES E MANNING, 93RD
JOHN R MANRHO, SM
CHARLES G MANROSE, 448TH
JOHN W MANSFIELD, 489TH
EVERETT W MANSIR, 44TH
FRANCIS A MANZA, 467TH
SAM MARAVICH, HDQ
ANTHONY F MARCELLI, 392ND
ROBERT E MARCELLUS, 453RD
JAMES MARCHIONE, 93RD
VIRGIL W MARCUM, SM
MAX MARCUS, 453RD
EDWARD J MAREVKA, 361FG
CARL E MARINO, 445TH
JACK MARINOS, 44TH
JOHN J MARIO, 467TH
COL ANTHONY J MARIS RET, 467TH
LTC JAMES R MARIS RET, 392ND
ROBERT MARJORAM, SM
BERNARD J MARKEY, 466TH
DR CLARON E MARKHAM, 44TH
LTC VERNON C MARKHAM RET, 445TH
HAROLD W MARKLE, 458TH
ROGER S MARKLE, 44TH
CARL H MARKOVER, 93RD
JOHN A MARKS, 445TH
CHARLES K MARLATT, HDQ

LEROY J MARLEAU, 93RD
RAY I MARNER JR, 44TH
MICHAEL M MAROTTA, 489TH
2NDLT KIMBERLY K MARQUARDT, 458TH, AM
ALBERT MARQUEZ, 448TH
PHILLIP F MARQUEZ, 467TH
STANLEY L MARR, 93RD
HENDERSON R MARRIOTT JR, 491ST
JAMES W MARSH, 446TH
ROBERT A MARSH, 466TH
B D MARSHALL, 458TH
CLAYTON F MARSHALL, 466TH
JAMES W MARSHALL JR, 445TH, 489TH
LYLE C MARSHALL, 392ND
WILLIS W MARSHALL JR, 389TH
NORMAN J MARSHANK, 446TH
GLEN E MARSTELLER, 445TH
EDWARD S MARSTON, 458TH
EILEEN E MARSTON, SM
MAJ ALBERT A MARTIN RET, 44TH
ALBERT S MARTIN, 448TH
LTC CECIL S MARTIN RET, 389TH
CHARLES D MARTIN, 392ND
HAROLD J MARTIN, 389TH
JAMES F MARTIN, 389TH
JAMES R MARTIN, 453RD
JEWEL B MARTIN, 93RD, AM
JOHN B MARTIN, 458TH
JOHN C MARTIN JR, 389TH
JOHN P MARTIN, 445TH
JOHN R MARTIN, 466TH
LESTER C MARTIN, 458TH
COL LLOYD J MARTIN RET, 445TH
DR O G MARTIN, 453RD
ROY G MARTIN, 93RD
SHERMAN A MARTIN, 93RD
WILLIAM A MARTIN, 93RD
WILLIAM B MARTIN, 491ST
WILLIAM MARTIN JR, 489TH, 466TH
COL WILLIAM M MARTIN RET, 448TH
WILLIAM T MARTIN JR, 389TH
EUGENE B MARTINEAU, 453RD
JOSEPH A MARTINEAU, 445TH
DAVID F MARTINEZ, 445TH
VICTOR J MARTINI, 453RD
CHARLES MARTYKAN, 491ST
MICHAEL J MARTZ SR, 93RD
THEODORE MARUSCHAK, 489TH
JOHN E MARVILL, 453RD
FRANCIS C MARX, 448TH
LT JOHN A MARX, 93RD, AM
LTC ROBERT C MARX RET, 453RD
LTC ROBERT L MARX, 93RD, AM
COL EDWARD H MARXEN JR RET, 446TH
FRED J MARZOLPH, 44TH
LAWRENCE G MASEK, 453RD
NICHOLAS MASLONIK, 445TH
HAROLD J MASLYN, 446TH
HARLEY B MASON, 389TH
HENRY MASON, HDQ
JEAN T MASON, 448TH, AM
JOHN B MASON, 458TH
LTC THOMAS L MASON RET, 446TH
CAPT FRED A MASSARO RET, 458TH
BERNARD MASSING, 466TH
EUGENE E MASSY, 453RD
COL EMIL B MASTAGNI RET, 491ST
PHILIP MASTANDREA, 467TH
ANTHONY J MASTRADONE, 44TH
SAM MASTROGIACOMO, 445TH
COL GEORGE MATECKO RET, 392ND, 453RD
CHARLES Q MATEER, 458TH
LTC LORN W MATELSKI RET, 392ND
WALTER J MATESKI, 392ND
MILAN R MATEYKA MD, 392ND
ALFRED G MATHER, 489TH
FRANK G MATHEWS, 466TH
GEORGE M MATHEWS, 448TH

LYMAN H MATHEWS, 389TH
LTC WILBUR J MATHIAS RET, 448TH
LUCIEN L MATHIEU, 93RD
DANIEL V MATLOCK, 93RD
JIM H MATNEY, 467TH, AM
MAJ JOHN MATT RET, 392ND
ELWOOD A MATTER, 445TH
GEORGE MATTES, 446TH
CHARLES A MATTHEWS, 445TH
WILLIAM A MATTHEWS, 458TH
ROBERT N MATTINGLY, 489TH
LTC BERNARD H MATTSON RET, 448TH
ROBERT L MATTSON, 492ND, 467TH
ROY H MATTSON, 389TH
WILLIAM F MATTULKE, 467TH
JOHN R MATUS, 446TH
GAZA J MATYUS, 446TH
DOYLE M MATZ, 458TH
GERARD W MATZE, 458TH
CHALON MAULDING, 389TH
YVONNE MAULE, 44TH, AM
LTC DAVID B MAUTNER RET, 491ST
GLENN R MAXIE, 453RD
LAURENCE L MAXTON, 448TH, AM
DOROTHY C MAXWELL, 448TH, AM
RICHARD E MAXWELL, 453RD, HDQ
ALVIN F MAY, 467TH
EVELYNNE MAY, 448TH, AM
HORACE L MAY, 445TH
KENNETH R MAYER, 446TH
WARREN H MAYER, 389TH
WILLIAM L MAYER, 389TH
LAMAR C MAYFIELD, SM
LADY MAYHEW, HM
ROY M MAYHEW, 93RD
KENNETH E MAYO, 446TH
CARL L MAYS, 489TH
DAVID B MAZER, 467TH
EDWARD MAZER, 44TH
DUKE MAZEROV, 445TH, 389TH, 355TH
STEVE J MAZNIO, 467TH
JOHN MAZUR, 448TH
LTC VINCENT MAZZA RET, 445TH
RICHARD H MCADAMS, 448TH
GEORGE E MCALISTER, 44TH
A D MCALLISTER JR, 448TH
RONALD L MCALLISTER, 448TH
ROBERT MCANULTY, 458TH
JAMES C MCATEE, 44TH
LEO R MCBRIAN, 389TH
CHARLES C MCBRIDE, 448TH
WILLIAM G MCCABE, 448TH
JOHN K MCCAIN, 458TH
JACK J MCCANNA, 389TH
DANIEL E MCCARTHY, 93RD
FRANK J MCCARTHY, 467TH
WESLEY H MCCARTNEY, 445TH
VERE MCCARTY, 446TH
DAVID E MCCASH, 44TH, 96CW
JOHN W MCCLANE JR, 44TH
DONALD H MCCLELLAN, 491ST
DON R MCCLELLAND, 389TH
WILLIAM L MCCLELLAND, 491ST
EDWARD F MCCLOSKEY, 491ST
JAMES B MCCLOSKEY, 93RD
SAMUEL MCCLUNG, 446TH
RALPH W MCCLURE, 453RD
C W MCCONNELL, 392ND
CARLTON H MCCONNELL, 445TH
CLAUDE H MCCONNELL OD, 458TH
C MCCOOL, 491ST
EDWARD J MCCORMACK, 467TH
ROBERT H MCCORMACK, 445TH
ROBERT J MCCORMACK, 389TH
EDWARD MCCORMICK, 445TH
HAROLD L MCCORMICK, HDQ
MARVIN V MCCORMICK, 445TH
PATRICK F MCCORMICK, 458TH
COL JOHN T MCCOY RET, SM
KENNETH C MCCOY O D, 389TH
ROBERT L MCCOY, 448TH

HOWARD I MCCRACKEN, 491ST
WILLIAM C MCCRACKEN, 389TH
HAROLD F MCCRAY, 458TH, 389TH
HENRY C MCCRAY, 445TH, 458TH, 389TH
DONALD F MCCREA, 389TH
RALPH R MCCREADY, 466TH
FRANK A MCCRORY, 458TH
JAMES P MCCRORY, 492ND
THOMAS E MCCUE, 466TH
CM/SGT BILL J MCCULLAH RET, 448TH
HAL E MCCULLOUGH, 44TH
JOHN P MCCURDIE, 389TH
JACK MCDANIEL, 448TH
ARTHUR J MCDERMOTT, 445TH
JOHN J MCDERMOTT, 458TH
C L MCDONALD, 489TH
H W MCDONALD, 458TH
HAROLD W MCDONALD, 93RD
LTC JOSEPH C MCDONALD RET, 458TH
LEO MCDONALD, 392ND
MAURICE A MCDONALD, 445TH
THOMAS E MCDONALD, 458TH, AM
RALPH A MCDONOUGH, 355FG
EUGENE F MCDOWELL, 453RD
JOHN A MCDOWELL, 389TH
EDGAR A MCDUFF, 458TH
GUY MCELHANY, 491ST
KENTON E MCELHATTAN, 458TH
DENNIS J MCELHINNY, 453RD
WILLIAM F MCELROY, 389TH
JOSEPH T MCELVEEN SR, 467TH
PATRICK J MCEVOY, 392ND
ROBERT B MCEWEN, 467TH
JAMES D MCFARLAND, 392ND
ROBERT S MCFARLANE, 44TH
JOHN D MCGEARY, 491ST
W C MCGINLEY, 392ND
EDWIN J MCGINTY, 466TH
WILLIAM J MCGONAGLE, 389TH
JOHN E MCGOUGH, 453RD
LTC DANIEL A MCGOVERN RET, SM
WILLIAM P MCGOVERN, 467TH
JOHN L MCGOWAN, 93RD
CHARLIE M MCGOWEN, 392ND
LESTER S MCGOWN, 448TH
JEAN F MCGRATH, 489TH, AM
DAN MCGREW, 448TH
PATRICK J MCGUCKIN, 389TH
GEORGE H MCGUHY, 489TH
JOHN F MCGUIRE SR, 491ST
ROBERT E MCGUIRE, SM
GARL D MCHENRY, 445TH
JOHN J MCHUGH, 389TH
ROBERT D MCINTYRE, 491ST
DAVID MCKALIP, 466TH
COL DESCO E MCKAY RET, 445TH
CHARLES H MCKEE, 93RD
CHARLES N MCKEE, 93RD, AM
M KEITH MCKEE SR, 458TH
OSCAR P MCKEEVER, 445TH
ROBERT B MCKEEVER, 93RD
JOHN W MCKELVEY, 389TH
E J MCKENNEY, 44TH
DEE W MCKENZIE, 491ST
JACK M MCKENZIE, 453RD
ROBERT L MCKENZIE, 467TH
THOMAS H MCKIERNAN, 458TH, 93RD, 466TH
LYNN D MCKIM, 392ND
ALBERT J MCKINNAN, 448TH
DONALD W MCKINNEY, 44TH
F HUGH MCKINNEY, 448TH
CONELY N MCKINNISH, 389TH
ARCHIBALD M MCLACHLEN, SM
HUGH R MCLAREN, 389TH, AM
HENRY J MCLARREN, 458TH
FRANK B MCLAUGHLIN, 389TH
E G MCLEAN, 458TH
GEORGE E MCLEAN, 93RD
L P MCLENDON JR, 389TH
M D MCLENDON, 448TH
ROBERT MCLOUGHLIN, 448TH, 93RD

C D MCMAHON, 392ND
F THOMAS MCMAHON, 446TH
HAROLD R MCMAHON, 492ND
JAMES H MCMAHON, 93RD
NEIL F MCMANAMON, 446TH
JAMES H MCMASTER, 44TH
E E MCMECHEN, 491ST
HUBERT L MCMILLAN, 392ND
PAUL L MCMILLEN, 458TH
ROBERT E MCMILLEN, 448TH
JOHN MCMULLEN, 489TH
HELEN L MCMULLIN, 44TH, AM
BAILEY A MCNAIR, 448TH
RUSSELL D MCNAIR, 466TH
MICHAEL J MCNAMARA, 491ST
MYRON C MCNAMARA, 458TH
RAYMOND L MCNAMARA, 44TH
HAROLD H MCNEELY, 458TH
E K MCNEW, 491ST
GEORGE F MCNULTY, 93RD
C FRANK MCPHILLIPS, 491ST
T J MCQUEEN, 458TH
EDDIE T MCQUELLON, 467TH
LTC THOMAS L MCQUOID RET, 489TH, 448TH
WILLIAM C MCRORIE, 445TH
ALFRED F MCSHEEHY JR, 491ST
JOHN E MCSHERRY, 453RD
KENNETH R MCVEE, 453RD
ROBERT J MCVEIGH, 389TH
ROBERT E MEAD, 445TH
STELL MEADOR, 389TH
ROBERT E MEAGHER, 491ST
FRANCIS P MEANEY, 458TH
SCOTT MEANS, 448TH, AM
MARION L MECHLING, 445TH
CLAUDE V MECONIS, 466TH
WILLIAM E MEDEIROS, 389TH
LOUIS E MEDLOCK, 446TH
FRANCIS R MEDUNA, 466TH
BEN MEEDS, 453RD
ARTHUR F MEFFORD, 446TH
BURTON A MEGLITSCH, 491ST
COL WILLIAM B MEHARG RET, 448TH
HARRY W MEHOLLIN, 491ST
WILLIS A MEIER, 445TH
JAMES E MEINER JR, 44TH
JOSEPH E MEINTEL, 453RD
JOHN E MEINTZER, 448TH
WALTER S MEISTER, 392ND
PHILIP H MEISTRICH, 453RD
JERRY MEJEUR, 448TH
JOHN MELLECKER, 467TH, AM
HARRY K MELLINGER, 491ST
EDWARD G MELLO JR, 466TH
H CLAY MELLOR, 448TH
LTC DAVID E MELLOTT RET, 448TH
NORMAN J MELLOW, 392ND
GERALD MELMOOD, 93RD
HOWARD E MELSON, 44TH
ALBERT T MELTON, 389TH
CHARLES A MELTON, 458TH
EDWARD MENARCHIK, 392ND
ROBERT A MENWEG, 492ND
PAUL E MENZENSKI SR, 489TH
DAVID MERCADO, 491ST
CHARLES H MERCER, 44TH
HOMER E MERCER, 453RD
JACK MERCER, 389TH
JACKSON C MERCER, 445TH
VIRGINIA L MERCER, 44TH, AM
WAYNE D MERCER, 491ST
G C MERKET, 466TH
COL CHARLES T MERRILL RET, 93RD
JOHN W MERRILL, 389TH
HARRY C MERRITT, 466TH
HOWARD L MERTZ, 44TH
JOHN MESARCH, 491ST
GRANVILLE E MESEKE, 93RD
HOWARD MESNARD, 93RD
JOHN C MESSERSCHMITT, 389TH
DONALD A MESSICK, 446TH
FRED MESSINA, 446TH
DONALD P METCALF, 491ST
JOSEPH R METCALF, 491ST
GENE L METTS DDS, 446TH

JOHN METZ, 491ST
RAYMOND METZ, 458TH
ALBERT G METZGER, 448TH
GEORGE MEUSE, 491ST
ROBERT D MEUSE, 389TH
ANDREW G MEYER, 453RD
DELVIN MEYER, 448TH
ELWYN A MEYER, 44TH
JEROME J MEYER, 489TH
JOHN E MEYER, 466TH
JOSEPH T MEYER, 448TH
ROBERT A MEYER, 445TH
ROBERT F MEYER, 448TH
ROBERT G MEYER, 446TH
LTC WALTER J MEYER JR RET,
453RD
WILLIAM J MEYER, 389TH
LTC GERALD L MEYERS RET,
445TH, 446TH
GERALD W MEYERS, 491ST
JOSEPH G MEYERS, 44TH
PAUL E MEYERS, 93RD
ROBERT A MEYERS, 467TH
VERNON C MEYERS, 44TH
WILLIAM C MEYERS, 389TH
FRANK A MIANO, 489TH
SAM S MICELI, 44TH, 492ND
EDGAR W MICHAELS, 44TH
LOUIS A MICHALAK, 458TH
GEORGE W MICHEL, 392ND
RAYMOND E MICHELS, 93RD
MERLIN L MICHELSON, 491ST
WALTER J MICHON, 491ST
GERALD E MICKEL, 466TH
WARREN E MICKELSON, 93RD
ROGER MICKLETHWAITE, SM
COL WILLIAM B MICKLEY RET,
44TH, 389TH, HDQ
KENNETH C MICKO, 467TH
WILLIAM D MIDDLEBROOKS, 44TH
DOROTHY L MIDDLETON,
453RD, AM
NORWOOD C MIDDLETON, HDQ
GILBERT A MIERITZ, 389TH
HENRY R MIERZEJEWSKI, 446TH
HENRY MIHALY, 491ST
LOWELL MIINCH, 389TH
CARL E MIKEL, 466TH
CM/SGT FRED MIKLASEVICH RET,
389TH
HENRY C MIKOL, 44TH, 95TH
STANLEY L MIKOLAJCZYK, 93RD
COL THOMAS J MILBURN RET,
448TH
FRANKLIN W MILES, 448TH
JOHN E MILIGAN, 458TH
ALLEN P MILLER SR, 93RD
ALLEN W MILLER, 44TH
ANDREW J MILLER SR, 93RD
BURR MILLER, 445TH
CHESTER V MILLER, 389TH
CWO4 CLAIR L MILLER RET,
453RD
DARWIN MILLER, 448TH
ELTON A MILLER, 458TH, HDQ
LTC ERRETT D MILLER RET,
453RD, 466TH
FRED J MILLER, 389TH
M/GEN FREDERIC H MILLER RET,
491ST, 2CW, HDQ
FREDERIC L MILLER, 458TH
GEORGE P MILLER, 448TH, 491ST
GERALD K MILLER, 458TH
JACK C MILLER, 448TH
JOSEPH MILLER, 448TH
LESTER F MILLER, 448TH
LOUIS J MILLER, 44TH
PETER P MILLER, 389TH
RICHARD E MILLER SR, 467TH
ROGER A MILLER, 466TH
COL SAMUEL F MILLER RET,
445TH
STEVEN D MILLER, SM
COL THOMAS E MILLER RET,
448TH
VIRGEL W MILLER, 467TH
WALTER R MILLER, 389TH
WAYNE A MILLER, 44TH
JOHN L MILLIKEN, 44TH

WARREN T MILLIKEN, 93RD
SAMUEL MILLMAN, 93RD
CHARLES H MILLS, HDQ
JAMES W MILLS JR, 491ST
REX MILLS, 453RD
MURRAY MILROD, 392ND
ROBERT J MINARICK, 458TH
MAJ MAX W MINEAR RET, 446TH
HUGH C MINER, 467TH
REGINALD R MINER, 445TH
CHARLES F MINICH, 453RD
RUSSELL I MINICK, 448TH
FATHER MARSHALL V MINISTER,
93RD
JACOB H MINK, 492ND
KEITH B MINK, 448TH
HAROLD E MINNICK, 446TH,
489TH
ROBERT H MINOR, 458TH
EDWARD L MIRKIN, 44TH
WILBERT G MISHLER, 491ST
ARTHUR MISKAR, 445TH
MICHAEL W MISKEWICH, 491ST
ELMO E MISNER, 445TH
MICHAEL J MISSANO, 389TH
LTC JAMES I MISURACA RET,
448TH
GILBERT H MITCH, 466TH
JOHN P MITCHEL, 466TH
ANTHONY MITCHELL, 44TH
DONALD F MITCHELL, 392ND
DUANE E MITCHELL MD, 44TH
EDWIN S MITCHELL, 448TH
EUGENE T MITCHELL, 492ND,
445TH
J W MITCHELL JR, 389TH
JOSEPH R MITCHELL, 93RD
LEONARD C MITCHELL, 489TH
LESLIE R MITCHELL, 446TH
M M MITCHELL, 489TH
MIKE MITCHELL, 458TH
WILLIAM F MITCHELL, 492ND,
14CW
MICHAEL MITNICK, 453RD
CHARLES G MIXSON JR, 446TH
JOSEPH E MLYNARCZYK, 448TH
ROBERT C MOBLEY, 389TH
WILLIAM R MODENE, 466TH
WALTER MODJESKA, 448TH
HARRY MOEDINGER, 389TH
JUDY MOHNEY, 492ND, AM
STANLEY J MOHR JR, 466TH
JOHN A MOIR, 489TH
E MAX MOISANEN, 448TH
MARC MOLDAWER MD, 453RD
ROBERT G MOLDENHAUER,
489TH
WILLIAM MOLES, 392ND
COL JOSEPH A MOLLER RET,
448TH
WILLIAM W MOLLER, 389TH
JAMES MOLLO, 453RD
PATRICIA MOLLOY, 458TH, AM
ROBERT A MOMBERG, 489TH
WARREN D MONAGHAN, 446TH
JOHN B MONFORT, 453RD
EUSEBIO E MONTANO, 458TH
HENRY MONTEGARI, 389TH
MARIO MONTRESOR, 491ST
DALE L MONTROSS, 389TH,
491ST
RICHARD M MOODY, 448TH
ALAN A MOORE, 453RD
B C MARGUERITE MOORE,
392ND, AM
DANNY R MOORE, 467TH
DAVID G MOORE, 93RD
DONALD F MOORE, 389TH
F DANIEL MOORE, 445TH
FRANCIS C MOORE, 44TH
GEORGE W MOORE, 44TH
HAROLD B MOORE, 389TH
B/GEN HOWARD W MOORE RET,
44TH
J R MOORE, 448TH
JOHN R MOORE, 389TH
JOSEPH L MOORE, 389TH
B/GEN LEON A MOORE JR RET,
445TH

LILLIAN MEADOWS MOORE, HDQ
MEREDITH MOORE, 458TH
PHILIP D MOORE, 467TH
RICHARD J MOORE, 458TH
ROBERT C MOORE, 466TH
ROBERT T MOORE, 446TH
WARREN C MOORE, 491ST
MELLICENT S MOORHEAD, 492ND
LEON H R MOQUIN, 467TH
OLGA M MORA, 93RD
JOSEPH A MORABITO, 489TH
EDWARD J MORAN, 392ND
EDWIN MORAN, 448TH
HOMER L MORAN, 93RD
JOSEPH W MORAN, 453RD
WILLIAM E MORAN, 458TH
GORDON W MOREHEAD, 458TH
MANUEL MORENO, 445TH
ROCCO V MOREO, 389TH
CHARLES E MORGAN, 445TH
DAVID N MORGAN, SM
FRANKLIN R MORGAN, 489TH
JACK B MORGAN, 44TH
JAMES E MORGAN, 389TH
JOHN W MORGAN, 389TH
JOSEPH A MORGAN, 492ND
KENNETH MORGAN, 389TH
MICHAEL L MORGAN, 93RD, AM
RUSSELL L MORGAN, 93RD, AM
WILLIAM F MORGAN, 445TH
TED J MORGENTHALER, 44TH
ROBERT N MORIN, 453RD
DUANE M MORK, 361ST
COL CHESTER H MORNEAU RET,
489TH, 389TH
CLARENCE B MORRIS JR, 467TH
FRANK E MORRIS, 489TH
GILBERT F MORRIS, 448TH
HAROLD L MORRIS, 489TH
HENRY A MORRIS, 491ST
JAMES E MORRIS, 389TH
JOHN W MORRIS, 389TH
MERLE S MORRIS, 448TH
OLIVER L MORRIS, 453RD
QUENTIN L MORRIS, 93RD
WALTER D MORRIS, 93RD
WILLIAM F MORRIS, 44TH
WILLIAM R MORRIS, 448TH
ALLAN L MORRISON, 44TH
DONALD K MORRISON, 93RD, AM
EDWARD J MORRISON, 489TH
LTC RICHARD I MORRISON RET,
458TH
WARREN E MORRISON, 44TH
WILLIAM R MORRISON, 458TH
DANTE MORRONI, 453RD
DEAN F MORROW, 467TH
BOYD M MORSE, 489TH
LOYD F MORSE, 448TH
PERRY A MORSE JR, 44TH
JAMES F MORTIMSON, 458TH
CALVIN T MORTON, 466TH
JAMES L MORTON, 389TH
WILLIAM G MORTON, 44TH
KENT C MOSELEY DDS, 448TH
CHARLES H MOSGAR, 453RD
RALPH S MOSHER, 458TH
JOHN L MOSIER, 93RD
SAMUEL MOSKOWITZ, 446TH
CARL M MOSS, 389TH
WILLIAM T MOSS, 489TH
CALVIN C MOSTELLAR, 448TH
HAZEL W MOTLEY, 389TH, AM
LTC JOHN C MOTT RET, 446TH
ROY A MOTTNER, 44TH
LOUIS J MOTTS, 446TH, 458TH
KENNETH MOULDEN, 448TH
JOHN A MOULDER, 467TH
RAYMOND H MOULTON, 389TH
ROBERT C MOUNT, 448TH
WAYNE G MOUNTFORD, 467TH
ROBERT W MOUNTSIER, 44TH
MILTON MOUTON, 448TH
MAJ LEO L MOWER RET, 466TH
DEAN MOYER, HDQ
LEONARD R MOYER, 453RD
ROBERT MOYER, HDQ, AM
COL DAN T MUAT RET, 389TH
JACK MUCHNIK, 466TH

ROBERT L MUDGET, 448TH
ALLEN O MUELLER, 44TH
FREDERICK E MUELLER, 93RD
THOMAS D MUFF, 44TH
RICHARD J MUFFOLETTO, 467TH
JOHN J MUKA, 392ND
CARL J MULA, 466TH
FRANK MULCONREY, 453RD,
467TH
LTC JAMES E MULDOON RET,
392ND
FRANCIS P MULEADY, 467TH
JAMES A MULHALL, 389TH
JOSEPH G MULHERAN, 467TH
JOHN V MULHOLLAND, 453RD
RITA A MULKERN, 466TH, AM
EDGAR J MULLEN, 491ST
ALBERT A MULLER, 467TH
HENRY MULLER III, 93RD
ROBERT H MULLER, 445TH
DONALD O MUNDALE, 389TH
ROBERT F MUNDELL, 44TH
DONALD P MUNDT, 389TH
ROBERT MUNDY JR, 466TH
WALTER J MUNDY, 467TH
DARYL H MUNGER, 389TH
ROBERT E MUNK, 44TH
MILTON L MUNRO, 44TH
WILLIAM L MUNRO, 491ST
H CAMERON MURCHISON, 453RD
DR GRIFFIN MURPHEY, SM
CHARLES E MURPHY, 491ST
EDWARD A MURPHY, 458TH
EDWARD J MURPHY, 458TH
JAMES L MURPHY, 458TH
ROBERT E MURPHY, 467TH
THOMAS X MURPHY, 448TH
MELVIN C MURRACK, 44TH
CLAUDE MURRAY, SM
DONALD F MURRAY, 466TH
DONALD L MURRAY, 445TH
BROTHER EDMUND MURRAY,
389TH
JACK W MURRAY, 467TH
JAMES J MURRAY, 392ND
ROBERT E MURRAY JR, 453RD
ROBERT H MURRAY, 445TH
JAMES F MURTA, 466TH
VINCENT J MUSCARNERA, 492ND
GRP CAPT RET JOHN
MUSGRAVE, SM
ABNER G MUSSER JR, 445TH
CHARLES W MUSSETT, 491ST
JOSEPH N MUSURACA, 448TH
VINCENT N MUTI, 489TH
DONALD L MYERS, 445TH
JAMES I MYERS, 489TH
JAMES L MYERS, 445TH
JOSEPH G MYERS, 355FG
LAWRENCE P MYERS, 392ND
ROY & RAMONA MYERS, 453RD
WILLIAM E MYERS, 448TH
EDMUND MYLES, 489TH
LESTER NAASTAD, 453RD
FRANK A NACCARATO, 446TH
RICHARD D NACE, 448TH
JOHN A NACEY, 466TH
DEAN V NADEAU, 93RD
JOHN E NAGLE, 489TH
JACK E NAIFEH, 93RD
GEORGE E NAMEY, 453RD
ELIZABETH E NAPIER, 489TH, AM
JAMES P NAPOLEON, 446TH
BENJAMIN J NAPOLITANO, 491ST
JOHN C NAPOLITANO, 445TH
DAVID H NASH, 467TH
FRANCIS NASHWINTER, 392ND
RICHARD H NASON, 445TH
ARNOLD J NASS, 445TH
DAVID NATHANSON, 44TH, HDQ
RAYMOND J NATHE, 389TH
WILBERT J NAUGHTON, 458TH
WILLIAM R NAY, 445TH
FRANKLIN NAYLOR, 448TH
TOMMY NEAL, 491ST, 389TH
DAVID M NEALE, SM
PETER G NEARHOS, 458TH
MARK R NEARY MD, 453RD
JOHN K NEAST, 93RD

RUSSELL J NEATROUR, 453RD
ELDEN J NEDEAU, 44TH
JULIUS NEEDELMAN, 458TH
JAMES E NEEDHAM, 458TH
WORTH E NEEL, 446TH
CHARLES G NEELY, 458TH
LOY L NEEPER, 44TH
GIRARD NEFCY, 93RD
KENNETH NEIDENTHAL, 93RD
THOMAS J NEILAN, 453RD
ARLIN E NEILL, 389TH
KENNETH R NEITZKE, 491ST
DONALD O NELL, 453RD
FRED B NELLUMS, 44TH
JOHN K NELMS, 93RD
CECIL H NELSON, 491ST
CHARLES NELSON, 448TH
CLAIR R NELSON, 445TH
DONALD R NELSON, 445TH
ERIK A NELSON, 491ST, 44TH
JOSEPH C NELSON JR, 446TH
KENNETH R NELSON, 448TH
LLOYD M NELSON, 453RD
LOWELL B NELSON, 458TH
MAYNARD NELSON, 93RD, AM
MILTON NELSON, 389TH
ODIS E NELSON, 44TH
ROBERT E NELSON, 453RD
ROBERT J NELSON, 467TH
THOMAS A & MARY ANN NELSON,
453RD, 492ND, 467TH
WILFORD W NELSON, 93RD
WILLIAM C NELSON, 491ST, 389TH
WILLIAM C NEMCHOCK, 489TH
JOHN W NEMETH, 489TH
VICTOR F NEMETZ, 389TH
COL MICHAEL J NERI RET, 44TH
GEOFFREY T NESE, 466TH, AM
BERNEIL M NESS, 453RD
WILLARD F NESTER, 491ST, 93RD
WINKIE VAN DYKE NETTLETON,
HDQ
GEORGE R NETZEL, 453RD
BERNARD NEUMANN, 448TH
LTC CLARENCE W NEUMANN
RET, 93RD
LTC WILLIAM K NEUMANN RET,
389TH
COL CHARLES A NEUNDORF RET,
392ND
RICHARD L NEURER, 448TH
WALTER NEUSTADT JR, 392ND
DON C NEVILLE, 458TH
WILLIAM P NEWBOLD, 44TH
GEORGE NEWBURGER, 491ST
HENRY L NEWELL, 458TH
JAMES K NEWHOUSE, 467TH
R T NEWMAN, 446TH
BERNARD J NEWMARK, 458TH
DONALD NEWSHOLME, 491ST
LTC SID A NEWSOM RET, 491ST
E WILLIAM NEWTON, 491ST
FIELDER N NEWTON, 389TH
GENE NEWTON, 491ST
JOHM M NEWTON, 491ST
THOMAS C NEWTON, 445TH
SHIRLEY NICELY, 389TH, AM
RALPH A NICHOLAS JR, 448TH
CHARLES H NICHOLS, 389TH
EARL H NICHOLS, 466TH
GAIL L NICHOLS, 392ND
LAWRENCE C NICHOLS, 445TH
MATTHEW NICHOLS, 466TH
MILTON A NICHOLS, 448TH
ROBERT E NICHOLS, 492ND
FRANCIS S NICHOLSON, 389TH
WILLIAM J NICHOLSON, 458TH
ALVIN G NICKERSON, 448TH
HERBERT C NICKLAUS, 453RD
E B NICOLINI, 491ST
RALPH G NIELAND, 453RD
DONALD NIELSEN, 458TH
ROBERT P NIELSON, 458TH
HASKALL NIMAN, 392ND
HOWARD B NISBET, 93RD, HDQ
ALBERT L NIX, 458TH
RALPH W NIX, 489TH
COL ROBERT O NIXON RET,
458TH

JAMES V NOBLE, 448TH
MILO NOBLE, 466TH
WILEY S NOBLE, 3SAD
AUSTIN NOBLES, 446TH
J WILSON NODEN, 467TH
DALLAS NOFFSINGER, 453RD
JOSEPH F NOGAN, 467TH
GEORGE O NOKES, 489TH
BENJAMIN F NOLAN, HDQ
WEAVER J NOLAND, 491ST
WILFORD A NOLEN, 491ST
ARTHUR T NOONAN, 453RD
MERLYN W NORBY, 392ND
BERNARD NORDENSTROM,
446TH
LTC HAROLD NORDLICHT RET,
361FG
REV EDWARD J NORKETT, 491ST
DOROTHY ADCOCK NORMAN,
389TH, AM
FRANK NORMAN, 458TH
JOE B NORRELL, 489TH
ARTHUR L NORRIS, 389TH
CHARLES NORRIS, 44TH
CHARLES E NORRIS, 389TH
LIDA B COWAN NORRIS, HDQ
COL WILLIAM H NORRIS RET,
453RD
ARNO NORRMAN, 389TH
ROBERT A NORSEN, 44TH
JOHN A NORTAVAGE, 445TH
ANTHONY M NORTH, SM
BENTON T NORTH, 445TH
ALBERT L NORTHRUP JR, 448TH
DONALD A NORTON, 389TH
FRANKLIN P NORTON, 491ST
ELWOOD & LUCILLE NOTHSTEIN,
466TH
DOMINIC J NOTTE, 491ST
EDWARD R NOVAK, 467TH
ALEXANDER NOVICKOFF, 389TH
EUGENE J NOWAK, 446TH
JOHN C NOWAK, 44TH
LEON J NOWICKI, 389TH
STEPHEN T NUCKOLS, 389TH, AM
THEODORE NUSSBICKEL, 466TH
DANIEL NYBAKKEN, 491ST
JAMES H NYE, SM
LTC JOHNSON A NYE JR RET,
HDQ
HENRY NYKAMP, 93RD
RICHARD W NYMAN, 458TH,
355FG
EDWARD F O'BRIEN, 466TH, AM
FRANK J O'BRIEN, 491ST
JACK W O'BRIEN, 448TH
JAMES E O'BRIEN, 44TH
JAMES J O'BRIEN, 93RD
JOSEPH D O'BRIEN, 446TH
RICHARD C O'BRIEN, 458TH,
44TH, 466TH
PATRICK J O'CARROLL, 466TH
JOSEPH G O'CONNELL, 453RD
DANIEL F O'CONNOR, 93RD
JAMES F O'CONNOR, 446TH
STEPHEN O'CONNOR, 389TH
WALTER J O'CONNOR, 389TH
AL R O'DONNELL, 448TH
EUGENE D O'DONNELL, 458TH
JOHN J O'DONNELL, 466TH
RAYMOND P O'DONNELL, 389TH
THOMAS J O'DWYER, 453RD
DONALD R O'FEE, 445TH
JOHN E O'GRADY, 93RD
J S O'GWIN, 93RD
HENRY P O'HAGAN, 93RD
THOMAS J O'HALLORAN, 445TH
JOHN D O'LEARY, 453RD
WALTER A O'LOUGHLIN, 489TH
LTC MALCOLM L O'NEALE JR RET,
389TH
WILLIAM J O'NEIL, 453RD, 93RD,
44TH
JOHN H O'NEILL, 448TH
THOMAS A O'NEILL, 445TH
DONALD W O'REILLY, 44TH, 491ST
DON J O'ROURKE, 448TH
WILLIAM J O'SHAUGHNESSY,
491ST, 448TH

LTC HARLAN G OAKES RET,
466TH
HARRY W OAKES, 392ND
DONALD R OAKLEY, SM
J OAKLEY, SM
ALBERT G OARD, 492ND
JAMES M OBEREMBT, 491ST
LTC ROBERT E OBERSCHMID
RET, 93RD
JOSEPH P OBICI, 93RD
MERLIN D ODEGAARD, 445TH
JOHN G ODER, 467TH
KARL R OESTERLE, 466TH
FLOYD C OGLESBY, 445TH
JOE OLANDESE, 466TH
JAMES OLD, 445TH
L C OLDHAM JR, HDQ
DONALD J OLDS, 453RD, SM
ODO OLIVA, 453RD
FRANK J OLIVE, 445TH
ALBERT OLIVEIRA, 491ST
WILLIAM D OLMSTEAD, 489TH
DAVID J OLNEY, 458TH, AM
JAMES E OLNEY, 458TH
ARTHUR W OLSON, 392ND
BEN OLSON, 466TH
ERLING A OLSON, 392ND
SM/SGT KENNETH D OLSON,
448TH
KENNETH R OLSON, 389TH
MILTON OLSON, 448TH
RICHARD C OLSON, 467TH
EDWARD J ONDRASIK, 448TH
PERRY ONSTOT, 392ND
MARILYN N OONK, 446TH, AM
GERARD M OPITZ, 389TH
ARCHIE E OPLINGER, 458TH
LEON OPPIS, 453RD
WARREN E OPPMANN, 489TH
ANDREW W OPSATA, 389TH
NANCY OPSATA, 389TH, AM
FRANK OREHOWSKY, 44TH
DAVID ORENBACH, 392ND
WILLIAM L ORIENT, 93RD
ALLEN R ORR, 453RD
SANTOS ORTEGA JR, 458TH
BEN ORTENBERG, 392ND
COL HARRY L ORTHMAN RET,
492ND, 44TH
VERONICA P ORZECHOWSKI,
445TH, AM
JOHN A OSBORN, 448TH
WILLIAM C OSBORNE, 466TH
MARK OSMENT, 392ND
CARL F OSMOND, 44TH
MILTON V OSNES, 44TH
TONY OSOJNICKI, 492ND, 467TH
RAY OSTERMAN, 93RD
ORLAND H OSWALD, 93RD
DONALD J OSWELL, 446TH
ALBERT J OTERO, 93RD
WILFRED J OTT, 389TH
LTC ROBERT H OTTMAN RET,
445TH, 2CW
BERNARD L OVERFELT, HDQ
H R OVERHOLT, 392ND, 492ND
CHARLES A OVERSTREET, 491ST
COL ROY W OWEN JR RET, 44TH
LEWIS W OWENS, 467TH
ROGER G OWENS, 389TH
TODD L OWENS, 446TH
CASIMER OZAR, 44TH
WALTER J PAC, 458TH
JAMES T PACE, 489TH
JOHN E PACE JR, 93RD
WINFORD R PACE, 453RD
JOSEPH R PACHUTA, 389TH
MARION S PACIOREK, 44TH
LTC KENNETH Q PADDOCK RET,
392ND
VINCENT M PADILLA, 448TH
EARLE C PAGE JR, 467TH
JOHN PAGE, SM
MARCUS G PAGE, 445TH
MIKE PAGE, SM
FRED C PAINE, 446TH, 93RD
CHARLES E PAINTER, 445TH
FRANK A PALADINO, 448TH
VINCENT J PALE, 453RD

ROBERT PALESTRI, 93RD
RICHARD PALKA, 93RD
LTC JOHN A PALLER RET, 491ST
COL JAMES L PALLOURAS RET,
445TH, HDQ
ARTHUR C PALMER, 448TH
GEORGE M PALMER, 93RD
LEWIS V PALMER, 489TH
OTIS M PALMER, 453RD
SAMUEL PALMER, 44TH
VINCENT A PALMER, 466TH
GUY C PANNELL, 93RD, 389TH
MAX C PAPUGA, 458TH
DONALD I PARCELLS, 453RD,
445TH
EDWARD J PARCIAK, 448TH
EDWARD PARETTI, 448TH
SAM PARISI, 93RD
NEIL E PARK DDS, 93RD, 389TH
COL PAUL L PARK RET, 446TH
DAVID H PARKE, 453RD
JOHN R PARKE, 389TH
BRUCE H PARKER, 466TH
CHARLES M PARKER, 453RD
EARL S PARKER, 392ND
EUGENE D PARKER, 467TH
FRANK S PARKER, 453RD
LTC GEORGE H PARKER RET,
466TH
HENRY P PARKER, 453RD
COL JACK PARKER RET, 448TH
JAMES C PARKER, 445TH
JOEL PARKER, 44TH
JUDY PARKER, 467TH, AM
LEWIS W PARKER JR, 14CW
THEODORE PARKER, 491ST
WILLIAM C PARKER JR, 491ST, AM
LTC RICHARD J PARKES RET,
445TH
RICHARD N PARKES, 445TH, AM
ARCHIE O PARKS, 446TH
EARL M PARKS, 448TH
GEORGE W PARKS, 458TH
ROBERT T PARKS, 389TH
BEN PARNELL, 492ND, AM
BERNARD PAROLY, 392ND
JACK C PARRISH, 93RD
ROLLAND L PARROTT, 445TH
LTC THOMAS B PARRY RET, 93RD
EDWARD A PARSONS, 491ST
GEORGE F PARSONS, 93RD
PHILIP H PARSONS, 453RD
THOMAS S PARSONS, 44TH
JAMES W PARTRIDGE, 389TH
LTC RAYMOND B PARTRIDGE
RET, 446TH
W R PARTRIDGE, 44TH
STEVEN M PASSNER, SM
ROBERT E PATEK, 458TH
T/SGT THEODORE P PATEREK
RET, 491ST
VINCENT J PATLA JR, 446TH
WALTER M PATRICK, 44TH
WALTER E PATSCHEIDER, 453RD
BRUCE R PATTERSON, 445TH, AM
DAVID & JOAN PATTERSON,
445TH
DAVID PATTERSON, SM
EARL S PATTERSON SR, 448TH
HAROLD F PATTERSON, 491ST
COL JAMES R PATTERSON RET,
448TH
WILLIAM A PATTERSON, 446TH
DANIEL C PATTON, 445TH
GEORGE T PATTON, 56FG
LTC JOHN M PATTON JR RET,
446TH
NOLAN G PATTON, 467TH
WALLACE W PATTON, 445TH
MARGARET N PAUL, SM
LTC MARVIN M PAUL RET, 492ND,
467TH
WILLIAM L PAUL, 44TH
JAMES H PAULEY, 445TH, 458TH
PAUL F PAULI, 489TH
JAMES A PAULMANN, 453RD
HERBERT H PAULSON, 466TH
BRUCE H PAULY, 44TH, HDQ
DONALD PAUMEN, 446TH

BRUNO PAUSSA, 445TH
HERBERT L PAUSTIAN, 93RD
JOHN E PAUTLER, 467TH
EUGENE F PAUZE, 93RD
JOHN R PAXSON, 448TH
JAMES L PAYNE, 446TH
LAURA H PAYNE, HDQ, AM
MELVIN K PAYNE, 448TH
LAWRENCE S PEABODY, 93RD
LTC STUART M PEACE JR RET,
466TH
HERMAN A PEACHER, 458TH
MAJ CLOYD E PEACOCK RET,
445TH
RALPH E PEACOCK, 489TH
ARTHUR R PEARCE, 491ST
DELMO M PEARCE, 448TH
J A PEARCE DDS, 458TH
JESSE E PEARCE, 446TH
LTC ALBERT V PEARSON RET,
446TH
LTC ELMER W PEARSON RET,
93RD
JOHN T PEARSON, 392ND,
492ND
LEO L PEARSON JR, 446TH
C F PEASE, 389TH
FRANK H PEASE, 389TH
ROSCOE PEASE JR, 467TH, 93RD,
492ND 479TH
WILLARD O PEASE JR, 445TH
DARRELL G PECK, 93RD
FRANCIS J PECK, 44TH
LTC JOHN W PECK RET, 44TH
WILBUR J PECKA, 44TH
ALBERT H PEDE, 389TH
HENRY PEDICONE, 448TH
ROBERT E PEDIGO, 453RD
DAVID A PEDRICK, 446TH
HARRY M PEEK, 446TH
LEROY PEELER, 458TH
VICTOR F PEGG, 93RD
JOSEPH D PEGRAM, 491ST
KENNETH M PEIFFER, 491ST
ROBERT L PEIPERT, 389TH
ROBERT L PELLICAN, 466TH
JOSEPH O PELOQUIN, 44TH
PAUL O PELOQUIN, 93RD
JACK D PELTON, 445TH
CLYDE D PEMBERTON JR, 489TH
LTC HAL PENDLETON RET, 44TH
LEO Z PENN, 458TH
WILLARD T PENNINGTON, 392ND
GARNER A PENNOCK, 93RD
JAMES B PENTZ, 466TH
FRANCIS T PEPIN, 93RD
FRANKLIN C PEPPER, 453RD
ANGELO PERCACCIOLO, 448TH
FRANK D PERDUE, 93RD
LTC ERNEST PEREZ RET, 93RD
CHARLES J PERKINS, 445TH
FAY E PERKINS, 467TH
LOUIS B PERKINS, 446TH
W DALE PERKINS, 466TH
JAMES C PERRIN JR, 458TH
EDWARD J PERRO, 453RD
JOHN J PERRONE, 489TH
CHARLES W PERRY, 446TH
HERBERT E PERRY, 458TH, HDQ
COL JAMES R PERRY JR RET,
44TH
JOSEPH PERRY, 389TH
PATRICK J PERRY, 491ST
PAUL J PERRY, 492ND
WALLACE E PERRY, 491ST
ROLAND F PERSON, 467TH
DOMINICK E PESCE, 93RD
WILLIAM J PESCHKE, 389TH
EUGENE M PETAGINE, 448TH
JAMES L PETEETE, 458TH
CHARLES B PETERS, 458TH
HELEN PETERS, 458TH, AM
JAMES PETERS, 44TH
JAMES F PETERS, 467TH
MARSHA KOORNDYK PETERS,
389TH, AM
RALPH E PETERS, 458TH
ROBERT W PETERS, 445TH
WADE D PETERS, 44TH

MAY DELLE PETERSEN,
467TH, AM
CARL D PETERSON, 466TH
CARL M PETERSON, 467TH
COL CHARLES H PETERSON RET,
389TH
CLIFFORD L PETERSON, 392ND
COBERN V PETERSON, 458TH
DEAN E PETERSON, 448TH
DONALD L PETERSON, 44TH
EDWIN R PETERSON, 445TH
JIM PETERSON, 453RD
MARY J PETERSON, 448TH, AM
NEWELL H PETERSON, 489TH
OSMON N PETERSON, 467TH
RICHARD A PETERSON, 389TH
ROBERT G PETERSON,
453RD, AM
ROBERT W PETERSON, 467TH
ROY A PETERSON JR, 389TH
WALTER E PETERSON, 448TH
MIKE R PETIX, 466TH
GEORGE PETRIK, 44TH
GEORGE PETRILYAK, 93RD
JOHN G PETROCELLI, 389TH
KENNETH A PETRY, 491ST
ROBERT W PETTERSEN, 466TH
GEORGE CLYDE PETTEY, 93RD
JOHN W PETTEY, 389TH
HARVEY P PETTIT, 467TH
NEAL W PETTIT, 448TH
WILLIAM J PEVELER, 445TH
PAUL F PFENNINGER, 453RD
JOSEPH R PFIFFNER, 458TH
BEN J PFISTER, 448TH
PAUL H PFLUG, 389TH, 453RD
WILLIAM J PFLUM MD, 453RD
CHESTER A PHELAN, 389TH
GEORGE A PHELPS, 392ND
HOWARD K PHILIPS, 446TH
EDWIN W PHILLIPS, 489TH
GEORGE A PHILLIPS JR, 446TH
GERALD D PHILLIPS, 453RD
JOHN W PHILLIPS, 453RD
NORMAN PHILLIPS, 446TH
R H PHILLIPS, 44TH
WILLIAM G PHILLIPS, 466TH
RUSSELL C PHILPOTT, 93RD
HARRY A PICARIELLO, 491ST
ROY J PICHT, 458TH
RICHARD S PICK, 44TH
FRANK M PICKERING, 489TH
LOUISE M PICKERING, 467TH, AM
JAMES C PICKETT, 446TH
FRED L PIELA, 44TH
HOWARD W PIER JR, 389TH
ARTHUR M PIERCE, 389TH
DONALD G PIERCE, 453RD
ROBERT G PIERCE, 44TH
JEFF PIERCY, 389TH
RALPH PIETRANGELO, 389TH
PAUL W PIFER MD, 446TH
JAMES PIKE, 448TH
L T PILAND, 467TH
THEDA W PILLOW, 445TH, AM
WILLIAM Z PIMM, 389TH
MARVIN L PINKERTON, 466TH
ROBERT J PINTER, 467TH
GEORGE H PINZGER, 466TH
CHARLES A PIPER, 392ND
S L PIPER, HDQ
ROBERT F PIPES, 466TH
ACHILLE PIRRI, 4FG
ALBERT F PISHIONERI, 446TH
ARNOLD A PISKIN, 458TH
MICHAEL PITASSI, 361FG
MICHAEL PITASSI, 361FG
JAMES R PITCHER, 446TH
RICHARD L PITTENGER, 389TH
WILSON H PITTS, 491ST
FRANK PIWOWARSKI, 466TH
ALFRED A PIZZATO, 458TH
JOSEPH R PLACHY, 445TH
MILTON M PLANCHE, 392ND
H MICHAEL PLANKA, 445TH
EUGENE C PLANKEY, 458TH
PHILIP PLASKON, 44TH
NICHOLAS B PLASMATI, 453RD
LTC WILMER A PLATE RET, 489TH

LYLE P PLATNER, 445TH, 448TH
LTC CHARLES A PLATT RET, 448TH
CHARLES J PLATZ, 445TH
GEORGE C PLAYER, 392ND
S A PLEDGER, 448TH
FRANK T PLESA, 445TH
RALPH W PLETCHER, 466TH
WILLIAM V PLETCHER, 389TH
ALEX PLISHKA, 491ST
BILL PLOEN, 445TH
FELIX C PLOVIE, 491ST
PRESTON F PLUMB, 446TH
EDWARD S POCZTOWSKI, 458TH
HAROLD S PODOLSKY, 448TH
THEODORE PODRAZA, 389TH
HARVEY L POFF JR, 458TH
HUGO A POFI JR, 93RD
LTC ALBERT F POGUE RET, 466TH, 458TH
ERNEST J POHLE, 389TH
PAUL R POITRAS, 453RD, 392ND
FRANCIS E POKORNY, 448TH, AM
BARUYR A POLADIAN, 448TH
WARREN J POLAND, 453RD
FRANK J POLEC, 458TH
COL WARREN A POLKING RET, 392ND
THOMAS C POLLIARD, 458TH
CHARLES J POLLMAN, HDQ
FLORENCE STAFINSKY POLLNER, HDQ
GERALD A POLZIN, 492ND
BERNARD S POMERANTZ, 389TH
LEONARD PONDER, 446TH
EMILIO A PONTILLO, 489TH
MRS C K POOL, 458TH, AM
CHARLES H POOL, 458TH, AM
NORMAN C POORMAN, 448TH
EDWARD POPEK, 392ND
FRANCIS L POPHAM, 389TH
WILLIAM F POPPE, 44TH
SAMUEL B POPPEL, 392ND
FREDERICK POPPER, 458TH
THADDEUS C POPRAWA, 389TH
THOMAS E PORTA, 491ST
BURL L PORTER, 445TH
DONALD L PORTER, 93RD
EUGENE T PORTER, 491ST
FREDERICK R PORTER, 467TH
LAWRENCE W PORTER, 445TH
ROBERT L PORTER, 466TH
ROBERT W PORTERFIELD, 489TH
WALLACE A PORTOUW, 489TH
ALFRED D PORTSMORE, 445TH
STEPHEN M POSNER, 389TH, 445TH
MARCUS L POTEET JR, 491ST
EDWARD M POTTER, 445TH
EDWARD S POTTER, 389TH
JACK POTTLE, 389TH
RAMSAY D POTTS, 93RD, 453RD
PETER POULAS, 453RD
PANOS L POULOS, 458TH
THOMAS G POVEY, 445TH
EDGAR J POWELL, 467TH
EDWARD S POWELL, 93RD
HOLLIS C POWELL JR, 392ND
NORMAN A POWELL, 44TH
ROBERT W POWELL, 445TH
WILLIAM I POWELL, 446TH
JOE C POWER, 389TH
BERNARD R POWERS, 491ST
MAJ DAVID B POWERS RET, 389TH
HARRY H POWERS, 93RD
JAMES C POWERS, 491ST
JOHN T POWERS, 448TH
ORVILLE W POWERS, 389TH
LLOYD W PRANG, 453RD
CHARLES H PRATT, HDQ
JOHN C PREDARI, 389TH
JOHN L PREDGEN, 489TH
DONALD J PRESCOTT, 467TH
R L PRESCOTT JR, 445TH
LTC RICHARD J PREZIOSE RET, 93RD
A J PRIBUSH, 389TH
CONSTANCE M PRICE, 489TH, AM

DONALD PRICE, 389TH
JAKE D PRICE JR, 445TH
ORA M PRICE, 389TH
LTC ARTHUR L PRICHARD RET, 467TH
JACK W PRILEY, 467TH
ROY J PRIMM, 458TH
JEROME S PRINCE, 445TH
RICHARD C PRINCE, 389TH
TONY PRINS, 93RD
GEORGE A PROCUNIAR, 467TH
GEORGE D PROLLOCK, 467TH
ROBERT N PROMEN, 491ST
DR WILLIAM D PROPPE, 466TH
HENRY M PROPPER, 392ND
BERTRAND J PROST, 392ND
PETER PROTICH, 448TH
TONY PROVENZANO, 489TH
SAM M PROVINE, 448TH
BERNARD L PRUEHER, 389TH
REV DONALD F PRUITT, 93RD
JACK C PRUITT, 389TH
JAMES R PRUITT, 448TH
ARNOLD A PRYOR, 467TH
DONALD V PRYOR, 445TH
ANTHONY A PUCA, 389TH
BEATRICE B PUCH, HDQ
CHARLES PUCHALSKI, 389TH
GERALD L PUCILLO, 467TH
COL FLOYD J PUGH RET, 467TH
ERNEST PUGLISI, 44TH
CECIL L PULLEN, 448TH
RICHARD I PULSE, 458TH
JOHN N PUPPO, 489TH
THOMAS F PURCELL, 389TH
NORMAN E PURDY, 44TH
BETSY SCHWEPPE PURSH, HDQ, AM
JAMES PUSATERI, 458TH
LTC STANLEY J PUSKO RET, 491ST
LAWRENCE C PUTGENTER, 448TH
STEPHEN PUTZIGER, 392ND
E J PYLE, 458TH
LARRY T PYLE, SM
HAROLD J PYNE, SM
RAY R PYTEL, 445TH
EARL QUACKENBUSH JR, 458TH
ROMAINE C QUACKENBUSH, 445TH
JOHN L QUAIL JR, 392ND, 44TH
LOUIS J QUARTERMAN, 491ST
ALBERT E QUERBACH, 445TH
LEONIL E QUESNEL, 389TH, 453RD
ARMOND N QUIGLEY, 448TH
WILLIAM L QUIGLEY, 448TH
COL RICHARD M QUIMBY JR RET, 93RD
REV JOSEPH E QUINLAN OMI, 445TH
ROBERT A QUINLIVAN, 93RD
ARTHUR J QUINN, 93RD
LOUIS F QUINN, 392ND
CHARLES W QUIRK, 458TH
JOSEPH F QUIRK JR, 446TH
FRANK J RAAB, 389TH
NICK P RABAGIA JR, 448TH
HAROLD C RABIDEAU, 458TH
JUDITH M RABSEY, 389TH, AM
KENNETH J RACHAU, 93RD
WILFRED R RACINE, 458TH
LEE W RACKLEY, 389TH
ARNOLD RADDE, 448TH
LTC HUBERT F RADFORD RET, 93RD
THOMAS K RADO, 453RD
EDWARD A RADOSEVICH, 445TH
NICK RADOSEVICH, 453RD
NORMAN E RAEBER, 453RD
NORMAN E RAEBER, 453RD
DR STANLEY I RAFALO, 93RD
DANIEL C RAGAN, 446TH
JOHN F RAGIN JR, HDQ
JOHN H RAINEY, 445TH, 489TH
EDITH RAINWATER, 467TH, AM
JOHN R RAINWATER, 448TH

RAY LYNN RAINWATER, 467TH, AM
ROSS A RAINWATER, 467TH, AM
KENNETH RAISCH, 489TH
CHARLES A RAJDA, 389TH
GEORGE E RAKE DC, 93RD, 389TH
SIDNEY W RALEY, 446TH
CARL G RAMBO, 445TH
R J RAMBOSKY, 467TH
GEORGE RAMERMAN, 458TH
FRANCIS X RAMIE, 489TH
JOE R RAMIREZ, 467TH
PAT RAMM, SM
RICHARD I RAMP, 445TH
DR W K RAMSTAD, 458TH
WILLIAM V RAND, 44TH
ALFRED S RANDALL, 492ND
JOHN C RANDALL, 453RD
MILTON F RANDALL, 458TH
WALTER B RANDALL JR, 489TH
HARDING W RANDLETT, 93RD
DONALD A RANEY, 458TH
DONALD F RANSOM, 448TH
EINO J RANTA, 392ND
DAVID RAPOPORT, 445TH
ANTHONY RAPP, 93RD
HERMAN L RAPP, 458TH
LTC WILSON A RAPP RET, 467TH
J L RASCH JR, 93RD
MELVIN N RASMUSSEN, 458TH
WILLIAM RASMUSSEN, 445TH
ROBERT J RASP, 389TH
PATRICK S RASPANTE, 448TH
ALBERT RATNER, 491ST
GEORGE H RAUH, 445TH
KARL H RAUSCH, 445TH
DALE E RAUSCHER, 44TH
HERBERT RAVIS, 44TH
JOHN M RAWLINGS, 44TH, 466TH, 458TH
DAVID J RAWLINS, SM
CARRY D RAWLS, 458TH
HARRY N RAWLS, 492ND
CHARLES W RAY, 44TH
RALPH H RAY, 445TH
SIDNEY L RAY, 445TH
DAN I RAYMOND, 389TH
VINCE RE, 467TH
HAROLD A READ JR, 466TH
ALEXANDER READE, 466TH
DANIEL J READING, 453RD
DOMENIC P REALI, 467TH
HARRIS A REAMES, 446TH
ROBERT J REASONER, 44TH
JULIUS REBELES, 448TH
ALVIN H REBSAMEN, 489TH
BASIL D RED JR, 445TH
D S REDABAUGH, 389TH
JOE W REDDEN, 446TH
DAVID G REDFERN, 491ST
GLEN F REDMOND, 44TH
PHILIP P REDMOND, 489TH
JAMES D REDUS, 44TH, 489TH
CLAUDE W REECE, 389TH
CLYDE E REECE, 392ND
CHARLES A REED, 93RD
CLIFFORD C REED JR, 458TH
DARRELL E REED, 445TH
DAVID B REED, 93RD
DONALD F REED, 392ND
FRANK A REED, 445TH
JOHN A REED JR, 445TH, 492ND
WILLIAM R REED, 446TH
RALPH F REEDER, 448TH
LAWRENCE R REEP, 448TH
JAMES & EDNA REEVES, HDQ
CHARLES E REEVS, 489TH
FLOYD W REFSAL, 392ND
LOUIS REGA, 466TH
BERNARD C REGAN, 467TH
T/SGT EDWARD REGAN RET, 93RD
THOMAS G REGAN, 389TH
WILLIAM B REGISTER, 458TH
JOHN T REHAK, 445TH, 4FG, HDQ
DAVID W REICH SR, 389TH
STANLEY REICH, 44TH
WALTER E REICHERT, 44TH

ROBERT D REICHLE, 453RD, 93RD
HOWARD E REICHLEY, 445TH, 389TH, 466TH
JAMES W REID JR, 93RD
JUANITA REID, 453RD, AM
JAMES G REIDY, 453RD
EDWARD J REILLY, 93RD
JOHN J REILLY, 491ST
JOSEPH M REILLY, 467TH
W DONALD REILLY, 93RD
RUSSELL REINDAL, 448TH
HERBERT REINDERS, 453RD
VIRGIL REINDERS, 467TH
COL ROLLIN C REINECK RET, 93RD, HDQ
EDWARD E REINHARDT, 446TH
ELMER H REINHART, 44TH
ROBERT J REINTGEN, 453RD, AM
HERBERT REIS, 453RD
WILLIAM REISS, 446TH
ROLAND L RENAUD, 467TH
WILLIAM A RENDALL, 44TH
RETO RENFER, SM
ROBERT K RENN, 458TH
ROBERT W RENNER, 389TH
MITCHELL P RENO, 446TH
MAX H RENOV, 389TH
ROBERT J RENTSCHLER, 448TH
J FRED RENTZ, 467TH
RALPH L RENZI, 491ST
COL JOHN REPOLA RET, 389TH
ARMAND P RESCIGNO, 492ND
THOMAS F RETO, 466TH
CHARLES W REUS, 453RD
MAJ JOSEPH H REUS RET, 445TH
MAJ JOHN D REWEY RET, 467TH
JOHN O REX, HDQ
FLOYD C REYNOLDS, 448TH
GEORGE A REYNOLDS, 458TH, AM
H MAXEY REYNOLDS, 44TH
JAMES E REYNOLDS, 392ND
LAWRENCE A REYNOLDS, 93RD
ROBERT J REYNOLDS, 466TH
WILLIAM E REYNOLDS, 93RD
CAPT FRANK J REZEK RET, 93RD
RAY J RHOADES, 93RD
MAJ JOHN M RHOADS RET, 389TH
LOUIS P RHOADS, 467TH
CLIFFORD B RHODES, 453RD
JOHN L RHODES, 44TH
RICHARD S RHODES, 445TH
OTIS L RHONEY, 445TH
ALDO A RICCI, 453RD
ANTHONY P RICCIO, 491ST
DR JOHN W RICE JR, 467TH
MARTIN A RICE, 93RD
MARY GILL RICE, SM
PETER J RICE, 389TH
RICHARD P RICE, 491ST
MAJ ROBERT RICE RET, 93RD
WILLIAM T RICE, 466TH
WILLIAM W RICE, 392ND
GEORGE F RICH JR, 453RD, 389TH
ROBERT H RICHARDS JR, 392ND
SARA L RICHARDS, 389TH, AM
WILLIAM M RICHARDS, 389TH
COL WILLIAM W RICHARDS RET, 446TH
CHARLES E RICHARDSON, 93RD
H E RICHARDSON, 389TH
JAMES A RICHARDSON, 44TH
LTC W H RICHESON JR RET, 392ND
MAJ DONALD L RICHISSIN RET, 445TH
JOHN B RICHMOND, 448TH
GEORGE C RICHNER, 392ND
JOHN J RICKEY, 392ND
ROBERT A RICKS, 44TH
CARL U RIDDLE, 467TH
WILLIAM I RIDDLEBERGER, 392ND
WILLIAM B RIDGWAY, 467TH
JEAN J RIDLEY, 445TH
LESLIE W RIDLEY, 448TH
BERTHA M RIEDEL, AM

JAMES E RIEDEL, 446TH
HERMAN B RIEKER, 492ND
VINCENT L RIEL, 446TH
H C RIEPENHOFF, 448TH
LAWRENCE P RIESEN, 458TH
GEORGE M RIESS, 93RD
CLELL B RIFFLE, 389TH
WILLIAM C RIGG, 491ST
WILLIAM W RIGGLE, 492ND
KENNETH F RIGGS, 93RD
COL JAMES D RIGLEY JR RET, 458TH
VERNON W RIGSBEE, 467TH
DR EMIL F RIHA, 392ND
ALBERT J RILEY, 392ND
H O RILEY, 448TH
JUDGE RICHARD J RINEBOLT, 4FG
CHARLES R RINEHIMER, 446TH
RONALD L RING JR, 389TH
FRANK RINGHOFFER, 458TH
ALFRED P RINKE, 392ND
RICHARD M RINTO, 491ST
ELEANOR BARTMESS RIORDAN, 44TH, AM
JOHN J P RIORDAN, 448TH
GEORGE A RISKO, 491ST
J A RISLEY, 446TH
EDWIN W RITTER, 93RD
EDWARD M RITTS, 466TH
DENNIS RIVA, SM
RAMO F RIVA, 458TH
ARTHUR L RIVKIN, 466TH
DOMINIC J RIZZO, 446TH
LTC HAROLD D ROACH RET, 446TH
WILLIAM E ROACH, 355TH
BONNY E ROARK, 448TH
WILLIAM R ROAT, 446TH
HOWARD H ROBB, 44TH
E PAUL ROBBINS, 389TH
EDWARD E ROBBINS, 458TH
MRS EVERETT M ROBBINS, 491ST, AM
CHARLES F ROBBS, 489TH
STANLEY J ROBENS, 392ND
PERRY M ROBERSON, 453RD
RICHARD C ROBERT, 453RD
WILLIAM & HAZEL ROBERTIE, 44TH
CHARLES L ROBERTS, 389TH
CHARLES L ROBERTS, 93RD
LTC CLAYTON R ROBERTS RET, 44TH
DANIEL O ROBERTS, 458TH
EARL J ROBERTS, 453RD
JOHN F ROBERTS, 458TH
JULIAN L ROBERTS, 466TH
KEITH E ROBERTS, 392ND
LEWIS E ROBERTS, 458TH
MERTON J ROBERTS, HDQ
WILLIAM F ROBERTS, SM
GEORGE S ROBERTSON, 448TH
JASPER ROBERTSON, 467TH
JIMMY T ROBERTSON, 389TH
RICHARD S ROBERTSON, 458TH
NOREL B ROBEY, 453RD
ANTONIA ROBINSON, 392ND, AM
BERL ROBINSON, 492ND
CLARK L ROBINSON, 389TH
JOHN H ROBINSON, 445TH
RUSSELL M ROBINSON, 453RD
WALTER J ROBINSON, 467TH
WILLIAM E ROBINSON, 458TH
M/SGT WINFRED ROBINSON, 458TH
DAVID W ROBISON, 93RD
MELVIN J ROBISON, 466TH
WILLIAM G ROBISON, 446TH
RONALD ROBSON, 466TH
RALPH E ROBY, 389TH
HAROLD J ROCHE, 489TH
COL JOHN R ROCHE RET, 93RD
JOHN W ROCHE, 466TH
THOMAS M ROCKETT, 389TH
WILLARD A RODERMEL, 458TH
F WALTER RODGERS, 489TH

FREDERICK V RODGERS, 392ND, 492ND

H LEWIS RODGERS, 453RD

CMS ERNIE RODRIGUEZ RET, 389TH

JOSEPH N RODRIGUEZ, 448TH

PEDRO T RODRIGUEZ, 44TH

EDWARD L ROETTELE JR, 458TH

CALVIN H ROEVER, 392ND

ELI ROFFWARG, 448TH

RAYMOND J ROGALA, 453RD

EUGENE ROGERS, 466TH

KENNETH L ROGERS, 489TH

ROBERT S ROGERS, 453RD

TOURIDA A ROGLEDI, 453RD

MANUEL M ROGOFF, 389TH

HAROLD C ROHMER, 453RD

CLASON L ROHRER, 491ST

JOHN C ROHRSSEN, 466TH

ERIC A ROKICKI, 458TH, AM

RICK & CECELIA ROKICKI, 458TH

JAMES A ROLLO, 467TH

RICHARD D ROLLO, 453RD

ED E ROLOFF, 445TH

PETER A ROMANO, 448TH

JOHN ROMEO, 44TH

COL ELMER J ROMIGH JR RET, 466TH

JIM ROMITO, 445TH

FRANCIS P RONDINONE, 491ST

JAMES E RONSICK, 93RD

MERAL O ROOD, 467TH

LTC VERNON J ROOD RET, 467TH

CHARLES W ROOF, 458TH

DONALD W ROOT, 491ST

JOSEPH J ROSACKER, 93RD

MAJ PHILIP E ROSE RET, 392ND

WARREN T ROSEBOROUGH, 492ND, 467TH

EUGENE D ROSEN, 44TH, 446TH

EDWARD G ROSENBERG, 453RD, 389TH

EDWIN ROSENBERG, 44TH

JOHN E ROSENBERG, 392ND

PHILIP ROSENBERG, 448TH

IRVING J ROSENBLUM, 453RD

CARL B ROSENDAHL, 489TH

ROBERT ROSENDAHL, 491ST

TIMOTHY J ROSENDAHL, 489TH, AM

HERBERT ROSENKOFF, 466TH

COL JOHN J ROSENOW RET, 93RD

BURT L ROSS, 389TH

JOHN G ROSS, 453RD

JOHN P ROSS, 458TH

MIRIAM ROSS, 445TH, AM

SHELDON B ROSS, 466TH

LTC WILLIAM O ROSS RET, 448TH

BILL A ROSSER, 44TH

ROBERT ROSSITER, 93RD

WALTER E ROSSON, 389TH

ROBERT G ROTEN, 93RD

JOHN E ROTH, 389TH

JOHN M ROTH, 453RD

JOSEPH E ROTH, 466TH

A E ROTHCHILD, 467TH

CECIL T ROTHROCK, 392ND

MARILYN ROTHSCHILD, 467TH, AM

ROBERT R ROTTMAN, 466TH

HERMAN H ROTZ, 458TH

FREDERICK J ROUGHAN, 445TH

LTC JOSEPH D ROURE RET, 93RD

W G ROW, 93RD

HARRY E ROWAN, 389TH

CLAIR D ROWE, 448TH

JOHN C ROWE, 448TH

EDWIN F ROWEHL, 467TH

GARY ROWELL, SM

CHARLES B ROWLEY JR, 93RD

CLEO H ROWLEY, 389TH, 489TH

LYNNE ROWLEY, 467TH, AM

STANLEY I ROWSON, 489TH, 93RD

EARL A ROY SR, 467TH

GAYLON J ROYER, 489TH

JAMES H ROYER JR, 446TH

VICTOR F ROYS, 448TH

MAJ MORRIS ROYSTER RET, 466TH

LESTER W ROZDALOVSKY, 491ST

LTC ROBERT N RUARK RET, 458TH

HAROLD C RUBENDALL, 467TH

EDWARD M RUBICH, 389TH

LTC DAVID S RUBIN RET, 392ND, 44TH, 491ST

ALBERT F RUBY, 44TH

CLARE F RUBY, 467TH

CAROLYN RUCK, 448TH, AM

GALE M RUCKER, 491ST

PETER RUDD, SM

CATHY RUDDEK, 466TH, AM

B J RUDDER, 458TH

HERBERT RUDH, 445TH

EDMUND J RUDNICKI, 389TH

STEVE RUDNYK, 93RD

CHESTER RUDZEWICZ, 458TH

ROBERT C RUFFCORN, 467TH

JOHN S RUGGERI, 492ND

DOMENICK R RUGGIERO, 389TH

FRANK A RUGGIERO, 453RD

ROBERTO RUIZ, 389TH

IRWIN A RUMLER, 489TH

LUTHER D RUMMAGE JR, 448TH

DALE E RUMMENS, 448TH

GEORGE J RUNBLAD JR, 453RD

E RALPH RUNDELL, 458TH

REV THEODORE RUNYAN, 448TH

HARRY E RUPELT, 489TH

WALTER H RUPP, 389TH

RICHARD O RUSCH JR, 389TH

JERRY J RUSS, 448TH

CHARLES C RUSSELL, 467TH

CHARLES F RUSSELL, 445TH

CHARLES H RUSSELL, 93RD

H J RUSSELL, 44TH

HERBERT W RUSSELL JR, 44TH

JAMES B F RUSSELL, 466TH

JOHN P RUSSELL SR, 489TH

RAY J RUSSELL, 93RD

ROBERT J RUSSELL, 445TH

ROBERT H RUSSELL, 389TH

FRANK P RUSSO, 453RD

ORLANDO J RUSSO, 453RD

S J RUSSO MD, 491ST

SANTO RUSSO, 44TH

CHARLES N RUST, 448TH

JOSEPH R RUSTIC, 458TH

JAMES RUTHERFORD, 93RD

COL JAMES E RUTHERFORD RET, 93RD

FRANK E RUTLEDGE, 389TH

GENE B RYAN, 446TH

J STEPHEN RYAN, 458TH

JOSEPH M RYAN, 466TH

LEO W RYAN, 453RD

RICHARD G RYAN, 93RD

CHARLES S RYDER, 458TH

JULIOUS E RYON JR, 448TH

ELBERT T SABLOTNY, 466TH, 467TH

HENRY J SABORSKY, 446TH

COL ROLAND E SABOURIN RET, 392ND

FRANK SACCO, 445TH

PHILIP SACHER, 392ND

M/SGT RUSSELL E SACKREITER RET, 93RD

GEORGE W SADLER, 93RD

ROBERT SAFFIR, 448TH

VANGELO S SAFOS, 44TH, 491ST

ROBERT M SAGE, 453RD

JOHN A SAGER, 448TH

PHILIP C SAGI, 458TH

JOHN SALADIAK, 44TH

HOBART S SALE, 448TH

ROBERT J SALER, 392ND

JOSEPH D SALISBURY, 445TH

RICHARD S SALMANSOHN, 448TH

ALFRED SALOTTI, 448TH

EUGENE A SALTARELLI, 466TH

JOHN J SALVATORELLI, 448TH

FREDERICK C SAMMETINGER, 467TH

C F SAMPSON, 389TH

JOHN A SAMSELL, 392ND

GEORGE A SAMUDIO, 389TH

HAROLD SAMUELIAN, 44TH

SVERRE JACK SAMUELSEN, 491ST

KENNETH A SAMUELSON, 453RD

FRANK L SANBORN JR, 458TH

MICHAEL S SANCHES, SM

DR ORLANDO J SANCHEZ, 458TH

LTC CHRIS SAND JR RET, 44TH

EDWARD A SAND, 93RD

ROBERT K SANDAHL, 446TH

JACK C SANDERS, 453RD

JOHN & JANICE SANDERS, HDQ

OTTO B SANDERS, 392ND

WILLIAM V SANDERS, 458TH

HAYES SANDERSON, 446TH

J EVERETT SANDERSON, 445TH

JAY SANDLER, 446TH

DR ROBERT B SANDS, 453RD

EDWARD SANICKI, 467TH

LILLIAN F SANSBURN, 448TH, AM

RUDOLPH D SANTINI, 44TH

ROY J SANTORO, 492ND, HDQ

JOSEPH L SAPIENZA, 93RD

LTC HUBERT E SARGENT JR RET, 466TH

CAPT L M SARKOVICH RET, 448TH

JOHN J SARRIS, 93RD

JOSEPH A SASSANO, 93RD

TERRANCE O SATHER, 445TH

ROBERT SATTER, 453RD

JOSEPH J SAVAGO, 446TH

JAMES A SAWYER, 389TH

MARVIN W SAWYER, 445TH

MAURICE J SAXTON, 446TH, 93RD

COL FRED E SAYRE RET, 389TH

HAROLD P SBROCCO, 446TH

WINTON T SCAFIRE, 445TH

LTC EUGENE D SCAMAHORN RET, 491ST

JAMES E SCANLON, 93RD

JAMES J SCANLON, 453RD, 4FG

CHARLES H SCARBOROUGH, 466TH

GENO SCARIOT, 458TH

RICHARD P SCHAD, 492ND

WILLIAM N SCHAEFER, 93RD

FRANK N SCHAEFFER, 44TH

RICHARD F SCHAFER, 389TH

WESLEY R SCHAFER, 392ND

MARY WILLIAMS SCHALLER, 93RD, AM

C DONALD SCHARF, 392ND

ROBERT J SCHARF, 458TH

WILLIAM P SCHARRSCHMIDT, 467TH

FLORA SCHATTE, 44TH, AM

LTC ROY E SCHAUER RET, 446TH

ROBERT I SCHAUSEIL, 458TH

DR PAUL G SCHAUWECKER, 448TH

MORTON R & MARILYN SCHECTER, 467TH

CHARLES J SCHEER, 445TH

ELVIN N SCHEETZ, 44TH

PAUL R SCHEETZ, 445TH

WALTER A SCHEIBER, 458TH

ARTHUR W SCHEID, 491ST

LAWRENCE J SCHEIDING, 458TH

WARREN E SCHERBERT, 489TH

ROGER V SCHERER, 467TH

LOUIS SCHERZER, 453RD

LTC LEONARD SCHEY RET, 489TH

WILLIAM B SCHISSLER, 389TH

MAJ A MICKEY SCHLEICHER RET, 93RD

RICHARD A SCHLEIF, 491ST

JOHN H SCHLICHER JR, 448TH

RICHARD SCHLIEF, 467TH

BENJAMIN H SCHLOSSER, 445TH

ALVIN E SCHMEDEMANN, 93RD

JACK M SCHMID, 448TH

JOHN E SCHMIDBAUER, 467TH

CONRAD J SCHMIDT, 458TH

JACK J SCHMIDT, 445TH

LOREN A SCHMIDT, 489TH

THEODORE J SCHMIDT, 446TH

A LORRAINE SCHMITZ, 389TH, AM

C J SCHMITZ, 467TH

RUSSELL N SCHNAUFER, 453RD

JAMES R SCHNEIDER, 458TH

JOHN J SCHNEIDER, 448TH

RAYMOND G SCHNEIDER, 93RD

HAROLD SCHNEIDERMAN, 466TH

ROBERT SCHNELLE, 491ST

ABRAHAM SCHNITZER, 445TH

JOHN J SCHOENING, 453RD

EDWARD SCHOESSLER, 44TH

VICTOR L SCHOLTEN, 458TH

HENRY J SCHOLZ, 446TH

ARNOLD SCHONBERG, 491ST

ABE H SCHONIER, 93RD

JEROME N SCHORR, 492ND, 467TH

GEORGE T SCHOTT, 458TH

CLARENCE W SCHRADER, 448TH

WILLIAM P SCHRADER, 361ST

LTC JAMES O SCHRECK RET, 446TH

MARTIN H SCHRECK, 389TH

DONALD J SCHREITER, 489TH

EDWARD N SCHROEDER, 448TH

HENRY L SCHROEDER, 466TH

JOHN D SCHROEDER, 445TH, 389TH

NORMAN N SCHROEDER, 44TH

TOM SCHROETER, SM

WALTER A SCHUCH, 458TH

ROY SCHULBACH, 93RD

ROBERT E SCHULER, 489TH

WILLIAM M SCHULER, 44TH, 93RD, 389TH, 392ND

AARON C & SALLY SCHULTZ, 389TH

EDWARD K SCHULTZ JR, 448TH

JAMES R SCHULTZ, 446TH

JOHN W SCHULTZ, 467TH

JOSEPH S SCHULTZ, 458TH

CHARLES J SCHULZ, 448TH

WILBERT G SCHULZ, 392ND

GENEVA E SCHULZE, 458TH, AM

CHARLES A SCHUPP 111, 389TH

HENRY W SCHUSSLER JR, HDQ

GLENN G SCHUSTER, 458TH

GEORGE C SCHUTZE, 392ND

KEITH C SCHUYLER, 44TH

PATRICIA SCHWAB, 466TH, AM

EDWARD G SCHWARM, 44TH, HDQ

EDWARD G SCHWARTZ, 446TH, 491ST

EDWARD S SCHWARTZ, 392ND

FREDERICK A SCHWARTZ, 446TH

MORRIS A SCHWARTZ, 453RD

RALPH J SCHWARTZ, 491ST

RAYMOND J SCHWARTZ, 448TH

JOSEPH A SCHWARZGRUBER, 93RD

ROBERT W SCHWELLINGER, 389TH

FRANK J SCHWERMIN, 389TH

RUSSELL J SCIANDRA, 389TH

EVELYN R SCIGULINSKY, 44TH, AM

FRANK M SCIMECA, 458TH

GEORGE W SCOREY JR, 93RD

BILLIE H SCOTT, 489TH, AM

CARLTON SCOTT, 445TH

DAVID A SCOTT, 392ND

JAMES H SCOTT, 458TH

JOHN W SCOTT, 446TH

LARREL C SCOTT, 448TH

M/SGT PERRY W SCOTT RET, 93RD

RICHARD C SCOTT SR, 93RD

RUSSELL E SCOTT, 467TH

SAMUEL E SCOTT, 453RD

SAMUEL E SCOTT, 467TH

THOMAS W SCOTT, 93RD

VAN B SCOTT, 448TH

WALTER V SCOTT, 453RD

WILLIAM D SCOTT, 44TH

WILLIAM J SCOTT, 392ND

MAJ LEONARD G SCRIVEN RET, 446TH

ROBERT I SEAGLE, 389TH

BETTY HOUSTON SEAL, 44TH, AM

EDWIN J SEALY, 458TH

WILLIAM H SEAMAN, 458TH

ALLEN E SEAMANS, 389TH

RICHARD H SEARER, 458TH

FREDERICK T SEARLE, SM

LLOYD H SEARLE, 448TH

LTC WILLIAM H SEARLES RET, 448TH

WALTER E SEASTROM, 489TH

M T SEBASTIAN, 448TH

HAROLD S SECOR, 93RD

JOHN E SEDERLUND, 458TH

LAWRENCE SEDLACEK, 93RD

J FRED SEGALLA, 467TH

STANLEY A SEGER, 492ND

ELMER SEIDL, 467TH

HAROLD L SEIDL, 492ND

JOHN M SEIFERT JR, 392ND, AM

PAUL A SEIFERT, 492ND

MAJ ROBERT B SEIGH RET, 389TH

ROBERT S SEILER, 467TH

ELVERN R SEITZINGER, 492ND

DEREK R SELF, SM

ROBERT C SELLERS, 458TH

HOWARD A SELLKE, 445TH

IRVIN M SELM, 44TH

TERRIE NELSON SELTZER, 491ST, 389THAM

WILLIAM M SELVIDGE, 389TH

FERDINAND A SENGSTACK, 491ST

JERALD R SENTER MD, 458TH

WALTER S SERAFIN, 458TH

EDWARD J SERBIN, 44TH

CHARLES SERWITZ, 467TH

BARBARA M SESSA, 466TH, AM

KENNETH SEVERI, 458TH

JOHN G SEVERSON, 93RD

LAVERNE F SEVILLA, 491ST

WILLIAM S SEWARD, 93RD

WALTER SEWITSKY, 446TH

ARTHUR P SEYLER, 458TH

EUGENE H SHABATURA, 93RD

F W SHACKELFORD, 453RD, 392ND

PHILLIP SHADY, 467TH

THOMAS A SHAFER, 445TH

DELBERT E SHAFFER, 458TH

JOSEPH H SHAFFER SR, 446TH

COL J C SHAHBAZ RET, 491ST

MERVIN M SHANK, 467TH

WILLIAM O SHANK, 445TH

DONALD W SHANKLIN, 466TH

GEORGE L SHANKS, 446TH

ROLAND C SHANKS, 93RD

HORACE SHANKWILER, 445TH

DONALD R SHANNON, 458TH

JAMES D SHANNON JR, 446TH, HDQ

RAY SHANNON, 389TH

WILLIAM F SHANNON, 458TH

ALEXANDER E SHANOSKI, 458TH

JAMES SHAPCOTT, 448TH

JACKIE SHAPIRO, 448TH, AM

SEYMOUR I SHAPIRO MD, 458TH

EDWARD C SHAPLEY, 392ND

FLETCHER E SHARP, 491ST

RICHARD M SHARP, 458TH

FRANK A SHARPE, 491ST

MELVIN SHARPE, 489TH

LEWIS S SHARPLESS, 467TH

LEO L SHARPNACK, 44TH, 389TH, 492ND

LTC LLOYD C SHARRARD RET, 445TH

COL AMOS B SHARRETTS RET, 466TH

THOMAS V SHAUGHNESSY, 467TH

CARL R SHAUT, 467TH

MERLIN M SHAVER, 445TH

HOWARD P SHAW, 453RD

JUDGE JAMES I SHAW, 453RD

JOHN P SHAW, 448TH

OLIVER A SHAW, 466TH

ROBERT P SHAW, 44TH

ARTHUR SHAY, 445TH

ROBERT C SHEA, 458TH

GEORGE R SHEAFFER, 458TH
MERVIN J SHEAFFER, 445TH
HAROLD F SHEAHAN, 389TH
MALCOLM H SHEALY, 458TH
BOB C SHEARER, 445TH
FRANCIS X SHEEHAN, 448TH
ROBERT D SHEEHAN, 467TH
COL ELVIN M SHEFFIELD RET, 448TH
WESLEY SHEFFIELD, 492ND, 93RD
RICHARD W SHELDON, 44TH
WILLIAM L SHELDRICK, 467TH
COL EDWARD L SHELEY RET, 446TH
ALBEN K SHELTON, HDQ, 458TH
WILLIAM O SHELTON JR, HDQ
GEORGE E SHENEFIELD, 458TH, 467TH, 489TH
THOMAS W SHEPHERD, 44TH
HELEN HANSON SHEPPARD, HDQ
RICHARD F SHERBURNE, 489TH
MICHAEL T SHERIDAN, 467TH
EDWARD S SHERMAN, 448TH
ELMER R SHERMAN, 489TH
ERIC SHERMAN, 446TH
J H SHERMAN DDS, 491ST
M/SGT JOHN H SHERMAN RET, 93RD
THOMAS D SHERMAN, 453RD
LTC JAMES L SHERRARD RET, 467TH
MORTON B SHERWOOD, 389TH, 44TH
ROBERT H SHERWOOD, 389TH
JOHN SHIA, 448TH
GEORGE SHIARAS, 491ST
STANLEY L SHIBOVICH, 389TH
ELLSWORTH H SHIELDS, 458TH
VERNON E SHIELDS, 392ND
BARRY J SHILLITO, 445TH
LEE H SHINN, 93RD
MAHLON C SHIPLEY, 93RD
ROBERT L SHIPLEY, 489TH
KEITH E SHIRK, 389TH
MYRON G SHIVER, 466TH
LTC FOY L SHOEMATE RET, 491ST
LTC ALEXANDER J SHOGAN RET, 448TH
KENNETH L SHOOK, 446TH
JOHN H SHOPE, 492ND
JOHN M SHORT, 489TH
LLOYD V SHORT, 458TH
COL ALBERT J SHOWER RET, 467TH
EDWARD E SHROYER, 489TH
M/GEN ANTHONY T SHTOGREN RET, HDQ
FRED E SHUBECK, 93RD
DEAN F SHUEY, 467TH
IRVING L SHUFFLER JR, 453RD, 93RD, 389TH, 392ND
ELTON M SHULL, 448TH
JERRY SHULMAN, 453RD
GORDON L SHUPP, 458TH
CHARLES J SHY, 467TH
COL WILLIAM M SHY RET, 491ST
VANCE L SIBERT, 392ND
ALEXANDER S SIDIE, 389TH
ANTHONY SIDOROWICZ JR, 448TH
DONALD L SIEBERT, 44TH, HDQ
VIRGINIA A SIEGFRIED, 392ND, AM
HARRY E SIEGRIST, 453RD
HARRY SIEMENS, 492ND
WILLIAM C SIEMS, 65FW
STANLEY A SIEVERTSON, 458TH
GABRIEL SIGNORELLI, 458TH
WALLACE N SIGWORTH, 389TH
LTC MILES L SIKES JR RET, 446TH
WILLIAM F SIKORA, 467TH, 489TH
SIDNEY SILINSKY, 466TH
CHRISTOPHER M SILLS, 389TH, AM
GREGORY U SILLS, 389TH, AM
JAMES M SILLS, 466TH
STEPHEN J SILLS, 389TH, AM

LTC WALTER H SILLS RET, 93RD
WILLIAM R SILLS SR, 389TH
ROBERT J SILVA, 492ND
EDWARD SILVER, 458TH
ROBERT G SILVER JR, 448TH
JOSEPH E SILVERBERG MD, 489TH
JOSEPH SILVEY, 445TH
CAPT JOHN E SILVIS RET, 448TH
JOYCE K SIMARD, HDQ, AM
CHARLES F SIMCOX, 467TH
JAMES F SIMES, 458TH
GEORGE SIMKINS, 467TH
DEWAYNE G SIMMONDS, 446TH
HERBERT E SIMMONS, 445TH
JESSE E SIMMONS, 453RD
OLIVER N SIMMONS, 467TH
HAROLD O SIMMS, 466TH, 44TH
HENRY G SIMON, 467TH
TAFFE S SIMON, 445TH
U B SIMONEAUX, 458TH
ALFRED SIMONINI JR, 491ST
DERALD A SIMONIS, 492ND
WILBUR E SIMONS, HDQ, AM
CLIFFORD W SIMONSON, 445TH
IRA L SIMPSON, 389TH
PATRICK B SIMPSON, 389TH, AM
WILLIAM H SIMS, 44TH
BENJAMIN W SINCLAIR, 492ND
J B SINCLAIR, 453RD
LOUIS SINGER, 389TH
THEODORE A SINGERMAN, 448TH
WILLIAM T SINGLETON, 392ND
ROBERT I SINN, 445TH
ROBERT J SINSABAUGH, 458TH
JOHN J SIPEK, 56FG, 479TH
JOHN SIPOS, 458TH
JOSEPH SIROTNAK, 458TH
ALLAN SIRRELL, SM
CLETUS A SISLEY, 445TH
DALE L SISSON, 389TH
JOSEPH J SIVON, 489TH
ARTHUR C SJOLUND JR, 458TH
COL ALVIN D SKAGGS RET, 448TH
RICHARD SKATTIE, 44TH
JACK T SKEELS, 93RD
FRANK W SKELDON, 489TH
THEODORE B SKERRITT, 489TH
LTC LESTER J SKIDMORE RET, 458TH
MAJ F C SKIFFINGTON RET, 489TH
JAMES C SKILTON, 467TH
WILLIAM D SKINNER, 93RD
JOSEPH J SKOMRO, 492ND, 44TH, 445TH
EDWARD E SKUBA, 448TH
E C SLACK, 448TH
COL HOWARD W SLATON RET, 458TH
EDWARD SLATTERY, 489TH
DALE W SLAYTER, 392ND
COLIN SLEATH, SM
LEE D SLESSOR, 389TH
HARTZEL C SLIDER, 93RD
FLOYD E SLIPP, 392ND
DR ALFRED V SLOAN JR, 445TH
RAY E SLOAN, 467TH
WALTER H SLOAN, 466TH
MEYER SLOTT, 491ST
ROBERT C SLUSHER, 445TH
WALTER J SMALLEY, 466TH
RICHARD H SMART, 44TH
MAGNE SMEDVIG, 467TH
JOE E SMELT, 93RD, AM
WALTER E SMELT, 93RD
EDWARD C SMERTELNY, 453RD
NICHOLAS SMETANA, 458TH
ADRIAN G HANRI SMIT, 93RD, AM
ALLAN B SMITH, 389TH
BARRY A SMITH, 458TH, AM
BEAUFORD R SMITH, 44TH
BLAIR G SMITH, 491ST
JUDGE C DOUGLAS SMITH, HDQ
CARLTON W SMITH, 467TH
CECIL L SMITH, 453RD
CHESTER SMITH, 445TH
CHRISTOPHER J SMITH, 389TH
COL CLARK S SMITH RET, 389TH

DR DON D SMITH, 466TH
DONALD W SMITH, 445TH
EARL R SMITH, 466TH
EDWARD M SMITH, 93RD
ERIC W SMITH JR, 445TH
ERNEST L SMITH, 446TH
ERNEST T SMITH MD, 491ST
EXCEL I SMITH, 389TH
FELIX M SMITH DVM, 491ST
FRED B SMITH, 491ST
G ELLIOTT SMITH, 467TH
GEOFFREY W SMITH, SM
GEORGE A SMITH, 453RD
GEORGE J SMITH, 445TH
MAJ GLENN M SMITH RET, 453RD
HAROLD E SMITH, 489TH
HAROLD L SMITH, 467TH
HAROLD W SMITH, 448TH
HENRY J SMITH, 93RD
HERMAN W SMITH, 489TH
HERSCHEL L SMITH, 492ND
IRVINE G SMITH, 44TH
JAMES C SMITH, 458TH
JAMES L SMITH, 448TH
JAMES M SMITH, 458TH
JAMES W SMITH, 392ND, 492ND
JOAN BENNS SMITH, SM
JOHN F SMITH, 491ST
JOHN L SMITH, 458TH
KENNETH R SMITH, 389TH
LELAND J SMITH, 489TH
LEONARD H SMITH, 466TH
LEROY A SMITH, 448TH
LLOYD T SMITH, 93RD
LLOYD W SMITH, 453RD
LOUIS SMITH, 93RD
LOUIS SMITH, C/O E ROSENBLOOM, 93RD
LOUIS H SMITH JR, 389TH
LUCIAN R SMITH JR, 466TH
MYRON G SMITH, 93RD
O K SMITH, 448TH
LTC RICHARD B SMITH RET, 389TH
RICHARD E SMITH, 44TH
RICHARD L SMITH, 466TH, AM
ROBERT A SMITH, 446TH
ROBERT E SMITH, 448TH
ROBERT E SMITH, 458TH
ROBERT S SMITH, 491ST
ROBERT W SMITH, 389TH
ROBERT W SMITH, 466TH
RONALD O SMITH, 453RD
SHERIDAN R SMITH, 93RD
THEODORE R SMITH, 93RD
W B SMITH, 445TH
WADE W SMITH, 445TH
WALTER B SMITH, 448TH
LTC WILLIAM E SMITH RET, 392ND
WILLIAM G SMITH, 445TH
WILLIAM J SMITH, 467TH
WILLIAM O SMITH SR, 389TH
COL WILLIAM R SMITH RET, 489TH
WILTON W SMITH, 466TH
LOWELL D SMOTHERS, 467TH
WILLIAM W SNAVELY, 448TH
HARRY R SNEAD, 44TH
MAJ VERYL L SNEATH RET, 448TH, 93RD
MAJ WALTER R SNEDDEN RET, 446TH
LTC GOMER J SNEDDON RET, 93RD
ELLIS E SNEE JR, 445TH
JOHN W SNIDER, 448TH
GEORGE W SNOOK, 445TH
RAY N SNOOK, 491ST
DEAN B SNOW, 491ST
EDWARD H SNOW, 466TH
GEORGE R SNOWDEN, 466TH
JAMES E SNOWDEN, 458TH
E MAX SNYDER, 458TH
EDWARD J SNYDER, 466TH
ERVIN R SNYDER, 446TH, 489TH
GEORGE E SNYDER, 458TH
H WALLACE SNYDER, HDQ
NATHAN H SNYDER, 467TH
PHILIP A SNYDER JR, 453RD

ROBERT E SNYDER, 389TH
ROBERT L SNYDER, 467TH
RUSSEL E SNYDER, 389TH
P W SOANES, SM
JOSEPH H SODER, 446TH
THEODORE Z SOKOLOWSKI, HDQ
EDWIN P SOKOLSKI, 467TH
ARCHIE M SOLATKA, 44TH
E A SOLBERG, 448TH
WILFRED R SOLLENBERGER, 491ST
EDWARD SOLOMON, 44TH
MORTON SOLOMON, 467TH
RIDD J SOLOMON, 448TH
ALBERT H SOLTAU, 453RD
COL JOSEPH I SONNENREICH RET, 453RD
HARRY SONNTAG, 491ST
DEAN M SORELL, 491ST
NEAL E & PAT SORENSEN, 489TH
ALLEN H SORENSON, 93RD
WILLIAM J SORGEL, 445TH
ERNEST G SORRENTINO, 467TH
LENDEN SOUDER, 389TH, 491ST
CHARLES A SOUTER, 491ST
MARIE SOUTH, 93RD, AM
STEPHEN A SOVIAR, 445TH, 93RD
CHARLES D SPADONE, 492ND
ALPHONSE J SPAHN, 445TH
LTC JOSEPH G SPARE RET, 448TH
LEO W SPARKMAN, 458TH
LUTHER S SPARKS, 489TH
WILLIE D SPARKS, 492ND
COL FRED D SPARREVOHN RET, 93RD
DONALD B SPARROW, 491ST, AM
WILLIAM SPARTICHINO, HDQ
RALPH SPAZIANI, 489TH
DANIEL D SPEARS, 392ND
JUDY SPEED, SM
HAROLD G SPEER, 453RD
MAURICE E SPEER, 458TH
MARVIN H SPEIDEL, 446TH
MIKE F SPELLAZZA, 445TH
JAMES SPENCE, 467TH
DONALD SPENCER, 93RD
EDWARD A SPENCER, 93RD
EUGENE P SPENCER, 389TH
GEORGE F SPENCER, 458TH
JULIUS E SPENCER, 458TH
REV LEE R SPENCER, 491ST
LELAND C SPENCER, 93RD
RONALD D SPENCER, 467TH
WALLACE J SPENCER, 93RD
E J SPENSER, 44TH
HUBERT A SPERANZA, 491ST
HARVEY SPIEGEL, 489TH
NATHAN SPIELVOGEL, 445TH
GAETANO SPINELLI, 392ND
JOSEPH L SPIROFF, 467TH
FRED SPITZER, 458TH
MAURICE SPITZER, 458TH
COL THURMAN SPIVA RET, 446TH
LTC J L SPOONER RET, 389TH, 446TH
ROBERT C SPRAGUE, 467TH
W C SPRATT, 458TH
RICHARD H SPRENKLE, 448TH
MERLE E SPRING, 453RD
R W SPROWLS, 392ND
JEROME A SPRY, 467TH
WILLIAM J SPULAK, 458TH
DEAN H SPURGEON, 44TH
W W SPURR, 448TH
EDWARD L SQUIRES, 44TH, 389TH, 392ND
SARAH M ST CLAIR, 448TH, AM
BASIL J ST DENNIS, 448TH
LESLIE E ST JOHN, 466TH
GERALD ST LEGER BARTER, SM
GORDON K STACKEL, 93RD
WALTER C STACKHOUSE, 458TH
JOSEPH STADT, 445TH
GUENTER H STAEDICKE, 467TH
J M STAFF, SM
LTC HORST A STAHL RET, 491ST
ROBERT C STAHL, 93RD
LTC ROY D STAHL RET, 445TH

CARL STAMMER, 453RD
FRANK E STANEK, 389TH
DAVID R STANFIELD, 458TH
HENRY T STANFORD, 44TH
JOHN W STANFORD, 448TH
WILBUR S STANFORD JR, 392ND
CECIL D STANLEY, 467TH
SMS CHARLES S STANSBERY RET, 491ST
MARTIN J STANTON, 56FG
SCOTT J STANTON, 44TH, AM
JOSEPH B STAREK, 448TH
MARY R STAREK, 448TH, AM
M/SGT BRUCE D STARNER RET, 458TH
WILLIAM R STARNES, 491ST
ROBERT R STARR, 389TH
ALVIN J STASNEY, 392ND
VETO J STASUNAS, 458TH
MELVIN E STATES, 389TH
MELVIN F STAUDT, 93RD
CLIFTON B STAUFF, 466TH
JOHN O STAVENGER, 489TH
COL B E STEADMAN RET, 466TH
JEROME M STEDMAN, 93RD
ARTHUR D STEELE, 448TH
DR JAY STEELE, 44TH
RICHARD E STEELMAN, 93RD
EDWARD J STEEVE, 489TH
HOWARD S STEFFEY, 467TH
FRANK T STEGBAUER, 44TH
PAUL R STEICHEN, 93RD
FRED E STEIN, 453RD
WALTER D STEIN, 389TH
LYLE W STEINBERG, 448TH
DALE M STEINER, 458TH
WILLIBALD P STEINER, 445TH
JEFF H STEINERT, 389TH
LEROY A STEINGRABER, 453RD
JERMANE M STEINHAUER, 445TH
ALBERT STEININGER, 489TH
JOHN A STEININGER, 492ND
BERNARD STELZER, 448TH
NEAL F STEMBRIDGE, 453RD
JOHN STEMMERMANN, 448TH
DON D STENABAUGH, 489TH
LTC RICHARD M STENGER RET, 489TH
JOSEPH J STEPAN, 446TH
LTC BILLY W STEPHAN RET, 445TH
LTC DALE J STEPHENS RET, 392ND
EDWARD L STEPHENS, 93RD
EUGENE R STEPHENS, 453RD
GREGORY A STEPHENS, 93RD, AM
HOWARD E STEPHENS, 458TH
LOUIS M STEPHENS, 392ND
LTC SIDNEY A STEPHENS RET, 448TH
TOM Y STEPHENS, 389TH
D D STEPHENSON, 467TH
HOLLIS STEPHENSON, 467TH
HARRY M STEPHEY, 491ST
IVAN C STEPNICH, 44TH, HDQ
FRANCIS B STEPP, 93RD
LEE R STEPP, 93RD
THOMAS STERANKO, 467TH
LOUIS STERN, 392ND
SOL STERN, 453RD
MARTIN S STERNBERG MD, 466TH
MICHELE STERRETT, 458TH, AM
EUGENE P STETZ, 448TH
ANDREW J STEVENS, 389TH
CLETUS I STEVENS MD, 389TH
EVERETT R STEVENS, 467TH
JEFFREY L STEVENS, 467TH
JOHN E STEVENS, 467TH
LEWIS S STEVENS, 458TH
DOUGLAS R STEVENSON, 446TH
MARY JEAN STEVENSON, 467TH, AM
BENNIE L STEWART, 446TH
BRADY C STEWART, 491ST
CARROLL & PEGGY O'MARA STEWART, 93RD, 93ARC
DEAN B STEWART JR, 491ST

156

M/SGT JACK O STEWART RET, 392ND

JAMES C STEWART, 65FW

JAMES M STEWART, 445TH, 453RD, 2CW

JOSEPH STEWART, 44TH

MARION M STEWART, 44TH, AM

NELSON R STEWART, 458TH

THOMAS R STEWART, 44TH

COL WALTER T STEWART RET, 93RD

WILLIAM C STEWART, 44TH

WILLIAM R STEWART, 448TH

NORMAN J STICKNEY, 491ST

LTC MAX A STIEFEL RET, 44TH

ALFRED A STIFF JR, 448TH

PAUL STIKELEATHER, 466TH

THOMAS J STILBERT, 453RD

ROBERT L STILES JR, 491ST

VERNON STILLWAGON, 392ND

LEWIS B STILWELL, 389TH

RALPH L STIMMEL, 445TH

CHARLES O STINE, 445TH

ROBERT J STINE, 44TH

AUSTIN F STIRRATT, 458TH

FRANCIS C STISULIS, 448TH

WILBUR & JEANE M STITES, 453RD

CARL E STODDARD, 44TH

CLYDE B STOKES, 491ST

FRANCIS W STOKES, 467TH

KENT STOKES, 453RD, AM

MILTON & LUCILLE STOKES, 453RD

MAJ WOODROE H STOKES RET, 93RD

DIANA FAIR STONE, 458TH, AM

LLOYD E STONE, 445TH

ROBERT M STONE JR, 467TH

LTC ROBERT N STONE RET, 389TH

ROGER L STONE, 389TH

WESTCOT B STONE, 466TH

KENNETH G STORIE, 389TH

LOUIS H STORMER, 491ST

ELEANOR & WILLIAM STORMS, HDQ

CALEB M STOUT, 453RD

FRANK E STOUT JR, 453RD

LTC ROBERT G STOUT RET, 389TH

JACK O STOVER, 492ND

PAUL R STOVEY, 453RD

RALPH H STOWE, 458TH

H L STRACENER, 491ST

GEORGE E STRAND, 458TH

JACK D STRANDQUIST, 458TH

WILLIAM S STRANGE, 44TH

JOHN STRANGWARD, SM

JACK D STRATTON JR, 467TH

JAMES E STRAUB, 453RD

ROBERT L STRAUSBAUGH, 392ND

JOHN M STRAUSS, 489TH

KENNETH R STRAUSS, 491ST

WALTER C STRAWINSKI, 445TH

HENRY J STREAT JR, 491ST

MILTON STREMPEL, 445TH

NORMAN L STRICKBINE, 389TH

JOHN C STRICKER, HDQ

MAJ FRED E STRICKLAND RET, 453RD

GLASSELL S STRINGFELLOW, 448TH

GEORGE H STRIPE, 389TH

EDWARD J STRISOVSKY, 491ST

DONALD E STROH, 44TH

ERWIN J STROHMAIER, 44TH, 492ND

PAUL M STROICH, 93RD

FREDERICK A STROMBOM, 93RD

RAYMOND E STRONG, HDQ

WILLIAM H STRONG, 44TH

WILLIAM W STRONG JR, 446TH

RICHARD B STROSNIDER, 458TH

HAROLD D STROUD, 448TH

C D & MARY STROUP, 389TH

ROBERT S STRUBLE, 44TH

HERBERT K STRUCK, 458TH

EUGENE C STRUCKHOFF, 492ND, 467TH

VIOLA STRYKER, 458TH, AM

ERSKINE H STUBBS, 44TH

HARRY C STUBBS, 44TH, 458TH

LEWIS STUBITS, 467TH

LESLIE STUCKEY JR, 458TH

RICHARD L STULTZ, 389TH

J J STUMBAUGH, 389TH, 453RD

CHARLES T STUMPF, 389TH

KARL STUPSKI, 392ND, AM

LAWRENCE J STUPSKI, 392ND, AM

STANLEY J STUPSKI, 392ND

ROBERT J STURENFELDT, 458TH

PAUL B STURGILL, 445TH

MALCOLM B STURGIS, 489TH

EARL STURTEVANT, 491ST

RICHARD M STYSLO, 448TH

ADAM J SUBJECK, 44TH

F C SUCHOCKI, 446TH

GEORGE SUCHORSKY, 448TH

LTC ROBERT W SUCKOW RET, 445TH

JAKE P SUDDATH, 492ND

LTC MYRON G SUDEROW AF RES, 93RD

LEON H SULKOWSKI, 445TH

HENRY P SULLIVAN, 389TH

JOHN J SULLIVAN, 448TH

JOHN L SULLIVAN, 93RD

JOHN W SULLIVAN, 392ND

JOSEPH M SULLIVAN, 44TH

JOSEPH P SULLIVAN, 389TH

PHILIP A SULLIVAN, 392ND

RAYMOND E SULLIVAN, 453RD

LTC RAYMOND W SULLIVAN RET, 489TH

THOMAS A SULLIVAN, 93RD

WALTER J SULLIVAN, 446TH

ERNEST SULTEMEIER, 445TH, 2CW

JULIUS N SUMMA, 467TH

VERA HEARD SUMMERS, HDQ

PAUL B SUMMEY, 389TH

RAYMOND E SUMRELL, 448TH

EDWARD W SUNDER JR, 491ST

EDWARD A SUPKO, 392ND

W R PAUL SURBAUGH, 446TH, 489TH

WILLIAM D SURFACE, 492ND, 467TH

MARVIN F SUROVY, 448TH

ELZE W SURRATT, 445TH

EDMUND M SURVILLA, 453RD

WILLIAM R SUSA, 489TH

ARTHUR R SUTER, 492ND

STEPHEN A SUTHERLAND, 489TH

ALEXANDER L SUTO, 466TH

WARREN K SUTOR, 389TH

RUPERT C SUTPHIN, 392ND

PAUL E SUTTER, 389TH

ELMER J SUTTERS JR, 458TH

COL JAMES L SUTTON RET, 446TH

RICHARD K SUTTON, 453RD, 467TH

WILBERT J SUWYN, 446TH

MICHAEL SVETICH, 445TH

VERNON R R SWAIM, 93RD

JOSEPH J SWANER, 491ST

JOSEPH A SWANICK, 445TH

ROBERT C SWANK, 44TH

CARLTON H SWANSON, 489TH

JOSEPH E SWANSON, 458TH

VINCENT H SWANSON, 466TH

WAYNE B SWANSON, 453RD

GEORGE W SWARTZ, 458TH

WILLIAM A SWARTZ, 458TH

COL JACK SWAYZE RET, 448TH

JACKIE SWEARINGEN, 467TH, AM

R L SWEARNGIN, 445TH

FRANCIS A SWEE, 392ND

CLINTON C SWEENEY, 453RD

F ROGER SWEENEY, 467TH

PHILIP J SWEENEY, 392ND

CHARLES H SWEETING, 389TH

CARL H SWENSON, 467TH

ROBERT S SWENSON, 93RD

STANLEY SWIENCKI, 448TH

GEORGE J SWIFT, 448TH

HERBERT E SWIFT, 4FG

ROBERT N SWIFT, 458TH

GILBERT E SWINBURNSON, 44TH

JOHN R SWINDLER, 93RD

THOMAS SWINT, 467TH

LTC PAUL SWOFFORD RET, 445TH

ROBERT L SWOFFORD, 445TH

MAX SYKES, 489TH

ROBERT J SYKES, 44TH

COL WILLIAM H SYPHER RET, 446TH

LAWRENCE SYVERSON, 453RD

CLIFFORD S SYVERUD, 445TH, 389TH

JOHN C SZABO, SM

JOSEPH SZELIGA, 448TH

ANDY SZERDI, 392ND

JOSEPH SZOPO, 448TH

TED J SZUMSKI, 44TH

REX L TABOR, 466TH

WAYNE TABOR, 466TH

GEORGE TACHUK, 93RD, AM

JOSEPH TADDONIO OD, 93RD, 491ST

ANDREW J TALAFUSE, 466TH

ELMER P TALBOT, 389TH

HELEN M TALBOT, 453RD, AM

JOHN H TALBOT JR, 453RD, AM

MARK E TALBOT, 453RD, AM

FRED W TALLEY, 453RD

VIRGIL C TALLY, 466TH

LTC TIMOTHY M TAMBLYN RET, 389TH, 489TH

JOHN M TANGORRA, 453RD

TSGT CARL J TANNER JR RET, 93RD

GORDON E TANNER, 453RD

SYLVIA E TANNER, 492ND, AM

HARRY TANZER, 467TH

JACK TARDIEU, 446TH

CHRISTIAN TAREAU, SM

THOMAS M TARPLEY JR, 458TH

LESTER C TARRANT, 389TH

RAYMOND T TATE, 446TH

FREDERICK P TAWNEY, 389TH

BILLIE TAYLOR, 467TH, 392NDAM

CHARLES H TAYLOR, 489TH

CHARLES W TAYLOR JR, 44TH

GLENN E TAYLOR, 466TH

JACK S TAYLOR, 491ST

JOHN F TAYLOR, 491ST

JOHN J TAYLOR, 492ND, 467TH

MAX A TAYLOR, 445TH

LTC ODIS F TAYLOR RET, 458TH

OWEN P TAYLOR, 93RD

ROBERT L TAYLOR, 44TH

THOMAS P TAYLOR JR, 448TH

VAN R TAYLOR, 458TH

COL WILLIAM B TAYLOR III RET, 44TH

COL ROBERT H TAYS JR RET, 392ND

WAYNE A TEALE, 445TH

RAY S TEATER, 392ND

CAPT GLENN E TEDFORD RET, 93RD, 448TH

WILBUR TEESDALE, 453RD

EDWARD R TEEVAN, 389TH

HERMAN E TEGTMEYER, 467TH

GEORGE D TELFORD, 44TH

LTC ALBERT TELSON RET, 489TH

VITALIS L TEMPEL, 389TH

PROF HOWARD TEMPERLEY, BG

GEORGE W TEMPLE, 44TH

MICHAEL F TEMPLER, 453RD, AM

VICTOR G TEMPLER JR, 453RD

LEONARD A TENET JR, 392ND

JAMES C TENNANT, 389TH

JOHN C TERBRACK, 93RD

WILLIAM H TERHUNE, 448TH

PATRICK J TERRANOVA, 448TH

EDWIN R TERRY SR, 466TH

WILLIAM A TERRY, 466TH

MARC TERZIEV, 453RD

BENJAMIN R TESCHON, 491ST

GLENN A TESSMER, 93RD

HANK TEVELIN, 466TH

GAYLORD A THAYER, 458TH

HARRY B THERIOT, 448TH

FLOYD E THIBODEAU, 489TH

MARCEL J THIBODEAU, 489TH

ALBERT L THOMALE, 453RD

CLIFFORD W THOMAS, 453RD

DANIEL B THOMAS, 392ND, AM

LTC DOWNEY L THOMAS RET, 448TH

FRANK THOMAS, 453RD

LTC HARRY E THOMAS RET, 392ND

J FRED & ELVA THOMAS, 392ND

J SHERMAN THOMAS, 448TH

JAMES E THOMAS, 466TH

JOHN E THOMAS, 491ST

KEITH R THOMAS, SM

ROBERT W THOMAS, 489TH

ROGER J THOMAS, 44TH

THOMAS J THOMAS DDS, 446TH

WILLIE THOMAS, 467TH

WORTH J THOMAS, 392ND

CARWIN A THOMASON, 392ND

ARNOLD R THOMPSON, 467TH

CHARLES O THOMPSON JR, 448TH

LTC DAVID W THOMPSON RET, 93RD

DONN G THOMPSON, 466TH

ELTON L THOMPSON, 93RD

EVERT R THOMPSON, 458TH

FRANK S THOMPSON, 458TH

GLEN D THOMPSON JR, 93RD

HOWARD E THOMPSON, 93RD

J ROBERT THOMPSON, 392ND

JACK E THOMPSON, 445TH, AM

JAMES B THOMPSON, 446TH

JOHN R THOMPSON, 453RD

LEO L THOMPSON, 446TH

LESLIE M THOMPSON, 466TH

RUSSELL A THOMPSON MD, 466TH

THOMAS A THOMPSON, 445TH

TRUET B THOMPSON, 93RD

WILLIAM M THOMPSON, 445TH

OLIVER J THOMSEN, 44TH

CATHY THOMSON, SM

JOSEPH W THORLEY, 93RD

JAY W THORNBURGH, 392ND, 44TH

NEWELL B THORNOCK, 44TH

EARL THORNSEN, 453RD

M/SGT JESSE J THORNTON, 93RD

LEONARD V THORNTON, 448TH

WILLIAM H THORPE, 446TH

ILA THUNBERG, 389TH, AM

JOSEPH M THURING, 453RD

JACK E THURMAN, 446TH

COL N D THURMAN RET, 453RD

EUGENE B THURSTON, 446TH

DONALD C TIBBETTS, 467TH

HOWARD R TIBBITTS, 458TH

RUSSELL TICKNER, 491ST

JOHN R TIERNEY, 448TH

JOSEPH F TIERNEY, 392ND, 14CW

WILLIAM F TIERNEY JR, 445TH

THOMAS TIGHE, 466TH

JOSEPH W TIKEY, 466TH

GILBERT B TILGHMAN, 389TH

ARTHUR H TILLETT, 44TH

NORMAN N TILLNER, 44TH

CHARLES W TILTON, 44TH

KENNETH L TIMMONS, 392ND

ROBERT T TIMS, 445TH

ROCCO TINARI, 453RD

HOWARD C TINKHAM, 458TH

GLENDON D TINSLEY SR, 361FG

MICHAEL TIPPLE, SM

GLEN A TISHER, 453RD

RALPH G TISSOT, 93RD

LESLIE C TOBEY, 389TH

DONALD J TOBIAS, 489TH

M L TOCKEY, 491ST

WILFRED J TOCZKO, 389TH

CARL L TODD, 93RD

DONALD C TODT, 448TH

IRVIN E TOLER, 448TH

JOHN TOLJANIC, 446TH

RAYMOND C TOLL, 491ST

JAMES A TOLLEFSON, 491ST

DR R B TOLSON, 489TH

LEONARD E TOMASKI, 467TH

WALTON TOMBARI, 448TH

JAMES N TOMBLIN, 44TH

JOSEPH J TOMBLIN, 458TH

SAMUEL L TOMPSON, SM

FLOYD G TONEY, 389TH

JOHN H TONEY, 44TH

E C TONN, 453RD

MOLLIE TOOLE, 491ST, AM

HARRY V TOOTELL, 466TH

JAMES V TOOTELL, 491ST

M LEE TOOTHMAN DDS, 446TH

ROY R TORCASO, 458TH

VINCENT K TORFIN, 448TH

CHARLES TORNO, 44TH

JOHN A TORODE, 491ST, 392ND

WALTER TORONJO JR, 446TH

LTC FRANCIS E TORR RET, 445TH

LTC PAUL TORRETTI RET, 467TH

ALEX J TOTH, 44TH

COL ROBERT H TOUBY RET, 445TH, 93RD, 389TH, 453RD

ALBERT L TOUCHETTE, 467TH

MAURICE E TOW, 453RD, 445TH

HARRY L TOWER JR, 93RD

THOMAS J TOWLE JR, 448TH

DONALD C TOYE, 445TH

LTC JOHN C TRACEY JR RET, 492ND

WILLIAM E TRACY, 466TH

DR ROBERT B TRADER, 44TH

EDWARD TRAFFORD, SM

MELVIN G TRAGER, 93RD, 44TH

AL TRAICOFF, 467TH

LTC JAMES H TRAINOR RET, 93RD

RAYMOND F TRAPP, 491ST

ROBERT E TRAPP, 93RD

MAJ WILLIAM V TRASK RET, 392ND

GURSON TRAUB, 389TH

ROBERT B TRAUTMAN, 458TH

EDWARD E TRAYLOR, 453RD

WILLIAM O TREBING, 491ST

BOB B TREDWAY, 93RD

WILLIAM J TREHAL, 448TH

ROLAND E TRENT, 448TH

ROBERT L TRESLER, 492ND, 445TH

DR EDNA TREUTING, 448TH, AM

M/GEN ROCKLY TRIANTAFELLU RET, 389TH

LESLIE L TRIBBETT, 392ND

ELWYN M TRIGERO, 446TH

GEORGE TRIGILIO, 392ND

FRANK H TRINDER, 489TH, 389TH

SAMUEL J TRIPI, 389TH

EDWARD A TRIPOLD, 467TH

ROY E TRIPP, 361FG

PAUL E TRISSEL, 389TH

ROBERT C TRITLE JR, 389TH

DURWARD A TRIVETTE, 458TH

LEE A TROGGIO, 445TH

ROBERT V TROMBLY, 491ST

VIRGIL E TROMBLY, 445TH

LARRY S TROMER, 466TH

CECIL M TROSTLE, 93RD

GLENN D TROSTLE, 491ST

RICHARD R TROUSDALE, 93RD

CHARLES M TROUT, 492ND, 467TH

T JOHN TROWBRIDGE, 458TH

CHARLES E TROY, 389TH

HERBERT E TRULOVE, 389TH

LESTER C TRUMP, 446TH

GUS M TSIMPINOS, 448TH

ALLAN T TUCCI, 467TH

JOHN P TUCHOLSKI, 389TH

DEWITT C TUCKER, 445TH

DOYLE W TUCKER, 448TH

GORDON F TUCKER, 467TH

LEROY H TUCKER, 445TH

COL ROBERT C TUCKER RET, 445TH

WILLIAM P TUCKER, 446TH

ALICE C TUCKWILLER, 389TH, AM

DAVID E TUCKWILLER, 389TH

JAMES R TUDOR, 392ND
DENO C TULINI, 44TH
JOSEPH J TULLY, 93RD
WILLIAM V TUMELAVICH, 445TH
J W TUNE, HDQ
HORACE TURELL, 445TH
FELIX P TURKOVITZ, 458TH
MAJ ROBERT B TURNBULL RET,
  492ND, 44THAM
DAVID TURNER, SM
DEWEY E TURNER, 458TH
DONALD E TURNER, 44TH
HARLYN G TURNER, 446TH
JAMES B TURNER, 453RD
JIM TURNER, SM
JOHN R TURNER, 453RD
LARRY C TURNER, 491ST, AM
MYRON E TURNER, 392ND
SHELBY O TURNER MD, 44TH
THOMAS D TURNER, 491ST
JERRY M TURRENTINE, 93RD
VINCENT J TURRO, 453RD
NORMAN C TUSSEY, 93RD
GUY E TWEED, 491ST
ROBERT G TWEED, 446TH
EDMUND S TWINING JR, 392ND
ROBERT C TWYFORD, 467TH
M/SGT JOHN T TYBOROSKI RET,
  445TH
JACK TYER, 93RD
M/GEN HAL C TYREE JR RET,
  44TH
BRUCE UCHITEL, SM
HELEN M UEBELE, 467TH, AM
WEB UEBELHOER, 445TH
FRANK A UHLMAN JR, 467TH
JACK K UMPHREY, 458TH
RUSSELL S UNANGST, 93RD
KAROL L UNDERWOOD, 448TH
KENNARD UNDERWOOD JR,
  466TH
KENNETH P UNDERWOOD, 446TH
PETER E UNDERWOOD, SM
ROGER L UNDERWOOD, 489TH
ERWIN M UNGER, 445TH
JACK W UNVERFERTH, 491ST
CENTRE UNVERSAW, 361ST
JOHN J URBAN, 392ND
WARD C URBOM, 446TH
ROBERT USSAK, 448TH
JORDAN UTTAL, HDQ
GRACE A VADAS, 389TH, AM
ODELL B VADEN, 389TH
JOHN G VAHLE, 445TH
JAMES E VAISEY, 44TH
MANUEL J VALENCIA, 466TH
ANTHONY J VALENTE, 453RD
LOUIS VALENTI, 446TH
JULIUS E VALENZANO, 458TH
KENNETH S VALIS, 446TH
JAMES B VALLA, 389TH
RUSSELL A VALLEAU, 492ND
ARTHUR J VALOIS, 389TH
JOHN J VAN ACKER, 491ST
JOSEPH M VAN BIBBER, 458TH
DALE R VAN BLAIR, 448TH, 389TH
MARY CATHERINE VAN BLARGAN,
  458TH, AM
JOHN W VAN BOGELEN, 445TH
HENRY H VAN CLEAVE, 491ST
ROBERT D VAN CLEAVE, 453RD
DOMINQUE VAN DEN BROUCKE,
  SM
HARRY E VAN DORIEN, 458TH
DAVID P VAN DYKE, 44TH
NANCY LUCE VAN EPPS, 44TH
HOMER VAN FLETEREN, 446TH
JAMES VAN GINKEL, 466TH
LAWRENCE VAN KURAN,
  458TH, AM
RON R VAN SICKLE, SM
RIP VAN SKY, 458TH
ANDREW VAN SLOT, 466TH
JOHN L VAN WINKLE, 489TH
ARTHUR H VANDERBEEK, 458TH
JAMES VANDERHEIDE, 467TH
ELMER C VANGSNESS, 93RD
HARRY M VASCONCELLOS,
  392ND

MAJ CARLOS VASQUEZ RET,
  93RD
DANIEL VASQUEZ, 44TH, AM
SMS EMUEL E VASSEY JR RET,
  392ND
D THROOP VAUGHAN, 3SAD
EDWARD L VAUGHAN, 445TH
HENRY A VAUGHAN, HDQ
CALVIN C VAUGHN, 445TH
HERBERT VAUGHN, 467TH
WILLARD G VAUGHN, 445TH
LAWRENCE A VECCHI, 445TH
BEN E VEGORS, 448TH, 489TH
LTC LOUIS D VEHSLAGE RET,
  458TH
AURELE E VEILLEUX, 453RD
MAX F VEITCH, 44TH
ROGER A VEITCH, 44TH, AM
ROBERT H VENECK, 93RD
ALBERT C VENIER, 392ND
WILLIAM M VERBURG, 445TH
JOHN VERCLER, 453RD
JOHN F VERDESCHI, 446TH
FRANK L VERMEIREN, 458TH
WARREN B VERNIER, 453RD
JOHN E VERNOR, 445TH
J GARRETT VERPLANCK, 489TH
JOHN E VESSELS, 445TH
HEAROL R VETETO, 93RD
CLYDE F VETTER, 492ND
CARON VEYNAR, HDQ, AM
GLADYS & MILTON VEYNAR, HDQ
LCDR VANCE VEYNAR, HDQ, AM
COL ROBERT E VICKERS JR RET,
  392ND
NORMAN A VICKERY, 44TH
WILLIAM A VICKERY, 448TH
ROBERT & ISABELLE VICTOR,
  453RD
JOSEPH C VIG, 445TH
GEORGE VILLELLA, 44TH
RODRIC L VILLEMAIRE, 467TH
JOHN W VINCENT, 392ND
PAUL VINCENT, 389TH
COL ROBERT W VINCENT RET,
  458TH
COL WILLIAM L VINETTE RET,
  389TH
WILLIAM H VINEY, 389TH
LAWRENCE VINOVICH, 93RD
WILLIAM H VINTON, 445TH
SAM J VIOLA, 467TH
FRANK J VIRANT, 491ST
WILLIAM VISLOCKY, HDQ
WILMER VOELKER, 389TH
CURT M VOGEL, 458TH
DANIEL J VOIGHT, 453RD, AM
ROBERT W VOIGHT, 453RD, AM
WILLIAM VOIGHT, 453RD
RICHARD K VOILES, 458TH
ARTHUR VOLINI, 467TH
ROBERT R VOLKMAN SR, 361FG
JAMES F VOLLMER, 389TH
WILBERT VOLLMER, 453RD
ROBERT H VOLONTE, 445TH
ARLIE H VON TERSCH, 448TH
E KEITH VOORHEES, 491ST
WILLIAM V VOORHEES, 448TH
ALFRED A VOSKIAN, 453RD
EUGENE J VOSSMER, 453RD
JOHN A VOWVALIDIS, 448TH
CHARLES T VOYLES, 491ST
MARTIN R VOYVODICH, 491ST
EUGENE M VREELAND, 491ST
ANTHONY VUOLO, 445TH
JOHN B WAAG, 458TH
PHYLLIS WACKFORD, 489TH, AM
BARBARA S WADE, 448TH, AM
ODIS F WAGGONER, 492ND
ALEX WAGNER, 489TH
ARTHUR J WAGNER, 93RD
CHARLES H WAGNER, 44TH
CM/SGT CLARENCE E WAGNER
  RET, 466TH
EDWIN E WAGNER, 93RD
HAROLD L WAGNER, 93RD
JAMES F WAGNER, 448TH
JAMES M WAGNER, 445TH
JOE WAGNER, 458TH

RICHARD C WAGNER, 448TH
ROBERT A WAGNER, 466TH
THOMAS W WAGNER, 389TH
LTC HARRY T WAGNON RET,
  489TH
IVES J WAHRMAN, 446TH
LEONARD H WAINICK, 458TH
DEAN L WAKELEE, 392ND
J STANFORD WAKEMAN, 446TH
JAMES T WAKLEY, 491ST
FREDERICK M WALD, 392ND
SMYTH WALDEN JR, SM
COL EDWIN L WALDO RET, 44TH
LEONARD C WALDO, 392ND, 44TH
FRANK WALDRON, 491ST
WILLIAM A WALDRON, 93RD
WARD L WALHAY, 458TH
ABRAM B WALKER, 44TH
CHARLES L WALKER, 445TH
DANIEL G WALKER, 458TH
LTC EVERETT G WALKER RET,
  458TH
FLOYD L WALKER, 445TH
GEORGE C WALKER JR, 445TH
HAROLD A WALKER, 458TH
ION WALKER, 467TH
JACK WALKER, 448TH
JOHN D WALKER JR, 453RD
JOHN H WALKER, 44TH
KIRKE WALKER, 446TH
RALPH S WALKER, 453RD
SANDERS B WALKER JR, 445TH
WILLIAM R WALKER, 446TH
JOSEPH A WALKO SR, 389TH
LTC EDWARD M WALL RET,
  489TH, 448TH
WILLIAM J WALL, 392ND
ALEX S WALLACE, 453RD
ALEX S WALLACE, 453RD
WO CLINTON E WALLACE RET,
  458TH
GEORGE WALLACE, 458TH
GRIER S WALLACE, 453RD
M/SGT WILLIAM L WALLACE RET,
  392ND
DAVIS S WALLBRIDGE, 445TH
CHARLES C WALLER, 491ST
ROY E WALLER, 489TH
AL A WALLS, 453RD
DAVID WALPOLE, SM
JAMES K WALSER, 453RD
COL H BEN WALSH RET, 389TH
DR JOSEPH WALSH, 445TH
THOMAS F WALSH, 458TH
LTC BERNARD W WALTER RET,
  389TH
JAMES E WALTER, 466TH
LINDA L WALTER, SM
N J D WALTER, HM
ALLEN R WALTERS, 453RD
JOHN E WALTERS, 392ND
CAREY J WALTON JR MD, 492ND
LTC FRANCIS L WALTON RET,
  491ST
LEE WALTON, 389TH
HARRY R WALZ, 392ND
EVERARD P WANDELL, 448TH
KENNETH H WANDER, 445TH
LTC DELMAR WANGSVICK RET,
  453RD
WAYNE M WANKER, 448TH
POLLY WANN, 448TH, AM
RICHARD L WANN, 446TH
LTC EDMUND A WANNER RET,
  445TH
EUGENE B WANNER, 445TH
RICHARD T WARBOYS, 56FG
CHARLES A WARD JR, 453RD
DENHAM WARD, 448TH
JAMES M WARD, 389TH
LOYD WARD, 489TH
RAYMOND B WARD, SM
ROGER G WARD, 445TH
WILLIAM T WARD, 458TH
MARY ANN WARNER, 93RD, AM
RONALD G WARNER, 446TH
VICKI L WARNING, 466TH, AM
CALVIN J WARREN, 489TH

MEL WARREN, 458TH, AM
MILLARD R WARREN, 445TH
SAMUEL E WARREN, 458TH
DAVID P WARRILOW, 389TH
CHARLES J WARTH, 44TH
GEORGE A WASHBURN, 44TH
WILLIAM VAN N WASHBURN,
  467TH
EDWARD K WASHINGTON, 392ND
LTC FIELDING L WASHINGTON
  RET, 458TH
JOSEPH J WASIL, 389TH
EARL E WASSOM, 466TH
LTC IRVING D WATERBURY RET,
  466TH
RAY S WATERS, 448TH
THOMAS J WATERS, 445TH,
  389TH
FRANK L WATHEN, 93RD
GEORGE A WATKINS, 448TH
MALTBY F WATKINS MD, 392ND
T M WATKINS JR, 389TH
EDWIN C WATSON, 491ST
FRANK S WATSON, 467TH
MAURICE L WATSON, 458TH
ROBERT S WATSON, 389TH
THEODORE R WATSON, 466TH
THOMAS F WATSON, 93RD
LTC NORMAN B WATTEN RET,
  93RD
MILTON R WATTERS, 93RD
JAMES WATTS, 389TH, 491ST
WAVERLY FLYING GROUP, SM
CLAIR J WAY, 491ST
WILLIAM D WAYLAND, 389TH
DONALD WAYNE, 489TH, 65FW
SAM D WEAKLEY MD, 458TH
FRED L WEATHERLY, 453RD
CALVIN C WEAVER, 389TH
CHARLES I WEAVER, 489TH
GEORGE J WEAVER, 389TH
HANOVER WEAVER, 448TH
KENNETH E WEAVER, 448TH
LYMAN F WEAVER, 392ND
LTC WALTER W WEAVER RET,
  467TH
FRANK W WEBB, 492ND
LOUIS A WEBB, 93RD
RODNEY E WEBB, 448TH
COL JOHN L WEBER RET, 458TH
JOHN R WEBER, 446TH
PHILBERT N WEBER, 448TH
DONALD E WEBSTER DVM, 458TH
KENNETH E WEBSTER, 445TH
PAUL L WEBSTER MD, 453RD
W E WEBSTER, 445TH
JOSEPH L WECKESSER, 445TH
WALTER C WECKESSER, 392ND
HENRY W WEDAA, 467TH
ERNEST L WEDDELL SR, 445TH
JAMES H WEDDING, 458TH
JAMES E WEDDLE, 445TH
OSCAR F WEED, 392ND
LTC DALE R WEES RET, 389TH
FRED E WEGGE, 389TH
HOWARD WEHNER, 93RD
GEORGE L WEIDIG SR, 44TH
EDWARD J WEIDNER, 466TH
GENE WEIGANT, 491ST
HENRY J WEIGEL, 448TH
WILLIAM J WEILAND, 458TH
LTC CHARLES WEINBERG RET,
  389TH, 96CW
GEORGE J WEINBERGER, 448TH
BEN WEINER, 466TH
HILDA SAVAGE WEINER, 4FG, AM
SAMMY S WEINER, 445TH
STANLEY B WEINER, 489TH
IRA P WEINSTEIN, 445TH
MORTON WEINSTEIN, 44TH
LTC EDWARD E WEIR RET, 93RD
JEROME WEISBERG, 453RD
EDWARD D WEISERT, 93RD
SEYMOUR WEISMAN, 93RD
CHARLES J WEISS, 93RD
JOHN B WEISS, 93RD
DANIEL WEISSMAN, 491ST
ARTHUR N WEISZ, 448TH
ALBERT E WEITZ, 458TH

JOHN B WELCH JR, 458TH
WALTER M WELCH, 389TH
JOSEPH R WELCH-SNOPEK,
  392ND, AM
JAMES R WELDING JR, 453RD
WILLIAM L WELLMAN, 489TH
COL CECIL M WELLS RET, 453RD
CHARLES E WELLS, 389TH
IRA WELLS, 448TH
MELVIN L WELLS, 458TH
VERNON G WELLS, 389TH
LTC JOHN C WELSH RET, 466TH
RALPH T WELSH, 448TH
ALLEN J WELTERS, 467TH
DR BERNARD H WELTMAN, 467TH
JACK H WENDLING, 466TH
GEORGE WENICK, 389TH
AUGUST E WENNERSTROM JR,
  445TH
HENRY A WENTLAND, 389TH
ALVIN WERBALOWSKY, 389TH
GERARD D WERDELL, 491ST
PAUL W WERMUTH JR, 446TH
GERTRUDE BLUE WERNDLI, HDQ
EDWARD C WERNER, 453RD
WOODROW W WERNER, 466TH
GENE WESLOCK, 467TH
ROBERT W WESSALE, 491ST
BEN WESSEL, 453RD
RICHARD WESSEL, HDQ, 44TH
WALLACE WESSELS, 466TH
CLARA WEST, 389TH, AM
DONALD E WEST, 93RD
GLEN L WEST, 445TH, AM
PAUL WEST, 389TH, AM
STEVE WEST, 389TH, AM
LTC JOSEPH W WESTBROOK JR
  RET, 392ND
LTC MELVIN D WESTBROOK RET,
  466TH
ROBERT F WESTCOTT, 44TH
COL RICHARD T WESTENBARGER
  RET, 389TH, HDQ
PETER H WESTER, 389TH
CHARLES H WESTERLUND,
  445TH
NANCY L WESTGATE, 448TH, AM
QUENTIN WETTEROTH, 446TH
ROBERT J WEXLER, 453RD
JOHN R WEYLER, 467TH
KEITH WHALEY, 446TH
ALBERT T WHEATON, 44TH
HARRY L WHEATON, 445TH
KENNETH A WHEELER, 448TH
WILLIAM C WHEELER, 453RD
WILLIAM O WHEELER, 448TH
MAJ JOHN B WHEELIS JR RET,
  446TH, 492ND
A P WHEELOCK, 467TH
CHARLES D WHEELWRIGHT,
  392ND
EDWARD B WHELAN, 489TH
CAPT RALPH W WHIKEHART RET,
  445TH
LUCIAN A WHIPPLE JR, 448TH
MORELL E WHIPPLE, 458TH
DEARL WHITAKER, 448TH
RICHARD A WHITBECK, 93RD
ALFRED S WHITE, 389TH
CARL WHITE, 458TH
E E WHITE JR, 467TH
EDWIN D WHITE, 392ND
LTC HARRY A WHITE RET, 392ND
HARRY E WHITE, 446TH
JOHN A WHITE, 448TH
JOHN F WHITE, 446TH
JOHN R WHITE, 453RD
OSCAR L WHITE, 389TH
RAYMOND E WHITE, 93RD
STANLEY L WHITE, 392ND
WALTER E WHITE JR, 492ND
DONALD M WHITED, 93RD, 491ST
DONALD D WHITEFIELD, 44TH,
  389TH, 445TH, 492ND
KAYLOR C WHITEHEAD, 453RD
MR RALPH WHITEHEAD, SM
WILLIAM G WHITELEY, 453RD
DONALD WHITFORD, 392ND
LARRY J WHITING, 445TH

MERLIN E WHITLEY, 389TH
HUBERT S WHITLOCK, 389TH
W HARRY WHITLOCK, 445TH
SIDNEY WHITMAN, 93RD
WILLIAM L WHITNEY, 93RD, 389TH
DONALD WHITTAKER, 453RD
HORACE F WHITTAKER, 389TH
JOSEPH B WHITTAKER, 392ND, HDQ
JOSEPH B WHITTAKER, HDQ
HIRAM W WHITTLE, 467TH
LTC JAMES L WHITTLE JR RET, 44TH
THOMAS R WHOLLEY JR, 458TH
FREDERICK WICHMAN, 448TH
NORBERT J WICK, 392ND
ROBERT S WICKENS, 392ND
ROBERT W WICKHAM, 446TH
WILLIAM G WICKHAM, 44TH
ARTHUR A WICKS, 467TH
DOUGLAS J WICKWAR, SM
ERNEST G WIENER, 392ND
RAYMOND C WIER, 93RD
GEORGE E WIGFIELD, 453RD
WILLIAM M WIKE, 44TH
SID WILBY, SM
EDWIN E WILCOX, 458TH
FRANKLIN J WILD, 389TH
NELSON BUDD WILDER, 446TH
LEE WILDERMUTH, 93RD, AM
EDWIN L WILDS, 458TH
J WILDS, SM
MELVIN V WILE, 389TH
A EDWARD WILEN, 453RD
ALVIN WILENSKY, 458TH
MARY K WILEY, SM
DENNIS W WILFAHRT, 392ND
JAMES R WILGUS, 445TH
CLAYTON C WILKENING, 458TH
LESLIE A WILKERSON, 44TH
WILLIAM G WILKIE, 389TH
ROBERT A WILKINS, 392ND
ANDREW J WILKINSON, SM
RICHARD L WILKINSON, 93RD
WILLIAM WILKINSON, 489TH
BILL R WILKS, 458TH
A R WILLIAMS, 445TH
BALSER R WILLIAMS, 389TH
CARL L WILLIAMS, 458TH
CLYDE G WILLIAMS, 392ND
MAJ CURTIS C WILLIAMS RET, 467TH
DONALD K WILLIAMS, 458TH
DWIGHT L WILLIAMS, 489TH
GEORGE E WILLIAMS, 466TH
HAROLD E WILLIAMS, 93RD
HARRY L WILLIAMS, 491ST
J W WILLIAMS JR, 446TH
JACK A WILLIAMS, 445TH
LTC JAMES B WILLIAMS RET, 44TH
JOHN W WILLIAMS, 492ND
KENDRICK L WILLIAMS, 93RD
LAWRENCE A WILLIAMS, 93RD
MARGUERITE R WILLIAMS, 44TH, AM
RAYMOND O WILLIAMS, 491ST
RICHARD F WILLIAMS, 392ND
ROBERT B WILLIAMS, 458TH
ROBERT C WILLIAMS, 389TH
ROBERT H WILLIAMS, 446TH
THOMAS P WILLIAMS JR, 44TH
WILLIAM A WILLIAMS, 492ND
WILLIAM H WILLIAMS, 93RD
WILLIAM J WILLIAMS OD, 467TH
ALLEN D WILLIAMSON, 453RD
DON R WILLIAMSON, 392ND
FLOYD B WILLIAMSON, 453RD
LORRAINE P WILLIFORD, 492ND, AM
MELVIN B WILLIS, 466TH, 96CW
ROY S WILLIS, 448TH
WILLIAM H WILLIS, 467TH
ROBERT H WILLOUGHBY, 446TH
DONALD D WILLS, 453RD, 467TH
CHARLES C WILLSON JR, 491ST
JAMES J WILNO, 489TH
F C WILSDORF JR, 445TH
ALFRED R WILSON, 44TH

BRADFORD P WILSON, 445TH
BRYANT WILSON, 448TH
FORREST G WILSON, 467TH
G HARWOOD WILSON, 446TH
HAIG WILSON, 491ST
LTC HENRY M WILSON RET, 467TH
HERBERT J WILSON MD, 44TH
JAMES N WILSON, 445TH, AM
JERRY B WILSON, 93RD
JOHN E WILSON, 44TH
JOHN H WILSON JR, 389TH, 93RD
JULIAN K WILSON, 453RD
TRUMAN D WILSON, 445TH
WILLIAM WILTROUT, 389TH
DONALD E WIMBISCUS, 445TH
JACK J WIND, 44TH
EDWIN WINER, 44TH
LTC LINDLEY A WING RET, 467TH
JUSTUS J WINGARD JR, 445TH
THOMAS J WINGARD, 453RD
CHARLES L WINGO, 448TH
RALPH L WINGROVE, 446TH
EDWARD WINICK, 453RD
EDWARD J WINKLER, 392ND
DONALD N WINN, 93RD
EUGENE T WINN, 446TH
HARRY C WINSLOW, 453RD
RANDOLPH J WINSMAN, 389TH
DAN WINSTON, 491ST
BRUCE B WINTER, 448TH
EDWARD WINTER, 466TH
STANLEY L WINTER, 448TH
JOHN WINTERBOTTOM, SM
NORMAN WINTERBOTTOM, SM
M/SGT CLARENCE R WINTERS RET, 448TH
DANA S WINTERS, 458TH
L A WIPFLER, 392ND
CARL WIRGES, 389TH
ARTHUR G WIRTH, 492ND
BAYLOR B WISE, 489TH
KENNETH W WISE, 389TH, 453RD
DAVID J WISEHART, 389TH
BERT H WISEMAN, 453RD
JOHN C WITHERSPOON, 467TH
JAMES T WITHEY, 445TH
LTC ALBIN A WITKOWSKI RET, 446TH
GEORGE WITT, 489TH
HERMAN M WITT, 93RD
RICHARD T WITTON, 453RD
LTC ROBERT B WITZEL RET, 453RD
WILLIAM B WIVELL, 448TH
JOHN WLODARSKI, 491ST
JOSEPH F WOERNER, 489TH
LTC RUSSELL K WOINOWSK RET, 466TH
LAWRENCE A WOJCIK, 389TH
FRANK S WOLCOTT, 466TH
FRANK E WOLF, 466TH
JOSEPH R WOLF, 44TH
NEIL S WOLF, HDQ, AM
RAYMOND A WOLF, 93RD
DR HARRY O WOLFE JR, 448TH
COL LAWRENCE J WOLFE RET, 448TH
ROBERT W WOLFE, 453RD
ARTHUR H WOLKEN, 93RD
RALPH F WOMBACHER, 489TH
THOMAS S WONNELL, 492ND
CLIFTON E WOOD, 389TH
GEOFFREY R WOOD, 448TH
GORDON A WOOD, 44TH
JOHN B WOOD, 489TH
LEONARD A WOOD, 361FG
ROBERT J WOOD, 458TH
RODNEY WOOD, 466TH
WAYMON B WOOD, 448TH
RALPH E WOODARD, 453RD, 389TH
FREDERICK WOODBECK, 93RD
CHARLES M WOODBURY, 466TH
JOHN A WOODFORD, 458TH
LTC EDWARD J WOODHOUSE RET, 93RD
DAVID WOODROW, SM
GRANVILLE C WOODRUFF, 446TH

LEE J WOODS, 492ND, 448TH
ROLAND G WOODS, 445TH
ROSS D WOODS, 389TH
WILLIAM V WOODS, 453RD
LTC W D WOODSON RET, 93RD
CLAYTON WOODWARD, 389TH
HERBERT N WOODWARD JR, 458TH
COL VALIN R WOODWARD RET, 458TH
JOHN I WOODWORTH, 458TH
ROBERT D WOOFTER, 389TH
ROBERT W WOOLLEN, 93RD
JOHN H WOOLSEY JR DVM, 389TH
ROBERT WOOLSON, 44TH
JOHN WOOLWAY, 453RD
KIM WORDEN, 448TH, AM
LTC JOHN A WORHACH RET, 389TH
GUY V WORLOCK, 93RD
FRED J WORTH SR, 466TH
MAJ FRED D WORTHEN RET, 93RD
JOSEPH J WOZNIAK, 445TH
FRED WRABLIK, 93RD
SHELTON J WRATH, 491ST
ROBERT H WRAY, 389TH
RUSSELL J WRAY, 491ST
CHARLES C WRIGHT, 458TH
DANIEL D WRIGHT, 467TH
SM/SGT HERBERT A WRIGHT RET, 491ST
HERBERT O WRIGHT, 453RD
COL JAMES F WRIGHT RET, 44TH
RICHARD D WRIGHT, 491ST
COL ROBERT L WRIGHT RET, 389TH
ROBERT R WRIGHT, 93RD
STUART WRIGHT, SM
THOMAS X WRIGHT, 453RD
WALTER H WRIGHT, 458TH
ZANE D WRIGHT, 446TH
WILLIAM H WRIGHTS JR, 44TH
LTC WILLYS D WUEST RET, BG
RICHARD D WULLSCHLEGER, 392ND
CARL C WUNDERLICH, 448TH
ERNEST C WURM, 93RD
WARREN C WURM, 489TH
JOHN P WYATT, 389TH

DAVID G WYLDE, 489TH
LTC JAMES M WYLIE RET, 93RD, 446TH
JOHN L WYNN, 458TH
LTC JOSEPH YANDIAN RET, 467TH, 489TH
MARLIN YANDT, 445TH
CHARLES A YANT, 448TH
CHARLES L YARGER, 446TH
ROBERT J YARISH, 458TH
ROBERT K YARLING, 2CW
HAL YATES, 389TH
JOHN YATSKO, 448TH
CARL K YEAGER, SM
ROBERT L YELLAND, 491ST
CHARLES E YELTON, 489TH
DON E YERBY, 448TH
D KEITH YERTY, 458TH
PHILIP YESSIAN, 93RD
COL FRANK N YOCHEM JR RET, 446TH
COL HARRY D YODER RET, 44TH
S ALFRED YORK, 93RD
JOHN W YOST, 392ND, 93RD
WALTER P YOST, 44TH
EDWARD C YOUNG JR, 389TH
EUGENE W YOUNG, 458TH
GLENN D YOUNG, 467TH
IVO R YOUNG, 453RD
JAMES D YOUNG, 44TH
JAMES G YOUNG, SM
JAY YOUNG JR, 448TH
JAY S YOUNG, 467TH
MEWIN NEELY YOUNG, 392ND
ROBERT H YOUNG, 389TH
ROBERT L YOUNG, 446TH
ROBERT L YOUNG, 389TH
RUSSELL E YOUNG, 446TH
WILLIAM A YOUNG JR, 44TH
WILLIS H YOUNG JR, 489TH, 448TH
JOHN E YOUNGBERG, 492ND
FRED B YOUNGBLOOD, 448TH
CHARLES YOUREE, 93RD
RAY A YOW, 458TH
ERNEST YUHAS, 446TH
THOMAS YURCINA, 491ST
STEPHEN S YURIK, 44TH
MICHEL YUSPEH, 44TH
STAN ZABOROWSKI, 448TH

LTC PETER A ZAHN RET, 392ND
JOSEPH T ZAK, 93RD
STANLEY ZAK, 491ST
CHESTER J ZALESKI, 467TH
THOMAS P ZALUSKY JR, 467TH
ARTHUR E ZANDER, 448TH
KENNETH R ZAREMBA, 467TH
EDWARD V ZAUCHA, 491ST
JOSEPH N ZBIKOWSKI, 467TH
EDWARD J ZDUNSKI, 453RD
SAMUEL ZEARFOSS, 93RD
ROBERT L ZEDEKER, 458TH
WALTER J ZEE, 44TH
JOHN T ZEIEN, 446TH
THEODORE E ZELASKO, 458TH
DONALD ZELDIN, 448TH
JOHN ZELINKA, 467TH
MILTON H ZELON, 445TH, AM
ROBERT ZEMAN, 93RD
JOHN W ZGUD, 44TH
DONALD G ZIEBELL, 448TH
RALPH W ZIEHM, 392ND
BRUCE E ZIGLER, SM
JOHN P ZIMA, 448TH
REV ALEX ZIMMER, 389TH
ROBERT E ZIMMER, 446TH, AM
EARL L ZIMMERMAN, 389TH
GENE G ZIMMERMAN, 448TH, AM
L SAYLOR ZIMMERMAN JR, 458TH
ROBERT P ZIMMERMAN, 453RD
ELDEN E ZINK, 445TH
MICHAEL R ZINKA, 448TH
SAMUEL ZINN, 93RD
FREDERICK G ZIRK, 93RD
COL FRANK P ZITANO RET, 389TH
JOHN ZITNAK, 458TH
JOSEPH F ZITO, 458TH
MORTON ZIVE, 93RD
ALBERT A ZIZZI, 489TH
EDWARD ZOBAC, 445TH, AM
CHARLES F ZODROW, 93RD
WILLIAM H ZOELLER, 445TH
JOSEPH H ZONYK, 448TH
WILLIAM F ZOSKE, 467TH
FRANK G ZOUBEK, 458TH
GABRIEL S ZSIGO, 93RD
MARY LOUISE ZUBIALDE, 448TH, AM
LTC MAX ZUCKERMAN RET, 44TH
STANLEY C ZYBORT, 392ND

Back row, L to R: 1st Lt. Frank Glut, Copilot (KIA); 1st Lt. William Lozowski, Pilot (KIA); 1st Lt. Arthur Scheicher, Bombardier; 1st Lt. Anthony Marulli, Navigator. Front row, L to R: S/Sgt. John Corradetti, Nosegunner; S/Sgt. Cornelius Carter, Tailgunner (KIA); T/Sgt. Seymour Weisman, Engineer; T/Sgt. Paul Colby, Radio (KIA); T/Sgt. James Seger, Waistgunner (KIA). (Courtesy of William Lozowski)

SECOND AIR DIVISION VETERANS

Front row, L to R: Lyle Platner, Pilot; Milt Ehman, Bombardier; Robert Shaw, Navigator; Robert Powell, Copilot. Back row, L to R: Rudy Jensen, Waist Gunner; John Reed, Waist Gunner; Don Bertels, Tail Gunner; "Red" Ryan, Ball Gunner; Vern Reid, Radio Operator; Wade Stroup, Engineer. (Courtesy of Rudy Jensen)

Publisher's Note: All members of the 2nd Air Division Association were invited to write and submit biographies for inclusion in this publication. The following are from those who chose to participate. The biographies were printed as received, with only minor editing. The publisher regrets it cannot accept responsibility for omissions or inaccuracies within the following biographies.

HARRY C. AARON (MOE), was born June 24, 1922 in Cumberland, MD. Enlisted in the Air Force on Nov. 4, 1942. His military training included Armament School at Lowry Field and Gunnery School at Laredo, TX. He was assigned to B-24's group with training at Casper, WY. After completion of training, he was assigned to the 489th Bomb Group and the 846th Bomb Sqdn. and flew 11 missions as a waist gunner.

Most memorable experience was being sent back to the States at Christmas in 1944. He was honorably discharged on Nov. 14, 1945 with the rank of staff sergeant and received the Air Medal.

After discharge he enrolled in Shephard College, graduated and married his college sweetheart, Geraldine Clark. They have four children and six grandchildren. After 32 years of service to the state of Maryland, he took his retirement to spend more time with his family and grandchildren.

FRANK W. AARONSON JR., was born in Mt. Holly, NJ on July 19, 1924. Enlisted in the USAAF Dec. 7, 1942; graduated navigator, Selma Field, LA in February 1944; assigned to the 445th Bomb Group 701st Sqdn. He joined crew at Casper, WY; picked up plane at Topeka, KS; flew to England April 1944 and completed 30 missions.

Was honorably discharged December 1962 with the rank of USAR captain. Received the Distinguished Flying Cross and four Air Medals.

Married with three children and 13 grandchildren. He retired from private business as a petroleum distributor that his sons now run. He resides in Florida for six months of the year and in New Jersey for other six months.

JOE LELAND ABERNATHY, was born in Pulaski, TN Dec. 7, 1925. Enlisted in USAAC Oct. 12, 1943 as cadet. Served with the 8th Air Force 2nd Air Div., 467th Bomb Group, 790th Bomb Sqdn.

Military locations/stations: Rackheath England, March Field, Miami, FL, Panama City, FL and more. Participated in the battles at Germany, crossing Rhine Bulge and Ardennes. Memorable experience: Berlin bombed Tuile; flying his first mission on the *Witchcraft*. He flew 22 bombing missions including one on Dec. 24, 1944.

Honorably discharged Nov. 8, 1945, he received the Air Medal with two clusters, ETO and other war-time medals.

Married with three children. He retired as engineer from the Pacific Telephone Company after 34 years.

LEONARD ABRAMOWITZ (LEN), was born Dec. 12, 1920 in Canton, MA. Enlisted Oct. 15, 1942 while attending Franklin Union Institute/Pharmacy College. Commissioned second lieutenant, Class 44B at Eagle Pass, TX. Graduate CIS Randolph Field, and instructor at Perrin Field, TX.

Assigned to 489th Bomb Group, he completed his 35th combat mission as pilot of the 458th Bomb Group's illustrious B-24 Liberator *Final Approach.* Flew 123 combat strikes, 113 missions without an abort. Downed by AA and interned as POW until May 1945.

Various assignments to stateside bases, Japan Self Defense Force, UK and Hawaii. Awards included Air Medal with four Oak Leaf Clusters, five European Campaign Stars, Commendation Medal, Purple Heart, Presidential Unit Citation and POW Medal.

After November 1966 USAF retirement, he entered real estate, landman and retired as Realtor, Texas-Oklahoma licensed broker in 1986.

HERBERT ACHTERBERG, was born Nov. 14, 1921 in St. Joseph, MI. Inducted into the USAAC in February 1943. Assigned to the 466th Bomb Group, Alamagordo, NM as Group HQ draftsman in the fall of 1943.

Arrived in England, via the steamship *Queen Mary,* March 1944. Active member of the 466th Flying Deck Glee Club and as such, performed extensively at both U.S. and British military bases as well as churches and theaters including Rainbow Corner in London.

In May 1944 received the one and only ever "Mouse Medal" as administered by His Majesty's Ministry of Mice & Rats, for the meritorious destruction of vermin by order of Lord Pushface.

Returned to U.S. via *War Weary* B-24 July 1945 for a

first time meeting with his 14 month old son, Gus. Was honorably discharged late August 1945 at Ft. Sheridan, IL.

Currently retired and serving as village trustee, Stevensville, MI.

DONALD L. ACKERMAN SR., was born Aug. 10, 1919, Plainfield, NJ and joined the USAAC Aug. 31, 1941. Graduated Flight School Class 42-D, Moultrie, GA. Advanced flying instructor and squadron commander April 1942-March 1944. Flew 17 missions B-24s, 506th Bomb Sqdn., 44th Bomb Group, Shipdham, England, June 1944 until war's end. Lost engine on mission #2 over Germany. Made lead crew after mission #12.

Participated in battles: Rhineland, Ardennes, Central Europe. With 5th Air Force, Japan and Korea, July 1948-September 1951. Instructor Air Science University of Buffalo, NY, 1955-1958. Command pilot Aug. 20, 1957. Commander Denham AFB, England November 1958-November 1961. Retired with 21 years service Aug. 31, 1962 with the rank major, total flying time 3,728 hours.

Received BS and MS in administration. Taught and administrated Duval County School System, Jacksonville, FL. Retired again June 9, 1981.

Married Portia Spalding Nov. 5, 1943. Has two children, Don Jr. and Jan Brundick and four grandchildren: Katie, Korey, Kasey Ackerman and Emerson Spalding Brundick. Major Ackerman died suddenly June 7, 1991. His spouse resides in Atlantic Beach, FL.

JAMES M. ACKERMAN, was born in Paterson, NJ. Sept. 18, 1919. Entered the service Oct. 3, 1940, 258th FA. Accepted for Aviation Cadet training January 1943. Graduated Class of 1943, K, December 1943. Assigned to Crew 2317 as co-pilot, B-24, 8th Air Force, 392nd Bomb Group, 577th Bomb Sqdn., Wendling, England.

Completed 12 missions and was shot down on the 13th (their first lead mission) Lyon, France June 23, 1944. Burned and bailed out, was captured and held POW at Rheims, France until liberated by Patton's 5th Div. Sept. 1, 1944.

Married 50 years to Madeleine, they have four children: Judith, Ron, Jeffrey and Jon; 10 grandchildren and three great-grandchildren. Retired in Virginia after 30 years with the Bendix Corporation. Now enjoying life and memories.

JAMES L. ADAMS, was born Sept. 26, 1920 in Rector, AR. Enlisted in the USAAC April 3, 1942, 8th Air Force, 93rd Bomb Group 330th Sqdn. Stationed at Muroc, Hamilton Field, Marfa, TX, Hardwick, England (93), Barksdale AFB, Randolph Field, Ellington, etc.

Participated in EAME Campaign, first pilot B-24s, completing 34 missions. He says there were to many memorable experiencs to list but feels most of them left part of themselves over there.

Adams was honorably discharged Sept. 26, 1968 with the rank of lieutenant colonel. He received the Distinguished Flying Cross, Air Medal with four Oak Leaf Clusters and other war-time medals.

Married Dec 10, 1943, he has four sons and two granddaughters. Currently retired and enjoying life.

JOHN H. ADAMS, was born on Jan. 10, 1918 and lived in Hamden, CT before graduating from Yale in 1941. His navigation training was at Turner Field, Albany, GA with the Class of 42-6, following which he was assigned to the 41st Anti-Submarine Sqdn. at Westover Field, MA.

After six months in B-25s, his squadron was sent to Langley Field, VA, trained in B-24s and sent to Gander, Newfoundland for North Atlantic patrol. Reassigned in the Spring of 1943 to cover the Bay of Biscay with the RAF Coastal Command, these AAF squadrons were later disbanded with the personnel reassigned to the 8th AAF.

Adams had 17 mission credits for his 1250 hours of patrol time but was shot down on Nov. 13, 1943 while flying with the 392nd Bomb Group and spent 18 months in Stalag Luft 1.

Married to Dorothy Wheeler Adams for over 46 years, they have three children and five grandchildren. He was in personnel management with United Aircraft, where he was assistant personnel manager for the Hamilton Standard Division, before going into education and retiring as a school headmaster in 1983 in Santa Barbara, CA.

ORA R. ADAMS, was born in Eldora, IA March 1, 1924. Entered the USAAC on Feb. 15, 1943. Trained in heavy bomber armament at Buckley and Lowry Fields, CO and Aerial Gunnery at Harlingen Field, TX. Assigned to a B-24 Bomber crew as an armorer-gunner at Gowen Field, ID. Flew with others of the 453rd Bomb Group, via the southern route to an 8th Air Force Base at old Buckingham, England in late 1943.

Completed tour of 31 combat missions against Germany from February 1944, to June 1944. He was honorably discharged from service in October 1945. He was awarded the Distinguished Flying Cross, four Air Medals, and four European Campaign Stars.

Attended Iowa State College 1946-1949, obtaining a degree in landscape architecture. Served 35 years with the Housing Authority and Planning Commission, Nashville, TN. Retired in 1985.

Married Kathleen Robertson Oct. 4, 1946, they have two daughters, a son, and three grandchildren.

ELLIOTT W. ADCOCK (TINY), was born in Dickson, TN on Nov. 27, 1913, son of James J. and Elizabeth Adcock.

Enlisted in the USAAF in Detroit, MI, July 4, 1942. Reported to Camp Atterbury, IN, then Jefferson Barracks, MO; Davis Monthan Field, AZ; Biggs Field, TX; Lowry Field, NJ.

Boarded the *Queen Elizabeth* for trip to England. Served with the 389th Bomb Group, 564th Bomb Sqdn. Stationed at Hethel, Norwich, Norfolk, England. Was mess sergeant of both enlisted and officers mess.

He was honorably discharged August 1945 at Charleston, SC. He was awarded the Presidential Unit Citation for Ploesti.

Adcock passed away in April 1973. He is survived by his wife, Eleanor Young Adcock.

Information submitted by his sister, Dorothy A. Norman, Dickson, TN, also an Associate Member of the 2nd Air Div.

BOYD D. ADSIT, was born Sept. 4, 1924 Hot Springs, AR and grew up in Topeka, KS. Trained in Texas and joined 578th Sqdn., 392nd Bomb Group, Wendling, England in October 1944 as first pilot. Flew 27 missions before V-E day. On 6th mission in early January 1945, bailed out over Alsace-Lorraine. Some minor injuries to crew, but all made it back to Wendling to continue flying together.

After several "trolley missions" (sight-seeing missions over the bombed areas), returned to U.S. with ground personnel aboard in June 1945, via Iceland and Greenland, flying a war-weary B-24. Japan surrendered before any of crew saw further action.

Adsit went on to college and law school, served 25 years as FBI Agent, 16 years as Real Estate Broker and retired in 1992.

The crew enjoyed a reunion in Dayton, OH in 1984. All members present, but two have since passed on.

ALBERT C. AHLERS (HAP), was born Oct. 14, 1925 in Toledo, OH. Enlisted in the USAAF Dec. 29, 1943. Military stations/locations included: El Paso, TX; Sioux Falls, SD and Chatham Field, Savannah, GA.

Assigned to the 389th Bomb Group, 8th Air Force, he flew B-24s. Being a chief armor gunner and being placed in all the gun positions, one of the worst things was all the flak from enemy fire. Stationed in Hethel, England, most all his "missions" were flown over the Rhineland and Central Europe.

Honorably discharged at Ft. Bliss, TX Jan. 30, 1946 with the rank staff sergeant. He received the Good Conduct Medal, Air Medal, Meritorious Unit Award, and WWII Victory Medal.

Married Mary Weasel Nov. 8, 1952 in Toledo, OH. They had one son, two daughters and four grandchildren.

Ahlers passed away suddenly Nov. 30, 1992. He was very proud of his service to his country and the Air Corps.

CARL W. AHRENDT, was born Hiawatha, KS on Sept. 5, 1921. Enlisted in the USAAC June 22, 1942 as a flight line and engine mechanic with the 2nd Air Div. Military stations/locations: Goldsboro, NC; Patterson, NJ; Wendover, UT; Sioux City Air Base, Sething, England, Station 146.

Memorable experience was ground crew at Sething, England, 448th Bomb Group, 715th Sqdn. and the German bombings and strafing on base.

Honorably discharge Sept. 5, 1945 with the rank of sergeant. He was awarded the Good Conduct, EAME Theater Medal and the WWII Victory Medal.

Married Oct. 8, 1943, has four children. He is now retired.

EUGENE A. AICHROTH, was born Sept. 27, 1915 in London, England. Emigrated to the USA December 1928. Drafted into the Coast Artillery April 1941 for one year. Discharged to re-enlist into the Regular Army in order to transfer to the USAAC in August 1941.

Sent to Jefferson Barracks, St. Louis, MO. Completed Link Trainer instructors course and was instructor at Advanced Flying School, Turner AFB, Albany, GA. Entered Aviation Cadets, SAACC, San Antonio, TX in 1943. Primary training Chickacha, OK, Class 43-J. Disqualified because of dangerous landings.

Entered Radio School, Scott Field, IL, radio operator, tech sergeant, 8th Air Force, Rackheath, England, November 1944 to June 1945. Had opportunity to renew acquaintance with his English grandmother. Flew 26 missions and received Air Medal.

Discharged October 1945, enlisted in USAFR June 6, 1949, and received honorable discharge on Dec. 5, 1952. He married Lillian Woodruff, whom he met while in St. Louis, MO, and they have two children.

Retired from Long Island Lighting Company in 1976. Enjoys writing as one of several hobbies.

CHARLES AILLET, was born June 7, 1922 in Lafayette, LA. Served in U.S. Naval Air Corps; graduated USN V-5 pre-flight, Athens, GA in November 1942. Entered the USAAC Jan. 27, 1943. Stationed at Chicago, IL radio operator; Sioux Falls, SD, Advanced Radio School; graduated Flex Gunnery, Kingman, AZ on April 12, 1943.

He completed 31 missions with the 458th Bomb Group from May 1, 1944 to February 1945. Was forced down on continent near Brussels in September 1944. Returned to base two days later, left aircraft (B-24) at St. Trund, Belgium, all four engines feathered.

Honorably discharged Sept. 12, 1945 with the rank of tech sergeant. He was awarded the Air Medal with five Oak Leaf Clusters, five Battle Stars and several Campaign Medals. Crew awarded Distinguished Flying Cross. Flew as Lead Class A radio operator.

Married Lucille Gankendorff Aug. 4, 1945, they have three children: Linda (Mrs. Kelly Younger), Cynthia Ann Aillet and Larry Aillet; and two grandchildren, Jessica and Michael Charles Younger.

ANTHONY ALBINO, was born in Blue Island, IL Jan. 18, 1922. Enlisted in the USAAF April 21, 1943. Basic training, Engineering and Gunnery schools at Keesler Field, MS. Met with assigned crew and completed overseas training at Chatham Field, GA. Obtained B-24s at Langley Field, VA, destination, England.

Stationed at Wendling, England with 392nd Bomb Group, 578th Bomb Sqdn., AAF Station 118. Flew supply mission to Wessel for troops across the Rhine and 34th and 35th missions to Northern France, Royens.

Was honorably discharged Oct. 12, 1945 with the rank of tech sergeant. He received the Air Medal with five Oak Leaf Clusters. Married to Edna and has one son, Charles.

Retired in late 70s and became very active in the Colombo Club, the largest Italian club west of the Mississippi with 800 members. Past president of the club and now on board of directors.

HARRY J. ALBRIGHT, was born Aug. 8, 1921. Entered USAAF Sept. 23, 1941. While in service, attended Airplane Mechanics School at Keesler Field and 8th Bomber Command Gunnery School near King's Lynn in England.

Reported for duty with the 330th Bomb Sqdn. of the just-forming 93rd Bomb Group at Barksdale Field, LA on March 22, 1942. Was a member of "Ted's Traveling Circus" until his rotation back home on Dec. 2, 1944.

Assigned to a combat flight crew as flight engineer, flew first combat mission on D-day, June 6, 1944, and last mission on Aug. 14, 1944. Volunteered for detached service with the Air Transport Command. Made 18 trips to France and Belgium hauling aviation gas using "war-weary" B-24s.

Returned to Hardwick Oct. 3, 1944 and worked as squadron engineer until rotation back to the States.

After his leave he saw duty at Kelly Field and at EEAB at Enid, OK. While at Enid, Germany capitulated and the "point system" was instituted. He was honorably discharged on May 28, 1945 with 156 discharge points.

Received the Distinguished Flying Cross, five Air Medals, Good Conduct Medal, Presidential Unit Citation, American Defense Service Medal, WWII Victory Medals and the EAME Theatre Ribbon with nine Battle Stars.

While he was stationed at Kelly Field, he married his childhood sweetheart and had five children and nine grandchildren. He retired in 1983 and at present is living in his hometown of Ewen, MI.

MAX K. ALDWORTH, was born Eau Claire, WI. Enlisted in the USAAF March 23, 1943. Assigned to the 8th Air Force, 2nd Div., 713th Group. Stationed at Miami Beach, FL; Sioux Falls Radio School Sioux Falls, SD; Yuma Gunnery School and crewed up at March Field, CA and ended up at Seething Field, Norwich, England.

Memorable experience was first sight of ME 262s. Had frontal attack and they got the deputy lead who came down on the bricket lead. They were flying left wing off the bricket. Only three chutes were seen from the two B-24s. He participated in the Ardennes, Rhineland and Central Europe campaigns.

Was honorably discharged Nov. 10, 1945 with the rank of tech sergeant. He received the Air Medal with two Oak Leaf Clusters.

Married Phyllis and has two sons, two daughters and eight grandchildren. He is a retired letter carrier for the U.S. Postal Service. He and Phyllis keep very busy with their many interests and are enjoying retirement.

BERT F. ALEXANDER, was born June 23, 1918 in Checotah, OK. Transferred from 12th Field Artillery to Aviation Cadet, Pilot, Class of 43-A. B-24 transition at Alamogordo, NM. Joined Ted's Travelling Circus, 330th Sqdn. May 1943. The group was deployed to Benghazi, North Africa and on their third mission, covering the invasion of Sicily, they missed the airdrome on return and bailed out over the Libyan Desert. Survived 10 days before rescue of six of the 10-man crew.

Completed 25 missions (one as waist gunner to Weiner-Neustadt, Austria) Feb. 28, 1944. Rotated Stateside December 1944. Co-pilot C-54s flew occupation troops into Japan 1945. Married Shirley in 1947. Discharged as master sergeant at Randolph AFB.

Recalled as first lieutenant C-47 pilot in support of Berlin Airlift. Back to master sergeant at Waco, TX November 1950. Captain, flying TB-50s at Mather Navigator School. Progressed through B-29s at Lake Charles SA-16s Air Rescue in Okinawa, B-36s at Biggs AFB, and B-52s at Seymour-Johnson, NC.

Retired November 1960. Was rewarded the Distinguished Flying Cross, Air Medal with three Oak Leaf Clusters, Purple Heart, European Theatre Ribbon with three Battle Stars, Pacific Campaign, China Service Medal and Distinguished Unit Citation with one Oak Leaf Cluster.

Worked as an administrator for Sacramento County, CA, retiring in 1979.

CARL I. ALEXANDERSON (CIA), was born in Jamaica, Long Island, NY July 9, 1924. Enlisted in USAAC Nov. 11, 1942 after completing high school. Took basic training in Miami Beach, FL, then was assigned to B-17 Crew

Chief Training Program in Amarillo, TX for six months. Lockheed Factory School in Burbank, CA for six weeks.

Small Arms Training at Salt Lake City. Gunnery School was completed at Davis-Monthan Field, Tucson, AZ in October 1943. Assigned to combat crew training on B-24s at that station, where 491st Bomb Group originated.

Departed USA for England May 8, 1944 with factory fresh aircraft via South America and Africa. Flew 15 missions from Metfield and 15 from North Pickenham as flight engineer-gunner. Completed tour Nov. 8, 1944. "TDY" 313th Troop Carrier Group.

Discharged October 1945 with the rank of staff sergeant. He received the Distinguished Flying Cross, Air Medal with three Oak Leaf Clusters, Good Conduct Medal and the ETO Campaign Medal with four Bronze Stars. Continued education under GI bill, acquiring aircraft and engine, 2nd class radio telephone and pilot license with seaplane rating.

Retired 1984 after 30 years with General Electric Corporate Air Transport Operation. Served five years as vice president of the 491st Bomb Group, one year executive vice president 2nd Air Division Association, president, 1987-88 and four years executive committee.

Married Louise Joyner Oct. 31, 1945. Has one son, three daughters and eight grandchildren.

JOHN E. ALFRIEND, was born June 30, 1925. Enlisted in the USAAF Sept. 2, 1943. Assigned to the 8th Air Force, 93rd Bomb Group, 328th and 329th Bomb Sqdns. as a tail gunner. Stationed at Keesler Field, MS; Harlingen Field, TX; Pueblo, CO and Hardwick, England.

Participated in Central Europe, Ardennes; North France and Rhineland campaigns. He will always remember all the flack at Magdeburg Sept. 11, 1944. He flew 25 missions over Germany.

Received honorable discharge Oct. 25, 1945 at Sioux Fall, SD. He received the Air Medal with four Oak Leaf Clusters and the ETO Ribbon with four Battle Stars.

Alfriend is married with one daughter. Retired from Mobil Oil Corporation.

PETER J.D. ALLATT, was born June 30, 1924 London, England and reared in New York City. Volunteered for the USAAF Aviation Cadet Program in July 1942 and entered Enlisted Reserve Corps, Dec. 8, 1942 with security clearance of "co-belligerent alien." Trained as pilot in SEFTC, graduated June 27, 1944 Class 44-F, George Field, Lawrenceville, IL. Posted to B-24 Transition, Chanute AAF and OTU at Charleston AAF, SC.

Flew B-24 with crew from Mitchell AAF, NY to England (northern route), attached to 328th Sqdn, 93rd Bomb Group, Hardwick, February through May 1945. Logged 17 missions, encountering the ME-262 from time to time. Returned, via same route, May 1945. Enrolled in ORC after release from AD October 1945. Flew A-26, C-119 and C-124 at Stewart AFB, NY.

Graduated from college, finally, in 1951. Activated for Vietnam incident in 1968 for 18 months. Placed on Retired List as major, June 30, 1984. Total time: 41 years, six months, 22 days, of which 20 were "satisfactory." He was awarded two Air Medals, EAME with stars, AF Longevity and Vietnam Service medals.

Civilian occupation was aviation insurance and reinsurance broker. He has two daughters and one son.

EDGAR J. ALLEN, was born on a farm in Cloud County, KS, Feb. 28, 1922. Entered the USAAC Feb. 3, 1943 as an Aviation Cadet and graduated as a pilot Dec. 5, 1943. Took B-24 transition at Liberal, KS combat crew training at Colorado Springs, CO and Mountain Home, ID.

Assigned to the 93rd Bomb Group, July 1944. After

eight missions became lead pilot. Finished 30 missions April 1945. After returning to the U.S. was assigned to Ferry Command, Long Beach, CA. Beginning September 1946, served four years in Flight Service at McChord AFB, WA. During Korean War served with 1503rd ATW, Tokyo, then 463rd Troop Carrier Wing, Memphis, TN. Released from active duty August 1953 as major and squadron commander. He received the Distinguished Flying Cross, Air Medal with four Oak Leaf Clusters, Korea, ETO with four stars and other war-time medals.

Married Thelma Moody (from London and whose family emigrated to America in January 1948) September 1948. They have three children and six grandchildren.

EVERETT S. ALLEN, was born Sept. 16, 1920 Portsmouth, NH. Enlisted Oct. 9, 1942 at Ft. Devens, MA; Cochran Field, Macon, GA, basic training; Courtland, AL, Dec. 15, 1942 and Seymour-Johnson, NC, Aircraft Mechanic School April 7, 1943; Aug. 31, 1943 Ft. Myer, FL Gunnery School (four trained on YB-40). Received Wings Dec. 7, 1943.

Ten day delay en route to Salt Lake City for assignment on Dec. 30, 1943, B-24 training as tail gunner. Ireland April 21, 1944. Combat June 6, 1944 with 458th Bomb Group, Horsham St. Faith, England. Shot down June 29, 1944. Memorable experience was three week Dutch Underground and POW forced march across Germany.

Honorable discharge Oct. 27, 1945 with the rank of staff sergeant. He received the Air Medal with two Oak Leaf Clusters and the POW Medal.

Married for over 47 years. Now retired.

GERALD O. ALLEN (JERRY), was born Monroe, MI Oct. 20, 1918. Graduated Cleveland Heights High School 1936. Received BS from Ohio State University in 1940 and Juris Doctorate in 1942. Enlisted USAAC Oct. 26, 1942. Stationed at Keesler Field, MS, basic training; Birmingham Southern College, aviation student; Maxwell Field, pre-flight; Union City, TN; Primary Flight Training; Newport, AR, Basic Flight Training; Valdosta, GA, Advanced Flight Training; Smyrna, TN, B-24 Transition; and Pueblo, CO Combat Crew Training.

Joined 458th Bomb Group, 755th Bomb Sqdn., July 1944. Flew lead pilot for 25 missions. Promoted to captain. Returned to U.S. May 1945. Released from active duty August 1945. Active reserves 1947-1950. Recalled for active duty October 1950. Base operations and medical-evacuation pilot at Rhein/Main AFB. Returned to Inactive Reserves June 1952.

Received Distinguished Flying Cross with one Oak Leaf Cluster, Air Medal with four Oak Leaf Clusters, European Campaign with four Battle Stars, Germany Occupation Medal and several other campaign medals.

Married Elizabeth Carlson on Oct. 24, 1942. Has one daughter and one grandson.

HENRY W. ALLEN (HANK), was born Sept. 7, 1919 in Freeport, ME. Enlisted in 152nd Field Artillery Dec. 5, 1940. Transferred to Corps of Engineers March 5, 1942, commissioned second lieutenant June 19, 1942. Transferred to Air Corps as first lieutenant Feb. 26, 1943. Qualified as navigator Jan. 15, 1944 at Selman Field, LA.

Assigned May 10, 1944 to 392nd Bomb Group (Henderson's crew) at Wendling, England. Made squadron navigator 578th Sqdn. Oct. 30, 1944 and was promoted Jan. 25, 1945 to captain. Flew 27 combat missions.

Retired from Reserves in 1972 with the rank of lieutenant colonel. He received the Air Medal with three clusters and five European Campaign Stars.

Married the late Lillian Sylvester, Jan. 18, 1944. They had four children and seven grandchildren.

He attended the University of Maine, University of Missouri and John Hopkins. Received AB 1948, AM 1949 in geology from the University of Missouri. Taught at University of Missouri, Wellesley College and University of Maine. 1957 to 1983 worked as geologist for Martin Marietta Corporation, retiring as chief geologist of Martin Marietta Cement. Resides in Conway, AR.

LYNN D. ALLEN, O.D., was born July 13, 1925 in Pontiac, MI. Enlisted in the USAAF, 8th Air Force, July 13, 1943. Gunnery, Ft. Myers, FL; OTU Casper, WY and Rackheath 467th Bomb Group, 489th Sqdn. Participated in the battles at Ardennes, Rhineland and Central Europe.

Most memorable experience was being in London when three V2s hit within a few blocks. Received honorable discharge in February 1946 with the rank of sergeant. He received three Battle Stars, Air Medal with two Oak Leaf Clusters and Presidential Unit Citation.

Married, he has two daughters and four grandchildren.

He attended school on the GI bill and became an Optometrist in 1950. At present, he is a county clerk/register of deeds for Oakland County, MI.

PAUL SEVERN ALLEN, was born Nov. 11, 1917 Greenville, SC. Operated movie theaters in North and South Carolina. Enlisted in the USAAC Sept. 27, 1941. Basic training at Keesler Field, MS where he remained as chief clerk operating base theaters, supervising the booking of movies and arranging concerts, vaudeville acts and personal appearances of celebrity personalities.

He attained the rank of technical sergeant. In 1944 he requested a reduction in rank to private so that he could enter Aerial Gunnery School at Laredo, TX. Upon graduation, he enrolled in Air Mechanics School in order to qualify as flight engineer. Assigned to the 8th Air Force, 2nd Div., for combat duty in the European Theatre.

Completed 21 combat air missions by V-E day in B-24 Bombers. Duties were flight engineer and radar counter measures equipment operator. Upon his return to the States, he was assigned to Alamogordo, NM to await discharge. While there he worked with Special Services arranging entertainment for base personnel.

He was honorably discharged at Ft. Bragg, NC Separation Center on Sept. 16, 1945. His awards included the Air Medal and the EAME Campaign Medal with seven Bronze Stars.

After his discharge and before retirement, he became Chamber of Commerce Executive in Hickory, NC; partnership in furniture manufacture and fund raiser at Lenoir Rhyne College in Hickory.

Married Marjorie Ann Fitch and they have two sons and two grandchildren. He and Marjorie are enjoying retirement in their home on Lake Hickory.

JULIO R. ALONSO (HAP), was born June 27, 1918 in Collinsville, OK. Parents born in Spain. Arrived in England October 1944. Stationed at "Old Buck" (Buckingham) near Attleborough East Anglia with the 453rd Bomb Group, 732nd Sqdn. Completed 26 bombing missions as waist gunner armorer.

Honorably discharged October 1945 with the rank of

staff sergeant. Received the Air Medal with three Oak Leaf Clusters and the European Theatre of Operations Ribbon with three Battle Stars.

Married Gladys E. Earhart of Westminster, MD in 1953. One son, William R. Alonso, a biochemist PhD research scientist.

Obtained commercial pilot's license in 1948. Crop duster pilot for five years. 1953-1960 civilian flight instructor training pilots for the Air Force. In December 1960 obtained airline transport pilots license and flew as co-pilot and flight engineer with Airlift International, Inc. until December 1981 retirement.

January 1983 through 1993 air traffic assistant with FAA at Atlanta Air Route Traffic Control Center.

GERALD ALPORT, was born in Chicago, IL April 6, 1925. Entered USAAF May 1943. Basic training Sheppard Field, TX; AM School Keesler Field, MS; Gunnery School Laredo, TX; crew assignment Gowen Field, ID May 1944. Joined 466th Bomb Group, 786th Bomb Sqdn., September 1944. First mission Oct. 6, 1944. Completed 35th mission April 5, 1945. Returned to ZI May 12, 1945.

Attended Engine Specialist School, Chanute Field, IL July 1945. Honorably discharged at Truax Field, WI Oct. 15, 1945 with the rank of staff sergeant.

Married high school sweetheart Sept. 8, 1946. Has two children and two grandchildren. Freight traffic manager for 28 years. Retired Aug. 31, 1990.

EINO ALVE, was born April 21, 1921, Newfield, NY. Enlisted in the USAAC in March 1940. Served the next three years in Panama Air Depot as an aircraft engine overhaul mechanic.

Graduated twin engine pilot training, December, Class 43-K, Lubbock, TX. Assigned a crew and new B-24 at Lincoln, NE to begin combat operations with the 453rd Bomb Group, 733rd Sqdn. effective July 1944 at Old Buckingham, Attleborough, UK. Competed 35 combat missions. Awarded the Distinguished Flying Cross, five Air Medals and five European Campaign Stars.

Returned to USA May 1945 to join the Air Force Reserves, retired as lieutenant colonel after 24 years. Attended Cornell Agricultural College. Operated a dairy farm for 35 years. Married Edna Saikkonen, June 1945 and has four daughters and five grandchildren. Also served the community as justice of the peace for 14 years and as an assessor for 10 years.

GENE P. ALVORD, was born in Detroit, MI on May 17, 1919 and raised primarily in Chicago, IL. Entered the Armed Forces Oct. 9, 1941 as a private. Was promoted through the ranks, eventually holding every rank up to master sergeant, then entered the Aviation Cadet Program, graduating as a second lieutenant navigator in June 1943.

Flew in B-24s all through the war in Europe. Assigned to the 93rd Bomb Group at Hardwick and flew all over Europe, England, France, Germany, Russia, Italy and Africa. First mission, Ploesti finished first tour (25 missions) in February 1944. Finished second tour in September 1944 (35 missions).

Returned to the USA and stayed in the Air Force, re-

tired as lieutenant colonel in 1965. Received the Silver Star, two Distinguished Flying Crosses, five Air Medals and one Purple Heart plus 31 assorted campaign medals and ribbons and six different wings.

Went to work for the state of Washington, graduated University of Maryland and took master's at University of Washington and doctorate at another school.

Married April 19, 1973 to Helen Stone and has six children, nine grandchildren and numerous great-grandchildren. Presently retired in Tacoma, WA.

HAROLD A. AMES, was born Nov. 21, 1919 in Morrice, MI. Entered the service Oct. 16, 1942. Served with 567th Bomb Sqdn., 389th Bomb Group(H), 8th Air Force in England. Also navigator 1034, 12th TAC rec. Korea.

Participated in action in Air Offensive Europe and Normandy campaigns. Flew 13 missions, then shot down June 21, 1944 near Temple Hoff, Berlin. Four crew members were killed and Ames was wounded in leg by 20mm explosive. Spent 35 days in Herman Goring Hospital, Berlin, then two more months in another POW hospital, moved to several POW camps. Spent five days and six nights in box car with 46 men and no food. Was bombed twice. Arrived Nuremburg Feb. 14, vermin ridden straw mattresses on floor. Twelve slices of bread and bowl of beet top soup per day for 245 men. April 3, 1945, marched to Mooseburg where they were released.

Discharged Aug. 21, 1945. Received the Purple Heart, Air Medal with four Oak Leaf Clusters, American Campaign Medal, WWII Victory Medal, Air Offensive Europe and Normandy, Normandy Service Medal, United Nations Service Medal, POW Medal, American Campaign Medal and National Defense. Was recalled for Korea and flew 37 mission in B-26.

Has wife and two sons. He is retired from the IRS.

PAUL C. ANDERSEN, was born Oct. 26, 1917 in Redfield, SD. Enlisted in the USAAC on Sept. 7, 1940. Promoted through the ranks to staff sergeant and entered OCS at Aberdeen, MD, graduated Dec. 12, 1942 as a second lieutenant, assigned to the 389th Bomb Group at Biggs Field, El Paso, TX as ordnance officer to the 564th Bomb Sqdn.

In June of 1942 the group completed combat training and was assigned to the 8th Air Force in England. On Sept. 5, 1944 on a combat mission in a B-24 bomber, he was shot down over Karlsruhe, Germany and spent the rest of the war in a German prison camp at Stalag Luft 1 Barth, Germany.

Duty stations after the war included Turner Field, Albany, GA; Enid AFB, OK; Barksdale Field, LA; Goodfellow Field, TX; Eielson AFB Alaska; Bryan AFB, TX; Chanute AFB, IL; Walker AFB, NM; Air Command and Staff School, Maxwell AFB, AL; Malmstrom AFB, MT; Goose Bay, Labrador and the last duty assignment as commander of the 533rd Strategic Missile Sqdn. at McConnell AFB, KS.

Retired as lieutenant colonel on Feb. 1, 1970. Married July 1, 1946 to Mildred Metz and has three children and two grandchildren.

ARTHUR G. ANDERSON, was born July 11, 1922 in Tacoma, WA. Enlisted in the USAAC June 4, 1942 and reported for active duty March 1, 1943. Took primary flight training at Chickasha, OK; basic at Garden City, KS; and graduated as second lieutenant at Frederick, OK, Class of 44-D. Transition at Ft. Worth, TX and crew assembly at Savannah, GA.

Left New York City Oct. 30, 1944 by convoy on the Uruguay with 15 crews for Liverpool. Four crews joined the 467th Bomb Group at Rackheath near Norwich. Flew his first mission with the 788th Bomb Sqdn. on December 4 and

his last (26th mission) on April 25 (12 days before V-E day). On June 13, flew back to the Azores, Newfoundland and Bradley Field with crew and 10 ground personnel.

Married Jean Miller Aug. 14, 1945 and left the service in December 1945. Had three children and three grandchildren. Retired from Burkhart Dental Supply as branch manager and vice president in 1984. Lost Jean in 1985 and married Jane Butler in 1986. Presently lives in Yakima, WA.

BURKE ANDERSON, was born July 1, 1921 in Adel, IA. Entered the USAF September 1942, served with 489th Bomb Group. Stationed at Camp Dodge, IA; Lincoln, NE; Lowry Field, Davis-Monthan, Salt Lake City. Was tail gunner with 8th Air Force.

Discharged September 1945 with the rank of staff sergeant. Received the Air Medal with three clusters.

Married and has two daughters and four granddaughters. He is retired.

JAMES J. ANDERSON, was born Aug. 22, 1920 in Plainview, MN. Entered the service May 26, 1943, 8th Air Force, 2nd Div., 453rd Bomb Group, 735th Sqdn. Stationed at Harlingen, TX, Gunnery School, Tonapah, NV (flight training).

Participated in Northern France, Ardennes and Rhineland campaigns. Completed 35 missions to Germany, France and Holland.

One of his worst experiences was the result of American bombers (B-24s) not from the enemy fighters. From his position as a nose turret gunner and about 60 seconds before releasing bombs, he had a feeling that this was going to be his last mission. They were in the lead squadron with the high right squadron right over them with bomb bays open and their 500 pounds bombs ready to drop. A radio conversation between his squadron and the high right squadron was to no avail. The bombs were released, two just missed his right wing. Two other American bombers were struck and lost.

Discharged Oct. 30, 1945 with the rank of staff sergeant. Received the Air Medal with four Oak Leaf Clusters, American Theater Ribbon, EAME Ribbon and three Bronze Stars.

Married to Sandy and has two sons by a previous marriage and four grandchildren. He is retired.

LLOYD E. ANDERSON, was born May 19, 1920 in Tularosa, NM. Joined the USAAC on Oct. 3, 1941. Graduated from A.M. School, Sheppard Field in March 1942. Joined the 93rd Bomb Group at Barksdale Field. Moved to Fort Myers, Grenier Field, Fort Dix and embarked on the Queen Elizabeth, Aug. 31, 1942. Stationed at Alconbury and Hardwick, England. In North Africa at Tunis, Benghazi, Tripoli and Marrakech. Returned to States on May 28, 1945.

"Ted's Traveling Circus" took part in 11 campaigns, received two Presidential Citations, flew 391 missions and had two Medal of Honor recipients. Received the Bronze Star and amassed 155 discharge points. Met an Army girl, Janie Luckey, in Havleston, England (where he spent three Christmas's). They were married in New York in 1947 and have three children. Janie died of cancer in 1987. He is a retired mechanical engineer.

PAUL I. ANDERSON, was born May 27, 1916 in Des Moines, IA. Entered military service through the courtesy of the local selective service board on Feb. 17, 1941 at Fort Des Moines, IA. (This was over a year before Ft. Des Moines became the home of the WACs.)

Assigned to Co. G, 20th Inf. Regt. at Ft. Warren, WY; 19 months later entered aviation cadet training at "Saad Sac," TX; washed out of pilot training at Sparton School of Aeronautics, Tulsa, OK, February 1943. Accepted in bombardier training and graduated from Big Spring, TX in August 1943.

Crewed up at Mt. Home, ID and then ferried a new B-24 from Forbes Air Base to Prestwick, Scotland via South America and Africa arriving in Prestwick on Feb. 17, 1944.

Flew 32 missions on the Gedehus crew with the 389th Bomb Group, 567th Sqdn. Their roughest mission was April 22 to Hamm, Germany. Returned after dark with German fighter planes taking pot shots at B-24s flying with formation lights on. Instead of landing at their base at Hethel, they landed at old Buck. Their navigator, who had not accompanied them on their journey, thought they had been shot down. When they returned to their base by truck, their navigator was quite relieved.

Returned to "ZI" August 1944. Returned to civil life in October 1945 in Boise, ID. Began working for the Union Pacific Railroad as a brakeman. October 1951 saw him being called back to the Air Force for a period of 17 months. Did not have to serve overseas.

Returned to the UPRR and promoted to conductor in 1953. Retired from UPRR in 1977 and is now the proud stepfather to seven children, grandfather of 24 and great-grandfather to 11 and a lot more to come.

RALPH N. ANDERSON, was born March 25, 1925 in Racine, WI. Entered the USAAC Feb. 22, 1943. Stationed at Wendover, UT and Rackheath, England. Commissioned Sept. 15, 1943 and completed his missions Aug. 11, 1944.

Retired in 1971 with the rank lieutenant colonel. Received the Distinguished Flying Cross, Air Medal with four clusters, Presidential Unit Citation, four Battle Stars, and Reserve Medal with one cluster.

Married since 1947, he has three sons. Two served as officers in the Navy and one as officer in USAF.

LLOYD B. ANDREW JR., was born Nov. 30, 1923 in Joliet, IL. Entered the USAAC on March 23, 1942. Pilot, second lieutenant, Class 43-D, Stockton, CA. Stationed at Sacramento, CA, B-25; Hobbs, NM, B-17; Boise, ID, B-24. Accepted at Tonopah, NV to England via South America and Africa, arriving February 1944.

Participated in Air Offensive Europe, Normandy and air combat over North France. AVON bombing, lead pilot, completed 32 mission with 458th Bomb Group.

Discharged July 10, 1945 on points with the rank first lieutenant.

Graduated Purdue University, 1948 mechanical engineer. Worked three years Phillips Petroleum. Joined Ethyl Corp. 1951 and retired as executive vice president and chief financial officer in 1989. Active in community work and as board member of Ethyl Corp.

Married Frances Burdell on Dec. 31, 1948. They have two daughters, one son and three grandchildren.

MARVIN E. ANDREWS, was born Sept. 24, 1919 in Kansas City, MO and raised there. He entered the service June 13, 1943. After Armor and Gunnery School, was assigned to B-24 crew as armor gunner at Pueblo Airbase, CO for crew training.

Shipped to England on the *Queen Elizabeth* in June 1944. Assigned to 446th Bomb Group, Bungay England. A week later re-assigned to 1409 AAFBU Leuchars Jct. Scotland. Flew seven missions there as a top turret gunner.

On Oct. 1, 1944 was assigned to 859th Sqdn., 492nd Bomb Group. Carpetbagger operations. On Dec. 18, 1944, the 859th Sqdn. was assigned to detached service with 2641st Special Group, 15th Air Force at Brindizi, Italy. Flew 35 missions there as tail gunner until V-E day.

Discharged Sept. 2, 1945 as staff sergeant. Retired from Graybar Electric Co. after 32 years as a salesman. Married June 29, 1946 to Stella Burch. Has one son, daughter and two grandchildren.

SAMUEL T. ANGUISH, was born July 26, 1917 in Oneida, NY. Drafted into the infantry, June 13, 1942, transferred to Aviation Cadets Air Corp. Training at SE Command, graduated pilot training, Columbus, MS, Class 43-H. B-24 training Montgomery, AL, first pilot. Assigned crew at Salt Lake City, UT. Crew training, SW, flew southern route to England.

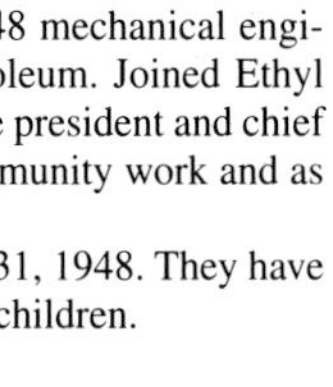

Assigned to 448th Bomb Group, April 1944. Selected for lead crew after 10 missions and completed 30th mission Oct. 17, 1944. Set up lead crew section at 448th and promoted to captain. Memorable experiences: division lead; 25 mission to Keil; Col. Knorre C/P; bombed component plant - target Victory, claimed best bombing of week.

Returned to the States Jan. 21, 1945. Released from active duty Nov. 30, 1945 with the rank of captain. Remained in the reserves and retired July 26, 1977 with the rank of lieutenant colonel. Received four Distinguished Flying Crosses, Air Medals and several ribbons.

Married Sept. 4, 1943 to Elaine Roberts. Has two sons, one daughter and five grandchildren. He is retired and enjoys woodworking, gardening and golfing.

GEORGE M. APGAR JR., was born Sept. 12, 1921 in Newark, NJ and entered military service March 5, 1943 at Fort Dix, NJ. Transferred to Miami Beach, FL for basic training, then to Chanute Field, IL to AAF Technical Training Command. Next he went to Coronaca Air Field in South Carolina, where he joined the 50th Station Complement Squadron commanded by Maj. Frank H. Haynes, then to Newport News, VA where he embarked on a liberty ship, the USS *General John Pope* to England.

They were attached to the 44th Bomb Group(H) at Shipdham AFB #115, East Anglia, England. It was from this base, commanded by Gen. Leon W. Johnson, that the aircraft which led the raid on the Ploesti Oil Fields departed. He was given the Congressional Medal of Honor.
Returned to the U.S. aboard the *Queen Mary*, arriving at New York City, then honorably discharged from the Air Force at Sioux City, IA in October of 1945. Returned home, married and has two children.

He started his own auto repair shop in Chester, NJ in June of 1946. In 1950 he took on a GMC truck franchise, adding a Jeep franchise in 1955. For 40 years he ran a successful business, selling out in 1984 and retiring. He still lives in Chester, NJ in the same house he bought in 1948.

EDWARD W. APPEL, was born April 14, 1917 in Onamia, MN and was raised on a farm in Redfield, SD. Joined USAAC July 29, 1940 as a private. Was promoted through the ranks to staff sergeant, then entered Aviation Cadets Aug. 4, 1942 and graduated May 20, 1943 as second lieutenant, Class of 43-E West Coast Training Center, Stockton Field, CA, where he had previously been crew chief and flight chief as enlisted man.

Trained as a pilot in B-25s, B-17s and B-24s. Flew B-24 bomber to 8th Air Force via South America, Africa and on up to England. Flew combat against Germany in B-24s from February 1944 to Sept. 5, 1944 when shot down on 30th and last mission while bombing railroad yards at Karlsruhe. After about three months of evasion behind the lines, finally escaped first part of December of 1944.

Went back to England to 8th and volunteered for P-47 fighters with the 56th Fighter Group. Flew fighters escorting bombers, dive bombing and strafing until again being shot down strafing Muldorf Airfield, east of Munich on April 16, 1945. Again escaped after nearly being caught by German soldiers several times and made it back through to American lines. Got back to Paris and the war was over.

Returned to the U.S. aboard an LST composed entirely of ex-POWs and evaders in May of 1945. Left the service in December of 1946, but stayed in the Reserves. Retired as a lieutenant colonel.

Received two Distinguished Flying Crosses, five Air Medals, four European Campaign Stars, the Purple Heart and several other ribbons.

Married April 10, 1950 to home-town girl, Crystal Crook and had five children (all grown now) and 10 grandchildren. In civilian life was in fuel, oil and gas business and retired in April of 1984. Still flying a rag wing Oironca which he restored in 1983.

CARL W. APPELIN, was born in McNeal, AZ on April 18, 1916, of immigrant parents from Finland. Learned the English language in the first grade in 1922, graduated from high school in 1934.

Volunteered into the USAAC in 1943. Received Navigator's Wings and Flight Officer's Bars Class 44-3 at Hondo, TX in 1944. Joined A. Oliver Hurst's B-24 crew in Fresno, CA and transitioned at Muroc, CA in 1944.

Sailed to England assigned to 44th Bomb Group, 67th

Bomb Sqdn., Shipdham, 1944. Flew 35 memorable missions. Received 36th mission credit, compliments of a general command pilot, after aborting an 8th AAF lead mission into enemy territory, December 1944. Assigned to ATC 1945, flew 13 Atlantic crossings and a super-secret flight to Guam.

Received a BA in mining engineer from the University of Arizona, 1950. Worked in Mexico, Australia, AK, Canada and U.S. mining. Received an honorary degree, Mining Engineer, 1972 from the University of Arizona. Served as chief of U.S. Uranium Ore Reserves for 12 years with AEC, ERDA and DOE. Retired after his old heart gave out after a coronary bypass in 1980. On April 15, 1993, he had surgery for abdominal aortic aneurysm.

Married Martha L. Sewell, Aug. 14, 1948. Has a son, two daughters and six grandchildren.

JOE L. ARAIZA, was born May 21, 1920 in Brownsville, TX. Joined the USAAC June 9, 1940. Volunteered for B-24 aircraft mechanics course and Aerial Gunnery School, Harlingen, TX, April 1943.

Sent to Davis-Monthan Field, AZ, April 1944 where he met his B-24 flight crew. They picked up a B-24 at Topeka, KS and then to Preswick, Scotland and by train to Bungay, East Anglia and on to Flixton Air Base, Suffolk, England. Assigned to the 705th Bomb Sqdn., 446th Bomb Group.

His first mission was Orly Field, Paris, France and his last one was Politz, synthetic oil refinery, Germany, June 20, 1944. After the war he stayed in the Air Corps in the aircraft maintenance field, retiring September 1969 as a senior master sergeant after 29 years. Then he joined the U.S. Postal Service until he retired October 1992 after 24 years.

RONALD JOSEPH ARBAUGH, was born Feb. 24, 1924 in Zanesville, OH. Entered service in 1943, trained in Eastern Training Command at A&E and Gunnery schools. Assigned in March 1944 to Westover Field as flight engineer on Harold Anderson's Liberator crew for operational training.

Thence to Langley Field for low altitude bombing training. Thence via Bangor, Goose Bay, Keflavik, Valley and eventually to Attlebridge, 466th Bomb Group. Flew tour on Anderson's crew (lead crew) also the "gas missions," trolly flights and "homerun."

Was tech sergeant and the youngest member of the crew. Was checked-out as qualified emergency pilot. Discharged in 1945, retired as sales representative in 1979 after 26 years with Marathon Oil Company.

Active in 2nd Air Division Association as group treasurer. Also member of many civic organizations. Arbaugh passed away May 1, 1993. Survived by wife, Irene; son, Joe Jr.; one brother; one sister; and seven grandchildren.

HENRY ARIAS SR., was born in Brooklyn Nov. 9, 1921. Married Antonia Bermudez on Nov. 1, 1942. They have two sons and two granddaughters. Reported for Army duty on Nov. 14, 1942. Transferred to Air Force a year later. Trained as a ball gunner at Harlingen AFB. Joined a crew and they were sent to Charleston AFB for combat training.

Completing their training, they shipped out on the

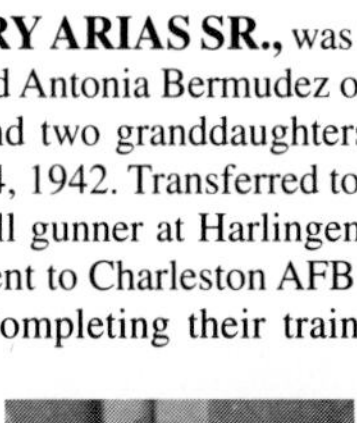

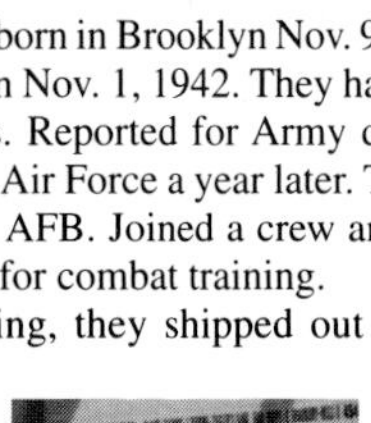

Queen Elizabeth for the ETO. Arrived there in May 1944 and was assigned to the 2nd Div., 458th Bomb Group and 754th Sqdn. They flew 35 missions with pilot, Warren G. Cook. Their last combat flight was on Dec. 10, 1944.

Was awarded the Air Medal with three Oak Leafs and the Distinguished Flying Cross. His rank was staff sergeant.

He is now a retired machinist, still married to the same girl and has two married sons living close by.

ROBERT E. ARMBRUSTER, was born June 4, 1920 in Cedarburg, WI. Entered the USAAC on June 16, 1943. Basic training at Miami Beach, FL; college training detachment, University of Alabama; navigation preflight, San Antonio, TX; advanced navigation, Ellington Field, TX; combat crew training, Mountain Home, ID.

Participated in combat operation with the 8th Air Force, Horsham St. Faith, England, 458th Bomb Group, 754th Bomb Sqdn. (B-24). Discharged Nov. 26, 1945, Sioux City AAF Base, IA with the rank second lieutenant.

Married Mary Aileen (Behnke) and has four children and five grandchildren. He is a retail jeweler.

PAUL E. ARMENTROUT, was born Feb. 7, 1920 near Anita, IA. Enlisted in the USAAC Cadet Program in October 1942 at Portland, OR. February 1943 he was assigned to Lowry Field, then Springfield State Teachers College in Missouri for three months.

Commissioned second lieutenant as pilot April 1944, transition B-24, Ft. Worth, crewed at Lincoln, joined 2nd Air Div., 8th Air Force, 446th Bomb Group, 706th Sqdn., Station 125, Bungay, England. After 17 missions as wing crew, was assigned to group as lead crew. Most memorable mission was leading 2nd Air Div. Wesel, Germany on March 24, 1945 at tree top level supplying Paratroops and Glider Airborne Infantry. The 446th lost three planes and crews #2 and #3, planes went down over target, 20 B-24s were also lost on this mission.

After V-E day he returned to the States for retraining to be reassigned to the Pacific. After peace was signed in Japan, he was discharged in December 1945 and assigned to active duty reserve. Retired Feb. 7, 1980 as lieutenant colonel. Returned to work at Sears in 1946, married and has four children. Home is McMinnville, OR, home of the Spruce Goose.

HENRY ARNAUD, Arnaudville, LA. Joined the National Guard in 1940 and the USAAC in July 1941. Served with 703rd Sqdn., 445th Bomb Group, 2nd Air Div., Tibenham, England.

Memorable experiences: 27 1/2 missions over Europe from March 6, 1944 to May 28, 1944; Ludwigshafen mission; and landing in Sweden.

Discharged Aug. 27, 1945 with the rank of staff sergeant. He received the Air Medal with two clusters and the Distinguished Flying Cross.

Married and has four children. Attended LSU from 1945-1949, BS in Petr. engineering. Currently retired from Unocal Corp.

CALVIN D. ARNETT, was born Sept. 10, 1924 in Detroit, MI and enlisted in the USAAC in March 1943, shortly after graduating from Southeastern High School.

Graduated pilot, second lieutenant, Class 44G at Walnut Ridge, AR. Assigned co-pilot in Daniels B-24 crew and proceeded to England. Assigned to 466th Bomb Group, 786th Sqdn. at Attlebridge in December 1944.

Completed 16 missions. Plane was shot down once with a severed fuel line but was able to land without incident in Antwerp, Belgium. Later, after repairs, while taxiing for takeoff, had about two feet torn from end of left wing from colli-

sion with a guy wire. Apparently no serious damage since they proceeded to take off and the plane flew without difficulty.

Discharged Oct. 9, 1945 with the rank of second lieutenant. Received three Air Medals and three European Campaign Stars. After V-E day had points to request inactive duty October 1945 and graduated University of Michigan with BS in engineering and later received MBA from U of M in 1958.

Retired from Ford Motor Co. after 25 years in various assignments and later retired from the Defense Logistics Agency after 5 years. Married Marjorie Littlefield in June 1948. They have five children and two grandchildren.

CHARLES W. ARNETT, was born Sept. 5, 1919, Franklin, AZ; drafted June 1942 and sent to Aircraft Mechanics School, Wichita Falls, TX. Accepted for pilot training in Class 43-H, graduating as pilot Aug. 30, 1943 at Seymour, IN. Assigned B-24 transition, Montgomery, AL and combat crew training in Tucson, AZ and Alamogordo, NM. Accepted a new B-24J in Harrington, KS and flew to England as part of newly formed 492nd Bomb Group in April 1944.

Shot down on third combat mission May 19, and crash landed in Holland. Liberated from POW status April 30, 1945. Discharged September 1945, recalled February 1951, after graduating with BS from Brigham Young University.

Served in MATS, SAC, and Communications, with overseas tours in Icelnd, Japan, and Vietnam. Retired April 1968 as lieutenant colonel.

Married June 15, 1945 to Anna Laurene Liljenquist, has seven children and 30 grandchildren. Life is wonderful.

ALFRED ASCH (AL), was raised on a small farm in Beaverton, MI. He joined the USAAC in September 1941 and graduated from Flying School as a pilot the following April with the Class of 42D. He was then assigned to the 93rd Bomb Group with B-24s. Al was soon flying combat against the Nazis in late 1942 with the 8th Air Force in England. The early high altitude bombing missions were generally without fighter escort and with small formations (24 B-24s, and many times smaller as airplanes were lost without replacements), the group was "mauled" by the Luftwaffe.

On the first mission over Lille, France on Oct. 8, 1942, the group was hit by heavy flak and was attacked by German fighters from every point on the compass (360°). Al was flying with Joe Tate and their B-24 received numerous 20mm hits with one rupturing a fuel line in the bomb bay. The engineer, A.F. Moses, held back some of the fuel from the ruptured line using his bare hands. Joe's oxygen system was shot out and he was saved from passing out with a walk-around oxygen bottle. Moses did superficial repairs on the fuel leak with emery paper and friction tape with his frost-bitten hands. The crew made an emergency landing at a sod fighter field on the west coast of England with two flat tires, the nose and right main gear. The crew had all the combat seasoning they cared for that day.

After that mission, Al received his own crew and airplane, *Wham Bam,* and went with the 93rd to North Africa and the Libyan Desert to help defeat the German forces led by Field Marshal Rommel. After completing 28 combat missions, Al returned to the U.S. with four other officers and helped organize the 455th B-24 Bombardment Group. Following flying combat in Italy with the 455th against the Nazis, Al held several positions in the AAC and accepted a regular officer appointment. Along with this, he earned his master's degree from the University of Pittsburgh. He had earned a bachelor of science degree from Central Michigan University, Mt. Pleasant, MI. Al remained active as a flyer, earned his Command Pilot Wings and helped introduce automation to the Air Force starting in the early 1950s. He retired as a full colonel in 1958 and worked for 16 years as a systems engineer for the automation of air traffic control functions by the FAA.

ROBERT I. ASH (BOB), was born in Lake Charles, LA on Feb. 13, 1919. Married Lucielle Winzenried. Has a step-daughter, three step-grandchildren and one step great-grandchild.

Entered the military by joining Co. L, 156th Inf., National Guard in Lake Charles, LA on Sept. 25, 1940. Inducted into federal service (regular Army) on Nov. 25, 1940. Transferred to the USAAC on Aug. 28, 1941 and was assigned to Randolph Field, TX. Serviced aircraft as crew chief, also airplane and engine mechanic.

Transferred to South Plains Army Air Field, Lubbock, TX as line chief, 1942-1943. Also served as base technical inspector while stationed at SPAAF. Completed Aerial Gunnery School at Harlingen, TX in 1944. Was assigned to a B-24 bomber crew as flight engineer. Their pilot was Bert Minor. Assigned to the 458th Bomb Group, 754th Bomb Sqdn. located at Horsham St. Faith near Norwich, England. Flew 32 combat missions against Germany on the B-24 bomber.

Returned to the States June 23, 1945. Received honorable discharge from the service on Sept. 12, 1945 as tech sergeant. Awarded the Air Medal with four Oak Leaf Clusters, European Medal with three Bronze Stars, American Campaign Medal, American Defense Medal, Good Conduct Medal, WWII Victory Medal and the Certificate of Valor.

Retired from Olin Corp., Lake Charles, LA on Aug. 1, 1982 as associate process automation and control engineer.

WILLIAM T. ASH, was born in Eureka Springs, AR on Aug. 18, 1922. While hitchhiking through Florida in February 1941, he tried to enlist in Air Force, and every other branch of the service, at Jacksonville. All turned him down, they had filled their quotas for that period. When war came along, he decided they could draft him.

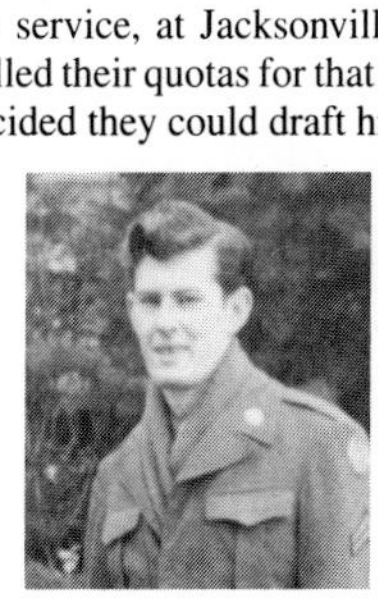

Sworn in at Camp Joseph T. Robinson, Little Rock, AR and put in Air Force November 1942. Basic training at Keesler Field; Air Force Radio School at Sioux Falls, SD; Advanced Radio School, Tomah, WI; ORTC Goldsborough, NC; Camp Shanks, NY.

Left New York on *Empress of Russia,* could not keep up with convoy, sailed back to New York unescorted. A week later boarded *Mauretania* and sailed to England, September 1943. Assigned to 52nd FCS of 65th FW Saffron Waldron. Assisted with air sea rescue of planes ditching in English Channel, gave lost planes compass bearings to home bases, etc. Manned radio stations at Southminster and Southwold on the channel. At end of war was flown to Weisbaden, Germany, Y-80 Airfield, they needed some radio operators.

Discharged Feb. 7, 1946 with the rank of corporal. Married Muriel McGaughey Nov. 3, 1946. Has one son, one daughter, one grandson. Wife deceased July 12, 1992. Retired independent insurance agent of 35 years. Cassville, MO has been his home since 1950.

GEORGE T. ASHEN, was born March 7, 1922 in Gievres, France. He came to the USA as a small boy and was raised in Denver, CO and educated at Regis College. He enlisted in the USAAC in August 1942, became an aviation cadet and completed his training as a bombardier in Victorville, CA in mid-1944.

Their crew was assembled and trained at March Field, CA and thereafter was assigned to the 8th Air Force in England. He was stationed at Wendling, England with the 392nd Bomb Group, 577th Sqdn. He completed 13 missions with the 392nd Bomb Group. Flew to targets over Berlin, Stettine on the Oder River, targets in Germany and targets along the French Coast.

He was discharged in December 1945 and after his discharge he attended St. Louis University and graduated the School of Law in 1948. He was admitted to the BAR of Missouri and Colorado and practiced in both states. He presently practices law in the state of Colorado.

He is married and has five daughters and six grandchildren.

JAMES O. AUMAN (JIM), was born and raised in St. Marys. He was educated in the St. Marys Church Catholic School System and also attended training programs at the Boys' Club.

On Dec. 4, 1941, just prior to WWII, he enlisted into the USRAAF. His first duties took him to the West Coast where he graduated from the required aviation mechanic courses at the Merced AFB Flying Training School in mid-1942. He served the next year on the flight line maintaining single-engine aircraft.

He was promoted to staff sergeant early in 1943 and advanced to heavy bomber flying training in Arizona, Wyoming, and New Mexico. Later that year he transferred to the European Theater of Operations with a crew of 10 and a B-24 Liberator aircraft just off the assembly line.

In England, Jim served with the 466th Bomb Group, 2nd Air Div. of the 8th Air Force near a small town called Attlebridge. His combat missions took place over Nazi-occupied Continental Europe and included the invasion of Normandy, France. Was honorably discharged from the service in June 1945 with the rank of staff sergeant.

Married Edna Dippold "Snookie" in 1945, also from St. Marys, at the Air Force Rehabilitation Hospital at Pawling, NY. They have four daughters: Peggy, Kathie, Barby and Patty. With them, their husbands and eight grandchildren, they have every day assistants with the operation of their neighborhood grocery store.

JUNIOR O. AUSTIN, was born July 29, 1921 in Fort Gibson, OK. Married Jacqueline Matthews on July 13, 1946. Has two sons, one daughter and five grandchildren.

Went to a civilian school on aircraft and engines at J.C. Sacramento, CA. Joined the USAAC on Aug. 5, 1942. Basic training at Mather Field, Sacramento, CA. Stayed at Mather Field for a period of time. Was crew chief on AT7s and C60s training navigators. Transferred to Selman Field at Monroe, LA on C60s. From there went to Richmond, VA on P47s Fighters as crew chief, and instrument spec. Later went to England as replacement 453rd Bomb Group, 734th Bomb Sqdn. with B-24s at Old Buckingham. Was crew chief assistant on mail call and Hollywood and Vine.

Received the Good Conduct Medal, European Theater Campaign Air Medal, five Bronze Stars, which is one Silver Battle Star, stayed in England until war was over in Europe. Went to Long Beach Air Transport. Discharged at Sheppard Field, TX in October 1945 with rank tech sergeant.

Junior now lives in Greely Hill, CA near Yosemite National Park.

JOSEPH M. AUTOBEE, was born Feb. 16, 1924 in Avondale, CO. Entered the USAAC in June 1943. Served with 448th Bomb Group as ball turret gunner at Buckley, Lowry, Harlingen, Lemoore, March Field and England. Completed 20 missions over enemy occupied territory from Seething Air Base.

Memorable experiences: his group was on last mission to drop last bombs over Europe on April 25, 1945,

Salsburg; meeting lone survivor of one aircraft on mission April 4, 1945 after 44 years.

Discharged Oct. 31, 1945 with the rank staff sergeant. Received the Sharp Shooter, Certificate of Valor, Gunners Wings and Air Medal with two Oak Leaf Clusters.

Married Aurora Raigoza April 15, 1950. They have one son and two daughters. Retired from Federal Civil Service after 40 years, worked for Boeing in Wichita as a sheet metal mechanic. Keeps busy taking and bringing home grandchildren from school.

ROBERT C. BACHER (BOB), was born in West View, PA on March 16, 1924. Married his high school May queen, Faith A. Geipel, in June 1947. They have a son, two daughters and three grandchildren. Entered the USAAC on May 17, 1943 after attending two years at Penn State. Graduated April 1944 from the PAM AM - Air Corps Navigation School, Coral Gables, FL.

Started flying combat missions August 1944 for the 491st Bomb Group, North Pickenham. He bailed out his fifth mission, September 13, over France. Bailed out again on the seventh mission, October 9, over France. He then joined Captain Burdkin's lead crew. On December 28, 13th mission, flying with a makeup crew, crashed at Manston Air Base returning from Germany.

Returned to the USA in April 1945 and then flew with the ATC between Puerto Rico and South America until discharged Dec. 27, 1945. Returned to Penn State for his engineering degree and joined the Bell of Pennsylvania and Bell System June 1947. He retired after 41 years, March 1988 as the vice president, Operations, Keystone Region for Bell Atlantic.

HENRY J. BACKOWSKI, was born Sept. 15, 1922 in Cleveland, OH. Joined the 8th Air Force, 2nd Air Div., 445th Bomb Group, 700th Sqdn., 492nd Bomb Group, 36th Bomb Sqdn. Stationed in Tibenham, North Pickenham, Chettington, England.

Participated in the ETO, 8th Air Force, Battle of Piccadilly. Will always remember the mud, rain, fog and 18 hour days. His twin brother, Chester R. Backowski, served overseas with him.

Discharged Oct. 15, 1945 with the rank staff sergeant. Received all the usual medals and awards.

Backowski retired from Pan American World Airways in 1991.

GEORGE W. BACON, was born May 10, 1923 and enlisted in USAAC in November 1940. Stationed at McDill Field for two months, transferred to Orlando Air Base, 1941 and assigned to 3rd Recon Sqdn. Moved to Mitchell Field, Long Island, NY and performed anti-submarine patrol.

Attended Bendix Turret School, March and April 1942; moved to Westover Field, Chicopee, MA, anti-subpatrol. Went to Gunnery School in Las Vegas, July-August 1942. Moved to Gander Bay, Newfoundland, April 1943, then Devenshire, England.

Transferred to 2nd Air Div., 392nd 579th Sqdn., Wendling. He flew as tail gunner. On his 30th and last mission, March 8, 1944, to Berlin, he flew as bombardier. He

was sent to the 448th Bomb Group at Seething as Gunnery instructor.

On May 10 he boarded the Isle de France in the harbor from Glascow, Scotland to return to the States. Spent his last year at Westover Field with the 112th, AAF Base Unit. Received the Distinguished Flying Cross, Air Medal with three Oak Leaf Clusters, American Defense Medal, American Theater, European Theater with a Battle Star. Discharged June 30, 1945.

Married Geraldine Towne July 6, 1945 in the "Little Church Around The Corner," New York City.

Recalled during Korean War in 1950 and assigned to 91st Reconn Wing (SAC) Barksdale AFB. Transferred to Ramey AFB with the 55th Strategic Reconn Group, 2nd Air Force (SAC). Promoted to tech sergeant and released Aug. 24, 1951.

Had three children: George W. Bacon III (killed in Angola Feb. 14, 1976), Gail T. and Heidi Lindsey. Also one grandson, Jesse George Wilcox. Retired May 1988 after 40 years with Anderson Little Co.

WARREN BACZIK, was born Oct. 21, 1923 in New York City, NY. Entered the USAAC on March 24, 1943. Served with the 87th Inf.

Discharged Nov. 29, 1945 with the rank tech 4. Received the Combat Infantry Badge.

Baczic is retired.

CHARLES H. BADER, was born June 22, 1915 in Perkasie, PA. Inducted May 1941 at Aberdeen Proving Grounds, one year, entered Navigation School, Selman Field Monroe, LA. Graduated May 1, 1943 and sent to Langley Field, training in B-24. Sent to Wendling Air Base in 1943 to the 392nd Air Base.

He had 21 operational missions, two division leads, three wing leads, four group leads, five deputy leads and seven squadron leads as mickey navigator. On 19th mission a defective flare defected into plane and he was one of four, out of 12 men, who escaped. The mission was over Schwapish Hall, AF Germany.

Discharged June 1, 1945, Westover Field, MA with the rank first lieutenant. Received the Air Medal, Distinguished Flying Cross with four stars and two Oak Leaf Clusters on military ribbon.

Married Eleanor Swartz on July 5, 1945. Has three children and nine grandchildren. Retired from Westinghouse Electric and moved to Pocono Mountains, PA.

HOMER H. BADGETT (BUS), was born in Mt. Vernon, IL Sept. 3, 1921. Joined the USAAC Glider Pilot Program in September 1942. In April 1943, he transferred to the Aviation Cadet Program, Class 43-K. Graduated in October 1943, was trained to fly B-24 Liberators and assigned to a combat crew as co-pilot.

Flew a B-24 with his crew to England via South America and Africa to join the 8th Air Force. Flew 15 missions with the 453rd Bomb Group and two missions with the 389th Bomb Group. On the 17th mission, his B-24 was shot down by German flack. He managed to evade German capture with the help of the French Underground until rescued by British/Canadian forces.

After returning to the U.S., he flew a B-24 with the Training Command. Later he became a C-54 pilot with the Air Transport Command. He received an Air Medal with an Oak Leaf Cluster. First Lt. Badgett separated from Scott Field, IL on Oct. 14, 1945.

Married in 1950 to Ruth Sharman of Medina, NY. Has two daughters and two grandchildren. Became an electronic design engineer and science teacher after the war. Retired, his hobby is computers.

LESTER J. BAER, was born Nov. 21, 1920 in Dubuque, IA. Entered the USAAC April 1942, served with 2nd Air Div. Memorable experience was landing the aircraft with two engines out.

Retired March 30, 1970, Dover AFB with the rank lieutenant colonel.

Married to Camilla Kerns Baer and has a son, daughter, step-daughter, six grandchildren and nine great-grandchildren. He is retired.

RICHARD F. BAILEY, was born May 30, 1922 in Moline, IL. Entered the USAAF Sept. 15, 1943. Was tail gunner in B-24 with 453rd Bomb Group, 735th Sqdn. Stationed at Keesler Field; Laredo, TX; Pueblo, CO; Old Buckingham, England.

Completed 35 combat missions from Sept. 8, 1944 to Feb. 24, 1945. Discharged Oct. 6, 1945 with the rank staff sergeant. Received the Air Medal and four Oak Leaf Clusters.

Retired from Deere and Co. He is a widower with three children and three grandchildren.

CLARENCE E. BAKER, was born 1919 in Malden, MA. Entered the USAAC in 1942. Airplane Mechanic, Biloxi, B-25 specialist, bombardier, Childress. During the ETO, with 15th Air Force, 376th Bomb Group, 513th Bomb Sqdn., Italy and with 8th Air Force, 44th Bomb Group, 67th Bomb Sqdn. in England.

Memorable experience was flying the "All American" (B-24s) to Owl's Head last fall and relived the past, including Ploesti.

Discharged in 1946 with the rank first lieutenant. Received the Distinguished Unit Badge, Air Medal and three Oak Leaf Clusters, European Service Medal and the Distinguished Flying Cross.

Married in 1945, widowed in 1982 and has a son, daughter and three grandsons. He is a retired master electrician.

FRANCIS BOYD BAKER (FRANK), was born in Bergholz, OH on Aug. 30, 1923. Married Belle Langley from Boise, ID in 1945. They have two sons. Entered the USAAC on March 17, 1943. He attended Airplane Mechanic School in Gulfport, MS; Gunnery School in Laredo, TX and Boise, ID; Supercharger Specialist School in Lynn, MA.

Left Topeka, KS for European Theater Operation on April 14, 1944 with a short stop over at Station #238 in Cluntoe Northern Ireland before being assigned by special order to the 466th Bomb Group(H) Station HQ, 784th Bomb Sqdn., Station #120 Attlebridge, England.

Flew B-24s as top turret gunner and engineer on planes nicknamed *Betty* and *The Parson's Chariot.*

Received Air Medal from GO #109 HQ 2nd BD, Distinguished Flying Cross from GO #128 HQ 2nd BD and the EAME Service Medal.

Returned to Ohio in 1945 and worked in the family owned coal mine and at Timken Roller Bearing Plant until health forced his retirement in 1980. He passed away in 1981 after a long illness.

JAMES R. BAKER, was born in Dana, IL on Oct. 9, 1924 and entered Illinois State University in September 1942. Was drafted into the USAAC on May 6, 1943. Basic training in Miami Beach; Radio School, Sioux Falls, SD; Gunnery School, Yuma, AZ; and flight crew training in Boise, ID.

Landed in England after D-day and began flying missions with the 2nd Div., 44th Bomb Group, 68th Sqdn. on Joe Gillespie's crew. Flew 35 missions including the supply mission to paratroopers who had jumped across the Rhine. The only mission he was attacked by enemy fighters was his last one, April 7, 1945. He played trombone and sang with volunteer swing band at Shipdham.

Returned to the States on V-E day aboard the SS *Brazil*, landing in Boston. After furlough, reported to Santa Ana, CA for reassignment to a band at Lackland, San Antonio. Discharged Oct. 1, 1945 at Ft. Sam Houston with rank of tech sergeant. Received Air Medal with four Oak Leaf Clusters.

Re-entered Illinois State University, finishing with BS in music education, August 1948 and later MS in education at Northern Illinois University. Taught school for 37 years as a band and choral director ending career in DeKalb, IL.

Met Marian Healy of rural Kankakee at Illinois State and they were married June 1948. They have two married daughters and three grandsons. They enjoy traveling, volunteering, family and church activities in retirement.

LOVELL EUGENE BAKER JR., was born Feb. 27, 1924, Wood, VA. Joined the Aviation Cadet Program in 1943 and trained in Texas, transitioned to B-24 combat crew training at Casper, WY. In January 1945, he was assigned to the 466th Bomb Group, 2nd Air Div., 8th Air Force, Attlebridge, England. He flew combat as air craft commander from March 2, 1945 to April 18, 1945. Was then assigned to Sioux City Field in June 1945. Married Mildred (Mickey) Mooty there Sept. 8, 1945.

After short assignments to Colorado Springs and Great Bend, KS, he left active duty to help with the family dairy and beef business in Alabama. In 1949 he returned to the University of Alabama to finish his bachelor's degree and was recalled to active duty in 1951. He stayed on active duty as an ROTC instructor, finished a master's degree and was granted a regular commission in 1956.

Was stationed at Orly Air Field in Paris, France from 1955-1958 in a variety of duties. He was transferred to Dover AFB, DE and stationed there from 1958-1962 where he flew C-124s and C-133s. From 1962-1965 he was stationed in Chateauroux, France with the 322nd Air Div., mainly as a forward air controller. His last assignment on active duty was in the ROTC department of Bradley University, 1965-1968, until his retirement.

His awards included the Air Medal with three Oak Leaf Clusters and numerous theater and Campaign Ribbons. He returned to Montgomery, AL where he worked in private industry and for the state of Alabama until 1987.

Baker passed away Jan. 29, 1993, Montgomery, AL. He is survived by his wife, Mickey, a daughter, two grandsons, two brothers and three sisters.

M.S. BALDWIN (STAN), was born in St. Louis, MO on Dec. 20, 1921. Started active duty Feb. 23, 1943. Basic training at Jefferson Barracks, MO. College Training Detachment at Jamestown, ND. Preflight at Santa Ana, CA. Navigation School at Hondo, TX. Commissioned a second lieutenant April 22, 1944. Operational training at Davis Monthan Field at Tuscon, AZ on crew of which S.R. Williamson was the pilot and H.O. Sandbeck was the co-pilot.

Was assigned to the 448th Bomb Group in summer of 1944. After three missions was assigned to a lead crew as pilotage navigator. Had to fly these missions in the nose turret, but had not been to Gunnery School-interesting. After Sid Williamson was made a lead pilot was returned to that crew with which he finished his tour. This crew lead the 2nd Div. on their last mission, Feb. 23, 1945. Flew 30 missions of which 24 were lead. Air Medal with three clusters and the Distinguished Flying Cross, the latter didn't catch up with him until after release from active duty.

After release from active duty in June of 1945, he enrolled in the engineering school at Washington University, St. Louis. After graduation in 1949, he joined Westinghouse Electric Corp. for which he worked as an electrical engineer until retirement in March of 1985. Still active professionally, doing some teaching and technical writing and is available as a consultant. Is a Fellow of the Institute of Electrical and Electronic Engineers (IEEE) and a registered professional engineer in three states.

Stan is married and has seven children and 12 grandchildren. Keeps in contact with many of the crew members, especially the Sanbecks and the flight engineer, Larry Keeran, and some of the gunners. Sid Williamson died many years ago, but Baldwin still exchanges Christmas cards with his widow.

JOHN F. BALES JR., was born Dec. 19, 1923 in Caldwell, ID. Enlisted October 1942 at Gieger Field, Spokane, WA while attending University of Idaho in Moscow, ID. Entered AAC at Lowry Field, Denver, CO. Houghton, MI as aviation student; Nashville, TN for classification; Montgomery, AL for pre-flight; Americus, GA for primary flight training in PT-17s; Greenville, MS for basic in BT-13s. Stewart Field, USMA NY for advance flight training in AT-10s. Commissioned February 1944 with Class 44-B. Orders were for light bomber and dive bomber assignment. To Salt Lake City, UT for further orders.

Assigned to B-24 as co-pilot and sent to Casper, WY for training. Further crew training done at McCook, NE, then Topeka, KS to prepare for overseas assignment.

Flew the North Atlantic landing in Ireland. After further training on flying in the UK, assigned to the 492nd Bomb Group, 859th Sqdn. where he flew 10 missions over Europe. Due to heavy losses, the 492nd was dispersed with crews going to various groups in the 2nd Div. He was assigned to the 467th at Rackheath and flew three more missions. The last flown on Aug. 18, 1944 when they crashed six miles from Norwich, England on their return from their target over Germany where they had been shot up. In the crash, the top turret dropped, killing five of their crew. He was driven in his seat, under the instrument panel. As a result, his hips, legs, ankles, ribs, right arm and head received numerous fractures. The crash rendered him unconscious for two weeks. He was told a British soldier gave him whole blood at the scene. For the next year and a half, he was in a body cast in various military hospitals in the States.

Discharged February 1946 with the rank of captain. He became active in the Reserves in Spokane, WA. Received the ETO Battle Ribbons, Air Medal and Purple Heart.

Retired from IBM Corp. in 1982 after 32 years in sales management. Then as a general contractor, built medium priced homes. He is now a semi-retired R.E. and Mortgage Loan Broker. Married and has four children, three step-children and seven grandchildren. Bales enjoys fishing and traveling with his wife, Pauline, in their 5th wheel. One summer on a two month trip, they visited three former crew members and their wives.

WILBUR A. BALLENTINE, was born Aug. 15, 1923 in Houston, TX; graduated high school in 1940; entered active duty as aviation cadet December 1942; rated pilot and commissioned second lieutenant at Altus, OK in October 1943.

Trained as B-24 pilot and joined 489th Bomb Group in Wendover, UT in February 1944. Crew flew B-24 via South America and Africa to Halesworth, England in May 1944. Completed combat tour with 489th Bomb Group as pilot, squadron lead crew, with the rank of captain in September 1944.

Awarded the Distinguished Flying Cross, Air Medal with three clusters and ETO Ribbon with four Battle Stars. Received Army Commission in 1947; BS degree in aero engineering, Texas A&M 1951. Completed USAF Experimental Flight Test Pilot School and served six years as Experimental Test Pilot, Edwards AFB, 1953-1960. Served as research and development officer on space systems programs and as program manager of a manned space flight experiments program. Retired in 1968 with the rank of colonel.

Married high school sweetheart, Helen E. Hutchison, October 1943. Has a son and daughter and six grandchildren.

CARL E. BALLY, was born May 21, 1921 in Ashland, OH. Entered the service Oct. 12, 1942, radio gunner. Stationed at Jefferson Barracks, Madison, WI, Tyndall Field, Clovis, NM, Biggs Field, Pueblo, Westover, Langley, Tibenham, Ellington Field.

On their 24 mission, Nov. 26, 1944, their pilot was killed by fighters on bomb run. On third mission their plane was thrown into flat spin by prop wash with full bomb load, pilot and co-pilot worked together to get out of it. Discharged Sept. 12, 1945 with the rank tech sergeant. Received the Air Medal with three clusters and the Distinguished Flying Cross.

Has wife, Fran, two children and one grandson. Retired, he works two days at golf course.

THOMAS K. BAMFORD, was born Oct. 9, 1923 in Kansas City, MO and raised in Dallas, TX. Joined the Army Air Corps, Jan. 18, 1943; attended Radio Operator School,

Scott Field, IL; Radio Mechanic School, Madison, WI; Radar Mechanic School, Boca Raton, FL; Radar Trainer School, Langley Field, VA.

From June 1944 until June 1945, stationed at Alconbury, England, with the 482nd Bomb Group, and Hardwick, England with the 93rd Bomb Group (B-24s). Served as the supervisor of the Mickey Radar Trainer Section. Discharged Nov. 3, 1945 as a sergeant.

Obtained BA degree from University of Missouri and commissioned a second lieutenant in the very first class of Air Force ROTC in June 1948. Graduated from University of Texas Law School in 1951. Served in the Reserve and the Texas Air National Guard from 1946 until 1980. Served as Wing Staff Judge Advocate, State Judge Advocate General of Texas and Chief Judge of the Texas Court of Military Appeals. Retired from the Air Force Reserve as a colonel in 1980.

Has practiced law in Dallas, TX from 1951 through the present date, and still serves as judge of the Texas Court of Military Appeals. Married Sept. 8, 1956 to Ina E. Ellis and has two sons, one daughter and five grandchildren.

WALTER E. BANDLOW, was born Feb. 6, 1919 in Southbridge, MA and raised in Benton Harbor, MI. Enlisted in the USAAC while attending Georgia Tech. Inducted at Camp Shelby, MS Oct. 10, 1941. Graduated from Aircraft Machinist School at Chanute Field, IL. Assigned as an instructor at the University of Wisconsin and at Chanute Field Aircraft Machinist schools.

Sent to England in late 1943 and assigned to the 470th Sub Depot attached to the 467th Bomb Group(H) at Rackheath Air Base, Station 145 five miles from Norwich Norfolk, East Anglia.

Discharged as staff sergeant, Nov. 10, 1945, returned to college and graduated with a BS in industrial education. Taught High School for nine years. Received an MA degree from Western Reserve University. Was supervisor of apprentice training at ALCOA Cleveland for seven years. Retired after 20 years from the National Acme Company in 1984.

Returned to school for an associate degree in computerized numerical control in 1989. Presently teaching classes in the Acme-Gridley Multiple Spindle Bar Machine.

Married Majorie L. Grahl, July 23, 1945, has one daughter, four sons and nine grandchildren. Resides in Lakewood, OH.

ANDREW BANKO, was born April 1, 1923 in Elkhorn, WV and grew up in Carbondale, PA. Married Evelyn Biciocchi, from Washington, DC, October 1949. They have four sons, three daughters and eight grandchildren.

Was inducted into the USAAC, March 1, 1943. After basic training in Atlantic City, NJ, he attended Aircraft Armament School at Buckley and Lowry Fields, outside Denver, CO. Aerial Gunnery School followed at Kingman, AZ. In August 1943, he was transferred to Clovis, NM to become one of the initial cadres (Aircrew 406) of the 466th Bomb Group, 784th Sqdn. Combat training was completed at Alamogordo, NM.

Departed from New York City on the *Queen Mary* on March 1, 1944, exactly one year after induction, for England, Attlebridge Station. Flew 30 combat missions from March to June 1944. Received the Distinguished Flying Cross, four Air Medals and three European Campaign Stars.

Returned to the U.S. in September 1944 and spent R&R at Atlantic City. Gunnery Instructor's School followed at Laredo, TX. He remained there as an instructor until wars end and was discharged October 1945.

After service he returned to his former job as a civilian with the Army Signal Corps in Washington, DC. Attended George Washington University while continuing to work. Retired from the government in January 1979. Spent next 12 years in home improvement business and is now semi-officially retired.

CLEON M. BARBER, was born in Meadville, PA on Sept. 8, 1919; enlisted in AAF Dec. 13, 1941; graduated from AM School, Chanute Field, IL. Met Ernest H. Barber and was shipped out together. From then on they were known as C.M. and E.H. and are still known that way today.

Along with 23 other men they were the first to attend Camp Legion at Willow Run for specialized training on B-24s. Then to Davis Monthan at Tuscon, AZ for on line experience. Chosen there for 578th, 392nd B.G. Cadre. Next to Air Force School of Applied Tactics in Orlando and Montebrook, FL. Back to Alamogordo, NM.

Overseas in 1943 to 2nd Air Div., 8th Air Force at Wendling, England. Started maintaining one B-24 with five mechanics, ended the war crewing two B-24s with two AMs. Made master sergeant in 1943. Flew home in 1945 and completed his service inspecting aircraft for the Air Transport Command at Wilmington, DE where he was honorably discharged on Oct. 1, 1945.

Retired from Talon Inc. and 39 years as a Star Route mail contractor. He lives with his wife, Evelyn, at Townville, PA.

ERNEST H. BARBER, entered the AAC at Ft. McPherson near Atlanta, GA on Feb. 3, 1942. He attended Air Corp Technical School at Chanute Field, IL for 18 weeks of training and then five weeks specialist training at Ford Bomber Plant in Ypsilanti, MI. Soon after he was assigned to Davis Monthan Field, Tucson, AZ where he joined the 392nd Bomb Group as a crew chief on B-24s in the 578th Bomb Sqdn. and was on the original cadre.

They also flew as instructor engineer training new air crews. He had over 90 hours in the air. Upon leaving Tucson he went to Biggs Field, TX and then on to Alamogordo Army Air Base for the remainder of his training in the States.

Arrived at Wendling, England on Aug. 1, 1943. Lost two planes and crews then finished the first air crew on their base with 25 missions. Then 13 days later he lost the plane with his new air crew. Finished another air crew with 25 missions and received the Bronze Star Medal for no aborts. He lost two more planes and air crews within three days. Barber and his ground crew went on to help finish a number of air crews and finished with 143 missions without an abort.

He returned to the States in June 1945 and was discharged at Ft. McPherson on Sept. 17, 1945.

JAMES B. BARBER, was born Sept. 28, 1925 in Salisbury, NC. Enlisted in the AAC (aviation cadets) on June 30, 1943. Gunnery training, Panama City, FL. Completed 31 missions with 66th Bomb Sqdn., 44th Bomb Group, Shipdham, England.

Discharged Oct. 26, 1945, Greensboro, NC with the rank staff sergeant. Received the Air Medal with four Oak Leaf Clusters.

Married since 1953 to Inez Hensley. Retired as national dealership manager with Chrysler Corp., but still consults.

BRUNO L. BARBI, was born in Cles Trentino, Italy on Dec. 14, 1921 and emigrated to USA with his mother in 1931. Lived in Brooklyn for two years, moved to New Jersey in 1933 and still lives there. Graduated from high school in 1941 and was drafted in 1942. After testing was placed in the AAF; sent to Gunnery School, Fort Myers, FL; Radio School, Salt Lake City, UT; 1st phase training, Tuscon, AZ; 2nd phase training, Alamogorda; 3rd phase training, Clovis, NM.

Completed 30 missions bombing targets in ETO, Air Offensive Europe, Normandy and Southern France. On way to Kinming, China to join the 14th Air Force, they were forced to bail out of plane (it had been sabotaged) over the jungles of Nigeria. One man had broken ankle, all others okay.

Returned to the States and stationed at Edwards AFB, Muroc, CA to be radio instructor for B-29 crews. Discharged September 1945 with the rank tech sergeant. Received the Air Medal with three Oak Leaf Clusters, Distinguished Flying Cross, Good Conduct, WWII Victory Medal, EAME Service Medal with three Battle Stars and the American Campaign Medal.

Went into the Schiffli Embroidery Mfg. industry. Was self-employed for 36 years, retiring in 1986. Now plays golf and travels.

STEVE F. BARILICH, was born Aug. 27, 1924 in South Bend, IN. Drafted April 21, 1943 in the USAAF and assigned to the 467th Bomb Group, 790th Sqdn., 2nd Air Div. Stationed at Kerns Field, UT; Mountain Home, ID; Wendover Field, UT; and Rackheath, England.

Participated in American Theater, Air Offensive Europe, Normandy, Northern France, Rhineland, Ardennes-Alsace and Central Europe. His memorable experience was D-day, June 6-8, 1944.

Discharged Oct. 21, 1945 with the rank sergeant. He received awards/medals for the above battles.

Married Oct. 4, 1947 to Gizella Domnanovich. Retired and enjoys married life, two children and five grandchildren.

HENRY M. BARKER (HANK), was born Jan. 7, 1925, Johnson City, TN. Entered the USAAF, May 6, 1943, Ft. Oglethorpe, GA. Pilot Class 44-H, Sept. 8, 1944, Moody Field, Valdosta, GA, basic training, St. Petersburg, FL.

B-24 co-pilot "Old Buckingham" Norfolk, Suffolk, England, 2nd Air Div., 453rd Bomb Group, 735th Sqdn., 8th Air Force. B-24 co-pilot flight officer 1945, 4th Ferrying Group, Memphis, TN. Project officer/detachment commander, command Operation "Creek Party" Rhein-Main AB, Germany. Air National Guard, TN, 1967-1973.

Memorable experiences: 453rd Bomb Group B-24 Liberators 24,000, April 7, 1945, target Geesthacht, Germany shell loading plane; two ME 262 jet fighters shot down three B-24 bombers in the squadron (lead squadron) just ahead of them.

Discharged Oct. 19, 1946 with the rank second lieutenant USAAF and retired Oct. 1, 1973 with the rank lieutenant colonel, USAF, RET. Received the Air Medal and ETO Ribbon with two Battle Stars.

Attended Dartmouth College, Class of 1945, graduated Washington and Lee 1949. Retired April 1977 from Knox County Govt., personnel director. Married Aug. 19, 1950 to Marilyn Ackerson Barker, who passed away Sept. 5, 1986. He has three children and three grandchildren.

LEWIS E. BARLEY, was born Feb. 6, 1917 in Millgrove, IN. Entered the USAF July 1942, instrument specialist. Stationed at Sheppard Field, Chanute Field, McClellan Field, Old Buck with 453rd Bomb Group, 467th Sub Dep. Station 144.

Discharged Nov. 21, 1945 with the rank tech sergeant. Received six medals.

Has wife, Trudy; daughter, Kay; son, Jeff; and two grandchildren. Retired from Owens Illinois, Inc., Toledo, OH after 42 years.

HARVEY P. BARNARD JR., was born Sept. 19, 1913 in Harrisburg, PA; cadet, USMA, 1933, graduated second lieutenant in 1938. Entered USAAC, August 1939 and later the USAF. Commanded 93rd Bomb Group, 8th Air Force, England 1944.

Memorable experiences: led 2nd Div. six times in 1944: Hamburg, Burnburg, Ludwigshaven, Kassel, Zellerfeld and Minden.

Retired June 1946 with the rank of colonel. (Physical

disability with tuberculous retirement). Received the Croix de Guerre (Palme), Air Medal with Bronze Star and the Distinguished Flying Cross.

After retirement from Air Force, spent 35 years in the airline business, last 10 years as president of Florida Airlines. Retired in 1980 and now plays golf, does community service, church work and enjoying life.

Married to Frances C. Chase Oct. 18, 1938. Has four children, 11 grandchildren and four great-grandchildren.

ALBERT R. BARNES (ROHL), was born June 24, 1920 in Tekoa, WA. Enlisted May 1942; commissioned communication officer, Yale University in December 1943. Attended Boca Raton Radar School, then assigned to 458th Bomb Group, 755th Sqdn. as radar maintenance officer, July 1944.

Most memorable experience was with the 458th Bomb Group. He designed a blind landing system using H2X Mickey Blind Bombing Radar components. This was installed in a small house constructed on a bomb trailer. He trained the control tower officer to recognize blips on the scope and directed the pilots to the runway. Best day was 36 planes in 35 minutes with 100 foot ceiling and 1/2 mile visibility.

Returned to States June 1945 and assigned to Biggs Field as radar maintenance officer. Discharged from Fort Bliss February 1946 as captain.

Sales engineer and district manager 22 years with General Electric. Electrical contractor, San Jose, CA for 20 years. Barnes and wife, Evelyn, celebrated their 50th anniversary in February. They have two sons and two granddaughters.

JOSEPH M. BARNES, was born July 26, 1920 in Wapello, IA and attended Cornell College, American Institute of Business and Drake University. Worked at Bankers Trust Co., Des Moines, IA before enlisting in the Army Air Corps, Nov. 23, 1942. Graduated navigator, second lieutenant, Class 44-7, Hondo, TX. Assigned to 392nd Bomb Group, 578th Sqdn. Wendling, September 1944.

Completed 35 missions in B-24s and returned to the U.S. May 1945. Awarded Air Medal with five Oak Leaf Clusters. Separated from active duty as first lieutenant October 1945 and resigned from the Reserves in 1952. Retired as senior vice president and trust officer of First Interstate Bank, Mason City, IA, Dec. 31, 1985, after 45 years in banking.

Married Ardeth A. Lettow, Feb. 19, 1943 and has two daughters, three grandchildren, and one great-grandchild. He and his wife continue to reside in Mason City, IA.

ROBERT C. BARNES, was born on May 15, 1923 in Hoverfield, MA. Attended school in Haverhill until 8th Grade, then was enrolled at Moses Brown School in Providence, RI where he graduated in June 1942. Enrolled at Brown University in the summer of 1942, graduating with Class of 1948.

Joined the Air Corps as an aviation cadet and completed pilot training with the Class of 44-3. Was assigned as a co-pilot to the 702nd Sqdn., 445th Bomb Group, stationed in England. Completed 25 missions as a co-pilot and was given his own crew as pilot for the remaining 10 missions. Flew his missions from July 1944 through March 1945.

Was re-called back into the Air Force in 1950 and assigned to combat crew training at Langley AFB in B-26. Later in 1951 was re-assigned to training command as an instructor in the B-29 Transition School, Randolph AFB, TX. Received two Distinguished Flying Crosses and five Air Medals during his combat tour in WWII.

Married to Nancy Barnes and has two sons, David and Thomas. They live in Massachusetts for six months and in Clearwater, FL for the other six months.

JAMES BARRETT, was born Jan. 2, 1925. Entered AAF Jan. 10, 1943; Radio School at Sioux Falls, SD; Gunnery School, Yuma, AZ. Assigned to B-24 crew in October 1944. Transition training at Casper, WY.

Sent to 8th Air Force in England and assigned to 330th Sqdn., 93rd Bomb Group, near Norwich. Flew 18 combat missions over Central Europe. Received EAME Ribbon with two Bronze Stars and two Air Medals. Discharged Dec. 2, 1945 with the rank tech sergeant.

Graduated from St. Cloud, MN, Dec. 2, 1949. Worked as a carpet rep for 25 years. Started a retail carpet business and is still active in it.

Married Ruth Kopriva in 1952 and has nine children and 29 grandchildren.

JOHN A. BARRON, was born May 5, 1925 in Fredricktown, PA. Entered the Air Force June 24, 1943. Basic training at Greensboro, NC; Keesler Field, MS for Airplane Mechanic School; Gunnery School at Harlingen, TX; Biggs Field, TX for overseas training and assigned to B-24s.

Stationed at Tibenham, England, assigned to 703rd Sqdn., 445th Bomb Group as an assistant engineer gunner. Completed 35 missions, the one he remembers most was Kassel, Germany mission. Returned to the States in April 1945 and spent R&R at Santa Ana Army Air Base, CA, then sent to Chanute Field, IL for Electronic School, while there the war ended.

Discharged Oct. 21, 1945 with the rank of staff sergeant. Received the Air Medal and Silver Oak Leaf Cluster.

Retired from USX. Married 40 years on Aug. 15, 1993. Has one son, two daughters and eight grandchildren.

RUDIE C. BARTEL, began his Air Force career in August 1942 as an aviation cadet. Graduated from Ellington AFB as a navigator; followed by a partial tour in B-24 bombers based in England during 1943/44 (partial tour as a result of being a POW in Germany for a year). After return to the ZI in June 1945, Lt. Bartel attended pilot training (Class 46-D). After a short tour as navigation instructor at Chanute Field, IL, Lt. Bartel was discharged from the Air Force. After six months he requested recall and was assigned to the Strategic Air Command. Flew in B-29, B-50 and B-47 bombers from 1947-1955 with the 97th and 43rd Bomb Wings.

Attended Airborne Electronics School, Keesler AFB. Followed with assignments at Richards Gebaur AFB; 5th Air Force in Japan; Westover AFB, MA until retirement from service August 1963 with 21 years.

Civilian positions with National Scientific Labs, Census Bureau, Navy Department, HQ USAF Data Automation Directorate in 1967, Air Staff R&D Directorate in 1977, 7th Communications/Computer Group in the Pentagon Computer Center in 1988. Retired Oct. 30, 1990 with 47 years total military/federal service.

Married to the former Shirley Richardson and blessed with nine children: Richard, Sharon, James, Betty, Steven, Timmie (deceased), Marjorie, Mary and Michael. Bowie, MD has been home since 1963 with short vacations on his farm near San Antonio, TX.

WESLEY J. BARTELT, was born May 22, 1922 in Milwaukee, WI. Moved to Pewaukee, WI at age 16 and helped run family farm. Graduated June 1941 and worked at Langley Field as a model builder. Returned to Wisconsin in June 1942 and enlisted in the USAAC, September 1942. Graduated Pilot School, Columbus, MS Class 44-D.

Sent to England September 1944, assigned to 489th Bomb Group. Reassigned to 453rd Bomb Group in November. Flew 22 Missions. Was shot down by Russian fighters over Lotz, Poland on March 15, 1945. Returned to Group April 1, 1945. Reassigned to 467th Bomb Group.

Returned to States by flying War Weary back. Separated service at Greensboro, NC in October 1945 with the rank first lieutenant. Received the Air Medal with three clusters and ETO with four Battle Stars.

Moved to Florida October 1945. Started first scuba diving resort in America at Marathon, FL. Business and home destroyed by hurricane Donna in 1960. Relocated to Kissimmee, FL. Developed RV resort. Retired and divorced in 1982. Has three daughters. Remarried June Basile 1985 and live in Fort Pierce, FL.

CARL C. BARTHEL, was born March 13, 1917 in Arbutus, MD. Entered the service Aug. 7, 1941, USAAC, USAF, 93rd Bomb Group, 329th Bomb Sqdn., HQ 2nd Air Div. Stationed at Alconbury, Bungay, Hardwick, Bengasi, Tunis.

Stayed in the Air Force after WWII with the Air Training Command at Keesler AFB, Scott AFB, James Connally AFB, Mather AFB. With the Air Force Academy at its beginning. With European Communications Area at Ramstein, Germany and Wiesbaden, Germany and Scott AFB. Memorable experience was low level raid on Ploesti, Rome, D-day.

Retired Aug. 31, 1970 with the rank of colonel to Upperco, MD. Received Legion of Merit with 20 Oak Leaf Clusters, Bronze Star Medal, Silver Star, Distinguished Flying Cross, Air Medal, Croix de Guerre and AFLSA with 11 Oak Leaf Clusters.

Married Joan L. Thomas at Kettringham Hall in 1944 (deceased). Later married to Helene Zborowski in 1982. Has two children by first marriage. He is retired.

ANTON BARTOLE (BUD), was born 1923 in North Dakota. Engineer and waist gunner on Joseph Bell's crew. After combat, flew night missions to Sweden until war ended.

Building contractor in Vancouver, WA; then construction supervisor for government. Married Ardis and has three children. Now retired in Lake Havasu City, AZ.

CLARENCE W. BARTON, was born Nov. 10, 1922 in Richmond, VA. He grew up in Huntington, WV and enlisted in the AAC June 1942. Was called to active duty as AC January 1943. Primary training, Tulsa, OK and commissioned as second lieutenant pilot, February 1944.

His crew ferried a B-24 to Ireland in August 1944 and was assigned to 93rd Bomb Group, 328th Sqdn. at Hardwick, England. Completed 35 missions in March 1945.

Received the Air Medal and Distinguished Flying Cross. Was assigned to the OSS as a staff pilot and stationed in London and Paris. Returned to USA in December 1945 and discharged as captain. (Probably the last man in the 8th Air Force to leave Europe.)

Met his wife, Betty Roberts, on a blind date during primary training in Tulsa, OK. They were married January 1946. Attended Oklahoma State University and graduated with a BSME in May 1949. They have two children. Retired from Dresser Engineering Co. as VP engineering July 1982 and lives in Tulsa.

The eight living members of his nine man crew have had reunions in 1989, 1991 and 1992.

RICHARD E. BATEMAN, was born in 1924. Entered the Army in April 1943, transferred to USAAF Aviation Cadet Program in 1943. Qualified for pilot, navigator or bombardier and chose navigation because of USAAF needs and request.

Graduated AAF Navigation School, Monroe, LA in 1944; phase training, Casper, WY AAB. Joined the 8th Air Force, 458th Bomb Group in fall 1944. Flew combat missions until V-E day, May 8, 1945. Received Air Medal, three Oak Leaf Clusters, three Battle Stars on ETO Ribbon for Ardennes, Rhineland, and Central Europe Battles.

Has degrees from University of California and University of Washington. Engineer at the Boeing Co. and jet propulsion laboratory. Trajectory engineer for lunar orbiter project at Boeing and Mariner Mars in 1971 and Mariner Venus-Mercury 1973 at jet propulsion laboratory. Retired 1989, principal engineer at Boeing with 36 years service in military and space assignments.

Married Marilyn J. Roehlen in 1945 and has two children, Marc and Lisa.

VERNON A. BAUMGART, was born May 14, 1915 in Appleton, WI. Joined the USAAC March 25, 1942. Finished pilot training Feb. 16, 1943 at Pampa, TX. Began B-24 phase training; assigned a crew at Tucson, AZ; and completed B-24 training at Pueblo, CO.

Assigned to the 93rd Bomb Group at Benghazi, North Africa, August 1943. After one combat mission with the 93rd from North Africa was reassigned to the 392nd Bomb Group at Wendling and flew 24 more missions with them. Some of these missions included the Frisian Islands, Diversion, Kiel, Gotha and culminated in leading the mission to Fredrichshafen, German (the 392nd's most costly mission, out of 29 aircraft only 10 returned).

Returned to the States in August 1944 with rank of captain. Stayed in the Air Force for 21 years with tours at Westover AB, MA; Clarks AB, Philippines; Bolling AB, Washington, DC; Griffins AB, NY; Taiper, Taiwan and retired from Elgin AFB, FL in April 1963 with the rank of lieutenant colonel. Was awarded the Distinguished Flying Cross and Air Medal with four Oak Leaf Clusters. Flew many aircraft from the P-51 Mustang through the B-29 and 500 hours in jets.

Moved back to Wisconsin in 1967, worked at civilian job for 10 years until retirement in 1977. Married for 51 years, now a widower with a son, two daughters and one granddaughter. Main recreation consists of taking trips on a touring motorcycle all over the U.S. and Canada and attending military reunions.

RICHARD C. BAYNES (DICK), was born May 6, 1924 in Mansfield, PA. Enlisted USAAC in November 1942. Pilot training, Southeast Training Command, graduated Turner Field, Albany, GA, Class of 43-K. Maxwell Field, AL for B-24 Transition and crew training at Biggs Field, El Paso, TX.

Flew to England via the northern route in June of 1944. Assigned to the 466th Bomb Group, 787th Sqdn. Started flying combat missions July 11. Flew 35 combat missions, plus six gas hauling missions, flying gas to Generals Patton and Montgomery. Flew 35th mission Nov. 1, 1944.

Assigned as instructor at B-24 Transition School, Liberal, KS, then instructor at Instrument Flying Instructors School, Lubbock, TX. Discharged October 1945. Awarded Distinguished Flying Cross, Air Medal with three Oak Leaf Clusters.

Graduated from Rensselaer Polytechnic Institute, Troy, NY then worked for Revere Copper and Brass for 27 years, VP Marketing and Sales, then with Reading Tube Corp as VP Marketing and Sales. Now self-employed as manufacturers representative. Remained in Air Force Reserve and retired as colonel in 1976.

Married in 1950, has three married children and two granddaughters.

ELROY W. BEANEY, was born in Rochester, NY on Aug. 24, 1921. Joined the USAAC as an aviation cadet, Aug. 4, 1942. After classification in Nashville, TN, went to pilot training in Decatur, AL, Walnut Ridge, AR, completed advanced training at Seymour, IN and commissioned as pilot April 29, 1943.

Pilot transition for B-24, Smyrna, TN. Assigned to 18th Anti-Sub Sqdn., Langley Field, VA on July 4, 1943. Transferred July 20, 1943 to 24th Anti-Sub Sqdn., Westover, MA until Sept. 17, 1943 when transferred to 2nd Air Force for reassignment at Kearney, NE. Joined the 467th Bomb Group, Nov. 6, 1943, assigned to 790th Sqdn.

Departed for England March 2, 1944 for the ETO. Flew first mission on April 24, 1944 and completed tour of 35 missions on July 21, 1944. Left England Sept. 4, 1944.

Assigned to Victorville, CA as part of the 2nd Air Div. Training Command and flew B-24s training navigators for the Pacific Theater. Transferred to Transport Command July 6, 1945 for C-54 transport transition. Assigned Nov. 13, 1945 to Middle Atlantic Div. Air Transport, Wilmington, DE, flying North Atlantic to Europe and Africa until Feb. 18, 1946.

State duty at Westover AAB, MA until discharge Jan. 1, 1947 with the rank captain.

Married his high school sweetheart, Dona Henry, on Sept. 21, 1943. They have three married daughters and three grandchildren. Retired in 1982 from advertising sales and sales management.

CHARLES W. BEARD, entered the USAAC as bomber pilot after graduating from Flying School in Columbus, MS in August 1943. He also graduated from Georgia Military College.

Beard was pilot of B-24 bomber *Big Fat Mama* of the 492nd Bomb Group, 856th Sqdn, an outfit that lost more B-24 bombers than any other group in the 8th Air Force in a three month period. He was the group from beginning until it was disbanded in August 1944. He flew 20 daylight bombing missions with the 492nd Group.

Flew 10 night missions to finish his tour and return to the States as a flight instructor in September 1944. He was honorably discharged with the rank of captain. His awards include the Distinguished Flying Cross, four Air Medals, Meritorious Service Unit Plaque, American Defense Service Medal, Croix de Guerre with Palm and the WWII Victory Medal with four Bronze Stars for Air Offensive Europe, Normandy, Northern France and Rhineland.

JESSE T. BEARD, was born July 7, 1921 in Hardinsburg, KY. Joined the USAAC on Aug. 17, 1942. Stationed at SAACC, Harlingen, San Angelo, Ovalde, TX. Received some pilot and bombardier training; Armor Gunnery School, Buckley Field, CO; and Gunnery School, Harlingen, TX.

His memorable experience was serving with the 458th Bomb Group. Discharged Sept. 30, 1945 at Randolph Field with the rank of staff sergeant. He received the Air Medal with four Oak Leaf Clusters, ETO with four stars, Good Conduct and clasp and the Victory Medal.

Married Brucie Moorman and has four daughters and one son. He is a farmer, president of Farm Bureau (three years), town mayor, co-publisher of weekly newspaper and member of Order of Washington, Colonial Society and Americans of Royal Descent.

WILLIS H. BEASLEY (BILL), was born in Denver, CO on April 13, 1922. Inducted into the USAAC Sept. 8, 1942. Entered active service on Feb. 25, 1943. Received basic training at San Antonio, TX. Other stations: El Reno, OK; Sheppard Field, TX; Laredo AAF, TX; Salt Lake City, UT; Biggs Field, TX; Alamogordo, NM.

Assigned to 492nd Bomb Group, 857th Bomb Sqdn., North Pickenham, England as armorer gunner, tail position

on B-24J. Completed 17 missions, interned in Sweden June 20, 1944.

Received Air Medal with one Oak Leaf Cluster, five Campaign Stars. Stationed at Kingman, AZ and Pueblo, CO AAF. Discharged Oct. 26, 1945 with the rank of staff sergeant, then entered the Reserves as second lieutenant.

Retired after 40 years with the Public Service Co. as senior customer relations representative.

Married Norma M. Pearson in December 1944. They have three sons, five grandsons and one granddaughter.

ROBERT J. BEATSON, was born July 3, 1922, Ludlow, MA. Enlisted Jan. 8, 1941, Springfield, MA, D Co., 104th Inf., 26th Div. Transferred to aviation cadets, summer of 1942. Assigned to Kelly Field, TX and received Navigator's Wings April 22, 1943, Hondo, TX.

Assigned to heavy bombers (B-24); trained at Tucson, AZ; El Paso, TX; Pueblo, CO; Alamogordo, NM and Topeka, KS. Flew first bombing mission Sept. 9, 1943, Abbeville Airfield. Completed 30 missions May 8, 1944, one month before invasion.

Received the Distinguished Flying Cross with one Oak Leaf Cluster, Air Medal with three Oak Leaf Clusters, Purple Heart (Berlin, Germany, April 29, 1943) and the Presidential Unit Citation which was awarded to 392nd for bombing accuracy (Gotha, "Big Week" February 1944).

Returned to States and pilot training. Received pilot's license in 1945. Flew PT-17s in primary at Curtis Field, Brady, TX and AT-6s in basic at Moore Field, Mission, TX. The end of Pacific hostilities brought discharge in September 1945. Returned to Georgetown University, Washington DC and graduated in 1948.

Worked 35 years as investigator for Secret Service, FBI, congressional committees and Maryland schools. Worked eight years handling storage and retrieval of sensitive computer data.

Married Sylvia and has five children: Mary Anne, Jane, Robert, Michael, David and eight grandchildren.

FRED BECCHETTI, was born in New Mexico on March 31, 1924. Joined the USAAC in 1942. Bombardier cadet training. Won wings at Big Spring, TX, Class 43-16, Nov. 13, 1943. In England May 1, 1944. 445th Bomb Group, 702nd Sqdn., Tibenham.

Flew 35 missions, including D-day, St. Lo breakout, Berlin, three in a row to Munich and a bail-out over Norwich on 32nd mission, July 31. Received four Air Medals and Distinguished Flying Cross. Back to the States September 1944. Became bombardier instructor for U.S. Chinese cadets at Carlsbad, NM, until discharge Nov. 13, 1945.

Back to school on GI bill and received BS and MA degrees from University of Missouri in 1949; PhD studies in Spanish, University of New Mexico. Taught high school 1950-1961 in Benson, AZ where he served as mayor 1958-1961. Diplomatic service for 27 years in Latin America with U.S. Information Agency, 1962-1989.

Married Vivienne Fleissner on Dec. 28, 1946. They have five children.

Now retired in Fairfax, VA, he writes a little and does watercolors.

FRANK W. BECK, was born June 4, 1924 and joined the USAAF Aviation Cadet Program in 1943. When the program was cut back, he continued flying as armorer gunner and was assigned to B-24s with the 458th Bomb Group; stationed at Santa Ana, CA; Lowry Field, CO; Harlingen, TS; and Norwich, England. Flew a total of 27 combat missions.

Memorable experiences: flying 200th mission as crew member of *Final Approach* on March 9, 1945; bomb runs on ball bearing plants in Germany; and mission to bomb Remagen Bridge in Battle of Bulge on June 14, 1945 and missed it by a mile.

Discharged Nov. 6, 1945 with the rank staff sergeant. He received the European-Middle Eastern Service Ribbon and Rhineland, Ardennes, and Central Europe Campaign Ribbons.

Retired in 1986 at the age of 62 from management of major insurance company. Now plays golf and enjoys life.

EDWIN D. BECKER, was in Elizabeth, NJ on March 6, 1925 and raised in Westfield, NJ. Entered the USAAC on April 4, 1943 and graduated as aerial navigator at Coral Gables in April 1944. Joined Joe Lates' crew at McGowan Field for operational training; subsequently, ferried a B-24J to 8th Air Force.

Joined 733rd Sqdn., 453rd Bomb Group in August 1944. Flew his first mission intended for Berlin on Aug. 27, 1944, but was recalled just after reaching enemy territory. Finally reached Berlin Feb. 26, 1945 on 30th and last mission.

Returned to the States and after training at Ellington Field and assignment to Selman Field as navigation instructor, was discharged as first lieutenant on Sept. 26, 1945. Received five Air Medals and three European Campaign Stars.

Obtained his AB from Harvard in 1948 and MS in industrial engineering from Columbia in 1956. After several manufacturing positions, finished industrial career at M&M/ Mars, retiring in 1982. Taught engineering at Union County College, NJ until 1987. Now lives in Jackson Hole, WY.

Married Doris Oneal in May 1953, she passed away August 1986.

LESTER W. BECKER, was born Oct. 4, 1922 in Merrill, WI and joined the USAAF on Dec. 22, 1942. Inducted at Fort Sheridan, IL; Air Craft Warning School, Camp Crowder, MO; general duty at Drew Field, Tampa, FL.

Departed Oct. 21, 1943 for ETO and arrived Nov. 3, 1943 on troop convoy as a replacement at Hethel AB, Norwich, England, sheet metal worker, 463rd Sub. Depot. At end of war in Germany, he went to North Africa and was stationed at Cazes Air Base outside of Casablanca. Worked out of operations as a line taxi driver. Departed Africa on Aug. 27, 1945 and arrived in the States Aug. 30, 1945.

Memorable experiences: ETO watching planes form overhead, headed to Germany on D-day; trolly run over Germany to see to see bomb damage from our bombers; first plane ride, trip from England to Africa aboard a B-17; trip from Africa to States aboard a C-54; serving aboard the Flat Top USS *America*.

Discharged Nov. 8, 1945, Truex Field, Madison, WI with the rank of corporal. Received the EAME Ribbon with six Bronze Stars, American Theater Ribbon and the Good Conduct Medal.

Married on Feb. 1, 1946, wife passed away on May 18, 1988. He is retired. Has one son who served four years in the Navy.

DR. RALPH S. BECKER, was March 4, 1925 and joined the USAF June 1943. Stationed at Maxwell Field, AL; Tyndall Field, FL; San Marcos, TX; Davis Monthan AB. Served with 2nd Div., 44th Group, 66th Sqdn. in Shipdham, England.

Participated in Bulge, Rhine crossing, Berlin, Munich. Completed 23 missions. Memorable experiences: 1200 plane raids on Berlin, low raids and Rhine crossing, landing in England with nose gear up; first attacks by German jet fighters; V-E day in England; navigating C-47 full of 9th AF guys from Wales to Mass. via Iceland, Greenland.

Discharged September 1945 with the rank second lieutenant. Received the Air Medal with two Oak Leaf Clusters, European Theater Operations, North Africa.

Attended University of Vermont after discharge in late 1945, received BS degree, MS degree from University of New Hampshire in 1950, PhD degree in chemistry from Florida State University in 1955. Has published 130 articles, two books in three languages and is guest lecturer in most countries of Europe, Asia and South America. Professor Emeritus, University Houston and professor New University Lisbon, Portugal.

Has three children: Sherryl, Janet and Scott.

LUTHER L. BEDDINGFIELD, was born July 29, 1923 in East Flatrock, NC. Enlisted Oct. 12, 1942 and entered the service January 1943, USAAC, navigator, 2nd Air Div. 392nd Sqdn. Stationed at Miami Beach, FL; University of TN, Nashville; Monroe, LA; Fort Myers, FL; Davis Monthan; Wendling; Miami Beach, Ellington Field, Ferry Command Memphis, TN.

L L BEDDINGFIELD JR

Completed 33 missions. Participated in D-day. Was discharged January 1946 with the rank of first lieutenant. He received the Distinguished Flying Cross, Air Medal with three Oak Leaf Clusters, ETO, five Battle Stars.

Married in 1945 and has two daughters and one son. He is retired and enjoys traveling, reading, Lions Club and American Legion, Post 126.

DANIEL BEIGHTOL, was born Sept. 2, 1921 in Erie, PA. Joined the USAAC on Aug. 8, 1942. Went to Keesler Field Air Mechanics School; Consolidated Air School, San Diego on B-24s; Gunnery School, Harlingen, TX; phases in Boise and Pocatello, ID. Then to the 93rd Bomb Group as an engineer on James Dourghetty's crew.

Went overseas November 1943 and came back October 1944. Most memorable mission was Aug. 8, 1944 when they were sent to mark a target for B-17s near Coen, France in thick fog. Marked the target okay, but received over 81 hits on their plane. The pilot was doing evasive action Beightol had never seen before. His top turret seat was unsnapped and he stayed in the turret by bracing his feet on the foot rest and doing a lot of praying.

After four missions, their crew was assigned as a lead crew and lead other groups on missions. Discharged Sept. 18, 1945 with the rank tech sergeant. He received the Distinguished Flying Cross, four Air Medals and the Unit Citation.

Retired, he is a widower with four sons.

EARL D. BELISLE, was born in 1921 in Amery, WI. Entered the USAAC in January 1943 and trained in SE Command. Joined Joseph Bell's crew as co-pilot in Apirl 1944.

After combat, he flew two night missions to Sweden until war ended. Returned to ZI in new B-24. Was discharged in August 1945.

Married and has five children. He is an air traffic controller in Chicago and Minneapolis, MN where he now lives.

PETER STEPHEN BELITSOS, was born July 18, 1922 in Washington, DC and was raised in Lynn, MA. Enlisted in the USAAC as an aviation cadet in November 1942, graduating with Class 44-B as a pilot at Columbus, MS.

Married to Ida Arvanites on February 13 while on 10 day delay en route to Westover Field, MA; completed transition as co-pilot on Lt. Edward Speers' crew in May; assigned

---

to 445th Bomb Group in June; flew 21 missions with Ed Speers, flew 22nd mission with Lt. Palmer Bruland over Kassel September 27. Was shot down and spent the remainder of the war as a POW in Stalag 1 during which time a son, Stephen Peter, was born on November 30.

Returned home, still married to Ida and has four grandchildren.

JOSEPH N. BELL, was born 1919 in Virginia. Pilot of B-24 crew from April 15, 1944. Flew to England in July and completed 35 combat missions over Europe plus four gas trucking missions to France from the 467th at Rackheath by March 1945.

Returned to the States via ship, stayed in the Air Force as pilot until 1963, flying many types of airplanes at many locations doing many kinds of jobs. Retired as lieutenant colonel.

Married Helen and has one married son. Lives near Ashland, VA.

WALTER M. BELL, was born on a farm May 10, 1916 in Lee County, SC. Graduated from Climson College in 1940 with a second lieutenant commission in the Infantry Reserve.

Called to duty on March 5, 1942 into the infantry. After a year of marching asked for a transfer to the Air Corps for pilot training. Graduated with pilot wings on Nov. 3, 1943. Sent to B-24 Transition School at Smyrna, TN. Received crew at Westover Field and crew trained at Savannah.

Given a B-24 and sent to Wales. Then to Ireland for course taught by combat veterans. August 1944 was sent to the 392nd Bomb Group, Wendling, England. Completed 35 missions. Received Air Medal and Distinguished Flying Cross.

Crew returned to States and he remained as squadron operation officer. Returned to farming in 1945. In 1966 went to work with South Carolina Farm Bureau. Retired in 1981.

WESLEY BELLESON, was born in Jewell, IA on April 8, 1923. Married his college sweetheart, Laverne Lenke, on Nov. 20, 1944 at Lowry Field, Denver. Enlisted in the USAAC on Nov. 19, 1942. Took basic training at Kearns Field, UT.

Assigned to Armour School at Buckley Field, Denver. Later moved to Lowry Field, Denver for further training. Was assigned to Gunnery School at Tyndall Field, FL. Completed that phase and sent to Boise, ID for crew assignment. Ended up in Tonopah, NV for crew training.

Left States on Jan. 15, 1944 flying southern route via Brazil, Africa, Morroco and Wales. Arrived at Horsham St. Faith, Jan. 31, 1944. Completed 30 missions, left England arriving States Sept. 16, 1944, R&R in Miami for first furlough.

Assigned back to Lowry Field and instructed tail turret. Went to Garden City, KS awaiting discharge which was Oct. 8, 1945 at Sioux Falls, SD with the rank of staff sergeant.

Owned men's clothing store for 29 years and retired in 1975.

RALPH L. BELWARD, was born Sept. 15, 1917 in Norwalk, CT and grew up in New Canaan. Two years college before joining the Army Air Corps Oct. 1, 1940 as a private. Promoted through the ranks until acceptance in Corps Aviation Cadets, Class 44-B, graduated as second lieutenant, Turner Field, GA.

Trained as pilot for multi-engine aircraft. Was instructor pilot at Albany, GA. Assigned Westover for B-24 train-

ing and crew assignment. To Mitchell Field for new B-24J. Flew it to England via Labrador, Greenland, Iceland, Scotland; thence replacement center for combat crew assignment; further training. Assigned to 489th Bomb Group Halesworth. Flew combat against Germany, mostly in the *Ripper*. Dropped supplies for Patton. Had a couple of lucky escapes. Flew 22 missions before being ordered to Tucson for B-29 training.

Received the American Defense Medal, Bronze Star, European Theater Ribbon, North France Campaign, Bronze Star, Germany Campaign, Air Medal and two Oak Leaf Clusters, American Theater and Victory Ribbons, Good Conduct and others.

After release from 489th was attached to Continental Air Command, then to 1st Air Force. Served in many capacities: food/laundry service officer. Also inspector general's team, finally administration services. Retired as lieutenant colonel.

Married June 1, 1951 to Virginia Vern Voboril. No children of their own, but 10 children lived with them for various reasons and times, bringing much happiness to all.

JAMES F. BELWOOD, was born Feb. 9, 1919 in Marshall, MO. Had pilot training in Class 43-G, Transition in B-24s, Montgomery, AL. Was assigned a newly trained crew and completed phase training at Clovis, NM.

Picked up a new B-24G at Mitchell Field and flew the southern route to England in March 1944. Was assigned with crew to 330th Bomb Sqdn., 93rd Bomb Group at Hardwick. Crew flew first mission April 11, 1944 and all the original crew except their bombardier flew a total of 34 missions in 80 days. That must rank up there somewhere near the shortest completed tour. Thank the Lord no one sustained an injury during the tour. God bless that Pratt & Whitney, 1400 hours in the B-24 without losing an engine to any cause. Returned to States and Langley Field, flying B-24s for navigational trainees until his discharge in 1946.

He married a girl from Norwich, began a career in insurance and started a family only to be recalled in 1951 to Randolph for transition training in B-29s. On to Travis with his crew assigned to 9th Bomb Group. Assigned finally to B-36s in the 5th Strat Recon Wg H at Travis and finally back to civilian life November 1953.

Now retired with time to find old friends and comrades and hope any who see this will drop me a line.

EUGENE E. BENNETT, joined the USAAC as air cadet at age 19 in July of 1942. Received wings and second lieutenant commission in November of 1943. Joined the 56th Fighter Group, 62nd Sqdn., 8th Air Force in England in April of 1944.

On May 4, 1944 on combat mission number seven, destroyed one FW 190 in the vicinity of Nordhausen, Germany. Because of no enemy aircraft to be found, was ordered to begin bombing and strafing ground targets.

Parachuted on June 7, 1944 from P-47 at 7:30 a.m. near Argentan, France, about 100 miles west of Paris. Was strafing German tanks when they returned the fire by cutting the engine oil lines. Was hidden in French farms by the Resistance and took part in their activity until August 6th when Patton's boys went by on their way to Berlin. Was MIA for 60 days as an evader.

Promoted to first lieutenant in September of 1944. In October returned to the USA to become instructor of French pilots learning to fly the P-47 in combat. In August 1945 was released from the service, but signed to the active reserve.

In May 1948, took part in organizing the 137th Fighter Sqdn. of the NYANG at White Plains, NY. Was extended federal recognition in three positions: flight commander of "B" flight, aircraft maintenance officer and automotive main-

tenance officer. Promoted to captain May 1950. In June 1951 promoted to operations officer and was called from civilian job to organize the 137th for Korea but orders were canceled.

In January 1952 was promoted to squadron and base commander at Westchester County Airport. Orders for promotion to lieutenant colonel by state of New York were denied by National Guard Bureau in 1952, but in June 1954 was promoted as commander of the 105th Fighter G. Resigned from USAF and Air Guard with 20 years service in July of 1962.

HUGH M. BENNETT, was born April 23, 1923 in Interlaken, NY. He enlisted Jan. 16, 1943 at Ft. Niagara, NY. Assigned to 854th Bomb Sqdn., 491st Bomb Group as radio operator Crew #48.

Basic training at Atlantic City, NJ and Greensboro, NC; Gunnery School, Laredo, TX; and Radio School, Salt Lake City, UT. Assigned to Dave Hicks crew September 1943 at Tucson, AZ, then on to Blythe, CA and Pueblo, CO where 491st Bomb Group was formed.

Arrived in England May 15, 1944, mission #1 was June 2 and mission #31 was Sept. 11, 1944. Completed 31 missions over occupied Europe from Metfield and North Pickenham, England. Discharged Oct. 13, 1945, Laredo, TX with the rank tech sergeant. Received the Air Medal and the Distinguished Flying Cross.

Married and has five children, 11 grandchildren and two great-grandkids. Retired from Ford Motor Co. after 28 years in 1985, then moved to Florida.

ROY E. BEQUETTE, was born Feb. 24, 1923 in Casper, WY. Joined the Army in January 1943 and completed basic training in Coast Artillery. In May 1943, entered aviation cadet training at Maxwell Air Field. Commissioned as pilot in January 1944 at Moody Field, GA. Joined the 8th Air Force, 446th Bomber Group, 704th Sqdn. at Flixton, England in May 1944.

Flew 30 combat missions, 11 as lead crew. Awarded the Distinguished Flying Cross, Air Medal with four Leaf Clusters, ETO Ribbon with four Battle Stars. Returned to States January 1945. Separated from the service on Nov. 16, 1945 with the rank first lieutenant.

Married in May 1947 to Clara. They have three great children and four wonderful grandchildren - all boys. Retired in 1986 from freight forwarding business. Now spends winters in Tucson and the rest in Washington playing golf.

LEROY C. BERG (RED), was born in Superior, WI on Feb. 20, 1924. He entered the service December 1942 and had basic training in St. Petersburg, FL. Took a course in aircraft mechanics at Amarillo, TX; advanced mechanics at Lockheed-Vega Plant, Burbank, CA; small arms training at Kerns, UT. Went to Seymour Johnson Field, NC for further training, then sent to Fort Dix, NJ as a replacement where he joined the 453rd Bomb Group, 733rd Sqdn.

Left for England December 1943 on the *Queen Elizabeth*. Promoted to sergeant at Old Buckingham. Being on the ground crew one of the things he did was paint names on B-24s: *Heavenly Body, Star Eyes, Porky* and *Ruth Marie*.

Discharged from service Oct. 16, 1945 at Truex Field, Madison, WI. Most memorable experience was having Jimmy Stewart fly the plane he worked on.

Worked 42 years for the Burlington Northern Railroad. Retired and enjoys traveling with his lovely wife, the former Gloria Flayton. They have eight children and 18 grandchildren.

ANDREW H. BERGER, was born April 25, 1922 in Tow, TX and raised on a farm. Joined the USAAC on Oct. 30, 1942 and was assigned to Waco Army Air Field. Was sent to Sheppard Field Flight Engineer School Feb. 2, 1943 and finished July 15, 1943. Attended Gunnery School at Tyndall Field, FL Aug. 15, 1943 to Oct. 14, 1943. Was assigned to a combat crew Dec. 2, 1943. Trained at Davis Monthan Field and Biggs Field until Feb. 18, 1944.

Overseas on March 11, 1944. Arrived in England March 29, 1944. Flight engineer B-24 Liberator, 8th AF, 2nd Air Div., 448th Bomb Group, 713th Bomb Sqdn., Seething Airfield, Norwich, England. Completed 30 combat missions and received the Air Medal with four Oak Leaf Clusters. Was assigned to the 448th Bomb Group on April 26, 1944. Returned to the States April 1, 1945. Assigned to Army Air Base until discharged Sept. 18, 1945 with the rank staff sergeant.

Returned to farming and retired in 1987.

ROBERT M. BERGER, was born 1920 in Perry, OK. He attended PHS and Oklahoma A&M. Was called to active duty with the 45th Inf. Oklahoma National Guard in September 1940. Became first sergeant, Btry. C, 158th FA. Joined aviation cadets September 1942, graduated Class 43F, transferred from P-51 transition to B-24s in July 1943. Was assigned as co-pilot to the crew of the *Jungle Princess* (Don Clover's crew). Flew 22 missions with 392nd Bomb Group, 2nd Air Div., 8th Air Force, September 1943 to March 1944. Shot down and POW to end of war.

Called back to active duty with the 45th Inf. Div. in Korea and stayed on active duty until retirement, Dec. 10, 1969, as colonel, USA. Wore pilots wings, Combat Infantry Badge and Airborne Wings. His medals included the Legion of Merit, Soldiers Medal, Air Medal with three clusters and the Joint Service Commendation Medal and the Army Commendation Medal with three clusters.

Served overseas four times, was Army advisor to the Texas and California National Guard. Married to Jean Dudley of Perry, OK, they have three daughters, four grandsons, one grand-daughter and one great-grandson. Colonel and Mrs. Berger live in Fair Oaks, CA. Since retirement has worked as a construction inspector.

SYLVESTER P. BERGMAN, was born Jan. 29, 1920 and raised on a farm in Ardmore, OK. He joined the Signal Corps on Sept. 6, 1940 and was promoted through the ranks to tech sergeant. He joined the Air Corps in Orlando, FL in March 1943 as a pilot trainee. He went through training as a tech sergeant and graduated at Seymour, IN in the Class of 44-A. Took transition in B-24s at Smyrna, TN and crew training was completed at Westover Field, MA.

Left for England from Langley Field, VA through Goose

Bay, Labrador. Was assigned to the 389th Group, 566th Sqdn. Flew his first mission August 1944 to St. Lo, France. The other 29 missions were flown to Germany. He took lead crew training at Hethel, England after 15 missions.

Closest scrape with death was when an 88 shell went through the horizontal stabilizer. The fuse, luckily, was set for altitude instead of contact. Saw a lot of German jets but was bypassed for other groups.

Separated from the Air Corps as a captain in June 1945, with the only crew from Barracks Section 8 to complete all their missions for the entire war. He received an Air Medal with a Silver Cluster and a Distinguished Flying Cross.

Married Virginia P. Wagner in September 1941. They have six children, 12 grandchildren and two great-grandchildren. Retired from the U.S. Post Office in 1980 and lives in Ardmore, OK.

OTEY R. BERKELEY

OTEY R. BERKELEY, was born in Detroit, MI on March 6, 1925. Entered the Army Air Force on June 23, 1943. Took basic training at Keesler Field, Biloxi, MS. Attended Ordnance School, Kerns, UT and was assigned to 846th Sqdn., 489th Bomb Group, Wendover, UT.

Went to Halesworth, England with the 8th Air Force. He worked in Ordnance, loading bombs, handling fuses, etc. Came back to USA, December 1944 with group, the first to be rotated from the 8th Air Force to the Pacific. Stationed at Great Bend, KS, Tucson, AZ and Fairmount, NE.

The end of the Pacific hostilities came and he was discharged in November 1945 at March Field. Attended Michigan State and moved to Cleveland, OH. Spent 34 years as sales rep with Nickel Plate, Norfolk Western and Norfolk Southern.

Married Ruth Hunter in 1951 and has a son, daughter and four grandsons.

JACK B. BERKLEY

JACK B. BERKLEY, was born at Tescott, KS on June 25, 1924. Entered the USAAC at Jefferson Barracks, MO on Feb. 23, 1943. Was stationed at Hunting, WV; San Antonio, TX; Ballinger, TX; San Angelo, TX; Victoria, TX, graduated from Pilot School (44-F); Savannah, GA; Wendling, England; Houston, TX.

Went to England in October 1944. Flew 31 combat missions over Europe when war ended. He was co-pilot in the Robert K. Crowell crew in the 576th Sqdn. of 392nd Bomb Group of 2nd Air Div. of 8th Air Force.

Memorable experience was flying the mission in March 1945 when 8th Air Force dropped supplies to Montgomery after he crossed the Rhine. When war ended in Europe in May 1945, their crew flew a new plane back to the States via Iceland. Was discharged on Nov. 7, 1945 with the rank of first lieutenant. Received the Air Medal with four Oak Leaf Clusters, ETO Ribbon with three Battle Stars and one Overseas Bar.

Returned to the University of Kansas and graduated in June 1948. Entered the banking business at the Bank of Tescott, Tescott, KS and is still director there. He is presently chairman of the Stockton National Bank, Stockton, KS; Farmers & Merchants Bank of Hill City, KS; Trego-Wakeeney State Bank, Wakeeney, KS; and Rooks County State Bank, Woodston, KS.

Married Eloise Schroeder on June 27, 1944. Has two sons, one daughter and six grandchildren. Married Barbara Booker on Oct. 24, 1978. Still using his flight training, he flies his own 1988 Mooney MK20K (252) turbo-charged and retractable gear.

HAROLD BERMAN

HAROLD BERMAN, was born 1917 in Haverhill, MA. Re-enlisted in the Air Corps in 1940, following three years in infantry. Completed Navigation School at Kelly Field in February 1942 and remained there and at Hondo, TX as in-

structor navigator until an August 1943 transfer to Clovis, NM AB. There he was assigned as squadron navigator with the newly formed 466th BG cadre.

Following staff combat training at Pinecastle, FL, the cadre joined ground elements at Salt Lake City and flight crews at Alamogordo, NM. While there he married Joy Wimberley from San Antonio. When combat ready the group flew to Attlebridge, England and was assigned to the 2nd AD. During March through November 1944 he flew 30 missions earning the Distinguished Flying Cross and five Air Medals.

Following release from active duty in 1945, he owned and operated a used car business in San Antonio. In 1947 Berman returned to active duty as a captain in the new USAF and became a triple rated navigator, bombardier and radar operator a few years later. For 10 years he flew in B-36s followed by two years in B-52s. Asking for and receiving a transfer to missile duty, he was assigned to the Boeing Company at Cape Canaveral for 18 months of Minuteman Missile training. His final assignment before retirement as a lieutenant colonel in 1964 was as a launch branch officer with the 44th Missile Wing, Ellsworth AFB, SD.

He spent the next 12 years as a realtor and tax consultant in San Antonio where he is now fully retired. He has two children and four grandchildren.

CARROLL BERNER

CARROLL BERNER, was born on a farm near Lidgerwood, ND in December 1919. Primary education was in one room prairie school. Army AC, February 1943 and graduated from Lubbock, TX, Dec. 5, 1943. Transition to B-24s at Liberal, KS.

Flew a B-24 to England via Labrador and Iceland. Assigned to 328th Sqdn., 93rd Bomb Group. First mission Sept. 10, 1944. The next day Magdaburg, a mission to remember. Flew a total of 35 missions including a supply drop at Nijmegen, 18 planes departed and two returned home unharmed. Received five Air Medals.

Married Delta Knight in February 1946 and has two sons, Geoffry and Steven. Earned an engineering degree at USC and worked in flight test/management at Teledyne Ryan, SD for 20 years.

In June 1975 he married June Everett. Retired in November 1979 from Reserves as lieutenant colonel. Presently semi-retired real estate broker.

JACK E. BERNER

JACK E. BERNER, was born Dec. 27, 1923 in Kalamazoo, MI. Enlisted Dec. 11, 1942 in the USAAC, 8th Air Force, 467th Bomb Group, 791st Bomb Sqdn., 2nd Air Div. Stationed at Boise, ID; Salt Lake City, UT; Lincoln, NE; Norwich, England, Rackheath APO 558; Miami, FL; Homestead, FL and Panama City.

Participated in Northern France, Normandy, German Air Offensive and Europe campaigns. Completed 30 missions as B-24 armorer gunner. Discharged May 27, 1945 with the rank staff sergeant. Received Overseas Service Bar, EAME Theater Ribbon, four Battle Stars and Air Medal with four Oak Leaf Clusters.

He is married and worked at insurance agency for 35 years.

ARTHUR BERNSTEIN

ARTHUR BERNSTEIN, was born April 21, 1920 in Philadelphia, PA. Enlisted July 1942 in the USAAF going from enlisted man to adjutant. Attended general school, then to OCS. Sent to England in October 1943 and joined HQ staff, 2nd Air Div. at Ketteringham Hall. Served until discharge as public relations officer.

Discharged November 1945 with the rank of captain. Married 51 years, he has three daughters, four grandchildren and four great-grandchildren. Retired in 1982 as CEO of refrig. mfg. co.

JAMES W. BERRY (BILL)

JAMES W. BERRY (BILL), joined the Air Corps as a private April 1941. Volunteered for and graduated as staff sergeant Army Glider Program. Then entered Aviation Cadets and graduated with Class 43-K in December 1943, Seymour, IN.

Assigned as co-pilot Crew #16, 844th Sqdn. of 489th Bomb Group (B-24s) January 1944. Flew the *Lynda Lee* from Kansas to Halesworth, England, via South Atlantic. Flew first combat mission with 8th Air Force on Memorial Day, 1944. Flew low-level mission #639, resupply of USAF in Nijmegen area, Sept. 18, 1944. Wounded by rifle bullet while flying at altitude of 100'. This was his 27th and last mission. Spent one year in various hospitals.

Discharged Sept. 19, 1945 with the rank first lieutenant. Received the Distinguished Flying Cross, Air Medal with three Clusters and the Purple Heart.

Flying a Cessna 150 on regular basis today. Practicing law in Oklahoma City, OK since 1947. Married since 1945, has two children, three grandchildren and one great-grandchild.

WILLIAM A. BERRY JR.

WILLIAM A. BERRY JR., was born Sept. 20, 1920 in Portsmouth, VA. Enlisted in the USAAC on March 25, 1942 from Bath, NC. Graduated pilot, Class 43-C. Joined 389th Bomb Group, Sept. 19, 1943. Upon completion of 39 missions with 389th and 93rd Bomb Group, assigned to 34th Group, 3rd Air Div.

After temporary duty with 492nd Bomb Group, he returned to U.S., released from active duty with rank of captain on May 17, 1945. Received the Distinguished Flying Cross with one Oak Leaf Cluster, Air Medal with four Oak Leaf Clusters, two Campaign Stars and one Presidential Citation.

Married May 29, 1943 to Betty Goette of Lakeland, FL. Has three sons, one granddaughter and six grandsons.

RONALD W. BERRYHILL

RONALD W. BERRYHILL, was born in Sanger, CA on July 16, 1923. Attended University of California at Berkeley until enlisting in the USAAC Aug. 11, 1942. Graduated Navigation Class 43-14 at Selma Field, LA. After graduation and crew training at Pueblo, CO, he was sent to Radar School at Langley Field, VA in 1943.

Sent to 482nd Bomb Group Alconbury, England in March 1944 for additional training as mickey operator. Flew 30 missions as lead radar navigator with 389th, 489th and 448th Bomb Group in B-24s. After tour sent to 2nd Air Div. HQ as radar advisor. Later sent back to 482nd Bomb Group as instructor. Returned home May 10, 1945. Reassigned as radar instructor in B-29s at Boca Raton, FL AAB. Discharged September 1945 at Beale AAB, CA.

Recalled for Korean War and flew 23 mission tour with 307th Bomb Wing from Okinawa. Discharged from Air Force as captain. Received the Distinguished Flying Cross, nine Air Medals and various other ribbons.

Married Gloria Cooper on Dec. 10, 1943 and has two sons and nine grandchildren.

ANTONIO E. BERTAPELLE

ANTONIO E. BERTAPELLE, was born June 28, 1923. Joined the USAAF on Dec. 13, 1941. Arrived at Tibenham Air Field with the 53rd Station Complement Sqdn. on Sept.

14, 1943. In December was transferred to the 462nd Sub-Depot and worked in the hangar as an airplane and engine mechanic.

In June 1945, the entire Sub-Depot was transferred to the Air Transport Command at Casablanca, Morocco. Returning to the States in November, he was discharged in January 1946 and married. In April 1949, he re-enlisted in the USAF. After assignments at Chanute AFB, IL and Lowry AFB, CO, he retired on April 1, 1966 with the rank of senior master sergeant.

He and wife, Lois, make their home in Commerce City, CO. They have five children and 11 grandchildren.

FRANK J. BERTRAM, was born April 8, 1921 in Paterson, NJ. Enlisted Oct. 30, 1942 in the USAAF, navigator. Stationed at Ellington Field, TX, Hondo, TX, Caspar, WY, Pueblo, CO with 445th Bomb Group, Tibenham, England.

Crash landed in England after severe battle damage, second air battle and bailed out Sept. 27, 1944, Kassel. Was captured by enemy and taken as POW to Stalag Luft #1.

Discharged September 1945 with the rank first lieutenant. Received the Air Medal with two clusters, Purple Heart and POW Medal. He completed 19 missions.

Married 50 years and has three children and six grandchildren. Currently retired and enjoys golfing, traveling and reading.

JOHN F. BEST, was born May 22, 1925 in Milford, MA. Took basic in Greensboro, NC; Radio School in Sioux Falls, SD; Gunnery School, Yuma, AZ; crew assembly at Westover Field, MA and phase training in Charleston, SC. Joined the 453rd Bomb Group at Old Buckingham in October 1944. Flew 35 missions between Nov. 2, 1944 and March 24, 1945.

They were forced down three times during their tour and once made a forced landing just outside of Brussels, Belgium. They lost one crew member during their tour and two were wounded, both on their first mission. Returned to the States on the SS *Paraguay* in a convoy and landed in New York on V-E day to an amazing welcome. He was still 19 but a much older 19.

Discharged in October 1945 and returned to Boston College, graduating in 1948. Received master's degree in 1950 and spent the next 38 years working in the Boston Public Schools at the high school level, the last 17 of those years as a high school principal.

Married in 1952 to Sally O'Brien of Boston and they raised two sons and four daughters. Retired from the school system in 1987 and sold real estate until this year.

RICHARD H. BEST (DICK), was assigned to the 448th Bomb Group, 713th and 714th Sqdn., Crew #46 as navigator. John C. Rowe was first pilot. Was stationed at Seething, England from August 1944 to April 1945.

Completed 35 missions and discharged with the rank first lieutenant. After discharge was employed with General Motors in various capacities until retiring in 1982.

Lives with his wife Shirley in Flushing, MI.

RAYMOND A. BETCHER, was born March 23, 1922 in Detroit, MI and lived in Roseville until drafted January 1943. Was inducted at Fort Custer, MI; basic at Clearwater, FL; Mechanics School at Gulfport, MS; B-24 School at Willow Run, MI.

Joined the 790th Sqdn., 467th Bomb Group (B-24s) at Salt Lake City, UT. Overseas training at Wendover, UT and arrived at Rackheath March 10, 1944. Joe Ramirez was their crew chief on Witchcraft which completed 130 missions without an abort. Others on the crew were George Dong, Joe Vetter, Walter Elliott, and Oliver Omundson. Was given a Meritorious Achievement Certificate by Gen. Kepner on the

100th mission. The war ended while on delay en route to Greensboro, NC and was discharged Sept. 29, 1945.

FAA aircraft and engine license 1946. Worked at Wayne University, Detroit, MI, Dana Corp., Toledo, OH and Borg Warner Corp. Pontiac, MI. Retired in 1981.

Married Doris Torrey of Mt. Clemens, MI on Aug. 29, 1943 and has one son, two daughters and four grandchildren.

RAYMOND W. BETHEL, was born Nov. 11, 1924 in Lockbourne, OH. Entered the USAAC April 9, 1943. Aviation Cadet, Class 44-A, commissioned second lieutenant, graduating as pilot SE Training Command, Moody Field, Valdosta, GA. Flew 35 missions, 8th Air Force, 2nd Air Div.

From September 1944-November 1944, 489th Bomb Group (B-24s), 844th Bomb Sqdn., Halesworth, England. Transferred to 44th Bomb Group(H) (B-24s), 67th Sqdn., November 1944-April 1945 and last flight was March 8, 1945.

Memorable experiences: Jan. 16, 1945-landing in Paris, France after mission to Dresden, Germany due to bad weather in England; Feb. 25, 1945-landing in Brussels, Belgium due to weather; having privilege and pleasure of being pilot of excellent crew: Joseph Bonneau, Willis Abrams, Joseph Andreotta, Melvin R. Coughenour, Hobbs Williams, Stanley Wirth, Eugene Root and Robert Moore.

Discharged June 27, 1945 with the rank first lieutenant. Received the Air Medal with four clusters and three Battle Stars (Northern France, Germany, Ardennes).

Graduate Ohio State University. Physician (M.D.), practiced internal medicine in Columbus, OH 1951-1992 when he retired. Married and has five children and two grandchildren.

BERT A. BETTS, was born Aug. 16, 1923 in San Diego, CA. Graduate of Hoover High School. Enlisted in USAAC, July 1942; aviation cadet in Western Flying Training Command; commissioned as second lieutenant, pilot Oct. 1, 1943.

Joined 458th Bomb Group, 755th Sqdn., Crew 76 at Boise, ID, then to Tonopah, NE. Flew B-24 to Norwich, England via Brazil and Dakar arriving January 1944. Co-pilot/pilot for 30 missions over enemy occupied Europe, flying the last two missions on D-day. Awarded the Distinguished Flying Cross, Air Medal and four Oak Leaf Clusters.

Instructor and tested airplanes in engineering at Pecos, TX, then to ATC Long Beach, CA. After discharge in October 1945, he graduated from California Western University in business administration; received CPA certificate in November 1950, principal in accounting firm Bert A. Betts & Co.

Elected treasurer of California in 1958 and served until 1967. Received the City of Louisville Award from MFOA of United States and Canada as the most outstanding fiscal officer in those two nations in 1963.

CHARLES L. BEVINS, was born May 12, 1920 in Pittsburg, KS. Entered the USAAF Oct. 27, 1942. Upon graduating from Gunnery School, he flew on a B-24 via South America, Africa and then to England. He flew as a tail gunner on a B-24, completing 31 missions.

Rotated back to the States on the *Queen Mary*. Was gunnery instructor until time of discharge. Discharged Sept. 8, 1945 with the rank staff sergeant. Received the Distinguished Flying Cross, Air Medal, three Oak Leaf Clusters, European Campaign Medal, three Battle Stars and several others.

Married Helen Watts June 29, 1941 and has three children, three grandchildren and two great-grandchildren. Retired as administrative assistant of nursing service.

ROBERT BEVIS, D.M.D. (BOB), was born in 1922 and raised in Arcadia, FL. He joined the USAAC in 1942 and graduated from Flight School in 1943 in Class of 43-G at Lubbock, TX. Bevis was a member of the 453rd Bomb Group stationed at Boise, ID.

Flew B-24 bombers via South America, Africa and on to England. Completed 30 missions on D-day against Germany lasting from February 1944 to June 1944 flying B-24s. Received the Distinguished Flying Cross, Air Medal with three Oak Leaf Clusters and two European Campaign Stars. Was discharged in 1945 as a first lieutenant.

Married Suzanne Williams and they have three children. He received his DMD at the University of Louisville and practiced in Arcadia, FL 30 years. Now retired and enjoying his three grandchildren.

MARTIN F. BEZON, was born on Nov. 8, 1921 in Port Henry, NY. He enlisted in the USAAF on Dec. 7, 1942.

Military locations and stations included Albuquerque, NM; Santa Ana, CA; Boca Raton, FL. He was with the 467th Heavy Bomb Group, Lead Sqdn. He was shot down over Berlin on his 18th mission on March 18, 1945. They reached Poland after being shot down. Bezon spoke polish and was able to communicate with the Russians. After seven weeks they flew a battered B-24 from Russia to Bori, Italy.

Received the American Campaign Medal, National Defense Service Medal, EAME Campaign Medal, WWII Victory Medal, Korean Service Medal, Air Medal with three Oak Leaf Clusters, and the Distinguished Flying Cross.

Was discharged in October 1945 and recalled in January 1950, and discharged again in July 1952 with rank of first lieutenant.

Married in October 1948 and was married 28 years. Had three children, one son and two daughters, plus seven grandchildren. His wife passed away with cancer. She never saw any of her grandchildren.

Bezon is now retired and lives in Port Henry, NY. He is watching his grandchildren grow, has a small garden and just enjoys life in the Adirondacks.

J. RAY BICKEL, was born on Dec. 1, 1922 in Myerstown, PA. He attended college two years and enlisted in the Aviation Cadet Program on Nov. 6, 1942. Received basic training in Miami Beach and Augustana College.

Was assigned as a pilot in Tulsa, OK. Graduated from San Marcos Navigation School as a second lieutenant, class of 44-3, on Feb. 26, 1944. Assigned to B-24 crew training at Westover, MA, then to 467th Bomb Group, 790th Sqdn. at Rackheath, England.

Bickel completed 35 combat missions and was awarded the Distinguished Flying Cross and the Air Medal with three Oak Leaf Clusters. He returned to the States and flew with Air Transport Command until he was discharged on Oct. 11, 1945 with rank of first lieutenant. He also retired from the Air Force Reserve with rank of lieutenant colonel.

Completed his BS degree at Penn State University in 1947. He married Lucy Bamberger and they have one son, Jonathan.

He taught vocational agriculture for 33 years, retired in 1983 and resides in Richland, PA.

ALBERT H. BIEL, was born on Sept. 8, 1922 in San Jose, CA. Enlisted in the USAF on Oct. 15, 1942.

He was a pilot with the 732nd Sqdn., 453rd Bomb Group. He received cadet training, Class 43-K, Eastern Training Command, Nashville, TN; Maxwell Field AFB, Lakeland, FL; and Courtland AB, Seymore, ID.

Biel participated in battles in England in the 8th Air Force, 453rd Bomb Group, 732nd Sqdn., Crew 201. Flew 35 missions, Germany, Europe, France, etc.

His memorable experiences included battle damage on Nov. 21, 1944 and two similar damages, but not as bad.

Received the Distinguished Flying Cross and five Air Medals. He was discharged on June 14, 1945 with rank of first lieutenant.

Biel married Claire Irene on April 11, 1942 and they have four daughters, Christine, Irene Marie, Barbara A., and Rosemary.

He is now retired.

BEDFORD BRUCE BILBY, was born on Aug. 5, 1918 in Omaha, NE and enlisted in the U.S. Army as a private on Jan. 19, 1942 at Fort Crook, NE.

Completed mechanic course at Chanute Field, IL; pilot training, Class 43-C, commissioned second lieutenant, USAAC; assigned to 389th Bomb Group, B-24 co-pilot with 567th Sqdn.

June 1943 assigned to UK, two months temporary duty in North Africa, participated in historic low level attack on the Ploesti, Rumania Oil refineries. After 10 missions, checked out with his own crew.

March 1944 completed 25 mission combat tour. Most missions flown without fighter escort. From 1944-1945 flew 25 top secret missions, Scotland/Sweden, transporting Norwegians and U.S. internees to the UK. Was credited with 25 more combat missions.

April 1945 returned to the U.S., Air Transport, Ferry Command. From 1945-1949 flew Trans-Pacific routes, C-54 aircraft commander, instructor/check pilot. During eight-month period (1947-1948) flew 116 missions, Berlin Airlift "Operation Vittles."

1949-1952 was wing chief pilot, Westover AFB, MA. Flew scheduled North Atlantic routes to UK, Germany, Thule, Greenland and other Arctic bases. Volunteered for SAC, B-36 aircraft commander, select crew, 2,000 hours, four years. Volunteered for Guam in 1956 as director of Operations Air Defense.

1958-1959: Command and Staff College, Maxwell AFB, AL; 1959-1960: division inspector general, Tinker AFB, OK; 1960-1962: commander NORAD Control Center, Roswell, NM; 1962-1964: commander, 874th Aircraft Control and Warning Sqdn. near Zaragoza, Spain. While in Spain he attended 2nd Air Div. reunion in Norwich, UK. 1964-1966: commander 604 Aircraft Control and Warning Sqdn., Freising, Germany; 1966-1968: commander NORAD Control Center, Tyndall AFB.

Retired from active duty in July 1968 as lieutenant colonel, with 8,000 flying hours. Received two Distinguished Flying Crosses, eight Air Medals, American Campaign Medal, American Defense Medal, Asiatic-Pacific Campaign Medal with six Bronze Stars, Presidential Distinguished Unit Citation, WWII Victory Medal, Army of Occupation-Germany, Medal for Humane Action, two Air Force Commendation Medals and Good Conduct Medal.

Bilby married wife, Lowana, in October 1946. They have one son, one daughter, and three grandchildren. He is an active real estate associate for the state of Florida. They reside in Vero Beach, FL.

GLENN W. BINDER, was born on March 10, 1920 in Table Rock, NE. Enlisted in the Air Force on April 2, 1942.

Served with the 389th Bomb Group. He was a B-24 pilot and flew four-engined aircraft and commanded crew. Served 14 months overseas in England and North Africa and nine months in the South Pacific, flew 45 missions.

Binder also served as assistant operations officer of Pathfinder Sqdn. in England. Was in charge of training and scheduling of missions. During his second tour he served as assistant operations officer of bomber command in South Pacific.

Military locations and battles included Luzon, South Philippines, Air Combat Borneo, Sicily Air Offensive Europe, Rome-Arno, Ploesti, Normandy, Northern France, and Philippine Liberation.

Received the Distinguished Flying Cross with one Oak Leaf Cluster, Air Medal with three Oak Leaf Clusters, three Overseas Bars, EAME Ribbon with six Battle Stars, Asiatic-Pacific Ribbon with four Battle Stars, Philippine Liberation and American Theater Ribbon and Presidential Unit Citation. Discharged on Feb. 6, 1946 and discharged from the Reserves on April 1, 1953 with rank of major.

Married Bernice Avery in 1949, they had two children. Bernice died in 1981. Married Lora Gray in 1982, they have six children and 10 grandchildren. He is a retired farmer and resides in Pawnee City, NE.

LUTHER S. BIRD, was born on Nov. 25, 1921 in Greenville, SC. He resigned Clemson College ROTC program in January 1942 and joined the AAC Aviation Cadet Pilot program. Received wings and commission on Dec. 7, 1942, Class of 42-K.

Served as co-pilot on the *Martin Red Cap* crew from June-September 1942 and as pilot from October-December 1942. They flew 14 missions on the B-24 *Bomerang* and nine missions in *El Toro.*

They were in the 328th Sqdn., 93rd Bomb Group (Ted's Traveling Circus) from June-December 1942. They participated in the Aug. 1, 1942 low level mission to Ploesti, two missions to Weiner Neustadt, Austria, Danzig, Poland, and Oslo, Norway. They were shot down on Dec. 22, 1942 on his 23rd mission that was to Osnabruck, Germany and he served 16 months as a POW at Stalag Luft 1.

Went on duty in the Air Force Reserve in January 1947, retiring as a lieutenant colonel in November 1981.

Received six Campaign Stars, Distinguished Flying Cross, Air Medal with three Oak Leaf Clusters, Distinguished Service Medal, Prisoner of War Medal and Presidential Unit Citation.

Returned to college in January 1947 completing MS and Ph.D. degree in Genetics at Texas A&M University. Served on the staff of the Texas A&M University system for 36 years researching for genetic control of diseases and insects in cotton, retiring as Professor Emeritus in February 1986. Was voted Man of the Year in Service to Texas Agriculture in 1982.

Bird married Bernice Allen in August 1947, they have twin daughters and four grandchildren. They have continued to reside in Bryan, TX for 45 years.

CHARLES R. BISHOP, was born on May 16, 1924. Joined the AAC on Feb. 5, 1943 shortly after graduating from Lincoln High School in Ferndale, MI.

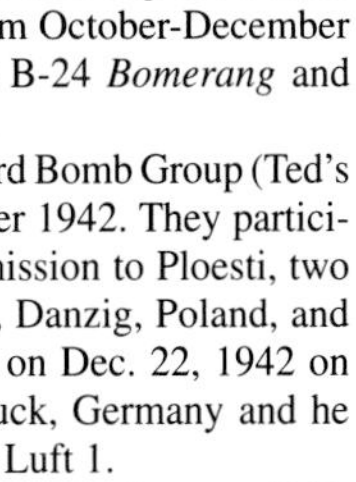

Received basic training in St. Petersburg, FL in the jungle area called "Tent City." Shipped out to Lowry Field, CO to Air Force Technical School for airplane armament course and graduated on Dec. 6, 1943 after nine weeks of schooling. Then to Laredo, TX for Aerial Gunnery School. Received his wings on Feb. 14, 1943.

Next stop was Hammer Field, Fresno, CA. Reprocessed and received his shots and 6-3 physical before being assigned to a crew.

Left California for Tonopah, NV where he was assigned his crew. They received their overseas training there, flying practice bombing missions and air to ground gunnery; also air to air sleeve targets. They shipped out to Hamilton Field, CA where they received their orders and destination for overseas. Hollis H. Hunt was their pilot.

They embarked on the USS *Uruguay* for Liverpool, England. From there to Northern Ireland for advanced training before entering combat. Returned to air base on outskirts of Norwich, England called Hardwick, where their crew completed 30 missions, 26 as lead in 329th Bomb Sqdn., 93rd Bomb Group.

Bishop was discharged on V-J day, Aug. 14, 1945 at Fort Sheridan, IL. Returned to the States on the *Il de France* from Chorley, England. They were the first ship to enter New York that was in England on V-E day, May 8, 1945.

Awarded the Air Medal with one Silver Oak Leaf Cluster, European Theatre Ribbon with one Silver Star, and Presidential Citation.

Returned to Ferndale, MI after discharge where he worked in the building industry with his father until he built his own home. He then joined his brother in the tool and die business until he moved to Naples at the age of 49. After three years in his own custom cabinet business, he obtained a real estate license and still holds an active license in Naples, Fl where he has lived for the last 20 years.

Bishop has been married to a girl from Pontiac, MI for 47 years and they have a son 27 years old who holds a bachelor's degree in law enforcement.

DWIGHT W. BISHOP, was born on Dec. 8, 1921 in Pleasant Dale, NE. Attended the University of Nebraska from 1938-1940. In 1941 he went to Stockton, CA and was drafted on Nov. 13, 1942.

Received his flight training in Georgia. Graduated on Nov. 3, 1943, B-24 training at Smyrna, TN. Received crew training at Casper, WY and Pueblo, CO. Overseas staging at Lincoln, NE. Flew to Ireland via New Hampshire and Goose Bay, Labrador. Went to Stone, England June 5, 1944 and assigned to the 453rd Bomb Group.

Bishop's first mission was on June 24, 1944. PFF lead crew training in September 1944. Completed his tour on Jan. 21, 1945 with rank of captain. Received the Air Medal with four Oak Leaf Clusters.

Arrived in the U.S. on March 12, 1945. After various assignments he was discharged on Sept. 28, 1945.

Bishop married Doris E. Berg on May 22, 1944. They have one daughter, one son, and three granddaughters.

He graduated from UCLA in 1947; received his CPA license in 1951. He was employed by Hussmann Refrigeration, Los Angeles Branch financial manager and retired in 1982. He and his wife reside in Dewey, AZ.

GORDON D. BISHOP, was born on March 20, 1922 in Eastern Kansas and was raised on a farm. In the fall of 1942 he enlisted in the AAC as an aviation cadet.

After training in Missouri, Kansas and Texas, he received flight officer appointment as gunner and bombardier on Dec. 4, 1943. In January 1944 he was assigned to George A. Linko's B-24 crew at Gowen Field, ID. April saw the crew delivering a new Liberator to England.

Bishop was assigned to the 446th Bomb Group, 705th Bomb Sqdn. The crew's third mission was D-day, Normandy, as the 446th lead the entire 8th Air Force. He completed 31 missions on Aug. 14, 1944. He instructed bombardier cadets until war's end.

He remained active in the Reserves, retiring in 1982 as a lieutenant colonel.

After release from active duty he attended college and taught for 35 years. Was married in March 1944 to Joan (Joanne) Ratliff and they have one son, one daughter and three grandchildren.

STANLEY J. BISKUP (STAN), was born on March 22, 1920 in Chicago, IL. He married Joan B. Palasz on July 28, 1945, they have four sons, a daughter (all graduates of Illinois universities), and four grandchildren.

Enlisted in the AAC on Aug. 29, 1940. Completed a course in airplane mechanics at Chanute Field, IL in June 1941. Was assigned to Wheeler Field, Hawaii and was there when the Japanese struck on Dec. 7, 1941.

Biskup attained rank of sergeant before returning to the States in January 1943 for aviation cadet training. Was classified navigator at Santa Ana, CA. Attended Las Vegas Gunnery, Mather Field, and Ellington Field Navigational Schools. Graduated second lieutenant on Dec. 4, 1943 and was assigned to the 489th Bomb Group, B-24s at Wendover Field, UT.

Was grounded with a bad cold on Feb. 23, 1944 when his crew crashed attempting a three-engine landing. The co-pilot was killed and the others badly injured.

Completed training with another crew and navigated

the southern route via South America and Africa to the 8th Air Force in England. Was shot down by flak on June 2, 1944 near Dieppe, France returning from his third mission. Target was German airfields near Paris. Only four out of 10 parachuted from the burning plane. Biskup spent almost 11 months in Stalag Luft III, Nuremburg and Mooseburg German Prison Camps. He was on two forced marches before being liberated by General Patton's 3rd Army on April 29, 1945.

Returned to civilian life in November 1945, completing five and one-quarter years in the service.

HOWARD E. BJORK, was born on Jan. 23, 1921 in Jamestown, NY. Enlisted in USAAF Oct. 7, 1942. Was also in the USAF. Graduated as bombardier, Class of 43-9, Deming AFB.

Served with the 392nd Bomb Group, 8th AF in WWII and many other locations. Wounded on March 2, 1944 and spent several months in the hospital. Was in Navigation School at San Marcos, TX at war's end.

Re-enlisted as tech sergeant in May 1946 and served on flight line on B-29s, B-36s and B-52s. Spent several years at Ellsworth AFB and Amarillo AFB, TX.

Retired Dec. 31, 1963 as SMGT. Promoted to WO1 after eight years in inactive Reserve. Was NCOIC of Quality Control when he retired in Amarillo and has been there ever since. Received the Purple Heart, Air Medal, ETO with one Battle Star.

Took flight training under the GI bill. Ratings were commercial, multi-engine, instrument and CF1 and CF11. Worked at local Pomtex Plant for 17 years and is now fully retired.

Married on June 16, 1945 in San Antonio, TX and has six children, 16 grandchildren and three great-grandchildren. He enjoys playing golf, riding horses and, in general, enjoying life and family.

FRANCIS M. BLACKWELL, was born on Feb. 21, 1925 in Orangeburg, SC. Entered the Army in March 1943. Was sent to Kessler for basic and AM School. Gunnery School at Harlingen, crew training at March.

A fast four and one-half days' trip on the *Queen Mary,* they were then assigned to the 467th Bomb Group (H) at Rackheath. After completing his tour he was sent to Sioux Falls, SD, then to Alamogordo. Was discharged in October 1945.

Re-enlisted in the Air Corps in 1946. Subsequently, he flew a tour in the 307th Bomb Wing as a flight engineer as part of the UN effort. Getting used to bombing at night was difficult. Was in air refueling and 8th Air Force until 1964, then Vietnam.

Married Hazel C. Young at Plattsburgh AFB, NY in November 1960. They had one daughter, Dawn Allyn, born in December 1962. Blackwell retired after 25 years as an E-9 flight engineer.

ROBERT W. BLAKENEY, was born on June 19, 1923 in Newton, MA. Enlisted in USAF Sept. 1, 1942. Served in North Africa, Italy and Bengasi.

Was waist gunner, B-24, with 44th Bomb Group, 67th Sqdn. Shot down Aug. 16, 1943 on Foggia, Italy mission. Survived crash landing in Reggio di Calabria. Escaped Germany prison in Sulmona, Italy; 25 days behind the enemy lines; then Canadian 5th Army.

Received Silver Star, Air Medal, Distinguished Unit Citation, POW Medal, Good Conduct Medal, and Africa-Middle East-Italy Campaign Medal with three Battle Stars. Discharged Nov. 5, 1945 with rank of tech sergeant.

Married Eileen Derocher on April 14, 1945, they have one son, Steve, one daughter, Cindy, plus three grandsons: Ian, Brett and Robert.

178

Graduated from Boston College in 1949 and Boston College Law School in 1952.

Retired after 37 years as a trial attorney. Now active in volunteer and church work.

HAZEL IRENE BLISS, was born on Jan. 26, 1919 in Gresham, OR. Enlisted March 10, 1943. Served as WAAC, then WAC, HQ Sqdn., 2nd Air Div. attached to 315th Signal Corps in Norwich, England.

Military locations and stations included Camp Shanks, Port of Debarkation; Des Moines, IA, basic training; Ft. Devins, MA, training overseas battalion of 600 WAC to go to ETO; Norwich, England; Old Cotton, Horsham, St. Faith (English Barracks), then to Ketteringham Estate.

Memorable experiences were the camaraderie of fellow service personnel, saying good-by to Statue of Liberty as they sailed on *Acquatania* to ETO, and spending a few hours in a fox hole.

Received WAC Service Medal, ETO Ribbon, and Good Conduct Medal. Discharged on Aug. 30, 1944 with rank of corporal.

Married in ETO and divorced 25 years later. Has three daughters and six grandsons. She is retired but house-sits for animals when folks want to vacation but not put pets in kennels. Resides in Milwaukie, OR.

HOWARD F. BLOHM, was born on Dec. 24, 1918 in Adrian, MI. Enlisted in AAC on Sept. 12, 1940. Attended Aircraft Mechanic School at Chanute Field, IL. Graduated in April 1941. Appointed instructor of aircraft hydraulics and taught at Chanute Field, IL.

Helped start a new school at Keesler Field, MS in September 1941. Started a new school at Gulfport, MS in 1942. Reached the rank of staff sergeant. Assigned office candidate, Boca Raton, FL in February 1943. Transferred to Yale University, New Haven, CT. Graduated June 14, 1943, commissioned second lieutenant. Assigned to Gowen Field, ID for B-24 training, engineering officer.

Transferred to 467th Bomb Group, 789th Bomb Sqdn., on Feb. 8, 1944 and went to England in March 1944. Received Squadron Citation for 49 missions without loss of aircraft or crew from April 17-June 20, 1944. Promoted to first lieutenant on April 15, 1944. Transferred to 389th Bomb Group, 564th Sqdn. on Sept. 2, 1944.

Participated in Air Offensive in Europe, Normandy, Northern France, Ardennes, Rhineland, and Central Europe campaigns. Received the American Defense Service Medal, EAME Service Medal with six Battle Stars. Discharged on Dec. 12, 1945.

Married hometown girl on June 17, 1943. They have three girls and one boy. He is proud of all of them.

Retired from Stauffer Chemical Company on May 15, 1983. Now enjoying life.

EDWARD J. BLOOM, was born on Dec. 11, 1920 in Red Bank, NJ. Enlisted in USAF in December 1942. Was pilot, B-24, 2nd Air Div., 389th Bomb Group, 566th Sqdn.

Locations and stations included Eastern Command pilot training; B-24 transition, Maxwell Field, AL; radar training; then overseas.

As a pilot, B-24, flew 35 combat missions (225 hours) over Europe. Flew one deputy group lead, five deputy squadron leads. Made 12 three-engine landings and one crash landing due to flak with no injuries. Flew high ranking officers on inspection tour over Europe. (Has a diary of each mission he flew, listing date of mission, target, flight time, bomb load, flak damage, plus a resume of the complete mission and observations). First mission was Sept. 26, 1944 and 35th mission was March 17, 1945.

Received Air Medal with six Oak Leaf Clusters, EAME

Ribbon with two stars, Good Conduct Ribbon and recommended for Distinguished Flying Cross. Discharged in July 1945 with rank of captain.

Presently a widower, has three married sons, and eight grandchildren. He is a retired postmaster and is presently working in civil service as a golf course ranger.

MALVIN N. BLOTCHER, was born on Nov. 29, 1923 in Boston, MA. Enlisted in USAAC, 8th Air Force, Oct. 30, 1942. Went from Ft. Devens, MA to Atlantic City for basic training.

Military locations and stations included Goldsboro, NC (Airplane Mechanical School); Baltimore, MD (Glen L. Martin Factory School, B-26); Ft. Myers, FL (Gunnery School); Salt Lake City (assignment); Clovis, NM (1st phase training); Pueblo, CO (2nd and 3rd phase); Herrington, KS, picked up B-24 and took southern route to England. After combat training in Ireland was assigned to 446th and had 10 missions over Europe. Then the 44th and went on to do 20 more missions. Thirty-day leave and then reported to Atlantic City for R&R. Next was Biloxi, MS, then on to Chanute Field and finally discharged from there on Sept. 25, 1945 with rank of staff sergeant.

Memorable experiences were controls shot out and he repaired them in flight; and bombed England. Received Air Medal with four Oak Leaf Clusters, Distinguished Flying Cross, Good Conduct Medal and Presidential Unit Citation.

His first wife is deceased. They had a son, daughter, two granddaughters and one step-grandson. Second wife, Sara Sarney Blotcher; one step-son, one step-daughter, three step-granddaughters, one step-great-grandson, and two step-great-granddaughters.

RALPH BLOWER, was born on July 21, 1918 in Gloster, OH. Enlisted in Air Force in 1941, aircraft mechanic, 492nd Bomb Group.

Military locations and stations included Westover, Mitchel Field, three years in England until 1945. Participated in Battle of the Bulge and hauled fuel to Patton. Memorable experiences were bombings and surrender of the Germans.

Received the Presidential Citation, Expert Rifle, European Theater, Air Force Commendation and Good Conduct Medal. Discharged in 1945 with rank of sergeant.

Lost his wife to cancer in 1992. Has one son, one daughter and five grandchildren. Retired after 45 years in the paper business.

ALLEN BLUM, was born on Oct. 18, 1917 in Monroe, MI. Classified 4-F in draft, physical disabilities. Volunteered for limited service as airplane mechanic at Chanute Field, IL where they discovered he had a pilot's license procured from government training in the early 1930s. Eventually, he was commissioned at George Field, IL.

After flying a B-24 to Ireland he was assigned to 458th Bomb Group a few days after D-day. They had many chilling experiences, such as gliding into base with all four feathered and empty tanks; caught fire four times; passed between two hangars trying to land in dense fog with a crippled plane; delivered first load of gas to Patton; and many more. Attained rank of captain with 755th Sqdn. All his crewmembers lived, but some were wounded.

His wife and one of his sons are deceased. Still living are one son and one daughter. Spent 42 years as a local volunteer fireman where they averaged 1,000 calls per year. He is still doing volunteer work.

DONALD E. BODIKER, was born on March 28, 1922 in Dayton, OH. Enlisted in AAC in March 1943, 8th AF, 2nd Air Div., navigator B-24. Military location in Seething, England. Participated in battles in Europe December 1944-May 1945, completing 22 missions.

His most memorable experience was crash landing on his second mission near Ostend, Belgium (no casualties).

Awarded Air Medal four times, European Campaign with two stars. Discharged in October 1945 (on points) with rank of first lieutenant.

Graduated in 1949 from University of Cincinnati as a mechanical engineer.

He and wife, Virginia, have a son, Tom; one daughter, Susan; and seven grandchildren. Retired in January 1986 as vice-president of engineering with the Badger Company, Cambridge, MA. Enjoys playing golf seven days a week.

FRANCIS S. BODINE, was born on Aug. 3, 1920 in Voltaire, ND. Grew up on family farm in North Dakota. Attended local schools and graduated as valedictorian of high school class. Active in sports and band.

Entered AAC Flying Cadet Program in March 1941. Graduated as pilot and commissioned in November 1941. Served as flight instructor. In 1944 flew as bomber lead crew pilot with 8th Air Force, 844th Sqdn., 489th Bomb Group, European Theatre. Later trained as aircraft maintenance officer (1947) and served in that capacity at Eglin AFB Proving Ground and in Korea. Progressed to group operations officer and deputy group commander, 18th Fighter Bomb Group during combat tour (67 combat missions, P-51) in Korea. Served with U.S. Army Chemical Corps engineering group on design of special purpose munitions (1952). Served as air staff planning officer, HQ USAF (1953).

Master's degree in business administration, Harvard graduate, June 1957; BS degree in aeronautical engineering, University of Minnesota, June 1950; Air Command and Staff School, 1953; Air War College, 1961; Maintenance Officers Training Course, 1947.

Received Distinguished Flying Cross, Air Medal with four Oak Leaf Clusters, two DSU Citations. Retired July 1, 1966 with rank of lieutenant colonel.

Married, has six children and nine grandchildren. Retired twice: after 25 years, four months in Air Force and 17 years with General Mills, Inc. Active in flying club and has current commercial pilots license, instrument rated, has over 4,700 hours. Enjoys family, travel, church work, raising flowers, reading, hunting and fishing, golfing and bowling.

BRUNO F. BODZIAK (BEN), was born on Feb. 25, 1916 in Adams, MA. Entered service in January 1941 as member of National Guard, which was federalized into active duty. Applied for cadet training in 1943, was accepted and had primary in Tulsa, basic in Independence, advance in Frederick and graduated in December 1943, Class of 43-K.

Flew as co-pilot and received pre-combat training at Casper, WY. Flew to England via South America, Africa, then to England. Assigned to 703rd Sqdn. of 445th Bomb Group, B-24s and completed 30th mission on Aug. 11, 1944. On one mission after coming back and landing, discovered that the plane was pierced with about 250 holes from flak, but no control cables were hit, nor none of the oxygen or hydraulic lines.

Discharged in August 1945. Received the Distinguished Flying Cross, four Air Medals and several other ribbons.

After discharge went to his hometown of Adams where he pursued getting an airline pilot job. Was unsuccessful whereby he moved to California and went into the real estate business and worked at it until retirement in 1982.

Ben is retired and lives in beautiful Leisure World in Seal Beach, CA with his wife, Helen, and close to his family, two sons, one daughter and four grandchildren.

LEONARD DONAT BOISCLAIR, was born on Sept. 3, 1921 in West Warwick, RI. Enlisted in USAF in Massachusetts, staff sergeant, gunner B-24, 566th Sqdn., 389th Bomb Group.

Military locations and stations included gunnery training in the States and flew to England. Flew 25 missions. Raided Rumanian oil fields on Aug. 1, 1943, 130 men went and only 24 returned. After 25 completed missions he re-

turned to the States, was married and voluntarily returned for the completion of three more missions.

Discharged Aug. 28, 1945. Received Distinguished Flying Cross, Air Medal with Oak Leaf Cluster.

Married former Dorothy Kettelle. They had one daughter, Donna; one son, Dana, and three grandsons.

He was a very humble, proud American who gave life his all. A true gentleman, a best friend, a loving husband and father. He succumbed to cancer on Jan. 1, 1991 after fighting it for many years. A true hero to everyone who knew him.

ARCADE BOISSELLE, was inducted at Ft. Devens, MA on Dec. 27, 1942; basic training, Miami Beach; transferred to Scott Field, IL in February 1943. Graduated from Radio Operator School and Mechanic School. Transferred to Harlingen Gunnery School in July 1943 for six weeks. Graduated latter part of August, reported to Salt Lake City, UT for crew formation. Assigned to Crew Y-156. Transferred to Mt. Home, ID, then to Wendover Field, UT.

Reassigned to 859th Sqdn. of the 492nd Bomb Group after they were taken off heavy bombardment due to heavy casualties. The 859th Sqdn. was later assigned to Brindisi, Italy to perform carpetbagger missions to Yugoslavia where they were given the Presidential Unit Citation.

Flew 13 heavy bombardment missions from April 12 to May 8, then transferred to Harrington, England where he flew 22 carpetbagger missions to France, England, Belgium, Holland and Denmark. One of the missions in heavy bombardment was to Epinal, France where they hit a POW prison camp, knocking down the walls and allowing some of the prisoners to escape, some of which were gathered in by the French Underground.

Returned to the zone of interior; Atlantic City, NJ for R&R; TDY Scott Field, IL. Gunnery instructor at Laredo, TX; Yuma, AZ AFB; Tyndall Field, FL; transferred to Maxwell Field, AL for separation on Oct. 9, 1945 with rank of tech sergeant.

After getting out of service, returned to work for a public electric utility company. Retired in January 1978 after 38 years service. Presently 78 years old, lives with his wife. They have two sons and four grandchildren.

HOWARD L. BOLDT, was born on Sept. 1, 1920 in Houston, TX. Enlisted in AAC on Oct. 19, 1942 as a private. Graduated AM School at Keesler Field, MS on June 16, 1943. Attended Consolidated Vultee School in San Diego, CA and Gunnery School at Laredo, TX.

Assigned to 383rd Combat Training School, Peterson Field, Colorado Springs, CO as flight engineer and top turret gunner. In July 1944, assigned to 445th Bomb Group, 702nd Sqdn. at Tibenham.

Shot down on Sept. 27, 1944 on a mission to Kassel, Germany. Received multiple wounds and sent to Stalag IXC at Obermasfield, Germany. Liberated by 11th Armd. Div. in April 1945.

Discharged from Beaumont General Hospital, El Paso, TX on May 6, 1947 with rank of master sergeant. Married Dorothy Elizabeth Tubb on June 6, 1941. They have a son and daughter, and four grandchildren.

ERNEST J. BOLDUC, was born on June 11, 1924 in Lawrence, MA. Enlisted in November 1942. Called to active duty in USAAF Cadet Program in March 1943.

Commissioned second lieutenant in June 1944 as bombardier/navigator. Took phase training in Pueblo, CO. Assigned to 734th Sqdn., 453rd Bomb Group in September 1944. Completed 25 missions on April 9, 1945.

Memorable experiences include two 500 lb. bombs hung up in the bomb bays after "bombs away." after let down and over the English Channel, he had to release them while standing over open bomb bays without a parachute since the chest chutes got in the way; getting hit by flak in the helmet and flak vest over Magdeburg, still has the piece of flak as it landed on his navigation table after dropping off his chest; almost getting hit by another plane while forming over the channel at 10,000 feet, they dived to avoid the oncoming plane and leveled off at about 2,000 feet, racked the ship and had to abort, during the dive the only people who could move were the pilots, nose gunner and Bolduc.

Discharged October 1945 with rank of first lieutenant. Awarded the Air Medal with three Oak Leaf Clusters.

Resides in Armonk, NY.

CHARLES H. BOOTH JR., was born on Nov. 23, 1919 in New Kensington, PA. Enlisted in U.S. Army on Dec. 18, 1941, flying cadet. Served with 458th Bomb Group(H).

Military locations and stations included Sikeston, MO; San Angelo, TX; Lubbock, TX; Victorville, CA; Hobbs, NM; Casper, WY; Tonopah, NV; Horsham St.Faith, England; Big Springs, TX.

Flew 30 combat missions, wounded in action, March 8, 1944, Berlin; command pilot, assistant group operations officer, Horsham St. Faith, Norwich; squadron commander, Big Springs AAB, TX.

Discharged Dec. 9, 1945. Retired from Reserves Nov. 23, 1979 with rank of colonel. Received Distinguished Flying Cross, Defense Service Cross, Air Medal with six Battle Stars, Purple Heart, and various theatre ribbons.

Married Laura Lee Benner of Bryan, OH. They have seven children: Laura L. Monteverde, Suzi J. Cochran, Mary K. Friday, Charles H. Booth III, Elizabeth A. Rotzler, Barbara J. Weil, Harvey F. Booth, and 19 grandchildren.

Charles is president of Burrell Group, Inc. and Omega Transworld, Ltd.

WILLIAM P. BOOTH, was born in May 1924 in Carsondale, PA. Graduated from Scranton THS in 1941, attended Pennsylvania Upstater until February 1942, Philadelphia and Levittowner.

Joined USNR on April 1, 1943. Basic training in Miami Beach; Radio School, Scott; Gunnery School, Tyndall; crew assignments at Westover, Mitchell, Goose Bay, Nutts Corner, Stone, Bungay.

Served with the 446th Bomb Group, 105th Sqdn., USN VR-24 in P.T. Lyautey during Korea, assigned SP, MAA, Dog Catcher. Flew B-24s.

Qualified as a Caterpillar on 29th mission, Sept. 26, 1944 in Hamm, 24,500 feet, hit by flak, captured and taken to Luft IV.

On Black Death March. Twelve member crew included Mullery, Kallstrom, Jones, Watt, Lengel, Gold, Cochrane, Bush, Cotton, Haugen, Booth. Charron didn't make mission. The rest were POWs.

Discharged in October 1945 with rank of tech sergeant. Awarded European Theatre Operation Medal, Air Medal with four Oak Leaf Clusters, Prisoner of War Medal and Caterpillar Medal.

Retired in 1977 from a U.S. Government position.

D.H. BORCHERDING (DUTCH), was born on Feb. 18, 1920 in New Haven, MO. Enlisted in USAAC in September 1942.

Trained at Las Vegas, Lowry Field and in Idaho. Assigned to B-17 crew in September 1943. With 93rd Bomb Group in England where retrained and assigned to B-24. Crashed in Holland on 11th mission, Jan. 30, 1944. Their plane went down with wheels up and skidded through four fields and skipped across three canals before plane came to halt in fourth field and tipped nose down. Only injury was when a 50-caliber spent shell fell from top turret and hit one of the sergeants on the nose. Six of crew were captured and four escaped, with two getting to Sweden and two to Switzerland. Borcherding spent time at Stalag VI at Hedykruge; Stalag IV, Keifheide; M-Stammlager XIII-D, Nurnburg; VII-A, Moosburg until liberated by Patton's forces on April 27, 1945.

He remembers the march from Nurnberg to Moosburg (120 kilometers), they were near Holtzhusen on April 13 when they received news of President Roosevelt's death. They moved out of the town, gathered on a large hill and one of the members of the march blew taps while all stood at attention.

Discharged in October 1945. Received Air Medal with Oak Leaf Cluster. Married and has two sons. Was a sports writer from 1948 through July 30, 1990, when retired.

In 1983, he and wife, Delores, made the same trip, by car, where the Germans marched them from Nurnberg to Moosburg. Went into the same barns in which the Germans kept them on the march between the two camps.

In June 1992, they took a trip to 93rd Bomb Group base, followed by a trip to The Netherlands to visit crash site in field where their B-24 ended.

He is retired and doing lots of Red Cross work.

PAUL J. BORDEWICH, was born on Dec. 9, 1917 in Thief River Falls, MN. Enlisted in USAAF on July 18, 1942. Was a gunner in 5th Air Force and 8th Air Div.

Received basic training at Sheppard Field, TX; Gunnery School at Las Vegas, NV; Armament School at Salt Lake City, UT; picked up crew and trained together at Tucson, AZ; bombing practice at Alamogordo, NM.

Got new plane and equipment at Topeka, KS; left for South Pacific from San Francisco, CA on May 18, 1943; stationed at Port Moresby, New Guinea with 5th Air Force, 90th Bomb Group on June 26, 1943; armament instructor, Casper, WY, March 1944; picked up crew in Casper on July 17, 1944; flew new plane to England, 8th Air Force, on Aug. 3, 1944; assigned to 389th at Hethel.

Completed 28 missions over Germany. Flew first mission Sept. 5, 1944, Karlsruhe and 28th mission on April 21, 1945, Salzburg, Austria.

Discharged July 14, 1945 with rank of staff sergeant. Received Distinguished Flying Cross, Air Medal with Oak Leaf Cluster.

Married and had four children, 16 grandchildren, and two great-grandchildren. Was widowed. Re-married, retired, and enjoying golf and traveling.

HERBERT C. BORGMANN, was born on May 20, 1923 in Athol, KS. Enlisted in USAAF on Dec. 7, 1942 at Kansas City, MO. Sent to Jefferson Barracks, MO for basic, then to East Lansing, MI for CTD. Spent time at SAACC San Antonio; primary flight training in Pine Bluff, AR; basic flight training in Independence, KS.

Graduated from pilot training, Class 44-E, Pampa, TX. Graduated B-24 training at Liberal, KS; sent to Lincoln, NE for his crew. Completed phase training at Casper, WY and proceeded by troop train to New Jersey. Sailed to England on the Il de France. Assigned to 330th Bomb Sqdn., 93rd Bomb Group at Hardwich, England.

Discharged in 1969 with rank of lieutenant colonel. Received Air Medal with one Oak Leaf Cluster.

Graduated with BS from University of Kansas, 1947. Worked for Swift and Co., Edible Oil Co., 1947-1972. Owned part of a tank truck line, 1972-1976. Worked for Wins Paper Products, 1976 until now. Still working as a manufacturer representative and enjoying it.

Married Erline Shotwell, August 1945, one daughter Nancy Jean. Married Dorothera Ray in 1971, no children. Married Billie Boydston in July 1983. They love playing golf and traveling together. They enjoy their combined three children, six grandchildren and one great-grandson.

DAVID DUFF BORLAND, was born on May 24, 1924 in Pittsburgh, PA. Enlisted in USAAF as aviation cadet on June 26, 1942.

After receiving training at several service schools, he went overseas as a radio operator gunner where he was assigned to the 566th Sqdn., 389th Bomb Group. After completing his tour of duty, he returned to the States and was assigned to a B-29 crew at Biggs Field, El Paso, TX.

Discharged Oct. 5, 1945 with rank of tech sergeant. Received the EAME Service Medals, Distinguished Unit Badge, Air Medal with three Oak Leaf Clusters.

Married on Jan. 11, 1946, they have two children, Nancy and David, and three grandchildren, Brian, Megan and Julian.

After discharge he worked for Westinghouse Electric Corp. for 24 years and later retired as executive vice-president of the Freedom Forge Corp. of which he still remains a director.

MELVIN L. BORNE, was born on July 16, 1923 in Covington, KY, one of eight children. Inducted into the USAAF on Feb. 10, 1943. Joined 453rd Bomb Group, 734th Sqdn. in July 1943.

Arrived Old Buckingham Air Base, Attleborough, England Dec. 21, 1943. Transferred to 733rd Bomb Sqdn. worked as aircraft mechanic, 747s, maintained two B-24s and one P-47 formation monitor aircraft. Flew with Jimmy Stewart on occasion in lead aircraft, *114 Whiskey Jinkles,* their aircraft to Scotland. Total sorties: 6,655, total tonnage: 15,804, claim to fame: 733rd Sqdn. completed 82 consecutive missions without a loss (a record).

Discharged on Oct. 16, 1945 at Gore Field, MT with rank of sergeant. Received six Battle Stars. Retired and writing his autobiography and one novel of fiction.

Memorable experience: The girl he fell in love with, in 1944 in Norwich, and he were separated at the end of his tour of duty in June 1945. While at the second Air Div. reunion in 1987, he was featured in an article about the unsung heroes, the ground crews. Through that article he found that she had moved to Australia and had seven children. Her husband had died 10 years before. They met back in Norwich in late 1987 and were married Jan. 4, 1988 in her garden in Melbourne, Australia, with her children present and other guests. He had no children and his life long dream had been answered, a fairy tale romance produced by a devastating war.

Note: They were both on national TV in Australia and the article appeared in all the papers there and back in Norwich, England. Betty has been here several times but gets homesick for her children and 13 grandchildren. Melvin is going to join her shortly. At present he is trying to get his two books published: *Justice* and his autobiography, *My Life.* It contains 80 pages about Old Buck and how the people there helped them, as Yanks thrown into a war on foreign soil, survive the hardest Christmas in their young lives in 1943.

ROBERT G. BORST (BOB), was born on Nov. 1, 1922 in Delhi, NY. Graduated from high school and joined the USAAF in February 1943.

Received basic training in Miami Beach, FL; Air Gunnery School in at Tyndall Field, Panama City, FL; and received air gunners wings on completion of training. Went to

---

Bombardier Navigator School in San Angelo, TX from November 1943-March 1944. Graduated with Class 44-4 and received rank of second lieutenant. Had heavy bomber training at Gowen Field, Boise, ID from March-May 1944.

Assigned to 8th Air Force, 466th Bomb Group, 787th Sqdn. at Attlebridge, England in mid-June 1944. Shot down by German fighter planes over Northern Holland on Aug. 15, 1944 on his 13th combat mission bombing German airfield at Vechta, Germany. Shot down on return after bombing. Parachuted into a farm field and was contacted by Dutch Underground who hid him in several places for eight months.

Liberated on April 13, 1945 by Canadian Army Forces. Turned over to U.S. Forces within a few days. Returned to States in June 1945.

Discharged in October 1945 with rank of first lieutenant. Received Air Medal with one Oak Leaf Cluster, Victory Medal and Good Conduct Medal.

Married to Eileen and they have four children, four grandchildren and one great-granddaughter. Retired in July 1986 from private business as customer service manager for Electro-therm, Inc., Laurel, MD.

FRANK T. BOSTWICK, was born on Nov. 14, 1925 in Shreveport, LA. Enlisted in USAAC on Nov. 10, 1943. Took basic training at Sheppard Field, Wichita Falls, TX; Gunnery School at Laredo, TX as tail gunner. Assigned to air crew at Lincoln, NE and took combat training at Gowen Field, Boise, ID.

Assigned to 466th Bomb Group, 786th Sqdn. at Attlebridge in August 1944. Completed 35 missions and participated in battles and campaigns of Northern France, Ardennes, Rhineland, and Central Europe.

Discharged on Oct. 23, 1945 with rank of staff sergeant. Received four Bronze Battle Stars and Air Medal with four Bronze Clusters.

Married Louise Wilson on Jan. 22, 1949. They have four children and 10 grandchildren. Retired from United Gas Pipe Line Company in Houston, TX on June 1, 1986 after 38 years service.

BRONA D. BOTTOMS, was born on June 3, 1922 in Newby, TX. Joined USAAC on Oct. 5, 1942. Received basic training at Ellington Field, TX; B-24 A&E at Keesler Field, MS; and Gunnery School at Laredo, TX. Joined Tom Keene's combat crew at Boise, ID on Sept. 5, 1943.

Assigned to crew 55, 714th Sqdn., 448th Bomb Group at Sioux City, IA on Sept. 14, 1943. Departed the States on Nov. 14, 1943 with destination, 8th Air Force in England via South America and Africa, arriving in Seething, England on Nov. 24, 1943. Flew first combat mission on Dec. 30, 1943. Completed 30 missions as engineering gunner with lead crew 55 on June 22, 1944, including mission on D-day.

Departed United Kingdom for ZOI in November 1944. Attended Gunnery Instructor's School at Laredo, TX and was assigned to Walla Walla AFB for the duration as gunnery instructor.

Discharged on Sept. 20, 1945 with rank of staff sergeant. Received Distinguished Flying Cross, Air Medal with three Oak Leaf Clusters, four European Campaign Stars, and other miscellaneous ribbons.

Graduate of business college and Drafting School in Houston, TX. Retired from Gulf Oil, Port Arthur, TX in 1982 after 32 years. He and wife, Lynette, are enjoying their grandchildren, traveling and playing golf during their retirement.

GERARD J. BOUCHER (GERRY), was born on Aug. 6, 1922 in Attleboro, MA. Enlisted in USAAC Cadet Program in March 1943 while attending Wentworth Institute at Boston, MA. Graduated as a bombardier on July 1, 1944 at Carlsbad, NM, followed by overseas training in B-24s at Walla Walla, WA.

Flew 21 combat missions, last 12 as lead crew bombardier with 458th Bomb Group at Horsham St. Faith in Norwich, England.

Discharged in November 1945 and returned to Wentworth to complete electrical and electronic course of study.

Married Jane Coogan, of Attleboro, on June 20, 1953. They have three children and eight grandchildren.

Retired in November 1982 from Skinner Valoe Division of Honeywell, Inc., New Britain, CT after 30 years as manager of engineering test laboratory. Resides in Westerly, RI.

ROBERT BOUTAIN, was born on Nov. 23, 1910 in Pennsylvania. Enlisted in 6th Field Artillery on May 15, 1938, then USAAF.

Sent to Bolling Field, TX on flight line mechanic on B-18A two-engine bomber until June 1941, then to Sheppard Field, TX about October 1941 to give training to new enlistees. Then in May 1942 transferred to army base close to New York City where four troop ships were boarded for Ireland, then on train to England. Staging area for two months repairing guns, then sent to 2nd Air Div., 8th Air Force, 330th Sqdn., 93rd Bomb Group on flight line on B-24 bombers close to Norwich, England. Then to Africa in 1943 and back to the States in October 1944.

Retired on June 30, 1959 after 21 years. Received the Good Conduct Award (6th), United Stated Defense Medal with five stars, American Campaign Ribbon, European Theater with 10 stars, WWII Victory Ribbon, Occupation Japan, 1946, National Defense Ribbon, Air Force Longevity (five awards), Aerial Engineer Wings, plus more.

He and wife, Alice, are in their 80s and in good health, no aches or pains. Have been living in a health resort in the state of Washington for 20 years, five miles from Morton, in the country with trees all around.

ROWE D. BOWEN JR. (DOC), was born on June 8, 1918 and raised on a Georgia farm. Graduated in Class of 1936 from Register High School, and Abraham Baldwin Agricultural College in 1938.

Enlisted as an aviation cadet on Nov. 5, 1941. Received pilot training in Southeast Training Command. Advanced training in T-6s at Napier Field, AL where he received his wings (Class 42-F) and commission on July 3, 1942.

Instructed at Turner Field, GA, Twin Engine Advanced Pilot Training School until October 1943, when he was transferred to SAAF, Smyrna, TN for B-24 transitions. Then to Salt Lake City, UT for crew assignment and trained with crew at Casper AFB, WY from early January-early April 1944.

Flew southern route to England and was assigned to Tibenham Air Base, England, 445th Bomb Group. The first morning at Tibenham, one of his crew members, Sgt. Murwin H. Cook, Johnson City, NY, volunteered to replace a sick crew member on another crew. That crew did not return from the mission.

Flew one tour of combat, then transferred to HQ 2nd Combat Wing on Nov. 13, 1944 as a controller. Reassigned

to 445th Bomb Group on March 31, 1945 as 703rd Sqdn. commander (Jimmy Stewart's cadre squadron). Flew two additional missions, then V-E day, May 8, 1945.

Survived four airplane crashes, including a bailout. Arrived back in the States on June 8, 1945 and reassigned to MATS.

Separated from active duty on Aug. 31, 1953. Received Distinguished Flying Cross, Air Medal with three Oak Leaf Clusters and European Campaign Medal with six Battle Stars. Retired as a lieutenant colonel (USAFR).

Did various things the next 25 years, a crop duster, flight instructor, auto parts manager, and postman. Now retired.

Had three marriages, one daughter and one granddaughter by second marriage. Does volunteer work one day a week at Moody AFB, GA.

WILLIAM H. BOWEN, was born on Oct. 6, 1922 in Lemoyne, PA. Enlisted in AAC on Jan. 6, 1943. Served with 8th Air Force, 392nd Bomb Group.

Military locations and stations included ETO, Wendling, England. Flew 30 combat missions over Germany from July 12, 1944 to Feb. 15, 1945. Bailed out when bomber was hit with flak on 7th mission, July 21, 1944.

On Dec. 24, 1944, his crew, "The Benson Crew," participated in the largest air armada in the history of the world. There were over 2,000 bombers and 936 fighter escorts on this date. They were off on Christmas Day.

Discharged on Sept. 16, 1945 with rank of staff sergeant. Received Distinguished Flying Cross, Air Medal with three Oak Leaf Clusters and Caterpillar Pin.

Married Sarah Critchley on April 8, 1945. They have one son, one daughter and two grandchildren. He is retired from state service.

LAWRENCE S. BOWERS (LARRY), was born on Dec. 2, 1922 on a farm near Moreland, GA. Attended Georgia Tech as co-op. Entered service on April 3, 1943 and completed basic and Airplane Mechanics School at Keesler Field, MS and gunnery at Harlington, TX. Joined Miners crew in Casper, WY to complete training.

Picked up B-24 at Willow Run, MI and flew to Lincoln, NE. Went from there to Bangor, ME and to Ireland for ETO training on May 29, 1944.

Joined 445th Bomb Group, 702nd Sqdn. and completed 19 missions over Germany. They were hit by flak on their 12th mission and crash-landed in England.

On Kassel mission on Sept. 27, 1944 they were shot down by FW-190s in the greatest loss of men and planes in WWII and their co-pilot and radio operator were killed. The rest of them bailed out and were captured by Germans. He spent three months in Stalag Luft IV and on Christmas Day started a four-month march ahead of the Russians through Germany. On April 26, 1945 they were marched into the 104th Field Artillery.

Discharged on Oct. 13, 1945 with rank of tech sergeant. Received EAME Ribbon with five Bronze Stars, Air Medal with two Oak Leaf Clusters, Purple Heart, and Good Conduct Medal.

After discharge returned to Georgia Tech in 1948 to complete schooling for BSME degree.

Married Mary Alexander in 1949. They have four children and six grandchildren. Retired and doing consulting work.

HOBERT G. BOWLBY, was born on Jan. 20, 1925 in Connellsville, PA. His family moved to Ohio where he later graduated from Wellsville High School in 1942.

Drafted into the Army on Nov. 11, 1943. He left basic training to enter the Aviation Cadets in Springfield, MO. This program was later cancelled sending him to Gunnery School at Harlingen, TX. Assigned to the B-24 air crew, piloted by Lt. Bernard Fishman, they completed their crew training at Gowen Field, Boise, ID. December 1944 found them onboard ship bound for England.

They arrived at Tibenham, base for the 8th Air Force

B-24s, flying in the 445th Bomb Group. He completed 24 missions as nose gunner, held the rank of staff sergeant, and was awarded the Air Medal with three Oak Leaf Clusters. After V-E day the crew returned in June 1945 to the States where Bowlby was stationed at Langley Field, VA until his discharge in November of that year.

Married Jean Cowles on Jan. 24, 1946. He lived in Chester, WV for 16 years. In April 1962, along with their four children, they moved to Concord, CA where they still reside. They have nine "super" grandchildren whom they are thoroughly enjoying.

WILLIAM C. BOYANOWSKI, was born on May 14, 1926 in New Cumberland, PA. Enlisted in USAAC Aviation Cadet Program on Jan. 25, 1944.

Received basic training at Keesler Field, Biloxi, MS. Aerial Gunnery School, Tyndall Field, FL. Overseas training, Casper, WY.

In January 1945 the crew joined the 445th Bomb Group, 700th Sqdn. at Tibenham, England. Flew missions to Perleberg, Duneberg, Memmingen, Germany, Passau, Czechoslovakia, and Salzburg, Austria as a tail gunner.

Married Dorothy Ann Pallini in June 1945. They have four daughters, one son and 14 grandchildren.

After a short stay at Sioux Falls, SD he transferred to Harlingen, TX. Discharged in January 1946. Re-enlisted and served another tour in the Air Force. Then went to work for the Department of Air Force as civil service at Olmstead AFB, PA. Career assignment, Directorate of Material Management. In October 1956 transferred to Norton AFB, CA. There he supervised development of the SM-65 Atlas Missile spare parts program.

Mid-1961 returned to Olmstead AFB, PA as a part of their electronics management staff. In June 1966 moved with that position to Kelly AFB, TX where he retired in October 1979.

A life member of the DAV and a member of the 2nd Air Division Association.

ROBERT B. BOYD, was born on Dec. 1, 1916 in Findlay, OH. Enlisted in USAAC on Nov. 7, 1941. First class at Aviation Cadet Center, Class 42-F. Trained in Gulf Coast Command as pilot. Completing combat training at Colorado Springs he was assigned a new B-24 to ferry to England. Participated in battles in Normandy, Rhine and Germany.

Memorable experiences: first mission, Claspres, France in idiot seat; over Gelsenkichen when tail gunner wounded above eye from shrapnel; Dec. 26, 1944, Neiderllahnstien when 88 shell stuck unexploded in trailing edge of wing; abandoning mission at Cologne due to fuel problem; Nurenburg, the last after the requirements were upped from 25 to 35, each time after he was on downside numbers; and being first to complete tour with original crew, Feb. 21, 1945.

Retired as Reserve Officer, major, in December 1961.

Returned to class room teacher for 15 more years. Married and had three children. They retired to Grand Junction in 1977 to enjoy the beauty and many hobbies of that area. His wife, Suzi, was a very good portrait artist. She died in 1983.

Retired, he enjoys gardening, digging for dinosaurs, hunting, fishing, and preserving wild life. In June 1993 over 100 of the 466th met in a reunion at Colorado Springs and dedicated a plaque on Memorial Wall the AF Academy in memory of 333 fallen comrades.

ROBERT N. BOYLE, was born on July 3, 1920 in Trenton, NJ. Enlisted in June 1942. Received pilot wings, Ellington Field, in October 1943; then B-24 transition.

Flew southern route with 489th Bomb Group to join 8th Air Force in early May 1944. His crew completed a 32-mission tour with no aborts. Returned to Trenton on Christmas Eve 1944.

Went to Smyrna as B-24 instructor. During this duty he married Alice. She is still with him. They have three children and three grandchildren. His Army "career" ended on Sept. 19,1945.

Was executive vice-president of The Home Rubber Company when he retired in mid-1985. Has been busy every since with various volunteer activity.

In April 1992, they moved to a Total Care Retirement Community in Lititz, PA and they continue to keep busy. He's glad he had the WWII experience but would not want to do it again. In June 1993, he went on a 3,100 mile trip to visit his crew members: Corey, Murph, Starnes and Klugh. In July and August he also visited Landis and Rable.

FLOYD H. BRADLEY JR. (PETE), was born on Oct. 16, 1923. Graduated from Merchantville High School, NJ in 1940 and from George School, PA in 1941. After one and a half years at Duke University he was called to active duty with the USAAC in February 1943.

Graduated in March 1944 from San Marcos Navigation School, Lt. Bradley joined Chuck Walker's B-24 crew in Casper, WY.

From June 1944 to January 1945, flew 35 combat missions with the 445th Bomb Group in Tibenham, England. Returning home he served as an instructor navigator on B-32s in Fort Worth until his discharge in October 1945.

Married his college sweetheart, Carol Lake, on March 10, 1945. They have three children and four grandchildren.

Graduated from Rutgers University in June 1948 and worked for the Prudential Insurance Company in Newark, NJ for 34 years. He and his wife reside in Little Silver, NJ.

HERBERT A. BRADLEY JR., was born on Nov. 13, 1920 in Cleveland, OH. His parents were Herbert A. and Kathryn R. Griffith Bradley.

Enlisted in USAAC in July 1942, aviation cadet (bombardier). Military locations and stations included Nashville AFB, Nashville, TN; Santa Ana AAB, Kirtland Field, Albuquerque, ETO 453rd Bomb Group, San Angelo AAB, Gowen Field AAB.

Participated in Air War Europe, 8th Air Force, 453rd Bomb Group, 733rd Sqdn., January-August 1944, B-23 Liberators. Flew total of 32 missions.

Memorable experience: May 8, 1944 their group led entire 8th Air Force to Brunswick, Germany. Attacked by 200 German fighters. Their plane, *Flak Hack,* was shot up but made it back to England where crew bailed out and pilot crashed plane at Watton Air Base near their base at Old Buckingham.

Discharged in September 1945 with rank of first lieutenant. Received Distinguished Flying Cross, presented personally by Major Jimmy Stewart (movie actor) who was their 453rd Bomb Group operation officer; Air Medal with three Oak Leaf Clusters; ETO Ribbon with Battle Star (Air War Europe); American Theater Ribbon; Victory Ribbon and Caterpillar Club.

Married Mary Cynthia Bradley. They have a daughter, Janice Renee DeMoss, and two grandchildren, James Bradley DeMoss and Amanda Marie DeMoss. Retired as Oklahoma branch manager for Collegiate Cap and Gown Company, Champaign, IL.

JOSEPH F. BRADLEY, was born on March 7, 1922 in Lyndhurst, NJ. Entered the service on Jan. 13, 1943. Assigned to basic training at Fort Dix, NJ and Miami, FL. Attended Radio School in Chicago and Gunnery School in

Tyndall Field, FL. Met crew in Chatham Field, GA. From there to the 93rd Bomb Group, 328th Sqdn. in Hardwick, England.

Sept. 21, 1944, while flying as radio operator on the 10th mission to Coblenz, Germany, their B-24, *The Naughty Nan,* was involved in a mid-air collision with another B-24 from the 330th Bomb Sqdn. near the little town of Inglemunster, Belgium. Four from their plane: E.E. Johnson, pilot (deceased 1983); S. Mikolajczyk, co-pilot; C.D. Johnson, flight engineer; and Bradley parachuted to safety. No one else survived from either plane.

Returned to England where, after a couple of months, he was sent to Radar School near London. Flew 20 more missions as radar operator and upon completion of the 30th mission, returned to the U.S. in April 1945 and was discharged in September 1945 at Greensboro, NC.

Served as teacher and administrator for 31 years in Rockaway Township, NJ (home of Picatinny Arsenal and R.D.-Patriot Missile).

In 1972 he and his wife went back to Belgium to thank the people of Inglemunster for all the help given to them in 1944.

Retired in 1984 to Brick, NJ near a lovely shore. After 40 years met the survivors of the *Naughty Nan.* Meets with them and their wives annually at their conventions, plus other times throughout the year and consider them family.

One last important thought: Lt. A. Kibler, New York; Sgt. M. Conaway, Delaware; Sgt. O. Bregman, Massachusetts; and Sgt. Lee Grafe, Idaho; along with the crew of the 330th Bomb Sqdn., Lt. C. Mullin, Minnesota; Lt. E. Morgan, Indiana; Lt. M. Guisti, California; Sgt. J. Picard, engineer; Sgt. D. Strait, gunner; Sgt. L. Miller, gunner; C.J. Johns, gunner; and M.H. Unnderdahl, radio operator, should be remembered at this writing. They all died many years ago on Sept. 21, 1944, but they will never be forgotten.

LLOYD H. BRANDENBURG JR., was born on July 4, 1924 in Sturgis, MI. Entered Army Air Force on March 23, 1943. Served at Keesler Field, MS; Laredo, TX for Gunnery School; Casper, WY for combat crew training.

Assigned as engineer on B-24. Further training at McCook, NE. Left for overseas from Goose Bay. Landed in Ireland. More school, then assigned to 856th Bomb Sqdn., 492nd Bomb Group at North Pickenham, England.

Flew seven missions. Transferred to 406th Bomb Sqdn. Bailed out from mechanical problems on Oct. 13, 1944 (Friday). Completed 39 missions total.

Discharged with rank of tech sergeant. Received Good Conduct Medal, European Theater Ribbon with five Battle Stars, Air Medal with five Oak Leaf Clusters.

Married and has three children. Now retired.

ROBERT B. BRATZEL SR., was born on July 31, 1924 in Habana, Cuba. Lived there 10 years, then raised in Fort Lauderdale, FL. Joined the Army Air Corps on Dec. 10, 1942.

Pilot training in Southeastern Training Command, graduated with Class 44-E from Columbus, MS. Completed B-24 transition in Boise, ID. Went overseas and was assigned to the 67th Sqdn., 44th Bomb Group, Shipdham Airfield, early January 1945.

Flew 15 combat missions in B-24s before the end of European conflict. Returned to U.S. on first flight of returning 8th Air Force crews. Reassigned to Clovis Air Base, NM as an instructor pilot on B-29s until discharge on Oct. 10, 1945 with rank of captain.

Received Air Medal with two Oak Leaf Clusters, ETO and three stars.

Married to Virginia (Ginny) Morton Green and has five children and stepchildren, and seven grandchildren. Spent 45 years in the title insurance field and as real property attorney.

ALFRED C. BRAUER, was born on Sept. 5, 1920 in Newton, KS. Enlisted in USAAC in September 1941, aviation cadet. App. 1942, Class 42-D. Served as flight commander with 458th (H) Bomb Group, 754th Sqdn.

Memorable experience was on April 22, 1944 on mission over Hamm, Germany, loss of planes from their squadron and group over England, Germans followed them back after dark.

Discharged from active duty in January 1946 and Air National Guard in 1948. Received American Defense Service Medal, American Theater Service Medal, Air Medal with three Oak Leaf Clusters and Distinguished Flying Cross.

Has wife, one son and three grandchildren. Retired and living in Cincinnati, OH.

GEORGE M. BRAUER, was born on Feb. 24, 1920 on a farm near Oakford, IL. Joined Air Corps on March 30, 1942. Graduated from pilot training on Feb. 5, 1943. Received training in B-17s and B-24s.

Flew 29 missions in 8th Air Force from Dec. 11, 1943-May 1, 1944. Was instructor pilot in B-24s and B-29s from July 1944 until the end of the war.

Discharged on Oct. 30, 1945 with rank of first lieutenant. Received Distinguished Flying Cross, Presidential Unit Citation, Air Medal with three Oak Leaf Clusters.

Received BS in Agriculture from University of Illinois in 1947 and has been engaged in pork production since then. Is the principal owner of Brauer Pork, Inc., a family owned business. His son and two daughters are involved in the management of Brauer Pork.

Received Master Farmer Award in 1971. Inducted into the Pork Producers Hall of Fame in 1989.

Married Ruth Brinhoff on May 24, 1958. They have three children, Barbara, Nancy, and James and eight grandchildren.

FRED S. BRAUSE JR., was born on July 27, 1924 in Denver, CO. Joined the U.S. Army on July 31, 1942 as a navigator in B-24s and was in the 446th Bomb Group, 705th Sqdn.

Received his gunner's wings at Las Vegas, NV and his navigator wings at Ellington Field in Texas. Flew 35 combat missions in the 8th Air Force in 1944 and left the service in 1945. Received Air Medal with three Oak Leaf Clusters and the Distinguished Flying Cross.

Thereafter, he returned to Muhlenberg College where he received his Bachelor of Arts degree and went to Columbia Law School. When the Korean War broke out he returned to the service where he served in MATS. While serving during the Korean War he became a legal officer as well as a procurement officer. Remained in the Reserves for 18 years and retired in 1962.

Met his wife, Hilda Karsif, and married her in Philadelphia in 1954. They have four children: two boys and two girls, two of whom are lawyers, one an aviator, and one teaches the handicapped in Texas. Has one granddaughter whose mother worked for the British Airlines and is English.

Ran for the New Jersey State Senate on the Republican ticket, as well as the New Jersey Assembly, in the 1960s. Was admitted to the New Jersey Bar in 1952 and was recently named as one of those who had served 40 years in the New Jersey Bar. Is a member of the Middlesex County Bar Association. Recently incorporated the 446th Bomb Sqdn. as a charitable organization in New Jersey in 1986. He is still practicing law and resides in Edison, NJ.

MARTIN BREDVIK, was born on April 17, 1920 in Sitka, AK. Graduated from Sitka High School in 1938. Entered University of Washington in 1938, working summers in Alaska as a commercial fisherman.

Joined 205th Coast Artillery (AA), Washington National Guard, Nov. 16, 1939. Inducted into federal service on Feb. 3, 1941. Entered Aviation Cadet Program in Class 43-D at San Antonio in 1942. Graduated Class 43-16 as second lieutenant navigator at Selman Field, Monroe, LA. Completed RTU training at Muroc (now Edwards AFB). Picked up a new B-24 and flew to England.

Assigned to the 466th Bomb Group, 785th Sqdn. at Attlebridge in April 1944. Flew 33 missions, the last three as a lead navigator. An Army SNAFU had his leave orders as an overseas assignment to Alaska. He flew the Aleutions with the 54th Troop Carrier Sqdn.

Discharged from active duty on Nov. 16, 1945. Received the Distinguished Flying Cross, four Air Medals, and three Combat Stars.

Graduated from University of Washington in 1948 in electrical engineering. Obtained professional engineering license in state of California.

Retired from Boeing as a manufacturing engineer supervisor, having various patents, and having designed some on the biggest tools in the world, i.e. the assembly tools for the 747th wing panels.

Presently a volunteer as a Washington State University Master Gardener, and is active in the local Mushroom Society.

FRANCIS W. BRENNAN,

was born on Nov. 18, 1919 in Newark, NJ. Enlisted in USAAF on Jan. 13, 1942. Served with 44th Bomb Group, 506th Sqdn.

Military locations and stations included Orlando, FL; Ellington Field; Big Spring, TX; Casper, WY; and Shipdham. Participated in the European Campaign. Shot down over Germany, interned in Stalag Luft I.

Discharged on Nov. 30, 1945 with rank of first lieutenant (post-discharge promotion to captain). Received the Air Medal and POW Medal.

Married Betty Kirkwood on Feb. 19, 1944, had three children (one now deceased) and two grandchildren. He is now retired.

ROBERT W. BRENNAN,

was born on June 5, 1925 in Rochester, NY. Served in 8th Air Force, 2nd Air Div., 392nd Bomb Group, 576th Sqdn.

Military locations and stations included Miami, FL; Denver, CO; Las Vegas, NV; Mt. Home, ID; Topeka, KS; and Wendling, England. Wounded by flak over Dortmund, Germany on Jan. 28, 1945. Flew 34 combat missions, armorer and nose gunner on B-24.

Discharged on Oct. 20, 1945 in Rome, NY with rank of staff sergeant. Received Purple Heart and Air Medal with four Oak Leaf Clusters.

Married on Aug. 23, 1947 and has six children. Started and operated refrigeration business, Ancoma, Inc. Mechanical Contractor, Inc., for 42 years. Retired in June 1991.

JEAN FREDERIC BRESSLER,

was born on July 13, 1919 in York, PA. Enlisted in the Air Force on Oct. 21, 1941 at Barksdale Field, LA. Was assigned to 44th Bomb Group, 67th Sqdn.

Group went to AAF 115, Shipdham, Norfolk about Oct. 10, 1942. On June 28, 1943 landed at Benina Main AF, Benghazi, Libya as the only S-2 clerk for the 44th Bomb Group in Africa. Lost about 15 pounds. Was then the 14th Wing at Shipdham. Made tech sergeant in October 1943, assigned to A-2 in the wing.

Discharged on Sept. 5, 1945 with rank of tech sergeant. Received the Bronze Star on April 11, 1944 from General Johnson.

Married Gloria Decker on April 27, 1946 (an old "flame"). They have two children, Kathy and Pam, and two grandchildren.

Retired from Metropolitan Edison Company on July 31, 1979 as division meter supervisor, with 41 years credit. Resides in York, PA.

WALTER BRESSLER,

was born on Feb. 20, 1923 in Unionville, PA. Joined the Air Force in 1942 and trained as a mechanic in various schools in the U.S.

Started flying in 1943 as a mechanic gunner on B-24. Went to England as a replacement to the 8th Air Force, 448th Bomb Group, 713th Sqdn.

Flew seven missions. Bailed out April 1, 1944 and landed in Northern France. Escaped over the Pyrenees Mountains with help of French Underground. Entered Spain, got

help from U.S. Government, returned back to England, then back to the States.

Discharged in December 1945 with rank of staff sergeant. Received Air Medal and Purple Heart.

Married Ruth on April 17, 1948. Has two sons, one daughter and five grandchildren. Retired in June 1986 as a mechanic from local utility company. Resides in Centre Hall, PA.

JAMES P. BREWTON,

was born on Jan. 5, 1919 in Zenoria, LA. Joined the Army on Feb. 8, 1938 as private. Promoted through the ranks to first sergeant, Co. C, 36th Armd. Inf., 3rd Armd Div. in Camp Polk, LA.

Entered cadet training in 1942, commissioned second lieutenant on Sept. 15, 1943 at Big Spring, TX as bombardier, then to B-24 phase training at Casper, WY assigned to 467th Bomb Group at Wendover, then to England with that group. After flying five missions was transferred to the 389th Bomb Group as a Pathfinder crew. Was with the 389th until the 564th Bomb Sqdn. was split up and the crew was transferred to 453rd Bomb Group. Flew 25 Pathfinder missions.

Returned to the States for Thanksgiving 1944. Served at Big Spring AFB; Midland AFB and Mather AFB, completed Navigator School in November 1945.

Discharged in Jan. 14, 1947 with rank of captain. He was recalled for the Korean War. Received Distinguished Flying Cross with Oak Leaf Cluster, Air Medal with three Oak Leaf Clusters, Good Conduct Medal, American Defense, EAME Campaign Medal with four Battle Stars, American Theater Campaign Medal, Victory Medal, Occupation Japan Medal, Korean Service Medal and United Nations Medal.

Worked for Lockheed Missiles and Space Co. in Sunnyvale, CA. Retired in January 1978.

MICHAEL BRIENZA,

was born in 1916 in Flushing, OH and attended ground school aviation training (CPT) at Linsley Institute, Wheeling, WV. Enlisted in the USAAC in January 1942. Appointed an aviation cadet at Fort Hayes, Columbus, OH; Santa Ana, pre-flight training; Oxnard, primary training; Bakersfield, CA for basic training; graduated, Class 43-D, at Luke Field. Commissioned a second lieutenant in the Air Corps.

Was a co-pilot on a B-17; to Casper, WY for phase training, and at Gowen Field, Boise, ID. Assigned a B-24 crew and served as first pilot. From there to England, Metfield and North Pickenham with the 491st. Flew 35 missions from Aug. 3-Dec. 31, 1944.

Upon leaving England in January 1945, was an instructor pilot on a B-24. Was in the Reserves for eight years.

Married and father of four. Now takes his two grandchildren flying in his Cessna 182.

O. HULON BRIGGS,

was born on April 1, 1918 in Caswell County, NC. Enlisted on May 5, 1942 at Ft. Bragg, NC. Basic training at Keesler Field, Biloxi, MS.

Graduated Aircraft Armorers Course AAFTS, Buckley Field, CO, 1942. Graduated Aerial Gunnery Course AAFES, Ft. Myers, FL, 1943. In Boise, ID assigned to crew, 453rd Bomb Group, 735th Sqdn. Then to Pocatello, ID for first phase training; March Field, CA for second and third phase

training. Left December 1943 for Old Buckingham, England by way of South America and Africa.

Flew 30 missions as top turret gunner over Europe, first mission was Feb. 6, 1944 and 30th mission was July 24, 1944. Then to Dundee, Scotland and flew 13 night sorties to Norway, dropping equipment to Underground (Aug. 14-Sept. 27, 1944). Sailed from England on Nov. 6, 1944 arriving in New York on Nov. 17, 1944.

Memorable experiences: On fifth mission Lt. Adams, pilot, was hit by flak on head and co-pilot had to fly plane back to base; on another mission the top turret dome was blown off, hit by flak.

Graduated AAF Gunnery Instructors School, Laredo, TX in 1945, then to Ft. Myers as gunnery instructor to Chinese pilots.

Discharged Sept. 9, 1945, Ft. Bragg, NC. Received EAME Campaign Medal with four Bronze Service Stars, Air Medal with six Oak Leaf Clusters and Distinguished Flying Cross.

After discharge attended Tri-State College, Angola, IN. Graduated in 1950 with a degree in mechanical engineering. After a career with AT&T he retired. Since retirement has done consulting work, woodworking, and volunteer charitable work.

Living with wife in Graham, NC. They have two daughters (one married), and one married son with the only grandchild.

JOHN BRADFORD BRINSON III,

was born on April 24, 1921 in Monticello, FL. Enlisted on Sept. 1, 1942. Served in USAAC, 2nd Air Div.

Graduated pilot, second lieutenant, Class 44-E at Seymore, IN. Assigned as co-pilot on B-24 crew. Assigned to 467th Bomb Group, 790th Sqdn., at Norwich, England. Flew 23 combat missions.

Discharged with rank of second lieutenant and received three Air Medals.

In October 1945 returned to college, received M.D. degree. Married Joyce Curry on May 17, 1964, two children: John, born in 1966 and Joy, born in 1971 and died in 1990.

He is a physician in family practice in Monticello, FL.

JAMES F. BROCK,

was born on March 2, 1922 in Waco, TX. Enlisted on Oct. 22, 1943 as aviation cadet in the Army.

Military locations and stations included Camp Walters, TX; Gulfport, MS; Harlingen, TX; Tonapah, NV; and with 467th Bomb Group, 789th Sqdn., Norwich, England. Participated in battles in Central Europe, Ardennes, and Rhineland.

Memorable experience was when two engines were shot out on same side on Christmas Day 1944 over Belgium. They aborted the bombs, turned around and landed safely in Brussels. The plane that took over their place was hit by fighters and went down. At the briefing it was thought Brock's crew were the ones lost. When they returned, their clothes had been taken up and telegrams were about to be sent out.

Discharged July 22, 1945 with rank of staff sergeant. Received EAME Campaign Medal with three Bronze Stars, Good Conduct Medal, Air Medal with five Oak Leaf Clusters and Victory Medal.

Married to wife, Winnie Dee, for 50 years. They have two sons, George and Jimmy, three grandsons and two granddaughters. Retired from the railroad and is manager of hotel in Groesbeck, TX.

SYLVAN BRODY (DAN),

was born on April 17, 1923 in Shreveport, LA. While wavering to enter the Glider Training Program and being drafted, a decision was made to enlist in the USAAF, Aug. 20, 1942.

Completed Class 42-46 in November 1942, Las Vegas Aerial Gunnery School, with rank of sergeant. Later he was assigned to 734th Sqdn., 453rd Bomb Group (H), 8th Air Force, 2nd Air Div., which flew out of Old Buckingham Airfield, Attlebourgh, England (ETO).

Flew in *Paper Doll,* and later, *Dolly's Sister.* Completed 30 missions as a right-waist aerial gunner, photographer, rank of staff sergeant.

Brody's first mission was on Feb. 5, 1944, Tours, France and last mission was on July 29, 1944, Balman, Germany. Pilot, Capt. Wendell Doug Faulkner, *Paper Doll's* and *Dolly's Sister's* crew, ground crew and others played a vital and supportive role in helping Brody to complete his tour successfully.

The 453rd Bomb Group (H), 8th Air Force became part of the 2nd Combat Wing, 2nd Air Div. The group was formed July 29, 1943, Gowen Field, Boise, ID. The group was comprised of the 732nd, 733rd, 734th and 735th Bomb Sqdns. The group was relocated to Old Buckingham, Attleborough, England, Station 144, December 1943.

The group was reported to be the first group to have completed 100 combat missions within five months in the ETO, July 29, 1944. Group completed its 259th mission, April 11, 1945, Amberg, Germany. Later in 1945 the group concluded its operations with a legacy of pride and memories.

The 8th Air Force, 2nd Air Div. flew 493 operational missions, 1,458 B-24 bombers were lost in combat missions, via air campaigns by German-Luftwaffe fighter planes, specifically FW 190s, ME-109s, JU-88s and flak emanating from anti-aircraft gunners and unfortunate crashes.

The 453rd Group flew 259 combat missions, 58 aircraft were missing in action, and 366 air crew members were lost in operational missions. One of crew's saddest losses was William S. Chappell, radio operator, who replaced another aircraft-radio operator. "Bill" was reported missing in an air campaign.

On ninth mission, flying over target, Friedrichshafen, Germany, 20,000 feet, *Paper Doll* encountered moderate flak, a piece of shrapnel missed Brody by several inches, which he saved as a souvenir.

On the 10th mission, the 453rd Group Commander, Col. Joseph A. Miller left the formation, during an attack by the Luftwaffe. It was reported he was made a German prisoner and he managed to escape. After WWII, Brody and Col. Miller met accidentally at March AFB Exchange. Col. Ramsey Potts replaced Col. Miller as the new group commander.

On the 11th mission, using a K-20 camera, Brody was credited as the only group aerial photographer to obtain pictures of strikes on the target, Munster, Germany.

On 14th mission *Paper Doll* was the lead plane flying over target, Watten, France, and incurred extensive damage, over 100 holes in a wing panel. *Paper Doll* was retired temporarily. Crew received new unpainted Liberator and named her, *Dolly's Sister.*

On 16th mission, May 8, 1944, flying over Brunswick, Germany, a group of 150 FW-190s and ME-109s attacked the group. Several planes were lost and several crashed in England. *Dolly's Sister* aerial gunners were credited with four German fighters. Staff Sgt. Ovando H. Gasaway reported two and a half kills, S/Sgt. Raymond C. Gibbons, S/Sgt. Robert E. Goudy and S/Sgt. Dan Brody reported probable each.

On 21st mission about 25 FW 190s attacked the group and the 453rd Group reported two B-24 planes were shot down.

D-day, June 6, 1944, on 22nd mission, Dolly's sister flew over the coast of St. Laurent, France, 15,000 feet. Encountered no enemy aircraft, nor did group observe fire from anti-aircraft gunners. Most of the action was on the ground.

On two missions, Brody's heater suit malfunctioned. On one mission he flew 11 hours in freezing temperature. Later hospitalized for a burned shoulder. Was given approval to fly with his crew. He felt the crew members depended on each other.

Tour ended on July 29, 1944 with 416 hours and 168 hours combat time in a B-24 which was respected by both the allies and enemies alike. He departed from the ETO, Aug. 31, 1944 and returned to the States. Was assigned to Base Photo-Lab, Will Rogers USAAF Base, Oklahoma City, OK. Had to make a decision to be removed from flying status or consider re-assignment as an aerial gunner-photographer in the South Pacific Theater; subsequently, he requested to be relieved from flying status.

Honorably discharged on Oct. 9, 1945 and enlisted in USAFR in 1949, received second lieutenant Reserves commission on May 28, 1951. Recalled to active duty as a social worker on June 4, 1951, assigned to March USAF Base Hospital, N/P Service, Riverside, CA.

Honorably discharged on Aug. 26, 1954 with rank of captain, remained in USAFR. Completed his MA degree in 1955 from University of Connecticut, School of Social Work. He retired from Reserves on April 17, 1983 with rank of colonel. Received the Distinguished Flying Cross, Air Medal with three Bronze Oak Leaf Clusters, Meritorious Service Medal, Good Conduct Medal, American Campaign Medal, EAME Campaign Medal with four Bronze Stars, WWII Victory Medal and the National Defense Service Medal. Reported eligible but never received the American Defense Service Medal, Korean Service Medal, Armed Forces Reserve Medal, and AF Longevity Service Award Ribbon.

While assigned to SAMSO (currently Space and Missile Systems Center, Los Angeles AFB, located in El Segundo, CA), he was credited for establishing a mental health clinic and awarded a meritorious medal.

From 1955-1967 worked as a social worker at the LBVA Medical Center, Long Beach, CA. Went into private practice, where he is currently the sole proprietor with Holistic Care Support System, Long Beach, CA. He is in the process of obtaining his Ph.D. His practice covers marriage-family counseling, consulting, and teaching. Married to his lovely wife, Felisa F. Brody. They reside in Long Beach, CA.

JESSE EUGENE BROOKS, was born on May 6, 1920 in Dothan, AL. Enlisted on Sept. 22, 1942. Attended Infantry School, Ft. Benning, GA, commissioned second lieutenant.

Served with 101st Inf. Regt., 26th Div.; transferred to USAAF in February 1943; graduated, Class 43-14, Big Springs Bombardier School. After graduation served with 790th Sqdn., 467th Bomb Group (H), 2nd Air Div., 8th Air Force.

Flew 30 combat missions as lead bombardier on B-24, *Wild Irish Rose;* six squadron leads, six groups; 14 Wing, two Div., two 8th Air Force leads. Participated in air offensive over Europe, Normandy and Northern France.

Memorable experiences: Combat mission returned to England after dark, trying to fly formation with lights, hundreds of four-engine bombers all over East Anglia, looking for their home bases. Turn on wing lights and German fighters shot you, turn them off and English Ack Ack shot you. Light runways and Germans bombed the bases.

Discharged on Jan. 14, 1947 with rank of lieutenant colonel. Received Distinguished Flying Cross twice, Air Medal with three Oak Leaf Clusters, Citation for outstanding performance in combat.

Married English Leading Aircraft woman, Edna Z. Head. They have two daughters, Eugenia and Michelle. Retired in 1963 from Bearing and Power Transmission career.

JOHN A. BROOKS III, graduated from West Point, 1941, earned pilot's wings in 1942. Became B-24 flight leader, squadron commander and deputy group commander. Deployed to 2nd Air Div. as 389th Bomb Group Operations Officer, May 1943. He led forces up to 500 B-24s against major strategic targets in Greece, Italy, Austria, France, Germany, Poland, and especially Romania where he led group of 17 B-24s on famous low level attack on Ploesti oil refineries.

After completing B-24 tour, he became one of a few pilots to fly combat in both bombers and fighters; creating and commanding special P-51 scouting force, preceding bomber streams over Europe, reporting route and target weather and enemy fighter formations. Once, together with his wingman, engaged in more than 100 enemy aircraft, destroying five, including German leader, dispersing enemy formations, thereby preventing any attack on B-24 force.

After three combat tours in Europe and Africa, headed for AF HQ there, 1948, individually promoted to colonel for helping create separate Air Force.

Graduated from Air War College (1950); served on faculty and in Korea. Became deputy commander, 20th Fighter Wing, in England, first fighter outfit with atomic delivery capability. Then commanded 36th Wing (Germany) with 150 supersonic F-100 fighters, and a matador missile squadron. Other flying assignments included test flying at Air Proving Ground Center and Tactical Air Warfare Center. Between flying jobs served again at AF HQ, United Nations Command in Korea, and Dept. of Defense. Also graduated from National War College in 1957.

Awards/Decorations: Distinguished Service Cross, Silver Star, four Legion of Merit, three Distinguished Flying Crosses, seven Air Medals, Joint Service Commendation Medal, two Commendation Medals, two Combat Readiness, French Croix de Guerre, and three other foreign decorations.

Married Janie in June 1941 who gave up her nursing career for motherhood. Betty, Johnny IV (Vietnam vet) and Carolyn are her decorations and awards along with 10 OLCs (grandchildren).

Second career evolved Country director, International Executive Service Corps, doing volunteer work, Brazil, Venezuela, and Caribbean, nine years, usually flying own airplane. IESC, founded by David Rockefeller, sends volunteer retired business executives to developing countries to teach American know-how to improve their standard of living. A very rewarding second career.

WILLIAM L. BROOKS, was born on April 10, 1920 in Whitesville, KY. Served with the 466th Bomb Group, 785th Sqdn., 96th Combat Bomb Wing (H).

Stations and locations included Attlebridge, Norfolk, England; Almagordo, MN; then San Antonio, TX. Flew 31 missions from March 24-July 5, 1944.

Discharged in 1945 with rank of lieutenant. Received the Distinguished Flying Cross and Air Medal with three Oak Leaf Clusters.

Married Dorothy Jean Rhoads on May 28, 1942.

Brooks passed away on Aug. 25, 1975.

CORTLAND L. BROVITZ, was born on Sept. 20, 1924. Enlisted in USAAC on Oct. 31, 1943.

Served with the 466th Bomb Group as navigator, Attlebridge, England and flew 30 missions.

Discharged on Sept. 21, 1945 with rank of first lieutenant. Received the Distinguished Flying Cross and Air Medal with clusters.

Married and has four children. He is a certified public accountant.

CARL L. BROWN (LEW), was born on Sept. 9, 1923 in Greenville, PA. Enlisted in USAAC on Jan. 1, 1943.

Basic training at Miami Beach, FL; Radio School, Scott Field, IL; Gunnery School, Fort Myers, FL. Assigned to Capt. Lou Jaques' crew in December 1943 as radio operator/gunner, received phase training on B-24s at Biggs Field, TX, then transferred to 492nd Bomb Group, 859th Sqdn. in Alamogordo, NM for third and final phase.

Departed for overseas on April 1, 1944 via southern route to North Pickenham, England. On May 12, 1944 was assigned to Lt. Ernie Haar's crew, "UMBRIAGO." Flew 24 missions before the 492nd was broken up. Their 859th Sqdn. was transferred to the 467th at Rackheath and became 788th Sqdn. Completed six missions for a total of 30, the last over Hamburg area on Oct. 6, 1944.

Returned to States in November 1944, transferred to ATC and assigned to China/Burma/India Theater in March 1945, based at Dacca, India, accumulating over 600 hours "Hump" time.

Memorable experiences include being greeted on the radio upon arrival at North Pickenham by Lord Haw Haw; first mission, Zietz, Germany on May 12, 1944; view on D-day mission of "Bridge of Ships" from England to Normandy; surviving the June 20, 1944 mission to Politz (into the Hornets' Nest) where 492nd lost 14 planes, 11 from 856th Sqdn.; mission when five bombs did not release over target, waiting instead until they were in traffic pattern over base, narrowly missing officers' mess hall, fortunately, disarmed.

Discharged on Oct. 29, 1945 with rank of tech sergeant. Received ETO Medal with four Bronze Stars, Distinguished Flying Cross, Air Medal with four Oak Leaf Clusters, Distinguished Unit Badge, Asiatic-Pacific Campaign Medal, Victory Medal and American Defense Medal.

Married Patricia Lalor on Aug. 14, 1948. They have one son, one daughter and four grandchildren. He retired in 1985 after 38 years in a career of data processing and payroll management with Owens-Illinois Glass, Inc.

EARL D. BROWN, was born on June 16, 1914 in Schuylkill Haven, PA. Following high school joined the 3rd Cavalry Band, Ft. Myer, VA on Sept. 21, 1933. Remained with band eight years until placed on a cadre to help organize one of the first Air Corps Bands ever, middle of October 1941 at Daniel Field, Augusta, GA.

With some new members and the band being in its best shape ever, they received notice of and alerted for overseas shipment. They shipped out from Camp Kilmer, NJ on the victory ship, *Sea Robin*. Assigned to Ketteringham Hall, 2nd Air Div., 8th Air Force. They were very proud of this assignment and wished it had been sooner.

It was their pleasure to be able to visit all fighter and bomber groups assigned to the 2nd Air Div. As the first sergeant and assistant band leader, he will never forget the 2nd Air Div., 8th Air Force.

Retired from USAF as master sergeant on July 31, 1956.

Married an army nurse, Lt. Jane E. Heintz, on June 2, 1943. They have one son, two daughters and three grandchildren.

EDWIN C. BROWN JR. (ED), was born on June 25, 1922 in Philadelphia, PA. Grew up on farms near Kennett Square and Coopersburg, PA. Graduated from Allentown High School in 1940. Attended Lehigh University September 1941-February 1943 and June 1946-June 1948. Graduated with a BSME.

Enlisted in Aviation Cadet Program in November 1942. Called to active duty in February 1943. Graduated as second lieutenant aerial navigator, San Marcos, TX, Class 44-4 in March 1944.

Married Sue H. Underhill, West Hartford, CT shortly after graduation. The newlyweds flew from New York to Denver, then by train to his first duty station, Casper, WY.

Attended B-24 OTU at Casper, WY and McCook, NE. Was in Bangor, ME en route to ETO on D-day. After ETO indoctrination was assigned to 491st Bomb Group, 854th Bomb Sqdn. Completed several combat missions prior to the St. Lo breakthrough. Flew as navigator on John Warczak's, Doug Hunt's, and Shelton "Red" Wrath's crews. Flew from both Metfield and North Pickenham. Completed 35 missions in December 1944.

Returned to States in January 1945. Assigned as instructor at Ellington Field, TX (V-E day happened here) and then on to the B-32 OTU Program, Tarrant Field, TX (V-J day happened here). Assigned to the active Reserve program in September.

After graduation from Lehigh University, joined Western Electric Company, Allentown, PA. In February 1949 was recalled to active duty. Attended Class 49-ACIS, Mather Field, CA. Spent next six years in various instructor and staff capacities at Ellington, Waco, and Harlingen AFBs. Then came a tour with the 58th Weather Recon. Sqdn., Eielson AFB, AK.

Air Force personnel finally discovered he had a BSME so he was assigned to the Flight Test Facility, Wright-Patterson AFB, OH as a flight test engineer. Was responsible for the extreme environmental test programs of the RF-101, F-101B, GAM-77, and early stages of the B-52H. This was followed by a 20-year military and civilian assignment to Eglin AFB, FL where he held many engineering and management positions in the Air Force's non-nuclear munitions development program.

Finally retired with the rank of lieutenant in July 1981 with a little over 39 years service to the USAF.

He and his wife, Sue, enjoy sailing throughout the Gulf of Mexico and the Bahamas. They have two sons, one daughter and four granddaughters. They reside in Niceville, FL.

IVAN D. BROWN (I.D.), was born on June 11, 1924 in Grant City, IA. Graduated from Greenfield High School, Greenfield, IA in May 1942 and joined the USAAC.

Assigned GDO from the cadet program, received his Silver Wings at Las Vegas Aerial Gunnery School. Went to war in 1944 as a ball turret gunner with the 844th Sqdn., 489th Bomb Group, completing 32 missions in 68 days on a B-24 over Europe.

Assigned to B-29-equipped 43rd Bomb Group at Davis-Monthan, AZ, then ordered to OCS. Earned Gold Bars on Dec. 20, 1947. Served on Guam as ordnance/munitions officer with 14th Air Ammunition Sqdn., became a radar observer and flew 28 missions in Korea with the 68th Fighter Sqdn., Lightning Lancers in F-94, Starfires, 1951-1952.

Upgraded to navigator at Mather AFB, CA, was ordered to Okinawa and assigned to the C-130, Hercules Flying 817th Troop Carrier Sqdn. Flew special forces deployment, resupply and evacuation missions in Vietnam. Carried external nuclear stored for Kadena-based quick-strike fighters and transported crews, parts and equipment for U-2, Smeaky-pete rendezvous.

Retired Jan. 31, 1964 with rank of major and worked in medical/electronics 25 years, retiring from Cordis Corporation in 1989. He is a dedicated ball turret gunner on the Collings Foundation restored B-24, All American.

Married Lillian G. Ballou of Chicago Heights, IL on Dec. 27, 1947. They have six children, 11 grandchildren and two great-grandchildren.

WILLIAM MARTIN BROWN, was born on July 19, 1920 in Omaha, NE. Enlisted in the USAAC on July 30, 1942 as an aviation cadet.

Graduated in December 1943 as a pilot, second lieutenant, Class of 43-K at Lubbock, TX. After four-engine training at Liberal, KS was assigned as B-24 pilot. Picked up crew at Lincoln, NE, then a new B-24-J at Topeka, KS and in July 1944, flew to England via Goose Bay, Labrador and Iceland. Assigned to 93rd Bomb Group, 328th Sqdn. at Hardwick.

Completed a tour of 35 missions. Returned to United States on April 3, 1945. Assigned to Pilot Instructor School and received his pilot instrument instructor certificate on July 27, 1945.

Discharged from active duty Nov. 12, 1945. Resigned from Reserves April 1, 1953.

Awarded the Distinguished Flying Cross, Air Medal with five Oak Leaf Clusters, EAME Ribbon with three Battle Stars and one Overseas Bar.

Retired on Aug. 1, 1980 from his position with the Union Pacific Railroad after 42 years of service.

WILLIAM R. BROWN, was born on July 26, 1923 in Indianapolis, IN and enlisted in USAAC in July 1943.

Military locations and stations included Gunnery School, Laredo, TX and Bungay, England from September 1944-March 1945.

On his first mission to OHM, Germany their ship incurred 20' hole from flak about three feet from left waist position, he was left waist gunner. They broke formation to fly home alone from Hamburg due to damaged engine.

Received an honorable discharge with rank of staff sergeant. Received Air Medal and ETO.

Has been married 47 years and has three children, four grandchildren and one great-grandchild. Retired and living in Ft. Lauderdale, FL.

REX L. BRUDOS, was born on Oct. 21, 1914 in Lake City, SD. Graduated from high school in 1933 at Veblen, SD. Attended SD State College and left there to join USAAC in September 1941.

Stationed at Thunderbird, Glendale, AZ. Graduated from Flying School at Stockton, CA, Class 42-D. Instructed gunners at Las Vegas in AT-6s.

Transferred to Kingman, AZ then to Del Rio, TX. Qualified in B-26s in one month. Sent to Ft. Worth, TX. Qualified in B-24s in three weeks. Picked up combat crew at Gowen Field. Sent to Wendover, UT. Final staging at Tonopah, NV.

Sent to Horsham-St. Faith, Norwich, England via South America, Africa. Flew 31 missions. First mission was first daylight raid on Berlin. Sent to Scotland, met King of Norway, returned to England, then to States.

Assigned to March Field as flight commander and base operations officer. Checked out in B-29s, transferred to McDill, Tampa, FL to inactive Reserve.

Awarded the Distinguished Flying Cross, Air Medals, WWII Victory Medal, American Defense Ribbon and EAME Theater Ribbon with Bronze Star.

Married to Margaret Sheridan by Father Junk at Air Base in Las Vegas.

FELIX B. BRUGNONI, was born on May 3, 1924 in Clifton, NJ. Joined USAAC on April 3, 1943 at Fort Dix, NJ.

Completed ground crew mechanic training and received further mechanic's training at Burtonwood Repair Depot, 21st School of Technical Training, RAF Station, Warrington, England. Served with 93rd Bomb Group, 330th Bomb Sqdn., Hardwick, England.

Discharged on Sept. 20, 1945 with rank of corporal. Received EAME Service Medal.

Married Irene Gorun and they have two children and four grandchildren. He is a retired postal clerk. They reside in Clifton, NJ.

BIRTO R. BRUMBY, was born on April 23, 1917 in Waco, TX. Enlisted in service on June 19, 1942 in St. Louis, MO and to active duty on Jan. 10, 1943 to SAACC for pilot training. Graduated as a pilot at Frederick AAF Base, Frederick, OK on Sept. 30, 1943.

Transition training in B-24 at Liberal, KS. Picked up his crew in Salt Lake City and trained as a crew in Blythe, CA. Sent to Norwich, England, 8th Air Force, 2nd Air Div., 458th Bomb Group, 755th Sqdn. After five missions, became lead crew and led the 8th twice to Munich. Numerous wing, division and group leads. Sent to Memphis, TN as operation officer in Ferry Command.

Discharged from active duty on Oct. 7, 1945, and from Reserves on Sept. 28, 1957 with rank of captain. Received Distinguished Flying Cross, Purple Heart, numerous Air Medals and Battle Stars.

Married Jean McGee on July 4, 1940. They have three children and five grandchildren.

Spent 30 years as petr. engr. along the Gulf Coast drilling and producing oil and gas wells. Also drilled two wells in Alaska and four in New Zealand. The last 10 years spent as a consulting engineer.

ALFRED F. BRUNNER (AL), was born on Aug. 1, 1923 in Milwaukee, WI. Enlisted in USAAC in May 1942 after one year at Marquette University in Milwaukee, WI.

Basic training at SAAC in March 1943. Cadet training at Ellington Field, Houston, TX. Bombardier training at Big Spring, TX, Class 43-15. Joined crew at Salt Lake City in November 1943. Phase training at Biggs Field, El Paso, TX. Served as instructor until May 1944.

Assigned to combat crew at Topeka, KS and flew to England. Arrived at 489th HB Group, B-24, at Halesworth. Assigned to 847th Bomb Sqdn. and finished in 845th Bomb Sqdn. Flew 34 combat missions. Returned to States in December 1944.

Retired from Air Force Reserves in 1970 as a major. Received Distinguished Flying Cross, Air Medal with three Oak Leaf Clusters, and European Theater Ribbon with four Battle Stars.

Married wartime sweetheart, Lila M. Malloy on July 1, 1945. They have two sons, two daughters, 12 grandchildren and one great-grandchild.

Completed studies and graduated from Marquette University in 1949. Has been in the construction field his entire life. Is semi-retired and resides in Wauwatosa, WI.

JOSEPH BRUNNER JR., was born on April 18, 1925 in Milwaukee, WI. Entered Army as aviation cadet on June 21, 1943, age 18+ years.

Subsequent training as follows: Keesler Field, AL; Nashville, TN; CTD at University of Vermont; pre-flight at Maxwell Field, AL; gunnery at Tyndall Field, FL; Bombardier School at Carlsbad, NM; Navigational School at Selman Field, LA. B-24 and crew assignment training at Mountain Home, ID.

Transferred to 389th Bomb Group, 564th Sqdn., Hethel Airbase near Norwich, England via the *Isle de France* ocean liner. Crew was a lead crew so extensive H2X and navigational procedure training was done. Was on as a deputy lead to the end of the war. Transfer orders to B-29 training and they flew B-24M back to the States. Training cut short with war's end in the Pacific.

Discharged Nov. 20, 1945 at age 20 with the rank F/O. Awarded Air Medal.

A few years of college engineering and marriage followed. His working career primarily in steel fabrication industry with most of his time in a supervisory capacity.

He is now a retired grandparent, happily involved with wife, children, grandchildren, friends and hobbies.

Most memorable experience has been his association with his comrades during those WWII years. He still thinks of those who were lost and gave their all. He remembers all the good and bad times. Honestly believes those were the best years of his life, the Good Lord willing.

CHESTER BRUZINSKI, was born on March 16, 1925 in Plaines, PA and grew up in Fairfield, CT. Inducted into the USAAF on Oct. 6, 1943 and sent to Greensboro, NC for basic training.

Went to Kingman, AZ for aerial gunnery in January 1944 and trained as a ball turret gunner, graduating in April 1944. Next came B-24 OTU training at Pueblo, CO and as-

signment as ball turret gunner with Lt. Peter Bakewell's crew. Completing training at Pueblo, went to Lincoln, NE to pick up a new B-24 for their flight overseas.

While en route to Europe on the northern route, they learned that they were to fly with the Mighty Eighth. After additional training in North Ireland they joined the 409th Sqdn., 93rd Bomb Group at Hardwick. Flew 35 combat missions from Aug. 28, 1944 to March 7, 1945. He was reassigned stateside, with 30-day leave at home, R&R at Atlantic City, NJ, then Gunnery Instructors School at Laredo, TX.

Memorable experiences: Nissen huts in winter; those cheerful wake-up calls for the day's exciting events; those exhilarating take-off runs in their gift-laden planes; and the steel confetti that was showered on them. Those were times that he will ever forget, but wouldn't trade those experiences for anything. He is proud to have been involved in a tiny way in the history of that time and to have had the privilege of flying with some great guys in the 2nd Air Div. of the Mighty Eighth.

End of war found him back in Pueblo, CO. Discharged on Oct. 26, 1945 at Sioux City, IA with rank of staff sergeant.

Received American Service Medal, ETO Service Medal, four Bronze Stars, and Air Medal with five Oak Leaf Clusters.

Retired and enjoys golfing, bowling, and gardening. Resides in Fairfield, CT.

FREDERICK VAN PELT BRYAN, was born on April 27, 1904 in Brooklyn, NY. Educated at Columbia College Law School. Enlisted in USAF in January 1942. Commissioned a first lieutenant.

Military locations and stations included Grafton Underwood, Grafton, Britain; then HQ 2nd Air Div., Ketteringham Hall, Norwich, and Norfolk. Was deputy chief of staff, 2nd Air Div., 1943-1945.

Discharged in March 1946 with rank of colonel. Received Legion of Merit, French Croix de Guerre, British Order of the British Empire.

Married wife, Denise, in 1945 and had two daughters, two grandsons and two granddaughters.

Was a founding trustee of 2nd Air Division Memorial Trust. U.S. District Judge of Southern District of New York from 1956 until his death on April 19, 1978.

PHILIP G. BUFFINTON, was born on Oct. 18, 1923 in Williamstown, MA where his father taught history at Williams College. Entered USAAF Aviation Cadet Program in January 1943.

Reported to Atlantic City, NJ, Syracuse University College Training Program in the spring of 1943. Reported to San Antonio, TX for pre-flight training in July 1943. Primary flight training at Coleman, TX. Basic at Greenville, TX.

Received wings and commission at Frederick, OK in March 1944 as part of Class 44-C. B-24 training in Liberal, KS and assembled crew at Bradley Field, CT in September 1944. Sailed to Scotland in October 1944. Reported to 93rd Bomb Group, 328th Sqdn. at Hardwick, England. Flew 19 missions over Germany, 13 as lead crew. Flew B-24 to States in May 1945. Reported to Sioux Falls, SD for B-29 training but with the end of Pacific hostilities was discharged in September 1945 with rank of first lieutenant. Received three Air Medals.

Married Rita Gagnier on Oct. 22, 1945. Has three daughters and one grandson.

Graduated from Worcester Polytechnic Institute in 1949, degree in engineering. Spent his business career in the insurance business in various capacities. Retired from State Farm Insurance Companies in 1987 as executive vice-president and ch. operating officer.

WAYNE HENRY BUHRMANN, was born on Feb. 23, 1923 near Princeton, NE. Enlisted in USAAC in September 1942 but was not called until Feb. 20, 1943 while attending Peru State Teachers College, Peru, NE.

Graduated a second lieutenant navigator and met his crew in Casper, WY. They flew to Hethel, England, first landing at Knotts Corner in Northern Ireland. After 19 and a half missions with the 8th Air Force, 389th Bomb Group, 2nd

Air Div., he was shot down over Germany on Nov. 26, 1944 and ended up in Stalag Luft I.

Discharged on Dec. 3, 1945 with rank of first lieutenant. Later retired from the Reserves with rank of captain. Received POW Medal, Purple Heart, and Air Medal with two Oak Leaf Clusters.

Married Joan Thickstun on Aug. 18, 1946. They have six children and five grandchildren.

Buhrmann finished his degree at Peru State Teachers College, taught for a few years, then went to work for Goodyear in Lincoln, NE acquiring an MS in education and BS in mechanical engineering along the way. He retired from Goodyear after 32 years as an engineer and development manager which included a stint in Northern Ireland and Brussels.

Lives with his wife on family farm in Nebraska.

DONALD F. BULS, son of Fred W. Buls, was born on May 12, 1922 in Garland, NE. Attended Lincoln High School and University of Nebraska. Enrolled in Lincoln Aviation Institute, employed by Curtiss Wright Aircraft Company, Buffalo, NY.

Enlisted in AAC in September 1942. Entered active duty in March 1943. Graduated in Class 44-F and received pilot wings in June 1944. Then went to B-24 School at Albuquerque and on to Casper, WY for B-24 crew training with a crew of nine eager airmen.

They delivered a brand new B-24 to the depot at Liverpool, England. From there he and his crew settled in with the 852nd Sqdn., 491st Bomb Group at North Pickenham, England.

They flew aircraft named, *Tally Ho* and *Fightin Gremlin*. After nine combat missions over Europe, the Germans sued for peace and they were returned to the States. Their group disbanded in the fall of 1945.

Their crew was a delight from start to finish. Members were: Kenneth Byers, 2nd pilot; James Turner, bombardier; Robert Dennett, navigator; Bob Croteau, Bud Moore, Ray Corris, Thomas Belk, Al Allison and Floyd Milliser.

Married Lea Wilcox in 1948. They have three daughters, Nancy, Holly, Becky, and seven grandchildren that are the light of their lives. They reside in Lincoln, NE.

DARRELL BURCHFIELD, was raised in New Mexico, riding horses and fishing, but gave that up to study art in Chicago. Then, came Pearl Harbor. He became a B-24 radio operator/gunner in the 491st Bomb Group.

From late 1944 to 1945, they flew to Berlin, Hamburg, Essen, Kiel, many marshalling yards, and to drop supplies, low level. All missions received intense flak.

Three feathered engines caused them to abort on one mission and to drop bombs and ammo into the Channel. They crash landed at a spitfire base and survived.

Another mission, an 88 knocked them out of formation over Essen, they crash landed just over Allied lines. No one jumped because of the angry Germans below. Again, they survived.

Darrell and his wife, Carol, live in Glendora, CA. They have four grown children and two grandchildren. He's a graphic designer and watercolorist and during the war he painted crew jackets and bombers.

JOHN A. BURKHARDT, was born on April 14, 1923 in Astoria, NY. Enlisted in USAAF on Nov. 25, 1942.

He was a flight engineer/gunner, 8th Air Force, 453rd Bomb Group, 734th Sqdn. Military locations and stations included Old Buckingham, England; March Field, Boise, ID and Laredo, TX. Participated in battles in Berlin, Blitz week in 1944, and D-day. Flew 30 missions. He was also Jimmy Stewart's flight engineer.

Memorable experiences were heat suit burns, frostbite, flak hits, gas lines hit, returning to England alone (out of formation) two or three times.

Discharged from USAAF on Sept. 28, 1945. Joined Air Force Reserve in 1950. Retired from Reserve on April 21, 1953 with rank of tech sergeant. Received B-24 Notre Dame Medal, B-24 Spirit of Notre Dame Medal, Air Medal with three Oak Leaf Clusters and Distinguished Flying Cross.

Has a wonderful wife, grown son who is an engineer and daughter who is a nurse.

Forced out to early retirement after 28 years with Eastern Airlines. Still working 15 days a month at Executive Gifts.

H. MARLIN BURKHART,
was born on July 22, 1922 in Marino, CO and drafted in June 1943.

After basic training, Pvt. Burkhart learned to repair fighter aircraft, heavy bombers, and to fire a 50 calibre machine gun. At Mountain Home AAF, ID Burkhart joined a 10-man crew. After training, this crew was assigned to Shipdham Air Base near Norwich, England. Burkhart was now a sergeant, the flight engineer and top turret gunner.

Completed 13 missions over Germany in a B-24 Liberator bomber. On the 14th mission he was shot down. Served out the remainder of the war in POW camp.

Awarded the Good Conduct Medal, Air Medal, POW Medal and Presidential Unit Citation.

Married Maroline Mae Saffel on Nov. 16, 1950. They have two children and two grandchildren. Retired from Gates Rubber Company after 40 years of service.

EUGENE K. BURSON,
was born on Oct. 11, 1920 in Banning, CA. Enlisted in USAF in June 1942. Air Force physical training instructor, Air Force Gunnery Schools, 93rd Bomb Group, Hardwick, England.

Military locations and stations included Lowry Field, Denver; Jefferson Barracks, St. Louis; Panama City, FL; Laredo, TX. Participated in battles in Europe.

Most memorable experience was coming home from a mission in 1945 and dropping four or five 250s through bomb bay doors onto runway in front of several hundred welcoming home boys.

Discharged in April 1946 with rank of captain. Received the Air Medal and Battle of Europe.

Has a wife, son and daughter. Retired from auto dealership in 1979.

EMMETT BASSETT BURTON (LUCKY),
was born on Jan. 9, 1921 in Owensboro, KY. Enlisted in the USAAC, USAF in 1939. Assigned 93rd Bomb Group, Hardwick and Benghazi as co-pilot and later as pilot on B-24. Initial training at Williams Field.

Continued flying after the war, 1,000 hours as B-47 pilot, Chenault AFB, 1952-1961. After training at Carswell in conjunction with General Dynamics, piloted B-58 Hustler, world's fastest bomber, and transferred to Grissom AFB. While at Grissom (1961-1969), member of the 305th Bomb Wing. His last position was chief of standardization at Grissom. Was also instructor pilot for the B-58.

Retired on July 31, 1969 with rank of lieutenant colonel. Received the American Campaign Medal, National Defense Medal, EAME Campaign Medal, Asiatic-Pacific Campaign Medal, Foreign Service-American Defense Medal, Good Conduct Medal, Victory Medal, Purple Heart, Military Merit, Air Medal, Air Force Commendation Medal, Combat Readiness Medal, and Distinguished Flying Cross.

Married high school sweetheart, Mary Josephine Westerfield, had four children, Robert, Patty, Betty Jo and Glen.

Burton died on Dec. 24, 1977 and is buried in the family plot at Rose Hill Cemetery, Owensboro, KY.

Because of the inspiration of his father, son, Robert, took pilot training and received his private license.

JESSE M. BURTON,
was born on Jan. 2, 1916 in Rockingham County, NC. Enlisted in Air Corps on Oct. 14, 1942. Was airplane armor gunner, 612, 44th Bomb Group, 67th Sqdn. (Mercer's Crew).

Military locations and stations included basic training at Fresno, CA, Buckley Field, CO, Armorer School, Tyndall Field, FL, Gunnery School, Salt Lake City, UT, Tucson, AZ, El Paso, TX and Flying School, Kilmer, NJ.

Participated in battles in Berlin, Brunswick, Rotenberg, Politz, two missions on D-day. Flew a total of 30 missions.

A memorable experience was on April 8, 1944 on way to Brunswick, very rough, Goering's hand-picked pilots flew through formation.

Discharged on Sept. 5, 1945 with rank of staff sergeant. Received Air Medal with three Oak Leaf Clusters, Distinguished Service Cross, and Good Conduct Medal.

Married on Aug. 11, 1946. Retired from textile company as planning supervisor after 41 years.

STEPHEN H. BURZENSKI,
was born on Sept. 1, 1917 in Pawtuckett, RI. Enlisted in Air Force on March 17, 1942. Served as B-24 crew chief 750, 714th Sqdn., 448th Bomb Group, 8th Air Force.

Military locations and stations included Norfolk, and Seething, England. Participated in battles over Ardennes, Air Offensive Europe, Central Europe, Normandy, Rhineland, and Northern France.

Discharged on Sept. 14, 1945 with rank of master sergeant. Received EAME Service Medal and Good Conduct Medal.

Married and has three children. Retired and is a collector and restorer of antique engines. Resides in De Bary, FL.

JOHN W. BUTLER,
was born on March 18, 1921 in East Boston, MA. Joined USAF on Aug. 1, 1943.

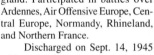

Military locations included England and Africa. Flew 25 missions, the last one on Feb. 12, 1943.

Discharged on Aug. 10, 1945 with rank of sergeant. Received Air Medal with three Oak Leaf Clusters, and Distinguished Flying Cross.

Married and has eight children. Retired and resides in Destin, FL.

RICHARD D. BUTLER,
was born on March 18, 1921 in San Diego, CA. Enlisted in USAAC on Jan. 19, 1942.

Served with 506th and 67th Bomb Sqdn., 44th Bomb Group. Participated in battles at Kiel, Ploesti, Naples/Foggia. His most memorable experience was with the 44th Bomb Group service.

Retired from the USAF on Feb. 1, 1971 with rank of colonel. Received Distinguished Flying Cross, Air Medals, etc.

He and his wife, Ardith, have six children.

GENE WRIGHT BUTTS,
was born on Dec. 3, 1924. Raised and educated in Los Angeles, CA. Joined the Air Force on his 18th birthday in 1942.

Received basic training at Fresno, CA; Armament School, Lowry Field, Denver, CO; Power Turret and Electric Gunsight School, Briggs Mfg. Company, Detroit, MI. Joined the 579th Sqdn., 392nd Bomb Group at Alamogordo, NM in May 1943.

POE was Camp Shanks, NY. Arrived in England via Scotland in July 1943 on the *Queen Mary*. The 392nd Bomb Group was at AAF Station 118, Wendling, Norfolk near Kings Lynn for over two years. His job in the 392nd was power turret and electric gunsight maintenance and repair

of U.S. Army MOS 678; check, adjust and repair cold weather and high altitude malfunctions.

The 392nd participated in, and was cited for their efforts in the Air Offensive Europe, Normandy, Northern France, Ardennes, Central Europe and the Rhineland Campaigns. The 392nd also received the Presidential Unit Citation.

In civilian life he worked for Delta Airlines and retired from Delta in 1981.

He now resides with his wife of 47 years, Audrey, in Escondido, CA.

JAMES M. BUZICK,
was born on Feb. 7, 1923 in Argusville, ND.

Enlisted in the USAAC on Sept.24, 1942. Discharged on Sept. 24, 1945 as staff sergeant, airplane armorer gunner. Completed 30 combat missions and four diversionary flights with the 577th Bomber Sqdn., 392nd Bomb Group, 8th Air Force from Sept. 9, 1943 to April 20, 1944. Officially credited with destruction of a JU-88 while returning from a mission to Gydnia, Danzig, Poland. Was a member of the lead crew of the 577th Sqdn.

Enlisted in the North Dakota Air National Guard on Dec. 14, 1949.

Ordered to active duty with USAF from April 1, 1951 to Dec. 21, 1952 during the Korean conflict. During this period he was a tech sergeant, Intelligence Operations Technician.

Re-enlisted in the North Dakota Air National Guard on Jan. 1, 1953. Had continuous service with them until May 4, 1980 when he was transferred to the Air Force Reserve (inactive status). Retired from USAF on Feb. 7, 1983, his 60th birthday. During his service with the Air National Guard he was a personnel officer, base comptroller and executive support staff officer, retiring as a lieutenant colonel.

Decorations: Distinguished Flying Cross, Air Medal with four Oak Leaf Clusters, Air Force Commendation Medal (June 17, 1975-Oct. 1, 1978), Meritorious Service Medal (Oct.2, 1978-May 3, 1980) EAME Medal and Good Conduct Medal.

Battles and Campaigns: Air Offensive Europe, Normandy, Northern France and Rhineland.

He is a widower with five married children. His civilian occupation was air technician with North Dakota Air National Guard from Dec. 14, 1949 to May 4, 1980, except for time recalled to active duty during Korean conflict. Retired May 4, 1980.

DANIEL R. BYNUM,
was born on Jan. 2, 1922 near Trinchera, Las Animas County, CO. Inducted into the U.S. Army in Los Angeles, CA on Nov. 18, 1942.

Entered active duty on Nov. 25, 1942 at Ft. McArthur, San Pedro, CA and assigned to the USAAC. Took basic training at St. Petersburg, FL and Clerical School at Fort Collins, CO.

Assigned to the Operations Section, 566th Bomb Sqdn. (H), 389th Bomb Group at Biggs Field, El Paso, TX in February 1943. Stayed in 566th Operations, except for a few months in Group Headquarters Operations, until Group returned to the U.S. in June 1945. Assigned to Officers' Laundry Unit at Charleston Air Base, SC from July-September 1945.

Discharged in September 1945 with rank of corporal at Sheppard Field, Wichita Falls, TX.

Married Helen E. Pittman on Jan. 12, 1942 in Compton, Los Angeles County, CA. They have two sons and seven grandchildren.

Retired in January 1982 as personnel management assistant of the Tonto National Forest headquartered in Phoenix, AZ.

ARTHUR W. CABLE SR., was born on Oct. 9, 1921 in Mount Vernon, NY. He was drafted into the regular U.S. Army on Sept. 18, 1942 and transferred to the USAAC. He graduated from New England Aircraft School.

He transferred to aviation cadet training. He graduated in class of 43-J on Nov. 3, 1943 as a second lieutenant He was assigned to B-24 training at Maxwell Field. Upon completion, he flew their B-24 and crew (via North Atlantic) to England. He joined the 93rd Bomb Group, 330th Bomb Sqdn. based at Hardwick, England in May 1944. He flew 30 missions over Europe, 12 as lead crew. First mission on D-day, last mission on Sept. 18, 1944. Full crew returned to the States in October 1944.

Cable enjoyed the whole experience of being in the Air Force. He received the Distinguished Flying Cross and four Air Medals. He was discharged on Oct. 14, 1945 with the rank of first lieutenant.

He married Margaret Winter on Aug. 14, 1954. They have three sons, one daughter and two grandchildren. He is enjoying retirement after 43 years with the International Paper Company.

JOHN V. CADDEN, was born on Dec. 30, 1923 in Morristown, NJ. He entered the USAAC on April 1, 1943. After basic training in Miami Beach, FL; Radio School at Scott Field, IL; and Gunnery School at Laredo, TX he was assigned to Lt. Stan Kriviks' B-24 crew as radio operator and flight trained at Westover Field, MA.

On completion, he relocated to the 8th Air Corp in England arriving late June of 1944 as replacements at the 445th Bomb Group, 702 Sqdn., Tibenham, England. He flew combat missions to Germany and France in July, August and September 1944, completed 19 and survived two crash landings that destroyed *Fearless Fosdick* and *Percy.*

Last mission flown was the disastrous Kassel, Germany raid of Sept. 27, 1944 and was on the only crew of the 702 Sqdn. to make it back to England that day, crash landing the *Percy* near the air base.

He received the Air Medal with two Oak Leak Clusters, Four Battle Stars and the Purple Heart. He was discharged on Sept. 27, 1945 with the rank of tech sergeant.

He married Eileen "Pat" Casey on June 27, 1953. They have three children and two grandchildren. He has been retired since 1990 and living in Avalon, NJ and spends the winter months in Palm Harbor, FL.

JOHN CAHILL, was born July 21, 1924 in Columbus, OH. Drafted in the USAAC in March of 1943. Graduated from Mechanic School at Keesler Field, MS and Gunnery School in Laredo, TX, then on to B-24 crew training in Casper, WY. From there he was sent to Hethel, England with the 389th Bomb Group, 565th Sqdn. Flew 35 missions with Anthony Gasbarre's crew as the aerial engineer gunner on the ship, *I've Had It.* He believes it was the only olive-drab plane in the group. The ship was cracked up by another crew overshooting the runway.

Their new plane was a B-24H and handled by the same excellent ground crew. He wishes he could recall the crew chief's name. The crew was sent overseas in May of 1944 and returned to the States the following December.

He obtained the rank of tech sergeant, received the Air Medal and three clusters, Distinguished Flying Cross and Group Citation. Was also a member of the Lucky Bastard Club.

Spent R&R in Santa Ana, CA, then to Hobbs, NM, Tyndall Field, FL and Smyrna, TN. Discharged Oct. 30, 1945 in Dayton, OH. He joined the Columbus, OH Div. of Fire in 1953 and retired in 1980.

Married with two daughters and seven grandchildren, all living in and around Columbus, OH.

STANFORD GAYLE CAIN, was born Feb. 3, 1925 near Hennessey, OK. Went into the Army Aug. 5, 1943; Radio School at Sioux Falls, SD; Gunnery School at Yuma, AZ; B-24 transition at Charleston, SC.

To England on the *Queen Mary;* assigned to the 446th Bomb Group, 707th Bomb Sqdn. in September 1944. Bailed out with William Woodburn's crew on Dec. 27, 1944 over Belgium after engine failure abort over Germany and lost second engine while trying to land in fog at Brusselles. Reassigned to Wallace Malone's lead crew. Flew on supply drop mission to Wesel. Completed 26 missions before V-E day. B-29 training at Fairmont, NE stopped on V-J day. Discharged Nov. 5, 1945.

After completing MSEE degree from Oklahoma A&M in 1950, worked for Atomic Energy Commission at Sandia National Laboratories in Albuquerque, NM and Livermore, CA for 37 years doing design engineering and testing on atomic weapons. Retired in 1990.

EDWARD A. CAIRNS, was born on Dec. 6, 1916, Clinton, MA. He enlisted into the USAAF at Ft. Devens, MA on July 2, 1942.

He was at these locations: Ft. Devens, MA; Miami Beach, FL; Lowry Field, CO for Bombsight-Auto-Pilot Maint. School; and Davis Monthan in Tucson, CO, where assigned as an original member of the 446th Bomb Group. He trained for overseas at Denver and flew to England on B-24 *Lady Luck* southern route arriving on Nov. 15, 1943. He spent his entire time as group section chief of auto-pilot maintenance. He left England on July 6, 1945 and boarded the *Queen Mary* in Scotland for the States. He was home on leave V-J day.

He was on trolley run in B-24 flying over Germany in May 1945 when Germany surrendered and saw lots of bomb damage such as bridges out and boats sunk.

Discharged on Sept. 28, 1945 with the rank of tech sergeant, he received the Bronze Medal.

He is married to Barbara (Hall) and they have two sons and two grandchildren. He is retired.

BYRON B. CALOMIRIS, was born on June 13, 1918. He enlisted in the USAAC on Dec. 11, 1942. Called to active duty as an aviation cadet for the Aircraft Maintenance Program on March 3, 1943.

Sent to Boca Raton, FL for basic training. Then reported to Yale University for technical training. Received commission as second lieutenant AUS in September 1943. Was ordered to Boeing Aircraft Factory for familiarization on the B-17G bomber.

Served with the 19th Bombardment Combat Crew Training Group at Pyote, TX for a few months before transfer to Pueblo AFB, CO. There he was assigned engineering officer for the 853rd Bomb Sqdn. of the 491st Bomb Group. The 491st was then in third phase training with B-24 aircraft in preparation for combat duty. He flew overseas with the group, arriving in England in May, 1944. At Pueblo, the group consisted only as an air echelon with ground staff officers attached. Upon arrival at Metfield in East Anglia, it was found that some of the ground staff positions were duplicated. As only a second lieutenant, he was outranked and had to assume the position of assistant engineering officer for the duration of his service in the ETO. He subsequently was promoted to the rank of first lieutenant prior to departure from England.

He was returned to the States on the *Queen Elizabeth* in July 1944 and received 30 days leave, during which time the Japanese surrendered. Upon return to duty he was shipped to McChord AFB in Tacoma, WA, where members of the group assembled for probable original intent to retrain in B-29s for Pacific duty. Due to the cessation of hostilities, they remained at McChord awaiting separation or re-assignment. Because he did not have the required points to qualify for separation, he was assigned to Gowan AFB in Boise, ID for further duty. He was separated from Gowan in November 1945 and accepted an AFR commission as a first lieutenant. He served in the reserves until 1956.

After separation from active duty in 1945, he returned to NYU and completed his studies towards a degree in aeronautical engineering. He was hired by Grumman Aircraft Engineering Corp., located at Bethpage, Long Island, NY where he remained for 30 years. In 1968 he was transferred to Los Angeles and took early retirement in 1977. He opted to remain in California where he now resides.

LARRY CALVERT, was a graduate of the University of Michigan before becoming an aviation cadet and commissioned as second lieutenant bombardier at Victorville, CA July 1943. He was sent to England with a B-24 crew and stationed at Seething Airfield, Norfolk.

Flew 17 missions with the 712th Bomb Sqdn., 448th Bomb Group, 8th Air Force. On the 17th mission (a second raid on Berlin without fighter protection) plane was seriously damaged over the German coast, and forced to land in Sweden. After six months internment, was flown to the States and reassigned to a B-29 Sqdn. headed for the Asian theater. Before training was complete, war ended.

Went to work as a flight test engineer for Douglas Aircraft. After 26 years with McDonnel Douglas, retired as a senior scientist working on the "Thor" first stage which was launching communication satellites at the time.

Joined the Station 146 Tower Association at Seething, England and hope to return there, as a visitor this time.

MIKE CAMBON, was born May 2, 1923 near Latrobe, PA, a coal mining town near Pittsburgh. He joined the USAAC in January 1943. He was commissioned as navigator at Selman Field, LA, then on to B-24 training at Casper, WY.

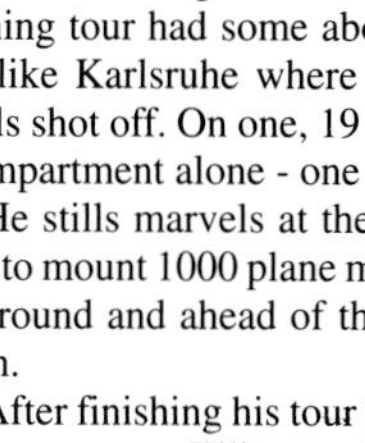
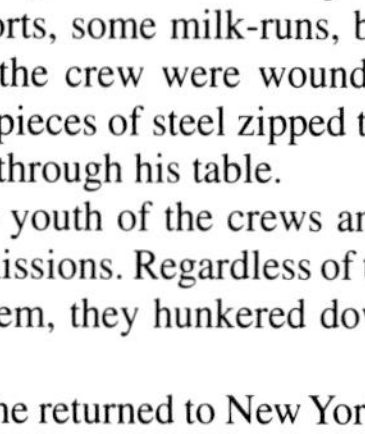

In July 1944, he joined 786th Sqdn., 466th Bomb Group at Attlebridge, England. On second mission, he survived crash landing after hitting tree while taking off. The remaining tour had some aborts, some milk-runs, but also many like Karlsruhe where the crew were wounded and controls shot off. On one, 19 pieces of steel zipped through his compartment alone - one through his table.

He stills marvels at the youth of the crews and their ability to mount 1000 plane missions. Regardless of the carnage around and ahead of them, they hunkered down and went in.

After finishing his tour he returned to New York, married, then went to Ellington, TX to retrain for Pacific duty. While there, the war ended and he was discharged September 1945.

He worked for awhile, then went to MIT for an engineering degree in 1952. He has two kids and is very proud of both. He enjoyed his work, traveled the world, retired in 1988, but still consults. He is also busy with volunteer work and a full social life. He learned to sail in England and still does.

H. ALBERT CAMPBELL, was born on Aug. 5, 1922 in Ottowa, IL.

He enlisted in the USAAC on July 20, 1942. He completed Aircraft Mechanics School at Sheppard Field, TX and graduated the second highest in his class. In November 1942

he attended Glen L. Martin School in Baltimore, MD for B-26.

In January 1943 he went to Fort Myers, FL for Gunnery School and advanced to staff sergeant. In February 1943 he went to MacDill Field at Tampa, FL as a B-26 engineer. In April 1943 he transferred to B-24 crew training as first engineer at Tucson, AZ. Then more training at El Paso, TX and Herington, KS. In September 1943 he joined the 389th Bomb Group, 566th Sdqn. and advanced to the rank of technical sergeant. They were the first replacement crew in the 389th and about their 12th mission became a lead crew. Out of the original crews only three finished, they being the fourth in the 389th to finish.

Their tour of missions was 28. On Nov. 5, 1943 over Munster, Germany he shot down an ME-109 and on April 11, 1944 over Oschersleben, Germany he shot down an FW-190. After his last mission on April 19, 1944, he was transferred to the 453rd Bomb Group, 733th Sdqn. as an instructor. At the 389th Bomb Group, he was awarded the Distinguished Flying Cross and the Air Medal with three Oak Leak Clusters.

He returned to the States on Aug. 1, 1944 and was married on Aug. 8, 1944. In October 1944, he attended Instructor School in Galveston, TX. In December 1944 he was assigned as a B-24 line chief at Kirtland Field in Albuquerque, NM. In March 1945 Kirtland Field was converted to B-29 training and he became a B-29 engineer in a flight test section.

On Dec. 13, 1945 he was discharged at Buckley Field, Denver, CO. He returned to being a glass blower for a neon sign company in Des Moines, IA until 1948. He went to college and in June 1952, he graduated from Iowa State College. In September 1952 he moved to Portland, OR and worked for various companies as a mechanical engineer and retired in 1984 and then did consulting engineering until 1988 and full retirement.

He is still married to that wonderful little girl he wed in 1944. They have three children whom they are very proud of. They have five wonderful grandchildren.

JOSEPH CAMPBELL, was born on Dec. 3, 1921 in Ohio. He enlisted on Sept. 22, 1942 at Wright/Patterson Field, Dayton, OH in the USAF.

He was stationed at Seymour Johnson, NC; Fort Myers, FL; Salt Lake, UT; Alamogorda and Clovis, NM. He was assigned to the 466th Bomb Group, 785th Bomb Sqdn., 2nd Air Div. He participated the 8th Air Force ETO. He was on the Booth (pilot) combat crew #503 of the 466th Bomb Group, 785th Sdqn. on the aircraft named *Jamaica* stationed in Attlebridge, England. The nose art was painted by Ralph Beggs of Lincoln, NE, the bombardier. M/Sgt Bailey was crew chief. They completed 19 missions in the *Jamaica.*

The crew was then trasferred to the Pathfinder aircraft in the 389th Bomb Group flying 30 combat missions in ETO. They had quite a few rough missions, a lot of flak and fighter damage, but they made it home.

Was discharged in September 1945. He married Marjorie on May 2, 1946 and they have five children. He is retired from Logan Clay Products in Logan, OH.

THOMAS W. CAMPBELL, was born on May 3, 1922 in Providence, RI. He enlisted in the USAAC in October 1942. His flying career began at Atlantic City for basic; CTD at Peabody College, TN; Maxwell Field for preflight; primary at Douglas, GA; basic at Macon, GA and graduated in Class 44-F Moody Field, Valdosta, GA.

He completed B-24 training at Buckingham Field, FL; OTU at March Field, CA and then on to the 8th Air Force in December 1944. He flew a tour with the 445th Bomb Group, 700th Bomb Sqdn. returning to the States in June 1945. He had two casual assignments at Sioux Falls, SD and Galveston, TX before separation in September 1945.

He continued flying after the war with the Air Reserve and Air Guard in P-51s, T-33s, F-84s, SA-16s, U-10s, C-54s, T-6s and T-29s. He retired from the Rhode Island Air Guards in May 1977 with the rank of lieutenant colonel.

On a mission in early 1945, the 445th Bomb Group was trailing the 389th Bomb Group when a mid-air collision involving four aircraft took place. The 389th gunners disabled an attacking FW-190 which crashed into the B-24 on the left of the lead ship causing the B-24 to crash into the lead, who in turn crashed into the B-24 on his right. All four aircraft went down at once. He shared this experience with an Air Guard navigator, Al Hall, who was in that 389th flight. Al was killed in an Air Guard crash a short time later.

He received four Air Medals, three European Campaign Stars and several other ribbons.

He married Margaret Ahearn in July 1944 and they have five children and six grandchildren. They are proud of them all.

THOMAS H. CANADY, JR., was born on Sept. 23, 1921 in Franklin, VA. He volunteered as aviation cadet in the USAAF in 1942. He received pilot training in Southeast Flying Training Command and graduated at Turner Field in Albany, GA in December 1943.

He checked out in B-24s at Maxwell Field, AL in early 1944 and picked up his crew at Salt City Replacement Center and went to Gowen Field in Boise, ID for combat crew training. They ferried factory fresh B-24 from Topeka, KS to Northern Ireland. After additional combat orientation, he was assigned to 754th Sqdn., 458th Bomb Group at Horsham St. Faith in Norwich, Norfolk. On the fourth combat mission aircraft sustained severe battle damage and limped home alone from Munich - a long four hours.

The remainder of tour had normal quota of exciting moments. He was cited for completing tour without aborting a mission. He also completed 11 "Truckin" missions in war-weary B-24s that had been reconfigured as makeshift tankers, hauling 80-octane gas to Montgomery and Patton armies in Northern France in the fall of 1944. He returned to the States in early 1945 and was assigned as a ferry pilot to 4th Ferry Command in Memphis, TN.

After the war he attended the Univeristy of Miami in Florida and received his bachelor's and master's degrees. He was recalled to active duty during the Korean War and flew as a pilot for several years in Troop Carrier and Military Air Transport Command before being tapped for duty as Assistant Air Attache to Indonesia. Following staff assignments in Pentagon and Vietnam, he was designated Air Attache to Spain. He served the last three years before retirement as Inspector General of the Defense Intelligence Agency. He is currently living in the Washington, DC area with his wife, Dorothya, who has shared his adventures for more than 40 years.

NORMAN J. CANFIELD, was born on April 17, 1918 in Faton Rapids, MI. He joined the USAAF in June 1942.

He was stationed at the following places: Camp Upton, Long Island, NY in June 1942; Miami Beach, FL; Buckingham Field in Fort Myers, FL; Key Field in Meridan, MS on the A-24s *Douglas Dauntless* as a radio gunner; in Myrtle Beach, SC on the B-26 *Martin Marauder*; MacDill Field in Tampa, FL B-26; in Tucson, AZ on B-24; in Pueblo, CO on B-24 with the 491st Bomb Group.

His memorable experiences include training in B-26 at MacDill when the motto was "One a day in Tampa Bay" (it took two hours to get to their mission on D-day target - took six hours to get home).

They took the scenic route to England on May 1, 1944 by way of: West Palm Beach, Trinidad, Belem, Brazil, Fortalisa, Brazil, Dakar, Africa, Marrekech, French Morocco, Newquay, England, Metfield, England after the bomb dump blew up North Peckingham, England. He flew 31 mission in ball turret and nose turret May 1, 1944 to Oct. 29, 1944. He was gunnery instructor in Laredo, TX and Walla Walla, WA from February 1945 to October 1945.

He received the European Campaign Ribbon with four Bronze Stars, the Air Medal with three Oak Leaf Clusters and the Distinguished Flying Cross. He was discharged in October 1955 with the rank of staff sergeant.

He married Helen Cumming on Sept. 29, 1950, they have a son and a daughter. He was a hotel manager and district director and retired from the hotel business in April 1983.

LYLE E. CARBAUGH, was born on Jan. 18, 1920 in Chadwick, IL. He enlisted in the USAAC on Oct. 17, 1941 at Fort Sheridan, IL, took basic training at Sheppard Field and remained there as clerk.

He embarked for ETO on April 6, 1943 and was sent to 21st Statistical Control at HQ 8th Air Force. He attained the rank of tech sergeant. He transferred to HQ 2nd Air Div. While there he was a chief clerk of the Statistical Section until being transferred to 1st Provisional Air Force on Nov. 18, 1944 at Vital, France.

On March 24, 1945, he was promoted from tech sergeant to second lieutenant as statistical officer. He remained with the 1st Provisional Air Force and 371st Fighter Group. Was relieved from active duty on Nov. 28 1945 and remained in the Reserve until December 1945 attaining the rank of captain.

He married Gertrude Schroeder of Houston, TX on Sept. 12, 1948 and they have three children and five grandchildren. He has worked for the same family (oil operator and rancher) since April 1, 1946 and still going strong.

WARREN G. CARDEN, was born on July 1, 1920 in Harlan County, KY. He worked as a coal miner from 1936 to 1941. He was inducted into the U.S. Army on Nov. 13, 1941 at Fort Thomas, KY. After basic training at Fort Bragg, NC in January 1942, he was sent to Fort Jackson, SC in the 30th Div., 118th Field Arty. and transferred to the 197th as staff sergeant.

His division moved to Camp Blanding, FL in the tall of 1942 where he trained recruits until the fall of 1943. He requested and received transfer to the USAAF. After Gunnery School at Harlingen, TX, he went to Salt Lake City, UT in December 1943, where he was assigned to the C.W. Johnson crew. He then went to Davis Monthan Field, Tuscon, AZ for training in B-24 in January 1944. The crew was selected by Col. Napier to join the 489th, Wendover Field, UT.

He was assigned to the 8th Air Force, 2nd Air Div., he flew via the southern route and landed at Holton Air Base, Halesworth, England. His first mission was May 30, 1944 to Oldenburg, Germany. He completed 32 missions. His last mission on Aug. 16, 1944 was saturated bombing which targeted the wooded area just across the Elbe River. He was sent back to the States with recommendation for tour in the Pacific.

After landing in Camp Shanks, NY he was sent to Miami, FL for 10 days of R&R. He then reported to Radio School in Scott Field, IL. In December he transferred to Truax Field in Madison, WI for on the job training in postal service.

He was awarded the American Campaign Medal, American Defense Service Medal, Expert Aerial Gunner, Crew Member Badge/Wings, ETO with four Bronze Stars, Air Medal with three Oak Leaf Clusters and the Distinguished Flying Cross. He was discharge on Nov. 13, 1945 with the rank of staff sergeant.

After discharge he returned to coal mining as foreman. During this time he became qualified through a home study course in the new field of air conditioning and moved to Atlanta, GA in 1952 to begin a new career. He worked for Aircond Atlanta for 32 years until he retired in 1984 as head dispatcher.

He and his wife Geneva Ulrich were married on Dec. 7, 1940. He had a daughter born at AAF base hospital on July 26, 1945. Also had a son born Feb. 27, 1949. Has three grandchildren and two great-grandchildren.

THOMAS CARDWELL (SCOTTY), was born in April 1923 in Philadelphia, PA. He entered the USAAC in November 1941 and was sent to Sheppard Field for basic, aircraft and engine training.

He trained as a B-24 flight engineer at San Diego, CA. Was assigned to the 44th Bomb Group (flying eight balls) in March 1942 to February 1945, flying missions from England and North Africa. Later service included B-29, B-50 and B-36s. He served with the 3rd Bomb Group in Korea receiving a direct commission. Later assignments included HQ, ARDC, participating in the initial "H" bomb tests.

He returned to Korea as Commander 6314th FMS, SAC, HQ. 15AF for building, testing and activation of the Minuteman ICBM and later served with the 90th and 44th SMWs. Also served with the 1st TFW and in Vietnam with 455th TFW. He retired as a lieutenant colonel in June 1973. He entered and is still engaged in law enforcement.

He received two Distinguished Flying Crosses, five Air Medals, two Air Force Commendation Medals, one American Campaign Star, eight European Campaign Stars, one Korean Campaign Star, three Vietnam Campaign Stars and several other ribbons including two Presidential Citations for Kiel and Ploesti.

He is married to Olive Shoemaker and they have four children and five grandchildren.

BERT CARLBERG (SWEDE),

was born in Meriden, CT and enlisted in the USAAC May 1943. Navigator, 67th Sqdn., 44th Bomb Group; CTD at University of Cincinnati; Navigation School, Selman Field; combat crew training, Mt. Home, ID.

Participated in Battle of Bulge, missions to Hamburg, Berlin, Magedeburg, Munich, Ruhr. His memorable experience was bailing out March 1, 1945 over St. Quintan, France, only survivor of original crew, Lt. Crandell was pilot.

Discharged January 1946 with the rank first lieutenant. He received the Air Medal with three clusters, ETO Campaign and Unit Citation.

Widowed, he has three children and one grandson. Retired as station manager with Scandinavian Airlines. Now working as branch manager, JFK Airport for security company Aviation Safeguards.

HARRY W. CARLS,

was born on July 9, 1921 in Altoona, PA. He enlisted in the USAAC on June 17, 1942. He arrived in England on May 2, 1944 as a pilot on a four engine B-24 and B-29 for 8th Air Force, 489th Bomb Group.

He was shot down over France. He received the EAME Campaign Medal with four Battle Stars, Air Medal with three Oak Leaf Clusters, and the Distinguished Flying Cross with one Oak Leaf Cluster.

He was discharged on Oct. 27, 1945 with the rank of captain. He joined the USAFR and retired on July 9, 1981 after 20 years and 14 days as a lieutenant colonel.

He is a member of the Caterpillar Club.

BILL CARLSON,

was born on Feb. 26, 1922 in Omaha, NE. He flew WACO PT-14s with CAA pilot training program prior to joining the USAAF in San Antonio, TX. He graduated from Cadet Corps Class 43-K and chose B-24 program in Liberal, KS.

In July 1944 he joined the 389th Bomb Group, 567th Squadron. He completed 35 missions in February 1945. He was awarded the Distinguished Flying Cross and five Air Medals. His next assignment was engineer officer and test pilot in Tonapah, NV, prior to discharge in August 1945.

He attended Iowa State College in 1946, graduating with degrees in electrical and mechanical engineering.

He retired from General Electric Company after 33 years service in engineering and sales management in Erie, PA and Bridgeport, CT. He resides in Laguna Niguel, CA. He is busy doing volunteer work and travels with his wife Beverly. They have two children, Julie Carlson Brooks a library director in Sandusky, OH and David Carlson, a photo editor with the South Orange County News in Mission Viejo, CA.

ROY W. CARLSON,

was born on Jan. 29, 1921 in Boston, MA. He joined the USAAC on June 11, 1942 and was inducted on Jan. 8, 1943, MOS No. 756 R/O and MOS No. 757 ROMG.

He was stationed at Old Buck Station 144, East Anglia, England. His memorable experience was seeing the Empire State Building in New York at night when returning from England on Nov. 4, 1944 in a C-54. He flew a 35 mission tour on a B-24 with the 453rd Bomb Group, 735th Squadron.

Carlson was awarded the Distinguished Flying Cross, Air Medal with three Oak Leaf Clusters and four Battle Stars.

He was discharged on Sept. 16, 1945 with the rank of tech sergeant.

He married Priscilla Hubbard (of Boston) on Feb. 10, 1945. They have five children and 10 grandchildren. He is retired after 40 plus years in the retail lumber yard business.

WILLIAM A. CARLSON,

was born on March 8, 1921 in Akron, OH. He enlisted in the USAAF on June 6, 1942 at Patterson Field, Dayton, OH as a navigator with the 8th Air Force.

He attended Navigation School at Selman Field, Monroe, LA. He returned from England to Westover Field. Carlson was with the 448th Bomb Group, 714th Bomb Squadron. He was in the air war over Europe, flew 33 missions from April through September 1944.

His memorable experience was on the ill fated Hamm Raid on April 20, 1944 and being shot down while on final approach. He bailed out at less than 2000 feet. They think they were hit by a JU-88.

He was awarded the Distinguished Flying Cross and the Air Medal with Clusters. He was discharged in September 1945 with the rank of first lieutenant.

He enrolled at Miami University, Oxford, OH. Married to Connie and they have three children and five grandchildren. Today, he is retired,

ARTHUR W. CARPENTER JR,

was born on Dec. 19, 1922 in Randolph, VT. He enlisted in the USAAF on Oct. 28, 1942. His basic training was at Miami Beach, FL. He took Airplane Mechanics at Amarillo, TX and preflight at San Antonio, TX. Gunnery School at Harlingen; Advanced Bombardiering at Midland (44-1).

Was commissioned as a second lieutenant and had crew training in Charleston, VA. He was assigned to the 93rd Bomb Group in England, flew 31 missions, 14 as lead bombardier and squadron bombardier including Air Force lead.

Carpenter received the Distinguished Flying Cross and the Air Medal with five clusters.

His memorable experience was mission when they fought off an attack of three ME-109s after losing an engine

and falling behind. They shot one down and returned ZO1 with group. In Korea he flew 15 missions and received one Air Medal.

Retired on Dec. 18, 1982 with the rank of lieutenant colonel. He retired from Union Carbide in 1985. Has been married for 47 years and has two children and four grandchildren.

JOHN S. CARROLL,

was born on March 4, 1923 in Memphis, TN and raised in the small town of Trimble, TN. After building B-25s for two years after high school, he was inducted into the USAAC on Dec. 3, 1943.

The first assignment after basic training at Miami Beach, FL was into the Aviation Cadet Program, however, this assignment ended in April 1944 when they were dismissed from the Aviation Cadet Program for the convenience of the government.

Gunnery training followed at Laredo, TX and crew training at Gowen Field in Boise, ID with assignment to Lt. Donald Rhinehart's crew as nose gunner. He arrived in England in February 1945 with eventual assignment to 445th Bomb Group, 702nd Sqdn. Their crew only flew four missions before V-E day with no casualties.

After his discharge in December 1945, he eventually became an industrial engineer and followed this profession until his retirement in 1988.

Recalled into the Air Force in 1951 and served 13 months with the 516th Troop Carrier Wing during the Korean situation.

In 1946 he married Lois Lee Wimmer, whom he met in Boise while in crew training. They have enjoyed 47 years of marriage. They have three children and six grandchildren.

RAPHAEL E. CARROW (RAY),

was born on Sept. 25, 1918 in Brooklyn, NY. He graduated from the University of Wisconsin, Class of 1940. He was drafted into the military service in July 1942. He entered aviation cadet training at Maxwell Field in Alabama.

He trained as a pilot in the Southeast U.S. graduating

Standing, L to R: T/Sgt. Joseph Piorkowski, Jr., Radio Operator; 1st Lt. Aubrey Cates, Pilot; 2nd Lt. Thomas P. Taylor, Co-Pilot; 2nd Lt. Jay Young, Jr., Bombardier-Navigator; T/Sgt. William L. Bullard, Engineer. Bottom row, L to R: S/Sgt. John S. Holombe, Gunner; S.Sgt. Chester L. Bolender, Gunner; S/Sgt. Walter Duma, Gunner; S/Sgt. Raul Romero, Gunner. (Courtesy of Aubrey P. Cates)

in the Class of 43-I at Columbus, MS as second lieutenant. He continued advanced training in B-24s at Maxwell Field in Boise, ID. He picked up factory new B-24 at Topeka, KS and flew it to Ireland with crew, stopping at Bangor, ME and Goose Bay, Labrador.

In England, he was assigned to the 445th Bomb Group, 700th Bomb Sqdn. at Tibenham. He flew 21 combat missions over Germany.

His memorable experience was being shot down in the infamous Kassil mission on Sept. 27, 1944. He was captured and became a prisoner of war at Stalag I, Barth, Germany until the end of the war in Europe.

He received three Air Medals, the Purple Heart and other ribbons. He was discharged in November 1945.

In civilian life, he pursued a career in real estate. Married and has four children and numerous grandchildren.

DAN J. CARTER, was born March 7, 1924 in Abilene, TX. He enlisted into the USAF in December 1943. He was assigned to the 2nd Air Force (Bombardier) as first lieutenant.

He was stationed at Big Springs, TX; Casper, WY; Halesworth, England with the 489th. Flew 35 missions over Europe.

Received the Air Force Medal and four Oak Leaf Clusters. He was discharged in August 1945 with the rank of first lieutenant.

He is married and they have two children and four grandchildren. He retired from Shell Oil Co. after 40 years. He enjoys golf, tennis and family activities.

ROBERT N. CARTER, was born Jan. 18, 1923 and entered the USAAC on Jan. 21, 1943 at Fort MacArthur, San Pedro, CA. Completed Aircraft Mechanics and Aerial Gunnery Schools. Assigned to B-24 flight crew as engineer, Salt Lake City, UT, December 1943.

After combat crew training, accepted New B-24J in Kansas. Flew it via South America and Africa to North Pickenham, England, 492nd Bomb Group, April 1944. Flew 27 missions. That group disbanded August 1944. Assigned to 448th Bomb Group at Seething, England. Flew six missions. Received five Air Medals with five European Campaign Stars. Returned to the States September 1944. Had enough points for discharge September 1945.

Re-entered service in USAF February 1948. Had numerous assignments in States and overseas to Guam, Libya, Turkey, and one tour of duty with 14th Combat Support Gp. C-47 Gatlin Gun Ships at Nha Trang Airport, Republic of Vietnam, October 1966-1967. Retired January 1969, USAF, master sergeant.

CHARLES E. CARY, was born Sept. 11, 1916 in Selma, CA. He enlisted in the USAAC in February 1942 as an aviation cadet at the West Coast Training Camp at the Victorville AAF, Biggsfield El Paso, TX.

He was stationed at Santa Ana, Santa Maria, CA; Lamoore, CA; Douglas, AZ; and Davis Monthan, AZ. He participated in these battles: Berlin, Bremen, Munster, Brunswick, Ludwig, Hapen, Innsbruck, Franfurt, Hamm, Ruher, Stettin, Zeitz, Emden and Soligen. He was a B-24 pilot with the 68th Sqdn., 44th Bomb Group. Flew 33 combat missions from July 1943 to July 1944. His memories of his service tour was the spirit of the Corps and camaraderie, D-day and surviving the tour.

He was awarded the EAME Campaign Medal with three Bronze Stars, the Air Medal with four Oak Leaf Clusters, the Distinguished Flying Cross and the Unit Citation with Oak Leaf Cluster. He was discharged on July 22, 1945 at Camp Beal, GA with the rank of first lieutenant.

He has been married to Virginia for 55 years and they have two daughters, Charlene and Barbara, and two grandchildren. He retired from the McKesson Robbins Sales in 1978.

JOHN F. CASCIO, was born on Feb. 7, 1918 and enlisted in the USAF on Nov. 11, 1942 as a navigator, 2nd Air Div. He graduated from Nav. School in San Marcos, TX and shipped out to Mt. Home, ID for B-24 transition. He left the States in November 1944 for Ft. Dix.

He arrived in England at Glasgow and entrained for Seething. He spent three weeks in flight orientation and flew his first mission over Neunkirchen on Jan. 3, 1945. Some of them were milk-runs; some were not including Berlin, Dresden, Kiel, Brunswick and Magdeburg. Dresden was the longest. He flew nine hours and 40 minutes and had to land in Belgium.

In 1945 he was assigned to B-29 as instructor navigator, but was discharged on Oct. 20, 1945 with the rank of lieutenant colonel. He received the Air Medal, three Oak Leaf Clusters, five campaigns for Silver Star and many more. He stayed in the Reserves and maintained flying proficiency in his 1034 MOS until 1974 when he retired from the Air Force in 1978.

He graduated from Cornell University with a Master's plus 30 hours. He started as a teacher and became a high school and elementary principal. He retired in 1980. He was married to Eleanor Schwerer (deceased) and has five children.

He plays golf, does woodworking and is currently the President of the Daytona Halifax Area of the Retired Officers Association.

NORMAN CASEY, was born on April 15, 1919 in Nekoosa, WI. He enlisted in the USAAC on July 28, 1941. He attended the Army Air Forces Technical School at Scott Field in Illinois. He graduated radio operator mechanic in 1942.

He departed New York Harbor on Aug. 31, 1942 on the *Queen Elizabeth*. Stationed at Alconbury Hill, England with the 93rd Bomb Group, B-24. He next moved to Hardwick from where he flew two missions over Germany.

Transferred to the 389th Bomb Group, 566th Sqdn., Hethel. Flew two missions from Benghazi, Libya. Returned to Hethel and was shot down over Bremen on the ninth mission on Dec. 20, 1943. He parachuted from his plane and was taken prisoner immediately. Spent 16 months at Stalag 17B, Krems, Austria.

Returned to the States on June 14, 1945. Was discharged on Oct. 8, 1945 at Cochran Field, Macon, GA with the rank of technical sergeant.

Received the American Defense Service Medal, EAME Campaign Medal, Air Medal and the Presidential Unit Citation.

He returned to Wisconsin Rapids, married Vivian Sullivan on May 25, 1946. They have five children and nine grandchildren.

EDGAR P. CASON, was born on Nov. 11, 1921 in Covington, KY. He was teaching at the Embry-Riddle School of Aeronatics in Florida when he joined the USAAC in the summer of 1942 and entered aviation cadets in December of that year. He graduated on Nov. 3, 1943.

He completed B-24 transition in February 1944 and flew a combat tour in the B-24s with the 467th Bomb Group at Rackheath, England during 1944. After completion of his tour, he instructed in B-24s at Nashville, TN until the end of the war. He graduated from Instrument Instructor School at Lubbock AAFB in December 1945. He completed PBY transition at Corpus Christi with the Navy in 1946. He instructed in B-25s at Keesler AFB for two years. He served in Japan for four years with the 475th Fighter Group, 8th Fighter Group flying P-51s during the Korean War.

He was a senior controller and operations officer in the 32nd Air Div. in Syracuse, NY in the early 1950s and then served at the Navy Special Devices Center in Sands Point, NY, where procedures were developed to use radar in the Lockheed Constellation as an airborne early warning aircraft.

Was assigned to McClellan AFB for activation of the first Air Force AEW&C organization using RC-121 aircraft. He was sent to Guam in 1957 as the squadron commander of an air defense unit for two years. His next assignment was with the Directorate of Flight Safety at Norton AFB and while there, he completed jet transition at Randolph AFB in 1959.

Cason served in the Pentagon for four years as the flight safety representative on the Air Staff and as the executive officer for the inspector general. He was director of Plans at Hickman AFB for two years. His last assignment was at HQ 7th & 13th Air Force in Udorn, Thailand conducting classified operations in Laos.

During his career he received two Distinguished Flying Crosses, four Air Medals, Bronze Star, Korean Presidential Citation and other ribbons.

He and his wife Ann were married in 1952 and they have three children.

MARTIN B. CASTLE, was born in St. Johns, MI and lived in Michigan all his life, graduating from Baldwin High School in 1938. In October 1942 he enlisted as a mechanic in the USAAF.

Basic training in George Field, IL and then to Lowry Field, Kingman Gunnery School, to here and there training to be; no, not a mechanic, but an aerial gunner. Their crew flew the southern route to England and made their first combat mission in December of 1943. Their last mission #24 was the one to Hamm, April 22, 1944 (plane crashed). Crew members and status are as follows: pilot, Paul T. Wilkerson, parachuted with no injuries; co-pilot, Clyde S. Sewell, fatal; navigator, Leroy A. Campbell, parachuted with major injuries; bombardier, Richard F. Sullivan, parachuted with major injuries; engineer George C. Gray, fatal; RO, Frank Terlesky, fatal; asst. engr., Robert L. Dotter, fatal; asst. RO, Norman S. Reed, fatal; gunner, Henry S. Bunting, parachuted with major injuries; gunner, Martin B. Castle, parachuted safely with no injuries; gunner, James R. Murray, fatal.

After the war he returned to Michigan and spent the rest of his life in Muskegon until he retired in 1984. He lives with his wife, Eileen, in Sun City, AZ and is very content there. Their six children are scattered across the USA, one each in Maine and California, two each in Michigan and Ohio. There are 13 grandchildren (two boys and 11 girls).

OLIN D. CASTLE, was born on Dec. 4, 1921 in Newark, OH. He enlisted on Jan. 28, 1942 in Columbus, OH in the Signal Corps basic training, then transferred to the USAAC.

He was stationed at Mitchell Field in New York, Westover Field in Massachussetts, Gander Lake in Newfoundland, Dunkeswell, England, Wendling, England and Scott Field, IL. He flew 280 hours Anti-Sub Patrol in 1942-1943, flew 19 missions with the 579th Sqdn, 392nd Group in 1943-1944.

Discharged Aug. 29, 1945 with rank tech sergeant. Called back to active duty from Army Reserve in September 1950. Was discharged on Dec. 31, 1952 with the rank of master sergeant.

Received the Distinguished Flying Cross, Air Medal with three Oak Leaf Clusters, American Campaign Medal with one Star, EAME Campaign Medal with two stars and others.

He and his wife has been married for 50 years and have four children and six grandchildren. He is a retired residential building from Columbus, OH.

AUBREY P. CATES, was born on Nov. 5, 1921 in Kaufman, TX.

He entered service on May 5, 1942 and was accepted

in the Air Force Aviation Cadet Pilot training. He graduated in Columbus, MS in Class 43-F on June 30, 1943.

He had B-17 transition flight training in Florida, later transferring to B-24s. He was assigned to crew as pilot and flew a B-24H to England in early 1944.

He was assigned to the 8th Air Force, 2nd Air Div., 448th Bomb Group, 713th Sqdn. in Seething, England. He flew 31 missions.

He received the Air Medal with three Oak Leaf Clusters and the Distinguished Flying Cross.

Married Myrtle Ann Allaire on Nov. 23, 1943, they have four children: Mary, Larry, Michael and Steven, and 12 grandchildren.

He retired from Boixe Cascade Corp. after 40 years in construction and building material management. He and his wife are enjoying their grandchildren, golfing, hunting and traveling.

WILLIS O. CATHCART JR., was born on Sept. 27, 1925 in Greenville, SC. He enlisted in the USAAF on Sept. 17, 1943 at Donaldson AFB in Greenville, SC.

He was with the 445th Bomb Group, 701st Sqdn., 8th Air Force flying B-24s at Base 124 in Tibenham, England. He was also stationed at Fort Bragg, Miami Beach, Laredo, TX, Denver, CO and Wichita Falls, TX.

Participated in campaigns at Ardennes and Central Europe, receiving Bronze Star for each. Also received Presidential Citation with two Oak Leaf Clusters and the Air Medal with one Oak Leaf Cluster.

Discharged Jan. 21, 1946 with the rank of staff sergeant.

He and his wife have been married for 50 years and have one son and two grandsons. He retired from Textile Manufacturing in 1986.

JAMES BARRON CAULFIELD, was born on Aug. 20, 1916 in Water Valley, MS. Attended the University of Mississippi and graduated May 28, 1938. Entered the USAAC at Keesler Field, MS on Sept. 26, 1942. After Keesler Field, he trained on Teletype at Gulfport Field, MS going to Pueblo, CO AFB, then to Wendover Field, UT. In February 1943 he went from Pueblo to Camp Kilmer, NJ where on March 7, 1943 sailed in convoy for unknown destination, which happened to be England, to rejoin the 506th Sqdn. already there with the 44th Bomb Group (H).

Duty at Shipdham Group Communications was until March 11, 1944 in personnel, then transferred to new base at North Pickingham, where the 492nd Bomb Group remained about four months. He with others were transferred to OSS Base at Cheddington, Bucks until Aug. 11, 1944 and moved to Harrington, North Hants on March 10, 1945 to be home sent home on July 8, 1945 by B-24 A/C.

Was discharged on Aug. 29, 1945 at Camp Shelby, MS with the rank of corporal.

He received the Unit Citation Kiel on May 14, 1943 and the Unit Citation Ploesti on Aug. 1, 1943 and many for group victories and war efforts.

Married his high school sweetheart, Caroline Anderson, on Aug. 10, 1945 while on furlough. They have one son, two daughters and eight grandchildren.

He worked as clergy and railway management for the Illinois Central Railroad and last worked for the Bank of Water Valley for 35 years. He retired from the bank in February 1980. He is enjoying family, church and traveling. He also enjoys various hobbies.

AUZIE EDWARD CEARNAL JR., was born Feb. 1, 1919 in Brownwood, TX. Received BS degree from Daniel Baker College in August 1941. Trained as pilot aviation cadet and received commission and wings at Stockton, CA in

the Class of 42-E. Instructed cadets in twin engine advanced in Roswell, NM and Yuma, AZ. Flew 30 missions with 389th Bomb Group, 565th Sqdn., Hethel, England June to September 1944.

Discharged from the service August 1945 and returned for two years in MATS during the Korean Conflict with service in Korea and Japan.

Married Marjorie Triplitt in April 1942. They have three sons: John, Lohn and Robert, and five grandchildren. Worked at Celanese Chem., McCarthy Chem., General Dynamics, LTV, and University of Texas at Arlington. Cearnal passed away Oct. 20, 1982.

JOHN CEASER, was born March 28, 1922 in Philadelphia, PA. He enlisted in the USAF on Aug. 5, 1943. He was with the 8th AAF, first lieutenant. AC AUS, Navigator 1034, Radar Operator 0141.

Was stationed in England, USA CIC Radar Instructor at Boca Raton, FL. He participated in the Air Offensive Europe, Central Europe, Invasion of France and was at Biscay Bay.

His memorable experiences were taking pride in successfully navigating 35 missions and relating his tales to his neices and nephews.

He was awarded the Distinguished Flying Cross, the Air Medal with six Oak Leaf Clusters and the EAME Campaign Medal with four Battle Stars.

Ceaser was discharged on Oct. 28, 1945 with the rank of first lieutenant.

He married Amelia in 1953. Ceaser passed away on March 8, 1993. He was an animal lover, avid reader, and historian.

WILLIAM F. CETIN, was born on Jan. 6, 1917 in Susy, WY. He joined the U.S. Army in March of 1936 and served as a platoon sergeant in Troop "A" of the 105th Cav. In 1940 the calvary was inducted into the 32nd Red Arrow Div., Btry. A, 126th Field Artillery.

He joined the USAAC on March 15, 1942 and went to Bombardier/Navigation School at Houston, TX and then to Bombardier School at Big Spring, TX. He graduated as second lieutenant on Jan. 5, 1943. He joined the 392nd Bomb Group at Tucson, AZ on March 3, 1943. From there, the group went on to finish its final phase of training at Alamogordo, NM. He flew to Wendling, England on Aug. 22, 1943.

Flew on the group's first mission to Abbeyville, Air Base in France as a deputy lead bombardier. All 30 of his missions were flown either as lead crew bombardier or deputy lead bombardier. The final mission was on Feb. 27, 1945 to Halle, Germany. It took 19 months to finish a 30 mission tour—that must have been some sort of record!

He received the Unit Citation, Distinguished Flying Cross with three Oak Leaf Clusters, Air Medal with five Oak Leaf Clusters, three Lead Crew Citations and other medals.

He was lead bombardier on six division leads, five wing leads, six group leads, nine squadron leads, four deputy leads. As squadron bombardier, he was also responsible for the training and indoctrination of lead crew bombardiers in the operation of the "Mickey" H2X radar equipment.

Some of his more notable missions were: Danzig, Poland (longest mission), three missions to Bremen, Germany, two missions to Hamburg, Germany, D-day the Groups' 100th mission, four Noball missions (Buzz Bomb sites) and Lauta, Germany on Jan. 6, 1945. The Lauta mission was a target opportunity. It was the largest aluminum plant in Germany, producing 75,000 tons of aluminum per year. All bombing results were good to excellent.

He and E. Lorraine Snyder were married in Houston,

TX on Sept. 26, 1942, they have one son, Bill Jr. After 11 years in the military service, Captain Cetin retired from the Air Corps on Jan. 7, 1947. He then went into the heating, air conditioning and sheet metal trade and after 32 years, retired as president and owner of Arrow Heating and Air Conditioning Company.

He now spends his summers at his summer home on the Flambeau River in Northern Wisconsin.

CLARENCE N. CHAMBERLAIN (BUD), was born on Aug. 30, 1922 in Pittsburgh, PA. He soon moved to Monmouth County, NJ. As an Asbury Park High School graduate, he entered Monmouth Junior College to prepare to enter West Point. Pearl Harbor intervened, however, and he joined the Aviation Cadet Pilot Class 43-J, graduating from Turner Field in Albany, GA.

After B-24 training, he flew the North Atlantic and became a 489th Bomb Group, 2AD, replacement crew in July 1944. Then on returning to the States with the 489th in December, he entered B-29 training.

Remained in service and spent eight years in operational flying until 1953 when he attended the Air Force Institute of Technology to complete his college education. The rest of his service life was spent in USAF R&D and Systems Management at Wright/Patterson AFB and the Pentagon from which he retired as a colonel in August 1970.

Married Ann Elizabeth Laird of Matawan, NJ on Feb. 22, 1945. They have three sons and four grandchildren. His post service career includes three years in New Zealand, working with the U.S. Antarctic Research Program, three years with an international engineering firm as a business development manager, four years as a general aviation manufacturing executive and a number of years, to the present, as a management consultant.

WAYNE C. CHAMBERS (ROCKY), was born on June 12, 1921 in Hamilton, KS. He joined the service in 1942 and served as a bombardier and later as a navigator during WWII. He flew 35 missions over Germany in a B-24.

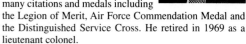

During his military career he was stationed at various "SAC" operations and in the mid-60s was assigned to the U.S. European Command in Germany. He was awarded many citations and medals including the Legion of Merit, Air Force Commendation Medal and the Distinguished Service Cross. He retired in 1969 as a lieutenant colonel.

Moved back to Eureka, KS and took over the family farm, raising registered Polled Herefords. In the 70s he served one term as Mayor of Eureka and in 1974 ran for the Kansas House of Representatives. He became highly involved in the community and the state through various organizations and was instrumental in promoting economic development for the area.

Married Lois M. Sturgeon in 1945 and had three daughters and 10 grandchildren. He passed away in Wichita, KS on Aug. 20, 1988.

ROBERT F. CHAPIN, was born Jan. 20, 1924 in Norwalk, OH. Enlisted Dec. 13, 1942 as pilot with 8th Air Force, 389th Bomb Group, 2nd Air Div., Eastern Cadet Program, Hethel Air Base, England. Completed 26 missions. His memorable experience was surviving combat.

Discharged Aug. 22, 1945 with the rank of second lieutenant. He received the Air Medal.

Has wife Troas, five children and 14 grandchildren. Retired - chairman of Chapin & Chapin Inc., heavy and highway construction firm.

BYRON D. CHAPMAN, was born on Aug. 15, 1923 on a rural route in Pond Creek, OK. He volunteered for the USAAC as a Radio Operator Gunner on Dec. 5, 1942.

He was stationed at Horsham St. Faith. Some of his memorable experiences were on his first mission to Bordeaux, France, they lost an engine because of mechanical failure as they were crossing the English Channel. They turned around and salvoed their bombs in the channel and

landed in Southern England. Their plane sustained heavy flak damage also at that time due to heavy anti-aircraft gun fire.

His awards and medals included the EAME Service Medal with four Bronze Battle Stars, Distinguished Flying Cross on July 26, 1944, Air Medal on April 7, 1944, and three Oak Leaf Clusters for Air Medal on May 10, 17, 24, 1944.

The name of their first plane was *Flying Circus*, he completed 31 missions. Was discharged on Sept. 30, 1945 with the rank of technical sergeant.

He married Mary Brien on Jan. 31, 1953, they have three daughters and five grandchildren.

OLIVER W. CHAPMAN, was born Oct. 24, 1921 in Waterloo, IA. He grew up in Phoenix, AZ. Joined the USAAC in November 1942 after trying to enlist from one coast to the other. He had worn glasses since the age of two and the Air Corps didn't like glasses. He finally got a waiver for navigator only and he wore glasses throughout his flying service.

Trained at San Marcos, TX Class 43-18. Commissioned second lieutenant, he joined his air crew in Colorado Springs. They picked up a new B-24H in Topeka, KS and flew the southern route across the Atlantic to GB as a replacement crew. Joined the 2nd Air Div., 492nd Bomb Group, 856th Sqdn. at N. Pickingham. He flew 25 missions with the 492nd before the group was disbanded due to the extreme losses in only 88 days.

In August 1944 the crew was sent with the 859th Sqdn. to the 801st Bomb Group (Carpetbaggers) at Harrington. This group was not a part of the 2nd Air Div. It was under the Composite Command. Shortly after arriving, the 801st Bomb Group was redesignated the 802nd Bomb Group, probably to conceal its activities and confuse the Huns.

Flew eight Carpetbagger missions (night single sorties) plus six tanker missions to supply gasoline to stalled forces at the Battle of the Bulge. Returned stateside in December 1944 with the rank first lieutenant.

Joined the Air Transport Command delivering C-46 aircraft to the South Pacific for the Ferry Command and the invasion of the Philippines. Discharged October 1945, he received the ETO with two stars, Air Medal with three Oak Leaf Clusters and the Distinguished Flying Cross.

He graduated from the University of Arizona in 1947 with a BS degree. Graduated from the American Institute for Foreign Trade in 1948. He married and has three children and five grandchildren. He had sales and management jobs with several major wood products corporations and in residential construction for 25 years and then owned two Taco Bells franchises for 16 years. He retired to SW Colorado in 1983. He enjoys traveling, golf and woodworking. In winter much of his time is spent removing snow at the 7800' elevation where he lives.

JAMES M. CHARLTON (CHARLIE), was born on March 2, 1923 in Davidson County, TN, as one of 12 children to Marsh and Lera Charlton. Was educated at Donelson High School, while working on his father's dairy. He entered the USAAF on Jan. 29, 1943 at Ft. Oglethorpe, GA.

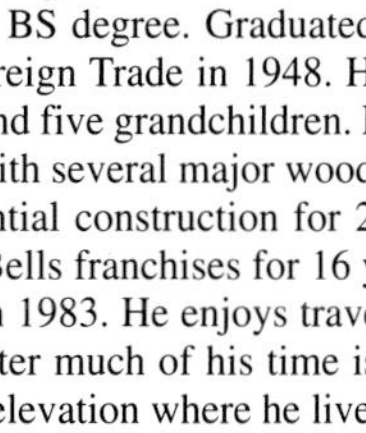
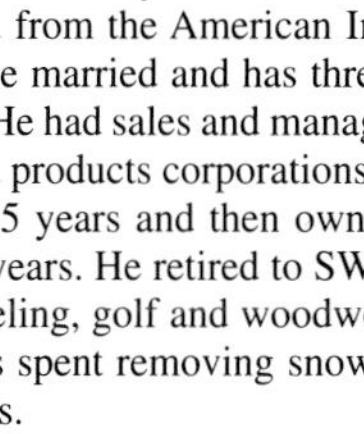

Received training at Miami Beach, FL; Gulfport, MS; Long Beach, CA, and Las Vegas, NV. Assigned as a B-24 engineer at Salt Lake and trained with Captain Hemrich's crew at Boise, ID. In May 1944 the crew flew a B-24 from Goose Bay Labrador to Nut's Corner, Ireland. They were attached to the 2nd Air Div., 458th Bomb Group at Horsham St. Faith near Norwich.

He flew 30 combat missions from May 25, 1944 to Nov. 30, 1944.

He received the Air Medal with four Oak Leak Clusters and the Distinguished Flying Cross. He was discharged in November 1945.

He and Gladys were married on June 9, 1947 in Nashville, TN. They have two sons, one daughter and six grandchildren.

Graduated from MTSU with a BS in 1951 at Murfreesboro, TN. He worked as a high school teacher, building contractor and computer draftsman. He retired in 1988.

FAY J. CHAUVIN, was born on May 16, 1919 in Montegut, LA an oil and sugar mill town. Drafted into the USAAC in June 1941 at Camp Shelby, MS; sent to MacDill Field in Tampa, FL with the 14th Recon Squad and trained as a bombardier.

In January 1942 he was sent to Barksdale Field, Shreveport, LA. The 14th Recon Squad was dissolved and a different squad was formed. From Barksdale he was sent as a staff sergeant bombardier to Ft. Myers, FL, Buckingham Field with Col. Haverson. Bombardiers had to be officers to be sent overseas, so he was sent to Drain Field, Lakeland, FL. There he flew as a bombardier on B-26 bombers (320th Bomb Group). On Sept. 14, 1942 he reported for duty at MacDill Field, Tampa, FL to the 21st Bomb Group. The slogan was "A Plane a Day in Tampa Bay."

He entered Aviation Cadet School, Nashville to Montgomery and graduated in Class 43-H. He was sent to Pilot School in Camden, SC. From Camden he was sent back to Nashville. Then he went to Gunnery School in Panama City, FL. He graduated Class 43-30 on July 27, 1943. He went to Selmon Field in Monroe, LA, graduated from Navigation School, Class 44-I on Jan. 15, 1944. He transferred to Roswell, NM and attended Bombardier School. He was sent to Lincoln, NE on April 14, 1944, then sent to Caspar, WY. He joined Liebrick crew in June 1944 at Casper, WY. A new 24-J was assigned to the crew in Topeka, KS.

On June 29, 1944, he navigated to Bangor, ME, Goose Bay, Iceland to Wales. He was sent to Shipdham, England. He joined the 68th Bomb Squad, 44th Bomb Group. He flew three missions with lead crews and 32 missions with Liebrick crew. He thought the three worst missions were his first missions, Aug. 8th 1944 to Hamburg, then Sept. 18, 1944, the low level mission to Best Holland (supplies for the Battle of the Bulge) and Kasselon on Oct. 7, 1944. His last mission was on Jan. 1, 1945.

He returned to the States in January 1945 on the *Queen Mary,* got married and then was sent to Ellington Field in Houston, TX. He was the assistant property officer of the base.

He was discharged in October 1945 at Camp Shelby, MS with the rank first lieutenant. He is retired and has five children and 12 grandchildren.

CARROLL WRIGHT CHEEK, was born on March 31, 1921 in Columbus, OH. He enlisted on Dec. 6, 1942 on Pearl Harbor night. He entered active duty on June 26, 1944 as an aviation cadet in the USAAC.

He was in combat with the 8th Air Force, 14th Combat Wing, 2nd Air Div., 392nd Bomb Group, 678th Sqdn. His recollections may be slightly altered by time, as exact dates are not available at this writing. He participated in air battles spanning late April 1944 until late October 1944. He flew 33 bomb missions as a lead pilot on latter missions.

Memorable experiences were numerous: The raids on Politz, Germany and surviving several waves of fighters. Hamburg on Aug. 6, 1944 suffering substantial battle damage, their bombardier was blinded and minor wounds to other crew members. The invasion on June 6, 1944, D-day, bombed ahead of troops. The Munich raids, Ruhr Valley and East Germany raids were especially costly in the loss of men and B-24s. The loss of comrades and friends are forever with him, especially the loss of the Edwin G. Clapper crew. Clapper radioed him, his buddy, for help while under attack. He could not turn around to help without endangering the lives of the other men in his squadron. He heard his final pleading as he was finished off.

The sight of his bombardier, Lt. Al Morse, with glass protruding from his head and eyes and witnessing the surgery removing the glass were very traumatic events. His memories include his thanks forever to the strength and support the English gave them in word and deed. The waves and salutes of the brave French Maquis as they received supplies during the night missions from the black, war-weary planes on missions to occupied Southern France.

The bombs crashing in London while riding in a cab and the rain of steel coming from the Hyde Park guns. The explosions of shell observed from a doorway of the Dorchester Hotel in London. His experiencing a buzz bomb overhead while visiting Buckingham on a Sunday morning and witnessing the direct hit on the Queen's Guards barracks. The Waterloo Station with all the little orphans or transplants with tears and identification tags. Having buddies (English kids) with them on Thanksgiving to feed and share with.

Listening to Glenn Miller in the Repair Hangar, sitting on ammunition boxes for seats. Praying with the Chaplain before and after missions. The great welcome the Red Cross gals gave them on return from a mission, especially Bertie Schmidt.

His awards include the Distinguished Flying Cross with one Oak Leaf Cluster, Air Medal with four Oak Leaf Clusters, several Battle Stars and the Group Presidential Citation. He has respect for those who died and those severely injured and qualified to wear the Purple Heart Medal.

Their mission to liberate Europe and defend Great Britain was critical to our freedom. He especially salutes the 757 casualties from the 392nd. Forever may their sacrifices be carved in the Granite of Time!

He was discharged in August 1945 with the rank of captain from the USAF.

He and Mabel have been married for 52 years. They have one son, Michael (an attorney) and two daughters, Susan Cheek Needler and Kathleen Cheek-Milby (professor of political science, Temple University, Tokyo, Japan). Susan has four children: Julie, Allyson, Lindsay and Michael. Kathleen has two children, James Dean and Nicholas.

Cheek is employed as Chairman and CEO of CWC Companies, Inc., an investment and management company. He serves as a director of several charitable organizations.

JAMES CHENAULT (JIM), was born in May 1924 at Long Beach, CA. He entered the Army in January 1943 at Fort MacArthur, CA. He graduated from Eastern Flying Training Command Class of 43-K at Freemen Field, Seymore, IN.

He crewed up as co-pilot on B-24 bombing crew. Phase trained with 489th Bomb Group at Wendover, UT. Joined 8th Air Force by way of southern route through South America and Africa. Completed 32 missions August 1944.

In process of transition to B-26 when European war ended. He separated from the Army in January 1947. Returned to the Army in November 1948 to make 126 trips to Berlin in C-54 on Berlin Airlift. Joined Strategic Air Command B-29 Group. Flew 32 missions during Korean War. He returned stateside and joined KC-97 Air Refueling Program at MacDill AFB, FL.

He was discharged from the Air Force in April 1952 with rank of captain.

GREGORY L. CHRIST, was born April 21, 1922 in Boston Run, PA. He enlisted in the USAAC Aug. 16, 1940. He was an aircraft armorer and aerial gunner.

He served with the 491st Bomb Group (H), 855th Bomb Sqdn. Locations and stations included Bolling Field, Washington, DC; Davis-Montham Field; Blyth; Medfield, U.K.; North Pickenham, U.K.

Memorable experiences: first mission south of Paris, they lost their first plane; their July 29, 1944 raid on Breman, instruments out, flak heavy, fighters, yet they had successful results.

Christ received the Distinguished Flying Cross, four Air Medals, four ETO Stars, plus several other ribbons.

Completed 31 missions and was discharged Sept. 12, 1945 with rank of technical sergeant.

Married Alice Ramage on June 18, 1955. They have no children. He is now retired and lives in Mahanoy City, PA.

H.H. CHRISTENSEN (CHRIS), was born on July 31, 1923 in Richfield, UT. He married Eleanor Brinton on Sept. 12, 1945. They have six children and 21 grandchildren. As a teenager he worked at the local airport in exchange for flying lessons. While still in high school he came in third out of 5,000 in competitive Civil Service examination and was appointed apprentice aircraft instrument mechanic.

He took Aviation Cadet examination two weeks after Pearl Harbor, the first day the age limit was lowered. Graduated as a reserve officer, second lieutenant, pilot, class 43C. Assigned as co-pilot to Bill Nading in Gerhart Provisional Group and crew, along with a new B-24D. Sent as a replacement to 93rd Bomb Group, Hardwick, England, but after two weeks he was transferred with airplane on June 25, 1943 to the new 389th Bomb Group, Hethel, England as an "experienced" crew. Flew Africa missions and the day after his 20th birthday survived Ploesti flying the last airplane across the Steaua Romana Refinery at Campina.

Promoted to pilot after returning to England and then squadron flight commander, captain (age 20) on Feb. 6, 1944. Completed combat on March 13, 1944 with four Air Medals and two Distinguished Flying Crosses. Appointed assistant group engineering officer and flew numerous test flights. Flew *Green Dragon* assembly aircraft many times. Was rated as maintenance engineering officer and engineering test pilot.

Transferred to Casper, WY and flew B-24 maintenance test flights until assigned as engineering test pilot in B-29 program at Albuquerque, NM. Flew many B-29 test flights, some more dangerous than combat.

After release from active duty, was assigned as engineering officer in Active Air Reserve and flew while studying engineering at the University of Utah, graduating in June 1949.

Career as an aeronautical engineer with General Electric in Automatic Flight Control Systems for 15 years and as a senior engineer with IBM, responsible for installation design and aircraft modifications for complex, special avionics systems.

He retired in February 1988 and has been involved with historical research for the 389th Bomb Group. Has lifelong participation in community and church activities.

EDWARD J. CHU, staff sergeant, tail gunner/armorer, was born on Oct. 23, 1925 in Gloversville, NY. He graduated from Gloversville High School in 1943. Volunteered for Aviation Cadet Program and entered the Air Force in early 1944.

Received basic training at Greensboro, NC; Aerial Gunnery School, Laredo, TX. Joined Lt. Gordon Brock's crew, training as tail gunner at March Field, CA. Assigned to 714th Bomb Sqdn., 448th Bomb Group (H), Seething, England. He flew 24 combat missions, the majority in B-24 Liberator, *My Buddie.*

He received the Air Medal with three Bronze Oak Leaf Clusters, EAME Campaign Medal with three Bronze Campaign Stars.

Returned to the USA in June 1945 and discharged in November 1945 at Rome AAF, Rome, NY.

Graduated in 1951 from Rensselaer Polytechnic Institute as chemical engineer. Employed as senior research engineer, National Gypsum Company, Buffalo, NY; last employment with Resistoflex Corporation, Roseland, NJ, as senior research engineer. He retired in 1989 as a plastics pro-

cess engineering manager. He holds six Teflon process patents.

Married Adelia (Dee) Slatt in 1969 and currently resides in Edinburg, NY.

HUBERT M. CHURCH, was born on Feb. 18, 1923 near Judsonia, AR. He joined the USAAC in December 1942 and was commissioned as a pilot at Pampa AFB, TX on Aug. 4, 1944.

At Casper, WY he received training as a B-24 co-pilot for replacement training units. He was assigned to the 458th Bomb Group, Norwich, England in February 1945.

About April 1945 he was asked to fly as a co-pilot for another co-pilot that was flying as first pilot on his first flight. The flight was routine until they returned onto final approach. They turned too soon, missing aligning with the runway. The first pilot yelled for a go-around procedure and pushed throttles forward. Then he began to do things the co-pilot did. The result was that they touched ground while Church was adjusting flaps and they were not on the runway. Looking at the airspeed indicator they were doing 155 mph. At that moment, the crew chief, acting as flight engineer, discovered the throttles had backed off because the first pilot had taken his hands off the throttles without locking them with friction locks. The crew chief shoved the throttles full forward and they bounced back into the air after rolling 2,000 feet on the ground.

In July 1945, they picked up a war-weary B-24 with 115 bomb symbols on its side and flew back to the USA via Wales, Iceland and Labrador with the original crew except its first pilot and navigator.

Discharged in September 1945, he received a civil engineering degree from the University of Kansas in 1948.

Church is married and they have four children. He retired from the Iowa Department of Transportation in 1988.

MICHAEL R. CIANO, was born on April 18, 1921 in Newark, NJ. He was drafted into the USAAC in June 1942. He served with the 702nd Bomb Sqdn, 445th Bomb Group, Tibenham AB, England; 989th Air Engineers, Kadena Air Base, Okinawa, B-29, April 1946-July 1947.

Other military locations and stations included Pope Field, NC; Biggs Field, TX; Casper AB, WY; Roswell AB, NM; Mogowan AB, Boise, ID. He participated in the European Air Offensive.

His memorable experiences include being shot down on April 12, 1944; POW in Stalag 17; Austria; 300 mile forced march and being liberated on May 3, 1945. He was discharged in November 1948 with rank of staff sergeant.

He is married, retired, and lives in Florida. They have no children.

CARL CITRON (CIT), was born on June 3, 1923 in Cleveland, OH. He attended Heidelberg College in Tiffin, OH in September 1941. Joined USAACR in the summer of 1942. They were told they could finish their college education before going on active duty.

Top row, L to R: Gibbs, Holtman, Hauger, Hershey, Johnson. Bottom row, L to R: Phillips, Derrick, Young, Lefever, Hicks and Brewer not in picture. (Courtesy of Raymond Hershy)

Entered active duty in February 1943 and spent two months in Biloxi, two months in Memphis, two months in San Antonio, and finally in the fall of 1943 he entered cadet training in San Antonio. He graduated with Wings (pilot) as a second lieutenant in June 1944.

He finally got into action in November 1944 at Attlebridge, B-24, 466th Group, 786th Sqdn. He completed 31 missions when the war ended. Flew home in June 1945 and was discharged in August 1945 with rank of first lieutenant. Received the Air Medal, five clusters-ETO.

Went back to college in September 1945 and graduated BSME in January 1948 from Case Institute of Technology in Cleveland, OH.

Spent one and one and a half years on the drawing board designing wire mill machinery, eight years selling power tools, and started his own business in New Jersey in February 1957. He sold the business in August 1991, but stayed on as general manager where he is presently employed in Oakland, NJ.

He married Georgia Reid on June 23, 1950. They have two boys, both engineers; one girl, who is a big time lawyer; and two grandchildren. They celebrated their 43rd wedding anniversary at the 466th Bomb Group Reunion in Colorado Springs in June 1993.

CARL W. CLADER, was born on April 11, 1916 in Wilkes Barre, PA. He graduated from Wheaton College in 1937 with a BA degree; received a Master of Science degree from Northwestern University in 1940. He began teaching biology and chemistry at New Trier Township High School, Winnetka, IL in September 1939.

Was sworn into the USAAC in June 1942 and entered as an aviation cadet in January 1943. He began pilot training in Camden, SC, followed by basic in Sumter, SC, and advanced in Albany, GA.

He was sent to Salt Lake City; then to Casper, WY as a B-24 co-pilot, where the 489th Bomb Group formed. He went to Wendover, UT, then Halesworth, England as education officer and co-pilot in the 846th Sqdn. He returned to Tucson, AZ and trained in B-29s.

Received the Air Medal and Oak Leaf Cluster, Victory Medal and the European Theater Medal. Was discharged in November 1945 with rank of first lieutenant, entered the Reserves and returned to New Trier High School, where he served as chairman of the science department, retiring in 1978.

Married Geraldine V. Benthey in August 1941 and has two daughters and two grandchildren. He enjoys playing tennis, and church work.

CLIMPSON B. CLAPP, was born on Nov. 20, 1922 in Indianapolis, IN. He enlisted in the USAAC in January 1943 as a navigator on B-24s.

Military locations included Hardwick, England with the 93rd Bomb Group, 328th Sqdn.

His memorable experiences included having a wing tip clipped by FW-190; and trolley mission over Germany.

Discharged in October 1945 with rank of second lieutenant. He has three children and six grandchildren. Retired, he enjoys hiking and bicycling.

ELMER W. CLAREY (BILL), was born on Oct. 25, 1916 in Omaha, NE. Joined the USAAC on Feb. 4, 1943 and served with the 492nd/467th Bomb Group, Rackheath, North Pickenham and Watton, England.

His memorable experiences include flying 31 missions as co-pilot; bailing out into the North Sea on May 29, 1944; rescued by Charles Halliday because Clarey couldn't get out of shroud lines.

Discharged on Oct. 10, 1945 with rank of captain. He received the Air Medal with three Oak Leaf Clusters, four European Campaign Stars, Victory in Europe Medal and the Distinguished Flying Cross.

He married his sweetheart (with the large black hat), Maxine, in 1946. He retired from United Airlines after 37 years as a flight dispatcher. He resides in Los Altos, CA. Belongs to the Caterpillar and Goldfish Club.

EDGAR D. CLARK, was born Oct. 1, 1916 in Dallas, TX. Since WWII has lived in Carthage, TX. Entered the USAAC in March 1942. First station was Tent City, Kelly Air Field, followed by Garner Field and then Kelly again. There were 18 from Kelly that volunteered for immediate overseas duty and specialized training. They were told that they would be commissioned before going overseas. How-

ever, they did not get their commissions until after training on RAF bases and successfully completing courses at the RAF School of Flying Control. They were then sent back to RAF bases to be certified flying control officers.

His first combat U.S. base was the 389th Bomb Group at Hethel. On Nov. 16, 1943, he was assigned to the 445th Bomb Group at Tibenham where he had a hard time securing the needed equipment and necessary repairs to the runways. They were still not ready when their first aircraft arrived.

On Dec. 23, 1943, he was transferred to the 453rd Bomb Group at Old Buckingham just before their aircraft arrived. After their first few missions he was transferred to the 44th Bomb Group at Shipdham. He later became the senior flying control officer and served there until they left for the States on June 15, 1945.

Flying Control not only contributed a very important part in the air war over Europe, but also, by their efforts, were able to save many lives of both the USAF and British air forces. It was a job of many duties and responsibilities. It wasn't always easy being a junior officer and operating under rules and regulations that were new to the Army Air Corps Field Commanders. The cooperation of the Flying Control at airbases, whether American or British, was remarkable and they could not have achieved what they did without it.

FORREST S. CLARK, was born on July 6, 1921 in Newark, NJ. He graduated from high school in Caldwell, NJ and from Rutgers University with an MA in English.

He joined the USAAC in October 1942. Assigned to basic training at Miami Beach and Radio School at Scott Field, IL. He graduated from Gunnery School at Harlingen, TX and was assigned to crew training at Clovis, NM and Biggs Field, El Paso, TX.

Memorable experiences: shooting at enemy fighters and parachuting from battle damaged B-24 Liberator.

Went to Europe in 1943, assigned to the 44th Bomb Group at Shipdham, England in September 1943. Flew combat missions from November 1943-April 1944. Shot down, went to Switzerland as an internee, escaped to France in December 1944 and came back to the USA in January 1945. He was assigned to Newark AFB and discharged at Fort Douglas, UT in October 1945 with rank of technical sergeant. He received the Air Medal with two Oak Leaf Clusters and the Purple Heart.

Married Ruth and has two children and two grandchildren. He retired after 36 years as a journalist and now does free lance writing.

GEORGE F. CLARK, was born on March 17, 1921 in Ames, IA. He joined the Army on Sept. 10, 1942 and received basic training at Camp Crowder, MO. Other locations were Buckley/Lowry Fields, CO; Harlingen/Laredo, TX; and Salt Lake City, UT. He flew with the 389th Bomb Group, 567th Sqdn., Hethal, England as a tail gunner B-24J.

On his 19th combat mission on July 25, 1944, over St. Lo, France, his plane was shot down by flak. He was captured by SS troops when he landed in parachute. The next several days he was transferred by foot and truck to different locations. On August 5 he was loaded on a train and on August 8, he and six others, escaped from the moving train, east of Chateau Thierry, France. He and fellow crew members walked and found a French farmer who helped and hid them until American Army was near. They made it back to Yank lines on August 28.

Sent back to England, then to the States, where he finished his service at Sioux City AB, IA, as a gunnery instructor. He was discharged Oct. 4, 1945 with rank of staff sergeant. He received the Purple Heart and Air Medal with two Oak Leaf Clusters.

He married in June 1945 and has four children. He farmed until his death on Aug. 16, 1978.

THAINE A. CLARK, was born on a farm in north central Kansas near the City of Concordia. He attended local grade and high schools and Kansas State College, graduating in 1940 with a degree in agriculture.

Inducted into the USAAC at Fort Riley on June 11, 1942 and went on active duty at the San Antonio Aviation Cadet Center. He trained at Ellington Field and Hondo Navigation School and was commissioned a second lieutenant on Aug. 5, 1943. He was assigned to the 448th Bomb Group being formed at Wendover, UT. The crew trained there and at Sioux City, IA, then flew their assigned plane to Seething, England via South America and Africa.

They flew 30 bombing missions from Dec. 30, 1943-

May 30, 1944. Memorable missions included the first to Ludwigshafen; the Berlin raid on March 8, 1944 and April 1, 1944, the fouled up one.

He spent the summer of 1944 in Northern Ireland at a base as a navigation instructor of incoming crews, and home at Gowen Field, ID, until the war ended.

Clark was awarded the Air Medal with three Oak Leaf Clusters; the Distinguished Flying Cross; and one Battle Star for the air battle of Europe. Was promoted to first lieutenant. He was discharged in September 1945 and was active in the Army Reserves until the fall of 1950.

In civilian life he taught agriculture courses in Kansas high schools and taught agriculture and biological science courses at Fort Hays, Kansas State University for 27 years, then retired in 1982.

He married Lucille Tibbetts in 1950 and they live in Hays, KS. They have one son, Kenneth, who is an attorney in Wichita and has five children.

WILLIAM K. CLARK, was born on May 25, 1925 in New Haven, CT. He enlisted in the USAAC in 1943. Graduated from Aircraft Armorers School, Buckley Field, Denver, CO; Aerial Gunners School, Laredo, TX. Received B-24 crew training at Gowen Field, Boise, ID and went overseas as replacement crew, 458th Bomb Group, 8th AF, Horsham St. Faith, England from Jan. 16-June 18, 1945.

Flew 19 missions, most at waist position. Returned to the USA and was assigned to separation center at Sioux Falls, SD, with discharge on Nov. 7, 1945 with rank of staff sergeant. He received the Air Medal with two Oak Leaf Clusters, Good Conduct Medal, and Campaign Medal with three stars.

Memorable experience: three of them were on their aircraft preparing for a mission when the plane was struck by bullets accidentally discharged from a gun on a nearby plane. They had a 5,000 lb. bomb load and a full complement of gasoline. In a panic they left the aircraft, and after several harrowing minutes, the plane blew up. This occurred on the morning of March 14, 1945 at Horsham St. Faith.

He married Jean Ruffer in 1950 and they have one son, two daughters, and six grandchildren. He worked for the New Departure Division of General Motors Corp. in Meriden and Briston, CT in the personnel department for 30 years. He is currently retired.

GEORGE MICHAEL CLEARY, was born on Jan. 20, 1920 in Taunton, MA. He joined the USAF on Aug. 30, 1942 as a radio operator and top gunner. Military locations included Biggs Field, El Paso, TX, and Norwich, England.

His memorable experiences included their first raid over Berlin; his 25th mission, plane on fire and crash landing after going over White Cliffs of Dover.

He was discharged on Sept. 14, 1946 with rank of technical sergeant. He received the Good Conduct Medal, Air Force Medal with three Oak Leaf Clusters, Silver Star and ETO Medal.

Cleary and his wife have three children, five grandchildren, and one great-granddaughter.

He is retired from government computer and resides in Lakeshore, MS.

CHARLES T. CLEATON, was born on Nov. 30, 1921 in Portsmouth, VA. They moved to Cleveland, OH in 1923. He enlisted in the USAAC on Jan. 20, 1942 and was stationed at Santa Ana and King City, CA; and Albuquerque, NM. Was commissioned in March 1943 and sent to Boise and Pocatello, ID.

Off to Hardwick, England in July 1943 as a bombardier and radar operator in the 93rd Bomb Group, 329th Sqdn. Flew 30 missions over Europe, a few of which were Berlin,

Paris, Oslo, Vegesack, Rjukan, Bremen, Emden, and Alencon, the most memorable one being D-day, June 6, 1944.

He was awarded the Distinguished Flying Cross with Oak Leaf, Air Medal with four Oak Leaf Clusters, European Theater Operation with two Battle Stars.

Returned to Boca Raton, FL in July 1944 and instructed radar. Was discharged on Sept. 20, 1945 with the rank of captain.

Married for 46 years and has three children, six grandchildren, and one great-grandchild so far!

He retired in 1987 and enjoys playing bridge, cruising, and spending time with his family.

JOHN W. CLERKIN, was born on Jan. 28, 1919 in North Vernon, IN. He entered the armed services on April 2, 1941 in the 139th Field Artillery, Cyclone Division. Transferred to Air Force as aviation cadet in 1942. He was commissioned as a navigator at San Marcos, TX.

Joined Russ Willer and crew for training at Clovis, NM; Salt Lake City and Alamagordo, NM. Went overseas with the 786th Sqdn., 466th Bomb Group. Flew 30 missions as a lead crew, some of which were memorable. On first mission had maps shattered by flak, wire to Gee Box was cut as if by a knife. Chest parachute was riddled. They always carried a couple of spare chutes after that. They had one mission just across the Channel and lost three engines. Made a crash landing at a fighter field near Dover. One mission was flown at 5,000 feet. They took out a bridge over the Loire River just before Patton's breakout.

Stayed on as assistant group navigator until his marriage in Norwich to Hannah Angland, an Irish lass from Cork, on Nov. 8, 1944. He returned to Indiana where he had several jobs.

Was elected county auditor and retired in 1984 from the Indiana State Board of Accounts. He still prepares income tax returns.

He and Hannah had five children: Ann Marie, high school teacher, deceased 1967; John J., deceased 1947 as an infant; Maureen, grade school principal in Lexington, KY; Dennis and Jerry, professional bridge players. They have one granddaughter, Amanda, a student at Indiana University.

HOWARD CLEVELAND, was born on July 18, 1918 in Vestal, NY. Enlisted in the USAAF Cadet Program in November 1942. Was commissioned a navigator at Selman Field, LA and joined the Bill MacFarland crew at Peterson Field, CO and Mt. Home, ID for B-24 OTU.

In July 1944 he flew a new B-24 by the northern route to Valley, Wales; then on to the 330th Bomb Sqdn., 93rd Bomb Group at Hardwick. He flew the first of 35 missions over Germany on Sept. 10, 1944 and the last on Feb. 25, 1945. He remembers well the tremendous effort of Dec. 24 and 25, 1944 when they flew in support of the troops in the Battle of the Bulge.

Returned on March 30, 1945 via C-54 from Prestwick, Scotland. After R&R at Atlantic City he was sent to Ellington Field, TX for refresher and assignment to B-29s in the Pacific. It never happened. Japan surrendered in August 1945 and he was discharged in October 1945.

Cleveland was recalled in October 1949 for the Korean War and spent the next three and a half years training navigators at Ellington Field, TX. He decided to stay with the USAF and spent the rest of his military career as a navigator and management engineer.

Retired in 1973 and lives in Germantown, TN with his wife of 52 years.

WILBUR LEE CLINGAN (WIB), was born on Aug. 4, 1920 in Springfield, MO. He enlisted in the USAAC on Jan. 2, 1942. He completed the Aviation Cadet Program and became a pilot with the 453rd Bomb Group, from Pocatello, ID until disbandment of the group.

Participated in action in Air Offensive Europe, Northern France, Normandy, Rhineland, Central Europe and Ardennes. Flew 30 missions including Berlin, Hamm, Hamburg, D-day, Wessel, etc.

Received the Distinguished Flying Cross with two Oak Leaf Clusters and the Air Medal with three Oak Leaf Clusters. Retired from the Air Corps Reserves on Aug. 4, 1980 with rank of colonel.

Married to Diana Booth and has daughter, Pamela, son, Jeffry, and four grandchildren. He is retired and active in the 2nd Air Division Association and the 453rd Bomb Group Association.

DONALD K. CLOVER, was born on Nov. 30, 1919 in Woodland, CA and enlisted in the USAAC on Sept. 1, 1941. Military locations and stations included Lubbock, TX, pilot class 43-C, Arizona, Kansas, and Wendling, England. He participated in 22 bombing missions with the 576th Sqdn., 393 Bomb Group, September 1943 to March 18, 1944.

Memorable experiences were the bombing missions over Germany, France, and Norway. He was a POW for 14 months.

Received the Air Medal with three Oak Leaf Clusters, Purple Heart and Presidential Unit Citation. He was discharged from the Air Corps Reserves in 1955 with rank of captain.

He married Anne Campoy on Sept. 1, 1946, they have three children and four grandchildren.

Retired, he resides in Woodland, CA.

EMIL CMAYLO (SMILEY), was born on July 4, 1918 in Akron, OH and was raised on a farm in Durhamville, NY. Following high school graduation he worked at Crucible Steele Company, Syracuse, NY.

Enlisted in the USAAC on May 23, 1941. Received basic training, followed by Armament School at Lawson Field, Fort Benning, GA, where he made sergeant. Other military assignments included Wendover, UT; Great Bend, KS; and Davis-Monthan Field, AZ. He arrived in England on April 21, 1944 with the 489th Bomb Group. Returned on Dec. 12, 1944 and discharged with rank of staff sergeant.

Married on June 7, 1947 and fathered three boys and three girls. Retired from Oneida Ltd. Silversmiths after 34 years, to tend his little farm and do more hunting and fishing.

Recalls with great pleasure, friends made during his service years. He contacted some after joining the 2nd Air Division Association.

Emil died of lung cancer on Oct. 18, 1988, survived by his wife, three sons, one daughter and seven grandchildren.

VICTOR EDWARD COCHRAN, was born in Sullivan County, MO and enlisted in the USAF in June 1942. He was a B-24 pilot, 489th Bomb Group, 2nd Division.

Military locations and stations included Biggs Field, El Paso, TX; Tulsa, OK; Independence, KS. He left from Topeka for Halesworth, England in May 1944. Flew 16 missions over Germany. Went down on his 16th mission and was interned in Sweden, then returned to the States for additional training.

He received the Air Medal, two stars, and European Theater Occupation Medal. Discharged on Sept. 13, 1945 with rank of first lieutenant.

Married Betty Stutler in December 1941. Their children are Vicky, David, and Martha. He is a retired college professor and farmer and loves big game hunting.

IRWIN B. COHEN, was born on March 23, 1922 in Philadelphia, PA. He entered the Aviation Cadet Program on March 5, 1943 and graduated from Victorville, CA Bombardier Class as second lieutenant.

Trained as bombardier at Blythe Air Base; Davis-Monthon and Langley Field, VA in B-24. He flew with Ed Appel to England and flew combat from February to September 1944. He was lead bombardier on 15 missions. Returned to the States as instructor at Midland, TX and Big Spring, TX.

Received two Distinguished Flying Crosses and five Air Medals, plus other ribbons. Was discharged in March 1945 with rank of first lieutenant.

Married Jan. 30, 1943 to Ann Rae Sommers, they have two children and four grandchildren. He is retired and lives in Boca Raton, FL.

SEYMOUR COHEN, was born on Sept. 19, 1916 in New York, NY. He enlisted in the Army Air Force on Aug. 6, 1941 and served with the 453rd Bomb Group, 733rd Bomb Sqdn.

Military locations included Camp Wheeler, GA; Kelly Field, TX; Ellington Field, TX; Midland, TX; Hondo, TX; Boise, ID; Pocatello, ID; March Field, CA; Old Buckingham, England; Boca Raton, FL; Langley Field, VA; Victorville, CA; and Yuma, AZ.

Participated in battles in Germany and occupied Europe, and the Normandy Invasion. He received the Distinguished Flying Cross, Air Medal with three Oak Leaf Clusters and three Battle Stars. He was discharged on Nov. 29, 1945 with rank of first lieutenant.

He is married and has three daughters and five grandchildren. He is a retired attorney and resides in Fairlawn, NJ.

ROYCE V. COLBY, was born on March 21, 1924 in Terril, IA. He graduated from Jackson, Minnesota High School in June 1942. Worked for the FBI, Washington, DC, before entering the USAAC Cadet Program on Sept. 15, 1943.

When the cadet program was discontinued, he was sent to gunnery training, Harlingen, TX AFB. Assigned to J.K. Wenzel crew for flight training, Casper, WY; then to England as replacements in 8th Air Force. Flew 27 combat missions with 491st Bomb Group (H).

Survived the Misburg mission on Nov. 26, 1944 by bailing out of damaged bomber; landed in friendly territory which had been liberated the previous day. Completed remainder of missions as radio operator. When hostilities ended in Europe, the crew flew back to the States and furlough. Reported to Santa Ana AFB for staging B-29 training. When hostilities ended in the Pacific, he was discharged on Oct. 15, 1945 with the rank of tech sergeant.

Received the Air Medal with three Oak Leaf Clusters, Purple Heart, Good Conduct Medal, European Medal with one Star; Victory Medal and Presidential Unit Citation.

After earning a BS degree from the University of Minnesota, he returned to the FBI with service in Dallas, TX; New York, NY; and Washington, DC. He retired in 1976 after 32 and a half years as a government agent. He now resides in North Carolina with his wife, Jeanette. They have five children and eight grandchildren.

HOWARD W. COLE, was born on June 23, 1922 in Mission, TX. He entered the USAAC in March 1942 as aviation cadet. After completing Gunnery School at Fort Meyers, FL and navigation training at Hondo, TX, he was commissioned a second lieutenant in June 1943.

Assigned to 735th Sqdn., 453rd Bomb Group, using B-24 type aircraft. After operational training at Pocatello, ID and March Field, CA, the group, including planes, went overseas to Old Buckingham at Attleborough, England. After 30 combat missions over Europe, he flew 14 additional missions with Col. Bernt Balchen's unit dropping supplies/agents to the Norwegian Underground.

Returning to the States, he flew with the Ferry Command delivering A-26s to Burma, then with the Air Transport Command from Travis AFB to the Philippines. He graduated from Meteorology School at Chanute AFB, IL. Was assigned as a weather forecaster the latter 17 years of service with assignments at Brooks AFB, TX; Albrook Field; Canal

Zone; and Patrick AFB, FL. He was weather reconnaissance officer at Yokota Field, Japan during the Korean conflict including typhoon reconnaissance using WB-29 aircraft, Reese AFB, TX; Lajes Field, Azores and Kelly AFB, TX.

Retired in July 1964 with the rank lieutenant colonel. Decorations include the Distinguished Flying Cross, Air Medal with five Oak Leaf Clusters, ETO Medal with two Battle Stars, Certificate for Meritorious Service in WWII, Air Force Commendation Medal, Service Ribbons for Rhineland, Ardennes-Alsace and Korea.

After retirement he taught school 15 years and worked as operations manager with Rural Water Supply Corporation for eight years. He retired at age 65, and resides in Leakey, TX.

Married Vera Kathryn Hawkinson on May 19, 1946, they have three daughters, four granddaughters and two grandsons.

LEONARD T. COLE, was born on May 8, 1918 in Jonesboro, AR and was raised in Missouri. He entered service at Jefferson Barracks, MO on Dec. 22, 1942. Completed basic training at Clearwater, FL and joined 26th Airdrome Sqdn. at Kearney, NE in January 1943. His squadron was a totally mobile unit designed as a forward operating unit attached to the 100th Bomb Group. The squadron was disbanded at Scott Field, IL in September 1943.

Volunteered for a bomber group being formed at Pocatello, ID. Completed training at March Field, CA and traveled to England on the *Queen Elizabeth.* Returned to the States in May 1945 and was discharged in October 1945 at Scott Field, IL.

Re-enlisted in the USAAC on Aug. 22, 1947 and served in Japan, Germany, Tripoli, Lybia, Taiwan, Philippines, and Vietnam. He had several Stateside assignments, the last being Homestead AFB, FL with the 31st TFW.

He was a member of the 453rd Bomb Group, 735th Sqdn. He retired from the USAF on July 1, 1974 with rank of chief master sergeant.

Married his high school sweetheart, Helen Elder, in November 1937. They have three sons, five grandchildren, and two great-grandchildren.

WILLIAM C. COLEMAN, was born on July 5, 1921 in Detroit, MI. He enlisted in the USAAC as aviation cadet, graduating in Class 44-10 at Ellington Field, TX as a flight navigator.

He was assigned to the 458th Bomb Group at Harsham/St. Faith, Norwich, England. Completed 13 missions as wing navigator with 752nd Sqdn. and 10 missions as lead navigator in the 755th Sqdn. He returned to the States and was assigned to the Air Transport Command at Casablanca, Morrocco.

Coleman received the Air Medal with two Oak Leaf Clusters and three Battle Stars. He was discharged on Oct. 9, 1946 with rank of first lieutenant (captain, Reserves).

Retired from Ford Motor Company after 40 years. He has a marvelous wife, Gerry; one ex-Marine brother; four children; eight grandchildren; and seven great-grandchildren. They reside in Green Valley, AZ.

Enjoys RV travel and has been in every state and still exploring this great country. He is very proud to have been associated with the great airmen of the 8th Air Force and to have served his country.

WILLIAM E. COLEMAN, was born on Oct. 6, 1922 in Johnson City, TN and enlisted in the Army Air Force in June 1942. He served with the 445th Bomb Group (H), combat in 703rd and 702nd Sqdns.

Military locations included various cadet training bases; graduated from pilot training at Columbus, MS, Class 45-E.

He participated in air battles of Western Europe from Tidenham Air Base. He was a B-24 pilot from January-May 1944.

His memorable experience was as described in an article, *English Channel Incident,* in the archives of 2nd Air Division Library in Norwich, England.

Received the Distinguished Flying Cross and four Air Medals. Was discharged in September 1945 with rank of first lieutenant, active duty and captain in Reserves.

Married and has four sons and nine grandchildren.

After working 43 years in the subcontracting business, having his own business for the last 27 years, he retired on Oct. 19, 1987 at age 65. He worked in advertising for about three years and now works as a full time "retiree" in the hardware business. As a hobby he enjoys watching the major divisions of NASCAR racing, a little golf and yard work.

HOMER L. COLEY, was born in Oklahoma and enlisted in the USAAF on Feb. 3, 1943 at Fort Sill, OK. Military locations included Sheppard Field, TX; Needles AFB, CA; Fresno AFB, CA; Brise Norton AFB, England; Pushan AFB, Korea; Mountain Home AFB, ID; Tolle Ordnance Depot, UT; Alexander AFB, LA; Otis AFA, MA; three tours to Vietnam with TAC; George AFB, CA; Myrtle Beach AFB, SC. He retired from Myrtle Beach July 1, 1973 with rank of technical sergeant.

Received the Bronze Star with two Oak Leaf Clusters. Also the Air Force Citation to accompany the Bronze Star Medal with V Device, which reads in part: "T/SGT Homer L. Coley distinguished himself by heroism as weapons supervisor when he drove through hostile fire to return his isolated comrades to safety."

Coley has resided in Oklahoma since 1963.

GEORGE M. COLLAR, was born on Nov. 24, 1917 in Jackson, MI. He joined the USAAF on June 2, 1942 as private in Enlisted Reserve. He was called to active duty as cadet on Jan. 5, 1943. He graduated as bombardier at Big Spring, TX in class of 43-18. Assigned to crew of 2nd Lt. Reginald Miner to train in B-24s at Casper, WY and Pueblo, CO. Flew overseas from Goose Bay to England via Iceland in May 1944.

Assigned to 445th Bomb Group at Tibenham, he flew his first mission on June 29, 1944. Shot down on famous Kassel mission of Sept. 27, 1944 while flying his 29th mission. Was captured and ended up at Stalag Luft I. He was liberated by the Russian army on May 1, 1945.

Received the Distinguished Flying Cross, four Air Medals, and three European Theatre Campaign Stars. He belongs to the American Ex-POWs, 8th Air Force Historical Society, 2nd Air Division Association, and is a director on the board of the Kassel Mission Memorial Association.

Married Florence Kaminski in July 1945, and they have two sons and five grandchildren. He is now retired as forging engineer and die designer, and resides in Tiffin, OH.

JOHN D. COLLINS, was born on Jan. 23, 1924 in Pine Bluff, AR. He married Evon Arledge in 1947, and they have two daughters, one son and two grandchildren.

Enlisted in the USAAC on Dec. 10, 1942. Received

basic training at Sheppard AFB, TX. He graduated from Gunnery School at Laredo, TX and B-24 AM School at Keesler Field, MS. He joined crew at Salt Lake City, UT in 1943 and took overseas training at Peterson Field, CO. Went overseas via southern route to Rackheath, England in 1944. Served as nose gunner on *Witchcraft,* a B-24, 790th Bomb Sqdn., 467th Bomb Group, 2nd Air Div. Volunteered a makeup mission on *Perils of Pauline* on Aug. 5, 1944, which was shot down. He successfully bailed out but was captured by Germans. Incarcerated at Stalag IV. He was a prisoner of war for nine months.

Returned to the States after liberation and was honorably discharged at Lackland AFB, TX in 1945. Re-enlisted in 1946 and retired as master sergeant in 1963.

Employed at National Aeronautics and Space Administration, Lyndon B. Johnson Space Center, Houston, TX in 1964 as aircraft maintenance inspector and flight engineer on various research and development aircraft. He retired in 1979.

RICHARD J. COMEY, was born on Nov. 18, 1919 in Cambridge, MA and enlisted in the USAC in October 1941. He was a pilot, flight leader, with the 66th Sqdn., 44th Bomb Group. Military locations included SEAFTC, England, Africa, Scotland, B-24 Training Command, and Boston Flight Service. He participated in battles in Britain, Sicily, Ploesti, Italy, and Europe. He flew 25 heavy bomb missions.

Received the Distinguished Flying Cross with two Oak Leaf Clusters, Air Medal with three Oak Leaf Clusters. He was discharged in December 1946 with rank of major.

Comey and wife, Charlotte, have three sons, Jack, David, and Bob. Richard is retired, living in Vermont, and is still able to ski, play tennis, hike and bike.

GEORGE W. CONDRY, was born on Sept. 29, 1920 in Providence, RI. He enlisted in the Aviation Cadet Program on Sept. 18, 1942, graduated Class of 44A in January 1944.

Assigned to crew FB333-AJ-24 as pilot, 8th Air Force, 467th Bomb Group, 789th Sqdn., Rackheath, England. Completed 35th mission on Dec. 29, 1944. Stayed with the group as assistant group operations officer until the war in Europe ended.

Received the Distinguished Flying Cross, Air Medal with six clusters, World War II Medal, American Campaign Medal, EAME Campaign Medal, and Air Force Reserve Medals.

Stayed in Reserves with retirement on Sept. 29, 1980. Served two years as CO of a reserve squadron. He attained the rank of lieutenant colonel, USAF, RET.

Married 29 years to his first wife who died in 1975. They raised two daughters. He has one grandson, Scott.

Has been married to his present wife since 1977. Now retired and living in Massachusetts. He is a member of the 2nd Air Division Association, 8th Air Force Historical Society, and Air Force Association. He has attended many 2nd Air Division Association conventions.

WILLIS G. CONKLE, was born on July 23, 1924 in Rogers, OH and entered the service on Nov. 14, 1943 at Fort Hayes, OH. Basic training was spent at Jefferson Barracks,

MO. After basics he was sent to Madison, WI for radio training, then went to Laredo, TX for Gunnery School. After that he was sent to Pueblo, CO for overseas training.

On arrival overseas he was assigned to the 448th Bomb Group, 715th Bomb Sqdn. Due to arrival overseas near the end of the war, they flew only two missions. One was to Bourdeaux, France and one to Salzburg, Germany. He returned to the States for reassignment to the Pacific Theater but the war ended so he was not sent.

Received the European-African-Middle East Medal, World War II Victory Medal and American Campaign Medal. He was discharged from Camp Carson, CO on March 6, 1946 with rank of sergeant.

Married Doris Olson on May 25, 1946. Married Margaret Shimek on Jan. 31, 1959. He has one daughter, three sons, two grandchildren and one great-grandchild.

He retired as a maintenance engineer from Carnation Company of Los Angeles, CA in 1989.

WALTER T. CONNEELY, was born on Nov. 29, 1920 in Sterling, IL. He enlisted in the USAAC on Dec. 8, 1941. Attended Airplane Mechanics School. As an aviation cadet, completed flight training and was commissioned on July 5, 1943 as second lieutenant bombardier, San Angelo, TX.

He was one of original crews of newly formed 453rd Bomb Group (B-24s), June 1943; combat ready, November 1943. They flew the southern route, travelling 10,000 miles to come 2,800 miles (single plane formation all the way) to England to join the 8th Air Force. They flew 16 missions, shot down by German Lufwaffe as they led the 8th Air Force on May 8, 1944. Interned at Stalag Luft #3. Eleven months later was liberated by Gen. George Patton Jr. on April 29, 1945 at Moosburg, Germany.

Went back to civilian life in September 1945. Formed the Conneely Brokerage Company. Retired in September 1986.

Married Patricia Curran on July 31, 1945. They have a daughter, Kim, and two grandchildren, Ben and Brianna.

LEE R. CONNER (LEROY), was born in October 1921 in Bonham, TX. He enlisted from Phoenix, AZ as Air Corps Cadet in May 1942. He was assigned to San Antonio, Texas Gulf Coast Training Command in October 1942. Graduated as a two-engine pilot in August 1943, Class 43H, at Altus, OK. Trained as pilot in B-24s at Liberal, KS and Tucson, AZ.

Flew B-24, Do-Bunny, to Wales via Goose Bay and Meeks Field. Flew his first mission on D-day, June 6, 1944. Completed 35 missions. Returned Stateside in December and in January 1945 was assigned as link trainer officer at Tarrant Field, Ft. Worth, TX.

Discharged in August 1945 with rank of first lieutenant. Received the Distinguished Flying Cross and five Air Medals.

Married Doris Christianson in December 1944. They have one son, two daughters and seven grandchildren. Worked in Minneapolis Air Route Traffic Control Center from February 1946 as controller, watch supervisor, area officer and military liaison officer until retiring in May 1977.

JAMES E. CONOLE, was born on Feb. 13, 1923 in Bennington, VT. He was raised on several dairy and trucking farms in New Hampshire and Maine. Attended schools in these states, plus his senior year at Dorchester High School.

He never lived with his mother and father, as his father contacted TB during WWI. At age 17, found his mother in Boston, MA and his father in a TB hospital in Rutland, MA, wanted to join the RCAF, answer was no. Was drafted at age 18. He told his mother they would be at war by December 1941. Joined USAAC Oct. 30, 1941.

Graduated from Aerial Gunnery School, Las Vegas, NV. Went up the ranks to sergeant, then went to cadet flying as flying sergeant. Since age seven, he had wanted to fly.

Stationed at different air bases including submarine patrol off Florida. He served in WWII with 8th Air Force (B-17s and B-24s) as armor/gunner. Shot down twice (in the English Channel and the jungles) and escaped the enemies, Germans and Japs.

Wounded on Nov. 26, 1943 over Bremen. Two-thirds of his body was frozen, 52 below zero, but he refused to turn back and disregarded his life to save the crew. Sent to a field hospital in England. He also served six or eight months in European Theater Occupation in 1943 and returned for invasion on D-day on June 6th. He was shot down a second time in the jungles of Burma and escaped the Japs. Wounded three times. Went to APT-CBI and flew the Hump supplies into China. Was attached to Merrill's Marauders and also the 13th and 14th Airborne as they dropped paratroopers between American and British troops to cut off Japs from taking Rangoon, Burma.

Was with the Flying Tigers, 88th Fighter Sqdn. and was wounded twice more for a total of five times. He was under the loud speaker waiting to go on B-29s when the war ended. He did occupation duties in CBI then, and Germany in 1946-1947. In 1947 he went to recruiting officers in Boston and Quincy, MA.

Married Joan C. O'Brien on Feb. 13, 1960, they have two daughters and five grandchildren.

His civilian job trade was A/R machinist and tool and die maker. He had to retire in 1976, at age 53, because of wounds and injuries received in WWII.

He belongs to five veterans' organizations. He and his wife reside in Kissimmee, FL.

JOHN B. CONRAD, was born on Aug. 23, 1920 in Dry Ridge, KY. He majored in business administration at the University of Kentucky and entered the Army Air Forces as an aviation cadet. He was commissioned as second lieutenant navigator on Oct. 16, 1943 at Monroe, LA.

He attended Pathfinder School at Langley Field, VA

and 482nd Bomb Group (PFF) at Alconbury, England. Assigned to the 2nd Bomb (later Air) Division, 8th Air Force, he flew a tour of 28 missions (three with the 44th Bomb Group and 25 with the 392nd Bomb Group). His mission lead credits include: three division leads, 10 wing leads, seven group leads, and seven deputy group leads.

Married Wanda E. McGill in 1945. They have three children and seven grandchildren. He built a career in the consultation and administration of employer-provided employee benefit plans (health, welfare and pension plans), retiring in 1987 at Lexington, KY as president of Professional Administrators Limited, a firm of 150 employees.

Conrad is a member of the Presbyterian Church, 8th Air Force Historical Society, Kentucky Historical Society, University of Kentucky Alumni Association, Sons of Confederate Veterans and Sons of the American Revolution.

He has been active in the affairs of the 2nd Air Division Association, 8th Air Force, since 1982. He has served as the 392nd Bomb Group vice-president, as a member of the Association's Executive Committee, as executive vice-president 1991-1992, as president 1992-1993 and again as president 1993-1994.

ROBERT E. CONRAD JR., was born on March 4, 1925 in Sunbury, PA. He enlisted in the Armed Forces on April 23, 1943 and was sent to Fort Riley, KS to complete 15 weeks basic training in Armored Infantry. Transferred to AAF Cadet Program in August 1944 and graduated on July 1, 1945 as second lieutenant navigator (childhood goal) at San Marcos, TX.

He further trained as navigator at Westover Field, MA and was assigned to B-24 crew. Their crew went to England in September 1944 via the *Mauretania,* and they were assigned to the 445th Bomb Group, 8th AAF. Completed tour of 30 missions (last half of them on lead crew) between October 1944 and April 1945.

Conrad returned to the USA in June 1945 and signed up for indefinite service; transferred to standby reserve and later to inactive reserve.

Received the Distinguished Flying Cross, Air Medal with four Oak Leaf Clusters, and ETO Ribbon with three Battle Stars. He was promoted to captain in July 1955 and transferred to Retired Reserve in March 1962.

Married Luella Yoder on Sept. 10, 1949, they have four children and eight grandchildren.

Received his BSME at Bucknell University in February 1950. Worked at Lycoming Division of Avco Corp., Bell Aircraft Corp., and GTE Sylvania Electronic Systems Division, retiring in March 1985. He resides in Williamsport, PA.

WARREN P. CONRAD, was born Jan. 2, 1923, Williamsport, PA and moved to Keokuk, IA at age 13. Enlisted June 1942 as aviation cadet. Received commission as second lieutenant upon completion of pilot training Class 43-I.

Attended B-24 transition training, Carswell AFB, TX. Assigned crew at Salt Lake City, UT, December 1943. Trained Tucson, AZ and as crew #86 with 489th Bomb Group at Wendover, UT. Group activated for overseas April 1944. Flew crew assigned aircraft to the UK by southern route. Stationed at Halesworth, completed combat tour of 32 missions and returned to USA September 1944.

Attended Communications School; served as communications officer Mountain Home AFB until separated November 1944. Followed aviation career with FAA first as traffic controller then as systems inspection pilot, retiring in 1978. He received the Distinguished Flying Cross and the Air Medal with three clusters. Concurrently served in Air National Guard units retiring as command pilot and major with 22 years of service.

Lived for most part in Ft. Worth, TX. Has a wife, three sons and five grandchildren.

THOMAS C. CONROY, was born on May 17, 1915 in Cochise County, AZ. Graduated with BS in 1937 from University of Arizona. Entered the Army on Aug. 16, 1940 at Fort Lewis, WA. Transferred to USAAC Flight School, Victorville, CA and graduated in September 1942.

He was assigned to the 566th Sqdn., 389th Bomb Group, 2nd Air Div., A/C 42-40691. *Fightin' Sam* crew: Capt. Conroy, pilot; 2nd Lt. Harley B. Mason, co-pilot; 2nd Lt. Harold Roodman, N; 1st Lt. Albert C. Ormsbee Jr., B; T/Sgt. Walter E. Taylor, R; T/Sgt. Robert W. McNair, AR; T/Sgt. Rudolph O. Anchondo, E; S/Sgt. Doyle L. Kirkland, AE; S/Sgt. Charles E. White, G; S/Sgt. Victor E. Scollin Jr., AG; M/Sgt. William H. Latta, line chief. All participated in the Ploesti raid.

Conroy was assigned to Sqdn. CO, 566th Sqdn., 389th Bomb Group, 2nd Air Div. Ops; 8th Air Force, Ops; USSAFE Ops; CO, 97th Airdrome Sqdn., Wiesbaden Air Field, Germany.

Exchange student, Naval General Line School, Newport, RI. Ch. Proof Test Div., Air Prov. Grnd. Cmd, Elgin AFB, FL; AF member, joint advanced study committee, JVS, Pentagon. Air University,Class of 1955; CO, 45th Ftr/Bomber Wing, Misawa AB, Japan.

Colonel Conroy died on Sept. 8, 1956 in flame-out of F-860 off Pacific Coast of Honshu, Japan. Awarded Legion of Merit, Distinguished Flying Cross with two Oak Leaf Clusters, Air Medal with three Oak Leaf Clusters, Silver Star and French Croix de Guerre.

DONALD R. CONWAY, was born on Feb. 6, 1923 in Lima, Peru. He was raised in San Francisco, CA.

He entered the USAAC on Dec. 1, 1942 from San Diego. Received basic training in Clearwater, FL. Attended Aircraft Mechanical School in Boston; Engine School in

Clifton, NJ; Turbo Supercharger School in Salt Lake City. Sent to Horsham St. Faith with the 458th Bomb Group, entered Gunnery School and became a spare gunner. Completed 30 missions and was discharged on June 5, 1945 and returned to San Diego.

Met and married Claire Hollobaugh while both were students at San Diego State College. Married for 45 years. They have five children, three boys and two girls. No grandchildren.

Conway earned a BA degree from the University of California at Berkeley; an MA degree from Middlebury College in Vermont and further graduate studies at International University, Mexico.

He has been and still is teaching at a state college in Massachusetts for more than 40 years.

ALFRED P. COOK, was born in Carlisle, KY on Jan. 13, 1924 and enlisted March 17, 1943. He served with the 8th Air Force, 748th Airplane Mechanic-gunner, 2nd Div., Keesler, Laredo, Boise, 446th HG, 707th Sqdn., Stat. 125 Bungay, England.

Participated in battles at Normandy, Northern France, Rhineland, Ardennes, Air Offensive Europe and Central Europe. Memorable experiences: his jump on 4th mission, broke his ankle; and on next to last mission when they were hit hard. He was flying nose turret and had 11 pieces of flack in the shield in front of his face. Their waist gunner was hit in the shoulder.

Discharged Sept. 23, 1945 with the rank of tech sergeant. He received the EAME Theater Ribbon with six Bronze Stars per WD GO #33/45, Good Conduct, Purple Heart and Air Medal with five Oak Leaf Clusters.

Married for 51 years, has four children, 15 grandchildren and 11 great-grandchildren. He retired as a health department plumbing inspector. His hobbies are woodworking and model WWII airplanes. He is active in Masonic order, is a member of the First Baptist Church and Caterpillar Club.

MARION E. COOK, was born May 19, 1925 in Tyro, MS and was raised on a farm in the Sardis area. Graduated from Sardis High School in May 1943 and enlisted in the Army Air Corp on May 18, 1943. He was in the cadet program for six months; went to Armanent School, Lowry Field, CO; Gunnery School, Tyndall Field, FL; then to Westover Field, MA.

Left for overseas October 1944; crew training at Hardwick, England with 2nd Air Div., 93rd Bomb Group, 328th Air Sqdn., B-24 Bomber, 8th Air Force. Memorable experiences were mission to Berlin and Munster. Two engines were shot out, one man dead and 128 holes in plane. Returned to the States after completing 33 missions.

Discharged on May 29, 1945, Randolph Field, TX with the rank of staff sergeant. He received the EAME with four Bronze Stars, Good Conduct, Air Medal with four Bronze Clusters and the Presidential Unit Citation.

Married May 4, 1946 to Irene M. Wisneski in Westfield, MA where they make their home. Employed with Stanley Home Products for 40 years, last 12 as manager of shipping room department. He retired in 1985. No children.

WARREN G. COOK, was born in Westmoreland, NY. He enlisted in the USAAC on Aug. 10, 1942. Was pilot of B-24, B-29, B-47, B-52.

Military locations/stations: SAACC, San Antonio; Primary Flying School, Corsicana, TX; Basic Flying School, Greenville; Advanced Flying School, Ellington Field; B-24 transition, Maxwell Field, AL; B-24 phase training, Charleston, SC; Horsham St. Faith, England, 754th Bomb Sqdn., 458th Bomb Group; Peterson Field, Courier Service; 15th Air Force HQ; Carswell AFB, TX, B-29 training; McGuire AFB, NJ, B-29 Photo Recon Sqdn.; Travis AFB, CA; Yakota AFB, Japan, B-29 bombing missions; Fairchild AFB, WA, B-29 Recon; Ellington Field, TX, 1037 training, bombing, nav. radar; Mather AFB, CA, for B-47 duty; Hunter AFB, GA, B-47 flying; (1959) Maxwell AFB, AL, Command/Staff School; 1960-66, Griffiss AFB, NY, B-52 416th Bomb Wing. Completed 36 missions (B-24) WWII, 40 mission (B-29) Korea.

Retired Jan. 1, 1966 with the rank lieutenant colonel. He received the Distinguished Flying Cross with Oak Leaf Cluster and the Air Medal with eight Oak Leaf Clusters.

Was state representative for United Services Life Ins. Co., Washington, DC until 1982 when he retired. He is married and has three sons and four daughters.

PAUL R. COOL, was born Sept. 22, 1919 in Syracuse, NY. He enlisted in the USAAC twice, Oct. 21, 1942 and June 30, 1946.

Military locations/stations: Aerial Gunnery School, Harlingen Field, TX; B-17 training, 331st Bomb Group, 461st Sqdn., Casper, WY; Aircraft Sheet Metal Course, Chanute Field, IL; 338th Photo Sqdn., Guam (1947).

Participated in air war over Europe, completing 37 missions. Memorable experience was coming back to England from Kassel raid safely, the 445th lost 16 airplanes from group.

Discharged Oct. 13, 1945 and again Oct. 8, 1947 with the rank of staff sergeant. He received the Air Medal with Oak Leaf Cluster, ETO Ribbon and Presidential Citation.

Cool and his wife, Antoinette, have two sons, Brian and David, and daughter, Gina. He is employed in paint and home sales, Lumber City, Van Nuys, CA.

JAMES G. COOLEY (JIM), was born Oct. 25, 1925 at Cohoes, NY, a mill town at the Mohawk and Hudson Rivers junction.

He married his high school girlfriend, Alice Luke, on Nov. 12, 1945. They have seven children and seven grandchildren.

During high school he joined the New York State Guard, Civil Air Patrol and enlisted in the Air Force Reserve for Aviation Cadet training. After induction on November 1943, he had basic training at Greensboro, NC; Gunnery School at Laredo, TX; and flight crew training at Tucson, AZ. As the tail gunner, his crew flew to Scotland on July 8, 1944. As a replacement crew they flew with 93rd Bomb Group, 409th Bomb Sqdn. out of Hardwick, starting their first mission on Aug. 13, 1944.

On August 21, Cooley spent his first Army three day pass in London. Their ninth mission on September 25 was a flak-filled venture to Koblenz. The struggle to get to and land at Brussels on only two engines was a thrill. The enemy had departed only one week before.

On his 19th birthday he flew his 13th mission. The 35-mission tour was completed on March 14, 1945, but he continued to fly through #39 on March 24.

Jim was discharged as staff sergeant on Sept. 20, 1945.

MYLES E. COOLIDGE, was born Aug. 8, 1918 in Arthyde, MN and enlisted in the USAAC on Dec. 22, 1939. Came up through the ranks, making master sergeant on July 2, 1942. He applied for pilot training and was accepted, entered and graduated with Class 43K-5 in December 1943 in Gulf Coast Training Command. RTU training at Casper, WY.

Overseas to England last of April 1944. Was shot down on 22nd mission in B-24 named *Bugs Bunny*. Spent nine months in prison camp in Germany. Stayed in the service and flew 196 combat hours in Korean Conflict. Flew at beginning of Vietnam Conflict. He flew 22 combat missions with 791st Bomb Sqdn., 467th Bomb Group from May 1944 to Aug. 13, 1944.

His memorable experience was being shot down by flak and getting out of the airplane after it blew up. He retired Oct. 1, 1963 with the rank of major. His awards include the Purple Heart and Air Medal.

He flew 18 years as corporate pilot for a total pilot time of 17,500 plus hours before retiring. He is a widower with six children.

ARTHUR I. COOPER, was born March 23, 1922 in Providence, RI. He enlisted Feb. 11, 1943. Branch of military, locations and stations: Armor OCS Ft. Knox, KY, February-May 1943; 2nd Lt. Inf. May 1943-November 1943; student officer (pilot training) Class 44-G December 1943-July 1944, B-24 stage training, Charleston, SC; Ft. Knox, KY; Ft. Chaffee, AR, 14th Armd. Div.; Central Flying Training Command; 389th Bomb Group, 565th Sqdn. 1945.

Participated in five and a half missions in ETO, January 1945-Feb. 19, 1945. A memorable experience was going down on sixth mission (Feb. 19, 1945) as co-pilot near Krefeld, Germany and was POW until April 29, 1945 in POW camps at Frankfurt, Wurzburg, Nurmberg and Mooseberg.

Was discharged in December 1945 with the rank of first lieutenant. He received the Air Medal and the POW Medal.

Married Margaret Heck on Aug. 20, 1943, they have three children and one grandson. He retired Feb. 28, 1990 as executive vice president and treasurer of American Automobile Association after 37 years of service.

CHARLES L. COOPER, was born Nov. 30, 1924 in Florence, SC. Joined the USAAC Nov. 13, 1942.

Graduated Aerial Gunnery School, Harlingen, TX, Feb. 13, 1943; graduated Aircraft Maintenance School, Biloxi, MS, June 1943; B-24 crew training, Boise, ID, July-August 1943; Cadet School, Utah State Agriculture College, September 1943-February 1944; pre-flight, Santa Ana, CA, March-April 1944; B-24 engines and hydraulics system instructor, Gowen Field, Boise, ID, May-August 1944; combat crew training, Gowen Field, September-December 1944; 700th Bomb Sqdn., 445th Bomb Group; 2nd Air Div.; 8th Air Force, December 1944-May 1945. Was shot down March 15, 1945, Zozzen Raid (14th mission). Completed 17 missions.

Discharged Oct. 25, 1945 with the rank tech sergeant. His awards include the Good Conduct Medal, Air Medal with three clusters, Marksman and Presidential Unit Citation.

His profession was income tax preparation and financial consulting. Retired Corporate CFO.

ARCHIE J. CORAN, was born April 5, 1923 in Detroit, MI and entered the service in February 1943 while attending Michigan State Normal College. He completed radio operator training at Sioux Falls, SD and aerial gunnery training at Kingman, AZ before assignment to B-24 crew and overseas training at Muroc, CA.

Promoted to tech sergeant after joining 453rd Bomb Group, 735th Sqdn. at Old Buckingham, England in May

1944. Completed 30 missions over Europe with last ten as lead crew. Received Air Medal with five Oak Leaf Clusters and Distinguished Flying Cross. Returned home and enlisted in Aviation Cadets. Was discharged from the service in late 1945 and returned to college.

Retired from Ford Motor Company in 1982 after 35 years in marketing and sales. Married Katherine in 1950 and has a son, daughter-in-law and three grandchildren.

ARTHUR J. CORBIN, was born May 27, 1923 in Columbus, OH. He enlisted in the service Nov. 7, 1942. Navigator, 8th Air Force, 93rd Group, Hardwick, England. He participated in three battles.

Discharged Nov. 30, 1945 with the rank first lieutenant, navigator. His awards include the Air Medal with four Oak Leaf Clusters, Victory Medal and ETO Ribbon with stars.

Married since June 23, 1945, has two children and seven grandchildren. He is a school board member, Ohio Gov. Alt Fuels Council, ham radio gen. lic., major, Civil Air Patrol, mission pilot, group safety off.

PAUL R. CORBISIERO, was born Jan. 7, 1922 in San Jose, CA and enlisted March 1942 in the USAAC. Graduated Dec. 1, 1943, second lieutenant pilot B-24, 453rd Bomb Group, Old Buckingham Air Field (England).

Participated in 30 missions, including D-day invasion week, in major cities in Germany including Hamburg, Dusseldorf, Cologne, Politz, Schwerin, Munich, Kassel.

Memorable experiences: Jimmie Stewart in command, B-24, Air Transport Command, Instructor School, back seat of AT-6, Cadet Program.

Discharged April 1945 with the rank of captain. He received four Air Medals and the Distinguished Flying Cross.

Married to Mary and has six children, nine grandchildren and two great-grandchildren. Retired as vice president of a teamsters local union in San Jose, CA, organizer and contract negotiator.

ANTHONY C. CORBO, was born Aug. 11, 1917 in Newark, NJ. Entered the service Feb. 20, 1941 and received basic training in infantry at Fort Benning, GA with Co. A, 29th Inf. Regt. Later was in post military police.

Transferred to Air Force and sent to Keesler Field, LA. Became airplane and engine mechanic. Assigned to Lt. Odie "Mike" Boyds crew as flight engineer. Took Gunnery at Laredo, TX. Then crew had training at Davis Monthan Field, Langley Field, then to Mitchell Field, NY for a new B-24H. They flew the southern route to Trinidad, Belem Fortalaza in South America, then to Dakar and Marrakech Africa to England. Assigned to 453rd Bomb Group (H) B-24s at old Buckingham Airfield of the Mighty 8th. Completed 31 missions and returned to the U.S.

Was discharged Sept. 13, 1945. Received the Distinguished Flying Cross, four Air Medals, EAME Campaign and three stars.

Married to Francine Magliese in July 1947, has one daughter, Michele, a high school teacher. Joined the Newark Police Dept. and became a detective and remained there until retirement.

JOHN CORLISS, was born Sept. 21, 1922 in Baltimore, MD and educated locally in the Roman Catholic School System, parochial and private. Attempted enlistment in the Navy after Pearl Harbor and was rejected on the basis of physical impairment. Was drafted into the Army Air Corps in 1942.

Graduated from Aircraft Armament School at Lowry Field in May 1943 with certified honorary distinction. In July 1943 joined the 707th Bomb Sqdn. Armament Shop as ground armorer for overseas training. Accompanied the 446th Bomb Group to Station 125, Flixton where he served in various capacities with several periods of detached service.

At the conclusion of European hostilities, was rotated to the States for training for duty in the Pacific. The cessation of war in the Pacific found this training still in the planning stage.

He continued his education at Loyola College and Johns Hopkins University to become a degreed research chemist with the Army Chemical Corps. In this work he published over 25 original scientific research reports, open and classified; received several honoraria and was listed in *Who's Who In The East*. He officially represented the American Microchemical Society at the Centennial Celebrations of the Society of Analytical Chemistry in London.

He retired in 1977 as chief chemist of his laboratory. He now finds work and interest as a deltiologist.

CLARENCE I. CORNELIUS, was born March 1, 1919 in Day County, SD and enlisted in the AAC September 1940, commissioned second lieutenant pilot, Stockton, CA in June 1943. He flew 30 combat missions with 446th Bomb Group, 705th Bomb Sqdn.

Participated in the first daylight raids on Berlin. Memorable experience was returning from aborted mission to Kiel, flying over the North Sea alone paralleling the coasts of Belgium, Holland etc.

Discharged October 1945 with the rank first lieutenant. He received the Distinguished Flying Cross, Air Medal and four others.

Married Doris J. Clemons and has two sons and two grandsons. He retired after 30 years with the Federal Aviation Administration. Doris has been active in the International Order of Rainbow for girls and Clarence has served as patron of Eastern Star twice and as master of two different Masonic lodges.

CHARLES CORNELL (BUD), was born in Baltimore, MD on June 7, 1924 and enlisted in the Army Sept. 23, 1942. Went to Aerial Gunnery School at Tyndall Field, FL and graduated Dec. 1, 1942. Went to Salt Lake City, UT and attended Radio-Operator School, graduated as radio operator/gunner on Feb. 1, 1943 with the rank of staff sergeant. Assigned to 8th Air Force on July 16, 1943, further assigned to 93rd Bomb Group(H), 328th Bomb Sqdn. Met the group in North Africa, flew several missions from there.

Returned to England in September 1943 and completed 26 missions. Returned to the States in June 1944 and taught gunnery at Fort Myers, FL. Discharged Oct. 24, 1945, joined the Baltimore City Fire Department on March 26, 1947 and went into Army Reserves. Received direct commission as second lieutenant in the USAF on June 21, 1949 as crash/rescue officer.

Recalled to active duty for Korean War, ordered to Japan on Nov. 9, 1951. Assigned as crash/rescue officer to Johnson Air Base, Tokyo, Japan on Jan. 7, 1952. Returned to States and released from active duty on Jan. 24, 1953. Returned to Fire Department and remained in Air Force Reserve until June 7, 1984, retiring with rank of captain.

Decorations include the Distinguished Flying Cross, Air Medal with three Oak Leaf Clusters, Purple Heart, Presidential Unit Citation, Good Conduct Medal, European Theater Medal with four stars, American Theater Medal, Victory Medal, National Defense Service Medal, Korean Service Medal with one star, Armed Forces Reserve Medal with one Hour Glass Device, Air Force Longevity Service Medal with nine Oak Leaf Clusters, United Nations Medal and Battle for Britain Medal (British).

Married Lavinia F. Roberts on Nov. 26, 1970, has four children and nine grandchildren. Retired from the Baltimore City Fire Dept. Oct. 23, 1983 with the rank of captain.

D. HULON CORNETTE, was born Jonesboro, GA on April 19, 1923. Joined the AAC on Oct. 24, 1942. Stationed first at Fort Myers, FL, second assignment was Gulfport, MS. Then sent to Tonopah, NV and assigned to 458th Bomb Group, 754th Bomb Sqdn., Crew 56.

His most memorable experience was training with Lt. Walt J. Raiter, his pilot and crew members of *Bomb-Totin-Mama*. They flew the southern route to Norwich, England arriving December 1943 and joined the 8th Air Force. The crew had flown 12 missions when on the 13th mission, Easter Sunday, April 9, 1944 their plane was shot down over Hamburg, Germany. German fighters killed three of their crew members and the rest of the crew became prisoners of war. He was a POW in Stalag 17-B for 13 months.

Received the Air Medal with one Oak Leaf Cluster, Purple Heart, Good Conduct Medal, ETO Medal and the POW Medal. He attained the rank of tech sergeant.

Married his childhood sweetheart, Jessie McConkey Cornette on Dec. 6, 1942. They have two sons and six grandchildren and three great-granddaughters. He became an insurance claims adjuster retiring in 1983 after 25 years service. He now enjoys life with his family, friends and church members. Cornette and his wife enjoy traveling, working in the yard, growing flowers and keeping their home attractive.

ANTHONY CORRADETTI (TONY), was born in Chester, PA on May 19, 1925. In 1943 he became 18 years old in May and graduated high school in June and was drafted into the Army Aug. 5th at Ft. Mead, MD. Went to basic at Miami Beach, FL, then to 27th CTD at University of Toledo, OH. Next to Gunnery School in Laredo, TX and crew training at Westover, MA.

Went overseas to the 467th Bomb Group, 789th Bomb Sqdn. (Rackheath, England). From there he flew 31 combat missions as a ball gunner and waist gunner. He returned to the States early in June of 1945 and after a 30-day furlough, he went to rehab at Greensboro, NC for a couple of weeks, then reassigned to Big Spring Air Base in Texas for about three months.

Discharged from Andrews Air Base on Oct. 31, 1945 with the rank of sergeant. His most memorable experience was the loss of a B-24 (Wolves Incorporated) off of their right wing on 21st mission of which six crew members were from the same hut he lived in. They had arrived at Rackheath about the same time and had about the same amount of missions. He was awarded an Air Medal with four Bronze Oak Leaf Clusters, the European Campaign Medal with three Battle Stars, Good Conduct Medal, American Theater Medal and a Victory Medal.

He married in September 1946 and has two sons and two grandchildren. He retired from Dupont Company in November of 1991.

CARMELO COSENTINO, was born Oct. 4, 1925 in Brooklyn, NY. Enlisted July 11, 1943 in the USAF, 392nd Bomb Group, 576th Bomb Sqdn. (H). Stationed at Greensboro, NC, Laredo, TX and Casper, WY.

Memorable experience was bombing Trier on Christmas Eve. Discharged Oct. 31, 1945 with the rank of staff sergeant. He received the Air Medal with two clusters, ETO and five Battle Stars.

Married since 1952, he has two children (one deceased) and three grandchildren. Retired as foreman at post office at Buffalo, NY Airport.

GEORGE COSTAGE, was born March 4, 1924 in Detroit, MI and enlisted in the USAAF March 22, 1943.

Military locations/stations: Miami Beach, Cadet; Tyndall Field Gunnery School; Davis Monthan, Tucson, AZ and Norwich, England. Assigned to the 458th Bomb Group, 754th Bomb Sqdn. Five Battle Stars for ETO.

It was a memorable experience serving in Korea and the whole war. Discharged Sept. 20, 1945 with the rank of staff sergeant. He received the ETO Ribbon, American Theater Ribbon, Good Conduct, Victory Medal and the Air Medal (5). He retired after Korea in 1964 as a captain.

Married on Feb. 28, 1955 to Nancy Tessmer. He retired from Detroit Fire Dept. in 1972, spent six years as commissioner and vice mayor of Safety Harbor, FL, and now travels the world.

GERALD L. COVEY, was born April 6, 1922 in Seattle, WA. He enlisted March 14, 1943, 8th Air Force, 2nd Air Div., 458th Bomb Group, 755th Sqdn. Commissioned a navigator, Ellington Field, Houston, TX in March 1944; B-24 training, Pueblo, CO. He completed 37 missions (seven volunteered).

Discharged September 1945 at Ellington Field with the rank first lieutenant. He received the Distinguished Flying Cross at Horsham St. Faith for mission flown in connection with Battle of the Bulge.

Married Barbara on April 10, 1949, has four children: Margaret, Carol, Richard and Larry. Retired as personnel manager from Hughes Aircraft.

JOSEPH T. COVONE, was born Oct. 18, 1921 in Trevose, PA. Enlisted August 1942 in the USAF as gunner/aerial engineer, 44th Bomb Group, 506th Sqdn., 93rd Bomb Group, 329th Sqdn. Stationed at Biloxi, MS; Pocatello, Boise, ID; Shipdham E. Hardwich, England.

Participated in 28 missions over Germany and occupied France while stationed in England. He flew with the R.A. Ponker crew on a B-24. On their third mission over Munster, Germany on Nov. 3, 1943, they were attacked by enemy fighters, seven crew were injured, crash landed back on base and spent 10 days in hospital.

Discharged September 1945 with the rank staff sergeant. He received the Distinguished Flying Cross, Air Medal with five Oak Leaf Clusters, Purple Heart, European Theater and American Theater Medal.

Married and has five children and eight grandchildren. Spends winters in Winter Haven, FL.

LIDA B. COWEN, was born in Argos, IN on Sept. 3, 1918; graduated Culver High School; enlisted in WAAC in February 1943. Basic training was at Ft. Oglethorpe, GA; Administration School at Conway, AR to 1st Separate Battalion at Ft. Devens, MA; to Camp Shanks on SS *Aquatania* to Scotland, to Horsham St. Faith, Norwich, July 1943. Housed at Old Catton in former RAF barracks where the ablutions block was a distance away.

Assigned to Statistical Control Section headed by L.C. Oldham. Rode back and forth to office on RAF bus that had to be entered and exited through large doors at the back.

Moved to Ketteringham Hall. Statistical Control Hut was isolated in the woods at the far end of the road, farthest from the Castle and the center of activities.

After V-E day, transferred to Istres, France until return to the States on the *Queen Mary*. Discharged Oct. 17, 1945 as staff sergeant.

While at Ketteringham, met Carroll L. Thompson, gunner stationed at Hethel. They danced and bicycled a lot the summer of 1944 before he returned to the States. They were

married Thanksgiving day 1945, had a dairy farm in Indiana until he died in 1974. They had five children and six grandchildren. In 1986 she married long time friend, Dave Norris, a Navy veteran.

JOHN P. COWGER (FLIP), was born April 18, 1922 in Dardanelle, AR. Enlisted in the Army as second lieutenant on June 4, 1942 while attending Wentworth Military Academy and Junior College. Transferred to Army Air Force September 1942 and graduated as a student pilot, second lieutenant in 43-K at Marfa, TX and assigned co-pilot on B-24 crew, accepted a new B-24 J at San Francisco, CA and flew to England.

Assigned to the 453rd Bomb Group, 734th Sqdn. at "Old Buck," Addleburg, England April 1943, completed 20 missions and went down and became a POW on the 21st mission where all the crew on his ship were killed except himself.

Received three Air Medals, two European Campaign Stars and the Purple Heart. He was repatriated, that is, prisoner exchange with the Germans in February 1945, before the war was over. Assigned to hospitals until the middle of 1945. Went back to flying status and then retired in October 1946 as disabled.

Retired from U.S. Government work, working for the selective service system, ending up as state director of selective service for the state of Arkansas in 1976. Married to Frances Bost on July 4, 1942 and has two sons and four grandchildren.

LUTHER C. COX, was born March 15, 1918, Baltimore, MD. Entered the AAC Flight Training May 28, 1941. Graduated April 11, 1942, Tunner Field, GA. Commissioned second lieutenant. Original member of 93rd Bomb Group, 328th Sqdn., Barksdale Field, LA, May 11th Page Field, FL, August 8 Grenier Field, NH, Sept. 6, 1942 orders to proceed to England.

Reported to Commanding General 8th Air Force. First group to fly formation across the North Atlantic non-stop. Sept. 10, 1942, Alconbury Air Base, England. Oct. 9, 1942 flew on first all-American raid against Lille, France. (10 missions ETO), Dec. 6, 1942 Group TDY to North Africa (Oran) and Middle East (Gambut - LG 139).

Was shot down on 21st mission, target Sousse, Tunisia, N.A. Two survivors, bombardier and navigator (Cox). They remained POWs until liberated by Gen. Patton on April 29, 1945. Mitchel Field, NY, Sept. 28, 1945.

Spent next 24 years in research and development commands. Retired Aug. 10, 1969. He received the Bronze Star (Valor), Purple Heart with Oak Leaf Cluster, Air Medal with three Oak Leaf Clusters, POW Medal, European Campaign Medal with seven Oak Leaf Clusters, Distinguished Unit Award with two Oak Leaf Clusters, Air Force Commendation Medal with Oak Leaf Cluster and several other ribbons.

Director Air Force JROTC programs for 16 years for a total of 45 years in uniform. Married Jeanene Haynes and has four children and nine grandchildren.

HARRY N. CRAFT, was born in 1923 and raised in Sharon, PA, son of an American steelworker and his Canadian bride. Commissioned as a navigator in January 1944 at Selman Field, LA. He joined RTU at Tonopah, NV and travelled to England with secret Azon bombing crews.

Flew 35 missions with 458th Bomb Group, six of them Azon, finishing on Christmas Day, 1944, at Horsham St. Faith. Awarded the Distinguished Flying Cross and Air Medals.

Graduated from Penn State in 1948; worked five years with Soil Conservation Service. Spent 42 years as general contractor, 14 as company president. Served 27 years in the

Reserve, retiring as lieutenant colonel with Air Force Academy Liaison Officer program. Devoted many years to the New Wilmington, PA School Board, to the Penn-Ohio Contractors' Association, church work, and to Rotary International's peace and goodwill programs.

Married Margaret Minteer in 1947 with whom he enjoys his family of four children and eight grandchildren.

JOE D. CRAFT, was born in Raleigh, MS on Dec. 8, 1921. Entered the Army Air Corps July 29, 1942 at Camp Shelby, MS. Transferred to Sioux Falls, SD via Miami Beach, where he became a radio operator mechanic. Attended Gunnery School in Las Vegas, NV and was assigned to the 453rd Bomb Group, Crew 41.

Entered the European Theater of Operations in December 1943, via the southern route, taking him through Trinidad, Natal, Dakar, Marrakesh and finally arriving in Old Buckingham, England.

Flew missions against Germany on the B-24 Liberator as tech sergeant. Received the Good Conduct Medal, Air Medal, Distinguished Flying Cross, four Battle Stars and three Oak Leaf Clusters. He finished his 30th mission after D-day, June 8, 1944, and returned to the States Sept. 21, 1944. He was honorably discharged Oct. 9, 1945 at Maxwell Field, AL.

Married to Melba New of Eagle Lake, TX, now resides on the Texas Gulf Coast. He has six children and 10 grandchildren.

WILLIAM C. CRAIG, was born Feb. 2, 1924 in Compton, CA. Drafted into the AAC Feb. 3, 1943. Sent to St. Petersburg, FL for basic training. After various assignments throughout Florida, he was accepted for Gunnery School at Panama City, FL. Upon completion of Gunnery School, he was sent to Westover Field, Holyoke, MA for crew assignment. Assigned to Lt. Marshall Modery's crew as nose gunner.

Completed 16 missions with the 491st Bomb Group, 852nd Sqdn. when V-E day happened. Received two Air Medals, three European Campaign Stars and the Presidential Unit Citation. Was discharged Nov. 15, 1945.

Retired from Pacific Telephone Company after 35 years in a marketing position. Since retiring he plays a little golf and does background acting in movies and television.

Was married Oct. 29, 1948 and has two children and three grandchildren.

WALTER N. CRANSON, was born July 14, 1920 in La Junta, CO. Joined AAC in February 1943. Trained as P-Shooter pilot Pine Bluff, AR (primary); Independence, KS

(basic) and Mission, TX (advanced). Received second lieutenant bars and wings in May 1944.

Assigned co-pilot B-24 crew, Lincoln, NE with hometown buddy, Tom Sisson as pilot. Combat training, Casper, WY. Ile de France to Scotland, February 1945. 392nd first mission March 8, 1945. Completed 15 missions in 48 days, last one, 8th flew (Hallein, Austria then over Berchtesgaden) through flak April 25, 1945 as Russian/American soldiers linked up on Elbe River, Torgan, Germany. Scariest takeoff, Rayon, France Sub pens April 14 with 8th's heaviest load, four one-tonners.

Flew 20 of them home, Wales, Iceland, Greenland to Bangar, ME, June 1, 1945. Married, discharged and home in September 1945.

Taught GI Ag five years, bought farm and raised nine kids (now has 30 grandchildren). He bought a cub cruiser and received commercial/instructor rating. Started Air Scouts. Was peace candidate for U.S. Senate 1966, 1968 and 1972. Made Journey for Peace Torgan and Russia in 1985 and 1990, celebrating link-up. Started Peace Academy Boot Stop 16 years ago. Challenging UFO non-believers and Kennedys/King assassination cover-uppers.

QUINNIE Q. CREWS, was born Samson, AL on April 1, 1917. Entered the service January 1942 and attended Aircraft Mechanics School, Keesler Field, MS and Aircraft Gun Turret School, South Bend, IN. Assigned to the 67th Bomb Sqdn., 44th Bomb Group, Barksdale Field, LA in mid-May, as a gun turret and gun sight mechanic.

Soon left for England on *Queen Mary* and assignment to Shipdham for 33 months. After V-E day and 30 day leave was reassembled at Sioux Falls, SD and assigned to a B-29 group at Clovis, NM. Discharged September 1945 as staff sergeant. Was employed with the Federal Civil Service, NAS Pensacola as Instrument Mechanic; Vitro Corporation, Eglin AFB, FL, Civil Service, Redstone Arsenal, AL and Eglin AFB, FL as a high speed camera technician.

Married Myrtice Williams on July 10, 1946 and has three daughters and five grandchildren.

Since retirement in August 1974 has been enjoying hobbies of gardening, wood and metal working and traveling.

VANCE E. CRIDLING, was born Oct. 15, 1916 in Maysville, MO. He enlisted in the USAAF, on Nov. 21, 1942, navigator B-24 (1034), 2nd Air Div., 8th AAF.

Military locations/stations: CTD Beloit, WI; Casper, WY, AAF; Las Vegas, NV; Hondo, TX (navigation training) Replacement Crew Training. His memorable experience was the German Campaign. He flew nine missions with 492nd Bomb Group (H) and 21 missions with 467th Bomb Group (H).

Discharged June 16, 1945 at Ft. McPherson, GA with the rank first lieutenant, active duty and as captain, Air Force Reserve. Received the Air Medal with four Oak Leaf Clusters and the Distinguished Flying Cross.

Cridling is a retired osteopathic physician and surgeon. He has a wife, Mildred.

HUBERT R. CRIPE, was born Oct. 20, 1920 in Bader, IL and enlisted August 1942 in the AAF, pilot, 2nd Div, 8th Air Force. Commissioned Roswell, NM, Class 43-E; joined 453rd Bomb Group, Pocatello, ID; trained at March Field November-December 1943.

Flew South American route to Old Buckingham, England. Bombed Gotha, Frankfurt, Aachemer, Berlin and Calais (four times). Was shot down March 6, 1944 (Berlin). Parachuted into Zuider Zee, POW for 14 months at Stalag Luft I.

Discharged in January 1945 with the rank of captain. He received the Air Medal and ETO Ribbon.

Married Louis A. Vollmer, has two children and two grandchildren. He is retired.

CALVIN D. CRISWELL, was born Jan. 17, 1924 in Adrian, MO. He joined the Army Air Force in October 1942 and served with the 458th Bomb Group, Horsham St. Faith England.

Criswell was discharged in October 1945 with the rank of tech sergeant. Retired and taking life easy.

HARRY G. CROSLAND, was born Oct. 7, 1919 in Palo Pinto, TX. Entered Army Air Corps as aviation cadet on April 18, 1942, graduated April 22, 1943 as second lieutenant, Class of 43-D at Ellington Field, TX.

Trained in B-24s and departed for England in November 1943 with 446th Bomb Group, 707th Sqdn. Flew 30 combat missions, finished tour May 1944. Sustained major battle damage to flak in France on 5th mission, losing #1 and #4 engines. Did wheels up landing on RAF fighter base at Hawkinge, England near Dover. No injury to crew.

Returned to States July 1944. Instructed crews in B-24s at Casper Army Air Base, Casper, WY and B-29s at Kirtland Field, Albuquerque, NM until end of war.

Discharged as a captain October 1946 at Lowry Field, Denver, CO. His medals include the Distinguished Flying Cross with one cluster, Air Medal with five clusters, and ETO Campaign. After discharge he spent several years in Air Force Reserve, highest rank attained was major.

Married Merle Gumm of Houston, TX on July 19, 1941. They have three children, 10 grandchildren and two great-grandchildren.

LUTHER B. CROSS, was born Feb. 13, 1924 in Marshall County, TN. Enlisted Nov. 4, 1942 in USAAF, engineer gunner. Military locations/stations: West Palm Beach, FL; Smyrna, TN; Newport, AR; Biloxi, MS; Colorado Springs, CO.

Participated in Air Offensive Europe. Memorable experience was flying southern route to Europe and his 35 combat missions over Europe.

Discharged Oct. 29, 1945 with the rank of staff sergeant. Received the Air Medal, Distinguished Flying Cross, Good Conduct, WWII Victory and the EAME Campaign.

His parents, William O. and Lacey Cross, and brother William R. are deceased. Luther is retired.

ALEX JEAN CROW, was born Aug. 20, 1922 in Raymondville, TX. Enlisted June 13, 1942 in the Army Air Corps; 4-engine pilot with 453rd Bomb Group, 734th Sqdn.; Old Buckingham, Norwich, England. Participated in Air War-Europe and invasion of Europe (D-day).

Memorable experiences: Piloting B-24 from Hamilton Field, CA to England via southern route. Completed 35 bombing missions as first pilot before his 22nd birthday (89 days between May 22-Aug. 18, 1944). On Aug. 6, 1944 he piloted a B-24 during a bombing raid on refinery in Hamburg, Germany. In 1971 he returned to Hamburg as construction manager to build an aluminum smelter on the site of the bombed out refinery and airplane factory. Found several unexploded American bombs during excavation.

Discharged November 1957 (Reserves) with the rank of captain. He received the Distinguished Flying Cross and Air Medal with five clusters.

Married nearly 50 years, has four children and three grandchildren. He retired in 1987 after 40 years in construction management.

WILLARD L. CRUM (BILL), was born Feb. 26, 1925 in Van Nuys, CA. Was drafted into the Army in June 1943 and was sent to AAF basic at Kearns, UT. Then to Aircraft Armament School, Lowry Field, CO. Next was Gunnery School at Harlingen, TX and from there was sent to Westover, MA where assigned to the B-24 crew of Lt. A.L. Berthelson at the ball turret.

Completed crew training in July 1944 and headed for the big war in a brand new B-24. They were assigned to the 566th Sqdn., 389th Bomb Group at Hethel. Flew their first mission August 30th to bomb the VI launch sites. Five months and 30 missions later, Jan. 28, 1945, was shot down over the Rhur and spent the rest of the war tramping all over western Germany, POW style. Was liberated by Pattons 3rd Army troops at Moosburgh and returned to Camp Lucky Strike in France on V-E day.

Arrived at home in June for 60 day furlough, reported back to the Mira Mar Hotel, Santa Monica, CA just in time for V-J day. Discharged with the rank of staff sergeant. Received the Air Medal with four Oak Leaf Clusters and the Purple Heart.

Went to Tech School on the GI bill to learn radio and the new thing, TV. Married in 1947 and raised a family of four. Currently has three fine grandchildren. Retired from Lockheed in 1987.

LYMAN CRUMRIN, was born July 17, 1922 near West Union, IL, a farming community. Entered the Army on Feb. 9, 1943 in the field artillery and later transferred to the Air Corps at Sheppard Field, TX. Graduated from Aerial Gunnery School at Laredo, TX and assigned to the Dempewolf crew and sent to El Paso, TX for B-24 crew training. The crew picked up a new plane at Topeka, KS and arrived at the 453rd Bomb Group in Old Buckingham, England in August 1944.

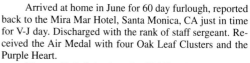

On the second mission over Coblenz, Germany, the plane and crew collided with a B-17 and had to land at the Manston, England crash field. After a few days at a rest home, the group was put on Pathfinder Crew training.

After Jan. 1, 1945, he was transferred to the 389th Bomb Group at Hethel, England, where he completed 28 missions on April 11, 1945, staying to bring a B-24 back to Dayton, OH, for experimental work on June 5, 1945. On June 12, 1945, he was discharged at Ft. Sheridan, IL.

Lyman is married and has one daughter and one son. He is now semi-retired on the farm with his son doing the farming.

CHARLES B. CUDD JR., was born Dec. 31, 1924 in Decatur, GA. Registered for the draft Dec. 31, 1942 and inducted in the Army Feb. 6, 1943. Was sent to Keesler Field AFB for basic training; flight engineer course and Gunnery School, Laredo, TX. Assigned to 2nd Lt. Wm. F. Gilbert's crew as flight engineer. Went to Gowen AFB at Boise, ID for OTU; troop train to Lincoln, NE to pick up a new B-24H, then to Banger, ME.

Received orders for overseas duty and sent the northern route: Goose Bay, Iceland and England. Assigned to 8th Air Force, 14th Combat Wing, 2nd Air Div., 44th Bomb Group and 64th Sqdn. Promoted to tech sergeant in 1944, flew his last mission (35th) on Aug. 3, 1944.

Arrived in the States Sept. 13, 1944 and married his high school sweetheart on Sept. 22, 1944. Reported back to Keesler Field AFB as a B-32 cruise control instructor. Reassigned to Drew AAF for discharge Oct.16, 1945 with the rank tech sergeant. Received the Air Medal with three Oak Leaf Clusters, Distinguished Flying Cross and two Battle Stars.

Completed his schooling, took flight training and received his private, commercial and flight instructor ratings and later on his instrument rating.

Enlisted in the AAF Reserve in 1946 and served at Dobbins AFB, Marietta, GA. Was promoted to master sergeant and recalled to active duty September 1950 at HQ&HQ Sqdn., Tinker AFB for one year. Left the Reserve Program in 1958.

Flew as a field service tech representative and product representative until 1972. At this time he had about 20,000 hours in the air and loved most of it. Now a retired locksmith and secretary/treasurer of a small family owned company.

He has a daughter, son and four grandchildren.

FRANK L. CUMMINGS, was born Jan. 3, 1924 in Minneapolis, MN. He enlisted on Jan. 31, 1942 in the Air Corps as navigator. Stationed in the USA, Great Britain and Korea. Flew 30 mission in B-24s with 392nd Bomb Group, July 1944-April 1945. Radar ground controlled bombing, Korea (1950-1951).

Discharged in August 1953 with the rank of captain. He received the Distinguished Flying Cross, Air Medal with six clusters and the Bronze Star Medal.

Cummings is married and has three children. Currently retired.

JAMES F. CUMMINGS, was a member of the 2nd Air Div., 448th Bomb Group, 715th Sqdn. Volunteered for Gunnery School in 1942. There were no openings so was sent to Electrical Engineering School in New York City. Worked as an electrician for a year, volunteered again, and was transferred to Gunnery School in 1943. Trained in Pueblo, CO and sent to England.

Arrived in England in November 1944. Flying out of an airfield near Seething, he flew missions to Eschweiler, Bingen, Offenburg, Koblenz, Aschaffenburg, Ehrang, Kaiserlautern, Merchernick, Remagen, Koblenz, Neunkichen, Achern, Wewieler, Magdeburg, Siegen, Kreinsen, Osnabruck, Misburg, Halle, Merchede, Harburg, Paderborn, Kiel, Gutersloh, Hanover, Berlin, Baumenheim, Stormede, Buchen and Wilhelmshaven. Completed his 35th mission March 30, 1945.

Returned to the States, leaving his crew in England. Married Avanelle in 1946. They have six children, 10 grandchildren and three great-grandchildren.

CARMAN CUNNINGHAM, was born Oct. 24, 1921 in Holland, MO. Enlisted June 4, 1942 in the USAAC, 8th Air Force, 2nd Air Div. Inducted at Fort Niagara, NY; basic training at Miami Beach, FL; Air and Engine School, Keesler Field, MS; specialist training at B-24 consolidated factory in San Diego, CA.

Participated in Air Offensive Europe, Ardennes, Central Europe, Naples-Foggia-Normandy, Northern France, Rhineland, Sicily, Air Combat, GO 33 WD 45.

Memorable experiences: buzz bomb and V2 attacks, being in Norwich and London during German bombing attacks, flight home via Wales, Iceland, LAB and Bradley Field, CT.

Discharged Aug. 30, 1945 with the rank of sergeant. He received the Distinguished Unit Badge WD GO #78 Nov. 15, 1943; EAME Service Medal and the Good Conduct Medal. Took up flying after his discharge. Last plane was a '47 Stinson

Married Genevieve Proppe on June 27, 1948. They have five children and eight grandchildren. Was operating engineer and retired in 1985 after 40 years.

JOHN F. CURCIO, was born in Brooklyn, NY on May 23, 1925. Worked at New Castle Army Air Base prior to entering the Army Air Corps September 1943. Completed Air Gunnery School at Tyndall Field, FL, assigned to Gabriel's Crew as tail turret gunner. Flew training missions from Charleston Air Base, SC, crew departed the States May 1944.

Started flying combat missions with 458th Bomb Group July 1944. In September the crew flew night training missions over England with the radio controlled Azon Bomb (experimental program), also flew gasoline to Gen. Patton's 3rd Army in France.

Resumed flying combat missions October, returning from most missions with battle damage from flak holes throughout their B-24s, without injury to crew members. Retrieved flak particle, 2 1/2 x 3" from his turret after 29th mission.

The most unforgettable experience of his life was when he assisted flight engineer, Wayne Walker, to release 1,000 pounder that was hung up near top of rack, holding on to his legs while he reached up with a stubby screwdriver to manually work the bomb holder at 25,000 feet near 40 below. The catwalk they were standing on looked like a thin string, and no parachute.

Completed 35 combat missions by Feb. 16, 1945. Was awarded Certificate of Valor, five Air Medals, ETO Medal with five Battle Stars and several other ribbons. Was proud to be a member of Gene F. Gabriel's crew, a fine bomber pilot. During R&R, had the honor of meeting Gen. Doolittle. Discharged September 1945 with the rank of staff sergeant.

Retired from Con-Rail after 35 years of service as clerk-yardmaster. Married to Ann Cowfer for 28 happy years. They live in Renovo, PA.

JOHN E. CURRAN, was born Nov. 23, 1924 in Pottsville, PA. Enlisted June 30, 1943, 8th Army Air Force, 2nd Air Div., 389th Bomb Group, 565th Sqdn. Stationed at Keesler Field, MS; Harlingen and Laredo, TX; Lincoln, NE; Boise, ID; Hethel, England; and Pueblo, CO as engineer/gunner.

Participated in action at Northern France, Rhineland and Central Europe. Discharged Jan. 8, 1946 with the rank of staff sergeant. Received all the usual awards and medals.

Curran and wife, Margaret, live in Harrisburg, PA. Worked 37 years with the Patriot-News Co. in Harrisburg, PA. He is now retired.

LOUIS T. CURTIS JR., was born Jan. 12, 1922 in Bellaire, TX. He entered the AAF on Oct. 5, 1942; basic training at Ellington Field, Houston, TX. Other training at Keesler, MS B-24 Mechanic School; Ypsilanta, MI B-24 Factory School; Laredo, TX Gunnery School.

Assigned to Lt. Eddie Bryson's crew as flight engineer, trained for overseas duty at Wendover, UT. Arrived Feb. 19, 1944 Rackheath Air Base, Norwich, England, home of 467th Bomb Group and 789th Sqdn. Flew 30 missions over Germany and France including first American raid on Berlin. Flew two missions to Normandy on D-day.

Received Wings, Good Conduct Medal with three Oak Leaf Clusters, Air Medal, European Theater Ribbon, Silver Star, Bronze Star and Distinguished Flying Cross. Discharged Oct. 15, 1945 with the rank tech sergeant.

Curtis and wife, Johnnie, have three children: Debbie, Mike and Randy and two grandchildren. Retired to Lake Livingston, TX where he enjoys fishing, hunting and gardening.

ORVILLE D. CURTIS, was born Aug. 28, 1920 in Newport, RI. He joined the AAC Aviation Cadet, Feb. 25, 1942, graduated Jan. 14, 1943 Pilot Class 43-A, Blytheville AAB, AR. Married his hometown sweetheart, Aurora Coutinho on Jan. 28, 1943 at Fort Adams, RI.

AAC Anti-Sub Patrol East Coast during 1943, 13th Anti-Sub Greniers Field, NH, 20th Anti-Sub in Gander Lake, NF and Mitchel Field, LI as co-pilot on B-25 and B-17.

October 1943 AAC Anti-Subs Sq. were disbanded, B-24 transition Casper, WY. On Dec. 14, 1943 was assigned to 489th Bomb Group, 845th Bomb Sqdn., Wendover, UT and in April 1944 moved to ETO, Halesworth. Flew on the 489th Bomb Group first combat mission over Germany May 30, 1944. After 10 missions became 845th Bomb Sqdn. training officer, flew several missions as check pilot with new crews on their first mission. Assigned to a crew August 1944. Completed 27 missions with 489th Bomb Group, eight missions with 44th Bomb Group, 506th Bomb Sqdn., finished mission #35 on Jan. 1., 1945.

Flew in Operation Truckin Aug. 30-Sept. 8, 1944, B-24s hauled flour and other food stuff to airfield in Orleans, France. Paris was starving, they made several runs.

Participated in ATO, ETO, Normandy, Northern France, Germany, Battle of the Bulge campaigns. Received the Air Medal and four clusters. Separated AAC on Aug. 17, 1945 as first lieutenant. Retired in 1983 after 33 years with EAIC a farmers co-op, artificial breeding of dairy cattle.

JOHN F. CUSHMAN, was born April 29, 1924 in Rochester, NY. Enlisted Dec. 12, 1942 in the USAAF, 448th Bomb Group, 2nd Air Div., 8th Air Force (pilot), Seething, England (Sta. 146).

Participated in action with the 8th Air Force from July 1944-January 1945 then ATC foreign transport group, Newcastle AAF, DE. Had many memorable experiences, but remembers most the crash in Belgium.

Retired in 1970 with the rank lieutenant colonel. He received six Air Medals along with all the usual medals and awards.

Married to a chemist and has two sons, one an enologist and the other a football coach. Retired, trial court judge, attorney and rancher.

DONALD W. CUTTER, was born June 18, 1918 in Groton, NY. Joined the USAAC on March 17, 1942. Took basic and aircraft mechanics at Keesler Field, MS and attended Glenn L. Martin Factory School, Baltimore, MD. Stationed at Boringuen Field, Puerto Rico, then attended Gunnery School at Ft. Myers, FL.

Formed crews and did overseas training at Tucson, AZ and Alamogordo, NM. Flew southern route to Britain and was assigned to 389th Bomb Group, 566th Bomb Sqdn. as flight engineer and top turret gunner. Had many memorable experiences, especially Hamm.

After tour was assigned to Chanute Field, IL as instructor in engine change. Discharged at Ft. Dix, NJ on Sept. 5, 1945 with the rank tech sergeant. Received the Distinguished Flying Cross, Air Medal with three clusters and the Presidential Unit Citation.

Retired in 1984 from aircraft mech. and quality control. Has a wife and two sons of whom he is very proud.

LESTER J. DAHN (LES), was born Dec. 25, 1921 in Albany, NY. Joined the USAAC on Aug. 19, 1942. After spending a couple of summers in the CMTC (Citizen's Military Training Camp) at Plattsburg, NY, he joined the Aviation Cadet Program in 1942.

After pilot graduation in Class 44-A, he was assigned to Lawson's crew where they flew 31 combat missions out of Halesworth, England in B-24s. Remained in the Air Force Reserves instructing reservists at Stewart AFB, NY. He retired after 22 years from Luke AFB, AZ with the rank of major. Received the Air Medal with four Oak Leaf Clusters, European Campaign with four stars, WWII Victory Medal and the CMTC Marksman Badge.

Memorable experiences were: first day on the base and seeing a B-24 land after a mission and thought it was a special plane as it had a red stripe down the top of the fuselage, then learning that the flight engineer who was sitting in the top gun turret had his head blown off by enemy fighters and the red was his blood; flying on two engines from Germany to Halesworth, England, flak denting pilot's seat; learning tool and die maker trade at IBM leading to perfect job at Garrett Corp. (now Allied Signal).

Has wife, Mary; sons: Fred, Mike, Jim and Dave; and daughters Debbie and Janeen. Retired USAF and Allied Signal. Retired, chairman of Senior Citizen Bingo.

FRED A. DALE, was born in Colfax, IL on Jan. 14, 1923. Enrolled at Illinois State Normal University in 1940. Enlisted in the armed forces on Nov. 17, 1942, called to active duty and assigned to the USAAC, March 11, 1943. Assigned to the 390th Service Sqdn. at Pueblo, CO.

Went overseas on the *Queen Elizabeth* on Aug. 8, 1943. Arrived in Glasgow, Scotland and by train to AAF 124 in Tibenham, England. Attended Link Trainer School and assigned to the 703rd Bomb Sqdn., 445th Bomb Group working with pilots and co-pilots on take-off and assembly formations in all types of weather. Was promoted to sergeant on Jan. 10, 1944.

Returned to USA after end of European Conflict on May 28, 1945; assigned to Sqdn. D, 563rd AAF BU, Homestead, FL. Discharged Oct. 10, 1945.

Enrolled at ISNU on GI bill and graduated in 1947 with a BS in education and taught business education subjects. Received a specialist degree in education and entered education administration. Was a superintendent of schools for 21 years. Married and has three children and six grandchildren. Retired in 1983 with 36 years in education.

JOHN K. DALGLEISH, was Born Dec. 15, 1921 in New Rochelle, NY. Sworn in as aviation cadet on Aug. 3, 1942, College Reserves to continue at Northeastern University, Boston, MA. Called to active duty April 16, 1943. Completed bombardier pre-flight, Ellington Field, TX; completed

aerial gunnery, Laredo, TX; graduated, bombardier advanced, Dec. 24, 1943, Big Spring, TX.

Assigned to a crew and flew transition in Casper, WY. Crew assigned to fly a B-24 the northern route non-stop to England arriving June 3, 1943. Assigned to the 489th Bomb Group, 845th Sqdn., Crew #2937. Completed 34 mission tour, Nov. 8, 1943. On various missions flew as bombardier, navigator and/or nose turret gunner.

Returned to stateside, assigned USAF instructor, later Air Force auditor. December 1944 graduated Northeastern University. Discharged Nov. 6, 1945 with the rank of first lieutenant. He received the EAME with three Battle Stars (Normandy, N. France and Germany), Distinguished Flying Cross and the Air Medal with three Oak Leaf Clusters.

While at Northeastern his fraternity house mother said of one date, "Kathleen Blair is the right girl for you." They were married and went to Ohio State University to earn an MASA. Retired after 42 years of professional fund raising for capitol and operational needs of organizations. They have four children and four grandchildren.

JOHN F. D'AMELIO, was born Sept. 8, 1920 in Waterbury, CT. Joined the AAF Sept. 1, 1942. Assigned to the 392nd Bomb Group; stationed at Sheppard Field, TX; schooling at Biggs Field, TX; Alamogordo, NM; Ford Willow Run; Salt Lake City, UT; Wendling, England.

Memorable experience was when on unassigned mission and plane was hit with flak. Discharged Sept. 27, 1945 with the rank staff sergeant.

Married with one child and one granddaughter. He is retired.

PORTER R. DANFORD, was born Nov. 6, 1913 in San Francisco, CA. Joined the Dental Corps AUS in April 1943. Stationed at Santa Maria; Tonopah, NV; Horsham St. Faith as group dental surgeon.

Memorable experience was flying a champagne mission to Rheims and returning with 2300 bottles for officers' club.

Discharged January 1946 with the rank of captain. He received the Presidential Unit Citation with leaf, ETO Ribbon and six Battle Stars.

Has three daughters, one son, two granddaughters and four grandsons. Retired in 1978. Enjoys duck hunting, fishing, travel and soaring (got his glider to 28,500' over S. Lake Tahoe).

BEN S. DANIEL, was born March 1, 1923 in Chicago, IL. Enlisted December 1942, 8th Air Force, 20th Combat Wing, 448th Bomb Group, 713th Bomb Sqdn. Stationed at Seething Airfield, Norwich, England.

Participated in the Battle of the Bulge and Battle of the Rhine. Memorable experience was forced landing in Mons, Belgium on second combat mission. Discharged November 1945 with the rank staff sergeant/rapid left waist gunner. Received the Air Medal, European Theater and three Battle Stars.

He had younger brothers who served in the Navy and Infantry. Daniel is a certified public accountant and senior partner of A.N. Schorn & Co.

HARRY H. DARRAH, was born June 23, 1919, Martins Ferry, OH. Enlisted Dec. 4, 1939 and assigned 17th Bomb Group, March Field, CA. When the 17th went on Tokyo Raid, transferred to the 1st Pursuit Sqdn. N.F. at Fort Benning, GA.

They were the first combat unit sent to England, arriving May 14, 1942, Newport, Wales, and they all carried passports. The RAF serenaded them at Kettering. Six of their A-20s were in the first ETO action with the RAF raiding Abbeville, Holland, July 4, 1942. November 1942, transferred to Division HQ Engineers Office at Norwich, where he spent many nights at the Lido Dance Hall. Transferred to 389th, Hethel, May 1944 as ground crew for *Delectable Doris*.

Upon returning to USA married Margaret Norman of Tacoma at Fort Lewis, WA on Oct. 4, 1944. They have two daughters and two grandsons. Retired 1975, he built giant scale R.C. aircraft on display at March AFB Museum.

GALE S. DAUDEL, was born in Maquoketa, IA on May 15, 1918. Entered the USAAC at Camp Dodge, IA on Nov. 13, 1942. Attended schools in the military ACFT Armt. 1943 and Ord. Clerical, 1943.

ETO to Tibenham, England Sept. 5, 1943 with ground crew of 1826th Ord., S&M Co. for the 445th Bomber Group. In May 1945 this group was part of the roster for the 830th Air Engineering Sqdn. along with other service groups. The 830th was disbanded July 24, 1945. He remained with 1826th Ord. for duration.

Discharged from service on Nov. 23, 1945, Fort Sheridan, IL with the rank of corporal. He received the Victory Medal, EAME Theater Ribbon, four Overseas Bars, one Service Stripe and the Good Conduct Medal.

Was employed at Rock Island Arsenal, Rock Island, IL for 38 years, retiring as a mechanical engineer technician for Quality Assurance Directorate in 1974. Married Vivian J. Clemens on Dec. 8, 1941. They had four children. Daudel passed away July 13, 1988. His widow is proud to be a life member of the 8th Air Force Historical Society Inc. *Submitted by his widow, Vivian J. Daudel.*

JAMES F. DAVEY, was born Nov. 25, 1924 in Townsend, MT. Enlisted March 17, 1943 in the USAAC, radio operator, top turret gunner with the 8th Air Force. Stationed at Atlantic City, NJ; Scott Field, IL; Tyndall Field, FL; and Westover Field, MA.

Participated in battle in Germany, France etc. Dropped supplies in Battle of Bulge. Memorable experience: bombed Munich, got shot up and crashed on first mission.

Discharged Sept. 15, 1945 with the rank tech sergeant. Received five Battle Stars, Air Medal and five clusters.

Davey is married and has three grown children and three grandchildren. He is retired.

CALVIN K. DAVIDSON, was born Sept. 9, 1924 in Oberlin, OH and raised there on a farm. Enlisted in the USAAC on Dec. 3, 1942. Originally relegated to be in the ground forces because of color blindness, but after attending Radio School at Scott Field, IL, was given a basic color test and then sent to Laredo, TX for Gunnery School.

After flight crew training at Davis-Monthan and Alamogordo Air bases, he picked up new B-24J at Lincoln, NE and flew the southern route to England. Assigned to the 93rd Bomb Group, 409th Sqdn. at Hardwick. Completed 31 missions including March 6, 1944 raid on Berlin and 30th mission on D-day. Received European Campaign Ribbon with three stars, four Air Medals, and the Distinguished Flying Cross.

Rotated back to the States in September of 1944 and became an instructor at Sioux Falls Radio School. Discharged immediately after V-J day and returned to the farm in Oberlin.

Retired in 1987. He is married with three children, six grandchildren and three great-grandchildren.

ERNEST T. DAVIS, was born March 15, 1920 in Bemis, TN. Joined the USAAF, March 1943, S.E. Training Command, 8th Air Force, England and USA, B-24s to B-29s. Completed 27 bombing missions ETO. Flew four years with Maryland Air National Guard after WWII.

Davis was discharged November 1945 and from the National Guard in 1950. Achieved the rank of first lieutenant and received the Air Medal with three Oak Leaf Clusters and the European Medal.

Has four children: Carol, Forrest, Paul and Michael. Retired but still flies his own plane.

GLENN L. DAVIS, was born March 20, 1925 in Findlay, OH. Enlisted May 3, 1943 in the USAAF, 14th Wing, 2nd Air Div., 392nd Bomb Group(H), 578th Sqdn. Stationed at Camp Perry, OH; Lincoln, NE; Bozeman, MT, 43-C-12; Radar School, Madison, WI; Aerial Gunnery Crew Training, Tucson, AZ; Laredo, TX; and Wendling, England.

He was discharged Dec. 11, 1945 with the rank of staff sergeant. Received the Air Medal with two clusters, Good Conduct Medal, ETO with two stars.

Married and has three sons and one grandson. Retired from Continental Can Co. in 1981. Now working for Atlanta Humane Society.

MARVIN RALPH DAVIS, was born in Lebanon, OH on Nov. 30, 1922. Entered the service on March 8, 1943 as an aviation cadet at San Antonio Aviation Cadet Center. Primary at Pine Bluff, AR; basic at Independence, KS; advance at Ellington Field, TX; and B-24 transition at Tarrant Field, TX.

Crew 57, the best crew in the service, was picked up at Gowen Field, ID and from Topeka, KS they flew their air-

craft over the northern route to Nutts Corner, Ireland. After combat crew training, reported to 467th Bomb Group in August 1944. Piloted 34 combat missions, all to Germany, and returned home at wars end.

Served two years during Korean War as production test pilot at North American Aviation. Completed college education with a PhD in management.

ROBERT T. DAVIS, was born Jan. 14, 1919 near Columbia, MO. Joined the USAAC September 1943. Went to Sheppard Field, TX for basic training; Harlingen, TX, Gunnery School; Pueblo, CO for crew training; Wichita, KS for combat crew assignment.

Arrived northern Ireland in June 1944 for refresher gunnery. With the 448th Bomb Group, arrived Seething, England in late June 1944. Flew 35 missions. Memorable experience was when they lost #4 engine on take-off with six 1,000 pound bombs. They managed to circle for emergency landing but missed runway because of strong cross wind. The grass area of field was rough and landing gear collapsed after about 300 yards. They skidded on belly to a stop, all bombs broke loose from ranks but, luckily, didn't explode.

Returned to USA in April 1945. After two weeks R&R in Miami Beach, he went to Laredo, TX for B-29 Gunnery School. Was discharged on points September 1945. Achieved the rank of staff sergeant.

VIRGINIA M. TOMLIN DAVIS, was born April 28, 1922 in St. Paris, OH. Enlisted Sept. 1, 1943, WAC, telephone operator 650, 311th and 315th Signal Co., stationed at Ft. Oglethorpe, GA; basic and 4th Service C, 315th Signal, Hetteringham, 311th Signal, Cambridge.

Memorable experiences were all the wonderful people of Blitz Hotel; working switchboard morning of D-day; and celebration on V-E day.

Discharged October 1945 with the rank private first class.

She received the EAME Theater Ribbon, Good Conduct, two Overseas Bars and the WAAC Service Ribbon.

Married and has four children: Douglas, Carl, Laura and Paula. She has seven grandchildren and one great-granddaughter. Retired from hospital.

WALTER S. DAVIS, was born in Evanston, IL on March 31, 1924. Entered USAAF in September 1942 while a sophomore at Northwestern University. From classification at Santa Ana, CA, completed cadet training at Ellington Field and Aerial Gunnery School at Harlingen, TX. Completed Navigation School at Hondo, TX and was crew assigned at Westover Field, MA.

Flew to 8th Air Force assignment over the northern route and posted at 489th Bomb Group, Halesworth, Buncher #8 in June 1944. Flew 22 missions in B-24 and was picked in December 1944 as experimental cadre to transfer whole 8th Air Force to Okinawa.

Formed new B-29 Group at Fairmont, NE, from which he was released from active duty. Most memorable mission was as a lead navigator for airborne invasion of Holland at Nijmegen in September 1944.

Married his college sweetheart, Betty Grede, on April 19, 1947. They have three sons, two daughters and 18 grandchildren.

Re-entered Northwestern University where he graduated with BS in 1947 and JD in law, 1950. After practicing in Chicago, was recalled during Korean War as B-29 combat crew. Transferred to Judge Advocate Dept. and released at Moody AFB, Valdosta, GA in 1952 when he and family moved to Milwaukee where he resumed practice of law and now heads 55-lawyer firm.

ERLING M. DAWES, was born in Coldspring, WY April 3, 1921 and was raised on ranches in Wyoming and Nebraska. Enlisted as an aviation cadet in May 1942; assigned to the Class of 43-G; graduated at Frederick, OK, July 29, 1943 as a second lieutenant.

Assigned to the 445th Bomb Group, 702nd Sqdn., Sioux City, IA as a co-pilot in August 1943. Went overseas with the 445th in November 1943. Flew 15 missions, was shot down in France April 1, 1944. Escaped and returned to England in September 1944.

Received three Air Medals, Purple Heart plus other ribbons. Separated from the service January 1953 as a captain. He is married with two children.

IRVING M. DAY JR., was born Nov. 13, 1922 in Schenectady, NY; educated in Montgomery County, MD schools; graduated with Class of 1940, Bethesda Chevy Chase High School. Enlisted in the USAAC Aviation Cadet program, Washington, DC in 1942.

Commissioned second lieutenant at Big Spring, TX, Army Air Corps Bombardier School, June 24, 1943. Took first phase training in B-18s, Clovis, NM; proceeded to bomb group training (B-24) with 446th Bomb Group, Lowry Field, Denver; assigned to crew of 2nd Lt. Sterling L. Tuck, 705th Bomb Sqdn.

Returned on leave to Washington, DC and married high school classmate, Marin Stoddard, Aug. 18, 1943. She accompanied him back to Denver. During third phase at Denver, the 446th lost three planes; en route to Bungay, England via South America and Africa, they lost two more.

Day's plane was shot down by flak near Dummer Lake, April 11, 1944, en route to Bernburg A/F on his 25th mission. Two planes were lost that day: *Brown Noser*, piloted by Lt. Kermit Fuchs (only bombardier survived) and *Werewolf. Princess O'Rourke* was piloted by Lt. Tuck (all 10 survived).

After 13 months as POW in Stalag Luft I, was released by Soviet forces and finally made it home to Marin. They have had 50 years of wedded bliss, have three children and five grandchildren. They reside on the shore of beautiful Deep Creek Lake in the hills of Western Maryland.

PHILLIP G. DAY, enlisted in the USAAC Enlisted Reserve for the Aviation Cadet program on his 18th birthday, May 22, 1942. Called to active duty on Feb. 21, 1943, completed pilot training on March 12, 1944 and was appointed and commissioned a temporary second lieutenant, Army of the U.S. and awarded an aeronautical rating of twin engine pilot.

Assigned to be a B-24 copilot, he crewed up with William A. Johnston in April 1944 and flew 100 hours in the Replacement Training Unit at Tonopah AAB, NV before sailing to England on July 3, 1944. Assigned first to the 492nd Bomb Group(H) where it flew no missions, the Johnston crew was transferred to the 467th Bomb Group(H) on Aug. 10, 1944.

Day flew his first combat mission on August 18 and his 35th on March 21, 1945 with battle participations of Northern France, Rhineland, Ardennes-Alsace and Central Europe. When his group flew supplies to Allied Ground Forces in France in September 1944, he flew 15 of those

missions with Johnston and other pilots of the 791st Bomb Sqdn.(H).

After 635 hours total B-24 time, 230 in combat and 90 as pilot or qualified dual, he returned to the States for R&R, then transitioned to Douglas C-47s to fly navigation cadets on principally over water and night training missions for over 200 hours. Relieved from active duty on Oct. 31, 1945, he returned to college to earn an industrial engineering degree after which he began his civilian occupation of oil and gas drilling and production engineering and management.

Was active in the Air Force Reserves until July 1958 and fully retired from business activities Jan. 1, 1991. Married May 19, 1944 to Lucille Webb, they have three sons, six grandsons and one granddaughter. He remains very active in the 467th Bombardment Group(H) Association, Ltd. as treasurer and editor/publisher of the association's newsletter, *Poop From Group.*

HARRY R. DEAN, was born Oct. 21, 1925 in Chicago, IL and raised on a farm in Mecosta, MI. Inducted into the Army on Jan. 19, 1944 at Big Rapids, MI. Volunteered for USAAC at Ft. Sheridan, IL. Attended basic training at Miami Beach, FL; Gunnery School at Laredo, TX; and phase training at Tonopah, NV. Assigned to Deany's crew as waist gunner. Crew was sent as replacements to 853rd Sqdn. of 491st Bomb Group at North Pickenham, England.

Returned to USA at end of war and was assigned to orderly room in Walla Walla, WA. Was discharged at Ft. Lewis, WA on March 1, 1946. Received Air Medal plus other service ribbons.

Married Ann Flachs Schafer on June 14, 1971. Has five children, five step-children and is grandfather to 14. Retired in 1981 after 35 years in building construction.

JOSEPH HENRY DEAN JR., was born Oct. 23, 1923 near Elkton, VA. Entered the USAAC on Feb. 17, 1943 after completing one year Aircraft Mechanic School at Virginia Polytechnic Institute. After training at Miami Beach, FL, Gulfport Field, MS and Harlingen, TX, he was assigned as flight engineer on 1st Lt. Floyd Harville's B-24 crew in the 489th Bomb Group.

On March 4, 1944, after completing additional training at Tucson, AZ and Wendover Field, UT, they were assigned a new B-24(H) #42-52698, *The Baby Doll.* The group departed Wendover Field, UT on April 13, 1944, flying the southern route via Fortaleza, Brazil and Dakar, Africa, to Halesworth, England.

Completed 34 missions during 269 combat flying hours as a technical sergeant, his decorations include the Distinguished Flying Cross, Air Medal with three Oak Leaf Clusters and the Good Conduct Medal. Service medals include the American Theater and the Europe-Africa-Middle Eastern Theater with five Bronze Stars (Rhineland, Air Offensive of Europe, Normandy, Northern France and Southern France).

Returning stateside by boat Dec. 22, 1944 with the group, he was sent to Central Instructors School at Laredo, TX. Upon completion, he was assigned to MacDill AFB, Tampa, FL. There he served as in-flight instructor on B-29s until Sept. 19, 1945, at which time, he re-enlisted in the Air Force Reserve at Byrd Field, Richmond, VA and departed immediately to Michigan.

He studied aeronautical engineering at the University of Michigan and has remained in the Detroit area, serving in the Michigan Air National Guard as a technical sergeant in charge of ground training and as a full time mechanic/inspector on Douglas B-26s and Republic F-84s, Nov. 3, 1946 to Nov. 2, 1952.

He was employed as an automotive engineer/writer at Central Engineering, Chrysler Corp. and Engineering Staff,

Ford Motor Co. He has studied computer programming at Henry Ford Community College.

Married to the former Helen Louise Hensley of Elkton, VA, they have one son, Michael Anthony Dean.

RICHARD M. DEAN (DICK), was born Sept. 4, 1920 in Grand Rapids, MI. Moved to Ann Arbor, MI in 1936 and entered the armed services in September 1942. He proceeded to Battle Creek, MI to complete written tests and then on to Biloxi, MS for basic training.

Was sent to Radio School at Truax AFB in Madison, WI. From there he went to Salt Lake City, UT at the fairgrounds for a refresher course and then on to Gowan AFB in Boise, ID where he joined a B-24 bomber crew which had already completed its first phase of training. He proceeded to March Field, Riverside, CA to finish 2nd and 3rd phase training, left there and picked up a new B-24 at Hamilton AFB near San Francisco.

Flew back across the U.S. to Florida and then took the southern route and on up to England in December 1943. Was stationed at old Buckingham AFB at Attleborough with the 8th Air Force. He was in the first daylight raid on Berlin. The crew's co-pilot was hit by flak on one mission but was not seriously injured. Oxygen tanks were knocked out on another mission and the plane left formation to return to the base alone without problems. Completed 32 bombing missions from January 1944 to June 11, 1944 and returned to the States September 1944.

Was assigned as Duty NCO in charge of a squadron at Tyndall Field, Panama City, FL until discharge in October 1945. He suffered fatigue but no injuries while serving with the Air Force. Discharged October 1945 with the rank tech sergeant, radio operator and gunner. Received the Distinguished Flying Cross, Air Medal with three Oak Leaf Clusters, European Battle Ribbon with four Battle Stars, and the Good Conduct Ribbon.

Married on May 11, 1991 to his present wife, June Marie. He has three sons and two daughters by a previous marriage and 13 grandchildren and six great-grandchildren. Retired from Ford Motor as a production supervisor after 27 years.

CHARLES E. DEARING, was born March 4, 1921 in New York City. Entered the service as aviation cadet on Jan. 19, 1942 and graduated as pilot, second lieutenant, class 42-K on Dec. 13, 1942, George Field, IL. Seriously injured in a May 1943, A-20 crash, it was January 1945 before he joined 564th Sqdn., 389th Bomb Group at Hethel, England. Flew missions until V-E day.

Remained on active duty and assigned to occupation duty at Oberpfaffenhofen and Furstenfeldbruck, Germany, 1946-1949. Served as wing adjutant, 314th Troop Carrier Wing, Sewart AFB, TN until 1953 when he joined the newly formed 63rd Troop Carrier Wing, flying C-124s at Donaldson AFB, SC. After a two and a half year tour in Japan (1954-1956) returned to Donaldson. Became Commander, 14th Troop Carrier Sqdn., C-124s until retirement as lieutenant colonel, April 1963.

Pursued variety of business interests until 1979 when he joined two Air Force (Medical Corps) retirees to distribute dialysis supplies to home kidney patients. Buy out of company led to final retirement in June 1987.

ANTHONY DE BENEDICTUS, was born Jan. 23, 1922 in Catskill, NY. Enlisted Sept. 20, 1940 in the USAAF as S/S aerial tail gunner with 2nd Air Div., 389th Bomb Group, 467th Sqdn. Stationed at Panama City, FL; Gunnery, Davis-Monthan, AZ; Biggs AF, El Paso; Hethel, England, B-24 Liberator.

Participated in 24 raids, shot down March 8, 1944, 2nd

Daylight, Berlin, lived with Dutch Underground until July 31, 1944. Crash landed in Netherlands, captured by Gestapo Aug. 12, 1944 in Antwerp, Belgium, was POW at Stalag Luft #4.

Discharged September 1946 with the rank staff sergeant. He received two Distinguished Flying Crosses and five Air Medals.

Married to Antoinette and has two daughters, Diane and Debra. Self-employed financial accounting, he is currently retired.

LOUIS J. DEBLASIO, was born March 21, 1921 in Brooklyn, NY. Enlisted in the USAAC on Sept. 23, 1942 and was sent to Randolph Field, TX as ground crew. Applied for cadet training and was accepted. Attended Norwich University in Vermont and qualified for pilot and bombardier. Completed Gunnery School, Tyndall, FL; Armorer School, Buckley Field, CO; assigned to Max Chandlers crew at Westover Field, MA.

Completed overseas training in B-24s, arrived in England in January of 1945. Assigned to the 506th Bomb Sqdn., the 44th Bomb Group flew seven combat missions including Berlin. On seventh mission, a low level (200-300 foot) mission, dropping supplies to ground troops at Wessel, Germany, they were shot down and crash landed. Out of nine men only Robert Vance (tail gunner) and DeBlasio (right waist gunner) survived the crash. They were both wounded and immediately captured by the Germans.

Liberated by the 2nd Armd. Div., who overran the town of Ahrlen, Germany, he spent seven months in the hospital. Discharged Nov. 5, 1945 from Macon Field Hospital in Georgia. Joined the Army Reserves and between active duty and reserves, he completed 22 years of service. Retired as CWO2 and received the Air Medal, Purple Heart, POW Medal, WWII Victory Medal, Good Conduct Medal, and European Theater Medal.

Married Agnes Colavito and has two children and four grandchildren.

MICHAEL J. DeBRINO, was born in Schenectady, NY on Sept. 22, 1919 and attended school there.

Enlisted in the USAAC Oct. 24, 1941; basic training at Ft. Dix, NJ; orientation at Jefferson Barracks, MO; then to Lowry Field, CO. Graduated from Air Corps Tech School as an aircraft armorer on March 21, 1942. Assigned to 329th Bomb Sqdn., 93rd Bomb Group, March 1942 at Barksdale Field, LA. Went to Ft. Myers, FL in May 1942 for antisubpatrol.

Left for overseas duty on Aug. 2, 1942, Alconbury, England, moved to Hardwicke, September 1942. While at Barksdale Field, he attended Chemical Warfare School. Became Gas NCO for 329th. In November 1943 he graduated from Consolidated Turret School, Kirkham, Blackpool. Their group participated in the African Campaign and Ploesti. They earned 11 Battle Stars plus DUB for Africa and Ploesti.

Memorable experience: On way back home, their plane made an emergency landing at Stornaway, Scotland and were there for eight days. When they finally arrived at Bradley Field, they were welcomed like "long lost heroes" by their buddies who thought they had perished in the cold ocean.

Returned to USA June 1945 via Bradley Field, CT. Went on 10 day furlough, then returned to Sioux Falls, SD, June 1945, then to Clovis, NM, August 1945. Back to Ft. Dix, NJ for discharge in September 1945. Received the American Defense Service Medal, WWII Victory Medal, DUB with cluster, EAME Service Medal and the Good Conduct Medal.

Married Oct. 10, 1946 to Mary Mizzero. They have three sons, one daughter and eight grandchildren. Retired from U.S. Postal Service.

FRANK DeCOLA, was born in East Brady, PA on April 20, 1921. Enlisted in the Air Force Oct. 19, 1942. After basic training in Miami, he reported to Amarillo, TX for AM training, graduated and was sent to Consolidated Aircraft in San Diego, CA for training on the B-24 Liberator. Graduated and went to the Modification Center in Tucson, AZ for more training on the Liberator. Was then sent to Wendover, UT to Gunnery School. Completed gunnery training and sent to Clovis, NM where he was assigned to a crew for training.

They were sent to Savannah, GA for further training, then ordered to Italy with the 15th Air Force. DeCola was left behind for minor surgery and later heard that his crew was lost in action. After recuperating from surgery, was sent to Pueblo, CO as a flight engineer instructor. Was there about six months, then requested combat duty. Assigned to a crew and in June 1944 was sent to England with the 8th Air Force, 2nd Div., 448th Bomb Group, 714th Sqdn. and flew as a flight engineer.

Completed 35 hectic missions in March 1945 and sent back to the States in April 1945. Discharged in June 1945 under the point system. Received the Distinguished Flying Cross, six Air Medals, campaign ribbons and various other ribbons.

Married Mary Sanesi in 1946. They have two sons and four grandchildren. He received two years further aviation training. Went into business for himself, retired in 1989 and is now cruising along at half throttle.

JOSEPH DeCUSATI, was born March 16, 1923 in New Haven, CT. Enlisted Dec. 1, 1942 in the USAAC. Attended Gunnery and Radio schools. Was assigned to 732nd Sqdn., 453rd Bomb Group, Old Buckingham, England with Lt. Eugene Mills crew. Participated in battles during March 1945 at Siegen, Gardelegen, Berlin, Hemmingstadt, Giebelstadt, Stormede, and Wilhelmshaven.

On seventh mission (flying aboard the *Linda Lou* over Wilhelmshaven), DeCusati was hit by a piece of flak that went through his arm and into his chest. He was the only member of his crew to be killed. According to the records, he was also the last man from the 732nd Sqdn. to be killed in action.

DeCusati was awarded the Air Medal and Purple Heart posthumously. *Submitted by his cousin, Andrew J. DeCusati.*

CHARLES R. DEEGAN, was born in Big Timber, MT on Dec. 20, 1923. Entered the Army and Aviation Cadets in 1943. Graduated Navigation School, Monroe, LA in September. Crew 61 training at Boise, Wendover and Tonopah. Took southern route itinerary to Norwich, 755th Bomb Sqdn., 458th Bomb Group, February 1944. Completed 30 missions D-day. Completed navigator instructor and pilot training when A-bomb drops ended active duty, October 1945, first lieutenant, Reserve.

Went to Montana State University, 1950 BS in health and education. Taught two years, recalled to active duty. Completed 50 night interdiction navigation missions in B-26, Korea in 1952; C-124 navigator, Moses Lake, WA, 1952 to 1955; tactical missiles, satellite operations and Minuteman R&D until retirement in 1969, lieutenant colonel, master navigator, senior missileman. Overseas tours in Korea (2) and Germany. Received the Distinguished Flying Cross with one Oak Leaf Cluster, Air Medal with six Oak Leaf Clusters, Commendation with one Oak Leaf Cluster and the Distinguished Unit Citation.

Married Bertie Gottlob in 1946. They had three sons and seven grandchildren. Bertie and one son are deceased.

Eleven seasons of commercial salmon trolling, Washington and Alaska. Activities now include bowling, golfing, and traveling.

ROSTEN R. DeFRATES, was born July 21, 1923 in Jacksonville, IL. Joined the AAF Jan. 11, 1943, Scott Field. Stationed at Amarillo, TX, Las Vegas, NV; Muroc, CA and ETO.

June 1944, #4 mission, Magdeburg, Germany-no fighter attacks but intense flak made up for that. Their engineer was killed on bomb run over target, #1 engine was hit and had to be feathered. They lost much of their fuel and all of their oxygen. Dropped to a lower altitude and headed for home. Leaving Holland, they were hit again by flak, losing #4 engine, pilot was hit by flak and lost tip of his fingers. Got within 20 miles of home when #3 engine quit. Crash landed at Horsham St. Faith.

Was put with a make-up crew for a low level mission to take emergency supplies to the English and 82nd Airborne trapped by the Germans. Was hit continually by small arms and lost hydraulic system and oxygen. Had to crank landing gear down manually to land. Upon landing was put on a train and transferred to the 9th Air Force, 322nd Bomb Group, 449th Bomb Sqdn. After moving to France the Red Cross told him his brother, Billy, was killed in Holland in September 1944 by a German anti-tank shell. To this day DeFrates wonders if he could have been only a few feet above him and still couldn't help his brother. Completed more than 35 more missions in the B-26 before the war ended.

Discharged Oct. 11, 1945 with the rank of staff sergeant. Received the Air Medal, Silver and Bronze Oak Leaf, Presidential Citation, ETO Ribbon with one Silver and one Bronze Star and the American Defense Medal.

Married Deloris June 1948, they have two sons and three grandchildren. He is retired.

GEORGE DeGROOT, was born Aug. 7, 1920 in Paterson, NJ. Completed high school and entered the service Sept. 7, 1942. Received basic training in Miami Beach, FL; aircraft training on B-17s at Amarillo, TX; B-24 training at Consolidated Voltee Aircraft Corp., San Diego, CA. After training was complete, he flew as flight engineer on shake down flights for about one month, then joined the 712th Bomb Sqdn., 448th Bomb Group at Sioux City, IA where their training began for overseas assignment.

Left the States for England in November 1943 and was stationed at Station #146, Seething, England where he was assistant crew chief and member of a ground crew on B-24s. His appointment to buck sergeant came before they departed for England. Received a total of seven citations with six Bronze Stars (Rhineland, Northern France, Normandy, Central Europe, Air Offense Europe and Ardennes). Discharged Oct. 12, 1945, Newark, NJ.

After the service he worked in two machine shops, first for nine years as assistant supervisor and die set-up man on punch presses and second as supervisor of machine shop for 34 years. Retired in 1984.

Married Oct. 7, 1943 and has a son, two daughters, one grandson and two granddaughters.

JOSEPH D. DEIGERT, was born April 3, 1925 in Baltimore, MD. Joined the USAAC Oct. 9, 1943. Stationed at Greensboro, NC; Sioux Falls, SD; Yuma, AZ; and Hethel Air Base, Norwich, England. Participated in air combat at Ardennes, Rhineland and Central Europe. He flew 22 missions over Germany.

Discharged Dec. 13, 1945 with the rank tech sergeant. Received the Air Medal with two Oak Leaf Clusters, Distinguished Unit Badge, American Theater Ribbon and the EAME Theater Ribbon.

Graduated from William and Mary College, he is an active land developer in Maryland. Married and has two sons.

DARIO A. DeJULIO, was born in Ontario, CA on Aug. 18, 1916. Enlisted in the USAAC in 1943; graduated Pilot School, Western Flying Training Command, Class 44-E from Pecos AAF Base, TX. Flew B-17s in Yuma AAF Base. Reassigned to B-24s and OTU at Charleston AAF Base, SC.

Overseas as a replacement crew on the *Queen Mary* to Glasgow, Scotland, then to Horsham St. Faith, Norwich,

England to the 752nd Bomb Sqdn., 458th Bomb Group(H). Flew 30 missions from November 1944 through April 1945. Received the Air Medal with four Oak Leaf Clusters, three campaigns with three Battle Stars. Had two engines shot out over Hamburg, Germany and managed to make it back to Norwich.

At war's end, he flew three trolley missions at low level, then brought plane back with passengers to Bradley Field AB CN. Assigned to Sioux City AB, IA as OIC in base processing. Left AAF in November 1945.

Was recalled for Korea in 1950. Served in Troop Carrier, McCord AB; Air Evac, Travis AB; Ferry Command, Long Beach AB; C-54 School, Great Falls AB; Rescue SA-16 School, Tampa AB; then crew training, Palm Beach AB; rescue assignment Fuerstenfeldbruck AB Germany (three years); March AFB. Retired June 1968 with the rank lieutenant colonel.

Civilian employment as advertising artist, art director at Western Lithograph Co., co-owner, packaging and label designer of Production Art Service Inc., and advisor for 10 years to Los Angeles Trade Tech College. Fully retired Jan. 1, 1979.

Married to Beverley Trank in 1939 and has a daughter, son and grandson.

ROBERT WM. DeKERF, was born on Aug. 10, 1922 in DePere, WI and was raised in Chicago, IL. Enlisted in the USAAF on Sept. 25, 1942. Prior to flight training at Wendover Field, UT, attended Engine A/C (B-24) and Gunnery schools. Assigned as a flight engineer/gunner to a crew and a new B-24H, A/C 252534. Was assigned to the 790th Sqdn. of the 467th Bomb Group, 96th Combat Wing, 2nd Air Div., 8th Air Force.

Ferried B-24 from Wendover, UT to Herington, KS for additional training, then on to Morrison Field, FL, en route to Rackheath, Norfolk, England. Completed 30 combat missions. Flew 29 of the 30 missions with his original crew on the now famous *Witchcraft* which flew over 100 missions without an abort. Discharged on Sept. 25, 1945.

Employed primarily by the Defense Dept. at various Defense installations until his retirement in January 1989. Married to Myra J. Tichan on Oct. 17, 1950. They have two daughters and two grandchildren. He was very fortunate to have flown 29 of his 30 missions with such a great air crew and such a dedicated ground crew. It was his good fortune to be able to be part of this great historical event and make so many lasting friends.

JOHN W. DeLURY, was born April 28, 1921 in Salt Lake City, UT. Moved to California in 1936, graduated with BS in economics, University of California, Berkeley in 1942. Joined the USAAC June 1942. Graduated second lieutenant, pilot, Class 43-K, Dec. 5, 1943, Yuma, AZ.

Assigned co-pilot on B-24 replacement crew for training at Muroc AAFB Jan. 1, 1944. Departed Hamilton Field on April 1, 1944 for overseas via the southern crossing, Natal to Dakar. Joined 453rd Bomb Group, 734th Sqdn. April 19 in Old Buckingham. Flew first mission on May 23; transferred temporarily to 389th Bomb Group for lead crew "Mickey" training. Completed 30 missions (including one bail out) on November 6.

Promoted to first lieutenant and awarded the Air Medal with three clusters and the Distinguished Flying Cross during tour. Arrived back in the States December 12. Joined Training Command at Merced AAFB as basic instructor in AT-6's. Reported to Camp Beale, CA July 21, 1945 for separation.

Followed career in purchasing management with H.J. Heinz (31 years) and FMC, Inc. (seven years). Married Helen Hartwell on Dec. 7, 1943, Oakland, CA. Remarried May 24, 1975 to Sandra Elliott. Retired 1983 to part-time consulting, growing roses, and enjoying three children, 10 grandchildren and four great-grandchildren.

WILLIAM J. DEMETROPOULOS, was radio operator gunner on B-24s attached to 714th Bomb Sqdn., 448th Bomb Group. Enlisted in the USAAC on Dec. 11, 1942. Processed at Ft. Sheridan, IL; basic training at Clearwater, FL; stationed at Scott Field, IL; Radio School.

Shipped to Gowen Field, Boise, ID; assigned to Crew 55 at Sioux City, IA. Received combat gear at Herington, KS and arrived at Morrison Field, FL. Flew southern route to Seething, England. Flew his first mission to Ludwigshaven, Germany on Dec. 30, 1943. Completed 30 missions on June 22, 1944.

Crew 55 received the Distinguished Flying Cross, Air Medal with three Oak Leaf Clusters, ETO Ribbon with three Battle Stars. Taught radio fundamentals at Truax Field, Madison, WI. Discharged from Truax on Sept. 20, 1945.

Married April 27, 1947 to Mary from Boston, MA. They have three children and four grandchildren. Retired from MILW Road RR after 31 and a half years as locomotive engineer. He is a member of the Masons, Consistory, and Tripoli Shrine Temple, VFW, Eastern Star and 2nd Air Division Association.

ROBERT LEE DeNEAL, was born Sept. 12, 1924 in Vermilion County, IL and reared on a dairy farm. Enlisted April 6, 1943 in the USAAF, 453rd Bomb Group. Attended Engineering School; Operations Clerk School, Fort Logan, CO. Saw action at Normandy, Northern France, Ardennes, Rhineland, Central Europe and Air Offensive Europe.

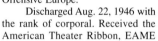

Discharged Aug. 22, 1946 with the rank of corporal. Received the American Theater Ribbon, EAME Theater Ribbon, six Bronze Battle Stars, WWII Victory Ribbon and the Good Conduct Medal.

After discharge, he finished high school, earned associate degree in accounting and was bookkeeper for auto agency until 1962. Appointed rural letter carrier, retired from route in 1984. Married Lela Mae Daniel, June 28, 1952. They had three sons: David, Dan and Dale; one daughter, Darla Finley; and nine grandchildren: Nancy, Stephanie, Stacy, Steven, Brian, Jonathan, Dustin, Diana, and Luke.

DeNeal was a member of 2nd Air Division Association and American Legion. He passed away Nov. 27, 1993.

WILLIAM J. DENTON JR., was born on Nov. 15, 1920 in Paris, TX. He joined the USAAC in September 1939. He was stationed at Randolph Field, worked through the ranks and was commissioned on Sept. 29, 1942 at Roswell Field, NM. Trained on a B-17, but was involved in a crash on take off at Biggs Field in El Paso, TX.

After recuperating, he was sent to B-24 training and given a crew at Biggs Field. He was sent to Denver, CO and assigned to the 389th. Left for overseas in June 1943. He was squadron leader on Danzog raid and later raids. After completing missions he became a combat training pilot in Ireland. On one such mission, his plane was the last one back from Ploesti. He had to cut the engines back into low to not run out of fuel. When he landed, all engines had quit. They had voted to go with the leaky tank.

He was active in the USAAC for 10 years and with the Reserve Corps for 31 years. Retired in June 1972 with the

rank of colonel. He was an airline pilot at United Airlines from which he retired in November 1980 as a captain. Accumulated 30,000 flight hours.

Married and has two sons, both of whom he is very proud of. One son is a commercial pilot and the other son is a lawyer.

CHARLES F. DERR, was born in November 1921 in Norristown, PA and educated at Michigan State University with a BS degree in mechanical engineering. He had flying training at Decator and Courtland, AL; Freeman Field, Seymour, IN and Chanute Field, IL.

Had combat experience in the 700th Bomb Sqdn., 445th Bomb Group from November 1944 through May 1945. He flew 26 combat missions as an airplane commander. He lost two crew members to enemy action and one was lost falling off of a bicycle. He received the Air Medal with four clusters and the Presidential Group Citation.

He returned to school, then married Mary Voorhees in 1946. They raised four successful children located coast to coast throughout the United States. He worked for Michigan Bell Telephone for 33 years, retiring in 1980 as assistant vice president. He moved to Pinehurst, NC, the golf capital of the world in 1986, and spends many days playing golf and volunteering at the local hospital and the local Hospice Chapter.

MERRITT E. DERR, was born on Jan. 16, 1920 in Emmaus, PA. He joined the USAAC on Jan. 14, 1942 in Allentown, PA. He was assigned to the 323rd Air Service Sqdn. in Savannah, GA. Applied for and was accepted as an aviation cadet, Class 43-F. Graduated as a pilot and was commissioned a second lieutenant at Yuma, AZ on June 22, 1943.

He was assigned to B-17 pilot training at Roswell, NM. Upon his completion of B-17 training, he was assigned to B-24 crew training at Boise, ID. He flew as co-pilot of B-24 replacement crew assigned to the 44th Bomb Group (H), 506th Sqdn. He arrived at Shipdham, England via South America and Africa in March 1944.

He completed 35 combat missions on Aug. 6, 1944. He received the Distinguished Flying Cross, four Air Medals, European Campaign Medal with four Battle Stars and several others. Returned to the States, was hospitalized at Pawling, NY until separation under the point system. He served in the Pennsylvania Air National Guard until 1960. Transferred to the Air Force Reserve and retired in 1969 as lieutenant colonel.

He and his wife Frances A. have one daughter and three grandchildren. He is retired.

ROLAND A. DESJARDINS (DESI), was born on Jan. 28, 1925 in New Bedford, MA. He entered the USAAC in July 1943. He completed bombardier/navigator training in May 1944 as second lieutenant at Childress, TX. He was assigned to flight crew at Westover Field, MA for B-24 training.

Arrived in Tibenham, England in October 1944 as replacements in the 445th Bomb Group, 702 Sqdn., 2nd Air Div. Flew 27 missions through the end of the war in Europe. Returned to Sioux Falls, SD until the Japan defeat. He returned from all 27 missions unscathed, however, all were memorable.

Released from active duty in October 1945 with the rank of first lieutenant. He received the Air Medal and Oak Leaf Clusters in addition to group awards.

He and Lillian M. Maye were married on April 27, 1946. They have four children and five grandchildren. He graduated from Northeastern University in Boston, MA with a BSME in 1951. He worked in aerospace and retired from the Boeing Helicopter Co. in 1986.

He enjoys family, Air Force reunions and traveling.

ROBERT P. DEVER, was born on Feb. 27, 1925 in Attleboro, MA. He enlisted into the USAAF on May 12, 1943 and discharged Oct. 30, 1945. Trained as a navigator at San Marcos AFB in Texas and graduated in June 1944.

Assigned to the 453rd Bomb Group (H), 8th Air Force in England, November 1944 and then to the 476th Bomb Group (H) about April 1945. He flew 25 missions as part of Virgil Smiths' crew. Most missions were flown in a B-24 named *Whiskey Jingles*. Where the name came from God only knows.

He was awarded the Air Medal with clusters. Was recalled to active duty during the Korean conflict. Served with the Air Transport Command at Westover AFB in Massachusetts and also with the 58th Fighter Bomber Group at K-2, Tagu, Korea from May 1951 to April 1952.

Total service this period was from Oct. 20, 1950 to Aug. 17, 1952. He retired from the Reserves on Dec. 1, 1968 after 25 years with the rank of major. He served in various assignments as a reservist.

He and his wife Rita have one son Robert. He is retired from a small consulting business.

ROY M. DEVLIN, was born on March 8, 1920, lived in the Milwaukee area until 1981, when they moved to Florida. Entered the service on Feb. 6, 1943 in Chicago, IL. Arrived at the USAAC Classification Center in Nashville, TN on Feb. 7, 1943.

Arrived at Selman Field, Monroe, LA on March 20, 1943 for Officers Training School. Entered pre-Flight Navigation School; Advanced Navigation School; assigned to Flight 22 and received wings. Was commissioned second lieutenant on Sept. 25, 1943. Reported to Davis Monthan Field in Tucson, AZ in October; Blythe, CA in October where he was assigned to a crew to prepare for overseas combat duty.

Went to Herington, KS Dec. 25, 1943, then Langley Field March 2, 1944 for radar navigator training on Pathfinder equipment. Left there on B-24J by way of Presque Isle, ME; Goose Bay, Labrador; Meeks, Iceland; Prestwick, Scotland; and Alconbury Air Base. After five weeks intensive training, was assigned to 44th Bombardment Group, 14th Bombardment Wing, 2nd Bombardment Div. of the 8th Air Force

Flew 25 combat missions over Germany and France. Received the ETO Medal with six Bronze Battle Stars, Air Offensive Europe, American Defense Medal, WWII Victory Medal, Air Force Reserve Medal, Air Medal with three Oak Leaf Cluster and the Distinguished Flying Cross.

Returned to Wisconsin in 1945 and to his apprenticeship at Chain Belt Company for Layout and Structural Erection. He and Elizabeth Coon were married on Sept. 29, 1943. They have a son, two daughters and five grandchildren. His son is also retired as captain from the Air Force after 21 years.

He retired from Rexnord as production manager of the Malleable Casting Division after 40 years with the same company. He remained in the Air Force Reserve, retiring in 1980 as lieutenant colonel at General Billy Mitchell Field in Milwaukee, WI. He enjoys the Florida sunshine and gardening, traveling and work with the church.

HARTLEY C. DEWEY, was born July 1, 1919, Manhattan, New York City, NY, joined the Army, May 22, 1942; transferred to the USAAC; commissioned as a pilot, June 22, 1943; transferred to USAF in July 1947. Had many assignments.

Stationed at Davis Monthan, AZ; Alamogordo, NM; Manduria, Italy; Bungay, England; Victorville, CA; Great Falls, MT; Seoul, Korea; Ent AFB, CO; Hickam AFB, HI; Langley AFB, VA.

Participated in Air Offensive Europe, Naples-Foggia, Southern France, Northern France, Rome-Arno, Western Europe, missions Regensburg and Polesti from Italy.

Completed his tour with a total of 39 missions. Released from active duty on Nov. 6, 1945. Became a grain broker on the Chicago Board of Trade in Illinois. In 1950 became a hotel manager in Carmel, CA.

Recalled to active duty on Feb. 5, 1951, sent to Korea as Psy war pilot. Was member of team negotiating release of USS *Pueblo* crew from North Korea and became assistant secretary, Armistice Affairs Division, Seoul, Korea. Returned to Langley AFB in 1969 as chief, Operational Plans Division, DSO HQ Tac. Retired on July 31, 1970 with the rank of colonel. Among his many medals were the Distinguished Flying Cross, Legion of Merit, Good Conduct and Air Medal with nine Oak Leaf Clusters.

Married Sally Glaser on Sept. 8, 1945. They have four married children: Deborah, Hartley F., Craig C. and Alan B.; seven grandchildren; and four great-granchildren. He enjoys working as Red Cross volunteer and updating family genealogy.

WILLIAM R. DEWEY, was born on Oct. 5, 1922 in Chicago, IL. He entered the USAAC on Oct. 6, 1942 as a private. He went through West Coast Flying Training Command as an aviation cadet. He cracked up a PT-22 Ryan in a forced landing caused by engine failure, washed back two classes, graduating Class 44-A as pilot, second lieutenant Marfa, TX.

Trained as a B-24 pilot, started flying combat missions from Tibenham, England with the 445th Bomb Group on Aug. 16, 1944. On Sept. 27, 1944, he survived the highest group loss in 8th Air Force history on mission to Kassel, Germany. Dewey's B-24 was one of six B-24s that safely landed back in England, 29 Liberators and 1 P-51 were destroyed by German fighters and 29 German planes were shot down in a five minute air battle.

He finished 30 combat missions over Germany as squadron lead pilot, assigned assistant group operations officer until return to ZO1, flying a war-weary B-24 over the Atlantic. He was discharged in October 1945. Received the Distinguished Flying Cross, five Air Medals and four European Campaign Stars.

Married Marilyn Alice Dewey on June 14, 1947, they have one son and two daughters and five grandchildren. He is still working as an executive recruiter.

TOMMIE FLOWERS DICKSON, was born on Nov. 22, 1921 in Rock Hill, SC. Enlisted into the USAAC on June 4, 1942 and called to active duty on Feb. 28, 1943.

Stationed at Miami Beach, FL; Nashville, TN; Ellington Field, Midland, TX; Laredo TX; Peterson Field, CO; Greensboro, NC; and Old Buck, East Anglia, 453rd Bomb Group, 732nd Sqdn., ball turret and waist gunner.

Participated in battles in Northern France, Ardennes, Rhineland and Central Europe. Was awarded the Air Medal with one Oak Leaf Cluster, EAME Campaign Medal with four Bronze Stars and the Purple Heart.

Was discharged on Oct. 26, 1945 with the rank of staff sergeant. Married and has two sons and six grandchildren. He is living in the beautiful mountains of West North Carolina and enjoying retirement.

HENRY X. DIETCH, was born Nov. 13, 1913 in Brooklyn, NY. He enlisted into the USAAC on June 7, 1943.

Stationed in Amarillo, TX, Camp Lee, VA; Metfield, England; North Pickenham, Norwich, Ketteringham Hall in England. Participated in the Battle of Britain.

Received the Good Conduct Medal, American Campaign Medal, EAME Campaign Medal with four stars and the WWII Victory Medal. Discharged the first time on April 8, 1945 as sergeant. Discharged the second time on Oct. 5, 1945 with the rank of second lieutenant.

Dietch is a member of Illinois Reserve Militia and Jewish War Veterans. He is a founding member of 2nd Air Division Association and helped organize Heritage League of the 2nd. He is a former and present member of numerous professional and civic organizations. Has had several publications and papers published from 1970 to 1979.

He writes a column for *The Star* and in recent years paints battle scenes in abstract form in acrylics. He is a retired judge and is presently serving as mediator and arbitrator.

RICHARD L. DIETRICK, was a B-24 tailgunner and met his crew (Hibbard's Crew) on the train from Salt Lake to Tucson in December 1943. They flew their first phase OTU there. Then the 2nd and 3rd phase at Wendover, where they joined the newly formed 489th Bomb Group, 844th Squadron.

They departed Wendover in April 1944 en route to England via Herington, KS; Morrison Field, FL; Trinidad, Belem, Natal Brazil, Dakar and Casablanca, Africa. Then on to Wales, England and on to their 8th Air Force Base in Halesworth, Suffolk.

They arrived in time to fly before D-day and participated in D-day. Flew in a lead crew in the 847th Sqdn., to Normandy, St. Lo, the resupply of the 82nd Abn. and 101st at Eindhoven and Nejmegan and numerous strategic targets in Hamburg, Bremen, Brunswick, Ludwigshaven, Ardennes, Koblenz, Munster and the Ardennes Bulge.

He finished his 30 missions with eight in the 448th at Seething and came back to the States in February 1945. Of his original crew that he flew over with, only six survived to come home.

PAUL R. DILLON, was born on Jan. 27, 1920 and raised on a family farm just west of Shiloh National Military Park near Michie, TN. He enlisted in the USAAC on Sept. 22, 1941. Started basic training at Camp Shelby, MS.

Graduated Class 2A Airplane Mechanics School at Keesler Field, MS in February 1942. Was assigned to the 409th Bomb Sqdn., 93rd Bomb Group as an airplance mechanic on B-24s and Transient Acft. He was a mechanic at Flying Central. He accompanied the 93rd from its activation at Barksdale Field, LA in February 1942 until its return from England in June 1945.

Was discharged on Aug. 31, 1945 at Camp Atterbury, IN with all the awards and decorations of 93rd Ground Support personnel.

Married his Tennessee sweetheart, Rachel Hurst on June 7, 1942. They had one son Michael, now deceased.

He re-enlisted in the USAAF and remained active until May 1965, retired on disability. Taught electronics in Selmer, TN, High School for 10 years, and retired again. He is presently active in RV travel club.

CARL M. DI MEDIO, was born on July 20, 1922 in Bronx, NY. He enlisted in the USAAF on Dec. 8, 1942.

He was with the 8th Air Force, 2nd Air Div., B-24, MOS 611 aerial gunner top turret. Stationed in Norwich, England, Old Buckingham Air Base with the 735th Bomb Sqdn. 453rd Bomb Group.

Flew 33 missions over Germany. Was shot down by flak batteries over Kassel, Germany and forced down at British Mosquito Air Field near Amiens, France. He received five Air Medals and four Campaign Stars. Discharged on Oct. 6, 1944 with the rank of staff sergeant.

Married on May 8, 1949 and widowed on July 14, 1980. He has one son and two daughters. A former police officer, he retired on July 1, 1983.

NELSON L. DIMICK (JR.), was born on Sept. 27, 1924 in Hanover, NH and raised in White River Junction, VT. Entered Aviation Cadet Training in October 1942 and graduated in February 1944 as a pilot, second lieutenant, Class 44-B. He was the youngest in his class, ie the Jr.

He flew to Goose Bay, to Nutt's Corner, North Ireland in a new B-24 in May 1944. Joined the 445th Bomb Group, 700th Bomb Sqdn., stationed at Tibenham, England. Flew 30 combat missions before being shot down on his 20th birthday on the notable Kassel Raid on Sept. 27, 1944, 35 bombers departed England and were attacked by waves of fighters within three minutes, 25 B-24s were shot down.

He was a POW at Stalag Luft I, Barth, Germany. Received the Distinguished Flying Cross, four Air Medals and the Purple Heart. Discharged in 1970 with the rank of captain after serving in the Reserves.

In 1949 he graduated from Cornwell University. In 1950 he married Gwendolyn Lane and they have three children.

FRANCIS J. DI MOLA, was born on Aug. 22, 1921 in Ridgewood, NY. After graduation from St. Francis Prep School in Brooklyn, he worked awhile, then joined the USAF on Aug. 22, 1942. Trained at Amarillo, TX, AM School and on to Chanute Field for instrument training.

Trained at Gowen Field, ID in March 1942. Became a cadre member of the 445th Bomb Group. Assigned as squadron instrument specialist and aircraft mechanic. Went overseas in 1943 and was stationed in Tibenham. Assigned to various other groups while serving in ETO (492nd and 490th) but stayed in touch with the 445th.

He received six citations, Good Conduct Medal and ETO. Was discharged on Oct. 17, 1945 with the rank of sergeant. His father was in WWI with the 69th from New York. His three brothers also served in the military and two in the Navy were wounded.

Went home October 1945, held various jobs until hired in 1950 with the New York Telephone Company. Retired in April 1984. A resident of New Milford, NJ for 37 years, moved to Sun City West, AZ in 1993.

He married Elizabeth Maggio on Sept. 1, 1946. They have a son, Louis; two daughters, Eleanor Dennis and Jennifer Di Mola. They are blessed with two granddaughters and four grandsons. Has been very active in the 2nd Air Div. Association and 8th AAF and served as president from 1989-1990.

FRED H. DINGELDEIN (DINK), entered the USAAC in 1943 and trained in armament. He was assigned to A.E. Cearnal crew as the nose gunner. Sent to the 389th Bomb Group (H) in June 1944. Completed 30 missions on Sept. 11, 1944. All 10 returned.

On their 6th mission to Politz, Germany, they encountered intense flak. A piece in the left side of his nose turret scratched his right cheek. He refused to stay in the hospital overnight so there was no Purple Heart. Was discharged in 1945 with the rank of staff sergeant. But then re-enlisted to B-29 crew. Dink was killed in a crash.

He received the Distinguished Flying Cross, Air Medal with three clusters, EAME Campaign Medal with four stars, American Theatre Ribbon, WWII Victory Medal and the Korean Service Medal.

EDWARD J. DITTLINGER, was born on July 30, 1923 in Robstown, TX. He entered the National Youth Administration in June 1940, studying aircraft engines at Duncan Field, San Antonio, TX. He accepted employment as a aircraft engine mechanic apprentice at Naval Air Station, Cor-

pus Christi, TX in January 1942. Was drafted into the USAAC in March 1943.

After basic training at Miami Beach, FL he went to Aircraft Mechanics School, Gulfport Field, MS. After graduation, he went to Gunnery School at Harlingen Field, TX. Assigned to a Bomber crew and received B-24 crew training at Davis Monthan, AZ.

Went overseas in April 1944, assigned to the 445th Bomb Group (B-24) at Tibenham, England. Flew as flight engineer, completed 35 missions, returned to the States and was discharged in September 1945. Joined the USAFR, completed 32 years of service and retired as a maintenance officer with the rank of CWO-4.

He married his high school sweetheart, Iline Zapalac in December 1943. They have a son, daughter and six grandchildren.

CHARLES C. DIXON, was born on June 25, 1923 in Connellsville, PA. He joined the USAAC on Feb. 17, 1943.

Assigned to the 448th Bomb Group, 713th Sqdn., power turret and gun sight specialist (678). Stationed at Lowry Air Base, Salt Lake City, UT; Wendover Air Base, Sioux City, IA; Seething Air Base, England and Sandia Air Base, NM.

Discharged Oct. 27, 1945 with the rank of corporal. He was awarded the EAME Campaign Medal with one Bronze Star and one Silver Star and the Good Conduct Medal.

Married his high school sweetheart. They have one daughter, two sons and seven grandchildren. He retired in 1987 after 40 years as manager of engineering in an electrical manufacturing company.

JAMES DOBRAVEC, was born on Sept. 28, 1918 in Lyons, IL. He enlisted in the USAAC on April 28, 1942 as an aerial gunner. Was with the 445th Bomb Group in Tibenham.

He flew combat missions from July 17, 1944 to April 15, 1945, almost all were on lead crew missions (Capt. A.C. Tracy's crew). Received the Air Medal with three Oak Leaf Clusters and four European Campaign Stars. He was discharged on July 4, 1945 with the rank of staff sergeant.

Dobravec enlisted in the USAFR in 1948. Flew as a tech sergeant flight engineer with the 437th Troop Carrier Wing based at O'Hare in Chicago. They flew Curtiss C-46 Commandos. The wing was activated in 1950 at the start of the Korean conflict and sent to Japan. They flew as part of combat cargo. He was discharged in 1952.

He married Ruth Graunke in October 1941. They have a son, James. Dobravec has been retired since 1984.

ODELL F. DOBSON, was born on March 11, 1922 in Schoolfield, VA. He enlisted in the USAAF on Aug. 19, 1942, the day of Dieppe Raid. He feared the war would be over before he got there. Washed out of cadets and too tall to be a gunner. He tried to transfer to paratroopers, but was refused.

To make a long story short, he forged flight surgeon's signature to Flight 64 physical stating height as 5' 10." Sent to Harlingen to Gunnery School. Assigned to Dick Rudd's crew as left waist gunner. Posted to 578th Sqdn. of 392nd Bomb Group.

Was shot down on the 13th mission in Hanover on Sept. 11, 1944, eight of the crew was killed. Confined to a German Army Hospital, Giessen, two POW hospitals, Obermassfeld and Meiningen. Was sent to Stalag Luft IV. He walked the last 87 days of the war ahead of the Russian advance. Was liberated by the British on May 2, 1945.

He married Barbara Killheffer on Oct. 14, 1950. They have two sons, one daughter and three grandchildren (another one on the way). He retired in 1986 as vice president of Claims, Mutual Savings Life.

WILLIAM F. DOERNER (BILL), was born on June 21, 1923 in Cleveland, OH. He joined the USAAF on Dec. 19, 1941. Basic training at Jefferson Barracks in Missouri. Assigned to the 14th Fighter Group, P-38s at Hamilton Field, CA. Went overseas to England on Aug. 16, 1942 and became a replacement gunner on B-24s with the 93rd Bomb Group, also known as "Ted's Traveling Circus."

He was on the Ploesti Oil Raid in Rumania, Aug. 1, 1943. He destroyed an ME-109, Macchi 202 and damaged a JU-88 over Foggia, Italy, Aug 16, 1943 and completed his 25th mission, Nov. 5, 1943 over Munster, Germany.

Was awarded two Distinguished Flying Crosses, six Air Medals, the Presidential Unit Citation for Ploesti, five European Campaign Stars and several other ribbons. He was part of a team of combat veterans headed by Col. George S. Brown, to instruct and prepare the newly arrived 446th and 448th Bomb Group for combat operations.

Returned to the States in March 1944 and was assigned as a gunnery instructor at Westover Field, MA and was discharged on May 18, 1945 with the rank of staff sergeant.

He married Josephine Zuccaro on Oct. 27, 1945, they have one daughter, Barbara. He worked for the Ford Motor Company in management and various capacities. Retired in March 1985 after 31 years with the company.

MICHAEL J. DONAHUE, was born on Sept. 19, 1923 in Emmett, MI. Joined the USAAF in April 1943, completed basic training in Florida, Radio School, Scott Field, IL and Gunnery School at Tyndall Field, FL.

At Westover Field, MA in December 1943, his crew was formed and assigned to the 8th Air Force, 93rd Bomb Group, 409th Sqdn. in Hardwick, England. On Friday 13, 1945 with a lead crew of 13, he completed his last mission to Worms, Germany.

His good memories are firing flares from the flight deck of *Balls of Fire*, the 93rd assembly ship. Flying the Glenn Miller Band to their airbase for a performance. The V-1 and V-2 Bombs exploding in London.

Received five Air Medals, ETO Medal, four Bronze Stars, Victory Medal, American Theater, Good Conduct Medal, Presidential Unit Citation and two lead crew Certificates of Commendation.

He returned to the States in February 1945. After flight training at Reno Army Airbase with the Air Transport Command, he was assigned to the Miami Airport where he remained until his discharge in November 1945.

He married Veronica Grace in 1948 and has four children and three grandchildren. He graduated in 1954 from U of D Dental School. He practiced dentistry in Midland, MI until his retirement in 1988.

VIRGIL H. DOPSON, was born on Dec. 12, 1920 in Madison, NE. Enlisted into the USAAF on Sept. 3, 1942. Basic training in Medical Corps, Camp Grant, IL; transferred to the Army Air Force via aviation cadet.

Completed Gunnery School in Harlingen, TX; Radio School, Sioux Falls, SD; then to Tucson, AZ for combat crew training. His crew flew new B-24 from Topeka, KS to Ireland, took the ferry to Scotland, on to Wendling and the 392nd Bomb Group, 576th Bomb Sqdn. Flew the first of his 30

missions on May 23, 1944 and his last mission on Dec. 6, 1944.

Flew in nose gunner togglier position and waist gunner. Was a member of Birdie Schmidt's crew. Discharged on July 28, 1945 with the rank of staff sergeant. He received the Air Medal with three Oak Leaf Clusters, Good Conduct and ETO with four stars.

He served in South Dakota Air National Guard from May 1947 to September 1954 until he was recalled to active duty at Rapid City AFB in South Dakota on March 1, 1950.

Married in March 1945 and has two married children. He retired from Montgomery Ward in 1985 as a group merchandiser after 31 years.

ROBERT M. DORRIETY, was born on Oct. 9, 1922 in Montgomery, AL. He enlisted in the USAAF on Oct. 6, 1942, pilot with the 489th Bomb Group, 2nd Div., 8th Air Force.

Stationed at Southeastern Training Command, OTU Charleston, SC, Halesworth, England and Davis Monthan in Tucson, AZ. He participated in the battles at Rhineland, Northern France and Normandy. Memorable experience was the barrage flak over Germany.

Separated on Oct. 6, 1945 and discharged on May 10, 1955 with the rank of first lieutenant. He was awarded the Air Medal with two Oak Leak Clusters and the EAME Campaign Medal with three Bronze Stars.

Married for 51 years and has two sons, one daughter and four grandchildren. He is retired and enjoys gardening and target shooting.

JOHN J. DOSKOCZ, was born on Aug. 26, 1915 in New York City and was employed by the Casey Jones School of Aeronautics in Newark, NJ as an instructor. He joined the USAAC in February 1943.

Trained in Alamorgordo, NM and sent with the 466th Bomb Group to Attlebridge, England. He was crew chief on the *Slick Chick*, a B-24. This plane was the lead ship for the first 25 missions and the first to set a record of 128 missions without a mechanical or personnel turnback.

He received the Bronze Star on Dec. 4, 1944 for meritorious achievement. Discharged on Oct. 6, 1945 and returned to New York. He was employed by Pan American Airways at Kennedy Airport for 35 years, retired and moved to Florida with his wife in 1979. He keeps busy as a volunteer, enjoys traveling, woodworking and has an active social life.

LEE DOTSON, was born on April 29, 1917 in Greenland, NH. He enlisted into the USAAF in Sept. 1940, Artillery A/A, Army Air Force engineer, gunner.

Was stationed at Greenville, Tyndall Field, Gowan, Tibenham and other places. Memorable experiences were Gotha, Hamburg, Frankfort, Berlin, Osnabruk; 445th Bomb Group; the B-24 *Conquest Cavalier.*

Discharged in July 1945 with the rank of staff sergeant. He received the Distinguished Flying Cross, Air Medal with clusters and the Purple Heart. Married to Jeanne and has three daughters. He is retired and living in Florida.

DAVID J. DOUGHERTY, was born on March 18, 1921 in Brooklyn, NY. Entered the USAAC on Sept. 2, 1942. Sent to basic training at Atlantic City, NJ. He was chosen for Aviation Cadet School, Class of 43-G, Kelly Field, TX. Earned his wings on July 29, 1943, Frederick, OK.

Transferred to Tucson, AZ; Blythe, CA, Liberal, KS and to the 491st Bomb Group. Went to England by way of South America and Africa to join the 2nd Air Div. Flew his first mission with the 491st on June 2, 1944. Finished his 31st mission on Sept. 11, 1944.

Received the Distinguished Flying Cross and the Air Medal. Was discharged in August 1945 with the rank of first

lieutenant. After his discharge he entered Fordham University, 1945 to 1949. After graduation he became partners with his brother, John, in the beverage business, Long Island, NY.

He and Edith Dempsey were married on Sept. 19, 1948. She was from Brooklyn, NY and he had met her through people he came to know while in England. They have married sons and four grandchildren. Retired in 1986 and has a vacation and retirement home in Naples, FL.

WILLIAM G. DOUGLAS, was born on Nov. 1, 1917 in Bluefield, WV. He enlisted in the USAAF on March 18, 1942 at Ft. Thomas, KY. Basic at Barksdale Field, LA and assigned to the 317th Service Group at Ft. Myers, FL.

Shipped overseas to Shipdham, England and was assigned to the 44th Bomb Group. Assigned to the newly activated 14th Combat Bomb Wing as wing sergeant major.

Received the Bronze Star, Good Conduct Medal, and the EAME Campaign Medal with seven Battle Stars.

Returned to the States on V-J day aboard the *Queen Elizabeth* and was discharged at Ft. George Meade on Sept. 8, 1945 with the rank of master sergeant. He enlisted in the USAFR and was recalled to active duty for the Korean Conflict, Sept. 11, 1951. Due to having four dependents, he was released from active duty.

Currently serves as president of Consolidated Brokerage Company, Bluefield, WV. Has 48 years in the business.

GERALD E. DOUGLASS, was born on Aug. 25, 1922 in Whitehall, NY. He enlisted in the USAAC after his examination for cadet training on June 1, 1942.

Trained Central Flying Command primary and basic in Oklahoma and advanced training at Victoria, TX. He graduated in June 1944, 40 single engine pilots assigned at once to 8th Air Force for replacement crews.

Was with the Hoover crew, 392nd Bomb Group, 578th Bomb Sqdn. Flew 19 missions before the war ended. Was assigned to Roswell, NM for B-29, elected to go home. Held reserve commission, served as squadron com. reserve, group operation staff Air Force liason officer.

Received the Air Medal with three clusters. Attained the rank of lieutenant colonel.

He and Barbara Wilcox were married in 1946. They have three daughters and one son who is an Army major.

Continued his education after the war was over and received his BS and MA degrees. Attended New York University, was a teacher, coach and school superintendent at Hamilton Central School, retired in 1980.

ARNOLD J. DOVEY, was born Jan. 3, 1918, Ely, MN and reared in suburban Philadelphia. Inspired by "Victory Through Air Power" and youthful interest in navigation, and after medical preparation to qualify, Dovey abandoned draft deferred employment and Drexel Engineering education, enlisting in 1942 in Air Corp Cadet Navigator Program.

Commissioned aerial navigator 1943. Trained with Anderson B-24 crew at six U.S. bases, last in Dec Langley Sea Search Attack Squadron. A Dr. Griggs announced there that crews assembled were to train with and fly the first 20, then (Top Secret Code Mickey), PFF Path Finder Force H2X equipped B-24s to the ETO. Griggs answer to the question

"Why us?" was "For you're navigators." This, then disbelieved, proved true at destination.

Declassified records reveal that British H2S then not in sufficient quantities for RAF needs or preferably superior equipment was essential for continuation of daylight bombing. Daylight losses experienced reaching targets obscured four-fifths of times were unacceptable. Dr. David T. Griggs was the Secretary of War Representative for crash development of greatly superior American H2X. The urgency explains the then not understood perilous winter weather North Atlantic routing over repeated objections of flight operations officers.

Dovey navigated the ice endangered no return option B-24 H2X Labrador to Iceland early February 1944 between layers of clouds without benefit of positions en route from visual celestial sightings, meteorological data, drift, H2X, reliable radio or other aids. He drew on basic meteorological training to reach Iceland surprisingly on course and time, but with great apprehensions because of weather inhibited navigation and enemy diversion measures. Safely landed, crew hoisted Dovey on shoulders from aircraft.

At Alconbury, England, 482nd Pathfinder Group, Dovey was separated from stateside crew explaining Griggs "For you're navigators" statement. Earned RAF Observer Wings training with British H2S at nearby Wyton RAF Pathfinder Headquarters. Assigned next to 66th Lead Crew BS, 44th-BG, 14th-CBW, 2nd AD to develop, refine and practice PFF crew coordination procedures with seasoned lead crews, to navigate them in combat clear of AA gun positions, to precisely position them for visual bombing and for blind release of bombs provide data to bombsight via bombardier.

On May 8, 1944, Dovey was shot down coordinating with 466th BG Lead Crew by twin engine intruder. Injured parachuting from the spin entering aircraft, Doven landed unconscious, awakening the next day with his left side paralyzed in 231 Station Hospital Trench Foot Ward. Ruby-eyed caterpillar pin was beside. Combat leads commenced six weeks later.

In August 1944, Dovey as H2X Group Navigator, initiated Mickey PFF operations at 392nd BG, then transferred to 14th CBW as wing H2X Navigator. He flew 23 combat lead H2X missions by V-E day, receiving DFC for Bremen, DFC cluster for Hamburg, Air Medal with three clusters, Caterpillar Pin and Wing Lead Crew Citations for Rheine, Hamburg again and six ETO Campaign Ribbons. Separated as first lieutenant soon after V-J day.

After separation Dovey embarked on a career in design and marketing of aircraft environmental control and bleed power ducting, leading a small operation through an 8-fold expansion into the world industry leader. He continues (1993) active in the same field as an independent contractor.

Dovey is reverently grateful for: having been qualified and being in the right places and times to make a difference countering Nazis with select lead crews, surviving the dangers while deeply regretting the necessity of periling innocents, the aviation influences carried into business, personal and family affairs. He married Cleome Van Huel in 1947 and has sons, Lee and Douglas (F-16 pilot).

JAMES E. DOWLING (JIM), was born in New York City, April 7, 1923. Moved to Smithtown, Long Island, NY at the age of six months. Returned to Smithtown after war and lives there today in Hamlet of St. James. Graduate of Class 44-4, Big Spring, TX, March 18, 1944 as bombardier navigator. Went to Pueblo, CO trained with crew of Lt. Ed Johnson in B-24s.

Shipped to England on *Queen Elizabeth*. Assigned to combat July 20, 1944, 11 missions. Shot down Sept. 27, 1944

on Kassel raid. Was POW at Stalag Luft I for eight and a half months.

Returned to the States July 3, 1944 and left the service August 1947. Received the Purple Heart, four campaign medals, Air Medal, POW Medal, and the Unit Citation for Croix de Guerre.

Elected to office of highway superintendent in 1960, still holding that position after 33 years. Married childhood sweetheart, Dorothy Owen, and has eight children and 18 grandchildren.

SAM DOWLING, was born July 12, 1924 in Titusville, PA. Enlisted March 1943 in USAAC as aerial gunner, 445th Bomb Group, 703rd Sqdn. Stationed at Miami Beach, FL; Keesler Field, MS; Harlingen, TX; Casper, WY; and Tibenham, England.

Participated in the Normandy, Northern France, Rhineland, Ardennes and Central Europe. Discharged September 1945 with the rank staff sergeant. Received the Air Medal with six Oak Leaf Clusters.

Married Grace Llewellyn and has six children and 12 grandchildren. Retired from the military after 22 years and from Federal Civil Service after 23 years.

CHRIS DRACOPOULOS (DRAKE), was born March 18, 1925 in Malden, MA. Inducted into Army, May 11, 1943. Assigned to President Hotel, Atlantic City, NJ; City College, NY; Greensboro, NC; then to ETO February 1944.

On special duty Station Defense, North Pickenham, England with 491st and 492nd Bomb Groups, February 1944 through July 1945. Was anti-aircraft gunner in base "gun pits" and with Special Services, he formed the 14 piece base band, The Rhythm Bombshells. He played drums, arranged for dances and entertainment on and off the base.

Discharged Oct. 27, 1945, formed dance band and played the Greater Boston area. Manager, NE branch Capitol records, Motorola TV distributor and last 27 years in sales management for Zenith TV distributor. Retired 1990 and is writing his autobiography and does volunteer work at Malden Hospital. Married since 1947 to Terry, they have a son, Chuck, and daughter, Dorri.

GUISTO E. DRAGONI, was born in Union City, NJ. Enlisted in the USAAC on Oct. 22, 1942 as airplane maintenance tech 750, 557th AAF BU, 734th Bomb Sqdn., 453rd Bomb Group. Stationed at Attleboro, England.

Participated in Normandy, Northern France, Ardennes, Rhineland, Central Europe and Air Offensive Europe campaigns. His memorable experience was serving as crew chief under Col. James Stewart.

Discharged Oct. 6, 1945 with the rank staff sergeant. Received the EAME Theater Ribbon with six Bronze Stars, Good Conduct and two Overseas Service Bars.

Attended Newark School of Engineering, Fairleigh Dickenson University, Dale Carnegie School, International Correspondence School. Was employed as sales engineer and New York manager for C&D Batteries for 40 years. Married Muriel Dege Sept. 8, 1945 and had a son, daughter and four grandchildren. Dragoni passed away Jan. 5, 1993. *Submitted by his widow, Muriel Dragoni.*

WALTER M. DRAKE, was born 1923 in Colorado. Enlisted in the USAAC, pilot of twin engine fighter. Stationed at SAAAB; Rankin Academy, Marana, AZ; Williams Field, AZ, Cadet Training, Hamilton Field, Wattisham, England and Ontario, CA.

Flew 68 combat missions with 8th Air Force, P-38s and P-51s. Every mission was a memorable experience.

Discharged September 1945 with the rank first lieutenant. Stayed in the Reserves for 25 years, retiring with rank lieutenant colonel. Received the Distinguished Flying Cross and Air Medal with nine clusters.

Married and has four sons. He is retired.

JOSEPH A. DRIGGS, was born in Spring Hill, WV on March 16, 1923. Entered the USAAC on July 5, 1943, completed basic training and Airplane Mechanic School on April 10, 1944 at Keesler Field, MS and Aerial Gunnery School at Tyndall Field, FL in June 1944. Arrived at Gowan Field, ID on Aug. 30, 1944 for overseas training with assigned crew, completed training on Nov. 18, 1944.

Was sent to England by troop ship and assigned to the 753rd Sqdn., 458th Bomb Group(H) at Horsham St. Faith near Norwich, England. Completed 22 missions as engineer gunner on a B-24 Liberator. Returned to the USA on June 17, 1945 and completed training course on B-29 on Sept. 27, 1945 at Davis Monthan Field, Tucson, AZ and discharged from there on Oct. 27, 1945.

Married on March 16, 1946 to Mary Alice Bibb and has two sons and two grandchildren. Retired from the C&P Telephone Company on Sept. 30, 1982 with 42 years of service.

ERROLL H. DRINKWATER, was born Sept. 17, 1921 in Dover-Foxcroft, ME. Graduated Foxcroft Academy Class of 40. Moved to Connecticut and was employed at Pratt Whitney. Enlisted in the USAAC Aug. 1, 1942 and went directly to Keesler Field for General AM training, then to Consolidated for B-24 familiarization. Cadre 389th Bomb Group, 565th Sqdn. at Biggs Field in El Paso, TX.

Staged for overseas at Lowry Field, Denver, CO. Loaded tools, spares etc. into *Vagabond King* (B24D) and himself on the *Queen Elizabeth*. Arrived England and Hethel Airfield on July 8, 1943. Crewed *Vagabond King, Spirit of 46, Spirit of 46 #2* and *S Sugar*. All were visual lead and all but the *King* got their crews home. End of war in ETO, new 24m for trip home, did shakedown hauling trolley runs and military govts. to Europe. Left Hethel May 19, 1945 loaded with HQ personnel and stuff. Iceland, Goose Bay and Bradley Field, CT. After R&R back to Charleston AB and DS to Ft. Dix AB to service C-47 ambulances from ETO.

Discharged Sept. 27, 1945 with the rank of master sergeant. Received nine Battle Stars and Bronze Star Medal. Memorable experience was when Col. James Stewart was command pilot on Spirit of 46.

Spent 45 years with United Technologies at assembly and test, installation development, experimental flight test and corporate research and development facilities. Now retired and lives in Portland, CT. Married Clara Ham in 1943 and has two sons and one daughter.

BERNARD F. DRISCOLL (BARNEY), was born Oct. 22, 1924. Raised on a farm south of Iowa City, IA. Enlisted Dec. 8, 1942, AAF Radio School, Chicago. Went to Gunnery School at Fort Myers, FL. Joined Kenneth R. Kleinshrot crew, Salt Lake City, October 1943; OTU Training, Casper, WY. Crew transferred to 467th Bomb Group, 789th Sqdn., Wendover, UT and picked up new B24H Herington, KS.

Flew southern route to Rackheath, England. First Mission was April 11, 1944. Six missions with 467th, including April 22 Hamm Mission. Crew transferred to 389th Bomb Group, 564th Sqdn. for PFF crew training. Balance of 30 missions flown as PFF lead crew. Original navigator was killed and lost two gunners with plane on fire. Crew transferred to 453rd Bomb Group, 733rd Sqdn. Completed missions Oct. 15, 1944.

Awarded the Distinguished Flying Cross, Air Medal with three Oak Leaf Clusters and Purple Heart. Returned to the States, Fort Worth AAF (later Carswell). Flew as radio operator with B-24 transition pilots. Discharged September 1945 with the rank tech sergeant.

Married Emeline Godley in 1947 and has three children and nine grandchildren. Spent greater portion of business life selling industrial electrical equipment in Houston, TX. Retired, now lives out in the timber 85 miles NW of Houston.

ROLAND B. DRISCOLL, was born Jan. 11, 1920 in Detroit, MI. Entered the USAAC Jan. 2, 1942. Sent to Fort Meade, MD; Jefferson Barracks, MO; Missouri Aviation Institute (Air Mechanic School) Class 25 in 1942; first cadre at Topeka Air Field, Topeka, KS; Lincoln Air Field, Lincoln, NE. Joined Air Cadet Program and attended University of Missouri, Columbia, MO.

At San Antonio, TX, was classified as surplus pilot. Attended Laredo Gunnery School, TX and assigned to 8th Air Force, England, 389th Bomb Group, 564th Sqdn., Hethel England. Completed 35 missions as flight engineer, B-24.

Memorable experience was flying at tree top level, dropping supplies to troops at Wesel, looking up over target area he saw a rooster atop a steeple. They failed to make proper run and were forced to make a second approach, losing their element of surprise and making them perfect targets from small arms fire. They lost #2 engine plus received many holes in the aircraft, but succeeded in dropping the vital supplies.

Discharged June 5, 1945 with the rank tech sergeant. Received the Air Medal with four Oak Leaf Clusters and EAME Theater Ribbon.

Married and has one son, two daughters and eight grandchildren. He is a retired school teacher.

EDWARD A. DROUIN, was born July 8, 1924, Tacoma, WA. Enlisted Dec. 3, 1942 in the USAAC, 1596th Ord. Co., 448th Bomb Group, Seething.

Memorable experience was the runway snow removal during the winters of 1943-44-45. Discharged Dec. 17, 1945, Marseille, France, with the rank T/4.

Retired from civil service at Puget Sound Naval Shipyard.

W.E. DRUMEL, was born February 1924. Enlisted in the USAAC May 1942. Completed basic air gunner training, March 1943. Assigned to Lt. Wm. Duffy's Crew for combat training, Tucson, AZ. Completed training at Pueblo, CO, July 1943.

Flew a new B-24 from Lincoln, NE to England. Arrived at 44th Bomb Group at Shipdham, October 1943. Completed 26 missions March 1944.

Awarded Air Medal with three Oak Leaf Clusters and Distinguished Flying Cross. Returned to USA August 1944. Attended Gunnery Instructor School, Laredo, TX. Served as instructor at Tyndall Field, FL until discharge September 1945.

Married October 1945 and has three children and seven grandchildren. Employed at Philadelphia Electric Co. as an apprentice pipe fitter, October 1946. Promoted to division supervisor, October 1964. Completed 40 years service, October 1986 and retired in 1987.

ROBERT J. DRUMMOND, was born Dec. 2, 1921 in Philadelphia, PA and grew up in Manoa, PA. Entered Army Air Corps on Aug. 4, 1942. After basic training in Miami Beach, went to Lowry Field, Denver for training as a power turret and computing gun sight specialist. Assigned to the 29th Bomb Group(H) at Gowen Field in Boise for further

training. A short time later the 29th Bomb Group was converted from B-17s to B-24s. This change in the parent group made a memorable change in the lives of all 445th Bomb Group personnel.

In April 1943, was assigned to the original cadre of the 702nd Bomb Sqdn., 445th Bomb Group(H), in the Armament Section. Completed final phases of training at Wendover, UT, Sioux City, IA and Watertown, SD, while progressing to tech sergeant.

Left from West Palm Beach to fly to Tibenham, England, with Lt. Sefton's crew in November 1943. Arrived at base on Christmas Eve. Served at Tibenham until June 1945. Returned to States and when the 445th Bomb Group was deactivated, transferred to Air Transport Command, at Homestead, FL, while waiting to be discharged on Oct. 27, 1945.

Married Oct. 26, 1946 to Catherine Fasy and has two sons, six daughters and 11 grandchildren. President of Drummond Scientific Co., Broomall, PA.

GEORGE DUBINA, was born in Willimantic, CT on March 27, 1918. Joined the National Guard Unit, Co. L, 169th Inf., 43rd Div. in 1940. Took the Aviation Cadet exam at Camp Shelby, MS in 1942; primary training, Helena, AR; commissioned second lieutenant August 1943, Class 43-H at Columbus, MS; B-24 transition at Maxwell AFB September 1943. Received first lieutenant grade at Casper, WY in March 1944.

Arrived in ETO flying a B-24, June 1, 1944. Completed 35 missions by November 1944 and was home for Christmas. Flew navigators at Victorville. CA until separated in May 1945. Memorable missions: second mission over St. Lo, Halle and the last five down Flak Alley (Ruhr). Received the Distinguished Flying Cross, Air Medal with four clusters and several other ribbons.

Married Alyce Lahiff of Troy, NH on June 25, 1946. Graduated from Parks Aero-Tech of St. Louis University, 1948. Retired from teaching in 1979.

ROBERT DUBOWSKY, was born Feb. 19, 1921 in Mineola, NY. Joined USAAC September 1942 and entered Aviation Cadet Program. Won pilots wings and commissioned second lieutenant Dec. 5, 1942. Flew 35 combat missions in B-24s with the 44th Bomb Group at Shipdham. Shot down on 33rd mission, bailed out near front lines.

Awarded the Distinguished Flying Cross, five Air Medals, Purple Heart and five European Battle Stars. Remained in service after WWII. Served with Military Air Transport Command, Training Command, USAF Security Service and Air Defense Command in flying, command and staff positions. Earned the aeronautical rating of command pilot. Attended University of Maryland and earned BS degree in military science. Attained the rank of lieutenant colonel.

Retired from Air Force 1964. Married Irma and has two daughters and two grandchildren. Presently does volunteer (Meals on Wheels) and docent at Air Force Space Museum. Lives in Satellite Beach, FL.

WILLIAM J. DUCEY, was born Jan. 6, 1923 in Flushing, Long Island, NY. Joined the USAAC as an aviation cadet on Feb. 28, 1943. After three years as an accounting major at St. Johns University, he attended Pre-flight School at Syracuse University. He graduated from Gunnery School at Laredo, TX after washing out of cadet training at Kelly Field, TX and was assigned to B-24s.

He trained at Pueblo, CO; Westover Field, MA and Langley Field, VA. Arriving in the ETO on April 27, 1944, he was assigned to 491st Bomb Group, 852nd Sqdn. stationed at Metfield and later at North Pickenham, Norfolk England. Flew 25 missions, 12 with Lt. Sparrow's crew on the *Lambsey Divey* (shot down over Misberg), 12 with Captain Cain's (lead crew) and one mission with Lt. Meglitsch, the last mission of the 8th Air Force.

During his service, Bill flew as a ball turret, waist and nose turret gunner, and received the air medal with three Oak Leaf Clusters, six Battle Stars and several other medals. He arrived back in the States on June 1, 1945 and was discharged on Aug. 6, 1945 as a staff sergeant.

Bill married Patricia A. Gorman on July 5, 1958 and has four children and four grandchildren. Retired in 1993 after 36 years as a self-employed certified public accountant, practicing and living in Massapequa, Long Island, NY.

MILTON D. DUCHARME, was born Aug. 5, 1915 in Detroit, MI. Enlisted in November 1941 in the USAAC. Military training: radio mech, Scott Field, IL; radar mech, Boca Raton, FL; Gee-H, AAF Station 102 Radar School Attachment, England.

Duty stations included Langley Field, VA June 1942-January 1944 NCO/1C. In fall of 1942 was on TDY for three months at Trinidad in support of a squadron (12 A/C) B-18s on ASW patrol duty. Worked with civilian tech reps. from Western Electric and Columbia University on development of tactical procedures in use of radar, MAD and sono buoy devices. At this time they had four squadrons identified as the anti-Submarine Sea Search Attack Group, soon to be dismantled and ASW equipment returned to the USN.

In Hethel there was a great deal of excitement around some B-24s that arrived daily. Soon became involved and became part of squadron going to Europe. They were equipped with the first 12 production radar sets, the APS-15 HAB (H2X). Within two weeks they were equipped, trained and on their way. Twelve A/C, 12 stories to tell. It took them 30 days, lost an engine, lost a radome, eight overnight stops due to weather and the tone of their special orders ie: the need to get to our destination with safety of the A/C over safety of personnel.

Captain Hylass had appointed Ducharme as NCO-1C at Alconbury and he retained the title. The radar building was new, to be destroyed by runaway A/C later, and wiped out a second time, in a similar manner. By this time they had an excellent lay-out, quite functional, all of which enabled them to provide timely response to the returnees needs.

As time went on they had acquired GEE-H, Loran and ECM. Was discharged Oct. 3, 1945 as master sergeant and was awarded the American Defense Service Medal, American Service Medal, Distinguished Unit Badge and the EAME Medal

Worked for MIT RadLab for one year. Project moved to Emerson Electric in St. Louis and he stayed with them 36 years as production engineer and program manager.

Has three married sons, three grandsons and one granddaughter. Member board manager local YMCA, participates in Y Indian Guide Program (a father and son program) was a national officer of YMCA Indian Guide organization. Loan executive to United Way 1971-72.

ROBERT G. DUCHARME, was born Sept. 8, 1925 in Mapleville, RI, joined the Aviation Cadet Reserves at 17 and reported for active duty, Fort Devans, MA, Oct. 25, 1943. Took basic at Greensboro, NC; Gunnery School; Laredo, TX; overseas training, Chatham Field, GA. Crew arrived Valley, Wales in new B-24J June 30, 1944. After combat training Greencastle, North Ireland, crew reported 445th Bomb Group, 701st Sqdn., Tibenham, England, July 26. Combat tour (as tail gunner) began Hamburg mission, August 6 and ended 35th mission to Zweibrucken, Jan. 7, 1945.

Memorable experiences: mid-air collision with another B-24 while forming. Five feet of left wing tip was crushed (knocking off nose turret on other B-24), overhead fuselage in waist section was chewed up by other 24's props and vertical stabilizers were bent over. Pilot regained control and after jettisoning everything that was loose, crew made it back to English crash strip.

Second memorable experience was missing disastrous Kassel raid, Sept. 27, 1944, when only seven of 445th's 37 planes made it back to Tibenham. His crew missed this one because they were on R&R leave.

He returned to States in March 1945, completed gunnery instructor's training at Laredo and was assigned to A-26 group, Marianna, FL. He was discharged Westover Field, MA Oct. 24, 1945.

Entered Goddard College on GI Bill and after 1951 graduation went to graduate school at Syracuse University for masters and PhD. Married and divorced twice, had three children with first wife. Professional career included 40 years as urban planner and environmental/economic consultant. He is now (1993) retired in Evanston, IL and busy with genealogy hobby, golf, travel, and enjoying children and two grandchildren.

ALLEN L. DUFF, was born Nov. 15, 1917 in Des Moines, IA. Enlisted April 5, 1943 in USAAC. Received Wings and commission Feb. 8, 1944. Served with 578th Sqdn., 392nd Bomb Group. Stationed at Casper, WY and Wendling, England, June 1944. Completed 35 missions as B-24 bomber pilot.

Discharged November 1945 with the rank captain, sqd. operations officer. Received the Air Medal, Silver Oak Leaf Cluster and the Distinguished Flying Cross.

Married Elizabeth on Oct. 28, 1942, has two children, four grandchildren and one great-granddaughter. He owns and operates 40 acres of walnuts in Visalia, CA.

ALLENBY K. DUKE, was born July 14, 1919 in San Antonio, TX. Graduated from Brackenridge High School, San Antonio, TX in 1937; joined the USAAF May 22, 1942; graduated as a bombardier with rank of second lieutenant on May 3, 1943, Class 43-17, Big Spring Bombardier School, Big Spring AFB, TX. He completed 17 combat missions in INB-24 Liberator bombers with the 389th Bombardment Group, 2nd Air Div., 8th Air Force, in England, from May 14, 1943-Aug. 8, 1944.

Served in the USAR from May 22, 1942 until he was called to active duty as a USAAF Aviation Cadet on Nov. 26, 1942. Went to Aerial Gunnery School; pre-Flight School, Houston, TX; and Bombardier School, Big Spring, TX. In January 1944 he was transferred to March Field, CA, a B-24 Liberator Transition School.

Was assigned to Lt. Clarence Craft Crew as bombardier and was in training until April 18, 1944. Was sent to the port of embarkation at Hamilton Field, San Francisco, CA. On April 23, 1944 boarded a troop train and traveled across the country to the port of embarkation at Camp Kilmer, NY.

On May 2, 1944 he boarded a troop ship with 3,000 troops and sailed out of New York Harbor past the Statue of Liberty. The troop ship was in the largest convoy of ships ever assembled to cross the Atlantic. Went through the Firth of Clyde and landed in Scotland on May 14, 1944. Boarded a train to England and was assigned to the 389th Bomb Group, 2nd Air Div., 8th Air Force. The 389th Bomb Group was located on Hethel Airfield near Norwich, England.

Flew 17 combat missions, seven as lead bombardier. Awarded a Lead Crew Commendation for the destruction of the aircraft repair hangars on the airfield at Scherwin, Germany on Aug. 4, 1944.

He was killed in action Aug. 8, 1944 on his 17th mission in the wing lead plane while synchronizing on a tactical support target in France. Was buried in the U.S. Cemetery at Cambridge, England. His body was moved to Mission Burial Park in San Antonio, TX after the war ended. He was married and had one daughter.

REUBEN D. DUKE (R.D.), was born Sept. 15, 1920 in Bandera County, TX. Joined the USAAF May 22, 1942; graduated as a bombardier with rank of second lieutenant on Dec. 3, 1943, Class 43-17, Big Spring Bombardier School, Big Spring AFB, TX. Completed 30 combat missions in B-24 Liberator bombers with the 389th Bomb Group, 2nd Air Div., 8th Air Force from May 14, 1943-Dec. 31, 1943. Achieved the rank of first lieutenant.

Participated in Air Offensive Europe, Northern France, Rhineland and Normandy campaigns. Received the Distinguished Flying Cross, Air Medal with four Oak Leaf Clusters, EAME Campaign Medal with four Bronze Service Stars. Received honorable discharge Sept. 18, 1945. Spent nine years in the Reserve unit at Brooks AFB, San Antonio, TX.

Memorable experiences: serving with his brother, A.K. Duke, in the USAAF from enlistment in the Reserves, May 22, 1942; active duty from Nov. 26, 1942; Aerial Gunnery School; Preflight Ground School through Bombardier School where they graduated as second lieutenants, Dec. 3, 1943. January 1944-both assigned to B-24 Liberator Bomber Transition School, March Field, CA, then assigned to different crews as B-24 bombardiers. Overseas assignment was to the 389th Bombardment Group, 2nd Air Div., 8th Air Force in England, arriving May 14, 1944. They were together until A.K.'s death from enemy anti-aircraft fire Aug. 8, 1944. A.K. was in the wing lead plane synchronizing on a tactical support target in France when he was killed on his 17th combat mission, seven missions were as lead bombardier.

R.D. completed 30 combat missions, 13 as the lead bombardier on pathfinder crew. He was the lead bombardier for one squadron lead, three group leads, three combat wing leads, and six combat division leads. Flew as lead bombardier for other groups that did not have pathfinder crews. Flew four missions with the 445th Bomb Group, four missions with the 453rd Group and five with his own 389th Group. Was credited with the destruction of a rail siding and the German Panzer Division parked on it. He was told at the briefing that this mission was at the personal request of Gen. Dwight Eisenhower to slow or prevent these critical German reinforcements from reaching our beach head in Normandy.

R.D. flew as bombardier in the lead plane which led the 8th Air Force, some 2,000 B-24s and B-17s, on a training mission over London, England, in 1944. His plane carried the only practice bomb and dropped it from 20,000 feet into the mouth of the Thames River. The training mission was testing a system designed to help prevent early bomb releases when bombing close ground support from high altitude for the Normandy Invasion front.

R.D. was in the 389th Bomb Group officers Club one evening when Lt. John Walsh, one of his 1938 high school classmates and the captain of the high school football team, walked up to him and said, "Hello Reuben, I just arrived in the 389th and have been assigned to your crew as bombardier-navigator." John and R.D. graduated together at Brackenridge High School in San Antonio, TX. John told him the way he became a bombardier-navigator. When John arrived in the 389th Group, the colonel called him and told him, "We need a bombardier-navigator for the Berger Crew, you are now a bombardier-navigator." John and R.D. flew on the same B-24 Liberator for 15 missions before R.D. finished his tour in December 1944. John was killed in January 1945 when a German fighter plane rammed the plane head-on.

R.D. flew as pathfinder bombardier in the division lead plane with the 445th Bomb Group after their 32 plane loss on Sept. 27, 1944 over Kassel. Only one plane returned to base, two others made crash landings at bases on the English Coast, 30 other planes were lost over enemy territory to enemy aircraft. This is a record loss in the USAF history for one group on a single mission. Their crew was told at the briefing that the 445th Bomb Group was chosen to lead the 2nd Air Div. on this mission to show the Germans that the 445th Bomb Group could not be destroyed. The 445th Group did not lose any planes on this mission.

He is married to Mary Louise Koehler and has four daughters, Anne, Lynne, Jeanne, and Gwynee.

TROY K. DUMAS, was born May 9, 1916 in McComb, OK. Entered the USAAC in August 1941, 448th Bomb Group, 715th Sqdn., Combat Intelligence of Seething, England. He spent approximately two years in States and various training stations.

Memorable experiences: seeing his group changed from last to first in bombing accuracy. He participated in European Campaign; B-24 Group; briefing and interrogation also photo interpetation.

Discharged October 1945 with the rank first lieutenant. Received all the usual medals and awards.

Has wife, Lola, three children, three grandchildren. Retired U.S. Army Corps of Engrs. Civil employment as real estate appraiser.

HAROLD DAVID DUNHAM, was born Nov. 4, 1923 in Cincinnati, OH. Enlisted in the Air Force Aug. 18, 1942; attended Gunnery School at Page Field, FL; promoted to staff sergeant. During phase training, passed cadet test and was to be held at Lincoln, NE, however, he was shipped to Topeka to replace tail gunner on a crew headed overseas.

Arrived England Oct. 9, 1943, joined 392nd Bomb Group, flew 28 missions, received four Air Medals, Distinguished Flying Cross and Unit Citation for Gotha Mission.

Returned to the States June 9, 1944, discharged Nov. 23, 1945, married Margaret Wright of Atlanta, GA. They have five daughters and five grandchildren. Retired from construction and is now CEO of Best Choice Home Health Care, working with two daughters, who are nurses.

Still communicates with six living crew members: P. Doug Ambrose, C.P. Winston Dorrell, Bombardier Joe Tierney, Nav. Vernon Lindberg, BT Earl Hall and L.W. Grant Oasheim.

JAMES J. DUNLAY, was born Aug. 4, 1917 in Kansas City, MO. Enlisted in the Air Corps Aug. 25, 1941. Stationed at Ft. Warren, WY as EM; cadet, Hondo, TX; crew training Biggs Field, TX; Pueblo, CO; England July 1943; Africa August 1943; Hardwick, England September 1943-August 1944; Flew 26 missions - one extra for Doolittle

Discharged November 1945 with the rank captain, squadron navigator, 20th and 2nd Wing, Watch Teams. Received the Distinguished Flying Cross, Air Medal with three Oak Leaf Cluster, Presidential Citation, pre-Pearl Harbor, American Defense Medal and ETO Theater.

Married and has three daughters and two sons. Dunlay is retired.

NORMAN R. DUNPHE, was born May 16, 1925 in Taunton, MA. Entered the USAAF Aug. 19, 1943 after completing his junior year at Taunton High School. Basic training at BTC #10, Greensboro, NC; Radio School, Sioux Falls, SD; graduated August 1944. Assigned to Yuma AFB for gunnery training, completing in September.

After 10 day leave went to Westover Field, Chicopee, MA for crew assignment; transferred to Charleston, SC for operational training. Finished mid-January 1945; picked up new B-24 at Mitchell Field, Long Island, NY; started for the U.K. by way of the northern route ie: Dow Field, Bangor, ME, Goose Bay, Labrador-BW #3 Greenland, Meeks Field, Iceland; landed in Wales. Assigned to 448th Bomb Group, 713th Sqdn. in Seething. Their crew, #611, flew 11 missions.

Most memorable mission was the last one, Landshut, Germany, April 16, 1945. Coming off the target they were being tracked pretty close by the flak. The mission to Berlin, March 1945, was also memorable. They lost part of their formation in the clouds, joined up with another group to complete the mission. Crew received Certificates of Valor. Finished with rank of staff sergeant. Received Air Medal, ETO Ribbon with three Battle Stars plus other ribbons.

Flew back to the States, June 1945. Following a 30 day leave made stops at Sioux Falls, SD, Albuquerque, NM, and Westover Field for discharge Dec. 3, 1945. Graduated Boston University, 1951; 29 years insurance underwriter; 12 years in radio broadcast business; starting third career as DJ.

Married Faith S. Spencer Aug. 28, 1948. Has three sons Stephen, Warren and Richard.

IRVING C. DUPUIS, was born Feb. 18, 1925 in Lake Linden, MI. Enlisted Aug. 4, 1943 in the USAAC, navigator, 2nd Air Div., 392nd Bomb Group, 576th Sqdn., Wendling, England. Participated in Rhineland and Central Europe campaigns. Memorable experience was dropping bombs on first mission.

Discharged Dec. 26, 1946 with the rank first lieutenant at Randolph Field, TX.

Married to Elizabeth and has six children and five grandchildren. He is a retired chemical engineer and worked 31 years for E.I. Dupont de Nemours & Co. His hobby is woodworking.

PAUL F. DWYER, was born in Somerville, MA on Feb. 25, 1921. Entered Aviation Cadet Program in August 1942. Graduated from Selman Field Navigation School, December 1943 as second lieutenant. B-24 OTU at Muroc, CA.

Flew South Atlantic route to England. Assigned to 713th Sqdn., 448th Bomb Group. Flew 30 missions. Received the Distinguished Flying Cross, Air Medal with three Oak Leaf Clusters.

Returned to USA in October 1944. Assigned to Walla Walla, WA AB as instructor. Discharged as first lieutenant, September 1945. Harvard College AB, 1948; University of Notre Dame Law School, JD, 1951; 25 years as an attorney for the U.S. Government; retired as chief counsel for subcommittee on health and safety of the U.S. House of Representatives, December 1984.

Married Katherine V. Murphy, January 1948 and has three sons and one daughter. They reside in Fredericksburg, VA.

HOWARD W. DYE JR. (DOER), was born in Franklin, NJ April 23, 1921. Attended Susquehanna University for two years where he met Martha Tribby and married in 1942. He has two daughters and three grandchildren from that marriage.

Entered the service Aug. 15, 1942 and Aviation Cadet Program shortly thereafter. Graduated as a second lieutenant pilot in Class 43-G at Turner Field, GA Southeast Training Command. Attended B-24 transition in the first class at Maxwell AFB, AL. Completed Phase I RTU crew training at Mountain Home, ID, and Phase II and III of OTU at Wendover Field, UT with 467th Bomb Group.

Deployed with the group to Rackheath, England as part of the 96th Combat Wing, 2nd Air Div. of 8th Air Force. Flew 35 combat missions (278 combat hours) as AC from April 11, 1944 to July 31, 1944, including two missions on D-day, June 6, 1944. His crew completed their tour with no injuries. He separated from AD Dec. 7, 1945 and joined the Air Force Reserve.

Joined the Air Reserve Technician Program in 1959 and served as instructor pilot, operations officer, squadron commander and four years as group commander at Westover

AFB, MA. Stayed with the Air Force in a military or civil service capacity until retirement in 1984 as executive officer in the 514th MAW Assoc., McGuire AFB, NJ which completed nearly 42 years of federal service. Military retirement was in 1973 as a command pilot with nearly 6,000 hours and the grade of colonel.

Decorations included the Distinguished Flying Cross, Air Medal with four Oak Leaf Clusters, WWII Medal, ETO Ribbon with four Battle Stars, American Campaign Ribbon, Dominican Republic Ribbon, Vietnam Campaign Ribbon and Air Force Reserve Medal.

After the loss of first wife in a tragic family auto accident in 1961, he married Anne McBain an Air Force Reserve nurse and has a son (in the Air Force since 1984), a daughter and one grandson. He and Anne are enjoying retirement in an adult community and traveling whenever possible.

DALE H. DYER, has been living in Blue Ridge, GA since 1948. Born Dec. 8, 1919 at Clearwater, KS. Attended Kansas State College 1938-1942, ROTC commission, infantry 1942.

Transferred to Air Corps and received pilot wings Class 43-F at Columbus, MS. Begin flying B-24 at Smyrna, TN and became flight instructor. Flew many pilot survivors of Ploesti oil field raid. Crew transition, Boise, ID.

Overseas August 1944 by SS *Brazil*. Stationed Horsham St. Faith, 458th Bomb Group, 8th Air Force, 26 missions, lead crew, rank captain. Received Distinguished Flying Cross at Pearberg bombing. Made gas hauls to France September 1944. Flew ground personnel over Germany and Rhine River after war ended.

During last 38 years has visited each crew member and kept in touch with six remaining. Married June 1945 and has four children and six grandchildren. Managed I.H. Implement and car business for 18 years. Retired from Dyer Realty after 28 years. Flew B-29s late 1945 and still flies Cessna Cardinal regularly and enjoys playing golf.

JAMES P. DYKE, was born Sept. 10, 1920 at Breckenridge, TX, raised and attended public schools at Walters, OK. Trained as private pilot through both basic and advanced civilian pilot training (CAA) while a student at Hardin-Simmons University, Abilene, TX from which he earned a BA degree in May 1942.

Enlisted as private USAAF Reserve Aug. 19, 1942. Called to active duty as aviation cadet (pilot) with Class 43-K Feb. 19, 1943. Primary School, Jones Field, Bonham, TX; Secondary, Greenville AAF, Greenville, TX; Advanced, Ellington AAF, TX; commissioned second lieutenant Dec. 4, 1943, rated pilot Dec. 5, 1943. Transition in B-24 aircraft at Ft. Worth, TX AAF; assigned a flight crew in Salt Lake City, UT and phase trained as a replacement crew at Biggs AAF, El Paso, TX. Flew northern route, Topeka, KS; Bangor, ME; Goose Bay, Labrador; Bluie West One, Greenland; Prestwick, Scotland, to deliver a B-24J to the ETO.

Assigned to Station 144, 733rd Sqdn., 453rd BG, 2nd W, 2nd AD, 8th AF, Norfolk, Old Buckingham, England on June 28, 1944. Flew first mission to Halle, Germany on July 7, 1944 and last mission to Minden, Germany on Oct. 26, 1944, completing 35 combat missions in 112 days (16 weeks) with 15 trips flown in the first 29 days of the tour. Awarded the Distinguished Flying Cross, Air Medal with three Oak Leaf Clusters, American Defense Medal, ETO Medal with four Bronze Battle Stars and the Victory Medal.

Credits success to a well-trained, disciplined, courageous and high performance flight crew, supported by a superior ground crew, who came back from the continent at times under less than ideal circumstances such as the loss of an engine and two superchargers on one mission. A crew which made it through an accidental feathering of two engines between Greenland and Scotland on the fly-over. A crew which, when slowed by B-17s in the pattern, made one of the very few go-arounds ever made at the Bluie West One strip; and the most simple, accurate and famous reply of any navigator in the 8th Air Force who, when crippled over Germany, replied to a request for an emergency heading with the singular response WEST!

Returned to ZI in January 1945; assigned to Courtland AAF, AL as an assistant base exchange officer. Released from active duty May 30, 1945, just after V-E day. Retained active reserve status with final rank of lieutenant colonel and terminal assignment as division personnel officer for the 832nd AD, TAC, Cannon AFB, Clovis, NM. Placed in retired catagory in 1980 with 38 years of active and reserve service. Awarded the Reserve Forces Medal with Hour Glass Device.

After release from active duty in 1945, pursued academic training as a university librarian. Received a BA in LS degree from the University of Oklahoma. Earned both masters and the PhD in Library Science from the University of Illinois. Held positions as chief librarian of Eastern New Mexico University, Portales, NM; Texas A&M University, College Station, TX; and New Mexico State University, Las Cruces, NM. Retired from New Mexico State in August 1988.

Served the 2nd Air Div. as a member of the Oversight Committee for the 2nd AD Memorial Library in Norwich, Norfolk County, England. Selected as an initial director for a 2nd AD Assoc. American Educational Foundation proposed as successor to the American Librarian Fund.

PHILIP ROSWELL EARL, was born Sept. 26, 1922 in Rochester, NY. Entered the USAAC February 1942. Had just begun his freshman year at Wesleyan University, CT and was in the living room of Delta Kappa Epsilon on "day of infamy" Dec. 7, 1941. His roommate helped him to decide the Air Corps was the service to join, which they both did in early 1942, continuing college until February 1943 when they were called to the college training detachments.

Went to Williamsport, PA and after two months there, went to Miami Beach for basic; primary at Arcadia, FL; Montgomery, AL secondary (BT-13s); Valdosta, GA (twin engine); Montgomery for transition (B-24s); Boulder, CO for pre-combat crew training; and finally overseas to England by boat.

Assigned to Wendling with the 392nd and flew 29 missions over Germany and one over France. Flew back to the States in April 1945 for redeployment which never happened as the atomic bombs brought about V-J day. Memorable experience was forced landing in Belgium and Naplam to France. Discharged September 1945 with the rank of first lieutenant. Received the Air Medal with five clusters.

Returned to Wesleyan in November 1945, graduated June 1947. Married in 1949 and has three sons and six grandchildren. His wife passed away in 1986. He remarried in 1988 to a widow with four grown children. Currently retired.

WALTER GLEN EASON, was born July 13, 1917 near Sardis, TN. Inducted Jan 18, 1943; basic in Miami Beach, FL. Attended several service schools: airplane and engine mechanic, Gunnery, B-24 Consolidated Aircraft Mechanic etc. before and during combat air crew training for overseas duty.

Served as flight engineer, gunner on B-24J Liberator, assigned to 389th Bomb Group, Hethel, England, July 22, 1944 to March 21, 1945 and flew 36 missions with same crew. Memorable experience was when a large shell, probably 88mm, went through wing (did not detonate) between fuselage and #3 engine at front of flap.

On rolls of the Lucky Bastard Club. Awarded Air Medal and four Oak Leaf Clusters, EAME Ribbon with three Bronze Stars. Returned to USA and attended Airplane Electrician School on the B-29. Discharged as tech sergeant Sept. 17, 1945, Maxwell Field, AL.

Returned to farming for one year but after seeing the world it is hard to "keepem" on the farm. Retired in 1980 as an automobile mechanic with Martin-Marietta, a defense contractor. Since 1988 has reunited with overseas air crew several times at various places in the USA. He has four children. Currently is retired.

GORDON L. EASTERBROOK, was born May 13, 1920 in Hackensack, NJ. Graduated from Leaneck High School in 1937 and was drafted in the USAAC in September 1943.

Flew 29 missions during WWII, the success of these missions were attributed to a baby shoe belonging to his son Dick. He believed that by having this shoe with him it would bring him good fortune. He believed in this concept so strongly that he named the original B-24 Liberator the *Shoe Shoe Baby*.

Was in the 8th Air Force, 445th Bomb Group, 700th Bomb Sqdn. Received many medals including the Distinguished Flying Cross, WWII Victory Medal, EAME Service Medal, American Defense Service Medal and Air Medal with three Oak Leaf Clusters. Participated in Normandy, Rhineland and Congo campaigns.

Discharged in 1945 and re-enlisted in 1950. Retired from the Air Force in 1967 with the rank master sergeant and went to work for Northrop Corp. and Civil Service.

Married Nov. 2, 1941 to Jane Pearson. They have five children, one adopted, 11 grandchildren and four great-grandchildren. Easterbrook passed away in March 3, 1985 in Bend, OR. *Submitted by his daughter Linda Perez.*

WILLIAM F. EASTLAND (MOE), was born in Sparta, TN on Aug. 14, 1923. Joined the USAAC on April 6, 1943 after completing one year of college. After basic, B-24 Mechanics and Aerial Gunnery schools, he joined a crew as flight engineer on a B-24 and went to England as a replacement crew in June 1944.

First assignment was 492nd Bomb Group and completed 12 missions prior to deactivation and transfer to 467th Bomb Group where he completed balance of 35 missions. Flew majority of missions in the *Feudin Wagon*. After completion of missions Jan. 7, 1945 was attached to a troop carrier unit in the 9th Air Force.

Returned to States March 17, 1945. After leave assigned as B-29 flying gunnery instructor until discharge on Oct. 3, 1945 with the rank tech sergeant.

He returned to college and graduated as a civil engineer, joined the Army Reserves as second lieutenant engineers and remained in Army Reserve for a total of 30 years. Progressed to rank of colonel. Worked as civil engineer with the U.S. Army Corps of Engineers for 38 years before retiring.

Married Helen Sparkman in 1949 and has one daughter and twin granddaughters.

HOWARD R. EBERSOLE, was born Feb. 8, 1922 and reared on a farm near Plymouth, MI. Radio operator in Merchant Marine, May 1940 to June 1942. Enlisted in Army Signal Corps, commissioned second lieutenant and married Mary, December 1942. Graduated pilot training Class 44-D, joined 392nd Bomb Group January 1945 and flew 16 missions.

Left service December 1945 and joined Michigan Air Guard, flying F-51s in 1948. Graduate, University of Michigan with BSEE. Recalled with Guard in January 1951. Flew 30 missions in F-51, 70 missions in F-86 in 18th Fighter Bombardier Group in Korea. Became regular Air Force officer, retired with the rank lieutenant colonel in January 1969.

Received the Silver Star, Distinguished Flying Cross, Air Medals, Commendation Medal, Korean Chungmoo with Gold Star. Duty stations include: Tyndall AFB, FL; Holloman AFB, NM; Elmendorf AFB, AK; Langley AFB, VA. He flew T-33, F-101, F-102, and F-106.

Ebersole and Mary had two sons. Lost the eldest in 1963 in airline accident. Mary passed away in 1973. He remarried and divorced twice. Has son by second wife in Mississippi. Now retired, he flies gliders, warbirds and is enjoying his three grandchildren.

HAROLD C. ECKELBERRY, was born Oct. 5, 1922 in Otsego, OH. Entered the USAAF on Aug. 4, 1942, flight engineer, 445th Bomb Group, 703rd Sqdn. Stationed at Tibenham, England 1943-1944. Completed 30 combat missions over France and Germany, lead crew.

Discharged Sept. 18, 1945 with the rank tech sergeant. He received the Air Medal and the Distinguished Flying Cross.

Married and has three children and six grandchildren. He is retired after being a service manager for 31 years at Lincoln-Mercury Ford Dealer.

RICHARD H. ECKMAN,
was born May 17, 1925 in Toledo, OH. Entered the USAAC July 17, 1943, served with 445th Bomb Group, 703rd Bomb Sqdn. as flight engineer/ gunner. Stationed at Davis-Monthan, Tucson, AZ; Keesler Field, MS; Laredo, TX; Tibenham, England.

Memorable experiences: being on the biggest air raid of the war, March 18, 1945, with over 1,300 heavy bombers and 700 fighters hitting Berlin; Christmas Eve of 1944 when downed in Lille, France. The town was liberated by British shortly before and they were the only Yanks there. Marlene Dietrich was there to entertain troops and when she heard the American Bomber crew was there, she insisted they all meet her back stage and join her for dinner at her hotel. She was a very gracious and beautiful lady.

Discharged Nov. 5, 1945 with the rank staff sergeant.

Married to Nelda and has daughter, Keely, and grandson, Erik (age 4). Retired, he is a full time baby sitter for grandson and loves it.

GEORGE ECONOMAKI,
was born Aug. 11, 1926 in Brooklyn, NY. Entered the USAAF April 2, 1943 (registered for draft at age 16). Served with 506th Sqdn., 44th Bomb Group, 8th AAF, 2nd Air Div. as radio operator, aerial gunner.

Radio School at Scott Field, IL; radio operations flight instructor, Pueblo, AFB, Pueblo, CO and overseas 1944-1945, Shipdham, England. Participated in Ardennes, Rhineland, Central Europe campaigns.

Discharged Oct. 26, 1945 with the rank of tech sergeant. Received the Air Medal with three Oak Leaf Clusters, ETO Ribbon and three Battle Stars.

He is a retired machinery salesman.

FREDERICK E. EDELL,
was born June 1, 1919 in Wallingford, CT. Entered the Air Corps Feb. 21, 1944, 389th Bomb Group. Stationed in Tonopah, NV Air Base, Laredo, TX and Hethel, England. Flew 21 combat mission in B-24 with 565th as a tail gunner.

Memorable experience: During his tour in England, he was asked to fly on a mission with another crew as their tail gunner was ill. What a surprize when they landed back at base, after dropping their bombs on Germany, to find his crew anxiously waiting his return. What a great group they were.

Discharged Nov. 3, 1945 with the rank staff sergeant. Received the Air Medal and campaign stars.

Married Emilie Matirko on Sept. 20, 1941. They have four children, six grandchildren and four great-grandchildren. Retired and lives in Stockton, CA. Would like to hear from crew mates.

WALTER ALLEN EDGEWORTH,
was born July 3, 1916 in Downers Grover, IL. Entered the USAAC on Dec. 12, 1941. Served with the 453rd Bomb Group, 733rd Bomb Sqdn., Lowry Field, Buckley Field, CO, and Old Buckingham.

Memorable experience was hitchhiking through England and Wales on furlough; and hearing the bells ring on Easter morning in 1944.

Discharged Sept. 4, 1945 with the rank sergeant. Received the ETO Medal with six Battle Stars.

Married 51 years and has two daughters and two grandchildren. He is currently retired.

GERALD D. EDWARDS (BARNEY),
was born June 23, 1923 in Akron, OH. Joined the USAAC Jan. 7, 1943. Basic training in Miami Beach; Airplane Mechanic School,

Seymour Johnson Field, Goldsboro, NC and Aerial Gunnery School, Fort Myers, FL. Shipped to Salt Lake City, UT and was assigned to a B-24 Bomber crew. Went from there to Biggs Field, TX for phase training.

Joined the 492nd Bomb Group in Alamogordo, NM as a replacement tail gunner on Lt. O'Sullivans crew. Flew overseas via Trinidad, South America and Africa, landing in Valley Wales before ending up at home base in North Pickenham, England. Flew his first mission on May 11, 1944, which was also the first mission of the 492nd Bomb Group. Flew his last mission on July 31, 1944. Was credited for shooting down a Messerschmitt 410 on a raid over Politz, Germany. Completed total of 30 missions.

Discharged Oct. 23, 1945 with the rank of staff sergeant.

Received the Distinguished Flying Cross, Air Medal with five Oak Clusters and four Battle Stars. Their plane was the *Irishmans Shanty* and they were the first crew to finish 30 missions in the 492nd Bomb Group.

Went to work for Goodyear Tire & Rubber Co., Akron, OH in December 1945 and retired in November 1979. Married Hazel in December 1958.

JOHN S. EDWARDS,
was born in Oakham, MA and graduated from Barre, MA High School. He is the son of a WWI veteran. Enlisted in May 1943, later served with the 703rd Bomb Sqdn., 445th Bomb Group, 2nd Air Div., 8th Air Force in England. Was a member of Lt. John Saunders crew and flew in B-24s. Was shot down on his 24th mission and bailed out over Germany. Was held POW at Dulag Luft, Stalag Luft III and Stalag VII.

Stationed in Tokyo, Japan when the Korean War broke out and was among the first American military to see action in July 1950. He served as company commander. In 1966 and 1967 his tour of duty was in Vietnam as battalion commander. He retired in 1972 with the rank of colonel.

After the war, he remained in the inactive reserve and attended college. Holds a bachelor's degree from the University of Nebraska and a master's in education from Boston University.

Edwards organized the NE New York Chapter Ex-POWs and was the first commander. Was elected first commander of the Dept. of New York and served as national commander 1989-1990. He organized the first Korean War Veterans Chapter in New York and was the first president. Served as the first elected president, Dept. of New York, Korean War Veterans Association. Was the chairman of the New York State Committee to design a memorial for all Korean War Veterans. After three years of hard work, a beautiful memorial was dedicated on June 25, 1990 in Albany, NY. Governor Cuomo was the principal speaker.

He is active in many community and civic projects. A member of the VFW, Post #357, DAV, American Legion, ROA (past chapter president), Tri-County Vietnam Veterans, Association U.S. Army (past chapter president), National Association of Atomic Veterans, chairman of the Red Cross Service to Military and Veterans Committee; 8th Air Force Historical Society, New York State Military Heritage Museum and advisor and member of numerous other committees and boards. His prime objective is to leave a legacy, school history books to contain a chapter on the veterans in the wars of this century, assist in making changes to the Geneva conventions, write a history of the Ex-POWs, as well as other projects that are underway.

Presently he is employed with the New York State Energy Office as director, Contingency Planning. He resides with his family in Niskayuna, NY.

ROBERT L. EDWARDS (BOB),
was born Jan. 21, 1922 in Barnardsville, NC. He began active duty with the USAAC on Feb. 25, 1943. After basic training at Keesler Field, MS, he completed a number of Air Corps training programs.

Arrived in England on Nov. 10, 1944 and served as a navigational radar mechanic with the 467th Bomb Group at Rackheath. Returned to the USA on June 15, 1945 and was discharged on Nov. 16, 1945 with the rank of corporal.

He received his BS degree at Berea College, KY, taught in high school, then obtained the MS and PhD degrees at North Carolina State University. Joined the faculty of Clemson University, SC in 1958 and retired as Professor Emeritus of Animal Science in 1986.

Married Dorothy Elizabeth Baldwin in 1951. They have a son and a grandson.

TOM N. EDWARDS,
was born March 30, 1923 in Logen, UT and grew up in Eldon, MO. He had two years of college at Missouri University. Joined the USAC as cadet in February 1943. Received his wings, Class 44-C in March 1944, Douglas, AZ.

Trained as B-24 bomber pilot, Albuquerque, NM and Tonopah, NV. He was A/C commander, had his crew with assigned plane for South Pacific. Five days later they were on troop carrier for England and 8th Air Force.

Started flying combat October 1944 and finished his tour of 35 missions in April 1945 on three engines. The crew was on leave on Nov. 26, 1944 when entire squadron was shot down on mission to Misburg.

After tour he flew weather scout for the 2nd Air Div. and RAF until war ended. Discharged in 1945 as first lieutenant. Received the Distinguished Flying Cross, six Air Medals, three European Campaign Stars, and the Presidential Citation.

Returned to Missouri University to graduate. Has had his own office in real estate in Fort Lauderdale, FL for the past 37 years.

Married March 5, 1949 to Nedra Covington and has three children, eight grandchildren and one great-grandson.

ARTHUR J. EGAN,
was born May 11, 1922 in Savage, MN. Entered the USAAF Nov. 3, 1942. Was on C.L. Bell Crew as the tail gunner. Stationed at Wendling, England, Panama, Canal Zone and Korea.

Joined the 392nd Bomb Group, 579th Bomb Sqdn. in March of 1944. On their fifth mission, April 12, their plane was damaged and limping home alone. Their two waist gunners bailed out near Dunkirk during evasive action by the crew. Their engineer was blown from his top turret and falling towards the open bombbay doors when the radio operator grabbed him by the leg and pulled him to safety (was killed later on May 28 by ground fire).

On 23rd mission their plane was damaged by groundfire and fighters on the way into, over the target and leaving the target which was the second Politz mission. They limped into Sweden safely on June 20, 1944.

Remained in the Air Force until wounded in Korea on second mission. Was medically retired in 1954 with the rank of staff sergeant. Received the Air Medal with three clusters and the Distinguished Flying Cross.

Has wife, Teddy; son, Bert; daughter, Robin; and grandson, John. Egan is a retired teacher.

ROBERT L. EGAN,
was born Jan. 29, 1918 in Minneapolis, MN. Was a peacetime selectee on April 9, 1941 and entered cadet program at time of Pearl Harbor. He trained in

the SE Command; commissioned Jan. 14, 1943 at George Field, IL; transition at Smyrna, TN; phase training at Davis-Monthan and Biggs Field.

Arrived Prestwick, Scotland July 7, 1943; assigned 93rd Bomb Group at Hardwick and sent to North Africa. Returned to United Kingdom in August and assigned to 392nd Bomb Group in September. An early mission was Gydnia, Poland and others were "The Big Week" on March 6 and 8 to Berlin.

Completed tour of 25 missions on March 21, 1944 and was pilot of first crew to complete tour in 577th Bomb Sqdn. Received the Distinguished Flying Cross, Air Medal and three Oak Leaf Clusters.

Spent remainder of war at Langley Field, VA as an instructor pilot. Was married to Rose Ahern on Sept. 19, 1944. Retired from the service in October 1945 as a captain. Has five children and nine grandchildren. Resides in Minneapolis.

VICTOR J. EHLERT, was born Aug. 5, 1919 in Kent, MN. Entered the USAAF Sept. 8, 1942, 8th Air Force, 2nd Air Div., 446th Bomb Group, 704th Sqdn. Stationed in England, etc. Participated in Air Offensive Europe, Northern France and Normandy campaigns. Completed 30 missions with James D. Shannon Crew.

Discharged Oct. 4, 1945 with the rank of staff sergeant. Received the Air Medal and three Oak Leaf Clusters, Distinguished Flying Cross, Good Conduct, American Defense, EAME Ribbon and the Victory Medal.

Married and has six children. He is a retired farmer.

CLEM C. EHMET, was born Jan. 8, 1921 in Newport, KY. Joined the USAAC Oct. 28, 1942, Ft. Thomas, KY. Left Nov. 11, 1942 for basic training in Atlantic City, NJ; Radio School, Sioux Falls, SD; Gunnery School, Laredo, TX. Assigned radio operator with B-24 Crew of Lt. D.B. Harris, trained at Alamogordo, NM and Herington, KS.

Assigned to 466th Bomb Group, 787th Sqdn. Sent overseas and stationed at Attlebridge, England. On the 5th mission, April 8, 1944, was shot down over Germany. After being loose for nine days was arrested by the Gestapo who held him for 10 days interrogation before releasing him to the Luftwaffe. Was interned as a POW for 13 months at Stalag 17B, Krems, Austria until repatriated and returned to the USA in May 1945. After R&R at Miami Beach was sent to Wright Patterson, Dayton, OH. Discharged Oct. 29, 1945.

Married Emma Marsch on Oct. 16, 1943.

WALTER H. EICHENSEHR, was born Feb. 16, 1920 in Altoona, PA. Enlisted April 14, 1943 in the USAF. Navigator, Class 44-5, assigned to 44th Bomb Group, 506th Sqdn. Stationed in Shipdham, England. Completed 35 missions over Europe in B-24 on Hal Tyree Crew.

Discharged October 1956 with the rank of captain. He received the Air Medal with four Oak Leaf Clusters. Memorable experience was Kassell raids in October 1944 and detached service in France to ferry war wearies back to England.

Married to Elaine and has four children, eight grandchildren and one great-grandchild. He is retired from Bell Telephone.

HENRY EIRICH, was born Oct. 11, 1920 in Newark, NJ and grew up in California. Drafted into the USAAC Sept. 22, 1942. Was assigned to Airplane School, Keesler Field, MS. After 19 weeks of schooling, transferred to B-24 Engine School, Ypsilanta, MI. Assigned to 445th Bomb Group, 700th Sqdn. at Mitchell Field, SD.

Left New York Oct. 27, 1943 on *Queen Mary*, arrived at Tibenham, England November 1943, served there 17 months, promoted to crew chief. Discharged with rank staff sergeant, McClellan Field, CA on Oct. 3, 1945. Received ETO Campaign Ribbon with Silver Star and one Bronze Battle Star, Distinguished Unit Badge, three Overseas Bars and one Service Stripe.

Married Lila Rakestraw Dec. 28, 1946 and has two sons. Worked for state of California as heavy equipment mechanics, retiring in 1981. Now farms five acres of almonds and enjoys his four grandchildren.

FRED J. EISERT, was born Sept. 8, 1916 in Long Island, New York. Enlisted April 23, 1941. Commissioned second lieutenant (pilot), Jan. 2, 1942, Barksdale Field, LA.

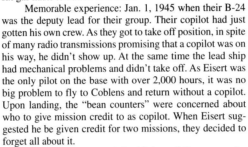

After 18 stateside assignments, was sent overseas with 755th Bomb Sqdn., 458th Bomb Group, Norwich, UK; Tripoli, Libya; Wiesbaden, Germany; Preswick, Scotland; Chateauroux, France. Flew 30 combat missions (most as lead crew) and six gas hauls to Patton in France.

Memorable experience: Jan. 1, 1945 when their B-24 was the deputy lead for their group. Their copilot had just gotten his own crew. As they got to take off position, in spite of many radio transmissions promising that a copilot was on his way, he didn't show up. At the same time the lead ship had mechanical problems and didn't take off. As Eisert was the only pilot on the base with over 2,000 hours, it was no big problem to fly to Coblens and return without a copilot. Upon landing, the "bean counters" were concerned about who to give mission credit to as copilot. When Eisert suggested he be given credit for two missions, they decided to forget all about it.

Discharged Nov. 30, 1968 with the rank lieutenant colonel. Received the WWII Victory, American Defense Service, Air Force Commendation, Air Medal with four Oak Leaf Clusters, EAME Campaign with four Bronze Service Stars, American Campaign, National Defense Service with one Bronze Service Star, Air Force Longevity Service Ribbon with one Silver Oak Leaf Cluster, Command Pilot and Missile Badge.

Lives in Dayton, OH. He is retired and does volunteer work and keeps busy with various hobbies.

ALLEN EK, was born Jan. 31, 1922 in Chicago, IL. Married Blaine Robin Oct. 4, 1947. Now lives in Schiller Park, IL and has one son, Elliot, daughter-in-law, Terry, and grandson, Eric.

Entered service Jan. 25, 1943 and received basic training at Wichita Falls, TX. Received college training at Oklahoma Baptist University in Shawnee, OK. Was sent to Laredo and Eagle Pass, TX for gunnery training. Pre-flight training was received at Ellington Field. Transferred to Midland, TX for bombardier training. Graduated Military Class 44-7.

First combat assignment was 453rd Bomb Group at Old Buckingham, Norwich, England. Memorable experience was flying all missions with a crew that kept them in flying condition through their tour. Completed 35 missions, 12 as bombardier and 23 as bombardier-navigator.

Received six Air Medals, three Campaign Stars and other medals. Discharged June 10, 1945 with the rank of first lieutenant.

Has been self-employed as tax accountant for the past 40 years.

S.J. ELDEN (SANDY), was born March 5, 1924 and raised in Detroit, MI. Shortly after graduation from high school, he entered the Army and was assigned to the Air Corp, receiving training as a munition handler and small arms mechanic. Was assigned to the 577th Bomb Sqdn., 392nd Bomb Group, then stationed at Alamogordo, NM then a dusty one horse town known for its daily 4 p.m. sandstorms. On Aug. 1, 1943, the heavily ladened *Queen Elizabeth* landed in Glascow and they entrained for Wendling. He became the clerk of their 30 man ordnance group, attaining the rank of sergeant.

Their work was rather mundane and ostensibly consisted mostly of being summoned from the movies each night, delivering bomb loads, waiting for the morning fog to lift and then hauling their booty back to the bomb dump through the haze. Of course there was the time when the alert came during their 200th mission party and the lieutenant and their cadre of non-coms "let the fellows continue their celebration." They laboriously loaded up 2,000 pounders, headed out; missed their mark in the fog, attempted a "U" turn and dropped a number of huge one tonners on the runway. An exciting evening was had by all.

After discharge in October of 1945, he completed college and law school; in 1951 moved to Ann Arbor, MI (home of the famous Wolverine football and basketball squads). After five years of private practice, he joined the city attorney's office (1956) was subsequently appointed municipal judge (1966) and then became a state court district judge, serving for the next 25 years. Though he retired Jan. 1, 1993, he still sits as a visiting judge throughout the State.

Married his childhood sweetie Sept. 8, 1946 and they have a married son and daughter.

LEROY W. ELFSTROM, was born in Minneapolis, MN Aug. 14, 1922. Lived there six years then moved to Frederic, WI where he graduated from High School in 1941. Drafted into the USAAC April 2, 1943 and after a year and a half of schooling was sent to England as radio operator on a B-24 crew. Completed 35 missions over Germany and had "points" for discharge July 1945.

Memorable experiences: Dec. 4, 1943 when coming home from mission to Bebra, Germany and they were forced to land (because of fuel shortage) in Brussels, Belgium the day after the Germans evacuated the city.

On return from St. Vith, Germany in March 1945, he was trying to dismantle three bombs that failed to drop when a German pilot flew by and they were "eye to eye." Elfstrom was a perfect target and thought it was fear causing him to tremble as he passed out. But his gas mask had become separated from the tube and the pilot came to check on him when Elfstrom failed to respond to his call. Got him back on oxygen, saving his life.

Was married Jan. 7, 1944 and has two sons and three grandchildren. He retired at 56 after 37 years service with Federal Aviation Association at Cleveland, OH and Bradford and Rockford, IL.

He enjoys traveling and his lake property in Wisconsin where they spend half their summers. At home he spends much time volunteering at the hospital and church.

GEORGE W. ELKINS, was born July 23, 1917 at Hammond, IN. Drafted into Army as private April 21, 1941; transferred to USAAC as cadet July 1, 1942; served with 448th Bomb Group, 2nd Air Div., 1092 (B-24 pilot).

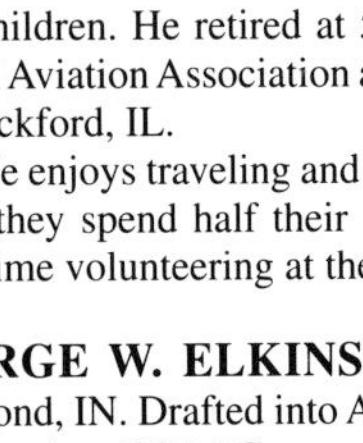
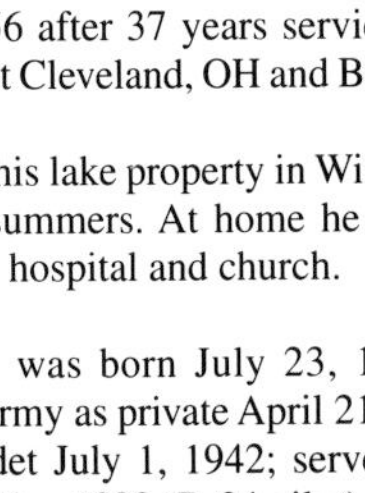

Was sent to Americus, GA for primary pilot training on Nov. 22, 1942. Commissioned at George Field, IL on May 28, 1943. After further training was attached to 448th Bomb Group at Sioux City, IA. On Nov. 26, 1943 group was sent to Seething, England. Was wounded on 11th mission over the continent by anti-aircraft fire. Completed 30 missions by June 26, 1944.

Discharged June 7, 1945 with the rank first lieutenant.

Received the Distinguished Flying Cross, Air Medal with three clusters, Purple Heart and several other ribbons.

Back in civilian life he was employed at Inland Steel Co., Chicago, IN for 36 years. Retired in 1982. Married Marguerite Juergens on Nov. 22, 1952. They have two daughters and four grandchildren.

KLEMMET ELLEFSON, was born at Washington Island, WI on Dec. 6, 1921. Enlisted USAAC in August 1942. Graduated Mechanics School, Keesler Field, MS; Gunnery School, Tyndall Field, FL; crew assignment and overseas training at Pueblo, CO. A Turkish Air Force captain trained with the crew.

Picked up new B-24 at Lincoln, NE. Delivered to Wales. Assigned to 466th Bomb Group, 787th Bomb Sqdn., Attlebridge. Flew first mission Sept. 8, 1944. On Sept. 23, 1944 while ferrying gasoline to Patton's tanks strayed over a pocket of Germans and the B-24 was damaged beyond landing safely. Skeleton crew parachuted safely while the airplane crashed into the emergency runway at Ipswich, England.

Discharged at Madison, WI on Oct. 13, 1945 on Roster #13, 13th man on the roster. Became a commercial fisherman for 25 years and then managed a mink farm until retirement in 1985. Highlight of working years was being in partnership with two brothers.

ROY E. ELLENDER, was born June 3, 1919, Rochester, NY. Joined the USAAC in February 1943. Served with 445th Bomb Group in Tibenham, England. Completed 27 missions over Germany as co-pilot in B-24 bomber. Shot down on Kassel mission Sept. 27, 1944.

Discharged March 15, 1946 with the rank first lieutenant. Received the Air Medal with three Oak Leaves and the Distinguished Flying Cross.

Married January 1946 to Marian Oriel. They have five children and seven grandchildren. Graduated from University of Roch. with a BSME degree in 1951. He is engineer in cardiac pacer company.

MEL ELLER, enlisted in 1942 from his Pontiac, MI home. After completing Gunnery School in Harlingen, TX and Armament School at Lowry Field, Denver, CO, he was assigned to a crew with Lt. Fred Thomas as captain. When phase training was completed in Boise, ID, the crew was sent to the 8th Air Force, becoming part of the 579th Sqdn. of the 392nd Bomb Group.

Upon discharge from service, he returned to Michigan, there the next 25 years were spent in the building field. In 1968 the family which consisted of wife, Barbara, and three children, moved to Harrisburg, PA where he became president of Morrison Laboratory, one of the largest contact lens manufacturers.

Retired in 1985 and now he and his wife spend their time visiting their three children and six grandchildren in Pittsburgh, Providence and Tampa.

He would enjoy hearing from his friends.

RALPH H. ELLIOTT, was born Jan. 20, 1922, Gilman, IL. Graduated University of Illinois in 1942. Pilot Wings

Class 43K, Brooks Field, TX, Dec. 5, 1943. B-24 transition Tarrant Field, TX. CCT Muroc Army AAF. England July 1944 assigned 8th Air Force, 467th Bomb Group, Rackheath. Completed 26 combat missions, 20 as lead crew.

Participated in Northern France, Ardennes, Rhineland and Central Europe campaigns. Lead 467th last mission WWII to Traunstein, Germany, April 25, 1945. Lead the 8th Air Force with Col. Shower CP, in fly-by for General Doolittle, May 1945. Made captain March 1945.

To Reserves October 1945. Received Distinguished Flying Cross and Air Medal with three Oak Leaf Clusters. Recalled to active duty 1952 to Chicago as chief, AFLC liaison officer with Army and Navy. To MacDill AFB, FL 1955 as AC in B-47 aircraft, SAC 305th Bomb Wing. To Bunker Hill AFB, IN 1969, with 305th as chief, Maintenance Analysis Division, B-58 Hustler.

Disability retirement as major in February 1966. Received two Air Force Commendation ribbons and Presidential Unit Citation. Resides in Tucson, AZ. Married Yvonne Bremer on Aug. 28, 1943, Waco Army Air Field, TX. Has four children and six grandchildren.

LEWIS N. ELLIS, was born June 12, 1915 in Chattanooga, TN. Entered the USAF, 8th Air Force, 2nd Div. 389th Group, Hethel Air Base, England. Completed 25 missions over Germany and North Africa. Memorable experience was Ploesti oil fields, Aug. 1, 1943.

Discharged in 1952 with the rank lieutenant colonel. Received the Distinguished Service Cross, Distinguished Flying Cross, five Air Med-  als, Presidential Unit Citation and France Croix de Guerre.

Married to Betty for 40 years and has four children. He is a retired stockbroker with Merrill Lynch.

HENRY WILLIAM ELLISON, was born Feb. 27, 1922 in Beasley, TX. Entered the USAAF Oct. 5, 1942, 2nd Air Div., 8th Air Force, 467th Bomb Group. Basic training at Ellington Field; Gunnery School, Laredo, TX; B-24 School, Biloxi, MS and Willow Run, MI; Wendover, UT; Rackheath, England; B-17 training Hobbs, NM.

Completed 32 missions in B-24 Liberator under Col. Albert Shower, Rackheath AB, Norwich, England. Flew two missions in Invasion of Normandy on D-day. Memorable experience was being the first airplane in their group to be hit by enemy fighter.

Discharged Sept. 21, 1945 with the rank of tech sergeant. Received the Distinguished Flying Cross, EAME Campaign Medal with four Bronze Stars and the Air Medal with four Oak Leaf Clusters.

Married to Mary Ana and is a proud great-grandpa. Retired from Electrical Workers Union IBEW 769, Phoenix, AZ. Retired second time after owning a diesel repair garage and towing service. Currently semi-retired, he keeps busy working for special friends when they need a hand.

ROBERT C. ELSTON (SKEETER), was born Oct. 2, 1922 in Kirksville, MO. Entered the USAAF Oct. 17, 1942, gunnery instructor. He was never assigned to a crew; however, Capt. H.N. Eldridge asked Elston to assist him in developing a gunnery practice range for the 492nd Bomb Group. He was with the 577th Sqdn., Wendling, England and managed the range. He was stationed there from January 1944 to June 1945. Most of the crew members knew him as Skeeter.

Participated in Normandy, Northern France, Ardennes, Rhineland, Central Europe and Air Offensive Europe campaigns. Discharged Oct. 22, 1945 with the rank tech sergeant. Received the EAME Ribbon with Silver Star, Bronze Star, Good Conduct Medal, Air Medal and the Unit Citation.

Married to Wanda for 47 years, has two daughters, four granddaughters and one grandson. Spent 34 years with Florida Federal Savings and Loan. Retired in 1982 as vice president and corporate secretary.

JOSEPH J. ELWOOD, was born March 28, 1924 in Chicago, IL. Entered the service December 1942. Stationed at Tyndall Field, Sheppard Field, Seething, England with the 448th Group.

Memorable experience was crash landing, Dec. 31, 1942; heavy flak April 29, 1943; June 6, support invasion of Europe. Discharged October 1945 with the rank of staff sergeant. Received the Air Medal and Distinguished Flying Cross.

Married Oct. 2, 1954, has wife, Mary, and daughter, Mary, and three grandchildren. He is retired.

JOHN O. EMBICH, was born in Tampa, FL on July 31, 1924. Married Nina L. Irvin in April 1950. They have one son, two daughters, 10 grandchildren and three great-grandchildren. Entered the USAAC June 1942; Gunnery School at Tyndall Field, FL; and Armory School at Lowry Field, CO.

Joined crew at Davis Monthan, AZ, then to 491st Bomb Group, 855th Bomb Sqdn. at Pueblo, CO and overseas to Metfield, England. Flew 31 missions from June to August. Helped move group to North Pickenham, returned to Lowry and other bases. Remained in Air Force at Panama, Northern Canada, Germany, Alaska.

Retired at Forbes AFB, KS in May 1963 as tech sergeant, missile ground support/calibration technician with 21 years. Worked as gunner, aircraft refueler, construction equipment mechanic and aircraft ground support mechanic.

Now retired in Colorado by Rocky Mountain National Park and volunteer at Senior Center and Museum.

EARLINE EMBREY, was running a sandwich shop in Coldwater, MS when WWII broke out. Uncle Sam came along and said that everyone had to move out of the town because of a dam that they were going to build and the town would be flooded. She decided to join the WAAC to help her country and to see the world. Was sworn in at Memphis, rode the train to Chattanooga, landed at Fort Oglethorpe for basic training, then to open up new camp at Fort Devens, MA.

Overseas duty: Landed at Firth of Mirth, Glasgow, Scotland and Stone England. First job in England was being the mail clerk. Had two furloughs to Scotland and went to Cambridge a few times and to London lots of times. Had a twin brother close to London.

One day she went bike riding with a couple of friends and as they started out the gate, they met Col. Sine on his bike and the three of them saluted, when the colonel saluted, he fell off his bike. When asked he said he was okay; but, the next day a note on the bulletin board said "No enlisted personnel shall salute an officer while riding a bike."

In July of 1945 she received orders to go home. Next was on a train going to Ft. Bragg, NC. Went on leave to go home (first time in two and a half years her folks ever saw her in uniform). After leave, went back to Fort Bragg, the Miami Beach for 30 days R&R, back to Fort Bragg for discharge and home.

She wouldn't take anything for her experience in the Army; they worked hard, but also had time to play. That combination brought about many memorable experiences for which she will always be grateful.

KENNETH W. ENGELBRECHT, was born May 21, 1922 at Onarga, IL; graduated from Watseka High School. Received BS in general engr./design major with University of Illinois, Class of 1953. Married Aug. 29, 1959 to Helen

Marie Hawthorne. Has two daughters, Penelope and Heidi. Retired and is battling Parkinson's disease.

Enlisted USAAF Oct. 3, 1940 at Chanute Field, IL, 5th School Sqdn. Enrolled in airplane Mechanics School, was instructor in propellers. Was next at Seymour Johnson Field, NC, 10th Air Base as supervisor of Propeller Branch Airplane Mechanics School. Assigned 715th Sqdn., 448th Bomb Group of the 2nd Air Div. Traveled by convoy, final destination was Seething Air Base, England, where as tech sergeant, he was a crew chief of B-24 bombers at Station 146.

Responded to request for volunteers for the infantry following D-day. Received ETO Badge with three Battle Stars and the coveted Combat Infanryman's Badge. Served in Germany with I Co. of 311th Div. Later was with occupation forces in Germany.

Having second most discharge points, he was on first truck out and returned via the *Queen Elizabeth* to New York City. Discharged Oct. 21, 1955 at Fort Sheridan, IL.

In 1973 he organized the first mini-reunion of the 448th to affiliate with the 2nd Air Division Association. He served as the 448th group's first president.

VICTOR ENGLERT, was born Oct. 5, 1920 and enlisted Oct. 28, 1942, Fort Sam Houston, San Antonio, TX. Basic training, Concho Field, San Angelo, TX; Airplane Mechanic School, Biloxi, MS; Gunnery School, Harlingen, TX. Training schools at Hammer Field and March Field, CA. Assigned to bomber crew Hamilton Field, CA, April 21,1944.

Landed in Scotland May 15, 1944. First bombing mission June 20, Politz, second mission to Berlin. Flak so heavy could hardly see planes in your group. German fighters in packs. Flew 30th mission New Years Eve in 1944. Member of C.H. (Kelly) Craft Crew. Lead Crew Commendation for destruction of target at Scherwin, Germany, Aug. 4, 1944.

Participated in Air Offensive Europe, Normandy, Rhineland, Ardennes, Northern France and Central Europe. Received the Distinguished Flying Cross with Oak Leaf Clusters, six Bronze Stars, Middle Eastern Theater and campaign ribbons. Discharged July 23, 1945, Fort Bliss, El Paso, TX as staff sergeant.

Married Dorothy Walker, Bangs, TX on Aug. 11, 1945. Has son Jerry Englert, wife, Linda, grandchildren: Shelly and Justin; son Billy Englert, wife, Joan, grandchildren: Scott and Bryan and step granddaughter, Jennifer Gallagher.

Retired from residential construction in 1979, Fort Stockton, TX.

JAMES A. ENNIS (SKINNEY), was born in Walker County, AL, April 26, 1916. Shortly thereafter moved to Illinois, attended school in Chicago and classes at Northwestern University. Enlisted in AAC at Chicago May 2, 1942. Was an aviation cadet, qualified as aerial gunner at Tyndall Field, FL, graduated as navigator second lieutenant, Class 43-16 at Selman Field, Monroe, LA on Dec. 4, 1943. Assigned to crew in Tonopah, NV; shipped over to England August 1944 on liner *Il de France*; assigned to 448th Bomb Group, 715th Bomb Sqdn., Seething, Sept. 4, 1944.

Flew three missions with 448th Bomb Group, was transferred to 93rd Bomb Group, HQ for 20th Combat Wing, trained on G.H. "Gee" system for navigation and bombing. Appointed lead navigator. Remainder of combat missions was leading the 20th Combat Wing Bomb Group. Received Distinguished Flying Cross, Air Medal with three Oak Leaf Clusters, ETO Campaign Ribbons and citations.

Moved west in 1954. Retired from United States Postal Service as superintendent of mails. Traveled full time eight years in a recreational vehicle hunting, fishing, shell-fishing in U.S., Canada and Mexico. Married Marie Willie March 13, 1943; they have three children and four grandchildren.

LLOYD LINWOOD ENNIS, was born July 2, 1923 in Roanoke Rapids, NC. Enlisted Oct. 21, 1942; entered active duty on Jan. 31, 1943, navigator, USAAF, served with 466th and 467th Bomb Groups, 96th Combat Wing. Initially he was in Pilot Robert W. Harrington's group.

Stationed in Allenbridge, Norwich, England, Watten Air Base, England, Northern France, Central Europe, Rhineland, Ardennes, Normandy and polar navigation in Alaska. Flew 30 missions. Also flew five missions with British Mosquitos, Watten Air Base, England. A memorable experience was mission to Dahlem, Germany on Dec. 23, 1944 to destroy Von Rundstedt's supply line (his squadron was only one to bomb assigned target). Discharged Feb. 13, 1947, Patterson Field, Dayton, OH with the rank captain AAF Reserve.

Was journeyman machinist then from 1966-1977 with U.S. Dept. of Labor as representative in Bureau of Apprenticeship and Training. Retired in October 1977 and is currently disabled with Alzheimer's disease. Has wife Susan, son Doug and daughters, Rebecca and Brenda.

RICHARD W. ENTWISTLE, was born May 8, 1919 in Portsmouth, NH. Joined infantry at Camp Edwards in December 1941; Gunnery School in 1943; nose gunner B-24, Casper, WY. April 1944 joined 8th Air Force, 389th Bomb Group, 567th Sqdn., Hethel, England.

Finished tour, returned to USA and was discharged August 1945. Memorable experience was when on a mission and another squadron flew through their formation—real scary. Received the Air Medal with cluster, Distinguished Flying Cross, European Theater of Operation.

Married in 1942 to Louise Etheridge and has two daughters. Divorced in 1950. Worked at National Aeronautics and Space Administration building frame supports for rockets. Moved to Miami in 1970 for 12 years and worked as diver for University of Miami on research vessel until retirement in 1985.

Entwistle passed away June 27, 1991, scuba diving in Bahamas with heart attack. *Submitted by Louise Etheridege.*

DONALD F. EPHLIN, enlisted as an aviation cadet at age 17 in September 1943 upon graduation from Framingham, MA High School.

He served as an aerial gunner on a B-24 in the 8th Air Force in England, completing 27 missions as a member of the Uncle Tom's Cabin (Capt. Tom Polliard) crew. They served as a lead crew much of the time, first with the 753rd Bomb Sqdn. and then as part of the 755th Bomb Sqdn. of the 458th Bomb Group. The crew returned to the States between V-E day and V-J day.

Ephlin retired as vice president of the United Auto Workers in 1989 after directing both the Ford and General Motors sections of the Union. He now serves as a senior lecturer at MIT in Cambridge, MA and as a consultant on labor management relations.

Married for 44 years to Theresa McKellick, they have three children and four grandchildren.

CARL E. EPTING JR., was born Newberry, SC on Aug. 12, 1921. Married his high school sweetheart, Margaret M. Parker on July 24, 1942. Has one son and two grandchildren. Entered military service on June 12, 1942 as second lieutenant, Infantry, Camp Wolters, Texas. Accepted for pilot training as student officer in April 1943.

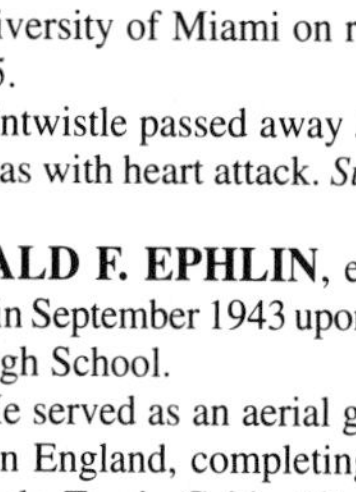
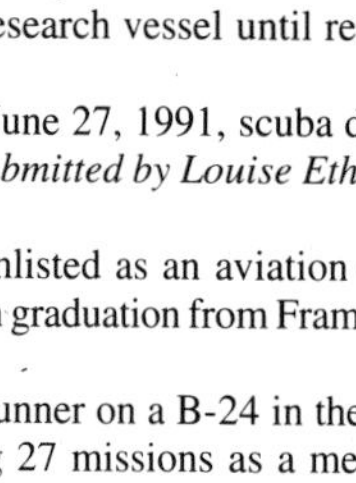

Completed pilot training at Frederick AAB, Frederick, OK on Dec. 5, 1943. Finished B-24 first pilot transition at Tarrant Field, Ft. Worth, TX in March 1944. Selected air crew at Hammer Field, Fresno, CA and completed POM at Muroc, CA (later Edwards AFB).

Assigned to 467th Bomb Group(H), 790th Bomb Sqdn., 8th Air Force at Rackheath near Norwich in July 1944. Completed 35 operational missions and six trucking missions between Aug. 9, 1944 and Feb. 21, 1945.

Returned to U.S. and after brief assignments at Tyndall Field, Panama City, FL and Chanute Field, IL was released from active duty on Nov. 17, 1945. Returned to civilian occupation as an architect and remained in the active USAF reserve program until 1968, retiring as lieutenant colonel. Retired from civilian work as vice president of a Florida based Savings & Loan Association in 1983. Now enjoying retirement with his wife of 50 years in Ormond Beach, FL.

CHARLES ERCEGOVAC, was born Oct. 27, 1916 in Chicago, IL. Enlisted December 1942 in the USAAC, B-24 pilot. Served with 96th Wing, 467th Bomb Group, 789th Sqdn. and flew combat missions from Rackheath, England.

Participated in battles of Normandy, Northern France, Germany and Air Offense of Europe. Discharged Dec. 30, 1946 with the rank of captain. Received Certificate of Valor and Air Medal with three Oak Leaf Clusters.

Has wife, Alida, and three children: Vicky, Mike and Chuck Jr. He is retired.

JACK M. ERICKSON, was born in Phoenix, AZ on Nov. 10, 1923 and raised in Oceanside, CA. Was employed at Mare Island Navy Yard from 1941 to February 1943. Married Florence O'Hara Jan. 18, 1943. Has two sons, Gary and James, and two grandsons, Tim and Stephen.

Drafted into USAAF in February 1943; basic training at BTC #8 at Fresno, CA; graduated Radio Operator/Mechanic School, Scott Field, IL on Nov. 2, 1943. Graduated Aerial Gunnery School at Tyndall Field, FL, January 1944. Completed Air Crew training at Westover Field, MA in May 1944. Departed Mitchell Field, NY for England in June 1944. Flew northern route via Labrador, Iceland to North Ireland. Crew assigned to the 445th Bomb Group, 701st Sqdn. at Tibenham, England.

Completed 11 missions over France and Germany. Shot down by FW 190s on Kassel Raid of Sept. 27, 1944. Parachuted and was captured upon landing. Interrogated at Dulag Luft then assigned to Stalag Luft IV at Kiefhiede, Germany in October 1944. Evacuated from Luft IV in February 1945 as Russian Forces advanced on the area. On forced march across North Germany until liberated by a British scout car while camped at a farm near Zarrentin, Germany. Made way to Laurenburg now in British Hands. Trucked to Emsdettin then flown to Brussels, Belgium in RAF Lancasters. Entrained for trip to Namur, Belgium and returned to USA control. Trucked to Camp Lucky Strike near LeHarve. Finally boarded the USS *Gen. Butner* for voyage to Hampton Roads, VA. Discharged at Santa Ana Air Base on Oct. 15, 1945 with the rank of tech sergeant.

Received the Air Medal with Oak Leaf Cluster, ETO Campaign with two stars, Victory Medal, POW Medal and the Good Conduct.

Worked 37 years for Pacific Telephone. Retired as a staff manager in San Francisco Nov. 30, 1983. Currently a member of AXPOW, Liberator Club, Air Force Association, 2nd Air Division Association and the Caterpillar Club.

Erickson and wife, Florence, have sons, Jim and Gary, and grandsons, Tim and Stephen.

ERIC E. ERICSON, was born Jersey City, NJ April 25, 1922; enlisted Avn/C October 1942; graduated Harlingen AAFGS 1944; graduated San Marcos AAFNS August 1944; assigned to Cadles Crew and trained at Boise for lead crew duty. Went to England aboard *Queen Mary*. Assigned 93rd Bomb Group(H), 328th Bomb Sqdn.

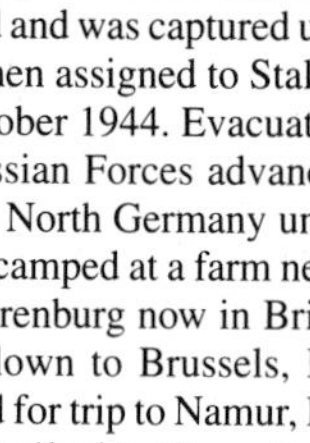
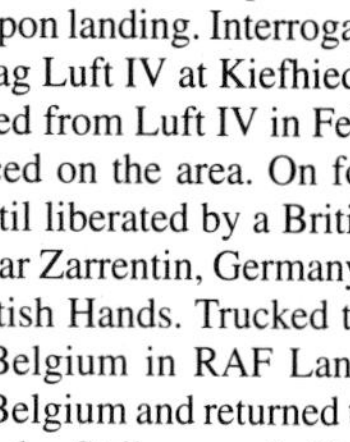

On second mission, Feb. 26, 1945, Berlin, Germany flying tail end Charlie, took a hit that wiped #3. Within 10 minutes #4 was likewise hit. They hit their baleout point on target three miles NE of Berlin some two hours after first being hit. Hit the Nylon at 3600 feet. Broke through approximately 900 feet.

After much transferring they flew via USSR C-46 from

Poznan Poland to Brest Litvosk. Took 35 mph express wood burning train to Kharkov then to Kiev and Poltava, the USAAF Airbase there.

Went via ATC to Teheran, Cairo, Athens, Naples, Marseilles, Paris and London. In 1992, two really great guys headed west, Sam Kesler, co-pilot and Bob Faulkner, nose gunner. They were down to eight. They flew North Atlantic with Bill Fisher's crew. Greatest thrill of his military career was to have his two tech sergeants run 35 yards, grab him by both hands saying, "Thank you for bringing us home." That was worth the 12 medals he accumulated. The 2nd ADA Journal carries their story a bit more.

LEWIS L. EUBANKS, was born in Mena, AR on March 14, 1922. Graduated from high school in Pauls Valley, OK. Entered the service on Oct. 26, 1942 as aviation cadet and received commission as second lieutenant bombardier at Midland, TX on Sept. 15, 1943.

Flew 30 combat missions with 389th Bomb Group, 8th Air Force from Hethel, England in B-24, *Delectable Doris*, piloted by Bill Graft. Assigned as instructor at Deming AFB, NM and applied for tour of duty in Pacific Theater. Was waiting for crew assignment in Lincoln, NE when the bomb was dropped on Japan in August 1945.

Received the Air Medal with three clusters, European Air Medal Ribbon with three Battle Stars, one Overseas Bar, Presidential Unit Citation, and the Distinguished Flying Cross. After discharge, he entered the University of Oklahoma in January 1946 and earned bachelor's, master's and doctor's degrees while teaching and coaching in public schools in Texas and Oklahoma.

Retired as superintendent of schools in 1987 at Midwest City, OK. Married Carol Foss of Pauls Valley, OK and has three daughters and seven grandchildren ranging in age from one year to 17.

JAMES W. EVANS, was born Elmira, NY on Jan. 20, 1924. Drafted 1943 Bombardier School, Midland, TX; assigned to George Bradley's crew with Bart Catanzaro, co-pilot; Roy Cook, gunner; Bob Cowan, top turret; Gus Duhon, ball turret; Dick McGough, navigator; EJ Pyle, radio; Louie Ratto, tail turret; and Allen Tuten, engineer.

Liberator transition at Tucson, Mt. Home and Boise. Flew a Liberator to England and assigned to Horsham St. Faith at Norwich. Completed a tour in December 1944 and stayed with the unit in Intelligence.

Discharged in November 1945 and recalled in June 1951. Retrained as all-weather radar intercept officer and assigned to all-weather fighters, super duty sport cars instead of trucks. Vietnam tour 1966, retired 1968.

Second career teaching high school fully retired 1984. Currently he and his wife have a home in Maine but spend a great amount of time in our RV touring North America.

LAWRENCE W. EVERETT, was born at Lacey, IA on Nov. 2, 1920; graduated from Iowa State University; enlisted in USAAC in September of 1942; called to active duty in Feb. 23, 1943 at Jefferson Barracks, MO. Spent time at the university, Santa Ana Air Base, Kingman, AZ Gunnery School and graduated from Bombardier School, Kirtland Field.

Crew assignment and training at March Field. Flew to England in July 1944. Assigned to 458th Bomb Group at Horsham St. Faith as a lead crew bombardier and flew 29 missions. Returned to U.S. in May of 1945. After a month of furlough, went to Sioux Falls, SD then Brownville, TX and discharged November 1945 with the rank of first lieutenant. Received the Good Conduct, Distinguished Flying Cross, Air Medal and three clusters, European Campaign and four stars.

Returned to Iowa State University and received BS degree. He returned to farming, currently retired. Married Beverly George in 1947, they have five children: Dr. Leslie Everett, Dr. George Everett, Rebecca Sinkler, Dr. Gordon Everett and Floyd Everett. There are 10 grandchildren.

ANDREW EWANUS, was born Nov. 20, 1919, Oliphant, PA. Entered the USAAC Dec. 16, 1941, 748th gunner, 2nd Air Div., 389th Bomb Group, 567th Sqdn. Credited with shooting down two aircraft, at JU-88 and a FW-190.

Discharged Sept. 29, 1969 with the rank master sergeant. Received the Distinguished Flying Cross, Air Medal and four clusters.

Married Maybelle and has a son, Andrew Jr.

HENRY A. FAGAN (HANK), was born on Feb. 2, 1920 in New York City. Enlisted in USAAC on July 27, 1942. Graduated as pilot, second lieutenant, Class 43-I at George Field, IL. Assigned co-pilot on B-24.

Assigned to new Bomb Group, 467th, forming at Wendover, UT as co-pilot on lead crew. Flew on B-24 to England via southern route. Flew four missions with 790th Sqdn. of 467th, then assigned to the Mickey (Pathfinder) Sqdn. 564 of 389th Bomb Group.

The 564th Sqdn. had only planes with radar so they were used by all groups in the 2nd Air Div. for lead purposes. Was wounded on 17th mission, leading a wing over Saarbrucken. Spent 10 days in Air Force hospital, then completed tour of 30 missions.

Reassigned to the States, stationed at Reno, Great Falls, Long Beach, Palm Springs, then to Guam, Philippines. Requested discharge in June 1947 with rank of first lieutenant. Received Distinguished Flying Cross, four Air Medals, Purple Heart and four European Campaign Stars.

Worked in sales promotion for publishing house, now retired. Married and resides in South Orange, NJ.

C.E. FAGER, Lt. Col., graduated pilot training March 10, 1943, commissioned 2nd Lt. USAAC Reserve and ordered to extended active duty.

After completing B-24 Liberator combat crew training, they picked up their new B-24 at Lincoln, NE and departed for the ETO., arriving in England on June 13, 1943 and was he assigned to the 389th BG (H), 567th BS (H).

The latter part of June 1943, the 389th along with the 44th and 93rd Bomb Groups. Ordered to North Africa to take part in Operation Tidal Wave and the Ploesti Raid of Aug. 1, 1943. (low level attack), which they barely survived.After Tidal Wave, went went back to England where he finished his combat tour, having flown his 25th and last combat mission on Feb. 6, 1943.

He was then transferred to the 87th Air Transport Sqdn. at Whorton Air Base in England. They provided air transport for Operation Overlord flying CB-24s and C-47 aircraft carrying personnel supplies of all sorts as well as thousands of gallons of gasoline. He also evacuated some wounded until November 1944 when he was rotated back to the Z of I.

Fager was assigned to the Air Transport Command flying out of Fairfield Army Airfield supporting the Pacific Campaign as well as flying the U.S. Army occupying force (11th Airborne Division) into Japan landing at Atsugi Air Field on Aug. 30, 1943.

Flew B-29s during the Korean War and B-36 Intercontinental Bombers for seven years logging 3,000 hours as A/C in global operations. When the B-36 was retired, he was assigned to the 389th Strategic Missile Wing, (ICBM), the First Combat Ready Intercontinental Ballistic Missile organization.

On March 31, 1962, he retired from the USAF via the 389th SMW. It seemed rather ironic, since he started with the 389th BG (H) that he would end with the 389th SMW 20 years later, thus having come full circle. He retired and lives in Cheyenne, WY.

ALBERT JOSEPH FALKE, was born on Oct. 11, 1924 in Attleboro, MA. Enlisted in USAAC on April 27, 1943. Armorer gunner with the 8th Air Force on B-24 Liberator. Stationed at Fort Devens, MA; Atlantic City, NJ; Lowry Field, CO; Laredo, TX; Westover Field, MA; Charleston, SC; Mitchell Field, NY and Bangor, ME.

From England flew 19 missions with his original crew. Flew seven with new crews from the States (green crews) and later saw action from a different location with the 15th Air Force in Italy. Flew 16 more missions with the 15th Air Force. Many battles were fought from the air over France, Germany, Italy, Yugoslavia, Hungary and Belgium.

Most memorable experiences were when a 20mm projectile flew around in his turret, knocking his oxygen mask off, on his 26th mission. Another time he had to go into the bomb bay to release a bunch of fragmentation bombs from the bomb shackles without his chest chute. Had to ditch in the English Channel and was shot at over the Regenburg A/C Plant and had to parachute over the Italian Alps. Made three missions on D-day and received credit for only one. Downed an FW-190 over Liepsig, Germany and another ME-109 over Halle, Germany. Walked over mine fields in Italy which were unknown to them at the time. Spent a couple of weeks with the British navy when 500 Americans were sent to Italy.

Had more than enough points to go home on. Discharged on Aug. 29, 1945 at Fort Devens, MA with the rank of staff sergeant. Received the Air Medal with 10 Oak Leaf Clusters. Was told he'd receive the Silver Star and the Soldier's Medal, but that's another story!

Met wife, Josephine Jamiel of Briston, RI on July 4, 1945 while home on leave before discharge. Married on Nov. 5, 1945. Through the years had a son and two daughters, Albert Joseph Jr., Joyce Ann and Deborah Jean. All are married and gave him three grandchildren: Sarah Beth, Cheryl Lynn and Michael Albert. Presently with the city of Miami and soon to be retired.

ANTHONY J. FALSONE, was born on Aug. 5, 1920 in Highbank, TX, near Marlin, TX. This town doesn't exist anymore. Volunteered in USAAC at Waco Army Air Field, Waco, TX in October 1942 as a cadet. Received basic training at Sheppard Field, Wichita Falls, TX; also San Antonio, Laredo, College Station and Midland, TX. Graduated from Bombardier School at Midland AAF in Class of 43-18.

Took crew training at Boise, ID. Went overseas with flight crew with Jack Ely as pilot. Removed from this crew and sent to navigator training with new radar navigation training. Joined new crew, since original crew was shot up and forced to bail out over the North Sea, two were rescued, Pilot Ely was captured, the rest were lost. Only the co-pilot is known to have been killed when he was dragged to his death by his plane.

Joined Frank Schwermin's crew and flew 20 missions. Shot down at St. Lo on 20th mission. They were flying at about 10,000 foot when hit by AA fire and forced to bail out when plane caught fire. Landed on German front lines and was immediately captured. Released from POW camp at Stalag VII-A at Moosburg.

Discharged in December 1945 as first lieutenant. Air Medal was presented to his parents while he was missing.

Married Frances Pauline Tusa of Waco in June 1946. Had three boys and two girls. Son, Steve, died at age 18.

He spent 22 years in the grocery business, one year in insurance and 18 years in car sales with a Ford Dealership in Waco. Retired in December 1987. Since then he does volunteer work, travels and visits the children and grandchildren.

WILLIAM R. FANNING, was born on Jan. 8, 1924 in Macon, GA. Married Winnifred "Honey" Hopkins on June 8, 1948. They have three sons and a daughter and four grandchildren.

He enlisted in the Air Force on Dec. 14, 1942 at Warner Robins AFB, GA. Completed Radio Operators School at Scott Field, IL and Aerial Gunnery School at Tyndall Field, FL. Was assigned to a B-24 bomber crew, completing first phase training at Davis Monthan Field, Tucson, AZ. Then assigned to 489th Bomb Group and completed second and third phase training at Wendover Field, UT.

The 489th flew their own aircraft via the southern route to England where they were based at Halesworth in East Anglia. After completing 31 combat missions (the 31st mission was Sept. 18, 1944), he was returned to the States on Oct. 25, 1944. Then transferred to the Air Transport Command. Was flown, again via the southern route, to the Assam Valley Base of Jorhat, India on March 19, 1945 where he completed 35 cargo missions over the Hump into China, flying on C-87s and C-109s.

T/Sgt. Fanning was returned to the States on Nov. 21, 1945 and honorably discharged on Nov. 26, 1945. Received the Distinguished Flying Cross, four Air Medals, four European Campaign Stars, one Asiatic-Pacific Campaign Star, Presidential Unit Citation, plus several other ribbons.

Now semi-retired after 36 years in sales management and marketing. Resides in Crescent, GA.

JAMES J. FARLEY JR., was born on July 31, 1912 in Providence, RI. Enlisted in service on May 22, 1942, 1105 Quartermaster, 638th Air Material Sqdn. USAA attached to 458th Bomb Group, 2nd Air Div.

Basic training at Westover, MA. Overseas in December 1942. Spent 31 months at AAF Station 123, Horsham St. Faith. Served with 56th Fighter Group at Horsham, and then with the 458th Bomb Group. In July 1945, R&R and redeployment.

Attached to 56th Fighter Group from April-July 1943, attached to 458th Bomb Group from January 1944-July 1945.

Discharged on Oct. 1, 1945 with rank of buck sergeant. Received Unit Meritorious Achievement Award, EAME Campaign, WWII Victory Medal and Good Conduct Medal.

Married in Norwich, England in October 1944. Will return in October 1994 for 50th Wedding Anniversary Celebration! He and his English bride raised four children, lost one in 1986. Others are doing well, same for mom and pop. He is now retired.

WALTER FARMER, was born on May 31, 1923 in Hill County, TX. Graduated from Corsicana High School, attended Navarro College. Enlisted in USAC Oct. 28, 1942, engineer on B-24. Flew 13 missions in the *Commanche.* Served in 448th Bomb Group, 714th Sqdn. Based at Seething, Norfolk, England from December 1943 to March 20, 1944. Plane downed over France by flak, parachuted and captured by Germans. Was prisoner of war 14 months, liberated by Russians. POW camp was Stalag Luft I, near Barth, Germany (off Baltic Sea).

Discharged on Nov. 5, 1945 with rank of tech sergeant. Received American Theatre Ribbons, EAME Theatre Ribbon with five Bronze Stars, Good Conduct Medal, Air Medal with one Bronze Cluster and Victory Medal.

Married Peggy O'Neal, they have one daughter, Susan Kheshtinejad. Currently resides in Duncanville, TX.

KEITH C. FARNER, was born in Cadillac, MI. Enlisted in AAF on Feb. 19, 1943.

Received his award for the services he performed the day his plane received 93 flak holes. He saved one of the crew members, George Bachleda. Flew 32 missions, all with the same crew. They have remained close for the past 50 years. They chose to remain a crew, rather than go up the ranks.

Discharged on March 7, 1945 with rank of staff sergeant. Received EAME Theater Ribbon with two Bronze Stars, Air Medal with three Oak Leaf Clusters, Distinguished Flying Cross and Overseas Service Bar.

Married Violet Oliver on June 27, 1954. They have four children and four grandchildren. Retired from auto work.

ROY J. FARNSWORTH, was born on March 14, 1921 in Clifton Springs, NY. Enlisted in USAAC on Aug. 12, 1942. Graduated at Columbia AFB, MS, in December 1943. Took B-24 transition at Maxwell Field, AL.

Left for England in June 1944, served as a pilot from August 1944 to February 1945 with the 445th Bomb Group, completing 35 combat missions over Germany. Memorable experience was returning to Kassel, Germany Sept. 22, 1944, day after their group (445th) suffered the largest loss in the 8th Air Force for one day with eight airplanes (all that was available). In March 1945 returned to Romulus, MI, Air Transport Command. Flew "war wearies" from England to Spokane, WA for Pacific Theatre modification.

Discharged from Fort Sheridan, IL on Oct. 5, 1945 with rank of first lieutenant. Received Distinguished Flying Cross, Air Medal with four Oak Leaf Clusters, European Theatre Ribbon with four Battle Stars.

Married Dorothy A. Rohr on Oct. 16, 1948 in Rochester, NY. Has one son, Roy Randall, one daughter, Martha Carolyn and three granddaughters. Became a Chevrolet dealer in Shortsville and Canandaigua, NY, retired in 1991.

FRANCIS A. FARRIS, was born on Dec. 6, 1922 in Paris, IL. Enlisted in USAAF on Jan. 5, 1943, air crew member, armor gunner, 714th Sqdn., 448th Bomb Group, 10 missions; PFF crew, 66th Sqdn., 44th Bomb Group, 20 missions.

Memorable experience as tail gunner on Capt. E.J. Hammer Jr.'s crew, aircraft B-24-H, *Lady from Bristol,* Dec. 24, 1943 to Feb. 14, 1945.

Discharged on Sept. 4, 1945 as staff sergeant. Received Distinguished Flying Cross, Air Medal with four Oak Leaf Clusters and four Battle Campaign Stars.

Married, with one son and two grandchildren. Retired and resides in Wolcottville, IN.

HARRIET S. FAU, was born on Dec. 9, 1913 in Brooklyn, NY. Joined WAAC in February 1943. Received basic training at Ft. Oglethorpe, GA. Then on to Nacogdoches, TX for further training. Was stationed at Buckingham Army Air Force, a Gunnery School, Ft. Myers, FL where she worked in the payroll department.

In August 1943 WAAC became WAC. On Feb. 12, 1944 boarded the Qu*een Mary* and went on to HQ, 2nd Air Div. at Norwich, England where she was assigned to Special Services Department. After V-J day was transferred to Istris, France, a veritable dust bowl. On Oct. 11, 1944 boarded the Queen Mary again and was on her way home. The most wonderful sight was seeing the Statue of Liberty once again.

Discharged on Oct. 21, 1945. As a civilian, worked as an insurance underwriter. Moved to Miami Beach in 1950. Retired at age 65, but continued to work part time for several years. Currently working as a teacher's aide.

JOHN HERBERT FAULDS, was born on June 30, 1919 in West Warwick, RI. Enlisted in USAAC in November 1942. Commissioned navigator at Selman Field, LA, B-24 training at El Paso, TX. Joined 446th Bomb Group, 707th Sqdn. in Bungay, England. Flew 35 combat missions.

Participated in Battle of Bulge and Battle of Europe. In Battle of the Bulge he flew supply mission at tree top

level to bring ammo, gas, etc. to glider troops near Aachen. Had engine shot out, put fire out, called May Day and escorted back to England by two PSIs which shot out flak tow. After missions got in Air Transport Command and ferried planes back to USA. Discharged in November 1945 with rank of first lieutenant. Received the Air Medal with five clusters.

Married in 1946 and has three daughters and six grandchildren. Retired from Chandler Evans Corp., as a design engineer of aircraft accessories. Was responsible for fuel pumps, helped in design of pumps in 727, SR71, 757, 767, 787, F-15, F-16, Air Bus, DC-9 and cruise missile C5A.

Volunteers for Cancer Society, drives patients, treasurer unit. Enjoys traveling and lots of social life.

CLYDE MONTANA FAULEY, was born on March 27, 1924 in Kalispell, MT. His father was a U.S. Park ranger in nearby Glacier National Park.

Clyde enlisted in the USAAC in November 1942 and was discharged in October 1945. Served in the 8th Air Force with the 466th Bomb Group as a nose-turret gunner/togglier during 1944. Flew all combat missions in B-24s piloted by Richard L. Bates and with same crew members on each mission!

His crew made a crash landing in a field in France on their seventh mission, nine days after D-day in 1944. The mission had been to the Renault Tank Factory where flak knocked out an engine on their bomber, Jamaica, which caused it to lag behind. A German fighter plane and flak knocked out another engine and damaged the plane which necessitated the forced landing. His entire crew made their way intact near enemy territory through the British invasion beachhead area and eventually to London via a liberty ship.

After several days at the Red Cross in London and after "buzz bombs" landed too close for comfort, the crew called their base at Attlebridge. "Missing in Action" reports had been prepared and crew belongings removed from their barracks. After several weeks in the Mulford Manor "Flac Home," Clyde and crew flew their remaining combat missions in a new B-24 named, *Times-A-Wastin.*

After receiving a BS degree in forestry from Montana State University, Clyde worked a couple of years on construction of air bases in the Arctic in Greenland (no forests)! He became a permanent U.S. Park Ranger in 1959. Served as district ranger and in fire and natural resources management positions in Yosemite, CA; Crater Lake, OR; Grand Canyon, AZ; and back to Glacier National Park, MT in 1971 where he had begun his National Park career.

From 1971 through 1975 he was also subject to emergency calls from the Western Fire Center in Boise, ID as a fire boss on an Inter-Agency fire overhead team and managed major forest and range fires in California, Nevada, Utah, Washington, Wyoming, Montana and Alaska. He retired from the National Park Service in 1983 after 30 years.

Married Rae Marie Price on Dec. 28, 1960. She also grew up in Glacier and retired from NPS in 1986 as secretary to the superintendent of Glacier National Park.

STEPHEN FECHO, was drafted into the infantry in October 1942 and sent to Camp Croft, SC and had six weeks basic training and seven weeks advanced training.

Applied to Air Force Cadets. Failed ARMA at Nashville, TN. Went to Keesler Field for basic training; Laredo, TX Gunnery School; Keesler Field Airplane Mechanics School; then to Salt Lake City for assignment. Colorado Springs for B-24 training with crew, became an engineer top turret gunner.

Went to Topeka, KS for plane; flew South America, Africa to England. Went to Cluntoe, Northern Ireland for gunnery training. Flew 30 missions with 466th Bomb Group, May 1944, including D-day. Finished in August 1944. Back to Keesler Field, airplane mechanics; Long Beach, CA, Douglas Plant airplane mechanics; Fairfield Suisun, CA, airplane mechanics on C-54s. V-J day on way to Okinawa, 11th Airborne into Japan. Enough points to get out. Hitch-hiked back to Fairfield Suisun, Mitchel Field, Long Island and released in October 1945.

FRANK W. FEDERICI,

was born on Dec. 15, 1923 in Illinois. Enlisted on Dec. 15, 1942, graduated navigator, Class 44-4, at San Marcos, TX. Assigned navigator on B-24 and to 445th Bomb Group, 700th Sqdn. at Tibenham, England in July 1944. Completed tour of 30 missions, nine as a lead navigator.

His most memorable experience was on a mission to Moosberg, Germany on Nov. 26, 1944. Pilot was killed by a 20mm, nose plexiglass blown out, co-pilot struggling with jammed rudder controls (pilot boots) until cleared by flight engineer. Bombardier and navigator knocked down when plexiglass was blown out. Sent bombardier to flight deck for first aid. He watched indices meet on bomb sight (bombardier had previously synchronized). He salvoed bombs and hit target. With maps blown away he was forced to navigate to Tibenham by recalling landmarks. With instrumentation now inoperative, co-pilot flew near another aircraft near traffic pattern to judge speed and altitude and smoothly landed the aircraft. All in a day's work!

After V-J day he was relieved from active duty in October 1945 and graduated from Northwestern University in 1948. Retired from General Electric Company after 28 years as an electrical engineer.

Married Ida Berns on April 11, 1944. They have three daughters and three grandchildren.

HAROLD W. FEICHTER,

was born on Dec. 6, 1918 in Ft. Wayne, IN. Joined USAAC on July 2, 1941. Military locations and stations included Lowry Field, Savannah, GA, 93rd Bomb Group in Hardwick, England.

Memorable experiences was service at Tobrok, Bengasie, Tunis, finished war in England. Discharged on Dec. 6, 1979 with rank of colonel. Received Presidential Unit Citation, 11 Battle Stars and Air Force Meritorious Medal.

He and his wife, Marilyn, have three children. He is a partner in a real estate company.

JOEY FELTEN,

was born in Middle Village, NY. Enlisted in USAAF on July 24, 1942. Was a tail gunner with the 453rd Bomb Group, 732nd Sqdn.

Served in 17 different locations and stations and completed 30 missions, July 1944. All missions were memorable, but most memorable was when they dropped ration coupons instead of bombs.

Discharged on Sept. 24, 1945 with rank of staff sergeant.

Received Distinguished Flying Cross and Air Medal with five Oak Leaf Clusters.

He and wife, Doris, have one daughter, Dorene. He retired from Western Electric Company after 38 years of service.

VICTOR J. FERRARI (VIC),

was born on Feb. 24, 1916. Enlisted as an aviation cadet on Jan. 12, 1942 at Maxwell AFB, AL. Received BS degree from Bloomsburg State and MS from University of Southern California.

Commissioned second lieutenant, Big Spring AAFBS, Class 43-1. Received navigation training at Hondo USAAF NS 43-7. Navigator crew member 392nd Bomb Group, 578th Sqdn., 8th Air Force.

Shot down over Holland on Nov. 13, 1943 when returning from a mission to Bremen. Was aided by Dutch-Paris Underground. Returned to London in May 1944. Reassigned to navigation schools at Monroe, LA and Ellington AFB, TX.

Remained on active duty 30-year tour. Retired in August 1971. Duty at Mather AFB, Saudi Arabia, assistant to the dean to USAF Academy, AFROTC, Notre Dame University, vice-commandant AFIT.

Received Air Medal, Presidential Unit Citation and Legion of Merit.

Second career with USAA, San Antonio, TX. Retired in June 1988. Assignments were chief of staff, president of USAA Federal Savings Bank. Now a consultant to USAA Educational Affairs.

GEORGE A. FERRELL,

was born on April 6, 1922 in Eufaula, AL. He joined the Army Air Force on Oct. 31, 1942 at Napier Field, AL after attending Auburn University for one year.

Trained at Keesler, Harlingen, and Gowen Field. Joined the 752nd Sqdn., 458th Bomb Group as engineer of Crew 8 at Tonopah. Began flying missions at Horsham St. Faith, England on March 8, 1944 (Berlin) on Wolves Lair. Finished last two of the 30-mission tour on D-day.

Returned to the USA and entered the Aviation Cadet Program as SAACC, TX and graduated a flight officer at Hondo as a B-29 flight engineer. The war's end brought a discharge at Roswell, NM on Oct. 16, 1945.

Graduated from Auburn University in May 1949, BSME and became an engineer with the Guidance and Control Lab of the Army missile and rocket program at Redstone Arsenal, Huntsville, AL in 1951. When Marshall Space Flight Center, NASA evolved in 1960, he was assigned to the Astrionics Lab.

Retired in 1977 after 31 years of service.

ROBERT L. FERRELL (BOB),

was born on Feb. 17, 1924 in Dothan, AL. Enlisted in USAAC at Napier Field on Dec. 15, 1942.

Military locations and stations included San Antonio, TX; Ellington Field, TX; Pueblo, CO; Lincoln, NE; Manchester, NH; Stone, England; and Norwich, England.

Shot down on Oct. 14, 1944 over Cologne. Spent rest of war in POW camp, Stalag Luft III, about which the movie, *The Great Escape*, was filmed. Leading the mission, 458th Bomb Group, 755th Sqdn., 96th Bomb Wing, 2nd Air Div., out of Horsham St. Faith RAF Base in Norwich, England.

While in POW Camp he was assigned duty of helping with dirt disposal on the tunnel-digging crews. Assignment was by Lt. Col. Albert Clark (later Lt. Gen.)

Discharged February 1946 with rank first lieutenant.

Received Good Conduct Medal, Purple Heart, ETO Ribbon with three Battle Stars, Victory Ribbon, Air Medal, plus 17 other awards and decorations for a total of 23.

After discharge went back to college to get BSME, three master's degrees and a Ph.D. Was a college professor and recalled for Korean War. Was a college graduate in Class of 1968. Retired in 1972.

Married Dorothy Carmichael (now deceased) on June 6, 1949. They had two sons, one a major, USAF pilot, and one a captain in U.S. Army Infantry. Also three grandchildren.

Now a corporate president and enjoys flying his two airplanes, one single engine and one twin engine.

ISAAC WARREN FESMIRE,

was born on Nov. 26, 1921 in Trezevant, TN. Enlisted in USAAC on July 29, 1942 as an aerial gunner. Served in England. Participated in ETO battle and flew 33 missions over Germany.

Discharged on Aug. 31, 1945 with rank of sergeant. Received Air Medal with six Oak Leaf Clusters.

He and his wife of 48 years, Helen, have four children. Fesmire is a retired school administrator.

JAMES J. FETTERLY,

enlisted in the USAF as a private on Nov. 23, 1942. Military locations and stations included basic training, St. Petersburg, FL; B-24 School, Keesler Field, MS; B-24 School, Willow Run Plant; Gunnery, Harlingen, TX; crew training, Casper, WY; crew training with 469th, Wendover, UT.

Received new B-24 from Willow Run in which they flew the southern route through Dakar, Africa to Halesworth, England. Completed 32 missions on *Pin Up Girl*, which was later shot down over Germany.

Sailed home on the *Queen Mary* on Oct. 2, 1944. Attended Instructor School at Laredo, TX and instructed at Tyndall Field until his discharge at Montgomery, AL.

Memorable experiences were Air Offensive of Europe, invasion of France and Southern France, Normandy invasion and Munich.

Discharged on Oct. 13, 1945 at Montgomery, AL with rank of tech sergeant.

Received European Medal with five Oak Leaf Clusters and the Distinguished Flying Cross.

Married and has five children. Currently retired.

LAWRENCE R. FICK,

was born on March 17, 1923 in Medford, OR. Enlisted in USAAF in October 1942, active duty in March 1943.

Graduated from Navigation School, San Marcos in April 1944. Replacement crew training at Peterson Field, CO. Flew B-23J to England via northern route. Assigned to 458th Bomb Group, Horsham St. Faith in July 1944. Flew 29 missions, 20 as lead crew navigator. Squadron navigator with 752nd Sqdn.

Returned to States after V-E day via Azores. Discharged in November 1945 at Portland, OR. Received Air Medal with three Oak Leaf Clusters, Distinguished Flying Cross and ETO Ribbon with four Battle Stars.

Married Marjorie Donaldson in 1947. They have one son, one daughter, and four grandchildren.

Completed forestry degree at Oregon State College and went to work for Oregon State Forestry Department. Retired after 40 years.

Co-authored book on history of rehabilitation of the Tillamook Burn. Continuing to work on historic files and photo record of forestry in Northwest Oregon.

BENJAMIN P. FIELDS, was born on Aug. 26, 1922 in Elnora, IN. Moved near Linton, IN after two years and lived there until drafted into the Army.

Enlisted in USAAC and entered active service on Oct. 21, 1942 after spending 18 months in the Civilian Conservation Corps. Sent to Fort Benjamin Harrison in Indianapolis, IN, Nov. 4, 1942. Placed in AAC and sent to Atlantic City, NJ for basic training, Nov. 7, 1942; Air Gunners School, Fort Myers, FL in January 1943; gun turret training Lowry Field, Denver, CO; armament training and air crew assignment at Boise, ID; and second and third phase training at Pocatello, ID.

Shipped overseas on *Aquatania,* landed in Scotland, from there to Hardwick, England and assigned to 328th Sqdn. of 93rd Bomb Group for more combat training.

Flew first mission with another crew as tail gunner, was wounded in left arm and spent 30 days in hospital. Sent back to squadron and flew the rest of his missions with crew. Flew missions to France, Germany, and the Ruhr Valley in Germany. Was shot down on sixth mission, Feb. 4, 1944, and taken prisoner. Spent 14 months and two weeks in three different POW camps until freed by Gen. Bernard Montgomery's 8th Army.

Travelled to Brussels, Luxemborg, Camp Lucky Strike, LeHarve where boarded boat for States. Landed in New York City; sent to New Jersey; Camp Atterbury, IN; Miami, FL for reassignment; then Chanute Field and George Field in Southern Illinois until discharged at Scott Field, IL on Nov. 27, 1945 with rank of staff sergeant. Received Air Medal, Purple Heart, Presidential Unit Citation and various other medals.

Has wife, three children, and seven grandchildren. Retired and resides in St. Anne, IL.

C.W. FINK SR. (CHUCK), was born on Nov. 8, 1922 in Deloit, IA. Enlisted August 1942 in AAC as aviation cadet, Class 43-K. After appendectomy was washed back to Class 44-B. Basic training at Lemoure AAB, CA; SAAAB (pre-flight training); Primary Flight School, Eagle Field, Dos Palos, CA; advanced training at Douglas, AZ; B-24 training, to England on QE. Flew 35 combat missions from Old Buckingham.

Most memorable experience was bringing B-24, Arrowhead, home with number three turbo charger shot out by flak; flew B-52 record setting non-stop jet flight around the world Jan. 16-18, 1957.

Discharged on July 31, 1968 with rank of lieutenant colonel. Received five Air Medals and Distinguished Flying Cross.

Married since 1947 and has three girls and one boy, all married. Still flying corporate aircraft, C-320, BE-35 and C-182s.

ELMER M. FISCHER, was born on May 3, 1925, Philadelphia, PA; graduated from high school and entered the Army in July 1943.

Stationed at Fort Meade, MD and Fort Eustis, VA. Transferred to AAF in November 1943, Miami Beach, FL; then Keesler Field, MS; Gulfport, MS; Florence AAB, SC as armorer; Tyndall Field, FL; Gunnery School; Lincoln AAB; Boise Field, ID, trained with Bernie Fishman's crew as tail gunner through October 1944.

Went to Topeka, KS for staging; Camp Miles Standish, POE, for overseas in December 1944. To 445th Bomb Group, Tibenham, England. After few days at Stone, England, started flying missions on third birthday of 8th Air Force, Jan. 28, 1945.

Flew 24 missions before V-E day. In May transferred to another group and flew home in June 1945 through Wales, Iceland, Labrador, and Bradley Field, CT to Fort Dix, NJ. After furlough went to Sioux Falls, SD then Great Bend, KS, August to October 1945.

Most exciting missions were first mission to Dortmund when bomb hung up in bomb bay and armorer had to release same; 13th mission, March 18, 1945, biggest day raid of war to Berlin; and 16th mission, Wesel, when supplied paratroops across Rhine at 200 ft. having been briefed to watch out for church steeples; April 1, 1945 when hit by own squadron with frag bombs, wounding two waist gunners and almost critically damaging plane.

Discharged from Sioux City, IA on Oct. 26, 1945 with rank of staff sergeant. Received Air Medal with three Oak Leaf Clusters, European Theater Ribbon and four Battle Stars.

Employed by R.M. Hollingshead, Camden, NJ 1945-46; entered Temple University 1946-49, graduated with BS in pharmacy June 1949. Entered USMCR, Willow Grove NAS, 1947-1949.

Employed by Smith, Kline and French Pharmaceutical Company 37 and a half years, June 1949-January 1986. Retired on Jan. 6, 1986.

Married to Jeanne since 1947, they have two daughters, Donna and Karen, and one grandchild, Olivia. Enjoys softball, Music Theater, tennis, aerobics, working around the house and church, building, repairing and working on grounds.

GILBERT W. FISHER, was born on June 23, 1917 in St. Joseph, MO. Enlisted in USAAC on Dec. 12, 1941 as aviation cadet, AAF Bakersfield and Santa Ana, CA.

Primary and basic training, Ontario, CA; advanced training, Roswell, NM. Flew 30 missions over Europe, B-24, 8th Air Force, 445th Bomb Group, 703rd Sqdn.

Most memorable experiences were first daylight raid over Berlin; 703rd Sqdn. operations officer with Jimmy Stewart; D-day missions; most damage sustained was 272 holes in aircraft with four injured crewmen, no aileron controls but landed safely.

Discharged on July 12, 1945 with rank of captain. Received Distinguished Flying Cross and Air Medal with five Oak Leaf Clusters.

He and wife, Kathleen, have one son, three daughters and three grandchildren. Retired as pilot from TWA after 32 plus years.

VIRGIL L. FISHER, was born on May 31, 1923 in Williams, IA. Joined USAAC on Feb. 25, 1943 in Des Moines, IA.

Basic training at Jefferson Barracks, MO; then to 310th College Training Detachment, Michigan State College, as aviation student. Then to San Antonio Classification Center and classified navigator. Pre-flight training at Ellington Field; flight training at San Marcos Air Base. Graduated second lieutenant in April 1944. Assigned to crew at Lincoln Air Base and B-24 training at Davis-Monthan Field, Tucson, AZ.

Sent as replacement crew to 8th Air Force in July 1944. Assigned to 458th Bomb Group. Flew wing crew and pilot navigator in lead crew. Completed 30 missions in April 1945. Transferred to 96th Combat Wing, also at Horsham Air Base. After V-E day returned to States, reported to Santa Ana Air Base. While there Pacific War ended.

Discharged on Nov. 18, 1945 with rank of first lieutenant. Received Air Medal with Oak Leaf Clusters and Distinguished Flying Cross.

Returned to Des Moines, IA where he married Catherine Brooke. They have three children and four grandchildren. Retired and does community volunteer work. Resides in Burnsville, MN.

JAMES EVERETT FITZGERALD, was born on Oct. 10, 1919 in Sheffield, AL. Enlisted in USAAC in November 1942. Pilot, 2nd Air Div., 8th Air Force, 389th Bomb Group.

Served in Hethel, England. Flew 35 missions over Germany. Most memorable experiences were landing on one wheel, coming home with just two engines, landing with top of tree in the bomb bay.

Airplane crew (all still living): pilot, James E. Fitzgerald; co-pilot, Dale R. Wees; navigator and bombardier, Steven J. Halcisak; tail turret gunner and armed bombs, Robert D. Booth; waist gunner, Laverne LaDoucuer (hospital after third mission), radio operator, Emanuel F. States; nose turret gunner, Charles E. Stumpf; waist gunner and ball turret, Wilfred E. Grenier; engineer top and waist turret gunner, James M. Flecher. Name of the plane was *Sleepy Time Gal.* Two other members of crew: Herman Greenspan, bombardier, was killed in Germany on another airplane. Emil C. Isert, engineer, flew about half the missions. Think he died about 10 years ago in Stockton, CA.

Discharged in August 1945 with rank of first lieutenant. Received Air Medal with three Oak Leaf Clusters.

Had two girls with first wife, Vivian, before her death. Also has three grandchildren. Retired from Duke Power Company and living with second wife, Dot, in Gastonia, NC.

LEWIS C. FLAGSTAD, was born on Feb. 9, 1924 in Superior, WI. Enlisted in December 1942 and entered service on Jan. 8, 1943 as a private. Basic training at St. Petersburg, FL; attended Armorerment School at Lowry Field, Denver; Gunnery School at Tyndall Field, FL. Graduated as an armorer gunner with rank of staff sergeant. Sent to Clovis, NM for crew assignment and then to Alamogordo, NM for training.

After completion of training sent via Goose Bay over North Atlantic to join replacement to 8th Air Force in England. Assignment was to 445th Bomb Group at Tibenham, England.

Most memorable experience was flying first mission to Munster, Germany with other crew, gun jam over Channel and engine knocked out by flak over Munster.

Returned to USA on May 19, 1945 and after furlough reported to Sioux Falls, then to B-29 Base, Pyote, TX.

Discharged on Oct. 17, 1945 with rank of staff sergeant. Received Good Conduct Medal, Air Medal and seven Campaign and Battle Stars.

Married Audrey Drinkwine on Jan. 31, 1953. They have two sons and six grandchildren. Retired railway clerk and union official.

JAMES M. FLEEHR, was born on June 30, 1924 in Duquesne, PA. Graduated from Duquesne High School in 1942 and enlisted in USAAF on July 31, 1943.

Served with 2nd Air Div., 389th Bomb Group, 565th Sqdn. Military locations and stations included basic training at Miami Beach, FL; Mountain Home, ID; Sioux Falls, SD; Hethel Army Air Force Base, Norwich, England; Las Vegas Army Air Force Base, Las Vegas, NV.

Flew 34 missions over Central Europe and Ardennes. Most memorable experience was crash of B-24 in La Grande, OR on a training mission. He was pinned in the wreckage. Co-pilot pulled him right out of his flight boots.

Discharged on Oct. 21, 1945 with rank of tech sergeant. Received Air Medal with four Oak Leaf Clusters, four European Campaign Stars, Bronze Service Stars, Good Conduct Medal and Presidential Unit Citation.

Married Irene Bodnar on May 7, 1947. They have two children and two grandchildren. Worked at U.S. Steel in chemical lab for seven years, then at U.S. Department of Energy, Bettis Atomic Power Lab as technician and supervisor for 32 years. Retired from Bettis in 1986. Really enjoying retirement.

Their B-24 crew, piloted by 1st Lt. Jim Fitzgerald, has a reunion every two years. They have all kept in touch since 1945. All crew members are still living.

ROBERT GORDON FLETCHER - In 1630, Robert Fletcher left Mattersey, England to begin the American Fletcher lineage in Concord, MA...314 years and 10 generations later, his grandson, a direct descendant, visited Mattersey again.

Robert Gordon Fletcher was born on March 27, 1923 in Los Angeles, CA. Joined the U.S. Army in 1942 as a private. Promoted through ranks to acting corporal, then joined Aviation Cadets. Graduated second lieutenant Class 44-B. Pilot training, George Field, IL. Served as B-24 pilot, Ft. Myers and Laredo Aerial Gunnery Schools.

After volunteering for 8th Air Force duty, trained with crew at Casper, WY. Served with 458th Bomb Group as combat pilot over Germany in 1944 with 300 plus combat hours.

At end of hostilities, retired as captain on Inactive Reserve. Received Distinguished Flying Cross, three Air Medals, four European Battle Stars, and several additional ribbons.

Returned to States, served as operations officer and squadron commander.

Graduated aeronautical engineer and served NASA in SIVB segment of C-1 moon vehicle.

WYNDHAM BURTON FLETCHER JR. (BUBBER),

was born on Feb. 16, 1924 in Indianola, MS. While attending University of Mississippi he tried to enlist in February 1942 but did not meet height or weight minimums. Finally accepted in October 1942 after consuming many bananas and much water!

Active duty in February 1943, basic at Miami Beach; April 1943, University of Alabama CTD preparation for air cadets. September 1943, air cadet classification, San Antonio, TX. Washed out for scarred lungs. To Buckley Field, CO for Armament School. From January-June 1944 at Buckingham Field, FL towing aerial targets for Gunnery School. July 1944-May 1945, 93rd Bomb Group, 328th Sqdn., 8th Air Force in England as armorer. Promoted to PFC by Act of Congress. Discharged in November 1945, Biggs Field, TX.

Memorable experiences: being shoulder to shoulder with Gen. Ted Timberlake loading parachute supply bundles in ball turret position for drop in Holland during operation Market Garden; the 45th reunion of 2nd Air Div. in Norwich, 1991, with very nostalgic visits to the Memorial Library and the 93rd Base at Hardwick; Spring 1993, Midwest 2nd Air Div. mini-reunion visit with two great guys, Myron Griffin, armorer 328th Sqdn. and Bob McKeever, crew chief of 409th Sqdn., 93rd Bomb Group.

Married Sarah Cliett in 1962. They have three daughters and one grandson. Retired in January 1992 from 46 years cotton farming in Indianola, MS.

THOMAS W. FLOYD,

was born on May 10, 1922 near Bismarck, IL. Joined the USAAC on July 10, 1942 as aviation cadet. After primary training at Parks Air College and basic training at Garden City, KS, Class 43-J, he graduated from Las Vegas Gunnery School. He was assigned to 859th Sqdn., 492nd Bomb Group, which trained at Alamagordo, NM and arrived at North Pickenham, England on April 27, 1944.

After 29 missions his squadron was transferred to 788th Sqdn., 467th Bomb Group where he completed 31st mission on Aug. 16, 1944 with the crew of Lt. Donald Prytulak. The most memorable experience was mission 15 on June 20, 1944 to Politz, Germany where the 492nd Bomb Group lost 14 planes to ME-210 and 410s.

Before being discharged he was transferred to the 3210th Engineer FF Co. at Santa Rosa, CA to fight fires often started by Japanese balloons all along the West Coast.

Discharged on Sept. 29, 1945 at Camp Beale, CA with rank of staff sergeant.

Received EAME Campaign Medal, Good Conduct Medal, Distinguished Flying Cross and Air Medal with three Oak Leaf Clusters.

After service he entered Southern Illinois University

and completed his MS degree in education. Later earned doctorate at University of Illinois.

Married in 1948 and has four children. Retired from Eastern Illinois University in 1984 after 34 years of teaching.

FRANCIS L. FLUHARTY,

was born in Mannington, WV. Enlisted in USAAF on Dec. 28, 1945. Was radio operator and photo lab technician. Military locations and stations included: Camp Crowder, MO; Drew Field, Tampa, FL; Jacksonville AAB; Dow Field, Bangor, ME; overseas to Attleboro, England. Back home to Fort Dix, NJ on May 23, 1945, 563rd AAFBU, Homestead, FL. Was assigned to Andrews AAFB in Washington for three months doing photo work for the office of War Info.

Participated in battles over Normandy, Northern France, Rhineland Air Offensive, Europe, Central Europe, and Ardennes campaigns. Most memorable experience was assignment to Andrews AAFB in Washington for three months just before discharge, doing photo work for the office of war information.

Discharged on Oct. 27, 1945 with rank of sergeant. Received EAME Campaign Medal with one Silver Star and one Battle Star.

Married Edith J. Kendall, they have one daughter Pamela J. Coulbourne and one son Francis Dean Fluharty. Retired from Consolidated Gas Transmission on Jan. 1, 1985. Still does some photo work. Resides in Vienna, WV.

SCOTT FOGG,

was born on July 7, 1913 in Nowata, OK. Grew up on a farm east of Nowata on a river bottom.

He found the country had plenty to offer, such as hunting, fishing, working, school and fresh air. The country schools went to eighth grade. Completed high school in town.

Joined the USAAF in Coffeyville, KS on Sept. 28, 1942. Since the new field was not ready, he was sent to Ft. Worth, TX for some of his basic training. Came back to Coffeyville to complete training, then sent to Keesler Field, MS for a course in aircraft mechanics; then to an Aerial Gunnery School in Laredo, TX. After Gunnery School he went to Mountain Home, ID for his first phase training. Whole new crew was formed there of which he was the engineer gunner.

March Field, CA was the next destination and the beginning of second phase training. His crew managed to get in one hour of flying time after they had been there one week. Weather was terrible for flying. He was pulled from crew and sent to Hamilton Field, CA to join a crew that was destined for overseas duty. Completed training the hard way, by doing 31 high altitude combat missions over France and Germany with crew 62 of the 458th Bomb Group.

Memorable experiences: all 31 bombing missions, losing an engineer on take-off, coming back from France on two engines, right foot stopping a piece of flak.

Discharged on Oct. 5, 1945 in Amarillo, TX with rank of staff sergeant. Received EAME Service Medal with three Bronze Stars, Air Medal with three Oak Leaf Clusters and Distinguished Flying Cross.

Married Carolyn Dixon on Oct. 20, 1936 and is still with her. No children came along. Retired after 25 years as a natural gas compressor plant operator from Enron Corporation of Houston, TX in 1972. Now, taking life easy.

CARSIE E. FOLEY,

was born on Jan. 30, 1924 in Jamestown, KY. Entered service on March 17, 1943 and served with 8th Air Force, 458th Bomb Group.

Military locations included Horsham St. Faith. Completed 30 combat missions, all in B-24.

Discharged on Nov. 22, 1945 with rank of staff sergeant. Received Distinguished Flying Cross, Air Medal with four Oak Leaf Clusters, EAME Campaign Medal, WWII Victory Medal and American Campaign Medal.

He and wife Blanche have two sons, Michael and Mark, and six grandchildren. Retired from IBM and resides in Lexington, KY.

ALEC FONTANA,

was born on March 25, 1922 in Hibbing, MN. Graduated from Hibbing High School in 1940 and migrated to Antioch, CA in 1941.

Inducted into military service, joining the USAAC on Jan. 16, 1943. Attained rank of staff sergeant as an aerial gunner. After training as a tail gunner was assigned to Lt. Keith Shirk's crew for B-24 crew training at Tonapah, NV. Assigned with crew to 389th Bomb Group, Hethel Air Base, England.

Completed tour of 34 missions from October 1944 through March 1945, having missed one mission. Hospitalized with a sprained ankle from playing basketball.

Returned to the U.S. in April 1945 and discharged at Camp Haan, CA on Sept. 29, 1945.

Married Elizabeth Machado, Oakley, CA on May 27, 1951 and resides in Antioch, CA.

BENJAMIN F. FOOTE (BEN),

was born on Aug. 21, 1921 in Wilkinsburg, PA. Married Marie Craig on Nov. 20, 1943. They reside in Redondo Beach, CA.

Graduated from the University of Pittsburgh in April 1942. Enlisted in Marines. Transferred to USAAC in December 1942, earmarked for aviation cadets. Aviation student at Butler University, Navigation Class 44-2, San Marcos, TX.

Sent to Wendling with Bill Kohl replacement crew in 192nd Bomb Group. Completed 30 missions May-September 1944. Earned Distinguished Flying Cross plus five Air Medals. Reassigned to 8th Air Force Headquarters, High Wycombe, as navigator on Combined Operational Planning Committee under Maj. Gen. Orvil Anderson. Returned to Orlando in June 1945 with USSTAF Evaluation Board to write and edit official publication on ETO air operations.

Separated as captain in January 1946. Settled in Arizona. Stayed in active Reserve and served as ROA national councilman and department president. As civilian, was featured sports writer for *Phoenix Gazette*, then press secretary to Arizona Gov. Sam Goddard.

Has been in California past 21 years as publicist and executive vice-president of J.C. Agajanian Enterprises, a motor racing entity.

Retired from USAF as reserve lieutenant colonel.

RALPH E. FORD,

was born on July 6, 1922 in Detroit, MI. Enlisted in USAAF in November 1942 as aviation cadet.

Began training in February 1943 and graduated from pilot training with Class 44-B, Turner Field, Albany, GA in February 1944. Assigned to Westover Field, MA for training as B-24 co-pilot. Flew B-24 with crew to England in June 1944. Assigned to 453rd Bomb Group, 732nd Sqdn.

First mission was on July 19, 1944; last mission on Feb. 6, 1945. Flew 15 missions as lead crew. Returned to U.S. and trained in various aircraft with the ATC.

Discharge in November 1945 at San Bernadino, CA with rank of first lieutenant. Received Air Medal with four Oak Leaf Clusters and European Campaign Ribbon.

Graduated as a mechanical engineer in 1950 and worked in that field for 35 years. Now retired. Married with six children and 10 grandchildren. Resides in Harper Woods, MI.

JAMES G. FORREST, was born on Jan. 3, 1923 in Nashville, TN. Enlisted in USAAC on March 7, 1941.

Military locations and stations: enlistment at Camp J.T. Robinson, AR; Bungay, Flixton, England. Participated in ETO Air Offensive and invasion of Europe. Completed 30 combat missions as tail gunner in B-24, one ME-109 confirmed, first daylight bombardment of Berlin.

Discharged at Tyndall Field, FL on May 18, 1945 with rank of staff sergeant. Received Distinguished Flying Cross and Air Medal with four Oak Leaf Clusters.

Has five children and is a retired electronic technician.

LARRY P. FORREST, was born on May 27, 1922 in Neligh, NE. Grew up in Bucklin, MO. Inducted into service in November 1942 at Fort Leavensworth.

Received basic training at St. Petersburg; gunnery training at Tyndall Field; A&E School, Sheppard Field. Assigned to B-24 crew, Boise, ID; phase training at Tonapah with 458th Bomb Group, 755th Sqdn.

Arrived at UK in late January 1944, Horsham St. Faith. Finished 30 mission tour June 5, 1944. Returned to U.S. in September 1944; R&R at Miami Beach then sent to Keesler Field, then to Laredo, TX for gunnery training.

Japan surrendered and war in Europe ended. Sent to Harlingen, TX. Discharged on Oct. 15, 1945.

Married on Sept. 18, 1948 and has four sons. Worked as trooper for Missouri Highway Patrol, for 33 years. Retired in 1982.

JOHN D. FOSTER, was born on May 30, 1923 in Los Angeles, CA. Entered the service at Fort McArthur, CA in 1942.

Sojourns as a radio operator include the following: St. Petersburg, FL; Clearwater, FL; Stevens Hotel, Chicago, IL; Sioux Falls, SC; Salt Lake City Air Base, UT; Wendover Gunnery School, UT; Gowen Field, ID (where the crew was formed); and finally, back to Wendover Air Base where the crew was assigned to the 489th Bomb Group and named their plane *Cover Girl*.

He flew 14 missions in the 489th while stationed at Halesworth, England; then 16 missions in the 93rd at Hardwick, England, flying on *Latrine Rumor*. He feels honored to have flown with the crew of *Cover Girl* and still marvels at their good fortune on the missions to Bretigny and Villacoublay, France. He is proud to have flown with two Congressional Medal of Honor recipients, Gen. Leon Johnson and Col. Leon Vance.

Mr. Foster graduated from Pepperdine University and the University of Southern California. He is married, has two children, and retired as a school administrator in 1981. He is presently raising avocados in Bonsall, CA.

RICHARD O. FOSTER, was born on April 17, 1919 in Grand Ledge, MI. Enlisted in USAAC on July 16, 1941.

Assigned to Scott Field, Belleville, IL. Applied for staff sergeant pilot training and graduated as a flight officer in Class 43-B. Assigned to 6th Tow Target Sqdn., Biggs Field, El Paso, TX. Transferred to Clovis, NM for make-up of the 466th Bomb Group. Flew the southern route to England to Attlebridge Base.

Completed 30 missions, then transferred to 25th

Bomb Group at Watton, flying British Mosquitoes, 15 missions.

Received four Air Medals, Distinguished Flying Cross and other medals. Returned to the U.S. in August 1945. Remained in Reserve Forces, assigned to Mobile Communications Sqdn. at Scott AFB as air traffic control officer, became commander, retired as lieutenant colonel on June 30, 1970.

Worked at the Defense Mapping Agency Aerospace Center and retired from there in September 1976.

Married and they have three children, five grandchildren and one great-grandchild.

ROBERT M. FOUST, was born on Sept. 23, 1924 in Ft. Worth, TX. Enlisted in the USAAF on Nov. 17, 1942 as a radio operator mechanic.

Sent to Mineral Wells, TX for two weeks for clothing, shots, etc., then returned to Ft. Worth AAB to fly and maintain radios on B-24s, transitional pilot training with rank private.

Signed up for Gunnery School and sent to Laredo, TX on March 1, 1943. Graduated as sergeant on a Friday and demoted to private first class on Monday and ordered to Lowry Field, Denver, CO for Armament School. Completed school on Sept. 21, 1943 as buck sergeant and ordered to Boise, ID for overseas training where he joined a crew for B-24 training. Sent to Topeka, KS to pick up B-24.

Left the States on Feb. 28, 1944 by the southern route to ETO. Assigned to 44th Bomb Group, 506th Sqdn. Flew 33 missions including D-day, June 6, 1944. Destroyed an FW-190 as a waist gunner. Received Air Medal with five Oak Leaf Clusters and Distinguished Flying Cross.

Returned to States on June 9, 1944. After leave went to Miami Beach for three months, then sent to Laredo for gunnery instructor and ended up at Harlingen, TX.

Discharged from Wichita Falls, TX on Sept. 10, 1945. After discharge returned to his Ft. Worth, TX home. Married and had two children and four grandchildren. Now retired from a TV Broadcasting Station in Ft. Worth, TX.

ROGER A. FOX, was born on March 1, 1917 in Wheatland, IA. Inducted into service on Jan. 6, 1942 at Fort Des Moines, IA.

Military locations and stations included Sheppard Field, TX; McClellan Field, CA; Airdrome, Alameda, CA; Camp Stockton, CA; Camp at San Bruno, CA; Aberdeen Proving Ground, MD; Halobird Motor Depot, Baltimore, MD; Santa Ana, CA; Las Vegas Air Base; Salt Lake; Biggs Field, El Paso, TX; Wendover Field, UT; Camp Shanks, NY; Glasgow, Scotland; Rackheath, England; Camp Joyce Kilmer; Camp Grant, IL and Sioux Falls, SD.

Participated in Air Offensive Europe, Normandy, Ardennes, Northern France, Rhineland and Central Europe. Memorable experiences: Going overseas on *Frederick Lyke's*, drive shaft broke and they were sitting ducks for a day until repaired; the three V-2 rockets that were shot over the base at supper time; the first buzz bombs over their base; German planes infiltrated their bombers on way home and bombed their runway; train trip from Camp Joyce Kilmer, they opened train windows and couldn't close them as they went through three tunnels and they looked like they were made up for a minstrel show.

Discharged on Dec. 28, 1945 with rank of first lieutenant.

He and wife Dorothy have one son Mark; one daughter Lynn; and grandchildren: Ian, Carrie and Laura. He is retired and resides in Lowden, IA.

WAYNE O. FOX, was born in 1921 in Cambridge, NE and raised in Colorado. Enlisted as an aviation cadet in December 1941 following first quarter exams at the University of Colorado.

Received wings and commission with Class 43-D at Roswell, NM. Trained as B-24 pilot at Clovis, NM. Assigned to the 446th Bomb Group at Lowry in Denver. Flew to England in the fall of 1943. After several 2nd Div. missions, his crew was transferred to the 482nd Pathfinder Group

and led 8th Air Force missions in both B-24s and B-17s in early 1944. In the fall of 1944 he was transferred to the 364th Mustang Fighter Group where he flew a few missions before being sent to the 5th Emergency Rescue Sqdn. where he flew escort and search missions until V-E day.

After discharge he returned to Colorado University. Married Denamae Dawson in 1947; graduated from the university with a BA in 1949 and an MA in 1950. Taught speech at the University of Hawaii until recalled to Air Force duty with the 11th Air Rescue Sqdn.

Returned with his wife, son and daughter to Colorado with teaching and Air Force Reserve assignments. Retired as lieutenant colonel from the Air Force in 1981 and from teaching a year later. Resides in Aurora, CO.

RICHARD H. FRANK (DICK), was born on Oct. 23, 1922 in Minneapolis, MN. Enlisted in USAAC on Dec. 15, 1942. Graduated second lieutenant pilot on May 24, 1944. Completed B-24 pilot training at Tarrant Field, Carswell AFB, NM.

Flew new B-24J to Valley, Wales. Assigned 703rd Bomb Sqdn., 445th Bomb Group. Flew five combat missions. Returned to USA in May 1945. Assigned to B-29 training, Roswell AAF. Discharged in 1946. Until May 1, 1951 he was a Reserve pilot, Wold-Chamberlin Field, Minneapolis, MN. Recalled to active duty, Fairchild AFB, WA. Assigned to Strategic Air Command.

Spent balance of active duty flying, primarily B-36 and B-52 aircraft, and operations staff officer. Completed 107 combat missions in B-52 aircraft during the Vietnam war. Retired as a lieutenant colonel on July 31, 1970. Awarded numerous medals including the Air Medal with four Oak Leaf Clusters.

Spent next 17 years in the life insurance and securities business, in sales and as regional manager. Retired in 1987 and now enjoys his wife, two sons and four grandchildren. Travels frequently, plays racquetball, flies light airplanes and is active in the Order of Dadelions. Resides in Gig Harbor, WA.

DONALD A. FRASER, was born on Sept. 12, 1922 in Freeland, MI. After school he worked for Michigan Bell Telephone Company until enlistment in USAAC in September 1942. Graduated as bombardier, second lieutenant, Class 43-16 at Midland, TX in November 1943.

Overseas in April 1944 to 458th Bomb Group at Horsham St. Faith, Norwich, England. Crew #80, a great bunch of fellows. Flew 30 missions, 25 as lead crew, from D-day to February 1945. Stayed as a squadron bombardier until end of war in ETO and flew home on last B-24 out of Horsham in June 1945.

Returned to Michigan Bell and retired after 40 years as an engineering supervisor.

Married in October 1942 to Carolyn Gregory. They have one son, one daughter and three grandchildren.

DONALD W. FRASER, was born on May 6, 1916 in Three Forks, MT. Moved to the Yellowstone National Park in 1919 and attended school there. Attended University of Montana, then entered service on March 3, 1942 at Fort Lewis, WA.

Served in U.S. Army Medical Corps one year as surgery technician at Fort McAndrew, Newfoundland. Entered USAAF, Class 44-4, Nashville, TN. Commissioned second lieutenant at Big Spring, TX. First assigned to 492nd (H) Bomb Group and flew five missions. Deactivated group, reassigned to 467th (H) Bomb Group, completed 30 lead missions and 28 gasoline sorties.

Retired on May 6, 1976 from USAFR with the rank first lieutenant. Received Distinguished Flying Cross with one Oak Leaf Cluster, Air Medal with four Oak Leaf Clusters, ETO Ribbon with four Battle Stars, American Theater Ribbon, Presidential Unit Citation, Victory Medal, Air Reserve Medal and Hour Glass (three Good Conduct Medals as EM) and Ready Reserve Medal.

Married Olga J. Garvey in 1942, they have one daughter, two grandsons, one granddaughter and one great-grandson. He is a retired assistant police chief and resides in Livingston, MT.

BURT FRAUMAN, was born on Sept. 4, 1922 in Chicago, IL. Joined the USAAC in November 1942. Commissioned as navigator at Selman Field, LA, then on to B-24 training with a great crew at Lincoln, NE.

In July 1944 joined 754th Sqdn., 458th Bomb Group, at Horsham St. Faith, England. On one mission, exceptionally heavy flak tore well over 200 holes in their plane, turning it into a flying sieve. Fortunately there were no major injuries. The aircraft was retired. When General Patton's tanks ran out of gas near Metz, they flew loads of gallon cans of gasoline to his troops. Highest award received was the Distinguished Flying Cross.

Often fighters and bombers could not return to base and made forced landings on the Continent. Two-man crews "repaired" these planes on site, but some needed major restorations. After completing their tour they spent a couple of months flying Liberators from fields in France, Belgium and Holland to a Sub Depot in England.

Volunteered to re-train for B-29 Pacific duty at Ellington Field, TX. While there the war ended and was discharged in November 1945.

Completed a degree in business administration from Northwestern University. Married Reva Kahn in 1952, whom he met when he moved to San Francisco in 1950. He is proud of his son and daughter. Both are mechanical engineers.

Established a business as a manufacturer's representative in electronics. Resides in Palo Alto, CA.

ZWINGLIO W. FRAUSTO, was born in El Paso, TX. Before the war started he was already a cavalry man with 12th Regt. in Fort Bliss.

Soon he was transferred to an air group in San Antonio. Next came Bombardier School where he received his wings and commission in January 1944. A few months later he was already flying out of Old Buckingham with the 453rd Group.

He was awarded the Air Medal with three Oak Leaf Clusters, European Campaign Medal with three Bronze Stars, American Defense Medal and, of course, the Victory Medal. In the process he also received his First Lieutenant Bars.

He remembers one special incident, a crash landing in Belgium (Germans were gone). Flak had knocked out one of the engines and landing gear was inoperative. Thanks to God and to their fine pilot and co-pilot, Cleary and McCardle, they all got out without a scratch.

He and his wife, Elena, have six children: Helene and her husband Ron Seitz; Emi Saylor; Neomi; Elizabeth and her husband Terry Sweet; Ernie and his wife Kirsti Frausto; John and his wife Nancy Frausto. They have eight grandchildren: David, Dana, Elizabeth, Erica, Nicholas, Abigail, Daniel and Jonathan.

WILLIAM J. FRAWLEY (BILL), entered the USAAC in 1942. Trained as navigator and assigned to A.E. Cearnal crew. Took air crew training at Blythe, CA. Assigned to 389th Bomb Group (H) on June 2, 1944.

Their seventh mission was Berlin, Germany. They threw everything they had at Frawley's group. They encoun-

---

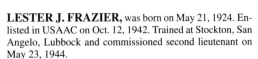

tered ME-210s, ME-109s, FW-190s and JU-88s. Frawley's group got three of the fighters.

Their ninth mission was the marshalling yards at Saarbrucken, Germany. They had to bomb PFF.

Folded wings in 1992 with rank of first lieutenant. Received Air Medal, EAME with five stars, American Campaign and WWII Victory Medal.

LESTER J. FRAZIER, was born on May 21, 1924. Enlisted in USAAC on Oct. 12, 1942. Trained at Stockton, San Angelo, Lubbock and commissioned second lieutenant on May 23, 1944.

Assigned first pilot B-24, Liberal, KS. Crew was Edward Linder, CP; Robert Robinson, N; Arthur "Hap" Hazard, B; Laurence R. McGrath, EG; Hervy Latour, ROG; Donald Penders, AG; Richard Leach, CG; James Sanders, CG; and Robert Rohde, CG.

Arrived in England in January 1945 and assigned to 392nd Bomb Group, completing 14 missions.

If there was a highlight to anyone's tour, his was getting to take a number of ground crews on trolley runs over Germany to see the results of their efforts and then flying AC #42-50390 home to the USA with a happy cargo of ground personnel and their full crew.

Married June Philbrick on Nov. 4, 1945. They have four children and 11 grandchildren. Retired from business in 1988 and now resides in Goodland, KS.

EUGENE FREED (GENE), was born on Feb. 6, 1922 in Philadelphia, PA. Enlisted in the U.S. Army in February 1942. After completing basic training he attended Infantry OCS at Fort Benning, GA.

Commissioned second lieutenant and assigned to 100th Inf. Div. as Regimental Anti-tank CO officer. Promoted to first lieutenant in January 1943. Transferred to USAAF in August 1943 to undergo pilot training in officer grade.

Earned pilot wings, Class of 44-D. Trained in B-24s at Montgomery, AL and March AFB, Riverside, CA. Assigned to 446th Bomb Group, 2nd Air Div., 8th Air Force in December 1944. Flew 17 combat missions. Returned to States shortly after V-E day.

End of hostilities brought about discharge in September 1945. Earned three Air Medals.

Married Lillian Gurland in October 1942. They have two sons, one daughter and seven grandchildren. After discharge he returned to family business enterprises and is still semi-active at age 72, after 49 years of various management duties.

GEORGE HARBERT FREEMAN, was born in 1919, reared and educated in Martin (Weakley County), TN. Eldest of three children of George H. Sr. and Willie M. Freeman.

Entered service in 1940 with Tennessee National Guard, Co. K, 117th Inf., federalized and stationed at Fort Jackson, SC. Held various duties until application accepted as avia-

---

tion cadet, USAAC. Eliminated and subsequently assigned as group sergeant major, 491st Bomb Group (H) forming at Pueblo, CO. Moved to Metfield, England and war service with group until demobilization in 1945.

After a short period of civilian life, re-entered Air Force as recruiter and personnel specialist at various stations in CONUS and Libya.

Retired in August 1970 as personnel superintendent, senior master sergeant (E-8), locating in Memphis, TN. Received Air Force Commendation Medal, Distinguished Presidential Unit Citation and various service awards.

Employed by J.C. Penney Company as stockroom manager for 10 years. Married to Frances Evelyn Wilmoth while assigned to Scott AFB. They have four daughters and one granddaughter. Active member of Bellevue Baptist Church.

GILBERT R. FREEMAN, was born on Dec. 8, 1920 in New York, NY; enlisted in Army on March 3, 1942; commissioned on Sept. 16, 1942 in USAAC.

Spent 34 months in European-African Theatre of Operations. Assignments ranged from HQ Fighter Command, HQ 8th Bomber Command and actual operational bomb groups including the 93rd Bomb Group which flew the low level raid on Ploesti, Romania; staff of the Petroleum Attache in London; and worked with and assisted an arm of our national security services. Was vice-chairman, Monmouth County Employer Support for Guard and Reserve; past president of 6,000 member New Jersey State Air Force Association; past president of Passaic-Bergen Chapter Air Force Association; past post commander of American Legion; member of VFW; member Retired Officers Association; member American Security Council; member Aviation Advisory Committee of ex-Congressman Harold C. Hollenbeck.

Commissioned on Feb. 20, 1987, National Defense Executive Reserve; assigned to U.S. Dept. of Energy; security clearance "Secret." Chairman of Air Force Academy selection committee for U.S. Senator Frank Lautenberg. Vice-chairman of Academy selection committee for U.S. Representative Marge Roukema. Consultant to U.S. Representative Jim Courter of House Armed Services Committee.

Discharged in March 1979. Received EAME Medal with four Battle Stars, Presidential Unit Citation with Oak Leaf Cluster, Combined Services Medal, Citation from Gen. Eisenhower, Victory Medal and American Campaign Medal.

He and wife Elsie have three sons and one daughter. Their son Bruce, is a colonel, USAF; son John Philip, is a lieutenant colonel, USAF (RET); daughter-in-law, Barbara is captain, USAFR; son George Richard is major, USAFR; ex-wife, a section officer in RAF; present wife built P-38s for Lockheed.

Gilbert is a senior program manager with New Jersey Department of Environmental Protection Agency.

J.B. FREEMAN, was born on Aug. 15, 1918 in Cleveland County, NC. Entered military service at Fort Jackson, SC from Rutherford County, NC in February 1942.

Assigned Savannah Army Air Force, GA in February 1943. Completed Gunnery School at Tyndall AAFB, FL in July 1942. Assigned 302nd Bomb Sqdn., 84th Bomb Group, Savannah AAFB, flying A-31 dive bombers. Assigned George A. Scheltens as pilot, Henry C. Vaughn as co-pilot Boise, ID, 1943. Trained on B-24s at Mountain Home, ID and Wendover, UT.

Assigned 392nd Bomb Group, 577th Sqdn. in January 1944. Flew 31 missions on aircraft, *Trips Daily*, and other aircraft. Completed missions in July 1944.

Discharged in September 1945 and re-enlisted on Nov. 9, 1945. Served in Korean and Vietnam Wars. Retired on May 1, 1972 with rank of chief master sergeant. Received Distinguished Flying Cross, Meritorious Service Medal, Air Medal with three Oak Leaf Clusters, Air Force Commendation Medal, Good Conduct Medal (Army), Good Conduct Medal (Air Force), American Defense Medal, American Campaign Ribbon, EAME Campaign Medal, WWII Medal, Army Occupation, National Defense, Vietnam Service Medal, Presidential Unit Citation, Air Force Outstanding Unit Award, Air Force Longevity, NCO Graduate Ribbon, Small Arms Expert Medal, Republic Vietnam, German Clasp, Good Conduct Clasp and Medal for Humane Action.

Married to Lena Warlick. They have two sons, one daughter, three grandchildren and two great-grandchildren.

CHARLES H. FREUDENTHAL, was born in 1916 in New York City. Enlisted in 16th Inf. from Worcester, MA on his 18th birthday.

Graduated from Midland Army Flying School in May 1942 and was assigned there and later to San Angelo as a bombardier instructor.

In early 1943 went to the 29th Bomb Group at Gowen

Field. That summer was transferred to the Webb Provisional Group at Pocatello AAB.

In December 1943 reported to the 489th Bomb Group, a B-24 unit forming at Wendover AAF, as group bombardier. The 489th joined the 8th Air Force in April 1944 and operated there until December 1944 when it was returned to the ZI for transition to B-29s. With the end of the war the group was inactivated.

Various stateside and overseas tours as an air inspector and public affairs officer occupied the ensuing years.

Retired in 1974 lieutenant colonel, USAF and settled in Vienna, VA with wife Helen and son Donald. He is a graduate of Southern Colorado State College, a past president of the 2nd Air Division Association and author of *A History of the 489th Bomb Group.*

THORPE L. FRIAR, was born on Nov. 8, 1924 in Grimes, IA and graduated from high school there. Entered service as a private. Received boot training for aviation cadet at Jefferson Barracks, MO, Feb. 14, 1943.

CTD at Beloit College, WI; classification at Santa Ana, CA for pilot training, Class 44-C. Primary at Thunderbird Field, Glendale, AZ. Basic and advanced multi-engine at Pecos AAB, TX. Graduated second lieutenant as pilot and sent to co-pilot B-17 School, Las Vegas AAB, NV.

Assigned to B-24 crew of E. Furnace at Gowen Field, Boise, ID. ETO replacement crew to 2nd Air Div. through Herington, KS, Camp Kilmer and liberty ship to Liverpool. Held for assignment at Stone; schooling at Clunto, Northern Ireland.

Flew first mission on Sept. 25, 1944 with 489th Bomb Group, 448th Bomb Sqdn. from Halesworth Base to Koblenz as crew co-pilot. Flew 35th mission on March 4, 1945 with 448th Bomb Group, 413th Sqdn. from Seething as replacement crew I.P. to Stuttgard. Also replacement crew inst. pilot to Berlin on Feb. 26, 1945.

Discharged on points July 2, 1945 with rank of first lieutenant. Received Air Medal with four Oak Leaf Clusters, ETO Ribbon with four stars, etc.

Graduated with BS in business administration, law major from Drake University in 1948. Numerous other specific trade education courses. Owner of several businesses, the primary one being Friar Brothers Adjusters as president, Des Moines, IA. Later authored computer program for field and strip mining soils restoration.

Flying interest alive but not current. Pre-retirement active in Masonry, Zig-Ga-Zig Shrine, Sertoma Club and Quiet Birdman. Now busy as secretary B of D, Mission Hills Condo Association. Now retired with wife Laurene at Clearwater, FL. They have one daughter.

DUDLEY E. FRIDAY, was born on Nov. 30, 1916 in Sabine Parish, LA. Grew up on a farm. After high school and two years at Louisiana State Normal College was drafted into the Army on Jan. 17, 1942. Accepted into the Aviation Cadet Program.

Graduated from Twin Engine Pilot School on June 29, 1943, Class 43-F at Seymour, IN. After B-24 transition and crew training, joined the 491st Bomb Group at Pueblo, CO in February 1944.

Flew the southern route with group to the U.K., arriving in May 1944. Flew on group's first mission on June 2, 1944. Completed 31 missions in 65 days, then back to ZI. Stayed in Air Force, serving in Japan, Korea and Alaska.

Retired on May 1, 1966 with rank of lieutenant colonel. Received Distinguished Flying Cross, four Air Medals, Army Commendation Medal, Air Force Commendation Medal and numerous other awards.

After military worked for Colorado State University in weather research. Now retired.

Married Doris R. Taylor of Albany, NY on May 2, 1952. They have two children, four grandchildren and one great-grandchild.

MURRAY D. FRIEDMAN, resides in York, PA. Born on April 25, 1923 in Jersey City, NJ. He joined the USAAF on Dec. 20, 1942.

Overseas units served with were the 93rd Bomb Group (H), 328th Sqdn. (H), 8th Air Force. He trained at Kirtland Field in the Class of 43-11 which lead to bombardier wings. Also trained at Monroe, LA where he attended Navigation School.

During his time with the 8th Air Force, which ran from March 1944 through September 1944, his operations included D-day, Berlin, Munich, Hamburg, and the other usual 8th Air Force hot spots. He was a member of the winning team of the IV Bombing Olympics which were held July 25, 1943 at Kirtland Field.

Separated from the service on Oct. 22, 1945 with rank of first lieutenant. Decorations included the Distinguished Flying Cross and Air Medal with five Oak Leaf Clusters. He was recalled for the Korean conflict during which time he served at HQ, 32nd Air Div. (Defense) at Syracuse, NY as division controller. Separated in 1953 with rank of major.

Graduated from Penn State University in 1947. His family includes his wife Nancy and children: Donald, Michael, Barbara and Stephen. He is presently managing partner of the accounting firm of Seligman, Friedman & Company, P.C. with offices in York, Harrisburg and Lancaster, PA.

He also serves as chairman of the Advisory Board of Penn State of York, chairman of Susquehanna Valley Regional Airport Authority, chairman of Air Transportation Authority of York County, and former president of the Penn State Nittany Lion Club Advisory Council.

JOHN L. FRIES (JACK), was born ca 1923. He was a nose gunner on Joseph Bell's crew (see J. Bell).

Fries died in 1971 in Niles, MI. Survived by wife Mary and son Chris who still live there.

WILFRED J. FRIGGE, was born on Dec. 13, 1921 in Dutton, MT. Enlisted in USAAF on Sept. 14, 1942.

Served as direction finder RO, 446th Bomb Group (H), Control Tower, 491st Bomb Group. Military locations and stations included Bungay, England, 446th Bomb Group, Metfield and North Pickenham, 491st Bomb Group.

Participated in battles of Normandy, Northern France, Ardennes, Rhineland, Central Europe and Air Offensive of Europe. Memorable experiences are too many to mention.

Discharged on Oct. 11, 1945 with rank of sergeant. Received EAME Theater Service Medal with six stars and two Presidential Unit Badges.

Married Maxine Harper, they have two boys, three girls and seven grandchildren. He is a retired farmer/rancher.

HAROLD W. FRITZLER, was born on July 24, 1922 in Herington, KS. Joined Air Corps as aviation cadet in August 1942. Graduated Class 44-2 as F/O Navigator, 491st Bomb Group.

Military locations and stations included Santa Ana, Las Vegas, Mather, March and North Pickenham. Flew 35 combat missions and was in two major crashes. Flew over and back via northern route.

Discharged on Nov. 24, 1945 with rank of second lieutenant. Received six Air Medals, Distinguished Unit Badge, ETO with four Battle Stars.

Married wife Florence on Sept. 17, 1949. They have one daughter and two grandchildren. He retired in 1983 as a traffic manager. Handyman, volunteer, Oregon State Defense Force, rank major. Active with Bomb Group Association. Resides in Portland, OR.

CURTICE B. FRY (C.B.), was inducted into USAAC on Jan. 16, 1943. Entered Keesler Field for basic training and Air Force Technical School where he graduated on June 24, 1943. Then to Ford Willow Run Air Frame School, received private first class and corporal ratings.

From there via Birmingham Modification Center, Topeka, KS; Salt Lake, arrived at Wendover Field, UT and assigned to 788th Bomb Sqdn., 467th Bomb Group.

Left Camp Shanks, NY on Feb. 27, 1944. Started missions about April 1944, lost their commanding officer, Maj. Salzarulo, after which the 788th Sqdn. became 801st Sqdn. stationed at Harrington, England.

They received stripped B-24s, painted black and called carpet baggers. He was picked as crew chief and promoted to staff sergeant. On the night of July 16, 1944 he lost his plane.

After several gasoline hauls to Belgium, good-bye England, as they picked up and flew to Italy. Brindisi was their base for awhile. Then to Rosignano, doing same type of work. It was all top secret with the OSS, delivering supplies and agents to French Underground and other supply drops, all at night.

After Germany surrendered they moved and finally the squadron split up. The war ended while they were at sea, so they were sent to Boston and arrived on Aug. 18, 1945.

Participated in Air Offensive Europe, Normandy, Northern France, Air Combat Balkans, GO 33 WD45 North Apennines, Po Valley and Rhineland campaigns. Discharged on Sept. 18, 1945. Received Good Conduct Medal, EAME Campaign Medal and the Distinguished Unit Badge.

Married Sally Peffer on Aug. 16, 1946. They have four children and six grandchildren. Retired from Santa Monica Unified School District, CA.

JOSEPH H. FULTON, was born on April 1, 1914 in Kiowa, KS. Joined USAAC in January 1942.

Was a member of the 2nd Air Division's 93rd Bomb Group (H) in England from September 1942 to June 1945, first at Alconbury Air Field and then at Hardwick Air Field near Norwich.

Reached England by way of the 3rd Staff Sqdn. at Fort Leavenworth, Miami Beach, Officer Candidate School, OCS Class of 1942, and as a passenger on the troop ship called the *Queen Elizabeth.* At war's end he was returned to civilian life on the *Queen Mary.*

The 93rd, a B-24 equipped group commanded by Gen. Ted Timberlake, became famous as Ted's Flying Circus. In Cambridge he had tea with George M. Trevelyan, the master of Trinity College, and dinner one night in December 1942 with the faculty of King's College and Lord John Maynard Keynes, the great economist whose theories were used by President Franklin D. Roosevelt in planning the New Deal.

Discharged in November 1945 with rank of first lieutenant. Received Good Conduct Medal and ETO.

Memorable experience was returning to England in the summer of 1992 for the 50th Anniversary of the 8th Air Force. Served from 1954-1962 as an SAC information service officer. He is single and a retired school teacher. Resides in Albuquerque, NM.

SHERMAN F. FUREY JR., was born on June 1, 1919 near Mackay, ID and was reared on a ranch in Central Idaho. He enlisted in the USAAC on July 21, 1941 as a private. His first duty station was Moffett Field, CA.

He was promoted through the ranks to staff sergeant and then entered aviation cadet pilot training in January 1943. Graduated on Dec. 5, 1943 as second lieutenant, Class of 43-K, Gulf Coast Training Command, Brooks Field, San Antonio, TX.

Trained as pilot in B-24s at Fort Worth Army Airfield, TX and Muroc Army Airfield, CA. Joined the 448th Bomb Group, 713th Sqdn. at Seething, England and flew 30 combat missions as pilot and lead crew pilot from Aug. 3, 1944 to Feb. 6, 1945.

Discharged in December 1945 with rank of captain. Received Distinguished Flying Cross, Air Medal with three Oak Leaf Clusters and three European Battle Stars (battles of France, Germany and Ardennes offensive).

Married Jo Ann Horton on Feb. 18, 1951, they have two daughters, Jan and Terrill, two sons, Stephen and Sherman III, and nine grandchildren.

Has been a lawyer for 46 years and is still practicing with his lawyer son, Sherman F. Furey III in Salmon, ID.

MIKE FUSANO, was born on Nov. 29, 1915 in Sylmar, CA. Enlisted in USAAC in February 1942.

Military locations and stations included Shipdham, England, 44th Bomb Group, 14th Combat Wing, 2nd Air Div. Participated in battle at Ploesti.

His most memorable experience was as a driver for Gen. Leon W. Johnson, plus many more experiences. Was discharged in August 1945 with rank of sergeant.

Married Catherine in 1945, they have four girls and one boy. He is a semi-retired olive grower.

CHARLES S. GABRUS (CHUCK), was born on July 28, 1923 in Hempstead, NY. He married a former USN WAVE, Olga D. Krapf, in 1948 and they have a son and daughter.

He graduated from high school in 1941 and entered the USAAC on Jan. 19, 1943. Assigned to the 489th Bomb Group, 844th Sqdn.

Received basic training in Atlantic City where he played left field on the Air Corps championship softball team for five months before being sent to Buckley and Lowery Fields for Armament School. After completion, he was assigned to Gunnery School at Tyndall Field, FL and then on to Wendover Field, UT. He was assigned to a flight crew but when the bombardier was killed in a crash while in training on a night flight, he and his co-pilot were assigned to another crew. Then, on to Tucson, AZ for more training. He left Morrison Field, FL for England and the 8th Air Force via South America and North Africa. Completed 31 missions and was grounded on the last mission on Aug. 26, 1944. Returned to the States on the USS *Saturnia,* arriving on Nov. 10, 1944.

In December 1944, after furlough, he reported to the convalescent hospital at Bowman Field, KY. Every two weeks he went on leave for two weeks because his records were lost. After four months his records were found and he was sent to Personnel Affairs School in New York (tough to take). Upon completion, he went from Truax Field, WI for shipping orders to Fort Lewis, WA. On June 9, 1945 he was assigned to a base unit at Chico Air Base, CA to fight forest fires up and down the coast of California. He was discharged on Sept. 11, 1945.

Received the Distinguished Flying Cross, Air Medal with three Oak Leaf Clusters and four European Campaign Stars. And he never missed a Thanksgiving at home.

In 1952 he built a home and in 1983, after 36 years, he retired from New York Telephone Company. Resides in East Meadow, NY.

ROSS W. GAINEY, was born on March 18, 1918 in Greene County, near Scotland, IN. Was drafted into service on March 12, 1941.

Went to Greenland in the infantry in October 1942. While in Greenland he signed up for Air Corps, was accepted, and came back to the States in January 1944. Went to Gunnery School at Tyndall Field, FL in spring of 1944.

Met and flew with his crew at Biggs Field near El Paso, TX in June and July 1944. On Aug. 10, 1944 their crew took off for Liverpool, England on a ship. Ten days later they landed at Liverpool. He was stationed at Norwich, 100 miles north of London.

In the 8th Air Force, 458th Bomb Group, 755th Sqdn. in a B-24 he flew his first mission on Oct. 5, 1944. Flew his last mission on April 10, 1945. Flew 27 missions over Germany. He was a nose gunner and 2nd engineer.

Discharged from service on Aug. 23, 1945 with rank of staff sergeant.

Worked at a Naval Ammunition Depot for 27 years, from 1947 to 1974. Has one daughter and three grandchildren, which are his pride and joy.

He loves that B-24 bomber. It brought him back home time after time.

JACOB E. GAIR (JACK), co-pilot, B-24, was born on April 1, 1922 in Pittsfield, MA. Hometown is Lee, MA. Attended University of Rochester, NY 1940-1943.

Enlisted in August 1942, called up in February 1943. Received cadet training at San Antonio, TX; Brady, TX; Winfield, KS; and Lubbock, TX (Class 44-D).

Married Peggy Lou Davis while in crew training at Pueblo, CO in August 1944. They have one daughter and two sons.

Arrived in United Kingdom in October 1944 by convoy. Flew 33 combat missions with 467th Bomb Group from Dec. 6, 1944 to April 25, 1945.

Discharged in November 1945 with rank of first lieutenant. Received five Air Medals. Returned to U.S. as passenger with 9th Troop Carrier Command mass flight via Iceland, Greenland and Labrador in July 1945.

Completed graduate studies in geology, 1949 (Ph.D., Johns Hopkins). Taught geology at University of Oregon from 1949-1952. Geologist with U.S. Geological Survey from 1952 until retirement in 1987. Worked mainly on metallic mineral deposits of Precambrian and early Paleozoic ages in Northern Michigan, Southern Appalachian Mountains, and Brazil.

Resides in Kensington, MD.

JOHN WALTER GALLAGHER JR. (WALT), was born Jan. 8, 1922 in Brooklyn, NY and joined the USAAF, July 2, 1942. Assigned to 445th Bomb Group, 702nd Bomb Sqdn., 8th USAAF as communications/cryptography. Stationed at Camp Upton, NY; Pawling AAFTTS, NY; Salt Lake, UT Replacement Depot; Sioux City, IA AFB; Watertown, SD AFB; Tibenham, England, ETO; Worcester, England; RAF Communications School, ATC Base, Nashville, TN, and Westover Field, MA AFB.

Memorable experiences: Meeting and associating with so many incredibly courageous young guys from all over the States. Living in a most memorable period of time, and never forgetting the terrible number of fellows that were lost.

Discharged Oct. 28, 1945 with the rank staff sergeant. Received the Distinguished Unit Badge, EAME Theater Campaign Ribbon with six Battle Stars.

Married Nancy Shanley May 20, 1950. They have five children and seven grandchildren. Retired as insurance broker in Garden City, NY and moved to Cape Cod. Has started a Sandwich Youth Lacrosse program for 5th through 8th grade boys. Enjoys traveling out West.

RUEZ R. GALLERANI, was born on Nov. 18, 1924 in Plymouth, MA. Enlisted in USAF on April 7, 1943 and served with 8th Air Force, 466th Bomb Group (H), 2nd Air Division. Military locations included Attlebridge, England. Participated in air battles over Germany.

Discharged in November 1945 with rank of sergeant. Received Good Conduct Medal, Air Medal, two Bronze Stars and European Theatre Medal.

Married and has two children, David and Marcella. Retired from Cape Auto Body after 42 years in business.

ROBERT A. GALLUP, was born on May 3, 1923 in Verona, IL. Enlisted in USAAC on April 1, 1942, went active on Aug. 12, 1942 and assigned to 445th Bomb Group, 700th Sqdn.

Received pre-preflight, Nashville, TN; preflight training, San Antonio; primary, Muskogee; basic, Enid and graduated on May 23, 1943 with Class 43-E at Pampa, TX. Sent to Tucson, then El Paso, Biggs Field for B-24 training, back to Tucson and got part of crew. Some training there, then to Pueblo, CO where he received rest of crew and more training. However, it proved not enough.

They went to England by southern route with brand new B-24J and arrived on Feb. 12, 1944. Plane went to one group, they went to 445th Bomb Group, 700th Sqdn. He made only two missions with crew and didn't have enough formation experience, flew co-pilot with Lt. Gabbe's crew for nine missions; got another crew and made 12 more missions before being shot down by flak over Munich. Made it to Switzerland and that is another story.

Discharged in September 1946 with rank of captain.

Married twice, two children from first marriage, six from second. Married 44 years. Retired, travelling, gardening, fishing and enjoying himself.

DONALD M. GANNETT, was born on April 28, 1922 in Lyons, NY. Enlisted in USAAC in August 1942, aviation cadet, Southeast Training Command, commissioned second lieutenant, pilot on Jan. 7, 1944. Assigned to Charleston, SC AAB, B-24 crew training through April 1944.

Completed 35 missions with 467th Bomb Group; co-pilot, D-day to Sept. 30, 1944; 1st pilot Oct. 1, 1944 to Jan. 5, 1945. 439th Troop Carrier Group, instructor pilot C-109. Flew war-weary B-24 to U.S. with skeleton crew via Marrakech, Dakar, Belem, Trinidad to West Palm Beach, FL.

Assigned Air Transport Command, Ferry Division. Checked out in P-47, P-51, P-63 and P-40. Ferry pilot on all from June 1945 until made inactive in March 1946.

Discharged from Air Force Reserve in December 1957 with rank of captain. Received Distinguished Flying Cross and Air Medal with three Oak Leaf Clusters.

Graduated from Cornell University in June 1947. Spent most of his career with a national advertising agency in New York City.

Married Betty Leresch in December 1945. They have two daughters, one son and six grandchildren. He is retired and enjoys playing golf in North Carolina.

DELBERT R. GARDNER, was born on May 6, 1923 in Wooster, OH and was raised in Willliamsport, PA and Elmira, NY. He enlisted in the USAAC on Dec. 30, 1941. Attended Aircraft Armament School at Lowry Field, CO where he was selected as an instructor after graduation.

He spent a year at Armament School as instructor, then served as an armorer with 16th Anti-Sub Sqdn., Charleston, SC. Embarked for England on March 1, 1944 with the 467th Bomb Group, B-24, and served as armorer with the group at Rackheath, England until V-E day. Transferred to 9th Air Force in France and was preparing for shipment to the Orient when the war ended, bringing discharge in September 1945.

For him, the war was mostly hard work, loading bombs and servicing guns at all hours of the day or night. After the war, he earned a BA and MA in English from Syracuse University and a Ph.D. in English from University of Rochester. Enjoyed a 20-year college-teaching career, then rounded out his professional career by working again for the Army for 13-plus years, this time as a training manager (Civil Service).

On June 20, 1968 he married Marilyn Hegarty, who has been the inspiration for many of the 20-odd poems and stories he has published. They have four children.

JESSE E. GARDNER, was born on May 15, 1920 in Bridgetown, TX. Entered aviation cadet training in USAAC on Sept. 20, 1942. Graduated from Bombardier School at Midland AAB, TX on May 13, 1943.

Aerial gunnery training and B-24 training at Wendover, UT; B-24 phase training at Boise and Pocatello, ID as a bombardier with Russell Reindal as first pilot on their crew.

Embarked on the *Queen Elizabeth* for England after leaving Camp Shanks, NY in October 1943. Stationed at Seething with 714th Bomb Sqdn., 448th Bomb Group. Their crew completed a tour of missions over Europe on June 4, 1944. He was awarded the Distinguished Flying Cross and the Air Medal, and returned to the USA.

Members of their B-24 crew included Russell Reindal, 1st pilot; Bernard Mattson, co-pilot; Jess Gardner, bombardier; Wilbur Phillips, navigator; Louis Donoso, engineer; Boyd Hatzell, radio operator; Paul Freeze, lower ball turret gunner; Ray Waters, waist gunner; Elden Farra, waist gunner; and David Avila, tail gunner.

Retired from Wichita Falls Post Office as assistant postmaster and from USAFR as major. During retirement, served as president of National Association of Retired Federal Employees, and AARP, Wichita Falls, Texas Chapters.

ROBERT S. GARDNER, was born on March 1, 1921 in Kansas City, MO. Enlisted in USAAF in 1942. Served with 8th Air Force, 392nd Bomb Group, 577th Bomb Sqdn. and 9th Air Force, 29th Air Disarmament Division. Was in Intelligence (S-2), Photographic Interpretation. Stationed in Alamogordo, NM; England; Ireland; Germany and France.

Participated in Air Offensive, European Campaign and EAME campaigns.

Discharged on Dec. 18, 1945 with rank of corporal. Received Bronze Service Star (Air Offensive European Campaign), Bronze Service Star (Central European Campaign), Campaign Ribbon for EAME Theatre, Victory Ribbon, four Overseas Service Bars and Good Conduct Medal.

Married Helen Reich on April 14, 1942. They have two sons and one granddaughter. Retired from U.S. Postal Service after 41 years service.

WELLS N. GARDNER, of Erie, PA, entered the service in April 1917. He served in the 56th Artillery in France for 16 months and was a veteran of the Argonne Campaign. Discharged in June 1919, having obtained the rank of corporal.

Between wars, Gardner was a railroad brakeman with the Pennsylvania Railroad for 10 years.

In October 1942 he re-enlisted and went overseas in May 1944 and served with crew 80, 458th Bomb Group, 755th Sqdn. A glider pilot before he became a gunner, Gardner completed a 30-mission tour in February 1945 and returned home. He was thought to have been the oldest air gunner on combat duty at 46 years of age.

Gardner was awarded the Air Medal with three Oak Leaf Clusters. He is now deceased. *Submitted by Donald A.Fraser.*

HERMAN S. GARNER, was born on Oct. 6, 1919 in Denton, NC. Enlisted in USAAC on Feb. 12, 1941, Maxwell Field, AL. Attended Gunnery School at Tyndall Field, FL and Buckingham Army Air Field, Fort Myers, FL. Volunteered for combat and trained in B-24 at Davis-Monthan Field, Tucson, AZ.

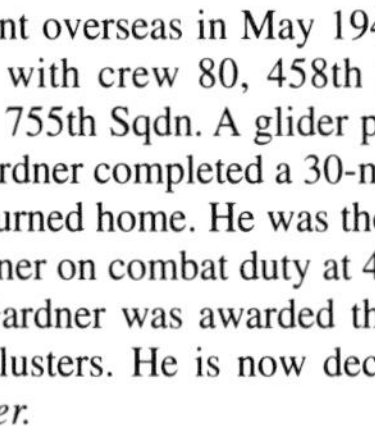

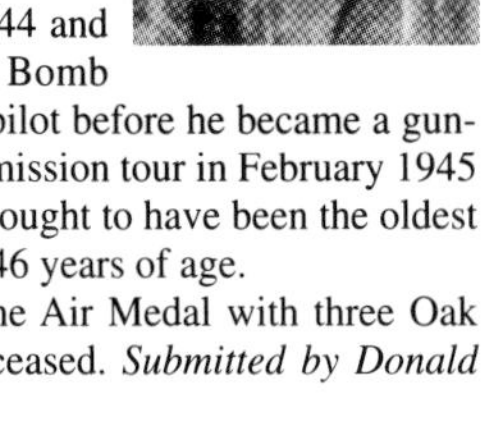

Assigned to 392nd Bomb Group at Wendling, England. Completed 35 missions in B-24s. First mission was D-day, June 6, 1944 and last mission on Oct. 25, 1944.

Returned to States on Dec. 8, 1944. Discharged at Fort Bragg, NC on Sept. 6, 1945 with rank of technical sergeant. Received Distinguished Flying Cross, Air Medal with three Oak Leaf Clusters and six European Campaign Stars.

Married Bessie Mae Kepley on Jan. 18, 1946. They have one daughter. He operated his own business from 1953 to 1977, at which time he retired.

EUGENE A. GARRETT, was born in Santa Monica, CA. Enlisted in USAAC on July 16, 1942, aviation cadet,

Class 44D, graduated as pilot, second lieutenant. Served with 467th Bomb Group, Rackheath, England. Flew 34 combat missions over Germany.

Discharged on Oct. 27, 1945 with rank of first lieutenant. Received three Battle Stars and Air Medal with four Oak Leaf Clusters.

Married Mary Ann Norstad on Jan. 31, 1948. They have five children and five grandchildren. He is a consultant and author.

HOWARD L. GARRETT (CHARLIE), was born on Sept. 8, 1924 in Porterville, CA. Enlisted in USAAF Ready Reserve on Oct. 24, 1942. Received basic training at Lincoln, NE; CTD, University of Nebraska; pre-flight at Santa Ana, CA; Gunnery School at Kingman, AZ; Bombardier School, Kirkland Field, Albuquerque, NM, Class 44-4. Graduated March 18, 1944.

Joined Lt. Henry M. Propper's B-24 crew at Lincoln, NE on April 14, 1944. Received crew training at Davis-Monthan Field, Tucson, AZ. Ferried a B-24 from Topeka, KS to England. Joined the 392nd Bomb Group, Wendling, England on July 26, 1944 as a replacement crew. He served with the 8th Air Force, 577th and 579th Squadrons.

Flew 29 missions over Europe, the last 14 they were a "GH" lead crew which he flew as an 8th Air Force qualified pilotage navigator. They had several hair-raising missions. The most memorable was a low-level supply drop to Arnheim, Holland on Sept. 18, 1944. This trip was a testimony to their crew and the "Old Bird" that brought them home safely 29 times.

After his discharge on Sept. 26, 1945, he attended Colorado School of Mines under the GI Bill of Rights. Graduated in May 1950 and joined Shell Oil as an exploration field geologist, working in the Western United States, Middle East, and South and Central America. Retired from Shell on Sept. 1, 1984 after 35 years.

On May 20, 1986, they had their 40th Crew Reunion at Atlanta, GA. Six of the original 10 crew were in attendance.

BEN C. GARSIDE III, was born on May 25, 1925. Enlisted in USAAC on March 5, 1943 as navigator with 389th Bomb Group. Served with 8th Air Force in Norwich, England and 5th Air Force in Kunsan, Korea. Participated in Rhineland, Central Europe and Central Korea campaigns.

Memorable experience: Monroe Harris and Garside ended up together in England. They were both on a mission to Parchim on April 4, 1945 and Harris was just a couple planes to his left in the formation. Garside happened to be looking right at his plane when it happened. A ME-262 pulled up behind Monroe and shot off one of his rudders. Harris' aircraft immediately stalled and went into a spin. Garside followed him down through the clouds and never did see any chutes. It wasn't until he saw him at home after the war that he learned he and two other crew members (out of 10) had been able to bail out. Garside was able to tell Monroe what happened outside as he did not know what hit him. On the inside, the wheel came right back in his lap. He had to put his feet up on the instrument panel and break the seat loose to get free. Monroe was not in the Class of 1943, but, in this case, close is good enough.

Discharged on Nov. 8, 1945. He graduated from Stanford University with a degree in economics. Life as a fundamentalist was short-lived as he was recalled for the Korean War and assigned to the 5th Air Force as aerial navigator on low level night intruder missions. Discharged Oct. 19, 1953 with rank of first lieutenant. Received Distinguished Flying Cross and Air Medal with three Oak Leaf Clusters.

Was in the securities business for 37 years analyzing and predicting markets. In 1970 got a secondary degree in computer programing. Married Charlyn Louise Pyles Sept. 4, 1949. They have four children: Pamela, Deborah, Victoria and Cynthia. He enjoys golfing, swimming and trout fishing.

LEE GARSON, was born on July 8, 1925 in Pittsburgh, PA. Moved to Akron, OH at age 14. Enlisted in USAAF and took basic at Amarillo, TX and Aerial Gunnery School at Kingman, AZ where he graduated. From there they were shipped to Biggs Field, El Paso, TX for crew formation and training for overseas. He was made tail gunner.

After completion they were assigned to temporary transport and as a crew they were shipped to Topeka, KS where they picked up a brand new B-24 to fly the northern route to England. There they were sent to Kiel Kiel, Ireland for additional gunnery training and mostly to wait for a spot to open at a base in England (they were told).

The great day came and they were assigned to the 445th Bomb Group, 702nd Sqdn. and immediately began their missions. They flew 30 missions in all, the last one to the Big B (Berlin). It was scary, but not too bad. They were made one of the lead crews which resulted in taking a long time to complete their missions.

Garson returned by ship and landed at Camp Kilmer, NJ the day before President Roosevelt died, April 11, 1945. He went on his 30-day leave with orders to report to Santa Ana, CA and head for the Pacific. He left Akron by train and wasn't more then 30 minutes away, at the next stop, when they heard about V-E day and almost turned back. Arrived at Santa Ana and all plans were up in the air. He was placed with the MPs until he was discharged on Oct. 25, 1945 with rank of staff sergeant.

Received EAME Theater Medal, Air Medal with four Oak Leaf Clusters and Good Conduct Medal.

His most memorable experience was the day they arrived back in the U.S. and the welcome they received at the pier in New York; also memorable was when he saw his family in Akron.

His children are Tom, Tim, Carolyn and daughter-in-law Pam. Pam and Tom have three splendid children: Ryan, Jennifer and Kate. Garson owns a boat rental and chartering business in Ft. Lauderdale, FL.

NICK E. GARZA, was born on Sept. 10, 1921 in Monterrey, Mexico. Enlisted in USAAC on Sept. 16, 1942. Served with the 506th Sqdn., 44th Bomb Group, Ground Crew Ordnance, 2nd Air Division. Military bases included Pueblo, Shipdham, North Pickenham, Cheddington and Alconbury. Sailed SS *Jean* March 8, 1943, with Rear Echelon.

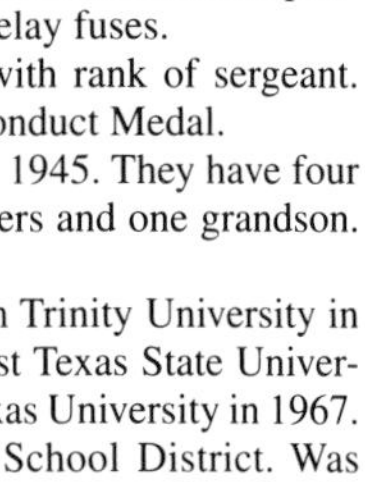

Campaigns included Sicilian, Naples Foggia, Normandy, Northern France, Ardennes, Rhineland, Central Europe and Ploesti Air Raid. Duties included loading and unloading bombs. Was one of two ground crewmen responsible for fusing one B-24 with time-delay fuses.

Discharged on Oct. 29, 1945 with rank of sergeant. Received EAME Medal and Good Conduct Medal.

Married Sarah Sears on April 6, 1945. They have four daughters, one son, five granddaughters and one grandson. They reside in San Antonio, TX.

Nick received a BS degree from Trinity University in 1949, master's degree from Southwest Texas State University in 1950, and graduate study at Texas University in 1967. Retired in 1982 from San Antonio School District. Was teacher, coach, principal, assistant superintendent for 37 years. Enjoys volunteer work with St. Paul's Parish and the Methodist Hospital.

O.H. GASAWAY (VAN), was born on Nov. 26, 1919 in Barnsdall, OK. Enlisted in Aviation Cadet Program on April 13, 1942. Eliminated in basic flight, went to Gunnery School in Las Vegas, NV and Armament School in Denver, CO. Crew was formed at Gowen Field, Boise, ID. Gasaway was as-

signed as tail gunner on Lt. W.D. Faulkner's crew, 734th Sqdn., 453rd Bomb Group.

Sent to March Field, Riverside, CA for phase training. On to Hamilton Field, San Francisco, CA. Assigned a new B-24 and immediately named her *Paper Doll*. Went by southern route to Old Buckingham, Attleborough, England. Flew his first mission on Feb. 5, 1944, made lead crew and flew a total of 30 missions.

Returned to Santa Monica, CA on Dec. 21, 1944. Based at George and Norton Air Bases. Discharged Sept. 11, 1945 with rank of staff sergeant. Received Distinguished Flying Cross and Air Medal with three Oak Leaf Clusters.

Married Tharon Waters on April 8, 1945. Retired and resides in Manhattan Beach, CA.

EUGENE GASKINS, was born in San Diego, CA. Enlisted in USAAC on June 11, 1942, 8th Air Force, 2nd Air Division. Military locations and stations included Keesler Field, MS; Las Vegas Aerial School; Wendover, UT; Sioux City, IA; and Seething, England.

From December 1943-August 1944-participated in Battle of Germany, Air Offensive France and Normandy. Every combat mission flown was a memorable experience, especially April 22, 1944, Hamm, Germany.

Discharged Sept. 4, 1945 with rank of staff sergeant. Received Distinguished Flying Cross, Air Medal with three Oak Leaf Clusters, three Battle Stars, and more.

Married Louise Kelly in June 1943. They have two children: Sharron Dianne and Robert Wayn. Gaskins is retired to the golf course, yard and hobby shop.

JOHN GATELY, was born on June 6, 1925 in Brooklyn, NY. Married Bernadette Planet in November 1950. They have five children, eight grandchildren and one great-grandson. His son, John P. Gately, is a lieutenant commander in the Navy and is currently flying an F-18 off the carrier, *Nimitz.*

John Gately enlisted in the USAAC in November 1943 upon graduation from high school. After basic training in Greensboro, NC he went to Aerial Gunnery School in Laredo, TX. From Laredo he went to Casper, WY for combat crew training in B-24 Liberators. Then flew new B-24s overseas via Iceland to 8th Air Force, joining the 44th Bomb Group, 67th Sqdn. in July 1944.

Flew 35 combat missions over Europe as a waist gunner on a B-24 Liberator. First mission was Aug. 26, 1944 and last mission was Feb. 28, 1945. Earned four European Campaign Stars and five Air Medals before returning to USA in April 1945 as a staff sergeant.

Entered Administrative Officer Candidate School at Maxwell Field, AL in June 1945, graduating as a second lieutenant in September 1945. Served one month as a second lieutenant at Maxwell Field, AL and was discharged in October 1945 after 23 months' service in USAAC at the ripe old age of 20. This was the end of his military and aviation career.

ERNEST M. GAVITT, was born on July 16, 1920 in Providence, RI. Enlisted in Air Force on Feb. 2, 1942. Attended Scott Field Radio School.

Arrived in England in August 1942 as replacement radio operator. Qualified for Air Force Cadet Program and returned to U.S. in December 1942. Commissioned navigator from Selman Field, LA and assigned to crew 717, B-24. Trained at Davis-Monthan Field, Tucson, AZ and Alamogordo, NM

April 1944, assigned to 857th Sqdn., 492nd Bomb Group, North Pickenham, England. On May 19, 1944 on mission to Brunswick, Germany, *Boomerang* was hit by German fighter fire. They crash landed in Holland, were taken prisoners and sent to Stalag Luft III, Sagan. He was liberated on April 29, 1945 by General Patton's forces in Moosburg, Germany.

Discharged from Air Force in August 1945 with rank of second lieutenant. Received European Theater Medal and Purple Heart.

Returned to Rhode Island and married Arline Crabtree. They have a son Scott, daughter Judy, and four grandchildren by Scott and his wife Lynda: Douglas, Heather, Amanda and Emily.

Retired in Rhode Island after 35 wonderful years with NCR Corporation, Dayton, OH.

He plans to visit old air base in England and crash site city in Holland on 50th Anniversary of last mission, with wife Arline, grandson Douglas and several members of crew. Also will visit gravesite of Sgt. Uriel Robertson who was killed in the crash. He is interred at U.S. Military Cemetery at Margraten, Holland.

RAYMOND R. GAWRONSKI, served in the USAAC. Technical schools included Airplane and Engines, Biloxi, MS from March-November 1943; Aerial Gunnery, Harlingen, TX, earned wings in December 1943, Transition B-24, Tucson, AZ, trained for flight engineer and top turret gunner from January-March 1944.

Ferried new B-24 to Europe in April 1944. Departed Grenier Field, NH to Goose Bay, Labrador to Reykjavik, Iceland, to Nuts Corner, Ireland. Assigned to 445th Bomb Group, 703rd Sqdn. in May 1944. Flew 25 combat missions.

Returned to U.S. in April 1945. From May-July 1945, assigned to B-29 program. Reported to Chanute Field, Rantoul, IL for Electrical Specialist and Central Fire Control School.

Received Honorable Discharge in August 1945 at Baer Field, Ft. Wayne, IN, with rank of technical sergeant. Received Aerial Gunners Wings, ETO Campaign Ribbon with two stars, Air Medal with four Oak Leaf Clusters, Good Conduct Medal, Victory Medal and Group Presidential Citation.

Dedicated to his wife Barbara; son Walter (Casey); and daughter Julia Ann. Thanks be to God.

NORBERT GEBHARD (GEB), was born on Nov. 20, 1920 in New Holstein, WI. Graduated from Sheboygan Falls, Wisconsin High School in June 1938. Served in CCC Northern Wisconsin from July 1938-1939.

Enlisted as private in USAAC in June 1941. Received basic training at Jefferson Barracks, MO. Completed Aircraft Armament School, Lowry Field, CO and assigned to Mather Field, CA on Dec. 6, 1941.

Sent to Aerial Gunnery School, Las Vegas, NV for training and instructor. Accepted for Aviation Cadet training, West Coast Command, Santa Ana, Ontario; and Bakersfield, CA for preflight, primary and basic. Graduated pilot and commissioned in March 1943 at Roswell, NM, Class 43-C.

Assigned to 389th Bomb Group, 565th Sqdn., Biggs Field, El Paso, TX; then to Denver for final phase. Flew northern route to Hethel, Norwich England in June 1943. Dispatched to Bengazi, Lybia for low level Ploesti, Romania oil field raid Aug. 1, 1943. Returned to England, then back to Tunis, Tunisia for 5th Army Landing Support. Back to England to complete 25 combat missions Feb. 2, 1944. Three months, B-17 and B-24 ferrying duty from Modification Depot, North Ireland to English bases. Returned to United States for B-24 and B-29 instructor training until inactive duty in June 1945.

Joined General Dynamics, Fort Worth Division, in Quality Assurance and retired after 35 years in 1983.

RICHARD F. GELVIN, was born on Dec. 21, 1922 in Topeka, KS. Entered Kansas University in 1941 (Aero Eng) and joined ROTC. Enlisted as aviation cadet Dec. 15, 1942. Graduated Navigation School, San Marcos, TX, Class 44-3-2 and commissioned second lieutenant.

Assigned to crew and departed with new B-24 for England and 8th Air Force on April 15, 1944 via southern route. Assigned to 700th Sqdn., 445th Bomb Group (H) May 24, 1944 and flew first mission on D-day, June 6, 1944. Became lead navigator and promoted to first lieutenant on June 10, 1944. Assigned acting squadron navigator Sept. 15, 1944. Completed 30 combat missions and returned to ZOI on Nov. 25, 1944.

Received assignment to Pilot Training Class 45-I and was in basic training, Moultre, GA at war's end. Relieved from active duty Nov. 2, 1945 and joined Reserve.

Entered aerospace industry in 1949 with Beech Aircraft Corp., Wichita, KS. Married Jane L. Skidmore on Aug. 16, 1952, they have a daughter, son (now master sergeant in AF) and three grandchildren.

Retired from Air Force Reserve June 12, 1968 as major. Received Distinguished Flying Cross, Air Medal with three clusters, French Croix de Guerre with Palm.

CLARENCE R. GENTLE, was born on Dec. 28, 1920. Entered USAAC with hopes of becoming a pilot. Washed out of pilots' training and went to Mechanics' School. Was flight engineer on B-24.

Left U.S. in January 1945 and assigned to 466th Bomb Group in England. Completed 16 missions and received five European Campaign Stars.

Remained in Air Force for 20 years and completed assignments in several U.S. bases, Panama Canal Zone and another tour in England.

Retired from the Air Force in 1964 and went to work for the Federal Government at Elmendorf AFB, Alaska. Retired a second time in 1977.

He participated in Battle of the Bulge, Madgeberg, Regansberg, etc. His most memorable experience was trying to bail out over Rotterdam and landing at Antwerp.

Clarence married Sibyl Moor. They have two sons, Russ and Dale, and one daughter Gay. He is enjoying retirement on a beautiful lake in Wasilla, Alaska and practicing his hobby of woodworking by making bowls, cutting boards and rolling pins in exotic woods. He gives things he makes to the women at church.

DONALD C. GEPHARD (DON), was born on Feb. 14, 1925 in Grover Hill, OH. Drafted in USAAC July 7, 1943 after completing high school. Was flight engineer on B-24 bomber, 392nd Bomb Group, 2nd Air Division. Received basic training at Miami Beach, MS; A/M school, Biloxi, MS; Gunnery School, Laredo, TX; phase training, Mountain Home, ID.

Arrived at Wendling, England (392nd Bomb Group) in February 1945 as a replacement crew (Hotchkiss crew). Flew six combat missions when war in Europe ended, then three trolley missions. Most memorable experiences were seeing front flak, German jets and seeing ruins after war ended.

Discharged on Feb. 6, 1946 with rank of staff sergeant. Received Air Medal, two European Theater (awarded to group while he was a member) and Good Conduct Medal.

Married Ann on April 8, 1961. They have two sons, two daughters and two grandsons. Gephard is retired from his own business founded April 1, 1954. Spends some time in Illinois, but mostly in Florida and Texas.

ELMO W. GEPPELT, was born on July 27, 1923 in Caddo, TX. Moved throughout the Midwest until Lamar High School in Houston. After three years of college, he enlisted

in the USAAC as an aviation cadet and graduated from San Marcos as a navigator and second lieutenant in the Class of 44-1.

He was assigned to a crew in Blythe, CA and sent to the 2nd Air Division in England. He became operational on June 10, 1944 and a lead crew navigator after four missions. After completing 30 missions (Feb. 9, 1945) he returned home as a first lieutenant, married Betty Lindauer and was assigned to Ellington Field where he completed Instructors' School and taught until being discharged.

Thereupon, he returned to the University of Kansas and completed a BS in electrical engineering. Also, upon discharge, he joined the Air Force Reserve and was active until completing 28 years of commission service and retired as a lieutenant colonel.

He received the Distinguished Flying Cross and the Air Medal with four Oak Leaf Clusters.

In civilian life he is a registered professional engineer and holds several patents. He has served as president of several corporations and is currently chairman/CEO of Delta Limited. He has been quite active in his church and in the Boy Scouts of America where he was awarded the Silver Beaver. He and wife Betty have two sons, a daughter, six grandsons and another grandchild on the way.

JOHN W. GERRITY, was born on Sept. 19, 1921 in Dallas, TX. Received private pilot license in 1939. Entered service as aviation cadet. Received primary training at Ft. Stockton, TX; basic at San Angelo, TX; twin engine advanced at Lubbock, TX, Class 43-K. Commissioned second lieutenant Dec. 5, 1943; B-24 transition, Tarrant AAF (now Carswell AFB, Ft. Worth, TX); crew phase training, Muroc AAF (now Edwards AFB Muroc, CA).

Assigned to 8th Air Force, 2nd Air Division, 96th Combat Wing, 466th Bomb Group, 785th Sqdn., crew 545, station 120, Attlebridge, Norfolk, England, approximately 10 miles WNW of Norwich, England.

Completed 35 missions over Germany and occupied territory from Aug. 7, 1944-March 4, 1945. After eight missions, crew trained for special night missions over Germany - code named Kings-X, from Sept. 1-Oct. 12 1944.

Their training involved engaging and evading searchlights over London at 20,000 ft., plus or minus 1,000 ft. They were told that they would not drop conventional bombs on Germany, but that their night missions would materially expedite the end of the war with Germany. Would like to know just what these missions would have entailed, if anyone can advise. Program cancelled after six weeks.

Returned to combat on Oct. 14, 1944. Four enlisted crew members relieved of combat after 27 missions. Crew awarded five Battle Stars, Air Medal with four Oak Leaf Clusters and Unit Citation. None of the 14 crew members suffered loss or injury.

Returned to USA in May 1945. Married and elected to remain in AAF until V-J day. Assigned to C-54 Douglas Skymaster Transition at Charleston, SC. Upon completion in July 1945, was assigned to Saipan in order to fly the many litter patients to Hawaii and U.S. mainland, expected, if necessary, to invade Japanese homeland. Separated from active service in September 1945 at Barksdale AAF, Shreveport, LA.

Entered Southern Methodist University, Dallas, TX. Received BSEE in 1948. Joined Union Carbide Corporation, Carbon Products Division, in Industrial Marketing. Retired in 1984 after 35 years. Resides in Houston, TX.

BOARDMAN G. GETSINGER JR. (GETS), joined the USAF in January 1943. Received aviation student training at St. Vincents College, Latrobe, PA; primary flying at Americus, GA; basic flying at Greenwood, MS; and completed twin engine pilot training with Class 44-E at Columbus, MS in May 1944.

Assigned as B-17 co-pilot to Buckingham Field, FL, Gunnery School and later in 1944 as B-24 co-pilot on crew of Donald Stuhmer for staging at Charleston, SC. Crew reported to 714th Sqdn., 448th Bomb Group, in Seething in November 1944 and after several missions was transferred as lead crew to 712th Sqdn., completing 23 missions by V-E day. Discharged as first lieutenant in October 1945.

"Gets" and Ruth Kinkel were married Sept. 17, 1942 and are parents of five children. Employed as communications manager for Connecticut public utility before retirement in 1982. He is a jazz musician and an artist.

C.W. GETZ (BILL), was born on March 8, 1924 in Fort Wayne, IN. Enlisted as an aviation cadet in the USAAC on May 5, 1942. Commissioned July 28, 1943. Flew 31 missions as first pilot, 491st Bomb Group. Combat tour in P-51s with 2nd Air Div. Scouting Force.

Retired from the USAF Nov. 1, 1962 with rank of lieutenant colonel. Received Legion of Merit, Distinguished Flying Cross, seven Air Medals, Air Force Commendation Medal, Presidential Unit Citation, campaign, theater and occupation ribbons.

Senior positions in industry and government from 1962-1980. Publisher, writer, consultant, property manager from 1980-present. Commercial pilot from 1988-1992. Author/publisher of two volume, *The Wild Blue Yonder: Songs of the Air Force.*

Received BA, ML and DBA degrees. Is past president of Society for Information Systems, Order of Dadelions, charter member of 2nd Air Division Association, 8th AFHS, life member of AFA, life member of 491st Bomb Group Association, 355th Fighter Group Association and Red River Valley Fighter Pilots Association.

Married JoLynn Green in 1946 (deceased 1974). Married Vicki D'Amico in 1976. Has three children: Charles, Jerilyn and Linda; and one grandson, Trevor.

RICHARD G. GHASTER, was born on April 4, 1925 in Findlay, OH. Enlisted in USAAC on Sept. 10, 1943. Military locations and stations included Scott Field, IL; Amarillo; Kingman; Biggs Field, El Paso, TX; Old Buckingham. Flew 35 missions from June 1944-December 1944 with the 8th Air Force, 2nd Air Division, 732nd Sqdn., 453rd Bomb Group.

Participated in battles of Normandy, Northern France, Ardennes and Rhineland. His most memorable experience was his first time flying in B-17 at Kingman Gunnery School when he crash landed in the desert during practice air to air.

Discharged on Oct. 22, 1945 at Tinker Field, Oklahoma City, OK with rank of staff sergeant.

Received Distinguished Flying Cross and Air Medal with three Oak Leaf Clusters.

Married in 1948 and has two sons and one daughter. Richard is a retired realtor.

RAYMOND C. GIBBONS, was born on April 30, 1922 in Cleveland, OH. Enlisted in USAAF Feb. 6, 1943. Served with 8th Air Force, 2nd Air Div., 453rd Bomb Group. Military locations and stations included ETO-Old Buckingham, Attleborough, England; Lowry Field; Las Vegas Aerial Gunnery School; Boise, ID Aerial Gunnery School; Laredo, Texas Instructor School.

Airplanes: *Paper Doll* and *Dolly's Sister* with Faulkner's crew. Was turret gunner on B-24 bomber. Completed 30 combat missions. His most memorable experience was being able to visit relatives in England when on leave.

Discharged Oct. 16, 1945 at Tyndall Field, FL with rank of staff sergeant. Received Distinguished Flying Cross, Air Medal, EAME Ribbon with three Oak Leaf (bronze) Clusters.

Married on Aug. 16, 1946 and had three lovely daughters and two beautiful granddaughters. Worked over 40 years making landing gears for airplanes.

Gibbons passed away Jan. 1, 1990.

RALPH L. GIDDISH, was born on March 6, 1923 in Atlanta, GA. Entered service in March 1943. Received basic training at Miami Beach, radio operator training at Scott Field, and gunnery training at Panama City. Assigned to B-24 crew with combat crew training at El Paso.

Crew ferried new B-24 to Scotland in June 1944. After United Kingdom radio procedure training in Ireland, was assigned to 67th Sqdn., 44th Bomb Group. Completed 32 combat missions safely, 10 of them as lead crew. Received Air

Medal with three Oak Leaf Clusters and Distinguished Flying Cross.

Returned to U.S. in February 1945. Completed B-29 gunnery instructor training at Laredo, TX. Trained B-29 crews at Chatam AFB until honorably discharged in October 1945.

Married with two children and four grandchildren. Retired after 33+ years from AT&T and after 12 years with IRS and U.S. Department of Education.

Enjoys gardening, theater and international travel.

WALTER RALPH GIESECKE, was born on Jan. 10, 1919 in Marble Falls, TX. He married in 1942, has a son, a daughter, and four grandchildren. He enlisted in the USAAC Dec. 16, 1941 and was promoted through the ranks to staff sergeant, then aviation cadet, and discharged in 1945 as a major.

His first assignment was 392nd Liberator Bomb Group (Heavy). Assigned to go to Wendling, England for combat operations as a squadron engineering officer. Later reassigned to 467th Liberator Bomb Group (Heavy) at Rackheath, England as a group engineering officer. Received Presidential Unit Citation and Bronze Star.

Returned to the U.S. at the end of WWII and became a businessman in the Central Texas area. Career included ranching, banking (chairman and CEO of two banks), supermarkets, lumber yard, buying and selling real estate and developing subdivisions. Still active at age 74 with no plans for retirement. Resides in Marble Falls, TX.

LAWRENCE G. GILBERT, was born on May 23, 1918 in Pleasant Lake, IN. Attended Tri-State College, Angola, IN, in aeronautical engineering. Learned to fly in CAA Civilian Pilot Training program. Entered aviation cadet training in 1941, graduating at Kelly Field in September 1941.

During 1942, flew submarine patrol in B-18s and instructed in B-17s and B-24s with 34th Bomb Group, training crews for assignment to newly forming combat groups. Assigned to initial cadre of 392nd Bomb Group in early 1943 at Tucson as group operations officer. Departed for England in July 1943 in advance of 392nd Group deployment for indoctrination training with experienced 8th Air Force bomber units.

Flew two combat missions as observer with B-17 groups and 24 missions with 392nd Group. Returned with the Group after V-E day on *Queen Mary.* Served in various command and staff assignments in Air Transport Command and Military Air Transport Service, including the Berlin Air Lift.

Married high school classmate, Marjorie Hardy, in 1945. They have one son, one daughter and four grandchildren. Retired to Winter Park, FL in 1961 with rank of colonel.

THOMAS D. GILBERT (GIL), was born on Jan. 19, 1921 in Rockford, IL. Entered the USAAC Sept. 1, 1942. After basic training in Jefferson, MO, was assigned to 93rd Bomb Group. Made first mission (in Tarfu) Aug. 1, 1943, Ploesti Oil Fields. Based in Bengazi, Libya. Moved to Hardwick, England.

Gilbert was shot down Sept. 15, 1943 over Yvette,

France (while crew member of *Bathtub Bessie* B-24 bomber, 93rd Bomb Group). Captured and held prisoner in Stalag 17B, Krems, Austria, for one year. Repatriated for burns and wounds received in last mission. Decorated with Air Medal, Distinguished Flying Cross, two Purple Hearts and other recognition medals. Chosen by Rockford, IL as their Outstanding War Hero.

After returning to the States, served 20 years as Loves Park, IL alderman. Was hearing officer for Secretary of State two years; 10 years as Cabinet Director at Admiral Corporation.

Retired in 1984 from sheriff's department with the rank of commander and continues to hold merit commissioner position for the sheriff's department.

Married Dorothy Humpal June 24, 1943. They have two daughters, one son and four grandchildren. They are happily retired in Loves Park and celebrated their 50th Wedding Anniversary on June 24, 1993.

MATHIAS GILLES, was born on May 9, 1923 in Chicago, IL. Entered service in March 1943. Was in 8th Air Force and served at Hethel Air Base. Was with 389th Bomb Group, 564th Sqdn. His memorable experiences include refueling of planes, towed disabled ones to hangars to gas, oil, oxygen, etc.

Discharged in October 1945 with rank of corporal. Received Good Conduct Medal, ETO, and five Battle Stars.

Married to Shirley and has four step-children and one of their own. Mathias is a driver for a bank. They reside in Evergreen Park, IL.

AMISA M. GILPATRICK, was born on April 15, 1921 in Glendo, WY. Enlisted in USAAC on Aug. 20, 1942. Attended Airplane Mechanics School in Laredo, TX. Joined Bob Lehr's crew in Pueblo, CO and arrived in England on June 22, 1944. Assigned to 752nd Bomb Sqdn., 458th Bomb Group, at Horsham St. Faith, Norwich, England.

Flew 35 missions over Europe as flight engineer on B-24. On third mission, target Berlin, two engines shut down. He feathered one runaway prop by using gasoline, jettisoning all loose equipment on plane to maintain altitude.

Received Air Medal with four Oak Leaf Clusters and European/African Service Medal with five Battle Stars. Arrived in U.S. on April 22, 1945.

Attended Tri-State University, graduated with a BS degree in civil engineering. Self-employed as engineer/land surveyor to date. Married Dec. 31, 1948 and they have three children. Resides in Vernon, NJ.

DOMINIC J. GIORDANO, was born on Oct. 10, 1922 in Brooklyn, NY. Attended Manhattan High School of Aviation Trades, graduating in 1941. Worked at Patterson Field, Fairfield, OH from August 1941 to March 1943 as an airplane and engine mechanic.

Entered the Air Force in March 1943. Received basic training in Clearwater, FL; Airplane Mechanics School, Keesler Field, Biloxi, MS; and Aerial Gunnery School in Harlingen, TX.

Participated in Normandy, Northern France, Ardennes, Rhineland and Air Offensive Europe campaigns.

After being assigned to a flight crew, he took phase training at Blythe, CA. Was shipped overseas in May 1944. Landed in Scotland, continued on to Ireland for more gunnery training, then shipped to Horsham St. Faith Air Field at Norwich, England. Flew 30 missions, last 10 as lead crew. Shipped back to the States in May 1945, landing in Atlantic City. Off to Chanute Field, IL for Instrument School.

Discharged from Randolph Field, TX in September 1945. Received Distinguished Flying Cross, Air Medal with five Oak Leaf Clusters, EAME with five Bronze Stars.

Married in Chicago, IL to Rose (Glorioso) Giordano, wife of 42 years. They have five children and six grandchildren. Attended reunion of surviving crew members in Sacramento, CA after 47 years. He retired from printing career in 1989.

FRANK GIOSTA, was born on June 26, 1925 in Arden, PA. Enlisted in service June 10, 1943. Received pre-aviation cadet training at Keesler Field; Gunnery School at Laredo, TX; and overseas training at Muroc. Served at Rackheath with 2nd Air Div., 467th Bomb Group, 790th Sqdn., 8th Air Force.

Frank participated in battles at Ardennes, Northern France, Central Europe and Normandy. His memorable experiences included the Berlin mission and flight home. Completed 33 combat missions.

Discharged on Oct. 21, 1945 with rank of sergeant. Received Air Medal with four Oak Leaf Clusters.

Frank was an only child so crew 51 was his adopted brothers and he remembers them all and keeps in touch with them. They were lucky that no one in their crew was wounded or injured.

Giosta has a mother, wife, two sons, and a daughter. He is a retired steel worker.

PATE E. GIVEN JR., was born on Sept. 4, 1922 in Memphis, TN. Enlisted in USAAC on Oct. 9, 1942 as a radio operator. Served with the 8th Air Force at Attlebridge. Participated in battles at Normandy, ETO, Air Offensive and Northern France.

Discharged Oct. 6, 1945 with rank of technical sergeant. Received Air Medal with three Oak Leaf Clusters and Distinguished Flying Cross.

Retired from Bendix Aerospace Systems Division and Magnavox Electronic Systems Division. He is now teaching art and painting.

CARL J. GJELHAUG, was born Feb. 3, 1924 in Washington, DC. Enlisted as private in Army Nov. 16, 1942 and left Georgetown University for aviation cadet training. Graduated as pilot and entered B-24 Transition, Chanute Field, IL. Received crew training at Walla Walla, WA. Shipped with crew to 8th Air Force in 1944 and assigned to 707th Sqdn., 446th Bomb Group, 2nd Air Div. at Bungay, England. Completed tour and flew crew home at end of war.

Assigned to B-29s and flew to FEAF with crew to 98th Bomb Wing, Yokota AB, Japan in 1950. Completed combat tour in Korea 1951. Reassigned to ZI and entered B-47 jet training. Flew B-47s eight years as pilot and instructor. Reassigned to B-52 and flew tour in SEA from Thailand and assigned as assistant director of operations. Flew B-52 12 years as pilot-instructor and assigned as squadron commander at Loring AFB, ME.

Returned to England in 1974 to 307th Strategic Wing, Mildenhall, Suffolk. Served three years as dept. commander for maintenance and chief logistics RC-135, KC-135, SR-71 and U-2 aircraft, Spooks. Returned to ZI to retire as lieutenant colonel on Dec. 1, 1977 with 35 years and 14 days of service.

Married 50 years to Evelyn, they have three children, eight grandchildren and one great-grandchild.

ROYCE BURTON GLENN (BEEZER), was born on Dec. 18, 1919 in Baird, TX. Attended Hardin-Simmons University, TX for four years and received BA degree in physics. Enlisted in Flying Cadets in July 1940. Received commission March 15, 1941 from Kelly Field, TX.

Instructed at Randolph Field, TX from March 1941 to July 1942; CCTS, Hendricks Field, Sebring, FL from July to September 1942; instructed four-engine pilots at Gowen

Field, Boise, ID from September 1942 to August 1943; overseas training August 1943 to January 1944; ETO (England) January-September 1944.

Attended Engineering Officer's School, Chanute Field, IL from October 1944 to April 1945. Stationed at Mountain Home AAB, ID as maintenance control officer. Glenn has 2700 hours total flying time, completed 31 combat missions from England, 230 combat hours; was experienced engineering maintenance office (MOS 4823); weight and balance officer (0911); additional MOS (1091, 1092, 4821); attended AAFSAT Orlando, FL, August and September 1943; and was operations office and squadron commander in heavy bomb group.

Discharged in 1946 with rank of major. Received Distinguished Flying Cross with one Oak Leaf Cluster, Air Medal with three Oak Leaf Clusters, ETO Ribbon with two Battle Stars, American Theatre Ribbon and American Defense Ribbon.

Married Marcia Gwinn in Boise on Nov. 15, 1945. They have two children, Michael and Margaret, and two grandchildren. He retired as officer in a savings and loan company.

DAVID P. GLICK, was born on Nov. 25, 1922 in Berkeley, CA and enlisted in USAAC in November 1942 while attending Pomona College.

Was activated in February 1943 and commissioned at Hondo Field, TX in March 1944 as a second lieutenant navigator. Joined his new B-24 crew at Biggs Field, TX. With training completed, the crew picked up a new B-24 at Topeka and flew to England via Iceland. Assigned to 489th Bomb Group at Halesworth in early June 1944.

Completed tour of 34 missions in October 1944, all flown in the B-24, *Sharon D,* which suffered only one injured crewman.

Was home by Christmas and next served as navigator instructor at Ellington Field, TX until separation from service in October 1945 as first lieutenant. Received four Air Medals and Distinguished Flying Cross.

Graduated from Pomona College in 1947 with degree in mathematics. Became involved with computers in pioneer days of 1957 while at Union Oil Company, and later completed career as programmer/analyst and computer sales support manager for NCR Corporation.

Married Patricia Allen in June 1947 and has three sons and two grandchildren. He continues to live in his native state of California.

NATHANIEL GLICKMAN (BUD), was born on April 18, 1922 in New York, NY. Joined the USAAC on June 25, 1942. Commissioned as a bombardier at Victorville, CA on July 31, 1943, then on to B-24 training at Tucson, AZ and Pueblo, CO.

Flew seven missions with the 328th Sqdn., 93rd Bomb Group, at Hardwick, England and was then transferred to the 66th Sqdn., 44th Bomb Group, a Pathfinder squadron at Shipdham, England.

Was wounded and bailed out over the English Channel on his 11th mission June 5, 1944. His command pilot, LTC Leon Vance Jr., received the CMH and he was awarded the Silver Star. Upon recovering from his wounds, he returned to flight status and completed 30 missions.

Was awarded Silver Star, two Distinguished Flying Crosses, five Air Medals, two Purple Hearts, four Battle Stars, two Presidential Unit Citations and the New York State Cross for Conspicuous Service. He retired as a captain.

Bud is married to the former Louisanne Kuffner von Dioszegh. They reside in Medford, OR. He retired as a corporate president in 1990 and is currently finishing his memoirs.

C. HOWARD GLOVER JR., was born on April 30, 1918 in Roswell, NM.

Entered the U.S. Army in 1941 after graduating from New Mexico State University with an ROTC commission. After two months, was assigned to flight training, earning pilot wings in 1942, Class 42-B. Served as flight instructor at various Texas bases until 1944. After completing flight crew training in B-24, reached the 448th Bomb Group in January 1945. Flew missions until the war was over in the ETO.

After the war, he served six years in ATC and MATS as base operations officer and chief pilot of Air Transport Wing.

Served five years in SAC as B-36 Aircraft Commander. Served nine years in comptroller field in Space Systems Division and Defense Atomic Support Agency, retiring as lieutenant colonel in October 1966.

Employed by Albuquerque Public Schools, retiring in 1983 as director of budget after 16 years of employment.

Married Lee Blundell in 1942. They have a son and two grandchildren.

FRANK C. GLUT, was born in Chicago, IL on Sept. 15, 1917. He married Julia Blasovits on Nov. 28, 1942. He joined the Army Air Force as a Cadet on Feb. 21, 1943. Their son, Donald, was born on Feb. 19, 1944 in Pecos, TX a week after receiving his Commission and checking out as a pilot on a B-24 Liberator.

Was sent to Hardwick Air Base, in Norwich, England. After making 24 missions in the 93rd Bomb Group, 328th Bomb Sqdn., was shot down over Benthe, Germany and was killed. Died on Feb. 3, 1945 at the age of 27.

He had received the Air Medal and the Purple Heart.

His remains were brought back to Chicago for burial on June 5, 1949, with full Military Honors.

JACK G. GNEITING, was born in Butte, MT on Aug. 5, 1919. Worked at Consolidated Aircraft located in San Diego, CA, building B-24 heavy bombers in 1941. After Pearl Harbor he joined the services. Had basic training at Fort Knox, KY then overseas to the Pacific in April 1942 with the 762nd Tank Bn.

While in the Pacific volunteered for Cadet Training and returned to the U.S. for training - attended USCC at Logan, UT then to Santa Ana AFB - then to Hondo, TX for Navigation School. Graduated August 1944. Formed their permanent crew at Tonopah, NV, then on to Hamilton Field, CA and then overseas to England. Flew 14 combat mission with 453rd Bomb Group and 466th Bomb Group.

Discharged in 1945 with the rank of second lieutenant. He was awarded the Asiatic-Pacific, European Theater and Air Medal.

Married Beatrice Greenfield May 1945 in London, England. They have three children. Retired in 1978 after 30 years with Mountain Bell Telephone.

JAMES V. GOAR, was born in Kirklin, IN on Dec. 30, 1919, enlisted in the USAAC three weeks after Pearl Harbor and spent a year at bases in Florida. After graduation from the Air Corps Administrative Officer Candidate school he joined the 392nd Bomb Group at Alamogordo, NM. He was with the 392nd for their entire 23-month stay at Wendling, serving as the 578th's Squadron Supply Officer and later was Group Transportation Officer.

He went to inactive duty as captain in 1945 and graduated from Earlham College, Richmond, IN in 1946. He then took the M.B.A. degree at Harvard University and was in

the newspaper business for a few years. He entered the real estate business in 1955 and is still active.

He co-edits the quarterly newsletter for the 392nd's Memorial Association and lives at 451 S. Harrison St., Frankfort, IN 46041.

HENRY J. GODEK, was born June 13, 1922 in Fitchburg, MA. He entered Civilian Pilot Training at Fitchburg State Teachers College on July 15, 1942, completed C.P.T. on Sept. 21, 1942 and was called to active duty.

Left Fort Devens, MA Sept. 28, 1942 and arrived at Roswell, NM Oct. 1, 1942. Then sent to Artesia, NM on Nov. 25, 1942 for pre-Glider Training. After completing training on Dec. 22, 1942 he left Artesia on Dec. 29, 1942 and arrived in Albuquerque, NM on December 30 where he stayed for one month. Arrived at 29 Palms, CA on Feb. 1, 1943, graduated from Glider School on March 11, 1943, and sent back to Albuquerque on March 15. In April the U.S. discontinued the glider program and he was honorably discharged as staff sergeant on May 12, 1943.

He was drafted on June 11, 1943 and left Fort Devens on July 3, 1943. Arrived in Biloxi, MS on July 5th. After basic training he was sent to Sioux Falls, SD arriving on Oct. 15, 1943. Started Radio School on Oct. 22, 1943 and on P.O.E. shipment Jan. 26, 1944, before finishing Radio School. Arrived at Scott Field, IL on Feb. 4, 1944 and then to Fort Dix, NJ on Feb. 18, 1944. Left Fort Dix and sailed from New York on the R.M.S.S. *Samaria* for England on Feb. 26, 1944. After 13 days at sea they arrived in Liverpool England on March 11th. From Liverpool to Stone, England. Next to North Pickerton and then Hethel.

Attached to the 389th Bomb Group on April 24th. June 6th (D-day) left Hethel to attend Radio School at the University of London. Saw first buzz bomb sent over London in Picadilly on June 17, 1944. Returned to Hethel on June 21st.

On Sept. 23, 1944 they celebrated their 200 bombing missions and paraded for Jimmy Doolittle, Gen. Spattz and Gen. Kepner.

April 12th started on leave for Ireland, but didn't get beyond Edinburgh, Scotland. While on train they heard of President Roosevelt's death. Returned to Hethel April 20, 1944.

On May 9th and 11th they took trips over Germany, France, Holland and other areas where their Liberators made history. May 28th, 1945 left Hethel for South Hampton to board the USS *Bienville* for trip home. Arrived in New York on June 7, 1945 and sent to Fort Dix. Given 30 day furlough on June 9th. Left Fort Devens for Charleston, SC. Left Charleston to join A.T.C. at Fort Dix, NJ. September 26, 1945 received orders to clear field for discharge. On Oct. 1, 1945 he ended up where he started from, with a lot of memories, but glad to be home.

Battles and campaigns include Air Offensive Europe, Normandy, Northern France, Central Europe, Ardennes and Rhineland.

He was awarded the Good Conduct Medal, Presidential Unit Citation, and EAME Ribbon with six Battle Stars.

HARRY GODGES, was born in Weirton, WV on Sept. 13, 1916. He enlisted in the USAAC on Jan. 6, 1942. Then went to AM School at Sheppard Field, TX. In Key Field, MS he worked as airplane mechanic, crew chief and flight chief. Promoted through the ranks to staff sergeant. Commissioned Oct. 16, 1943 at Miami Beach. He was discharged on Dec. 16, 1945 with the rank of captain.

Military locations and stations: Air Offensive Europe, Normandy, Northern France, Ardennes, Rhineland, and Central Europe.

Assigned to 453rd Bomb Group on Oct. 31, 1943 and arrived in England on Dec. 20, 1943 as assistant engineering officer becoming E.O. July 5, 1944. Left England with group in May 1945. Assigned to ATC Ferrying Div., Palm Springs, CA then to ATC Hqs., Cincinnati.

He was awarded the EAME Service Medal.

Harry married his high school sweetheart on June 20, 1941. They have two sons and four grandchildren. He graduated U.S.C. February 1949 as Industrial Engineer and went to work for ALCOA as I.E. then Production Superintendent. Retired on Jan. 1, 1983 and now enjoys golf and traveling.

LUTHER E. GODWIN JR. (LUKE), was born on Nov. 2, 1919 in Spartanburg, SC. He enlisted in the service in November 1936 serving with the U.S. Navy for four years, USAAC for six years and the U.S. Air Force for 15 years. He was a member of the 389th Bomb Group, 2nd Air Div. He was discharged in November 1966 with the rank of SM Sergeant.

Stationed at San Diego (Navy), Travis AFB, McGuire AFB, Eniwetok Atoll, Rhein Main (USAF). Participated in first Berlin Raids "D" Day and completed 35 missions.

His memorable experiences include searching for Amelia Earhart (1957 Navy), "D" Day, accidental dropping of bomb on RAF Field while landing (it didn't explode).

Luke was awarded the Distinguished Flying Cross, Air Medals, Purple Heart, Presidential Citation and Air Force Commendation.

He has four sons, Richard, Michael, Patrick and Timothy and one daughter, Sheralyn Sue. Worked with Air America in Asia. Presently builds and rents buildings. Owns his own paint and body shop and automotive garage.

KARL GEO. GOFF, was born on Oct. 3, 1921 in Burton, OH. Enlisted in U.S. Air Force on Oct. 14, 1942. Based at Tibenham, England, 445th Bomb Group, 703rd Sqdn. Flew 23 combat missions in B-24 bombers before being shot down and taken POW. Was in Stalag 7A, Germany from March 3, 1945 to April 29, 1945. Liberated by Patton's Army and sent to LeHavre, France (Camp Lucky Strike) for return to states. Attained rank of staff sergeant. Honorably discharged Oct. 10, 1945.

Participated in Rhineland-Ardennes Campaign.

Received Air Medal with one Oak Leaf Cluster, Purple Heart, and EAME Theatre Service Medal with one Bronze Star.

In August 1990, the 445th Bomb Group was belatedly awarded the Croix De Guerre Avec with Plume unit citation at the Second Air Division Reunion in Norwich, England.

Retired from managerial position with Middlefield Hardware, Middlefield, OH.

Married Barbara Harrington on July 8, 1948 and now lives in Bradenton, FL. Has two sons and two daughters, seven grandsons and seven granddaughters.

MARVIN THOMSON GOFF, was born in Angleton, TX on Nov. 2, 1918. Graduated from Angleton High School in 1937.

Enlisted USAAC 1941. Basic training Randolph Field, TX. Aircraft mechanics school, Chanute Field, IL. Mechanic, Mather Field, CA. Accepted as Aviation Cadet. Pre-flight, Kelly Field, TX. Primary, Pine Bluff, AR. Basic, Waco, TX. Washed out pilot training. Married Ida L. Davis and had two children, two grandchildren, one great-grandchild. Commissioned second lieutenant bombardier Midland, TX 1943.

Went to Clovis, NM for crew assignment. Assigned Clay Mellor crew and had training at Alamogordo, NM. Flew liberator to England via Natal, Dakar, and Marakesh.

Crew assigned to 713th Sqdn., 448th Bomb Group, Seething, England. Bailed out over northeast France on seventh mission, April 1, 1944. Five months with French underground. Picked up in August by advancing American Forces. Returned Midland, TX for navigation course. Attained rank of first lieutenant. Transferred Ellington Field, TX and discharged in late 1945.

Earned Doctor of Veterinary Medicine degree from Texas A&M in 1952 with a private practice in Houston, TX. Then Department of State Foreign Aid Program 1956-67. Served in Thailand, Yugoslavia, Republic of Mali (W. Africa) as advisor in livestock diseases and production. With U.S. Dept. of Agriculture 1967-80. Served as laboratory virologist, laboratory director, Ames, IA. Served as Assoc. Administrator for Veterinary Services, Washington, D.C. Retired to Angleton, TX 1980.

JOHN O. GOFFE, was born Sulphur, OK, Sept. 22, 1924, graduated high school May, 1942. Student Oklahoma University when entered Army, Feb. 14, 1943, 87th Inf. Div.,

five months, then entered Aviation Cadets, graduated Navigation School, Hondo AAF, TX, Oct. 13, 1944. Overseas as B-24 Navigator, 445th Bomb Group, 703rd Bomb Sqdn., 8th Air Force, Tibenham, England. Flew 14 missions, including last maximum effort raid on Berlin, March 18, 1945, also supply mission when U.S. 9th Army crossed Rhine River at Wesel, Germany, on March 24, 1945.

Awarded Air Medal with Oak Leaf Cluster, ETO Ribbon with three Battle Stars and Distinguished Unit Citation.

Inactive duty as first lieutenant in October, 1945. Stationed at 17 different bases in U.S. and overseas. Returned to Oklahoma University, received degree in Petroleum Geology. Worked as Geologist and Exploration Manager for Marathon Oil Co. for 30 years, worked in 13 states and overseas. Worked nine years for Pogo Producing Co., retired as VP.

Travels extensively, 50 states and 56 foreign countries. Plays golf and works on journal when not traveling. Married Judy Herrod, Nov. 8, 1952, one son is college professor, one son is sergeant in Army in Korea, and daughter is banker, grandchild on the way. Home is 12516 Arrowhead Terrace, Oklahoma City, OK 73120.

FRANK GOLDCAMP, was born in Pittsburgh, PA on March 14, 1925. He enlisted in the Air Force in April 1943 where he served as a pilot. Served with 492nd Bomb Group at North Pickenham, Leuchars Airfield Scotland and Hethel with 389th Bomb Group. Participated in 30 combat missions over France and Germany. All 30 combat missions and time with Carpet Baggers in Scotland were memorable experiences. He was discharged in July 1945 with the rank of first lieutenant.

Frank was awarded the Air Medal with Oak Leaf Cluster and ETO Ribbon with three Battle Stars.

Married Betty and they have 13 children, 25 grandchildren and 1 great-grandchild. Retired from LTV Steel after 36 years.

WOLFRED HAROLD GOLDEN, was born in Waurika, OK, Sept. 26, 1918. Entered Regular Army on Sept. 25, 1941 at Ft. Sill, OK as a draftee for one year. Received discharge nine days later after volunteering for three years in the Regular USAAC. Assigned to Shepherd Field, TX for basic training. Completed basic training and served as a clerk for one year. Transferred to Buckley Field, CO and attended Pursuit Armorer's School. Transferred to Hamilton Field, CA and was assigned to the Air Transport Command for six months, and to the Ferrying Command for six months. Attained rank of sergeant.

Passed preliminary exam for Aviation Cadet and transferred to Amarillo, TX for further testing. Upon completion of testing was advised no more pilots were needed at that time. Transferred to Kingman, AZ B-17 Gunnery School. Received training as lower ball turret gunner and transferred to Lincoln, NE Replacement Center. Transferred to Casper, WY for B-24 overseas training. Became B-24 tail gunner at Casper, WY and transferred to 453rd Bomb Group at Old Buckingham on Aug. 23, 1944. Completed 35 missions on March 5, 1945 and returned home on April 13, 1945. Discharged as staff sergeant at Camp Chaffee, AR on June 9, 1945.

Retired from Halliburton Services on Jan. 4, 1982 as senior auditor after more than 36 years service.

EDWARD GOLDSMITH, was born April 30, 1915 Chicago, IL. Enlisted in USAAC Oct. 27, 1942. Basic training at Eagle Pass, TX. Basic in the morning, worked on AT-6s in the afternoon.

Transferred to Keesler Field, Biloxi, MS February 1943. Graduated from Keesler Airplane Mechanics School June 22, 1943.

Assigned to the 700th Bomb Sqdn., 445th Bomb Group, Sioux City, IA B-24s. Sailed on the *Queen Mary* on Oct. 27, 1943 to Tibenham, England. Transferred to the 859th Bomb Sqdn., 492nd Bomb Group April 1944 before it arrived at North Pickenham.

When the 492nd was disbanded, August 1944 the 859th Sqdn. transferred to the 467th Bomb Group and became the 788th Bomb Sqdn. at Rackheath. Was there until end of war.

Returned on the *Queen Mary*, July 1945. Discharged from Davis-Monthan, Tucson, AZ on Oct. 12, 1945 as a sergeant.

Received Presidential Citation, ETO with six Bronze Stars, Meritorious Achievement, etc.

Presently married and retired.

HARRY GOLDSTEIN, was born in Newark, NJ Feb. 25, 1917. Harry was a singing waiter at the Town Talk Tavern in Newark, NJ. He enlisted in the U.S. Army Dec. 8, 1941.

He transferred to the USAAC and was stationed at Keesler Field in Biloxi where he trained as a gunner.

Originally attached to the 93rd Bomb Group, 409th Bomber Sqdn., he later transferred to the 458th Bomb Group (B-24), 754th Sqdn., stationed in Horsham St. Faith.

He was killed on his third mission on March 6, 1944 on a bombing raid of the Erkner Bearing Works. He was manning the left waist gun when the plane exploded in mid-air. Only the pilot Guy C. Rogers, and the Co-Pilot, Francis O. Proteau survived the explosion.

At the time of his death at age 27 he was the "old man" of the crew. *Compiled by his nephew, Mel Goldstein*

ERNEST W. GOODE, was born in Hopkinsville, KY on Dec. 13, 1922. He enlisted in the Army Air Force on Jan. 2, 1943. Graduated from Gunnery School on April 2, 1944. Served in Hethel England with 389th Bomb Group, 564th Bomb Sqdn., lead crew. Participated in 30 missions over France and Germany. He was discharged on Oct. 2, 1945 with the rank of staff sergeant.

His memorable experiences include Jimmie Stewart flying with them as command pilot and his pilot, Bob Arrington, getting killed.

He was awarded the Air Medal with five Oak Leaf Clusters.

Married in August 1947 and has two children. Retired after 45 years in industrial electronics.

KENNETH E. GOODING, was born in Cushing, OK, Dec. 7, 1922, entered service Jan. 13, 1943, USAAC, training: Salt Lake City, Wendover, UT, Tonopah, NV and Langley Field, VA.

Arrived in England on April 6, 1944 on the *Queen Elizabeth*, went to Northern Ireland for extra training. Assigned to Crew #68, waist gunner/armorer and assistant radio operator for 10 missions, Crew #74 25 missions, 448th Bomb Group, 715th Sqdn. Station #146, Seething, England. Com-

---

pleted 35 missions: 11th mission, Munich, Germany, their war weary B-24 used more than one-half fuel to target, they left formation, took straight course to Southern England/nearest field, ran out of fuel taxiing off runway. Eighteenth mission Bremen, Germany plane "RABDUCKIT" shot up, limped back to England, bailed out. twenty-second mission Kiel, Germany, he was hit by flak, saved by flak vest.

Awarded the Distinguished Flying Cross, five Air Medals, four European Campaign Stars, Good Conduct Medal and Certificate of Valor from 448th Bomb Group Commander, Col. Gerry Mason, also member of the Caterpillar Club.

Married Feb. 23, 1944 to school sweetheart Norma Wingfield and they have four children. Retired from owning/operating Mountain Resort in Southern California. Has lived in Idyllwild, CA since March 4, 1960.

ROBERT E. GORDON, was born Feb. 7, 1924 in Ft. Scott, KS. Enlisted in USAAC Aviation Cadet Program December 1942. Commissioned second lieutenant and received pilots wings April 1944 at Ft. Sumner, NM. B-24 transition training at Hirtland Field Albuquerque, NM and crew training at Mountain Home, ID. Was assigned to 466th Bomb Group, 787th Bomb Sqdn. at Attlebridge England in October, 1944. Flew 29 combat missions as pilot. Returned to USA flying B-24 "Sunshine Jane". Back via Iceland, Goose Bay and landing and leaving "Sunshine Jane" at Bradley Field, CT June 1945.

Separated from active duty fall of 1945 and returned to Kansas State University receiving MS Degree in Spring 1947.

Participated in the Battle of the Bulge.

His memorable experiences include crashing B-24 on take-off Christmas Eve 1944 enroute to mission supporting Battle of the Bulge.

Awarded the ETO and Air Medal with four Oak Leaf Clusters

Accepted commission, first lieutenant, in Regular USAF in fall of 1947. Assigned to SAC and flew B-29s with 301st Bomb Group until December 1954. Resigned Regular Commission for personal reasons December 1954. Worked for Boeing Aircraft Co. as B-47 tech. rep., McDonnell Aircraft as F-101 flight test engineer and finally Martin-Marietta Aerospace for 30 years in various engineering and procurement functions. Retired in March 1987.

Two sons and four step-sons, all successful in their own fields. Has traveled extensively and since retirement has been active in classic T-Bird restoration.

KENNETH M. GORRELL, was born Jan. 25, 1920 in Alberta, Canada. He finished college and enlisted in the USAAC in June 1940. He was assigned to Wheeler Field, HI and spent two years as engineering clerk in a fighter squadron. Attained the rank of staff sergeant.

After the Japanese attack he applied for pilot training and was accepted in the West Coast Training Command in 1942 and completed the program in the class of 43E. Then followed additional training in B-25s, B-17s and B-24s.

He was assigned to the 458th Bomb Group in September 1943 and flew to England with the group in January 1944. He flew 30 missions in Europe and spent his last three months in England as operations officer for the 752nd Sqdn.

He returned to the U.S. in September 1944; had miscellaneous assignments for one year and took a discharge in August 1945. Discharged with the rank of captain.

He was awarded the Pearl Harbor Ribbon, Pacific Theater Ribbon, Air Medal with four clusters, and Distinguished Flying Cross.

He then spent 36 years in the marketing division of Scott Paper Co.

In July 1943 he married Emma V. Eastburn of Philadelphia. They have three children and eight grandchildren.

G. LIONEL GOUDREAULT, was born in Haverhill, MA on Sept. 3, 1915. In 1941 he took the Civilian Pilot Training (CPT) offered free by the government and received a Private Pilot's license. In 1942 he joined the Aviation Cadets; was sent to the classification center at Nashville, TN. There, selected for pilot training and sent on to Maxwell Field at Montgomery, AL for pre-flight.

On to Avon Park, FL (primary); Macon, GA (basic);

Blytheville, AR (advanced TE). Graduated Class of 43H, and received Wings and commission at that station. Assigned operational training (OTU) at Wendover Field in Utah, and Gowen Field, Boise, ID. Went overseas on board ship out of New York (*Florence Nithingale*). Flew complete tour (30 missions) while based at Horsham St. Faith, near Norwich, England. Awarded the Distinguished Flying Cross, and the Air Medal with three Oak Leaf Clusters. Fortunate to complete missions with little, or no, damage.

Returned to U.S. and finished time at Randolph Field, TX and Kirtland AFB, at Albuquerque, NM. Released from active service on June 2, 1945 with rank of first lieutenant.

Back to grocery market operated by family. When that was swallowed up by large food chains, and later, malls, he found his "roots" in the good old U.S. Post Office from which he retired. He has one step-son, daughter-in-law and two grandchildren.

PAUL E. GOURD, was born in Haverhill, MA on April 12, 1918. He enlisted in the USAAC on April 11, 1942. Served with the USAAC (England) with 467th Bomb Group and 788th & 801/492nd Bomb Group; USAF (Fairchild) with 92nd Wing, and France Field with 37th Fighter Wing. Stationed at Wendover, Rackheath, Harrington, Maxwell, Smyra, Ellington, Hondo, Fairchild, Long Beach Reserve, Guam, Biggs, Saigon, Phocat Vietnam, Grissum, and Walker. Participated in battles in Europe and Vietnam. Discharged on March 31, 1970 with the rank of lieutenant colonel USAF.

Memorable experiences include aerial gunnery Harlingen, TX, Navigation - Marcos, Cruise Control Inst. Adv. Survival, B52 Castle, Intelligence Officer, Adv. Aerospace photo inter.

Awarded the Distinguished Flying Cross, Air Medal with four Oak Leaf Clusters, American, African with HGD, Distinguished Service Medal with one Bronze Star, Good Conduct Medal, Afouan with one Oak Leaf Cluster, SAEMR, Victory Service Medal with three Bronze Service Stars and many others.

Married to Jennie and they have seven children and fourteen grandchildren. He is presently retired.

CHARLES W. GRACE, was born in Kalamazoo, MI on Aug. 17, 1916. He served with the USAAC and USAF in Selfridge Field, MI; Hickman Field, HI; Offutt Field, NE; Otis AB, MA; Air Offense Europe, Northern France and Germany. Discharged on Aug. 31, 1957 (retired) with the rank of lieutenant colonel.

Participated in Normandy Invasion, D-day and the Bulge.

Memorable experiences include being pilot of first aircraft (B-24) to land on Normandy Beachhead.

Awarded the Distinguished Flying Cross with one Oak Leaf Cluster, Air Medal, EAME Theater Ribbon with four stars, American Defense Service Medal, American Campaign Medal and WWII Victory Medal.

He is presently widowed and has three children. He enjoys golf and traveling.

JAMES V. GRATTA, was born in Hingham, MA on Feb. 23, 1922. He enlisted in the service on July 17, 1942 and served with the 8th Air Force, 14th CBW, 44th Bomb Group, 506th Sqdn. Air Cadet training at Maxwell Field, AL; primary at Lakeland; ROM at Sioux Falls; radar at Madison, WI and Chanute Field, IL; gunnery at Yuma, AZ. He was discharged on Nov. 8, 1945 with the rank of tech. sergeant.

Participated in battles in Central Europe, Ardennes and Rhineland.

His memorable experiences include V.E. Day in London, first plane back from Europe, playing baseball, football and basketball at Sioux Falls, many fine friends and being with best crew in England.

He was awarded the Air Medal with one Oak Leaf Cluster, EAME Theatre with three Battle Stars, American Theatre Campaign Medal and Good Conduct Medal.

Married to Ruth and they have four children, Jamie, Nancy, Jim and Barbara. They also have nine grandchildren. Presently retired from construction - was a union carpenter and builder. Spends his winters at New Port Richey, FL.

CHARLES I. GRAVES, was born in Picayune, MS on Nov. 4, 1919. Enlisted in USAAC Aug. 20, 1941 at Camp Shelby, MS. Entered Keesler Aircorp Aircraft Technical School, Keesler AF Base Biloxi, MS 1941 and graduated March, 1942. Assigned to 93rd Bomb Group at Barksdale Field, moved to Ft. Meyers, FL Airbase, then they moved to Alconbury, England on Aug. 31, 1942. After few weeks, they moved to Hardwick Air Base for the duration. During this period promoted several times, finally to crew chief and a rating of tech. sergeant.

Received Bronze Star, two Presidential Group Citations, four European Campaign Stars, one African Theatre Campaign Award.

On leaving the military Aug. 31, 1945, joined Delta Airlines in October 1945 in operations. After serving in several departments, was promoted to station manager and served in this capacity for 28 years in Haiti, Ohio, Missouri and Indiana. Retired April 1, 1982 after 37 very enjoyable years.

Married to Jane Blake from Texas and a Delta Stewardess. Has five healthy children and two grandchildren. Today they live in Knoxville, TN. They travel a great deal, do some woodworking and since his wife is an artist she does enjoy her painting.

One of his most memorable experiences was in returning to their old airbase Hardwich, England this past March, 1993. This brought back many fond memories. Their Bomb Group, the 93rd, was also known as Ted's Flying Circus, was all B-24s. They had the honor of flying the most combat missions and the least losses of any group in the Mighty 8th AF.

GERALD GILBERT GRAY, was born March 3, 1919 in Vida, MT, enlisted December 1941, in USAAC after graduating from Concordia College in Moorhead, MN. As a second lieutenant he was assigned as bombardier to a B-24 D, 328th Bomb Sqdn., 93rd Bomb Group. Arrived in Alconbury, England Sept. 10, 1942.

As bombardier on "Double Trouble" flew 19 operational missions from Alconbury and from Libya, North Africa, before being shot down over Sousse, Tunisia on Jan. 19, 1943. Survived duration of war as prisoner, mostly in Stalag Luft III. Liberated in Moosburg, Germany in Spring, 1945. Final rank of first lieutenant. Died Jan. 30, 1978 in Portland, OR.

S.T. GRAY JR., was born Sept. 28, 1916 in Agnes, MS and was reared in New Augusta, MS. Married Trudie Mae Ainsworth of Bay Springs, MS on July 14, 1940. They have one son and four grandchildren.

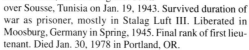

He volunteered for Flying Cadet Program and was sworn into the Army of U.S. on Aug. 19, 1942 at Camp Shelby, MS. Was called to active duty in March, 1943, and graduated from twin-engine pilot training and commissioned second lieutenant in the Class of 44-A at Pampa, TX. He completed B-24 transition at Liberal, KS and with his crew training in June, 1944, at Peterson Field, Colorado Springs, CO.

The crew rode the *Queen Elizabeth* to England and arrived at the 467th Bomb Group (H) as replacement, and assigned to 790th Sqdn. His first mission was July 31, 1944 and last (35) on Dec. 10, 1944. The WITCHCRAFT, (famous for holding record of 130 missions without aborting), was flown on majority of missions. Received Air Medal with five Oak Leaf Clusters and other usual medals.

His most memorable experience was a very near miss of a mid-air collision during assembly. The maneuver performed to avoid other planes was so violent that a bomb was shaken loose and knocked a bomb bay door off. The mission was completed.

On returning to the United States was assigned to a detachment of Proving Ground Command at Huntsville Arsenal, AL. There he flew the B-26, B-25, B-17, A-20 and AT-11, drop testing bombs until released from active duty Dec. 1, 1945.

Retired as postmaster at New Augusta, MS August 1983.

DAVID A. GREENE, was born July 4, 1922 in New York City, moved to southern New Jersey at age one. He saw his first up-close aircraft, a seaplane, at age three, when it landed on the Delaware River just off the beach at Penns Grove, NJ and taxied over to a local dock next to Dave's house. This one seemingly minor experience was the trigger mechanism between David and the flying machine.

At age seven Dave's family relocated in Brighton Beach, Brooklyn, NY. Dave finished at Abraham Lincoln High School and in September, 1941, started his first year at New York University (for engineering of course) but then came Pearl Harbor and all that was on his mind was how soon could he get into the USAAC and fly.

On Sept. 30, 1942, he was sworn into the USAAC Reserves as an Aviation Cadet candidate. On Jan. 1, 1943, Dave was sent to Miami Beach, FL for basic training. One month later he was shipped to Jamestown, ND, a college training detachment.

Three months later Dave was undergoing tests at the Santa Ana Classification Center in California; from there to Thunderbird Field in Scottsdale, AZ, for primary pilot training and after 26 hours of take-offs, landings, solo-rides, stalls and recovery, S-turns and mild acrobatics, he was suddenly ordered to report to Hondo Air Base, for advanced navigation training.

He graduated from Hondo Navigation School on March 18, 1943 and three days later reported in at Biggs Field, El Paso, TX where he began indoctrination into the B-24 Liberator combat training program.

On April 30, 1943, Dave and his crew, headed by their pilot Norby Wick, went to Topeka, KS, picked up their brand-new B-24J, and ten days later they took off to join the 8th Air Force in England. Their air route was from Topeka to Bangor, ME; to Goose Bay, Labrador; then over the North Atlantic to Keflavik, Iceland. Following a two-day weather delay, they took-off for Northern Ireland. After reaching Northern Ireland the crew remained there for several weeks of special training in combat navigation, combat operations and modification changes to their B-24, the crew eventually went on to Wendling, (East Anglia, England) the home base of the 392nd Bomb Group, (Heavy) joining the group on June 1, 1944.

Dave flew 30 combat missions with the last one on Jan. 7, 1945. On Nov. 4, 1944 his aircraft was hit by heavy concentrations of flak during the bomb-run near Hanover, Germany, losing two outboard engines, but they continued the run and dropped their bombs. After the longest 60 minutes of his life, the plane made a forced, crash landing just outside of Reims, France. No one on board was seriously injured, however, the pilot sustained a shrapnel injury to his shinbone at the time of "bombs away".

Dave and his crew were able to get back to Wendling on the third day following the crash and he continued flying combat missions and completed his tour but the rest of his crew was sent back to the states.

He was released from active duty on Oct. 8, 1945 and returned to New York University, graduated, entered Brooklyn Law School and graduated in 1951.

He remained in the Air Force Reserves, as a week-end warrior, flying out of Floyd Bennett Field and later out of Mitchell Field, then McGuire AFB and finally flying with the 904th MAC Group out of Stewart Field in Newburgh, NY. It was there on Jan. 24, 1968 when his MAC group was activated by President Johnson. He and the 904th MAC Group were released from active duty on July 30, 1969 and he retired from the Reserve program as a lieutenant colonel on Oct. 1, 1971.

Awarded the Distinguished Flying Cross and the Air

Medal with five Oak Leaf Clusters. He is a certified master navigator and flight examiner and has accumulated over 6400 hours of military flying.

David married in 1950 and later divorced. That marriage produced three daughters and two grandchildren. In January, 1962, he met Renee and they married on June 24, 1962. They have a daughter, Andrea, and a son, Spencer. Andrea is a practicing lawyer in New York City, married and the mother of a baby boy. Spencer is awaiting admission to medical school. Renee is an active travel agent and Dave still goes into his office three days a week, which allows him to get to the golf courses two or three days a week. He is presently on the Board of Directors and is Secretary of the 392nd Bomb Group Memorial Association, Inc. He is also on the Board of Directors for the New York, Southern Wing Chapter of the Eighth Air Force Historical Society and a member of the 2nd Air Division Association.

WILLIAM GREER, was born Oct. 18, 1924. Joined USAAC March 2, 1943. Flew 34 combat missions in Europe with 389th Bomb Group as armorer/gunner. Was wounded twice, once over Mainz, second time over Hannover, their 13th and roughest mission. Mr. Cpiptic notes say "flak was intense and extremely accurate, they sustained over 160 hits, B-24 on right wing received direct hit on bomb run - no shoots, Nov. 14, 1944". Plane was "Lucky Lady". They survived missions with severe flak damage, near mid-air collision with British bomber, engine failure on take off corrected while at tree top level, bombs dropped from group above them, and horrible weather.

Discharged in 1945. Graduated from New York University 1950. Married Edith Poppe Feb. 5, 1950. They have three sons, one daughter, and five grandchildren. Had a career in personnel management which included overseas travel. Ironically spent considerable time at a former target, Frankfurt, Germany. Retired from Richardson Vicks, division of Procter and Gamble, as director personnel administration, December 1986.

G. GREGORY (JEFF), was born Aug. 24, 1923 in Providence, RI. Raised in Deep River, CT. Joined the USAAC in February 1942, served as a private radio operator on anti-sub patrol off the East Coast of U.S. Entered Aviation Cadet Training and was commissioned second lieutenant Bombardier, Class 44-2 in February 1944. Served in the 467th Bomb Group, Rackheath, England. Flew 35 missions and returned to the states and was discharged September 1945 with the rank of first lieutenant (captain in AF Reserve).

Awarded the Air Medal with seven clusters.

Entered University of Pennsylvania Wharton School, graduated 1948, BS Economics. Recalled to active duty during Korean War. Discharged, entered sales work. Started own business in 1973. Sold business and retired in 1986. Lives in Garland, TX. Married Nov. 26, 1949 to Teresa Dillenscheider. They have one son and two grandchildren.

WILFRID E. GRENIER (BILL), was born in Biddeford, ME on May 17, 1925. He enlisted in the Air Cadets, USAAC on Aug. 9, 1943. Basic at Keesler Field, studied at University of Alabama, gunnery at Harlingen, TX and Mt. Home, ID, assigned to 565th Bomb Sqdn., 389th Bomb Group, Fitzgerald Crew, Hethel, England. Participated in battles in Ardennes, Rhineland, Central Europe and air combat Balkans. Discharged Oct. 25, 1945 with the rank of staff sergeant.

Awarded the EAME with four stars and the Air Medal with four clusters.

Married Doris Garon on Oct. 14, 1946 and they have five children and four grandchildren. Retired from Maremont Corp. after 39 years as industrial engineer and I.E. manager.

ROBERT GRIES, was born in Newark, NJ on Aug. 14, 1921. He enlisted in the USAAF on May 15, 1942 and served as navigator with 8th A.F., 2nd Air Div., 392nd Bomb Group, 577th Sqdn.

Stationed at Fort Dix, NJ; Sheppard Field, TX; and Selman Field Monroe, LA (class 43-5). Participated in the air battle of Britain. Discharged in September 1945 with the rank of first lieutenant.

His memorable experiences include first day raid on

Berlin; crash landing in England; longest 8th A.F. raid Gdynia Danzig.

Awarded the Air Medal with four Oak Leaf Clusters, Distinguished Flying Cross, Presidential Unit Citation and ETO Ribbon with one Battle Star.

Married and has three children and four grandchildren. Presently retired.

RICHARD E. GRIFFIN, was born in Rochester, NY on July 5, 1921. Served with 578th Bomb Sqdn. November 1944-June 1945. Co-pilot Bill Case crew, 26 combat missions.

After the war, back to school at University of Southern California. Graduated 1949. Remained active in the reserves - re-called to active duty in February 1951 at Norton AFB. Assigned to the Air Reserve activities in Japan and Korea for two and one-half years 1953-55. Five years with Continental Air Command, training reserves and National Guard. Five years Air Force Plant Representative operations at Northrop and North American Hq. Air Force Systems Command (1965-70) with time out for a full tour in Vietnam with the 460th Tactical Recon. Wing, 103 combat missions.

Commander, Defense Contract Admin. Services from 1971-75. Retired in November 1975. Eight years Director of Quality Assurance at a large aerospace firm.

Awarded the Legion of Merit, Distinguished Flying Cross, Air Medal with eight Oak Leaf Clusters, Bronze Star, Air Force Commendation Medal and numerous Theater Ribbons and Citations.

Married Shirley Jean on June 14, 1946. They have one daughter and two grandchildren. Presently retired.

BEN E. GRIMM, was born Sept. 27, 1924 and grew up in Rutherford, NJ. Joined the USAAC Oct. 17, 1942, and graduated Radio School, Scott Field, IL, and Gunnery School, Laredo, TX. Joined the 700th Bomb Sqdn., 445th Bomb Group at Sioux City, IA. Phase training at Sioux City and Mitchell, SD. Radio operator with crew #9 (Lt. H.M. Planka). Landed in England Thanksgiving Day 1943. Stationed at Tibenham, Norfolk. Flew combat tour (29 missions) December 1943-April 1944. Assigned as an instructor England and North Ireland; rotated back to Central Instructor School, Laredo, then taught Aerial Gunnery at AAB Yuma, AZ and Tyndall Field, FL, until discharge as tech. sergeant Oct. 10, 1945.

Awarded the Distinguished Flying Cross, Air Medal with three Oak Leaf Clusters, and two European Campaign Stars.

He earned his B.A. (English) at Washington & Lee University, Lexington, VA, and his M.S. (Library Science) at Columbia University, New York. Married Jean Bohrer in 1950; four children. Pursued his career as a public librarian and library consultant, retiring in 1986 as Director of the Jersey City Public Library system.

Married Lucy Ann Taylor in 1989. Together the couple has seven children and six grandchildren (so far). They retired to Virginia in February of 1991 where they now thrive.

RICHARD J. GRIMM (PETE), was born in Newark, NJ on Jan. 8, 1921. Entered the USAAC July 7, 1942 as an

aviation cadet unassigned. Graduated from Midland, TX in class 43-17. Upon graduation was sent to Westover Field, MA to be assigned to a crew. There he met a high school friend, Tom Harrocks, and they managed to get on the same crew.

Sent to 44th Bomb Group, 2nd Air Div., 8th Air Force and flew 35 missions, completing tour on his birthday, Jan. 8, 1945.

Returned to states for further training for service against Japan. War over before this could be accomplished, so returned home after discharge, and married Harrocks' sister, Joan.

He has nine children and eighteen grandchildren. Life is much simpler today.

ROY H. GRIMM, was born on Dec. 8, 1922 in Oxford, NC. He entered the service in February 1943. Transferred from Signal Corp. to Air Corp Radio Op. Gunner. Gunnery School, Laredo, TX. Served with 392nd Bomb Group, 578th Sqdn. in Wendling, England. Discharged on July 13, 1945 with the rank of staff sergeant.

His memorable experiences include flying 30 missions from July 31, 1944 to April 7, 1945. Sailed from England V.E. Day May 8, 1945.

Awarded the Air Medal with four clusters.

Married in 1951 to Virginia Hinson and has three children and three grandchildren.

Retired in 1981 from the construction industry. Now pursuing hobbies of gardening and woodturning.

TRUMAN L. GRISWOLD, was born in Lebanon, OH on Oct. 31, 1923. Enlisted in the Army Air Force Nov. 16, 1942. Served with the U.S. Air Force, 445th Bomb Group, 3rd Air Reserve Sqdn., 453rd Transport Wing. Stationed in Tibenham England, Misana AB Japan and Clark AB Philippines. Participated in WWII, Korean War and Vietnam War. Discharged on Feb. 1, 1977 with the rank of lieutenant colonel.

Memorable experiences include being only member of original 445th crew to complete combat tour.

Awarded Air Medal, Commendation Medal and Distinguished Flying Cross.

Married to Jeanne and they have two children. Presently retired.

GENE R. GROLL, was born June 13, 1924 in Toledo, OH. Enlisted in the USAAC Nov. 30, 1942. Attended Aircraft Gunnery School at Buckley Field, CO and Tyndall Field, FL. Was assigned to his crew in September 1943 at Tonopah, NV. He was a nose gunner on a new B-24 called "Wurf' Less". Went overseas with their plane and was the start of Group 458 stationed at Horsham St. Faith. He flew 10 missions on "Wurf' Less" and 22 missions on "Gas House Mouse". They flew four missions on D-day.

He received the Distinguished Flying Cross and the Air Medal with three Oak Leaf Clusters.

Attended Ohio State University. Married his wife in 1947. They have five children, nine grandchildren and one great-grandchild. He retired in 1986 as fire chief from the Oregon Fire Dept. They presently live in Florida in the winter and travel and fish the rest of the year.

WILLIAM L. GROS, was born in Springfield Center, NY on May 8, 1923. Married to Benetta F. Gaskin on Oct. 24, 1947. Has two daughters and four grandchildren.

Enlisted in the USAAC Sept. 23, 1941. Attended AF

Tech. School at Scott Field, IL graduating April 4, 1942. Assigned to 328th Bomb Sqdn., 93rd Bomb Group as a radio operator. Took part in anti-sub patrols during the summer until group assigned to 8th AF. As a crew member of "Eager Beaver", joined in the first squadron formation crossing of the North Atlantic in September. Entered combat on Nov. 9, 1942 and completed 31 missions from bases in the UK, Northern Africa and Libya. Returned to the U.S. in September 1943 and served as an instructor until war's end at Langley, Davis Monthan and Alamogordo. Was head of Communications Flight Training at the latter. Discharged Sept. 21, 1945.

Continued interest in aviation led to private pilot's license. Retired from electronic sales and service business in 1985.

CARL W. GROSHELL, was born on April 15, 1923 in Richmond, CA. Enlisted in the Army Air Force on Jan. 18, 1943. Stationed at Keesler Field, Lowry Field, Pueblo, Blythe and Tucson. Discharged on Oct. 24, 1945 with the rank of staff sergeant.

His memorable experiences include being shot down and captured on Nov. 26, 1944 in Misburg, Germany.

Awarded the Air Medal with three Oak Leaf Clusters. Presently retired.

SEYMOUR T. GROSSMAN, was born in Chicago, IL. Enlisted in the USAAC on Dec. 11, 1942 and served as clerk typist with 700th Bomb Sqdn., 445th Bomb Group. Stationed in Tibenham England, Keesler Field, OK, Wendover Field, Sioux City, Mitchell, SD. Participated in battle of Piccadilly. Discharged on Oct. 17, 1945 with the rank of corporal.

His memorable experiences include plane flight to England and liberty ship return to U.S.A.

Awarded the Good Conduct Medal and ETO.

Seymour is single and is presently a steel broker.

JOSEPH I. GROSSO, was born in Brooklyn, NY, Jan. 27, 1922. At 19 he moved to Coventry, CT where he still resides. At 21 he entered the AAF and attended Radio School at Scott Field, IL, and gunnery at Harlingen, TX. Phase training followed at Gowen Field, Boise, ID. Upon completion they ferried a B-24 from Grenier Field, NH to Cluntoe, Ireland - arriving June 1943. Assigned to the 389th Bomb Group, Hethel, England. He crashed on take off on his first mission, with full bomb load, and went down in France on his last. Completing 34 missions, he returned stateside flying radioman on C47s. He was discharged Oct. 25, 1945 as a technical sergeant.

He received the Distinguished Flying Cross, Air Medal with three Bronze Clusters, European Theatre Ribbon with three Campaign Stars, Presidential Unit Citation and other decorations.

Joe is presently a retired utility company marketing manager.

FERDINAND J. GUIDA (FRED), was born in Philadelphia, PA on July 13, 1924. He enlisted in the U.S. Air Force (8th) in May 1943 and served with the 458th Bomb Group at Horsham St. Faith and Norwich England. Graduate of Selman Field Navigation School, Monroe, LA in 1944. Flew 22 missions (from November 1944 to final one in May 1945). Discharged in November 1945 with the rank of first lieutenant lead navigator.

Awarded the Air Medal and European with Oak Leaf Clusters.

His father, Antonio, served in WWI and his brother, Louis, was killed off Okinawa April 1945, U.S. Navy, WWII. Presently semi-retired investment advisor plus musical show creator.

KENNETH L. GULLEKSON, was born Feb. 4, 1923 in a logging camp near Mesick, MI. Graduated from Mesick High School in 1941. He worked a short time at the Willow Run Bomber Plant building B-24s, before joining the USAAC in January 1943. Took basic training at Miami Beach. After graduating from Mechanics School at Sheppard Field, TX was sent to Tyndall Field, FL for Gunnery School. Was assigned to a crew at Salt Lake City, then went for crew training at Casper, WY. Was assigned a plane at Lincoln, NE.

Departed the states from Manchester, NH for England via Labrador and Greenland.

Was assigned to the 489th at Halesworth. Flew 35 missions as tail gunner, receiving the Air Medal with three Oak Leaf Clusters and the Distinguished Flying Cross. Returning to the states in December 1944, then assigned to Chanute Field, IL. Discharged September 1945.

Retired 1990 from the Detroit Public Library. Has four children, divides time between Cadillac, MI and Kansas City, FL. His wife's name is Mary.

PETER M. GUNNAR, was born in London, England, March 12, 1924. Educated at Phillips Exeter and University of Chicago, before called to service as an Aviation Cadet. After basic and flight training, graduated in Bombardier class 43-11 from Big Spring AAF. Assigned to 453rd Bomb Group (H) at Gowen Field, with later training at Pocatello and March Field. Went with original group to Old Buckingham, Norfolk. Later trained as navigator and completed a 32 mission tour in September 1944. Awarded a Distinguished Flying Cross and Air Medal and five Oak Leaf Clusters. After return to the States, volunteered for a second tour in B-29s and after training was discharged not long after V-E day.

Graduated from University of Chicago and Willamette University Law School and admitted to the Bar in 1950. Spent working career as a lawyer, judge, businessman, party politician, and author. Married Edith Fairham in 1949 and has three grown children.

JAMES T. GUNNELL, was born on June 12, 1919 in Detroit, MI. Enlisted in the USAF on June 22, 1942 and served as first lieutenant navigator with 8th AF, 2nd Air Div., 453rd Bomb Group, 732nd Bomb Sqdn. Finished cadet training at Selman Field, Monroe, LA; served overseas at Old Buck; with last station ATC Nashville, TN. Discharged on Nov. 30, 1945 with the rank of first lieutenant.

Participated in battles in Normandy, Northern France, Ardennes, Rhineland and Air Offense Europe.

His memorable experiences include being ditched on return from Munich July 11, 1944; crash landing at Ipswich; and crashing on December 1944 on return from Battle of the Bulge.

Awarded the Air Medal with three clusters, Purple Heart and three Battle Stars.

Married Lucille and they have one daughter, Jean and two sons, George and James. Retired from General Motors and lives in northern Michigan.

STANLEY GUTERMAN, was born on Sept. 4, 1922 in New York City. He enlisted in the USAAC in October 1942. Branch of Military, classifications: United States - Major Commands, training command, material command. Pacific, European, NE Air command, SAC and ADE. Overseas in England, Okinawa, Thule, Greenland, France and Puerto Rico. Discharged in October 1964 with rank of lieutenant colonel. Flew 4400 hours as master navigator.

As a navigator flew in B-24s, RB50s, C124s as well as AT-6, C-47, B-25s until retirement. Between wars and flying assignments served as a refueling officer, food service officer, commissary officer, club officer, retiring as director of material at Hancock Field, Syracuse, NY (1964). As a civilian he worked for U.S. Army and U.S. Air Force HQ giving worldwide assistance in services area. Retired in February 1984 from A.F. civil service as GS-13 chief of Air Force Food Service operations branch.

He has two grown daughters, Susan Dursant and Sandra Nissen.

Married to Barbara McKee of Atlantic City, NJ and is presently enjoying retirement at the blue-green waters and sea breezes at Panama City, FL.

EBODIO T. GUTIERREZ, was born ca 1923. Top gunner on Joseph Bell's crew (see J. Bell). Lived in Chicago, IL, believe he stayed there, married and has children.

EARL J. GUY JR., was born in Oak Park, IL on March 6, 1921. Enlisted in December 1942 at Fort Sheridan, IL with USAAF: A/C Boca Raton, FL; A/C Yale University, Connecticut; Kelly Field, TX; Shipdham England, 44th Bomb Group, 66th Bomb Sqdn. Discharged in August 1945 with rank of first lieutenant, 44th Bomb Group, 66th Bomb Sqdn.

Memorable experiences include flying several missions as a paddlefoot just to experience what the crews had to endure. His job was air sea rescue and flying equipment supply. His roommates were the best in the Army.

Married to Nancy T. Guy and has one son, Earl J. Guy III and one daughter, Sarah R. Newport. Retired chemical engineer with AT&T.

ROY E. GUY, was born Jan. 8, 1924 in San Diego, CA. Worked on B-24s in 1942 and entered the service in 1943. He graduated from pilot training and completed B-24 training in mid 1944. He was assigned to the 787th Bomb Sqdn., 466th Bomb Group, Attlebridge, England where he flew 14 combat missions.

He was shot down twice; the first time he parachuted from his severely damaged B-24 over England, the second time on Sept. 8, 1944 he crash landed near Metz, France and was captured. He was a POW in Stalag Luft I, Barth, Germany for the duration.

In 1947 he received a regular commission. Command and staff assignments included: air transport, atomic energy, education, Escape and Evasion/POW matters, personnel, maintenance, B-47 Squadron Commander, Assistant Air Attache, Thailand, Group Commander and Base Commander, Space and Missiles Systems Organization. Retired in 1972 after 30 years.

JAMES T. GWALTNEY (TWEET), was born in Surry County, VA on April 13, 1917. Entered the USAAC at Camp Lee, VA on April 7, 1942. Received aircraft and engine training at Keesler Air Base, MS and Lockheed Factory School, California. While training on B-17s at Gowan Field, ID he was transitioned to B-24s. There the 448th Bomb Group was activated and he was assigned to the 713th Bomb Sqdn. Following additional training he arrived at Seething, England November 1943 using the southern route from West Palm Beach, FL. Served as crew chief on "Fascinatin Lady" and other B-24s including the checked board.

After the war he returned with the 448th Bomb Group to the states through the Azores to El Paso, TX. Re-trained on B-29s for Pacific duty - Japan surrendered. Following discharge in September 1945 with the rank of master sergeant he first joined the Virginia Air Guard and second the USAF Reserve. Recalled for Korea in September 1950 and discharged in August 1952.

Remained in USAF Reserve and retired in 1977 USAF.

FRANK GYIDIK, was born on Nov. 18, 1919 in Binghamton, NY. Enlisted Jan. 7, 1942. Sent to Keesler Field, MS for basic training, and after basic sent to Newark, NJ to

Casey Jones School of Aeronautics. After completion of this course in Aviation Maintenance he was assigned to 63rd Fighter Sqdn. of the 56th Fighter Group at Mitchel Field on Long Island. The 63rd Sqdn. was sent to Bridgeport Airport, CT for further training. At this time he was assigned a crew chief on P-47 Thunderbolts until the end of the war.

Then the 56th Fighter Group embarked on Jan. 6, 1943 and arrived in England Jan. 11, 1943.

The bases in England were: RAF Base Wittering near Peterborough, then to Horsham St. Faith, Norwich, next to Halesworth and then to Boxted Base near Colchester.

Awards and medals received include Distinguished Unit Badge, Presidential Unit Citation with two Bronze Stars, European Theater with two Battle Stars and others such as WWII Victory and American Theater. He was discharged on Oct. 1, 1945 with rank of staff sergeant.

He married Althea Coats July 26, 1947. They have three children and three grandchildren.

After the war he resumed his flying (he was a pilot before the war) and has a commercial pilot certificate with the following ratings: Single Engine Land; Multi Engine Land and Multi Engine Sea.

He has an Amateur Radio License, call letters K2CWD. He is now retired from IBM Corporation, Endicott, NY and doing his hobbies - flying and amateur radio operating.

RICHARD H. HACKETT, was born Dec. 27, 1922 in New York City. Enlisted in the USAAC Nov. 16, 1942. Received his basic training in Miami. Was sent to Radio School at Truex Field, WI. From there to Gunnery School at Kingman, AZ. Crew make-up and training was completed in Casper, WY and Scottsbluff, NE. They picked up their B-24 in Herington, KS, on to West Palm Beach, FL and over the southern route to England.

Their first stop was Puerto Rico. He doesn't believe any of them ever heard of it before or knew exactly where it was. Little did he know that some years later he would end up living and working there. When they arrived in England their plane was taken away from them, after they had the nose painted "Ambling Okie". Pilot was from Oklahoma. They were assigned to the 93rd Bomb Group, 409th Sqdn. Completed 30 missions on May 11, 1944.

Awarded the Distinguished Flying Cross and the Air Medal with three clusters.

Returned to the states and assigned as an instructor on B-17s. Discharged with the rank of tech. sergeant on Oct. 26, 1945.

Married Elizabeth Markey from Charlotte, NC Sept. 2, 1948 and they have one daughter. Retired from Eastern Air Lines in 1986 and now lives in Warren, RI.

DANIEL HACKU, was born on March 9, 1925 in Wallingford, CT. He was inducted into the service in July 1943 and served with the USAAC. Stationed at Sioux Falls AAB, Horsham St. Faith and Savannah AAB. Daniel was discharged in September 1945 with the rank of staff sergeant.

He was awarded the Air Medal.

He is married and has two sons. Daniel is presently retired.

JOSEPH W. HAENN, was born in Philadelphia, PA in 1917. He was inducted into the USAAF on Feb. 4, 1943 and served with the 747th Aircraft as engine mechanic 467th Bomb Group. Stationed at Miami Beach, FL for basic training. Also stationed at DMAFB Tucson, AZ; Wendover, UT; and Rackheath England. Discharged on Oct. 11, 1945 with the rank of staff sergeant.

Participated in battles at Ardennes, Rhineland, Central Europe, Air Offensive Europe, Normandy, and Northern France.

His memorable experiences include the German night raid on Rackheath Airfield.

Awarded the Carbine Silver Star.

Married in 1942 and has one son and one daughter. Retired and lives with wife, Florence, in Florida. Active in VFW and volunteer work.

ARDIE HAGOPIAN, was born Nov. 5, 1925 in San Francisco, CA. Enlisted in the USAAC in January 1944 after graduating from high school. Was stationed in Amarillo, TX, then in Harlingen, TX for Aerial Gunnery School. He crewed-up in Casper, WY as a nose gunner on B-24s.

In February 1945 he left New York City on the *Ile de France* for Norwich, England where he was stationed with the 8th Air Force, 93rd Bomb Group. His crew flew 13 missions over Germany, and as they were preparing for the 14th mission - news came that the war was over.

Awarded the American Theater Ribbon, EAME Theater Ribbon with three Bronze Stars, Good Conduct Medal, Air Medal with one Bronze Cluster and the Victory Medal.

Upon returning from Europe he married Virginia (Jean) Lloyd and had four children and twelve grandchildren. He was a building contractor specializing in custom home construction. Enjoyed his work, gold mining and his grandchildren. Ardie Hagopian died Feb. 22, 1993.

HAROLD A. HAGOPIAN, was born on June 14, 1924 in Providence, RI. He joined the Air Force on March 9, 1943. Upon completion of Radio and Gunnery School, he was assigned to a B-24 liberator group for combat training in California before leaving for England in March of 1944. He completed 30 missions over Europe from Wendling with the 392nd Bomb Group with an unlimited number of missions during the 'D' Day campaign.

He was awarded the Air Medal with a Silver and one Oak Leaf Cluster.

He returned to the USA in April of 1944 and was assigned as a flight communication instructor until his discharge on Oct. 11, 1945. He joined the Air Force Reserve until his discharge in 1952.

He graduated from the University of Rhode Island with a BSEE followed by graduate work in Theoretical Physics and Guided Missile Instrumentation. He joined IBM Corporation in 1952 and served in various management assignments until his retirement in 1992 as a telecommunication consultant. Upon retiring, he started the Advanced Publishing Solution Company to market desktop publishing solutions as an IBM business partner.

He is married to Elizabeth Ann Jarvie and has three sons, Gregory, Creighton, and Richard and four granddaughters.

ROGER R. HAHN (BUZZY), was born June 3, 1924 at Eau Claire, WI. Enlisted in the USAAC after graduation from high school, June 1942. Took basic training at Atlantic City, NJ. Sent to Lowry Field, Denver, CO to Armament School - sent to Harlingen, TX for Gunnery School. Sent to Casper - WY and joined the rest of the crew.

They trained together as a crew and left Palm Beach, FL and traveled to England the southern route to South America, to Africa and then to England. They were assigned to the 734th Bomb Sqdn., 453rd Bomb Group, Station 144 Old Buckingham. Their ship was named *Diana-Mite*. Their crew finished 33 missions and returned to the States November 1944.

He was discharged 1945 and enlisted in the Air Corps

Reserve. He entered the field of law enforcement, married and settled in Augusta, WI and raised four children and has eight grandchildren. Recalled for the Korean War - July 1950. Sent to Travis Air Force Base, CA and assigned to an Air Police Investigation Unit. Discharged November 1951.

Retired from public service in 1985 with the rank of captain.

Returned to England in 1990 for reunion. Visited their old base, "Old Buck". Brought back the fondest of memories.

FREDRICK J. HAHNER, was born Oct. 30, 1920 in Jersey City, NJ. Enlisted in the Aviation Cadet program of the USAAC in October 1942.

Graduated as a second lieutenant pilot in April 1944 from the Columbus, MS Advanced Flying Training School.

Completed B-24 transition training at Maxwell Field, Montgomery, AL as an airplane commander.

Eventually in 1944 assigned to the European Theatre of Operations, 8th Air Force, 2nd Air Div., 2nd Wing, 448th Bomb Group, 715th Sqdn. based at Seething, England.

Flew 25 missions over Nazi occupied Europe and was awarded five Air Medals.

Discharged from the U.S. Air Force Reserve in September 1957.

Married to Mary Hynes Nov. 8, 1941. Has five children and seven grandchildren. Was employed by the Jersey City, NJ Police Dept. for 33 years. Retired as a deputy chief and served as police director for three years. Retired to Bradenton, FL in 1980.

WILLIAM E. HAILEY, was born in Houston, TX, on Sept. 30, 1922. Enlisted in Reserve and was called to duty on Feb. 17, 1943. Graduated in May, 1944, Frederick, OK, as second lieutenant pilot. Flew B-24s for 25 missions out of 453rd Bomb Group and 1 mission out of 466th Bomb Group, mostly as co-pilot and some as first pilot. Discharged in 1945 and returned to Baylor University, Waco, TX.

Captained 1946 Southwest Conference Championship basketball team at Baylor. Graduated in 1947 with Bachelor of Arts degree and in 1949 as Juris Doctor. Practiced law in San Antonio, TX, since 1949.

Married Eleanor Mansfield on June 24, 1951, and still happily married to her. Two sons, Mike Hailey, a writer, and Joel Hailey who practices law with his father. Deacon in Trinity Baptist Church, San Antonio, TX, since 1959. Resides at Lake Placid, TX, and at Angel Fire, NM.

GEORGE V. HALAPY, was born in Finleyville, PA on June 28, 1920. Inducted into the Army Air Force in July 1942 and served with the 93rd Bomb Group, 8th Air Force. Stationed at Biloxi, MS; Sioux Falls; Harlingen, TX; El Paso; Tucson; Scott Field; England and Africa. Participated in Air Offensive in Europe and Air Offensive in Italy. Discharged in September 1945 with the rank of staff sergeant.

Memorable experiences include D Day over France, terrible flak on 30th mission and getting off the ship in Boston.

Awarded the Distinguished Flying Cross and the Air Medal with three clusters.

Married and lives in Gibsonia, PA. Semi-retired as a meat cutter.

ALBERT P. HALL, was born on Sept. 23, 1921 in Boston. Enlisted June 1942 into the Air Force. Graduated Gunnery School at Tyndall Field. Assigned B-25s and trained for

Doolittle Tokyo Raid. Assigned pilot training. Assigned radio training and graduated. Assigned B-24 Combat Crew at Wendover Field. Assigned 489th Bomb Group and sent to Halesworth England with the 8th Air Force. Flew 25 combat missions over Germany. Shot down on last mission and managed to make it to Switzerland on two engines with no fuel left. Badly damaged. Escaped through French Underground and returned to group. Returned to the U.S. and assigned as gunnery instructor in Texas. Discharged September 1945 with the rank of tech. sergeant.

Awarded the Distinguished Flying Cross, five Air Medals, plus others.

Salesman for Westinghouse for 40 years and retired in 1984. He has one son and one granddaughter.

Considers it a privilege and honor to have served with the 8th Air Force. Among the most magnificent men he will ever know. God rest their dedicated and courageous souls. Because of their heroic sacrifice we are free to live in this glorious land.

EARL A. HALL, was born on Oct. 22, 1923 in Augusta, WI. Enlisted in the Army Air Force on Nov. 25, 1942 and stationed at Sioux Falls, SD; Harlingen, TX; and Wendling England. Discharged on Oct. 2, 1945 with the rank of staff sergeant.

Memorable experiences include 28 missions over Germany as ball turret gunner on Shaufhausen Switzerland bombing raid April 1, 1944.

Awarded the Distinguished Flying Cross, Air Medal with three clusters and 392nd Presidential Citation.

Married fifty years and has three sons, one daughter and six grandchildren. Worked for a tire company in Eau Claire, WI for 36 years as a tire builder. Retired in 1981 and now works part time for a station, pumping gas.

HAROLD B. HALL (BY), was born June 6, 1922 in Portage, UT. Joined the Aviation Cadet Program in August 1942 and completed bombardier training at Roswell, NM, class 43-12, August 1943. Completed 30 missions with the 458th Bomb Group, Horsham St. Faith, England on June 2, 1944, and returned to the U.S. in July 1944.

Completed pilot training and received pilots wings with class 45-E. Aloe AAF, Victoria, TX in August 1945. Assigned to the 502nd Tactical Group in Korea, January 1952 and returned to the U.S. January 1953. Subsequent assignments with the Directorate of Flight and all weather testing, Wright Patterson AFB; detached service with the Federal Aviation Agency, Washington, D.C.; Air Proving Ground command, Eglin AFB; and Headquarters Air Force Systems Command, Andrews AFB. Retired from Hq. USAF, Pentagon, July 1973.

Married Hazel Jennaway July 28, 1951. Has three daughters and four grandchildren.

As a member of a great crew, and as part of a huge armada of the 8th AF, for as far as one could see, combat missions over Germany, including six over and around Berlin, was a tremendous and often hair raising experience.

ALLAN P. HALLETT, was born April 22, 1926 in Clinton, MA. Entered service May, 1944 at Fort Devens, MA where he resided, as his father was civilian employee of the Post Engineers. Basic training at Biloxi, MS; Gunnery School at Harlingen, TX; crew assembled at Lincoln, NE; and combat crew training at Casper, WY. Picked up new B-24J at Topeka, KS.

Left for England February 1945 via northern route. In Greenland a month, due to overcast weather and hurricane force winds that blew engine covers off and put sand into engine intake ducts. When ready to leave, only two planes got off that day, and they were first. Was assigned to the 389th Bomb Group at Hethel. Flew just three combat missions before war ended. Returned to the States May, 1945. Served another year, discharged May, 1946 at Fort Devens, MA with rank of staff sergeant.

Employed by local paper manufacturing company for 36 years. Retired in 1988 as chief electrician. Married and has two children and three grandchildren.

HOWARD G. HALLGARTH, was born June 15, 1921. Married Hermina Helmich and has two sons, one daughter and five grandchildren. Joined Army Air Force and became a B-24 pilot. Assigned to 93rd Bomb Group, 409th Sqdn. in England. Flew 24 missions over Germany and returned home after Germany surrendered. Took reserve training and retired 1981 as a lieutenant colonel.

One of the memorable experiences was their first mission. He flew co-pilot with an experienced pilot (Frank Eiben). They went to Magdeburg Germany and Frank flew all the way until they reached the bomb run (I.P.). He was a tall fellow and he looked over to him and said (you got it Howie). Hallgarth was not use to flying co-pilot and looking across Frank to the lead plane and trying to stay in formation was difficult but kept his mind off the flak. Frank melted into the coffin seat with helmet and flak vest covering him. This was one of his last missions and he took extra precautions.

Awarded the Air Medal.

Retired - farming, apple orchard.

L. JACK HALLMAN, 8th A.F., 467th Bomb Group, 790th Sqdn., Crew 51, Rackheath England September 1944 to June 1945. Flew 32 missions as gunner on B-24 bomber.

Born July 1924, Lancaster, SC. Joined Air Force October 1943 at Shaw AFB Sumter, SC. Took basic training at Keesler Field, MS, Gunnery School at Laredo, TX. The crew had overseas training at Muroc AAF, Muroc, CA.

August 1944 sailed on *Ile de France* from New York to Liverpool England. At Rackheath flew first mission Nov. 9, 1944 and last mission April 25, 1945.

June 13, 1945 left ETO flying home to Azores Islands, 14th Gander Field Newfoundland, 15th Brunswick Naval Air Base, ME at 18:20 hours. Due to weather storm, command given... "Prepare to bail out." Plane carried 10 ground personnel as passengers. Many prayers were said, an opening in clouds appeared, revealing an airport. They landed safely. The base was built for two engine planes.

June 16, base had holiday to watch the combat, four engine, "Big Bird", take off for two hour flight to Bradley Field, CT. After three nights and 24:45 hours flying time, they celebrated and thanked God.

June to September enjoyed temporary duty at home. Discharged October 1945 at Greensboro AAF, NC.

Finished University of South Carolina in Civil Engineering in 1950. Married, reared four children. Retired, enjoying life in Charlotte, NC. Crew 51 continues to visit.

CHARLES R. HAM JR., was born Nov. 1, 1920 in Stuttgart, AR. He enlisted in the USAAC in August 1942 and served as pilot with 445th Bomb Group, 703rd Bomb Sqdn. at Tibenham England. Received cadet training on the West Coast. Discharged in September 1945 with the rank of captain.

Participated in European Theater Operation.

Memorable experiences include passes to London, seeing history, flying with his dog - Pippin.

Awarded the Air Medal with five clusters and the Distinguished Flying Cross.

Divorced and has two children. Retired - total disability.

JOHN D. HAMMER, was born Feb. 15, 1915 in Chicago, IL. Entered the USAAC on Dec. 31, 1940 in the 1st Flying Cadet Class for communications officers at Scott Field, IL. Sent to MacDill Field on May 15, 1941.

Received his commission on Aug. 15, 1941. Was assigned as group communications officer of the 44th Bomb Group. Served in this capacity for two and one-half years. The 44th Bomb Group was sent to England in 1942. They served at Shipdham in Norfolk. On temporary duty in 1943 with the 44th in North Africa at Oudna 1 near Tunis. Upon returning to the States in February 1943, served at Drew Field, Tampa as communications officer of the 89th Combat Crew Training Wing, and Barksdale Field as base communications officer. Was discharged as lieutenant colonel on Dec. 20, 1946.

Married on June 6, 1942 at Barksdale Field to Betty Brown of Christopher, IL. Has a daughter and two grandchildren.

STEPHEN T. HAMMOCK, was born April 19, 1921 in Cooledge, TX. Raised on a farm near Sudan, TX. Enlisted in Army Aviation Cadets Class 43-I. Eliminated while in Basic Flying School in a big pilot training cutback. Trained as a Radio Operator/Gunner. Flew 29 combat missions as radio operator/gunner on a B-24 in the 445th Bomb Group on Lt. Howard's crew.

Crashed Feb. 25, 1945 at Tibenham, England when returning from their 29th bombing mission. The #3 engine on fire was feathered and a full load of ten 1000 pound bombs still on board. As they came in for landing, the prop run away on #4 engine. Last thing he remembers was when the B-24 stalled.

In Army hospitals for two years, discharged as a disabled Veteran. Retired from U.S. Civil Service since 1981.

Awarded four Air Medals, two European Battle Stars and the Purple Heart.

GEORGE EARL HAMMOND, was born April 27, 1920 in Sayre, PA. He attended Pennsylvania State University for two years and on Jan. 21, 1942 he enlisted in the USAAC, and attended Bombardiers School at Victorville, CA, class of 42-11. George graduated a second lieutenant on Aug. 15, 1942.

His first station after graduation was Wendover, UT with the 382nd and GB (H), Army. S/N 0728273. On March 23, 1943, he was assigned as Group Bombardier of the 389th Bomb Group (B-24). In June of that year he accompanied that group to England and thence to Benghazi, North Africa where he participated in the Aug. 1, 1943 Low Level raid on the Ploesti Oil Refineries. He flew 29 combat missions over Europe, 17 of which were as lead bombardier.

He received the Distinguished Flying Cross with two Oak Leaf Clusters, Air Medals with five Oak Leaf Clusters, Unit Citations and the French War Cross and Star.

After discharge from the service, George attended Kansas State University. He worked at the Bendix Corp. in Kansas City, MO and retired in 1982 from Huck Manufacturing Company.

George and Marie Graham were married in September 1942. They have three children and seven grandchildren. The Hammonds reside on their farm in Kingsville, MO.

THERON D. HAMPTON, was born in Randle, WA Dec. 18, 1919. Family moved to Antioch, CA in 1923. Married Irene Beratto in November, 1942. Celebrated Golden Anniversary last year. Has daughter and son and two grandchildren.

Entered Army at Fort Ord, CA December, 1942. Went to St. Petersburg, FL for basic training; Chicago, IL for Aircraft Mechanic School; Detroit, MI for Engine School; Laredo, TX for Gunnery School; Tucson, AZ for first phase B-24 crew training; Wendover, UT for second phase. Flew B-24 to England as flight engineer in April, 1944 via South America and Africa to join 8th A.F. and 489th Bomb Group. Flew 32 combat missions; returned to U.S. in November, 1944. Was in Aviation Cadet training when war ended. Received discharge in October 1945 as tech. sergeant.

Awarded the Distinguished Flying Cross, Air Medal

with four Oak Leaf Clusters, and ETO Service Ribbon with three Battle Stars.

Recalled to active duty in Korean War, August, 1950. Flew 16 missions as B-29 gunner mechanic before crash landing. Returned to civilian life in August, 1951. Employed in aircraft industry until retirement in Santa Barbara, 1982.

EDWARD A. HANDY, was born Sept. 29, 1922 in Riverside, CT and enlisted in the USAAC April 13, 1942. After six months training and nine months aircraft mechanic work at Topeka AAB, volunteered for combat as aerial engineer-gunner on B-24. Sent to 8th AAF on Lt. Thaddeus Tedrowe's lead crew—the Luftwaffe's target-of-choice as the crew learned. Shot down en route to Hannover April 11, 1944. Sent to Stalag XVII-B where by coincidence, not heroism, became organizer and leader of tunnel-digging team (what **great** men **they** were) that eventually saved lives of five men in a four-day Gestapo search of the camp—the basis for play and movie "Stalag 17". After V-E day, was asked by Lt. Tedrowe to fly with him on an A-26 in Pacific Theater, but Hiroshima ended that.

Awarded the Air Medal, Purple Heart and European Theater Medal.

Went to MIT on GI Bill and became a city planner. Married Margaret Colaluca, first boss after going to work. Recently celebrated 41st wedding anniversary. One daughter, Jenifer.

THOMAS E. HANLEY III (IRISH), was born on May 5, 1925 in Chicago, IL. Inducted into the USAAC in June 1943 and served with the 458th Bomb Group, Horsham St. Faith England. Discharged in November 1945 with the rank of lieutenant.

Memorable experiences include navigating D.K. Williams' crew, lead crew 458th Bomb Group, squadron navigator, and 28 sorties.

Awarded the European Theater with clusters.

Married and has six sons, one of which is a lieutenant colonel USAF. Froze feet on mission in February 1945, double amputee. Volunteer help at VA hospital, Hines, IL.

RUSSELL J. HANSEN, was born July 7, 1922 at Hunter, ND. Enlisted in the USAAC Sept. 25, 1941 and was discharged Oct. 23, 1945 as tech. sergeant.

Attended Armament School at Lowry Field and was sent to help open Lubbock Army Air Field and South Plains Army Air Field. While there became an Aircraft Maintenance Technician and crewed planes used in training single, twin engine and transport glider pilots.

Was selected to attend Oklahoma A&M but after about one and one-half terms asked for combat duty and was sent to Gunnery School at Laredo. From there to Tonopah for air crew combat training and met the rest of Deany's Crew and became his engineer and top gunner.

They arrived at North Pickenham in late December 1944 and became part of the 853rd Sqdn. of the 491st Bombardment Group - "The Last and The Best". They flew three different planes - Hot Rock, Sweet Eloise and Going My Way?.

They flew 12 missions and was badly shot up over Rotterdam. Their radio operator was the only one wounded. Flak made a hole in the top turret between Hansen's left shoulder and ear on their second mission to Magdeburg on Feb. 15, 1945.

ROBERT HANSON, was born in Iron River, MI on May 25, 1924. Enlisted in the USAAF on Feb. 16, 1943 and served with the 466th Bomb Group, 784th Sqdn. - Ordnance Section. Basic in St. Petersburg, FL. Also stationed at Biggs Field, El Paso, TX; Alamogordo, NM and Salt Lake Air Base. Discharged Oct. 25, 1945 at Sioux City Air Base with the rank of sergeant.

Married on Sept. 20, 1945 and has five children. Retired in 1986 after 42 years as a mechanic and enjoys hunting, fishing and visiting his children.

ROBERT O. HANSON, was born Nov. 8, 1921 at York, WI. Entered service Sept. 9, 1942. Airplane Mechanics School, Keesler Field, MS. Consolidated B-24 Factory School San Diego, CA; Gunnery School, Harlingen, TX; sent to Gowen Field, Boise, ID and assigned to the original cadre of the 453rd Bomb Group as part of Model Crew #41 of the 734th Bomb Sqdn. as engineer gunner. Attended Army Air Force School of Applied Tactics at Pinecastle, FL. Phase training at Pocatello, ID and March Field, CA. Picked up new B-24 at Hamilton Field and flew southern route to Old Buckingham, England. Completed 32 missions and returned to the U.S. to spend limited time at several bases. Discharged Sept. 1, 1945. Achieved the rank of tech. sergeant.

Awarded the ETO Ribbon with three Battle Stars, Presidential Unit Citation, Air Medal with three clusters and the Distinguished Flying Cross.

Retired from Land O' Lakes Inc. after 43 years of service as controller of a division. Married April 24, 1942 to Mavis Hanson - two sons, one daughter, three grandchildren and three great-grandchildren.

Memorable experiences include the flight Southern Route to England. The March 6, 1944 mission to Berlin. The April 9, 1944 mission to Tutow where bad weather conditions caused a large number of aircraft to turn back. After extensive icing, they penetrated the front and joined a mixed formation to face heavy fighter attacks but completed the mission. According to the Mighty Eighth War Diary, only 106 out of 246 aircraft completed the mission with 14 aircraft lost. Also the June 6th D Day missions.

FRANK HANZALIK, was born on June 13, 1919 in Chicago, IL. Enlisted in the USAAF on Jan. 25, 1943 at Hondo, TX. Graduated as pilot, class 44-A Jan. 7, 1944. Primary at Sikeston, MO; basic at Coffeyville, KS; and advance at Pampa, TX. Discharged March 30, 1959 with the rank of captain.

Memorable experiences include 34 missions as co-pilot B-24, 453rd Bomb Group, 735th Bomb Sqdn. Forty missions (sorties) P-51 pilot, 359th Fighter Group, 368th Fighter Sqdn. Also remembers four of them flying P-51s, buzzing cows in East Anglia, and almost getting clobbered by high tension wires.

Awarded the Air Medal with seven clusters and Distinguished Flying Cross.

Married June 8, 1946 and has one son and three daughters. Also has six grandsons and one granddaughter. Presently retired and does babysitting, gardening and travels.

HAROLD HARDY, was born Aug. 4, 1922 in Duplin County near Kinston, NC. He was inducted into service at Fort Bragg, NC. After being classified, he was assigned to the Army Air Force and sent to Keesler Field in Biloxi, MS for basic training. He also spent six months in Airplane Mechanic School, then went to Laredo, TX for Aerial Gunnery School. After that, he went to Salt Lake Army Air Base in Utah for processing. After Salt Lake, he traveled to Boise, ID to be assigned to a crew as flight engineer and was sent with their crew to Casper, WY for OTU. He had more OTU in Alamogordo, NM where they joined the 466th Bomb Group. In early January, they received a new B-24 and left for Herington, KS for modification on their B-24. After a stop at Morrison Field in West Palm Beach, FL, they left in the middle of the night with sealed orders. An hour into their flight, they were allowed to open the orders and learned they were to take the southern route to Waller Field in Trinidad. After stops in Belim, Brazil; Fortaleza, Brazil and Dakar, Africa they were enroute to Marrakech, Morocco but had to make an emergency landing on a metal strip runway in Tindouf, Algeria. After three days in Algeria, they flew on to Marrakech and joined the rest of the crews. They spent three weeks there waiting for weather conditions to clear, then flew on to Attlebridge Station #120 where they trained mostly for a lead crew with PFF.

He flew 30 combat missions with the same pilot, Fred McConnell. They had a very good crew and no injuries. There was one mission he will never forget...they were heading for an attack on Marshalling Yards in Karlsruhe, Germany and were at 20,000 feet flying lead crew over the Channel when the auto pilot malfunctioned and put the plane into a straight dive. The pilot and Command Pilot were able to override the auto pilot and, in doing so, the two 1,000 pound bombs broke loose and crashed through the front bomb bay doors. They had to do something in order to land, so he crawled from the top turret and suspended himself in the bomb bay and knocked the doors loose with the bomb shackle. He had to do this without his parachute because of the narrow space in which he had to work.

They finished their 30 missions in early November, 1944 and came back by ship to New York. He spent two days at Camp Kilmer, NJ. He left the crew there and went to Fort Bragg for all new uniforms and was given a 30 day delay enroute to Miami Beach, FL for R&R.

From Miami, he went to Courtland Field, AL for reassignment. He applied for B-29 Flight Engineer and was sent to San Antonio Aviation Cadet Center in Texas for six weeks, then on to Amarillo, TX for mechanic school and finally to Hondo, TX for Cruise Control. He came up through the ranks to tech. sergeant. About ten days before he was to graduate as a second lieutenant, he was informed he had to sign up for an indefinite time or take discharge. He chose to take discharge for family reasons and was processed out at Fort Bragg, NC on Sept. 10, 1945.

After several years as a sales representative for Nabisco, he formed his own company in snack foods which he still operates. He is happily married with one daughter, one son and four grandchildren.

CHARLES L. HARKINS, was born Aug. 26, 1923 in Waco, TX. Graduated from Waco High School May, 1941. Entered Baylor University September 1941. Departed Waco and Baylor, March 1942 to enter Aviation Cadet Pilot training pre-flight at Kelly Field ("the Hill"). Washed out of pilot training, primary, at El Reno, OK June 1942. Then to bombardier/navigation pre-flight, Ellington Field. Graduated from bombardier training at Concho Field, San Angelo, TX Dec. 17, 1942, class 42-17. Ordered to 8th AF Personnel Hq. at Bolling Field. Instead of England, wound up at Gander Air Base, Newfoundland in 20th Anti-Sub Sqdn. Later squadron moved to Mitchell Field, Long Island. B-24 conversion training Casper, WY June 1943 through December 1943. More B-24 training at Wendover, UT January 1944 to April 1944. Then England and 8th A.F. with 489th Bomb Group. Flew 27 missions on lead crew. Group grounded! Aircraft taken away! Returned to U.S.A. December 1944 as a group. Commenced B-29 conversion training at Davis Monthan, Tucson February 1945 to June 1945. More training at Fairmont AFB, NE. Pacific War ended. Spent a short post war career at Clovis, NM, Herington, KS and Tampa, FL. Due to chaos and confusion of post-war armed forces, asked for and received his discharge at Fort Benning October 1946.

Held several sales jobs with various companies. Obtained a position in the purchasing department of a large natural gas company in Houston in January 1961. Retired in August 1985 as manager of pipeline purchasing. Now resides near Spring Branch, TX (20 miles north of San Antonio) with his wife "Flo" whom he married Nov. 28, 1943 at Casper AAB, WY.

WILLIAM J. HARKINS, JR., was born on Dec. 5, 1924 in Philadelphia, PA. He was inducted into the USAAC on March 3, 1943 and served as radio operator/gunner with 713th Sqdn., 448th Bomb Group, 20th Combat Wing. A.T.C. foreign and domestic. Discharged on Oct. 6, 1945 with the rank of tech. sergeant.

Pilot, flight engineer and he flew 33 missions in 101 days.

Awarded the Victory Medal, Air Medal with four clusters, Good Conduct Medal, ETO with four stars and American Theater.

Received BS in education at Westchester State University and master's degree from the University of Delaware. Married and has 10 grandchildren. Military war-gamer and collector. Retired, part-time benefit consultant.

RICHARD D. HARLAND, graduated Dec. 12, 1942 at Albuquerque, NM. Overseas B-17 training at Blythe, CA and advanced overseas B-17 training at Pyotu, TX. Twelve

crews were cut from overseas group due to lack of new B-17s. Stationed at Gowen Field, Boise, ID in March or April 1943. No assignment B-24 crew training. Flew about six weeks with various crews. Lots of dry runs and dropped some bombs with the Sperry Bomb Sight as volunteer.

Assigned as squadron bombardier to 458th Bomb Group, 753rd Bomb Sqdn. (June or July 1943).

Trained Boise, Salt Lake City, Midland, TX, Orlando, FL and Tonopah, NV.

Picked up new B-24s and equipment at San Francisco early December 1943. Flew to Miami, FL. Landed New York, Boston, Gander Island (five day storm), Scotland, Horsham St. Faith, Norwich, England about Jan. 10-15, 1944.

Flew 30 missions (most as lead bombardier). First three-four to Berlin, rest all over Europe. They used bombsight control on bomb run and dropped by group and/or squadron. Very few of his missions were with the same crew. He bombed for group and squadron commanders, operation officers, 2nd Air Div. flying officer - whoever was leading their group when he was flying.

Sometime after D Day 12(?) crews Flying Azore modified B-24s were assigned to the 753rd Sqdn. They dropped 1000 lb. bombs that were equipped with flairs and special bomb fins that allowed flight control with joy stick located by bombsight.

He flew two-three missions with commander (major) to bomb bridges behind German lines. Some success but not much. They trained at 10,000 ft. in states - at 18-22,000 ft. distortions by eye were too great to overcome and the bombardiers had a tendency to use joy stick too soon.

Picked up some kind of navigation certificate on gas runs to Lille France in October. He flew his last mission in late October or November 1944.

Arrived back in states sometime in January 1945 by boat. Reassigned to Nevada. He was in charge of training crew assignment of their daily activities scheduled from wake up to bed. He was one of the last officers to leave the closed base.

Assigned back to Gowen Field, Boise, sometime in October 1945.

Discharged mid-October and returned to University of Idaho. Finished his BA hours in January 1946.

GEORGE L. HARLOW, was born Feb. 19, 1924 in Waukegan, IL. Enlisted in USAAF in 1942 in November on Friday the 13th, taking the oath at 1300 in a group of 13 enlistees. Graduated Radio School Sioux Falls, SD and Gunnery School, Las Vegas, NV.

Assigned to Henry Bussing's crew forming the original 702nd Sqdn. of the 445th Bomb Group and traveled to England via Brazil, Africa and French Morocco. Flew combat against Germany in B-24s from Fall 1943 until shot down, leading group in the bombing of Gotha, Germany, Feb. 24, 1944. Group awarded Presidential Unit Citation for efforts and results. Prisoner of war Stalag Luft 6 in East Prussia, Stalag Luft 4 in Poland and spent three months of Winter 1944-1945 on forced march across Northern Germany to Stalag 357. Escaped to English lines April 1945 and flown to Army Hospital Oxford, England. Returned to Air Force duty October 1945.

Presently is a banker and lives in Waukegan, IL.

JOHN PAUL HARPER, was born Jan. 3, 1924 in Andrews, SC. Married Frances Jacqueline Cook, Nov. 21, 1943. Now has four children and four grandchildren.

Entered Army Air Force April 8, 1943 after one year at Presbyterian College, Clinton, SC. Trained at Tyndall Field, Salt Lake City, Sheppard Field, Lowry Field #2, and Pueblo.

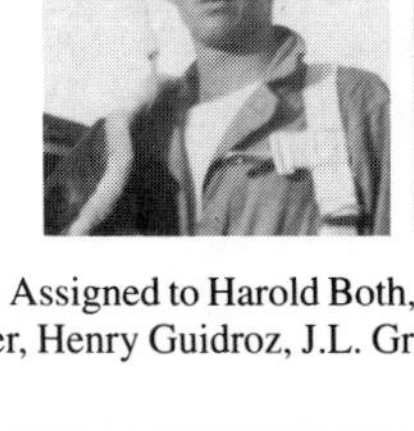

Assigned to Harold Both, Jr. crew (Frank Johnson, R.S. Carter, Henry Guidroz, J.L. Graham, Paul Duran, Ira Guinn, Allen Sabol, Ted Tucci) as a replacement B-24 crew in the 8th AF in England, 492nd Bomb Group at North Pickenham, 856th Sqdn.

Shot down on fifth mission over Kiel on Aug. 4, 1944. P.O.W. at Stalag IV. Left camp on Feb. 6, 1945 on the "Shoe Leather Express" forced march through Swinemunde, Uelzen, Magdeburg, Annsburg, to Bitterfeld.

Liberated on April 26, 1944. Sent to Camp Lucky Strike, then Le Harve. Returned to U.S. on Liberty Hull "Explorer".

Discharged as staff sergeant on Oct. 9, 1945. Completed education at North Carolina State University and retired in 1989 after 40 years in the paper industry.

C. HERBERT HARRIGAN, was born in Norristown, PA on July 1, 1921. He enlisted in the 8th Air Force, 2nd Air Division, 713th Sqdn., 448th Bomb Group (Heavy) in May 1942. From Nashville, TN through a dozen stations to Seething, Norfolk, England and thence back to Sioux Falls, SD where he was discharged on Oct. 28, 1945 with the rank of staff sergeant.

Served from Battle of the Bulge to Nazi surrender. His memorable experiences include in "Tail-end Charlie" B-24 over Kiel Canal; plane went into a spin (from turbulence, not the flak); pilot and co-pilot pulled them out (supposedly impossible). Also earned his pay by spotting barrage balloons over French coast that weren't supposed to be there. Kept them from nasty tangle.

Awarded the ETO, Air Medal with three Oak Leaf Clusters as armorer-gunner/enlisted bombardier.

Married Margaret Rowan Robinson with three stepchildren. Attended Columbia University's Pulitzer School (graduate) of Journalism on the GI Bill (previously made it through Dartmouth) and worked on Providence, RI, *Journal*; Richmond, VA, *News Leader*; and Philadelphia *Inquirer* before putting in almost 20 years in Sarasota. Presently retired editorial page editor (Sarasota Herald-Trib., Florida)

RUSSELL L. HARRIMAN, was born on Nov. 28, 1923 in Detroit, MI. Graduated Southwestern High January 1942. Hired into Ford Motor Co. March 1942 as an apprentice aircraft engine mechanic. Entered USAAC Jan. 7, 1943. Basic training St. Petersburg, FL. Aircraft Mechanics School, Keesler Field, MS. B-24 Specialists School, Willow Run, MI. Aerial Gunnery School, Laredo, TX. Flight Training as B-24 engineer Westover Field, MA. Joined Kaylor C. Whitehead's crew July 1944 at "Old Buckingham", 453rd Bomb Group, 734th Sqdn. Flew their first mission Aug. 8, 1944.

Memorable experiences include September 8th mission to Karlsruhe, Germany their aircraft was badly damaged and they were forced to land at a fighter field, recently liberated near Belgium. Spent three days repairing damaged fuel and hydraulic lines with the help of British aircraft mechanics and then flew their aircraft "Never Mrs." back to home base.

November 21, 1944 was another day he won't forget! Hamburg, Germany lost one engine on bomb run and then another after bombs away. Had little choice but to head for Sweden! Landed safely and spent the next three months in an internment camp. Was transferred to Stockholm March 1945 to work for the American Legation. After V-E day was selected to help ferry repaired aircraft back to England making the last trip July 7, 1945.

Awarded the Good Conduct Medal, four Air Medals, Victory Medal, and ETO with three Battle Stars.

Returned to Ford Motor Co. to continue a skilled trade apprenticeship that was completed in 1949. Transferred to management as a skilled trade supervisor, the last 13 years as a general supervisor.

Widower after 12 years of marriage. Raised four sons. Has been retired from Ford Motor since June 1980.

JOE L. HARRIS, was born on April 26, 1916 in Chrystal Falls, TX. Inducted into the Aviation Cadets on Oct. 1, 1941. Received second lieutenant and pilots wings on April 24, 1942; 1944 assigned B-24 Bomber Pilot with 8th A.F., 492nd Bomb Group. Stationed in Great Britain, Germany, Japan and Alaska. Retired on July 31, 1967 as lieutenant colonel USAF after 26 years of service.

Memorable experiences include flying 15 bomb missions over Germany and occupied countries in spring of 1944, No. 8 to Politz oil refinery. Three crew members wounded and extensive damage from fighter attack. No. 15 to same target - received major flak damage, one crewman wounded and made forced landing.

Awarded the Air Medal with one Oak Leaf Cluster, National Defense Service Medal, Humane Action Medal (Berlin airlift), WWII Victory Medal, American Defense Service Medal, etc.

Married Frances Armitage on April 25, 1942. He is a citrus grower and his hobbies are skeet shooting and hunting most American wild game.

KURT W. HARRIS, was born on Jan. 17, 1925 in Richwood, OH. He enlisted in the USAAC on July 17, 1943 as a radio operator and gunner on B-24 with the 2nd Air Division, 409th Bomb Sqdn., 93rd Bomb Group.

He was stationed at Miami Beach, FL; Sioux Falls, SD; Yuma, AZ and Hardwick, England. Participated in the Battles of Rhineland, Central Europe and the Ardennes. Flew 35 missions.

Harris was discharged on Oct. 18, 1945 with the rank of tech sergeant. He earned the EAME Campaign Medal with three Bronze Stars, the Air Medal with five Oak Leaf Clusters and the Overseas Bar.

Married and has two children and five grandchildren. Harris is retired.

ROBERT B. HARRIS (BOB), was born on Aug. 15, 1924 in Medford, MA. He joined the USAAF on March 6, 1943 at Fort Devens, MA as a radio operator and gunner.

He had basic training in Miami Beach, FL; Radio School at Scott Field, IL; Gunnery School at Yuma, AZ; crew training at Westover Field, MA; Charleston, SC; and Langley Field, VA.

He arrived with his crew at the 389th Bomb Group in Hethel, England in September 1944. He flew his 34th mission and last mission on April 14, 1945. He received the Air Medal with four Oak Leak Clusters and four European Campaign Stars. He served four months at Randolph Field, TX until his discharge on Oct. 12, 1945 with the rank of tech sergeant.

He was married on Feb. 4, 1949, they have three children and three grandchildren. He is retired and spends the three summer months at Lake Winnipesaukee in New Hampshire.

SAM HARRIS, was born on July 12, 1924 in Chicago, IL. He enlisted in the USAAC on Jan. 23, 1943. He was sent to Camp Crowder, MO to take a teletyping course. He was assigned to the 437th Troop Carrier Command Signal Center.

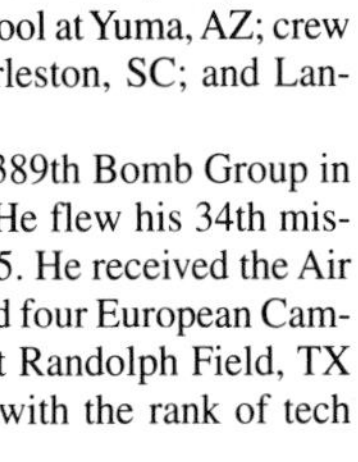

He took the Air Force examination and finally graduated as a bombardier at Midland Army Air Field. Was assigned to the crew at Westover Army Air Field. He went on to combat training at Chatam Army AFB in Georgia and then on to combat on the B-24 Liberator.

He flew 11 missions with the 93rd Bomb Group, 390th Bomb Sqdn. from Hardwick, England over Germany. His memorable experience was serving with the men on his crew, who were all responsible and talented at their jobs. The love and respect they had and still have for each other. They still meet every year.

He was recalled back during the Korean conflict for B-29 training in San Antonio Army Air Force in Texas. He was then assigned to Mountain Home Air Field in Idaho and then to SAAC for the remainder of the conflict.

Discharged from WWII as second lieutenant and from the Korean Conflict as first lieutenant. Received the Air Medal with one Oak Leaf Cluster, ETO and others.

He is married and they have three children and six grandchildren.

DEAN HARVEY HART, was born on Dec. 6, 1917 at Macksville, KS. He has been a resident of Garden City, KS since 1929. He joined the National Guard in December 1940. He transferred to the USAAC in the spring of 1942.

Commissioned as a pilot at Stockton, CA, Class of 43E on May 20, 1943. Went on to B-24 training at March Field, then he joined the 453rd Bomb Group, 734th Sqdn. In December 1943, he flew the south route to England. He was based at Old Buckingham and was shot down on his 18th mission over Germany.

He was interned at Stalag Luft III as a POW from May 8, 1943 until he was liberated at Moosberg on May 9, 1944. Memorable experiences include the march in blizzard conditions from Sagan and on to Moosberg; and seeing the Swastika come down and Old Glory going up at Moosberg when he was liberated.

He received the Purple Heart, and the Air Medal with three Oak Leaf Clusters. After returning to the States, he was discharged on Dec. 10, 1945 with rank of captain. He served in the Reserves for six years.

Married for 47 years and has four daughters and three grandchildren. Retired from the insurance and real estate business. Enjoys raising and racing bred quarter horses.

C. WADE HARTLEY, was born on Oct. 13, 1923 near Ava, MO. He entered the USAAC in May 1943. He completed Gunnery School at Harlingen, TX and was assigned to the 1st Air Force as a tail gunner on a B-24 crew.

Following overseas training in Georgia and Bastista Field, Cuba, part of his crew was sent to Stone, England. After gunnery refresher in North Ireland, he joined the 713th Sqdn., 448th Bomb Group in Seething, England in July 1944. The first mission on July 12th to Munich was a rough one. He completed 34 additional missions with varying lengths and problems. His Liberator crew exemplified teamwork.

Returned to the States late in December 1944. Later he attended Gunnery Instructor's School at Laredo, TX and when he was discharged in October 1945, he was an instructor at Fort Myers, FL. In 1946 he married Sybil Sell from his home town. He taught social studies in high schools for several years and worked a lot in industry, especially quality control. He is very proud of his daughter and son-in-law and his two granddaughters.

GENE G. HARTLEY, was born on Nov. 28, 1923 in New Hampton, IA. His family moved to San Diego, CA. He was a freshman at San Diego State College until becoming an Aviation Cadet, Class of 43K. He graduated a second lieutenant pilot and was assigned to B-24 training at Kirtland Field.

He was sent to March Field for operational training. The crew went to Hamilton Field, CA where they were as-

signed a new B-24. Their orders were to fly to England. The route was via Goose Bay, Greenland and Iceland.

Completed 35 combat missions as a B-24 pilot with the 389th Bomb Group. His most memorable experience was completing his tour. Received the Distinguished Flying Cross and the Air Medal with four Oak Leaf Clusters. He was discharged in August 1945 with the rank of first lieutenant.

Following the war, he returned to school, graduating from Pomona College in 1948. Retired from a career in public education in 1985. Married Nancy Hayter in 1952, they have three children. He has edited and published the 389th Bomb Group Newsletter since his retirement.

MORGAN E. HARTMAN, was born on Feb. 25, 1916, in Bennetville, MN. He joined the service as an infantry rifleman and then transferred to the USAAC.

Was stationed at Camp Roberts, CA; Hammer Field, CA and Old Buckingham, England with the 453rd Bomb Group. He received the Ex-POW Medal in 1989. His memorable experiences were: being shot down on March 8, 1944; being a POW for 14 months in Germany; first mission to Gotha on Feb. 24, 1944; flying in B-29s as a tail gunner in 1950 and 1951.

He was discharged on Nov. 11, 1945 in Santa Ana, CA with the rank of staff sergeant, returned to the service and retired on April 30, 1962.

Married on Oct. 20, 1948 (wife German ex-Munich), they have two sons.

HAROLD F. HARTNER, was born on Dec. 30, 1923 in New York City, NY. He joined the USAAF on Jan. 21, 1943 as an armorer gunner. Stationed at various U.S. Air Bases and schools and in Tibenham, England.

Was with the 445th Bomb Group, 702nd Sqdn. On Feb. 24, 1944 the 445th Group lost 13 of 25 B-24s to fighters during an hour long air battle on a mission to an aircraft plant at Gotha, Germany. They had their No. 1 engine shot out before they dropped their bombs.

On April 25, 1944 their ship had to leave the group near the German border due to a gas leak and they dropped their bombs on a target of opportunity, airfield, and they descended to ground level and hedge hopped across France.

Hartner received the EAME Campaign Medal, Distinguished Flying Cross, Air Medal with four Oak Leaf Clusters, three Bronze Service Stars, Air Crew Member Badge and the Good Conduct Medal. He was discharged on Sept. 19, 1945 with the rank of staff sergeant.

He married Geraldine M. Breen on June 24, 1950, they have five children and 12 grandchildren. Retired from the New York City Police as a lieutenant.

BROWNIE G. HARVATH, was born Sept. 6, 1920. Enlisted in the USAAC on March 5, 1941 in the 8th Air Force, 2nd Bomb Div., 96th Wing, 458th Group, 755th Squadron.

He first served in the Army Artillery Tank Destroyer Battalion, then transferred to the Army Air Force in 1943. Flew 30 bomb missions as a gunner over Europe. Was stationed at Norwich, Norfolk in England.

He received the Air Medal with five Oak Leaf Clusters, Distinguished Flying Cross, EAME Campaign Medal with four Bronze Stars and the Defense Service Ribbon. Discharged on July 5, 1945 with the rank of staff sergeant.

Married Lorine Wishard on April 12, 1945, they have five children and four grandchildren. Retired from the Chevron USA Oil Company.

Harvath waited almost half a century before receiving his DFC, which he earned so willingly and at great personal risk, in defense of his country. Many of his former crew members, as well as friends and family were there to share his moment.

ROBERT R. HARVEY, was born on June 24, 1922 in Newark, OH. He enlisted into the USAAC on Sept. 9, 1942. Was with the 491st Bomb Group, 855th Bomb Sqdn., 8th Air Force. Took basic at St. Petersburg, FL; AM School, Gulfport, MS; Vultee Factory in Nashville, TN; Gunnery School, Ft. Myers, FL; then to Tucson, AZ to form new bomb group.

Next to Pueblo, CO for Group training and final staging at Herington, KS; left Palm Beach, FL to go to South

America, Dakes W. Africa to Metfield, England. Second mission D-day. After 491st Group bomb dump blew up and heavy loss of 492nd at North Pickenham, they moved to North Pickenham. Finished tour October 1944, then home on *Queen Elizabeth*.

After Gunnery Instructor School, Laredo, TX was instructor at Pyote, TX until V-J day.

He received the Air Medal with three Oak Leaf Clusters, Distinguished Flying Cross and the EAME Campaign Medal with four Stars. Was discharged on Sept. 23, 1945 with the rank of staff sergeant.

He and Dot (his high school girlfriend) were married in 1943, they have three children and five granddaughters. Retired after 25 years as a flight instructor. Has a one man aerial photographer business. Currently lives on Canyon Rd, Granville, OH.

PAUL HARWOOD, was born on Aug. 17, 1923 in Clarksfield, OH. He joined the USAF on March 9, 1943 in Toledo, OH. He attended Aircraft Mechanics School in Gulfport, MS and Gunnery School in Kingman, AZ.

He joined the rest of the crew in Tucson, AZ for phase training. They picked up a new B-24 in Topeka, KS and flew it to England by the northern route. They arrived at Hardwick and were assigned to the 328th Bomb Sqdn., 93rd Bomb Group. He flew 35 missions and was awarded the European Theater Ribbon with five Bronze Stars and the Air Medal with five Oak Leaf Clusters.

Returned to the States and was discharged on June 7, 1945 with the rank of tech. sergeant.

He worked as a service manager at several auto dealerships. Joined the staff of the Lorain County Joint Vocational School as an auto mechanic instructor and retired from there in 1986.

Also served as Chief of the Rochester Volunteer Fire Dept. for 27 years. He and Nora Knapp were married on Dec. 7, 1943. They have three children and seven grandchildren.

JAMIEL HASSEN, was born on July 20, 1924. He joined the USAAC on April 27, 1943, completing aviation cadet training as a navigator, Class 44-6 and commissioned as a second lieutenant on April 22, 1944.

Arrived in England in July 1944 and assigned to the 492nd Bomb Group, 788th Sqdn. They were transferred to the 467th Bomb Group, 788th Sqdn. Flew his first mission on Aug. 16, 1944, then flew trucking missions from September to October 1944 and flew his 35th mission on April 9, 1945.

He was awarded the Air Medal with one Silver Oak Leaf Cluster, Air Force Commendation Medal, EAME Campaign Medal with three Bronze Stars and various other victory, campaign and longevity medals. He was released from active duty in July 1945.

He and Mary T. Codino were married in October 1948. He joined the California Air National Guard in 1949 and was recalled to active duty in October 1951.

Served in various assignments and positions that included Labrador, Greece and Germany. He retired from Hamilton AFB on Nov. 1, 1968 as a lieutenant colonel.

CLYDE W. HATLEY SR, was born on Oct. 13, 1921. He entered the USAAC on Aug. 19, 1942, flight engineer on a B-24. Crew training at Wendover Field in Utah, then to Seething, England in December 1943 to September 1944 with the 448th Bomb Group.

His first mission was early in January 1944. The first raid on Berlin was on March 6, 1944 and his last mission was on May 28, 1944 in Merseburge, Germany. He lost hose to oxygen mask on his last mission, but before he lost all his capability to see and think he realized what had happened and got the hose hooked up again. Just like a big light had been turned on.

He was awarded the Distinguished Flying Cross, Air Medal with three Oak Leaf Clusters, European Theater Medal and Good Conduct Medal. He was discharged on Sept. 7, 1945 with the rank of tech. sergeant.

He and Annie S. Sprouse were married on Aug. 14, 1948, they have one son and one daughter. He was co-owner of the Queen City Lumber & Supply Company for 48 years in Charlotte, NC.

PAUL V. HATTEN, was born on Sept. 19, 1921 in Cavittsville, PA. Enlisted in the USAAC Cadet Program on Sept. 25, 1942, inducted on Feb. 3, 1943 and attended basic training at Miami Beach, FL.

Attended Wittenberg College in Springfield, OH from Feb. 28, 1943 until July 10, 1943 for pre-cadet training. Shipped to San Antonio, TX Aviation Cadet Classification Center. Reclassified, and attended Aerial Gunnery School in Laredo, TX from Aug. 5, 1943 until Sept. 15, 1943. He attended combat training on B-24 at Gowen Field in Boise, ID as a ball gunner. He was shipped to Topeka Army Ari Base for overseas assignment. Departed for England on May 20, 1944 with a new B-24 via the northern route.

Spent several weeks in northern Ireland, Scotland and England preparing for combat. Arrived at Rackheath, England on June 17, 1944 and assigned to the 467th Bomb Group (H) Sqdn, 791st Crew 98th. Transferred to the 788th Sqdn. on Oct. 13, 1944. Flew his first mission on June 24th and his 33rd mission on Dec. 12, 1944.

They incurred intense flak nearly every mission. Flak damage was a memorable experience, but thanks to an excellent pilot, Charles J. White, they returned safely. An excellent fighter protection made their missions a lot safer. The loss of their co-pilot, Roy J. Doole (MIA) was a severe blow.

Discharged on Sept. 15, 1945 as a staff sergeant with the Distinguished Flying Cross and the Air Medal with three Oak Leaf Clusters.

He and Evelyn M. Weaver were married on July 3, 1943, they have five children and six grandchildren. After his return from the service, he returned to electrical contracting industry and retired in 1983. He and Evelyn celebrated their 50th wedding anniversary on July 3, 1993.

HERSHEL J. HAUSMAN, was commissioned in May 1944 and assigned to B-24 Transition School in Smyrna, TN. He was appointed 1st pilot and completed operational training at Walla Walla, WA. His crew was assigned to the 448th Bomb Group, 714th Sqdn. in Seething, England and completed 22 missions.

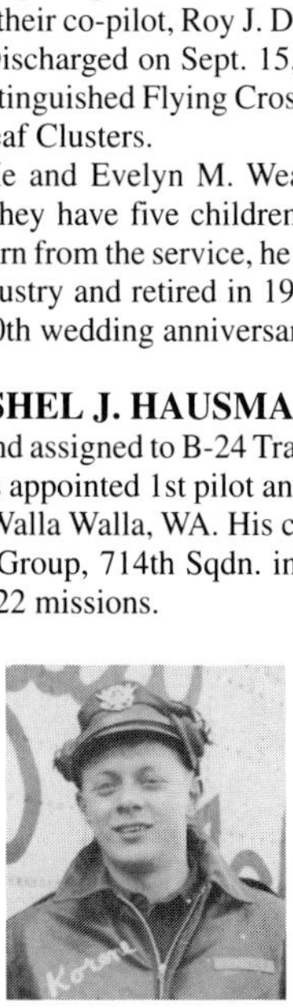
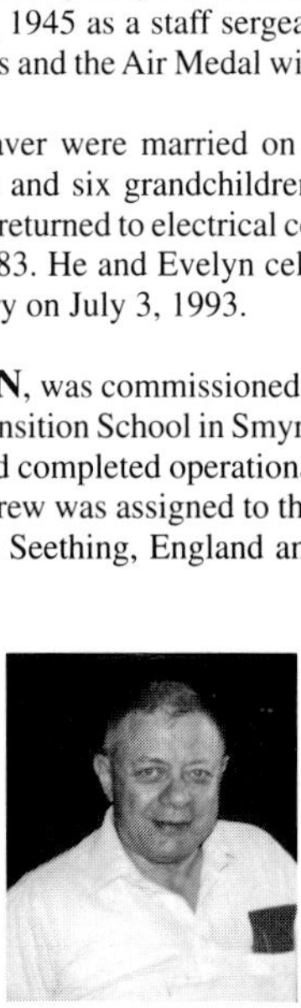

He left the service as a first lieutenant. Received his BS and MS degrees in 1948 and 1949 from the Carnegie Institute of Techology and the Ph.D. in Physics from the University of Pittsburgh in 1952. He served as Professor of Physics and Head of the Accelerator Laboratory at the Ohio State Univeristy in Columbus, OH from 1952 until his retirement in 1989.

He now holds the title of Professor Emeritus. He has been married for 49 years to his wife Korene and they have three children, Herbert, Sally and William, and a grandson, David.

STEVE HAVANEC, was assigned to basic training at Miami Beach, FL; AP Mechanics School at Keesler Field in Biloxi, MS; Aerial Gunnery in Harlingen, TX. He was assigned to B-24 combat crew training at Biggs Field in El Paso, TX, then to Topeka, KS for overseas departure; but went to Lincoln, NE and changed crews due to death in the family.

He flew overseas stopping at Rochester, NY; Grenier Field, NH; Rajavik, Iceland ending at Northern Ireland. Then on a ship across the Irish Sea to Scotland and train down to Halesworth, England. He became part of Crew #47, 845th Sqdn., 489th Bomb Group, APO #558, nine crew members are listed below. On Sept. 14, 1944, they were assigned to the B-24H, *Mizpah*, meaning "May the Lord watch between me and thee when we are absent one from the other." On Oct. 19, 1944, on it's 57th and last mission the *Mizpah* brought it's crew (not #47) home safely after losing its #4 engine over the target and the #3 was badly hit and losing oil, it crashed in nearby Beccles while attempting to land. On Oct. 24, 1944, they got a brand new B-24J for crew #47.

The nine crew members were: John P. Burns, (skipper) pilot, Rochester, NY; Floyd W. Bloethe, co-pilot, New York City, NY; Frederick J. Chico (Chic) Bombardier, Brooklyn, NY; Steve Havanec, flight engineer/waist gunner, Bridgeport, CT; Thomas V. Neal, radio operator to Oct. 3, 1944; Carmel C. Copley replaced Tom Neal on Oct. 3, 1944; Otto Bernard Geisler (Bernie) radio man/martin turret; Edward Janka, (Pollack) waist gunner, Chicago, IL; John P. Arbes, (Greek) nose gunner; Elizabeth, NJ, Frank R. Sparrow (Spatz) sperry ball then tail gunner.

Returned to the States in 1944 for Christmas. Changed from B-24 to B-29 at Davis Montham Field in Tucson, AZ, graduated from Amarillo, TX as a B-29 electronic engineer. Returned to Connecticut and married Veronica (Vera) Fellow of Stratford, CT on May 30, 1945. They both went to Tucson, where he completed combat crew training, then both went to Fairmont, NE for further combat crew training and departure to the South Pacific. Both of them went to Pueblo Air Base and finally discharged from Fort Devens, MA.

They have four sons, three daughters-in-law, three grandson, three granddaughters, one great-grandson and one great-granddaughter. They now live four (June to September) months in Shelton, CT and the remaining eight months in the Villages of Lady Lake, FL.

FRANCIS EARL HAWTHORNE, was born on Dec. 18, 1920 in Akron, OH and drafted in August 1942. Completed Aerial Gunnery training at Las Vegas, NV in December 1942 and Radio Operator Mechanics School in May 1943.

Upon completion of B-24 training, he was assigned with crew to the 389th Bomb Group, 566th Sqdn. to Hethel, England. Completed 30 missions. Was discharged in October 1945 and received the Distinguished Flying Cross, Air Medal with three Oak Leaf Clusters, Purple Heart with cluster and three European Campaign Stars.

Re-enlisted into the USAAF in October 1946. Served as communications cryptologic operator at various bases. Was sent overseas to Rio de Janiero, Brazil, Air Attache Office, then to Samun, Turkey and TUSLOG 3-2. Retired in November 1963 at Kelly AFB, HQ USAF Security Service, senior master sergeant with over 20 years of service.

Started his federal civilian career in January 1964, also attended evening classes at St. Mary's University. He graduated with a BA in history in 1966. During his Civil Service career, he earned several sustained Superior Performance Awards, Outstanding Performance Ratings, monetary awards and accolades for noteworthy leadership and achievement in career and career-related projects and programs.

He retired on April 31, 1991 as a Supply Systems Analyst, HQ Electronic Security Command with 48 years combined military and civilian service at Kelly AFB in San Antonio, TX.

He is married to the former Miriam Smith of Pratt, KS, they have two children, Kirkwood and Cynthia.

ALFRED G. HAYDUK, was born on May 5, 1916 in Chicago, IL. Private with Illinois National Guard in 1935. Attended Wright Junior College in Wabash, CO, graduated with a USMA in 1941, MBA at New York University in 1950.

From 42C was assigned to the 45th Bomb Group and flew an anti-sub patrol in the 7th AS Sqdn. and the 17th AS Sqdn. which became nucleus for the 491st Bomb Group. Then to the 8th Air Force in the spring of 1944, where they flew from pre-D-day until V-day. He had various assignments at the Pentagon, USMA and in the Air Defense Command.

Lt. Col. Carl Goldenburg took 491st from Pueblo to 8th AFB at Metfield. Goldie called #149 *The Old Lady* but never got it painted.

Retired as colonel at Ent AFB. Rceived the Legion of Merit Medal, the Distinguished Flying Cross, Air Medal, Distinguished Unit Badge, Air Force Commendation Medal, CDG and ribbons.

He married Vivian Stewart, they had four children. Vivian passed away in 1984. He married Louise R. Schottenheimer, a widow, in 1987 and she has one son.

EVERETT G. HAYES, was born on March 11, 1916 in New Haven, CT. He was raised in New Haven and Bethany and was employed by the Telephone Company until March 1942, when he joined the U.S. Army. He entered aviation cadets in the summer of 1942 and graduated in the June class of 43F as a 2nd Lt. Pilot.

He flew to England in a B-24 Bomber and did 30 combat missions with the 446th Bomb Group as a co-pilot/pilot against Germany. He was awarded one Distinguished Flying Cross and four Air Medals. Returned to the States and became a B-24 instructor pilot. Then joined the Ferry Command and flew B-24s, B-25s, A-26s, P-47s, P-51s, P-63s and P-40s within the States.

He received a commercial single/multi engine instructors rating and taught flying after leaving the service in 1945. Married Amelia Kollins in 1947 after leaving the service as a first lieutenant and served in the Reserves until the late 1950s, resigning as a major. He flew his wife over New York City from Connecticut in his Stearman in 1946. They drove to Albuquerque, NM in 1947 where he attended the University of New Mexico, graduating in 1952 as a mechanic engineer and was employed as a staff engineer at Sandia National Laboratories for 29 years. He retired in 1981. He has two sons, two daughters and two grandchildren. He enjoys traveling in his motor home, and his 15 acre mountain property, 26 miles from where he lives in Albuquerque.

HENRY R. HAYES, was born on Nov. 17, 1918 in Washington, DC. He joined the USAAF in November 1940, assigned to Ft. Devens, MA Post HQ Co., MP Platoon.

In April 1941 joined Flying Cadets Southeast Training Center, Class of 41-I. Commissioned as a second lieutenant in December 1941 at Turner Field, GA. Assigned to the 45th Bomb Group (L) at Grenier Field, NH, flying Douglas A-20s. Diverted to AS Operations (1942-1943), Atlantic Seaboard, based successively in Dover, DE and Jacksonville, FL. B-24 training at Langley Field, VA, then assigned to 4th USAF AS Sqdn. at Mitchell Field, NY.

In June 1943 the 4th AS Sqdn. was sent to Gander, Newfoundland; St. Evah, Cornwall, UK for operations with RAF Coastal Cmd. to fly patrols over Bay of Biscay. Transferred to 93rd Bomb Group(H), 2nd Air Div., 8th Air Force at Hardwick, assigned to Group HQ. Finished combat tour flying as deputy command pilot until August 1944 when he joined the 2nd AD Scouting Force. Completed his second tour just before V-E day in May of 1945.

Returned to the States, served in various duties with the Air Transport Cmd. until going inactive in May of 1946 with final status major, USAF RES (RET). He received the Distinguished Flying Cross with Oak Leaf Cluster, Air Medal with six Oak Leaf Clusters, Purple Heart, No. Atlantic and European Campaigns Stars etc.

Joined Pan American Airlines as a second officer/navigator in August 1946. Retired from there in 1978 as B-747 captain. Now flies only sailplanes.

He married Rosemary Hadden from Pasadena, CA on May 12, 1951, they have two daughters, Yvonne and Ruth.

RUSSELL D. HAYES, was born on Oct. 11, 1921 in Waterloo, IA. Joined the USAAC on June 11, 1942 as an aerial gunner. Stationed at Lowry and Biggs Field, Alamogordo, Hethel U.K. and Charleston, SC. Served with the 389th Bomb Group, 566th Bomb Sqdn. (H). Their aircraft was the B-24D, *The Little Gramper,* in which he and his crew flew 25 missions, including the Ploesti mission on Aug. 1, 1943. His last day of combat was on Feb. 14, 1944.

Returned to the States to Charleston, SC as a aerial gunnery instructor. He was discharged on Sept. 25, 1945 with the rank of tech sergeant.

His memorable experiences include: Ploesti on Aug. 1, 1943; the green country side of England; and the great people of the United Kingdom.

He received the Air Medal, Distinguished Flying Cross with Oak Leaf Clusters, Mid East Service Medal, Good Conduct Medal and the Presidential Unit Citation.

Married and has seven children. He worked at Standard Distribution for 34 years and retired in 1987. He passed away on Dec. 14, 1990.

JOSEPH W. HAYS, was born in 1924 in Bowie, TX. His family moved to Fort Worth, TX in 1925 where he still resides and manages his business forms distributorship. Started his Sophomore year at Texas Christian University, when he was called to active duty in January 1943.

Was in the Pilot Cadet Class 44F. He had completed 16 missions as co-pilot on John Vinski's crew when the war was over in 1945. Thanks to the GI Bill, he earned a degree in business from TCU in 1948. Married to Gloria, they have raised and educated two children and now are busy with their five grandchildren.

High in the highlights of his life is a crew re-union every two years since 1987. The last re-union was held at Las Vegas in fall of 1993. Three of his crewmates have passed away. You can bet they are missed.

ROBERT R. HAYZLETT, was born on March 22, 1921 in Loup City, NE. He was the son of Gilbert Warren and Maude Viola (Johnson) Hayzlett. Entered the USAAC Cadet Pilot Training Program in 1942, graduating with the Class of 43-I.

Was a Group Lead Pilot, B-24s in combat with the 458th Bomb Group, 96th Wing at Horsham St. Faith, Norwich, England, AAF Station 123. His assignment was from June 10, 1944 to Feb. 15, 1945. Completed a tour of 30 missions. Received the Distinguished Flying Cross, four Air Medals, three European Theater Campaign Stars.

A graduate of Air Command and Staff College, he completed post graduate Air Command and Staff, graduate of

Industrial College of the Armed Forces, graduate of Air Intelligence Courses Program. He retired from the USAF in 1968 with the rank of lieutenant colonel.

Hayzlett is a graduate of the University of Southern California, bachelor of engineering, registered professional engineer of California, received a MBA in general management and finance. He is a licensed commercial pilot, multi-engine, has lifetime standard junior college teaching credentials, California, in business administration and economics.

He is a retired publishing company executive, consultant and lecturer printing processes, contributor of articles to professional journals. He is listed in the Marquis *Who's Who in America*, Vol. 32, (1962-1963), *World Who's Who in Commerce and Industry,* 15th Edition, *Who's Who in the West,* 11th Edition, *Who's Who in the Midwest,* 17th Edition, *Who's Who in Finance and Industry,* Vol. 22 thru 28 and *Who's Who in California,* 14th Edition by Who's Who Historical Society.

Married Glendelle Mary Jaedike on Oct. 12, 1945. Their children are Robert Glen and Mark Randal.

BERNARD E. HEAD JR., was born on Sept. 27, 1925 in Uniontown, KY. Enlisted in the USAAF on Sept. 16, 1943 as an aerial gunner with the 854th Bomb Sqdn., 491st Bomb Sqdn., 8th Air Force.

Basic at Jefferson Barracks; gunnery at Harlingen, TX; crew training at Casper, WY; and ETO at North Pickenham, England. Participated in battles in Central Europe and Rhineland. His memorable experience was the last ditch sub/engine demolition and abortion of second mission with one engine out and the other one throwing oil.

He received the Air Medal, ETO Medal and Victory Medal. Discharged on April 6, 1946, Fort Lewis, WA with the rank of staff sergeant.

Completed ROTC at University of Kentucky. Recalled for Korean Conflict as munitions officer and retired from the USAFR as a major.

Married and has eight children and six grandchildren. He was a plant engineer and manager at the Lorillard Tobacco Co. in Greensboro, NC. He is retired!

H.L. HEAFNER JR., was born on Oct. 26, 1920 in Greenwood, MS. Inducted in the U.S. Army on Oct. 18, 1942 at Camp Shelby, MS. Basic training at Miami Beach, FL; Armament School at Lowry Field, Denver, CO; Gunnery School at Tyndall Field, FL and Myrtle Beach, SC.

Joined Lt. Catner's crew formed in the summer of 1943 in Boise, ID. Trained in B-24s in Casper, WY and Almorgarda, NM as a staff sergeant. His 10-man crew were all good friends and had great respect for each other then and still do (six are still living).

Their plane was named the *Play Boy.* T/Sgt. Pipes wrote a book about the crew called *Play Boy Crew* 1944-45. He was in the 466th Bomb Group, 8th Air Force.

They made 10 successful missions and were shot down on their 11th mission by FW 190s on the way back from Berlin on April 29, 1944. The tail gunner and top turret gunner shot down at least three and maybe more of the FW 190s.

T/Sgt. Pipes and Heafner escaped and stayed together at various places in Holland until the night of Feb. 27, 1945. That night they were raided on the farm of deBruin with four other Americans hiding there. They all escaped with most of their Dutch friends but he and Pipes were separated and he didn't see him again until the Canadians (Manitoba Dragons) liberated their section of Holland on April 5, 1945. They were in Paris for a while before coming back to good ole USA.

Heafner got back to Camp Shelby, MS and left there on V-E day with a 60 day free furlough. Discharged on Oct. 31, 1945 at Barksdale Field, LA. He received the Air Medal with one Oak Leaf Cluster and the Purple Heart.

He married Mary Louise Thibodeaux on June 20, 1947. They live in Orlando, FL.

CHARLES F. HEALY (CHUCK), was born on Feb. 12, 1920. Grew up in Marshall, MN, attended SDSU, graduated in 1942 with a BSEE degree. Joined the USAAC and was shipped off to San Antonio, TX for pre-flight; primary at Corsicana; basic at Greenville; advance at Fredrick, OK; and graduated pilot, Class of 44A. B-24 transition at Fort Worth and operational at Pueblo, CO.

Left Lincoln in July 1944. Flew the northern route via Goose Bay, Iceland and Valley Wales. Was assigned to the 458th Bomb Group, 753rd Sqdn. to (Azon) Norwich, England. He flew 11 missions as lead crew with the 755th Sqdn. He completed 30 missions and remained in the Reserve until October 1957.

Received the Air Medal with four Oak Leaf Clusters and Campaign Stars for five European campaigns. He ended up with the rank of captain.

Married his college sweetheart, Donna Dyste, on Aug. 7, 1943, they have three children and six grandchildren.

In civilian employment, he held an engineering position in Minneapolis, MN and finally a business of his own selling electronic and electrical equipment. He retired in 1987 leaving the business to his son. Now spends the summers in Minneosota and the winters in Naples, FL.

LEO E. HEBERT JR., was born on June 18, 1925 in Baltimore, MD. Joined the USAAC in September 1943 at Greensboro, NC for basic training. Took Radio Operator and Mechanic School in Sioux Falls, SD; Aerial Gunnery School in Yuma, AZ; and crew training on B-24s at Westover Field, MA during 1944.

He was shipped overseas to England on *Aquatania* in January 1945 and assigned to the 93rd Bomb Group, 409th Sqdn. in Hardwick for European Theater War Service. Flew 18 missions with Lt. Ollie Marmon's crew on a series of war-weary B-24s, including *Gambling Lady*. Most memorable were the targets to Magdeburg and Berlin, Germany.

Was finally assigned to a B-24H Liberator, a/c #42095204. His ground crew chief name it *Jitter's from Bitters* and applied the nose art accordingly with a large "Mug of British Beer." After V-E day they flew this back to the States on May 21, 1945 with the crew and 11 passengers via Iceland, Goose Bay, Labrador and Bradley Field, CT.

After R&R went to Sioux Falls, SD for assignment to Pacific Operation and training on B-29 Superfortress at Clovis, NM. He was discharged in December 1945 at Andrews Field with the rank of technical sergeant and received the Air Medal with two Oak Leaf Clusters.

He attended the University of Baltimore, received a BS in marketing and worked in construction management. He married Lorraine Stansbury in 1951, they have 10 children and 25 grandchildren.

MAURICE G. HEBERT, was born on Dec. 30, 1921 in Manchester, NH. Entered the USAAC on Aug. 26, 1942. After attending the Air Forces Technical School at Chanute Field in Illinois, he was assigned to the 389th Bomb Group on a

B-24 at Biggs Field, El Paso, TX, as chief sheet metal specialist with the 565th Bomb Sqdn., Lowry Field, CO.

He arrived at Hethel Airdrome on July 8, 1943. Flew to Benghazi, Libya via Oran, Algeria for the Ploesti "Operation Tital Wave" mission. Returned to Hethel in October 1943 and transferred to the 491st. Bomb Group, 852nd Bomb Sqdn. at Metfield, North Pickenham.

On June 18, 1945 he returned to the States with the Advance Echelon via Wales, Greenland, Labrador and landed at Westover Air Base in Massachuetts. He arrived on July 21, 1945 at McChord Field, WA, where the 491st was reassembled for B-29 training under the 464th Base Unit.

Discharged on Oct. 3, 1945 as sergeant at Fort Devens. He received ETO, EAME Campaign Medal with nine Battle Stars, two Presidential Distinguished Unit Citations with Oak Leaf Clusters, the WWII Victory Medal and the Good Conduct Medal.

He married Georgette T. LeBlanc on Sept. 28, 1946, they have two sons, Russell and Raymond, one daughter Susan and seven grandchildren. Hebert retired in 1990 as high school teacher/ coordinator.

FRANCIS EARL HEFFNER, was born on Oct. 3, 1923 in Detroit, MI. Enlisted in the USAAFR in 1942, then into active duty on Feb. 24, 1943. After Miami Beach, FL basic and cadet training assignments, he graduated from Selman Field, Monroe, LA as second lieutenant navigator on April 22, 1944.

He joined the B-24 heavy bomber crew at Peterson Field, CO on May 19, 1944. The crew completed training and ferried a B-24 across North Atlantic reaching England on July 30, 1944. From Sept. 11, 1944 until April 17, 1945, he flew 30 combat missions (22 as lead crew) with the 93rd Bomb Group at Hardwick. He led an attack on oil refineries at Magdeburg on March 3 and low level mission to resupply airborne troops crossing the Rhine River on March 24th.

He was awarded the Commendation Certificate for Magdeburg and five Air Medals. Discharged on Nov. 27, 1945 with the rank of first lieutenant.

He and Gini Pachuta were married in August 1958 and are living in Troy, MI. Resumed his education at Wayne State University in Detroit, MI earning a bachelor and master of science in mechanical engineering. He was employed at General Motors Research Laboratories on conventional and unconventional heat engines, with the last 19 years as assistant department head, Engine Research Department. He retired in 1987 after 39 and a half years.

JOSEPH P. HEGEDUS SR., was born in Buffalo, NY. He was drafted into the USAAC in December 1942 as a radio operator with the 2nd. Bomb Div. He took aerial gunnery at Laredo, TX and radio operator in Missouri.

He was in the Battle of Europe and earned four stars on his ETO Ribbon. His memorable experience was the first German jet he saw in 1943 or 1944. He also received the Air Medal with four clusters, Distinguished Flying Cross and the Presidential Citation. He was discharged in October 1945 with rank of tech sergeant.

He was married in 1945 and has one son, one daughter, four grandchildren and one great-grandson. He is retired.

CARL R. HEIN, was born on May 4, 1925 in San Juan, TX. After high school, he was an aircraft sheet metal mechanic at Kelly AFB in Texas. He entered the U.S. Army in September 1943.

After Gunnery School and OTU, he was assigned to Horsham St. Faith, Norwich England in the 458th Bomb Group, 752nd Bomb Sqdn. From July 1944 to March 1945, he flew 35 missions in B-24 as waist and tail gunner. He

earned the Air Medal with four Oak Leaf Clusters and eight other medals and ribbons.

He was in B-29 Gunnery Instructor School when the war ended. Was discharged in October 1945 with the rank of staff sergeant.

At college he met Sarah Ellen Smith, they were married on June 17, 1947. They have one daughter, three sons and five grandsons. He taught high school in 1949 and 1951 at Pharr, TX (PSJA).

He rejoined the USAF in July 1951. He received direct commission halfway through OCS. He completed a Meteorology course at UCLA. He was a Weather forecaster at Biggs AFB in Texas, Sondrestrom Air Base in Greenland and Harlingen AFB in Texas.

Was weather instructor at Harlingen and Chanute AFBs in Illinois. Graduated Air Force Advanced Management Program in DC with a MBA. He was a combat WX forecaster for Unified Alaskan Command, 1965-1967. His last duty was commander AFROTC at the University of New Mexico.

Retired in September 1969 with the rank of major. He taught math in Albuquerque schools and retired in September 1987.

FRANK JOHN HEINECKE, was born on Feb. 11, 1924 in St. Bernard, OH. He joined the Army on Nov. 14, 1942. Left Fort Thomas for Atlantic City for basic training. While in A/C he transferred to the USAC.

Went to Fort Myers, FL for Gunnery School. His second school was in Salt Lake City for Armament School, then sent to Boise, ID to join the 458th Bomb Group and Crew 73. He became first Armorer and a ball turret gunner. The 458th Bomb Group went to Tonapah, NV for group training, then left for England and ETO.

They named their aircraft (B-24 Liberator) the *Sqat 'n Droppit.* They became the lead crew of 755th Bomb Sqdn. Completed 31 missions over Europe and presented the Distinguished Flying Cross and the Air Medal with three Oak Leaf Clusters. His memorable experience was D-day.

Discharged on June 9, 1945 with the rank of staff sergeant. He started working in June 1940 and retired in 1990.

ROSCOE HEINS, was born on Sept. 15, 1917 at Corder, MO. He attended elementary and high school in Ruskin, NE and attended the University of Nebraska from 1934 to 1940. He was employed at Lockheed Aircraft, Burbank, CA until entering the USAF in February 1943.

He had gunnery training in Denver, CO and Las Vegas, NV; B-24 training in Boise, ID; took B-24 from Topeka, KS to Florida, Trinidad, Brazil, Africa and to Wales. Completed 16 missions with the 458th Bomb Group. Transferred to the 15th Air Force in June 1944. He completed 16 missions with the 459th Bomb Group in Cerighnola, Italy. He returned to the States in September 1944. Trained in B-29 gunnery at Las Vegas, NV and at Gulfport, MS until the end of the war in August 1945.

Received the Air Medal with two clusters. Returned to the University of Nebraska, graduating from College of Dentistry in 1949. He practiced in Poulsbo, WA for 35 years and still resides in that city. He has three children and four grandchildren.

RUSS HELLWIG, was born on Aug. 31, 1913 in St. Louis, MO. Inducted into the USAF on April 1, 1943. Basic training in St. Petersburg, FL. He was an "Honor Graduate" from the Army Air Force Technical Training Command, CO A&M, completing operations, engineering courses on July 17, 1943.

He joined the 448th Bomb Group, 715th Sqdn., at Wendover Field, UT. He departed the States on Nov. 23, 1943 arriving in England on November 29th. Participated in a formal ceremony take-over of Seething Air Field by the 448th. He played the National Anthem on drums with trumpeter "Irish" and cited in letter by 1st. Lt. McLaughlin, Special Services for fine work. Created Jazz Band, for active interest and helpful on many occasions.

He transferred to the 491st, 855th Sqdn., Metfield in April 1944 as chief engineering clerk and reserve drummer in group dance band. A bomb explosion moved the group to North Pickenham.

Awarded six Bronze Stars for Air Offensive Europe, Normandy, Northern France, Rhineland, Ardennes and Central Europe. Also received the Presidential Citation, three Overseas Bars. He flew back to the States on June 9, 1945 as acting first sergeant landing at Bradley Field, CT on June 22, 1945. He was discharged on Sept. 9, 1945 with the rank of staff sergeant.

He and his first wife, Evelyn Graham, (deceased) had three children, seven grandchildren and four great-grandchildren. He is now married to Mary Wiegers. Retired as classified advertising manager with the St. Louis Post-Dispatch in 1977.

TED HELWEG, was born on Oct. 3, 1924 in Chicago, IL. He trained in Texas; Wichita Falls; San Antonio (SACC); Ballinger; Sherman; and got his pilot wings at Houston, TX in April 15, 1944. His B-24 transition was in Fort Worth, TX and his crew training took place in Mountain Home, ID. Unlike Texas, Idaho had rocks in their clouds.

They joined the 330th Sqdn. of the Ploesti and tested and experienced 93rd Bomb Group in October 1944. By then the 8th Air Force bombers had the advantages of fighter support and improved equipment. The foggy winter weather and the improved flak barrages were their big operational challenges and the M-262 jet made its debut. They did lose one fine gunner who was flying as a volunteer substitute with another crew. While overall their crew had its share of flak holes, lost engines and scares, none were catastrophic. They were lucky.

On a "strategic" mission to the south of Europe, a leaky tank forced them to seek fuel on the way home. The emergency field was a fighter base with short steel-mat runways. With all possible flaps and drag, they looked like a goose trying to land in a water bucket. They crunched down with a great clatter of screeching metal (thought he forgot the wheels) and braked to a stop.

A jeep loaded with Brass roared out from operations and he climbed down to get his Distinguished Flying Cross for a super short-field landing. The award ceremony was brief and diminished by the greeting "You SOB, look what you did to my runway." The edges were bent up the entire length and it didn't help when two slats popped loose next to their nose wheel. They were given much abuse and just a few gallons to depart; downwind no less. On the short-field takoff, they even used the Put-Put at full power.

They were more than four hours overdue, when they landed at Hardwick. By custom, he had to reclaim his squatter's rights for the bunk by the window, a bicycle and a very precious stash of real chocolate cocoa and eggs.

As a wingman or deputy lead they flew 24 missions with just one abort. It was due to a Napalm bomb that ruptured in the bomb-bay at altitude. Everyone's eyes were watering from acrid fumes. Their gutsy engineer scooped the gook off the freezing fuselage walls with his bare hands while balancing on the catwalk in the open Bomb-bay. All electrical systems stayed off and no one smoked.

After he graduated from Minnesota in 1949, he spent his career in the computer business. He was recalled for Korea and transitioned into Mustangs and the new F-86s. Now retired and living in Manhattan near the UN Complex.

ALBERT A. HENKE, was born Jan. 31, 1918 in Saskatchewan, Canada. Entered the USAAF Dec. 2, 1941. Served with 467th Bomb Group, 789th Sqdn., 8th Air Force in ETO. Memorable experience was his final mission and rotation to States.

Discharged in 1945 with the rank first lieutenant. Received the Air Medal, Silver Cluster, ETO and three Battle Stars.

Married to Lenora and they make their home in Aberdeen, WA. He is retired.

THOMAS H. HENLEY, was born Feb. 3, 1920, Wetumka, OK; graduated Hondo, TX Navigation School; assigned 701st Sqdn., 445th Bomb Group as navigator. Had B-24 training in Pocatello, ID and Scribner, NE.

On Nov. 20, 1943 left the States and flew to Tibenham, England. Flew 30 missions on a lead crew and finished with eight second section leads, five group leads, five wing leads and one division lead. After completion of missions, he served six months as squadron navigator.

In December 1944 he returned to the States. Went to Medical School and took his residency in general surgery. Retired in December 1992. Henley has five children, five grandchildren and is enjoying life.

ROBERT A. HENN, was born Feb. 13, 1924 in New Rochelle, NY. Entered the USAAF December 1943. Served as pilot of B-24 with the 458th Bomb Group, 8th Air Force in England. Completed 24 combat missions.

Discharged from Reserve in 1964 with the rank of captain. Received three Battle Stars and three Air Medals.

Henn is married and has one son, two daughters and four grandsons. Currently retired and lives in New Bern, NC.

JOHN C. HENNING, was born June 17, 1923 in Philadelphia. He attended school in Philadelphia and Pine Grove, PA as well as University of Cincinnati. Received his wings and second lieutenant commission with Class 44-E at Pampa, TX.

As a B-24 pilot, he and his crew joined the 392nd Bomb Group and the 578th Sqdn. at Wendling, England in 1945. Although their missions were flown during the latter part of the war, some were memorable experiences. Included were: the first target requested by Russia (Swinemunde), a mission on the German General Staff HQ, a napalm attack, a low-level supply mission during the Rhine crossing, and the heaviest raid of the war on March 18th on Berlin. On another mission, most of the bombs went through the closed bomb bay doors and when the crew flew the 285th mission of the 392nd, the final mission of the war for the 8th Air Force.

They flew several missions and returned Stateside in aircraft #4450493 C-Bar. In later years, Air Force artist, Keith Hill, selected this plane for a painting representing the 578th Sqdn., copies of which today hang in U.S. and British museums. John returned to the U.S. as first lieutenant.

He spent 37 years with Stearns & Foster Co., retired in 1983 as vice president of corporate engineering. In 1945 he married Marylou Colonel. They have four children and two grandchildren.

HOWARD C. HENRY JR. (PETE), was born Pikeville, KY on June 26, 1920. Enlisted in the USAAC Aviation Cadets, Jan. 20, 1942; completed pilot training in Southeast Training Command, Nov. 10, 1942; graduated from Turner Field, Albany, GA as Pilot and Second Lieutenant, Class 42-J.

Instructed cadets in basic flying training at Bainbridge Army Air Field, Bainbridge, GA until assigned B-24 pilot training, November 1943. Upon completion, assigned 44th Bomb Group, 2nd Air Div., 8th Air Force at Shipdham, England, June 1944. Promoted to Captain, December 1944 and completed 32 missions, February 1945 with half as lead crew.

Returned to States and separated from service Nov. 10, 1945. Served 18 years in Air Force Reserve and promoted to Major July 1, 1955. Awarded Distinguished Flying Cross, five Air Medals and four Campaign Ribbons.

Enrolled New York University College of Engineering February 1946 and graduated with Bachelor of Mechanical Engineering degree, June 1949 and Master of Mechanical Engineering degree June 1950. Employed by New Departure Division General Motors Corp. June 1950 and retired at the end of June 1982 serving in management capacities the last 26 years.

Married Mary E. Lanier May 1, 1945 and has two married sons and one granddaughter. Henry is retired.

LEASK H. HERMANN, was born Oct. 9, 1921 in Waterloo, IA. Entered the USAAF and served as armorer gunner with the 93rd Bomb Group. Stationed at Buckley Field, Tyndall Field, Richmond, Wendover and Hardwick, England.

Memorable experience was first raid to Berlin on March 6, 1944 and sixth raid to Friedrichshaften, March 16, 1944. One engine out over France, was hit over target and bailed out. Landed in Switzerland (eight of crew landed in Austria), interned in Switzerland and escaped Dec. 1, 1944 to France.

Discharged Oct. 25, 1945 with the rank staff sergeant. Received the Air Medal and two Battle Stars.

Graduated from University of Northern Iowa, 1947. Was industrial engineer for 38 years, retired in 1986. Married Ruth Taplin in 1947 and has two sons and one grandson.

WALTER S. HERN JR., was born June 15, 1921 in White Sulphur Springs, WV. Enlisted in the USAAC July 9, 1940 and was sent to Ft. Slocum, NY for basic training, then to the Panama Canal Zone, France Field and assigned to the 6th Bomb Group. Since he was a ham radio operator prior to service, he was assigned as an aircraft radio operator where he attained the rank of staff sergeant. He was one of 500 selected to attend the Army's West Point Prep School in the Canal Zone. He became one of four finalists competing for two academy openings. Since he came in third, he applied for the Aviation Cadet Program.

Hern went through SAACC in Texas, then to primary, Class of 43K. He failed to pass and was assigned to the Bombardier DR Class 44-1. He was commissioned second lieutenant in January 1944 and assigned to a B-24 crew. After phase training in Tonopah, NV, he was shipped to England and assigned to the 446th Bomb Group (Bungay Buckeroos).

On Aug. 26, 1944 his aircraft was badly hit and abandoned near Ossendrecht, Holland. He evaded capture with the help of the Dutch Underground until liberation by Allied troops in November 1944, when he was returned to the States.

After separation from service in September of 1945, he received a BBA degree with management major from the University of Houston, TX. He worked for Shell Oil Co. until 1959 when he joined Beckman Instruments in California. He retired as a Beckman division controller in 1985.

Has been married for 47 years and has two grown children and one granddaughter. He and his wife have lived on a golf course in San Juan Capistrano, CA for the past 18 years.

TOMMY R. HERNANDEZ, was born in San Diego, CA on June 4, 1925. Entered the USAAC on Jan. 17, 1943 during his senior year of high school (lied about age). Basic training at Keesler Field, MS; Armorer School, Buckley and Lowry Field, Denver, CO; Gunnery School, Harlingen, TX and his first plane ride. Sent to Wendover Field, UT for crew assignment then to Davis-Monthan Field, AZ to meet his new crew members. More training at Alamogordo, NM; Lincoln, NE where they picked up new B-24J; Morrisson Field, West Palm Beach, FL.

Overseas to England via southern route, joined the "Flying Circus," 93rd Bomb Group, 409th Bomb Squadron, Hardwick on Jan. 21, 1944. Flew 34 combat missions; shot down two ME-109s; survived a crash landing at Manston on

his 13th mission and bailed out over Norwich on his 33rd mission. He is a member of the Caterpillar Club. Flew his 24th mission on his 19th birthday and believes that he was one of the youngest if not the youngest airman in the 2nd Air Div.

Flew two missions on D-day and received two Distinguished Flying Crosses, Air Medal with five Oak Leaf Clusters, Good Conduct, two Distinguished Unit Citations and five European Campaign Ribbons. Was discharged Oct. 17, 1945 with the rank staff sergeant.

Married his high school sweetheart, Catalina Brionez, on Easter Sunday, April 21, 1946. They have five children and four grandchildren.

JOSEPH F. HERRMANN, was born April 25, 1921 in Chicago, IL. Joined USAAF July 1942, ERC. Completed infantry basic training and assigned to Aviation Cadet, Class 43-I. Completed flight training, Southeast Training Command, graduating Oct. 1, 1943, Blytheville AAF, AR. Sent to Maxwell Field for B-24 pilot training, subsequently assigned to 44th Bomb Group (H) completing full tour of 31 missions in 72 days.

Received regular Air Force Comm., 1947. Served in SAC (7th Bomb Wing, 3rd Air Div., 92nd Bomb Wing) MATS-Air Rescue Service, Pers. Dist. Cmd. and CONAC:USAFE (7499th Support Group): SEA 35th TacFtrWg. Assignments included aircraft commander B-24, B-29, RB-50, C-47 and several others. Served as squadron and group commander, director operations and training, director personnel management, disaster preparedness officer and misc. other duties.

Received 18 awards and decorations, including the Distinguished Flying Cross, Bronze Star, Air Medal with three Oak Leaf Clusters, Meritorious Service Medal, Air Force Commendation Medal with one Oak Leaf Cluster, etc.

Married Doris Bain May 15, 1946 of Portland, OR and they had five children. Retired July 1, 1971 and worked for the John Hancock Financial Services 21 plus years as sales manager and special representative. Retired in grade of lieutenant colonel.

ALFRED HERSH, was born April 4, 1918, New York City, NY. Enlisted April 2, 1941, 13th Inf., Columbia, SC. Transferred into Air Corps April 1942 and went to Navigation School. Graduated April 1943 as second lieutenant and assigned to B-24s with crew at Wendling Air Field, England. Completed 29 missions from Dec. 22, 1943 to May 19, 1944 with the 392nd.

Memorable experience was participating in first American Air Force raid to Berlin on March 6, 1944. Discharged July 1945 with the rank first lieutenant. Received four air medals and the Distinguished Flying Cross upon completion of tour.

Married Anita Lobel in April 1945. They have two children and four grandchildren. Hersh is consultant in parochial school uniform company in New Jersey.

RAYMOND C. HERSHEY, was born Dec. 20, 1916, Little Falls, NJ. Drafted for one year as truck mechanic in Quartermaster Corps; trained as a pilot and graduated from Turner Field, Albany, GA, Class 43-D. Flew overseas with the 491st Bomb Group from Pueblo, CO to Metfield, England.

Thanks to the crew for their faith and dedication in the performance of their duties. The members were as follows: Russel Brewer, WG; Melvin Derricks, BG; Henry Gibbs, B; Fred Hicks, TG; Harold Holtman, Nav.; Malcolm Johnson,

P/Nav.; John Lefever, Radio Oper.; Werner Phillips, Flt. Crew Chief; William Van Riper, CP; Adrion Young, WG; Jack Hauger, CP after Van Riper was wounded and sent back to the States. Frank Boggiano was ground crew chief and did an excellent job of having the plane ready to go. No engines were lost during their tour.

Hershey married Elfriede Mund in 1945. They have three children and five grandchildren. Ray and Elfriede are retired and live at 315 Meadowridge Lane, Santa Rosa, CA.

FRED M. HESS JR., was born Sept. 21, 1924, Cincinnati, OH. Enlisted June 28, 1943 in the USAAC, Aviation Cadets. Basic training at Miami Beach, FL; transferred to Harlingen, TX for Gunnery School, graduating Feb. 5, 1944. Shipped to Utah for formation of 10-man crew under the command of second lieutenant Russel C. Anderson, pilot (KIA, Dec. 27, 1944).

After more training, picked up new B-24 and flew to Nuts Corner, Ireland via Grenier Field, New Hampshire and Goose Bay, Labrador. Flew 35 combat missions against France, Germany with the 453rd Bomb Group, 732nd Bomb Sqdn. July to Dec. 30, 1944. On mission to bomb a bridge south of Paris, they lost two engines over target, kept losing altitude and lost their formation. By the time the reached the north coast of France, they were at 10,000 feet heading for the south coast of England down to 5,000 feet. Bailed out near Ashford, England. All crew members survived.

Discharged Oct. 10, 1945 with the rank staff sergeant. Received the EAME Campaign Medal, Good Conduct and Air Medal with four Oak Leaf Clusters.

Hess has two sons, two daughters and nine grandchildren.

HERMAN H. HETZEL, was born Feb. 8, 1918 in Guthrie, OK. Joined the USAAC on Aug. 17, 1940 at March Field, CA. Served as aerial photographer and photographer lab technician with the 38th Recon Sqdn., 19th Bomb Group before WWII. Stationed at March Field, CA; Albuquerque, NM; Gowen Field, ID; Alamogordo, NM; Biggs Field, TX; Tonopah, NV; Horsham St. Faith, England.

The 38th formed into the 303rd Bomb Group, left them for aviation cadet training and washed out in 1943. Transferred to the 458th Bomb Group in Tonopah, NV for B-24 training. Left for England in January 1944 and arrived at Horsham St. Faith for bombing operation. Participated in Air Offensive Europe, Normandy, Northern France, Central Europe, Rhineland and Ardennes. Memorable experience was air flight to ETO and back to the States in a B-24 Liberator to Pyote, TX for B-29 training until Japan surrendered.

Discharged at Camp Chaffee, AR on Sept. 25, 1945 with the rank staff sergeant. Received the Good Conduct Medal, EAME Service Ribbons with one Silver Star and one Bronze Service Star.

Hetzel is single, retired from oil exploration and seismograph and lives in Guthrie, OK.

H.E. HETZLER (GENE), was born Feb. 26, 1922, St. Louis, MO. Entered the USAAC Oct. 10, 1942. Basic training at Jefferson Barracks, MO; CTD, Mt. Pleasant, IA; classification and pre-flight, Santa Ana, CA; primary, Ryan Field;

basic, Gardner Field; advanced, MAAF, TX. From March 1944-April 1944, 4th AFRD, Hammer Field, CA; 2nd AFRD, Lincoln, NE; RTU Gowen Field, Boise, ID; staging TAAF, Topeka, KS.

Flew overseas on *Party Girl* en route Grenier Field, NH; Goose Bay, Labrador; Meeks Field, Iceland; Valley, Wales. Assignment-Stone, England, July 16-24, 1944; Warrington, England; Clunto, Ireland. Served with 389th BG, 567th BS, August 1944-March 27, 1945, Hethel, Norwich, England.

Memorable experience was flying gasoline to Gen. Patton's Army in France. Plenty of champaign, brown bread and cheese. Discharged June 17, 1945 with the rank first lieutenant. Received the Air Medal with four Oak Leaf Clusters.

Married Ruth Jeanne Turley Nov. 8, 1946. They have four children and six grandchildren. He is semi-retired, still does some work in commercial real estate.

LARRY M. HEWIN, was born July 27, 1924, graduated Pilot Class 44-A, he received B-24 training at Liberal, KS and Colorado Springs. After flying his B-24 and crew overseas, he requested the 93rd and flew six combat missions and several supply missions with the 409th Sqdn. before being shot down (flying *Baggy Maggy*) Sept. 18, 1944 near Arnhem.

Was POW in Poland, Stalag Luft III, Nurnburg, and Moosburg. Returning stateside, he instructed in B-25s at Turner AFB and worked in base ops. at Wright Field until separation September 1946.

Graduated from Clemson and joined NACA, later transferred to Army Aviation Research and Development. Retired in 1974 as technical director of the Aviation Laboratories at Ft. Eustis. He continued reserve flying until 1957, departing as a major. He holds the Air Medal, Purple Heart, ETO with four stars, POW and several other ribbons.

He holds an MSA from GWU and a doctoral degree from William and Mary. Married to Barbara Mckay Woods with two children, James Bryant Hewin and Julie McKay Hewin.

JAMES O. HEY, was born April 22, 1918. Basic ROTC at University of Illinois. Entered service June 26, 1942, graduated from Fort Sill, OK Artillery School. Assigned to 83rd Div. Arty. Transferred to Air Force January 1943. Graduated George Field, IL 44F. Took transition training in Chanute Field. Picked up their new B-24M at Mitchell Field.

Flew across non-stop from Goose Bay, Labrador. They got their new plane assigned to them at their base. Flew 15 missions and flew back stopping in Iceland overnight. Memorable experience was the mission Col. Crawford was shot down dropping bombs N. Sea when Patton was running wild.

Discharged Oct. 4, 1945 with the rank of captain. Received three Air Medals and three Battle Stars.

Hey married sweetheart he met in the service, Roxy L. Ward. They have three sons, one daughter and 13 grandchildren. He is retired from wholesale ice cream industry.

WILLIAM HEYBURN II (BILL), was born Sept. 29, 1924 in Louisville, KY and has lived there all his life. Joined the USAF on July 3, 1943. Completed Radio School at Sioux Falls, SD in March of 1944 and Gunnery School at Yuma, AZ in May 1944.

Was assigned to Pueblo, CO for crew training with pilot Don Edkins. He was assigned to the 506th Sqdn., 44th Bomb Group in October 1944.

His number of missions was reduced to 13 because of a broken ankle suffered while playing basketball in January of 1945. They were very fortunate on their tour as the German Air Force was pretty much non-existent. Their closest call was after the war when they crashed a brand new plane while on a training flight. Even though it looked as though no one could survive it, all six members aboard lived to see some pretty gruesome pictures of the crash.

After the war, he worked in the farm equipment industry for five years and for the last 43 years has been with Mutual of New York as an agent. Has been active in many charitable causes as well as his church.

On June 10, 1944 he married Bonnie Barr of Louisville. They are active golfers and have a cottage in northern Michigan where they spend a lot of time in July and August. They have a daughter, Julie; son, Bill; and three lovely granddaughters: Chamie, Julie and Katie.

JAMES ROBERT HICKEY, was born Feb. 24, 1925, Wausau, WI. Entered the Army June 26, 1943; Army Infantry, March 1, 1944; and the USAF March 2, 1945. ASTP-North Camp Hood, TX, tank destroyer basic training; University of Illinois, Urbana, IL, engineering; Camp Granite, Mojave Desert, CA; Camp Carson, Colorado Springs; combat in Belgium, Holland, France and Germany; HQ & HQ Sqdn., 2nd Air Div., 8th Air Force, Ketteringham Hall, Norwich, England Sta. 149; Sioux Falls AFB, Sioux Falls, SD, Maxwell AFB, Montgomery, AL.

On Dec. 14, 1944, he was wounded by shell fire and transferred to England for Rehab. It was after this he was transferred to HQ & HQ Sqdn., 2nd Air Div., 8th Air Force at Ketteringham Hall. Shortly after the war ended was sent back to the States for discharge with the rank of corporal. Received the Purple Heart, Bronze Star, Expert Infantry Badge, Combat Infantry Badge, three Campaign Stars and several other ribbons.

On GI Bill he graduated from Lawrence University and went to work in the Research and Development end of the Specialty Paper Industry. (BS Chem.) He retired in 1977 as the VP R & D Nicolet Paper Co., a paper mill in Wisconsin. Since then spends his time with hobbies and at summer home in northern Wisconsin.

Has wife, Audrey; son, James R. Jr.; daughter, Mary; and one grandchild.

DONALD E. HICKS, was born Dec. 31, 1921 in Detroit, MI. Enlisted in Cadet Program July 13, 1942, graduated as pilot second lieutenant, November 1943, Ellington Field, TX. Assigned to Selman Field, LA for navigator training. Received Naval Aviator Wings in March 1944. Assigned to Keesler Field, MS for Air Sea Rescue training.

Assigned to 5th ERS Sqdn. at Halesworth, England. Flew 35 plus air-sea rescue missions. On one mission they picked up a fighter pilot five minutes after the call came, the speed was fortunate because he hadn't undone his chute leg straps and was being pulled under by that big sea anchor. They got a line around his chest and pulled him out of his chute. That made the Stars and Stripes. On another mission the North Sea was running at 20' waves. They followed a B-24 in, but it broke up on impact. They saw survivors, landed and were able to save two; but the sea was so rough, they couldn't get off. That night a British rescue boat rescued them. Discharged November 1945.

Married Mary Lee in June 1945 (passed away in 1986). They had two children and two grandchildren. Remarried to Marjorie Hatherley in October 1988 who gave him a family of five children and 13 more grandchildren.

Retired in 1982 as engineering group manager from General Motors.

ROGER F. HICKS, was born April 17, 1920 in Cementon, NY, raised in Belvidere, NJ. Took the Aviation Cadet exams and was sworn into the USAAC on Nov. 7, 1942. Called to active duty in February 1943. Graduated as a second lieutenant, Class of 44D on April 15, 1944 at Waco, TX.

Trained as a B-24 pilot at Liberal, KS. Attached to 458th Bomb Group, 752nd Sqdn., November 1944. Went down Jan. 17, 1945 on mission to destroy synthetic oil yards at Harburg, Germany. After V-E day ferried war weary B-24s back to England from Sweden. Returned to the States in July 1945 and was separated Dec. 16, 1945.

Joined the active reserves and was promoted to captain and flew C-119s and C-46s with the 512th Troop Carrier Wing, Newcastle, DE.

Married June 7, 1941 to Berdie Nunn, Hackettstown, NJ. Now has four children, eight grandchildren and four great-grandchildren.

WM. F. HICKS, was born Oct. 11, 1925, Harmon County, OK. Joined the USAAC, June 10, 1943. After a short stay in the Aviation Cadets was sent to Gunnery School at Harlingen, TX. Assigned to Lt. Raymond R. Swingle's B-24 crew and remained through training and 23 missions.

Crew was first assigned to the 453rd Bomb Group and transferred to 458th Bomb Group. He received the Air Medal with two Oak Leaf Clusters, ETO Ribbon with three Battle Stars. They flew back to the States in June of 1945 and he was discharged November 1945 with the rank staff sergeant.

In January 1946 he enrolled in the University of Oklahoma and attended until 1948. He farmed for part of 1948 and 1949. Married Mickie Young Dec. 27, 1949 and moved to Los Alamos, NM where he was employed by the Atomic Energy Comm. They are retired, but still living in Los Alamos, NM. They were blessed with a daughter, son and five grandchildren.

ROBERT E. HIEMSTRA, was born in Chicago, IL on Aug. 6, 1920; sworn in as aviation cadet; called to active duty, Oct. 25, 1942 and graduated from George Field, IL (twin-engine) with Class 43-H on Aug. 30, 1943. Assigned to the 458th Bomb Group at Wendover, UT. After training at Tonopah, NV moved with the 458th to Horsham-St. Faiths (Norwich). After 31 missions with the 752nd Sqdn., the last being on July 2, 1944, he returned to the States in September of 1944.

Memorable experiences: April 18, 1944 trip to Brandenburg when several 2nd BD groups entered a huge cloud bank at the same time and place on converging courses. After breaking out of clouds they found themselves all alone and joined two other lonely ships to fly a three ship formation back to Norwich from deep in Germany. The April 22, 1944 trip to Hamm and returning to Norwich after dark to find German fighters were waiting there. Just like Fourth of July fireworks back home!

Assigned to Albuquerque, NM and then to Palm Springs, CA to finish out the war. Discharged on Nov. 19, 1945 with the rank first lieutenant. Received the Distinguished Flying Cross, Air Medal with three clusters, ETO, three stars.

Returned to school, graduated from the University of Denver (BA 1948 and JD 1951) and admitted to the Colorado Bar.

Flew for Continental Air Lines from 1949 to 1980. He has now retired to Pensacola, FL with wife, Kathryn. They have two sons, one daughter and two grandchildren.

MORGAN G. HIGHAM, was born July 22, 1921 in Salt Lake City, UT. He joined the National Guard July 15, 1940, federalized March 3, 1941, sailed for the Philippines Dec. 6, 1941 and ended up in Hawaii. Returned to the States March 1942 for pilot training to become a staff sergeant pilot in Class 42-I, West Coast Training Command. Went to glider pilot training with a promise of a commission. Went back to pilot training in the Southeast Training Command and was commissioned second lieutenant Oct. 1, 1943 at Stuttgart, AR.

Trained in B-24s with the 467th Group at Mt. Home, ID and Wendover, UT. Flew to England out of Miami along the southern route. Flew 10 missions with the 467th group and was then transferred to the 489th group. On August 5 his plane was shot up on a mission to Brunswick, Germany and he was forced to bail out with his crew in the North Sea. He completed his tour of 32 missions on October 14 and returned back to the States with the 489th Group to transition into B-29s prior to going to the Pacific Theater.

Retired from the Army as a colonel March 31, 1979. Received the Distinguished Flying Cross, Air Medal with four clusters, and ETO Ribbon with four stars.

Married Ella Deane Jorgensen March 1945 and has three daughters and 10 grandchildren.

JOHN HILDEBRAN, was born March 3, 1920 in Cochranton, PA. Enlisted in Erie, PA in October 1942. Basic training at Duncan Field, TX; Gunnery School, Laredo, TX; Radio School, Sioux Falls, SD and Salt Lake. Joined Lt. Kremer's crew #549 as radio operator. Took B-24 training at Casper, WY and El Paso, TX.

Took new B-24 from Topeka, KS via southern route to England in spring of 1944. Flew 30 missions with 453rd Bomb Group, 732nd Bomb Sqdn. from May 23 to Aug. 9, 1944.

Taught gunnery in Harlingen, TX, then an MP in Independence, KS. Discharged Oct. 4, 1945 at Ft. Dix, NJ. Worked for Capital Airlines in Erie, then United Airlines in Miami and Ft. Lauderdale for nearly 35 years. Retired in 1981 to the hills of southeastern Oklahoma to a log cabin, where they feed deer, turkey, foxes, etc and love it.

Married Aida McElroy Sept. 28, 1944. They have two children, both in Florida.

LAWRENCE C. HILDEBRAND (LARRY), was born in Rural Ridge, PA, July 10, 1922. Entered the Aviation Cadets on Aug. 20, 1942 at Pittsburgh, PA on inactive duty. Called to active duty on March 1, 1943. Took navigation training at Selman Field, Monroe, LA. Graduated February 1944. Also took Gunnery School at Fort Myers, FL.

At Fresno, CA was assigned to B-24 crew. Took transition training at Muroc, CA. Assigned to 2nd Air Div., 392nd Bomb Group, 576th Sqdn. at Wendling, England in June 1944. Flew 35 missions ending on Jan. 10, 1945. Returned to the States. Assigned to Ellington Field, Houston, TX for deployment. Went to Hondo, TX for training August 1945. Discharged Oct. 1, 1945 as first lieutenant.

Graduated University of Pittsburgh June 1949. Held managerial positions with American Hardware (Servistar) from where he retired in 1974.

Married Rosemarie Fleming, June 1, 1951. They have three married daughters and six grandchildren.

GEORGE R. HILL, was born Aug. 4, 1918 in Kenosha, WI. Entered the USAAC Jan. 26, 1942. Stationed at Ft. Sheridan; basic at Jefferson Barracks, MO; Radio School, Scott Field, IL. Served with 44th Bomb Group, 67th Sqdn. in Shipdham, England, September 1942 to June 1945.

Memorable experience was his service in North Africa with the 44th and trips to the Holy Land, Paris, and Ploesti oil field. Discharged Sept. 8, 1945 with the rank master sergeant. Received the Bronze Star, Victory Medal and etc.

Married June 1946 to Mary. They have a son, Joseph, and daughter, Norean. Hill retired after 45 years in the radio TV business.

WILLIAM M. HILL (BILLY), was born July 27, 1921, Cape May, NJ and lived in Richmond, VA all his life. A graduate of University of Virginia in 1943, was captain of football in 1942. Joined USAAC in February 1943, received pilots wings at Lubbock Army Air Base in Class 44-D, completed B-24 training at Fort Worth, TX and Pueblo, CO.

Joined the 700th Sqdn., 445th Bomb Group in September 1944. Flew 35 missions over enemy territory. On Dec. 31, 1944 had two engines shot out flying over St. Vith (Battle of Bulge), was able to fly plane for over an hour and crash landed with no nose wheel at Valenciennes, France. No one was injured. Received Distinguished Flying Cross and six Air Medals.

In 1953 he married Ruth Nelson Johns. They had two sons and two daughters, eldest son Billy Jr. died running in the Marathon in Richmond in 1981. They have five wonderful grandsons. He works for Wheat, First Securities, senior vice president investments as a stockbroker. Chairman of committee to build Richmond's 12,500 seat coliseum. Past president of several clubs and organizations, just elected vice president of the Thomas Jefferson Society of the University of Virginia (members who graduated 50 years ago or more) still plays lots of tennis, handball, fishes and grows a vegetable garden.

SCOTT L. HILLIARD, was born Sept. 4, 1921 at Rockland, PA. Enlisted in the USAAF Aug. 22, 1942. Graduated from the schools in Aircraft Mechanics at Amarillo AAFB; Aircraft Mechanics at the B-24 factory San Diego; and Aerial Gunnery, Harlingen AAFB. Assigned as instructor engineer on B-24s at Clovis AAFB. Repeated requests for combat duty produced assignment to the 706th Bomb Sqdn., 446th Bomb Group then forming in July 1943 at Lowry AAFB.

In December 1943, the unit joined the 8th Air Force at Bungay, England. Flew first combat flight Dec. 22, 1943 and 31st (of a 30 mission tour) June 22, 1944. Served as B-24 mechanic-engineer at U.S. bases until discharged Oct. 6, 1945. Charter member of the DC Air National Guard, January 1946.

Recalled to active duty with that unit February 1951. Changed to Regular Air Force May 1951. Appointed warrant officer September 1953. Subsequently served as aircraft maintenance officer at bases in U.S., England, Germany, Philippines, and Vietnam.

Discharged September 1974 as CWO-4. Awarded the EAME Campaign Medal, three Bronze Battle Stars, Good Conduct Medal, Distinguished Flying Cross, four Air Medals, four Air Force Commendation Medals and numerous campaign-ribbons.

CARL E. HIMES, was born Sept. 13, 1924 in Coolsprings, PA. Drafted March 1943 in the USAAF. Basic at Clearwater, FL; Mechanic, Keesler Field; Gunnery, Harlingen, TX; crew training, Muroc, CA; 448th Bomb Group, Seething, England; Hydraulic School, Chanute, IL; B-17 crew chief, Dayton, OH.

Memorable experiences: losing power in #3 engine with four 2,000 lb. bombs over English Channel, hit storm and went into spin; hit in right aleron over Black Forest and it jammed straight up, Capt. Beall turned wheel over and flew back to England.

Discharged October 1945 with the rank tech sergeant. Received three Oak Leaf Clusters and Distinguished Flying Cross.

Himes is retired and lives in Englewood, OH.

BURTON J. HINCKLEY, was born Jan. 22, 1924 in Proctor, VT. Joined the service March 8, 1943; stationed in

Miami Beach, Scott Field, Harlingen, Wendling, England. Served as radio operator/gunner with the 8th AAF.

Memorable experience was low level mission over low-lands with 397th Bomb Group flying supplies to paratroopers. Completed 30 missions, Jan. 16, 1945. Discharged Sept. 28, 1945 with the rank tech sergeant. He received Air Medal and four clusters.

Married Jean in December 1945. They have one daughter and two granddaughters. Hinckley retired from the stained glass business.

LESTER E. HIX, was born Feb. 28, 1925 in Spencer, SD. Joined the USAAC, June 8, 1943 and called to active duty June 23, 1943, Ft. Crook, NE. Basic training, Jefferson Barracks, MO; airplane armorer, Lowry Field, CO; aerial gunnery, Harlingen Field, TX; and advanced training and crew formation Westover Field, MA.

Flew to Norwich, England and was assigned to the 467th Bomb Group, 789th Sqdn. Their plane was the *Miss Judy*. Memorable experience was 22nd mission, Oct. 14, 1944 when they were forced to bail out as an engine was on fire and could not be extinguished. As they hit the ground the Germans were firing at some of the crew. The pilot was killed while hanging in a tree, three others were wounded by gunshot wounds including Hix. From that point on they were prisoners until liberated April 26, 1945.

Discharged Oct. 14, 1945 with the rank staff sergeant. Received the Air Medal with three Oak Leaf Clusters, EAME Theater Medal, WWII Victory, Purple Heart and POW Medal.

Married and has three sons, one daughter, eight grandchildren and two great-grandchildren.

ANTHONY P. HMURA, was born July 3, 1923 in Worcester, MA. Entered the Air Corps in 1943. Attended Air Mechanic and Gunnery School 611-612. Was with the 445th Bomb Group, 703rd Sqdn. (Jimmy Stewart's outfit, operations officer).

Flew 28 combat missions in B-24s, Tibenham, England. Shipped to Sioux Falls, SD during second tour for B-29 training. Backed our troops on Desert Shield in 1992; helped to install monument at Worcester Common. Although was not in favor of war.

Discharged Oct. 10, 1945 with the rank staff sergeant. Awarded about 13 medals, including Battle Stars, clusters, Presidential Unit Citations and American Order of French Croix de Guerre. He is past commander of AMVETS.

Has four sons and four grandsons. Owner of Leader SKM Co. and Leader Construction Co. Ran for State Representative and Congress Congressional District. Still working harder than ever. Married 40 years, divorced.

GEORGE D. HOBKIRK, was born in Williamsville, IL Aug. 11, 1921. Married Sylvia Kaytis in 1945. Has one son and daughter and two grandchildren. Entered the USAAC as cadet graduating as navigator November 1943. Joined 467th Bomb Group at Wendover and went to Rackheath, England with them. Flew 30 missions from April 11, 1944 to June 24, 1944.

After war re-enlisted as master sergeant, recalled as navigator and flew 58 combat missions in B-29s with 19th Bomb Group during Korean Conflict. Retired from Air Force in 1962 after serving in HQ, 3rd Air Force, 86th Div. and MATS.

As civilian managed a Quilting Company and was analyst programmer for Aetna Life and Casualty. After wife died, he retired and moved to Orlando. Married Nancy Ching in September 1989 and moved back to Illinois.

RALPH F. HOEHN, was born Sept. 16, 1921 in Ottoville, Putnam County, OH. Enlisted in the USAAC October 1942. Stationed at San Antonio Aviation Cadet Center; primary flight training, Muskogee, OK; basic, Coffeeville, KS; advance twin engine training, Altus, OK; B-24 four engine training at Ft. Worth, TX, Liberal, KS and March Field, CA.

Their crew was among the first replacements to the 491st Bomb Group, 852nd Sqdn., 2nd Air Div. at Metfield, England and later moved to North Pickenham, north of London. Discharged October 1945 with the rank first lieutenant. Received Air Medal with Oak Leaf Clusters.

Married Alice M. Martz, Feb. 12, 1945. They have four children: Ed, David, Dan and Nancy. Retired February 1982 from Sohio Chemical, now B.P. Chemical.

FRANCIS J. HOFFMAN (FRANK), was born Jersey City, NJ on Oct. 8, 1924. Entered the Army February 1943; basic training at Miami Beach; A&E Mechanic, Casey Jones School of Aeronautics, Newark, NJ and Long Island, NY, September 1943; Flexible gunnery, Buckingham AAF, FL. Promoted to sergeant December 1943. Assigned to 884th Bomb Sqdn., 489th Bomb Group, Crew #9, Lt. Tankersley, pilot, January 1944, Wendover, UT. Upon completion of overseas training left for Camp Miles Standish, CT and POE Boston en route to England on the USS *Wakefield*, April 13, 1944.

Arrived Southampton and proceeded to RAF Station Holton near Halesworth. Upon arrival of the air eschelon, he was informed that his crew was disbanded. Temporarily assigned to base defense, awaiting crew assignment. Assigned to various crews, completing 27 missions when group was "stood down" to return to the States and retrain into B-29s. Completed overseas training with 489th (VH) Group as central fire control gunner at Davis-Monthan AAF, AZ when war ended. Was discharged from Sioux Falls, SD in October 1945.

Married Marge Cooke in 1947. They have eight children. While in the Reserves he received a direct commission of second lieutenant, November 1949. Recalled to active duty April 1951 as air police officer. Appointed captain Regular Air Force November 1956. Retired as lieutenant colonel May 1970.

Appointed chief of police, Glastonbury, CT, June 1970 and retired 17 years later to Florida. A happy triple dipper.

GEORGE D. HOFFMAN, was born Nov. 17, 1920, Pasadena, CA. Enlisted July 14, 1941 in the USAAF; graduated from pilot training at Stockton AAB, CA; and reported to Clovis AAB, NM for B-24 transition. Continued training at Lowry AAB, CO; Pueblo AAB, CO; Davis-Monthan AAB, AZ; and Blythe AAB, CA.

Overseas with the 491st through Herington, KS, etc. to Metfield, North Pickenham and Hethel in England. Upon return to ZO1, was assigned to 6th Ferry Command at Long Beach until WWII ended. Flew 47 combat missions, 35 with the 491st and 12 weather recon/VHF relay missions from Hethel.

Graduated from University of Southern California after WWII. Flew B-45 jet bombers during Korean Conflict. Was shot at and had a mid-air collision during the 50s and survived. Commanded a TAC Troop Carrier Sqdn. and a military airlift sqdn. During the MAC assignment, made numerous trips to Vietnam, Japan, Philippines, Korea and all points in between.

Retired Dec. 31, 1972 with the rank of colonel. Received the Air Force Commendation Medal, Distinguished Flying Cross, Air Medal with four Oak Leaf Clusters, Unit Citation with two Oak Leaf Clusters, Combat Readiness Medal with one Oak Leaf Cluster, American Defense Medal, American Campaign Medal, ETO Campaign Medal with four stars, WWII Victory Medal, National Defense Service Medal, Vietnam Campaign Medal and others.

Married and has two sons and one daughter. Retired from aerospace company in 1989 where he was a senior data management engineer. Began extensive travel in Great Britain in 1984 and continues to do so every two to three years spending two months there each trip.

RICHARD H. HOFFMAN, was born in West Virginia, Jan. 29, 1924; enlisted in the USAAC, Sept. 3, 1943; and attended Gunnery and Radio School. Assigned to original crew 9-1, 392nd BMGP, 579th Sqdn., Tuscon, AZ as a radio operator/gunner on Feb. 13, 1943.

Deployed to Wendling, England and was shot down on Nov. 5, 1943 over Munster, Germany and held at Stalag 17. Discharged as a tech sergeant on Nov. 9, 1945. Joined the USAFR in 1948 and was later commissioned as a second lieutenant. He volunteered for active duty in 1952 and spent much of his 30 year career as an intelligence officer, primarily in fighter/bomber groups in the U.S., Europe, Far East and Southeast Asia. He also saw duty as liaison with CIA. Lt. Col. Hoffman retired in 1974. Received the Meritorious Service Medal, Air Force Commendation Medal, Bronze Star, Purple Heart and many others.

Married Ruth J. Hastings in 1946 and has two children and two grandchildren. He is a writer and has drafted a manuscript about Stalag 17 POWs, their remarkable march across Austria and return to front line duty.

MARVIS T. HOGEN, was born Nov. 6, 1923 in Kadoka, SD. Enlisted in the Air Corps on Dec. 3, 1942. Graduated from Bombardier School on April 4, 1944 with the rank of flight officer. Went to England on a B-24 crew and flew 30 missions over Europe with the 453rd Bomb Group, 2nd Air Div., 8th Air Force.

His most memorable combat experience was the mission that bombed the Remagen bridge. The bombs were so close to target that they were sure that the bridge was destroyed. But it remained standing, the only bridge left on the Rhine River. The allied troops crossed this bridge in great numbers and it has been said that because it was left, WWII was shortened by six months and 10,000 American lives were saved. Shortly after the allied troops had crossed, the close bomb hits finally took their toll and the bridge collapsed.

Discharged on Oct. 13, 1945 with the rank first lieutenant. Received the Air Medal with four Oak Leaf Clusters.

Hogen opened his first hardware store, a business he still is involved in today. He opened other hardware stores, became involved in cattle ranching and wheat farming. He also was involved in South Dakota Republican politics, served in both houses of the state legislature, six years as Secretary of Agriculture and two years as state director of the Farm Home Administration.

Married Florence Brown, also from Kadoka, in 1943 while in Bombardier School in San Angelo, TX. They reside in Kadoka today and are active in the hardware business, ranching, farming and state politics. They have three sons, one daughter and five grandchildren.

DWIGHT NELSON HOHL, was born in Argyle, IA, Aug, 25, 1920. Enlisted in the USAAC in 1942 and received primary flight training Ft. Stockton, TX; basic flight training, San Angelo, TX; and advanced flight training, Pampa, TX. Graduated Aug. 4, 1944, Class 44-G as second lieutenant.

Overseas training Unit, Mt. Home, ID. Picked up new B-24 Topeka, KS. Flew northern route via Goosebay, Labrador and Iceland to England. Assigned to 445th Bomb Group, 702nd Bomb Sqdn., 8th Air Force, Tibenham, England. Flew missions over Germany until end of war 1945. Returned with B-24 to Sioux Falls, SD and Harlingen AFB, TX for discharge.

Recalled in 1950. Assigned Classification School, Lowry AFB, Denver, CO. Assigned officer in charge airman recall 14th Air Force, Warner Robins AFB, GA. Recalled 35,000 airmen for Korean War. Discharged June 1952. Married Freda Ball Jan. 19, 1951 and has a son, two daughters and three grandchildren.

EDWARD J. HOHMAN, was born in Pittsburgh, PA in 1923 and lived in Sharon, PA before entering the service in March 1943 at Miami Beach, FL.

After completing Air Force basic training, he attended Radio School at Scott Field, IL and completed gunnery training at Yuma, AZ. Assigned to combat crew #4566 and trained for combat at Peterson Field, Colorado Springs, CO. The crew flew to England in July 1944, joining the 491st Bomb Group, 852nd Bomb Sqdn.

Moved from Metfield to North Pickenham, they flew 27 missions. Their original pilot, Lt. Evan L. McClung, was killed on their seventh mission over Karlsruhe, Germany on Sept. 5, 1944.

Discharged at Sioux Falls, SD in October 1945 with the rank of tech sergeant. He followed a career in commercial art and was a freelance writer of greeting card verse and numerous articles for magazines and newspapers. He married Norma Jean McGilvray in 1966. They now reside in Hermitage, PA.

KENNETH C. HOLCOMB, was born Dec. 18, 1923 in Monroe, WI. Enlisted in USAAC Aug. 10, 1942. Graduated Radio School, Scott Field, IL and Aerial Gunnery School, Kingman, AZ. Assigned to Gowen Field, Boise, ID for flight crew training.

Assigned 2nd Air Div., 458th Bomb Group, Horsham, St. Faith Norwich, England, May 1944. Flew B-24s and abandoned damaged aircraft on 19th mission, July 20, 1944. Lived with Belgium underground until captured by Germans Aug. 18, 1944. Escaped during train derailment Sept. 4, 1944.

Returned to States for reassignment to 2nd Ferry Group, Air Transport Command, Wilmington, DE. Flew C-54s to Paris returning wounded infantry soldiers to hospitals in States.

Discharged Oct. 26, 1945 with the rank tech sergeant. Received the Air Medal and Purple Heart.

Graduated from University of Wisconsin in 1949 with BS in electrical engineering. Worked for public utility for 33 years. Retired May 1, 1983.

Married Alice Schenk on Aug. 11, 1943. They have two children and one grandchild.

FRED HOLDREGE, was born in Thermopolis, WY, Sept. 3, 1917. Enlisted in Army to attend West Point Preparatory School at Ft. Scott in 1936. Commissioned as second lieutenant CAC upon graduation from USMA and proceeded directly to pilot training.

Instructed in B-17s and B-24s before taking command on 790th Sqdn., 467th Group in October 1943. Led 790th Sqdn. until completion of combat missions at which time was reassigned to HQ 96th CBW.

Upon return to ZI proceeded to March Field for B-29 training for transfer to Pacific. Remained on active Air Force duty until retirement as colonel. Military awards include Air Medal with three clusters, Distinguished Flying Cross with cluster, Croix de Guerre and Legion of Merit with cluster. Flew numerous prop and jet aircraft in attaining command pilot rating.

Attained PhD at Ohio State University. Filled various assignments such as chief personnel Mgt AMC, professor of psychology, Air Force Academy, and chief Air Force Personnel Research Laboratory. Has lived in Durham, NC since 1970.

Married Jane Healy in June 1945. They have a son Mark.

FREDERICK J. HOLLIEN JR., enlisted Sept. 1, 1942 in the USAAC; served with 392nd Bomb Group, 578th Sqdn. as airplane mechanic gunner, 748, and engineer top turret gunner, B-24.

Participated in action in the EAME Theater Air Offensive. The crew's B-24 was named the *Laurie H.* after Hollien's daughter. Of the three married crew members, he was the only one with a child.

From his top turret gun position he was credited with shooting down two enemy aircraft. The best part of his crew was that all 10 men finished their missions with only one member, the navigator, getting a Purple Heart. Nine of the crew are still alive and they meet at the 2nd Air Division Association meeting.

Discharged July 19, 1945 with the rank of staff sergeant. Received the Distinguished Flying Cross and the Air Medal with five Oak Leaf Clusters.

Married 52 years to Lorraine and has four children and 14 grandchildren. Hollien retired after 30 years with the U.S. Postal Service. Has part-time job as a glass finisher, beer preferably!

WILLIAM J. HOLM, was born Dec. 30, 1920 in New York City and grew up near New Vernon, NJ. Graduated Morristown, NJ High School in 1939. Enlisted in USAAC in January 1942. Ordered to cadet training February 1943. Received wings and commission November 3, Moody Field, Valdosta, GA.

Trained with B-24s, Davis-Monthan, Tucson and with the original complement of the 491st Bomb Group, Pueblo, CO. Served as co-pilot, pilot, and later as assistant group training officer (853rd Sqdn. and Group HQ).

Flew with the group's 72 new B-24s to England in May 1944. Based at Metfield and North Pickenham. Flew group's first mission June 2 and on D-day. The crew's luck ran out June 20 at a no ball target in France. Nose turret was blown off and navigator and bombardier were lost. On the return to England, lost three engines and two gunners. Landed gear up among mines on beach near Folkstone. Lt. Holm suffered what later became a recurring back problem.

Assigned to group training office. Flew with new crews, some sorties, and sent to RAF Lancaster Base with 853rd Sqdn. Bombardier learn to learn evasive action tactics.

Returned to States January 1945. Trained GCA technicians McQuire AFB until inactive status on Sept. 10, 1945. Received five ETO Battle Stars, Air Medal and Presidential Unit Citation.

Returned to Army civilian personnel work, Navy Salary and Wage Administration. Retired as Labor-Management Relations officer at NASA's Kennedy Space Center, FL. Flies his North American (Air Force) L-17 for pleasure. Married with two daughters.

MAURICE O. HOLMEN (MO), was born July 9, 1922 in Upsala, MN and raised in Tucson, AZ. Interrupted studies at Phoenix Jr. College to join USAAC on March 1, 1943. Graduated Twin-Engine Advanced Class, 44-C, Stockton, CA, followed by B-24 Commander's School, Kirtland AFB, Albuquerque, NM. Combat crew training at Pueblo, CO then a slow boat to Europe and 35 missions with 715th Sqdn., 448th Bomb Group at Seething, England.

The two most difficult aspects of that tour were extreme weather conditions during winter of 1944-1945 and heavy losses from German ME-262 jet fighters. During Battle of the Bulge, they took off in zero visibility/zero ceiling weather. On 13th mission they experienced numerous mechanical problems after dropping bombs. They force landed in France; later returned to England, landing in blinding storm with 12" snow on ground, using ILS.

Was discharged with the rank of captain. Received five air medals and three battle stars.

Returned to Albuquerque on May 30, 1945. He married Berniece Byrd, who is a twin. They courted during Kirtland training. Attended University of New Mexico before establishing his own air conditioning contracting business.

Was recalled during the Korean War, 1951-1953, was air installations officer at Indian Springs AFB, NV. Entered Retired Reserve as captain and spent ensuing years in air conditioning business until 1985 retirement.

Father of six children and has five grandchildren. He is an elder in his church, past-mayor of Cochiti Lake, NM and travels in his 5th wheel RV. They winter in Arizona, Texas, Florida.

THOMAS GRANT HOLMES, was born Nov. 10, 1923 in Buffalo, NY. Enlisted in USAAC Feb. 1, 1943 while working for Chevrolet Aircraft Engine Plant. Stationed at Sheppard Field, TX; Peterson Field, CO. Assigned as flight engineer on B-24 crew and flew new B-24J to England.

Assigned to 392nd Bomb Group, 577th Bomb Sqdn. at Wendling, England. Participated in Air Offensive, Ardennes, Normandy, Northern France, Rhineland and Southern France. Completed tour of 35 missions. Received five Air Medals, Distinguished Flying Cross, five European Campaign Stars.

Discharged September 1945 and went on to build homes in Western New York area. Married Dawn Meyer July 12, 1947 and has four children and six grandchildren. He is semi-retired.

JOHN J. HOLZINGER, was born April 28, 1919 in Bethlehem, PA. Enlisted in the USAAC on Oct. 28, 1942. Graduated from Navigation School, Hondo, TX, Class 44-4. Assigned to 392nd Bomb Group, 578th Sqdn. in August 1994. Flew 33 missions as navigator with Robert H. Tays crew.

Received Air Medal with four Oak Leaf Clusters and four European Campaign Battle Stars. Separated in October 1945. Was recalled to active duty Oct. 8, 1950. Served with 48th Troop Carrier Sqdn. at Mitchell AFB, NY until Aug. 31, 1953. Separated with rank of captain. Retired from Reserves on July 1, 1964 with rank of major.

Retired from Bethlehem, Pennsylvania Police Department as captain in 1966. Retired from Bethlehem Steel Co. as supervisor in 1982.

Married Myra Mason at Kings Lynn, England on Dec. 22, 1944. Has one son and two grandchildren.

JOSEPH A. HOMSHER, was born Feb. 16, 1926 in Bryn Maws, PA. Enlisted April 15, 1944 in the USAAF, tail gunner. Served with 491st Bomb Group, Lt. Albert Fischer's crew. Stationed at Pickenham, UK, Good Fellow, Big Spring, McGuire, Forbes, and Beale.

Memorable experience was when heavy flak caused three B-24s to be emergency landed on continent in Holland. Was discharged December 1969 with the rank of major. Received the Air Medal, USAF Outstanding Procurement Officer, 1968.

Has BS in business administration from St. Joseph's University, PA, 1951; Air Force pilot training, Class 1953-A, commissioned second lieutenant; Bachelor of Law, Class of 1961 from LaSalle Extension University, Chicago, IL; Master of aerospace, operations and management, Class of 1968, University of Southern California; Air Force Contract Officer's School, 1963, chief, Base Procurement, 1964-1969; U.S. Dept. Justice, Ins. Supervisory contract specialist, Western Regional Office, 1971-1987.

Married Theresa A. Skowyra and has six children, all in good health and working in various career fields. Homsher has been retired since 1991.

WELLONS B. HOMUTH, was born Sept. 16, 1920 in Barrington, IL. Enlisted in the USAAC on Oct. 10, 1942, Aurora, IL. Sent to Sheppard Field, TX for airplane mechanic training. Volunteered for Gunnery School and sent to Glen L. Martin B-26 specialized training; to Fort Myers, FL for Gunnery School, Clovis, NM for B-24 flight engineer training; Lowry Field, CO to train with crew in 704th Bomb Sqdn., 446th Bomb Group.

Flew 30 missions and on 10th mission Feb. 24, 1944 to Gotha, Germany. Bailed out when plane was shot up and pilot killed. Finished missions and went to air base in Ireland as combat crew flight instructor. Back to the States for rest and deployment in December 1944. Various assignments in States until discharged at Truax Field, Madison, WI on Oct. 13, 1945 with the rank tech sergeant. Received the European Theater Ribbon, Good Conduct, Airplane Mechanic, Air Medal with three Oak Leaf Clusters and the Distinguished Flying Cross.

Worked as engineer for Illinois Bell Telephone Co. for 37 years until retirement in May 1982. Homuth married Marguerite 45 years ago, they have five children.

MARK R. HONTZ, was born Feb. 1, 1922 and enlisted in the Army Enlisted Reserve Corps while attending Lehigh University. Called to active duty in March 1943, he took infantry training at Camp Croft. Prior to completing training he applied for and was accepted for aviation cadet training. Graduated from the Pan American Airways Navigation School in Coral Gables, FL in April 1944.

Assigned to the B-24 crew of Lt. Leon Cwikla. After combat crew training the crew was given a B-24 to ferry to the ETO. Assigned to the 330th Sqdn. of the 93rd Bomb Group in September 1944. Second mission was on September 27 to Kassel. Completed tour of 35 missions in February 1945. Awarded the Air Medal with five Oak Leaf Clusters and four European Campaign Stars.

Graduated in 1948 from Lehigh University. Employed by Public Service Electric and Gas Co., Newark, NJ for 36 years, retiring in 1984 as manager of maintenance. During his working career he joined the Air Force Reserve and retired in 1982 with the rank of major.

Married Barbara Daugherty Oct. 13, 1946. They have four children: Sharyn, Mark, Garry and Robin, and nine grandchildren.

PAUL E. HOOD, was born Feb. 1, 1921 in Clare, IA and joined the service July 14, 1942. Stationed at Camp Roberts Inf.; aviation cadet, San Antonio and Waco; Armanent School, Denver; Gunnery School, Tyndall Field, FL. Served with 329th and 328th Bomb Sqdn., 93rd Bomb Group, Hardwick, England as armorer gunner, B-24.

Flew 35 combat missions over France, Germany, Rhineland, Ardennes, Central Europe, GO-40 WD45. Memorable experiences: lead crew crossing of Rhine, low level; as armorer gunner in pre-check of bombs before take-off, he found three bombs without pins, one a 500#, then had flat tire on take-off and crashed at end of field.

Discharged July 19, 1945 at Fort MacArthur with with rank of staff sergeant. Received five Oak Leaf Clusters, Air Medal GO11 HQ 2BD, EAME Campaign Medal, Marksman M1 Rifle (Camp Roberts).

Graduated University of Southern California, 1949 civil engineer, California State Dept. Water Resources for 34 years, assistant to district engineer of Los Angeles for 10 years. He retired in June 1983.

Married Martha Olsen Likness in August 1953. They have four sons, four daughters and two grandchildren. He enjoys bowling, golfing, horseracing, ball games, traveling and reunions.

BENJAMIN R. HOOKER JR., was born Jan. 31, 1923 in Broaddus, TX. Enlisted Jan. 25, 1943, Ordnance Dept. attached to USAAF. Basic at Miami Beach TTC; Ordnance School, Ft. George Wright, Santa Anita, CA; Wendover Field, UT; Tonopah, NV; St. Faiths Horsham, England. Served with 458th Bomb Group, 754th Sqdn.

Participated in action at Normandy, Northern France, Rhineland and Air Offensive Europe. Memorable experience was buzz bomb attacks, London; V2 Rocket attacks and friendships developed with English people.

Discharged Oct. 30, 1945 with the rank private first class. Received the American Theater, EAME with four Bronze Stars, Good Conduct and three Overseas Service Bars.

Married Betty Bridges Jan. 31, 1946. They have two children, Cecilia and Pamela, and four grandsons: Chad, Chris, Eric and Danny. Retired Oct. 1, 1983 after 37 years as photographer with local industry. Stays busy with church, gardening, crafts, etc.

ODELL HOOPER, was born March 18, 1923 in Hastings, OK. Entered the service Nov. 1, 1942, 8th Air Force, 453rd Bomb Group, 732nd Sqdn. Stationed at Sheppard Field, TX; Tyndall Field, FL; Boise, ID; and Riverside, CA.

Memorable experiences: bombing missions over Germany in B-24; bailed out over Holland after Berlin Raid and spent 14 months as prisoner of war.

Discharged Oct. 29, 1945 with the rank tech sergeant. Received the Purple Heart, Cross of Valor, POW Medal, ETO, Good Conduct and the Victory Medal.

Married since Feb. 8, 1947 to Imaree. They have one daughter, Patricia Ann Hooper. He is retired and lives in Duncan, OK.

EDWARD HOOTEN JR., was born Oct. 7, 1923 in Elizabeth, NJ. Graduated high school there in 1939; sworn into USAAC in March 1942 and called up in October. Active duty at Nashville, assigned pilot training, Southeast Command. Received pilot wings July 1943, Turner Field, GA; B-24 transition at Maxwell; then Wendover, UT. Assigned to 467th Bomb Group, 789th Sqdn.

Sent to England February 1944 as squadron assistant ops officer. Did 30 missions in command pilot slots beginning April 1944 and finished November 1944. Home as captain and assigned to Dow Field, Air Transport Command. Flew the Atlantic regularly.

Separated September 1945 on point system. Began Rutgers University the same month. Graduated BS, mechanical engineer in 1949. Joined du Pont Co's Eng'g Dept. in February 1950 in Construction Division at Niagara Falls. Various managerial assignments.

In 1972 transferred to Remington Arms Company, du Pont subsidiary at Bridgeport, CT. In 1976 he became vice president and director of production with seven U.S. plants and 7,000 employees. Retired at age 62 in April 1985 with 35 years service.

Is lifetime member ASME and licensed professional engineer, state of Delaware. Listed in *Who's Who in the East* and *Who's Who in Aviation and Aerospace.* Moved to Pensacola, FL in 1991 for weather and boating reasons. Has good wife, good kids, good health, good boat and enjoying life.

JAMES A. HOOVER, was born April 30, 1918 in Fayette County, KY. Entered the USAAC in January 1943 as cadet.

First mission was the toughest, they lost several B-24s out of 392nd Group. Memorable experience was flying the Atlantic when he came home.

Discharged November 1945 with the rank first lieutenant. Received the Air Medals and all the usual campaign medals and ribbons.

Married to Rebecca, has daughter, Susan Jenkins, and son, James Michael. He enjoys golfing, fishing and playing bridge.

MICHAEL CLARENCE HOOVER, was born Jan. 26, 1919 in Keene Twp., Ionia County, MI. Enlisted March 21, 1941, assigned to Field Artillery and USAAF, 1024, B-24 pilot. Stationed at Camp Roberts, CA; March Field, CA; Fort Hood, TX; Mojave Desert, CA; Liberal, KS; Salt Lake City, UT; Alamogordo, NM; Attlebridge, England, Long Beach, CA; Homestead, FL; and Travis, CA.

Assigned to 8th Air Force, 2nd Air Div., 466th Combat

Group, picked up new B-24H and flew southern route to England. Plane had serious defect and could not keep up with other B-24s. No one in the group knew what was wrong or how to correct it so plane was named *The Lemon.* The crew was assigned to a different aircraft. Later a factory representative found and corrected a misalignment of the tail rudders.

Memorable experience was group's #6 mission with severe fighter opposition on April 8, 1944, six planes lost, 21 KIA, 38 POW, other planes damaged and personnel wounded. Relieved of active duty Dec. 1, 1945 as a first lieutenant. Entered Inactive Reserve and retired from USAFR Jan. 26, 1979 with the rank of major. Received the Distinguished Flying Cross, Air Medal with three Oak Leaf Clusters, two Battle Stars, American Campaign Medal, WWII Victory Medal and Armed Forces Reserve Medal.

Attended Michigan State University for four years, graduated with a BS degree in electrical engineering. In June of 1950 was employed by the Electric Sorting Machine Co. (division of Geosource Inc.) was chief engineer from 1969-79, retired in 1980 and moved to Jacksonville, FL. For the past 10 years has been collecting genealogical information and making a book regarding the Hoover-Feuerstein families.

Married Pauline E. Appleby, Jan. 18, 1945, Long Beach, CA. They have no children.

MORRIS L. HOOVER, was born Sept. 18, 1923, Cincinnati, OH. Entered USAF January 1943, served with 8th Air Force, 2nd Air Div., 93rd Bomb Group, 330th Bomb Sqdn., stationed in Hardwick, England. Participated in the ETO.

Discharged November 1945 with the rank staff sergeant. He received the Air Medal.

Morris Hoover is a retired architect and his father Ed is a lawyer, Cincinnati, OH.

JEROME F. HOUGH, was born June 29, 1920 in Ann Arbor, MI. Enlisted in the USAAC in August 1940, four years mechanic, Southeast Training Command. Flew 31 missions in *Career Girl* with pilot Lt. Crowell, 576th Sqdn. as flight engineer from November 1944 to May 1945.

Discharged July 10, 1945 with the rank master sergeant. Received the Air Medal with four Bronze Oak Leafs, EAME Theater with four Bronze Battle Stars, American Defense and Good Conduct.

Married to Winnifred and has a son, daughter and one grandchild. Graduated with BSEE and was employed 29 and a half years, eng. staff, Ford Motor Company. Currently retired.

ROSS S. HOUSTON, was born Jan. 2, 1921 in St. Louis, MO. Entered the USAAF on Sept. 22, 1942, Aviation Cadet Navigation Aerial. Stationed at Selman Field, Monroe, LA; Tucson, AZ; Blythe, CA; Pueblo, CO; Medfield, North Pickenham, England.

Participated in aerial combat over France and Germany, completing 27 missions. Was shot down on 27th mission, Nov. 26, 1944, over Misberg, Germany. Was prisoner of war for six months at Stalag Luft 1, Barth, Germany.

Discharged Oct. 8, 1945 with the rank first lieutenant. Received four Air Medals, four Battle Stars, POW Medal and the Unit Citation.

Married Jean Teeling Nov. 22, 1947. Has four children and 10 grandchildren. He is retired and does volunteer work.

BARKEV A. HOVSEPIAN, was born in Hartford, CT on July 10, 1921. Enlisted in USAAF Aviation Cadets, July 1942 (ERC), Class 43-J (Pilot), graduated Radio School, Sioux Falls, SD. Assigned to crew at Westover AAF, trained at Charleston AAF and as lead crew, Langley Field, for H2X bomb/nav. Assigned to 466th Bomb Group, 787th Bomb Sqdn., 2nd Air Div., 8th AAF, tech sergeant, radio/ECM operator with 35 combat missions and three fuel haul missions

to Patton's Army, September 1944. Crash landed at Manston after preparing to ditch in channel. MIA for week. Received five Air Medals and European Campaign Battle Stars.

Graduated Wentworth Inst., Northeastern University, EE and BBA degrees. Founder of Massachusetts Chapter, 8AFHS; past president, 466th BGA; member AFA, 2ADA; past vice-president, 8AFHS; past president, NU Regional Alumni Chapter; chairman, Radiation Control Committee. Amateur radio, KLYYG; electronics instructor, Sylvania Tech School; representative to AF Facilities Group for Minuteman II, III, Peacekeeper (MX) missiles; Norton AFB, CA; Lic. Prof. Eng., Massachusetts. Retired from GTE (Sylvania) after 34 years.

Married to Pauline since 1951. They live in Needham Heights, MA and have one son, Mark Aram.

DAL A. HOWARD, was born in Neola, IA on June 20, 1921. Entered the USAF in January 1943. Was proud to be part of of the 567th Bomb Sqdn. and 389th Bomb Group. Pilot Clarence J. (Bud) Harmon was the best skipper in the 8th Air Force. Co-pilot, Huey Dumbar, was a P-51 pilot sent to help their skipper.

Returning to the USA, he was sent to B-29 training. V-J day left him wondering what to do; but with a tech sergeant rating, he decided to re-enlist. They were offering a 90 day re-enlistment leave plus a $300 bonus. He continued flying in the B-29s until 1950. Resigned from the USAF in 1951. Received the American Theater Operations, ETO Ribbon with three B Stars, Air Medal with one Oak Leaf Cluster, Good Conduct and the Unit Presidential Citation.

Has kept in contact with his pilot and after 45 years visited him in Sun City, AZ in 1989. After nine years in the Air Force, he worked in the Civil Service for the postal department. He retired in 1976 with 30 years of service with military credits at the age of 56.

Has attended many wonderful and memorable reunions of the 389th Bomb Group. They were privileged to attend two reunions in Norwich, England. What a thrill. Howard and wife, Betty, have two married sons and four grandchildren. Fort Madison, IA is their permanent home, but they enjoy winter in their Arizona home.

GEORGE T. HOWARD JR., was born Aug. 26, 1925 in Bradford, PA; graduating from high school, June 1943; enlisted in the USAAC; reported to Miami Beach in September 1943 to begin basic training in the Aviation Cadet Program. Transferred to Harlingen, TX in December 1943 for Aerial Gunnery School, then transferred to Lincoln, NE and assigned to Charles F. Healy B-24 crew.

Trained in Pueblo, CO in spring of 1944 and after picking up new B-24 in Lincoln, NE, flew to Valley, Wales via Bangor, ME, Goose Bay, Labrador and Reykjavik, Iceland. Assigned to 458th Bomb Group and flew first four missions as ball turret gunner and remaining missions as waist gunner. Trained as a lead crew in the 755th Bomb Sqdn. and completed 30 missions on April 10, 1945.

Returned to USA in May 1945 and after several temporary assignments in Santa Ana, CA; Amarillo and Wichita Falls, TX; and Denver, CO was discharged in October 1945 with the rank staff sergeant. Received Good Conduct Medal,

ETO Ribbon with four stars, Air Medal with four Oak Leaf Clusters. Most memorable experience was meeting his future wife in Brussels, Belgium, following an emergency landing on their 6th mission to Karlsruhe, Germany, Nov. 5, 1944. Following an exchange of Christmas cards in 1945, Liliane and Howard corresponded for three years and in February 1948, they were married. They have two children and a grandson.

Howard is currently retired and enjoys traveling and playing golf.

JOHN D. HOWARD, was born July 9, 1922 in a farming area near Paris, TX. Graduated from the Hondo, TX Navigation School on April 22, 1944 and received B-24 crew and operational training at Biggs Field, El Paso, TX. Joined the 466th Bomb Group at Attlebridge, England in August 1944.

The pilot of their crew was killed in a mid-air collision on Sept. 16, 1944 while flying as an observer on a practice mission with another crew. They were assigned another pilot and immediately flew two missions hauling gasoline to Patton's troops at Lille and St. Dizier, France. Later flew 30 combat missions, the last 10 being as pilotage navigator on a lead crew. Received flak damage on 17 of first 18 missions. On one mission received a direct hit through the right wing by an 88mm shell that failed to explode.

Attained the rank of first lieutenant and was awarded the Air Medal and four Oak Leaf Clusters. Participated in the battles of Northern France, Rhineland, Ardennes, and Central Europe receiving Bronze Stars for each.

Following discharge Oct. 31, 1945, he attended the University of Texas and received a degree in petroleum engineering in 1949. Worked in the Oil industry for 35 years retiring in 1984. Married Aug. 28, 1948 and has two children and three grandchildren.

ARTHUR W. HOWE, was born Dec. 31, 1920, Atlanta, GA. Enlisted in the USAAC, January 1941. Weather School at Chanute Field, IL; Hunter Field, Savannah, GA, 1941. In 1942 was assigned to HQ & HQ Sqdn., 8th Bomber Cmd. and shipped to England on HMS *Andes*. In April 1942, Pine Tree, Wycombe Abby, then assigned to HQ 2nd Bomb Wing Horsham St. Faith, Norwich. Set up Weather Station RAF, Hendon, in 1943 with M/Sgt. Wayne Pennypacker, 18th Weather Sqdn., Air Transport Cmd.

Returned to States November 1944 and discharged September 1945. Returned to Savannah and employed as plant manager, metal buildings. Attained BS degree, industrial arts, taught Savannah Tech and retired in 1986.

On Jan. 28, 1992, Wing Commander, GA Chapter, 8th AFHS, helped host the 50th anniversary celebration of the 8th founded in Savannah 1942. Returned to England in May 1992 and visited 2nd Air Division Library, Phyllis Dubois and staff. Visited with Tom and Robin Eaton. Revisited Horsham St. Faith, Hendon, and Wycombe Abby.

Married Dec. 27, 1944 to Martha Jo Brewer, has one daughter, Cindy Barnwell.

LEONARD R. HOWELL JR., was born May 19, 1925 in Valdosta, GA. Entered active service at Keesler Field, MS in June 1943. Graduated from cadet training as a navigator at Selman Field, LA, Oct. 28, 1944. Assigned to 389th Bomb Group (Hethel) about March 15, 1945.

Departed England for States May 20, 1945 (after having flown no missions). Was in B-29 navigation training at McDill Field, FL, when war ended. Released from active duty Dec. 2. 1945, not discharged, but put in Inactive Reserves. Ended war as second lieutenant.

Recalled to active duty June 1953. Stationed at Travis AFB, CA as navigator in Military Air Transport Service. Transferred to Wiesbaden AFB, Germany in May 1955.

Transferred to Air Force Academy as assistant professor of mathematics in August 1958. Went to Florida State University (Tallahassee, FL) under Air Force Institute of Technology program to pursue PhD in mathematics in June 1962. Graduated August 1965 and transferred to HQ USAF, stationed in Alexandria, VA. Transferred to AFIT Engineering School, Wright Paterson AFB, OH as associate professor of mathematics in June 1969. Retired from Wright-Paterson as lieutenant colonel in June 1972.

Married Sept. 2, 1944 to Myrtis Avera. They have four children and nine grandchildren. After retirement he taught mathematics for nine years at Valdosta State College, Valdosta, GA. Retired from there in 1981. Now fully retired.

RICHARD H. HOWELL, was born Dec. 29, 1925 in Cincinnati, OH. Entered the USAAC January 1944 as gunner. Served overseas with 445th Bomb Group, Tibenham, England.

Memorable experiences were getting lost over the English Channel at night on a training mission; the low-level tactical mission at Rhine crossing March 24, 1945; attempting to bomb Heligoland, March 20, 1945.

Discharged December 1945 with the rank staff sergeant. Received the Air Medal with two Oak Leaf Cluster. His brother was killed November 1944 in the battle of the Hurtgen Forest in Germany, 1st Inf. Div. (Rangers). Howell has been married 46 years and has six children and 11 grandchildren. He is a physician (M.D.) and has been in private practice for 40 years.

JOHN H. HOYLE, was born Aug. 7, 1923 in Woonsocket, RI. Enlisted Feb. 19, 1943 in the USAAC, airplane engine mechanic, 467th Bomb Group, 791st Bomb Sqdn. Stationed at Wendover Field, UT; Rackheath; Salina, KS; Sioux City, IA; and Sioux Falls, SD. Participated in Normandy, Rhineland, Northern France, Ardennes, Southern France, Air Offensive Europe and Central Europe.

Memorable experience was when the Germans followed the group back and bombed the air field. Discharged Oct. 24, 1945 with the rank sergeant.

He received the EAME Service, seven Bronze Stars and the Good Conduct.

Married and has three children and seven grandchildren. He is retired.

HUGH H. HOYT, was born Sept. 5, 1922 in Colchester, IL. Enlisted Oct. 1, 1942 and was activated Jan. 30, 1943 in USAAC, 4-engine pilot. Aviation Cadet, pilot, Gulf Coast Training Command, stationed at Old Buck with the 453rd Bomb Group, 732nd Bomb Sqdn. His memorable experience was surviving.

Discharged Sept. 14, 1945 with the rank first lieutenant.

Married June 1945 and has three children and seven grandchildren. He is retired.

RALPH L. HOYT JR., was born Sept. 4, 1922. Entered the USAAF Aug. 4, 1942. Stationed at Santa Anita, CA; Salt Lake City, UT; Mt. Home, ID; Wendover, UT; Tonapah, NV; Horsham St. Faith, Norfolk, England; Sioux Falls, SD; Albuquerque, NM and Ft. Smith, AR. Served as small arms weapons mechanic 511 with the 753rd Bomb Sqdn.(H), 458th Bomb Group(H), 8th Air Force.

Participated in Air Offensive Europe, Normandy, Rhineland, Ardennes, Northern France, Central Europe. Memorable experiences: their 753rd Sqdn. was first to use Azon bombing (radio controlled); D-day; flights; first raids on Berlin; and Battle of Bulge.

Discharged Sept. 19, 1945 with the rank aviation cadet. Received the Good Conduct Medal, American Service Ribbon, EAME Ribbon with one Silver Star, One Bronze Star, and the Victory Medal. Married Phyllis Knight March 27, 1943. They have three sons, seven grandchildren. Oldest son, Ron (20 years in Air Force) and youngest son, Jeff, received medical discharge after five and a half years in Air Force.

Worked 39 years for U.S. Postal Service, last 20 years as Postmaster, Rindge, NH. He retired in May 1985.

RICHARD J. HRUBY, was born Aug. 26, 1922 in Elizabeth, NJ. Entered the USAAC March 1942 at Ft. Dix, NJ. Served as combat pilot with 506th Sqdn., 44th Bomb Group, Shipdham, England. Trained at Pine Bluff, AR, Winfield, KS, Altus, OK, Smyrna, TN and Boise, ID.

Participated in air war in Europe from February 1944 to December 1944. Flew 31 missions, ditched B-24 on Berlin Mission in April 1944. All crew were saved. Discharged in 1945 with the rank first lieutenant. Received the Air Medal with three clusters and Distinguished Flying Cross with one cluster.

Married and has five children. He is semi-retired and lives in Mt. Holly, NJ and Middletown, VT.

JOSEPH J. HUBEN, was born Oct. 7, 1925 in Staten Island, NY. Entered the service Dec. 30, 1943. Served with 8th Air Force, U.S. Army, 467th Bomb Group (H), 791st Sqdn. Attended Gunnery School, Laredo, TX; Casper, WY; Rackheath, England.

Participated in action at Ardennes, Rhineland, Central Europe and North Apennines. Completed 30 combat missions. Discharged Nov. 20, 1945 with the rank sergeant. Received the Air Medal with four Oak Leaf Clusters, four Campaigns with four Battle Stars and New York State Conspicuous Service Cross.

Retired sergeant, New York City Police, private investigator and security director.

CHARLES A. HUDDLESTUN, was born Sept. 13, 1923 in East Liverpool, OH. Entered the USAAF March 28, 1943. Basic training at Kearns Field, Salt Lake City, UT; Armament training at Lowry and Buckley Fields, Denver, CO; gunnery training, Tyndall Field, Panama City, FL; Class of 43-46, November 1943.

Overseas training at Peterson Field, Colorado Springs, CO. Assigned to crew of Joseph D. Salisbury in Salt Lake City, UT. Flew southern route to Blackpool, England and arrived in April 1944. Flew 26 missions with 445th Group, 700th Sqdn., May 1944 to December 1944. Was hospitalized June 1944 for perforated ear drums. This let Joe Salisbury get ahead of him in missions. After Joe finished he flew as a replacement gunner with John French's crew for three missions.

Most memorable run was ill-fated raid on Kassel, Germany when the 445th was wiped out. They were fortunate and crashed at Rheims, France. This was his last and 25th mission. After returning to the 445th, his replacement had not yet arrived and he was slated for another mission on Oct. 15, 1944 to Dusseldorf, Germany. This made #26 and he was done. Received credit for a kill of an FW-190 on the Kassel raid. Left "merrie old England" on Dec. 6, 1944 by seas and arrived New York City Dec. 22, 1944. After a furlough, he reported to Santa Ana, CA, then assigned to Instructor's School in Laredo, TX. Then to Harlingen, TX to teach B-29 gunnery. War was winding down then and he was reassigned to Tinker Field, Oklahoma City. Discharged Oct. 3, 1945, Wright Patterson Field, Dayton, OH with the rank staff sergeant. Received the Distinguished Flying Cross, five Air Medals, European Ribbon with four Battle Stars and some lesser medals. Also a certificate in lieu of medal for the Croix de Guerre with Palme which was awarded to the 445th Group.

Married to Trecia A. Minor on Aug. 26, 1945. They have two sons, two daughters, seven grandchildren (one drowned) and two great-grandchildren. Retired after 30 years as chemist in water and waste-water treatment.

ROBERT D. HUDNALL, was born near Dayton, OH on Nov. 9, 1924. Graduated from high school in May and was inducted into USAAF in August 1943. Basic training at Miami Beach, FL; additional training at Chanute Field, IL; Aerial Gunnery School, Laredo, TX and Fresno, CA. Joined crew at March Field, CA and trained there as tail gunner.

Crew got a new B-24 at Hamilton Field, CA. Flew to Wales for combat training and then flew to Horsham St. Faith in England with 458th Bomb Group, 753rd Sqdn. They later were transferred to 755th Sqdn. as lead crew (Scott Hathorn now of Arizona was pilot). Flew 28 missions over Germany 1944-1945. Discharged October 1945.

Worked at NCR Dayton for 30 years as tool inspector. Then worked at G.M. Chevrolet Engine as lay-out inspector for 14 years. Retired May 1991. Married Norma on March 21, 1947. They have two daughters, two sons, three granddaughters and one grandson

JAMES C. HUDSON (JIM), was born June 18, 1921, Cheraw, SC. Enlisted in the Air Force Oct. 6, 1942, Columbia, SC for aviation training and began active duty Jan. 29, 1943. Basic training at Miami Beach, FL; classes at Maryville College, Maryville, TN; classification July 4, 1943, in Nashville, TN for pilot training; pre-flight at Maxwell Field, Montgomery, AL; primary flight training at Jackson, MS; basic flight training at Greenville, MS and advanced training at George Field, Lawrenceville, IL. Here he had the thrill of graduation, Class 44-D and received his wings.

In December 1944 he was sent on the New Amsterdam to North Pickenham, England in the 8th Air Force, 2nd Air Div., 491st Bomb Group. His memorable experience was returning from Berlin on three engines. He flew his crew and some passengers back to the States June 1945. Following a 30 day leave, was sent to McChord Field, Tacoma, WA, where the 491st was terminated.

Was made flight instructor at Gowan Field, Boise, ID, then sent to Army Finance School, St. Louis, MO and next to Air Tactical School, Panama City, FL. Next he was Special Services Officer at Roswell AFB until discharged in November 1947 with the rank of captain. Received the European Theatre and three Air Medals. He is now retired and lives near Murrells Inlet, SC.

Married Beverlie M. Derminer on Dec. 6, 1942. They have three sons, three daughters, 12 grandchildren and two great-grandchildren.

LEON C. HUGGARD, was born in Waverly, IA on Oct. 25, 1922 and raised on a farm near Plainfield, IA. Entered the USAAC on Jan. 26, 1943. Attended Radio Operator School at Camp Crowder, MO and Gunnery School at Laredo, TX. Continued crew training at Peterson Field, CO as radio operator. Charles S. Evans was crew pilot.

Crew assigned as replacement to 458th Bomb Group (B-24) at Horsham St. Faith in April 1944. Completed 30 mission tour and returned from England in March 1945. Reassigned for B-29 training prior to discharge September 1945.

Most memorable experience was August 1944 when, as a lead crew plane, they were in a mid-air collision with the deputy lead plane near Metz, France. Pilot Evans was able to fly their crippled plane *A Dog's Life* back to Woodbridge, England emergency field for a successful landing, with the right wing tip dragging on the runway.

Discharged Sept. 13, 1945 with the rank tech sergeant. Received the Air Medal with four Oak Leaf Clusters and ETO with five Battle Stars.

Married Gertrude Schukar in March 1947. Has a son, two daughters and seven grandchildren. Huggard retired from civil service, Dec. 31, 1982.

WALTER F. HUGHES, was born Jan. 27, 1922 near Goleta, CA and enlisted in the Air Corps July 1942. Pilot, Class 44-A, Marfa, TX, January 1944. He flew a new B-24 from Hamilton Field, CA to England. Crew was assigned to the 330th Sqdn., 93rd Bomb Group, August 1944. First mission, Sept. 10, 1944 and last mission (35th) April 8, 1945. Discharged on June 10, 1945 as first lieutenant. He earned the Distinguished Flying Cross, Air Medal with seven Oak Leaf Clusters and Unit and Theater decorations.

Lt. Peter Scott, the crew's co-pilot was killed over Hamburg on a mission on Nov. 21, 1944 and two crewmen were injured during a fighter attack on the 34th mission April 7, 1945. The crew participated in low level resupply missions to Montgomery's Rhine River Crossing on March 24, 1945.

Lt. Hughes returned to March Field to marry WAC Cpl. Violet Sasso on July 24, 1945. They have three children and two grandchildren. He was a veterinarian, specialized in Avian Medicine. He retired in 1990.

RICHARD P. HUMPHREY JR. (DICK), was born Nov. 11, 1925 in Tanner, AL. Enlisted May 1944 in the USAAC and served as tailgunner on B-24 Liberator bomber with the 389th Bombardment Group, 2nd Air Div. Gunnery School, Tyndall Field, FL. Participated in action in European Theater of Operations, Southern France, Rhineland and Central Europe. Discharged May 1945 with the rank tech sergeant. Received three Battle Stars.

Graduated from Auburn University with BS degree from School of Education; did graduate work on master's degree at Auburn and Mississippi State; holds achievement, standard and graduate diplomas from the Institute of Financial Education. Taught Lamar County High School, Vernon, AL for five years; entered savings and loan business in April 1963; active in numerous civic affairs. Was inducted into Birmingham Home Builders Hall of Fame after retiring. Taught Sunday School adult classes for 43 years at Methodist Church and is presently a volunteer in AARP as district director in Alabama District 4.

Married to former Mildred Skelton of Reform, AL. They have two children, daughter, Julie, and son, Richard. He is currently retired from Jefferson Federal and Loan Association after 25 years with the company.

LEW S. HURTIG, was born May 25, 1915 in Liberty Lake, WA. Enlisted July 13, 1943 in the USAF, 8th Air Force, 2nd Air Div., 458th Bomb Group. Basic training at Miami Beach; Radio School, Sioux Falls, SD; Gunnery School, Yuma; Operational, Walla Walla, WA.

Overseas to Norwich, Horsham, St. Faith, England. Completed 30 missions over Germany in B-24, *Top of the Mark*. Flew a six-man crew (with no machine guns) on April 14, 1945 to Point deGrave, France. They anticipated ack ack close to the target, but it never came. That few minutes of silence turned out to be the hairiest of his 30 missions.

Discharged Nov. 5, 1945 with the rank tech sergeant. Received the Good Conduct and Air Medal with four clusters.

Married Jean Rothenberg in 1950, had one son. Married Betty Malmedal, Jan. 18, 1952, has three sons and two grandsons. Hurtig is retired. Was a fuel delivery driver in winter and a commercial fisherman in the summer.

HAROLD W. HUTCHCROFT, was born Jan. 29, 1922. Entered the USAF Nov. 3, 1942. Graduated Cadet Class 44-B. B-24 transition, Ft. Worth, TX. Co-pilot training Tonapah, NV. Arrived England via ship. Assigned to 579th Sqdn., 392nd Bomb Group, later to 576th Sqdn. Returned to USA in May 1945.

Crew members: Pilot, C.O. Markuson; navigator, W.W. Gallagher (re-assigned); bombardier, E.R. Maceyra; engineer, P.L. Cain; radio, J.E. Burke; armament gunner, T.D. Monogham; waist gunners, J.B. Howard and E.R. Hunter; and tail gunner, J.E. Horn. On 34th mission they collided

with wing man due to inclement weather. Wing broke off between #3 and #4 engines. Engineer and Hutchcroft survived by parachuting. Discharged with the rank first lieutenant.

Married Mary Esther Spitzmiller in December 1945. Returned to family business and later owned/operated grain elevator. At present he is a real estate broker in Burlington, IA and resides in Middletown, IA. He is proud father of Kim, Lucia and Lon and grandfather of five children.

JOHN A. HUTCHINS, was born in Amesbury, MA, Aug. 29, 1924 and was raised in Merrimac, MA. He joined the USAAC on Dec. 7, 1942 as a private. He had basic training at Atlantic City, NJ and attended Radio School at Scott Field, IL.

Joined B-24 air crew of Capt. Fred Deneffe at Boise, ID. Also trained at Wendover, UT and Tonopah, NV. Received new B-24 and headed for overseas via South American, Africa to Horsham, St. Faith, 458th Bomb Group, 753rd Sqdn. in early 1944.

He completed 31 missions and returned to the USA in the fall of 1944. He was sent to Sioux Falls, AFB, SD where he met and married Ruth Christianson of Brookings, SD. They have one daughter and three grandchildren. Discharged from the Army Oct. 1, 1945 with the rank tech sergeant. He now resides in Dover, NH.

RUPERT I. HUTCHINSON, was born May 10, 1923 in Arlington, IN. Entered the USAAF Nov. 12, 1942. Was flight engineer with 491st Bomb Group in Pinkingham, England. His memorable experiences include: when he escaped from the Swiss after being held nine months as prisoner; and on all the bomb raids they went on.

Discharged Oct. 24, 1945 with the rank of tech sergeant. Received the Air Medal with two Bronze Stars, Bronze Star GO #109, EAME Theater with four Bronze Stars.

Married Alice E. Davis on May 20, 1951. They have one son, one daughter and two grandchildren. Hutchinson retired from Conrail after 37 years. Now enjoys doing whatever he wants to.

CARL C. HVAMBSAL, was born April 25, 1925 in Minot, ND. Enlisted July 23, 1943 in the USAAF as ground radio mechanic with the 2nd Air Div. Stationed at Amarillo Air Base, Traux Field, Shipdham St. 115 and Peterson Field. Participated in Normandy, Northern France, Ardennes, Rhineland, Central Europe and Air Offensive Europe.

Discharged Oct. 28, 1945 with the rank private first class. Received all the usual awards and ribbons.

Worked for Control Corp., Minneapolis, MN and is now retired. He has three daughters, five grandchildren and one great-grandchild.

VETO A. IAVECCHIA, was born in Philadelphia, PA on Aug. 3, 1920. He enlisted in the Army on July 23, 1942 and served with the field artillery (powder man 155 MM howitzer). Stationed at Fort McClelland, AL; Camp Edwards, MA; San Antonio, TX; El Reno, OK; San Angelo, TX; Westover, MA; and Hethel, England. Discharged on Sept. 12, 1945 with rank of first lieutenant bombardier-navigator.

Participated in seven combat missions, ETO, 8th Air Force, 389th Bomb Group.

Memorable experiences include crash landing in Sweden June 20, 1944 (interned seven months).

Awarded the Air Medal.

Married in 1944 and has five children. Retired in 1987 and enjoys playing golf.

ANGELO J. INDRE, was born March 6, 1924, in Shawmut, a small town near DuBois, PA. Inducted in the

USAAC in February 1943 and received his basic training at Keesler Field, MS. Assigned to Radio School at Scott Field in Illinois and upon graduation went on to Gunnery School at Tyndall Field in Florida. Promoted to sergeant at graduation in December 1943. Assigned to 2nd Air Force. Participated in refresher courses, assigned to a crew and transferred to Tucson, AZ. The crew was assigned a B-24 to complete a three month phase training program, and moved to Topeka, KS. Assigned to the 8th Air Force, the crew left the U.S. and ferried a new B-24 to England arriving on May 13, 1944. Sent to Ireland on May 27 for more training and refresher courses. Left Quanto, Ireland in a B-24, arriving at Bungay, England on June 4, 1944 and assigned to the 446th Bomb Group, 706th Bomb Sqdn.

Flew first mission on D-day June 6, 1944. Flew some grocery runs and the last of his 31 missions to Kiel Sept. 12, 1944. Received orders to return to the U.S. on Sept. 18, 1944. After arrival in the states, signed up with the Air Transport Command as a radio operator, navigator. Spent the rest of the war in the C.B.I. assigned with the 1332nd Sqdn. B, Air Transport Command, flying C-46s over the Hump. Completed 119 round trips. Returned home and was discharged at Indiantown Gap, PA Dec. 8, 1945. Angelo J. Indre passed away June 6, 1993 in DuBois, PA.

GEORGE ROBERT INSLEY, was born April 25, 1922, the third of five sons born of Charles and Harriet Insley at Roseburg, OR. George enlisted in the USAAC Jan. 8, 1942. Completed Aviation Cadet training, Class 43-B Waco, TX. Rank second lieutenant.

August 1943: Ferried B-24 Kansas to Labrador, across to Iceland then to England. Assignment: the 44th Bomb Group the 66th and 506th Sqdn.

First mission, six new crews joined forces with another group for their 'baptism of fire'. The target Gydenia, Poland, was the German battleship. George's position was low left and last in "Purple Heart" corner. They experienced their first flak, first sound of flak explosions.

First fighter attack, a running battle when twin engine fighters zeroed on their element. About 50 miles west of Denmark the fighters left, then all four of their engines quit! The engineer had been transferring fuel when the fighters attacked. After they left, the engineer asked the radio operator to shut off the transfer pumps, instead mistakenly the fuel shut off valves were turned off. Thankfully they didn't have to try their life rafts.

They flew additional missions for a total of 48, flying many lead positions.

Awarded two Flying Crosses and seven Air Medals.

1946-50: S.A.C. Castle Air Force Base where he flew B-29 and B-50.

1950: He took discharge from the Air Force as a major in the Reserves.

1951-1991: George flew for Wycliffe Bible Translators as a "Jungle Bush Pilot" in Peru and Brazil where he took missionaries in and out of tribal locations.

1957: George married Jeanne Forrer of Chicago, in the jungles of Peru. They have three children and eight grandchildren. After 40 years of volunteer service as a missionary pilot George is now living on his farm in Roseburg, OR. He and his wife have established a commercial greenhouse business in Roseburg, OR.

JOSEPH A. INTERMOR, was born in Brooklyn, NY on June 12, 1925. In July 1943 he enlisted in the USAAF and served as tail gunner with the 453rd Bomb Group, 732nd Bomb Sqdn., 8th Air Force. He was discharged in October 1945 with the rank of staff sergeant.

He served in the ETO, Old Buckingham and Norwich. Awarded four Battle Stars for ETO, Distinguished Flying

Cross and Air Medal with five clusters. Participated in 35 or 36 missions with the first being on July 7, 1944 and the last being Dec. 24, 1944. Participated in battles twice in St. Lo, twice in Kassel and three times in Munich.

Married to Margaret and they have five daughters and two sons. They also have 16 grandchildren. He is presently retired.

ARTHUR IRELAND (KEN), was born in Trenton, NJ on June 25, 1919. He was inducted into federal service on Jan. 27, 1941 with the New Jersey National Guard, horse drawn field artillery.

Transferred while at Fort Bragg to aviation cadet training in 1942. Graduated from pilot training with class of 43H. After assignment to 20th Tow Target Sqdn. transferred to 467th Bomb Group at Wendover Field.

Returned to the states after 35 missions in the ETO and was separated from the service in August of 1945.

Awarded the Distinguished Flying Cross and Air Medal with three Oak Leaf Clusters.

Rejoined the New Jersey Air National Guard as artillery air officer flying light observation aircraft. Placed on retired reserve June 1979 as captain AVS.

Retired to Florida from sales management in the electronics industry in 1980.

H. HARDING ISAACSON, was born in New York City, NY on April 29, 1921. He was accepted into the Aviation Cadets on June 22, 1942. Graduated Aerial Gunnery School, Laredo Air Force Base, TX and Armament School, Lowry Field, CO. Discharged on Sept. 23, 1945.

Assigned to 859th Sqdn., 492nd Bomb Group, 8th Air Force, North Pickenham, England. Participated in seven missions with 492nd. Thence to 788th Sqdn., 467th Bomb Group, Rackheath, Norfolk UK. Completed 30 missions with 467th as waist gunner. Five years with Air Force Reserve Mitchell Field, NY 514th Troop Carrier Wing. Commissioned in New York Guard, 11th Internal Security Bn., 7th Regt. Thirty years with Veteran Corps of Artillery, New York State Militia. Retired with rank of colonel.

Awarded the Air Medal with four Oak Leaf Clusters, New York State Conspicuous Service Cross, four Bronze Campaign Stars. Order of Polonia Restituta. Knight Commander, Order of St. Sava and Order of White Eagle (Jugoslavia). 492nd received Croix de Guerre and Distinguished Unit Citation.

JAMES H. ISBELL (JIM), was born in Union City, TN on June 2, 1914. After high school, Jim attended Union University a year and a half; then enlisted in the Army to attend West Point Prep School. He entered West Point in 1934; graduated in 1938. Flying training was at Randolph and Kelly Fields. With the great military build-up about that time moves were frequent and promotions rapid. In October 1943 Jim, then a lieutenant colonel, was named commanding officer of the last Liberator Group scheduled for activation—the 492nd.

In December 1943 the 458th Group Commander was hospitalized and had to be replaced—Jim got the job. Overseas movement began Jan. 1, 1944. By late February all elements were in place at Horsham St. Faith and the group was declared "operational". The first mission was to a target in Frankfort, the group commanding officer led. 8th Air Force operations over Germany became intense; 14 months later the 458th held a small celebration after completing its 200th mission over Germany. A few days later the wing commander sent Jim back to the U.S. on leave. Heading back, after 45 days, he was held at the port—clearly, the war was almost over.

Post-war assignments were: Hq. Training Command; Air War College, Hq. 3rd Air Force; Nat. War College; Hq. USAF; Hq. Alaska Air Command; Hq. CONAC. Retired March 31, 1967 with rank of brigadier general.

Participated in all battles of 8th Air Force from March 1, 1944 to March 10, 1945. Awards/medals: Legion of Merit (two); Distinguished Flying Cross (two); Air Medal (two); Bronze Star; Commendation Medal (two); French Croix de Guerre; ETO Ribbon; and American Defense Medal.

EMERSON Y. ISHMAEL, was born Fairborn, OH on Nov. 9, 1924. Joined the USAAC as aviation cadet on Aug. 5, 1943. Basic training Keesler Field, MS. College training detachment Butler University then sent to San Antonio, TX Cadet Center. Need for fewer cadets brought Radio School at Sioux Falls, SD. Air crew formed at Wichita, KS - B-24 crew training at Casper, WY. From Casper was sent to 458th Bomb Group - Horsham St. Faith. Flew 11 combat missions. Received Air Medal. Back to Sioux Falls May 1945 to go into B-29 training. End of hostilities in Pacific brought discharge January 1946.

Married Ruth Anna Shock June 8, 1946. Has two children and five grandchildren. Worked for National Cash Register 31 years and for Amber Heights City Schools 10 years. Retired July 1, 1988 as maintenance supervisor.

NICK JABBOUR, was born in Albany, NY during Woodrow Wilson's last year in office. He was raised in the "ghetto" before the term was born.

He enlisted at Stewart Field, NY in 1942. Was a corporal three times, busted twice and promoted (reluctantly) the third time to enter The Adjutant General's Officer Candidate School, where he was commissioned in 1943.

As a fresh second lieutenant was given a choice of going overseas or be subject to a courts martial for telling a major his motor pool stunk. Was selected as the first and only Group S-1 for the 491st Bomb Group in February 1944 before the Air Echelon arrived. Was the youngest and only 2nd lieutenent Group S-1, of the 14 bomber groups in the 8th Air Force. He considers working for Col. F.H. Miller Jr., the group commander, as the most educational and best experience of his life.

He had two tours in the Pentagon, and as a personnel staff officer was able to avoid the military staff schools.

In 1954 he completed graduate school at the University of Pittsburgh in Advanced Management at the request of his commanding general "to round off his rough edges". His second "best" tour was as AFROTC PAS at Colorado State University 1965-69. His detachment was the first ROTC Unit to ever win the Air Force Outstanding Unit Award. His annual A.F. Dining in at Colorado State University set a precedence not yet equalled. The President of the University and the Deans for the seven colleges attended all four Dining In's. His guest speakers each year were: Assistant Secretary of the Air Force Robert Charles; General Robert A. Breitweiser, USAF; General (then Colonel) "Chappie" James and General Lewis W. Walt, USMC, Deputy Commander of the Marine Corps, Class of 1936. His Aerospace Academic Achievement Award for each AFROTC senior with a 3.5 grade point average, presented by the appropriate College Dean was also an unprecedented event. Students and guests averaged over 600 each year.

He credits the Air Force and Dr. Alex S. Pow for his entire college education. He worked for four of the most brilliant and finest General Officers in the Air Force, and three who he ranked in the bottom 10%.

Married Ruth Seipel of Newburgh, NY and has two sons, Jack and Mark, and three grandchildren. Retired in 1973 as a colonel after 31 years of service. Lived in Solana Beach, CA for 17 years, where he became president of the Chamber of Commerce, and taught in the San Diego Community College system. Ultimately retired to Air Force Village West, Riverside, CA in October of 1989.

STANLEY F. JACEWICZ, was born in Pittsburgh, PA on May 3, 1916. He enlisted in the USAAC on Aug. 25, 1942 and served with the 554th AAF Base Unit as radio operator, 93rd Bomb Group. Discharged on Oct. 5, 1945 with the rank of tech. sergeant.

Participated in Air Offense Europe, Normandy, and Ted's Traveling Circus. Awarded the EAME Ribbon, three Battle Stars, Distinguished Flying Cross with three Oak Leaf Clusters and the Good Conduct Medal.

Married and living in Springfield, NH. Presently retired as police chief, Stafford Springs, CT in 1976.

EDGAR JACKSON, was born near Old Hickory, TN May 20, 1918 and was raised and graduated from Jackson County Central High School, Gainesboro, TN. Completed three years of Citizens Military Training Camps (CMTC) while in high school.

Joined the USAAC Sept. 20, 1940. Accepted as aviation cadet May 1942. Reported to Gulf Coast Training Area for training. Graduating in Aviation Cadet Class 43-9, Big Spring, TX as bombardier/navigator and commissioned second lieutenant June 24, 1943. After attending (B-29) Gunnery School at Lowry Field, CO he trained as B-24 crew member, flew with crew and new B-24 airplane to 8th Air Force via South America, Africa to England. Flying combat missions against targets in France and Germany, (flying two missions on June 6, 1944 D-day). Completed tour, 32 missions - 20 missions as lead crew with 453rd Bombardment Group located at Old Buckingham July 9, 1944. Transferred to 2nd CCRC Group (training) AAF Station in North Ireland. Training replacement crews arriving from U.S. November 1944, transferred to Air Disarmament Command (Prov) for short stay.

Departed UK Dec. 15, 1944 arriving U.S., Dec. 22, 1944 for Christmas. After WWII, Jackson was a career USAF officer, in addition to flying, performed duty as communications/air electronics officer until retirement Aug. 30, 1972, as lieutenant colonel. His awards include Distinguished Flying Cross, four Air Medals, Air Force Commendation Medal, four European Theater Campaign Stars, two Outstanding Unit Awards and several other service and theater ribbons.

Married Dec. 30, 1944 to former WWII Air Force Nurse Ruth M. Bannister, they have a daughter and son and two grandchildren.

JAMES HAMILTON JACKSON (HAM), was born Sept. 17, 1922, Richmond, OR. Wife, Autumn Stace Jackson. Children - two sons and a daughter, six grandchildren. 1940 to Oregon State College until entering the Aviation Cadet program February 1943. Graduated Navigation School at Hondo Class 44-3. Joined Tepfer's crew Gowen Field, picked up new B-24 at Topeka, proceeded to Nutt's Corner, Ireland. After U.K. Orientation assigned to 453rd Bomb Group flying aircraft "Lace", as lead navigator.

Awarded Distinguished Flying Cross, Air Medal with two Silver Clusters, four Campaign Stars and three Presidential Citations.

Returned to States April 1945. Flew Jezebel missions out of Lockheed Air Terminal in B-25. Back to Ellington to check out in AT-9 and 10s. Then to Lincoln for AT-6. Separated service October 1945. Realtor for 30 years.

JOSEPH M. JACKSON, was born May 10, 1925 in Philadelphia, PA. Took basic in Miami Beach, FL. After

graduating Gunnery School at Harlingen, TX, was sent to Tonopah, NV for overseas training with assigned crew. Upon completing training they were given a brand new B-24J, July 19, 1944 to deliver to Wales. Was sent to Ireland for refresher course in gunnery, after which he was assigned to the 44th Bomb Group at Shipdham, England. Their pilot flew two missions with an experienced crew. When he reached 35 missions, they had only flown 33. Rather than send them out with other crews, they were excused. He returned to the U.S. March 1945. Spent R&R at Santa Ana Army Air Base in California. Gunnery Instructor's School followed at Laredo, TX. He graduated the same day Japan surrendered. Was discharged Nov. 2, 1945 at Richmond, VA with rank of staff sergeant.

Memorable experiences include engine trouble over Holland, aborted mission on first 1000 plane raid over Berlin. Returned to completely fogged England. Landed on base five miles from tower pilot was talking to. Pilot was considering bailing out and heading plane out to sea.

Awarded the Air Medal with four Oak Leaf Clusters, Good Conduct Medal, American Theatre Ribbon, and EAME Theatre Ribbon.

Married to Lillian for 44 years and they have one son, Mark. He is presently a retired machinist.

WILLIAM E. JACKSON, was born in Weirton, WV on Sept. 11, 1922. Enlisted November 1942 in USAAC. Cadet pre-flight Maxwell Field, AL. Primary - McBride, MO. Basic - Greenville, MS. Advance - Lawrence Field, IL. Transition B-17 and B-24 Chanute Field, IL. Operational - Walla Walla, WA. Combat - first pilot 752nd Sqdn., 458th Bomb Group, Horsham St. Faith England. Twenty-five missions - twenty-three with his crew and two with new crews. Awarded the Air Medal with three Oak Leaf Clusters.

The luckiest day of his life was April 16, 1945 - bombing fuel storage, Landshut, Germany with I.P. in Czechoslovakia low level mission. 88 millimeter went through #3 engine and did not go off. A long trip back to Norwich.

His wife Carolyn died in November 1988. They had two daughters. Remarried December 1991 Vondie Bayne. Retired January 1985 chairman and president of Union Electric Steel Corp., Pittsburgh, PA. Presently lives in Newport Beach, CA.

Records show "My Bunnie II" transferred to another group. It did not leave Horsham St. Faith. He flew it back to the states with his crew and 10 passengers to Hartford, CT.

JOHN M. JACOBOWITZ, was born Feb. 23, 1917 in Streator, IL. Graduated from high school in 1935; University of Illinois, 1940; College of Medicine, University of Illinois (Chicago), 1950 (M.D.); Internship and Residency, Detroit, 1951-1952.

Joined the Air Force June 24, 1940, flying cadet, Class 41-A.

Assignments: Flying instructor February 1941-February 1944, Stockton Field, CA; B-24 transition, Kirtland AFB February-May 1944; C.O., 786th Bomb Sqdn. (H), 466th Bomb Group, June 1944-August 1945; deputy commander, Douglas AFB, August-September 1945.

Completed 25 missions as command pilot.

Awarded the Distinguished Flying Cross with Oak Leaf Cluster, Air Medal with three Oak Leaf Clusters, Air Force Reserve Medal, American Defense Medal, American Campaign Medal, ETO Medal with five stars and Victory Medal.

Obtained the rank of lieutenant colonel on Jan. 22, 1945. Returned to the U.S.A. on June 13, 1945. Discharged Feb.

2 , 1946. Served in the inactive reserves from 1946-1965 (20 year retirement).

General practice (medical), Three Rivers, MI 1952-1977. Medical director, G.M.C., Kalamazoo, MI 1978-1989. Married and has three sons.

DAVID L.G. JACOBS, was born on Aug. 20, 1923 in Chicago, IL. On Nov. 13, 1942 he was inducted into the Army reserves. March 1943 began active duty USAAF, radio operator gunner. Assigned to St. Petersburg, FL for basic training; Scott Field, IL for Radio School; Yuma, AZ for Gunnery School; Casper, WY for combat crew training, Class 7-7-44. Served with 8th Air Force, 44th Bomb Group, 67th Sqdn. August 1944-March 1945. Discharged on Oct. 26, 1945 with the rank of tech. sergeant.

Completed 35 missions when they finished their tour Feb. 23, 1945.

Awarded the Air Medal with four Oak Leaf Clusters and three European Combat Stars.

Obtained an undergraduate degree from DePaul University, Chicago, IL. Graduate degree from University of Missouri, Columbia, MO in 1950. Married and has two children.

Presently arbitrator, adjunct professor, semi-retired.

JOHN W. JACOBS, was born in 1921 at Sparta, KY, the son of a railroad station agent. At start of WWII was a boring mill operator with Wright Aeronautical. Became an aviation cadet in September 1942 training in the Southeast Command. Formed his B-24 crew at Casper, WY and flew the Atlantic, joining the 489th Bomb Group at Halesworth, England. Flew 35 noteworthy missions with every crew member flying every mission without substitution.

Later assigned as test pilot for chemical and bacteriological delivery. Flew most all military aircraft through B-47. Served at all levels of command from squadron to JCS in command and senior staff positions.

Married in 1947 to Marian Schneider now boasting six grown children with advanced degrees. Retired as colonel in 1971, last position Chief Comm./Electronics at Vandenberg AFB Space and Missile Test Center. Now resides in Riverside, CA.

ROBERT A. JACOBS, was born Sept. 26, 1919, and inducted into the U.S. Army from Los Angeles, CA in February 1940. After Pearl Harbor, he entered the Aviation Cadet program for navigation training graduating on July 25, 1943 as a second lieutenant at Selman Field, LA. His crew flew to the U.K. via Goose Bay in December 1943. The first 14 missions were flown with the 93rd Bomb Group at Hardwick. The last 16 missions were flown from Hethel, 389th Bomb Group, as a lead pathfinder navigator. Remaining in the Air Force, he earned a B.A. in Meteorology from UCLA, retiring as a colonel in May 1972. For 11 years he worked for Tenneco Corp. until September 1984.

Decorations include the Legion of Merit, two Distinguished Flying Crosses, four Air Medals, and three Air Force Commendation Medals.

Married Nancy R. Lacey of Norwich, May 1945. They have a son, two grandchildren, and two great-grandchildren.

HAROLD L. JAMES, was born Feb. 27, 1922 in Richardson, TX and reared in Temple, TX. Married Doris Ann Sunday of Waco, TX. One son, one daughter, and three grandchildren. Graduate of Texas A&M and George Washington Universities. Aeronautical engineer and certificated flight instructor.

He commenced flying as a civilian in June 1941 and graduated from the Aviation Cadets Class 42-J. Trained with the 389th Bomb Group and flew to his B-24 base at Hethel,

England June, 1943. Interned in Turkey following Aug. 1, 1943 low-level raid on Ploesti oil fields. Later, flew British-built Mosquito's with the 25th Bomb Group from Watton, England. Flying experience included 70 combat missions over Europe, two midair collisions, one crash landing, and one crash on takeoff.

Harold retired as a colonel in the USAF from his last assignment as U.S. Defense and Air Attache to Turkey in September 1975. He finally retired in 1987 as a mortgage banker.

THOMAS K. JAMES, was born in Wadesboro, NC on March 23, 1922. He enlisted in the USAAF in May 1943 and served as flight engineer. Basic training, Ft. Bragg, NC; Aircraft Mechanic School, Keesler Field, MS; Gunnery School, Harlingen, TX. Flight training with assigned crew at Tonopah, NV.

Was stationed at Hardwick, Norwich with the 93rd Bomb Group, 330th Sqdn.

Flew in all battles (35 missions) between Oct. 2, 1944 March 30, 1945.

Memorable experiences include flying below sea level at Death Valley; Ille de France - third largest ship transported him to England - no convoy. Bing Crosby on board - entertained troops. After missions came home on convoy. Halfway back to states when war in Europe ended. German sub surrendered to convoy before reaching U.S.

Awarded the Air Medal with five Oak Leaf Clusters and ETO Ribbon with Battle Stars. Discharged in May 1945 with rank of tech. sergeant. He was the first in Anson County, NC to be discharged on points.

Married and has two children. Retired in 1986 after 34 years at James River - Dixie Corp., Darlington, SC.

WILLIAM K. JANN (BILL), was born Sept. 1, 1925, Brooklyn, NY. Entered USAAC March 14, 1944 as a private. Flew 33 combat missions as top turret gunner on B-24s with the 448th Bomb Group, 713th Bomb Sqdn., 8th Air Force attaining the rank of staff sergeant before being rotated back to United States for furlough.

The end of Pacific hostilities resulted in discharge on Nov. 15, 1945 at which time, under the G.I. Bill, he attended Colorado University receiving BS degree in Mechanical Engineering in 1949. In 1970 during his civilian career he earned a MS degree from Oklahoma University. Concurrent with his exciting and challenging civilian career as chief engineer and later, Deputy Program Manager for the Army's high priority Pershing Missile System he maintained his military proficiency in the Army Reserve, retiring with the rank of colonel, Army Corps of Engineers. His highest military award was the Meritorious Service Medal while his civilian counterpart award was the Army's highest civilian Decoration for Exceptional Civilian Service.

Married April 23, 1949 in Hays, KS to Clare L. Delva, has three children and three grandchildren to date.

DONALD E. JANSS, was born Oct. 21, 1921 in Belle Plaine, IA, one of seven boys and two girls. He was inducted into the service Oct. 21, 1942 and was sent to Kalamazoo, MI, then to the 12th Armd Div., Camp Campbell, KY. Don

transferred to the Air Force in December 1942 and sent to Miami, FL. He received his CTD training at Coe College, Cedar Rapids, IA. Don received his navigator wings at Hondo, TX, and joined Crew 9313 in Casper, WY for B-24 training. The most memorable experience was having been hit hard by flak over Kiel bombing the Sub-Pens.

Don was discharged at Jefferson City, MO Oct. 22, 1945 as a 2nd Lieutenant. Don married Marian Hall Feb. 1, 1945. Three children were born. Don worked as a supervisor for a steel iron crew for steel bridges on the Chicago Northwestern Railroad for 46 years. He retired Oct. 20, 1986.

He enjoys his grandkids, golf, and meeting with his B-24 crew in yearly meetings.

DR. LOUIS JAQUES JR., was born in Hollywood, CA in 1914. Married Jacquelyn Burton in 1947 and they have three children. Commissioned Infantry ROTC Berkeley 1938, two weeks Cavalry 1939. Practiced Optometry before, between and after wars. Graduated Flying Class 41-G in September. Flight Instructor Stockton, CA two years; Bomb Pilots School 1943 Roswell, NM; B-24 instructor Smyrna, TN; filled quota to Biggs AFB then 492nd Bomb Group at Alamogordo, NM on the way to North Pickenham UK.

Flew five missions as lead pilot for 859th Bomb Sqdn., then assistant Group Operations Officer. Got his long-delayed sixth mission, to Bernburg July 7, 1944; he briefed it, flew as command pilot and joined the Caterpillar Club. Released from POW Stalag One by Russians in May 1945.

Recalled 1951: early warning, radar calibration, and ROTC Professor. Nine years in SAC Operations included twice ferrying C-123s to Vietnam.

Retired as lieutenant colonel May 1966 in Vista, CA.

BERNARD JOHN JAWORSKI SR. (BARNEY), served with the 714th Bomb Sqdn., 448th Bomb Group; stationed at Seething from August 1944 to May 1945. Completed 35 missions, received commission, second lieutenant, while flying in combat. Discharged after three years and 359 days of service.

Works as commercial printer, monotype keyboard and hot metal castor operator, does photo typesetting and commercial camera work. Served as coach and manager of Little League baseball teams. He enjoys playing golf and tennis. Has put two sons through four years of college at Indiana University.

MILTON L. JAY, was born in Newark, NJ on Oct. 25, 1923. Married Shirley Jaye and has two sons and one daughter.

Enlisted Nov. 21, 1942. Training schools attended: gunnery, navigation (non-rated), armament and central instructors schools. Became a B-24 armorer gunner. Crew flew to England, was assigned to the 458th Bomb Group and became a lead crew. Flew 30 missions with the 755th Bomb Sqdn. Returned to U.S. shortly after the war ended in Europe. Attended and graduated from central instructors school at Nueva Laredo, TX. Became a B-29 central fire control instructor. Remained in the Reserve when the war ended and was commissioned 2nd Lieutenant November 1948. Tours of active duty included serving as armament systems officer with ADC and SAC. Last assignment - education and training officer for the Northeast region of the Reserve Assist Program to the CAP. Also served as an instructor for the CAP Cadet Officer School at the Air University, Maxwell Field, AL.

Retired Oct. 25, 1983 as major.

DONALD N. JEFFERY, was born on Jan. 24, 1923 in Erie, PA. He enlisted in the USAAC in October 1942. Graduated Bombardment Armament and Gunnery School. Joined 489th Bomb Group, Gowen Field, December 1943. Assigned 847th Bomb Sqdn. B-24 crew training completed at Wendover Field. Group departed for England about March 22, 1944 via Herington, Morrison Field then southern route South America, Africa on to Hailsworth, England. Flew 23 combat missions over Europe. Returned to states in December 1944. Discharged October 1945.

Entered Aviation Cadets, Randolph Field, December 1949. Graduated Vance AFB, Feb. 10, 1951, 2nd Lieutenant and assigned 22nd Bomb Wing, 2nd Sqdn., March AFB. Flew B-29s then joined the 301st Bomb Group, 32nd Sqdn., Lockbourne AFB, OH. Flew several variants of B-47 as aircraft commander.

Retired Feb. 1, 1967 Westover AFB, a command pilot in the rank of major.

Married Rebecca Lay, March 28, 1951. Has four children and five grandchildren.

JAY H. JEFFRIES JR., was born in Denver, CO on May 27, 1919. Joined the 209th Coast Artillery (AA) February 1941 to fulfill his one year service. Transferred to the USAAC December 1941 as an aviation cadet. Graduated Class 43 H. Stationed at Salt Lake City, UT; Casper, WY; Alamogordo, NM; El Paso, TX; Topeka, KS; and West Palm Beach, FL. Then the southern route to England. Joined the 453rd Bomb Group (H), 732nd Bomb Sqdn. (B-24s) at Old  Buckingham, 8th Air Force, 2nd Air Div. First mission May 23, 1944. Finished 30 missions Aug. 9, 1944 (77 days). Returned to the USA September 1944. Discharged September 1945.

Received the Distinguished Flying Cross, four Air Medals, four Campaign Stars, Presidential Citation, and other ribbons. By the way, that one year service turned out to be five years, nine days.

Married Anna Jane Lane May 26, 1945 at Syracuse, NY. Then to Huntington Beach, CA. Clothing business 11 years, his own fish business 37 years (highly recommended). Happily married 48 years with six children and eleven grandchildren.

VERNON E. JEFFRIES (JEFF), was born on Oct. 24, 1916 in Laverne, OK and grew up in Tracy, CA. Married in May 1940 and has four children and six grandchildren.

Entered the USAAC October 1943. Assigned to CTD at Teachers College in St. Cloud, MN. From there to Preflight at Santa Ana, CA with the class of 44 C. Primary at Rankin Aeronautical Academy, Tulare, CA flying Stearmans. Flew BT-15s and AT-17s at basic, Leemore, CA then to Douglas, AZ, finishing in AT-9s.

Flew B-17s at Kingman, AZ and B-24s in Tonopah, NV. Sent to England fall of 1944 and assigned to 458th Bomb Group at Norwich. Served in the 754th and 755th Sqdns.

Flew 33 combat missions (20 as lead crew) (2 gas missions for Montgomery's Army).

In December 1944 shot down, landed at RAF Base Lille, France.

Received ETO Ribbon with four Battle Stars and the Air Medal with four Oak Leaf Clusters.

After discharge in 1945 attended Chiropractic College in San Francisco, received degree of D.C. in 1948, practiced two years and decided to return to Law Enforcement, became Chief of Police in Manteca, CA from 1952 to 1957.

In 1957 joined the District Attorneys Office in Stockton, CA where he retired after 20 years of service as an investigator.

DONALD R. JENKINS, was born in New Brunswick, NJ, May 1, 1923. Married Lavinia J. Burns, June 1947. Had four children; one deceased. Presently has a son, two daughters, and four grandchildren.

Entered the USAAC May 23, 1943. After several aviation student and cadet training programs, received training as a navigator at the Pan-American School at Coral Gables, FL and graduated April 22, 1944, Class 44-6 as a 2nd Lieutenant.

Flew a B-24 from the U.S. to England via the northern route. Joined the 44th Bomb Group, "Flying Eightballs", in July 1944. Flew 30 combat missions, 13 leads, from August 1944 to April 1945. The next to last mission was leading the 68th Sqdn. to Wesel, Germany to supply troops on the east bank of the Rhine River. Although the Second Air Div. lost 22 aircraft and crews, that day their squadron returned with minor damage and no casualties.

Received the Distinguished Flying Cross, five Air Medals and several ribbons.

Returned home April 1945; discharged as a first lieutenant Nov. 9, 1945.

Retired from Lafayette College after 40 years of mechanical engineering teaching and consulting. His wife and he presently live in Gilmanton Iron Works, NH.

WILLIAM S. JENKINS, was born on Feb. 28, 1919, in Amagansett, NY, a small village 17 miles from the end of Long Island.

Enlisted Jan. 15, 1942 and was sent to Camp Upton. From there he was sent to Mitchell Field to become part of the 315th Signal Corp. and took his basic training.

On Dec. 7, 1942, one year after Pearl Harbor, they were loaded on the *Queen Mary* with 11,500 other G.I.s and sailed for Scotland. They landed in Scotland and were loaded on a train and rode all night to Norwich, Norfolk.

They were assigned to the 2nd Bomb Div., 8th Air Force and set up headquarters at Old Catton. They later moved to the nearby airfield of Horsham St. Faith, finally moving across Norwich to Ketteringham Hall in December of 1943.

Returned to the U.S. in August 1945 and after 45 days of R&R was discharged September 1945.

Awarded the EAME Service Medal with two Bronze Battle Stars.

Married in October 1946 and moved to New Jersey. He has one son. Retired in 1975 and returned to his hometown of Amagansett.

THELO M. JENNY, was born on Sept. 2, 1920 in East St. Louis, IL. Enlisted in the U.S. Army Air Force in September 1941. Served in Shipdham from November 1942 to June 1945 as aircraft mechanic. Discharged on Oct. 2, 1945 with the rank of sergeant.

Retired from U.S. Army AVSCOM Civil Service.

ALDON H. JENSEN, was born Dec. 20, 1922 and reared on a farm near Massena, IA. Enlisted in USAAC April 20, 1942. Sent to Kelly Field August 20. Primary, basic and advanced flight training at Coleman, San Angelo (Goodfellow Field) and Eagle Pass, TX, respectively, receiving "Wings" and commissioned as second lieutenant April 22, Class of 1943D. Assigned to 392nd Bomb Group. Trained at Biggs Field, TX; Alamogordo, NM; Pueblo, CO; and Topeka, KS. Flew to England via Gander, Newfoundland and Prestwick, Scotland, arriving at Wendling Air Base August 20. First official mission was Oct. 4, 1943; last (30th) mission May 25, 1944. Stateside, instructed in B-24s and B-29s at Chatham

Air Force Base, Savannah, GA, from August, 1944 to August, 1945. Officially discharged from service Oct. 6, 1945.

Married Margaret McLaren Aug. 28, 1948. Has three children and three grandsons.

Obtained B.S. (1949) and M.S. (1950) degrees at University of Illinois and Ph.D. (1953) at Iowa State University. Faculty member at University of Illinois Jan. 1, 1954 until retirement Jan. 1, 1988.

ARTHUR H. JENSEN, was born in Richmond, IL on July 28, 1906. Enlisted in the USAAC on Dec. 23, 1942 and served with the 392nd Bomb Group H, 578th, as parachute rigger. Discharged on Oct. 17, 1945 with the rank of sergeant.

Stationed in England, Europe, and Wendling Air Base.

Battles participated in include Central Europe, Air Offensive Europe, and Ardennes.

Awarded the EAME Theater Service Medal and the Good Conduct Medal.

He married his wife in July 1945. They had no children. After discharge he went back to his old job at the milk producers association dairy as a relief man, truck driver, etc. After a few years he transferred to their garage as a mechanic. A short time later he became head mechanic and fleet superintendent. He retired in July 1970 as fleet superintendent. They had a fleet of about 40 trucks. His wife, Helen, passed away Dec. 27, 1992.

NORMAN W. JENSEN, was born July 26, 1921 in Brooklyn, NY. Moved to Albany, NY at age of six months. Drafted into service on Aug. 11, 1942, Fort Dix, NJ. Basic training, Miami Beach, FL; Photo Camera Repair School, Lowry Field, Denver, CO, Class 15-43; 86th CTD, Centenary College of Louisiana, Dodd College, June-September 1943; Classification at San Antonio, TX, September-November 1943; Preflight at Ellington Field, TX, November-December 1943; Advance at Childress, TX, January-May 1944; and bombardier training at Westover Field, MA, 112th AAFBU, 11 Sec., B-24J Bombardier-D.R. Navigator, June-September 1944.

European Theater - Sept. 17, 1944 return USA May 24, 1945. Awarded the EAME Theater Campaign Ribbon with three stars, Air Medal with five clusters and Silver Oak Leaf Cluster, Distinguished Unit Citation, New York State Conspicuous Service Medal and Victory Medal, WWII.

2nd Air Division, 445th Bomb Group, 702nd Sqdn. flew out of Tibenham, England. Thirty-five missions, including Hamburg, Hanover, Magdeburg, Kiel, Zossen, Dortmund, Duneberg, Cologne and twenty-seven other strategic targets.

Discharged Oct. 14, 1945 as a first lieutenant.

Retired in 1976 after 30 years with New York State Dept. of Transportation, Bureau of Soil Mechanics, Albany, NY as a principal draftsman.

Happily married 42 years to Bernice (Christiansen) Jensen. They have two children: Karen, who has two children, Brian and Rachel; and Roger, who has two children, Heather and Sarah.

Very busy with Veterans of Foreign Wars, Post 8692, Colonie, NY. Duties - chaplain, Membership Chairman, Youth Activities Chairman. Past Post Commander, 1973-

1975. Volunteer at Samuel S. Stratton Medical Hospital, Albany, NY as an organist for the patients, once a week - five years so far. Wife, Bernice, also volunteers, 14 years. They are both co-editors of their VFW Post newsletter. Choir director at Good Shepherd Lutheran Church, Colonie, NY for 20 years.

RUDOLF S. JENSEN (RUDY), was born in Hamburg, Germany on May 17, 1921. Came to U.S. at age of four. Attended public schools in Washington D.C. Joined AAF in 1943 and survived basic training in Miami Beach.

Assigned to the ATC, Love Field, TX. Requested transfer to a tactical unit and ended up at aerial gunner training facility in Laredo, TX. On to Lincoln, NE for crew assignment and back to Texas with nine great guys for overseas training at Biggs Field. Then to Topeka, KS—given a brand new 24H but ended up on a troop ship heading for Liverpool, England! Two weeks in Ireland and "ready" for combat in the 700th Sqdn. of the 445th Bomb Group at Tibenham. Scheduled to fly Sept. 27, 1944 to Kassel but were "scrubbed" for this, their fourth mission, because the crew was required to fly "night orientation" the night before. This Kassel mission turned out to be the worst loss in a single day for any group in the history of the 8th in WWII (31 planes out of 37 failed to return!!). They finished their tour of 35 in March 1945.

Awarded four Battle Stars and seven Air Medals (silver and gold). Discharged August 1945 with rank of staff sergeant.

He has three children and one grandson. Retired school administrator (34 years).

WILLIAM C. JENSEN, was an airplane mechanic working on B-24s with 579th Sqdn., 392nd Bomb Group. One of the planes he was assigned to was "Mac's Sack". He thinks #599 McGreager was the pilot.

Two memorable events: (1st) He pre-flighted "Mac's Sack" on its final mission with a different pilot and crew. It did not return. (2nd) The 579th Sqdn. was reduced to two B-24s which were transferred to the 578th. He was pre-flighting one of them when the 578th came to taxi them away.

A group of the engineering personnel were transferred to the 490th Bomb Group for a couple of days. Familiarization then work on B-17s. He later was assigned to an engine change crew and they thought they were the best in England.

On discharge he began working for Minneapolis Molire Co. Shipped tractors, combines, pickers, shellers, etc. to Colorado, Nebraska, Kansas, Wyoming and Utah. After 25 years they were bought out by White Motor. He elected to do something else and wound up selling auto parts for the next ten years. After that he spent the next 12 years working with his wife, operating a day care home.

It's been a good life, and, he thanks the Lord, he's still healthy.

ALLAN M. JOHNSON, was born in Marysville, CA on Oct. 21, 1923. Inducted into the Army Air Force on Feb. 3, 1943. Basic training at Biloxi, MS.

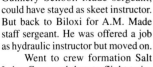

Next to Harlingen Field, TX, Gunnery School. Made sergeant, could have stayed as skeet instructor. But back to Biloxi for A.M. Made staff sergeant. He was offered a job as hydraulic instructor but moved on.

Went to crew formation Salt Lake, Crew and then to flight training McGowen Field in B-24s.

Picked up airplane in Topeka, KS and named it the "Dissepated Duck". Flew over southern route then to Wales. They took the plane away. The crew went to North Ireland for combat crew training.

Then to 715th Sqdn., 448th Bomb Group, Crew #75 the 5th replacement crew.

Shot down during 15th mission on June 21, 1944 in Berlin. Was POW in 10 different hospitals, military prison, stalag camps.

Liberated Barth, Germany Stalag I by Russians May 2. Spent 18 days with Russian military. Came across our lines May 20, 1945 in Brussells.

CECIL GRAY JOHNSON, was born in Nanafalia, AL on Feb. 26, 1922. In December 1942 he volunteered for the USAAC at the University of Alabama and was signed up by Col. Carpenter, one of the engineers who designed the fortress at Corregidor, Philippines. Johnson received basic training in Miami Beach, FL. From there he was sent to Clemson University, Clemson, SC; Classification Center, Nashville, TN; Preflight, Maxwell Field, Montgomery, AL; Primary, Jackson, MS; Basic, Greenville, MS; Advanced, George Field, IL (graduated); Transition, Chanute Field, IL; Sonora, CA; Crew Training, Walla Walla, WA; Hamilton Field, CA and Camp Kilmer, NJ; Norwich, England; Sioux Falls, SD; Galveston, TX; Fort McPherson, GA. Twenty combat missions over Germany.

His first ocean voyage was from New York to Glasgow aboard the top Netherlands flag ship, the *New Amsterdam*. This converted passenger ship was carrying a division of the U.S. Army across the Atlantic in storm and submarine stressed waters. A typical North Atlantic storm hit the ship and it had to head South to get out of the storm. Farther South the weather broke and they were able to sneak their navigator, Bosshardt, on the deck and with his octant and the stars located them going toward Gibraltar. Shortly after that they turned North and then they knew they were headed to Great Britain.

Upon landing in Glasgow, Scotland, they were assigned to the 2nd Air Div., 458th Bomb Group, Norwich, England. On their first mission Co-pilot Hecht was killed. After a few missions with superior ratings, Lt. Johnson and his crew were promoted to the lead squadron for further intensive training. In the winter and spring of 1945 they flew 20 combat missions over Germany.

Soon the war in Europe was over and Johnson and his crew were sent to Sioux Falls, SD, to train for B-32s. Shortly thereafter the "A" bomb fell and the whole war was over. From Sioux Falls, SD, Johnson was shipped to Galveston Air Base, TX, for a rest and from there to Fort McPherson, GA, to exit active duty status.

Awarded the Air Medal with two Oak Leaf Clusters and Lead Crew Commendation.

Discharged October 1945 with rank of first lieutenant.

Married in 1948 and has three children and two grandchildren. He retired in December 1991 after 37 years of service - Professor Emeritus, Georgia Institute of Technology, Professional Engineer. He enjoys writing and traveling and is very busy and productive in community work.

CLAIRE H. JOHNSON, was born in the state of Iowa June 3, 1917. Enlisted in the cadet program in October 1942. Attended the Ceder City College before reporting to Santa Ana, CA. Continued in the cadet program and graduated at Marfa, TX March 12, 1944. Completed B-24 transition crew training and was assigned to the 8th Air Force, 2nd Div., ETO. Completed 30 missions, then returned to the States.

After various assignments was assigned to the Asia area for one tour. Upon return, was assigned to the Air Training Command as an instructor pilot for six years.

Was assigned to SAC in 1956. Flew the KC-97 then transferred to the KC-135 which he flew until he retired in 1965. Finally completed an accounting degree at Indiana University in 1967. After graduation worked in the accounting area until 1985 when he retired.

Married Phyllis R. Bradely in 1969. They have a son Mark and a daughter Lynn. They continue to live in Colorado.

DALE L. JOHNSON, was born April 11, 1923 in Woodhull. Enlisted Dec. 5, 1942 in the USAAC. AM, Keesler Field, MS; Ford Factory School, Ypsilanti, MI; Gunnery School, Harlingen, TX. Served with 2nd Air Div., 93rd Bomb Group, 328th Bomb Sqdn., 8th Air Force.

Completed 30 missions from Hardwick, England on B-24, engineer on Buckner crew. His memorable experience was D-day.

Discharged Sept. 20, 1945 with the rank tech sergeant. Received the Air Medal with three Oak Leaf Clusters and the Distinguished Flying Cross.

Married Susan Perry on Oct. 13, 1945. They have three children and nine grandchildren.

He owned and operated an underground coal mine in Illinois. Retired as safety inspector of coal mines, state of Illinois.

DEAN H. JOHNSON, was born Nov. 30, 1922 in Lancaster, OH. After high school he attended Ohio State University in pre-med until February 1943 when he enlisted in the USAAC. Commissioned in April 1944 as aerial navigator at Selman Field, LA and assigned to B-24 crew (Frank Watson, pilot) at Biggs Field, TX.

Sent to England in August 1944 and assigned to 789th Sqdn., 467th Group of 8th Air Force at Rackheath, near Norwich. Flew a total of 30 missions to Germany (16 as lead crew in 791st Sqdn.) Received the Air Medal with four Oak Leaf Clusters and the Distinguished Flying Cross.

Following his discharge in September 1945, he returned to Ohio State University and received his medical degree in June 1950. He served an internship at Christ Hospital, Cincinnati, OH.

Dr. Johnson returned to active duty with the USAAF as a physician in July 1951. He served at Langley Field, VA and Wichita Air Force Base. Returned to civilian life in July 1953 and migrated to Concord, CA. Established himself in private practice as a GP; was active in many community projects; elected to and served for eight years as trustee on the Mt. Diablo Unified School District Board, one of California's largest districts with over 50,000 enrollments. He also designed and built three medical office buildings in Concord.

After finishing his tour in WWII, he married his college sweetheart, Frances L. Bell of Manchester, OH. They had two sons, six daughters and 20 grandchildren (as of September 1993). In 1971 he took a sabbatical from his practice and along with his wife and four children, joined the Peace Corps and served three years in Afghanistan as a Peace Corp Physician. This Afghanistan experience was and is most precious to all the Johnsons and to Dr. Johnson is only second to the intense pride that he has for his crew and his group and the 8th Air Force.

He retired in 1986 and has travelled extensively since then. Frances passed away in June 1993 following a massive stroke.

DELMAR C. JOHNSON, was born Jan. 21, 1920 in Regina, Sask., Canada. Moved to Camas, WA in 1926 and graduated from Camas High School in 1938. Married Lucille Bangs, March 6, 1943 at Tucson, AZ. They have three sons and two grandchildren.

Accepted for Aviation Cadet training in March 1942, Seattle. Commissioned second lieutenant/navigator January 1943 at Hondo, TX. Assigned to 392nd Bombardment Group (B-24s). After training at Alamogordo, NM, the group deployed from Topeka AAB to the 2nd Air Division, 8th Air Force at Wendling, England in August 1943.

Flew 19 missions over Germany and occupied Europe beginning September 1943. Shot down by FW-190s in March 1944, losing eight of their 10 crewman. Was POW in Stalag Luft III, Sagan; Stalag XIIID, Nurnberg and Stalag VIIA, Moosburg. Was liberated April 1945 by Gen. Patton's 3rd Army.

Inactive duty in Air Force Reserve from December 1945 until retired as lieutenant colonel. In hospital administration with the Veterans Administration from 1946 until retirement 1975.

DONALD A. JOHNSON, was born Hop Bottom, PA on Sept. 13, 1922. Graduated high school in 1940 and attended Mansfield State Teacher's College until April 1943 when he was called to active duty in the Air Force. Graduated from Navigation School in Monroe, LA, Class of 44-4.

Joined to crew of Charles Norris in Tucson, AZ and

flew to England in July 1944. Flew 35 combat missions with the 44th Bomb Group from September 1944 to April 1945. Crash landed twice during this time. Once at home base and once in Belgium.

Returned to USA with the bomb group June 1, 1945. Held the rank of first lieutenant when separated from service in September 1945. Received Air Medal with four clusters and ETO Ribbon with four stars. Retired from IBM Feb. 1, 1985. Was married to high school sweetheart while in Monroe. Has three children, seven grandchildren and one great-grandchild.

EDWARD C. JOHNSON, was born March 23, 1924 in Superior, WI. Enlisted Dec. 3, 1942 in the USAAC. Served with 2nd Air Division, 489th Bomb Group, 846th Sqdn. Stationed at St. Petersburg, Tyndall Field and Panama City, FL; Sheppard Field, Texas Tech, Lubbock, TX; Santa Ana, CA; Lincoln AB, NE; Davis-Monthan AB, Tucson, AZ; Amarillo AB, TX; Lackland AB; and Maxwell Field, Montgomery, AL.

Three weeks from commission when the atomic bomb was dropped on Japan. Stayed in reserve for 10 years. Participated in 23 missions in ETO during summer and early fall of 1944 (Normandy, Northern France and Rhineland campaigns). Late May of 1944 their plane iced up badly on a night flight from Goose Bay, Labrador to Nutts Corner, Ireland. They returned on three engines (flak damage) from Munich, Germany; their aircraft was alone in heavy cloud cover, landing 45 minutes after group at Halesworth. Returned from Coblenz, Germany mission, September 1944, with all hydraulics shot out by flak and also turbo damage. Had to crank out locks on main gear and kick out nose wheel. Despite all their flak damage on numerous missions, no crew members were hit physically.

Discharged Oct. 12, 1945 with the rank tech sergeant. Received the ETO Air Medal and clusters.

Johnson is semi-retired from the construction field. Married Eleanor Busse 43 years ago and has one daughter.

FRANK C. JOHNSON, was born Jan. 12, 1922 in Chicago, IL. Enlisted Nov. 22, 1942 in the USAAC, aviation cadet program, commissioned in 1944 as second lieutenant bombardier navigator. Stationed at North Pickenham, England, flying B-24 with 2nd Air Division, 492nd Bomb Group.

Memorable experiences: being shot down over Kiel, Germany; was POW for a year and was on the 300 mile march from Stalag III to Moosburg, Germany where the POWs were liberated. Discharged Nov. 22, 1945 with the rank of captain.

Married April 23, 1943, has one son, one daughter and four grandchildren. Johnson retired in 1989 and passed away Nov. 13, 1993.

FRANK HOLMES JOHNSON (BIG JOHN), was born July 17, 1923 in Brooklyn, NY. Grew up in Princeton-Lawrenceville area of New Jersey. Graduated from Princeton High School and one year of Industrial Art School. Entered service on Feb. 11, 1943 at Fort Dix, NJ. Basic training at Miami Beach; Armament School in Buckley and Lowry Field, Denver, CO; and Gunnery School, Tyndall Field, FL and Wendover, UT.

From pool at Salt Lake City, UT was assigned to Crew Y-4, 788th Bomb Sqdn., 467th Bomb. Group, B-24s at Wendover Field, UT. After several months of training, group was sent to Rackheath, England via Trinidad, Brazil, Dakar, Africa, Marrakech, Wales.

Flew 33 missions as left waist gunner, including Berlin, Munich, Brunswick, Mannheim, etc. Returned to the U.S. in September 1944 on the USS *Mariposa*. Went to Laredo,

TX for B-29 Gunnery Instructor's School. Assigned as instructor for B-29s at Las Vegas AFB until September 1945.

His memorable experiences include D-day and all the boats in the English channel; and getting shot up on May 10, 1944 over Brunswick, Germany by five Me-109s. Discharged from Fort Dix on September 26, 1945. Decorations include Flying Cross, four Air Medals and four European Campaign Stars.

Spent 33 years as a business representative for a labor union. Married to Rita Ernst and has five children and two grandchildren. He is retired.

FREDERICK M. JOHNSON, was born Feb. 12, 1924. Enlisted in the USAAC April 1943. Attended AM School, Keesler Field; Gunnery School, Harlingen; crew training, Casper, WY. Participated in Air Offensive of Europe. Flew 30 missions with 18 as lead crew. Was flight engineer on R.E. Oberschnid crew.

Discharged July 1945 with the rank tech sergeant. Received the Air Medal with five Oak Leaf Clusters, Air Offensive of Europe with five stars and the Good Conduct Medal.

Married To Betty Budd, they have five children and nine grandchildren. Their oldest son retired from Air Force. Johnson is a retired model maker from IBM and lives in Charlotte, NC.

GEORGE H. JOHNSON, was born Sept. 16, 1924, Minneapolis, MN; joined the USAAC in Chicago, IL on May 13, 1943; graduated as navigator and commissioned as second lieutenant, Class 44-6, San Marcos AAF, April 22, 1944.

B-24 RTU at Biggs AAF. Assigned to 93rd Bomb Group, 8th AAF at Hardwick, England and completed 30 combat mission tour as navigator with 409th and 329th squadrons from September 1944 to March 1945. Returned to pilot training at Goodfellow, Perrin and Enid AAFs and graduated as pilot with Class 46-B on Aug. 27, 1946. Separated as captain in December 1946.

Flew with Air Force Reserve while earning civil engineering degree (U of Minnesota) and then was recalled to active duty with SAC on May 1, 1951. Flew B-29s (9th Bomb Wing, Travis AFB), B-47s (376th Bomb Wing, Barksdale AFB) and B-52s (92nd Bomb Wing, Fairchild AFB and 4141st Bomb Wing, Glasgow AFB) from May 1951 to September 1963.

Earned MBA from the George Washington University in 1964. Served as operations officer and commander with RC130 and DC130 Recon units in Japan and Vietnam (1964-1970), followed by headquarters staff assignments in Recon plans and as comptroller. Retired as colonel Aug. 31, 1978.

Married former Shirley Sams on Sept. 4, 1948. They have four children and nine grandchildren.

HENRY K. JOHNSON, was born July 17, 1918 in Franklin, MA. Joined the Air Corps May 4, 1942. Stationed at Muroc, CA; Sioux Falls, SD; Laredo, TX; Harlingen, TX; Lincoln, NE. Joined Robert Tuchel's crew in 1943. Completed his 35th mission December 1944 at Wendling, with the 579th Sqdn., 392nd Bomb Group.

Memorable experience was emergency landing at Woodbridge with hydraulic system shot out. Was forced to send out SOS over channel. Discharged Sept. 15, 1945 with the rank tech sergeant. Received the Air Medal with six Oak Leaf Clusters and the Distinguished Unit Badge.

Married since Jan. 1, 1946, has one son. Retired in 1983 as postmaster of Townsend, MA.

HOWARD W. JOHNSON, was born Feb. 7, 1915, in New Britain, CT. Graduated from Princeton University in the Class of 1936. From 1937-1942, he was employed by

American Airlines in a variety of traffic management positions, with an occupational draft deferment.

After Pearl Harbor, he enlisted in the Army Aviation Cadets, graduating in the Class of 43G at Altus, OK as a second lieutenant pilot.

Prior to graduation, he married Ruth Marie Snowden, who shared his remaining U.S. training locations in the midwest and Wendover, UT where he was assigned a B-24 as aircraft commander. He named the plane *Ruth Marie*.

He flew a combat tour of 33 missions with the 790th Sqdn., 467th Bomb Group, 2nd Air Division from April 1944 to August 1944. Was promoted to first lieutenant and awarded decorations including the Distinguished Flying Cross and Air Medal with three Oak Leaf Clusters.

On his return to the States in September 1944, he was transferred to the Air Transport Command, flying the Atlantic to Paris regularly in C-54s and making one trip to India. After the war, he remained in the Air Force Reserve, retiring as a colonel in 1973.

Returned to work with American Airlines (post-war). Spent a year as co-pilot and the remainder of his service in various management positions in sales, traffic and flight schedule planning. On retirement in 1976, he did some aviation consulting work, and was a substitute teacher in the Stamford, CT High School System for four years.

Community service since retirement included Kiwanis Club (lieutenant governor); Coast Guard Auxiliary (Flotilla commander); and U.S. power squadrons. He is currently national chairman of the Weather Course Committee, with the rank of rear commander in USPS.

His first wife passed away in 1968. He married Gretta Stephenson Mellecker in 1971. Has a son, daughter, stepson, step-daughter, four step-grandchildren and one step-great-granddaughter.

JOSEPH S. JOHNSON, was born Aug. 20, 1922 in Ozark, AL. Enlisted Jan. 19, 1942 in the USAAC, USAF. Served with 389th Bomb Group, armor. Stationed at Maxwell AFB, McGowan AFB, Pocatello, Hethel and Pacific. Completed 30 combat missions (Berlin six times) on D-day.

Memorable experiences: D-day; badly shot up plane and crew, mission Oldenberg, Germany. Retired Aug. 31, 1964 with the rank lieutenant colonel AUS. Received four Air Medals, Distinguished Flying Cross, Combat Infantryman's Badge and the Commendation Medal.

Married Pattie B. Johnson and has four daughters. Farms, management, now mostly retired.

KENNETH W. JOHNSON, was born May 19, 1921 and was raised in the farming area of Phillips County, KS. Interrupted his pre-law studies at Wichita, KS to enlist in the USAAC in September 1942. Flew 34 missions with the 389th Bomb Group based at Hethel AAB, Norwich, England.

Discharged in September 1945 and began a farming and cattle operation. Became active in the VFW and served as state commander of Kansas in 1951-52. Served on President Eisenhower's Committee to employ the physically handicapped and participated in ceremonies to lay the cornerstone of the Eisenhower Complex at Abilene, KS in 1952.

Joined the USDA Soil Conservation Service in 1952 and retired Friday, April 13, 1984, exactly 39 years after returning from overseas (Friday, April 13, 1945).

Married to Beryl Schulke on May 31, 1942. They have three children, one foster son, six grandchildren and three great-grandchildren.

OLIVER D. JOHNSON, was born April 28, 1919, Philadelphia, MS and moved to Chase, LA, July 1919. Attended LA Tech University and entered U.S. Army April 8, 1941 and served in ground forces to December 1941 when he was

accepted aviation cadet and commissioned as second lieutenant, navigator, Selman Field, Monroe, LA, Class 44-3, February 26, 1942.

Assigned navigator on B-24 crew, 458th Bomb Group, 8th Air Force, 2nd Air Division based at Horsham St. Faith, Norwich, England. Flew 35 missions in European Theater. Received Air Medal and Oak Leaf Clusters. Discharged Nov. 3, 1945 as first lieutenant. Reserve duty to September 1957.

Married Harris (Penny) Winstead Aug. 10, 1945. They have one son and one grandson. Self-employed, he owns and operates Johnson Agri-business, Chase, LA.

RAYMOND D. JOHNSON (RAY), entered the USAAC as an aviation cadet in June 1942, graduated from pilot training on Nov. 3, 1943. He completed B-24 transition at Fort Worth, TX and combat crew training at Muroc, CA. In July 1944 his crew was assigned to the 392nd Bomb Group in England and flew 35 missions.

Upon return to the U.S. Ray was assigned as assistant base operations officer at March Field where he met Harriet Rumsch, an Army nurse stationed at Camp Haan. They were married in June 1947.

In January 1950, Ray graduated with a degree in business administration from the University of California in Berkeley. The major portion of his career was in county government management. After 10 years in Fresno County, he was selected to be the chief administrative officer of Santa Barbara, CA where he served until his retirement in 1980.

Ray remained in the Reserve of the Air Force with 18 years in the California Air National Guard and retired with the rank of colonel. Was awarded the Distinguished Flying Cross and Air Medal with four Oak Leaf Clusters. He was appointed by Governor Reagan to serve on two state advisory commissions.

In September 1993, he and his wife will become residents at Air Force Village West near March AFB, Riverside, CA.

ROLAND W. JOHNSON, was born Nov. 29, 1916 in Minneapolis, MN and was one of the original crew members of the 458th Bomb Group. The second lieutenant/bomber trained at Deming, NM, Boise, ID and Tonopah, NV, prior to assignment at Norwich, England.

Johnson's B-24J was shot down in the 8th Air Force's first daylight raid on Berlin, March 6, 1944 and with the crew, was forced to bail out over Holland. Captured by German soldiers, Johnson was sent to Stalag Luft I POW camp in Barth, Germany where he remained until liberated by the Russian army on May 2, 1945. Returning to the States, he served in the Air Force Reserve as a first lieutenant until honorably discharged in 1957.

An accountant for several years in private industry, Johnson was appointed a New Mexico State Bank examiner in 1965, serving for 20 years until retirement.

Roland and his wife, the former Rosemary Peloquin, were married in July 1946 and make their home in Albuquerque, NM. They have six children and six grandchildren.

STANLEY H. JOHNSON, was born Sept. 24, 1921, Salt Lake City, UT. Entered the service Jan. 5, 1942. Graduated

Aug. 27, 1942, aviation cadet, Class 42H, Army Air Corps, Air Force. Served with 714th Sqdn., 448th Group. Stationed at Gowen Field, Wendover, Seething, Victorville and Buckley Field.

Memorable experience was first raid on Berlin. He completing 30 missions with no casualties to crew. Discharged July 15, 1945 with the rank of captain. Received the Distinguished Flying Cross, Air Medal with three clusters and the European Medal.

Married with three children and nine grandchildren. He is retired from air traffic control.

STANLEY L. JOHNSON, was born Dec. 29, 1919 in Chicago, IL. Enlisted in the Army Aug. 11, 1942; honorable discharge from AAF Navigation School, Monroe, LA Sept. 24, 1943 to accept commission in AC-AUS. Entered active duty from AFER Feb. 6, 1943. Entry to active duty Sept. 25, 1943 as navigator 1034. Departed USA to ETO Jan. 13, 1944, arrived Feb. 1, 1944.

Participated in Normandy battles, Air Offensive Europe. Decorations and citations: Air Medal with one Bronze Oak Leaf Cluster with two Bronze Oak Leaf Clusters with three Oak Leaf Clusters; GO 283, 8th Air Force April 17, 1944; GO 366 HQ 8th Air Force May 8, 1944; GO 89 2nd Bomb Div. June 6, 1944; GO 369 HQ 8th Air Force May 15, 1944; Distinguished Flying Cross GO 122 HQ 2nd Bomb Div. July 8, 1944 EAME Theater Ribbon with two Bronze Battle Stars; one Overseas Service Bar.

Departed ETO to USA July 13, 1944 arrived July 15, 1944. Separated Oct. 13, 1945, Fort Sheridan, IL with the rank first lieutenant, navigator. B-24H "Envy of 'em all I and II, 8th Air Force, 2nd Air Div., 458th Bomb Group, 754th Bomb Sqdn., 96th Combat Wing, USAAF Station 123, Horsham St. Faith, Norwich, England. Completed 34 missions in a six month period. Made two missions on D-day, June 6, 1944.

After discharge completed college with an industrial engineering degree. Married Royna Rogers in 1946 and has one daughter and one granddaughter. He had 37 years service (1948-1985) with Metropolitan Sanitary District of Greater Chicago as mechanical engineer.

Johnson passed away Dec. 16, 1988.

WARREN DEAN JOHNSTON, was born March 18, 1921 in Ferndale, MI. Enlisted August 1942 and inducted March 4, 1943, Aviation Cadet Center, San Antonio basic training; pre-flight, Ellington Field; Aerial Gunnery, Harlingen; Navigation School, Hondo, TX; graduated Class 43-18, December 1943.

Gowen Field, Boise, ID, January 1944, B-24 staging crew: 1/LT James Monahan, pilot; 2/LT Gordon Morehead, co-pilot; 2/LT Warren Johnston, navigator; 2/LT William Baer, bombardier; S/SGT Kenneth Holcomb, radio operator; S/SGT Coburn Petersen, engineer; SGT Earl Knee, gunner; SGT Dennis Medley, gunner.

Received new B-24J in Topeka, KS, flew solo to Wales with overnight in Bangor, ME, Goose Bay, Labrador and Iceland. Assigned to 458th Bomb Group, 752nd Sqdn., Horsham, St. Faith, Norwich. First of 30 missions

, May 20, 1944, bombed French coast on D-day ahead of Allied troops.

Flew several missions to France also Cologne, Saarbrucken, Kiel, Munich, Freidburg, Ludwigshaven, Magdenburg, Lubeck, Dulman, Karlsruhe and big "B" (Berlin). All Germany. Transferred from original crew in July after 17 missions. Former crew was shot down over France next day. All became prisoners except tail gunner (killed jumping). Flew last 13 missions as squadron lead.

Navigation instructor, 1944, Brooks Field, San Antonio. Memorable experience were losing first crew; seeing fighters shoot down our bombers; getting hit with flak; bombers colliding in air; fully loaded planes not being able to take off and crashing.

Discharged October 1945 with the rank first lieutenant. Received the Air Medal with three Silver Clusters and the Distinguished Flying Cross.

Married former June Nicholson, Bellevue, MI on Nov. 26, 1942. They have two sons, two daughters, three grandsons, four granddaughters and one great-grandson. He started diaper service business in 1948 in Saginaw, MI and retired in 1982. Spends October-May in Horseshoe, TX and June-September in Frankenmuth, MI.

MARVIN A. JONAS, was born in Butternut, WI. Enlisted October 1943 in the USAAF. Stationed at Jefferson Barracks for basic; Gunnery at Las Vegas AAB; crew training, Biggs Field, El Paso, TX; served with 93rd Bomb Group, Hardwick, England.

Participated in Northern France, Rhineland, Ardennes and Central Europe campaigns. Second mission, badly shot up; 21st mission, badly shot-up, Aug. 11, 1944 flew new B-24 to Wales, went to Tiverton, Devan R&R.

Discharged Sept. 29, 1945 with the rank staff sergeant. Received the ETO Ribbon, four Battle Stars, Air Medal with five Oak Leaf Clusters.

Married over 44 years and has four children and seven grandchildren. A carpenter, he is semi-retired.

ROY JONASSON, was born March 4, 1906 in Pennsylvania. Married Mildred King May 24, 1942. Was inducted into the USAAC in March 1942, one day under 36. Jonasson was immediately nick-named "Jon." Was trained as an airplane mechanic at Sheppard Field, Wichita Falls, TX and then sent to the B-24 Specialist Training School at Camp Consair, San Diego, CA.

At Davis Monthan Field, Tucson, AZ, he was assigned to technical supply. Then from Biggs Field, El Paso, TX to Lowry Field, Denver, CO. Arrived at Hethel Airdrome, England, July 7, 1943, with the 564th Sqdn., 389th Bombardment Group.

Following his discharge Sept. 30, 1945, Roy went back to school. In 1951 they moved to Morro Bay, CA. Was employed by the State Highway as a soil analyst for 19 years. Although Roy is now an invalid and is 87 years old, he still hears from many of his GI friends. He was an active amateur radio operator, K6TOE. His other hobby was hunting for his GI friends so he could tell them of the 2nd Air Div. Assoc. This was a task of love for Jonasson has always said, "these boys are my family."

ALBERT JONES (ED), was born July 12, 1918 in Pottsville, AR. Lived and worked in Springfield, IL before entering the USAAC, September 1941. Was assigned to first class for airplane mechanics and taught at Keesler Field, MS. After Pearl Harbor, was assigned to the 340th Service Sqdn. with the 44th Bomb Group at a former RAF base at Shipdham, England near Norwich, Norfolk (8th Air Force).

Was in charge of the control tower alert crew, responsible for maintenance of visiting aircraft, also to the tower for updated location of all aircraft on the base. His prime responsibility was operation of a radio jeep equipped to communicate with the tower radio operator and the aircraft pilots. Continued on this job from August 1942 until leaving England at end of ETO in June 1945. After a short assignment with 2nd Air Force, he was separated on Oct. 31, 1945.

Married Emma Ruth Phillips and they have two children and two grandchildren. His post-military career was 41 years with the state and federal employment service, having retired in 1984.

ALBERT V. JONES, was born March 13, 1922 in Detroit, MI. Graduated from Cass Tech High School and worked at Briggs Aircraft riveting wings for A-20, Corsair, etc. Joined the USAAC as cadet, Class 44D and received commission as second lieutenant, pilot. Transitioned to B-24s at Chanute, IL with crew training at March Field, CA.

Shipped to Liverpool, England on USS Mt. Vernon and joined 445th Bomb Group, 703rd Sqdn. at Tibenham in December 1944. Flew 24 missions and after V-E day, flew B-24, *Plucky Lucky*, back to States.

Married in 1947 to Bernis L. McGowan. They have five children and to date six grandchildren. Earned degree in AERO at Northrup University. Worked 31 years as instrumentation engineer, 19 years at North American, Downey, CA and 12 years at Lockheed, Burbank/Sunnyvale, CA. Retired to Tulsa, OK in 1984 and built a home in the country to watch birds, etc.

EDWARD H. JONES, was born Aug. 7, 1922 in Chicago, IL. Enlisted December 1943 in USAF, Pilot 1092, 466th Bomb Group. Stationed at Wichita Falls; Nashville; Montgomery; Knoxville; Cape Girardeau, MO; Harlingen, TX; Malden; Albany; Lemoore, CA; March Field, CA; Hamilton Field, CA; Miles Standish, Boston; Attlebridge; Sioux Falls, SD; and Camp Beale, CA.

Memorable experiences: the low level mission over Germany; flying home through Wales, Iceland, Nova Scotia, in B-24 with crew and passengers. Flew 11 missions over Germany. Discharged September 1945 with the rank lieutenant, co-pilot B-24. Received the Air Medal.

Married Maxine and has two daughters Laura and Donna. Started with appliance/TV retail store in 1946, now owns and operates same company.

ELWOOD JONES JR. (MORRIS), was born Nov. 5, 1917, Council Grove, KS. Graduated high school in 1935 and Emporia State University in 1941. Entered the Aviation Cadet Corps at Fort Riley, KS in time for the pilot class of 43-E. After 30 hours of pilot training was ordered to Selman Field, LA (because of his eyes) for navigation training.

Commissioned Sept. 25, 1943 in the Class of 43-13. Reported to Tucson for crew formation; to Blythe, CA for OTU. Met his wife-to-be and her sister who were ANC nurses at Brooks Field. At Pueblo, CO joined other crews to form the 491st Bomb Group (H), B-24s; loaded up at Herington, KS and left by southern route for Africa.

Arrived at Dakar, Senegal in May 1944 and proceeded to Marrakech. Land's End and finally Metfield. First mission was bombing France to support D-day. Replaced the 492nd Group at North Pickenham. Completed 30 missions but missed the deadline so flew another five as a casual. While at Metfield he helped to form a dance band, the 491st Rhythm Bombshells.

Returned to the States on SS *America*, arrived in New York in February 1945, married his nurse, Doris Dillehay Jones, on March 7, 1945. They have two sons, Charles R. and Paul M.

Reported to USC in September for Graduate School and proceeded to follow a dual path, teacher and reserve officer. Retired from the Air Force as a major in 1977 and from teaching in 1978. Received the Distinguished Flying Cross from Gen. Leon Johnson, Air Medal with four clusters and ETO Ribbon with six stars. He is presently a senior activist.

EVERETT R. JONES JR., was born July 28, 1918 in Leitchfield, KY. Went into U.S. Signal Corps May 5, 1942

as a private, then entered Aviation Cadet Program Feb. 1, 1943 and graduated Nov. 3, 1943 as second lieutenant, Class 43-J, Southeast Training Command, Stuttgart, AR.

Trained as a B-24 pilot and flew B-24 bomber to England via northern route. Flew first seven combat missions with the 458th Bomb Group including two missions on D-day. Transferred to the 44th Bomb Group for lead crew training and returned to the 466th Bomb Group for completion of a combat tour on Dec. 30, 1944. While at the 466th, flew lead positions for the 2nd Air Div., 96th Combat Wing and for three different groups on 22 occasions.

Received the Distinguished Flying Cross, five Air Medals and four European Campaign Stars. Remained with the 466th Bomb Group after tour completion as an assistant group operations officer. Checked out on a war-weary P-47 fighter on the base and later bailed out of this same Thunderbolt on June 4, 1945 over England. Left the service Nov. 15, 1945 with the rank of captain.

Married Lois Gibbins and has two daughters. Began oil industry career in South Louisiana in 1946, presently he is an independent oil and gas producer in Dallas, TX. A trustee of the Southwest Engineering Foundation and a past president of both the Engineers Club of Dallas and the Dallas Petroleum Club.

HARLEY M. JONES, was born Sept. 19, 1923 in Tallapoosa, GA. Jones entered the USAAC in January 1943. His basic training was at Keesler Field, MS; Armament School, Lowry Field, CO; Gunnery School, Buckingham Field, FL. Some of his other stations include: Pocatella Field, ID; Stone AB, England; Tibenham AB, England; Turner Field, GA; Ft. McPherson, GA; Greenville AFB; Rabat, Morroco; Barksdale AFB, LA; Torrejon AFB, Spain; Vandenberg AFB, CA; and Barksdale AFB, LA.

Was sent to the 445th Bomb Group in England in January 1944 where on his 24th mission was shot down over France going after a buzz bomb installation. For the three months following, Jones lived with the French Underground before returning to the States in November 1944. He then proceeded to serve his country for 23 years in the Air Force before retiring as a chief master sergeant. Received the Purple Heart, Air Medal with three Oak Leaf Clusters, Air Force Commendation with one Oak Leaf Cluster and two Battle Stars.

He came out of retirement to join the U.S. Post Office where he enjoyed 10 years of service. Since 1983 he has been an active member of the VFW in Oviedo, FL.

He married Melba L. Loyd on June 1, 1946. They have two daughters, Pat and Susan, and four grandsons.

HENRY JONES (HANK), was born Santa Barbara, CA on Nov. 7, 1920 and lived on a farm in Goleta, CA. Joined the cadets April 1942. Pre-flight, SAACC, San Antonio; primary, Cuero, TX; basic, Randolph Field; advanced, Ellington Field, Houston, Class 43-E.

Bases: Moses Lake, WA, B-17; Gowan, Boise, B-24; Scottsbluff, NE, crew training; Casper, WY, overseas cadre. Flew new B-24 from Forbes/Topeka to England late 1943 via Palm Beach, Trinidad, Belem and Natal, Brazil, crossed South Atlantic to Dakar, Senegal, north to Marrakech, Morrocco, then W/O continent, to Newquay, Lands End.

Joined 702nd Sqdn., 445th Group, Tibenham, Norfolk early 1944. Flew CP first mission to Gotha, 445th lead with 26 planes, 12 returned, 54% lost and 34 more missions to go. Hamm railyards, returned at dusk with two injured. After Dover, dove for home and unloaded injured, whereupon "all hell" broke loose as JU-88s following, shot down many over our bases. "By becoming injured, our crew members had saved us." Lost two engines, gained 263 flak holes, returned home along. Engines replaced, all flak damage re-

paired and flew again three days later. He can't praise the ground crews enough.

Crew flew 35 missions. Received Air Medal with six clusters, ETO and the Distinguished Flying Cross. Of their original 21 crews, four survived intact.

He returned to his first love, farming, and worked for a public utility. Enjoying retirement, he has three college grad children who are his life.

J. LIVINGSTON JONES, was born July 3, 1920, Columbus, GA. Entered USAAF on Sept. 25, 1942; basic training at Miami Beach; gunnery training, Tyndall AFB, FL and armament training at Lowry AFB, CO. Had ear operation at Salt Lake City and could not be a heavy bomber gunner. Was given a military occupation title of general clerk.

Sailed to England on *Queen Elizabeth*, assigned to HQ 2nd Air Div. at Horsham St. Faith, HQ, later moving to Ketteringham Hall and assigned to the adjutant general section. Was assigned to collect all restricted, secret, etc. material which was no longer in force. Once a week this material was taken to a plant at Thetford where it was destroyed in a water vat and eventually made into water buckets, flower boxes, ash trays, etc. Otherwise he did general clerk work as sergeant.

Graduated from Georgia Tech with a bachelor degree of civil engineering in December 1949. Became a professional engineer in North Carolina. Retired in 1984 from engineering profession.

First marriage on Jan. 20, 1946 and had six children. Second marriage on July 15, 1978 to widow, Tina, with three children. Has 16 grandchildren.

JOHN H. JONES (JACK), was born March 27, 1919 in Boston, MA. Served with 392nd Bomb Group, 577th Sqdn. as squadron navigation officer March 1, 1943 to July 24, 1944. Lead navigator pathfinder 392nd August-December 1944. Flew 30 combat missions as lead navigator.

Participated in raids over Danzig, Norway, Bremen, Hamburg, Kassel, Hamm ETO. Was EM from March 1941 to May 1942, radio operator, 26th Inf. Div. Retired as lieutenant colonel March 1979, Air Force Reserve. Received the Distinguished Flying Cross with one Oak Leaf Cluster, Air Medal with three Oak Leaf Clusters, Presidential Unit Badge, EAME Campaign Ribbon with four Battle Stars plus several other ribbons.

Most memorable experience was mission to Kassel on Oct. 7, 1944, two engines shot out over target on "Umbriago" and crash landed at Brussels.

Married Dec. 11, 1942 to Catherine I. Orr (Betty). They have four children and five grandchildren. Jones is retired from flat glass distribution business in April 1987.

KENNETH D. JONES (DEACON), was born Janesville, WI on June 21, 1924. Sworn into Enlisted Reserves Nov. 29, 1942 with basic training at Miami Beach, FL, January 31, 1943. Classified for pilot training at San Antonio Cadet Classification Center. Earned silver wings at Twin Engine Flight School, Lubbock, TX, April 15, 1944. Given transition training in B-24s at Liberal, KS and combat training with bomber crew at March Field, CA.

Went overseas on *Queen Mary* to Hethel Air Base, 389th Bomb Group, home of the Green Dragons, Nov. 15, 1944. Flew 10 missions over 3rd Reich as wing man and then eight more missions as lead crew. Received three Air Medals and three Battle Stars.

At age 20 he flew B-24H home to USA on May 23, 1945. Assigned to Sioux Falls, SD and discharged as first lieutenant Sept. 25, 1945. Married Junice E. Hanewall Oct. 25, 1947 and has two sons and six grandchildren. Retired as police chief.

LEON ARLO JONES, was born June 2, 1925, Cresbard, SD. Enlisted Sept. 1, 1943, USAAF 611 tail gunner, 2nd Air Div. Stationed at Jefferson Barracks, MO; Fort Myers, FL; Chatham Field, GA; and Wendling, England.

Participated in Rhineland, Ardennes and Central Europe campaigns. Memorable experience was Dec. 2, 1944, a busy day at Bingen (392nd Bomb Group, 578th Bomb Squadron).

Discharged Nov. 9, 1945 with the rank staff sergeant. Received the Air Medal with two Oak Leaf Clusters and the Distinguished Unit Citation.

Has BS and MS, school administration for 10 years, bank officer 25 years, currently retired. Married June in August 1947, they have a daughter, son and four grandchildren.

RICHARD W. JONES, was born Jan. 12, 1924 in Samoa, CA. Drafted Feb. 4, 1943 in the Air Corps. Served as armorer gunner, air crew B-24, "White Lit'nin'." Trained at Gowen Field, Boise, ID to be a visual lead crew.

Stationed at "Bungay Buckeroo" Bungay, England with the 446th Bomb Group. First mission was April 6, 1944. Deputy lead to Col. Broger on D-day, June 6, 1943. Crew broke up in July and he finished rest of his missions training green crews/replacements. Completed 25 combat missions with 705th Bomb Sqdn.

Discharged Sept. 30, 1945, Camp Adair, OR with the rank staff sergeant. Received the Air Medal with three clusters and the Distinguished Flying Cross.

Retired and spending lots of money.

ROBERT L. JONES, was born Nov. 16, 1922 in Peoria, IL and raised in Wisconsin and Illinois. After two years of college, he joined the USAAC November 1942. Active duty January 1943 for basic, then into cadet training, Ellington Field, TX and graduated as bombardier, second lieutenant, Nov. 13, 1943 at Big Spring, TX.

Flew overseas to England in new B-24, April 1944 to Horsham St. Faith, Norwich, England, 458th Bomb Group, 755th Sqdn. Completed 31 combat bombing missions by Sept. 11, 1944 as first lieutenant, bombardier/navigator, after which completed several "gas" missions carrying 1,000 GI cans of gas for Patton's tanks.

Memorable experience was flying over Aachen, Germany in August 1944 where they took 330 flak hits and totaled B-24 on emergency field in England. Returned to States November 1944. Received the Distinguished Flying Cross, six Air Medals and two Combat Stars.

Completed college on GI Bill, graduating in summer of 1947 with PHB degree. Married to Janet since November 1947, has three children and one grandchild. Started his own business distributing school and office furniture in 1955 and is still active in business today along with two sons. Has lived in Redding, CA on the Sacramento River since 1979.

ROBERT T. JONES (BOB), was born June 26, 1922, Mansfield, OH and graduated from high school there. Entered the USAAC March 31, 1941 as a private at Ft. Hayes, Columbus, OH; sent to Chanute Field, IL for Technical School training April 1941. July 1941 assigned with 320th

School Sqdn. which was transferred to Sheppard Field, TX as permanent party. In August 1942 was transferred to Amarillo Field, TX with 418th School Sqdn. as permanent party. His duty assignment at both locations was administration with general mess office. In October 1943, he was transferred to Ft. Logan, CO for field training and processing for shipment to ETO.

Arrived in England on Dec. 18, 1943 and assigned to 1215th QM Co. attached to 389th Bomb Group, Hethel. He was assigned late March 1944 to Eastern Command USSTAF HQ Poltava, Russia to support shuttle bombing missions from 8th Air Force, England. Returned to England December 1944 and transferred to 9th Air Force Base Depot, February 1945. Compiegne, France and assisted in transferring depot to Erding, Germany from June to September 1945.

Returned to U.S. November 1945 and separated Nov. 17, 1945 upon transfer to Army Air Force Reserve with rank as tech sergeant. He retired as master sergeant, USAFR, July 1, 1965. Received numerous ribbons, four Campaign Stars and ETO Ribbon.

Married high school sweetheart, Martha J. Hunter on June 19, 1943 at Amarillo, TX. They have five children and 11 grandchildren. They celebrated their 50th wedding anniversary on June 19, 1993.

THOMAS F. JONES, was born Aug. 21, 1921 in Bigelow, AR. Graduated from Perryville High School in 1939. Entered USAAC as aviation cadet, Santa Ana, CA, March 1943. Graduated Bombardier Class 43-13, Sept. 11, 1943. Assigned bombardier on B-24 crew, picked up their plane at Mitchell Field, NY and flew to Lecce, Italy via Natal Dakar and Tunisia arriving March 1944. Assigned to 98th Bomb Group, 344th Sqdn. at Lecce, March 1944.

Completed 20 missions on the *Consolidated Mess*. Transferred to Norwich, England in early May of 1944 and flew 20 missions with the 458th Bomb Group, 754th Sqdn., 2nd Air Div., having bombed the same targets from both Italy and England. Awarded the Distinguished Flying Cross and Air Medal with two Oak Leaf Clusters in Italy and awarded the Distinguished Flying Cross and Air Medal with two Oak Leaf Clusters while serving with the 8th Air Force in England. Returned to Carlsbad, NM and discharged in 1945 at Camp Chaffee, AR.

Returned to work in family business, Perry County Abstract and Guaranty Company served as county and circuit clerk (Perry County) 17 years, retired on Dec. 31, 1980. Married Velda Lucille Padgett March 2, 1942 and has one daughter, Tommie Lou Jones Wingfield, one granddaughter, Wendy Kay Wingfield Grimes and one grandson, Mark Wingfield.

LARRY JOSEPH, was born Oct. 19, 1917 in Hollister, CA. Basic training in Fresno, CA; AAFTS Sioux Falls, SD; Gunnery School, Laredo, TX; overseas training on B-24s as waist gunner, Muroc, CA. When training was completed his crew was shipped to Hamilton AAFB, CA and then by train, bus and ship to Scotland on D-day.

He and his crew were assigned to the 735th Bomb Sqdn., 453rd Bomb Group at Old Buckingham, England. First mission was flown July 7, 1944 and the 35th mission was completed the first week of December 1944. During this tour he was given the rank of staff sergeant and awarded the Air Medal and Distinguished Flying Cross.

After discharge in September 1945, he worked for various companies and retired in 1982. He has three children, eight grandchildren and now resides in Woodinville, WA.

GEORGE G. JUDD, was born Feb. 1, 1922 in Cannonsville, NY. Entered the USAAF in March of 1943 as an aviation cadet. Trained as a navigator and assigned to a crew at Peterson Field in May of 1944.

Flew with a full crew in a new B-24 to England, landing at Worthington and from there was transferred to the 392nd Bomb Group. He flew his first mission on Aug. 4, 1944 to Kiel and on his fourth mission was wounded. Able to fly again on Oct. 9, 1944. His last mission was flown on March 24, 1945. After completing 35 missions, he was assigned to be group navigator.

After the war in Europe was over, he flew back to the States with a crew that had lost their navigator. He was preparing to go to the Pacific theater when the atomic bombs were dropped so at that time he was discharged. He returned to Cornell University to complete his education. Was finally discharged in 1953 after the end of the Korean War. Received the Purple Heart and Air Medal.

Married with two daughters and four granddaughters

HENRY F. JURGENS, was born May 8, 1925 in Queens, NY. Enlisted January 1943 in the USAAC. Served with the 392nd Bomb Group, 577th Bomb Sqdn. in England. Participated in the ETO - Wendling, England, Normandy, Northern France and Germany campaigns.

Was shot down Sept. 12, 1944, Hanover, Germany and became POW for eight months. Discharged September 1945 with the rank staff sergeant. Received Air Medal (2) Oak Leaf Clusters, ETO Medal with two Battle Stars, Good Conduct, POW Medal and Conspic. Service Cross.

A retired business executive, he has three sons.

ROBERT H. JURGENS (BOB), was born March 4, 1920 in Chicago, IL. Inducted into the Army, Dec. 26, 1942 at Camp Shelby, MS. Sent to Miami Beach, FL for basic training and assigned to the USAAC. Graduated from Mechanic School, Gulfport, MS, B-24 School Willow Run, MI and Gunnery School, Harlingen, TX.

Sent to Salt Lake City, UT and assigned to crew, then to Tucson, AZ for training. Reported to Wendover Field, UT and assigned to the 489th Bomb Group, 844th Sqdn., Crew 14 as engineer. Crashed March 8, 1944 and held up group until they recovered.

Flew southern route to England and completed 31 missions. Assigned to 312th Ferrying Sqdn., AAF19 flying B-24s ferrying supplies to their troops with pilot, co-pilot and radio operator. Sent back to U.S. to Maxwell Field, AL. Went to B-29 School at Seattle, WA. Then back to Maxwell Field.

Discharged Dec. 1, 1945. attained rank of technical sergeant. Awarded Distinguished flying Cross, Air Medal with three Oak Leaf Clusters, ETO Campaign Ribbon with three stars. Returned home and went into business with his father and retired in 1985.

JOHN JOSEPH KALLAS, was born May 28, 1924 in Phillips, WI. Graduated 1942 from North Beaver Township High School, Mount Jackson, PA. Enlisted in the USAAC on Sept. 2, 1942 at New Castle, PA.

Received Aircraft Mechanics training at Isaac Delgado Trade School in New Orleans and attended B-24 Specialist School at Ford Motor Co. Joined 392nd Bomb Group, 578th Sqdn. at Biggs Field, El Paso.

At Wendling served as crew member on "Double Trouble" and "Miss Minnie". After rejoining the 392nd Bomb Group in Charleston, transferred to ATC in New Castle AFB, and discharged Oct. 2, 1945 with rank of sergeant.

Served apprenticeships as cabinetmaker and electrician and became self-employed. Member of North Beaver Township Fire Dept. for eight years. April 16, 1955 employed by United Air Lines at San Francisco International Airport. Worked as sheet metal mechanic, cabinetmaker, foreman and maintenance specialist, retiring after 27 years.

Retired as captain of the South San Francisco Police Reserves after 28 years of service.

Retired 1992 as a self-employed contractor after 10 years.

Resides in South San Francisco with his wife of 46 years, Anne. Has daughter, Pamela Jean; grandson, Jon; and granddaughter, Jaqueline.

ARTHUR G. KALTENBACH, was born in Scioto County, OH on Nov. 28, 1920. He was inducted into the U.S. Army Air Force on Oct. 19, 1942 and served as radio operator with the 458th Bomb Group (H), 755th Sqdn. He was discharged on Nov. 15, 1945 with the rank of staff sergeant.

Military locations and stations include basic training at St. Petersburg, FL; Scott Field, IL; Yuma, AZ; and Casper, WY. Participated in 19 missions between December 1944 and April 1945.

His memorable experiences include bail out on May 2, 1945 at Oxford, England.

He was awarded the Air Medal, Good Conduct Medal and ETO.

Taught junior high math for 30 years in Dayton, OH. Graduated from Xavier University. Presently retired. Married to Norma Jean Raynard on Aug. 19, 1950 and they have one son and one daughter.

JOHN KANYUCK, was born in Glen Lyon, PA on Nov. 19, 1922. Same town as high school classmate, "Rick" Rokicki of 458th Bomb Group.

Married Rina Caporaletti of San Diego, CA. Has two daughters.

In January 1943 received basic training at Jefferson Barracks, MO. Attended Franklin Institute in Boston, MA for drafting engineer. Assigned to "Compliment Squadron" and sent overseas. Transferred to 389th Bomb Group Hq. at Hethel, England as draftsman, in September 1943. His job was to make and keep updated, all graphs and charts of the missions. He returned to the states June 5, 1945 for 30-day "Rehab" leave. Assigned to Air Transport Command, Washington National Airport, at the end of Pacific hostilities. On Oct. 5, 1945 received honorable discharge from Andrews Air Force Base.

He attended Michigan State University and General Motors Institute.

Retired, after 39 years, from Buick Motors Division, Flint, MI as a tool supervisor.

MORRIS KAPLAN, was born in Philadelphia, PA on Sept. 16, 1923. Joined Army Air Force in March 1941, and was sent to McDill Field for nine months. He was then shipped to Barksdale Field where he trained to be an airplane mechanic.

In September of 1942 he was sent with the 93rd Bomb Group, 328th Sqdn. to Alconberry Air Field in Huntington, England where they received their new B-24 planes. At this time he was a staff sergeant and was made crew chief of their plane the "Shoot Luke" and promoted to tech. sergeant. Approximately one month later he was made a master sergeant and their group was moved to Hardwick where they were advised they were leaving England and going to North Africa to bomb southern Italy. Their location was a field called L.G. 139 in Libya where they were stationed for approximately three months.

After that period they were sent back and forth between England and Africa on several occasions to do low level bombing.

In 1944, he was sent on temporary duty outside of London to Bovington Air Force Base to work on SCS 51 to install blind landing equipment at English and American bases and then check it by flying test patterns.

After the troops moved the Germans out of Paris, their headquarters was moved outside of Paris where he remained

until being shipped back to Greensboro, NC. He was discharged from the Army in September of 1945.

He married April 11, 1948 to Annette Hoffman and has three children and two grandchildren. He is a self-employed businessman.

CHRIS KARRAS, was born on June 5, 1924 in Chicago, IL. He was inducted into the service on Dec. 15, 1942 and was discharged on Dec. 22, 1945 with the rank of corporal. He served as armorer and airplane sheet metal worker.

Chris was stationed in the U.S. at Fresno, CA (basic training); Spearfish, SD (CTD); Santa Ana, CA (classification); Amarillo, TX; Chanute Field, IL (Sheet Metal School); and Seymour Johnson Field. Overseas he served with the 492nd Bomb Group (H), 491st Bomb Group (H), 853rd Sqdn. at Huntington Air Base and Airstrip B-53 Merville France. On T.D., returned to Huntington Air Base, Biarritz France, Army University 27R #2, back to Huntington and home for discharge.

He was awarded one Service Stripe, three Overseas Service Bars, American Campaign Medal, Good Conduct Medal, WWII Victory Medal and EAME Theater Ribbon with two Bronze Battle Stars.

Married to Deana Lynn and has a son by a previous marriage. Presently retired and paints landscapes full time (artist).

GERALD J. KATHOL, was born in Hartington, NE on Aug. 31, 1921. He enlisted in the Army Air Force on July 30, 1942 and served as pilot with the 445th Bomb Group, 702nd Sqdn., 8th Air Force.

He was discharged on Oct. 25, 1945 with the rank of first lieutenant.

Gerald was stationed in England and later Stalag III near Sagan, Poland. He participated in two bombing missions in the B-24 and was shot down on his second mission at Kassel Germany on Sept. 27, 1944.

His memorable experiences include being liberated by Gen. Patton's 7th Armor in April 1945.

He was awarded the Purple Heart, WWII Medal, European Campaign Medal and Prisoner of War Medal.

Married in 1945 and has four children. His wife died in 1975 and he re-married in 1977 and raised two more children. He is a petroleum geologist and engineer - independent producer.

SIDNEY KATZ, was born on May 19, 1925 in New York City, NY. He enlisted in the USAAC in June 1943 and was attached to the 467th Bomb Group, 790th Bomb Sqdn. in Rackheath, England. He was discharged on Oct. 5, 1945 with the rank of tech. sergeant.

Sidney was stationed in Miami Beach, Tyndall Field, FL, Buckingham Air Base, FL and Westover, MA. Participated in battles in the Air Offense Europe, Normandy, Northern France, Rhineland and Central Europe.

Flew 30 missions as radar counter measure operator including 3 missions as Sperry ball turret operator and 27 missions as radar counter measure operator (R.C.M.). He trained with R.A.F. for this assignment.

His memorable experiences include being assigned to fly in ship #29 5115 (B24-4J - 42 - 95115) on Dec. 29, 1944. While plane was on hardstand he was removed by officer of the day and replaced by another R.C.M. operator. The plane minutes later crash landed on take off with all aboard being killed.

Awarded the Air Medal with five clusters and five Battle Stars.

Widowed with three children and five grandchildren. Presently manufacturing shoulder pads for clothing.

THEODORE SAVA KAYAS (THE GREEK), was born on June 23, 1921 in New York City. He joined Citizens Military Training Camps at Camp Dix, NJ in 1939 and 1940.

Took basic at Randolph Field, TX; Heavy Bombardment Armorer School at Buckley Field and Lowry Field; Link Trainer at Kelly Field, TX. Went on to Harlingen and Pampa, TX. Then on to 8th Air Force via the HMS *Britannic* to the U.K., 100th Bomb Group and then to the 491st Bomb Group, 479th Sub-Depot at North Pickenham. Returned on the *Santa Paula* and discharged on Oct. 31, 1945 at Gowen

Field, ID. He also attended Gunright Maintenance School at Blackpool England.

His most memorable experience was the camaraderie and pleasant times with buddies and the people of Narborough, Swaffham, North Pickenham and Kings Lynn.

On a furlough to Scotland in the spring of 1944 he met Jessie Rae Anderson who later became his wife of 40 years. She died in 1988. He travels often to the U.K., Europe and Greece.

WILLIAM D. KEAN, was born in Mantua, NJ on Nov. 11, 1920. On Aug. 12, 1942 he enlisted in Flight Training (Cadet), USAAC, and served as pilot with the 489th Bomb Group, 8th Air Force, 2nd Air Div. He was discharged on Dec. 5, 1945 with the rank of first lieutenant.

Stationed at Jackson, TN; Walnut Ridge and Blytheville, AR; Wendover, UT; Laredo, TX; Boise, ID; and Halesworth, England. Participated in European Operations, "D" Day, 31 missions.

His memorable experiences include surviving the air black with airplanes, an unbelievable sight, on "D" Day.

Awarded the Distinguished Flying Cross, Air Medal and Campaign Medal.

Married Barbara on Nov. 18, 1944 and has two sons, William, Jr. and Bob and one daughter, Janice. Presently retired, golfing, gardening, playing bridge, dancing, etc.

KENNETH E. KEENE, was born June 21, 1918 in Connersville, IN and spent most of his life in Indianapolis. Enlisted in the USAAC Sept. 15, 1941, as a private. After A&E School, was promoted to corporal. Entered Aviation Cadets October 1942 and graduated June 1943 as a second lieutenant, class of 43E Southeast Training Command. Trained as a pilot in B-24s and flew two tours of combat in the 93rd Bomb Group and the 466th Bomb Group with a 30-day leave in the States between tours.

Helped organize Indiana Air Guard and was called to active duty January 1951 for Korean War with the 4th Fighter Intercepter Wing and became base commander at Kimpo, Korea. Called again to active duty in September 1961 during Berlin Wall crisis and became base commander at Chambley Air Base, France.

Completed four years on Secretary of the Air Force Reserve Policy Commission and retired in 1967 as brigadier general with 20 decorations including Distinguished Flying Cross. Has been in the Advertising Agency business since 1934.

Married July 1, 1945, to grade school/high school sweetheart, Virginia Lee Fowler, and has one son, Kenneth E. Keene, Jr.

LAWRENCE E. KEERAN, served with the 448th Bomb Group, 712th and 714th Sqdn. and served as engineer/gunner. He completed 35 missions. Retired from service on Aug. 25, 1965 after 22-1/2 years with the rank of tech. sergeant.

Assigned to the "Exp. Guided Missile" group at Eglin AFB, FL and went to the South Pacific on two atom tests. His base commander was Gen. Timberlake.

His civilian vocation was in material logistics with TRW Ispore Park, Redondo, CA. *Submitted by R. Cater Lee*

MYRON KEILMAN, is a native of Montana, and a graduate of the University of Montana. He earned his wings in Class 41-E, Kelly Field, TX, July 11, 1941. Assigned to Panama he flew B-18s, B-17s, LB-30s and B-24Ds in defense of the Panama Canal. Returning to the U.S., January 1943, he instructed in B-24s until assigned to the 392nd Bombardment Group.

Then to England with new B-24Hs, August 1943. On October 4 his squadron commander suffered a mid-air collision with a German fighter. That night Myron was assigned as the squadron commander. As command pilot he flew 43 combat missions. His airplanes were shot up, but he was never shot down. His group excelled in bombing accuracy.

In Korea, 1952-1953, he flew 50 missions.

The B-47 was the last operational airplane he flew. He has flown 30 different types of airplanes.

A full colonel, he retired in 1970. He and Blanche raised two aviators.

Myron has been awarded the Distinguished Flying Cross four times.

ABSOLAM H. KELLY, was born on Jan. 29, 1924 in Harlan County, KY (but has been an Indiana resident since the age of three months). He enlisted in the USAAC on Nov. 26, 1942 and served as radio operator and mechanic - Aerial Gunner School. He served with the 449th Bomb Group, 718th Sqdn. in Italy and the 44th Bomb Group, 68th Sqdn. in England. Discharged on Sept. 21, 1945 with the rank of tech. sergeant.

Military locations and stations include European Air Offensive, Naples-Foggia, Rome-Arno, Normandy, Air Combat Balkans, Northern France, Rhineland and Central Europe.

His memorable experiences include being a POW for 364 days at Stalag Luft #4 and his 86 day march across Northern Germany.

Awarded the EAME Theater Ribbon, Air Medal, Good Conduct Medal, ETO Ribbon, eight Bronze Stars and four Oak Leaf Clusters.

He was called up for examination about two years after WWII. He was awarded the order of the Purple Heart but has never received the medal.

Married to Mary Anderson on Feb. 28, 1953 and they have two children and three grandchildren. He is presently retired.

CHARLES A. KELLEY, was born July 19, 1918. He was a navigator on B-24, 446th Bomb Group, first with the 704th Sqdn. until his crew became MIA while he was in attendance at H2X (Mickey) School, then with the 705th Sqdn. After the war he was admitted to the Massachusetts bar and ultimately accepted a regular Air Force commission and retired as a JAG Colonel in 1972.

After retirement from the Air Force he served as an assistant attorney general and municipal court judge in Colorado, from the last of which positions he again retired to enjoy his five children and three grandchildren, albeit from afar since they are scattered throughout the country. His wife, Mary, died in 1979.

He was awarded the Legion of Merit with cluster, Distinguished Flying Cross, Air Medal with cluster, Air Force Commendation, Meritorious Service Medal, etc.

ERNEST KELLEY, was born in Huron, NY on Nov. 3, 1924. He enlisted in the service on March 23, 1943 at Ft. Niagara, NY and served with the 117th AAA Bn. at Camp Davis, NC. Transferred to Aviation Cadet Corp., Miami Beach. Discharged on Oct. 27, 1945 at Rome AAF Base as staff sergeant, flight engineer, 712th Sqdn., 448th Bomb Group.

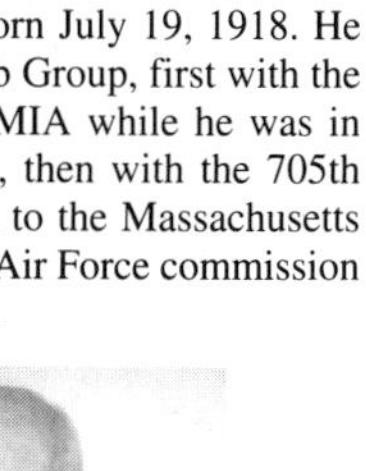

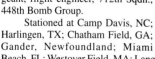

Stationed at Camp Davis, NC; Harlingen, TX; Chatham Field, GA; Gander, Newfoundland; Miami Beach, FL; Westover Field, MA; Langley Field, VA; and Iceland to England.

Participated in battles in Ardennes, Central Europe and Rhineland.

Memorable experiences: Shot down one ME 109 over Hamburg Germany on March 5, 1945 completing 30 missions April 25, 1945, Salzburg, Austria.

Awarded the Air Medal with five clusters, Bronze Oak Leaf, Good Conduct Medal and New York State Silver Cross.

He married his school pal, Leona, and they have five children. She died of cancer on May 7, 1991. Completed business college and received a Law & Accounting degree in May 1949. Presently retired after 13 years railroading and 30 years in paper printing trade. Now lives in Ocala, FL.

ERNEST KELLY, was born May 14, 1923 at Norridgewock, ME, a small town located on the Kennebec River. He joined the service January 1943 at Fort Devens, Ayer, MA, then on to Miami Beach for basic, was sent to Tyndall Field, FL for Aerial Gunnery School and then to Sheppard Field, TX for Aircraft Mech. School, joined his crew at Gowen Field, Boise, ID as their ball turret gunner.

They did their overseas training at Tonopah, NV in the 754th Bomb Sqdn., 458th Bomb Group. Flew overseas to England joining the 96th Combat Bomb Wing, 2nd Air Div., 8th Air Force at Horsham St. Faith in time to fly the March 6-8, 1944 Berlin missions.

He flew 31 missions as a staff sergeant, was decorated six times. Returned to the U.S. in October 1944. Spent R.R. at Atlantic City, NJ, went to Gunner Instructor's School at Laredo, TX. Volunteered for another combat tour in England, was sent to Blackland AAF Base, Waco, TX and then up to Grenier Air Field, NH where he was discharged Oct. 10, 1945.

He worked for N.E.T. Co. and later for AT&T as a P.B.X. installer for 38 years, retiring in 1984. He is now helping his son, John, in his antique business in Auburn and Buxton, ME.

ALBERT R. KEMP (BERT), was born March 13, 1921 on a farm near Potomac, IL. Graduated University of Illinois with B.S. 1942, M.S. 1947, and University of Wisconsin with Ph.D. 1950.

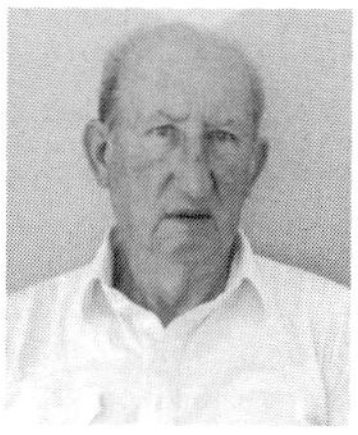

Drafted Sept. 15, 1942 into U.S. Army. Entered Aviation Cadet training graduating as Navigator Hondo, TX Air Base December 1943. Served 458th Bomber Group from October 1944 to end of the European phase of WWII as Radar Navigator. Received Distinguished Flying Cross, Air Medal and Battle Stars during 20 missions.

Married Lillian Bennett, 1942, two children; later divorced. Married Carol Clark Estes in 1975; together four children.

Twenty years research chemist for Dean Foods, then 19 years for Crest Foods retiring in 1986 as Vice President Technical Director. One patent.

Now enjoying RVing with Carol; sightseeing and exploring with their friends.

JOHN MARCUS KENDRICK JR., was born July 8, 1921 in Edwards, MS and enlisted in the Army on Aug. 4, 1939. Assigned to regiment at Schofield Barracks, Territory of Hawaii. Joined the 35th Inf. Band in 1940. Survived Japanese attack on Pearl Harbor, Dec. 7, 1941.

Began USAAC aviation training July 1942, completed Phase II B-24 training as a pilot and flight officer at Pueblo, CO in 1943. Temporarily assigned to 8th Air Force, 12th Combat Crew Replacement and Training Center, Cheddington, England. Later assigned to 389th Bomb Group, 564th Bomb Sqdn. at Hethel, England along with original nine crew members from 4-Engine Bomber School. Kendrick flew 11 missions to bomb the 3rd Reich, beginning Feb. 6, 1944. Participated in Big Week campaign to destroy Nazi airfields and aviation-related factories. Participated in first full-scale daytime attack on Berlin on March 6, 1944.

On second mission to Berlin, Kendrick's ship was hit by flak and crash landed in Friesland, Holland. Nine of the 11 crew members were able to exit the aircraft and pry the pilots from the mangled cockpit. A crowd of locals encouraged the crew to run before Nazi soldiers arrived assuring them the pilots were better off in enemy hands where they could receive medical attention. Kendrick was placed in Luftwaffe hospital at Leeuwarden, Holland where both his legs were amputated just above the knee. Was moved to hospital in Obermassfeld, Germany in May of 1944. Kendrick was repatriated back to the States in early 1945.

Discharged from active duty Feb. 28, 1947. His awards included the ETO Campaign Ribbon with star, Asiatic-Pacific Campaign Ribbon with star, Air Medal with Olive Leaf Cluster, WWII Victory Medal, American Defense Service Medal, American Theater Service Medal and the Purple Heart.

Kendrick chose to continue his education in law and passed the bar examinations in September 1949. Later was employed as a mail carrier with the U.S. Postal Service. Kendrick married Newelyn Walton in September 1955. He died of heart failure October 1969. Kendrick is survived by his children: Missy Powell, Vicky Mobley and J.M. Kendrick III.

EDWARD J. KENNEDY, was born in Ackman, CO, on March 11, 1921. He was raised on a farm at Yellow Jacket, CO. He attended an aviation engine course at Spokane Community College in Washington, and worked for Geiger Subdepot until he entered the service in February of 1943. His basic training took place in Gelena, WA, five miles from Geiger.

After basic training, was stationed at Felps Field. Transferred to Mountain Home Air Base in Idaho to train on B-24s. Departed for England in 1944 arriving on the English ship, *Moritina*. Was assigned the 755th Sqdn., 458th Group (B-24) at Horsham St. Faith as an aircraft inspector. Arrived back in the United States on the *Queen Mary* in 1945.

Edward married LaVern Swenk on March 16, 1946, and has four sons, eleven granddaughters and three grandsons. He retired from the Bureau of Indian Affairs in 1979.

HAROLD KENNEDY, waist gunner/assistant engineer, Pelton crew, 701st Sqdn., 445th Bomb Group, was born July 15, 1921 near Sewanee, TN, attended St. Andrews School, St. Andrews, TN, graduating in 1939. Education at the University of the South, Sewanee, was interrupted in 1941, when he began working at Glenn L. Martin.

Before enlistment in 1943, he was inspector on Martin's B-26. In 1943, he married Carolyn Hawkins of Sewanee. After Basic Training, Gunnery at Tyndall, and Mechanics at Sheppard, he joined Jack Pelton's crew in early 1944, training at Peterson Field. At Topeka, receiving a new B-24J, they named it "Briney Marlin". Departed Morrison Field April 15, 1944. Arriving in England, "Briney" went to a modification depot and the crew to the 445th Bomb Group.

First mission flown May 29 to Politz. Returning from Dessau, August 16, Pelton crash-landed at Woodbridge. "Sweetest Rose of Texas" had 150 holes in her, no radio and the trim tabs shot out in the full UP trim position. Finished ETO tour October 3, missing the Kassel mission by a 701st Sqdn. training class. Finished as gunnery instructor on B-29s at Barksdale.

Returning to civilian life, he finished his education, receiving a Master's Degree in History from Middle Tennessee State College, Murfreesboro. The rest of his life was spent as an educator at St. Andrews School and Battle Ground Academy. During his career, he taught English, Economics,

Sociology, American History and coached football, basketball and softball. His American History students gained insights from his first-hand descriptions of flying missions.

Harold Kennedy died Aug. 19, 1970 and is buried at Sewanee. *Submitted by his daughter, Mary Beth Kennedy Barnard*

JOHN R. KENNEDY, was born March 25, 1925 in Frederick, MD. Joined USAAC in February 1943. Commissioned a second lieutenant (pilot) at George Field, IL, then on to B-24 training at Charleston AFB, SC and Langley Field, VA.

In June 1944 joined the 489th Bomb Group at Halesworth, England. On Aug. 6, 1944 the 24th mission their aircraft "Cover Girl" was shot down near Hamburg Germany, all crew members bailed out and were POWs. Spent the rest of the war at Stalag Luft III (Saigon), Stalag XIIID (Nuernberg) and Stalag VIIA (Moosburg).

Liberation day came on April 29, 1945 by the 14th Armd. Div. of Gen. Patton's 3rd Army.

On return to the U.S.A. was discharged as a first lieutenant on Dec. 7, 1945.

Received the following medals: Purple Heart, Air Medal with three Oak Leaf Clusters, ETO with two Battle Stars, Victory (Germany), Good Conduct, and Prisoner of War.

Married Dec. 29, 1945, attended Vincennes University (AA 1947) and Purdue University (BSAE 1949). Has four children, two boys and two girls.

Enjoyed his working days as a research engineer at Fort Detrick, MD and chief engineering and plant management at National Animal Disease Laboratory at Ames, IA. Retired in 1979 and enjoys retirement of travel, videomaking and golf with his wife, Mary Ann.

RICHARD M. KENNEDY, was born on Nov. 23, 1921 in Cohoes, NY. Educated at primary and secondary schools in Cohoes, NY and Siena College, Loudenville, NY. Enlisted in the USAAF on Aug. 3, 1942 and was discharged as tech. sergeant on Sept. 5, 1945. Basic training, St. Petersburg, FL; graduated Radio Operator-Mechanic, Sioux Falls, SD January 1943; graduated Aerial Gunner School, Fort Meyers, FL March 1943; Promoted to staff sergeant and assigned as Radio Operator Gunner B-25 Group, Columbia, SC, assigned to B-24 Operational Training Unit, Davis-Monthan AAB; February 1944 joined 448th Bomb Group, 8th AAF Seething, England.

Thirty-five combat missions as Radio Operator Gunner 714th Bomb Sqdn., 448th Bomb Group. First mission was on June 27, 1944 - thirty-fifth mission on Nov. 9, 1944.

Flew Radio Operator on special assignment known as "Ackerman Relay" involving Radio Relay missions. Unit based at Hethel (389th Bomb Group). Tour dates - Nov. 10, 1944 to Feb. 10, 1945.

Decorations include Air Medal with five Oak Leaf Clusters, Good Conduct Medal, four Battle Stars for action in the Ardennes, Rhineland, Normandy and Northern France Campaigns.

Civilian Career - Post WWII to-date: December 10, 1945 - Inspector, Albany District, New York Fire Insurance Rating Organization - Promoted to Chief Inspector in 1950 - 1954 became District Manager, Albany District NYFIRO - 1957 advanced to Assistant Manager NYFIRO Headquarters, New York City with statewide responsibilities - 1967 left NYFIRO to join Middle Department Association, Philadelphia, PA as Assistant Executive Manager - 1968 became Executive Manager (CEO) of MDAFU - 1972 left MDAFU to form MDIA - Has served MDIA as owner, President from inception (July 1, 1972) to present date.

Air Force Associations - Life Member 8th AFHS, Member 2nd Air Division Association, elected to the post of Executive Vice President of the 2nd Air Division Association in November 1989 - elected President, 2nd Air Division Association, July 1990 and served two consecutive terms as President, 2nd Air Division Association - currently serving as 2nd Air Division Association Liaison Officer with the 8th Air Force Memorial Museum Foundation and the 8th Air Force Heritage Center. Actively serving as a member of the Board of Directors of the 8th Air Force Heritage Center, Savannah, GA.

Married Bobbie Bartling, Schenectady, NY. They have two daughters, Patti Beaver and Colleen Conlow. They also have five grandchildren, Cherokee, Seneca and Cheyenne Beaver and Tyler and Trevor Conlow.

BENTLEY KERN II, was born on March 1, 1919 in Winchester, VA. He enlisted in the Air Force in October 1941 and served as pilot with the 8th Air Force, 2nd Div., 2nd Wing. He was discharged in October 1945 with the rank of lieutenant colonel.

Southeast training - Maxwell Field; Craig Field, AL (graduate). Participated in the invasion in Europe and was in 33 missions with the last as C.O. of 564th Sqdn.

Awarded the Distinguished Flying Cross with Oak Leaf Cluster and the Air Medal with three clusters.

Married with two children and three grandchildren. Retired as apple grower. Presently semi-retired - running small retail business.

PERRY KERR, was born in Baird, TX on Aug. 4, 1925. From 1940 until war was declared in 1941, Perry corresponded with R.C.A.F. at age of 15. When war was declared against Germany and Japan, all enlistments into that organization by American citizens ended. Thus he had to wait until reaching the age of 17, where the opportunity arose to enlist in the USAAC Reserve. At the age of 18 and 5 days, Perry was called in to train as an aviation cadet in Class 44J. Washing out of Cadets, he became an armorer gunner and was sent to England and the 466th Bomb Group, 787th Bomb Sqdn. on the R.D. Koch crew, as the togalier. He flew 11 combat missions against Nazi oppressed Europe, earning the Air Medal and three Battle Stars to the ETO ribbon.

After the war was over, Perry was employed in the oil and gas industry, and still there as of Nov. 7, 1993.

KURT G. KERSTEN, was born Oct. 28, 1923 and raised in small town of Flat Rock, MI. Worked at Willow Run Bomber Plant after high school turning out B-24s and two years later flew aboard one as navigator. Entered service February 1943. Went through basic training and topographical school with Corp. of Engineers before transferring to Air Force. After CTD at Missoula, processing at Santa Ana, Gunnery School at Kingman, and commission at Hondo Navigation School, joined crew in Casper for training, followed by assignment to 704th Sqdn., 446th Bomb Group, Flixton Airfield, Bungay, England. Flew 13 combat missions before war ended. Was on biggest day raid of war (as per *The Stars and Stripes*) over "Big B" (Berlin) on March 18, 1945. Flew aboard "Ronnie" reported to have recorded the most missions of any Liberator in WWII.

Returned to U.S. for reassignment to Pacific Theater. After V.J. Day released to civilian life in December 1945.

Graduated from Michigan State University, married high school sweetheart, started having children and finished law night school while working as Claims Adjustor for U.S.F. & G. Insurance Company.

Practiced law in home town of Flat Rock for 33 years before being elected Judge of 33rd District Court, Wayne County, MI. Will serve until retirement in 1996. Son, James, took over law practice.

Early picture is with sister, an Army nurse, who came from France to meet in London for a short leave. Snap shot taken April 13, 1945. Black armband worn by sister was to commemorate Commander in Chief, President Franklin D. Roosevelt, who died the day before.

Married Lenore Kott in 1947 and has four children and four grandchildren.

WALTER W. KETRON, was born Sept. 18, 1922 in Kingsport, TN. Was attending Tennessee Wesleyan College on Pearl Harbor Day. Entered Army Aviation Cadet Pilot Training Class 43-J. Graduated Nov. 3, 1943 at Lubbock, TX commissioned second lieutenant. After B-24 Pilot School at Maxwell Field and combat crew training at Charleston, SC, flew northern route to England. Assigned to 566th Bomb Sqdn., 389th Bomb Group at Hethel May 9, 1944. Became a lead crew while flying 30 combat missions, fortunately with no injuries to any crew member.

Returned to Kingsport, married Jewell (Judy) Price. After short tour flying B-24s at Victorville, CA, transferred to ATC and flew C-54s on Pacific run and in support of "Operation Crossroads" - atomic bomb test. Released from AD December 1946 and recalled in April 1953 as C-54 pilot in MATS. Transferred to Strategic Air Command that fall and spent the next 15 years in air refueling operations (KB-29 and KC-135) while stationed at Dow, Bergstrom, Fairchild, Eielson, Kadena and Robins. Moved to Westover in 1968 for duty at Headquarters 8th Air Force. Retired June 1, 1970 rank of colonel. Judy and he are still married, have three sons, and six grandchildren.

CHESTER W. KIDD, JR. (C.W.), was born in Mecklenburg County, Charlotte, NC on Nov. 7, 1923. Married to Helen Fraizier Kidd for 51 years with four children, eight grandchildren, and five great-grandchildren.

Inducted into the military Feb. 19, 1943. First assigned to Navy and "talked my way out" which led to the USAAC. Attended Gunnery School at Harlingen, TX - "Hags"; graduated, Class 51-43 - Dec. 18, 1943, as a staff sergeant.

From July 1944 until November 1944, flew on a Liberator B-24 with 35 combat missions over France and Germany. In August, 1944, their 10th mission, the crew survived a crash landing. Fortunately, the only other close call was being knocked down by flak. Honorably discharged October 1945.

Has a working ranch with monthly rodeos. Operates successful abattoir, grading company, and motel at Myrtle Beach, SC.

Elected Sheriff of Mecklenburg County in November, 1982, reelected in 1986 and 1990—serving 462,000 people in this community for 10 years. Plans to run again in 1994.

JAMES N. KIDDER, was born on June 21, 1915 in Medford, MA. Enlisted in the Air Force on Aug. 1, 1942 and served as Air Force Aviation Cadet. Discharged on June 15, 1945 with the rank of captain.

Served in Santa Ana, CA to Las Vegas, NV for Gunnery School and then commissioned Navigator Class of 43-9 at San Marcos, TX to Boise, ID. Joined 445th, 703rd Sqdn. to Sioux City, IA to ETO in November 1943. Flew 30 missions. Finished tour August 1943 to I & E School 1944 and finally Jackson, MS as instructor when war ended.

Awarded the Distinguished Flying Cross with one cluster and the Air Medal with three clusters.

Married Aug. 1, 1940 to Priscilla Comins and has two sons, one daughter and five grandchildren. Has just retired from "Priscilla of Boston", manufacturer of wedding gowns, after 43 years in the business.

EARL E. KIEFFER, was born in Canton, OH on June 2, 1924. Graduated high school in June 1942. Worked at Republic Steel until he was drafted in April 1943. He was inducted at Columbus, OH, processed and sent to Jefferson Barracks, MO for basic training. From basic he was sent to Camp Kearns, UT Replacement Training Center. He spent four months at Kearns until placement with 467th Bomb Group, 790th Bomb Sqdn. He then went to Wendover Field, UT with the 467th Bomb Group for overseas training as a

squadron welder. In February 1944 he went with 467th to Scotland and on to Norwich, England to Rackheath Air Base. He held the rank of sergeant until demobilization in November 1945.

He was married in January 1946, received his pilot license in 1947, worked for Ford Motor Co. for 31 years before retiring in 1979, at age 55 and moved to Florida.

RICHARD B. KIMBALL, was born Greene, NY on April 22, 1917. Graduated from Syracuse University 1939. Turned down by Air Cadet Board 1941, tried again May 1942 and was accepted.

Married Edith Ticknor in 1941. Has four children and five grandchildren.

Eliminated from pilot primary training. Took primary navigation Selman Field, Monroe, LA, aerial gunnery Ft. Myers, FL, commissioned second lieutenant navigator from Selman February 1944. Joined crew Davis Monthan Field, Tucson, AZ, picked up new B-24 in Lincoln, NE, flew it to Ireland via Labrador. Joined 448th Bomb Group, 715th Sqdn. Seething, England June 6, 1945. Promoted lead crew after eight missions, joined an experienced crew, Kimball's first lead was 20th Wing. January 1945 promoted to captain and assigned as squadron navigator.

Received Distinguished Flying Cross January 1945 for leading several successful missions, and second Distinguished Flying Cross upon completing 30 missions. Received six Air Medals, ETO Medal with Battle Stars, and WWII Victory Medal. Separated from service at Fort Dix, NJ May 17, 1945.

One mission had flak go through navigation table shredding maps - no injury. One mission had flak go through bombardier's pant leg - no one injured. One mission came back from Germany on three engines. No. 3 engine feathered so no hydraulics, had to crank gear and flaps down, bomb bay door open and upon landing found left tire flat so plowed wheat for about 100 yards.

ROBERT E. KIMBALL, was born Nov. 1, 1922 in Omaha, NE. Entered the Army Air Force on Dec. 26, 1942. Spent most of 1943 in basic training, Armament School in Denver, CO, Gunnery School Laredo, TX, three phase trainings for combat in Midwest Air Fields. Flew to England with the 445th Bomb Group, 700th Sqdn. putting in 29 missions from Dec. 16, 1943 through April 24, 1944. Left England early October 1944. After brief leave spent time in Armor School, Denver, CO. Worked in military training office Amarillo, TX. Had to go fight forest fires in Idaho and Montana. Was discharged in early October 1945 with rank of staff sergeant.

Participated in air offensive of Europe and all German occupied territory.

Memorable experiences include taking a B-24 in on the belly at Grand Island, NE and being in 29 missions without a wound.

Awarded the ETO Ribbon with two Battle Stars, four Air Medals, Good Conduct Medal, Normandy Campaign Medal, Distinguished Flying Cross, and Unit Citation (which was not entered in record).

Married Rosemary E. Donahue on May 2, 1945 and they have three sons, two daughters-in-law and four grandchildren. After getting out of the service spent most of his time as a steel worker and welder. At age 62 had to retire because of heart and lives in Arvada, a suburb of Denver, CO.

LAURENCE B. KIMBROUGH, was born in Buhl, ID on Aug. 16, 1921. He was inducted into the USAAC in July 1942 and served as first lieutenant, B-24 first pilot, aircraft engineering officer. Discharged on Nov. 20, 1945 with the rank of first lieutenant.

Took pilot training in Texas, combat in 8th Air Force, England. Participated in D-day June 6, 1944, Air Offensive over Europe, German glider and parachute landing - Holland and Belgium Sept. 15, 1944. Participated in 32 missions.

His memorable experiences include being issued and signing for the B-24 (#898) at Wendover, UT. His crew flew the bomber to England and flew approximately 25 of their 32 missions in this plane while in the 489th Bomb Group. Of course, several other crews also flew the plane. After the 489th was deactivated it was transferred to the 392nd Bomb Group where it flew many more missions. Somewhere along the line the distinctive picture of "Terri Ann" was painted on the starboard side. After the B-24 received extensive battle damage and while making an emergency landing from 200 feet, he made a dead stick landing with no further damage to the plane.

Awarded the Distinguished Flying Cross with Oak Leaf Cluster, Air Medal with three Oak Leaf Clusters and four Battle Stars.

Married Eileen Keane and has five children and eight grandchildren. In 1949 he graduated from Oregon State College with B.S. in Mech. Engineering. Worked for 32 years, principally as a design engineer in the fields of aircraft, machine design, production tools, for the last 25 years. Was project engineer for many types of projects. Retired in March 1982.

EARL E. KINDER, was born on March 21, 1926 in Sharpsville, IN. He was inducted into the USAAC on Jan. 3, 1944 and served as armorer gunner with the 2nd Air Div. Discharged on Dec. 28, 1948 with the rank of staff sergeant.

Locations and stations include Tibenham England, Harlingen, TX and Davis, Monthan.

Participated in battles in Central Europe, North Appennies, Rhineland and French Campaign. His plane was shot down on the 10th mission, but no one was hurt as they landed in France.

Awarded the Air Medal with one Oak Leaf Cluster.

Married to Louise and they have one son, Steven. Retired, owner of his own sign business (now owned by son and grandson).

EDWARD W. KING, was born Jan. 13, 1923 in Pittsburgh, PA but grew up in Salamanca, NY. Won a scholarship to Cornell University, Arts & Sciences, but enlisted USAAF as an aviation cadet in 1942; active duty January 1943. Basic training in Atlantic City, NJ.

After basic, they were warehoused in the 63rd College Training Detachment in Burlington, VT for four months. To Nashville, TN and then on to pilot training at Maxwell Field, AL; Clarksdale, and then Greenville, MS; and George Field, IL where pilot's wings were pinned on April 15, 1944.

Two months of B-24 transition at Smyrna, TN; to Bradley Field, CT to assemble crew. Crew training at Charleston, SC during which a hurricane warning sent them flying to Cuba for sanctuary!

Off to England in October 1944, in a convoy, on a bouncing little tin can named "SS General Black". Their crew was assigned to the 467th Bomb Group (H), 789th Bomb Sqdn. at Rackheath. His first combat mission was to try to hit the bridge at Bingen am Rhine in November 1944. Through the next 30 missions they were shot up often but never shot down; all crew members survived without a casualty.

Many of their missions were flown as squadron deputy lead in a B-24 which had been named the "Massillon Tiger".

Their most notorious mission was flown in "The Tiger" to knock out a railroad bridge just northwest of Nienburg, Germany: flying as Deputy Lead, and without authorization and in violation of SOP, on the third or fourth 'no-bomb' run on it by their squadron they dropped their bombs, thereby inducing another plane in their squadron to also drop. They were the only ones to bomb the bridge—but they did such a fine job of it that after that pass the Group went on to the secondary target, Bielefeld. They went to Coombe House, Shaftsbury, Dorset, just before the final mission of the Group and of the war and celebrated VE Day in Shaftsbury.

After service he attended Cornell University in October 1944 and persevered there to earn a BA in 1947 and LLD Law Degree in 1949. Entered general law practice in Ithaca, NY in 1949 and is still at it—with no plans to retire.

Married a young lady from Denmark in 1948; divorced in 1973—25 years and three children: son a MD in Bennington, VT; one daughter a Spanish and French teacher in New York and the other a Psychologist in Montreal, Quebec Canada. Second marriage six years later to a Salamanca, NY lady.

EUGENE L. KING, was born in East Chicago, IN on Sept. 16, 1917. Met his wife-to-be, Mary Ann Krieter, in September 1946. Married Nov. 27, 1947. They have two sons and a daughter and eight grandchildren.

Entered Army Air Force Jan. 12, 1942. After basic training was sent to Chanute Field, IL for training as airplane and engine mechanic. After graduation was sent to Robins Field, GA. Worked on the line, engine test blocks. Was assistant flight engineer on Clo's ship. Applied for Cadet School. Had six months college at University of Buffalo. Washed out at SAACC along with 5000 others - no need for more pilots, navigators, bombardiers. Was sent to Gunnery School, Laredo, TX. From there to March Field, CA where he met his crew. He was the flight engineer on Capt. John B. Mattson's crew.

They flew 26 missions over Germany with the 446th Bomb Group, 706th Bomb Sqdn. Was discharged from Sioux Falls, SD on Oct. 7, 1945. Received the Air Medal with three Oak Leaf Clusters, EAME Medal with three Battle Stars and Good Conduct Medal.

Retired in 1979 from Inland Steel Co. after 43 years service.

F.C. KINGSBERY (JACK), was born May 26, 1922 at Santa Anna, TX. Attended Texas A&M for two years and entered the USAAC on Sept. 26, 1942. Trained at Ellington Field, TX; Biloxi, MS; Willow Run, MI; and Gunnery School at Laredo, TX.

Joined 458th Group, 754th Sqdn. at Wendover, UT, went to Tonopah, NV. Flew with Lt. A.C. Braver's crew to West Palm Beach, FL. Flew to New York by Eastern Air Lines and on to Scotland in Air Transport Command B-17 and by train to Horsham St. Faith at Norwich.

Was tech. sergeant crew chief on #692 that was the first B-24 in the group to fly 50 combat missions.

Flew home in June 1945 in a new B-24 and assigned as crew chief to a B-29 group at Pueblo, CO and discharged September 1945.

Finished Texas A&M in 1949 and married Evelyn Bruce in 1951 and has two boys and two girls, all Aggies, and seven grandchildren.

Still has ranching interest at Crystal City, TX and is president of Kingsbery Mfg. Corp.

He and Evelyn have traveled all over the world.

ALAN W. KINGSTON, was born in Gillett, WI on Sept. 18, 1921. Graduated with a master degree in educational administration from University of Wisconsin, 1952.

Commissioned as a LST lieutenant on October 1 and married Hazel V. Phillips on Oct. 2, 1943.

Has five sons living in Wisconsin with twelve grandchildren.

Joined the 453rd Bomb Group at March Field, CA in late December 1943.

Arrived at Old Buckingham England in January 1944. Flew 32 missions with 24 as a co-pilot and 8 as a first pilot.

On the Berlin mission on April 29, 1944 they lost two engines over the target. Increasing the power from the remaining engines used up a lot of gasoline and they ran out of gas about 70 miles from Great Yarmouth England. Ditching in the North Sea was a real challenge. Two crew members were unable to swim and he was able to keep them afloat until they were able to reach the air-sea rescue boat.

He received the Soldier's Medal for their rescue. Also received the Distinguished Flying Cross and three Air Medals.

Served 32 years in Department of Public Instruction as director of the division for school financial aids services.

FRANK T. KINKER JR., was born in Richmond, VA on Sept. 2, 1924. He enlisted in the Air Force on Feb. 18, 1943 and served as 612th Armorer Gunner with the 96th Combat Wing, 458th Bomb Group, 753rd Sqdn.

He was discharged on Sept. 25, 1945 with the rank of staff sergeant.

Military locations and stations include St. Petersburg, FL; Lowry Field, Denver, CO; Amarillo, TX; Laredo, TX; Salt Lake City, UT; Boise, ID; Wendover, UT; Tonopah, NV; Horsham St. Faith, England; and Miami Beach, FL. Participated in 30 combat missions with 8th Air Force.

His memorable experiences include being an original member of "Flak Magnet" with pilot Lt. Jack K. Umphery. They used three B-24s to make one mission.

Awarded the Distinguished Flying Cross, Air Medal with four Bronze Oak Leaf Clusters, Presidential Unit Citation, Good Conduct Medal with Oak Leaf Cluster, American Campaign Medal, EAME Campaign Medal with three Bronze Service Stars, WWII Victory Medal and Marksman Badge with Carbine Bar.

Has been married to Janet for 46 years and they have three sons. Presently retired and working harder than ever.

ROBERT W. KIRBY, was born in Pittsburgh, PA on Aug. 9, 1922. Enlisted on Aug. 31, 1942 with the Army Air Force, 489th Bomb Group and served as navigator. Discharged on Nov. 13, 1945 with the rank of first lieutenant.

Stationed at Selman Field, Monroe, LA; Wendover, UT; and Halesworth, England. Battles include Air War Northern France, D-day, West Germany.

Memorable experiences were D-day St. Lo, France, Munich, Cologne, St. Cyr.

Awarded the Air Medal with three Oak Leaf Clusters and the Distinguished Flying Cross.

Married and has three children. Presently a land agent with Columbia Gas System, Inc.

WILLIS H. KIRKTON (BILL), was born Oct. 6, 1925 at Gridley, IL. Married high school sweetheart Jan. 1, 1946 and raised three children, Carolyn, David and Barbara and has six grandchildren.

He joined the Air Cadets Sept. 30, 1943 at Chicago, IL. Did basic at Sheppard Field, TX - Gunnery School at Harlingen Air Base, TX - crewed up in Lincoln, NE and spent three months overseas training at David Monthan Field, AZ.

He left Topeka, KS January 1945 and arrived via Ulde France Ship at Scotland. Based at Rackheath England, 467th Bomb Group, 788th Bomb Sqdn. Flew six missions and transferred to 791st Bomb Sqdn. Flew back to U.S. June 1945 and was transferred to Harlingen, TX-reclassified to 501 and became 1st sergeant moving to Lackland Air Base in January 1946. Became 1st sergeant of the First Basic Training Class at that base.

He was discharged from Fort Sam Houston, TX May 6, 1946. Received the ETO, Good Conduct and Air Medal. He attended Eureka College where President Reagan attended.

He is presently owner of an auto parts wholesale business.

BERNARD B. KIRSCHNER, was born on Aug. 2, 1923 in Boston, MA. He enlisted in the Air Force on Dec. 7, 1942 and served as radio operator (751) with the 467th. Discharged in 1945 with the rank of private first class.

Participated in Air Offensive Europe, Normandy, France, and Rhineland. Awarded the EAME Ribbon.

Married to Phyllis and has one son, Harlan and one daughter, Joanne. Bernard is deceased.

MARSHALL L. KISCH, was born in St. Paul, MN on June 13, 1918. He enlisted in the USAAC, Medics, on April 22, 1942 and served as armorer gunner, waist, with the 2nd Air Div. He was discharged on Oct. 17, 1945 with the rank of staff sergeant.

Military locations and stations include: Little, AR Camp Robinson; Aurora, CO Lowry Field; Harlingen, TX; Seething, England; and Montgomery Field, Montgomery, AL.

His memorable experiences include crash landings (12), fighter attacks, induction and service in England.

He is married and has two daughters, two sons and eight grandchildren (three boys, five girls). He is retired after 50 years in wholesale meats.

SILAS HENRY KISER (HANK), was born Nov. 16, 1920. Volunteered for service with the USAAC. Reported for duty in January 1943. Graduated as a pilot and received his wings at George Field, IN. Assigned to Chanute Field for B-24 pilot training. Went to Charleston Army Air Base where his crew was assembled and trained for overseas duty. Crew was shipped overseas to England in December 1944 and reported to the 389th Bomb Group at Hethel and assigned to the 565th Sqdn. Completed 27 missions when war in Europe ended. Returned to U.S. and the war with Japan was over. Assigned to Reserve and released from active duty. Worked a few months and returned to college at Cornell University where he received his BME Degree in Engineering in June 1949.

Worked for DuPont Company and was assigned to help build and then operate the Atomic Energy's Savannah River Plant. Retired from DuPont in January 1984 and continues to live in Aiken, SC.

Members of his crew included Alan Hall - navigator, Hank Kiser - pilot, Chalon Maulding - co-pilot, Joseph Keplner - bombardier, Charles Rajda - tail gunner, Pat McGucklin - waist gunner, Willis Robinson - waist gunner, Clayton Wood - nose gunner, Joseph Woodruff, crew chief and Francis Connolly - radio operator. Six of the crew have maintained contact and meet approximately every two years and are still meeting.

Had the usual happenings such as flak damage, engine shot out, etc., but they made it back to the good old USA.

BERNARD F. KISSELL, was born May 11, 1919 in Bellows Falls, VT. Member of USAAC January 1943 to November 1945. Graduate of Armament, Aerial Gunnery and Aerial Navigation Schools. Commissioned second lieutenant at Ellington Field, TX October 1944. Ferried new B-24J from Mitchell Field, NY to England. Stationed at Horsham St. Faith in Norwich, England and flew combat missions with 753rd Bomb Sqdn., 458th Bomb Group as B-24 navigator. Ferried war-weary B24 from England to Bradley Field, CT.

Air Force April 1951 to May 1952, first lieutenant stationed at K-9 in Pusan, Korea and flew 55 combat missions with 730th Bomb Sqdn. as B-26 navigator. Received Distinguished Flying Cross, Air Medals and other appropriate awards.

Graduate of Colorado State University, B.E. Degree; Memphis State University, M.A. Degree and LL.B. Degrees. Retired from U.S. Navy Department as Senior Educational Consultant.

Married Patricia Jane Hurtgen Nov. 26, 1949 and has six children and eight grandchildren.

ALVIS O. KITCHENS, was born in Quitman, MS on Jan. 5, 1925. He enlisted in the Army Air Force on Aug. 13,

1943 and served in Amarillo, TX; Harlingen, TX; and Casper, WY. Assigned to the 445th Group in Tibenham, England. He completed 15 missions. Discharged on Oct. 18, 1945 with the rank of staff sergeant.

Kitchens was a POW in Germany. Awarded the EAME Theater Ribbon with one Silver Star, Air Medal with one Bronze Cluster and the Purple Heart.

He is married and has two children. Presently retired from the U.S. Post Office.

JACOB KLEIN, was born in New York City on Jan. 4, 1922. He enlisted in the Army Air Force on Dec. 7, 1942 and served as staff sergeant with the 445th, 2nd Air Div. Stationed at Camp Forrest, TN; Miami, FL; and England. Discharged on Sept. 25, 1945 with the rank of staff sergeant.

Participated in African and European battles. His memorable experiences include surviving being shot down on his 24th mission and his first parachute jump.

Awarded the Air Medal with three Oak Leaf Clusters and the P.O.W. Medal.

Married and has three children and six grandchildren. Presently retired and lives six months in Delray Beach and six months in New York.

KENNETH R. KLEINSHROT, was born in Middlefield, OH March 11, 1921. Married high school sweetheart Catherine Welch in Fort Worth, TX at Tarrant Field. Has seven children, ten grandchildren and three great-grandchildren.

Inducted July 18, 1942 in the U.S. Army Inf. at Camp Croft, SC for basic training. Transferred to Aviation Cadet Program September 1942. Graduated second lieutenant Class of 43-G as Pilot. July 29, 1943 Pampa, TX with Gulf Coast Training Command. B-24 Transition Training at Fort Worth, TX. Crew assembled Salt Lake City, UT. Joined the 467th Bomb Group at Wendover, UT. It was the last bomb group to go to England.

Flew to England via South America to Africa to base at Rackheath. Transferred to 389th Bomb Group at Hethel. Became lead crew in 564th Pathfinder Sqdn. (H2X). Flew six wing leads, ten group leads; last ten missions with 453rd Bomb Group.

Most memorable missions were to Hamburg, Germany April 22, 1944, D Day June 6, 1944 and Berlin June 21, 1944. Ended tour Oct. 15, 1944 as captain.

Received two Distinguished Flying Crosses, Air Medal with three Oak Leaf Clusters, and one EAME Medal with four Bronze Stars.

WALTON H. KLING, was born in Evanston, IL on Feb. 6, 1917. Drafted into the Air Force in September 1941 and served with the 2nd Air Div., 8th Air Force. Served at Hethel Field - Wyndham - England.

Served as ground officer with 389th Bomb Group, 566th Sqdn. Discharged in September 1945 with the rank of captain.

Married and has two children. He and his wife just celebrated their 50th anniversary. He is presently retired.

ALBERT C. KLIPPERT JR., was born Dec. 30, 1924, in Chicago, IL, enlisted in the USAAC in June 1943 after graduating from high school. Graduated pilot, second lieutenant, Class 44G at Altus, OK. Assigned co-pilot on B-24 crew, accepted a new B-24J at Topeka and flew to England. Assigned to 389th Bomb Group, 565th Sqdn. at Hethel January 1945.

Completed tour of 16 missions, parachuting out over France after fourth mission. Received one Air Medal, one European Campaign Star and Presidential Unit Citation and membership in the Caterpillar Club. After VJ Day, joined

the 437th Troop Carrier Wing Reserve at Orchard Airport (now O'Hare International).

Called to active duty in August, 1950. Assigned co-pilot, then pilot, flew a C-46 to Japan. Assigned to 85th Troop Carrier Sqdn. at Brady Field near Fukuoka. Flew 800 hours to Korea with cargo, paratroopers, etc. Received one Air Medal. Released from active duty as first lieutenant May 1952.

Retired from family floral business. Owned and flew a BC12D 1946 Taylorcraft. Married Bette Maus June 20, 1945, and has two children, four grandchildren, and one great-grandchild.

ORVILLE H. KLITZKE,

was born in Appleton, WI on Dec. 11, 1922. He enlisted in the 8th Air Force on Dec. 11, 1942 and served with the 2nd Bomb Div., 445th Bomb Group, 701st Bomb Sqdn. in Tibenham England. Discharged on Sept. 24, 1945 with the rank of staff sergeant.

Basic training in Clearwater, FL; mechanics at Gulfport, MS; gunnery at Las Vegas, NV. Participated in 33 missions to France and Germany from April 19, 1944 to July 29, 1944. After completing 33 missions sent to West Palm Beach then to Keesler Field as crew chief on B-17 rescue plane.

Awarded the Good Conduct Medal, ETO Medal, Air Medal with three clusters and the Distinguished Flying Cross.

Married to Bette and has one son, Brad and one daughter, Sue Hammond. Presently retired and working part time.

ROBERT C. KNABLEIN,

was born May 27, 1922, in Chicago, IL. Married high school sweetheart, Marjorie Bouzek, February 1944. Sworn in as USAAC Cadet in a mass swearing in of 1,200 cadets at Soldier Field, Chicago, June 26, 1942. Called to active duty Jan. 5, 1943, assigned pilot training Class 43-I, South East Training Command. Commissioned as a second lieutenant Blytheville, AR Oct. 1, 1943.

Trained as B-24 pilot Maxwell Field, Montgomery, AL. Assigned combat crew training Casper, WY. Flew aircraft #42-95122 via South Atlantic route to England. Assigned as replacement crew to the 8th Air Force, 44th Bomb Group, 68th Bomb Sqdn., Shipdham. Flew 31 combat missions against Germany from June 2, 1944 to Sept. 5, 1944. Memorable experience includes having 15 bombs (100 lbs. each) hang up in bomb bay on July 4, 1944. When they were released, the bomb bay doors went with them.

After completion of operational tour, assigned 302nd Transport Wing, 310th Ferrying Sqdn., 27th Air Transport Group. Flew gasoline and other supplies to advancing ground forces in France and Belgium.

Returned to the U.S.A. January 1945, assigned to fly gunnery students Fort Myers, FL, attended instrument instructors course Bryan, TX. Separated Sept. 25, 1945. Received Distinguished Flying Cross and Air Medal with three Oak Leaf Clusters.

Retired 1982 after 40 years with Western Electric, A.T. & T.

MARK I. KNAPP,

was born Sept. 11, 1923, New York City. Enlisted in USAAC, December 1942. After basic and flying training was commissioned as pilot, May, 1944. Assigned to B-24 combat crew training as co-pilot, July 1944.

In November 1944, crew joined the 445th Bomb Group at Tibenham, England. By VE Day had flown 28 missions. In June, 1945, they flew a war-weary B-24 to the U.S. Were prepared for redeployment to the South Pacific, but Japan surrendered. Was separated from service in October 1945.

Worked in aircraft engine development while acquiring an engineering degree; then was immediately recalled to active duty (during the Korean conflict) as Air Technical Intelligence Officer (captain).

Career included six years in engine development, seven

---

years in air technical intelligence, and twenty-three years with a prominent 'think tank' in Virginia.

Awarded Air Medal with three clusters and battle stars for Ardennes, Rhineland, and Central Europe.

Married and has four children.

LORIN G. KNIERIEMEN,

was born Aug. 31, 1922 in Bucyrus, OH. Attended high school in Sycamore, OH. Worked farm and meat packing.

Enlisted AAF Jan. 8, 1942. Basic and A.M. School, Sheppard Field, TX. B-24 Maintenance School, Consolidated Aircraft, San Diego. Sent to Sioux City for eventual assignment to combat group, was clerk in headquarters, made corporal and qualified for cadet. Santa Ana, CA - preflight, Tulare, CA - primary, Merced, CA - basic, Douglas, AZ - advanced. Graduated Feb. 8, 1944, second lieutenant pilot, Class 44-B.

Married Jean Curtis Feb. 14, 1944. B-24 crew training, Tonopah, NV. Norwich, England by boat. 467th Group, 790th Sqdn. Flew 33 missions and many practice missions from July 1944 to June 1945 as co-pilot. Received normal citations. Numerous flights in famous "Witchcraft", which had most missions (130) and no abortions. Flew "Witchcraft" to States after V.E. Discharged Nov. 6, 1945.

Note: Never had to land in B-24 without four engines operating. Several times had to leave formation due to shot out supercharger.

Graduated Toledo University in engineering Feb. 14, 1950. Worked U.S. Steel, Lorain, OH Feb. 15, 1950 to April 30, 1983 as Industrial Engineer.

Jean and he have two sons, both engineering graduates from Toledo University. Both have obtained master's degrees and are career officers in the service: one, Air Force; one, Corps of Engineers.

JOHN M. KNIZESKI JR.,

was born in Patchogue, NY on Nov. 12, 1923. He joined the USAAC Dec. 11, 1942, as a private. He received his gunners wings while in the Aviation Cadet Program. His overseas assignment was with the 445th Bomb Group where he flew 26 combat missions as a B-24 waist gunner. On his 13th mission he and crew members bailed out over France. He received three European Campaign Stars and Air Medal with three Oak Leaf Clusters.

S/Sgt. Knizeski returned to the U.S. and was assigned to Harlingen Field as a seaman aboard Army crash boats. He was honorably discharged on Oct. 25, 1945 and enlisted in the reserve program the same day. On June 25, 1969 he was honorably discharged as captain.

"John K" attended Massachusetts State College, Mohawk College, Columbia University and Post College. He retired from Memar International as their CEO. He married Elsie B. Gozelski in 1947 and has three children and six grandchildren. He and his wife reside in Freeport, ME.

FREDERICK J. KNORRE JR.,

was born in San Francisco in 1916.

He completed more than 26 years of active and reserve federal service. During WWII he was awarded the Distinguished Flying Cross with first Oak Leaf Cluster and the Air Medal with second Oak Leaf Cluster. He flew 20 combat missions with 150 combat hours, and earned seven Bronze Stars for campaign participation and was also awarded the French Croix de Guerre avec Palme. While serving with Rome Air Material Area, which was the culmination of his military career, he was awarded the Air Force Commendation Medal. Col. Knorre retired from the service in October 1963.

Additional awards and medals include the Air Medal with third Oak Leaf Cluster, American Defense Service Medal, EAME Campaign Medal with seven Bronze Stars

---

for campaign participation, Air Reserve Medal with three Oak Leaf Clusters, WWII Victory Medal and Army Commendation.

He and his wife, Evelyn, have one son and two daughters, four grandsons and one granddaughter. They are also blessed with three great-grandsons and one great-granddaughter. Presently working on home, yard, pool - visiting and being visited by family and Air Force friends. Attends reunions of the 446th Bomb Group each year and the 1938 Flying Class reunions every two years. He is a member of the 8th Air Force Historical Society and 2nd Air Division Association. Lives on San Francisco Peninsula and still has friends from kindergarten through college.

JOHN J. KNOX,

was born July 14, 1921 near Harrisburg, MO, a small farm town in the center of the state. Entered Army in August 1942 and shortly thereafter was transferred to USAAC. Went to Mechanic School at Lincoln, NE. Then Gunnery School at Fort Myers, FL. Got B-24 training at Tucson, AZ and Pueblo, CO. Arrived at 445th Bomb Group, 700th Sqdn. in February 1944. Flew first mission March 22. Believes that was one of his most memorable, as it was to Berlin. Flak was very heavy but wasn't hit by fighters that time. Soon found out what flak looked like, sounded like and would do. After tour returned to states and was discharged October 1945.

Awarded the Air Medal with clusters, Distinguished Flying Cross and a Bronze Star from Vietnam.

Enlisted Air Force March 1951 and retired after tour in Vietnam 1968.

Married wife, Vera, in 1949. Has one stepson and two grandchildren. Spends time now visiting with them and former crew members.

JOHN W. KNOX,

was born 1923 in Columbus, OH. Joined USAAC February 1943, basic training, St. Petersburg, FL; Gunnery School, Ft. Myers, FL; Flight Engineer School, Sheppard Field, TX on B-25s and 26s. Assigned to B-24 crew Peterson Field, Colorado Springs.

They were deprived of the experience of flying to England, but sailed on the *Queen Elizabeth II* with Glenn Miller's Band performing on deck daily.

Their crew in tact was assigned to 2nd Air Div., 445th Bomb Group, Tibenham, England. They flew several tough missions resulting in severe flak damage to their plane and on their eighth mission they were the unfortunate group that lost 31 of 35 planes when hit by 150 German fighters near Kassel, Germany, Sept. 27, 1944.

Five crew members survived as POWs; engineer and he (tail gunner) were injured badly from fighter gun fire and spent the duration in POW hospital near Meiningan, Germany.

He came home on *St. Mihiel* (hospital ship) June 1945. Married his high school sweetheart September 1945. They have three fine children, five grandchildren. He retired from Ohio Department of Taxation 1981, moved to Deerfield Beach, FL 1982 where they currently reside in a waterfront condo.

He is still in touch with their pilot, flight engineer and waist gunner.

MICHAEL M. KOCZAN (MIKE), was born Feb. 29, 1916 in Farrell, PA. Grew up in Cleveland/Parma, OH. Married Donna Wilgus Feb. 5, 1942, Bellefontaine, OH. Has one daughter, Kristin Elmore, Plano, TX; four grandchildren and two great-grandchildren.

Enlisted USAAC, 1st Transport Sqdn., Fairfield Air Depot, Wright/Patterson Field, Dayton, OH, April 6, 1939. Attended A/M Tech School, Chanute Field 1940 and slated to be instructor Keesler Field upon graduation. Last-minute change in shipping orders and he returned to Patterson Field. Re-organization in Air Corps and assigned 5th Transport Sqdn. then 5th Troop Carrier Sqdn.

His C-39 was among the first five ships to drop paratroopers at Fort Benning in 1941 when 82nd Airborne was activated. December 7th—eventful day—announced engagement and drove back to Patterson for duty as sergeant-of-the-guard. As he stepped through the guardhouse door it was announced Pearl Harbor had been bombed.

February/March 1942, assigned as flight chief, secret mission; departed Bolling Field, Washington D.C. under sealed orders.

June 1942, 5th Troop Carrier Sqdn. moved to Gen. Mitchell Field, Milwaukee to do transition work with civilian airline pilots. Decided on Aviation Cadets. Took the exam at Wright/Patterson and proceeded to Nashville for classification then to Maxwell Field for preflight with Class 43-I. Became cadet captain in primary flight training, Carlstrom Field, Arcadia, FL. Soloed in six hours but received no more instruction thereafter.

In June of 1943 sent to St. Petersburg, FL for reassignment, after four-five weeks to Miami Beach, waiting enrollment as engineering officer trainee at Harvard. Tired of waiting so went to headquarters and requested overseas combat duty in any capacity. On September 1st placed in charge of troop train headed for B-24 School, Willow Run plant Ypsilanti, MI.

Mid-November 1943 to Gunnery School, Harlingen, TX. February 1st to combat crew pool at Salt Lake City for two weeks, then to Gowen Field, Boise, ID for crew assignment.

Left Boise a week after D-day and spent a week in Lincoln, NE before departing for Reykjavik, Iceland after having made stops in Bangor, ME and Goose Bay, Labrador.

From Shannon to Greencastle, Ireland for some advanced gunnery then to Metfield, England to join the 855th Sqdn. of the 491st Bomb Group. Later, they replaced the 492nd at North Pickenham. Completed his 35 missions and departed for the States aboard the USS *Wakefield* in late February 1945.

After completion of processing at Camp Miles Standish he shipped to Miami Beach for a supposed-to-be two-week R&R before reassignment to Seattle for B-29 Flight Officer training.

Was scheduled to head for the out-west rocket proving grounds but opted for discharge on Sept. 6, 1945. Went to work in a retail appliance and general merchandise store where he spent three and one-half years. His activities have been mostly in sales, at commercial, industrial and retail levels. Also stints at being a P.I. for one of the oldest detective agencies; as an Outside Machinist on atomic subs; a corporate insulating contractor; operating engineer; spec writer; membership chairman, S.A.M. (Society for Advancement of Management); Special Rep. (Geo. S. May Co., management consultants). Is presently retired but still fairly active.

GEORGE P. KOERNER, was born in Cresco, PA on Oct. 31, 1917. Enlisted in the Air Force in November 1939. Basic training at Langley Field, VA. Assigned to 3rd Observation Sqdn. as radio operator. Flew missions for coast artillery at Fort Monroe.

Was transferred to Blythe, CA, flying for Gen. Patton when he was on maneuvers to go to Africa. While he was at Blythe he took his cadet exam at Santa Ana and was transferred to San Antonio, TX. Graduated Flying School at Waco, TX Class 43-I as F.O. Transferred to Clovis, NM to a B-24 crew as co-pilot. Went to Pueblo, CO for training and sent to Langley Field to fly radar navigators. April 1, 1944 left Langley for England, northern route, Goose Bay, Labrador. To Iceland and Belfast, Ireland. From there was assigned to 458th Bomb Group. Was in London when first V1 buzz bomb was sent over. They flew first Azon bombs, radio control September 1944. Gas tanks were put in the bombay. They carried gas to Patton going across France. Returned to U.S.A. February 1945. Joined the Reserve Forces. Retired Oct. 31, 1977 with the rank of major.

Married Anne Louise Sterner on Sept. 29, 1943. Has four children, seven grandchildren and one great-grandson.

JOSEPH F. KOHLER, was born in Wapakoneta, OH on Oct. 30, 1922. Enlisted in the USAAC in September 1942 and served with the 446th Bomb Group, 707th Bomb Sqdn., 8th Air Force, B-24 Liberators. Discharged in November 1944 with the rank of tech. sergeant.

Stationed at Chicago, Fort Myers, FL, Denver, CO, England and Africa. Participated in air war in Europe.

His memorable experiences include first raid on Berlin (accidently flew over the Eiffel Tower February 1944 at 300 ft.).

Awarded the Distinguished Flying Cross, five Air Medals, European Theater Medal, Presidential Citation, and Good Conduct Medal.

Married and has three girls and one boy. Retired to Florida from Ohio after 34 years with N.C.R. Corp. in Dayton, OH.

OLAF E. KOLARI, was born Jan. 7, 1919, in Gilbert, MN. He entered the Army in July 1942, but transferred to the USAAC, completing flight training at Frederick, OK, Class of 43I.

He transitioned into B-24s at Fort Worth, TX, and completed combat crew training at Colorado Springs, CO. He, and his crew, flew to England by way of South America and Africa. He flew his first mission to Politz, Germany in the 389th Bomb Group. After completing combat, he was assigned as a B-24 instructor pilot at Casper, WY and, later, a B-29 combat crew instructor at Albuquerque, NM.

He left active duty in October 1945, but remained in the Reserves, flying Mustangs and, later, jets with the 440th FBG, Minneapolis-St. Paul, MN. He left the Reserves in the middle of 1956.

Awarded the Air Medal with three Oak Leaf Clusters and the Distinguished Flying Cross.

He married Miriam D. Niemi on Nov. 11, 1943. They have five children and seven grandchildren. He is presently retired.

DONLEY RAY KOON, was born in Little Mountain, SC, June 21, 1924. Married Vera Blondell Hamm, April 5, 1953. Has a son and daughter, and three grandsons.

Was inducted into the USAAC at Fort Jackson, SC. Completed basic training at St. Petersburg, FL. Was assigned flight training at Reno, NV. Further trained at Mountain Home, ID and Casper, WY. Assigned to the 458th Bomb Group at Tonopah, NV. Left Nevada for Hamilton Field, CA to pick up new B-24s to fly to England via Brazil and Africa to their permanent assignment at the Army Air Force Station 123 Horsham Saint Faith, Norfolk County, England, Feb. 18, 1944.

Completed balance of 35 missions with one crash landing and one abandoned craft on the English coast. Returned to the U.S. on furlough. Reported to Santa Ana, CA for further assignments. Coming closer to the close of WWII, was transferred to Fort Bragg, NC. Discharged July 5, 1945.

Returned to Columbia, SC. Enrolled in electrical engineering with local utility company. Last years spent in supervision. Retired after 30 years of service.

E. BUD KOORNDYK, was born on Sept. 9, 1921 in Grand Rapids, MI, attended schools in this city until the attack on Pearl Harbor in December 1941. Married a local girl June M. Wolters upon his return from combat duty in Europe on Dec. 19, 1944. Has two sons and two daughters, all happily married and thirteen wonderful grandchildren.

After Pearl Harbor he enlisted in the USAAC as a private unassigned, remained at home until called into active duty on March 23, 1943.

Went through pilot training in the Gulf Coast Training Command and graduated as a second lieutenant in the class of 43-E. Took phase training in B-24s at Casper, WY and sent overseas to Norwich, England in mid 1943. Flew combat with both the 389th and the 93rd Bomb Groups and completed his tour of duty on D Day 1944 and was awarded the Distinguished Flying Cross with one cluster, Air Medal with four clusters and the Presidential Unit Citation.

Left active service December of 1945, returned to Grand Rapids and assisted in organizing a corporation involved in the selling and distribution of construction equipment and supplies with branches in Michigan, Ohio, Illinois and Wisconsin. Spent entire career as an officer in this corporation.

Joined the 2nd Air Division Association in 1953 and has served as group vice president of the 389th Bomb Group. Executive vice president and president of the 2nd Air Division Association. At the present time he serves as the American representative and governor on the Board of Governors of the Memorial Trust and Library in Norwich, England.

RAYMOND H. KOPECKY, was born Oct. 15, 1921 in Beasley, TX, on a farm, in Fort Bend County. Enlisted in the USAAC in April 1942, while attending Rice University. Graduated Bombardier, second lieutenant, Class 44-3, at Kirtland Field, NM. Continued training in H2X equipment at Boca Raton, FL, arriving in England in August 1944. Assigned to the 392nd Bomb Group, 379th Sqdn. at Wendling September 1944. Completed 15 missions as H2X operator by war's end in Europe. Received the Air Medal and Oak Leaf Cluster. After VE Day, was placed on inactive duty November 1945. Reentered Rice University, Houston, TX, and graduated from Rice with a degree in mechanical engineering in 1948. Resigned from the Reserves as first lieutenant in 1951.

Retired from Armco Steel Corporation, after 34 years of service, as assistant superintendent of mechanical maintenance. Married Norma Jean Heitmann, June 15, 1946 and has four children - one son, three daughters and four grandsons.

JAMES G. KOTAPISH SR., was born Sept. 27, 1919 in Cleveland, OH. Enlisted May 19, 1943, ordered to Nashville, TN, classified pilot. Entered Class 43-H Maxwell Field, LA; primary, LAMA Avon Park, FL; basic, Cochran Field, Macon, GA; advance, twin engine (TE) Blytheville, AR; Aug. 30, 1943 rated pilot and second lieutenant. Posted to Gowen Field, Boise, ID, attached to 734th Sqdn., 453rd Bomb Group (H) as co-pilot on Ray L. Sears' crew.

Phase training at March Field, CA; assigned to B24#41-29257, named *Spirit of Notre Dame-Shamrock,* crew chief

Sgt. Shaner. (Due to extensive battle damage, a replacement B24-H was re-christened with the same name and slightly different logo, a shield with Shamrock superimposed.)

Left Hamilton Field, San Francisco, CA and flew via Texas, Florida, Puerto Rico, South America, Africa and arrived at Old Buckingham, U.K. (Norfolk) third week of January 1944. February 10, 1944 they went on their first mission, to Gilze-Rijen Holland. They had failed to locate the 453rd formation and tacked onto another group as tail-end Charlie. A novice at the controls, he had to take over from the pilot on the bomb run, -40F temperature and a faulty heated suit had incapacitated him. Needless to say, his formation expertise grew rapidly in succeeding missions!

June 6, 1944, D-day, his 21st mission, saw a transfer from squadron lead to group lead crew Capt. Carter. They were over the beachhead 0620AM. On Aug. 6, 1944 flew a "plus one" to Hamburg, his 31st, to finish up the crews 30 mission quota, or goal. A crew commendation had been issued on June 15, 1944 for destruction of the bridge target at Le Port Boulet, France.

Missions accomplished: 16 Germany, 15 France and Holland. Combat awards: Distinguished Flying Cross, Air Medal with clusters, European Theatre Medal with Battle Stars, WWII Victory Medal and last but not least, Good Conduct Medal.

After flak leave, was "requested" by Col. Hubbard to "pilot the Officers Club out of troubled waters" where after many successful dance banquet missions as a "ground pounder" left on May 8, 1945, V-E day, with the group for Portsmouth Port, thence via troopship USS *Hermitage* to arrive in Boston, USA on May 23, 1945.

After 30 days of R&R went to Fort Dix, NJ and then to Rosecrans Field, St. Joseph, MO. Checked out in B25 and C46. On Dec. 7, 1945 separated from service, stayed in reserves and subsequently checked out in AT6 at Fort Knox, KY in 1947. Military MOS Nos.: 1092, 1051, 2120, 2161 plus single engine. 1946-49 graduated with BSCOM degree from Ohio University, Athens, OH.

1950 married BJ (Betty Jane) first and only wife. They have four children: Joan-teacher; Pattie-actress; Jimmie-endodontist and Dick-city of Cleveland commissioner; and four grandchildren.

1951 resigned from reserves with rank of captain. Still maintains pilot rating, second class physical.

Career included: marketing/sales manager; establishing and operating a distributorship for a corporation; a manufacturing agents organization; travel agency owner; heading up a number of professional organizations.

Member of: 2nd Air Division Association, 8th AFHS and DAV.

Retirement: Busy as Santa, aka James George, modeling, print and VHS movies; community theatre; travel, golf, fishing. Last, but not least, counting his blessings in life for the God given safety in combat, and the good memories of buddies and comrades, those living and those gone, who shared duty and love of our country. In their memory: "Let's Keep 'em Flying."

PETER KOWAL, was born July 11, 1919 in Clifton, NJ. Inducted June 13, 1941. Released as staff sergeant for flight training June 1942.

Commissioned second lieutenant (navigator) Sept. 25, 1943 Selman Field, Monroe, LA. Assigned Crew 33 753rd Bomb Sqdn., 458th Bomb Group, Tonopah, NV for B-24 OTU training.

Departed USA Jan. 18, 1944 to 458th Bomb Group at Horsham St. Faith England with 8th Air Force.

April 22, 1944 on 11th mission became POW when aircraft "Flak Magnet" was shot down over Hamm, Germany. Interned at Stalag Luft III, Stalag XIIID and Stalag VIIA. Liberated April 29, 1945.

Returned USA May 28, 1945, discharged first lieutenant Feb. 11, 1946.

Graduated New York University, BSME degree 1950. Employed by Amoco in Oklahoma.

Married Margie Barger 1952. They had a son and daughter. In 1956 took engineering position with E.I. DuPont in Delaware. Widowed 1961. Married Evelyn Crowl 1970 who had three daughters. They have eight grandchildren. Retired 1980.

EDWARD V. KOWALSKI, was born on June 25, 1921 in Brooklyn, NY. Before going into the service he worked for Bendix Aviation Co. as an operator doing internal and external grinding.

He was inducted into the Army Air Force in April 1943. Served as armorer tail gunner on B-24 with the 445th Bomb Group, 702nd Sqdn. Stationed at Tibenham Base, Tibbershore, England. Discharged on Sept. 14, 1945 with the rank of staff sergeant.

Basic training - Miami Beach, FL; Gunnery School - Laredo, TX; Armory School - Denver, CO; and Crew training - Boise, ID. Their commander of 445th Bomb Group was Col. Jimmy Stewart. He flew lead ship.

Served as tail gunner on Webster's crew. Flew plane the northern route from Bangor, ME to Greenland. Twenty planes took off - two crashed into the mountains - two lost in Arctic Ocean. They took the ball turret out, it was his turn to stay on the ground (18 missions). Capt. Webster and crew were shot down. Got a week's pass to go to Scotland, when he got back to the base he found out the group got wiped out over Kassel. He was assigned to Capt. Hall's crew and flew ten more missions.

Awarded the Air Medal with four Oak Leaf Clusters and EAME Campaign Medal with four Bronze Service Stars. Participated in 28 missions.

Married Eileen Balvin on Feb. 7, 1943. They have two sons, two daughters, two grandsons, nine granddaughters, and two great-grandchildren. Retired in Florida. Enjoys traveling and pitching horseshoes.

FRANK KOZA, was born Oct. 7, 1922, Lawrence, MA, raised Andover, MA. Enlisted USAAC, Nov. 10, 1942, entered Aviation Cadet Pilot Training March 25, 1943. Graduated Jan. 7, 1944 as second lieutenant, Class 44-A Brooks Field, TX. B-24 pilot transition, Liberal, KS, OTU at Colorado Springs, CO.

Departed for England in new B-24 J, June 29, 1944. Assigned to 8th Air Force, 392nd Bomb Group. First mission Aug. 6, 1944, Hamburg. Thirteenth mission, Friday, Sept. 13, 1944 to Schwabish Hall AF, Germany. Twenty-sixth mission Dec. 2, 1944 to Bingen, Germany, lost six of nine squadron aircraft to approximately 60 FW-190s and ME-109s. Thirty-fifth, last mission, Jan. 13, 1945.

Awarded Distinguished Flying Cross, five Air Medals, and four European Campaign Medals.

Continued actively flying with USAFR MATS and Troop Carrier units. Retired as lieutenant colonel, Feb. 2, 1969.

Worked for FAA as tower controller, retired as facility manager, June 14, 1977. Also flew with FAA flight standards. FAA commercial multi-engine pilot license with instrument rating.

Married hometown sweetheart, Helen E. Martinson, R.N., Jan. 5, 1946, has two sons, one daughter and three grandchildren.

ROBERT KRAFT, was born in Buffalo, NY on May 3, 1925. Married Carole M. Randall on June 8, 1945. Has one son and two grandsons.

Entered USAAC, April 1943. After basic at Miami Beach, attended Aerial Gunnery School at Tyndall Field, FL. Transferred to Westover, MA for replacement crew training. In England, flew as left waist gunner in B-24s in the 492nd Bomb Group, 16 missions, from June to August 1944. And in the 467th Bomb Group, 19 missions, from August to December 1944. Returned to Tyndall Field and became gunnery instructor.

Discharged in October 1945 at Las Vegas AAF with rank of staff sergeant. Reenlisted in May 1947.

Attended Flight Engineer School at Chanute AFB, IL and Randolph AFB, TX in 1951. Had crew training in B-29s at Topeka, KS in 1952. Flew 16 missions, over Korea, with the 93rd Bomb Sqdn., Okinawa from February to August 1953. Served 11 years in SAC with the 97th Air Refueling Sqdn., flying KC-97Gs at Biggs and Malmstrom AFBs. Transferred to 58th Air Rescue at Wheelus AB, Libya, flying HC-97s from August 1964 to November 1966. Returned to Hill AFB, UT until retirement October 1968 with rank of master sergeant.

Awarded Distinguished Flying Cross, five Air Medals, five ETO Ribbons and several other medals.

WILLIAM ROHAN KRAHAM, was born May 14, 1923 in Cooperstown, NY; attended Columbia University until entering pilot training with the USAAC in 1942.

Winning pilot wings in 1943, he completed B-24 transition at Fort Worth and combat training at Colorado Springs by early 1944.

He flew missions as B-24 aircraft commander with the 700th Sqdn., 445th Group, 2nd Air Div. of the 8th Air Force, based at Tibenham, Norfolk, in East Anglia, England.

Wounded, with loss of left leg on a June 12, 1944 mission, he was rehabilitated at Walter Reed Hospital in Washington, D.C.

In 1945 he requested return to flight duty, and he was one of four similarly challenged pilots who were restored to flight status by Gen. H.H. Arnold. He served as an instructor and training officer with the 3rd Air Force at Drew and MacDill Fields in Florida until his disability retirement in 1946.

Upon completion of college and law school he was admitted to the Bar in 1952. He continues in law, and early in 1993 he was pleased to complete another mission: a victory as counsel for an American client before the Queen's Bench (Court) in Norwich, just a few miles from his old bomber base at Tibenham.

As an adjunct to less strenuous lawyering via mediation and arbitration, he also writes: fact and fiction, and is a member of the Aviation/Space Writers Association, and the American Institute of Aeronautics and Astronautics.

Married, with two sons, a daughter, and seven grandchildren, he and his wife have their principal home in Rockville, MD.

HAROLD E. KREN (HAL), was born in San Francisco, CA on Sept. 10, 1920. Graduated from the University of California, Berkeley in 1941 and from Deming AAF in the class of 44-2. Flew 35 missions as bombardier in 8th Air Force B-24s with the 466th Bomb Group out of Attlebridge, England, receiving the Distinguished Flying Cross, five Air Medals and four European Campaign Stars.

Postwar, returned to San Francisco and embarked on career in financial and administrative management. That vocation, along with college teaching, has kept him occupied ever since, although he did remain active in the Air Force Reserve and retired with the rank of lieutenant colonel.

His primary employment has been with small to medium size engineering and research organizations, followed by a 20 year period of self-employment as a business consultant and investor.

Today, he is pretty much retired - being married to the former Marilyn Williams, trying to keep track of six adult children and four grandchildren.

ADOLPH R. KRIEGER, was born on Feb. 20, 1921 in New Troy, MI. Enlisted in the USAAC on Aug. 15, 1942. Stationed at San Antonio, TX; Laredo, TX; Pueblo, CO; Westover, MA; Metfield; North Pickenham; England. Discharged on Sept. 13, 1945 with rank of staff sergeant.

A washed out cadet at Spartan School at Tulsa, was sent to gunnery at Laredo, TX, then on to Salt Lake City, to join the crew of 1st Lt. Harold Burdekin. From there on to Pueblo, CO for first phase training as a crew. To Westover Field, MA for their second phase training. To Langley Field, VA for lead crew training, and by way of LaGuardia, NY and MATS to England, and a replacement center.

Three of the crews were sent to the 491st Bomb Group, one to each squadron to replace a lost crew. They flew their first mission July 7, 1944, a JU-188 plant at Oschersleben, and their last and thirty-first mission on Feb. 6, 1945 to Magdeburg.

Their worst mission was their first, and almost their last with a lot of flak, running low on fuel, seeing the white cliffs of Dover lust ahead, and barely making it back to base.

He was the nose gunner and armorer on their plane "So Round, So Firm, So Fully Packed".

Awarded the Air Medal with four Oak Leaf Clusters, European Theatre Ribbon with one Silver Battle Star, two Overseas Service Bars, one Service Stripe and Good Conduct Medal.

He has one daughter and is presently retired from Zenith TV.

GORDON M. KROEBER, was born June 12, 1923 at Napoleon, ND, enlisted in the USAAC Nov. 7, 1942. He was commissioned at Frederick, OK Class 44-E, completed B-24 transition at Liberal, KS, and operational training at Casper, WY as pilot of Crew 9317. Crew was assigned to the 854th Sqdn., 491st Bomb Group Feb. 20, 1945. Returned to USA June 19, 1945 flying 44-40226, "Mah Aikin Back". He was relieved from active duty Oct. 14, 1945, remained in the reserve and Air National Guard, and retired in 1968 as lieutenant colonel.

He returned to the University of North Dakota in 1945 and earned degrees in accounting, liberal arts, and civil engineering by 1950. Employed by the highway department, the adjutant general's office and the University of North Dakota, in that order, he retired in 1989 and lives in Grand Forks, ND. He met and married Margaret Mary Butler while attending University of North Dakota and their six children are also University of North Dakota graduates.

C. WALTER KRONBETTER, was born Sept. 13, 1924 in Hope, KS. Joined the USAAC March 30, 1943. Completed B-24 Airplane Mechanics Course at Keesler Field, Biloxi, MS and received his aerial gunner wings at Laredo, TX.

Their crew picked up their new B-24 at Topeka, KS and flew to England. Assigned to the 448th Bomb Group, 712th Sqdn., Crew #17 at Norwich May, 1944.

Completed a tour of 32 missions and returned to USA November 1944. Then he became an aviation cadet. After Japan surrendered he had enough points to receive a discharge and was discharged Oct. 11, 1945 without completing his pilot's training.

Retired from Chardon Rubber after 50 years as manager of design engineering. He worked there six months prior to entering the Air Corps.

Married Mary Etta Kolberg April 4, 1948 and has one daughter, one son and three grandchildren.

LEON S. KRUSZEWSKI (LEE), was born June 5, 1924 in New Bedford, MA and joined the USAAC as an Aviation Cadet in January 1943. Became an armorer/gunner and flew 16 missions with the 491st Bomb Group of the 8th Air Force. On one mission was shot down over Essen but landed over the lines in Allied territory and on another mission made a crash landing on the coast of England.

In 1948 went back into the service and then graduated from the Counter-Intelligence Corps School and then served

as a Russian interpreter with the rank of tech. sergeant for three years in Berlin in charge of all rail traffic to West Germany until 1952. While in Berlin met Marjorie Ruth Elkins who was with the U.S. State Dept. and married in November 1952.

Graduated from Rutgers University in 1956 and then lived in Alaska for several years before moving to Southern California and spending 30 years in the investment business as a stockbroker and retired to live in Sun City Palm Springs.

DONALD K. KUHN, was born in Dubuque, IA, July 5, 1923, attended schools in Mason City, IA. He entered the Army Air Force as Aviation Cadet Aug. 13, 1942. On completion of flight training, he was commissioned second lieutenant, Feb. 26, 1944. He flew 30 lead crew missions with the 445th Bomb Group, 8th Air Force, May 1944 to January 1945. Don flew over 6500 hours in B-24, C-47, C-54, SB-17, OA-10, B-29, B-50, B-47 and B-52 aircraft.

Among his decorations are the Distinguished Flying Cross, the Airman's Medal, five Air Medals, two Air Force Commendation Medals, five European Campaign Battle Stars and the Knight of the Crown of Belgium.

He retired as lieutenant colonel in May 1965.

Don served as an Aeronautical Information Analyst with the Defense Mapping Agency in St. Louis, MO from December 1965 to January 1986. Married to Dorothea Lloyd, he has one son, Maj. David Kuhn, USA, and two grandsons.

DONALD E. KUNKLE, 1st Lt., was born at Peru, IN on July 28, 1922. Entered Purdue University in 1940. Enlisted in Air Force in December 1942. Earned wings April of 1944. After B-24 training at Chanute Field, IL and Pueblo, CO left for England with crew in December 1944.

After completion of missions returned to USA and was discharged October 1945. Returned to Purdue and graduated as BSME in June 1947. Married Caroline B. Gordon in 1948 and now has two sons and four grandchildren.

Spent 35 years working in engineering and management including building and managing a factory in Brazil South America. Retired to South Carolina in 1982.

WALTER K. KURK, was born on April 8, 1919 in Chicago, IL. Enlisted in the U.S. Army on Feb. 4, 1942 and served with the 8th Air Force, 448th Bomb Group, 714th Sqdn. as navigator. Stationed at Seething, England. Discharged in January 1953 with the rank of first lieutenant.

His memorable experiences include six months service in 1st Special Service unit. As lead navigator in B-24 on 23rd mission over Rostock, Germany, they were forced down in Sweden and interned in Mullsjo, Sweden.

Awarded the Air Medal with three clusters, Battle Ribbons, EAME Campaign Medals with three stars, American Campaign Medal and Victory Medal WWII.

Widower with two children and two grandchildren. Presently retired.

WILLIAM D. KYLE JR., was born March 2, 1918, in Butte, MT. Entered USMA, West Point, NY, July 1, 1939. Earned pilot wings, class 42-K. Commissioned second lieutenant upon graduation from USMA, Jan. 19, 1943. Assigned

446th Bomb Group November 1943. Served as 706th Sqdn. Operations Officer, 706th Sqdn. Commander, 446th Operations Officer. Returned with 446th to CONUS at end of war. Awarded two Distinguished Flying Crosses, four Air Medals and one French Croix de Guerre during 446th tour.

After the war, continued serving in the military. Flew combat with 307th Bomb Group in Korean War. Served in Air Force in various staff and command positions, primarily in Strategic Air Command. Retired on April 1, 1972, as colonel.

Married Grace B. Shay on Jan. 20, 1943. Has two children and four grandchildren. Presently member of the United Savings Bank Board of Directors and volunteer with several charitable organizations in Ogden, UT.

HENRY A. LAFORET, was born May 15, 1924 and raised in Detroit, MI. He entered the USAAC on Feb. 25, 1943 and had basic training in Miami Beach. Sent to pilot school at Maxwell Field then to primary at Douglas; basic at Macon, GA; advance twin engine training at Valdosta, Class of 44-C; sent to Maxwell Field for B-24 training; put on crew at Westover Field and sent to Savannah.

Shipped to England, 445th Bomb Group, and arrived day after Kassel raid, Sept. 28, 1944.

Achieved rank of first lieutenant pilot and received the Distinguished Flying Cross, five Air Medals, ATO-ETO two Battle Stars, Victory Medal and Honorary Croix de Guerre. Discharged just before Pacific War ended. Graduated with degrees in metallurgical engineering, industrial management, and MBA from University of Chicago.

Laforet married Veronica Masterson in 1949; they have two sons, three daughters and six grandchildren. Became president of various foundries, spent two years as consultant in Spain and retired in Vero Beach, FL.

FRED LAKNER, was born June 10, 1921, Lock Haven, PA. Enlisted July 18, 1942 in the USAAF, then USAF; was an AAF pilot Class 43-J; in combat served with 8th Air Force, 2nd Air Div., 93rd Bomb Group.

Shot down on 29th mission Feb. 24, 1945 and held POW at Neuburg-Moosburg.

Discharged July 1968 with the rank of lieutenant colonel. He received the European Campaign with four Bronze Stars, Air Medal with three Oak Leaf Clusters, Prisoner of War Medal, Purple Heart with five Battle Stars, and WWII Victory Medal.

Lakner and his wife Betty have one son and a granddaughter. He resides in Altoona, PA.

ROBERT W. LAMBERT (BOB), was born in Columbus, OH Feb. 15, 1924. Was an aircraft engine mechanic at Wright Patterson Air Field prior to joining the USAAC Feb. 18, 1943. Graduated from Scott Field, IL as a radio operator mechanic.

After training with a crew on B-24s, flew to England and was assigned to the 453rd Bomb Group (734th Wing), stationed in Old Buckingham near Attleburgh. Completed 30 missions over France and Germany with a number of very close calls, he feels very fortunate to have survived.

He received an honorable discharge in October 1945.

Awarded the Distinguished Flying Cross, four Air Medals and several other medals and ribbons.

Attended Ohio State University and graduated in engineering in 1949. Joined the DuPont Company in their textile fibers department and after a number of plant assignments retired in Wilmington, DE as a business analysis manager in December 1982.

Lambert married Mary Ann on Sept. 9, 1946, they have three children Gary, Mike and Lori, and one grandchild Paul. He currently belongs to the 453rd Bomb Group Association and the 2nd Air Division Association.

HAROLD PETE LAMBOUSY, was born in Crowley, LA on April 7, 1923. Joined USAAC November 1942; attended A M Mechanics and Gunnery schools.

Flight crew assembled at Wendover Field, UT. They trained at McGowen Field in Idaho, then Nevada and California. He was a flight engineer and belonged to the 754th Bomb Sqdn., 458th Bomb Group, stationed at Tonopah.

Sent overseas to Horsham St. Faith, England. Shot down on a Berlin mission and captured. A POW for 15 months in Stalag Luft VI and Stalag Luft IV. Later forced into a march of 500 miles, ending up in Halle, Germany. When liberated, was flown to La Harve, France for recuperation for seven weeks. Then sent back to the States and spent several months in a hospital in Miami.

Discharged Nov. 2, 1945 with the rank of staff sergeant.

He married Audrey Gigout June 8, 1947. They have three children and five grandchildren. Lambousy retired in 1977 after 33 years as a technical drafting instructor.

ARTHUR J. LAMONTAGNE, was born Sept. 28, 1923 in Northampton, MA. Enlisted in the USAAF Jan. 24, 1943; he served as a pilot with Central, 93rd Bomb Group, 2nd Air Div.

Military locations/stations: USCTD, Syracuse NY; SAAC, San Antonio; Parks Air College, E. St. Louis; Winfield, KS; Lubbock, TX; Hardwick England, 93rd Bomb Group. Participated in 22 missions over Germany; 328th (M) Sqdn., five as copilot; 329th Sqdn., 22 as head crew copilot.

Memorable experiences: He remembers the friendliness of the English people, and comraderie of fellow crews. He received four Air Medals, European Campaign Stars and Presidential Unit Citation.

Discharged Oct. 8, 1945 with the rank of second lieutenant.

Lamontagne attended Amherst College, Amherst, MA. Married and has four children while involved in the automobile business followed by 30 years in real estate business. He is now retired and spends six months in Massachusetts and six months in Florida.

DONALD E. LANCE, was born Aug. 20, 1920 in Mills River, NC. He joined the USAAC in January 1942 in Asheville, NC; was sent to Fort Jackson, SC, then to Jefferson Barracks, MO. He went to Chanute Field, IL for Airplane Mechanics School, then applied for aviation cadet and was eliminated two weeks before graduation.

He went to Tyndall Field, FL for aerial gunner training; Tucson, AZ for crew training; to Alamogordo, NM and

then Lincoln, NB. Went from Langley Field, VA to the 8th Air Force, 93rd Bomb Group in England. His first mission was May 1944, they finished 31 missions in a B-24 in July 1944.

Assigned to the Air Sea Rescue from Mitchell Field, NY as a seaman on an 82 foot patrol boat. Lance was stationed at 20 places; 16 in the U.S., three in England and one in Ireland.

Discharged at Fort Bragg, NC, September 1945. He is now retired.

HOWARD D. LANDERS, was born in Danville, AL on May 24, 1918. He entered the Armed Services Feb. 18, 1942 and after basic training in Aberdeen Proving Grounds in Maryland, was assigned to the 68th Sqdn., 44th Bomb Group at Shreveport, LA.

He landed in England Sept. 10, 1942 and was stationed at Shipdham with the 44th Bomb Group. Transferred to the 492nd Bomb Group, Group Ordnance, North Pickenham, Feb. 27, 1944. After the 492nd was dismantled he was sent back to the 44th for rations and quarters.

Transferred to the 392nd Bomb Group until time came to return to the USA on the point system, which was about two and a half months. After return to the USA, furlough and rest period at Miami Beach, FL, was assigned to a B-29 Gunnery School, Fort Meyers, FL and remained there until discharged Sept. 16, 1945.

Landers married Sarah Jacobs Aug. 14, 1948 and has a son and a grandson.

LLOYD R. LANDIS, was born in Salford, PA on Sept. 30, 1924. Inducted in the USAAF at New Cumberland, PA on April 14, 1943; engineer gunner, 489th Bomb Group, 847th Sqdn.

Received basic training at Miami Beach, FL; Embry Riddle School of Aviation, Florida, Gunnery School, Tyndall Field, FL; sent to Salt Lake City for assignment; Davis Monthan Field, Tucson, AZ for phase training on the B-24; Wendover, UT for more phase training; Herington, KS to pick up plane and make modifications.

Sent to England via the southern route; South America, Africa, Wales, then to base at Halesworth, England, arriving May 3, 1944. He flew 32 combat missions and was awarded the Air Medal, three Oak Leaf Clusters and Distinguished Flying Cross.

Memorable experience: While flying a mission in the top turret, an unopened bundle of chaff hit the turret and shattered the plexi-glass dome and put quite a large hole in it. He was very scared, he thought he had it.

He returned to the U.S. on the *Queen Mary* on Oct. 11, 1944. Reassigned to Keesler Field, MS on Nov. 16, 1944 for mechanic's course on the C-46; George Field, Lawrenceville, IL, May 7, 1945 for mechanic's course on C-46 until discharged on Nov. 5, 1945.

Landis worked as a furnace operator in a steel tubing mill retiring Dec. 31, 1986 at the age of 62. Married 43 years to Arlene; they have five children and eight grandchildren.

FORREST E. LANE, was born Sept. 29, 1915 at Beresford, SD. His first year of college, 1933-34, at Univer-

sity of Minnesota; second year, 1935, at Compton Jr. College, in California. Attended Optometry School at SCCO in Los Angeles and worked nights at Bullocks in Los Angeles. He was deferred induction into the Army to finish school.

Joined the USAF and reported to Santa Ana Dec. 7, 1942; assigned to Mather Field Navigation School Class 43-U. Eventually assigned to 446th Bomb Group at Lowry Field, joined crew of a new B-24H *El Toro*. Flew to England (Bungay). Flew 30 missions including three times over Berlin. Was awarded four Air Medals and the Distinguished Flying Cross.

Served as intelligence officer with the 458th at Norwich. Here, he learned that all 360 degree approaches to Berlin were covered by at least 500 heavy caliber flak guns.

Married Faunice Wilson Jan. 13, 1945 and was discharged in the fall the same year with the rank of first lieutenant; Reserve, captain. Has two children: Julie Carter, who is expecting first child, Fresno, CA; and Forrest W. Lane, Bend, OR.

Lane spent 37 years in practice in Antioch, CA; sold out Aug. 1, 1989 and retired to Arnold, CA in the Sierra Nevadas Dec. 28, 1993. Loves retirement.

HAROLD H. LANE, was born May 28, 1924, Gate City, VA. Enlisted in the USAACR November 1942 while a freshman at LMU, Harrogate, TN. Called for active duty Richmond, VA, April 12, 1943.

Graduated second lieutenant, Pilot Training Class 44-A, Jan. 7, 1944, George Field, IL. Assigned co-pilot B-24 crew February 1. Crew flew a new B-24 from Mitchell Field, NY via Dow Field, ME; Labrador, Iceland arriving Valley Wales May 6, 1944. Arrived Hethel, England by train May 9, 1944. Assigned 566th Bomb Sqdn. within the 389th Bomb Group, 2nd Air Div., 8th Air Force.

Flew first combat mission May 23 and 30th and final mission Aug. 13, 1944. Aircraft sustained many flak and fighter hits, but there were no crew injuries. Crew was disbanded Aug. 21, 1944 and soon returned to the U.S. Awarded the Distinguished Flying Cross and three Air Medals. He received a fourth Air Medal as a C-54 pilot on the Berlin Airlift. Retired lieutenant colonel Jan. 31, 1965; retired again Aug. 31, 1980 after 15 years as an officer with the Bank of America.

Married Helen Davis Oct. 11, 1947; has one son, two daughters and one grandson. Helen died in 1966. He married Dolores Lee, March 4, 1967; has four stepchildren and four step-grandchildren.

ROBERT E. LANE (BOB), was born March 16, 1920 in Woodford County, Versailles, KY and raised in Fayette County, Lexington, on a farm. Decided to pursue professional baseball rather than college upon graduating from high school, but this was cut short when the draft started in September 1940.

Enlisted October 1940 in the U.S. Army and was assigned to the 38th Infantry Div., Camp Shelby, MS. After becoming a tech. sergeant was accepted as a cadet at the Army Air Force Officer Candidate School, Class of 42-E Army Air Forces Technical Training Command, Miami Beach, FL. Graduating a second lieutenant, was assigned to the 392nd B-24 Bomb Group as adjutant of the 578th Sqdn. original cadre, Tucson, AZ and then to Wendling, England July 1943 serving as the 578th Sqdn. executive officer until the end of the war in 1945.

Married a few days after V-E day in England, May 1945, to Lt. Marilyn Haglund, air evacuation flight nurse, 9th Air Force. After five years service was discharged with the rank of major and joined the Reserves.

Attained some degree of higher education through Mississippi Southern College, Hattisburg, MS; Industrial War

College, Wayne University, Detroit MI; Air University, USAF Gunter AFB, AL.

After WWII went to work for Standard Oil Company, Kentucky, as sales representative in 1946. Was recalled to active duty in 1950 and served in the Far East-Korean War with the Air Force Material Command. Returned home from Japan 1952, reverted back to reserve status and Standard Oil Company.

Retired Air Force Reserves as a lieutenant colonel in 1980 and retired from Standard Oil Company of California in 1982 after many years as one of their marketing managers. Still married after 48 years, has five daughters and 13 grandchildren.

CRYSTAL LANG, was born Feb. 5, 1924 in New York, NY. Enlisted April 1943; aviation cadet, graduated Selman Field, LA, second lieutenant, Class 44-C as a navigator.

Flew 35 missions with 448th Bomb Group, 714th Sqdn. stationed in Seething, England. Returned to U.S. in December 1944 and was trained as cruise control officer on B-29s.

Assigned to permanent party at Randolph Field where he was separated in September 1945 with the rank of first lieutenant. Received one Distinguished Flying Cross, five Air Medals and three European Campaign Stars.

Returned to Harvard College where he graduated with an AB Degree in June 1946. Entered construction field where he performed varied duties in his own business, and later as an executive for John W. Ryan Construction Co., and lastly with Turner Construction Co. until retiring in 1991.

Lang married Joan Schuster on Nov. 29, 1949. They have two children and three grandsons.

ROGER LEWIS LANIER, was born in White Plains, GA in 1919. He served in the USAAF 1942-1945; serial number, 34197687; 93rd Bomb Group, 329th Bomb Sqdn.; rank, sergeant; airplane and engine mechanic on B-24 heavy bombers.

Military locations/stations before foreign service: Barksdale Field, LA; Combat Training Field, Ft. Myers, FL. After foreign service: Sioux Falls, SD and Albuquerque, NM. Foreign service: stationed in England two years and nine months at Hardwick Air Base near Norwich.

Group took part in the following: Normandy, Naples-Foggia, Egypt-Libya, Tunisia-Sicily, Air Offensive Europe, air combat, Central Europe-Northern France, Rhineland-Ardennes.

Memorable experience: low level bombing of Ploesti oil fields in Romania. They took heavy losses of men and bombers. One hundred and seventy-five B-24 bombers took part with about 100 returning to friendly bases. Many of those were heavily damaged.

Group citations: Distinguished Unit Badge, EAME Service Medal, two Silver Stars, one Bronze Star.

He married Doris Taylor in Atlanta, GA on June 4, 1946. They have three daughters and five grandchildren. Lanier retired June 1, 1983 after 42 years with Georgia Power Co. He and Doris live on a private lake near Athens, GA, which was formally part of their family farm; children and families return home often to visit, keeping their lives full.

PAUL E. LANNING, was born April 5, 1920 in Darlington, PA. Entered the USAAC Aug. 11, 1943 and attended Army Air Corps Cadet Training Miami Beach, FL.

Participated in 31 tough combat missions in WWII. He saw Col. John Herboth rammed by an ME-109 and saw the deputy taken down also. They flew off the wing off the deputy at Duneberg, Germany. Later, they were hit, lost gas and had to crash land in France.

Lanning stayed on reserve status after WWII and went voluntarily back in during the Korean War and served as a

crew chief. Received a serious whiplash in his back when brakes on his C-82 failed. Remembers having frost bitten feet as his heated suit failed.

Discharged Oct. 15, 1945 with the rank of tech. sergeant. Awarded Air Medal and four clusters; Good Conduct Medal, Presidential Unit Citation, four clusters, European Campaign Medal and the Victory Medal.

Lanning is retired. He has a daughter and two sons.

WILLIAM F. LANTZ, was born in Hutchinson, KS Aug. 25, 1924. He enlisted in the USAAF Feb. 3, 1943; served as flight engineer on B-24, 8th Air Force, 2nd Air Div.; Harlingen Gunnery, Keesler Field; Pueblo AAFB Westover Field, crew training.

Participated in Ardennes, Central Europe, Air Offensive Europe, Normandy, Northern France and Rhineland campaigns.

Flew 30 missions, pathfinder crew in ETO, May 1944-February 1945. Essen-Mainz, Ludwigshaven were tough targets.

Discharged Aug. 29, 1945 with the rank of tech. sergeant. Received Air Medal with four Oak Leaf Clusters.

Lantz went to college on the GI Bill, and after 35 years as a Kansas school teacher, retired.

He is married, has three children, seven grandchildren and two great-grandchildren.

BERT J. LAPOINT III, was born Oct. 19, 1922 in Newark, NJ. Enlisted Dec. 31, 1942 in the USAAC. Served in the 713th Bomb Sqdn., 448th Bomb Group, 20th Combat Wing, 8th Air Force. Attended Photo School, photographer 941, camera tech.

Military locations/stations: Camp Dix, NJ; Miami Beach, FL, Lowry Field, CO; Casper, WY; Salt Lake City, UT; Sioux City, IA; Seething, England; Pueblo, CO, B-29s when war ended.

Participated in Normandy, Northern France, Central Europe, Ardennes, Rhineland, Air Offensive Europe.

Discharged Oct. 27, 1945 with the rank of staff sergeant. Awarded American Theater Service, three Overseas Service Bars, Victory Medal, Good Conduct Medal, EAME with six Bronze Stars.

Married his childhood sweetheart of Hillside, NJ, V. Jean Chesney and had three children: twin daughters, Barbara and Sherry and a son David. They have eight grandchildren and one great-grandchild.

LaPoint retired after working for Westinghouse in Newark, NJ for 40 years.

PHILIP D. LARIVIERE (P.D.), was born July 26, 1922 in Fort Collins, CO. After two years of naval astronomy and navigation at the University of California signed up for aerial navigation training with the Air Corps in April 1942.

Shipped with 50 cadets to Rio Hato, Panama for advanced training with operational squadron flying LB-30s on submarine patrol. After commissioning in 1943 served as navigator/observer in B-17s and navigator/cannoneer in the B-25G until squadron deactivated.

He became navigation instructor at Galveston, TX to war-weary 8th Air Force veteran navigators tagged for the Pacific. Opted for combat duty and was accommodated swiftly with assignment to the 448th Bomb Group, Seething in November 1944 and flew 23 missions with Bill Redeen's crew before hostilities ended.

Married his college sweetheart, the lovely Florence Mary Heckel upon separation from the Air Force in October 1945 with the rank of first lieutenant. They have four wonderful children and one grandchild. Retired from a career in radiation physics in 1987, and currently assists his wife in wetlands conservation work.

HAROLD R. LARSON, was born in Boston, MA on April 1, 1917. Joined USAAC as aviation cadet, completed flight training and commissioned March 20, 1943 as second lieutenant pilot, George Field, IL; 43-C.

Military locations/stations: Gowan Field, Casper-Mitchell, SD; Tibenham, England; in SAC Smoky Hill, KS.

Flew 29 missions in B-24s, 445th Bomb Group from Tibenham, England. Recalled in Air Force, 1952, Korean conflict, flew B-29s in SAC.

He received Air Medal with four clusters, Distinguished Flying Cross, Presidential Unit Citation and Air Offensive.

Larson married Marge Snow on June 8, 1946; they have two daughters, and five grandchildren. He retired from elevator business.

RICHARD A. LARSON, was born Aug. 5, 1919 in Concordia, KS. Enlisted in the Air Force Jan. 25, 1942; served as a pilot with the 506th Sqdn., 44th Bomb Group, Pathfinders, 482nd Bomb Group.

Military locations/stations: Shipdham, East Anglia, Benghazi, Tunis, Alconburg. First mission was Ploesti, Wiener Neustadt-Foggia.

Memorable experiences: forced landing Palermo, Sicily, due to battle damage and wounded after Wiener Neustadt raid. Flying into cumulus nimbus cloud off coast of France. Twice leading 2nd Air Div. while in Pathfinders, pilot of first B-24 over Berlin.

Went to reserve status September 1945; discharged from Reserves 1954 with the rank of major. He received Distinguished Flying Cross, Air Medal with three clusters and Presidential Unit Citation.

On April 9, 1943 he married in Clovis, NM and has two sons and four grandchildren. Retired Jan. 1, 1990 after 43 years of farming.

ELWOOD LASH, was born on Flag Day, June 14, 1920 in Hamburg, PA. Joined the USAAC in July 1943; basic training and Flight Engineering School at Keesler Field, MS; Gunnery School at Harlingen, TX; then to Tonopah, NV for crew assignment.

He was flight engineer on Keith Shirk's crew which was a replacement crew and sailed over on *IL-de-France*. Had a refresher course in Ireland then to Hethel; was in 566th Sqdn., 389th Bomb Group. Most missions were on *Shady Lady*.

First of 34 missions was to Kassel. Need he say more, they finished March 9, 1945. Came back several times on three engines. Sailed home on *Queen Elizabeth* with 4,000 wounded aboard. Was then assigned to Chanute Field, IL.

Discharged in October 1945. Received all campaign ribbons along with Air Medal with five Oak Leaf Clusters.

Married for 52 years on Christmas 1992; has two children and five grandchildren. He has worked in sales since WWII.

DARRELL W. LATCH, was born Nov. 13, 1924 in Decatur, IL. Enlisted March 1, 1943 in the USAAC; gunner (tail), 2nd Air Div., 8th Air Force, 458th Bomb Group (H).

Military locations/stations: Boston; Colorado Springs; Tonopah, NV

Discharged Sept. 20, 1945 with the rank of staff sergeant. Received Purple Heart, Air Medal with four Oak Leaf Clusters and Distinguished Flying Cross.

Latch attended the University of Wisconsin and made a career in insurance. He is now a consultant: insurance management and underwriting. He has one son, Mark.

LYLE B. LATIMER, was born June 15, 1917 on a southwest Iowa farm. Enlisted in the USAAC at Ft. Crook, NE,

June 16, 1942; Armorer School, Lowry 2, CO, Sept. 10, 1943; Gunnery School, Harlingen, TX, Dec. 10, 1943.

B-24 crew formed at Casper, WY, Jan. 12, 1944; Joseph F. Herrmann, command pilot; Latimer, tail gunner. Flew B-24 Topeka, KS to Valley Wales, southern route May 2, 1944.

Assigned May 28, 1944 to 44th Bomb Group, 67th Sqdn.; a respected, tested unit with two citations from FDR. First of 31 missions on D-day, June 6, 1944; 72-day tour ended Aug. 15, 1944. All raids had some danger potential with our roughest being, Politz, Berlin, Kiel (two), Munich (two) and Hamburg (Tray hit by flak). Awarded Distinguished Flying Cross and Air Medal (four clusters). Left ETO (on *Queen Elizabeth-1*) Oct. 10, 1944; Laredo, TX AAF gunnery taught until discharge June 25, 1945.

Married June 2, 1946; has four children and five grandsons. Retired July 15, 1982 after 45 years of teaching.

WALTER LAUT, went into service from Ozone Park, NY in January 1943; Miami Beach, basic training; Fort Myers, FL, Gunnery School; AC Mechanics, Sheppard Field, TX; advance training gunnery, Tyndall Field, FL; formed 489th Bomb Group Wendover, UT.

Went overseas March 1944. Flew 32 missions as waist gunner and nose turret gunner. Started first mission May 31, 1944; completed 32 on Aug. 14, 1944.

Returned to States and went to Tyndall Field, FL as a turret instructor. Discharged September 1945.

Went back to work for the A and P Tea Co. as a store manager until 1972 when he retired. Have since traveled Europe and the U.S., has been back to the base in England on three occasions. Once for a group reunion in Florida.

MICHAEL A. LAVERE, was born in New York City, March 14, 1925. Joined Aviation Cadets February 1943; preflight assignments at Keesler Field, Nashville, Ellington Field, and 39th CTD, Presbyterian College, Clinton, SC. Trained as a celestial navigator and meteorologist by Pan American Aviation at University of Miami, Coral Gables, FL; graduated second lieutenant, Class 44-6, April 1944.

Joined crew 5278 at Lincoln AAF, NE, took combat crew training at Mountain Home, ID and Peterson Field, CO; then proceeded to Topeka AAF, KS to ferry a new B-24 to POE Grenier Field, NH. Took North Atlantic route to Valley, Wales for combat duty in England.

Joined 458th Bomb Group at Horsham St. Faith. Flew 36 missions as a B-24 navigator. During two missions, tested Azon bombs. Promoted to first lieutenant May 1944. Flew two gasoline delivery flights to Gen. Patton's tank units. After V-E-day flew 12 "trolley mission" flights over Germany.

Navigated a B-24 to Bradley Field, CT, June 7, 1945. Assigned to Fort Dix, NJ then to AAF Redistribution Station, Greensboro, NC. The Pacific War ended and he was discharged December 1945. Received Air Medal and three Oak Leaf Clusters, EAME Theater Ribbon with four Bronze Stars, Purple Heart and one Overseas Service Bar.

LaVere married July 1949; has a son, a daughter and four granddaughters. Has lived in Southern California since 1948. Retired from the engineering profession, April 1988 after 40 years service with various aerospace companies.

STEPHEN V. LAWNICKI, was born Dec. 11, 1923, Chicago Heights, IL. Enlisted March 10, 1943 in the USAAF; attended B-24 Mechanics School, Keesler Field, Biloxi, MS; Gunner School, Laredo, TX; next to Gowen Field, Boise, ID; Topeka, KS, picked up a new B-24 and then to Grenier Field, Manchester, NH.

Flew the northern route overseas, assigned to the 448th Bomb Group, 712th Bomb Sqdn., stationed at 146 in Seething, England. While flying turret on a mission, July 16, 1944 over Saarbucken, Germany, was hit by flak and wounded in the right rib cage. Spent three months at the 231st station hospital, then to the U.S. to AAF Convoy Hospital, Santa Ana, CA. Crew completed all missions. Completed 13 missions.

Discharged April 17, 1945 with the rank of staff sergeant. Received European Theater Campaign Ribbon with two Bronze Stars, Air Medal with one Oak Leaf Cluster and Purple Heart.

Lawnicki has a wife and two sons. He retired from Sears in Illinois and moved to Oregon in 1979.

WALTER V. LAWRENCE (TEX), was born May 30, 1924 in Kemah, TX. Entered the NYA program at the Naval Air Sta., Corpus Christi, TX. Discharged from civil service to join AAF Sept. 26, 1942, Ellington Field, TX as airplane mechanic. Later attended B-24 aerial engineer training, Keesler Field, MS and aerial gunnery at Harlingen, TX.

Crew training at Davis Monthan AAB, AZ; Blythe AAB, CA; continued to Will Rogers Field, OK and Forbes AAB, KS where a new B-24, Lyndi, carried the crew via South America and Africa to England and the 506th Sqdn. of the 44th Bomb Group. He flew combat missions as assistant engineer gunner from April 22, 1944 until shot down June 29, 1944 over Magdeburg, Germany.

Was POW at Stalag IXC, Luft IV and marched for 52 days to Stalag 357 where he was liberated by the English on April 21, 1944. Was hospitalized at Oxford until May 6; arrived in London for V-E day and in New York on May 30, 1945.

Discharged Oct. 22, 1945 with the rank of tech sergeant. He received the usual citations plus the Air Medal and Purple Heart.

Married Letha June Brooks on Oct. 19, 1947, they have three daughters and seven grandchildren. He worked as auto mechanic, carpenter and plumber for several years then operated and managed a church camp for 30 years at Arkansas, KS. Retired in 1986 and enjoys his hobbies of carpentry and amateur radio.

ROBERT S. LAWSON (BOB), was born April 18, 1914; attended New York University and entered service March 25, 1942. Commissioned through Quartermaster OCS Sept. 25, 1942. Commanding officer of the 1132nd QM Co. attached to 44th Bomb Group, Shipdham and became base quartermaster for almost two years.

War concluded, returned to fabric business in New York then to Los Angeles, retired in 1980 to travel extensively and has visited over 100 countries. Formerly active in the Air Force Association becoming national director.

As reservist he was affiliated with the new Air Force Academy, returning as the liaison officer coordinator for the Los Angeles area. The academy relationship remains very close after 30 years, and so does continued involvement with the British community.

Married Ruth Triefus Betterman, they have four children and three grandchildren.

MILES R. LEAGUE, was born June 22, 1921 in Greenville, SC. Obtained a private pilot's certificate while attending Erskine College in May 1941; completed an advanced civilian pilot training course June-September 1941 at Furman University, Greenville, SC. He received notice "to join one of the air arms" after Pearl Harbor, Dec. 7, 1941. He joined the USAAC as an aviation cadet Jan. 16, 1942 and was commissioned second lieutenant, Reserve, and awarded pilot wings Nov. 25, 1942.

Assigned to Davis Monthan Army Air Field, AZ; Alamogordo and Clovis, NM and Topeka, KS for B-24 training. With training completed April 1943, he was issued a new B-24 at Topeka and orders for England. In early May 1943 his crew joined the 409th Bomb Sqdn., 93rd Bomb Group at Hardwick, England as the first replacement crew and new airplane since the 93rd Bomb Group deployed to England in 1942.

Participated in combat missions out of England and North Africa, including the low-level mission to Ploesti oil refineries, Romania; and the first bombing mission of Weiner Neustadt, Austria, aircraft factories. On his 13th mission which was Gydnia, Poland severe flak knocked his crew out of formation (deputy lead) on the bomb run, but made solo bomb run nevertheless; assessed aircraft damage (two engines out, many fuel leaks, etc.); decision was made to make emergency landing on southern tip of Sweden. Interned for three months, he was one of four American pilots exchanged for four German pilots.

He rejoined the 409th Bomb Sqdn., 93rd Bomb Group, resumed combat mission and was on his 23rd mission (25 mission tour) Feb. 25, 1944 when shot down and bailed out. Was captured near Saarbrucken, Germany and remained POW, Stalag Luft I, Barth, Germany, until liberated by Russian army May 5, 1945.

Returned to U.S. early June 1945 and married fiance, Ora Gibson, June 30, 1945. Placed on inactive reserve January 1946. Recalled to active duty February 1948 to compete for a regular Air Force commission which he received October 1949.

A command pilot, he served in staff and mostly command assignments including Vietnam; Ellsworth AFB, SD; Carswell AFB, TX; FEAF and Johnson Air Base, Japan; Davis Monthan AFB, AZ; Mactan AB, Philippines; Saigon, Vietnam; Langley AFB, VA; Wheeler AB, HI.

Retired with the rank of colonel, USAF, in February 1974. Received the Distinguished Flying Cross, Air Medal with five Oak Leaf Clusters, Purple Heart, Bronze Star, ETO with eight Battle Stars and others.

Enjoys golfing, swimming, volunteer work, travelling, church choir and social activities. He is married with no children.

ROY D. LEAVITT, was born Sept. 14. 1919 in Pleasanton, KS. Enlisted in the U.S. Army Nov. 30, 1941 as private, 3rd Armored Div.

Served mostly as material procurement officer in Air Training Command and Air Material Command.

He retired after 26 years active duty with the rank of lieutenant colonel, July 31, 1967. He received the Distinguished Flying Cross, Air Medal with three clusters, ETO Ribbon with four battle stars.

Married and has two children, Randy and Tracy. He is a management consultant.

HARRY M. LEE, was born Oct. 3, 1924 in Newton Grove, Sampson County, NC. Enlisted June 4, 1943 in the USAAF, 2nd Air Div., 2nd Combat Wing, 453rd Bomb Group, 734th Sqdn. as radio operator-gunner.

Military locations/stations: Keesler Field, MS; Scott Field, IL; Yuma, AZ; March Field, CA; Old Buckingham, England. Flew 18 combat missions on B-24s with Lt. (later Col.) George Matecko's crew, 734th Sqdn. 453rd Bomb Group.

Memorable experience: collided with Lt. Flatt's ship on Feb. 6, 1945 over England while forming. His crew completed mission, Flat's crew went down, no survivors.

Discharged Nov, 8, 1945 with the rank of tech sergeant. He received Air Medal with two Oak Leaf Clusters.

He married Mary Lee Thompson Aug. 25, 1945, they have three children and four grandchildren. Lee graduated from Wake Forest University Law School June 1951 and has practiced law in Clinton, NC since that time and continues to practice law today.

JOHN L. LEE JR., was born in Baltimore, MD, June 8, 1922. Joined the USAAC in 1942 and became part of a combat crew on a B-24. Was sent to England as part of the 93rd Bomb Group in January 1945.

The German fighters were not as numerous as earlier

in the war, but they were still able to inflict a great deal of damage. There was no evidence of a shortage of anti-aircraft ammo and they experienced the first jet fighters (ME-262).

After the war, he returned to civilian life, but remained in the Reserves. Worked for Martin Marietta in management; graduated from the University of Baltimore with a Juris Doctor Degree; returned to active duty in 1968 with the Air Force and retired in the grade of colonel in 1982.

Married Elizabeth (Betty) and raised two sons and two daughters, who in turn gave them 14 grandchildren. He and his wife now live in Florida, play a lot of golf and like to travel.

R. CATER LEE, was born in Gordon, GA, July 24, 1921 and raised in Savannah, GA. Entered the USAAC April 1942; sent to Kelly Field, San Antonio, classified bombardier. Sent to Ellington Field, Houston, then Midland where he graduated in Class 43-2; then sent to Hondo AFB for navigation where he graduated in Class 43-9.

Joined 448th B-24 group at Wendover Field, UT, July 1943; moved to England with them November 1943 and completed 30 mission tour May 22, 1944. Returned to USA in August and assigned to the Air Transport Command. Discharged January 1946.

Joined 117th Aircraft Control and Warning National Guard Sqdn. in 1948 in Savannah. Mobilized January 1951 and served at Smyrna AFB, Smyrna, TN and Tyndall Field, Panama City, FL. Discharged May 1952.

He married his long term sweetheart Sara McLarry in June 1943, they have one daughter, two sons and seven grandchildren. They moved to Birmingham, AL in August 1942 where he spent the remainder of his business life in a company he founded in 1966.

WILLIAM W. LEESBURG, was born Aug. 20, 1922 in Wheelersburg, OH. Joined the USAAC as an aviation cadet Sept. 17, 1942 and received his pilot wings as a second lieutenant on April 15, 1944. Trained as a B-24 airlift commander and flew 31 missions over Germany in 1944 and 1945 as a member of the 389th Bomb Group located at Hethel Air Field, England.

Served most of remaining career in the Strategic Air Command as a B-47 and B-52 airlift commander, B-52 squadron commander and director of B-52 operations. Completed over 100 missions over Vietnam.

Memorable experiences: was flying right wing when a German fighter broke through the formation, scored a direct hit on his lead and the B-24 literally exploded in his face, almost taking Leesburg B-24 with it; low-level mission, 100 feet or lower, March 24, 1945, to Wessel, Germany, dropping supplies; ready to taxi on his 32nd mission when word came to shut down because war had ended; flying home from England in a war-weary B-24 and flying over the Statue of Liberty, she was the first to welcome them home.

Retired as a colonel Oct. 1, 1977 with over 35 years service. Awards include Distinguished Flying Cross, Air Medal with 11 Oak Leaf Clusters, Bronze Star with one Oak Leaf Cluster and Meritorious Service Medal with one Oak Leaf Cluster.

Leesburg married July 11, 1942 to Doris J. Wright from Wheelersburg, OH, and reared six children. He loved all of it.

FELIX B. LEETON, was born March 3, 1921 in Lee County, AR and raised in Springfield, TN. Two years at the University of Tennessee, joined the USAAF July 3, 1942; pilot training at Maxwell Field, AL; Dorr Field, FL; Bainbridge, GA and Moody AFB, GA; Nov. 3, 1943 Class 43-J. Crew assignment Salt Lake City; phases, Blythe, CA. Left New York City May 2, 1944 on transport *Mitchell*, ar-

riving Glasgow May 15. After Escape School, he was assigned to the 389th Bomb Group.

Hitched ride on weather ship June 6, 1944 for D-day show. Flew 30 missions in 93 days. Most memorable missions included: Hamburg, Berlin, Munich, Bremen, Brunswick, Berlin recall, and an abort after penetration, landed with three engines, instrument conditions.

Watched first big V-1 attack on London June 21 from roof of a Cromwell Road Hotel; and back on September 10 for the first V-2 hit. After return, flew B-24s at Buckingham Field, FL; Victorville, CA; and Westover, MA; A-26 transition; AMOT School at Chanute Field.

Left active duty December 1946 from Ft. Worth AFB, TX as a captain. Received Distinguished Flying Cross, Air Medal with three Oak Leaf Clusters, ETO with four Bronze Stars.

He received BS degree in mechanical engineering. Retired 1984 from Allis Chalmers. Organizations include ASME, IEEE, Phi Sigma Kappa Fraternity, NSPE, LSPE, TSPE, Mensa, 2nd Air Division Association.

Married to Frances Caldwell Nov. 5, 1944, has five children and five grandchildren. Widowed in 1981, married Marjorie Triplitt Cearnal May 7, 1983.

ALBERT H. LEIGHTON, was born May 6, 1919 in Berlin, NH and reared in Pawtucket, RI. Enlisted June 2, 1939 in the USAAC at Chanute Field, IL; graduated Photo School, Lowry Field, CO, Aug. 30, 1940; instructor, staff sergeant (Photo School); appointed aviation cadet June 1942, graduated Class 43-C (pilot) Gulf Coast Training Center and commissioned second lieutenant AC (Res) March 20, 1943. Assigned to 389th Bomb Group, 567th Sqdn., Biggs Field, TX as co-pilot for Max van Benthuysen crew.

Became first pilot November 1943. Completed 30 mission tour on May 30, 1944 as captain, flight comm. Awarded Distinguished Flying Cross, Air Medal with three Oak Leaf Clusters, EAME with two bronze stars and other ribbons.

Memorable experiences: His forced landing on the beach at Lahinch, CO. Clare, Ireland on July 10, 1943 after nursing B-24 with leaking fuel cells across the Atlantic. Evading JU-88s over the Bay of Biscay when returning from Africa, October 1943.

Returned stateside July 1944 and married "Pat" Manning in Denver, CO, Aug. 6, 1944. Has three children: Jacqueline, Pamela and James, and three grandchildren.

Graduated photo pilot course at Lowry Field, CO, Feb. 5, 1945 and assigned to Deming AAF as base photo officer on March 28, 1945.

Released from active duty in December 1945 but remained active in the Air Force Reserve. Retired as lieutenant colonel on Feb. 1, 1969.

He attended University of Denver (business administration) and was employed in sales and purchasing, retiring in May 1985.

GEORGE E. LEININGER, was born Sept. 10, 1923. He enlisted in the USAAC Jan. 21, 1943 and served in the 8th Air Force, 445th Bomb Group, 700th Sqdn. Military locations/stations: Sioux City, IA; Lowry Field, Denver, CO; Laredo, TX., Norwich, England.

Flew southern route to England, Puerto Rico to South America, Africa to England. He flew 29 missions as tail gunner; flew all missions with same crew. Memorable experience: April 22, 1944 Koblenz, Germany, took off 3:45 p.m. and approached field 10:00 p.m., German fighters followed them as they were landing and 14 aircraft crashed.

Discharged Oct. 26, 1945 with the rank of staff sergeant. Awarded Distinguished Flying Cross, American Order French Croix de Guerre, Air Medal with three Oak Leaf Clusters, Unit Citation, NYS Conspicuous Service Cross.

Married Lucille Mohrmann, his high school sweetheart, June 11, 1944, they have three children and three grandchildren.

Leininger owned Aronca Aircraft. He was a member of Local 740, New York Millwrights as millwright machinery erector, and has been retired for seven years.

WILLIAM D. LEMKOWITZ, was born in Patterson, LA on March 12, 1915 and raised in Cutoff, LA. Graduated Louisiana State University with BS degree in electrical engineering; worked in south Louisiana oil fields until August 1940. Entered military service as first lieutenant Aug. 12, 1940 at Ft. McClellan, AL; assigned to various stations in U.S. until August 1943. Transferred to 8th Air Force with duty station AAF 123, Bungay, 446th Bomb Group, August 1943 until January 1944.

Assigned AAF 125, Horsham St. Faith, 458th Bomb Group as base ordnance officer and commander 1686th Ordnance S & M Co., January 1944. Retained this position until reorganization of base support units, under Bradley Plan, April 1945. Assigned various duties, squadron commander, ordnance officer, until reassignment to States July 1945.

Transferred to USAF summer 1945; served in various command and staff positions. Released from active duty January 1946; returned to active duty September 1946, served with ordnance department in various staff positions with Army of Occupation of Europe, October 1946-May 1949. Returned to States May 1949; served as PMS and T (Asst) at University of Minnesota, and Louisiana Polytechnic Institute.

Retired from Air Force January 1963. Taught high school math for one and a half years; worked civil service, Kelly AFB, from October 1964 until retirement March 1980.

Lemkowitz married Louella Faleout on Aug. 28, 1937; has eight children, four boys and four girls; 15 grandchildren and five great-grandchildren.

JOHN RAY LEMONS JR., was born Nov. 4, 1919 in Dallas, TX. Reported to Camp Wolters Feb. 3, 1943; assigned to Air Force at Miami Beach; graduated Gunnery School, Ft. Myers and Aircraft Mechanics School, Sheppard Field. Then assigned to B-24 bomber combat crew at Peterson Field, CO.

Next assignment June 1944, overseas, 8th Air Force. After special training in Ireland, assigned to the 445th Bomb Group at Tibenham. Flew eight missions as engineer gunner in various positions.

Three tough missions: first, Hamburg, third, Dessau, then Sept. 27, 1944 when shot down on the infamous Kassel mission. After harrowing experiences with civilians at capture, spent remainder of the war in prison camps in Poland, Germany and Austria. Liberated April 29, 1945 by Gen. Patton. Many years later, learned that of four crew members KIA, three were killed by local people after capture.

Returned to States in June and was discharged in October 1945.

BURTON H. LENHART, was born Dec. 14, 1919 in Lockport, NY. Went into service November 1942 as aviation cadet (pilot) training. Preflight at SAAC San Antonio, TX; primary training at Chickashay, OK. When pilots weren't

needed from his particular class only six of 36 made it through. Lenhart wasn't one of the six. He was given three choices and picked Radio School, remaining on flying status as radio/gunner.

Attended Radio School, Sioux Falls, SD; Gunnery School, Yuma, AZ; crew training, Casper, WY.

Flew B-24 overseas via Labrador, Greenland, Iceland to England; got lost between Iceland and England, found way by short wave code radio. They were forced to land in Brussels, Belgium with three motors and full bomb load just hours after capturing airfield. Each of his 35 missions were lasting experiences.

Discharged October 1945 with the rank of tech. sergeant. He received six Air Medals, ETO Ribbon with two Battle Stars and the Good Conduct Medal.

Married for 45 years and has two daughters, two sons and three granddaughters. He spent 38 years in the television and appliance business (two stores) and is now retired.

JAMES T. LENNON, was born Oct. 10, 1918 in Montclair, NJ. Entered the service Feb. 3, 1942 at Ft. Dix, NJ and attended Radio and Gunnery Schools. Assigned to Westover Field, Langley Field and Hethel, England. Participated in battles at Ardennes, Central Europe, Northern France and Rhineland.

Memorable experiences: At Westover and his crew was to fly in the morning when their engineer told the pilot, Bob Herington, the plane (No. 44) was unfit to fly. They were then scheduled to fly making night landings. Number 44 was back out on the line in front of them. After the second time around it blew up in front of them.

Discharged with the rank of tech. sergeant. Received Air Medal with four Oak Leaf Clusters, EAME Service Medal and Good Conduct Medal.

JAMES A. LENOIR, was born Sept. 14, 1923 in New Castle, DE. He was inducted February 1943 in the USAAC; armorer/gunner. Basic training at Sheppard Field; Radio School, Scott AFB, IL; Armor School, Lowry AFB, CO; Gunnery School, Buckingham Field; crew placement, Westover AFB, MA; phase training, Chatham Field; POE, Mitchell Field; Instructor School, Laredo Field; B-29 gunnery instructor, Buckingham Field.

Took northern route to England; flew 35 missions from September 1944 to February 1945. His memorable experience was low level mission dropping supplies to the troops in Holland.

Discharged October 1945 with the rank of staff sergeant. Received six Air Medals, three ETO Battle Stars and Good Conduct Medal.

Married to Catherine 44 years; they have six children and 10 grandchildren. He retired from Hercules Inc. after 45 years.

BERNARD A. LEPOER, was born Oct. 31, 1924 in Petersham, MA. Enlisted April 5, 1943 in the USAAC; flight maintenance gunner.

Military locations/stations: Miami, Keesler Field; Laredo; Fresno; Muroc; Hamilton Field; Camp Kilmer, NJ; Northern Ireland; Rackheath, England; Chanute Field; Columbus, OH.

Departed for overseas June 29, 1944. He participated in battles at Rhineland, Ardennes, Northern France. Returned to the States April 19, 1945.

Discharged Oct. 27, 1945, Columbus, OH with the rank of tech. sergeant. Awarded Good Conduct Medal, Air Medal with four Oak Leaf Clusters, EAME Ribbon with three Battle Stars.

LePoer married in 1945 and has three children, four grandchildren and two great-grandchildren. He is retired.

RUSSELL R. LESLIE, was born July 8, 1922 in South Bend, IN, graduated from high school 1940. Enlisted in the USAAC on Dec. 17, 1941. By-passed technical school after four months basic training at Jefferson Barracks, MO and was assigned as A/C mechanic, Perrin, FL.; Sherman, TX early 1942 and was promoted to sergeant by September; attended Aerial Gunnery School at Harlingen, TX, December 1942; assigned to 389th Bomb Group 565th Sqdn. as assistant crew chief Biggs Field, El Paso, TX, early 1943.

He was sent overseas, after training at Lowry Field, CO, on *Queen Elizabeth* arriving at Hethel Air Drome on his 21st birthday. After six months as assistant crew chief, volunteered as replacement gunner, flight engineer.

Completed 30 missions May 30, 1944, rotating stateside September 1944. He was an instructor at Keesler Field, MS before going to Pre-flight School, San Antonio, TX to become flight engineer (second lieutenant) on the new B-32 a/c of which only a few were made. The class was cancelled after four months, then assigned as flight chief until discharged September 1945 with the grade of tech. sergeant.

Received Air Medal with three Oak Leaf Clusters, Distinguished Flying Cross and several Battle Stars to other Air Campaign Medals.

Married September 1947 after re-enlistment March 1947 and discharged 1950. He has three sons (who were in the Air Force at the same time), three daughters and 12 grandchildren at the present time.

Leslie retired from the Air Force Reserves as master sergeant and civil service technician. Two of his sons are also retired from the Air Force (1992). He has been retired since age 59.

GEORGE E. LETLOW, born in Navasota, TX; enlisted 1943 in the USAAC; 8th Air Force, 2nd Air Div., 448th Bomb Group, 713 Sqdn. Stationed at Seething, England; Boise, ID; Wichita Falls and San Antonio, TX, Scott Field, IL.

Participated in 35 combat missions in France, Holland, Low Lands, but mostly Germany. Memorable experience was staying alive. Discharged 1945 as a staff sergeant turret gunner, stayed in the Reserves and retired 1966 with the rank first lieutenant. Received six Air Medals and three Battle Stars.

Married for 44 years, has one surviving child and one grandson. He is retired and resting.

OLEN F. LEVELL JR., was born in Staunton, VA on July 3, 1916. Enlisted in Aviation Cadets Dec. 9, 1942, Class of 43-I. Graduated from Pampa, TX as a second lieutenant; trained in B-24 at Liberal, KS as pilot; was transferred to Salt Lake City where he picked up his crew. RTU in Westover Field, MA and from there joined 8th Air Force in England.

He completed tour and was the last squadron commander of the 576th Sqdn., 392nd Bomb Group, Wendling, England.

Flew in the Air Force Reserve for several years and retired in December 1953 as a major. He received the Air Medal and five clusters, Distinguished Flying Cross and one cluster and the ETO Ribbon.

Levell retired from PPG, Industries after 42 years. Married Martha Jane Carter in 1938, they have two children and three grandchildren.

ISRAEL LEVINE (IZ), was born in New York City on Aug. 30, 1923. He took a military leave from the City College of New York and joined the USAAC on Feb. 27, 1943. After basic training at Atlantic City, NJ, he entered the Aviation Cadet Program, graduating from the AAC Advanced Navigation School at Selman Field, LA in September 1944. Assigned to B-24 training at Chatham Field, GA he and his crew flew a B-24 to England, joining the 389th Bomb Group

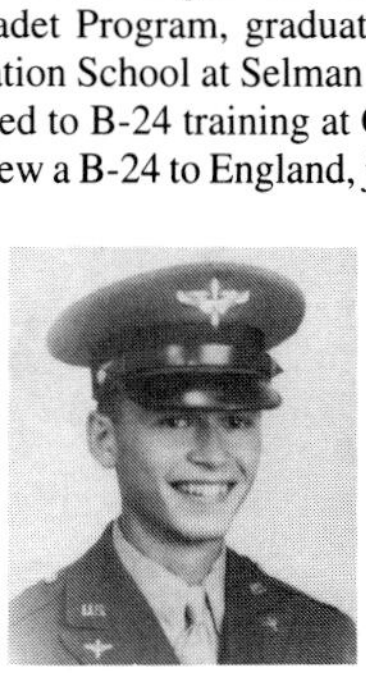

at Hethel, arriving in time to take part in the Battle of the Bulge.

From Dec. 30, 1944 until the end of hostilities in Europe, he flew 32 missions, including Operation Varsity, the low-level run into Germany in the face of heavy ground fire to supply British ground forces during the crossing of the Rhine. Another memorable mission was his first, when the B-24 took a flak hit and returned from the target area alone and almost out of fuel with a "hung" 2,000-pound bomb that refused to be jettisoned over the North Sea drop area. When the bomber touched down at Hethel, the bomb dropped out and "chased" the aircraft down the runway until it ran out of steam. Needless to say, the bomb did not explode.

He retired as a second lieutenant in October 1945 and holds the Air Medal and three Oak Leaf Clusters, three Battle Stars and other ribbons. Since the war he has been a magazine writer, editor and public relations executive. He is the author of 13 books.

Was married on June 23, 1946 to the former Elaine Michael of Monroe, LA whom he met while in Navigation School. They have two children and two grandchildren.

ROBERT M. LIBBY, was born Jan. 7, 1926 in Newton, MA. Enlisted Feb. 1, 1944 in the 8th Army Air Force, 445th Bomb Group, 702nd Bomb Sqdn.

Stationed at Laredo, TX; Mt. Home, ID; and Tibenham, England. He flew 28 missions in B-24s over Europe as a waist gunner. Memorable experience was when he bailed out on 15th mission, Etain, France; returned to England.

Discharged Nov. 6, 1945 with the rank of staff sergeant. He received the Good Conduct Medal, Air Medal with three Bronze Oak Leaf Clusters and ETO Service Medal.

Libby married Elaine Knowlton Feb. 18, 1950. He is retired.

LEE M. LINDERMUTH, was born May 20, 1922 Market Street, Auburn, PA. Enlisted Philadelphia, PA, June 9, 1941 in the Army of the U.S., Air Corp, Regular Army. Attended Mechanic and Engineering Schools at Love Field, Dallas, TX; Tucson AB, Tucson, AZ; San Diego AB, Fresno, CA; Langley Field, VA; Westover Field, MA; Cherry Point, NC (Special Gunnery School).

Participated in battles at Normandy, Northern France, Rhineland, Ardennes, Central Europe and Air Offensive Europe. Among his memorable experiences is his voyage on Liberty Ship from New York to England (stranded in the middle of the Atlantic for three days); and returning on the *Queen Mary* to New York.

Was discharged Sept. 21, 1945 from the Separation Center at Sioux Falls, SD; an aircraft mechanic with the rank of sergeant. Awards received include the EAME Service Medal, American Defense Ribbon and Good Conduct Medal.

On July 28, 1943 he married Helen P. Herring; they have two sons: Terry Lee and Gary Lee; and a granddaughter Cathy Lee. Lindermuth is retired.

WILLIAM J. LINDOPP, was born in East Providence, RI on Sept. 11, 1911. He enlisted November 1942 in the USAF, 492nd Bomb Group, 857th Sqdn., crew 717. Stationed at Lowry AFB Tucson, AZ; Alamogordo, FL; South America to Africa and England Air Base, North Pickenham, Swaffum, England.

Memorable experience was when taken prisoner of war on May 19, 1944.

Discharged November 1945. He received World War II Efficiency Honor and Fidelity Medal, EAME, Air Medal and American Campaign Medal.

Lindopp married in 1941, had two children, son James G. and daughter Paula A.L. Solinger. Lindopp passed away Aug. 15, 1980. *Submitted by Mrs. Wm. J. Lindopp.*

JOHN A. LINFORD, was born in Oakland, CA on Sept. 2, 1922. Entered pilot training in USAAF, graduating Class 44-C Marfa, TX. After B-24 transition at Kirtland Field, he completed operational training at Mountain Home, ID. His crew No. 7155 was assigned to 445th Bomb Group from October 1944 to June 1945 at Tibenham. Flew last 15 of 34 missions as lead crew.

With five ETO Battle Stars, five Air Medals and a Presi-

dential Unit Citation, he left the Air Corps in July 1945 with the rank of captain.

He re-entered U.C. Berkeley and received his BS, ME in 1947. After seven years with Scott Co., he founded his own engineering and mechanical contracting firm. For 33 years he served as a national ski patroller and he is current IFR-Commercial pilot flying his Cessna 320 E.

John is a past president of the Rotary Club of Oakland, of the International Fellowship of Flying Rotarians and of several trade organizations. In 1984 he landed his twin Cessna at Tibenham, England following a transatlantic flight. The Norwich Gliding Club uses the runways which are still in excellent condition.

From his marriage on March 15, 1944 to Louise Talcott, there are three children and six grandchildren.

JOSEPH LINSK, was born Nov. 30, 1919 in New York City. He enlisted in the USAAF on Aug. 30, 1943 and served as a pilot, heavy bomb group, 2nd Air Div.; attended pilot training southeast, Maxwell Field, Clarkesdale, MS; Newport, AR; George Field, Lawrenceville, IL

He flew a total of 31 combat missions and participated in the bombing raids over Liepzig, Berlin and Hamm (Germany). Was commended for crash landing a disabled B-24 on the last (31st) mission to Saarbrucken. Landed in England with engine sputtering because all fuel had been consumed. Name of the plane, *Final Approach* has become famous because it flew over 100 missions without any mechanical abortions.

Was discharged Aug. 5, 1945 with the rank of first lieutenant. Awarded the distinguished Flying Cross, Air Medal with three Oak Leaf Clusters and ETO Campaign Ribbon.

Married Lillian 51 years ago, they have two daughters. Graduated from CCNY, BS; Brooklyn College, MA degree; Polytech Institute of Brooklyn, Ph.D. Today, he teaches chemistry at a Catholic high school.

NORMAN B. LINVILLE, was born Oct. 29, 1923 in Bourbon County, KY between Paris, KY and Ruddlesmill, KY. He joined the USAAF on Nov. 10, 1942; basic training, Miami Beach, FL; Gunnery School, Ft. Myers, FL; ORTC, Atlantic City, NJ.

Departed the USA for ETO May 27, 1943; joined 68th Sqdn, 44th Bomb Group on May 29. Finished tour with 34 missions September 1944. Went to NATO for Ploesti raid but did not go on the mission because another crew had taken their aircraft and were shot down. Shot down on one mission that claimed five of seven aircraft in their squadron. Linville was on Capt. Gildart's crew.

He was awarded the Air Medal with three Oak Leaf Clusters, Distinguished Flying Cross, six Battle Stars, three Unit Citations plus other ribbons. He was awarded the Distinguished Flying Cross at 20 missions and flew 14 missions after, without ever getting one Oak Leaf Cluster to his Air Medal. Shot down one enemy fighter and crash landed once.

Now retired and living in Brandon, FL, has three children living nearby. His wife is deceased.

ERNEST DALE LITTLE, was born in Benkelman, NE on Nov. 6. 1921. Entered USAAC Sept. 11, 1942, Fort Logan, CO; basic training, Kearns, UT; Air Gunnery School, Las Vegas, NV; Radio School, Salt Lake City, UT; first phase combat training, Tucson, AZ; second phase, Alamogordo, NM; third phase, Clovis, NM. Overseas staging, Lincoln, NE to Morrison Field, Miami, FL.

Overseas route: Puerto Rico, Trinidad, Belem, Brazil, Natal, Brazil. Ascension Island, Accra, Ghana (Africa). From

Accra on way to Khartoum, Sudan, on way to 14th Air Force in China under Gen. Chennault, plane lost three engines, bailed out, picked up from jungles and went to Kano, Nigeria. Ordered back to States, four crew members hospitalized in Puerto Rico with malaria fever on way home.

Rejoined his crew at Lowry Field, Denver, CO. Assigned 446th Bomb Group, 705th Bomb Sqdn. and retraced their route back to Dakar, Africa then to Marrakech, Morocco. Their last long flight to Station 125, Bungay, (Flixton) England.

Flew first of 30 missions Jan. 11, 1944. Lost their navigator, Lt. Homer S. Gentry, KIA, April 11, 1944, Bernberg, Germany. Flew last mission on May 12, 1944. Discharged Sept. 24, 1945, received Air Medal with three Oak Leaf Clusters, Distinguished Flying Cross, European Campaign Ribbon with three campaign stars and others. Little got his private pilot's license after discharge.

Married his high school sweetheart, Helen Louise Daugherty, Aug. 29, 1941. They have a son, daughter and six grandchildren.

RICHARD E. LITTLEFIELD, was born Dec. 22, 1924 in Sidney, OH. He enlisted in the USAAC February 1943; served as armor gunner in the 8th Air Force, 2nd Air Div. Attended Armament School, Lowry, Buckley at Denver, CO; Gunnery School, Laredo, TX; assigned B-24 crew at Salt Lake City November 1943; accepted new B-24 Mitchell Field, March 1944.

Flew to England, assigned to 445th Bomb Group. Participated in Air Offensive Europe, Normandy, Rhineland and Northern France. Flew 11 missions, first one April 19, 1944. Crew transferred to the 389th Bomb Group, flew 14 missions for a tour of 25 on Aug. 11, 1944.

Discharged October 1945 with the rank of staff sergeant. Awarded the Distinguished Flying Cross, four Air Medals, four Bronze Battle Stars and ETO Ribbon.

Returned to Toledo, OH; attended University of Toledo. Worked at Sun Oil Company as lab supervisor, retiring in 1983. He married Marjorie Lampley Dec. 3, 1948, they have one son, three daughters, six grandsons and one granddaughter expected on St. Patrick's Day 1994.

LESTER J. LITWILLER, was born May 1920 in Hopedale, IL. Enlisted in May 1942 in the USAAF, Class 43-D. Training was all in Texas. Served in England, 93rd Bomb Group, 389th Bomb Group.

All battles were in Europe. Two missions on D-day; six of seven to Berlin area.

Discharged July 1945 with the rank of captain of lead crew with mickey equipment. He received five Air Medals and two Distinguished Flying Crosses.

Married with five children. He is a retired stock broker.

HENRY M. LIVELY, was born April 16, 1923 in a one room log cabin near Lietchfield, KY. Enlisted in USAAC Nov. 6, 1942; attended Aircraft and Engine Mechanic School at Gulfport, MS; Aerial Gunnery School at Laredo, TX. Joined B-24 flight crew at Boise, ID in June 1943. Crew joined 445th Bomb Group, 702nd Bomb Sqdn. at Sioux City, IA in July 1943.

Left for overseas in late November 1943 and arrived Tibenham, England in December 1943. Bailed out over Germany on Feb. 24, 1944 while on mission to Gotha. Was incarcerated in Stalag Luft VI in East Prussia to July 1944, then Stalag Luft IV in East Pomerania to Feb. 6, 1945. Spent two months and 20 days walking approximately 540 miles from Stalag Luft IV to a point on the Mulde River near Bitterfeld, Germany where the Germans turned them over to the American Army on April 26, 1945. After trip back to States and a 30 day leave, was assigned to a technical intelligence unit out of Wright Field, where he worked on German FW-190, ME-109, ME-262 and Italian Macchi 202 aircraft until discharged Nov. 13, 1945.

Worked and attended school for two and one-half years; then re-entered USAF, retired in 1968 as a chief warrant officer, grade W-4.

Spent next 20 years as a stock and bond broker with a New York Stock Exchange listed firm. Retired from that position in 1989. He married Ceserina "Nina" Campana Dec. 30, 1951, they have one daughter and two grandchildren.

ARTHUR LIVINGSTON JR., was born in Paterson, NJ, Dec. 23, 1922. Entered USAAF Jan. 30, 1943; attended Armorer School at Buckley, Field, CO and on to Gunnery School at Kingman, AZ graduating as sergeant. Sent to newly formed 446th Bomb Group at Lowry Field, CO; assigned as ball turret gunner on Shore's crew of *The Worrybird*. During 10 days leave prior to going overseas, married high school sweetheart Elsie Holdsworth.

Left zone interior October 1943 and flew southern route arriving England November 16. Flew first mission to Bremen December 16; completed 26 missions on April 27, 1944. Extra one required when tour was increased to 30 from 25. Assigned Combat Crew replacement Center at Northern Ireland and ran the "jeep skeet" range. December 1944, assigned to Air Disarmament Unit and sent to France and into Germany. Dismantled German jet aircraft and sent to Wright Field for evaluation.

Sailed for home August 1945 and discharged from Ft. Dix Sept. 13, 1945 with the rank of tech sergeant. Awarded Distinguished Flying Cross, Bronze Star, Air Medal with three Oak Leaf Clusters, ETO with three Battle Stars, Occupation of Germany, Victory Medal and Medal of French Liberation.

He retired in 1978 after 30 years as owner of a boat and sports store. He has three children and eight grandchildren.

JAMES L. LIVINGSTON, was born Oct. 13, 1923 in Jacksonville, FL. Enlisted in the USAAC Nov. 9, 1942; basic training in Miami Beach, FL; Gunnery School in Ft. Myers, FL.

Departed New York May 27, 1943. Assigned to 506th Bomb Sqdn., 44th Bomb Group in England as a spare gunner. Completed 30 missions on B-24s. In November 1943, he was on a short mission over France; they had dropped their bombs and ran into some heavy flak. Their plane was hit pretty bad. Livingston was flying tail gunner and turned around, looked back and there were no waist gunners. He made his way to the cockpit and only the pilot was there. The pilot told him to get the nose gunner back to the cockpit; the three of them made it back to the base okay.

Returned to the U.S. Sept. 21, 1944 and discharged Sept. 15, 1945. Received the Distinguished Flying Cross, four Air Medals, EAME Service Medal with Silver Star and the Distinguished Unit Badge.

He was a paper cutter and worked for the railroad in Denver, CO; moved to Miley, SC and did sawmill work.

Re-entered service in 1948; served four and a half years in Germany and married a wonderful girl. Returned to the States; had a son born in March 1954. Discharged Dec. 1, 1958.

Worked for the state of Florida until 1963; moved to Savannah, GA in December 1963 where he worked as a warehouse manager until retirement June 1989.

ROBERT LLOYD, was born April 22, 1922 in Herminie, PA. Entered service February 1943; basic training in Miami Beach; went to school, became a flight engineer on the B-24.

Sent to England to the 448th Bomb Group at Seething, Norwich. Started flying missions May 1944. Was a staff ser-

geant and flew 34 missions over France, Belgium, Holland, Germany.

Returned to the States from England February 1945, sent to Ft. Worth AAF as an instructor. He was discharged October 1945. Received Distinguished Flying Cross, six Air Medals and two Purple Hearts.

In September 1992, he returned to Seething with 62 other veterans for a reunion with the 448th Bomb Group. He is now retired from Westinghouse Electric, air condition maintenance.

RICHARD D. LODGE, was born in Oak Park, IL on Jan. 29, 1922. Enlisted in the USAAC in Baltimore, MD on Nov. 5, 1942 and earned pilot wings in Class 44-C.

Assigned to 467th Bomb Group as B-24 pilot, he flew 27 missions over France and Germany, most of them by flying *The Monster*. (Paintings of a buxom black-haired beauty, carrying a bomb in her left arm, decorated both sides of the nose.) He received Air Medal with three Oak Leaf Clusters; EAME with three Battle Stars for Rhineland, Central Europe and Ardennes campaigns; and Victory Medal.

After appointment to Officers Reserve Corps on Oct. 6, 1945, he returned to University of Maryland where he had been a freshman engineering student when bombs fell on Pearl Harbor.

Married to Chun Yung Kyung in Seoul; they have one daughter, Barbara Anne, born on Tachikawa AFB. Retired from the USAFR on June 6, 1973 with the rank of major. He is a registered professional engineer.

LOUIS LOEVSKY, was born March 8, 1920. Enlisted U.S. Army Air Corps Dec. 26, 1941. Graduated Aviation Mechanic School, Keesler Field, Biloxi, MS and B-26 Specialist School, Baltimore, MD. "Washed out!"...pilot training, Corsicana, TX. Graduated Navigation School, Hondo, TX, November 1943. Joined 8th Air Force, 466th Bomb Group, 786th Bomb Sqdn., Clovis, NM. Stationed at Attlebridge, England.

On March 22, 1944 the 466th Bomb Group flew its first mission to Berlin. Our B-24, *Terry and the Pirates,* was hit by flak over Berlin and lost #1 propeller. A mid-air collision ensued with *Terry* losing props #2 and #3, and the *Brand* B-24 lost its tail, causing it to go into a tight spin. Because of the centrifugal force, only two *Brand* crew members managed to get out of their aircraft. A waist gunner ripped open his chest pack chute and payed it out into the slip stream, and it popped him out of the plane. About a year after his 13 months POW incarceration, he ended his life by putting a gun in his mouth and pulling the trigger. The co-pilot, C. Wayne, Beigel, was clawing his way to the bomb bay to bail out when the *Brand* aircraft exploded and blew him out of the plane. Len Smith, bombardier, was trapped in the *Terry* nose turret since the electrical and manual systems to operate the turret had been rendered inoperable by the crash. The turret would not turn so that its doors could open to let Len out. Len had sustained substantial injury. For me to extricate Len from his predicament was most difficult, since he was in shock and kept removing his gloves (at -35°F or below) and his oxygen mask (at 23,500'). Putting his mask and gloves back on repeatedly while trying to spring a nose turret door, put an arm around his chest and pull him out was quite an achievement. Eventually, Lou got Len out, and released the bombs in train. Thirteen of 20 crew members were KIA, five *Terry* and eight *Brand*.

After assisting Len to bail out, our pilot, "Bill" Terry yelled, "Hey, Lou...wait for me!" I waited until he left the control column and started across the flight deck, then I bailed out through the bomb bay. Distrusting the Germans, I free fell and saw one parachute open above me, which had to be Terry's. While free-falling I realized that with the "H" (Jewish) on my dog tags, I risked being shot as a spy, if I ripped them off and threw them away...and risked being shot as a Jew if I left them on and fell into the hands of the Gestapo or S.S. I left them on. While free-falling I thought of the gross of condoms scattered in every pocket of every uniform..."my parents will think they raised a sex fiend."

When I finally opened my parachute...thinking it safe, I soon found I was being shot at from the ground. Slipping and spilling air, I became an instant expert in maneuvering the chute...despite admonitions to keep our "cotton-pickin' hands" off the shroud lines. I got away from a small camp where they were shooting at me toward another small camp where they were not. Selecting a small tree in Berlin, crossed my legs for posterity, crashed branches clean off one side of the tree, chute caught on top, my feet whipped over my head, back injured, blacked out briefly, came to with toes touching ground, heels off. A home guard (Volkstrum), shaking...had gun in my ribs, repeating: "Pis-tole?, pis-tole?" Two Wehrmacht troops appeared and took over my custody. While still getting out of the parachute harness, three S.S. arrived, apparently from the small camp where they had been shooting at me. The S.S. argued with the Wehrmacht, they wanted to take custody of me (and since my parents sometimes talked Yiddish, I could understand). Fortunately, the two Wehrmacht troops retained my custody.

As they marched me through the streets of Berlin to their headquarters, the angry civilian mob were yelling in perfect American, "string him up," "hang him," "lynch him," they wanted a necktie party. As they were closing in the Wehrmacht troops had to draw their sidearms to keep the ugly lynching mob at bay.

I believe that "Bill" Terry was shot from the ground as he floated down in his parachute or possibly the civilians "took care of him."

Prisoner of War at Stalag Luft III, Sagan, Germany until Russians got close in January 1945. Evacuated at 2:00 a.m. in a freezing blizzard. Reached Stalag VII A, Moosburg, by marching in sub-zero weather, and crammed into (40 and 8) box-cars. We were improperly clothed or fed; our conditions were unsanitary and inhumane. Imagine hundreds of American officers and enlisted men lined up evacuating their bowels when the train stopped at a station in full view of German women and children. We were treated like swine.

We were liberated by Gen. Patton's troops on April 29, 1945.

Joe Greenberg, flight engineer of *Terry and the Pirates* folded his wings in early 1993. Fifty years after the mid-air collision, the three survivors of both crews are C. Wayne Beigel (*Brand* crew), Len Smith and Lou Loevsky (*Terry* crew). Lou lives in North Caldwell, NJ with a lovely lady, his sexy wife, Molly.

EDWARD T. LOGAN, was born July 10, 1922 in Cheshire, CT. He enlisted Nov. 2, 1942, served in the 8th Air Force, 93rd Bomb Group, 330th Sqdn. Stationed at Hardwick. Flew 11 missions, then interrupted by an appendix operation.

All of his service time was a memorable experience. Discharged Nov. 19, 1945 with the rank of second lieutenant and awarded the Air Medal.

Married Helen Coley, April 22, 1944, they have five children; nine (soon to be 10) grandchildren. He is semi-retired after 25 years with NCR. Now owns a telephone interconnect business, operated by his son Coley Logan.

GRAHAM A. LOGAN JR., was born in Selma, AL on Jan. 18, 1924; graduated Albert G. Parrish High School, June 1942. Enlisted in the Air Corps at Craig AFB, AL in October 1942; trained as radio operator, Air Corps Tech School, Stevens Hotel, Chicago and as aerial gunner, Buckingham AFB, Fort Myers, FL.

Joined James L. Erwin B-24 crew, Clovis AFB, NM in November 1943. Trained at Clovis, Pueblo AFB, CO and Langley AFB, VA; picked up B-24 at Mitchell AFB, NY in February 1944 and flew to England. Assigned to the 8th Air Force, 453rd Bomb Group, 735th Bomb Sqdn., Old

Buckingham. Flew 33 combat missions and returned to U.S. in September 1944.

Entered officers training, Fort Benning, GA in November 1946 and was commissioned second lieutenant Signal Corps, May 1947.

Served overseas in Korea, Gen. MacArthur's Headquarters, Japan; Eniwetok Island, Okinawa; Puerto Rico and Vietnam. Major assignments in U.S. were chief, DA Cryptographic Center, Pentagon; Combat Developments Command, Fort Leavenworth, KS; chief, Signal Division Field Command Defense Atomic Support Agency, Sandia Base, NM; and director, Communication Operation Department Signal School, Fort Gordon, GA.

Military awards are Legion of Merit with cluster, Distinguished Flying Cross, Air Medal with three clusters, Joint Service Commendation Medal, Army Commendation Medal with cluster and nine other theater and service medals.

Retired as colonel July 1971 with over 28 years service. Since retirement, employed as navy auditor, and for 14 years the central accounting officer for Fort Gordon.

Married his high school sweetheart, Nell Chappelle, September 1945; they have two sons and seven grandchildren. He and his wife make their home in Augusta, GA.

JAMES J. LONG, was born Dec. 7, 1924 in Barnesboro, PA. On Dec. 11, 1942 he enlisted in the USAAF, 453rd Bomb Group and 466th Bomb Group, 2nd Air Div., 8th Air Force; basic training, Miami Beach; aviation student, Akron University; pre-flight, San Antonio, TX; primary flight, Ballinger, TX; basic flight, Sherman-Dennison, TX; twin engine advanced, Ellington Field, TX; B-24 flight, Fort Worth, TX; operations, Tucson, AZ.

Sent to England January 1945, stationed at Attleborough and Attlebridge. Flew 16 missions with the 453rd Bomb Group. He was transferred to the 466th Bomb Group where he flew one mission before the end of the war. He took part in the battles of Ardennes, Central Europe and Rhineland. Participated in fly back to U.S. via Wales, Iceland, Labrador, arriving Bradley Field, CT, June 1945.

Discharged Oct. 8, 1945 with the rank of first lieutenant; B-24 pilot MOS 1092. He received the Air Medal with two clusters.

Long has one son (deceased), one daughter and seven step-children. Retired owner/operator of Long Funeral Home, Inc., Barnesboro, PA. He is enjoying retirement with his wife Susie.

ORVILLE K. LONG, was born Oct. 19, 1919 at Forest Lake, MN and was raised on a dairy farm. He graduated from high school at Forest Lake on June 1, 1939. He joined the Army Air Corps Jan. 21, 1941 as a private and went through Airplane Mechanics School at Chanute Field, IL. Entered aviation cadets in September 1942 and graduated as a pilot and second lieutenant on May 20, 1943 in the Class of 43-E at Stockton Field, CA.

He trained as a pilot in B-24s at Tarrant County Airport (now Carswell AFB), Ft. Worth, TX. After a short training period with the 459th Bomb Group at Tucson, AZ, transferred to an RTU (Replacement Training Unit) at Gowen Field, Boise, ID where he picked up his combat crew.

Flight to England in a B-24 as aircraft commander via Goose Bay, Labrador landing at Knotts Corner, Northern Ireland on July 4, 1944. After pre-combat training he joined the 453rd at Old Buckingham.

Lt. Long flew 30 combat missions over Germany as a lead pilot. Last mission was Brunswick, Germany on March 31, 1945.

After receiving the Distinguished Flying Cross, four Air Medals, four Campaign Stars, and a promotion to captain, he returned to the States on the French liner *Ile de France*.

He separated from the service on Aug. 27, 1946. Subsequently recalled on April 1, 1951, he flew P-51s, B-29s, B-36s, B-47s and the Lockheed C-130 before retiring on June 1, 1967 as a lieutenant colonel in the USAF.

He married on Air Force nurse, 1st Lt. Lovey Telenson, on Nov. 26, 1952 at March AFB, Riverside, Ca. They have five children and 10 grandchildren.

WILLIAM S. LONG, was born Jan. 17, 1921 in Portland, OR. He graduated from the University of Idaho in June 1942 and enlisted in the USAAC in August 1942. He was sent to Santa Ana, February 1943; completed navigator training, Hondo, TX as second lieutenant March 1942; assigned Caspar, WY for combat crew training; then with his crew to 392nd Bomb Group, Wendling, England July 1943.

Ditched on 19th mission, Sept. 11, 1944 and returned to U.S. January 1945. Assigned Santa Monica Redistribution Station and Ft. George Wright, until placed on active reserve April 1946. Recalled April 1951 with 22nd Bomb Group, March AFB, CA. He served until February 1953; continued in reserve and retired as lieutenant colonel January 1981.

Married May 1943 to Viola Miller; they have two children and three grandchildren. Acquired master of social work degree from the University of Southern California, June 1948.

He retired from California Department of Mental Health after 31 years of various treatment, supervisory and administrative duties.

JOSEPH LONGO, was born Jan. 22, 1924 in Racine, WI. He attended Armorer School at Lowry Field, Gunnery School at Harlingen, TX and overseas training at Tucson, AZ. He was attached to the 448th Bomb Group at Seething.

He flew 30 missions and received the Distinguished Flying Cross, Purple Heart with cluster, Air Medal with four clusters and the European Theater of Operations Medal with four Battle Stars. He was discharged as a staff sergeant in 1945.

Longo received a BS, MS, and doctorate in vocational-technical administration. He married his wife, Phyllis, in 1948, they have two sons, one daughter and five granddaughters. He retired from the Milwaukee Area Technical College as special assistant to the district director in 1983.

Dr. Longo remained in the Wisconsin Air National Guard after the war as a reservist and retired in 1970 as a lieutenant colonel.

ANTON J. LOOMAN

ROBERT MELTON LOONEY, enlisted February 1943 in the USAAF; received advanced twin-engine training, Columbus, MS; co-pilot training, Panama City, FL. He joined the 564th Sqdn., 389th Bomb Group at Hethel Air Base, Norwich, England in February 1945.

Flew five missions, including the last bombing mission of the 8th over Selzburg. His memorable experience was his first bombing mission. B-17s erred on base peg, made correction and bombed through B-24s. The squad in front of them lost five out of nine planes.

Discharged Oct. 9, 1945 with the rank of second lieutenant. Married 45 years, he has four children and seven grandchildren. He retired at 71 and is now playing golf and gardening.

ALEX K. LOPEZ, was born Aug. 17, 1921. He enlisted in the USAAF on Nov. 9, 1942 at Camp Cook in California; went to Douglas, AZ and after basic training, he went to Mechanics School, then to Pickenham, England where he was assigned to the 93rd Bomb Group (H).

He was assigned to the plane named *Rage in Haven*. They stayed there until the end of the war in June 1945. His memorable experience was when a German fighter plane came out of the sun and strafed our air base and bombed four airplanes.

In 1951 enlisted for Korea as a motor pool mechanic. He was discharged in August 1952 with the rank of corporal. Awarded Good Conduct Medal, European Campaign Medal and Presidential Unit Citation.

After the service, Lopez took a test to become a street car conductor, in 1957 changed over to bus driver. He retired in 1982.

Lopez is married and has one daughter.

JAMES H. LORENZ, was born Dec. 3, 1923 in Elkhart, IN. He enlisted in the USAAC on Nov. 28, 1942 while attending Kalamazoo College; graduated pilot, second lieutenant, Class 44-C at Marfa, TX. Assigned co-pilot on B-24 crew, accepted a new B-24J at Topeka and flew to England, where he was assigned to the 466th Bomb Group, 785th Sqdn. at Attlebridge in August 1944.

He completed a tour of 35 missions, last five as instructor pilot taking new crews on their first missions. Received five Air Medals, five European Campaign Stars and Presidential Unit Citation.

After V-E day, he had points to request inactive duty July 1945; graduated from the University of Michigan in 1948. Resigned from reserves as captain in September 1957.

He retired from Union Carbide Corporation after 35 years as a chemist and director of renewable energy contracts. Married Mary Burton Oct. 14, 1950 and has two children and three grandchildren.

IRVING ROBERT LORING, was born Nov. 1, 1924 in Madison, WI. Enlisted in the USAF December 1942 as navigator/bombardier. Assigned to 93rd Bomb Group, 409th Sqdn. 2nd Air Div., Hardwick, England.

Memorable experiences: combat with 8th Air Force over Europe and his first mission to Berlin; dropping supplies at 100 feet at crossing of Rhine.

Discharged September 1945 with the rank second lieutenant. Received the Air Medal and ETO.

Married Adeline and has four children and four grandchildren. Graduated from University of Wisconsin. Loring is currently retired.

JOHN F. LOSEE, was born in Providence, RI on Sept. 13, 1914. Called to active duty upon the induction of the 152nd Observation Rhode Island National Guard, Nov. 25, 1940 as a second lieutenant pilot. Served the next two years with tow target, observation and reconnaissance units and rose to captain rank.

Attended Four-engine (B-17) School, Lockbourne Air Base, OH. Then to heavy bomb RTU (B-24) at Clovis, NM. Picked there to command embryo 856th Sqdn., 492nd Bomb Group (H), Oct. 24, 1943. Combat flight training at Alamogordo, NM, and promoted to major.

Departed April 11, 1944 from WPB via the southern route to the United Kingdom, 8th Air Force, 2nd Air Div., Northern Pickenham, England. On the seventh mission, June 20, 1944 while leading 492nd group, observed the shoot down of the entire 11 aircraft of the 856th squadron of which I was the commanding officer. Continuing as group air commander and as one of four additional aircraft taken out over the target (Politz), severely damaged, landed at Malmo, Sweden to become interned. Through U.S. Air Attache, Stockholm, managed early repatriation and return to England. Found 492nd group to be disbanded. Sought return to combat unit, assigned 1st Div., 92nd Bomb Group (H) (B-17); forced to bail out first return mission over Belgium. On return to England flew (a record) four successive missions. Transferred 3rd Air Div., 96th Bomb Group (H) (B-17), no position vacancy. Transferred 3rd Air Div., 95th Bomb Group (H) (B-17). Assigned commanding officer 335th Sqdn., promoted to lieutenant colonel.

Following Germany's surrender, returned to the U.S. Attended Instrument Instructors School, Byron, TX. Assigned director of training and operation, Columbus, MS.

Probably the only 8th Air Force officer to command both B-17 and B-24 squadrons, fly four successive combat missions, serve in all three air divisions, four groups, 8th Air Force, become highest ranking internee-Sweden, voluntarily obtain early repatriation-Sweden and voluntarily return to combat following repatriation.

Departed active duty July 30, 1946 for opportunity in civilian aviation. Received the Silver Star (Politz mission), Distinguished Flying Cross, four Air Medals, Croix de Guerre, American Defense Service Medal with one Bronze Star, EAME with six Bronze Stars, Presidential Unit Citation, American Campaign Medal and Victory Medal of World War II.

Spent the next thirty-five years in corporate aviation. He is retired, married with five children and six grandchildren.

CHARLES F. LOTSCH was born Jan. 25, 1923 in New York City. Enlisted Dec. 8, 1942 while attending Polytechnic Institute of Brooklyn as a mechanical engineering student. Completed aviation cadet training and was commissioned second lieutenant on April 7, 1944 at San Marcos AAF Navigation School.

Assigned navigator on a B-24 crew, and trained at Casper, WY. New B-24J flown from Topeka to Stone, Wales. Crew assigned to 93rd Bomb Group, 409th Sqdn. at Hardwick, July 30, 1944.

Completed 30 combat missions, including two air division leads, two wing leads and eight group leads. Awarded

Air Medal and four clusters. He was discharged in June 1945 as first lieutenant.

He returned to college and graduated June 1947 with a bachelor of mechanical engineering degree. After a 43 year career in engineering and management positions, he retired from Certainteed Corporation as director of engineering in October 1990.

Lotsch married Doris Shuster, Aug. 5, 1950; they have three children and two grandchildren.

GEORGE W. LOUTSCH, was born Feb. 22, 1917 in St. Paul, MN. He joined the U.S. Army in 1942 and transferred to the Air Corps Cadet Program in 1943. He graduated from the Pan American School of Navigation, University of Miami on April 22, 1944 and commissioned a second lieutenant.

He flew 29 combat missions with the 93rd Bomb Group from Hardwick, England. His most memorable mission was as lead navigator on the Rhine Crossing supply mission with Col. Brown, command pilot.

Received Distinguished Flying Cross, Air Medal with three Oak Leaf Clusters and four European Campaign Stars. He continued in the Reserves retiring in 1966 with the rank of major.

Loutsch completed 32 years with the USDA retiring in 1973 as assistant director of personnel. He married Maree Muller on Jan. 5, 1946 in St. Paul, MN; they have seven children and eight grandchildren. He resides in Greenbelt, MD.

THOMAS STAFFORD LOVE JR., was born Oct. 5, 1920 in Ashville, NC. He enlisted in the USAAC on Jan. 3, 1942 and served in the 2nd Air Div. HQ.

Military locations/stations: Horshman St. Faith and Ketterham Hall and Old Catton in Norwich, Norfolk, England-three years.

Was discharged in August 1945 with the rank of sergeant.

Love married twice, has three sons and two granddaughters. Private investments in Dallas, TX occupy his time today.

ANDREW STEVENSON LOW JR., began his military career on June 1, 1936 in his hometown of Westerly, RI when he enlisted as a private in the local National Guard Unit, Battery E, 243rd Coast Artillery (HD). Thirty-five years later, he was placed on the retired list, USAF, as a major general.

Born to Scottish immigrant parents, Andy completed public schools, attended Rhode Island College of Education for three years, was accepted to enter West Point after multiple tries, with waivers for color blindness and underweight standards.

Upon graduation in 1942, he entered pilot training, despite his earlier waivers. Permitted to graduate and accept pilot's wings, he was medically classified, "Limited service, unfit for combat." Despite this, he completed four-engine pilot and all phases of combat-crew training on the B-17. Pulled off his crew for medical reasons, he was designated instructor at Casper, WY, in a B-17 RTU.

"Found" by the newly-designated commander of the 453rd Bomb Group (H), who promised to "handle" the "limited service" problem, he reported to Pocatello as assistant group operations officer after a 10-day course on the B-24.

Next training phases were at March Field, from which he departed in January for Old Buckenham, East Anglia. The 453rd was a unit of the 2nd Combat Wing, 2nd Air Div., the mighty eighty!

As staff officer, then commander, 735th Sqdn., and finally as director of operations, he flew principally as a command pilot, at Wing, Division, and once leading the entire 8th Air Force, while still a captain. He was promoted to major just two years after graduating from West Point.

On July 31, 1944, while leading the 2nd Air Div. against Ludwigshaven (his 16th mission), his PFF aircraft was brought down by anti-aircraft fire. He was taken POW as he landed east of the Rhine River.

After a difficult interrogation, and despite serious burn wounds, he was transferred to the infamous Stalag Luft III, from whence had come the "great escape" some five months earlier. After hospitalization, he was incarcerated in North Compound, a British POW Camp. As a major, AC, he was given command of a barracks and became a member of the camp council.

On Jan. 25, 1945, the camp was evacuated in the face of the oncoming Russians. A six-day hike in below-freezing temperatures took heavy casualties in both the prisoner ranks and the German guards. The route of march was choked by refugees fearing the approaching enemy. Reaching a railhead, Muskow, the prisoners were transferred to railway cars, and began a retreat to Nuremburg, passing through Dresden en route. A week later Dresden was heavily bombed.

In Nuremburg, the POWs were quartered in barracks a scant three kilometers (1.86 mile) from the main railroad station. The prisoners' council protested the location as a shield to a military objective. On Feb. 20, 1945, the mighty 8th attacked the city, that night the RAF followed, and on the 21st the 8th returned. Miraculously, none of the prisoners of war received serious wounds as shrapnel and falling flak peppered the compound, bringing plaster ceilings down in some barracks.

Responding to the POWs charges of disregarding the Geneva convention quarantees, the camp was evacuated, and in 10 days the march to Moosburg (91 miles) was completed.

On April 29, 1945, the 14th Armd. Div., USA, overran the camp, and the liberation was complete. Major Low, USAAC, returned to CONUS and began a long career in military-politico assignments. He served long years in Strategic Air Command, culminating in his command of the 40th Bomb Wing (B-47).

Many years of his career were spent in the Pentagon, and finally on March 1, 1971, he was placed on the retirement roster as a major general, almost 35 years after his enlistment as a private.

As Andy says, "In retrospect, I have seen it all!"

GERALD LOWENTHAL, was born in November 1919 in Elkhart, IN. He enlisted Oct. 17, 1941 in the USAAF; original cadre, 506th Bomb Sqdn.; graduated OCS June 15, 1942, Miami, FL.

Military locations/stations: Wendover Field, UT; Pueblo, CO; Shipdham U.K.; LeBorget, Paris, France; Nancy, France; Munich, Germany.

Memorable to him is seeing the damage done by the Air Force in Germany.

Discharged in Jan. 1, 1946 with the rank of captain. He received 13 Battle Stars, Unit Dist. Ribbon with Oak Leaf Cluster and the American Theater Campaign Medal.

Lowenthal is married, has three children, three grandchildren and three boxers (dogs). He is retired and enjoys restoring a 1966 Rolls Royce.

FRANKLIN D. LOWN JR., was born in Cotulla, TX, July 23, 1920. Most of his pre-college school years were spent in San Antonio, TX graduating from Harlandale High School in 1937. He entered Texas A & M University, College Station, TX in the fall of 1937 and graduated with a BS degree in agriculture education in June 1941.

Immediately following graduation from the university, Lown was appointed as an aviation cadet in the USAAC. He was commissioned a second lieutenant in February 1942 after successfully completing pilot training at Randolph AAF and Brooks AAF in Texas.

After completion of bomber combat crew training, he was assigned to a combat group training for overseas deployment and moved with the 93rd Bomb Group to England in September 1942. After flying 25 combat missions (approximately 200 combat flying hours) in B-24 type aircraft over France, North Africa, Sicily, Italy and Germany; Lown was shot down over Brest, France April 16, 1943, was captured immediately and remained a POW until liberation in April 1945.

Lown was on continuous active duty with the USAF from July 1941 until retirement in 1970. He served in many and varied assignments from squadron level to HQ USAF and organization of the Joint Chiefs of Staff. The majority of Lown's military service experience was as a staff officer in a supervisory capacity from branch chief to deputy chief of staff at the major air command level. He served in the Washington, DC area for five years on the Joint Staff and HQ USAF Staff. His overseas service (other than WWII) included a tour (33 months) in Norway on the NATO staff of Allied Air Forces Northern Europe, two and one half years with HQ, USAF, Europe at Wiesbaden, Germany, and a Southeast Asia tour (one year) with HQ, 7th Air Force in South Vietnam. He completed his third tour on the staff of Headquarters Tactical Air Command, Langley AFB, VA upon retirement Aug. 31, 1970.

Service schools attended by Lown while in the Air Force included the Air Tactical School at Tyndall AAF, FL, 1947; the Air Command and Staff School, Maxwell AFB, AL, 1951; the jet indoctrination course, Craig AFB, AL 1954; the air weapons course, Maxwell AFB, Alabama 1955; and the Armed Forces Staff College, Norfolk, VA 1958.

While in the Air Force, Lown was a command pilot with over 5,500 flying hours in over 15 different aircraft types. His awards and decorations include the Legion of Merit with one Oak Leaf Cluster, Distinguished Flying Cross, Air Medal with three Oak Leaf Clusters, Joint Service Commendation Medal, Purple Heart, American Defense Service Medal, American Campaign Medal with Bronze Service Star, EAME, Army of Occupation Medal with Airlift Device, National Defense Service Medal with one Bronze Service Star, Vietnam Service Medal with two Bronze Stars and the Air Force Longevity Service Award with five Oak Leaf Clusters. He was authorized to wear the Italian pilots wings by the Italian Air Force. Retired Aug. 31, 1970 with the rank colonel.

Immediately following retirement from the USAF, Lown entered the Graduate College at Texas A & M University and completed the requirements for a master's degree in education psychology and a vocational counselor certificate. He took a position with the Bryan Independent School District in August 1971 to develop a computer model for a system approach to placement and follow-up for former vocational education students. In the fall of 1973, Lown was given the job to coordinate the computer processing of administrative activities for the Bryan Independent School District. This involved the operation of a remote job entry terminal at Bryan High School and processing data from the business office and 14 schools in the district. This data involved finance, bills payable, inventory, personnel, utilities, student attendance accounting, student scheduling, student grade reporting, attendance zones, bilingual and other data for specified needs. He remained in this position until he retired from the system in June 1986.

He is the son or Mr. and Mrs. Franklin D. Lown (deceased) of Brenham, TX. He is married to the former Marceia Jolley of Fort Worth, TX. They had three sons: David, John and Kevin, deceased. Lown and his wife currently reside in Bryan, TX.

BILL LOZOWSKI, was born in Northern Wisconsin, April 7, 1921. Joined the Army in 1942; commissioned a pilot while at Blackland Air Base, TX; and advanced to Liberator bomber pilot. He married the beautiful Iris Thompson of Waco on July 9, 1944 in El Paso.

In August 1944 Bill and crew departed from Topeka, KS to become part of the 93rd Bomb Group, 328th Sqdn., Hardwick Airdrome, Norfolk, England.

After completing over 25 missions to Germany, Bill and his crew were sent to an English mansion for some R&R. While the amenities were wonderful there, Bill was anxious to return to Hardwick and complete more missions so he could eventually return home to his wife who was expecting their first baby in April.

On Feb. 3, 1945, which was their 30th mission, a problem with No. 3 engine developed, and they had difficulty feathering it. They salved their bombs to lighten their load, when suddenly, they were hit by flak. They began losing altitude rapidly and the order to "bail out" was given. Six crew members were able to bail out, but some were too close to the ground for their parachutes to open and they perished. Bill was among those. There were three survivors who became prisoners of war for the duration of the war. The deceased were temporarily buried in a cemetery at Benthe,

Germany; Bill was later returned to his final resting place in Weyerhauser, WI.

Bill's son, also named Bill, is a scientific specialist for Cyclotron Targets at the University of Indiana and has two daughters, Dana and Jennifer. *Writen and submitted by his niece, Carol Lozowski Gerard.*

LENARD H.E. LUDWIG, was born Sept. 25, 1914 at Alcester, SD. He enlisted in the USAAC on Feb. 5, 1942 at Ft. Des Moines, IA as a private. He was promoted to corporal (T) on June 1, 1942 in the 44th Bomb Group as a teletype operator.

He departed for overseas duty in September 1942 aboard the *Queen Mary.* Ludwig entered Officer Candidate School and was commissioned second lieutenant on Oct. 8, 1943 and served with HQ 2nd Air Div., 8th Air Force and served as technical supply officer.

Decorations and service ribbons received during his overseas tour were: Normandy, Air Offensive Europe, Northern France, Rhineland, Ardennes, Central Europe, EAME and Good Conduct Medal. He returned to the U.S. and was separated as first lieutenant, USAAC at Sioux Falls, SD on Nov. 9, 1945

He owned and operated Ludwig Insurance Àgency in Yankton, SD for 35 years. Lenard married Gladys Johnson on July 15, 1945 and has two sons and seven grandchildren. He passed away Sept. 1, 1980.

JOHN L. LUFT, was born Oct. 16, 1920, Tremont, IL. Drafted Sept. 7, 1942, took basic infantry training at Camp Wheeler, GA. Cadets application received; went to S.E. Training Command November 1942. Graduated pilot training at George Field, IL, Aug. 30, 1943. (43H). Joined 458th Group for co-pilot training (B-24) at Boise, then to Wendover and Tonapah.

Left the States as group in January 1944, to Horsham St. Faith, England. Completed required 31 missions; sent to Lynam, England; then to Chartres, France to haul gas and cargo (B-24) close to front lines. Once they R.O.N. at St. Trond, Belgium. The next morning they went from town to base; everything gone but their planes. In England discovered Germans had recaptured St. Trond overnight; by-passed us.

Spent Christmas and New Years, 1944, on USS *Richardson* coming home for leave; then sent to Waco for Instructors School, then to Memphis, TN, ATC Ferry Command.

After release in December 1945, farmed and worked for the State Highway Department. Since retiring, he keeps busy gardening, fishing, and traveling.

CLARENCE A. LUHMANN, was born April 27, 1922 in Northrop, MN and grew up on a farm. He enlisted in the USAAF on Aug. 21, 1942 with training at Santa Ana, CA.; Twenty-nine Palms, CA; Pecos, TX; Williams Field at Chandler, AZ; Casper, WY.

Flew overseas with a new B-24, southern route to England and assigned to the 445th Bomb Group, 703rd Sqdn. Flew 35 missions as a co-pilot. First mission May 15, 1944 and last mission Aug. 5, 1944.

Returned to USA in August 1944 and was given medical retirement with the rank of first lieutenant. He received the Air Medal with clusters and the Distinguished Flying Cross.

Married Winnefred Ottman, Sept. 25, 1943, they have three daughters and eight grandchildren. He is now retired from farming and construction work.

ROBERT J. LUMPKIN, was born May 8, 1923 in Richmond, VA. He joined the USAAF on Feb. 25, 1943; basic

training, Miami Beach, FL; Aerial Gunnery School, Las Vegas, NV; Bombardier School, Carlesbad, NM; crew training, Tonopah, NV.

He received orders for England, 8th Air Force; stationed at Old Buckingham. Flew 30 combat missions as bombardier in B-24, lead crew. After completing his missions he was sent to Midland AAB, TX for retraining for Pacific War.

When the war ended, he was discharged at Goldsboro, NC, October 1945 with the rank of first lieutenant.

He returned to school at the University of Richmond receiving a BS degree in English and education. Attended Graduate School and received his law degree. Spent nine years with the Federal Bureau of Investigation. Retired from the Department of Defense as chief trial attorney at Defense General Supply Center, Richmond, VA.

Lumpkin passed away April 29, 1993. He is survived by his wife, six children, five stepchildren and 15 grandchildren.

ROY A. LUNDQUIST, was born in Chicago, IL on Feb. 27, 1921 and grew up in Evergreen Park, IL. He entered the USAAF on Oct. 15, 1942. After basic training at Jefferson Barracks, he was sent to Armament School at Lowry Field. After further training at Las Vegas and Davis Monthan AFB, his crew left the States from Lincoln, NE on Sept, 12, 1943 in a new B-24 and flew to Scotland, then to Norwich.

Flew 25 missions with the 567th Sqdn., 389th Bomb Group. On the 25th mission they were hit over Palia De Calais and two engines were knocked out; but they managed to reach Ipswich in England. After crash landing, the crew escaped and the plane burned, everything was burnt except the engines. They went home on R&R for 90 days, and returned to England for a few more missions, then back to the States again until the war ended.

He received the EAME with five Bronze Stars, Air Medal with three Oak Leaf Clusters and the Distinguished Flying Cross.

Lundquist was married in Las Vegas Feb. 27, 1943. He has two children, five grandchildren and two great-grandchildren.

WILL LUNDY, was was born Aug. 10, 1917 in Malad, ID, then returned to the family hometown of Lancaster, CA where he grew up. After graduating from UCLA, he was drafted on Nov. 11, 1941 and immediately enlisted for three years.

He graduated from Keesler Field, MS as aircraft mechanic; assigned to 44th Bomb Group, 67th Sqdn. at Barksdale Field, LA. Went overseas on *Queen Mary* and was permanently based at Shipdham, England, Oct. 10, 1942.

Served as assistant crew chief for two years, promoted to assistant inspector August 1944. Returned to the U.S. via combat B-24 *Iron Corset* which completed 129 missions, most missions of any Liberator in the 44th Bomb Group, and probably in the 2nd Div. Flights made from Valley, Wales, Iceland, Greenland and Bradley Field, CT.

Was discharged the end of September 1945.

EDWARD T. LUSZCZ, was born Aug. 13, 1921 in Youngstown, OH. He was drafted into the Army Signal Corps on Sept. 22, 1942.

Stationed in Camp Crowder, MO where he trained as radio operator and promoted to tech/4 sergeant before transferring to USAAC on April 1, 1943.

Went through aviation cadet training in Santa Ana AB (preflight); Tulare, CA (primary); Merced, CA (basic) and

graduated in Douglas, AZ as multi-engined pilot in February 1944 (Class 44-B).

Trained as B-24 co-pilot at Muroc, CA and departed for England on the *Queen Elizabeth,* arriving in Glasgow, Scotland on D-day, June 6, 1944. Flew 35 missions over France, Germany, Austria and Belgium from Seething Air Base, 712th Bomb Sqdn., 448th Bomb Group.

Returned home to USA on Christmas Day, 1944; assigned to Bryan Instrument Flying School, Bryan, TX, where he became instrument instructor. He was discharged on Aug. 2, 1945 with the rank of first lieutenant. Received three European Campaign Stars, Distinguished Flying Cross and Air Medal with four Oak Leaf Clusters.

Graduated from Youngstown (OH) College with a BS degree in physics in 1948; and Syracuse (NY) University with a MS degree in physics in 1951. Retired from Northrop Corporation, Anaheim, CA in 1986.

Married to Jane, they have five children, eight grandchildren and one great-grandchild.

WILLIAM B. LYBARGER, was born Sept. 9, 1922 in Albuquerque, NM; worked for Consolidated Aircraft, San Diego; entered service in January 1943.

As a tech. sergeant, he was B-24 radio operator in Gus Konstand's 711 lead crew, serving in the 857th Sqdn. of the ill-fated 492nd Bomb Group and 68th Sqdn., 44th Bomb Group.

Lybarger's plane force-landed at Best, Holland, Sept, 18, 1944, and about his 28th combat mission, was shot down over Kaiserslautern on December 28th-five survived, seven were killed. As POW of Stalag XIII D, Nuremberg, he made a cold, forced march in January to VII A at Moosburg. He was liberated on April 29, 1945.

He attended college, married Phyllis Lutz; had daughters, Cynthia and Cheryl, and lived in Santa Clara, CA. He was a Lockheed reliability analyst at the time of his death, Oct. 9, 1969. He is buried in the veterans' section of the Oak Hill Cemetery, San Jose, CA.

GEORGE H. LYMBURN, During World War II, he was a pilot of the four-engine B-24. On a Berlin mission, his plane was hit by flak and burst into flames. He crash landed the bomber and was captured. During the next 14 months as a POW, he formed a theater group. His interest in theater has continued from that moment to the present time.

Has over 50 films including *The Natural* with Robert Redford; *Lover Come Back, The Outsider, A Gathering of Eagles, Get Crazy, Mr. Mom, Under Pressure, Forever One, Still Smokin, The Man Who Never Was* and *War Hunt.*

All major networks including *Cagney and Lacey, The Grace Kelly Story, Concrete Beat* and *Buffalo Bill,* commercials for Sunnyside-Up Productions, Pepsi Cola, Playboy Channel, and Ripley. Appeared in 18 Playhouse 90 productions with Paul Newman, George C. Scott, Charles Bronson, Richard Boone and Anthony Quinn.

Stage credits include: Broadway, *Stalag 17, Cyrano de Bergerac* with Jose Ferrer. Summer theater, seven years as resident actor. Plays, over 60 total parts as a summer stock actor, including appearances with Richard Kiley, Christopher Plummer, Olivia de Haviland, and Tony Perkins. Best actor award, Walter Burns in *The Front Page.*

Education: Yale Drama School, The Neighborhood Playhouse, The American Theater Wing, Rollins College-B.A. in Theater Arts; UCLA-graduate division motion pictures.

Special Abilities: Golf (seven handicap), mime/dance, all sports, photography, fencing, film producer.

To fly, to be a pilot. Ah, that was the lofty ambition of many young men raised in the 1920s and 30s. It certainly was Lymburn's.

Remember those wonderful balsa wood airplane kits? For ten cents? All the precious hours carving them out with razor blades, applying the dope, the sandpaper, the paint, and the decals? Then flying them on WWI missions? Wonderful!

And the movies; *Ceiling Zero, Dawn Patrol, Test Pilot*. How they did flame the imagination.

Did you ever read the pulp magazine, *G-8 and His Battle Aces*? More inspiration!

Yet, somehow after graduating from high school, Lymburn ended up working at Woolworths in Plymouth, MA. A grounded job.

December 7, 1941, the world would never be the same. Nor would any of their lives. Most significantly to him at the time, the age to be an aviation cadet was dropped from 21 to 18, and two years of college waived.

Lymburn was in line saying, "Where do I sign up?"

Seldom do we have the opportunity as adults to reach back into those childhood dreams and bring them to reality.

His solo flight in a PT-17 was more than he imagined. He was a WWI Ace, looking for the Red Baron. He laughed with joy. He went around twice because he could not or would not stop.

He was flying! He was a pilot!

Graduating in the Class of 43-B, Lymmburn was assigned to a cadre forming the 445th Bomb Group.

His crew went to England in December of 1943. There were 16 original crews in the 701st Sqdn. Six months later, only two had survived. The rest were either dead or prisoners of war.

On March 6, 1944, his crew flew on the first major daylight raid to Berlin. It was his crew's 12th mission.

A few moments after dropping their bombs they received a direct hit from flak. The plane caught fire, the crew bailed out. Theirs was one of 68 bombers to be shot down on that single day.

When Lymburn went to the bomb bay to jump, he found he was paralyzed. By now the ship was in a steep spiral. He struggled back to the controls and knew if he drew one more breath, he would die. Terror went through his body like an electric shock.

He managed to pull the plane out of its spiral, level it off, and crash land in a field. A group of civilians took him captive and he was interned the next 14 months as a POW in Stalag Luft I.

He had no fear of flying his missions. That adage in the Bible is a fact, "Pure love drivest out fear." And Lymburn truely loved to fly. That love was driven out by terror. It is quite true when one says, "The first casualty of war is innocence."

Innocence is what so many of them lost at the age of 20, 21 or 22. And for him, having lost that quality, his life was forever altered. Innocence is a most precious thing.

In 1983 Lymburn's son, Bruce, found a picture of the plane *God Bless Our Ship* that crashed landed in Germany. The Luftwaffe had taken pictures of the B-24 and one found its way into Roger Freeman's *The Mighty Eighth*.

Through the encouragement of his son, Lymburn had the unusual opportunity to redeem himself and gain a bit of that innocence back.

For 40 years he had been holding the belief he should have bailed out of the aircraft.

On March 6, 1984, exactly 40 years later to the day, Lymburn did parachute from a plane. His son Bruce and God were his witnesses.

JOHN P. LYNES, was born Feb. 5, 1922 in Elizabeth, NJ. He enlisted in the USAAC on March 11, 1942 and served the 2nd Air Div., 445th Bomb Group.

Military locations/stations: Tibenham, Norwich, England.

Discharged Jan. 17, 1946 with the rank of staff sergeant. Awarded Purple Heart, Air Medal and Croix de Guerre.

Married Marguerite and has three children: Joanne, Robert and Martha. Lynes passed away Dec. 5, 1991.

RAYMOND LYTLE JR., was born in Mount Sterling, PA on Nov. 27, 1923. Entered the USAAC in December 1941; attended Airplane Mechanic School at Chanute Field; after graduating sent to Las Vegas to Aerial Gunnery School, was kept there as an instructor; from there to Kingman, AZ and opened the school there. From Arizona, he volunteered for overseas duty, went to Hamilton Field in San Francisco, to West Palm Beach to Trinadad, Bellem, South America, to Dakar, Africa to Mearkech, Africa; to Horsham St. Faith.

He completed a 35 mission tour. Returned to States and discharged at Fort Sam Houston, TX, Sept. 30, 1945 with the rank of staff sergeant. Received Distinguished Flying Cross, Air Medal with five Oak Leaf Clusters and several other medals.

After 29 years he retired (due to throat cancer) as an account executive at a television station. Now partner and he are running small chocolate truffle company.

Lytle married Pearl Daugherty in 1943; they have a daughter Darlene and two granddaughters, Raylene and Jennifer.

JOSEPH LEON LYVERS, was born March 6, 1923 in Nelson County Kentucky. Attended school at Holy Cross, KY. Enlisted in USAAF on Oct. 21, 1942 at Fort Benjamin, Harrison, IN. Received basic training at Smyrna, TN. Graduated from Aircraft Mechanics School July 6, 1943 at Seymour Johnson Field, NC, where he also secretly married his hometown sweetheart, Marie Miles. After nine children, 12 grandchildren and two great-grandchildren, they are still happily married. From there he went on to Aerial Gunnery School at Buckingham Field, Fort Myers, FL.

Upon graduation spent seven days and nights on the good old coal burning military train to Wendover, UT, for crew assembly and combat training on B-24 type aircraft with the 467th Bomb Group. Upon completion all crews were assigned new aircraft and headed for England via South America, Africa, and French Morocco arriving in England 10 days after starting. Then to their combat base at Rackheath in East Anglia.

After several months which included air raids, buzz bombs, V-bombs, threats of German invasions, D-day and 31 missions, he returned to the good old U.S. wearing with his Silver Wings the Distinguished Flying Cross, Air Medal with three clusters and Purple Heart which he felt he didn't deserve after he saw what some others had to pay for the same award.

Furlough and unwind time before being sent to good old Laredo, TX for gunnery instructor training, which he had very little need for in his next assignments at Muroc, CA and Wenatchee, WA. By this time they were discharging and he had enough points to qualify for separation at Patterson Field, OH on Oct. 9, 1945.

Lyvers is a retired school teacher.

FLOYD H. MABEE, was born in Lafayette, NJ on June 9, 1920. Entered service Feb. 14, 1942; basic, Keesler Field, MS; assigned to new 93rd Bomb Group at Barksdale Field, LA. Attended flight engineer course. Crews were formed when the group moved to Fort Myers, FL. Training was flying submarine patrol over the Gulf of Mexico. Group was sent to Grenier Field, NH and picked up new B-24D's. Named theirs, *Shoot Luke*.

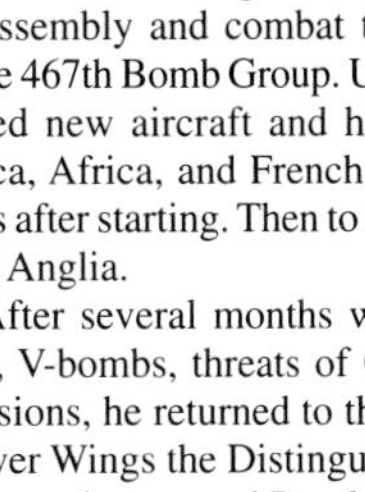

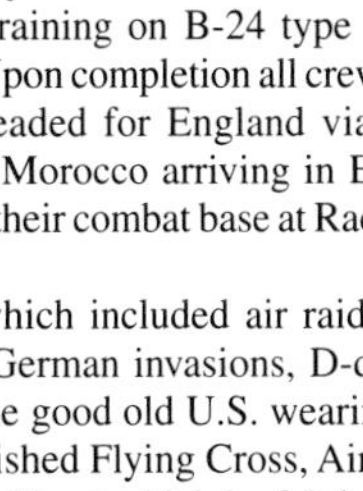

The 93rd was first group to fly overseas Sept. 7-9, 1942. Arrived at Alconbury, England. First mission Oct. 9, 1942. They were told to pack-up light as they were going away for 10 days. On Dec. 7, 1942 landed at Tafaroui, North Africa. It rained constantly and they lost one plane in the mud. Then flew to LG-109 in the Libya desert. The 10 day trip turned out to be three months, with no extra clothes. February 1943, he was promoted to tech sergeant/flight engineer.

On Feb. 25, 1943 they flew back to their new base Hardwick, England. March 18, 1943 was their big mission, Vegesack, Germany, with other B-24 groups and B-17 groups. They were under fighter attack an hour and forty-five minutes. The group took off again June 25, 1943 to Benchazi, Libya. They flew long missions, then July 19, 1943 the marshalling yards at Rome. On Aug. 1, 1943, they flew the Ploesti mission. That made 36 missions for him, and six of his original crew flew back to the States.

Mabee was sent to Pueblo, CO, group transferred to Westover Field, MA and he received promotion to master sergeant/flight chief, July 1944. Was discharged on points July 1, 1945. Awarded two Distinguished Flying Cross Medals, six Air Medals, Purple Heart and Good Conduct Medal. The 93rd Bomb Group received two Unit Citations.

Married Dorothy, July 4, 1944, they have one son and two grandchildren. He retired July 25, 1975 with 30 years government service, worked with the Department of Defense, chief of police.

DANTE J. MACARIO (DAN), served with 712th Sqdn. Primary crew assignment: nose gunner; secondary, waist gunner. Air ratings: first, gunner/radio operator; second, gunnery instructor.

Was with the 448th Bomb Group, 712th Sqdn. at Seething from July 9, 1944 to April 26, 1945. Completed 30 missions. First pilot was Sidney Williamson.

Years of service: active duty, two and one-half years; National Guard, eight months; Reserves, six years. He attained the rank of staff sergeant.

Macario is a building contractor. Married to Katheryn (Kitty). He enjoys golf and gardening. *Submitted by R. Carter Lee.*

RALPH L. MACCARONE, was born in Tuckahoe, NY, May 20, 1924. He entered the USAAC on June 23, 1942 after graduating high school. Following basic training in Atlantic City was assigned to the Pratt-Whitney Engine School in Flint, MI. Following graduation was transferred to Warner Robbins Field in Macon, GA to join replacements to the 8th Air Force in England.

First assignment was at the Honington Air Depot 595, later transferred to the 812th Air Engineering Sqdn., 375th Service Group at Rackheath. Was instrumental with opening the base for arrival of the 467th Bomb Group from the States. Served as ground support crew specializing in sheet metal structural repairs and rose through the ranks to staff sergeant.

Returned to the USA on July 11, 1945 and reclassified for redeployment to the South Pacific. Hostilities ceased and was discharged from Tucson, AZ.

Continuing his education and entering the automotive industry, he retired from Chrysler Corporation after 34 years in various management capacities. Married Agnes G. Intrieri, Nov. 2, 1947; they have a son, Ralph L. III, a daughter, Elena, and two grandchildren. He and his wife now reside in Southfield, MI

GORDON WILLIAM MACDONALD, was born Nov. 20, 1917 in Hardwick, VT. After an unsuccessful try at joining the Royal Canadian Air Force in 1940, enlisted in the 172nd Inf. Regt. of the 43rd Inf. Div. on Feb. 4, 1941. After a year as an infantryman was able to transfer to the USAAC. After being stationed at Nashville, TN, then Maxwell Field, AL, was assigned to the Southeast Training Command for pilot training. Received primary training at Arcadia, FL, basic at Macon, GA and graduated from advanced training at Blythville, AR and received his commission and Silver Wings on Aug. 30, 1943.

After B-24 transitional training at Smyrna, TN, was assigned to the "best crew in the 8th Air Force" at Salt Lake City, UT. Received operational training at Davis Monthan AFB, AZ and Pueblo AFB, CO before departing for overseas assignment in the spring of 1944. Flew new "Ford" B-24 via southern route (Trinidad, Brazil, Dakar, Morocco to

Metfield, UK). Missing in action on July 12, 1944, returned to England December 1944 and the USA January 1945.

In the spring of 1946, after attending Engineering School in Washington and instructing Chinese Air Force officers in instrument flying, attended Aerobatic School at Waco, TX and the "famous" Instrument School at Bryan, TX.

He was ordered overseas to Manila via Japan and was eventually assigned to 19th TCS at Hickam Field, Territory of Hawaii. Flew inter-island and various Pacific routes including Christmas Island, Fiji, Guadalcanal and Australia until 1948, and then spent one year on the Berlin Airlift.

After service at various stations in the U.S., separated from USAF at Carswell AFB, TX in early 1950. Attended Texas Technological University 1950-1954, graduating with a degree in architecture. After various stints in architectural offices in New York and California, including his own practice, retired as architect in 1987.

MALCOLM J. MACGREGOR, was born Feb. 24, 1923 in Albany, NY and was raised in Delhi, NY. Drafted in the Army and assigned to the 82nd Combat Engineers January 1943. Transferred to the USAAC in April; graduated as a second lieutenant bombardier, Class of 43-J, Big Spring, TX. Trained with a replacement crew in B-24s from January to April 1944 in Boise, ID and flew to Scotland via Iceland in a B-24, *The Heavenly Body*.

He flew his first mission on D-day. Flew 17 missions as a nose turret navigator and 17 as a deputy lead bombardier with the 445th Bomb Group. He flew with six different crews and was shot down on his 34th mission, to Kassel, Germany, Sept. 27, 1944. They lost 31 out of 35 bombers and 118 killed. This was the highest loss rate of any group on one mission. He spent the rest of the European war in Stalag Luft IA, Barth, Germany.

Discharged October 1945 with the rank of first lieutenant. Received Distinguished Flying Cross, Air Medal with three clusters, Purple Heart, ETO Ribbon with five Battle Stars and POW Medal.

Married Betty on July 8, 1945 and has four children and three grandchildren. He is now retired.

OAK MACKEY, was born July 22, 1922 near Okemah, Okfuskee County, OK; thus, they called him Oak. Entered Aviation Cadets January 1943, graduated April 1944 as a second lieutenant. Assigned as a co-pilot on a consolidated B-24 at Tonopah, NV, May-August 1944. Shipped overseas to England, August 1944 and assigned to the 392nd Bomb Group at Wendling, Norfolk.

First combat mission was to Hamm, Germany, October 2. Promoted to first lieutenant in December, 1944. Flak damage to the airplane on many missions. Crashed Jan. 10, 1945 at the 448th Bomb Group airfield; two runaway propellors, frosted windshields on landing approach; no crew injuries. Flew 35th and last mission April 7, 1945. Saw a Republic P-47 shoot down a Messerschmitt jet-propelled ME-262. Shipped back to the States in May 1945 and was discharged Aug. 13, 1945.

Employed as an airline pilot from May 1946 to July 22, 1982. He was with Republic Airlines from April 1950 to July 1982 (32 years). Retired at age 60.

Married Maxine Moore on Aug. 6, 1949, they have six children, six grandchildren and one great-grandson.

ROBERT L. MAGER, was born Nov. 9, 1924 in Chicago, IL. Entered the USAAF March 1943. Military locations/stations: Miami Beach; University of Buffalo, NY; Denver, CO; Laredo, TX; Hethel, England.

Memorable experience: Being assigned to combat duty with the 2nd Air Div., 389th Bomb Group, 565th Sqdn., Janu-

ary 1945 to June 1945. Being proud of honorably serving his country when needed.

Discharged Feb. 18, 1946 with the rank of staff sergeant. He received WWII Victory Medal, EAME with two Battle Stars, American Campaign Medal, Presidential Unit Citation and Good Conduct Medal.

Married Sept. 19, 1954 to Elsie F. Heenan, they have three children and three grandchildren. S/A Illinois State Police, Retired.

ARTHUR C. MAGILL, was born Feb. 28, 1917 in Scott City, KS. Went to Montreal in late summer of 1941 and enlisted with the British Air Ministry for radio location work. England, schooling, posted to the CHL early warning station RAF Torness Point.

The U.S. Government broke his enlistment and he joined the Army Signal Corps in London on Oct. 19, 1942. After the "shuffle," he settled down in 8th Air Force, 93rd Bomb Group (H), 409th Sqdn. as a "gee" mechanic.

February 1944 detached service to RAF Great Malvern to help construct a synthetic echo generator. May 1, 1944, transferred to the 4th Air Force. Spent a couple of months at MIF for more construction and it all came together in California.

Discharged, Lincoln, NE, Nov. 19, 1945 with the rank of tech sergeant.

Employed by Standard Oil of Indiana in the oil exploration and research departments for 30 years. Retired April 1977 and now lives in the pine woods of Montgomery County, TX with his wife Sandra.

CLEM L. MAHER, was born July 2, 1920 in O'Fallon, MO. Enlisted October 1942; pilot wings, Class of 44-C, Western Flying Training Command.

Overseas orders July 1944 to 448th Bomb Group, 8th Air Force in B-24 Liberator bomber.

Completed 35 combat missions (last Feb. 27, 1945). Decorated seven times, three battle stars. One emergency parachute jump. Flak damage at Worms, Germany, Jan. 13, 1945, on 27th mission. One close to out-of-control landing; several "engine out" landings. He is member of the Caterpillar Club.

Most thrilling mission was Operation Market Garden (A Bridge to Far), 9th mission. Oil reservoir hit with machine gun fire while in formation at 600 feet (yes, that's 600 feet, not 6,000!), spraying oil on hot engine parts. Stayed in formation, dropped cargo, started a climbing 180 and feathered. Climbed to 7,000 and landed at base in England.

Married Patricia Sweeney, December 1946; they have four daughters. He is a certified public accountant/lawyer. CPA in several states; attorney-at-law in Missouri, District of Columbia and Florida.

Partner in Price Waterhouse until June 1981. Adjunct professor of taxation, Washington University (St. Louis) 1982 and 1983; incorporator, president and CEO of A.G. Edwards Trust Company, 1983-1986 and 1987-1989. Now retired.

CLAUDE L. MAINE (LUCKY), was born July 11, 1925 in Gowanda, NY. Air Cadets Feb. 10, 1942; voluntary induction Feb. 9, 1943. Served USAAC/Air Force, gunner, ball turrett with 467th Bomb Group, 789th Sqdn.

Military locations/stations: Colorado Springs, CO; Laredo, TX; Jefferson Barracks, MO; Atlantic City, NJ; Nashville, TN. Participated in raids on France; Le Culot, Belgium; Kiel, Germany; Lutzendorf, Germany; Munich, Germany, all others in dispute.

Memorable experience was being shot down on 19th birthday, freed from Barth, May 1945 by Russians. (Records of one tour, 30 missions, lost in St. Louis fire.) He was discharged Nov. 6, 1945 with the rank of staff sergeant.

Married twice, raised five girls. Retired, 100 percent VA disability.

GEORGE J. MAKIN JR., was born in Wilkes-Barre, PA on June 11, 1921. Entered the service on March 15, 1942, after working at the Glenn L. Martin Aircraft Company. His pre-flight training was at Santa Ana, CA and he graduated from Victorville Bombardier School, Class of 42-15. After being assigned to B-17s and YB-40s until April 1943, he was transferred to the 389th Bomb Group, B-24s. Following tran-

sition training at Lowry Field, CO, he was sent to Hethel, England.

Within days, the 389th group was transferred to the African Theater to fly raids from Bengazi, Libia. On July 19, 1943 and Aug. 11, 1943, he flew the first raid on Rome and the historic low level attack on the Ploesti, Romania, oil fields. Makin returned to Hethel to complete a total of 28 missions. After serving as assistant group armament officer, he returned to the U.S. to enter pilot training. Upon graduation he was assigned to Midland, TX, as a pilot for student bombardiers. He later flew for the Maryland National Guard.

Awarded Distinguished Flying Cross with Oak Leaf Cluster, Air Medal with five Oak Leaf Clusters, Presidential Unit Citation, American Campaign Medal and EAME.

After military service, he graduated from the University of Maryland and taught school for 30 years.

Married the girl next door, Martha McKelvey, in December 1944 in the Air Force Chapel at San Antonio, TX.

ROBERT S. MALLICK JR., was born Nov. 30, 1923 in Meadville, PA. From high school he enlisted on Oct. 23, 1942 as an Air Force Cadet. Graduated Twin Engine School, Columbus, MS; co-pilot on B-24.

Flew 21 combat missions with 453rd Bomb Group, transferred to 467th. Participated in battles of Ardennes, Central Rhineland, Southern Europe, European Theater, four Battle Stars. Memorable experience: when his crew was shot at and engine was out, they landed at A-92 Saint Trond's, Belgium for three days.

Returned home June 1945. He received the Air Medal with three Oak Leaf Clusters and Good Conduct Medal.

Final discharge from Reserves in 1951 with the rank of second lieutenant from F/O enlisted man.

Married high school sweetheart, close to 50th anniversary now; has two fine sons. Retired from Duquesne Light Company at Pittsburgh, PA. He is a cattle rancher in Arkansas.

GIRD M. MALONE, was born Jan. 26, 1924 in Haynes, AR (Lee County). Entered USAAF Jan. 18, 1943 at Camp Joseph T. Robinson, AR.

Military locations/stations: Miami Beach; Buckley Field; Lowry Field, Denver, CO; Wendover Field, UT; Seething, England. Participated in battles at Southern France, Normandy, Northern France, Ardennes, Rhineland, Central Europe, and Air Offense Europe.

Memorable experiences: Dropping supplies at tree top level from a B-24; when Gen. Patton crossed the Rhine River; breaking a wing tip when they hit a tree, but made it back to the base safely; watching anti-aircraft flak underneath their plane when they were on a mission; serving as a tail gunner; going overseas as a gunnery instructor.

Discharged Oct. 7, 1943 with the rank of staff sergeant. Received EAME and Good Conduct Medal.

Lives in Orange, TX, since 1965. Married and has eight children and 16 grandchildren. Worked with Veterans of Foreign Wars and other veteran's organizations for 25 years, 18 years as quartermaster Post 2775 VFW, served as post commander and district commander.

STRATIS J. MALOUKIS JR., was born Sept. 12, 1924 at Fort Sam Houston Station Hospital. Graduated from Central Catholic High School, San Antonio, TX in 1943. Drafted July 17, 1943 into the USAAC; basic training at Buckley Field, Denver. Armament training at Lowry AAF and Aerial Gunnery School at Harlingen AAF; combat crew training at Davis Monthan AAF at Tucson, AZ.

Flew overseas and joined 392nd Bomb Group; flew on 22 combat missions. Awarded the Purple Heart Medal on 22nd mission.

Returned to the States for further hospitalization. Stayed in the Air Force for 25 years, retired in 1968. Returned to San Antonio and is presently working civil service at Randolph AFB.

Life member of Military Order of the Purple Heart, 8th Air Force Historical Society and 392nd Bomb Group Memorial Association.

He and his wife Frances will celebrate 36 years of marriage on Feb. 2, 1994.

IRVING MANIN, was born March 2, 1922. Enlisted June 1942; graduated pilot, second lieutenant, Class 43-F. Co-pilot B-24, 713th Sqdn., 448th Bomb Group, Seething.

Completed 35 missions. Next assigned as controller AC&W. Sqdn., Okinawa. Released from active duty April 1947. Became controller FAA.

Recalled October 1948; flew 152 missions, C-54s, Berlin Airlift. Released from active duty January 1950, Returned Air Traffic Controller at New York Center. Recalled August 1951, B-29 aircraft commander. Flew 28 missions Korean Conflict.

Released August 1953. He was awarded Distinguished Flying Cross, Air Medal with six clusters, European Campaign Medal with three stars, Army of Occupation Medal, Humanitarian Service Medal, Korean Service Medal and United Nations Medal for Korean service.

Stayed New York Center until retired GS-14, team supervisor, March 1977.

Attended college while working full time and graduated Dowling College with BA degree, Adelphi University with two MBAs.

Married Arlene Zaidberg October 1950; has one son, one daughter and five granddaughters.

EARL R. MANN, was born in Stony Creek, CT Feb. 27, 1921. Entered active service on Sept. 1, 1942. After basic training at Keesler Field, MS started Mechanic School at Sheppard Field, TX and completed advanced training at Willow Run, Ypsilanti, MI. Receiving a diploma for service and maintenance course B-24E.

At Biggs Field in El Paso, TX he was assigned to the 578th Bomb Sqdn. and 392nd Bomb Group. He was sent to Alamogordo, NM to complete his training and left for Europe aboard the *Queen Mary* on July 25, 1943, arrived in Wendling, England on July 30, 1943. At Wendling his group was cited for distinguished and outstanding service in 100 combat missions over Europe.

Returned to the USA on June 8, 1945. Worked for United Technology for 31 years and is now retired. Married Jean E. Altermatt, June 19, 1945.

EVERETT MANSIR (RED), was born Aug. 31, 1924 in Pittston, ME. Entered the USAAC on April 27, 1943. Military locations/stations: Basic training, Atlantic City, NJ; Armorer Gunnery School, Lowry, CO; Aerial Gunner School, Laredo, TX; 44th Bomb Group, Shipdham, England; gunnery instructor, Ft. Myers, FL.

Memorable experience was mission on Sept. 13, 1944 to Hall, Germany Air Field. Received heavy flak damage 100-150 holes, gas leaking into bomb bay, radio man hit in leg by flak, P-38 escorted to Laon Air Field, left plane and hitchhiked to Paris. Spent escape money then returned to Shipdham and completed 34 bomb missions with 67th Sqdn., 44th Bomb Group.

Discharged Oct. 23, 1945 with rank of staff sergeant. Awarded EAME with four Bronze Stars, Air Medal with three Oak Leaf Clusters and Distinguished Flying Cross.

Married and has three children and three grandchildren and soon expecting twins. Retired and busy as ever.

CARL E. MARINO, 445th Bomb Group, 701st Sqdn. was born May 29, 1922 in Lafayette, CO. Entered USAAF Oct. 13, 1942; served as engineer, 2nd Air Div.

Military locations/stations: Midland, TX; Harlingen, TX; Salt Lake Replacement Base; Davis Monthan, Tucson, AZ; Pocatello Idaho Air Base; Wendover, UT; Sioux City, IA; Oct. 27, 1943-June 17, 1945, Tibenham, England, Station #123; Fort Dix, NJ; Palm Springs AB, CA.

Participated in battles at Normandy, Northern France, Ardennes, Rhineland, Central Europe and Air Offensive Europe. Memorable experiences were D-day and Battle of Bulge air drops.

Discharged Oct. 20, 1945 with the rank of staff sergeant. Received EAME Ribbon with six Bronze Stars and Distinguished Badge.

Married and has three children. Marino is retired.

ANTHONY J. MARIS, was born in Lodi, CA March 13, 1921. Entered the USAAC on Nov. 1, 1942. Completed Flexible Gunnery School, Kingman, AZ; Bombardier School, Deming, NM. Assigned and served as group lead bombardier in the 467th Bomb Group, 8th Air Force, stationed at Rackheath, England. Participated in the Rhineland, Ardennes-Alsace, Northern France and Central Europe campaigns.

Returned to the U.S. at end of European War for reassignment to B-29s. At end of hostilities transferred into Air Force Reserve and then to U.S. Army Reserve in 1956. Completed training as an artilleryman. Attended and graduated from basic and Advance Artillery School and Command and General Staff College. While assigned to the 91st Div. served as battery, battalion, regimental and brigade commander and as the assistant division commander of the 91st Div.

Retired as a colonel in January 1976. Received Legion of Merit, Distinguished Flying Cross, Air Medal with three Oak Leaf Clusters, Army Commendation Medal, Army Reserve Meritorious Achievement Medal and others.

In addition to active reserve duty, he taught English for 23 years at high school. Has BA and MA in English and history. Retired 1982.

Married Elpis Apostolos of Sacramento on Oct. 27, 1946, they have two sons, a daughter and two grandchildren.

JAMES R. MARIS (JIM), was born in 1919. Flight trained in the Southeast Training Command, receiving his wings in 43-G. He trained in B-17s, but was transferred into B-24s. He flew with the 392nd and his second mission was D-day. After 30 missions he flew with the first tow target and gunnery flight in A-35s, P-47D's and A-20s as maintenance and test flight officer.

In December 1944 he returned stateside and flew multi-engine test at Smyrna, TN. He separated in September 1946 to go to the Currey School of Aeronautics to obtain his CAA certificates. He was recalled for the Korean conflict and functioned as an education officer for a Mobile Training Development Squadron. He was discharged Nov. 10, 1952.

He completed his degree in education at the University of Illinois and joined the Purdue University Department of Aviation Technology as the first instructor in the new aviation program. He became department head and later became the assistant to the Dean of the School of Technology. He retired in 1984.

Maris and his wife, Lucille, celebrated their 50th wedding anniversary on Jan. 16, 1993. They have four daughters: Cathy, Nancy, Susan and Vickie, and six grandchildren. He is still active in aviation as an advisor to the student flying club and has constructed two custom built aircraft, a

Starduster Two and a Quickie 2. He is still active with the Air Force Association, the local communicator.

VERNON C. MARKHAM, was born Aug. 15, 1918 in Evansville, IN. Drafted April 5, 1941. He was married to Lillian Ann Meyer on Dec. 21, 1941.

Entered Aviation Cadet Training September 1942 and graduated May 28, 1943 in Class 43-E at Turner Field, GA. In August he was assigned to the 445th Bomb Group, 700th Sqdn. and departed for England in October.

Flew his airplane and crew arriving in Tibenham in November 1943. He named his airplane *Lillian Ann* for his wife. As first pilot he flew 10 missions and as the lead crew pilot, 20 missions. His first was Dec. 16, 1943 to Bremen and his last, D-day, June 6, 1944.

On Feb. 13 he crash-landed his airplane, enemy flak destroyed three engines. He was awarded a Distinguished Flying Cross. On February 24 his first deputy lead was to Gotha, Germany. They received the Presidential Citation for this mission.

Missions completed, he was reassigned to 2nd Bomb Wing staff. After the initial invasion he was released and returned home in September 1944.

October 1947, he accepted a regular commission. Most assignments were within research and development command. He retired May 1, 1970 as a lieutenant colonel.

RAY I. MARNER JR. was born Oct. 29, 1922 in Iowa. He attended the University of Iowa from 1940 to 1942 and entered the USAAF on Aug. 4, 1942. He joined the 506th Bomb Sqdn., 44th Bomb Group on Oct. 21, 1942 at Pueblo Air Base, CO.

Went to England with the ground echelon of the 506th Bomb Sqdn. in February 1943 on the SS *Chantilly* and arrived Shipdham Aerodrome in March 1943. Was squadron mail clerk from March 1943 to April 1944 and squadron personnel supply sergeant from April 1944 until discharged on Sept. 8, 1945.

Married LaVonne Gaffney on Feb. 14, 1948, they have five children and eight grandchildren. Presently resides in Iowa City, IA.

He owned and operated a drug store in Lone Tree, IA for 25 years, and then joined the staff of the Farmers and Merchants Savings Bank of Lone Tree. He retired as executive vice president of this bank in July of 1991.

JAMES W. MARSH, was born May 24, 1919 in Toledo, OH. Inducted Nov. 14, 1941, as a private in the infantry; served as bombardier with the 446th Bomb Group (H), 705th Bomb Sqdn.

Military locations/stations: Lowry Field, CO; Station #125, England; C.P. Wheeler, GA; Ellington Field, TX; Childress AFB, TX.

Memorable experiences: Parachuting from bomber over Germany, his chute didn't open at 2,500 feet; finally was able to free chute about 1,000 to 1,200 feet above ground landing in a pine tree. Forced march with fellow krieges from Stalag Luft III to Spremberg, Germany in the winter of 1944.

Discharged Dec. 3, 1945 with the rank of first lieutenant. Retired from Air Force Reserve May 24, 1979.

Awarded Air Medal with two Oak Leaf Clusters, Prisoner of War Medal, American Service Medal, American Defense Medal, EAME with Silver Star, Air Force Reserve Medal, Air Force Reserve Longevity Bar and WWII Victory Medal.

Married to Charlotte 50 years on June 3, 1993. They have two sons: Thomas and Christopher, and six grandchildren.

He retired as a postal supervisor with 34 years service in 1974 and is now enjoying life.

BENJ. D. MARSHALL, was born Dec. 23, 1920 in Elm Creek, NE. Enlisted USAF June 2, 1942 as aviation cadet.

Military locations/stations: Cedar Falls, IA; Boise, ID; England. Memorable experiences: Hauling gas to Patton; starting engine on B-24 by windmilling on runway with other three.

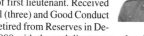

Discharged Oct. 10, 1945 with the rank of first lieutenant. Received Air Medal (three) and Good Conduct Medal. Retired from Reserves in December 1980 with the rank lieutenant colonel.

Married 50 years to wife Louise; they have two children, one boy and one girl. .

CLAYTON FRED MARSHALL, was born July 11, 1924 in Canton, OH. Enlisted in USAAC on June 1, 1943 while attending Ohio State University. Became a flight engineer on a B-24 crew, assigned to 466th Bomb Group, 785th and later 784th Sqdn. at Attlebridge, August 1944.

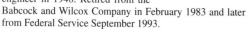

Completed tour of 30 combat missions and was discharged as a technical sergeant. Returned to Ohio State and graduated as an industrial engineer in 1948. Retired from the Babcock and Wilcox Company in February 1983 and later from Federal Service September 1993.

Married Mary Abbott June 7, 1947; they have two daughters and two grandchildren.

WILLIS WOOD MARSHALL, was born at grandparents home, Island Ford, VA on Dec. 1, 1924. At the time his parents lived near Gettysburg, PA. Lived in Pennsylvania until 1937 when his father moved to Baltimore to obtain a job.

Entered USAAC Feb. 19, 1943 in the Aviation Cadet Program. Basic at Miami Beach; college training at St. Xavier University, Cinn., SAACC; Mechanics School at Keesler Field; Factory School, San Diego; Gunnery School at Harlingen, TX; phase training at March Field. Went to England November 1944, 389th Bomb Group, Hethel.

Flew seven missions as regular crew then 11 as a lead crew. Returned to USA late May 1945 to Sioux Falls, then back to Harlingen.

Rose to the rank of tech. sergeant and flew as flight engineer, top turret. Discharged on Oct. 27, 1945 at Randolf Field. Received four Battle Stars, Air Medal with two Oak Leaf Clusters, Good Conduct Medal and one Overseas Bar.

Married Charlotte Venis from London, England; they have three children, six grandchildren and three great-grandchildren. Moved back to Pennsylvania in 1953 and worked as a plumber until retirement in 1988.

NORMAN J. MARSHANK, was born March 4, 1925 at Los Angeles. Enlisted in USAAC at 17 and called in at 18 for pilot training. Graduated, Douglas, AZ (44-B). Trained with B-24 crew at Muroc, CA and began combat missions as co-pilot on June 20, 1944. Checked out as first pilot after 13th mission.

While awaiting orders to return to USA after 31st mission, was advised that crews now had to fly 35 missions. Shot down near Frankfort on 34th and spent six and one-half months as guest of German government. Liberated April 29, 1945 near Munich by Patton's 3rd Army.

Joined father's manufacturer's representative business in late 1945 and is still active as chairman with youngest son as president. Also has one other son and a 17-year-old grandson who starts Yale University in September 1993.

Still very active in tennis and paddle tennis and socially involved with lady he unsuccessfully proposed to in 1945.

GLEN E. MARSTELLER, was born April 25, 1921 in Youngstown, OH. During senior year at Miami University, Oxford, OH, was called to active duty. Aviation cadet pilot training in February 1943; graduated second lieutenant, pilot at Freeman Field, IN, Class of 44-C.

After B-24 flight training, arrived 445th Bomb Group, Tibenham, England Sept. 27, 1944. Assigned first pilot in the 700th Bomb Sqdn. Completed 35 missions and awarded five Air Medals and European Campaign Stars. Returned to U.S. on April 1, 1945; attended, graduated and became an instructor at Aircraft Maintenance Officer Training School at Chanute Field, IL.

Separated from Air Force active duty May 2, 1947 with rank of captain. Completed college education and became an industrial engineer. Retired from LTU Steel, East Chicago, IN on May 1, 1983. Married Jean Raub on March 15, 1944; they have three children, four grandchildren and one great-grandchild.

EDWARD MARSTON, was born Jan. 26, 1919 at Lubec, ME, the most eastern town in the U.S. Lived on lighthouses on the Maine coast until going into the service. Received notice to the service on June 3, 1941. Assigned to the 25th Air Base Sqdn. at Westover Field in Springfield, MA. Promoted to staff sergeant in August 1943. Worked in the engineering office at Westover.

Transferred to England in October 1943. In January assigned to 458th Bomb Sqdn. Worked in personnel office. Returned to U.S. on July 4, 1945. Discharged on Sept. 1, 1945.

Went to Coyne Electric in Chicago, 1945. In 1947 went to work for Otis Elevator Company, worked same until 1981. Worked on construction, maintenance and retired as local representative in Bangor, ME. Married to Jane Fahey in 1948. Has two children, one of each. Wife died of cancer January 1988.

ALBERT A. MARTIN, USAF (Ret.) was born April 5, 1918 in Gallup, NM. Entered the service in March 1942; commissioned Dec. 17, 1942.

Military locations/stations: Midland, TX; Anti-Sub Patrol, Westover Field, MA and Langley Field, VA; Anti-Sub Patrol, 19th ARON, 1st Bomber Command, ETO 8th Air Force; 44th Bomb Group, 2nd Air Div., 8th Air Force; 449th Bomb Group, 15th Air Force, completed 50 combat missions (first officer to complete the "50 mission tour" in 449th Bomb Group).

Rotated back to U.S. Then July 18, 1944-Sept. 22, 1944, bombardier instructor course, Midland, TX; bombardier instructor, Kirtland AFB, NM and Victorville Air Field, CA; HAAF, Hobbs, NM; Patterson Field, OH, administrative office (2120), intelligence officer (9300). Separated Jan. 15, 1947.

Recalled for Korea Sept. 2, 1952, radar observer; Okinawa, 370th Bomb Sqdn., 307th Bomb Wing; navigator (1035) lead crew, instructor crew (B-47) 338th Bomb Sqdn., 96th Bomb Wing, 413th Bomb Sqdn., squadron navigator, 96th Bomb Wing SAC Dyess AFB, TX. Disability retirement Sept. 19, 1963 with the rank of major.

Received Presidential Unit Citation, Distinguished Flying Cross, Air Medal with four Oak Leaf Clusters, Air Force Longevity Service Award Ribbon with two Oak Leaf Clusterv, American Campaign Medal with one Bronze Star, EAME with three Bronze Stars, WWII Victory Medal, National Defense Service Medal, Korean Service Medal, United Nations Service Medal and Air Force Armed Forces Expeditionary Medal.

Married Marie E. on July 26, 1954. Has two daughters, Joanne and Barbara. Retired educator.

JAMES F. MARTIN (PEEPER), was born Sept. 23, 1922 in Deming, NM. Enlisted in the 7th Cavalry, U.S. Army on Jan. 3, 1942. Transferred to the USAAC. Rated as a bombardier May 13, 1943. Phase training at Davis Monthan, AZ and Blythe, CA. Joined the 567th Bomb Sqdn. flew on a pathfinder crew and was appointed the squadron bombardier. Completed tour in early 1945. On return to the Zone Interior, volunteered for a tour in the Pacific in the single tailed B-24. Didn't get there!

Completed Single Engine Flying school at Williams AFB in July 1949. Flew a combat tour in Korea in F-86s, participated in the blockade of Cuba flying F-106s and served as the air liaison officer to the Vietnamese Airborne Brigade in the Republic of Vietnam. Completed the Vietnamese Parachute School, helped develop the heliborne assault program and flew combat support for the brigade in the 0-1, Bird Dog.

Retired Sept. 30, 1969 as a colonel.

JOHN MARTIN, was born Oct. 11, 1924 in Wooster, OH. Graduated high school June 1942; enlisted Aviation Cadets June 1942; called up in January 1943. Basic training at Miami Beach, January 1943; aviation students, Concord State Teachers College, Athens, WV; cadet classification, Nashville, TN classified for pilot training. Pre-flight cadet training, Maxwell Field, AL, Class of 44B; primary flight training, Darr Aero Tech, Albany, GA; basic flight training, Greenwood, MS; advanced twin-engine flying training, Columbus, MS. Graduated Feb. 8, 1944, commissioned a second lieutenant. Operational training, Pueblo, CO, B-24 co-pilot; assigned to 458th Bomb Group, November 1944.

Memorable experience: lost an engine going into target, lost altitude and dropped below bomber formations. They dropped bombs which fell all around them-scary!

Completed 30 combat missions by April 1945. Checked out as first pilot but war ended before being assigned crew. Awarded five Air Medals and three ETO Campaign Battle Stars.

After the war, John, attended the College of Pharmacy at the University of Michigan at Ann Arbor, MI. He received the degree of BS in pharmacy in 1949, and followed a career in retail pharmacy. He is now retired and lives in Aurora, OH.

He married his high school sweetheart, Elizabeth Loretta Findlay, on July 22, 1944. They have one son and two grandsons. Martin is a retired Pharmacist.

LESTER C. MARTIN, was born July 29, 1921 in Brewton, AL. Entered the USAAC April 7, 1942 and accepted in aviation cadets December 1942. Training in Southeast Maxwell Bennettsville, SC; Shaw Field and graduated Class 43-I from Turner Field. Back to Maxwell for B-24 transition and then to Salt Lake City for formulation of crew. Operational crew training was at Casper, then flew a new B-24G from Topeka via Grenier Field, Goose Bay, Meeks Field, Iceland to Nutts Corner, Ireland.

Assigned to 458th Bomb Group at Horsham St. Faith where on his third mission was very fortunate to recover from a mid-air collision and to return to the base safely. The remainder of the tour was relatively uneventful.

Returned to the States in September 1944 and stayed in until January 1947, spending time instructing B-24s at Courtland, AL and in ATC from May 1945 until discharge flying out of Westover Field on regular run to Paris. Received

Distinguished Flying Cross with one Oak Leaf Cluster and Air Medal with three Oak Leaf Clusters.

Flew with Pan American and Eastern a few years but was caught in RIFS with each at the end of the Korean conflict. Worked with Monsanto Textiles at Pensacola, FL and Greenwood, SC, retiring at Greenwood in 1982. Was involved in real estate until another retirement in June 1993.

Married Katherine "Martin" (maiden name); has three children.

LLOYD J. MARTIN

was born Dec. 5, 1918 in Wichita, KS. Entered USAF Feb. 28, 1941, served as pilot in Europe during WWII. Memorable experience was the Gotha mission, Feb. 24, 1944.

Discharged Aug. 1, 1970 with the rank of colonel. Awarded Legion of Merit with two Oak Leaf Clusters, Distinguished Flying Cross with two Oak Leaf Clusters, Air Medal with three Oak Leaf Clusters, Commendation Ribbon and French Croix de Guerre.

He is retired.

ROBERT A. MARTIN,

was born May 14, 1916 in Spokane, WA. Volunteered November 1940, assigned to 17th Inf., Presidio of Monterey, CA. Transferred to USAAF February 1942.

Pilot training at King City, Chico and Stockton, CA, where commissioned October 1942, Class 42-J. Married same day. Flew B-24s, B-26s, A-26s, P-38s and AT-11. Flew bombing approach at Bombardier School, Deming, NM.

Combat training Fort Worth, TX; Boise, ID; Sioux City, IA. Stationed Norwich, England with 714th Sqdn. 448th Bomb Group, 8th Air Force, WWII.

Returning from an aborted mission on March 5, 1944, his B-24 was hit by heavy flak. With one engine left, he landed in a field near Niort, France. Evaded capture and escaped to Spain.

Returned to U.S. under Project R; served in 6th Ferry Group, ATC, Long Beach, CA delivering planes to Africa, India, Australia and U.S. Discharged Jan. 15, 1946. Awarded Air Medal with Oak Leaf Cluster, Purple Heart, EAME Theater Ribbon with two Bronze Stars and the Winged Boot. Established contact with all his French benefactors in 1946.

Returned to Bakersfield, CA where he became owner of the Q-Ne-Q Drive-In for 10 years. Later became a partner in Kern Battery Manufacturing Company until his retirement in 1982.

Diagnosed with leukemia in 1985; achieved remission, but passed away in October 1988 after a recurrence. Survived by his wife, Jeane, two children and four grandchildren.

SHERMAN A. MARTIN,

was born in Oak Park, IL on Oct. 5, 1917. His elementary and high school days were spent in the Quad-cities (Davenport, Rock Island, Moline, East Moline). He studied journalism in high school and Bradley University. Entered the USAAC in February 1942, received basic at Sheppard Field, TX, and joined the 93rd Bomb Group (B-24) April 1942 at Barksdale Field, LA. During the 93rd's three-month final training at Fort Myers, FL he married Rene Marre; they have three daughters and nine grandchildren.

His first British station was RAF Alconbury. Later the 8th Air Force organized the three air divisions and the 93rd was moved to RAF Hardwick. He spent several months on special assignment when the 329th Bomb Sqdn. was sent to RAF Bungy. In addition to NCO public relations duties, he was scheduling and equipment manager for the 15-piece base dance band.

He returned to the U.S. with the 93rd and was assigned to the PR office at Sioux City Air Base with discharge on Labor Day 1945. He completed 29 years as an Air Force

civilian in technical writing and editing assignments with the Joint Atomic Weapons Publications Board, Joint Task Force Two, Iranian Gendarmerie Communications and Human Resources Laboratory with retirement in March 1978 at Brooks AFB, TX.

JOSEPH A.A. MARTINEAU,

was born March 28, 1922 in Seattle, WA. Enlisted at McChord Field, WA, April 24, 1942. Commissioned on April 12, 1943, AAFAFS, Stockton, CA, Class of 43-D. Assigned to 29th Bomb Group, Gowen Field, Boise, IA, April 12, 1943; trained as co-pilot in B-17s and transition to pilot in B-24s. Assigned to 445th Bomb Group, 701st Bomb Sqdn., "C" flight, July 14, 1943, Sioux City, IA.

Trained at Satellite Field, Scribner, NB then flew to Europe. Arrived England, Dec. 1, 1943, transferred to 445th Bomb Group base at Tibenham and flew missions December 13, Kiel; December 16, Bremen; December 20, Bremen. Wounded Dec. 20, 1943, returned to States and spent all but six months in hospitals. Assigned temporary limited duty with "observer" flying status to Rapid City Army Air Base under project 066.

Separated O'Reilly General Hospital, Springfield, MO; disability retirement on Jan. 28, 1946.

Married to Annabelle; has six children and 11 grandchildren. Attended Gonzaga University, Spokane, and Seattle University, Seattle, WA.

He is retired from his career as association management and legislative consultant and is completing 28 years and 11 months as city council member of Houghton and Kirkland, WA.

THEODORE MARUSCHAK (TED),

was born in Houtzdale, PA, March 11, 1919; graduated from Altoona High School in 1937 and Altoona School of Commerce in 1940.

Inducted into the Army Dec. 10, 1941, graduated from Army Air Corps Technical School at Keesler Field, Biloxi, MS in 1942 as airplane mechanic.

Graduated from Gunnery School at Laredo, TX, completed combat crew training at Casper, WY and Mountain Home, ID as flight engineer and top turret gunner on the B-24.

Completed tour of duty (32 sorties) with the 489th Bomb Group, 847th Sqdn. in European Theater of Operations between dates of May 31 and Aug. 15, 1944.

Honorably discharged as tech sergeant on Oct. 1, 1945. Received Distinguished Flying Cross and Air Medal with three Oak Leaf Clusters.

Married Gladys Shipstead in 1952. Worked at several large consulting engineering firms before retiring from U.S. Borax as senior engineering designer in 1981 after 16 years. Enjoys travelling, fishing and visiting.

HARLEY B. MASON,

was born Feb. 17, 1920 in Caruthers, CA. Enlisted in the USAAC Oct. 25, 1941 and commissioned as a second lieutenant pilot in February 1943 at Ellington Field in Houston, TX.

Assigned to the 366th Bomb Sqdn., 389th Bomb Group in June 1943. Flew a total of 18 missions in *Fightin' Sam* in Germany, Romania (Ploesti raid), and France (Cognac). Shot down over St. Nazaire, France on Dec. 5, 1943 and was a POW for approximately 18 months at Dulag Luft in Barth, Germany.

Honorably discharged on Aug. 26, 1946. Received Distinguished Flying Cross and two Oak Leaf Clusters.

Married for 45 years to Rachel and resides outside of Fresno, CA where he has farmed for over 40 years (now retired). Has one son, Roger; one daughter, Pat; and two grandchildren, Stephanie and Jason.

JOHN B. MASON,

was born July 16, 1924 in Greeneville, TN. Entered USAAC April 1943. After basic training, completed aerial gunnery training at Laredo, TX; then crew assignment and training at March Field, CA.

In May 1944 was assigned to the 752nd Sqdn. 458th Bomb Group, 8th Air Force, Horsham St. Faith, Norwich, England. He flew tail gunner on B-24s for 32 combat missions. Returned to the USA on Oct. 10, 1944. Attended Gunnery Instructors School at Laredo, TX and instructed B-24 and B-29 gunnery at Harlingen Army Air Field, TX.

Discharged Oct. 26, 1945 at San Antonio, TX. Awarded the Distinguished Flying Cross, four Air Medals and three European Campaign Stars. Recalled for two years during Korean War (1950-1952).

Retired July 1986 after 30 years as an instrument technician at Arnold AFB, TN. Resides in Tullahoma, TN.

SAM MASTROGIACOMO,

was born Jan. 23, 1922 to Italian immigrants in Philadelphia, PA. Entered the USAAF on Nov. 9, 1942, tail gunner on the B-24 BTO in the 8th Air Force, 445th Bomb Group.

Memorable experience was mission over Gotha, Germany on Feb. 24, 1944. They were hit by ME-109, FW-190 and ME-210. Planes on both sides were blowing up and coming down. He could see the target, the ME aircraft factory. When the bombs hit, he could see the factory and planes almost completely destroyed.

There was an explosion in Mastrogiacomo's turret. He was stunned and could feel a stinging hot pain in the back of his nect. Something red and sticky was running down his neck. Just then one the gunners came running back and he was laughing and said, "You're OK. It's hydraulic fluid."

Saw a FW-190 coming right up on their tail. He was so close Mastrogiacomo could see the grim look on pilot's face. He immediately hit the firing button and blew him apart. This picture will live in his mind forever. Thirteen of the 25 planes sent on mission were shot down. The Gotha mission was the longest, continuous fighter battle ever recorded, two hours and 40 minutes.

Discharged August 1977 with the rank of master sergeant. Awarded the Air Medal with four Oak Leaf Clusters and Presidential Unit Citation.

He and his wife Jean have four girls and three sons. Retired as a/c mechanic and machinist.

LORN W. MATELSKI,

was born Dec. 21, 1923 in La Crosse, WI. Entered the USAAC Dec. 7, 1942, then the USAF. Military locations/stations: Enid and Altus, OK; Mt. Home, ID; Wendling, England and many others.

Graduate of Command and Staff College, Squadron Officer School, Academic Instructor School; taught at Carthage College, Northwestern University-Evanston, Gateway Technical College.

Memorable experience: While stationed at the USAF Academy I, he met Col. White (astronaut) a week after he had walked in space.

He was assigned to USAF Academy for 10 years as a liaison officer. Spent 41 years in the USAF, active and reserve. Retired with the rank of lieutenant colonel Dec. 21, 1983.

Awarded the Air Medal, European Campaign with three stars, Longevity Medal, Victory Medal and others.

Received a BS and MS degrees; further work in graduate mathematics at University of Buffalo, NY. Retired as a high school principal, also chairman of the board of an insurance corporation.

Married, has five children and 10 grandchildren. Today he is a circuit court bailiff.

WALTER J. MATESKI, was born Jan. 11, 1922 in Downers Grove, IL. Joined the USAAC Nov. 4, 1942; 392nd Bomb Group, 578th Bomb Sqdn.

Waist gunner on SaBourin crew. Ed Moron (tail gunner) and he had same laundry mark on military clothing, M-7128-odds 10,000 to one happening.

Flew 32 missions. Had crash landing at base in England. No casualties, nine men of 10 man crew still living.

Married and has a son and two grandsons. Retired from AT&T 1981 with 40 years service. He is proud to be part of 2nd Air Division Association and 8th Air Force.

FRANK MATHEWS, was born April 28, 1924 in Printer, WV. Entered USAAC June 16, 1941 at Fort Hayes, OH. Basic, Jefferson Barracks, MO, 1941; Aircraft Mechanic School, Sheppard Field, TX, 1942-1943; Armor School, Lowry Field, CO, 1943; gunnery instructor, Kiel, Ireland, January 1944-July 1944.

Assigned to 466th Bomb Group, 784th Sqdn, Capt. Weiser's crew as an extra. Weiser was promoted to command pilot, and was killed on a practice mission 1944.

Participated in battles at Northern France, Rhineland and Germany. Two missions to marshalling yard, Karlsruhe.

Discharged July 4, 1945 with the rank of tech sergeant. Awarded Air Medal with Silver Cluster and Certificate of Valor.

Retired from Consolidated Rail as superintendent.

JOHN MATT (Matishowski), was born in Yonkers, NY, Jan. 26, 1924. Entered aviation cadet training March 1943; graduated at Selman Field, Monroe, LA in Navigator Class 44-4. Assigned to 576th and 579th squadrons, 392nd Bomb Group at Wendling. Flew as lead navigator and completed 28 missions.

After WWII served in weather reconnaissance and transport squadrons. Served as radiological safety officer at Enewetak in 1958, then joined the White House Squadron at Bolling and Andrews AFB and, for a time, navigated the presidential aircraft *Columbine.*

Awarded the Distinguished Flying Cross and four Air Medals and retired as major in 1963.

He then joined the FAA and became an operations inspector assigned to PanAm. At his second retirement in 1986, he was U.S. member of the North Atlantic System Planning Group, a part of the International Civil Aviation Organization (ICAO). Given Distinguished Career Service Award.

Author of *Crewdog,* a saga of a young American, about the WWII generation's exploits.

Married 1955 to Priscilla Park and has two daughters and four grandchildren.

ELWOOD A. MATTER, was born Nov. 5, 1919 in Sunbury, PA. Entered USAAC on March 21, 1942; served as aerial gunner B-24. Military locations/stations: Peterson Field, CO; Seymour Johnson, NC; Tyndall Field, FL. 44th Bomb Group, 506th Bomb Sqdn., England.

Memorable experience: Two low level supply missions. Holland and Rhine River crossing near Wesel, Germany. Received Purple Heart over Holland. Completed 26 missions.

Discharged Sept. 30, 1945 with the rank of staff sergeant. Awarded Purple Heart, Air Medal with three Oak Leaf Clusters, Good Conduct, ETO with four Battle Stars and Air Force Reserve Medal. Joined Air Force Reserve, retiring Nov. 5, 1979 with the rank of master sergeant.

Married Aug. 24, 1943; wife deceased in 1989. Has two children and three grandchildren. Retired postmaster, 1979.

CHARLES ALLAN MATTHEWS, was born in Thomaston, GA on March 5, 1922. Attended Gordon Military College and Georgia Tech. Joined the infantry as a commissioned officer in March of 1942. Was transferred to the USAAC in September 1942. After pilot training was assigned to the 445th Bomb Group in Boise, ID.

Flew B-24s over occupied Europe for a total of 31 missions. First mission was Dec. 22, 1943 and last one May 29, 1944.

Retired as a captain in December 1945. Received two Distinguished Flying Cross Medals, five Air Medals, Purple Heart, four European Campaign Stars.

Married in Augusta, GA on Oct. 4, 1947. Has three children and two grandchildren.

WILLIAM A. MATTHEWS, was born Oct. 24, 1925 in Tuscaloosa, AL. Enlisted in the USAAF, 8th Air Force, 2nd Air Div. on Oct. 25, 1943. Active duty, Jan. 8, 1944 Fort Sam Houston, TX; assigned to Sheppard Field, TX for six weeks basic. Assigned to Laredo, TX for six weeks Gunnery School; Pueblo, CO as replacement tail gunner on Charles E. Mitchell crew. Completed training with crew.

From Pueblo assigned to Lincoln, NE, where they picked up a new B-24, flew to Grenier Field, Manchester, NH, then North Atlantic route to European Theater of Operations, British Isle (Wales). Assigned to Norwich, England, Horsham; 458th Bomb Group, 755th Bomb Sqdn. crew 60.

Completed tour with 25 combat missions. While returning from a mission to Berlin, where they encountered heavy flak and had extensive damage, they crash landed in Belgium where they were picked up and returned to England to complete their tour.

Returned to States June 2, 1945, after leave was assigned to Lackland Air Base, San Antonio, TX where he was assigned as clerk. Served in this capacity until discharge Oct. 25, 1945. Awarded Air Medal with four Bronze Clusters, ETO with four Bronze Stars and Good Conduct Medal.

Married to Jackie; has two sons, William C. and Charles E.; one daughter, Linda G. He retired in 1987 as real estate developer and building contractor.

ROBERT L. MATTSON, was born Nov. 24, 1922 in San Francisco, CA. Enlisted in the USAAC on Sept, 25, 1942; basic training Stockton, CA; aircraft engine mechanic, Boeing School Aeronautics, Oakland, CA; Armament School, Lowry Field, Denver, CO 1943; B-24 Bomber Group training, Biggs Field, El Paso, TX; joined 492nd Bomb Group for overseas training Alamogordo, NM.

Transferred to 8th Air Force, 2nd Air Div., North Pickenham, England; commenced flying combat missions May 12, 1944 as gunner. His so called claim to fame; bailed out twice into North Sea.

May 29, 1944, returning from Politz, Germany, mis-

sion unable to reach England, forced to bail out. Wearing Mae West spent one hour 30 minutes in water waiting for Air Sea Rescue launch. All crewmen saved except bombardier, he didn't jump.

Mattson flew 22 missions with 492nd Bomb Group. Group dissolved Aug. 13, 1944, after "record" losses. With 492nd he earned Air Medal with two clusters, three Campaign Medals with appropriate Battle Stars and promotion to staff sergeant. Transferred to 467th Bomb Group.

On Aug. 16, 1944, flew practice mission over North Sea. As guns were test fired his plane was sprayed by bullets from malfunctioning top turret gun in the plane below them, setting bomb bay on fire. Of the 11 men on board, seven, including Mattson, bailed out. Five were picked up alive. The pilot and three others were in plane when it exploded.

Once again Mattson was in the water with a Mae West; Air Sea Rescue boat took three hours 10 minutes to get to him. Miracles do happen!

He left service in 1945; met, then married Patricia A. Morton; they have four sons and six grandchildren.

GAZA J. MATYUS, was born March 22, 1916. Inducted into the Army Aug. 31, 1942; attended Airplane Engine Mechanic School at Seymour Johnson Field; Gunnery School at Tyndall Field, Panama City, FL; assigned to B-24 Bomber crew as ball turret gunner at Pueblo, CO. Took combat training at Westover Field, MA.

Arrived in Bungay, England, April 24, 1944. His crew was assigned to the 446th Bomb Group, 704th Sqdn. Flew 31 missions. Departed to the States Oct. 26, 1944.

Stationed at Chanute Field, IL. Assigned as instructor, taught fundamentals of airplane power plants in the phase of trouble shooting. Also, engine changes on B-29 bombers.

Discharged Oct. 7, 1945 with the rank of staff sergeant. Awarded the Distinguished Flying Cross, Air Medal with three Oak Leaf Clusters, European Theater Ribbon with four Bronze Stars.

One year in the 4th Coast Artillery at Fort Amador in 1935. One year in Air Corps at Albrook Field both assignments in the Panama Canal Zone. Retired at age 60, 1976, from Bell Aero Systems.

He married Elizabeth Barnes April 12, 1947; they have two sons.

DOYLE M. MATZ, was born Nov. 22, 1921 in Grayville, IL. Inducted in the USAAC Jan. 22, 1943; served as flight engineer with the 458th Bomb Group.

Crossed Atlantic on *Billy Mitchell* and came back to U.S. on *Queen Mary.* He was stationed at Horsham St. Faith, and completed 30 missions.

Discharged Sept. 17, 1945 with the rank of tech sergeant. Received Air Medal with four Oak Leaf Clusters.

Married November 1946 to

Eloise Ridemour. They have a son and daughter. Matz is retired from farming.

DONALD MAULE

286

ROY M. MAYHEW, was born Dec. 3, 1921 in Urbana, IL. Entered the USAAC Feb. 19, 1941; served as bombsight mechanic with the 93rd Bomb Group (H), 2nd Air Div., 8th Air Force.

Military locations/stations: Hardwick, England (home base), Middle East, Gambet, Egypt, Benghazi, Libya, Tunis, Tunisia.

Discharged Sept, 15, 1945 with the rank of tech sergeant. Received 14 Battle Stars, EAME, Unit Citation and Bronze Star.

Married July 31, 1946 and has three children (two boys, one girl) and five grandchildren. Working at HWH Corp., Moscow, IA.

DAVID B. MAZER, was born Dec. 5, 1917 in New Jersey. Entered Field Artillery July 28, 1941. Transferred to the AAC and commissioned as navigator October 1943 from Hondo, TX.

Military locations/stations: Fort Bragg, NC; Mather Field, CA; Camp Luna, NM; San Antonio, TX; Hondo, TX; Wendover, UT; Norwich, England; Santa Monica, CA. Joined the 467th Bomb Group in Wendover, UT. Flew as a group to Rackheath, England. Completed 31 missions on Oct. 9, 1944 as a lead navigator.

Returned to the States, December 1944 and served as information and education officer, West Coast Training Command until discharge on Nov. 11, 1945 with the rank of first lieutenant. Received ETO, Bronze Star, Air Medal with three Oak Leaf Clusters and Distinguished Flying Cross.

Completed last year of school in 1947 from Colorado School of Mines as metallurical engineer.

Worked at Curtiss Wright Corporation for six years and then became owner and president of Bennett Heat Treating Company in New Jersey. After 25 years, sold out and retired to Tucson, AZ.

His wife Dorothy and he have been traveling and enjoying an active life. They frequently visit their son Richard, his wife Diane, and grandson Sam, in Half Moon Bay, CA.

EDWARD MAZER, was born in Pittsburgh, PA, Dec. 18, 1922. Entered USAAF Nov. 11, 1942; basic training, Keesler Field, MS; radio operator training, Scott Field, IL. Finished gunnery training Las Vegas, NV; met with crew at Blythe Field, CA and began training on B-24 Liberator bomber. Finished training Davis Monthan Field, Tucson, Az.

Left for the British Isles from Topeka, KS, flying as a passenger on a B-17 Flying Fortress. Arrived in Preswick, Scotland, December 1943. Transferred to Shipdham, England where he flew 30 missions over occupied Europe. Last mission was June 2, 1944. Bombed the coast of France in preparation for D-day. Sent back to States August 1944.

Became a radio operator and gunnery instructor at Westover Field, MA. Finished his Air Force duty there. Discharged September 1945 with the rank of tech sergeant. Received the Distinguished Flying Cross, Air Medal with three Oak Leaf Clusters.

Married Jean Sigal Dec. 15, 1946; they have three children and five grandchildren. Mazer is a retired salesman.

GEORGE JAY McARTHUR (MAC), was born Jan. 8, 1910 in Wilford, Fremont County, ID. Enlisted in Army March 22, 1944; stationed for training at Tyndall Field, FL; LeMoore, CA; Walla Walla, WA. Squadron formed at Hamilton Field, CA, Nov. 13, 1944.

Left Fort Standish, NJ Dec. 4, 1944; arrived Glasgow, Scotland Dec. 14, 1944. Went to Horsham St. Faith, Norwich, England. Assigned 458th Bomb Group, 753rd Bomb Sqdn. Completed 21 missions as tail gunner on B-24s.

Returned to States, discharged as staff sergeant October 1945, Davis Monthan Field, Tucson, Az. Received European Campaign Ribbon with three Bronze Stars, Good Conduct Ribbon, Air Medal with two Oak Leaf Clusters.

April 7, 1945, received Token of Award for mission flown over Krummel, Germany under difficult conditions.

Married Colleen Miller Feb. 13, 1944, they have four sons, four daughters, 29 grandchildren, 28 great-grandchildren and nine great-great-grandchildren. Mac passed away July 1979.

LEO R. McBRIAN, was born March 25, 1920 in Ridon, CA. Entered USAF January 1942 at Stockton Field. Served as bombardier in the 389th Bomb Group, 2nd Air Div.

Military locations/stations: Victorville AFB; Davis Monthan, Tucson, AZ; Biggs AFB, El Paso, TX; Lowry Field, Denver, CO. Hethel AFB, Norwich, England; Benghazi AFB, North Africa; Muroc AAB, CA.

Flew 31 missions. Memorable experience was when shot down over Malta (Rome raid).

Discharged June 1945 with the rank of first lieutenant. Awarded Purple Heart, Distinguished Flying Cross, Air Medal with three Oak Leaf Clusters.

Married to Betty; they have two daughters, one son, one grandson and two great-grandsons. Retired newspaper publisher.

VERE A. McCARTY, was born April 10, 1917 in Condon, OR. Enlisted April 5, 1942, Portland, OR as private (AC) AUS. Graduated from Bombardier School, San Antonio AAB, Class 43-7, May 13, 1943 as second lieutenant rated bombardier.

Joined the 446th Bomb Group at Lowry AAB, Denver, July 1, 1943 where the group staged for combat service. Flew with group in new B-24H to join the 2nd Air Div. in October 1943. Base was Flixton, Bungay, Station 125. He was bombardier for O.W. "Pappy" Henderson, B-flight leader for the 706th Sqdn.

Memorable experience was participating as lead bombardier for the 706th Sqdn. supporting troops landing at Normandy and following his group leader who led the entire 8th Air Force on that occasion.

Served as 706th Sqdn. bombardier for a short time and as a staff bombardier for the 20th Combat Wing at Hardwick until rotating home in late November 1944.

Separated at Fort Lewis, WA, June 6, 1945. Received Distinguished Flying Cross with Oak Leaf Cluster and Air Medal with three Oak Leaf Clusters.

Returned to raising cattle and wheat until he was employed by the state of Oregon's Department of Veterans' Affairs. Retired after nearly 30 years as a division administrator of that department in December 1978. Served as 446th group vice president for the 2nd Air Division Association for six years.

Married Marie Garrow in Portland, Dec. 27, 1942. Their daughter Kathleen was born while he was in cadet training. They also have six sons and 12 grandchildren. Now retired and does quite a bit of traveling with Marie.

CARLTON H. McCONNELL, was born Sept. 1, 1922 at Mangham, LA. Student at Louisiana State University immediately prior to enlisting as an aviation cadet Jan. 24, 1942.

Commissioned second lieutenant Sept. 5, 1942, Albuquerque, NM; bombardier Class 42-12. Instructor Big Spring AAF, TX, September 1942-May 1943. OTU training in U.S. with 445th Bomb Group until November 1943. Flew combat from England as lead bombardier with 701st and 703rd squadrons, 445th Bomb Group, promoted to captain in August and returned to the U.S. in November 1944. Reassigned to Big Spring AAF in early 1945 and separated from the service in November 1945.

McConnell was recalled to active duty for the Korean conflict in September 1950, became a regular officer the same year and remained for a career in the Air Force. He retired as a lieutenant colonel in 1969, one year after completing a tour as the commander of the Vietnam District, USAF Postal and Courier Service.

Received Distinguished Flying Cross, Air Medal with three Oak Leaf Clusters, Bronze Star, Air Force Commendation Medal with two clusters and Presidential Unit Citation.

Received BS degree, Louisiana State University; MA degree, Stanford University.

McConnell was married to his college sweetheart, Betty Owen, in the Albuquerque base chapel, Sept. 5, 1942 following commissioning ceremonies. In retirement they reside in Baton Rouge, LA, and have their own Mom and Pop real estate business.

CLAUDE HARDISON McCONNELL, was born May 28, 1924 in Lewisburg, TN and raised on a farm. Inducted Jan. 20, 1943; joined the USAAC in April; sent to Gulf Port for basic training; Keesler Field, MS for air engineering on B-24 Liberators; Laredo Field, TX for gunnery. Crew was assembled in Lincoln, NE with orders to report to Pueblo, CO to begin flight training. Returned to Lincoln, NE and assigned a new B-24J to deliver by northern route: Goose Bay, Greenland, Iceland; Valley, Wales.

Kill Kill, Ireland for ETO indoctrination; Horsham St. Faith, 458th Bomb Group. 754th and moved to 755th as lead crews, No. 60. Flew 32 combat missions and five gas hauls for Patton's Army from May 1944 to 1945.

Memorable experience was March 17, 1945 (27th mission) to Berlin, Germany. Received direct hit to #3 engine, propeller broke off cutting through the nose of plane. They fell 10,000 feet over target, bombs raining all around and increasing amount of flak from 19,000 feet down to 9,000 feet. Took a heading for Hanover, Germany and limped across front lines near Brussels on two engines and approximately 75 gallons of fuel remaining for #1 and #4 engines. RAF flew in next morning and rescued them, by noon the German air force strafed the field, killing seven Americans.

Returned to U.S. on R&R and reported for B-29 training as flight engineer Chanute Field, IL, July 1945. Awarded Oak Leaf, Bronze Star, two Air Medals and five European Campaign Stars.

Discharged September 1945 with the rank of tech. sergeant. Attended Northern Illinois College of Optometry, Chicago, IL. He and his wife, Dr. Mary Jane McConnell, have practiced together for 40 years in North Carolina. They have three children and three grandchildren. Retired 1990, but continues to do eye missions to third world countries.

His crew, No. 60 "Heaven Can Wait," held its first reunion May 1992 at Branson, MO, with 50 percent attending, others folded wings.

ROBERT H. McCORMACK, was born July 19, 1925 in West New York, NJ. Moved to New York City before age one. Joined USAAF Oct. 5, 1943; basic training, Greensboro, NC; graduated Radio School in Sioux Falls, SD, July 19, 1944.; graduated Gunnery School at Yuma, AZ Sept. 16, 1944; crew training at Mt. Home, ID; assigned as radio operator to Ed Potter crew.

Battle of Bulge caused acceleration of crew training, arrived in England in February in a new B-24 from Topeka via Iceland. Crew assigned to 702nd Sqdn. of 445th Bomb Group and discovered plenty of war saved for them. First mission Essen, March 21, 1945; last, Salzburg April 25, 1945. R&R in June 1945 then back to Sioux Falls awaiting Pacific assignment when Japan surrendered. Completed service as a ground station radio operator at March Field, CA. Discharged from there March 16, 1946.

Married Nancy Potts in 1949, they have two sons, one daughter and three grandchildren. Put in 24 years as a New York City firefighter, retired in 1975. Worked other jobs until full retirement in North Carolina in 1989. His wife passed away in 1991.

He had no knowledge of the 2nd Air Division Association until 1982, when he and his wife saw a poster on a wall during a visit to the *Queen Mary* in Long Beach, CA. Always had wondered what became of the money donated in 1945. After joining the association, he discovered that the money could not have been better spent than for the Memorial Library in Norwich. He visited the library and the base at Tibenham in May 1992. Unlike most, the 445th base still exists due to the Norfolk Glider Club operating there. They treated them like VIPs.

ROBERT J. McCORMACK, was born February 1924; drafted February 1943; graduated Hondo, January 1944 as navigator.

He flew 30 missions from Hethel; 389th Bomb Group spring and summer 1944 on Ketron's crew, no aborts, no injuries.

McCormack is spending his retirement with the Forest Service in Arizona. His grandchildren enjoy the following story the most.

His crew was flying over Germany when nature's call demanded attention. Having no acceptable receptacle, he hooked up to a portable oxygen, crawled through the tunnel to the bomb bay where he took off his parachute, Mae West vest, dropped his flight coveralls, electric flying suit, pant and shorts. By reaching between the bombs to hang onto the bomb rack with one hand, feet shackled with clothes and crouching on the narrow catwalk and rear end over the bomb bay doors, nature had its way. The plane was bouncing around from turbulence, mighty scary. At 22,000 feet and 20° below zero things froze quickly so when the bomb bay doors opened, he successfully pooped on Germany.

EDWARD McCORMICK (MAC), was born in Simsbury, CT, March 28, 1921. Employed at Pratt and Whitney Aircraft Corporation 1939; joined USAAC Aug. 28, 1942; was classified a "bypass specialist," went straight to a flight line maintenance organization as an aircraft mechanic.

Entered B-24 training as flight engineer October 1944 and was assigned to the 445th Bomb Group, Tibenham, England. Discharged Nov. 3, 1945 and re-enlisted USAF, March 1949.

Spent the next 25 years in various assignments in the aircraft maintenance field. Retired from the USAF as an aircraft maintenance superintendent in the grade of chief master sergeant, September 1974.

He is one of a select few that has served in the military during three wars the U.S. was engaged in during this century: World War II, Korea and Vietnam.

PATRICK McCORMICK, was born in Minnesota in 1921. Entered the service in October 1942; served the 8th Air Force, 458th Bomb Group. Military locations/stations: Kelly Field, Uvalde, TX; Goodfellow AFB, Lubbock; Horsham St. Faith. Completed 35 missions from May 1944 to April 1945.

Discharged in August 1945 and received the Air Medal and Purple Heart.

He and his wife, Margaret Anne, have four children: Patrick, Micheal, Kathleen and Mary Beth. He is retired.

HOWARD I. McCRACKEN, was born Nov. 5, 1921 in Lorain, OH. Entered the USAF May 22, 1942; served the 491st Bomb Group, 2nd Air Div.; Southeast Training Company, Metfield and Pickenham, England. Flew Air Offensive over Europe.

The news of the attack on Pearl Harbor changed his plan to join the RAF in Canada that day in December 1941. He enlisted in the USAAC being assured that enlisted men received preferential appointments for pilot training if they passed the required tests. This he did and was on the "waiting list." Meanwhile, he spent several months in England with an engineering group, then returned stateside for pre-flight training at Maxwell Field, AL. After graduating with the Class of 43-J, he flew new Liberators from Topeka, KS to Ireland.

Most memorable missions: mission to Eindhoven where Capt. Hunter's plane went down, his ship was flying next to McCracken's; the St. Lo area; over Achen, Germany when his crew's waist gunner, Lloyd Hubbard, was wounded. Two engines were shot out and with deteriorated weather, they were forced to land at Woodbridge using Fido. That was Nov. 16, 1944 and his 35th mission. Within the 35 missions, his crew crossed the English Channel seven times on three engines and three times on two engines.

He was discharged January 1946 with the rank of captain, USAFR. Awarded Distinguished Flying Cross, Air Medal with five Oak Leaf Clusters, European and American Defense Medals, five Campaign Stars and Presidential Unit Citation. According to McCracken his bomb group, the 491st, 853rd Sqdn, was the last to go into combat service and considered to have the best record and the most missions in the shortest time.

He is married and has four children and three grandchildren. McCracken is retired.

WILLIAM C. McCRACKEN, was born June 20, 1924 in Warrenton, MO. Enlisted in the Army Signal Corps, Dec. 4, 1942. Attended Signal Corps Radio and Radar Schools and transferred to Air Corps, September 1943. Attended Air Corps Radio and Gunnery Schools before signing on as radio operator/gunner with B-24 crew for OTU at Tucson, Az. Crew was assigned a new B-24 at Topeka in January 1945 and flew North Atlantic route to England, whereupon was assigned to 389th Bomb Group, 564th Sqdn., Hethel Aerodrome.

Trained as a lead crew, credited with six combat and three trolley missions before flying back to States on May 18, 1945. Was assigned to combat crew squadron as acting first sergeant at Clovis, NM for overseas crew replacements until March 1946, but elected to be discharged and served in Air Force Reserve until retirement in July 1959 as a first lieutenant public information officer.

Owned and operated Bilmac Press, Inc., a printing and office products business in Warrenton, MO until sold on Dec. 30, 1986. McCracken is actively involved in real estate and securities investments at present time. He tries to do some fishing and boating at his lake-side home away from home on Pinnacle Lake (a carbon coy of Golden Pond) about 70 miles from his permanent residence in St. Louis County, MO. Seems he is more busy today than ever before and enjoying it more.

He has a beautiful wife, one wonderful step-daughter, five wonderful grandchildren and two handsome great-grandsons; for the most part living very close by, whom they enjoy very much. (Two granddaughters are away at college but come home often.) He is enjoying excellent health, a full social life and as the song goes "Everything is wonderful."

HAROLD F. McCRAY, was born December 1919 on a farm in Dixon, IL. Entered U.S. Army January 1942; sent to Camp Robinson, Little Rock, AR for infantry training. May 1942 to Duncan Field, San Antonio, TX; Radio School and 1080th Signal Co. service group, August 1942, Kelly Field AT 6 Radio Maintenance.

In 1943, Waycross, GA Air Base, Daniel Field. Camp Shanks, NY, arrived May 1943 Hethel Airdrome, Norwich, England, 389th Bomb Group. Then Attlebridge, install communications, Tibenham also, then Cranwell Airdrome, Lincolnshire VHF Radio School. Back to 2nd Air Div. for B-24J installation blind landing systems, then 2nd Air Div. tech. inspector, communications. 1944 D-day flight line, Rockheath Airdrome.

November, attached to RAF Leicester East Airdrome, communications coordinator practice bombing range until May 1945. Then to 56th Fighter Group, Saffron Walden, on to Hinxton Hall Guard gate MP. November, home to U.S. on *Queen Mary*, discharged Dec. 3, 1945.

Married Verna Katke, October 1941 in Rockford, IL. They have a son, two daughters, and four grandchildren. Owned and operated Hammond Organ store 14 years; organ service 43 years. He is now semi-retired and trailering in Florida winters. He has been back to Norwich three times.

DONALD F. McCREA, was born Jan. 21, 1920 in St. Ignatius, MT. Entered the U.S. military Dec. 3, 1941 at Ft. Douglas, Salt Lake City, UT.

Service record: One month in U.S. Army. 1942, Jefferson Barracks, St. Louis, MO, basic training; Chanute Field, IL, airplane mechanics; 1942 Indianapolis, IN, aircraft engine specialist; 92nd Fighter Sqdn., Dale Mabry Field, Tallahassee, FL; Muroc, CA; Santa, CA, engine specialist; 330th Fighter Sqdn., 329th Fighter Group, Glendale, CA; San Diego, CA, engine specialist. 1943, Gulf Coast Flying Command Class of 43-I, pilot training; 34th Bomb Group, Blythe, CA, co-pilot B-24 aircraft. 1944, 389th Bomb Group, Hethel, England, co-pilot B-24, flew 30 missions. 1945, Laredo, TX, Gunnery School, pilot; ATC 4th Ferrying Group, 554th BU, Memphis, TN, pilot; ATC 7th Ferrying Group, Great Falls, MT, pilot.

Discharged October 1945 with the rank of first lieutenant. Awarded Distinguished Flying Cross, Air Medal with three clusters, European Campaign Medal.

Most interesting mission was bombing an airfield in Paris, France. As they passed over the city of Paris, the flak started to burst all around and through the formation. They could hear the thump, thump. The flak was dense and intense. It covered the entire formation. He expected to see someone go down, but it didn't happen. All aircraft returned to base safely, but full of holes. They had 15 holes in the fuselage. No one was seriously injured. He retrieved a momento, a shell piece two inches by four inches that fell at his feet.

Married to Margaret Myers, they have a son, daughter and grandson.

JAMES P. McCRORY, was born April 11, 1915 in Hobart, LA. Entered USAAF at Dallas, TX Jan. 25, 1943. Took basic training at Tent City, St. Petersburg, FL. Went to High Speed Radio School for 22 weeks at Camp Crowder, MO., Gunnery School at Harlingen, TX. Went to Salt Lake City for crew assignment and arrived at Peterson Field, Colorado Springs on December 25 for crew training. Left U.S. April 11, 1944 and arrived England April 25, 1944 via South America, Dakar and Marrakech.

Went to Ireland for three weeks for specialized training. Arrived at 492nd Bomb Group (H) on May 25 as first replacement crew for the group. Made first combat mission May 30, 1944. Flew 24 daylight missions, including two on D-day, and also to Politz, Munich, Kiel, Brunswick, Hamburg and Paris. Transferred to 801/492nd Bomb Group (Carpetbaggers) and made eight night missions plus six gasoline missions to 3rd Army in Belgium.

Received the Distinguished Flying Cross, Air Medal with three Oak Leaf Clusters and five Battle Stars. Returned to U.S. Nov. 19, 1944. Went to Miami Beach for R&R and to Ft. Worth AAFB to fly as radio operator for Pilot Transition School. Discharged at Ft. Sam Houston, TX Sept. 18, 1945.

He has one daughter and five sons, two step-daughters, 11 grandchildren and one great-grandchild.

BILL J. McCULLAH (BILLY THE KID), was born Nov. 3, 1923 in Springfield, MO. Inducted U.S. Army Jan. 23, 1943; reassigned Air Corps. Combat volunteer, aerial gunner. Gunnery, Harlingen, TX, graduating "top gun." Armament, Denver, CO; assigned Crew 11, 712th Bomb Sqdn. 448th Bomb Group, (B-24s) Boise, ID. First armorer; ball/nose turret gunner.

November 1943, flew to 8th Air Force via South America, opening Seething Air Base, England. Flew first group mission to Osnabruck, Germany Dec. 21, 1943. Lead crew, 30 missions, 22 Germany, one Poland, seven scattered. Seventeen missions nose turret (eight bomb releases), four ball, four tail, four waist. Last mission, Paris, June 26, 1944, top turret. Aircraft: *Boomerang* and *Little Sheperd* (Kills, Focke Wulf 190) First Berlin mission, plus two more; including major city "triples."

Discharged USAAC Oct. 23, 1945. Received Distinguished Flying Cross, four Air Medals, Purple Heart, two European Campaign Stars, two Presidential Unit Citations and several ribbons.

Recalled USAF Nov. 26, 1950 (Korean conflict). Flew 10 years. ICBMs 1960-1976. (Minuteman I, II and III; missile superintendent, technical advisor to chief of maintenance)

Retired USAF June 26, 1976 with rank of chief master sergeant after 29 years service. Married May 29, 1948 to Nina Ruth (Sally) Wood. They have two sons.

HAROLD W. McDONALD,

was born Sept. 12, 1916 in Cannon City, CO. Entered the USAF Dec. 22, 1942; navigator 2nd Air Div., 458th Bomb Group, 755th Sqdn.

Military locations/stations: Selman Field, LA; Wendover, UT; Tonapah, NV; Horsham St. Faith, England; March Field, CA. Participated in battle of Europe. First three missions were over Berlin, Germany.

Memorable experiences: Coming home on two engines; first mission over Berlin; coming back from a mission with German fighters following them home.

Discharged December 1945 with the rank of major (in reserves). Awarded Distinguished Flying Cross, Air Medal with clusters and ETO.

Married 55 years to Orva, they have one son Gary. Now retired, he enjoys working in the garden and yard, fishing and traveling.

EUGENE F. McDOWELL,

was born Nov. 19, 1921 at Detroit, MI. Entered service March 1942 as second lieutenant, infantry. Assigned 31st Inf. Div.; applied for flight training and entered preflight training November 1942. Obtained pilot rating in July 1943 at Lubbock, TX, Class 43-G, Gulf Coast Training Command.

Joined the 453rd Bomb Group, 732nd Sqdn. at Pocatello, ID. Flew B-24 to England via South America and Africa. Flew combat from February 1944 to September 1944, completing 30 missions, last seven as lead crew pilot. Served as mission controller at 2nd Combat Wing until end of hostilities, returning stateside August 1945.

Discharged February 1946 as a captain. Awarded two Distinguished Flying Cross Medals, four Air Medals, Purple Heart, six European Campaign Stars and other medals.

Married Frances Stringer in June 1942, they have one son. Sold Pressure Vessel manufacturing business and retired in 1991.

JOHN A. McDOWELL,

was born Aug. 21, 1925 at Washington, PA. Enlisted in the USAAC Reserve Aug. 17, 1943 and was called to active duty on March 14, 1944. Completed basic training at Keesler Field, Biloxi, MS and was sent to Gunnery School at Tyndall Field, Panama City, FL. After completing the gunnery course as an Emerson nose turret gunner, he was issued orders to Westover Field, MA to be crewed.

After processing was completed, they were sent to Chatham Field, GA for overseas training. Upon completion they were flown from National Airport, Washington, DC on March 14, 1945 (one year to the date of entering service) to Prestwick, Scotland where they were assigned to the 389th Bomb Group, 564th Bomb Sqdn. at Hethel.

His MOS was changed from 611 to 612 and was advanced to staff sergeant.

Wiley S. Parsons was the pilot of McDowell's crew.

He flew four missions with Parsons, then the war was over and he was discharged on April 12, 1946.

Married Barbara Meyers from Chahalis, WA. They have four children and eight grandchildren. Developed a casualty insurance agency in Seattle, WA which has been sold. McDowell is now retired in Everett, WA.

EDGAR A. McDUFF,

was born Aug. 11, 1924 in Milan, MO. Enlisted April 1943; basic training, Miami Beach, FL and 17th Airborne Div., Camp Mackall, NC (rifleman) until January 1944. To Army Air Corps February 1944; attended/instructed at Aerial Gunnery School, Harlingen, TX through July 1944. Trained with assigned crew at Mountain Home Army Air Base, ID until October 1944.

Sent to Norwich (Horsham St. Faith) England, November 1944 as staff sergeant/armorer gunner in 458th Bomb Group. Completed 33 combat missions, commencing Dec. 25, 1944 (Pronsfled/ground support). Battle damages: January and February 1945, Magdeburg synthetic oil plant/marshalling yards; and March 1945, Osnabruck marshalling yards. Final mission April 25, 1945, Bad Riechenhall rail yards.

Returned to U.S. July 1945 and discharged October 1945 from Santa Ana Army Air Base, CA.

Married Anna Schutte, 1950, they have two sons, two daughters, seven grandchildren. Resided in China Lake and Ridgecrest, CA from 1947.

Retired 1981 from Naval Weapons Center, China Lake, CA as safety specialist after 33 years civilian service. Died April 1993 in Oklahoma while traveling of stroke (in 1991) and subsequent complications.

GUY E. McELHANY,

was born Dec. 16, 1923 in Stockton, CA Joined USAAC on Feb. 26, 1943; completed basic training at Sheppard Field, TX; sent to Scott Field, IL, Radio School; then to Gunnery School at Fort Myers, FL. Assigned to B-24 crew in Charleston, SC; then to 8th Air Force in England, 491st Bomb Group, 855th Bomb Sqdn.

After 11 missions with original crew he was sent to London to RCM School. Upon completion he was returned to the 491st and flew the balance of his tour (30 missions) with several different crews. He found this vastly different; not knowing anyone on the crew put a whole new dimension on the missions.

Discharged Aug. 13, 1945 with the Air Medal and five clusters. He joined the staff of the county assessor and completed college at night. In 1962 resigned his position as chief appraiser/assistant assessor to become founder and president of the Financial Center Credit Union, from which he retired at the end of 1989. Today he devotes much of his time assisting elderly with financial considerations.

He currently resides in Stockton with his wife of 50 years. They have four children, six grandchildren and two great-grandchildren.

KENTON E. McELHATTAN (KENT),

was born in Knox, PA, Aug. 2, 1922. Enlisted in USAAC Aug. 22, 1942 after Franklin Commercial College. Basic training, Clearwater, FL; Technical School, Chanute Field, IL. Instructor at Chanute, May 1943 and qualified for Army Specialized Training Program; chemistry at University of Illinois; engineering at Ripon College; then University of Michigan Medical School. Requested combat duty after first semester. Trained at Wichita Falls, TX; Tyndall Field, FL; and Gowan Field, ID.

Aerial flight engineer (748), assigned B-24 nose turret gunner (611). Crew flew B-24 serial #44-50798 to Wales.

Assigned to 8th Air Force, 458th Bomb Group, 752nd Sqdn. Horsham St. Faith, England. Seven combat missions.

Bronze Star for only European Napalm Bomb Mission, Pointe Grave, France, April 15, 1945, and Air Medal. Flew last heavy bomber mission in Europe, April 25, 1945, target Bad Reichenhall, Austria. Flew trolley missions after V-E day and pilot check outs as flight engineer.

Crew flew B-24 to USA in June 1945. B-29 training aborted due to V-J day. Discharged November 1945 with the rank of sergeant.

Married high school classmate, Florence Ditty, July 9, 1946. Has son Kent, a daughter Elaine, and seven grandchildren. He is chairman of Industrial Scientific Corporation.

DENNIS J. McELHINNY,

was born March 20, 1924. Entered USAC March 20, 1943; 2nd Air Div., 8th Air Force. Aircraft and Engine Mechanic School, Keesler Field, MS; Aerial Gunnery School, Harlingen, TX; airplane propeller mechanic, Chanute Field, IL.

Participated in Normandy, Northern France, Ardennes and Rhineland campaigns. Memorable experiences: was when his crew was formed at Westover Field, MA, picked up a new B-24 at Mitchell Field, NY and flew to Goose Bay, Labrador. About 12 hours after arrival they were ordered to depart to make room for additional B-24s from the States. They finally landed at Bellfast, almost out of gas. Missions to Berlin, Hamburg, Ruhr Valley and Battle of the Bulge were also very memorable.

Discharged Oct. 1, 1945 with the rank of tech sergeant from Randolph Field, TX. Received EAME with four Bronze Stars and Air Medal with four Bronze Clusters.

Retired from his own insurance agency.

WILLIAM F. McELROY,

was born Jan. 9, 1922 in Pittsburgh, PA. Entered USAF July 6, 1942; airplane and engine mechanic on B-24s; 389th Bomb Group, 566th Sqdn. Stationed at Keesler Field, AAFTD Ford Motor Company; Hethel Field, Norwich, England. Participated in Air Offensive Europe, Ardennes, Naples Foggia, Normandy, Northern France, Sicily GO 33 WD 45, Rhineland GO 33 WD 45.

Discharged Sept. 29, 1945 with the rank of sergeant. Received Distinguished Unit Badge, GO 78 43; EAME and Good Conduct Medal.

Married to Lorraine, no children. Retired in 1983 after 32 years with Bethlehem Steel. Residing in Miami, FL since 1951.

JOSEPH T. McELVEEN SR.,

was born in Sumter County, Lynchburg, SC on Dec. 30, 1922. Entered the USAAF Feb. 11, 1943; armorer gunner, 8th Air Force, 2nd Air Div., 790th Bomb Sqdn., 467th Bomb Group. Stationed at St. Petersburg, FL; Lowry Field, Denver CO; Tyndall Field, Panama City, FL; Gowan Field, Boise, ID; Rackheath, England.

Participated in Air Offensive over Europe, Central Europe, Normandy, Northern France, Rhineland and Ardennes campaigns. On their eight mission, over Munich, Germany, they crashed landed at a base other than their own trying to make an emergency landing. McElveen was hospitalized from July to October from this crash. He flew on four missions after this.

Discharged Oct. 3, 1945 with the rank of staff sergeant. Awarded EAME with one Silver Star and one Bronze Service Star, Purple Heart, Air Medal, WWII Victory Medal and American Campaign Medal.

Married to Elizabeth in Boise, ID, April 12, 1944. They have two children, Martha and Joseph T. Jr., both attorneys in Sumter; four grandchildren Kate, Elizabeth, Joseph T. III and Joseph Tyler.

He owns and operates Empire Cycle Company selling Yamaha motorcycles, Schwinn bicycles, Toro and Lawn-Boy lawn mowers and other related items.

JAMES D. McFARLAND, was born Nov. 25, 1923 in Harrisburg, PA. Enlisted in the USAAC in February 1942 and served with the 11th Air Force Bomber Command in Alaska and the Aleutian Islands from May 1942 to February 1943 when he returned to the States to attend aviation cadet pilot training schools. He was commissioned and rated as a multi-engine pilot on Feb. 8, 1944. He was then assigned to March Field, CA for crew formation and B-24 transition training; after which he served with the 576th Sqdn., 392nd Bomb Group at Wendling, England from June 1944 to April 1945, completing 35 missions during that period.

On his fifth mission, July 21, 1944, to Oberpfaffenhofen, returned alone on three engines and crash landed in southern England, after being under frequent attack for three and a half hours, with one dead, one wounded and one with a nervous breakdown. On his 16th mission, Oct. 14, 1944, to Cologne, had two engines shot out on the same side and crash landed on a farm in eastern Belgium.

After finishing his tour he returned to the States in April 1945 and was discharged Nov. 6, 1945 with the rank of first lieutenant. Received Asiatic-Pacific Theater Ribbon with one Bronze Star, EAME with four Bronze Stars, Air Medal with five Oak Leaf Clusters, American Theater Ribbon, Good Conduct Medal (enlisted) and three Overseas Service Bars.

He then got his commercial pilot multi-engine land license and entered Penn State University, graduating in February 1950 with a degree in aeronautical engineering. He subsequently worked for Boeing-Vertol, General Electric Missile and Space Division and the Department of Defense Naval Air Development Center.

He retired in January 1989 and is still happily married (since Oct. 24, 1945) with three children and six grandchildren.

JOHN E. McGOUGH, was born Oct. 30, 1922 in Altoona, PA. Drafted Jan. 22, 1943, reserve enlistment Dec. 3, 1949; reserve recall to active duty Sept. 3, 1950. Served USAAC, Ordnance Dept., 2nd Air Div, 8th Air Force; U.S. Army Trans. Corps, operations sergeant PRR Rwy. Shop Bn. and chief clerk TRADS.

Military locations/stations: New Cumberland, PA; Jefferson Barracks, MO; Salt Lake City, UT; Tucson, AZ; Pocatello, ID; March Field, CA; Ft. Dix, NJ; Old Buckingham, England and Ft. Eustis, VA; Wilmington, DE.

Memorable experience was being assistant section chief in charge of night loading of bombs in the 735th Sqdn., 453rd Bomb Group at Old Buckingham, England.

Discharged Oct. 4, 1945, WWII, with the rank of staff sergeant, assistant section chief; May 17, 1952 with the rank of sergeant first class (P) operations sergeant. Received Bronze Star, Good Conduct, WWII Victory Medal and EAME Service Medal.

Married Oct. 14, 1950 to M. Teresa and has two sons, James V. and John W. Retired after four years employment with OPA and VA and 34 years RR service with PRR, Penn Central and Conrail. Today he enjoys hunting, fishing, bowling and traveling.

LESTER SAMUEL McGOWN, was born Sept. 2, 1923. Drafted May 1943, armored force trans to Army Air Force. Military locations/stations: Fort Knox, KY; Jefferson Barracks, MO; Harlingen, TX; Walla Walla, WA. Ended up in England with 448th Bomb Group, 714th Sqdn.

Flew first mission Jan. 7, 1945; second mission Jan. 15, Aschaffenburg. Completed 21 missions. Memorable experience was when crash landed (out of gas) B-24 #224 eight miles north of Dunkirk on coast.

Discharged Nov. 1, 1945 with the rank of sergeant. Received Air Medal and clusters, Good Conduct Medal and ETO awards.

Married in 1948 to Joyce Brooks. Raised seven children, five boys and two girls. Now retired after 21 years as service station operator.

HOWARD S. McGUFFIE, was born in 1923, Monticello, MS. Waist gunner on Joseph Bell's crew (see J.

Bell) Discharged in 1945, painter for Dow Chemical in Freeport, TX and in Louisiana and Mississippi until 1985.

Married and has two children. Now living in Jonesville, LA in a nursing home. McGuffie suffered serious stroke seven years ago.

GARL D. McHENRY, was born Sept. 26, 1924 in Huntington, In and was raised in Markle, IN. Entered AAF March 9, 1943; basic in St. Petersburg, FL; ROM training at Sioux Falls, SD; and aerial gunnery training at Laredo, TX. Assigned to B-24 crew 2366 and trained at Casper, WY.

Flew southern route to England and completed 31 bombing missions to Germany and France with 702nd Sqdn, 445th Bomb Group, 8th Air Force between May 20, 1944 and July 29, 1944. Bailed out on mission 32 and sprained ankle.

Received Distinguished Flying Cross, Air Medal and three clusters. Became gunnery instructor and air depot typist at Yuma, AZ. Discharged as a tech. sergeant Oct. 11, 1945.

Received BSRE from ITC in 1949 and was employed by ITT on the Bomarc Missile Project. Retired from TRW as a servo engineer in 1987.

Married Millicent R. Swaidner and has a daughter, son and three grandchildren.

JOHN J. McHUGH, was born Nov. 21, 1921 in Pittsfield, MA where he was raised. Entered the service July 27, 1942. A&E School, Lincoln AFB, Lincoln, NE; Electrical Specialist School, Chanute Field, IL; 567th Sqdn., 389th Bomb Group, Biggs Field, TX; 1943-1945 Hethel Norfolk, England.

U.K. technical sergeant, electrical specialist. Discharged Sept. 27, 1945.

Attended Wentworth Institute, Boston; Coyne Electrical School, Chicago. Government licenses: aircraft and engine mechanic, general radio tel., ham radio, flight engineer, pilot.

Aircraft electrician UAL SFO, one year; aircraft electrician BOAC JFK, three years; Pan American airways, 30 years. Retired 1982 as flight engineer B-747.

He has two daughters (nurses) and one son (KC-135 aircraft commander).

ROBERT D. McINTYRE, was born Feb. 8, 1921 in Conway Springs, KS. Entered the USAAC in July 1942 as a cadet. Served in the 491st Bomb Group, 853rd Sqdn.

Military locations/stations: Pampa Field, Pampa, TX; San Antonio, Kelly Field; Cimmaron Field, Cimmaron; Strother Field, Winfield, KS. Participated in the European Theater. Memorable experience was being shot down on 29th mission, Nov. 26, 1944. Was discharged October 1945 with the rank of first lieutenant.

Married Carol Corr Nov. 27, 1942 and has four daughters and three grandchildren. He was in the implement business and a truck dealer for 26 years. Now retired and farming.

DESCO E. McKAY, was born June 22, 1925 in Spades, IN. He enlisted in 1943 as an aviation cadet after graduation from high school in Fairland, IN. Completing Bombardier School at Carlsbad, NM, he was commissioned and sent to Tonopah, NV for training on B-24s.

Arriving in England, his crew was assigned to the 8th Air Force, 445th Bomb Group at Tibenham in East Anglia. Upon return to States he attended Bombardier Instructor School at Midland, TX.

After World War II he graduated in engineering from Purdue University and became a member of the Air Force Reserve's 434th Wing in Indiana. His business career was with AT&T's Western Electric Company in Indianapolis in engineering and purchasing management assignments.

McKay served in flying, personnel, comptroller and logistics assignments in the Air Force Reserve. He has been national vice president for Air of the Reserve Officers Association (ROA), has chaired ROA's national budget committee and strategic long range planning committee. He was promoted to colonel in 1971 and completed 33 years of service both in AT&T and the Air Force Reserve.

CHARLES H. McKEE, was born May 23, 1925 in Buena Vista, VA. Entered USAAC September 1943 and served as an aerial gunner.

Military locations/stations: Camp Lee, VA; Miami Beach, FL; Tyndall Field, FL; Peterson Field, CO; Hardwick Air Base, England; Sioux Falls, SD; Las Vegas (Henderson Field), NV. Assigned to 93rd Bomb Group, 330th Bomb Sqdn., 8th Air Force. Memorable experience was his first mission, Ludwigshaven.

Discharged Oct. 13, 1945 with the rank of staff sergeant. Received Good Conduct Medal, Air Medal with three Oak Leaf Clusters, Victory Medal and European Theater Ribbon.

Married and has two sons. Retired from CSX Railway.

OSCAR PATRICK McKEEVER, was born Oct. 15, 1920 in Fort Madison, IA, a railroad town and home of the Iowa State Penitentiary.

Joined the USAAF on July 8, 1940 and was sent to Chanute Field, Rantoul, IL. After spending four years in permanent party, requested Cadet School, but failed physical because of color blindness. Then, requested Gunnery School and graduated at Harlingen, TX.

Assigned crew at Lincoln, NE and did overseas training at Mountain Home, ID. Sent to Omaha, NE where they were assigned a new B-24M and flew to England. Arrived there February 1945 and assigned to the 445th Bomb Group, 702nd Bomb Sqdn. Crew was credited with 11 missions before the war ended. Returned to the States in an older war bird B-24J to retrain in B-29. His memorable experience was meeting his brother Tom at the Air Force Supply Depot in England.

Received discharge on Aug. 12, 1945.

ROBERT L. McKENZIE, was born in Eldred, PA. Joined USAAC in December 1942 after graduating from Clarion (PA) State College and teaching high school and coaching basketball one school year.

Entered primary pilot training in Vernon, TX; basic at Enid, OK; graduated from multi-engine advanced training at Frederick, OK with Class 43-I and commissioned Oct. 1, 1943. B-24 transition training at Liberal, KS and combat crew training at Casper, WY.

Assigned to 467th Bomb Group, 790th Sqdn. at Rackheath, England. Flew 35 mission tour in European Theater of Operations starting July 21, 1944 and finishing Jan. 16, 1945. Most memorable mission was Hamburg, Germany, Aug. 6. 1944. Flak so heavy approaching target it seemed impossible to penetrate and survive, but somehow managed. Otherwise, had plane battle damage several times, but no aborted missions or crew injuries.

Also flew gasoline missions to Clastres, France to supply Gen. Patton's rapid advancement toward Berlin. Returning from missions often proved hazardous due to low ceilings, visibility, limited navigational facilities and heavy traffic.

Discharged Oct. 13, 1947 following two years of recruiting duty.

Earned masters degree at St. Bonaventure University and retired from public school counseling in Jamestown, NY in January 1985. Has winter residence in Cape Canaveral, FL.

THOMAS H. McKIERNAN, enlisted May 5, 1942; graduated as pilot, Class of 43-F. Assigned as B-24 instructor pilot with 382nd Group at Pocatello and Muroc Army Air Bases. Joined the 458th Bomb Group at Horsham St. Faith on March 2, 1944. Transferred to 93rd Bomb Group at Hardwick on April 15 to become a G-H lead crew. Assigned to 466th Bomb Group at Attlebridge on August 1.

After bombing tour was diverted from Port, assigned to 316th TC Group as instructor pilot in C-109. Assisted with drop of paratroopers from C-47 at Battle of the Bulge, then returned to the U.S.

Served in Korea with 61st TC Wing, and flew 296 missions in Vietnam with 21st TASS. Returned from Vietnam and received a medical retirement as lieutenant colonel on Oct. 1, 1968. Received Silver Star, three Distinguished Flying Cross Medals, Bronze Star, 26 Air Medals and the Air Force Commendation Medal.

He married Marie Sturm in August 1946. They have two children and three grandchildren.

CONLEY NEWTON McKINNISH, was born March 22, 1921 in Asheville, NC. Enlisted September 1942 in the USAAF. On Norwich, England, joined 389th Bomb Group, 2nd Air Div., 8th Air Force, B-24 bombers. Completed 30 missions and participated in battles in Germany and France. Discharged September 1945 with rank of staff sergeant.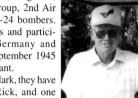

Married Athene Clark, they have two sons, Rock and Rick, and one daughter Rita. Retired from Olin Corp, Ecusta Paper and Cellophane Plant in 1980. Now a beef cattle farmer.

MELBURNE DEKALB McLENDON, was born April 21, 1921 in Atlanta, GA. Entered USAAC July 1942; served in the 8th Air Force, 448th Bomb Group, 715th Sqdn.

After training, was sent to Seething, England where he flew 30 missions over France and Germany. Shot down on 30th mission, held in prison camp for three and a half months.

Discharged Oct. 10, 1945 with the rank of staff sergeant. Melburne and his four brothers: George, Jack, Frederick and James served their country at the same time, four in the Navy and one in the Army Air Forces.

Married to Jacqueline K., they have two children, Kirk and Loyce, and two grandchildren. Received his education at the University of Georgia School of Law, LLB degree, and practiced law for 36 years. He retired in 1986. Has traveled extensively in Europe, Asia, South Pacific, Australia, New Zealand, U.S. and Canada.

HAROLD R. McMAHON, was born July 25, 1923 in Woodsfield, OH and raised in Macedonia, OH and graduated local high school 1941.

Entered USAAC Dec. 29, 1942; attended various training schools, including Davis Monthan and Blythe Air Base. Eventually assigned to 492nd Bomb Group (H) at Biggs Field, TX.

After phase training, sent to England via southern route. Flew 26 missions out of North Pickenham with the ill-fated 492nd. After its disbandment, August 1944, was sent on detached service with the 15th Air Force to Brindisi, Italy as part of a "carpetbagger" outfit, flying 27 clandestine missions into the Dalmation Coast area on the Adriatic Sea, for a total of 53 combat missions.

Awarded four Air Medals, four Battle Stars and several other ribbons. Discharged as a tech. sergeant May 25, 1945.

Married September 1945. Remarried July 1, 1967 to Martha Blouch. Has three children and eight grandchildren. After two careers, retired in 1985 in Westlake, OH.

JAMES H. McMAHON, was born December 1923 in The Bronx, NY and enlisted Dec. 27, 1941 in the USAF. Served at March Field and Hamilton Field, CA; attended Las Vegas Flexible Gunnery School, Las Vegas, NV in 1942, Class 42-45.

Assigned to B-17s with the 43rd Sqdn., 29th Bomb Group at Gowen Field, Boise, ID. Flew the ball turret; transferred to B-24s at Davis Monthan Field, Tucson, AZ in 1942. Did phase training in Tucson, Alamogordo, and Clovis. His brother, Thomas, was a 306th Bomb Group tail-gunner with the 329th Sqdn. and was shot down on Jan. 13, 1943 over Lille.

Requested overseas duty and left Herington, KS in August 1943; joined the 330th Sqdn., 93rd Bomb Group; flew 32 missions with the 329th & 409th Sqdns. of the 93rd Bomb Group. Flew first mission on Oct. 18, 1943 and last mission on June 21, 1944 when force landed in Sweden on the way home from Berlin. Every mission was a battle for survival. Escaped from Sweden in December 1944.

Returned to the States on Dec. 31, 1944 and was medically discharged at the Mitchell Field Old Cantonement Hospital on May 5, 1945. His brother, S/Sgt. Thomas, returned from a POW camp in 1945. His cousin, T/Sgt. William C. Lilienthal Jr., of the 92nd Bomb Group was killed in action over Solingen on Dec. 1, 1943.

McMahon became a U.S. Treasury Department officer in 1950. Later became a NYC police detective with the Manhattan West Detective Division of the NYC Police Department. Retired with line of duty injuries. Became an undercover agent with the TRA for several years and then moved to California.

Earned an AA degree from Orange Coast College, Costa Mesa, CA and BA degree from the California State University. Began a teaching career and earned special education degrees from the University of California at Irvine and San Diego State University.

Awards and decorations include the Distinguished Flying Cross, Air Medal with three Oak Leaf Clusters and Purple Heart. The 93rd Bomb Group earned two Presidential Citations and many campaign stars. Also received the New York state Conspicuous Service Cross with a Gold Cross as well as several awards from NYC Police Dept.

He is a California licensed private investigator and also employed by the Sonoma County California sheriff's department. Married Helen Wells in Newport Beach, CA in 1966. They have a daughter Shauna.

HUBERT L. McMILLAN, was born near Millersview, TX, Sept. 27. 1918, one of nine children of a sharecropper. Joined Signal Corps, 2nd Inf. Div. on Oct. 14, 1940. November 1942 he qualified for flight training; attended Flight School; graduated Sept. 1, 1943; commissioned second lieutenant with wings.

Four-engine transitional training at Ft. Worth, TX, April 1944; southern route to England and joined 579th Sqdn., 392nd Bomb Group at Wendling. Flew 30 missions over Germany and German occupied territory. Completed last mission September 1944. With co-pilot, flight engineer and radio operator was shipped to Lyneham, England to fly approximately 15-20 gas haul missions to fast moving ground troops in Europe.

As pilot on first mission to Politz, flak over target was spectacular, they lost six aircraft. On another mission with #3 engine out, entered landing pattern when one crewman reported three bombs still in bomb bay, while talking to him, McMillan heard a dull thud three times. Crewman said, "Oh, never mind."

On a mission flying deputy lead, three bombs on bottom of one section hung, rest of bombs jammed against them, to avoid a catastrophe bombardier and squadron bombardier moved bombs back of bulkhead behind bomb bay and replaced pins.

Another mission, #1 engine knocked out, signaled copilot to feather #1. Due to misunderstood communication #4 engine feathered. Lost so much speed group flew on. On way back alone three Me-109s flew a perfect pursuit curve on them but for reasons unknown never fired a shot.

Unforgettable mission, damaged hydraulic system, control tower sent his crew to neighboring field. Had to hand crank gear down, landed without brakes, coasted to end of runway before plane stopped. Being late returning to Wendling Air Base, enlisted men reported quarters cleaned out in readiness for new crew.

Upon returning to States, sent to Alabama as instructor, was given job as flight testing B-24s that had been through maintenance. Discharged May 1945 on point system.

After discharge, married, settled down to livestock farming for 36 years. Retired 1980, spends retirement traveling, fishing, enjoying family.

EARL K. McNEW, was born May 28, 1918 in Holton, IN. Married Irma Jeffries in April 1941. When he was drafted in January 1943, his daughter was 10 months old and his son was born four months later.

Sent to Ft. Lewis, WA. In May 1943, transferred to Air Corps and sent to Kearns, UT. Commissioned navigator, May 1944, at Hondo, TX. B-17 training at Ellington Field, TX. In August 1944, joined 852nd Bomb Group at North Pickenham, England. After five months transferred 853rd Bomb Group. After finishing tour of 30 missions returned to Houston, TX, May 1945.

Received Distinguished Flying Cross and Air Medal with four Oak Leaf Clusters. Discharged as first lieutenant, November 1945 at Columbus, IN.

Farmed one year then went to Purdue. Received BA degree in 1949 and after teaching three years went back to Purdue for MS degree in 1953. His family consists of his wife of 52 years, five children, 13 grandchildren and seven great-grandchildren. Retired in Tucson, Az.

EDWARD T. McQUELLON JR., was born April 26, 1920 in Peoria, IL. Entered the USAAF April 1943; served 467th Bomb Group, 789th Sqdn.

Stationed at Rackheath, England; flew 30 missions in ETO.

Discharged August 1946; discharged from Reserves June 1956. Achieved rank of first lieutenant.

Married Eleanor Henrick Aug. 7, 1941; one son, deceased. Owns and operates Eddie McQuellon Plumbing and Heating Company.

THOMAS L. McQUOID, enlisted in the USAAC 1942; Aviation Cadet 1943-44; assigned B-24 Liberator, heavy bombers. Combat crew co-pilot, 489th and 448th Bomb Groups, 8th Air Force, England, 1944-45. Completed 35 missions over Germany and occupied Europe.

Awarded six Air Medals, ETO with four stars, WWII Victory Medal, three Air Force Commendations and Outstanding Unit Citation. Separated USAAC 1945, recalled 1951.

Graduated Arkansas Tech University, Graduate School, University of New Mexico. Retired 1968 as lieutenant colonel. Real estate broker and appraiser 1970-91.

Organizations: The Military Order of the World Wars; Youth Leadership Foundation; The Halifax River Yacht Club,

Daytona Beach, FL; and the 2nd Air Division Association. In 1990, attended a reunion of all 10 B-24 Liberator crew members known as "Shroyer's Crew."

Tom and Betsy (Gill) were married in O'Fallon, IL, May 17, 1952. They have one son, Tom Jr.

WILLIAM C. McRORIE, was born April 1923 in Flint, MI. Entered the USAF November 1942. Southeast Training Command (pilot training) single engine fighter, graduated, then B-24 co-pilot training in Florida.

Second Air Div., 8th Air Force, Europe, Norwich, England (Tibenham) 445th Bomb Group B-24s. Fifteen missions European Theater, credit for nine, others recalled or had plane trouble. One crash landing.

Memorable experience: Helgioland, Germany, leader shot down by AA and extensive damage to all planes in squadron, bombs fell into sea by radio bomb release when leader hit March 20, 1945.

Flew 20 or more low level tour missions with ground crews aboard to view destruction of Hitler's reich. After war in ETO was over in May 1945, trained in B-29s for invasion of Japan which never happened due to atomic bomb.

Discharged October 1945 from active duty; USAF Reserve, April 1983. Achieved rank of major. Awarded Air Medal.

Married, has four children and seven grandchildren. He is retired executive of Buick Motor Div., General Motors Corporation after 39 years.

ROBERT J. McVEIGH, was born April 22, 1920 in North Ireland. Entered USAAC Oct. 6, 1941; served as armorer gunner, 2nd Air Div.

Stationed Hethel, England, 389th Bomb Group, 567th Sqdn. Participated in the Air War over Europe from October 1943 to Feb. 24, 1944. Shot down, POW at Stalag Luft VI and IV. Finished 15 missions (14 and a half).

Discharged Oct. 5, 1945 with the rank of staff sergeant. Received Air Medal with two Oak Leaf Clusters, Purple Heart, EAME with two Bronze Stars, American Defense Medal, POW Medal and Good Conduct Medal.

His wife Wanda was a Navy nurse; they have one daughter Eileen. He is a retired plant manager living now in Rancho Bernardo, CA.

ROBERT E. MEAD, was born on Sept. 21, 1924 and raised in Bucklin, KS. He enlisted in the USAAC while he was in high school. After graduation he joined the Aviation Cadet Program at the University of North Dakota.

After Preflight School at Santa Ana, CA, he was sent to Lowry Field in Denver, CO for Armament School. After gunnery training at Tyndall Field, FL, he joined Robert L. Thompson crew at Mt. Home, ID.

In January 1945 he flew a new B-24 to England via the northern route. He was assigned to the 445th Bomb Group, 703rd Sqdn. at Tibenham. He flew bombing missions over Europe till V-E day.

Returned to the States on May 25, 1945 on a war weary B-24 that had to be put in a military junk yard in Greenland on the way home. Was discharged on Feb. 12, 1945 at Fort Dix, NJ with the rank of staff sergeant. He has four children and three grandchildren.

LILLIAN GRACE MEADOWS, was born on Aug. 11, 1918 in Mancelona Township, MI. She entered the WAAC in March 1943 at Miami, FL. Basic training was at the Cantonment area at Daytona Beach, FL; Army Administration School at Steven Austins State Teachers College, Nacogdoches, TX; trained on the job for Cryptography at Galena Field in Spokane, WA and was stationed there for one year.

She re-enlisted as a WAC. Had overseas training in Fort Oglethorpe, GA and then embarked on the transport ship *Argentina* out of New York. Was underway 13 days in a convoy destined for Scotland. Went to Stone, England for assignment to the 2nd Air Div., B-24 Liberator's Headquarters as a Cryptographer at Kettering Hall. After D-day, she was sent to Oxford University to learn English Code. Then back to 2nd Air Div., 315th Signal Corps.

At war end, she transferred to First Aid Division with B-17s. Returned to the States in July 1945 and was discharged with the rank of T/5.

She married Harry Moore in June 1946. They have three sons, one daughter and six grandsons. They reside in Miami, FL.

JOSEPH E. MEINTEL, was born on May 16, 1924 in Altoona, PA. He enlisted Dec. 10, 1942 in the USAAC 1092 lead pilot four engine. Received Wings, Class 43-I at Aloe AAF at Victoria, TX. Got his crew and trained at March Field, CA, then went to the 453rd Bomb Group, 735th Sqdn. with the 8th Air Force to Attleboro, England.

Participated in the Battle of the Bulge and numerous other ones in Europe. Memorable experiences: landing on a "metal landing mat" and leaving a "shot up" (many holes) B-24 in Brussels; flying back from Europe (three Red-lined Engines) dropping bomb load and landing below London as #3 prop and the entire front of the engine was gone, they had no radio and they were led into a 2400 ft. fighter strip by English Fighter planes. The ceiling was less than 100 feet. They blew a tire, the engine and prop were replaced and the aircraft had to be stripped of its armament to fly it out.

He received the Presidential Unit Citation, Air Medal with clusters and the European Theatre Ribbon. He was discharged in December 1945.

Graduated from Penn State in September 1949 as an engineer and has had a career in engineering and management in both the private sector and the government. He vested with General Electric and plans to retire from the government early in 1994.

There are eight members of their lead crew that are still living and they think the most of any crew in the 2nd. Air Div.

Married Gloria McClain from Altoona, PA about 50 years ago. They have three children: Mark, Gretchen and Christopher.

HARRY K. MELLINGER, was born on Sept. 12, 1923 in Lebanon, PA. He enlisted as an aviation cadet on April 15, 1943. He was commissioned a second lieutenant bombardier at VAAF on July 1, 1944 and was assigned to the 491st Bomb Group, 8th Air Force on Nov. 18, 1944.

Flew 27 missions, 10 as lead bombardier. Memorable missions were Magdeburg (5), Berlin (2), Homburg and Dresden.

His awards included the Distinguished Flying Cross, four Air Medals and the Presidential Unit Citation. Discharged on Sept. 29, 1945, he re-enlisted in the USAACR.

Was called to active duty on May 7, 1951 during the Korean conflict and served as a R&D engineering officer at Wright/Patterson AFB for 21 months. He retired from the USAFR as a lieutenant colonel on July 30, 1972.

After WWII he graduated from Penn State University with a BS in aeronautical engineering. He was employed in Air Force Civil Service for 11 years as an engineer at WPAFB and automatic data processing manager at Olmstead AFB. He joined the Philco Corporation in April 1960 with 28 and a half years in engineering, marketing and sales positions. He retired in September 1988.

Married to Alice Stiles, has one son, one daughter and a grandson from a previous marriage.

NORMAN J. MELLOW, was born on Feb. 14, 1920 in San Mateo, CA. He enlisted in the USAAC on Oct. 23, 1941; assigned to 392nd Bomb Group, 578th Sqdn.; left Topeka, KS on Aug. 13, 1943 for Presque Isle, ME; then to Gander Field in Newfoundland; to Prestwick, Scotland, where landed in a cow pasture; then on to Wendling.

Memorable experiences: dancing with Adele Astaire (Lady Charles Cavendish) in London's Rainbow Corner; Oct. 9, 1943-4th mission, Capt. Edwards crew (Ford's Folly) and JU-88 encounter; April 11, 1944-16th mission, Capt. Edwards crew and ME-109 attack.

Discharged Sept. 11, 1945 with the rank tech sergeant. Received the Air Medal with three Oak Leaf Clusters, Distinguished Flying Cross, Good Conduct Medal, American Defense Service Medal and EAME Campaign Medal.

Mellow and wife Alberta (Bert) have two sons, a daughter, 11 grandchildren and two great-grandchildren. He is enjoying his retirement, traveling and square dancing.

CHARLES A. MELTON (CHARLEY), was born on April 9, 1919 in Omaha, NE. He entered active duty with the USAAC on Sept. 16, 1940 with 203rd; Aviation Cadet, 1942 to 1943; then assigned to the 458th Bomb Group at Wendover, UT after B-25 and B-17 training in 1943.

Moved to England, Horsham St. Faith as group in January 1944. Completed 30 missions on June 6, 1944 on D-day aboard the aircraft *Paddlefoot*.

Returned to the States in September 1944. Flew radar students from Victorville, CA until his release from active duty in November 1945. Worked for Bekins Van & Storage in California until 1959. Then with the FAA as a regional training officer until he retired in 1980.

Married his high school sweetheart on June 6, l939, they have three sons, two daughters and also raised his nephew, whose father was killed in action in World War II. They have 12 grandchildren.

Lives in the same town where he attended high school and was later married. He is retired from the FAA (U.S. Civil Service) and from the USAFR.

GEORGE W. MERCER, was born on Feb. 12, 1919 in Livingston, TX. He enlisted into the USAAC on Jan. 15, 1942, assigned to 2nd Air Div., 44th Bomb Group. Was with the 1646th Ordinance Supply and Maintenance Co. in England from 1942 until 1945.

Memorable experience was loading and unloading bombs and small arms ammunition at supply points.

Mercer received the Good Conduct Medal and the ETO Ribbon. He was discharged on Oct. 18, 1945 with the rank of sergeant.

He was killed in a car accident in March 1993. His wife Virginia is living in Marquez, TX and their daughter, Claryce Mercer lives in Pasadena, TX.

GRANVILLE E. MESEKE (CHICK), was born on May 13, 1921 in Vandalia, IL. He entered the USAAC on Jan. 6, 1942 as an aircraft armorer gunner 612. Stationed at Sheppard Field, TX for basic; Lowry Field, CO, Armorer School; and joined 93rd Bomb Group at Ft. Myers, FL.

Memorable experiences: crossing the Atlantic on the

Queen Elizabeth with some 19,000 other troops; joining the crew of *Little Lady* as tail gunner and getting hit by fighters on first mission, lost left rudder to 20mm cannon fire but got home okay. The most memorable day was Aug. 1, 1943, North Africa for the Ploesti oil field mission. While passing over target, their plane tipped up on a wing to go around a big fireball-tail turrent got pretty warm as they went by. The trees were waving in their propwash they were so low. They headed for Turkey and made a hot landing, overran the end of the runway, but everything was okay.

Discharged on June 4, 1945 at Camp Beal, CA with the rank of staff sergeant. Received two Distinguished Flying Crosses, four Air Medals, seven Campaign Stars and two Unit Presidential Unit Citations and other medals.

Married Aileen Bridge on Feb. 27, 1946, they have two sons, two daughters and seven grandchildren. He is retired from Civil Service (Navy) since 1980. Enjoys traveling, gardening and life to the fullest.

JOSEPH R. METCALF, was born on April 12, 1922 in Brocton, IL. He joined the USAAC on Dec. 6, 1939, stationed at Schoen Field, Ft. Benjamin Harrison, 1939 to July 1941. Transferred to the 42nd Material Sqdn. at Davis Monthan Field, Tucson, AZ in July 1941 and made first sergeant in September 1941. On Dec. 7, 1941 he transferred to Muroc Dry Lake, CA.

Applied for Flying Cadet School and was accepted in Class 43-F at Randolph Field; primary training, Coleman, TX; basic and advanced training, Waco, TX; graduated on June 26, 1943 and was sent to Lockbourne, OH to fly B-17s. In September 1943 he transferred to Davis Monthan Field, Tucson, AZ to fly B-24s with the 855th Sqdn., 491st Bomb Group.

He was sent to England in May 1944, his crew (Ragged but Right) was a lead crew, and flew every fourth mission. First at Metfield, near Norwich. After bomb dump blew up, he was transferred to North Pickenham close to Kings Lynn.

Flew 30 missions over Germany. His most memorable mission was on Nov. 26, 1944, their plane was leading group to bomb oil refinery at Misberg, Germany. They lost 16 of the 28 planes to fighters.

He returned to States in January 1945. Was assigned to Air Transport Command at Love Field and Civilian Airport, El Paso, TX. Discharged in September 1945, he was awarded the Distinguished Flying Cross and the Air Medal on several occasions.

Graduated from the University of Arizona in 1948. Worked for Sears for 31 years, managing stores in El Centro, Ventura, Tucson and the South Coast Plaza Store in Costa Mesa, CA until retirement in 1978. Married Margaret Cunningham from Tucson, June 25, 1943; they spend summers in Pinetop, AZ and winters in Tucson, AZ.

JOHN METZ (N.M.I.), was born on Jan. 4, 1922 in Buhl, ID and raised in a rural farming community. Shortly after graduation from high school, he joined the USAAC on July 30, 1940.

Promoted through the ranks to staff sergeant first aircraft mechanic and was crew chief on the AT-9 trainer at Mather Field, CA. Was then assigned to Class 42-J for pilot training at Santa Maria, CA. After 72 hours of flight training, was washed out.

Applied for overseas duty and sent to aircraft armament training. On Dec. 4, 1943, he shipped out of Camp Kilmer, NJ and arrived at Liverpool, England on Dec. 15, 1943. He was assigned to the 389th Bomb Group at Hethel until the 491st Bomb Group arrived, then assigned to 491st-853rd Sqdn. Armament on Aug. 15, 1944, Metfield Station #366 and promoted to technical sergeant as a power turret mechanic.

His memorable experience was the Bomb Dump Explosion where they lost many aircraft.

Left North Pickenham on June 17, 1945 flying B-24 back to States via Meek's Field, Iceland, Greenland, and Goose Bay, Labrador. He was scheduled for re-assignment to the Pacific Theater, when the "A" bombs were dropped on Japan, resulting in his discharge on Sept. 22, 1945.

After returning to the States, he worked with a manufacturing company that had built B-17 parts during the war, then worked briefly as an aircraft mechanic for Western Airlines. In 1947 he signed on with the California Department of Transportation as a heavy equipment mechanic. After 36 years, he retired as an equipment superintendent III.

RAYMOND METZ, was born on Sept. 20, 1923 in Detroit, MI; graduated from Northeastern High in January 1942; and drafted into the USAAC in March 1943. Had basic at St. Petersburg, Fl; Radio School, Scott Field, IL; gunnery training at Tyndall Field, FL; crew training at Charleston, SC.

They crossed the ocean on the *Queen Elizabeth,* arriving June 5th and after orientation in Ireland, were assigned as replacements to the 458th Bomb Group, 754th Sqdn. at Horsham, St. Faith. Flew their first mission on July 6th to Kiel, Germany. They flew several "gasoline" runs during September. Illness caused Metz to fall behind the crew on missions. The crew completed its 35th mission on December 10, Metz made up his last two missions on December 25 and 27 flying with other crews.

He married Martha Moos on his return to the States. Was assigned to Fort Worth, TX flying with pilots on "cross countrys," then as a radio instructor for B-32 Devastator crews. He was discharged in October 1945. He has two sons and two daughters. An electrician, his last 20 years were with Ford Motor Company.

GEORGE MEUSE, was born in 1924 in Boston, MA. He enlisted in the U.S. Army in November 1942 and commissioned as a second lieutenant USAAF as pilot in January 1944.

Flew a B-24 to ETO then assigned to the 854th Sqdn., 491st Bomb Group, 8th Air Force. He was shot down on his 12th mission over Misberg, Germany on Nov. 26, 1944. He was a POW at Stalag Luft 1 until he was liberated by the Russians on May 1, 1945.

He remained on active duty, flying first postwar B-29 overseas deployment in 1947. He completed 60 missions in a B-29 over Korea in 1950 and 1951. He flew F8F Bearcat with the 1st Fighter Sqdn., Bien Hoa, VNAF 1958 to 1959. He retired from the USAF in 1965 with the rank of lieutenant colonel.

Meuse and his wife Florence have four daughters. After he graduated from UNO in Omaha, NE, he worked for Brandeis Department Stores, retiring as vice president. He operated airport and flying services in Osage Beach, MO and enjoys water sports. Their children are all married and they cherish visits from their eight grandchildren.

ROBERT D. MEUSE, was born on March 11, 1924 in Reading, MA. He enlisted in the USAAC in 1942 and received basic military training in Atlantic City, NJ. Transferred to Massachuestts State College (now University of Massachusetts) in Amherst, MA as an aviation student.

Became an aviation cadet at Maxwell Field, Montgomery, AL and completed flight training at Stuttgart Army Air Base in Stuttgart, AR and received his commission as second lieutenant. He was assigned to the 8th Air Force, 389th Bomb Group, 567th Sqdn. Flew 32 missions from Hethel, England. He remained in the Air Force Reserve after his discharge and was promoted to captain. Received the Air Medal with many clusters.

He attended the Boston University and joined Hughes Aircraft Company in 1954 as a quality engineer. He retired after 35 years with Hughes in 1989. Presently in retirement and is a recording engineer with his own company, Meuse Audio Arts, recording Symphony Orchestras for delayed FM Classical Radio Broadcast.

ROBERT A. MEYER, was born on Nov. 13, 1924 in Pittsburgh, PA. He reported for USAAF basic training in January 1943 at Keesler Field, MS; followed by CTD classification; pilot preflight training was at San Antonio, TX.

He graduated from advance twin-engine flight training as a pilot, second lieutenant, Class 44-D at Pampa, TX. Transferred to B-24 transition at Fort Worth, TX, followed by RTU training (Crew 7495) at Casper, WY.

In December 1944 he flew a Ford built B-24 with crew to the 8th Air Force via the northern route. He was assigned to the 445th Bomb Group, 701st Sqdn. He completed about 15 missions by V-E day. Was awarded the Air Medal and the ETO Badge with two Battle Stars. Flew the B-24 home via northern route with flight crew and 10 ground crew members. Reported for B-29 transition at Roswell, NM. On V-J day, training was halted and he was discharged in November 1945.

He married Charlotte Bramer on June 18, 1945, they have five children and 10 grandchildren.

ROBERT G. MEYER, was born on Oct. 7, 1923 in Brooklyn, NY. He enlisted in the USAAC in November 1942. Attended Air Gunnery at Ft. Myers, FL and Air Mechanics at Keesler Field, Biloxi, MS. He remembers flying with the greatest group of men ever assembled.

Discharged on May 11, 1945 with the rank of staff sergeant. He received the Distinguished Flying Cross and the Air Medal.

Married Shirley Massey in 1945, they have two sons, one daughter, eight grandchildren and two great-grandchildren. He has been retired from the U.S. Postal Service since 1978.

PAUL E. MEYERS, was from Fort Wayne, IN and about 19 years old when he was in the USAAC. His nickname in the 93rd Bomb Group was "Recruit." He served as the left waist gunner and armorer on a B-24 Liberator, assigned to the 328th Bomb Sqdn. at Hardwick, England in October 1944. They saw quite a bit of flak on their tour but not too many enemy fighters.

Memorable experience was when a ME-262 came barrelling through their formation and never fired a shot. He was just showing off. Some of their roughest targets were Hemburg, Munster and Magdeburg synthetic oil plants. They had nine minutes of flak on each mission to Berlin. Flew his last mission on April 8, 1945.

After the war he served an apprenticeship as a plumber/steamfitter and worked as as industrial pipefitter for 14 years, then took a managerial job at International Harvester where he retired as a maintenance general foreman. In between times, he joined the Indiana Air National Guard and their unit was called to active duty in February 1951. He served 21 months as Section Head of the Armament Section of a Fighter Interceptor Squadron during the Korean War. Received six Air Medals, three Battle Stars on the ETO Ribbon and a Presidential Unit Citation with one cluster.

All of crew except two are members of the 2nd Air Division Association. Five of them attended the 1992 Las Vegas convention. It was the first time he has seen or spoken to any of them since 1945 (47 years), so it was a joyous reunion for all.

Meyers is married and has seven children and 18 grandchildren. Retired he spends summers on a lake in Northern Indiana and winters at Siesta Key in Sarasota, FL.

EDGAR W. MICHAELS, was born on July 20, 1923 in Pittsburgh, PA. His military service was February 1943 to September 1945, with the rank of first lieutenant. MOS aerial navigator B-24 with the 8th Air Force.

He trained at Ellington Field, TX; San Marcos, TX;

Harlingen, TX and Pueblo, CO. ETO was in Shipdham, England with the 44th Bomb Group, 506th Sqdn. He was missing in action in occupied France. His awards include the Air Force Medal, Purple Heart and the ETO.

Michaels was a navigation instructor at March AFB, Riverside, CA in 1945. Presently CEO Chairman with Hinkel/Hofmann Co., Pittsburgh, PA.

Married Norma Barker in 1950, they have three children: Laura Rubinoff (husband, Edward), James Michaels (wife, Beth) and Gary Michaels (wife, Joan). They are all presently living in Potomac, MD.

LOUIS A. MICHALAK, was born on Aug. 16, 1921 on a farm near Tarentum, PA and graduated from high school in 1939. He was inducted into the military service on Sept. 4, 1942; took basic and airplane mechanics schooling in B-24s at Keesler Field, MS. Then on to Ford Willow Run for more mechanical B-24 training.

Served at the following bases: Birmingham Modification, Kelley, TX; Love, TX; Casper, WY; Gowen Field, ID. Transferred to the 754th Sqdn., 458th Bomb Group at Tonopah, NV in October 1943. Arrived in England, Horsham, St. Faith on Feb. 1, 1944 as a sergeant mechanic on the flight line. They were also assigned other duties, such as CQ, KP and guard.

Returned to the States in June 1945 and discharged at Patterson Field, OH on Oct. 12, 1945 with the rank of sergeant.

Married Helen L. Landowski in August 1947, they have three children and one grandchild. He was employed at a Glass Manufacturing Plant for 42 years in various clerical and production positions. Has been retired since 1983 and enjoys gardening, hunting, fishing and reading.

GEORGE W. MICHEL, was born on June 10, 1924 in Saginaw, MI. Drafted into the USAAC in March 1943, radio operator and gunner with the 8th Air Force, 392nd Bomb Group, 576th Bomb Sqdn. Stationed at Scott Field, IL; Laredo, TX; Eagle Pass, TX; Blythe, CA; Wendling; Selfridge Field. Flew nine and a half missions from June 11, 1944 to July 11, 1944. His plane was damaged over Munich, ended up in Switzerland and he escaped with the help of the FFI.

Discharged in November 1945 with the rank of tech sergeant. He received the Air Medal with clusters.

Married Colleen Vanderslice on June 25, 1949, they have six children and 19 grandchildren. Received a BS degree in civil engineering and has a career in international locations (Europe and South America) in product design, manufacturing and marketing.

WARREN E. MICKELSON, was born on Jan. 14, 1923 in Day County, SD. Inducted into the USAAC in March 1943; basic training at Sheppard Field, TX; Aircraft Mechanics at Keesler Field, MS; Gunnery at Tyndall Field.

Was assigned on a crew as aerial engineer gunner at Westover Field, MA. Took overseas training at Savannah, GA, including one week at Batista Field, Cuba. Ferried a new B-24J to Ireland and joined the 93rd Bomb Group, 330th Sqdn. at Hardwick, England, where he completed 35 missions on Feb. 3, 1945.

Returned to Santa Ana, CA for re-assignment to Ft. George, Wright, WA, where he was discharged in November 1945. His most memorable mission was his 32nd to Harburg. There was severe flak damage, causing loss of two engines, fuel and electrical lines, guns and ammo were jettisoned. He decided to try to get home rather than to Sweden or bail out. He just made it across the channel, where they crashed short of emergency air drome with 300 to 400 flak damage holes.

Mickelson received the Distinguished Flying Cross, Air Medal with cluster, ETO, etc.

294

He is a retired chief engineer for a Natural Gas Utility and resides in Lincoln, NE. Married 40 years to Jane Nelson; they have two daughters and one granddaughter.

KENNETH C. MICKO (KEN), was born on Aug. 24, 1922 and raised in St. Paul, MN. He attended St. Thomas College until February 1944, when he enlisted in the USAAC. In May he received his pilot's wings at Ft. Sumner, NM Twin Engine School and one week later he married his high school sweetheart.

Spent June and July as co-pilot on B-17s at Gunnery School in Las Vegas, NV. He transferred to B-24s and took RTU at Walla Walla, WA before departing to England. Was assigned to the 467th Bomb Group at Rackheath near Norwich.

Flew 19 complete missions over Germany before being shot down on the 20th over Berlin. Flak exploded in bomb bay about 30 seconds after "bombs away." Parachuted down and was captured immediately after landing on the sidewalk in downtown Berlin. His oldest daughter was born on the same day, March 18th. They lost four crew members and he and the remaining members spent the rest of the war in Stalag Luft I near Barth, Germany. Was liberated by an advance unit of the Russian army near the end of the war and all prisoners were flown out to France by the 8th Air Force in B-17s and B-24s.

Has owned his own manufacturing company since 1976 and still manages a few hours of work each day in between rounds of golf.

NORWOOD C. MIDDLETON, was born on May 26, 1918 in Sumter, SC. He enlisted in the U.S. Army VOC Program in June 1942 and was commissioned a second lieutenant in the Quartermaster Corps in December 1942 at Fort Lee, VA. He had training at Luke, AZ; Santa Maria, CA; Baker, OR and Pueblo, CO air bases.

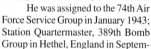

He was assigned to the 74th Air Force Service Group in January 1943; Station Quartermaster, 389th Bomb Group in Hethel, England in September 1943; assistant division quartermaster, HQ, 2nd Air Div., 8th Air Force, Ketteringham Hall in March 1944 until he was redeployed in August 1945.

Commissioned as a first lieutenant in August 1943 and promoted to captain in March 1944. Was appointed captain of the Air Corps in January 1947. Was discharged from the USAFR in May 1955 and received six European Campaign Stars.

Retired from the Roanoke (Virginia) *Times and World-News* in 1983 after 22 years as managing editor. He married Lucille Hood on June 28, 1941; they have two sons and two granddaughters.

HENRY R. MIERZEJEWSKI, was born on Dec. 22, 1920 in Wilmington, DE. He enlisted into the USAAC on March 22, 1943. He was a flight engineer and top turret gunner with the 446th Bomb Group, 704th Sqdn., stationed at Miami Beach, FL; Harlingen, TX; Keesler Field Biloxi, MS; Walla Walla, WA; Pyote, TX; and Bungay, England.

He participated in battles in Central Europe, Rhineland and Ardennes. Completed 23 combat missions. He did the nose art work on the B-24-M-44-50775 *Mighty Mouse*. Was discharged on Oct. 31, 1945 with the rank of technical sergeant. He received the ETO Ribbon and Air Medal with two Oak Leaf Clusters.

He is married to Gladys and they have a son Joseph, also in the Air Force, now living in Ft. Lauderdale, FL. Retired from the DuPont Co. since 1983. He had heart surgery

in 1987 (no more fishing or golfing). He does some poster work for his church, friends, etc.

STAN MIKOLAJCZYK (MIKE), was born on March 29, 1922 in Brooklyn, NY. He enlisted into the USAAC in November 1942. He graduated pilot training at Moody Field, GA in March 1944. He trained as a B-24 co-pilot at Savannah, GA and arrived at ETO in June 1944.

Assigned to the 93rd Bomb Group, 328th Sqdn., Ted's Flying Circus. On Sept. 21, 1944, he was in a mid-air collision with a 330th Sqdn. B-24, only his flight deck survived. Flew an additional 16 missions to complete his tour.

Returned to the States in March 1945 and was assigned to fly MATS and FTM until his separation from the service in October 1945 at Mitchell Field, NY.

Married the girl next door (Dorothy) in June 1948. They have two sons, one daughter, daughter-in-law and a grandson. Received his BBA degree from Fordham University in May 1950. He worked as an accountant for a New York City firm and subsequently became a CPA and partner of the firm. He retired in 1988.

JOHN E. MILIGAN, was born on Aug. 23, 1918 in Toledo, OH. He became a member of the USAAC, the Ohio National Guard 112th Observation Sqdn. in Cleveland, OH. His unit was called into active duty on Nov. 25, 1940. He was stationed at Pope Field, Ft. Bragg, NC.

Patrolled Atlantic waters and became part of the 15th Anti-Sub Squad based at Langley Field, VA. He attended Air Mechanics School at Chanute Field in Illinois and took care of all types of aircraft from Piper Cubs, Taylor Craft; Stinsons, 0-47, Lockheed Vegas, B-25s and B-24Ds.

Anti-Submarine Group patrolled the Atlantic Coast from Maine to Cuba. Next was sent to Tonopah, NV and Wendover Field, UT. He became a member of the 458th Bomb Group H, 754th Sqdn., where he was crew chief on Ship #42-100366 for the entire war period that they were overseas.

The *Mizpah* was a lead ship for over 50 missions and it finished with 88 missions to its credit. At the wars end, he was privileged to fly it back to the States. With a crew of 10 and 10 passengers, *Mizpah* was one of three original ships out of 70 to return to the States.

While home on leave, he married his childhood sweetheart, JoAnn. After leave he was sent to Grand Island, NE to work on B-29 bombers with the 8th Air Force. When the war ended with Japan, he was discharged on Sept. 4, 1945. He never received the Bronze Star that should have been forthcoming.

He attended the University of Toledo College of Pharmacy and received his BS degree in Pharmacy. He is still active in his store in Toledo, OH, where they made their home and raised their two sons, Steve and Tom.

ALLEN W. MILLER (BILL), was born on July 9, 1924 in Robinson, IL. On April 30, 1943 he entered the service at Camp Ellis, IL with the 361st Combat Engineers. He transferred to the Air Force one year later at Tyndall Field, FL.

Following training he was assigned to Lt. Roger Markels crew on a B-24 at Shipdham Field, Norwich, England with the 67th Sqdn. During service, he was the recipient of the EAME Campaign Medal with two Bronze Stars, Air Medal with Oak Leaf Clusters, Victory Medal, Good Conduct Medal and the Presidential Unit Citation.

In 1945, he returned to the States and was discharged on Nov. 16, 1945 at Maxwell Field, Montgomery, AL. Since that time he has been in the welding business and is currently the owner of Bill's Welding. On Jan. 25, 1993, he and his wife, the former Marcella Mitchel, celebrated their 50th wedding anniversary. They have two sons and three grandsons. They live west of Evansville in Mt. Vernon, IN. Miller is semi-retired.

ERRETT D. MILLER, was born on Nov. 16, 1923 in East Palestine, OH. He enlisted as an aviation cadet on Nov. 11, 1942 after graduating high school in June 1940 at High Point, NC. Completed aviation cadet training and graduated as a second lieutenant pilot, Class 44-D at Lubbock, TX.

Assigned to B-24 training at Liberal, KS and then to combat crew training in Boise, ID. After completion was sent to England on the *Queen Mary* with 15,000 other troops and assigned to the 453rd Bomb Group. He flew 15 missions over Germany.

Was awarded two Air Medals and three Combat Stars. He returned to the States in June 1945 and was assigned to the 4th Ferrying Group, ATC, Long Beach, CA after 30 days of rest and relaxation. He flew C-54s and various other aircraft until his release from active duty in September 1946.

Attended North Carolina State College, graduating in June 1951. He returned to the family business and retired in 1990. He maintained active reserve status with the local USAFR Squadron, serving as training officer and local commander. He retired from active status as lieutenant colonel in 1972. He is very active statewide in Jaycees and Kiwanis, serving as local president of each. He is a 22 gallon blood donor with the America Red Cross.

Has been married to Helen I. Pierce since July 4, 1945. They have three children and six grandchildren. His hobbies are square dancing, traveling, camping and genealogy.

JOSEPH MILLER, was born on Nov. 1, 1916 in Brooklyn, NY. He joined the USAC in December 1942. Took basic in San Antonio, TX and was commissioned as a bombardier at Kirtland Field, NM and then went on to radar H2X training at Boca Raton, FL.

His first few missions with the 8th Air Force were at Alconbury, England. Then he was transferred to the 448th Bomb Group at Seething, England. The pilot of the crew was Ed Jones. They were shot up enough on two missions to have to land in Belgium and leave the planes. Fortunately, they suffered no casualties.

He was in the battles of Balkans, Rhineland, Central Europe, Northern France and the Ardennes. Discharged with the rank of first lieutenant, he received the Distinguished Flying Cross and the Air Medal.

After his discharge he married Nan; they have five children and eight grandchildren.

Entered into the restaurant business and then the sales field in wines and liquors. After relocating to Texas he had a successful sales career with an importing firm, the W.A. Taylor Company. He retired from business in 1982 as a vice president of the company. Now happily retired, he plays golf, does some traveling and attends the 2nd Air Div. and 448th Bomb Group re-unions.

LESTER FRED MILLER, was born on June 19, 1917 in Dearborn County, IN. His early education was in Indiana and high school in Cincinnati, OH. Attended the University of Minnnesota from 1936 to 1940, majoring in petroleum engineering. Entered the USAAC as an aviation cadet in January 1942 and received his commission and pilot wings at Turner Field, GA in November 1942.

Entered B-17 pilot training; assigned duty as an instructor in B-17s for a short period of time; assigned to the 448th Bombardment Group, a B-24 unit, as squadron operations officer. Deployed with the 448th Bombardment Wing of the 8th Air Force to England, completed two combat tours and flew 33 bombing missions in the ETO. Following the end of the WWII, Gen. Miller entered the inactive Reserve force. In 1947 he received a regular commission and returned to active duty.

Served a tour of duty in Air Training Command; in 1951 entered Strategic Air Command (SAC) HQ in the office of the directorate of plans; January 1955 was assigned to the 7th Air Div., England as the director of plans.

Returned to the States and was assigned to Biggs AFB, TX as director of Material, 97th Bombardment Wing. In October 1958 he was assigned to Fairchild AFB, WA as vice commander of the 92nd Bombardment Wing and one year later became commander. In July 1962 was reassigned to SAC HQ as deputy director of personnel.

He commanded the 6th Strategic Aerospace Wing at Walker AFB, NM from June 1965-July 1966. Was assigned as deputy chief of staff, personnel at HQ Air Training Cmd., Randolph AFB, TX; August 1967 he became chief of staff, Air Training Cmd.; assigned as director of personnel training and education, deputy chief of staff, personnel, HQ USAF, Washington, DC in August 1968.

His decoration include the Distinguished Service Medal, Legion of Merit with two Oak Leaf Clusters, Distinguished Flying Cross with one Oak Leaf Cluster, Air Medal with three Oak Leaf Clusters, Army Commendation Medal with one Oak Leaf Cluster, American Campaign Medal, the EAME Campaign Medal, WWII Victory Medal, National Defense Service Medal with one Service Star, the Air Force Longevity Service Award Ribbon with four Oak Leaf Clusters and the Croix de Guerre with Silver Gilt Star (France).

At the time of his retirement, he had attained the rank of major general. He married Everdine Fox Miller on Oct. 9, 1946, they have four children: Lester Fred Jr., Andrew Stephen, Anne Christine and John Michael.

RICHARD E. MILLER SR., was born on Sept. 27, 1924 in New York City, NY. He moved to Bridgeport, CT in 1936 and was inducted into the USAAF at Fort Devens, MA in April 1943. After basic training in Miami Beach and various technical schools at Scott Field, IL; Madison, WI; Boca Raton, FL and Langley Field, VA, he became a radar mechanic on high altitude bombardment equipment. The equipment was nicknamed Mickey and used only on the lead airplanes.

Shipped overseas from New York aboard the liner *Aquatainia* in September 1944. After a seven day cruise of dodging German subs, they arrived at the Firth of Forth, Scotland, from where he was sent to the 467th Bomb Group in Rackheath. He returned to the States in September 1945 and was re-assigned to B-29s in Salina, KS.

Received the Good Conduct Medal and the EAME Campaign Medal with three Battles Stars. He was discharged in September 1945 with the rank of Sergeant.

Has spent most of civilian life in sales. Was owner of two hardware stores and is currently semi-retired. Has been married twice, currently to Bernadette Mullin. He has two sons and four granddaughters.

ROBERT B. MILLER, was born on Oct. 14, 1914 in Clinton, IL. Enlisted in the USAAF in 1939 and attended the U.S. Military Academy. Rotated to Shipdham with the 44th Bomb Group in 1942 and returned to States in October 1944. He completed 30 missions as commander with the 389th Bomb Group at Hethel. His final 10 years of service was in the Strategic Air Command in command of B-47 and B-52 units.

Retired in 1965 with the rank brigadier general, he received the Silver Star, Distinguished Flying Cross with two Oak Leaf Clusters, Air Medal with three Oak Leaf Clusters and the French Croix de Guerre.

Spent a second career in California as a bank trust officer. He resides with his wife Helen in a retirement center in San Diego, CA.

SAMUEL FORD MILLER, was born in 1917 in Surrey County, NC. He received a AB degree from Elon College in North Carolina in 1938. He was principal of North Carolina Elementary School from 1940-1941. In 1942 he enlisted into the USAAC, following a Pearl Harbor attack.

Graduated from Aviation Cadet Flying School as a pilot in 1943. First combat mission of the 445th Bomb Group, 2nd Air Div., 8th Air Force was in December 1943 and his last combat mission in Munich in April 1944, he was the first to complete his tour.

Notable missions: Berlin on March 6, 1944 and Gotha, Schweinfurt. Awarded the Legion of Merit, Distinguished Flying Cross, five Air Medals and Presidential Unit Citation.

He received a BS degree from the Air Force Institute of Technology in 1949 and a MBA degree from the Ohio State University in 1950. He retired from the USAF in 1968 following a career as contracting officer and procurement specialist.

Married for 53 years to Louise Pate of Statesboro, GA. They have four children, two daughters and two sons (both Air Force Pilots). They have seven grandchildren (one an Air Force Academy graduate). Miller owns and operates a tree farm near Tullahoma, TN.

WILLIS L. MILLER, was born on Feb. 3, 1921 in Akron, OH. His family moved to Long Beach, CA in August 1921 where he was raised. He enlisted in the USAAC in 1941 and called into cadet training in the Class of 42K.

Received his pilot wings from Stockton Field, CA in December 1942. He trained in B-24s at Albuquerque, NM. Crew trained at Muroc Army Air Base (now Edwards Air Base). Arrived in Europe in 1944 joining the 392nd Bomb Group, 577th and later the 579th Sqdn. based at Wendling, England. He became a lead pilot after eight missions and completed 30 missions. A memorable mission was flying lead in the 577th Sqdn. on a low flying mission dropping bundles to paratroopers in Best, Holland.

Returned to the States and was assigned to the Ferrying Command. He received two Distinguished Flying Crosses, six Air Medals, seven European Campaign Battle Stars and one Unit Citation. Discharged from the USAAC in August 1945 with the rank of captain.

He and Dorothy Murdy were married on June 22, 1945. They have seven children and 14 grandchildren. His oldest granddaughter received an appointment to the Air Force Academy, Class of 1997 and hopes to fly.

Went to the University of California, Davis. Later went into ranching, was a principle in County National Bank and a director and chairman of the Southern California Federal Land Bank for 26 years. Now developing industrial, commercial and auto agencies in Westminster, CA.

JOHN L. MILLIKEN, was born on July 4, 1921 in Buffalo, NY. He received a BS at Queens College, NY in June 1942. He was commissioned a second lieutenant pilot at Lubbock, TX, Class of 43-I in September 1943.

Flew his first mission on D-day, June 6, 1944 as a 1st pilot on a B-24 with the 44th Bomb Group. He was shot down on his last mission (31st), nine weeks later on Aug. 13, 1944 over Northern France and taken prisoner for 12 hours, then escaped and spent four days walking thru German front lines.

He graduated as a pilot aerial photo officer at Lowry Field, CO in March 1945. During the Army Occupation of Japan in 1946-1949, he was a member of the 8th Photo Recon. Sqdn. He graduated as ECM Observer in March 1951 at Biloxi, MS. He graduated a pilot AOB at Mather AFB in September 1953 and got off from active duty.

He was a Reserve Pilot of a C-124 in 1955 to 1968 at Travis and McClellan AFB. Retired in 1968 with the rank of major. From 1968 to present he has been a car dealer, real estate broker and with a trucking company in Sacramento, CA.

He received two Distinguished Flying Crosses, four Air Medals, one Purple Heart and a POW Medal. He still flies and has a twin Comanche and travels to Europe every year.

SAMUEL MILLMAN (SAM), was born on March 11, 1918 in Philadelphia, PA. Joined the USAAC in 1940 and trained in airplane mechanics at Casey Jones School of Aeronautics in Newark, NJ and at the Pratt & Whitney Engine School in Flint, MI.

Volunteed for flying duty and was sent to Biggs Field, TX for crew assignment and overseas training. In the summer of 1944, he shipped out to Hardwick, England and was assigned to the 409th Sqdn., 93rd Bomb Group.

He flew combat against Germany aboard the *Gambling Lady* and *Tabasco Keeds* (B-24s) from Sept. 18, 1944 to March 21, 1945 as a flight engineer and upper Martin gunner in "Ted's Flying Circus" (Gen. Ted Timberlake). He completed 35 bombing missions and was never shot down or seriously injured. He kept a diary of his combat missions which was published. Millman received the Air Medal with five Oak Leak Clusters.

He married Betty Cherner on June 25, 1948, they have three sons and four granddaughters.

CHARLES H. MILLS, was born on April 9, 1916 in Bridgeton, NJ. Enlisted in the U.S. Army Signal Corps on Feb. 12, 1942. Stationed at Ft. Dix, NJ; Mitchell Field, NY; Horsham St. Faiths and Ketteringham Hall. His memorable experience was the German bomber appearing outside their orderly room at Horsham.

Received the American Theater, German Occupation, EAME Campaign, Good Conduct Medal, ETO and the WWII Victory Medal. He was discharged on Dec. 5, 1945 with the rank of first lieutenant.

He and his wife Madeleine have two daughters, one son and several grandchildren. Today he is taking life easy after two open heart surgeries. He sells advertising specialties, mostly by telephone, to established customers.

JAMES REX MILLS, was born in September 1925 in Lawrence, KS. Enlisted into the USAAC in June 1943; active duty in October 1943 and took basic training in Amarillo, TX. He had aerial gunnery in Harlingen, TX, crew training in Colorado Springs, CO.

Assigned to Norman J. Putman crew, flew B-24J Lincoln, NE to England via Greenland, Iceland, arriving in Wales in July 1944. He was assigned to the 453rd Bomb Group, 733rd Bomb Sqdn. in Old Buckingham, Attleboro.

Trained as ball gunner, Mills was disappointed to find them removed from the B-24s to allow heavier bomb loads and deeper penetration into Germany. He flew as a waist gunner. The crew completed their 35 missions in January 1945. All members except the co-pilot (Dettenmayer) returned to the States in February 1945. Dettenmayer, always chaffing with lumbering bombers, had arranged to join a fighter squadron and remained to complete a tour of duty in P-47s.

Stateside Mills attended Central Gunnery Instructors School, Laredo, TX with final training in B-29s, Pueblo, CO before being separated from service October 1945 in Lincoln, NE.

JAMES W. MILLS, was born on Dec. 7, 1910 in Caddo, OK. Joined the Air Force in March 1941. Stationed at Brooks Field, TX; in February 1942 transferred to Lubbock, TX and promoted to staff sergeant.

He was commissioned at OCS at Miami Beach, FL, June 1942 as second lieutenant with his first assignment in the San Antonio Cadet Detachment. He was an adjutant of the Cadet Detachment at Lubbock, TX from November 1942 until March 1944. He was sent to England in April 1944, assigned to the 491st Bomb Group at Metfield.

He and Capt. John Price acted as station defense officers. When the Metfield Bomb Dump blew up, the 491st Bomb

Group was moved to North Pickenham and he went to squadron duty as adjutant of the 853rd, later as captain, and was made executive officer of the 853rd Bomb Sqdn. After V-E day, they returned to the States. Japan surrendered while he was on a 30 day leave; then he was assigned to McChord Field as assistant base adjutant.

Mills was discharged from the service in 1945 with the rank of captain. He married Jimmie Lee Layton on May 9, 1943. They have one son Kenneth and one daughter Deanna Brooks and two granddaughters and two grandsons.

MURRAY MILROD, was in aviation cadet training at Selman Field in Monroe, LA; gunnery instruction in Fort Myers, FL and back to Monroe for advanced training, graduating as a navigator.

Then on to Langley Field in Virginia for Mickey training. He was sent to County Tyrone, Ireland for further radar training. Had an appendectomy there and was detached from his crew. Sent to the 392nd Bomb Group, 577th Sqdn. at Wendling. But most of his missions were flown with other squadrons. He flew the famous mission that bombed Switzerland by mistake. Was bunkmate of President John Conrad.

Returned to the States after the war with the rank of first lieutenant. He spent most of his life on Long Island, NY. He is married to Helen; they have four children and two grandchildren. He worked for H.I.S., a principal apparel manufacturer, rising to vice president.

He is now retired and lives in Lake Worth, FL.

ROBERT J. MINARICK, was born on Oct. 6, 1922 in Midland Park, NJ. He enlisted in the USAAC on Sept. 26, 1942 as a flight engineer. Stationed at Sheppard Field, TX and had Gunnery School, Fort Myers, FL. His memorable experiences include: flying three missions in Brunswick, Germany; being in Hamm, Germany on April 22, 1944 and returning after dark; June 11, 1944 bombing run, R/R bridge at 6500 feet.

He received the Distinguished Flying Cross, Air Medal with three Oak Leaf Clusters, ETO with three stars and the Presidential Unit Citation with one Oak Leaf Cluster. He was discharged on Oct. 31, 1945 with the rank of staff sergeant.

He and his wife, Joan are retired in North Carolina. They have four children and 11 grandchildren. He enjoys boating, fishing and going to the beach.

REGINALD R. MINER, was born on Oct. 29, 1920 in Hammondsport, NY. He moved to Teaneck, NJ in 1931; graduated from Teaneck High School in 1938; from Alfred University, NY with a BS in ceramic engineering in 1943. He enlisted in the USAAC in 1943.

Began active duty in the USAAC on March 5, 1943 and graduated from Twin Engine Advanced at Moody Field in Valdosta, GA in Pilot Class 43-J as a second lieutenant on Nov. 3, 1943.

He completed B-24 transition at Smyrna, TN in January 1944 and trained with his crew in Casper, WY and Pueblo, CO. He picked up a new B-24 in Topeka, KS and flew it to the UK via Goose Bay, Labrador and Iceland, landing at Valley, Wales on May 30th.

He and his crew were assigned to the 445th Bomb

Group, 702nd Sqdn. in Tibenham and flew his first mission on June 25th.

His crew flew its first squadron lead on his 9th mission and was shot down by FW-190s on his 20th mission, while leading the high right squadron on the Kassel Mission of Sept. 27, 1944. He spent the rest of the war as a POW at Stalag 1 in Barth, Germany. He was discharged on Dec. 23, 1945 with the rank of captain.

He married Martha Perry of Stonington, CT on Feb. 27, 1943. They have four children and four grandchildren. He spent 36 years working for the Carborundum Company Refractories Division in the super refractories business. He and Martha now live on the shores of Lake Keuka, one of New York's Finger Lakes in active retirement.

JACOB H. MINK, was born on June 30, 1921 in Volney, VA. Enlisted in the service on Nov. 27, 1942; assigned to 8th Air Force, 492nd Bomb Group, 858th Sqdn.

He was stationed in North Pickenham, England and flew 13 missions as an engineer gunner in ETO on B-24 with Miller's crew. He remembers being shot down over Hamburg, made it to Sweden on June 18, 1944.

Received two Air Medals and was discharged on Nov. 25, 1945 with the rank of E-5 tech sergeant.

Married Helen on April 16, 1945, they have one son Jerry and one daughter Joyce. He is retired from the General Motors Company as a dealer.

HAROLD E. MINNICK (HAL), was born in Muncie, IN. He was in the Class of 43-C in Douglas, AZ; went to B-24 transition at Clovis, NM; joined the 446th Bomb Group at Lowry Field, CO in August 1943.

Assigned to 706th Bomb Sqdn. and made "C" Flight Commander/Lead Crew. He was assigned crew, trained and departed for the 8th Air Force at Bungay, England in a B-24 aircraft #41-29141 by the southern route. They named the aircraft *Kill-Joy* and flew 22 missions.

Promoted to captain and transferred to newly arrived 845th Bomb Sqdn. 489th Bomb Group in May 1944. He flew 11 missions in a lead position with the 489th Bomb Group. He returned to the States in October 1944 and was assigned to B-24 instructor pilot at Smyrna AAB, TN and Tyndall AFB, Florida until he was released on points on July 31, 1945.

Was recalled as captain on Aug. 1, 1950 as a pilot and weather officer. He served with the SAC, TAC, ATC, AWS and MAC. The last five years, he served as an aircraft commander and OPS officer, 4MAS at McChord AFB, WA in C-141s. He retired from the USAF with the rank of lieutenant colonel in August 1970.

MICHAEL JOSEPH MISSANO, was born on Oct. 7, 1912 in Brooklyn, NY. He enlisted into the USAAC on April 7, 1942 and eventually reached the grade of technical sergeant.

He was trained as an aerial gunner, airplane crew chief and an aircraft mechanic at AAFGS at Tyndall Field, FL. In October 1943 he was sent to England and served in the ETO as a waist gunner on the B-24 Liberator *Betty Jane* in the 8th Air Force. He was assigned to the 389th Bombardment Group, 565th Sqdn.

His missions included Air Offensive Europe, Normandy, Northern France and Germany. In early September 1944, after flying more than 30 missions, he was shot down over Holland. On Sept. 11, 1944 he was captured by the German Army and spent the duration of the war in a POW Camp in Germany. He was honorably discharged on Aug. 26, 1945 with the rank of tech sergeant. Missano was honorably discharged from the USAAC and returned home to East Meadow, Long Island, NY.

He earned the Distinguished Flying Cross, Bronze Star

Medal, Air Medal with four Oak Leaf Clusters, Presidential Unit Citation (Distinguished Unit Badge), Good Conduct Medal, American Campaign Medal, the EAME Campaign Medal with three Bronze Service Stars, the WWII Victory Medal and the Prisoner of War Medal.

On Sept. 7, 1947 he married Santa Maria Pisciotta. They reside in East Meadow, Long Island, NY. They have four daughters and eight grandchildren. He retired in 1977 after owning and operating a service station for over 30 years. He was a loving husband, father and grandfather. Missano passed away on Oct. 28, 1990.

J.W. MITCHELL JR.,

was born on Aug. 8, 1922 in Cedar Hill, TX. He entered the USAAC in January 1943; basic training at Sheppard Field. Wichita Falls, TX; Gunnery School, Laredo, TX; aircraft mechanics in Biloxi, MS; air crew training in Blythe, CA.

Assigned to A.E. Cearnall crew and sent to England in May 1944. He was assigned to the 389th Bomb Group (H), 565th Sqdn. in Hethel as a flight engineer gunner. Their first mission was on June 11, 1944. He had completed 30 missions in September 1944.

Returned to the States in October 1944. He entered the cadet program in December 1944. Took B-29 flight engineer training at Amarillo AFB in Texas. Was awarded the Distinguished Flying Cross, Air Medal with three Oak Leaf Clusters, EAME Campaign with four Bronze Stars, American Theatre, WWII Victory Medal, National Defense Service Medal, United Nations Service Medal and the Korean Service Medal. He was discharged in September 1945 with the rank of technical sergeant.

Entered SMU November 1945; graduated MBA, major professional accounting. Passed CPA exam and practiced accounting in Texas for 35 years. Was recalled to the USAF in 1951 and served two years in Tokyo, Japan as a first lieutenant, management analyst.

Married Lottie Rae George Aug. 24, 1941, they have four children, nine grandchildren and seven great-grandchildren. He is presently a rancher in Teague, TX.

JOSEPH R. MITCHELL,

was born on Dec. 30, 1918 in Buckingham, IA. He took pilot training in the Southeast Training Command as a student officer in the Class of 43-K. Trained in Jackson, Greenville and Columbus, TN, and for transition in B-24s at Maxwell Field. He had crew training at Westover Field, MA.

On June 24, 1944, he joined the 330th Sqdn., 93rd Bomb Group. He flew 30 missions of which 13 was on wing and 17 as a lead crew in H2X equipped planes. On July 21 in Munich, he lost all turbo power at 27,000 feet above the clouds and spiraled down to 10,000 feet where they returned home to base alone expecting an attack any moment. They lead the 2nd Air Div. on mission to Ludswighaven in August 1944. They received a Wing Citation by Gen. Timberlake on bombing Hanover, Germany on Dec. 12, 1944. He had flown his 30th mission by Jan. 6, 1945.

Returned to the States and went to B-24 Instructors School in Smyrna, TN. Then was transferred to B-29s at Davis Monthan Field, AZ.

He was discharged in May 1947 with the rank of major in the Reserves.

Finished college in 1947 with a degree in animal science, ISU Ames, IA. He worked five years with the Metropolitan Life Farm Loans; 10 years as a self-employed real estate and insurance agent; many years farming and raising pure bred black Angus cattle.

Has been married for 52 years and raised four children. They have eight grandchildren. He quit flying at the age of 65 with no accidents. He has been retired for three years in Fountain Hills, AZ.

JOSEPH MLYNARCZYK,

was born on March 3, 1916 in Detroit, MI, the renowned MOTOWN. He joined the USAAC on Feb. 2, 1942. He received aircraft mechanical electrical specialist training at Chanute Field, IL.

Stationed at Langley AFB, VA. Weeks later, he took cadet examination and pilot training at Gulf Coast Training Command. He graduated in 1943 Class F as a Flight Officer. He took B-24 training at Pueblo, CO. He was assigned a crew and was transferred to Seething, England with the 713th Sqdn. 448th Bomb Group.

On his third mission, eight bombers of the 448th were lost over Germany. His bomber lost two engines, but he was able to baby one engine back to England. Another mission was especially rough over Cologne and Karlsrum as they flew without a fighter escort. The remaining tour was routine with no aborts. He made second lieutenant in 1944 and first lieutenant a week later. Completed 35 missions in February 1945.

Was sent home for R&R, then back to Randolph Field, TX for B-29 training. Transferred to Love Field, TX where he ferried various aircraft to U.S. bases. He went to West Palm Beach, FL for C-54 and C-97 training.

Took a discharge in 1948 and enlisted as a master sergeant. Had recruiting duty in Detroit, MI where he met his wife. They were married in 1949 and they have two wonderful children, Jim and Sue. He was transferred to Rhine Maine, Germany for the Berlin Air Lift. After that, he had a stint at Brookley AFB, AL.

Took a discharge in 1952 for some civilian life, but got recalled to Westover AFB, MA in 1952 as a first lieutenant to ferry government personnel to Germany and France. He was later transferred to Barksdale AFB, LA refueling tankers.

He took his disrcharge in 1954 to civilian life. He retired as draftsman at General Motors Tech Center, Warren, MI in 1977. Spending his "golden years" golfing, flying and travelling over the country.

STANLEY J. MOHR JR.,

was born on April 22, 1925 in Bellevue, KY. He was drafted into the USAAF on Aug. 26, 1943. He trained as armorer gunner at state side Army Air Force fields in Amarillo, Buckingham, Lowry Field and Gowen Field.

Sailed to England in December 1944 and was assigned to the 466th Bomb Group, 785th Sqdn. at Attlebridge Air Base northwest of Norwich, England with "Wygonik, Pilot and Saltarelli, Co-Pilot" crew.

Flew 26 missions on B-24 Liberator through May 1945 in Ardennes, Rhineland and Central Europe campaigns. He flew back to the States in June 1945.

Received the Air Medal with three Oak Leaf Clusters and three Bronze Stars for the above battles. He was discharged on Oct. 25, 1945 with the rank of staff sergeant.

On return to civilian life, he studied accounting and worked in that occupation with Fairbanks, Morse & Co., Dravo Corporation and for the past 11 years to present with Comp. Care Centers of Northern Kentucky. He has been a resident of Ft. Thomas, KY for 38 years. He and his wife, Jo Ann have six children, four daughters and two sons.

WILLIAM W. MOLLER,

was born on Nov. 16, 1922 in Mapleton, IA. He grew up in Sioux City, IA attending the public schools. After high school graduation, he worked for Boeing in Wichita, KS and Martin Aircraft in Omaha, NE. where he enlisted in the USAAC on Nov. 13, 1942.

After the usual testing, college training detachment, he received his navigation wings at San Marcos, TX. Then on

to El Paso, TX to join a crew for phase training. The crew picked up a Ford built B-24 at Topeka, KS and flew it to Ireland by way of Goose Bay, Labrador. They were assigned to the 389th Bomb Group at Hethel Field in July 1944.

He flew one and a half missions, then joined the Caterpillar Club and spent the rest of the war in Stalag Luft I. He was liberated by the Russians in May 1945 and flown to France. He arrived back in the States on June 17, 1945. Obtained and assignment of pilot training and graduated advanced single engine in the P-47. He was then assigned to the 72nd. Liaison Sqdn. at Langley Field, VA.

Returned to Sioux City, IA and married his high school sweetheart. He took helicopter flight training at San Marcos, TX and returned to Virginia and flew helicopters until his discharge in June 1948.

Moller received a BS degree from the University of Southern California in June 1958.

He and his wife had two children, one son and one daughter. They celebrated their 46th Wedding Anniversary in 1993.

He retired from Lockheed Missile & Space Co. in 1987. Moller and his wife, Janet are active in many endeavors.

JOHN B. MONFORT,

was born on Jan. 20, 1924 in Alton, IL. He enlisted in the USAAF on Dec. 8, 1942.

He took Gunnery School at Tyndall Field, FL; aircraft mechanics at Keesler Field, MS; and was stationed at Gowen Field in Idaho. He was with the 453rd Bomb Group, 733rd Sqdn. in Old Buckingham, England from Sept. 10, 1944 to March 15, 1945.

Monfort remembers the accidental ignition of flare in flight deck during preflight inspection; it finally burned out without causing a fire or explosion. He received the Air Medal with five Oak Leaf Clusters. Was discharged on Sept. 2, 1945 with the rank of technical sergeant.

He is married and they have two children. He retired from the USAF as a civilian employee.

HENRY MONTEGARI,

was born on June 18, 1916 in Brooklyn, NY. He enlisted into the USAAF on Aug. 1, 1942; assigned to 389th Bomb Group, 566th Sqdn., 2nd Air Div., radio operator, control tower operator VHF D/F operator.

Stationed at Truax Field, Chanute Field, Biggs Field, Lowry Field, Langley Field and Hethel Air Base in England. Was with the 566th Sqdn., 2nd Air Division as a ground crew VHF D/F operator. His memorable experience was the returning of an aircraft to Hethel, being followed by German planes.

He received the ETO Service Medal, Good Conduct Medal, WWII Victory Medal, Presidential Unit Citation and the American Defense Service Medal. He was discharged on Sept. 6, 1945 with the rank of staff sergeant. And today he is retired!

ALAN A. MOORE,

was born on April 18, 1920 in Cleveland, OH. He joined the 82nd Div. Inf. on May 26, 1942 and on July 28, 1943, he went into the USAAC.

He was in Old Buckingham, England and his memorable experience was meeting and chatting with Gen. Eisenhower (not about the war) while in Europe. Spent one year as a German prisoner at Stalag Luft I on Baltic Sea. Was discharged on Nov. 21, 1945 with the rank of second lieutenant.

Moore and his wife have been happily married for 50 years; they have one son, one daughter and a grandson just graduating from college.

DANNY ROY MOORE,

was born on Aug. 9, 1925 in Haynesville, LA. He enlisted into the USAAC on May 9, 1943 as a radio operator and gunner.

He attended Radio School in Sioux Falls, SD; basic training at Amarillo Air Base in Texas; Gunnery School in

Yuma, AZ; flight crew training in Tonopah, NV; then joined the 467th Bomb Group.

Flew 14 combat missions as lead crew in the 791st Bomb Sqdn. Hildesheim, Germany low level 8,800 foot raid. Lead bomber on Feb. 22, 1945, took heavy flak and made an emergency landing in England after rudder trim tab shot away and destroyed target.

He was awarded the Air Medal with one Oak Leaf Cluster, Special Crew Citation for leading group and destroying ammunition dump at Zwiesel, Germany on April 20, 1945. Experienced explosion shock wave from 19,500 feet over the target (fireball). Was discharged on Nov. 22, 1945 in Rackheath, England with the rank of technical sergeant.

Has been married twice and has two sons and two daughters. A self-employed civil engineer, he served a four year term as a Louisiana State Senator.

F. DANIEL MOORE, was born on Sept. 21, 1924 in Troy, NY. He joined to USAAC on Feb. 6, 1943. After basic training at Miami Beach, FL, he was assigned to AAFTT Det., Buick Motor Division in Flint, MI. Graduated in June 1943 as aircraft engine mechanic. Assigned to the 445th B-24 Bomb Group, 703rd Bomb Sqdn. at Wendover, UT. Group transferred to Sioux City, IA for training.

In November 1943 the group was shipped overseas to northeast England, joining the 2nd Air Div. Group disbanded after return to States in May 1945. Assigned to ATC in Dover, DE. Immediately, detached to school at Lockheed Aircraft in California. End of Pacific hostilities brought his discharge in October 1945 with the rank of sergeant.

Attended night classes to obtain an electronics engineer degree. Retired from a Specialty Steel Company after 35 years, the last 10 as chief test engineer.

He married his high school sweetheart, Anne V. Heenan, while on leave June 17, 1945. They have one son (who passed away at age 18), a married daughter and two granddaughters. His hobbies are golf, photography and travel in USA by train.

GEORGE MOORE, was born on Feb. 12, 1920 in Rochester, NY. He entered the USAAC on March 18, 1942 and did his basic training at Keesler Field in Mississippi. He attended Cook and Baker's School at Barksdale Field, LA and went to Mess Sergeant's School there.

Joined the 44th Bomb Group, 67th Bomb Sqdn. as 1st cook. He was sent on advance assignment, as sergeant in charge, to Will Rogers Field in Oklahoma to set up a kitchen and troop train. Went to ETO in September 1942 in England and spent some time in Cheddington, Shipdham and Norwich. His memorable experience was in London on the Wednesday they got bombed, hit Paddington Station, was at the Fleming Hotel.

Returned to Sioux Falls, SD in 1945. Went to Pratt, KS and from there to Fort Dix for discharge on Sept. 6, 1945. He received the Good Conduct Medal, American Defense Service Medal, EAME Campaign Medal with nine stars, the WWII Victory Medal and the Presidential Unit Citation with one Oak Leaf Cluster.

Returned to Eastman Kodak and held several supervisory jobs, retiring in 1981, after 42 years of service. Retired as an assistant food service manager of the Kodak Park Division, serving 32,000 people each day.

Married his high school sweetheart, Virginia Woodruff on June 4, 1942. They have one son, two daughters and seven grandchildren.

He is a member of the Pioneer Club and the Kodak Management Club and enjoys hunting, fishing and playing.

HAROLD B. MOORE, was born on Feb. 22, 1917 in Mt. Olivit, KY. He enlisted into the USAAC on June 25, 1941. Was in the Mechanized Calvary and later transferred to Aviation Cadet in May 1942 for Bombardier School. Stationed at Santa Ana, CA; Albuquerque, NM; Hethel, England; Banghazi, Libya; and Tunis.

Participated in Air Offensive Europe, Sicily, Italy, Southern France, Northern France, and Rhineland. His memorable experience was the raid on Ploesti oil refineries in Romania on Aug. 1, 1943.

Was discharged on Oct. 27, 1945 with the rank of first lieutenant. He received two Distinguished Flying Crosses, four Air Medals, Presidential Unit Citation and the EAME Campaign Medal.

Moore and Nancy L. Portwood were married in December 1945. He is retired.

JOSEPH L. MOORE, was born on Aug. 30, 1921 in Boston, MA. He enlisted December 1940 with the 26th Inf. Div., 101st FA, and then in March 1943 transferred to the USAAF. Stationed at many different locations during his service tour. He was a member of William W. Leesburgs crew.

Completed 31 missions in ETO. His memorable experience was the crossing of the Rhine River in April 1945. He was discharged on Sept. 12, 1945 with the rank of technical sergeant. Received the Air Medal with five Oak Leaf Clusters.

Moore is married and has three sons and three daughters. One son served in Vietnam and son in Desert Storm. He is retired and enjoys golfing and enjoys life with his wife.

ROBERT C. MOORE, was born on March 19, 1916 in Paris, IL and was raised in Georgetown, IL. He joined the USAAC on May 13, 1935 as a private at Chanute Field, IL. He completed airplane mechanics and instrument specialist courses and served as an instructor on aircraft instruments.

In May 1939 he was released from the USAAC to accept Civil Service position at Fairfield Air Depot in Fairfield, OH (now Fairborn) as an instrument overhaul mechanic. In March 1941 he transferred to Wright Field, Dayton, OH as project engineer on aircraft engine instruments.

He entered Aviation Cadet Program in October 1942. Graduated as second lieutenant, Class 43-G, Southeast Training Command at Turner Field, Albany, GA. Trained as a B-24 pilot at Maxwell Field in Montgomery, AL. He was assigned to the 466th Bomb Group, in Attlebridge, England. Flew 29 combat missions (17 missions as lead pilot) between Oct. 6, 1944 and April 21, 1945. He flew five gas haul missions prior to combat.

Received the Distinguished Flying Cross and Air Medal with three Oak Leaf Clusters.

In October 1945 he returned to Civil Service position at Wright Patterson AFB. He was recalled to active duty May 8, 1951 and was released Oct. 19, 1954 with the rank of major.

He then resumed his Civil Service Career at Kelly AFB in San Antonio, TX. He retired in May 1970 after completing a total of 35 years Federal Service (Military & Civil Service combined).

He married Audrey E. Meredith on July 27, 1940, they have one son.

CHARLES K. MORAN, was born 1918 in Salado, TX. He graduated from the University of Texas in 1940 and enlisted in the service on May 23, 1942, second lieutenant (navigator). June 1942 to August 1943, he was with the 11th Air Force (Aleutian Islands), the 404th Bomb Sqdn.

Completed 52 combat missions in a B-24D; September 1943 to October 1944 pilot training, B-24 School and crew training. From October 1944 to June 1945, he was with the 8th Air Force, 448th Bomb Group in Seething, England as a pilot (AC) assistant squadron ops officer and squadron leader (Gp. Co "Young Charlie" in Westover).

From 1945 to 1948, B-29 School, Air Staff School, various staff assignments. From 1948 to 1952, he attended AFROTC University of Utah, and BYU. From 1952 to 1966, KC-97 (air tanker) AC Operations Officer and Squadron Commander. From 1966 to 1971, he was a communications staff officer, Commander European GEEIA Wing.

He married Naomi Tullis from Houston, TX. On July 1, 1971, he retired after 30 years, four months and 21 days with the rank of colonel.

EDWARD J. MORAN, was born on Sept. 20, 1922 in Chicago, IL. On Sept. 20, 1942, he enlisted in the USAAC with the 392nd Bomb Group.

Attended Gunnery School, Tyndall Field and Ireland; Armament School at Lowry Field; operations in Wendling, England, Berlin, Brunswick, Munich and Hamm. Completed a total of 30 missions.

Retired on May 1, 1968 with the rank of technical sergeant. Received the Distinguished Flying Cross, Air Medal with three Oak Leaf Clusters and two Battle Stars.

Married to Bettie Nee Sumner. She is an artist and they have an art gallery and antique shop in Albuquerque, NM.

JOHN A. MORAN, was born on June 3, 1925 in Pittsburgh, PA. He joined the USAAC on Aug. 4, 1943.

Because pre-flight classes were full, he took two stints in basic training and an automatic wash-out. On July 22, 1944, after 32 weeks of training as a radio operator at Sioux Falls, SD and six weeks in Flexible Gunnery School in Yuma, AZ, he was sent to Lancastershire, England in the replacement pool for "The Carpetbaggers" who were attached to the OSS and flew night operations in conjunction with the RAF.

After successfully bombing the marshalling yards at Deutchburg, Germany, with over 100 bullet holes, two burned out engines, all props hit and landing gear destroyed, their crippled B-24 carried them back across the English Channel, where they crash landed at a coastal emergency field. The plane was declared un-repairable and scrapped.

The remainder of the war was spent flying covert operations with the RAF and OSS.

GORDON W. MOREHEAD (BUD), was born Oct. 10, 1920 in Crookston, MN. He entered the USAAC in April 1943 at San Antonio, TX. Graduated from advanced twin engine flight training at Waco, TX in the Class of 44-A.

Assigned to Boise, ID for B-24 transition training. Crew flew a B-24 to Scotland, where he was assigned to the 458th Bomb Group (B-24) at Horsham St. Faith in England. Bailed out over Belgium while on his 20th mission (Eisenach, Germany) on July 20, 1944. Was in a POW Camp at Barth, Germany until May 1945.

Returned to the States via troop ship *General Buckner* on June 20, 1945. He was assigned to Turner Field, GA in August 1945 as a B-25 pilot and instructor pilot. Transferred to Mather Field in Sacramento, CA in June 1946. Discharged on May 29, 1947 with the rank of captain. Received the Air Medal with three Oak Leaf Clusters and the ETO Ribbon with three Campaign Stars.

He married Doris S. Suthers in January 1944. They had four children (two deceased) with one daughter and one son living. There are four grandchildren. He graduated from the University of California, Davis with a BS degree in 1951. Employed by the U.C. Agriculture Extension Service as a farm adviser from 1951 to 1988. He is retired and presently operates and manages a partnership pear orchard at Elk Grove, CA.

ROCCO V. MOREO, was born April 17, 1921 in Inwood, Nassau County, NY. He was inducted into the service on Sept. 29, 1942 as a radio operator mechanic. Participated in Normandy, Northern France, Central Europe, Air Offensive Europe, China and Central Burma campaigns.

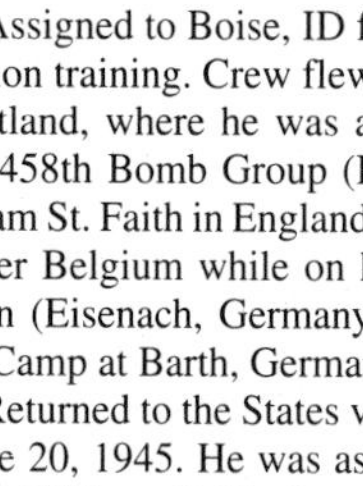

Was assigned to the European Theater of Operations and served in the dual capacity of communications technican and aerial gunner. Returned to the States upon completion of mission and was re-assigned in the Air Transport Command for service in the China Burma India Theatre of Operations in the capacity of Airborne Communications Specialist.

He received the American Campaign Medal, EAME Campaign Medal, Victory Medal, Good Conduct Medal, Air Medal with three Bronze Clusters, Distinguished Flying Cross, Meritorius Unit Award and the Asiatic Pacific Theater. Was discharged on Dec. 1945 with the rank of technical sergeant.

He is married and has five children (lost one child in an auto accident). He is retired.

JACK B. MORGAN, was born on Sept. 23, 1925 in Key West, FL. Enlisted into the USAAC on Aug. 14, 1941 with the 66th Bomb Sqdn., 506th Bomb Sqdn., 44th Bomb Group. Stationed at Jefferson Barracks, MO; Glendale, CA; Barksdale Field, LA, Shipdham, England and MacDill AFB, FL.

His memorable experiences was Shipdham (1942 to 1945), assistant crew chief B-24 named *Downd de Hatch.*

Retired in 1963 with the rank of E/8. Morgan and his wife Hazel have two children and five grandchildren. He is a retired schoolteacher.

JOHN W. MORGAN, was born on June 28, 1923 in Pittsburgh, PA. Enlisted into the USAAF on Aug. 10, 1942. Assigned to 389th Bomb Group, 567th Sqdn. and in various training bases, then went to Hethel, England.

Attended Radio School in Sioux Falls, phase, El Paso, Tucson, combat in Hethel, England. Participated in low level mission, Ploesti on Aug. 1, 1943 (first mission) and lost half of crew. Flew as replacement, finished one tour including four trips to Berlin. Volunteered for second tour and got shot down on 42nd mission on Sept. 28, 1947.

His memorable experience was Ploesti, Berlin, being shot down, POW Camp, transfer from Luft 4 to 1 in boxcars and the Russian overtaking the camp.

Morgan received two Distinguished Flying Crosses, seven Air Medals, Battle Stars and the Presidential Unit Citation. He was discharged on Sept. 15, 1945 with the rank of staff sergeant.

Worked at TWA for 11 years as a flight radio operator (based in Cairo, Egypt for six years); Philadelphia Flight Service Station in 1958 and ended up as the assistant manager at Philadelphia; transferred to Wilkes-Barre, PA and retired as manager in 1987. Also bought a farm in 1957 and is still in the Christmas tree business.

He is presently single and has three daughters and four grandchildren.

TERRANCE MORIARTY (MORRY), was inducted into the USAAC in 1943. He trained in armament and was assigned to A.E. Cearnal crew as tail gunner. Was sent to Hethel, England to 389th Bomb Group.

There were two missions that stand out to him. At Brunswick, Germany there was intense flak. One piece came through his tail turret barely missing him. The second mission was in Hamburg. All the shells to his tail guns were exploded except one. They were all jumpy and nervous. They flew eight long missions in 11 days.

Discharged with the rank of staff sergeant. He was awarded the Distinguished Flying Cross, Air Medal with three Oak Leaf Clusters, EAME Campaign Medal with four stars, American Theatre and the WWII Victory Medal.

HAROLD L. MORRIS, was born on Aug. 25, 1923 at Poverty, in McLean County, KY. He was inducted in a Japanese Church in Sacremento, CA on April 19, 1943. Basic at Fresno, CA; Keesler Field, MS for aircraft mechanic training; assigned to the 489th Bomb Group at Wendover, UT.

Sent to Halesworth, England as an aircraft mechanic on B-24 Bombers. Spent a lot of days and nights repairing aircraft, engines, changing engines, etc. Saw a lot of aircraft crash, explode, run together, etc. They kept them running and ducking.

Saw Joe Kennedy Jr's aircraft explode in mid-air just east of their base. It took him 40 plus years to find out who was on the Navy Plane being accompanied by a British Mosquito bomber, who feathered an engine and landed on their base.

Came back to the States in the fall of 1944. Married Martha L. Jackson on Dec. 25, 1944. Was discharged on Nov. 23, 1945 at Westover Field, MA with the rank of sergeant.

HENRY A. MORRIS, was born on May 12, 1924 in Trenton, NJ. He joined the USAAC on Nov. 27, 1942 as a private. Trained as a gunner, he was promoted through the ranks to staff sergeant.

Arrived in England in July 1944, a member of the 491st Bomb Group, 852nd Sqdn. Flew 14 missions as a member of Lt. Sparrow's crew, most of them aboard the B-24 *Lambsy Divey*. Was shot down on Sept. 12, 1944 over Misburg, Germany. The *Lambsy Divey* took a direct hit and exploded. Morris was blown out of the plane and the only crew member to survive. He parachuted and was beaten and almost hung by civilians. Rescued by German military, he spent the rest of the war in Stalag Luft IV and Stalag IIA until liberated on April 29, 1945.

Married Jennie Sola on Aug. 15, 1948; they had three children: Joseph, Henry Jr. and Maria. Morris passed away on Dec. 1, 1964. *This account was written by his son, Henry Jr.*

OLIVER L. MORRIS, was born on July 27, 1921. Enlisted into the USAF on Jan. 8, 1942. His memorable experience was Briton, Air Offensive Europe and D-day.

Discharged on Aug. 11, 1945 with the rank of staff sergeant. He was awarded the Distinguished Flying Cross and Air Medal with seven Oak Leaf Clusters.

Retired, but works every day in stock farming.

MELVIN M.L. MORRISON, was born on Dec. 23, 1920 in Oil City, PA. He enlisted in the USAAC on Oct. 12, 1942 in Akron, OH. Trained as an aircraft gunner and assigned to the 93rd Bomb Group from Hardwick.

First mission was on March 2, 1944. He was involved in a crash on takeoff on March 3, 1944 killing three crew members. After recuperating from his injuries, he returned to combat as a replacement gunner. When he finished his 30 missions on Sept. 26, 1944, he stayed on the base and worked in supply.

He returned to the States on the *Queen Mary* which arrived on March 11, 1945. Discharged on Sept. 7, 1945. After the war he returned to Akron and worked in the rubber industries.

He married Violet Hutchinson, they have two children, four grandchildren and one great-grandchild.

DANTE MORRONI, was born on Oct. 16, 1913 in Smithmill, PA. Enlisted in the USAAF on Dec. 26, 1942, Fort Dix, NJ. Basic training at Miami Beach, FL; Radio Operator School at Scott Field, IL; Gunnery School at Davis Monthan Field, Tucson, AZ. Assigned to 453rd Bomb Group, 735th Bomb Sqdn., 2nd Air Div.

After short stays in Pueblo, CO and Clovis, NM, he joined Lt. Irwins's crew in Langley Field, VA. Then later to the 8th Air Force by the southern route. He flew his first on April 27, 1944 and last mission on July 25th and two missions on D-day.

Saw his share of planes go down: a B-17 on his second mission; lead plane with more than 10 men with a collapsed left wing after a direct hit; and a plane split apart behind the wings.

A memorable experience was when returning from a mission a B-24 at 6 o'clock high gained on them, tail gunner said "What the hell's he doing?" Navigator behind Morroni yelled, "Go down, go down." As Morroni looked up and ducked his head, that B-24 was about 5' away when they dropped like a high speed elevator.

Participated in the battles at Normandy, Northern France, Rhineland and Air Offensive Europe. Completed 32 missions, two as ball turret gunner and 30 nose/togalier.

Received the Distinguished Flying Cross, Air Medal with three Oak Leaf Clusters, Good Conduct Medal and the ETO Ribbon with four Battle Stars. Was discharged on Oct. 27, 1945 with the rank of technical sergeant.

He is married to Josephine, they have two children, Joseph and Carol, and four grandchildren. He was an Ironworker for 40 years, retired in 1979.

JAMES L. MORTON, was born on July 23, 1921 in Greenville, SC. Enlisted in the service on April 11, 1942. Assigned to the 389th Bomb Group, 566th Bomb Sqdn. as a radio operator, ETO. Participated in Normandy, Air Offensive Europe, Northern France campaigns.

His memorable experience was finishing his 30th mission. Received the Distinguished Unit Badge, Air Medal with three Oak Leaf Clusters, Distinguished Flying Cross and the ETO Service Medal with three Bronze Stars. Was discharged on Sept. 13, 1945 with the rank of tech sergeant WWII, and retired Nov. 30, 1966 from 31st Inf. Cixie Div. with the rank of captain U.S. Army.

He and Ida May Adair were married on June 17, 1941, they have three children and five grandchildren.

He is retired from South Central Bell Telephone Co. and has retired from the U.S. Army Signal Corps.

CHARLES H. MOSGAR, was born on July 17, 1909 in Victoria, TX. Enlisted into the U.S. Army on March 9, 1942 at Fort Lewis, WA, then converted to the USAF in 1947.

Was with the 2nd Air Div. at Old Buckingham. He was crew chief on three bombers from January 1944 to April 1945. Memorable experience was the crews returning all shot up, engines out and one wheel down.

Received all of the ordinary campaign medals and ribbons. Served in all a total of 21 years. Discharged in September 1945, he re-entered the service three weeks later.

Married and has two sons, they live in Spokane, WA. He enjoys keeping up home plus his lake property and helping his neighbors when he can.

RALPH S. MOSHER, was a first lieutenant in the USAAC. He joined in July 1943, was commissioned as a navigator at Ellington AFB in Houston, TX. Based at Horsham St. Faith pre-war air drome, Norwich, England with the 458th Bomb Group.

Completed 35 missions over Germany. The first mission was on Oct. 9, 1944 at Koblenz and his 35th mission on March 17, 1945, Hanover. On his third mission to Cologne, they lost an engine just 15 minutes short of the target. Struggling alone with determination, they continued and dropped their 8,000 pounds of bombs on the central railroad yard. His pilot, Ronald Beckstrom could have aborted the mission, but chose to do the courageous thing. Being modest as he was, he probably never reported his actions. All of the Air Force people were very high performance soldiers. They can all be very proud of their accomplishments.

They lost an engine four times (which means flying home alone). Once they came home with over 200 flak holes in the plane, one man wounded in the arm (flak suit prevented chest wounds). Their many experiences were broad and wild, but over all they were very lucky compared to some.

They were a good team, they did not smoke, drink or chase bad women (probably were classified as dull people). But together they pulled off very tricky maneuvers. He is bragging about the whole 8th Air Force.

Discharged in May 1945. Received engineering degree from the University of New Hampshire in 1949. He is married with three daughters and three grandchildren. He resides in Bear Island, NH.

JOHN L. MOSIER, was born on July 18, 1922 in Enough, MO. Enlisted into the USAF on Nov. 11, 1942, assigned to the 8th Air Force, 93rd Bomb Group, 330th Bomb Sqdn. as an engineer gunner.

Stationed at Miami Beach, FL; Gulfport, MS; Kingman, AZ and Hardwick, England. Completed 32 missions from mid-1943 to mid-1944. Had numerous memorable experiences.

Mosier received the Distinguished Flying Cross, Air Medal with five Oak Leaf Clusters and Presidential Unit Citation with one Oak Leaf Cluster.

He was discharged on Oct. 9, 1945 with the rank of staff sergeant.

He and his wife have one daughter, one son and three grandchildren. He retired after a massive heart attack in 1977.

CARL M. MOSS, was born on May 18, 1923 in Cincinnati, OH, moved to Michigan and graduated from Fordson High School in Dearborn, MI. He worked at Willow Run

Bomber Plant in 1942 and joined the USAAF in February 1943.

Basic training at "Tent City" St. Petersburg, FL; Radio School at Scott Field, IL; Aerial Gunnery School at Las Vegas, NV; then crew training at Muroc, CA. He flew a new B-24 from Hamilton Field, CA to West Palm Beach, FL with stops at Phoenix, AZ; Midland, TX and Macon, GA.

Flew overseas out of West Palm Beach, FL to Trinidad, Belem Brazil, Natal Brazil, Dakar Africa, Merrakesh to Blackpool, England. Combat Training School at North Ireland and then assigned to the 453rd Bomb Group at Old Buckingham, England. He flew his first combat mission on May 22, 1944. His ninth mission was on D-day, June 6th.

On June 15, 1944, transferred to Hethel, England to the 389th Bomb Group to train as a pathfinder (Mickey) crew. On his 17th mission to Munich on July 11, 1944, the B-24 was hit by flak, damaging the fuel tank and lines, left formation and headed back to England. Running out of fuel, bailed out near Lille, France and captured by the Luftwaffe Ground Force. He was held in the Citadel at Lille, France.

Transferred to Frankfort, Germany and spent seven days in solitary confinement, then sent to Dulag Luft at Wetzler. Railroads through Berlin to Stalag Luft 4 between Kiefheide (railroad station) and the town of Grostychow near the Baltic Sea. He was roughed up by German Guards with dogs on a seven kilometer walk/run from railroad station to camp.

At Luft 4, until Feb. 6, 1945, then forced to march out of camp as the Russian Army units were approaching. The beginning of the 86 day ordeal known as "The Black March." He was liberated by the British on May 2, 1945 after approximately a 600 mile journey (while hiding out in a Polish barn). Then on to Camp Lucky Strike, France (to fatten up), then on to a ship to Boston, MA.

Was discharged in November 1945 from San Antonio, TX. Graduated from Michigan State University in 1950. He was a director of Sales for Replacement Systems International. He is living in Williamson, MI with his wife Mary, they have three children: Michael, John and Joann. He is currently Commander of Mid Michigan Chapter of American EX-POWs, lifetime member of the 8th Air Force Historical Society and 2nd Air Division Association.

WILLIAM THOMAS MOSS, was born on Dec. 21, 1923 in Granville County, Oxford, NC. He enlisted into the USAF on June 12, 1943. Stationed at Keesler Field in Biloxi, MS and Davis Monthan Field in Tucson, AZ. He was with the 8th Air Force in Halesworth, England and participated in numerous bombing missions over Germany.

Moss was discharged on Nov. 26, 1945 with the rank of sergeant. He received the Air Medal. He is married and has two children, one son and one daughter. Currently retired.

CALVIN C. MOSTELLER, was born on July 18, 1918 in Lincoln County, in Lincolnton, NC. Enlisted into the USAAC on Oct. 19, 1942 as an engineer gunner. After basic training, he attended schools in Amarillo, TX; San Diego, CA and Laredo, TX. Was then assigned to the 448th Bomb Group as an engineer gunner.

In November 1943, the 448th Bomb Group arrived at Seething (Station 146). While he was hospitalized, his crew was shot down. Upon his recovery, he was assigned to the Crew 48, 714th Sqdn. Was on Berlin Raid on April 29, 1944, also the Marshalling Yards at Hamm, where while trying to land after dark, JU-88s infiltrated the formation and shot down a number of B-24s.

After completing mission tour, he returned to the States and was assigned to Helicopter School, Chanute Field, IL. Was hanger chief until his discharge on Oct. 19, 1945 with the rank of staff sergeant. He received the Distinguished Flying Cross, four Air Medals, four European Campaign Stars, Good Conduct Medal, WWII Victory Medal and the American Campaign Medal.

He and Mary Pinkie Holbrooks were married on Nov. 14, 1947. They have no children. He is retired from the North Carolina Forest Service.

KENNETH MOULDEN, was born on Jan. 6, 1923 in Tivoli, NY. He joined the USAAC in October 1942 as a private, after qualifying for the Aviation Cadet Program. Following basic training in Atlantic City, NJ, he entered Bombardier School in Big Spring, TX and graduated on June 24, 1943, Class 43-9.

He received further training at air bases in New Mexico, Arizona, California and Virginia. He arrived in England as part of a B-24 bomber crew by way of South America and Africa. From Seething Air Field near Norwich, he flew 30 combat missions over Europe. After several missions as a bombardier, he received training as dead reckoning navigator and then he performed the duties of a navigator bombardier on a number of missions.

He received campaign ribbons for the Air Offensive of Europe, Battle of Normandy and Battle of Northern Europe. His most memorable experience was participating in the bombing of the Normandy beachhead on D-day, June 6, 1944. He was discharged in November 1945 with the rank of first lieutenant.

Entered the University of Bridgeport and graduated in 1949. He and Phyllis Cummings were married on Aug. 25, 1951 and they have one son Stuart.

Spent several years in business, then became a teacher and taught for 27 years in Milford, CT. He lives in Woodbridge, CT and enjoys travel and community work.

RAYMOND H. MOULTON (MOOSE), was born on June 24, 1921 in Worcester, MA. Enlisted in the USAAF in November 1942, bombardier/navigator with the 389th Bomb Group. Stationed in Santa Ana, CA; Deming AFB in Blythe and in Hethel, England.

Flew five combat mission in a B-24J. Used his own bomb sight to take out a large facotry at Gotha on Feb. 24, 1944.

Moulton was discharged in October 1945. Received the POW Medal, Purple Heart, Air Medal and the ETO Medal.

He was married in Deming, NM in May 1943 and has one son, one daughter and three granddaughters. He is retired at Glen Echo Lake in Charlton, MA.

ROBERT C. MOUNT, was born on Dec. 14, 1921 in Lost Nation, IA. Entered the USAAF in August 1942, attended Radio School in Sioux Fall, SD, 1943 and Flex Gunnery, Harlingen, TX in 1944.

Spent 10 months with 8th Air Force, 448th Bomb Group on Capt. A. Donald Johnson Crew as tail gunner. Flew 21 missions from August 1944 until war ended. Spent about 10 months in Korea with 8th Fighter Bomb Wing, working on electronics.

He received the Air Medal with two Oak Leaf Clusters, Air Force Commendation Medal, Air Force Outstanding Unit Award with two Oak Leaf Clusters, Korean Service Medal with two Bronze Stars (1952-1953), ETO with four Bronze Stars and the United Nations Service Medal. Retired in 1967 with the rank of E-6 after 20 years of active service from 552 AEW at McClellan AFB.

Mount is married and has seven children. He worked for 17 years in civil service on aircraft electronics systems and retired from civil service in 1983. His hobby is amateur radio.

LEO L. MOWER, was born on March 5, 1922 in Fountain Green, UT. Enlisted in the Utah National Guard on Sept. 15, 1940. On March 3, 1941 the guard became a part of the U.S. Army at Camp San Luis Obispo, CA.

A few days after Pearl Harbor, he requested a transfer to the Aviation Cadet Program and became part of Class 43-D at the San Antonio Army Air Corps Training Center on Aug. 3, 1942. From there it was to Cimarron Field west of Oklahoma City for primary; Coffeyville, KS for basic; Altus, OK for advanced twin engine training; and commission as a second lieuteant.

Thence to Tarrant Field in Fort Worth, TX for B-24 training. From there to Gowan Field, Boise, ID, for final check rides and a combat crew. Next to Casper, WY for crew training, followed by Alamogordo, NM to join the 466th Bomb Group. Their final destination was to Attlebridge, England via South America, Africa and Valley, Wales.

Crew #609 flew it's first mission on March 23, 1944. They were to have many close calls, but they came through them in good stead. Their most satisfying mission was the D-day mission on June 6, 1944. The 466th Bomb Group was among the first groups over the invasion coast.

On June 21st and their 24th mission, they were on a bomb run towards the Fredrichstrasse railroad station in the Berlin area when their plane was very critically damaged by a flak burst in the bottom of #3 engine, followed shortly by severe damage from five cannon hits and from many machine gun rounds from attacking German fighters. They were able to feather the engine and to get their bombs on the target while their gunners, assisted by P-38s, damaged at least two German fighters.

With two wounded crew members and very extensive plane damage, to include non-functional electric and hydraulic systems, they fortunately made it to the southern coast of Sweden where a crash landing almost completely destroyed their plane. Some six months later, they were able to leave Sweden and return to England.

For him, it was back to the States as a AT-6 instructor and then release from active duty as the end of the war drew near. He later rejoined the Utah National Guard from which he retired as a major many years later.

After his release, he and his wife Mildred enrolled at Utah State University, where she graduated with a degree in elementary education and he graduated with a degree in industrial education. They taught in Salina, UT before moving to Salt Lake City, UT in 1962. Mildred continued teaching in the elementary schools, while he taught drafting for nine years in the Olympus High School before transferring to the new Cottonwood High School for his final 11 years.

He and his wife has been retired for several years. Their two sons and their families of four and five live nearby. Traveling has been a pleasurable part of their retirement years.

DEAN E. MOYER, was born on Jan. 12, 1915 in Harmony, PA. Joined the service in May 1941 and was sent overseas in August 1942. He obtained the rank of master sergeant and was chief NCO in charge of ordnance activities and supply for the 2nd Air Div. of the 8th Air Force.

He returned to the States on June 21, 1945 and was discharged on June 28 with the Bronze Star among his citations. He joined the 2nd Air Division Association in 1950, serving as secretary in 1959, president in 1960 and treasurer from 1961 to 1964 and 1969 through 1993. He owned a retail kitchen business for 30 years, retiring in 1991.

He and his wife, Deanie were married on July 14, 1945 and they reside in Evans City, PA. They have three children: Robert, a telecommunications engineer; Barbara, an occupational therapist; and Maxine, an administrative assistant; and six grandchildren.

LEONARD R. MOYER, was born on Dec. 11, 1923 in Amelia County, VA. He joined the USAAC on Nov. 11, 1942. He had pre-flight at Santa Ana, CA and graduated from Bombardier School at Deming, NM on Aug. 9, 1943.

Was assigned to the 732nd Sqdn., 453rd Bomb Group with the Phase I training at Pocatello, ID. The Phase II and Phase III training was at March Field, CA. This newly formed group of B-24 aircraft flew to England via South America and Africa to become a part of the 2nd Air Div. in England in Febraury 1944.

On April 9, 1944, while on Hamby's crew's 11th mission, they lost two engines on the left side due to ME-109 fighters. This action took place over the Baltic Sea and Denmark. Unable to continue the mission, they landed in Sweden and he was interned for six months.

Received the Air Medal with one Oak Leaf Cluster for combat service in the ETO. In November 1944 he returned to the States and served as an instructor at Midland, TX and Smyrna, TX. On V-J day he was on orders to go to a Bomb Disposal School. The orders were cancelled and he was transferred to the active reserve. He remained active in the Air Force Reserve and was discharged as a lieutenant colonel on Aug. 29, 1971.

He retired from the U.S. Postal Service in May 1988 and is enjoying life with the lady he married in 1943. They have been blessed with one daughter and two grandsons. Also spends time gardening, traveling, VOLKS marching and traveling.

ALLEN O. MUELLER, was born on July 11, 1919 in Hooper, NE. He joined the USAAF on Oct. 26, 1943 at Fort Crook, NE. Assigned to the 506th Sqdn., 44th Bomb Group. Basic training at Jefferson Barracks, St. Louis, MO.

Went overseas and participated in Southern France, Normandy, Northern France, Ardennes, Rhineland, Air Offensive Europe and Central Europe campaigns.

Received the EAME Campaign Medal with seven Bronze Stars, Good Conduct Medal, Overseas Service Bars and the WWII Service Medal. He was discharged on Oct. 31, 1945 with the rank of corporal.

Married in March 1946, they had three daughters and eight grandchildren. His wife passed away in 1970. He married again in 1972. He was farming and now raises registered polled Shorthorn cattle.

JOHN MUKA, was born on Jan. 22, 1925 in Chicago, IL. He was inducted into the USAAF as an aviation cadet on July 21, 1943. Basic training at Miami Beach, FL, college training at Geneva College, Beaver Falls, PA. Classified as a bombardier at Nashville, TN; pre-flight training at Maxwell Field, AL; Aerial Gunnery at Tyndall Field, Panama City, FL. Washed out of Advanced Bombardier School in August 1944 at Carlsbad, NM. After being crewed up as a 611 B-24 waist gunner and overseas training at Mountain Home, ID, he was assigned to the 392nd Bomb Group, 377th Bomb Sqdn., 8th Air Force at Wendling, England.

On Jan. 28, 1945, while on a bombing mission to Dortmand, Germany their plane sustained flak damage causing it to collide with another plane in the formation, both planes going down and exploding. Due to his injuries, he was put into a German hospital until he was liberated by the 8th Inf. Div. on April 14, 1945. On Nov. 1, 1945 he was given a medical discharge from Gardiner General Hospital, Chicago, IL.

Married on May 8, 1948 to June; they have five children. He retired in July 1988 as a mechanical design engineer.

JACK MURE SR., was born on April 30, 1924 in Jackson, MI. He enlisted in to the USAAC on Dec. 27, 1942 as an armorer gunner with the 453rd Bomb Group, 732nd Sqdn., 2nd Air Div.

He was stationed at Old Buckingham Airfield in Buckingham, England flying B-24s. Completed 35 missions from June 1944 to November 1944 with Pilot C. Fink and ship *Arrowhead.*

Mure received the Air Medal and Distinguished Flying Cross. He was discharged in October 1945 with the rank of staff sergeant.

Married Phyllis Shehan in 1947; they have six children. He is retired and is enjoying fishing and snowmobiling.

MELVIN C. MURRACK, was born on Oct. 19, 1924 in Racine, WI. He enlisted into the USAAC on Nov. 6, 1942 and reported for active duty on Jan. 28, 1943. Was an aerial armorer gunner with the 8th Air Force, 44th Bombardment Group, 506th Sqdn. Stationed at Sheppard Field, TX; basic training, Lubbock, TX; CTD in Santa Ana, CA; pre-flight, Thunderbird Field, IL; primary at Buckley Field, CO; Armament School, Las Vegas, NV; Aerial Gunnery School, Colorado Springs and Mountain Home, ID.

Crew training was in North Ireland, then to Shipdham, Norfolk, England. Participated in Central Europe, Ardennes, Rhineland and Northern France campaigns. He was given credit for five in the point system. His first mission was Sept. 8, 1944 and his final mission was March 23, 1945. He finished his combat tour without a scratch.

Murrack received the EAME Campaign Medal and the Air Medal with four Oak Leaf Clusters. None of their crew ever received the Distinguished Flying Cross they were supposed to get as a lead crew. Was discharged on Oct. 5, 1945 with the rank of staff sergeant.

He and Marily Crilley were married on July 27, 1946. He and his lovely wife have two daughters and two wonderful grandsons. He retired in 1977 as bank president, organized a financial & business consulting firm which he deactivated in 1992, retiring for the second time.

DONALD L. MURRAY, was born on Oct. 4, 1923 in Lewisburg, PA. Enlisted in the USAAC on Jan. 14, 1942. Basic training and airplane mechanic course at Keesler AAB, Biloxi, MS. Completed B-25 specialist course at North American Aviation in Santa Monica, CA. In September 1942 was sent to A/C training in Nashville, TN and Maxwell Field, AL. On July 31, 1943 he graduated with Class 43-11 at Victorville, CA as a second lieutenant bombardier and assigned to a crew at Clovis, NM.

They picked up a B-24 in Lincoln, NE and flew overseas via the southern route to Trinidad, Belem and Fortaleza, South America. Over to Dakar and Marrakech, Africa, landing in Newquay, England on Jan. 12, 1944.

They started flying missions with the 445th Bomb Group, 702nd Sqdn. at Tibenham (20th Wing, 2nd Div., 8th Air Force) on March 18. They were shot down on their 3rd mission over Muenster, Germany on March 23, 1944, bombing Wehrmacht troop assembly areas, prior to Allied Invasion of June 6, 1944.

He was a POW from March 23, 1944 to Jan. 26, 1945 at Stalag Luft III in Sagan, Germany. The Russians were advancing on Sagan so the Luftwaffe marched them out on a cold night on Jan. 26, 1945. The "death march" of three weeks of two feet of snow to Spremberg, close to Berlin. Here they boarded a train of box cars and were transported to Stalag VII-A in Moosburg. Things got very rough from Jan. 26 to April 29, 1945, when they were liberated by General Patton's 3rd Army troops. They flew to France and was shipped home on the USS *Gen. Gordon.*

He received the Good Conduct Medal, American Defense Medal, POW Medal, ETO Medal with one Battle Star and the WWII Victory Medal. He was discharged on Nov. 20, 1945 with the rank of first lieutenant

He and Mary Lee Ervine were married on Oct. 8, 1945; they have four children, two sons and two daughters and five grandchildren. He retired after 41 years as a first class lineman and metering technican for Citizens Electric Co. in Lewisburg, PA. Retirement is great!

JAMES J. MURRAY (JIM), was born on Feb. 2, 1922 in Bakersfield, CA. He enlisted into the USAAF on Aug. 21, 1942. He was an aviation cadet, basic gunner and assistant radio operator on B-24s.

Stationed at Santa Ana AAB at Hancock Field, Santa Maria; Amarillo, TX Radio School; Scott Field, IL, Radio School; Harlingen, TX Air Gunnery School; Colorado Springs Phase Training; Wendling, England with the 392nd Bomb Group. Then back to the Santa Ana AAB for discharge.

Participated in Ardennes, Central Europe, Northern France and Germany campaigns. His memorable experience was seeing his first B-24 blown up right next to them. Also being made a lead crew flying mission #30 - the last one!

He received Ardennes Medal, ETO and five Air Medals. Discharged on Oct. 5, 1945 with the rank of staff sergeant.

Murray and his wife Carmen have been married for 42 years; they have three daughters and six grandchildren.

He is retired from agriculture and is now in Agricultural Real Estate.

ROBERT E. MURRAY JR., was born on Aug. 9, 1924 in Pittsburgh, PA. Enlisted in the USAAC on Nov. 29, 1942, Allentown, PA. Was assigned to the 453rd Bomb Group, 732nd Sqdn., 2nd Air Div.

Basic training in Miami Beach, FL; Gunnery School, Laredo, TX; phase training in Pueblo, CO and Westover Field, MA. Completed 30 mission as a nose and waist gunner, Old Buckingham, England. Attended Air Gunner Instructor School, Laredo, TX; was instructor at Ft. Myers, Fl.

His memorable experience was engine failure and returning to base alone; jettisoned guns and ammuntions over Zuider Zee; mid-air collision near their aircraft; low altitude mission to St. Lo on July 25, 1944 afforded rare view of smoke and fire on ground; New Year's Day 1945 when lead plane slid off frozen runway and struck two parked planes, nine of the crew were killed.

He received the Air Medal and the ETO Medal. Discharged on Oct. 20, 1945 with the rank of staff sergeant. He is married and has two children and three grandchildren. Attended college under the GI Bill and worked for 35 years as an insurance adjuster. He is retired!

ROBERT H. MURRAY (BOB), was born on March 18, 1924 in Flint, MI. Entered the USAAC on Dec. 19, 1941; attended the National School of Aeronautics, Kansas City, MO in 1942; gunnery training at Harlingen, TX; and trained in B-24s.

He was assigned to the 448th Bomb Sqdn., 445th Bomb Group. Was shot down on April 12, 1944 (listed as MIA) and avoided capture with the Belgian underground.

Was assigned to a B-26 Sqdn. as an instructor for the French Air Force until WWII ended in 1945. He re-enlisted and was assigned to the 21st Troop Carrier Sqdn. C-54s, flew as flight engineer on B-29s, C-97s, C-124s and C-133s and now has a powerplant and private pilots license. Retired from the USAF Dec. 31, 1962.

He married Gloria C. Mikel and they have three daughters and one son, who is a master sergeant in the USAF. He retired from McDonnell Douglas April 30, 1989 with the last five years on the AH64 Apache Helicopter. Now lives in Dewey, AZ.

ABNER G. MUSSER JR., was born on Oct. 25, 1917 in South Bend, IN. Enlisted in USAAC on April 2, 1937 at Harrisburg, PA. Basic training, 1st. Air Base Sqdn., Langley Field, VA; transferred to 2nd Bomb Group, 20th Sqdn.; armanent and bomb sight maintenance course at Lowry Field, CO. He qualified as an unlisted bombardier late in 1939.

Transferred to the 25th Bomb Group at Langley, the Group moved to Boringuen (Ramsey) Field, Puerto Rico, then to the 40th Bomb Group at Ramsey. The Group moved to Panama in 1942. A couple of months at Guatamala City, GA, then to Salina, Equador, South America flying patrol to the Rock.

Back to the States for B-29 training, then transferred to Biggs Field for OTU training in B-24s. Sent to the 445th Bomb Group in Tibenham, England. He flew 26 missions of which 16 were either lead or deputy lead.

Earned the Distinguished Flying Cross, five Air Medals, Purple Heart and other campaign medals. He was discharged in 1945 with the rank of first lieutenant.

Married in January 1946. They have four children, including a pair of twins, and 11 grandsons.

He retired from the supermarket business 10 years ago. His sons are operating four stores at the present time.

VINCENT N. MUTI, was born on Nov. 21, 1916 in Ramsey, NJ. Worked at the local post office as clerk and carrier. Entered the USAAF on April 1, 1943 at Ft. Dix, NJ. After basic training in Atlantic City, NJ, he went to Aircraft

Armament School at Lowry Field, CO also to Aerial Gunnery School in Harlingen, TX.

Stationed in England with the 8th Air Force. They were engaged in the Invasion of Normandy, Northern France, Germany Campaign and Air Offensive Europe. His position was tail gunner on B-24, *Lusty Lib*. After many flights he was wounded over Munich, Germany on July 21, 1944. He was in a hospital in England, then sent home for discharge on April 25, 1945 with the rank of staff sergeant.

Their lead plane flew 21 missions before he was wounded. They belonged to the 847th Bomb Sqdn., 489th Bomb Group. He received the EAME Campaign Medal with four Bronze Stars, the Air Medal with two Oak Leaf Clusters, Purple Heart, Aviation Badge, Gunner Medal, and Good Conduct Medal.

He is married to Doris; they have two children, three grandchildren and two great-grandchildren. He retired from the U.S. Post Office and resides in Port Richey, FL.

DONALD L. MYERS, was born on July 23, 1923 in Kay County, OK. His birth was near the two quarter sections of lands claimed and homesteaded by his two grandparents in the last Oklahoma Land Run on Sept. 16, 1893. He received his early education in a two room country school and attended Oklahoma State University prior to joining the USAAF in January 1943.

He received his commission and wings at Childress Army Air Field on Feb. 5, 1944, Class of 44-2. After graduation from aviation cadets, he received radar bombardier and navigational training at Langley Field, VA. After which he was sent to the 8th Air Force and was assigned to the 482nd Pathfinder Group at Alconbury in May 1944. He was transferred to the 445th Bomb Group at Tibenham in August 1944.

He completed an operational combat tour of 30 missions as a lead crew member in March 1945. After completion of tour, he was assigned to the 482nd Bomb Group as an instructor, and remained with the 482nd until this group departed from England.

He received two Distinguished Flying Crosses, five Air Medals, six European Campaign Stars and several other ribbons. He remained in the Air Force Reserve after his WWII service and retired as a lieutenant colonel.

After his discharge from active service in September 1944, he returned to Oklahoma State University and graduated in January 1948, he went to work for Cities Service Oil Company (now Occidental Petroleum Corporation). He held various positions in the accounting and auditing areas during approximately 35 years of service with this company. He retired from the position of Audit Manager, International Auditing in June 1982. He is a certified public accountant (CPA).

He and Ida Madaline Etherington were married on Dec. 31, 1971. They maintain a winter home in Tulsa, OK and a summer home in Mill Creek, WA. He has two sons, both MDs and surgeons, one step-daughter and six grandchildren.

JOHN H. NACEY, was born on March 10, 1923 in New York City, NY.

He enlisted in the USAAF on March 31, 1942. Assigned to the 466th Bomb Group, 785th Bomb Sqdn. as an aircraft armorer gunner. Flew 22 missions over Germany from Sept. 1, 1944 to April 1945.

His memorable experience was on Jan. 16, 1945 when they bombed Dresdan, Germany, and when they landed in Paris.

Nacey was discharged on Sept. 22, 1945 with the rank of staff sergeant.

He received the Air Medal with two Oak Leaf Clusters and the ETO Ribbon.

He is retired.

JAMES P. NAPOLEON, was born on Sept. 25, 1923 in Chicago, IL. He enlisted in the USAAC on March 1, 1943. Was stationed in Mississippi, Texas, Wyoming, California and England. He remembers the completion of his 35th combat mission on Oct. 25, 1944, the target being the airfield in Neumunster, Germany.

Napoleon received the Distinguished Flying Cross, Air Medal, European Campaign Stars and the Presidential Unit Citation. He was discharged on April 1, 1945 with the rank of staff sergeant.

He has been married for 46 years and has two children. He completed 30 years of service with the Illinois State Police. He is retired.

BENJAMIN J. NAPOLITANO, was born on June 10, 1925 in Ozone Park, Queens, NY. He enlisted in the USAAC in August 1943. He took basic training in Miami Beach, FL; trained as a tail gunner on B-24s at Gunnery School, Laredo, TX; assigned to a crew at Salt Lake City, UT in December 1943; transition training took place at Biggs Field, El Paso, TX.

In June 1944 they flew to Prestwick, Scotland and eventually were assigned as a replacement crew to 804th Sqdn., 491st Bomb Group, Metfield, East Anglia. They relocated to Northern Pickenham after a bomb dump explosion destroyed the airfield.

He remembers the crash landing at Brussels, Belgium and numerous air battles. Completed his tour 35 missions and returned to the States in December 1944. Was discharged on Nov. 19, 1945 with the rank of staff sergeant. received the Distinguished Flying Cross, five Air Medals, five Battle Stars, ETO Medal, American Campaign Medal, WWII Victory Medal and the Good Conduct Medal

He received his bachelor's degree in accounting from Adelphi University in Long Island, NY and was the controller for the International Division of UST Inc. He returned to the U.K. a number of times related to business.

He and Helene Stark were married in 1955, they have four children and two grandchildren. He retired March 1, 1993 after 30 years of service with the UST. He resides in Stanford, CT.

EARLE P. NASE, was born on Nov. 23, 1923 in Souderton, PA. He enlisted in the USAAC on Dec. 14, 1942 and graduated in the Class 44-C, pilot in March 1944. Stationed at Randolph AFB, Molesworth/ Alconbury, England, Bolling AFB, Andrews AFB and the Air Force Headquarters, Pentagon.

He completed 35 missions as a B-24 pilot with the 8th Air Force, 453rd Bomb Group, 733rd Sqdn. on Jan. 15, 1945. Was a pilot on a C-54 in the Berlin Airlift on 252 coal hauling trips to Berlin in November 1948 to August 1949 from Celle, West Germany. He is a qualified instructor pilot or pilot on the following aircraft: B-29, B-24, C-54, C-119, T-29, C-131, C-45, C-47, T-33, U-3, U-4, PT-19, BT-13 and UC-78.

Was separated from active duty in January 1950. He was a pilot for Capital Airlines from June to November 1950. Recalled to active duty in November 1950 as a first lieutenant. He retired from the USAF on Oct. 31, 1968 with the rank of lieutenant colonel.

Received BS degree from University of Maryland, 1957. Nase was a market researcher with the Omni Jet Trading Floor in Rockville, MD from June 1969 to January 1990. He and Marcy Worrell were married on July 22, 1978. He has one daughter, Christine, from a previous marriage in 1945. He resides in Carlisle, Pa and has three grandchildren.

FRANCIS NASHWINTER, was born on Aug. 3, 1921 in Drifting, PA. He entered the USAAC on July 21, 1942. After basic training at St. Petersburg, FL he was assigned to the USAAF Technical School at Keesler Field, MS.

Graduated as an airplane mechanic on Dec. 22, 1942. Was sent to San Diego, CA to Consolidated Aircraft Corp. on a B-24 familiarization course on Feb. 3, 1943. Next to Gunnery School at Laredo, TX where he flunked his eye test and was grounded. Joined the 392nd Bomb Group at Alamogordo, NM. Arrived at Wendling, England on Aug. 1, 1943.

After almost two years in England as a line mechanic, he returned to the States and was discharged in October 1945 with the rank of corporal.

He married Erna Brose on June 29, 1946, they have one daughter and one granddaughter. Worked for 39 years as an auto mechanic, retiring in 1983. He resides in Sanborn, NY.

ARNOLD J. NASS, was born on Feb. 7, 1920 near Suring, WI. He enlisted in the USAAC on July 24, 1941. Was promoted through the ranks to staff sergeant and accepted in the Cadet Corp on Jan. 22, 1943. Took pilot training at Ballinger, Sherman and Houston, TX where he was assigned to Carlton Kleeman's crew at Clovis, NM. He trained in B-24s at Blythe, CA; Langley Field, VA and Clonto, Ireland before joining the 701st Sqdn., 445th Bomb Group at Tibenham by way of the northern route.

Flew the first of 19 missions as Kleeman's co-pilot on May 7, 1944, the first of 16 missions as a pilot of *Sweetest Rose of Texas* of July 2, 1944 and the last of his 35 missions on Aug. 9, 1944. He returned to the States on Sept. 21, 1944. He completed Instructors School at Smyrna, TN and instructed students in B-24 at Fort Worth, TX and former instructors in B-29 at San Antonio, TX.

Was discharged on Feb. 18, 1946 with the rank of captain. He entered the oil and gas exploration business in Dallas, TX in 1947 and remained active in it as an employee, general partner and founder of three companies through 1988.

He and Rose Mary have been married for nearly 52 years and have six children and nine grandchildren.

DAVID NATHANSON, was born on Dec. 10, 1917 in Dallas, TX. He joined the service on May 31, 1941, Ordnance Department, aviation ordnance officer, automotive officer on the staff.

Stationed at Army Air Force Station #115, England, Ft. Sill, OK and Aberdeen Proving Ground. His memorable experiences were his activities involved with D-day; sailing to and from England on the two Queens; serving with the 44th Bomb Group for 28 months; and the HQ Group of the 2nd Air Div. for six months.

Nathanson received the Distinguished Unit Badge with one Oak Leaf Cluster, ETO Ribbon with seven Bronze Stars, American Defense Service Medal and the WWII Victory Medal. He was discharged on Dec. 27, 1945 with the rank of captain.

He is married to Maxine, they have one daughter Nancy Louise, son Paul David and two granddaughters. He is retired.

RAYMOND J. NATHE, was born on June 12, 1919 in Sargent Co., ND. Inducted in the Infantry from Milwaukee, WI in May 1941; transferred to the USAAC in February 1942; commissioned as second lieutenant navigator and assigned to the 389th Bomb Group in 1943. He became captain in

December 1943 and transferred to the 482nd Bomb Group as an instructor in December 1943.

Flew 30 missions including Ploesti on Aug. 1, 1943 and a night mission to Berlin in December 1944. He received the Distinguished Flying Cross with Oak Leaf Cluster. Was discharged in October 1945.

Nathe married Ruth Brorstrom, they have four children and 10 grandchildren. He is a retired design engineer, now living in Marblehead, OH.

RUSSELL J. NEATROUR, was born on Oct. 18, 1922 in Johnstown, PA. Enlisted in the USAAC on Nov. 13, 1942 and later transferred to the USAAF. Stationed at Miami Beach, basic; 60th CTD at University of Pittsburgh; Nashville, TN for classification; Maxwell Field, AL, Preflight School; Helena, AR, primary pilot training; Malden, MO, basic training; Stuttgart, AR, advanced two engine; 2nd Air Div., 453rd Group, 732nd Sqdn.; Sioux Falls, SD; Galveston Air Base, TX; and Ellington Field, Houston, TX.

His memorable experience was the first take off in fog during the Battle of the Bulge and didn't get back to home base for four days, he stayed at the Navy Base in Western England.

Neatrour received the Air Medal with four Oak Leaf Clusters. Was discharged on Nov. 18, 1945 at Ellington Field, TX with the rank of first lieutenant.

He and Marguerite Montgomery were married on June 26, 1943. They have two daughters and three grandsons. He retired at the age of 60 from the York Division Borg-Warner Corp. Was a supervisor in the machining department. Moved to Sebring, FL in 1982 after retiring.

JULIUS NEEDELMAN, was born in July 1918 in New York City, NY. Enlisted in the USAAC in June 1942 as an aviation cadet. Stationed at Nashville, TN; Monroe, LA; Boise, ID; Tonopah, NV with the 2nd Air Div., then on to Horsham St. Faith in Norwich, England.

He flew nine combat missions over Europe. Plane was shot up and he made a forced landing in Sweden, April 9, 1944, and was interned for six months. Was recalled to active duty in 1952. Flew 40 combat missions over North Korea from Pusan South Korea with the 5th Air Force.

Needelman received six Air Medals and the Distinguished Flying Cross. He retired from the Active Reserve on July 1, 1978 with the rank of lieutenant colonel.

He is married and they have three children and six grandchildren. He is a retired motion picture distributor.

CHARLES G. NEELY (CHUCK), was born on Oct. 2, 1922 in Chattanooga, TN. He lived in Nashville from 1924 to 1983. He enlisted in the USAAC in 1942. He graduated from Mechanics School at Maulden, MO in 1943; multi-engine training in Biloxi in 1944; washed out cadets in 1944; aerial gunnery graduate, Harlingen, TX; completed B-24 operational training at Gowen AFB in Boise, ID. He was assigned to the 753rd Bomb Sqdn., 458th Bomb Group, 8th Army Air Force in Horsham St. Faith, England December 1944 as a top turret gunner and assistant flight engineer.

Neely flew 22 missions and received the Air Medal with three Oak Leaf Clusters, three Campaign Battle Stars and the Good Conduct Medal. Returned to the States in July 1945 to Nellis AACB, Las Vegas, NV in B-29 Flight Engineer Training. Was discharged on Oct. 10, 1945 with the rank of staff sergeant.

Received a BS degree from Tennessee Technological University in March 1949. Was employed with the General Motors Acceptance Corp. for 32 years and a licensed real estate agent from 1977 to 1986. He enjoys traveling and sports activities. Married Dorothy L. Yates (passed away in 1973), then married Betty L. Martin. He has three step-children and 11 grandchildren. He retired to Cookeville, TN for its diversity of beauty.

GIRARD NEFCY, was born on Aug. 31, 1921 in Driftwood, PA. Enlisted in the USAAC on Nov. 27, 1942 as an aviation cadet and pilot. Military stations and locations: basic training, Miami Beach, FL; college training detachment, Clinton, SC; Classification Center, Nashville, TN; pre-flight training, Maxwell Field, AL; primary flight training, Clarksdale, MS; basic flight training, Greenville, MS; advanced flight training, Lawrenceville, IL; Chanute Field, IL; crew training, Westover Field in MA; Savannah, GA; and combat operation, Hardwick Field, England.

Participated in Rhineland bombing and Central Europe area. He remembers that after five missions with his original crew, they were chosen for lead crew training because of their excellent bombardier. At that time, he still wanted to become a fighter pilot (every young flier's dream), so, by choice, he left the crew to become a spare co-pilot, so he could finish all his missions sooner as a pre-requisite to qualify for fighter training. The war ended before he could complete his tour. He had so many close calls that he never really expected to return.

Nefcy received the Air Medal with Oak Leaf Clusters. Was discharged on Dec. 14, 1945.

After the war, he went back to the University of Detroit and finished Engineering School. Mechanical engineering 1947, MS automotive engineering 1949, MBA, University of Michigan, 1970.

Married in 1947, they have 14 children, all grown up now. He retired from the Ford Motor Co. in 1984.

The original crew has been holding regular reunions since 1945 in various parts of the country. They have a trophy, a picture of a B-24 from the Ford Archives annealed on metal, that circulates for the host of the reunion to keep that year. It's always a great party.

KENNETH WILLARD NEIDENTHAL, was born on Sept. 19, 1921 in Brewster, OH. Enlisted in the USAAC in 1942. Assigned to the 93rd Bomb Group (H), 328th Bomb Sqdn. stationed at Lowry Field, CO on Oct. 21, 1942; altitude training record, Salt Lake City, UT, Dec. 18, 1942; Wendover Aerial Gunnery School, Davis Monthan Field Gunnery School, March 27, 1943; Army Air Base, Pueblo, CO, 804th Bomb Sqdn., June 6, 1943; European and North African Theaters of Operation with the 328th Bomb Sqdn., Liberator Base, London.

Returned to the States, 29th Altitude Training Unit, 78th Flying Wing, San Antonio.

His memorable experience was photographically recorded in *The Story of The 93rd Bombardment Group*. The photo caption "Lucky Miss" says it all, describing the hit over Kiel on Dec. 13, 1943 by flak beside Neidenthal's waist gunner location.

Neidenthal received the Distinguished Flying Cross, Air Medals and three Oak Leaf Clusters. Was discharged in 1945 with the rank of staff sergeant.

Married Mary Jean Dunlevy (passed away in 1973), they have three sons: Wally, Gary and Randy. He attended the Ohio State University, graduating with an engineering degree and worked for the Ranco Controls, Battelle Memorial Institute and became chief engineer of the Federal Gas Company and retired from Vipco, a division of Crane Plastics as their chief engineer.

In 1988, he and JoAnn Baker were married and reside in Columbus, OH. They enjoy their families, attend air shows, visited the Liberator and other activities.

DONALD O. NELL, was born July 24, 1925 in Medford, MA. Enlisted in the USAAC on July 8, 1943 and called to active duty Feb. 1, 1944. Assigned to 453rd Bomb Group, 733rd Bomb Sqdn. Basic training at Greensboro, NC; Flex Gunnery School, Harlingen, TX; and crew training at Pueblo, CO.

Participated in action at Ardennes, Central Europe and Rhineland. Memorable experience was Jan. 1, 1945. His crew was one of the first to get off the ground. Ice on wing and stablizer surfaces was very heavy. About six more from group took off, then one crashed and blew up, remainder of planes stayed on the ground and mission was cancelled.

Discharged Nov. 7, 1945 with the rank staff sergeant. Received the ETO with three Battle Stars, Air Medal with three Oak Leaf Clusters, American Theater, Good Conduct and the WWII Victory Medal.

Married Joyce Baker on Aug. 27, 1955. They have two children, Scott and Barb; and grandson Austin William Kanner. Nell is retired.

FRED B. NELLUMS, was born on March 28, 1918 in Spring Hill, TN. Enlisted in the USAF on April 16, 1941. Attended Mechanic School at Chanute Field; Gunnery School, Laredo, TX; joined the 19th Anti-Sub at Langley Field, flew from Langley to Gander Bay Newfoundland, to Preswick, Scotland, then to Dunkswell, England and made several anti-sub patrols.

Was assigned to the 66th Bomb Sqdn., 44th Bomb Group at Norwich, England. As an engineer gunner he flew 35 missions over France and Germany. He was shot down once over the English Channel, parachuted out and landed on the English Coast.

He received the Distinguished Service Cross, Good Conduct Medal, Air Medal with three Oak Leaf Clusters, Distinguished Flying Cross, EAME Campaign Medal with one Bronze Star and the Purple Heart. He was credited with three enemy fighters. He was discharged on May 30, 1945 with the rank of staff sergeant.

Nellums is married and has one son, a daughter and two sisters. He is retired and enjoys doing charity work.

CARL W. NELSON (POP), entered the service in 1943 and trained in aircraft mechanics and gunnery. He was assigned to the A.E. Cearnal crew as waist gunner. Sent to the 389th Bomb Group (H), 565th Sqdn. at Hethel, England and put on combat status on June 2, 1944.

His 22nd mission was the most memorable. Flak was very intense, they were hit five times and counted 139 holes in the waist compartment. One piece cut his parachute harness in the small of his back. No one was hurt.

Nelson completed 30 missions in 91 days and returned to the States. Was discharged with the rank of staff sergeant. He received the Distinguished Flying Cross, Air Medal with three Oak Leaf Clusters, EAME Campaign Medal with four stars, American Theatre Ribbon and the WWII Victory Medal.

RONALD L. NELSON, was born on June 12, 1912 in Cherokee, IA. Enlisted in the USAAC on Dec. 10, 1941. Stationed at the Army Air Base in Ft. Myers, FL and attended Gunnery School in Las Vegas, NV. He was assigned to the 409th Sqdn., 93rd Bomb Group.

One of his most memorable experience was the Epic Flight of the Night Raider over Germany. This story was published in the June 26, 1943 edition of *Liberty Magazine* detailing his experiences during his tour in Germany.

He received the Purple Heart and the Air Medal and attained the rank of staff sergeant. Nelson was killed in action on April 16, 1943. His brother Maynard, B-24 pilot, 15th Air Force completed 51 missions; brother Russell, 1st Army was Purple Heart recipient and his brother Llye, 27th Inf. Div. also received a Purple Heart.

THOMAS A. NELSON, was sworn into the USAAF in July 1942. Due to no openings available for aviation cadets in communication, he was assigned to armament. Was called to active duty in December 1942; sent to basic training at Valley Forge Military Academy; advanced training, Yale University. Graduated from the Aviation Cadet Program in May 1943 and commissioned a second lieutenant. Assigned to the 701st Sqdn., 445th Bomb Group at Gowen Field, ID. Trained at Wendover, UT and Sioux City, IA until hospitalized for six weeks. Temporarily assigned to aircraft accident investigation at Sioux City following recovery from illness.

In October 1943, he was assigned to the 733rd Sqdn., 453rd Bomb Group at March Field, CA and departed with the 453rd Bomb Group for the U.K. in December 1943.

In March 1944, half of the 733rd was re-assigned as the 859th Sqdn., 492nd Bomb Group at Old Buckingham. He went with the 859th to North Pickenham in April and became squadron armament officer, first lieutenant. In August 1944 the 859th was redesignated as the 788th Sqdn., 467th Bomb Group and moved to Rackheath. In July 1945 departed UK for redeployment at Sioux Falls, SD and released from active duty in December 1945.

He attended Los Angeles City College, Associate in Arts, 1942; University of Southern California, BS in EE, 1949; MS in EE, 1953 and also received a certificate in business management from the Graduate School of Mgmt., 1970.

Was employed in engineering and management at the Los Angeles Water and Power in 1944 to 1980. He is currently a consulting engineer, transportation consultant, author of rail transportation articles, editor of monthly rail transportation publication from 1980 to present.

VICTOR F. NEMETZ, was born on May 27, 1921 in Czechoslovakia. His family immigrated to New Jersey. He entered the service with SAW Battalions in Florida, transferred to aviation engineers and served in Colorado, Oklahoma, Louisiana, Alaska and England.

While with the 949th Topo engineers helped print secret maps for the Normandy invasion. After his plane was shot down over occupied France, he got his crew back to England with the help of Slovak forced laborers and the French underground. He then joined the 389th Bomb Group in Hethel, England as a tail gunner in the Parke crew.

Aside from combat, the most memorable experiences include: meeting a free Slovak lieutenant whose family house was destroyed during the raid on Most, Czechoslovakia; meeting "Father Beck" while bringing in a cab load of girls to celebrate V-E day; turning the 566th sergeants' hut into a darkroom, developing several hundred rolls of film for returning crews; being one of the "Bloody 800" transferred from Sioux Falls, SD to Harlingen, TX; hiring a German immigrant mason who was filling in bomb craters on sub pens while Nemetz was bombing them; and shooting at a ME262 on last mission.

Was discharged as a staff sergeant and received commission as second lieutenant for saving crew in occupied France. Served active duty tours during the Cuban missile and Berlin crises. Retired as a major of the USAFR in 1970 and as a Facilities Engineer in 1986.

He and his wife, Valentine, have three daughters and four grandchildren.

BERNARD NEUMANN, was born on Jan. 7, 1918 in Minneapolis, MN. Joined the USAF as an armor gunner on Aug. 21, 1942. Stationed at Amarillo; Denver; Tonapah; Santa Ana; Harlingen; and Seething, England. He was with the 714th Bomb Sqdn., 448th Bomb Group.

His memorable experience was flak, flak, and more flak in his 29 combat missions. His crew flew 15 missions as a lead crew, crew #56.

Received the Air Medal with three Bronze Stars, Presidential Unit Citation and the Good Conduct Medal. He was discharged on Oct. 10, 1945 with the rank of staff sergeant.

He is married, and they have three children and four grandchildren. He is retired.

CLARENCE W. NEUMANN (BILL), was born on Nov. 7, 1920 in Detroit, MI. Joined the USAAC on March 23, 1942. He graduated from navigator training, Hondo Field, TX and commissioned a second lieutenant on Jan. 28, 1943. Trained as a navigator in B-24 and completed crew training at Lincoln Field, NE in May 1943.

Flew to ETO with the Gerhardt Provisional Group and assigned to the 328th Bomb Sqdn., 93rd Bomb Group in Hardwick, England in June 1943. During subsequent tour with the 93rd Bomb Group made two trips (Detached Service) to North Africa, flying combat missions from Bengasi, Libya and Tunis.

Flew several missions from Hardwick, then he was transferred to the 814th Bomb Sqdn., 482nd Bomb Group (Pathfinders). He trained with the British "Stinky" Radar and

H2X "Mickey" Radar. He flew combat missions with Hinchman crew leading Groups of the 2nd Air Div., until March 22, 1944. He then served as radar navigator instructor until August 1944, when he returned to the ZI and Langley Field, VA as radar instructor and radar intelligence.

Neumann was discharged from the service in December 1945. He returned to school at the University of Detroit. Was recalled to active duty in July 1948 and trained as a meteorologist. During the Korean War, he flew 50 missions in a B-26 from Kimpo Army Air Field plus three weather recon missions in the B-29.

He received the Distinguished Flying Cross, six Air Medals, two Presidential Unit Citations and several other Service Awards. He retired as a lieutenant colonel in December 1964.

Married Dolores June Twamley on Feb. 9, 1943; they have one son, Jeffrey.

WILLIAM K. NEUMANN (BILL), was born on June 18, 1922 in Yonkers, NY. Entered the USAAC on Nov. 18, 1942. After basic training in Atlantic City, NJ, attended Weather Observer School at Chanute Field, IL, transferred to Aviation Cadets and graduated as a second lieutenant with Class 44F at Freeman Field, IN. He was assigned to B-24 transition training in Smyrna, TN; followed by RTU training at Charleston, SC.

He flew a B-24 via northern route to England in March 1945. He was assigned to the 389th Bomb Group in Hethel, England. They had completed six missions when the war ended in Europe. He flew a B-24 back to Windsor Locks, CT in May 1945.

Transferred to Active Reserve in September 1945. Flew trainers P-47, C-47 and B-25 aircraft with the Reserve and New York Air National Guard until re-activated in March 1951 for the Korean War, as a finance officer. He also flew C-47s during a two year tour at March AFB and Travis AFB in California. Joined the California Air National Guard in October 1953 and flew trainers, F-51, T-33 and F-86 ADL aircraft.

Other assignments included comptroller operations officer and flying safety officer. Transferred to the 944th Troop Carrier Group (AFRES) in February 1963. Flew C-119 aircraft and held flying safety assignments until he was assigned to Inactive Reserve in October 1969.

He retired as a lieutenant colonel and command pilot in October 1973. He received the Air Medal, EAME Campaign Medal and several other ribbons.

He worked in Aerospace Industries for nearly 40 years, mainly in purchasing positions at Rohr, Lockheed and Ciba-Geigy. Was married to Joan Hoganson for 23 years. After her death in October 1973, he married Laura Beck. He has three step-children, two children and 12 grandchildren.

DON C. NEVILLE, was born on Aug. 24, 1925 at Hartselle, AL. Volunteered for the USAAC Cadet Program in April 1944. He completed basic training at Keesler Field in Biloxi, MS. Was advised after basic that Cadet Program discontinued. He attended Gunnery School at Tyndall Field in Panama City, FL. Was assigned as an upper turret gunner on a B-24. His crew assignment and overseas training at Westover Field in Springfield, MA.

His crew flew new B-24 overseas through Labrador, Greenland, Iceland and Wales. Was assigned to 754th Sqdn., 458th Bomb Group at Horsham St Faith near Norwich, England. First mission to Regensburg, Germany. He crashed shortly after take off on April 14, 1945 on the second mission. Five members of his seven man crew were killed. He spent the next year in Army Hospitals recuperating from the crash.

He was discharged from the service in April 1946. Retired from the Marshall Space Flight Center in Huntsville, AL in 1974 after 26 years of service. He is married and has one daughter and one grandson.

WILLIAM P. NEWBOLD, was born on June 16, 1920 on a Bucks County farm near Langhorne, PA. He joined the USAAC on June 16, 1941. He qualified for cadet training at Barksdale Field, LA and eventually joined the newly formed 506th Sqdn., (B-24) at Pueblo, CO as a navigator.

He arrived in England in February 1943 and served out of Shipdham, East Anglia, Tunis and Benghazi, North Africa with the 8th Air Force, 44th Bomb Group, 506th and 67th Sqdns. He was sent to Africa twice and returned once. His more prominent missions, 15 and one half total, was the May 14, 1943 raid on the Kiel, Germany submarine pens and the 14 hour low level Ploesti strike of Aug. 1, 1943.

His most memorable mission was his last. It was the Wiener Neustadt raid of Oct. 1, 1943 where he replaced a Ploesti casualty of the 67th Sqdn. They were six hours away from Africa on the I.P. as fighters attacked head on, on fire and spinning, the aircraft came apart in the air. Seven of the 10 crew members perished.

Thence, they were captured and put in solitary confinement for 17 days, hospital (Obermasfeld), Stalag Luft III, prison escape efforts forced them to march to Moosburg and subsequently to return to the U.S. control on April 29, 1945. He escaped from this to head from Paris via Patton's Red Ball Express arriving on V-E day.

Returned to the States in June 1945 then sent to Ellington Field, TX to re-train for Pacific duty. When the war ended, he was dispatched to Mather Field, CA as an O.C. Instrument Training Department.

Was discharged on Jan. 13, 1947 with the rank of captain. He received the Distinguished Flying Cross, Air Medal with four Oak Leaf Clusters, Purple Heart, Prisoner of War Medal, Presidential Unit Citation with one Oak Leaf Cluster, EAME Theatre Ribbon with eight Bronze Stars, WWII Victory Medal and other ribbons.

He went to Dretzel for a BS degree in engineering. He retired in 1982 as an R&D and test engineer in the General Electric Space Program.

Married to Elizabeth, they have three sons and four grandchildren. They reside in Langhorne, PA.

HENRY L. NEWELL, was born on Sept. 28, 1921. He joined the USAAF on May 25, 1942. Took pilot training in South East Training Command and graduated from Twin Engine Flying School at George Field, IL in Class 43-I. Went to Maxwell Field, AL for B-24 pilot training, then sent to Casper, WY and three months training with crew.

In late April picked up new B-24 at Topeka, KS and flew to Nuts Corner, North Ireland with stops at Manchester, NH, Goose Bay, Labrador and Iceland. Assigned to the 458th Bomb Group, 754th Sqdn. at Horsham St. Faith, Norwich, England. All crew members survived 32 missions and returned home safely.

He is married, has three sons and one granddaughter and lives in Winchester, KY.

ROBERT T. NEWMAN (BOB) was born on Nov. 7, 1924 in Farmville, VA. Was drafted into the Army on March 20, 1943 and was assigned to the USAF for basic training at Miami Beach, FL, then sent to Seymore Johnson Field Aircraft Mechanics School (light and medium bombers). Graduated #4 in his class and sent to Aviation Cadets in Miami Beach, FL. Was eliminated from Cadet Training and sent to

Gunnery School at Tyndall Field, FL in February 1944. Trained in ball turret in B-17s. Upon his graduation, he was sent to Westover Field, MA as a flight engineer, top turret on B-24s

His next stop was England, 8th Air Force, 446th Bomb Group, 706 Sqdn., stationed at Bungay. Completed 35 missions over Germany between Oct. 31, 1944 to March 10, 1945.

He received the Air Medal with five Oak Leaf Clusters, and the ETO Medal with three Battle Stars. Returned to the States in April 1945 and was assigned to Smyrna AFB near Nashville, TN and was discharged at Maxwell Field in September 1945 with the rank of tech sergeant.

Newman attended the University of Virginia, graduated in 1949 with a BS in chemistry. Was employed by Southern Railway as Chemist in Research & Test Department. (Southern Railway later became part of Norfolk Southern). He retired as chief chemist at Norfolk Southern in December 1986.

Married Margaret Farmer on June 26, 1950. They have two daughters, one son and two grandchildren. He and Margaret now reside in Soddy-Daisy, TN near Chattanooga, TN. He enjoys traveling, woodworking and stamp collecting.

SID NEWSOM, was born on Nov. 5, 1916 in Oakland, CA. He graduated from the University of California in Berkeley in 1940 with a degree in military science and the rank of second lieutenant in the Army Infantry Reserves. Upon entering active duty in February 1941, he became a member of the Ski Troops, 87th Mountain Inf. at Camp Hale, CO.

To fulfill his life long dream to fly, he transferred to the 2nd Air Force, graduating in the Class 44-B in Frederick, OK. After completing 4-Engine School at Fort Worth, TX and combat crew training at Casper, WY, he went to England in August 1944, where he was assigned to the 491st Bomb Group at Swaffam, England.

Newsome was proud to have served his country in WWII as a lead pilot flying B-24s, completing 28 missions over Germany. He participated in the Rhine Crossing. On one mission, flying low at 50 feet, his plane was riddled with bullet holes but he and his crew were unhurt. Another mission ended in a forced landing on the street of a small town in northern France due to the damage of two engines. At the end of the war, he flew many trips over Germany and the Rhine to enable ground personnel to assess the damage.

After resuming civilian life, he was called back to serve his country in the USAF during the Berlin Airlift. He taught ROTC at the University of California in Berkeley and later was transferred to Alaska, where he flew B-29s to remote sights involved in national security. Spent his last years of active duty with HQUSAF, Pentagon and then San Antonio, TX. After 29 years, he retired from active duty. He took a position heading a Junior ROTC unit, Compton High School, CA for the next 16 years.

On May 11, 1993, Newsome died at the age of 76 years. He received the Distinguished Flying Cross, Air Medal with three Oak Leaf Clusters and two Combat Stars, as well as the love and affection of his wife of 54 years, five children, 10 grandchildren and five great-grandchildren. He is missed, but they are grateful that he lived such a long and eventful life in service to his country.

FIELDER N. NEWTON, was born on Sept. 23, 1923 in Farrell, PA. Enlisted in the USAAC while attending Penn State and was inducted on May 17, 1943. After basic training at Atlantic City, he was assigned to Slippery Rock College and from there through classification, Preflight at Maxwell Field, Primary Flight, Gunnery School and graduated as a second lieutenant navigator from Selman Field on Aug. 7, 1944.

He joined the JC Dodman crew at March Field and trained on B-24s before being assigned to the 389th Bomb Group at Hethel, England. He flew as a lead crew from December 1944 through the War's end completing 17 missions. He returned a B-24 to the States with crew and 10 passengers via Azores and Gander Lake to Bradley Field, CT.

His memorable experience was flying back from Berlin on three engines and landing at Hethel with only 50 gallons of fuel. He received the Air Medal with two Oak Leaf Clusters, the EAME Campaign Medal with four Stars, the American Campaign Medal, the WWII Victory Medal and the Presidential Unit Citation.

Newton was discharged on Dec. 8, 1945 with the rank of first lieutenant. Received the Air Medal with two clusters, European Campaign with four stars, American Campaign, Victory Medal and the Presidential Unit Citation.

He returned to Penn State and received a mechanical engineering degree in 1948. Worked in steel industry sales until he retired in 1988. He and Marjorie Cherry were married on Aug. 12, 1944, they have four sons and seven grandchildren.

THOMAS C. NEWTON, was born in Grand Rapids, MI. Inducted into the USAAC about November 1942 at Fort Custer, MI.

Was sent to Camp McCoy, WI for short basic. Requested transfer to the Air Force late in 1943; sent to Jefferson Barracks, MO; re-assigned to Bradley Field, CT; and joined the Army AFB Unit. In the fall of 1944 was transferred overseas to join the 445th Bomb Group at Tibenham, England.

Worked in the field operations office until V-E day. V-E day was celebrated with the inclusion in a "Trolley Mission." This was a sight seeing mission in a B-24 to Frankfort and back up the Rhine River at 500 feet altitude. He served with 20 men on holding party to clear base. Then back to the States on the *Queen Mary.*

His memorable experience was seeing Colonel Stewart when he visited their office to see Major Critchfield.

When points reached 50, he was discharged. Newton received the Good Conduct Medal, Amerian Theater Medal, WWII Victory Medal and the European Theater Ribbon with two Bronze Stars.

Newton and Vivienne Carpenter were married in 1956. He is retired.

DONALD NIELSEN, was born on May 17, 1922 in Fresno, CA. Enlisted in the USAAC as a navigator. Was sent over to Horsham St. Faith at Norwich, England and assigned to the 458th Bomb Group, 753rd Sqdn. He participated in the Normandy Invasion of Europe.

Nielsen completed 31 combat missions over Europe. Received the Distinguished Flying Cross and the Air Medal with three Oak Leaf Clusters. Retired from the USAF with the rank of major.

Married to Billee, they have three daughters and one son. He is a retired electrical engineer with the Pacific Gas & Electric Co.

ALBERT L. NIX, was born on Sept. 6, 1911 in Wibaux, MT. Enlisted in the service on March 20, 1942 and assigned to the 754th Sqdn., 458th Bomb Group (H), 2nd Bomb Division, 96th Wing, 8th Air Force.

Nix was an aerial gunner and his plane crashed on May 8, 1944 at Horsham, England. Of the 10 man crew, only four survived. He spent a year in the hospital at Walla Walla, WA.

Was discharged on March 21, 1945 with the rank of staff sergeant. He was a post master at Wibaux, MT for 27 years, retiring on Jan. 5, 1973. He is married and has five children and 13 grandchildren.

ROBERT O. NIXON, was born on Feb. 14, 1922 in Pittsburgh, PA. Enlisted in the Army in August 1942, sergeant. Attended Navigation Flying School, commissioned second lieutenant, Army Air Corps. Flew 32 missions as lead crew with the 458th Bomb Group, ETO, captain. He flew B-29 Bombers and C-119 combat cargo as a master navigator, completing 35 missions. During Korean Conflict, he was chief navigator with the 13th Air Force Unit in Taipai 1968-1969 and Commander of Support Unit in the Vietnam War.

Memorable experiences: First Berlin Raid, Bloody

Monday, lead navigator on Beezer Glenn's crew, completed 31 missions from February to August 1944. Lead 42 aircraft via South America, Africa to England. Did not drop bombs on last mission on July 24, 1944 at St. Low.

Nixon received the Legion of Merit, two Distinguished Flying Crosses, 12 Air Medals, Meritorious Service Medal, Joint Service Commendation Medal, Air Force Commendation Medal, Presidential Unit Citation, Combat Readiness Citation, Air Force Reserve Meritorious Service Medal, all of the area service medals, WWII, Korea and Vietnam with Battle Stars. He was discharged in August 1973, after 31 years of service with the rank of colonel, USAF, Division Chief Mobility Div. JCS.

His wife Marilyn passed away in 1990. He has one daughter, two sons and four grandchildren. He was a college professor and worked in business and management and business computer application.

J. WILSON NODEN, was born on Sept. 30, 1924 in Lambertville, NJ. While attending Rutgers University in 1943, he was drafted into the Transportation Corps. Noden passed the exam for Aviation Cadets and became a navigator as second lieutenant at Ellington Field, TX in September 1944.

After phase training at Mt. Home, ID, he flew to Rackheath with the 467th Bomb Group via Goose Bay, Labrador. Flew 12 missions, mostly milk runs. After the war he flew home and returned to Rutgers Undergraduate and Law School.

Was appointed to the New Jersey Judiciary in 1959. Became semi-retired in 1991 and currently sits two days per week on Judicial recall. He married an English girl, Cecily Horne, after a blind date in New Jersey. They have three great children.

BENJAMIN F. NOLAN, was born on June 22, 1917 in New York City, NY. He was a border patrolman on the Mexican Border, when he entered the Army in April 1942. After graduation from the Military Police Officer Candidate School, he was attached to the 8th Air Force in England, serving at Hethel, Morley Hall and Ketteringham Hall, where he was an assistant 2nd Air Division Provost Marshal.

Later, he commanded criminal investigation (CID) agents operating in East Anglia, France and Belgium. He was awarded the Army Commendation Medal, and upon his discharge as a first lieutenant, he had four European Campaign Stars.

After the war, he was an assistant United States Attorney in New York City and elected a judge in 1972 and re-elected in 1982. In retirement, he serves by assignment as trial judge and a lecturer at judicial seminars.

In 1943 he married Agnes Wynne. They have one daughter, Carol Nolan; two sons, Robert and James Nolan; and five grandchildren: Christopher, Vivian, Kelly, Erin and Bryan.

JOHN H. NORDBY, DMD, was born in May 1921 in Millville, MA. He enlisted in the USAF in March 1943 as a second lieutenant bombardier B-24 with the 467th Bomb Group.

Was with the 8th Air Force in Rackheath, England. His memorable experience was the trolley missions at war's end and seeing the air devastation of Germany. Was discharged in December 1945 at Randolph Field, TX.

Nordby is married and has two sons. He is a retired dentist.

CHARLES E. NORRIS, was born on June 4, 1915 in Jacksonville, FL. Enlisted in the USAAC on April 4, 1941 and assigned to G Co., 124th Inf., Camp Blanding. On Jan. 13, 1942 he was with G Co, 124th Inf., Fort Benning, GA. He was assigned to the 2nd Air Division, Pilot Class 43-E and sent to Hethel, England and the ETO. His memorable experience was April 22 night mission with the 389th Bomb Group, 567th Sqdn.

Norris received the Distinguished Flying Cross, Air Medal with three Oak Leaf Clusters and the ETO Ribbon. He was discharged on July 30, 1945 with the rank of first lieutenant.

Married Jean Phillips on June 3, 1952, they have one son, William J. and a daughter, Cora. He is retired and living the "Life Of Riley" in St. Augustine, FL.

JOSEPH W. NORRIS, was born on Nov. 28, 1918. Joined the USAF in 1941. His memorable experiences include the B-24 they were testing over Wendover, UT got into a three and one half turn spin and although the pilots managed to get it back on the ground (it was truly a miracle), the plane was so severely damaged, it never flew again. Consequently the crew had to pick up a shiny new B-24 in Wichita before heading over to England to join the 2nd Air Division, 489th Bomb Group at Halesworth.

He flew 32 missions on the B-24 *St. Louis Woman*. Norris received the Distinguished Flying Cross. He was discharged in 1967 with the rank of lieutenant colonel. His career was mostly with the Strategic Air Command. He helped pioneer the jet air refueling age and served as a USAF Advisor to the Vietnamese Air Force at Tan Son Nhut Air Base, 1966-1967 during the Vietnamese War.

Norris passed away on May 9, 1990; he is survived by his wife, Frances Scott Norris, daughter, Ginger Lane and son, Randall Norris.

WILLIAM H. NORRIS, was born on Jan. 31, 1922 in Philipsburg, PA. He joined the 104th U.S. Cavalry at the age of 17, at the Pennsylvania National Guard.

The Guard was Federalized in 1941 and he traded his horse for a motorcycle. He was later accepted into the USAAC and graduated from pilot training at Ellington Field, TX in Class 43-C.

He trained in B-26s, then B-24s which he and crew flew to England and were joined with the 735th Sqdn., 453rd Bomb Group. Following their 30 missions, he and some of the crew flew supply missions into Belgium, taking gasoline to Gen. Patton's 3rd Army.

Norris made the USAF his career, flying the Berlin Air Lift and the Greenhouse Atomic Project. After retraining in jet fighters, he flew some 42 different aircraft, retiring as a colonel in 1964.

He and his wife, Priscilla, live in Albuquerque, NM. They have four children and six grandchildren.

ROBERT A. NORSEN, was born on Oct. 25, 1917, a farm kid. Attended University of Minnesota, Santa Maria February 1940, Randolph, Kelly, Class 40-F. Back to Randolph, Sebring B-17, May 1942 to Barksdale, 44th Bomb Group, 68th Sqdn. B-24 pilot.

His first combat was: Sub Patrol of the Gulf of Mexico. Was pilot of crew to sink the one sub, taken by the 44th Bomb Group, July 1942. He flew the northern route as Ops O&A flight lead, 68th Sqdn. with 44th Bomb Group moved to Shipdham, England, October 1942. Flew the *Spirit of '76* and moved to Operations with the 68th Sqdn., then Group, planning missions, flying as a substitute pilot, managing modifications to the plane, planning and flying missions and training until December 1943. Transferred to Wing Operational Engineering. Teamed with others to develop twin nose guns, pilots windows, ammo supplies, finally the low nose turret. He took a B-24 with a "chin" turret and all the other mods on it under Gen. Doolittle's orders. The low "chin" turret made a B-24 fly, fight and look better but it was too late to change the B-24 production.

Was assigned procurement manager, the B-36, Wright Field. The first of these six engined bombers was still in the factory when the "A" bomb ended the war. Believing that the war was over, he opted for Air Reserve and civil life. Bad guess.

In the Reserves and in his own business since. They miss the military. The best times and best people were there. Donna, Linda, Steve, Marc and five grandchildren.

Verbatim: "Today I believe we former military owe those who did not live to return with us, our best efforts to guide lives on earth. Our WWII fight for freedom is far from over. The world is in no less a problem. The freedom we lived for, they died for, is being destroyed by too many people, by little regard for earth's limitations, by crime, by religious idiocy, by poor or false education. World wide, most young grow without suitable role models, without the wonderful 'imprinting' most of us were given at home, in school, in church and in our military experience. Instead they have TV, street fighting, drugs, starvation, political turmoil, disregard for quality of life.

The problem is urgent. Your advice expressed loud and clear can make a difference. Your guidance of kids can help. We who lived thru WWII, we who have seen this amazing part of history have little time left to help fly this space ship, Earth. Give it your all!"

JOHN A. NORTAVAGE, was born on Nov. 23, 1915 in Windy Harbor, Schuylkill County, PA. Enlisted in the USAAF on Jan. 21, 1943 and assigned to the 2nd Air Division, 702nd Sqdn. and joined the 445th Bomb Group at Wendover, UT.

Participated in action at Northern France, Rhineland, Air Offensive Europe, Ardennes, Central Europe, Normandy. Remembers buzz bombs, bomber raids on London, flying overbase (Tibenham).

He received the Good Conduct Medal, EAME Service Medal and the Distinguished Unit Badge. Was discharged on Aug. 31, 1945 with the rank of corporal.

Nortavage is married and has one son, two daughters and four grandchildren. He is retired and has attended some of the 445th Bomb Group Re-unions.

ELWOOD W. NOTHSTEIN (BILL), was born on Oct. 29, 1925 in Ashley, PA. He was inducted into the Army in January 1944. After basic training at Miami Beach, FL, he entered Aerial Gunnery School at Harlingen, TX.

Trained as a crew member at Gowen Field, Boise, ID and following preparations for overseas, shipped out of Boston for Liverpool. Was assigned to the 466th Bomb Group in December 1944 and flew in combat from Jan. 31, 1945 to April 8, 1945.

He completed 27 missions and received the Air Medal with three clusters and an ETO Ribbon with three Battle Stars. Was discharged in November 1945 and re-enlisted in 1947.

Post war service included Alaska, Puerto Rico, Goose Bay, Labrador as well as eight stateside bases. The final nine years were with the 98th Bomb Wing at Lincoln, NE. He repaired and taught instrument, auto-pilot and bombing systems on B-36, B-50 and B-47 aircraft, retiring from active duty on Oct. 31, 1965.

From November 1965 to December 1985, he was employed as a service technician with the Eastman Kodak. He and Lucille Ebner were married on Dec. 3, 1950 and they have three children and four grandchildren.

EDWARD R. NOVAK, was born on Nov. 7, 1917 in Chicago, IL and joined the USAAC on April 9, 1942. He attended Radio School at Scott Field, IL; Radar in Boca Raton, FL; OCS in Miami Beach, FL and commissioned as second lieutenant on April 16, 1943, Intelligence, Harrisburg, PA; Security and Censorship, Ft. Belvoir, VA and Advanced Security School in UK.

Joined the 467th Bomb Group, 790th Sqdn., Asst. S-2, January 1944 at Wendover, England and served as base counter intelligence officer. He assisted in the planning, briefing and interrogation of bombing missions; squadron censor; custodian of and maintained updated battle zone maps in war room for the use of Col. Shower, staff and visiting dignitaries.

He was an accounting major at Loyola University in Chicago, IL. Worked 50 years in publishing from circulation clerk to president with stints as comptroller, advertising space salesman, general sales manager and publisher mostly with construction industry publications. Worked several years with Price, Waterhouse and retired in 1982 from McGraw-Hill. Now semi-retired doing some advertising sales and market consulting.

He and Janet Bednarz were married on Nov. 22, 1941 and have one son and three grandchildren.

ALEXANDER NOVICKOFF, was born on July 27, 1924 in Harwick, PA and enlisted in the USAAC on May 18, 1943. Took aerial gunnery at Fort Myers, FL; combat training at Casper, WY; airplane and engine mechanics at Lincoln, NE; propeller mechanic at Chanute Field, IL. He was sent to Hethel, East Anglia, England. He was assigned to the 566th Bomb Sqdn., 389th Bomb Group and flew 30 missions.

Targets were Saarbrucken, Laupheim, Metz, Munich, St. Lo, Bremen, Ludwigshafen, Paris, St. Malo and Hamburg. His memorable experience was fighting off the FW-190's over Halle, Germany.

He received the EAME Campaign Medal with three Bronze Stars, Distinguished Unit Badge, Distinguished Flying Cross, Air Medal with three Bronze Oak Leaf Clusters and the Good Conduct Medal. He was discharged on Oct. 28, 1945 at Patterson Field, OH with the rank of staff sergeant.

He and Vera Bahur were married on Aug. 9, 1953 and have one daughter. He retired from the coal mining industry as a Pennsylvania Mine Examiner.

MELVIN TOM NOVOTNY, was born on Sept. 4, 1920 in Gary, IN. He joined the USAAC on Sept. 3, 1942 and was stationed at Fort Harrison, IN; Camp Luna, NM; Houlton ATC; Keesler Field, Harlingen, TX; Topeka, KS; and Shipdham, England.

He received the Good Conduct Medal, ATO, ETO and WWII Victory Medals. Was discharged on Oct. 16, 1945 with the rank of private first class.

He and Doreen Bird were married in England in 1945. They have four children and four grandchildren. He is retired.

ALLEN NYE (JACK), was born in September 1919 in Ida Grove, IA and attended the University of Iowa. He joined the USAAC as an aviation cadet in Communications in November 1941.

After he was commissioned in March 1942, he attended four schools in advanced electronics. He joined HQ 2nd Air Division in England in June 1943 as a division radar officer, supervised introduction of new electronic bombing, naviga-

tion and electronic countermeasure systems into the B-24 Bomber units.

Following WWII, he married Kathleen Davis of Des Moines, IA; they have two children and two grandchildren. He completed an engineering degree at the University of Illinois.

Recalled in June 1949 for the Berlin Airlift, then served in Strategic Air Command as a wing electronics officer on new B-36 and B-50 Wings. He was transferred to the Air Research and Development Command and was involved for 12 years at Wright-Patterson and Eglin AFBs in development of bombing, navigation and reconnaissance systems for new aircraft.

When he retired as a lieutenant colonel in 1965, he was a deputy chief of project office supervising development of ST-71 reconnaissance aircraft.

He received the Legion of Merit Medal.

HENRY J. NYKAMP, was born on Nov. 15, 1923 in Hunterdon County, NJ on a farm. He reported for service on July 3, 1943 at Fort Dix, NJ. Basic training was at Greensboro; Armorer School at Lowry Field; gunnery training at Buckingham Air Field. His crew was assembled at Westover Field then went to Chatham Field for training as a crew.

Overseas flight from Mitchell Field, Long Island via northern route to Valle, Wales on July 3, 1944. He flew 35 missions on the George Bridgeman crew with the 409th Bomb Sqdn., 93rd Bomb Group from Aug. 1, 1944 to Jan. 6, 1945. He returned to the States and Gunnery Instructor School and was assigned to Tyndall Field until Oct. 13, 1945.

Was discharged with the rank of staff sergeant. He received the Air Medal with six Oak Leaf Clusters and was supposed to receive the Distinguished Flying Cross but never did.

Scariest mission was Nov. 21, 1944 to Hamburg, Germany. They had battle damage to fuel tanks and lost most of their fuel. Not enough fuel to get across the Channel, so landed at a fighter base in Liege, Belgium. Their crew has stayed in contact with each other over the years.

He is married and they have one son and two daughters. He worked in the retail meat business. He is active in Veterans Organizations and neighborhood affairs. He devotes his time to travel, grandchildren, golf and gardening.

HARLAN E.G. OAKES, was born Feb. 21, 1910, Massac County, IL. Joined CMTC Infantry, 1926, horse cavalry 1935, Illinois National Guard 1935-1937, USAAF second lieutenant 1942, USAFR California Air National Guard 1947.

Stationed at Miami Beach 1942; Sqdn. Adj. Basic Training Sqdn. 1942; AAFIS Harrisburg, PA 1943; 2nd AF Dyersburg, TN 1943; original cadre formation 466th Bomb Group, Clovis, NM 1943; overseas with 8th AF 1944-45. Sqdn. S-2 (two volunteer missions) RAF Int. School 1944-45; AAF Res. 1946-47 and 1951-1969; California Air NG 1947; 1951 Korean recall. Retired as lieutenant colonel, USAFR in 1969.

Memorable experience was low level mission, 500 feet, bomb run, Normandy June 10, 1944. Participated in action in Europe, Northern France, Normandy etc.

Attended Central Y Jr. College, 1929-30; Crane College, 1930; Northwestern University, 1935-36 journalism major. After 50 years in broadcasting and advertising, retired as broadcasting executive in 1979.

Married Mary Jane Shank of Indianapolis, IN in 1950. They have two children and two grandchildren. He is a member of TROA.

JAMES M. OBEREMBT, was born Oct. 13, 1921 in Parkston, SD. Joined the USAAC Sept. 8, 1942. Stationed at

San Antonio, Brady, TX; Liberal, KS AFB; Tonopah AB and others. Assigned to 491st Bomb Group, 2nd Air Div. Oberembt completed 18 missions. A memorable experience was second mission over Belgium-Germany border when 88 shell went through gas tank.

Discharged October 1945 with the rank second lieutenant. He received the Air Medal with two clusters.

Married and has three children. Graduated with a BS degree in 1948 from University of South Dakota. Employed with the Internal Revenue Service, he retired after 35 years.

ROBERT E. OBERSCHMID, was born in St. Paul, MN on May 22, 1921. Joined the Air Corps in July 1942, entered pilot training in February 1943 and graduated as a second pilot in December 1943. Flew a B-24 and crew to Hardwick, England (93rd Bomb Group) in August 1944. Completed 30 missions, 18 lead and 12 wing. Returned to the States and separated in September 1945.

Recalled to active duty in December 1948. Flew B-17s in Recon of the South Pacific, reassigned to Strategic Air Command as a B-29 and then a B-50 aircraft commander. Served in Korea and Japan during Korean War. Assigned to U.S. Embassy Germany in 1956 and the Pentagon, Washington, DC in 1959. Commander Air Force Munitions Test Center, UT in 1963-65 and staff officer to commander in Chief Pacific until retirement in 1967. Received two Distinguished Flying Crosses, six Air Medals, Commendation Medals from Joint Chief of Staff, USAF, USA - et al.

Married Jean Scannell in August 1947 and has three children and seven grandchildren.

JAMES E. O'BRIEN, was born May 25, 1919 in Donora, PA. Graduate of Monongahela, PA High School; State Teachers College, PA, 1941 with BS in education; School of Social Work, University of Pittsburgh, 1948, master, social work.

Enlisted June 2, 1941 Aviation Cadets, graduated February 1942 and commissioned second lieutenant. Assigned to 44th Bomb Group, Barksdale Field, LA. Completed 21 bombing missions over occupied Europe and Germany before being taken POW May 14, 1943, Kiel, Germany. Spent next 23 months moving around to various camps in Germany.

Returned to the States and assigned to San Antonio Personnel Depot, Kelly Field, from where he was separated in October 1945. Received the Distinguished Flying Cross, Air Medal with three Oak Leaf Clusters, EAME Ribbon with Unit Presidential Citation, WWII Victory Ribbon, Air Force Longevity Service Award, American Theater Ribbon, Air Force Reserve Ribbon and POW Ribbon. Retired from the USAFR in 1973 with the rank of colonel.

Married since June 12, 1946 to Elsie B. Schultz. They had twin daughters, Judith and Joyce (Joyce passed away in 1987.) Employed as teacher, branch director and summer camp director of the Brashear Association in South Side, Pittsburg. He has been an active member and officer in the Eastern Ohio Chapter of the National Association of Social Workers and is also active in many civic and social committees dealing with community health and welfare.

EUGENE O'DONNELL, was born May 10, 1923 in Buhl, MN. Joined the Air Corps in November 1942 and received his wing at Pecos, TX in March 1944. Assembled with crew and trained as co-pilot at Pueblo, CO. Lost his best buddy (who would have been his future brother-in-law) in a training crash there.

Flew a B-24 to England, more training in Ireland, then assigned to the 458th Bomb Group at Norwich, England. Flew with four different crews. Had several memorable missions. Hit a high speed stall and fell several thousand feet over Berlin. Once, couldn't gain altitude on take-off, jettisoned over bombs in a field in England. On another mission,

the plane flying right wing, received a direct flak burst and went down over Germany.

His bombing missions were interrupted for a month to fly diesel fuel to France. Landed at his brother's P-38 base only to find his brother had been shot down the previous day. Completed 35 missions then remained in the Air Force after the war. Flew with ATC out of Paris, France and Reinmain, Germany, clearing out bases in Casablanca, Tripoli, Cairo, and Daharan, Arabia. Left the Air Force Reserves in 1950 with the rank of captain.

Married and has three children, eight grandchildren and one great-grandchild. Developed land and built thousands of homes in Houston, TX before retiring.

RAY O'DONNELL, was born March 11, 1923 in Ormsby, PA. Joined the USAAC in Nov. 11, 1942. After graduating Gunnery School in Harlingen, TX was sent to Denver, CO for armament training then to Blythe, CA for B-24 training. His crew joined the 389th Bomb Group in December of 1943.

Gotha, Germany was his most unforgettable mission. He was a tail gunner on Joe Mestemaker's crew. The target was a ME-109 plant and several groups participated in the raid. His group had a maximum effort contingent of 31 bombers. They scored direct hits on the target and were under continuous attacks for two and a half hours. His crew returned with only 15 bombers and the group took a toll of 38 German fighters.

Was discharged June 11, 1945 with the rank staff sergeant. His awards for 30 missions were Distinguished Flying Cross, Air Medal with five clusters, two Bronze Battle Stars and a Presidential Unit Citation.

O'Donnell has three children, he is presently retired and lives in Sharon, PA.

DONALD R. O'FEE, was born Nov. 1, 1925 in Jersey City, NJ. While in his senior year in high school, he enlisted in Aviation Cadet Program. Entered the USAAC Oct. 13, 1943. Trained as Aerial Gunner, Tyndall Field, FL; B-24 crew training, Boise, ID.

Arrived in England in January 1945, was assigned to 445th Bomb Group and flew as nose gunner. Was shot down Feb. 27, 1945 on mission over Halle, Germany while bombing railroad marshalling yards. Liberated April 17, 1945 after escaping mortar barrage on POW encampment. Observed first ME262 enemy jet fighter take off on capture.

Discharged with rank of sergeant. Awarded Air Medal and Purple Heart.

Married Sept. 11, 1948 to Jean Wiley and has four children and five children and five grandchildren. Semi-retired after varied business careers.

FLOYD C. OGLESBY, was born Dec. 28, 1923 in Luverne, IA. Spent most of his growing up years in Mason City, IA. Joined the USAAC on March 5, 1943. Training: Miami Beach, FL; Sheppard Field, TX; Tyndall Field, FL; and Casper, WY.

Tail gunner on Robert Ottman's B-24 crew. Flew the southern route to England and landed in Wales on April 30, 1944. He joined the 445th Bomb Group, 703rd Sqdn. at Tibenham Airbase.

His crew flew two missions on D-day. Never saw so many bombers and fighters in the air as on that eventful day. Near miss on a mid-air collision.

Had many anxious moments during his 30 mission tour but, during his life he has been one of those individuals who was lucky enough to be in the right place at the right time, so he was able to get home to the USA physically unscathed. Navigator, John Hennessy, stayed on as a training navigator for new crews and was killed in a flying accident. The crew had great love, respect, and admiration for John.

Discharged Oct. 10, 1945. Returned to Mason City and married his childhood sweetheart, Gwen, Dec. 10, 1945. He has four daughters and 13 grandchildren. He received his BA from the University of Northern Iowa 1950 and his MA from Western Michigan University. Runner-up 1950 NCAA Wrestling Tournament.

Taught school and coached wrestling and football in Iowa and Battle Creek, MI. Employed at Kellogg Community College as dean of students and counselor. Elected to Battle Creek City Commission for 12 years and served as mayor for three years.

JOHN EDMUND O'GRADY, was born May 19, 1919 in Frankfort, NY. Enlisted Dec. 10, 1940. Embarked from Fort Slocum, April 1941 to Oahu, TH. Reported to Co. A, 3rd Engineers at Schofield Barracks. Pitched for Beavers which which prompted a delay to sign up for a cadre to the Philippines. Applied for Air Corps staff sergeant pilot training, delayed by the Japanese attack on Oahu, Dec. 7, 1941. Received orders to report to West Coast for pilot training, Class 43-A, at Santa Ana, Hemet, Bakersfield and Roswell. Appointed Flight Officer 212 and assigned to B-24 training at David Monthan and Biggs Field. Pilot of Crew #15. Departed for England, July 1943 on unescorted *Queen Elizabeth.*

Crew #15 rushed to Libya, via ATC, to join 389th Bomb Group but upon arrival at Benghazi was placed on Detached Service with 345th Sqdn., 98th Bomb Group. On Aug. 1, 1943, he flew first mission as copilot for the 98th with pilot, Lt. Blevins in *Snake Eyes.* Harold B. Moore, bombardier and six enlisted men of Crew #15 plus a 389th navigator made up balance of the B-24 D's roster. Colonel "Killer" Kane led the mission in *Hail Columbia.* Crippled by flak at the target, *Snake Eyes* ran the gauntlet of fighters and aerial bombs on the return trip. Lack of fuel forced *Snake Eyes* and three other 24s to land in Syracuse, Sicily at an RAF fighter strip. Lt. Blevens was signalled to land first due to extensive damage. Flaps out and the left tire gone flat caused *Snake Eyes* to pile up on a stone wall, ending 13 hour 24 minute mission. All participants were awarded the Distinguished Flying Cross with higher honors to many. Joined the 389th for one mission and returned to England. Reported to the 93rd Bomb Group, 409th Sqdn. Finished 28th mission in April 1944.

Assigned to 448th Bomb Group as first lieutenant. Served as training officer under Col. "Gerry" Mason and flew one additional mission (29th) to France after D-day. Returned to States to instruct at Liberal, KS. Opted out on points July 1945.

Married Jean in 1951 and worked as industrial photographer. Earned BA in education, Syracuse University, MA, State University, Albany, NY. Coordinator social studies at South Colonie School System. Retired in 1980. "Ham" N2DGE. QTH Schenectady, NY. Visited Ploesti, Romania, August 1, 1993 and stood at the site of the final IP, Floresti, 50 years later. Pilgrimage accomplished!

THOMAS J. O'HALLORAN, was born in Buffalo, NY, but grew up in the Boston, MA area. He graduated from high school having previously enlisted, underage, in the 26th Inf. of the Massachusetts Guard. While still underage he entered

the Army Air Force. He flew his 30 mission tour with 703rd Bomb Sqdn., 445th Bomb Group.

His most memorable mission being Kassel, Germany. Following his combat tour, he served as an instructor at a B-29 OCTU. He received a direct commission as a second lieutenant. Following the war he continued in the inactive reserve until 1957.

Decorations include the Distinguished flying Cross, four Air Medals, ETO with six Bronze Stars, Distinguished Unit Citation, Croix de Guerre avec Palme.

Graduated from Holy Cross College and spent 32 years with the Ford Motor Company, achieving the rank of executive. He married Barbara C. Mahoney in June of 1950, they have five children and 14 grandchildren.

SEYMOUR OHLSTEIN, was born Jan. 28, 1924 and enlisted November 1942. He struggled to get into the Air Corps because of his flat feet and was afraid of being classified limited duty (he wanted combat). Went to Radio School, then Gunnery School.

Shipped to Boise, ID where he and Stepnich formed the basis of a crew. Joined the 44th Bomb Group in Shipdham on Nov. 3, 1943. On the fourth mission, when the ship was severely damaged and the armorers refused to go into the bomb bay, he opened the bomb bay doors manually, took off his chute and managed by experimentation to drop the arming, hung-up, anti-personnel bombs. He lost his oxygen bottle and he somehow crawled back to the radio room. As a result of those actions they survived that raid. The pilot and copilot recommended him for the Silver Star, no follow up. He volunteered for five extra missions and was promised a second Distinguished Flying Cross and fourth Air Medal, but nothing came of it. Taught Gunnery School at Tyndall Field for 11 months and was discharged October 1945.

Married Ruth Kulman May 31, 1947. Now has two daughters and five grandchildren. Retired from the diamond business January 1989.

ODO OLIVA, was was born April 27, 1923 in Newport, RI, but has lived in Lockport, NY for 67 years. Joined the USAAC in January 1943, went to pre-Meteorology School at Haverford College for six months, but ended up as a flight engineer on a B-24 with E. Miller's crew.

Went to England on the *Queen Mary* January 1945 and completed 16 missions over Germany with the 453rd Bomb Group in Attleboro, the 466th Bomb Group at Attlebridge. Returned to the States with *Damifino* in June 1945.

Flying has always been in his life having completed about 2100 missions between Buffalo and Detroit in his 41 years with General Motors until retirement in June 1982. Vacation flying has taken him and wife to Europe six times, Hawaii four times, and trips to Alaska, China/Hong Kong, Australia/New Zealand, Barbados, Russia/Finland, Canadian Rockies, plus many parts of the States. Seven of the Miller crew meet yearly at various locations in the States.

FRANK J. OLIVE (JIM), was born June 13, 1917 in E. Alton, IL. Enlisted in USAAC June 1943. After completing basic training and college detachment training was classified as aviation cadet for navigation training. Graduated,

August 1944 as 2nd lieutenant, Class of 44-11 Pan American Contract School, Coral Gables, FL.

Combat training was completed at Casper, WY with the Richard Mardis crew. This crew then suffered a take-off crack up that caused a delay before Olive was reassigned to the Robert Meyers crew and to the 445th Bomb Group, 700th Sqdn. at Tibenham, England.

With the defeat of Germany, he returned to the States and was on orders to report for B-29 duty when the Japanese war ended. Received two European Campaign Stars and the Air Medal. Separated from service Nov. 10, 1945 at Randolph Field, TX.

Married high school sweetheart, Sara B. Seabaugh, February 1940. Has a son, two daughters and nine grandchildren

WILLIAM D. OLMSTED, was born May 15, 1920 in Virgil, NY. Basic training October 1942 at Atlantic City. To Lincoln, NE for Aircraft Mechanic School; Detroit for engine specialist; then to Salt Lake City for assignment. Signed up for Gunnery School in Wendover; assigned to 489th B-24 Group as first engineer, Boise, ID; one phase then to Wendover for three phases.

Left for England by southern route in New B-24 named *Cover Girl.* After 15 missions, crew transferred to 93rd for G H lead crew training. Finished 30 missions in November 1944. Back to States in January 1945. Signed for Pacific tour (B-24s) to Tyndall Field, FL for gunnery refresher course.

Germany surrendered in May 1945. Olmstead finally got out in October 1945. Signed up for three years inactive duty. Never did regret this experience, career ended with tech sergeant rating.

Married Marie Schmidt of Buffalo.

ARTHUR W. OLSON, was born June 24, 1921, Lemont, IL. Graduated high school; joined the service Dec. 26, 1942 and and went to three months of Army Adm. School. Stationed at Biggs Field AFB, El Paso, TX; Alamogordo AFB, NM, 8th AF Station 114, Wendling England, U.K.

Memorable experiences: encountering hurricane at Homestead AFB of ATC in September 1945; serving with 392nd Bomb Group(H) in England when D-day operations ran; Gotha, Germany air raid on Feb. 24, 1944; and serving with a great bunch of Air Force guys and officers.

Discharged Oct. 9, 1945 with the rank of sergeant. Received the Good Conduct, ETO Ribbon, Unit Presidential Citation and ETO Arm Hashes.

Married Dorothy (deceased July 1964), remarried June 1970 to Lee. He has five children and nine grandchildren. Employed as RR frt. claims head clerical investigator until retiring on Sept. 1, 1985.

RICHARD C. OLSON, was born May 9, 1922 in Perrysburg, NY.

Graduated Gowanda High School in 1939. Entered service Dec. 7, 1942 at Fort Dix, NJ, transferring to aviation cadets in February 1943, Class of 43-K at SAACC. After Primary Flight School, Parks Air School, Sikeston, MO; Basic Flight School, Coffeville, KS. Transferred to Armorer School, Lowry Field, CO for convenience of government; Gunnery

School at Laredo, TX and combat crew training at Casper, WY with the crew of Joe Bell.

Completed the training and was assigned to 8th AF at Rackheath, England in 467th Bomb Group(H), 789th Bomb Sqdn.(H). Participated in Air Offensive Europe, Northern France, Rhineland, Ardennes-Alsace and Central Europe campaigns. Flew 42 missions over France and Germany from July 5, 1944 through March 17, 1945 on B-24s as tail gunner.

Promoted through combat to staff sergeant, he returned to States in April 1945 for discharge at Atlantic City, NJ in June 1945. Received Air Medal with four Oak Leafs.

Married Marcella Trampert Oct. 24, 1942. They have four boys, the first born on Jan. 5, 1945, his 25th mission. They were divorced in 1970. Married Sara Toland and lives in Depew, NY. He retired from New York State Tax Dept. as auditor on Jan. 2, 1986. He has 16 grandchildren and four great-grandchildren.

PERRY O. ONSTOT, was born Jan. 11, 1922, Maryville, MO. Raised on a farm at Lamar, MO. Enlisted in USAAF, Aug. 8, 1942 and served on inactive duty until Feb. 2, 1943 when he entered Cadet Class of 43-K at San Antonio, TX. Completed primary flight training at Stamford, TX, proceeded to basic flight training at Garden City, KS, washed out then transferred to Air Force Technical Armament School at Lowry Field, CO. Upon completion, proceeded to Army Air Force Aerial Gunnery School at Tyndall Field, FL, and then proceeded to Westover Field, MA for assignment to a flying crew of a B-24.

Trained with flying crew of B-24 at Chatham Field, GA. Upon completion proceeded with crew to Mitchell Field, NY to pick up new B-24 to ferry to England. Upon arrival in England, the crew was assigned to 2nd Air Division of the 8th Air Force, 392nd Bomb Group, 578th Sqdn. Flew 35 combat missions as waist gunner/armorer over German occupied Europe. Attended American Power Turret School on bombsighting and harmonization at Blackpool. England. Completed 35 combat missions on April 9, 1945.

Departed England on May 19, 1945 to return to the U.S. Received honorable discharge as staff sergeant on July 15, 1945 at Jefferson Barracks, MO. Awarded Air Medal with five Oak Leaf Clusters, Good Conduct Medal, four Bronze stars with five Oak Leaf Clusters for Northern France, Central Europe, Rhineland and Ardennes campaigns.

Attended University of Missouri 1945-1948, received BS in agriculture. Taught vocational agriculture at Carl Junction High School, Carl Junction, MO 1948-1952. Served as Agronomist/Sales promotion manager with W.R. Grace & Co., 1952-62; fertilizer specialist with ESSO Chemical Co., NY, 1962-65; vice president, marketing with ESSO Chemical, Philippines 1965-71; private consultant, Fertilizer Marketing, 1971-1992 in Indonesia, Sri Lanka, Thailand, Burma, India, Nigeria, Turkey, Malaysia, and the People's Republic of China (based in Hong Kong).

Retired in 1992 now lives in Kansas City, MO. Has three children and four grandchildren.

WARREN E. OPPMANN, was born June 8, 1921 in Croydon, PA. Enlisted in the USAAC Jan. 5, 1942. After extensive weapons training, he volunteered for Aerial Gunnery School, Las Vegas, NV. Graduated a sergeant and assigned to 11th Anti-Sub Squadron flying B-25s along the Atlantic Coast, Maine to Virginia as observer and armorer gunner. This military duty was interrupted when their squadron was transferred to Wendover, UT for B-24 training. Upon completion was assigned to Tampa, FL then overseas to Halesworth, England.

The first mission they flew in combat was Bretiney Airfields near Paris as squadron lead, their B-24 encountered

105 flak holes on that mission. On second mission, June 6, 1944 D-day, crew witnessed the greatest armada of planes and ships ever assembled. Flak was very intense.

Completed tour of duty flying 26 missions with Maj. Jack D. Pritchard's crew in the 489th, 2nd Bomb Div., 8th Air Force, but due to bureaucratic mishap, he didn't receive his Distinguished Flying Cross until 45 years later with the tremendous assistance of Lt. Col. Ret. Charles H. Freudenthal and Col. Chester H. Morneau, Ret., both 2nd Air Division members.

At long last the military chain of command admitted the error and corrected the official records. Oppmann received the full military recognition to which he was due when the DFC was presented as part of a ceremony conducted at the 438th Military Airlift Wing's Review Day and parade on June 2, 1989 at McGuire AFB, Wrightstown, NJ. Major Pritchards crew of 13 men flew division lead on four of the 26 bombing missions as well as numerous other lead positions.

ANDREW OPSATA, entered the USAAC June 1941, Fort Lewis. Sent to Moffett Field as private and started pilot training when war broke out. Went to Santa Ana, Phoenix, Bakersfield and Victorville, where he graduated in Class 42-K. Sent to Tucson to fly B-24s. Became first pilot and first lieutenant. Six weeks there, Clovis and Alamogordo.

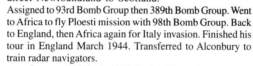

Left for England in B-17s due to B-24 shortage. First group to fly direct Newfoundland to Scotland. Assigned to 93rd Bomb Group then 389th Bomb Group. Went to Africa to fly Ploesti mission with 98th Bomb Group. Back to England, then Africa again for Italy invasion. Finished his tour in England March 1944. Transferred to Alconbury to train radar navigators.

Returned to USA in 1945. Back to Victorville then Long Beach Ferry Group. Flew MATS from Stockton, on to Topeka to ferry group and traffic officer. Discharged as major in 1947.

Best part of his life and would be glad to do it all over again.

WILLIAM L. ORIENT, was born April 29, 1921 in the Pittsburgh, PA area. Enlisted as an aviation cadet, after classification at Nashville. Pre-flight at Santa Ana; primary at Santa Maria, "the washout." Back through Radio School at Sioux Falls, SD; Gunnery at Yuma, AZ; operational training at Davis Monthan, Tucson, AZ to 93rd Bomb Group in England.

After going through three pilots and "walking home" four times, the crew was broken up at 28 missions. He finished the next six as extra and replacements. Flew home with 93rd Bomb Group and after R&R leave, back to Sioux Falls with the 8th Air Force. On V-J day he was sent to Pyote, TX for B-29 training. Thanks to the bomb, Orient didn't have to go to the Orient. Sent to Fort Bliss for discharge, rode the bus to Tucson that night and married the girl he met while stationed there. They have four daughters and seven grandchildren. A general contractor for about 40 years, he still likes Tucson and the Old Air Corps.

SANTOS ORTEGA JR., was born Dec. 12, 1918, Holbrook, AZ. Was radio operator mechanic/gunner, 458th Bombardment Group (H). Stationed at Fort MacArthur, CA; Wichita Falls, TX; Laredo, TX; Sioux Falls, SD; Presidio of Monterey, CA; Lincoln, NE; Casper, WY; Kilmer, NY; Horsham St. Faith, England; Smyrna, TN and Davis Monthan Field, AZ. Participated in Ardennes, Rhineland and Central Europe campaigns. Completed 31 missions.

Memorable experience was returning home to the good ole USA and landing at Bradley Field, CT. Discharged Oct. 5, 1945 with the rank tech sergeant. Received the EAME Ribbon, Air Medal with four Oak Leaf Clusters and the Good Conduct Medal.

Married to Maxine Ruiz since June 22, 1942. They have three children: Terry, Andrea and Cathy. Worked 40 years for North American Aviation/Rockwell International as technician instructor, tech. repairman, engineer and aerospace executive. Retired in 1988. Presently resides in Downey, CA, Desert Springs, CA or Holbrook, AZ.

HARRY L. ORTHMAN, was born July 5, 1922 in Richmond, CA. Joined the USAAC in November 1941 as a private. Graduated from Flying School in December, 1942 at Moody Field, GA, Class 42-K. After approximately one year of flying Anti-Sub patrols out of Langley Field, CA, became a charter member of the 492nd Bomb Group.

Went to England with the 492nd as a lead crew pilot in May 1944. Flew 13 missions as a lead crew pilot. Promoted to captain. Transferred to the 44th Bomb Group when the 492nd was deactivated in August 1944. Flew 17 missions as lead crew pilot with 44th completing his tour in January 1945.

Reserve status 1946 to 1950 attending University of California, Berkeley. Recalled August 1950. Flew five years with 97th Bomb Wing (SAC) as select crew aircraft commander. Three years overseas on planning staffs of HQ, 3AF, England, and HQ, USAFE, Germany. Five years, Director of Operations, HQ, USAF, Pentagon. Five years, Secretary of the Air Force Special Projects Office, Los Angeles AFS. Five years as deputy systems program director, F-15 program office, Wright-Patterson AFB. Retired as colonel in April 1974.

1974-1985, management consultant to various aerospace companies.

EMIL S. OSOJNICKI, was born April 29, 1923 in Keewatin, MN. Graduated high school in 1941, attended Hibbing Jr. College 1941-42. Enlisted in USAAF January 1943. Pre-flight at SAACC, San Antonio, TX; primary and basic training, followed by advance at Pecos, TX with Class 44-C. Assigned to Kirtland Field, Albuquerque, NM, B-24s. Arrived ETO September 1944, assigned to 392nd Bomb Group. Completed 35 missions in 1945.

Back to USA and assigned to Enid, OK. Left the service October 1945. Attended University of Minnesota with help of GI Bill and graduated in 1949 with BSEE.

Married Marion Comstock in 1948. They have two sons and two daughters. Emil passed away February 1971 at age 47. Internment at Fort Snelling National Cemetery, St. Paul, MN. Son Mark was chopper pilot for Vietnam 1970-1971. *Submitted by brother Tony Osojnicki.*

TONY D. OSOJNICKI, was born Dec. 6, 1916 in Biwabik, MN. Grew up in Keewatin, MN. Engaged to Violet Vukmir in 1941. Enlisted in AAF July 1942. Called to active duty January 1943. Pre-flight at SAACC, San Antonio; primary at Cuero, TX; basic at Waco, TX; advance, Blackland, Waco, TX; graduated Class 43-K Dec. 5, 1943.

Sent to Biggs Field, El Paso, TX for B-24 phase training. Transferred to Alamagordo, NM as part of new bomb group, 492nd. April 1944 flew southern route to ETO. Arrived at North Pickenham, England in May 1944. In August 1944 their 859ths Sqdn. transferred to 467th Bomb Group, 788th Sqdn. at Rackheath where he completed remainder of 35 missions. Left Scotland for USA on Queen Mary. After

30 day leave assigned to Forth Worth, TX as air craft maintenance officer on B-32s. Left the service December 1945.

Married to Violet in Cuero, TX on June 12, 1943. Has two daughters, Jean and Bette.

THOMAS O. OWEN (TOMMY), was born Feb. 17, 1924 in Roseboro, NC and attended high school in Pineville, KY. Joined the service June 10, 1942 with active duty on Nov. 3, , 1942. Served with 732nd Sqdn., 453rd Bomb Group, 2nd Air Div., 8th AAF. Graduated as navigator, San Marcos, TX, combat crew training at Casper, WY.

Memorable experience was when group after turning at rally point had a head on with aircraft of 492nd Bomb Group, both aircraft lost. Completed tour of 30 missions (last 14 as a lead crew) at Dessau, Germany on Aug. 16, 1944. Finished active duty as radar bomber/navigator instructor at Boca Raton, FL and Williams Field, AZ.

Discharged Sept. 5, 1945 as first lieutenant and from the Reserves on Feb. 17, 1984 with the rank of lieutenant colonel. Received the Distinguished Flying Cross, Air Medal with three Oak Leaf Clusters, American Theater and ETO.

Graduated from Vanderbilt University in 1948 with a degree in history and economics and a MA from the University of Kentucky. Began a coaching career at Amory, MS in 1948; at Montgomery Bell Academy, Nashville, TN in 1953; joined the Vanderbilt staff in January 1971 with assignment of varsity receiver coach.

Married to Nell Stephens of Charlotte, NC, they have a daughter Lee and a son Steve.

ROGER G. OWENS, was born Nov. 11, 1922 in Livingston, KY. Enlisted Jan. 20, 1943 in the USAAF, 2nd Air Div., 556th Air Sqdn., 389th Bomb Group. Completed 24 combat missions in the ETO.

Discharged Sept. 15, 1945 with the rank staff sergeant.

Owens is married and has one son and one daughter. He is a realtor in Clearwater, FL.

WILLIAM R. OWNBEY, was born July 20, 1916 in Asheville, NC. Joined the USAAC May 8, 1942, stationed at Ft. Jackson, SC. Participated in Ardennes, Central Europe, Air Offensive Europe, Normandy, Norther France, North Apennines and Rhineland campaigns.

Volunteered to go to the continent. The mission was to take the bomb beam to the front. The U.S. had been bombing their own men since they only had smoke signals. When commanding officer was taken to hospital, Ownbey was next highest officer. His orders not to be taken captive with this equipment. If he had to, well, blow it all up. He ended up in the Battle of the Bulge.

Discharged Sept. 10, 1945 with the rank staff sergeant. Received the Campaign Medal with seven Bronze Stars, Good Conduct Medal and Bronze Star Medal.

Married to Ruth Wood and had one son, three grandchildren and three great-grandchildren. He passed away March 15, 1993.

WINFORD PACE, was born May 23, 1918 at Salem, MO. Enlisted in the USAAC on July 8, 1942 for pilot training but was eliminated in primary flight training in Florida. Then assigned to Radio School at Scott Field, IL during which time he was married on Nov. 1, 1943. Then on to Gunnery School at Harlingen, TX.

From there he was sent to B-24 overseas training at Peterson Field, CO as right waist gunner. In July 1944 was assigned to the 453rd Bomb Group, 734th Sqdn. at old Buckingham Field, England. His most memorable experience of his 35 rough missions was Mission #23, Oct. 17, 1944, while bombing the Marshalling Yards at Cologne, Germany. Flak was very heavy and one shell came through

the bomb bay and exploded above the plane sending it into a dive. His pilots brought it under control making it to Belgium where the crew bailed out. Pace was wounded, landed in a river and pulled out by the Belgium people. They took him to a convent where the doctor attended his wound.

Finished his missions on Feb. 22, 1945 then shipped back to the States. After a furlough he reported to Miami Beach for reassignment. He received an early discharge due to the point system on June 3, 1945 at Jefferson Barracks, MO with the rank of staff sergeant.

He has two boys, two girls and eight grandsons. He retired from the building trade in 1980 and enjoys farm life and travelling.

KENNETH Q. PADDOCK, son of George W. and Ilka Lee Wilson Paddock was born Dec. 5, 1915 in Vigo County, IN. He grew up in Clark County, IL and graduated from the University of Illinois in 1938 with a BS degree in Agriculture and a reserve commission in the Coast Artillery Corps. Paddock taught vocational agriculture in Fountain County, IN prior to becoming a flying cadet in 1941 at Parks Air College and Randolph Field. He served as tactical officer at Maxwell Field before attending Navigation School as a second lieutenant.

Paddock was assigned to the 34th Bomb Group (B-17s), became group navigator and was promoted to captain. He then transferred with group staff to the 392nd Bomb Group in February 1943. He was promoted to major in August 1944 and served as group navigator until the group was deactivated in September 1945.

Received the Distinguished Flying Cross by Brig. Gen. Leon Johnson, commander of the 14th Combat Wing for aerial leadership; Purple Heart on Nov. 5, 1943 after mission on Munster; Air Medal with three Oak Leaf Clusters; and two French Croix de Guerres.

After the war Paddock served with the Air Transport Command and was crew supervisor for the Globester crews in Cairo, Egypt. He received his regular Air Force Commission in 1947 and taught Air Force ROTC at Purdue University for three years. In 1951 he earned bombardier and radar operator ratings at Mather Field and was assigned to the 22nd Bomb Wing at March AFB, flying B-29s and then B-47s. In 1954 he was promoted to lieutenant colonel and became director of Wing Intelligence. In 1955 Paddock was transferred to Rabat, Morocco, and then Wheelus AFB, Libya where he was commander of HQ Sqdn., 17th Air Force. He transferred to Dow AFB, ME in 1959 and was director of Combat Operations for the B-52 Wing.

He married Bridget M. White of London, England in December 1946 and has four daughters and eight grandchildren. After military retirement in January 1961, Paddock taught math and science in New Hampshire for 15 years. In 1976 he moved to Anchorage, AK where he became ground superintendent at the University of Alaska.

Paddock retired in November 1982 to the coast of Maine where he enjoys sailing, kayaking and gardening. Incidentally, when Paddock was navigation training officer for the North Atlantic Division, Air Transport Command, Major Leo George Clarke, the division navigator, was working to get advance ratings for navigators the same as Air Force pilots. The Pentagon approved senior navigator rating but disapproved request for command navigator rating. However, they stated they might look with favor on some more suitable title. When Major Clarke discussed his problem with Paddock, Paddock suggested master navigator, which was accepted by the Pentagon.

JAMES L. PALLOURAS SR., was born in New York City on Nov. 26, 1921. He left Manhattan College, School of Engineering to enlist as an aviation cadet for pilot training in

the USAAC the day after Pearl Harbor was attacked. On Aug. 5, 1942 he was commissioned a second lieutenant.

In December of 1943 he landed with the air echelon of the 445th Bombardment Group. As group engineering officer he was responsible for the maintenance and supply of 75th Combat ready B-24 aircraft. His additional duty was Station S-4. Towards the end of 1944 Major Pallouras was transferred to the 2nd Air Div. as assistant A-4.

He rotated to the States as A-4 in the latter part of June 1945 on the *Queen Mary*. The European war had ended a month previously. Personnel had earmarked him for assignment to the 20th Air Force, stationed on Guam after a 30 day leave in the States. However, the Japanese in early August 1945 surrendered and Lt. Col. Pallouras separated from the service shortly thereafter to work for New York State.

In February 1951, Col. Pallouras was recalled to active duty with the New York Air National Guard as A-4 of the 106th Bombardment Wing (SAC). In June 1952 he was integrated into the regular Air Force as an officer. His other overseas tours included a seven month temporary duty tour as A-4 of the 96th Bomb Wing which bombed North Korea from B-29s and a three year assignment with the American Embassy in Paris, France as executive officer to an Army major general.

After 21 years attending six different colleges, Col. Pallouras received his BS degree, cum laude, in June 1960. In 1965, having completed 20 years of active service, Col. Pallouras retired. During this period he was presented with numerous awards and decorations, both U.S. and foreign. He returned to work for the port authority of New York and New Jersey, a bi-state agency and again retired in 1975. Col. Pallouras presently resides in Melbourne, FL.

VINCENT ALLEN PALMER JR., was born Rochester, NY on Oct. 6, 1925. Entered the service Dec. 7, 1943 at Camp Upton, NY and qualified for cadet training January 1944. Released by general order April 3, 1944.

Gunnery training at Laredo, TX and assignment for combat training at Davis Monthan in Tucson. Assigned William J. Grey crew. Arrived Great Britain after seven day trip on *Ile de France* January 1945. Completed 21 combat missions from Attlebridge with last B-24 named *Rabbit Habit*. Nose gunner-togalier 466th Bomb Group, 786th Bomb Sqdn. Discharged on Nov. 30, 1945 from Biggs Field, El Paso as staff sergeant.

Married, semi-retired. Has wife Eleanor and sons, Craig and Scott. Resides in Pultneyville, NY, south shore Lake Ontario. Outside interests: member of National Ski Patrol, Republican County Chairman; sailing-represented USA 1955 International Gold Cup, Holland, Dragon Class and various boards and community activities.

DONALD I. PARCELLS, was born in Minnesota and New Milford, CT was his hometown. Enlisted as USAAC cadet Feb. 20, 1943. Commissioned pilot Stuttgart AAF, AR on June 25, 1944. Arrived England Sept. 15, 1944 after crossing on SS *Mauritania*. Assigned as co-pilot to lead crew 735th Bomb Sqdn., 453rd Bomb Group, Old Buckingham.

A memorable mission led a deep penetration into Germany. After dropping bombs, they headed for home. Thrilled to a magnificent sight—hundreds of B-24s and B-17s streaming contrails, and following them, hundreds of RAF Lancasters and Halifaxes filled the sky delivering more Christmas presents to Hitler. Inspecting their plane, found numerous flak holes. A thumb sized piece stopped in the instrument panel inches from his chest.

Completed 25 missions. In May 1945 was assigned to B-29 School, Pratt, KS. Discharged October 1945 with the rank first lieutenant. Received the ETO Ribbon, Air Medal with four Oak Leaf Clusters and the Presidential Unit Citation.

Graduated from college and married his sweetheart. They have three wonderful children. After 32 years in the insurance industry, he retired. Continues to travel, returned to England and Germany many times. He is a member of 8th Air Force Historical Society and the 2nd Air Division Association.

JACK PARKER, was born Dec. 11, 1922 in Shidler, OK. Joined the USAF July 15, 1941. Stationed at Seething Air Base, England; Rhein, Main, Germany; Osan AFB, Korea; Travis AFB, CA; HQ, MAC-V, Saigon, Vietnam; Ft. Mason, San Francisco, CA.

Assigned as pilot to crew #2, 712th Sqdn., 448th Bomb Group, July 1943 at Wendover, UT. Completed 30 missions in May 1944 without any Purple Hearts on crew. As pilot on stripped down B-29, he set time and distance record in August 1945. Gen. LeMay broke it two weeks later. Assigned as chief, Movements Div., HQ, MAC-V, Saigon, 1967-68.

Discharged Dec. 1, 1972 with the rank colonel. Received the Legion of Merit, Distinguished Flying Cross, Commendation Medal, Air Medal, Medal of Merit and Bronze Star.

Married Helen Fox in 1945; they have two sons and two grandchildren. Employed as manufacturers rep. of medical equipment.

JAMES C. PARKER, was born Nov. 23, 1919 in Philadelphia, PA and enlisted in the USAAC on Jan. 12, 1942 at the Custom House in Philadelphia. After receiving his initial training in the U.S., he flew to England on a B-24 Liberator. He was assigned as an engineer gunner on the B-24 Liberator and stationed with the 702nd Sqdn., 445th Bomb Group in Tibenham, England.

He flew 14 successful combat missions from England. On the 15th mission to Fredrickshafen they lost two engines and electric power and made an emergency landing in Switzerland. The crew was interned in Switzerland. On October 15 Jimmy Parker and Ed Winkle made an escape from Switzerland with the help of the FFI and the OSS. It took five days for them to work their way back to France and then to England. Jimmy Parker finished his tour of duty as staff sergeant and was discharged on Oct. 8, 1945 from Westover Field in Massachusetts. He was awarded the Air Medal, European Campaign Medal, Presidential Unit Citation, Good Conduct Medal and the American Campaign Medal.

After leaving the service he received a BS degree from Temple University in accounting. Married Isabel Duncan on Dec. 5, 1947 and has one son. Retired from the automobile business in 1984. Currently, a widower living with his son, daughter-in-law and two grandchildren in Douglasville, GA. He is enjoying all the pleasures of retirement.

THEODORE PARKER (TED), was born East Boston, MA on Aug. 30, 1925. Enlisted in the USAAC in July 1943. Became a B-24 waist gunner and in June 1944 flew a brand new B-24 to England and joined the 491st Bomb Group.

Most memorable mission was to Cologne where they got shot up pretty bad and Parker took a piece of flak through his neck. They crash landed in Belgium and were MIA for several weeks. Took part in the low level mission to Holland in September 1944. From the waist he tossed out bundles of food and ammo through the hatch. Fired at Germans on the ground with waist gun. Counted 300 bullet holes in plane on return to base at North Pickenham.

Received a medical discharge as staff sergeant in September 1945. Was awarded the Air Medal, Purple Heart and three European Campaign Stars.

Married Phyllis Pesce, December 1945 and has three daughters and seven grandchildren.

RICHARD J. PARKES, was born on June 16, 1921 in Lyons, PA. He enlisted in the USAAC on Aug. 24, 1942, received his basic training at Keesler Field, MS and trained as navigator at San Marcos Field, TX.

On Jan. 24, 1944, now a second lieutenant, he left Morrison Field, FL via the southern route to Tibenham, England, arriving at the 445th Bomb Group. Lt. Parkes became a lead navigator in the 700th Squadron. He flew 30 combat missions in B-24s from February to July 1944, receiving the Distinguished Flying Cross and three Air Medals. Promoted to first lieutenant. After his tour Parkes became an instructor stationed in Ireland, and returned to the States on Dec. 13, 1944.

After the war Lt. Parkes joined the Air National Guard until being called to active duty again for the Korean War. He was assigned to the 6167th Air Base Group, K-16, Seoul, Korea. He flew 68 combat missions there in B-26s, C-46s, and C-47s and received another Distinguished Flying Cross and three more Air Medals.

After Korea Parkes joined the Air Force Reserve at NAS Willow Grove, PA and was called to active duty again for the Cuban Missile Crisis at MacDill AFB. Subsequently he became a master navigator serving as squadron navigator for the 326th Troop Carrier Sqdn., 912th Group flying C-119s and later C-141s at Dover AFB. He retired on May 1, 1971, having attained the rank of lieutenant colonel with 28 years service.

Parkes married the former Ruth Spohn on Oct. 16, 1943. They are both retired and reside in Kutztown, PA. They have two children and two grandchildren.

BERNARD PAROLY (NMI), was born Aug. 3, 1923, Bronx, NY. Appointed aviation cadet, Oct. 1, 1943; pre-flight at (SAAC) San Antonio Aviation Cadet Center; primary, Brayton Flying School, Cuero, TX; basic, Waco, AAF; Wings and commission, Class 43-1, Blackland AAF, transition into B-24 at Tarrant AAF, Fort Worth. Trained combat crew at Colorado Springs.

Was issued a "Ford" B-24J Serial #44-41097 at Lincoln, NE. Flew to 8th Air Force in England (southern route). Assigned to 576th Sqdn., 392nd Bomb Group, Wendling. Was airplane commander on 30 strategic bombing raids, including Orleans, Bremerhaven, Bremen, Politz, Kiel, Munich; 15 missions were as lead element. Made three-engine-forced landing south of London, during mission of June 4, 1944. Participated in tactical bombing of German forces in support of D-day invasion June 6. Total combat hours, 220.

After completing combat missions, flew gas supply plane to Patton's tanks and fighter planes on the continent. Decorations include Distinguished Flying Cross, Air Medal with three Oak Leaf Clusters, Presidential Unit Citation, European Theater Ribbon with four Battle Stars and the Victory Medal.

Upon return to States, qualified as an aircraft mainte-

nance officer and weights and balance officer at Chanute Field where he separated from the service Aug. 4, 1945 with the rank first lieutenant.

Has been self-employed as designer and expert on sewn products, such as ladies handbags and various sport and gym bags. Still active in own business in New Haven, CT. Married while at Waco to Rhoda (Fallick), childhood sweetheart. Has two daughters, two sons-in-law and four grandchildren.

ROLLAND L. PARROTT, was born Nov. 2, 1924 at Vancouver, WA. Entered USAAC November 1942. Graduated from Navigation School at San Marcos, TX August 1944. Joined the Bernie Fishman crew and went through RTU training at Gowen Field, Boise, ID.

They proceeded to England in December 1944 and were assigned to the 445th Bomb Group. Flew only seven missions and was then sent to Radar Bombardier/Navigator School at Alconbury, England. After completing that training returned to the 445th and was training with a lead crew when the war ended. Returned to the States and was completing Radar Instructors School when the war in the Pacific ended.

Married Rita Ankeny, Nov. 3, 1946 at Caldwell, ID. Has one son and two grandsons. Spent most of working career in insurance, specializing in Workers Compensation. Now lives in Caldwell, ID, playing a lot of golf (not very well) and enjoying his family.

THOMAS B. PARRY, was born in Georgetown, KY, July 7, 1916. Called to active duty in 1941 as an infantry lieutenant, transferred to flight training and received his Wings with Class 43-H. Flew 33 missions as first pilot of a B-24 lead crew with the 330th Sqdn., 93rd Bomb Group from April to August 1944. Remaining in England, he ferried all type aircraft from P-51s to B-17s and married a Russian-Latvian refugee before returning to the U.S. and leaving the service in 1945.

Recalled to active duty for the Korean War, he flew B-

29s before going to Korea to fly L5s. Flew KC97 tankers in SAC before escaping into TAC in time to fly C130s in combat in Vietnam.

Retired in 1969 as a lieutenant colonel with three Distinguished Flying Crosses and seven Air Medals. He started serious traveling and has visited 85 countries and island groups. Now resides in Holyoke, MA.

PHILIP H. PARSONS, was born June 9, 1921 at Hugoton, KS. Joined the service June 16, 1942. Went through pilot training in the Central Training Command and graduated at Ellington Field, Houston, TX. Took transition in B-24s at Liberal, KS, then to Tonopah, NV for training with his crew.

Flew with crew in B-24 from Hamilton Field to Goose Bay, Lab., Iceland and Scotland. After training at Loe Ney Northern Ireland, was sent to "Ole Buck" 453rd Group as a replacement crew. He flew 14 missions as a wing man and then went into training for lead crew. Flew 16 missions as a lead pilot.

Memorable experiences: led the 8th Air Force on a mission to Gardelegen, Germany on March 15, 1945 with some 2,500 planes behind them.

Discharged in August 1945 with the rank of captain.

Received the Distinguished Flying Cross, five Air Medals and four European Campaign Stars. Married in 1946 and had two children and five grandchildren. Married Barbara in 1988 and has a stepson.

THOMAS S. PARSONS (TOM), was born March 24, 1924 in Niles, MI. Joined the USAAF on Nov. 16, 1942. Served with 44th Bomb Group (H), 68th Sqdn. and completed 31 8th Air Force combat missions. Singular experience as pinch hitting bombardier/gunner. Flew with nine pilots including Dimpfl, Marcoulier, Murphy, Principe and Weaver.

Memorable experiences: 14th mission on June 20, 1944 to Politz, flew 2nd ADA lead with Morcoulier, 492 Bomb Group virtually destroyed; 15th mission June 21 to Berlin with Principe; 16th mission on July 6, 1944, alone to Kiel with Murphy in *Southern Comfort II*, skip-bombed sub pens and destroyed two; 17th mission July 7 to Bernburg with Principe in Flak Alley.

Discharged Sept. 15, 1945 with the rank staff sergeant. Received the Distinguished Flying Cross, Air Medal with three Oak Leaf Clusters and others.

Married Sara Perry, they have five children, eight grandchildren and four great-grandchildren. Retired (Associate Dean Emeritus) California State University; president, Georgia Chapter, 8th Air Force Historical Society, and trustee, 44th Heritage Memorial Group.

WALTER PATSCHEIDER, was born March 1, 1925 at Lynn, MA, entered U.S. Army as private June 1, 1943, then volunteered for aviation cadets. Graduated Bombardier Class 44-9. Joined Elmer Mitchell B-24 crew at Charleston AFB.

Departed U.S. on *Queen Mary,* October 1944, to 453rd Bomb Group. Flew first mission November 5. Only survivor of Mitchell plane crash, December 28. Trained as "Mickey" operator and joined Owen Hopper crew, February 1945. Was captured by Germans March 31 after parachuting from burning plane. Walked, hitchhiked across Holland guarded by WWI "retreds" who begged food along the way. Guards surrendered May 2 when British tanks approached. Returned to U.S. through Camp Lucky Strike. Discharged Nov. 14.

Recalled to active duty to Japan in November 1948. Assigned to 610th Aircraft Control and Warning Sqdn. for three years as radar maintenance officer. Stationed with family on remote site in Sea of Japan during Korean War. Worked for General Electric in U.S., Japan and Germany. Received commendation from Apollo 11 crew for support of first lunar landing. Discharged September 1953 with the rank captain.

Married Sally Morse over 47 years ago and has five daughters, 15 grandchildren and two great-grandchildren.

DAVID G. PATTERSON, was born Aug. 13, 1920, Oakland, CA. Was university student when entered active duty June 1942 as second lieutenant, U.S. Signal Corps. After stint at Ft. Monmouth, NJ, Signal School and over a year of maneuvers with Armored Forces at Desert Training Center, CA, finally obtained a transfer to USAAC, October 1943. Graduated from Pilot School, Pampa, TX, Class of 44-F.

Served with 445th Bomb Group, December 1944-May 1945 (Tibenham, England). Earned Air Medal and three Battle Stars. On mission near Berlin was shot up, crash landed in Poland, interned by the Russians. Eventually "liberated," and returned courtesy of USAF ATC to home base. En route back, met his brother Capt. John Patterson, OSS Commando, for short "hello" in France.

Returned to States May 1945. After war's end, resumed studies, graduated from Stanford University with engineering degree and advanced business degree (MBA). Spent following years in engineering and management. Since then, involved as CEO, later board chairman of family held real estate management corporations (California).

Married to Joan, they have children,step-children and grandchildren widely scattered throughout the western states. Still active in flying, outdoor sports, volunteer work and business. Past President and currently serving as secretary, 2nd Air Division Association.

EARL S. PATTERSON (PAT), signed up for Aviation Cadet Program while working for the Glen L. Martin Co. in the industrial engineering department building B-26 bombers.

Called to active duty July 1943 and proceeded to Latrobe, PA for college training, ground school at Montgomery, AL (cadet adjutant); then to Gunnery School at Panama City, FL and then to Midland Airfield, Midland, TX where he graduated as a second lieutenant and bombardier of Class 44-12.

Assigned to the best crew ever to fly the B-24 bomber with training at Boise, ID. Along with Patterson, the crew consisted of Lt. Forest E. McCready Jr., Lt. Eddie O. McLaughlin Jr., Lt. Harold D. Pittenger, Merle L. Law, Pat H. Cochran, Claude E. Lamoy Jr., Arthur J. Helganz, Eugene T. Short, and Darwin D. Dague. Assigned to the 8th Air Force, 2nd Air Division, 20th Combat Wing, 448th Bomb Group, 713th Bomb Sqdn. He flew 22 missions over Germany. The 448th was known to have one of the best accuracy records in the 8th Air Force.

Returned to the States in June 1945 as a first lieutenant. Was assigned to administrative work as a surplus property officer (MOS 2120). Closed and sold out Sioux Falls, SD, Kearney, McCook, and Lincoln AFBs in Nebraska.

Entered pilot training at Randolph AFB, TX in June 1946 in Class 46-F. Was promoted to rank of captain in November 1946. After pilot training was assigned to Yakota AFB, Japan for occupation duty. In addition to flying, he had the assignment as commanding officer of the 5th Air Force Searchlight and Radar Maintenance Team reporting directly to Gen. White, CG 5th Air Force. This assignment required travel throughout the entire Far East Command of the 5th Air Force.

Participated in the start of the Korean conflict and later reassigned to the Strategic Air Command and returned to the States.

After assignment to the SAC someone at the top got the great idea to rotate the air groups every 90 days or so to a new base all over the world and when the group exceeded a divorce rate of over 60 percent, he departed the Air Force and was promoted to the rank of major at separation. Awarded the Distinguished Flying Cross, Air Medal with clusters, Purple Heart and other citations. His file indicates a letter from the commanding general 314th. Air Division in Japan recommending him for the Soldiers Medal for his being a major factor in saving the lives of pilots, Lt. William R. Casteel and Lt. William Edwards who were seriously injured in Japan.

He became a general contractor and land developer. For the period of 1966 to 1970 he had a position with the engineering division of the Army-Air Force Exchange Service developing the new concept of shopping malls on many Army Posts and Air Bases. That assignment was completed after being assigned as the assistant chief of engineering, Vietnam area at the grade of GS-13.

He returned to the general contracting and land developing business which his sons are following today. He entered partial retirement in 1984 and now is acting as a consultant to contractors, developers, and owners in matters relating primarily to site work, utilities, wetlands problems as well as commercial building of shopping centers and office buildings. He has no plans for total retirement.

Married Winona Marie Bobo and raised a family consisting of one daughter and three sons (daughter became a captain in the Air Force and her husband is presently Lt. Col. Melvin P. Hoke, USAF).

DANIEL CLARK PATTON, was born May 12, 1924 in Gibsonville, NC. Enlisted June 1943 in the USAAF, 703rd Sqdn., 445th Bomb Group, 8th Air Force. Flew 24 missions as flight engineer on B-24 from Tibenham, England. Was shot down over Germany, captured, and POW for three months. Was liberated by Gen. George Patton's 3rd Army in May 1945.

Discharged October 1945 with the rank of tech sergeant. Received the Purple Heart, Air Medal with three clusters.

Attended Elon College, NC and married Violet Stone on Dec. 14, 1946. They have three children and five grandchildren. He is president of DC Patton Construction Co., Elon College, NC.

JOHN M. PATTON JR., was born April 20, 1918 in Morganton, NC. Enlisted USAAF, Air Cadet, October 1942 and reported for basic training January 1943. Military locations/stations: Miami Beach, Tenn Poly-Cookeville five months; classification: pilot one month, primary, basic, two months; advance, two months; graduated, second lieutenant in March 1944.

Flew 28 missions to Germany with the 446th Bomb Group, 8th AAF, ETO, 15 as lead crew and balance as wing man. All missions were exciting and scary.

Discharged June 19, 1978 with the rank lieutenant colonel. Received the Air Medal with three Oak Leaf Clusters, ETO Ribbon with three clusters.

Married and has two sons, both in the military (one in Air Force). Patton is retired and enjoys playing tennis and having a good time.

MARVIN M. PAUL, was born Feb. 5, 1920 in Beallsville, PA. Enlisted in the USAAC on Dec. 8, 1941. Upon completing Air Plane Mechanics School at Keesler Field, MS in May of 1942, he was stationed at Windsor Locks, CN until pilot training.

Commissioned as a pilot, May 28, 1942, he then completed B-24 pilot training at Casper, WY. His crew was assembled and assigned a new B-24, *Bold Venture.* They joined the 492nd Bomb Group in Alamogordo, NM and departed Morrison Field, FL, April 14, 1944, arriving in England at North Pickenham Base.

Flew 23 missions with the 492nd until the group was disbanded, then assigned to the 467th Bomb Group where he became squadron leader. On the 27th mission, they crash landed. Returned to the States November 1944 and was relieved of active duty. Assigned to the Reserves Oct. 17, 1945. He received the Distinguished Flying Cross, four Air Medals and various campaign stars.

Married April 2, 1945 to Lois Ann Langenbacher, they have a son, daughter and four grandchildren. Paul is a retired lieutenant colonel.

BRUCE H. PAULY, was born Nov. 11, 1920, Washington, DC. Army (Coast Artillery) ROTC cadet at VPI, September 1937-June 1941. Received BS in mechanical engineering June 1941. Immediately enlisted in USAAC as aviation cadet for six months engineering officer training at Chanute Field, IL.

Assigned to 44th Bomb Group (H), MacDill Field, FL, December 1941, just then receiving its first "Liberators" (all-black LB-30s still wearing RAF insignia). Served as 44th Group Engineering officer February 1942 to November 1943 in USA, England, Libya and Tunis. Station S-4, Shipdham, England November 1943-April 1944.

Director of maintenance, 2nd Air Div. April 1944-May 1945 at Division HQ, Ketteringham Hall, England. Last active duty position as AFSC Maintenance Division, Wright Field, OH. Retired from USAFR November 1980 with the rank lieutenant colonel. Received the Legion of Merit, Bronze Star, Croix de Guerre.

Married Dorothy B. Rollins June 20, 1945, they have daughter Margaret M. Price. Retired from civilian engineering career in industry December 1982. He is a member of the 2nd Air Division Association.

EUGENE F. PAUZE, was born in Hartford, VT on Jan. 23, 1917. Inducted into the service from New Hampshire on Aug. 13, 1942. Attended Army Air Forces Technical School at Chanute Field, IL. Graduated from Teletype maintenance course November 1942.

Went overseas in May 1943. Assigned to 8th Air Force,

93rd Bomb Group (B-24) Hardwick, England. Worked at 93rd HQ as Teletype operator to rank of corporal. Actively two plus years with the 93rd, posting credits to his service record, viz.

Battles and campaigns: Air Offensive Europe, Tunisia, Sicily-Naples-Foggia, Rome-Arno, Normandy, Northern France, Rhineland, Ardennes, Central Europe, Air Combat Balkans.

Honorably discharged at Fort Devens, MA, Sept. 11, 1945. Received the Good Conduct Medal, EAME Theater Campaign Ribbon, Presidential Unit Citation and the American Defense Medal.

Returned to USA via B-24 "Home Run/Project" May 1945. Re-assigned 2nd Air Force HQ, Colorado Springs, Teletype operator. Currently a retired cost accountant. He married Virginia Rae in May 1953, they have one son and two grandsons.

HERMAN A. PEACHER, was born June 16, 1917 in Laclede, MO. Graduated from Laclede High School in 1935. Joined Civilian Conservation Corps Camp as caterpillar driver and mechanic in 1939 for 14 months. He was employed by Consolidated Aircraft from August 1940 through September 1942, manufacturing parts for B-24, PBY and B-32.

He returned to Missouri and volunteered for USAAC on Nov. 2, 1942. Attended basic training at Coffeville, KS. Graduated AM School at Keesler Field and Gunnery School, Laredo, TX; attended first phase training in Boise, ID. Group 458 was formed. Completed 2nd and 3rd phase training in Tonopah, NV.

Flew overseas ATC B-17. Rejoined group, Horsham St. Faith. Flew first mission, first attempt to bomb Berlin on March 3, 1944. Second mission to Berlin on March 8. Ran out of gas and crashed at Walton, England.

On the 12th or 13th mission, April 22, 1944, they were shot down. The target was a huge marshaling yard in Hamm, Germany. He spent approximately four months in a POW hospital in Obermasfelt. Afterwards, he was transferred to Luft IV. In December 1944, he was moved to Barth, Luft I. A few days before the end of the war, they were liberated by the Russians. He was discharged from service on Nov. 2, 1945.

Married Jan. 5, 1946. Has two sons, two grandsons and one granddaughter. Employed at Naval Air Station North Island in San Diego from May 11, 1946-May 11, 1974 as an aircraft and engine mechanic. After 42 years he was awarded both the Purple Heart and POW medals.

CLOYD E. PEACOCK, was born Dec. 17, 1922 in Scott County, IN and raised there on a farm. Joined the USAAC Oct. 14, 1942. Was an aviation cadet, completed flight training, and commissioned May 20, 1944 as a second lieutenant bombardier at Midland Field, TX.

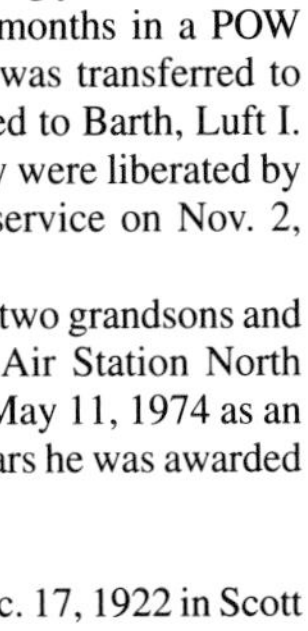

Flew 26 combat missions in B-24s with the 445th Bomb Group from Tibenham, England. Was discharged with a BS degree in mathematics and physics, taught high school one year then recalled into the USAF in May 1951. Soon was assigned to SAC and on combat crews in B-29s and B-47s in the 68th, 40th and 100th Bomb Wings for some time.

Assigned to the Air Force Representative Office at the Lockheed Aircraft Company Marietta, GA doing flight testing in C-130s, C-140s, and C-141s for three years. Completed Command and Staff College, then assigned to Los Angeles AFS doing missile and space systems analysis in advanced planning for five years until retiring in October 1968 with the rank of major.

Returned to college, got an MS degree in physics, taught college and high school mathematics, physics and computer science until 1990 when he retired second time. Married May 24, 1944 to Julia Goff, he has two daughters and four grandchildren.

CLARENCE F. PEASE (SKIP), was born Oct. 24, 1923, San Bernardino, CA. Joined the USAF Dec. 17, 1941. Military locations include March AFB; Sheppard Field, TX;

463rd Sub Depot, Hethel, England; 389th Bomb Group, 565th Sqdn. Assigned propeller shop at Hethel with repeated requests for combat assignment. Attended full-time Gunnery School on base, working regular shift. Combat request finally approved December 1944 and given engineer position.

Flew 17 missions with crews where existing engineer evidenced problems or was wounded. Flew as co-pilot on slow flights to run overhauled engines and any missions possible. Flew top turret gunnery position, waist four times and tail turret once. On March 25, 1945 had low level supply mission in Wessel, Germany. Took over lead April 7, 1945 on Duneberg/Neumunster raid after lead and deputy lead aircraft were knocked down by ME-109. Discharged Aug. 13, 1945 with the rank of tech sergeant.

Received private pilot license after discharge in 1946. Has owned three planes including J-3 Cub, Ercoupe and currently a Pitts S-2A in which he has flown in acrobatic competition. He is on board of directors of Evergreen International Aviation, McMinville, OR. Membership in Confederate Air Force and National Biplane Association. Member of lead crew of *All American,* a fully restored B-24 by the Collings Foundation.

Married Zona Jan. 1, 1946; they have four children and three grandchildren. Held position with Prudential Ins. Co., retiring as senior VP Oct. 31, 1988.

ROSCOE I. PEASE JR., was born Sept. 26, 1919 at Racine, WI. Enlisted in the USAAC Aug. 27, 1941. Transferred from the glider training program to flight training at Helena, Newport and Stuttgart, AR. Graduated with Class 43-K and received commission as a second lieutenant on Dec. 5, 1943. Transition to B-24 Liberators at Maxwell Field, AL, then joined the crew with whom he would fly a combat tour of 35 missions over enemy occupied Europe, at Westover Field, MA. From there they flew a new B-24 over the northern route to England. En route they listened to Gen. Eisenhower make his D-day speech.

Assigned to the 93rd Bomb Group for less than a month, they moved to the decimated 492nd Bomb Group from which they survived nine combat missions before that group was disbanded. Then on to the 788th Bomb Sqdn., 467th Bomb Group at Rackheath, England; there completed 35 missions. Crew intact with the exception of their bombardier who had the misfortune to be shot down during a practice mission. The next move was a second tour with the 479th Fighter Group escorting the heavies that he had recently left. He had only flown two missions when hostilities ended and he was returned to Fort Sheridan, IL for separation.

On Oct. 17, 1945, he accepted a commission in the Reserves and completed 38 years subsequently with the Wisconsin Air National Guard. Retirement was reached Sept. 26, 1979 with the rank of lieutenant colonel. Upon separation from active duty, he attended Marquette University in Milwaukee, WI. Taught elementary and high school for 17 years, retiring in 1985.

Married Bette Allyne Watkins of Horning, Norfolk, England while stationed at Ipswich with the fighter group 48 years ago, June 30, 1945. Has two daughters and three grandchildren.

WILBUR J. PECKA, was born June 7, 1918 in Cicero, IL. Enlisted Jan. 25, 1942 in the USAAC, Aviation Cadets, Kelly Field, TX. Stationed at Clovis, NM; Topeka, KS; Salina, KS; Selman Field, Monroe, LA; Davis Monthan AB, Tucson, AZ; Reykjavik, Iceland; Shipdham, England.

Memorable experiences: when his crew was selected for the secret Cocker Mission and sent to Iceland; Nov. 13, 1943 when returning from bombing mission over Germany, badly damaged with three lost engines and crash landed in Holland. All 10 crewman survived but almost immediately were taken prisoners by Nazi. Interned at Stalag I POW Camp for 18 months before being liberated by Russian army in May 1945.

Discharged Dec. 26, 1945 with the rank first lieutenant. Received the Purple Heart, five unit citations with Oak Leaf Clusters.

Married 1st Lt. Karoline Schreiber July 21, 1945, they have son Jeffrey who was a Green Beret in Vietnam War. Pecka retired as VP after 47 plus years with At&T Bell System Service.

HENRY L. PEDICONE, was born June 23, 1923 in Bronx, NY. Joined the USAAF Nov. 14, 1942, Intelligence Specialist 631. Stationed Sioux City, IA and Seething, England. Graduated from Administrative and Technical Clerk School in L.A., 1943; Intelligence School, Salt Lake City, UT, 1943; assigned to 715th Bomb Sqdn., S-2 Section. Then assigned to Intelligence Section, 448th Bomb Group HQ as section chief.

Discharged Oct. 20, 1945 with the rank sergeant. Received the Meritorious Unit Award, ETO Ribbon with Bronze and Silver Star.

Married Oct. 22, 1949 to Theresa Padova. They have seven children and 14 grandchildren. Co-owner in supply company, H. Pedicone & Sons, Inc. for 25 years, then went into real estate. Currently semi-retired real estate broker.

ROBERT E. PEDIGO, was born Oct. 20, 1923 at Indianapolis, IN. Worked as an 18 year old precision machinist for one year cutting gears for the Norden Bombsight. Enlisted in the USAAC Oct. 30, 1942. Completed Armorer and Aerial Gunnery Schools. Did phase training in dive bombers, then on to phase training on B-24s. Assigned to 453rd Bomb Group, 735th Sqdn.

Also spent a while in Aviation Cadets. They flew a new B-24 to England; but, was assigned to another B-24, *Silent Yokum,* and did 30 missions with it. Their first mission was May 22, 1944 and their last was Sept. 8, 1944. Battles were: Normandy, Northern France, Rhineland and Air Offensive of Europe.

Discharged on points Sept. 9, 1945 with the rank staff sergeant. Received the Distinguished Flying Cross, five Air Medals and four Bronze Stars.

Married Helen Wood May 3, 1943. They have two sons, four grandchildren and three great-grandchildren. He retired from Naval Avionics, Indianapolis, IN.

JOSEPH D. PEGRAM, was born Ponder, TX on May 23, 1924. Entered the service on June 18, 1943 and was discharged on July 24, 1945. After Armor School, Aerial Gunnery in Las Vegas, he was assigned to Lester Bridges crew, which included: CP, William Rigg; N, William Hamilton; B, Gordon Walker; E, George Taylor; RO, Martin Voyvodich; G, Douglas Rodewald; G, Clair Way; and G, Ed Wallace.

They were issued a B-24 with equipment and flew to Scotland, where the plane and equipment was placed in a replacement pool. Their crew was assigned to the 2nd Air Div., 491st Bomb Group, 852nd Bomb Sqdn. with Pegram as right waist gunner. They commenced flying missions August 1944.

On Sept. 12, 1944 they were hit by flak. He saw Sparrows plane with part of a wing shot off, go down in flames and spotted one parachute. Their plane had rudders and ailerons blown off the tail, busting the turret. An engine was shot up and had to be feathered. Ed Wallace was thrown out of the turret into the tunnel. The lock was blown off the waist door, causing Pegram to be partially blown out the R.W. window. While clutching the window with his knees wrapped around the waist gun, he was struck by flak. It passed through both hips and his spine.

Lester Bridges flew their crippled plane to safety. He is a superb pilot and Pegram would not be here if it wasn't for his exceptional skills as a pilot. The rest of the crew went on to complete 30 missions before returning to the States. Pegram spent nine months lying paralyzed on his back while recuperating from several operations.

He married one of his nurses following his discharge. They settled in his home state of Texas and relocated to Cincinnati, OH in 1951.

Christmas 1991 he received a letter from William Rigg, his first correspondence from his crew in many years. He joined the 2nd Air Div. in attending the reunion in Las Vegas in 1992. He is honored to have been part of such a great and caring crew.

KENNETH M. PEIFFER, was born 1925 in Quentin, PA. Enlisted September 1943 in the USAAC. Sent to Miami Beach, FL on Jan. 17, 1944 for basic training and from there to Harlingen, TX for Gunnery School. From there to Tonopah, NV for training in B-24s in Lt. Wynns crew as tail gunner. He was then sent to Fort Dix and overseas to Great Britain. Name of the plane was *Grease Ball*.

Next to North Pickenham to the 491st Bomb Group, 854th Bomb Sqdn. On their 11th mission they were shot down on the Misburg raid. He was the only survivor. He spent nine weeks in a hospital and after six months was liberated by Gen. Patton at Moosburg. Went to Camp Lucky Strike and then home.

Discharged Dec. 12, 1945 with the rank staff sergeant. Received the Air Medal, Purple Heart, POW Medal, Unit Citation, Good Conduct Medal, ETO and two Battle Stars and the American Defense.

Has wife Anna and son Ken Jr. Peiffer is retired.

ROBERT L. PELLICAN, became second lieutenant Cavalry Reserve upon graduation from University of Illinois in 1939.

Started active duty July 1941 and temporarily assigned to Air Corps at Jefferson Barracks, MO. From October 1941 to August 1943 was at Keesler Field, Biloxi, MS doing desk work.

June 1943, transferred permanently from Cavalry to Air Corps. He requested flying training but was disapproved. September 1943, McClelland AB, Sacramento, CA; October 1943, assigned to 61st Station Complement Sqdn. at Attlebridge with duty as Base S1. This duty extended to July 1945. October-November 1943, B-24s were flying anti-submarine missions over Bay of Biscay. December 1943, Seabees expanded Attlebridge. The 466th Bomb Group arrived January 1944. Continued S1 duties: mission counts, promotions, decorations, payroll and general service record. May 1944 assumed command of the 61st Station Complement Sqdn. July 1945 sailed home on *Queen Mary* from Scotland.

Employed at Butler Brothers and Ben Franklin Stores doing budgetary accounting work until retirement 1982. Pellican and his wife celebrated their 50th wedding anniversary in 1993.

JOSEPH O. PELOQUIN, was born Nov. 10, 1923 in Saco, ME. Joined the military Oct. 1, 1942; attended Airplane Mechanic School at Sheppard Field, TX; Airplane Engine School at Wrights Aeronautical in Patterson, NJ; Wendover Aerial Gunnery School in Wendover, UT. Trained on B-24 Liberator as flight engineer.

At Alamogordo, NM, Langley Field, VA on sub-patrol prior to being assigned to 8th Air Force at 44th Bomb Group in England. Bailed out on second mission over France May 11, 1944. Evaded until Aug. 13, 1944 after being liberated by American troops.

Separated from service April 26, 1945. Now retired from Portsmouth Naval Shipyard as a submarine pipefitter after 28 years of government service. He and his wife reside in Biddeford, ME.

PAUL O. PELOQUIN, was born June 12, 1919 in Cadott, WI. Entered the regular Army Oct. 31, 1939, 3rd Inf. Regt., Line Co. Stationed at Ft. Snelling, MN; Kelly Field March 28, 1942; AFTD Coleman, TX April 1942; AFPS (BN) Ellington Field, TX, June 1942, and AAFNS Hondo, TX, October 1942 to October 1943.

Participated in action at Sicily, Air Offensive Europe, Normandy, Northern France, Naples, Foggia.

Memorable experiences: going to Berlin on March 22, 1944; sojourn to North Africa in 1943 to battle sand, insects and Germans; Hardwick, England with 93rd Bomb Group, 409th Sqdn.

Flew two tours with 93rd Bomb Group from June 30, 1943 to Oct. 4, 1944. Became lead navigator on second tour. Was never shot down but came home alone quite often. Most trying mission was to Olso, Normandy on Nov. 16, 1943. They nearly froze to death (no heated suits at that time).

Suffered from TB during combat. After two years in hospital was retired from service at Fitzsimmons Hospital on Aug. 11, 1947 with the rank of captain. He received the Distinguished Flying Cross.

Married on Oct. 31, 1944 to his high school sweetheart. They had seven children (two deceased). Peloquin is retired but still does small plumbing repairs, mostly lawn sprinklers. Enjoys fishing for trout.

ERNEST PEREZ, was born May 25, 1922 in Santa Paula, CA. He joined the USAAC in October 1942. Was commissioned as a navigator in Hondo, TX in April 1944. Assigned to the 329th Bomb Sqdn., 93rd Bomb Wing from September 1944 to June 1945. Flew 23 combat missions, eight as a lead crew navigator.

Assigned in 1946 to a Military Mission to Cali, Colombia and taught the first students rated as navigators by the Colombian Air Force. From July 1948 to February 1949 he served in the Berlin Airlift as a navigator and squadron supply officer.

Completed his high school in 1948 by correspondence courses. Subsequently attained a BA degree in 1955 from Sacramento State College and MA degree in 1957 from Stanford University.

Served as an instructor, 1950-53. Flew over 5,000 hours. His assignments were varied with 10 years overseas. Memorable experiences: tour with 93rd Bomb Group; military observer in El Salvador/Honduras Conflict in 1970; duty with B-47 units, Strategic Air Command, 1958-63; Vietnam tour, 1971.

Retired from the Air Force in May 1972 as a lieutenant colonel. He was hired by Santa Clara County, CA in May 1972. He retired from the county in April 1990 as a director of the county's Equal Opportunity Program.

Was married in Norwich, England on May 20, 1945 to Stella Smith, who was serving in the British Navy. They live in San Jose, CA and have a daughter, four sons and eight grandchildren.

CHARLES W. PERRY, was born March 19, 1920 in Indianapolis, IN. Enlisted Oct. 15, 1942, USAAF. Assigned to McKeny's crew at Denver as ball turret gunner with 446th Bomb Group, 706th Bomb Sqdn., 2nd Air Div. Stationed at Key Field, MS; Clovis, NM; Denver, CO (Lowry 1).

Went to England with the original group, flew 29 missions. Was shot down on a Berlin mission flying replacement as nose gunner and taken POW near Helmstedt, Germany. Was interned at Stalag VI and Stalag IV. Was liberated at Torgau on the Elbe River.

Returned to the States in June and was discharged Oct. 8, 1945 with the rank staff sergeant. He received the Air Medal with three Oak Leaf Clusters and the Distinguished Flying Cross. Married he has one daughter. Perry is a tax consultant.

GENE D. PERSON, was born March 17, 1923 on a farm west of Burnside, IA. Graduated Gowrie High School and attended Iowa State University. Entered the service Oct. 28, 1943 as an Air Force Cadet. Trained at Amarillo AFB, TX; Keesler AFB, Biloxi, MS; Tyndall AFB, Panama City, FL; Charleston AFB, Charleston, SC; Westover AFB, MA; and Mitchel AB, NY.

Flew from Presque Isle AB, ME to Goose Bay, Labrador; Meeks Field, Iceland; Woodbury AB; Valley Wales AB; Attlebridge AB with 787th Bomb Sqdn. 466th Bomb Group. Missions included Wilmenshaven, Brunswick, Tirstrup, Ploen, Kemul, Litchfelt, Recklin, Regensburg, Rayon, Landshut, Karlsbad and Salzburg. Flew first mission in *Hardluck*, five missions in *Earthquake Magoon* and six missions on *Joker*. Discharged March 7, 1945, Wright-Patterson AFB.

Occupation after service: R/W agent AT&T, Chicago, IL; Tobin Pkg. Co., hog buying dept. and security, Hormel Pkg. Co., Purchasing and Comptometor Depts. Retired from the Cure-81 Ham Dept. after working for Tobins & Hormels for 31 years. Also owned Ft. Dodge Lawnmower Service & Sales for five years; Devil Rapids Hunting and Fishing Lodge on Churchil River in Saskatchewan, Canada for four years while working at Hormels. Retired when he was 58 years of age.

Married Naomi Johnson in July 1946. She passed away in 1972 and he married Anne Beadle in February 1974. Children: Mark, Sheree Pandil, Sheila Collins, Randy, Jeff, Thomas and Dan. Spend summers in Manson, IA and winters in Donna, TX.

RAYMOND PETERS, was born in Monticello, IA on Aug. 31, 1917. Enlisted in the service Aug. 22, 1941, 2nd Cavalry C-Troop T/5 Ft. Riley, KS. Cavalry was disbanded July 1942 and was assigned to Med. Detachment, 2nd Armd. Div., Ft. Riley, KS. Joined the USAAC, December 1942.

Sent to Santa Ana, CA; Oxnard, CA; Marana, AZ; Marfa, TX; Albuquerque, NM; and Pueblo, CO. Went overseas in 1944 as co-pilot of B-24. Stationed with 458th Bomb Group, 755th Bomb Sqdn. at Horsham St. Faith, Norwich, England. Completed 29 missions.

Discharged September 1945, Leavenworth, KS with the rank first lieutenant. Married and has two children. Worked for IDOT for 36 years. Peters passed away April 27, 1988.

CLIFFORD L. PETERSON, was born Jan. 26, 1920 in Anoka, MN and was raised on a farm near Minneapolis. Joined the USAAC as aviation cadet in Baltimore, MD, March 25, 1942. Graduated from Flying School as pilot, second lieutenant, March 25, 1943, Class 43C, Columbus, MS. Trained in B-17 at Boise, ID and B-24 at Pocatello, ID.

Sent overseas as B-24 crew pilot, October 1943, assigned to 392nd Bomb Group, 578th Bomb Sqdn. at

Wendling, England, November 1943. Flew as pilot of B-24 crew until shot down on March 18, 1944, mission #18 to Fredrichshafen, Germany. Captured and interned as POW in Stalag Luft III and Stalag Luft VII A until liberated April 29, 1945.

Remained on active duty at Smyrna, TN and Davis Monthan AFB, Tucson, AZ as base recruiting officer and ground training officer. In October 1950, trained in B-29 at MacDill AFB, Tampa, FL. Assigned to 307th Bomb Group in Okinawa, January 1951. Flew as B-29 pilot on 32 combat missions to Korea until November 1951. Assigned to MacDill AFB and Barksdale AFB, LA.

Left service in 1955 with the rank of major. Received the Distinguished Flying Cross, Air Medal with six Oak Leaf Clusters, Purple Heart, POW Medal, Distinguished Unit Citation, WWII Victory Medal, ETO Ribbon with six Campaign Ribbons, Far East Air Force Ribbon and Korean Service Medal.

Was general manager, Morrison Cafeteria Restaurant Co., 1955-1985. Retired September 1985. Member of reunion groups of American Ex-POWs, 8th Air Force Historical Society, 2nd Air Division Association, 392nd Bomb Group Memorial Association. Served on board of directors of 8AFHS for eight years and one year as national president. Served two years as president of Florida Chapter, 8AFHS.

Lives with his wife Mary in Winter Park, FL.

GEORGE B. PETERSON, was born Dec. 24, 1921 on a farm near McCanna, ND. Joined the USAAF Oct. 28, 1942. Departed overseas Feb. 25, 1944. Flew with the 453rd Bomb Group, 735th Bomb Sqdn. as a flight engineer and top turret gunner on Lt. Lovell's crew.

Peterson was KIA when their B-24H (*Gypsy Queen*) was shot down May 8, 1944 on the raid to Brunswick, Germany. Two crew members survived and were held as POWs. He is survived by his mother, father, two sisters and a brother who was serving in the Army in Europe. *Submitted by his cousin, Bob Peterson.*

NEWELL H. PETERSON (PETE), was born Nov. 25, 1921 in Martell Twp., Pierce County, WI. Joined USAAC April 15, 1942 as waist gunner. Attended Airplane Mechanics School, Roosevelt Field, Long Island, NY; Radio Operator and Mechanics, AAFTS, Scott Field, IL; Gunnery School LAAF, Laredo, TX; Davis Monthan AB, Tucson, AZ; Wendover Field, UT; Halesworth, England; Harlingen Gunnery School instructor, Harlingen, TX.

Memorable experiences:

July 7, 1944-target was a factory which manufactured fuselages for JU-88s in Aschersleben, Germany. Peterson stood at right waist window and watched both fighters and bombers going down in smoke and flame. A 20mm cannon knocked off the dome of a top turret and also the gunner's head. Blood from top turret way back to tail, almost like paint. They lost 39 bombers and six fighters that day and the Germans lost 114 fighters.

Aug. 13, 1944-mission in Seine area. Flak was moderate-heavy but accurate. The *Lynda Lee II* received 119 holes. A piece of flak came up through the bottom of the ship and went through his A-3 bag which was right beside his feet, just missing his knees.

Discharged June 8, 1945 with the rank staff sergeant. Received the Distinguished Flying Cross, Air Medal with three Oak Leaf Clusters and EAME Ribbon with Battle Star.

Married Mable E. Marker in 1948, they have four children: Ramona, Dennis, Daniel and Angela; eight grandchil-

dren; and two great-grandchildren. Oldest son Dennis was killed in Vietnam. Peterson worked in a rubber factory, hardware store clerk and farmed. Currently is retired.

JOHN G. PETROCELLI (PETE), was born Conemaugh, PA, May 16, 1919. Moved to Altoona, PA in 1926. Entered USAAC Dec. 10, 1941. Attended Air Corps Schools at Biloxi, MS and Farmingdale, NY. Was member of cadre out of Tucson that formed 389th Bomb Group.

Attained rank of master sergeant; was crew chief of B-24 Liberator *Fightin' Sam* that saw action in Middle East, Africa and Europe. *Fightin Sam* flew whole war without aborting a mission. The 389th Bomb Group participated in Ploesti Oil Field Raid Aug. 1, 1943. Among first groups to bomb Rome. Over 300 missions were flown by 389th Bomb Group.

Petrocelli received the Presidential Unit Citation, Bronze Star Medal, ETO Ribbon with nine Campaign Stars and other ribbons.

After war Petrocelli opened and operated two automotive radiator, cooling systems, air conditioning works for 30 years before retiring. Married Nancy Ferguson on Dec. 22, 1942 and has three daughters and two grandchildren. His wife passed away in May 1973.

JAMES C. PICKETT, was born April 27, 1924 in Finchville, KY. Enlisted in the USAF July 8, 1942. Assigned to the 446th Bomb Group, 705th Sqdn., Bungay. Completed 35 missions in ETO.

Discharged Dec. 31, 1972 with the rank brigadier general (KYANG). Received the Distinguished Flying Cross, Air Medal with three clusters and ETO Ribbon.

Married and has two children. Pickett is currently retired.

RALPH PIETRANGELO, was born Jan. 25, 1917 in Rhodesdale, OH and enlisted in the USAAC on Dec. 17, 1940. Was an aviation cadet, completed flight training, and commissioned Feb. 22, 1943 as a second lieutenant navigator at Hondo, TX.

Flew 28 combat missions with the 389th Bomb Group from Hethel, England, Tripoli and Benghazi, North Africa. Most memorable missions were Rome RR yards, Italy, first mission July 19, 1943; Ploesti Oil Field Aug. 1, 1943; Berlin March 22, 1944; and his last mission Oldenburg, Germany, May 30, 1944.

Separated from the service Dec. 17, 1946 with the rank of major. He received the Distinguished Flying Cross with Oak Leaf and five Air Medals.

Married Anna G. and has one son and two grandchildren. He is presently retired.

ROBERT J. PINTER, was born Oct. 12, 1918 in Youngstown, OH. Joined the USAAC on Sept. 4, 1941. Stationed at Cherry Point, NC; Hammer Field, New Bern, NC; Alameda Naval Base; Rackheath Air Base, crew chief 2-B-24.

Memorable experiences: was almost lost on Anti-Sub Patrol; picked to inspect bomb damage in Frankfort, Germany two weeks after Gen. Patton went through.

Discharged Sept. 20, 1945 with the rank master sergeant. Received the EAME Theater Ribbon with six Bronze Stars, American Theater Ribbon, American Defense Medal, Good Conduct Ribbon, Bronze Star Medal and anti-Sub Squadron HQ 44.

Married Nov. 27, 1947 to Dorothy Kornyak. There were no children. He managed a grocery store for 40 years, now retired.

CHARLES A. PIPER, was born July 31, 1921 in New Castle, NH. Enlisted Oct. 22, 1942 in the USAAC. Stationed at Hethel England with 389th Bomb Group, 564th Pathfinder Sqdn. and Wendling, England with 392nd Bomb Group, 564th Sqdn. Completed 24 combat missions, ETO as tail gunner.

Memorable experience was being shot down on 24th mission on April 29, 1944 during Berlin raid.

Discharged Aug. 19, 1945 with the rank of staff sergeant. Received the Distinguished Flying Cross, Air Medal with five clusters, Purple Heart, POW Medal, Good Conduct with clasp and numerous campaign medals.

Married with four children, six grandchildren and five great-grandchildren. Retired as of Jan. 1, 1969 after Korea, USAFR and civil service.

ALBERT F. PISHIONERI, was born in Hillsville, PA on Jan. 30, 1921. CDT St. Vincent College, Latrobe, PA; Nashville Classification Center; Armament School, Buckley Field, CO; Air Gunnery School, Harlingen, TX; OTU, Westover, MA.

Flew B-24L to Dow Field, ME then Goose Bay Labrador and Iceland, October 1944, Holyhead, Wales. Next by rail to Bungay, home of the 446th Bungay Buckeroos (B-24s). Flew ball turret gunner on *Patriotic Patty.*

Flew his first mission to Minden, Germany on November 25 and completed his 35th mission to Landshut, April 16, 1945. Back to the States on May 23, 1945, rehabilitated at Santa Ana, CA and Pampa Air Base, TX.

Discharged from Lubbock Air Base, TX on Oct. 11, 1945. Retired from St. Vincent College after 40 years of teaching in 1985.

Married Lillian E. Frichtel, Nov. 27, 1947. His family includes Felicia, Larry and Rich. He is now enjoying life with his two granddaughters who live just around the block from him in Freehold, NJ.

RICHARD L. PITTENGER (DICK), was born April 11, 1916 in Richland County, Shelby, OH. Enlisted Oct. 7, 1942 in the USAAC, Air Force, Ohio Air Guard. Stationed in San Antonio, Ft. Stocton, San Angelo, Class 43-K Waco, TX, Liberal, KS, Casper, WY and with the 8th AAF, 389th Bomb Group in Norwich, England.

Completed 35 missions. Retired January 1972 with the rank lieutenant colonel. Received the Distinguished Flying Cross, Air Medal with four clusters, ETO with four stars, WWII Victory, AF Longevity Service Medal with Oak Leaf Cluster, AFRM with Hour Glass and National Defense Medal.

Married since January 1937.

WILSON H. PITTS, was born June 10, 1925 in Winston-Salem, NC and enlisted Aug. 17, 1943. Assigned to 8th Air Force, 491st Bomb Group, 853rd Sqdn. (B-24s). Stationed at Westover Field, MA; North Pickenham, England; Keesler Field, MS; Gunnery School, Tyndall Field, FL; Chatham Field, GA; and Langley Field, VA.

Participated in five major European Battles and completed 21 combat missions (B-24). Memorable experience was low level supply drop to paratroopers in Holland, five wounded, crash landed in England; became POW on 21st mission.

Discharged Oct. 29, 1945, Greensboro, NC and later achieved the rank colonel AFR (RET). Received three Air Medals, five major Battle Stars and POW Medal.

Married Mary E. Ragland June 29, 1946, has two sons and seven grandchildren. Retired as AT&T Co. security officer. Now owns restaurant and health food store in Winston-Salem, NC.

MILTON M. PLANCHE, was born Jan. 7, 1920 in Brooklyn, NY and enlisted in the USAAC March 1942. Graduated as navigator, second lieutenant, Class 43-3 at Hondo, TX. Assigned 392nd Bomb Group at Tucson, AZ in April 1943. Trained at Alamogordo, NM. Group accepted first of B-24Hs at Topeka, KS. Assigned to John Reade's crew 578th Sqdn. August 1943. Completed 28 combat missions in May 1944; included a memorable North Sea Diver-

sion, Oct. 4, 1943; Kjeller, Norway, Nov. 18, 1943; Gotha (the big one for 392nd), Feb. 24, 1944; Erkner (Berlin), May 8, 1944 and Politz (Stettin), May 29, 1944.

Inactive duty, June 1945. Received BBA from Pace College, NY in 1950; MBA from Hofstra College, NY, 1959. Left the inactive Reserve with rank of major.

Retired from Shell Oil Co. with 45 years service with various group Co's. Married Mary Bernice James, Uvalde, TX, Feb. 13, 1943. They have one son (helicopter pilot in Vietnam), one lovely daughter and six grandchildren.

WARREN A. POLKING, was born on a farm just west of Breda, IA on Dec. 9, 1917 in the middle of the night in a howling blizzard. The only light was from a kerosene lamp, water was carried from a well about 30 yards away and heated on a stove burning corn cobs. Dr. Jones, who aided in the delivery, drove out from town in his horse and buggy on a dirt road clogged with snow drifts.

Polking's mother was a schoolteacher and a graduate of the University of Iowa. She had a major "I" in womens' intercollegiate sports. His father was a farmer, banker and small businessman.

Two of his brothers served in the USAAC in WWII, his sister's husband was in the Army Infantry. His third and younger brother lost his life in 1951 piloting a USAF jet interceptor F-86D fighter.

Prior to WWII he was flying instructor, flight commander, engineering officer at Randolph Field, TX. Then instructor, flight commander, Provisional Group Commander, B-17 and B-24 combat crew training.

In January 1943, he had the privilege of becoming the first commander of the 578th Bombardment Sqdn. (H), 392nd Bomb Group, which he helped organize, train, and lead in combat, their first mission being on Sept. 9, 1943 on which he flew.

Flew 25 combat missions as command pilot on division wing, group, and squadron leads, to targets in Germany, France, Holland, and Norway, the last being to Erfurt, Germany on July 20, 1944.

While assigned as commander of the 578th, he was promoted from captain to major in April of 1943 and to lieutenant colonel in March 1944.

Having volunteered for a second combat tour, went to the States for a 30 day leave and just before getting on the *Queen Mary* to return to England, he was ordered to the Training Command where he served in different command and staff positions.

Then back to England to fly with the British Royal Air Force for a year, flying just about every type aircraft in the RAF.

After duty in the States, assigned to the U.S. Embassy, Paris, France, working in the military foreign aid program. Married Miss Dette Hagan from Shreveport, LA on July 26, 1951 in Paris where they spent three wonderful years.

After that a year in the Air War College, then four years in the Pentagon, one year in Air Force policy planning and three years in joint strategic planning, office of the Joint Chiefs of Staff.

Then several years in Tokyo, Japan, and back to Randolph AFB where he suffered a heart attack and lengthy hospitalization, requiring his retirement from the Air Force in October 1966. He had achieved the rank of colonel in Paris in 1951 and was a command pilot with a Green Card Instrument Rating.

After spending some time at their home on the Texas coast, they moved to Mexico where they spent 15 years getting well. Dette resumed her oil painting and it was a great 15 years. They left Mexico in January 1982 for California where they lived in the San Francisco and San Diego areas, with long trips to Europe and a year near New Orleans.

After being treated for lung cancer in San Diego, they came to San Antonio in 1988 and are still there. They try to make the 2nd Air Div. and 392nd Bomb Group reunions where they find so great the renewal and keeping alive of the friendships of their old comrades in arms and their loved ones.

LEONARD PONDER, was born July 27, 1922 in East Point, GA. Grew up there until he joined the USAAC in November 1942. His basic training was at Miami Beach, FL.

From there to Gulfport, MS for Mechanical School and from there to Nevada for aerial gunnery training. Then to Denver, CO for bomber training. Assigned to the 8th Air Force, 446th Bomb Group as a flight engineer.

Arrived in England after flying the southern route: South America, Africa and Europe. Completed 14 combat missions, but on his 15th mission, March 22, 1944, target-Berlin, his plane was hit by flak and lost formation. Landed on an island (Gotland) in the Baltic Sea and was interned in Sweden for the duration of the war.

Returned home to his wife; they now have three children and three grandchildren. Retired after 43 years with the Western Electric Company, now known as AT&T Co. in June 1984.

EMILIO A. PONTILLO, was born June 10, 1921 in Clearfield, PA. He entered the USAAF on Feb. 8, 1943. Enlisted July 22, 1942, Air Force Cadet. Stationed at Casper, WY, phase training; Biloxi, MS, basic training and airplane mechanics; Harlingen, TX for Gunnery School and training.

Assigned to 489th Bomb Group, 845th Sqdn., Halesworth, England. His first mission was July 6, 1944, Kiel, Germany and his last (35th) mission was Nov. 6, 1944. On their 10th mission, with new pilot Capt. Allen, they had a belly landing coming back from Rouen, France. Their target was gas storage tanks. Their nose wheel would not go down and not enough time to crank the nose wheel manually when they came in for landing, one engine out.

Discharged Oct. 5, 1945 with the rank tech sergeant, flight engineer, gunner. Received the Distiguished Flying Cross, Air Medal with three Oak Leaf Clusters. EAME Service Medal with three Bronze Stars.

Married with four children and five step-children. He is semi-retired from real estate sales.

EDWARD POPEK, was born March 1, 1922 near Wild Rose, WI, the youngest of nine children. Two brothers had enlisted in the Air Force but neither qualified for flight training but insisted that kid-brother should fly. Enlisted in Air Force Reserve in September 1942 and reported to SAAC in San Antonio in March 1943. Completed flight training, commissioned January 1944, assigned to four engines at Liberal, then sent to Casper to prepare for combat.

Flew a replacement to Wales. Was assigned to 577th Sqdn., 392nd Bomb Group. Flew first mission in August 1944 and 35th in March 1945.

Returned to Milwaukee, tended bar, sold real estate, moved to Kansas City to attend the University. Graduated with MA, history and government, taught in secondary schools for 32 years until retiring in 1984.

Greatest impression was being part of a huge Air Force as demonstrated in 1,000 plane raids with a bomber stream extending from England to Berlin.

Popek is married, has twin daughters, both doctors in Houston.

THADDEUS C. POPRAWA, was born Jan. 20, 1923 in Detroit, MI; drafted March 23, 1943; basic at St. Petersburg, FL; CTD University of Alabama, SAC Kelly Field, TX; Aerial Gunnery, Laredo, TX; navigation pre-flight, Ellington Field, TX; Nav. Advanced School, San Marcos,m TX; B-24 phase training, March Field, CA; .

To ETO aboard the *Queen Mary* November 1944; assigned to 564th Sqdn., 389th Bomb Group, Hethel. Completed 30 missions December 1944-April 1945 as wing crew (several as deputy lead) including three to Berlin, emergency landing in Belgium at RAF base.

Flew home June 1945, Wales, Azores, Goose Bay, Conn. After 30 days R&R, Sioux Falls, SD. Was discharged October 1945. Earned BSME degree from University of Detroit, February 1951. Worked for all the car companies in Detroit.

Married to Virginia, February 1979, no children. His hobbies are golf, bridge, and skiing. He resides in Fraser, MI summers and winters in Florida.

FREDERICK R. PORTER, was born Oct. 30, 1918 in Detroit, MI.

Joined the USAAC June 4, 1943. Basic training in Lincoln, NE; ordinance training in Santa Ana, CA; and then replacement pool in Salt Lake City, UT. The 467th was in third phase training when he arrived at Wendover, stationed at Rackheath, UK.

His brother Don flew with the 9th Air Force and was also stationed in England. He managed to fly his plane to Rackheath from his base. The rationale which permitted this was that he brought the chaplain from his base to confer with our chaplain. Porter later received word from home that he had been shot down over France. There was later word that he was a prisoner of war. He was liberated by Gen. Patton's army and visited Porter at Rackheath one more time before going home.

After a month of leave at home, the group went to Sioux Falls, SD to be reassigned to the Pacific Theater of Operations. Fortunately the war ended before that reassignment took place.

The 467th Bomb Group (H) consisted of four bomb squadrons and various support activities. Porter was in the 790th Bomb Sqdn.

Discharged Oct. 23, 1945 with the rank of corporal. Received the EAME Ribbon and the Good Conduct.

Married since April 28, 1946 to Connie, they have three sons and eight grandchildren. Porter retired from Ford Motor Co. in 1985.

MARCUS L. POTEET JR., was born Aug. 6, 1922 in Lincoln, NE. Joined the USAAC Feb. 10, 1943, MOS 1034 (B-24) navigator. Stationed at Sheppard Field, TX; Jamestown, ND; Santa Ana, CA; Ellington Field, Houston, TX; Gowen Field, Boise, ID; San Marcos, TX.

Assigned to 852nd Sqdn., 491st Bomb Group, North Pickenham, UK; McChord Field, Tacoma, WA; navigator on Randolph's crew.

Memorable experience was getting hit by flak at Macdeburg, Germany on March 3, 1945. Managed to limp back to England. Lost one engine and most of power in another. Landed at Woodbridge, damage to the plane was so severe that the ship was used for spare parts.

Discharged Oct. 8, 1945 with the rank second lieutenant. Received three Air Medals, two European Battle Stars and the Presidential Unit Citation.

Married Feb. 17, 1951 to Virginia Lee. They have a daughter, Mary Poteet, who is a lawyer in Anchorage, AK, and two grandchildren, Katie and Jennie. Poteet retired after 30 years with Goodyear, Lincoln, NE; also owned, farmed, manager of 2,700 acres in Nebraska.

JACK T. POTTLE, was born July 2, 1924 in Burnham, MO.

Drafted in USAAC June 1943. Stationed at Keesler Field; Tyndall Field, Sananch AAFB, Hethel Field, England and Fort Myers, FL.

Memorable experience was April 7, 1945 mission to Duneberg.

Discharged December 1945 with the rank tech sergeant. Received the Distinguished Unit Citation, WWII Victory Medal, Good Conduct Medal, ETO with four Battle Stars and American Campaign

Married and has three children and six grandchildren. Pottle is retired.

NORMAN A. POWELL, was born July 29, 1923 in Carmel, ME near Bangor. Joined the USAAC in January 1943. Basic training at Keesler Field; Field Baking Camp Lee; Cooking Bomber Base, New Orleans; Orderly BOQ, Brookly Field, Mobile; Camp Kilmer and overseas to Greenock, Scotland.

Arrived at Shipdham, Norfolk, England in October 1943. DRO at Combat Officers' Mess until March of 1945 when he went to Wiltshire Plains for training as an infantry rifleman. He broke his ankle and heel on the obstacle course and spent nearly six months in hospitals in England and USA.

Went to Husson College and University of Maine and became a business education teacher in Maine and later in Vermont. Now lives at birthplace with his lovely wife of 40 years. Their four children live in New York City, San Francisco and two in Vermont.

WILLIAM FREDERICK POWELL, was born Feb. 10, 1923, Whistler, AL. Entered the service Oct. 24, 1942. Received basic and aviation mechanics training at Keesler Field, MS. Trained on B-24 aircraft at Willow Run, MI; graduated Aerial Gunnery at Harlingen, TX; sent to Salt Lake City, UT where crew was formed (his position: flight engineer and tail gunner); then on to Sioux City, IA to become part of 445th Bomb Group, 702nd Bomb Sqdn.

Further training at Boise, ID and finally Watertown, SD qualified their crew in September or October 1943 for a new B-24H, later christened *Big Time Operator* (BTO). Departed USA November flying southern route: Puerto Rico, South America, Africa. Arrived Tibenham, Norfolk County, England to begin combat operations December 1943.

Their short spell of good luck ended Easter Sunday, April 9, 1944 en route to target, Tutow, when their liberator took a direct hit from a 20mm cannon. Unable to stay in formation and with questionable gas supply, their pilot was faced with three choices: going down behind enemy lines, the icy Baltic, or trying to make Sweden. He wisely chose the latter. Fortunately, with the help of a heads up navigator, he was successful.

After six months internment, they were smuggled in November from Sweden to England by the Carpet Baggers and received orders to return to America.

Discharged Oct. 24, 1945. Decorations include the EAME Service Ribbon with four Bronze Stars, Air Medal, Oak Leaf Cluster and Presidential Unit Citation.

Three days after discharge he married Lataine Houston, a native of Union, MS. They have three children, seven grandchildren and three great-grandchildren. As of today they are still living the American dream.

CHARLES HENRY PRATT, was born in Warsaw, NY on May 1, 1915 and moved to Shreveport, LA in 1938. Was drafted April 1942; basic in Louisiana; trained at Fort Monmouth, NJ as a radio repairman in the 315th Signal Corps.

He was sent to Scotland on the *Queen Mary* on which trip during a storm the ship nearly turned on her side. Their company was sent to Horsham St. Faiths, Norwich, England attached to the 2nd Air Div., later moved to Ketteringham Hall. At close of war in Europe their company was the only one in the division scheduled to go directly to the Pacific without returning to the United States. Japan surrendered when they were at the point of embarkation.

While returning to the States on the *Queen Mary* he assisted in issuing the ships paper. He was discharged in October 1945 as a tech sergeant after three years overseas.

Married Louise E. Culbertson on July 3, 1941. They have one son Craig and two grandchildren, Christopher and Kimberly. After working for United Gas Pipe Line Co. for 40 years he retired as supervisor of drafting and computer drafting. Pratt now lives in Shreveport, LA where he is active in church and various organizations.

JOHN L. PREDGEN (PREDGE), was born in Staunton, IL on Jan. 23, 1921. Entered the USAAC in August 1942. Received pilot training at Nashville, TN, Americus, GA and graduated from Blytheville, AR as second lieutenant, Class 43-J. He was sent to Salt Lake City for assembling of the crew and to B-24 bombardment training at Casper, WY.

Their crew #2937 flew to Goose Bay over the Atlantic to Preswick, Scotland. Assigned to Halesworth, England and flew 34 missions with the 489th Bomb Group, 845th Sqdn. The 25th mission to Groesbeek, Holland was the worst. They crash landed at Woodbridge.

Predgen returned to the States December 1944. He received the Distinguished Flying Cross, three Air Medals and several others. Served in Korea 1952 in AACS.

Married Peggy Fettinger on May 20, 1955. He has three children and four grandchildren. Predgen is currently retired.

ADOLF J. PRIBUSH, volunteered for the USAAC in 1942. He was assigned as radio operator with the Auzie E. Cearnal crew. Their first mission was June 11, 1944 with the 389th Bomb Group (H) at Hethel, England. In addition to radio his job was to handle the bomb doors on the bomb run. The crew said they knew how the flak was by his actions. If it was intense, the doors were closed immediately after bombs away and he would say "Let's get out of here." On their 22nd mission their instruments were shot out and he had to take radio fixes to aid in navigation.

Completed 30 missions and returned to the States in October 1944 with the tech sergeant. Pribush received the Distinguished Flying Cross, Air Medal with three clusters, EAME Campaign with four stars, American Theater and the WWII Victory Medal.

ORA M. PRICE, was born Nov. 7, 1924 in Oblong, IL. Was drafted April 1943 in the USAAC. Basic at Greensboro, NC; ASTP, University of Maine; Armament School, Lowry Field, CO; Gunnery School, Harlingen, TX; phase training, Charleston, SC.

Arrived in Hethel, England November 1944 with the 389th Bomb Group, 565th Sqdn., was waist gunner on B-24s. Completed 30 plus missions and then R&R, Santa Ana, CA.

Discharged Oct. 11, 1945, Scott Field, IL with the rank staff sergeant. Received the Air Medal with four clusters.

Has BS from Utah State Ag. College. Married and has two sons and one daughter.

Retired after 33 years, fisheries biologist with Illinois Dept. of Conservation. He says he wouldn't take a million dollars for experiences, but wouldn't give a dollar to go through it again.

ARTHUR L. PRICHARD, was born Oct. 9, 1920 in Gaylord, MI. Attended schools in this area. Enlisted in the USAAC May 1942. Graduated from George Field, Lawrenceville, IL in July 1943. Assigned as a right seat pilot in B-24s in 467th Bomb Group.

Went overseas with original cadre in March 1944. Flew combat against Germany from April to August 1944. June 12, 1944 went down when bomb load blew up. Was first allied bomber to land in Normandy after invasion.

Returned to States in September. Taught Chinese cadets in AT6, flew C-47 2nd Air Force Air Transport, flew B-17s, B-25s, B-29s, C-45s and towed gliders in C-46s. Was glider instructor in CG4A and CG-15s. Retired as lieutenant colonel. Awarded the Distinguished Flying Cross with one Oak Leaf Cluster, Air Medal with three Oak Leaf Clusters and the ETO Medal with Battle Stars.

Married Irene Palmer on March 13, 1943, no children.

ROY J. PRIMM, entered the USAAC in December 1942. Went to Engineering/Technical School in Colorado, joined the 458th Bomb Group, 755th Bomb Sqdn. in Wendover, UT. Overseas training in Tonopah, NV.

Arrived Station 123, Horsham St. Faith, Norwich, England January 1944. Worked with engineering/crew chiefs/mechanics in total maintenance of squadron aircraft.

Most memorable of all experiences was April 1945 "low-level" trolley mission over Nazis Germany with targets like Hamburg, Osnabruck, Hamm, Dortmund, Munich, Frankfurt, Cologne, etc.; to witness the complete devastation of enemy, made all the months of sacrifice, sweat and toil worthwhile.

Spent 24 years with Lanier, Atlanta, GA and 24 years with Philips Lighting. He is now retired. Married 47 years to Sue, they have a son Tom (Captain in U.S. Air) and two grandsons Christopher and Matthew.

JEROME S. BERNSTEIN-PRINCE, was born Nov. 1, 1921 in Baltimore, MD. Was accepted for pilot training in USAAC by letter from President Roosevelt, July 1941. Cadet training in Montgomery, AL; pilot training in Ocala, FL; AT-6 training in Greenville, MS. Graduated advance flight training, second lieutenant, Georgefield, IL.

Served nine months, twin engine anti-submarine patrol over Atlantic coast. Dropped depth charges on German sub in coastal waters off South Carolina Coast. Graduated heavy bomber pilot training from Gowan Field in Boise, ID.

Flew with crew of 10 men via North Africa to England. Stationed near Tibenham, England, February 1944 at the 445th Heavy Bombardment Group HQ. Flew 35 bombing missions over Europe without serious casualty.

Returned to the States on the *Queen Mary* in October 1944. Recalled 1951 to 1953 and was active in Korean War with rank of captain. Received the Distinguished Flying Cross, 445th Commendation, Croix de Guerre, Air Medal with three Oak Leaf Clusters and others.

Retired in Oregon and is writer of exciting WWII novels. Married twice, he has three children and two grandchildren.

RICHARD C. PRINCE, was born June 28, 1921 in Jerome, AZ. After two and a half years of engineering study at the University of Arizona, Tucson, he joined the USAAC in January 1943. Undertook cadet pilot training in California and Arizona and graduated in Class 44C, March 1944.

Joined B-24 crew as co-pilot at March Field, CA and then assigned to 389th Bomb Group in Hethel, England in July 1944. Completed tour of 35 combat missions over Germany without serious mishap. Ferried a plane load of fighter pilots back to USA June 1945.

Discharged November 1945 at McClellan Field, Sacramento, CA. Completed education and received BS in EE at University of California, Berkeley in 1948. Joined Bechtel Corp., an engineering construction firm based in San Francisco. After 35 years with this firm and extensive world travel, he retired in 1983.

Married while in college and before joining USAAC, he has five children and 12 grandchildren.

WILLIAM D. PROPPE, was born in Portland, OR on Jan. 4, 1923. Called up for active duty as a cadet in spring of 1943. Sent to KSTC, Emporia for CTD. Trained in Gulf Coast Command, Class of 44E at San Antonio, Muskogee, Coffeeville, Frederick, Liberal and finally at Tucson Davis-Monthan.

Flew B-24 to England via Goose Bay in January 1945. Assigned to 466th Bomb Group (H) 785th Sqdn. Flew 18 missions as deputy squadron lead, great crew members, awarded three Battle Stars and three Air Medals. Survived three missions to Berlin and a direct hit in the left wing over Essen. Shell exploded 20 feet above the Martin turret with no damage to crew.

Flew B-24 home via Iceland. Brief time in ATC, Long Beach. Discharged on points November 1945 as first lieutenant.

Degrees from Oregon State, Stanford and the University of Portland. Spent 40 great years as a pedagogue and administrator. Married and has three children and several grandchildren.

PETER PROTICH, was born Aug. 11, 1917 in Philadelphia, PA. Moved to Maple Shade, NJ in 1921. Enlisted in the USAAC Dec. 10, 1941. A/M School then England in August 1942. Aviation Cadet in U.S. in 1943, second lieutenant pilot, Class 44B. B-24 transition, Smyrna, TN and was assigned his own crew.

Assigned to 715th Bomb Sqdn., 448th Bomb Group in England in July 1944. Completed 35 combat missions over Germany. One forced landing in France and one Belgium. Both times bringing the damaged B-24 over the battle lines to land in allied territory. "Week End Warrior" after the war and worked at the Philadelphia Naval Air Experimental Station.

Completed course at Georgetown University School of Foreign Service majoring in psychological warfare and Georgetown University School of Languages and Linguistics specializing in the Serbo-Croatian language and the history and culture of the people of Jugoslavia.

Recalled to active duty for Korean War, attached to the Jugoslav Desk, Voice of America which included live radio broadcasts to Jugoslavia in both English and the Serbo-Croatian language. Then Tripoli, Libya as psychological warfare officer and language intelligence officer chief of psychological warfare team covering the Balkan area. Also a pilot in the Air-Sea Rescue unit flying the SA-16 seaplane. Travelled extensively in the North African and Mediterranean area from Casablanca and Marrakech to the island of Cyprus for staff studies. 1965 active reservist assigned to HQ USAF, Washington, DC as Intelligence staff officer.

Retired in 1972 as lieutenant colonel with 30 good years active and reserve.

Protich is a professional violinist and piano technician. Married Elizabeth Uherko 1945. They have one daughter Elizabeth and two grandchildren, Scott and Laura.

JACK C. PRUITT, was born July 27, 1917 in Osceola, TX, a small town south of Dallas, TX. Graduated from Baylor University in Waco, TX in 1940. Became an aviation cadet

in the Class of 41-H. After Pearl Harbor he became a flight instructor of aviation cadets in Advance Flying School in Lubbock, TX. He requested combat duty and became a B-24 bomber pilot. He assembled his combat crew in Clovis, NM. After training the navigator in the new radar navigation program at Langley Field, VA, he flew the North Atlantic route to England in a B-24 equipped with radar navigational aids installed.

In April 1944 he joined the 565th Sqdn., 389th Bomb Group, stationed in Hethel near Norwich, England. He flew B-24 bombers on 32 missions, two on D-day, and his crew was credited with four and a half German fighter planes knocked out of the skies with no injuries to his crew.

He then returned to the States and became an instructor in B-29s at the Kirtland AAB, Albuquerque, NM training crews for combat in the Pacific combat zone. While stationed at Kirtland, the war ended. He requested and received his discharge in December 1945 with the rank of captain. Received the Distinguished Flying Cross, Air Medal with four clusters and many campaign ribbons.

Pruitt returned to his home in Hillsboro, TX with his wife and entered into the business, civic and social life of the community. He has two sons, of whom he is very proud, four grandchildren and one great-grandchild. He is semi-retired, but still leads a busy life and enjoys traveling with his wife of 52 years.

DONALD V. PRYOR, was born in Bridgewater, ME on Dec. 14, 1924. Grew up in Medford, MA and played on the high school soccer and basketball teams. While attending Tufts University, played Freshman basketball and Varsity soccer. Enlisted in the USAAC in June 1943. After aviation cadet training at Ellington Field, completed navigation training at San Marcos, TX in July 1944. Crew assignment and training was at March Field, CA.

Arrived in England aboard the *Queen Mary*, November 1944. Joined the 445th Bomb Group (B-24) in Tibenham. His pilot, Richard Klopfenstein was killed on his orientation mission to Hanau with another crew. His original crew co-pilot, Lyman Bates, was killed on a training mission, days before last mission of war to Salzburg.

Received five Air Medals, three European Campaign Stars and 445th Group Presidential Citation and 445th Group Croix de Guerre with Palm. Separated in August 1945 at Greensboro, NC, where he had started with basic training.

Returned to Tufts University and graduated in 1948. Pryor has three children and one grandchild. In 1970s he became vice president of the Chelsea Clock Co. In the 1980s started his own clock company, Quincy Ltd. He moved back to Maine in 1992.

DONALD PRYTULAK (PUTCH), was born Dec. 14, 1916 in Darby, CT. Grew up in Connellsville, PA. Joined the USAAC in September 1939 as a private. Promoted through the ranks to staff sergeant, then entered Aviation Cadets in December 1942, graduating from Valdosta August 1943 as a second lieutenant, Class 43H.

After training in Alamogordo on April 1, 1944 with a 19 year old navigator, he flew his B-24 via South America, Dakar, and on to N. Pickenham, England. He completed 29 missions with the 492nd Bomb Group before its remaining planes and men were reassigned. His final two missions were out of Rackheath. On one mission, his group of B-24s had to join the gaggle in the wrong position, as another group was in their slot. That entire group of 14 planes was shot out of the air—from the position that should have been his groups.

Returned to the States September 1944. Spent time at Victorville and Bakersfield before being assigned to Berlin and C-47s in May 1945. Flew Berlin Airlift April-September 1948. After assignments at Sherman, TX and Lowry AFB, CO, was stationed at Yokota, Japan in RB-50s. Experienced rockets fired at him and MIGS being scrambled while recon over Russia. Another flight had him bring back an RB-50 that had lost 89 inches of horizontal stabilizer due to an escaping life raft. This earned him the "Order of the Able Aeronaut" award.

Before his retirement from Turner AFB, GA as a major on Sept. 30, 1960, he had received two Distinguished Flying Crosses, six Air Medals, four European Campaign Stars and many other ribbons.

Married Shirley A. English on October 2, 1943. They had two married daughters and four grandsons. He passed away Nov. 10, 1989. *Submitted by his daughter Lorraine Prytulak Williford.*

BEATRICE B. PUCH, was born in Paterson, NJ on Oct. 7, 1916, the sixth of nine children. She enlisted in the Women's Army Auxiliary Corps in August 1942 and began a long and distinguished career which spanned 26 years and included service in the ETO during WWII and culminating with her retirement at Randolph AFB, TX in March of 1968 with the rank master sergeant.

Her military service included assignments at Ft. Des Moines, IA; HQ, 2nd Bomb Wing (B-24 Liberator) in the United Kingdom (which was subsequently known as the 2nd Air Div.) and the 40th Bomb Wing, 1st Air Div. in Southern France. While in Europe she also served as assistant to the supply officer, WAC Detachment, HQ USAFE, Germany.

Upon her return she had assignments to Mitchell AFB, where she re-enlisted and performed duties at HQ, Continental Air Command, Logistics as a member of the Women's Air Force. After assignments to Larson AFB and Long Beach Municipal Airport, she proceeded to duty at Ramstein, Germany as a first sergeant. While there she attended the NCO Academy and was one of three honor graduates in a class of 150 and was the recipient of the Commandant's Award. She subsequently served as first sergeant of the WAF School Sqdn. at Lackland AFB and of the WAF Sqdn. at Randolph AFB. In the year prior to her retirement, she served as NCOIC of Administration for the Special Services Unit as Randolph AFB. She retired March 1, 1968.

Master Sgt. Puch's decorations include the ETO Ribbon with six Battle Stars, Commendation Medal, Good Conduct Medal with clasp and two knots, WWII Victory Medal, American Theater Ribbon and the Longevity Ribbon with four clusters.

She is a resident of Universal City, TX and is the owner-operator of the Enchanted Cottage Florist and Ceramic Shop in Schertz, TX.

FLOYD J. PUGH, was born Dec. 31, 1920. Enlisted in the USAAC on Aug. 6, 1942 and graduated pilot Class 43K and commissioned second lieutenant Dec. 5, 1943, Pampa, TX. Assigned co-pilot, B-24, Wendover AAF, Wendover, UT with 467th Bomb Group, 791st Sqdn. Departed the States for England via southern route arriving Rackheath, UK.

Participated in the groups first combat mission, groups first mission to Berlin and first mission on D-day. Finished 30 missions June 1944. Sustained a few flak holes and one feathered engine. Cold sweat memories: Splasher five rendezvous. Just memories: British designed three cushion cot for a bed; steak for chow after first Berlin mission, 100 mission party with the fallen cake.

Returned stateside via *Mariposa* in September 1944. Assigned to Victorville, CA flying radar trainees. Discharged into active reserve September 1945 (troop carrier). Recalled February 1951 (Korea) Strategic Air Command. Retired from the USAF September 1972.

Married Anne Copley in May 1947, they have two daughters and five grandchildren.

CECIL L. PULLEN (VERN), was born in Foss, OK on Oct. 29, 1923. Graduated from Elk City, Oklahoma High School in May 1941. After one year with the FBI in Washington, DC, he enlisted in the USAAC as air cadet. Was commissioned second lieutenant July 31, 1944 after graduation from Navigation School at San Marcus, TX AAF. He was assigned to Ken Wheeler's crew on B-24 aircraft at Walla Walla, WA.

November 1944 arrived at Seething, England; assigned to 713th Sqdn., 448th Bomb Group; transferred December 1944 to 712th Sqdn. as a lead crew with radar. Flew a total of 24 combat missions in Europe.

He received the Distinguished Flying Cross, four Air Medals and three Battle Stars. He was promoted to first lieutenant March 1945. After European hostilities ceased, he was assigned to B-29 training at Great Bend, KS until the surrender of Japan.

Married Anita Lou Maltbie from Seminole, OK on June 17, 1950. They have two sons. Currently resides in Edmond, OK. He is semi-retired in the insurance business.

THOMAS F. PURCELL, was born Nov. 22, 1917 at Valatie, NY. Graduated Class of 42K, Lubbock, TX in November 1942. Was one of the original pilots with the 453rd Bomb Group, 733rd Sqdn. Trained at March Field, Riverside, CA.

Went overseas to Old Buckingham, England in January 1944. Was wounded on 8th mission on March 15, 1944 to Brunswick. Transferred to 389th Bomb Group 564th Pathfinder Sqdn. Was shot down on 17th mission June 20, 1944 by flak over Politz. Spent seven months in Stalag Luft 3 at Sagan, Poland. When Russians were sure to overrun the camp at the end of January 1945, the Germans marched ten thousand POWs 50 miles to Spremburg then loaded them into freight cars and sent them to Moosburg (Stalag 7A) where they stayed until liberated on May 1, 1945. He stayed in the reserves until 1956 when job transfer forced his retirement.

Purcell and his wife Helen celebrated their 50th anniversary on May 8, 1993. They have five children and four grandchildren. Their residence is in Wellesley, MA.

NORMAN E. PURDY, was born Oct. 15, 1916 in Hamilton County, OH and raised on a farm. Graduated from high school in 1934; attended Wilmington College, OH and taught school until he joined the USAAC in September 1941 as aviation cadet. Completed pilot training and commissioned a second lieutenant.

Assigned to 393rd Bomb Sqdn. at Mitchell Field, Long Island. Flew B-25s on anti-sub patrol. Moved to Westover Field than to Langley Field.

Flew to Scotland and continued to fly anti-subpatrol in the Bay of Biscay. Crew was assigned to 44th Bomb Group. Flew his first combat mission in November. His last three missions were the first three daylight raids on Berlin. After tour was finished, he was assigned to the 445th Group at Tibenham as briefing officer.

Returned to the States and was flight instructor at Charleston, SC, then assigned to the Air Transport Command.

Left the service in 1945 and worked at Allis Chalmers, then went to Miami University to continue his education. He received a BS in education, double major in industrial arts. Worked for the Queen City Flying Service as an instructor pilot.

Returned to school for his MS degree and was principal, superintendent, curriculum coordinator, and 4H agent. Retired from education and from the Extension Service in 1979 and has been a full-time farmer since.

Married Helen on April 26, 1942 and has two daughters, Jill and Barbara, and three grandchildren.

STANLEY J. PUSKO, was born on Jan. 14, 1919 in Chicago, IL. Joined the USAAC as an aviation cadet in April 16, 1942. Commissioned as a navigator at Hondo, TX in July 1943. First assignment was with the 17th anti-Sub-Sqdn. flying B-25 bombers out of Cuba on sub-patrol before the Navy took over.

Assigned to the 491st Bomb Group, 854th Sqnd. Flew the southern route to England as staff navigator at Metfield and later at North Pickenham. Spent his tour developing flight plans and briefing air crews on their missions.

Memorable experiences: First mission on D-day. Was impressed and awed at the historical sight of seeing the channel crawling with ships and the sky alive with aircraft as the invasion started. Market-Garden was another impressive mission on which he flew as deputy lead, a low-level mission in support of troops.

Stayed in England from May 1944-May 1945. Flew most of his missions as lead or deputy lead. Completed 30 missions and received the Distinguished Flying Cross, Air Medal with four clusters. Stayed in the Air Force and assigned to the Strategic Air Command, flying on a select crew as an atomic weapons qualified crew on B-29 and B-50 aircraft. Later became a nuclear weapons squadron commander of three different units. Later was assigned to Strategic Air Command HQ as a nuclear weapons and conventional weapons staff officer.

Retired July 1, 1967 with the rank lieutenant colonel.

E.J. PYLE, was born in Bruno, AR on Aug. 24, 1923. Entered the Air Force Feb. 1, 1943 after attending Arkansas Tech University in Russellville. After basic at Keesler Field was assigned to Radio Operator School, Scott Field. Following graduation was assigned to Gunnery School, Tyndall Field, FL. Joined Bradley Crew No. 1874 in Salt Lake City, trained at Tucson and Boise.

Arrived in England in May 1944, assigned to 458th Bomb Group. Completed 35 missions in November and returned to States in January 1945. Served as Gunnery instructor on B-32 at Fort Worth until end of hostilities.

Continued education at the University of Arkansas, graduating in 1953. Retired in 1986 from Kraft Foods after serving 33 years in various management capacities.

Married Betty Harris in September 1946. They have two daughters, Linda and Deborah.

LARRY T. PYLE, was born Jan. 12, 1921 in Ogden, UT. Joined the USAAC March 16, 1942. Stationed at various stateside locations. Discharged with the rank of staff sergeant. Currently lives in El Cerrito, CA.

RAY R. PYTEL, was born 1920 on a farm near Green Bay, WI. Family friend's use of farm aroused interest in flying. Later took courses in airplane mechanics and civilian pilot training in 1940 provided a commercial license.

Enlisted in the USAAF February 1942, pilot training put on hold due to 4th grade academic background, meanwhile took airplane mechanics course at Keesler Field, MS and Willow Run, MI; Gunnery and Submarine Observer, Laredo, TX; plus a stint on U-boat patrol with the Caribbean area during 1943.

Sent to the 8th Air Force's 445th Bomb Group via Brazil and Africa as aerial engineer. Completed 33 combat mission by Oct. 3, 1944. Assigned to Truax Field, WI as line chief until discharge Sept. 20, 1945.

Awards include the Distinguished Flying Cross, Air Medal with three Oak Leaf Clusters, four Battle Stars as well as the 445th Bomb Group's Presidential Citation and the French Croix de Guerre.

Received a degree in business administration and accounting from the University of Idaho. Employed by state of Wisconsin as consumer frauds investigator and unfair trade practices auditor until 1965, then cost accounting and budgets manager with Olin Corporation and finally as parking and transportation accounting manager with the University of Wisconsin in Madison until retirement in 1985.

JOHN E. QUEENAN JR. (JACK), was born June 6, 1921 in Burlington, NJ. He has a twin brother Martin John Queenan. They attended school together, played basketball and football together and after graduating from high school in 1939, both went to work for John A. Roebling & Sons. The twins were initiated together in Burlington Council K of C and engaged in joint gymnastics at the YMCA.

They decided to enter the Air Corps at the same time, filing their applications in Newark on March 28 and were called to active duty in 1942.

"Jack" participated in Air Offensive Europe, Normandy and Northern France as a pilot. Was discharged Oct. 19, 1945 with the rank of first lieutenant. He received the Air Medal and four Oak Leaf Clusters and the Distinguished Flying Cross.

Jack is a lawyer. His wife Bea passed away Nov. 6, 1991.

ALBERT E. QUERBACH, was born Jan. 18, 1920 in Hanston, KS. After two years of college, he enlisted in the USAAC on Nov. 12, 1941 and was assigned to Sheppard Field, TX. After completing Air Mechanic School, he worked on the line on B-17s at MacDill Field, FL. Transferred to the Aviation Cadet Corps in September 1942. Completed pilot training at Pampa, TX on July 29, 1943. After B-24 transition at Liberal, KS, he was assigned a crew and had replacement crew training at Clovis, NM and Langley Field, VA.

Left Langley with a new B-24-H, equipped with Pathfinder and a crew having two Mickey navigators and two Mickey technicians. Arrived Alconbury, England and assigned to the 445th Bomb Group, 702nd Sqdn. Flew first mission as co-pilot on lead crew, July 24, 1944 and 35th and last mission on Feb. 28, 1945. During his whole tour, he didn't have a mission abort, a crew member injured or an engine failure. He saw a lot of bad things happen to other crews but by the luck of the draw, didn't happen to them.

Returned to the USA with the rank of captain in April 1945. Was assigned to Liberal Army Airfield as a pilot instructor, then moved to Hondo Army Airfield where he continued instructing until the B-24 program closed down in December 1945. Was assigned to the Air Material Command at Wright Field where he remained until he separated from the service in December 1946.

Returned to the family farm near Hanston, KS where he still resides with his wife Dorothy. They have two sons, Robert and Edward.

ARTHUR F.J. QUINN (ART), was born in Brooklyn, NY on April 18, 1922. Drafted into the Medical Corps on

Dec. 12, 1942. Served one-half year and transferred to the USAAC in May 1943. Took cadet pilot training at Lincoln, NE and Santa Ana, CA; Radio School at Sioux Falls, SD; and Gunnery at Yuma, AZ.

Assigned as a radio operator/gunner on a B-24 at Hardwick (Norwich) England, January 1945. Flew 12 combat missions with the 93rd Bomb Group, 409th Bomb Sqdn., 2nd Air Div., 8th Air Force, Gen. Ted Timberlake's "Traveling Circus." Reassigned to the ZOI in June 1945. Was at Davis Monthan AB, Tucson, AZ when war ended. Discharged with the rank of first sergeant on Nov. 23, 1945. Was awarded the Air Medal with cluster, Good Conduct Medal, ETO, Victory Medal and credit for downing a ME-109. Married the "girl next door" Dorothy E. Downs on Nov. 9, 1946. They have four daughters, two sons and 12 grandchildren. Retired in Lancaster, PA where his family is all around him. Had a 42 year career in transportation with railroad and trucking companies. Served as a salesman and held several managerial positions. Presently enjoying leisure time at home, watching the grandchildren participate in various sport and school endeavors, playing golf, bowling, and several other hobbies.

HUBERT F. RADFORD, was born Jan. 27, 1920. Joined the Army, 9th Infantry Div., Dec. 5, 1940. Transferred to USAAC as aviation cadet July 1942; graduated, Midland AAF in April 1943 as bombardier, second lieutenant. Joined B-24 crew at Davis Monthan AFB, AZ, later assigned 409th Sqdn., 93rd Bomb Group, October 1943. Flew first five combat missions on B-24D, *Teggie Ann*.

Flew several group leads and one air division lead. Completed missions with 8th Air Force, March 23, 1944. Joined 15th Air Force, 449th Group, Italy. Flew lead or deputy lead most every mission. From May 17, 1944 through June 11, 1944, flew 15 missions, nine on consecutive days.

Retired 1962 as lieutenant colonel. Decorations included five Air Medals, Purple Heart and Distinguished Flying Cross.

Married Mary Creech, 1944; one son, one grandson. He tries to visit England or some other European country each year.

JOHN F. RAGIN JR., was born Feb. 18, 1919 in Hawkinsville, Ga. Entered the Army Oct. 15, 1941; served with 315th Signal Corps aviation in USA and European Theater of Operations and supervised the installation, repair and maintenance of telephone and telegraph communications, including switchboards and carrier terminal equipment. Also assigned work to crews and supervised up to 32 linemen, installers, construction men and maintenance men. Installed and maintained telephone and telegraph communication between divisions and groups as well as at headquarters Ketteringham Hall.

Military locations/stations: Ft. Monmouth, NJ; Bearfield, Ft. Wayne, IN; Old Catton, England; Horsham St. Faith; Ketteringham Hall

Discharged Oct. 23, 1945 with the rank of tech sergeant.

Married 48 years; has two sons, one daughter and four grandchildren. Retired after 42 years with AT&T.

JOHN R. RAINWATER, was born May 23, 1923 in Clayton, NM. Entered the USAAF March 31, 1943; served as tail gunner, B-24.

Military locations/stations: Ft. Bliss, TX; Tonopah, NV; Sheppard Field, TX; Amarillo AFT, TX; Laredo, TX and others.

Completed 35 missions on B-24; twice flew as crew member; below sea level (Death Valley and Holland). His crew lost hut mates on the day they left to return home (German jets).

Discharged Sept. 21, 1945 with the rank of staff sergeant. Received Air Medal with five Oak Leaf Clusters (35 missions) Air Offense Europe, Rhineland, Northern France, Ardennes and other.

Married Agnes Burns; they have a son, Warren; two daughters, Terry and Becky; and four grandchildren. He is retired.

GEORGE RAMERMAN, was born Oct. 15, 1923 in Zillah, WA. Entered the USAAF Jan. 19, 1943; served 526th Air Force, supply technician; 405th clerk typist; 458th Bomb Group, 754th Sqdn.

Military locations/stations: Walker, KS; Herington, KS; Horsham St. Faith, England; Orlando, FL as an instructor. Participated in battles at Rhineland.

Discharged Feb. 17, 1946 with the rank of tech sergeant. Awarded ETO Theater Medal, WWII Victory Medal, American Theater Service Medal and Good Conduct Medal.

Married Phyllis Terpstra May 22, 1947; they have a daughter, a son and two grandchildren. Retired in 1985 after 42 years as a Ford dealer parts manager.

FRANCIS X. RAMIE, was born Jan. 5, 1914 in Ogdensburg, NY. Graduated from St. Mary's Academy, June 25, 1933. Married Helen Dolores Costello Sept. 17, 1939. He was inducted into the USAF at Camp Upton, Long Island, Jan. 11, 1943. After basic training he was classified as limited service due to a punctured right ear drum. Assigned to Lawson General Hospital, Atlanta, GA, medical technician course. Completed this course and assigned to 90 Church Street, New York City, staying at Hotel Albert in Greenwich Village, NY.

At 90 Church Street he gave shots, vaccinations, and took blood pressure of new inductees into the service. After six weeks, was sent to Mitchell Field, Long Island. Assigned to the 20th Anti-Submarine Group, returning from Newfoundland.

Later was sent to Casper, WY, where the 20th changed its name to 847th Bomb Sqdn. and part of the 489th Bomb Group. Trained at Wendover Field, UT, and then to England, arriving in 1944. While in England set up a field hospital, and was the medical NCO in charge of three wards: medical, surgical and VD ward. Was chosen ward master on evening shift by flight surgeon, supervising four technicians.

Discharged Oct. 8, 1945 with the rank of corporal. Received EAME Ribbon, four Bronze Stars and Good Conduct Medal. Returned to Long Island with a wife and young baby daughter. Ramie claims it was a great experience he will never forget.

He is the proud father of two daughters and one son, and has one grandson and three granddaughters. Retired from Dairy Barn Milk Stores of Long Island in February 1979.

RICHARD I. RAMP, was born in Columbia City, IN on March 22, 1922. Enlisted March 2, 1943.

Military locations/stations: AAF basic training 521, St. Petersburg, FL; Photo Lab Tech 945 School, Lowry Field, CO; Armorer Gunner 612, Ft. Myers, FL; Air Field, Boise, ID; Gowen Field, where B-24 crew was formed; Air Field at Tibenham, Norfolk, England, Dec. 25, 1944.

Participated in 20 missions over France and Germany with the 445th Bomb Group and 702nd Bomb Sqdn. Memorable experience: March 18, 1945, Berlin mission. His crew hit by flak as they left target and had to fly home by themselves. When they got home they found a piece of flak that had stopped the engine. Ramp still has that piece of flak.

Discharged Nov. 9, 1945 with the rank of staff sergeant. Awarded Air Medal with two Oak Leaf Clusters, EAME Service Medal, Good Conduct Medal, American Theater Service Medal and WWII Victory Medal.

Married March 10, 1944 at Will Rogers Air Base, Oklahoma City, OK, to Viola Anne Binder. Has one daughter, Paula Mary Heintzelman, born Oct. 18, 1946; two grandsons: Joseph J. Heintzelman, serving in the U.S. Navy stationed on Guam; and Craig Alan Heintzelman, deceased.

He retired from the U.S. Post Office in 1984. Operated antique shop until 1992. Moved to Brodenton, FL, in July of 1992 and lives in a mobile home park. He and his wife are interested in park activities. They have family living in Brodenton.

DONALD A. RANEY, was was born Feb. 3, 1923 in Loogootee, IN. Enlisted February 1943, served in the 8th Air Force as a tail gunner in the 458th Bomb Group, 752nd Bomb Sqdn.

Basic training, Florida; A.M. School, Seymour-Johnson, NC; Gunnery School, Ft. Myers, FL.

Participated in the invasion of France flying sorties for Patton's Army at St. Lo. Memorable experience: Patton's breakthrough in France and bombing ball bearing at Hamburg, Germany.

Discharged September 1945 with the rank of staff sergeant. Received Distinguished Flying Cross and Air Medal with three clusters.

He is married and has four children. A mail carrier December 1945 to June 1972, he is retired after 28 years.

WILSON A. RAPP, was born Feb. 15, 1916 in Rochester, NY. Enlisted USAAC Jan. 2, 1942, aviation cadets and served as navigator.

Military locations/stations: Maxwell Field then Navigation School at Selman Field, Monroe, LA, graduated Class 43-D and assigned B-24s. Flew plane and crew to South America, Africa to England. Assigned to 467th Bomb Group (H) in 8th Air Force at Rackheath, England.

After 15 missions (including first 8th Air Force raid on Berlin), was transferred to 98th Bomb Group (H) in Lecce, Italy. Memorable missions here were three to Munich, five to Ploesti oil fields, Marseille, France (sub pans). Completed 50 mission tour, reassigned to Selman Field as navigation instructor.

Rapp had three brothers also in the service; one in the Marines, one with Patton's 3rd Army, and one a navigator on B-47s.

Retired as lieutenant colonel from Air Force Reserves. Awarded Distinguished Flying Cross, Air Medal with three Oak Leaf Clusters, European Campaign Medal with seven Battle Stars, American Campaign Medal, Purple Heart and two Presidential Unit Citations.

Just celebrated golden wedding anniversary with Betty. He retired from dairy industry as pasteurizer. He is active in VFW and community activities.

JACOB L. RASCH JR., was born Jan. 26, 1922 in New Orleans, LA. Entered the USAAF Nov. 23, 1942, served the 329th Bomb Sqdn., 93rd Bomb Group in England.

Military locations/stations: Keesler Field, Biloxi, MS; Lowry Field, Denver, CO; Boise, ID; Wendover Field, UT.

Completed 23 missions; shot down on 24th. Captured by Germans and spent one year as prisoner of war.

Discharged Sept. 21, 1945 with the rank of staff sergeant. Received four Air Medals, Prisoner of War Medal, and Presidential Unit Citation.

He is married and has one son. Retired from Gulf Oil Corporation and now lives is Atlanta, GA, currently a real estate agent.

HARRY N. RAWLS, was born Feb. 20, 1921 in Weakley County, TN. Entered service Oct. 2, 1942 at Fort Oglethorpe, GA. Completed basic training and graduated from Aircraft and Engine Mechanic School at Keesler Field, Biloxi, MS, May 1943. Then to Factory Specialist School at Willow Run, MI; Gunnery School at Laredo, TX; assigned flight engineer on B-24 Salt Lake City, UT, December 1943. Assigned to No. 705, 857th Bomb Sqdn., 492nd Bomb Group, pilot M.M. Heber, Biggs Field, El Paso, TX, January 1944. Crew received new silver aircraft No. 44-40071. April 1944 went to Herington, KS, where they painted aircraft naming her the *Sweat Box*. Left the States flying the southern route: Florida; Puerto Rico; Trinidad; Natal, Brazil; Dakar, Africa, up coast of Spain to Wales to North Pickenham, England. A new group and a new field arriving on or about April 17, 1944.

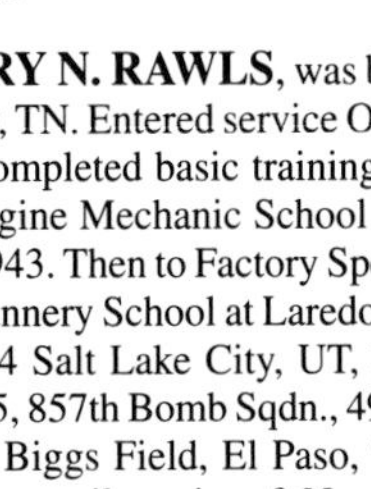

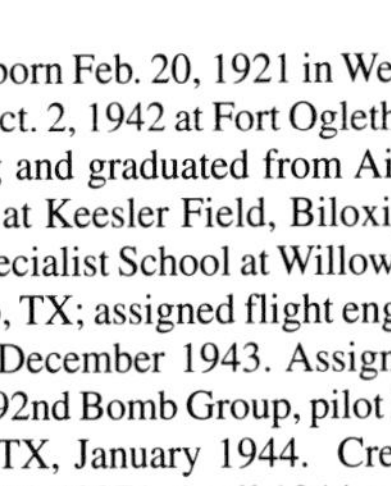

Flew first mission May 11, 1944. On 16th mission, June 20, flying *Say When* to Politz, Germany, had heavy damage from enemy aircraft and flak, losing No. 4 engine completely. Also was on receiving end of bombs from plane above, one hit nose wounding gunner and one bomb in left wing, fuel lines leaking. Forced to head to Sweden rather than ditch in the Baltic. Interned in Sweden until July 13, 1945. After end of war in Europe returned to U.S. for assignment but war in Pacific ended. Sent to Brooks Field, San Antonio, TX, and on Nov. 2, 1945 was separated from service with rank of sergeant first class.

In 1947, joined the Tennessee National Guard serving with an engineer company. Retired 1965 with the rank of captain. Received the Good Conduct, Air Medal with three Oak Leaf Clusters, ETO Ribbon with two Oak Leaf Clusters and Presidential Unit Citation.

Retired from CSX Railroad in 1986 after 32 years. His wife, the former Katherine Martin, and he live in Paris, TN. They have two daughters, Sandra and Cindy, and two grandsons, Mark and Mason.

SIDNEY LEE RAY, was born in Claiborne Parish, LA. Entered service July 3, 1942, served the 8th Air Force. Military locations/stations: Casper, WY; Salt Lake City, UT; Sioux City, IA; Tibenham, England.

Memorable experience: 445th Bomb Group bringing in 703rd Sqdn. Commander Jimmie Stewart and his men after a combat mission.

Discharged Oct. 22, 1945 with the rank of corporal. Awarded 445th group medals for service over seas.

He is married and now retired.

DAN RAYMOND, was born Oct. 26, 1924, at Spokane WA. Graduated high school in San Francisco January 1943. Basic training and A & E School, Keesler Field, Biloxi, MS. Gunnery School at Laredo, TX. Second Air Force phase training as flight engineer at Casper, WY. Assigned to the 389th Bomb Group, 566th Bomb Sqdn. at Hethel, East Anglia, May 1944.

Flew 31 missions. At Halle, Germany, on July 7, 1944, his crew was the only survivor of four B-24s hit by nine FW-190s. Despite heavy damage they were able to land at Hethel. At Humieres, France, they received 87 flak holes from the waist back.

Discharged Oct. 20, 1945 with the rank of tech. sergeant. Awarded Air Medal with three Oak Leaf Clusters, and Distinguished Flying Cross.

Following combat and a year in the Air Transport Command at Miami, he went to the University of California at Berkeley, graduating with a bachelor of science degree. His employment was with the State Compensation Insurance Fund of California where he was promoted to district manager in 1954. He managed different district offices until 1978 when he was transferred to the executive offices in San Francisco.

Raymond retired in 1979 and presently resides in Arcata, CA. He has three step-children from his second marriage.

VINCENT C. RE, was born July 3, 1925, in Cincinnati, OH. Upon entering the Air Force in September 1943, he took basic training at Amarillo, TX and entered cadet training at Iowa State Teachers College. Attended Gunnery School at Yuma, AZ and was assigned to Boise, ID for overseas training.

He was assigned to the 467th Bomb Group at Rackheath, England late in 1944. Most missions flown as a lead crew with the 791st Sqdn. Flew missions until late April 1945, as top turret gunner.

Married and has three children and in 1953 started the successful Business Machines Inc. Photography being one of his foremost interests turned into another business which is being operated currently.

JULIUS REBELES, was born Aug. 2, 1922 in Elyria, OH. Graduated from Belden High School May 1941. Drafted into USAAC in January 1943. Basic training at Miami Beach, FL; graduate of Aircraft Armorer School, Denver, CO and also Gunnery School at Buckingham Field, Ft. Myers, FL. Instructed gunnery there until late December 1943. Sent to England in early February 1944 and was assigned to the 448th Bomb Group at Seething as a replacement gunner.

His first mission was the first daylight raid on Berlin.

He completed 36 missions then taught gunnery training at Seething. Returned to the States in late March 1945 and was discharged in June 1945 as a staff sergeant. Awarded Distinguished Flying Cross, Air Medal with six Oak Leaf Clusters, ETO Ribbon and six stars.

He graduated from Miami University, Oxford, OH in June 1949 with a bachelor of science degree in education. He instructed at Chalker High School in Southington, OH from 1949 to 1954, then at North Olmsted High School in North Olmsted, OH until his retirement in 1977. He taught industrial arts, graphics arts, physical education and also coached basketball. Since his retirement he is a world traveler.

JOE W. REDDEN, was born July 31, 1920, in Hamilton County, TX. Joined USAAC in 1942 and commissioned bombardier at San Angelo, TX, Class 43-4 on March 11, 1943.

Following six weeks DR Navigation School, had duty as bombardier instructor in both B-25 and B-24 aircraft until being assigned to 446th Bomb Group, 8th Air Force, 2nd Air Div. in July 1944.

Flew 30 combat missions, the last 20 as a lead bombardier earning the Distinguished Flying Cross and Air Medal with four Oak Leaf Clusters along with a Lead Crew Commendation for leading group mission to Sinzig, Germany on Dec. 26, 1944.

Returned to States April 1945, and discharged at Miami Beach, FL on Oct. 30, 1945. Completed BBA degree at University of Texas in June 1947. Recalled for two years during Korean conflict and afterwards continued in reserve program and retired as lieutenant colonel in 1968.

Civilian work was in sales and sales management and retired Dec. 31, 1984. Enjoys golf, a full social life and one son, Joe Jr., and his family all living in Houston, TX. Celebrated 50th wedding anniversary Dec. 24, 1993.

RALPH F. REEDER, was born Nov. 15, 1922 in St. Louis, MO. Grew up in Granite City, IL, attended one year at University of Illinois, then to service February 1943.

Attended Armament School at Buckley Field, Denver, CO and Power Turret School at Briggs Manufacturing Company, Detroit, MI and classified as power turret specialist.

Was with the 448th Bomb Group, 712th Sqdn. at Seething from November 1943 to June 1945.

Discharged October 1945; awarded six Bronze Stars.

Graduated from Westminster College, Fulton, MO in 1949. Employed in engineering at Emerson Electric Company of St. Louis where work was on aircraft armament systems and missiles. He retired in 1986.

Married in 1947, has four children and 12 grandchildren. Widowed in 1983, he remarried in 1986.

He and his wife enjoy flying around in their Piper Arrow plane.

JAMES HINTON REEVES, was born May 11, 1919 in Moultrie, Colquitt County, GA. Joined the service in 1942 where he held every enlisted rank from private through master sergeant. Was given a direct appointment from rank of master sergeant to second lieutenant by Major General William P. Kepner, commanding general of 2nd Air Div. of 8th Air Force. Retired with the rank of major.

Attended Engineering and Operations School at Ft. Logan, CO.

Went overseas as member of 14th combat Wing and merged with 2nd Combat Wing which became 2nd Air Div. He saw the 2nd Div. grow from three bomber groups to 14 bomber groups (B-24) and five fighter groups.

Served as chief clerk in operations section of 2nd Air Div. before receiving a direct appointment. Continued to serve as officer in operations. Published a booklet on air craft accidents for which he was awarded the Bronze Star Medal.

Reeves has been very active in the 2nd Air Div. since its organization; served as vice president of headquarters, 2nd Air Div. and later as president of 2nd Air Division Association.

During this 45 year span his wife, Edna, and he have had the pleasure of associating with some of the finest people in the world. In his opinion the 2nd Air Division Association is the finest veterans organization in existence today. They founded and support a memorial library in Norwich, England in memory of the over 6,300 comrades of the 2nd Air Div. who paid the supreme sacrifice. This memorial is one of the finest in existence today.

Since separation from the service, Reeves has operated a retail furniture store and real estate business in Moultrie, GA, Kelly Reeves Furniture Company and Kelly Reeves Property Rentals. His wife and he are semi-retired and his businesses are operated by their two sons, Grover and Roy.

CHARLES E. REEVS, was born Sept. 25, 1916 in Rhinelander, WI and drafted in 1941. Transferred from Inf. Div. 6 to Air Corps and 2nd Air Div., 8th Air Force, 489th Group. Training at Santa Ana, CA; Ellington Field, San Luis Obispo, and Casper, WY.

Stationed at Halesworth, England, he participated in the Battle of the Bulge. Navigator on B-24, flew 30 missions over Europe from June 1944 through December 1944. Memorable experience was getting  back to the U.S. and having a malted milk and a hamburger.

Discharged June 1945 with the rank of first lieutenant. Awarded Distinguished Flying Cross and Air Medal with five clusters.

Reevs is married and has five children. He is Retired.

BERNARD C. REGAN (BUD), was born July 8, 1920 in Kansas City, MO. Was inducted into Army on Aug. 29, 1942 at Fort Leavenworth, KS. After basic training in Clearwater, FL, he was assigned to USAAC and sent to Madison, WI for Radio Operator School, Nov. 16, 1942-March 6, 1943.

March 14, 1943, assigned to a base in Meridian, MS; June 1943, sent to Westover Field, Springfield, MA to train on B-24s as radio operator; assigned to crew with Charles E. Deardorff, pilot.

Departed from Dow Field, Bangor, ME in new B-24J and arrived in Norwich, England, July 14, 1944 and assigned to 467th Bomb Group, 790th Bomb Sqdn., APO No. 558.

July 25, 1944, operational first mission, St. Lo, France; Dec. 2, 1944, 34th and last mission, Bingen, Germany. Departed from Preswick, Scotland and arrived Jan. 10, 1945, New York City. After 15 day leave was sent to Santa Ana, CA for three weeks and then assigned to Lubbock, TX AFB.

Discharged Sept. 25, 1945 at Jefferson Barracks, MO with the rank of tech. sergeant.

Awarded Air Medal with three clusters and Presidential Unit Citation.

Married high school sweetheart, Edna K. Sage, April 12, 1947; they have a son, granddaughter and grandson. He is retired.

EDWARD B. REGAN, was born Sept. 13, 1920 in Rosedale, KS. Enlisted Oct. 20, 1941; sent to Jefferson Barracks, St. Louis (KP); Mechanic School, Keesler Field, Biloxi, MS; training on the B-24D then to Ft. Myers, FL, "tent city" and formed their crew. Near Manchester, NH received their plane *Thar She Blows*.

Flew to Newfoundland, stop over then to Scotland. There they learned the difference between a shilling or quarter, "What's a farthing?" Their first home was near Bungay,

England. There the crew met King George and he inspected their plane.

After some regular missions, they were sent to Africa. Trips over Sicily and Italy, train station in Rome. Next he carried a souvenir from Ploesti, Romania. That trip finished their third B-24 with a new plane and crew. On their last trip from Italy, they saw a crescent of ships heading for the night landing. He flew 27 missions with the 329th Sqdn., 93rd Bomb Group.

Back home he was assigned to a training group in Savannah, GA on B-24s. He had a few hours training on the B-29 before retiring.

Discharged July 24, 1945 with the rank of tech sergeant. Received Purple Heart with first Bronze Oak Leaf Cluster, Air Medal with four Bronze Oak Leaf Clusters, Distinguished Flying Cross with first Bronze Oak Leaf Cluster and Distinguished Unit Badge. His crew was awarded the Lead Crew Certificate of Commendation.

He and wife Lou have five sons and two daughters. Now retired, he is a member of the 2nd Air Division Association, Veterans of Foreign Wars and Optimist Association.

DAVID W. REICH, was born June 9, 1923 in Winston-Salem, Forsyth County, NC. Entered USAAF in February 1942, aviation cadet, pilot-bomber, ETO. Stationed at Maxwell Field, Cape Girardeau, MO; Malden, MO; Stuttgart, AR; Tucson, AZ; Norwich, England. Served with 564th Sqdn., 389th Bomb Group, 8th Air Force.

Memorable experience was his first and last mission and flights to and from England. Discharged November 1945 with the rank of lieutenant. Received Air Medal.

He married Polly Wilson Nov. 24, 1945, they have one son and four grandchildren. He is retired from the transportation industry.

JAMES W. REID, JR., was born in Tulia, TX. He enlisted in the Army Air Corps in December 1942 at the age of 19 while going to Texas A&M College.Reid returned in 1946 to finish his degree in petroleum engineering.

Assigned to the 93rd Bomb Group, 330th Sqdn., piloted B-24s. Stationed at Gowen, Hardwick, Jones Fld., Perrin, Lubbock AAF, Ft. Worth AAF.

Reid returned to the States Easter Sunday, 1945. He went to 4th Ferry in Memphis, TN, and attended Instructor Instrument School in Lubbock AAF. Ferried war-weary B-24s to junk yards and ferried L-5s and C-54s.

His memorable experiences include four trucking and 35 combat missions.

Battles and campaigns: N. France, Ardennes, Central Europe, Germany.Discharged December 1945 as a 1st Lt. Received the Distinguished Flying Cross and Air Medal with five Oak Leaf Clusters.

Reid is married with four sons, two daughters, (one son is deceased), 12 grandchildren, two great grandchildren. His father was in WW I as a Jenny Pilot and WW II as Link Trainer Instructor.

EDWARD J. REILLY, was born April 2, 1923 in Syracuse, NY. Attended public schools, left Holy Cross Seminary, Notre Dame University in December 1942 to join USAAC. Pilot training throughout most of 1943, washed out. Santa Ana. Transferred to Radio School, Scott Field. Graduated, top quartile. Won gunner's wings on B-17s at Yuma. Joined combat crew at Charleston AFB, Autumn 1944. This time, Libs.

Assigned to 93rd Bomb Group, 409th Bomb Sqdn. at Hardwick, England in February 1945. Shot down ME-262 jet within 20 feet of their nose turret on second mission near Augsburg. Bill Deutch, nose gunner from Detroit and Flight Engineer Bill (Ben) Franklin from Birmingham in the Martin upper scored the kill.

Attacked by FW-190s. Saved by P-47 Thunderbolt escorts. The "jug" saved their lives; loved the sight of "Little Brother" at wing tip. Her eight 50s were more deadly than all Reilly's turrets.

Discharged November 24, 1945 from March Field. No decorations except for Air Medal and two campaign stars for the ETO duty.

Did four years in three at St. Bonaventure University. Married in senior year to Marjorie Cook, a Canadian transplant at Great Lakes Steel in Syracuse. Graduate studies, Fordham University. Began five year teaching career, 1950 in New York City, then upstate. Then to National Fire Sprinkler Association for next 30 years. Last six as president.

Reilly has great wife, six children, 15 grandchildren and one great-granddaughter. Retired April 1985. Youngest son, Dan, career officer in USAF, Tinker AFB.

RUSSEL O. REINDAL, was born July 2, 1915 on a farm near Alden, MN and lived there until drafted into Army in July 1941. Was transferred to the USAAC after about a week. Entered cadets and graduated as pilot Luke Field, AZ, Class 43-D.

Assigned pilot of B-24 and his crew formed at Pocatello, ID. They went to Seething, England AFB November 1943 where assigned to 448th Bomb Group, 714th Sqdn.

Completed 30 missions in June 1944. Remained at Seething as assistant operations officer until November 1944.

Returned to the States and attended Instrument School at Bryan, TX. Instructed various bases, served as pilot to Alaska and later base flight officer at Great Falls, MT.

Discharged December 1946. Retired from reserves as major in 1960.

Married Martha Buckner Jan. 6, 1946; they have four children and seven grandchildren. Retired to farm near Scarville, IA and is still actively farming.

ROLLIN C. REINECK, was born April 7, 1920 and raised in California. Graduated Kelly Field navigation training in June 1942. Deployed with 93rd Bomb Group to England in September 1942.

Completed first combat tour April 5, 1943 (among first to finish) and assigned 2nd Air Div. HQ as staff navigator. Deployed to Pacific as staff navigator for 73rd Bomb Wing HQ (B-29s) in 1944. Most memorable experience: surviving.

Graduated from University of California and accepted regular commission in 1947. Post war assignments included flying training, Strategic Air Command HQ, Bomber Command HQ (Korean War), Air Force HQ, Joint Chiefs of Staff, Pacific Air Force HQ Director, Nuclear Field Operations, Kirtland AFB, Director, Program Control, Minuteman Missile System.

Retired from USAF with rank of colonel. Awards include Legion of Merit, Distinguished Flying Cross, Air Medal with five Oak Leaf Clusters, Bronze Star Medal, Commendation Medal with one Oak Leaf Cluster and various campaign ribbons (ETO with three Battle Stars, Pacific with three Battle Stars and Korean War).

Colonel Reineck retired in 1970 and now resides in Kailua, HI with his wife Esther.

ROBERT K. RENN, was born Oct. 10, 1920 in Sunbury, PA. Enlisted Army Aviation Cadet Corps Oct. 12, 1942, entered pilot training, received wings and commission, Class 43-H, Blytheville, AR. Completed B-24 training Tonopah, NV. The 458th Bomb Group (H) left New Years Day, 1943, for New York and England.

Arrived Horsham St. Faith, Norwich, England February 1944. First mission in March was memorable by virtue of the unknown. D-day will remain "THE" missions; flew three sorties back to back. Completed 31 missions by the end of June and received the Distinguished Flying Cross and Air Medal with three Oak Leaf Clusters.

Returned to the States in August 1944. Became instructor pilot B-25s and A-26s, transferred to Philippines flying B-25s and operations control officer. Spent 29 years associated with the Air Force, retiring as wing comptroller rank of lieutenant colonel.

In 1945, married Marty; they have two children, three grandchildren and make their home in Arlington, TX. Member of the 2nd Air Division Association for many years enjoying reunions here and England. Friendships and camaraderie have made the association a great organization.

J. FRED RENTZ (JAKE), was born Oct. 15, 1924 in New Castle, PA. Enlisted USAAC November 1942; attended SAAC, Coleman, Sherman and graduated as pilot from Pampa, TX in Class 43-K. Trained at Wendover Field with 467th Bomb Group and went to England (Rackheath) with group as a co-pilot. Finished 30 missions July 1944, first crew in group to do so.

Returned to States and married high school sweetheart Suzanne Shannon in July 1944. Discharged August 1945 with the rank of first lieutenant. He received the Distinguished Flying Cross and Air Medal with three clusters.

Received BS degree in electrical engineering from Carnegie Tech, Pittsburgh, PA, September 1948; and MS degree from Caltech, Pasadena, CA, June 1949. System engineer on guided missiles for North American Aviation, Downey, CA for five years. Returned to New Castle, PA where family operated daily newspaper in 1954. Retired as publisher in March 1988.

Has two children: Bruce with wife Sue; Nancy with husband Charles Blakely (both children and son-in-law are ordained Presbyterian ministers); and four grandchildren. Suzanne died in June 1990 after a long illness. Married Barbara Pagach Mayer April 1992. Has traveled extensively since.

JOHN REPOLA, was born April 4, 1921 in Paterson, NJ. Joined the Air Force in April 1942 as an aviation cadet. After being commissioned in July 1943 was sent to the United Kingdom as a member of the 467th Bomb Group then transferred to the 389th Bomb Group as a member of a Pathfinder crew. Became staff bombardier after flying 30 combat missions and earning two Distinguished Flying Crosses and four Air Medals.

After the U.K. experience he was sent to the Philippines with the 9th Bomb Group. Returned in 1946 to join the 2nd Bomb Group in Tucson, AZ, attended and graduated AOB school. Joined the 509th Bomb Wing, Roswell, NM. Stayed in Roswell and became the staff observer in the 47th Air Div. Attended the Air Staff College and then reported to HQ 8th Air Force at Westover AFB, MA as the operations staff director, then executive officer for operations.

Retired in March 1966 with the rank of colonel. Became deputy director of the Boston Poverty Program, subsequently became director of the Massachusetts Division of Employment Security. Left government service to become business manager for a large law firm from which he retired in 1985.

JOHN O. REX, was born Feb. 21, 1923 in Philadelphia, PA. Entered Army Jan. 26, 1943 at Fort Dix to Aberdeen Proving Grounds. Graduated Cadre Training School to Camp Forrest, TN, joining 513th Ord. (HM) Co. and participated in field maneuvers. Moved to Fort Breckenridge, KY for overseas shape-up; to Camp Shanks and thence to Liverpool via SS *Argentina* in an August 1943 convoy.

First U.K. station was Roudham Road, Norfolk. Assigned military police duties in East Harling and vicinity. Transferred to 987th Military Police Co. of 2nd Bomb Group, quartered at Morley Hall with Detachment B. Morley Hall

was the 231st Station Hospital. Assigned foot and mobile patrol of the town and villages of S.W. Norfolk. In April 1945 transferred to 1192nd Military Police Co. in Norwich. The 987th was to be redeployed to Zone Interior and 1192nd was part of 3rd Air Div. Remained in Norwich patrolling, doing investigations, clerking and you name it. One of the last 12 Americans to leave Norwich, Norfolk in December 1945. Transferred to Honington Suffolk. Almost one of the last to leave Suffolk Jan. 13, 1946.

Memorable experiences: coming to the aid of two GIs who had been jumped by five Irish laborers and assisting in tossing one of the Irish blokes off the foundry bridge into the Wensum River in Norwich; and his relationships with the East Anglians.

Discharged on his mother's birthday Jan. 28, 1946, with the rank of private first class.

He married Mary Ottey in May 1950; they have two sons, one daughter and two grandchildren. He is retired.

HAROLD M. REYNOLDS, was born Jan. 3, 1920 in Richmond, VA. Enlisted Sept. 20, 1940; 246th C.A. Vangus. Transferred to Air Force January 1943; received bombardier wings, Class 43-9, Big Spring, TX, June 1943.

Completed combat tour October 1941; 35 missions with 44th Bomb Group, 506th Sqdn., Shipdham, Norfolk, England. Discharged Oct. 25, 1945, with the rank of first lieutenant. Received Distinguished Flying Cross and Air Medal with three Oak Leaf Clusters.

He has two sons, Harold M. Jr. and Douglas S.; and five grandchildren. He is retired.

JERRY M. REYNOLDS JR., was born March 2, 1920 in Bude, MS. Attended Bowling Green University (Kentucky), enlisted in the USAAC Jan. 8, 1942. Was accepted as aviation cadet from Enid AAF, OK and assigned to Cuero AAF, TX, Class 43-H, for training but washed out just prior to graduation. Declined bombardier and navigator programs, completed Gunnery School at Tyndall AAF, FL and Armorer School at Lowry AAF, CO. Joined Lt. Harold B. Dane's B-24 crew in Boise, ID for final phase training.

Arrived in the ETO June 4, 1944, and assigned to the 754th Sqdn., 458th Bomb Group, Horsham St. Faith, England. Completed tour of 30 missions with lead crew #67, participating in the Normandy, Northern France, Rhineland, Ardennes and Central Europe campaigns.

He had accumulated 99 "points" and was discharged at Beale AAF, CA July 29, 1945. Awarded five Air Medals and five Battle Stars along with the EAME Medal, American Campaign and WWII Victory Medals.

Completed a civilian pilot training program to obtain a private license with intent to enter the brand new USAF. Fatally injured in an aircraft accident while on a training flight Sept. 12, 1947. *Submitted by George A. Reynolds.*

RAY RHOADES, was born Jan. 3, 1920, in Lincoln NE. Graduated from the University of Nebraska in 1942. Worked for U.S. Rubber in Pennsylvania until joining the USAAC in November 1943. Completed Aviation Cadet Program in Class 44-C as a navigator.

Joined the B-24 crew of J.W. Reid in Boise, ID. Arrived at Hardwick on Aug. 9, 1944. Trained and flew with 93rd Bomb Group, 330th Sqdn.

Completed 35 combat missions from September 1944 to February 1945. Received major flak damage on many missions and made emergency landings at RAF emergency fields. Had the pleasure of circling the Eiffel Tower in a two-ship formation at one half the height of the tower while flying food to France.

Flew home in a C-54. Married Mary Smyth in Omaha, NE on Feb. 15, 1947.

Retired from Nebraska Public Power District as power production manager in 1985. Has three daughters and four grandchildren.

JOHN L. RHODES, was born Dec. 9, 1917 in Webb, CO. Entered USAAC May 26, 1942; tail gun, 44th Bomb Group, 67th Sqdn. Served Herring's crew, Shipdham, England. Flew 34 missions over Europe June 9 to Nov. 20, 1944. Crash landed Laun, France on 29th mission; got back to finish missions.

Discharged Oct. 13, 1945 with the rank of staff sergeant. Awarded ETO with four Battle Stars, Air Medal with three Oak Leaf Clusters and Distinguished Flying Cross.

He and his wife Wilma have five sons and one daughter. He is retired.

ALDO A. RICCI, was born Aug. 19, 1922 in New York City, NY. Joined USAAC as aviation cadet on Oct. 30, 1942. Class 44-C. Graduated from Navigator School, Selman Field, Monroe, LA, first in class. Assigned to Lt. Arthur D. Barre's B-24 crew at Tonopah, NV. Flew B-24 via North Atlantic route: Labrador, Iceland, and Wales. Crew was assigned to 2nd Air Div., 453rd Bomb Group, 735th Sqdn., 8th Air Force at Old Buckingham, Station No. 144, England.

Completed 35 combat missions from Aug. 26, 1944 to Feb. 24, 1945. Crew landed on continent twice, and crash landed Bungay, England, two engine return.

Discharged May 30, 1945 with the rank of first lieutenant. Awarded Air Medal with four Oak Leaf Clusters.

Married to Maryann Bellino on Dec. 11, 1948; they have two children, Donna and Bruce, and grandson Jason.

Business career in conveyor belting and power transmission sales with several companies. In 1981 formed Al Ricci Associates, Incorporated and was successful in operating a power transmission sales organization. He sold his business to associate in 1992. Currently retired and travels. Still actively down hill skiing, golfing, bowling, fine furniture making and visits Florida in March and April.

PETER J. RICE, was born Aug. 1, 1914 in New York City, NY. Served in the 8th Air Force, 389th Bomb Group, 567th Sqdn. Statined at Camp Upton, Miami Beach; Scott Field; Biggs AAF; Lowry Field; Harlingen, TX.

Participated in action at Ploesti; Kjeller, Norway; and his 25th mission Feb. 20, 1944 to Brunswick. Discharged June 30, 1945 with the rank of tech. sergeant. Received Distinguished Flying Cross with cluster, Air Medal with four clusters and EAME.

He and his wife Kathleen have a son Kevin and a daughter Suzanne. He is a retired pipe fitter since 1981.

ROBERT T. RICE, was born Jan. 30, 1919 at Newton, MA. Drafted Feb. 5, 1942 into U.S. Army with basic at 4th Armored Div. Pine Camp, NY. Accepted into Aviation Cadets May 1942; completed aerial gunnery June 1943; commissioned as bombardier, Midland AAF, October 1943 as member of combat crew. Joined 330th Bomb Sqdn., 93rd Bomb Group April 1944 with Jack Jennings as pilot.

His 11th mission was June 6, D-day; completed 33 missions July 24, 1944. Relieved from active duty June 1945; awarded Distinguished Flying Cross and Air Medal with three Oak Leaf Clusters.

Was recalled from the reserves January 1948 to 330th Bomb Sqdn., 93rd Bomb Group. B-29 at Castle AFB, member of Dick Butler's "A" Bomb crew. Awarded Aircraft Observor Wings 1037 (bomb/nav/radar) Mather AFB, 1952. Completed 13 missions B-29 with 28th Bomb Sqdn., 19th Bomb Group, Korean War. Flew last sortie before truce 1953. With A/C Gene Smith, received 4th Oak Leaf Cluster to Air Medal. Assigned Air University, Maxwell AFB, June 1955. Awarded USAF Commendation Medal.

Retired from active duty August 1964 as major. Retired from AESCO Steel, Incorporated, Montgomery, AL in August 1982. Rice married Janet Guilford, his high school sweetheart, on Dec. 20, 1941. They have three children, eight grandchildren and one great-grandson.

WILLIAM H. RICHESON, was born in 1920 at Bowling Green, KY. Entered cadets May 1941, graduated Kelly Field, TX, Class 42-A. Assigned Navigation School at Kelly and Hondo, TX. Accumulated 1700 flying hours before transferring October 1943 to Smyrna, TN for B-24 training and then combat training at Blythe, CA.

Assigned 392nd Bomb Group, Wendling, England, May 1944. Completed 35th combat mission Nov. 1, 1944. Returned to ZI for helicopter training. Assigned Pacific Theater May 1945. Flew four combat missions in B-17 before wars end.

Post war assignments: Japan, Wright Patterson, Guam. Discharged April 1947; recalled 1948. Assigned MacDill AFB. Follow on assignments: Lakenheath, England, Dow AFB, HQ 16th Air Force, Spain and HQ SAC, Offutt AFB. Retired from military May 1963.

Began civil service career October 1963. Retired as deputy director of Budget, HQ ATC, Randolph AFB, TX, December 1982. Married Virginia Schaeufele of Kansas. They have two children and grandchildren.

JOHN B. RICHMOND, was born Aug. 20, 1923 in Nappanee, IN. Enlisted in USAAC on June 6, 1942. After basic training and Radio School, passed examination for aviation cadets and was assigned to Southeast Training Command, Class 43-F. Had primary flight training at Tuscaloosa, AL; basic at Newport, AR; advanced at Seymour, IN. Assigned as co-pilot on B-24 crew at Boise, ID and then Pocatello for transition training.

Departed U.S. in November 1943 on *Queen Elizabeth* and subsequently assigned to 448th Bomb Group at Seething, England. Flew 30 missions from January through May 1944 and was awarded Air Medal with three clusters and the Distinguished Flying Cross.

Married Mary Robison while attending Northwestern University from which he graduated in 1948. Worked 20 years at Johnson Wax, then 23 at his own company in Tennessee. He has three children and five grandchildren, all living in Murfreesboro, TN.

GEORGE C. RICHNER, was born Dec. 24, 1923 at Twinsburg, OH. Joined Air Corps in December 1942. Called up in February 1943 to Miami Beach, FL to begin cadet training. Completed Navigational School at Selman Field, Monroe, LA, May 1944, Class of 44-7. Met his crew at Lincoln, NE, May 1944, and transitioned at Casper, WY.

Crossed the Atlantic on the USS *Brazil* to the 392nd Bomb Group, 576th and 579th Sqdns. Completed his 35 missions March 14, 1945, none without apprehension. Returned to the U.S. April 1945 on the *Il De France*. R&R at Santa Ana, CA. Discharged June 1945.

Returned home to a partnership in a family business. Married with two children and two grandchildren. Now retired and involved in volunteer work, hobbies and family.

JOHN J. RICKEY, was born in Brooklyn, NY on Nov. 2, 1923. Worked for the Corporation Trust Company before enlisting in the USAAC, September 1942. Graduated from Aerial Gunnery School at Ft. Myers, FL. Went to Salt Lake

City, UT and graduated from Armament School. Flew B-17s at Boise, ID and later transferred over to B-24s.

Shipped overseas to Wendling, England, Oct. 8, 1943. Assigned to 392nd Bomb Group, 578th Sqdn. Flew 31 missions aboard *G.I. Jane* from 1943 to 1944. Shot down one ME-109. Most harrowing experience was landing B-24 with ball turret down at 45 degree angle with the ball gunner still in it.

Came back to U.S. in 1944 as an instructor on B-32s. Discharged from Ft. Dix, NJ in 1945. Awarded Air Medal with five Oak Leaf Clusters, Distinguished Flying Cross, Presidential Unit Citation with one Oak Leaf Cluster and recently received the Conspicuous Service Cross with two clusters from New York state.

Worked for the post office for 38 years before retiring. Graduated from New York City College, married with five children and two grandchildren.

WILLIAM I. RIDDLEBERGER III, was born in Charles Town, WV on Jan. 18, 1920. Graduated from high school in 1938, joined the USAAC Oct. 3, 1940. Graduated from Technical School at Chanute Field, Il as airplane mechanic in August 1941. He was assigned to 78th School Sqdn., Moffett Field, CA. Promoted through the ranks to staff sergeant. He entered the aviation cadet training April 17, 1943; graduated from Pilot School at Stockton Field, Stockton, CA, Feb. 8, 1944. Trained with a crew in B-24 and transferred to the 8th Air Force, 392nd Bomb Group, June 6, 1944.

Flew first mission on July 7, 1944. The target on his 13th mission was Kiel, Germany. Lt. Paul Barton, his pilot, was killed by flak. Riddleberger returned the plane to base. The crew was assigned another pilot, Louis Stephens, and on their 19th mission they were shot down over Mainz, Germany and became prisoners of war. They were both in a hospital and later sent to a prisoner of war camp. He was sent to Stalag Luft I; transferred in December 1944 to a hospital at Bad Soden, Germany. The American forces liberated the hospital in April 1945. They were transferred to Valley Forge General Hospital on May 2, 1945.

Riddleberger was discharged March 22, 1946 with the rank of first lieutenant. Received Purple Heart, Air Medal, POW and European campaign.

He and his wife Kathryn have a daughter, a son, and five grandsons. He is retired.

WILLIAM BRYANT RIDGWAY, was born Feb. 12, 1919 in Jackson, MS. Entered the Air Force Oct. 10, 1941; served as advanced single engine flying instructor and B-24 pilot with 467th Bomb Group, 8th Air Force.

Military locations/stations: Pre-flight, Montgomery, AL; primary, Decatur, AL; basic, Greenville, MS; advanced, Spence Field, Moultrie, GA; B-24, Smyrna Field and March Field; 467th Bomb Group, 2nd Air Div., 8th Air Force.

Participated in 14 air raids over Germany from Dec. 15, 1944 to June 15, 1945. Memorable experience: first or second mission carried four 2,000 pound bombs for bridge in Germany. Dropped. One bomb hung in bomb bay. Bomb dislodged on landing. Pulled up and went around. No problem. Bomb slid to end of runway. No damage.

Discharged September 1945 with the rank of captain.

Ridgway married Mary Juanita Wallace; they have five children. He is retired.

LESLIE W. RIDLEY, was born June 15, 1922 in Sandpoint, ID. Entered the USAF Oct. 21, 1942 and served as a radio mechanic. Stationed at Fort Douglas, Camp Kearns, Sioux Falls, SD; Wendover, UT; Sioux City, IA; Camp Shanks; Seething, England.

Memorable experience: Field bombed twice and strafed by 20mm cannon. Two buzz bombs exploded close by. Sailed on both *Queen Mary* and *Queen Elizabeth*. Served with the 448th Bomb Group, 713th Sqdn.

Discharged Oct. 11, 1945 with the rank of corporal. Awarded Sharpshooter, Presidential Citation and earned Good Conduct Medal but never received one.

Married in 1943, wife died 1969. Remarried and divorced. He has two sons, one daughter and four grandchildren. Retired in 1986 and now enjoys golfing, bowling and traveling.

GEORGE RIESS, was a waist gunner. *Submitted by Herbert C. Borgmann.*

ALBERT J. RILEY (AL), was born in Utica, NY on April 30, 1922. He entered the USAAC in 1942 after completing basic training in Atlantic City and aerial gunnery training at Tyndall Field in Panama City, FL. He went on for more training at Lowry Field, Denver, CO and completed his advanced armored gunnery training at Alamogordo Field, NM.

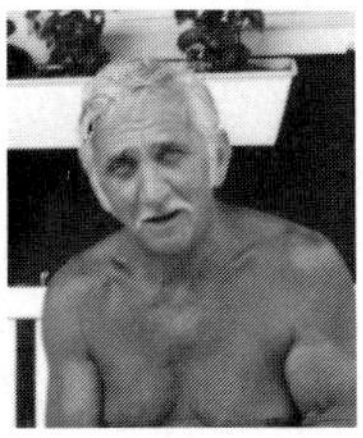

Arrived Wendling Field, England, a member of the 392nd Bomb Group, 576th Bomb Sqdn. in September 1943. He was a ball turret gunner, one of the original members of Capt. Barnes' crew.

Riley would have completed his tour of duty after his 30th mission; however, on May 19, 1944, just after completing his last bombing mission over Brunswick, Germany and just two and a half hours from landing in England, he was shot down. He was taken as a prisoner of war and spent the next nine months in Stalag Luft IV. For the next three months he was part of a forced march in which POWs participated. He was liberated by the British army on May 15, 1945.

He was awarded the Distinguished Flying Cross, four Air Medals, POW Medal and Conspicuous Service Medal, New York state.

Married Anne Haskell Sept. 3, 1942. They have seven children and 11 grandchildren. He retired from the New Telephone Company after 35 years of service.

JUDGE RICHARD J. RINEBOLT, was born Sept. 14, 1922 in Bradner, OH and grew up in Findlay, OH. Attended Northwestern University for two years and on Sept. 2, 1942, enlisted as an aviation cadet in the USAAC. Went through pilot training in Class 44-A receiving pilot's wings and second lieutenant commission on Jan. 7, 1943 at Moore Field, Mission, TX. Following RTU training in P-51s was sent to England and in July 1944 was assigned to the 4th Fighter Group located at Debden in Essex.

The 4th Fighter Group had been formed in September 1942 from the 71st, 121st and 133rd Eagle Sqdns. and by the end of WWII had been credited with destroying more than 1,000 German aircraft of which total he contributed one. After 30 missions and surviving a bad crash, he returned to the U.S. in March 1945 ending up as a P-47 instructor.

After release, he stayed in the reserves retiring as a lieutenant colonel in the JAG. He received the Air Medal with three Oak leaf Clusters.

Rinebolt received his law degree from Ohio Northern University in 1948 after which he practiced law and served as assistant and county prosecuting attorney. He became a judge in 1977, serving until retirement in 1990.

Married Ruth C. Murphy Oct. 1, 1955; she is now deceased. He has two sons, David and Tom; one daughter Ann; and three grandchildren: Christine, Danny and Jesse. He is still an active pilot, and president of the association of the 4th Fighter Group.

GEORGE A. RISKO, was born Nov. 21, 1923 in Roscoe, PA. Joined the USAAC Sept. 2, 1942, served as navigator (1034), 491st Bomb Group, 855th Bomb Sqdn., 2nd Air Div., 8th Air Force. Assigned Metfield, North Pickenham, England.

Flew 28 missions, 18 wing (Burk), 10 lead (Forsha); wounded on 28th bombing tactical targets near Caen. Recalls continuous maximum efforts following D-day and missions over France and Germany to defeat Nazi war effort.

Discharged Nov. 19, 1945 with the rank of first lieutenant. Received Distinguished Flying Cross, Air Medal with three Oak Leaf Clusters. ETO Ribbon with four Campaign Stars and Purple Heart.

Married Lucrezia, he is a retired engineer.

RAMO F. RIVA, enlisted in the USAAC which later became USAAF. Stationed at Maxwell Field and Gunter Field, AL. Then sent to Casey Jones School of Aeronautics in New Jersey. From there he was sent to Wendover Field, UT and Tonopah, NV. Flew from Goose Bay, Labrador to Norwich, England and became master sergeant, was in England for 18 months.

One of two flight chiefs with a master sergeant rank stationed in Norwich, England with 755th Bomb Sqdn. and 458th Bomb Group. Responsible for the operation of the hangar with maintenance personnel for 50 and 100 hour inspections; also major repairs were done in the hangar. He test flew B-24s with pilots to make sure that all repairs were properly made.

His hat goes off to all crew chiefs, airplane mechanics and airplane technicians for a super job working long hours in keeping the B-24s in top flying condition. He was in Norwich, England when the V-2 bomb was used. They were dropped on the field and in the city of Norwich.

After the war in Europe, he was sent to Wichita, KS for B-29 schooling. He was offered a warrant officer commission but chose to be discharged, September 1945. Received ETO Ribbon with three Battle Stars, American Defense Ribbon with two Battle Stars, Good Conduct Medal, Marksman Medal and a Meritorious Achievement Award which was signed by Gen. Peck and Col. Hersberg.

Married Lillian Alegi in 1950. He has three children: Brenda Ruggiero, Randy Riva and Cynthia Sullivan; and is a proud grandfather of six children. He has been in the restaurant business for 46 years and is semi-retired.

HOWARD H. ROBB, was born June 19, 1921 in Moscow, MI. Moved to Montpelier, OH 1927. Graduate of Montpelier High School 1939. Moved to Jackson, MI 1940, employed by Sparks-Withington Co., Horn Div., became tool and die maker, 1940-1953; went on to Mechanical Products, 1953-1964; started own laundromat, 1959-1985, retired.

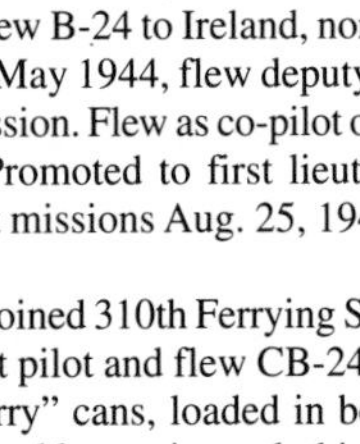
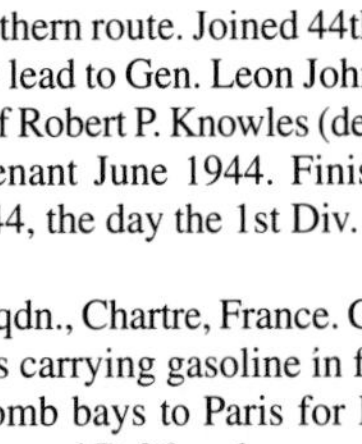

Volunteered 312th Coast Artillery July 1942, entered aviation cadet training January 1943. Commissioned second lieutenant Dec. 5, 1943. Trained with B-24 crew at Casper, WY. Flew B-24 to Ireland, northern route. Joined 44th Bomb Group May 1944, flew deputy lead to Gen. Leon Johnson D-day mission. Flew as co-pilot of Robert P. Knowles (deceased) crew. Promoted to first lieutenant June 1944. Finished 31 combat missions Aug. 25, 1944, the day the 1st Div. entered Paris.

Joined 310th Ferrying Sqdn., Chartre, France. Checked out first pilot and flew CB-24s carrying gasoline in five gallon "jerry" cans, loaded in bomb bays to Paris for Patton's tanks; and later winter clothing and B-26 replacement crews to Florence, Belgium during the Battle of the Bulge.

Entered ZOI Jan. 3, 1945. Released July 1945. Awarded Distinguished Flying Cross and Air Medal with three Oak Leaf Clusters.

Married to Norma Tom in 1941; they have three children and seven grandchildren.

ELMER PAUL ROBBINS (ROBBIE), was born Aug. 5, 1924 in New Bedford, MA. Inducted May 21, 1943 in the

USAAF; Class 44-9, Selman Field, LA, navigator. Joined 389th Bomb Group, 567th Sqdn., 8th Air Force, Hethel, England January 1945 on Ned Ansel's crew.

Flew 22 missions. April 14, 1945 knocked down by bombs from B-17s, three of crew lost. He evaded for four days before reaching allied lines. Target, Royan, France.

He retired from the USAFR in 1969 with the rank of lieutenant colonel. Received three Air Medals, Purple Heart, ETO Ribbon with three Battle Stars.

Graduated from Harvard. He married Elizabeth Wood Nov. 26, 1945; they have one son Eric.

EVERETT MAX ROBBINS, was born June 21, 1922 in Triplett, MO. Drafted from Jackson County, MO, October 1942. Stationed at Kearns, UT; Scott Field, IL; Las Vegas, NV; Blythe, CA. Assigned to crew at Davis Monthan Field, Tucson, AZ August 1943. February 1944, assigned to 853rd Bomb Sqdn., 491st Bomb Group, Pueblo, CO. Flew from Herington, KS to England with the group.

Fourth mission, June 11, 1944, plane ditched in English Channel, five crew members lost. He completed 30 missions: Normandy, Northern France, Air Offensive Europe, Rhineland, Ardennes and Central Ardennes campaigns.

Returned May 1945 and discharged as tech. sergeant on July 21, 1945 from Jefferson Barracks, MO. Returned to Jackson County, MO, married Doris Koch and they have two sons, two daughters and 11 grandchildren. Both sons are Vietnam veterans.

Robbins did farm and factory production work. Parkinson's disease forced him to retire in 1982. He died Nov. 24, 1991, at his home in Buckner, MO and is buried in the country cemetery near his birth place.

STANLEY J. ROBENS, (formerly Stanley J. Rubenstein until 1949 when he changed his last name) was born March 30, 1922 in Little Rock, AR. Entered the USAAC April 2, 1941. Stationed at Scott Field, IL; Keesler Field, MS; Kelly Field, TX; Laredo Gunner School, TX; Westover Field, MA; Wendling, England, serving with the 392nd Bomb Group, 576th Bomb Sqdn.

Flew 16 missions over Germany in B-24 as tail gunner. Shot down on 16th mission and was prisoner of war in Germany. He never knew how he got shot down because there were no fighters in the area. He joined the Liberator Club 38 years later, and received a flier on a new book about the air combat of his group. Robens called the author who read him the following passage: "A tragic accident spoiled an otherwise perfect mission when one of the group's ships was accidently shot down by one of the other formations' B-24s during a test firing of the 50 caliber machine guns."

Discharged Oct. 3, 1945 with the rank of staff sergeant. Received Air Medal with one cluster, Purple Heart, European Theater with three clusters and Good Conduct Medal.

Robens and his wife Vickie have a daughter Linda and a son Mark. A graduate of the University of Oklahoma, 1949, with a BA degree in psychology, he is semi-retired in 36th year in life insurance business as an agent.

CLAYTON R. ROBERTS, was born Oct. 1, 1922 in Gasport, NY, a small rural community near Buffalo. Joined the USAAC October 1942. Was an aviation cadet, Class 44-E, completed pilot training and commissioned second lieutenant at Columbus Field, MS. Received B-24 co-pilot training Harlingen, TX; B-24 pilot training Maxwell Field, AL; crew assignments at Westover Field, MA; and overseas crew training at Chatham Field, GA. Delivered a new B-24J to Valley Wales and reported to the 68th Bomb Sqdn., 44th Bomb Group at Shipdham, England. Returned to States May 1945 delivering B-24 to Bradley Field, CT.

Served 19 years in SAC as crew member, instructor pilot, squadron operations officer, deputy base commander and deputy inspector general, at 305th 306th, 307th Bomb Groups, 72nd Bomb Wing, and HQ 15th and 8th Air Forces. Awarded Air Medal with clusters, ETO Ribbon with five Battle Stars, Army Commendation, Air Force Commendation with cluster and eight others. Received BS degree at Sacramento State College, CA. Retired as colonel in August 1965. Completed 26 years second career in federal civil service in January 1992.

He is still awed by the way his generation performed as teenagers and early 20 year olds. As a pilot, he was the oldest crew member, 21 years. His tail gunner was the youngest, 18. This typified the bomber crews that did the impossible, daylight precision strategic bombing which brought the two most powerful military forces the world had ever known to their knees. He will be forever proud to have served.

CLARK L. ROBINSON, was born Dec. 31, 1922 in Chillicothe, OH. Was a freshman at Miami University, Dec. 7, 1941; enlisted Wright Field. Aviation cadet: Keesler, University of Chattanooga, Nashville, Maxwell, Bennetsville, Bush, and Moody. Pilot, second lieutenant, Class 44-E. B-17 transition, Ft. Myers, FL; co-pilot B-24, Savannah, GA.

Flew to United Kingdom via Iceland where he was snowed in 21 days. Joined 389th Bomb Group at Hethel. Dropped 2,000 pound bomb on runway. Selected for lead crew training.

On March 24, 1945 was shot down and crash landed on low level varsity haul/Rhine Crossing. Evacuated on Winston Churchill's C-47. April 7, 1945, took over 8th Air Force lead when ME-109 rammed CO John Herboth. He was awarded the Distinguished Flying Cross.

Returned to U.S. via Greenland. Received BFA from Miami University in 1948. Was advertising art director, McCann-Erickson; executive art director, Fuller & Smith & Ross; group head, Cunningham & Walsh; vice president/creative director, Ketchum, MacLeod & Grove; senior vice president, Friedlich, Fearon & Strohmeier; president, Robinson, Donino and West; president, Clark L. Robinson, Inc.

Married Beatrice Barna June 14, 1947. They have five children: Laura, Drew, Diane, Kevin and Kerry; and four grandchildren: Corky, Nicholas, Isabel and Robert.

JOHN HAROLD ROBINSON, was born Oct. 14, 1921 in Jackson, TN and resided in Memphis, TN. Inducted into the Army Nov. 26, 1942, assigned AAF, Keesler AFB, aircraft mechanic, Laredo, TX, gunnery staff sergeant. AEG on B-24s, Salt Lake City, UT; Boise, Pocatello, ID; assigned 703rd Sqdn., 445th Bomb Group, Sioux City, IA and sent to Tibenham, England.

Flew 30 missions between Nov. 25, 1943 and May 13, 1944; original aircraft *Bullet Serenade* 42-64439, second was *Tennessee Dottie* 41-28652. Returned from ETO September 1944, Keesler, AFB; assigned senior instructor cargo C-46.

Discharged Oct. 16, 1945 at Maxwell AAF, AL. Received Distinguished Flying Cross, Air Medal with three clusters, ETO, three Battle Stars, Presidential Group Citation, Croix de Guerre with Palms, Good Conduct Medal and WWII Victory Medal.

Married to Virginia Elizabeth Marbury over 52 years, they have three daughters and one son. He is the author of *A Reason To Live*; professional engineer; president AME Engineers Association; retired engineering manager, Kraft, Corporation; Witco, Corporation; Scouter Woodbadge; president of Tennessee 8th AFHS; AFA director and member American Legion.

DAVID W. ROBISON, was born March 2, 1923 in New Castle, PA. Entered USAAC Dec. 4, 1942 at Erie, PA. After basic training, Armorer and Gunnery School, he was assigned to Ralph Schneck's lead crew with the 445th Bomb Group, 702nd Sqdn. as a tail gunner. Trained at Watertown, SD and flew to Tibenham, England by the southern route on *Sin Ship*, 427601.

Flew 30 missions. First mission was Dec. 31, 1943, in southwestern France; attacked by ME-109s and most of B-24 crews ran out of ammunition. Second mission was to Brunswick Jan. 11, 1944; 60 bombers lost. Third mission over coast of France, they got accurate flak and first holes in *Sin Ship*. Fourth to Brunswick and two more missions in *Sin Ship* over coast of France. Another crew was flying *Sin Ship* when it was shot down Feb. 16, 1944. His crew transferred to 93rd Bomb Group, 329th Sqdn. Feb. 17, 1944. Their new plane, *Connie*, was equipped to bomb through clouds. Seventh mission was March 13, 1944, first with the 93rd. D-day was their 19th and after that most of their missions were bombing through overcast; and their 30th and last mission was on June 20, 1944, St. Martin, France, a rocket site. They received heavy accurate flak, 27 holes in plane and #4 engine on fire. Crew was ready to jump when fire blew out.

Discharged Oct. 20, 1945 with the rank of staff sergeant. Received four Air Medals and Distinguished Flying Cross. Married Louise Barnhouse Nov. 10, 1947; they have four boys, one girl and eight grandchildren. Worked as machinist and tool maker and is now retired.

HAROLD J. ROCHE, was born Oct. 28, 1923 in Hartford, CT. Entered USAAF Nov. 6, 1942; served with the 489th Bomb Group, 845th Sqdn., 2nd Air Div., 8th Air Force.

Stationed with the 8th Air Force at Halesworth, England. Participated in Air Offensive Europe and 28 combat missions over enemy territory. His most memorable raid was on Ludwigshaven and supply drop to paratroopers in Holland, 50 percent of squadron shot down.

Discharged Oct. 21, 1945 with the rank of staff sergeant, top turret gunner. Awarded four Air Medals, Battle Stars for Air War Europe and Normandy invasion.

Married with four married children and one grandchild. Retired from ITT Hartford Insurance Group.

JOHN ROCHE (DUTCH), was born in Baltimore, MD July 26, 1925. Entered U.S. Army at Ft. George Meade, MD Oct. 21, 1943. Assigned USAAF basic training in Miami Beach, FL; attended Gunnery School at Tyndall Field, Panama City, FL; the transported by train to Lincoln, NE. Crew was formed and assigned as nose gunner. B-24 crew training, Gowen Field, Boise, ID, Westbrook crew #5002; sent to Topeka AAF, KS and assigned to B-24J (42-50714) July 1944.

Flew aircraft to European Theater via Grenier Field, Manchester, NH; Goose Bay, Labrador; Reykjavik, Iceland; Bluie West One, Greenland; Nutts Corner, Northern Ireland; Stone, England; back to Ireland for gunnery training. Assigned 785th Bomb Sqdn., 466th Bomb Group, 96th Combat Wing, 8th Air Force, Station 120, Attlebridge, England.

Flew 35 combat missions, 216 combat hours, 178,000 pounds bombs dropped from Aug. 26, 1944 to March 20, 1945, waist gunner missions 1-9 and togglier/nose gunner missions 10-35.

Returned to U.S. in May 1945 on USS *General Squire* and landed Boston Harbor on Mother's Day May 12, 1945.

Assigned AAF Redistribution Center in Greensboro, NC from June 1945 to October 1945. Discharged Oct. 19, 1945 with the rank of staff sergeant. Awarded Air Medal with four Oak Leaf Clusters, ETO with four Bronze Service Stars, American Campaign Medal, Good Conduct Medal, WWII Victory Medal and Certificate of Valor.

Married Mary Cecelia May on July 26, 1947. They have six daughters and 13 grandchildren. He worked for IBM Corporation from March 1948 to May 1987 in various staff and management positions. Presently, he is the primary caregiver for his wife, a diagnosed Alzheimer's patient.

RICHARD G. ROESING, was born Feb. 6, 1921. Graduated Toledo University June 1942 and went to work at the Champion Spark Plug Company, engineer department, Toledo, OH. After Pearl Harbor, joined USAAF Jan. 1, 1943 at San Antonio, TX. Commissioned second lieutenant, Class 44-B, Houston, TX. Stationed at Jones Field, Starkville Flying School, 65 hours, Bonham, TX; P and W Majors Air Force Flying School, 71 hours, Greenville, TX; Ellington Flying School, 73 hours, Houston, TX; Liberal, KS Flying School, 82 hours, B-24 transition.

He was a B-24 co-pilot with the 93rd Bomb Group Hardwick, England. Had 15 or 16 missions over Germany and V-E day came, sent home and discharged July 11, 1945.

Returned to Champion Spark Plug Company and was sent to Pittsburgh, PA sales department and retired in 1982 after 40 years. Married 47 years to Shirley, a wonderful woman who died Aug. 5, 1993. He has two boys, two girls, one granddaughter and three grandsons. Today he enjoys fishing and taking care of his children's home in Naples, FL.

MANUEL M. ROGOFF, was born Feb. 11, 1917 in Mt. Pleasant, PA. Joined military June 24, 1940. Motor School instructor, Infantry, Ft. Benning, GA. Joined Air Force July 1942, commissioned bombardier Midland Air Base, TX, 1943. Trained at Davis Monthan, Tucson, AZ and Casper, WY Air Base. Joined 389th Bomb Group, 567th Bomb Sqdn., 8th Air Force, B-24s, Norwich, England.

On first mission blew up heavy water plant, Rujukan, Norway. Bailed out Jan. 7, 1944 south of Paris, France. Severley burned on face and hands. Patient at Valley Force General Hospital. Assigned to the Greater Pittsburgh Air Force Command. Released Jan. 16, 1946. He was awarded the Purple Heart and Air Medal.

Still active. President Leetsdale Auto Incorporated. Married Irma E. Schaffer Sept. 5, 1944. Two children: Lawrence J. and Cynthia R. Abrams. They reside in Pittsburgh, PA.

EDMUND A. ROKICKI (RICK), was born in Glen Lyon, PA on April 18, 1924. Married high school sweetheart, Cecelia M. Maguda, January 1946; they have a son, a daughter, and two grandchildren.

He entered the USAAC on March 3, 1943, after attending one year of Embry-Riddle Aeronautical University in Coral Gables, FL (since relocated to Daytona Beach). After basic training in Miami Beach, was assigned to Embry-Riddle to continue aviation training. Graduated military Class 21-43-A2 and sent to Kelly Field, TX to join replacements to 8th Air Force in England.

First assignment was the 96th Bomb Group (B-17) at Snetterton-Heath in early October 1943. Transferred to 458th Bomb Group (B-24) at Horsham St. Faith at end of December 1943. Completed balance of 25 mission tour as flight engineer. Assigned to ground support crew until departure from England. Returned to the USA on furlough and reported to B-29 training as flight engineer at Clovis, NM. The end of Pacific hostilities brought discharge on Nov. 11, 1945.

He completed further aviation training and received the following Federal Licenses: Aircraft & Engine, Radio-Telephone, Flight Engineer and Pilot License. Joined United Airlines in July 1946. Retired in 1985 after nearly 39 years, the last 30 being in various management capacities.

EDMUND E. ROLOFF (EDDIE), was born near Ritzville, WA Feb. 22, 1920. Entered USAAC April 13, 1942. Basic at Sheppard Field, TX; Radio School at Scott Field, IL; Aerial Gunnery School at Harlingen, TX where upon graduation was assigned as instructor.

Assigned to bomber crew July 1943 and trained at Boise and Pocatello, ID; Sioux City, IA and Mitchell, SD. November 1943, left for England via South America and Africa.

First mission was to Bremen, Germany Dec. 16, 1943. Last and 30th to Berlin April 29, 1944. Following combat he was transferred to Northern Ireland to help train newly arriving crews in the art of gunnery.

He arrived back in the U.S. aboard *The Acquitania* Sept. 21, 1944, and was stationed at Scott Field, IL. Spent a month at the AAF rest camp at Lake Lure, Asheville, NC and was stationed at McClellan Field, CA when he was discharged Sept. 25, 1945 as tech. sergeant.

He received Distinguished Flying Cross, Air Medal and Letter of Commendation from commanding officer 700th Sqdn., 445th Bomb Group for March 15, 1944 mission over Brunswick.

After discharge he worked as accountant one year, operated a used car business for seven years, flew duster and spray planes for 15 years, cruised timber, appraised real estate and bought and sold land.

Married Sue Maicrak October 1945. They have one son. He is still active working and managing their 100 acre Douglas Fir Tree Farm. He would like to hear from war-time friends and associates at 424 O'Farrell, Olympia, WA 98501.

ELMER J. ROMIGH JR., was born Sept. 27, 1920 in Houston, TX. Joined the USAAC March 19, 1942 as an aviation cadet. Reached the grade of colonel and retired July 1, 1968.

Graduated from Flying School, Class 43-B, Feb. 16, 1943 and received wings, commission and wife on that day. Six months, 6th Tow Target Sqdn. Then B-17 training, then to B-24s and the 466th Bomb Group in Alamogordo, NM. Issued B-24H, 42-52598, *Guess Who's Here,* and flew it through South America to Dakar, to Attlebridge in England.

Flew with the group on the first mission, Berlin, March 22, 1944. Completed 32 missions and returned to the States in August 1944. Ended flying in 1952 and served 19 years as a civil engineer. Served in Korea and in the northern jungle of Thailand to start construction of a fighter base during the Vietnam conflict. Romigh was awarded the Distinguished Flying Cross, four Air Medals, two Bronze Stars, plus campaign and service medals and ribbons.

He has three children, seven grandchildren and two great-grandchildren. His wive passed away in 1978.

HERMAN ROOKS, was born Aug. 28, 1921 in Washington, GA. He served as navigator on Joseph Bell's crew, 789th Bomb Sqdn., 467th Bomb Group, Rackheath, Norfolk, England.

Received BS degree, Berry College; MA degree, University of Wisconsin. Married Daphine Lummus and have two children: Joe and Leland. Professor of history and economics at Berry College 1946-1953; Gulf Coast Community College 1960-1979. President, Florida Association of Community Colleges, 1971. Retired and residing in Panama City, FL.

WARREN J. ROSEBOROUGH, 0817274 was born Feb. 27, 1921 in Pittsburgh, PA. Graduated pilot second lieutenant USAAC Dec. 5, 1943. Flew 35 missions in B-24s, 16 with 492nd Bomb Group and 19 with 467th Bomb Group (H), 2nd Air Div.

His crew included: himself, pilot; 2nd Lt. Castel Reed 0819871 co-pilot; Seymour Freeman 0709325 navigator; Leo F. Johnson 0706882 bombardier (six missions); Sgt. Jack W. Priley 37548931 eng/gun; Pfc. Joseph C. Domino 32995171 ball turret; Cpl. Billie F. Lewis 34725018 radio; Pfc. Allen J. Young 31380660 waist gunner; Sgt. Kenneth A. Dowell 31293398 armor/tail gun; Pfc. Robert Kraft 12217696 waist gun. All returned safely to the U.S.

EDWARD GUSTAV ROSENBERG, was born June 13, 1925 in Cleveland, OH. Enlisted July 10, 1943 in USAAC; MOS 514, ECM operator/Pathfinder. Stationed at Greensboro, NC, basic; Sioux Falls, SD; Citadel, Charleston, NC; Attleboro, Old Buck; Radar School at Luton, England, U.K.

Flew 27 missions with 732nd Bomb Sqdn., 453rd Bomb Group, Oct. 12, 1944 to March 30, 1945. Eight missions with 389th Bomb Group April 2, 1945 to June 5, 1945. Participated in all air battles in ETO and three campaigns in Korea.

Memorable experience: Shot down over Cologne, Germany October 1944. Walked out and started over again on Oct. 25, 1944 with 732nd Bomb Sqdn, Gelsen Kirchen, Germany. Two years of hell in Korea June 1951 to August 1953.

Retired June 30, 1980 as lieutenant colonel with 37 years service with the USAF. He received Air Medal with five clusters, ETO, four Bronze Stars, Good Conduct Medal, Meritorious Service Medal, four Presidential Citations, three Air Force Commendation Medals, German Occupation Medal and more.

He has a wife Bernice; a son Karl; a daughter Deborah Ann; and one grandson Woody. He is retired and enjoys fishing, golfing and hunting.

CARL B. ROSENDAHL (ROSIE), was born Jan. 16, 1922 in Georgetown, CT. Inducted into Army Jan. 16, 1943 and assigned to USAAC. Graduated from Radio School, Sioux Falls, SD and Gunnery School, Harlingen, TX. Assigned to 489th Bomb Group, 844th Sqdn., crew #14 as radio operator/gunner, Wendover, UT.

Flew with group to ETO and started combat operations May 30, 1944. Completed tour of 30 plus missions. Flew B-24, ferrying supplies with pilot, co-pilot and engineer to troops in Europe. Transferred to transportation group, flying C-47 before being returned to States for reassignment.

Assigned to Lockbourne AFB as radio operator, B-17s, then transferred to Grenada, MS and assigned to HQ personnel and finance.

Received "ruptured duck" of discharge Oct. 12, 1945 with the rank of tech. sergeant. Awarded Air Medal with three Oak Leaf Clusters, Distinguished Flying Cross and ETO Campaign Ribbon with three stars.

Returned home and became production/inventory control manager of wire mill and retired in 1984 after 43 years service.Married Helen in 1947; they have three boys (two are married) and one granddaughter.

JAMES M. ROSSMAN, was born Aug. 20, 1922 in Atlanta, GA. Grew up in Tampa, FL, graduated from Hillsboro High School and enlisted in the USAAC Jan. 7, 1942. Graduated from pilot training June 1943, Class 43-F at Douglas, AZ. Spent two months School of Aviation Medicine at Randolph Field, TX. Assigned as co-pilot on B-24; destination, 8th Air Force in England.

Assigned to be a replacement crew with 44th Bomb Group which participated in the low level bombing of Ploesti oil fields. Flew 30 missions over Germany with this group. Had a number of close calls on these raids with one resulting in a crash landing in Southern England. No injuries but the aircraft demolished. Returned to U.S. August 1944 and spent remainder of service as an instructor pilot.

Discharged November 1945 with the rank of first lieutenant. Received Distinguished Flying Cross, five Air Medals, two Presidential Unit Citations and campaign ribbons.

Married to Elizabeth Powell and has three sons. Lifetime career as a general lines insurance agent in Florida and now retired.

JOSEPH E. ROTH, was born Jan. 15, 1918 in Connersville, IN. Entered Army, 38th Div. April 17, 1941 and transferred to USAAF; 8th Air Force, 2nd Air Div., 466th

Bomb Group, 785th Sqdn.; class, aircraft and engine mechanic, 747.

Military locations/stations: Smyrna, TN; Goldsboro, NC; Dearborn, MI; Kearns, UT; Alamogordo, NM; and Attlebridge, England.Memorable experience was when he received recognition for 100 missions on *Slick Chick* B-24 which he maintained as a member of the ground crew.

Discharged Sept. 16, 1945 with the rank of sergeant. He was awarded the Good Conduct Medal.

Graduated as ME from Tri-State University. Married Elizabeth Thornbury Aug. 30, 1958; they have two children and four grandchildren. He is retired.

A.E. ROTHCHILD (ROCKY), was born Dec. 18, 1916 near Mankato, KS. Enlisted November 1942 and graduated as a pilot January 1944 at Turner Field, Albany, GA. Left Langley Field, VA July 4, 1944 with a brand new B-24J for England. Subsequently assigned to 467th Bomb Group, 790th Sqdn. at Rackheath, where he achieved rank as captain and served as operations officer from November 1944 until the end of the war. He completed 30 combat missions.

He was discharged November 1945. Medals received include Distinguished Flying Cross, Air Medal with six Oak Leaf Clusters and Presidential Citation for first successful hit on submarine pens at Pointe De Grave, France. He was group command pilot on this mission. Was ranking officer on orders from Gen. Doolittle of the strategic bombing survey conducted in Germany at the end of the war in the ETO.

He moved to West Des Moines, IA in 1949 where he began his career as a home builder and land developer. On Sept. 25, 1993 he celebrated his 50th wedding anniversary with his wife Ida. He enjoys his four children and five grandchildren and is an avid hunter and fisherman.

CECIL T. ROTHROCK, was born Nov. 9, 1921 in Athens, PA. Enlisted in the USAAC March 1942 while attending Northeastern University, Boston, MA. Classification, airman gunner; 8th Air Force, 14th Bomb Wing, 2nd Air Div.

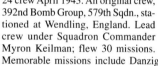

Assigned Harrison Cassell's B-24 crew April 1943. An original crew, 392nd Bomb Group, 579th Sqdn., stationed at Wendling, England. Lead crew under Squadron Commander Myron Keilman; flew 30 missions. Memorable missions include Danzig, Bremen, Hamburg, Kiel Canal, D-day.

His best memories are of the companionship of the crew. Bombardier, William Cetin, lives in Sturtevant, WI. They have remained friends, fishing and hunting buddies, for the past 50 years.

Discharged April 1945 with the rank of staff sergeant. Awarded Distinguished Flying Cross with Oak Leaf Cluster, Air Medal, Silver Cluster and Bronze Cluster, Presidential Unit Citation and four Battle Stars.

Entered Cornell University, Ithaca, NY September 1945. Transferred to Law School, University of Nebraska, LLB in 1951. Naval Air Reserve during the Korean conflict. Admitted Nebraska Bar, 1951; Wisconsin Bar, 1954. Senior partner, Rothrock and Kendall, still practicing.

Married Mary Steadman August 1946; they have three boys, one girl and 10 grandchildren.

JOSEPH D. ROURE (DAN), was born Dec. 21, 1921, Staten Island, NY; grew up in Flatbush, Brooklyn. Working with FBI in Washington (fingerprint technician) when America entered WWII. Applied for Aviation Cadets and was eventually inducted September 1943. Basic training, eliminated aircrew potential, Greensboro, NC, sent to Radar School, Tampa.

Applied for aerial gunnery, completed Tyndall Field, FL ("Gunner of Class" 44-32) August 1944. B-24 crew training, Chatham AAF, GA; flew new B-24 to England February 1945; 14 missions (including Rhine crossing and rammed by FW-190), 328th Bomb Sqdn., 93rd Bomb Group, staff sergeant by V-E day. Pratt Field, KS for B-29, Pacific Theater, but war ended.

Enlisted in reserve, returned to Washington, later New York City police. Applied for USAF commission as wartime first-three-grader, appointed second lieutenant February 1950. Reserve unit activated 1951, over age (29) for other rated training, applied for Electronic Countermeasures Officer Course, graduated Keesler AFB, MS July 1952. Thirty-five Douglas RB-26 electronic reconnaissance sorties, Kimpo AB, Korea, 1952-53. Later assigned Martin RB-57D2 high-altitude strategic reconnaissance, Laughlin, AFB, TX; flew (65,000 feet) out of England and Turkey, 1959 and 1960. Other SAC assignments (including 93rd Bomb Wing, Castle AFB, CA), and HQ 7th Air Force, Tan Son Nhut AB, Saigon, 1968-69.

Entered EB-66 (radar suppression) training, flew 101 sorties from Takhli RTAFB, Thailand until retirement as lieutenant colonel June 1970. Awarded Distinguished Flying Cross, Bronze Star, Air Medal with seven Oak Leaf Clusters, Air Force Commendation with Oak Leaf Cluster and other theater and service ribbons.

He lived in England until 1981 when he returned to Staten Island house he was born in. Now writing memoirs, travel, some amateur theater acting. He has two daughters, two sons and five grandchildren.

HARRY E. ROWBOTTOM, (name now Rowan), was born Aug. 29, 1918 in Evansville, IN; resident of Oklahoma City, OK since 1960. Entered active duty Jan. 17, 1941 as private, HQ Btry., 2nd Bn., 139th FA, 38th Div., Indiana National Guard.

Transferred to USAAF in mid-1942 and as aviation cadet went through Santa Ana, CA, Aero, Polaris graduating as second lieutenant/pilot from Marfa, TX, Class 43-F. Completed B-17 transition training at Hobbs, NM. After one of those military fiascoes and several months of towing targets, was assigned a B-24 crew at Boise, ID; completed combat crew training there.

Then assigned to 566th Sqdn., 389th Bomb Group. Completed tour of 35 missions, June 28, 1944 to Nov. 9, 1944. Crew Members: Bick Summey (cp, Purple Heart), then Hank Fagan (cp); Bruce Adams, (Magellan); Walt Bielanski (bomb aimer, Purple Heart); Charles Blue (flight engineer, deceased); Joe Grosso (Marconi); Max Heither (nose turret, deceased); Dean Dahlke (left waist); Ernie Pohle (right waist); Frank Carney (tail turret).

Recalled September 1948. Flew 106 round trips on Berlin Airlift. Began participation in Air Force Reserve in early 1950s, retiring as lieutenant colonel in 1967. Flew as facilities flight check pilot with the FAA, 1960-75.

JOHN C. ROWE, was born Dec. 11, 1922 in Promise City, IA and raised in Monroe, SD. Joined USAAC in Los Angeles, CA, July 31, 1942. Called for active duty February 1943. Reported to San Antonio Classification Center on February 12, 1943. Pilot training at Coleman, TX; Sherman, TX and Amarillo, TX. B-24 training at Liberal, KS and Boise, ID.

His crew picked up a new B-24J at Topeka, KS. Flew northern route to 8th Air Force via Maine, Labrador, Greenland, Iceland, and Ireland. Assigned to 448th Bomb Group, Seething, England.

Flew first mission Aug. 25, 1944. Completed 35 mission March 11, 1945. Returned to States April 1945 and discharged as first lieutenant, July 1945.

Completed education Drake University, Des Moines, IA. Rehired by Bank of America, retired June 30, 1982 as vice president, Los Angeles main office. Married May 15, 1953 to Agnes Keane and has one daughter.

CHARLES B. ROWLEY JR., was born Oct. 14 1923 in Cleveland, OH. Entered the USAAF February 1943. Military locations/stations: Nashville, TN; Montgomery, AL; Atlantic, GA, Sioux Falls, SD; Yuma, AZ; 93rd Bomb Group Hardwick, England; and Patterson Field, OH.

Memorable experiences: dropping supplies Arnhem, September 1944; and first day weather cleared allowing Air Force to battle Germans in Battle of the Bulge.

Discharged August 1945 with the rank of tech. sergeant. Received Air Medal with five clusters and Presidential Unit Citation.

He is married, has two children and one grandson. Senior vice president of Paine Webber, Incorporated.

HAROLD C. RUBENDALL, was born April 14, 1923 in Oberlin, KS. Entered USAAF Aug. 13, 1943; 612 (armored gunner), 2nd Air Div., 8th Air Force; Rackheath, 467th Bomb Group.

Military locations/stations: inducted at Leavenworth; basic, Sheppard Field, TX; Armorer School, Buckley Field, Denver, CO; gunner, Laredo, TX; Mountain Home, ID, left New York Harbor on *Ile De France* to Glasgow to Rackheath.

Participated in the Battle of the Bulge. He survived miraculous takeoff in fog and subsequent crash landing on return Dec. 29, 1945. Flew 23 missions.

Discharged Nov. 2, 1945 with the rank of staff sergeant. Awarded Good Conduct Medal, Air Medal with three Oak Leaf Clusters, EAME Theater Medal.

He is married and has two daughters and one son. Retired after 42 years in natural gas measurement and production; living in Sublette, KS.

DAVID S. RUBIN, was born in New Haven, CT, Feb. 9, 1918. Received BA degree in economics, Yale 1939 and MS degree in accounting, Columbia University Graduate School of Business 1941.

Entered Army Aug. 9, 1941, Fort Devens, MA. Basic training at Camp Grant, IL; Medical Corpsman, Fort Stevens, OR; commissioned second lieutenant, Nov. 13, 1942 after graduating from Quartermaster OCS, Fort Lee, VA. Assigned to 1063rd QM Co. Serv. Gp. (Avn.), Baer Field, IN; Syracuse AAB, NY; Fort Dix AAB, NJ; and Camp Miles Standish, MA. Assigned to 8th Air Force, 2nd Bomb Div. in December 1943. In 1217th QM Co. Serv. Gp. (Avn.), 392nd Bomb Group at Wendling, England, and 1132nd QM Co. Serv. Gp. (Avn.), 44th Bomb Group at Shipdham, England, for about 10 months each.

At end of tour, was quartermaster and purchasing and contracting officer for the 44th Bomb Group. Discharged from service on Dec. 13, 1945 as first lieutenant, Air Corps. Promoted to captain in reserve.

Recalled to active duty January 1951 as chief, Purchasing and Contracting Div., HQ, Continental Air Command, Mitchell AFB, NY. Transferred to Wiesbaden, Germany in October 1953 with several different assignments in the 7290th Procurement Sqdn., HQ USAFE. Transferred in July 1956 to the London Air Procurement Office (LAPO) as chief, production branch, and deputy chief, LAPO. Promoted to major in July 1958.

One year in training with industry program at Republic Aviation and Sperry Rand; held various positions in the Propulsion Directorate, Ballistic Systems Division, Los Angeles Air Force Station and Norton AFB, CA; assigned to HQ Air Force Systems Command; Research and Development and Base Procurement Div.; DCS Procurement and

Production. Promoted to lieutenant colonel. Retired from active duty, Oct. 15, 1970.

Received Meritorious Service Medal, Air Force Commendation Medal with Oak Leaf Cluster and 11 other campaign or service medals and ribbons.

Married Doris Kessler of Richmond, VA, July 22, 1945. He has a son Martin and a daughter Peggy Borkon, and two grandsons, Andrew and Matthew Borkon.

CLARE F. RUBY, was born March 6, 1919 in Midland, MI. Reared in Saginaw, MI and graduated high school there in 1938. Drafted and entered USAAC training on July 15, 1943.

Was assigned to Air Corps Cadet Program and attended Marietta College at Marietta, OH. They had cadet uniforms and 10 hours pilot flying training while there. At graduation, they were told Air Corps did not need any more flight officers so the whole class was sent to Gunnery School.

Ruby was sent to Yuma AAFB and graduated as a B-24 tail gunner. Went to England with crew and was assigned to 467th Bomb Group, 389th Sqdn. at Rackheath near Norwich, December 1944. He flew 32 combat missions and was on the last mission flown by his crew when the war ended in ETO.

After Japan surrendered, he had enough points to be discharged on Aug. 27, 1945. Received five Air Medals, five Campaign Stars, one Silver Battle Star and one Overseas Service Bar.

Worked 32 years for U.S. Postal Service and retired as an accounting technician on March 6, 1978. Married on May 3, 1941 to Reva I. Hoag; they have three children and four grandchildren. They now live in Florida.

STEVE RUDNYK, was born Aug. 31, 1922 in Butler, PA. Enlisted Detroit, MI October 1942, Aviation Class 44-B; basic training Miami Beach, FL, quarters, Haddon Hall. College training detachment Danville, KY; Maxwell Field for aptitude tests. Pilot primary Decatur, AL (PT-17s) Courtland, AL. Basic flight (BT 13s) twin engine advanced George Field, Lawrenceville, IL. (AT-10s) Savannah, GA. B-24 Flight School, Chatham Field. Assigned co-pilot on George Bridgeman's crew. Overwater navigator and gunnery Batista Field, Havana, Cuba. Mitchell Field, NY, R&R June 1944.

New B-24J to Iceland and Wales. Assigned 409th Sqdn., 93rd Bomb Group. Flew some missions with Bridgeman crew, transferred to Capt. Louis Novotny's crew. Lead ship Magdeburg raid Sept. 11, 1944, 25th mission for Novotny's crew. Shot down, jumped and was captured. On to Stalag Luft I, Barth on the Baltic. Eight months later released by the Russians, last of April 1945.

Made way across Germany on the ground to Allies and on to Paris with Dave Miles and three others. Later shipped home from Camp Lucky Strike on a liberty ship, *The Jonathan Elmer.* Arrived Camp Kilmer, NJ, and home to Detroit for R&R and V-J day. Discharged Camp Kilmer October 1945.

Met and married Geraldine, moved to Arizona 1949. Have four children Ted, Rich, Terry and Patricia; five grandchildren and one on the way. In Detroit until Christmas 1949; Phoenix, AZ until 1963; Scottsdale to 1987; Fountain Hills to present. Owned bar 1950 to 1958, real estate broker 1957 to 1993.

JOHN P. RUMANCIK, was born in Crucible, PA, Oct. 13, 1925. On Oct. 13, 1943, he enlisted in the USAAC as an aviation cadet. After basic training in Biloxi, MS, he was assigned to Gunnery School at Tyndall Field, FL. He continued advanced gunnery and flight training at Ft. Myers, FL, and Charleston, SC, where he was assigned the position as tail gunner on the B-24.

He flew to Wendling, England where he was attached to the 8th Air Force, 392nd Bomb Group, 576th Sqdn. where he completed eight combat missions. Following V-E day, he flew back to the USA and was assigned to Ft. Myers, FL for B-29 gunnery training for Pacific duty.

After V-J day, he was discharged from Maxwell Field, AL on Feb. 5, 1946 with the rank of staff sergeant.

In 1950 he married Lucy O'Brochta; they have two sons, one daughter and two grandchildren. He retired in January 1986 after 37 years service as postmaster of Crucible, PA.

LUTHER DEE RUMMAGE JR., was born May 29, 1923 in High Point, NC. Volunteered December 1941, graduated Aerial Gunnery and Flight Engineer Schools for B-24s.

Assigned to the 448th Bomb Group, 713th Sqdn. in Seething, England. Wounded during his third mission over France and shot down over England on mission #12. Mission #13, April 25, 1943, shot down near Mannheim, Germany and taken to prison farm to work.

With help of Belgium underground, he made it into Switzerland and was prisoner until escaped into France. Stayed with French underground until he made contact with American 7th Army. He was flown home Dec. 23, 1943. He had been missing in action for nine months. What a Christmas present for his folks!

He was discharged October 1945. Entered North Carolina State University and then went back into the Air Force before marrying in 1947.

Stationed in U.S. and Europe until retiring August 1963 as chief master sergeant. He settled in Asheboro, NC and raised four children. Worked as engineer for Burlington Industries in Greensboro, NC until retiring in 1986. Now spends retirement traveling the 50 states and visiting his seven grandchildren. His wife and children are very proud of his accomplishments while serving his country. He is a loving husband and father.

DALE E. RUMMENS, was born Dec. 30, 1922 in Esterville, IA. Entered the USAAC Jan. 30, 1943; tech. sergeant, armorer/gunner. Joined group and crew at Wendover, UT, 448th Bomb Group, 712th Sqdn., Crew #6 in August 1943.

Went to Keesler for basic; Kingman for gunnery; Lowry for armorer; 8th Air Force, Seething, England November 1943.

Participated in Air Offensive Europe, 11 missions: Brunswick, Toton, Gotha, Munster, Kiel, Frankfort, Berlin, and Fredrickshaven.

Memorable experience: Trip to Europe on *Queen Elizabeth,* KP duty whole voyage, battle damage, interned Sweden, Easter Sunday, April 9, 1943 to Oct. 20, 1944, returned England and USA.

Discharged Nov. 3, 1945 with rank tech sergeant. Awarded Purple Heart, Air Medal with one Oak Leaf Cluster, Battle Star for Air Offensive Europe and WWII Victory Medal.

Married March 1951 to Joyce Pease Fuller; they have two sons, one daughter and seven grandchildren. Both sons served Air Force during Vietnam. In 1980, he retired after 33

years with Los Angeles Department of Water and Power as iron worker and supervisor. Now living in fresh mountain air near Tahoe Lake, CA and enjoying life and family. In 1983 returned to England for reunion of 2nd Air Div. The British people were as super then as in the war years.

CHARLIE F. RUSSELL, was born March 15, 1919 in Stroud, OK. Entered the USAAC July 9, 1942; served 8th Air Force, 2nd Air Div, 445th Bomb Group.

Primary flight training for gliders, armorer gunner training, Lowry Field, CO; Harlingen, TX. Participated in Air Offensive Europe, Normandy, Northern France. Flew 30 missions. Shot up but never shot down, went to Munich three times.

Discharged Oct. 4, 1945 from Sheppard Field with rank of staff sergeant with gunners wings. Awarded ETO Service Medal, three Battle Stars, Distinguished Flying Cross and Air Medal with three Oak Leaf Clusters.

Married 1946, has two children. Retired from General Dynamics of Fort Worth after 37 years. Enjoying retirement in Ft. Worth, TX.

HERBERT W. RUSSELL JR., was born May 27, 1922 in Annapolis, MD. On Aug. 25, 1942, he entered USAAF; served 8th Air Force, 44th Bomb Group, 68th Sqdn.

Military locations/stations: basic training, Miami Beach FL; Aerial Gunnery School, Ft. Myers, FL; Salt Lake City, UT; Airplane Mechanic School, Kessler Field, Biloxi, MS; left for Tucson, AZ where crews were formed, had first phase training in Tucson; second and third phase training, Pueblo, CO. Getting a new B-24D, they left Kansas for England via the northern route. Presque Isle, ME; Goose Bay, Labrador, Meeks Field, Iceland; Preswick and Stornoway, Scotland. Then on to England, landing in Shipdham, home of the 44th Bomb Group.

Assigned to the 68th Sqdn., was in Bks. 220th from September 1943 through September 1944. Flew 35 combat missions over Germany as an engineer gunner on B-24 Liberator. Participated in action at Munster, Kiel, Bremen, Berlin, Politz etc. (35 in all).

Back in the States, he was discharged Sept. 17, 1945 with rank of staff sergeant.

Received Good Conduct Ribbon, Air Medal with three Oak Leaf Clusters, Distinguished Flying Cross, EAME Theater Ribbon with four Battle Stars and Presidential Unit Citation with Oak Leaf Cluster.

Russell is retired.

JAMES B.F. RUSSELL, was born in Savannah, GA on March 23, 1923. Attended North Georgia College, 1940-42. Enlisted in Aviation Cadet Program November 1942 and reported for active duty January 1943. Trained as student pilot in Eastern Flying Training Command. Graduated as second lieutenant, Class 44-B at George Field, IL.

Assigned as co-pilot on Harold E. Anderson's Liberator crew at Westover Field in March 1944. Arrived in England in August 1944. Flew combat out of Attlebridge, 466th Bomb Group. Advanced to lead crew. Completed tour of 30 missions.

Separated as first lieutenant in August 1945. Attended Georgia Tech under GI Bill. Became land surveyor and worked for county as road construction superintendent. Now manages family-owned timber lands.

Married to Elinor McCarthy; they have three children: Mary Malinda, Bo (Jr.), Carolyn Lettetia. No grandchildren, yet.

FRANK P. RUSSO, was born March 18, 1926 in Winchester, MA. Graduated Winchester High School June 1943 and was employed by General Electric, Boston, MA until he was inducted at Fort Devens, Ayer, MA on March 20, 1944.

Basic training, Greensboro, NC; Attended Gunnery School, Tyndall Field, FL; and OTU training as a nose gunner on B-24s, Charleston, SC. About November 1, 1944, boarded *Queen Mary* in New York for overseas.

At Old Buckingham, England, was assigned to the 453rd Bomb Group and rose to the rank of staff sergeant. Completed 29 bombing missions over Germany.

He was discharged Dec. 19, 1945 at Westover Field, Springfield, MA. Recipient of the Air Medal with three Oak Leaf clusters, ETO Ribbon with three Battle Stars and Good Conduct Medal.

Owned and operated an auto repair shop with his brother-in-law until his retirement, April 1988. He married Carmela Cila in January 1945; they have one daughter Leslie Ann and three grandsons.

JAMES E. RUTHERFORD, was born Feb. 12, 1922 on a farm in Decatur County, near Greensburg, IN. Married June 20, 1942 to Virginia Bean and has one daughter Linda.

Inducted into service on Sept. 26, 1942. Received basic training in Denver, CO; gunnery training at Las Vegas, NV. Flew to England July 1943 as a tail gunner on a B-24 bomber.

In August 1943 spent time in Africa on detached service with the 8th Air Force. On Oct. 1, 1943, he was wounded on a bombing mission from North Africa to Weiner Neustadt, over the railroad yards. He was with the 93rd Bomb Sqdn.

Received medical discharge on Feb. 24, 1945 with the rank of staff sergeant. He was awarded the Air Medal, Silver Star and Purple Heart.

Worked for the U.S. Postal Service retiring in 1977 after 32 years. Following the death of his wife, Virginia, Rutherford married Kathryn Braley in 1985. She has four children and eight grandchildren.

JAMES E. RUTHERFORD (JIM), was born April 11, 1921 in Mart, TX. After two years of college, he entered aviation cadets, where he was a cadet officer at each station. He graduated as second lieutenant, Class 43-K, from Ellington Field, TX. He then trained in B-24s at Liberal, KS. Then as crew first pilot, he flew B-24 *Little Chum* (named after his wife, Dorothy Wemple) from Topeka, KS to the European Theater of Operations.

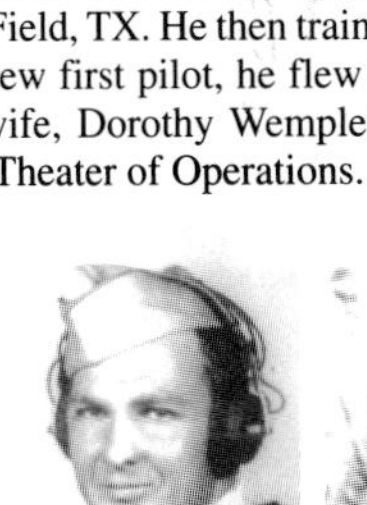

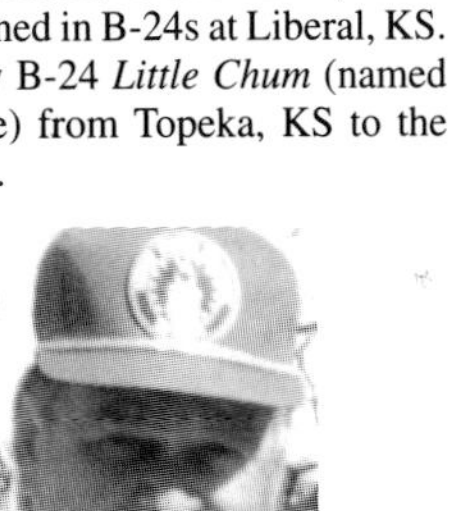

He flew as the lead pilot in the 329th Bomb Sqdn., 93rd Bomb Group, 2nd Air Div, 8th Air Force, England. After 30 combat missions, he sailed for the USA on V-E day. Voluntarily discharged July 25, 1945, he returned to his home in Waco, TX.

After recall to active duty as a captain in 1951, he served as instructor pilot in ATC in Texas until 1955; rescue aircraft commander in Alaska until 1958; base operation officer at Larson AFB, Washington; radar operations at Roswell AFB, NM; Keflavik AFS, Iceland in IDC; Norton AFB, CA in ADC; Luke AFB, AZ in ADC; Qui Nhon, Vietnam as air field commander; HQ 7th Air Force at Ton Son Nhut in Plans.

He retired from Luke AFB as a lieutenant colonel in August 1968. He has been a real estate broker in Glendale and Phoenix since 1970. He and "little chum" celebrated their golden wedding anniversary May 7, 1992. They parented three children and have two grandsons.

LEO W. RYAN, was born June 1, 1918 in Walla Walla, WA. Entered USAAF Jan. 5, 1942; served as bombardier with the 2nd Air Div.

Military locations/stations: Wichita Falls; Barksdale Field; Midland; Old Buckingham, England. He flew 28 missions over Germany. Shot down on 28th mission June 21, 1944 and prisoner of war until April 29, 1945.

Discharged October 1945 with the rank of first lieutenant. Awarded Purple Heart, Air Medal with three Oak Leaf Clusters, Distinguished Flying Cross and POW Medal.

Ryan is single and now retired.

ELBERT T. SABLOTNY (AL), was born on May 12, 1922 in Cleveland, OH. He entered the USAAC in June 1942 as a private and promoted through the ranks to master sergeant. After gunnery training at Fort Myers, FL and Airplane Mechanics School in Amarillo, TX.

He entered Aviation Cadet in April 1943, graduated as second lieutenant navigator on Jan. 15, 1944 from Hondo, TX. He was assigned to the 111th at Langley Field, VA in B-17s from March 1st to April 22, 1944.

Went to the 8th Air Force via the northern route and was assigned to the Station 102 for more training. Was assigned to the 466th Bomb Group heavy B-24s and then to the 467th, 791st Sqdn. to complete 30 combat missions. Then he was transferred to Station 102 as an instructor in March 1945 to May 29, 1945.

Returned to the States on a furlough, then went to Victorville, CA for B-29 training. Joined the Inactive Reserves and was released from active duty in November 1945 as a first lieutenant. He received two Distinguished Flying Crosses, five Air Medals and five European Campaign Stars.

He and Mary Ellen Brown were married on Sept. 20, 1947. They have a son Jim, daughter Mary Beth, and two grandchildren, Tim and Laurie.

ROLAND E. SABOURIN, was born on Nov. 8, 1919 in Haverhill, MA. He enlisted in the USAAC in March 1942 as a pilot in the Aviation Cadet Program in the Class 43-E with the 2nd Air Div.

He took B-24 training in Boise, Wendover, UT and mickey training at Langley AFB. He was assigned to the 392nd Bomb Group, 578th Bomb Sqdn., 2nd Air Div. from April 1944 to November 1944, completing 32 combat missions.

Received the Air Medal, Bronze Star, Distinguished Flying Cross and the Legion of Merit. He was discharged on Aug. 1, 1946 at Grenier Field, NH. He graduated from the University of New Hampshire in 1950. Was immediately recalled and went through Navigation School for the B-47 program. Was stationed at Savannah, GA, Tampa, FL and Shreveport, LA; and in Morocco. He was an instructor in B-52s at Castle Merced, CA; was on the Target Planning Staff at SAC HQ; did a tour in South Vietnam, then back to SAC HQ for four more years.

Retired as commander of the 544th ARTW on Aug. 1, 1974. Was shot at, shot up, but never shot down. His memorable experience was flying on Col. Kielmans' Wing on a mission that aborted. They made a hot approach and landing - nose gear not down and locked. They had all the engines cut-off, no chance to go around, went off the end of the runaway. Col. Rendel chewed on him for so long, he thought he would require surgery.

He and his wife, Genevieve have one son Ronald and two grandsons. He is retired.

PHILIP SACHER, was born on June 21, 1924 in Brooklyn, NY. He was drafted into the USAAF in April 1943 as a flight engineer/top turret gunner on a B-24, heavy bomber.

Went to Wendling, England with the 392nd Bomb Group, 577th Bomb Sqdn. in December 1944. He participated in the battles in the Ardennes, Rhineland and Central Europe.

Received the Air Medal with three Oak Leaf Clusters and the Presidential Unit Citation with two Oak Leaf Clusters. Was discharged in October 1945 with the rank of tech/sergeant.

He received his BS degree from New York University. He is a retired senior vice president of a stock brokerage company and president of Medical Transportation Corp. of America. He is a widower, has one married son. He is retired.

RUSSEL E. SACKREITER, was born on Aug. 25, 1919 in Montevideo, MN. He grew up in Rochester, MN and worked at Consolidated Aircraft Corp for two years prior to enlisting in the USAAC on Oct. 5, 1942.

He completed basic training at BTC #8 in Fresno, CA. He graduated from Flexible Gunnery School in Harlingen, TX in August 1944. Joined Terry Aton's B-24 crew at Lincoln AAF, NE. The crew completed phase training at Mountain Home AAF, ID in December 1944. The crew processed through the staging area at Topeka AAF, KS and traveled by troop train to the PQE at Camp Miles Standish near Boston, MA.

Their crew departed for the ETO on Troop transport *Ile de France* without escort. After processing through Stone, England the crew was assigned to the 328th Bomb Sqdn., 93rd Bomb Group at Hardwick, England. He flew his first mission on Feb. 14, 1945 and his last mission on April 17, 1945. He flew a total of 23 missions; 11 missions as a left waist gunner and 12 missions as a radar operator jamming German radar controlled flak guns. He was a tech/sergeant when he arrived back in the States on June 11, 1945.

After 30 days furlough and an R&R at Santa Ana AAF, CA, he was assigned to Buckley Field, CO. He decided to make the service a career and remained in for nearly 30 years, retiring on Oct. 1, 1972 as a master sergeant. He was assigned to recruiting duty in Youngstown, OH for the next five years.

During that time he met and married Leona E. DeWalk; they celebrated their 47th wedding anniversary on March 16, 1993. He was promoted to master sergeant on April 1, 1951. In the subsequent years, he served a tour in Hawaii, two in Europe and five years on ROTC duty at the University of Missouri as the sergeant major of Detach 440.

He received the Air Medal with three Oak Leaf Clusters, EAME Medal with three Bronze Battle Stars, American Campaign Medal, WWII Victory Medal, Meritorous Service Medal, Air Force Commendation Medal, Air Force Longevity Service Award with one Silver Oak Leaf Cluster and one Bronze Oak Leaf Cluster, Good Conduct Medal, AF Good Conduct Medal with three Bronze Oak Leaf Clusters and the National Defense Service Medal with one Bronze Star from 1945 to 1972.

He moved back to Columbia, MO after retiring at Richards-Gebaur AFB, MO. He worked for a local firm as a purchasing agent for 16 years, retiring from that position in 1988. He and his wife have one son and a daughter; they are both teachers.

JOSEPH SADT, was born on Jan. 31, 1924 in Brooklyn, NY. He enlisted in the USAAF on Nov. 28, 1942 as a radio operator and mechanic with the 445th Bomb Group, 701st Sqdn.

He attended Radio School in Chicago, IL, went to Tibenham, England and then back to Wendover Field in Utah. In the latter part of 1944, their field was straffed at about 2 a.m., just missing the bomb dump. He was out that night at the planes near the dump, serving under his superior, W/O Dunn.

Sadt participated in Ardennes, Central Europe, Normandy, Air Offensive Europe, Northern France and Rhineland campaigns. He received the Distinguished Unit Badge and ETO Ribbon . Was discharged on Oct. 15, 1945 with the rank of corporal.

Married to Evelyn, they have two daughters. He is retired, active at the senior center, where he holds classes in weaving and woodworking.

ROBERT M. SAGE, was born on July 6, 1924 at Monmouth, IL to Clara and Arthur Sage. They moved to Rochelle, Il where on Nov. 19, 1942, he enlisted in the

USAAC as a private. He attended Airplane Mechanic School at Keesler Field in Mississippi.

He had Advance Airplane Mechanic School at Ford Willow Run Plant in Michigan on B-24 bombers. He had gunnery training at Harlingen, TX; earned his gunnery wings and promotion to sergeant; was assigned to the air combat crew as flight engineer on Flank Tarbell crew at Boise, ID. Completed crew training at March Field, CA and was assigned to a B-24J and departed for the ETO by way of the southern route on Dec. 22, 1943.

He arrived at Old Buckingham Air Base with the 453rd Bomb Group, 735th Bomb Sqdn., 2nd Air Div., 8th Air Force in England on Jan. 14, 1944. He flew 27 combat missions against Germany. While he was on a mission to Politz, Germany on June 20, 1944 and flying the waist gun position on Lt. Donald Kolb's crew, the aircraft received extensive damage from ground fire and was forced to land in neutral Sweden and internment.

He was returned to England and back to the 453rd Bomb Group on Oct. 26, 1944. He was awarded a crew citation and the Distinguished Flying Cross for the destruction of the target at Politz, Germany. Returned to the States and married Elizabeth Rucker on July 14, 1945. They have one son, two daughters and eight grandchildren.

He was discharged from active duty on Aug. 22, 1945. Was recalled to service while a member of the Reserves on July 30, 1950 and he served until July 31, 1953 as a training flight engineer for C-46 Troop Carriers. While he was with the 8th Air Force in England, he was awarded the Distinguished Flying Cross, the Air Medal with three Oak Leaf Clusters, the EAME Ribbon with four Battle Stars.

JOHN SALADIAK, was born on Dec. 10, 1917 in Pittsburgh, PA. He earned his wings in the Canadian Air Force in 1941. He served as a navigator with the Canadian Air Force, RAF and USAAF.

He was with the 44th Bomb Group and was a navigator in a Liberator on the Aug. 1, 1943 raid on Ploesti. On this raid he flew with Edward Mitchell (pilot), Donald Decker (co-pilot), Julio Castellotti (waist gunner), Henry Flister (tail gunner), James Kipple (bombardier), David Collie (waist gunner), Robert McAdams (flight engineer and top turret gunner). He and all his crew were interned in Turkey.

He was awarded the Distinguished Flying Cross for extraordinary achievement while participating in operations against the Ploesti oil refineries. Back in England he was stationed at Shipdham. He was married in East Dereham Parish Church on Nov. 25, 1944. After returning to the States in 1945, he stayed in the USAF until 1948, when he was honorably discharged as a first lieutenant. He had injuries which plagued him for many years and eventually led to the amputation of his right leg.

He graduated from Dequesne University with a BS degree and worked for about 20 years as a field agent for the Internal Revenue Service. He retired in 1984. He has enjoyed travelling in Eastern and Western Europe and spends much time reading and listening to classical music.

JOSEPH D. SALISBURY, was born on Sept. 25, 1918 in Medina, OH. He graduated from Columbus North High School in 1936 and Ohio State University in 1942. Was commissioned on June 15, 1942, when he was sworn in with 3500 other ROTC cadets by Lt. Gen. Lewis B. Hershey.

He reported to the Field Artillery Training Center in Ft. Bragg, NC. He married Juanita on July 28, 1942 on his first leave. Transferred to the USAAC. Received his wings on Oct. 1, 1943 and was sent to Ft. Worth, TX for B-24 pilot transition training; crew training was at Peterson Field, CO. He reported to the 445th Bomb Group, 700th Bomb Sqdn. in May 1944.

His first mission was on May 31st, his second mission was on D-day over Caens, France. Over Berlin on June 21, 1944, he took extensive flak damage. He trailed a B-17 formation to enemy coast coming out over a seething North Sea with two engines shot out, a runaway propeller on third and the fourth running out of fuel. He ditched in 12' to 15' waves. Five of nine crewmen perished. The remainder of the crew were rescued after 22 hours by a British Royal Navy launch.

After R&R in England, he returned to complete 30 missions. The crew members who lost their lives were: William J. Diercks, Joe Farino, John R. Koppitz, Ensign M. Tunstall and Angelo C. Vetri.

The saddest occasion was meeting the only four of 39 planes from the 445th Bomb Group, which flew the Kassel mission of Sept. 27, 1944. This translated into roughly 300 group personnel, who failed to return to base including the 700th CO and several from my quonset hut.

He is extremely proud of the 445th Bomb Group, which was awarded the Croix de Guerre avec Palm by the French government as well as a Presidential Unit Citation.

After his discharge, he returned to the College of Veterinary Medicine, graduating with the DVM degree in 1949. He spent 37 years in Public Health investigating disease transmissible between man and animal. He is now retired. Salisbury has been married for over 51 years and has three children and four grandchildren.

EUGENE A. SALTARELLI, was born on Feb. 22, 1923 in Buffalo, NY. He enlisted in the USAACR in November 1942, while attending Buffalo State Teachers College. Was called to active duty in February 1943, graduating as a pilot, second lieutenant, Class 44-E at Valdosta, GA. As a co-pilot on a B-24 crew, he flew 27 missions in the 466th Bomb Group, 785th Sqdn. at Attlebridge.

He received the Air Medal with three Oak Leaf Clusters, two European Campaign Stars and the Presidential Unit Citation. After V-E day, he remained at Attlebridge to assist in closing down the base. He flew back to the States landing at Bradley Field, CT at the end of July 1945.

Was discharged from active duty in November 1945. Received a bachelor of mechanical engineering degree from the University of Detroit in June 1949 and a master of science degree in mechanical engineering from Northwestern University in June 1950. He was employed by the Westinghouse Bettis Atomic Power Laboratory as an engineer in the design and initial testing of the first nuclear powered submarines commissioned for the U.S. Navy.

He retired in 1988 after 38 years in the power engineering and construction industry. When he retired, he was senior vice-president of the Power Engineering for Brown and Root, Inc. in Houston, TX.

Married Jean Marie Cray on Nov. 25, 1950 and has six children and 11 grandchildren.

JOHN A. SAMSELL, was born on June 24, 1922 in Moosic, PA. He joined the USAAF in September 1940. Graduated from Aircraft Maintenance School, Chanute Field, IL in April 1941. He was assigned to operations and engineering with the 16th Pursuit Group (P-40s) in Panama prior to the Pearl Harbor attack.

Graduated as pilot in the Class 44-B. He joined the B-24 crew of John Beder as a co-pilot in June 1944. He reported to the 392nd Bomb Group at Wendling, England in August 1944. After a dozen missions, he was assigned as lead crew. While completing a 30 mission tour, he participated in the Battle of the Bulge and the Crossing of the Rhine.

Samsell was discharged in August 1945 with the rank of first lieutenant. He married Dolores Zenker in 1946. He enjoyed a career in packaging and shipping supply business in New Jersey for 43 years. The last 28 years as president of Central Jersey Steel Strapping Co. until retiring in January 1989. During the past 20 years, he has traveled extensively to all parts of the world.

GEORGE A. SAMUDIO, was born on Jan. 4, 1926 in Casco, WI. He joined the USAAF on Jan. 31, 1944; basic training at Keesler Field; Gunnery School at Tyndall Field, FL; and overseas training in Charleston, SC.

He was assigned to the 389th Bomb Group, 564th Bomb Sqdn., 2nd Air Division. His memorable experience was the low level trolley missions as host to ground personnel. His awards include the Air Medal, EAME Campaign Medal, American Campaign Medal, Distinguished Unit Badge, WWII Victory Medal, National Defense Service Medal, Armed Reserve Forces Meritorious Service Ribbon and others. Was discharged on May 2, 1946 with the rank of staff sergeant.

Joined the Air National Guard in 1958 as a Federal Civil Service Technican. Served as fire chief at the Toledo Express Airport 180th TFG and at Buckley Field, Co and Nellis AFB as crash rescue fire fighter. He retired in 1985 as SMSGT.

He and his wife Alberta adopted two boys in 1958, Albert and Frederick, who now reside in Denver, CO. Samudio and his wife enjoy roller skating and touring the USA in their motor home.

FRANK L. SANBORN JR., was born on Sept. 6, 1923 in Middletown, CT. Joined the USAAF on Feb. 8, 1943. After basic training in Miami Beach, FL, he trained as a radio operator and mechanic in Sioux Falls, SD. He attended Gunnery School in Harlingen, TX.

Joined the air crew at March Field, CA. He was assigned to the 458th Bomb Group, 96th Wing, 8th Air Force at Horsham St. Faith, England on May 13, 1944. Completed 35 combat missions plus eight gas missions to the 5th Army in France.

He received the Air Medal with five Oak Leaf Clusters, ETO Medal, Certicificate of Valor and the Meritorious Achievement Award. He remembers flak, buzz bombs and V-2 rockets. He returned to the States on Feb. 27, 1945. He trained new men at Laredo, TX and Pueblo, CO. He was discharged on Oct. 18, 1945 at Mitchell Field, NY.

He married Lorraine F. Fournier on Oct. 14, 1950. They have two sons, one daughter and two grandchildren. He worked for Northeast Utilities for 40 years, 15 of those years as a lineman and 25 years in various supervisory positions in electric operations. He retired in 1986.

ORLANDO J. SANCHEZ (JOSE), was born on June 15, 1921 in Guerrero, Tamps, Mexico. He spent his early childhood in his ancestral home, The Trevino Fort in San Ygnacio, Zapata Co, TX. He attended school in Laredo, TX and in Corpus Christi, TX where he graduated from Corpus Christi High School in 1941. He later attended Corpus Christi Junior College until October 1942, when he volunteered to join the USAAC.

After finishing an airplane mechanics course at the Army Air Forces Technical Training Command in Gulfport, MS, he was transferred to Kingman Army Airfield in Kingman, AZ, where he graduated as an aerial gunner on Sept. 13, 1943.

From Kingman, AZ he was assigned to Boise Air Base in Boise, ID; where the 458th, B-24 Combat Group was being organized. He became a member of Lt. Wilfred F. Tooman's lead crew #22, 753rd Sqdn.

The 458th Bomb Group trained in Wendover, UT and Tonapah, NV until December 1943, when it left for England to join the US Army 8th Air Force. Their base in England was Horsham St. Faith Airdrome in Norwich. While flying with the 458th, his crew had two B-24 airplanes, the *Bomb Ah Dear* and *Lassie Come Home*. His crew position was nose gunner, but he also substituted as an engineer flying with different crews.

After D-day lead crew 22 having finished their missions, volunteered, along with other crews from the 458th Bomb Group, to join a highly classified project. This involved guiding radio-controlled, explosive laden robot B-17s from a mother plane to targets in occupied German. These crews joined the 388th B-17 Bomb Group at Knettishall Air Base near Thetford. The operation was carried out from a satellite base at Winfarthing-Fersfield Army Airdrome. Crew 22 was flying a B-17G, *Pappy's Bad Boys* as their mother ship to guide the robots. Their targets were V-2 sites and submarine installations in Northern Germany. These missions were carried out without fighter escort.

At Fersfield, the USN Coastal Command were experimenting with Aizon Bombing. On one occasion, Sgt. Ray Wilson, Sgt. O.J. Sanchez and Sgt. E.T. Karrels, all members of crew 22, were called to help a pilot and co-pilot fly a B-24 bomber to Fersfield from a Navy base. R. Wilson was the radioman, O.J. Sanchez the engineer and Karrels the tail gunner. This B-24 bomber was to be fitted out as a robot for the USN.

On Aug. 12, 1944, the USN Lt. Joseph P. Kennedy Jr. as pilot and USN Lt. Wilford J. Willey as co-pilot flew this robot off the base. A USN Vega Ventura bomber flew as the mother plane to guide the robot. Contact was made by radio between the robot and the mother plane and everything checked out. As the robot approached the village of Beccles, where they would turn over the controls to the mother plane and parachute to the field below, the robot mysteriously exploded ending the lives of both fliers.

Crew 22 flew many successful missions until the end of the war. Sanchez was awarded the Air Medal with three Oak Leaf Clusters, ETO Medal with six Campaign Stars and three group citation Medals.

He returned to the States in September 1945. In January 1946, he enrolled in Texas Chiropractic College in San Antonio, TX and graduated four years later as a Doctor of Chiropractic. He established his practice in Corpus Christi, TX. In 1955, he married Miss Eulalia Cantu from Woodsboro, TX, they have two sons and two daughters. He is still working full time.

JACK SANDERS, was born on Jan. 1, 1921 in Tulsa, OK. He entered the USAAC on Jan. 1, 1942, joining the 125th Observation Sqdn., Air National Guard and stationed at Fort Sill, Lawton, OK. He applied for flight training and was accepted for pilot training, starting at San Antonio, TX and working through the central training command. He graduated from twin engine training at Altus, OK Air Base in the Class of 43-E.

His first assignment was to a special group of B-17 bombers in training at Scotts Bluff, NE. The crews were commanded by West Point graduates. After a few weeks of training, the crews were dismantled and he was sent to Casper, WY and Boise, ID for B-24 training. After the training period at Boise, Casper and Scotts Bluff, he became aircraft commander and assembled his crew.

The B-24 aircraft *Black Jack* and Sanders' crew departed West Palm Beach, FL on Dec. 17, 1943. Their destination was Fortaleza, Brazil. Upon receiving their orders, they proceeded to Marrakech, Morocco and on to Prestwick, Scotland and their assignment to the 453rd Bomb Group, 734th Sqdn. to Old Buckingham, England.

The *Black Jack* flew her first mission on March 16, 1944 to Friedrichshafen and continued on to complete a tour of 31 missions, the last mission on June 29, 1944 to Kothen. The toughest mission was the April 22nd strike at Hamm, Germany and the night return to base. Ten minutes before a safe return to Old Buck, a German fighter rose up from the cover of darkness and clobbered them from the rear, taking out the two inboard engines and severely damaging #1. They crashed at Tibenham, about 2215 and by the Grace of God, they walked away, even the wounded.

He was awarded the Distinguished Flying Cross with one Oak Leaf Cluster.

Upon returning to the States, he was assigned to B-29 training at Kirtland Field, NM. After returning to civilian life, he returned to the Air National Guard, 125th Fighter Sqdn., flying P-51 Mustangs. He married his high school sweetheart, Helen Johnson. They have been married for 51 plus years and have one son Gary and one grandson Jeffrey. He is retired after 45 years of fire protection and fire prevention services. He and his wife reside in their hometown of Tulsa, OK.

JOHN L. SANDERS, was born on Jan. 31, 1916 in Lamar County, TX. He enlisted with the USAAC as a technical inspector with the 2nd Air Division.

He arrived in UK with the 60th Compliment Sqdn. in Horsham, Norwich. He was later transferred to HQ at Ketteringham Hall. His memorable experiences were meeting and visiting some wonderful English families on voyage to England; and the viscous storm in the mid-Atlantic they were in.

Sanders received the ETO Medal. He was dishcarged in October 1945 with the rank of first lieutenant and as a captain in the Reserves.

He and Janice Caldwell were married on May 31, 1942. They have two daughters, one grandson and one great-grandson. He is retired after 11 years in aircraft work and 17 years as a paint contractor.

J. EVERETT SANDERSON (SANDY), was born on May 15, 1920 in Bakersfield, CA. He enlisted in the USAAC May 26, 1942 from the University of Montana. CTD at Texas A&M; SAACC; Navigation School at Ellington. Joined B-24 crew of Pilot Ed Wanner at Peterson Field, then shipped on *Queen Elizabeth* to Scotland and the 445th Bomb Group, 700th Sqdn. at Tibenham in June 1944.

Flew 30 combat mission, all but the first seven as deputy, squadron, or group lead crew. His memorable experiences: waiting at base for ill fated Kassel mission on Sept. 27, 1944 when only 4 of 35 planes returned and being briefed by Lt. Col. James Stewart for experimental six ship element bombing.

Sanderson received the Distinguished Flying Cross, Air Medal and Oak Leaf Clusters, and the EAME with Bronze Service Stars. He was discharged on June 18, 1945 with the rank of first lieutenant.

He and his wife Barbara have been married for 50 years. They have three children and five grandchildren. He retired after 35 years as a forest ranger and supervisor for the U.S. Forest Service.

JAY M. SANDLER, was born on March 22, 1922 in New York, NY. He enlisted September 1942 while he was a student at Ohio State University. After graduating, he was inducted on April 8, 1943.

After accelerated pre-flight at Maxwell Field, AL; he received primary pilot training at Camden, AR; basic training at Greenville, MS and advanced twin-engine at Columbus, MS in Class 43-K. He was commissioned as a pilot in November 1943 and assigned to B-24 Combat Crew Training School at Casper, WY.

Was assigned overseas on March 3, 1944, where he flew B-24 110043 to England via Topeka, KS; Morrison Field, West Palm Beach, FL; Borinquen Field, Puerto Rico; Belem, Brazil; Dakar, French West Africa and Ireland. Joined the 8th Air Force, 446th Bomb Group, 706th Sqdn. in Bungay, England. His first combat mission was on May 7, 1944. Was commissioned as a first lieutenant on June 3rd. He flew D-day mission with the 446th Bomb Group and was selected to lead the entire 8th Air Force on that day. He completed combat tour with his 31st mission on July 20, 1944. It was believed to be the shortest time from induction to a completed tour.

On return to the States, he flew radar training missions from Victorville, CA until his discharge on Aug. 3, 1944. He received the Distinguished Flying Cross and the Air Medal with three Oak Leaf Clusters.

He married Estelle Bergelson in 1953; they have one son Dale.

EDWARD SANICKI, was born on Jan. 1, 1924 in Niagara, WI. He enlisted in the USAAC on Dec. 13, 1942 as a pilot; was in Class 44-C at Blythville, AR; then assigned to the 467th Bomb Group at Rackheath, England.

Finishing his combat tour of 35 missions, he received the Air Medal with Oak Leaf Clusters and was discharged in December 1945.

He is married and has three children. Sanicki is a retired vice-president of a life insurance company.

HUBERT E. SARGENT JR., was born on Aug. 22, 1920 in Concord, NH and grew up in Montpelier, VT. Attended Norwich University, Northfield, VT. Graduated from Flying School at Blackland Army Air Field in Waco, TX, Class of 43-A.

Went to B-17 School at Lockbourne AFB, OH; joined the 466th BG at Clovis, NM; went to Gunnery and Instrument schools at Davis-Monthan AAF; joined the 2nd Air Div. in England at Attlebridge early in March 1944 and became squadron OPS officer. Flew 30 missions as command pilot in B-24s.

Returned to the States in March 1945; went to Counter Intelligence School at Holabird Signal Depot; sent to Linz, Austria with Counter Intelligence Corp.; accepted regular commission and was transferred to Weisbaden, Germany. Flew the Berlin Air Lift from Weisbaden to Berlin for three months.

Returned to the States in 1950 and he commanded a MATS C-97 Strato-Cruiser Sqdn, at Westover AFB, MA. Attended Command and Staff School at Maxwell Field, AL; spent three years at MATS HQ at Andrews AFB in Maryland; went to Northeast Air Command HQ, St. Johns, Newfoundland, again in manpower.

Returned to the States in 1957 to TAC and became commander of a troop carrier squadron at Pope AFB, NC, then assistant wing operations officer. Transferred to 9th Air Force HQ at Shaw AFB, SC for four years and commanded the Air Force Combat Airlift Support Unit at Fort Benning, GA in 1964 to 1966.

Retired at Maxwell AFB in July 1966. Was awarded the Distinguished Flying Cross with Oak Leaf Cluster, Air Medal with Silver Oak Leaf Cluster, Medal for Humane Action and the Air Force Commendation Medal.

Moved to Gastonia, NC and was employed by Wix Corp. He retired in 1983 and now plays golf and travels. He spends part of each summer on Cape Cod, his wife's home, and the winter in Florida. They have one son and two grandsons. He frequently participates in the 2nd Air Division of the 8th Air Force Amateur Radio Net on Tuesday mornings. His call sign is K4QPX.

JOSEPH A. SASSANO, was born on Dec. 21, 1922 in Akron, OH. He enlisted in the USAF in 1941 and was assigned to the 93rd Bomb Group as a navigator. Stationed at Hondo, TX; Idaho; and Hardwick, England. Participated in action in Germany.

Sassano was discharged in 1946 with the rank of second lieutenant and received the Air Medal and several other medals.

He is married, and they have four children. He is retired.

JAMES A. SAWYER, was born on March 19, 1923 in Limestone County, TX. He completed pilot training at Frederick, OK on Oct. 1, 1943 and trained as a co-pilot with the Steve Bridges crew. He arrived at the 565th Sqdn., 389th Bomb Group in early March 1944 and assigned as a co-pilot to Kelly's crew.

Flew his first mission on March 5, 1944, was promoted to pilot after his 14th mission on April 13th when Kelly completed his missions. Sawyer flew his 30th and last mission on June 2, 1944. Was an instructor pilot until he was discharged in the fall of 1945.

Worked for Union Carbide for nine years, before going to work for the FAA as an Air Traffic Controller in El Paso Center. Now retired from Houston ARTCC and living in Dickinson, TX.

He is married to Olga Oliver and they are the proud parents of one son and two daughters.

HAROLD P. SBROCCO, was born on June 15, 1924 in Brooklyn, NY. He enlisted in the USAAC on Nov. 28, 1942. Took his basic training in Miami Beach, FL and was assigned as a DI. After 10 months was sent to Greensboro, NC, then two months later was reclassified and sent to AM School, then to Gunnery School and Engineers School on B-24s.

Was assigned to a crew, then sent to Mitchell Field in Long Island, NY for overseas training, sent to 8th Air Force in Bungay, England and to Flexton Air Field to 446th Bomb Group, 705th Bomb Sqdn. He flew 21 missions on the plane named *Shady Sadie.* He was discharged on Nov. 18, 1945.

He married his teenage sweetheart, Josephine M. DePietro on Oct. 5, 1946. They have three sons, three daughters and 13 grandchildren. He lost Josephine on Feb. 26, 1967 and with the help of his family, was able to raise the children. He married Florence E. Golankiewicz on Nov. 29, 1992, and she has four grandchildren.

JAMES J. SCANLON, was born on June 17, 1924 in Denver, CO. He joined the USAAC on Aug. 6, 1942. Graduated from Pilot Class 43-K from Pampa, TX. Transition in B-24 at Liberal, KS. Picked up his crew at Hamer Field, CA; took operational crew training at Tonopah, NV. At the age of 19, he had a bomber crew ready to go to war. He flew a new B-24 from Hamilton Field, CA to Nuts Corner, Ireland via Labrador and Iceland. Was assigned to the 453rd Bomb Group, 734th Sqdn. in Old Buckingham, England. He completed 35 missions with his original crew. The last B-24 mission was Berlin on Feb. 26, 1945.

Joined the 4th Fighter Group, 335th Sqdn. on Feb. 28th. Trained in P-51 Mustangs, then flew combat until the war ended. Was over Berlin in a B-24 on Feb. 26th and 42 days later he was over Berlin in a P-51 Mustang.

Retired on April 1, 1975 after 32 years, seven months and two days of military service. He had been assigned to most all major commands, including combat in both bombers and fighters, while flying 45 different military airplanes, including 4-engine bombers and transports, twin engine bombers and transports; single engine fighters; multi and single engine jets and numerous military training planes and many civilian airplanes, while logging 12,000 hours.

Was assigned to the following military commands: SAC, TAC, Air Defense Command, Air Material Command, Systems Command, Training Command, Joint U.S. Taiwan Defense Command, 8th Air Force, 5th Air Force etc.

He is married and has eight children. He continued in the aviation business after his retirement from the USAF. He is one lucky aviator!

BENJAMIN C. SCHAEFER, was born on Jan. 14, 1925 in Cincinnati, OH. He enlisted in the USAAC in June 1943. Was with the 748th, 2nd. Air Division. Went into the cadet program while attending Iowa State Teachers College; Engine Mechanic School, Amarillo, TX; Gunnery School, Fort Myers, FL; Flight Engineer School, Westover Air Base, MA.

Joined up with the 389th Bomb Group in Norwich, England in 1945. He participated in the battles of the Rhineland and Central Europe.

His most memorable flight was his first mission. They were flying tail end "Charlie" in the low group, target was Wilhemshaven Docks. As they were approaching their I.P., the lead group was over the target and flack was heavy. It looked like they were going to be flying through a wall of flack. The lead group's bombs didn't drop. They made a 360

degree turn. The flack stopped! This was to be an electronic bomb drop, which didn't work for the lead group. They dropped their bombs off their group's bombardier. The lead group fell in behind them and the flack again was very intense. The lead group took a lot of flack that day. They had his admiration and thanks.

He received the American Theater Ribbon, EAME Theater Ribbon with two Bronze Stars, Good Conduct Medal, Distinguished Unit Badge and the WWII Victory Medal. Was discharged on Feb. 20, 1946 with the rank of technical sergeant.

He and Helen were married on Nov. 4, 1944. They have two daughters and one son. He is retired from General Electric Jet Engines after 37 years of service. He is active in the Masonic and Eastern Star Order. He does volunteer work for the Shriners Burns Hospital and is a member of the Syrian Shrine and the Valley of Cint Scottish Rite. He enjoys travelling and is currently ill with terminably cancer.

FRANK N. SCHAEFFER, was born on Dec. 6, 1921 in Milwaukee, WI. He graduated from Washington High School and enlisted in the USAAC on Sept. 15, 1942. He attended Airplane Mechanics School at Sheppard Field, TX; Aerial Gunnery School at Tyndall Field, FL.

He is credited with six missions as engineer on Lt. Bernard J. Komasinski's B-24 crew with the 506th Sqdn., 44th Bomb Group. He bailed out of a burning plane over enemy occupied territory on a mission to LaPerthe, France on Aug. 8, 1944. Was able to evade capture with the aid of French resistors for three weeks until he was liberated by General Patton's 3rd Army on Aug. 28, 1944 at Orbais l'Abbaye, Marne, France.

He returned to the States and graduated from Willow Run Factory School. Worked with a B-17 ground crew and flew gunner training flights as an engineer at Laredo, TX. He ended his service career as an orderly room clerk in a basic training squadron at Sheppard Field, TX.

Was discharged on Nov. 29, 1945 with the rank of staff sergeant. He received the Air Medal, EAME Medal, two Bronze Battle Stars, Good Conduct Medal and the WWII Victory Medal.

He worked as a machining inspector at General Electric and Chrysler Corp. until retiring in 1983. He is single.

ELVIN N. SCHEETZ, was born on Feb. 5, 1925 in Allentown, PA. He entered the USAAC on April 13, 1943. Had basic training in Miami Beach, FL; Mechanics School at Keesler Field, MS; and Gunnery School at Tyndall Field, FL.

Was assigned to train on a B-24 crew in Lincoln, NE. From there to Mt. Home, ID and Peterson Field, CO. After training with a crew, they went to Topeka, KS and received a new B-24. From there they went to Westover, MA to Labrador, Iceland, Ireland and then to England. He was assigned to the 44th Bomb Group. After being there for about two months, he was transferred with a large group, that consisted of all ranks and crew positions.

They left with a British convoy to Naples, Italy. At Naples, he was picked up by a B-25 and flown to Corsica and assigned to the 321st Bomb Group, 446th Sqdn. He was shot down on his 32nd mission over the Brenner Pass at Campo, Italy and bailed out.

Was discharged on Nov. 3, 1945 with the rank of staff sergeant. He received the Air Medal with two Oak Leaf Clusters, Purple Heart, POW Medal, and the EAME Campaign Ribbon with four Bronze Stars.

He and Jean B. Bachman were married on Aug. 4, 1945. They have one daughter and two grandchildren. He is retired from the IBEW as an electrican and previously was a supervisor for National Steel Corp.

WALTER A. SCHEIBER, was born on Jan. 31, 1922 in New York City, NY. He joined the USAAC on March 18, 1943. After Radio School at Scott Field, IL and Aerial Gunnery School at Laredo, TX, he was assigned to B-24 crew training at Muroc Field, CA.

He joined the 752nd Sqdn., 458th Bomb Group at Horsham St. Faith in July 1944 and flew his first mission on Aug. 4, 1944. He flew 35 missions over Germany, France, Belgium, Holland and Luxemburg. He crash landed once in France on Dec. 31, 1944, after his plane lost two engines over Coblenz. The pilot intended to return to base to keep a New Year's Eve date, but was persuaded not to try by an armed and determined flight engineer.

Scheiber was discharged on Sept. 8, 1945. He attended Columbia Law School on the GI Bill. He is married and has four children and five grandchildren. Spent the years from 1947 to 1991 as a lawyer, businessman and government official. He is retired and consulting in the Washington, DC area.

WARREN E. SCHERBERT, was born on June 2, 1924 in Milwaukee, WI. He enlisted in February 1943; took basic in Miami Beach, FL; Airplane Mechanics School, Keesler Field; Gunnery School, Harlingen, TX; combat crew training, Westover Field, MA. Was assigned to the 489th Bomb Group, 844th Sqdn. as a flight engineer with the 8th Air Force, Halesworth, England.

Was also stationed at these stations: Topeka, KS; Lincoln, NE; Amarillo, TX. He went to B-29 Engineer School, Davis Montham Field in Tuscon, AZ. Completed 30 missions from July to December 1944 in ETO.

His memorable experiences was on Aug. 16, 1944 at Magdeburg when his Bomb Group 489th had bombs dropped on them by the 446th Bomb Group. They had both reached the target at the same time. He was flying top turret when he looked up and saw 100# bombs falling on them. Lt. Walter Springer's plane was hit and blew up, only two crew members survived. The next experience was on Sept. 18, 1944 at Groesbeck, Holland on low level mission at 200 feet. They lost three planes in his group. The small arms fire was intense - one plane hit the church steeple and one hit a dyke. Their plane was hit many times by small arms fire. Just seeing the Germans on the ground at that altitude and shooting at them was unbelievable.

He received the ETO Unit Citation, Good Conduct Medal, Air Medal with four Oak Leaf Clusters and three Battle Stars. He was discharged on Oct. 18, 1944 with the rank of technical sergeant.

He was married on Oct. 9, 1948 and has three children. He is a retired tool and die maker.

JOHN H. SCHLICHER JR (JACK), was born on April 2, 1922 in Allentown, PA. He enlisted on Sept. 15, 1942; was assigned to the 448th Bomb Group, 715th Sqdn. as a navigator, stationed at Seething, England. Completed 31 missions.

He received the Air Medal with three Oak Leaf Clusters and the Distinguished Flying Cross. He was discharged on Sept. 15, 1945 with the rank of first lieutenant.

He and Blanche Stowe were married on March 23, 1945. They have one son, John E. Schlicher is retired from General Dynamics as an engineering chief, with the R&E Department.

BEN H. SCHLOSSER, was born on Feb. 17, 1919 at Tamaqua, PA. He enlisted into the USAAF on June 26, 1943 as an aerial engineer. Stationed at Greensboro, NC; Biloxi, MS; Harlingen, TX; Boise, ID; Kirtland, NM and Tibenham, England.

Assigned to the 445th Bomb Group, 701st & 703rd Sdqn. He particapted in the Battles of the Ardennes, Rhineland and Central Europe. His memorable experience was on April 2, 1945 when the bombs were dropped through the right wing.

Schlosser received the EAME Medal with three Bronze Stars, Good Conduct Medal, Air Medal with three Bronze Clusters and one Overseas Bar. Was discharged Oct. 25, 1945 with the rank of tech sergeant.

He and Mary H. Piches Simer were married on March 30, 1948; they have three daughters. He is retired.

JACK J. SCHMIDT, was born on March 19, 1924 in Milwaukee, WI. He enlisted into the USAAC in March 1943.

He was in Amarillo, TX; LaGrande, OR; Santa Ana, CA; Hondo, TX; and Mt. Home, ID where he met his B-24 crew. After three months in Mt. Home, went to Tibenham, England to join the 8th Air Force, 445th Bomb Group, 700th Sqdn.

His memorable experience was flying 12 missions and bombing Berlin twice. Was discharged in September 1945 with the rank of flight officer.

Schmidt is married and has two children. He is a graduate of the University of Wisconsin. Spent 40 years in the industrial relations field plus he moonlighted as a teacher for 10 years for the University of Wisconsin and the Carthage College. He retired in 1991.

JAMES R. SCHNEIDER, was born in Benwood, WV March 15, 1918. Entered USAAC March 1943 after attending Miami and Ohio State Universities. After completing basic training in Clearwater, FL was assigned to Lowry Field, Denver, CO. After completing bomb sight maintenance training, was assigned to the 458th Bomb Group at Wendover Field, UT. In January 1944, he went overseas with the 458th Bomb Group at Horsham St. Faith, England.

Returned to USA in May 1945 and reported for B-29 training at Kirtland Field, Albuquerque, NM. The end of Pacific hostilities brought his discharge in November 1945.

He returned to the Timken Company as a mechanical engineer and retired in 1983 after 40 years service; the last 35 years in various management capacities.

Married Mina Belle Hostetler in March 1983. He has two sons and three grandchildren.

EDWARD SCHOESSLER, was born Sept. 2, 1921 in Portland, OR. Joined the USAAC August 1942; basic training at Sheppard Field, TX; went to San Diego, CA to consolidated B-24 factory for crew chief training. Formed an air crew with Lt. Parks as pilot; in 1943, they joined the 8th Air Force, 2nd Div., 44th Bomb Group, 67th Sqdn.

Completed 25 missions as a flight engineer. Became a B-24 instructor, in instruments and hydraulics at a mobile training unit in England. Was sent to Mt. View Air Base, Boise, ID in September 1944 as an instructor. Discharged September 1945.

Received the Distinguished Flying Cross, four Air Medals, and two European Campaign Stars.

Married Irene Rose Muth on May 11, 1943 and has a daughter, son, four grandchildren and one great-grandchild. He was a mechanic for United Air Lines, San Francisco; retired in 1979. Presently lives in Sutter, CA with his wife of 50 years.

ARNOLD SCHONBERG, was born in New York City, Oct. 15, 1922. Completed civilian pilot training program on J3 seaplane while attending New York University, 1942. Enlisted in USAAC as aviation cadet Feb. 3, 1943. Completed twin engine pilot training at George Field, IL, Feb. 8, 1944 and commissioned second lieutenant, Class 44-B. Served as flight instructor for two months at George Field, then entered B-24 training unit at Chatham Field, GA, then to Langley Field, VA for radar training.

Left Langley July 7, 1944, to deliver B-24 to England via North Atlantic route to Valley, Wales. Assigned to 491st Bomb Group, 8th Air Force at Metfield; moved to North Pickenham when bomb dump exploded, where he completed a tour of 31 combat missions.

Delivered B-24 to Windsor Locks, CT and left service at Ft. Dix as first lieutenant July 7, 1945. Awarded Distinguished Flying Cross, six Air Medals, Presidential Unit Citation, five ETO Battle Stars, Conspicuous Service Cross New York State, plus others.

Holds FAA commercial pilot ratings for single engine land and sea, multi-engine land, instrument and presently flying twin engine aircraft. Operates beef cattle farm near Utica, NY.

Married Charlotte Hill Feb. 5, 1956; has daughter Jane and son Jeffrey.

WILLIAM P. SCHRADER, was born Jan. 1, 1921 in Maplewood, MO. Entered the service Oct. 19, 1942. Served with 361st Fighter Group, 375th Fighter Sqdn., aircraft armorer.

Military locations/stations: Bottisham, England; Little Walden, England; Chievres, Belgium; Brugelette, Belgium; Cambridgeshire. Participated in Air Offensive Europe, Normandy, Northern France, Rhineland, Ardennes and Central Europe campaigns.

Discharged Nov. 14, 1945 with rank of corporal. Was awarded six Bronze Stars.

He is a widower, now retired.

EDWARD SCHROEDER (EDDIE), served at Seething December 1943 to April 1945; with the 448th Bomb Group, 712th Sqdn., assigned to crew No. 5 with First pilot, Robert Ayrest. His primary crew assignment was assistant engineer; secondary assignment, right waist gunner. Completed four missions.

Memorable experiences: December 1943 flight from Marrakesh to England, bad weather, head wind instead of tail wind. Got over occupied France and ground fire shot them up. Got to England and crash landed, plane burned up, co-pilot was injured by gunfire. Rest of crew OK. On Feb. 10, 1944, a near miss over England, seven were killed and three bailed out.

Upon completion of missions in England, he was with 448th, 2nd Air Div. as mechanic. Highest rank achieved at Seething was staff sergeant. He served three years active duty and holds membership in the 2nd Air Division Association and 8th Air Force Historical Society.

Schroeder's civilian vocation: journeyman electrician, part-time musician in dance band and music arranger. Married to Kathryn (Kay).

CHARLES J. SCHULZ, after completing training at San Antonio Aviation Cadet Center was sent to Radio School at Sioux Falls, SD; Gunnery School at Yuma, Az; then phase training with crew at Biggs Field, TX and assigned to B-24 bombers.

Arrived at Norwich, England and assigned to 448th Bomb Group, 715th Sqdn. June 1944. Completed 35 missions as radio/gunner March 1945. Flew last mission with different crew as replacement radio operator. Lost one engine, oxygen system destroyed and severe flak damage.

After finishing tour returned to U.S. and was assigned

to Waco, TX AAB as a control tower operator. Discharged in September 1945 SAAC and returned to New York.

September 1946 joined New York Police Department and at a Veteran's Day Parade met fellow police officer that flew as engineer on near fatal 35th mission. Completed 20 years with New York Police Department and then joined the DEA where he retired after 26 years of federal service. Married to wife, Therese, in 1948 and fathered four sons. Currently busy traveling and enjoying his nine grandchildren.

JOHN W. SCHULTZ, was born Dec. 22, 1920 in Minneapolis, MN. Entered USAAF; 8th Air Force, 467th Bomb Group; co-pilot, B-24, *My Ideal,* commissioned December 1943.

Stationed at San Antonio, TX; primary, Corsicana, TX; basic, Enid, OK; Advanced, Frederick, OK; Salt Lake City; Casper, WY; Rackheath, Norwich, England. After return, one month Miami R&R; Laredo, TX; Georgia; final ferry command, Memphis, TN.

Participated in two missions D-day; Berlin, Hamburg. Discharged September 1945 with the rank of first lieutenant. Received the Distinguished Flying Cross.

Married June 1943, has two sons, one daughter and five grandchildren. Retired in 1978 from career as a pharmaceutical salesman, and after much traveling, lives in Estero, FL and spends summers in Minnesota.

GILBERT E. SCHULZE, was born Oct. 12, 1920 in Cincinnati, Oh and was raised in Hamilton, OH. Joined Army Aviation Cadets in August 1942 and graduated May 20, 1943 as second lieutenant, Class 43-E, Stockton Field, CA. Pilot training was in B-24s at Boise, ID and Tonopah, NV.

January 25, 1944, arrived at Horsham St. Faith, England. Flew 31 combat missions over Europe with the 754th Sqdn., 458th Bomb Group. Promoted to captain and made assistant group operations officer and flight instructor to replacement crews. In September 1944, he flew to France as liaison officer between the 96th Wing, 8th Air Force, England and the 9th Air Force HQ in Paris, France. He was to inspect certain air fields to determine if they could accommodate the bombers ferrying supplies from England to France for the ground troops. Flying into Paris also meant flying through the Eiffel Tower in the single engine C-61.

He returned to the USA Nov. 30, 1944 and instructed at both Courtland Field, AL and at Smyrna Field, TN. He was discharged in October 1945. Awards included the Distinguished Flying Cross, Air Medal with five Oak Leaf Clusters and a Silver Star.

He became a chiropractor and married Geneva Reynolds from Hamilton in Tonopah, NV on Dec. 3, 1943. They lived in Sidney, OH with their two sons and a daughter until he became the victim of a fatal auto accident in 1965.

CHARLES A. SCHUPP III, was born May 8, 1924 in Middletown, NY. Entered service Jan. 22, 1943; took basic at Miami Beach, FL; completed Airplane Mechanics School, Amarillo, TX and B-24 Engine Specialist School at Willow Run, MI. Graduated Gunnery School, Laredo, TX and joined the Willard Wilkerson crew for phase training at Biggs Field, TX.

Departed June 1, 1944 for the ETO arriving just before D-day. He and his crew were detained in Ireland until after the invasion was begun. He reached the 389th Bomb Group, 565th Sqdn. at Hethel, England in mid-June. The first of 30 missions was flown on July 6, 1944. He was the second engineer gunner on his aircraft, one of the group's pathfinders and a reserve engineer for his group.

Upon return to the U.S. and R&R leave, he graduated as an instructor from Laredo, TX and finished out the war as an instructor of gunnery and engineering at Westover Field, Springfield, MA. He was discharged Sept. 19, 1945 holding four Battle Stars, Air Medal with four clusters and the Distinguished Flying Cross.

As a civilian he married and has one son. He holds several degrees and is a retired media specialist of the Middletown New York Enlarged School District. He has served as director and officer in several organizations and is presently completing his 45th year as an active fire fighter in his city's Fire Department where he attained the rank of captain.

EDWARD G. SCHWARM, was born Oct. 16, 1922 in Milwaukee, WI. Halfway through his education as an electrical engineer at the University of Wisconsin, he joined the USAAC engineering officers' cadet training program in late 1942. He was commissioned at Yale in November 1943. After assignments at bases in Fort Worth and Clovis, he became a member of the 2nd Air Division.

At Ketteringham Hall he headed a B-24 nose armament redesign program which resulted in four lead B-24s being modified to that configuration to improve target acquisition capability. Upon completion of that project he was assigned as assistant engineering officer of the 506th Sqdn., 44th Bomb Group at Shipdham where he remained until the end of European hostilities, returning to the U.S. as part of the fly-back of the 8th Air Force in June 1945. He served at Pueblo AFB until October, when he was separated as a reserve officer.

He married his college sweetheart, Erla, and returned to the University of Wisconsin to complete his degree in electrical engineering. His work has been principally in aerospace electronics with assignments as system engineer for the K-bombing system used on B-36 and B-47s; program manager for several flight simulators including the DC-8, built by Link Aviation; president of Applied Dynamics, Inc.; special projects director at MIT for the Apollo Spacecraft Guidance and Navigation System; and is now in private consulting practice. He holds 10 patents for electronic equipment. Schwarm has his commercial pilot's license and flew actively until recently.

He and Erla travel extensively having toured the South Pacific, the Indian Ocean and Antarctica within the past four years. When not traveling they cruise on their sailboat, go downhill skiing or enjoy their year-round home on Cape Cod. They have three children and four grandchildren.

FREDERICK A. SCHWARTZ, was born in New York City, Aug. 29, 1922. Entered Aviation Cadet Program while attending college September 1942; activated February 1943. Trained as pilot in Southeast Command at Chester Field, MO; Malden AAF, MO; Napier AAF, AL; graduating Class 44-G as single-engine pilot. With emphasis on strategic bombing, assigned to B-24 Pilot Training School. Sailed overseas with crew January 1945 on SS *Aquitania* for duty with 446th Bomb Group, 707th Bomb Sqdn., Bungay, Flixton.

Flew 28 combat missions, being shot down by flak battery during Holzwickede mission March 14, 1945. Bailed crew out after crossing bomb line, all members returning safely. With war over in ETO, he served briefly in the Ferry Command, Long Beach AAF, CA.

Discharged Dec. 19, 1945. Awards include Distinguished Flying Cross, Air Medal with three Oak leaf Clusters, ETO Battle Ribbon with three stars.

Married to Annabel Bassett, July 22, 1956; two daughters, three sons and eight grandchildren. Lost youngest son, Douglas, aged 19 in 1987. In his memory established the Douglas J. Schwartz Living Foundation which awards greenhouses to deserving institutions for purposes of horticultural therapy. Also continues active as chairman of advertising agency.

MORRIS A. SCHWARTZ, was born Nov. 26, 1923 in Newark, NJ. Entered USAAF in 1943; navigator, 2nd Air Div., 493rd Bomb Group, 733rd Sqdn. Military locations/stations: Navigator School, Selman Field; crew training, Tonopah, NV; 493rd Bomb Group, Old Buckingham, East Anglia.

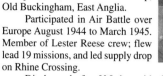

Participated in Air Battle over Europe August 1944 to March 1945. Member of Lester Reese crew; flew lead 19 missions, and led supply drop on Rhine Crossing.

Discharged after V-J day with the rank of captain. Awarded Distinguished Flying Cross and Air Medal with nine clusters.

Married Shirley and has three daughters: Susan, Rebecca and Judy; and four grandchildren. Retired end of 1993 from executive vice president of operations, Revlon, North America.

ROBERT W. SCHWELLINGER, was born June 3, 1921 in Toledo, OH. Entered USAAC Jan. 27, 1942; aviation cadet, second lieutenant Nov. 25, 1942; 389th Bomb Group, 8th Air Force.

Military locations/stations: W/CTE; Ontario; Lancaster; Victorville; Hethel; Pueblo. Participated in Ploesti low level; Bengashi; Air Offensive Europe. Memorable experiences: crash landing El Paso, TX; and Ploesti low level.

Discharged June 15, 1945 with the rank of captain. Awarded Distinguished Unit Citation, Air Medal with four Oak Leaf Clusters; DFS with Oak Leaf Cluster.

Married, he is retired.

DAVID A. SCOTT, was born May 23, 1923 in Massachusetts and moved to Westminster, MD at age nine. Attended Johns Hopkins University and enlisted in the USAAC October 1942. Completed pilot training and was commissioned at Turner Field, Albany, GA, Feb. 8, 1944. After B-24 transition training was assigned pilot of crew at Gowen Field, Boise, ID.

Arrived Wendling, England July 1944 and completed 35 missions with 392nd Bomb Group in March 1945. Remained with 577th Sqdn. and assisted in new crew orientation. Returned home as pilot of stripped down experimental B-24 in June 1945. Was discharged August 1945 with the rank of first lieutenant. Made pilgrimage to Norwich Library and Wendling Memorial in 1985.

Retired in 1985 as president of a metal specialties manufacturing company. Married Betty Billingslea in 1947 and has four children and nine grandchildren.

THOMAS W. SCOTT (SCOTTY), was born April 23, 1923 in Clearfield, IA. Entered USAAC cadets in 1943. They had too many cadets so went to Gunnery School in Laredo, TX. Joined Emil Kengle's crew in 1945; crew training at Charleston, SC.

Arrived England October 1945. Flew 35 missions over Germany as nose gunner with 93rd Bomb Group. Memorable experience: low level (300 feet) dropping supplies to paratroop and glider troops crossing Rhine River, Spring of 1945.

Returned to U.S. and was discharged October 1945 with the rank of staff sergeant.

Returned to Simpson College and graduated 1948. Spent 35 years selling for Schering Corporation. Retired January 1990 and moved just outside Flagstaff, AZ.

He is married, has two children and eight grandchildren. Keeps busy gardening in summer and woodworking in winter.

LEONARD GILMORE SCRIVEN, was born Jan. 11, 1920 in Lincoln, NE. Entered the USAAC Aug. 3, 1942; basic training at Kearns Training Center near Salt Lake City, UT. Assigned to Lowry Air Base, CO for Bomb Sight Maintenance School. This included training in the automatic pilot unit. Went next to Officers Candidate School at Valley Forge, PA and Yale University at New Haven, CT. Commissioned a second lieutenant on March 11, 1943. Then transferred to Salt Lake City Air Base, then to Alamogordo, NM and finally to Tucson, Az where he joined the 446th Bomb Group (H) for training on the B-24 and then on to Lowry Air Base to prepare for overseas duty. Assigned to Flixton Air Drome, Bungay, England in October 1943.

He was the OIC of the automatic pilot shop and bombsight vault until wars end. Promoted to first lieutenant March 1, 1944 and then to captain Aug. 17, 1944. Returned to the USA in July 1945 and assigned to Sioux Falls, SD.

While in England, his enlisted personnel and he maintained both the A-5 Auto Pilot and Sperry Bombsight made by Sperry; also the Norden Bombsight and the C-1 Auto Pilot made by Norden. They held the best bombing record for three months running for each type of equipment. They were also the only unit to use the altitude control unit due to their ability to properly maintain it; and to train the pilots to use it.

At the end of WWII in Europe, he was assigned to Wright-Patterson Air Base, OH working with automatic flight control equipment.

He was released from active duty in March 1946. Tried civilian life and soon found that he was better suited for military life. Enlisted as a tech. sergeant May 29, 1947 and assigned to Elmendorf Air Base, AK. The USAAC was renamed the USAF in 1947. He was promoted to master sergeant May 16, 1950. Returned to the USA in July 1951 and assigned to Ellsworth AFB, Rapid City, SD. Requested recall to commissioned status and was recalled to the grade of captain in August 1952. Transferred to Lowry AFB, CO for Advanced Armament School. Transferred to Hahn AFB, Germany in July 1953 as squadron armament officer with the 50th Fighter Bomber Wing. He was next assigned as the base vehicle maintenance officer then as the commanding officer of the Base Motor Vehicle Squadron. Returned to the USA in July 1957 and assigned to Wright-Patterson AFB, OH as deputy chief of transportation. Applied for school at Sheppard AFB, TX where he received certificate of graduation from the Chicago School of Transportation. He was next transferred to Moody AFB, GA in December 1960 as the commanding officer of the transportation squadron.

Retired from the USAF in November 1963 with the rank of major. Received the Bronze Star for meritorious service; Good Conduct Medal; EAME Medal; American Campaign Medal; WWII Victory Medal; Occupation Medal, Germany; National Defense Medal; Armed Forces Reserve Medal; Air Force Longevity Service Award with four Bronze Oak Leaf Clusters; 20th Combat Wing Award of Distinction.

Scriven entered civil service at Hill AFB as a GS-5, then promoted to GS-11 as chief of transportation of hazardous cargo. Retired from Hill AFB, UT in January 1982. Total federal service, 39 and one-half years.

Married to Mary Ann, they have one son Edward and five grandchildren.

EDWIN J. SEALY, was born in Lynbrook, NY on May 17, 1924. Attended Lafayette College. Enlisted USAAC in 1942. Basic, Miami Beach, FL; college, Cleveland, OH; preflight, Maxwell Field, AL; primary, Ocala, FL; basic, Bainbridge, GA; advanced, Turner Field, Albany, GA; transition, Maxwell; crew training, Chatham Field, GA.

Assigned to 458th Bomb Group (H), 753rd Sqdn. at Horsham St. Faith AB, Norwich, England in August 1944. Flew gasoline to Lille, France. Began combat missions October 1944; flew 35 missions and received usual decorations. One crash landing in Lille, but no injuries. Completed tour in April and sailed for U.S. on V-E day. After rehabilitation in Atlantic City, received honorable discharge on V-J day.

Became special agent for Associated Aviation Underwriters in New York. Moved to Cleveland, OH in 1948, joining Davis and Dissette, Inc. as agent. Became president of this firm in 1963. Merged this company with three others in 1977 to form Insurance Management Services, Inc. and served as president and CEO. Sold this company to Robinson-Conner and became senior vice president of successor firm until retirement in 1989.

Obtained CPCU designation in 1952 and ARM designation in 1973. Served as national president of Society of CPCU in 1978-1979. Since retirement has served as expert witness and also as adjunct professor at Kent State University.

Married Mary Jo Barclay in 1969 (second); has three

children, three stepchildren and seven grandchildren. Hobbies include tennis, golf, cross-country skiing and has performed in over 30 community theater productions.

WILLIAM H. SEAMAN (BILL),
was born Oct. 25, 1920 in Lueders, TX. Enlisted Oct. 5, 1942; basic training, Randolph Field, TX; Armament School, Lowry Field, Denver, CO; graduated as second lieutenant from AAFTTC Tech School, Yale University, New Haven, CT, July 8, 1943, Class 18-42-AS.

Assigned to 29th Bomb Group at Gowen Field, Boise, ID. Original member of the 458th Bomb Group cadre. Other duty stations were Camp Seven Miles, Spokane, WA; Kearns, UT; Wendover, UT; Tonopah, NV.

Discharged Nov. 9, 1945 with the rank of first lieutenant. Graduated from Texas Christian University, Fort Worth, TX in 1948 with a degree in geology. Retired October 1982.

Married Lucy A. Ligon on Oct. 27, 1950; they have two sons, a daughter and five grandchildren.

RICHARD H. SEARER,
was born Sept. 25, 1925 in Tyrone, PA. He entered the USAAC Dec. 23, 1943 and took basic training at Greensboro, NC; Aerial Gunnery School at Harlingen, TX; replacement crew training at Chatham Field, Savannah, GA. Going to England in August 1944, he was assigned to the 458th Bomb Group (H) B-24s, 753rd Sqdn. at Horsham St. Faith.

He flew 35 missions as a nose gunner and "toggled" bombs with Ed Sealy's crew. Completed his tour April 8, 1945. Discharged on Oct. 23, 1945 with the rank of staff sergeant. Received Air Medal with four Oak Leaf Clusters and four ETO Bronze Battle Stars.

He graduated from Dickinson College, Carlisle, PA with a BS degree and from the Pittsburgh Institute of Mortuary Science with a Mortuary Science degree. He is the owner and operator of the Richard H. Searer Funeral Home, Incorporated of Tyrone, PA.

Married to Ann Graham on June 14, 1952; he is the father of three children and the grandfather of eight.

HAROLD SECOR,
was born Sept. 22, 1919 in Savannah, NY. Entered the military December 1941, assigned to the 93rd Bomb Group, 328th Sqdn.; R.O. and gunner, crew #8.

Military locations/stations: basic, Keesler Field; Barksdale Field. Ft. Myers, FL, anti-sub patrol. Group flew non-stop Gander to Prestwick, September 1942. Alcanberry, England; Oran, Tunisa; Gambut, Lybia; Hardwick, England. Flew 26 plus missions on *Ball of Fire Jr.*, Joe Tate's ship. Worst battle, first Vegesek mission. Shot down April 16, 1943 over Brest; POW for two years plus (Stalag 17B).

Discharged October 1945 with the rank of tech sergeant. Received Presidential Unit Citation, Distinguished Flying Cross, Air Medal with three Oak Leaf Clusters, Purple Heart, POW Medal, Good Conduct Medal, ETO with four Battle Stars, American Theater with one Battle Star and WWII Victory Medal.

Married to Erma J.; he is retired from a lumber company.

PAUL A. SEIFERT,
was born in Quincy, IL Aug. 5, 1921. Enlisted in USAAC September 1942. Called to active duty February 1943. After cadet training, graduated as a bombardier Class 44-5 at Big Spring, TX AAF. After crew training at Langley Field went to more school at Boca Raton, FL in the operation of airborne radar for bombing and navigation.

Assigned overseas to 492nd Bomb Group at Harrington, England and the 857th Night Bombing Sqdn. The black B-24s would release target indicators for the main force of England's Royal Air Force bombers to drop on.

Flew 21 lead bombing missions over major industrial targets and four missions dropping spies and supplies to the underground in Denmark and Norway.

Discharged August 1945 with the rank of first lieutenant. Received Distinguished Flying Cross and three Air Medals.

Married in 1952, he is proud of his six children and 15 grandchildren. Retired Oct. 15, 1991 after 44 years in the clothing business.

ELVERN SEITZINGER,
was born Aug. 13, 1922. Enlisted in USAAF Nov. 12, 1942. Appointed aviation cadet Dec. 3, 1942. Graduated from Pilot School, Moody Field, GA with Class 43-H, Aug. 29, 1943. Took B-24 flight training at Maxwell Field, AL. Assigned to a crew at Salt Lake City November 1943. Started training as a crew at Davis Monthan Field, AZ December 1943. Crew joined the 856th Bomb Sqdn. of 492nd Bomb Group at Alamogordo, NM January 1944. Crew reassigned to one of cadre pilots and Seitzinger was assigned to Pete Val Predas' crew as a co-pilot.

Arrived North Pickenham, England, 8th Air Force, 2nd Air Div., 14th Combat Wing in April 1944. Flew his first five missions as pilot or co-pilot with various crews. On May 24, Jerry Kuntz broke his arm and Seitzinger was assigned to that crew as pilot. On his 14th mission, June 20, 1944, to Politz, they were attacked by fighters and forced to land in Sweden, the only aircraft of the 856th to survive the attack. Released from internment Nov. 7, 1944.

Arrived back in the States via England, Dec. 3, 1944. Served various squadron assignments and went on terminal leave Nov. 11, 1946.

He retired from the General Electric Company April 1, 1985 as special manufacturing engineering with 38 years service.

WILLIAM MAYHEW SELVIDGE,
was born Sept. 6, 1916 in Ardmore, OK, the son of George P. and Toy Mayhew Selvidge. He had a sister and a brother. He attended Ardmore Public Schools, received an AB and LLB from the University of Oklahoma. In January 1942 he joined the USAAC as an aviation cadet, receiving his commission and wings at Lubbock, TX, Class 42-J.

Following B-24 training at Tarrant Field, Ft. Worth, TX and Davis-Monthan Field, Tucson, AZ, he and his crew joined the 389th Bomb Group at Biggs Field, El Paso, with subsequent training at Lowry Field, Denver. On June 20, 1943, he flew his crew from Newfoundland to England.

Missions were flown from Benghazi, Libya and Hethel, England. All members of the crew completed the combat tour, which included the Aug. 1, 1943 low-level attack on Ploesti.

Upon returning to the States he married Frances Shafer of Denison, TX on Nov. 17, 1944. They now live in Houston, TX where he retired following a 39 year career as an Exxon Company USA petroleum land man. They have one son Bill, a doctor who practices family medicine in Chapel Hill, NC.

LUPE H. SERVIN,
was born March 24, 1924 in Port Chicago, CA. Entered USAAC Feb. 22, 1943. Military locations/stations: Wichita Falls, TX; Fort Myers, FL; Salt Lake City, UT; Bungay, England.

Completed 35 missions as flight engineer/gunner on B-24 stationed in Bungay, England. First mission was on D-day. His twin brother, John Servin, was on the same B-24

bomber with him. They were with the 446th Bomb Group, 705th Sqdn. stationed in Bungay, England. They had many battles with German fighters over enemy territory. When the war ended they were returned to Williams AFB in Chandler, AZ and assigned as crew chiefs at the base.

Discharged Oct. 24, 1945 with the rank of staff sergeant. Received Air Medal with three clusters, Distinguished Flying Cross, ETO Ribbon, and Good Conduct Medal.

Married 47 years, he has one son, two daughters and five grandchildren. He is a retired construction superintendent.

ABRAHAM CHARLES SERWITZ,
was born May 14, 1923 in Brooklyn, NY. Entered USAAC August 1943 as an aviation cadet. Military locations/stations: Arcadia, FL, primary; Courtland, AL, basic; George Field, IL, advanced (and instructor); Springfield, MA, Langley Field; Rackheath, East Anglia.

Participated in three battles over Europe from June 1944 to April 1945. Flew 35 missions with no aborts in B-24s.

Memorable experience: On raid to Zossen, Germany, lost one engine, left group, lost second engine. Just made it over the battle lines and landed at a fighter base with zero gas left.

Discharged June 1945 with the rank of first lieutenant (pilot). Received air Medal with five clusters, European Theater with two clusters and American Theater.

Married 48 years and has three children and nine grandchildren. Retired Dec. 31, 1981.

KENNETH LEROY SEVERI,
was born Nov. 8, 1915 in Franklin, MN. Entered the military service Nov. 23, 1940. He completed two schools of flying as a would-be glider pilot until the program was discontinued by the military. Later graduated from Armament, Flexible Gunnery and Instructor's Schools. He and his crew flew to the British Isles via the northern route in a new B-24 bomber. They became one more crew in the 458th Bomb Group and completed 31 combat missions.

Following graduation from Instructors School, he taught gunnery at Las Vegas, NV and then was sent to Ft. Snelling, MN where he received his discharge July 21, 1945 with the rank of staff sergeant. Awarded Distinguished Flying Cross, Air Medal with four Oak Leaf Clusters, Air Offensive Europe, Normandy, Northern France and Rhineland.

He farmed with his brother until about 15 years ago when he retired. He is a member of VFW Post 8459 Fairfax, MN, and is a member of the Firing Squad.

JOHN G. SEVERSON,
was born Nov. 7, 1921 in Akron, OH. In February 1943 he entered the USAAF; pilot, 2nd Air Div., 8th Air Force.

Stationed overseas at Hardwick, England. Flew 30 missions from August 1944 to March 18, 1945. Memorable experience: Dec. 24, 1944, right rudder shot off on bomb run, but finished the run and returned to base and landed without a problem.

Discharged June 1945 with the rank of first lieutenant. Received Air Medal with four Oak Leaf Clusters.

Married 48 years, has three children and seven grandchildren. He retired after 25 years at Eastman Kodak Company.

J. CALVIN SHAHBAZ,
was born in Gary, IN, Jan. 19, 1924. He enlisted in the USAAC in 1942 as an aviation cadet. After graduating from Bombardier School in March 1944, was assigned to the 491st Bomb Group in England, flying B-24s.

Shot down over Berlin on 28th mission. Evaded to Poland, hidden by Polish underground, joined up with Russian forces, spent time at the front with their tank units and finally transported via boxcar to Odessa. Detained in Odessa and eventually returned to England via Italy.

After return to the States, flew on B-29s for eight years. Graduated from Navigator and Radar School in 1955 and assigned as navigator on the Air Force's first B-52 crew.

In 1961 attended Air Command and Staff College; after graduation, in various staff assignments in SAC (total of 23 years in SAC), including SAC HQ. In 1969 assigned to the Air Force IG as chief, comptroller branch and in 1972 assigned to HQ, AAFES, Dallas, as director of inspection and audit.

Retired in 1973 as colonel. Decorations include: Legion of Merit, Distinguished Flying Cross, Air Medal with three Oak Leaf Clusters, Purple Heart, Air Force Commendation Medal with three Oak Leaf Clusters.

GEORGE L. SHANKS, was born Nov. 10, 1921 in Poplargrove, OH. June 3, 1941, entered the military, serving with the 45th Inf., 1941-1942; 1942-1945, AAAFGS-HAAF, Harlingen, TX; 8th Air Force.

Participated in ETO, 707th Sqdn., 446th Bomb Group, 2nd Air Div.

Participated in battles at Rhineland, Central Europe, Ardennes. Memorable experience: Lost *Lil Snooks* March 2, 1945; bailed out, over lines; St. Louis, *Le Bitche*.

Discharged Sept. 4, 1945 with the rank of staff sergeant. Awarded EAME Theater with seven Bronze Stars and Air Medal with three Oak Leaf Clusters.

He married October 1957 and has three children and two grandchildren. Retired from General Motors after 35 years; he farms part time.

ROLAND C. SHANKS, was born in Washington Township, Carroll County, IN. He entered the USAAC Feb. 5, 1943. Military locations/stations: St. Petersburg, FL; Lowry Field, CO; Tyndall Field, FL; Westover Field, MA; Charleston, SC; Hardwick, England with the 93rd Bomb Group.

Memorable experiences: The first flight he took in Gunnery School, Tyndall Field, FL. Receiving his crew member wings upon graduation from Flexible Gunnery Class 43-52, Tyndall Field, FL and completing his 30 combat missions with the 93rd Bomb Group.

Discharged Oct. 20, 1945 with the rank of staff sergeant. He received five Air Medals and four campaign stars.

Shanks is single; he has a sister and 98-year old mother as of this date. He retired from the Department of the Army, Department of Defense.

HORACE SHANKWILER, was born July 12, 1920 in Detroit, MI. Joined the USAAC July 1943; after training he assembled his B-24 crew at Westover Field, MA before embarkation on USS *Mauratania* for England.

Devastation caused by the Kassel Raid prompted his orders as replacement in the 445th Bomb Group at Tibenham, England. He flew 12 missions, was made lead pilot and completed 25 missions, piloting a B-24 home to the States in May 1945.

Memorable experience: Safely landing all men aboard from a bombing mission to Koblentz, Germany, with only two engines and the rudder missing.

Discharged November 1945 after receiving the Air Medal with three Oak Leaf Clusters and the Distinguished Flying Cross.

Married Dorothy Rinkus in 1942; she passed away in 1987. In 1988 he married Jane Vance Hartman and together they have three sons, one daughter and seven grandchildren.

Retired from Sherwin Williams, "Shank" lives in Hot Springs Village, AR where he serves many philanthropic and community groups, golfs and is now working to form an 8th Air Force Historical Society Chapter in Arkansas.

DONALD SHANNON, was born Oct. 26, 1921 in St. Paul, MN. Enlisted in USAAC May 28, 1942 and called to active service Feb. 25, 1943. After training, flew with his crew in a new B-24 to England via South America and Africa.

Assigned to 458th Bomb Group, 753rd Sqdn. at Horsham St. Faith, Norwich in May 1944. Completed 36 missions as flight engineer/top turret on B-24 *Howling Ban-*

shee. Was reassigned to Victorville AFB in California as flight engineer and section crew chief, training new crews. One emergency jump while at Victorville.

Discharged, married Shirley Webber and returned to University of Minnesota in 1945. Graduated with degree in aero engineering, worked five years at Boeing in Seattle. Resigned to found own business as master distributor of jet fuel filtering products in Washington, Oregon and Alaska. Retired and sold business in 1985. Remains in Seattle and spends his time golfing, skiing, hunting and fishing.

JAMES G. SHAPCOTT, was born Dec. 1, 1922 in Eddington, PA. Entered USAAC Jan. 1, 1943. Military locations/stations: Harlingen, TX; Langley Field; Miami Beach; Keesler Field; Clovis, NM; Seething, England with 448th Bomb Group, 712th Sqdn.

Completed 30 missions April 24, 1944 to Aug. 12, 1944; pilot, B. Wade (great pilot and great crew).

Discharged Oct. 17, 1945 with the rank of staff sergeant. Received Distinguished Flying Cross, Air Medal with three Oak Leaf Clusters, ETO Theater Medal with three Battle Stars and Good Conduct Medal.

Married to Minerva for 43 years; they have a son and a daughter. Currently retired in Florida.

HAROLD SHAPIRO, was born Jan. 1, 1924 in New York City. Joined USAAF after graduating high school in June 1943. Took basic training in Harlingen, TX; radio operator, mechanic gunner. Shipped overseas on *Queen Mary* to Norwich, England, home of the 448th Bomb Group.

Participated in raids over Central Europe, Rhineland, Normandy and Southern France before being shot down on fifth mission. Spent 10 months in Stalag Luft IV. After liberation by Russians, went home to his family in Los Angeles. Awarded Purple Heart and POW Medal.

Married Jackie Gottlieb and had two great kids, Marc and Stephanie. He lived and worked in the Los Angeles area until his death of multiple sclerosis on July 24, 1971.

MEL SHARPE, was born Sept. 20, 1918 in Brooklyn, NY. He volunteered after graduating from New York University in June 1942. After completing cadet training was commissioned as a second lieutenant, bombardier on Nov. 12, 1943 at Midland Field, TX.

He flew 32 combat missions in B-24s with the 489th Bomb Group from Halesworth, England. He participated in the D-day invasion of France.

After being deactivated as a first lieutenant in November 1945, he was employed as director of purchasing for Castro Convertible Corporation of New Hyde Park, NY. He received the Distinguished Flying Cross, four Air Medals, and Campaign Stars for the battles of Normandy, Northern France and Germany.

He retired in 1985 and presently resides with his wife Dolly in Columbus, NJ.

LEWIS S. SHARPLESS, was born March 27, 1918 in Minneapolis, MN. Entered USAAC May 2, 1942. Military locations/stations: Buckley Field; Lowry Field; armament instr., armorer, 467th Bomb Group, 790th Sqdn., Norwich, England.

Participated in action at Normandy, Northern France, Rhineland, Central Europe and Ardennes.

Discharged Oct. 22, 1945 with the rank of sergeant. He was an expert rifleman.

Married, he has four children and four grandchildren.

Retired after 51 years selling full range of stationery supplies.

LLOYD C. SHARRARD, was born August 1918 in Riley, MI; lived on farm, attended University of Michigan, entered service as aviation cadet, July 1941. Pilot Class 42-B, Luke Field, AZ. Trained as B-24 pilot, flew to United Kingdom by southern route in 1943 with Capt. James Stewart as commander, 703rd Sqdn., 445th Bomb Group.

Flew 30 missions over Germany, through usual fighters and flak, shook up and shot at many times but unscathed. Returned to U.S. in 1944 and attended Aerial Photographic School, Lowry, CO.

Instructor pilot on B-29s, 1945-46, at Clovis, NM. Starting 1947 through 1965, long association with Strategic Air Command, staff material officer SAC HQ, Omaha, 7th Air Div., United Kingdom, 2nd Air Force HQ, Barksdale, LA. Aircraft commander, operations officer, 913th AR Sqdn., Barksdale, LA.

Retired as lieutenant colonel in January 1965. Received Distinguished Flying Cross and Air Medal with three Oak Leaf Clusters.

Married Betty, his high school sweetheart, in January 1945, they have two daughters and two sons. On retirement moved to Eugene, OR. Owner/partner of equipment rental 1966-77. Fully retired January 1978 to traveling, golf, boating, hunting, fishing, skiing, poker, bridge and gardening. Still going strong in 1993.

AMOS B. SHARRETTS, was born June 12, 1915 in New York City. Entered the New York National Guard, Oct. 10, 1940, 101st Cavalry; U.S. Cavalry January 1941 through April 1942. Graduated Aviation Cadet School Dec. 13, 1942, pilot, second lieutenant.

Military locations/stations: Ft. Devens, MA; MacDill AFB, FL; Alamogordo AAB, NM; Lake Charles AAB, LA; Attlebridge AAB, England with the 466th Bomb Group, 787th Bomb Sqdn. Participated in the ETO, Air Offensive over Europe, Northern France, Rhineland, Normandy, and Central Europe. Completed 31 operational missions.

Relieved from active duty Aug. 6, 1945; retired from USAFR, June 12, 1973 with the rank of colonel. Awarded Distinguished Flying Cross, Air Medal with three Oak Leaf Clusters, EAME Theater Ribbon with four Battle Stars, American Defense Service Medal and Air Force Commendation Medal.

Married to Louise Hoy, they have two children and three grandchildren. He is a retired lawyer.

MERLIN M. SHAVER, was born in Jackson, MI on Dec. 7, 1923 and was raised in rural Charlotte, MI. He entered the USAAC on March 1, 1943; took basic training at Miami Beach, FL; assigned to Mechanic School at San Antonio, TX; assigned to 53rd STA. Compl. Sqdn. at Atterbury Air Base in Indiana.

Arrived in England at Tibenham Air Base on Sept. 13, 1943 to await the arrival of the 445th Bomb Group, transferred to the 700th Sqdn. Returned to the States June 8, 1945. Reassigned to ATC at Palm Springs, CA.

Discharged September 1945 with the rank of corporal. Awarded EAME Theater Ribbon with one Silver Battle Star and one Bronze Battle Star and three Overseas Service Bars.

Married June Ruddock on Jan. 19, 1942; they have five children, 30 grandchildren and 28 great-grandchildren. He and his wife have lived in Marshall, MI, the past 30 years. Retired in 1989 having served in a management capacity of a Ford dealership for nearly 30 years and owning two small businesses.

JAMES I. SHAW, was born July 8, 1918 in Wapakoneta, OH. On Feb. 10, 1941 entered the USAAC; served as bombardier, 8th Air Force, 453rd Bomb Group, 2nd Air Div. Received commission April 1, 1942, Albuquerque, NM; training command until Dec. 20, 1943.

Military locations/stations: Ellington Field; Lowry

Field; Albuquerque, NM; Kirtland; Pocatello, ID; Boise, ID; March Field, CA; Old Buckingham, England.

Flew 19 air missions over Europe from February 1944 through April 1945. Memorable experiences: Dropping parachute bundles from altitude of 200 feet from B-24. Shaw was appointed the group bombardier when the group was formed in June 1943 and served in that capacity until the 453rd terminated on V-J day.

Discharged Aug. 6, 1945 with the rank of major. Received Air Medal with three clusters and Distinguished Flying Cross.

He is married and has two daughters and one son. Practiced law in Ohio from April 1, 1948 until Feb. 2, 1967; prosecuting attorney for 10 years,; judge for 14 years. Retired as judge Oct. 1, 1981 and lives at Hilton Head Island, SC.

OLIVER ABBOTT SHAW, was born April 16, 1918 at Winona, MS. Graduated University High School, Oxford, MS in 1934. Platoon leaders class, U.S. Marine Corps, Quantico, VA in 1938. Ole Miss boxing team, featherweight, 1937-1938. Graduated, BA with distinction, mathematics and physics, 1938. Joined USAAC May 1940. Pilot training Class 41-A at Love Field, Dallas, TX.

Navigation training at Coral Gables and at Barksdale. Navigation instructor at Turner, Selman, Ellington and Mather. Revised the navigation pre-flight curriculum at Maxwell Field, 1942.

Joined original cadre of the 466th Bomb Group at Clovis, NM as group navigator. Flew southern route to Attlebridge, England, March 1944. Combat tour as squadron navigator of the 786th Sqdn. Led 15 missions out of 30; two additional missions with Bernt Balchens' squadron.

Upon return to the U.S., rejoined the Navigation Schools as curriculum officer. Assigned George Washington University for post-graduate study of mathematical statistics 1946-1948. Comptroller directorate at the Pentagon, 1948. Instructor in planning and statistics at the Comptroller's Course, Air University 1949-1950.

Riffed in the "Johnson-Cut" 1950. Recalled as operations analyst, HQ 2nd Air Force, 1951. Retread combat crew training, Ellington Field, 1952. Heart attack, September 1952.

Administrator for basic research in statistics and probability theory, Air Force Office of Scientific Research, HQ Air Research and Development Command, 1953-1963. Retired 1963.

Employed at Federal Aviation Agency, Army Computation Laboratory, The Boeing Company, Army Aviation Command and Army Tank Automotive Command.

Married 1943 to Eleanor Craft Strowd, a tennis player and graduate of Ole Miss and University of North Carolina Library School. From this union came four children: Jo Ann (Benninghove) a primary school teacher in Westminster, MD; John, all SEC. second baseman, now a pacemaker salesman in Shelbyville, KY; Terry, an artist, living in Olympia, WA; Judy (Thompson) a pharmacist in Jackson, MS. There are eight grandchildren.

Memorable experiences: (First tactical experience) On Dec. 10, 1941, one of 15 navigation instructors sent to the West Coast to stop the Japanese invasion. Assigned to the 12th Recon. Sqdn., with Lt. Sullivan, Geiger Field, Maj. Kenneth Walker, commanding.

Maj. Walker's welcome included the information that his squadron included only one navigator and that his pilots were all inexperienced and got nervous out of sight of land. The squadron was flying search missions 600 miles into the Pacific. Now, with three navigators he could form three crews for a three day rotation.

The crew assigned to fly the next day had Earl Biggers from Meridian, MS for bombardier. Since Earl was a close friend, I volunteered to fly the next day. Earl's first words were, "Artie, you should feel at home here; Lt. Nice was one of your students, you already know Sullivan and me, and the squadron bombardier is Eddie Mack Morgan, a classmate from your home town, Oxford, MS."

After Earl introduced the rest of the crew, I asked, "What kind of planes do we have?" Earl replied, "We have two B-10s, two B-12s, one B-18 and one B-17." I asked "Which plane do we have tomorrow?" The pilot replied, "Tomorrow we have the B-17." I said that I would like to go out and look it over, because I had never seen a B-17. The co-pilot said that he would like to go with me because he had never seen one either. Shaw asked, "What kind of a pilot are you?" He replied, "I'm a P-40 pilot, I just got here from Langley Field last night."

Sequel: That night there was an eight inch snowfall that closed the airfield to flying for two days. The third day (Sunday) was the day Nice was to be navigator. The B-17 lost an engine between Yakima and Seattle and returned to Geiger. About 200 yards from the end of the run way, it crashed and burned. Two gunners escaped.

Two years later, while at Kearns AFB, I encountered Eddy Mack Morgan and asked him what happened with my crew. He said that on their very first bomb run, on a Japanese battleship, Macassar Sea, they were shot down. I asked about Maj. Walker, and he replied that Maj. Walker became the first Air Corps general to be killed. He flew into a mountain in Australia.

How the system works: I came aboard the 466th Bomb Group as group navigator at its inception at Clovis, NM. We trained at Pine Castle, Kearns, and Alamogordo. The last big simulated combat mission was an attack on Colorado Springs, involving a fly-by of the airport at Amarillo, and a rendezvous with the 467th Bomb Group about half way between Amarillo and Colorado Springs.

Col. Pierce, the group commander, was the lead pilot with Lt. Harold Berman, the squadron navigator of the 785th Sqdn., navigating. Shaw was in the deputy lead position with Eddy Anastasio, 786th Sqdn. commander, as pilot.

Lt. Berman flew a perfect course, including the rendezvous. Following the rendezvous, Col. Pierce made an obvious, but inexplicable attempt to follow the 467th. This involved a turn of about 270 degrees. By the time we completed the turn, the 467th was out of sight. We turned back toward the IP, held that course for about five minutes, then turned due north. We passed 25 miles east of Colorado Springs now obscured by an overcast. We flew north almost up to the point of no return.

When we got back to Alamogordo, I asked Berman what had happened. He said that Col. Pierce had asked for a heading to the IP. He flew that heading for a few minutes, said, "You're lost. I'm taking over the navigation," and turned north.

The next day Col. Pierce came to me and said that Gen. Peck had called and asked him what went wrong with the mission. He had replied, "The navigation." Gen. Peck asked, "What are you doing about it?" and he had replied "I replaced the group navigator." Then he asked me, "Whom do you think should replace you?"

I answered, "Lt. Drebert." So Lt. Drebert went to England as group navigator, and I replaced him as squadron navigator of the 786th Sqdn.

Some other exciting missions: I flew three exciting missions as nose turret gunner. (Berlin) we had a near head-on collision with a Messerschmidt; we had the left inboard engine destroyed, by flak, a fragment striking my left eyebrow; and we had to bomb the secondary target (Cologne). On another mission, as a result of fire aboard the aircraft, we returned from Saarbrucken alone.

GILBERT S. SHAWN, Lt. Col., was born July 25, 1921, in New York City, NY. Joined the Air Force directly as cadet in Class 43-E. Took pilot training in Gulf Coast training command.

Flew as first pilot in B-24, C-47, C-54, B-25. Served in two wars, WWII and Korea. Reserve pilot in peace time with heavy time in C-47s. Retired from Air Force in 1980.

Flew combat with the 445th Bomb Group, 702nd Bomb Sqdn., which was headed by Jimmy Stewart. In Korea flew C-47s with HQ Sqdn. of 5th Air Force.

In WWII flew B-24s and was shot down on mission to Zwickau. Parachuted into Belgium where with friends and the underground worked his way to Sedan, France (before the invasion). Time behind enemy lines was six months.

Civilian employment: was president of Warsaw Studio and retired in 1981. Joined the Peace Corps and served in Kenya, Africa.

Married to beautiful actress, Melba Rae (deceased) and has one son, Eric Shawn, who is a reporter for Channel 5 of the Fox Broadcasting Company. Currently resides in New York, but has lived in Portugal and Africa.

ROBERT D. SHEEHAN, was born in Bradford, PA on May 12, 1920, and was raised in Tulsa, OK. He enlisted early in 1942 and was called in October 1942 reporting to SAACC. He completed pilot training in 43G at Frederick, OK, and then went on to B-24 Transition School at Tarrant Field in Fort Worth, TX. He was assigned to the 467th Bomb Group, 790th Sqdn. at Wendover, UT. They flew their own plane to Rackheath, near Norwich, England.

He completed 30 lead crew missions between April 11, 1944, and November 10, 1944. The 467th Bomb Group had the best group bombing record during the war throughout Europe. His crew led the 8th Air Force twice and the 2nd Air Div. six times.

Discharged Sept. 1, 1945, he received two Distinguished Flying Cross Medals and eight Air Medals.

Still partially active as managing partner of Sheehan Pipe Line Construction Company, a 90 year-old construction company started by his grandfather. Sheehan and his wife Rosemary have two children and two grandchildren. They recently celebrated their 50th wedding anniversary.

RICHARD F. SHERBURNE, was born May 23, 1923 in Quincy, MA. Enlisted Oct. 21, 1942 in the USAAF. Military locations/stations: Maxwell Field, pre-flight B-24 transition; B-29 transition, 489th Bomb Group, 846th and 847th Sqdns., 8th Air Force.

Flew B-24 to England via Labrador and Iceland. Memorable experiences: Low level mission to drop supplies to troops in Holland. Flew food to Orleans For FFI and buzzed Eiffel Tower; crash landed B-24, *Lonesome Polecat,* in England coming back from mission.

Discharged Nov. 12, 1945 with the rank of first lieutenant. Received Air Medal with one Oak Leaf Cluster, EAME Service Medal, American Theater Service Medal and the WWII Victory Medal.

Married, wife deceased, and has one daughter, one granddaughter and one grandson. His son-in-law is in NOH Air National Guard; grandson in CAP.

Retired mechanical engineer; has BSME degree from Northeastern University.

ERIC H. SHERMAN, was born July 21, 1919 in Evanston, IL. Entered U.S. Army March 3, 1942, aviation cadet; graduated pilot Class 42-J at Roswell, NM, Oct. 30, 1942.

Military locations/stations: B-24 transition and Bomb Group assignment Davis Monthan, Tucson; AZ, El Paso, TX; Biggs Field; Lowry Field, Denver, CO. Assigned to 446th Bomb Group, 705th Bomb Sqdn. ETO November 1943-July 21, 1944.

Flew 28 missions as lead pilot and shot down on his last mission, July 21, 1944. Prisoner of war until April 1945. Memorable experiences: Leading group on second wave over D-day and leading group on Berlin mission, March 6, 1944.

Discharged Jan. 6, 1946 and entered reserves. Retired from reserves in 1980 as lieutenant colonel. Awarded Purple Heart, Distinguished Flying Cross, Air Medal with five clusters, POW Medal, and ETO Ribbon.

Married Ethel in 1942; they have a daughter, son, five grandchildren and four great-grandchildren. Retired from

Pacific Bell Telephone Company in 1980. Enjoys golf, gym, home chores and attending 2nd Air and 446th Bomb Group reunions.

ROBERT SHERMAN, was born Dec. 29, 1920 in Galway, NY. Entered Air Force Sept. 8, 1942. Aircraft Mechanics School, Amarillo, TX; Aerial Gunnery School, Wendover, UT. Crew training, Pueblo, CO. Arrived with John Hendrick's crew, 564th Bomb Sqdn., 389th Bomb Group, Hethel, England, September 1943.

On 11th mission to Berlin, Germany, March 8, 1944, plane was crippled by flak and crash landed in German occupied Holland. Pilot Kendrick was severely injured and Copilot Stephen Judd killed. Sherman, was one of five (of 11) who escaped capture. They were rescued by Dutch Underground and hidden 13 months among Dutch families until freed by Canadian Army.

Returned to States April 1945. Discharged Oct. 31, 1945, Rome, NY. Awarded Air Medal with one Oak Leaf Cluster, EAME Theater Medal with one Campaign Star.

Married Corinne Maines in 1945; they have one daughter Barbara and two grandchildren, Robert and Rhonda. Was a heavy equipment operator for highway construction contractor until retiring in 1982. He resided in Northville, NY, prior to his death in 1990. *Submitted by Edward J. Chu.*

ELLSWORTH SHIELDS, was born Nov. 9, 1924 in Antigo, WI. Inducted April 23, 1943, at Ft. Sheridan, IL. Basic training, Sheppard Field, TX; Air Force radio operator training, Sioux Falls, SD; Aerial Gunnery School, Yuma, AZ. Flew to England, arriving July 20, 1944. Stationed at Horsham St. Faith Air Base, 458th Bomb Group, 752nd Sqdn.

Participated in 35 bombing missions; also, eight gasoline support flights to France for Gen. Patton's tanks and armored vehicles. First mission Aug. 24, 1944, last mission April 7, 1945. Recalls especially the 20th mission to Dortmund, when after bombs away, the B-24, *Lucky One,* got hit hard by flak. Four crew members were wounded, they dropped out of formation, lost two engines and crashed behind our lines, near Montpelier, France. All survived. He also remembers narrow escapes in fog, clouds, fighter, and flak encounters. Especially enjoyed two "rest" leaves in beautiful English mansions.

Discharged Oct. 7, 1945. Graduated University of Wisconsin, 1948. He married Joyce in 1950; they have three children. Forty-two year vocation in insurance and investments; CLU, 1974, sales vice president. Retired in Jan. 1, 1990.

BARRY J. SHILLITO, was born in Dayton, OH, Jan. 1, 1921. Attended, University of Dayton and UCLA. Pre-WWII pilot. Married Eileen Cottman Dec. 2, 1942, while in USAAC pilot training. Pilot Class 43-E, South East. Flew P-40s and was transitioning in P-51s when required to become B-24 copilot.

After phases, flew B-24 to England via South America. Assigned to the 445th Bomb Group, 703rd Sqdn. Was shot down on fourth mission en route to Ludwigshaven. Captured and was POW at Stalag Luft I.

Program manager, Air Force Fighter Fire Control Sys-

tems, Wright Field, 1949-53; director material/marketing, Hughes Aircraft 1953-57. President, Houston Fearless, 1957-61. Founding president, Logistics Management Institute, 1961-68; Assistant Secretary of the Navy, 1968-69; Assistant Secretary of Defense, 1969-73; president, Teledyne Ryan Companies, 1973-77. Vice president, Teledyne and chairman Teledyne International, 1977-85. Retired 1985. Presently, corporate director. He has five children and 10 grandchildren.

ROBERT L. SHIPLEY, was born March 29, 1924 in Bristol, VA. Entered USAC Aug. 8, 1942; four engine pilot, B-24; 489th Bomb Group, 8th Air Force. Stationed at Maxwell Field, AL; Newport, AR; Blytheville, AR; England; Fort Myers, FL.

Participated in action, Air Offensive Europe, Southern France, Normandy, Northern France. Discharged Nov. 16, 1945 with the rank of major. Received Air Medal with three Oak Leaf Clusters, Distinguished Flying Cross; EAME Theater Medal with four Bronze Stars.

He is married and has four children, two step-children and 11 grandchildren. Realtor and real estate agent for 48 years.

KEITH E. SHIRK, was born May 21, 1922 in Grundy County, IA. Entered the service February 1943 and graduated from Aviation Cadets at Frederick, OK and commissioned second lieutenant Jan. 7, 1944. Transition training in B-24 at Liberal, KS. Met crew and did operational training at Tonapah, NV. Shipped to England and assigned to 389th Bomb Group. Flew 35 missions with same crew from October 1944 to March 1945 with no injuries to any of crew.

Shirk was discharged July 19, 1945, returned to college and graduated with a BS in civil engineering in December of 1947. He spent 35 years as a structural engineer in Des Moines, IA and retired in May 1987 from the presidency of "Higgins Shirk & Colvig" Architects & Engineers, having designed the structure for several of the important buildings in Des Moines and Omaha.

Married Ann Hellmich May 19, 1945; they have four children and eight grandchildren.

LLOYD SHORT, was born in Saginaw, MI, March 10, 1925. Entered USAAC March 8, 1943.

Assigned 8th Air Force, 458th Bomb Group, Horsham St. Faith near Norwich, England. Member of Thomas Pollard's crew, *Uncle Tom's Cabin;* flew 27 missions, about 15 as lead navigator at all levels, squadron through division, plus six gas hauls.

Participated in battles of Northern France, Ardennes, Rhineland, Central Europe.

Discharged Nov. 3, 1945 with the rank of first lieutenant. Received Air Medal with three clusters, Distinguished Flying Cross and EAME Theater Medal with four Bronze Stars.

Short is married and has six children. Retired after 16 years teaching; high school principal, seven years; and school superintendent, 13 years.

ALBERT J. SHOWER, was born June 16, 1910 in Madison, WI. Attended University of Wisconsin, 1930-31, graduated USMA West Point, 1935. Flight training, Randolph, Kelly Fields. Pilot rating October 1936; assigned 26th Attack Sqdn., Wheeler Field, HI.

Lieutenant colonel AUS 1943, served one year in South Pacific area. May to August 1943 Commander Shower provisional group of 44 B-17 crews, took 12 crews and B-17 aircraft to Africa August 1943. Assigned to 467th Bomb Group B-24s at Wendover September 1943. As group commander October 1943 took group to Rackheath, Norfolk in

March 1944. Flew 30 missions with group, returned with group to ZI, July 1945.

Received five Air Medals, four Distinguished Flying Cross Medals and the Bronze Star. Commanded various B-29 groups in SAC. Served with logistics command, retired February 1961.

Employed by General Motors-Delco Electronics Division in reliability-quality control department until he retired in 1971. Real estate broker to date.

Married Feb. 10, 1936 to Damaris Smith; they have three children, eight grandchildren and one great-grandson.

ELTON M. SHULL, was born Oct. 27, 1919, Texas County, OK. Inducted Feb. 2, 1942, Hutchinson, KS; assigned to ordnance attached to AAF. Started preflight October 1943; graduated Army Air Force Navigation School, Hondo TX, June 24, 1944. Assigned to Crew B-16 at March Field for heavy bombardment training; met Betty Jean Nickel while at March.

Transferred to Hamilton November 24; December 9 boarded ship for ETO, arrived December 17. Assigned to 713th Sqdn., 448th Bomb Group, AAF Station #146, Seething, England. Completed 18 missions. Left June 17 for States and arrived June 20, 1945.

Awarded Air Medal with two Oak Leaf Clusters, EAME Ribbon with three Bronze Stars, and one Overseas Bar. Discharged from active duty Dec. 17, 1945, transferred to retired USAFR, Aug. 1, 1970, rank of major.

Married Betty Jean July 8, 1945; they have two children and three grandchildren. Retired, he enjoys yard work, model airplanes and traveling.

WILLIAM M. SHY (BILL), was born in Cumbarland Gap, TN, Oct. 6, 1917. Commissioned as second lieutenant, Infantry, from University of Tennessee ROTC. Class of 1938. Entered active duty with 24th Infantry, Fort Benning, GA, Dec. 10, 1940. Transferred to Air Corps in 1942 and received pilot training in grade as a first lieutenant student officer at Shaw and Moody Fields. Flew anti-submarine patrol (B-34, B-18, and B-25) throughout the Caribbean in 1943, and the B-24 with 491st Bomb Group, 8th Air Force out of the United Kingdom during the remainder of WWII, except for period of TDY with 14th Combat Wing HQ and six weeks TDY with 9th TAC and 1st Army in Belgium and Germany.

Stateside service was divided between Pentagon, SAC and service schools. Served second overseas tour in the United Kingdom from 1948 to 1951. Served as Air Force liaison officer to the House of Representatives, United States Congress from 1952 to 1954. Chief of Air Force Aides for Eisenhower Inauguration activities. Attended several service schools including the Armed Forces Staff College in 1951. Was happily entrenched as 43rd Bomb Wing (B-47 and KC-97) deputy commander for operations when selected to attend the Air War College at Maxwell AFB (Class of 1957-58). This "education" bought a tour of duty in the Directorate of plans, at SAC HQ, Offutt AFB, NE. Attended the B-52G and H Combat Training School at Castle AFB. Subsequent assignments included base and vice wing commander of the 72nd Bomb Wing at Ramey AFB, Puerto Rico; Commander of the 416th Bomb Wing at Griffiss AFB, NY; and the 42nd Bomb Wing at Loring AFB, ME. All three wings flew the B-52G and KC-135 in various size squadrons. Was combat crew and instructor pilot qualified in the B-52G.

Held commercial pilot rating in single and multi-engine land, Boeing 707-720 and instruments. Flew a few missions over Vietnam from Guam and Thailand with crews TDY from 8th Air Force in 1968 and 1969. Assigned to 8th Air Force HQ as assistant chief of staff for operations from 1968-1970.

Shy met his wife, Ada, an "army brat," while attending

a dinner party given by his regimental commander (her father) at Camp Croft, SC in 1941. They have two daughters and four grandchildren.

Has approximately 7,000 hours flying time and 30 years service. Retired in the grade of colonel, Feb. 1, 1970. His decorations include the Legion of Merit with one Oak Leaf Cluster, Distinguished Flying Cross, Air Medal with three Oak Leaf Clusters, Army and Air Force Commendation Medals with clusters, Distinguished Unit Citation, plus campaign and theater awards.

ALEXANDER S. SIDIE, was born May 25, 1924, in Post Falls, ID. Entered USAAC June 1943; served as navigator. Upon graduating from high school in June 1943, he entered the Aviation Cadet Program and completed his training as a navigator at Hondo, TX in July 1944. From Hondo, he went to Pueblo, CO and joined the Raymond DuFlon crew for training in the B-24. Survived a mid-air collision with a P-47 during its mock attack on his crew's formation. Their bombardier, John Whittaker, was taking his turn in the top turret at the time and suffered facial lacerations as the P-47 slammed across the top of them. The P-47 spun in and its pilot did not appear to have bailed out.

Arrived in England via ship convoy in October 1944 and flew 33 missions (two with other crews) from Hethel. Memorable experience: Parachute supply drop to troops crossing the Rhine; they had to go through the ground twice as they would have run into the parachute of the preceding group.

Discharged October 1945 as first lieutenant. Received Air Medal and usual awards for flying 33 mission in the 8th Air Force.

Returned home in June 1945 and married his high school sweetheart, Lois White. They have four children and two grandsons. He owns a pharmacy in Bothell, WA.

HARRY E. SIEGRIST, was born June 11, 1921, in Clarksburg, WV and attended school in Glenville, WV. He joined the Army Aug. 27, 1942; entered Bombardier Cadet Program and graduated June 24, 1943.

Flew first combat mission with 453rd Bomb Group, February 1944. Was one of lead crews with 735th Sqdn. with Lt. Col. James Stewart as command pilot. Completed 33 missions August 1944. Pilot was Capt. William Norris.

Memorable experiences: Counting 308 holes in B-24 *Squeegee* after one mission; B-24 night raid over Hamm, Germany; stuck in B-24 bomb bay with doors open and no chute on; toggling bombs over Germany; seeing the Statue of Liberty in 1944.

Closed Gulfport AFB, MS, 1946. Assigned to Okinawa and then to Philippines in 1948. Transferred all black troops from Philippines to Okinawa. Transferred to Japan 1950. Flew 64 combat missions (B-26s) to Korea. In 1953, commander, bombardier and radar refresher programs, Sheppard AFB, TX. In 1954 project officer renovation Moore AFB, TX; 1955, attended Navigation School, Harlingen AFB, TX; 1956-1960, staff and base civil engineer, Taipei, Taiwan for M/Gen. Fred Dean.; 1960-1965, 30th Air Div., director of facilities support over five bases.

Retired as major on Jan. 31, 1965. Received 13 medals and ribbons, three Distinguished Flying Cross Medals and eight Air Medals. Director of adult migrant education program, Santa Rosa, TX 1965 through 1967; 1967-1984, civil service USAF as family housing officer at several bases. Retired June 1984.

He married his college sweetheart and had four children. Wife Flossie (McIe) passed away Dec. 16, 1987. On June 24, 1989, he married Mary E. Logan Alexander.

GABRIEL SIGNORELLI, was born Feb. 22, 1922 in New Orleans, LA. Entered USAAC October 1942; served as radio operator, 2nd Air Div., 458th Bomb Group. Military locations/stations: Keesler Field, MS; Sioux Falls AB; Santa Ana, CA; Thunderbird Marana Field; Yuma AB; Pueblo AB; Horsham, England.

Participated in the European Theater of Operations. Flew 30 combat missions with a great crew. Discharged October 1945 with the rank of tech. sergeant. Received Air Medal with four Oak Leaf Clusters.

Attended Louisiana State University for BS degree. Married, has four children and eight grandchildren. Today he enjoys fishing, golfing, honeydoing, etc.

SIDNEY SILINSKY, was born April 16, 1922 in New Brunswick, NJ. Entered USAAF Sept. 10, 1942; served with the 466th Bomb Group, 784th Sqdn. Military locations/stations: Aircraft School, Amarillo, TX; cadre to form 466th Bomb Group, Alamogordo, NM; B-24 Factory School, San Diego, CA; Attlebridge, England.

Participated in Air Offensive Europe, Normandy, Northern France, Rhineland, Ardennes and Central Europe campaigns. Memorable experience: Meeting Eisenhower and Jimmy Doolittle.

Discharged Oct. 31, 1945 with the rank of staff sergeant. Awarded EAME Theater Ribbon with six Bronze Stars, Presidential Citation and Good Conduct Medal.

Married to Bonnie; they have one daughter, one son and six grandchildren. He is retired.

WILLIAM RICHARD SILLS SR., was born March 11, 1923 in Hartford City, IN. Entered USAAF March 16, 1943 and served as an engineer on a B-24. Basic training, Clearwater, FL; AM School 412 TSS, Keesler Field, MS; Gunnery School, Laredo, TX; B-24 Crew 2954 at Casper, WY.

Participated in the European Theater of Operations. B-24, Hethel, England, 389th Bomb Group, 565th Bomb Sqdn. Flew 33 missions over Germany and occupied territory. Returned from second mission (Leipzig) with 118 holes in plane but no one hurt. On one aborted target, chose a random target which turned out to be large ammunition dump, was almost blown out of sky.

Discharged Oct. 2, 1945 with the rank of staff sergeant. Received Distinguished Flying Cross, Air Medal with three Oak Leaf Clusters, EAME Campaign Medal and four Battle Stars.

Married Jan. 11, 1945 to Margaret Bowen; they have five sons, two daughters and 17 grandchildren. He retired from 3M Company, April 1, 1988, maintenance electronics journeyman electrician.

Today he and his wife enjoy spending time with their children and traveling.

FREDERICK B. SIMARD, was born Aug.. 17, 1922, in Northampton, MA. On Dec. 9, 1941, he entered USAAF. Was in Chemical Warfare attached to HQ. Participated in the European Theater of Operations. Stationed at Horsham and Ketteringham Hall, Norwich, England.

Memorable experiences: Watching for planes to return after raids; the many friends made; returning to USA on *Queen Elizabeth*.

Discharged Oct. 10, 1945, with the rank of private first class.

Married to Joyce Kelf, an English girl, for 48 years; had one son and three grandchildren. Worked for his father in the dry cleaning business in Greenfield, MA. Headed for California in 1953. Was supervisor for ITT Barton Instrument, 30 years. Retired 1980.

Simard passed away June 20, 1992.

HENRY G. SIMON, was born June 29, 1924, in Pittsburgh, PA. Entered the USAAF Jan. 22, 1943; served 8th Air Force, 467th Bomb Group (H), 791st Bomb Sqdn. Assigned Station #145, Rackheath, England. APO 558. Flew 30 mission in Air Offensive Europe; lead crew.

Memorable experience was flying mission over beach on D-day, June 6, 1944.

Discharged May 3, 1945 with the rank of staff sergeant. Awarded ETO Ribbon with three Bronze Stars, Good Conduct Medal, Distinguished Flying Cross and Air Medal with four Oak Leaf Clusters.

Married in 1948 and has three daughters and six grandchildren. Retired as general manager of retail chain.

TAFFE S. SIMON, entered USAF March 1942, air gunner, radio operator, radar operator, Served all over the USA and with the 8th Air Force in England. Participated in ETO and battles at Ardennes, Rhineland, Central Europe, Alsace.

Memorable experience: #3 engine getting hit on 18th mission, Madgeburg, March 2, 1945, went down in Votel, Holland and slept in a windmill for four days.

Discharged 1945, recalled for Korean war. Received WWII Victory Medal, EAME Theater Medal with four stars, Good Conduct Medal and Air Medal with four Oak Leaf Clusters.

He is divorced, has two children, one granddaughter and one great-granddaughter. Retired in Oklahoma City, OK.

IRA L. SIMPSON, was born March 11, 1924 in Jackson, MS. Joined USAAC in November 1942. Basic training, Miami Beach, FL; CTD training, James Milligan University, Decatur, IL; preflight, Santa Ana AAB,; navigation training, Hondo AAF, Hondo, TX; B-24 training, Charleston, SC.

In August 1944, assigned 389th Bomb Group, Hethel, England. Shot down on 20th mission, parachuted into Holland and captured by Germans. After release from prisoner-of-war camp, returned to U.S.

Remained in Air Force for 20 years; served in SAC with 307th Bomb Group and a joint command; retired with rank of major. Received Purple Heart, Air Medal, Commendation Medal and various other campaign medals.

Married in 1945, has three sons. Worked for major corporation for 23 years retiring in 1986. Works with various veteran's organizations at present.

THEODORE A. SINGERMAN (TED), was born in Buffalo, NY, May 30, 1922. Volunteered for the USAAF in 1943, graduated Class 44-B. Did basic at Atlantic City, sent to Geneva College at Beaver Falls, PA; then Montgomery, AL and graduated twin engine pilot, Albany, GA. Wanted a P-38 or A-20 but sent to Westover, MA as a co-pilot B-24.

Flew with Capt. Ed Malone, a B-24 instructor, they were a lead radar ship. They joined the 448th Bomb Group, but also flew with 389th, 445th and 93rd groups. Completed 30 missions, three in France, 27 in Germany. Assigned statewide, 2nd Ferry Command, Wilmington, DE.

Widower of Dorothy, he has two sons and four grandchildren. Still actively working as a manufacturer's agent in New York State.

JOHN J. SIPEK (SI), was born in Chicago, IL, Sept. 27, 1920. Graduated from Catholic Technical High School in 1938. He attended a National Defense Course in sheet metal welding and auto mechanics for two years. Enlisted in the USAAC on Dec. 8, 1941, and after basic training at Jefferson Barracks, MO, was assigned to a service squadron as a propeller specialist. In June 1942 he moved to Dow Field, Bangor, ME and serviced B-17s of the 91st, 92nd and 303rd Bomb Groups for their flight to England.

December 1942 he was at Grenier Field, Manchester, NH, packing equipment for overseas. Arrived at Kings Cliffe, England, Jan. 12, 1943, with 56th Fighter Group as a member of a mobile repair unit, and performed third echelon maintenance on P-47s. Group was moved to Horsham, St. Faith, Halesworth and Boxted. In September 1943 he passed the mental, physical examination and the Aviation Cadet Examining Board but was notified by his commanding officer that he had a critical MOS number and could not be released.

During 1943 and 1944, he attended technical training schools pursuing courses in general hydraulics, super charger, P-38 crew chief, hydromatic and electric propellers. In May 1944 transferred to 479th Fighter Group at Wattisham as crew chief of mobile repair unit performing third echelon maintenance on P-38 and P-51s. He returned to the USA on USS *Enterprise* and was discharged on Dec. 6, 1945 as a staff sergeant.

He married Alice Lempke on Oct. 12, 1946. He has three children and four grandchildren.

JOSEPH V. SIVON, was born March 5, 1918, Cleveland, OH. Joined USAAC May 1942; went to Bombsight Maintenance and Automatic Pilot School at Lowry Field,

Denver; assigned to B-26 Bomb Group cadre, Plant City, FL. Applied for aviation cadet, accepted, and graduated from Twin Engine Flying School, Blytheville, AR, Class 44-B.

Assigned to B-24 cadre being formed at Wendover, UT, as second lieutenant. Replaced a co-pilot in the 489th Bomb Group which was in the final phase of training. Went to England the southern route. Flew 32 missions including D-day. Returned to the States on the *Queen Mary*.

Transferred to Appalachicola Gunnery School and checked out as first pilot. Then transferred to Victorville (George AAF) served as assistant armament officer. Left service after V-E day.

ARTHUR CARL SJOLUND JR., was born Dec. 16, 1925 in Duluth, MN. Entered the USAAC Jan. 24, 1944 at Fort Snelling. Basic at Biloxi, MS; Gunnery School at Laredo, TX and Charleston AFB. After advanced gunnery was sent to air base at Horsham St. Faith, Norwich, England. Assigned to the 458th Sqdn.

Completed 27 missions over Germany. Had a few close encounters and scares before being discharged Nov. 17, 1945 with the rank staff sergeant. Received the Air Medal and three Oak Leaf Clusters.

Married Marjorie on May 19, 1951. They have four sons and three grandchildren. After 20 years in the shade and drapery business, he retired.

FRANK W. (SKRZYNSKI) SKELDON, was born July 29, 1922, in the Buffalo, NY area. A graduate of Buffalo Technical High School. Entered service in January 1943; attended Pre-flight School at Ellington Field, Houston, TX; Gunnery School at Laredo, TX; and received his commission as a second lieutenant bombardier at Midland, TX, Class 43-14.

Flew 32 combat missions with the 489th Bomb Group, 847th Sqdn. of the 2nd Air Div. out of Holton Field, Halesworth, England. HRH Prince Bernhard of Holland flew combat mission 13 with Skeldon's crew (Crew 89) on June 21, 1944, over Siracourt, France. HRH became an honorary bombardier at the "Gathering of the Eagles '91" ceremony held on June 14, 1991, at Maxwell AFB, Montgomery, AL. HRH was presented with his bombardier wings by Skeldon on behalf of all bombardiers of the USAFs.

Skeldon received the Distinguished Flying Cross, Air Medal with three Oak Leaf Clusters four Bronze Stars to the European Campaign Ribbon.

After his service career, he received his associates and bachelor of science degrees from the University of Buffalo. Employed as a design engineer at Bell Aircraft Company in the Buffalo area prior to and after military service. He retired from design liaison engineering assignments with Textron Marine Systems at the Naval Base at Panama City, FL, where he now spends all time "goofing off."

ROBERT E. SLATER, was born Dec. 24, 1923, in Peru, IN. Enlisted in the USAAC Dec. 7, 1942. Graduated pilot, Class 44-F at Stuttgart, AR. Assigned co-pilot B-24, served with 567th Sqdn., 389th Bomb Group, 2nd Combat Wing, 2nd Air Div., 8th Air Force based at Hethel near Norwich, England. Completed 21 missions.

Served in the reserves; honorably discharged July 31, 1957, with the rank of captain. Awarded Air Medal with two Oak Leaf Clusters, European Theater Medal with three Battle Stars and Presidential Unit Citation.

Attended Stevens Institute of Technology, Hoboken, NJ. A mechanical engineer, he served in various engineering positions with several firms. Retired in 1988. Currently dealer in antiques and collectibles in Schenectady, NY.

Married Katherine Stathis, June 30, 1944; they have one daughter Joan.

HOWARD W. SLATON, was born Sept. 19, 1917 in Town Creek, AL. BS (military engineering) from U.S. Military Academy in 1942. Attended various military schools including Command and General Staff College 1945, Air War College, 1962 and Foreign Service Institute in 1954.

Military locations/stations: all over SAC; Cuba, Uruguay, two tours in England, two tours in Latin America.

Flew 31 missions with 458th Bomb Group, England; DCO, 509th Bomb Wing, Pease AFB, NH (B-47s); Air War College; Defense Attache, Uruguay; Air Attache, Cuba, Haiti, Dominican Republic.

Discharged October 1970 with the rank of colonel. Awarded Legion of Merit, two Distinguished Flying Cross Medals and four Air Medals.

Married to Chris, they have three children: Pat, Hal and Sally; and three grandchildren: Christy Lee, David and Kelley Slaton.

LEE D. SLESSOR, was born May 9, 1920 in Fort Collins, CO. Joined USAF Sept. 30, 1941; commissioned pilot, USAFR April 19, 1943; joined 389th Bomb Group (B-24) April 1943 in second phase training.

Flew to England as co-pilot June 1943; flew to North Africa June 1943. Participated in Aug. 1, 1943, low level mission to Ploesti oil fields. Returned to England mid-August 1943. Finished combat tour April 1944 as first pilot.

Discharged Sept. 12, 1945 with the rank of first lieutenant. Awarded Distinguished Service Cross, Distinguished Flying Cross, Air Medal with three Oak Leaf Clusters, Unit Citation, ETO with star and Asiatic-Pacific Campaign Medal.

Slessor is married and has three children. Worked in production, management and purchasing, retired June 1984. Enjoys fishing, golfing and woodworking.

ALFRED V. SLOAN JR., was born Dec. 24, 1921 in New York, NY. Entered the USAAC April 14, 1943; served with 8th Air Force, 445th Bomb Group.

Assigned U.S. Air Station #124, Tibenham, Norfolk, England from October 1943 to June 1945. Memorable experience was winning division football championship in 1944.

Discharged Oct. 28, 1945 with the rank of staff sergeant. Received three overseas stripes, six campaign stars, two unit awards: Presidential Unit Citation and Croix de Guerre.

He and his wife Anita have one son Alfred (III). Sloan is a college professor at State University of New York.

MEYER SLOTT, was born May 26, 1922. Inducted into the U.S. Army Dec. 23, 1942 and sent to Camp Maxey, TX. Served 102nd Inf. Div. Medical Corps for 10 months, transferred to USAAF for flight training. Early in 1944, he was sent to Harlingen AFB for gunnery training. In April 1944, he was transferred to Tonopah, NV for crew training. From April 10 to June 10 his crew trained on B-24. Then sent to

Boston by train and to England by ship, arriving there July 1944.

After a few weeks of training flights, they started tour of missions over Germany on August 16 and completed that tour of 35 missions June 16, 1945. Remained in England for about three more months and aided other flight crews with training and equipment.

Returned to USA May 1945. Attended Instructors School at Laredo, TX. Discharged October 1945 with the rank of staff sergeant. Awarded Air Medal with four clusters.

He is married and has two children and three grandsons. A pharmacist, he remains active.

ROBERT C. SLUSHER, was born Dec. 30, 1921 in Lexington, MO. Entered USAF January 1942; served as bombardier with the 2nd Air Div. Stationed in Tibenham, Norfolk County, England.

Discharged August 1946. He was awarded the Distinguished Flying Cross and Air Medal with Oak Leaf Clusters.

He has a wife, two daughters, and three grandchildren. Slusher is a retired petroleum engineer.

WALTER E. SMELT, was born Sept. 16, 1925 in Tampa FL. Entered USAAF Sept. 16, 1943; assigned to 2nd Air Div. Stationed at Camp Blanding, FL; Tyndall Field, FL; Chatham Field, GA; Hardwick, England.

He participated in many air raids, particularly remembering his first mission to Suchluchtern, Germany.

Discharged September 1945 with the rank of staff sergeant. Received Air Medal with two Oak Leaf Clusters.

Married in 1950, he has four children and 14 grandchildren. Retired after 44 years with Graybar Electric.

EDWARD C. SMERTELNY, was born July 21, 1924 in Michigan City, IN. In January 1943, entered USAAC and served as flight engineer and gunner. Stationed at St. Petersburg, FL; Gulfport, MS; Kingman, AZ; Muroc Dry Lakes; and England.

Flew 31 combat missions over Europe. Memorable experience was May 30, 1944 when wounded from shrapnel, crash landed their plane, *Zeus,* at the base.

Discharged September 1945 with the rank of staff sergeant. Received Distinguished Flying Cross, Air Medal with five clusters, Purple Heart and several other medals.

Four members of the family were in the service. He is retired and living in the high desert not too far from Muroc Dry Lakes, now Edwards Air Base.

NICHOLAS SMETANA, was born Feb. 16, 1914 in Elkhorn, WV. On April 22, 1943 entered USAAC; served with the 458th Bomb Group, 755th Sqdn. Stationed at Horsham, St. Faith, 123, Norwich, England; flew 35 combat missions.

Memorable experiences: Released single shackle hung bomb with a screw driver and no chute; plane making a deadstick landing; returning to England over an English air field; the flak holes received on missions.

Discharged Sept. 4, 1945, with the rank of staff sergeant. Awarded Distinguished Flying Cross, four Air Medals and Good Conduct Medal.

The oldest of seven, he moved to Binghampton, NY from Elkhorn, WV. In 1933, he worked as a hydraulic machine operator in a shoe factory.

He retired from IBM after 14 years.

BEAUFORD R. SMITH, was born in Straight Creek, KY on June 29, 1922. Entered USAAC April 19, 1941; served with the 66th Bomb Sqdn., 44th Bomb Group. Stationed at Exter and Shipdham, England. Participated in anti-subpatrol, Exter, England, 8th Air Force. Flew 22 missions. All missions were memorable, but most memorable was when he bailed out (France).

Discharged Sept. 27, 1945 with the rank of tech. sergeant, flight engineer. Awarded Air Medal with three Oak Leaf Clusters and 8th Air Force, Distinguished Flying Cross.

Married Barbara K. and they have one son, Don. He is retired from OSS.

C. DOUGLAS SMITH (CHARLES D.), was born in Santa Barbara County, CA, Jan. 5, 1903. He was practicing law in Santa Barbara when he enlisted in the Army as a private and was inducted July 22, 1942. After completing basic training and half way through officer training at Fort Riley, he was commissioned a first lieutenant in the Judge Advocate Generals Department.

After graduating JAGD School and while serving as the judge advocate at Fitzsimmons General Hospital, he was assigned to the 8th Air Force in November 1943, where he served as assistant judge advocate to Lt. Col. Allen Clark at 2nd Air Div. HQ, rising to the rank of major, during which time he also met his present wife, Constance Richardson.

After the war he resumed his law practice in Santa Barbara and was appointed a superior court judge in 1959 where he served until his retirement in 1971.

CLARK S. SMITH, was born Oct. 17, 1917, La Farge, WI. He joined the Army Sept. 26, 1940; took aviation cadet exam in early 1942 and was commissioned Jan. 7, 1943. Went to Gowen Field and Pocatello AAB in Idaho for B-24 crew training, flying as a navigator. A provisional group was formed at Topeka, KS and in November 1943 he joined the 389th Bomb Group at Hethel, England as a replacement crew.

Shot down by fighters on a mission to Gotha, Germany, Feb. 24, 1944, and became a prisoner of war at Stalag Luft I until the end of the war.

He returned to the States, married Jean Nelson while on R&R leave in August 1945.

After navigation refresher and Radar School, again saw duty as a combat crew in B-29, B-50, B-36 and B-47 aircraft.

He was a member of the Strategic Air Command (SAC) from October 1948 until his retirement as a colonel in 1967.

He and his wife have son Bradley. Smith is retired and lives in Sun City West, AZ.

DONALD W. SMITH, was born Oct. 4, 1920 in Eau Claire, WI. In July 1942, entered USAAF; served as bombardier with 445th Bomb Group. Assigned Tibenham Station, England. Flew 30 missions over Europe.

Discharged November 1945, captain, Reserves. Received Distinguished Flying Cross and Air Medal with five clusters.

Married, he has two children. He is retired and resides in Madison, WI.

EDWARD M. SMITH, was born April 27, 1922 in Paonia, CO. Joined regular Army April 5, 1941, Ft. Logan, CO. After completing training, he was assigned as flight engineer with E.P. Monroe, pilot; F.M. Loos, co-pilot; W.E. Britt, navigator; J.B. Wilson, bombardier; G.W. Woodard, radio operator; B.B. McComas, armorer gunner; A.H. Karels, nose gunner; G.K. Hutchinson, tail gunner. They picked up a new plane in Lincoln, NE, via northern route to Ireland, then to England with the 93rd Bomb Group, 328th Bomb Sqdn in July 1944.

They learned about war on their second mission over Coblenz, Germany. Flak hit them pretty hard and #2 engine started smoking. They dropped bombs in the river trying to hit barges. Britt was standing on his flak suit which took a direct hit. Karels had a scratch on the left thigh. They lost altitude and headed home. Smith had to kick the nose wheel out, but landed OK; they had over 200 holes in the plane.

He completed 35 missions and made tech. sergeant. Discharged May 22, 1945.

Completed A.P. School, worked for Boeing for 15 and a half years in Wichita, KS, and spent 20 years with United Air Lines at San Francisco. He retired in 1987.

His first wife Mickey died in 1982. Married Millie Harless in 1984. They live in Sacramento.

ERIC W. SMITH JR., was born Aug. 15, 1916 in St. Louis, MO. Enlisted in the USAAC as an aviation cadet at Hickam Field, Honolulu, Territory of Hawaii. He washed out of pilot training in 1942, then completed Gunnery School near Kingman, AZ and finally bombardier training at Kirtland Field just outside Albuquerque, NM in Class 44-3. He received his wings and his commission on Feb. 26, 1944 at a post ceremony presentation. As Gen. R.M. Ramey pinned on the wings, he

commented that Lt. Smith had just gotten his wings and would immediately get them clipped. Smith and his bride-to-be, Micki Kaiser from Rochester, NY, were then married by the post chaplain. The ceremony was very successful because they celebrated their 50th anniversary in February 1994.

Smith was then ordered to Westover Field, MA, then Chatham Field, Ga, and on to the 702nd Sqdn., 445th Bomb Group near Tibenham, England. By this time, Smith was flying as a DR navigator.

On his 11th combat mission, Smith became a statistic...he was shot down by ME-109s and FW-190s near Kassel, Germany on what was later billed as the highest group loss in the 8th Air Force history. He was lucky to get out of his crippled and burning B-24. After a night in hiding, Smith was captured the next day by Volks Police, interrogated at Dulag Luft and eventually incarcerated in Stalag Luft near Barth, Germany.

He was liberated May 1, 1945 by the Russians, returned to the U.S., deactivated and has lived happily ever since.

ERNEST L. SMITH, was born in Halstead, KS, Nov. 3, 1923. Enlisted USAAC Dec. 7, 1942; basic training St. Petersburg, FL; Radio School, Truax Field, Madison, WI; Aerial Gunnery School, Harlingen, TX. B-24 crew training, Clovis, NM; Langley Field, VA; Mitchell Field, Long Island.

Assigned to 705th Sqdn., 446th Bomb Group Flixton-Bungay, England, First mission Rathenow, Germany, April 17, 1944. Shot down on 17th mission to Mulhausen, Alsace, France; Lt. Eugene T. Winn's crew. Prisoner of war Stalag IV and I, April 17, 1944 to May 8, 1945.

Discharged Oct. 13, 1945, with the rank of tech. sergeant. Received Air Medal with two Oak Leaf Clusters.

Retired May 25, 1988, after 33 years of public school

teaching. Kansas Air National Guard member for 26 years, senior master sergeant.

Smith's younger brother, Allen D. Smith, was a member of the 101st Airborne Inf. Div., a veteran of The Battle of the Bulge.

EXCEL I. SMITH JR., was born Nov. 1, 1921 in Snyder, TX. Entered USAAF as a private Feb. 12, 1941, at Goodfellow Field, San Angelo, TX; transferred Perrin Field, Sherman, TX.

Staff sergeant adm. appointed officer candidate February 1942; graduated and commissioned at Miami Beach, FL, June 1942. Assigned SAAAB San Antonio June 1942, squadron and group commander until June 1943. Entered flight training Stamford, TX, June 22, 1942.

Basic, Winfield, KS; advanced twin, Waco, TX; B-24 trans. Ft. Worth; trained combat crew, Casper, WY; received new B-24 at Topeka, KS, first pilot and flew from Manchester, NH to Goose Bay, Iceland.

In Valley, Wales he was assigned to the 565th Sqdn., 389th Bomb Group, Hethel, 2nd Air Div. Flew 17 missions; two group leads, two Air Medals. Lost engine while leading group, 25,000, fell through entire formation. Lost engine over Zider Zee, co-pilot feathered wrong engine.

Discharged November 1945, continued in Reserves for five years, reached rank of captain. Awarded two Air Medals and Expert 45 Pistol.

Married Aug. 22, 1942 to Elizabeth Miller in Coleman, TX. Has one son, one daughter, six grandchildren, and one great-grandchild.

Smith and his wife own and operate a ranch on the Colorado-New Mexico border assisted by their son and grandsons.

GEORGE ALLEN SMITH, was born Aug. 5, 1918 in Port, OK. Entered USAAF in June 1940. Military locations/stations: Brooks Field; Ellington; Tucson AB; Idaho; March Field; England with 453rd Bomb Group, 735th Sqdn. After Europe stationed at Great Falls, MT, preparing to go and fight Japan. War ended so he stayed in USA.

Discharged May 28, 1945 with rank of master sergeant; re-enlisted, final discharge June 1954. Awarded European Theater Medal and Good Conduct Medal.

Married 48 years, has four children, 10 grandchildren and one great-grandchild.

Still working and helping his boys with their businesses.

HENRY J. SMITH, was born Oct. 7, 1924 in Scranton, PA. Volunteered in the USAAF Feb. 5, 1943. Trained Laredo, TX, Gunnery School; assigned to B-24 crew and trained at Peterson Field, Colorado Springs. Flew to Prestwick, Scotland via southern route.

Crew assigned to 93rd Bomb Group, 409th Sqdn. Flew 25 missions, 16 over France and nine over Germany including invasion beachhead, June 6, 1944.

Bailed out over Magdeburg, Germany after plane, hit by flak, caught fire on Sept. 11, 1944. Prisoner of war in Pomerania until Feb. 6, 1945 when Russian Army invaded Germany. Approximately 8,000 Air Force enlisted crew walked 500-600 miles east and south. His group was liberated at Bitterfeld, Germany, April 26, 1945.

Discharged Oct. 31, 1945 with the rank of staff sergeant. He was awarded three Air Medals.

Earned private pilot license via GI bill. Bought a Navy Stearman, his dream. Rolled it around the sky for six months;

then got serious and worked for Commercial Credit Corporation 38 years. Retired May 1986.

Married Evelyn, Oct. 4, 1961; they have two daughters, Kim and Candace.

In memory of: 1st Lt. David Yous, bombardier (didn't bail out); 2nd Lt. James M. Harrison, Mickey operator (unknown); T/Sgt. Robert A. Weander, radio operator (shot by civilians); and S/Sgt. John J. Hodgeman, gunner (shot by civilians).

JAMES W. SMITH, was born in San Diego, CA, May 4, 1924. On Aug. 8, 1942, entered USAAC; October 1942, Las Vegas Gunnery School. 1942/43, B-24D A/C Davis Monthan, Tucson, AZ; Alamogordo, NM; Pueblo, CO; Casper, WY; Topeka, KS.

August 1943, B-24H to England via Iceland. September 1943, 392nd Bomb Group, 578th Sqdn., Wendling Station #118. Tail gunner on five diversion missions and 18 combat missions. In January 1944 to 482nd Bomb Group, 814th Sqdn. (PFF) Pathfinders, Alconbury, Station #102; 12 missions in B-24H lead with H2X "Mickey." April to September 1944 flew B-24H and B-17G's on H2X and "Gee" day and night training flights over France on experimental "Mickey" missions. October 1944 to March 1945 Carpetbaggers 801/492nd Bomb Group, 858th Sqdn., Harrington, Station #179.

Night (Maquis) missions, also night bombing and leaflet missions into France. Returned to ZI April 1945.

Discharged June 1945 as staff sergeant. Received Distinguished Flying Cross, Air Medal with four Oak Leaf Clusters, ETO with five Battle Stars, American Defense with star, American, Pacific Theater, Occupation of Japan, WWII Victory. Unit Citations: Presidential (two, 392nd/482nd); Crox de Guerre (one, 492nd); Czechoslovakian War Medal (one, 492nd).

Married Celia W. Crane, Dec. 16, 1945. They have a daughter, Carolyn Morgan; and grandchildren, Clayton and Travis. Retired owner, Mountain Relay Company, radio communication sites in Southern California.

JOHN L. SMITH, was born at Harrisburg, PA, on Dec. 8, 1924; moved to Massachusetts in 1940. Entered USAAC on July 7, 1943 via Fort Devens, MA. Assigned to basic training at Greensboro, NC; attended Airplane Mechanics School at Keesler Field, Biloxi, MS; trained in aerial gunnery at Laredo AAFB in Laredo, TX.

Flight crew was formed at Lincoln AAFB in Lincoln, NE. Assigned to Gowen Field, Boise, ID, for indoctrination and learning to fly as a crew. Entire crew went overseas on a "Liberty" ship, arriving in England on Aug. 23, 1944.

Flight crew (Hodges Flak Dodgers): Pilot Willie E. Hodges (deceased), Virginia; Co-pilot Milton Krough (deceased), New Mexico; Bombardier Alfred A. Pizzato, Illinois; Navigator James Ginn, Ohio, now Kentucky; Radioman Jack Gideon, Iowa (wherabouts unknown); 1st Engineer Bennett Martin, Ohio (whereabouts unknown); 2nd Engineer John L. Smith, Massachusetts; Armorer Walter Dennard (deceased), Georgia; Ball Turret Frederick J. Honold, New Jersey; Tail Gunner Joseph T. Sirna (deceased), Maryland.

Assigned to 2nd Air Div., 96th Combat Wing, 458th Bomb Group, 754th Bomb Sqdn. at Horsham St. Faith in Norwich, England. Flew 35 combat missions over Germany, France and Belgium. In addition, crew flew gasoline to Gen. Patton's troops after tour of duty completed.

Upon arriving home from overseas, he was assigned to B-29 electronic training at Chanute Field, IL; part way through the course, Japan surrendered and he was sent to Grenier Field in Manchester, NH, where he was discharged on Oct. 8, 1945.

Upon graduating from Wentworth Institute and Northeastern University, both in Boston, MA, he worked as a consulting engineer for 42 plus years before retiring in December 1989.

Married November 1948, he has two daughters, one son and seven grandchildren.

KENNETH R. SMITH, was born in Laurel, OR, May 16, 1924, a third generation Oregonian. Graduated from St. Helens High School, St. Helens, OR, class of 1942. Inducted

June 17, 1943 at Portland, OR and reported to Fort Lewis, WA, July 1, 1943.

Basic training at Biloxi, MS; next to Lowry Field, Denver, CO for Armament School; then to Tyndall Field, FL, for gunnery training. Next came a break, nine days travel time and a nine-day leave which took him home to Oregon and back to Springfield, MA for crew assignment.

Assigned to Bill Leesburg's crew and off to Charleston, SC. Overseas trip to Liverpool was 13 days across the North Atlantic. Visited by his brother, Ronald Smith twice while at Hethel. He served with field artillery while on the continent. Enjoyed his weeks rest leave with his brother in London.

Completed 30 missions from Dec. 5, 1944 to end of war in Europe. Discharged at Sioux Falls, SD, Oct. 25, 1945 with the rank of staff sergeant.

Retired in 1982 from paper industry as steam plant engineer with 33 years service.

LEANARD SMITH

LEROY A. SMITH JR. (JACK), was born in Wray, CO, Oct. 3, 1916. Graduated South High School, Denver, CO. Attended University of Denver and University of Colorado. Enlisted as cadet USAAC December 1941. Flying School, Santa Ana, Dos Palos and Merced in California; Marana, AZ, graduated as pilot and commissioned second lieutenant at Douglas, Az. Checked out as first pilot B-24 Liberator, Clovis, NM. Joined 446th Bomb Group, Lowry Field, Denver, CO as assistant operations 705th Sqdn.

Flew southern route South America, Ascension Island, Africa to 8th Air Force, England. Arrived Station #125, Bungay (near Norwich), November 1943.

As staff pilot, he flew combat missions in command position with lead crews. Transferred to 448th Bomb Group station #146 Seething as operations officer 713th Sqdn. Completed first combat tour. Had short leave in States.

He returned to Seething for second combat tour. Became group operations officer. In addition to bombing missions, flew supplies to pocketed paratroopers in Holland (treetop level). Also, flew potatoes and flour to Paris the day after its liberation.

After V-E day became group and base commander. Closed base and returned it to the British. Supervised return of ground personnel to States. Based at Sioux Falls, SD and Salina, KS.

Separated late August 1946 with the rank of lieutenant colonel. Was awarded two Distinguished Flying Cross Medals, six Air Medals, American Campaign Medal, European Campaign Medal with seven major Battle Stars, WWII Victory Medal and the French Croix de Guerre with Bronze Star.

Married to Mary Syler Miller and Eileen Eckland Way, both deceased. Four children and 11 grandchildren. Founder and CEO of the L.A. Smith Company, Scottsbluff, NE and Carroll, IA. Retired 1982.

LOUIS SMITH, was born Nov. 14, 1919 in Boston, MA. Entered military service Feb. 18, 1942. Served with the 93rd Bomb Group, 330th Bomb Sqdn.; air combat crew, air gunnery instructor. Stationed at Scott Field, IL; Fort Myers, FL;

Charleston AB, SC; Benghazi, Africa; Alconbury, England; Hardwick, England.

He joined the 93rd at Fort Myers, FL, before the group went to England. Flew with Gen. Ramsey Potts (at that time, major) on most of his tour of 25 missions. On low-level Ploesti raid, Aug. 1, 1943, his position as gunner was in the nose of the B-24D where twin guns had been installed. Maj. Potts led the flight of 12 planes. Being in the nose, he was probably the first man in the flight over the target. That mission still brings him scary dreams even after 50 years. He thanks the good Lord for bringing him through and letting him fly with Maj. Potts.

Discharged May 26, 1945 with the rank of staff sergeant. Awarded Distinguished Flying Cross with Oak Leaf Cluster, Air Medal with four Oak Leaf Clusters; EAME Theater Medal with Battle Stars and Good Conduct Medal.

His wife Ethel is deceased; he has a daughter Judith, one grandson and one granddaughter. Retired, he spends six months in Florida and six months in Massachusetts.

RICHARD B. SMITH (DICK), was born Jan. 14, 1921 near Belgrade, NE, where he graduated from high school in 1938. He enlisted in the Air Corps in 1941 and graduated from Flight School in November 1942. He took B-24 training at Fort Worth, TX and picked up his crew in Tucson, AZ early in 1943. His crew trained with the initial cadre of the 389th Bomb Group and finished its combat with that group.

On the bomb run over Ploesti, the plane took a direct hit in the bomb bay gas tank through the open bomb bay doors. The plane filled with fumes, but miraculously, did not catch fire. During the transfer of fuel from that tank, Curtis Callahan, the radio operator, saved as much fuel as possible by laying on the catwalk and plugging holes from fragments of the explosive shell with his fingers. The plane still had about 100 gallons of gas back over Benghazi. Another exciting ride resulted from the loss of #1 and #2 engines to flak after bombs away over Bremen. Cloud cover helped the crew to get back to the channel without further damage. Loss of rudder trim to the same flak complicated the trip home. Heading to Hethel was maintained by banking into the good engines.

After the war, Dick flew for a time with Capitol Airlines, then got back into the Air Force and retired as a lieutenant colonel in 1962.

His second career consists of three years as a professor of insurance at Northeastern University and 15 years in the home office of Aetna Life and Casualty.

His wife of more than 40 years died in 1985, he is now married to his high school sweetheart who also lost a mate of more than 40 years. His family now consists of her three daughters and three grandchildren.

He has just begun to fly his home-built *Cosy Classic,* a 200 mph airplane with a range of over 1,000 miles. The *Cosy Classic* is of course equipped with two vertical tail fins.

ROBERT W. SMITH, was born Nov. 30, 1923, in Arcola, IL. He joined the service Feb. 19, 1943. Assigned to 466th Bomb Group, 784th Sqdn., stationed at Attlebridge.

He went overseas as a bombardier with Lt. Robert Wightman's crew, completing 15 missions with this crew.

Transferred to the lead squadron with Capt. George Maxton's crew where he flew 12 lead missions as pilotage navigator. Several later missions were visual and received good bombing results leading to all of their officers receiving the Distinguished Flying Cross. All crew members of both crews returned home safely.

Discharged Oct. 20, 1945, with the rank of first lieutenant. Received Air Medal with three clusters; Distinguished Flying Cross, EAME Theater Medal with four Bronze Battle Stars.

Smith is retired and living near Hanover, IN, with his wife Dorothy of 41 years. They have four children and six grandchildren.

He is a graduate of DePauw University, Greencastle, IN; a career in various sales positions for 40 years in Indianapolis and Carmel, IN. Now active in Hanover Presbyterian Church, Madison, IN, and Jefferson County (IN) historical organizations, traveling and other hobbies.

WADE W. SMITH, was born April 6, 1918 in Youngstown, OH. Enlisted Aug. 1, 1942, active duty May 29, 1943, USAAF. Basic training at Camp Fannin, TX; transferred to Army Air Corps; attended schools at Keesler Field, MS and Tyndall Field, FL. Training at Westover Field, MA on B-24s. Departed for England July 16, 1944.

Assigned to 8th Air Force, 2nd Air Div., 445th Bomb Group (B-24s). Completed 35 missions, served as aerial gunner or flight engineer. Returned to U.S. in March 1945 on furlough.

Assigned to Chanute Field, IL; completed Electrical School and became instructor on electrical systems (B-29s).

Discharged Sept. 23, 1945 with the rank of staff sergeant. Awarded Air Medal with five Oak Leaf Clusters, ETO Ribbon with three Bronze Stars.

Employed in steel industry management until retirement in 1979.

Married in 1947, his wife is deceased. He has a son and one grandson. He spends five months per year in Florida.

WILLIAM EDWARD SMITH, was born Oct. 2, 1922 in Oak Park, IL. Joined the USAAF Sept. 5, 1942; called to active duty Feb. 24, 1943, became an aviation cadet on Aug. 1, 1943. Earned wings as a pilot at Ellington Field, TX on April 15, 1944, in Class 44-D. Commissioned as a second lieutenant. Earned aeronautical ratings (wings) as a senior pilot in 1953 and as a command pilot in 1960.

Sent to B-24 Transition School at Ft. Worth AAF; Gowen Field, Boise, ID; then went to England on the SS *Mount Vernon*. Assigned to the 392nd Bomb Group, 576th Bomb Sqdn. His crew flew 26 combat missions. Memorable experiences were his 16th mission to Berlin on March 18, 1945; and 19th mission, a low-level resupply to paratroopers, four glider troops that had just crossed the Rhine River on March 24, 1945.

Transferred to Air Transport Command; brought a new B-24 back to Windsor Locks, CT, via Iceland, Greenland and then home. Subsequently went to B-24 Instructors School and then the war was over.

Released from active duty Sept. 20, 1945 with the rank of first lieutenant. Retired as a ready reservist on Oct. 2, 1969, as a lieutenant colonel.

Received Air Medal with three Oak Leaf Clusters, Good Conduct Medal, ETO and American Theater Medal, and WWII Victory Medal.

Smith volunteered to go back on active duty during the Korean War from May 1, 1951 to Jan. 30, 1953.

Married Kay C. Cumby Dec. 1, 1946 (she passed away Sept. 5, 1958), they had two sons. On March 6, 1959, he married Mary A. Raines.

Graduated from SMU in January 1948. Retired January 1986 as a vice president of a Dallas based property and casualty company.

WILLIAM J. SMITH, was born Jan. 15, 1926 in Franklin, PA. Entered USAAF Jan. 14, 1944; served with 8th Air Force as aerial gunner with the 467th Bomb Group, 390th Bomb Sqdn, 2nd Air Div. in Rackheath, England. Stationed at Keesler Field, Biloxi, MS; Tyndall Field, Gunnery School, Mitchell Field, NY; Chatham Field, GA; Harlingen, TX; Fort Dix, NJ; Bradley Field, CT; Scotland, Rackheath, England; Azores; Sioux Falls, SD; Fort Sam Houston, TX.

Participated in battles of Ardennes, Rhineland and Central Europe. Memorable experiences: Landing back at base when an electrical malfunction wouldn't release their bombs over the target. Landing on one engine. On a mission over Germany seeing one of their B-24 shot down, saw three chutes.

Discharged March 16, 1946 with the rank of sergeant. Awarded Good Conduct Medal, Air Medal, WWII Victory Medal, American Campaign Medal, EAME Theater Medal with three Bronze Stars.

Married Shirley J. Graham on July 27, 1946; they have one son Gary J. and two grandchildren. He retired from Joy Technologies, Inc., Franklin, PA, after 46 years service.

VERYL L. SNEATH, was born April 24, 1924 in St. Petersburg, FL; graduated from St. Petersburg Senior High in 1942; enlisted U.S. Army, November 1942. Basic training, Miami Beach (Army Air Corps). Graduated Aircraft Armorer School, Buckley/Lowry Fields, 1943 and sent to England.

Assigned to 328th Bomb Sqdn., 93rd Bomb Group, 2nd Air Div., January 1944; transferred to 1595th Ord. S&M Co., AAF Station #146, April 1944; reassigned to 713th Bomb Sqdn., 448th Bomb Group, 2nd Air Div., July 1944 as a bombsight/automatic pilot mechanic. Hitchhiked a ride with the 714th Bomb Sqdn. to Ludwigshaven and back Aug. 26, 1944.

Returned to Sioux Falls, SD. Discharged as private first class at Tucson, AZ, October 1945.

Attended St. Petersburg Junior College and worked for the U.S. Postal Service, 1946-47. Re-enlisted USAAF, May 1947; graduated Army OCS, February 1948, commissioned second lieutenant Ord Corps. Served in Korean Police Action 1950-52, then in France 1955-58.

Returned to Korea in 1959, KMAG, then Germany, 1960, 7th ATC, Vilseck, returned to Ft. Benning, GA, 1963, deputy maintenance officer and retired as a major in July 1965. Received Good Conduct Medal, Parachute Badge, Glider Badge and Army Commendation Medal for military service and awarded twice the Commander's Award for civilian service with the federal government.

Employed as depot maintenance liaison officer for an Army Depot 1966, deputy maintenance officer, Kaiserslautern Army Depot, FRG, 1970, reassigned to Navy, detailed as deputy base maintenance officer of U.S. Marine Base, Quantico, VA, 1975, transferred to military district of Washington, (chief, program/budget, DCSLOG), 1979, and reassigned as logistics management specialist, DCSLOG U.S. Army, Pentagon, 1982, retiring in January 1986.

Married Michelle R. Rangeard in 1957.

JOHN WILLIAM SNIDER, was born Sept. 13, 1924 at Middleport, OH, an Ohio River town. Enlisted in USAAF at Patterson Airfield in August 1942, called to active duty March 1943 after spending one semester at Miami University in Oxford, OH. Graduated from Bombardier School at Albuquerque and commissioned second lieutenant on April 1, 1944. Became part of B-24 crew at Tonopah, NV, in June 1944.

Assigned 8th Air Force's 448th Bomb Group (H) at Seething in September 1944. First mission was the disastrous September 27 mission to Kassel and last mission was 8th's last mission to Salzburg on April 25, 1945. Crew survived several incidents including a landing in a burning B-24 and a mid-air collision with a B-17 but was never damaged by enemy action.

Released from active duty in October 1945 and returned to school as a physics major at Miami in 1946. Promoted to captain during Air Force Reserve duty in 1956.

Earned AB and MA degrees at Miami and Ph.D. at Ohio State. Returned to Miami to teach physics and have been there ever since, having become Professor Emeritus upon retirement in 1992, an even half century after first enrolling at the university.

GEORGE W. SNOOK, was born Dec. 26, 1920 in Ashland, OH. Entered military service Oct. 26, 1942; served with the 8th Air Force, 445th Bomb Group, 702nd Sqdn. Stationed at Jefferson Barracks, MO; Lincoln, NE; Wendover Field, basic, Sioux City; Tibenham, England.

Memorable experience: On their 13th mission to Ovanlenburg, Germany, they were hit by flak. Large hole inside of airplane, lost hydraulic fluid, landed plane tail first, nose wheel damaged; walked away.

On June 27, 1944, he completed his 30th mission. Ran Sergeant's Club until war was over. Discharged Sept. 5, 1945 with the rank of tech. sergeant, flight engineer. Received Distinguished Flying Cross, Air Medal with three clusters.

Married to Barbara for 32 years; they have four children and four grandchildren. Retired after 38 years with electric utility.

RAY A. SNOOK, was born Nov. 18, 1924 in Portland, OR. Entered USAAC in 1943; served as radio operator/air gunner. Stationed at Keesler Field, MS for basic; Radio School, Sioux Falls, SD; Gunnery, Yuma, AZ; and overseas North Pickenham AB, United Kingdom.

Participated in the battles of Ardennes, Rhineland, Central Europe. Memorable experience: Loss of aircraft, *Flying Jackass*, at Marston due to battle damage on mission and the crash of a British Lancaster on top of aircraft as it was parked at Marston, destroying it.

Discharged in 1946 with the rank of tech. sergeant. Received Air Medal with cluster, Good Conduct Medal, American Theater Medal, Presidential Unit Citation, ETO Medal and WWII Victory Medal.

Married to Betty, they have a son, Marc R.; daughters, Kathy, Melody and Lisa; five grandchildren; and two great-grandchildren.

He is retired and currently a major in the National Guard Reserve.

ELEMUEL M. SNYDER (LEM), was born April 2, 1923 in Ockley, IN. Joined USAAF November 1942. Military locations/stations: 64th College Training Detachment, Mississippi State College, Starkville; SAACC, testing pilot, navigator, bombardier; pilot primary training, Bonham, TX; pilot basic training, Greenville, TX; pilot advanced training multi-engine, Ellington Field, Galveston, TX; pilot B-24 transition training, Liberal, KS; crew formation and Training Center, Pueblo, CO; Overseas Departure Center, Topeka, KS; 2nd Div., 458th Bomb Group, 754th Sqdn., Norwich, England; B-29 transition, Las Vegas, NV; USAAFR Troop Carrier Base, Columbus, IN.

Memorable experiences: Replacing crew navigator who passed out on first mission due to hyper-ventilation; crew selection for lead crew and radar training; finding his crew flew deputy lead to Bad Reichenhall, Germany, on the last mission day over Europe in WWII, April 25, 1945; two return trips to 2nd Air Div. Memorial with his wife (getting the red carpet treatment by Phyllis DuBois, Martin Levett and their associates at the memorial); being asked to donate a copy of his personal, pilot log book to 2nd Air Div. Memorial.

Resigned in 1951 with the rank of first lieutenant. Awarded Air Medal. His son also received Air Medal from Vietnam.

He received a degree in air transportation engineering from Purdue University in January 1949. Started wholesale electronics business and sold it to become vice president of a tag manufacturing company. The next 20 years he managed, consolidated or merged allied paper converting companies, and the last 20 years consulted on materials management in variety of industries including major airlines. Today he is semi-active in materials management consulting. He collects and classifies "old hand tools" and makes presentations to school history classes. He is also active in service clubs for fun and frolic and fund-raising programs.

Married Marilyn Wrightsman, Jan. 12, 1946; they have three daughters, one son, three grandsons, and five granddaughters.

ROBERT E. SNYDER (BOB), was born in Ridgefield Park, NJ, April 13, 1919. Inducted in Army, Fort Dix, NJ, October 1942. Attended Radio School, Sioux Falls, SD; Radar School, Boca Raton, FL in 1943. He was at Seymour Johnson Field, NC before going to England in the fall of 1943.

Assigned to 389th Bomb Group, 565th Sqdn. at Hethel, England and also to RAF Base at Cheddington to work on Jostle (anti V2 equipment).

With other Yanks he visited an English family in Luton, Beds. on weekend passes (visited again in 1976), also London. On furlough, visited Scotland.

Took a flight over Germany to see damage done by 8th Air Force. Served 18 months in the Air Force in England, ending as a staff sergeant.

He returned to the USA in May 1945, landing at Bradley Field; married Florence Leavenworth June 11, 1945 in Rochester, NY. They have a son, daughter, and two grandsons.

RUSSELL E. SNYDER, was born May 17, 1923, in Lafayette, IN. Drafted into the Army Jan. 20, 1943, transferred to the Air Corps at Drew Field, FL; volunteering for the 2032nd Engineer Aviation Fire Fighting Platoon.

With 10 weeks of Fire Fighting School in New Orleans, LA, and after a five-day furlough, they sailed for Hethel on the *Queen Mary*, arriving Nov. 20, 1943; assigned to 389th Bomb Group.

Memorable experiences: The excitement on D-day, their planes returning from the Hamm raid; one of their planes hitting the radar shack; the tour of Germany after hostilities.

Being attached to the 2nd Air Div., he received six European Campaign stars.

Retired from TRW Steering in 1988. Married Mary 47 years ago and have a daughter, four sons and 12 grandchildren. He feels it was a privilege to have been a small part of such a great organization.

PHILIP SOLOMON, was born June 2, 1917 in New York; lived in New Jersey and later in Washington, DC. Was a civilian employee in the office of Quartermaster General.

Enlisted in the USAAF March 1942; trained at Maxwell Field, AL; Bennetsville, SC; Monroe, LA, where he received navigator's wings in June 1943. Remained there as an instructor until assigned to 445th Bomb Group, part of a new B-24 wing forming at Sioux City, IA, where he met Capt. Jimmy Stewart also joining the 445th.

After training at Watertown, SD, they flew their own planes to England via the southern route (South America and Africa), arriving in December 1943.

On April 12, 1944, on 24th mission, they were shot down over eastern Belgium where Solomon bailed out and landed on a cow. Fortunately he made immediate contact with the Underground, minutes before arrival of a German search party.

He eventually got down to the Swiss border, which he crossed about midnight of June 1, in time for his birthday, June 2.

Received Air Medal with three Oak Leaf Clusters and Purple Heart.

After relief from active duty September 1945, worked in New York office of the FCC until moving to Los Angeles in 1953. Retired as controller of Paramount Paint Company in 1982.

He and Claire were married May 4, 1943. For their first anniversary, Solomon was missing in action in Belgium. They had two sons; their one surviving son, Barry, now lives in Salt Lake City. They have two grandchildren, a boy and a girl.

NEAL E. SORENSEN, was born Aug. 22, 1920, in Petersburg, MN. Enlisted in the USAAC Oct. 22, 1942 as a private. An aviation cadet in 1943, he graduated as a second lieutenant navigator in February 1944.

His combat consisted of 23 bombing missions and five combat time "flour sack" missions with the 489th Bomb Group (B-24), 8th Air Force at Halesworth. Sorensen trained in B-29s at Tucson, AZ, and Fairmont, NE, before the A-bomb ended the war.

Upon graduation from the University of Minnesota in 1948, he entered the printing business, but continued active in the reserves. Neal eventually became president and CEO of Beddor Companies, a seven-company conglomerate. Restless in retirement in 1987, he bought into a start-up web printing company.

As a Mats (Mac) qualified navigator, he won his last combat ribbon (Vietnam) in 1966 on a supply mission to Da Nang. He retired a lieutenant colonel in 1969.

He married Patricia J. Robertson June 17, 1947; they have one daughter, two sons and three granddaughters.

HERSHALL E. SPAULDING, was born May 26, 1918 in Moscow, OH. Drafted in the USAAF Sept. 8, 1942; 1596th Base Unit; 703rd Bomb Sqdn, 445th Bomb Group. Stationed at Seymour Johnson, NC; Chanute Field, IL; Sioux City, IA; Tibenham, England where he was airplane instrument specialist on B-24s.

Participated in battles of Northern France, Rhineland, Central Europe, Ardennes, Air Offensive Europe. Memorable experience: Graduating from AM Course at head of class on April 14, 1943, two days before first baby was born in Maysville, KY.

Discharged Sept. 15, 1945 with the rank of sergeant. Received Good Conduct Ribbon, Distinguished Unit Citation, EAME Theater Medal with six Bronze Stars.

He married Marjorie Clift Sept. 27, 1941; they have four children and nine grandchildren. He was employed at Allis-Chalmers Manufacturing Company as turret lathe operator from November 1940 until drafted; returned there after discharge and was promoted to data processor in early 1950s, to tool designer in 1960s, to maintenance foreman in 1970s. He was forced to retire in 1980 due to ill health, and passed away Aug. 17, 1986.

HAROLD GLENN SPEER, was born Oct. 25, 1925 in Poor Fork, KY. Dec. 2, 1943, entered USAAF. Military locations/stations: Chatham Field, GA and Old Buckingham Field, England.

Memorable experience: Alerted for seven missions, flew four missions which were turned back when the weather closed in on the target. Discharged April 19, 1946 with the rank of sergeant T-5.

Speer re-entered the service October 1950 at Waco, TX, as an aviation cadet at James Connelly AFB, TX, graduated in Class 51-G at Williams Field, Chandler, AZ, as a jet fighter pilot. Stationed at Luke Field, AZ; Chaumont AFB, France flying patrol along the Iron Curtain; Kelly Field, TX; Malstrom AFB; Alaskan Air Command; finally at Nellis AFB. Honorably discharged with the rank of captain. Awarded ETO Campaign Medal, American Service Ribbon and others.

Married Ruby Catherine Cox; they have five children and 10 grandchildren. Speer has been a Ford salesman at Ted Russell Ford for 22 years.

MAURICE E. SPEER, was born Jan. 25, 1916, in Marathon, TX. He entered the U.S. Army June 2, 1937 and served until 1943. Military locations/stations: Texas A&M; University of Arizona; 2nd Air Div., England; Williams AFB; Mather AFB; Las Vegas AFB; Orlando, FL, AFB; Philadelphia, Mats; Elmendorf AFB; Bergstrom AFB.

Participated in European Theater of Operations, 1944-1945; 458th Bomb Group, 2nd Air Div., 8th Air Force. Memorable experiences: Combat missions over Europe; rescue operations in Alaska; Azon bombing over Europe in 1944.

Retired Oct. 30, 1964 with the rank of lieutenant colonel. Received six Air Medals, Distinguished Flying Cross and various safety awards of units commanded.

In 1992, he retired from Pima Community College as director of purchasing. Now living in Tucson, AZ.

MARVIN H. SPEIDEL, was born in Elizabeth, NJ, July 3, 1921. Entered the USAAC Jan. 29, 1943 and trained at Miami Beach, FL; Gulfport, MS; Long Beach, CA. After a short stint with the ATC came Gunnery School at Indian Springs, NV (Las Vegas) and assignment to Lt. Charles Irwin's crew as flight engineer/top turret gunner. Following phase training at Tucson, AZ, flew northern route via Manchester, NH; Goose Bay, Labrador; Meeks Field, Iceland, and Nutts Corner, Ireland.

Joined 446th Bomb Group, 706th Bomb Sqdn. of the 8th Air Force and flew 31 missions between June and September 1944. Discharged Oct. 12, 1945. Received Distinguished Flying Cross, four Air Medals, four ETO Battle Stars and several other ribbons.

Received B/SC and M/ED in physical education and enjoyed a highly successful career as teacher and gymnastics coach, retiring in 1985. Now serves as 446th Bomb Group vice president to 2nd Air Division Association and editor of New Jersey Chapter, 8th Air Force Historical Society News.

Married Margaret L. Gall in May 1948; they have two daughters and one granddaughter.

EDGAR SPENCER (JAY), was born April 11, 1918 in Abbott, NM. He was drafted into the Infantry Nov. 5, 1940, and was stationed at Elmendorf Field, AK when the war started. He volunteered for cadet training and was commissioned as a pilot on Sept. 1, 1943. After B-24 transition training, he was sent to the 44th Bomb Group, 67th Sqdn. in Shipdham, England in 1944, where he completed 35 combat missions as first pilot.

In January of 1945 he returned to the U.S. and in May started first pilot transition training on B-29s. Separated from

the service in August 1945 with the rank first lieutenant when a combat-related injury resulted in permanent grounding. He was awarded the Air Medal with four Oak Leaf Clusters.

His first wife, Laura E., died in December 1988 after 49 years of marriage. In 1990, he married Estelle R. Voelker. They each have one grown son amd Estelle has two grandchildren.

GAETANO SPINELLI (GUY), was born in Albanella, Italy, June 20, 1924; emigrated with his parents to the U.S. at five years of age. Arriving in New York, December of 1929, they settled in Boston, MA, where he spent his childhood and adult life.

He enlisted in the USAC in November 1942; basic training, Atlantic City, NJ; attended Armament School, Denver, CO; then assigned to 8th Air Force, 2nd Air Div., 392nd Bomb Group, 578th Sqdn. First stationed in El Paso, TX; and Alamogordo, NM; he subsequently departed New York for Wendling, England.

After armoring B-24s for campaigns over Normandy, Central Europe and Germany, he was honorably discharged as corporal on Oct. 11, 1945, from Wilmington, DE. Awarded Distinguished Unit Badge, 8th Air Force EAME Service Medal and Good Conduct Medal.

Married in 1950 to Madeline Juliano, they now reside in Dorchester. He has two sons: Guy Jr., a doctor of internal medicine; and Stephen, a cable television executive. In addition, Guy Jr. and his wife Rosemonde have blessed him with three grandchildren.

Spinelli worked as a machinist for several years before entering the Boston Police Department where he made a 34-year career as a police officer. He now enjoys golf and traveling.

THURMAN SPIVA, was born May 11, 1918, near Stella, MO. Enlisted USAAC May 16, 1942, called to active duty Nov. 10, 1942. Commissioned second lieutenant and navigator Mather Field, CA, July 31, 1943, and assigned to 446th Bomb Group.

Flew overseas November 1943 for assignment to 8th Air Force at Bungay, England. Attacked by four German fighters off Brest Peninsula, France, on flight from Merrakesh, Morrocco, to England. Aircraft received extensive damage and crew awarded combat mission credit later on March 16, 1944, for that flight. Received Distinguished Flying Cross, four Air Medals and four European Campaign Battle Stars while completing 29 combat missions ending on April 29, 1944.

Received regular Air Force commission in 1946. After Pentagon tour, AFIT schooling at University of Missouri, four years as instructor and staff duty at AF Navigation School, Mather AFB, CA, and attendance command and staff course was assigned to B-47 wing at Chennault AFB, LA. Spent 14 of next 17 years in crew and staff assignments in Strategic Air Command. Retired as colonel, Beale AAB, CA, Nov. 30, 1972.

Returned to college and worked as tax consultant from 1976 to 1993.

Married Feb. 8, 1945, to Mary V. Fisher, three sons and two grandsons.

ROBERT W. SPROWLS, was born March 3, 1925 in Washington, PA. Enlisted in the USAAF in April 1943; graduated second lieutenant from Bombardier School in December 1943. After radar training in Boca Raton, FL, and Langley Field, VA, assignment was made to the 8th Air Force in England.

After a brief period in the 482nd and 44th Bomb Group, assignment was made to the 392nd Bomb Group at Wendling. Completed 22 lead missions as a H2X radar operator. Memo-

rable experience was last combat mission flown by the 8th Air Force. Heavy flak was encountered and due to damaged controls a very skillful emergency landing was made in Belgium by his pilot.

He returned to the States in June 1945, and was discharged October 1945. Received Distinguished Flying Cross and Air Medal with two Oak Leaf Clusters.

GORDON K. STACKEL, was born June 12, 1924, in Sellersville, PA. Drafted into the USAAC April 1943; graduated from Armament and Gunnery Schools receiving staff sergeant rank. Assigned to B-24 crew as a tail gunner and attached to the 93rd Bomb Group, 409th Bomb Sqdn., May 1944.

Second mission flown was D-day, which was an overwhelming experience. Next 24 missions flown targeted industrial railroad marshalling yards and supporting ground troops. On 27th mission, he was wounded over Liege, Belgium. Stackel's fellow crew members and a Lt. Pearson, who was assigned to Stackel's crew for this one mission as a bombardier and who Stackel only spoke to one time and never met or talked or heard of since, helped save Stackel's life. Was told at a later time that the anti-aircraft gunner crews, whose exploding shells wounded him, were women.

Awarded Air Medal with three Oak Leaf Clusters, Distinguished Flying Cross and Purple Heart.

Married Ann Farkas in July 1949. They have four daughters, one son, 10 grandchildren and two great-grandchildren. He is retired from the United States Postal Service, Spring Hill, FL, where he also lives.

CLEMENT LOWREY STAFFORD JR., was born April 22, 1925 in Greensboro, NC. Entered USAF February 1944.

Was stationed at San Marcos, TX and Gulfport, MS. He was discharged May 1944 with the rank of second lieutenant.

Stafford passed away Oct. 10, 1979.

ROY D. STAHL JR., was born Aug. 4, 1921 in Pontiac, IL. Joined the USAAC from the 33rd Div. Nat. Guard in 1942. Graduated from Bombardiers School at Childress, TX AAB on July 15, 1943. Was assigned to the 701st Bomb Sqdn., 445th Bomb Group, Aug. 17, 1943, went to Tibenham, England with that organization arriving Dec. 1, 1943.

Completed 30 missions May 1, 1944. Most memorable was third mission to Asnabruck, Germany Dec. 22, 1943 when they were badly shot up. Their navigator was killed and they crash landed near Marston. Awarded the Silver Star and Purple Heart for his part on that mission. Flew most missions in same plane they flew overseas, *Conquest Cavalier*.

Returned to the U.S. and trained future bombardiers at Pueblo AAB, CO until the war's end. Separated in 1946 and recalled to active duty in 1951. Served Kimpo and Taegu air bases in Korea 1952-53; France 1954-58; Eielson AB, AK 1962-64; Ton Son Nhut AB, Vietnam 1968-69. Retired from active duty May 1973 as a lieutenant colonel.

Married with two daughters and three grandchildren. Currently is retired.

MARTIN J. STANTON, was born Feb. 1, 1913 in Bayonne, NJ. Drafted Sept. 28, 1942. A stroke of luck twice got him in the 62nd Fighter Sqdn. of 56th Fighter Group. When going to Ft. Dix, his friend, Charley Griffen, fixed it so Stanton went to 322nd Fighter Sqdn. on Oct. 1, 1942. When there, a lieutenant of the 62nd came and asked him to join his outfit. Stanton said yes and on Nov. 1, 1942, he was in the 62nd. Went to Kilmer, NJ on Dec. 26, 1942, and on Jan. 6 left on *Queen Elizabeth* for England.

Arrived Greenoch January 12 and Kings Cliffe on January 14. Went to Horsham St. Faith and the 56th started its career. The 56th went through the war flying P-47s and was the leading outfit in planes shot down, 674 total in air combat.

Left service on Oct. 16, 1945 with the rank of sergeant. Received Distinguished Unit Badge with Oak Leaf Cluster and EAME Theater Medal.

Stanton is single. He is retired and lives in Bayonne, NJ.

CHARLES O. STARCHER, was born in Logan, OH Jan. 20, 1923, son of Ralph and Hattie Starcher. He graduated from Logan High School in 1941

and same summer enlisted in the USAAC. After training as a radio man was assigned to the Liberator bomber *Flying Cock*.

On his last mission on a raid on Tripoli, Jan. 15, 1943, the *Flying Cock* was hit by enemy fire. They were over water and all crew thought the plane was going down. S/Sgt. Starcher and three other crew members bailed out and were never heard from. The rest of the crew got the plane back to Bengasi about 200 miles from their base.

ROBERT R. STARR, was born April 25, 1920 in East St. Louis, IL. Entered USAAF April 1, 1943. Military locations/stations: Biloxi, MS; Harlingen, TX; Hethel, England; Chanute Field, IL.

Participated in the European Theater of Operations, Hethel, B-29 F/E training. Many memorable experiences, including mail call from home and scenes in flight.

Discharged Oct. 1, 1945 with the rank of tech. sergeant. Awarded Air Medal with four clusters, European Theater and Presidential Unit Citation.

Retired after 35 years as FAA inspector of airlines, TWA.

VETO J. STASUNAS, was born Sept. 18, 1924 in Athol, MA. Drafted in March 1943 after completing freshman year at Boston College. Sent to Miami Beach for basic training. While there, transferred to USAAC. Commissioned as navigator at Selman Field, Monroe, LA, in 1944; sent to Casper, WY for B-24 training.

Following a 13-day boat trip to Liverpool, England, ended up at Horsham St. Faith (458th Bomb Group). After completing 31 missions, flew back to USA landing at Bradley Field, CT, via the Azores and Newfoundland. Was on troop train when Japan surrendered. Ended up in Nashville, TN.

After discharge, went back to Boston College to complete his undergraduate (BS) and graduate (MS) studies. Later received Ph.D. in chemistry from University of Connecticut.

Married in 1950, raised four children, worked for several large companies in research, production and management capacities. Retired in 1987.

JOHN O. STAVENGER (JACK), was born May 19, 1921, Rock County, MN. Graduated from high school, 1938. Entered active duty military service, Jan. 6, 1941, Minnesota National Guard, 215th Coast Artillery, AA, Rank private first class.

Stationed Kodiak Island when Pearl Harbor was at-

tacked, served as communications section truck driver. Applied for pilot training mid-1942; exams taken in Anchorage. Departed Kodiak Christmas Day, 1942; arrived San Antonio Cadet Center mid-January, 1943. Commissioned second lieutenant, pilot, Nov. 3, 1943, Class 43-J, Waco, TX. B-24 training, Liberal, KS. Assigned crew, Lincoln, NE. Crew training, El Paso, TX; assigned B-24, Topeka, KS. Flew crew to England, August 1944.

Assigned 489th Bomb Group, Halesworth. Flew 16 combat missions. Departed England with group, November 1944. Separated service as first lieutenant in October 1945 from Tucson, AZ. Awarded three Air Medals.

Married Audrey Nelson on July 1, 1944. They have one daughter Joan; two granddaughters, Cathy and Lisa; and son-in-law Gary Sethney. Retired from the jewelry business in 1982.

BASIL J. ST. DENNIS, was born in Little Falls, MN, Jan. 19, 1924. Worked on Liberators at Northwest Airlines Holman Field Modification Center nine months 1942-43. Entered Army May 19, 1943, at Ft. Snelling, CTD at Spearfish, SD; pre-flight at Santa Ana; advanced navigation Hondo, TX. OTU at Mt. Home, ID. Shipped to Seething, England, Station #146 flying 16 missions in Liberator's crew *Homas Redcaps*, 448th Bomb Group.

Returned to Minneapolis, MN, and to Northwest Airlines. Recalled November 1950, flew 41 missions, 91st Strat. Recon. Wing Yokata Japan. Released August 1952, Fairchild, WA.

Returned to Northwest Airlines Transportation Services Department, retiring at Seattle 1987.

Married Mildred Loverud; they have two children, Douglas and Melodee; and one grandchild, Lisa.

Enjoyed reunions in Tucson, Santa Ana, Savannah, Omaha and Seething, England. A retired navigator finding the local libraries in and around Vancouver, WA.

ARTHUR DALE STEELE, was born Aug. 19, 1920 in Hebron, NE. Entered the U.S. Army in February 1941 and completed cadet training as a bombardier at Midland, TX in April 1943. Completed 30 missions with Crew #1, 712th Bomb Sqdn., 448th Bomb Group in June 1944. Of the 60 original crews that went to England in December 1943, only 10 crews completed their mission requirements.

Mustered out in September 1945. After a stint as a civilian photographer, he volunteered to return to the USAF for the Korean War. Flew with 345th Sqdn., 98th Bomb Wing in B-29s, and retired in September 1967 as a major with 27 years service. In the ensuing years, among other duties, served as an airborne controller in EC-121s on Cape Cod, MA, and as manpower officer.

After retirement worked for 14 years as a claims deputy for the state of Nebraska, retiring for good in 1982.

Married to Frances Richmond, April 3, 1946. They have five children, seven grandchildren and two great-grandchildren.

PAUL R. STEICHEN, was born Oct. 1, 1918 in Dwight, IL. Graduated Marquette University, College of Journalism, Class of 1941. Dispatcher, DuPont TNT Plant, Joliet, IL, until

entering service September 1942. Stationed at Miami, FL; Hiram College, OH; San Antonio, Houston, San Angelo, San Marcos, El Paso, TX.

Assigned to 93rd Bomb Group, Hardwick, England. Completed 35 missions as a navigator, September 1944 to April 1945. Pawling, NY, Army Air Corps Convalescence Hospital as public relations director.

Discharged Dec. 2, 1945 with the rank of first lieutenant. Received four Air Medals and the Purple Heart.

Married his college sweetheart, Jean Kane, from Dubuque, IA. They have five daughters and three sons.

He was a pioneer in manufacturing and sale of automatic merchandising vending machine industry 1945 to retirement in 1988. Steichen is vice president of 2nd Air Division Association in charge of 93rd Bomb Group.

LYLE W. STEINBERG, was born Jan. 6, 1918 in Ogdensberg, NY. Entered service on Oct. 29, 1942; served with the 8th Air Force, 448th Bomb Group, 712th Sqdn, Crew 14. Stationed at Norwich, England, he flew 31 missions.

Discharged Sept. 7, 1945 with the rank of staff sergeant. Awarded Air Medal with three Oak Leaf Clusters, Distinguished Flying Cross and EAME Theater Medal.

Steinberg married on May 5, 1945. He has six children.

CLARENCE H. STEINERT (JEFF), was born in Jersey City, NJ on April 23, 1921. Entered the USAAC March 6, 1943, and graduated from Selman Field AAF Navigation School in Class 43-17 after earning aerial gunnery wings at Tyndall Field, FL.

Via celestial navigation to Ireland from Goose Bay, Labrador, he arrived in England on D-day, and was assigned to the 389th Bomb Group (B-24) at Hethel. After completing 35 combat missions and two gas missions to supply Gen. Patton's army, he returned to become a navigation instructor at San Marcos AAF.

The end of hostilities brought discharge on Nov. 6, 1945 with the rank of first lieutenant. Received Distinguished Flying Cross, four Air Medals and four European Theater Campaign Stars.

Married Mary Schepis Dec. 26, 1943; they have a son, two daughters, and two grandchildren.

LEROY A. STEINGRABER, was born April 13, 1924, River Grove, IL. Enlisted in the USAAC Nov. 19, 1942; basic training, Biloxi, MS; B-24 Aircraft and Engine Mechanics School, Ann Arbor, MI; Gunnery School, Harlingen, TX. On to Idaho and the formation of the 453rd Bomb Group, 735th Sqdn., being assigned to Lt. William's Crew #77 as flight engineer and gunner.

January 1944, arrived in Norwich, England. While on 28th mission, they were shot down 50K outside Berlin on June 21, 1944. Prisoner of war life began, then liberation day, April 29, 1945, by Gen. Patton's tank corps.

Discharged Oct. 20, 1945 as tech. sergeant. Awarded Distinguished Flying Cross, five Air Medals, three Battle Stars.

Married Violet Reynolds in September 1943. They have three sons, one daughter, 10 grandchildren and one great-grandchild.

Steingraber retired to Arizona in 1988 after 40 plus years as a brick and stone mason in Illinois and California.

JOHN A. STEININGER, was born Oct. 23, 1924 in York, PA. Jan. 23, 1943, volunteered for induction at Harrisburg, PA. Processed at New Cumberland then sent to Atlantic City, NJ for basic training. After seven weeks, sent to Ft. Monmouth, NJ, radio training, 13 weeks, then went to Lincoln AB, NE for 14 weeks additional training.

Sent overseas Feb. 1, 1944 until July 13, 1945. Was ground crew member of 856th Bomb Sqdn., 492nd Bomb Group until fall of 1944. Reassigned to 36th Bomb Sqdn. until end of war.

Discharged at Greensboro, NC, Oct. 2, 1945, with the rank of private first class. Received EAME Theater Medal with seven Bronze Stars.

Returned to Landisburg High School Oct. 5, 1945, to complete education. Graduated June 1946, re-enlisted Aug. 1, 1946, Harrisburg, PA, Army Air Force. Served in Panama until Feb. 8, 1947. Demobilization AR 615-365, Nov. 7, 1946.

Completed molder apprenticeship and retired after 30 years in the Beth Steel Foundry at Steelton, PA. Rural mail carrier at Shermans Dale from 1979 to 1986, now retired.

Married, divorced and remarried, he has one daughter.

RICHARD M. STENGER, was born Nov. 22, 1918 in Franklin County, PA. Enlisted June 1942 in aviation cadets, graduating second lieutenant and pilot November 1943, Class 43-J. Trained Maxwell, Montgomery, AL; Bennettsville, SC; Shaw, Sumter, SC; Turner, Albany, GA. First phase training, Casper, WY; B-24 co-pilot. Completed phase training newly formed 489th Bomb Group (H), Wendover, UT.

Flew April 1944 with group to European Theater, Halesworth, England, 8th Air Force, 2nd Air Div. Flew first operational bombing mission over Germany May 30, 1944, completing 32 mission combat tour Aug. 6, 1944. Performed additional duty tour with group HQ, returning USA Oct. 16, 1944.

Assigned Harlingen Field, TX, as B-24 pilot flying aerial gunnery students and training B-24 co-pilots until relieved from active duty July 1945. Remained active in Air Force Reserve, including tour as liaison officer Air Force Academy, retiring as lieutenant colonel November 1978. Received Distinguished Flying Cross and Air Medal with four clusters.

Married Beverly M. Moser May 30, 1942; they have two daughters, two granddaughters and one grandson.

He retired from machinery manufacturer Pangborn Corporation, Hagerstown, MD, as international branch manager, July 1981.

BILLY WHITE STEPHAN, was born in Pittsburgh, PA, Feb. 27, 1924. Enlisted USAAC Dec. 12, 1942 while attending Georgia Tech. Graduated pilot, second lieutenant, Class 44-C, Moody Field, GA. Completed B-17, then B-24 transition and combat crew training.

Arrived 445th Bomb Group, Tibenham, England, evening of disastrous Kassel mission, September 1944. Thought for a moment he was wrong in wanting a combat assignment rather than IP job at Moody. Completed tour of 26 missions.

Spent 1946-1949 Far East. Returned with his bride, Elaine, reported to B-29s, 509th Bomb Group, Roswell, NM. Went to B-47s in 1952 after training spent seven years with 44th Bomb Group, Chennault AFB, LA. In 1960 after B-52 training reported Seymour Johnson AFB, NC.

Retired Aug. 1, 1965 with the rank of lieutenant colonel. Received four Air Medals, three Oak Leaf Clusters, ETO three Battle Stars and Victory Medal.

Completed degree at Omaha University and moved to Dallas, TX in 1966. Retired from civilian employment in 1990. He married Elaine Miller in 1949; their five wonderful children have presented them with 13 grandchildren to date.

LOUIS M. STEPHENS, was born Jan. 10, 1921, Palestine, OH. Entered USAAC, pilot training in Southeast Command, graduated June 1943, Spence Field. B-24 training at Pocatello.

Reported to 578th Bomb Sqdn., 392nd Bomb Group about Oct. 8, 1943 (day Buckman crew missing in action at Vegesak) with complete crew minus one pilot. Flord George transferred from Fletcher's crew to fill vacancy. First mission Nov. 3, 1943 and last mission of tour March 24, 1944. Home for 30 days after volunteering for second tour.

Returned to 578th Sqdn. to fly first mission with Edwards July 13, 1944. Replaced Barton, killed in action, and flew first mission with new crew August 11. Shot down September 1944 at Mointz. In German hospitals and prisoner of war camps until liberated April 1945. Renewed acquaintance with many 392nd Sqdn. people while in POW camps.

Discharged April 1946 with the rank of captain. Received the Distinguished Flying Cross, Air Medal with five clusters and Purple Heart.

Married to Delores with two sons, Larry and Terry (deceased). Civilian employment, Air Force at W-P AFB and defense logistics agency at Gentile AFS, 1948-1986. Retired in Englewood, OH.

SIDNEY A. STEPHENS, was born June 17, 1917 in Largo, FL. Drafted into the Army June 17, 1941 as a private. Was commissioned a second lieutenant in the armored force April 11, 1942 after completion of OCS, Ft. Knox, KY. Entered pilot training, Class 43-C, Maxwell Field, AL, graduating March 1943, Moody Field, GA.

First pilot duty B-17, then B-24s. After completing the combat crew training phases, was assigned to 449th Bomb Group, Bruning, NE, as crew commander, deploying overseas late November 1943 via the southern route from Morrison Field, FL, arriving Grottaglie, Italy, December 1943. First combat mission January 1944.

After 15 missions, he and his crew were transferred from 15th Air Force to 8th Air Force in England, March 1944 and assigned to 712th Bomb Sqdn., 448th Bomb Group, Seething, England. After local indoctrination, was made a lead crew. Completed 34 missions and returned to U.S. September 1944 and qualified in B-29s. Requested release from active duty December 1945.

June 1946 was tendered regular officer commission and recalled to duty, serving in various capacities from squadron through major air command, retiring June 1969. in permanent grade of lieutenant colonel, USAF.

Received Distinguished Flying Cross, Bronze Star, four Air Medals, three Commendation Medals, five European Campaign Stars, one Far East Campaign Star and 10 other ribbons/medals.

DORE D. STEPHENSON (STEVE), was born in Estelline, TX, "Hall County" on Sept. 14, 1918. Inducted Dec. 3, 1941, Ft. Bliss, TX.

Cadet training at San Antonio, TX; Cimmeron Field, OK; Winfield, KS; Altus, OK; B-24 transition at Ft. Worth AAF, TX; combat training at Wendover Field, UT. Served in ETO at Rackheath, England, with the 467th Bomb Group (H), 2nd Air Div., 8th Air Force.

His group issued new B-24 and flew over as a group through South America-North Africa, then to England. He flew in group's first mission, April 10, 1944. Flew 35 missions completing them the first week in July 1944.

Memorable experience: May 8, 1944, flying mission to Brunswick and six enemy fighters hit their B-24 near bomb run. Despite extensive damage they managed to cripple back to their base and landed safely with only one man slightly injured.

Shipped back to the USA on *Queen Mary* October 1944. Served at 11 stations until discharged October 1945 at Ft. Sam Houston, TX with the rank of first lieutenant. Received Distinguished Flying Cross with one Oak Leaf Cluster, Air Medal with three clusters and ETO Ribbon with three Bronze Stars.

Married Jerry Ann Harelson, June 1942; they have two daughters and five grandchildren. He is retired, worked 34 years at Los Alamos, NM, as equipment operator and superintendent of department.

IVAN C. STEPNICH, was born Dec. 16, 1916, Toroda Creek, WA. Drafted March 11, 1942, Fort Lewis, WA and immediately applied for the aviation cadets. He was accepted Class 43-D and graduated April 22, 1943, Lubbock Army Flying School. His first assignment was co-pilot on a B-17 combat crew, Gowen Field, Boise, ID. Later he was re-assigned a B-24 pilot and formed a new combat crew.

This crew joined the 2nd Div., 44th Bomb Group, Shipdham, England, Nov. 3, 1943. Thirty combat missions were flown from January to May 24, 1944. Memorable were Berlin, Brunswick and Friedrichshafen missions. Most memorable was total destruction of a Messerschmidt factory in Furth, Germany, Feb. 25, flak barrage. The B-24 was knocked out of formation and barely made the English coast for an emergency landing. The most unusual mission was April 1, bombing of Schaffhausen, Switzerland. Upon tour completion the next assignment was engineering modification officer at 2nd Div. HQ. This resulted in taking a modified B-24, *Hap Hazard*, on a state wide tour.

Discharge was effected at MacDill Field, FL, Nov. 5, 1946, with the rank of major. He received two Distinguished Flying Cross Medals, four Air Medals and Purple Heart.

Married Ruth Halsey, Nov. 1, 1947. Retired Dec. 16, 1992, as a building automation consultant.

THOMAS STERANKO, was born Port Carbon, PA, May 8, 1922. Enlisted Sept. 21, 1942, USAAC and served as an aircraft mechanic. Stationed at Bowman Field, KY; Sedalia, MO; Mt. Home, ID; Wendover, UT; Rackheath, England. Graduated Curtiss Wright Technical Institute, Glendale, CA; graduated B-24 Specialist School, San Diego, CA.

Memorable experience was representing Station #145, Rackheath, with group engineering officer Maj. Giesecke, worked with other bases in development, preparation and implementation of dropping jelly bomb over Germany using B-24 ferry tanks and P-51 wing tanks. Bomb was 80 percent high octane fuel, 20 percent fels napta soap and had a phosphorus fuse.

To give Wesley Bartelt crew, who was assigned to fly *Normandy Queen* (B-24) back to the USA, confidence, Steranko as a squadron inspector volunteered to fly back as assistant flight engineer and crew chief. He and his crew were shot down over Russia and came back through the underground and assigned to 467th Bomb Group. Aircraft was called *Normandy Queen* because it landed on Normandy beach on D-day, due to enemy action.

Discharged Oct. 17, 1945 with the rank of master sergeant. Received Bronze Star and ribbons related to European Theater of Operations and six Battle Stars.

Married Anna Hatala in 1949; they have two sons, Robert and Roland; and four grandchildren: Justin, Robert Jr., Renee and Ryan.

He has A&P, radio license with FAA, also certified FAA inspector. Worked for Boeing Helicopters for 33 years and held several management positions in quality assurance department. Retired 1985.

FRANK T. STERBENZ, was born Nov. 24, 1921, in California, PA, the son of Frank and Rose Sterbenz. He graduated from East Pike Run High School in 1939, and was inducted into the service in 1942 at New Cumberland, PA.

After being stationed at Wendover Field, UT, he served as a bombardier with the 489th Bomb Group, 844th Bomb Sqdn., at Halesworth Field, England, aboard the B-24H *Fay-Day* (#42-94874).

The crew departed for their 13th mission on Sunday, June 25, 1944, at about 1600 hours, en route to Villacoublay, France. They could not gain altitude because of engine trouble and had to return. *Fay-Day* crashed upon landing and Lt. Sterbenz perished along with most of the crew.

In his last letter of June 23, 1944, he hoped that the war would end soon. He is fondly remembered by his family.

JOHN E. STEVENS (JACK), was born in Worcester, MA, Dec. 17, 1919. Entered Army Aviation Cadets (pilot) Jan. 15, 1942, and graduated from Columbus, MS, on Jan. 14, 1943.

Assigned to the 7th Anti-Submarine Sqdn., based in Trinidad, BWI, he flew anti-submarine missions throughout the Caribbean area from March until July 1943. In November he and his crew were transferred to the 467th Bomb Group at Wendover, UT, and landed at Rackheath Airfield, near Norwich, England, in March 1944.

After completing 13 missions with the 8th Air Force, the crew was transferred to the 98th Bomb Group (15th Air Force) at Lecce, Italy. He flew another 38 missions and participated in the return of Allied airmen who had been POWs in Bulgaria.

After WWII, he served as military government officer, information and education officer, associate professor of air science and tactics, squadron commander, personnel services officer and base administrative officer.

He and Lucile Harshman were married in Indianapolis on Sept. 25, 1948, and have four daughters.

BENNIE L. STEWART, was born May 27, 1921, in Hutchinson, KS. Entered USAF September 1942. Stationed at Randolph Field, Wichita Falls, Salt Lake City, Gowen Field. Assigned to 446th Bomb Group, 707th Sqdn. Memorable experiences: Flying his first operational mission on D-day and making three dangerous passes over Bricy Orleans Airfield.

Discharged May 1945 with the rank of tech. sergeant, radio operator/gunner (B-24). Received Air Medal with four Bronze Stars and Distinguished Flying Cross.

Married September 1949; has two boys, two girls and 16 grandchildren. Retired from teaching high school.

NELSON R. STEWART, was born in Sebree, KY. Entered USAF February 1942; graduated Cadets Class 43-E, Stockton, CA. Served as pilot, B-25, B-17, B-24, C-124. Assigned Horsham St. Faith, England. Flew 30 combat missions, 458th Bomb Group.

Memorable experiences: Kiangwan AFB, Shanghai, China, and other locations. Haneda, Japan; took discharged at Nanking, China, April 1948, with the rank of first lieutenant to fly for China National Aviation Corporation. Upon discharge in March 1954, he had achieved rank of captain.

Received Distinguished Flying Cross, Air Medal with three Oak Leaf Clusters.

Married Margaret Lee Preston Dec. 28, 1940. They have three sons: Lawrence, Brett and Gregory. He is retired.

WALTER TRAVIS STEWART SR., was born Nov. 8, 1917 in Benjamin, UT. Enlisted Sept. 27, 1941, Flying Cadet, CA; Aero, Ontario, CA. Commissioned with wings April 24, 1942, Victorville AAFB, CA as pilot four-engine B-24. Stationed at Barksdale Field, LA; Manchester, NH; Hardwick and Hethel, England; Benghazi, Libya; Tunis; 93rd Bomb

Group, 330th Sqdn., 2nd Combat Bomb Wing, Kirtland, NM; Roswell, NM. B-29, war ends, liaison officer with Civil Air Patrol, Reno, NV.

Flew 32 missions: Bay of Biscay, France, Germany, Holland, Italy, Sicily, Ploesti (low level).

Memorable experiences: Spent half a day with the Queen and two princesses as a speaker in Sandringham, England, Jan. 19, 1944. Flew the *Boomerang* to USA to tour ball bearing plants in New England.

Discharged Oct. 26, 1946, Marysville, CA. Served five years active duty, 25 years Air Force Reserve. Received Air Medal with four Oak Leaf Clusters, Distinguished Flying Cross, Silver Star, Presidential Unit Citation, plus campaign ribbons.

Married Ruth Francis Dec. 14, 1944, Salt Lake Temple. They have five children: Walt Jr., Scott, Sally, Alexandra, Sam; 20 grandchildren and counting.

Graduated University of Utah, 1947 BA (speech), 1949 JD (law); didn't like law practice, formed Walt Stewart Construction. Hired on to teach LDS Seminary for 17 years in high school, and at prison and a boy's school. Retired 1983 to the 40-acre farm and home where he was born. Raises gourmet beef and enjoys family, children and grandchildren.

PAUL STIKELEATHER, was born Nov. 12, 1920 at Indianapolis, IN. Inducted Nov. 7, 1942, at Fort Harrison, IN. Went to Miami Beach, FL for basic training; sent to Alamogordo, NM to the 466th Bomb Group, was made mail clerk for the squadron.

Sent to England March 4, 1944, arriving March 8, 1944, at Attlebridge, England at a B-24 base, 785th Sqdn. Transferred in 1945 to Co. K, 101st Inf., due to the Battle of the Bulge.

Discharged January 1946 at Camp Atterbury, IN. Received Good Conduct Medal, Distinguished Unit Badge, Combat Infantry Badge, WWII Victory Medal, two Bronze Stars and one Bronze Cluster.

After returning home, married an English girl from North Tibenham (near Attlebridge) Norfolk, England, Feb. 14, 1947. They have three daughters and two grandchildren. Retired after working for two heating and sheet metal firms as warehouse foreman.

RALPH L. STIMMEL, was born Nov. 2, 1916 on his grandfather's farm, Green Springs, Frederick County, seven miles from Winchester, VA. Enlisted in the USAAC Sept. 3, 1942, and became an aviation cadet. Graduated May 28, 1943, pilot, second lieutenant, Class 43-E at Moody Field, Valdosta, GA. Graduated July 14, 1943, as a B-24 pilot at Smyrna, TN, and assigned to 29th Bomb Group, Gowen Field, Boise, ID, as pilot of crew 71. Transferred July 31, 1943 to the 445th Bomb Group, 703rd Sqdn., Sioux City, IA.

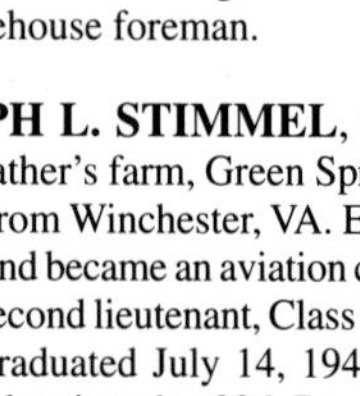
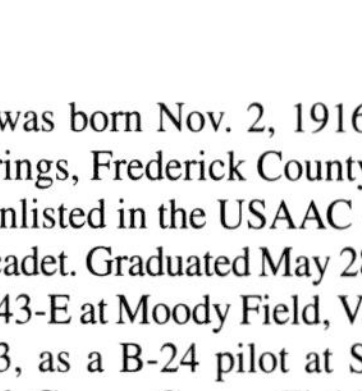

Nov. 30, 1943, landed at Tibenham, England; assigned 8th Air Force. Dec. 20, 1943, first combat mission, Bremen, Germany. Feb. 24, 1944, 12th mission, Gotha, Germany (group Presidential Citation); March 6, 1944, 13th mission, first daylight air raid on Berlin, Germany by 8th Air Force; April 30, 1944, 30th mission, Siracourt, France. Crew 71 was first crew in 703rd Sqdn. to complete the tour of duty of 30 missions.

Assigned squadron test pilot and assistant operations officer. Oct. 1, 1944, promoted to captain. Jan. 15, 1945, transferred to ATC, 559th AAF, Nashville, TN; then to Romulus, MI, March 11, 1945. May 1945, he was sent to Instrument Flying School (four engine), Homestead, FL, and was retained as an instrument flying instructor until discharge in December 1945 from active duty. Spent next six years in the active reserve in Philadelphia, PA. Received Air Medal and three Oak Leaf Clusters, Distinguished Flying Cross, six European Campaign stars and a Presidential Group Citation.

Finished college, got a BS degree in mechanical engineering, Drexel University and textile engineering at Philadelphia College of Textiles and Science.

Married Genevieve Reavis; has two daughters, one son and one grandson. He serves as deacon, and an elder in Presbyterian Church in Winchester, VA.

WILBUR D. STITES, was born Feb. 13, 1922, at LaRose, IL, son of Leslie and Ethel Kohl Stites. Enlisted in USAAC at Peoria, IL, summer of 1942. Reported for duty Oct. 1, 1942, Ft. Sheridan, IL.

After basic training, college training detachment, and processing at San Antonio, TX, was removed from Aviation Cadet Program because of an over supply of candidates for pilot, bombardier, and navigator training. Sent to Aerial Gunnery School at Tyndall Field, FL. Upon completion was assigned as ball turret gunner on Phillips' crew in 484th Bomb Group, Harvard, NE. Completed combat phase training, but due to a minor back injury, was hospitalized when group shipped out. They went to 13th Air Force in Italy. Assigned as left waist gunner on Bill Lofton's crew at Peterson Field, CO, in early 1944. Crossed the Atlantic on the *Queen Elizabeth*, arriving in Scotland in June.

Assigned to 453rd Bomb Group at Old Buckingham. First mission July 31, 1944, and flew six in a row. Shot down on 23rd mission Oct. 17, 1944, parachuting into Belgium about a mile inside American occupied territory. Returned to duty and completed 35 missions with the 453rd group. Returned to States in March 1945 on USS *West Point*.

Honorable discharge as staff sergeant, August 1945 at Ft. Sheridan, IL.

Graduated from University of Illinois (journalism degree) in 1951. Spent five years with Illinois Department of Conservation as news release writer, magazine editor, and pioneer in radio and TV programming. Joined Wisconsin Conservation Department in 1956 and retired in 1984 after 28 years service, primarily as producer-host of "Wisconsin Outdoors," series of radio-TV programs broadcast on stations in Wisconsin and surrounding states.

Married Jeane Sorchych at DePue, IL, April 21, 1945. Children: Wilbur Jr., and Linda Stites Bennett; grandchildren: Ben and Katherine Stites.

WOODROE H. STOKES, was born Jan. 15, 1917, Greer, SC. Enlisted as aviation cadet Oct. 2, 1941. Sent to Montgomery, AL, for basic training and to Turner Navigation School at Albany, GA. Graduated May 23, 1942; was commissioned second lieutenant and assigned to 93rd Bomb Group (H) at Page Field, Ft. Myers, FL. Assigned to B-24 bomber crew, 329th Sqdn. Other crew members were assigned as they arrived.

They trained and did submarine patrol in the Gulf of Mexico and the Caribbean. Group left Florida and went to Manchester, NH; were assigned new B-24, after breaking in went to Newfoundland on their first leg flight to Scotland. Flew as a group to Scotland, then to Alcumbury, England. After a few days were assigned to Hardwick, their permanent base. The 93rd Bomb Group was first B-24s to be assigned to 8th Air Force in England. Oct. 8, 1942, flew first combat mission, continued as the weather allowed.

Three squadrons of the group were sent to Egypt to bomb German Army in North Africa; 329th Sqdn. stayed in England and flew special bad weather missions.

Early June, the entire group of flying crews were sent to Lybia to bomb Romania oil wells at low level and Sicily and Italy for the ground invasion. Returned to England early September 1943. Stokes had completed his tour of combat and was assigned 2nd Air Div. as one of division navigators.

February 1944 returned to U.S., assigned to Officers Gunnery School which was being organized to train gunnery officers at Ft. Myers, FL. In July the school was transferred to Laredo, TX. After VE-day, he went on inactive duty, Aug. 5, 1945. Remained in reserves and retired May 1972 with rank of major. Received Distinguished Flying Cross, Air Medal with four Oak Leaf Clusters and two Battle Stars.

Married; he has a son, daughter, three grandchildren and one great-grandchild. Retired, having worked in schools, 1945-1979, teaching and administration.

LLOYD E. STONE, was born June 19, 1922 in Dexter, NM, and raised on a farm. Entered cadet program August 1942. Pilot training, Oklahoma, Kansas, California, Texas, Idaho, Arizona. Commissioned second lieutenant, pilot wings, Waco, TX. B-24 transition, Liberal, KS; overseas training with crew at Boise, ID. Sent with crew to 701st Bomb Sqdn., 445th Bomb Group, Tibenham, England.

Flew 26 missions as aircraft commander (pilot) in France and Germany. Flew home B-24 with crew by Azores, Newfoundland, Bradley Field, CT.

Trained as pilot on B-24, B-25, C-47, C-46, C-45 and trainer planes.

Discharged January 1947 as captain. Received Air Medal with three Oak Leaf Clusters, Distinguished Unit Citation, American Theater Ribbon, WWII Victory Medal, EAME Theater Medal with three Battle Stars.

Married Mary Lois Sadler April 26, 1944; they will celebrate their 50th wedding anniversary in 1994. They have two sons. One son was an Air Force Academy graduate (deceased) and the other son is a Vietnam veteran. He is retired.

ROBERT N. STONE, was born in Haverhill, MA, July 3, 1920. Enlisted USAAF Sept. 17, 1943. After a short time at Gunter Field as a tech. inspector, entered aviation cadet program to become a pilot. Graduated from Turner Field, GA, Dec. 5, 1943. After training with B-24 crew at Peterson Field, CO, joined 389th Bomb Group, 565th Sqdn.

On 19th mission over Munich, B-24 sustained serious damage to engines, and navigator and Stone were wounded by heavy flak thrown up that day. Unable to continue flight in safety of the group, diverted to Switzerland and landed at Basel. Received excellent medical attention, and after a month in hospital, joined other internees at Davos in Eastern Switzerland.

After the war, was recalled to active duty with 103rd Fighter Group, CT ANG 1951. Extended that tour of duty to indefinite status, and in 1947 accepted a commission in regular component of USAF. Served as maintenance officer, material officer, and maintenance staff officer through career. Served at Kirtland AFB, NM; Kwajalein, MI; Eniwetok, MI; Hickam AFB, HI; Clark AB, Philippines; Nakhon Phanom Royal Thai AFB, Thailand and retired as lieutenant colonel May 1, 1974, after tour as maintenance staff officer at Mather AFB, CA.

Received Bronze Star, Purple Heart, Meritorious Service Medal with one Oak Leaf Cluster, Air Medal with two Oak Leaf Clusters, Air Force Commendation Medal, Army Commendation Medal and numerous other theater ribbons.

Married Betty J. McCoull of his hometown Jan. 19, 1946; they have one son, Douglas N. Stone. Now retired and living in Carmichael, CA.

ROBERT G. STOUT (BOB), was born July 25, 1921, Parkersburg, WV. Joined 389th Bomb Group, Biggs AAF, TX, early 1943 from an Army Ordnance School, complete with orange piping on cap, to be a bomb loader (had yet to see a bomb). First order, after being introduced to a bomb was, "Get rid of that orange piping and sew on the blue!". After practicing bomb loading and a pause at Lowry AAF for review by President Roosevelt, arrived RAF Hethel, England, July 1943.

Flew as a spare gunner in any position needed with many different crews. Did a tour—worked in group gunnery. Appointed gunnery officer January 1945. TDY'D early Spring 1945 to attend Gunnery Officers School, Laredo, TX. Return to England nixed by V-J day.

Ordered after R&R Atlantic City, to Las Vegas, NV, to take a group of replacement gunners to the Pacific. They made it to the port—VJ-day sent them back to Las Vegas. Remained until separation.

After terminal leave, became a master sergeant in 1946 and was assigned gunnery duties with SAC units. Involved—B-29 gunnery training programs to include operation of OQ radio controlled target planes. Briefly with the Frangible Bullet (B-29/P-63) program at Alamogordo, NM. Spent much time TDY deployed overseas, (mostly to England, but not Norwich area). After TDYing as group gunnery officer with 22nd Bomb Group to England was back to HQ 15th Air Force, March AFB, CA, when Korea hit in 1950. TDY'd to Yokota, Japan, working to set up bomber command. Returned to be a second lieutenant again, as armament operations officer (new name for gunnery officer). Later to Japan finally ending up on Okinawa.

After Okie it was NAV/RADAR/BOMB upgrading, Ellington, TX; and Mather, CA (with B/RB-66 included). Assigned to a TAC unit (17th Bomb Group) Hurrburt Field,, Eglin, FL. In 1958 Shaw AFB, SC, in WB-66 WX Recon, (unusual Wg two squadrons WB/RB-66s and two squadrons RF-101s). June 1960 to HQ 17th Air Force, Ramstein, Germany (was there when the wall went up and in Berlin when it came down).

Lucked-out, was able in 1964 to sail stateside with his family (wife and three boys) on the last crossing of the *USS United States*. A stint at TAC, command manpower programmer, then assignment air staff—Pentagon, manager program 2 (Tactical Forces ie, TAC/USAFE/PACAF/V-N) manpower resources preceded return to Ramstein, Germany to wind up his military hitch.

Retired (lieutenant colonel) August 1975 after 32 and one-half (ENL/OFF) years duty. Signed on for a hitch with Mobil Oil Corporation, California, and again retired in 1989.

Active with volunteer work at the nearby Air Patch, San Bernardino. He is also member of the Orange Empire Retired Officers Club (TROA) and the Elks Lodge Charity Projects in his community.

WILLIAM S. STRANGE, enlisted in the USAC Sept. 27, 1939 and was discharged Oct. 5, 1945. Took recruit training at Randolph, San Antonio and was assigned there until January 1943. In 1943 was assigned to Sheppard, Wichita Falls for Mechanics School. Next was sent to B-25 Factory School in Inglewood, CA then to Tyndall at Panama City, FL for Gunnery School, then finally to Gowan Field, Boise, ID.

At basic was assigned to B-24 combat crew: pilot, Fred E. Stone; Lt. Merritt E. Derr, co-pilot; Lt. Andrew J. Patrichuck, navigator; Lt. Emory R. Lundy, bombardier; T/Sgt. Charles J. Brown, engineer; T/Sgt. Samuel M. Cervellera, radio operator; gunners all S/Sgts., Rober M. Foust; Marsil Merenitz, Robert E. Ryan and William S. Strange.

After more training overseas, they were assigned to the 506th Sqdn., 44th Bomb Group, 2nd Air Div., 8th Air Force near Shipdham, England. Lt. Lundy left their crew to become a navigator. Strange flew 22 missions. The first to Hamm, Germany on April 22, 1944 and the last to France on June 27, 1944, when he became a POW.

JAMES E. STRAUB, was born Sept. 7, 1923 in Chicago, IL. Lived and went to schools in Chicago until age 19, when he enlisted in USAAF Sept. 12, 1942. Went to Air Forces Technical School, Sheppard Field, TX. Then to Boeing Flying Fortress School, Seattle, WA. Joined 453rd Bomb Group at Walla Walla, WA. Then to March Field, CA for more training. Then to POE, Camp Kilmer, NJ.

Left for England Dec. 14, 1943 aboard *Queen Elizabeth*. Arrived Glasgow, Scotland Dec. 20, 1943. The 453rd Bomb Group was assigned Station #144 at Old Buckingham near Norwich, England. He was assigned 733rd Bomb Sqdn. as a line mechanic where he worked for a year and a half servicing B-24 aircraft before and after missions. Reached rank of sergeant while in England.

Memorable experiences: Sweating out their aircraft while they were on missions; visiting friends in Yorkshire, England; flight over Germany to see the damage bombing had done; and being in London during air raids.

After cessation of hostilities, returned to USA aboard *Queen Mary*. Then to Sioux Falls, SD where he was discharged Sept. 23, 1945 with the rank sergeant.

He is still living and working in Chicago, IL, area.

FREDERICK A. STROMBOM, was born in Chicago, IL on July 30, 1923; spent half of his life on a farm near Ogema, WI. Enlisted in Chicago in the USAAC Dec. 14, 1942. Had finished two years at Illinois Institute of Technology. Completed aviation cadet flight training and graduated as second lieutenant, pilot, Class 44-C, Stockton, CA.

Flew co-pilot on B-17s at Yuma, AZ, then assigned as co-pilot on B-24s at Peterson Field, CO. Arrived Hardwick, England, July 24, 1944, assigned 330th Bomb Sqdn., 93rd Bomb Group. Completed tour of 30 missions on lead crew April 5, 1945. Squadron training officer from Feb. 28, 1945 until flying the *Maulin Mallard* B-24D back to Bradley Field on May 28, 1945. Assigned to B-29s Pratt, KS.

Discharged December 1945. Attended University of Minnesota, receiving BS degree in aeronautical engineering December 1948. Joined Army National Guard December 1953, became helicopter pilot, and retired March 15, 1968.

Married July 10, 1948, Inez Trebil; they have three daughters, one son and three grandchildren. Own S&L Manufacturing Corporation in Ogema, WI.

RAYMOND E. STRONG, was born Oct. 8, 1919, grew up in South Bend, IN; attended College of Commerce and worked for Bendix Aviation before being drafted in August 1941. Sent to Sheppard Field, TX and in Spring 1942, sent to Air Corps Administration OCS. Commissioned, sent to England, and assigned to HQ, 2nd Bomb Wing, in October. The wing grew from a small staff with two bomb groups to become the 2nd Air Div. with a large staff, 14 bomb groups and five fighter groups.

Served 32 months (two at Old Catton, 12 at Horsham and 18 at Ketteringham Hall) at HQ as assistant adjutant general attaining rank of major.

After the war, graduated from University of North Carolina, worked for Standard Oil, returned to university for graduate study in 1949 and never left. Retired as university registrar. Achieved rank of colonel in Army Reserve.

Married Ruth in 1950, has daughter and two grandchildren. One of the original seven organizers and past president of 2nd Air Division Association.

HAROLD D. STROUD, was born Aug. 20, 1924 in Fredonia, KS. Entered USAAC Feb. 12, 1943; armorer, MOS-678. After tech. training, joined 448th at Wendover.

Memorable experiences: Crash landing at Belem on way over; on flight line during intruder raid at Seething; and being part of 448th from start to finish.

Discharged Oct. 21, 1945 with the rank of staff sergeant.

Married Berra Ewen, July 23, 1951. He is a retired teacher and semi-active farmer.

RICHARD L. STULTZ, was born Feb. 17, 1924 in Fincastle, IN. Entered U.S. Army in 1943. Took basic training in the paratroops in North Carolina. Four weeks later, he volunteered out and went into the 389th-564th Air Force Sqdn. Sent to Scott Field, IL for schooling in radio and codes. Then sent to Gunnery School, Harlingen, TX; then to Peterson Field, CO where he was assigned to B-24 crew as tail gunner. After two months training, the crew flew from Topeka, KS to England.

After reaching England, they were sent to Hethel AB which was called Lucky Hethel. Completed 31 missions over Germany. Wounded over Hamburg, Germany.

Returned to Camp Kilmer, NJ, April 1945. Discharged as staff sergeant at Tinker Field, OK. Received Purple Heart, Air Medal plus four Oak Leaf clusters.

Married Rosemary Trosper, Aug. 23, 1943. They have one son, four daughters and 15 grandchildren. Retired in 1986 after 41 years with R R Donnelley and Sons in Crawfordsville, IN.

STANLEY J. STUPSKI, was born April 28, 1919. Entered service March 1941. Accepted into the Army Air Corps for cadet training and sent to Santa Ana, CA. Attended Roswell, NM, Flying School where he was commissioned as bombardier. Sent to Tucson, AZ after gunnery training where he joined crew.

Sent overseas July 1943 where he joined 579th Sqdn., 392nd Bomb Group. Memorable experience: Gotha, Feb. 24, 1943, and his 25th mission to Friederickshafen Nov. 11, 1943. The plane was damaged and their navigator wounded. He was amazed they were able to make it back to Wendling.

Living in Jacksonville, FL, with his wife of 50 years. They have five sons and six grandchildren. He is retired and disabled.

ROBERT SUCKOW (BOB), was born June 26, 1919 in Plymouth, WI. Enlisted in USAAC Jan. 25, 1941. Stationed at Chanute Field; TDY Lowry Field; Air Corps Administrative Clerical School; Officer Candidate School, Miami Beach; stationed at Scott Field as administrative officer, one and one-half years; pilot training in grade of first lieutenant; six months later multi-engine pilot; B-24 transition at Fort Worth; staging, Mountain Home, ID. Served with 445th Bomb Group in ETO, operations officer and command pilot. B-29 transition.

Awards include the Air Medal, two Oak Leaf Clusters, four Campaign Ribbons with stars, Good Conduct and three theater ribbons.

After six years of active duty, stayed in active reserve for 18 years. Reserve instructor every week, active duty two weeks each year. Graduated from college 1952. After 35 years of corporate activity went into independent management consulting. Perform workshops and seminars on human resource development subjects. Still flying with multi-engine and instrument ratings. Re-certified for flying after by-pass heart surgery in 1978. A professional speaker high-lighting staying healthy after heart surgery, including motivational and good communication skills. Enjoying life to the fullest.

Married, he has two daughters, one son and five grandchildren.

RAYMOND E. SUMRELL, was born Oct. 29, 1924 in New Bern, NC. Enlisted in USAAC Nov. 11, 1942. Graduated second lieutenant from bombardier training Dec. 24, 1943, Big Spring AAF, TX, Class 43-18. Assigned B-24 crew and sent to Biggs Field, El Paso, TX for operational training.

Went overseas Spring 1944 and assigned 712th Sqdn., 448th Bomb Group, based at Seething, near Norwich, England. Completed 35 combat missions.

Released from active duty Sept. 15, 1945. Received Air Medal with four Oak Leaf Clusters and Distinguished Flying Cross.

Entered University of North Carolina at Chapel Hill. Received bachelor of law degree, 1949 and entered private practice New Bern, NC. Served as county prosecuting attorney 1950-1954; judge of county recorder's court 1954-1962. Engaged in private practice continuously since 1962.

WILLIAM R. SUSA, was born May 2, 1921, Vestaburg, PA. Enlisted August 1942, inactive; February 1943, active. Served in the USAAC, pilot, 2nd Air Div., 489th Bomb Group. Military locations/stations: Preflight, Maxwell Field, Montgomery, AL; primary training, Fletcher Field, Clarksdale, MS; Basic Flight School, Newport, AR; twin engine training, Stutgart, AR, graduating second lieutenant; B-24 training, Maxwell Field; joined crew Westover Field, Springfield, MA; crew training, Fort Dix, NJ.

Boarded *Queen Mary* landed in Scotland June 5, 1944; oriented North Island, joined 489th June 27, 1944. Stationed Halesworth, England. Flew 28 missions over France and Germany.

Memorable experiences: On a mission to Ascherleben they were late getting off due to radio problems. They joined up with another crew. Hit by fighters before reaching turning point knocking out #4 engine, damaging #3 engine. Watched dogfights between B-24s and fighter planes with planes going down all around them. Flew to turning point, flew to I.P., flying straight while group was taking evasive action from flak. Flew to target, dropped bombs with group, then home to England. Bullets had knocked out hydraulic line on outside of landing gear strut. Forced to land short, using brakes once and turning off runway. They killed engines and had to be towed in.

Discharged November 1945 with the rank of first lieutenant. Received Air Medal with three clusters.

After discharge moved family to California; and after losing his loving wife, his tour of duty was raising four young children. He retired in 1981 after 32 years at McDonnell Douglas Aircraft. He enjoys gardening and raising orchids.

ARTHUR R. SUTER, was born April 13, 1923, in Guttenberg, NJ. Enlisted Oct. 6, 1942; USAAC, armorer gunner, 856th Bomb Sqdn., 492nd Bomb Group, 2nd Air Div. Military locations/stations: England, Korea, Japan, Germany, Alaska and numerous stateside locations.

Flew 13 missions, May-June 1944; shot down during 13th mission on June 20, 1944.

Retired Aug. 31, 1964 with the rank of master sergeant. Received Air Medal with Oak Leaf Cluster, National Defense Service Medal, WWII Victory Medal, Occupation Medal-Japan, Occupation Medal-Germany, American Campaign Medal, Good Conduct Medal with Silver Loop, Alaskan Air Command Commendation Medal and Air Force Commendation Medal.

Retired, he is a widower.

STEPHEN A. SUTHERLAND, was born Oct. 7, 1924 in Stockton, CA. Volunteered January 1943 while a student at University of California, Berkeley. Bombardier School, Deming, NM. Graduated second lieutenant (0 780445) Class 44-8 (Jan. 10, 1944).

Overseas to Halesworth, England, October 1944, 489th Bomb Group, 844th Bomb Sqdn. Flew four missions and returned to States December 1944 with 489th and completed B-29 training just prior to atomic bomb.

Highlight of stay in England was reunion with only (and older) brother, PFC Armorer Arliss Harold Sutherland, who was with the 78th Fighter Group stationed at Duxford. Arliss had been in England approximately two years and early in 1945 took a commission as second lieutenant in Army Corps of Engineers and served six months in Army of Occupation in Austria. Both Arliss and Stephen were discharged in December 1945.

Graduated from Oregon State, Corvallis, OR, August 1949.

Married December 1947; has three sons and seven grandchildren. Lived in Elko, NV, 1953-1986. Elected Elko County Commissioner 1968-1972. State Farm Insurance agent 1961-1986. Retired 1986 and moved to Twin Falls, ID.

WARREN K. SUTOR, was born Jan. 12, 1922, in Zurich, KS. Basic, St. Petersburg, FL; Gunnery School, Panama City, FL; Armament School, Lowry AFB, Denver, CO. Shipped out to Salt Lake City, UT, where he was assigned to a crew. Training mission, Tucson, AZ; Casper, WY, then shipped out to Herington, KS and picked up new plane.

Flew to England via Newfoundland, Greenland, Iceland and Belfast then on to Norwich, England, 389th Bomb Group, Hethel Air Base. Flew first mission Nov. 16, 1943. Shot down on 8th mission over Ludwigshaven, Germany, Jan. 7, 1944. five crewmen lost their lives; four escaped and one was taken prisoner of war. Sutor managed to escape through Shelburn escape route on March 23, 1944; took 78 days to complete his 8th mission (a very long day).

Returned to States and worked out of the MIA/POW office in Pentagon, giving lectures to new crews. After invasion they had no further use for his services, rest of time at Muroc, CA and was discharged October 1945.

Now residing in Kansas City, MO.

MICHAEL SVETICH, entered USAAF Sept. 9, 1942. Military locations/stations: Mather AFB; Lowry Field; Las Vegas; Davis Monthan; Tibenham; 445th Bomb Group.

Completed 35 missions; three over Berlin but only two counted. Memorable experience: Last mission, was happy to land on English soil.

Discharged June 2, 1945, with the rank of staff sergeant. Received Air Medal with clusters and Distinguished Flying Cross.

Married 57 years and has four children and nine grandchildren. Retired, 23 years.

VERNON SWAIM (RED), was born near Rose Lake, ID, October 1924; moved to Lewiston 1940. After a year of college there, enlisted in USAAC, December 1942. In CPT/WTS until active service October 1943. Basic and gunnery at Buckley and Harlingen Fields before D-day. RTU with Merle King's crew at Westover Field.

Flew North Atlantic in new B-24K to Holyhead, and assigned to 93rd/328th at Hardwick, November 1944 until V-E day. Completed 21 missions as non-lead and lead crew. Flew back across through Iceland, Goose Bay, etc. joined B-29s at Pratt, KS, until V-J day.

Discharged February 1946 as staff sergeant in Denver. Graduated 1950 and 1959 from Northern Idaho and OSC, Corvallis. Taught high school math/science until 1963.

Returned to Bonneville Power as specifications/construction engineer until 1986 retirement. Bicycle Oregon each September, canoe, hike, etc. near Vancouver, WA.

JOSEPH E. SWANSON, was born Feb. 21, 1913, in Southampton, Long Island, NY. Entered USAF May 20, 1942; assigned to 2nd Air Div., 8th Air Force, 458th Bomb Group. Military locations/stations: Utica, NY; Camp Upton, Long Island; Miami Beach, FL; Fort Bragg, NC, 793rd Tech. School; Seymour Johnson Field, NC, Lockheed Vega Service School; Burbank, CA, Prov. Sqd. F; Salt Lake City, UT; Gowen Field, Boise, ID; Wendover, UT; Tonopah, NV; Norwich, England, Horsham St. Faith; Sioux Falls, SD; Paterson Field, CO; Rome, NY.

Memorable experience: he will never forget his three years, four months service time. B-24J3, #395 tail wind, assistant crew chief; B-24J3, August 1944 to September 1945, crew chief.

Discharged Oct. 20, 1945 with the rank of staff sergeant. Received Silver and Bronze Star, Good Conduct Medal, American Campaign Medal, EAME Theater Medal and WWII Victory Medal.

Married to Betty, they have two sons, and three grandchildren. He is retired.

ROBERT N. SWIFT, entered USAF Sept. 15, 1942; bombardier, 458th Bomb Group, 753rd Sqdn., 8th Air Force. Military locations/stations: Gowen Field, ID; Wendover, UT; Tonopah, NV; cadet at Big Spring, TX.

Memorable experiences: Shot down on March 6, 1944 (Berlin), prisoner of war 14 months, Stalag Luft I. Parachuted from B-24 just seconds before it crashed about 50 feet from him. Plane was in a flagtspin.

Discharged Jan. 16, 1946 with the rank of second lieutenant.

Married, he has two sons and one daughter. Retired from fruit farming (mainly grapes).

H. THOMAS SWINT, was born Aug. 21, 1922 in LaGrange, GA. Joined Army Sept. 24, 1940 and was sent to Fort Ord, CA. April 1941, transferred to 79th School Squadron, Moffett Field, Sunnyvale, CA. Worked on B-T-13s; joined 467th Bomb Group, February 1944.

Flew overseas to Rackheath, AAF Station #145, East Anglia. Left 467th February 1945, attached to Inf. S-2 Plt. in 65th Div.; he was a lousy soldier, a fair air mechanic and scared in combat.

Memorable experiences: Flying to England via South America and Africa; flying gas in jerry cans in B-24 to Clastres, France, September 1944 to Patton's tanks.

Discharged Sept. 26, 1945 from Fort Dix, NJ, with rank of tech. sergeant. Received usual ETO ribbons and Combat Infantry Badge while attached to 65th Inf. Div. in Austria.

Swint and wife Shirley J. have three children and six grandchildren. He is a retired newsman.

ROBERT LEE SWOFFORD, arrived in England Jan. 2, 1944 by way of South America and Africa. Flew tour of 30 missions approximately half as squadron lead pilot.

Memorable experiences: Leading a mission on the bridge of Caen on D-day; and when they lost both right engines to four ME-109s over Berlin. Got back to England (alone) but ran out of fuel over an airport. Put it down in a wheat field with considerable damage to the aircraft but none to the crew.

Finished military career flying transport from New York to Paris Oct. 28, 1945 Received Distinguished Flying Cross with Oak Leaf Cluster and Air Medal with five Oak Leaf Clusters.

Flew 36 plus years for Capital Airlines and United Airlines from DC-3s to 747s.

ROBERT J. SYKES (BOB), was born Nov. 11, 1923 in Macel, MS. Entered USAAC May 30, 1942, after graduating from high school. Graduated from ACFT Armorer Course and Flexible Gunnery School and was shipped to Gowen Field in Boise, ID. Was placed on flying status as aerial gunner and assigned to B-24 crew. February 1944, his crew departed from Morrison Field, FL and arrived in ETO March 12, 1944.

Assigned 44th Bomb Group, 67th Bomb Sqdn., Shipdham, England, where he served as B-24 gunner and armament technician until V-E day. After flying back to the States, was stationed at Alamogordo, NM until separated at end of hostilities with Japan.

Received bachelor of science degree in 1949 and a master of education degree in 1952. After serving in field of education 36 years he retired in 1986.

Married Roxie Griffin Aug. 25, 1950; they have two children and two grandchildren.

WAYNE TABOR, was born in Newton, IA on Dec. 23, 1918. Enlisted January 1940 and graduated from Chanute Field as aircraft engineer. First stationed at McChord Field, WA assigned to 12th Bomb Group (M). As cadre member flew with B-17 and B-24 groups until assigned to 466th Bomb Group (B-24). Was a waist gunner on John Brown's "Polaris" crew and stationed at Attlebridge, England.

Flew first mission over Berlin on March 22, 1944. Completed 30 missions on June 14, 1944. Awarded the Distinguished Flying Cross, Air Medal with three Oak Leaf Clusters and two European Battle Stars. Memorable experiences were being hit by German fighters and terrifying flak explosions.

Discharged as staff sergeant in December 1944 and graduated from Iowa State University in 1950. In sales and management for 35 years.

Married Carlene Dupre and has one son, one daughter, two step-daughters and four grandchildren.

JOSEPH TADDONIO JR., was born Dec. 18, 1920, East Boston, MA. Enlisted in the Air Force in September 1942. Left Salina, KS in B-24E (ball turret) to Bengasi, Libya in August 1943. Joined 376th Bomb Group and in February 1944 joined the 93rd Group, Hardwick, England.

Participated in battles at Naples, Foggia; Rome, Arno; Air Combat, Balkans; Air Combat, Europe; Normandy; Northern France; and Air Offensive Europe, England.

Memorable experience was flying with 9th in Middle East; 12th in North Africa; 15th in N. Africa and Italy; and 8th in England. Completed a total of 40 missions.

Discharged July 1945 with the rank staff sergeant. Received the Distinguished Flying Cross and Air Medal with six clusters. Received official credit for one ME-109, Nov. 2, 1943, Weiner Neustadt, Austria.

Taddonio is a retired optometrist.

VIRGIL C. TALLY, was born in North East, PA June 23, 1925. Enlisted in ERC, June 1943, one day before 18th birthday. Called to active duty September 1943. After basic training in Miami Beach, FL, was assigned to Flexible Gunnery School at Tyndall Field, FL. After graduation, assigned as tail gunner on B-24 crew at Westover Field, MA.

After OTU, crew flew a new B-24 from Mitchell Field, NY to Ireland. Reassigned to 466th Bomb Group at Attlebridge. Flew 25 combat missions as both wing crew and lead crew.

Received four Air Medals and four European Campaign Stars.

Returned to USA in March 1945. After graduation from Instructors School at Laredo AFB, TX, assigned to Buckingham Field, FL as air to air gunnery instructor on B-24s and B-29s. Discharged Oct. 23, 1945.

Married June Rolla in July 1947, they have a son, daughter and four grandchildren. June passed away in 1992. Retired in 1988 after 40 years in the transportation field.

TIMOTHY M. TAMBLYN, was born Nov. 8, 1919 in Narberth, PA. Joined ROTC September 1938, July 9, 1942, USAAC as aviation cadet then USAF as lieutenant colonel. Stationed at gulf coast flying training command; Wendover, UT Army Air Field; Halesworth, England (8th Air Force); Carlsbad, NM Army Air Field.

Memorable experiences: experimental mission for chemical warfare service at Dugway Proving Ground, Utah; to England via South Atlantic route; all his 35 missions especially Hamburg, Kiel, Munich, Ruhr Valley, Aschersleben;

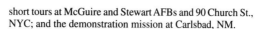

short tours at McGuire and Stewart AFBs and 90 Church St., NYC; and the demonstration mission at Carlsbad, NM.

Retired Dec. 12, 1971 with the rank lieutenant colonel, USAFR. Received the Air Medal with five Oak Leaf Clusters, USAF Commendation Medal, two Distinguished Unit Citations, EAME Medal with five Battle Stars.

Married Mary Louise Prophet on Feb. 18, 1950. They have a daughter Erica, son Tyler, daughter Cynthia and identical twin granddaughters, Bonnie and Kimberly.

Civilian employment: corporate officer and board director of New York City bank; trustee of three charitable foundations northern New Jersey; retired police commissioner; elected councilman of Saddle River, NJ; and now trying to cope with retirement (not easy).

CARL J. TANNER JR., was born in Traverse City, MI on March 12, 1923. Went back to high school in October 1945 and graduated June 7, 1946. Enlisted in the USAAF on Jan. 13, 1942. Took basic training at Jefferson Barracks, MO. Entered Radio Operators & Mechanics School, Scott Field, IL in March and graduated with Class 33 on July 28, 1942.

Boarded the *Queen Elizabeth* in New York Harbor on Aug. 31, 1942. After seven days they sailed up the Clyde River in Scotland. Boarded a train for Alconberry, England, their first base. Later their squadron, the 329th, moved to Bungay and the rest of the 93rd Bomb Group moved to Hardwick. Their squadron joined the group later. The 93rd Ted Timberlake's Flying Circus had four B-24 squadrons: 328th, 329th, 330th and 409th. He worked as a radio mechanic and rose in rank to staff sergeant in 27 months from enlistment.

Flew back to the States in a B-24. Left on May 22, 1945, flew to Wales for overnight, on to Iceland for three day stay, to Labrador to gas up, on to Dow Field, ME where they stayed overnight, then to New Hampshire where they left their plane. Took 30 days leave, then went to Sioux Falls, SD. Sent next to Galveston, TX where he stayed until the Pacific War ended.

Was discharged on September 28 at Fort Sheridan, IL and called back to active duty on May 6, 1951 during the Korean War. Spent two years with 55th Air Weather Sqdn. at McClellan AFB, Sacramento, CA. Worked as a communications line chief on B-29s before being assigned to the 31st Air Rescue Sqdn. at Clark AFB in the Philippines. Went TDY to Okinawa to fix B-50s planes for the 34th Air Rescue Sqdn. He was TDY for 55 days earning the Korean and United Nations Awards.

After three years in the Philippines, he was sent to Loring AFB, ME on March 16, 1956, his first B-52 base. Spent time at Nellis AFB, NV and George AFB, CA before flying to Vietnam in October 1963. Was stationed at Danang for one year as quality control inspector. Next went to Wurtsmith AFB at Oscoda, MI to work on the B-52. His last base before retiring was Nellis AFB, NV where he was to work on the F-111. It never arrived until one year later, so he never got to work on it as he retired Jan. 31, 1968 with the rank of tech sergeant.

Married to childhood sweetheart, Elsie M. Smith, on June 16, 1946. They have six children living out of seven, 15 grandchildren and three great-grandchildren.

HARRY TANZER, was born Nov. 10, 1924 in Holyoke, MA. Attended school in South Hadley and Chicopee. Was at the opening dedication of Westover in the late 30s and graduated from Chicopee High in 1942. Attended College of William and Mary, Williamsburg, VA, 1942-43. Aviation Cadet Class 44-A, Maxwell Field, Decatur (PT-17) and eliminated at Courtland.

Went to Liaison Pilot School at Waco, TX and again eliminated (depth perception); Scott Field, IL for radio; Yuma

for Gunnery; assigned to crew at Westover; OTU at Charleston, SC. All expense trip paid for by U.S. Government on the *Acquatania* late 1944. Assigned to 467th Bomb Group at Rackheath in 1945. Flew 22 missions and was then discharged on Nov. 10, 1945.

Received the Air Medal with three Oak Leaf Clusters, ETO Ribbon and three Battle Stars.

Graduated William and Mary in 1949 and taught school before being recalled and sent to Goose Bay, Labrador 1951-1952. Graduated University of Miami, FL in 1955. Opened a small business and sold it to become an agent for Metropolitan Life Ins. Co. Worked as agent in Miami, sales manager in Tallahassee, FL and moved to California in 1965 where he was a sales manager and received his Charter Life Underwriter Degree in 1967. Moved to Yucca Valley, CA in 1976 where he now is semi-retired, working as Metlife Rep. and does substitute work in school.

Married in 1962 to Ruth Von Breuning of Easton, PA, no children. He had two brothers who also survived WWII. Tanzer is active in Yucca Valley Lions Club, Masonic Lodge, Friends of the Library, amateur radio operator (W6CYK) and a member of 2nd Air Division Association and 8th Air Force Historical Society. Tanzer displays his WWII souvenirs at various conventions.

JACK D. TARDIEU, was born March 3, 1924 in Redding, CA and raised in Los Angeles and Piedmont, CA. Joined the USAAF December 1942. After A&E and Gunnery schools, was assigned and trained as an engineer gunner with a crew in South Carolina. Assigned to B-24M (446th Bomb Group, 704th Bomb Sqdn.) and headed for England.

When the war ended he had completed 11 missions. Received two Air Medals, one Bronze Oak Leaf, American Theater, EAME, three Bronze Stars plus WWII Victory Medal. Was discharged as a staff sergeant at March Field, Dec. 10, 1945.

Worked as a manufacturing engineer in various aerospace companies ending with United Tech Co. He retired in 1983. Married Barb Haran June 20, 1953 and has eight children and 13 grandchildren. Retired in Grants.

OWEN PHILLIPS TAYLOR, was born April 11, 1922, Miccosukee, FL and grew up in Jacksonville, FL. Served with CCC Feather Falls, CA October 1940-March 1941. Enrolled Florida Southern College in Summer of 1941. Enlisted USAAC, Dec. 16, 1941. Assigned to Instructor Armament School at Lowry and Buckley Fields, CO.

Sent to England November 1943 and January 1944 was assigned armorer duty (sergeant) 328th Sqdn. 93rd Bomb Group (B-24), Hardwick. Discharged September 1945.

Graduated Jacksonville Junior College in 1947. Joined Florida Air National Guard, worked as a caretaker until activated October 1950, 159th Fighter Sqdn., George AFB, CA and Misawa, Japan; 7th Bomb Wing SAC, Carswell AFB, TX, 1953; SAC HQ Offutt, NE, 1957; Naha, Okinawa 1961; Shaw, SC 1963; Tachikawa, Japan 1966. Retired as E9, July 1969. BA elementary education; MA reading education University of South Florida (Tampa); reading teacher, Pasco County seven years.

Married Anne Wood on April 23, 1948. Retired and living in Bartow, FL.

RAY S. TEATER, was born Nov. 30, 1921 at Wheeling, WV; drafted June 1942; basic at St. Petersburg; Airplane Mechanics School, Gulfport, MS; C-47 Factory at Long Beach, CA; Aerial Gunnery School at Las Vegas; first and

second phase bomber training at Gowen Field; third phase at Wendover, UT.

Overseas October 1 in a new B-24 via Goose Bay and Iceland. Assigned to 392nd at Wendling in November 1943. Flew first bombing mission December 1943 and last mission the 31st in July 1944. Signed up for another tour in order to get a furlough home for 30 days. Had a happy reunion with his new wife. Didn't have to go back for extra tour.

After four months R&R at Fort Logan, CO in fall of 1944, was assigned to alert crew at Truax Field March 1945. Their daughter, and only child, was born at Truax Base Hospital on June 8, 1945. Was discharged Sept. 23, 1945 at Truax with the rank of staff sergeant. Received the Distinguished Flying Cross, Air Medal with three Oak Leaf Clusters and ETO Medal.

Back to Wheeling for nine years, moved to Salt Lake in 1954. Worked for Texaco for 17 years then moved back to Wheeling in 1971 and operated family landscape business for 17 years. Retired in 1986. Has been golfing and gardening since.

GLENN E. TEDFORD, was born Jan. 5, 1923 in Wichita Falls, TX. Graduated high school in 1940; enlisted at Brooks Field Sept. 13, 1940; graduated Radio School, Scott Field in 1941; went to Lubbock in 1942. Went to Santa Ana, CA for preflight and became a flying sergeant. Advanced, Luke Field, Phoenix, AZ; primary, Hamet, CA; basic at Mintor Field, Bakersfield, CA. Graduated as flight officer April 1943 and sent to Gowen Field, Boise, ID to fly B-24 and became first pilot.

Received his crew at Boise and flew before going overseas, eight hour missions and a lot of days flew 16 hours (eight hours in and eight hours out).

They were put in a provisional group as replacements for crews shot down at Ploesti. Joined 93rd Bomb Group at Hardwick, England.

Flew first mission Dec. 11, 1943 and 30th mission March 23, 1944. They were almost shot down on bomb run over Berlin and lost two engines on March 6, 1944. Transferred to 448th Bomb Group as group training officer. On D-day, June 6 he flew his 31st mission. Discharged with the rank of captain. He received the Distinguished Flying Cross and six Air Medals.

Married Sept. 16, 1944 to Katherine Foster. They have one son Walter and two granddaughters.

Tedford was sales and service manager and travelled over most of the world, vice president and half owner of company with 235 employees at the time of selling the company.

GEORGE W. TEMPLE, was born Aug. 6, 1922 in Brattleboro, VT. Later moved to Staten Island, NY where he attended grade school and high school. Joined the cadets April 1942 and attended Navigation School at Selman Field, graduating in Class 43-2, Feb. 6, 1943. Went through B-24 transition and arrived in the 8th Air Force, 44th Bomb Group in June.

Went TDY with the group, a week later, to Benghazi, Libya. They covered the Sicilian Campaign and flew on their primary mission Aug. 1, 1943. The low-level (150' bombing altitude) raid on the oil refineries of Ploesti, Romania. Returned safely from it, but was shot down two raids later over Foggia, Italy on August 16. Spent three weeks as a POW in a Catholic hospital in Potenza. Escaped, along with five other airmen, when the hospital was blown up by B-25s. They all made it safely, some to Tunis and those of the 8th AF to England.

In the Spring of 1944 he gave escape and evasion lectures and instructed navigation in the summer. In January 1945 he began single engine pilot training. Lacked one week of graduating when the war was over.

Received his BSEE in August 1953 after completing a 21 month Korean recall. That duty was in the 301st Bomb Wing on B-29s.

His industrial career was with Thermatomic Carbon Company, finishing as plant manager. Took early retirement in 1980.

Has been married for 49 years to Irvie Lee Humble; they have four children, 10 grandchildren and three great-grandchildren.

JOHN C. TERBRACK JR., was born Jan. 13, 1912 in Nora, LA. Joined the service Oct. 30, 1942. Received first Markmanship Medal, Aerial Gunnery Aug. 27, 1943; graduated Gunnery School, Aug. 28, 1943; school at Biggs Field, TX; Sept. 27, 1943, first flight in B-24; Received second Markmanship Medal, Jan. 10, 1944. Left Mitchell Field to ferry B-24 to England via South America, Africa. Completed 32nd mission on July 25, 1944.

Participated in Normandy, Northern France and Air Offensive Europe campaigns. Memorable experience was Jan. 22, 1944 when on night navigation flight in Atlantic was lost for a few hours in the Bermuda Triangle. Finally got out by floodlight from shore.

Discharged Oct. 18, 1945 with the rank staff sergeant. Received the EAME Ribbon with three Bronze Stars, Good Conduct Medal, Air Medal with four Oak Leaf Clusters and the Distinguished Flying Cross.

Has wife, son, daughter and granddaughter. Employed with American Auto Association AAA Road Service.

GAYLORD A. THAYER, was born Sept. 23, 1915 in Iowa Falls, IA. Enlisted April 1945. Assigned to 8th Army Air Force, 752nd Bomb Sqdn., 458th Bomb Group, Norwich, England. Participated in Normandy, Northern France, Rhineland, Ardennes, Central Europe and Air Offensive Europe campaigns.

Memorable experience was V-E day offensive. Discharged Sept. 28, 1945 with the rank of sergeant. Received the EAME Ribbon and the Good Conduct Medal.

Was Harding County executive director ASCS County Office, Iowa Falls, IA until retiring Dec. 31, 1977. Now does volunteer work.

MARCEL J. THIBODEAU, was born Aug. 12, 1920 in Dayton Twp., MN and grew up in Pine City, MN. Joined the USAAC Nov. 5, 1942 at Ft. Snelling, MN. Basic at Brooks Field; AM School, Sheppard Field; Spec. Sc. Chanute; Wendover Field, UT where 489th Bomb Group was formed.

Sent to Halesworth, England with 845th Bomb Sqdn. in April 1944 and returned December 1944. Went to Tucson, AZ on B-29 advanced training Clovis, NM and Tinker, OK. Back to Tucson in preparation for Okinawa. War ended so was sent to Lincoln/Omaha, NE.

Discharged Nov. 7, 1945 at Sioux City, IA with the rank of sergeant.

Married June 1946 and has two daughters, one son and six grandchildren. Retired from McDonnell Douglas in 1982.

ALBERT L. THOMALE, was born April 9, 1921 on a farm near New Rockford, ND during that winter's worst snow blizzard. Worked one year at Lockheed Aircraft Corp. in Burbank, CA before being drafted into the USAAC on Oct. 8, 1942. Attended Med. Bombardment Aircraft School, Sheppard Field, TX. He qualified for acceptance to flight crew status, then sent to Martin Aircraft Factory in Baltimore, MD for specialized training on the B-26 bomber (M).

Ordered to Aerial Gunnery School at Tyndall Field, FL; dispatched to Salt Lake City, UT for assignment; dispatched to Gowen Field, ID to make up the 453rd Bombardment Group, 733rd Bombardment Sqdn. They were rushed through three phases of training. One at Gowen Field, ID and the additional two at March AFB, CA. Then dispatched to Hamilton AFB, CA to pick up their new B-24 aircraft.

Made several shake-down flights and then headed for England (via the long route). Stopped at Natal, Brazil where they spent Christmas Day. Next stop was Dakar, Africa and last stop was an air field near Old Buckingham, England. The same day that they arrived "Berlin Sally" (on her infamous radio broadcast) welcomed their commander, Col. Joe Miller and group to England and said, "We'll be seeing you soon" which was to have been a threat; but as it turned out, "they surely did see us, for 31 missions and felt our payloads—bomb after bomb after bomb."

HARRY E. THOMAS JR., was born Aug. 25, 1922 in Florence, SC. Volunteered for Aviation Cadet training January 1942. Took preflight at Kelly Field; primary at Pine Bluff, AR; basic at Waco, TX; transferred to Bombardier training at Ellington and graduated Midland April 1943.

Completed crew training in B-24 at Tucson and Blythe. Picked up new B-24 H in Lincoln, NE in October 1943. Completed 33 heavy missions and shot down July 7, 1944 with an added 10 months visit with the German POW camps.

Stayed in ORC until 1965 and full retirement Aug. 25, 1982 with the rank lieutenant colonel. Received the Distinguished Flying Cross, Purple Heart, Air Medal with five clusters, and the Distinguished Unit Citation.

Sept. 1, 1992 was his toughest mission yet. He had major surgery (nine hours) having found golf ball size tumor in bladder wall. He is doing great now. Always thinks, "Lord help me to remember that nothing is going to happen today that you and I together cannot handle."

Thomas has completed a book, *33 and then 10,* now retired and lives in Florence, SC. Married over 50 years and has five grandchildren.

JAMES FRED THOMAS, was born Sanford, NC on May 26, 1919. Joined the Air Force Enlisted Reserve at Fort Bragg on May 18, 1942. Active duty at Nashville Classification Center on Oct. 28, 1942. Maxwell Field for preflight training January 1943. Primary, basic and advanced flight training at Camden, AR, Greenville and Columbus, MS, graduating with Class 43J on Nov. 3, 1943.

Back to Maxwell Field for B-24 transition training. Through Salt Lake City for crew assignment, and on to Boise for RTU mid-February to mid-April. To Lincoln, NE to pick up new B-24 which was flown to Bangor, ME, and Goose Bay, Labrador to Nutts Corner, Ireland, to Stone, England for assignment. Arrived 392nd Bomb Group on May 12, 1944 and was assigned to 579th Sqdn.

Flew first combat mission May 24, 1944. Flew 30th mission Aug. 1, 1944, a period of 70 days which included two three day passes to London and a seven day "flak" leave. Sound easy? Consider 200 flight hours during a period when the 579th Sqdn., alone, lost 11 planes and crews. Worst mission: Bernberg, Germany July 7, 1944; a day when 44 bombers were lost, including six from the 392nd Bomb Group and 12 from the 492nd Bomb Group while flying in one formation.

Returned to USA September 1944 and after R&R at Miami Beach, was assigned to B-24 flying at Victorville, CA AAB November 1944 until May 15, 1945 when he was released from service.

He joined United Airlines June 29, 1945 and after co-pilot training was assigned to LaGuardia, NY for two years. Transferred to Midway at Chicago where he was promoted to DC-3 and DC-4 captain in 1951. Spent 17 years flying DC-3, DC-4, CV-340, DC-6, DC-7 and French Caravelle S-240 out of Midway and O'Hare Fields. Checked out on Boeing 720 and transferred to Los Angeles September 1964 where he flew the B-720, DC-8, DC-10 and B-747 until retirement December 1984. Married Myrtle McFarland August 1940 and has a son, daughter and three grandchildren. He and present wife of 28 years, Elva, live in retirement in Huntington Beach, CA.

JOHN E. THOMAS, was born Dec. 29, 1925, Pensacola, FL. Joined the service December 1943; basic training at Miami Beach, FL; Gunnery School at Laredo, TX and joined his crew in Boise, ID and took combat training.

Stationed at North Pickenham, England with 8th Air Force in July 1944. Was left waist gunner of Lt. Art Pearce's crew, 491st Bomb Group, 853rd Sqdn. His first mission to Hannover, Germany was a memorable experience. Nobody had told them about the intensity of the flak. He saw two bombers explode.

Flew 28 missions before his discharge September 1945 with the rank of staff sergeant. Received the Air Medal with three clusters.

Married to Helen and has three sons, one daughter and four grandchildren. He is retired.

WORTH J. THOMAS, was born Oct. 19, 1924 in Lee County, NC. Enlisted in the USAAF April 7, 1943. Was nose gunner on B-24 with 392nd Bomb Group, 577th Bomb Sqdn. Stationed at Wendling, England from August 1944 to February 1945.

Completed 35 missions over Germany. Participated in Normandy Campaign and Battle of the Bulge.

Memorable experiences: dream before 10th mission, shot up over target on fire; hit in bomb bay, hydraulic system shot out, 150 holes, emergency landing.

Discharged Oct. 23, 1945 with the rank of staff sergeant. Received the Air Medal and six Oak Leaf Clusters.

Married April 1946 and has two sons. Thomas is currently retired.

CARROLL L. THOMPSON, was born Concordia, KS on Jan. 31, 1922. Graduated from Norway High School and was inducted into the USAAF Sept. 25, 1942 at Leavenworth, KS. Basic training in Kearns, UT to various Gunnery schools in Las Vegas, Lowry Field, Denver, CO; Harlingen, TX; Salt Lake City, UT; assigned to a crew at Davis-Monthan, Tucson, AZ; to Hethel AFB (389th) Norwich July 1943.

Flew tour of missions as ball turret gunner. Received Distinguished Flying Cross and Air Medal with three Oak Leaf Clusters. Returned to States September 1944, gunnery instructor at Laredo and "pickled planes" at Garden City, KS until discharged in September 1945 with rank of staff sergeant.

On Thanksgiving Day, he married WAC Lida B. Cowen whom he had met in England while at Hethel and she at adjacent 2nd Air Div. HQ at Ketteringham. They had five children, oldest of whom was killed in plane crash while pilot instructor at Vance AFB in 1972.

Thompson had a dairy farm in Indiana until he died in April 1974 of an undiagnosed ailment which later was discovered to be sleep apnea.

CHARLES O. THOMPSON JR., was born Oct. 14, 1925, Oklahoma City, OK. Attended University of Oklahoma for BA in 1950. Joined the USAF Dec. 20, 1943 (ERC). Stationed at Fort Sill, OK; Sheppard AFB, Wichita Falls, TX; Harlingen AFB, TX; Lemoore AFB, CA; Walla Walla AFB, Walla Walla, WA; Hamilton AFB, CA; Camp Kilmer, NJ; Stone, England; Seething, England, Station 146, 8th AF; Bradley Field, CT; Camp Chafee, AR; Sioux Falls, SD; Deming AFB, NM and Randolph AFB, San Antonio, TX.

Participated in Ardennes, Rhineland and Central Europe campaigns. Memorable experiences: the character, loyalty, courage and compassion of officers and enlisted; 448th Bomb Group first mission crash land; flak, fighter attacks, air-sea rescue, ground crew, napalm bomb, low level mission, Wesel, Germany.

Discharged Dec. 21, 1945 with the rank staff sergeant. Received the EAME Theater Ribbon with three Battle Stars, Air Medal with two Oak Leaf Clusters, American Theater Ribbon, Victory Medal, Good Conduct Medal and one Overseas Bar.

Married 39 years to Jerry, they have two daughters, Cynthia and Kathleen; son Charles III; three granddaughters and three grandsons. Employed with Sherwin-Williams, Employers Insurance of Wausau, Bridgestone/Firestone Tire & Rubber Co. in sales, management and production. Retired May 1, 1993.

GLEN D. THOMPSON JR., was born Aug. 19, 1925 in Healdton, OK. Joined the USAAC Sept. 23, 1943. Assigned to 329th Bomb Sqdn., 93rd Bomb Group as armorer gunner. Stationed at Amarillo, TX; Harlingen, TX; Lincoln, NE; Casper, WY; Topeka, KS; Hardwick, England.

Memorable experiences: flew six missions before 19 years of age; low level mission over Arnheim to resupply 82nd Airborne - 101st Airborne Sept. 18, 1944; completing 30 missions as lead crew; and receiving three commendations from Gen. Timberlake.

Discharged Oct. 25, 1945 with the rank staff sergeant. Received the Air Medal with four Oak Leaf Clusters, ETO Medal with four Battle Stars, American Theater Ribbon and the WWII Victory Medal. Was recalled March 1951 for Korean Conflict, discharged November 1951.

Married 44 years to Mary B. Wood, they have three children and seven grandchildren. Retired after 30 years with the postal service.

WILLIAM MARSHALL THOMPSON, was born Oct. 21, 1920 in Mt. Gilead, NC and was inducted Nov. 19, 1942 at Ft. Bragg, NC. Was assigned to the Air Corps and sent to Keesler Field, MS for basic training. Completed Aircraft Mechanic School in May 1943 and was sent to Willow Run Plant, Ypsilanti, MI for advanced training. Was then sent to Replacement Center in Salt Lake City, assigned to 445th Bomb Group, 703rd Sqdn. at Wendover Field, UT.

Went to Sioux City, IA for overseas training then to Tibenham, England in October 1943. Served there until 445th Bomb Group returned to States in May and June 1945. Served with ATC unit, New Castle Air Base until discharged as a sergeant September 1945.

Since then, he has farmed, raised beef cattle, tobacco and melons in Jackson Springs, NC. Married Sarah Ruth Currie May 13, 1942 and has a daughter, son and two grandsons.

NEWELL B. THORNOCK, was born Oct. 18, 1919 in Bloomington, ID and enlisted Aug. 11, 1942 in the USAAF as radio operator gunner and air operations specialist. Stationed at Sioux Falls, SD; Harlingen, TX; Tucson, AZ; El Paso, TX; Pueblo, CO; Benghazi, Libya; Turis, Tunisia; Shipdham, England.

Participated in Air Offensive Europe, Rome Arno, Sicily, Normandy, Northern France, Ardennes, Rhineland and Central Europe campaigns. His memorable experience was just being associated with 67th Bomb Sqdn., 44th Bomb Group.

Discharged Sept. 18, 1945 with the rank tech sergeant. Received the EAME Service Medal, Good Conduct, Victory Medal and group citations.

Thornock is married and has seven children. He is a retired school bus driver.

WILLIAM F. TIERNEY JR., was born Feb. 10, 1924 in New York City. Married Anne T. in December 1949. Enlisted in the USAAC while attending Niagara University. Active duty in February 1943. Went through pilot training with the Southeast Training Command, graduating as second lieutenant, George Field, IL, May 23, 1944.

B-24 transition, Harlingen, TX; crew training, Gowan Field, ID and assignment to 445th Bomb Group, 8th Air Force in November 1944. Flew 24 missions.

Returned to States June 1945 and shipped to Long Beach, CA. Was assigned to 7th Ferrying Div. Separated October 1945. Graduated Fordham University, New York City, June 1948. Volunteered for Berlin Airlift in September 1948. Assigned to 509th Bomb Group, Roswell, NM as tech supply officer, GDO January 1950. Separated June 1950.

Returned to civilian life as career salesman, regional manager, general manager for major paper companies from 1952 until retirement in 1989. Presently works part-time for previous customer and has an 18 golf handicap.

JOSEPH WM. TIKEY, was born in Sharon, PA on Nov. 9, 1920. Received pilot wings with Class of 43-D in April

1943. Flew to Attlebridge, England with the original 466th B-24 group in February 1944. Was a lead Pathfinder pilot and along with 96th Wing Commander Gen. Peck led the 2nd Air Div. twice (once leading the 8th Air Force over Germany). Led many successful missions unscathed.

After 30 missions was a stateside B-24 pilot instructor and later a B-29 pilot instructor at Maxwell Field until V-J day. Discharged in December 1945 with the rank of major. Received the French Croix de Guerre Avec Etole d'argent (with Palme) from President DeGaulle, two Distinguished Flying Crosses, six Air Medals and several other ribbons.

Received an aeronautical engineering degree from Carnegie Tech in March 1948. Married Cathie Boyle and spent 37 years with Sperry Gyroscope in various management positions. Has five children and six grandchildren.

Was valedictorian of his high school class, first to solo in his primary class, King of Hearts at Tech in 1947, member of Theta Tau (honorary engineering fraternity) at tech and a bowling Gold Medal winner in 1991 and a golf Gold Medal winner in 1992 and 1993 in the St. Louis Senior Olympics.

NORMAN N. TILLNER, was born Dec. 4, 1924, Long Beach, CA. Spent childhood, schooling and early work history in Southern California, including driving truck on construction of Blythe Army Air Base. Joined USAAC, April 1943. Basic, Fresno, CA; Armament School, Lowry Field, Denver, CO; Gunnery School, Laredo, TX. Next assignment, Blythe USAAB as member of combat air crew (Pete Henry, pilot).

Overseas by boat, New Jersey to Scotland. Assigned to 67th Sqdn., 44th Bomb Group, 14th Wing, 2nd Air Div. May 1944. Flew eight missions after D-day in June, wounded over Magdeburg, June 29, 1944. When combat ready again, was unable to rejoin crew. By boat to 15th Air Force, Italy, assigned 756th Sqdn., 459th Bomb Group, November 1944. Between instructing skeet and 50 cal. machine gun, flew five more missions prior to Europe war end.

Flew back to States in war weary B-24, by way of North Africa and Azores. On return expected assignment in South Pacific but while home on leave, that was concluded. Discharged September 1945 with the rank staff sergeant. Received the Air Medal, Purple Heart, ETO Ribbon and seven Campaign Stars.

Worked at North American Aircraft, building B-45s and modifying F-86s for use in Korea. Plant engineer for Hallamore Electronics, retired as captain from Costa Mesa Fire Dept., carried mail for U.S. Postal Service, currently camera store clerk.

Married June 1, 1957 to Joyce Blackmon. They have one son Chad.

RALPH G. TISSOT, was born Nov. 29, 1922 in Chestnut Hill, PA. Enlisted March 18, 1941 in the USAAC. Assigned to 330th Bomb Sqdn., 93rd Bomb Group (H). Stationed at McDill Field, Tampa, FL; Barksdale Field, LA; Ft. Myers, FL; Hardwick, England. Completed 28 bombing missions over Europe as engineer/gunner.

Memorable experiences: crashing on take-off with delay bombs (all survived) at Hardwick, England; being shot-up by flak, ditched everything into English Channel, landed safely on grass fighter field in Southern England with only gas fumes in tanks.

Discharged Aug. 1, 1945 with the rank staff sergeant. Received the Distinguished Flying Cross, Air Medal with three Oak Leaf Clusters, American Defense Service Medal, EAME Service Medal with six Bronze Stars, Presidential Unit Citation and Good Conduct Medal.

Married to Ruth and has son Ralph Jr., daughter-in-law Debbie Penny Backer Tissot and grandchildren Aaron M. and Sasha M. Returned to Air Force during Korean War and discharged second time Aug. 16, 1965 with the rank master sergeant, USAF (RET).

JOHN TKACHUK, was born in Cleveland, OH on Sept. 19, 1918. Graduated from Lincoln High School in June 1936 and was employed with the Kroger Grocery and Baking Co. Attended Fenn College (Cleveland State) with studies in aeronautical engineering.

Entered service on July 7, 1942. Had basic training at Atlantic City and graduated from Bombardier and Gunnery School at Wendover, UT. Was a tech sergeant as flight engineer and assigned to the 8th Air Force, 2nd Air Div., 93rd Bomb Group, 329th Sqdn. and flew to England in the fall of 1943.

Tkachuk was killed in action on Dec. 20, 1943. He had achieved the rank of tech sergeant and awarded the Purple Heart. His twin brother George Tachuk (Tkachuk) served with the U.S. Army 75th Inf. Div. 575th Sig. Co. in the ETO.

IRVIN E. TOLER, was born Oct. 30, 1920 in Tulare County, CA. Grew up on a farm and later in Sequoia National Park. Was student at college of Sequoias and University of California, 1939-42. Joined the USAAC (air cadet-pilot); trained at Dos Pacos and Merced, CA and La Junta, CO; commissioned May 1943; bomber training at La Junta and Sacramento (B-25s); Hobbs, NM (B-17s); Boise, ID; Sioux City, IA; and Herington, KS (B-24s).

Flew via South America and Africa to England. Assigned to 448th Bomb Group, 2nd Air Div., 8th Air Force at Seething, Norfolk. Flew 30 missions over Europe. Was first crew to complete tour with all crew members alive. Transferred to 487th Bomb Group, 3rd Air Div. at Lavenham Suffolk as director of training and assistant operations officer.

Awarded the Distinguished Flying Cross, five Air Medals, five European Campaign Stars and Presidential Unit Citation. Was discharged with the rank of captain.

Returned to University of California, Berkeley and received BS degree in forestry and engineering. Worked for timber industry as forester/land manager, 1947 to date.

Married Marilyn Tyler Dec. 27, 1953, has daughter Shannon and son Brett. They live at Burney, CA.

JAMES N. TOMBLIN, was born Nov. 29, 1924 in Morristown, TN. Joined the USAAC February 1943. Completed navigator training Coral Gables, FL on April 22, 1944. Commissioned a second lieutenant.

Phase training at Gowan Field, Boise, ID. Assigned new B-24J in Topeka and flew seven missions with 44th Bomb Group, including dropping supplies to paratroopers at Arnhem, Netherlands. Shot down September 1944. POW in Germany in Stalag Luft

III, in forced march to Moosburg and Stalag VIIA, north of Munich. Liberated April 29, 1945, by tanks of 7th Armd. Div. attached to Gen. Patton's 3rd Army.

Discharged December 1945 and received the Air Medal, two ETO Campaign Stars and Purple Heart.

Attained BS and MBA, retired from Air Force Reserve as major in 1969. Employed by NCR as computer systems analyst and manager of Microcode Development. Retired June 1987. Taught computer science 10 years in Community College.

Married Leah Ruth Marsh, 1954. Has one child, Neal Alan.

HARRY L. TOWER JR., was born April 9, 1912 in Westdale, MA. Entered the Air Force July 23, 1942. Stationed at Fort Dix; Scott Field; Harlingen, TX; Davis-Monthan; Biggs Field; Hardwick, England; Miami Beach and Louisville. Completed 28 missions over the continent as a radio operator.

Memorable experience was his 22nd mission when they had three engines shot out, into cloud cover, limped back across channel and crash landed. No one was injured.

Discharged Aug. 31, 1945 with the rank tech sergeant. Received the Air Medal and Distinguished Flying Cross.

Has a beautiful wife, two children and six grandchildren. Tower has always drawn pictures and painted in various media and continues to do so.

JOHN CHARLES TRACEY JR., was born in Kansas City, MO July 2, 1923. Graduated from Hale H. Cook Elementary School, Soldan High School, BS in aeronautical engineering from Air Force Institute of Technology and MBA in R&D Management from University of Chicago. Entered USAAC July 20, 1942, aviation cadets, Jan. 3, 1943, graduated from Brooks Field as second lieutenant on Oct. 1, 1943. Joined B-24 crew in Mountain Home, ID for training.

Flew 17 missions over Germany as copilot then got his own crew. On his 20th mission over Munich, July 11, 1944, lost #2 at target and #3 losing power and could not keep up with group. Elected to crash land in Switzerland. Escaped from Swiss Prison Camp into France and U.S. control November 1944.

Retired March 31, 1967 from Satellite Test Center, Sunnyvale, CA as test director of Satellite Program.

JAMES H. TRAINOR, was born Aug. 31, 1924 in Belt, MT. Joined USAAF December 1942. Military locations include: pilot training, Class 44-E, Lubbock, TX; B-24 transition training, Ft. Worth, TX; Boise, ID; 93rd Bomb Group, Hardwick.

Completed 29 missions and achieved the rank of lieutenant colonel. Discharged August 1945 and recalled March 1951. Discharged second time in September 1954.

Married in 1945. Returned to EWCE at Cheney, WA graduating with BA in 1947. Started career in education. Recalled in March 1951 to fly B-29s and B-50s prior to attending School of Aviation Medicine. Returned to classroom after September 1954 for discharge.

Graduated from USC with MS in education. Moved to northern California, owned and operated cattle and horse ranch. Retired from USAFR. Retired from career in education in 1983 to pursue full-time ranch operation along with back country outfitting.

WILLIAM J. TREHAL, was born Sept. 7, 1923 at McCook, NE to William Walter and Esther A. Ebert Trehal. Attended McCook Schools and McCook Community College, 1947-1948. Married Elaine (who had three children) and they had two more. Currently have 14 grandchildren, two step-grandchildren and two great-granddaughters.

Was sworn into the Army Jan. 29, 1943, Fort Logan near Denver, CO. Basic training at Kearns, UT where they learned the Air Force song. Went to Brookings State College at Brookings, SD where they learned Army administration. Some of the stations he was stationed at were: Santa Maria, CA; Pendleton, OR; Great Falls, MT; Camp Shanks, NY, where they boarded the USS *Alexander* for trip across the Atlantic.

Docked in Grenock, Scotland about the third week in October 1943. It was a sunny day and the pastel colored homes were a welcome sight after a scary trip (enemy submarines were after them). They went to Norwich, Rackheath and later to Seething Air Base. Their duty was to supply the 448th Bomb Group and its four squadrons: 712, 713, 714 and 715.

The officers and men supplying the 448th Bomb Group: Lt. Col. Frank Cruixshank, Capt. Nesmith, 1st Lt. McRae, Lt. Anderson, M/Sgt. Herbert Marshall; W/O Howard K. Hadley; Roy Howland; Tyrone Anthony; Mike Franko; Jack Wolf; Johnson; Charles Gordon; James Tierney; Robert Shorty Asbury; Chris Thompson; Charles Andrews, Walley Wendler, Clyde Vickers, Ted Clark, Frank Stiklis, Robert W.

Fox, "Hope" Amadi, Bob Hit, James Wade, Robert F. Whitney, George Kuhnle, Elmer Swanson, William J. Trehal, Frank Sower.

Propeller Shop: O'Brien, Finley, C.B. Francisco, Foley, Indian Shirley, Dowell Price, Emil Martini and Carmelo Cuozzi.

ROBERT LEWIS TRESLER, was born March 23, 1920 in Gill, CO and raised in Eden, WY, a very rural area in Western Wyoming.

Military locations and stations: bombardier training and navigator with the Class of 43-15 Childress, TX, B-24 crew training at Westover, MA. Assigned to 492nd Bomb Group, England and flew 17 missions, then transferred to 445th Bomb Group. Most of his missions were flown as pilotage navigator on various lead crews. He was very impressed with the tremendous coordination of efforts to make the invasion of Normandy a success. With the day being so cloudy there was only an occasional break in the clouds and all they could see were rows and rows of ships—truly an amazing sight.

Discharged Sept. 16, 1945 with the rank first lieutenant. Received the Distinguished Flying Cross, European Service Medal, Air Medal with three Oak Clusters.

Married Shirley Tresler (deceased) and has son Roger, daughter Linda Zullig and two grandchildren, Tina and Johnny Zullig. Presently married to Patt. He is retired from career of agronomist with Soil Conservation Service of USDA. His hobbies include mycology, hunting and fishing.

ROCKLY TRIANTAFELLU, was born Oct. 17, 1917 in Daytona Beach, FL. Joined the USAAC Jan. 12, 1942, commissioned bombardier Dec. 12, 1942. Stationed at Roswell, UK, Libya, Mather, SAC, TAC, SHAPE, Vietnam, PACAF, Pentagon.

Memorable experience was three crash landings in B-24, including one in Turkey after bombing Ploesti. Was interned and later escaped. Returned to UK for 20 more missions.

Discharged March 1, 1972 with the rank major general. Received three Distinguished Service Medals, two Legion of Merit, two Distinguished Flying Crosses, five Air Medals, Croix de Guerre with star, Vietnam Air Cross and Master Wings (4300 hours flight time).

Married in 1946 to Ruth Anne Zahn; they have two daughters. He is a consultant with Mitre Corp.

ROBERT C. TRITLE JR., was born September 1924. Lived in many States before graduation from East High in Des Moines, June 1942. Arrived in California and joined USAAC Cadets in November 1942. Was called to active duty May 1943. Completed several technical school locations and was assigned bomber crew position as armorer-gunner. Saw duty in ETO on a B-24J while assigned to 389th Bomb Group in 8th Air Force.

Karlsruhe was his last successful mission, arrived in Switzerland September 1944. Returned to U.S. April 1945 and was assigned to Western Technical Training Command at Lowry Field. Took honorable discharge November 1945, returned to Denver to wed a lovely young lady in December 1945 and took her home to California.

In June 1946 he hired on with Pacific Bell Telephone and later re-enlisted into the USAF. With the Korean War starting, he was recalled to active duty and assigned into Air Depot Command as military wire chief. Constructed and made operational wire communications at an air base near Casablanca.

Returned home April 1953 and resumed career at Pacific Telephone. Retired from management June 1982 after 36 years service. Married 48 years and has three children.

DURWARD A. TRIVETTE, was born March 15, 1924, entered the USAAC February 1943, attended Radio Operators School in Salt Lake City, UT. Upon completion assigned to Gowen Field, ID where flight crews were being selected for a new B-24 Bomb Group known as the 458th. Became a part of the 752nd Sqdn., Crew 11.

First phase flight training was completed at Gowen Field. Became the first bomb group to be stationed at Tonopah Air Base, UT. Completed final flight training in December 1943. Assigned new B-24H, serial #41-28709 (later named Lucky Strike) at Hamilton Field, CA. Flew to England via Brazil and Africa for permanent assignment at AAF Station 123 Horsham St. Faith Norwich, England.

Began operational tour March 3, 1944. Wounded on 20th mission, Brunswick, Germany on May 19,1944. Spent the next few months at 231st Station Hospital. Returned to flight status in September 1944. Assigned to gasoline runs to France September 18-20, 1944. Flew 30th mission on Nov. 16, 1944. Received Distinguished Flying Cross, Air Medal with three Oak Leaf Clusters and Purple Heart. Discharged in September 1945.

Married Doris Flammer on Jan. 23, 1945. They have two sons, Larry and Bill, and five grandchildren.

LEE A. TROGGIO, was born May 27, 1921 in Laredo, Bleggio, Italy. Entered the service April 1942. Stationed at Keesler Field; Scott Field; Sioux City, IA; Tibenham, Atlantic City, and Scribnor, NE. Was assigned to 8th Air Force, 401st Bomb Sqdn., 445th Bomb Group.

Memorable experiences: serving in the 8th Air Force; V-1s, V-2s, enjoyed the warm hospitality of the English and Scottish people.

Discharged October 1945 with the rank of sergeant. Received the ETO, Good Conduct and awards for five campaigns.

Troggio is owner and president of Troggio's Inc. Restaurant (employs 80 persons and seats 600 persons). He is retired.

CECIL M. TROSTLE, was born Feb. 10, 1919 in near Jewett, IL, moved near Brocton, IL and finally to Oak Park, IL. Joined the USAAC Dec. 4, 1941 and went directly to Ft. Sheridan, Jefferson Barracks, Chanute Field and to Specialist School at the General Electric Plant in Lynn, MA.

Reported in to the 328th Bomb Sqdn., 93rd Bomb Group at Ft. Myers, FL in May 1942. The ground echelon transferred to Ft. Dix, NJ; then on the *Queen Elizabeth* to Prestwick, Scotland and by train to Alconbury, England. The group moved to Hardwick Air Base and time was spent on the maintenance crew of the *Ball of Fire*.

In 1944 he became the crew chief on (B-24-11), later named *Top Hat,* and crewed this aircraft 88 missions without an abort. After four additional missions, the aircraft was transferred to the 329th Bomb Sqdn. and his crew was assigned a lead aircraft which flew 26 missions. The original aircraft was returned to the 328th, Bomb Sqdn. and continued to 123 missions.

Vivid memory of D-day with all available aircraft lined up on approaches to main run-way near midnight, with running lights on and engines running.

Discharged Nov. 11, 1945 with the rank tech sergeant. Received the Bronze Star.

Trostle is retired from Northern Illinois Gas Co. He is the last of 12 children.

CHARLES M. TROUT, was born April 6, 1921 in lower Lancaster County, PA. Raised on a farm until 1938 then went to work for Pennsylvania Railroad as a trackman and a machinist helper. Called to Army Service on Aug. 1, 1942. Took basic training at St. Petersburg, FL. Then went to Aircraft Mechanic School at Gulfport Field, MS; Republic Training Detachment in Long Island, NY then to 320th Fighter Sqdn. at Westover Field, MA.

Took B-24 training; went to Tyndall Field for Gunnery

School; and Salt Lake City to get placed on a bomber crew (B-24) with Lt. William Prewitte, pilot, assigned to 492nd Bomb Group, 859th Sqdn., crew #916 at Alamogordo, NM. Was a flight engineer and gunner flying over Europe. Made 22 missions. Lost two planes and bailed out twice into the North Sea, May 29, 1944 and Aug. 16, 1944 (half of crew lost).

Returned to USA in September of 1944 and a few months stay in Louisville, KY hospital. then on to Ft. Worth, TX as a service record clerk until discharged at Indiantown Gap, PA on Sept. 15, 1945. Returned to civilian life and back to work. He enjoys life with wife and family. Presently lives in Westfield, PA.

LESTER C. TRUMP, was born April 14, 1923 in Reading, PA. Joined the USAAF, pilot, 446th Bomb Group, 707th Sqdn. Cadet locations: Nashville, TN; Montgomery, AL; Cape Giradeau, MO; Stutgart, AR; Malden, MO. Officer locations: Salt Lake City, UT; Tucson, AZ; Bungay, England. POW locations: Dulag Luft; Miengen Hospital; Obermasfeld Hospital; Stalag Luft III.

Participated in invasion of Europe, invasion of Southern France, completed 25 missions before being shot down on Aug. 24, 1944. His squadron led 8th Air Force in the invasion of Europe on D-day. Received the Purple Heart, Air Medal with three clusters, POW medal, European Theater with one Arrowhead and two stars and the American theater Ribbon.

Discharged Nov. 18, 1945 with the rank first lieutenant. He is married and has four children. They live at Spring Valley Lake, CA. Trump is retired and enjoys cards, golf and fishing from the back porch.

ALLAN T. TUCCI, was born April 1, 1925 in Verona, NJ. Entered the USAAF in September 1943 and assigned to 8th Air Force, 467th Bomb Group, 791st Sqdn.

Discharged Oct. 19, 1945 with the rank of staff sergeant. He received the Air Medal with three clusters (Northern France, Southern France and Germany).

Married and has five children, seven grandchildren and one great-grandchild. Tucci is retired and lives in Orange, CA.

JOHN P. TUCHOL'SKI, was born Roslyn Heights, Long Island, NY on June 24, 1922. Joined the service in July of 1942 and requested Air Force. Reception Center was Camp Upton, NY. From there to Keesler Field, Biloxi, MS for basic training, sent to Washington State College for Radio and Gunnery School, completed in December 1942 and assigned to the 389th Bomb Group, Davis-Monthan Field, Tucson, AZ. Assigned to a crew as a radio operator with the rank of tech sergeant. Further training at Biggs Field, TX and Lowry Field, then sent to ETO.

Sent from England to Benghazi, Libya where they started their first combat mission. Crew was shot down on third mission (July 12, 1943) on a raid to Italy. They returned in time for practice for the August 1, Ploesti mission which they participated in.

Returned to England in September for a few missions and then to Tunis. Returned to England where they completed their tour of 25 combat missions.

Discharged Sept. 25, 1945 with the rank tech sergeant. Received the Distinguished Flying Cross with one Oak Leaf

Cluster, Air Medal with four Oak Leaf Clusters, Good Conduct and the ETO with five Battle Stars.

Married May 16, 1943, Lowry Field, Denver, CO. They have two daughters and five grandchildren. Tucholski owns and operates a funeral home.

GORDON F. TUCKER, was born Jan. 30, 1921 in Windsor, VT. Enlisted Aug. 3, 1942 in the USAF. Stationed at Sioux Falls, SD; Valley Forge; Yale University; Boca Raton; Rackheath, Norfolk, England; and March Field, CA.

Memorable experience was serving as group radar officer, 467th Bomb Group from January 1944 until August 1945 and as base radar instructor at March Field from August 1945 to November 1945.

Discharged November 1945, captain, squadron commander; Reserves, White River Jct., VT 1946-1952; major in USAFR until about 1960. Received all the usual awards and decorations.

Worked 32 years for NE Telephone Co., various plant, staff, engineering and network assignments. Retired 1978 as network manager, design for Vermont toll facilities.

Married since July 15, 1943 and they have a son and daughter.

WILLIAM V. TUMELAVICH, was born July 14, 1923 in Carbondale, PA, a coal mining town. In 1943 he took infantry basic training at Camp Croft, SC. Transferred to Army Air Force. Graduated Gunnery School at Harlingen, TX. Joined his crew and sent to Casper, WY for transition training on the B-24.

After completion of training, the crew embarked for England on the QE-1. Crew assigned to the 445th Bomb Group, 703rd Sqdn. at Tibenham on Sept. 27, 1944. Completed 31 combat missions over Europe as a top Turret and waist gunner.

When war in Europe ended, was reassigned to Las Vegas for remote gunnery training on the B-29. Japan surrendered before training began. Discharged at Las Vegas in October 1945.

Married WAC corporal in August 1945. They have two children, six grandchildren and two great-grandchildren. Tumelavich retired from glass factory after 35 years of service. At the present time, Bridgeton, NJ is home.

JOHN I. TURNBULL (JACK), was born in Baltimore, MD on June 30, 1910. He graduated from the Johns Hopkins University in 1932 after only three years. A fine athlete, he was named a three year, First Team All-American in Lacrosse.

In 1931 he became a licensed pilot and in 1940 became a pilot in the 104th Observation Sqdn. Maryland National Guard.

In 1943 he joined the 492nd Bomb Group in B-24s at Blythe, CA. Flew as command pilot on eight missions with the 492nd at North Pickenham and served as Group Operations officer. In August 1944 he moved to the 44th Bomb Group at Shipdham. On October 18 as command pilot on a mission to Leverkusen, Germany Turnbull was killed in a collision with another B-24. There were two survivors, S/Sgts. George Encimer and Cecil Scott.

Turnbull was awarded the Distinguished Flying Cross, four Air Medals and the Purple Heart.

DONALD E. TURNER, was born May 7, 1920 in Depue, IL. Joined the USAAC Aug. 14, 1940. Graduated from Armor School, February 1941; joined the 15th Bomb Sqdn. (L); graduated from NCO Gas School and flew to Mitchel Field, NY for submarine duty.

Boarded ship to England April 1942. The 15th Bomb Sqdn. made the first raid on Germany July 4, 1942, starting the war with the Germans. Transferred to the 44th Bomb Group, 66th Bomb Sqdn. and was armor gunner on the waist for nine raids. Transferred to North Ireland, 3 R&T School as a gunnery teacher.

Memorable experience: On the first raid on Germany, Feb. 26, 1943, he ran into trouble. Coming off the target, they picked up FW-190 and ME-109 fighters. He felt a jerk of his head. Coming to, the waist gunner had strapped a new mask on him. Back on his feet, he noticed his oxygen hose had been cut into and he had passed out. This cut in the hose was just a inch or so from his neck.

Returned to the States August 1944 and discharged June 1945 with the rank staff sergeant (75% disabled). Received the American Defense, American Theater, European Theater with two Oak Leafs, Air Medal, Good Conduct (Army), WWII Victory Medal, two Presidential Unit Citations and Army of Occupation.

October 1945 went to Bradley University, Peoria, IL for Watchmakers and Diamond Setters School. Married October 1947 to Betty Humphrey of Glenwood, IA. They have one son. Turner is now retired.

DWIGHT L. TURNER SR., was born in Greensboro, NC on April 25, 1918. He completed high school. Participated in ROTC for four years, North Carolina State College, graduating with BS in textile chemistry and received second lieutenant commission in the Army Quartermaster Corps on May 31, 1941. Was primarily stationed at Fort Bragg, NC where promoted to first lieutenant on June 26, 1942.

Volunteered for pilot training and assigned to Class SE 43-G; proceeded to pre-flight at Maxwell Field, AL; primary at Lodwick Aviation Military Academy, Avon Park, FL; basic at Cochran Field, Macon, GA; advanced at Moody Field, GA; and received his pilot's rating July 28, 1943.

Four-engine transition training at Maxwell Field in October 1943; assigned to 39th Bomb Group at Davis-Monthan Field, AZ; transferred to 34th Bomb Group (H), Blythe AAF, CA for combat crew training. Joined the 491st Bomb Group (H) on Jan. 28, 1944, Pueblo AAB, CO, further assigned to 852nd Bomb Sqdn.

1st Lt. Turner and his crew arrived in England early in May 1944 stationed at Metfield, England (Station 366). Participated in first combat mission on June 2, 1944 which was a strike on Bretigny Air Field, France. Piloting a B-24J named Pappy's Persuader, Turner and his crew completed 31 combat missions without a scratch. Last mission was Aug. 27, 1944.

Returned to the States in January 1945 and spent his last year of active duty at many different locations. Before leaving active duty on Nov. 30, 1945 at Camp Blanding, FL, he had obtained the rating of instrument pilot instructor and qualified as first pilot in advanced four engine air transport training. Last promotion was that of captain in the Air Corps Reserve in 1946.

Received the Distinguished Flying Cross, Air Medal with three Oak Leaf Clusters, American Defense Service Medal, American Campaign Medal, EAME Campaign Medal with four Battle Stars (Air Offensive Europe, Normandy, Northern France and Rhineland campaigns), WWII Victory Medal and Distinguished Unit Citation.

Married Doris Dent of Macon on June 26, 1943. They had two sons and a daughter: Dwight Jr., Tom and Cathy, and six grandchildren.

Turner enjoyed a long and fruitful career as a textile salesman with Dupont. He passed away Nov. 18, 1990 in Columbus, GA. *Submitted by his eldest grandson, Mark.*

EDMUND S. TWINING JR., was born Sept. 19, 1915 in New York, NY. Enlisted January 1943 in the USAAB, Aviation Cadets. Stationed at San Antonio Aviation Center, Ft. Stockton, TX; San Angelo, TX; Lubbock, TX; Liberal, KS; Salt Lake City, UT; McCook, NE; Casper, WY; Topeka, KS; AFTAC, Orlando, FL.

Assigned to 8th Air Force, 2nd Air Div. Participated in ETO, completed 30 missions over Germany and France. He shot down five German fighters.

Discharged September 1945 with the rank of captain, USAAF.

He received five Air Medals, Distinguished Flying Cross, ETO Medal with stars and his crew had two Purple Hearts.

Married and has two sons and four grandchildren. Twining is retired.

JOHN F. TYBOROSKI, was born Sept. 13, 1924 in Marlin, TX. Entered USAAC on Nov. 10, 1942, College Station, Texas A&M. Stationed at Keesler Field, MS; Laredo Field, TX; Boise, ID; Casper, WY; Topeka, KS; Scott Bluff, NE. Flew B-24 to England, station at Tibenham #124.

Memorable experience was combat flight over Germany in B-24 and his 18 months in Europe.

Discharged Oct. 21, 1945 with the rank tech sergeant. Received the Good Conduct Medal, Air Medal, ETO Medal, Aviation Badge, Distinguished Unit Badge, French Croix de Guerre and EAME Ribbon.

He has two daughters, Jeraldine and Rose Marie, five grandchildren and three great-grandchildren.

Retired USAF, 30 years, M/Sgt. flight engineer. Total flight time-17,500 hours.

WEB L. UEBELHOER, was born on April 6, 1917 in Fort Wayne, IN on the day the U.S. declared war on Germany in WWI. He graduated from the University of Alabama in 1941. Entered pilot training on Oct. 1, 1941 in the Class of 42-D. He instructed single and twin engine advanced.

He went overseas with the 492nd Bomb Group, 8th Air Force. First mission was also the first for the 492nd Bomb Group. They ran out of gas, one engine operating, for a belly landing near East Whitering in Southern England. After D-day, he was transferred to the 445th Bomb Group, where the crew was made a radar lead ship. He completed his tour of duty with the 445th Bomb Group.

His claim to fame was on Sept. 27, 1944 when the 445th put up 31 B-24s on a mission to Kassel, Germany. They were jumped by 100 to 150 fighters. With the exception of four, the remaining 27 aircraft were shot down. This crew was one of the four to return to base at Tibenham.

He retired on April 6, 1977 with the rank of lieutenant colonel. He received five Air Medals, two Distinguished Flying Crosses and nine Campaign Stars.

He married Helen Brudi in 1943. They have three children, two grandchildren and two great-grandchildren. He was employed by Pan American Airways on the North Atlantic route. He has spent the last 20 years as an Elementary School Teacher.

JACK K. UMPHREY, was born on May 13, 1922 in Birmingham, AL. He entered the Aviation Cadet Training Program in March 1942. Graduated as a pilot, second lieutenant, Class of 43-B in Blytheville, AR in February 1943.

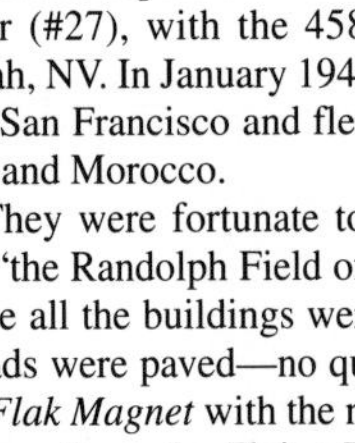
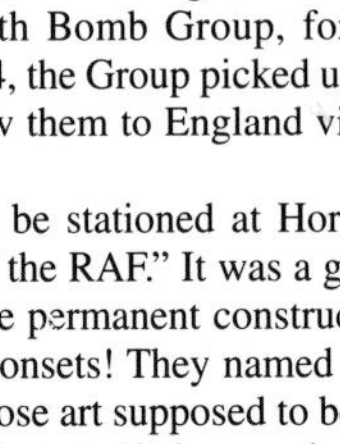

Was a flight commander in new A-20 group at Will Rogers Field in Oklahoma City, then went to B-17 and B-24 transition. In September 1943, he was assigned as crew commander (#27), with the 458th Bomb Group, forming in Tonapah, NV. In January 1944, the Group picked up new B-24s in San Francisco and flew them to England via Brazil, Africa and Morocco.

They were fortunate to be stationed at Horsham St. Faith, "the Randolph Field of the RAF." It was a great base because all the buildings were permanent construction and the roads were paved—no quonsets! They named their airplane *Flak Magnet* with the nose art supposed to be like the shark mouth on the Flying Tiger P-40, but on the B-24, it looked more like a friendly whale than a shark lumbering down the runway.

Flew 30 combat missions from March to May 1944, including six to Berlin. The *Flak Magnet* was shot down while they were on leave and they named their new airplane *Flak Magnet II* (which was shot down after they finished their missions). They were the first crew in the 458th Bomb Group to finish a tour and the first to finish without an abort jump (used three airplanes on one mission to keep their non-abort string going). Did various flying and comptroller assignments, mostly in SAC, until his retirement in 1964.

He was awarded two Distinguished Flying Crosses, Bronze Star, four Air Medals, Army and Air Force Commendation Medals, plus many service medals.

His civilian career consisted of 24 years in the Air Force Budget at the Pentagon. Was selected for Senior Executive Service (SES). Headed Air Force Acquisition Funds; later headed Operating and Military Personnel Funds. Then made Deputy Director of Air Force Budget eight years before retiring in May 1988. All in all, he had 46 great years in the USAF.

President Reagan personally awarded him the rank of Distinguished Executive in the SES. His other awards include the Presidential Meritorious Executive Award, Air Force Exceptional Civilian Service Medal, Department of Defense Meritorious Civilian Service Medal and two Air Force Meritorious Civilian Service Medals, as well as numerous SES performance bonuses and outstanding performance awards.

Married Mary Theresa Lee in Denver, CO in November 1953; they have two children and one grandchild.

KAROL L. UNDERWOOD, was born on Jan. 29, 1924. His hometown was in Versailles, IN. In 1942 while he was attending Purdue University, he enlisted in the USAAC, graduated as a bombardier on Sept. 2, 1944 and made second lieutenant in Victorville, CA.

He completed 14 missions with the 448th Bomb Group in the 8th Air Force, based at Seething near Norwich, England.

He finished college after the war ended and worked for Borden, Inc. until his retirement. Married Lois Harrison of Versailles on April 2, 1944. They have a daughter, son, four grandchildren and five great-grandchildren.

KENNARD UNDERWOOD, was born on May 23, 1922 in Auburn, NY. He enlisted into the USAAF as a aviation cadet in September 1942 and graduated as a navigator in April 1944 at the Hondo AAF in Texas.

He picked up a B-24 in Boise, ID on May 6, 1944; flew the northern Atlantic route Topeka/Valley (Wales) RAF, July 18, 1944. Was assigned to the 466th Bomb Group, 787th Bomb Sqdn., 8th Air Force, Attlebridge on Russell Thompson crew. Completed 35 missions. Participated in Battle of the Bulge.

Memorable experiences: three days in Paris in January 1945; Feb. 22, low level lead squadron; railroad station at Celle, Germany; gas hauling to Patton's tanks; drew pubbing map around Attlebridge, issued to the new crews.

Underwood received the Air Medal with four Oak Leaf Clusters and five European Campaign Battle Stars. He was discharged in June 1945 with the rank of first lieutenant.

Married Nancy Wadsworth in June 1947. They have two children and two grandchildren. He graduated as mgt. engineer at Rensselaer Polytech in June 1949. Travelled Brazil and Venezuela with Caterpillar Tractor. He joined the GM Terex Division and retired as a manager of government sales in Washington, DC in 1985.

KENNETH P. UNDERWOOD (K.P.), was born on Sept. 15, 1923 in Clarksburg, WV. He enlisted into the USAAC in the Aviation Cadet Program on Dec. 1, 1942 and was called to active duty on March 2, 1943, while a sophomore at Potomac State College, Keyser, WV. Preflight in San Antonio, TX; pilot training at Corsicana and Greenville, TX; multi-engine advance at Altus, OK; awarded his wings and second lieutenant bars with the Class of 44-A in January 1944.

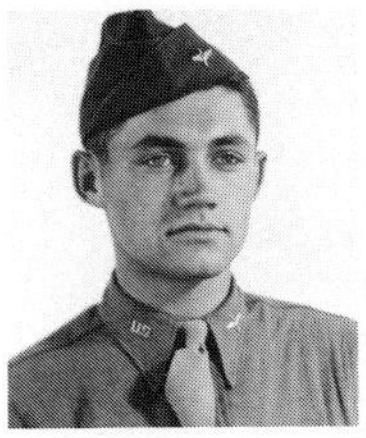

In mid August 1944, after training in B-24s at Liberal, KS; Colorado Springs, CO; and Mt. Home, ID; he and his new crew flew a "right-off-the-assembly-line" B-24 from Topeka, KS to the ETO via Labrador, Iceland and Wales.

Was assigned to the 704th Sqdn., 446th Bomb Group at Bungay, and immediately found himself and his group involved in a "grocery run." Instead of bombs they were hauling flour and medicines to Orleans in France. The "on-the-deck" grocery run was soon over and his 30 combat missions were completed on March 18, 1945.

Was discharged in June 1945 as a result of victory in Europe. He received two Distinguished Flying Crosses, five Air Medals and various Campaign Ribbons.

Married Ann Phillips on June 14, 1947; they have three children and four grandchildren.

JORDAN R. UTTAL,
was born on July 30, 1915 in New York City, NY. He graduated from New York University in June 1935. Enlisted into the Signal Corps/Air Corps on Dec. 29, 1941 as radar operator. As a staff sergeant, he left for Air Corps OCS in August 1942, transferred to Harvard Graduate Business School and commissioned as a second lieutenant, statistical control officer on Dec. 5, 1942.

Went overseas in May 1943 to 2nd Bomb Wing HQ as an assistant statistical control officer. Soon after, he met, and subsequently wooed and married, the lovely British lady, Joyce Christie King, assistant to the Red Cross Field Director, Horsham St. Faith.

In February 1944, he was re-assigned to become division photo officer to improve bomb strike coverage for determination of bombing accuracy. In November 1944, with the rank of major, he was re-assigned as a division statistical control officer with chief emphasis on bombing accuracy analysis.

Uttal received the Bronze Star, the Croix de Guerre and several other ribbons. He returned to the States in August 1945 after 27 months overseas. Was discharged in November 1945 to resume his marketing career in the food industry. In 1948 he and six others founded the 2nd Air Division Association. Later, he served two terms as president and 17 years as a member of the Board of Governors of the Memorial Trust of the 2nd Air Division USAAF located in Norwich, England.

FRANK C. VADAS,
was born on Aug. 25, 1917 in Allentown, PA where he resided his entire life. He enlisted into the USAAC on April 2, 1942. After basic training at Ft. Eustis, VA, he was sent to Honolulu, HI for coast artillery duty.

Returned to the States in September 1943 for Airplane Mechanics School at Keesler Field, MS; Factory School in Willow Run, MI and Gunnery School at Tyndall Field, FL. Was sent as a flight engineer to Westover Field, MA to meet the rest of his crew. After transitional at Charleston, SC his crew was assigned a B-24 at Mitchell Field, NY and they left for England on March 8, 1945. They arrived at Hethel Air Field, Norwich on March 21, 1945 and flew his first mission on April 3rd.

With the war winding down, crew was sent home on May 13, 1945 arriving at Bradley Field, CT and on to Ft. Dix, NJ and a 30 day furlough. Was then sent to Sioux Falls for reprocessing to the Pacific when the point system allowed for his discharge.

He married Grace Spisak of New Brunswick, NJ on Oct. 30, 1943. They have three children and two grandchildren. Returned to Allentown where he was employed by Western Electric/Bell Labs. Vadas passed away on July 3, 1991.

JAMES E. VAISEY,
was born on Jan. 13, 1926 in Rochester, NY. He enlisted into the USAAF on July 19, 1943 and entered into active service on Feb. 4, 1944. He received gunnery training at Laredo, TX in the Sperry Ball Turret and received overseas training at AAB in Pueblo, CO.

Was shipped overseas in October 1944 and assigned to

the 14th CBW, 44th Bomb Group, 506th Bomb Sqdn. stationed near Shipdham. As the Sperry turrets were removed from the B-24, he flew the first three missions as a waist gunner, the remaining 21 missions were flown in the nose turret.

He received the Air Medal, Unit Citation with one cluster and the Theater Ribbon with three Bronze Stars. His most memorable experience was surviving a spin in a B-24 from 9000 feet, while he was returning from a mission to Karlsruhe on Dec. 11, 1944. The pressure was so great from the spin that no one was able to exit the plane, but the pilot and co-pilot pulled it out with about 100 feet to spare.

Married Drucilla in 1956; they have one daughter and two grandchildren.

ARTHUR J. VALOIS,
was born on March 19, 1920 in New Bedford, MA. He enlisted into the USAF on Oct. 1, 1941. Stationed at Keesler; Kelly; Lowry and Casper, WY. He was with the 389th Bomb Group, 567th Sqdn at Hethel Field in Norfolk, England. Completed 33 combat missions.

His memorable experience was when their B-24 crashed while training on a night bombing mission from Casper, WY in April 1944. His crew bailed out but the pilot and co-pilot were killed in the crash.

Valois received the Good Conduct Medal, American Defense Service Medal, Distinguished Flying Cross, Presidential Unit Citation, Air Medal with three Oak Leaf Clusters, and the EAME Service Medal with three Bronze Stars. He was discharged on Sept. 8, 1945 with the rank of staff sergeant.

Married Mary Donth on June 2, 1945; they have one daughter. He is retired and does volunteer work at a museum, visitors center and is also a walking tour guide.

JAMES B. VALLA (JIM) or (VAL),
was born on Nov. 6, 1923 in St. Paul, MN a first generation American born Norwegian, joined the USAAC on Dec. 26, 1941, just 18 days after Pearl Harbor. He was a volunteer gunner, he trained while at Hethel Airdrome in England.

He flew eight missions as a "spare" flying with any crew that needed him. During early March, he joined the Gudehus crew as a nose turret gunner and flew the 22 additional missions needed to complete a tour of 30, two of which were on D-day, across the Normandy Beach Landing.

Returned to the States during August 1944, he became an instructor in B-24 bomb racks at Lowry Field out of Denver. He was discharged in September 1945 and returned to the Twin Cities. He re-enlisted into the USAAC in May 1947 and remained until he was able to retire in the grade of master sergeant with 20 years of active duty.

He now lives in Tampa, FL. Valla is married and has four children and five grandchildren.

JOHN VAN ACKER (JACK),
was born on April 19, 1922 in Albany, NY. He enlisted into the USAACR on Oct. 14, 1942, while attending Pratt Institute. Was called to active duty in March 1943. He had basic training at Atlantic City, CD at Penn State and cadet training in the Southeast Command graduating as a pilot in April 1944.

Completed Aircraft Commander School at Smyrna, TN

and flew his first of 22 combat missions in the Battle of the Bulge with the 491st Bomb Group. He believed in and practiced a tight formation flying. He had two emergency landings in Belguim, received three Air Medals, three European Campaign Stars and a Unit Citation. Flew the 491st's oldest B-24 (113 missions) back to the States in May 1945 as a first lieutenant.

As a Pratt graduate industrial designer, he has had design work exhibited in the Museum of Modern Art. He also worked as liason engineer on the F84F and the Thunderbird team aircraft and was associated with the firm that designed the interior of the first jet passenger plane, the 707.

He retired from Addressograph-Multigraph after 27 years in industrial design management positions, working on various types of business machines.

Married Margaret Smolen on Aug. 12, 1950. They have three daughters and five grandchildren.

DALE R. VAN BLAIR,
was born on June 17, 1921 in Quincy, IL. He enlisted into the USAAF in November 1942. A graduate of Armorers School in Buckley Field, CO and Harlingen Aerial Gunnery School in Texas.

Assigned as a tail gunner to B-24 crew, then sent to England with the 448th Bomb Group in December 1943. He flew 13 missions with the 448th Bomb Group before the crew transferred to the 389th to fly as a lead crew on the Pathfinder B-24. On his fifth PFF mission leading the 466th to Berlin on April 29, 1944, they ditched in North Sea because of flak and fighter damage. Was grounded because of injuries. He was discharged in October 1945.

Blair received his AB degree from Quincy College in 1949. He received his MA degree from Drake University in 1956. He was a media specialist at the Southern Illinois University in Edwardsville, IL in 1976. He taught High School English until 1965, then served as an English Department chairman at BTHS West, Belleville, IL until his retirement in 1982.

Married Mary E. Stickler in 1949. They have two daughters, Debbie and Karen, and one granddaughter Elizabeth.

JOHN VAN BOGELEN,
was born on March 16, 1923 in Grand Haven, MI. He enlisted into the USAAF on Nov. 24, 1942. Stationed at Tibenham, England with the 8th Air Force, 445th Bomb Group, 703rd Bomb Sqdn. He flew 30 combat missions as a radio operator over Germany, France and Belgium.

His memorable experience was being assigned to a "great crew" #76. He received the Air Medal, Distinguished Flying Cross, WWII Victory Medal, European Campaign and others. Van Bogelen was discharged on Oct. 24, 1945 with the rank of technical sergeant.

Married Esther Grubham in 1947. They have a son Douglas and an adopted daughter Carole. He practiced public accounting in Santa Monica, CA for 40 years, until retiring in 1989.

LEON ROBERT VANCE JR.,
was born on Aug. 11, 1916 in Enid, OK. Attended University of Oklahoma for two years before entering Military Academy, West Point. Was commissioned as second lieutenant in infantry June 1939. Was accepted for pilot training in the summer of 1940. On graduation, he served first as a flying instructor and then as a Squadron Commander.

In December 1942 was appointed director of flying at Basic Flying School, Strother Field, KS. In November 1943 was appointed deputy commander with the 489th Bomb Group at Wendover, UT. Helped form group and went to UK with it April 1944. Action for which award was made occurred while Lt. Col. Vance was on his second mission and acting as group leader in B-24H, 42-94830.

After a period in hospital, Lt. Col. Vance was to be returned to the USA for further treatment. The C-54, 42-

107470, in which he was travelling disappeared on the flight between Iceland and Newfoundland. Besides the Medal of Honor, he received the Silver Star, Air Medal, Purple Heart, WWII Victory Medal, American Defense Service Medal, American Campaign Medal, EAME Campaign Medal with one Bronze Service Star and Aviation Badge.

He was a lieutenant colonel upon his death on July 26, 1944. He is survived by his wife Georgette Drury Brown and his daughter Sharon Drury Vance (Kierman) for whom he named his first plane *The Sharon-D*.

WILLIAM L. VANCE JR. (CHUB), was born on Sept. 12, 1920 in Asheville, NC. He was the only son of William and Etta Vance. He entered the service in July 1943 and trained at Gulfport, Tyndall Field, Westover Field and Charleston before going overseas in September 1944 with the 8th Air Force to Tibenham, England. Was with the 445th Bomb Group, 701st Bomb Squadron and was a tail gunner on a B-24 Liberator.

Was a graduate of Lee H. Edwards High School and the Nashville Aircraft College and was well-known in his hometown for amateur boxing, having received the Western North Carolina Golden Gloves Award in 1942. He always had a guitar and enjoyed pickin' and singing with several local buddies.

He and Vera Tweed were married in the Fall of 1941. They had one daughter who was 18 months old when he was killed. His plane was shot down on a bombing mission to Misburg, near Hanover, Germany on Nov. 26, 1944. Heavy aircraft action took place in the vicinity of the target and his plane was attacked by two fighter planes. Although two parachutes were reportedly seen emerging from the plane, none of the crew ever appeared on POW lists and all were presumed dead.

He was awarded the Air Medal with one Oak Leaf Cluster and the Purple Heart, posthumously. His remains were returned to Asheville for burial in June 1949. *Submitted by his daughter Judy Vance Garren.*

ARTHUR H. VANDERBEEK, was born on April 16, 1923 in Gloversville, NY. He entered the USAAC on Jan. 21, 1943 after attending one and a half years at Clarkson College of Technology in Potsdam, NY.

After basic training, he went through Gunnery School at Fort Myers, FL; navigation training at Selman Field, LA; graduated as a second lieutenant; and assigned to a crew at Langley Field, MD.

He flew the northern route via Greenland and Iceland to England. The crew was assigned to the 458th Bomb Group at Horsham St. Faith, England. Completed 35 missions and a number of gas runs in support of Gen. Patton. Returned to the States in May 1945 as a first lieutenant and was discharged.

Returned to Clarkson College of Technology and graduated as a mechanical engineer in June 1949. He entered the U.S. Customs Service in April 1950 as a customs appraiser and was a treasury representative in Montreal, Canada and a criminal investigator in Detroit, MI. He worked as a chief appraiser in northern New York until his retirement in 1985. He now deals part-time in antiques.

Married Geraldine J. Norman on Oct. 19, 1946. They have three sons, three daughters and five grandchildren.

JAMES VAN GINKEL, was born on Feb. 27, 1923 in Prairie City, IA. He enlisted into the USAAC in August 1942, but was not called to active duty until January 1943. Went through San Antonio Aviation Cadet Center (SAACC) and

several flight schools in Texas and received his wings and his commission with Class 44-B in Lubbock, TX.

Was a flight instructor for a short time at Waco Army Air Field in Texas and then sent to England as a co-pilot on a B-24 with Paul Dickerman's crew and assigned to the 466th Bomb Group, located at Attlebridge. Paul Dickerman was killed in a mid-air collision over England on Sept. 16, 1944 after only two missions. Ginkel flew the remaining 35 missions as pilot, completing his tour on March 22, 1945.

Returned to the States and was assigned to the 6th Ferry Group at Long Beach, CA until his discharge in December 1945 with the rank of first lieutenant.

He and Marvel Crumpacker were married in 1953. They have three children: James, Jane and John. His work included special agent with the FBI and law practice in Atlantic, IA.

HARRY M. VASCONCELLOS, was born on Nov. 15, 1917 in Des Moines, IA. He enlisted in the Army Medical Corps - Air Force on Thanksgiving Day in 1940. Assigned to the 392nd Bomb Group in European Theater.

His memorable experience was being a replacement for the 8th Air Force in Wendling, England. When he asked how many missions he would have to fly, the response was "35, don't worry, you'll never make it."

He completed 35 missions and was discharged in February 1946 with the rank of captain.

Married Edythe Anderson on Aug. 12, 1942. They have two sons and three grandchildren. He is retired.

CARLOS VASQUEZ, was born on July 24, 1922 in Edinburg, TX. He joined the USAAC on July 7, 1942. He completed glider pilot training and entered Pilot School in August 1943: primary at Mira Loma Flight Academy in Oxnard, CA; basic at Lemoore AAF, CA; advanced at LaJunta AAF, CO on B-25s. Was commissioned on Jan. 7, 1944.

Had B-24 training at Kirtland Field, Albuquerque, NM and completed his B-24 combat training at Tonopah AAF, NV. He was assigned to the 330th Bomb Sqdn. (H), 93rd Bomb Group (H) in Hardwick, England in July 1944 as an aircraft commander. Was among the first crews to transport food and supplies to France in support of General Patton's forces on Sept. 3 & 4, 1944.

Participated in Operation Market Garden on Sept. 18, 1944. He completed 35 combat missions on Jan. 31, 1945.

He was awarded the Distinguished Flying Cross, Air Medal with five Oak Leaf Clusters, four Battle Campaign Stars and other medals. He had Senior and Command Pilot ratings.

Remained in the military as a pilot, serving in several positions including instructor and test pilot, engineering officer, supply officer (squadron, depot and command level). He qualified in over 48 military aircraft. Retired June 1, 1963 where he served as assistant chief, Equipment Division for MATS (MAC).

He attended various colleges and universities; his major was in economics and business administration; his minors were in real estate and Spanish. He was awarded four national honor academic awards.

Hobbies include: astronomy, gemology and lapidary. He is a professional securities and real estate investor and enjoys world travel.

Married Nadine M. Murphy on Dec. 24, 1943; they have one daughter, Carla Nadine.

EMUEL E. VASSEY JR., was born on April 5, 1921 in Pacolet Mills, SC. He enlisted in the USAAC on Jan. 23, 1941 in Brevard, NC. Had basic training at Maxwell; Aerial and Engineer School in Chanute.

He was assigned as a crew chief in 1942 at Tyndall Field on O-46s, AT-6s, AT-18s, M-37s (English version of a B-34); Buckingham Field, he crewed B-34s and met his wife-to-be from Winter Harbor, ME.

In 1943 in Mt. Home, ID, he joined B-24 combat crew training as a flight engineer/top turret gunner, Wendover Field then advanced flight training. In 1944 he arrived at Wendling Field, England with the 392nd Bomb Group, 578th Bomb Sqdn. for special combat training. His first mission was on April 12th and his last two missions (#31 & #32) were over St. Lo.

He returned to the States and after a break in service from 1945-49, he re-enlisted into the USAF maintenance, TAC F-5s, flight engineer, SAC B-29s, B-50s, B-36s, KC-97s, PACAF RB-29s, KB-50s, MATS/MAC C-130s, C-141s and C-5s. He retired as a SMSGT after 29 years of service, including Korea, Vietnam and other brush fires.

Married Elinor Blance on September 23, 1944. They have four children, 13 grandchildren and four great grandchildren.

WILLARD E. VAUGHN, was born on Nov. 3, 1922 in New York City, NY. He enlisted in the USAAC on Feb. 19, 1942 in New York City, NY at the age of 19. Eventually went to San Antonio Aviation Cadet Center. He attended Preflight School at Ellington Field in Houston, TX.

Graduated from Bombardier School at Childress AAF in Texas in the Class of 43-7 on May 13, 1943. Was one of the original members of the 445th Bomb Group, 701st Sqdn. based at Sioux City Air Base. The Group flew B-24 Liberators over the "Southern Route" to England in November 1943 and was based at Tibenham. His crew completed 30 missions and volunteered for a second tour of duty. He left Liverpool, England on D-day morning of June 6, 1944 and returned to Tibenham, England in August after spending time with family in the States. He did not fly any more missions because of combat fatigue.

After returning to the States the second time, he was an instructor at several air bases and his last assignment was as bombsite maintenance and Autopilot officer at Tonopah Army Air Base in Tonopah, NV. He was discharged on Nov. 23, 1945 with the rank of first lieutenant.

He received the Distinguished Flying Cross, Air Medal with three Oak Leaf Clusters, Distinguished Unit Citation, the Group was awarded the French Croix de Guerre with Palm for "helping to liberate French Territory."

He is married and they have two daughters, three grandchildren and two great-grandchildren. He is semi-retired.

MAX F. VEITCH, was born on Sept. 23, 1924 in Toledo, OH. He enlisted into the USAAC on Nov. 30, 1942. He was a radio operator gunner with the 8th Air Force. He flew a B-24 out of the 44th Bomb Group to Shipdham, England.

Completed 17 missions and was shot down on the 18th mission. He parachuted over Germany and was taken POW. Eight of his crew were killed in action.

Received the Air Medal with two Oak Leaf Clusters and the Purple Heart. He was discharged on Oct. 29, 1945 with the rank of technical sergeant.

He is married and has five children. He is retired and resides in Toledo, OH.

ROBERT H. VENECK, was born on Nov. 4, 1923 in Omaha, NE. He enlisted into the USAAF on June 19, 1942, bombsight and auto pilot mechanic. Stationed at Lowry Field, CO; Patterson Field, OH; Grenier Field, NH. Assigned to 93rd Bomb Group 330th Sqdn., Hardwick, England.

His memorable experience was flight checking auto pilots; seeing the D-day air armada; serving 28 months overseas with the 8th Air Force; flying over Germany after surrender and seeing the total destruction of the cities and etc.; flying to the States on May 22, 1945 in a B-24H Liberator; landing at Bradley Field, Windsor Locks, CT.

Received the Distinguished Unit Badge, Good Conduct Medal, and 11 Campaign Battle Stars. He was discharged on Sept. 16, 1945 with the rank of staff sergeant.

Married and has five children and many grandchildren. Retired since 1990.

In his leisure time he likes to fly his Beech Sport for fun and attends conventions. He visited London and Hardwick in May 1990.

ALBERT C. VENIER, was born on May 15, 1921 in Ogdensburg, NY and joined the USAAC at Clarkson College on Oct. 7, 1942. Following basic training in Atlantic City, he went to Santa Ana Preflight School and finally to Kirtland Field Bombardier School, graduating as a flight officer in the Class of 44-8.

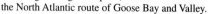

Phase training was at Casper. Overseas destination was the 392nd Bomb Group, 577th Sqdn. at Wendling arriving via Topeka, KS and the North Atlantic route of Goose Bay and Valley.

Most memorable mission was the Wesel resupply in March 1945. He also has a very graphic recall of standing on the runway of Lille, France watching "The Mighty Eighth" Air Armada pass over climbing to altitude. He completed 12 missions by V-E Day and was discharged in October 1945. He returned to Clarkson graduating in October 1947.

After 24 years of various corporate management positions in New York City and New Jersey, he returned to northern New York and the building supply business in Massena.

In 1974 he completed 32 years in the USAFR with the rank of lieutenant colonel.

MERLIN H. VERBURG (MERLE), was born on Aug. 21, 1920 in Grand Rapids, MI. Graduated from Grand Rapids High School and attended Michigan State University before being called to serve his country at the outset of WWII. Volunteered to join the USAF and was inducted into the service at Santa Ana, CA AFB on March 2, 1942.

Served overseas for 24 months with the 8th Air Force, 2nd Air Div., 389th Bomb Group. Was a bombardier on B-24s and completed 11 combat missions, a total of 105 combat hours, 500 military flying hours while he was stationed in England and Africa.

On Nov. 26, 1943 while returning from low level raids over Ploesti oil fields in Bremen, Germany, his plane was shot down and he was forced to bail out. He was fortunate to be seen by the Dutch underground; they helped him to avoid capture for five weeks. Then on Jan. 4, 1944 was interned by the Germans at Stalag Luft I and liberated by the Russians about May 1, 1945. He was returned to allied control and processed at camp "Lucky Strike" outside Paris.

Was discharged from the service shortly after the war was over; however, stayed in the Reserves and was retired as a lieutenant colonel on Aug. 21, 1988. His life was forever changed by his imprisonment, but he avoided talking about his wartime experiences.

Verburg was founder and president of Merlex Stucco, Inc. of Orange, CA in 1963. His company has been recognized for its quality and service in the building industry for 30 years.

He was diagnosed with (ALS) Lou Gherigs disease January 1992. He fought this disease with courage and denial. He never stopped fighting and never quit work. His last day at work was only five days before his passing on July 23, 1993. A man who loved family, his manufacturing business, golf and the outdoors. He was the quinticential volunteer for charitable causes. Merle gave 100% of himself to life. He is survived by his wife, Mary Verburg.

JOHN VERCLER, was born on April 15, 1921 in Chenoa, IL. He enlisted into the USAAF on July 15, 1942. He was a medic. stationed at Gowen Field, ID; Miama Beach, FL; Camp Sheridan, IL; Camp Barkley, TX; Kelly Field, TX; Keesler Field, MS; Camp Robinson, AR; Stevens Hotel, Chicago, IL; Scott Air Base, IL; Harlingen Field, TX.

Overseas to Old Buckingham, England. He participated in the American Theater and European Theater.

Assigned to 453rd Bomb Group, 733 Sqdn., Joe Lutes Crew with Max Stout as co-pilot. First mission Aug. 27, 1944 and 30th and last mission Feb. 24, 1945. On Jan. 1, 1945, they hit the ground on take off bending outer four feet of left wing up 45,° but still finished mission to Remagan Bridge with bent wing. There were only seven planes in their group that day.

Vercler received the Air Medal with five Oak Leaf Clusters, the American Theater Ribbon, European Theater Ribbon, WWII Victory Medal and the Good Conduct Medal. He was discharged on May 26, 1945 with the rank of staff sergeant.

He and his wife, Josephine, have five children. He is retired and enjoys farming and cattle feeding.

Five members, along with four wives, attended the Oct. 27-28, 1993 reunion at Minden, NE.

JOHN F. VERDESCHI, was born on Jan. 2, 1924 in New York City, NY. He applied for enlistment into the USAAF in November 1942. Was advised that flying status enlistments were closed and advised to request induction to Army and then requested transfer to Air Force. Was then assigned to combat engineers at Camp Swift, TX.

Was transferred to Air force at San Antonio Aviation Cadet Center. Training from SAACC to primary at Ellington Field, Houston to Harlingen, TX, advanced, Childress, TX. Graduated Class of 44-2. Transition at Westover Field, MA.

Assigned to B-24s which they flew to England. Assigned to the 446th Bomb Sqdn., 704thth, Base 125 Bungay. He completed 35 missions and then returned to the States November 1944. Had various assignments until his discharge in September 1945.

His memorable experiences: the first flak leave in London and talking to the British citizens living in the underground after having been bombed out of their homes. Their acceptance, determination and lack of complaint left an indelible impression. - Also watching a 500 pound bomb come loose on take-off from plane in front of them and skipping down the runway.

He was awarded the Air Medal with three Oak Leaf Clusters and the Distinguished Flying Cross.Was discharged in September 1945 with the rank of first lieutenant.

Married Esther Kelly on June 18, 1945. They have four children and five grandchildren. He is retired from sales management.

FRANK L. VERMEIREN, entered the service on March 27, 1941. His first assignment was with the 1st Cavalry, Fort Bliss, TX. He entered pilot training in 1942, graduated in July 1943. He acquired the grade of first lieutenant in 1944.

He attended primary, basic and advanced pilot training; B-17 transition course; officer administration course; and supply officer course. During WWII, he served in the European Theater of Operations; subsequent to WWII, he had served overseas tour in England, Iceland and Japan. Particapted in the Normandy, Northern France and Europe Air Offensive Campaigns.

Completed 30 missions with the 458th Bomb Group and the 466th Bomb Group. He received the Distinguished Flying Cross, Air Medal with three Oak Leaf Clusters, Good Conduct Medal with five Bronze Loops, Army of Occupation Medal, EAME Medal, WWII Victory Medal, American Defense Service Medal, National Defense Service Medal and the AF Longevity Service Award with four Bronze Oak Leaf Clusters. He was discharged on May 31, 1963 with the rank of first lieutenant.

After retiring from the USAF, he took a position with the Aeronautical Chart and Information Center in St. Louis, MO. Retired after 17 and a half years from the Defense Mapping Agency Aerospace Center on Jan. 8, 1982.

He and his wife were married on Nov. 11, 1948, and they have three children and four grandchildren. They enjoy traveling and camping.

WILLIAM F. VICROY, was born on Nov. 28, 1925 in Dayton, OH. He enlisted into the USAAC as an aviation cadet on Nov. 15, 1943. He was inducted at Fort Benjamin Harris, IN and was sent to Keesler Field, MS for basic training; Harlingen, TX for Gunnery School; and B-24 training at Boise, ID.

Served as a tail gunner with the 453rd Bomb Group and the 466th Bomb Group while stationed in Attlebridge and Old Buckingham in England.

He flew 16 missions and was discharged on Feb. 2, 1946 with the rank of sergeant. He and his wife, Dorothy, were married on March 13, 1950. He is the father of four children and has eight grandchildren. He is retired now and taking life easy.

ROBERT W. VINCENT, was born on July 9, 1920 in Creek Village, OK. He graduated from Oklahoma A&M in 1941. He entered active duty in September 1941 in the infantry as a second lieutenant. He joined the USAAC in 1943. Received his wings in the Class of 43-K. Checked out PT-17, BT-13, AT-17, AT-6, C-47, B-25, C-54 and L-1. He trained in B-24 at Muroc. Flew 35 combat missions, five "Truckin" and two weather missions with the 458th Bomb Group. Was assigned to the Azon Project (radio controlled bombs). The Azon aircraft was named *A Dog's Life*.

Was involved in an incident that several military historians described as unparalleled in WWII. During a mission to the Metz, he discovered the group was lining up on a friendly target. He advised the group leader but was rebuffed. He broke formation and led his element, and another element followed, bombing the correct target. Historians named the action, "Vincent's Rebellion."

Was threatened with a court-martial, vindicated by General Patton and was promoted. He received the Distinguished Flying Cross, Soldiers Medal, Air Medal with four Oak Leaf Clusters, EAME Medal with six Campaign Bronze Service Stars and other service medals.

His interesting assignments: project officer for infrared satelite, U-2 support and NATO. Overseas in England, Saudi Arabia, Japan, Turkey and Germany. Career officer, he retired in 1971. His retirement activities are college student, doctoral candidate ABD, OSU. He is a National Commander for Scabbard and Blade. Received the DOD Distinguished Service Award in 1986. Designated honorary B.G. He retired with the rank of colonel.

Presently serves on several foundation boards. He is married to his hometown sweetheart, Pattie Jean West, they were married in 1942. They celebrated their 50th last year with their five children and five grandchildren. He is a member of the Order of Dadelions, AF Historical Foundation, MOWW, 4th Cavalry SVR, TROA, DAV, Sons of Union Veterans (GAR). He is on the board of directors of Scabbard and Blade Corporation.

WILLIAM HARVEY VINEY, was born on Nov. 1, 1919 in Bryn Mawr, PA. He graduated from Upper Darby High School, PA in 1937. Enlisted into the USAAC on Nov. 1, 1940. Basic training, weather observer training and duty at Langley Field, VA through April 9, 1942.

Was appointed an aviation cadet and transferred to Santa Ana, CA for preflight evaluation and training program. Graduated from Victorville AAF, CA as a second lieutenant bombardier on Jan. 23, 1943. He was assigned to Selman Field, LA Navigational School, graduating as a bombardier/ navigator on May 22, 1943.

Assigned as navigator on Lt. Gregory Perron's B-24

crew for combat phase training at Biggs Field, El Paso, TX and Herington Air Field, KS, June through August 1943. He and his crew departed from Herington on Sept. 2, 1943 on a new B-24. Flew via Bangor, ME; Iceland; Prestwick, Scotland to the 567th Bomb Sqdn., 389th Bomb Group; located at Hethel, England arriving on Oct. 6, 1943.

From November 1943 through February 1944, he flew 10 missions as a navigator on his original crew with the 567th Bomb Sqdn. on B-24s *Touch of Texas* and *Fighting Sam* with Greg Perron and Sam Blessing as pilots. (Bombardier Lt. Gwimond and Navigator Lt. Viney were together since El Paso, TX.) They were transferred to William H. Wambold's lead crew of the 566th Bomb Sqdn. on Feb. 18, 1944. They flew together as a deputy and lead crew team for squadron, section and 389th Bomb Group lead missions on Wambold's B-24J *Princess Konocti* plane for 16 combat missions through May 19, 1944.

One of Viney's saddest memories was the loss of Captain Everal A Gwimond, Bombardier, flying his 30th and final combat tour mission with Lt. Marcus Vincent Courtney on June 6, 1944, "D-day in Europe." Gwimond was assigned as a replacement bombardier on Courtney's crew, which was the 389th Bomb Group deputy lead B-24 for the first mission of the day. Courtney's plane crashed about one half hour after take-off. The cause was not known. The crew was listed as killed in action. Viney and Gwimond were like two brothers and worked closely together as a team on the ground and in flying. Both made first lieutenant and captain on same dates. Viney flew four other missions with the Vaughan, Colt and Berger crews for his total of 30 combat tour missions, finishing on July 2, 1944. He was assigned to 2nd Combat Wing HQ as acting wing navigator until his departure from England. He arrived back in the States on Nov. 6, 1944.

His memorable experiences during his combat tour were: the quality and courage of air and ground crew members; the close-knit kinship of these members; the friendliness of the English people; meeting and visiting his great aunt and cousins living near London while on pass or leave; the horror of war and losing known crew members shot down; and having officer's like Ted Timberlake, Jimmy Stewart, Milton Arnold, Robert Miller, Tom Conroy, Jack Dieterle and Bob Schwellinger flying with his crew as "Mission Commanders" on some of the roughest missions over Europe.

He was released from active duty to a reserve unit in September 1945. He attended San Jose State College in California through December 1948. He was recalled to active duty for Weather Officer School at Chanute AFB, IL graduating in November 1949. His active duty tours were in Japan from 1950 to 1951; Korea from 1951 to 1952; U.S. from 1952 to 1957 (graduated from University of California at Berkley with a BA degree during this period); Germany from 1957 to 1958 and back to the States from 1958 to 1959.

His primary duties were: weather forecasting; weather detachment commander; staff weather briefing officer and advisor and flying. He maintained his flying status in various Air Force planes including the "Turbo-prop Jets" and he became a senior navigator in 1956.

He and Mary Lenora Hensley of Houston, TX were married on Nov. 2, 1942 in Victorville Base Chapel. They have two sons, two daughters and five grandchildren. He retired as a major on permanent physical disability status in September 1959. He and Mary celebrated 50 years of marriage in November 1992. He "thanks God" that he was not wounded in WWII or the Korean War.

WILLIAM H. VINTON, was born on May 28, 1917 in Chicago, IL. He had four years of High School with ROTC training, four year enlistment in the Illinois National Guard. He was an employed Railroad Conductor and was drafted into the service on Aug. 30, 1943.

After basic training and Army Air Force cadet training, he was one of 36,000 re-assigned for convenience of the Government to aerial gunnery training. He graduated in flexible and turret gunnery and was assigned to a B-24 bomber crew for overseas training. His crew was assigned to the 2nd Air Division, 8th Air Force, 445th Bomb Group at Tibenham Air Field in England.

He completed 34 missions as top turret and waist gunner from Dec. 5, 1944 to April 25, 1945 with the same crew members, all of them returning safely to the States together at the end of European hostilities. After furlough was assigned armor gunnery training.

End of the Pacific hostilities, brought his discharge on Sept. 18, 1945 with the rank of staff sergeant. He received Cadet Wings, Gunner Wings, Air Medal with four Oak Leaf Clusters, ETO with three stars, American Campaign Medal, Presidential Unit Citation Medal, Good Conduct Medal and the WWII Victory Medal.

Returned to civilian employment as a railroad conductor, completed 39 and a half years in the railroad industry, retiring in 1980. Married Florence Dragert on March 19, 1949; they have two children, Vicki and William, and five grandchildren.

WILLIAM VISLOCKY, was born on Feb. 5, 1917 in Pittsburgh, PA. He enlisted into the service on Jan. 19, 1942 at Maxwell Field, AL. Stationed at Selma Field, LA; RTU in Tucson, AZ; Ocala, FL; and Pocatello, ID.

He was sent overseas with the 389th Bomb Group. Completed 25 missions by April 1944. Then to Combat Staff Int. HQ, 2nd Air Div. Advanced nav. training, Ellington Field, TX. Flew missions over France, Germany, Austria and Italy. Crash landed at H.B. on return from mission. Participated in the battles of Normandy, Northern France, Germany, Air Offensive Europe, Naples, Foggia, Central Europe and Ardennes.

Received the EAME Medal, American Campaign Medal, Distinguished Flying Cross Medal, Air Medal with three Oak Leaf Clusters and the Distinguished Unit Citation. Was discharged in January 1946 with the rank of captain. Retired from the Reserve as a lieutenant colonel in February 1971.

He and wife Mary have son Mark and daughter Debra. They have three grandchildren: Mark Jr., Nicholas and William. He is a semi-retired travel agent.

CURT M. VOGEL, was born on Oct. 19, 1916 in Altenburg, MO. He graduated from the University of Missouri Law School in June 1941. He enlisted as a cadet in the USAAC in April 1942. He graduated as a pilot at Stockton, CA in May 1943.

He was a pilot of a B-24 with the original 458th Bomb Group, 755th Sqdn. Crew 74 named the plane *Rough Riders*. He left Tonopah, NV in January 1944 and flew the southern route to Horsham St. Faith, Norwich, England. He completed a tour of 30 missions by June 5, 1944.

He received the Air Medal with three Oak Leaf Clusters and the Distinguished Flying Cross. Practiced law in Perryville, MO until he was recalled into the Korean War. Served in 1951 in Korea as an assistant Judge Advocate in the 5th Air Force. Resigned from the Reserves with the rank of captain in 1953.

Returned to Perryville, MO to practice law, including eight years as a prosecuting attorney and about 12 years as an associate circuit judge. He retired at the age of 70.

Married Billie Jean Bumgarner on Feb. 7, 1941. They have five children and seven grandchildren. All three sons have served a tour in the military and one of them in combat in Vietnam.

LEONARD PAUL VOGT, was born on Aug. 25, 1921 in Baltimore, MD. He attended Strayers Business College for certification in accounting. Worked for Crosse and Blackwell in Baltimore before he enlisted in the service.

He began basic training at Sheppard Field, TX. His extensive training took him to airfields in California, Alabama, Florida, Mississippi and Tennessee. He became a B-24 pilot and he flew to Rackheath, England, where he became attached to the 467th Bomb Group (H), 790th Bomb Sqdn. in May 1944.

He completed 32 missions and was awarded the Air Medal with three Oak Leaf Clusters and the Distinguished Flying Cross.

Returned to the States and assigned as a flight instructor until June 1945. He returned to active duty at the beginning of the Korean War acting as a co-pilot.

On his last mission he was lost with all the crew members over the sea of Japan on March 28, 1951. He was promoted posthumously to captain and awarded the Air Medal with four Oak Leaf Clusters.

He was married to Verda Bewerman on Jan. 31, 1943. They had two sons, Paul Angelo and Mark Douglas.

WILLIAM J. VOIGHT, was born on Jan. 21, 1921 in Santa Rosa, CA. When the war was declared in December 1941, he started work at Mare Island Navel Ammo. Depot loading 5" AA shells.

He became an ordinance first class in charge of filling house with 80 people. He had to quit his job in order to enlist in the USAAC on Nov. 11, 1943. He went into pilot training, but was transferred into gunnery with 3600 other trainees. He started with MOS 521 basic, then to 612 gunner and then to 748 aerial engineer gunner. He took basic at Buckley Field, CO; Gunnery School at Yuma, AZ; and crew training at Pueblo, CO.

Went overseas with Lt. J.E. Baier's crew in November 1944. They became part of the 453rd Bomb Group, 735th Sqdn. He flew 18 bomb missions, six chaff missions. In April 1945, their crew was transferred to the 467th Bomb Group in Norwich. All crews with less than 15 missions were sent stateside to be re-assigned to the Pacific. The only flying they did was with the 467th, a few trolley missions and then flew the bomb group home.

All missions were memorable in as much as not one crew member got the Purple Heart. The war in the Pacific ended and he was discharged at an AAF separation base in San Bernardino, CA on Oct. 17, 1945 with the rank of staff sergeant. He received the Air Medal with three Oak Leaf Clusters, Good Conduct Medal and several others.

He married his high school sweetheart, Beatrice V. Cleaveland on Feb. 1, 1941. They have three sons, one daughter, 11 grandchildren and seven great-grandchildren.

He worked as a service manager for various auto dealerships and also owned his own repair shop. From 1978 to 1988, he worked as a millwright for a Metal Fab Co. in Portland, OR. He is retired and enjoys hunting, fishing and life.

ROBERT R. VOLKMAN SR., was born on March 23, 1924 in Wilmington, DE. He was inducted into the USAAC on Jan. 20, 1943 as a MOS 1055, U.S. 8th Air Force, as a cadet, Class 44-A and a Mustang pilot.

Took flight training in Southeast and flew in England and Belgium, with the 361st Fighter Group, 376th Fighter Sqdn. Sent to St. Lo, Arnhem/Nigmegan, Kassel, Sept. 27, 1943. Completed 61 missions. Memorable experience was surviving crash landing in England when his P-51 threw a rod.

Volkman received seven Air Medals, five Campaign Medals, Polish Cross and American Victory. He was discharged on Aug. 17, 1945, charter pilot in Delaware Air Guard, captain and flight leader.

Married Jane Coucill on Sept. 7, 1946; they have two sons, one daughter and four grandchildren. He was a graduate mechanic engineer for 30 years in the Dupont Engineer Dept. He is retired and enjoys travel. Has a cottage in Cape May, NJ. Enjoys attending the 8th Air Force and the 361st Fighter Group re-unions.

ARLIE H. VON TERSCH, was born on Sept. 16, 1920 in Cottonwood, ID. He enlisted in the USAAF on July 28, 1942. Assigned to the 2nd Air Div., 8th Air Force, 715 Sqdn., 448th Bomb Group as right waist armorer gunner on B-24.

They flew out of Seething, England and on their 20th mission in August 1944, their plane was hit by flak. He was captured by Germans, traveled some of the way in a box car to Stalag Luft IV near the Baltic Sea. In February 1945 the camp was moved away from Russians, walking on shoe leather express for 89 days, nearly 700 kilometers. Was liberated in May 1945 and weighed about 90 pounds.

Tersch was awarded the Air Medal with three Oak Leaf Clusters, three Battle Stars, POW Medal and the American Theater Service Medal. Was discharged on Oct. 23, 1945 with the rank of staff sergeant.

He retired in 1982 from the Burlington Railroad in Spokane, WA.

WILLIAM V. VOORHEES, was born on April 4, 1919 in Freehold, NJ. Entered the Armed Services via the draft in June 1941. He served in the Infantry at Camp Wheeler, Macon, GA and Ft. Bragg, Fayetteville, NC.

After Pearl Harbor, he was transferred to the USAAC cadet training in Santa Ana, CA and completed navigation

training at Mather Field, Sacramento, CA. Received his Navigators Wings and Commission on July 10, 1943.

Was assigned to the 712th Sqdn., 448th Bomb Group at Wendover Field in Utah. Moved to the Sioux City AAF Base in September 1943. Left for England in November 1943 via South America and Africa and arrived at Seething in Norfolk in December 1943.

Flew 30 missions as navigator completing his tour on May 31, 1944. He was awarded the Distinguished Flying Cross and four Air Medals. Returned to the States and was stationed at Boca Raton AAB in Florida for Radar Navigation Training.

While there, he married his wife Ruth. Was transferred to Victorville AAB, CA as an instructor and then to Williams AAF Base in Chandler, AZ. Was discharged in October 1945 with the rank of first lieutenant. Received the Distinguished Flying Cross and four Air Medals.

He has three children and two grandchildren. Worked for 34 years in marketing and management for NCR Corp.

ED WAGNER, was born in Arkansas City, KS. Enlisted in service on Aug. 1, 1941.

He served with the 434th Inf., 28th Div., as a rifleman. Military locations included Amtigua, BWI with 93rd Bomb Group, 409th Sqdn., 8th Air Force. Flew 32 missions over France and Germany

Received the Distinguished Flying Cross and Air Medal with four Oak Leaf Clusters. Discharged Sept. 3, 1945 with rank of staff sergeant. Retired and spends his time loafing.

JAMES M. WAGNER, was born in Cambridge, MA and raised in Arlington, MA. Joined the USAAC in February 1943. Received basic training in Florida; Armament School at Lowry Field, CO; Aerial Gunnery School at Harlingen, TX; bomber crew training at Casper, WY.

Wagner flew with a B-24 bomber crew to England. Assigned to the 445th Bomb Group, 701st Sqdn. Flew 23 missions over France and Germany. Crashed on the shores of England on second mission, losing their bombardier, waist gunner and radio man. On his 23rd mission to Munich, Germany, they were hit over the target and crashed in Belgium. All of the crew were captured except Wagner. He was able to escape and lived with the Belgium Underground Resistance.

He was given Belgium passports and civilian clothes. All personal and military identification was taken away. He was later sold to the German Gestapo by a double agent and was taken prisoner as a spy. He was in civilian clothes with no military identification and Belgium passport.

Wagner was put in a political prison. The cell was about eight feet by 10 feet. His cell mates were a German SS trooper, a German marine and a Belgium man who had fought for the Germans. They were all sentenced to death. All the people who were prisoners were one day taken and loaded into freight cars to be taken to Germany. With the threat that the Germans were going to shoot all prisoners, Wagner made his escape and returned to Brussels.

After the English liberated the city, he returned to England and to the USA. He was discharged with rank of technical sergeant.

He married his lovely wife, Rita. They have a wonderful son and daughter, James and Maureen.

W. ROBERT WAGNER, was born on Feb. 2, 1921 in Alma, MI, a son of Winton and Mildred (Smith) Wagner. Enlisted in the Air Force and was a bombardier with the 466th Bomb Group, serving during World War II as a first lieutenant with the B-24 Sqdn. of the 8th Air Force. Discharged in 1945 with rank of first lieutenant.

He married Mary O. Bongard on April 27, 1946. They

had a son, Scott; a daughter, Carol; and six grandsons. Wagner was a commercial artist for 33 years, retired in 1986. Was a member of the Parchment United Methodist Church and the Trout Unlimited Club of Kalamazoo.

Wagner died on July 2, 1993 at the age of 72 at his home in Kalamazoo, MI.

JAMES T. WAKLEY, was born on Feb. 17, 1921 in Springfield, OH. He enlisted in the USAAC and served as a pilot, first lieutenant, 491st Bomb Group.

Military locations included North Pickenham, Metfield, England and Davis Monthan Field, Tucson, AZ. Participated in battles of D-Day, Paris, Munich, Kiev and Hamburg. His most memorable experience was crashing on his first mission to Paris. Also crashed on his 24th mission to Munich because they were out of gas.

Discharged in June 1945 with rank of first lieutenant. Received the Distinguished Flying Cross and Air Medal with five clusters.

He and wife Mary have a daughter Nadine and two sons, Gary and Martin. Wakley is chairman of Marmac Corporation in Parkersburg, WV.

LEONARD C. WALDO, was born on Nov. 27, 1922 in Detroit, MI. Enlisted in USAF on Oct. 21, 1942 as a cadet.

Trained as navigator at Selman Field, LA; operational training at Peterson Field, Colorado Springs, CO. ETO bases included Wendling and Shipdham. Served with the 14th Combat Wing, 392nd and 44th Heavy Bomb Groups. Flew 30 missions, 24 as lead navigator with six different crews.

Discharged from active duty on point system June 18, 1945. Received Distinguished Flying Cross with two clusters, Air Medal with four clusters, ETO Medal and five Battle Stars.

His education includes: Engineering at Lawrence Institute of Technology, Michigan; Industrial Relations at University of California, Los Angeles; and Economics at University of San Francisco.

Has worked as an electrical engineer for a telephone company, general engineering contractor (road building and land development), and as a management consultant.

He and his lovely wife Rosemarie have two sons and four grandchildren. They enjoy traveling worldwide, reading, classical music, hiking and gardening. They reside in San Mateo, CA.

CHARLES L. WALKER (CHUCK), was born on Aug. 6, 1918 in Anna, IL. Grew up in Boulder, CO and was a student at the University of Colorado when the war started. Volunteered for the Aviation Cadet Program in the spring of

1942. Went through Southwest Training Command and on to Liberal, KS for B-24 pilot training, then to Casper, WY for crew training and on to England in June 1944.

Flew 35 combat missions with the 700th Sqdn., 445th Bomb Group, 8th Air Force. His crew had the distinction of completing their tour by putting the 100th mission on the *Bunnie*, which was reported to be the first B-24 in the 8th Air Force to complete 100 missions. He stayed with the 445th in a non-combat capacity until May 1945.

Received a regular commission in the Air Force in 1947. Served in Korea from May 1951-1952 with the 67th Tactical Reconnaisance; Athens, Greece and Chateauroux, France with Logistics Command.

Retired in May 1967 with rank of lieutenant colonel. Awarded the Distinguished Flying Cross, Bronze Star, five Air Medals, three Commendation Medals and several other ribbons.

Married Maxine Burnett on March 1, 1946 and they have two children and one grandson.

Pursued several business interests before retiring to the golf course in 1984. He has been active in the 2nd Air Division Association for several years. Resides in Dallas TX.

ION S. WALKER, was born on Dec. 12, 1906 in Olivet, MI. Served in the Air Force, Administration, 467th Bomb Group, 2nd Air Div.

Military locations included Randolph Field, TX; Enid, OK; Spokane, WA; Mountain Home, ID; Wendover Field, UT and Norwich, England. Discharged on Jan. 1, 1967 with rank of colonel.

Married Eileen and they have one daughter Cheryl Walker. He is now retired.

JOHN H. WALKER, was born on Jan. 1, 1924 in Taylorsville, MS. Entered USAAC in February 1943 after attending Mississippi College for one and a half years. Received basic training at Keesler Field, MS; Air Force Technical School at Keesler Field; transferred to B-24 Factory School at consolidated plant in San Diego, CA; Gunnery School at Laredo, TX; crew assignment at Lincoln, NE; and on to Pueblo, CO for crew training.

Went overseas from Camp Kilmer, NJ to 8th Air Force assignment, 44th Bomb Group, 66th Bomb Sqdn. in Shipdham, England. Completed 25 missions.

Came back to the States for a 30-day furlough, then to Fort Myers, FL for B-29 training. The war ended before that training began, so was transferred to Turner Field, GA for discharge in October 1945 with rank of technical sergeant. Received Air Medal with four Oak Leaf Clusters, Good Conduct Medal, European Theatre of Operations and Sharp Shooter Medal.

Memorable experiences: first mission, lead ship got direct hit and he had to take over lead. Smoke bomb stuck in bomb bay but S/Sgt. Thompson remedied the situation by getting in the bomb bay and releasing it, great relief from smoke. Nose wheel gave away on landing after mission causing much excitement.

Married his high school sweetheart, Sara Ford, in June 1944. They had a son and a daughter, Chloe Giloberg and John H. Walker Jr., and six grandchildren. Sara died of cancer in 1980, and John remarried in 1987 to Carolyn.

Retired in 1986 after 41 years service with the Mississippi Department of Education as state director of Child Nutrition. Resides in Clinton, MS.

SANDERS B. WALKER JR., was born on Sept. 15, 1922 in Fulton County, GA. Graduated from Georgia Military College, Milledgeville, GA in 1942. Was inducted into the Army at Ft. McPherson, Atlanta, GA in December 1942. Was sent to Keesler Field, Biloxi, MS where he was a drill instructor in basic training. Went through Aircraft Mechanics School and was sent to Harlingen, TX for gunnery training. Shipped to Clovis, NM for flight crew training and then to Salt Lake City, UT where the crews were formed and then sent to Alamogordo, NM for overseas flight training in B-24s.

The crew went to Lincoln, NE where they picked up a new B-24J and flew it to England via the southern route. They were shot down on their third mission, captured and spent 13 and a half months in a German prison camp. He is a

survivor of the infamous "Heydekrug Death March." They belonged to the 445th Bomb Group, 702nd Sqdn. stationed at Tibenham, England. As far as Sanders knows, the whole crew survived the ordeal.

Discharged at San Antonio, TX in October 1945 with rank of technical sergeant. Received Air Crew Wings, Good Conduct Medal, Marksmanship Medal and AP Mechanic Medal.

He is married and has two sons. Walker is a farmer.

H. BEN WALSH, was born on Sept. 25, 1919 in Hampton, IA. Educated at Iowa State College and University of Maryland. Entered the military in November 1940, commissioned in September 1941. After B-17 training, assigned Davis-Monthan as cadre for 389th Bomb Group. Departed for overseas in June 1943.

While operating out of Libyan Desert he was shot down by fighters on July 19, 1943. Parachuted into the Mediterranean and was rescued by British near nightfall. He was hospitalized on Malta, rejoined the group and completed first combat tour at the end of 1943. Remained in United Kingdom for second combat tour. Assigned to 458th Bomb Group, 2nd Air Div. HQ and 14th Bomb Wing at Shipdham. Flew last combat mission to Wurzburg on March 22, 1945.

Following WWII he was an air attache to Sweden; NATO (Washington-Paris-Belgium); SAC; TAC HQ USAF. Retired as colonel in January 1970. Received numerous decorations including the Legion of Merit, two Distinguished Flying Crosses, four Air Medals, Purple Heart, Meritorious Service Medal, Croix de Guerre with Palm (French), and Knighthood of the Royal Order of the Sword (Sweden).

LEE E. WALTON, was born in Hastings, MI and lived most of his life in Jackson, MI. Enlisted in service in May 1943. Served with the 389th Bomb Group in Hethel, England. Flew 18 missions over France, Belgium and Germany. Memorable experience was when their aircraft was bombed six times. Only one of the crew was wounded (not serious).

Discharged in November 1945 with rank of first lieutenant. Received Air Medal with clusters and Presidential Unit Citation.

Married in 1945 and has five children and seven grandchildren. Retired and lives in Michigan and Florida.

LESTER D. WALTON, was born on Feb. 1, 1922 in Huntington County, IN. Lester joined the USAAC May 29, 1942 and was inducted at Fort Benjamin Harrison, Indianapolis.

Received basic training at Keesler Field, Biloxi, MS. Following basic, received training at Camp Consair, San Diego, CA; Las Vegas Gunnery School, Las Vegas, NV; Davis-Monthan Field, Tucson, AZ; Biggs Field, El Paso, TX; and Lowry Field, Denver, CO. Assigned to a crew piloted by Capt. Max VanBenthuysen. Crew picked up their B-24 in Lincoln, NE and flew overseas from Bangor, ME.

On the flight overseas, their plane lost radio contact and they were forced to crash land on a beach at Lahinch, Ireland. A ceremony and dedication of a plaque memorializing the 50th Anniversary of this event was held July 9-10, 1993.

The crew was assigned to the 567th Sqdn., 389th Bomb Group, stationed at Hethel Air Field near Norwich, England. Lester was the flight engineer-gunner. Flew from North Africa on the Weiner Neustadt Mission; Ploesti Oil Field Mission; and missions over many sites in Germany, Austria, France, Norway and Holland. Completed his tour of duty May 29, 1944. Received the Distinguished Flying Cross and Air Medal with three Oak Leaf Clusters.

Returning to the States and assigned as a flight gunnery instructor for several weeks, then entered the Cadet Training Program in preparation to becoming a pilot. Was stationed in Enid, OK when the war ended and was discharged Sept. 8, 1945 from Camp Atterbury, IN.

Married Mary Phyllis Smith of Warren, IN on June 23, 1945. They have two daughters and two grandchildren. They have resided in Marion, IN since 1947.

Lester retired from the U.S. Postal Service in 1983. He enjoyed traveling and had visited every state but Alaska. He especially enjoyed the 1983 reunion of the 2nd Air Division Association in Norwich, England. Following the reunion he was able to visit Lahinch, Ireland where he had crash landed in 1943, and met two of the people who had witnessed the crash. He loved playing golf, oil painting, flower gardening, and working in his church.

Lester had Non-Hodgkins Lymphoma which he battled valiently for four and a half years, and died in his home in Marion, IN on Feb. 11, 1993.

DELMAR H. WANGSVICK, was born on Feb. 20, 1915 in Mott, ND. Enlisted in the USAAC at Fort Snelling, MN on Feb. 19, 1942, one day before his (disqualifying) 27th birthday. Commissioned as a second lieutenant and rated as a navigator at Hondo, TX AAF on Sept. 26, 1942. Served as a squadron navigator at Gowen Field, Boise, ID; Pocatello AAB and March Field, CA before deploying with the 453rd Bomb Group to England in 1943. Flew 30 combat missions over Europe, including 10 lead missions, before returning to the U.S. in 1945. Relieved from active duty at Camp Beale, CA.

In 1952 he re-entered active duty and was assigned to MATS before being transferred to Weather Recon at Eielson AFB, AK. Flew 115 Polar missions and 85 Aleutian missions. Returning to the "lower 48" in 1957, he flew in tanker aircraft at MacDill and McGuire, and was assigned to SAC HQ at Offutt AFB, NE in 1963 where he served in "Positive Control" until 1968, at which time he was assigned to Intelligence in the 319th Bomb Group at Grand Forks AFB, ND where he retired on May 1, 1970. Received the Air Medal with four clusters, Air Force Commendation Medal with one cluster, Outstanding Unit Award, and numerous campaign medals.

He is a member of the American Legion, Air Force Association, 2nd Air Division, and is a life/perpetual member of Reserve Officers Association, the Retired Officers Association, and Military Order of the World Wars.

He and wife Doris live in Key West, FL and have five children.

RICHARD L. WANN, was born in Elwood, IN, son of Clifford H. and Lula Wann. Grew up on a family farm near Summitville. Enlisted in the USAAF on Oct. 15, 1942. Graduated as a pilot, second lieutenant, in May 1944. Served with the 446th Bomb Group, B-24, *Lil Snooks*, as crew commander.

Shot down Feb. 3, 1945 on a mission to Magdeburg, Germany. Bailed out near Zweibrucken. Landed in no-man's land between front lines and evaded capture for seven days. Placed in Heppenheim Prison Hospital due to injuries. The German commandant expressed that he hated Americans' guts and treated them accordingly with physical abuse, threats, lack of food, care and medical attention. Wann was liberated on March 27th by the 7th Army. He was awarded the Purple Heart.

Married to Ruth Proctor of Elwood, IN. Graduated from Purdue University with a BS and MS. Received honor of "Purdue Old Master" in 1965.

Civilian career was spent in education and engineering management. Retired in 1982 after 30 years service as division manager with Firestone, Akron, OH. Returned to Elwood, IN in 1987.

In July 1990 he met one of his original Waffen SS captors when he visited relatives near Portland, OR. He was the only captor to treat him humanely as a POW. His first statement was, "Germans human - war no good for no man."

CHARLES A. WARD (CHUCK), was born on April 8, 1921 in Chattanooga, TN. After attending the University of Tennessee for two years, he joined the USAAC as an aviation cadet on Jan. 5, 1942.

Graduating as a pilot and second lieutenant in Class 42H, Moody Field, GA, he was transferred to the Central Instructors School at Maxwell, Field, AL. After instructing for seven months in a Twin Engine Advanced School, he was sent to a B-26 Transition School. The entire class was sent to an abbreviated B-24 Transition School and then to various OTUs for the build-up of B-24 combat groups. Ward and his crew joined the 453rd Bomb Group at March Field, picked up their aircraft and flew the southern route to Old Buckingham in December 1943. They were the first crew to complete the required 30 missions.

Remained in the Air Force for 24 years as both a pilot and a civil engineer. Was the resident engineer in charge of construction of an air base in France and later the chapel at the Air Force Academy in Colorado.

Left the Air Force in 1967 as a lieutenant colonel to join an engineering design and construction firm in Philadelphia where he remained for 17 years, retiring in 1984 as corporate vice-president for International Operations. Currently resides in Williamsburg, VA.

LOYD WARD, was born on Aug. 20, 1921 in Morgan County, AL. Enlisted in the USAAF as an aviation cadet Oct. 16, 1942. Reported to Miami Beach in January 1943. Entered S.E. Training Command; received pilot wings and second lieutenant commission Feb. 8, 1944, Class 44B, in Illinois.

Flew new B-24 to England via Goose Bay and Iceland in August 1944. Flew 11 combat missions with 489th Bomb Group. Returned with 489th in December 1944 and trained in B-29s with 489th.

Discharged Oct. 26, 1945 with rank of first lieutenant. Received Air Medal, American Campaign Medal, EAME Campaign Medal with two Battle Stars, WWII Victory Medal, National Defense Service Medal, Korean Service Medal with four BBS and United Nations Service Medal.

Recalled to service in August 1950 and served two years as army aviator, first lieutenant. Spent one year (April 1951-1952) in Korea as liaison pilot. Flew several years during 1960s and 1970s as commercial pilot for corporations and his own air taxi service.

Married Hazel Brooks in June 1945 while at Davis-Monthan Field, Tucson, AZ. They have one daughter and two grandchildren.

He is retired from the U.S. Postal Service and real estate. Resides in Decatur, AL.

SAMUEL E. WARREN, was born on Feb. 22, 1923. Enlisted in service at Camp Blanding on Nov. 5, 1942. Attended Gunnery School at Fort Myers, FL. Joined the group at Boise, ID and trained at Tonopah, NV. Served with the 752nd Sqdn., 458th Bomb Group as a ball turret gunner.

Left for overseas Jan. 25, 1944 and returned Sept. 17, 1944. Was stationed at Biloxi, MS and California.

Discharged Oct. 18, 1945 at Drew Field, Tampa, FL with the rank staff sergeant.

EDWARD K. WASHINGTON, was born on March 28, 1923 in Hampshire County, WV. Enlisted in USAAF Nov. 9, 1942 at Greensboro, NC as a pilot with 392nd Bomb Group, 579th Sqdn. Graduated S.E. Flying Training Command,

Stewart Field, NY; AAF Flying Station 118, Wendling, England. Participated in battles at St. Lo, Munich, Hanover, Hamburg and Holland Low Level Supply. Completed 30 combat missions.

Discharged July 12, 1947; again after Korean service Nov. 29, 1953; then retired from Reserves June 4, 1966. Received EAME Theatre Medal with four Battle Stars, Air Medal with three Oak Leaf Clusters and Distinguished Flying Cross.

He and wife Lucy have three children: John, Ed and Bryan; and six grandchildren. Retired as Superior Court Judge of North Carolina.

EARL E. WASSOM, was born on Sept. 20, 1923 in Blackwell, OK. Enlisted in Army Air Corps Cadet Training on Aug. 9, 1942. Graduated as a pilot and commissioned as second lieutenant, Class 43K, Dec. 4, 1943.

Stationed at Liberal, KS for B-24 transition training; Casper, WY for phase and crew training; Station 120, Attlebridge, England with 8th Air Force, 466th Bomb Group (H), 785th Sqdn. Flew 35 combat missions into Germany, eight gasoline transport hauls into France during combat tour. Received five Air Medals, Purple Heart, four European Campaign Stars and the Distinguished Unit Citation.

The original crew remained intact for the entire tour of duty and completed their combat assignment together. Assigned to the Air Transport Command, Ferry Division and flew C-47s, B-24s, B-25s, A-26s and P-38s. Discharged in November 1945.

Received BA from Southern Nazarene University; MA from East Tennessee State University; Ph.D. from Oklahoma State University. Served career as clergyman and educator. Is Professor Emeritus and Dean Emeritus of Academic Services, Western Kentucky University.

Lives in Bowling Green, KY. Married April 19, 1946 to Cynthia Elizabeth Johnson. They have two children and five grandchildren.

RAY STONER WATERS, was born on July 9, 1922 in Maiden, NC. Enlisted in USAAF in September 1942. Served as engineer gunner, 448th Bomb Group, 714th Sqdn., Crew 52. Stationed at Keesler Field Engineering School; Laredo, TX Gunnery School; Pocatello Phase Training and Seething Air Base, England.

Participated in air battles over Germany, France, etc. Words can't describe the memorable experiences of 30 missions.

Discharged in October 1945 at Gowen Field, Boise, ID with the rank staff sergeant. Received Good Conduct Medal, Air Medal with clusters and Distinguished Flying Cross.

Married Eva Cline on Aug. 18, 1944. They have five children: Richard, Judy, Steve, Joan and Tim; eight grandchildren and two great-grandchildren: Cindy, Beverly, Angela, Robert, Melissa, Mark, Megan, Kendra; Amanda and Jesse.

Ray is a retired furniture designer, and is taking loving care of his disabled sweet wife Eva.

MALTBY WATKINS (FOXIE), was born on Jan. 3, 1924 in Ft. Myers, FL. Enlisted in USAAF in March 1943. Served as an aerial gunner with 8th Air Force, 392nd Bomb Group, 576th Sqdn. in Wendling, Germany.

Flew 30 combat missions between August 1944 and March 3, 1945. Discharged in September 1945 with rank of staff sergeant. Received Air Medal with Oak Leaf Clusters.

Married 44 years and has three children and three grand-

children. Retired after 35 years of practice as a medical doctor.

FRANK S. WATSON, was born on Oct. 27, 1918 in Hillsboro, TX. Enlisted in the 133rd FA, 36th Inf. Div., Texas National Guard on Oct. 25, 1940 and was mobilized Nov. 25, 1940.

Appointed an aviation cadet April 3, 1943. Commissioned as second lieutenant and rated pilot on Feb. 8, 1944 at Pampa, TX AAF. Received transition training in B-24s at Ft. Worth, TX AAF. Upon completion, was assigned a crew at Lincoln, NE. Underwent combat crew training at Biggs Field, El Paso, TX. In August 1944 he was assigned to the 789th Sqdn., 467th Bomb Group, Station 145, Rackheath, England.

After 12 missions his crew was designated as a lead crew. He flew lead on one group mission and nine squadron missions. Was deputy lead on one wing mission, three group missions and four squadron missions. Completed 30 combat missions on April 9, 1945. Returned to the U.S. in May 1945 and was separated in July 1945. Received Air Medal with four Oak Leaf Clusters and Distinguished Flying Cross.

Joined the USAFR and was retired as lieutenant colonel in 1962. After separation from the service he became an air traffic controller with the FAA, later becoming a training officer and liaison officer to USAF with the FAA in Albuquerque, NM.

Presently enjoys golfing, fishing, travelling and yearly reunions with his crew.

He is married to the former Etoile Roach of Goldthwaite, TX. They celebrated their 51st wedding anniversary July 3, 1993. They have one son, Frank Stephen, a lieutenant colonel in the USAF, stationed at Peterson AFB, CO.

FRED L. WEATHERLY, has many very fond and loving memories concerning his time in the USAF. He was able to go on and finally retire from the U.S. Government, and being a disabled veteran, he is very well taken care of.

Weatherly stays in touch with most of his crew and they have had two reunions and hope to have another one in 1994. They made 30 missions without any serious trouble and he can remember most of them just like they were yesterday.

He believes that one of the most remembered occasions was when they were coming in on final approach, and as he had left the tail at this time, he and the two waist gunners noticed that there was a big round hole through the left main landing gear strut. They asked the pilot, Whitey (as they called him), to set the plane down on the right wheel and hold it up as long as possible. He did just that, Lordy, what a pilot! He served with the 453rd.

GEORGE J. WEAVER JR. (JIM), was born in 1922 in Dayton, OH. Enlisted in USAAC on Oct. 28, 1942 as an aviation cadet. Stationed at Patterson Field, OH; Keesler Field, MS; Mississippi State College, Starkville, MS; pre-flight training at Santa Ana, CA; primary training at Glendale, AZ; basic at Marana, AZ; advanced training at Douglas, AZ; combat crew training at Mountain Home, ID. Served with 8th Air Force, 2nd Air Div., 389th Bomb Group, 564th Sqdn.

Participated in Battle of the Bulge; flew 20 bombing missions, including Berlin, Magdeburg, Swinemunde, Wessel, crossing the Rhine River; last mission of the 8th Air Force on April 25, 1945.

Memorable experiences: Crash landing at Mountain Home after losing engines one and two on take-off. Nearly crashing into the channel trying to get under the clouds and losing the formation in the clouds. Low level mission to Wessel to drop supplies to ground troops; after they crossed the Rhine River and being on the pivot when the 389th missed the drop point and had to circle around and come in the second time. Being in Paris, France within two weeks after it

was liberated. Being in London on V-E day and Phoenix on V-J Day. Flying a brand new B-24 home through Iceland.

Discharged Sept. 21, 1945. Received Air Medal with two Oak Leaf Clusters, Good Conduct Medal, and EAME Medal.

Married high school sweetheart, Ludy Gubser, after graduating from flying school in 1944. Settled in Dayton, OH and has three sons and two grandsons.

Spent 21 years in hardware business. Began work with the U.S. Civil Service in 1966 as contract negotiator-specialist. Retired from Wright Patterson AFB in 1966. Sold real estate until 1993, then retired again. Enjoys some traveling in his travel trailer, but Dayton, OH is still home base.

WALTER C. WECKESSER, was born on Sept. 9, 1920 in Little Falls, NY. Inducted in USAAC Sept. 10, 1942 as electronic specialist. Took basic training in Miami Beach, FL. Went to Amarillo, TX for A.M. School; Chanute Field, IL for Electronic School and attended two supercharger schools while in England.

He will never forget D-Day with all the C-47s and gliders going over their field. Went overseas on *Queen Mary*. Arrived in United Kingdom July 30, 1943. Came back on *Queen Mary* June 20, 1945.

Discharged in October 1945 at Rome, NY with rank of staff sergeant. Received ETO Medal with six European Campaign Stars and Distinguished Unit Citation.

Retired and resides in Little Falls, NY. Weckesser married June 28, 1947 and has a son and a daughter.

HENRY W. WEDAA, was born on Feb. 15, 1924 in Atlantic City, NJ. Enlisted in USAAC as a bombardier in January 1943. Served with the 467th Bomb Group. Military locations included multiple U.S. stations and Rackheath, England. Participated in pre-D-day and post-D-day battles. His most memorable experience was surviving the war!

Discharged in September 1945 with rank of first lieutenant. Received the Distinguished Flying Cross, Air Medal with three Oak Leaf Clusters and ETO Ribbon.

He is divorced, has four children and is still working.

JAMES E. WEDDLE, was born on Feb. 9, 1924 in Norfolk, VA. Enlisted in USAAC Feb. 6, 1943. Served with the 2nd Air Div., 445th Bomb Group, 702nd Bomb Sqdn. Received basic training at Miami Beach; Radio School at Scott Field, IL; Gunnery School at Kingman, AZ; phase training at Casper, WY.

Completed 12 missions over Germany: St. Lo, Breman, Munich, Saarbrucken, etc. and France. Was wounded on Aug. 9, 1944 over Saarbrucken when his plane crashed in England about 15 miles from base.

Discharged Nov. 30, 1944 with rank of technical sergeant. Received Air Medal with Oak Leaf Cluster and Purple Heart.

Married and has two children and two grandchildren. He is proud of them all. Retired in 1988 from general contracting business. Enjoys traveling, hunting, fishing and a full social life.

OSCAR F. WEED, was born in Missouri and lived, from age 10, in Longview, WA. He joined the USAAC in July

1942. Graduated from Aviation Cadets in June 1944, second lieutenant, Class 44E, Ellington Field, Houston, TX. Trained as pilot on B-24s at Liberal, KS. Trained combat crew at Boise, ID. Processed to overseas duty in December 1944.

B-24 crew consisted of Lts. Oscar F. Weed, pilot; Bernard Healey, co-pilot; William Trask, navigator; Claude Washabaugh, bombardier; Sgts. Eugene Gorman, flight engineer; Eldon Yoak, radio operator; Robert Erfurth, armament and nose turret; James Laird, top turret; Ralph Higgins, waist gunner; and John Kolodziejski, tail turret.

Joined 577th Sqdn., 392nd Bomb Group in January 1945. Later assigned to 579th lead squadron Among others, flew mission to Berlin on March 18, 1945. Returned to U.S. June 6, 1945. Joined troop carrier squadron in Portland, OR as reserve officer on part-time duty.

Graduated from Oregon State University with BS in forestry degree. Retired from Weyerhauser Company in 1982, vice-president region operations. Currently resides on the Southern Oregon Coast, North Bend, OR.

Married Mary Louise Marcelline on Feb. 6, 1944. They have three sons, one daughter and seven grandchildren.

FRED E. WEGGE, was born on Dec. 11, 1924 in Jasonville, IN. Enlisted in USAAC on May 29, 1943, as aviation cadet, bombardier. Assigned to the 389th Bomb Group, 564th Sqdn. Military locations included Deming, NM; Mountain Home, ID; Hethel, England; Sioux Falls, SD and Walla Walla, WA.

Participated in battles over Ardennes, Central Europe and Rhineland. Flew 16 missions. Discharged Aug. 22, 1946 from Ft. Lewis, WA with rank of second lieutenant. Received Air Medal with one Oak Leaf Cluster, EAME Service Medal with three Bronze Stars, American Theatre Service Medal and WWII Victory Medal.

Married Jeanetta Ver Mulm on Nov. 10, 1946. They have two children. He retired Jan. 8, 1988 after working as a railroad clerk for 38 and a half years.

GEORGE L. WEIDIG SR., was born on July 29, 1925 in Zanesville, OH. Entered the USAAC on Sept. 1, 1943 and was promoted to the rank of staff sergeant as tail gunner on a B-24 bomber.

Basic training was at Sheppard Field, TX; gunnery training at Harlingen, TX; phase training at Davis-Monthan Field, AZ. He was then assigned to the crew of Hal Tyree. His crew, the winners of a contest in efficiency, was given the prize of a leave with a B-24 bomber to take them anywhere they wished to go and return in 48 hours.

After this they left for overseas, picking up a plane in the East. They flew the northern route, landing in Nuts Corner Island. They then went to Shipdham. The 44th Bomb Group, 506th Sqdn. completed 35 missions.

Discharged on Oct. 19, 1945. Married Faye V. Patton of Winchester, VA in the Army Chapel at Greenville, MS. He has lived in Winchester, VA since being discharged. Has three children and six grandchildren.

SAMMY S. WEINER, was born on Dec. 29, 1919 in San Bernardino, CA. Enlisted in the USAAC with his childhood and lifetime friend, Ross L. Oakley, on Oct. 17, 1941, who also survived a B-26 assignment with the 8th Air Force. They graduated from Radio School, Scott Field, IL in March 1942.

After many instructional assignments with B-17 and B-24 groups, he was assigned overseas in June 1944 to the 445th Bomb Group, 702nd Sqdn. as an ROG technical sergeant at Tibenham, England. On his 20th mission, Sept. 27, 1944, they were shot down, with 27 other B-24s, by ME-109s and FW-190s on their way home from Kassel, Germany. Sammy was one of three of their crew who survived. After parachuting safely he was captured and sent to Oberousal for interrogation and processing. On Oct. 3, 1944 he was sent to Stalag Luft #4 until February 1945, when the camp was evacuated by foot. After two days of the march, two of them (at night) escaped from the column, Feb. 15, 1945. They were recaptured on March 1st, then processed and sent to Griefswalde on March 7th until April 15th, then to Stalag Luft #1 until the camp was liberated by the Russians on May 1, 1945.

Shipped back to the States in June 1945 and discharged Sept. 24, 1945. Received the Purple Heart, given to his mother posthumously, European Campaign Air Medal with Clusters and the POW Medal.

Married Teri on March 2, 1947. They had a son, Michael, who also spent four years in the USAF (the last year in Vietnam). They lost their son to cancer four years after his discharge at the age of 29. Other than the loss of their son, they have been extremely happy all their married years. They are now retired from real estate.

IRA P. WEINSTEIN, was born on June 10, 1919 in Chicago, IL. Enlisted Aug. 7, 1942, aviation cadet at Ellington Field, Childress, TX, bombardier/DR navigator, Pathfinder crew flying B-24 Liberators. Assigned to 445th Bomb Group, 702nd Bomb Sqdn., Tibenham, England.

Flew 25 missions (last 10 as a Pathfinder crew). Was shot down on the notorious Kassel raid on Sept. 27, 1944. Group lost 28 of 36 planes. Weinstein bailed out through the nose wheel hatch. His parachute harness caught on bomb sight. Chinned himself back into the airplane, unhooked his chute and finally got free of the plane at about 2,000 feet. He was captured and interrogated at Oberusal and interned at Stalag Luft 1, Barth, Germany.

Discharged in December 1945 with rank of first lieutenant. Received Distinguished Flying Cross, Air Medal with Oak Leaf Cluster, Purple Heart with Oak Leaf Cluster, Presidential Citation, Distinguished Unit Citation, POW Medal, Good Conduct Medal, American Theatre Victory Medal and French Croix de Guerre.

Married to Norma; they have two children and two grandchildren. They reside in Glencoe, IL and Palm Beach, FL.

Life member of the Ex-POW Association, 8th Air Force Historical Society, life member of 2nd Air Division Association, 8th Air Force Jewish War Veterans, 8th Air Force Memorial Museum Foundation, B-24 Liberator Association, International B-24 Liberator Club, Caterpillar Association, Air Force Association, Bombardiers Inc., Purple Heart Association, 8th Air Force Heritage League, 2nd Air Division Heritage League, American Air Museum, Air Force Museum. President of Schram Advertising Agency in Chicago since 1945.

NICHOLAS WEISGARBER (NICK), was born in 1917 in Trenton, NJ. Enlisted in CCC at age 18. Attended Arizona State College and joined National Guard. Was activated and sent to Panama when WWII began.

Transferred to USAAC and trained as bombardier. Assigned to 466th Bomb Group, B-24s, and stationed at Attlebridge, England. He flew 32 missions as a member of John Brown's "Polaris" crew. He remained in the Air Force and served in the Korean War and was a SAC member.

Retired as captain and awarded the Distinguished Flying Cross, Air Medal with three Oak Leaf Clusters, plus other medals during his career.

After Air Force retirement he was a correctional officer at Folsom Prison. Nick enjoyed all types of sports. He was the father of Margaret and Paul Weisgarber and an adopted son Tom. Nick had two brothers, John and Matt, and a sister Regina.

Nick passed away in 1991.

CHARLES J. WEISS JR., was born on Nov. 26, 1920 in San Antonio, TX. Joined the USAAC Nov. 28, 1941 as an aviation cadet (comm), then assigned to newly formed 93rd Bomb Group at Barksdale Field, LA.

Received OTU training in Florida and sent overseas to

England as a commissioned officer. Flew 15 combat missions and shot down two FW-190 fighters. He was shot down over St. Nazaire, France (German Submarine Pens) but the pilot managed a controlled "crash" in Southern England.

Married an English girl, Elsie Neal. They celebrated their 50th Wedding Anniversary in July 1993. Received BS degree from University of Maryland.

Served 15 years with Air Force Office of Special Investigations and retired in 1963 as lieutenant colonel. Then went with the Defense Intelligence Agency, Research and Development, until receiving a position with the U.S. Department of State as director of Technical Security for all Embassies world-wide.

Instrumental in the detection and neutralization of the Soviet and Eastern Block technical intelligence efforts directed against U.S. Embassies. Served 13 years and retired from the Foreign Service in 1976 as FSRU-2. Decorations and campaigns: Air Medal, Presidential Unit Citation, EAME with four clusters, American, American Defense Service Medal, Army of Occupation (Germany), National Defense Medal, Air Force Reserve Medal, Air Force Outstanding Unit Award, WWII Victory Medal, Air Force Longivity Service Award with four Oak Leaf Clusters and the Air Force Commendation Medal.

IRA WELLS (WELKOWITZ), was born on Oct. 11, 1923 in Staten Island, NY. Enlisted Oct. 5, 1942. Called to active duty Jan. 30, 1943 while attending Wagner College. Completed tour of 35 missions as armorer/nose turret gunner with 448th Bomb Group, 714th Bomb Sqdn. at Seething on March 18, 1945. Awarded Air Medal with Silver Oak Leaf Cluster

Graduated from Wagner College in 1948 and received MA degree from New York University in 1949.

Married Mildred Katz July 13, 1949. They have two children and two grandchildren.

Retired in 1981 after 33 years as high school teacher of social studies in the New York City Board of Education schools. Resides in Staten Island, NY.

JOHN C. WELSH JR., Attack Helicopter Troop, 107th Armd. Cav. Regt., is cited for his long and distinguished service to his country, state and community from April 1940 to his retirement in July 1980. He enlisted in the Ohio National Guard on April 8, 1940 and on Oct. 15, 1940 he entered the active military service of the U.S. He became an aviation cadet on June 7, 1942 and on March 20, 1943 was commissioned a second lieutenant, Air Corps. He served as a pilot in the Air Offensive Europe, Northern France, Ardennes and Rhineland Campaigns for which he was awarded the Distinguished Flying Cross and the Air Medal with four Oak Leaf Clusters. He was relieved from active duty on Nov. 18, 1945 as a captain.

He was a member of the Officer Reserve Corps, Army Air Corps until recalled to active duty in the USAF on April 11, 1951 and served as a fighter and bomber pilot in the Korean War until Oct. 12, 1953, having been promoted to major. He then served in the Inactive Air Force Reserve until he was reappointed a captain in the 121st Fighter Interceptor Wing, Ohio Air National Guard, on Dec. 8, 1955. He was separated from the Air National Guard on Nov. 17, 1960 and assigned HQ Continental Air Command, USAF. He was promoted to lieutenant colonel in the Air Force Reserve in 1966.

Chief Warrant Officer Welsh was appointed a CW2 in the Ohio Army National Guard on Dec. 10, 1970 and served continuously until July 1980. He functioned as a Fixed Wing and Rotary Wing pilot and was outstanding in aerial gunnery in an Attack Helicopter unit. He held ratings of Master U.S. Air Force Aviator and Master Army Aviator. Chief Warrant Officer Welsh's more than 40 years of loyal and dedicated service have brought distinct credit on himself, the Armed Forces of the U.S. and the State of Ohio.

BERNARD H. WELTMAN, was born on Oct. 16, 1923 in Brooklyn, NY. Entered USAAC as aviation cadet Feb. 22, 1943. Basic training at Atlantic City, NJ; student (CDT)

Lafayette College, Easton, PA; classification, Nashville, TN; pre-flight, Maxwell Field, AL; primary flight training, Hawthorne, SC; gunnery training, Buckingham Field, FL; navigation training, Selman Field, Monroe, LA; phase training, Gowen Field, Boise, ID; overseas movement, casual pool, replacement and training squadrons; combat with 8th Air Force, ETO, 467th Bomb Group, 790th Sqdn., Rackheath, Norfolk, England. Completed 35 combat missions as navigator.

Returned to U.S. for reassignment/separation, Atlantic City, NJ; June 27, 1949-April 28, 1961: Air Force Reserve. Discharged from Reserve with rank of captain.

Received BS in biochemistry in 1946 from City College of New York using GI Bill. Graduated from New York University College of Dentistry, DDS, in June 1950. Practiced dentistry in Brooklyn and Staten Island, NY. Recently retired after 43 years of practice.

Married Helen Shapiro in June 1950. They have a son, a daughter and four grandchildren. Resides in Staten Island, NY.

JACK H. WENDLING, Harrisburg, IL, entered flight training from the University of Minnesota in April 1943, graduating in January 1944, the youngest second lieutenant/pilot in the Air Corps. He was a collegiate springboard diver, designated for fighters, scratched by bomber losses of late 1943. Completed B-24 transition, was first to solo and first to gain instrument card. Shipped out as co-pilot for frequent requests for transfer to fighters.

Flew North Atlantic, arrived 466th Bomb Group in July 1944. Pilot and navigator were removed from crew for mutual mistrust. Crew was assigned to Heath Carriker, experienced on B-25s, B-17s and B-24s before assigned to 466th Bomb Group, accumulating 12 missions as fill-in. Cortland Brovitz was added as navigator. Matching experienced pilot with well-qualified co-pilot and navigator led to immediate selection as a lead crew, and shortly, wing lead.

Following Carriker's tour, the crew was assigned to a flak-happy West Pointer to enhance the latter's record. Leads were downgraded to squadrons for the last 12 missions.

Wendling was awarded the Distinguished Flying Cross for 29 lead missions and airmanship, in concert with Carriker, successfully returning a heavily flak-damaged aircraft from Dec. 23, 1944 Dahlen/Junkerath mission with Roberson, 785th CO command pilot, on the jump seat. Volunteered for 25th Bomb Group to fly Mosquitos with 466ers, Dick Foster and Bob Greenwood.

Returned to college for aeronautical engineering at war's end. Recalled in 1949 by Air Force Chief of Staff, assigned to Wright-Patterson AFB for three years. Resigned for civilian position in Air Force Intelligence.

Retired early to hunt, fish and ski in Idaho. Annual event is reunion with Carriker crew survivors.

HENRY A. WENTLAND, was born on Sept. 23, 1923 in New York, NY. Joined the USAAC as a 19 year old. Graduated from Class 44G as pilot, second lieutenant in Frederick, OK and assigned as a flight instructor. Received B-24 transition training in Casper, WY in winter of 1944.

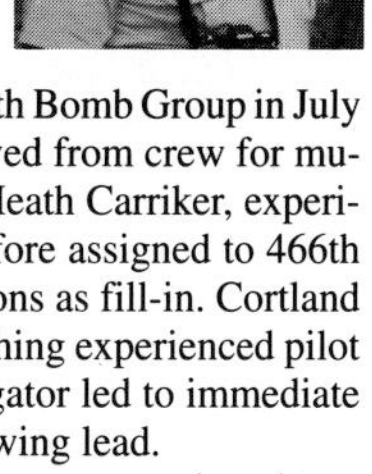

Assigned to 564th Sqdn., 389th Bomb Group, Hethel, England in February 1945 and flew 14 combat missions. Three trolley missions followed V-E day and on May 19, 1945, with 20 souls onboard, took off in a new B-24M for Bradley Field, CT via Stornaway, Scotland; Iceland; Goose Bay, Labrador and Bangor, ME. B-29 pilot training, Dalhart, TX to August 1945 and to inactive status Oct. 7, 1945.

Graduated from New York University. Married Eleanor Weiss on May 29, 1948. They have two children and three grandchildren.

Retired from New York Telephone as a district sales manager and moved to Cape Cod, MA for sailing, flying, tennis, golfing...

EDWARD C. WERNER, was born on Sept. 27, 1922 in Detroit, MI. Enlisted in USAAC on June 5, 1942. Graduated as second lieutenant/pilot, Class 43K, Marfa, TX, on Dec. 5, 1943. Served with the 453rd Bomb Group. Flew 35 missions including D-day and 50 missions over Korea.

Retired in September 1966 with rank of lieutenant colonel, after 12 years active duty and 12 years in the Reserve. Received the Distinguished Flying Cross and Air Medal with seven clusters.

Has three daughters and two grandsons. Retired and living in a Florida swamp in Hernando, FL.

MELVIN D. WESTBROOK, was born on Sept. 2, 1922 in Genoa, NE. He was drafted into the Army in October 1942. Graduated as a pilot, second lieutenant in Class 43K at Frederick, OK. Trained for first pilot on B-24 at Liberal, KS.

Picked up his crew at Lincoln, NE and trained at Gowen Field in Boise, ID. Took a new B-24 to England. Assigned to 466th Bomb Group, 785th Sqdn. at Attlebridge in July 1944.

Completed tour of 35 missions, including two gas missions for Patton and two missions to Sweden for OSS. Received six Air Medals, five ETO Stars and Presidential Unit Citation.

Married Barbara Warner on June 2, 1946 and had three children: Chris, Kevin and Anne.

Stayed in Reserves for 28 years and retired in 1982 with rank of lieutenant colonel.

After 20 years of being a licensed contractor, he founded his own company, Westbrook Construction, and was successful for an additional 20 years.

QUENTIN K. WETTEROTH, was born on May 29, 1920 in St. Louis, MO. Entered service on Aug. 5, 1943. Received basic training at Omaha, NE; Radio School at Sioux Falls, SD; then to Gunnery School at Yuma, AZ. Took overseas training at Walla Walla, WA.

Went overseas to England by boat. Their crew was assigned to the 446th Bomb Group, 705th Sqdn. and flew 32 missions. They had some milk runs, tough ones, and shoot-us-up ones, but their crew came through okay.

Flew their plane back to the States, went on leave and married a wonderful girl. While en route to the West Coast the Japanese war ended. Was phased out at Peterson AFB, Denver, CO and discharged on Oct. 25, 1945.

They proudly present their daughter and son, plus seven wonderful grandchildren. Retired in 1977 and enjoying every minute. Resides in Affton, MO.

WILLIAM C. WHEELER, was born on April 14, 1919 in Lynville, KY. Enlisted in USAAF at Louisville, KY in October 1942. Received basic training at Biloxi, MS; primary training at Ellington Field; gunnery training at Laredo, TX; bombardier/navigator training at Midland, TX.

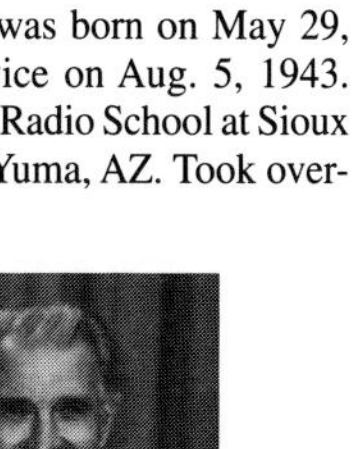

Commissioned second lieutenant, Class 44A, March 18, 1942. Military locations and stations included Peterson Field, Colorado Springs, CO; Old Buckingham, Attleborough, England. Assigned to 453rd Bomb Group, Lt. Fischer's crew, as bombardier. Flew 36 missions: three to France, one to Norway and 32 to Germany.

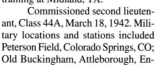

Memorable experiences included travel and sightseeing in England; enemy flak over Dessav, Koblenz-Kassel; forced landing in Brussels in September 1944.

Discharged on June 10, 1945 at Camp Atterbury, IN with rank of first lieutenant. Received Air Medal with five Oak Leaf Clusters.

Married Mary Frances Freeman on Oct. 13, 1947. They have two children and three granddaughters. Retired in 1981 from service station operated with brother, Terry Wheeler, for 36 years in Paoli, IN. Since retiring they have enjoyed traveling the USA and Canada.

RALPH W. WHIKEHART, graduated from Bombardier School, Class 43-7, first class, Childress, TX. Flew with the 8th Air Force, 445th Bomb Group, 701st Sqdn. as lead bombardier in December 1943. On Feb. 20, 1944, the beginning of "big week,"the 445th Bomb Group, led by Maj. Jimmie Stewart, attacked the aircraft factory at Brunswick, Germany. After fierce opposition, the target was severely damaged. Capt. Whikehart and Maj. Stewart were awarded the Distinguished Flying Cross at the recommendation of Gen. Hodges.

On March 6, 1944 the 445th led the 2nd Air Div. on the first massive raid on Berlin, Germany flying deputy lead. He became the first B-24 bombardier to drop bombs on Berlin. On April 20, 1944 he flew deputy lead on mission #18 to France. Due to a malfunctioning CI auto-pilot near the French Coast, the mission commander turned the lead over to Whikehart's crew and he attempted a PDI bomb run. Near the target a flak burst hit the #4 engine and another hit the nose, blowing plexiglass all over Whikehart and cutting his face badly. Bleeding severely, he recovered in time to readjust the bombsight and get the bombs on target. At "bombs away" a 105mm scored a direct hit in the nose turret and blew it to pieces, killing the observer and detonating some of the 50-caliber ammunition. The bombsight and other equipment were lost out of the gaping hole. Whikehart's right shoulder was struck by exploding ammunition and his flak suit, parachute harness, and Mae West were completely shredded and blown off. Capt. Henley, the navigator, pulled him back in after getting the hydraulic fluid out of his eyes. He managed to get his feet under Whikehart and pull him along the catwalk up to the flight deck. He administered first aid to Whikehart, who was blinded and cut by shrapnel. Losing altitude rapidly, they threw everything overboard. With instruments and hydraulics gone they could only lower the left gear. The pilot made a perfect crash landing!

Whikehart was hospitalized three months then returned to the States. After 18 months in Valley Forge General Hospital, he was retired on physical disability Jan. 23, 1946. He received the Silver Star, Distinguished Flying Cross, Air Medal with four Oak Leaf Clusters, Purple Heart, Presidential Unit Citation and French Croix de Guerre with Palm.

Whikehart married Dorcas on June 23, 1945 in the Fort Meyer Chapel. He was in full body and arm cast (sick as a dog). Of their four sons, two are pilots. One son Mark Andrew died on a combat mission in Vietnam in 1970.

After service he returned to work at the U.S. State Department, setting up military assistance advisory groups and was liaison with the Pentagon.

DEARL WHITAKER, was born on Oct. 16, 1924 in Acorn, KY. Enlisted in the USAAF on Aug. 20, 1942. Attended Airplane Mechanic School at Lincoln, NE and Gunnery School at Kingman, AZ. Assigned to Crew 35, 713th Sqdn., 448th Bomb Group at Boise, ID. Completed training at Sioux City.

Drew new airplane and followed southern route to England. They missed the landing at South England and crash landed in Wales; no injuries. Flew 35 missions, completing number 30 and 31 on D-day.

He was technical sergeant and received the Distinguished Flying Cross and Air Medal with four Oak Leaf Clusters. Re-enlisted and went to OCS in 1947.

Whitaker had a break in the service and was Kentucky State policeman for six years. Returned to the Army and retired as a major in 1971.

Worked as administrative assistant to the county judge until elected mayor of Somerset, KY in 1973. Fully retired in November 1982.

He has one daughter. Whitaker is now married to Lela Price of Somerset, which is their home, and they have a condo in Clearwater, FL.

OSCAR L. WHITE, was born on Nov. 11, 1914 in Goodway, AL. Married Margie Bush in August 1941 and has five children, 10 grandchildren and two great-grandchildren.

After service schools at Keesler and Las Vegas, he was assigned to the 565th Sqdn., 389th Bomb Group as a B-24 flight engineer. His crew left Bangor, ME in June 1943 and arrived at Bengazi, North Africa to join the 9th Air Force. Flew six missions and was in the hospital when his crew was shot down on the seventh mission. After three months he was able to hitch-hike to Hethel, England Base. Assigned to 8th Air Force Operations as clerk for rest of tour.

Received the EAME Service Medal with four Bronze Stars, Good Conduct Medal, Air Medal and Distinguished Unit Badge.

Discharged with rank of sergeant at Ft. McClellan on Sept. 18, 1945. He is now retired and resides in Eight Mile, AL.

STANLEY L. WHITE, was born on Oct. 8, 1915 in Grayson County, KY. Inducted into the service on Oct. 3, 1942 at Fort Benjamin Harrison, IN. After basic training at Jefferson Barracks, MO, he graduated from Aeronautical University in Chicago and the B-24 Airframe Assembly School at the Ford Plant in Willow Run, MI.

Assigned to the 392nd Bomb Group in Alamogordo, NM and arrived in Wendling, England on Aug. 1, 1943 with ground support group. Was assistant squadron inspector with 576th Squadron.

Returned to the USA after V-E day (round trip onboard *Queen Mary*). After a furlough, assigned to Charleston Army AFB, Charleston, SC. Discharged at Patterson Field, OH on Sept. 24, 1945.

Received MA from Indiana University in 1949. Was history teacher and department chairman at Ottawa Township High School. Retired in 1972. Married Muriel Reynolds on June 14, 1952. They have one daughter, Nanette.

THOMAS WHITE, was born on Oct. 7, 1921 in Long Island, NY. Enlisted in USAAF on Aug. 18, 1942. Was flight engineer and gunner with 8th Air Force, 392nd Bomb Group.

Military locations and stations included Fort Dix, NJ; Miami, FL; Gulfport, MS; Tucson, AZ; Alamogordo, NM; Topeka, KS; Wendling, England; and Pueblo, CO. He flew 32 missions in Air Offensive Europe in 14 months.

Discharged Sept. 15, 1945 with rank of staff sergeant. Received Air Medal with four Oak Leaf Clusters, Distinguished Flying Cross, European Service Medal, Good Conduct Medal and WWII Victory Medal.

Married Velma Henegar, Pueblo, CO in 1945. They have two daughters, and one son (deceased). Thomas is retired from the Nassau County Police Department. Resides in Medford, OR (five years).

WALTER E. WHITE JR., was born on Dec. 12, 1923 in Austin, TX. Enlisted in USAAF in February 1942. Military locations and stations included Kelly AFB; Harlingen, TX; El Paso, TX; Alamogordo, NM; Biloxi, MS and Jackson.

Discharged in October 1945 with rank of staff sergeant. Recalled to USAFR in May 1951 and discharged in June 1952 with rank of technical sergeant.

He was a tail gunner on Lt. Hammond's crew, Ruptured Duck, 856th Sqdn. Only three crew members and two crews completed 30 missions in the 492nd Bomb Group.

Received the Distinguished Flying Cross, three Air

Medals, American Defense Medal and European Medal with three Battle Stars. The good Lord and the fortune of war looked after him.

He and wife Joyce have two sons, Maj. Brian White and Clark White, a chemical engineer. Walter is retired and they reside in Austin, TX.

WILLIAM HARRY WHITLOCK, was born on Jan. 15, 1922 in Lake City, SC. Was drafted on Oct. 16, 1942. Received basic training at Miami Beach, FL. Graduated from Armament School, Buckley Field, Denver, CO and Gunnery School, Fort Myers, FL. Trained in dive bombers at Key Field, MS. Transferred to Scribner AFB near Lincoln, NE for overseas training in B-24 bombers. Was assigned to a crew and to the ball turret.

Flew the southern route via Belem, Brazil and Daker, Africa on Nov. 18, 1943 to Tibbenham AFB in England, about 18 miles from Norwich. Assigned to the 445th Bomb Group, 701st Sqdn.

Flew 30 missions over Europe, most missions in the ball turret. Was never wounded or shot down, just scared.

Returned to the U.S. on Sept. 15, 1944 and discharged on Sept. 24, 1945 in Amarillo, TX. Was awarded the Air Medal with three Oak Leaf Clusters, Distinguished Flying Cross and Distinguished Unit Citation.

Came home, married and has four children and 11 grandchildren. Became part owner of a Western Auto store. Went to Francis College in 1979, received degree in history. Taught history eight years. Now retired.

SIDNEY D. WHITMAN, was born on Jan. 24, 1917 in Erath County, TX. After high school and two years junior college he entered the service with a National Guard unit in November 1940. Transferred to the Air Force in February 1942. Went to several technical schools and then assigned to a flying crew as flight engineer on a B-24 in Clovis, NM in 1943.

Went overseas in February 1944 from Mitchell Field, NY via Florida, Puerto Rico, South America and Africa.

Assigned to 93rd Bomb Group, 8th Air Force. Flew 32 combat missions over Europe in a B-24 from May 6 to July 25, 1944. Received the Distinguished Flying Cross, Air Medal with four Oak Leaf Clusters, three European Campaign Stars and other ribbons.

Returned to the States on Sept. 5, 1944 and was sent to Davis-Monthan Field, Tucson, AZ. Assigned to B-29 planes. This state made a total of 38 states he had either been in or was stationed in.

Discharged Aug. 3, 1945 and returned to Stephenville, TX, engaging in electrical work. Married on Feb. 17, 1944. They have three children and three grandchildren.

WILLIAM L. WHITNEY (BILL), was born on March 22, 1923 in Norwich, NY. Entrained at Binghamton, NY May 20, 1942 with four young men to go for induction AVS at Fort Niagara, NY. All were aviation cadets and received commissions.

Graduated from Luke Field, Phoenix, AZ on June 22, 1943. Schooled as fighter pilot and assigned as co-pilot of a B-24. Phase training at Smoky Hill, Salina; Wichita and Topeka, KS.

Went to England on the *Queen Elizabeth*, docking in the Firth of the Clyde, Grennock, Scotland. Went by train to Hethel near Norwich, England. Assigned to the 389th Bomb Group, 565th Sqdn. The flak, FW-190s and ME-109s forced bail-out on their 8th mission, a raid to Gotha, Germany. Controls were shot out of their hands and plane continued on auto-pilot.

Parachuted down on west side of Rhine near Bonn. Greeted on ground by civilians who said, "For you the war is

over." From there, interrogation at Frankfurt and a train ride to Stalag Luft #1 at Barth on the Baltic Sea, about 100 miles north of Berlin.

Russians freed the camp on May 1, 1945. Bill was glad to see them, as he had become a POW on Feb. 24, 1944. As camp was about to be liberated, he contracted pneumonia and pleurisy. Recovered rapidly with freedom and was flown to France and the USA through the hospital system. With the war ended, he was relieved from active duty.

Discharged Jan. 6, 1946 with rank of first lieutenant. Received Air Medal with Bronze Star, European Theater with Bronze Star, Purple Heart and POW Medal.

Attended Agriculture School at Cornell. Took horseshoeing and blacksmithing to shoe standard-bred horses, raced with his father. After a few years he turned to horseshoeing as life's endeavor.

Now enjoying retirement in Verona, NY and Pompano Beach, FL with his wife, the former Fran Childs.

JOSEPH B. WHITTAKER, was born on Dec. 22, 1917 in Hollidaysburg, PA. Enlisted in USAAF on July 1, 1940. He was a bombardier with the 392nd Bomb Group, 2nd Air Div., 8th Air Force. Promoted to 14th CBW as wing bombardier, then to the 2nd Air Div. HQ as division bombardier. Was one of the first flying officers of the 392nd Div. Bombardiers from April 17, 1944 to V-E day. Worked under Maj. Gens. James Hodges and William Kepner.

Flew 17 missions with the 392nd Bomb Group and then was grounded when he went to 2nd Air Div. HQ. However, he flew two missions with 392nd Bomb Group on D-day. Memorable experience was Nov. 18, 1943 Oslokjeller mission, Norway.

Discharged in January 1946 with rank of lieutenant colonel. Received Distinguished Flying Cross, Legion of Merit, Air Medal, French Croix de Guerre with Gold Star, Good Conduct Medal, Pre-Pearl Harbor and five Campaign Ribbons.

He is widowed and has two sons and two daughters. Retired after 42 year career as explosive engineer.

JAMES L. WHITTLE JR. (JACK), was born on Sept. 14, 1921 in Baltimore, MD. Called to active duty in March 1943. Took primary, basic and advance flight training in Central Command. Graduated as second lieutenant, pilot, Class 44E at Twin Engine Advance in Lubbock, TX. Took B-24 phase training at Pueblo, CO and headed for England in October 1944.

Assigned to 8th Air Force, 2nd Air Division, 14th Combat Wing, 44th Bomb Group, 506th Sqdn. stationed near Shipdham. Flew 28-30 combat missions, mostly as co-pilot, but also flew several missions as first pilot. While on local flight after V-E day, they crashed at Watton Air Base and destroyed the aircraft. All survived with various degrees of injuries. Returned to the U.S. in July 1945 and elected to remain on active duty until September 1947.

Returned to University of Maryland and Johns Hopkins University on a part-time basis, but after two years took job at Edgewood Arsenal while flying T-6s on weekends as a flight commander in Baltimore Reserve Sqdn.

Recalled to active duty in May 1951 as captain because of the Korean War. Assigned to Bomber Flight Test at Wright-Patterson AFB in Dayton and participated in Atomic Energy Commission project. Later assigned to Furstenfeldbruck, Germany in 5th Tow Target Sqdn. While there he married Vera Lowe from Catonsville, MD.

In February 1956 attended the University of Maryland and received his BS degree in military science. Was assigned to the 552nd Airborne Early Warning and Control Wing at McClellan AFB, Sacramento, CA.

Spent 18 months at a radar site on Mt. Hebo in Oregon.

Their daughter, Valerie, was born there. Was awarded the Air Defense Command "Expert" rating as a weapons controller.

Returned to Sacramento in 1961 where he continued to fly the EC-121 and U-3A. In 1965 he spent four months TDY in Vietnam and Taiwan.

Retired at McClellan AFB in November 1966 as a lieutenant colonel. For approximately five years after retirement he flew, instructed in and towed sailplanes at Truckee, CA on weekends and qualified for a commerical glider pilot and instructor rating.

During the week he started restoring vintage Ford Thunderbirds as a hobby which ultimately became a full-time business. At the same time, he attended college part-time and earned a BS degree in business administration in 1970 at Sacramento State University and two years later he earned an MBA from Golden Gate College.

Unfortunately, his wife, Vera, died in 1973 after a relatively short illness. Their daughter, Valerie, still lives in Sacramento.

Awards and medals: Air Medal with five Oak Leaf Clusters, Good Conduct, American Defense Service, American Campaign, EAME Campaign with three Bronze Stars, WWII Victory, Army of Occupation-Germany, Armed Forces Reserve and Vietnam Service.

THOMAS R. WHOLLEY JR.,
was born on Feb. 11, 1915 in New Bedford, MA. He was inducted into the service on June 17, 1943 and joined active service on July 1, 1943. He served as Fire Fighter (383) with the 2016th Eng. Avn. F/F Plt., 458th Bomb Group. Wholley was discharged on Nov. 11, 1945 with the rank of staff sergeant.

Military locations/stations included Bradley Field and Horsham St. Faith, England.

He was awarded the American Theatre Medal, EAME Ribbon, Good Conduct Medal, Bronze Star and Victory Medal.

Returned from England June 1945, furloughed and was assigned to Biggs Field, El Paso, TX and discharged from Ft. Bliss on Nov. 11, 1945.

Member of New Bedford Fire Department at time of entry in service. Returned to Fire Department December 1945. Retired after 28 years on April 1, 1970.

Graduated from Secretary School 1952; LaSalle University Correspondence School, Chicago, IL 1955.Public Accountant and tax consultant 47 years, Office Manager of TV and Appliance store 16 years after retirement.

Married Marion J. Booth on April 22, 1946. They have three daughters, one son and two grandchildren. Is now volunteer docent and lecturer for the New Bedford Whaling Museum.

NORBERT J. WICK,
was born Nov. 13, 1921 in Lockport, NY. Joined Air Force in November 1942 and commissioned pilot December 1943 at Altos, OK. B-24 training in Ft. Worth and crew training at Biggs Field, El Paso. Picked up new plane at Topeka, KS for delivery to Prestwick Scotland. Assigned to 392nd Bomb Group, 579th Sqdn. Flew 31 missions. The 31st was the bad one, lost #4 engine, #3 was losing oil pressure, they limped back to France with a P51 escort. No serious injuries.

Returned to the States. Was discharged in September 1945 as first lieutenant. He received the Distinguished Flying Cross, Air Medal with four Oak Leaf Clusters and Purple Heart.

Transferred to AT6s for instrument flying in Bryan, TX. Instructed Chinese cadets in Marana, AZ until war ended. Retired in 1985 and now spends the winters in Florida in their motor home.

Married in March 1945 and has two children.

ROBERT S. WICKENS,
was born on Jan. 6, 1918 in Ludington, MI. Enlisted in the USAAC on May 15, 1942 at Santa Fe, NM. He was discharged on Sept. 15, 1945 with the rank of technical sergeant, radio operator-gunner.

Military locations, stations included Wichita Falls, TX; Scott Field, IL; El Paso, TX; Gowen Field, Boise, ID; Wendling Base, Wendling, England with the 392nd Bomb Group.

Participated in European Theatre of Operations from June 1944 until January 1945.

Memorable experiences include bailing out over southern England on the way back from Munich raid.

Awarded the Distinguished Flying Cross, Air Medal with three clusters, Good Conduct Medal, European Theater Operations and several Battle Stars.

He flew with pilot, Art Benson's crew, 579th Bomb Sqdn., 392nd Bomb Group in B-24s. Completed 30 missions. They were a lead crew for the 392nd Bomb Group.

Married to Mary Ann Franey for 45 years. They have one daughter, Mary Louise. He is presently retired from the U.S. Postal Service after 29 years. His wife taught school for 29 years.

EDWIN E. WILCOX,
was born Aug. 8, 1920. Enlisted as aviation cadet on July 18, 1942 in Rochester, NY. Ordered to Nashville, TN March 1943. Transferred to Maxwell Army Air Force Eastern Flying Command at Montgomery, AL Class of 43K. Then to Tuscaloosa, AL; Greenwood, MS; and Blytheville, AR. Received wings and commission on Dec. 4, 1943.

In Salt Lake City assigned to B-24 crew. Went to Blythe, CA for crew training. Troop train from California to New Jersey for ship convoy to England.

Joined the 458th Bomb Group, 755th Sqdn. in May 1944. Completed 25 missions. First sortie June 10, 1944 Chateaudan, France. Last sortie April 25, 1945 Bad Reichenhall, Germany. Notable missions: St. Lo, France and Berlin, Germany. After V-E day he was transferred to the 19th Photo Sqdn. Flew F-9C aircraft, a modified B-17 for photo mapping.

Transferred from England to Foggia, Italy.

Photo mapped Sicily, Yugoslavia and Greece.

When number came up, they flew a F-9C back to West Palm Beach, FL by way of North Africa, South America and Puerto Rico.

Separated at Camp Blanding, FL Nov. 28, 1945.

Returned to Taylor Instrument Co. in Rochester, NY.

In August 1953, married Helma Holtz, a school teacher, who lived just around the corner. They now have four grown daughters, three sons-in-law and three grandchildren. He is retired from Eastman Kodak Co. They are planning to build a year-round second home on a beautiful lake in the Adirondack Mountains in northern New York State.

WILLIAM G. WILKIE,
was born Dec. 18, 1923 in Mansfield, LA to George and Ella Wilkie. Entered USAAF on Nov. 6, 1942. Basic training at Brooks Field, TX. Promoted through the ranks to staff sergeant.

Assigned to Jack Pruitt's crew, *The Bon Voyage.* Boarded *Queen Mary* in New York in March 1944 to England with 8th Air Force, 2nd Div., 389th Bomb Group.

Flew 33 missions on B-24 Liberator in ETO.

Received Air Medal, three Oak Leaf Clusters and Distinguished Flying Cross.

Returned to U.S. in October 1944 on *Queen Mary.*

Married high school sweetheart, Margie Holland, on Oct. 14, 1944.

Stationed at Keesler Field, Biloxi, MS as instructor in mechanics until discharge from Air Force on Oct. 21, 1945 at Barksdale AFB.

Worked in oil production until retirement in May 1986 in Smackover, AR. Has two daughters, one son, eight grandchildren and two great-grandchildren. Hobbies include gardening, fishing, and hunting. William loves to travel.

BILL R. WILKS,
was born April 8, 1922 in Albertville, AL. Graduated Albertville High School and enlisted in USAAC Oct. 12, 1942 with three best friends, like brothers.

Basic training B-24 Base at Smyrna Air Base, TN. 1943 transferred to Greenwood, MS and served as a dispatcher for one year. With information that two of guys he enlisted with were shot down and POW, he volunteered for Aerial Gunnery School Laredo, TX. He did not feel good being stateside. Did final phase of training Pueblo, CO.

Stationed at Horsham St. Faith Air Base in Norwich, England. Participated in battles of Rhineland and Central Europe (ETO). April 14, 1945, loaded heavy with special bomb load, they went down. Crashed five miles from runway. He was only survivor, six crew members killed. Possibly had mid-air collision. One other B24 went down the same morning in the same location.

Hospitalized 4210 U.S. Army Hospital Plant for two months during the time the war ended. Discharged Nov. 28, 1945 Maxwell Field, AL as sergeant and received Purple Heart.

1948 hired as Southeast salesman for Hester Battery Co. out of Nashville, TN. Opened own business, Wilks Tire & Battery in 1952. They now have two stores, Albertville and Gadsden. He has two sons which run their family business and he and his wife consult and work part-time. They have three grandsons.

DONALD K. WILLIAMS,
was born Nov. 30, 1923. Enlistment: Aviation Student & Cadet, Nov. 27, 1942 to April 15, 1944. Officer and first pilot April 15, 1944 to Nov. 27, 1945.

Received training at West Coast Training Command; basic indoctrination, Fresno, CA; Aviation student, Utah State Agri. Cult. College, Logan, UT; pre-flight, Santa Ana, CA; primary flight training, Tulare, CA; basic flight training, Taft, CA; advanced twin engine flight training, Pecos, TX; B-24 four engine transition training, Albuquerque, NM; and crew assemble and assimilation, Walla Walla, WA.

Combat experience - ETO September 1944 to June 1945. Sent to England by boat the end of September 1944. Sent to 489th Bomb Group, Halesworth, Nov. 1, 1944, deactivated group. Arrived at 458th Bomb Group, Horsham St. Faith, end of November 1944, assigned to 753rd Sqdn. Flew first mission as co-pilot with Lt. Vincent - aborted on takeoff. Flew first complete mission early December with Lt. Vincent's crew. Flew six missions with own crew in 753rd Sqdn. during Battle of the Bulge.

Transferred to 755th Sqdn. as lead crew, serving as Squadron, Group, Wing, and Division Leads; in 18 more missions and 1 abort until the end of the war in Europe. Transferred at Europe war's end to 754th Sqdn. In June of 1945 they flew back from Europe to Bradley Field, MA with Capt. Warren E. Cook and 10 enlisted ground personnel via Ireland, the Azores, Newfoundland, Boston. Crew disbanded, and was sent to Camp Grant, IL, and on to Sioux Falls Air Corps Base.

Married Arlayne Arnold on May 12, 1944. They have five children - Thomas, Patricia, Laurie, Jeanne and Elizabeth. Patricia has two children - Jenna and Alex. Retired retail jeweler and gemologist after 45 years. Served in various school and county political positions; state occupational offices and as a volunteer fireman 31 years.

DWIGHT WILLIAMS,
was born June 25, 1923 in Detroit, MI. Enlisted USAAC on Dec. 15, 1942, schools-link trainer, armament (B-24 and B-29) and gunnery. Assigned to Bob Thomas's crew in Topeka, KS July 1944, assigned to 489th Bomb Group, 844th Sqdn. at Norwich, England October 1944. Flew four missions - group sent to states for B-29 training. Discharged Dec. 22, 1945 with the rank of staff sergeant.

Received the American Theater,

Victory Medal and EAME Ribbon with one Bronze Battle Star.

Two years at Lawerance Tech. in Detroit. Became tool and die designer/checker in various job shops around Detroit area.

Married and has two sons, five daughters and ten grandchildren. Retired October 1984.

GEORGE EMERY WILLIAMS, was born on Feb. 22, 1924 in Lexington, ME. Inducted into the USAAC on April 12, 1943 and was discharged on Oct. 23, 1945 with the rank of technical sergeant. Served with the 466th Bomb Group, 787th Bomb Sqdn.

Stationed at 12 Air Force bases in the USA plus ETO. Memorable experiences include flying 31 missions with planes badly damaged at times but none of their crew members were injured.

Awarded the EAME Ribbon with three Bronze Stars and the Air Medal with four Oak Leaf Clusters.

Married 48 years to Ellen Maree, and they have a son and a daughter. Retired after 42 years with the CF&I Steel Plant.

JACK A. WILLIAMS, was born in Portsmouth, Hants County, England Oct. 18, 1917. Became naturalized citizen summer of 1943 in Sioux City, IA. Joined USAAC August 1942, as a private, promoted through the ranks to technical sergeant. Completed an eight week course at Lowry Field, CO and a six weeks course at Gowen Field, Boise, ID, on power operated gun turrets.

Later in England attended a specialized course on electrical gunsights. Directly supervised work of six power turret men, also served as power turret and gunsight instructor for approximately 26 months. Selected to fly and solve turret and bomb rack problems which occurred in the air but not on the ground.

After the war enrolled in Northeastern University and earned an associates degree in electronics and a BBA in engineering and management. Joined Raytheon Co. as an engineer working there 35 years until retirement.

After the war he married Barbara G. Akers, June 17, 1945. They have four sons, one daughter and three grandchildren.

JAMES B. WILLIAMS JR., was born Nov. 14, 1919, Sunset, TX. Entered the Army Aviation Cadet Program April 1942. Completed pilot training and commissioned second lieutenant Turner Field, GA, April 1943.

Joined a B-24 aircrew at Davis Monthan, AZ in May 1943. Finished combat crew training Biggs Field, TX September 1943. After ferrying a new B-24 from Willow Run to Prestwick Scotland, arrived in England October 1943. After processing through Cheddington, the crew was transferred to a former Sub-patrol base where B-24 formation flying training was received until the 8th Air Force B-24 combat units returned from North Africa. December 1943 assigned to the 68th Bomb Sqdn., 44th Bomb Group, Shipdham, England.

Completed 30 combat missions May 19, 1944, from which he received the Distinguished Flying Cross and four Air Medals. Participated in the first Berlin mission, and 44th Bomb Group's highest aircraft loss mission April 8 to Brunswick, Germany, but not without considerable battle damage.

June 1944 transferred to 8th Air Force Service Command flying B-24 and C-47 transport missions supporting the June 6 invasion of continental Europe.

Returned to US, October 1944 and spent the next 23 years of his military career in the Military Airlift Command. Retired USAF with rank lieutenant colonel.

KENDRICK L. WILLIAMS, was born on March 31, 1920. He was inducted into the Air Force on Oct. 3, 1941 and was discharged on Sept. 26, 1945 with the rank of sergeant. Served with the 93rd Bomb Group, 329th Sqdn., Ted's Flying Circus.

Military locations, stations: Sheppard Field, TX; Barksdale, LA; Ft. Myers, FL; and Norwich, England (Sept. 7, 1944-May 26, 1945).

Married to Mary, and they have three sons and two grandchildren. Employed as air mechanic Pennzoil Refinery for 45 years until retirement in 1985. Hobbies include hunting, fishing and gardening.

LAWRENCE A. WILLIAMS, was born Dec. 13, 1923, in Fredonia, NY. He entered the USAAF on Jan. 21, 1943, at Fort Niagara, Youngstown, NY. Preflight training, Ellington Field, Houston, TX, February to June 1943; Gunnery School, Laredo Army Air Base, Laredo, TX (July-September 1943); Ellington Field, Houston, TX; Bombardier Training at Midland AAFB, TX (September 1943-January 1944). Graduated as flight officer. Overseas training at Peterson Field, Colorado Springs, CO (February-April 1944).

While overseas, he served with 8th Air Force, 2nd Air Div., 93rd Group (H), 409th Sqdn., at Hardwick (Norwich), England. Williams flew 30 bombing missions over Germany and occupied Europe in B-24 Liberators. From May 29 to Aug. 15, 1944, his missions included: Tutow, Metz, Pas de Calais (3), St. Andre A/D, Orleans A/D, Hamburg, Berlin, Buc Airdrome, Fiefs, L'Isle Adam, Gien, Peronne, Augsburg, Munich, Saarbrucken (2), Montagne (2), Grentemville, Schmalkalden, St. Lo Area (2), Ludwigshaven, Melun, Montereau, Coulommiers, Dijon Longvic, and Wittmundhafen.

Upon returning from ETO, he was an instructor at Midland Army AFB, TX, and at the Army AFB in Deming, NM, and Childress, TX.

Honorable discharge in November 1945 in Amarillo, TX as second lieutenant. His awards included: Air Medal with three Oak Leaf Clusters, Distinguished Flying Cross, Bronze Star to ETO.

Parents: Ethel and G. Arthur Williams, sisters: Dora Coykendall and Frances Young. Married Theresa Dubnicki on July 25, 1953.

Williams retired in 1971 after 30 years from Office Staff Allegheny Ludlum Steel Corp., Bar Products Division, Dunkirk, NY. He enjoys traveling, photography, carpentry, music, and theater.

THOMAS P. WILLIAMS JR., was born June 24, 1921, Atlanta, GA. Resides in Little Rock, AR. Graduated Hendrix College 1942, joined Aviation Cadet Program same year. After basic training at Sheppard Field and CTD at Texas Tech., completed preflight at Santa Ana, Flexible Gunnery School at Kingman. Graduated from Victorville Bombardier School, Class 43-18 followed by radar navigation training at Langley, Boca Raton and Alconbury, England.

Assigned 44th Bomb Group, 2nd Air Div., and flew 21 lead missions as "Mickey" navigator with 506th and 68th Bomb Sqdns.

Awarded Air Medal with two Oak Leaf Clusters and Distinguished Flying Cross. Recalled in 1950 and served in the 136th M&S Group, 5th Air Force, Korean War. Discharged with rank captain.

Married Betty in 1947 and has three children and six grandchildren. Spent entire business career in insurance. Holds Chartered Life Underwriter Designation and Life Membership in Million Dollar Round Table. Enjoys grandchildren, travel and is active in civic affairs and his church. In 1987 visited 44th Bomb Group site at Shipdham and 2nd Air Division Memorial Library in Norwich.

WILLIAM J. WILLIAMS, was inducted into the USAAC in November 1940 and graduated Pilot Class 43-G from Marfa, TX. He was discharged on Aug. 6, 1945 with the rank of captain; Williams served with the 8th Air Force, 467th Bomb Group, 791st Bomb Sqdn. as a pilot.

Stationed in East Anglia near Norwich.

Participated in 30 missions. Awarded five European Campaign Stars, five Air Medals and one Oak Leaf Cluster.

Back to Optometry College when discharged. Retired as optometrist after 35 years practicing in southern California. Married to Betty in June 1943 and they celebrated their 50th anniversary last June 12th. They have four children and nine grandchildren. Presently living in Laguna Hills, CA and enjoys traveling, golfing and volunteer work.

WILLIAM H. WILLIS, was born in Clayton, DE on March 29, 1925. He enlisted in the USAAC in September 1943 and served as armorer gunner with the 467th Bomb Group. He was discharged in November 1945 with the rank of staff sergeant.

Military locations, stations: Miami, FL; Lowry Field, Denver; Fort Myers, FL; Chatham Field, GA; and Rackheath, England. Participated in bombing missions over Germany.

Memorable experiences include being shot down Feb. 16, 1945 and being held POW until April 29, 1945 when liberated by Patton's army.

Awarded the Good Conduct Medal plus Ex-POW Medal and others.

Married 47 years to Betty Wessel Willis. He is presently retired.

FRED C. WILSDORF JR., was born in Linden, TN on Jan. 20, 1923. He enlisted in the USAAC in June 1943 and served as engineer gunner with the 445th Bomb Group. Discharged on Oct. 13, 1945 at Chanute Field, IL with the rank of technical sergeant.

Military locations, stations: Inducted - Fort Oglethorpe, GA in June 1943; basic training - Gulfport, MS; A.M. School - Biloxi, MS; Factory AM School - San Diego, CA; Gunnery School - Kingman, AZ; Aerial Engineer, combat crew training - Tucson, AZ; overseas lectures, shots and etc., Topeka, KS; 445th Bomb Group, 702nd Sqdn., Tibenham, England November 1944 to June 1945.

Flew twenty-nine combat missions and six trolley missions after war ended. Back in the states June 1945, Miami Beach, FL for reassignment.

Participated in Rhineland, Ardennes and Central Europe battles.

Memorable experiences include tree top level mission, supplies to paratroopers on March 23, 1945.

Awarded the Air Medal with three Oak Leaf Clusters, Victory Medal and Good Conduct Medal.

Married to Dorothy and they have three children - Benno Wilsdorf, Terry Wilsdorf and Chris Hammond. He also has one grandson, Jordan Hammond. Presently retired but working every day.

BRYANT S. WILSON, was born in Adrian, MI in June 1919. Enlisted in the Air Force in November 1942 and served with the 2nd Air Force, 448th Bomb Group, 712th Sqdn. Discharged Oct. 31, 1945 with the rank of first lieutenant (captain reserves).

Military locations, stations: Trained in Midland, TX; Laredo, TX; Boise, ID with bombardiers. Battles participated in were Normandy, Northern France, Rhineland and Air Offensive Europe. He completed 32 missions.

Memorable experiences include D-day and three-plane crash at base in Seething Norwich England.

Awarded the Distinguished Flying Cross, Air Medal and four Oak Leaf Clusters.

Was married in 1947 to Ella Mae; they have three sons - Martin, Jeffrey and Andrew. Taught school for 35 years until retirement in 1982.

G. HARWOOD WILSON, was born June 24, 1918 in Spencer, MO. He was inducted into the service on Feb. 8, 1944 and served in the Army Air Force. He was discharged on Nov. 4, 1945 with the rank of staff sergeant. Military locations/stations: Laredo, TX and Pueblo, CO.

Memorable experiences include being top turret gunner on 28 missions. Went into a spin over channel. Pulled out at 8000 feet. Dropped 10,000 feet first. Paul Armentrout was pilot.

Awarded the Air Medal with three Oak Leaf Clusters.

Married Madeline on June 9, 1941; they have one son, Carl, born in 1946. He is presently retired.

JERRY B. WILSON, was born in Jefferson County, IL on July 29, 1922. Drafted Oct. 3, 1942, served six months in the 96th Inf. Div., Camp Adair, OR.

Then aviation cadet training. Graduated as second lieutenant as a bombardier/navigator April 1, 1944 at Victorville, CA.

Flew 30 combat missions as a navigator in a B-24 over Germany with the 93rd Bomb Group.

Received Distinguished Flying Cross, five Air Medals, four European Battle Stars plus several other medals.

Married his childhood sweetheart, Betty Youngblood. They have four children and seven grandchildren.

After WWII he stayed in the reserve and was recalled to active duty in 1951. Served in Korea as a clothing sales officer with the 5th Air Force.

Retired from the Air Force Reserve as a lieutenant colonel.

His entire civilian life was in the grocery business. He retired in 1988.

JULIAN K. WILSON, was born May 17, 1923 in Ogden, UT. In 1937 his family moved to Burbank, CA. Graduation from Burbank High 1941, worked as a skin fitter P-38 Interceptor line. Entered service Jan. 23, 1943. Basic training Biloxi, MS, followed by schooling in armament technology Buckley and Lowry Fields. Joined 453rd Pocatello, ID. Trained March Field, CA, going with the ground troops to Old Buckingham Air Base December 1943. Was armorer in the 735th Sqdn. until the 453rd disbanded. Next served as postal office worker with the Air Transport Command in Long Beach, CA. Was discharged Oct. 19, 1945 with rank of sergeant.

Attended UCLA, AB 1950, MA 1951. Married Mary Jean Suttner July 22, 1949. Two children, Joanne and Thomas. Worked in field of secondary science education as a science teacher, advisor, consultant, and supervisor. Participated in teacher training at the University of California at Northridge. Retired in February 1982.

LINDLEY A. WING, was born Feb. 7, 1920 at Visalia, CA. Enlisted in "D" Co., 185th Inf. in 1936. Attained the rank of first sergeant in 1940.

On Aug. 18, 1942 he graduated from Ft. Benning, GA and was posted to Camp Roberts, CA as an instructor and platoon leader.

In April of 1943 he transferred to the Army Air Force. Assigned to pilot Class 43-K he received his wings and was sent to Tonapah for training in B-24 aircraft. He was then assigned to the 467th Bomb Group, 8th Air Force. Upon completion of 35 missions he was ordered to Western Flying Command and released from active duty in 1945.

Recalled in 1951 he elected to remain in the service and served at Hamilton AFB, Okinawa, Travis AFB,

Keflavick Iceland, and Travis AFB where he retired on Jan. 1, 1968.

He now resides in Cameron Park, CA with Mabel his wife of 47 years.

J.J. WINGARD JR. (JESS), was born in Greenville, SC on May 12, 1923. He served in the USAAF and was stationed at Maxwell Field, Boise, ID and Tibenham, England with the 8th Air Force, 2nd Air Div., 445th Bomb Group, 703rd Sqdn. He was discharged in September 1945 with the rank of second lieutenant.

Participated in four air raids over Germany.

Memorable experiences include the flak and German fighters.

Awarded the European Theatre Medal and others.

Married to "Honey," they have three children, Mike, Susan and Joyce. They also have six grandchildren. Presently retired and enjoys playing golf and traveling.

HARRY C. WINSLOW, was born in Punxsutawney, PA on April 28, 1921. Raised in Kittanning, PA; graduated from Kittanning High School in 1939. Was in junior year at Penn State when Pearl Harbor was bombed. Quit school at mid-year and enlisted, vision precluded flight training. Completed Armament School, commissioned July 24, 1942. Completed Bombsight Maintenance course, both at Lowry Field, Denver, CO. Briefly stationed at Hill AFB, Ogden, UT and Pueblo, CO.

Arrived in ETO Aug. 27, 1943 with a sub depot group; stationed at Tibenham. With the help of Mike Phipps, was moved to 2nd Combat Wing; then with the patience of John Driscoll, became a gunnery officer. Joined the 453rd Bomb Group when the group arrived at Old Buckingham.

In the summer of 1944 was sent stateside to Gunnery School in Laredo, TX. When finished was given observer's rating and pay raise; flight pay. Returned to "Old Buck" in October 1944. Finished with 40 missions; picked up Air Medal with six Oak Leaf Clusters.

Returned to states with group. Discharged in Fall of 1945. Found the job market had no openings for old gunners; decided to make a living "Playing the Horses. Disaster!"

In 1948 enrolled at Colorado School of Mines; graduated with degree in Petroleum Engineering in 1951. Worked for Argo Oil Corp. until they were purchased by Atlantic Richfield in 1962. Opened business in San Antonio, in Natural Gas Measurement and consulting. Consulting, that's when your wife hands you your hat each morning and says, "get out there and see what you can find today."

Married, six children and eight grandchildren.

Memorable experiences: (1) Watching Bob Coggeshall flying his airplane in daylight; and his bicycle in darkness. (2) Flipping coins with Jim Shaw for the last drop of Vitalis.

DAN WINSTON, was born in New York City on May 13, 1916. He was inducted into the Air Corp on April 13, 1942 and later served in the Air Force. Stationed at Ft. Totten, New York City; OSC, Miami Beach; Grenier Field, New Hampshire; and ETO with the 8th Air Force. Discharged in February 1946 with the rank of captain.

Memorable experiences include walking out of a B-25 five minutes after take-off when both engines quit at 1,200 feet and the pilot started them up and returned to base.

Awarded the American Theater Medal, European Theater Medal and the Victory Medal.

He has one daughter and one son. Presently a sales executive.

EDWARD W. WINTER, was born in Hempstead, NY on Oct. 31, 1924. Enlisted in the Air Corps in December 1942 and served with the 466th Bomb Group, 784th and 785th Sqdns. Discharged in October 1945 with the rank of first lieutenant. Military locations, stations: Attlebridge, England.

In a recent relocation, his Air Corps file was misplaced. See biography, John Welsh, Crystal River, FL 34929; they were a lead crew of which John was pilot, he, the navigator.

Awarded the Distinguished Flying Cross, Air Medal with three Oak Leaf Clusters and the Good Conduct Medal.

Married Anne Williams, Feb. 9, 1957. They have three daughters and five grandchildren. Presently retired after employment as an architect.

JOHN CRAWFORD WITHERSPOON (III), was born Sept. 3, 1917 in Farmville, VA, reared in Rock Hill, SC and graduated from Iowa State in 1940. Married June Verna Thompson from Ontario, Canada in 1940. Joined Air Force February 1943, trained at Keesler Field, MS; graduated from Air Force Radio School, Sioux Falls, SD October 1943; assigned to B24's 2nd Air Force, 467th Bomb Group at Wendover Field, UT Nov. 1, 1943.

Sailed with Group, arriving Rackheath, England, 8th Air Force, March 1944. Staff Sergeant and Radio Maintenance Line Chief 790th Sqdn. Attended two weeks RAF School for VHF. Attended one week's Armed Forces Leave Course, Cambridge University. Trolley Mission for ground forces, Europe, forestry tour guide over Black Forest. After V-E day, by B24 to U.S., scheduled for Pacific Theatre when WWII ended. Separated Oct. 23, 1945.

Resumed Forestry career. Elected Elder, Presbyterian Church. Assistant State Forester, South Carolina, stressing forest fire prevention and originating photo of hand cradling a little tree, widely reproduced totalling more than 12 million impressions, including Newsweek Magazine which captioned the photo "Smokey's ally" June 2, 1952 issue. Joined Forest Industry Associations in Washington DC and Atlanta, GA, advisor to filming "The Paper Forest" which won world Sweepstakes award at the World Forestry Congress in Madrid, Spain in 1966. Joined International Paper Company in 1971, serving the last seven years as Regional Manager of Corporate Affairs. Retired 1983. One daughter, one son, three granddaughters.

JAMES T. WITHEY (JIM), was born March 7, 1924 in Saugus, MA. Married to Dorothy Barr Merrill, widow of his cousin, first lieutenant, 83rd Chemical Bn. attached to the Rangers, killed at Anzio beachhead, 1944. Has two stepsons, two daughters and 10 grandchildren.

After graduating from Peterborough, NH High School in 1942, joined the USAAC, washed out of Pilot Training in Camden, AR, via Nashville, TN and Maxwell Field, AL. Then to Navigation School via Ft. Myers, FL and Gunnery School, graduating in Class of 44-3 at Selma Field, Monroe, LA.

Joined J.D. Pelton crew 148-52 at Colorado Springs, CO, then to Kansas to pick up new plane and to England via the Southern Route. After seven missions left the Pelton crew to become Group Lead Navigator for the next twenty-two missions. This completed that crew's tour needing one more mission. Flew with Don Reynolds crew, September 27 to Kassell, crash landed spending balance of war at Stalag Luft 1. Discharged as captain, Indian Head Gap, PA, and went to college. Graduation BSME from University of New Hampshire, Class of 1949.

Next 27 years, resided in New Jersey, working for Curtis Wright and Reaction Motors (Thiokol). Designed and Project Engineer on Atlas and Mercury Booster Disconnect Valves, Production Manager on 'Peak Power' Electrical Systems, using jet engines plus other products including F-15 Engine.

'Retired' in 1973, moving back to New Hampshire. Presently partners with son-in-law, (Withey-Crook Associates) owning Withey Press Printing Company in Seabrook, NH and residing, with wife (of 48 years) at Kittery, ME.

ALBIN A. WITKOWSKI, was born Dec. 18, 1915 in Stevens Point, WI. Commissioned as a second lieutenant on Feb. 28, 1942 at Lowry Field, CO. After completing the armament course he later completed the bomb sight maintenance and bombardier training programs.

He joined Chuck Haney's crew for B-24 training at the Davis-Monthan Field, Tucson, AZ. In May 1944 they were assigned to the 705th Sqdn., 446th Bomb Group at Bungay, England.

After 29 missions he became a squadron bombardier

(staff) with duties including practice bombing with individual bombardiers. As such, they drew friendly fire - 22 flak holes with one near miss - nipping the back of his garrison cap. Made his 30th mission shortly after.

His awards and ribbons consisted of the Distinguished Flying Cross, Air Medal with three Oak Leaf Clusters, Occupation of Japan, etc.

On April 20, 1947, he separated from active duty and remained in the reserves until 1967 attaining rank of lieutenant colonel.

He has one daughter who lives nearby. Now retired after 32 years in insurance career.

JOHN WLODARSKI, was born in Milwaukee, WI on June 7, 1918. He enlisted in the USAAC Aviation Cadet Program in May 1942 while a student at Marquette University College of Engineering and employed in a defense industry. Classified for navigation training he was sent to Selman Field, Monroe, LA for basic and advanced training, graduating in October 1942 and commissioned a second lieutenant.

Sent to Davis-Monthan Field, Tucson, AZ he was assigned to a crew for training in B-24s. From there he was sent to Blythe, CA for further crew training and then on to Pueblo, CO where the 491st Bomb Group was formally started. After the necessary training and receipt of the new B-24 the crew flew by way of Florida, South America, and North Africa to Met Field in England. Flew on the 854th Sqdn., 491st Bomb Group first mission in June 1944 and then completing 34 missions by Nov. 30, 1944.

There were many memorable missions, such as the first mission where the "puffs of flak" looked intriguing and almost pretty until hearing the shrapnel against the plane and finally realizing it could develop into a dangerous situation. Another was the mission to Hamburg, Germany where individual six-plane formations attacked targets. The anti-aircraft fire was unusually heavy. After dropping the bomb load, the formation dove away from the target reaching red-line speed, the pilot not realizing his instruments were shot-up and not reading correctly. They made it back with quite a bit of damage. However, the most exciting and satisfying mission was the low-level flight dropping supplies to troops trapped at Eindhoven and Nijmegen, Netherlands. It was a real spectacle seeing young boys on roof tops and people in the streets waving their hearts out at the low flying bombers. But it was also sad and disheartening to lose friends on this mission. Overall, flying the required missions was a satisfying accomplishment.

He received the Distinguished Flying Cross, five Air Medals, and the usual campaign ribbons with stars. Returning to the USA he taught "cruise control" for B-29s and was finally discharged in October 1945.

Resumed his studies in engineering at Marquette University graduating in 1946. Worked temporarily for General Electric in Chicago, IL and then to NACA (National Advisory Committee for Aeronautics) Langley Field, VA doing basic research in supersonic aerodynamics as applied to jet engines. After eight years at Langley Field, he transferred to the U.S. Army Missile Command - Redstone Arsenal in Huntsville, AL. Work there was in Research and Development on missiles and rockets. Most of the development work was spent on wire-guided, anti-tank missiles with the last years spent developing and fielding the Tow Missile System. Retirement from civil service was in January 1980. After a few years of engineering consulting the second retirement was made and now time is spent travelling, golfing, yard-work and just loafing.

He is married to Margaret Kash of Lynchburg, VA and has three daughters and a son. One grandchild, a boy, who is the apple of his grandfather's eye.

The war was a dreadful thing but an experience they now appreciate as having made them responsible human beings in a hurry.

FRANK S. WOLCOTT, was born in Billings, MT on Oct. 7, 1917. Married college sweetheart, Betty Lyons, Oct. 4, 1942. She passed away in 1975 and he remarried Phyllis Davis Spragg May 25, 1977. He had one son and three daughters by Betty.

He graduated from college in June of 1942 with an ROTC commission in the Infantry, and was ordered to active duty on June 25, 1942. He applied for and got pilot training reporting to Randolph Field in February of 1943. He went through pilot training in grade and got his wings in October 1943. Went overseas to England as a copilot on a B-24 in February 1944. Flew 18 missions as a copilot and on the second mission of D-Day started flying first pilot. On finishing his combat tour was made an assistant squadron operations officer and later assistant group operations officer. He was in the 466th Bomb Group from Clovis, NM until it was phased out. He was a captain when separated. Now a retired airport manager.

Awarded the Distinguished Flying Cross and Air Medal with three clusters.

FRANK E. WOLF, was born on May 26, 1921 in Gary, IN. Inducted into the Air Force on June 28, 1941 and was discharged on July 31, 1961 with the rank of captain (highest war time rank).

Memorable experiences: Troopship - Pacific Dec. 7, 1941; pilot training 1942-1943; B-24 pilot - 33 missions; bombardier-navigator radar training 1948; national defense service - Asiatic-Pacific.

Awarded one Battle Star, American Theater Medal, ETO with five Battle Stars, WWII Victory Medal, American Defense Medal and Air Medal with four Oak Leaf Clusters.

Presently retired.

RAYMOND A. WOLF, was inducted into the Army Air Force, 93rd Bomb Group on Aug. 12, 1941 and was discharged September 1945 with rank of technical sergeant.

Military locations, stations: Rantoul, IL; Sarasota, FL; Hardwick England; Libya; Keesler Field, MS.

Battles participated in: Naples-Foggia-Tunisian Campaign; Egypt-Libya; Air Offensive Europe; all combat theaters; Sicilian Campaign; and Ploesti Raid.

Awarded the Good Conduct Medal, EAME with seven Battle Stars, Distinguished Flying Cross, Air Medal with two Oak Leaf Clusters and Presidential Unit Citation.

Presently retired.

ROBERT W. WOLFE, was born on May 28, 1914 in Brooklyn, NY. Drafted into the USAAC on Feb. 1, 1943 and discharged Oct. 28, 1945 with the rank of technical sergeant, 8th Air Force.

Stationed in Texas, Florida and Old Buckingham England.

Completed 35 missions with the worst being the Berlin Mission in July 1944 as flight engineer.

Awarded the Distinguished Flying Cross, Air Medal with three clusters, Good Conduct Medal and European Theater of Operation Medal.

Married and has four children and six grandchildren. Presently chairman of the board - Cache Creek Foods.

R.F. WOMBACHER (JEFF), was born on Jan. 16, 1916 in Hills, IA (Iowa City, IA). Entered service at Jefferson Barracks, MO and then to Selman Field at Monroe, LA. Served with 489th Bomb Group, 846th Sqdn. Discharged in June 1945 with the rank of first lieutenant.

Military locations, stations: Wendover, UT and Davis Monthan Field, Tucson, AZ.

After going through three phases of training, they left the U.S. in their own B-24 from Miami Beach, FL. They were not allowed to open their overseas destination folder until they were out over the sea one hour. The pilot opened the orders and announced over the intercom that they were going to England. After stopping in South America and Africa they landed at Halesworth, England.

On D-day they flew three missions over France, knocking out bridges, road intersections, railroad marshalling yards etc. After flying with a crew he had trained with for three missions and six combat missions, he was placed on a lead crew that led the 489th Group and several others. After flying 25 missions with them he was 2 missions short of a complete tour of 35 missions. He elected to stay in England and fly two missions rather than go back to the U.S. with the crew who were scheduled to go into B-29 training.

He was awarded the Distinguished Flying Cross Medal for leading successfully on numerous missions. He returned on his own in February 1945 and was discharged in July 1945 at Jefferson Barracks, MO. He was also awarded the Air Medal with one cluster.

He was one of five brothers in the service at the same time. A brother bombardier in the 8th Air Force, a brother that was an ambulance driver in the European Theater, a brother who was in the Navy, and a brother who was a mechanic in Texas and Louisiana during the war.

His mother sweat out the period where she had four sons in heavy combat during the war. He admired her very much for that. They all came home safely and he has to think her daily prayers and attending mass daily had a lot to do with that.

After the war he went back to work for Sears Roebuck & Company. Later he started his own business, Jeff's Music Company. He had juke boxes, wired music and vending machines. Later he went into real estate, selling homes and commercial property. Presently retired in Iowa City, IA.

ROBERT J. WOOD, was born in Alhambra, CA on Sept. 26, 1922. He was inducted into the Air Corps in August 1943 and served as staff sergeant with the 458th Bomb Group, 754th Sqdn. Discharged in October 1945.

Stationed in Horsham St. Faith. Participated in the ETO. Memorable experiences: Live red - red flare on flight deck.

Awarded the Air Medal with clusters.

Married and has four children, 10 grandchildren and seven great-grandchildren. Presently retired.

RALPH E. WOODARD, was born in Nelsonville, OH, May 27, 1921, graduated from Logan High School, Logan, OH, 1939. Enlisted in Aviation Cadet Program, June 1942, began cadet training, West Coast Flight Training Command, November 1942. Received wings and second lieutenant commission October 1943, married Virginia Williams, Springfield, OH, Oct. 8, 1943. Returned to B-24 training at Kirtland AFB, NM, and Muroc AFB, CA. Departed Hamilton AFB, San Francisco with B-24 and crew flying southern route to England. Left B-24 "Down the Hatch" at Liverpool and reported to the 453rd Bomb Group (H) at Old Buckingham. Flew 15 missions before transfer to 389th Bomb Group (H) at Hethel for Pathfinder Training. Shot up on 17th mission, to Munich, but able to stay airborne until bailout near Lille, France. Captured by Luftwaffe and was prisoner at Stalag Luft 1 at Barth for 10 months plus 1 month under Russian care and hospitality. Separated from active duty November 1945.

Co-owner, with family, Woodard Auto Service 1946-1952, graduated Wittenberg University 1953, BS Physics major/Math minor. Employee at Wright Patterson AFB 1953-1961 as physicist in Nuclear Research Facility. Studied at Oak Ridge School of Reactor Technology 1956-1957; Director of General Physics Research Lab 1961-1969 WPAFB. One of four civilians selected to attend Industrial College of the Armed Forces in Washington, D.C. 1969-1970, simultaneously earning an MBS at George Washington University. Retired WPAFB, 1979. Retired from Air Force Reserves with rank of colonel.

Awarded the Air Medal with one Oak Leaf Cluster, POW Medal and ETO Campaign Ribbon with five stars.

GEORGE BRYANT WOODS, a WWI flight commander in the 28th Pursuit Sqdn., was shot down behind German lines and was a POW. Afterward, he graduated from Harvard, worked in Wall Street, and with Bell Aircraft until he was re-commissioned a Major in 1940, entering active duty February 1941.

He joined the 93rd at Ft. Myers in April 1942. He designed the coat-of-arms of the 93rd. He went with the 93rd to Alconbury, as Air Intelligence. While not retaining his pilot rating, he did become officially rated as a gunner and flew several missions there and elsewhere.

He transferred to North Africa (about a month before the 93rd went to Tafaroui) to the 320th Bomb Group (M), B-26s, as Group Air Intelligence for the invasion. In February 1943, promoted to lieutenant colonel, he was assigned to Air Chief Marshall Tedder for the air planning of the Sicily Invasion, and subsequently reassigned to Air Plans for Force 343 for the Sicily Invasion. Later he was made assistant chief of staff A-2 of the 12th Air Support Command. Back home, he served at WPAFB and was promoted to full colonel in 1946.

On separation he returned to Wall Street, but shortly left again to become special assistant to the Undersecretary for Procurement under Secretary Symington. He died from an untimely heart attack in the early 1950s.

WILLIAM V. WOODS, was born Feb. 14, 1924 in Detroit, MI, raised in Chicago, IL. Married Marie Ellen Ryan March 6, 1948. They have two daughters and four grandchildren.

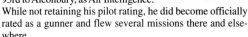

Drafted into military service Feb. 10, 1942. Sent to Fort Belvoir, VA, for basic training in army engineers. Applied for pilot training upon completion of basic training. Accepted and assigned to the 60th College Training Detachment, Air Crew at Pittsburgh University. Upon completion sent to Nashville where he was "washed" out of flying because of a stigmatism. Sent to Truax Field for training and then to England arriving in March 1943, assigned to 453rd Bomb Group, 735th Bomb Sqdn. and Joe Mieles ground crew as aircraft mechanic (M.O.S. 747) servicing B-24s.

Hostilities ended in May 1945. After 30 day furlough at home sent to Great Falls, MT and attached to ATC until war's end. Was discharged on Oct. 18, 1945 as corporal.

Was a journeyman tool & die maker for 18 years for Honeywell and a tool & die designer for Victor Comptometer & Signode Corps. until retirement in 1992.

W.D. WOODSON (BILL), was born in Kentucky; entered service from Florida 1941. Graduated Flight School Class of 1942-J. Had three phases combat training as first pilot B-17s. Became flight instructor in B-24. Joined 409th Sqdn. of 93rd Bomb Group July 1943 in Bengasi. Returned Hardwick, England for complete combat tour.

Memorable missions include Oslo Oct. 18, 1943; Bremin December 16 and Dec. 20, 1943; Berlin March 6, 1944 and finally Mulhouse May 11, 1944. Losses were so heavy in 1943 and early 1944 that they refrained from making close friendships with flight personnel. On one occasion, his left wingman was cut in two at the waist windows.

He received two Distinguished Flying Crosses and four Air Medals.

Retired from Air Force as lieutenant colonel. He is grateful to God for - SURVIVAL - that NONE of his crew was injured - and that Prat and Whitney built such super engines.

CLAYTON G. WOODWARD, was born in Portland, OR on July 13, 1909. Drafted into the service on April 3, 1942 and served with the 567th Sqdn., 389th Bomb Group,

2nd Air Div., 8th Air Force. Discharged on Sept. 5, 1945 with the rank of master sergeant.

Military locations, stations: Presidio of Monterey, Tent City, Davis Monthan, AM School, Perry Institute Yakima, WA, Davis Monthan, Biggs El Paso then Lowry then to Hethel England.

Participated in Sicilian Air Combat Balkans, Naples-Foggia, Air Offensive Europe, Normandy, Northern France, Ardennes, Rhineland, Central Europe GO 33 WD 45.

There were many incidents each day that caused much apprehension. One that occurred when the mission was returning to their base and Germans were shooting down their planes.

Awarded the Distinguished Unit Badge WD 78 45, EAME Service Medal and Good Conduct Medal.

Has lived alone since 1984 but has a daughter, granddaughter and grandson and great-grandchildren, twins, a boy and a girl, all living in Stockton. Presently retired.

JOHN H. WOOLSEY, was born in San Francisco, CA on July 14, 1923. Enlisted in the Air Corps in the spring of 1943 and served with the 8th Air Force as navigator on B-24, 389th in Hethel England. Discharged on Oct. 24, 1945 with rank of first lieutenant.

Military locations, stations: Wichita Falls, Texas Tech, Ellington Field, Gowen Field, San Marcos, Goodfellow Field, and San Angelo.

Participated in Normandy GO 33 WD 45, Northern France GO WD 45 and Central Europe GO 40. Awarded the Air Medal with four Oak Leaf Clusters.

Following his discharge in 1945 he completed four years at Kansas State College and received a degree in Veterinary Medicine. He immediately went back to his home state of California where he conducted 40 years of Equine practice in Santa Rosa, CA. He has retired but continues to raise, race and breed rare horses.

ROBERT B. WOOLSON, was born on June 26, 1920 in Detroit, MI. Enlisted in the USAAC, February 1942 while attending The Citadel, Military College of South Carolina. Graduated Pilot second lieutenant Class 43A, Stockton, CA. Completed three phases on B-26 trying for fighters. After being assigned Tallahassee Fighter Pool all fighting pilots in pool were assigned enmasse as B-17 and B-24 co-pilots. Took B-24 phase training at Pueblo, CO. Crew picked up the last "pink" B-24 in Lincoln, NE and flew to Enfidaville, North Africa 376th Bomb Group, 513th Sqdn.

Completed five missions from Tunisia 12th Air Force, moved to San Pancrazio, Italy, completed seven missions 15th Air Force. Participated in crew transfer from 15th Air Force to 8th Air Force. Assigned 44th Bomb Group, 66th Bomb Sqdn., Shipdham, East Anglia, England. Completed 35 combat missions in 8th Air Force. Received Distinguished Flying Cross, five Air Medals, four European Campaign Battle Stars, Presidential Unit Citation. Flew two missions over Normandy V.E. day, June 6th. 1946 to 1948 Photomapping Officer Liaison 29th Engr. Topo Bn. and 5th Recon. Group Post Hostilities Mapping Program, Philippines. Last ten years performed duty of Base Civil Engineer, Foster AFB, TX; Chambley, France; Wheelus, Tripoli, and Pope AFB, NC. Retired lieutenant colonel, April 1962.

Returned to Victoria, TX. Obtained insurance and real estate brokerage license specializing in residential sales, syndication of investment properties and property management. Married Frances M. Dysart, May 7, 1955. Two sons, three grandsons.

GUY V. WORLOCK, was born in Utica, NY on Sept. 26, 1920. Entered the service on Aug. 26, 1942 and was discharged Sept. 28, 1945 with the rank of corporal.

Basic training Westover Field, MA. Left on *Queen Mary* Dec. 7, 1942. Arrived Hardwick England Dec. 16, 1942. Left Hardwick June 12, 1945. Arrived New York on *Queen Mary* June 20, 1945.

Bombardier Recon. School in England. All service with 93rd Bomb Group at Hardwick.

Married Jane A. Campbell June 5, 1942. They have

one daughter and two grandchildren. Retired after 23 years with Blue Cross as claims manager.

FREDERICK D. WORTHEN (DUSTY), was born on May 25, 1923 in St. Paul, MN. Enlisted in USAAC Aviation Cadet Program, Nov. 12, 1942. Graduated from Victorville AAB as bombardier/navigator, second lieutenant, April 1, 1944.

Air crew assembled in Lincoln, NE. Trained in B-24s in Boise, ID. Picked up airplane in Topeka, KS. Flew to England in July 1944 via Labrador, Greenland, Iceland and Wales. Assigned to 8th Air Force, 93rd Bomb Group, 328th/329th Sqdns. Flew 23-1/2 missions.

On Jan. 28, 1945, on a mission to Dortmond, Germany, with two engines out and propellers windmilling and a third engine failing, they bailed out near Haamstede, Holland. All captured within two hours. That night they started a trip back through Dortmond, it was devastated. Then ten days of solitary confinement at Oberursel. Next to Hurnberg, Stalag XIII-D. On April 4, started forced march to Moosburg, Stalag VII-A. Liberated April 29, 1945.

Married Connie Woolley July 7, 1945, has two daughters, Janet and Jill and two grandchildren, Eric and Dena. Left active duty Nov. 11, 1945. Retired from the reserves in 1983 as a major. Retired from the architectural and building construction business, Oct. 28, 1988. Currently resides in Burbank, CA.

ROBERT H. WRAY, was born on Oct. 1, 1921 in Atwood, IN. Joined the USAAC - radio operator on Aug. 11, 1942 and began active service on Feb. 5, 1943. Discharged Sept. 19, 1945 with the rank of technical sergeant.

Military locations, stations: Montgomery, AL; Sioux Falls, SD; Hethel England; and Boise, ID.

Memorable experiences include mission to Hanover - over 200 flak holes in plane. He flew 35 missions.

Awarded the Air Medal with four clusters and other ribbons. Married and has four children and five grandchildren. Presently retired.

JAMES F. WRIGHT (JIM), was born in Elizabeth, NJ on July 9, 1921. Enlisted as private, USAAC, May 8, 1942. February 28, 1943 began aviation cadet training Maxwell Field, AL. Completed primary flying, Lakeland, FL. Transferred, due to bombardier shortage, to bombardier training. Graduated second lieutenant bombardier - navigator, May 20, 1944, San Angelo, TX.

To bomber command Westover Field, MA, then Charleston, SC. Then 68th Sqdn., 44th Bomb Group, 8th Air Force, Oct. 25, 1944. Made first lieutenant, lead bombardier, completing 29 missions, including last of 44th, April 25, 1945. Received Distinguished Flying Cross, four Air Medals, Presidential Unit Citation, three European Theatre Battle Stars, other awards.

To Sioux Falls, SD, for B-29 training. War ended. Discharged October 1945. Married Marion G. Cubberley, Nov. 16, 1945. Two sons, Robt. Bruce and Wm. Scott.

Continued service in Air Force Reserve, retiring as colonel, commanding 9256th Air Reserve Sqdn., with 39+ years service.

JAMES M. WYLIE, was born Aug. 6, 1921 in Apollo, PA. Has two sons, two daughters and six grandchildren.

Entered USAAC on March 9, 1942. Graduated from pilot training on Feb. 16, 1943 (43-B Turner Field).

Started B-24 training at Davis Monthan, Tucson, AZ. Assigned to cadre, 446th Bomb Group, 705th Sqdn. as co-pilot on model crew. Group trained at Lowry Field, and deployed to ETO October 1943 as pilot of the former model crew.

Flew 30 missions, half with 446th, half with 93rd Pathfinder crew. Promoted to captain, 1944. Returned to states October 1944. Entered B-29 training early 1945.

Spent 22 years in USAF, retired July 1964 as lieutenant colonel. Flew B-24, B-17, B-29, B-50 and B-47, as well as support tubes C-47, T-33, L-20, etc.

Employed by Commonwealth of Pennsylvania in department of welfare, 20 years. Received B.A. Shippensburg University in August 1965; MGA, University of Pennsylvania Wharton School, June 1970.

Was awarded two Distinguished Flying Crosses, four Air Medals, and USAF Commendation Medal as well as ETO Campaign with three Battle Stars. Rated command pilot and AOB (1953).

Now fully retired - does some traveling and some volunteer literacy work.

JOHN L. WYNN, was born of Shawnee ancestors on his mother's side, and early in life he was raised in the tradition of the Shawnee warrior. He lived the early part of his life in the Shawnee homeland of Ohio. His grandparents and great-grandparents on his mother's side were among the remnants of Tecumhsas survivors who scattered into the hills of Virginia and West Virginia after their defeat and the death of their leader.

Upon graduation from high school he enlisted in the United States Cavalry, and shortly thereafter, transferred to the USAAC. Prior to entering the cadet flying program he qualified as a flying sergeant and non-commissioned observer as well as an instructor in every phase of the Air Mechanics School at Chanute Field, IL.

He qualified and received training under the academy extension program in 1942, and upon entering the flying cadet program he was classified for bombardier training in conflict with his previous sergeant pilot status. He graduated from the bombardier course in 1943 and was commissioned a second lieutenant.

At the time of his graduation he was relieved of bombardier status and assigned to set up the school for commissioned B-29 flight engineers. Upon completion of this duty he was given the choice of remaining in the B-29s as a flight engineer or reverting to bombardier status. He chose the latter and joined the crew with which he would fly combat at Casper, WY. He completed 37 missions in the B-24 Liberator while assigned to the 2nd Air Div., 96th Bomb Wing, 458th Bomb Group, 754th Bomb Sqdn., of the 8th Air Force, ETO.

In 1963 he was inducted into the Aero Space Hall of Fame at San Diego, CA. Prior to his retirement from the USAF in 1963 he had served in WWII, the Korean Conflict and Vietnam. He had qualified for nine sets of wings which were as follows: Enlisted Pilot, Observer, Technical Observer, Air Crew Member, Aerial Gunner. His commissioned wings included: Bombardier, Navigator, Flight Engineer and Aircraft Observer Bombardment.

He was awarded 32 service medals among which were the Distinguished Flying Cross and the Air Medal with three Oak Leaf Clusters.

During his tour of combat in the ETO he shot down two ME-109s, and it is with some degree of reflection that this account of the happenings during his tour with the 458th is related. All of the instances are factual, however, the events may or may not be chronically correct. The personalities and actions of the individual crew members are quite vivid in memory and provide a vivid and accurate picture of one crew as it wends its way through the rigors of combat.

ROBERT J. YARISH, was born in Phillips, WI on March 14, 1923. Entered USAAC on Jan. 31, 1943. After basic training in Miami Beach, he attended the University of Arkansas Air Corps College Training Program. Reclassified as clerk/

typist and attended college at Ft. Collins, CO. Then on to Salt Lake City, Wendover and Tonopah with 458th Bomb Group. Flew to Horsham St. Faith with ATC as advance echelon for 753rd Sqdn. Operations.

Returned to the States on V-E day, May 1945, and discharged November 1945 from Ashburn General Hospital, McKinney, TX and from service.

Employed past 36 years as owner-manager of several credit bureaus and collection agencies in Northern Wisconsin. Married his high school sweetheart Miriam while in Arkansas. They have four children and six grandchildren. He hunts in Montana and Wisconsin and fishes in Canada. Visits family around the country several times a year and enjoys still being relatively steadily employed.

HORACE YATES (HAL), was born March 11, 1915 in Donaldsonville, GA. Enlisted November 1942 in the USAAC and was assigned to the 389th Bomb Group, 567th Bomb Sqdn., stationed at Savannah, GA.

Completed 31 missions. Made lead on third mission. Tail shot off; lost nose twice; lost two engines twice; and crash landed twice in Southern England and bailed out.

Discharged November 1945 with the rank of captain. Received six Air Medals and two Distinguished Flying Crosses.

Yates and wife Lois have five children: Bill, Polly and Sarah (twins), John and Don. After 50 years in auto parts business, he retired.

KEITH YERTY, was born Dec. 4, 1911. Joined the USAAF on April 20, 1943. Stationed at Headquarters, Wendover, UT; Tonopah, NV; Salt Lake City, UT (458th Bomb Group); Horsham, St. Faith, England.

Discharged Oct. 30, 1945 with the rank of sergeant. Married Maude Wallace Sept. 11, 1938 and Maude Dieddec Dec. 19, 1989. He has two sons and three grandchildren. Yerty retired after 37 years with Hastings Mfg. Co.

HARRY D. YODER, was born in Boyertown, PA. Was inducted in the service in January 1942. Graduated from Twin Engine Flying School March 1943 and immediately assigned to B-24 Transition School in Tucson, AZ. Was assigned to two theaters of operation during WWII. First to North Africa for Mediterranean Theater and later assigned to the 2nd Air Div. for the European Theater. Was assigned to four Air Forces while overseas, ie 9th, 12th, 15th and the 8th.

Assigned to the 1st Replacement Depot, Cairo, Egypt, and later to the 376th Bomb Group, 513th Sqdn. Combat missions were flown from Tunis and Libya. Missions were flown to the Balkans, Northern Italy, Germany and Vienna,

Austria (Weiner-Neustadt) two missions requiring 750 gallons of fuel carried in the forward bomb bay from Tunis. Later moved to San Pancrazzio, Italy, was selected as an exchange crew and transferred to the 2nd Air Div., 8th Air Force. His missions with the 8th Air Force were to important targets including several to Berlin.

Flew a total of 38 missions, 20 in the Mediterranean Theater and 18 with the 8th Air Force. All missions were rough and especially to Berlin and the Rhur Valley - Essen - the Krupp Gun plant.

Was a career officer and retired with 30 years of service. His decorations include the Legion of Merit with Oak Leaf Cluster, Distinguished Flying Cross, Air Medal with eight Clusters, Mediterranean Theater of Operations, ETO, Berlin Airlift Medal and Army Commendation Medal.

Subsequent to his retirement, he worked for Lockheed-Georgia Co., President and owner Boyertown Auto Body Works, Inc. and currently is doing consulting work.

WALTER P. YOST, was born in Allentown, PA. Enlisted in the USAAC on Dec. 2, 1942. Trained at Miami Beach, FL; Gunnery School, Laredo, TX; Armorment School, Buckley Field, Denver, CO; and bomber training at Tucson, AZ.

Assigned to B-24 crew and flew 30 missions with the 44th Bomb Group, 506th Sqdn. at Shipdham, England. Received four Air Medals and four European Campaign Stars. Returned to USA after completing missions and assigned to Gunnery Instructor School at Harlingen, TX. Discharged October 1945 with the rank staff sergeant.

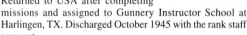

After discharge from service, graduated from Muhlinberg College in 1949. Retired from United Counties Trust Co. after 30 years as a bank manager. Married to Dorothy September 1946, have three children and five grandchildren.

EUGENE YOUNG, was born July 20, 1918 in McAlester, OK. Joined the USAAC December 1941. Based at 31 locations (sometimes on detached service). Was briefly in the Glider Pilot Program then in Armament and Gunnery schools. Survived crash at Pocatello. Eventually was ball turret gunner in 755th Bomb Sqdn., 458th Bomb Group at Horsham St. Faith.

Participated five battles: Rhineland, Air Offensive Europe, Normandy, Northern France and Ardennes. He has vivid memories of when plane was hit at Tutow and throwing loose equipment out. They returned to England on two engines, thanks to excellent pilots. Also remembers three occasions of getting rid of hung up bombs (always the right rear bomb bay), the last time on their final mission.

Received the Distinguished Flying Cross, Air Medal with clusters and Silver Service Star. Returned in January 1945 and after being hospitalized at Santa Ana was discharged in June 1945.

A graduate of Oklahoma University. He is married with five children and three grandchildren.

WILLIAM A. YOUNG JR. (ART), was born Dec. 31, 1919 in Philadelphia, PA. Enlisted in the USAAC Sept. 4, 1941. Assigned to the 8th Air Force, ETO, England (1943-44) and with 13th Air Force, PAC 1946-47).

Memorable experiences: as navigator with 68th and 66th Sqdns. of 44th Bomb Group and flying 35 missions.

Discharged with the rank lieutenant colonel, USAFR. Received the Distinguished Flying Cross, Air Medal and three Oak Leaf Clusters.

WILLIS HAROLD YOUNG JR., was born Jan. 21, 1921 in Washington, DC. Enlisted July 14, 1942 in the USAAF. Assigned to the 8th Air Force, 2nd Air Div., 489th Bomb Group, Halesworth, England and with the 448th Bomb Group in Seething, England.

Participated in Air Offensive Europe, Northern France, Normandy, Rhineland, and Ardennes. As a B-24 co-pilot, he flew 28 missions against Germany. Was shot down over Germany and spent four months as POW.

Discharged Dec. 2, 1945 with the rank first lieutenant. Received the EAME Theater Ribbon with five Battle Stars, Air Medal with three Oak Leaf Clusters, and two Overseas Service Stars.

Young is a widower with three grown children and four grandchildren. He retired to Vero Beach, FL and is healthy and happy.

MICHEL YUSPEH (MIKE), was born Oct. 27, 1920 in New Orleans, LA. Joined the A/C Air Force March 24, 1942. Stationed at Maxwell, Tyndall Field, Keesler, Peterson, Shipdham, Lowry and others.

Memorable experiences: Mission #25, Nov. 6, 1944, when bomb stuck in bomb bay-put on portable oxygen bottle and manually tripped the bomb release and it fell someplace in France. Mission #27, Nov. 10, 1944, was in top turret getting some sun when they were hit with a lot of flak. Top of turret was blown off and a piece of shrapnel pierced his flak helmet and lodged in the rubber ear cup of fight helmet. His face was scratched and he was knocked out for a short period of time.

Discharged in September 1945 with the rank of tech sergeant. Received the Distinguished Flying Cross, Air Medal with four Oak Leaf Clusters, Meritorious Service, Good Conduct Medal, EAME Theater Medal with four Battle Stars and the WWII Victory Medal.

Married to Rose Fay; they have two children, Alan and Larry, and two grandchildren, Andrew and Margaret.

LEROY M. ZACH, was born April 29, 1925 in Swisher, IA. Enlisted July 28, 1943 in the USAAF. Served with the 466th Bomb Group, 787th Sqdn., 2nd Air Div., 8th Air Force. Stationed in Attlebridge, England B-24 Bomber Base.

Participated in the European Theater. Memorable experience was Dec. 23, 1944 when he flew low level support to Battle of the Bulge. The flak was very intense.

Completed 26 missions before his discharge on Oct. 22, 1945 with the rank of tech sergeant. Received the Air Medal with three Oak Leaf Clusters and two Battle Stars.

Married to Ruth and has two children, Susan and Catherine and four grandchildren. Has degree in mech. Engr. from Iowa State University. Career in engr. and engr. mgmt. Zach is retired and lives in Davenport, IA and Venice, FL.

GEORGE O. ZEIBER, entered the U.S. Military in August 1943 as an aviation cadet. Went to Radio School in Sioux Falls, SD; Gunnery School at Yuma; then to Lincoln, NE where crews were formed. His crew went to Casper, WY for flight training.

Upon completion was sent to England, 8th Air Force at Rackheath for 35 missions over Germany plus hauling gas to Army in France. Returned home April 1945, had 21 days furlough, then reported to Miami Beach for reassignment to Fort McPherson, GA.

With enough points, he was discharged in June 1945 with the rank tech sergeant. Zeiber lives in Lewisburg, PA.

DONALD G. ZIEBELL, was born June 4, 1924 in Oshkosh, WI. Graduated Oshkosh High School in 1941. Employed as dental technician apprentice 1941-1943.

Enlisted USAAFR in February 1943. Graduated Laredo Aerial Gunnery School and Midland Bombardier School, Class 44-4. Flew overseas to Seething, England with new B-24H in July of 1944. Flew 16 missions as bombardier nose gunner with Lt. Hillman's crew, 448th Bombardment Group (B-24s). Received two Air Medals and a certificate of valor. Retired as second lieutenant USAAFR May 22, 1945. Received BS Lawrence University in 1949. Taught school for 25 years. St. John's Military Academy, Delafied, WI, 11 years. Retired from teaching in 1986.

EARL L. ZIMMERMAN, was born Dec. 24, 1923 in Marion, IN. Joined the USAAC in June 1942, attended Radio and Gunnery School. Joined 389th Bomb Group at Tucson, AZ, phase training, departed with Group for ETO, June 1943, returned with 389th, June 1945.

Mid-air collision, June 1943 while practicing for Ploesti. Flew first mission and last mission with 389th Bomb Group, Maleme, Crete and Salsbury, Germany. Six months vacation in Ankara, Turkey, via Ploesti until escape in December 1943.

Flew black Libs, Operation Ball, out of Leuchars, Scotland, dropping supplies to the Norwegian underground at night during Spring of 44. Retired from Air Force, May 1964, the last 15 years as a special agent, OSI.

Married an English beauty and has two children. Self-employed as a security consultant.

THEODORE R. ZIMMERMAN, was born in Kutztown, PA on Feb. 25, 1923. Enlisted in Harrisburg, PA in November 1942. Graduated pilot, second lieutenant, Class of 44E at Lubbock, TX. Combat crew training at Pueblo Field, CO. Was married at Pueblo in August 1944.

Assigned Station 146, Seething, 448th Bomb Group, 715th Bomb Sqdn. on Nov. 8, 1944. Reported MIA on Jan. 7, 1945 on Achern mission in aircraft, *Daisy Mae,* no further report was ever received. *Submitted by his brother Gene G. Zimmerman of Kempton, PA. Would greatly appreciate any information of any crew member of Daisy Mae.*

ELDEN EUGENE ZINK, was born Jan. 7, 1921 in Dayton, OH and married Patricia Ortengren Oct. 25, 1944. They have one son, three daughters and 11 grandchildren. Entered the USAAC Oct. 14, 1942; attended Casey Jones School of Aeronautics, Newark, NJ; Aircraft Mechanics Roosevelt Field, NY; Bell Aircraft P-39 Maintenance, Buffalo, NY; Flexible Gunnery School, Kingman, AZ.

On July 2, 1943 started B-24 air crew training at Salt Lake City, UT; Boise, ID; Sioux City, IA; Mitchell, SD; Lincoln, NE. Was assigned to the 445th Bomb Group, 700th Bomb Sqdn. Arrived Tibenham, England, Station 124 on Thanksgiving Day 1943. He flew 30 missions as gunner/flight engineer, finishing April 24, 1944.

Received two Distinguished Flying Crosses, five Air Medals, four European Campaign Stars and the Presidential Citation.

Transferred to the 492nd Bomb Group, 857th Bomb Sqdn. as air crew instructor. Returned to the States Oct. 8, 1944, R&R at Miami Beach. Assigned to Keesler Field, MS; Chanute Field, IL as supervisor/instructor. Discharged Sept. 6, 1945 as staff sergeant.

Retired Feb. 17, 1976 after 30 years as project engineer for Research and Development at Wright Patterson AFB, Dayton, OH.

FREDERICK G. ZIRK, was born May 4, 1919 in Brooklyn, NY. Enlisted in the USAAC on April 10, 1942. Attended Weather School, Grand Rapids, MI; Radio Operator Mechanic School, Sioux Falls, SD; Gunnery School, Yuma, AZ. Was assigned to a B-24 air crew for training and sent to Charleston, SC; Roosevelt Field, NY; Mount Pelier, VT.

Overseas on Feb. 4, 1945 bound for England via Newfoundland, Greenland, Iceland to England. Eventually assigned to the 329th Sqdn. of the 93rd Bomb Group, Norwich, England, "Teds Travelling Circus." Completed 17 air combat missions over Germany including Brunswick, Regensburg, Hanover, Berlin, Wilhelmshaven, Battle of the Rhein and the Central Europe Campaigns. Their B-24 aircraft was known as the *Picadilly Virgin*. Crew members: pilot, Lt. Joseph McGhan; co-pilot, Lt. Robert Wright; radio operator/mechanic/gunner, Frederick G. Zirk; waist gunners, Gerry Geonnotti and Wilson Good; ball gunner, George Vancavage; and tail gunner Paul Greenwald.

Discharged Oct. 29, 1945 with the rank of tech sergeant. Received the Air Medal with clusters, European Medal with clusters, American Theater Medal, WWII Victory Medal and the Good Conduct Medal.

Married to Edna A. Antoska (cadet nurse). They have three children: Rick, Lauren and Debbie. Zirk retired from New York Government and resides in Naples, FL.

FRANK P. ZITANO, was born March 15, 1921 in New York City. Enlisted Sept. 2, 1942 in the USAAC. After completion of bombardier/navigator training, he joined crew, and they were sent to England to the 389th Bomb Group, 564th Sqdn. based at Hethel.

On very first mission they were badly shot up and forced to land at a recently captured base in France. Their crew was returned to Hethel by way of Antwerp and Brussels, Belgium. Got it again on their second mission and had to land in Brussels. Rest of tour went fairly well, and they returned stateside at the end of the war in Europe.

Recalled to active duty in early 1950. Flew 35 combat missions (B-29s). Decided on a career in the Air Force. Flew B-47s then B-52s. Had combat tours in Vietnam and retired in 1970 with the rank of colonel.

Received the Air Medal with 10 Oak Leaf Clusters, three Unit Citations, Air Force Commendation, ETO, Korea and Vietnam Service.

Married 49 years and has four daughters. These days he does much volunteer work and travels extensively with his wife Jo.

JOHN ZITNAK, was born May 30, 1924 in Doniphan, Ripley County, MO. Enlisted Nov. 6, 1942 in the USAAF. Assigned to the 754th Sqdn., 458th Bomb Group. Stationed at Sheppard Field, Wichita Falls, TX; G.L. Martin, MD; Ft. Myers, FL; Chanute Field, IL; and Kirtland Field, NM.

Participated in Air Offensive Europe, Normandy, Northern France and Southern France. Memorable experience was April 25, 1944 raid, Mannheim, Germany.

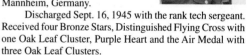

Discharged Sept. 16, 1945 with the rank tech sergeant. Received four Bronze Stars, Distinguished Flying Cross with one Oak Leaf Cluster, Purple Heart and the Air Medal with three Oak Leaf Clusters.

Married Betty Deen in 1951, they had one son (deceased) and one daughter.

Zitnak is retired from GM and returned to his hometown Doniphan, MO in 1980. Now keeps busy with volunteer work.

ROBERT W. ZOBAC, was born Feb. 1, 1920 in Chicago, IL. Enlisted in the USAAC on July 31, 1943. Stationed at Jefferson Barracks, MO. He entered the Aviation Cadets, Class 44-C at Washington University on Sept. 9, 1943 but was washed out in early 1944.

On June 1, 1944, after gunnery training at Harlingen, TX, he qualified as a combat crew aerial gunner. He was transferred to Mountain Home, ID where on Sept. 20, 1945, he qualified for Class I flying crew. His flight crew became a part of the 2nd Air Div., 445th Bomb Group upon their arrival at Tibenham, England on Jan. 14, 1945. From Feb. 16 to April 20, 1945, he flew 13 combat missions against targets in Germany and Czechoslovakia as a left waist gunner in the *Asbestos Alice*, a B-24M Liberator (Ser. #44-50525) with the 700th Sqdn. and subsequently was awarded the Air Medal with Oak Leaf Cluster. V-E day, May 8, 1945, ended his service with the 445th Bomb Group and he was transferred to the AAF Base Sioux Falls, SD on May 23, 1945. With the surrender of Japan and the end of WWII, he was honorably discharged Nov. 19, 1945 with the rank of sergeant.

While stationed in Sioux Falls, he met and eventually married Agnes Call on Nov. 26, 1946. Moving back to Chicago, he worked in insurance and various product sales and clerical positions until the time of his fatal heart attack on Sept. 12, 1977, in Justice, IL. He is survived by his wife Agnes; sons, Edward and Gregory; and five grandchildren. *Submitted by Edward Sobac.*

STANLEY C. ZYBORT, was born in Ansonia, CT on Aug. 13, 1919. Enlisted in the USAAF. Assigned to the 392nd Bomb Group, 577th Sqdn. Stationed at Maxwell AFB, Keesler Field and Wendling England.

Was shot down over Germany, was a POW and received Purple Heart. Discharged Dec. 23, 1946 with the rank staff sergeant.

Married Mildred R. Rabb in 1946. Currently retired and lives winters in Little Silver, NJ and summers in Pompano Beach, FL.

1st Lt. H.C. 'Pete' Henry, Pilot of Henry's crew, 1944. (Courtesy of H.C. Henry)

Earl Garrigas and Russell Leslie, 1943-44 in England. (Courtesy of Russell R. Leslie)

"My Everlovin' Gal," B-24, 44th BG. (Courtesy of Albert (Ed) Jones)

INDEX

The biographies, Roll of Honor and Roster were not indexed since they appear in alphabetical order in their respective sections.